American Casebook Series
Hornbook Series and Basic Legal Texts
Black Letter Series and Nutshell Series

of

WEST PUBLISHING COMPANY
P.O. Box 64526
St. Paul, Minnesota 55164–0526

Accounting

FARIS' ACCOUNTING AND LAW IN A NUTSHELL, 377 pages, 1984. Softcover. (Text)

FIFLIS' ACCOUNTING ISSUES FOR LAWYERS, TEACHING MATERIALS, , approximately 750 pages, 1991. (Casebook)

SIEGEL AND SIEGEL'S ACCOUNTING AND FINANCIAL DISCLOSURE: A GUIDE TO BASIC CONCEPTS, 259 pages, 1983. Softcover. (Text)

Administrative Law

BONFIELD AND ASIMOW'S STATE AND FEDERAL ADMINISTRATIVE LAW, 826 pages, 1989. Teacher's Manual available. (Casebook)

GELLHORN AND LEVIN'S ADMINISTRATIVE LAW AND PROCESS IN A NUTSHELL, Third Edition, 479 pages, 1990. Softcover. (Text)

MASHAW AND MERRILL'S CASES AND MATERIALS ON ADMINISTRATIVE LAW—THE AMERICAN PUBLIC LAW SYSTEM, Second Edition, 976 pages, 1985. (Casebook) 1989 Supplement.

ROBINSON, GELLHORN AND BRUFF'S THE ADMINISTRATIVE PROCESS, Third Edition, 978 pages, 1986. (Casebook)

Admiralty

HEALY AND SHARPE'S CASES AND MATERIALS ON ADMIRALTY, Second Edition, 876 pages, 1986. (Casebook)

MARAIST'S ADMIRALTY IN A NUTSHELL, Second Edition, 379 pages, 1988. Softcover. (Text)

SCHOENBAUM'S HORNBOOK ON ADMIRALTY AND MARITIME LAW, Student Edition, 692 pages, 1987 with 1989 pocket part. (Text)

Agency—Partnership

DEMOTT'S FIDUCIARY OBLIGATION, AGENCY AND PARTNERSHIP: DUTIES IN ONGOING BUSINESS RELATIONSHIPS, 740 pages, 1991. Teacher's Manual available. (Casebook)

FESSLER'S ALTERNATIVES TO INCORPORATION FOR PERSONS IN QUEST OF PROFIT, Third Edition, 339 pages, 1991. Softcover. Teacher's Manual available. (Casebook)

HENN'S CASES AND MATERIALS ON AGENCY, PARTNERSHIP AND OTHER UNINCORPORATED BUSINESS ENTERPRISES, Second Edition, 733 pages, 1985. Teacher's Manual available. (Casebook)

REUSCHLEIN AND GREGORY'S HORNBOOK ON THE LAW OF AGENCY AND PARTNERSHIP, Second Edition, 683 pages, 1990. (Text)

SELECTED CORPORATION AND PARTNERSHIP STATUTES, RULES AND FORMS. Softcover. Approximately 900 pages, 1991.

STEFFEN AND KERR'S CASES ON AGENCY-PARTNERSHIP, Fourth Edition, 859 pages, 1980. (Casebook)

STEFFEN'S AGENCY-PARTNERSHIP IN A NUTSHELL, 364 pages, 1977. Softcover. (Text)

Agricultural Law

MEYER, PEDERSEN, THORSON AND DAVIDSON'S AGRICULTURAL LAW: CASES AND MATERIALS, 931 pages, 1985. Teacher's Manual available. (Casebook)

List current as of June, 1991

Alternative Dispute Resolution

KANOWITZ' CASES AND MATERIALS ON ALTERNATIVE DISPUTE RESOLUTION, 1024 pages, 1986. Teacher's Manual available. (Casebook) 1990 Supplement.

RISKIN AND WESTBROOK'S DISPUTE RESOLUTION AND LAWYERS, 468 pages, 1987. Teacher's Manual available. (Casebook)

RISKIN AND WESTBROOK'S DISPUTE RESOLUTION AND LAWYERS, Abridged Edition, 223 pages, 1987. Softcover. Teacher's Manual available. (Casebook)

American Indian Law

CANBY'S AMERICAN INDIAN LAW IN A NUTSHELL, Second Edition, 336 pages, 1988. Softcover. (Text)

GETCHES AND WILKINSON'S CASES AND MATERIALS ON FEDERAL INDIAN LAW, Second Edition, 880 pages, 1986. (Casebook)

Antitrust—see also Regulated Industries, Trade Regulation

FOX AND SULLIVAN'S CASES AND MATERIALS ON ANTITRUST, 935 pages, 1989. Teacher's Manual available. (Casebook)

GELLHORN'S ANTITRUST LAW AND ECONOMICS IN A NUTSHELL, Third Edition, 472 pages, 1986. Softcover. (Text)

HOVENKAMP'S BLACK LETTER ON ANTITRUST, 323 pages, 1986. Softcover. (Review)

HOVENKAMP'S HORNBOOK ON ECONOMICS AND FEDERAL ANTITRUST LAW, Student Edition, 414 pages, 1985. (Text)

POSNER AND EASTERBROOK'S CASES AND ECONOMIC NOTES ON ANTITRUST, Second Edition, 1077 pages, 1981. (Casebook) 1984–85 Supplement.

SULLIVAN'S HORNBOOK OF THE LAW OF ANTITRUST, 886 pages, 1977. (Text)

Appellate Advocacy—see Trial and Appellate Advocacy

Architecture and Engineering Law

SWEET'S LEGAL ASPECTS OF ARCHITECTURE, ENGINEERING AND THE CONSTRUCTION PROCESS, Fourth Edition, 889 pages, 1989. Teacher's Manual available. (Casebook)

Art Law

DUBOFF'S ART LAW IN A NUTSHELL, 335 pages, 1984. Softcover. (Text)

Banking Law

BANKING LAW: SELECTED STATUTES AND REGULATIONS. Softcover. 263 pages, 1991.

LOVETT'S BANKING AND FINANCIAL INSTITUTIONS LAW IN A NUTSHELL, Second Edition, 464 pages, 1988. Softcover. (Text)

SYMONS AND WHITE'S BANKING LAW: TEACHING MATERIALS, Third Edition, 818 pages, 1991. Teacher's Manual available. (Casebook)

Statutory Supplement. *See Banking Law: Selected Statutes*

Business Planning—see also Corporate Finance

PAINTER'S PROBLEMS AND MATERIALS IN BUSINESS PLANNING, Second Edition, 1008 pages, 1984. (Casebook) 1990 Supplement.

Statutory Supplement. *See Selected Corporation and Partnership*

Civil Procedure—see also Federal Jurisdiction and Procedure

AMERICAN BAR ASSOCIATION SECTION OF LITIGATION—READINGS ON ADVERSARIAL JUSTICE: THE AMERICAN APPROACH TO ADJUDICATION, 217 pages, 1988. Softcover. (Coursebook)

CLERMONT'S BLACK LETTER ON CIVIL PROCEDURE, Second Edition, 332 pages, 1988. Softcover. (Review)

COUND, FRIEDENTHAL, MILLER AND SEXTON'S CASES AND MATERIALS ON CIVIL PROCEDURE, Fifth Edition, 1284 pages, 1989. Teacher's Manual available. (Casebook)

COUND, FRIEDENTHAL, MILLER AND SEXTON'S CIVIL PROCEDURE SUPPLEMENT. Approximately 475 pages, 1991. Softcover. (Casebook Supplement)

FEDERAL RULES OF CIVIL PROCEDURE—EDUCATIONAL EDITION. Softcover. Approximately 700 pages, 1991.

FRIEDENTHAL, KANE AND MILLER'S HORNBOOK ON CIVIL PROCEDURE, 876 pages, 1985. (Text)

KANE AND LEVINE'S CIVIL PROCEDURE IN CALIFORNIA: STATE AND FEDERAL Approxi-

Civil Procedure—Cont'd

mately 550 pages, 1991. Softcover. (Casebook Supplement)

KANE'S CIVIL PROCEDURE IN A NUTSHELL, Third Edition, 303 pages, 1991. Softcover. (Text)

KOFFLER AND REPPY'S HORNBOOK ON COMMON LAW PLEADING, 663 pages, 1969. (Text)

LEVINE, SLOMANSON AND WINGATE'S CALIFORNIA CIVIL PROCEDURE, CASES AND MATERIALS, . Approximately 550 pages, 1991. Teacher's Manual available. (Casebook)

MARCUS, REDISH AND SHERMAN'S CIVIL PROCEDURE: A MODERN APPROACH, 1027 pages, 1989. Teacher's Manual available. (Casebook) 1991 Supplement.

MARCUS AND SHERMAN'S COMPLEX LITIGATION–CASES AND MATERIALS ON ADVANCED CIVIL PROCEDURE, 846 pages, 1985. Teacher's Manual available. (Casebook) 1989 Supplement.

PARK AND MCFARLAND'S COMPUTER-AIDED EXERCISES ON CIVIL PROCEDURE, Third Edition, approximately 200 pages, 1991. Softcover. (Coursebook)

SIEGEL'S HORNBOOK ON NEW YORK PRACTICE, Second Edition, Student Edition, 1068 pages, 1991. Softcover. (Text)

Commercial Law

BAILEY AND HAGEDORN'S SECURED TRANSACTIONS IN A NUTSHELL, Third Edition, 390 pages, 1988. Softcover. (Text)

EPSTEIN, MARTIN, HENNING AND NICKLES' BASIC UNIFORM COMMERCIAL CODE TEACHING MATERIALS, Third Edition, 704 pages, 1988. Teacher's Manual available. (Casebook)

HENSON'S HORNBOOK ON SECURED TRANSACTIONS UNDER THE U.C.C., Second Edition, 504 pages, 1979, with 1979 pocket part. (Text)

MURRAY'S COMMERCIAL LAW, PROBLEMS AND MATERIALS, 366 pages, 1975. Teacher's Manual available. Softcover. (Coursebook)

NICKLES' BLACK LETTER ON COMMERCIAL PAPER, 450 pages, 1988. Softcover. (Review)

NICKLES, MATHESON AND DOLAN'S MATERIALS FOR UNDERSTANDING CREDIT AND PAYMENT SYSTEMS, 923 pages, 1987. Teacher's Manual available. (Casebook)

NORDSTROM, MURRAY AND CLOVIS' PROBLEMS AND MATERIALS ON SALES, 515 pages, 1982. (Casebook)

NORDSTROM, MURRAY AND CLOVIS' PROBLEMS AND MATERIALS ON SECURED TRANSACTIONS, 594 pages, 1987. (Casebook)

RUBIN AND COOTER'S THE PAYMENT SYSTEM: CASES, MATERIALS AND ISSUES, 885 pages, 1989. Teacher's Manual Available. (Casebook)

SELECTED COMMERCIAL STATUTES. Softcover. Approximately 1800 pages, 1991.

SPEIDEL'S BLACK LETTER ON SALES AND SALES FINANCING, 363 pages, 1984. Softcover. (Review)

SPEIDEL, SUMMERS AND WHITE'S COMMERCIAL LAW: TEACHING MATERIALS, Fourth Edition, 1448 pages, 1987. Teacher's Manual available. (Casebook)

SPEIDEL, SUMMERS AND WHITE'S COMMERCIAL PAPER: TEACHING MATERIALS, Fourth Edition, 578 pages, 1987. Reprint from Speidel et al., Commercial Law, Fourth Edition. Teacher's Manual available. (Casebook)

SPEIDEL, SUMMERS AND WHITE'S SALES: TEACHING MATERIALS, Fourth Edition, 804 pages, 1987. Reprint from Speidel et al., Commercial Law, Fourth Edition. Teacher's Manual available. (Casebook)

SPEIDEL, SUMMERS AND WHITE'S SECURED TRANSACTIONS: TEACHING MATERIALS, Fourth Edition, 485 pages, 1987. Reprint from Speidel et al., Commercial Law, Fourth Edition. Teacher's Manual available. (Casebook)

STOCKTON'S SALES IN A NUTSHELL, Second Edition, 370 pages, 1981. Softcover. (Text)

STONE'S UNIFORM COMMERCIAL CODE IN A NUTSHELL, Third Edition, 580 pages, 1989. Softcover. (Text)

WEBER AND SPEIDEL'S COMMERCIAL PAPER IN A NUTSHELL, Third Edition, 404 pages, 1982. Softcover. (Text)

WHITE AND SUMMERS' HORNBOOK ON THE

Commercial Law—Cont'd

UNIFORM COMMERCIAL CODE, Third Edition, Student Edition, 1386 pages, 1988. (Text)

Community Property

MENNELL AND BOYKOFF'S COMMUNITY PROPERTY IN A NUTSHELL, Second Edition, 432 pages, 1988. Softcover. (Text)

VERRALL AND BIRD'S CASES AND MATERIALS ON CALIFORNIA COMMUNITY PROPERTY, Fifth Edition, 604 pages, 1988. (Casebook)

Comparative Law

BARTON, GIBBS, LI AND MERRYMAN'S LAW IN RADICALLY DIFFERENT CULTURES, 960 pages, 1983. (Casebook)

GLENDON, GORDON AND OSAKWE'S COMPARATIVE LEGAL TRADITIONS: TEXT, MATERIALS AND CASES ON THE CIVIL LAW, COMMON LAW AND SOCIALIST LAW TRADITIONS, 1091 pages, 1985. (Casebook)

GLENDON, GORDON AND OSAKWE'S COMPARATIVE LEGAL TRADITIONS IN A NUTSHELL. 402 pages, 1982. Softcover. (Text)

Computers and Law

MAGGS AND SPROWL'S COMPUTER APPLICATIONS IN THE LAW, 316 pages, 1987. (Coursebook)

MASON'S USING COMPUTERS IN THE LAW: AN INTRODUCTION AND PRACTICAL GUIDE, Second Edition, 288 pages, 1988. Softcover. (Coursebook)

Conflict of Laws

CRAMTON, CURRIE AND KAY'S CASES–COMMENTS–QUESTIONS ON CONFLICT OF LAWS, Fourth Edition, 876 pages, 1987. (Casebook)

HAY'S BLACK LETTER ON CONFLICT OF LAWS, 330 pages, 1989. Softcover. (Review)

SCOLES AND HAY'S HORNBOOK ON CONFLICT OF LAWS, Student Edition, approximately 1100 pages, November 1991 Pub. (Text)

SIEGEL'S CONFLICTS IN A NUTSHELL, 470 pages, 1982. Softcover. (Text)

Constitutional Law—Civil Rights—see also First Amendment and Foreign Relations and National Security Law

ABERNATHY'S CASES AND MATERIALS ON CIVIL RIGHTS, 660 pages, 1980. (Casebook)

BARRON AND DIENES' BLACK LETTER ON CONSTITUTIONAL LAW, Third Edition, 440 pages, 1991. Softcover. (Review)

BARRON AND DIENES' CONSTITUTIONAL LAW IN A NUTSHELL, Second Edition, 483 pages, 1991. Softcover. (Text)

ENGDAHL'S CONSTITUTIONAL FEDERALISM IN A NUTSHELL, Second Edition, 411 pages, 1987. Softcover. (Text)

FARBER AND SHERRY'S HISTORY OF THE AMERICAN CONSTITUTION, 458 pages, 1990. Softcover. Teacher's Manual available. (Text)

GARVEY AND ALEINIKOFF'S MODERN CONSTITUTIONAL THEORY: A READER, Second Edition, approximately 575 pages, 1991. Softcover. (Reader)

LOCKHART, KAMISAR, CHOPER AND SHIFFRIN'S CONSTITUTIONAL LAW: CASES–COMMENTS–QUESTIONS, Seventh Edition, approximately 1650 pages, 1991. (Casebook) 1991 Supplement.

LOCKHART, KAMISAR, CHOPER AND SHIFFRIN'S THE AMERICAN CONSTITUTION: CASES AND MATERIALS, Seventh Edition, approximately 1250 pages, September, 1991 Pub. Abridged version of Lockhart, et al., Constitutional Law: Cases–Comments–Questions, Seventh Edition. (Casebook) 1991 Supplement.

LOCKHART, KAMISAR, CHOPER AND SHIFFRIN'S CONSTITUTIONAL RIGHTS AND LIBERTIES: CASES AND MATERIALS, Seventh Edition, approximately 1250 pages, September, 1991 Pub. Reprint from Lockhart, et al., Constitutional Law: Cases–Comments–Questions, Seventh Edition. (Casebook) 1991 Supplement.

MARKS AND COOPER'S STATE CONSTITUTIONAL LAW IN A NUTSHELL, 329 pages, 1988. Softcover. (Text)

NOWAK AND ROTUNDA'S HORNBOOK ON CONSTITUTIONAL LAW, Fourth Edition, approximately 1275 pages, August, 1991 Pub. (Text)

ROTUNDA'S MODERN CONSTITUTIONAL LAW: CASES AND NOTES, Third Edition, 1085 pages, 1989. (Casebook) 1991 Supplement.

VIEIRA'S CONSTITUTIONAL CIVIL RIGHTS IN A NUTSHELL, Second Edition, 322 pages,

Constitutional Law—Civil Rights—Cont'd

1990. Softcover. (Text)

WILLIAMS' CONSTITUTIONAL ANALYSIS IN A NUTSHELL, 388 pages, 1979. Softcover. (Text)

Consumer Law—see also Commercial Law

EPSTEIN AND NICKLES' CONSUMER LAW IN A NUTSHELL, Second Edition, 418 pages, 1981. Softcover. (Text)

SELECTED COMMERCIAL STATUTES. Softcover. Approximately 1800 pages, 1991.

SPANOGLE, ROHNER, PRIDGEN AND RASOR'S CASES AND MATERIALS ON CONSUMER LAW, Second Edition, 916 pages, 1991. (Casebook)

Contracts

CALAMARI AND PERILLO'S BLACK LETTER ON CONTRACTS, Second Edition, 462 pages, 1990. Softcover. (Review)

CALAMARI AND PERILLO'S HORNBOOK ON CONTRACTS, Third Edition, 1049 pages, 1987. (Text)

CALAMARI, PERILLO AND BENDER'S CASES AND PROBLEMS ON CONTRACTS, Second Edition, 905 pages, 1989. Teacher's Manual Available. (Casebook)

CORBIN'S TEXT ON CONTRACTS, One Volume Student Edition, 1224 pages, 1952. (Text)

FESSLER AND LOISEAUX'S CASES AND MATERIALS ON CONTRACTS—MORALITY, ECONOMICS AND THE MARKET PLACE, 837 pages, 1982. Teacher's Manual available. (Casebook)

FRIEDMAN'S CONTRACT REMEDIES IN A NUTSHELL, 323 pages, 1981. Softcover. (Text)

FULLER AND EISENBERG'S CASES ON BASIC CONTRACT LAW, Fifth Edition, 1037 pages, 1990. (Casebook)

HAMILTON, RAU AND WEINTRAUB'S CASES AND MATERIALS ON CONTRACTS, 830 pages, 1984. (Casebook)

KEYES' GOVERNMENT CONTRACTS IN A NUTSHELL, Second Edition, 557 pages, 1990. Softcover. (Text)

SCHABER AND ROHWER'S CONTRACTS IN A NUTSHELL, Third Edition, 457 pages, 1990. Softcover. (Text)

SUMMERS AND HILLMAN'S CONTRACT AND RELATED OBLIGATION: THEORY, DOCTRINE AND PRACTICE, 1074 pages, 1987. Teacher's Manual available. (Casebook)

Copyright—see Patent and Copyright Law

Corporate Finance—see also Business Planning

HAMILTON'S CASES AND MATERIALS ON CORPORATION FINANCE, Second Edition, 1221 pages, 1989. (Casebook)

OESTERLE'S THE LAW OF MERGERS, ACQUISITIONS AND REORGANIZATIONS, Approximately 1100 pages, 1991. (Casebook)

Corporations

HAMILTON'S BLACK LETTER ON CORPORATIONS, Second Edition, 513 pages, 1986. Softcover. (Review)

HAMILTON'S CASES AND MATERIALS ON CORPORATIONS—INCLUDING PARTNERSHIPS AND LIMITED PARTNERSHIPS, Fourth Edition, 1248 pages, 1990. Teacher's Manual available. (Casebook) 1990 Statutory Supplement.

HAMILTON'S THE LAW OF CORPORATIONS IN A NUTSHELL, Third Edition, 518 pages, 1991. Softcover. (Text)

HENN'S TEACHING MATERIALS ON THE LAW OF CORPORATIONS, Second Edition, 1204 pages, 1986. Teacher's Manual available. (Casebook)

Statutory Supplement. *See Selected Corporation and Partnership*

HENN AND ALEXANDER'S HORNBOOK ON LAWS OF CORPORATIONS, Third Edition, Student Edition, 1371 pages, 1983, with 1986 pocket part. (Text)

SELECTED CORPORATION AND PARTNERSHIP STATUTES, RULES AND FORMS. Softcover. Approximately 900 pages, 1991.

SOLOMON, SCHWARTZ AND BAUMAN'S MATERIALS AND PROBLEMS ON CORPORATIONS: LAW AND POLICY, Second Edition, 1391 pages, 1988. Teacher's Manual available. (Casebook) 1990 Supplement.

Statutory Supplement. *See Selected Corporation and Partnership*

Corrections

KRANTZ' THE LAW OF CORRECTIONS AND PRIS-

Corrections—Cont'd

ONERS' RIGHTS IN A NUTSHELL, Third Edition, 407 pages, 1988. Softcover. (Text)

KRANTZ AND BRANHAM'S CASES AND MATERIALS ON THE LAW OF SENTENCING, CORRECTIONS AND PRISONERS' RIGHTS, Fourth Edition, 619 pages, 1991. Teacher's Manual available. (Casebook)

ROBBINS' CASES AND MATERIALS ON POST-CONVICTION REMEDIES, 506 pages, 1982. (Casebook)

Creditors' Rights

BANKRUPTCY CODE, RULES AND OFFICIAL FORMS, LAW SCHOOL EDITION. 909 pages, 1991. Softcover.

EPSTEIN'S DEBTOR-CREDITOR LAW IN A NUTSHELL, Fourth Edition, 401 pages, 1991. Softcover. (Text)

EPSTEIN, LANDERS AND NICKLES' CASES AND MATERIALS ON DEBTORS AND CREDITORS, Third Edition, 1059 pages, 1987. Teacher's Manual available. (Casebook)

LOPUCKI'S PLAYER'S MANUAL FOR THE DEBTOR-CREDITOR GAME, 123 pages, 1985. Softcover. (Coursebook)

NICKLES AND EPSTEIN'S BLACK LETTER ON CREDITORS' RIGHTS AND BANKRUPTCY, 576 pages, 1989. (Review)

RIESENFELD'S CASES AND MATERIALS ON CREDITORS' REMEDIES AND DEBTORS' PROTECTION, Fourth Edition, 914 pages, 1987. (Casebook) 1990 Supplement.

WHITE'S CASES AND MATERIALS ON BANKRUPTCY AND CREDITORS' RIGHTS, 812 pages, 1985. Teacher's Manual available. (Casebook) 1987 Supplement.

Criminal Law and Criminal Procedure—see also Corrections, Juvenile Justice

ABRAMS' FEDERAL CRIMINAL LAW AND ITS ENFORCEMENT, 866 pages, 1986. (Casebook) 1988 Supplement.

AMERICAN CRIMINAL JUSTICE PROCESS: SELECTED RULES, STATUTES AND GUIDELINES. 723 pages, 1989. Softcover.

CARLSON'S ADJUDICATION OF CRIMINAL JUSTICE: PROBLEMS AND REFERENCES, 130 pages, 1986. Softcover. (Casebook)

DIX AND SHARLOT'S CASES AND MATERIALS ON CRIMINAL LAW, Third Edition, 846 pages, 1987. (Casebook)

GRANO'S PROBLEMS IN CRIMINAL PROCEDURE, Second Edition, 176 pages, 1981. Teacher's Manual available. Softcover. (Coursebook)

HEYMANN AND KENETY'S THE MURDER TRIAL OF WILBUR JACKSON: A HOMICIDE IN THE FAMILY, Second Edition, 347 pages, 1985. (Coursebook)

ISRAEL, KAMISAR AND LAFAVE'S CRIMINAL PROCEDURE AND THE CONSTITUTION: LEADING SUPREME COURT CASES AND INTRODUCTORY TEXT. Approximately 745 pages, 1991 Edition. Softcover. (Casebook)

ISRAEL AND LAFAVE'S CRIMINAL PROCEDURE—CONSTITUTIONAL LIMITATIONS IN A NUTSHELL, Fourth Edition, 461 pages, 1988. Softcover. (Text)

JOHNSON'S CASES, MATERIALS AND TEXT ON CRIMINAL LAW, Fourth Edition, 759 pages, 1990. Teacher's Manual available. (Casebook)

JOHNSON'S CASES AND MATERIALS ON CRIMINAL PROCEDURE, 859 pages, 1988. (Casebook) 1991 Supplement.

KAMISAR, LAFAVE AND ISRAEL'S MODERN CRIMINAL PROCEDURE: CASES, COMMENTS AND QUESTIONS, Seventh Edition, 1593 pages, 1990. (Casebook) 1991 Supplement.

KAMISAR, LAFAVE AND ISRAEL'S BASIC CRIMINAL PROCEDURE: CASES, COMMENTS AND QUESTIONS, Seventh Edition, 792 pages, 1990. Softcover reprint from Kamisar, et al., Modern Criminal Procedure: Cases, Comments and Questions, Seventh Edition. (Casebook) 1991 Supplement.

LAFAVE'S MODERN CRIMINAL LAW: CASES, COMMENTS AND QUESTIONS, Second Edition, 903 pages, 1988. (Casebook)

LAFAVE AND ISRAEL'S HORNBOOK ON CRIMINAL PROCEDURE, Second Edition, Student Edition, approximately 1200 pages, December, 1991 Pub. (Text)

LAFAVE AND SCOTT'S HORNBOOK ON CRIMINAL LAW, Second Edition, 918 pages, 1986. (Text)

LOEWY'S CRIMINAL LAW IN A NUTSHELL, Sec-

Criminal Law and Criminal Procedure—Cont'd

ond Edition, 321 pages, 1987. Softcover. (Text)

LOW'S BLACK LETTER ON CRIMINAL LAW, Revised First Edition, 443 pages, 1990. Softcover. (Review)

SALTZBURG'S CASES AND COMMENTARY ON AMERICAN CRIMINAL PROCEDURE, Third Edition, 1302 pages, 1988. Teacher's Manual available. (Casebook) 1991 Supplement.

VORENBERG'S CASES ON CRIMINAL LAW AND PROCEDURE, Second Edition, 1088 pages, 1981. Teacher's Manual available. (Casebook) 1990 Supplement.

Domestic Relations

CLARK'S HORNBOOK ON DOMESTIC RELATIONS, Second Edition, Student Edition, 1050 pages, 1988. (Text)

CLARK AND GLOWINSKY'S CASES AND PROBLEMS ON DOMESTIC RELATIONS, Fourth Edition. 1150 pages, 1990. Teacher's Manual available. (Casebook)

KRAUSE'S BLACK LETTER ON FAMILY LAW, 314 pages, 1988. Softcover. (Review)

KRAUSE'S CASES, COMMENTS AND QUESTIONS ON FAMILY LAW, Third Edition, 1433 pages, 1990. (Casebook)

KRAUSE'S FAMILY LAW IN A NUTSHELL, Second Edition, 444 pages, 1986. Softcover. (Text)

KRAUSKOPF'S CASES ON PROPERTY DIVISION AT MARRIAGE DISSOLUTION, 250 pages, 1984. Softcover. (Casebook)

Economics, Law and—see also Antitrust, Regulated Industries

GOETZ' CASES AND MATERIALS ON LAW AND ECONOMICS, 547 pages, 1984. (Casebook)

MALLOY'S LAW AND ECONOMICS: A COMPARATIVE APPROACH TO THEORY AND PRACTICE, 166 pages, 1990. Softcover. (Text)

Education Law

ALEXANDER AND ALEXANDER'S THE LAW OF SCHOOLS, STUDENTS AND TEACHERS IN A NUTSHELL, 409 pages, 1984. Softcover. (Text)

YUDOF, KIRP AND LEVIN'S EDUCATIONAL POLICY AND THE LAW, Third Edition, approximately 1000 pages, August, 1991 Pub. (Casebook)

Employment Discrimination—see also Gender Discrimination

ESTREICHER AND HARPER'S CASES AND MATERIALS ON THE LAW GOVERNING THE EMPLOYMENT RELATIONSHIP, 962 pages, 1990. Teacher's Manual available. (Casebook) Statutory Supplement. 1991 Supplement.

JONES, MURPHY AND BELTON'S CASES AND MATERIALS ON DISCRIMINATION IN EMPLOYMENT, (The Labor Law Group). Fifth Edition, 1116 pages, 1987. (Casebook) 1990 Supplement.

PLAYER'S FEDERAL LAW OF EMPLOYMENT DISCRIMINATION IN A NUTSHELL, Second Edition, 402 pages, 1981. Softcover. (Text)

PLAYER'S HORNBOOK ON EMPLOYMENT DISCRIMINATION LAW, Student Edition, 708 pages, 1988. (Text)

PLAYER, SHOBEN AND LIEBERWITZ' CASES AND MATERIALS ON EMPLOYMENT DISCRIMINATION LAW, 827 pages, 1990. Teacher's Manual available. (Casebook)

Energy and Natural Resources Law—see also Oil and Gas

LAITOS' CASES AND MATERIALS ON NATURAL RESOURCES LAW, 938 pages, 1985. Teacher's Manual available. (Casebook)

SELECTED ENVIRONMENTAL LAW STATUTES—EDUCATIONAL EDITION. Softcover. Approximately 1075 pages, 1991.

Environmental Law—see also Energy and Natural Resources Law; Sea, Law of

BONINE AND MCGARITY'S THE LAW OF ENVIRONMENTAL PROTECTION: CASES—LEGISLATION—POLICIES, 1076 pages, 1984. Teacher's Manual available. (Casebook)

FINDLEY AND FARBER'S CASES AND MATERIALS ON ENVIRONMENTAL LAW, Third Edition, approximately 750 pages, 1991. (Casebook)

FINDLEY AND FARBER'S ENVIRONMENTAL LAW IN A NUTSHELL, Second Edition, 367 pages, 1988. Softcover. (Text)

RODGERS' HORNBOOK ON ENVIRONMENTAL LAW, 956 pages, 1977, with 1984 pocket part. (Text)

Environmental Law—Cont'd

SELECTED ENVIRONMENTAL LAW STATUTES—EDUCATIONAL EDITION. Softcover. Approximately 1075 pages, 1991.

Equity—see Remedies

Estate Planning—see also Trusts and Estates; Taxation—Estate and Gift

LYNN'S AN INTRODUCTION TO ESTATE PLANNING IN A NUTSHELL, Third Edition, 370 pages, 1983. Softcover. (Text)

Evidence

BROUN AND BLAKEY'S BLACK LETTER ON EVIDENCE, 269 pages, 1984. Softcover. (Review)

BROUN, MEISENHOLDER, STRONG AND MOSTELLER'S PROBLEMS IN EVIDENCE, Third Edition, 238 pages, 1988. Teacher's Manual available. Softcover. (Coursebook)

CLEARY, STRONG, BROUN AND MOSTELLER'S CASES AND MATERIALS ON EVIDENCE, Fourth Edition, 1060 pages, 1988. (Casebook)

FEDERAL RULES OF EVIDENCE FOR UNITED STATES COURTS AND MAGISTRATES. Softcover. 381 pages, 1990.

FRIEDMAN'S THE ELEMENTS OF EVIDENCE, Approximately 310 pages, 1991. Teacher's Manual available. (Coursebook)

GRAHAM'S FEDERAL RULES OF EVIDENCE IN A NUTSHELL, Second Edition, 473 pages, 1987. Softcover. (Text)

LEMPERT AND SALTZBURG'S A MODERN APPROACH TO EVIDENCE: TEXT, PROBLEMS, TRANSCRIPTS AND CASES, Second Edition, 1232 pages, 1983. Teacher's Manual available. (Casebook)

LILLY'S AN INTRODUCTION TO THE LAW OF EVIDENCE, Second Edition, 585 pages, 1987. (Text)

MCCORMICK, SUTTON AND WELLBORN'S CASES AND MATERIALS ON EVIDENCE, Sixth Edition, 1067 pages, 1987. (Casebook)

MCCORMICK'S HORNBOOK ON EVIDENCE, Fourth Edition, Student Edition, approximately 1200 pages, January 1992 Pub. (Text)

ROTHSTEIN'S EVIDENCE IN A NUTSHELL: STATE AND FEDERAL RULES, Second Edition, 514 pages, 1981. Softcover. (Text)

Federal Jurisdiction and Procedure

CURRIE'S CASES AND MATERIALS ON FEDERAL COURTS, Fourth Edition, 783 pages, 1990. (Casebook)

CURRIE'S FEDERAL JURISDICTION IN A NUTSHELL, Third Edition, 242 pages, 1990. Softcover. (Text)

FEDERAL RULES OF CIVIL PROCEDURE—EDUCATIONAL EDITION. Softcover. Approximately 700 pages, 1991.

REDISH'S BLACK LETTER ON FEDERAL JURISDICTION, Second Edition, 234 pages, 1991. Softcover. (Review)

REDISH'S CASES, COMMENTS AND QUESTIONS ON FEDERAL COURTS, Second Edition, 1122 pages, 1989. (Casebook) 1990 Supplement.

VETRI AND MERRILL'S FEDERAL COURTS PROBLEMS AND MATERIALS, Second Edition, 232 pages, 1984. Softcover. (Coursebook)

WRIGHT'S HORNBOOK ON FEDERAL COURTS, Fourth Edition, Student Edition, 870 pages, 1983. (Text)

First Amendment

SHIFFRIN AND CHOPER'S FIRST AMENDMENT, CASES—COMMENTS—QUESTIONS, Approximately 760 pages, 1991. Softcover. (Casebook) 1991 Supplement.

Foreign Relations and National Security Law

FRANCK AND GLENNON'S FOREIGN RELATIONS AND NATIONAL SECURITY LAW, 941 pages, 1987. (Casebook)

Future Interests—see Trusts and Estates

Gender Discrimination—see also Employment Discrimination

KAY'S TEXT, CASES AND MATERIALS ON SEX-BASED DISCRIMINATION, Third Edition, 1001 pages, 1988. (Casebook) 1990 Supplement.

THOMAS' SEX DISCRIMINATION IN A NUTSHELL, Second Edition, approximately 400 pages, 1991. Softcover. (Text)

Health Law—see Medicine, Law and

Human Rights—see International Law

Immigration Law

ALEINIKOFF AND MARTIN'S IMMIGRATION: PROCESS AND POLICY, Second Edition, approximately 1090 pages, 1991. (Casebook)

Statutory Supplement. *See Immigration and Nationality Laws*

IMMIGRATION AND NATIONALITY LAWS OF THE UNITED STATES: SELECTED STATUTES, REGULATIONS AND FORMS. Softcover. Approximately 450 pages, 1991.

WEISSBRODT'S IMMIGRATION LAW AND PROCEDURE IN A NUTSHELL, Second Edition, 438 pages, 1989, Softcover. (Text)

Indian Law—see American Indian Law

Insurance Law

DEVINE AND TERRY'S PROBLEMS IN INSURANCE LAW, 240 pages, 1989. Softcover. Teacher's Manual available. (Coursebook)

DOBBYN'S INSURANCE LAW IN A NUTSHELL, Second Edition, 316 pages, 1989. Softcover. (Text)

KEETON'S CASES ON BASIC INSURANCE LAW, Second Edition, 1086 pages, 1977. Teacher's Manual available. (Casebook)

KEETON'S COMPUTER-AIDED AND WORKBOOK EXERCISES ON INSURANCE LAW, 255 pages, 1990. Softcover. (Coursebook)

KEETON AND WIDISS' INSURANCE LAW, Student Edition, 1359 pages, 1988. (Text)

WIDISS AND KEETON'S COURSE SUPPLEMENT TO KEETON AND WIDISS' INSURANCE LAW, 502 pages, 1988. Softcover. Teacher's Manual available. (Casebook)

WIDISS' INSURANCE: MATERIALS ON FUNDAMENTAL PRINCIPLES, LEGAL DOCTRINES AND REGULATORY ACTS, 1186 pages, 1989. Teacher's Manual available. (Casebook)

YORK AND WHELAN'S CASES, MATERIALS AND PROBLEMS ON GENERAL PRACTICE INSURANCE LAW, Second Edition, 787 pages, 1988. Teacher's Manual available. (Casebook)

International Law—see also Sea, Law of

BUERGENTHAL'S INTERNATIONAL HUMAN RIGHTS IN A NUTSHELL, 283 pages, 1988. Softcover. (Text)

BUERGENTHAL AND MAIER'S PUBLIC INTERNATIONAL LAW IN A NUTSHELL, Second Edition, 275 pages, 1990. Softcover. (Text)

FOLSOM, GORDON AND SPANOGLE'S INTERNATIONAL BUSINESS TRANSACTIONS—A PROBLEM-ORIENTED COURSEBOOK, Second Edition, approximately 1240 pages, 1991. Teacher's Manual available. (Casebook) 1991 Documents Supplement.

FOLSOM, GORDON AND SPANOGLE'S INTERNATIONAL BUSINESS TRANSACTIONS IN A NUTSHELL, Third Edition, 509 pages, 1988. Softcover. (Text)

HENKIN, PUGH, SCHACHTER AND SMIT'S CASES AND MATERIALS ON INTERNATIONAL LAW, Second Edition, 1517 pages, 1987. (Casebook) Documents Supplement.

JACKSON AND DAVEY'S CASES, MATERIALS AND TEXT ON LEGAL PROBLEMS OF INTERNATIONAL ECONOMIC RELATIONS, Second Edition, 1269 pages, 1986. (Casebook) 1989 Documents Supplement.

KIRGIS' INTERNATIONAL ORGANIZATIONS IN THEIR LEGAL SETTING, 1016 pages, 1977. Teacher's Manual available. (Casebook) 1981 Supplement.

WESTON, FALK AND D'AMATO'S INTERNATIONAL LAW AND WORLD ORDER—A PROBLEM-ORIENTED COURSEBOOK, Second Edition, 1335 pages, 1990. Teacher's Manual available. (Casebook) Documents Supplement.

Interviewing and Counseling

BINDER AND PRICE'S LEGAL INTERVIEWING AND COUNSELING, 232 pages, 1977. Softcover. Teacher's Manual available. (Coursebook)

BINDER, BERGMAN AND PRICE'S LAWYERS AS COUNSELORS: A CLIENT-CENTERED APPROACH, 427 pages, 1991. Softcover. (Coursebook)

SHAFFER AND ELKINS' LEGAL INTERVIEWING AND COUNSELING IN A NUTSHELL, Second Edition, 487 pages, 1987. Softcover. (Text)

Introduction to Law—see Legal Method and Legal System

Introduction to Law Study

HEGLAND'S INTRODUCTION TO THE STUDY AND PRACTICE OF LAW IN A NUTSHELL, 418 pages,

Introduction to Law Study—Cont'd

1983. Softcover. (Text)

KINYON'S INTRODUCTION TO LAW STUDY AND LAW EXAMINATIONS IN A NUTSHELL, 389 pages, 1971. Softcover. (Text)

Judicial Process—see Legal Method and Legal System

Jurisprudence

CHRISTIE'S JURISPRUDENCE—TEXT AND READINGS ON THE PHILOSOPHY OF LAW, 1056 pages, 1973. (Casebook)

Juvenile Justice

FOX'S JUVENILE COURTS IN A NUTSHELL, Third Edition, 291 pages, 1984. Softcover. (Text)

Labor and Employment Law—see also Employment Discrimination, Workers' Compensation

FINKIN, GOLDMAN AND SUMMERS' LEGAL PROTECTION OF INDIVIDUAL EMPLOYEES, (The Labor Law Group). 1164 pages, 1989. (Casebook)

GORMAN'S BASIC TEXT ON LABOR LAW—UNIONIZATION AND COLLECTIVE BARGAINING, 914 pages, 1976. (Text)

LESLIE'S LABOR LAW IN A NUTSHELL, Second Edition, 397 pages, 1986. Softcover. (Text)

NOLAN'S LABOR ARBITRATION LAW AND PRACTICE IN A NUTSHELL, 358 pages, 1979. Softcover. (Text)

OBERER, HANSLOWE, ANDERSEN AND HEINSZ' CASES AND MATERIALS ON LABOR LAW—COLLECTIVE BARGAINING IN A FREE SOCIETY, Third Edition, 1163 pages, 1986. Teacher's Manual available. (Casebook) Statutory Supplement.

RABIN, SILVERSTEIN AND SCHATZKI'S LABOR AND EMPLOYMENT LAW: PROBLEMS, CASES AND MATERIALS IN THE LAW OF WORK, (The Labor Law Group). 1014 pages, 1988. Teacher's Manual available. (Casebook) 1988 Statutory Supplement.

Land Finance—Property Security—see Real Estate Transactions

Land Use

CALLIES AND FREILICH'S CASES AND MATERIALS ON LAND USE, 1233 pages, 1986. (Casebook) 1991 Supplement.

HAGMAN AND JUERGENSMEYER'S HORNBOOK ON URBAN PLANNING AND LAND DEVELOPMENT CONTROL LAW, Second Edition, Student Edition, 680 pages, 1986. (Text)

WRIGHT AND GITELMAN'S CASES AND MATERIALS ON LAND USE, Fourth Edition, 1255 pages, 1991. Teacher's Manual available. (Casebook)

WRIGHT AND WRIGHT'S LAND USE IN A NUTSHELL, Second Edition, 356 pages, 1985. Softcover. (Text)

Legal History—see also Legal Method and Legal System

PRESSER AND ZAINALDIN'S CASES AND MATERIALS ON LAW AND JURISPRUDENCE IN AMERICAN HISTORY, Second Edition, 1092 pages, 1989. Teacher's Manual available. (Casebook)

Legal Method and Legal System—see also Legal Research, Legal Writing

ALDISERT'S READINGS, MATERIALS AND CASES IN THE JUDICIAL PROCESS, 948 pages, 1976. (Casebook)

BERCH AND BERCH'S INTRODUCTION TO LEGAL METHOD AND PROCESS, 550 pages, 1985. Teacher's Manual available. (Casebook)

BODENHEIMER, OAKLEY AND LOVE'S READINGS AND CASES ON AN INTRODUCTION TO THE ANGLO-AMERICAN LEGAL SYSTEM, Second Edition, 166 pages, 1988. Softcover. (Casebook)

DAVIES AND LAWRY'S INSTITUTIONS AND METHODS OF THE LAW—INTRODUCTORY TEACHING MATERIALS, 547 pages, 1982. Teacher's Manual available. (Casebook)

DVORKIN, HIMMELSTEIN AND LESNICK'S BECOMING A LAWYER: A HUMANISTIC PERSPECTIVE ON LEGAL EDUCATION AND PROFESSIONALISM, 211 pages, 1981. Softcover. (Text)

KEETON'S JUDGING, 842 pages, 1990. Softcover. (Coursebook)

KELSO AND KELSO'S STUDYING LAW: AN INTRODUCTION, 587 pages, 1984. (Coursebook)

KEMPIN'S HISTORICAL INTRODUCTION TO AN-

Legal Method and Legal System—Cont'd

GLO-AMERICAN LAW IN A NUTSHELL, Third Edition, 323 pages, 1990. Softcover. (Text)

MEADOR'S AMERICAN COURTS, 113 pages, 1991. Softcover. (Text)

REYNOLDS' JUDICIAL PROCESS IN A NUTSHELL, Second Edition, approximately 310 pages, 1991. Softcover. (Text)

Legal Research

COHEN'S LEGAL RESEARCH IN A NUTSHELL, Fourth Edition, 452 pages, 1985. Softcover. (Text)

COHEN, BERRING AND OLSON'S HOW TO FIND THE LAW, Ninth Edition, 716 pages, 1989. (Text)

COHEN, BERRING AND OLSON'S FINDING THE LAW, 570 pages, 1989. Softcover reprint from Cohen, Berring and Olson's How to Find the Law, Ninth Edition. (Coursebook)

Legal Research Exercises, 3rd Ed., for use with Cohen, Berring and Olson, 229 pages, 1989. Teacher's Manual available.

ROMBAUER'S LEGAL PROBLEM SOLVING—ANALYSIS, RESEARCH AND WRITING, Fifth Edition, approximately 520 pages, 1991. Softcover. Teacher's Manual with problems available. (Coursebook)

STATSKY'S LEGAL RESEARCH AND WRITING, Third Edition, 257 pages, 1986. Softcover. (Coursebook)

TEPLY'S LEGAL RESEARCH AND CITATION, Third Edition, 472 pages, 1989. Softcover. (Coursebook)

Student Library Exercises, 3rd ed., 391 pages, 1989. Answer Key available.

Legal Writing and Drafting

CHILD'S DRAFTING LEGAL DOCUMENTS: MATERIALS AND PROBLEMS, 286 pages, 1988. Softcover. Teacher's Manual available. (Coursebook)

DICKERSON'S MATERIALS ON LEGAL DRAFTING, 425 pages, 1981. Teacher's Manual available. (Coursebook)

FELSENFELD AND SIEGEL'S WRITING CONTRACTS IN PLAIN ENGLISH, 290 pages, 1981. Softcover. (Text)

GOPEN'S WRITING FROM A LEGAL PERSPECTIVE, 225 pages, 1981. (Text)

MARTINEAU'S DRAFTING LEGISLATION AND RULES IN PLAIN ENGLISH, 155 pages, 1991. Softcover. Teacher's Manual available. (Text)

MELLINKOFF'S LEGAL WRITING—SENSE AND NONSENSE, 242 pages, 1982. Softcover. Teacher's Manual available. (Text)

PRATT'S LEGAL WRITING: A SYSTEMATIC APPROACH, 468 pages, 1990. Teacher's Manual available. (Coursebook)

RAY AND COX'S BEYOND THE BASICS: A TEXT FOR ADVANCED LEGAL WRITING, Approximately 425 pages, 1991. Softcover. Teacher's Manual available. (Text)

RAY AND RAMSFIELD'S LEGAL WRITING: GETTING IT RIGHT AND GETTING IT WRITTEN, 250 pages, 1987. Softcover. (Text)

SQUIRES AND ROMBAUER'S LEGAL WRITING IN A NUTSHELL, 294 pages, 1982. Softcover. (Text)

STATSKY AND WERNET'S CASE ANALYSIS AND FUNDAMENTALS OF LEGAL WRITING, Third Edition, 424 pages, 1989. Teacher's Manual available. (Text)

TEPLY'S LEGAL WRITING, ANALYSIS AND ORAL ARGUMENT, 576 pages, 1990. Softcover. Teacher's Manual available. (Coursebook)

WEIHOFEN'S LEGAL WRITING STYLE, Second Edition, 332 pages, 1980. (Text)

Legislation—see also Legal Writing and Drafting

DAVIES' LEGISLATIVE LAW AND PROCESS IN A NUTSHELL, Second Edition, 346 pages, 1986. Softcover. (Text)

ESKRIDGE AND FRICKEY'S CASES AND MATERIALS ON LEGISLATION: STATUTES AND THE CREATION OF PUBLIC POLICY, 937 pages, 1988. Teacher's Manual available. (Casebook) 1990 Supplement.

NUTTING AND DICKERSON'S CASES AND MATERIALS ON LEGISLATION, Fifth Edition, 744 pages, 1978. (Casebook)

STATSKY'S LEGISLATIVE ANALYSIS AND DRAFTING, Second Edition, 217 pages, 1984.

Legislation—see also Legal Writing and Drafting—Cont'd

Teacher's Manual available. (Text)

Local Government

FRUG'S CASES AND MATERIALS ON LOCAL GOVERNMENT LAW, 1005 pages, 1988. (Casebook)

MCCARTHY'S LOCAL GOVERNMENT LAW IN A NUTSHELL, Third Edition, 435 pages, 1990. Softcover. (Text)

REYNOLDS' HORNBOOK ON LOCAL GOVERNMENT LAW, 860 pages, 1982, with 1990 pocket part. (Text)

VALENTE AND MCCARTHY'S CASES AND MATERIALS ON LOCAL GOVERNMENT LAW, Fourth Edition, approximately 1000 pages, December, 1991 Pub. Teacher's Manual available. (Casebook)

Mass Communication Law

GILLMOR, BARRON, SIMON AND TERRY'S CASES AND COMMENT ON MASS COMMUNICATION LAW, Fifth Edition, 947 pages, 1990. (Casebook)

GINSBURG, BOTEIN AND DIRECTOR'S REGULATION OF THE ELECTRONIC MASS MEDIA: LAW AND POLICY FOR RADIO, TELEVISION, CABLE AND THE NEW VIDEO TECHNOLOGIES, Second Edition, 657 pages, 1991. (Casebook) Statutory Supplement.

ZUCKMAN, GAYNES, CARTER AND DEE'S MASS COMMUNICATIONS LAW IN A NUTSHELL, Third Edition, 538 pages, 1988. Softcover. (Text)

Medicine, Law and

FISCINA, BOUMIL, SHARPE AND HEAD'S MEDICAL LIABILITY, 487 pages, 1991. Teacher's Manual available. (Casebook)

FURROW, JOHNSON, JOST AND SCHWARTZ' HEALTH LAW: CASES, MATERIALS AND PROBLEMS, Second Edition, approximately 1225 pages, 1991. Teacher's Manual available. (Casebook)

FURROW, JOHNSON, JOST AND SCHWARTZ' BIOETHICS: HEALTH CARE LAW AND ETHICS, Reprint from Furrow et al., Health Law, Second Edition. Softcover. Teacher's Manual available. (Casebook)

FURROW, JOHNSON, JOST AND SCHWARTZ' THE LAW OF HEALTH CARE ORGANIZATION AND FINANCE,Reprint from Furrow et al., Health Law, Second Edition. Softcover. Teacher's Manual available.

FURROW, JOHNSON, JOST AND SCHWARTZ' LIABILITY AND QUALITY ISSUES IN HEALTH CARE, Reprint from Furrow et al., Health Law, Second Edition. Softcover. Teacher's Manual available. (Casebook)

HALL AND ELLMAN'S HEALTH CARE LAW AND ETHICS IN A NUTSHELL, 401 pages, 1990. Softcover (Text)

JARVIS, CLOSEN, HERMANN AND LEONARD'S AIDS LAW IN A NUTSHELL, 349 pages, 1991. Softcover. (Text)

KING'S THE LAW OF MEDICAL MALPRACTICE IN A NUTSHELL, Second Edition, 342 pages, 1986. Softcover. (Text)

SHAPIRO AND SPECE'S CASES, MATERIALS AND PROBLEMS ON BIOETHICS AND LAW, 892 pages, 1981. (Casebook) 1991 Supplement.

Military Law

SHANOR AND TERRELL'S MILITARY LAW IN A NUTSHELL, 378 pages, 1980. Softcover. (Text)

Mortgages—see Real Estate Transactions

Natural Resources Law—see Energy and Natural Resources Law, Environmental Law

Negotiation

GIFFORD'S LEGAL NEGOTIATION: THEORY AND APPLICATIONS, 225 pages, 1989. Softcover. (Text)

WILLIAMS' LEGAL NEGOTIATION AND SETTLEMENT, 207 pages, 1983. Softcover. Teacher's Manual available. (Coursebook)

Office Practice—see also Computers and Law, Interviewing and Counseling, Negotiation

HEGLAND'S TRIAL AND PRACTICE SKILLS IN A NUTSHELL, 346 pages, 1978. Softcover (Text)

MUNNEKE'S LAW PRACTICE MANAGEMENT: COURSE MATERIALS, Approximately 630 pages, 1991. (Casebook)

STRONG AND CLARK'S LAW OFFICE MANAGEMENT, 424 pages, 1974. (Casebook)

Oil and Gas—see also Energy and Natural Resources Law

HEMINGWAY'S HORNBOOK ON THE LAW OF OIL AND GAS, Third Edition, Student Edition, approximately 700 pages, Aug., 1991 Pub. (Text)

KUNTZ, LOWE, ANDERSON AND SMITH'S CASES AND MATERIALS ON OIL AND GAS LAW, 857 pages, 1986. Teacher's Manual available. (Casebook) Forms Manual. Revised.

LOWE'S OIL AND GAS LAW IN A NUTSHELL, Second Edition, 465 pages, 1988. Softcover. (Text)

Partnership—see Agency—Partnership

Patent and Copyright Law

CHOATE, FRANCIS AND COLLINS' CASES AND MATERIALS ON PATENT LAW, INCLUDING TRADE SECRETS, COPYRIGHTS, TRADEMARKS, Third Edition, 1009 pages, 1987. (Casebook)

MILLER AND DAVIS' INTELLECTUAL PROPERTY—PATENTS, TRADEMARKS AND COPYRIGHT IN A NUTSHELL, Second Edition, 437 pages, 1990. Softcover. (Text)

NIMMER, MARCUS, MYERS AND NIMMER'S CASES AND MATERIALS ON COPYRIGHT AND OTHER ASPECTS OF ENTERTAINMENT LITIGATION—INCLUDING UNFAIR COMPETITION, DEFAMATION, PRIVACY, ILLUSTRATED, Fourth Edition, approximately 1175 pages, 1991. (Casebook) Statutory Supplement. See *Selected Intellectual Property*

SELECTED INTELLECTUAL PROPERTY AND UNFAIR COMPETITION STATUTES, REGULATIONS AND TREATIES. Softcover.

Products Liability

FISCHER AND POWERS' CASES AND MATERIALS ON PRODUCTS LIABILITY, 685 pages, 1988. Teacher's Manual available. (Casebook)

NOEL AND PHILLIPS' CASES ON PRODUCTS LIABILITY, Second Edition, 821 pages, 1982. (Casebook)

PHILLIPS' PRODUCTS LIABILITY IN A NUTSHELL, Third Edition, 307 pages, 1988. Softcover. (Text)

Professional Responsibility

ARONSON, DEVINE AND FISCH'S PROBLEMS, CASES AND MATERIALS IN PROFESSIONAL RESPONSIBILITY, 745 pages, 1985. Teacher's Manual available. (Casebook)

ARONSON AND WECKSTEIN'S PROFESSIONAL RESPONSIBILITY IN A NUTSHELL, Second Edition, approximately 500 pages, 1991. Softcover. (Text)

MELLINKOFF'S THE CONSCIENCE OF A LAWYER, 304 pages, 1973. (Text)

PIRSIG AND KIRWIN'S CASES AND MATERIALS ON PROFESSIONAL RESPONSIBILITY, Fourth Edition, 603 pages, 1984. Teacher's Manual available. (Casebook)

ROTUNDA'S BLACK LETTER ON PROFESSIONAL RESPONSIBILITY, Second Edition, 414 pages, 1988. Softcover. (Review)

SCHWARTZ AND WYDICK'S PROBLEMS IN LEGAL ETHICS, Second Edition, 341 pages, 1988. (Coursebook)

SELECTED STATUTES, RULES AND STANDARDS ON THE LEGAL PROFESSION. Softcover. Approximately 720 pages, 1991.

SMITH AND MALLEN'S PREVENTING LEGAL MALPRACTICE, 264 pages, 1989. Reprint from Mallen and Smith's Legal Malpractice, Third Edition. (Text)

SUTTON AND DZIENKOWSKI'S CASES AND MATERIALS ON PROFESSIONAL RESPONSIBILITY FOR LAWYERS, 839 pages, 1989. Teacher's Manual available. (Casebook)

WOLFRAM'S HORNBOOK ON MODERN LEGAL ETHICS, Student Edition, 1120 pages, 1986. (Text)

Property—see also Real Estate Transactions, Land Use, Trusts and Estates

BERNHARDT'S BLACK LETTER ON PROPERTY, Second Edition, approximately 375 pages, 1991. Softcover. (Review)

BERNHARDT'S REAL PROPERTY IN A NUTSHELL, Second Edition, 448 pages, 1981. Softcover. (Text)

BOYER, HOVENKAMP AND KURTZ' THE LAW OF PROPERTY, AN INTRODUCTORY SURVEY, Fourth Edition, approximately 660 pages, 1991. (Text)

BROWDER, CUNNINGHAM, NELSON, STOEBUCK AND WHITMAN'S CASES ON BASIC PROPERTY LAW, Fifth Edition, 1386 pages, 1989. Teacher's Manual available. (Casebook)

Property—Cont'd

BRUCE, ELY AND BOSTICK'S CASES AND MATERIALS ON MODERN PROPERTY LAW, Second Edition, 953 pages, 1989. Teacher's Manual available. (Casebook)

BURKE'S PERSONAL PROPERTY IN A NUTSHELL, 322 pages, 1983. Softcover. (Text)

CUNNINGHAM, STOEBUCK AND WHITMAN'S HORNBOOK ON THE LAW OF PROPERTY, Student Edition, 916 pages, 1984, with 1987 pocket part. (Text)

DONAHUE, KAUPER AND MARTIN'S CASES ON PROPERTY, Second Edition, 1362 pages, 1983. Teacher's Manual available. (Casebook)

HILL'S LANDLORD AND TENANT LAW IN A NUTSHELL, Second Edition, 311 pages, 1986. Softcover. (Text)

KURTZ AND HOVENKAMP'S CASES AND MATERIALS ON AMERICAN PROPERTY LAW, 1296 pages, 1987. Teacher's Manual available. (Casebook) 1991 Supplement.

MOYNIHAN'S INTRODUCTION TO REAL PROPERTY, Second Edition, 239 pages, 1988. (Text)

Psychiatry, Law and

REISNER AND SLOBOGIN'S LAW AND THE MENTAL HEALTH SYSTEM, CIVIL AND CRIMINAL ASPECTS, Second Edition, 1117 pages, 1990. (Casebook)

Real Estate Transactions

BRUCE'S REAL ESTATE FINANCE IN A NUTSHELL, Third Edition, approximately 270 pages, 1991. Softcover. (Text)

MAXWELL, RIESENFELD, HETLAND AND WARREN'S CASES ON CALIFORNIA SECURITY TRANSACTIONS IN LAND, Fourth Edition, approximately 750 pages, October, 1991 Pub. (Casebook)

NELSON AND WHITMAN'S BLACK LETTER ON LAND TRANSACTIONS AND FINANCE, Second Edition, 466 pages, 1988. Softcover. (Review)

NELSON AND WHITMAN'S CASES ON REAL ESTATE TRANSFER, FINANCE AND DEVELOPMENT, Third Edition, 1184 pages, 1987. (Casebook)

NELSON AND WHITMAN'S HORNBOOK ON REAL ESTATE FINANCE LAW, Second Edition, 941 pages, 1985 with 1989 pocket part. (Text)

Regulated Industries—see also Mass Communication Law, Banking Law

GELLHORN AND PIERCE'S REGULATED INDUSTRIES IN A NUTSHELL, Second Edition, 389 pages, 1987. Softcover. (Text)

MORGAN, HARRISON AND VERKUIL'S CASES AND MATERIALS ON ECONOMIC REGULATION OF BUSINESS, Second Edition, 666 pages, 1985. (Casebook)

Remedies

DOBBS' HORNBOOK ON REMEDIES, 1067 pages, 1973. (Text)

DOBBS' PROBLEMS IN REMEDIES. 137 pages, 1974. Teacher's Manual available. Softcover. (Coursebook)

DOBBYN'S INJUNCTIONS IN A NUTSHELL, 264 pages, 1974. Softcover. (Text)

FRIEDMAN'S CONTRACT REMEDIES IN A NUTSHELL, 323 pages, 1981. Softcover. (Text)

LEAVELL, LOVE AND NELSON'S CASES AND MATERIALS ON EQUITABLE REMEDIES, RESTITUTION AND DAMAGES, Fourth Edition, 1111 pages, 1986. Teacher's Manual available. (Casebook)

O'CONNELL'S REMEDIES IN A NUTSHELL, Second Edition, 320 pages, 1985. Softcover. (Text)

SCHOENBROD, MACBETH, LEVINE AND JUNG'S CASES AND MATERIALS ON REMEDIES: PUBLIC AND PRIVATE, 848 pages, 1990. Teacher's Manual available. (Casebook)

YORK, BAUMAN AND RENDLEMAN'S CASES AND MATERIALS ON REMEDIES, Fifth Edition, approximately 1200 pages, September, 1991 Pub. Teacher's Manual available. (Casebook)

Sea, Law of

SOHN AND GUSTAFSON'S THE LAW OF THE SEA IN A NUTSHELL, 264 pages, 1984. Softcover. (Text)

Securities Regulation

HAZEN'S HORNBOOK ON THE LAW OF SECURITIES REGULATION, Second Edition, Student Edition, 1082 pages, 1990. (Text)

RATNER'S SECURITIES REGULATION IN A NUT-

Securities Regulation—Cont'd

SHELL, Third Edition, 316 pages, 1988. Softcover. (Text)

RATNER AND HAZEN'S SECURITIES REGULATION: CASES AND MATERIALS, Fourth Edition, 1062 pages, 1991. (Casebook) Problems and Sample Documents Supplement.

Statutory Supplement. *See Securities Regulation, Selected Statutes*

SECURITIES REGULATION, SELECTED STATUTES, RULES, AND FORMS. Softcover. 1331 pages, 1991.

Sports Law

SCHUBERT, SMITH AND TRENTADUE'S SPORTS LAW, 395 pages, 1986. (Text)

Tax Practice and Procedure

GARBIS, RUBIN AND MORGAN'S CASES AND MATERIALS ON TAX PROCEDURE AND TAX FRAUD, Third Edition, approximately 700 pages, October, 1991 Pub. Teacher's Manual available. (Casebook)

MORGAN'S TAX PROCEDURE AND TAX FRAUD IN A NUTSHELL, 400 pages, 1990. Softcover. (Text)

Taxation—Corporate

KAHN AND GANN'S CORPORATE TAXATION, Third Edition, 980 pages, 1989. Teacher's Manual available. (Casebook)

SCHWARZ AND LATHROPE'S BLACK LETTER ON CORPORATE AND PARTNERSHIP TAXATION, Approximately 500 pages, September, 1991 Pub. Softcover. (Review)

WEIDENBRUCH AND BURKE'S FEDERAL INCOME TAXATION OF CORPORATIONS AND STOCKHOLDERS IN A NUTSHELL, Third Edition, 309 pages, 1989. Softcover. (Text)

Taxation—Estate & Gift—see also Estate Planning, Trusts and Estates

MCNULTY'S FEDERAL ESTATE AND GIFT TAXATION IN A NUTSHELL, Fourth Edition, 496 pages, 1989. Softcover. (Text)

PENNELL'S CASES AND MATERIALS ON INCOME TAXATION OF TRUSTS, ESTATES, GRANTORS AND BENEFICIARIES, 460 pages, 1987. Teacher's Manual available. (Casebook)

Taxation—Individual

DODGE'S THE LOGIC OF TAX, 343 pages, 1989. Softcover. (Text)

GUNN AND WARD'S CASES, TEXT AND PROBLEMS ON FEDERAL INCOME TAXATION, Second Edition, 835 pages, 1988. Teacher's Manual available. (Casebook) 1991 Supplement.

HUDSON AND LIND'S BLACK LETTER ON FEDERAL INCOME TAXATION, Third Edition, 406 pages, 1990. Softcover. (Review)

KRAGEN AND MCNULTY'S CASES AND MATERIALS ON FEDERAL INCOME TAXATION—INDIVIDUALS, CORPORATIONS, PARTNERSHIPS, Fourth Edition, 1287 pages, 1985. (Casebook)

MCNULTY'S FEDERAL INCOME TAXATION OF INDIVIDUALS IN A NUTSHELL, Fourth Edition, 503 pages, 1988. Softcover. (Text)

POSIN'S HORNBOOK ON FEDERAL INCOME TAXATION, Student Edition, 491 pages, 1983, with 1989 pocket part. (Text)

ROSE AND CHOMMIE'S HORNBOOK ON FEDERAL INCOME TAXATION, Third Edition, 923 pages, 1988, with 1989 pocket part. (Text)

SELECTED FEDERAL TAXATION STATUTES AND REGULATIONS. Softcover. Approximately 1560 pages, 1992.

Taxation—International

DOERNBERG'S INTERNATIONAL TAXATION IN A NUTSHELL, 325 pages, 1989. Softcover. (Text)

KAPLAN'S FEDERAL TAXATION OF INTERNATIONAL TRANSACTIONS: PRINCIPLES, PLANNING AND POLICY, 635 pages, 1988. (Casebook)

Taxation—Partnership

BERGER AND WIEDENBECK'S CASES AND MATERIALS ON PARTNERSHIP TAXATION, 788 pages, 1989. Teacher's Manual available. (Casebook) 1991 Supplement.

BISHOP AND BROOKS' FEDERAL PARTNERSHIP TAXATION: A GUIDE TO THE LEADING CASES, STATUTES, AND REGULATIONS, 545 pages, 1990. Softcover. (Text)

SCHWARZ AND LATHROPE'S BLACK LETTER ON CORPORATE AND PARTNERSHIP TAXATION, Approximately 500 pages, September, 1991 Pub. Softcover. (Review)

Taxation—State & Local

GELFAND AND SALSICH'S STATE AND LOCAL TAXATION AND FINANCE IN A NUTSHELL, 309 pages, 1986. Softcover. (Text)

HELLERSTEIN AND HELLERSTEIN'S CASES AND MATERIALS ON STATE AND LOCAL TAXATION, Fifth Edition, 1071 pages, 1988. (Casebook)

Torts—see also Products Liability

CHRISTIE AND MEEKS' CASES AND MATERIALS ON THE LAW OF TORTS, Second Edition, 1264 pages, 1990. (Casebook)

DOBBS' TORTS AND COMPENSATION—PERSONAL ACCOUNTABILITY AND SOCIAL RESPONSIBILITY FOR INJURY, 955 pages, 1985. Teacher's Manual available. (Casebook) 1990 Supplement.

KEETON, KEETON, SARGENTICH AND STEINER'S CASES AND MATERIALS ON TORT AND ACCIDENT LAW, Second Edition, 1318 pages, 1989. (Casebook)

KIONKA'S BLACK LETTER ON TORTS, 339 pages, 1988. Softcover. (Review)

KIONKA'S TORTS IN A NUTSHELL: INJURIES TO PERSONS AND PROPERTY, 434 pages, 1977. Softcover. (Text)

MALONE'S TORTS IN A NUTSHELL: INJURIES TO FAMILY, SOCIAL AND TRADE RELATIONS, 358 pages, 1979. Softcover. (Text)

PROSSER AND KEETON'S HORNBOOK ON TORTS, Fifth Edition, Student Edition, 1286 pages, 1984 with 1988 pocket part. (Text)

ROBERTSON, POWERS AND ANDERSON'S CASES AND MATERIALS ON TORTS, 932 pages, 1989. Teacher's Manual available. (Casebook)

Trade Regulation—see also Antitrust, Regulated Industries

MCMANIS' UNFAIR TRADE PRACTICES IN A NUTSHELL, Second Edition, 464 pages, 1988. Softcover. (Text)

OPPENHEIM, WESTON, MAGGS AND SCHECHTER'S CASES AND MATERIALS ON UNFAIR TRADE PRACTICES AND CONSUMER PROTECTION, Fourth Edition, 1038 pages, 1983. Teacher's Manual available. (Casebook) 1986 Supplement.

SCHECHTER'S BLACK LETTER ON UNFAIR TRADE PRACTICES, 272 pages, 1986. Softcover. (Review)

Trial and Appellate Advocacy—see also Civil Procedure

APPELLATE ADVOCACY, HANDBOOK OF, Second Edition, 182 pages, 1986. Softcover. (Text)

BERGMAN'S TRIAL ADVOCACY IN A NUTSHELL, Second Edition, 354 pages, 1989. Softcover. (Text)

BINDER AND BERGMAN'S FACT INVESTIGATION: FROM HYPOTHESIS TO PROOF, 354 pages, 1984. Teacher's Manual available. (Coursebook)

CARLSON AND IMWINKELRIED'S DYNAMICS OF TRIAL PRACTICE: PROBLEMS AND MATERIALS, 414 pages, 1989. Teacher's Manual available. (Coursebook) 1990 Supplement.

DESSEM'S PRETRIAL LITIGATION: LAW, POLICY AND PRACTICE, Approximately 615 pages, 1991. Softcover. (Coursebook)

DEVINE'S NON-JURY CASE FILES FOR TRIAL ADVOCACY, 258 pages, 1991. (Coursebook)

GOLDBERG'S THE FIRST TRIAL (WHERE DO I SIT? WHAT DO I SAY?) IN A NUTSHELL, 396 pages, 1982. Softcover. (Text)

HAYDOCK, HERR, AND STEMPEL'S FUNDAMENTALS OF PRE-TRIAL LITIGATION, 768 pages, 1985. Softcover. Teacher's Manual available. (Coursebook)

HAYDOCK AND SONSTENG'S TRIAL: THEORIES, TACTICS, TECHNIQUES, 711 pages, 1991. Softcover. (Text)

HEGLAND'S TRIAL AND PRACTICE SKILLS IN A NUTSHELL, 346 pages, 1978. Softcover. (Text)

HORNSTEIN'S APPELLATE ADVOCACY IN A NUTSHELL, 325 pages, 1984. Softcover. (Text)

JEANS' HANDBOOK ON TRIAL ADVOCACY, Student Edition, 473 pages, 1975. Softcover. (Text)

LISNEK AND KAUFMAN'S DEPOSITIONS: PROCEDURE, STRATEGY AND TECHNIQUE, Law School and CLE Edition. 250 pages, 1990. Softcover. (Text)

MARTINEAU'S CASES AND MATERIALS ON APPELLATE PRACTICE AND PROCEDURE, 565 pages, 1987. (Casebook)

Trial and Appellate Advocacy—Cont'd

NOLAN'S CASES AND MATERIALS ON TRIAL PRACTICE, 518 pages, 1981. (Casebook)

SONSTENG, HAYDOCK AND BOYD'S THE TRIALBOOK: A TOTAL SYSTEM FOR PREPARATION AND PRESENTATION OF A CASE, 404 pages, 1984. Softcover. (Coursebook)

WHARTON, HAYDOCK AND SONSTENG'S CALIFORNIA CIVIL TRIALBOOK, Law School and CLE Edition. 148 pages, 1990. Softcover. (Text)

Trusts and Estates

ATKINSON'S HORNBOOK ON WILLS, Second Edition, 975 pages, 1953. (Text)

AVERILL'S UNIFORM PROBATE CODE IN A NUTSHELL, Second Edition, 454 pages, 1987. Softcover. (Text)

BOGERT'S HORNBOOK ON TRUSTS, Sixth Edition, Student Edition, 794 pages, 1987. (Text)

CLARK, LUSKY AND MURPHY'S CASES AND MATERIALS ON GRATUITOUS TRANSFERS, Third Edition, 970 pages, 1985. (Casebook)

DODGE'S WILLS, TRUSTS AND ESTATE PLANNING–LAW AND TAXATION, CASES AND MATERIALS, 665 pages, 1988. (Casebook)

MCGOVERN'S CASES AND MATERIALS ON WILLS, TRUSTS AND FUTURE INTERESTS: AN INTRODUCTION TO ESTATE PLANNING, 750 pages, 1983. (Casebook)

MCGOVERN, KURTZ AND REIN'S HORNBOOK ON WILLS, TRUSTS AND ESTATES–INCLUDING TAXATION AND FUTURE INTERESTS, 996 pages, 1988. (Text)

MENNELL'S WILLS AND TRUSTS IN A NUTSHELL, 392 pages, 1979. Softcover. (Text)

SIMES' HORNBOOK ON FUTURE INTERESTS, Second Edition, 355 pages, 1966. (Text)

TURANO AND RADIGAN'S HORNBOOK ON NEW YORK ESTATE ADMINISTRATION, 676 pages, 1986. (Text)

UNIFORM PROBATE CODE, OFFICIAL TEXT WITH COMMENTS. 839 pages, 1990. Softcover.

WAGGONER'S FUTURE INTERESTS IN A NUTSHELL, 361 pages, 1981. Softcover. (Text)

WATERBURY'S MATERIALS ON TRUSTS AND ESTATES, 1039 pages, 1986. Teacher's Manual available. (Casebook)

Water Law—see also Energy and Natural Resources Law, Environmental Law

GETCHES' WATER LAW IN A NUTSHELL, Second Edition, 459 pages, 1990. Softcover. (Text)

SAX, ABRAMS AND THOMPSON'S LEGAL CONTROL OF WATER RESOURCES: CASES AND MATERIALS, Approximately 975 pages, 1991. (Casebook)

TRELEASE AND GOULD'S CASES AND MATERIALS ON WATER LAW, Fourth Edition, 816 pages, 1986. (Casebook)

Wills—see Trusts and Estates

Workers' Compensation

HOOD, HARDY AND LEWIS' WORKERS' COMPENSATION AND EMPLOYEE PROTECTION LAWS IN A NUTSHELL, Second Edition, 361 pages, 1990. Softcover. (Text)

MALONE, PLANT AND LITTLE'S CASES ON WORKERS' COMPENSATION AND EMPLOYMENT RIGHTS, Second Edition, 951 pages, 1980. Teacher's Manual available. (Casebook)

WEST'S LAW SCHOOL ADVISORY BOARD

The Supreme Court of the United States 1990–1991

From left to right, Justice John Paul Stevens, Justice Harry A. Blackmun, Justice Anthony M. Kennedy, Justice Thurgood Marshall, Justice Byron R. White, Chief Justice William H. Rehnquist, Justice Antonin Scalia, Justice Sandra Day O'Connor and Justice David H. Souter.

This photograph is reprinted with the permission of National Geographic Society/Supreme Court Historical Society.

CONSTITUTIONAL RIGHTS AND LIBERTIES

CASES–COMMENTS–QUESTIONS

Seventh Edition

By

William B. Lockhart
Professor of Law, University of California, Hastings
Dean and Professor of Law Emeritus, University of Minnesota

Yale Kamisar
Henry K. Ransom Professor of Law, University of Michigan

Jesse H. Choper
Dean and Earl Warren Professor of Public Law,
University of California, Berkeley

Steven H. Shiffrin
Professor of Law, Cornell University

This book is an abridgement of Lockhart, Kamisar, Choper & Shiffrin's "Constitutional Law, Cases—Comments—Questions, Seventh Edition".

AMERICAN CASEBOOK SERIES®

WEST PUBLISHING CO.
ST. PAUL, MINN., 1991

This is an abridgement of Lockhart, Kamisar, Choper & Shiffrin's *"Constitutional Law, Cases—Comments—Questions, Seventh Edition"*, West Publishing Co., 1991.

American Casebook Series, the key symbol appearing on the front cover and the WP symbol are registered trademarks of West Publishing Co. Registered in U.S. Patent and Trademark Office.

Printed in the United States of America

Library of Congress Cataloging-in-Publication Data

Constitutional rights and liberties : cases, comments, questions / by William B. Lockhart ... [et al.]. — 7th ed.
p. cm. — (American casebook series)
Includes index.
ISBN 0-314-88940-X
1. Civil rights—United States—Cases. I. Lockhart, William B. II. Series.
KF4748.C66 1991
342.73'085—dc20
[347.30285] 91-36746
CIP

ISBN 0-314-88940-X

L.K.C. & S. Rights & Lib. 7th Ed. ACB

Preface

Casebooks are teaching tools, and this is no exception. What distinguishes this book is its commitment to the proposition that a student's understanding of constitutional law is greatly enriched by exposure to a variety of competing perspectives drawn from the best of legal scholarship. To that end, we have reproduced many selections from the literature or woven them into notes and questions that follow almost every main case.

The problem in preparing this edition has been to figure out a way to integrate more than five new years of cases and articles and to produce a book that not only reflects recent doctrine and the modern commentary, but also gives a strong sense of how we got to where we are today, and to do all this without producing an oversized monster. To achieve this goal, we paid heed to the adage that selection is the most important part of editing.

That insight is especially applicable to the materials on freedom of expression and association. The time is long past that effective teaching about the first amendment can be accompanied with materials that produce snippets from every free speech case ever decided by the United States Supreme Court. Our overall strategy has been to pick the great teaching cases and to give them detailed treatment.

The freedom of expression materials have been restructured in some significant respects without compromising the overall design of the chapter. The most important decision involved the placement and selection of cases involving unconventional forms of communication. We have added a wonderful teaching case, *Clark v. Community for Creative Non-Violence* (involving sleeping in the park) and placed it after the draft card burning case (*O'Brien*) and the flag burning cases, (*Johnson* and *Eichman*), and immediately before *Arcara* (formerly in section nine), (a case finding no first amendment issue presented despite the forced closing of a bookstore). The placement of these materials in section two of the chapter will not only allow a ready comparison of the issues surrounding pornography and racist speech with those raised by draft card burning and flag burning, but also makes possible an early exploration of the distinctions between content regulations and time, place, and manner regulations. The materials are designed to facilitate discussion of which tests apply when and whether the different tests—*O'Brien*; time, place and manner; "exacting scrutiny"—are helpful guides to first amendment doctrine. The materials also invite an early exploration of the question of how dissenters without ample funds can communicate their messages and whether the legal system adequately responds to their needs.

We have made a number of other changes that should tighten the organization. For example, we have placed *Tinker* (the black armband case) with other school cases, such as *Pico* (library book selection) and *Hazelwood* (school newspapers). We have taken *Connick v. Meyers* out of the "private speech" subsection and placed it with the burgeoning flood of public employee cases. The latter move will also connect *Greenmoss* (the credit reporting case) with the commercial speech cases and squarely raise issues about the definition of commercial speech and its underlying doctrinal coherence. Of course, many may wish to teach these and other cases in different places and we have maintained our policy of making it easy for instructors to reorganize the materials as they prefer. We are well aware that the first amendment can be organized in *many* different ways.

So too with equal protection. We have restructured the materials on gender discrimination; gathered the materials on poverty in one place; and moved illegitimacy after gender discrimination (because some instructors will find it desirable to raise the gender discrimination issues lurking in the illegitimacy context). We have returned to some older cases because we think they teach better than the new ones. (See, for example, the cases on aliens.) In the main, however, we have adhered to the same basic structure of the chapter.

Since the last edition was published, there have been a large number of dramatic changes in the church and state area. We have revised the basic free exercise of religion materials significantly, in light of the momentous Peyote Case (*Unemployment Division v. Smith*). Because of the receding significance of the *Lemon* analysis and the emergence of Justice O'Connor's "endorsement" test and Justice Kennedy's contrasting "coercion" standard, we have made *Wallace v. Jaffree* and *Allegheny County v. ACLU*—two cases that spell out these contrasting new approaches and bring them to the fore—the main cases in their respective subsections of the establishment clause materials.

The "newness" of the 150-page "right of 'privacy' " section (Ch. 3, § 2) is evidenced by the fact that of the twelve main cases in the section, six were decided since the last edition was published: *Bowers v. Hardwick* (the first Supreme Court case addressing the constitutionality of a law criminalizing homosexual activity); *Cruzan v. Director, Missouri Dep't of Health* (the Court's first "right to die" case); *Michael H. v. Gerald D.* (which raises the important and difficult question of how one determines the appropriate level of generality in defining rights, an issue also presented in *Cruzan* and *Hardwick*); and three significant recent abortion cases: *Hodgson, Thornburgh* and *Webster.*

The nature and scope of the *Cruzan* decision is explored in a long series of Notes & Questions, second in depth and comprehensiveness only to the many Notes & Questions accompanying *Roe v. Wade.* A number of substantial extracts from the literature also appear in the material following *Hardwick* and *Michael H.* In general, we think it fair to say, the cases in the "right to 'privacy' " section have been given uniquely intensive treatment.

We are well aware that virtually all other constitutional law and civil liberties casebooks completely exclude the "death penalty" cases, but we continue to believe that they belong in a constitutional law casebook. (See Ch. 3, § 4.) Although nominally "cruel and unusual punishment" material, the "death penalty" cases are striking illustrations of standards and methodology in due process adjudication. Older material in this section has been significantly pruned to make room for the new, e.g., Justice Scalia's provocative concurring opinion in *Walton v. Arizona*.

The cut-off date for this book is March 1, 1991. Significant cases handed down during the last three months of the 1990–91 Supreme Court Term appeared in a supplement published in the summer of 1991. Important developments thereafter will appear in annual supplements.

Case and statute citations, as well as footnotes, of the Court and commentators have been omitted without so specifying; other omissions are indicated by asterisks or by brackets. Numbered footnotes are from the original materials; lettered footnotes are ours. The composition of the Court on any date may be obtained by consulting the Table of Justices in Appendix A, originally prepared by Professor John J. Cound, a compilation of basic biographical data on all the individuals who have ever served on the Court.

Over the years, in the course of preparing seven editions, we have become indebted to many teachers (and students) of constitutional law for their valuable suggestions and insights. The contributions to the first edition by Carl A. Auerbach, John C. Cound and Terrance Sandalow persist to date. The book reviews of Ira C. Lupu, Robert B. McKay, Lester J. Mazor, Charles W. Quick, Norman Relich, Christopher D. Stone, William W. Van Alstyne and Lawrence G. Wallace have all been very helpful, as have the criticisms and suggestions of Vincent A. Blasi, Arthur E. Bonfield, Mary I. Coombs, Frank I. Goodman, Kenneth Karst, Michael E. Smith, Laurence H. Tribe, and Jonathan Varat. Our thanks go also to Dianne Catchot and Jennifer Smith, for the excellent secretarial assistance they have provided, too often under great stress.

William B. Lockhart
Yale Kamisar
Jesse H. Choper
Steven H. Shiffrin

October, 1991

*

Summary of Contents

*

Table of Contents

Table of Cases

The principal cases are in bold type. Cases cited or discussed in the text are roman type. References are to pages.

Table of Authorities

For authorities from which extracts have been taken page numbers appear in bold; page numbers for other authorities appear in roman.

Frickey & Farber, The Jurisprudence of Public Choice, 65 Texas L.Rev. 873 (1987), 566

Fried, Affirmative Action After City of Richmond v. J.A. Croson Co.: A Response to the Scholars' Statement, 99 Yale L.J. 155 (1989), 1033

Fried, C., Testimony before House Subcommittee on Civil and Constitutional Rights (1989), 543

Fried, Metro Broadcasting, Inc. v. FCC: Two Concepts of Equality, 104 Harv.L.Rev. 107 (1990), 1049

Friedman, ed., Argument: The Oral Argument Before the Supreme Court in Brown v. Board of Education, (1969), 1273

Friendly, H., Minnesota Rag (1981), 603

Friendly, F., The Good Guys, The Bad Guys and the First Amendment (1975), 695

Friendly, F. & Elliott, The Constitution: That Delicate Balance (1984), 158, 519, 628, 787

Friendly, H., The Dartmouth College Case and the Public–Private Penumbra (1969), 1217

Friendly, "Some Kind of Hearing," 123 U.Pa.L.Rev. 1267 (1975), 373

Friendly, The Bill of Rights as a Code of Criminal Procedure, 53 Calif.L.Rev. 929 (1965), 123, 132

Frug, Argument as Character, 40 Stan.L.Rev. 869 (1988), 789

Frug, The City as a Legal Concept, 93 Harv.L.Rev. 1057 (1980), 753

Galanter, Religious Freedom in the United States: A Turning Point? 1966 Wis.L.Rev. 217, pp. 917, 929

Galebach, A Human Life Statute, 7 Human Life Rev. 3 (1981), 1280

Gara & Dorsen, Free Speech, Property, and the Burger Court: Old Values, New Balances, 1982 Sup.Ct.Rev. 195, p. 795

Gardner, Illicit Legislative Motivation as a Sufficient Condition for Unconstitutionality Under the Establishment Clause, 1979 Wash.U.L.Q. 435, p. 841

Garrett, Federal Tax Limitations on Political Activities of Public Interest and Educational Organizations, 59 Geo.L.J. 561 (1971), 669

Garvey, Children and the First Amendment, 57 Tex.L.Rev. 321 (1979), 688

Garvey, Children and the Idea of Liberty, 68 Ky.L.J. 809 (1979–80), 250, 370

Garvey, Churches and the Free Exercise of Religion, 4 Notre D.J.L.Eth & Pub.Pol. 567 (1990), 850

Garvey, The Power and the Duties of Government, 26 San Diego L.Rev. 209 (1989), 590

Gegan, De Jure Integration in Education, 11 Cath.Law. 4 (1965), 1045

Gelfand, Living Will Statutes: The First Decade, 1987 Wisc.L.Rev. 737, p. 290

Gellhorn, American Rights (1960), 410

Gellhorn and Canby, Physician Advertising: The First Amendment and the Sherman Act, 1978 Duke L.J. 543, p. 575

Gerety, Children in the Labyrinth: The Complexities of Plyler v. Doe, 44 U.Pitt.L.Rev. 379 (1983), 1188

Gerety, Doing Without Privacy, 42 Ohio St.L.J. 143 (1981), 155, 244

Gershman & Koffler, The New Seditious Libel, 69 Corn.L.Rev. 816 (1984), 624

Gerwitz, Choice in the Transition: School Desegregation and the Corrective Ideal, 86 Colum.L.Rev. 728 (1986), 993

Gewirtz, Remedies and Resistance, 92 Yale L.J. 585 (1983), 965, 987, 997

Gey, The Apologetics of Suppression, 86 Mich.L.Rev. 1564 (1988), 463, 512

Giannella, Lemon and Tilton: The Bitter and the Sweet of Church–State Entanglement, 1971 Sup.Ct.Rev. 147, p. 863

Giannella, Religious Liberty, Nonestablishment, and Doctrinal Development—Part I. The Religious Liberty Guarantee, 80 Harv.L.Rev. 1381 (1967), 910, 913

Gibson, The Supreme Court and Freedom of Expression from 1791 to 1917, 55 Fordham L.Rev. 263 (1986), 375

Gilbert, Theories of State Action as Applied to the "Sit–In" Cases, 17 Ark.L.Rev. 147 (1963), 1226

Gillette, Plebiscites, Participation, and Collective Action in Local Government Law, 86 Mich.L.Rev. 930 (1988), 30

Ginsburg, D., Afterword, 40 U.Chi.L.Rev. 243 (1973), 379, 387

Ginsburg, R., Some Thoughts on Autonomy and Equality in Relation to Roe v. Wade, 63 N.C.L.Rev. 375 (1985), 177

Girdner & Loftis, The Great Betrayal (1969), 954

Givelber, The Application of Equal Protection Principles to Selective Enforcement of the Criminal Law, 1971 U.Ill.L.F. 88, p. 971

Glennon & Nowak, A Functional Analysis of the Fourteenth Amendment "State Action" Requirement, 1976 Sup.Ct.Rev. 221, p. 1227

Godofsky & Rogatnick, Prior Restraints: The Pentagon Papers Case Revisited, 18 Cum.L.Rev. 527 (1988), 620, 624

Goebel, History of the Supreme Court of the United States: Antecedents and Beginnings to 1801 (1971), 13, 55

Goldberg, E., Mr. Justice Harlan, The Uses of History, and the Congressional Globe, 15 J.Pub.L. 181 (1966), 1112

Goldberger, A Reconsideration of Cox v. New Hampshire: Can Demonstrators Be

Required to Pay the Costs of Using America's Public Forums?, 62 Tex.L.Rev. 403 (1983), 643

Goldberger, Judicial Scrutiny in Public Forum Cases: Misplaced Trust in the Judgment of Public Officials, 32 Buffalo L.Rev. 175 (1983), 548

Goldman, A Doctrine of Worthier Speech: Young v. American Mini Theatres, Inc., 21 St. Louis U.L.J. 281 (1977), 561

Goldstein, The Asserted Constitutional Right of Public School Teachers to Determine What They Teach, 124 U.Pa.L.Rev. 1293 (1976), 688

Goodale, Moodhe & Imes, Reporter's Privilege Cases in Communications Law (1984), 774

Goodale, The Press Ungagged: The Practical Effect on Gag Order Litigation of Nebraska Press Association v. Stuart, 29 Stan.L.Rev. 497 (1977), 629

Goodman, De Facto School Segregation: A Constitutional and Empirical Analysis, 60 Calif.L.Rev. 275 (1972), 962, 975, 995, 1004, 1059

Goodman, Professor Brest on State Action and Liberal Theory, 130 U.Pa.L.Rev. 1331 (1982), 1264

Goodman, Racial Imbalance in the Oakland Public Schools: A Legal Analysis (1966), 993, 1004

Goodman & Abrams, End of an Era? The Decline of Student Press [Rights], 1988 Duke L.J. 706, p. 682

Goodpaster, The Integration of Equal Protection, Due Process Standards, and the Indigent's Right of Free Access to the Courts, 56 Ia.L.Rev. 223 (1970), 1168

Gordon, The Nature and Uses of Congressional Power Under Section Five of the Fourteenth Amendment to Overcome Decisions of the Supreme Court, 72 Nw.U.L.Rev. 656 (1977), 1275

Gordon, The Unconstitutionality of Public Aid to Parochial Schools, in The Wall Between Church and State (Oaks ed. 1963), 872

Gordon & Tenenbaum, Conclusive Presumption Analysis: The Principle of Individual Opportunity, 71 Nw.U.L.Rev. 579 (1977), 1196

Gorfinkel & Mack, Dennis v. United States and the Clear and Present Danger Rule, 39 Calif.L.Rev. 475 (1951), 406

Gottlieb, In The Name of Patriotism: The Constitutionality of "Bending" History in Public Secondary Schools, 62 N.Y.U.L.Rev. 497 (1987), 688

Graglia, Disaster By Decree (1976), 1002

Graglia, Racially Discriminatory Admission to Public Institutions of Higher Education, in Constitutional Government in America (Collins 3d 1980), 1023, 1045

Graglia, The Brown Cases Revisited: Where Are They Now?, 1 Benchmark 23 (Mar.–Apr. 1984), 966

Graham, Our "Declaratory" Fourteenth Amendment, 7 Stan.L.Rev. 3 (1954), 71

Graham, The "Conspiracy Theory" of the Fourteenth Amendment, 47 Yale L.J. 371 (1938), 124

Grano, Free Speech v. The University of Michigan, Academic Questions (Spring 1990), 522

Grano, Judicial Review and a Written Constitution in a Democratic Society, 28 Wayne L.Rev. 1 (1981), 168, 182, 243, 962

Greenawalt, All or Nothing at All: The Defeat of Selective Conscientious Objection, 1971 Sup.Ct.Rev. 31, p. 917

Greenawalt, Criminal Coercion and Freedom of Speech, 78 Nw.U.L.Rev. 1081 (1984), 419, 420, 457

Greenawalt, Free Speech Justifications, 89 Colum.L.Rev. 119 (1989), 386

Greenawalt, Insults and Epithets: Are They Protected Speech?, 42 Rutgers L.Rev. 287 (1990), 522

Greenawalt, Judicial Scrutiny of "Benign" Racial Preference in Law School Admissions, 75 Colum.L.R. 559 (1975), 1047

Greenawalt, O'er the Land of the Free: Flag Burning as Speech, 37 UCLA L.Rev. 925 (1990), 542

Greenawalt, Religion as a Concept in Constitutional Law, 72 Calif.L.Rev. 753 (1984), 914

Greenawalt, Speech, Crime, and the Uses of Language (1989), 420, 457, 487

Greenawalt, Speech and Crime, 1980 Am.B.Found.Res.J. 645, pp. 396, 410, 420

Greenawalt, The Unresolved Problems of Reverse Discrimination, 67 Calif.L.Rev. 87 (1979), 937, 1043

Greenberg, Capital Punishment as a System, 91 Yale L.J. 908 (1982), 301, 326

Greenspan & D. Cohen, Conscientious Objection, Democratic Theory, and the Constitution, 29 U.Pitt.L.Rev. 389 (1968), 919

Gressman, The Constitution v. The Freund Report, 41 Geo.Wash.L.Rev. 951 (1973), 54

Gressman & S. Shapiro & Stern, Supreme Court Practice (6th ed. 1986), 59

Grey, Civil Rights v. Civil Liberties: The Case of Discriminatory Verbal Harassment, Soc.Phil. & Pol'y (Spring 1991), 522

Grey, Do We Have an Unwritten Constitution?, 27 Stan.L.Rev. 703 (1975), 181, **186,** 458

Grey, The Constitution as Scripture, 37 Stan.L.Rev. 1 (1984), 181

Griswold, Absolute is in the Dark—A Discussion of the Approach of the Supreme

Kanowitz, "Benign" Sex Discrimination: Its Troubles and Their Cure, 31 Hast.L.J. 1379 (1980), 1084
Kanowitz & Klinger, Can a State Rescind Its Equal Rights Amendment Ratification: Who Decides and How? 28 Hast.L.J. 979 (1977), 45
Kaplan, Administering Capital Punishment, 36 U.Fla.L.Rev. 177 (1984), 314
Kaplan, Comment on School Desegregation, 64 Colum.L.Rev. 223 (1964), 966
Kaplan, Equal Justice in an Unequal World: Equality for the Negro—The Problem of Special Treatment, 61 Nw.U.L.Rev. 363 (1966), 955
Kaplan, Segregation Litigation and the Schools—Part II: The General Northern Problem, 58 Nw.U.L.Rev. 157 (1963), 993, 1004
Karst, "A Discrimination So Trivial": A Note on Law and the Symbolism of Women's Dependency, 35 Ohio St.L.J. 546 (1974), 1071
Karst, Boundaries and Reasons: Freedom of Expression and the Subordination of Groups, 1990 U.Ill.L.Rev. 95, pp. 518, 522
Karst, Equality and Community: Lessons From the Civil Rights Era, 56 Not.D.Law. 183 (1980), 753
Karst, Equality as a Central Principle in the First Amendment, 43 U.Chi.L.Rev. 20 (1975), 646, 777
Karst, Foreword: Equal Citizenship Under the Fourteenth Amendment, 91 Harv.L.Rev. 1 (1977), 177
Karst, Freedom of Intimate Association, 89 Yale L.J. 624 (1980), 757
Karst, Not One Law at Rome and Another at Athens: The Fourteenth Amendment in Nationwide Application, 1972 Wash.U.L.Q. 383, p. 996
Karst, Paths to Belonging: The Constitution and Cultural Identity, 64 N.C.L.Rev. 303 (1986), 267
Karst, Public Enterprise and the Public Forum: A Comment on Southeastern Promotions, Ltd. v. Conrad, 37 Ohio St.L.J. 247 (1976), 689
Karst, The Costs of Motive-Centered Inquiry, 15 San Diego L.Rev. 1163 (1978), 985
Karst, The Fifth Amendment's Guarantee of Equal Protection, 55 N.C.L.Rev. 541 (1977), 931, 1153
Karst, The Freedom of Intimate Association, 89 Yale L.J. 624 (1980), 183, 245
Karst, Woman's Constitution, 1984 Duke L.J. 447, p. 1072
Karst & Horowitz, Presidential Prerogative and Judicial Review, 22 U.C.L.A.L.Rev. 47 (1974), 45
Karst & Horowitz, Reitman v. Mulkey: A Telophase of Substantive Equal Protection, 1967 Sup.Ct.Rev. 39, p. 1233
Karst & Horowitz, The California Supreme Court and State Action Under the Fourteenth Amendment: The Leader Beclouds the Issue, 21 U.C.L.A.L.Rev. 1421 (1974), 1234
Karst & Van Alstyne, Sit-Ins and State Action—Mr. Justice Douglas Concurring, 14 Stan.L.Rev. 762 (1962), 1228
Karst & Van Alstyne, State Action, 14 Stan.L.Rev. 3 (1961), 1226
Katz, Note on the Constitutionality of Shared Time, 1964 Relig. & Pub.Or. 85, p. 920
Katz, Privacy and Pornography, 1969 Sup.Ct.Rev. 203, p. 466
Kaufman & Bittker, Taxes and Civil Rights: "Constitutionalizing" the Internal Revenue Code, 82 Yale L.J. 51 (1972), 666, 1242
Kauper, Book Review, 41 Texas L.Rev. 467 (1963), 923
Kauper, Penumbras, Peripheries, Emanations, Things Fundamental and Things Forgotten: The Griswold Case, 64 Mich.L.Rev. 235 (1965), 153
Kauper, Prayer, Public Schools and the Supreme Court, 61 Mich.L.Rev. 1031 (1963), 836
Kauper, Public Aid for Parochial Schools and Church Colleges, 13 Ariz.L.Rev. 567 (1971), 871
Kauper, Religion and the Constitution (1964), 893, 911
Kauper, Schempp and Sherbert: Studies in Neutrality and Accommodation, 1963 Relig. & Pub. Or. 3, p. 845
Kauper, Segregation in Public Education, 52 Mich.L.Rev. 1137 (1954), 963
Kay, Equality and Difference: The Case of Pregnancy, 1 Berkeley Women's L.J. 1 (1985), 1072
Kay, Models of Equality, 1985 U.Ill.L.Rev. 39, p. 1072
Kelly, Clio and the Court: An Illicit Love Affair, 1965 Sup.Ct.Rev. 119, p. 125
Kelsey, The Ninth Amendment of the Federal Constitution, 11 Ind.L.J. 309 (1936), 146
Kennedy, R., McCleskey v. Kemp: Race, Capital Punishment and the Supreme Court, 101 Harv.L.Rev. 1388 (1988), 339
Kernochan, On Constitutionalism and the Antecedents of Judicial Review, in Dowling & Gunther, Constitutional Law (7th ed. 1965), 13
King, The Judicial Status of the Fetus: A Proposal for Legal Protection of the Unborn, 77 Mich.L.Rev. 1647 (1979), 178, 179
Kinoy, The Constitutional Right of Negro Freedom, 21 Rutg.L.Rev. 387 (1967), 1204
Kirkland & Ferris, Fairness—The Broadcaster's Hippocratic Oath, 34 Cath.U.L.Rev. 605 (1985), 705

CONSTITUTIONAL RIGHTS AND LIBERTIES

CASES–COMMENTS–QUESTIONS

Seventh Edition

*

Chapter 1

NATURE AND SCOPE OF JUDICIAL REVIEW

SECTION 1. ORIGINS, EARLY CHALLENGES, AND CONTINUING CONTROVERSY

"Whoever hath an absolute authority to interpret any written or spoken laws, it is he who is truly the lawgiver, to all intents and purposes, and not the person who first spoke or wrote them."

—Bishop Hoadly's Sermon,
preached before the King,
1717.

MARBURY v. MADISON

5 U.S.(1 Cranch) 137, 2 L.Ed. 60 (1803).

[Thomas Jefferson, an Anti-Federalist (or Republican), who defeated John Adams, a Federalist, in the presidential election of 1800, was to take office on March 4, 1801. On January 20, 1801, Adams, the defeated incumbent, nominated John Marshall, Adams' Secretary of State, as fourth Chief Justice of the United States. Marshall assumed office on February 4 but continued to serve as Secretary of State until the end of the Adams administration. During February, the Federalist Congress passed (1) the Circuit Court Act, which, inter alia, doubled the number of federal judges and (2) the Organic Act which authorized appointment of 42 justices-of-the-peace in the District of Columbia. Senate confirmation of Adams' "midnight" appointees, virtually all Federalists, was completed on March 3. Their commissions were signed by Adams and sealed by Acting Secretary of State Marshall, but due to time pressures, several for the justices-of-the-peace (including that of William Marbury) remained undelivered when Jefferson assumed the presidency the next day. Jefferson ordered his new Secretary of State, James Madison, to withhold delivery.

[Late in 1801, Marbury and several others sought a writ of mandamus in the Supreme Court to compel Madison to deliver the commissions. The Court ordered Madison "to show cause why a mandamus should not issue" and the case was set for argument in the 1802 Term.

[While the case was pending, the new Republican Congress—incensed at Adams' efforts to entrench a Federalist judiciary and at the "Federalist" Court's order against a Republican cabinet officer—moved to repeal the Circuit Court Act. Federalist congressmen argued that repeal would be unconstitutional as violative of Art. III's assurance of judicial tenure "during good behavior" and of the Constitution's plan for separation of powers assuring the independence of the Judiciary. It "was in this debate that for the first time since the initiation of the new Government under the Constitution there occurred a serious challenge of the power of the Judiciary to pass upon the constitutionality of Acts of Congress. Hitherto, [it had been the Republicans] who had sustained this power as a desirable curb on Congressional aggression and encroachment on the rights of the States, and they had been loud in their complaints at the failure of the Court to hold the Alien and Sedition laws unconstitutional. Now, however, in 1802, in order to counteract the Federalist argument that the Repeal Bill was unconstitutional and would be so held by the Court, [Republicans] advanced the proposition that the Court did not possess the power." [a]

[The Repeal Law passed early in 1802. To forestall its constitutional challenge in the Supreme Court until the political power of the new administration had been strengthened, Congress also eliminated the 1802 Supreme Court Term. Thus, the Court did not meet between December, 1801 and February, 1803.]

[On] 24th February, the following opinion of the court was delivered by CHIEF JUSTICE MARSHALL: * * *

No cause has been shown, and the present motion is for a mandamus. The peculiar delicacy of this case, the novelty of some of its circumstances, and the real difficulty attending the points which occur in it require a complete exposition of the principles on which the opinion to be given by the court is founded. * * *

1st. Has the applicant a right to the commission he demands? * * *

Mr. Marbury, [since] his commission was signed by the President and sealed by the Secretary of State, was appointed; and as the law creating the office gave the officer a right to hold for five years, independent of the executive, the appointment was not revocable, but vested in the officer legal rights, which are protected by the laws of his country.

To withhold his commission, therefore, is an act deemed by the court not warranted by law, but violative of a vested legal right.[b] * * *

2dly. If he has a right, and that right has been violated, do the laws of his country afford him a remedy?

The very essence of civil liberty certainly consists in the right of every individual to claim the protection of the laws, whenever he receives an injury. One of the first duties of government is to afford that protection. * * *

The government of the United States has been emphatically termed a government of laws, and not of men. It will certainly cease to deserve this high appellation, if the laws furnish no remedy for the violation of a vested legal right. * * *

[W]here the heads of departments are the political or confidential agents of the executive, merely to execute the will of the president, or rather to act in

a. 1 Warren, *The Supreme Court in United States History* 215 (1922).

b. Consider Van Alstyne, *A Critical Guide to Marbury v. Madison,* 1969 Duke L.J. 1, 8: "[T]here is clearly an 'issue' of sorts which preceded any of those touched upon in the opinion. Specifically, it would appear that Marshall should have recused himself in view of his substantial involvement in the background of this controversy. * * * Proof of the status of Marbury's commission not only involved circumstances within the Chief Justice's personal knowledge, it was furnished in the Supreme Court by Marshall's own younger brother who had been with him in his office when, as Secretary of State, he had made out the commissions."

cases in which the executive possesses a constitutional or legal discretion, nothing can be more perfectly clear than that their acts are only politically examinable. But where a specific duty is assigned by law, and individual rights depend upon the performance of that duty, it seems equally clear that the individual who considers himself injured, has a right to resort to the laws of his country for a remedy.[c] * * *

It remains to be inquired whether,

3dly. He is entitled to the remedy for which he applies? This depends on,

1st. The nature of the writ applied for; and,

2dly. The power of this court.

1st. The nature of the writ. * * *

This writ, if awarded, would be directed to an officer of government, and its mandate to him would be, to use the words of Blackstone, "to do a particular thing therein specified, which appertains to his office and duty, and which the court has previously determined, or at least supposes, to be consonant to right and justice." Or, in the words of Lord Mansfield, the applicant, in this case, has a right to execute an office of public concern, and is kept out of possession of that right.

These circumstances certainly concur in this case.

Still, to render the mandamus a proper remedy, the officer to whom it is to be directed, must be one to whom, on legal principles, such writ may be directed; and the person applying for it must be without any other specific and legal remedy.

1st. With respect to the officer to whom it would be directed. The intimate political relation subsisting between the President of the United States and the heads of departments, necessarily renders any legal investigation of the acts of one of those high officers peculiarly irksome, as well as delicate; and excites some hesitation with respect to the propriety of entering into such investigation. Impressions are often received without much reflection or examination, and it is not wonderful that in such a case as this the assertion, by an individual, of his legal claims in a court of justice, to which claims it is the duty of that court to attend, should at first view be considered by some, as an attempt to intrude into the cabinet, and to intermeddle with the prerogatives of the executive.

It is scarcely necessary for the court to disclaim all pretensions to such a jurisdiction. An extravagance, so absurd and excessive, could not have been entertained for a moment. The province of the court is, solely, to decide on the rights of individuals, not to inquire how the executive, or executive officers, perform duties in which they have a discretion. Questions in their nature political, or which are, by the constitution and laws, submitted to the executive, can never be made in this court.

But [what] is there in the exalted station of the officer, which shall bar a citizen from asserting, in a court of justice, his legal rights, or shall forbid a court to listen to the claim, or to issue a mandamus, directing the performance of a duty, not depending on executive discretion, but on particular acts of congress, and the general principles of law? * * *

c. Consider Redlich, *The Supreme Court—1833 Term*, 40 N.Y.U.L.Rev. 1, 4 (1965): "[T]he Court could have ruled that, since the President had the power to appoint the judges, he also had the power to deliver the commissions which was in a sense the final act of appointment. Viewed as a component of the act of appointment, the delivery of the commissions could have simply been considered as lying within the discretion of the President."

This, then, is a plain case for a mandamus, either to deliver the commission, or a copy of it from the record; and it only remains to be inquired,

Whether it can issue from this court.

The act to establish the judicial courts of the United States authorizes the supreme court "to issue writs of mandamus, in cases warranted by the principles and usages of law, to any courts appointed, or persons holding office, under the authority of the United States." [d]

The secretary of state, being a person holding an office under the authority of the United States, is precisely within the letter of the description; and if this court is not authorized to issue a writ of mandamus to such an officer, it must be because the law is unconstitutional, and therefore absolutely incapable of conferring the authority, and assigning the duties which its words purport to confer and assign. * * *

In the distribution of [the judicial power of the United States] it is declared that "the supreme court shall have original jurisdiction in all cases affecting ambassadors, other public ministers and consuls, and those in which a state shall be a party. In all other cases, the supreme court shall have appellate jurisdiction."

It has been insisted, at the bar, that as the original grant of jurisdiction, to the supreme and inferior courts, is general, and the clause, assigning original jurisdiction to the supreme court, contains no negative or restrictive words, the power remains to the legislature, to assign original jurisdiction to that court in other cases than those specified in the article which has been recited; provided those cases belong to the judicial power of the United States.

If it had been intended to leave it in the discretion of the legislature to apportion the judicial power between the supreme and inferior courts according to the will of that body, it would certainly have been useless to have proceeded further than to have defined the judicial power, and the tribunals in which it should be vested. The subsequent part of the section is mere surplusage, is

d. § 13 of the Judiciary Act of 1789 provided: "That the Supreme Court shall have exclusive jurisdiction of all controversies of a civil nature, where a state is a party, except between a state and its citizens; and except also between a state and citizens of other states, or aliens, in which latter case it shall have original but not exclusive jurisdiction. And shall have exclusively all such jurisdiction of suits or proceedings against ambassadors or other public ministers, or their domestics, or domestic servants, as a court of law can have or exercise consistently with the law of nations; and original, but not exclusive jurisdiction of all suits brought by ambassadors or other public ministers, or in which a consul, or vice consul, shall be a party. And the trial of issues of fact in the Supreme Court in all actions at law against citizens of the United States shall be by jury. The Supreme Court shall also have appellate jurisdiction from the circuit courts and courts of the several states, in the cases hereinafter specially provided for; and shall have power to issue writs of prohibition to the district courts, when proceeding as courts of admiralty and maritime jurisdiction, and writs of mandamus, in cases warranted by the principles and usages of law, to any courts appointed, or persons holding office under the authority of the United States."

Consider Van Alstyne, supra, at 15: "Textually, the provision regarding mandamus says nothing expressly as to whether it is part of original or appellate jurisdiction or both, and the clause itself does not speak at all of 'conferring jurisdiction' on the court. The grant of 'power' to issue the writ, however, is juxtaposed with the section of appellate jurisdiction and, in fact, follows the general description of appellate jurisdiction in the same sentence, being separated only by a semicolon. No textual mangling is required to confine it to appellate jurisdiction. Moreover, no mangling is required even if it attaches both to original and to appellate jurisdiction, not as an enlargement of either, but simply as a specification of power which the Court is authorized to use in cases which are *otherwise* appropriately under consideration. Since this case is not otherwise within the specified type of original jurisdiction (e.g., it is not a case in which a state is a party or a case against an ambassador), it should be dismissed."

entirely without meaning, if such is to be the construction. If congress remains at liberty to give this court appellate jurisdiction, where the constitution has declared their jurisdiction shall be original; and original jurisdiction where the constitution has declared it shall be appellate; the distribution of jurisdiction, made in the constitution, is form without substance.

Affirmative words are often, in their operation, negative of other objects than those affirmed; and in this case, a negative or exclusive sense must be given to them, or they have no operation at all.

It cannot be presumed that any clause in the constitution is intended to be without effect; and, therefore, such a construction is inadmissible, unless the words require it. * * *

The authority, therefore, given to the Supreme Court, by the Act establishing the judicial courts of the United States, to issue writs of mandamus to public officers, appears not to be warranted by the Constitution;[e] and it becomes necessary to inquire whether a jurisdiction so conferred can be exercised.

The question whether an Act repugnant to the Constitution can become the law of the land, is a question deeply interesting to the United States; but, happily, not of an intricacy proportioned to its interest. It seems only necessary to recognize certain principles, supposed to have been long and well established, to decide it.

That the people have an original right to establish, for their future government, such principles as, in their opinion, shall most conduce to their own happiness, is the basis on which the whole American fabric has been erected. The exercise of this original right is a very great exertion; nor can it nor ought it to be frequently repeated. The principles, therefore, so established, are deemed fundamental. And as the authority from which they proceed is supreme, and can seldom act, they are designed to be permanent.

This original and supreme will organizes the government, and assigns to different departments their respective powers. It may either stop here, or establish certain limits not to be transcended by those departments.

The government of the United States is of the latter description. The powers of the legislature are defined and limited; and that those limits may not be mistaken, or forgotten, the constitution is written. To what purpose are powers limited, and to what purpose is that limitation committed to writing, if these limits may, at any time, be passed by those intended to be restrained? The distinction between a government with limited and unlimited powers is abolished, if those limits do not confine the persons on whom they are imposed, and if acts prohibited and acts allowed, are of equal obligation. It is a proposition too plain to be contested, that the constitution controls any legislative act repugnant to it; or, that the legislature may alter the constitution by an ordinary act.

Between these alternatives there is no middle ground. The constitution is either a superior paramount law, unchangeable by ordinary means, or it is on a

e. Consider Van Alstyne, supra, at 31: "It can be plausibly argued, however, that the Article III division of judicial power between appellate and original jurisdiction served a useful purpose other than that insisted upon by Marshall. Had Congress *not* adopted the Judiciary Act of 1789 or taken any other action describing Supreme Court jurisdiction, the division itself would have provided a guideline for the Court to follow until Congress was inclined to act." See also id. at 30–33.

By Marshall's interpretation of Art. III, may Congress authorize the Court to exercise appellate jurisdiction in cases involving foreign consuls? See *Bors v. Preston,* 111 U.S. 252, 4 S.Ct. 407, 28 L.Ed. 419 (1884).

level with ordinary legislative acts, and, like other acts, is alterable when the legislature shall please to alter it.

If the former part of the alternative be true, then a legislative act contrary to the constitution is not law: if the latter part be true, then written constitutions are absurd attempts, on the part of the people, to limit a power in its own nature illimitable.

Certainly all those who have framed written constitutions contemplate them as forming the fundamental and paramount law of the nation, and consequently, the theory of every such government must be, that an act of the legislature, repugnant to the constitution, is void.

This theory is essentially attached to a written constitution, and is, consequently, to be considered, by this court, as one of the fundamental principles of our society. It is not therefore to be lost sight of in the further consideration of this subject.

If an act of the legislature, repugnant to the Constitution, is void, does it, notwithstanding its invalidity, bind the courts, and oblige them to give it effect? Or, in other words, though it be not law, does it constitute a rule as operative as if it was a law? This would be to overthrow in fact what was established in theory; and would seem, at first view, an absurdity too gross to be insisted on. It shall, however, receive a more attentive consideration.

It is emphatically the province and duty of the judicial department to say what the law is. Those who apply the rule to particular cases, must of necessity expound and interpret that rule. If two laws conflict with each other, the courts must decide on the operation of each.

So if a law be in opposition to the constitution; if both the law and the constitution apply to a particular case, so that the court must either decide that case conformably to the law, disregarding the constitution; or conformably to the constitution, disregarding the law; the court must determine which of these conflicting rules governs the case. This is of the very essence of judicial duty.

If, then, the courts are to regard the constitution, and the constitution is superior to any ordinary act of the legislature, the constitution, and not such ordinary act, must govern the case to which they both apply.

Those then who controvert the principle that the constitution is to be considered in court, as a paramount law, are reduced to the necessity of maintaining that courts must close their eyes on the constitution, and see only the law.

This doctrine would subvert the very foundation of all written constitutions. It would declare that an Act which, according to the principles and theory of our government, is entirely void, is yet, in practice, completely obligatory. It would declare that if the legislature shall do what is expressly forbidden, such Act, notwithstanding the express prohibition, is in reality effectual. It would be giving to the legislature a practical and real omnipotence, with the same breath which professes to restrict their powers within narrow limits. It is prescribing limits, and declaring that those limits may be passed at pleasure.

That it thus reduces to nothing what we have deemed the greatest improvement on political institutions, a written constitution, would of itself be sufficient, in America, where written constitutions have been viewed with so much reverence, for rejecting the construction. But the peculiar expressions of the Constitution of the United States furnish additional arguments in favor of its rejection.

The judicial power of the United States is extended to all cases arising under the Constitution.

Could it be the intention of those who gave this power, to say that in using it the Constitution should not be looked into? That a case arising under the Constitution should be decided without examining the instrument under which it arises?

This is too extravagant to be maintained.

In some cases, then, the Constitution must be looked into by the judges. And if they can open it at all, what part of it are they forbidden to read or to obey?

There are many other parts of the Constitution which serve to illustrate this subject.

It is declared that "no tax or duty shall be laid on articles exported from any State." Suppose a duty on the export of cotton, of tobacco, or of flour; and a suit instituted to recover it. Ought judgment to be rendered in such a case? Ought the judges to close their eyes on the Constitution, and only see the law?

The Constitution declares "that no bill of attainder or ex post facto law shall be passed."

If, however, such a bill should be passed, and a person should be prosecuted under it, must the court condemn to death those victims whom the Constitution endeavors to preserve?

"No person," says the Constitution, "shall be convicted of treason unless on the testimony of two witnesses to the same overt act, or on confession in open court."

Here the language of the Constitution is addressed especially to the courts. It prescribes, directly for them, a rule of evidence not to be departed from. If the legislature should change that rule, and declare one witness, or a confession out of court, sufficient for conviction, must the constitutional principle yield to the legislative act?

From these, and many other selections which might be made, it is apparent, that the framers of the constitution contemplated that instrument as a rule for the government of courts, as well as of the legislature.

Why otherwise does it direct the judges to take an oath to support it? This oath certainly applies in an especial manner, to their conduct in their official character. How immoral to impose it on them, if they were to be used as the instruments, and the knowing instruments, for violating what they swear to support!

The oath of office, too, imposed by the legislature, is completely demonstrative of the legislative opinion on this subject. It is in these words: "I do solemnly swear that I will administer justice without respect to persons, and do equal right to the poor and to the rich; and that I will faithfully and impartially discharge all the duties incumbent on me as ______, according to the best of my abilities and understanding agreeably to the constitution and laws of the United States."

Why does a judge swear to discharge his duties agreeably to the constitution of the United States, if that constitution forms no rule for his government? If it is closed upon him, and cannot be inspected by him?

If such be the real state of things, this is worse than solemn mockery. To prescribe, or to take this oath, becomes equally a crime.

It is also not entirely unworthy of observation, that in declaring what shall be the supreme law of the land, the constitution itself is first mentioned; and not the laws of the United States generally, but those only which shall be made in pursuance of the constitution, have that rank.

Thus, the particular phraseology of the Constitution of the United States confirms and strengthens the principle, supposed to be essential to all written constitutions, that a law repugnant to the constitution is void; and that courts, as well as other departments, are bound by that instrument.

The rule must be discharged.[f]

"We are under a Constitution, but the Constitution is what the judges say it is."

—Charles Evans Hughes,
Speech, 1907.

Comments and Questions

Further Historical Context

CHARLES WARREN, 1 *The Supreme Court in United States History,* 232, 242–43 (1922): "Contemporary writings make it very clear that the Republicans attacked the decision, not so much because it sustained the power of the Court to determine the validity of Congressional legislation, as because it enounced the doctrine that the Court might issue mandamus to a Cabinet official who was acting by direction of the President. In other words, Jefferson's antagonism to Marshall and the Court at that time was due more to his resentment at the alleged invasion of his Executive prerogative than to any so-called 'judicial usurpation' of the field of Congressional authority. [It] seems plain [that Marshall might] have construed the language of the section of the Judiciary Act [to escape the necessity] to pass upon its constitutionality. Marshall naturally felt that in view of the recent attacks on judicial power it was important to have the great principle firmly established, and undoubtedly he welcomed the opportunity of fixing the precedent in a case in which his action would necessitate a decision in favor of his political opponents."

MORRIS COHEN, *The Faith of a Liberal* 178–80 (1946) (written in 1938): "The section of [the] Act of 1789 which Marshall declared unconstitutional had been drawn up by Ellsworth, his predecessor as Chief Justice, and by others who a short time before had been the very members of the constitutional convention that had drafted its judicial provisions. It was signed by George Washington who had presided over the deliberations of that Convention. Fourteen years later, John Marshall by implication accused his predecessor on the bench, the members of Congress such as James Madison, the Father of the Constitution, and President Washington, of either not understanding the Constitution (which some of them had drawn up), or else wilfully disregarding it. [To] a secular historian, it is obvious that John Marshall was motivated by the fear of impeachment if he granted the mandamus or dared to declare the Republican

f. Six days later, the Circuit Court Act Repeal Law was held to be constitutional. *Stuart v. Laird,* 5 U.S. (1 Cranch) 299, 2 L.Ed. 115 (1803). After *Marbury,* the Court did not hold an act of Congress unconstitutional until *Dred Scott v. Sandford,* 60 U.S. (19 How.) 393, 15 L.Ed. 691 (1857).

Judiciary Repeal Act of 1802 unconstitutional. Having thus refused aid to his fellow Federalists ousted from offices created for them by a 'lame duck' congress, he resorted to a line of sophistical dicta to get even with his political enemy, as indeed he did also in the *Aaron Burr* case. In his letter to his colleague Chase, Marshall offered to abandon judicial supremacy in the interpretation of the Constitution in return for security against impeachment." [g]

Text of the Constitution

Is the doctrine of "judicial review," which gives the Court power to declare an act of a coordinate branch of the government unconstitutional, compelled because a contrary rule "would subvert the very foundation of all written constitutions"?

WILLIAM VAN ALSTYNE, *A Critical Guide to Marbury v. Madison,* 1969 Duke L.J. 1, 17: "[E]ven in Marshall's time (and to a great extent today), a number of nations maintained written constitutions and yet gave national legislative acts the full force of positive law without providing any constitutional check to guarantee the compatibility of those acts with their constitutions [e.g.,] France, Switzerland, and Belgium (and to some extent Great Britain where Magna Carta and other written instruments are roughly described as the constitution but where acts of Parliament are not reviewable)." [h]

Does the "judges' oath" provision (Art. VI, cl. 3) furnish the necessary textual support for the doctrine of judicial review?

JUSTICE GIBSON, dissenting in *Eakin v. Raub,* 12 S. & R. 330 (Pa.1825): [i] "The oath to support the Constitution is not peculiar to the judges, but is taken indiscriminately by every officer of the government, and is designed rather as a test of the political principles of the man, than to bind the officer in the discharge of his duty: otherwise, it were difficult to determine, what operation it is to have in the case of a recorder of deeds, for instance, who, in execution of his office, has nothing to do with the Constitution. But granting it to relate to the official conduct of the judge, as well as every other officer, and not to his political principles, still, it must be understood in reference to supporting the Constitution, only as far as that may be involved in his official duty; and consequently, if his official duty does not comprehend an inquiry into the authority of the legislature, neither does his oath. * * *

"But do not the judges do a positive act in violation of the Constitution, when they give effect to an unconstitutional law? Not if the law has been

g. In 1804, the House impeached Justice Chase due, inter alia, to what the Republicans believed to be Chase's partisan Federalist activities and statements both on and off the Bench. After a lengthy trial in the Senate, the constitutional majority to convict was not obtained. It was generally assumed that, if the effort had been successful, Marshall and other Federalist judges would suffer the same fate. See generally 1 Warren, supra, ch. 6. For a further account of *Marbury,* see 3 Beveridge, *The Life of John Marshall* 105–156 (1919).

h. Consider Cohen, supra, at 185: "Nor is it necessary to consider in detail the argument that this power is necessary for a federal system. The Swiss constitution is a perfect example of a federal system without the judiciary having such power. The late Justice Holmes said, 'I do not think the United States would come to an end if we lost our power to declare an Act of Congress void. I do think the Union would be imperiled if we could not make that declaration as to the laws of the several states.'"

For discussion of the modern growth of various forms of judicial review in other countries—Australia, Austria, Canada, Cyprus, Denmark, Germany, India, Italy, Japan, Norway, Sweden, Turkey, Yugoslavia—see Cappelletti, *Judicial Review in Comparative Perspective,* 58 Calif.L.Rev. 1017 (1970).

i. This opinion is widely regarded as the most effective answer of the era to Marshall's reasoning supporting judicial review.

passed according to the forms established in the Constitution. The fallacy of the question is, in supposing that the judiciary adopts the acts of the legislature as its own; whereas, the enactment of a law and the interpretation of it are not concurrent acts, and as the judiciary is not required to concur in the enactment, neither is it in the breach of the constitution which may be the consequence of the enactment; the fault is imputable to the legislature, and on it the responsibility exclusively rests."

What of Art. III, § 2, cl. 1, extending "the judicial Power" "to *all* cases * * * arising under this Constitution"?

ALEXANDER BICKEL, *The Least Dangerous Branch* 5–6 (1962): "[W]hat the Constitution extends to cases arising under it is 'the judicial Power.' Whether this power reaches as far as Marshall wanted it to go—namely, to reviewing acts of the legistalure—is the question to be decided. What are the nature and extent of the function of the Court—the judicial power? Is the Court empowered, when it decided a case, to declare that a duly enacted statute violates the Constitution, and to invalidate the statute? Article III does not purport to describe the function of the Court; it subsumes whatever questions may exist as to that in the phrase 'the judicial Power.' It does not purport to tell the Court how to decide cases; it only specifies which kinds of case the Court shall have jurisdiction to deal with at all. Thus, in giving jurisdiction in cases 'arising under * * * the Laws' or 'under * * * Treaties,' the clause is not read as prescribing the process of decision to be followed. The process varies. I cases 'under * * * the Laws' courts often leave determination of issues of fact and even issues that may be thought to be 'of law' to administrative agencies. And under both 'the Laws * * * and Treaties,' much of the decision concerning meaning and applicability may be received ready-made from the Congress and the President. In some cases of all three descriptions, judicial decision may be withheld altogether[j]—and it is for this reason that it will not do to place reliance on the word 'all' in the phrase 'all cases * * * arising * * *.' To the extent that the Constitution speaks to such matters, it does so in the tightly packed phrase 'judicial Power.'

"Nevertheless, if it were impossible to conceive a case 'arising under the Constitution' which would not require the Court to pass on the constitutionality of congressional legislation, then the analysis of the text of Article III made above might be found unsatisfactory, for it would render this clause quite senseless. But there are such cases which may call into question the constitutional validity of judicial, administrative, or military actions without attacking legislative or even presidential acts as well, or which call upon the Court, under appropriate statutory authorization, to apply the Constitution to acts of the states."

What of the supremacy clause (Art. VI, cl. 2)?

HERBERT WECHSLER, *Toward Neutral Principles of Constitutional Law*, 73 Harv.L.Rev. 1, 3–5 (1959): "Judge Hand [*The Bill of Rights* 28 (1958)] concedes that under this clause 'state courts would at times have to decide whether state laws and constitutions, or even a federal statute, were in conflict with the federal constitution' but he adds that 'the fact that this jurisdiction was confined to such occasions, and that it was thought necessary specifically to

j. See Sec. 2 infra, "Political Questions."

provide such a limited jurisdiction, looks rather against than in favor of a general jurisdiction.'

"Are you satisfied, however, to view the supremacy clause in this way, as a grant of jurisdiction to state courts, implying a denial of the power and the duty to all others? This certainly is not its necessary meaning; it may be construed as a mandate to all of officialdom including courts, with a special and emphatic admonition that in binds the judges of the previously independent states. That the latter is the proper reading seems to me persuasive when the other relevant provisions of the Constitution are brought into view.

"Article III, section 1 [represented] one of the major compromises of the Constitutional Convention and relegated the establishment vel non of lower federal courts to the discretion of the Congress. None might have been established, with the consequence that, as in other federalisms, judicial work of first instance would all have been remitted to state courts. Article III, section 2 goes on, however, to delineate the scope of the federal judicial power, providing that it 'shall extend [inter alia] to all Cases, in Law and Equity, arising under this Constitution * * *' and further, that the Supreme Court 'shall have appellate jurisdiction' in such cases 'with such Exceptions, and under such Regulations as the Congress shall make.' Surely this means, as section 25 of the Judiciary Act of 1789 took it to mean, that if a court passes on a constitutional issue, as the supremacy clause provides that it should, its judgment is reviewable, subject to congressional exceptions, by the Supreme Court, in which event that Court must have no less authority and duty to accord priority to constitutional provisions that the court that it review. And such state cases might have encompassed every case in which a constitutional issue could possibly arise, since, as I have said, Congress need not and might not have exerted its authority to establish 'inferior' federal courts.

"If you abide with me thus far, I doubt that you will hesitate upon the final step. Is it a possible construction of the Constitution, measured strictly as Judge Hand admonishes by the test of 'general purpose,' that if Congress opts, as it has opted, to create a set of lower courts, those courts in cases falling within their respective jurisdictions and the Supreme Court when it passes on their judgments are less or differently constrained by the supremacy clause than are the state courts, and the Supreme Court when it reviews their judgments? Yet I cannot escape, what is for me the most astonishing conclusion, that this is the precise result of Judge Hand's reading of the text."

Did Judge Hand concede too much in reading the text of the supremacy clause to empower state courts to decide the constitutionality of *federal* statutes? If so, is Chief Justice Marshall's reference to Art. VI persuasive?[k]

k. Consider C. Black, *The People and The Court* 23–25 (1960): "[T]he most impressive thing in firming the claims of judicial review is the operation of our history since its beginning. And the most striking thing about this history is that the other departments of government, preeminently Congress, have operated under the assumption (and not through mere oversight, for the assumption has in several epochs been passionately challenged) that judicial review is an authentic part of our system of government. One of the most decisive Congressional expressions of this assumption, of special interest because it was passed by the First Congress, is the 25th Section of the first federal Judiciary Act [which] explicitly recognizes and provides for review of state court decisions by the Supreme Court, and lays it down with certainty that the Supreme Court may, by reversing a state judgment that has upheld a state law as against constitutional attack, hold state laws unconstitutional. But it says more than that. It clearly recognizes, first, that the validity of a "treaty or statute of * * * the United States' may be drawn in question in a state court and that the decision of the state court may be 'against their validity.' It then goes on to say, not only that the Supreme Court may review such a judgment, but that it may be 'reversed or

WILLIAM VAN ALSTYNE, supra, at 20–22: "The phrase 'in pursuance thereof' might as easily mean '*in the manner prescribed by this Constitution,*' in which case acts of Congress might be judicially reviewable as to their procedural integrity, but not as to their substance. An example of this more limited, procedural, judicial review is found in *Field v. Clark* [143 U.S. 649, 12 S.Ct. 495, 36 L.Ed. 294 (1892)], It is, moreover, far more common in other countries than is substantive constitutional review. * * *

"The phrase might also mean merely that only those statutes adopted by Congress *after* the re-establishment and reconstitution of Congress pursuant to the Constitution itself shall be the supreme law of the land, whereas acts of the earlier Continental Congress, constituted merely under the Articles of Confederation, would not necessarily be supreme and binding upon the several states. Under this view, acts of Congress, like acts of Parliament, *are* the supreme law and not to be second-guessed by any court, state or federal, so long as they postdate ratification of the Constitution.[36]

"* * * *Assuming that an act repugnant to the Constitution is not a law 'in pursuance thereof' and thus must not be given effect as the supreme law of the land, who, according to the Constitution, is to make the determination as to whether any given law is in fact repugnant to the Constitution itself?* [T]he supremacy clause itself cannot be the clear textual basis for a claim by the judiciary that this prerogative to determine repugnancy belongs to it.

"[The phrase] could mean merely that the people should regard the Constitution with deep concern and that *they* should act to prevent Congress from overstepping the Constitution. It might even imply, moreover, a right of civil disobedience or serve as a written reminder to government of the natural right of revolution against tyrannical government which oversteps the terms of the social compact. Such a construction would be consistent with philosophical writings of the period, consistent with the Declaration of Independence, and consistent also with the view of some antifederalists of the period." [l]

affirmed' in that Court. If the Supreme Court may 'affirm' a state judgment holding a federal law invalid, then the Supreme Court obviously may, in such a case at least, hold a federal law invalid. So much is beyond cavil on the face of the statute. [But] does it not seem likely that it was also assumed that the federal courts were empowered to pass and would pass, in all cases within their jurisdiction, on the validity of the state laws? Actually, the absurdity of the contrary assumption, in the context of the Judiciary Act of 1789, is even greater than this bare statement makes it appear. For that Act provided (as the law still provides) that parties from different state could sue and be sued in the federal courts. So the hypothesis that the state courts might, while the federal courts might not, pass on the validity of federal statutes, would necessarily imply that parties who were citizens of the same state could appeal to the federal Constitution in court, while those who were citizens of different states could not. This is sheer lunacy—but to clear the members of the First Congress (as they deserve to be cleared) of this charge of lunacy, we have to assume that they took it for granted that the federal constitutional validity of state and federal laws could be passed on by all courts, state and federal."

36. For a careful elaboration of this point, see 2 Crosskey, *Politics and the Constitution* 990–1007 (1953).

As distinguished from acts of Congress, treaties were binding upon the several states according to this view merely by having been entered into "under the Authority of the United States," and irrespective of whether they were approved by the Senate as it was proposed to be established pursuant to the new Constitution.

l. Much has been written on the matter of "historical original intent" in respect to judicial review—generally examining pre-Convention judicial precedents in England and the colonies, statements of the framers both within and outside the Constitutional Convention (see especially Alexander Hamilton in Nos. 78 and 80 of *The Federalist* (1788)), and debate during the ratification period—arriving at conflicting conclusions. See, e.g., Beard, *The Supreme Court and the Constitution* (1912); Berger, *Congress v. The Supreme Court* (1969); Boudin, *Government by Judiciary* (1932); Corwin, *The Doctrine of Judicial Review*

The Court as "Final" Arbiter

THOMAS JEFFERSON, writing in 1804, 8 *The Writings of Thomas Jefferson* 310 (1897): "The Judges, believing the [Sedition Law] constitutional, had a right to pass a sentence of fine and imprisonment; because that power was placed in their hands by the Constitution. But the Executive, believing the law to be unconstitutional, was bound to remit the execution of it; because that power has been confided to him by the Constitution. The instrument meant that its co-ordinate branches should be checks on each other. But the opinion which gives to the Judges the right to decide what laws are constitutional, and what not, not only for themselves in their own sphere of action, but for the Legislative and Executive also in their spheres, would make the Judiciary a despotic branch."

ANDREW JACKSON, veto message in 1832 on act to recharter Bank of United States (the constitutionality of which had earlier been upheld by the Court), 2 Richardson, *Messages and Papers of the Presidents* 576, 581–82 (1900): "It is as much the duty of the House of Representatives, of the Senate, and of the President to decide upon the constitutionality of any bill or resolution which may be presented to them for passage or approval as it is of the supreme judges when it may be brought before them for judicial decision. The opinion of the judges has no more authority over Congress than the opinion of Congress has over the judges, and on that point the President is independent of both. The authority of the Supreme Court must not, therefore, be permitted to control the Congress or the Executive when acting in their legislative capacities, but to have only such influence as the force of their reasoning may deserve."

ABRAHAM LINCOLN, inaugural address in 1861, 2 Richardson, supra, at 5, 9–10: "I do not forget the position assumed by some that constitutional questions are to be decided by the Supreme Court, nor do I deny that such decisions must be binding in any case upon the parties to a suit as to the object of that suit, while they are also entitled to very high respect and consideration in all parallel cases by all other departments of the Government. And while it is obviously possible that such decision may be erroneous in any given case, still the evil effect following it, being limited to that particular case, with the chance that it may be overruled and never become a precedent for other cases, can better be borne than could the evils of a different practice. At the same time, the candid citizen must confess that if the policy of the Government upon vital questions affecting the whole people is to be irrevocably fixed by decisions of the Supreme

(1914); Crosskey, *Politics and the Constitution in the History of the United States* (1953); Goebel, *History of the Supreme Court of the United States: Antecedents and Beginnings to 1801* (1971); Haines, *The American Doctrine of Judicial Supremacy* (2d ed. 1932); Nelson, *Changing Conceptions of Judicial Review: The Evolution of Constitutional Theory in the States, 1790–1860,* 120 U.Pa.L.Rev. 1166 (1972). Warren, *Congress, the Constitution, and the Supreme Court* (1925). For brief discussion see Levy, *Judicial Review, History, and Democracy: An Introduction,* in Judicial Review and the Supreme Court 1–12 (1967); Kernochan, *On Constitutionalism and the Antecedents of Judicial Review,* in Dowling & Gunther, Constitutional Law 19–31 (7th ed. 1965). For the view that "strict intentionalism" is not a "tenable approach to constitutional decisionmaking," see Brest, *The Misconceived Quest for the Original Understanding,* 60 B.U.L.Rev. 204 (1980).

For review of the broader historical setting, see Bailyn, *The Ideological Origins of the American Revolution* (1967); Wood, *The Creation of the American Republic, 1776–1787* (1969).

Court, the instant they are made in ordinary litigation between parties in personal actions the people will have ceased to be their own rulers, having to that extent practically resigned their Government into the hands of that eminent tribunal. Nor is there in this view any assault upon the court or the judges. It is a duty from which they may not shrink to decide cases properly brought before them, and it is no fault of theirs if others seek to turn their decisions to political purposes."

Are these views inconsistent with *Marbury?* Does *Marbury* decide anything more than that *"the Court may refuse to give effect to an act of Congress where the act pertains to the judicial power itself"?* Van Alstyne, supra, at 34. Than that the Court claimed the power of judicial review "only in the defensive sense of safeguarding the Court's original jurisdiction from congressional enlargement"? Strong, *Judicial Review: A Tri-Dimensional Concept of Administrative-Constitutional Law,* 69 W.Va.L.Rev. 111, 249 (1967).

If the Court upholds the constitutionality of a federal statute, may the President refuse to enforce it because be believes it to be unconstitutional May he refuse to enforce it on this ground after Congress has enacted it but before it comes before the Court? May he refuse to enforce it on this ground if Congress overrides his veto? May the President continue to enforce a statute (e.g., by pressing charges for its violation) after the Court has held it unconstitutional? May he refuse to return property that the Court has held was unconstitutionally seized? If Congress forbids the President from taking certain action, may he do so on the ground that Congress' restriction is unconstitutional? Even after the Court has upheld its constitutionality?

LEARNED HAND, *The Bill of Rights* 11–15 (1958): "[L]et us try to imagine what would have been the result if the power [of judicial review] did not exist. There were two alternatives, each prohibitive, I submit. One was that the decision of the first 'Department' before which an issue arose should be conclusive whenever it arose later. That doctrine, coupled with its conceded power over the purse, would have made Congress substantially omnipotent, for by far the greater number of issues that could arise would depend upon its prior action. * * *

"As Hamilton intimated, every legislator is under constant pressure from groups of constituents whom it does not satisfy to say, 'Although I think what you want is right and that you ought to have it, I cannot bring myself to believe that it is within my constitutional powers.' Such scruples are not convincing to those whose interests are at stake; and the voters at large will not usually care enough about preserving 'the balance of the Constitution' to offset the votes of those whose interests will be disappointed. [But] the second alternative would have been even worse, for under it each 'Department' would have been free to decide constitutional issues as it thought right, regardless of any earlier decision of the others. Thus it would have been the President's privilege, and indeed his duty, to execute only those statutes that seemed to him to be constitutional, regardless even of a decision of the Supreme Court. The courts would have entered such judgments as seemed to them consonant with the Constitution; but neither the President, nor Congress, would have been bound to enforce them if he or it disagreed, and without their help the judgments would have been waste paper.

"For centuries it has been an accepted canon in interpretation of documents to interpolate into the text such provisions, though not expressed, as are essential to prevent the defeat of the venture at hand; and this applies with especial force to the interpretation of constitutions, which, since they are designed to cover a great multitude of necessarily unforeseen occasions, must be cast in general language, unless they are constantly amended. If so, it was altogether in keeping with established practice for the Supreme Court to assume an authority to keep the states, Congress, and the President within their prescribed powers. Otherwise the government could not proceed as planned; and indeed would almost certainly have foundered, as in fact it almost did over that very issue.

"However, since this power is not a logical deduction from the structure of the Constitution but only a practical condition upon its successful operation, it need not be exercised whenever a court sees, or thinks that it sees, an invasion of the Constitution."

May a Congressman vote against a bill because he believes it to be unconstitutional even though the Court has held to the contrary? May the President veto such a bill on this ground? If the Court has upheld the constitutionality of a federal criminal statute, may a subsequent President grant pardons to all persons convicted under it (see Art. II, § 2, cl. 1)? If the President altogether refuses to "receive Ambassadors and other public Ministers" (see Art. II, § 3), may the Court order him to do so? Or should the "supremacy" of judicial review at least be limited to those decisions that do not "interfere with the procedural machinery of Congress or the federal executive"? Buchanan, *Judicial Supremacy Reexamined: A Proposed Alternative,* 70 Mich.L.Rev. 1279, 1304 (1972). See Sec. 2 infra—"Political Questions." Is there a distinction between *state* and federal officials in respect to the binding nature of the Court's decisions?

COOPER v. AARON (1958), set forth more fully, Ch. 10, Sec. 2, IV: "Article VI of the Constitution makes the Constitution the 'supreme Law of the Land.' In 1803, [*Marbury*] declared the basic principle that the federal judiciary is supreme in the exposition of the law of the Constitution, and that principle has ever since been respected by this Court and the Country as a permanent and indispensable feature of our constitutional system. [Every] state legislator and executive and judicial officer is solemnly committed by oath taken pursuant to Art. VI, ¶ 3 'to support this Constitution.' * * * Chief Justice Marshall spoke for a unanimous Court in saying that: 'if the legislatures of the several states may, at will, annul the judgments of the courts of the United States, and destroy the rights acquired under those judgments, the constitution itself becomes a solemn mockery * * *.' *United States v. Peters,* 5 Cranch 115, 136. A Governor who asserts a power to nullify a federal court order is similarly restrained." [m]

Cooper involved the refusal of Arkansas officials to abide by federal court decrees requiring school desegregation. In contrast, if the Court *upholds* the constitutionality of a state law, may that state's supreme court subsequently rule that the state law violates the Constitution? Would the state court's ruling "annul the judgment" of the Supreme Court? See Tribe, *American Constitutional Law* 27–33 (1978).

m. For criticism and defense of this "judicial supremacy" analysis, see Farber, *The Supreme Court and the Rule of Law: Cooper v. Aaron Revisited,* 1982 U.Ill.L.Rev. 387.

Judicial Review and Democracy

ALEXANDER BICKEL, supra, at 16–20: "The root difficulty is that judicial review is a counter-majoritarian force in our system. [W]hen the Supreme Court declares unconstitutional a legislative act or the action of an elected executive, it thwarts the will of representatives of the actual people of the here and now; it exercises control, not in behalf of the prevailing majority, but against it. That [is] the reason the charge can be made that judicial review is undemocratic.

"Most assuredly, no democracy operates by taking continuous nose counts on the broad range of daily governmental activities. * * * Nevertheless, although democracy does not mean constant reconsideration of decisions once made, it does mean that a representative majority has the power to accomplish a reversal. This power is of the essence, and no less so because it is often merely held in reserve.

"It is true, of course, that the process of reflecting the will of a popular majority in the legislature is deflected by various inequalities of representation and by all sorts of institutional habits and characteristics, which perhaps tend most often in favor of inertia.[n] Yet, impurities and imperfections, if such they be, in one part of the system are no argument for total departure from the desired norm in another part. * * *

"No doubt ['interest' or 'pressure groups'] operate forcefully on the electoral process, and no doubt they seek and gain access to and an effective share in the legislative and executive decisional process. Perhaps they constitute also, in some measure, an impurity or imperfection. But no one has claimed that they have been able to capture the governmental process except by combining in some fashion, and thus capturing or constituting (are not the two verbs synonymous?) a majority. They often tend themselves to be majoritarian in composition and to be subject to broader majoritarian influences. And the price of what they sell or buy in the legislature is determined in the biennial or quadrennial electoral marketplace. * * * Judicial review works counter to this characteristic.

"It therefore does not follow from the complex nature of a democratic system that, because admirals and generals and the members, say, of the Federal Reserve Board or of this or that administrative agency are not electorally responsible, judges who exercise the power of judicial review need not be responsible either, and in neither case is there a serious conflict with democratic theory. For admirals and generals and the like are most often responsible to officials who are themselves elected and through whom the line runs directly to a majority. What is more significant, the policies they make are or should be interstitial or technical only and are reversible by legislative majorities * * *—a fact of great consequence. Nor will it do to liken judicial review to the general lawmaking function of judges. In the latter aspect, judges are indeed something like administrative officials, for their decisions are also revers-

n. For a forceful position "that there can be no automatic and blanket equation of Congress or the Executive branch with the voice of the people," see M. Shapiro, *Freedom of Speech*, 17–25 (1966). Consider Krislov, *The Supreme Court and Political Freedom* 20 (1968): "If one analyzes the actual rules of behavior in the so-called democratic units of government, we find that they also have mixed aspects, with the possibility—sometimes the actuality—of minority control. The power of the Rules Committee, the filibuster, and the Senate are obvious shortcomings; [the] operational consequences of seniority, and the population base of districts likely to maintain continuity in representation are more veiled aspects." See also Kommers, *Professor Kurland, The Supreme Court, and Political Science*, 15 J.Pub.L. 230 (1966).

ible by any legislative majority—and not infrequently they are reversed.[o] Judicial review, however, is the power to apply and construe the Constitution in matters of the greatest moment, against the wishes of a legislative majority, which is, in turn, powerless to affect the judicial decision."

JESSE CHOPER, *The Supreme Court and the Political Branches: Democratic Theory and Practice,* 122 U.Pa.L.Rev. 810, 830–32 (1974): "In the main, the effect of judicial review in ruling legislation unconstitutional is to nullify the finished product of the lawmaking process. It is the very rare Supreme Court decision on constitutionality that affirmatively mandates the undertaking of government action. To make the point in another way, when the Supreme Court finds legislative acts unconstitutional it holds invalid only those enactments that have survived the many hurdles fixed between incipient proposals and standing law.

"The significance of this [is] that most of the antimajoritarian elements that have been found in the American legislative process [are] negative ones. They work to *prevent* the translation of popular wishes into governing rules rather than to *produce* laws that are contrary to majority sentiment. [S]enators representing only fifteen percent of the population may hold sway in the upper house; but their real impact (as is obviously the case with the filibuster as well) is to halt ultimate action rather than facilitate it. For the enactment of law also requires the concurrence of the lower [house]. Furthermore, within each legislative chamber, the ability of the committees and their chairmen and minority members—and frequently of the lobbies and other interest groups as well—to circumvent the majority will of the assembly is most saliently manifested in obstructing the process rather than in making laws. The more formidable task usually is not to stall or defeat a proposal but to organize the requisite support among the dispersed powers so as to form a coalition for its passage. * * *

"Thus, although exceptions exist, '[a] distinguishing feature of our system, perhaps impelled by heritage of sectional division and heterogeneity, is that our governmental structure, institutional habits, and political parties with their internal factional divisions, have combined to produce a system in which major programs and major new directions cannot be undertaken unless supported by a fairly broad popular consensus. This normally has been far broader than 51 percent and often bipartisan as well.' [Consequently,] when the Supreme Court, itself without conventional political responsibility, says 'thou shalt not' to acts of Congress, it usually cuts sharply against the grain of majority rule. The relatively few laws that finally overcome the congressional obstacle course generally illustrate the national political branches operating at their majoritarian best while the process of judicial review depicts that element of the Court's work and that exertion of federal authority with the most brittle democratic roots.[59] "

o. Compare Bishin, *Judicial Review in Democratic Theory,* 50 So.Cal.L.Rev. 1099, 1110 (1977): "Closer examination suggests [that] not all of the decisions that such officeholders make can, in fact or theory, be reversed by majoritarian action. [It] must be remembered [that] Congress—especially the Senate—is so structured that representatives of only a minority of the people can prevent the passage of legislation which would overturn prior decisions * * *. Wherever the position of such a minority coincides with the [judge's or administrative officer's] position, therefore, the Constitution gives the principle of reversibility no effect at all."

59. Although no detailed examination of the legislative systems in the states and their political subdivisions has been ventured here, the same conclusion appears to have substantially similar merit in respect to the Court's overturning the laws they produce.

"THE MOST CELEBRATED FOOTNOTE IN CONSTITUTIONAL LAW": FOOTNOTE 4 OF THE *CAROLENE PRODUCTS* CASE

UNITED STATES v. CAROLENE PRODUCTS CO., 304 U.S. 144, 58 S.Ct. 778, 82 L.Ed. 1234 (1938), upheld the constitutionality of a federal statute that prohibited the shipment in interstate commerce of "filled milk," a product compounded with fat or oil so as to resemble milk or cream. Appellee argued that the legislation violated both the commerce and due process clauses. The government countered that appellee's product was an impure, adulterated substance that posed a danger to the public. Writing for the Court, JUSTICE STONE took the position that economic regulatory legislation, such as the statute at issue, was entitled to a presumption of constitutionality and should be upheld if supported by any rational basis. Under this approach, the challenged legislation easily passed constitutional muster.[a] In the course of writing his opinion, JUSTICE STONE dropped a footnote (fn. 4) that has been called "the most celebrated footnote in constitutional law" [b] and "the great and modern charter for ordering the relations between judges and other agencies of government."[c] That footnote (case citations omitted) reads as follows:

"There may be narrower scope for operation of the presumption of constitutionality when legislation appears on its face to be within a specific prohibition of the Constitution, such as those of the first ten amendments, which are deemed equally specific when held to be embraced within the Fourteenth.

"It is unnecessary to consider now whether legislation which restricts those political processes which can obviously be expected to bring about repeal of undesirable legislation, is to be subjected to more exacting judicial scrutiny under the general prohibitions of the Fourteenth than are most other types of legislation [referring to cases dealing with restrictions on voting rights and freedom of expression and political association].

"Nor need we enquire whether similar considerations enter into the review of statutes directed at particular religions or national or racial minorities[:] whether prejudice against discrete and insular minorities may be a special condition, which tends seriously to curtail the operation of those political

a. "The plaudits accorded [footnote 4] are matched by the disregard of the case itself." G. Miller, *The True Story of Carolene Products,* 1987 Sup.Ct.Rev. 397, 398. This is unfortunate, points out Professor Miller, id. at 398–99, "because [the case] is interesting in its own right and because its facts shed light on the meaning of the footnote. The statute upheld in the case was an utterly unprincipled example of special interest legislation. The purported 'public interest' justifications so credulously reported by Justice Stone were patently bogus. [It] is difficult to believe that members of the Court were unaware of the true motivation behind this legislation. That they should nevertheless vote to uphold the statute strongly suggested that all bets were off as far as economic regulation was concerned. Footnote four, in this light, can be seen as indicating that the Court intended to keep its hands off economic regulation, no matter how egregious the discrimination or patent the special interests motivation. Rational basis scrutiny of [this sort] could not be taken seriously if it precluded judicial protection of individual liberties. By separating economic and personal liberties, Justice Stone suggested that the Court might really mean what it said about deference to the legislative will in economic cases. Two-tiered scrutiny did much more than facilitate the categories entitled to exacting judicial review. It also freed the forces of interest group politics from the stumbling block of the federal courts."

See also, Komesar, *Taking Institutions Seriously,* 51 U.Chi.L.Rev. 366, 416 (1984): "It does not take much scrutiny to see the dairy lobby at work behind the passage [of] the 'filled milk' act. Indeed, [it] is not too uncharitable [to] suggest that concern for the dairies' pocketbooks rather than for the consumer's health best explains the dairy lobby's efforts."

b. Justice Powell, *Carolene Products Revisited,* 82 Colum.L.Rev. 1087 (1982).

c. Fiss, *The Forms of Justice,* 93 Harv.L. Rev. 1, 6 (1979).

processes ordinarily to be relied upon to protect minorities, and which may call for a correspondingly more searching judicial inquiry."

1. *Removing "impurities" in the democratic process. Carolene Products* was concerned about the impurity of appellee's product and the need to exclude it from interstate commerce, but, observes, **J. A. BALKIN**, *The Footnote,* 83 Nw. U.L.Rev. 275, 283 (1989), "*Carolene Products* is also about another type of purity and impurity, another type of inclusion and exclusion—that which affects the democratic process. *Carolene Products,* especially in its famous footnote, is concerned with impurities in the democratic process caused by adulteration of the means of political deliberation (the subject of the footnote's second paragraph) or by the exclusion of discrete and insular minorities from full political participation (the footnote's third paragraph). According to the logic of the footnote, certain groups are shut out of the democratic process, relegated to the periphery. They are, to use, Professor Birmayer's expression, 'insider-outsiders'—persons subject to the power of the political community yet excluded from participation within it.[25] The goal of *Carolene Products* is to restore them to their rightful place within the polity through judicial supervision of the results of the democratic process. The role of the judiciary is to exclude legislation which is the result of impurities in the process, and by this exclusion, include those persons previously excluded, or prevent their future exclusion."

2. *"Revers[ing] the spin of the countermajoritarian difficulty."* Ackerman, *Beyond Carolene Products,* 98 Harv.L.Rev. 713, 714–15 (1985), sees the case and footnote 4 as a "brilliant" effort "to turn the Old Court's recent defeat into a judicial victory": "*Carolene* promises relief from the problem of legitimacy raised whenever nine elderly lawyers invalidate the legislative decisions of our elected representatives. The *Carolene* solution is to seize the high ground of democratic theory and establish that the challenged legislation was produced by a profoundly defective process. By demonstrating that the legislative solution itself resulted from an undemocratic procedure, a *Carolene* court hopes to reverse the spin of the countermajoritarian difficulty. For it now may seem that the original legislative decision, not the judicial invalidation, suffers the greater legitimacy deficit."

3. *Did footnote 4 replace one kind of "judicial activism" with another? Does it cause us to return to another "kind of substantive due process?* Consider the remarks of JUSTICE LEWIS POWELL, fn. b supra, at 1089–91 (1982): "Unlike Holmes, Stone lived to see—and indeed helped to preside over—the passing of the *Lochner* era. The well-known turning point came in 1937, when the Court upheld the constitutionality of a state minimum wage law for women [in *West Coast Hotel Co. v. Parrish,* p. 85 infra]. *Carolene Products* was an otherwise unremarkable decision in the same line. But Footnote 4, as interpreted by many commentators, represented a radical departure of its own. Far from initiating a jurisprudence of judicial deference to political judgments by the legislature, Footnote 4—on this view—undertook to substitute one activist judicial mission for another. Where once the Court had championed rights of property, now—according to some—it should view its special function as the identification and protection of 'discrete and insular minorities.' Where the Court before had used the substantive due process clause to protect property rights, now it should use the equal protection clause—a generally forgotten provision that Holmes once

25. Brilmayer, *Carolene, Conflicts and the Fate of the "Insider-Outsider,"* 134 U.Pa.L. Rev. 1291, 1294 (1986).

dismissed as 'the usual last resort of constitutional arguments'—as a sword with which to promote the liberty interests of groups disadvantaged by political decisions.

"The difference—or so runs the argument—is that protection of minority rights occurs in the name of correcting defects of *process,* defects that may have prevented minorities from gaining for themselves a fair bargain in the political arena. The theory is that the Court—in so protecting minority interests—does not risk imposing its own substantive values and distributive preferences on the Constitution and on the people of the United States.

"* * * Stone referred to discrete and insular minorities in a sentence, divided by a colon, in which he had referred earlier to racial, ethnic, and religious groups. Examining the textual evidence only, I think it would be a plausible reading that these are the only kinds of groups to which the term 'discrete and insular' was intended to refer. In the normal operation of the political process, the term then would suggest that *some* racial, religious, and ethnic groups are not treated fairly and equally. Courts therefore should apply strict scrutiny to laws 'directed at' these disadvantaged groups.

"This idea has intuitive appeal, and it has been widely accepted. But it too may require some form of limitation in its application. In our uniquely heterogeneous society there are countless groups with some claim to being racial, ethnic, or religious. Over our history many have been minorities, ineffective in politics, and often discriminated against. But these conditions do not remain static. Immigrant groups that once were neglected have become influential participants in the political process. One reasonably may doubt the capacity of courts to distinguish wisely among them or determine which groups—at a given time and place—operate effectively within our politics. One also must inquire how far a court may go in determining when a law, nondiscriminatory on its face, fairly may be considered as 'directed at' a particular group.[d]

"The problem is this: in a democratic society there inevitably are both winners and losers. The fact that one group is disadvantaged by a particular piece of legislation, or action of government, therefore does not prove that the process has failed to function properly. To infer otherwise—that the process has been corrupted by invidious discrimination—a judge must have some *substantive* vision of what results the process should have yielded. Otherwise he has no way to know that the process was unfair.

"Here I must pause to wonder. If I am correct about the implicit link between a substantive judgment and a malfunction of process, then one may inquire whether we have not returned in some cases to a kind of substantive due process. And one also may wonder what Stone—who had fought so vigorously against substantive due process—would have had to say about this."

4. *Is Carolene's conception of the impact of prejudice "underinclusive"?* Should courts protect groups that are "anonymous and diffuse" rather than "discrete and insular"? Is "discretness and insularity" likely to be a source of

d. Does *Carolene* require that "neutral rules" be strictly scrutinized? Would such scrutiny be contrary to its reasoning? See Brilmayer, fn. 25 supra, at 1307–09. Professor Brilmayer concludes, id. at 1334: "*Carolene*'s cruelest hoax is its suggestion that, once the discriminatory rules are invalidated, our political process problems are over. But, as any excluded person surely realizes, after putting the illusion of *Carolene* to one side, discriminatory rules are only a small part of a very large problem. They are only the first hurdle in a long road to political participation and equality. *Carolene*'s approach has led us seriously astray. It suggests that only discriminatory rules have process defects."

important bargaining advantage, not disadvantage, for a group involved in pluralist American politics? Consider BRUCE ACKERMAN, supra, at 731–32, 745: "*Carolene*'s empirical inadequacy stems from its underinclusive conception of the impact of prejudice upon American society. It is easy to identify groups in the population that are not discrete and insular but that are nonetheless the victims of prejudice as that term is commonly understood. Thus, the fact that homosexuals are a relatively anonymous minority has not saved the group from severe prejudice.[e] Nor is sexism a nonproblem merely because women are a diffuse, if discrete, majority. Prejudice is generated by a bewildering variety of social conditions. Although some *Carolene* minorities are seriously victimized, they are not the only ones stigmatized; nor is it obvious that all *Carolene* minorities are stigmatized more grievously than any other non-*Carolene* group. Why should the concern with 'prejudice' justify *Carolene*'s narrow fixation upon 'discrete and insular' minorities?

"The answer seemed easy in a world in which members of the paradigmatic *Carolene* minority group—blacks—were effectively barred from voting and political participation. [As] we move beyond the pariah model, however, anonymous or diffuse minorities will increasingly emerge as the groups that can raise the most serious complaints of pluralist disempowerment.

"* * * [A]s long as we use *Carolene* rhetoric to express our constitutional concerns with racial equality and religious freedom, we will find ourselves saying things that are increasingly belied by political reality. While constitutional lawyers decry the political powerlessness of discrete and insular groups, representatives of these interests will be wheeling and dealing in the ongoing pluralistic exchange—winning some battles, losing others, but plainly numbering among the organized interests whose electoral power must be treated with respect by their bargaining partners and competitors. * * *

"* * * [I]f we are to remain faithful to *Carolene*'s concern with the fairness of pluralist politics, we must repudiate the bad political science that allows us to ignore those citizens who have the most serious complaints: the anonymous and diffuse victims of poverty and sexual discrimination who find it most difficult to protect their fundamental interests through effective political organization."[f]

MARTIN v. HUNTER'S LESSEE

14 U.S. (1 Wheat.) 304, 4 L.Ed. 97 (1816).

[Lord Fairfax, a Virginia citizen, willed his Virginia land known as the Northern Neck of Virginia to his nephew, Martin, a British subject resident in England. In 1789, Virginia, acting pursuant to state laws confiscating lands owned by British subjects, granted land in the Northern Neck to Hunter. The latter brought an action of ejectment against Martin. The Virginia district court ruled for Martin, whose claim was fortified by the anti-confiscation clauses

e. Earlier in his article, id. at 729, Professor Ackerman notes that he "propose[s] to define a minority as 'discrete' when its members are marked out in ways that make it relatively easy for others to identify them. [In] contrast, other minorities are socially defined in ways that give individual members the chance to avoid easy identification. A homosexual, for example, can keep her sexual preference a very private affair and thereby avoid much of the public opprobrium attached to her minority status. It is for this reason that I shall call homosexuals, and groups like them, 'anonymous' minorities and contrast them with 'discrete' minorities of the kind paradigmatically exemplified by blacks."

f. The impact of the *Carolene Products* footnote is further discussed at many points in the materials, especially Chs. 3 and 6.

of the treaties of 1783 and 1794 with Great Britain. But the Virginia Court of Appeals reversed, holding that (1) the state's title to the Northern Neck had been perfected before any treaty and (2) in any event, a 1796 Act of Compromise between the Fairfax claimants and the state claimants, formally adopted by the Virginia legislature, had settled the matter against Martin.

[Acting for the purchasers of the Fairfax estate, John Marshall, then a member of the Virginia legislature, had negotiated the compromise. Since he and his brother had organized a syndicate which purchased 160,000 acres of Northern Neck from Martin in 1793, Marshall had a great interest in the case's outcome.

[In *Fairfax's Devisee v. Hunter's Lessee,* 11 U.S. (7 Cranch) 603, 3 L.Ed. 453 (1813), the Supreme Court (Marshall, C.J., not participating) reversed the Virginia Court of Appeals, ruling that Virginia had not perfected title to Northern Neck prior to the grant to Hunter and that therefore the Treaty of 1794 confirmed the title remaining in Martin. Neither Story, J.'s majority opinion nor Johnson, J.'s dissent mentioned the Act of Compromise.

[The cause was remanded to the Virginia Court of Appeals with instructions to enter judgment for appellant, but that court refused to obey the Supreme Court's mandate. All four judges then sitting maintained that in so far as it extended the appellate jurisdiction of the Supreme Court to "this court," § 25 of the Judiciary Act was unconstitutional. Judge Roane—Marshall's arch political enemy—and Judge Fleming (the two judges sitting when the court had decided the case against Martin on the merits) contended further that even if the Judiciary Act were valid the case had not properly been before the Supreme Court since the Virginia decision turned not upon a treaty, but "upon another and ordinary ground of jurisdiction—the act of compromise."

[The case again came to the Supreme Court, Marshall again not sitting.[a]]

STORY, J., delivered the opinion of the court. * * *

The third article of the constitution is that which must principally attract our attention. [A]ppellate jurisdiction is given by the constitution to the supreme court, in all cases [within "the judicial power of the United States"] where it has not original jurisdiction; subject, however, to such exceptions and regulations as congress may prescribe. [W]hat is there to restrain its exercise over state tribunals, in the enumerated cases? [If] the judicial power extends to the case, it will be in vain to search in the letter of the constitution for any qualification as to the tribunal where it depends. It [is] plain, that the framers of the constitution did contemplate that cases within the judicial cognisance of the United States, not only might, but would, arise in the state courts, in the exercise of their ordinary jurisdiction [pointing to the supremacy clause]. Suppose, an indictment for a crime, in a state court, and the defendant should allege in his defence, that the crime was created by an ex post facto act of the state, must not the state court [have] a right to pronounce on the validity and sufficiency of the defence? [It] was foreseen, that in the exercise of their ordinary jurisdiction, state courts would incidentally take cognisance of cases

a. For further exploration of the historical background, see 4 Beveridge, *The Life of John Marshall* 144–61 (1919); 2 Crosskey, *Politics and the Constitution* 785–817 (1953); Myers, *History of the Supreme Court* 231–41, 270–73, 278–82 (1925); 1 Warren, *The Supreme Court in United States History* 442–53 (1922). For excellent briefer treatments, see Hart & Wechsler's *The Federal Courts and the Federal System* 442–46 (2d ed. 1973); Note, *Judge Spencer Roane of Virginia; Champion of States' Rights—Foe of John Marshall,* 66 Harv.L.Rev. 1242, 1248–51 (1953).

arising under the constitution, the laws and treaties of the United States. Yet, to all these cases, the judicial power, by the very terms of the constitution, is to extend. It cannot extend, by original jurisdiction, if that was already rightfully and exclusively attached in the state courts, which (as has been already shown) may occur; it must, therefore, extend by appellate jurisdiction, or not at all. It would seem to follow, that the appellate power of the United States must, in such cases, extend to state tribunals * * *

It has been argued, that such an appellate jurisdiction over state courts is inconsistent with the genius of our governments, and the spirit of the constitution. That the latter was never designed to act upon state sovereignties, but only upon the people, and that if the power exists it will materially impair the sovereignty of the states, and the independence of their courts. [But the Constitution] is crowded with provisions which restrain or annul the sovereignty of the states, in some of the highest branches of their prerogatives. The tenth section of the first article contains a long list of disabilities and prohibitions imposed upon the states. [The] language of the constitution is also imperative upon the states, as to the performance of many duties. It is imperative upon the state legislatures, to make laws prescribing the time, places and manner of holding elections for senators and representatives, and for electors of president and vice-president. And in these, as well as some other cases, congress have a right to revise, amend or supersede the laws which may be passed by state legislatures. When, therefore, the states are stripped of some of the highest attributes of sovereignty, and the same are given to the United States; when the legislatures of the states are, in some respects, under the control of congress, and in every case are, under the constitution, bound by the paramount authority of the United States; it is certainly difficult to support the argument, that the appellate power over the decisions of state courts is contrary to the genius of our institutions. The courts of the United States can, without question, revise the proceedings of the executive and legislative authorities of the states, and if they are found to be contrary to the constitution, may declare them to be of no legal validity. Surely, the exercise of the same right over judicial tribunals is not a higher or more dangerous act of sovereign power.

Nor can such a right be deemed to impair the independence of state judges. It is assuming the very ground in controversy, to assert that they possess an absolute independence of the United States. In respect to the powers granted to the United States, they are not independent; they are expressly bound to obedience, by the letter of the constitution * * *.

The argument urged from the possibility of the abuse of the revising power, is equally unsatisfactory. [From] the very nature of things, the absolute right of decision, in the last resort, must rest somewhere—wherever it may be vested, it is susceptible of abuse. [A]dmitting that the judges of the state courts are, and always will be, of as much learning, integrity and wisdom, as those of the courts of the United States (which we very cheerfully admit), it does not aid the argument. It is manifest, that the constitution has proceeded upon a theory of its own, and given or withheld powers according to the judgment of the American people, by whom it was adopted. We can only construe its powers, and cannot inquire into the policy or principles which induced the grant of them. The constitution has presumed (whether rightly or wrongly, we do not inquire), that state attachments, state prejudices, state jealousies, and state interests, might sometimes obstruct, or control, or be supposed to obstruct or control, the regular administration of justice. * * *

This is not all. A motive of another kind, perfectly compatible with the most sincere respect for state tribunals, might induce the grant of appellate power over their decisions. * * * Judges of equal learning and integrity, in different states, might differently interpret the statute, or a treaty of the United States, or even the constitution itself: if there were no revising authority to control these jarring and discordant judgments, and harmonize them into uniformity, the laws, the treaties and the constitution of the United States would be different, in different states, and might, perhaps, never have precisely the same construction, obligation or efficiency, in any two states. The public mischiefs that would attend such a state of things would be truly deplorable * * *.

On the whole, the court are of opinion, that the appellate power of the United States does extend to cases pending in the state courts; and that the 25th section of the judiciary act, which authorizes the exercise of this jurisdiction in the specified cases, by a writ of error, is supported by the letter and spirit of the constitution. [It] is an historical fact, that this exposition of the constitution, extending its appellate power to state courts, was, previous to its adoption, uniformly and publicly avowed by its friends, and admitted by its enemies, as the basis of their respective reasonings, both in and out of the state conventions. It is an historical fact, that at the time when the judiciary act was submitted to the deliberations of the first congress, composed, as it was not only of men of great learning and ability, but of men who acted a principal part in framing, supporting or opposing that constitution, the same exposition was explicitly declared and admitted by the friends and by the opponents of that system. It is an historical fact, that the supreme court of the United States have, from time to time, sustained this appellate jurisdiction, in a great variety of cases, brought from the tribunals of many of the most important states in the Union,[b] and that no state tribunal has ever breathed a judicial doubt on the subject or declined to obey the mandate of the supreme court, until the present occasion. * * *

[The Court next rejected the contention that the case was not properly before it because the Virginia decision turned on the Act of Compromise.]

We have not thought it incumbent on us to give any opinion upon the question, whether this court have authority to issue a writ of mandamus to the court of appeals, to enforce the former judgments, as we did not think it necessarily involved in the decision of this cause.

It is the opinion of the whole court, that the judgment of the court of appeals of Virginia, rendered on the mandate in this cause, be reversed, and the judgment of the district court [be] affirmed.

JOHNSON, J. It will be observed, in this case, that the court disavows all intention to decide on the right to issue compulsory process to the state courts; thus leaving us, in my opinion, where the constitution and laws place us—supreme over persons and cases, so far as our judicial powers extend, but not asserting any compulsory control over the state tribunals. In this view, I acquiesce in their opinion, but not altogether in the reasoning or opinion of my brother who delivered it. * * *

b. See, e.g., *Clerke v. Harwood,* 3 U.S. (3 Dall.) 342, 1 L.Ed. 628 (1797) (state law in conflict with treaty). The first Supreme Court decision holding a state law unconstitutional was *Fletcher v. Peck,* 10 U.S. (6 Cranch) 87, 3 L.Ed. 162 (1810) but the case arose in a lower federal court.

Notes and Questions

1. *Was the judgment executed?* Charles Warren reports that the Court "decided to avoid the chance of further friction" with the Virginia Court of Appeals "and accordingly, instead of issuing a second mandate to that Court, it issued its process directly to the District Court [in] which the suit had been originally instituted," 1 Warren, supra, at 450.[c] See also Dodd, *Chief Justice Marshall and Virginia 1813–21,* 12 Am.Hist.Rev. 776, 779 (1907), claiming that the United States marshal was eventually ordered to execute the judgment of the Supreme Court. But William Crosskey insists that execution of judgment was neither issued nor required. Under the Virginia practice, he contends, the proceeding under which the case was brought "served much the same purpose in settling points of law in dispute in land-title controversies, as does a modern action for a declaratory judgment," 2 Crosskey, supra, at 786. Moreover, he adds, "upon the peculiar facts of the case, execution of the judgment would have been a completely vain proceeding; for Hunter could at once have brought a successful action to recover possession again, based on the compromise. There was not a word in the Supreme Court's decision that forbade it." Id. at 806 n.[d]

2. COHENS v. VIRGINIA, 19 U.S. (6 Wheat.) 264, 5 L.Ed. 257 (1821)—which sustained the Court's appellate jurisdiction under § 25 of the Judiciary Act to review state criminal proceedings, and is generally viewed as reaffirming and "supplementing" *Martin,* see 2 Warren, supra, at 10—has stronger historical links with *McCulloch v. Maryland,* 17 U.S. (4 Wheat.) 316, 4 L.Ed. 579 (1819), see 4 Beveridge, *The Life of John Marshall* 343 (1919).

Appellants were found guilty in a Virginia court of selling lottery tickets in violation of state law. Their defense was that the lottery was organized by the City of Washington, under a congressional statute authorizing the lottery. On appeal to the Supreme Court, they were met with the contentions that the Court had no jurisdiction to review a state criminal case and, in any event, Congress had no power to permit the sale of lottery tickets in a state which prohibited such sale. On the jurisdictional point, Virginia argued that (1) if when the state is a party the Supreme Court has original jurisdiction, this grant excludes appellate jurisdiction; (2) federal courts cannot take original jurisdiction over criminal cases, since that rightfully belongs to the courts of the state whose laws have been violated; (3) consequently, the Supreme Court has no jurisdiction at all. As in *Marbury,* MARSHALL, C.J., used the occasion to express a broad view of the Court's powers, but decided the case on a narrow ground in favor of the Jeffersonians—the federal statute authorizing a lottery had no effect outside the City of Washington.

The case was decided at a time when the state autonomy and states' rights generally were being boldly proclaimed. Two years earlier, most southern and western states had vehemently denounced the decision in *McCulloch v. Mary-*

c. In respect to its appellate jurisdiction, 28 U.S.C.A. § 2106 presently empowers the Court to "remand the cause and direct the entry of such appropriate judgment, decree or order, or require such further proceedings to be had as may be just under the circumstances."

d. For post-*Martin* instances of state court resistance to Supreme Court orders and various efforts to secure compliance see Murphy, *Lower Court Checks on Supreme Court Power,* 53 Am.Pol.Sci.Rev. 1017 (1959); Warren, *Federal and State Court Interference,* 43 Harv.L. Rev. 345 (1930); Beatty, *State Court Evasion of United States Supreme Court Mandates During the Last Decade of the Warren Court,* 6 Val.L.Rev. 260 (1972); Notes, 67 Harv.L.Rev. 1251 (1954), 56 Yale L.J. 574 (1947). On the theory of "interposition," see Note, *Interposition vs. Judicial Power—A Study of Ultimate Authority in Constitutional Questions,* 1 Race Rel.L.Rep. 465 (1956).

land, invalidating a state tax on the Bank of the United States. Indeed, in disregard of *McCulloch* and in defiance of a federal circuit court injunction, the state auditor of Ohio had enforced his state's tax on the Bank by entering its vaults, seizing whatever specie and notes he could find, and conveying them to the state treasurer. See 1 Warren, supra, at 514–30. And only a year before *Cohens,* in the hot debate which finally resulted in the Missouri Compromise, "constant fears were expressed by Southern statesmen lest Marshall's broad views of the 'necessary and proper' clause of the Constitution might support Congressional interference with the States on the subject of slavery," 2 Warren, supra, at 2–3. "The final settlement" of the existence and powers of the Bank of the United States and the extension of slavery in the new states "were felt to depend largely upon the future trend of the Supreme Court," id. at 4.

In the course of his "immortal Nationalist address," 4 Beveridge, supra, at 343, Marshall said: "When we consider [the] nature of our constitution; the subordination of the state governments to that constitution; the great purpose for which jurisdiction over all cases arising under the constitution and laws of the United States, is confided to the judicial department; are we at liberty to insert in this general grant, an exception of those cases in which a state may be a party? Will the spirit of the constitution justify this attempt to control its words? We think it will not. We think a case arising under the constitution or laws of the United States, is cognizable in the Courts of the Union, whoever may be the parties to that case. * * *

"In many states, the judges are dependent for office and for salary on the will of the legislature. [When] we observe the importance which that constitution attaches to the independence of judges, we are the less inclined to suppose, that it can have intended to leave these constitutional questions to tribunals where this independence may not exist * * *.

"[A] constitution is framed for ages to come, and is designed to approach immortality, as nearly as human institutions can approach it. Its course cannot always be tranquil. It is exposed to storms and tempests, and its framers must be unwise statesmen indeed, if they have not provided it, so far as its nature will permit, with the means of self-preservation from the perils it may be destined to encounter. No government ought to be so defective in its organization, as not to contain within itself, the means of securing the execution of its own laws against other dangers than those which occur every day. Courts of justice are the means most usually employed; and it is reasonable to expect, that a government should repose on its own courts, rather than on others."

SECTION 2. POLITICAL QUESTIONS

Does the principle of judicial review comprehend the Court's acting as "final arbiter" on *all* constitutional questions presented by a case properly within its jurisdiction? Or are some constitutional issues inappropriate for judicial resolution and thus "nonjusticiable"?

In 1902 Oregon amended its constitution to allow the people to enact laws through an initiative process. In 1906 an initiative was passed taxing certain classes of corporations. Pacific States Telephone and Telegraph Company objected to the tax on the ground that the initiative process violated the federal constitution's guarantee to each state of a republican form of government (Article IV, section 4). In essence the company argued that the initiative process is democratic, not republican. In addition, the company argued that the tax violated the equal protection clause of the fourteenth amendment and fundamental rights making it not in accordance with the "law of the land" (Art. VI).

PACIFIC STATES TEL. & TEL. CO. v. OREGON, 223 U.S. 118, 32 S.Ct. 224, 56 L.Ed. 377 (1912), per WHITE, C.J., held that the case presented a political question and was "therefore not cognizable by the judicial power but solely committed by the Constitution to the judgment of Congress: "On the surface, the impression might be produced that [the equal protection claim and the claim about fundamental rights] are addressed to some inherent defect in the tax or infirmity of power to levy it without regard to the guarantee of a republican form of Government. But this is merely superficial, and is at once dispelled by observing that every reason urged to support the two [claims] is solely based on § 4 of Art. IV and the consequent inability of the State to impose any tax of any kind which would not violate the Fourteenth Amendment or be repugnant to the law of the land if in such State the initiative or referendum method is permitted. * * * "In other words, the [telephone company's arguments proceed] upon the theory that the adoption of the initiative and referendum destroyed all government republican in form in Oregon.[a] This being so, the contention, if held to be sound, would necessarily affect the validity, not only of the particular statute which is before us, but of every other statute passed in Oregon since the adoption of the initiative and referendum. And indeed the propositions go further than this, since in their essence they assert that there is no governmental function, legislative or judicial, in Oregon, because it cannot be assumed, if the proposition be well founded, that there is at one and the same time one and the same government which is republican in form and not of that character.

"Before immediately considering the text of § 4 of Art. IV, in order to uncover and give emphasis to the anomalous and destructive effects upon both the state and national governments which the adoption of the proposition implies, as illustrated by what we have just said, let us briefly fix the inconceivable expansion of the judicial power and the ruinous destruction of legislative authority in matters purely political which would necessarily be occasioned by giving sanction to the doctrine which underlies and would be necessarily involved in sustaining the propositions contended for. First. That however perfect and absolute may be the establishment and dominion in fact of a state government, however complete may be its participation in and enjoyment of all its powers and rights as a member of the national Government, and however all the departments of that Government may recognize such state government, nevertheless every citizen of such State or person subject to taxation therein, or owing any duty to the established government, may be heard, for the purpose of defeating the payment of such taxes or avoiding the discharge of such duty, to assail in a court of justice the rightful existence of the State. Second. As a result, it becomes the duty of the courts of the United States, where such a claim is made, to examine as a justiciable issue the contention as to the illegal existence of a State and if such contention be thought well founded to disregard the existence in fact of the State, of its recognition by all of the departments of the Federal Government, and practically award a decree absolving from all obligation to contribute to the support of or obey the laws of such established state government. And as a consequence of the existence of such judicial authority a power in the judiciary must be implied, unless it be that anarchy is

a. "Consider Tribe, *American Constitutional Law* 99 (2d ed. 1988): "[I]f a court found that a particular feature of state government rendered the government unrepublican, why could not the Court simply declare that feature invalid?"

to ensue, to build by judicial action upon the ruins of the previously established government a new one, a right which by its very terms also implies the power to control the legislative department of the Government of the United States in the recognition of such new government and the admission of representatives therefrom, as well as to strip the executive department of that government of its otherwise lawful and discretionary authority.

"Do the provisions of § 4, Art. IV, bring about these strange, far-reaching and injurious results? That is to say, do the provisions of that Article obliterate the division between judicial authority and legislative power upon which the Constitution rests? In other words, do they authorize the judiciary to substitute its judgment as to a matter purely political for the judgment of Congress on a subject committed to it and thus overthrow the Constitution upon the ground that thereby the guarantee to the States of a government republican in form may be secured, a conception which after all rests upon the assumption that the States are to be guaranteed a government republican in form by destroying the very existence of a government republican in form in the Nation?

"We shall not stop to consider the text to point out how absolutely barren it is of support for the contentions sought to be based upon it, since the repugnancy of those contentions to the letter and spirit of that text is so conclusively established by prior decisions of this court as to cause the matter to be absolutely foreclosed.

"[T]he leading and absolutely controlling case [is] *Luther v. Borden,* 7 How. 1, 12 L.Ed. 581 (1849). [In deciding which of two contending forces was the lawful government of Rhode Island], [t]he Court said: '[T]he fourth section of the fourth article of the constitution of the United States provides that the United States shall guarantee to every State in the Union a republican form of government, and shall protect each of them against invasion; and on the application of the legislature or of the executive (when the legislature cannot be convened) against domestic violence.

" 'Under this article of the constitution it rests with Congress to decide what government is the established one in a State. For, as the United States guarantee to each State a republican government, Congress must necessarily decide what government is established in the State before it can determine whether it is republican or not. And when the senators and representatives of a State are admitted into the councils of the Union, the authority of the government under which they are appointed, as well as its republican character, is recognized by the proper constitutional authority. And its decision is binding on every other department of the government, and could not be questioned in a judicial tribunal. It is true that the contest in this case did not last long enough to bring the matter to this issue; and as no senators or representatives were elected under the authority of the government of which Mr. Dorr was the head, Congress was not called upon to decide the controversy. Yet the right to decide is placed there, and not in the courts.'

" 'Pointing out that Congress, by the act of February 28, 1795 (1 Stat. 424, c. 36), had recognized the obligation resting upon it to protect from domestic violence by conferring authority upon the President of the United States, on the application of the legislature of a State or of the Governor, to call out the militia of any other State or States to suppress such insurrection, it was suggested that if the question of what was the rightful government within the intendment of § 4 of Art. IV was a judicial one, the duty to afford protection from invasion and to suppress domestic violence would be also judicial, since those duties were inseparably related to the determination of whether there was a rightful government. If this view were correct, it was intimated, it would follow that the delegation of authority made to the President by the act of 1795 would be void as a usurpation of judicial authority, and hence it would be the duty of the courts, if they differed with the judgment of the President as to the manner of discharging this great responsibility, to interfere and set at naught his action; and the pertinent statement was made: 'If the judicial power extends so far, the guarantee contained in the constitution of the United States is a guarantee of anarchy, and not of order.'" * * *

Turning from *Luther,* the Court said "It is indeed a singular misconception of the nature and character of our constitutional system of government to suggest that the settled distinction which the doctrine just stated points out between judicial authority over justiciable controversies and legislative power as to purely political questions tends to destroy the duty of the judiciary in proper cases to enforce the Constitution. The suggestion but results from failing to distinguish between things which are widely different, that is, the legislative duty to determine the political questions involved in deciding whether a state government republican in form exists, and the judicial power and ever-present duty whenever it becomes necessary in a controversy properly submitted to enforce and uphold the applicable provisions of the Constitution as to each and every exercise of governmental power.

"How better can the broad lines which distinguish these two subjects be pointed out than by considering the character of the defense in this very case? The defendant company does not contend here that it could not have been required to pay a license tax. It does not assert that it was denied an opportunity to be heard as to the amount for which it was taxed, or that there was anything inhering in the tax or involved intrinsically in the law which violated any of its constitutional rights. If such questions had been raised they would have been justiciable, and therefore would have required the calling into operation of judicial power. Instead, however, of doing any of these things, the attack on the statute here made is of a wholly different character. Its essentially political nature is at once made manifest by understanding that the assault which the contention here advanced makes it not on the tax as a tax, but on the State as a State. It is addressed to the framework and political character of the government by which the statute levying the tax was passed. It is the government, the political entity, which (reducing the case to its essence) is called to the bar of this court, not for the purpose of testing judicially some exercise of power assailed, on the ground that its exertion has injuriously affected the rights of an individual because of repugnancy to some constitutional limitation, but to demand of the State that it establish its right to exist as a State, republican in form.

"As the issues presented, in their very essence, are, and have long since by this court been, definitely determined to be political and governmental, and embraced within the scope of the powers conferred upon Congress, and not therefore within the reach of judicial power, it follows that the case presented is not within our jurisdiction, and the writ of error must therefore be, and it is, dismissed for want of jurisdiction."

Notes and Questions

1. Consider Bonfield, *The Guarantee Clause of Article IV, Section 4: A Study in Constitutional Desuetude,* 46 Minn.L.Rev. 513, 554 (1962): "Even if the

Pacific Telephone case would bar federal courts from enforcing the guarantee, it does not bar state courts from doing so since the Supreme Court does not control state court jurisdiction. In enforcing it, a state court would be fulfilling the obligation imposed on the state to maintain such a government." [b] Do you agree?

2. Suppose the Court had decided that the constitutionality of the initiative process was not a political question. Should it have declared the initiative process unconstitutional? In making the decision, should it have consulted the subjective intentions of the framers? [c] What if the subjective intentions of the framers were that their subjective intentions not be consulted? [d] Would the Court have to look in any event at the intellectual tradition from which the term *Republican* was taken? Does the structure of the Constitution offer any assistance in approaching the question?

Suppose a city or a state employed a technology which allowed citizens to enact legislation in their homes on all issues presented to the legislature? Suppose that the city or state assured that the technology was available to all and that legislative debates on the issue were fully aired. Constitutional? [e]

3. Although the Court holds in this circumstance [f] that Congress is the appropriate body to decide whether a state has a republican form of government, the concept of republicanism may be important to other problems of constitutional interpretation. In attempting to secure ratification of the Constitution, *The Federalist Papers* maintained that the Union was a republic solidly grounded in republican principles. In Federalist # 10, for example, Madison argued that the Constitution afforded protection against factions by which he meant "a number of citizens whether amounting to a majority or a minority of the whole, who are united and actuated by some common impulse of passion, or of interest, adverse to the rights of other citizens, or to the permanent and aggregate interests of the community." The Union could control faction because of its republican character: "The two great points of difference between a democracy and a republic are: first the delegation of the government, in the

b. See generally Linde, *When is Initiative Lawmaking Not "Republican Government"?*, 17 Hast.Con.L.Q. 159 (1989).

c. Consider Eule, *Judicial Review of Direct Democracy*, 99 Yale L.J. 1503, 1523 (1990) ("It is idle (but fun nonetheless) to speculate how the delegates might have responded to a proposal that the Constitution contain provisions for initiatives and referenda. Such devices were virtually unknown to them. But everything about the tone of the Convention suggests that they would have looked upon such a scheme 'with a feeling akin to horror' "); A. Hacker, *Congressional Districting* 7–8 (1963) ("The assemblage at the Philadelphia Convention was by no means committed to popular government, and few of the delegates had sympathy for the habits or institutions of democracy. Indeed, most of them interpreted democracy as mob rule and assumed that equality of representation would permit the spokesmen for the common man to outvote the beleaguered deputies of the uncommon man."). See also e.g., R. Hofstadter, *The American Political Tradition* 3–21 (1973). For general discussion of the Guarantee Clause, see Wiecek, *The Guarantee Clause of the United States Constitution* (1972); Bonfield, supra Note one; Eule, supra at 1539–48.

d. See J. Powell, *The Original Understanding of Original Intent*, 98 Harv.L.Rev. 885 (1985).

e. For relevant discussion, see e.g., Barber, *Strong Democracy* (1984); Eule, supra fn. c, particularly at 1544–1545; Gillette, *Plebiscites, Participation, and Collective Action in Local Government Law*, 86 Mich.L.Rev. 930 (1988); Linde, supra note b, at 166; Sirico, *The Constitutionality of the Initiative and Referendum*, 65 Iowa L.Rev. 637 (1980); Note, *Lousy Lawmaking: Questioning the Desirability and Constitutionality of Legislating By Initiative*, 61 S.Cal.L.Rev. 733 (1988).

f. For the suggestion that the states as states may have protection under the guarantee clause against some forms of congressional action, see Tribe, supra note a, at 398; Merritt, *The Guarantee Clause and State Autonomy: Federalism for a Third Century*, 88 Colum.L.Rev. 1 (1988).

latter, to a small number of citizens elected by the rest; secondly, the greater number of citizens and greater sphere of country over which the latter may be extended."

Large republics guard against faction, he argued, because they afford a greater probability of "fit characters" being elected and because the diversity of parties and interests make it less likely that factions could gain control. He concluded: "In the extent and proper structure of the Union, therefore, we behold a republican remedy for the diseases incident to republican government. And according to the degree of pleasure and pride we feel in being republicans ought to be our zeal in cherishing the spirit and supporting the character of federalists."

If the Union is itself a "republican" government, should interpretation of the Constitution be guided by an understanding of the meaning of republicanism?

Does it matter that the opponents of the Constitution argued that it violated republican principles and that Madison had distorted the meaning of republicanism to suit his ends? From their perspective, to put it in modern terms, Republicanism was a form of participatory democracy in which citizens collectively pursued the common good.

For the contention that republicanism is a repressed, but important, theme in the Constitution and that it deserves greater prominence, see Michelman, *Law's Republic,* 97 Yale L.J. 1493 (1988); Michelman, "*Foreword: Traces of Self-Government,*" 100 *Harv.L.Rev.* 4, 16 (1986). For the contention that the Constitution should be interpreted against a background of "Madisonian Republicanism," see Sunstein, *Beyond the Republican Revival,* 97 Yale L.J. 1539 (1988); Sunstein, *Interest Groups in American Public Law* 38 Stan.L.Rev. 29 (1985).[g]

BAKER v. CARR

369 U.S. 186, 82 S.Ct. 691, 7 L.Ed.2d 663 (1962).

JUSTICE BRENNAN delivered the opinion of the Court.

[Appellants sought a federal declaratory judgment that the apportionment of the Tennessee General Assembly violated fourteenth amendment equal pro-

g. The focus on republicanism in law has stimulated a blizzard of commentary. See, eg., Symposium: *The Republican Civic Tradition,* 97 Yale L.J. 1493 (1988) (comments on articles by Michelman and Sunstein by Abrams, Bell & Bensal, Brest, Epstein, Fitts, Kerber, Macey, Mashaw, Powell, Sullivan); Symposium: *Roads Not Taken: Undercurrents of Republican Thinking in Modern Constituional Theory,* 84 Nw.U.L.Rev. 1 (1989) (articles by Conrad, Cornell, Howe, McWilliams, Presser, Rose); Symposium: *Republicanism and Voting Rights,* 41 U.Fla.L.Rev. 409 (1989) (articles and commentaries by L. Alexander, Baker, Cook, Farber, Levinson, Mensch & Freeman, Michelman, Minow & Minow, Sandalow); Tushnet, *Red, White, and Blue, A Critical Analysis of Constitutional Law,* (1988); G. Alexander, *Time and Property in the American Republican Legal Culture,* 66 N.Y.U.L.Rev. 273 (1991); Eule, supra fn. c; Fallon, *What Is Republicanism and Is It Worth Reviving,* 102 Harv.L.Rev. 1695 (1989); Horwitz, *Republicanism and Liberalism in American Constitutional Thought,* 29 Wm. & Mary L.Rev. 57 (1987) (with comments from Hartog, Simon, Tushnet, and White, id. at 75–112); Sherry, *Civic Virtue and the Feminine Voice in Constitutional Adjudication,* 72 U.Va.L.Rev. 543 (1986). Much of this scholarship echoes and builds upon a debate among historical scholars. See, eg., Pocock, *The Machiavellian Moment,* (1975); Wood, *The Creation of the American Republic 1776–1787* (1969); Appleby, *Republicanism in Old and New Contexts,* 43 Wm. & Mary Q. 20 (1986); Kramnick, *The "Great National Discussion": The Discourse of Politics in 1787,* 45 Wm. & Mary Q. 3 (1988); Pocock, *"Between Gog and Magog: The Republican Thesis and the Ideologia Americana,"* 48 Journal of the History of Ideas 325 (1987); Shalhope, *Republicanism and Early American Historiography,* 39 Wm. & Mary Q. 334 (1982).

tection "by virtue of the debasement of their votes." They alleged that, although the state constitution allocated representation on a population basis, no reapportionment law had passed since 1901. They further sought an injunction against any further elections under the 1901 scheme and] until the General Assembly enacts a valid reapportionment, the District Court should either decree a reapportionment by mathematical application of the Tennessee constitutional formulae to the most recent Federal Census figures, or direct the appellees to conduct legislative elections, primary and general, at large. * * *

[W]e hold today only (a) that the court possessed jurisdiction of the subject matter; (b) that a justiciable cause of action is stated upon which appellants would be entitled to appropriate relief; and (c) [that] the appellants have standing to challenge the Tennessee apportionment statutes. Beyond noting that we have no cause at this stage to doubt the District Court will be able to fashion relief if violations of constitutional rights are found, it is improper now to consider what remedy would be most appropriate if appellants prevail at the trial.

Jurisdiction of the Subject Matter

The District Court was uncertain whether our cases withholding federal judicial relief rested upon a lack of federal jurisdiction or upon the inappropriateness of the subject matter for judicial consideration—what we have designated "nonjusticiability." The distinction between the two grounds is significant. In the instance of nonjusticiability, consideration of the cause is not wholly and immediately foreclosed; rather, the Court's inquiry necessarily proceeds to the point of deciding whether the duty asserted can be judicially identified and its breach judicially determined, and whether protection for the right asserted can be judicially molded. In the instance of lack of jurisdiction the cause either does not "arise under" the Federal Constitution, laws or treaties (or fall within one of the other enumerated categories of Art. III, § 2), or is not a "case or controversy" within the meaning of that section; [a] or the cause is not one described by any jurisdictional statute. Our conclusion that this cause presents no nonjusticiable "political question" settles the only possible doubt that it is a case or controversy. Under the present heading of "Jurisdiction of the Subject Matter" we hold only that the matter set forth in the complaint does arise under the Constitution and is within [a statute conferring federal court jurisdiction].

An unbroken line of our precedents sustains the federal courts' jurisdiction of the subject matter of federal constitutional claims of this nature. [Unlike] many other cases in this field which have assumed without discussion that there was jurisdiction, all three opinions filed in *Colegrove v. Green,* 328 U.S. 549, 66 S.Ct. 1198, 90 L.Ed. 1432 (1946), discussed the question. Two of the opinions expressing the views of four of the Justices, a majority, flatly held that there was jurisdiction of that subject matter.[b] * * *

a. This topic is considered in Ch. 9, Sec. 1.

b. *Colegrove* affirmed dismissal of a suit by voters in Illinois congressional districts, that had much larger populations than others, to enjoin the forthcoming election on federal constitutional and statutory grounds. Frankfurter, J., joined by Reed and Burton, JJ., held that the applicable congressional apportionment statute did not require equality of population in districts. He also felt that the case should be "dismissed for want of equity" because the issue was "of a peculiarly political nature and therefore not meet for judicial determination." The result of judicial interference might be elections-at-large—"a mode that defies the direction of Congress for selection by districts * * *. In the exercise of its power to judge the qualifications of its own members, the House may reject a delegation of Representatives-at-large. Article I, § 5, Cl. 1." "[T]his controversy concerns matters that bring courts into immediate and active relations with party contests. * * * Courts ought not to enter this political thicket." Art.

JUSTICIABILITY

[I]t is argued that apportionment cases, whatever the actual wording of the complaint, can involve no federal constitutional right except one resting on the guaranty of a republican form of government, [Art. IV, § 4,] and that complaints based on that clause have been held to present political questions which are nonjusticiable. [But appellants'] claim that they are being denied equal protection is justiciable, and if "discrimination is sufficiently shown, the right to relief under the equal protection clause is not diminished by the fact that the discrimination relates to political rights." *Snowden v. Hughes,* 321 U.S. 1, 11, 64 S.Ct. 397, 402, 88 L.Ed. 497. [B]ecause there appears to be some uncertainty as to why [Guaranty Clause] cases did present political questions, and specifically as to whether this apportionment case is like those cases, we deem it necessary first to consider the contours of the "political question" doctrine.

[I]n the Guaranty Clause cases and in the other "political question" cases, it is the relationship between the judiciary and the coordinate branches of the Federal Government, and not the federal judiciary's relationship to the States, which gives rise to the "political question."

We have said that "In determining whether a question falls within [the political question] category, the appropriateness under our system of government of attributing finality to the action of the political departments and also the lack of satisfactory criteria for a judicial determination are dominant considerations." *Coleman v. Miller,* 307 U.S. 433, 454–455, 59 S.Ct. 972, 982, 83 L.Ed. 1385. The nonjusticiability of a political question is primarily a function of the separation of powers. Much confusion results from the capacity of the "political question" label to obscure the need for case-by-case inquiry. Deciding whether a matter has in any measure been committed by the Constitution to another branch of government, or whether the action of that branch exceeds whatever authority has been committed, is itself a delicate exercise in constitutional interpretation, and is a responsibility of this Court as ultimate interpreter of the Constitution. To demonstrate this requires no less than to analyze representative cases and to infer from them the analytical threads that make up the political question doctrine. We shall then show that none of those threads catches this case.

Foreign relations: There are sweeping statements to the effect that all questions touching foreign relations are political questions. Not only does resolution of such issues frequently turn on standards that defy judicial application, or involve the exercise of a discretion demonstrably committed to the executive or legislature; but many such questions uniquely demand single-voiced statement of the Government's views. Yet it is error to suppose that every case or controversy which touches foreign relations lies beyond judicial cognizance. Our cases in this field seem invariably to show a discriminating analysis of the particular question posed, in terms of the history of its management by the

I, § 4 of the Constitution confers "upon Congress exclusive authority to secure fair representation by the States in the popular House." If Congress fails, "the remedy ultimately lies with the people."

Rutledge, J., concurred in the result, believing the issues to be "justiciable" but that the case should be dismissed for want of equity due to "the gravity of the constitutional questions" and "the possibilities for collision [with] the political departments of the Government."

Black, J., joined by Douglas and Murphy, JJ., dissented, believing the apportionment to be unconstitutional: "[I]t is a mere 'play on words' to refer to a controversy such as this as 'political' in the sense that courts have nothing to do with protecting and vindicating the right of a voter to cast an effective ballot."

For *Colegrove's* formal demise, see *Wesberry v. Sanders.*

political branches, of its susceptibility to judicial handling in the light of its nature and posture in the specific case, and of the possible consequences of judicial action.[c] For example, though a court will not ordinarily inquire whether a treaty has been terminated, since on that question "governmental action [must] be regarded as of controlling importance," if there has been no conclusive "governmental action" then a court can construe a treaty and may find it provides the answer. * * *

While recognition of foreign governments so strongly defies judicial treatment that without executive recognition a foreign state has been called "a republic of whose existence we know nothing," and the judiciary ordinarily follows the executive as to which nation has sovereignty over disputed territory, once sovereignty over an area is politically determined and declared, courts may examine the resulting status and decide independently whether a statute applies to that area. * * *

Dates of duration of hostilities: [H]ere too analysis reveals isolable reasons for the presence of political questions, underlying this Court's refusal to review the political departments' determination of when or whether a war has ended. Dominant is the need for finality in the political determination, for emergency's nature demands "A prompt and unhesitating obedience," *Martin v. Mott,* 12 Wheat. 19, 30, 6 L.Ed. 537 (calling up of militia). [But] deference rests on reason, not habit. The question in a particular case may not seriously implicate considerations of finality—e.g., a public program of importance (rent control) yet not central to the emergency effort. Further, clearly definable criteria for decision may be available. In such case the political question barrier falls away * * *.

Validity of enactments: [*Coleman*] held that the questions of how long a proposed amendment to the Federal Constitution remained open to ratification, and what effect a prior rejection had on a subsequent ratification, were committed to congressional resolution and involved criteria of decision that necessarily escaped the judicial grasp. Similar considerations apply to the enacting process: "The respect due to coequal and independent departments," and the need for finality and certainty about the status of a statute contribute to judicial reluctance to inquire whether, as passed, it complied with all requisite formalities. *Field v. Clark,* 143 U.S. 649, 672, 676–677, 12 S.Ct. 495, 497, 499, 36 L.Ed. 294. But it is not true that courts will never delve into a legislature's records upon such a quest: If the enrolled statute lacks an effective date, a court will not hesitate to seek it in the legislative journals in order to preserve the enactment. The political question doctrine, a tool for maintenance of governmental order, will not be so applied as to promote only disorder. * * *

It is apparent that several formulations which vary slightly according to the settings in which the questions arise may describe a political question, although each has one or more elements which identify it as essentially a function of the separation of powers. Prominent [is] found a textually demonstrable constitutional commitment of the issue to a coordinate political department; or a lack of judicially discoverable and manageable standards for resolving it; or the impossibility of deciding without an initial policy determination of a kind clearly for nonjudicial discretion; or the impossibility of a court's undertaking independent resolution without expressing lack of the respect due coordinate branches of

c. See generally Henkin, *Viet-Nam in the Courts of the United States: "Political Questions,"* 63 Am.J.Int'l L. 284 (1969).

government; or an unusual need for unquestioning adherence to a political decision already made; or the potentiality of embarrassment from multifarious pronouncements by various departments on one question.

Unless one of these formulations is inextricable from the case at bar, there should be no dismissal for non-justiciability on the ground of a political question's presence. The doctrine of which we treat is one of "political questions," not one of "political cases." The courts cannot reject as "no law suit" a bona fide controversy as to whether some action denominated "political" exceeds constitutional authority. * * *

But it is argued that this case shares the characteristics of decisions that constitute a category not yet considered, cases concerning [Art. IV, § 4]. We shall discover that Guaranty Clause claims involve those elements which define a "political question," and for that reason and no other, they are nonjusticiable. In particular, we shall discover that the nonjusticiability of such claims has nothing to do with their touching upon matters of state governmental organization.

Republican form of government: Luther v. Borden, 7 How. 1, 12 L.Ed. 581, though in form simply an action for damages for trespass was, as Daniel Webster said in opening the argument for the defense, "an unusual case." The defendants, admitting an otherwise tortious breaking and entering, sought to justify their action on the ground that they were agents of the established lawful government of Rhode Island, which State was then under martial law to defend itself from active insurrection; that the plaintiff was engaged in that insurrection; and that they entered under orders to arrest the plaintiff. The case arose "out of the unfortunate political differences which agitated the people of Rhode Island in 1841 and 1842," and which had resulted in a situation wherein two groups laid competing claims to recognition as the lawful government. * * *

Clearly, several factors were thought by the Court in *Luther* to make the question there "political": the commitment to the other branches of the decision as to which is the lawful state government; the unambiguous action by the President, in recognizing the charter government as the lawful authority; the need for finality in the executive's decision; and the lack of criteria by which a court could determine which form of government was republican.

But the only significance that *Luther* could have for our immediate purposes is in its holding that the Guaranty Clause is not a repository of judicially manageable standards which a court could utilize independently in order to identify a State's lawful government. The Court has since refused to resort to the Guaranty Clause—which alone had been invoked for the purpose—as the source of a constitutional standard for invalidating state [or congressional] action. [See] *Pacific States Tel. & T. Co. v. Oregon,* 223 U.S. 118, 32 S.Ct. 224, 56 L.Ed. 377 (claim that initiative and referendum negated republican government held nonjusticiable); *Highland Farms Dairy v. Agnew,* 300 U.S. 608, 57 S.Ct. 549, 81 L.Ed. 835 (claim that delegation to agency of power to control milk prices violated republican government, rejected).

[In] *Georgia v. Stanton,* 6 Wall. 50, 18 L.Ed. 721, the State sought by an original bill to enjoin execution of the Reconstruction Acts, claiming that [the] Acts "Instead of keeping the guaranty against a forcible overthrow of its government by foreign invaders or domestic insurgents [are] destroying that very government by force." Congress had clearly refused to recognize the republican character of the government of the suing State. It seemed to the Court that the only constitutional claim that could be presented was under the Guaranty

Clause, and Congress having determined that the effects of the recent hostilities required extraordinary measures to restore governments of a republican form, this Court refused to interfere with Congress' action at the behest of a claimant relying on that very guaranty. * * *

We come, finally, to the ultimate inquiry whether our precedents as to what constitutes a nonjusticiable "political question" bring the case before us under the umbrella of that doctrine. [We find none] of the common characteristics which we have been able to identify * * *. The question here is the consistency of state action with the Federal Constitution. We have no question decided, or to be decided, by a political branch of government coequal with this Court. Nor do we risk embarrassment of our government abroad, or grave disturbance at home if we take issue with Tennessee as to the constitutionality of her action here challenged. Nor need the appellants, in order to succeed in this action, ask the Court to enter upon policy determinations for which judicially manageable standards are lacking. Judicial standards under the Equal Protection Clause are well developed [to determine] that a discrimination reflects *no* policy, but simply arbitrary and capricious action.

This case does, in one sense, involve the allocation of political power within a State, and the appellants might conceivably have added a claim under the Guaranty Clause. [Although it] could not have succeeded it does not follow that appellants may not be heard on the equal protection claim which in fact they tender. * * *

Reversed and remanded. * * *

JUSTICE WHITTAKER did not participate in the decision of this case.

JUSTICE DOUGLAS [who joined the Court's opinion], concurring. * * *

So far as voting rights are concerned, there are large gaps in the Constitution. Yet the right to vote is inherent in the republican form of government * * *.[2] That the States may specify the qualifications for voters is implicit in Article I, Section 2, Clause 1 * * *. It is, however, clear that by reason of the commands of the Constitution there are several qualifications that a State may not require [referring to the fifteenth and nineteenth amendments, as well as equal protection].

It is said that any decision in cases of this kind is beyond the competence of courts. Some make the same point as regards the problem of equal protection in cases involving racial segregation. [The] constitutional guide is often vague, as the decisions under the Due Process and Commerce Clauses show. The problem under the Equal Protection Clause is no more intricate.

There are, of course, some questions beyond judicial competence. Where the performance of a "duty" is left to the discretion and good judgment of an executive officer, the judiciary will not compel the exercise of his discretion one

2. The statements in *Luther* that this guaranty is enforceable only by Congress or the Chief Executive is not maintainable [and are] contrary to [the] modern decisions of the Court that give the full panoply of judicial protection to voting rights. * * *

Moreover, the Court's refusal to examine the legality of the regime of martial law which had been laid upon Rhode Island is indefensible, as Mr. Justice Woodbury maintained in his dissent. * * *

What he wrote was later to become the tradition, as expressed by Chief Justice Hughes in *Sterling v. Constantin,* 287 U.S. 378, 401, 53 S.Ct. 190, 196, 77 L.Ed. 375: "What are the allowable limits of military discretion, and whether or not they have been overstepped in a particular case, are judicial questions."

way or the other (*Kentucky v. Dennison,* 24 How. 66, 109, 16 L.Ed. 717), for to do so would be to take over the office.

Where the Constitution assigns a particular function wholly and indivisibly [3] to another department, the federal judiciary does not intervene. None of those cases is relevant here. * * *

JUSTICE CLARK, concurring.

[An] examination of Table I accompanying this opinion conclusively reveals that the apportionment picture in Tennessee is a topsy-turvical of gigantic proportions. This is not to say that some of the disparity cannot be explained, but when the entire table is examined—comparing the voting strength of counties of like population as well as contrasting that of the smaller with the larger counties—it leaves but one conclusion, namely that Tennessee's apportionment is a crazy quilt without rational basis. * * *

Although I find the Tennessee apportionment statute offends the Equal Protection Clause,[d] I would not consider intervention by this Court into so delicate a field if there were any other relief available to the people of Tennessee. But the majority of the people of Tennessee have no "practical opportunities for exerting their political weight at the polls" to correct the existing "invidious discrimination." Tennessee has no initiative and referendum. [T]he legislative policy has riveted the present seats in the Assembly to their respective constituencies, and by the votes of their incumbents a reapportionment of any kind is prevented. The people have been rebuffed at the hands of the Assembly; they have tried the constitutional convention route, but since the call must originate in the Assembly, it, too, has been fruitless. They have tried Tennessee courts with the same result,[9] and Governors have fought the tide only to flounder. It is said that there is recourse in Congress and perhaps that may be, but from a practical standpoint this is without substance. To date Congress has never undertaken such a task in any State. * * *

Finally, we must consider if there are any appropriate modes of effective judicial relief. [One] plan might be to start with the existing assembly districts, consolidate some of them, and award the seats thus released to those counties suffering the most egregious discrimination. Other possibilities are present and might be more effective. But the plan here suggested would at least release the stranglehold now on the Assembly and permit it to redistrict itself. * * *

[It] is well for this Court to practice self-restraint and discipline in constitutional adjudication, but never in its history have those principles received sanction where the national rights of so many have been so clearly infringed for so long a time. National respect for the courts is more enhanced through the

3. The category of the "political" question is, in my view, narrower than the decided cases indicate. * * *

Georgia v. Stanton involved the application of the Reconstruction Acts to Georgia—laws which destroyed by force the internal regime of that State. [The] question was no more "political" than a host of others we have entertained. See, e.g., *Pennsylvania v. West Virginia,* 262 U.S. 553, 43 S.Ct. 658, 67 L.Ed. 1117; *Youngstown Sheet & Tube Co. v. Sawyer,* 343 U.S. 579, 72 S.Ct. 863, 96 L.Ed. 1153 (1952); *Alabama v. Texas,* 347 U.S. 272, 74 S.Ct. 481, 98 L.Ed. 689.

Today would this Court hold nonjusticiable or "political" a suit to enjoin a Governor who, like Fidel Castro, takes everything into his own hands and suspends all election laws? * * *

d. Clark, J., "not being able to muster a court to dispose of the case on the merits," joined the Court's opinion.

9. It is interesting to note that state judges often rest their decisions on the ground that this Court has precluded adjudication of the federal claim.

forthright enforcement of those rights rather than by rendering them nugatory through the interposition of subterfuges. * * *

JUSTICE STEWART, concurring.

The separate writings of my dissenting and concurring Brothers stray so far from the subject of today's decision as to convey, I think, a distressingly inaccurate impression of what the Court decides. * * * Contrary to the suggestion of my Brother Harlan, the Court does not say or imply that "state legislatures must be so structured as to reflect with approximate equality the voice of every voter" [or] that there is anything in the Federal Constitution "to prevent a State, acting not irrationally, from choosing any electoral legislative structure it thinks best suited to the interests, temper, and customs of its people." * * * My Brother Clark has made a convincing prima facie showing that Tennessee's system of apportionment is in fact utterly arbitrary—without any possible justification in rationality. My Brother Harlan has, with imagination and ingenuity, hypothesized possibly rational bases for Tennessee's system. But the merits of this case are not before us now. * * *

JUSTICE FRANKFURTER, whom JUSTICE HARLAN joins, dissenting.

The Court today reverses a uniform course of decision established by a dozen cases [which] reflected the equally uniform course of our political history regarding the relationship between population and legislative representation—a wholly different matter from denial of the franchise to individuals because of race, color, religion or sex. Such a massive repudiation of the experience of our whole past in asserting destructively novel judicial power demands a detailed analysis of the role of this Court in our constitutional scheme. Disregard of inherent limits in the effective exercise of the Court's "judicial Power" not only presages the futility of judicial intervention in the essentially political conflict of forces by which the relation between population and representation has time out of mind been and now is determined. It may well impair the Court's position as the ultimate organ of "the supreme Law of the Land" in that vast range of legal problems, often strongly entangled in popular feeling, on which this Court must pronounce. The Court's authority—possessed of neither the purse nor the sword—ultimately rests on sustained public confidence in its moral sanction. Such feeling must be nourished by the Court's complete detachment, in fact and in appearance, from political entanglements and by abstention from injecting itself into the clash of political forces in political settlements.

[The claim in this case] is hypothetical and the assumptions [on which it rests] are abstract because the Court does not vouchsafe the lower courts—state and federal—guidelines for formulating specific, definite, wholly unprecedented remedies for the inevitable litigations that today's umbrageous disposition is bound to stimulate in connection with politically motivated reapportionments in so many States. In such a setting, to promulgate jurisdiction in the abstract is meaningless. It is as devoid of reality as "a brooding omnipresence in the sky" for it conveys no intimation what relief, if any, a District Court is capable of affording that would not invite legislatures to play ducks and drakes with the judiciary. [One] of the Court's supporting opinions, as elucidated by commentary, unwittingly affords a disheartening preview of the mathematical quagmire (apart from divers judicially inappropriate and elusive determinants) into which this Court today catapults the lower courts of the country without so much as adumbrating the basis for a legal calculus as a means of extrication. Even assuming the indispensable intellectual disinterestedness on the part of judges in such matters, [t]o charge courts with the task of accommodating the incommensurable factors of policy that underlie these mathematical puzzles is to attribute, however flatteringly, omnicompetence to judges. * * * Considering the gross inequality among legislative electoral units within almost every State, the Court naturally shrinks from asserting that in districting at least substantial equality is a constitutional requirement enforceable by courts [and] implies that geography, economics, urban-rural conflict, and all the other non-legal factors which have throughout our history entered into political districting are to some extent not to be ruled [out]. To some extent—aye, there's the rub. In effect, today's decision empowers the courts of the country to devise what should constitute the proper composition of the legislatures of the fifty States. * * *

We were soothingly told at the bar of this Court that we need not worry about the kind of remedy a court could effectively fashion once the abstract constitutional right to have courts pass on a statewide system of electoral districting is recognized as a matter of judicial rhetoric, because legislatures would heed the Court's admonition. This is not only a euphoric hope. It implies a sorry confession of judicial impotence in place of a frank acknowledgment that there is not under our Constitution a judicial remedy for every political mischief, for every undesirable exercise of legislative power. The Framers carefully and with deliberate forethought refused so to enthrone the judiciary. In this situation, as in others of like nature, appeal for relief does not belong here. Appeal must be to an informed, civically militant electorate. In a democratic society like ours, relief must come through an aroused popular conscience that sears the conscience of the people's representatives. [From] its earliest opinions this Court has consistently recognized a class of controversies which do not lend themselves to judicial standards and judicial remedies. To classify the various instances as "political questions" is rather a form of stating this conclusion * * *.

The Court has been particularly unwilling to intervene in matters concerning the structure and organization of the political institutions of the States. * * *

The cases involving Negro disfranchisement are no exception to the principle of avoiding federal intervention into matters of state government in the absence of an explicit and clear constitutional imperative. For here the controlling command of Supreme Law is plain and unequivocal. * * *

The present case [is], in effect, a Guarantee Clause claim masquerading under a different label. But it cannot make the case more fit for judicial action that appellants invoke the Fourteenth Amendment rather than Art. IV, § 4, where, in fact, the gist of their complaint is the same. * * *

At first blush, this charge of discrimination based on legislative underrepresentation is given the appearance of a more private, less impersonal claim, than the assertion that the frame of government is askew. Appellants appear as representatives of a class that is prejudiced as a class, in contradistinction to the polity in its entirety. However, the discrimination relied on is the deprivation of what appellants conceive to be their proportionate share of political influence. * * * Hardly any distribution of political authority that could be assailed as rendering government nonrepublican would fail similarly to operate to the prejudice of some groups, and to the advantage of others, within the body politic. [T]he real battle over the initiative and referendum, or over a delegation of power to local rather than statewide authority, is the battle between forces whose influence is disparate among the various organs of government to whom power may be given. [What] Tennessee illustrates is an old and still widespread method of representation—representation by local geographical division, only in part respective of population—in preference to others, others, forsooth, more appealing. Appellants contest this choice and seek to make this Court the arbiter of the disagreement. * * * Certainly, "equal protection" is no more secure a foundation for judicial judgment of the permissibility of varying forms of representative government than is "Republican Form." * * *

The notion that representation proportioned to the geographic spread of population is so universally accepted as a necessary element of equality between man and man that it must be taken to be the standard of a political equality preserved by the Fourteenth Amendment—that it is, in appellants' words "the basic principle of representative government"—is, to put it bluntly, not true. However desirable and however desired by some among the great political thinkers and framers of our government, it has never been generally practiced, today or in the past. It was not the English system, it was not the colonial system, it was not the system chosen for the national government by the Constitution, it was not the system exclusively or even predominantly practiced by the States at the time of adoption of the Fourteenth Amendment, it is not predominantly practiced by the States today. Unless judges, the judges of this Court, are to make their private views of political wisdom the measure of the Constitution—views which in all honesty cannot but give the appearance, if not reflect the reality, of involvement with the business of partisan politics so inescapably a part of apportionment controversies—the Fourteenth Amendment [provides] no guide for judicial oversight of the representation problem. * * *

[In] all of the apportionment cases which have come before the Court, a consideration which has been weighty in determining their nonjusticiability has been the difficulty or impossibility of devising effective judicial remedies in this class of case. An injunction restraining a general election unless the legislature reapportions would paralyze the critical centers of a State's political system * * *. A declaration devoid of implied compulsion of injunctive or other relief would be an idle threat. Surely a Federal District Court could not itself remap the State [and] the choice of elections at large as opposed to elections by district, however unequal the districts, is a matter of sweeping political judgment having enormous political implications, the nature and reach of which are certainly beyond the informed understanding of, and capacity for appraisal by, courts.

In Tennessee, moreover, the *McCanless* [case] said, "There is no provision of law for election of our General Assembly by an election at large over the State." 200 Tenn., at 277, 292 S.W.2d, at 42. Thus, a legislature elected at large would not be the legally constituted legislative authority of the State. [A] federal court cannot provide the authority requisite to make a legislature the proper governing body of the State of Tennessee. * * *

Dissenting opinion of JUSTICE HARLAN, whom JUSTICE FRANKFURTER joins.

[I]n my opinion, appellants' allegations [do not] show an infringement by Tennessee of any rights assured by the Fourteenth Amendment. Accordingly, I believe the complaint should have been dismissed for "failure to state a claim upon which relief can be granted." [Thus], we need not reach the issues of "justiciability" or "political question" * * *.

In the last analysis, what lies at the core of this controversy is a difference of opinion as to the function of representative government. It is surely beyond argument that those who have the responsibility for devising a system of representation may permissibly consider that factors other than bare numbers should be taken into account. The existence of the United States Senate is proof enough of that. To consider that we may ignore the Tennessee Legislature's judgment in this instance because that body was the product of an asymmetrical electoral apportionment would in effect be to assume the very conclusion here disputed. Hence we must accept the present form of the Tennessee Legislature as the embodiment of the State's choice, or, more realistically, its compromise, between competing political philosophies. The federal courts have not been empowered by the Equal Protection Clause to judge whether this resolution of the State's internal political conflict is desirable or undesirable, wise or unwise. * * *

The claim that Tennessee's system of apportionment is so unreasonable as to amount to a capricious classification of voting strength stands up no better under dispassionate analysis.[e] * * *

The suggestion of my Brother Frankfurter that courts lack standards by which to decide such cases as this, is relevant not only to the question of "justiciability," but also, and perhaps more fundamentally, to the determination whether any cognizable constitutional claim has been asserted in this case. [Those] observers of the Court who see it primarily as the last refuge for the correction of all inequality or injustice, no matter what its nature or source, will no doubt applaud this decision and its break with the past. Those who consider that continuing national respect for the Court's authority depends in large measure upon its wise exercise of self-restraint and discipline in constitutional adjudication, will view the decision with deep concern. * * *[f]

POWELL v. McCORMACK, 395 U.S. 486, 89 S.Ct. 1944, 23 L.Ed.2d 491 (1969): Petitioner was elected to the House of Representatives for the 90th Congress. Although he met the age, citizenship and residence requirements of Art. I, § 2, cl. 2, he was not permitted to take his seat pursuant to a House resolution after a Select Committee "reported that Powell had asserted an unwarranted privilege and immunity from the processes of the courts of New York; that he had wrongfully diverted House funds for the use of others and himself; and that he had made false reports on expenditures of foreign currency to the Committee on House Administration." Powell sought, inter alia, a federal declaration that his exclusion was unconstitutional and that his salary be paid by the Sergeant-at-Arms. The lower courts dismissed the complaint.

The Court, per WARREN, C.J., reversed, (Stewart, J., dissenting on the ground that the case was moot) holding that the claim did not present a political question. It rejected the contention—after lengthy examination of the pre-Constitutional Convention precedents of the English Parliament and American colonial assemblies, the debates at the Constitutional Convention and state conventions, and the early and more recent congressional precedents—that Art. I, § 5, cl. 1 ("Each House shall be the Judge of the * * * Qualifications of its own Members") contained a "textually demonstrable constitutional commitment" to the House of "judicially unreviewable power to set qualifications for membership and to judge whether prospective members meet those qualifications." "In order to determine whether there has been a textual commitment to a co-ordinate department of the Government, we must interpret the Constitu-

e. In his opinion and in an appendix to it, Harlan, J., challenged Clark, J.'s original formula for determining how many representatives each county presently had. He then demonstrated that no feasible formula "could provide proportionately equal 'total representation' for each of Tennessee's 95 counties," and argued the relevancy and legitimacy of factors other than numbers, e.g., "a proper balance between urban and rural interest," "the size of a county in terms of its total area," "the location within a county of some major industry," "various economic, political, and geographical considerations," and deferring reapportionment "in the interest of stability of government."

f. For detailed consideration of the reapportionment problem, see Ch. 6, Sec. 4, I, A.

tion. [Our] examination of the relevant historical materials leads us to the conclusion [that] the Constitution leaves the House without authority to *exclude* any person, duly elected by his constituents, who meets all the requirements for membership expressly prescribed in" Art. I, § 2.[g]

"Had the intent of the Framers emerged from these materials with less clarity, we would nevertheless have been compelled to resolve any ambiguity in favor of a narrow construction of the scope of Congress' power to exclude members-elect. A fundamental principle of our representative democracy is, in Hamilton's words, 'that the people should choose whom they please to govern them.' As Madison pointed out at the Convention, this principle is undermined as much by limiting whom the people can select as by limiting the franchise itself. * * * Unquestionably, Congress has an interest in preserving its institutional integrity, but in most cases that interest can be sufficiently safeguarded by the exercise of its power to punish its members for disorderly behavior and, in extreme cases, to expel a member with the concurrence of two-thirds." The Court expressed no view on what limitations may exist on Congress' power to "expel or otherwise punish" a member, under Art. I, § 5, cl. 2 once he has been seated.[h]

"Respondents' alternate contention is that the case presents a political question because judicial resolution of petitioners' claim would produce a 'potentially embarrassing confrontation between coordinate branches' of the Federal Government. But, [our interpretation of Art. I, § 5] falls within the traditional role accorded courts to interpret the law, and does not involve a 'lack of respect due [a] coordinate branch of government,' nor does it involve an 'initial policy determination of a kind clearly for nonjudicial discretion.' *Baker.* Our system of government requires that federal courts on occasion interpret the Constitution in a manner at variance with the construction given the document by another branch. The alleged conflict that such an adjudication may cause cannot justify the courts' avoiding their constitutional responsibility. * * *

"Nor are any of the other formulations of a political question 'inextricable from the case at bar.' *Baker.* Petitioners seek a determination [for] which clearly there are 'judicially manageable standards.' Finally, a judicial resolution of petitioners' claim will not result in 'multifarious pronouncements by various departments on one question.' For, as we noted in *Baker,* it is the responsibility of this Court to act as the ultimate interpreter of the Constitution. * * *

"Petitioners seek additional forms of equitable relief, including mandamus for the release of Petitioner Powell's back pay. The propriety of such remedies,

g. For a contrary conclusion, see Dionisopoulous, *A Commentary on the Constitutional Issues in the Powell and Related Cases,* 17 J.Pub.L. 103 (1968). Consider Sandalow, in *Symposium,* 17 U.C.L.A.L.Rev. 164, 172–73 (1969): "The most striking feature of the Court's review of history [is] that not until the *Powell* case can one find any suggestion that courts are empowered to sit in judgment on the question whether the House or Senate exceeded their authority in excluding a person elected to membership. [Having] begun by asking the right question, whether there was a 'constitutional commitment of the issue' to the House, the Court proceeded to answer a quite different one, whether the 'qualifications' which Article I, Section 5 authorized the House to 'judge' were only those specified in Article I, Section 2 (and perhaps elsewhere in the Constitution). The opinion reflects, in short, a classic instance of confusion between 'jurisdiction'—the power to decide—and 'the merits'—the correctness of decisions."

Query: Could Congress enact a mandatory retirement age for its members?

h. For the view that Congress may expel a member for any reason it wishes and that the expulsion is not subject to judicial review, see Ellis, *Powell v. McCormack and the Power to Expel: Some Unanswered Questions Regarding the Framers' Intent,* 5 Ga.L.Rev. 203 (1971).

however, is more appropriately considered in the first instance by the courts below." [i]

Notes and Questions

1. *"Judicially manageable standards."* COLEMAN v. MILLER stated: "[T]he question of a reasonable time [for the pendency of a constitutional amendment before the states involves] an appraisal of a great variety of relevant conditions, political, social and economic, which can hardly be said to be within the appropriate range of evidence receivable in a court of justice and as to which it would be an extravagant extension of judicial authority to assert judicial notice. [T]hese conditions are appropriate for the consideration of the political departments of the Government. The questions they involve are essentially political and not justiciable." If the *Coleman* question was "political" for this reason, what of the questions in *Baker* and *Powell?* What of the questions in the *School Segregation Cases*? Is this a helpful test by which to determine justiciability?

2. *Foreign relations.* GOLDWATER v. CARTER, 444 U.S. 996, 100 S.Ct. 533, 62 L.Ed.2d 428 (1979), summarily reversed a court of appeals decision that the President had power to terminate a treaty with Taiwan without congressional approval. REHNQUIST, J., joined by Burger, C.J., and Stewart and Stevens, JJ., believed "that the controversy [is] a nonjusticiable political dispute. [W]hile the Constitution is express as to the manner in which the Senate shall participate in the ratification of a Treaty, it is silent as to that body's participation in the abrogation of a Treaty. In this respect the case is directly analogous to *Coleman.* [In] light of [the] fact that different termination procedures may be appropriate for different treaties, the [case] 'must surely be controlled by political standards.' [T]he justifications for concluding that the question here is political [are] even more compelling than in *Coleman* because it involves foreign relations—specifically a treaty commitment to use military force in the defense of a foreign government if attacked. [W]e are asked to settle a dispute between coequal branches of our government, each of which has resources available to protect and assert its interests, resources not available to private litigants outside the judicial forum."

POWELL, J., concurred because of "prudential considerations": "[A] dispute between Congress and the President is not ready for judicial review unless and until each branch has taken action asserting its constitutional authority. [Since] Congress has taken no official [action], we do not know whether there ever will be an actual confrontation between the Legislative and Executive Branches."

But "reliance upon the political-question doctrine is inconsistent with our precedents. [First,] the text of the Constitution does not unquestionably commit the power to terminate treaties to the President alone. Second, there is no 'lack of judicially discoverable and manageable [standards.]' Resolution of the question may not be easy, but it only requires us to apply normal principles of interpretation to the constitutional provisions at issue. [This] case 'touches' foreign relations, but the question presented to us concerns only the constitution-

i. Powell was re-elected to the 91st Congress. Pursuant to a House resolution, he was seated but fined $25,000 and denied all prior seniority. Would a suit challenging this action present a "political question"?

Suppose a defeated House candidate brings an action challenging the House's seating of his opponent—who is a 23 year-old alien who has never resided outside of the District of Columbia since coming to the United States?

See generally *Symposium,* 17 U.C.L.A.L.Rev. 1 (1969).

al division of power between Congress and the President. [Finally,] [i]nterpretation of the Constitution does not imply lack of respect for a coordinate branch. *Powell.* * * * [2]" [a]

BRENNAN, J., who would have affirmed on the merits, dissented: "[T]he political question doctrine restrains courts from reviewing an exercise of foreign policy judgment by the coordinate political branch [but] the doctrine does not pertain when a court is faced with the *antecedent* question whether a particular branch has been constitutionally designated as the repository of political decisionmaking power. Cf. *Powell.* The issue of decisionmaking authority must be resolved as a matter of constitutional law, not political discretion; accordingly, it falls within the competence of the courts." [b]

3. *Controversial nature of subject matter.* Should this be an important criterion for determining "political questions"? If so, was it omitted from the *Baker* "checklist"? Consider Finkelstein, *Judicial Self-Limitation,* 37 Harv.L. Rev. 338, 344 (1924): "There are certain cases which are completely without the sphere of judicial interference. They are called, for historical reasons, 'political questions'. [The term] applies to all those matters of which the court, at a given time, will be of the opinion that it is impolitic or inexpedient to take jurisdiction. Sometimes this idea of expediency will result from the fear of the vastness of the consequences that a decision on the merits might entail." See generally Bickel, *The Least Dangerous Branch* 183–98 (1962). Compare Weston, *Political Questions,* 38 Harv.L.Rev. 296, 298–99 (1925): "[T]he courts in the obligatory exercise of unquestioned jurisdiction walk every day upon ground still shaken by the conflict of public opinion."

4. *"Textually demonstrable constitutional commitment."* (a) *Amending process.* (i) Concurring in *Coleman v. Miller,* Black, J., joined by Roberts, Frankfurter and Douglas, JJ., stated that Art. V "grants Congress exclusive power [over] the amending process" and that Congress "is under no duty to accept the pronouncements upon that exclusive power by this Court." Does this distinguish *Coleman* from *Baker*? From *Colegrove* (see note 1 after *Wesberry v. Sanders,* p. 1377 infra)? From *Powell*? Does the language of Art. V support Black, J.? Suppose Congress submitted a proposed constitutional amendment to the states and provided that no black could participate in the state ratification process? See generally Tribe, *A Constitution We Are Amending: In Defense of a Restrained Judicial Role,* 97 Harv.L.Rev. 433 (1983); Dellinger, *The Legitimacy of Constitutional Change: Rethinking the Amendment Process,* 97 Harv.L.Rev. 386 (1983).

(ii) In *Coleman,* the Court held that "the question of the efficacy of ratifications by state legislatures, in the light of previous rejection or attempted withdrawal, should be regarded as a political question pertaining to the political departments, with the ultimate authority in the Congress in the exercise of its control over the promulgation of the adoption of the Amendment." Does this also apply to the question of whether a state legislature, which has already

2. *Coleman* is not relevant here. [The] proposed constitutional amendment at issue in *Coleman* would have overruled decisions of this Court. Thus, judicial review of the legitimacy of a State's ratification would have compelled this Court to oversee the very constitutional process used to reverse Supreme Court decisions. In such circumstances it may be entirely appropriate for the Judicial Branch of government to step aside. * * *

a. Marshall, J., concurred in the result.

b. Blackmun, J., joined by White, J., dissented. They "would set the case for oral argument and give it the plenary consideration it so obviously deserves."

ratified a proposed amendment, may subsequently rescind that ratification? [c]

(iii) If, pursuant to Art. V, "the legislatures of two-thirds of the several states" apply to Congress to "call a convention for proposing amendments" and Congress ignores the application, is an action for a mandatory injunction "nonjusticiable"? See Bonfield, *The Dirksen Amendment and the Article V Convention Process,* 66 Mich.L.Rev. 949, 976–85 (1968).

(b) *Impeachment.* Does Art. I, § 3, cl. 6—"The Senate shall have the sole power to try all impeachments"—"demonstrably commit" final constitutional decision "to a coordinate political department"? Consider Berger, *Impeachment: The Constitutional Problems* 105–06, 117–18, 120 (1973): "Like the three qualifications of Art. I, § 2(2) [in *Powell*], impeachment, by Art. II, § 4, is limited to three grounds, 'treason, bribery, or other high crimes and misdemeanors,' * * *. Although impeachment was chiefly designed to check Executive abuses and oppressions, there was no thought of delivering either the President or the Judiciary to the unbounded discretion of Congress. This is attested by the Framers' rejection of the unfettered removal by Address [formal request of Congress], by their rejection of 'maladministration' because that was 'so vague' as to leave tenure, 'at the pleasure' of the Senate, and by the substitution of 'high crimes and misdemeanors' with knowledge that it had a 'limited' and 'technical meaning.' * * * 'Limits' on Congress determined by Congress itself would be no limits at all. [I]f it be assumed that the 'sole power to try' conferred insulation from review, it must yield to the subsequent Fifth Amendment ['due process' provision]." See also Rezneck, *Is Judicial Review of Impeachment Coming?* 60 A.B.A.J. 681, 682–83 (1974): "Nothing in the text of the Constitution expressly bars judicial review of an impeachment conviction. On the contrary, Art. III provides that the 'judicial Power' of the [federal courts] 'shall extend to all cases, in Law and Equity, arising under this Constitution.' [If, in *Powell*], the constitutional provision that 'Each House shall be the Judge of the Elections, Returns and Qualifications of its own Members' did not commit the final determination of Powell's exclusion to the House of Representatives, why should the language on impeachment be read to commit final decision of all impeachment questions to the Senate? The grant of power to 'judge' is at least as comprehensive as a power to 'try,' but it did not prevent judicial review in *Powell.* [Moreover, the] use of the word 'try' suggests a limited, not absolute, measure of finality for decisions of the Senate in an impeachment proceeding. [The] 'trial,' in which the facts are determined, is different from an 'appeal' or other mode of review in which questions of law are resolved in an appellate court." [d]

Compare Black, *Impeachment: A Handbook* 54–55, 61–62 (1974): "If the Supreme Court [were] to order reinstatement of an impeached and convicted president, there would be, to say the least, a very grave and quite legitimate

c. For varying views on this issue, both as to justiciability and the merits, see Kanowitz & Klinger, *Can a State Rescind Its Equal Rights Amendment Ratification: Who Decides and How?* 28 Hast.L.J. 979 (1977); Comment, *The Equal Rights Amendment and Article V: A Framework for Analysis of the Extension and Rescission Issues,* 127 U.Pa.L.Rev. 494 (1978); Note, *The Process of Constitutional Amendment,* 79 Colum.L.Rev. 109 (1979).

d. See also Karst & Horowitz, *Presidential Prerogative and Judicial Review,* 22 U.C. L.A.L.Rev. 47, 52 n. 26 (1974): "[T]he more one thinks of the process as a 'legal' proceeding, with, for example, 'high Crimes and Misdemeanors' given a highly particularized definition, the more one is inclined to look favorably on judicial review. As one gives greater emphasis to the propriety of considering political factors in the impeachment process, the more that process appears to be something the courts should leave alone."

doubt whether that decree had any title to being obeyed, or whether it was [as] widely outside judicial jurisdiction as would be a judicial order to Congress to increase the penalty for counterfeiting. To cite the most frightening consequence, our military commanders would have to decide for themselves which president they were bound to obey, the reinstated one or his successor. [It] would be most unfortunate if the notion got about that the Senate's verdict were somewhat tentative. [No] senator should be encouraged to think he can shift to any court responsibility for an unpalatable or unpopular decision. [Further,] if a removed president tried [judicial review], and had his case (as would almost surely happen) dismissed for want of jurisdiction, he might be able, though quite wrongly, to persuade a part of the people that he had been denied his rightful day in court."

Suppose a federal judge seeks judicial review of his impeachment and conviction on the ground that he was denied the right to counsel in the proceeding? That many Senators were personally prejudiced against him? That he was impeached because of his race? Because of his political affiliation? Suppose a disappointed candidate for judicial appointment seeks judicial review of the President's failure to nominate him, alleging the foregoing reasons?

(c) *Regulating the militia.* In GILLIGAN v. MORGAN, 413 U.S. 1, 93 S.Ct. 2440, 37 L.Ed.2d 407 (1973), students at Kent State University sought various relief against government officials to prevent repetition of events that had occurred on that campus in May 1970. The court of appeals instructed the federal district court to evaluate the "pattern of training, weaponry and orders in the Ohio National Guard" so as to determine whether it made "inevitable the use of fatal force in suppressing civilian disorders." The Court, per BURGER, C.J., reversed, relying heavily on Art. I, § 8, cl. 16—which grants to Congress "the responsibility for organizing, arming and disciplining the Militia (now the National Guard), with certain responsibilities being reserved to the respective States"—and on federal legislation enacted pursuant thereto: "[T]he nature of the questions to be resolved on remand are subjects committed expressly to the political branches of government. [It] would be difficult to think of a clearer example of the type of governmental action that was intended by the Constitution to be left to the political branches [or] of an area of governmental activity in which the courts have less competence. The complex, subtle, and professional decisions as to the composition, training, equipping, and control of a military force are essentially professional military judgments, subject *always* to civilian control of the Legislative and Executive Branches [which] are periodically subject to electoral accountability." [e]

(d) Do *Baker, Powell, Coleman* and *Gilligan* establish that the "political question" doctrine is "a function of the separation of powers"—presently confined exclusively to "the relationship between the judiciary and the coordinate branches of the Federal Government"? That the other *Baker* criteria—includ-

e. Blackmun, J., joined by Powell, J., concurred: "This case relates to prospective relief in the form of judicial surveillance of highly subjective and technical matters involving military training and command. As such, it presents an '[inappropriate] subject matter for judicial consideration,' for respondents are asking the District Court, in fashioning that prospective relief, 'to enter upon policy determinations for which judicially manageable standards are lacking.' *Baker.* [On] the understanding that this is what the Court's opinion holds, I join that opinion."

Douglas, Brennan, Stewart and Marshall, JJ., dissented because "this case is now moot."

ing "judicially manageable standards" (note 1 supra) and "effective judicial remedies" (note 5 infra)—are all subsumed within this specific principle? See Jackson, *The Political Question Doctrine: Where Does It Stand After Powell v. McCormack, O'Brien v. Brown and Gilligan v. Morgan,* 44 U.Colo.L.Rev. 477 (1973). If so, and if the political branches specifically authorize the Court to decide the question, may (should) the Court do so? See Choper, *Judicial Review and the National Political Process* 405–15 (1980). See also note 4, after *Poe v. Ullman,* p. 1328 infra.

For the view that the leading political question cases have *not* "involved abstention from judicial review, or other extraordinary deference" to the political branches—i.e., that the Court has *not* held that the other branches' "determinations were binding on the courts 'right or wrong,' constitutional or unconstitutional"—but rather involved the Court's either "accept[ing] decisions by the political branches [as being] within their constitutional authority," or "refus[ing] some (or all) remedies for want of equity," see Henkin, *Is There a Political Question Doctrine?* 85 Yale L.J. 597 (1976). See also Note, *A Dialogue on the Political Question Doctrine,* 1978 Utah L.Rev. 523.

(e) O'BRIEN v. BROWN, 409 U.S. 1, 92 S.Ct. 2718, 34 L.Ed.2d 1 (1972), per curiam, stayed judgments which had adjudicated the merits of challenges to "recommendations of the Credentials Committee of the 1972 Democratic National Convention regarding the seating of certain delegates to the convention that will meet three days hence": "[N]o holding of this Court up to now gives support for judicial intervention in the circumstances presented here, involving as they do, relationships of great delicacy and essentially political in nature. [It] has been understood since our national political parties first came into being as voluntary associations of individuals that the convention itself is the proper forum for determining intra-party disputes as to which delegates shall be seated. [While] the Court is unwilling to undertake final resolution of the important constitutional questions presented without full briefing and argument and adequate opportunity for deliberation, we entertain grave doubts as to the action taken by the Court of Appeals." [f]

Douglas, White and Marshall, JJ., would have denied the stays, MARSHALL, J., joined by Douglas, J., believing that "the doctrine of 'political questions' was fashioned to deal with a very different problem, which has nothing to do with this case. [T]he full convention of the National Democratic Party [is] most assuredly not a coordinate branch of government to which the federal courts owe deference within the meaning of the separation of powers or the political question doctrine.

"Moreover, it cannot be said that 'judicially manageable standards' are [lacking]. The Illinois challenge requires the court to determine whether certain rules adopted by the National Party for the selection of delegates violate the First and Fourteenth Amendment rights of Illinois [voters]. The California challenge requires the court to determine whether the votes of party members were counted in accordance with the rules announced prior to the election and, if not, whether a change in the rules after the election violates the constitutional rights of the voters or the candidates." [g]

f. Brennan, J., concurred in the result.

g. See also *Cousins v. Wigoda,* 419 U.S. 477, 95 S.Ct. 541, 42 L.Ed.2d 595 (1975) (first amendment right of political party to conduct its convention).

Does *O'Brien* suggest a revival of Frankfurter, J.'s view in *Colegrove* and *Baker?*

5. *Effective judicial remedies.* To what extent should "the difficulty or impossibility of devising effective judicial remedies" influence "justiciability"? How effective (seemly?) were the possible remedies available in *Baker*? What remedies could (should) a court afford in the various situations discussed in the above notes?

6. *"Judicial restraint" and the political process.* Consider Frank, *Political Questions,* in Supreme Court & Supreme Law 36, 46 (Cahn ed. 1954): "[T]he basic objective of a plan of government ought to be to put the responsibility for the decision of questions some place, and [the] political question doctrine is useful when it operates to put responsibility at the best place, and is harmful when it puts the decision no place. [W]hat happens in the redistricting cases is that the responsibility, if not taken by the court, is transferred to a body which has a completely vested interest in the maldistricting." Does this adequately respond to Frankfurter, J.'s "appeal must be to an informed, civically militant electorate" argument? Compare Auerbach, *The Reapportionment Cases: One Person, One Vote—One Vote, One Value,* 1964 Sup.Ct.Rev. 1, 2: "It is paradoxical [for] the advocates of judicial self-limitation to criticize the Court for helping to make majority rule effective, because the case for self-restraint rests on the assumption that the Court is reviewing the legislative acts of representatives who are put in office and can be turned out of office by a majority of the people. Since malapportionment destroys this assumption, judicial intervention to remove this obstacle to majority rule may be less intolerable than the self-perpetuation of minority rule."

7. *Presidential war-making power.* (a) If a draftee seeks a federal declaratory judgment that American participation in a particular armed conflict is "unconstitutional in that it was not initially authorized or subsequently ratified by Congressional declaration," is the question "justiciable"? See opinions of Marshall and Douglas, JJ., in *Holtzman v. Schlesinger,* 414 U.S. 1304, 1316, 94 S.Ct. 1, 8, 38 L.Ed.2d 18, 28 (1973)—and lower court decisions and opinions of Supreme Court justices dissenting from denials of certiorari cited therein. Consider Velvel, *The War in Viet Nam: Unconstitutional, Justiciable, and Jurisdictionally Attackable,* 16 Kan.L.Rev. 449, 480 (1968): "The proposition that a court may not rule on the issue [because] the question is 'political' [is] at best very dubious, since it denies the court the power to delineate the authority of the various branches of government. Since *Marbury,* it has been clear that this power is a major part of the courts' role in the constitutional scheme." Does this satisfy the *Baker* criteria? Are there "judicially manageable standards"? Consider Cox, *The Role of Congress in Constitutional Determinations,* 40 U.Cinc.L.Rev. 199, 204 (1971): "[O]ne might formulate a workable principle for delimiting the President's power to engage in military activities overseas, but the task is far from easy. Should the rule permit the use of troops to protect the lives of United States citizens in a foreign country until they can be safely evacuated? Should it permit sending arms with which another nation may defend itself against foreign aggression? Sending 'technicians' to give battlefield instructions in the use of sophisticated weapons? Sending instructors? Sending support troops to protect the bases where logistic support is delivered but to fight only when themselves attacked? If, through gross miscalculation, measures that the rule permits result in armed combat on a sizeable scale, what then may the Executive do, without a declaration of war, to protect the lives of United States soldiers and the national interest during a process of disengagement? May the adverse effects

of declaring war upon international relations be taken into account in determining whether the declaration is essential? These are only a few of the pertinent questions." Are there "effective judicial remedies"? Would the Court inevitably be drawn into directing and supervising the conclusion of the war (cf. *Gilligan*)?

(b) Even if there are "political question" considerations lurking, what of the *Baker* "inadequate political redress" factor? Consider W. Schwartz & McCormack, *The Justiciability of Legal Objections to the American Military Effort in Vietnam,* 46 Tex.L.Rev. 1033, 1047 (1968): "It is about as unlikely that a President will, absent judicial intervention, dilute his power by acknowledging the authority of Congress to control the commitment of troops to combat as it was that the state legislators would have weakened their power base through reapportionment. Thus, as in *Baker,* since the political process is itself impaired by the challenged action, there is compelling practical need to restore the effectiveness of the responsible political branch." Is this situation distinguishable from *Baker* because here, if the Court does not intervene, the responsibility is left "to a body (Congress) which has a completely vested interest in" preserving the constitutionally *proper* political authority? Consider Moore, *The Justiciability of Challenges to the Use of Military Forces Abroad,* 10 Va.J.Int'l L. 85, 95–96 (1969): "[S]ince these constitutional claims are intended to resolve a dispute about the relative role of Congress and the Executive and not to apply some constitutional prohibition limiting total governmental power to act, such as the Bill of Rights, if there are institutional checks other than judicial determination which each branch exercises on the other it is certainly relevant to the abstention decision. [O]nce a major commitment of troops abroad has been made, Congress could refuse to appropriate funds or to conscript the necessary troops, could censure the President as the House did President Polk for his Mexican War activities, or could even institute impeachment proceedings against the President. And short of these checks, Congress can hold public hearings and mobilize public opinion in a manner which can have a major impact on Executive discretion."

Compare Hughes, *Civil Disobedience and the Political Question Doctrine,* 43 N.Y.U.L.Rev. 1, 16 (1968): "Congress of course might assert that the President has usurped [the power to declare war], but if the courts refused to resolve the dispute we [might] then be presented with a political choice about taking sides but not with a legal question for resolution. If the Constitution reserves powers to Congress in such a way that disputes can be envisaged between Congress and the President, and if the courts tell us that they have no power to resolve such disputes, we can only conclude that such provisions in the Constitution are of no more than hortatory significance." If the President rejects Congress' assertion of authority, what is the likelihood that he will abide by the Court's "resolution of the dispute"? Are the Court's decisions—at least on issues of this nature—of "more than hortatory significance"? See Choper, note 4(d) supra, at 305–08. Compare Ratner, *The Coordinated Warmaking Power—Legislative, Executive and Judicial Roles,* 44 So.Cal.L.Rev. 461, 483 (1971): "Judicial jurisdiction [may] be appropriate to ameliorate the impeachment confrontation that would probably result from presidential defiance of a congressional directive to limit or terminate hostilities. Though a president who defies Congress may also defy the Court, he is more likely to acknowledge the jurisdiction of an impartial and respected tribunal or yield to the pressure of combined legislative and judicial opposition." [h]

(c) If a person is prosecuted for draft evasion—or if a draftee is court martialed for refusing an order to engage in combat and seeks federal habeas corpus—may he obtain an adjudication of the war's constitutionality? Consider Tigar, *Judicial Power, The "Political Question Doctrine," and Foreign Relations,* 17 U.C.L.A.L.Rev. 1135, 1177–78 (1970): "[It is] the duty of the Court to consider the legality of a detention by consideration of all the legal rules which are conceded to be operative under the Constitution, laws and treaties of the United States. This determination does not necessarily involve the Executive in litigating the validity of its claim to possess lawfully the power it exercises in conducting a war: it says only that so long as the Executive stays out of the federal courts, its 'right to be let alone' is perhaps arguable, but when it comes into court it must be bound by the rules fashioned by the judiciary and the Congress for the protection of litigants' rights."

(d) If a draftee, ordered to the "battle zone," asserts deprivation of due process because his participation will constitute a "war crime" under principles of international law thus subjecting him to punishment by an international tribunal, does his suit for injunction present a "political question"? Is the case distinguishable from those discussed above?

SECTION 3. CONGRESSIONAL REGULATION OF JUDICIAL POWER

Beginning with the Judiciary Act of 1789, Congress has enacted various statutes defining the Supreme Court's jurisdiction. For example, it was not until 1914 that the Court was authorized to review state court decisions holding state laws violative of the Constitution. The Court's original jurisdiction, which typically comprises only a handful of cases each year (mainly concerning "controversies between two or more states"), is presently governed by 28 U.S.C.A. § 1251. The most important current provisions respecting the Court's appellate jurisdiction are 28 U.S.C.A. §§ 1254 (federal courts of appeals) and 1257 (state courts).

---

§ 1254. Cases in the courts of appeals may be reviewed by the Supreme Court by the following methods: (1) By writ of certiorari granted upon the petition of any party to any civil or criminal case, before or after rendition of judgment or decree; (2) By certification at any time by a court of appeals of any question of law in any civil or criminal case as to which instructions are desired, and upon such certification the Supreme Court may give binding instructions or require the entire record to be sent up for decision of the entire matter in controversy.

§ 1257. Final judgments or decrees rendered by the highest court of a State in which a decision could be had, may be reviewed by the Supreme Court by writ of certiorari, where the validity of a treaty or statute of the United States is drawn in question or where the validity of a statute of any State is drawn in question on the ground of its being repugnant to the Constitution, treaties or

h. See also Powell, J., concurring in *Goldwater v. Carter,* note 2 supra: "The spectre of the Federal Government brought to a halt because of the mutual intransigence of the President and the Congress would require this Court to provide a resolution pursuant to our duty 'to say what the law is.' *Marbury.*"

laws of the United States, or where any title, right, privilege or immunity is specially set up or claimed under the Constitution, treaties or statutes of, or any commission held or authority exercised under, the United States. * * *

Sections 1254 and 1257 previously provided for a form of appeal that required the Court to determine some classes of cases on their merits. Congress removed this form of jurisdiction because it concluded that the Court was in the best position to decide which cases were worthy of its attention. For discussion of the Court's exercise of discretion, see Section 4 infra.

EX PARTE McCARDLE

74 U.S. (7 Wall.) 506, 19 L.Ed. 264 (1869).

[On February 5, 1867, Congress empowered federal courts to grant habeas corpus to persons restrained in violation of the Constitution, treaty, or federal law. Appeal could be to the Supreme Court. McCardle—imprisoned by the military government of Mississippi pursuant to the Reconstruction Acts for publishing "incendiary and libelous" articles—"alleging unlawful restraint by military force," sought habeas corpus which was denied by the Circuit Court. He appealed to the Supreme Court, apparently presenting it with the opportunity finally to reach the merits of the Reconstruction laws' constitutionality. However, in 1868, after argument but before decision, Congress (over President Johnson's veto) passed the following act:] "That so much of the act approved February 5, 1867 [as] authorized an appeal from the judgment of the Circuit Court to the Supreme Court of the United States, or the exercise of any such jurisdiction by said Supreme Court, on appeals which have been, or may hereafter be taken, [is] hereby repealed."

* * * Argument was now heard upon the effect of the repealing act.

The CHIEF JUSTICE [CHASE] delivered the opinion of the Court.

[T]he appellate jurisdiction of this Court is not derived from acts of Congress. It is, strictly speaking, conferred by the Constitution. But it is conferred "with such exceptions and under such regulations as Congress shall make."

It is unnecessary to consider whether, if Congress had made no exceptions and no regulations, this court might not have exercised general appellate jurisdiction under rules prescribed by itself. From among the earliest acts of the first Congress [was the Judiciary Act of 1789 which] provided for the organization of this court, and prescribed regulations for the exercise of its jurisdiction.

[In] *Durousseau v. United States* [6 Cranch, 307 (1810)], particularly, the whole matter was carefully examined, and the court held, that [the] judicial act was an exercise of the power given by the Constitution to Congress "of making exceptions to the appellate jurisdiction of the Supreme Court." "They have described affirmatively," said the court, "its jurisdiction, and this affirmative description has been understood to imply a negation of the exercise of such appellate power as is not comprehended within it."

The principle [thus] established, it was an almost necessary consequence that acts of Congress, providing for the exercise of jurisdiction, should come to be spoken of as acts granting jurisdiction and not as acts making exceptions to the constitutional grant of it.

The exception to appellate jurisdiction in the case before us, however, is not an inference from the affirmation of other appellate jurisdiction. It is made in terms. * * *

We are not at liberty to inquire into the motives of the legislature. We can only examine into its power under the Constitution * * *.

What, then, is the effect of the repealing act upon the case before us? * * * Jurisdiction is power to declare the law, and when it ceases to exist the only function remaining to the court is that of announcing the fact and dismissing the cause. And this is not less clear upon authority than upon principle. [J]udicial duty is not less fitly performed by declining ungranted jurisdiction than in exercising firmly that which the Constitution and the laws confer.

Counsel seem to have supposed, if effect be given to the repealing act in question, that the whole appellate power of the court, in cases of habeas corpus, is denied. But this is an error. The act of 1868 does not except from that jurisdiction any cases but appeals from Circuit Courts under the act of 1867. It does not affect the jurisdiction which was previously exercised.

The appeal [must] be dismissed for want of jurisdiction.[a]

Notes and Questions

1. *Extent of the decision.* (a) In *Ex parte Yerger,* 75 U.S. (8 Wall.) 85, 19 L.Ed. 332 (1869), also challenging the Reconstruction Acts, the Court, upholding its appellate jurisdiction by writ of certiorari in a habeas corpus proceeding based on pre-1867 legislation, said of *McCardle*: "The effect of the Act was to oust the court of its jurisdiction of the particular case then before it on appeal, and it is not to be doubted that such was the effect intended. Nor will it be questioned that legislation of this character is unusual and hardly to be justified except upon some imperious public exigency." More recently, Douglas, J., joined by Black, J., stated: "There is a serious question whether [*McCardle*] could command a majority view today." *Glidden Co. v. Zdanok,* 370 U.S. 530, 605 n. 11, 82 S.Ct. 1459, 1501–02, 8 L.Ed.2d 671, 718–19 (1962).

(b) How great an incursion into the Court's jurisdiction did *McCardle* really permit? Consider Ratner, *Congressional Power Over the Appellate Jurisdiction of the Supreme Court,* 109 U.Pa.L.Rev. 157, 180 (1960): "The statute [did] not deprive the Court of jurisdiction to decide McCardle's case; he could still petition the Supreme Court for [an original] writ of habeas corpus * * *. The legislation did no more than eliminate one procedure for Supreme Court review of decisions denying habeas corpus while leaving another equally efficacious one available." [b]

(c) Does *McCardle* stand for the proposition that Congress may *completely* deprive the Court of power to review certain federal questions? Apart from *McCardle,* does Congress have this power? The power to deprive the Court of *all* appellate jurisdiction? If not, what is the meaning of the "Exceptions" language

a. For an historical account, see Fairman, *Reconstruction and Reunion, 1864–88, Part One,* c. X (1971).

b. For criticism of the *McCardle* rationale because the Court (1) dismissed the case "for want of jurisdiction" despite the existence—as evidenced by *Yerger*—of an alternative source of jurisdiction, and (2) treated the Repealing Act as making an "exception" to the Court's Art. III appellate jurisdiction when, in fact, it only repealed a portion of the 1867 act which had created a special right of appeal not previously authorized by statute, see Van Alstyne, *A Critical Guide to Ex Parte McCardle,* 15 Ariz.L.Rev. 229 (1973).

in Art. III? Is it "that Congress may except certain cases otherwise subject only to the Court's appellate jurisdiction *by adding them to the Court's original jurisdiction*"? Van Alstyne, *A Critical Guide to Marbury v. Madison,* 1969 Duke L.J. 1, 32. It is that the Constitution *itself* only grants appellate jurisdiction in "all the other cases before mentioned" and that Congress may make "Exceptions" to this by adding to the appellate jurisdiction cases that Art. III has assigned to the original jurisdiction? For the position that this clause was intended to permit congressional control of the Court's appellate jurisdiction only as to questions of fact, not questions of law, see Merry, *Scope of the Supreme Court's Appellate Jurisdiction: Historical Basis,* 47 Minn.L.Rev. 53 (1962); Berger, *Congress v. The Supreme Court* 285–86 (1969).[c]

Consider Ratner, supra at 171–72: "It is reasonable to conclude [that the Constitutional] Convention gave Congress authority to specify * * * orderly procedures and to modify the jurisdiction from time to time in response to prevailing social and political requirements, within the limits imposed by the Court's essential constitutional role. It is not reasonable to conclude that the Convention gave Congress the power to destroy that role. Reasonably interpreted the clause means 'With such exceptions and under such regulations as Congress may make, not inconsistent with the essential functions of the Supreme Court under this Constitution.' "

What is the Court's "essential constitutional role"? Consider Ratner, *Majoritarian Constraints on Judicial Review: Congressional Control of Supreme Court Jurisdiction,* 27 Vill.L.Rev. 929, 935, 956 (1982): "The supremacy clause of article VI mandates one supreme federal law throughout the land, and article III establishes the Supreme Court as the constitutional instrument for implementing that clause. [As] such, its essential functions under the Constitution are: 1) ultimately to resolve inconsistent or conflicting interpretations of federal law, and particularly of the Constitution, by state and federal courts; 2) to maintain the supremacy of federal law, and particularly the Constitution, when it conflicts with state law or is challenged by state authority." Compare Redish, *Congressional Power to Regulate Supreme Court Appellate Jurisdiction Under the Exceptions Clause: An Internal and External Examination,* 27 Vill.L.Rev. 900, 907 (1982): "I might well agree, as a policy matter, that Congress should not possess the power to tamper with performance of the Supreme Court's role, [but] I can find no constitutional basis for erecting such a limitation." See also Rice, *Congress and the Supreme Court's Jurisdiction,* 27 Vill.L.Rev. 959, 962–81 (1982). Contrast Sager, *Constitutional Limitations on Congress' Authority to Regulate the Jurisdiction of the Federal Courts,* 95 Harv.L.Rev. 17, 57 (1981): "The Court must be available to superintend *state compliance* with federal law unless Congress provides effective review elsewhere within the *federal* judiciary."[d]

(d) Suppose that McCardle had been released by the court below and, after the government appealed to the Supreme Court, Congress passed a statute commanding the Supreme Court to resolve all pending habeas corpus appeals in

c. See also *Luckenbach S.S. Co. v. United States,* 272 U.S. 533, 47 S.Ct. 186, 71 L.Ed. 394 (1926) (upholding statute limiting Supreme Court review of Court of Claims decisions to questions of law); *Barry v. Mercein,* 46 U.S. (5 How.) 103, 12 L.Ed. 70 (1847) (Supreme Court review of action based on diversity of citizenship unavailable because action did not involve minimum monetary value required by statute).

d. For a detailed study of the background and debates in the Constitutional Convention and during the ratification process, reaching a similar conclusion, see Clinton, *A Mandatory View of Federal Court Jurisdiction: A Guided Quest for the Original Understanding of Article III,* 132 U.Pa.L.Rev. 741 (1984).

favor of the government? Cf. *United States v. Klein,* 80 U.S. (13 Wall.) 128, 20 L.Ed. 519 (1872). See generally Sedler, *Limitations on the Appellate Jurisdiction of the Supreme Court,* 20 U.Pitt.L.Rev. 99, 102–07 (1958). Suppose Congress resolved to impeach any justice who decided otherwise? Enacted a statute that no law may be declared unconstitutional on less than a $^2/_3$ vote of the justices?

2. *Legislative proposals.* From the early nineteenth century, there have been numerous congressional attempts to limit the Supreme Court's appellate jurisdiction over various issues.[e] Since the late 1970s, the most prominent have concerned abortion, school prayer, and busing for school integration. See Baucus & Kay, *The Court Stripping Bills,* 27 Vill.L.Rev. 988 (1982); fn. i infra.

Suppose Congress sought to deny Supreme Court appellate jurisdiction in any case brought by a black? Is this distinguishable from the recent proposals? What role do other constitutional provisions play in respect to the "Exceptions and Regulations" clause? See Tribe, *Jurisdictional Gerrymandering: Zoning Disfavored Rights Out of the Federal Courts,* 16 Harv.Civ.Rts.-Civ.Lib.L.Rev. 129, 141–46 (1981); Sager, note 1(c) supra, at 78–80. Compare Bator, *Congressional Power Over the Jurisdiction of the Federal Courts,* 27 Vill.L.Rev. 1030, 1034–37 (1982).

3. *Proposal for a National Court of Appeals.* In 1972, a committee chaired by Professor Paul Freund, appointed by Chief Justice Burger "to study the case load of the Supreme Court," proposed, inter alia: "The establishment [of] a National Court of Appeals, [with] seven judges drawn on a rotating basis from the federal courts of appeals and serving staggered three-year terms. This Court would have the two-fold function of (1) screening all petitions for certiorari and appeals that would at present be filed in the Supreme Court, referring the most review-worthy [to] the Supreme Court [and] denying the rest; and (2) retaining for decision on the merits cases of genuine conflict between circuits (except those of special moment, which would be certified to the Supreme Court)." Federal Judicial Center Study Group, *Report on the Case Load of the Supreme Court* (1972).

Does this recommendation of the "Freund Report" comport with Art. III? Consider C. Black, *The National Court of Appeals: An Unwise Proposal,* 83 Yale L.J. 883, 885–86 (1974): "A court that can finally determine, *for the whole nation,* questions over the whole range of federal law, without the possibility of further review, is a 'Supreme Court' in everything but name, and the Constitution provides for *one* Supreme Court, quite as clearly as it provides for one President. This National Court of Appeals * * * would (in its own unreviewable discretion) be a 'Supreme Court,' for the entire nation, *on the full and final merits* of all questions where, in its own view, an intercircuit conflict happened to have arisen."[f] Compare Freund, *Why We Need the National Court of Appeals,* 59 A.B.A.J. 247, 251 (1973): "[T]he appellate jurisdiction of the Supreme Court, from 1789 to the present day, has never extended by law over the full range of cases to which it might extend under Article III. [F]or a long time there was a special jurisdictional amount requirement for review of circuit court decisions, [and] for a century criminal cases could reach the Supreme Court from the circuit courts only on a certificate of division in the circuit court. Review of state court decisions depended on how the state court decided a federal question;

e. See Elliott, *Court-Curbing Proposals in Congress,* 33 Not.D.Law. 597 (1958); Nagel, *Court-Curbing Periods in American History,* 18 Vand.L.Rev. 925 (1965).

f. See also Gressman, *The Constitution v. The Freund Report,* 41 Geo.Wash.L.Rev. 951 (1973); Note, *The National Court of Appeals: A Constitutional "inferior Court"?* 72 Mich.L. Rev. 290 (1973).

thus for a time, when workmen's compensation was held unconstitutional in a state court, there was no possible review in the Supreme Court. Were all these tribunals—the circuit courts and the state courts—the Supreme Court, in violation of Article III?" Contrast Black, supra, at 886: "[These] examples [are] one and all broadly and crucially distinguishable for they excepted from or regulated the exercise of the uniquely 'supreme' appellate review rather than providing an alternative supreme appellate review—just what we cannot do if we are to have 'one Supreme Court.' " [g]

4. *Limitation of lower federal court jurisdiction.* It is settled that Congress, having power to establish lower federal courts, may also prescribe and limit their jurisdiction. *Sheldon v. Sill,* 49 U.S. (8 How.) 441, 12 L.Ed. 1147 (1850).[h] Thus it was not until 1875 that these courts were given general jurisdiction to decide questions arising under the Constitution, treaties or federal statutes. The Norris-LaGuardia Act greatly restricted federal courts from issuing injunctions in "labor disputes" and from enforcing "yellow-dog" contracts. See *Lauf v. E.G. Shinner & Co.,* 303 U.S. 323, 58 S.Ct. 578, 82 L.Ed. 872 (1938). The Emergency Price Control Act of 1942 provided that validity of price regulations could be judicially tested only in the specially created Emergency Court of Appeals (thus excluding all other lower federal and state court jurisdiction) with review by the Supreme Court. See *Lockerty v. Phillips,* 319 U.S. 182, 63 S.Ct. 1019, 87 L.Ed. 1339 (1943) (upheld validity of provision denying district courts power to enjoin enforcement of the Act); *Yakus v. United States,* 321 U.S. 414, 64 S.Ct. 660, 88 L.Ed. 834 (1944) (upheld validity of district court criminal prosecution for violation of price regulation in which defendants were not permitted to challenge the regulation's validity on the ground that, under the Act, they should have challenged it in the Emergency Court); *Bowles v. Willingham,* 321 U.S. 503, 64 S.Ct. 641, 88 L.Ed. 892 (1944) (upheld the enjoining of state court proceedings under the Act). Suppose that the Emergency Price Control Act had provided that *no* court, state or federal, could test the regulations? That they could be tested only in state courts? With no Supreme Court review?[i] That the federal courts must enforce the Act without regard to the validity of the regulations? See generally Hart, *The Power of Congress to Limit the Jurisdiction of Federal Courts: An Exercise in Dialectic,* 66 Harv.L.Rev. 1362 (1953); Choper, *Judicial Review and the National Political Process* 389–93, 398–404 (1980).

g. For a proposal "to leave with the present Court final jurisdiction for review of constitutionality, transferring finality [for nonconstitutional] judicial review to one or more separate judicial bodies," see Strong, *The Time Has Come to Talk of Major Curtailment in the Supreme Court's Jurisdiction,* 48 N.C.L. Rev. 1 (1969).

h. But see T. Eisenberg, *Congressional Authority to Restrict Lower Federal Court Jurisdiction,* 83 Yale L.J. 498 (1974); cf. Redish & Woods, *Congressional Power to Control the Jurisdiction of Lower Federal Courts: A Critical Review and a New Synthesis,* 124 U.Pa.L.Rev. 45 (1975).

i. This was the substance of a bill by Rep. Tuck in 1964 respecting legislative reapportionment, see McKay, *Court, Congress, and Reapportionment,* 63 Mich.L.Rev. 255 (1964); of a bill by Sen. Helms in 1979 respecting voluntary prayers in public schools, see 125 Cong.Rec. 54128–65; and of a Senate Judiciary Committee proposal in 1968 respecting the admission of confessions deemed voluntary by the state courts in state criminal prosecutions, see S.Rep. No. 1097, 90th Cong., 2d Sess. (1968).

For the view that, at a minimum, all cases comprehended within the judicial power as described in Art. III must be vested in *some* federal court, see 1 Crosskey, *Politics and the Constitution in the History of the United States* 610–18 (1953); Goebel, *History of the Supreme Court of the United States: Antecedents and Beginnings* 240–46 (1971).

May Congress, as urged by Pres. Nixon in 1973, bar all federal courts—for approximately one year—from issuing or implementing any order that students be bused so as to effectuate racial desegregation in public schools? See Note, *The Nixon Busing Bills and Congressional Power,* 81 Yale L.J. 1542–58 (1972); Bell, *Congressional Response to Busing,* 61 Geo.L.J. 963–78 (1973).

SECTION 4. DISCRETIONARY REVIEW

In the words of Vinson, C.J., 69 S.Ct. vi (1949), the Supreme Court is not "primarily concerned with the correction of errors in lower court decisions. In almost all cases within the Court's appellate jurisdiction, the petitioner has already received one appellate review of his [case]. If we took every case in which an interesting legal question is raised, or our prima facie impression is that the decision below is erroneous, we could not fulfill the Constitutional and statutory responsibilities placed upon the Court. To remain effective, the Supreme Court must continue to decide only those cases which present questions whose resolution will have immediate importance far beyond the particular facts and parties involved." [a]

UNITED STATES SUPREME COURT RULES

Rule 10. Considerations Governing Review on Certiorari

.1. A review on writ of certiorari is not a matter of right, but of judicial discretion. A petition for a writ of certiorari will be granted only when there are special and important reasons therefor. The following, while neither controlling nor fully measuring the Court's discretion, indicate the character of reasons that will be considered: (a) When a United States court of appeals has rendered a decision in conflict with the decision of another United States court of appeals on the same matter; or has decided a federal question in a way in conflict with a state court of last resort; or has so far departed from the accepted and usual course of judicial proceedings, or sanctioned such a departure by a lower court, as to call for an exercise of this Court's power of supervision. (b) When a state court of last resort has decided a federal question in a way that conflicts with the decision of another state court of last resort or of a United States court of appeals. (c) When a state court or a United States court of appeals has decided an important question of federal law which has not been, but should be, settled by this Court, or has decided a federal question in a way that conflicts with applicable decisions of this Court. * * *

Notes and Questions

1. *Appraisal of the standards.* Can the standards articulated in Rule 10 be improved? Consider Blumstein, *The Supreme Court's Jurisdiction—Reform Proposals, Discretionary Review, and Writ Dismissals,* 26 Vand.L.Rev. 895, 906–07 (1973): "Surely if petition screening itself were based on 'recognized principles,' the Court would develop more precise rules to govern its own management of the

a. But see McElwain, *The Business of the Supreme Court as Conducted by Chief Justice Hughes,* 63 Harv.L.Rev. 5, 13 (1949): "[H]e was interested in preventing grave miscarriages of justice, and occasionally he would recommend the grant of certiorari in a case of no public importance whatever simply because the decision below was unjust, unreasonable, or plainly wrong." See also Chief Justice Warren, *Attacks Freund Study Group's Composition and Proposal,* 59 A.B.A.J. 721, 729 (1973): "There are many instances where the Court, without granting plenary review, has summarily reversed, remanded, or taken other direct action to achieve what the justices conceived to be essential justice."

process. [Rather] than institutionalizing the viewpoint [that] the Court had a restricted role, the ambiguity of the jurisdictional legislation merely transferred from the Congress to the Court the locus of decision-making authority as to what cases would be heard, and simultaneously transformed a very substantial portion of the Court's work into outright political decision-making." See further, fn. b infra.

2. *Proper judicial discretion.* What considerations beyond those outlined in Rule 10 should be pertinent ("proper," "principled") to the granting of certiorari? Consider Harper & Rosenthal, *What The Supreme Court Did Not Do In The 1949 Term—An Appraisal of Certiorari,* 99 U.Pa.L.Rev. 293, 299, 300 (1950): "[T]he Court, in determining whether the issue involved is of the required importance, may, and indeed perhaps should in some instances, consider whether the time is one for decision of the particular question. [Further], a justice [might] very properly vote for denial because persuaded that if the writ were granted, five or more justices might decide the issue wrongly. It is altogether understandable that a justice who has strong convictions about a case of public importance might prefer to have the decision of an inferior court stand rather than to have it authenticated in affirmance by the highest Court." [b]

MARYLAND v. BALTIMORE RADIO SHOW, INC.

338 U.S. 912, 70 S.Ct. 252, 94 L.Ed. 562 (1950).

Opinion of JUSTICE FRANKFURTER respecting the denial of the petition for writ of certiorari. * * *

A variety of considerations underlie denials of the writ, and as to the same petition different reasons may lead different Justices to the same result. This is

b. Compare Henkin *On Drawing Lines,* 82 Harv.L.Rev. 63, 90–91 (1968): "Surely the Court did not consider the question [in *Mora v. McNamara,* 389 U.S. 934, 88 S.Ct. 282, 19 L.Ed.2d 287 (1967), of the constitutionality of United States military activity in Vietnam,] 'unimportant.' Rather, [one] is tempted to guess that the Court recognized that if it heard the case it could not give the relief requested. Even if the Justices privately thought that the President exceeded his constitutional authority in sending Mr. Mora to fight in Vietnam, it would not so declare and presume to restrain the President. Nor would the Court adjudicate claims that acts of the political branches violate international law. If it heard the case, the Court would have to decide that the issues are 'political questions' and not justiciable; or, that even if the war is illegal, Mora is not justified thereby in refusing to serve and therefore the legality of the war is not properly in issue; or that the war is not in fact illegal. Any of these judgments might be less politic than a decision not to hear the case at all, might give the impression that the Court supports the political branches in the Vietnam war, and might make the Court itself a target of the national malaise. Denying certiorari may well have been the better part of valor. [Or the] Justices might at least like to keep open the possibility of intervention rather than read themselves out 'forever.'" Contrast Hughes, *Civil Disobedience and the Political Question Doctrine,* 43 N.Y.U.L.Rev. 1, 15 (1968): "Those who advocate civil disobedience have, I think, some warrant for saying that a dearth of reasoned opinions on the political question doctrine in its application to issues that surround the war in Vietnam leaves them without a satisfactory response to their challenge. And by a satisfactory response I do not of course mean one that agrees with the petitioner nor one that will enable neat predictions to be made in the future, but only one which presents a reasoned justification for the denial of his claim." See also Rehnquist, J., dissenting from denial of certiorari in *Ratchford v. Gay Lib,* 434 U.S. 1080, 98 S.Ct. 1276, 55 L.Ed.2d 789 (1978): "[T]he existence [of] discretion does not imply that it should be used as a sort of judicial storm cellar to which we may flee to escape from controversial or sensitive cases."

In addition to articles referred to in this section, examining and criticizing the Court's exercise of its certiorari jurisdiction, see Harper & Etherington, *What the Supreme Court Did Not Do During the 1950 Term,* 100 U.Pa. L.Rev. 354 (1951); Frankfurter & Hart, *The Business of the Supreme Court at October Term, 1934,* 49 Harv.L.Rev. 68 (1935); Frankfurter & Fisher, *The Business of the Supreme Court at October Terms, 1935 and 1936,* 51 Harv.L.Rev. 577 (1938).

especially true of petitions for review on writ of certiorari to a State court. Narrowly technical reasons may lead to denials. [For detail, see Sec. 5 infra.] A decision may satisfy all these technical requirements and yet may commend itself for review to fewer than four members of the Court. Pertinent considerations of judicial policy here come into play. A case may raise an important question but the record may be cloudy. It may be desirable to have different aspects of an issue further illumined by the lower courts. Wise adjudication has its own time for ripening.

Since there are these conflicting and, to the uninformed, even confusing reasons for denying petitions for certiorari, it has been suggested from time to time that the Court indicate its reasons for denial. Practical considerations preclude. [The] time that would be required is prohibitive, apart from the fact as already indicated that different reasons not infrequently move different members of the Court * * *.[c] It becomes relevant here to note that failure to record a dissent from a denial of a petition for writ of certiorari in nowise implies that only the member of the Court who notes his dissent thought the petition should be granted. * * *

Notes and Questions

1. *Certiorari and the "rule of four."* Should a justice who voted against certiorari—strongly believing that argument and decision would squander the Court's time—refuse to participate in deciding the merits? If so, suppose there were only four votes to grant certiorari and the other five justices feel this way? Suppose the five who voted against certiorari did so because they felt the case did not satisfy jurisdictional requirements?

Consider Leiman, *The Rule of Four,* 57 Colum.L.Rev. 975, 988 (1957): "The work and the working relationships of the Court are liable to be adversely affected if a majority of the Justices are forced to decide cases which they are convinced are not proper ones for the Court to decide." Does this argument ignore both the basis for the "rule of four" and the interests of the litigants in those cases which are argued on the vote of only four justices? Or does (should) the rule of four only obligate the Court to *hear* rather than to *decide*? See generally Comment, 105 U.Pa.L.Rev. 1084 (1957). Consider Stevens, J., concurring in *New York v. Uplinger,* 467 U.S. 246, 104 S.Ct. 2332, 81 L.Ed.2d 201 (1984): "The Rule of Four is [a] device for deciding when a case must be argued, but its force is largely spent once the case has been heard. At that point, a more fully informed majority of the Court must decide whether some countervailing princi-

c. Consider Harper & Pratt, *What The Supreme Court Did Not Do During the 1951 Term,* 101 U.Pa.L.Rev. 439, 443 (1953) "[A]ssuming that it is impractical to give reasons in [many cases], what of [the] suggestion of a fairly complete explanation occasionally so that the 'accumulated explanations would make familiar the canons which guide the Court.'" Contrast Frankfurter & Hart, *The Business of the Supreme Court at October Term, 1933,* 48 Harv.L.Rev. 238, 276 (1934): "Virtually all the desiderata urged for statements of reasons for denials [of certiorari] would be attained by statements of reasons for grants; nor in the context of a full statement of the case would brevity be inconsistent with illumination." See also Hart, *The Business of the Supreme Court at the October Terms, 1937 and 1938,* 53 Harv.L.Rev. 579, 588 (1940): "[Giving reasons for grants'] great value lies in avoiding the natural misapprehension which results when cases appear in the reports in which, on the face of the opinion, certiorari seems to have been granted on grounds irreconcilable with the declared standards. Not to state the fact that review followed a claimed conflict of decision permits the inference that it was warranted by the intrinsic importance of the issues alone, or, particularly where the judgment is reversed, that it was induced by a mere showing of probable error."

ple outweighs the interest in judicial economy in deciding the case." [d]

2. *Dismissal of the writ.* When the Court feels on oral argument, or upon further study, or due to the occurrence of intervening factors, that the basis upon which certiorari was granted no longer exists, the Court may "dismiss the writ as improvidently granted." See Stern & Gressman & S. Shapiro, *Supreme Court Practice* 93–288 (6th ed. 1986). Is the interest of the litigants any different here than in the situation posed in note 1? Is the operation of the "rule of four" any different? Suppose the four justices who voted to grant continue to want the case heard? Compare *Triangle Imp. Council v. Ritchie,* 402 U.S. 497, 91 S.Ct. 1650, 29 L.Ed.2d 61 (1971) with *Burrell v. McCray,* 426 U.S. 471, 96 S.Ct. 2640, 48 L.Ed.2d 788 (1976). Is there ever justification for dismissing the writ after the Court has rendered a decision on the merits? Cf. *Rice v. Sioux City Memorial Park Cemetery,* 349 U.S. 70, 75 S.Ct. 614, 99 L.Ed. 897 (1955).

SECTION 5. PREREQUISITES TO FEDERAL JURISDICTION AND JUDICIAL REVIEW: AN INTRODUCTION

Under Art. III, federal judicial power extends only to resolving "cases" and "controversies." Thus, federal courts are precluded from giving "advisory opinions" or deciding "moot" cases. In determining whether there is a "case or controversy" capable of and suitable for resolution by federal courts, parties asserting particular contentions must have "standing"; at a minimum, they must allege "such a personal stake in the outcome of the controversy as to assure that concrete adverseness which sharpens the presentation of issues." [a] Further, claims must be asserted at a time when they are "ripe" for adjudication: "a hypothetical threat is not enough"; [b] "determination of [the] constitutionality of legislation in advance of its immediate adverse effect in the context of a concrete case involves too remote and abstract an inquiry for the proper exercise of the judicial function." [c]

Because all these matters must be resolved before a federal court may consider the merits of a constitutional contention, they could profitably be explored in detail here. But their consideration is often intertwined with and requires understanding of the substantive constitutional provision in issue. Thus, their presentation is deferred to Ch. 9 when students will be better equipped to comprehend and evaluate them.

A number of additional requirements must also be satisfied for federal judicial review of state court decisions. While these are considered at length in courses on Federal Courts, the most important are briefly described below.

CHARLES ALAN WRIGHT—FEDERAL COURTS

738–52, 759–60 (4th ed. 1983).

The state court decision to be reviewable must be that of the highest court of the state in which a decision could be had. [Even] a trial court decision is

d. For consideration of the view "that the Rule of Four must inevitably enlarge the size of the Court's argument docket and cause it to hear a substantial number of cases that a majority of the Court deems unworthy of review," see Justice Stevens, *The Life-Span of a Judge-Made Rule,* 58 N.Y.U.L.Rev. 1 (1983).

a. *Baker v. Carr,* Sec. 2 supra.

b. *United Public Workers v. Mitchell,* p. 1345.

c. *International Longshoremen's and Warehousemen's Union v. Boyd,* 347 U.S. 222, 74 S.Ct. 447, 98 L.Ed. 650 (1954).

reviewable in the United States Supreme Court if there is no higher state court to which the party can resort. [If] discretionary review is available in some higher state court, such review must be sought, no matter how unlikely it may seem that it will be granted. * * *

Review can only be had of "final judgments or decrees." [T]he Court has been liberal, and has even been willing to regard a letter from the clerk of the state court to the appellant, refusing to docket his appeal, as being a judgment of the state court. * * *

The limitation of review to "final" judgments is consistent with the general aversion of the federal courts to piecemeal review. Thus the same principles that determine what is a final judgment of a district court, reviewable in a court of appeals or, in some instances, directly in the Supreme Court, are generally applied in determining what is a final judgment of a state court. * * *

It might be supposed that the requirement of finality would be given stricter application in reviewing state court decisions, since they involve potential conflict between the courts of two different governments [but there is no such evidence].

The Court decides for itself whether the decision of the state court is a final judgment. [The] test, as in other instances where finality must be determined, is increasingly a pragmatic one [and] has been that judgment is not final for purposes of review, though it settles the important issue in the case, if it leaves open something not merely ministerial that might itself raise a federal question.[36]

In recent years the Court has departed strikingly from this traditional view. As it said in *Cox Broadcasting Corp. v. Cohn,*[37] "as the cases have unfolded, [t]here are now at least four categories [of] cases in which the Court has treated the decision on the federal issue as [final] without awaiting the completion of the additional proceedings anticipated in the lower state courts."

The first of [these] includes those cases in which [for] one reason or another the federal issue is conclusive or the outcome of further proceedings preordained.[38] The second category is the cases in which the federal issue [will] survive and require decision regardless of the outcome of future state proceedings.[39] The third category is those situations [in] which later review of the federal issue cannot be had, whatever the ultimate outcome of the case.[40]

The fourth of the *Cox* categories was described by the Court as "those situations where the federal issue has been finally decided in the state courts with further proceedings pending in which the party seeking review here might

36. *Republic Natural Gas Co. v. Oklahoma,* 334 U.S. 62, 68 S.Ct. 972, 92 L.Ed. 1212 (1948).

37. 420 U.S. 469, 502–503, 95 S.Ct. 1029, 1037, 43 L.Ed.2d 328 (1975). [See generally Note, *The Finality Rule for Supreme Court Review of State Court Orders,* 91 Harv.L.Rev. 1004 (1978).]

38. As examples the Court cited *Organization for a Better Austin v. Keefe,* 402 U.S. 415, 418 n. 1, 91 S.Ct. 1575, 1577 n. 1, 29 L.Ed.2d 1 (1971); *Mills v. Alabama,* 86 S.Ct. 1434, 16 L.Ed.2d 484, 384 U.S. 214 (1966); *Local No. 438 v. Curry,* 83 S.Ct. 531, 536–537, 9 L.Ed.2d 514, 371 U.S. 542, 550–551 (1963); *Pope v. Atlantic C.L.R. Co.,* 73 S.Ct. 749, 750, 97 L.Ed. 1094, 345 U.S. 379, 382 (1953).

39. As examples the Court cited *Brady v. Maryland,* 373 U.S. 83, 85 n. 1, 83 S.Ct. 1194, 1195 n. 1, 10 L.Ed.2d 215 (1963); *Radio Station WOW, Inc. v. Johnson,* 326 U.S. 120, 126–127, 65 S.Ct. 1475, 1479–1480, 89 L.Ed. 2092 (1945); *Forgay v. Conrad,* 6 How. 201, 47 U.S. 201, 12 L.Ed. 404 (1848).

40. As examples the Court cited *North Dakota State Bd. of Pharmacy v. Snyder's Drug Stores, Inc.,* 414 U.S. 156, 94 S.Ct. 407, 38 L.Ed.2d 379 (1973); *California v. Stewart,* 384 U.S. 436, 498 n. 71, 86 S.Ct. 1602, 1640 n. 71, 16 L.Ed.2d 694 (1966) (decided sub nom. *Miranda v. Arizona*).

prevail on the merits on nonfederal grounds, thus rendering unnecessary review of the federal issue by this Court, and where reversal of the state court on the federal issue would be preclusive of any further litigation on the relevant cause of action rather than merely controlling the nature and character of, or determining the admissibility of evidence in, the state proceedings still to come. In these circumstances, if a refusal immediately to review the state court decision might seriously erode federal policy, the Court has entertained and decided the federal [issue]." [41]

The *Cox* case itself was held reviewable as falling in the fourth category. The state court had rejected a federal constitutional challenge to a state law authorizing damage suits against the press for publishing the names of rape victims. The state court had sent the case back for trial. The defendants might win at trial on nonfederal grounds, [but] this would leave on the books the unreviewed decision of the highest state court rejecting the constitutional challenge. Delaying final decision of the constitutional claim until after trial would leave unanswered an important question about freedom of the press, while if the Supreme Court took the case and sustained the constitutional claim—as it in fact did—the litigation would be at an end. * * *

The substantial federal question must have been raised in a proper and timely manner in the state courts. "No particular form of words or phrases is essential, but only that the claim of invalidity and the ground therefor be brought to the attention of the state court with fair precision and in due time. * * *" [48]

[T]imeliness [is] largely a matter for the state to regulate by its own procedural rules. Failure to raise the question at the stage of the proceedings required by state law will preclude review, unless the state rule is regarded as an attempt to evade decision of the federal question or permits no fair opportunity to assert the question.[50] [Even] if the question has been properly raised in the trial court, the party may be held to have waived it by failing to preserve it on appeal or by appealing to the wrong court. It is too late to raise a federal question by petition for rehearing to the state appellate court,[54] except where the decision of that court has unexpectedly given rise to a federal question that the party seeking review has had no previous opportunity to assert and could not fairly have anticipated.[55]

41. As examples the Court cited *Miami Herald Publishing Co. v. Tornillo,* 418 U.S. 241, 247 n. 6, 94 S.Ct. 2831, 2834 n. 6, 41 L.Ed. 2d 730 (1974); *Mercantile Nat. Bank v. Langdeau,* 371 U.S. 555, 558, 83 S.Ct. 520, 522, 9 L.Ed.2d 523 (1963).

[Compare *Flynt v. Ohio,* 451 U.S. 619, 101 S.Ct. 1958, 68 L.Ed.2d 489 (1981) (5–4) (state court's rejection of magazine publisher's equal protection claim of "selective and discriminatory prosecution" for disseminating obscenity is not a "final judgment" since "there has been no finding of guilt and no sentence imposed" and "there is no identifiable federal policy that will suffer if the state criminal proceeding goes forward").]

In two other recent cases the Court has found a state judgment sufficiently final for review though the judgment was hardly final in any traditional sense and does not seem to fit into any of the four *Cox* categories. See *National Socialist Party of America v. Skokie,* 432 U.S. 43, 97 S.Ct. 2205, 53 L.Ed.2d 96 (1977), and *American Export Lines, Inc. v. Alvez,* 446 U.S. 274, 100 S.Ct. 1673, 64 L.Ed.2d 284 (1980).

48. *New York ex rel. Bryant v. Zimmerman,* 278 U.S. 63, 67, 49 S.Ct. 61, 63, 73 L.Ed. 184 (1928); *Street v. New York,* 394 U.S. 576, 581–585, 89 S.Ct. 1354, 1360–1362, 22 L.Ed.2d 572 (1969).

50. *National Mut. Building & Loan Ass'n v. Brahan,* 193 U.S. 635, 24 S.Ct. 532, 48 L.Ed. 823 (1904); *Reece v. Georgia,* 350 U.S. 85, 76 S.Ct. 167, 100 L.Ed. 77 (1955).

54. *Herndon v. Georgia,* 295 U.S. 441, 55 S.Ct. 794, 79 L.Ed. 1530 (1935).

55. *Missouri ex rel. Missouri Ins. Co. v. Gehner,* 281 U.S. 313, 50 S.Ct. 326, 74 L.Ed. 870 (1930); *Brinkerhoff-Faris Trust & Savings*

To all of these rules [there] is a salutary and sensible exception. If the highest court of the state in which decision could be had actually decides the federal question, it is reviewable in the Supreme Court regardless of when it was first presented. * * *

The most important, and most difficult, limitation on Supreme Court review of state court decisions has been well stated by Justice Jackson: "This Court [will] not review judgments of state courts that rest on adequate and independent state grounds. [The reason] is found in the partitioning of power between the state and federal judicial systems and in the limitations of our own jurisdiction. Our only power over state judgments is to correct them to the extent that they incorrectly adjudge federal rights [and] not to revise opinions. [I]f the same judgment would be rendered by the state court after we corrected its views of federal laws, our review could amount to nothing more than an advisory opinion." [57]

In the early years such a limitation was imposed on the Court by the proviso to section 25 of the Judiciary Act of 1789 * * *. This proviso was eliminated when that section of the statute was amended in 1867. It seems entirely plausible that Congress intended by eliminating the proviso to open the whole case for review by the Supreme Court, if there is a federal question in the case sufficient to take the case to the Supreme Court. Such a broad review may well be constitutional. [In] the landmark case of *Murdock v. Memphis* [60] the Court held [however] that no such drastic change in its jurisdiction had been accomplished by the 1867 revision. This case, and others which have built on it,[61] lay down two fundamental propositions. The Court will not review a case, even though it contains a federal question, if there is an adequate state ground that supports the decision of the state court. Further, the Court will accept as binding upon it the state court's decision of questions of state law.

[Thus] there can be no review if the state court has decided the case exclusively on some ground of state law, and has never reached a federal question present in the case. Nor can there be review where the state court has decided both the state and federal questions, if its decision of the federal question was unnecessary in the light of its disposition of the state question. But if the state court has decided the case entirely on the federal question presented, the Supreme Court can review, even though there was a state question in the case that could have been the basis for decision. In such a case, if the state court's resolution of the federal question is erroneous, the Supreme Court will remand the case to the state court, which can then pass on the state question.[70] And it is held, though on shaky theoretical ground, that where a state statute incorporates federal law by reference, the Supreme Court may review a state court decision as to that statute, pass on the federal question that is incorporated by reference, and remand for the state court to reconsider its interpretation of the statute in the light of the Supreme Court's interpretation of the underlying federal law.[71]

Co. v. Hill, 281 U.S. 673, 50 S.Ct. 451, 74 L.Ed. 1107 (1930).

57. *Herb v. Pitcairn,* 324 U.S. 117, 125–126, 65 S.Ct. 459, 463, 89 L.Ed. 789 (1945).

60. 87 U.S. (20 Wall.) 590, 22 L.Ed. 429 (1875).

61. *Berea College v. Kentucky,* 211 U.S. 45, 29 S.Ct. 33, 53 L.Ed. 81 (1908); *Fox Film Corp. v. Muller,* 296 U.S. 207, 56 S.Ct. 183, 80 L.Ed. 158 (1935).

70. *Orr v. Orr,* 440 U.S. 268, 275–277, 283–284, 99 S.Ct. 1102, 1109–1110, 1114, 59 L.Ed. 2d 306 (1979); *Indiana ex rel. Anderson v. Brand,* 303 U.S. 95, 58 S.Ct. 443, 82 L.Ed. 685 (1938).

71. *Standard Oil Co. of California v. Johnson,* 316 U.S. 481, 62 S.Ct. 1168, 86 L.Ed. 1611 (1942). See Greene, *Hybrid State Law in the Federal Courts,* 1970, 83 Harv.L.Rev. 289; Note, *Supreme Court Review of State Interpre-*

In order to bar Supreme Court review, the state ground must be "adequate." [72] If there is no fair and substantial support in the facts for the state court's ruling on the state ground, the Supreme Court can disregard it.[73] A new state rule cannot be invented for the occasion in order to defeat the federal claim.[74] It has been said that if the state court's refusal to consider the merits of a case is based on a rule "more properly deemed discretionary than jurisdictional" this does not bar review in the Supreme Court.[75] Even a state procedural rule of general applicability may be thought not an adequate state ground if it is so strict that it interferes unduly with the presentation of federal questions.[76] * * *

The question of the adequate state ground was much confused by the decision in *Henry v. Mississippi.*[79] [The] Court first recognized the adequate state ground rule but drew a distinction between state substantive grounds and state procedural grounds, and declared it to be settled that "a litigant's procedural defaults in state proceedings do not prevent vindication of his federal rights unless the State's insistence on compliance with its procedural rule serves a legitimate state interest." [83] This indicates that the Court could review the case if it found that the state rule served no legitimate state interest. [But the Court] saw some reason to think that counsel might [as] a matter of strategy [have] deliberately bypassed the [state's procedural rule. If so], Henry would be deemed to have forfeited his state court remedies. The case was, accordingly, remanded to the state court to determine whether there had been such a waiver.

[The] case clearly must be studied in any consideration of the doctrine of the adequate state ground but the few obscure cases in which it has since been invoked go in opposite directions [90] and suggest that *Henry* was not a significant

tations of Federal Law Incorporated by Reference, 1953, 66 Harv.L.Rev. 1498.

72. Bice, *Anderson and the Adequate State Ground,* 1972, 45 S.Cal.L.Rev. 750; Hill, *The Inadequate State Ground,* 1965, 65 Col.L.Rev. 943; Sandalow, *Henry v. Mississippi and the Adequate State Ground: Proposals for a Revised Doctrine,* 1965 Sup.Ct.Rev. 187; Comment, *Supreme Court Treatment of State Procedural Grounds Relied on in State Courts to Preclude Decision of Federal Questions,* 1961, 61 Col.L. Rev. 255; Note, *The Untenable Nonfederal Ground in the Supreme Court,* 1961, 74 Harv.L. Rev. 1376.

73. *Ward v. Board of County Com'rs,* 253 U.S. 17, 40 S.Ct. 419, 64 L.Ed. 751 (1920).

74. *NAACP v. Alabama ex rel. Flowers,* 377 U.S. 288, 293–302, 84 S.Ct. 1302, 1306–1311, 12 L.Ed.2d 325 (1964); *NAACP v. Alabama ex rel. Patterson,* 357 U.S. 449, 78 S.Ct. 1163, 2 L.Ed.2d 1488 (1958); *Staub v. Baxley,* 355 U.S. 313, 78 S.Ct. 277, 2 L.Ed.2d 302 (1958); see *Parrot v. Tallahassee,* 381 U.S. 129, 85 S.Ct. 1322, 14 L.Ed. 2d 263 (1965).

75. *Sullivan v. Little Hunting Park, Inc.,* 90 S.Ct. 400, 396 U.S. 229, 24 L.Ed.2d 386 (1969).

76. *Brown v. Western Ry.,* 338 U.S. 294, 70 S.Ct. 105, 94 L.Ed. 100 (1949); *Douglas v. Alabama,* 380 U.S. 415, 420–423, 85 S.Ct. 1074, 1078–1079, 13 L.Ed.2d 934 (1965). See Comment, *Procedural Protection for Federal Rights in State Courts,* 1961, 30 U.Cin.L.Rev. 184.

Professor Hill, n. 72 above, at 971–977, argues that neither the *Brown* case, nor any other, supports the proposition stated in the text.

79. 85 S.Ct. 564, 379 U.S. 443, 13 L.Ed.2d 408 (1965). The case is extensively considered in the articles by Hill and Sandalow, note 72 above.

83. 85 S.Ct. at 567, 379 U.S. at 447. One commentator thinks this proposition "amply supported by previous case law," Sandalow, note 72 above, at 229, while another can find "no suggestion" of it in the earlier cases, Hill, note 72 above, at 988. The distinction between substantive and procedural grounds is said to be insignificant in Wechsler, *The Appellate Jurisdiction of the Supreme Court: Reflections on the Law and the Logistics of Direct Review,* 1977, 34 Wash. & Lee L.Rev. 1043, 1054.

90. See *Camp v. Arkansas,* 92 S.Ct. 307, 404 U.S. 69, 30 L.Ed.2d 223 (1971), in which the Supreme Court reversed because of remarks by the prosecutor in his summation, though no objection had been made in the trial court. The state court refused to consider the point because of the lack of objection but the Supreme Court cited *Henry* for the proposition that "petitioner's alleged procedural default does not bar consideration of his constitutional claim in the circumstances of this case."

Compare *Monger v. Florida,* 92 S.Ct. 1163, 405 U.S. 958, 31 L.Ed.2d 236 (1972), where the break with the past * * *.

It is often difficult to determine whether there is an adequate state ground [because] of failure of the state decision to indicate with sufficient clarity whether that court was relying on a federal ground or a state ground. [One] remedy in such a situation is for counsel to seek clarification from the state court * * *.

Where there is no such clarification from the state court, four techniques are available to the Supreme Court: (1) since the burden is on the party invoking the jurisdiction of the Supreme Court to establish that that Court has jurisdiction, it may dismiss if its jurisdiction is ambiguous; (2) it may vacate the judgment below and remand so that the state court will have an opportunity to clarify what it has ruled; (3) it may continue the case to give the parties an opportunity to apply to the court below for clarification; or (4) if it considers that any state ground that might be advanced for the decision is insubstantial, it may take jurisdiction and decide the federal question.

[But in MICHIGAN v. LONG, 463 U.S. 1032, 103 S.Ct. 3469, 77 L.Ed.2d 1201 (1983), the Court, finding it "appropriate to reexamine our treatment of this jurisdictional issue in order to achieve the consistency that is necessary," decided to "disfavor further requests to state courts for clarification [and] require a clear and express statement that a decision rests on adequate and independent state grounds. * * * Accordingly, when [a] state court decision fairly appears to rest primarily on federal law, or to be interwoven with the federal law, and when the adequacy and independence of any possible state law ground is not clear from the face of the opinion, we will accept as the most reasonable explanation that the state court decided the case the way it did because it believed that federal law required it to do so."]

The Supreme Court does not ordinarily sit to decide questions of fact. [On] review of decisions of state courts, the stated rule is that "all those matters which are usually termed issues of fact are for conclusive determination by the State courts * * *." Perhaps this is so, but only by an ingenious redefinition of what constitutes a question of fact. Only a year before the statement just quoted a unanimous Court had said: "The duty of this Court to make its own independent examination of the record when federal constitutional deprivations are alleged is clear, resting, as it does, on our solemn responsibility for maintaining the Constitution inviolate." In making such an independent examination the Court recognizes that it is reviewing the facts. It has said that "this Court will review the finding of facts by a State court where a Federal right has been denied as the result of a finding shown by the record to be without evidence to support it; or where a conclusion of law as to a Federal right and a finding of fact are so intermingled as to make it necessary, in order to pass upon the Federal question, to analyze the facts." Since cases do not come to the Supreme Court from the state courts unless they involve some claim of a federal right, the exceptions seem quite broad enough to swallow up the announced rule against review of state court fact determinations.

state court's dismissal of an appeal because notice of appeal had been given after the oral entry of judgment but before the written order was expressly held to be an adequate state ground, over the dissent of three justices who relied on *Henry*. * * *

These seem to be the only cases in which the Court has discussed *Henry* with regard to its power to review state law decisions.

Professor Hill has observed that "*Henry* has never been overruled, but seems relatively moribund." Hill, *The Forfeiture of Constitutional Rights in Criminal Cases*, 1978, 78 Col. L.Rev. 1050, 1052.

Chapter 2

SUBSTANTIVE PROTECTION OF ECONOMIC INTERESTS

PREFATORY NOTE

Most of the remaining chapters are concerned with constitutional limitations on governmental power, independent of limitations arising out of the distribution of powers within the federal system. Some of the limitations are identical, or nearly so, whether applied to the state or federal governments, but are based on different sources. The major limitations on the federal government are found in the Bill of Rights and in Art. I, § 9, while those on state government are based largely on the thirteenth, fourteenth, and fifteenth amendments and on Art. I, § 10. But the fourteenth amendment has now been held to impose on the states most of the limitations the Bill of Rights imposes on the federal government.

These materials do not deal with all limitations based on the federal Constitution but only those of major significance and difficulty. State constitutions include additional limitations on state government, some similar to federal limitations though occasionally interpreted differently, and some quite dissimilar in terms and purposes. Study of the federal limitations should provide adequate training and background for handling the state-imposed limitations with professional skill.

SECTION 1. ORIGINS OF SUBSTANTIVE DUE PROCESS AS A LIMITATION ON GOVERNMENTAL POWER

INTRODUCTION

One important concern of this and later chapters is the extent to which the due process clauses of the fifth and fourteenth amendments may be invoked to impose limits on the *substance* of governmental regulations and other activities, as well as to govern the *procedures*—the due process—by which government affects "life, liberty and property." That these clauses embody *any* limits on the substance of legislation requires some initial explanation, since their terms refer only to "process."

Professor Edward S. Corwin traced the origin and evolution of due process as a substantive limitation on governmental power in a series of articles[a], later revised in his *Liberty Against Government* (1948).[b] This book, concerned primarily with judicial evolution of concepts designed to limit government regulation of property and economic interests, provides a valuable background for understanding, as well, some of the underpinnings for the later use of the due process clause and first amendment to limit governmental interference with the more basic personal liberties.

Space limits preclude detailed study here of the judicial search for tools by which to limit governmental power, culminating in the "substantive due process" concept. Here we only sketch, by suggestive excerpts, some of the more significant steps.

I. JUDICIAL RESPONSE TO PHILOSOPHICAL LIMITS ON GOVERNMENTAL POWER

CALDER v. BULL, 3 U.S. (3 Dall.) 386, 1 L.Ed. 648 (1798), is remembered, not for its refusal to interfere when a state legislature set aside a court ruling, but for two opinions that expressed opposing views on the nature and source of limits on government power:

"CHASE, JUSTICE. "I cannot subscribe to the omnipotence of a State legislature, or that it is absolute and without control; although its authority should not be expressly restrained by the constitution, or fundamental law of the state. The people of the United States erected their constitutions, or forms of government, to establish justice, to promote the general welfare, to secure the blessings of liberty, and to protect their persons and property from violence. The purposes for which men enter into society will determine the nature and terms of the social compact; and as they are the foundation of the legislative power, they will decide what are the proper objects of it. The nature and ends of legislative power will limit the exercise of it. This fundamental principle flows from the very nature of our free republican governments, that no man should be compelled to do what the laws do not require; nor to refrain from acts which the laws permit. There are acts which the federal, or state, legislature cannot do, without exceeding their authority. There are certain vital principles in our free republican governments, which will determine and overrule an apparent and flagrant abuse of legislative power; as to authorize manifest injustice by positive law; to take away that security for personal liberty, or private property, for the protection whereof the government was established. An act of the legislature (for I cannot call it a law), contrary to the great first principles of the social compact, cannot be considered a rightful exercise of legislative authority. The obligation of a law in governments established on express compact, and on republican principles, must be determined by the nature of the power on which it is founded. A few instances will suffice to explain what I mean. A law that punished a citizen for an innocent action or, in other words, for an act, which, when done, was in violation of no existing law; a law that destroys, or impairs, the lawful private contracts of citizens; a law that makes a man a judge in his own cause; or a law that takes property from A and gives it to B: It is against all reason and justice, for a people to intrust a legislature with SUCH powers;

a. Corwin, *The Doctrine of Due Process of Law Before the Civil War,* 24 Harv.L.Rev. 366, 460 (1911); Corwin, *The Basic Doctrine of American Constitutional Law,* 12 Mich.L.Rev. 247 (1914); Corwin, *The "Higher Law" Background of American Constitutional Law,* 42 Harv.L.Rev. 149, 365 (1928–1929).

b. Republished in *Corwin on the Constitution, Vol. III,* on *Liberty against Government,* edited by Richard Loss (1988).

and therefore, it cannot be presumed that they have done it. The genius, the nature, and the spirit, of our State governments, amount to a prohibition of such acts of legislation; and the general principles of law and reason forbid them. [To] maintain that our Federal, or State legislature possesses such powers, if they had not been expressly restrained, would, in my opinion, be a political heresy, altogether inadmissible in our free republican governments." [a]

"Iredell, Justice. [If] a government, composed of legislative, executive and judicial departments, were established, by a constitution which imposed no limits on the legislative power, the consequence would inevitably be, that whatever the legislative power chose to enact, would be lawfully enacted, and the judicial power could never interpose to pronounce it void. It is true, that some speculative jurists have held, that a legislative act against natural justice must, in itself, be void; but I cannot think that, under such a government any court of justice would possess a power to declare it so.

"[I]t has been the policy of all the American states, which have, individually, framed their state constitutions, since the revolution, and of the people of the United States, when they framed the federal constitution, to define with precision the objects of the legislative power, and to restrain its exercise within marked and settled boundaries. If any act of Congress, or of the legislature of a state, violates those constitutional provisions, it is unquestionably void. [If], on the other hand, the legislature of the Union, or the legislature of any member of the Union, shall pass a law, within the general scope of their constitutional power, the court cannot pronounce it to be void, merely because it is, in their judgment, contrary to the principles of natural justice. The ideals of natural justice are regulated by no fixed standard: the ablest and the purest men have differed upon the subject; and all that the court could properly say, in such an event, would be that the legislature (possessed of an equal right of opinion) had passed an act which, in the opinion of the judges, was inconsistent with the abstract principles of natural justice. * * *"

Notes and Questions

1. Compare Lord Coke in *Dr. Bonham's Case,* 8 Co. 113b, 118a, 77 Eng.Rep. 646, 652 (1610): "And it appears in our books, that in many cases, the common law will controul Acts of Parliament, and sometimes adjudge them to be utterly void: for when an Act of Parliament is against common right and reason, or repugnant, or impossible to be performed, the common law will controul it, and adjudge such Act to be void." For commentary on the influence of the Coke dictum, see Corwin, *Liberty Against Government* 34–40 (1948).

2. For philosophical origins of the Chase viewpoint, see Corwin, *Liberty Against Government* 10–57 (1948); Corwin, *The "Higher Law" Background of American Constitutional Law,* 42 Harv.L.Rev. 149, 365 (1928–1929). For the extent to which similar viewpoints crept into judicial opinions and decisions between the revolution and 1830, see Corwin, *Liberty Against Government* 58–67 (1948): "The truth is that Iredell's tenet that courts were not to appeal to natural rights and the social compact as furnishing a basis for constitutional decisions was disregarded at one time or another by all of the leading judges and advocates of the initial period of our constitutional history, an era which closes about 1830."

a. Dean Ely interpreted Chase, J.'s, opinion as a philosophical, not a constitutional, argument. See Ely, *On Discovering Fundamental Values,* 92 Harv.L.Rev. 5, 26–27 n. 95 (1978).

3. *Other early reflections of natural law.* Some early decisions combined the Chase philosophy in *Calder* with broad interpretations of the contract clause, which barred state laws impairing the obligation of contracts. FLETCHER v. PECK, 10 U.S. (6 Cranch.) 87, 3 L.Ed. 162 (1810), held that the contract clause prevented legislative annulment of the title of purchasers in good faith, who bought land from grantors who had obtained it by a corruptly-secured legislative grant. To reach this result, the Court construed "contract" to include an "executed contract" or grant of land. MARSHALL, C. J.'s, concluding paragraph revealed the role played by the Chase philosophy: "It is, then, the unanimous opinion of the court, that, in this case, the estate having passed into the hands of a purchaser for a valuable consideration, without notice, the state of Georgia was restrained, either by general principles which are common to our free institutions, or by the particular provisions of the Constitution of the United States, from passing a law whereby the estate of the plaintiff in the premises so purchased could be constitutionally and legally impaired and rendered null and void."

JOHNSON, J., concurring, invoked natural justice reasoning: "I do not hesitate to declare that a state does not possess the power of revoking its own grants. But I do it on a general principle, on the reason and nature of things: a principle which will impose laws even on the deity."

Similarly, TERRETT v. TAYLOR, 13 U.S. (9 Cranch.) 43, 3 L.Ed. 650 (1815), per STORY, J., invoked natural justice philosophy and unnamed constitutional provisions to bar Virginia from claiming title to church property under a statute authorizing its sale and the use of the proceeds for the poor of the parish: "[T]hat the legislature can repeal statutes creating private corporations, or confirming to them property already acquired under the faith of previous laws, and by such repeal can vest the property of such corporations exclusively in the state, or dispose of the same to such purposes as they may please, without the consent or default of the corporators, we are not prepared to admit; and we think ourselves standing upon the principles of natural justice, upon the fundamental laws of every free government, upon the spirit and the letter of the constitution of the United States, and upon the decisions of most respectable judicial tribunals in resisting such a doctrine."

During this same period the state courts were protecting vested property rights against legislative interference through a variety of rationales similar to that in *Calder*. See Corwin, *Liberty Against Government* 65–82 (1948).

II. THE SEARCH FOR A CONSTITUTIONAL BASIS

The philosophical grounds asserted in those early cases for protecting economic interests from legislative power could not long prevail in the face of the growing acceptance of the federal and state constitutions as the only sources of judicially enforceable limitations on legislative power. See Corwin, *Liberty Against Government* 173 (1948): "The doctrine of vested rights attained its meridian in the early thirties, when it came under attack from two sources. The first [was] the notion that the written constitution, being an expression of popular will, was the supreme law of the State and that judicial review could validly operate only on that basis; the second was the related idea, which is connoted by the term 'police power'—that legislation which was not specifically forbidden by the written constitution must be presumed to have been enacted in the *public interest.* Confronted with these doctrines, the champions of the doctrine of vested rights were compelled to find some clause of the written constitution which could be thrown about the doctrine or else to abandon it."

Before the adoption of the fourteenth amendment in 1868, the federal constitution provided little basis for challenging state regulation of economic interests. The Bill of Rights applied only to the federal government [a], and the Court soon narrowed the scope of the contract clause,[b] considered infra Sec. 3. Corwin observed that the *Charles River Bridge* opinion seemed designed to discourage resort to the federal constitution to escape regulation of economic interests: "It is well settled by the decisions of this court, that a state law may be retrospective in its character, and may divest vested rights; and yet not violate the constitution of the United States, unless it also impairs the obligation of a contract." "Thus it *became more and more evident that the doctrine of vested rights must, to survive, find anchorage in some clause or other of the various State constitutions.*" Corwin, *Liberty Against Government* 89 (1948).

With federal constitutional grounds not available to protect against most encroachments on economic interests, lawyers and state judges resorted to the "due process" and "law of the land" clauses of state constitutions. These provisions originally referred to proceeding in accordance with the law and accepted legal procedure.

"The 'law of the land' clause of the early State constitutions was usually a nearly literal translation of the famous chapter 29 of the Magna Carta of 1225, the Magna Carta of history.[c] [The] phrase 'due process of law' comes from chapter 3 of the statute of 28 Edward III (1355) which [reads]: 'No man of what state or condition he be, shall be put out of his lands or tenements, nor taken, nor imprisoned, nor disinherited, nor put to death, without he be brought to answer by due process of law.'

"In his Institutes Coke asserts the complete identity in meaning of the two expressions, which he explains as signifying 'due process of the common law,' that is, 'indictment or presentment of good and lawful men [or] writ original of the common law.' Both phrases, in short, were intended to consecrate certain methods of trial; and neither bore any reference to those principles of 'common right and reason' which Coke had invoked in *Dr. Bonham's Case.*" Corwin, *Liberty Against Government* 90–91 (1948).[d]

Professor Corwin pointed out how the state courts began to evolve out of these clauses a substantive limitation on legislative power, aimed first at special legislation designed to affect the rights of specific individuals, and then applied to general legislation interfering with vested rights. See Corwin, *The Doctrine*

a. *Barron v. Mayor & City Council,* 32 U.S. (7 Pet.) 243, 8 L.Ed. 672 (1833).

b. *Proprietors of Charles River Bridge v. Proprietors of Warren Bridge,* 36 U.S. (11 Pet.) 420, 9 L.Ed. 773 (1837) (state grant of right to operate toll bridge did not imply obligation not to authorize competing bridge); *West River Bridge Co. v. Dix,* 47 U.S. (6 How.) 507, 12 L.Ed. 535 (1848) (state grant of exclusive right to operate toll bridge does not bar state from acquiring it by eminent domain); *Stone v. Mississippi,* 101 U.S. (11 Otto) 814, 25 L.Ed. 1079 (1880) (vital public interest permits state to ban lottery business 3 years after it granted 25 year charter).

c. Corwin quoted "its rendition" in the 1780 Massachusetts constitution: "No subject shall be arrested, imprisoned, [or] deprived of his property, [his] life, liberty, or estate, but by the judgment of his peers or the law of the land."

d. The earliest state cases involving a "law of the land" clause found in it no substantive limitation on legislative power. One interpreted it as meaning simply an act of the state legislature, and the other held it to require a jury trial in serious cases. *State v. ———,* 2 Haywood (N.C.) 29, 38 (1794); *Zylstra v. Charleston,* 1 Bay (S.C.) 382 (1794).

of Due Process of Law Before the Civil War, 24 Harv.L.Rev. 366, 460 (1911); Corwin, *Liberty Against Government* 89–115, 173–74:

"Again the ingenuity of Bench and Bar were equal to the exigency. Most State constitutions contained from the outset a paraphrase of chapter 29 of Magna Carta, which declared that no person should be deprived of his 'estate' 'except by the law of the land or a judgment of his peers'; and following the usage of the Fifth Amendment of the United States Constitution, more and more State constitutions came after 1791 to contain a clause which, paraphrasing a statute of Plantagenet times, declared that 'no person shall be deprived of life, liberty or property without due process of law.' By the outbreak of the Civil War a more or less complete transference of the doctrine of vested rights and most of its Kentian corollaries had been effected in the vast majority of the State jurisdictions. One exception was Kent's distinction between the power of 'regulation,' which he conceded the State, and that of 'destruction,' which he denied it unless it was prepared to compensate disadvantaged owners. The division of judicial opinion on this point was signalized in the middle fifties, when the New York Court of Appeals, in the great *Wynehamer* case, stigmatized a State-wide prohibition statute as an act of destruction, in its application to existing stocks of liquor, which was beyond the power of the State legislature to authorize *even by the procedures of due process of law.* In several other States similar statutes were sustained in the name of the 'police power.'" [e]

WYNEHAMER v. PEOPLE, 13 N.Y. 378 (1856) held by a divided court that a New York prohibition statute violated the state due process clause as applied to the sale of liquor owned at the time of the enactment of the statute. Professor Corwin commented on *Wynehamer* in *Liberty Against Government* 103, 114–15:

"In *Wynehamer,* [the] court was confronted with a frankly penal statute which provided a procedure, for the most part unexceptionable, for its enforcement. That statute was nonetheless overturned under the due 'process of law' clause, which was [plainly] made to prohibit, regardless of the matter of procedure, a certain kind or degree of exertion of legislative power altogether. The result serves to throw into strong light once more the dependence of the derived notion of due process of law on extra constitutional principles; for it is nothing less *than the elimination of the very phrase under construction from the constitutional clause in which it occurs.* The main proposition of [*Wynehamer*] is that the legislature cannot destroy by any method whatever what by previous law was property. But why not? To all intents and purposes the answer of the court is simply that 'no person shall be *deprived* of life, liberty or *property.*' * * *

"In less than twenty years from the time of its rendition the crucial ruling in *Wynehamer* was far on the way to being assimilated into the accepted constitutional law of the country.[f] The 'due process' clause, which had been intended originally to consecrate a *mode of procedure,* had become a constitutional test of ever increasing reach of *the substantive content of legislation.* Thus was the doctrine of vested rights brought within the constitutional fold, although without dominating it. For confronting it was the still-expanding concept of the police power."

e. All extracts from *Liberty Against Government* are reprinted with permission of the publisher, copyright © 1948, Louisiana State University Press.

f. Corwin was referring here to the broad principle exemplified by *Wynehamer*; its actual ruling on state liquor prohibition was rejected by all states but one. See id. at 107.

III. FOURTEENTH AMENDMENT

Historical background. The history of the Civil War amendments, particularly the fourteenth, insofar as that history relates to the problems considered in this and later chapters, is thoroughly treated elsewhere. See, e.g., Fairman, *Does the Fourteenth Amendment Incorporate the Bill of Rights? The Original Understanding,* 2 Stan.L.Rev. 5 (1949); Bickel, *The Original Understanding and the Segregation Decision,* 69 Harv.L.Rev. 1 (1955); Frank & Munro, *The Original Understanding of "Equal Protection of the Laws"* 1972 Wash.U.L.Q. 421 (where other historical studies are cited). Only the barest outline is feasible here.

The thirteenth amendment forbidding involuntary servitude was ratified in 1865, but freeing the slaves did not produce the fruits of freedom, due to the "Black Codes" and other repressive measures.[a] The plight of the blacks and their need at the time was reflected in the Civil Rights Act of 1866, which recognized "all persons born in United States" as United States citizens,[b] and gave to "such citizens, of every race or color, without regard to any previous condition of slavery [the] same right, in every State and Territory in the United States, to make and enforce contracts, to sue, be parties, and give evidence, to inherit, purchase, lease, sell, hold, and convey real and personal property, and to full and equal benefit of all laws and proceedings for the security of person and property, as is enjoyed by white citizens."[c]

Even while that 1866 Civil Rights Act was awaiting enactment, action was under way designed, in part at least, to remove existing doubts as to the power of Congress to enact such legislation. One week after the Senate passed the Civil Rights Act,[d] the Congressional Joint Committee on Reconstruction submitted to both houses of Congress its early version of a fourteenth amendment authorizing Congress to enact laws to protect equal rights.[e] After Congress passed the Civil Rights Act in April[f] over a presidential veto based in part on the view that Congress lacked power to enact the law,[g] the Joint Commission on Reconstruction hammered out a revised proposal that added privileges and immunities, due process, and equal protection provisions as limitations on the states, and authorized Congress to enact legislation to "enforce this article."[h] After further modifications, the most important being the addition of the first sentence relating to citizenship,[i] Congress approved the fourteenth amendment in June, 1866[j] and sent it to the states for ratification.

Ratification was completed in 1868 after bludgeoning the southern states to ratify as a condition for their representation in Congress.[k] Two years later the fifteenth amendment was ratified. Five years later the Court rejected 5 to 4 an

a. See Stephenson, *Race Distinction in American Law* 35–66 (1969 ed.); Myrdal, *An American Dilemma* (1962); Maslow & Robison, *Civil Rights Legislation and the Fight for Equality, 1862–1952,* 363, 366–67 (1953). Frank & Munro, supra, at 444–46.

b. With two exceptions not relevant here.

c. 14 Stat. 27 (1866), 42 U.S.C.A. §§ 1981–1983.

d. Cong.Globe, 39th Cong., 1st Sess. 606 (1866).

e. Fairman, supra, at 21.

f. Cong.Globe, 39th Cong., 1st Sess. 1809, 1861 (1866).

g. Id. at 1860.

h. Fairman, supra, at 41–43.

i. For commentary on this addition see Graham, *Our "Declaratory" Fourteenth Amendment,* 7 Stan.L.Rev. 3 (1954).

j. Cong.Globe, 39th Cong., 1st Sess. 2545, 3042, 3149 (1866).

k. 14 Stat. 428, 429 (1867); Suthon, *The Dubious Origin of the Fourteenth Amendment,* 28 Tul.L.Rev. 22, 32 (1953).

attempt to invoke its privileges and immunities, due process, and equal protections clauses to protect economic interests.

IN RE SLAUGHTER–HOUSE CASES, 83 U.S. (16 Wall.) 36, 21 L.Ed. 394 (1873), per MILLER, J., upheld a legislatively-granted monopoly to operate slaughter-houses in the New Orleans area, subject to letting others use the facilities at state-regulated fees. The Court viewed this as an "appropriate, stringent, and effectual" means to "remove from the more densely populated part of the city, the noxious slaughterhouses and large and offensive collections of animals, [and] to locate them where the convenience, health and comfort of the people require," [a] but that was not the basis for its rejection of the challenge to the monopoly under the privileges and immunities clause of the fourteenth amendment:

"[I]n the light of this recapitulation of events, [and] on the most casual examination of the language of these amendments, no one can fail to be impressed with the one pervading purpose found in them [all]; we mean the freedom of the slave race, the security and firm establishment of that freedom, and the protection of the newly-made freeman and citizen from the oppressions of those who had formerly exercised unlimited dominion over him. * * *

"We do not say that no one else but the negro can share in this protection. [I]f other rights are assailed by the states which properly and necessarily fall within the protection of these articles, that protection will apply, though the party interested may not be of African descent. But [in] any fair and just construction [of] these amendments, it is necessary to look to the purpose which we have said was the pervading spirit of them all, the evil which they were designed to remedy * * *.

"The first section of the fourteenth article, to which our attention is more specially invited, opens with a definition of citizenship—not only citizenship of the United States, but citizenship of the states. * * * 'All persons born or naturalized in the United States, and subject to the jurisdiction thereof, are citizens of the United States and of the state wherein they reside.' [T]he distinction between citizenship of the United States and citizenship of a state is clearly recognized and established. Not only may a man be a citizen of the United States without being a citizen of a state, but an important element is necessary to convert the former into the latter. He must reside within the state to make him a citizen of it, but it is only necessary that he should be born or naturalized in the United States to be a citizen of the Union. * * *

"The language is, 'No state shall make or enforce any law which shall abridge the privileges or immunities of citizens of the United States.' It is a little remarkable, if this clause was intended as a protection to the citizen of a state against the legislative power of his own state, that the word citizen of the state should be left out when it is so carefully used, and used in contradistinction to citizens of the United States, in the very sentence which precedes it. It is too clear for argument that the change in phraseology was adopted understandingly and with a purpose.

a. See Hovenkamp, *Technology, Politics and Regulated Monopoly: An American Historical Perspective,* 62 Tex.L.Rev. 1263, 1295–1308 (1984), for a dramatic historical account of the legislative conversion of the fragmented, unhealthful, mislocated New Orleans slaughtering industry into a well-placed, price-regulated public utility monopoly open to every butcher to use, which solved the health problem and drastically reduced the price of beef.

"Of the privileges and immunities of the citizen of the United States, and, of the privileges and immunities of the citizen of the state, and what they respectively are, we will presently consider; but we wish to state here that it is only the former which are placed by this clause under the protection of the federal Constitution, and that the latter, whatever they may be, are not intended to have any additional protection by this paragraph of the amendment."

The opinion distinguished Article IV privileges and immunities mandating equal treatment to citizens of other states. It noted that apart from a few express limitations, such as the prohibition on ex post facto laws, bills of attainder, and laws impairing the obligation of contracts, "the entire domain of the privileges and immunities of citizens of the states [lay] within the constitutional and legislative power of the states, and without that of the federal government. Was it the purpose of the Fourteenth Amendment by the simple declaration that no state should make or enforce any law which shall abridge the privileges and immunities of *Citizens of the United States,* to transfer the security and protection of all the civil rights [from] the states to the federal government? And where it is declared that Congress shall have the power to enforce that article, was it intended to bring within the power of Congress the entire domain of civil rights heretofore belonging exclusively to the states?

[Such] a construction [would] constitute this court a perpetual censor upon all legislation of the states, on the civil rights of their own citizens, with authority to nullify such as it did not approve as consistent with those rights as they existed at the time of the adoption of this amendment. [When] these consequences are [so] great a departure from the structure and spirit of our institutions; [when] in fact it radically changes the whole theory of the relations of the state and federal governments to each other and of both these governments to the people; the argument has a force that is irresistible, in the absence of language which expresses such a purpose too clearly to admit of doubt.

"We are convinced that no such results were intended by the Congress which proposed these amendments, nor by the legislatures of the states which ratified them.[b]

"The argument has not been much pressed in these cases that the defendant's charter deprives the plaintiffs of their property without due process of law, or that it denies to them the equal protection of the law. The first of these paragraphs has been in the Constitution since the adoption of the Fifth Amendment, as a restraint upon the federal power. It is also to be found in some form of expression in the constitutions of nearly all the states, as a restraint upon the power of the States.

b. Here the opinion added:

"[L]est it should be said that no such privileges and immunities are to be found if those we have been considering are excluded, we venture to suggest some which owe their existence to the federal government, its national character, its Constitution, or its laws.

"One of these is well described in *Crandall v. Nevada,* 73 U.S. (6 Wall.) 35, 18 L.Ed. 745 [1867]. It is said to be the right of the citizen of this great country, protected by implied guarantees of its Constitution, 'to come to the seat of government to assert any claim he may have upon that government, to transact any business he may have with it, to seek its protection, to share its offices, to engage in administering its functions.' * * *

"The right to peaceably assemble and petition for redress of grievances, the privilege of the writ of habeas corpus, are rights of the citizen guaranteed by the federal Constitution. The right to use the navigable waters of the United States, however they may penetrate the territory of the several states, all rights secured to our citizens by treaties with foreign nations, are dependent upon citizenship of the United States, and not citizenship of a state. [To] these may be added the rights secured by the thirteenth and fifteenth articles of amendment, and by the other clause of the fourteenth."

"[U]nder no construction of that provision that we have ever seen, or any that we deem admissible, can the restraint imposed by the state of Louisiana upon the exercise of their trade by the butchers of New Orleans be held to be a deprivation of property within the meaning of that provision.

"[In] the light of the history of these amendments, and the pervading purpose of them, which we have already discussed, it is not difficult to give a meaning to [the equal protection] clause. [We] doubt very much whether any action of a state not directed by way of discrimination against the negroes as a class, or on account of their race, will ever be held to come within the purview of this provision. It is so clearly a provision for that race and that emergency, that a strong case would be necessary for its application to any other."

FIELD, J., dissented.[c] "The amendment does not attempt to confer any new privileges or immunities upon citizens, or to enumerate or define those already existing. It assumes that there are such privileges and immunities which belong of right to citizens as such, and ordains that they shall not be abridged by State legislation. If this inhibition has no reference to privileges and immunities of this character, but only refers, as held by the majority of the court in their opinion, to such privileges and immunities as were before its adoption specially designated in the Constitution or necessarily implied as belonging to citizens of the United States, it was a vain and idle enactment, which accomplished nothing, and most unnecessarily excited Congress and the people on its passage. With privileges and immunities thus designated or implied no State could ever have interfered by its laws, and no new constitutional provision was required to inhibit such interference. The supremacy of the Constitution and the laws of the United States always controlled any State legislation of that character. But if the amendment refers to the natural and inalienable rights which belong to all citizens, the inhibition has a profound significance and consequence. * * *

"The terms, privileges and immunities, are not new in the amendment; they were in the Constitution before the amendment was adopted. They are found in [Art. IV, § 2.] In *Corfield v. Coryell*, 6 Fed. Cas. 546 (No. 3,230) (C.C.E.D. Pa. 1825) Mr. Justice Washington said he had 'no hesitation in confining these expressions to those privileges and immunities which were, in their nature, fundamental; which belong of right to the citizens of all free governments.' [In] the discussions in Congress upon the passage of the Civil Rights Act repeated reference was made to this language of Mr. Justice Washington. It was cited by Senator Trumbull with the observation that it enumerated the very rights belonging to a citizen of the United States set forth in the first section of the [act].

"The privileges and immunities designated in [Art. IV, § 2] are, then, according to the decision cited, those which of right belong to the citizens of all free governments. [What] the clause in question did for the protection of the citizens of one State against hostile and discriminating legislation of other States, the fourteenth amendment does for the protection of every citizen of the United States against hostile and discriminating legislation against him in favor of others, whether they reside in the same or in different [States].

"This equality of right, with exemption from all disparaging and partial enactments, in the lawful pursuits of life, throughout the whole country, is the distinguishing privilege of citizens of the United States. To them, everywhere, all pursuits, all professions, all avocations are open without other restrictions

c. Chase, C.J., and Swayne and Bradley, J., joined this dissent. Bradley, J., joined by Swayne, J., also dissented, asserting violation of due process and equal protection.

than such as are imposed equally upon all others of the same age, sex, and condition. The State may prescribe such regulations for every pursuit and calling of life as will promote the public health, secure the good order and advance the general prosperity of society, but when once prescribed, the pursuit or calling must be free to be followed by every citizen who is within the conditions designated, and will conform to the regulations. This is the fundamental idea upon which our institutions rest, and unless adhered to in the legislation of the country our government will be a republic only in name."

Notes and Questions

1. *Objectives of privileges and immunities and citizenship provisions.* An historical study protests that the *Slaughter-House* opinion flies in the face of the congressional purpose for inserting the citizenship sentence. Graham, n. i, supra, at 23–26: "Significantly, no one observed that while citizenship was made dual in this first sentence, only the privileges or immunities of 'citizens of the United States' were specifically protected in the second sentence against abridgment by the states. The reason for this apparent oversight is that ever since Birney's day, opponents of slavery had regarded all important 'natural' and constitutional rights as being privileges and immunities of *citizens of the United States.* This had been the cardinal premise of antislavery theory from the beginning, and this had been the underlying theory and purpose of Section One from the beginning. The real purpose of adding this citizenship definition was to remove any possible or lingering doubt about the freedman's citizenship."

2. *Resulting scope of privileges and immunities.* Professor McGovney paraphrased the clause as interpreted: "No State shall make or enforce any law which shall abridge any privilege or immunity conferred *by this Constitution, the statutes or treaties of the United States* upon any person who is a citizen of the United States." He then commented, "This narrower construction [renders] it an idle provision, in that it only declares a principle already more amply and more simply expressed in the constitution." McGovney, *Privileges or Immunities Clause, Fourteenth Amendment,* 4 Iowa Law Bull. (now Iowa L.Rev.) 219, 220, 221 (1918).

3. *The "idle provision."* The restrictive interpretation given the privileges and immunities clause in *Slaughter-House* has been consistently followed. Except for one quickly-overruled case,[d] the Court has never invalidated state legislation under the fourteenth amendment privileges and immunities clause. On a few occasions a minority of the Court invoked the clause. For details and analysis see Tribe, *American Constitutional Law* 418–26 (1978).

4. *Echoes of Calder and natural justice.* One year after resisting the Field philosophy in *Slaughter-House,* Miller, J., writing for eight justices, echoed *Calder.* Without referring to the Constitution, *Loan Ass'n v. Topeka,* 87 U.S. (20 Wall.) 655, 22 L.Ed. 455 (1875) struck down a tax designed to finance a bonus to attract a private manufacturer to Topeka, as "purely in aid of private or personal [objects] beyond the legislative power and [an] unauthorized invasion of private right: [The] theory of our governments, state and national, is opposed to the deposit of unlimited power anywhere. [There] are limitations on such power which grow out of the essential nature of all free governments. Implied reservations of individual rights, without which the social compact could not exist, and which are respected by all governments entitled to the name. No

d. *Colgate v. Harvey,* 296 U.S. 404, 56 S.Ct. 252, 80 L.Ed. 299 (1935), overruled by *Madden v. Kentucky,* 309 U.S. 83, 60 S.Ct. 406, 84 L.Ed. 590 (1940).

court, for instance, would hesitate to declare void a statute [which] should enact that the homestead now owned by A should no longer be his, but should henceforth be the property of B." Clifford, J., dissented on much the same basis as did Iredell, J., in *Calder.*[e]

5. *Creative dicta.* Two closely related factors played important roles in the emergence of substantive due process. (1) Lawyers in speeches, treatises, articles and briefs strongly advanced the *laissez faire* concept of government, often urging the due process clause as a constitutional limitation on governmental regulation of business. See the remarkable study of the influence of lawyers in this respect in Twiss, *Lawyers and the Constitution* 18–173 (1942). (2) Supreme Court justices in dissenting opinions, and state courts, strongly reflected these views, until majority opinions sustaining state regulation began also to recognize that the due process clause imposes some limits on the regulatory power of government. See Corwin, *Liberty Against Government* 129–152 (1948).

The Court held fairly firm on its strong position against interference with legislative policy issues as it sustained regulation of the rates of grain elevators in *Munn v. Illinois* (1876)[a] and of railroads in *Railroad Com'n Cases* (1886).[b] Similarly *Mugler v. Kansas* (1887)[c] and *Holden v. Hardy* (1898)[d] upheld state laws putting liquor dealers out of business and imposing maximum eight-hour days for underground mines and smelters, but in dicta intimated availability of due process protection from laws having "no real or substantial relation" to the public health, morals or safety, or invading "rights secured by the fundamental law," or "not in conformity with natural and inherent principles of justice."

ALLGEYER v. LOUISIANA, 165 U.S. 578, 17 S.Ct. 427, 41 L.Ed. 832 (1897) was the first reasoned decision[e] actually to hold that the substance of economic legislation violated the due process clause. It struck down a Louisiana law forbidding effectuation in Louisiana of an insurance policy entered into outside the state with an unapproved insurance company on property located within the state. While the ruling related to jurisdiction to regulate,[f] the opinion by Peckham, J., contained much broader dicta, often repeated later: "The 'liberty' mentioned in that amendment [is] deemed to embrace the right of the citizen to be free in the enjoyment of all his faculties, to be free to use them in all lawful ways; to live and work where he will; to earn his livelihood by any lawful calling; to pursue any livelihood or avocation; and for that purpose to enter into all contracts which may be proper, necessary, and essential to his carrying out to a successful conclusion the purposes above mentioned."

---

e. Because *Topeka's* federal jurisdiction rested on diversity the Court was able to achieve this result on non-constitutional grounds. See *Liberty Against Government* 129 (1948); Tribe, *American Constitutional Law* 563–64 (2d ed. 1988).

a. 94 U.S. (4 Otto) 113, 24 L.Ed. 77 (1876).

b. 116 U.S. 307, 6 S.Ct. 1191, 29 L.Ed. 636 (1886).

c. 123 U.S. 623, 8 S.Ct. 273, 31 L.Ed. 205 (1887).

d. 169 U.S. 366, 18 S.Ct. 383, 42 L.Ed. 780 (1898).

e. One year earlier *Missouri Pac. Ry. Co. v. Nebraska,* 164 U.S. 403, 17 S.Ct. 130, 41 L.Ed. 489 (1896), held, without further reasons, that a state requirement that a railroad permit construction on its right of way of a private grain elevator not intended to serve the public violated due process by "taking [private property] for the private use of another." Cf. Introduction, Sec. 4 infra.

f. Later cases cut back substantially on the *Allgeyer* jurisdiction ruling. See, e.g., *Alaska Packers Ass'n v. Industrial Acc. Com'n,* 294 U.S. 532, 55 S.Ct. 518, 79 L.Ed. 1044 (1935); *Osborn v. Ozlin,* 310 U.S. 53, 60 S.Ct. 758, 84 L.Ed. 1074 (1940); *Watson v. Employers Liab. Assur. Corp.,* 348 U.S. 66, 75 S.Ct. 166, 99 L.Ed. 74 (1954).

LOCHNER v. NEW YORK

198 U.S. 45, 25 S.Ct. 539, 49 L.Ed. 937 (1905).

MR. JUSTICE PECKHAM delivered the opinion of the Court.

[The Court held invalid a New York statute forbidding employment in a bakery for more than 60 hours a week or 10 hours a day.]

The statute necessarily interferes with the right of contract between the employer and employees. [The] general right to make a contract in relation to his business is part of the liberty of the individual protected by the 14th Amendment. [*Allgeyer.*] The right to purchase or to sell labor is part of the liberty protected by this amendment. [W]hen the state [legislature] has passed an act which seriously limits the right to labor or the right of contract in regard to their means of livelihood between persons who are sui juris (both employer and employee), it becomes of great importance to determine which shall prevail,—the right of the individual to labor for such time as he may choose, or the right of the state to prevent the individual from laboring, or from entering into any contract to labor, beyond a certain time prescribed by the [state].

It must, of course, be conceded that there is a limit to the valid exercise of the police power by the state. [Otherwise] the 14th Amendment would have no efficacy and the legislatures of the states would have unbounded power. [In] every case that comes before this court, therefore, where legislation of this character is concerned, and where the protection of the Federal Constitution is sought, the question necessarily arises: Is this a fair, reasonable, and appropriate exercise of the police power of the state, or is it an unreasonable, unnecessary, and arbitrary interference with the right of the individual to his personal liberty, or to enter into those contracts in relation to labor which may seem to him appropriate or necessary for the support of himself and his family? Of course the liberty of contract relating to labor includes both parties to it. The one has as much right to purchase as the other to sell labor.

This is not a question of substituting the judgment of the court for that of the legislature. If the act be within the power of the state it is valid, although the judgment of the court might be totally opposed to the enactment of such a law. But the question would still remain: Is it within the police power of the state? and that question must be answered by the court.

The question whether this act is valid as a labor law, pure and simple, may be dismissed in a few words. There is no reasonable ground for interfering with the liberty of person or the right of free contract, by determining the hours of labor, in the occupation of a baker. There is no contention that bakers as a class are not equal in intelligence and capacity to men in other trades or manual occupations, or that they are not able to assert their rights and care for themselves without the protecting arm of the state. [They] are in no sense wards of the state. Viewed in the light of a purely labor law, with no reference whatever to the question of health, we think that a law like the one before us involves neither the safety, the morals, nor the welfare, of the public, and that the interest of the public is not in the slightest degree affected by such an act. The law must be upheld, if at all, as a law pertaining to the health of the individual engaged in the occupation of a baker. It does not affect any other portion of the public than those who are engaged in that occupation. Clean and wholesome bread does not depend upon whether the baker works but ten hours per day or only sixty hours a week. [There] is, in our judgment, no reasonable foundation for holding this to be necessary or appropriate as a health law to safeguard the public health, or the health of the individuals who are following the trade of a baker. * * *

We think that there can be no fair doubt that the trade of a baker, in and of itself, is not an unhealthy one to that degree which would authorize the legislature to interfere with the right to labor, and with the right of free contract on the part of the individual, either as employer or employee. In looking through statistics regarding all trades and occupations, it may be true that the trade of a baker does not appear to be as healthy as some other trades, and is also vastly more healthy than still others. To the common understanding the trade of a baker has never been regarded as an unhealthy one. [Some] occupations are more healthy than others, but we think there are none which might not come under the power of the legislature to supervise and control the hours of working therein, if the mere fact that the occupation is not absolutely and perfectly healthy is to confer that right upon the legislative department of the government. [It] is unfortunately true that labor, even in any department, may possibly carry with it the seeds of unhealthiness. But are we all, on that account, at the mercy of legislative majorities? A printer, a tinsmith, a locksmith, a carpenter, a cabinet maker, a dry goods clerk, a bank's, a lawyer's, or a physician's clerk, or a clerk in almost any kind of business, would all come under the power of the legislature, on this assumption. No trade, no occupation, no mode of earning one's living, could escape this all-pervading power, and the acts of the legislature in limiting the hours of labor in all employments would be valid, although such limitation might seriously cripple the ability of the laborer to support himself and his family. In our large cities there are many buildings into which the sun penetrates for but a short time in each day, and these buildings are occupied by people carrying on the business of bankers, brokers, lawyers, real estate, and many other kinds of business, aided by many clerks, messengers, and other employees. Upon the assumption of the validity of this act under review, it is not possible to say that an act, prohibiting lawyers' or bank clerks, or others, from contracting to labor for their employers more than eight hours a day would be invalid. * * *

It is also urged, pursuing the same line of argument, that it is to the interest of the state that its population should be strong and robust, and therefore any legislation which may be said to tend to make people healthy must be valid as health laws, enacted under the police power. If this be a valid argument and a justification for this kind of legislation, it follows that the protection of the Federal Constitution from undue interference with liberty of person and freedom of contract is visionary, wherever the law is sought to be justified as a valid exercise of the police power. Scarcely any law but might find shelter under such assumptions. [Not] only the hours of employees, but the hours of employers, could be regulated, and doctors, lawyers, scientists, all professional men, as well as athletes and artisans, could be forbidden to fatigue their brains and bodies by prolonged hours of exercise, lest the fighting strength of the state be impaired. We mention these extreme cases because the contention is extreme. We do not believe in the soundness of the views which uphold this law. [The] act is not, within any fair meaning of the term, a health law, but is an illegal interference with the rights of individuals, both employers and employees, to make contracts regarding labor upon such terms as they may think best, or which they may agree upon with the other parties to such contracts. Statutes of the nature of that under review, limiting the hours in which grown and intelligent men may labor to earn their living, are mere meddlesome interferences with the rights of the individual, and they are not saved from condemnation by the claim that they are passed in the exercise of the police power and upon the subject of the health of the individual whose rights are interfered with, unless there be some fair ground, reasonable in and of itself, to say that there is material danger to the public health, or to the health of the employees, if the hours of labor are not curtailed. * * *

This interference on the part of the legislatures of the several states with the ordinary trades and occupations of the people seems to be on the increase. [It] is impossible for us to shut our eyes to the fact that many of the laws of this character, while passed under what is claimed to be the police power for the purpose of protecting the public health or welfare, are, in reality, passed from other motives. We are justified in saying so when, from the character of the law and the subject upon which it legislates, it is apparent that the public health or welfare bears but the most remote relation to the [law].

It seems to us that the real object and purpose were simply to regulate the hours of labor between the master and his employees (all being men, sui juris), in a private business, not dangerous in any degree to morals, or in any real and substantial degree to the health of the employees. Under such circumstances the freedom of master and employee to contract with each other in relation to their employment [cannot] be prohibited or interfered with, without violating the Federal Constitution. * * *

JUSTICE HOLMES dissenting: * * *

This case is decided upon an economic theory which a large part of the country does not entertain. If it were a question whether I agree with that theory, I should desire to study it further and long before making up my mind. But I do not conceive that to be my duty, because I strongly believe that my agreement or disagreement has nothing to do with the right of a majority to embody their opinions in law. It is settled by various decisions of this court that state constitutions and state laws may regulate life in many ways which we as legislators might think as injudicious, or if you like as tyrannical, as this, and which, equally with this, interfere with the liberty to contract. Sunday laws and usury laws are ancient examples. A more modern one is the prohibition of lotteries. The liberty of the citizen to do as he likes so long as he does not interfere with the liberty of others to do the same, which has been a shibboleth for some well-known writers, is interfered with by school laws, by the Postoffice, by every state or municipal institution which takes his money for purposes thought desirable, whether he likes it or not. The 14th Amendment does not enact Mr. Herbert Spencer's *Social Statics.* [Some] of these laws embody convictions or prejudices which judges are likely to share. Some may not. But a Constitution is not intended to embody a particular economic theory, whether of paternalism and the organic relation of the citizen to the state or of laissez faire. It is made for people of fundamentally differing views, and the accident of our finding certain opinions natural and familiar, or novel, and even shocking, ought not to conclude our judgment upon the question whether statutes embodying them conflict with the Constitution of the United States.

[I] think that the word "liberty," in the 14th Amendment, is perverted when it is held to prevent the natural outcome of a dominant opinion, unless it can be said that a rational and fair man necessarily would admit that the statute proposed would infringe fundamental principles as they have been understood by the traditions of our people and our law. It does not need research to show that no such sweeping condemnation can be passed upon the statute before us. A reasonable man might think it a proper measure on the score of health. Men whom I certainly could not pronounce unreasonable would uphold it as a first instalment of a general regulation of the hours of work. * * *

JUSTICE HARLAN (with whom JUSTICE WHITE and JUSTICE DAY concurred) dissenting:

[Whether] or not this be wise legislation it is not the province of the court to inquire. Under our systems of government the courts are not concerned with the wisdom or policy of legislation.

[The opinion quoted from writers on health problems of workers, pointing out that long hours, night hours, and difficult working conditions, such as excessive heat and exposure to flour dust, were injurious to the health of bakers, who "seldom live over their fiftieth year."]

We judicially know that the question of the number of hours during which a workman should continuously labor has been, for a long period, and is yet, a subject of serious consideration among civilized peoples, and by those having special knowledge of the laws of health.

We also judicially know that the number of hours that should constitute a day's labor in particular occupations involving the physical strength and safety of workmen has been the subject of enactments by Congress and by nearly all of the states. Many, if not most, of those enactments fix eight hours as the proper basis of a day's labor.

I do not stop to consider whether any particular view of this economic question presents the sounder theory. [It] is enough for the determination of this case, and it is enough for this court to know, that the question is one about which there is room for debate and for an honest difference of opinion. There are many reasons of a weighty, substantial character, based upon the experience of mankind, in support of the theory that, all things considered, more than ten hours' steady work each day, from week to week, in a bakery or confectionery establishment, may endanger the health and shorten the lives of the workmen, thereby diminishing their physical and mental capacity to serve the state and to provide for those dependent upon them.

If such reasons exist that ought to be the end of this case, for the state is not amenable to the judiciary, in respect of its legislative enactments, unless such enactments are plainly, palpably, beyond all question, inconsistent with the Constitution of the United States. * * *

SECTION 2. THREE DECADES OF CONTROL OVER LEGISLATIVE POLICY

From *Lochner* in 1905 to *Nebbia* in 1934, infra, the Court frequently substituted its judgment for that of Congress and state legislatures on the wisdom of economic regulation interfering with contract and property interests.[a] It relied mainly upon the due process clauses of the fifth and fourteenth amendments, with occasional resort to the equal protection clause. Between 1899 and 1937, after excluding the civil rights cases, 159 Supreme Court decisions held state statutes unconstitutional under the due process and equal protection clauses and 25 more statutes were struck down under the due process

a. See Pound, *Liberty of Contract,* 18 Yale L.J. 454 (1909); Brown, *Due Process of Law, Police Power, and the Supreme Court,* 40 Harv. L.Rev. 943 (1927).

clause coupled with some other provision of the Constitution. B. Wright, *The Growth of American Constitutional Law* 154 (1942).

The Court most freely substituted its judgment for that of the legislature in labor legislation, regulation of prices, and limitations on entry into business. It was most tolerant in the regulation of trade and business practices.[b] A few examples will suffice to show the extent to which the Court interfered with legislative policymaking in economic regulation. With regularity Holmes, J., dissented from this use of the due process clause, joined later by Brandeis and Stone, JJ., and Hughes, C.J.

1. *Control over hours of labor.* We have already seen how the Court barred control over the hours of labor, even in an industry where long hours threatened health. *Lochner* (1905). But in 1908 the Court sustained regulation of work hours for women in *Muller v. Oregon,* 208 U.S. 412, 28 S.Ct. 324, 52 L.Ed. 551 (1908), basing the decision on special considerations relating to women, and in 1917 the Court overruled *Lochner* 5 to 3 in sustaining a regulation of work hours for men in manufacturing establishments. *Bunting v. Oregon,* 243 U.S. 426, 37 S.Ct. 435, 61 L.Ed. 830 (1917). In *Muller* the majority was influenced by the so-called "Brandeis brief," which furnished the Court with overwhelming documentation justifying regulation of hours of labor for women. Felix Frankfurter, Esq., successfully followed the same technique in *Bunting.* See 208 U.S. at 419–20, and 243 U.S. at 433; Bikle, *Judicial Determination of Questions of Fact Affecting the Constitutional Validity of Legislative Action,* 38 Harv.L.Rev. 6, 13 (1924).

2. *Control over anti-union discrimination.* At an early date the Court struck down labor legislation forbidding discrimination by employers for union activity and requiring employees to sign "yellow dog" agreements not to join a union. *Adair v. United States,* 208 U.S. 161, 28 S.Ct. 277, 52 L.Ed. 436 (1908) (5th amendment); *Coppage v. Kansas,* 236 U.S. 1, 35 S.Ct. 240, 59 L.Ed. 441 (1915) (14th amendment).

Adair held that for Congress to forbid an interstate railroad to discharge an employee for union membership denied due process. For the Court, Harlan, J., who had dissented in *Lochner,* relied upon the liberty of contract approach in *Lochner* and equated the right of an employee to quit his employment with "the right of the employer, for whatever reason, to dispense with the services of the employee." McKenna and Holmes, JJ., dissented. *Coppage,* per Pitney, J., rejected the claim that the legislature could protect employees from being required to sign yellow dog contracts to obtain or keep needed employment.

These restrictive decisions were distinguished away in *Texas & N.O.R.R. v. Brotherhood of Ry. & S.S. Clerks,* 281 U.S. 548, 50 S.Ct. 427, 74 L.Ed. 1034 (1930) and *NLRB v. Jones & Laughlin Steel Corp.* (1937). They were finally expressly overruled in *Phelps Dodge Corp. v. NLRB,* 313 U.S. 177, 61 S.Ct. 845, 85 L.Ed. 1271 (1941) and *Lincoln Fed. Labor Union v. Northwestern Iron & Met. Co.* (1949), Sec. 3 infra.

3. *Regulation of wages.* Six years after the Court had upheld regulation of hours of labor, it held 5 to 3 that regulation of wages violated due process. *Adkins v. Children's Hosp.,* 261 U.S. 525, 43 S.Ct. 394, 67 L.Ed. 785 (1923) (fifth amendment); *Murphy v. Sardell,* 269 U.S. 530, 46 S.Ct. 22, 70 L.Ed. 396 (1925) (14th amendment); *Morehead v. People of New York ex rel. Tipaldo,* 298 U.S.

b. See summary of such cases in *Nebbia v. New York,* 291 U.S. 502, 527–529, 54 S.Ct. 505, 511–13, 78 L.Ed. 940, 950–53 (1934), infra.

587, 56 S.Ct. 918, 80 L.Ed. 1347 (1936) (same). Not until 1937 were these decisions overruled in *West Coast Hotel Co. v. Parrish,* Sec. 3 infra, where the Court expressly recognized the unequal bargaining position of workers, and that the wisdom of debatable policy is for the legislature.

4. *Regulation of prices.* The Court also held that regulation of prices for commodities and services violated due process except for a limited class labeled "business affected with a public interest." [c] *Tyson & Bro.—United Theatre Ticket Offices v. Banton,* 273 U.S. 418, 47 S.Ct. 426, 71 L.Ed. 718 (1927) (theatre tickets); *Ribnik v. McBride,* 277 U.S. 350, 48 S.Ct. 545, 72 L.Ed. 913 (1928) (fees of employment agency); *Williams v. Standard Oil Co.,* 278 U.S. 235, 49 S.Ct. 115, 73 L.Ed. 287 (1929) (gasoline prices); cf. *Chas. Wolff Packing Co. v. Court of Industrial Relations,* 262 U.S. 522, 43 S.Ct. 630, 67 L.Ed. 1103 (1923) (compulsory arbitration of wages). *Nebbia v. New York* (1934) severely limited these rulings and they were expressly overruled in *Olsen v. Nebraska ex rel. Western Ref. & Bond Ass'n* (1941), both in Sec. 3 infra.

5. *Limitations on entry into business.* The Court also relied on the "liberty of contract" concept to strike down legislation limiting entry into a business, despite strong demonstrations of need for such limitations. *New State Ice Co. v. Liebmann,* 285 U.S. 262, 52 S.Ct. 371, 76 L.Ed. 747 (1932) (invalid to deny entry into ice business without a finding of "necessity" and that existing facilities are not "sufficient to meet the public needs"); *Louis K. Liggett Co. v. Baldridge,* 278 U.S. 105, 49 S.Ct. 57, 73 L.Ed. 204 (1928) (invalid to limit new entrants into pharmacy business to pharmacists; *Adams v. Tanner,* 244 U.S. 590, 37 S.Ct. 662, 61 L.Ed. 1336 (1917) (invalid to ban private employment agencies that charge fees paid by employees).

In 1973, *North Dakota State Board v. Snyder's Drug Stores,* Sec. 3 infra, overruled *Liggett.* While no cases precisely like *Adams* or *New State Ice* have arisen, the Court in 1963 asserted in effect that *Adams* had been overruled when it unanimously sustained a state prohibition on engaging in the debt adjusting business. See *Ferguson v. Skrupa,* Sec. 3 infra.

SECTION 3. DECLINE OF CONTROL OVER LEGISLATIVE POLICY

NEBBIA v. NEW YORK

291 U.S. 502, 54 S.Ct. 505, 78 L.Ed. 940 (1934).

JUSTICE ROBERTS delivered the opinion of the Court.

[After a year's legislative study of the New York dairy industry, in 1933 New York enacted a law that regulated minumum and maximum retail milk prices, which the Court sustained 5 to 4:]

[Under] our form of government the use of property and the making of contracts are normally matters of private and not of public concern. The general rule is that both shall be free of governmental interference. But neither property rights nor contract rights are absolute; for government cannot exist if the citizen may at will use his property to the detriment of his fellows, or

c. See McAllister, *Lord Hale and Business Affected with a Public Interest,* 43 Harv.L.Rev. 759 (1930); Hamilton, *Affectation with Public Interest,* 39 Yale L.J. 1089 (1930); Finkelstein, *From Munn v. Illinois to Tyson v. Banton: A Study in the Judicial Process,* 27 Colum.L.Rev. 769 (1927).

exercise his freedom of contract to work them harm. Equally fundamental with the private right is that of the public to regulate it in the common interest.

[T]he guaranty of due process, [demands] only that the law shall not be unreasonable, arbitrary, or capricious, and that the means selected shall have a real and substantial relation to the object sought to be attained. [A] regulation valid for one sort of business, or in given circumstances, may be invalid for another sort, or for the same business under other circumstances, because the reasonableness of each regulation depends upon the relevant facts.

[The opinion here summarized many different kinds of business and property regulations and controls previously sustained against due process attacks.]

The legislative investigation of 1932 was persuasive of the fact [that] unrestricted competition aggravated existing evils and the normal law of supply and demand was insufficient to correct maladjustments detrimental to the community. The inquiry disclosed destructive and demoralizing competitive conditions and unfair trade practices which resulted in retail price cutting and reduced the income of the farmer below the cost of production. [The Legislature] believed conditions could be improved by preventing destructive price-cutting by stores which, due to the flood of surplus milk, were able to buy at much lower prices than the larger distributors and to sell without incurring the delivery costs of the latter. In the order of which complaint is made the Milk Control Board fixed a price of 10 cents per quart for sales by a distributor to a consumer, and 9 cents by a store to a consumer, thus recognizing the lower costs of the store, and endeavoring to establish a differential which would be just to both. In the light of the facts the order appears not to be unreasonable or arbitrary, or without relation to the purpose to prevent ruthless competition from destroying the wholesale price structure on which the farmer depends for his livelihood, and the community for an assured supply of milk.

But we are told that because the law essays to control prices it denies due process. Notwithstanding the admitted power to correct existing economic ills by appropriate regulation of business, [the] appellant urges that direct fixation of prices is a type of regulation absolutely forbidden. [The] argument runs that the public control of rates or prices is per se unreasonable and unconstitutional, save as applied to businesses affected with a public interest; that a business so affected is one in which property is devoted to an enterprise of a sort which the public itself might appropriately undertake, or one whose owner relies on a public grant or franchise for the right to conduct the business, or in which he is bound to serve all who apply; in short, such as is commonly called a public utility; or a business in its nature a monopoly. The milk industry, it is said, possesses none of these characteristics.

[W]hat constitutional principle bars the state from correcting existing maladjustments by legislation touching prices? We think there is no such principle. The due process clause makes no mention of sales or of prices any more than it speaks of business or contracts or buildings or other incidents of property. The thought seems nevertheless to have persisted that there is something peculiarly sacrosanct about the price one may charge for what he makes or sells, and that, however able to regulate other elements of manufacture or trade, with incidental effect upon price, the state is incapable of directly controlling the price itself. This view was negatived many years ago. *Munn v. Illinois,* [Sec. 1 supra].

[T]here is no closed class or category of businesses affected with a public interest, and the function of courts in the application of the Fifth and Fourteenth Amendments is to determine in each case whether circumstances vindicate the challenged regulation as a reasonable exertion of governmental authority or condemn it as arbitrary or discriminatory. The phrase "affected with a public interest" can, in the nature of things, mean no more than that an industry, for adequate reason, is subject to control for the public good. [There] can be no doubt that upon proper occasion and by appropriate measures the state may regulate a business in any of its aspects, including the prices to be charged for the products or commodities it sells.

So far as the requirement of due process is concerned, and in the absence of other constitutional restriction, a state is free to adopt whatever economic policy may reasonably be deemed to promote public welfare, and to enforce that policy by legislation adapted to its purpose. The courts are without authority either to declare such policy, or, when it is declared by the legislature, to override it. If the laws passed are seen to have a reasonable relation to a proper legislative purpose, and are neither arbitrary nor discriminatory, the requirements of due process are satisfied. [If] the legislative policy be to curb unrestrained and harmful competition by measures which are not arbitrary or discriminatory it does not lie with the courts to determine that the rule is unwise. With the wisdom of the policy adopted, with the adequacy or practicability of the law enacted to forward it, the courts are both incompetent and unauthorized to deal.

[If] the lawmaking body within its sphere of government concludes that the conditions or practices in an industry make unrestricted competition an inadequate safeguard of the consumer's interests, produce waste harmful to the public, threaten ultimately to cut off the supply of a commodity needed by the public, or portend the destruction of the industry itself, appropriate statutes passed in an honest effort to correct the threatened consequences may not be set aside because the regulation adopted fixes prices reasonably deemed by the Legislature to be fair to those engaged in the industry and to the consuming public. And this is especially so where, as here, the economic maladjustment is one of price, which threatens harm to the producer at one end of the series and the consumer at the other. * * *

JUSTICE MCREYNOLDS [dissented, joined by Van Devanter, Sutherland, and Butler, JJ.]:

[P]lainly, I think, this Court must have regard to the wisdom of the enactment. At least, we must inquire concerning its purpose and decide whether the means proposed have reasonable relation to something within legislative power—whether the end is legitimate, and the means appropriate. * * *

The court below [has] not attempted to indicate how higher charges at stores to impoverished customers when the output is excessive and sale prices by producers are unrestrained, can possibly increase receipts at the farm. * * *

Not only does the statute interfere arbitrarily with the rights of the little grocer to conduct his business according to standards long accepted—complete destruction may follow; but it takes away the liberty of 12,000,000 consumers to buy a necessity of life in an open market. It imposes direct and arbitrary burdens upon those already seriously impoverished with the alleged immediate design of affording special benefits to others. To him with less than 9 cents it says: You cannot procure a quart of milk from the grocer although he is anxious to accept what you can pay and the demands of your household are urgent! [Grave] concern for embarrassed farmers is everywhere; but this should neither obscure the rights of others nor obstruct judicial appraisement of measures proposed for relief. The ultimate welfare of the producer, like that of every other class, requires dominance of the Constitution.

Notes and Questions

1. *The Nebbia rationale.* (a) Did *Nebbia* appear to retain any degree of judicial review over legislative policy in state economic regulation? What standards of judgment did *Nebbia* suggest the Court would apply? May the makeup of the majority explain the standards advanced in the opinion?

(b) *Interests justifying price controls; sources of information.* Do you see any significance in the type of interests the Court found sufficient to justify price controls in *Nebbia?* In the sources relied upon by the Court to establish the factual basis for justifying price regulation?

2. *A standard in transition.* (a) WEST COAST HOTEL CO. v. PARRISH, 300 U.S. 379, 57 S.Ct. 578, 81 L.Ed. 703 (1937), sustained 5 to 4 a state regulation of women's wages, overruling earlier decisions. The opinion, per HUGHES, C.J., devoted substantial space to the reasons for regulation of women's wages: "What can be closer to the public interest than the health of women and their protection from unscrupulous and overreaching employers? [The] Legislature of the state was clearly entitled to consider [the] fact that [women] are in the class receiving the least pay, that their bargaining power is relatively weak, and that they are the ready victims of those who would take advantage of their necessitous circumstances. The Legislature was entitled to adopt measures to reduce the evils of the 'sweating system,' the exploiting of workers at wages so low as to be insufficient to meet the bare cost of living, thus making their very helplessness the occasion of a most injurious competition. [Even] if the wisdom of the policy be regarded as debatable and its effects uncertain, still the Legislature is entitled to its judgment.

"[The] exploitation of a class of workers who are in an unequal position with respect to bargaining power and are thus relatively defenseless against the denial of a living wage is not only detrimental to their health and well being, but casts a direct burden for their support upon the community [which] is not bound to provide what is in effect a subsidy for unconscionable employers. The community may direct its law-making power to correct the abuse which springs from their selfish disregard of the public interest."

(b) Compare UNITED STATES v. CAROLENE PRODUCTS CO., 304 U.S. 144, 58 S.Ct. 778, 82 L.Ed. 1234 (1938), per STONE, J., finding due process not violated by a federal statute excluding "filled milk" (non-milk fats added) from interstate commerce: "[R]egulatory legislation affecting ordinary commercial transactions is not to be pronounced unconstitutional unless in the light of the facts made known or generally assumed it is of such a character as to preclude the assumption that it rests upon some rational basis within the knowledge and experience of the legislators. * * *

"Where the existence of a rational basis for legislation whose constitutionality is attacked depends upon facts beyond the sphere of judicial notice, such facts may properly be made the subject of judicial inquiry, and the constitutionality of a statute predicated upon the existence of a particular state of facts may be challenged by showing to the court that those facts have ceased to exist. [B]y their very nature such inquiries, where the legislative judgment is drawn in question, must be restricted to the issue whether any state of facts either known or which could reasonably be assumed affords support for it." Black, J., withheld concurrence in the foregoing portion of the opinion.

(c) Did *Carolene* indicate an intention in 1938 to retain the Court's power to strike down economic legislation in appropriate cases? See McCloskey, *Economic Due Process and the Supreme Court: An Exhumation and Reburial,* 1962 Sup. Ct.Rev. 34, 37. What kind of a test of validity would the Court apply?

(d) *United States v. Darby* (1941), unanimously held FLSA's minimum wage and overtime rate regulations valid under due process on the authority of *West Coast Hotel* without further discussion or justification. Were the reasons for sustaining regulation of women's wages in *West Coast Hotel* so clearly applicable to men's wages as to call for no further justification? Or had the standard for judicial review of interference with "freedom of contract" so changed as to require no justification?

3. *Renunciation of former due process philosophy.* (a) OLSEN v. NEBRASKA, 313 U.S. 236, 61 S.Ct. 862, 85 L.Ed. 1305 (1941), upheld a Nebraska statute fixing maximum fees for employment agencies. DOUGLAS, J.'s, unanimous opinion [a] bluntly rejected the state court's reliance on *Ribnik v. McBride,* 277 U.S. 350, 48 S.Ct. 545, 72 L.Ed. 913 (1928), which had held a similar statute violated due process: "The drift away from *Ribnik* has been so great that it can no longer be deemed a controlling authority. [The Court summarized several cases overruling earlier due process rulings.] These cases represent more than scattered examples of constitutionally permissible price-fixing schemes. They represent in large measure a basic departure from the philosophy and approach of the majority in *Ribnik.* The standard there employed [was] that the constitutional validity of price-fixing legislation, at least in absence of a so-called emergency, was dependent on whether or not the business in question was 'affected with a public interest'. [That] test, labelled by Mr. Justice Holmes in his dissent in [*Tyson*] as 'little more than a fiction', was discarded in *Nebbia.*

"The *Ribnik* case, freed from the test which it employed, can no longer survive. But respondents maintain that the statute here in question is invalid for other reasons. They insist that special circumstances must be shown to support the validity of such drastic legislation as price-fixing, that the executive technical and professional workers which respondents serve have not been shown to be in need of special protection from exploitation, that legislative limitation of maximum fees for employment agencies is certain to react unfavorably upon those members of the community for whom it is most difficult to obtain jobs, that the increasing competition of public employment agencies and of charitable, labor union and employer association employment agencies have curbed excessive fees by private agencies, and [that] there are no conditions which the legislature might reasonably believe would redound to the public injury unless corrected by such legislation.

"We are not concerned, however, with the wisdom, need, or appropriateness of the legislation. Differences of opinion on that score suggest a choice which 'should be left where [it] was left by the Constitution—to the states and to Congress.' *Ribnik,* dissenting opinion. There is no necessity for the state to demonstrate before us that evils persist despite the competition which attends the bargaining in this field. In final analysis, the only constitutional prohibitions or restraints which respondents have suggested for the invalidation of this legislation are those notions of public policy embedded in earlier decisions of this Court but which, as Mr. Justice Holmes long ago admonished, should not be read into the Constitution. [Since] they do not find expression in the Constitution, we

a. McReynolds, J., the last of the four *Nebbia* and *West Coast Hotel* dissenters, retired two days before *Darby* and two months before *Olsen.*

cannot give them continuing vitality as standards by which the constitutionality of the economic and social programs of the states is to be determined."

Is the absence in *Olsen* of any judicial explanation of the need to regulate employment agency rates significant? Were there reasons in 1941 to be less skeptical of the *Olsen* expression of no concern over "the wisdom, the need, or appropriateness of the legislation" than of the similar statement in *Nebbia* in 1934?

(b) After *Olsen* the Court consistently repudiated *Lochner*-type reasoning in rejecting substantive due process challenges to economic regulation.[b]

4. *Social, as distinct from economic, regulation.* WHALEN v. ROE, 429 U.S. 589, 97 S.Ct. 869, 51 L.Ed.2d 64 (1977), per STEVENS, J., upheld a New York law requiring those who fill prescriptions for specified harmful drugs to send copies to the New York Department of Health, where the information, including the patient's name, was to be retained on computers for five years under strict non-disclosure regulations: "There was a time when [the state's inability to demonstrate the need for patient identification] would have provided a basis for invalidating the statute. *Lochner.* [The] holding in *Lochner* has been implicitly rejected many times. State legislation which has some effect on individual liberty or privacy may not be held unconstitutional simply because a court finds it unnecessary, in whole or in part. For we have frequently recognized that individual States have broad latitude in experimenting with possible solutions to problems of vital local concern.

"The New York statute challenged in this [case] is manifestly the product of an orderly and rational legislative decision. It was recommended by a specially appointed commission which held extensive hearings on the proposed [legislation]. There surely was nothing unreasonable in the assumption that the

b. *Lincoln Fed. Labor Union v. Northwestern Iron & Metal Co.,* 335 U.S. 525, 69 S.Ct. 251, 93 L.Ed. 212 (1949), per Black, J., sustained a state right-to-work law that barred employers' pro-union discrimination: "This Court beginning at least as early as 1934, when [*Nebbia*] was decided, has steadily rejected the due process philosophy enunciated in the *Adair-Coppage* line of cases. [Just] as we have held that the due process clause erects no obstacle to block legislative protection of union members [see Sec. 2, note 2, par. 3 supra], we now hold that legislative protection can be afforded non-union workers."

Day-Brite Lighting v. Missouri, 342 U.S. 421, 72 S.Ct. 405, 96 L.Ed. 469 (1952), per Douglas, J., sustained a requirement that employees have four hours off work with full pay in order to vote: "The liberty of contract argument pressed on us is reminiscent of the philosophy of [*Lochner, Coppage, Adkins v. Children's Hospital*] and others of that vintage. Our recent decisions make plain that we do not sit as a super-legislature to weigh the wisdom of legislation nor to decide whether the policy it expresses offends the public welfare. * * * The judgment of the legislature that time out for voting should cost the employee nothing may be a debatable one. [But] if our recent cases mean anything, they leave debatable issues as respects business, economic and social affairs to legislative decisions." Jackson, J., dissented and Frankfurter, J., concurred in the result without opinion.

Similarly, *Ferguson v. Skrupa,* 372 U.S. 726, 83 S.Ct. 1028, 10 L.Ed.2d 93 (1963), per Black, J., unanimously spurned a due process challenge to a state law that barred all but lawyers from the business of debt adjusting: "Under the system of government created by our Constitution, it is up to the legislatures, not the courts, to decide on the wisdom and utility of legislation. [The] doctrine that prevailed in *Lochner, Coppage, Adkins* and like cases [has] long since been discarded. We have returned to the original constitutional proposition that courts do not substitute their social and economic beliefs for the judgment of legislative bodies, who are elected to pass [laws]. [Arguments that] the business of debt adjusting has social utility [are] properly addressed to the legislature, not to us." Harlan, J., concurred in the judgment on the ground that "[this] measure bears a rational relation to a constitutionally permissible objective."

For similar rulings and opinions see *Williamson v. Lee Optical of Okl.,* 348 U.S. 483, 75 S.Ct. 461, 99 L.Ed. 563 (1955); *North Dakota State Bd. v. Snyders' Drug Stores Inc.,* 414 U.S. 156, 94 S.Ct. 407, 38 L.Ed.2d 379 (1973).

patient identification requirement might aid in the enforcement of laws designed to minimize the misuse of dangerous drugs. For the requirement could reasonably be expected to have a deterrent effect on potential violators as well as to aid in the detection or investigation of specific instances of apparent abuse. At the very least, it would seem clear that the State's vital interest in controlling the distribution of dangerous drugs would support a decision to experiment with new techniques for control. For if an experiment fails [the] legislative process remains available to terminate the unwise experiment." [c]

ABSTENTION EXCEEDING HALF A CENTURY

When faced with substantive due process challenges to economic legislation after 1940, the Court's actual decisions gave full effect to its strong opinions repeatedly asserting that on such matters legislative policy is for the legislature, not the courts. Not since 1937 has the Court struck down economic legislation as violating substantive due process;[a] and only in rare instances have individual justices withheld their approval of opinions renouncing power under the due process clause to review the wisdom, need, or soundness of such legislation.[b]

Referring to the foregoing due process decisions, and to a similar line of equal protection decisions,[c] Professor McCloskey concluded in 1962: "[T]here could be little doubt as to the practical result: no claim of substantive economic rights would now be sustained by the Supreme Court. The judiciary has abdicated the field." [d]

Has the Court "abdicated?" Has it renounced all substantive due process review power over economic legislation? Or has the Court hedged its opinions sufficiently to enable it, without recanting, to reassert substantive due process if it ever concludes that a legislative economic enactment is devoid of any arguable justification? [e]

With such questions in mind, consider DUKE POWER CO. v. CAROLINA ENVIRONMENTAL STUDY GROUP, INC., 438 U.S. 59, 98 S.Ct. 2620, 57 L.Ed. 2d 595 (1978). *Duke Power,* per BURGER, C.J., upheld the Price-Anderson Act's limit on the aggregate liability for a single nuclear incident in the atomic energy industry to the amount available through private insurance ($60 million) plus the $500 million indemnification undertaken by the federal government: [f] "[I]t is clear that Congress' purpose was to remove the economic impediments in order to stimulate the private development of electric energy by nuclear power while simultaneously providing the public compensation in the event of a catastrophic nuclear incident. The liability limitation provision thus emerges as a classic

c. For cases applying stricter scrutiny to legislation impinging on a limited category of "fundamental" personal rights, see Ch. 3, Sec. 2. However, *Whalen* ruled that the New York law did not unduly impinge on the right to privacy.

a. The last substantive due process decision invalidating economic legislation was *Thompson v. Consolidated Gas Utilities Corp.,* 300 U.S. 55, 57 S.Ct. 364, 81 L.Ed. 510 (1937), where the regulation was viewed as taking property for a private purpose.

b. See the Harlan concurrence in *Ferguson v. Skrupa,* and the Jackson dissent and Frankfurter concurrence "in the result" in *Day-Brite Lighting.*

c. For the equal protection cases relating to economic regulation see Ch. 6, Sec. 1.

d. McClosky, *Economic Due Process and the Supreme Court,* 1962 Sup.Ct.Rev. 34, 38.

e. Cf. Wonnell, *Economic Due Process and the Preservation of Competition,* 11 Hast. Const.L.Q. 91 (1983) (a strongly reasoned argument that substantive due process should be extended to protect "free and open competition for society's lawful occupations [as] a constitutional value" that could invalidate legislation enforcing monopoly conditions, absent a sufficiently strong state interest).

f. Stewart, Rehnquist and Stevens, JJ., concurred in the result without reaching the merits.

example of an economic regulation—a legislative effort to structure and accommodate 'the burdens and benefits of economic life.' *Usery v. Turner Elkhorn Mining Co.,* 428 U.S. 1, 96 S.Ct. 2882, 49 L.Ed.2d 752 (1976). 'It is by now well established that [such] legislative Acts [come] to the Court with a presumption of constitutionality, and that the burden is on one complaining of a due process violation to establish that the legislature has acted in an arbitrary and irrational way.' Ibid. That the accommodation struck may have profound and far-reaching consequences, contrary to appellees' suggestion, provides all the more reason for this Court to defer to the congressional judgment unless it is demonstrably arbitrary or irrational.

"When examined in light of this standard of review, the Price-Anderson Act, in our view, passes constitutional muster. The record before us fully supports the need for the imposition of a statutory limit on liability to encourage private industry participation and hence bears a rational relationship to Congress' concern for stimulating the involvement of private enterprise in the production of electric energy through the use of atomic power; nor do we understand appellees or the District Court to be of a different view. Rather, their challenge is to the alleged arbitrariness of the *particular figure* of $560 million, which is the statutory ceiling on liability. The District Court aptly summarized its position: 'The amount of recovery is not rationally related to the potential losses, [which] could well be many, many times [that] limit.'

"Assuming, arguendo, that the $560 million fund would not insure full recovery in all conceivable circumstances,—and the hard truth is that no one can ever know—it does not by any means follow that the liability limitation is therefore irrational and violative of due process. The legislative history clearly indicates that the $560 million figure was not arrived at on the supposition that it alone would necessarily be sufficient to guarantee full compensation in the event of a nuclear incident. Instead, it was conceived of as a 'starting point' or a working hypothesis. The reasonableness of the statute's assumed ceiling on liability was predicated on two corollary considerations—expert appraisals of the exceedingly small risk of a nuclear incident involving claims in excess of $560 million, and the recognition that in the event of such an incident, Congress would likely enact extraordinary relief provisions to provide additional relief, in accord with prior practice."

Notes and Questions

1. *The standard of review.* Was the standard of review that *Turner Elkhorn* and *Duke Power* asserted with no dissenting voices—"demonstrably arbitrary or irrational"—consistent with the opinions from *Olsen* (1941) to *Snyder* (1973)? In forecasting future decisions on such issues, is it significant that *Duke Power* used four pages to explain why Price-Anderson was not "arbitrary or irrational" and hence "passes constitutional muster?"

(b) Did "arbitrary or irrational" mean something different in 1978 than from 1905 (*Lochner*) to 1934 (*Nebbia*)? *North Dakota State Board v. Snyder's Store* (1973), supra, per Douglas, J., in overruling *Liggett Co. v. Baldridge* (1928) [Sec. 2, note 5 supra] to uphold a requirement that pharmacies be owned by pharmacists, noted that " 'a pronounced shift in emphasis since [*Liggett*]' had deprived the words 'unreasonable' and 'arbitrary' of the meaning which *Liggett* ascribed to them." Realistically, what appears to be the standard after *Duke Power?*

2. *Substance or style?* Does *Duke Power* portend a difference in the results of due process challenges to economic regulation, or does it reflect only a different pattern of opinion writing?

3. *Protection of "personal" rights.* The Court gives far stricter scrutiny and greater constitutional protection to some *personal* rights, often viewed as "fundamental," than to *economic* or *social welfare* interests. This development is considered primarily in Ch. 3, Sec. 2, and Ch. 6, Sec. 4.

4. *Equal protection.* The rise and fall of judicial protection of economic and social welfare interests under the equal protection clause is similar to that under due process, though equal protection issues involve somewhat different concerns and values. See Ch. 6, Sec. 1.

5. *Substantive due process under state constitutions.* Most state constitutions include due process clauses identical or similar to that in the fourteenth amendment. Not all state courts, whose interpretations and applications of their own state constitutions are not ordinarily subject to Supreme Court review, have followed the Court's lead in leaving economic policy decisions to the legislature. A few have continued to follow the Court's 1905–1934 approach, invalidating under state due process clauses economic legislation that the Supreme Court would have upheld.[f]

SECTION 4. "TAKING" OF PROPERTY INTERESTS

INTRODUCTION

The fifth amendment limits the federal government's power of eminent domain: "nor shall private property be taken for a public use without just compensation." Similarly the due process clause has long been held to require a state to compensate the owner when it takes property for a public use,[a] and to forbid taking property for a private use, even with compensation.[b] Space limits do not permit consideration of the extensive body of law relating to eminent domain. Two aspects only are considered here: (1) What are the limits, if any, on the purposes for which property may be taken, even with compensation? (2) Under what circumstances may, or should, a regulation be considered a "taking" that requires compensation?

I. PURPOSE OF "TAKING"

BERMAN v. PARKER, 348 U.S. 26, 75 S.Ct. 98, 99 L.Ed. 27 (1954), per Douglas, J., unanimously upheld the District of Columbia Redevelopment Act, which authorized the Redevelopment Agency to acquire and assemble, by eminent domain or otherwise, real property "for the redevelopment of blighted territory (and) the prevention, reduction, or elimination of blighting factors." The Agency was empowered to transfer such property to public agencies for

f. The cases to 1958 are found in Paulsen, *The Persistence of Substantive Due Process in the States,* 34 Minn.L.Rev. 91 (1950); Hetherington, *State Economic Regulation and Substantive Due Process of Law,* 53 Nw.U.L.Rev. 13, 226 (1958). A few such decisions continue. See, e.g., *Gillette Dairy, Inc. v. Nebraska Dairy Products Bd.,* 192 Neb. 89, 219 N.W.2d 214 (1974) (milk price control); *Condemarin v. University Hospital,* 775 P.2d 348 (Utah 1989) (limitation on state liability).

a. See *Chicago, B. & Q.R. Co. v. Chicago,* 166 U.S. 226, 241, 17 S.Ct. 581, 586, 41 L.Ed. 979, 986 (1897).

b. *Missouri Pac. Ry. Co. v. Nebraska,* 164 U.S. 403, 17 S.Ct. 130, 41 L.Ed. 489 (1896).

streets, utilities, recreational facilities and schools; and to lease or sell the remainder, preferably to a private redevelopment company, under terms that required the lessee or purchaser to conform to the redevelopment plan adopted by the National Capital Planning Commission. The Court found no fifth amendment violation in the Agency's taking by eminent domain a well-maintained department store posing no blight or health problem itself, located in a redevelopment area where roughly two-thirds of the dwellings were beyond repair or otherwise blighted:

"The power of Congress over the District of Columbia includes all the legislative powers which a state may exercise over its affairs. We deal, in other words, with what traditionally has been known as the police power. [Subject] to specific constitutional limitations, when the legislature has spoken, the public interest has been declared in terms well-nigh conclusive. In such cases the legislature, not the judiciary, is the main guardian of the public needs to be served by social legislation. [This] principle admits of no exception merely because the power of eminent domain is involved. The role of the judiciary in determining whether that power is being exercised for a public purpose is an extremely narrow one.

"Public safety, public health, morality, peace and quiet, law and order—these are some of the more conspicuous examples of the traditional application of the police power to municipal affairs. Yet they merely illustrate the scope of the power and do not delimit it. Miserable and disreputable housing conditions may do more than spread disease and crime and immorality. They may also suffocate the spirit * * *; make living an almost insufferable burden. They may [be] a blight on the community which robs it of charm, which makes it a place from which men turn. * * *

"We do not sit to determine whether a particular housing project is or is not desirable. The concept of the public welfare is broad and inclusive. The values it represents are spiritual as well as physical, aesthetic as well as monetary. It is within the power of the legislature to determine that the community should be beautiful as well as healthy, spacious as well as clean, well-balanced as well as carefully patrolled. In the present case, the Congress and its authorized agencies have made determinations that take into account a wide variety of values. It is not for us to reappraise them. If those who govern the District of Columbia decide that the Nation's Capital should be beautiful as well as sanitary, there is nothing in the Fifth Amendment that stands in the way.

"Once the object is within the authority of Congress, the right to realize it through the exercise of eminent domain is clear. For the power of eminent domain is merely the means to the end. [Here] one of the means chosen is the use of private enterprise for redevelopment of the area. Appellants argue that this makes the project a taking from one businessman for the benefit of another businessman. But the means of executing the project are for Congress and Congress alone to determine, once the public purpose has been established. The public end may be as well or better served through an agency of private enterprise than through a department of government—or so the Congress might conclude. We cannot say that public ownership is the sole method of promoting the public purposes of community redevelopment projects. * * *

"In the present case, Congress and its authorized agencies attack the problem of the blighted parts of the community on an area rather than on a structure-by-structure basis. That, too, is opposed by appellants. They maintain that since their building does not imperil health or safety nor contribute to the making of a slum or a blighted area, it cannot be swept into a redevelopment plan by the mere dictum of the Planning Commission or the Commissioners. The particular uses to be made of the land in the project were determined with regard to the needs of the particular community. The experts concluded that if the community were to be healthy, if it were not to revert again to a blighted or slum area, as though possessed of a congenital disease, the area must be planned as a whole. It was not enough, they believed, to remove existing buildings that were insanitary or unsightly. It was important to redesign the whole area so as to eliminate the conditions that cause slums—the overcrowding of dwellings, the lack of parks, the lack of adequate streets and alleys, the absence of recreational areas, the lack of light and air, the presence of outmoded street patterns. It was believed that the piecemeal approach, the removal of individual structures that were offensive, would be only a palliative. The entire area needed redesigning so that a balanced, integrated plan could be developed for the region, including not only new homes but also schools, churches, parks, streets, and shopping centers. [Such] diversification in future use is plainly relevant to the maintenance of the desired housing standards and therefore within congressional power."

Notes and Questions

1. *Historical development.* For a study of the rise and fall of limitations on the exercise of the power of eminent domain see Note, *The Public Use Limitation on Eminent Domain: An Advance Requiem,* 58 Yale L.J. 599 (1949). The Court found a "public use" or "public purpose" limitation on the taking of private property, even for compensation, in the fifth amendment and in the due process clause of the fourteenth amendment. Id.; Dunham, *Griggs v. Allegheny County in Perspective: Thirty Years of Supreme Court Expropriation Law,* 1962 Sup.Ct. Rev. 63, 65. Prior to 1946 the condemnation of private land normally was justified on one of two grounds: (1) "public use" of the property in the sense of actual subjection of the property to use by a segment of the public, or (2) the purchase of the land to eliminate a public evil and thus for a "public purpose." Id. at 66–67.

2. *"Taking" to lessen concentrated land ownership.* HAWAII HOUSING AUTHORITY v. MIDKIFF, 467 U.S. 229, 104 S.Ct. 2321, 81 L.Ed.2d 186 (1984), per O'CONNOR, J., upheld the use of eminent domain to lessen the concentration of fee simple land ownership, inherited from Hawaii's early feudal land tenure system. In the 1960's the Hawaii legislature found that 72 private owners owned 47% of Hawaiian land, and the state and federal government 49%, leaving only 4% for all other private owners. On Oahu, the most urbanized island, 22 landowners owned 72.5% of the fee simple titles. The legislature found, as summarized by the Court, that such concentrated land ownership was "responsible for skewing the State's residential fee simple market, inflating land prices, and injuring public tranquillity and welfare." The resulting Land Reform Act authorized "eligible tenants" from residential tracts of at least five acres to invoke the Hawaii Housing Authority's (HHA) power to acquire the fee owners "right, title and interest" at a "fair market value" set by negotiation between the lessee and the lessor or by condemnation trial, and then to sell that fee title interest to the tenant-lessee.[a]

a. An "eligible tenant" was one who "owns a house on the lot, has a bona fide intent to live on the lot or be a resident of the State, shows proof of ability to pay for a fee interest in it, and does not own residential land elsewhere nearby." The HHA was authorized to proceed under the Act only when 25 such eligible tenants from the tract, or those from

In upholding the Act over the challenge that such taking was not for a public use, the Court relied heavily on *Berman* from which it concluded, "The 'public use' requirement is thus coterminus with the scope of a sovereign's police powers. There is, of course, a role for courts to play in reviewing a legislature's judgment of what constitutes a public use, even when the eminent domain power is equated with the police power. But the Court in *Berman* made clear that it is 'an extremely narrow' one. [Where] the exercise of the eminent domain power is rationally related to a conceivable public purpose, the Court has never held a compensated taking to be proscribed by the Public Use Clause.

"On this basis, we have no trouble concluding that the Hawaii Act is constitutional. The people of Hawaii have attempted, much as the settlers of the original 13 Colonies did, to reduce the perceived social and economic evils of a land oligopoly traceable to their monarchs. The land oligopoly has, according to the Hawaii Legislature, created artificial deterrents to the normal functioning of the State's residential land market and forced thousands of individual homeowners to lease, rather than buy, the land underneath their homes. Regulating oligopoly and the evils associated with it is a classic exercise of a State's police powers. We cannot disapprove of Hawaii's exercise of this power.

"Nor can we condemn as irrational the Act's approach to correcting the land oligopoly problem. The Act presumes that when a sufficiently large number of persons declare that they are willing but unable to buy lots at fair prices the land market is malfunctioning. When such a malfunction is signalled, the Act authorizes HHA to condemn lots in the relevant tract.

"[When] the legislature's purpose is legitimate and its means are not irrational, our cases make clear that empirical debates over the wisdom of takings—no less than debates over the wisdom of other kinds of socioeconomic legislation—are not to be carried out in the federal courts. Redistribution of fees simple to correct deficiencies in the market determined by the state legislature to be attributable to land oligopoly is a rational exercise of the eminent domain power. Therefore, the Hawaii statute must pass the scrutiny of the Public Use Clause:" [b]

II. "TAKING" THROUGH REGULATION

PENN CENTRAL TRANSP. CO. v. NEW YORK CITY

438 U.S. 104, 98 S.Ct. 2646, 57 L.Ed.2d 631 (1978).

JUSTICE BRENNAN delivered the opinion of the Court.

[Pursuant to New York City's Landmarks Preservation Law, the Preservation Commission designated Grand Central Terminal, owned by Penn Central, as a "landmark." It denied Penn Central a certificate of "appropriateness" to construct a 55 story office building resting on the roof of the Terminal, cantilevered to preserve the existing Terminal facade. The Commission emphasized the harmful effect of the proposed construction on the dramatic view of the Terminal from Park Avenue South.[a] Choosing not to modify its proposal, or to use its right under New York laws to transfer its unused landmark site

half the lots in the tract, whichever is less, filed applications with HHA for the remedy provided by the Act.

b. Marshall, J., did not participate.

a. "[To] balance a 55-story office tower above a flamboyant Beaux-Arts facade seems nothing more than an aesthetic joke. Quite simply, the tower would overwhelm the Terminal by its sheer mass. The 'addition' would be four times as high as the existing structure and would reduce the Landmark itself to the status of a curiosity."

development rights to one or more of its eight nearby lots, Penn Central unsuccessfully challenged in the New York courts the constitutionality of this application of the Landmarks Law. The Court upheld the Law as applied.]

[The issue is] whether the restrictions [upon] appellants' exploitation of the Terminal site effect a "taking" of appellants' property for a public use within the meaning of the Fifth Amendment, [made] applicable to the States through the Fourteenth.[25]

A. [W]hat constitutes a "taking" for purposes of the Fifth Amendment has proved to be a problem of considerable difficulty. While this Court has recognized that the "Fifth Amendment's guarantee [is] designed to bar Government from forcing some people alone to bear public burdens which, in all fairness and justice, should be borne by the public as a whole," *Armstrong v. United States,*[b] this Court, quite simply, has been unable to develop any "set formula" for determining when "justice and fairness" require that economic injuries caused by public action be compensated by the government, rather than remain disproportionately concentrated on a few persons. See *Goldblatt v. Hempstead,* 369 U.S. 590, 594, 82 S.Ct. 987, 8 L.Ed.2d 130 (1962). Indeed, we have frequently observed that whether a particular restriction will be rendered invalid by the government's failure to pay for any losses proximately caused by it depends largely "upon the particular circumstances [in that] case." *United States v. Central Eureka Mining Co.,* 357 U.S. 155, 168, 78 S.Ct. 1097, 2 L.Ed.2d 1228 (1958), see *United States v. Caltex, Inc.,* 344 U.S. 149, 156, 73 S.Ct. 200, 97 L.Ed. 157 (1952).

In engaging in these essentially ad hoc, factual inquiries, the Court's decisions have identified several factors that have particular significance. The economic impact of the regulation on the claimant and, particularly, the extent to which the regulation has interfered with distinct investment-backed expectations are, of course, relevant considerations. See *Goldblatt.* So, too, is the character of the governmental action. A "taking" may more readily be found when the interference with property can be characterized as a physical invasion by government, see, e.g., *United States v. Causby,* 328 U.S. 256, 66 S.Ct. 1062, 90 L.Ed. 1206 (1946), than when interference arises from some public program adjusting the benefits and burdens of economic life to promote the common good.

"Government hardly could go on if to some extent values incident to property could not be diminished without paying for every such change in the general law," *Pennsylvania Coal Co. v. Mahon,* 260 U.S. 393, 413, 43 S.Ct. 158, 67 L.Ed. 322 (1922), and this Court has accordingly recognized, in a wide variety of contexts, that government may execute laws or programs that adversely affect recognized economic values. * * *

[I]n instances in which a state tribunal reasonably concluded that "the health, safety, morals, or general welfare" would be promoted by prohibiting particular contemplated uses of land, this Court has upheld land-use regulations that destroyed or adversely affected recognized real property interests. See *Nectow v. Cambridge,* 277 U.S. 183, 188, 48 S.Ct. 447, 72 L.Ed. 842 (1928). Zoning laws are, of course, the classic example, see *Euclid v. Ambler Realty Co.,* 272 U.S. 365, 47 S.Ct. 114, 71 L.Ed. 303 (1926) (prohibition of industrial use);

25. As is implicit in our opinion, we do not embrace the proposition that a "taking" can never occur unless government has transferred physical control over a portion of a parcel.

b. 364 U.S. 40, 49, 80 S.Ct. 1563, 4 L.Ed.2d 1554 (1960). *Armstrong* found a "taking" in the destruction of a materialman's lien when, on default of the builder, the government took possession of boats he was building for the United States.

Gorieb v. Fox, 274 U.S. 603, 608, 47 S.Ct. 675, 71 L.Ed. 1228 (1927) (requirement that portions of parcels be left unbuilt); *Welch v. Swasey,* 214 U.S. 91, 29 S.Ct. 567, 53 L.Ed. 923 (1909) (height restriction), which have been viewed as permissible governmental action even when prohibiting the most beneficial use of the property. See *Goldblatt.*

Zoning laws generally do not affect existing uses of real property, but "taking" challenges have also been held to be without merit in a wide variety of situations when the challenged governmental actions prohibited a beneficial use to which individual parcels had previously been devoted and thus caused substantial individualized harm. *Miller v. Schoene,* 276 U.S. 272, 48 S.Ct. 246, 72 L.Ed. 568 (1928), is illustrative. In that case, a state entomologist, acting pursuant to a state statute, ordered the claimants to cut down a large number of ornamental red cedar trees because they produced cedar rust fatal to apple trees cultivated nearby. Although the statute provided for recovery of any expense incurred in removing the cedars, and permitted claimants to use the felled trees, it did not provide compensation for the value of the standing trees or for the resulting decrease in market value of the properties as a whole. A unanimous Court held that this latter omission did not render the statute invalid. The Court held that the State might properly make "a choice between the preservation of one class of property and that of the other" and since the apple industry was important in the State involved, concluded that the State had not exceeded "its constitutional powers by deciding upon the destruction of one class of property [without compensation] in order to save another which, in the judgment of the legislature, is of greater value to the public."

Again, *Hadacheck v. Sebastian,* 239 U.S. 394, 36 S.Ct. 143, 60 L.Ed. 348 (1915), upheld a law prohibiting the claimant from continuing his otherwise lawful business of operating a brickyard in a particular physical community on the ground that the legislature had reasonably concluded that the presence of the brickyard was inconsistent with neighboring uses. * * *

Goldblatt is a recent example. There, a 1958 city safety ordinance banned any excavations below the water table and effectively prohibited the claimant from continuing a sand and gravel mining business that had been operated on the particular parcel since 1927. The Court upheld the ordinance against a "taking" challenge, although the ordinance prohibited the present and presumably most beneficial use of the property and had, like the regulations in *Miller* and *Hadacheck,* severely affected a particular owner. The Court assumed that the ordinance did not prevent the owner's reasonable use of the property since the owner made no showing of an adverse effect on the value of the land. Because the restriction served a substantial public purpose, the Court thus held no taking had occurred. It is, of course, implicit in *Goldblatt* that a use restriction on real property may constitute a "taking" if not reasonably necessary to the effectuation of a substantial public purpose, see *Nectow;* or perhaps if it has an unduly harsh impact upon the owner's use of the property.

Pennsylvania Coal is the leading case for the proposition that a state statute that substantially furthers important public policies may so frustrate distinct investment-backed expectations as to amount to a "taking." There the claimant had sold the surface rights to particular parcels of property, but expressly reserved the right to remove the coal thereunder. A Pennsylvania statute, enacted after the transactions, forbade any mining of coal that caused the subsidence of any house, unless the house was the property of the owner of the underlying coal and was more than 150 feet from the improved property of another. Because the statute made it commercially impracticable to mine the coal, and thus had nearly the same effect as the complete destruction of rights claimant had reserved from the owners of the surface land, the Court held that the statute was invalid as effecting a "taking" without just compensation. [See] generally Michelman, *Property, Utility, and Fairness: Comments on the Ethical Foundations of "Just Compensation" Law,* 80 Harv.L.Rev. 1165, 1229–1234 (1967).

Finally, government actions that may be characterized as acquisitions of resources to permit or facilitate uniquely public functions have often been held to constitute "takings." *Causby* is illustrative. In holding that direct overflights above the claimant's land, that destroyed the present use of the land as a chicken farm, constituted a "taking," *Causby* emphasized that Government had not "merely destroyed property [but was] using a part of it for the flight of its planes." See [also] *United States v. Cress,* 243 U.S. 316, 37 S.Ct. 380, 61 L.Ed. 746 (1917) (repeated floodings of land caused by water project is taking). See generally Michelman, [supra at 1226–1229]; Sax, *Takings and the Police Power,* 74 Yale L.J. 36 (1964).

B. [A]ppellants do not contest that New York City's objective of preserving structures and areas with special historic, architectural, or cultural significance is an entirely permissible governmental goal. [They] do not challenge any of the specific factual premises of the decision below. They accept for present purposes both that the parcel of land occupied by Grand Central Terminal must, in its present state, be regarded as capable of earning a reasonable return, and that the transferable development rights afforded appellants by virtue of the Terminal's designation as a landmark are valuable, even if not as valuable as the rights to construct above the Terminal. In appellants' view none of these factors derogate from their claim that New York City's law has effected a "taking."

[First, they] urge that the Landmarks Law has deprived them of any gainful use of their "air rights" above the Terminal, [entitling] them to "just compensation" measured by the fair market value of these air rights.

[T]he submission that appellants may establish a "taking" simply by showing that they have been denied the ability to exploit a property interest that they heretofore had believed was available for development is quite simply untenable. Were this the rule, this Court would have erred not only in upholding laws restricting the development of air rights, see *Welch,* but also in approving those prohibiting both the subjacent, see *Goldblatt,* and the lateral, see *Gorieb,* development of particular parcels. "Taking" jurisprudence does not divide a single parcel into discrete segments and attempt to determine whether rights in a particular segment have been entirely abrogated. In deciding whether a particular governmental action has effected a taking, this Court focuses rather both on the character of the action and on the nature and extent of the interference with rights in the parcel as a whole—here, the city tax block designated as the "landmark site."

Secondly, appellants [argue that the New York law] effects a "taking" because its operation has significantly diminished the value of the Terminal site. Appellants concede that the decisions sustaining other land use-regulations, which, like the New York City law, are reasonably related to the promotion of the general welfare, uniformly reject the proposition that diminution in property value, standing alone, can establish a "taking," see *Euclid* (75% diminution in value caused by zoning law); *Hadacheck* ($87^1/_2$% diminution in value). [But] appellants argue that New York City's regulation of individual landmarks is fundamentally different from zoning or from historic-district legislation because the controls imposed by New York City's law apply only to individuals who own selected properties.

Stated baldly, appellants' position appears to be that the only means of ensuring that selected owners are not singled out to endure financial hardship for no reason is to hold that any restriction imposed on individual landmarks pursuant to the New York City scheme is a "taking" requiring the payment of "just compensation." [It] is true [that] both historic-district legislation and zoning laws regulate all properties within given physical communities whereas landmark laws apply only to selected parcels. But, contrary to appellants' suggestions, landmark laws are not like discriminatory, or "reverse spot," zoning: that is, a land-use decision which arbitrarily singles out a particular parcel for different, less favorable treatment than the neighboring ones. See 2 Rathkopf, *The Law of Zoning and Planning* 26–4 and 26–4–26–5, n. 6 (4th ed. 1978). In contrast to discriminatory zoning, which is the antithesis of land-use control as part of some comprehensive plan, the New York City law embodies a comprehensive plan to preserve structures of historic or aesthetic interest wherever they might be found in the [city].

Next, appellants observe that New York City's law differs from zoning laws and historic-district ordinances in that the Landmarks Law does not impose identical or similar restrictions on all structures located in particular physical communities. It follows, they argue, that New York City's law is inherently incapable of producing the fair and equitable distribution of benefits and burdens of governmental action which is characteristic of zoning laws and historic-district [legislation]. It is, of course, true that the Landmarks Law has a more severe impact on some landowners than on others, but that in itself does not mean that the law effects a "taking." Legislation designed to promote the general welfare commonly burdens some more than others. The owners of the brickyard in *Hadacheck,* of the cedar trees in *Miller,* and of the gravel and sand mine in *Goldblatt,* were uniquely burdened by the legislation sustained in those cases.[30] Similarly, zoning laws often affect some property owners more severely than others but have not been held to be invalid on that account. * * *

[T]he New York City law applies to vast numbers of structures in the city in addition to the Terminal—all the structures contained in the 31 historic districts and over 400 individual landmarks, many of which are close to the Terminal. Unless we are to reject the judgment of the New York City Council that the preservation of landmarks benefits all New York citizens and all structures, both economically and by improving the quality of life in the city as a whole—which we are unwilling to do—we cannot conclude that the owners of the Terminal have in no sense been benefited by the Landmarks Law. Doubtless appellants believe they are more burdened than benefited by the law, but that must have

30. Appellants attempt to distinguish these cases on the ground that, in each, government was prohibiting a "noxious" use of land and that in the present case, in contrast, appellants' proposed construction above the Terminal would be beneficial. We observe that the uses in issue in *Hadacheck, Miller,* and *Goldblatt* were perfectly lawful in themselves. They involve no "blameworthiness, [moral] wrongdoing or conscious act of dangerous risk-taking which induce[d society] to shift the cost to a pa[rt]icular individual." Sax, *Takings and the Police Power,* 74 Yale L.J. 36, 50 (1964). These cases are better understood as resting not on any supposed "noxious" quality of the prohibited uses but rather on the ground that the restrictions were reasonably related to the implementation of a policy—not unlike historic preservation—expected to produce a widespread public benefit and applicable to all similarly situated property.

been true, too, of the property owners in *Miller, Hadacheck, Euclid,* and *Goldblatt.* * * *

C. [A]ll we thus far have established is that the [law] is not rendered invalid by its failure to provide "just compensation" whenever a landmark owner is restricted in the exploitation of property [interests], to a greater extent than provided for under applicable zoning laws. We now must consider whether the interference with appellants' property is of such a magnitude that "there must be an exercise of eminent domain and compensation to sustain [it]." *Pennsylvania Coal.* That inquiry may be narrowed to the question of the severity of the impact of the law on appellants' parcel, and its resolution in turn requires a careful assessment of the impact of the regulation on the Terminal site.

Unlike the governmental acts in *Goldblatt, Miller, Causby, Griggs,* and *Hadacheck,* the [law] does not interfere in any way with the present uses of the Terminal. Its designation as a landmark not only permits but contemplates that appellants may continue to use the property precisely as it has been used for the past 65 years: as a railroad terminal containing office space and concessions. So the law does not interfere with what must be regarded as Penn Central's primary expectation concerning the use of the parcel. More importantly, on this record, we must regard the [law] as permitting Penn Central not only to profit from the Terminal but also to obtain a "reasonable return" on its investment.

Appellants, moreover, exaggerate the effect of the law on their ability to make use of the air rights above the Terminal in two respects. First, it simply cannot be maintained, on this record, that appellants have been prohibited from occupying *any* portion of the airspace above the Terminal. [Nothing] the Commission has said or done suggests an intention to prohibit *any* construction above the Terminal. The Commission's report emphasized that whether any construction would be allowed depended upon whether the proposed addition "would harmonize in scale, material and character with [the Terminal]." Since appellants have not sought approval for the construction of a smaller structure, we do not know that appellants will be denied any use of any portion of the airspace above the Terminal.[34]

Second, to the extent appellants have been denied the right to build above the Terminal, it is not literally accurate to say that they have been denied *all* use of even those pre-existing air rights. Their ability to use these rights has not been abrogated; they are made transferable to at least eight parcels in the vicinity of the Terminal, one or two of which have been found suitable for the construction of new office buildings. Although appellants and others have argued that New York City's transferable development-rights program is far from ideal, the New York courts here supportably found that, at least in the case of the Terminal, the rights afforded are valuable. While these rights may well not have constituted "just compensation" if a "taking" had occurred, the rights nevertheless undoubtedly mitigate whatever financial burdens the law has imposed on appellants and, for that reason, are to be taken into account in considering the impact of regulation.

On this record we conclude that the application of New York City's [law] has not effected a "taking" of appellants' property. The restrictions imposed are substantially related to the promotion of the general welfare and not only permit

34. Counsel for appellants admitted at oral argument that the Commission has not suggested that it would not, for example, approve a 20-story office tower along the lines of that which was part of the original plan for the Terminal.

reasonable beneficial use of the landmark site but afford appellants opportunities further to enhance not only the Terminal site proper but also other properties.[36] * * *

JUSTICE REHNQUIST, with whom The Chief Justice and Mr. Justice Stevens join, dissenting.

[The] question in this case is whether the cost associated with the city of New York's desire to preserve a limited number of "landmarks" within its borders must be borne by all of its taxpayers or whether it can instead be imposed entirely on the owners of the individual properties.

[While] neighboring landowners are free to use their land and "air rights" in any way consistent with the broad boundaries of New York zoning, Penn Central, absent the permission of appellees, must forever maintain its property in its present state. The property has been thus subjected to a nonconsensual servitude not borne by any neighboring or similar properties.

Appellees have thus destroyed—in a literal sense, "taken"—substantial property rights of Penn Central. While the term "taken" might have been narrowly interpreted to include only physical seizures of property rights, "the construction of the phrase has not been so narrow. The courts have held that the deprivation of the former owner rather than the accretion of a right or interest to the sovereign constitutes the taking." *United States v. General Motors Corp.*, 323 U.S. 373, 378, 65 S.Ct. 357, 89 L.Ed. 311 (1945). [An] examination of the two exceptions where the destruction of property does *not* constitute a taking demonstrates that a compensable taking has occurred here.

1. As early as 1887, the Court recognized that the government can prevent a property owner from using his property to injure others without having to compensate the owner for the value of the forbidden use. *Mugler v. Kansas,* 123 U.S. 623, 8 S.Ct. 273, 31 L.Ed. 205 (1887). [Thus], there is no "taking" where a city prohibits the operation of a brickyard within a residential city, see *Hadacheck,* or forbids excavation for sand and gravel below the water line, see *Goldblatt.* Nor is it relevant, where the government is merely prohibiting a noxious use of property, that the government would seem to be singling out a particular property owner. *Hadacheck.*[8] * * * Appellees are not prohibiting a nuisance. [Instead], Penn Central is prevented from further developing its property basically because *too good* a job was done in designing and building [it].

2. Even where the government prohibits a noninjurious use, the Court has ruled that a taking does not take place if the prohibition applies over a broad cross section of land and thereby "secure[s] an average reciprocity of advantage." *Pennsylvania Coal.* It is for this reason that zoning does not constitute a "taking." While zoning at times reduces *individual* property values, the burden is shared relatively evenly and it is reasonable to conclude that on the whole an individual who is harmed by one aspect of the zoning will be benefited by another.

36. We emphasize that our holding today is on the present record which in turn is based on Penn Central's present ability to use the Terminal for its intended purposes and in a gainful fashion. The city conceded at oral argument that if appellants can demonstrate at some point in the future that circumstances have changed such that the Terminal ceases to be, in the city's counsel's words, "economically viable," appellants may obtain relief.

8. Each of the cases cited by the Court for the proposition that legislation which severely affects some landowners but not others does not effect a "taking" involved noxious uses of property. See *Hadacheck; Miller; Goldblatt.*

Here, however, a multimillion dollar loss has been imposed on appellants; it is uniquely felt and is not offset by any benefits flowing from the preservation of some 400 other "landmarks" in New York City. Appellees have imposed a substantial cost on less than one one-tenth of one percent of the buildings in New York City for the general benefit of all its people. It is exactly this imposition of general costs on a few individuals at which the "taking" protection is [directed.] *Armstrong.*

[The] benefits that appellees believe will flow from preservation of the Grand Central Terminal will accrue to all the citizens of New York City. There is no reason to believe that appellants will enjoy a substantially greater share of these benefits. If the cost of preserving Grand Central Terminal were spread evenly across the entire population of the city of New York, the burden per person would be in cents per year—a minor cost appellees would surely concede for the benefit accrued. Instead, however, appellees would impose the entire cost of several million dollars per year on Penn Central. But it is precisely this sort of discrimination that the Fifth Amendment prohibits.

[A] taking does not become a noncompensable exercise of police power simply because the government in its grace allows the owner to make some "reasonable" use of his property. "[I]t is the character of the invasion, not the amount of damage resulting from it, so long as the damage is substantial, that determines the question whether it is a taking." *Cress,*[c] 243 U.S. 316, 328, 37 S.Ct. 380, 61 L.Ed. 746 (1917). *Causby.* * * *[d]

Notes and Questions

1. *Balancing judgments?* (a) Earlier decisions led thoughtful commentators to conclude that in determining whether a regulation constituted a "taking" the "extent of the diminution of the owner's rights must be weighed against the importance of that diminution to the public,"[a] and that "[c]ourts have never been able to develop [a] standard more meaningful than balancing the public need against the private cost."[b] For a helpful critique of such a balancing approach, see Michelman, supra, 80 Harv.L.Rev. at 1193–96, 1234–35.

(b) Is such balancing consistent with *Penn Central?* Did *Penn Central* "demonstrat[e] a method by which competing social and individual interests might be weighed"? Did it "balance public necessity and legitimacy of the regulation against the degree of physical invasion and economic harm"? See Note, 11 Conn.L.Rev. 273, 290 (1979). Or did *Penn Central* reflect "a belief that given the validity of the governmental interest asserted, the nature of the interest plays no further role in determining whether a taking has occurred," and that "[a]ny nondiscriminatory enactment reasonably related to a goal within the police power will be subjected only to a test of economic impact"? See 92 Harv.L.Rev. at 229.

c. Compensation required for damage to property when a federal dam raised water level in tributary stream, causing frequent overflows in one case and loss of water power for mill in the other.

d. On the "taking" issue, see generally—in addition to articles cited in *Penn Central*—Kratovil & Harrison, *Eminent Domain—Policy and Concept,* 42 Calif.L.Rev. 596 (1954); Dunham, *Griggs v. Allegheny County in Perspective: Thirty Years of Supreme Court Expropriation Law,* 1962 Sup.Ct.Rev. 63; Sax, *Takings, Private Property and Public Right,* 81 Yale L.J. 149 (1971); Note, *Zoning,* 91 Harv.L.Rev. 1427, 1462–86 (1978); 92 Harv.L.Rev. 222–32 (1977). For later scholarly commentaries on taking issues, kindled by the more recent takings decisions, see note 3 following *Nollan v. Calif. Coastal Com'n,* infra.

a. Kratovil & Harrison, fn. d supra, at 609.

b. Dunham, fn. d supra, at 76.

(c) What *ought* the standard to be? *Should* the extent of economic harm that can be imposed without compensation depend on the degree of importance of an admittedly valid governmental interest?

2. *Economic impact on claimant.* What factors appear relevant to deciding whether the "economic impact of the regulation on the claimant" suffices to support a judgment of "taking?" Does *Penn Central* mean that, absent the use of private property for "uniquely public functions," an economic impact will not suffice if the regulation permits continuation of the property's pre-regulation uses and a "reasonable return" on the investment? What kinds of problems are likely to arise from basing such decisions on factors like "reasonable return on investment, "investment-backed expectations," and "primary expectation concerning use?" Cf. 92 Harv.L.Rev. at 231.

3. *The "bundle of rights."* (a) The Eagle Protection Act [16 USCA § 668(a)] forbad the taking, sale, possession or transportation of bald or golden eagles, or parts thereof, except for possession or transportation of eagles or parts obtained prior to the Act. ANDRUS v. ALLARD, 444 U.S. 51, 100 S.Ct. 318, 62 L.Ed.2d 210 (1979), per BRENNAN, J., unanimously ruled application of the ban to sales of commercially traded Indian artifacts containing eagle parts taken before the Act did not violate the taking clause: [a]

"[Where] an owner possesses a full 'bundle' of property rights, the destruction of one 'strand' of the bundle is not a taking, because the aggregate must be viewed in its entirety. Compare *Penn Central.* [In] this case, it is crucial that appellees retain the rights to possess and transport their property, and to donate or devise the protected birds.

"[In] the instant case, it is not clear that appellees will be unable to derive economic benefit from the artifacts; for example, they might exhibit the artifacts for an admissions charge. At any rate, loss of future profits—unaccompanied by any physical property restriction—provides a slender reed upon which to rest a takings claim. Prediction of profitability is essentially a matter of reasoned speculation that courts are not especially competent to perform."

(b) Might the contraband nature of eagle parts in 1979 have influenced the result? Consider the Court's closing comment: "Regulations that bar trade in certain goods have been upheld against" taking claims, citing the decisions ruling that the prohibition-day ban was not a taking when applied to the sale of pre-prohibition liquor.[c]

4. *Permanent physical occupation.* LORETTO v. TELEPROMPTER MANHATTAN CATV CORP., 458 U.S. 419, 102 S.Ct. 3164, 73 L.Ed.2d 868 (1982), per MARSHALL, J., found a "taking" in a New York law that, as applied, authorized cable TV installations for tenants of privately-owned apartment houses. The cables, permanently attached to the roofs and outside walls by bolts, screws and other means, were subject to a one-time $1 payment to the landlord:

"When faced with a constitutional challenge to a permanent physical occupation of real property, this Court has invariably found a taking.[5] [To] the

a. Burger, C.J., concurred only in the judgment.

c. See *Jacob Ruppert, Inc. v. Caffey,* 251 U.S. 264, 40 S.Ct. 141, 64 L.Ed. 260 (1920); *James Everard's Breweries v. Day,* 265 U.S. 545, 44 S.Ct. 628, 68 L.Ed. 1174 (1924).

5. Professor Michelman has accurately summarized the case [law]: "[The] modern significance of physical occupation is that courts, while they sometimes do hold nontrespassory injuries compensable, *never* deny compensation for a physical takeover. The one incontestable case for compensation (short of formal expropriation) seems to occur when the government [or] the public at large, 'regularly' use, or 'permanently' occupy, space or a thing [theretofore] under private ownership."

extent that the government permanently occupies physical property it effectively destroys" the rights to possess, use and dispose of it. "The owner has no right to possess the occupied space himself [or] to exclude the occupier." It "denies the owner any power to control the use of the property [or] to dispose of [it] by sale, [since] the purchaser will be unable to make any use of" it.

"Our holding today is very narrow. We affirm the traditional rule that a permanent physical occupation of property is a taking. In such a case, the property owner entertains an historically-rooted expectation of compensation, and the character of the invasion is qualitatively more intrusive than perhaps any other category of property regulation. We do not, however, question the equally substantial authority upholding a State's broad power to impose appropriate restrictions upon an owner's *use* of his property."

BLACKMUN, J., joined by Brennan and White, JJ., dissented: "Modern government regulation exudes intangible 'externalities' that may diminish the value of private property far more than minor physical touchings. ["Precisely] because the extent to which the government may injure private interests now depends so little on whether or not it has authorized a 'physical contact,' the Court has avoided per se takings rules resting on outmoded distinctions between physical and nonphysical intrusions. As one commentator has observed, a takings rule based on such a distinction is inherently suspect because 'its capacity to distinguish, even crudely, between significant and insignificant losses is too puny to be taken seriously.' Michelman, [supra. 80 Harv.L.Rev. at 1227].

"In sum, history, teaches that takings claims are properly evaluated under a multifactor balancing test. By directing that all 'permanent physical occupations' automatically are compensable, 'without regard to whether the action achieves an important public benefit or has only minimal economic impact on the owner,' the Court does not further equity so much as it encourages litigants to manipulate their factual allegations to gain the benefit of its per se rule. I do not relish the prospect of distinguishing the inevitable flow of certiorari petitions attempting to shoehorn insubstantial takings claims into today's 'set formula.' "

5. *Regulating harmful activities: Pennsylvania Mining revisited.* KEYSTONE BITUMINOUS COAL ASS'N v. DeBENEDICTIS, 480 U.S. 470, 107 S.Ct. 1232, 94 L.Ed.2d 472 (1987), per STEVENS, J., upheld 5 to 4 Pennsylvania's Subsidence Act (§ 4) that forbade mining bituminous coal "so as to cause damage as a result of the caving in, collapse or subsidence of" public buildings, human dwellings, cemeteries, perennial streams, impoundments of water, aquifers supplying public water systems, and coal refuse disposal areas, unless the current owner of the structure consents and the resulting damage is fully repaired or compensated. Applying the Act, Pennsylvania required 50% of the coal under protected structures to be kept in place. The Court affirmed denial of an injunction against enforcing the Act:

"Unlike the Kohler Act [in] *Pennsylvania Coal,* the Subsidence Act does not merely involve a balancing of the private economic interests of coal companies against the private interests of the surface owners. The Pennsylvania Legislature specifically found that important public interests are served [by] 'providing for the conservation of surface land areas which may be affected in the mining of bituminous [coal], to aid in the protection of the safety of the public, to enhance

Michelman, *Property, Utility, and Fairness: Comments on the Ethical Foundations of "Just Compensation" Law,* 80 Harv.L.Rev. 1165, 1184 (1967) (emphasis original). See also L. Sackman, *Nichols' Law of Eminent Domain* 6–50, 6–51 (rev. 3d ed. 1980); Tribe, *American Constitutional Law* 460 (1978).

the value of such lands for taxation, to aid in the preservation of surface water drainage and public water supplies and generally to improve the use and enjoyment of such [lands].'

"[With] regard to the Kohler Act, the Court believed that the Commonwealth had acted only to ensure against damage to some private landowners' homes. Justice Holmes stated that if the private individuals needed support for their structures, they should not have 'take[n] the risk of acquiring only surface rights.' [d] Here, by contrast, the Commonwealth is acting to protect the public interest in health, the environment, and the fiscal integrity of the area. That private individuals erred in taking a risk cannot estop the State from exercising its police power to abate activity akin to a public [nuisance].

"[The] public interest in preventing activities similar to public nuisances is a substantial one, which in many instances has not required compensation. The Subsidence Act, unlike the Kohler Act, plainly seeks to further such an interest. Nonetheless, we need not rest our decision on this factor alone, because petitioners have also failed to make a showing of diminution of value sufficient to satisfy the test set forth in *Pennsylvania Coal* and our other regulatory takings cases.

"Diminution of Value and Investment–Backed Expectations

"The second factor that distinguishes this case from *Pennsylvania Coal* is the finding in that case that the Kohler Act made mining of 'certain coal' commercially impracticable. In this case, by contrast, petitioners have not shown any deprivation significant enough to satisfy the heavy burden placed upon one alleging a regulatory taking. For this reason, their takings claim must fail.

"[The] test to be applied in considering this facial challenge [to the Subsidence Act] is fairly straightforward. A statute regulating the uses that can be made of property effects a taking if it 'denies an owner economically viable use of his land * * *.' Petitioners thus face an uphill battle in making a facial attack on the Act as a taking.

"The hill is made especially steep because petitioners have not claimed, at this stage, that the Act makes it commercially impracticable for them to continue mining their bituminous coal interests in western Pennsylvania. Indeed, petitioners have not even pointed to a single mine that can no longer be mined for profit. The only evidence available on the effect that the Subsidence Act has had on petitioners' mining operations comes from petitioners' answers to respondents' interrogatories. [The] total coal in [petitioners'] 13 mines amounts to over 1.46 billion tons. [Section] 4 requires them to leave less than 2% of their coal in place. But, as we have indicated, nowhere near all of the underground coal is extractable even aside from the Subsidence Act. The categories of coal that must be left for § 4 purposes and other purposes are not necessarily distinct sets, and there is no information in the record as to how much coal is actually left in the ground *solely* because of § 4. We do know, however, that petitioners have never claimed that their mining operations, or even any specific mines, have been unprofitable since the Subsidence Act was passed. Nor is there evidence that mining in any specific location affected by the 50% rule has been unprofitable. * * *

"The parties have stipulated that enforcement of [the] 50% rule will require petitioners to leave approximately 27 million tons of coal in place. Because they

d. As in *Kohler,* the surface owners in *Keystone* had acquired only surface rights and had waived any claims for damages caused by removal of the coal.

own that coal but cannot mine it, they contend that Pennsylvania has appropriated it for the public purposes described in the Subsidence Act.

"This argument fails for the reason explained in *Penn Central* and *Andrus.* The 27 million tons of coal do not constitute a separate segment of property for takings law purposes. [When] the coal that must remain beneath the ground is viewed in the context of any reasonable unit of petitioners' coal mining operations and financial-backed expectations, it is plain that the petitioners have not come close to satisfying their burden of proving that they have been denied the economically viable use of that property. The record indicates that only about 75% of petitioners' underground coal can be profitably mined in any event, and there is no showing that petitioners' reasonable 'investment-backed expectations' have been materially affected by the additional duty to retain the small percentage that must be used to support the structures protected by § 4." [e]

REHNQUIST, C.J., dissented, joined by Powell, O'Connor, and Scalia, JJ. The dissent asserted that the "nuisance exception" to the taking clause was a "narrow exception" to prevent a "misuse or illegal use," and was not applicable to a "legal and essential use, an attribute [of] ownership:"

"[The] Subsidence Act [is] much more than a nuisance statute. The central purposes of the Act, though including public safety, reflect a concern for preservation of buildings, economic development, and maintenance of property values to sustain the Commonwealth's tax base. We should hesitate to allow a regulation based on essentially economic concerns to be insulated from the dictates of the Fifth Amendment by labeling it nuisance regulation.

"[More] significantly, our cases have never applied the nuisance exception to allow complete extinction of the value of a parcel of property. Though nuisance regulations have been sustained despite a substantial reduction in value, we have not accepted the proposition that the State may completely extinguish a property interest or prohibit all use without providing [compensation.]

"[The] Court's refusal to recognize the coal in the ground as a separate segment of property for takings purposes is based on the fact that the alleged taking is 'regulatory,' rather than a physical intrusion. On the facts of this case, I cannot see how the label placed on the government's action is relevant to consideration of its impact on property rights."

6. *Conditioning a building permit on beachfront easement.* (a) NOLLAN v. CALIFORNIA COASTAL COM'N, 483 U.S. 825, 107 S.Ct. 3141, 97 L.Ed.2d 677 (1987), per SCALIA, J., held invalid as an uncompensated taking the Commission's condition that to secure a permit to replace their small beachfront cottage with a house nearly five times larger, the Nollans must grant a public easement to pass laterally across the eight foot strip of beach between their sea wall and the mean high tide line. After regulations authorized such conditions, similar easements had been required of all shorefront developments on the same tract. The Commission found that "a wall of residential structures" would "burden" public use of the nearby shorefront by preventing the public from "realizing that a coastline exists nearby they have every right to visit" to which the public had access from two public beaches one-fourth mile south and one-third mile north of Nollan's property:

e. The Court [rejected] the contention that the Subsidence Act violated the contract clause by not allowing the owners of the mining interest to hold the surface owners to their contractual waiver of liability for surface damage. The Court invoked the "strong public interest in preventing this type of harm, the environmental effect of which transcends any private agreement between private parties." See Section 5, infra.

"Had California simply required the Nollans to make an easement across their beachfront available to the public on a permanent basis in order to increase public access to the beach, rather than conditioning their permit to rebuild their house on their agreeing to do so, we have no doubt there would have been a taking. [Given that] requiring uncompensated conveyance of the easement outright would violate the Fourteenth Amendment, the question becomes whether requiring it to be conveyed as a condition for issuing a land use permit alters the outcome. We have long recognized that land use regulation does not effect a taking if it 'substantially advance[s] legitimate state interests' and does not 'den[y] an owner economically viable use of his land.'[3] [The] Commission argues that among these permissible purposes are protecting the public's ability to see the beach, assisting the public in overcoming the "psychological barrier" to using the beach created by a developed shorefront, and preventing congestion on the public beaches. We assume, without deciding, that this is so—in which case the Commission unquestionably would be able to deny the Nollans their permit outright if their new house (alone, or by reason of the cumulative impact produced in conjunction with other construction) would substantially impede these purposes, unless the denial would interfere so drastically with the Nollans' use of their property as to constitute a taking. See *Penn Central.*

"The Commission argues that a permit condition that serves the same legitimate police-power purpose as a refusal to issue the permit should not be found to be a taking if the refusal to issue the permit would not constitute a taking. We agree. Thus, if the Commission attached to the permit some condition that would have protected the public's ability to see the beach notwithstanding construction of the new house—for example, a height limitation, a width restriction, or a ban on fences—so long as the Commission could have exercised its police power (as we have assumed it could) to forbid construction of the house altogether, imposition of the condition would also be constitutional. Moreover (and here we come closer to the facts of the present case), the condition would be constitutional even if it consisted of the requirement that the Nollans provide a viewing spot on their property for passersby with whose sighting of the ocean their new house would interfere. Although such a requirement, constituting a permanent grant of continuous access to the property, would have to be considered a taking if it were not attached to a development permit, the Commission's assumed power to forbid construction of the house in order to protect the public's view of the beach must surely include the power to condition construction upon some concession by the owner, even a concession of property

3. Contrary to Justice Brennan's claim, our opinions do not establish that these standards are the same as those applied to due process or equal protection claims. To the contrary, our verbal formulations in the takings field have generally been quite different. We have required that the regulation "substantially advance" the "legitimate state interest" sought to be achieved, *Agins v. Tiburon,* 447 U.S. 255, 260, 100 S.Ct. 2138, 2141, 65 L.Ed.2d 106 (1980), not that "the State *'could rationally have decided'* the measure adopted might achieve the State's objective."

Justice Brennan relies principally [on] equal protection [and] due process cases in support of the standards he would adopt. [For details see n. 1 of the Brennan dissent.] But there is no reason to believe (and the language of our cases gives some reason to disbelieve) that so long as the regulation of property is at issue the standards for takings challenges, due process challenges, and equal protection challenges are identical; any more than there is any reason to believe that so long as the regulation of speech is at issue the standards for due process challenges, equal protection challenges, and First Amendment challenges are identical. *Goldblatt,* [supra], does appear to assume that the inquiries are the same, but that assumption is inconsistent with the formulations of our later cases. [Note 3 appears later in the opinion.]

rights, that serves the same end. If a prohibition designed to accomplish that purpose would be a legitimate exercise of the police power rather than a taking, it would be strange to conclude that providing the owner an alternative to that prohibition which accomplishes the same purpose is not.

"The evident constitutional propriety disappears, however, if the condition substituted for the prohibition utterly fails to further the end advanced as the justification for the prohibition. [The] lack of nexus between the condition and the original purpose of the building restriction converts that purpose to something other than what it was. The purpose then becomes, quite simply, the obtaining of an easement to serve some valid governmental purpose, but without payment of compensation. [In] short, unless the permit condition serves the same governmental purpose as the development ban, the building restriction is not a valid regulation of land use but 'an out-and-out plan of extortion.'

"The Commission claims [that] we may sustain the condition at issue here by finding that it is reasonably related to the public need or burden that the Nollans' new house creates or to which it contributes. The Nollans' new house, the Commission found, will interfere with 'visual access' to the beach. That in turn (along with other shorefront development) will interfere with the desire of people who drive past the Nollans' house to use the beach, thus creating a 'psychological barrier' to 'access.' [These] burdens on 'access' would be alleviated by a requirement that the Nollans provide 'lateral access' to the beach.

"[It] is quite impossible to understand how a requirement that people already on the public beaches be able to walk across the Nollans' property reduces any obstacles to viewing the beach created by the new house. It is also impossible to understand how it lowers any "psychological barrier" to using the public beaches. [We] therefore find that the Commission's imposition of the permit condition cannot be treated as an exercise of its land use power for any of these purposes. Our conclusion on this point is consistent with the approach taken by every other court that has considered the question, with the exception of the California state courts [citing over 20 cases].

"Justice Brennan argues that imposition of the access requirement is not irrational. In his version of the Commission's argument, the reason for the requirement is that in its absence, a person looking toward the beach from the road will see a street of residential structures including the Nollans' new home and conclude that there is no public beach nearby. If, however, that person sees people passing and repassing along the dry sand behind the Nollans' home, he will realize that there is a public beach somewhere in the vicinity. The Commission's action, however, was based on the opposite factual finding that the wall of houses completely blocked the view of the beach and that a person looking from the road would not be able to see it at all.

"Even if the Commission had made the finding that Justice Brennan proposes, however, it is not certain that it would suffice. [Our] cases describe the condition for abridgement of property rights through the police power as a '*substantial* advanc[ing]' of a legitimate State interest. We are inclined to be particularly careful about the adjective where the actual conveyance of property is made a condition to the lifting of a land use restriction, since in that context there is heightened risk that the purpose is avoidance of the compensation requirement, rather than the stated police power objective."

BRENNAN, J., dissented, joined by Marshall, J.:

"The Court imposes a standard of precision for the exercise of a State's police power that has been discredited for the better part of this century. [Even] under the Court's cramped standard, the permit condition imposed in this case directly responds to the specific type of burden on access created by appellants' development.

"[The] Commission has sought [to] balance private and public interests and to accept tradeoffs: to permit development that reduces access in some ways as long as other means of access are enhanced. In this case, it has determined that the Nollans' burden on access would be offset by a deed restriction that formalizes the public's right to pass along the shore. In its informed judgment, such a tradeoff would preserve the net amount of public access to the coastline. The Court's insistence on a precise fit between the forms of burden and condition on each individual parcel along the California coast would penalize the Commission for its flexibility, hampering the ability to fulfill its public trust mandate.

"Even if we accept the Court's unusual demand for a precise match between the condition imposed and the specific type of burden on access created by the appellants, the State's action easily satisfies this requirement. [Those] persons who go down to the public beach a quarter-mile away will be able to look down the coastline and see that persons have continuous access to the tidelands, and will observe signs that proclaim the public's right of access over the dry sand. The burden produced by the diminution in visual access—the impression that the beach is not open to the public—is thus directly alleviated by the provision for public access over the dry sand. The Court therefore has an unrealistically limited conception of what measures could reasonably be chosen to mitigate the burden produced by a diminution of visual access. * * *

"In reviewing a Takings Clause claim, we have regarded as particularly significant the nature of the governmental action and the economic impact of regulation, especially the extent to which regulation interferes with investment-backed expectations. *Penn Central.* The character of the government action in this case is the imposition of a condition on permit approval, which allows the public to continue to have access to the coast. The physical intrusion permitted by the deed restriction is minimal. The public is permitted the right to pass and re-pass along the coast in an area from the seawall to the mean high tide mark. This area is at its *widest* 10 feet, which means that *even without the permit condition,* the public's right of access permits it to pass on average within a few feet of the seawall. [The] intrusiveness of such passage is even less than the intrusion resulting from the required dedication of a sidewalk in front of private residences, exactions which are commonplace conditions on approval of development." [a]

(b) *Heightened scrutiny.* Might the majority's heightened scrutiny of the relationship between the easement condition and the impact of the proposed building on "public access" be explained by the nature of the taking—permanent physical occupancy? Cf. Michelman, *Takings 1987,* 88 Col.L.Rev. 1600, 1607–1613 (1988); Note, 102 Harv.L.Rev. 992, 997–99 (1989). Or might it portend requirement of tighter means-end relationships whenever conditions on land development raise taking issues—or perhaps even when other types of regulations raise taking issues? Cf. *Note, Taking a Step Back: A Reconsideration of the Takings Test of Nollan v. California Coastal Commission,* 102 Harv.L.Rev. 448 (1988).

(c) *Germaneness.* For consideration of the germaneness approach in the light of other similar issues, see Sullivan, supra at 1462–68.

a. Blackmun, J., dissenting, protested the "close nexus" for permit conditions and could find no taking under "traditional taking analysis." Stevens, J. also filed a dissent.

(d) *Commentaries.* For wide-ranging, critical analyses of recent developments in the law of takings, see *The Jurisprudence of Taking,* 88 Col.L.Rev. 1581–1794 (1988), a collection of articles by nine leading scholars, which grew out of a Dartmouth College conference on the taking issue in the light of the 1987 decisions, primarily *Keystone, Nollan,* and *First English Lutheran Church,* infra. For a thoughtful consideration of the relationship of the public trust concept to the *Nollan* situation, see Finnell, *Public Access to Coastal Public Property: Judicial Theories and the Taking Issue,* 67 N.C.L.Rev. 627, 660–66 (1989).

7. *Remedies for regulatory taking: inverse condemnation.* (a) In FIRST ENGLISH EVANGELICAL LUTHERAN CHURCH v. COUNTY OF LOS ANGELES, 482 U.S. 304, 107 S.Ct. 2378, 96 L.Ed.2d 250 (1987), the church had sued in a California court for damages only, alleging uncompensated taking of its recreation property by an "interim ordinance" that denied it all use of the property by forbidding all construction in an "interim flood protection area." Nearly six years' later, the California courts reached a final decision that upheld a nonsuit [a] based on a California precedent that under similar circumstances "mandamus or declaratory relief, rather than inverse condemnation, is the appropriate relief," because of the "chilling effect" of a compensation judgment upon the "exercise of police regulatory powers" and "the need for preserving a degree of freedom in the land use planning function." [b] The Supreme Court, per REHNQUIST, C.J., reversed, holding 6 to 1 that if the regulation were found to be a taking, "invalidation of the ordinance without payment of fair value for the use of the property during [a considerable period of years] would be a constitutionally insufficient remedy:"

"In this case the California Court of Appeal held that a landowner who claims that his property has been 'taken' by a land-use regulation may not recover damages for the time before it is finally determined that the regulation constitutes a 'taking' of his property. We disagree, and conclude that in these circumstances the Fifth and Fourteenth Amendments to the United States Constitution would require compensation for that period. * * *

"[The] Court has recognized in more than one case that the government may elect to abandon its intrusion or discontinue regulations. [The] landowner has no right under the Just Compensation Clause to insist that a 'temporary' taking be deemed a permanent taking. But we have not resolved whether abandonment by the government requires payment of compensation for the period of time during which regulations deny a landowner all use of his land.

"In considering this question, we find substantial guidance in cases where the government [only] temporarily exercised its right to use private property [during World War II. There] was no question that compensation would be [required.]

"These cases reflect the fact that 'temporary' takings which, as here, deny a landowner all use of his property, are not different in kind from permanent takings, for which the Constitution clearly requires compensation. [In] the present case the interim ordinance was adopted by the county of Los Angeles in January 1979, and became effective immediately. Appellant filed suit within a month after the effective date of the ordinance and yet when the Supreme Court of California denied a hearing in the case on October 17, 1985, the merits of

a. The California Supreme Court denied review of the Court of Appeals affirmance of the nonsuit.

b. *Agins v. Tiburon,* 24 Cal.3d 266, 276–77, 157 Cal.Rptr. 372, 378, 598 P.2d 25, 31 (1979), affirmed on other grounds 447 U.S. 255, 100 S.Ct. 2138, 65 L.Ed.2d 106 (1980).

appellant's claim had yet to be determined. The United States has been required to pay compensation for leasehold interests of shorter duration than this. The value of a leasehold interest in property for a period of years may be substantial, and the burden on the property owner in extinguishing such an interest for a period of years may be great indeed. Where this burden results from governmental action that amounted to a taking, the Just Compensation Clause of the Fifth Amendment requires that the government pay the landowner for the value of the use of the land during this period. Cf. *United States v. Causby* ('It is the owner's loss, not the taker's gain, which is the measure of the value of the property taken'). Invalidation of the ordinance or its successor ordinance after this period of time, though converting the taking into a 'temporary' one, is not a sufficient remedy to meet the demands of the Just Compensation [Clause]."

"Once a court determines that a taking has occurred, the government retains the whole range of options already available—amendment of the regulation, withdrawal of the invalidated regulation, or exercise of eminent domain. [We] merely hold that where the government's activities have already worked a taking of all use of property, no subsequent action by the government can relieve it of the duty to provide compensation for the period during which the taking was effective."

STEVENS, J., dissented: "Contrary to the Court's implications, the fact that a regulation would constitute a taking if allowed to remain in effect permanently is by no means dispositive of the question whether the effect that the regulation has already had on the property is so severe that a taking occurred during the period before the regulation was invalidated.

"[While] virtually all physical invasions are deemed takings, see e.g., *Loretto; Causby,* a regulatory program that adversely affects property values does not constitute a taking unless it destroys a major portion of the property's value. This diminution of value inquiry is unique to regulatory takings. [I] am willing to assume that some cases may arise in which a property owner can show that prospective invalidation of the regulation cannot cure the taking—that the temporary operation of a regulation has caused such a significant diminution in the property's value that compensation must be afforded for the taking that has already occurred. For this ever to happen, the restriction on the use of the property would not only have to be a substantial one, but it would have to remain in effect for a significant percentage of the property's useful life. In such a case an application of our test for regulatory takings would obviously require an inquiry into the duration of the restriction, as well as its scope and severity.

"[The] policy implications of today's decision are obvious and, I fear, far reaching. Cautious local officials and land-use planners may avoid taking any action that might later be challenged and thus give rise to a damage action. Much important regulation will never be enacted, even perhaps in the health and safety area.[c] "

(b) Should *First English* be viewed as leaving unresolved whether compensation is required if "a local government [enacts] an expressly temporary, say three-year building moratorium to allow time for study of a problematic situa-

c. While not joining the foregoing portions of the Stevens dissent, Blackmun and O'Connor, JJ., joined Parts I and III of the dissent, which argued (I) that the complaint did not sufficiently allege an unconstitutional taking, and (III) that the church should have been required to exhaust its remedies in the state courts by "demanding invalidation of the ordinance prior to seeking this Court's review of California procedures."

tion, and then actually [lifts] the moratorium at the expiration of three years?" Consider Professor Michelman's analysis in *Takings 1987,* supra at 1614–1621.

SECTION 5. CONTRACT CLAUSE

ALLIED STRUCTURAL STEEL CO. v. SPANNAUS

438 U.S. 234, 98 S.Ct. 2716, 57 L.Ed.2d 727 (1978).

JUSTICE STEWART delivered the opinion of the Court.

[In 1963 Allied adopted a pension plan based on earnings and length of employment. Pension rights vested when an employee worked to age 65, or 15 years to age 60 or 20 years to age 55. Those who quit or were terminated before vesting had no pensions rights. Pensions were payable only from Allied's pension fund to which it made yearly payments based on actuarial predictions. Allied informed its employees that the plan implied no assurance against dismissal and that it retained the right to terminate the pension plan at any time for any reason, subject to use of the funds assets to pay vested pensions in a specified order of priorities.

[A 1974 Minnesota Act required employers with pension plans, who went out of business in Minnesota, to provide full pensions to all its Minnesota employees who had worked 10 years or more, and to pay a "pension funding charge" sufficient to buy deferred annuities for any pension fund deficiency. As a first step in closing its 30 employee Minnesota operation, Allied terminated 11 employees, 9 of whom had worked for Allied over 10 years, but not long enough to have vested pension rights. Under the Act, Allied's "pension funding charge" was $185,000. The Court held 5 to 3 that this application of the Act violated the contracts clause.]

The Act substantially altered [the company's contractual relationships with its employees] by superimposing pension obligations upon the company conspicuously beyond those that it had voluntarily agreed to undertake. But it does not inexorably follow that the Act, as applied to the company, violates the Contract Clause. * * *

Although it was perhaps the strongest single constitutional check on state legislation during our early years as a Nation, the Contract Clause receded into comparative desuetude [with] the development of the large body of jurisprudence under the Due Process Clause.[12] Nonetheless, the Contract Clause remains part of the Constitution. It is not a dead [letter.]

[The] Contract Clause does [not] "prevent the State from exercising such powers as are vested in it for the promotion of the common weal, or are necessary for the general good of the public, though contracts previously entered into between individuals may thereby be affected. This [police power] is paramount to any rights under contracts between individuals." *Manigault v. Springs,* 199 U.S. 473, 480, 26 S.Ct. 127, 50 L.Ed. 274 (1905).[a] As Mr. Justice Holmes succinctly put the matter [in] *Hudson Water Co. v. McCarter,* 209 U.S.

12. Indeed, at least one commentator has suggested that "the results might be the same if the contract clause were dropped out of the Constitution, and the challenged statutes all judged as reasonable or unreasonable deprivations of property." Hale, *The Supreme Court and the Contract Clause,* 57 Harv.L.Rev. 852, 890–91 (1944).

a. *Manigault* held the contract clause did not bar legislation that authorized a riparian owner to dam a creek to facilitate reclamation of lowlands, in violation of his contract with another riparian owner. Cf. *Union Dry Goods Co. v. Georgia Public Service Corp.,* 248 U.S. 372, 39 S.Ct. 117, 63 L.Ed. 309 (1919) (contract clause not violated by statute authorizing utili-

349, 357, 28 S.Ct. 529, 52 L.Ed. 828: "One whose rights, such as they are, are subject to state restriction, cannot remove them from the power of the State by making a contract about them. The contract will carry with it the infirmity of the subject matter."

If the Contract Clause is to retain any meaning at all, however, it must be understood to impose *some* limits upon the power of a State to abridge existing contractual relationships, even in the exercise of its otherwise legitimate police power. The existence and nature of those limits were clearly indicated in a series of cases in this Court arising from the efforts of the States to deal with the unprecedented emergencies brought on by the severe economic depression of the early 1930's.

In *Home Building & Loan Assn. v. Blaisdell,* 290 U.S. 398, 54 S.Ct. 231, 78 L.Ed. 413 (1934), the Court upheld [a] mortgage moratorium law that Minnesota had enacted to provide relief for homeowners threatened with foreclosure. Although the legislation conflicted directly with lenders' contractual foreclosure rights, the Court there acknowledged that, despite the Contract Clause, the States retain residual authority to enact laws "to safeguard the vital interests of [their] people." In upholding the state mortgage moratorium law, the Court found five factors significant. First, the state legislature had declared in the Act itself that an emergency need for the protection of homeowners existed. Second, the state law was enacted to protect a basic societal interest, not a favored group. Third, the relief was appropriately tailored to the emergency that it was designed to meet. Fourth, the imposed conditions were reasonable.[b] And, finally, the legislation was limited to the duration of the emergency.

The *Blaisdell* opinion thus clearly implied that if the Minnesota moratorium legislation had not possessed the characteristics attributed to it by the Court, it would have been invalid under the Contract Clause of the Constitution. These implications were given concrete force in [cases] that followed closely in *Blaisdell's* wake.[c] * * *

The most recent Contract Clause case in this Court was *United States Trust Co. v. New Jersey,* [infra]. In that case the Court again recognized that although the absolute language of the Clause must leave room for "the 'essential attributes of sovereign power,' necessarily reserved by the States to safeguard the welfare of their citizens," that power has limits when its exercise effects substantial modifications of private contracts. Despite the customary deference courts give to state laws directed to social and economic problems, "[l]egislation adjusting the rights and responsibilities of contracting parties must be upon reasonable conditions and of a character appropriate to the public purpose justifying its adoption." Evaluating with particular scrutiny a modification of a contract to which the State itself was a party, the Court in that case held that legislative alteration of the rights and remedies of Port Authority bondholders violated the Contract Clause because the legislation was neither necessary nor reasonable.

ty to charge rates fixed by commission higher than pre-existing contract rate).

b. *Blaisdell* stressed that the law did not impair the mortgage indebtedness, that the ultimate right to foreclosure and a deficiency judgment remained, that interest continued to accrue, and that the mortgagor must pay the rental value to be applied to taxes, insurance, and interest.

c. The Court briefly stated the rulings in three cases that found contract clause violations shortly after *Blaisdell*: *W.B. Worthen Co. v. Thomas,* 292 U.S. 426, 54 S.Ct. 816, 78 L.Ed. 1344 (1934); *W.B. Worthen v. Kavanaugh,* 295 U.S. 56, 55 S.Ct. 555, 79 L.Ed. 1298 (1935); *Treigle v. Acme Homestead Ass'n,* 297 U.S. 189, 56 S.Ct. 408, 80 L.Ed. 575 (1936).

In applying these principles, the first inquiry must be whether the state law has, in fact, operated as a substantial impairment of a contractual relationship.[16] [Minimal] alteration of contractual obligations may end the inquiry at its first stage. Severe impairment, on the other hand, will push the inquiry to a careful examination of the nature and purpose of the state legislation.

The severity of an impairment of contractual obligations can be measured by the factors that reflect the high value the Framers placed on the protection of private contracts. Contracts enable individuals to order their personal and business affairs according to their particular needs and interests. Once arranged, those rights and obligations are binding under the law, and the parties are entitled to rely on them.

Here, the company's contracts of employment [included] the pension plan. The company's maximum obligation was to set aside each year an amount based on the plan's requirements for vesting. The plan satisfied the current federal income tax code and was subject to no other legislative requirements. [The] company [had] no reason to anticipate that its employees' pension rights could become vested except in accordance with the terms of the plan. It relied heavily, and reasonably, on this legitimate contractual expectation in calculating its annual contributions to the pension fund.

The effect of Minnesota's [Act] on this contractual obligation was severe. The company was required in 1974 to have made its contributions throughout the pre-1974 life of its plan as if employees' pension rights had vested after 10 years, instead of vesting in accord with the terms of the plan. Thus a basic term of the pension contract—one on which the company had relied for 10 years—was substantially modified. The result was that although the company's past contributions were adequate when made, they were not adequate when computed under the 10-year statutory vesting requirement. The Act thus forced a current recalculation of the past 10 years' contributions based on the new, unanticipated 10-year vesting requirement.

Not only did the state law thus retroactively modify the compensation that the company had agreed to pay its employees from 1963 to 1974, but it did so by changing the company's obligations in an area where the element of reliance was vital—the funding of a pension [plan].[18] [The company was] forced to make all the retroactive changes in its contractual obligations at one [time].

Thus, the [statute] nullifies express terms of the company's contractual obligations and imposes a completely unexpected liability in potentially disabling amounts. [Yet] there is no showing in the record before us that this severe disruption of contractual expectations was necessary to meet an important

16. [The] narrow view that the Clause forbids only state laws that diminish the duties of a contractual obligor and not laws that increase them, a view arguably suggested by *Satterlee v. Matthewson,* 2 Pet. 380, 7 L.Ed. 458, has since been expressly repudiated. *Detroit United Ry. v. Michigan,* 242 U.S. 238, 37 S.Ct. 87, 61 L.Ed. 268; *Georgia Ry. & Power Co. v. Decatur,* 262 U.S. 432, 43 S.Ct. 613, 67 L.Ed. 1065. Moreover, in any bilateral contract the diminution of duties on one side effectively increases the duties on the other.

The even narrower view that the Clause is limited in its application to state laws relieving debtors of obligations to their creditors is, as the dissent recognizes, completely at odds with this Court's decisions. See generally Hale, 57 Harv.L.Rev. 512, 514–16 (1944).

18. In some situations the element of reliance may cut both ways. Here, the company had relied upon the funding obligation of the pension plan for more than a decade. There was no showing of reliance to the contrary by its employees. Indeed, Minnesota did not act to protect any employee reliance interest demonstrated on the record. Instead, it compelled the employer to exceed bargained-for expectations and nullified an express term of the pension plan.

general social problem. The presumption favoring "legislative judgment as to the necessity and reasonableness of a particular measure," *United States Trust Co.,* simply cannot stand in this case.

[Whether] or not the legislation was aimed largely at a single employer,[20] [which closed one of its Minnesota plants and attempted to terminate its pension plan,] it clearly has an extremely narrow focus. It applies only to private employers [who] have established voluntary private pension plans, [and] only when such an employer closes his Minnesota office or terminates his pension plan. Thus, this law can hardly be characterized, like the law at issue in the *Blaisdell* case, as one enacted to protect a broad societal interest rather than a narrow class.

Moreover, [this] legislation, imposing a sudden, totally unanticipated, and substantial retroactive obligation upon the company to its employees, was not enacted to deal with a situation remotely approaching the broad and desperate emergency economic conditions of the early 1930's—conditions of which the Court in *Blaisdell* took judicial notice.[24] * * *

This Minnesota law simply does not possess the attributes of those state laws that in the past have survived challenge under the Contract Clause of the Constitution. The law was not even purportedly enacted to deal with a broad, generalized economic or social problem. Cf. *Blaisdell.* It did not operate in an area already subject to state regulation at the time the company's contractual obligations were originally undertaken, but invaded an area never before subject to regulation by the State. It did not effect simply a temporary alteration of the contractual relationships of those within its coverage, but worked a severe, permanent, and immediate change in those relationships—irrevocably and retroactively. And its narrow aim was leveled, not at every Minnesota employer, not even at every Minnesota employer who left the State, but only at those who had in the past been sufficiently enlightened as voluntarily to agree to establish pension plans for their employees. * * *

JUSTICE BRENNAN, with whom Justice White and Justice Marshall join, dissenting.[e] * * *

[The Minnesota Act] does not abrogate or dilute any obligation due a party to a private contract; rather, like all positive social legislation, the Act imposes new, additional obligations on a particular class of persons. In my view, any constitutional infirmity in the law must therefore derive, not from the Contract Clause, but from the Due Process Clause of the Fourteenth Amendment.

[The Act was] designed to remedy a serious social problem arising from the operation of private pension plans. [Not] only would employers often neglect to furnish their employees with adequate information concerning their rights under the plans, leading to erroneous expectations, but because employers often failed to make contributions to the pension funds large enough adequately to fund their plans, employees often ultimately received only a small amount of those benefits they reasonably anticipated. [Denial] of all pension benefits not because of job related failings but only because the employees are unfortunate

20. [See *Malone v. White Motor Corp.,* 435 U.S. 497, at 501 n. 5, 98 S.Ct. 1185, 55 L.Ed.2d 443 (1978)].

24. This is not to suggest that only an emergency of great magnitude can constitutionally justify a state law impairing the obligations of contracts. See, e.g., *Veix v. Sixth Ward Building & Loan Assn.,* 310 U.S. 32, 39–40, 60 S.Ct. 792, 84 L.Ed. 1061 [1945]; *East New York Savings Bank v. Hahn,* 326 U.S. 230, 66 S.Ct. 69, 90 L.Ed. 34; *El Paso v. Simmons,* 379 U.S. 497, 85 S.Ct. 577, 13 L.Ed.2d 446 (1965).

e. Blackmun, J., did not participate.

enough to be employed at a plant that closes for purely economic reasons is harsh indeed. [The] closing of a plant is a contingency outside the range of normal expectations of both the employer and the employee. [Although] the Court glides over this fact, it should be apparent that the Act will impose only minor economic burdens on employers whose pension plans have been adequately funded. [An] adequate pension plan fund would include contributions on behalf of terminated employees of 10 or more years service whose rights had not vested. Indeed, without the Act, the closing of the plant would create a windfall for the employer, because, due to the resulting surplus in the fund, his future contributions would be reduced. * * *

[The] Act does not impose 'sudden and unanticipated' burdens. [The] existence of the Act's duties—which are similar to a legislatively imposed requirement of severance pay measured by the length of the discharged employees' service—is simply one of a number of factors that the employer considers in making the business decision whether to close a plant and terminate the employees who work there.

[The] Act does not relieve either the employer or his employees of any existing contract obligation. Rather, the Act simply creates an additional, supplemental duty of the employer, no different in kind from myriad duties created by a wide variety of legislative measures which defeat settled expectations but which have nonetheless been sustained by this Court. For this reason, the Minnesota Act, in my view, does not implicate the Contract Clause in any way. The basic fallacy of today's decision is its mistaken view that the Contract Clause protects all contract-based expectations, including that of an employer that his obligations to his employees will not be legislatively enlarged beyond those explicitly provided in his pension plan.

A. Historically, [the] Contract Clause was not intended to embody a broad constitutional policy of protecting all reliance interests grounded in private contracts. It was made part of the Constitution to remedy a particular social evil—the state legislative practice of enacting laws to relieve individuals of their obligations under certain contracts—and thus was intended to prohibit States from adopting "as [their] policy the repudiation of debts or the destruction of contracts or the denial of means to enforce them," *Blaisdell.* But the Framers never contemplated that the Clause would limit the legislative power of States to enact laws creating duties that might burden some individuals in order to benefit others.

B. [It] is nothing less than an abuse of the English language to interpret, as does the Court, the term "impairing" as including laws which create new duties. While such laws may be conceptualized as "enlarging" the obligation of a contract when they add to the burdens that had previously been imposed by a private agreement, such laws cannot be prohibited by the Clause because they do not dilute or nullify a duty a person had previously obligated himself to perform.[7] * * *

C. [More] fundamentally, the Court's distortion of the meaning of the Contract Clause [threatens] to undermine the jurisprudence of property rights

7. In *Georgia Ry. & Power Co. v. Decatur, Detroit United Ry. v. Michigan,* [fn. 16 supra], and in dictum in other cases, this Court embraced, without any careful analysis and without giving any consideration to *Satterlee v. Matthewson,* the contrary view that the impairment of a contract may consist in "adding to its burdens" as well as in diminishing its efficacy. These opinions reflect the then-prevailing philosophy of economic due process which has since been repudiated. See *Ferguson v. Skrupa.* In my view, the reasoning of *Georgia Ry.* and *Detroit United Ry.* is simply wrong.

developed over the last 40 years. The Contract Clause, of course, is but one of several clauses in the Constitution that protect existing economic values from governmental interference. The Fifth Amendment's command that "private property [shall not] be taken for public use, without just compensation" is such a clause. A second is the Due Process Clause, which during the heyday of substantive due process, see *Lochner,* largely supplanted the Contract Clause in importance and operated as a potent limitation on Government's ability to interfere with economic expectations. Decisions over the past 50 years have developed a coherent, unified interpretation of all the constitutional provisions that may protect economic expectations and these decisions have recognized a broad latitude in States to effect even severe interference with existing economic values when reasonably necessary to promote the general welfare. At the same time the prohibition of the Contract Clause, consistently with its wording and historic purposes, has been limited in application to state laws that diluted, with utter indifference to the legitimate interests of the beneficiary of a contract duty, the existing contract obligation.

Today's conversion of the Contract Clause into a limitation on the power of States to enact laws that impose duties additional to obligations assumed under private contracts must inevitably produce results difficult to square with any rational conception of a constitutional order. [The] validity of such a law will turn upon whether judges see it as a law that deals with a generalized social problem, whether it is temporary (as few will be) or permanent, whether it operates in an area previously subject to regulation, and, finally, whether its duties apply to a broad class of persons. The necessary consequence of the extreme malleability of these rather vague criteria is to vest judges with broad subjective discretion to protect property interests that happen to appeal to them.

[There] is nothing sancrosanct about expectations rooted in contract that justify according them a constitutional immunity denied other property rights. Laws that interfere with settled expectations created by state property law (and which impose severe economic burdens) are uniformly held constitutional where reasonably related to the promotion of the general welfare. * * *

Notes and Questions

1. *Contract vs. other property rights.* (a) In what respects, if any, is there a significant difference in the Court's review of economic legislation when challenged under the contract clause as compared to due process? Consider particularly (1) the professed standard of review, (2) the degree of deference to the legislature or strictness of judicial scrutiny, (3) the Court's willingness to hypothesize state purposes to justify the legislation. Cf. 92 Harv.L.Rev. 94–99 (1978).

(b) Ought the degree of constitutional protection from legislative interference differ as between preexisting contract interests and preexisting noncontractual property interests?

2. *Legislatively-added burdens.* Did *Allied Steel* soundly interpret the contract clause to protect against "impairment" by legislatively-added burdens that increase those stated in the contract? Would it have made a difference in the law's validity if it had added a burden of sounder *funding* of the contractual pension benefits without adding to the *benefits*? Cf. *Connolly v. Pension Benefit Guaranty Corp.*, 475 U.S. 211, 106 S.Ct. 1018, 89 L.Ed.2d 166 (1986) (a taking clause decision).

3. *Impairment of government contractual obligations.* One year before *Spannous,* UNITED STATES TRUST CO. v. NEW JERSEY, 431 U.S. 1, 97 S.Ct. 1505, 52 L.Ed.2d 92 (1977), per BLACKMUN, J., applied the contract clause to invalidate, 4 to 3,[a] New Jersey and New York laws repealing earlier statutory commitments with Port Authority bond holders not to use revenues pledged as security for the bonds for any railroad facility that was not self-supporting: The purpose of the repeal was to enable the Port Authority to lessen traffic problems by increasing use of mass transit through subsidizing commuter service with revenues from higher bridge and tunnel tolls:

"[The] Contract Clause is not an absolute bar to subsequent modification of a State's own financial obligations. As with laws impairing the obligations of private contracts, an impairment may be constitutional if it is reasonable and necessary to serve an important public purpose. In applying this standard, however, complete deference to a legislative assessment of reasonableness and necessity is not appropriate because the State's self-interest is at stake. [If] a State could reduce its financial obligations whenever it wanted to spend the money for what it regarded as an important public purpose, the Contract Clause would provide no protection at all.[25] * * *

"Mass transportation, energy conservation, and environmental protection are goals that are important and of legitimate public concern. Appellees contend that these goals are so important that any harm to bondholders from repeal of the 1962 covenant is greatly outweighed by the public benefit. [We] can only sustain the repeal of the 1962 covenant if that impairment was both reasonable and necessary to serve the admittedly important purposes claimed by the State."

The Court considered the repeal "unnecessary" because the need could have been satisfied by a "less drastic modification", such as to "exclude the additional bridge and tunnel tolls from the revenue use limitation," or to encourage use of mass transit by changes in the tax and toll structures for autos. It viewed the repeal also as "unreasonable" because the need for increased mass transit had long been recognized, and the repealed 1962 commitment "was specifically intended to protect the pledged revenues and reserves against the possibility that such concerns would lead the Port Authority into greater involvement in deficit mass transit."

BRENNAN, J., joined by White and Marshall, JJ., dissented: "[Today's decision] remolds the Contract Clause into a potent instrument for overseeing important policy determinations of the state legislature. At the same time, by creating a constitutional safe haven for property rights embodied in a contract, the decision substantially distorts modern constitutional jurisprudence governing regulation of private economic interests.

"[The] Court's various alternative proposals [are] not responsive to New York's and New Jersey's real environmental and traffic problems, [and] intrude

a. Blackmun did not participate in *Spannaus,* but Powell and Stevens, who had not participated in *U.S. Trust Co.* joined the *Spannaus* majority, making a majority of 6 justices voting in the 1970s to revitalize the contract clause.

25. For similar reasons, a dual standard of review was applied under the Fifth Amendment to federal legislation abrogating contractual gold clauses. "There is a clear distinction between the power of the Congress to control or interdict the contracts of private parties when they interfere with the exercise of its constitutional authority, and the power of the Congress to alter or repudiate the substance of its own engagements when it has borrowed money under the authority which the Constitution confers." *Perry v. United States,* 294 U.S. 330, 55 S.Ct. 432, 79 L.Ed. 912 (1935).

the Court deeply into complex and localized policy matters that are for the States' legislatures and not the judiciary to resolve.

"[I] can neither understand nor accept the Court's characterization of New Jersey's action as unreasonable. The Court [strictly] applies a novel standard for reviewing a State's attempt to relieve its citizens from unduly harsh contracts entered into by earlier legislators. Such 'an impairment may be constitutional if it is reasonable and necessary to serve an important public purpose.' [T]his apparently spontaneous formulation virtually [assured] frustrating the understanding of court and litigant alike[17] * * *."

4. *"Incidental effect" of regulation.* EXXON CORP. v. EAGERTON, 462 U.S. 176, 103 S.Ct. 2296, 76 L.Ed.2d 497 (1983), per MARSHALL, J., unanimously held that a ban on oil and gas producers passing a severance tax increase on to consumers did not violate the contract clause even though pre-existing contracts required consumers to reimburse producers for all severance taxes:

"[T]he pass-through prohibition did not prescribe a rule limited in effect to contractual obligations or remedies, but instead imposed a generally applicable rule of conduct designed to advance 'a broad societal interest,' *Allied Steel,* protecting consumers from excessive prices. The prohibition applied to all oil and gas producers, regardless of whether they happened to be parties to sale contracts that contained a provision permitting them to pass tax increases through to their purchasers. The effect of the pass-through prohibition on existing contracts that did contain such a provision was incidental to its main effect of shielding consumers from the burden of the tax increase.

"Because the pass-through prohibition imposed a generally applicable rule of conduct, it is sharply distinguishable from the measures struck down in *United States Trust* and *Allied Steel. United States Trust* involved New York and New Jersey statutes whose sole effect was to repeal a covenant that the two States had entered into with the holders of bonds issued by The Port Authority of New York and New Jersey. Similarly, the statute at issue in *Allied Steel* directly 'adjust[ed] the rights and responsibilities of contracting parties,' quoting *United States Trust.* * * *

"Alabama's power to prohibit oil and gas producers from passing the increase in the severance tax on to their purchasers is confirmed by several decisions of this Court rejecting Contract Clause challenges to state rate-setting schemes that displaced any rates previously established by contract. * * * And if the Contract Clause does not prevent a State from dictating the price that sellers may charge their customers, plainly it does not prevent a State from requiring that sellers absorb a tax increase themselves rather than pass it through to their customers."

5. *Legislation increasing employer's liability to fund pension benefits.* (a) Contrast *Spannaus* with CONNOLLY v. PENSION BENEFIT GUARANTY CORP., 475 U.S. 211, 106 S.Ct. 1018, 89 L.Ed.2d 166 (1986). [T]he federal Multiemployer Pension Plan Amendments Act (MPPAA) of 1980, implemented

17. The Court's newly announced standard of review, like all such formulations, can merely hope to suggest the direction that a court's inquiry should take, and the relative weight to be afforded a constitutional right. But particular words like "reasonable" and "necessary" also are fused with special meaning. [The] Court's new test [represents] a most unusual hybrid which manages to merge the two polar extremes of judicial intervention, [Until] today one would have fairly thought that as a matter of common sense as well as doctrine, state policies that are "necessary to serve an important public purpose" a fortiori would be "reasonable." * * *

ERISA's[a] 1978 objective to protect anticipated retirement benefits by requiring employers who withdraw from a multiemployer pension plan to pay into that plan's fund the withdrawing employer's "proportionate share" of the plan's "unfunded vested benefits," calculated as the difference between the plan's vested benefits and the current value of its assets at the time of withdrawal. The 1960 trust agreement creating the multiemployer Operating Engineers Pension Plan provided that no individual employer under the plan "has any liability to provide the benefits established by this Plan beyond [its] obligation" to make the contributions specified in the applicable collective bargaining agreement, even though the Pension Fund "does not have the assets to make the benefit payments." The Court, per WHITE, J., rejected the claim that this statutory "withdrawal liability" was a "taking" in violation of the withdrawing employers' property rights under the trust agreement:

"[H]ere, the United States has taken nothing for its own use, and only has nullified a contractual provision limiting liability by imposing an additional obligation that is otherwise within the power of Congress to impose. [The] Act safeguards the participants in multiemployer pension plans by requiring a withdrawing employer to fund its share of the plan obligations incurred during its association with the plan. This interference with the property rights of an employer arises from a public program that adjusts the benefits and burdens of economic life to promote the common good and, under our cases, does not constitute a taking requiring Government compensation.

"[The] final inquiry [is] whether the MPPAA has interfered with reasonable investment-backed expectations. Appellants argue that the only monetary obligations incurred by each employer involved in the Operating Engineers Pension Plan arose from the specific terms of the Plan and Trust Agreement between the employers and the union, and that the imposition of withdrawal liability upsets those reasonable expectations. Pension plans, however, were the objects of legislative concern long before the passage of ERISA in 1974, and surely as of that time, it was clear that if the PBGC exercised its discretion to pay benefits upon the termination of a multiemployer pension plan, employers who had contributed to the plan during the preceding five years were liable for their proportionate share of the plan's contributions during that period. It was also plain enough that the purpose of imposing withdrawal liability was to ensure that employees would receive the benefits promised them. When it became evident that ERISA fell short of achieving this end, Congress adopted the 1980 amendments. Prudent employers then had more than sufficient notice not only that pension plans were currently regulated, but also that withdrawal itself might trigger additional financial obligations. 'Those who do business in the regulated field cannot object if the legislative scheme is buttressed by subsequent amendments to achieve the legislative end.'

"[The] employers in the present litigation voluntarily negotiated and maintained a pension plan which was determined to be within the strictures of ERISA. We do not know, as a fact, whether this plan was underfunded, but Congress determined that unregulated withdrawals from multiemployer plans could endanger their financial vitality and deprive workers of the vested rights they were entitled to anticipate would be theirs upon retirement. For this reason, Congress imposed withdrawal liability as one part of an overall statutory scheme to safeguard the solvency of private pension plans. We see no constitu-

a. Employees' Retirement Income Security Act of 1980, 29 U.S.C.A. §§ 1381–1453.

tionally compelled reason to require the Treasury to assume the financial burden of attaining this goal."

(b) Had the withdrawal liability been based on state legislation attacked under the contracts clause would the Court have reached the same result? How might the reasoning have differed? What are the likely similarities? Are there distinctive roles for each clause?

6. *The law summarized.* For a unanimous summary of the controlling considerations in modern contract clause cases see Blackmun, J.'s, opinion in *Energy Reserves Group, Inc. v. Kansas Power and Light Co.,* 459 U.S. 400, 103 S.Ct. 697, 74 L.Ed.2d 569 (1983).

Chapter 3

PROTECTION OF INDIVIDUAL RIGHTS: DUE PROCESS, THE BILL OF RIGHTS, AND NONTEXTUAL CONSTITUTIONAL RIGHTS

SECTION 1. NATURE AND SCOPE OF FOURTEENTH AMENDMENT DUE PROCESS; APPLICABILITY OF THE BILL OF RIGHTS TO THE STATES

I. THE "ORDERED LIBERTY—FUNDAMENTAL FAIRNESS," "TOTAL INCORPORATION" AND "SELECTIVE INCORPORATION" THEORIES

Twining v. New Jersey, 211 U.S. 78, 29 S.Ct. 14, 53 L.Ed. 97 (1908); *Palko v. Connecticut,* 302 U.S. 319, 58 S.Ct. 149, 82 L.Ed. 288 (1937); and *Adamson v. California,* 332 U.S. 46, 67 S.Ct. 1672, 91 L.Ed. 1903 (1947), rejected the "total incorporation" view of the history of the fourteenth amendment, the view—which has never commanded a majority—that the fourteenth amendment made all of the provisions of the Bill of Rights fully applicable to the states.[a] But *Twining* recognized that "it is possible that some of the personal rights safeguarded by the first eight Amendments against National action may also be safeguarded against state action, because a denial of them would be a denial of due process" or because "the specific pledge of particular amendments have been found to be implicit in the concept of ordered liberty and thus through the Fourteenth Amendment, become valid as against the states" (*Palko*). And the Court early found among the procedural requirements of fourteenth amendment due process certain rules paralleling provisions of the first eight amendments. For example, *Powell v. Alabama,* 287 U.S. 45, 53 S.Ct. 55, 77 L.Ed. 158 (1932), held that defendants in a capital case were denied due process when a state refused them the aid of counsel. "The logically critical thing, however," pointed

a. *Palko,* which held that the fourteenth amendment did not encompass at least certain aspects of the double jeopardy prohibition of the fifth amendment, was overruled in *Benton v. Maryland* (1969), discussed below. The *Twining-Adamson* view that the fifth amendment privilege against self-incrimination is not incorporated in the fourteenth was rejected in *Malloy v. Hogan* (1964), discussed below. *Griffin v. California* (1965), Part IV infra, subsequently applied *Malloy* to overrule the specific holdings of *Twining* and *Adamson,* which had permitted comment on a defendant's failure to take the stand at his criminal trial. These later decisions, however, were still consistent with the rejection of the "total incorporation" interpretation.

out Harlan, J., years later, "was not that the rights had been found in the Bill of Rights, but that they were deemed * * * fundamental." [b]

Under the "ordered liberty"—"fundamental fairness" test, which procedural safeguards included in the Bill of Rights were applicable to the states and which were not? Consider Cardozo, J., speaking for the *Palko* Court: "[On reflection and analysis there] emerges the perception of a rationalizing principle which gives to discrete instances a proper order and coherence. The right to trial by jury and the immunity from prosecution except as the result of an indictment [are] not of the very essence of a scheme of ordered liberty. To abolish them is not to violate a 'principle of justice so rooted in the traditions and conscience of our people as to be ranked as fundamental.' [What] is true of jury trials and indictments is true also, as the cases show, of the immunity from compulsory self-incrimination. This too might be lost, and justice still be [done.] [c]

"We reach a different plane of social and moral values when we pass [to those provisions of the Bill of Rights] brought within the Fourteenth Amendment by a process of absorption. These in their origin were effective against the federal government alone. If the Fourteenth Amendment has absorbed them, the process of absorption has had its course in the belief that neither liberty nor justice would exist if they were sacrificed. This is true, for illustration, of freedom of thought and speech. Of that freedom one may say that it is the matrix, the indispensable condition, of nearly every other form of freedom.

b. *Duncan v. Louisiana* (dissent joined by Stewart, J.), discussed below.

c. As pointed out in fn. a supra, the fifth amendment privilege against self-incrimination was subsequently held to be fully applicable to the states via the fourteenth amendment. So was the sixth amendment right to jury trial in criminal cases. *Duncan v. Louisiana* (1968), discussed below.

The above language in *Palko* and language in *Adamson,* infra, and other cases are susceptible of the interpretation that when the Court held that a particular Bill of Rights guarantee was not "incorporated into," or implicit in, fourteenth amendment due process it was *completely* "out." But such a reading of these cases seems unsound. Typically the Court dealt with state procedures transgressing the "outer edges," rather than the basic concept, of a particular Bill of Rights guarantee. It seems most doubtful that in sustaining such challenged procedures the Court was authorizing the states to abolish completely—or to violate the "hardcore" of—e.g., the protection against double jeopardy, or the privilege against self-incrimination, or the right to trial by jury in criminal cases. Rather the Court probably meant that the state rules did not violate the fourteenth amendment because the Bill of Rights guarantee invoked by defendant did not apply to the states *to the full extent* it applied to the federal government. To hold that a particular provision of the Bill of Rights is not *totally* "incorporated," i.e., not binding on the states *in its entirety,* is not to say it is *completely "out"* of the fourteenth amendment. See generally Henkin, *"Selective Incorporation" in the Fourteenth Amendment,* 73 Yale L.J. 74, 79 & n. 18, 80–81 (1963).

At issue in *Palko* was not whether a state could completely disregard the basic notion against twice putting a person in jeopardy for the same offense, but a Connecticut statute permitting prosecution appeals "upon all questions of law arising [in criminal trials] with the permission of the presiding judge." Thus, elsewhere in the opinion the Court asked: "Is *that kind of double jeopardy* to which the [Connecticut] statute has subjected [appellant] *a hardship so acute and shocking* that our polity will not endure it? [What] the answer would have to be if the state were permitted *after a trial free from error* to try the accused over again or to bring another case against him, we have no occasion to consider." (Emphasis added).

Nor should *Adamson* be read for the proposition that a state could make it a felony for a person to "plead the fifth" or for a defendant to refuse to take the stand. Rather the Court merely sustained a California provision infringing upon the *periphery* of the guarantee by allowing comment upon a defendant's failure to explain or to deny evidence against him.

Nor, as the Court later emphasized in *Duncan,* discussed below, did *Maxwell v. Dow* (1900), discussed below, hold that a state could abolish trial by jury *altogether* in criminal cases; only that fourteenth amendment due process did not prevent a state from trying a noncapital defendant before a jury with fewer than 12 persons.

* * * Fundamental too in the concept of due process, and so in that of liberty, is the thought that condemnation shall be rendered only after trial. The hearing, moreover, must be a real one, not a sham or pretense [discussing *Powell* which] did not turn upon the fact that the benefit of counsel would have been guaranteed to the defendants by [the] Sixth Amendment if they had been prosecuted in a federal court [but on] the fact that in the particular situation laid before us [the aid of counsel] was essential to the substance of a hearing."

The "total incorporation" position received its strongest support in the *Adamson* dissents. In the principal dissent, Black, J., joined by Douglas, J., observed: "I cannot consider the Bill of Rights to be an outworn 18th Century 'strait jacket' as the *Twining* opinion did. Its provisions may be thought outdated abstractions by some. And it is true that they were designed to meet ancient evils. But they are the same kind of human evils that have emerged from century to century wherever excessive power is sought by the few at the expense of the many. In my judgment the people of no nation can lose their liberty so long as a Bill of Rights like ours survives and its basic purposes are conscientiously interpreted, enforced and respected so as to afford continuous protection against old, as well as new, devices and practices which might thwart those purposes. I fear to see the consequences of the Court's practice of substituting its own concepts of decency and fundamental justice for the language of the Bill of Rights as its point of departure in interpreting and enforcing that Bill of Rights. If the choice must be between the selective process of the *Palko* decision applying some of the Bill of Rights to the States, or the *Twining* rule applying none of them, I would choose the *Palko* selective process. But rather than accept either of these choices, I would follow what I believe was the original purpose of the Fourteenth Amendment—to extend to all the people of the nation the complete protection of the Bill of Rights. To hold that this Court can determine what, if any, provisions of the Bill of Rights will be enforced, and if so to what degree, is to frustrate the great design of a written Constitution.

"Conceding the possibility that this Court is now wise enough to improve on the Bill of Rights by substituting natural law concepts for the Bill of Rights, I think the possibility is entirely too speculative to agree to take that course. I would therefore hold in this case that the full protection of the Fifth Amendment's proscription against compelled testimony must be afforded by California. This I would do because of reliance upon the original purpose of the Fourteenth Amendment.

"[T]o pass upon the constitutionality of statutes by looking to the particular standards enumerated in the Bill of Rights and other parts of the Constitution is one thing; to invalidate statutes because of application of 'natural law' deemed to be above and undefined by the Constitution is another. 'In the one instance, courts proceeding within clearly marked constitutional boundaries seek to execute policies written into the Constitution; in the other they roam at will in the limitless area of their own beliefs as to reasonableness and actually select policies, a responsibility which the Constitution entrusts to the legislative representatives of the people.' " [d]

d. Dissenting separately in *Adamson*, Murphy, J., joined by Rutledge, J., "agree[d] that the specific guarantees of the Bill of Rights should be carried over intact into [the fourteenth amendment but was] not prepared to say that the latter is entirely and necessarily limited by the Bill of Rights. Occasions may arise where a proceeding falls so far short of conforming to fundamental standards of procedure as to warrant constitutional condemnation in terms of a lack of due process despite the absence of a specific provision of the Bill of Rights." In this connection, consider fn. e infra.

Responding, Frankfurter, J.'s concurrence in *Adamson* stressed the "independent potency" of the fourteenth amendment due process clause, maintaining that it "neither comprehends the specific provisions by which the founders deemed it appropriate to restrict the federal government nor is confined to them":[e] "Between the incorporation of the Fourteenth Amendment into the Constitution and the beginning of the present membership of the Court—a period of 70 years—the scope of that Amendment was passed upon by 43 judges. Of all these judges only one, who may respectfully be called an eccentric exception, ever indicated the belief that the Fourteenth Amendment was a shorthand summary of the first eight Amendments theretofore limiting only the Federal Government, and that due process incorporated those eight Amendments as restrictions upon the powers of the States. [To] suggest that it is inconsistent with a truly free society to begin prosecutions without an indictment, to try petty civil cases without the paraphernalia of a common law jury, to take into consideration that one who has full opportunity to make a defense remains silent is, in de Tocqueville's phrase, to confound the familiar with the necessary.

"[Those] reading the English language with the meaning which it ordinarily conveys, those conversant with the political and legal history of the concept of due process, those sensitive to the relations of the States to the central government as well as the relation of some of the provisions of the Bill of Rights to the process of justice, would hardly recognize the Fourteenth Amendment as a cover for the various explicit provisions of the first eight Amendments. Some of these are enduring reflections of experience with human nature, while some express the restricted views of Eighteenth-Century England regarding the best methods for the ascertainment of facts. The notion that the Fourteenth Amendment was a covert way of imposing upon the States all the rules which it seemed important to Eighteenth Century statesmen to write into the Federal Amendments, was rejected by judges who were themselves witnesses of the process by which the Fourteenth Amendment became part of the Constitution. [A]t the time of the ratification of the Fourteenth Amendment the constitutions of nearly half of the ratifying States did not have the rigorous requirements of the Fifth Amendment for instituting criminal proceedings through a grand jury. It could hardly have occurred to these States that by ratifying the Amendment they uprooted their established methods for prosecuting crime and fastened upon themselves a new prosecutorial system.

"Indeed, the suggestion that the Fourteenth Amendment incorporates the first eight Amendments as such is not unambiguously urged. [There] is suggested merely a selective incorporation of the first eight Amendments into the Fourteenth Amendment. Some are in and some are out, but we are left in the dark as to which are in and which are out. Nor are we given the calculus for determining which go in and which stay out. If the basis of selection is merely that those provisions of the first eight Amendments are incorporated which commend themselves to individual justices as indispensable to the dignity and

e. See also Friendly, *The Bill of Rights as a Code of Criminal Procedure,* 53 Calif.L.Rev. 929, 937 (1965): "[N]o facile formula will enable the Court to escape its assigned task of deciding just what the Constitution protects from state action, as *Estes v. Texas,* 381 U.S. 532, 85 S.Ct. 1628, 14 L.Ed.2d 543 (1965), where no 'specific' could be invoked, showed [for] procedural due process, and *Griswold v. Connecticut* [Sec. 2 infra] demonstrated for substantive due process." Consider, too, *In re Winship,* Part IV infra, holding that "proof beyond a reasonable doubt is among the essentials of due process" over the protest of dissenting Justice Black that nowhere in the Bill of Rights could he find any command that conviction of crime or adjudication of delinquency requires such a high standard of proof.

happiness of a free man, we are thrown back to a merely subjective test. [In] the history of thought 'natural law' has a much longer and much better founded meaning and justification than such subjective selection of the first eight Amendments for incorporation into the Fourteenth. If all that is meant is that due process contains within itself certain minimal standards which are 'of the very essence of a scheme of ordered liberty,' *Palko,* putting upon this Court the duty of applying these standards from time to time, then we have merely arrived at the insight which our predecessors long ago expressed. * * *

"A construction which gives to due process no independent function but turns it into a summary of the specific provisions of the Bill of Rights [would] deprive the States of opportunity for reforms in legal process designed for extending the area of freedom. It would assume that no other abuses would reveal themselves in the course of time than those which had become manifest in 1791. Such a view not only disregards the historic meaning of 'due process.' It leads inevitably to a warped construction of specific provisions of the Bill of Rights to bring within their scope conduct clearly condemned by due process but not easily fitting into the pigeonholes of the specific provisions.

"* * * Judicial review of [the Due Process Clause] of the Fourteenth Amendment inescapably imposes upon this Court an exercise of judgment upon the whole course of the proceedings in order to ascertain whether they offend those canons of decency and fairness which express the notions of justice of English-speaking peoples even toward those charged with the most heinous offenses. These standards of justice are not authoritatively formulated anywhere as though they were prescriptions in a pharmacopoeia. But neither does the application of the Due Process Clause imply that judges are wholly at large. The judicial judgment in applying the Due Process Clause must move within the limits of accepted notions of justice and is not to be based upon the idiosyncracies of a merely personal judgment."

Notes and Questions

1. Are Frankfurter and Black, JJ., each more persuasive in demonstrating why the *other's* test is subjective, ill-defined and unilluminating than in explaining why his own is *not*?

2. *Escape from the "idiosyncrasy of a personal judgment".* If, as Frankfurter, J., insists, the *Palko-Adamson* test is not based upon "the idiosyncrasies of a merely personal judgment," *whose* moral judgments furnish the answer? And *where* and *how* are they discoverable? The opinions of the progenitors and architects of our institutions? The opinions of the policy-making organs of state governments? Of state courts? The opinions of other countries? Of other countries in the Anglo-Saxon tradition? See Kadish, *Methodology and Criteria in Due Process Adjudication—A Survey and Criticism,* 66 Yale L.J. 319, 328–333 (1957). What judgments were relied on in *Palko* and *Adamson?* In *Rochin v. California,* Part III infra?

3. *History.* Historical research has produced ample support—and ample skepticism—for the "incorporation" theory. Compare 2 Crosskey, *Politics and the Constitution,* chs. XXXI, at 1083, XXXII, at 1119 (1953); Flack, *The Adoption of the Fourteenth Amendment* (1908); and Guthrie, *The Fourteenth Article of Amendment to the Constitution of the United States* (1898) with tenBroek, *The Antislavery Origins of the Fourteenth Amendment* (1951); Fairman, *Does the Fourteenth Amendment Incorporate the Bill of Rights? The Original Understanding,* 2 Stan.L.Rev. 5 (1949); Graham, *The "Conspiracy Theory" of the*

Fourteenth Amendment, 47 Yale L.J. 371 (1938). For brief but incisive criticism of both Black, J.'s position and Professor Fairman's attack, see Kelly, *Clio and the Court: An Illicit Love Affair,* 1965 Sup.Ct.Rev. 119, 132–34.

Is further historical search likely to do more than "further obscure the judicial value-choosing inherent in due process adjudication which can proceed with greater expectation of success if pursued openly and deliberately rather than under disguise"? Is due process more a moral command than a jural or historical concept? Ought it be? See Kadish, supra, at 340–41.

Although the Court continued to apply the "*Palko* selective process" approach to the Bill of Rights, DUNCAN v. LOUISIANA, 391 U.S. 145, 88 S.Ct. 1444, 20 L.Ed.2d 491 (1968) (holding the sixth amendment right to jury trial applicable to the states via the fourteenth amendment), no longer employed the Cardozo-Frankfurter terminology (e.g., whether a particular guarantee was "implicit in the concept of ordered liberty" or required by "the 'immutable principles of justice' as conceived by a civilized society") but instead inquired whether the procedural safeguard included in the Bill of Rights was "fundamental to the *American scheme of justice*" (emphasis added) or "fundamental *in the context of the criminal processes maintained by the American states*" (emphasis added). As WHITE, J., noted for the *Duncan* majority (fn. 14), the different phraseology is significant:

"Earlier the Court can be seen as having asked, when inquiring into whether some particular procedural safeguard was required of a State, if a civilized system could be imagined that would not accord the particular protection [quoting from *Palko*]. The recent cases, on the other hand, have proceeded upon the valid assumption that state criminal processes are not imaginary and theoretical schemes but actual systems bearing virtually every characteristic of the common-law system that has been developing contemporaneously in England and this country. The question thus is whether given this kind of system a particular procedure is fundamental—whether, that is, a procedure is necessary to an Anglo-American regime of ordered liberty. It is this sort of inquiry that can justify the conclusions that state courts must exclude evidence seized in violation of the Fourth Amendment, *Mapp v. Ohio* [Part IV infra] [and] that state prosecutors may not comment on a defendant's failure to testify, *Griffin v. California* [fn. a supra]. [Of] each of these determinations that a constitutional provision originally written to bind the Federal Government should bind the States as well it might be said that the limitation in question is not necessarily fundamental to fairness in every criminal system that might be imagined but is fundamental in the context of the criminal processes maintained by the American States.

"When the inquiry is approached in this way the question whether the States can impose criminal punishment without granting a jury trial appears quite different from the way it appeared in the older cases opining that States might abolish jury trial. A criminal process which was fair and equitable but used no juries is easy to imagine. It would make use of alternative guarantees and protections which would serve the purposes that the jury serves in the English and American systems. Yet no American State has undertaken to construct such a system. Instead, every American State, including Louisiana, uses the jury extensively, and imposes very serious punishments only after a trial at which the defendant has a right to a jury's verdict. In every State, including Louisiana, the structure and style of the criminal process—the supporting framework and the subsidiary procedures—are of the sort that naturally complement jury trial, and have developed in connection with and in reliance upon jury trial." [f]

Because the *Duncan* Court believed that "trial by jury in criminal cases is fundamental to the American scheme of justice," it held that it was guaranteed by the fourteenth amendment: "The guarantees of jury trial in the Federal and State Constitutions reflect a profound judgment about the way in which law should be enforced and justice administered. A right to jury trial is granted to criminal defendants in order to prevent oppression by the Government. Those who wrote our constitutions knew from history and experience that it was necessary to protect against unfounded criminal charges brought to eliminate enemies and against judges too responsive to the voice of higher authority. The framers of the constitutions strove to create an independent judiciary but insisted upon further protection against arbitrary action. Providing an accused with the right to be tried by a jury of his peers gave him an inestimable safeguard against the corrupt or overzealous prosecutor and against the compliant, biased, or eccentric judge. If the defendant preferred the common-sense judgment of a jury to the more tutored but perhaps less sympathetic reaction of the single judge, he was to have it. Beyond this, the jury trial provisions in the Federal and State Constitutions reflect a fundamental decision about the exercise of official power—a reluctance to entrust plenary powers over the life and liberty of the citizen to one judge or to a group of judges. Fear of unchecked power, so typical of our State and Federal Governments in other respects, found expression in the criminal law in this insistence upon community participation in the determination of guilt or innocence. The deep commitment of the Nation to the right of jury trial in serious criminal cases as a defense against arbitrary law enforcement qualifies for protection under the Due Process Clause of the Fourteenth Amendment, and must therefore be respected by the States."

HARLAN, J., joined by Stewart, J., dissented: "Even if I could agree that the question before us is whether Sixth Amendment jury trial is totally ['incorporated into' the fourteenth amendment] or totally 'out' [see Sec. II infra], I can find in the Court's opinion no real reasons for concluding that it should be 'in.' The basis for distinguishing among clauses in the Bill of Rights cannot be that [only] some are old and much praised, or that only some have played an important role in the development of federal law. These things are true of all. The Court says that some clauses are more 'fundamental' than others, but [uses] this word in a sense that would have astonished Mr. Justice Cardozo and which, in addition, is of no help. The word does not mean 'analytically critical to procedural fairness' for no real analysis of the role of the jury in making procedures fair is even attempted. Instead, the word turns out to mean 'old,' 'much praised,' and 'found in the Bill of Rights.' The definition of 'fundamental' thus turns out to be circular.

f. See also Powell, J., concurring in the companion 1972 "jury unanimity" cases of *Johnson v. Louisiana* and *Apodaca v. Oregon,* discussed below: "I agree with Mr. Justice White's analysis in *Duncan* that the departure from earlier decisions was, in large measure, a product of a change in focus in the Court's approach to due process. No longer are questions regarding the constitutionality of particular criminal procedures resolved by focusing alone on the element in question and ascertaining whether a system of criminal justice might be imagined in which a fair trial could be afforded in the absence of that particular element. Rather, the focus is, as it should be, on the fundamentality of that element viewed in the context of the basic Anglo-American jurisprudential system common to the States. That approach to due process readily accounts both for the conclusion that jury trial *is* fundamental and that unanimity *is not.*"

"[Jury trial] is of course not without virtues [but its] principal original virtue—[the limitations it] imposes on a tyrannous judiciary—has largely disappeared. [The] jury system can also be said to have some inherent defects, which are multiplied by the emergence of the criminal law from the relative simplicity that existed when the jury system was devised. It is a cumbersome process, not only imposing great cost in time and money on both the State and the jurors themselves, but also contributing to delay in the machinery of justice. [That] trial by jury is not the only fair way of adjudicating criminal guilt is well attested by the fact that it is not the prevailing way, either in England or in this country.

"[The majority recognizes that not every, or any particular, criminal trial before a judge alone is unfair, or less fair than one held before a jury.] I agree. I therefore see no reason why this Court should reverse the conviction of appellant absent any suggestion that his particular trial was in fact unfair, or compel the State of Louisiana to afford jury trial in an as yet unbounded category of cases that can, without unfairness, be tried to a court.

"[In] sum, there is a wide range of views on the desirability of trial by jury, and on the ways to make it most effective when it is used; there is also considerable variation from State to State in local conditions such as the size of the criminal caseload, the ease or difficulty of summoning jurors, and other trial conditions bearing on fairness. We have before us, therefore, an almost perfect example of a situation in which [the states should serve as laboratories.] [Instead,] the Court has chosen to impose upon every State one means of trying criminal cases; it is a good means, but it is not the only fair means, and it is not demonstrably better than the alternatives States might devise."

Although the Court has remained unwilling to accept the total incorporationists' reading of the fourteenth amendment, in the 1960s it "selectively" "incorporated" or "absorbed" more and more of the specifics of the Bill of Rights into the fourteenth amendment. As White, J., observed in *Duncan*:

"In resolving conflicting claims concerning the meaning of this spacious [fourteenth amendment] language, the Court has looked increasingly to the Bill of Rights for guidance; many of the rights guaranteed by the first eight Amendments to the Constitution have been held to be protected against state action by the Due Process Clause of the Fourteenth Amendment.[g] That clause now protects [the] Fourth Amendment rights to be free from unreasonable searches and seizures and to have excluded from criminal trials any evidence illegally seized; the right guaranteed by the Fifth Amendment to be free of compelled self-incrimination; and the Sixth Amendment rights to counsel, to a speedy and public trial [*Klopfer v. North Carolina,* 386 U.S. 213, 87 S.Ct. 988, 18 L.Ed.2d 1 (1967); *In re Oliver,* 330 U.S. 257, 68 S.Ct. 499, 92 L.Ed. 682 (1942)], to confrontation of opposing witnesses [*Pointer v. Texas*, 380 U.S. 400, 85 S.Ct. 1065, 13 L.Ed.2d 923 (1965)] and to compulsory process for obtaining witnesses

g. See also Black, J., joined by Douglas, J., concurring in *Duncan*: "[I] believe as strongly as ever that the Fourteenth Amendment was intended to make the Bill of Rights applicable to the States. I have been willing to support the selective incorporation doctrine, however, as an alternative, although perhaps less historically supportable than complete incorporation [because it] keeps judges from roaming at will in their own notions of what policies outside the Bill of Rights are desirable and what are not. And, most importantly for me, the selective incorporation process has the virtue of having already worked to make most of the Bill of Rights' protections applicable to the States."

[*Washington v. Texas,* 388 U.S. 14, 87 S.Ct. 1920, 18 L.Ed.2d 1019 (1967)]." [h]

II. SHOULD THE "SELECTED" PROVISION APPLY TO THE STATES "JOT–FOR–JOT"? "BAG AND BAGGAGE"?

In the 1960s, the Court seemed to be "incorporating" not only the basic notion or general concept of the "selected" provision of the Bill of Rights, but applying the provision to the states *to the same extent* it applied to the federal government. Thus, Brennan, J., observed for a majority in *Malloy v. Hogan,* 378 U.S. 1, 84 S.Ct. 1489, 12 L.Ed.2d 653 (1964): "We have held that the guarantees of the First Amendment, the prohibition of unreasonable searches and seizures of the Fourth Amendment, and the right to counsel guaranteed by the Sixth Amendment, are all to be enforced against the States under the Fourteenth Amendment *according to the same standards that protect those personal rights against federal encroachment.* [The] Court thus has rejected the notion that the Fourteenth Amendment applies to the States only a 'watered-down, subjective version of the individual guarantees of the Bill of Rights.' " (Emphasis added.) And White, J., put it for a majority in *Duncan:* "Because we believe that trial by jury in criminal cases is fundamental to the American scheme of justice, we hold that the Fourteenth Amendment guarantees a right of jury trial in all criminal cases which—*were they to be tried in a federal court*—would come within the Sixth Amendment's guarantee." (Emphasis added.)[i]

The federal guarantees, protested some justices, were being incorporated into the fourteenth amendment "freighted with their entire accompanying body of federal doctrine" (Harlan, J., joined by Clark, J., dissenting in *Malloy v. Hogan*); "jot-for-jot and case-for-case (Harlan, J., joined by Stewart, J., dissenting in *Duncan*); "bag and baggage, however securely or insecurely affixed they may be by law and precedent to federal proceedings" (Fortas, J., concurring in *Duncan*).

Justice Harlan was the most persistent and powerful critic of the *Malloy–Duncan* approach to fourteenth amendment due process. "The consequence," he maintained in his *Malloy* dissent, "is inevitably disregard of all relevant differences which may exist between state and federal criminal law and its enforcement. The ultimate result is compelled uniformity, which is inconsistent with the purpose of our federal system and which is achieved either by encroachment on the State's sovereign powers or by dilution in federal law enforcement of the specific protections found in the Bill of Rights."

Concurring in the result in *Pointer v. Texas,* 380 U.S. 400, 85 S.Ct. 1065, 13 L.Ed.2d 923 (1965) (holding that the Sixth Amendment right of an accused to confront the witnesses against him applies in its entirety to the states via the

h. In the area of criminal procedure, the Court has come very close to incorporating all of the relevant Bill of Rights guarantees. But still on the books, is a lonely exception. *Hurtado v. California,* 110 U.S. 516, 4 S.Ct. 111, 28 L.Ed. 232 (1884), refusing to apply to the states the fifth amendment requirement that prosecution be initiated by grand jury indictment. For an overview of the development and application of the selective incorporation doctrine see Israel, *Selective Incorporation Revisited,* 71 Geo.L.J. 253 (1982).

i. See also Justice Marshall's opinion for the Court in *Benton v. Maryland,* 395 U.S. 784, 89 S.Ct. 2056, 23 L.Ed.2d 707 (1969) (the validity of the state conviction "must be judged not by the watered-down standard enumerated in *Palko,* but *under this Court's interpretations of the Fifth Amendment double jeopardy provision* "). (Emphasis added.) Consider, too, Justice Black's concurring opinion in *Duncan* and Justice Goldberg's concurring opinion in *Pointer v. Texas* (1965), infra, both responding to Justice Harlan's repeated criticism of the "selective incorporation" approach.

Fourteenth), Justice Harlan observed that " 'selective' incorporation or 'absorption' amounts to little more than a diluted form of the full incorporation theory. Whereas it rejects full incorporation because of recognition that not all of the guarantees of the Bill of Rights should be deemed 'fundamental,' it at the same time ignores the possibility that not all phases of any given guaranty are necessarily fundamental."

Dissenting in *Duncan*, HARLAN, J., joined by Stewart, J., protested: "Today's Court still remains unwilling to accept the total incorporationists' view of the history of the Fourteenth Amendment. This, if accepted, would afford a cogent reason for applying the Sixth Amendment to the States. The Court is also, apparently, unwilling to face the task of determining whether denial of trial by jury in the situation before us, or in other situations, is fundamentally unfair. Consequently, the Court has compromised on the ease of the incorporationist position, without its internal logic. It has simply assumed that the question before us is whether the Jury Trial Clause of the Sixth Amendment should be incorporated into the Fourteenth, jot-for-jot and case-for-case, or ignored. Then the Court merely declares that the clause in question is 'in' rather than 'out.'

"The Court has justified neither its starting place nor its conclusion. If the problem is to discover and articulate the rules of fundamental fairness in criminal proceedings, there is no reason to assume that the whole body of rules developed in this Court constituting Sixth Amendment jury trial must be regarded as a unit. The requirement of trial by jury in federal criminal cases has given rise to numerous subsidiary questions respecting the exact scope and content of the right. It surely cannot be that every answer the Court has given, or will give, to such a question is attributable to the Founders; or even that every rule announced carries equal conviction of this Court; still less can it be that every such subprinciple is equally fundamental to ordered liberty."

In the 1970s matters were brought to a head by the "right to jury trial" cases: *Baldwin v. New York*, 399 U.S. 66, 90 S.Ct. 1886, 26 L.Ed.2d 437 (1970) (no offense can be deemed "petty," thus dispensing with the fourteenth and sixth amendment rights to jury trial, where more than six months incarceration is authorized); *Williams v. Florida*, 399 U.S. 78, 90 S.Ct. 1893, 26 L.Ed.2d 446 (1970) ("that jury at common law was composed of precisely 12 is an historical accident, unnecessary to effect the purposes of the jury system"; thus 6-person jury in criminal cases does not violate sixth amendment, as applied to the states via fourteenth);[a] and the 1972 *Apodaca* and *Johnson* cases, discussed below, dealing with whether unanimous jury verdicts are required in criminal cases.

Dissenting in *Baldwin* and concurring in *Williams*, HARLAN, J., maintained: "[*Williams*] evinces [a] recognition that the 'incorporationist' view of the Due Process Clause of the Fourteenth Amendment, which underlay *Duncan* and is now carried forward into *Baldwin*, must be tempered to allow the States more elbow room in ordering their own criminal systems. With that much I agree. But to accomplish this by diluting constitutional protections within the federal system itself is something to which I cannot possibly subscribe. Tempering the rigor of *Duncan* should be done forthrightly, by facing up to the fact that at least

a. But *Ballew v. Georgia*, 435 U.S. 223, 98 S.Ct. 1029, 55 L.Ed.2d 234 (1978), subsequently held that a state trial in a non-petty criminal case to a jury of only five persons did deprive a defendant of the right to trial by jury guaranteed by the sixth and fourteenth amendments.

in this area the 'incorporation' doctrine does not fit well with our federal structure, and by the same token that *Duncan* was wrongly decided.

"[Rather] than bind the States by the hitherto undeviating and unquestioned federal practice of 12-member juries, the Court holds, based on a poll of state practice, that a six-man jury satisfies the guarantee of a trial by jury in a federal criminal system and consequently carries over to the States. This is a constitutional *renvoi.* With all respect, I consider that before today it would have been unthinkable to suggest that the Sixth Amendment's right to a trial by jury is satisfied by a jury of six, or less, as is left open by the Court's opinion in *Williams,* or by less than a unanimous verdict, a question also reserved in today's decision.[b]

"[These decisions] demonstrate that the difference between a 'due process' approach, that considers each particular case on its own bottom to see whether the right alleged is one 'implicit in the concept of ordered liberty,' and 'selective incorporation' is not an abstract one whereby different verbal formulae achieve the same results. The internal logic of the selective incorporation doctrine cannot be respected if the Court is both committed to interpreting faithfully the meaning of the federal Bill of Rights and recognizing the governmental diversity that exists in this country. The 'backlash' in *Williams* exposes the malaise, for there the Court dilutes a federal guarantee in order to reconcile the logic of 'incorporation,' the 'jot-for-jot and case-for-case' application of the federal right to the States, with the reality of federalism. Can one doubt that had Congress tried to undermine the common law right to trial by jury before *Duncan* came on the books the history today recited would have barred such action? Can we expect repeated performances when this Court is called upon to give definition and meaning to other federal guarantees that have been 'incorporated'?

"[I]t is time [for] for this Court to face up to the reality implicit in today's holdings and reconsider the 'incorporation' doctrine before its leveling tendencies further retard development in the field of criminal procedure by stifling flexibility in the States and by discarding the possibility of federal leadership by example."

In the companion cases of *Apodaca v. Oregon,* 406 U.S. 404, 92 S.Ct. 1628, 32 L.Ed.2d 184 (1972) and *Johnson v. Louisiana,* 406 U.S. 356, 92 S.Ct. 1620, 32 L.Ed.2d 152 (1972), upholding the constitutionality of less-than-unanimous jury verdicts in state criminal cases, eight justices adhered to the *Duncan* position that each element of the sixth amendment right to jury trial applies to the states to the same extent it applies to the federal government, but split 4–4 over whether the federal guarantee *did require* jury unanimity in criminal cases. State convictions by less than unanimous votes were sustained only because the ninth member of the Court, newly appointed POWELL, J., read the sixth amendment as requiring jury unanimity, but—taking a Harlan-type approach—concluded that *this feature* of the federal right is not "so fundamental to the essentials of jury trial" as to require unanimity in state criminal cases as a matter of fourteenth amendment due process:[c]

b. Cf. Frankfurter, J., for the Court in *Rochin v. California* (1952) (discussed in Part III infra): "Words being symbols do not speak without a gloss. [T]he gloss may be the deposit of history, whereby a term gains technical content. Thus the requirements of the Sixth and Seventh Amendments for trial by jury in the federal courts have a rigid meaning. No changes or chances can alter the content of the verbal symbol of 'jury'—a body of twelve men who must reach a unanimous conclusion if the verdict is to go against the defendant."

c. But *Burch v. Louisiana,* 441 U.S. 130, 99 S.Ct. 1623, 60 L.Ed.2d 96 (1979), subsequently held, without a dissent on this issue, that conviction by a nonunanimous *six-person* jury

"[I]n holding that the Fourteenth Amendment has incorporated 'jot-for-jot and case-for-case' every element of the Sixth Amendment, the Court derogates principles of federalism that are basic to our system. In the name of uniform application of high standards of due process, the Court has embarked upon a course of constitutional interpretation that deprives the States of freedom to experiment with adjudicatory processes different from the federal model. At the same time, the Court's understandable unwillingness to impose requirements that it finds unnecessarily rigid (e.g., *Williams*), has culminated in the dilution of federal rights that were, until these decisions, never seriously questioned. The doubly undesirable consequence of this reasoning process, labeled by Mr. Justice Harlan as 'constitutional schizophrenia,' may well be detrimental both to the state and federal criminal justice systems." [d]

BRENNAN, J., joined by Marshall, J., dissented: "Readers of today's opinions may be understandably puzzled why convictions by 11–1 and 10–2 jury votes are affirmed [when] a majority of the Court agrees that the Sixth Amendment requires a unanimous verdict in federal criminal jury trials, and a majority also agrees that the right to jury trial guaranteed by the Sixth Amendment is to be enforced against the States according to the same standards that protect that right against federal encroachment. The reason is that while my Brother Powell agrees that a unanimous verdict is required in federal criminal trials, he does not agree that the Sixth Amendment right to a jury trial is to be applied in the same way to State and Federal Governments. In that circumstance, it is arguable that the affirmance of the convictions [is] not inconsistent with a view that today's decision is a holding that only a unanimous verdict will afford the accused in a state criminal prosecution the jury trial guaranteed him by the Sixth Amendment. In any event, the affirmance must not obscure that the majority of the Court remains of the view that, as in the case of every specific of the Bill of Rights that extends to the States, the Sixth Amendment's jury trial guarantee, however it is to be construed, has identical application against both State and Federal Governments." [e]

III. BODILY EXTRACTIONS: ANOTHER LOOK AT THE "DUE PROCESS" AND "SELECTIVE INCORPORATION" APPROACHES

As noted earlier, Justice Harlan maintained that "the difference between a 'due process' approach [and] 'selective incorporation' is not an abstract one whereby different formulae achieve the same results." But he made this observation in the context of the applicability to the states of the sixth amendment right to trial by jury, which had, or was thought to have, a relatively rigid meaning. Most language in the Bill of Rights, however, is rather vague and

in a state criminal trial for a nonpetty offense did violate the sixth and fourteenth amendment rights to trial by jury.

d. See also Powell, J., joined by Burger, C.J., and Rehnquist, J., dissenting in *Crist v. Bretz,* 437 U.S. 28, 98 S.Ct. 2156, 57 L.Ed.2d 24 (1978) (holding that federal rule as to when jeopardy "attaches" in jury trials applies to state cases). Consider, too, Burger, C.J.'s separate opinion in *Crist v. Bretz* and Rehnquist, J.'s separate opinion in *Buckley v. Valeo,* maintaining that "not all of the strictures which the First Amendment imposes upon Congress are carried over against the States by the Fourteenth Amendment, [but] only the 'general principle' of free speech."

e. In a separate dissent, Stewart, J., joined by Brennan and Marshall, JJ., protested that "unless *Duncan* is to be overruled," "the only relevant question here is whether the Sixth Amendment's guarantee of trial by jury embraces a guarantee that the verdict of the jury must be unanimous. The answer to that question is clearly 'yes,' as my Brother Powell has cogently demonstrated."

general, at least when specific problems arise under a particular phrase. In such cases, does dwelling on the literal language simply *shift the focus of broad judicial inquiry* from "due process" to e.g., "freedom of speech," "establishment of religion," "unreasonable searches and seizures," "excessive bail," "cruel and unusual punishments," and "the assistance of counsel"? See Friendly, *The Bill of Rights as a Code of Criminal Procedure,* 53 Calif.L.Rev. 929, 937 (1965); Israel, fn. h supra, at 336–38; Kadish, *Methodology and Criteria in Due Process Adjudication—A Survey and Criticism,* 66 Yale L.J. 319, 337–39 (1957); Wechsler, *Toward Neutral Principles of Constitutional Law,* 73 Harv.L.Rev. 1, 17–18 (1959). Cf. Nowak, *Due Process Methodology in the Postincorporation World,* 70 J.Crim.L. & C. 397, 400–01 (1979) (arguing that decisions based on specific guarantees tend to rely on definitional analysis and fail to explore the interests at stake).

In considering whether the right to counsel "begins" at the time of arrest, preliminary hearing, arraignment, or not until the trial itself, or includes probation and parole revocation hearings or applies to juvenile delinquency proceedings, deportation hearings or civil commitments, or, where the defendant is indigent, includes the right to *assigned* counsel or an assigned psychiatrist at state expense, how helpful is the sixth amendment language entitling an accused to "the assistance of counsel for his defense"? Is the specificity or direction of this language significantly greater than the "due process" clause?

To turn to another cluster of problems—which form the basis for this section—in considering whether, and under what conditions, the police may direct the "pumping" of a person's stomach to uncover incriminating evidence, or the taking of a blood sample from him, without his consent, do the "specific guarantees" in the Bill of Rights against "unreasonable searches and seizures" and against compelling a person to be "a witness against himself" free the Court from the demands of appraising and judging involved in answering these questions by interpreting the "due process" clause?

ROCHIN v. CALIFORNIA, 342 U.S. 165, 72 S.Ct. 205, 96 L.Ed. 183 (1952) arose as follows: Having "some information" that Rochin was selling narcotics, three deputy sheriffs "forced upon the door of [his] room and found him sitting partly dressed on the side of the bed, upon which his wife was lying. On a 'night stand' beside the bed the deputies spied two capsules. When asked 'Whose stuff is this?' Rochin seized the capsules and put them in his mouth. A struggle ensued, in the course of which the three officers 'jumped upon him' and [unsuccessfully] attempted to extract the capsules. [Rochin] was handcuffed and taken to a hospital. At the direction of one of the officers a doctor forced an emetic solution through a tube into Rochin's stomach against his will. This 'stomach pumping' produced vomiting. In the vomited matter were found two capsules which proved to contain morphine. [Rochin was convicted of possessing morphine] and sentenced to sixty days' imprisonment. The chief evidence against him was the two capsules."

The Court, per FRANKFURTER, J., concluded that the officers' conduct violated fourteenth amendment due process: "This is conduct that shocks the conscience. Illegally breaking into the privacy of the petitioner, the struggle to open his mouth and remove what was there, the forcible extraction of his stomach's contents—this course of proceeding by agents of government to obtain evidence is bound to offend even hardened sensibilities. They are methods too close to the rack and the screw to permit of constitutional differentiation.

* * * "Due process of law, as a historic and generative principle, precludes defining, and thereby confining, [civilized] standards of conduct more precisely than to say that convictions cannot be brought about by methods that offend 'a sense of justice.' It would be a stultification of the responsibility which the course of constitutional history has cast upon this Court to hold that in order to convict a man the police cannot extract by force what is in his mind but can extract what is in his stomach.

"[E]ven though statements contained in them may be independently established as true[,] [c]oerced confessions offend the community's sense of fair play and decency. So here, to sanction the brutal conduct which naturally enough was condemned by the court whose judgment is before us, would be to afford brutality the cloak of law. Nothing would be more calculated to discredit law and thereby to brutalize the temper of a society."

Concurring, BLACK, J., reasoned that the fifth amendment's protection against compelled self-incrimination applied to the states and that "a person is compelled to be a witness against himself not only when he is compelled to testify, but also when as here, incriminating evidence is forcibly taken from him by a contrivance of modern science." He maintained that "faithful adherence to the specific guarantees in the Bill of Rights insures a more permanent protection of individual liberty than that which can be afforded by the nebulous [fourteenth amendment due process] standards stated by the majority."

DOUGLAS, J., concurring, also criticized the majority's approach. He contended that the privilege against self-incrimination applied to the states as well as the federal government and because of the privilege "words taken from [an accused's] lips, capsules taken from his stomach, blood taken from his veins are all inadmissible provided they are taken from him without his consent. [This] is an unequivocal, definite and workable rule of evidence for state and federal courts. But we cannot in fairness free the state courts from the [restraints of the fifth amendment privilege against self-incrimination] and yet excoriate them for flouting the 'decencies of civilized conduct' when they admit the evidence. This is to make the rule turn not on the Constitution but on the idiosyncracies of the judges who sit here." [a]

---

a. *Irvine v. California,* 347 U.S. 128, 74 S.Ct. 381, 98 L.Ed. 561 (1954), limited *Rochin* to situations involving coercion, violence or brutality to the person. In *Irvine* the police made repeated illegal entries into petitioner's home, first to install a secret microphone and then to move it to the bedroom, in order to listen to the conversations of the occupants—for over a month. Jackson, J., who announced the judgment of the Court and wrote the principal opinion, recognized that "few police measures have come to our attention that more flagrantly, deliberately, and persistently violated the fundamental principle declared by the Fourth Amendment as a restriction on the Federal Government," but adhered to the holding in *Wolf v. Colorado* (1949) (Part IV infra) that the exclusionary rule in federal search and seizure cases is not binding on the states. (*Wolf* was overruled in *Mapp v. Ohio* (1961) (Part IV infra)). Nor did Jackson, J., deem *Rochin* applicable: "However obnoxious are the facts in the case before us, they do not involve coercion, violence or brutality to the person [as did *Rochin*], but rather a trespass to property, plus eavesdropping."

Because of the "aggravating" and "repulsive" police misconduct in *Irvine,* Frankfurter, J., joined by Burton, J., dissenting, maintained that *Rochin* was controlling, not *Wolf.* (He had written the majority opinions in both cases.) Black, J., joined by Douglas, J., dissented separately, arguing that petitioner had been convicted on the basis of evidence "extorted" from him in violation of the self-incrimination clause, which he considered applicable to the states. Douglas, J., dissenting separately, protested against the use in state prosecutions of evidence seized in violation of the fourth amendment.

Breithaupt v. Abram, 352 U.S. 432, 77 S.Ct. 408, 1 L.Ed.2d 448 (1957), illustrated that under the *Rochin* test state police had considerable leeway even when the body of the accused was "invaded." In *Breithaupt,* the police took a blood sample from an unconscious person who had been involved in a fatal automobile collision. A majority, per Clark, J., affirmed a manslaughter conviction based on the blood sample (which showed intoxication), stressing that the sample was "taken under the protective eye of a physician" and that "the blood test procedure has become routine in our everyday life." The "interests of society in the scientific determination of intoxication, one of the great causes of the mortal hazards of the road," outweighed "so slight an intrusion" of a person's body.

Dissenting, Warren, C.J., joined by Black and Douglas, JJ., deemed *Rochin* controlling and argued that police efforts to curb the narcotics traffic, involved in *Rochin,* "is surely a state interest of at least as great magnitude as the interest in highway law enforcement. [Only] personal reaction to the stomach pump and the blood test can distinguish the [two cases]."

Douglas, J., joined by Black, J., dissented, maintaining that "if the decencies of a civilized state are the test, it is repulsive to me for the police to insert needles into an unconscious person in order to get the evidence necessary to convict him, whether they find the person unconscious, give him a pill which puts him to sleep, or use force to subdue him."

Nine years later, even though in the meantime the Court had held in *Mapp v. Ohio,* Part IV infra, that the federal exclusionary rule in search and seizure cases was binding on the states and in *Malloy v. Hogan,* supra, that the fifth amendment's protection against compelled self-incrimination was likewise applicable to the states, the Court still upheld the taking by a physician, at police direction, of a blood sample from an injured person, over his objection. SCHMERBER v. CALIFORNIA, 384 U.S. 757, 86 S.Ct. 1826, 16 L.Ed.2d 908 (1966). In affirming the conviction for operating a vehicle while under the influence of intoxicating liquor, a 5–4 majority, per BRENNAN, J., ruled: (1) that the extraction of blood from petitioner under the aforementioned circumstances "did not offend 'that "sense of justice"' of which we spoke in *Rochin,*" thus reaffirming *Breithaupt;* (2) that the privilege against self-incrimination, now binding on the states, "protects an accused only from being compelled to testify against himself, or otherwise provide the State with evidence of a testimonial or communicative nature and that the withdrawal of blood and use of the analysis in question did not involve compulsion to these ends"; and (3) that the protection against unreasonable search and seizure, now binding on the states, was satisfied because (a) "there was plainly probable cause" to arrest and charge petitioner and to suggest "the required relevance and likely success of a test of petitioner's blood for alcohol"; (b) the officer "might reasonably have believed that he was confronted with an emergency, in which the delay necessary to obtain a warrant, under the circumstances, threatened 'the destruction of evidence' "; and (c) "the test chosen to measure petitioner's blood-alcohol level was [reasonable and] performed in a reasonable manner."

Dissenting, Black, J., joined by Douglas, J., expressed amazement at the majority's "conclusion that compelling a person to give his blood to help the State to convict him is not equivalent to compelling him to be a witness against himself." "It is a strange hierarchy of values that allows the State to extract a human being's blood to convict him of a crime because of the blood's content but proscribes compelled production of his lifeless papers." [a]

Notes and Questions

1. In light of *Rochin, Breithaupt* and *Schmerber,* when courts decide constitutional questions by "looking to" the Bill of Rights, to what extent do they proceed, as Black, J., said in *Adamson,* "within clearly marked constitutional boundaries"? To what extent does resort to these "particular standards" enable courts to avoid substituting their "own concepts of decency and fundamental justice" for the language of the Constitution?

2. Did *Mapp* and *Malloy,* decided in the interim between *Breithaupt* and *Schmerber,* affect any justice's vote? Did the applicability of the "particular standards" of the fourth and fifth amendments inhibit Black, Douglas or Brennan, JJ., from employing their own concepts of "decency" and "justice" in *Schmerber?* After *Schmerber,* how much force is there in Black, J.'s view, concurring in *Rochin,* that "faithful adherence to the specific guarantees in the Bill of Rights assures a more permanent protection of individual liberty than that which can be afforded by the nebulous standards stated by the majority"?

3. For other recent illustrations of standards and methodology in due process adjudication, see the "death penalty" cases (although nominally "cruel and unusual punishment" cases), Sec. 4 infra. See also the "right of privacy" cases, Sec. 2 infra.

IV. THE RETROACTIVE EFFECT OF A HOLDING OF UNCONSTITUTIONALITY

In recent years, the Court has considered the retroactive effect of a holding that a law or practice is unconstitutional primarily in the context of criminal procedure decisions.[a] Rejecting what it called the Blackstonian Theory that a new ruling merely sets forth the law as it always existed, *Linkletter v. Walker,* 381 U.S. 618, 85 S.Ct. 1731, 14 L.Ed.2d 601 (1965), took the position that "the Constitution neither prohibits nor requires retrospective effect," [b] and that a determination of the effect of a judgment of unconstitutionality should turn on

a. Warren, C.J., and Douglas, J., dissented in separate opinions, each adhering to his dissenting views in *Breithaupt.* In a third dissent, Fortas, J., maintained that "petitioner's privilege against self-incrimination applies" and, moreover, "under the Due Process Clause, the State, in its role as prosecutor, has no right to extract blood from [anyone] over his protest."

a. In none of these cases, apparently, did the Court seriously consider applying the new constitutional ruling "purely prospectively," i.e., not even giving the litigant in the very case the benefit of the decision. "Pure prospectivity" raises "difficult problems concerning the nature of a court's functions; persuasive arguments can be made that courts are badly suited for the general determination and proclamation of future rules and, indeed, that for them to do so violates the Constitution's grant to the judiciary only of power over 'cases' and 'controversies.'" 80 Harv.L.Rev. 140 (1966). Another frequently made point, although it may carry less weight in the criminal procedure area, is that "if the Supreme Court begins regularly to announce new rules prospectively only, petitioners, knowing they will be unlikely to benefit personally, will be deterred from pressing for the new rules." Id.

b. "If an unconstitutional statute or practice effectively never existed as a lawful justification for state action [perhaps the dominant view in the era between the Civil War and the Depression], individuals convicted under the statute or in trials which tolerated the practice were convicted unlawfully even if their trials took place before the declaration of unconstitutionality; such a declaration should have a fully retroactive effect, and previously convicted individuals should be able to win their freedom through the writ of habeas corpus. Alternatively, if a judgment of unconstitutionality affects only the case at hand [a view which also had support], the legality of the convictions of individuals previously tried is not affected. In *Linkletter,* the Court rejected both extremes." Tribe, *American Constitutional Law* 29–30 (2d ed. 1988).

"the prior history of the rule in question, its purpose and effect," "whether retrospective operation of the rule will further or retard its operation" and what adverse impact on the administration of justice retroactivity would be likely to have.

The prime purpose of *Mapp v. Ohio,* 367 U.S. 643, 81 S.Ct. 1684, 6 L.Ed.2d 1081 (1961) (imposing the exclusionary rule on the states), emphasized the *Linkletter* Court, was to deter future police misconduct and this purpose would not be advanced by applying the rule to cases which had become "final" (i.e., direct appellate review had been exhausted) prior to the overturning of *Mapp.* The Court recognized that it had given full retroactive effect to some recent law-changing decisions—such as *Gideon v. Wainwright,* 372 U.S. 335, 83 S.Ct. 792, 9 L.Ed.2d 799 (1963) (establishing an absolute right to appointed counsel at least in all serious criminal cases) and the coerced confession cases—but, unlike *Mapp,* the principles in those cases "went to the fairness of the trial—the very integrity of the fact-finding process. [Here] the fairness of the trial is not under attack."

Relying upon the *Linkletter* analysis, STOVALL v. DENNO, 388 U.S. 293, 87 S.Ct. 1967, 18 L.Ed.2d 1199 (1967), set forth a framework for determining whether a new ruling should be given retroactive effect. The "criteria guiding the resolution of the question," observed the *Stovall* Court, "implicate (a) the purpose to be served by the new standards, (b) the extent of the reliance by law enforcement authorities on the old standards, [and] (c) the effect on the administration of justice of a retroactive application of the new standards."

Prior to *Linkletter, Mapp* had already been applied to cases still pending on direct appeal, so the only issue considered by *Linkletter* was whether *Mapp* should be applied to a collateral attack upon a conviction. In applying the *Linkletter* standard, however, *Stovall* and subsequent cases did not draw a distinction between final convictions attacked collaterally and those challenged at various stages of direct review.

Moreover, in limiting the retroactive effect of new rulings, cases applying the *Linkletter–Stovall* standard selected different "starting points." Because *Miranda v. Arizona,* 384 U.S. 436, 86 S.Ct. 1602, 16 L.Ed.2d 694 (1966), was viewed as not primarily designed to protect the innocent from wrongful conviction, *Johnson v. New Jersey,* 384 U.S. 719, 86 S.Ct. 1772, 16 L.Ed.2d 882 (1966) held that the new rule in *Miranda* affected only cases in which *the trial began* after the date of that landmark decision. Because the use of improper lineups could be challenged on due process grounds even if the new ruling on lineups were not applied retroactively, *Stovall,* supra, declined to give retroactive effect to *United States v. Wade,* 388 U.S. 218, 87 S.Ct. 1926, 18 L.Ed.2d 1149 (1967), the case that established a right to counsel at certain pretrial lineups. But this time the Court selected a different "starting point": the new lineup ruling affected only those pretrial identification procedures *conducted* in the absence of counsel *after the date* of the decisions.[c]

Selection of the date of the challenged *police conduct* as the starting point indicated that *police reliance* on the overturned rule was a major factor in

c. Although "at first glance the prospectivity rule appears to be an act of judicial self-abnegation," "in reality," observes F. Allen, *The Judicial Quest for Penal Justice: The Warren Court and the Criminal Cases,* 1975 U.Ill.L.F. 518, 530, such a rule "encourages the making of new law by reducing some of the social costs." See also Haddad, *Retroactivity Should Be Rethought: A Call for the End of the Linkletter Doctrine:* 60 J.Crim.L.C. & P.S. 417, 439 (1969): "The alternative to the prospective-only technique is a more conservative approach to constitutional criminal procedure. [Detailed requirements] such as those laid down in *Miranda* would no longer be possible."

retroactivity disputes. In this respect, DESIST v. UNITED STATES, 394 U.S. 244, 89 S.Ct. 1030, 22 L.Ed.2d 248 (1969) is hardly surprising. *Desist* held that *Katz v. United States,* 389 U.S. 347, 88 S.Ct. 507, 19 L.Ed.2d 576 (1967) (overruling *Olmstead v. United States,* 277 U.S. 438, 48 S.Ct. 564, 72 L.Ed. 944 (1928) and holding that wiretapping and other forms of electronic surveillance are subject to Fourth Amendment restraints) should be given what the Court called "wholly prospective application," i.e., applied only to *police activity* occurring *after* the date of the *Katz* decision.[d]

The *Desist* Court saw no significant distinction for retroactive purpose between direct review and collateral attack. All of the reasons for making *Katz* prospective only, observed the Court, per STEWART, J. (author of the *Katz* opinion), "also undercut any distinction between final convictions and those still pending on direct review. Both the deterrent purpose of the exclusionary rule and the reliance of law enforcement officers focus upon *the time of the search,* not any subsequent point in the prosecution as the relevant date." (Emphasis added.)

JUSTICE HARLAN wrote a powerful dissent. Two decades later, this dissent seems a good deal more significant than the opinion of the Court in that case. "[A]ll 'new rules' of constitutional law," maintained Harlan, "must, at a minimum, be applied to all those cases which are still subject to direct review by this Court at the time the 'new' decision is handed down." Observed Harlan:

"[We release a prisoner] only because the Government has offended constitutional principle in the conduct of his case. And when another similarly situated defendant comes before us, we must grant the same relief or give a principled reason for acting differently. We depart from this basic judicial tradition when we simply pick and choose from among similarly situated defendants those who alone will receive the benefit of a 'new' rule of constitutional law.

"[If] a 'new' constitutional doctrine is truly right, we should not reverse lower courts which have accepted it; nor should we affirm those which have rejected the very arguments we have embraced. Anything else would belie the truism that it is the task of this Court, like that of any other, to do justice to each litigant on the merits of his own case. It is only if each of our decisions can be justified in terms of this fundamental premise that they may properly be considered the legitimate products of a court of law, rather than the commands of a super-legislature."

RETHINKING RETROACTIVITY: HARLAN'S VIEWS COME TO THE FORE

Relying heavily on Justice Harlan's reasoning in *Desist,* a 5–4 majority found the distinction between final convictions and those still pending on direct review persuasive for retroactivity purposes and applied it in SHEA v. LOUISIANA, 470 U.S. 51, 105 S.Ct. 1065, 84 L.Ed.2d 38 (1985). The case arose as follows: When read his *Miranda* rights, Shea asserted his right to counsel. The questioning session was terminated, but the next day, before Shea had communicated with a lawyer, the police again read him his rights. This time he agreed to talk and confessed. The confession was admitted into evidence and Shea was convicted. While his appeal was pending, the Court handed down *Edwards v.*

d. The Court recognized that "[o]f course, Katz himself benefited from the new principle announced [on the date of the *Katz* decision], and [to] that extent the decision has not technically been given wholly prospective application. But [this] is an 'unavoidable consequence of the necessity that constitutional adjudications not stand as mere diction.' "

Arizona, 451 U.S. 477, 101 S.Ct. 1880, 68 L.Ed.2d 378 (1981), holding that a custodial suspect's rights are violated when the government uses a confession obtained by police-instigated interrogation—without counsel present—after the suspect has requested a lawyer. The Court, per BLACKMUN, J., held that Shea was entitled to the benefit of the *Edwards* ruling:

"[It is argued] that drawing a distinction between a case pending on direct review and a case on collateral attack produces inequities and injustices that are not any different from those [we purport] to cure. The argument is that the litigant whose *Edwards* claim will not be considered because it is presented on direct-review will be just as unfairly treated as the direct-review litigant whose claim would be bypassed were *Edwards* not the law. The distinction, however, properly rests on considerations of finality in the judicial process. The one litigant already has taken his case through the primary process. The other has not. For the latter, the curtain of finality has not been drawn. Somewhere, the closing must come.

"[It is also argued] that in every case, *Edwards* alone excepted, reliance on existing law justifies the nonapplication of *Edwards.* [But] there is no difference between the petitioner in *Edwards* and the petitioner in the present case. If the *Edwards* principle is not to be applied retroactively, the only way to dispense equal justice to Edwards and to Shea would be a rule that confined the *Edwards* principle to prospective application unavailable even to Edwards himself."

Dissenting JUSTICE WHITE, joined by the Chief Justice and Rehnquist and O'Connor, JJ., maintained that "the attempt to distinguish between direct and collateral challenges for purposes of retroactivity is misguided":

"Under the majority's rule, otherwise identically situated defendants may be subject to different constitutional rules, depending on just how long ago now-unconstitutional conduct occurred and how quickly cases proceed through the criminal justice system. The disparity is no different in kind from that which occurs when the benefit of a new constitutional rule is retroactively afforded to the defendant in whose case it is announced but to no others; the Court's new approach equalizes nothing except the numbers of defendants within the disparately treated classes.

"The majority recognizes that the distinction between direct review and habeas is problematic, but justifies its differential treatment by appealing to the need to draw 'the curtain of finality' on those who were unfortunate enough to have exhausted their last direct appeal at the time *Edwards* was decided. Yet the majority offers no reasons for its conclusion that finality should be the decisive factor. When a conviction is overturned on direct appeal on the basis of an *Edwards* violation, the remedy offered the defendant is a new trial at which any inculpatory statements obtained in violation of *Edwards* will be excluded. It is not clear to me why the majority finds such a burdensome remedy more acceptable when it is imposed on the state on direct review than when it is the result of a collateral attack. The disruption attendant upon the remedy does not vary depending on whether it is imposed on direct review or habeas; accordingly, if the remedy must be granted to defendants on direct appeal, there is not strong reason to deny it to prisoners attacking their convictions collaterally. Conversely, if it serves no worthwhile purpose to grant the remedy to a defendant whose conviction was final before *Edwards,* it is hard to see why the remedy should be available on direct review.

"[The retroactivity principles set forth in *Linkletter*] provide a rational framework for thinking about the question whether retroactive application of any particular decision makes sense—that is, whether the benefits of retroactivity outweigh its costs. Because the Court [determined last Term] that the relevant considerations set forth in *Linkletter* (the purpose of the new rule, the extent of law enforcement officials' justifiable reliance on the prior rule, and the effects on the criminal justice system of retroactivity) dictate nonretroactive application of the [*Edwards* rule] [in collateral attacks on criminal convictions], I cannot join in the majority's conclusion that that rule should be applied retroactively to cases pending on direct review at the time of our decisions in *Edwards.*"

Notes and Questions

1. *Rejection of the "clear break" exception.* Answering a question left open in the *Shea* case, *Griffith v. Kentucky,* 479 U.S. 314, 107 S.Ct. 708, 93 L.Ed.2d 649 (1987), applied *Batson v. Kentucky* to all convictions not final at the time of the ruling even though *Batson,* which held that a defendant may establish a prima facie case of racial discrimination in the selection of a petit jury on the basis of the prosecution's use of peremptory challenges, was "an explicit and substantial break with prior precedent." "The fact that the new rule may constitute a clear break with the past," observed a 6–3 majority, "has no bearing on the 'actual inequity that results' when only one of many similarly situated defendants receives the benefit of the new rule."

2. *Adoption of the other part of Harlan's approach to retroactivity. What constitutes a "new rule"?* There were two parts to Justice Harlan's approach to retroactivity. He believed that new rulings should always be applied retroactively to cases on *direct* review (a view adopted in *Shea*), but that generally new rulings should not be applied retroactively to cases on *collateral* review. In *Teague v. Lane,* 489 U.S. 288, 109 S.Ct. 1060, 103 L.Ed.2d 334 (1989), seven justices adopted Harlan's basic position with respect to retroactivity on collateral attack. However, there was no clear majority as to what the exceptions to this general approach should be.

A four-justice plurality, per O'Connor, J. (joined by Rehnquist, C.J., and Scalia and Kennedy, JJ.), identified two exceptions: A new ruling should be applied retroactively to cases on collateral review only (1) if it "places 'certain kinds of primary, private individual conduct beyond the power of the criminal lawmaking authority to proscribe'" or (2) if it mandates "new procedures without which the likelihood of an accurate conviction is seriously diminished." As to what constitutes a "new rule," Justice O'Connor noted for four justices that generally "a case announces a new rule when it breaks new ground or imposes a new obligation" on government or "if the result was not *dictated* by precedent existing at the time the defendant's conviction became final." Is this an unduly broad definition of a "new rule"? How often are results *dictated* by existing precedent?

SECTION 2. THE RIGHT OF "PRIVACY" (OR "AUTONOMY" OR "PERSONHOOD")

Introductory Note

"Whether as substantive due process or as Privacy, 'fundamentality' needs elaboration, especially with respect to the weight particular rights are to enjoy in the balance against public good. Justices Stone and Cardozo suggested that the freedoms of speech, press and religion required extraordinary judicial protection against invasions even for the public good, because of their place at the foundations of democracy and because of the unreliability of the political process in regard to them. If other rights—those to be described as within the Rights of Privacy—are also to be specially guarded against the democratic political process, similar or other justifications must be found—if there are any. Perhaps unusual respect for autonomy and idiosyncrasy as regards some 'personal' matters is intuitively felt by all of us, including Justices; that such deference is 'self-evident' is not self-evident."

—Henkin, *Privacy and Autonomy,* 74 Colum.L.Rev. 1410, 1428–29 (1974).

As noted in Lupu, *Untangling the Strands of the Fourteenth Amendment,* 77 Mich.L.Rev. 981, 1029–30 (1979), "unlike the all-inclusive theory of the *Lochner* era that held all liberties equally inviolable, and unlike the procedural due process theory that assesses the weight of any protected interest in a refined way for purposes of 'balancing' [Sec. 5 infra], [what might be called] modern substantive due process theory has a distinct all-or-nothing quality to it. Most liberties lacking textual support are of the garden variety—like liberty of contract—and thus their deprivation is constitutional if rationally necessary to the achievement of a public good. [See, e.g., *Williamson v. Lee Optical Co.,* p. 935 fn. b infra]. Several select liberties, on the other hand, have attained the status of 'fundamental' or 'preferred,' with the consequence that the Constitution permits a state to abridge them only if it can demonstrate an extraordinary justification." A notable example is *Roe v. Wade,* infra, where the Court held that the "right of privacy" encompassed "a woman's decision whether or not to terminate her pregnancy" and thus certain restrictions on abortion could be justified "only by a 'compelling state interest.'" See also *Shapiro v. Thompson,* p. 1150 infra, which can be viewed as a "right to travel" case, which, in the course of invalidating a one-year durational residence requirement for welfare, rejected the argument that "a mere showing of a rational relationship between the waiting period and [administrative governmental] objectives will suffice [for] in moving from state to state [appellees] were exercising a constitutional right, and any classification which serves to penalize the exercise of that right, unless shown to be necessary to promote a *compelling* governmental interest, is unconstitutional." As Lupu observes, ibid., "[b]ecause the review standard for ordinary liberties is so deferential, and the standard for preferred liberties so rigid, outcomes are ordained by the designation of 'preferred' [or 'fundamental'] or not."

Regulations dealing with "fundamental rights" call for "strict scrutiny" review just as government classifications based upon what have come to be known as "suspect" criteria trigger "strict" equal protection review. "[T]here is a case to be made for a significant degree of judicial deference to legislative and administrative choices in some spheres. Yet the idea of strict scrutiny acknowledges that other political choices—those burdening fundamental rights, or suggesting prejudice against racial or other minorities—must be subjected to close analysis in order to preserve substantive values of equality and liberty. Although strict scrutiny in this form ordinarily appears as a standard for judicial review, it may also be understood as admonishing lawmakers and regulators as well to be particularly cautious of their *own* purposes and premises and of the effects of their choices." Tribe, *American Constitutional Law* 1451 (2d ed. 1988).

Not infrequently, as in *Skinner v. Oklahoma* (discussed immediately below), which is an "equal protection" case in form, and which never mentioned any "right of privacy," but to which "the development of a constitutionally protected 'right of privacy' in sexual matters can be traced," Nowak, Rotunda & Young, *Constitutional Law* 736 (2d ed. 1983), a decision can be viewed as either an "equal protection" or a "fundamental rights" (or "substantive due process") case.

Indeed, observes Lupu, at 983–84, "the tangling [of 'liberty' and 'equality'] is most apparent and most serious when viewed in its relationship to the so-called 'fundamental rights' developments in both equal protection and due process clause interpretation. In the sense used here, fundamental rights include all the claims of individual rights, drawn from sources outside of the first eight amendments, that the Supreme Court has elevated to preferred status (that is, rights which the government may infringe only when it demonstrates extraordinary justification). [Which] new rights properly derive from the liberty strand, and which from the equality strand? [6] Sometimes the Court tells us; other times it does not. Often, members of the Court agree upon the preferred status of an interest but disagree about its textual source.[7] On occasion, members of the Court concede that an interest has no textual source, yet battle still over which strand of the fourteenth amendment protects it from state interference." [8]

SKINNER v. OKLAHOMA, 316 U.S. 535, 62 S.Ct. 1110, 86 L.Ed. 1655 (1942), per DOUGLAS, J., held violative of equal protection Oklahoma's Habitual Criminal Sterilization Act, which authorized the sterilization of persons previously convicted and imprisoned two or more times of crimes "amounting to felonies involving moral turpitude" and thereafter convicted of such a felony and sentenced to prison. (Petitioner, previously convicted of "chicken-stealing" and robbery, had again been convicted of robbery.) Expressly exempted were embezzlement, political offenses and revenue act violations. Thus a person convicted three times of larceny could be subjected to sterilization, but the embezzler could not—although "the nature of the two crimes is intrinsically the same" and they are otherwise punishable in the same manner. The Court recognized that "if we had here only a question as to a State's classification of crimes, such as embezzlement or larceny," no substantial federal question would be presented. "But the instant legislation runs afoul of the equal protection clause" because—

"We are dealing here with legislation which involves one of the basic civil rights of man. Marriage and procreation are fundamental to the very existence and survival of the race. [In] evil or reckless hands [the power to sterilize] can cause races or types which are inimical to the dominant group to wither and disappear. There is no redemption for the individual whom the law touches. [He] is forever deprived of a basic liberty.[a] We mention these matters [in]

6. Compare *Roe v. Wade* [infra] (due process) with *Eisenstadt v. Baird* [infra] (analogous interests protected by the equal protection clause), and *Loving v. Virginia* [infra] (analogous interests protected by the due process clause) (alternative ground).

7. The reference is to *Griswold v. Connecticut* [infra], in which Bill of Rights' penumbras, the ninth amendment, and "pure" substantive due process compete for attention.

8. In *Shapiro v. Thompson,* the majority held that the equal protection clause protected the right to travel, while Justice Harlan in dissent believed that the due process clause was the relevant shield. A similar doctrinal dispute split the Court in *Zablocki v. Redhail* [infra], where the majority held that the equal protection clause protected the right to marry. Justice Powell, in a concurring opinion, felt the right found its source in the due process clause.

a. The Court began its opinion by observing: "This case touches a sensitive and important area of human rights. Oklahoma deprives certain individuals of a right which is emphasis of our view that strict scrutiny of the classification which a State makes in a sterilization law is essential, lest unwittingly, or otherwise, invidious discriminations are made against groups or types of individuals in violation of the constitutional guaranty of just and equal laws. [When] the law lays an unequal hand on those who have committed intrinsically the same quality of offense and sterilizes one and not the other, it has made as invidious a discrimination, as if it had selected a particular race or nationality for oppressive treatment." [b]

STONE, C.J., concurred in the result: "[I]f we must presume that the legislature knows—what science has been unable to ascertain—that the criminal tendencies of any class of habitual offenders are transmissible regardless of the varying mental characteristics of its individuals, I should suppose that we must likewise presume that the legislature, in its wisdom, knows that the criminal tendencies of some classes of offenders are more likely to be transmitted than those of others. And so I think the real question [is] not one of equal protection, but whether the wholesale condemnation of a class to such an invasion of personal liberty, without opportunity to any individual to show that his is not the type of case which would justify resort to it, satisfies the demands of due process.

"There are limits to the extent to which the presumption of constitutionality can be pressed, especially where the liberty of the person is concerned [referring to his famous *Carolene Products* footnote, Ch. 1, Sec. 1] and where the presumption is resorted to only to dispense with a procedure which the ordinary dictates of prudence would seem to demand for the protection of the individual from arbitrary action. Although petitioner here was given a hearing to ascertain whether sterilization would be detrimental to his health, he was given none to discover whether his criminal tendencies are of an inheritable type. * * *

"Science has found and the law has recognized that there are certain types of mental deficiency associated with delinquency which are inheritable. But the State does not contend—nor can there be any pretense—that either common knowledge or experience, or scientific investigation, has given assurance that the criminal tendencies of any class of habitual offenders are universally or even generally inheritable. In such circumstances, inquiry whether such is the fact in the case of any particular individual cannot rightly be dispensed with. [A] law which condemns, without hearing, all the individuals of a class to so harsh a measure as the present because some or even many merit condemnation, is lacking in the first principles of due process." [c]

Notes and Questions

1. *Did the Lochner era haunt the Skinner Court?* Why was *Skinner* "unrestrained in its vigorous protection of a nontextual liberty, yet cautious in its grounds that went no farther than the particular case at hand"? To what extent does *Skinner's* "1942 vintage" explain why the Court preferred "a

basic to the perpetuation of a race—the right to have offspring."

b. As for *Buck v. Bell,* 274 U.S. 200, 47 S.Ct. 584, 71 L.Ed. 1000 (1927), upholding a sterilization law applicable only to mental defectives in state institutions, "it was pointed out that 'so far as the operations enable those who otherwise must be kept confined to be returned to the world, and thus open the asylum to others, the equality aimed at will be more nearly reached.' Here there is no such saving feature."

c. In a separate concurrence, Jackson, J., agreed that the hearings provided are "too limited [to] afford due process" and also agreed with the Court that the classification denies equal protection.

relatively narrow equal protection ground of decision to a broader preferred liberty theory that would have impugned all involuntary sterilization schemes"? No matter how serious the issue, was the Court unwilling to reinstate "substantive activism" a short five years after its repudiation? See Lupu, supra, at 1019.

2. *To what extent was Skinner colored by the Court's concern that the statute invited prejudiced action against powerless minorities?* Consider Tribe, supra, at 1465–66: "Clearly prominent [in] *Skinner* was [the Court's] concern to protect within the realm of personal autonomy 'one of the basic civil rights of man,' the right to reproduce. Yet the Court's opinion makes evident an even greater preoccupation with the notion that the state's classifications had been promulgated with their harshest effect against a relatively powerless minority, that of lower-class, as opposed to white-collar, criminals. [Although] not willing to characterize the group discriminated against as automatically deserving the protection of special judicial scrutiny, the Court combined allusion to the invidiousness of discrimination against the class with discussion of the fundamental right involved. Indeed, since that right—personal autonomy in reproductive matters—had not previously been held fundamental, it seems likely that the *Skinner* Court was moved to give the right such a status, and thereby to assure the most rigorous scrutiny of future governmental intrusions into the reproductive realm, in large part *because* of fear about the invidiously selective and ultimately genocidal way in which governmental control over that realm might tend to be exercised—a fear illustrated by the facts of *Skinner* itself.

"[*Skinner*] is the leading instance in which a new star appears to have been added to the firmament of preferred freedoms primarily because of concerns about invidious discrimination and majoritarian domination. Such concerns of course move to center stage once we are prepared to treat the classification employed by government as so plainly invidious or prejudiced that, quite without regard to the nature of the choice burdened or the interest unequally distributed, strict scrutiny seems required if any semblance of equal justice under law is to be preserved. The theory of invidious or suspect classification [Ch. 7, Secs. 2–3,] thus takes us beyond *Skinner* to a realm in which, even without finding a fundamental right, our tolerance will be at low ebb."

"[In *Griswold,* Douglas, J.,] skipped through the Bill of Rights like a cheerleader—'Give me a P . . . give me an R . . . an I . . .,' and so on, and found P–R–I–V–A–C–Y as a derivative or penumbral right."

—Dixon, *The "New" Substantive Due Process and the Democratic Ethic: A Prolegomenon,* 1976 B.Y.U.L.Rev. 43, 84.

GRISWOLD v. CONNECTICUT

381 U.S. 479, 85 S.Ct. 1678, 14 L.Ed.2d 510 (1965).

JUSTICE DOUGLAS delivered the opinion of the Court.

Appellant Griswold is Executive Director of the Planned Parenthood League of Connecticut. Appellant Buxton [is] Medical Director for the League at its Center in New Haven—a center open [from] November 1 to November 10, 1961, when appellants were arrested.

They gave information, instruction, and medical advice to *married persons* as to the means of preventing conception. * * * Fees were usually charged, although some couples were serviced free.

The statutes whose constitutionality is involved [are] §§ 53–32 and 54–196 of the General Statutes of Connecticut (1958 rev.). The former provides: "Any person who uses any drug, medicinal article or instrument for the purpose of preventing conception shall be fined not less than fifty dollars or imprisoned not less than sixty days nor more than one year or be both fined and imprisoned." Section 54–196 provides: "Any person who assists, abets, counsels, causes, hires or commands another to commit any offense may be prosecuted and punished as if he were the principal offender." The appellants were found guilty as accessories and fined $100 [each].

Coming to the merits,[a] we are met with a wide range of questions that implicate the Due Process Clause of the Fourteenth Amendment. Overtones of some arguments suggest that *Lochner* should be our guide. But we decline that invitation * * *. We do not sit as a super-legislature to determine the wisdom, need, and propriety of laws that touch economic problems, business affairs, or social conditions. This law, however, operates directly on an intimate relation of husband and wife and their physician's role in one aspect of that relation.

The association of people is not mentioned in the Constitution nor in the Bill of Rights. The right to educate a child in a school of the parents' choice—whether public or private or parochial—is also not mentioned. Nor is the right to study any particular subject or any foreign language. Yet the First Amendment has been construed to include certain of those rights. [See] *Pierce v. Society of Sisters,* 268 U.S. 510, 45 S.Ct. 571, 69 L.Ed. 1070 (1925) [and] *Meyer v. Nebraska,* 262 U.S. 390, 43 S.Ct. 625, 67 L.Ed. 1042 (1923).[b] [T]he State may not, consistently with the spirit of the First Amendment, contract the spectrum of available knowledge. The right of freedom of speech and press includes not only the right to utter or to print, but the right to distribute, the right to receive, the right to read and freedom of inquiry, freedom of thought, and freedom to teach—indeed the freedom of the entire university community. Without those peripher-

a. For resolution of the issue of standing, see p. 1322 infra.

b. Consider Nowak, Rotunda and Young, *Constitutional Law* 635 (3d ed. 1986): In both *Meyer,* invalidating a state law forbidding all grade schools from teaching subjects in any language other than English, and in *Pierce,* holding a state law requiring students to attend public schools violative of due process, "the majority [per McReynolds, J.] found that the law restricted individual freedom without any relation to a valid public interest. Freedom of choice regarding an individual's personal life was recognized as constitutionally protected. These decisions may only have reflected the attitude of the Court towards government regulation during the apex of 'substantive due process.' While these decisions might today be grounded on the first amendment, their existence is important to the growth of the right to privacy. If nothing else, they show a historical recognition of a right to private decision-making regarding family matters as inherent in the concept of liberty."

Consider, too, Lupu, supra, at 988–89, commenting that although *Meyer* and *Pierce* "can be, and at times have been, rerationalized, as attempts to protect values derived from the first amendment," the most recent reliance on these cases, citing e.g., *Moore v. East Cleveland,* infra, and *Roe v. Wade,* infra, "have stressed their nontextual underpinnings of protected interests in family autonomy. The survival of those two cases in that form suggests that the only durable objection to the *Lochner* era's handiwork is that it generally selected the 'wrong' values for protection." See also Hutchinson, *Unanimity and Desegregation: Decisionmaking in the Supreme Court, 1948–58,* 68 Geo.L.J. 1, 49–51 (1979) (Frankfurter, J., long an outspoken critic of the McReynolds opinions in *Meyer* and *Pierce,* warned that the method used in these cases could just as easily produce "another *Lochner*"); Posner, *The Uncertain Protection of Privacy by the Supreme Court,* 1979 Sup.Ct. Rev. 173, 195–96 ("under ostensible modern test of substantive due process," *Meyer* was "incorrectly decided"; its citation in "privacy" cases shows "survival of substantive due process despite frequent disclaimers.")

al rights the specific rights would be less secure. And so we reaffirm the principle of the *Pierce* and the *Meyer* cases.

In *NAACP v. Alabama* [p. 727 infra], we protected the "freedom to associate and privacy in one's associations," noting that freedom of association was a peripheral First Amendment right. [In] other words, the First Amendment has a penumbra where privacy is protected from governmental intrusion. In like context, we have protected forms of "association" that are not political in the customary sense but pertain to the social, legal, and economic benefit of the members. *NAACP v. Button*, 371 U.S. 415, 83 S.Ct. 328, 9 L.Ed.2d 405 (1963). [W]hile [association] is not expressly included in the First Amendment its existence is necessary in making the express guarantees fully meaningful.

The foregoing cases suggest that specific guarantees in the Bill of Rights have penumbras, formed by emanations from those guarantees that help give them life and substance. Various guarantees create zones of privacy. The right of association contained in the penumbra of the First Amendment is one, as we have seen. The Third Amendment in its prohibition against the quartering of soldiers "in any house" in time of peace without the consent of the owner is another facet of that privacy. The Fourth Amendment [is another]. The Fifth Amendment in its Self-Incrimination Clause enables the citizen to create a zone of privacy which government may not force him to surrender to his detriment. The Ninth Amendment provides: "The enumeration in the Constitution, of certain rights, shall not be construed to deny or disparage others retained by the people."

The Fourth and Fifth Amendments were described in *Boyd v. United States,* 116 U.S. 616, 630, 6 S.Ct. 524, 532, 29 L.Ed. 746 (1886), as protection against all governmental invasions "of the sanctity of a man's home and the privacies of life." We recently referred in *Mapp v. Ohio* to the Fourth Amendment as creating a "right to privacy, no less important than any other right carefully and particularly reserved to the people."

We have had many controversies over these penumbral rights of "privacy and repose." [*Skinner* and other cases] bear witness that the right of privacy which presses for recognition here is a legitimate one.

The present case, then, concerns a relationship lying within the zone of privacy created by several fundamental constitutional guarantees.[c] And it concerns a law which, in forbidding the *use* of contraceptives rather than regulating their manufacture or sale, seeks to achieve its goals by means having a maximum destructive impact upon that relationship. Such a law cannot stand in light of the familiar principle [that] a "governmental purpose to control or prevent activities constitutionally subject to state regulation may not be achieved by means which sweep unnecessarily broadly and thereby invade the area of protected freedoms." *NAACP v. Alabama.* Would we allow the police to search the sacred precincts of marital bedrooms for telltale signs of the use of contraceptives? The very idea is repulsive to the notions of privacy surrounding the marriage relationship.[d]

c. Did the Court omit the free exercise clause of the first amendment? Like religious beliefs, are beliefs in the areas of marriage, procreation and child rearing "often deeply held, involving loyalties fully as powerful as those that bind the citizen to the state"? Will the choice of whom to marry or whether or not to have a child, once taken, "have as strong an impact on the life patterns of the individuals involved [as] any adoption of a religious belief or viewpoint"? See Heymann & Barzelay, *The Forest and the Trees: Roe v. Wade and Its Critics,* 53 B.U.L.Rev. 765, 773–74 (1973).

d. But consider *Posner,* fn. b supra, at 194: "Such a search would indeed be an invasion of

We deal with a right of privacy older than the Bill of Rights * * *. Marriage is a coming together for better or for worse, hopefully enduring, and intimate to the degree of being sacred. It is an association that promotes a way of life, not causes; a harmony in living, not political faiths; a bilateral loyalty, not commercial or social projects. Yet it is an association for as noble a purpose as any involved in our prior decisions.

Reversed.

JUSTICE GOLDBERG, whom THE CHIEF JUSTICE and JUSTICE BRENNAN join, concurring.

I [join the Court's opinion]. Although I have not accepted the view that "due process" as used in the Fourteenth Amendment includes all of the first eight Amendments, I do agree that the concept of liberty protects those personal rights that are fundamental, and is not confined to the specific terms of the Bill of Rights. My conclusion [that] it embraces the right of marital privacy though that right is not mentioned explicitly in the Constitution [1] is supported both by numerous decisions [and] by the language and history of the Ninth Amendment [which] reveal that the Framers of the Constitution believed that there are additional fundamental rights, protected from governmental infringement. [The] Ninth Amendment [was] proffered to quiet expressed fears that a bill of specifically enumerated rights could not be sufficiently broad to cover all essential rights and that the specific mention of certain rights would be interpreted as a denial that others were protected.

[While] this Court has had little occasion to interpret the Ninth Amendment,[6] "[i]t cannot be presumed that any clause in the constitution is intended to be without effect." [To] hold that a right so basic and fundamental and so deep-rooted in our society as the right of privacy in marriage may be infringed because that right is not guaranteed in so many words by the first eight amendments to the Constitution is to ignore the Ninth Amendment and to give it no effect whatsoever. * * * I do not mean to imply that the Ninth Amendment is applied against the States by the Fourteenth [nor] to state that the Ninth Amendment constitutes an independent source of rights protected from infringement by either the States or the Federal Government. Rather, the Ninth Amendment shows a belief of the Constitution's authors that fundamental rights exist that are not expressly enumerated in the first eight amendments and an intent that the list of rights included there not be deemed exhaustive.[d]

privacy in a conventional sense. But it would be a justifiable invasion if the statute were not otherwise constitutionally objectionable. This case can be seen by imagining that the statute in question forbade not contraception but murder and that the police had probable cause to believe that the suspected murderer had secreted the weapon to his mattress. Furthermore, even if some methods of enforcing the Connecticut statute [violated the Fourth Amendment], that would mean only that the statute was difficult to enforce. [As] the facts of *Griswold* show, the State could enforce the statute without invading anyone's privacy, simply by prosecuting, as accessories, the employees of birth-control clinics."

1. [This Court] has never held that the Bill of Rights or the Fourteenth Amendment protects only those rights that the Constitution specifically mentions by name. * * *

6. [It] has been referred to as "*The Forgotten Ninth Amendment,*" in a book with that title by Bennett B. Patterson (1955). Other commentary [includes] Redlich, *Are There "Certain Rights * * * Retained by the People"?* 37 N.Y.U.L.Rev. 787 (1962), and Kelsey, *The Ninth Amendment of the Federal Constitution,* 11 Ind.L.J. 309 (1936). * * *

d. See generally Note, *The Uncertain Renaissance of the Ninth Amendment,* 33 U.Chi.L. Rev. 814 (1966); Paust, *Human Rights and the Ninth Amendment; A New Form of Guarantee,* 60 Corn.L.Rev. 231 (1975).

[While] the Ninth Amendment—and indeed the entire Bill of Rights—originally concerned restrictions upon *federal* power, the subsequently enacted Fourteenth Amendment prohibits the States as well from abridging fundamental personal liberties. [In] sum, the Ninth Amendment simply lends strong support to the view that the "liberty" protected by the Fifth and Fourteenth Amendments from infringement by the Federal Government or the States is not restricted to rights specifically mentioned in the first eight amendments.

[The] entire fabric of the Constitution and the purposes that clearly underlie its specific guarantees demonstrate that the rights to marital privacy and to marry and raise a family are of similar order and magnitude as the fundamental rights specifically protected.

[Surely] the Government, absent a showing of a compelling subordinating state interest, could not decree that all husbands and wives must be sterilized after two children have been born to them.[e] Yet by [the dissenters'] reasoning such an invasion of marital privacy would not be subject to constitutional challenge because, while it might be "silly," no provision of the Constitution specifically prevents the Government from curtailing the marital right to bear children and raise a family. [I]f upon a showing of a slender basis of rationality, a law outlawing voluntary birth control by married persons is valid, then, by the same reasoning, a law requiring compulsory birth control also would seem to be valid. In my view, however, both types of law would unjustifiably intrude upon rights of marital privacy which are constitutionally protected.

In a long series of cases this Court has held that where fundamental personal liberties are involved, they may not be abridged by the States simply on a showing that a regulatory statute has some rational relationship to the effectuation of a proper state purpose. [The] State, at most, argues that there is some rational relation between this statute and what is admittedly a legitimate subject of state concern—the discouraging of extra-marital relations. It says that preventing the use of birth-control devices by married persons helps prevent the indulgence by some in such extra-marital relations. The rationality of this justification is dubious, particularly in light of the admitted widespread availability to all persons [in] Connecticut, unmarried as well as married, of birth-control devices for the prevention of disease, as distinguished from the prevention of conception. But in any event, it is clear that the state interest in safeguarding marital fidelity can be served by a more discriminately tailored statute, which does not, like the present one, sweep unnecessarily broadly, reaching far beyond the evil sought to be dealt with and intruding upon the privacy of all married couples. * * *

* * *

JUSTICE HARLAN, concurring in the judgment.

I [cannot] join the Court's opinion [as] it seems to me to evince an approach [that] the Due Process Clause of the Fourteenth Amendment does not touch this Connecticut statute unless the enactment is found to violate some right assured by the letter or penumbra of the Bill of Rights. [W]hat I find implicit in the

e. Compare Comment, *Population Control—The Legal Approach to a Biological Imperative,* 1 Ecol.L.Q. 143, 167 (1971): "It is not completely clear [whether] Justice Goldberg's vaguely defined marital and family rights include the right to unlimited procreation. Clearly, one family right which is not protected against legislative control is the right to decide how many spouses to have. By custom Americans have one spouse and many children but there would seem to be little difference between legislative control of the number of spouses and the number of children." See also Note, *Legal Analysis and Population Control: The Problem of Coercion,* 84 Harv.L.Rev. 1856 (1971).

Court's opinion is that the "incorporation" doctrine may be used to *restrict* the reach of Fourteenth Amendment Due Process. For me this is just as unacceptable constitutional doctrine as is the use of the "incorporation" approach to *impose* upon the States all the requirements of the Bill of Rights. * * *

[T]he proper constitutional inquiry in this case is whether this Connecticut statute infringes the Due Process Clause of the Fourteenth Amendment because the enactment violates basic values "implicit in the concept of ordered liberty." For reasons stated at length in my dissenting opinion in *Poe v. Ullman* [discussed below], I believe that it does. While the relevant inquiry may be aided by resort to one or more of the provisions of the Bill of Rights, it is not dependent on them or any of their radiations. The Due Process Clause of the Fourteenth Amendment stands, in my opinion, on its own bottom.

[While] I could not more heartily agree that judicial "self restraint" is an indispensable ingredient of sound constitutional adjudication, I do submit that the formula suggested [by the dissenters] for achieving it is more hollow than real. "Specific" provisions of the Constitution, no less than "due process," lend themselves as readily to "personal" interpretations by judges whose constitutional outlook is simply to keep the Constitution in supposed "tune with the times".

[Judicial self-restraint will] be achieved in this area, as in other[s], only by continual insistence upon respect for the teachings of history, solid recognition of the basic values that underlie our society, and wise appreciation of the great roles that the doctrines of federalism and separation of powers have played in establishing and preserving American freedoms. Adherence to these principles will not, of course, obviate all constitutional differences of opinion among judges, nor should it. Their continued recognition will, however, go farther toward keeping most judges from roaming at large in the constitutional field than will the interpolation into the Constitution of an artificial and largely illusory restriction on the content of the Due Process Clause.

[Dissenting in POE v. ULLMAN, 367 U.S. 497, 523, 81 S.Ct. 1752, 6 L.Ed.2d 989 (1961), which failed to reach the merits of the constitutional challenge to the Connecticut anti-birth control statute, Harlan, J., had maintained that the statute, "as construed to apply to these appellants, violates the Fourteenth Amendment" because "a statute making it a criminal offense for *married couples* to use contraceptives is an intolerable and unjustifiable invasion of privacy in the conduct of the most intimate concerns of an individual's personal life." Harlan, J., "would not suggest that adultery, homosexuality, fornication and incest are immune from criminal enquiry, however privately practiced," but "the intimacy of husband and wife is necessarily an essential and accepted feature of the institution of marriage, an institution which the State not only must allow, but which always and every age it has fostered and protected. It is one thing when the State exerts its power either to forbid extra-marital sexuality altogether, or to say who may marry, but it is quite another when, having acknowledged a marriage and the intimacies inherent in it, it undertakes to regulate by means of the criminal law the details of that intimacy."

[Although the state had argued the constitutional permissibility of the moral judgment underlying the challenged statute, Harlan, J., could not find anything that "even remotely suggests a justification for the obnoxiously intrusive means it has chosen to effectuate that policy." He deemed "the utter novelty" of the statute "conclusive." "Although the Federal Government and many States have at one time or another [prohibited or regulated] the distribution of contraceptives, none [has] made the *use* of contraceptives a crime. Indeed, a diligent search has revealed that no nation, including several which quite evidently share Connecticut's moral policy, had seen fit to effectuate that policy by the means presented here."

[Because the constitutional challenges to the Connecticut statute "draw their basis from no explicit language of the Constitution, and have yet to find expression in any decision of this Court," Harlan, J., deemed it "desirable at the outset to state the framework of Constitutional principles in which I think the issue must be judged":

["[Were] due process merely a procedural safeguard it would fail to reach those situations where the deprivation of life, liberty or property was accomplished by legislation which by operating in the future could, given even the fairest possible procedure in application to individuals, nevertheless destroy the enjoyment of all three. [I]t is not the particular enumeration of rights in the first eight Amendments which spells out the reach of Fourteenth Amendment due process, but rather [those concepts embracing] rights 'which [are] *fundamental;* which belong [to] the citizens of all free governments.'

["[T]hrough the course of this Court's decisions [due process] has represented the balance which our Nation, built upon postulates of respect for the liberty of the individual, has struck between that liberty and the demands of organized society. [The] balance of which I speak is the balance struck by this country, having regard to what history teaches are the traditions from which it developed as well as the traditions from which it broke. That tradition is a living thing. A decision of this Court which radically departs from it could not long survive, while a decision which builds on what has survived is likely to be sound. No formula could serve as a substitute, in this area, for judgment and restraint.

["[The] full scope of the liberty guaranteed by the Due Process Clause cannot be found in or limited by the precise terms of the specific guarantees elsewhere provided in the Constitution. This 'liberty' is not a series of isolated points pricked out in terms of [the] freedom of speech, press, and religion; [the] freedom from unreasonable searches and seizures; and so on. It is a rational continuum which, broadly speaking, includes a freedom from all substantial arbitrary impositions and purposeless restraints [and] which also recognizes, what a reasonable and sensitive judgment must, that certain interests require particularly careful scrutiny of the state needs asserted to justify their abridgment. Cf. *Skinner.*"] [f]

JUSTICE WHITE, concurring in the judgment.

In my view this Connecticut law as applied to married couples deprives them of "liberty" without [due process] guaranteed by the Fourteenth Amendment against arbitrary or capricious [denials]. Surely the right [to] be free of regulation of the intimacies of the marriage relationship, "come[s] to this Court with a momentum for respect lacking when appeal is made to liberties which derive merely from shifting economic arrangements." *Kovacs v. Cooper* [discussed infra] (opinion of Frankfurter, J.).

The Connecticut anti-contraceptive statute deals rather substantially with this relationship. [And] the clear effect of these statutes, as enforced, is to deny disadvantaged citizens of Connecticut, those without either adequate knowledge or resources to obtain private counseling, access to medical assistance and up-to-date information in respect to proper methods of birth control. In my view, a

f. See also the extracts from this dissent in fn. e, note 6 following *Roe v. Wade,* infra.

statute with these effects bears a substantial burden of justification when attacked under the Fourteenth Amendment.

An examination of the justification offered, however, cannot be avoided by saying that the Connecticut anti-use statute invades a protected area of privacy and association or that it demeans the marriage relationship. The nature of the right invaded is pertinent, to be sure, for statutes regulating sensitive areas of liberty do, under the cases of this Court, require "strict scrutiny," *Skinner,* and "must be viewed in the light of less drastic means for achieving the same basic purpose." But such statutes, if reasonably necessary for the effectuation of a legitimate and substantial state interest, and not arbitrary or capricious in application, are not invalid under the Due Process Clause. [There] is no serious contention that Connecticut thinks the use of artificial or external methods of contraception immoral or unwise in itself, or that the anti-use statute is founded upon any policy of promoting population expansion. Rather, the statute is said to serve the State's policy against all forms of promiscuous or illicit sexual relationships, be they premarital or extramarital, concededly a permissible and legitimate legislative goal.

[But] I wholly fail to see how the ban on the use of contraceptives by married couples in any way reinforces the State's ban on illicit sexual relationships. * * * Perhaps the theory is that the flat ban on use prevents married people from possessing contraceptives and without the ready availability of such devices for use in the marital relationship, there will be no or less temptation to use them in extramarital ones. This reasoning rests on the premise that married people will comply with the ban in regard to their marital relationship, notwithstanding total nonenforcement in this context and apparent nonenforcibility, but will not comply with criminal statutes prohibiting extramarital affairs and the anti-use statute in respect to illicit sexual relationships, a premise whose validity has not been demonstrated and whose intrinsic validity is not very evident. At most the broad ban is of marginal utility to the declared objective. A statute limiting its prohibition on use to persons engaging in the prohibited relationship would serve the end posited by Connecticut in the same way, and with the same effectiveness, or ineffectiveness, as the broad anti-use statute under attack in this case. I find nothing in this record justifying the sweeping scope of this [statute].

JUSTICE BLACK, with whom JUSTICE STEWART joins, dissenting.

[There are] guarantees in certain specific constitutional provisions which are designed in part to protect privacy at certain times and places with respect to certain activities. [But] I think it belittles [the Fourth] Amendment to talk about it as though it protects nothing but "privacy." [The] average man would very likely not have his feelings soothed any more by having his property seized openly than by having it seized privately and by stealth. [And] a person can be just as much, if not more, irritated, annoyed and injured by an unceremonious public arrest by a policeman as he is by a seizure in the privacy of his office or home.

One of the most effective ways of diluting or expanding a constitutionally guaranteed right is to substitute for the crucial word or words of a constitutional guarantee another word or words, more or less flexible and more or less restricted in meaning. This fact is well illustrated by the use of the term "right of privacy" as a comprehensive substitute for the Fourth Amendment's guarantee against "unreasonable searches and seizures." * * *[1] I like my privacy as well as the next one, but I am nevertheless compelled to admit that government has a right to invade it unless prohibited by some specific constitutional provision.

[This] brings me to the arguments made by [the concurring justices]. I discuss the due process and Ninth Amendment arguments together because on analysis they turn out to be the same thing—merely using different words to claim for this Court and the federal judiciary power to invalidate any legislative act [that] it considers to be arbitrary, capricious, unreasonable, or oppressive, or this Court's belief that a particular state law under scrutiny has no "rational or justifying" purpose, or is offensive to a "sense of fairness and justice." If these formulas based on "natural justice" [are] to prevail, they require judges to determine what is or is not constitutional on the basis of their own appraisal of what laws are unwise or unnecessary. [I] do not believe that we are granted power by the Due Process Clause or any [other] provisions to measure constitutionality by our belief that legislation is arbitrary, capricious or unreasonable, or accomplishes no justifiable purpose, or is offensive to our own notions of "civilized standards of conduct." Such an appraisal of the wisdom of legislation is an attribute of the power to make laws, [a] power which was specifically denied to federal courts by the [Framers].

Of the cases on which my [Brothers] rely so heavily, undoubtedly the reasoning of two of them supports their result here—[*Meyer* and *Pierce*]. *Meyer* [relying on *Lochner,*] held unconstitutional, as an "arbitrary" and unreasonable interference with the right of a teacher to carry on his occupation and of parents to hire him, a state law forbidding the teaching of modern foreign languages to young children in the schools.[7] [*Pierce,* per McReynolds, J.] said that a state law requiring that all children attend public schools interfered unconstitutionally with the property rights of private school corporations because it was an "arbitrary, unreasonable, and unlawful interference" which threatened "destruction of their business and property." Without expressing an opinion as to whether either of those cases reached a correct result in light of our later decisions applying the First Amendment to the States through the Fourteenth, I merely point out that the reasoning stated in *Meyer* and *Pierce* was the same natural law due process philosophy which many later opinions repudiated, and which I cannot accept. Brothers White and Goldberg also cite other cases [which] held that States [could not] pass unnecessarily broad laws which might indirectly infringe on First Amendment [freedoms.] Brothers White and Goldberg now apparently would start from this requirement [and] extend it limitlessly to require States to justify any law restricting "liberty" as my Brethren define "liberty." This would mean at the very least, I suppose, that every state criminal statute—since it must inevitably curtail "liberty" to some extent—would be suspect, and would have to be justified to this Court.

1. The phrase "right to privacy" appears first to have gained currency from an article written by Messrs. Warren and (later Mr. Justice) Brandeis in 1890 which urged that States should give some form of tort relief to persons whose private affairs were exploited by others. *The Right to Privacy,* 4 Harv.L. Rev. 193. * * * Observing that "the right of privacy presses for recognition here," today this Court, which I did not understand to have power to sit as a court of common law, now appears to be exalting a phrase which Warren and Brandeis use in discussing grounds for tort relief, to the level of a constitutional [rule].

7. In *Meyer,* in the very same sentence quoted in part by my Brethren in which he asserted that the Due Process Clause gave an abstract and inviolable right "to marry, establish a home and bring up children," Justice McReynolds asserted also that the Due Process Clause prevented States from interfering with "the right of the individual to contract."

My Brother Goldberg has adopted the recent discovery [12] that the Ninth Amendment as well as the Due Process Clause can be used by this Court as authority to strike down all state legislation which this Court thinks violates "fundamental principles of liberty and justice," or is contrary to the "traditions and collective conscience of our people." [One] would certainly have to look far beyond the language of the Ninth Amendment to find that the Framers vested in this Court any such awesome veto powers over lawmaking. [The Ninth] Amendment was passed [to] limit the Federal Government to the powers granted expressly or by necessary implication. [This] fact is perhaps responsible for the peculiar phenomenon that for a period of a century and a half no serious suggestion was ever made that [that] Amendment, enacted to protect state powers against federal invasion, could be used as a weapon of federal power to prevent state legislatures from passing laws they consider appropriate to govern local affairs. * * *

I realize that many good and able men have eloquently spoken and written [of] the duty of this Court to keep the Constitution in tune with the times [but I] reject that philosophy. The Constitution makers knew the need for change and provided for it. [The] Due Process Clause with an "arbitrary and capricious" or "shocking to the conscience" formula was liberally used by this Court to strike down economic legislation in the early decades of this century, threatening, many people thought, the tranquility and stability of the Nation. See, e.g., *Lochner*. That formula, based on subjective considerations of "natural justice," is no less dangerous when used to enforce this Court's views about personal rights than those about economic rights. [So] far as I am concerned, Connecticut's law as applied here is not forbidden by any provision of the Federal Constitution as that Constitution was written, and I would therefore affirm.

JUSTICE STEWART, whom JUSTICE BLACK joins, dissenting.

[I] think this is an uncommonly silly law. As a practical matter, the law is obviously unenforceable, except in the oblique context of the present case. As a philosophical matter, I believe the use of contraceptives in the relationship of marriage should be left to personal and private [choice]. As a matter of social policy, I think professional counsel about methods of birth control should be available to all, so that each individual's choice can be meaningfully made. But we are not [asked] whether we think this law is unwise, or even asinine. We are asked to hold that it violates the United States Constitution. And that I cannot do.

In the course of its opinion the Court refers to no less than six Amendments [but] does not say which of these Amendments, if any, it thinks is infringed by this Connecticut law. [As] to the First, Third, Fourth, and Fifth Amendments, I can find nothing in any of them to invalidate this Connecticut law, even assuming that all those amendments are fully applicable against the States. [The] Ninth Amendment, like its companion the Tenth [was] simply to make clear that the adoption of the Bill of Rights did not alter the plan that the *Federal* Government was to be a government of express and limited powers, and that all rights and powers not delegated to it were retained by the people and the individual States. Until today no member of this Court has ever suggested that the Ninth Amendment meant anything [else].

12. See Patterson, *The Forgotten Ninth Amendment* (1955). Mr. Patterson urges that the Ninth Amendment be used to protect unspecified "natural and inalienable rights." The Introduction by Roscoe Pound states that "there is a marked revival of natural law ideas throughout the world. Interest in the Ninth Amendment is a symptom of that revival."

* * *

What provision of the Constitution, then, does make this state law invalid? The Court says it is the right of privacy "created by several fundamental constitutional guarantees." [I] can find no such general right of privacy in the Bill of Rights, in any other part of the Constitution, or in any case ever before decided by this Court.[7]

At the oral argument [we] were told that the Connecticut law does not "conform to current community standards." But it is not the function of this Court to decide cases on the basis of community standards. [If], as I should surely hope, the law before us does not reflect the standards of the people of Connecticut, the people of Connecticut can freely exercise their true Ninth and Tenth Amendment rights to persuade their elected representatives to repeal it. That is the constitutional way to take this law off the books.

Notes and Questions

1. *Is Douglas, J.'s argument logical?* Consider Henkin, *Privacy and Autonomy,* 74 Colum.L.Rev. 1410, 1421–22 (1974): "Although it is not wholly clear, Justice Douglas's argument seems to go something like this: since the Constitution, in various 'specifics' of the Bill of Rights and in their penumbra, protects rights which partake of privacy, it protects other aspects of privacy as well, indeed it recognizes a general, complete right of privacy. And since the right emanates from specific fundamental rights, it too is 'fundamental,' its infringement is suspect and calls for strict scrutiny, and it can be justified only by a high level of public good. A logician, I suppose, might have trouble with that argument. A legal draftsman, indeed, might suggest the opposite: when the Constitution sought to protect private rights it specified them; that it explicitly protects some elements of privacy, but not others, suggests that it did not mean to protect those not mentioned."

2. *Did Griswold successfully avoid "renewing the romance" with "substantive due process"? Griswold,* observes Lupu, at 994, "provided the severest test for a Court determined to advance chosen values [without] renewing the romance with the dreaded demon of substantive due process. [Douglas, J.,] drew upon the incorporation legacy, rather than a doctrine of 'naked' substantive due process, and tortured the Bill of Rights into yielding a protected zone of privacy that would not tolerate a law banning contraceptive use by married couples. Justice Goldberg's reliance upon the ninth amendment [was] equally disingenuous in its attempt to avoid the jaws of substantive due process. Only Justices White and Harlan were willing to grapple directly with the fearful creature, and concluded that a law invading marital choice about contraception violated the due process clause itself, independent of links with the Bill of Rights. Shocking though that analysis may have been at the time, subsequent developments seem to have confirmed the White-Harlan view, and not the magical mystery tour of the zones of privacy, as the prevailing doctrine of *Griswold* [referring to *Moore v. East Cleveland* (1977), infra]."

3. *Emanations-and-penumbras theory and "economic" vs. "personal" rights.* Do any of the Justices analytically distinguish between "economic" and "personal" rights? Or is the distinction "only self-imposed"? Consider Kauper, *Penumbras, Peripheries, Emanations, Things Fundamental and Things Forgotten: The Griswold Case,* 64 Mich.L.Rev. 235, 253 (1965).

7. [The] Court does not say how far the new constitutional right of privacy announced today extends. I suppose, however, that even after today a State can constitutionally still punish at least some offenses which are not committed in public.

4. *"Privacy" or "equality"?* "Seen in the context of the Warren Court's general jurisprudence," observes M. Shapiro, *Fathers and Sons: The Court, the Commentators, and the Search for Values,* in The Burger Court 218, 228 (V. Blasi ed. 1983), "the fact situation in [*Griswold*] was crucial. The living law of Connecticut was that middle-class women received birth control information and purchased birth control supplies, and the Connecticut statute was enforced only to block the operation of birth control clinics that would bring these services to the poor. *Griswold* was an equality not a privacy decision * * *."

5. *Skinner and Griswold taken together.* Consider Tribe, supra, at 1340: "Taken together with *Griswold,* which recognized as equally protected the individual's decision *not* to bear a child, the meaning of *Skinner* is that *whether one person's body shall be the source of another's life must be left to that person and that person alone to decide.* That principle seems to collide in the abortion cases [infra] with a command that is no less fundamental: *an innocent life may not be taken except to save the life of another.*"

Griswold invalidated a ban on the *use* of contraceptives by *married* couples. EISENSTADT v. BAIRD, 405 U.S. 438, 92 S.Ct. 1029, 31 L.Ed.2d 349 (1972), overturned a conviction for violating a Massachusetts law making it a felony to *distribute* contraceptive materials, *except* in the case of registered physicians and pharmacists furnishing the materials to married persons. Baird had given a woman a package of vaginal foam at the end of his lecture on contraception. He was not charged with distributing to an unmarried person. No proof was offered as to the recipient's marital status. The crime charged was that Baird had no license, and thus no authority, to distribute to anyone. The Court, per BRENNAN, J., concluded that, since the statute is riddled with exceptions making contraceptives freely available and since, if protection of health were the rationale, the statute would be both discriminatory and overbroad, "the goals of deterring premarital sex and regulating the distribution of potentially harmful articles cannot reasonably be regarded as legislative aims." "[V]iewed as a prohibition on contraception per se" the statute "violates the rights of single persons under the Equal Protection Clause." For, "whatever the rights of the individual to access to contraceptives may be, the rights must be the same for the married and the unmarried alike":

"If under *Griswold* the distribution of contraceptives to married persons cannot be prohibited, a ban on distribution to unmarried persons would be equally impermissible. It is true that in *Griswold* the right of privacy in question inhered in the marital relationship. Yet the marital couple is not an independent entity with a mind and heart of its own, but an association of two individuals each with a separate intellectual and emotional make-up. If the right of privacy means anything, it is the right of the *individual,* married or single, to be free from unwarranted governmental intrusion into matters so fundamentally affecting a person as the decision whether to bear or beget a child. On the other hand, if *Griswold* is no bar to a prohibition on the distribution of contraceptives, the State could not, consistently with [equal protection,] outlaw distribution to unmarried but not to married persons. In each case the evil, as perceived by the State, would be identical, and the underinclusion would be invidious."

WHITE, J., joined by Blackmun, J., concurred, emphasizing that "the State did [not] convict Baird for distributing to an unmarried person [but because] Baird had no license and therefore no authority to distribute to anyone."

"Given *Griswold,* and absent proof of the possible hazards of using vaginal foam, we could not sustain [Baird's] conviction had it been for selling or giving away foam to a married person. Just as in *Griswold,* where the right of married persons to use contraceptives was 'diluted or adversely affected' by permitting a conviction for giving advice as to its exercise, so here to sanction a medical restriction upon distribution of a contraceptive not proved hazardous to health would impair the exercise of the constitutional right. That Baird could not be convicted for distributing [foam] to a married person disposes of this case. Assuming arguendo that the result would be otherwise had the recipient been unmarried, nothing has been placed in the record to indicate her marital status." [a]

Burger, C.J., dissented, "see[ing] nothing in the Fourteenth Amendment or any other part of the Constitution that even vaguely suggests that these medicinal forms of contraceptives must be available in the open market. [By] relying on *Griswold* in the present context, the Court has passed beyond the penumbras of the specific guarantees into the uncircumscribed area of personal predilections."

Notes and Questions

1. *Does Eisenstadt offer a new rationale for Griswold?* Did *Eisenstadt* decide one of *Griswold* 's open issues—the constitutionality of a ban on the use or distribution of contraceptive devices that excluded from its reach the married couple—"by assertion, without a pretext of reasoning"? Wellington, *Common Law Rules and Constitutional Double Standards,* 83 Yale L.J. 221, 296 (1973), so charges: "[W]hether the 'different classes' (married, not married) are [as *Eisenstadt* states] 'wholly unrelated to the objective of the statute,' depends on whether, as *Griswold* insists, the marriage relationship is important to that aspect of liberty that the Court calls privacy. How, then, [could the Court write *Eisenstadt* the way it did] without offering a new rationale for *Griswold*[?]" *Cf.* Gerety, *Doing Without Privacy,* 42 Ohio St.L.J. 143–44 (1981).

2. *Griswold "unmasked"?* Consider Posner, *The Uncertain Protection of Privacy by the Supreme Court,* 1979 Sup.Ct.Rev. 173, 198: "*Griswold* had at least attempted to relate the right to use contraceptives to familiar notions of privacy by speculating on the intrusive methods by which a statute banning the use of contraceptives might be enforced. This ground was unavailable in [*Eisenstadt*] because the statute there forbade not the use, but only the distribution, of contraceptives. [*Eisenstadt*] is thus a pure essay in substantive due process. It unmasks *Griswold* as based on the idea of sexual liberty rather than privacy." Cf. Perry, *Abortion, the Public Morals, and the Police Power,* 23 U.C.L.A.L.Rev. 689, 705–06 (1976).

3. *Griswold and Eisenstadt extended.* As pointed out in Tribe 1339, "the effect of *Eisenstadt v. Baird* was to single out as decisive in *Griswold* the element of reproductive autonomy, something the Court made clear in 1977, when it extended *Griswold* and *Baird* " in CAREY v. POPULATION SERVICES INTERN., 431 U.S. 678, 97 S.Ct. 2010, 52 L.Ed.2d 675 (1977), to invalidate a New York law which allowed only pharmacists to sell non-medical contraceptive devices to persons over 16 and prohibited the sale of such items to those under 16. (The Court relied in part on the 1973 *Abortion Cases,* infra.) In striking

a. Douglas, J., who joined the Court's opinion, also concurred on free speech grounds. Powell and Rehnquist, JJ., did not participate.

down the restriction on sales to adults, BRENNAN, J., spoke for six justices; in invalidating the ban on sales to those under 16, he spoke for a four-justice plurality.

As for the restriction on distribution to adults, "where a decision as fundamental as that whether to bear or beget a child is involved, regulations imposing a burden on it may be justified only by compelling interests, and must be narrowly drawn to express only those interests"—and the Court found none of the state interests advanced (e.g., protecting health, facilitating enforcement of other laws) to be "compelling." [a] The state argued that *Griswold* dealt only with the *use* of contraceptives, not their manufacture or sale, but read "in light of its progeny, the teaching of *Griswold* is that the Constitution protects individual decisions in matters of childbearing from unjustified intrusion by the State."

As for the ban on sales to those under 16, Brennan, J., joined by Stewart, Marshall, and Blackmun, JJ., applied a test "apparently less rigorous than the 'compelling state interest' test applied to restrictions on the privacy rights of adults"—restrictions inhibiting privacy rights of minors are valid "only if they serve 'any significant state interest [that] is not present in the case of an adult.' *Planned Parenthood v. Danforth,* infra]." The plurality then rejected what it called "the argument [that] minors' sexual activity may be deterred by increasing the hazards attendant on it," pointing out that that argument had already been rejected by the Court in related areas.[b]

Powell, J., concurred in the judgment, observing that by restricting not only the kinds of retail outlets that may distribute contraceptives, "but even prohibit[ing] distribution by mail to adults"—"thus requiring individuals to buy contraceptives over the counter"—the New York provision "heavily burdens constitutionally protected freedom." He saw "no justification for subjecting restrictions on the sexual activity of the young to heightened judicial review"—"a standard that for all practical purposes approaches the 'compelling interest' standard"—but concurred in the invalidation of the "distribution to minors" restriction on narrow grounds.[c]

---

a. The Court recognized, however, that "other restrictions may well be reasonably related to the objective of quality control," and thus "express[ed] no opinion on, for example, restrictions on the distribution of contraceptives through vending machines."

b. Nor was the restriction on the privacy rights of minors "saved" by another provision authorizing physicians to supply minors with contraceptives. As with limitations on distribution to adults, "less than total restrictions on access to contraceptives that significantly burden the right to decide whether to bear children must also pass constitutional muster. [This provision] delegates the State's authority to disapprove of minors' sexual behavior to physicians, who may exercise it arbitrarily * * *."

c. White, J., concurred in the invalidation of the restriction on minors "primarily because the State has not demonstrated that [the restriction] measurably contributes to the deterrent purposes which the State advances as justification for the restriction."

Stevens, J., too, concurred only in the judgment with respect to the restriction on minors: "[The State's] central argument is that the statute has the important *symbolic* effect of communicating disapproval of sexual activity by minors. [Although] the State may properly perform a teaching function, [an] attempt to persuade by inflicting harm on the listener is an unacceptable means of conveying a message that is otherwise legitimate. The propaganda technique used in this case significantly increases the risk of unwanted pregnancy and venereal disease. It is as though a State decided to dramatize its disapproval of motorcycles by forbidding the use of safety helmets. One need not posit a constitutional right to ride a motorcycle to characterize such a restriction as irrational and perverse."

Rehnquist, J., dissented, observing that if those responsible for the Bill of Rights and Civil War Amendments could have lived to know what their efforts had wrought "it is not difficult to imagine their reaction." Burger, C.J., dissented without opinion.

ORAL ARGUMENTS IN THE ABORTION CASES *

* * *

THE COURT: [I]s it critical to your case that the fetus not be a person under the due process clause? [W]ould you lose your case if the fetus was a person?

SARAH WEDDINGTON [on behalf of appellant Roe]: Then you would have a balancing of interests.

THE COURT: Well you say you have [that] anyway, don't you? * * *

THE COURT: [If] it were established that an unborn fetus is a person, [protected by] the Fourteenth Amendment, you would have almost an impossible case here, would you not?

WEDDINGTON: I would have a very difficult case. * * *

THE COURT: Could Texas constitutionally, in your view, declare [by] statute [that] the fetus is a person, for all constitutional purposes, after the third month of gestation?

WEDDINGTON: I do not believe that the State legislature can determine the meaning of the Federal Constitution. It is up to this Court to make that determination. * * *

ROBERT FLOWERS [on behalf of appellee]: [I]t is the position of the State of Texas that, upon conception, we have a human being; a person, within the concept of the Constitution of the United States, and that of Texas, also.

THE COURT: Now how should that question be decided? Is it a legal question? A constitutional question? A medical question? A philosophical question? Or, a religious question? Or what is it?

FLOWERS: [W]e feel that it could be best decided by a legislature, in view of the fact that they can bring before it the medical testimony * * *.

THE COURT: So then it's basically a medical question?

FLOWERS: From a constitutional standpoint, no, sir. * * *

THE COURT: Of course, if you're right about [the fetus being a person within the meaning of the Constitution], you can sit down, you've won your case. * * * Except insofar as, maybe, the Texas abortion law presently goes too far in allowing abortions.

FLOWERS: Yes, sir. That's exactly right. * * *

THE COURT: Do you think [you have] lost your case, then, if the fetus or the embryo is not a person? Is that it?

FLOWERS: Yes sir, I would say so. * * *

THE COURT: Under State law [there] are some rights given to the fetus?

FLOWERS: Yes, sir.

THE COURT: And you are asserting these rights against the right of the mother. [And] that's wholly aside from whether the fetus is a person under the Federal Constitution. * * *

FLOWERS: Yes, sir. * * *

THE COURT: I want you to give me [a] medical writing of any kind that says that at the time of conception the fetus is a person. * * *

* These extracts are taken from 75 *Landmark Briefs and Arguments of the Supreme Court of the United States: Constitutional Law* 807–33 (Kurland & Casper ed.).

FLOWERS: [I] find no way [that] any court or any legislature or any doctor anywhere can say that here is the dividing line. Here is not a life; and here is a life, after conception. Perhaps it would be better left to that legislature. * * *

THE COURT: Well, if you're right that an unborn fetus is a person, then you can't leave it to the legislature to play fast and loose dealing with that person. [I]f you're correct, in your basic submission that an unborn fetus is a person, then abortion laws such as that which New York has are grossly unconstitutional, isn't it?

FLOWERS: That's right, yes.

THE COURT: Allowing the killing of people.

FLOWERS: Yes, sir. * * *

[Rebuttal argument of Weddington]

THE COURT: [I] gather your argument is that a state may not protect the life of the fetus or prevent an abortion [at] any time during pregnancy? Right up until the moment of birth? * * *

WEDDINGTON: [T]here is no indication [that] the Constitution would give any protection prior to birth. That is not before the Court. * * *

THE COURT: Well, I don't know whether it is or isn't. * * *

ROE v. WADE

410 U.S. 113, 93 S.Ct. 705, 35 L.Ed.2d 147 (1973).

JUSTICE BLACKMUN delivered the opinion of the Court.

This Texas federal appeal and its Georgia companion, *Doe v. Bolton,* [infra,] present constitutional challenges to state criminal abortion legislation. The Texas statutes [are] typical of those that have been in effect in many States for approximately a century. The Georgia statutes, in contrast, have a modern cast and are a legislative product that, to an extent at least, obviously reflects the influences of recent attitudinal change, of advancing medical knowledge and techniques, and of new [thinking]. The Texas statutes [make procuring an abortion a crime except] "by medical advice for the purpose of saving the life of the mother."

[Jane] Roe alleged that she was unmarried and pregnant [and] that she was unable to get a "legal" abortion in Texas because her life did not appear to be threatened by the continuation of her pregnancy.[a] [The district court held the

a. Who was "Jane Roe"? Her real name was Norma McCorvey. Shortly after *Roe* was decided, she revealed who she really was. She explained then that she was an unmarried woman who had become pregnant as a result of a gang rape. She had tried to get an abortion, but had been unable to pay the price ($650) demanded by a doctor she finally found who was willing to perform an abortion. Because she did not want to subject to "public ridicule" a young child she had from a previous marriage, Ms. McCorvey's one condition for going ahead with the legal challenge was that she remain anonymous. See Bobbitt, *Constitutional Fate* 165 (1982); Friendly & Elliott, *The Constitution: That Delicate Balance* 202–04 (1984). But, as noted in Tribe, *Abortion: The Clash of Absolutes* 5 (1990), a decade and a half after *Roe* was decided "McCorvey explained, with embarrassment, that she had not been raped after all; she had made up the story to hide the fact that she had gotten 'in trouble' in the more usual way. Many reacted with dismay. How could the heroine of the most important abortion rights case have deceived the advocates of such rights?" Comments Tribe: "Few asked why [McCorvey] had felt a *need* to deceive them. In a different sort of society the life she would have faced as an unwed mother might not

Texas abortion statutes unconstitutional, but denied the injunctive relief requested. Roe appealed.]

[R]estrictive criminal abortion laws [like Texas'] in effect in a majority of States [today] derive from statutory changes effected, for the most part, in the latter half of the 19th century. [The Court then reviewed, in some detail, "ancient attitudes," "the Hippocratic Oath" which forbids abortion, "the common law," "the English statutory law," and "the American law." Subsequently, it described the positions of the American Medical Association, the American Public Health Association, and the American Bar Association. Thus,] at common law, at the time of the adoption of our Constitution, and throughout the major portion of the 19th century, [a] woman enjoyed a substantially broader right to terminate a pregnancy than she does in most States today. * * *

Three reasons have been advanced to explain historically the enactment of criminal abortion laws in the 19th century and to justify their [continuance].

It has been argued occasionally that these laws were the product of a Victorian social concern to discourage illicit sexual conduct. Texas, however, does not advance this justification [and] it appears that no court or commentator has taken the argument seriously.

[A] second reason is [that when] most criminal abortion laws were first enacted, the procedure was a hazardous one for the woman. [But] medical data indicat[es] that abortion in early pregnancy, that is, prior to the end of first trimester, although not without its risk, is now relatively safe.

[The] third reason is the State's interest—some phrase it in terms of duty—in protecting prenatal life. Some of the argument for this justification rests on the theory that a new human life is present from the moment of conception. * * * Only when the life of the pregnant mother herself is at stake, balanced against the life she carries within her, should the interest of the embryo or fetus not prevail. [In] assessing the State's interest, recognition may be given to the less rigid claim that as long as at least *potential* life is involved, the State may assert interests beyond the protection of the pregnant woman alone.

[It] is with these interests, and the weight to be attached to them, that this case is concerned.

The Constitution does not explicitly mention any right of privacy. [But] the Court has recognized that a right of personal privacy, or a guarantee of certain areas or zones of privacy, does exist under the Constitution. In varying contexts the Court or individual Justices have indeed found at least the roots of that right in the First Amendment, *Stanley v. Georgia* [p. 465 infra]; in the Fourth and Fifth Amendments; in the penumbras of the Bill of Rights, *Griswold;* in the Ninth Amendment, id. (Goldberg, J., concurring); or in the concept of liberty guaranteed by the first section of the Fourteenth Amendment, see *Meyer.* These decisions make it clear that only personal rights that can be deemed "fundamental" or "implicit in the concept of ordered liberty," are included in this guarantee of personal privacy. They also make it clear that the right has some extension to activities relating to marriage, *Loving;* procreation, *Skinner;* contraception, *Eisenstadt;* family relationships, *Prince v. Massachusetts* [discussed at p. 900 infra]; and child rearing and education, *Pierce.*[b]

have been nearly so lonely. In such a society she might not have made up a story about how she became pregnant. In such a society she might not even have chosen an abortion."

b. Do these parental rights permit parents to forbid public school teachers from imposing corporal punishment on their children? See *Ingraham v. Wright* (1977), Sec. 5, II infra.

This right of privacy, whether it be founded in the Fourteenth Amendment's concept of personal liberty [as] we feel it is, [or] in the [Ninth Amendment], is broad enough to encompass a woman's decision whether or not to terminate her pregnancy. The detriment that the State would impose upon the pregnant woman by denying this choice altogether is apparent. Specific and direct harm medically diagnosable even in early pregnancy may be [involved]. Psychological harm may be imminent. Mental and physical health may be taxed by child care. There is also the distress, for all concerned, associated with the unwanted child, and there is the problem of bringing a child into a family already unable, psychologically and otherwise, to care for it. In other cases, as in this one, the additional difficulties and continuing stigma of unwed motherhood may be involved. All these are factors the woman and her responsible physician necessarily will consider in consultation.

On the basis of elements such as these, appellants and some amici argue that the woman's right is absolute and that she is entitled to terminate her pregnancy at whatever time, in whatever way, and for whatever reason she alone chooses. With this we do not agree. [The] Court's decisions recognizing a right of privacy also acknowledge that some state regulation in areas protected by that right is appropriate. [A] state may properly assert important interests in safeguarding health, in maintaining medical standards, and in protecting potential life. At some point in pregnancy, these respective interests become sufficiently compelling to sustain regulation of the factors that govern the abortion decision.

[Where] certain "fundamental rights" are involved, the Court has held that regulation limiting these rights may be justified only by a "compelling state interest," and that legislative enactments must be narrowly drawn to express only the legitimate state interests at stake.

[Appellee argues] that the fetus is a "person" within the language and meaning of the Fourteenth Amendment. [If so,] appellant's case, of course, collapses, for the fetus' right to life is then guaranteed specifically by the Amendment.

[The] Constitution does not define "person" in so many words. [The Court then listed each provision in which the word appears.] But in nearly all these instances, the use of the word is such that it has application only postnatally. None indicates, with any assurance, that it has any possible pre-natal application. All this, together with our observation that throughout the major portion of the 19th century prevailing legal abortion practices were far freer [than] today, persuades us that the word "person," as used in the Fourteenth Amendment, does not include the unborn. [Thus,] we pass on to other considerations.

The pregnant woman cannot be isolated in her privacy. She carries an embryo and, later, a fetus. [The] situation therefore is inherently different from marital intimacy, or bedroom possession of obscene material, or marriage, or procreation, or education, with which *Eisenstadt, Griswold, Stanley, Loving, Skinner, Pierce,* and *Meyer* [were] concerned.

[Texas] urges that, apart from the Fourteenth Amendment, life begins at conception and is present throughout pregnancy, and that, therefore, the State has a compelling interest in protecting that life from and after conception. We need not resolve the difficult question of when life begins. When those trained [in] medicine, philosophy, and theology are unable to arrive at any consensus, the judiciary, at this point in the development of man's knowledge, is not in a position to speculate as to the answer.

[W]e do not agree that, by adopting one theory of life, Texas may override the rights of the pregnant woman that are at stake. We repeat, however, that the State does have an important and legitimate interest in preserving and protecting the health of the pregnant woman [and] that it has still *another* important and legitimate interest in protecting the potentiality of human life. These interests are separate and distinct. Each grows in substantiality as the woman approaches term and, at a point during pregnancy, each becomes "compelling."

With respect to [the] interest in the health of the mother, the "compelling" point, in the light of present medical knowledge, is at approximately the end of the first trimester. This is so because of the now established medical fact that until the end of the first trimester mortality in abortion is less than mortality in normal childbirth. It follows that, from and after this point, a State may regulate the abortion procedure to the extent that the regulation reasonably relates to the preservation and protection of maternal health. Examples of permissible state regulation in this area are requirements as to the qualifications of the person who is to perform the abortion; [as] to the facility in which the procedure is to be performed, [and] the like. This means, on the other hand, that, for the period of pregnancy prior to this "compelling" point, the attending physician, in consultation with his patient, is free to determine, without regulation by the State, that in his medical judgment the patient's pregnancy should be terminated. If that decision is reached, the judgment may be effectuated by an abortion free of interference by the State.

With respect to [the] interest in potential life, the "compelling" point is at viability [which "is usually placed at about seven months (28 weeks) but may occur earlier, even at 24 weeks."] This is so because the fetus then presumably has the capability of meaningful life outside the mother's womb.[c] State regula-

c. Earlier in its opinion, 410 U.S. at 160, the Court described the point "at which the fetus becomes 'viable' " as the point that the fetus is "potentially able to live outside the mother's womb, albeit with artificial aid." *Planned Parenthood v. Danforth* (1976) (other aspects of which are discussed infra), per Blackmun, J., upheld a Missouri abortion statute defining "viability" as "that stage of fetal development when the life of the unborn child may be continued indefinitely outside the womb by natural or artificial life-supportive systems." In rejecting contentions that the Missouri statute unduly expanded the *Roe* Court's definition of "viability," failed to contain any reference to a gestational time period, and failed to incorporate and reflect the three stages of pregnancy, the Court observed: "[W]e recognized in *Roe* that viability was a matter of medical judgment, skill, and technical ability, and we preserved the flexibility of the term. [The Missouri statute] does the same. [I]t is not the proper function of the legislature or the courts to place viability, which essentially is a medical concept, at a specific point in the gestation period. The time when viability is achieved may vary with each pregnancy, and the determination of whether a particular fetus is viable is, and must be, a matter for the judgment of the responsible attending physician. [The statutory definition] merely reflects this fact."

Consider, too, *Colautti v. Franklin*, 439 U.S. 379, 99 S.Ct. 675, 58 L.Ed.2d 596 (1979), per Blackmun, J., striking down on "void for vagueness" grounds a Pennsylvania provision requiring use of a statutorily prescribed technique when the fetus is "viable" or when there is "sufficient reason to believe that the fetus may be viable": "[The provision] subjects the physician to potential criminal liability without regard to fault. [I]t is not unlikely that experts will disagree over whether a particular fetus in the second trimester has advanced to the stage of viability. The prospect of such disagreement, in conjunction with a statute imposing liability for an erroneous determination of viability, could have a profound chilling effect on the willingness of physicians to perform abortions near the point of viability in the manner indicated by their best medical judgment." (White, J., joined by Burger, C.J. and Rehnquist, J., dissented, disagreeing with the Court's interpretation of the statute).

On similar analysis, the *Colautti* majority held "void for vagueness" a provision requiring that "the abortion technique employed shall be that which would provide the best opportunity for the fetus to be aborted alive so tion protective of fetal life after viability thus has both logical and biological justifications. If the State is interested in protecting fetal life after viability, it may go as far as to proscribe abortion during that period except when it is necessary to preserve the life or health of the mother.

Measured against these standards, [the Texas statute] sweeps too broadly [and] therefore, cannot survive the constitutional attack made upon it here.

[In] *Doe* [infra], procedural requirements contained in one of the modern abortion statutes are considered. That opinion and this one [are] to be read together.[67]

This holding, we feel, is consistent with the relative weights of the respective interests involved, with the lessons and examples of medical and legal history, with the lenity of the common law, and with the demands of the profound problems of the present day. The decision leaves the State free to place increasing restrictions on abortion as the period of pregnancy lengthens, so long as those restrictions are tailored to the recognized state interests. The decision vindicates the right of the physician to administer medical treatment according to his professional judgment up to the points where important state interests provide compelling justifications for intervention. Up to those points, the abortion decision in all its aspects is inherently, and primarily, a medical decision, and basic responsibility for it must rest with the physician. If an individual practitioner abuses the privilege of exercising proper medical judgment, the usual remedies, judicial and intra-professional, are available. * * *

JUSTICE STEWART, concurring.

In 1963, this Court, in *Ferguson v. Skrupa* [p. 87 fn. b supra], purported to sound the death knell for the doctrine of substantive due process, [but] [b]arely two years later, in *Griswold,* the Court held a Connecticut birth control law unconstitutional. In view of what had been so recently said in *Skrupa,* the Court's opinion in *Griswold* understandably did its best to avoid reliance on the

long as a different technique would not be necessary to preserve the life or health of the mother."

Colautti reaffirmed that the determination of "viability" is "a matter for medical judgment" and that that point is reached "when, in the judgment of the attending physician on the particular facts of the case before him, there is a reasonable likelihood of the fetus' sustained survival outside the womb, with or without artificial support. Because this point may differ with each pregnancy, neither the legislature nor the courts may proclaim one of the elements entering into the ascertainment of viability—be it weeks of gestation or fetal weight or any other single factor—as the determinant of when the State has a compelling interest in the life or health of the fetus."

Does the *Roe-Danforth-Colautti* approach to viability focus more on the physician's right to practice medicine than on the patient's right of privacy? Do medical advances in extrauterine gestation threaten the *practicability* of the woman's right to choose abortion? May the state assert its interest in potential life to whatever extent biotechnological advances enable a fetus to survive outside the womb, *no matter how early in its development*? Should the Court limit the definition of viability to the reasonable likelihood of survival outside the womb *without* technological support, thus designating a period in which a woman's decision to abort would be immune from state intervention? But where would we draw the line? Is an incubator a form of technological support? Should the focus of the abortion inquiry be not on the existing state of medical technology, but on the state of fetal development—the point at which a fetus becomes a "thinking, conscious being" (said to be between 19 and 30 weeks after conception)? See generally Notes, 27 U.C.L.A.L.Rev. 1340 (1980), 29 U.C.L.A.L.Rev. 1194 (1982). See also Justice O'Connor's dissent in *Akron v. Akron Center for Reproductive Health,* infra; and the notes following *Akron.*

67. Neither in this opinion nor in *Doe* do we discuss the father's rights, if any exist in the constitutional context, in the abortion decision. No paternal right has been asserted in either of the [cases]. North Carolina, for example, requires written permission for the abortion from the husband when the woman is a married minor [and] if the woman is an unmarried minor, written permission from the parents is required. * * *

Due Process Clause of the Fourteenth Amendment as the ground for decision, [but] it was clear to me then, and it is equally clear to me now, that the *Griswold* decision can be rationally understood only as a holding that the Connecticut statute substantively invaded the "liberty" that is protected by the Due Process Clause of the Fourteenth Amendment. As so understood, *Griswold* stands as one in a long line of pre-*Skrupa* cases decided under the doctrine of substantive due process, and I now accept it as such.

[The] Constitution nowhere mentions a specific right of personal choice in matters of marriage and family life, but the "liberty" protected by the Due Process Clause of the Fourteenth Amendment covers more than those freedoms explicitly named in the Bill of Rights. [As] recently as last Term, in *Eisenstadt,* we recognized "the right of the *individual,* married or single, to be free from unwarranted governmental intrusion into matters so fundamentally affecting a person as the decision whether to bear or beget a child." That right necessarily includes the right of a woman to decide whether or not to terminate her pregnancy. [It] is evident that the Texas abortion statute infringes that right directly. [The] question then becomes whether the state interests advanced to justify this abridgment can survive the "particularly careful scrutiny" that the Fourteenth Amendment here requires.

The asserted state interests are protection of the health and safety of the pregnant woman, and protection of the potential future human life within her. These are legitimate objectives, amply sufficient to permit a State to regulate abortions as it does other surgical procedures, and perhaps sufficient to permit a State to regulate abortions more stringently or even to prohibit them in the late stages of pregnancy. But such legislation is not before us, and I think the Court today has thoroughly demonstrated that these state interests cannot constitutionally support the broad abridgment of personal liberty worked by the existing Texas law. * * *

JUSTICE DOUGLAS, concurring [in *Doe* as well as in *Roe*].

While I join the opinion of the Court, I add a few words.

[The] Ninth Amendment obviously does not create federally enforceable rights. [But] a catalogue of [the rights "retained by the people"] includes customary, traditional, and time-honored rights, amenities, privileges, and immunities that come within the sweep of "the Blessings of Liberty" mentioned in the preamble to the Constitution. Many of them in my view come within the meaning of the term "liberty" as used in the Fourteenth Amendment.

First is the autonomous control over the development and expression of one's intellect, interests, tastes, and personality. These are rights protected by the First Amendment and in my view they are absolute * * *.

Second is freedom of choice in the basic decisions of one's life respecting marriage, divorce, procreation, contraception, and the education and upbringing of children. These rights, unlike those protected by the First Amendment, are subject to some control by the police power. [They] are "fundamental" and we have held that in order to support legislative action the statute must be narrowly and precisely drawn and that a "compelling state interest" must be shown in support of the limitation. * * * [4]

4. My Brother Stewart, writing in the present cases, says that our decision in *Griswold* reintroduced substantive due process that had been rejected in [*Skrupa*]. There is nothing specific in the Bill of Rights that covers [the marital relation]. Nor is there anything in the Bill of Rights that in terms protects the right of association or the privacy in one's association. [Other] peripheral rights are the right to educate one's children as one

[Third] is the freedom to care for one's health and person, freedom from bodily restraint or compulsion, freedom to walk, stroll, or loaf. These rights, though fundamental, are likewise subject to regulation on a showing of "compelling state interest." * * * Elaborate argument is hardly necessary to demonstrate that childbirth may deprive a woman of her preferred life style and force upon her a radically different and undesired future.

[Such reasoning] is, however, only the beginning of the problem. [V]oluntary abortion at any time and place regardless of medical standards would impinge on a rightful concern of society. The woman's health is part of that concern; as is the life of the fetus after quickening. These concerns justify the State in treating the procedure as a medical one.

[T]he Georgia statute outlaws virtually all such operations—even in the earliest stages of pregnancy. In light of modern medical evidence [it] cannot be seriously urged that so comprehensive a ban is aimed at protecting the woman's health. Rather, [this ban] can rest only on a public goal of preserving both embryonic and fetal life.

The present statute has struck the balance between the woman and the State's interests wholly in favor of the latter. [We] held in *Griswold* that the States may not preclude spouses from attempting to avoid the joinder of sperm and egg. [I]t is difficult to perceive any overriding public necessity which might attach precisely at the moment of conception.

* * *

[The] protection of the fetus when it has acquired life is a legitimate concern of the State. Georgia's law makes no rational, discernible decision on that score. For under the Act the developmental stage of the fetus is irrelevant when pregnancy is the result of rape or when the fetus will very likely be born with a permanent defect or when a continuation of the pregnancy will endanger the life of the mother or permanently injure her health. When life is present is a question we do not try to resolve. While basically a question for medical experts, [it is], of course, caught up in matters of religion and morality. * * *

JUSTICE WHITE, with whom JUSTICE REHNQUIST joins, dissenting [in *Doe* as well as in *Roe*].

At the heart of the controversy in these cases are those recurring pregnancies that pose no danger whatsoever to the life or health of the mother but are nevertheless unwanted for any one or more of a variety of reasons—convenience, family planning, economics, dislike of children, the embarrassment of illegitimacy, etc. The common claim before us is that for any one of such reasons, or for no reason at all, and without asserting or claiming any threat to life or health, any woman is entitled to an abortion at her request if she is able to find a medical advisor willing to [perform it].

The Court for the most part sustains this position [and] simply fashions and announces a new constitutional right [and], with scarcely any reason or authority for its action, invests that right with sufficient substance to override most existing state abortion statutes. The upshot is that the people and the legislatures of the 50 States are constitutionally disentitled to weigh the relative importance of the continued existence and development of the fetus on the one hand against a spectrum of possible impacts on the mother on the other hand.

chooses, and the right to study the German language. These decisions with all respect, have nothing to do with substantive due process. One may think they are not peripheral rights to other rights that are expressed in the Bill of Rights. But that is not enough to bring into play the protection of substantive due process. * * *

As an exercise of raw judicial power, the Court perhaps has authority [but] in my view its judgment is an improvident and extravagant exercise of the power of judicial review * * *.

JUSTICE REHNQUIST, dissenting. * * *

I have difficulty in concluding [that] the right of "privacy" is involved in this case. [Texas] bars the performance of a medical abortion by a licensed physician on a plaintiff such as Roe. A transaction resulting in an operation such as this is not "private" in the ordinary usage of that word. Nor is the "privacy" which the Court finds here even a distant relative of the freedom from searches and seizures protected by the Fourth Amendment.

[If] the Court means by the term "privacy" no more than that the claim of a person to be free from unwanted state regulation of consensual transactions may be a form of "liberty" * * * I agree [with] Mr. Justice Stewart [that that "liberty"] embraces more than the rights found in the Bill of Rights. But that liberty is not guaranteed absolutely against deprivation, but only against deprivation without due process of law. The test traditionally applied in the area of social and economic legislation is whether or not a law such as that challenged has a rational relation to a valid state objective. [If] the Texas statute were to prohibit an abortion even where the mother's life is in jeopardy, I have little doubt that such a statute would lack a rational relation to a valid state [objective].[d] But the Court's sweeping invalidation of any restrictions on abortion during the first trimester is impossible to justify under that [standard]. As in *Lochner* and similar cases applying substantive due process standards to economic and social welfare legislation, the adoption of the compelling state interest standard will inevitably require this Court to examine the legislative policies and pass on the wisdom of these policies in the very process of deciding whether a particular state interest put forward may or may not be "compelling." The decision here to break the term of pregnancy into three distinct terms and to outline the permissible restrictions the State may impose in each one, for example, partakes more of judicial legislation than it does of a determination of the intent of the drafters of the Fourteenth Amendment.

The fact that a majority of the States, reflecting after all the majority sentiment in those States, have had restrictions on abortions for at least a century seems to me as strong an indication there is that the asserted right to an abortion is not "so rooted in the traditions and conscience of our people as to be ranked as fundamental." Even today, when society's views on abortion are changing, the very existence of the debate is evidence that the "right" to an abortion is not so universally accepted as the appellants would have us believe.

[By] the time of the adoption of the Fourteenth Amendment in 1868 there were at least 36 laws enacted by state or territorial legislatures limiting abortion. [The] only conclusion possible from this history is that the drafters did not intend to have the Fourteenth Amendment withdraw from the States the power to legislate with respect to this matter. * * *

DOE v. BOLTON, 410 U.S. 179, 93 S.Ct. 739, 35 L.Ed.2d 201 (1973), the companion case to *Roe v. Wade,* sustained, against the contention that it had been rendered unconstitutionally vague by a three-judge district court's interpre-

d. Is it "irrational" or "invalid" for a state to weigh the *possibility* (or even *probability*) that the mother will die without an abortion against the *certainty* that the fetus will not survive with one and then to legislate against abortions in such situations?

tation, a Georgia provision that permitted a physician to perform an abortion when "based upon his best clinical judgment that an abortion is necessary." (The district court had struck down the statutorily specified reasons: because continued pregnancy would endanger a pregnant woman's life or injure her health; the fetus would likely be born with a serious defect; or the pregnancy resulted from rape.) "The net result of the District Court's decision," observed the Court, "is that the abortion determination, so far as the physician is concerned, is made in the exercise of his professional, that is, his 'best clinical,' judgment in the light of all the attendant circumstances. He is not now restricted to the three situations originally specified. Instead, [the] medical judgment may be exercised in light of all factors—physical, emotional, psychological, familial, and the woman's age—relevant to the well-being of the patient. All these factors may relate to health. This allows the attending physician the room he needs to make his best medical judgment. And it is room that operates for the benefit, not the disadvantage, of the pregnant woman."

However, despite the fact that the Georgia statute was patterned after the American Law Institute's Model Penal Code (1962), which had served as the model for recent legislation in about one-fourth of the states, the Court, per Blackmun, J., invalidated substantial portions of the statute. Struck down were requirements (1) that the abortion be performed in a hospital accredited by the Joint Commission on Accreditation of Hospitals (JCAH); (2) that the procedure be approved by a hospital staff abortion committee; and (3) that the performing physician's judgment be confirmed by independent examinations of the patient by two other physicians.

As for (1): There is no restriction of the performance of nonabortion surgery in a hospital not accredited by the JCAH. This requirement is also invalid "because it fails to exclude the first trimester of pregnancy, see *Roe*. [As] for (2), [we] see no constitutionally justifiable pertinence [for] the advance approval by the abortion committee. We are not cited to any other surgical procedure made subject to committee approval as a matter of state criminal law. The woman's right to receive medical care in accordance with the licensed physician's best judgment and the physician's right to administer it are substantially limited by this statutorily imposed overview." As for (3), the two-doctor concurrence, "the statute's emphasis [is] on the attending physician's 'best clinical judgment that an abortion is necessary.' That should be sufficient. [No] other voluntary medical or surgical procedure for which Georgia requires confirmation by two other physicians has been cited to us."

COMMENTARY ON THE *ABORTION CASES:* (A) WHY THE CASES WERE WRONGLY DECIDED; (B) HOW A BETTER OPINION REACHING THE SAME RESULT MIGHT HAVE BEEN WRITTEN; AND (C) WHAT LIGHT THE CASES SHED ON THE NATURE OF THE BURGER COURT'S ACTIVISM

1. *The linkage between the abortion decision and the privacy cases.* Consider SUSAN ESTRICH & KATHLEEN SULLIVAN, *Abortion Politics: Writing for an Audience of One,* 138 U.Pa.L.Rev. 119, 125–27 (1989): "The privacy cases rest, as Justice Stevens recognized, [concurring in *Thornburgh,* p. 205 infra], centrally on ' "the moral fact that a person belongs to himself [or herself] and not others nor to society as a whole." ' Extending this principle to the abortion decision follows from the fact that '[f]ew decisions are * * * more basic to individual

dignity and autonomy' or more appropriate to the 'private sphere of individual liberty' than the uniquely personal, intimate, and self-defining decision whether or not to continue a pregnancy [quoting from Blackmun, J., for the Court, in *Thornburgh.*].

"In two senses, abortion restrictions keep a woman from 'belonging to herself.' First and most obviously, they deprive her of bodily self-possession. [P]regnancy increases a woman's uterine size 500–1,000 times, her pulse rate by ten to fifteen beats a minute, and her body weight by 25 pounds or more. Even the healthiest pregnancy can entail nausea, vomiting, more frequent urination, fatigue, back pain, labored breathing, or water retention. There are also numerous medical risks involved in carrying pregnancy to term * * *. In addition, labor and delivery impose extraordinary physical demands, whether over the six to twelve hour or longer course of vaginal delivery, or during the highly invasive surgery involved in a cesarean section, which accounts for one out of four deliveries.

"By compelling pregnancy to term and delivery even where they are unwanted, abortion restrictions thus exert far more profound intrusions into bodily integrity than the stomach pumping the Court invalidated in *Rochin v. California* [p. 403 supra] or the surgical removal of a bullet from a shoulder that the Court invalidated in *Winston v. Lee* [470 U.S. 753, 105 S.Ct. 1611, 84 L.Ed.2d 662 (1985)]. 'The integrity of an individual's person is a cherished value of our society' [*Winston*] because it is so essential to identity; as former Solicitor General Charles Fried, who argued for the United States in *Webster* [p. 213 infra], recognized in another context: '[to say] that my body can be used is [to say] that I can be used.' "

2. *The precedents relied on by Roe.* Taken together, maintain Heymann & Barzelay, *The Forest and the Trees: Roe v. Wade and Its Critics,* 53 B.U.L.Rev. 765, 772 (1973), the *Meyer–Pierce–Skinner–Griswold–Eisenstadt* line of cases "clearly delineate a sphere of interests—which the Court now groups and denominates 'privacy'—implicit in the 'liberty' protected by the fourteenth amendment. At the core of this sphere is the right of the individual to make for himself—except where a very good reason exists for placing the decision in society's hands—the fundamental decisions that shape family life: whom to many; whether and when to have children; and with what values to rear these children." But see Regan, *Rewriting Roe v. Wade,* 77 Mich.L.Rev. 1569, 1639 (1979): "[The *Meyer–Eisenstadt* line of cases which Heymann & Barzelay say] establish a 'realm of private decision as to matters of marriage, procreation and child rearing' [are] a rag-tag lot. Most of them either claim to be or are best understood as being primarily about something other than marriage, procreation and child-rearing." [a] Moreover, continues Regan, supra, at 1641–42: "Whether or not the cases from *Meyer* to *Eisenstadt* establish a right of family-related freedom-of-choice, none of these cases involves a state interest remotely like the interest in protecting 'potential' but *already conceived* human life. Accordingly none of those cases establishes or even suggests that the right of family-related freedom-of-choice is weighty enough to overcome the state's interest in forbidding abortion."

Consider, too, Epstein, *Substantive Due Process by Any Other Name: The Abortion Cases,* 1973 Sup.Ct.Rev. 159, 170–72: "If we must hazard an attempt to

a. See also Ely, *The Wages of Crying Wolf: A Comment on Roe v. Wade,* 82 Yale L.J. 920, 931–32 n. 79 (1973); Noonan, *The Root and Branch of Roe v. Wade,* 63 Neb.L.Rev. 668, 672–73 (1984).

find the common thread which runs through [the *Meyer–Eisenstadt* line of cases], it might well be the principle of classic liberalism: the state is entitled to restrict the liberty of any individual within its jurisdiction only where necessary to protect other persons from harm. [But] the general principle will have only an empty exception if 'harm to another' does not cover the death of another person. Let it be accepted that the unborn child is a person (or even is to be treated like one), and it is clear beyond all question that the abortion cases fall not within the general rule that protects the liberty of each person to do as he pleases but within the exception that governs the infliction of harm to others. And the case, moreover, becomes instantly distinguishable from that posed by the state regulation of contraception, because no one claims that there is a person before conception."

3. *Does Roe reflect the same circular reasoning of the earlier substantive due process cases?* Consider JOSEPH GRANO, *Judicial Review and a Written Constitution in a Democratic Society,* 28 Wayne L.Rev. 1, 24 (1981): "*Roe* reflects the same circular reasoning and the same subjectivity that plagued the Court's earlier noninterpretivist efforts [referring to *Allgeyer* and *Lochner*].[b] The right to terminate a pregnancy can be deemed fundamental only if the fetus is not regarded as a form of life entitled to protection. No *a priori* moral principle can resolve the question of the fetus' status. By declaring the woman's right 'fundamental,' however, the Court necessarily rejected the legislative judgment that fetal life deserves protection. At this point, some might object that the Court merely concluded that public opinion was too divided to justify such a restraint on the woman's choice, but this conclusion went to the weight of the state's interest. The Court's test required that it first decide whether a fundamental right was implicated, and it could not do this, any more than it could in *Allgeyer* or *Lochner,* or any more than Justice Harlan could in *Poe v. Ullman,* without making its own moral assessment of the activity in question, an assessment not subject to demonstration by analytic reasoning."

4. *"Privacy" or "autonomy"—or "fundamentality"?* "[T]he Right of Privacy" observes LOUIS HENKIN, *Privacy and Autonomy,* 74 Colum.L.Rev. 1410, 1427 (1974), "aggravates uncertainties in the jurisprudence of individual rights and public goods under the Constitution. We had had two categories of constitutional rights, with those of the first amendment 'fundamental,' 'preferred.' Now we have restored independent importance to 'liberty-autonomy,' with an additional bifurcation of its own. Most aspects of an individual's life are not 'fundamental,' and in these his liberty is subject to the police power of federal and state governments, with presumptions of statutory validity, and a heavy, generally hopeless, burden on a resisting individual to show that a regulation has no conceivable public purpose, or that there is no rational relation between means and ends. Some, fewer, aspects of individual life are 'fundamental,' constitute a zone of prima facie autonomy (called Privacy), are presumed sacrosanct, and will bow only to a compelling public good clearly established. We are not told the basis—in language, history, or whatever else may be relevant to constitutional interpretation—for concluding that 'liberty' includes some individual autonomy that is 'fundamental' and much that is not. We are not told what is the touchstone for determining 'fundamentality.' We are not told why Privacy satisfies that test (unless Privacy is a tautology for fundamentality). [What] is it that makes my right to use contraceptives a right of Privacy, and

b. For extensive commentary on the "interpretivist"/"noninterpretivist" debate generated by *Roe,* see p. 180 infra.

fundamental, but my right to contract to work 16 hours a day or to pay more for milk than the law fixes, not a right of Privacy and not fundamental? [c] Is it, as some suspect, that the game is being played backwards: that the private right which intuitively commends itself as valuable in our society in our time, or at least to a majority of our Justices at this time, is called fundamental, and if it cannot fit comfortably into specific constitutional provisions it is included in Privacy?"

5. *Should "'privacy' semantics" be abandoned in cases such as Roe?* One reason the Court utilizes the "privacy" terminology, observes Perry, *Substantive Due Process Revisited,* 71 Nw.U.L.Rev. 417, 440–41 (1976), is "precisely *because* it obfuscates what is actually going on in a case like *Roe.* Abandoning the privacy approach for the analytical framework set forth herein would require the Court to unmask the methodology and function of substantive due process for all to see, something the Court has been rather shy to do." See also Lupu, *Untangling the Strands of the Fourteenth Amendment,* 77 Mich.L.Rev. 981, 1032–33 (1979): "If the 'naked' substantive due process decisions had to be summed up in a brief capsule, rights of 'familial choice' would be a far more accurate description than rights of 'privacy.' But rights of 'familial choice' stand starkly naked, since no amount of Bill of Rights penumbra-fashioning can responsibly lead to 'family rights' as a protected category." [d]

6. *Was the state's justification for interference with individual decision a "moral" one? A "religious" one?* Professor Henkin asks, supra, at 1431–32: "Once, [the] promotion and protection of morals was clearly a proper concern of government; does the Right of Privacy imply that it is no longer? While the rights to use contraceptives, to have an abortion, to read obscene materials, were held not offset by hypothesized, particular public goods, were they not all essentially 'morals legislation'? And does it essentially all come down to the Court's saying [in effect] that these are not 'the law's business'? Does the Constitution, then, permit government to be only utilitarian not 'moral'? Or, if that inference is unwarranted, which morals may society promote, by what means? How much attention may it give in legislation to national history, to ancestral or contemporary religion, to the prevailing morality of the time?"

But compare Cox, *The Role of the Supreme Court* 113–14 (1976): "My criticism of *Roe* is that the Court failed to establish the legitimacy of the decision by not articulating a precept of sufficient abstractness to lift the ruling above the level of a political judgment based upon the evidence currently available from the medical, physical and social sciences. Nor can I articulate such a principle—unless it be that a State cannot interfere with individual decisions relating to

c. Posner, *The Uncertain Protection of Privacy in The Supreme Court,* 1979 Sup.Ct.Rev. 173, 199, maintains that in the sense "privacy" is used in *Eisenstadt* and *Roe*—what is private is "simply what the Court thinks should not be subject to public control"—"the right to follow the occupation of one's choice without hindrance from government could equally well be regarded as an aspect of the right of privacy. The Justices who thought that the Constitution protected the right of employer and employee to set the terms of employment without government interference simply lacked the wit to justify their belief in the language of privacy." But see Craven, *Personhood: The Right To Be Let Alone,* 1976 Duke L.J. 699, 701–02 ("a right of 'personhood' can be given meaningful protection without awakening the long dormant shade of *Lochner*"; "the term, which originated with Professor Paul Freund, includes elements of the concepts of individuality, autonomy, and privacy, but none of these words is sufficient").

d. See, too, Dixon, *The 'New' Substantive Due Process and the Democratic Elite,* 1976 B.Y.U.L.Rev. 43, 84–85: "[A]lthough the privacy label is tossed about loosely as though it had some intrinsic meaning, [*Griswold* and *Roe* involved] not ['privacy,' but] a particular freedom of action. [B]ecause 'privacy' has no single, generally accepted meaning, the mold remains pure *Lochner.*"

sex, procreation, and family with only a moral or philosophical State justification: a principle which I cannot accept or believe will be accepted by the American people.[e] The failure to confront the issue in principled terms leaves the opinion to read like a set of hospital rules and regulations, whose validity is good enough this week but will be destroyed with new statistics upon the medical risks of childbirth and abortion or new advances in providing for the separate existence of a foetus."

"*[A]ll* normative judgments," observes Tribe, *American Constitutional Law* 1350 (2d ed. 1988), "are rooted in moral premises; surely the judgment that it is wrong to kill a two-week old infant is no less 'moral' in inspiration than the judgment, less frequently made but no less strongly felt by many of those who make it, that it is wrong to kill a two-day old fetus. Archibald Cox seems correct, therefore, when he concludes that *Roe* must be wrong if it rests on the premise that a state can never interfere with individual decisions relating to sex or procreation 'with only moral justification.' But it is clear that *Roe* rests on no such premise."

Is the judgment that it is wrong to kill a two-day old fetus a moral judgment or a *religious* one? Consider Richards, *Constitutional Privacy, Religious Disestablishment, and the Abortion Decisions,* in *Abortion: Moral and Legal Perspectives* 148, 171–73 (Garfield & Hennessey eds. 1984): "The implicit premises" of the argument that "the fetus is in all stages of pregnancy a moral person on a par with normal persons" "surely are specific religious or metaphysical assumptions about the fetus at all points having an individual soul: the soul requiring baptism for release from original sin (so that killing prior to birth has disastrous religious consequences for the soul); [and] the like." But an argument requiring specific religious assumption to bridge the gap between potential personhood and actual personhood, maintains Professor Richards, "is exactly the kind of endorsement of nonneutral values by the state which the religion clauses forbid." See also Emerson, *The Power of Congress to Change Constitutional Decisions of the Supreme Court; The Human Life Bill,* 77 Nw.U.L.Rev. 129, 131 (1982); Law, *Rethinking Sex and the Constitution,* 132 U.Pa.L.Rev. 955, 1026 n. 249 (1984).

Although shortly after *Roe* was decided he suggested it, Professor Tribe now rejects the view that the interest in fetal life is "intrinsically religious, or at least that the inescapable involvement of religious groups in the debate over abortion" renders the subject "proper only for decision by the woman herself." See Tribe, *Treatise* 1349–50. According to Tribe, such a view, inter alia, "appears to give too little weight to the value of allowing religious groups freely to express their

e. Consider Harlan, J., dissenting in *Poe v. Ullman:* "[T]he very inclusion of the category of morality among state concerns indicates that society is not limited in its objects only to the physical well-being of the community, but has traditionally concerned itself with the moral soundness of its people as well. Indeed to attempt a line between public behavior and that which is purely consensual or solitary would be to withdraw from community concern a range of subjects with which every society in civilized times has found it necessary to deal. The laws regarding marriage which provide both when the sexual powers may be used and the legal and societal context in which children are born and brought up, as well as laws forbidding adultery, fornication and homosexual practices which express the negative of the proposition, confining sexuality to lawful marriage, form a pattern so deeply pressed into the substance of our social life that any Constitutional doctrine in this area must be built upon that basis.

" * * * If we had a case before us which required us to decide simply, and in abstraction, whether the moral judgment implicit in the application of the present statute to married couples was a sound one, the very controversial nature of these questions would, I think, require us to hesitate long before concluding that the Constitution precluded Connecticut from choosing as it has among these various views. [But we] are not presented simply with this moral judgment to be passed on as an abstract proposition."

convictions in the political process" and "underestimates the power of moral convictions unattached to religious beliefs on this issue." But which moral convictions are "attached" to religious beliefs and which are not? Are people who hold strong religious beliefs likely to *call them* moral convictions? And to believe sincerely that they *are* moral convictions? The judgment that it is wrong to kill a two-month or two-week old child is universally held in our society, but a great many people, religious as well as nonreligious, do not consider it wrong to kill a two-day or two-week or two-month old fetus. No general agreement exists about the previability stage at which a fetus becomes, or should be regarded as, a human being with independent moral claims. Indeed, it may be said, and Professor Olsen has, *Unravelling Compromise,* 103 Harv.L.Rev. 105, 127 (1989), that "[a]bsent an appeal to an external authority, any determination of the beginning of human life can be criticized as arbitrary." If the view that it is wrong to kill a two-day old fetus may properly be called a *moral* judgment, then what religious conviction, if any, may not be called that?

7. *Is there no reality in the womb, only theories? More about whether a fetus is a "person."* In one passage, protests Noonan, *The Root and Branch of Roe v. Wade,* 63 Neb.L.Rev. 668, 672–73 (1984), "the [*Roe*] court spoke of the unborn before viability as 'a theory of life,' as though there were competing views as to whether life in fact existed before viability. The implication could also be found that there was no reality there in the womb but merely theories about what was there. [To] judge from the weight the Court gave the being in the womb—found to be protectible in any degree only in the last two months of pregnancy—the Court itself must have viewed the unborn as pure potentiality or a mere theory before viability. The Court's opinion appeared to rest on the assumption that the biological reality could be subordinated or ignored by the sovereign speaking through the Court."

But consider MacKinnon, *Reflections on Sex Equality Under Law,* 100 Yale L.J. 1281, 1315 (1991): "[T]he only point of recognizing fetal personhood, or a separate fetal entity, is to assert the interests of the fetus *against* the pregnant woman. * * * Even well toward the end of pregnancy, the view that the fetus is a person vaults over [the medically uncertain gestation-birth process] in a way that is unrealistic and dangerous for the birthing woman, who can be made invisible and chattel in a situation in which she is deeply implicated. * * * Personhood is a legal and social status, not a biological fact. [In] my opinion and in the experience of many pregnant women, the fetus is a human form of life. It is alive. But the existence of sex inequality in society requires that completed live birth mark the personhood line. If sex equality existed socially—if women were recognized as persons, sexual aggression were truly deviant, and childrearing were shared and consistent with a full life rather than at odds with it—the fetus still might not be considered a person but the question of its political status would be a very different one."

Consider, too, Olsen, note 6 supra, at 128: "The value of life is not a simple attribute of any particular life form, something that can be discovered. Culturally created, the value of life rests on social meanings, and, importantly, on sexual politics. Fetal life has value when people with power value it." Professor Olsen's conclusion is "nicely put," comments Tribe, *Abortion: The Clash of Absolutes* 119 (1990), "but is it a valid conclusion? The same thing once was said of slaves: the value of black Americans was less than the value of white Americans in the view of people with power. It once was said of women, who were deemed property * * *. And it once was said of some infants and may be said even today, by some, about the severely deformed. For most of us, though, it makes overwhelming sense nonetheless to respond: *That doesn't make it right.* The members of these other groups, degraded sometimes by the law, simply *are* human beings even though 'people with power' may try to deny it. We must be able to import into the law some moral view from a perspective external to that of those with power, or we will be trapped in a moral world of, by, and for the powerful."

8. *Could compromise have been achieved through federalism? Should each state be allowed to define "person" for itself?* Commenting on the Burger Court's attitude toward federalism in the 1970's, Sandalow, *Federalism and Social Change,* 43 Law & Contemp Prob. 35, 38 (1980), observes: "[T]he Court's failure to concede any role to the states in mediating the conflicts generated by the most important social change of the decade—indeed, its seeming unawareness that the denial of such a role required justification or even comment—is a remarkable demonstration of the extent to which a unitary system of government has evolved in the United States. [T]he Court's response to the most important legal issues arising during the past decade demonstrates how deeply embedded the assumption has become that the nation, not the states, is responsible for responding to important issues of social change." Could compromise have been achieved in the abortion area through federalism? Consider CARL SCHNEIDER, *State–Interest Analysis in Fourteenth Amendment "Privacy" Law: An Essay on the Constitutionalization of Social Issues,* 51 Law & Contemp. Probs. 79, 113–14 (1988):

"[A] local-choice policy would help remove several unduly divisive issues—abortion is an obvious example—from national politics. It would allow citizens who felt strongly about family law issues to affect their state's law without imposing on states whose citizens felt differently. * * * Abortion provides a test case * * *. In the early 1960's, an abortion-reform movement, propelled by a host of powerful forces and establishment organizations, rapidly gained momentum. Between 1967 and 1971, seventeen states, including California and New York, reformed their abortion laws. California's new statute was moderate in tone but made abortion readily available; New York's instituted a scheme quite close to that eventually enacted in *Roe.* The legislative debates [were] exemplary—earnest essays in morals and politics. It was at this point that the Court intervened with *Roe v. Wade.*

"Had the Court not acted, I suppose the political process would have continued to deal with abortion. A number of states, particularly Northern and coastal states, would have adopted reforms [which] would have made abortion virtually as available as it is today. A number of other states, particularly Southern and Western states, would not have done so. Neither pro- nor anti-abortion groups would have been entirely happy. But parties to a compromise rarely are, and both sides would have had much to be satisfied with. Abortions would have been available to anyone able to travel and to pay for the abortion. (Recall that even today many states do not pay for abortions for the poor and there is evidence that private philanthropy has done so instead.) Yet where anti-abortion feelings were strongest, the state would have expressed them. And because abortion would not have been given the national forum and the national publicity which *Roe* provided, a divisive and distorting influence would probably have been kept out of national politics."

The *Roe* Court balked at the notion that "by adopting one theory of life" a state "may override the rights of the pregnant woman that are at stake."

Professor Schneider suggests that the Court erred. Did it? Should the question of when a person comes into being be decided in each state by the democratic political process? Consider LAURENCE TRIBE, *Abortion: The Clash of Absolutes* 126–28 (1990):

"Without giving each fetus constitutional protection (and thereby barring states from allowing abortion), the Court could still overrule *Roe* and permit states to use a 'human life' declaration as a justification for restricting abortion. In states that had such a declaration, the Supreme Court could then find protection of human life to be a sufficient—a 'compelling'—reason to restrict abortion rights. This is probably the regime that most of those who oppose *Roe* would like to have in its stead.

"But what would such a world look like? What if a woman conceives in a state that regards her fertilized ovum as a person, say, Missouri, but wishes to travel to a state that chooses fetal viability or even birth as the relevant line defining personhood? Can the state in which she conceived forcibly restrain her so that she does not 'kidnap' the person that lives inside her en route to the 'murder' she plans for it? The state could probably do just that if the Constitution permitted it to regard the fetus as a baby temporarily trapped inside its mother.

"[The] fetus as chamelon—now it's a person, now it's not—makes the woman less than a full person in some states but not in others. It seems both too totalitarian and too bizarre to contemplate seriously. If the embryo is not a full person in California or Hawaii or New York, then it can't be a full person in Missouri or Utah or Georgia either."

See also Estrich & Sullivan, note 1 supra, at 151 & n. 123: "The right to abortion should not depend on where you live and how much money you have for travel. * * * Even if only ten or eleven states were to preclude abortion within their borders, many women would be held hostage there by the combination of geography, poverty, and youth. This situation would be no more tolerable than the enforcement of racial segregation in a 'mere' ten or eleven states in the 1950s."

But consider, Schneider, supra, at 115: "[I]f anti-abortionists are correct that fetuses are human beings, then criminalizing abortion is entirely within the range of the ordinary assumption that government has the power and even the duty to define and protect what it plausibly takes to be human life and that citizens may and should elect a government that will do so. Only by judicially imposing the view that fetuses are not human did *Roe* make abortion a right and foreclose its opponents from exercising their otherwise commonplace power to act through the government to protect what they plausibly take to be human life. Yet, in no other area has the government been thought unauthorized to define 'life.' And when impositions of this kind are made by judicial constitutional decisions, they disturbingly state, at various levels of explicitness, that the losing side's views are illegitimate [citing Calabresi, note 9 infra]."

9. *The impact of Roe on a pluralistic society.* Consider Calabresi, *Ideals, Beliefs, Attitudes, and the Law 95–97 (1985):* "[When] the Court proclaimed [that] anti-abortion beliefs as to commencement of life, *whether true or not,* are not part of our Constitution [it] made that Constitution unacceptable to the holders of these beliefs. It said to highly defensive groups composed in significant part of recent immigrants that their highest beliefs [are] not part of *our* law as represented by its most fundamental statement, the Constitution. [This] was

catastrophic because it reinforced doubts which the holders of anti-abortion beliefs already had about their full acceptance in American society.

"[*Roe*] opened wounds one wishes were closed. The decision made it impossible for the opposing views to live with each other, and created a situation in which one side seemed to need to *win* over the other. And, while that may be the side the Court supported, the losers will not quickly forget their exclusion (just as they have not forgotten their treatment as recent immigrants) to the detriment of our pluralistic society."

10. *Constitutional values prohibiting abortion: a defense of Roe even assuming that the fetus is a person.* Agreeing with Professor Ely (see p. 183 infra) that "constitutional argument ought to be based on values that can be inferred from the text of the Constitution, the thinking of the Framers, or the structure of our national government," DONALD REGAN, note 2 supra, at 1618–42, maintains that such constitutional argument against laws prohibiting abortion may be made, based on three constitutional values: "non-subordination, freedom from physical invasion, and equal protection":[f]

"The non-subordination value that is implicit in the bad-samaritan principle of the common law[g] is at the core of the thirteenth amendment [which] speaks not merely of slavery, but of 'involuntary servitude.' * * * Unwilling pregnancy is not slavery in its fullest sense, [but] it certainly involves the disposition and coercion of the (intensely) personal service of one 'man' for another's benefit. The second value, freedom from physical invasion or imposed physical pain or hardship, is embodied in the eighth amendment and also plainly counts among those fundamental values of our society which are traditionally subsumed under fifth and fourteenth amendment due process. [There] is no other case, I believe, in which the law imposes comparable physical invasion and hardship as an obligation of samaritanism. * * *

"[E]ven if those parts of our tradition which forbid subordination or physical invasion have historically included an exception for abortion laws, the exception is impermissible. It creates an inequality that is inconsistent with an even more fundamental part of our tradition, reflected in the equal protection clause and the due process clause of the fifth amendment.

"[To] see the equal protection problem, we must look at abortion in a broader context. Life in society [provides] many opportunities to be a good or bad samaritan. The objection to an anti-abortion statute is that it picks out certain potential samaritans, namely women who want abortions, and treats them in a way that is at odds with the law's treatment of other potential samaritans. Women who want abortions are required to give aid in circumstances where closely analogous potential samaritans are not. And they are

f. As Professor Regan acknowledges, his article builds on an argument made in Thomson, *A Defense of Abortion,* 1 Phil. & Pub.Aff. 47 (1971).

g. At the outset of his article, id. at 1569, Professor Regan contends that "abortion should be viewed as presenting a problem in what we might call 'the law of samaritanism,' that is, the law concerning obligations imposed on certain individuals to give aid to others. It is a deeply rooted principle of American law that an individual is ordinarily not required to volunteer aid to another individual who is in danger or in need of assistance. [I]f we require a pregnant woman to carry the fetus to term and deliver it—if we forbid abortion, in other words—we are compelling her to be a Good Samaritan. [I]f we consider the special nature of the burdens imposed on pregnant women by laws forbidding abortion, we must eventually conclude that the equal protection clause forbids imposition of these burdens on pregnant women." Regan refers to "the established principle that one does not have to volunteer aid" as the "bad-samaritan principle," id. at 1572.

required to give aid of a *kind* and an *extent* that is required of no other potential samaritan.

"[I]t is important that the inequality of treatment between pregnant women and other potential samaritans touches on the constitutional values of nonsubordination and freedom from physical invasion. A woman who is denied an abortion is compelled to serve the fetus and to suffer physical invasion, pain, and hardship. [That it can plausibly] be argued that the Constitution prohibits this imposition outright, [surely] means that any inequality of treatment we can point to becomes harder to justify. * * *

"Other reasons for the Court to give the abortion problem special attention are related to the suspect classification idea. Only women need abortions. [T]he one potential samaritan who is singled out for specially burdensome treatment is a potential samaritan who must, given human physiology, be female. Why is this important?

"First, any inequality that flows from an unchosen and unalterable characteristic is likely to be specially resented. [Since] pregnancy happens only to women, and since no one has any choice about whether to be a woman, susceptibility to pregnancy (and to being in the position of wanting an abortion) is a nonchosen characteristic. (It is not an unalterable characteristic, since a woman might have herself sterilized, but this method of altering the characteristic itself involves a significant physical invasion.)

"It might be objected that even if susceptibility to pregnancy is an unchosen characteristic, pregnancy itself is not, and that laws attaching unpleasant consequences to pregnancy therefore do not interfere with women's controlling their own destinies. [But] the only method of avoiding pregnancy with certainty requires, for many people, extraordinary self-denial [and] does not, to my mind, eliminate the force of the suggestion that pregnancy is often sufficiently 'unchosen' so that laws specially disadvantaging pregnant women limit women's control of their lives, are justifiably resented, and deserve more-than-minimal judicial attention.[h]

"[M]ost legislatures would defend laws against abortion on the ground that they protect human life (or potential life). [But the] inequality between the

h. Consider MacKinnon, *Roe v. Wade: A Study in Male Ideology,* in *Abortion: Moral and Legal Perspectives* 45, 46–48 (Garfield & Hennessey eds. 1984): "Feminist investigations suggest [that women do not significantly control sex]. Feminism has found that women feel compelled to preserve the appearance—which, acted upon, becomes the reality—of male direction of sexual expression, as if it is male initiative itself that we want: it is that which turns us on. Men enforce this. It is much of what men want in a woman. * * *

"Under these conditions, women often do not use birth control because of its social meaning, a meaning we did not create. Using contraception means acknowledging and planning and taking direction of intercourse, accepting one's sexual availability, and appearing nonspontaneous. It means appearing available to male incursions. A good user of contraception is a bad girl. She can be presumed sexually available and, among other consequences, raped with relative impunity. (If you think this isn't true, you should consider rape cases in which the fact that a woman had a diaphragm in is taken as an indication that what happened to her was intercourse, not rape. 'Why did you have your diaphragm in?') * * * I wonder if a woman can be presumed to control access to her sexuality if she feels unable to interrupt intercourse to insert a diaphragm; or worse, cannot even want to, aware that she risks a pregnancy she knows she does not want. * * * Sex doesn't look a whole lot like freedom when it appears normatively less costly for women to risk an undesired, often painful, traumatic, dangerous, sometimes illegal, and potentially life-threatening procedure, than it is to protect oneself in advance. Yet abortion policy has never been explicitly approached in the context of how women get pregnant; that is, as a consequence of intercourse under conditions of gender inequality; that is, as an issue of forced sex."

treatment of pregnant women and the treatment of other potential samaritans who are not required to undertake burdens (often very much smaller burdens) in order to save life is too great. The inequality trenches on two distinct constitutionally protected interests—the interest in non-subordination and the interest in freedom from serious physical invasion. In addition, the inequality disadvantages a class that is defined by a non-chosen characteristic (whether sex or unwanted pregnancy) and that has suffered from a history of discrimination. This is more than any reasonable American legislature would tolerate. * * *

"Perhaps the greatest advantage of my argument is that it makes it possible to avoid the question of whether the fetus is, or may be treated by the state as, a person. Justice Blackmun claims at one point that the Court need not decide 'when life begins'. But his general argument [seems] plainly to assume that the fetus is *not* a person until the point of viability (at the earliest). Indeed, Blackmun elsewhere suggests that if the fetus were a person within the meaning of the fourteenth amendment, the woman's claim to an abortion would be foreclosed by the Constitution itself.

"On the last point, I think Blackmun is mistaken. [The] people who need the assistance of potential samaritans in ordinary samaritan cases are persons under the fourteenth amendment, and yet the general common law bad-samaritan principle is not unconstitutional.

"[My] argument, unlike Blackmun's, does not depend on refusing to allow the state to regard the fetus as a person. Everything I have said is consistent with the assumption that the fetus is a person. Other persons are allowed to die when potential samaritans are authorized by the bad-samaritan principle to deny aid. The personhood of the fetus, even if it be conceded, is not an adequate reason (indeed it is no reason at all) for treating the pregnant woman differently from other potential samaritans.

"[M]y argument justifies more clearly than the Court's argument [its] conclusion that abortion may not be forbidden even in the third trimester when the life or health of the mother is at stake. If the problem is ultimately one of balancing, as the Court's opinion suggests, it is not clear why the state's compelling interest (as the Court describes it) in protecting the potential life of a fetus already capable of 'meaningful life outside the mother's womb' (in the Court's phrase) is outweighed even by the woman's life, much less by her health. On my approach, however, the matter is clear. Even the reader who rejects my general conclusions must admit that there is no other case in which we would even consider requiring one individual to sacrifice his life or health to rescue another." [i]

11. *Prohibiting the government from "coercing intimate acts."* The argument that a state may not compel a pregnant woman to be "a Good Samaritan" is questioned by Bobbitt, *Constitutional Fate* 163 (1982): "This argument seems to treat the embryonic child as a stranger who merely happens to be inconveniently placed proximate to the mother. There is much law, however, for the proposition that one owes a duty of care to one's child. This puts us back in the position of deciding when a child's life begins, a position the *Roe* Court was doctrinally forced to take in its argument despite its disclaimers and one which

i. For criticism of Regan's argument, see Alexander, *Modern Equal Protection Theories: A Metatheoretical Taxonomy and Critique,* 42 Ohio St.L.J. 3, 40–42 n. 114 (1981). See also Bobbitt, note 11 infra; Davis, *Abortion and Self-Defense,* in *Abortion: Moral and Legal Perspectives* 186 (Garfield & Hennessey eds. 1984) (hereinafter referred to as "*Abortion*"); P. Foot, *Killing and Letting Die,* in *Abortion* 175, 184–85; Michaels, *Abortion and the Claims of Samaritanism,* in *Abortion* 213.

sound constitutional decision ought to avoid completely." Professor Bobbitt proposes a somewhat different "ethical argument [that] avoids the necessity for this determination" and one that "would decide *Roe*" (id. at 160–65): "Government may not coerce intimate acts. Stated generally, does anyone really doubt this? * * * Whatever else may be an intimate act, carrying a child within one's body and giving birth must be a profoundly intimate act."

12. *"Privacy" or "sex equality"?* "Nothing the Supreme Court has ever done," observes Law, *Rethinking Sex and the Constitution,* 132 U.Pa.L.Rev. 955, 981 (1984), "has been more concretely important for women [than the decision in *Roe*]. Laws restricting abortion have a devastating sex-specific impact." Yet, as Professor Law notes, not only was the abortion decision not grounded on the principle of sex equality, the plaintiffs in *Roe* and *Doe* did not even challenge the abortion restrictions as sex discriminatory. But there seems to be a growing consensus that the best argument for the right to abortion is based on principles of sex equality rather than due process.[j] CATHARINE MacKINNON, Note 7 supra, at 1319, puts it powerfully:

"Because the social organization of reproduction is a major bulwark of women's social inequality, any constitutional interpretation of a sex equality principle must prohibit laws, state policies, or official practices and acts that deprive women of reproductive control or punish women for their reproductive role or capacity. * * * Women's right to reproductive control is a sex equality right because it is inconsistent with an equality mandate for the state, by law, to collaborate with or mandate social inequality on the basis of sex, as [denials of abortion through criminalization or lack of public funding where needed] do. This is not so much an argument for an extension of the meaning of constitutional sex equality as a recognition that if it does not mean this, it does not mean anything at all.

"Under this sex equality analysis, criminal abortion statutes of the sort invalidated in *Roe* violate equal protection of the laws. They make women criminals for a medical procedure only women need, or make others criminals for performing a procedure on women that only women need, when much of the need for this procedure as well as barriers to access to it have been created by social conditions of sex inequality. Forced motherhood is sex inequality. Because pregnancy can be experienced only by women, and because of the unequal social predicates and consequences pregnancy has for women, any forced pregnancy will always deprive and hurt one sex only as a member of her gender."

13. *In Roe did the woman patient take a back seat to the male physician?* In *Roe,* maintains ANDREA ASARO, *The Judicial Portrayal of the Physician in Abortion and Sterilization Decisions,* 6 Harv. Women's L.J. 51, 53–55 (1983), Justice Blackmun "subsumed the woman's right to privacy within the ambit of the doctor-patient relationship, and ultimately subordinated her interest to the physician's. [For] Blackmun, the key issue was quite simply one of medical discretion, in other words: '[F]or the period of pregnancy prior to the "compelling" point, the attending physician, in consultation with his patient, is free to

j. See Calabresi, note 9 supra, at 87–114; Tribe, *Treatise* at 1353–55; R. Ginsburg, *Some Thoughts on Autonomy and Equality in Relation to Roe v. Wade,* 63 N.C.L.Rev. 375, 382–86 (1985); Karst, *Foreword: Equal Citizenship Under the Fourteenth Amendment,* 91 Harv.L. Rev. 1, 57–59 (1977); Law, supra, at 987–1002, 1020–1028; Olsen, note 6 supra, at 117–26; Schauer, *Easy Cases,* 58 S.Cal.L.Rev. 399, 431 n. 83 (1985); Strauss, *Discriminatory Intent and the Taming of Brown,* 56 U.Chi.L.Rev. 935, 990–98 (1989); Sunstein, *Why the Unconstitutional Conditions Doctrine Is An Anachronism (With Particular Reference to Religion, Speech and Abortion*), 70 B.U.L.Rev. 593, 617–20 (1990).

determine [that], in his medical judgment, the patient's pregnancy should be terminated.' Interestingly, the abortion decision is characterized here neither as primarily the woman's nor as fundamentally or initially a moral or personal one. Blackmun's perspective is clinical, and the woman patient has taken a back seat to the male physician-protagonist. [Concluding his *Roe* opinion, Justice Blackmun states]: '[The] decision vindicates the right of the physician to administer medical treatment according to his professional judgment up to the points where important state interests provide compelling justifications for intervention. Up to these points, *the abortion decision in all its aspects is inherently, and primarily, a medical decision, and basic responsibility for it must rest with the physician.*' [Emphasis added by Ms. Asaro.] Blackmun has neglected even to mention the pregnant woman as party to the abortion decision! The state, the physician, and the court have displaced Ms. Roe altogether."

14. *Protection of the viable fetus.* Did *Roe* assume that the mother's interest in her life or health predominates over the identical interests of the viable fetus? If so, why? Should the interests of mother and viable fetus be weighed equally in resolving conflicts between them? If, for example, continued pregnancy threatens a mother's life or health at a time when her unborn child is viable, should we first consider separating them by a procedure designed to minimize the risks to both? Yes, answers King, *The Juridical Status of the Fetus: A Proposal for Legal Protection of the Unborn,* 77 Mich.L.Rev. 1647, 1682–89 (1979): "[W]hether the fetus is a 'person' is irrelevant to whether it should have legal protection.[k] [The] capacity to have independent existence points to viability instead of birth as the determinative moment in development. [V]iable fetuses merit all protection currently given the newborn infant." [l]

But consider Comment, 27 U.C.L.A.L.Rev. 1340, 1348 n. 45 (1980): "Professor King's proposal that "the competing interests in the life of the viable fetus and the pregnant [be] balanced on an issue-by-issue basis" "implies that the viable fetus has constitutional rights at least equivalent to those of the pregnant woman. It is in direct conflict with *Roe.* If adopted, the proposal would create a deterrent against carrying a pregnancy to term even to the woman who wants her child as well as to the child's father, because after fetal viability there would be no guarantee that in the case of a contest between the life of the unborn child and the pregnant woman, the woman's life would prevail."

Given *Roe's* acceptance of the state's interest in protecting "potential life," does the constitutional right recognized in *Roe* encompass the right to have the fetus destroyed? Consider Tribe, *Toward a Model of Roles in the Due Process of Life and Law,* 87 Harv.L.Rev. 1, 4 n. 24 (1973): "Since the procedures for removal of a viable fetus typically present the same risks to the woman whether the fetus is saved or destroyed, it seems questionable that the Court actually

k. Cf. *Ely,* fn. a supra, at 926: "[T]he argument that fetuses lack constitutional rights is simply irrelevant. For it has never been held or even asserted that the state interest needed to justify forcing a person to refrain from an activity, *whether or not that activity is constitutionally protected,* must implicate either the life or the constitutional rights of another person. Dogs are not 'persons in the whole sense' nor have they constitutional rights, but that does not mean the state cannot prohibit killing them: It does not even mean the state cannot prohibit killing them in the exercise of the First Amendment right of political protest. Come to think of it, draft cards aren't persons either [referring to *United States v. O'Brien* (p. 524 infra)]."

What Professor Ely's argument overlooks, maintains Comment, 29 U.C.L.A.L.Rev. 1194, 1205 (1982), "is that if the fetus is not a separate human being, then it is a part of the woman's body. This is not true of [dogs and] draft cards. [A] law that forbids the destruction of draft cards [does] not impinge upon the right of privacy with respect to procreation."

l. See fn. c. to the *Roe* opinion.

intended to mandate a choice in favor of the latter. The only situations in which a justification for such a choice could be plausibly advanced would be those involving a troublesome deference to the woman's desire to preserve her mental health by assuring that the unwanted fetus be killed."

Are there other plausible reasons for the woman's desire to have the unwanted fetus destroyed? If "mental and physical health may be taxed by child care," may she also wish to avoid the economic burden of sustaining the viable fetus (or is "prematurely born child" the more accurate term?) until other people (or the state) assume this burden? Does *Roe* obligate the state to assume the financial burden at once? See Note, 7 U.C.Davis L.Rev. 432, 451 (1974).

If the woman's right in *Roe* does not encompass destruction of the viable fetus, may the state require a pregnant woman to submit to blood transfusions where necessary to "save the life" of the viable fetus? See King, supra, at 1683. If the woman's right in *Roe* does not encompass destruction of the viable fetus, to what extent does (should) it oblige the pregnant woman to delay abortion until viability? See Vieira, *Roe and Doe: Substantive Due Process and the Right of Abortion,* 25 Hast.L.J. 867, 875 (1974).

15. *The "peculiar nature" of the Burger Court's activism.* Unlike the Warren Court, [whose] justices' doctrinal compromises "took place against a background in which the direction of constitutional development was both clear and, to many, inspiring," observes VINCENT BLASI, *The Rootless Activism of the Burger Court,* in *The Burger Court: The Counter-Revolution that Wasn't* 198, 212–13 (V. Blasi ed. 1983), the *Roe* justices "could not plausibly justify their decision as the working out of a theme implicit in several previous decisions, still less as the vindication of values deeply embedded in the nation's constitutional tradition. The Court's opinion in *Roe* is best characterized as an ad hoc comparison of material interests: the woman has an interest in avoiding the physical and psychological burdens of an unwanted pregnancy and childbirth; the state has an interest in protecting the woman's health and the potentiality of life represented by the fetus. Grounded not on principle but on contingent considerations, these interests either grow or diminish during the course of the pregnancy, and in fact change as technological developments alter the capacity to sustain a fetus outside the womb. No effort was made in the *Roe* opinion to relate the woman's burdens to more general conceptions of choice-making capacity, bodily integrity, nonsubordination to other human beings, or equality of treatment. Similarly, no effort was made to assess the state's claim to regulate in terms of the much mooted dispute over whether government is entitled to enforce moral precepts.

"[T]he peculiar nature of the Burger Court's activism can be seen from the fact that even so fundamental an issue as abortion was treated by this Court as a conflict of particularized, material interests—a conflict that could be resolved by accommodating those interests in the spirit of compromise. Thus, third trimester abortions can be prohibited but earlier abortions cannot. The state cannot prohibit all abortions outright, but can refuse to fund them [see *Maher v. Roe* and *Harris v. McRae,* infra], even while funding the alternative of childbirth and thereby encouraging pregnant women to forgo the abortion option. The woman's husband cannot veto her choice to have an abortion [*Planned Parenthood v. Danforth,* infra] but a minor's parents can do so under certain limited circumstances. These doctrinal lines are not necessarily incoherent. But each has in fact taken on a highly arbitrary character because in grappling with the issues that followed in *Roe*'s wake, the justices were unable to draw upon any sort of theory, or vision, or even framework for determining the contours of the right they had recognized. Each variation on the abortion issue was treated by the Court as an isolated, practical problem."

ROE v. WADE AND THE DEBATE IT STIRRED OVER "INTERPRETIVIST"/"NONINTERPRETIVIST" CONSTITUTIONAL DECISIONMAKING[a]

1. Consider Lupu, *Constitutional Theory and the Search for the Workable Premise,* 8 Dayton L.Rev. 579, 583 (1983): "*Roe* clarified, as had no other case

a. Although the materials in this section inevitably overlap to some extent with the preceding set of Notes & Questions, it seems useful to focus separately on the general constitutional debate generated by the 1973 *Abortion Cases.*

"Interpretivism" indicates that "judges deciding constitutional issues should confine themselves to enforcing norms that are stated or clearly implicit in the written Constitution"; "noninterpretivism" indicates that "courts should go beyond that set of references and enforce norms that cannot be discovered within the four corners of the document." Ely, *Democracy and Distrust* 1 (1980). "What distinguishes interpretivism from its opposite is its insistence that the work of the political branches is to be invalidated only in accord with an inference whose starting point, whose underlying premise, is fairly discoverable in the Constitution. That the complete inference will not be found there—because the situation is not likely to have been foreseen—is general common ground." Id. at 1–2.

"Noninterpretivism," comments Van Alstyne, *Interpretations of the First Amendment* 94 n. 27 (1984), "signals a frank resolve to detach judicial review from the Constitution itself by stipulating it purports not to be interpreting the Constitution. It may say too much about the current condition of constitutional scholarship that 'noninterpretivism' is willingly adopted as a mode of describing one's own work in constitutional law. If there were not writers who evidently welcome its fit, [one] might have supposed that its use was limited and purely pejorative."

As might be expected, there is disagreement over the appropriate terminology. Dean Bennett prefers the term "originalists" to describe those who "argue that constitutional language, understood in light of the substantive intentions or values behind its enactment, is the sole proper source for constitutional interpretation," because this term "better captures the static pretense of the approach that seems to me to be its principal flaw." Bennett, *Objectivity in Constitutional Law,* 132 U.Pa.L. Rev. 445, 446 & n. 3 (1984). "On the other side of the debate are 'noninterpretivists' or 'nonoriginalists' who believe it is legitimate for judges to look beyond text and original intention in interpreting constitutional language," but they "are divided on what particular sources should replace or supplement originalist sources and on how to justify their use." Id. at 446.

Fallon, *A Constructivist Coherence Theory of Constitutional Interpretation,* 100 Harv.L.Rev. 1189, 1211 (1987), divides "interpretivists" into two camps: "On one side stand 'originalists.' [They] take the rigid view that only the original understanding of the framers' specific intent ought to count. On the other side, 'moderate interpretativists' allow contemporary understandings and the framers' general or abstract intent to enter the constitutional calculus."

Professor Fallon has some unkind words for "originalism," id. at 1211, 1214: "[Its] purity proves its undoing, because originalism cannot satisfy the standards that it sets for itself. The problem is that arguments from text and the framers' intent cannot be kept independent of other kinds of factors that originalists, with their conception of what the rule requires, insist on excluding. [The] questions of when, how, and to what extent the rule-of-law ideals associated with a written constitution should accommodate needs for adaptation and change are notoriously difficult. [It] is a normative deficiency of originalism that its premises deny any scope whatever for accommodation."

Nor is Professor Fallon a fan of "moderate interpretivism," id. at 1215, 1217: "[It] also fails to provide a viable theory. [It] recognizes the legitimacy of arguments of original as well as contemporary meaning and of specific as well as general intent. But this recognition raises the problem of how to decide which meaning or which type of intent should govern in any particular situation. * * * Recognition that moderate interpretivism relies on factors besides text and history—and in particular that judges must make delicate moral and political judgments to determine the contemporary meaning of numerous constitutional concepts and the level of abstraction at which the framers' intent ought to be stated—reveals the theory as failed in its own terms."

since World War II, the Supreme Court's willingness to reach results which no defensible interpretivist position could support. Although rhetorically tied to the meaning of 'liberty' in the fourteenth amendment due process clause, and loosely aligned with the penumbral analysis developed in *Griswold, Roe* cut fundamental rights adjudication loose from the constitutional text. [There followed] a vast array of doctrinal, methodological, and theoretical inquiries into the outcome in *Roe.* More or less detached from the case itself, these scholarly efforts offered a variety of justifications for noninterpretive review—natural law underpinnings of the 1787 Constitution, [the] search for enduring or traditional unwritten norms, [and] judicial manifestation of consensus morality."

2. Ely, *Democracy and Distrust* 2–3 (1980), suggests why "interpretivism may be entering a period of comparative popularity": The first is that *Roe,* "the clearest example of noninterpretivist 'reasoning' [in] four decades," "forced all of us who work in the area to think about which camp we fall into, with the result that a number of persons would today label themselves interpretivists who had not previously given the choice much notice. The second may be that, *Roe* notwithstanding, the Burger Court is by and large a politically conservative Court—or at least more conservative than its predecessor. This means that observers who might earlier have been content to let the justices enforce their own values (or their rendition of society's values) are now somewhat uneasy about doing so and are more likely to pursue an interpretivist line, casting their lot with the values of the framers."

3. *What happened on January 22, 1973?* "The subject of abortion," observes ROBERT BORK, *The Tempting of America* 111 (1990), "had been fiercely debated in state legislatures for many years. It raises profound moral issues upon which people of good will can and do disagree * * *. Whatever the proper resolution of the moral debate, * * * few people imagined that the Constitution resolved it. In 1973, a majority of the Supreme Court did imagine just that in *Roe v. Wade.*" Continues Judge Bork, id. at 111–12, 116:

"In an opinion of just over fifty-one pages, Justice Blackmun, writing for [the majority], employed the right of privacy to strike down the abortion laws of most states and set severe limitations upon the states' power to regulate the subject at all. From the beginning of the Republic until that day, January 22, 1973, the moral question of what abortions should be lawful had been left entirely to state legislatures. The discovery this late in our history that the question was not one for democratic decision but one of constitutional law was so implausible that it certainly deserved a fifty-one page explanation. Unfortunately, in the entire opinion there is not one line of explanation, not one sentence that qualifies as legal argument. [Nor has the Court] ever provided the explanation lacking in 1973. It is unlikely that it ever will, because the right to abort, whatever one thinks of it, is not to be found in the Constitution. * * *

Grey, *Do We Have an Unwritten Constitution?*, 27 Stan.L.Rev. 703 (1975), probably originated the use of the "interpretivist-noninterpretivist" terminology, but he now thinks these labels "distort the debate": "If the current interest in interpretive theory [does] nothing else, at least it shows that the concept of interpretation is broad enough to encompass any plausible mode of constitutional adjudication. We are all interpretivists; the real arguments are not over whether judges should stick to interpreting, but over what they should interpret and what interpretive attitudes they should adopt. Repenting past errors, I will therefore use the less misleading labels 'textualists' and 'supplementers' for, respectively, those who consider the text the sole legitimate source of operative norms in constitutional adjudication, and those who accept supplementary sources of constitutional law [such as 'conventional morality']." Grey, *The Constitution as Scripture,* 37 Stan.L.Rev. 1 (1984).

"Attempts to overturn *Roe* will continue as long as the Court adheres to it. And, just so long as the decision remains, the Court will be perceived, correctly, as political * * *. *Roe,* as the greatest example and symbol of the judicial usurpation of democratic prerogatives in this century, should be overturned. The Court's integrity requires that."

But consider LAURENCE TRIBE, *Abortion* 99: "Judge Bork says that 'the right to abort, whatever one thinks of it, is not to be found in the Constitution.' In a sense this is obviously right. Indeed, not one of the words 'abortion,' 'pregnancy,' 'reproduction,' 'sex,' 'privacy,' 'bodily integrity,' and 'procreation' appears anywhere in [the] Constitution.[b] But neither do such phrases as 'freedom of thought,' 'rights of parenthood,' 'liberty of association,' 'family self-determination,' and 'freedom of marital choice.' Yet nearly everyone supposes that at least some of these dimensions of personal autonomy and independence are aspects of the 'liberty' which the Fourteenth Amendment says no state may deny to any person 'without due process of law.'

"The 'right to abortion' was first *announced,* it's true, in *Roe v. Wade.* [But the] 'right to privacy,' whatever its outer bounds, was suggested as early as 1923 in the case of *Meyer v. Nebraska. Roe* was simply the first case in which the general question of state regulation of abortion was squarely considered by the Supreme Court. To argue that for this reason, the Constitution does not protect the right to abortion, or that it did not do so until January 22, 1973, is no better than to argue that it does not protect the 'right to contribute money to a political campaign.' Although that right was not *announced* until the Supreme Court's 1976 decision in *Buckley v. Valeo* [p. 777 infra], it is beyond doubt that the right is, and has long been, a right protected by the free speech guarantee of the First Amendment."

4. Consider JOSEPH GRANO, *Judicial Review and a Written Constitution in a Democratic Society,* 28 Wayne L.Rev. 1, 25, 59 (1981): [An objection to criticisms of *Roe*] might be that the Court's poor choice of methodology is not a valid argument against noninterpretivism. The truth, however, is that the Court's methodology is basically all there is. Noninterpretivism is a methodology of *fundamental* rights, [for] no one maintains that the judiciary should require "compelling" reasons for all laws, including those that prohibit swindling or murder. Noninterpretivism's first requirement is that the judiciary separate that which is fundamental from that which is not, and it is this very task that requires the judiciary to take normative and moral positions that cannot be demonstrated.

"[*Roe*] is as wrong as the proposed constitutional amendment to protect the fetus, and for the same reason: it seeks to bind succeeding generations to our generation's thinking, or at least to the thinking of a segment of it. Through the Supreme Court, our generation has dictated to future generations that they can prohibit abortions only by mustering the requisite super-majority to amend the Constitution. [*Roe*] is just one example of judicial noninterpretivism, a methodology that permits the judiciary to decide the difficult moral issues of our time under the rubric of constitutional law. Whether the issue be abortion, the right of the family or unrelated individuals to share living quarters,[c] [or] the right to a

b. On the other hand, the *Lochner* Court did rely on words that appeared in the Constitution. As Professor Tribe notes elsewhere, see *Treatise* at 771, "the *Lochner* error" "was not in invoking a value the Constitution did not mark as special; the text evinces the most explicit concern with 'liberty,' 'contract,' and 'property.' The error lay in giving that value a perverse content."

c. See *Moore v. East Cleveland,* p. 241 infra.

greater share of the wealth, every noninterpretivist decision recognizing one of these claims adds, in effect, a new provision to the written constitution and thereby imposes an additional moral restraint on subsequent generations.[267]"

5. *Are the Abortion Cases "bad constitutional law" or "not constitutional law"?* Consider JOHN ELY, *The Wages of Crying Wolf: A Comment on Roe v. Wade,* 82 Yale L.J. 920, 935–37, 939, 943, 947–49 (1973): "What is unusual about *Roe* is that the liberty involved is accorded [a] protection more stringent [than] that the present Court accords the freedom of the press explicitly guaranteed by the First Amendment. What is frightening about *Roe* is that this super-protected right is not inferable from the language of the Constitution, the framers' thinking respecting the specific problem in issue, any general value derivable from the provisions they included, or the nation's governmental structure. Nor is it explainable in terms of the unusual political impotence of the group judicially protected vis-á-vis the interest that legislatively prevailed over it.[d]

"[The] problem with *Roe* is not so much that it bungles the question it sets itself, but rather that it sets itself a question the Constitution has not made the Court's business. It *looks* different from *Lochner*—it has the shape if not the substance of a judgment that is very much the Court's business, one vindicating

267. Noninterpretivism is sometimes defended by positing horribles that only noninterpretivism can correct. Professor Karst, for example, invited us to imagine legislation prohibiting marriage: "All would agree—even Justice Rehnquist, I suppose—that an arbitrary denial by the state of the freedom to marry would violate the Fourteenth Amendment." Karst, *The Freedom of Intimate Association,* 89 Yale L.J. 624, 667 (1980). Thus, extremely confident, Karst concluded, "*Of course* there is a right to marry." Id. [I] am quite certain I do not agree. I cannot conceive of a legislature prohibiting marriage, but the reason is that I cannot foresee the circumstances that would prompt such legislation. Presumably, however, such a decision would occur only after some event convinced a majority or supermajority of the population that marriage should be banned. Assuming such a society (again, one we cannot really conceive), it cannot be obvious that such a ban should be struck down as unconstitutional. "Ah!," you answer, "but suppose the legislature passes such a law without popular support?" Anyone who believes that noninterpretivism or anything else in constitutional law, or in any other law, can safeguard society from such a legislature is welcome to his views, for I have nothing further to say to such a person. Cf. Ely, *Democracy and Distrust* 182 (1980) (discussing hypothetical law banning gall bladder operations) * * *.

d. Elsewhere in his article, id. at 933–35, Professor Ely argues that Justice Stone's suggestion in his famous *Carolene Products* footnote that the Court provide extraordinary constitutional protection for " 'discrete and insulate minorities' unable to form effective political alliances" does not apply to *Roe*: "Compared with men, very few women sit in our legislatures, [but] *no* fetuses sit [there]. Of course they have their champions, but so have women. The two interests have clashed repeatedly in the political arena, and had continued to do so up to the date of [*Roe*], generating quite a wide variety of accommodations. [Justice Stone's suggestion] was clearly intended and should be reserved for those interests which, as compared with the interests to which they have been subordinated, constitute minorities usually incapable of protecting themselves. Compared with men, women may constitute such a 'minority'; compared with the unborn, they do not."

Professor Ely's challenge of the appropriateness of judicial intervention in *Roe* "is misguided, however," maintains Bennett, *Abortion and Judicial Review,* 75 Nw.U.L.Rev. 978, 995–96 n. 71 (1981), "because it assumes that fetuses are political actors—indeed a political minority—whose 'powerlessness' is relevant to assessing the Court's appropriate role in the abortion controversy. Each political system must define, explicitly or implicitly, the universe of relevant political actors. [But] outside the abortion context there are no indications that fetuses are considered relevant political actors. [E]ven within the context of abortion-related issues, the suggestion that fetuses are a part of the larger political community appears, as in Ely's formulation, only incidentally and as part of the abortion discussion. It is, of course, possible for a legislature to take into account interests outside its own political community. [But] with fetuses, as with other interests outside the relevant universe of political actors, the legislative process can only take them into account insofar as relevant political actors subsume those interests into their own."

an interest the Constitution marks as special—and it is for that reason perhaps more dangerous. Of course in a sense it is more candid than *Lochner*. But the employment of a higher standard of judicial review, no matter how candid the recognition that it is indeed higher, loses some of its admirability when it is accompanied by neither a coherent account of why such a standard is appropriate nor any indication of why it has not been satisfied.

"[*Roe* is] a very bad decision. [It] is bad because it is bad constitutional law, or rather because it is *not* constitutional law and gives almost no sense of an obligation to try to be. [The] point that often gets lost in the commentary, and obviously got lost in *Roe*, is that *before* the Court can get to the 'balancing' stage, *before* it can worry about the next case and the case after that (or even about its institutional position) it is under an obligation to trace its premises to the charter from which it derives its authority. A neutral and durable principle may be a thing of beauty and joy forever. But if it lacks connection with any value the Constitution marks as special, it is not a constitutional principle and the Court has no business imposing it."[e]

6. *Is it a question of "inventing" a new right, or of the state having to justify an invasion of liberty?* Consider the remarks of Professor Tribe in Choper, Kamisar & Tribe, *The Supreme Court: Trends and Developments 1982–83* (1984) at 215: "[The *Roe* Court] is said to have invented the right to abortion. [To quote Professor Ely], *Roe* was not just *bad* constitutional law, it was not constitutional law at all. I have never found it easy to understand what that criticism means in this context. Once one concedes that the word 'liberty' has substantive content in its application against the states through the Fourteenth Amendment—and it must, if any substantive provisions of the Bill of Rights are to be enforced against the states through the Fourteenth Amendment—it becomes not a question of inventing a new right, but of asking what the justification is for a state intrusion into what is indisputably an aspect of someone's personal liberty."

Cf. WALTER DELLINGER & GENE SPERLING, *Abortion and the Supreme Court: The Retreat from Roe v. Wade,* 138 U.Pa.L.Rev. 83, 90–91 (1989): "[One may argue] that the abortion right is not fundamental because, at 'the most specific level,' abortion itself, it does not fit within a historical tradition of protection. [But the] goal of constitutional jurisprudence cannot be to inquire whether the narrowest or most specific aspect of an activity in question has specific support. The task, rather, is to identify the historical values underlying the constitutional principle at stake and to inquire whether the current activity must be protected to realize those values.

"The framers said nothing specific about hysterectomies and did not even contemplate the issue when drafting the Fourteenth Amendment, but concentrating on their opinion of reproductive surgery would be inappropriate when assessing a statute that unjustly compelled unnecessary hysterectomies or prohibited necessary [ones]. A court that invalidated such a law would not be 'creating a new constitutional right to hysterectomy-choice,' but merely applying the established constitutional rule that deeply intrusive laws restricting liberty must be justified by a compelling governmental reason."[f]

e. See also Forrester, *Are We Ready for Truth in Judging?,* 63 A.B.A.J. 1212 (1977); Lusky, *By What Right?* 14, 16–17, 20 (1975); Monaghan, *The Constitution Goes to Harvard,* 13 Harv.Civ.Rts.-Civ.Lib.L.Rev. 116, 131 (1978); Posner, *The Uncertain Protection of Privacy in the Supreme Court,* 1979 Sup.Ct. Rev. 173, 199–200.

f. For more on the levels of generality in the definition of rights, see the notes following *Michael H. v. Gerald D.,* p. 250 infra; *Bowers*

7. *"The Constitution" vs. "the original Constitution."* "[H]ow," asks Michelman, *Commentary* (panel discussion), 56 N.Y.U.L.Rev. 525, 532 (1981), "is it arguably an offense or violation of the Constitution for the New York legislature to do what it did in *Lochner* or for a state legislature to criminalize abortion? [M]y answer to that question is: There is no argument that I can see to the effect that those statutes violate the original Constitution. The argument has to be that they violate the Constitution—meaning the original Constitution with all the interpretive precedents that have arisen in the course of the judicial attempt to carry out the office of the Court, which is to decide hard cases under the Constitution when they arise."

8. *Should the legitimacy of Roe be debated in terms of "institutional continuity"?* Consider Bennett, *Objectivity in Constitutional Law*, 132 U.Pa. L.Rev. 445, 486 (1984): "My point is not that *Roe* was rightly decided, but that the debate about whether the Supreme Court could legitimately invalidate laws prohibiting abortion is often misconceived. Viewed as a question of judicial objectivity, the legitimacy of *Roe* turns not on whether there is some authoritative basis on which the Court can substitute its value judgment for that of the legislature but on whether the Court can successfully define its opinion as a natural outgrowth of what it has received. [The legitimacy of *Roe*] should be debated in terms of institutional continuity and of its substantive merits and not by reference to one or another dubious and inevitably incomplete standard of authoritativeness. In contrast to *Roe,* the state legislative apportionment cases, favorites of Ely, seem much less justifiable in terms of institutional continuity."

9. *Why noninterpretive review is a "necessary postulate" for constitutional adjudication.* Consider ROBERT SEDLER, *The Legitimacy Debate in Constitutional Adjudication,* 44 Ohio St.L.J. 110, 118–19, 122 (1983): "The Court has not viewed interpretive review as a tenable methodology for determining the meaning and application of the Constitution. Rather, it has viewed noninterpretive review as a necessary postulate for constitutional adjudication under the Constitution. The Court, therefore, has engaged in noninterpretive review throughout its history, convinced that its actions were legitimate and consistent with the Court's function under our constitutional system. [The] meaning of a constitutional provision develops incrementally, and that provision's line of growth strongly influences its application in particular cases.[167] The framework within which constitutional decision making has operated, then, is a significant constraint on the results that the Court will reach when it is engaged in that decision making.

"[The] argument that noninterpretive review is fully supportive of constitutional governance established by the Constitution proceeds as follows: (1) The overriding principle in the structure of constitutional governance established by the Constitution is the limitation on governmental power. (2) Many of the limitations on governmental power designed to protect individual rights that are contained in the Constitution are broadly phrased and open ended, and these

v. Hardwick, p. 257 infra; and *Cruzan v. Director, Missouri Dep't of Health,* p. 272 infra.

167. * * * [B]y the time the Court decided *Roe,* constitutional protection for reproductive freedom had been firmly established. [I]t would not have been inconsistent with the line of growth of constitutional protection for reproductive freedom for the Court to have held that the asserted governmental interest in protecting potential human life was constitutionally more important than the woman's interest in reproductive freedom. [But] because the Court had previously held that reproductive freedom is entitled to constitutional protection, the holding in *Roe,* extending that protection to the abortion decision, was fully consistent with the line of growth of constitutional protection for reproductive freedom.

majestic generalities directed toward the protection of individual rights are a part of our constitutional tradition.[g] (3) [Thus these limitations on governmental power] contained in the Constitution are broadly phrased and open ended, these limitations cannot be fully operable in contemporary society as a limitation on governmental power if their meaning is determined solely or even primarily by referring to values purportedly constitutionalized by the framers at an earlier time. (4) Therefore, given items (1) and (3) above, noninterpretive review is not only legitimate, but is also a necessary postulate for constitutional adjudication under our constitutional system."

10. *The "pure interpretive model" of constitutional adjudication vs. adjudication going beyond the norms implicit in text and original history.* Consider THOMAS GREY, *Do We Have an Unwritten Constitution?* 27 Stan.L.Rev. 703 (1975), who rejects the view that constitutional adjudication must rest on values derived by normal process of textual interpretation from the written Constitution—what he calls "the pure interpretive model"—as too narrow to capture the full scope of legitimate judicial review. He maintains, id. at 710–14, that "numerous and important substantive constitutional doctrines" would seem "unjustified under a consistently applied pure interpretive model of judicial review. First and most obvious is virtually the entire body of doctrine developed under the due process clauses of the 5th and 14th amendments. If those clauses can be seen as having any specific normative content attributable to their framers, it is probably only that given to them by Mr. Justice Black. In his view, due process requires only that deprivations of life, liberty or property be authorized by law duly enacted, rather than carried out by arbitrary executive action.

"[W]hat many regard as the core of due process doctrine—its flexible requirement of 'fundamentally fair' procedures in criminal and civil proceedings—cannot be reconciled with the interpretive model. These doctrines are developments of the 'living constitution' concept *par excellence.* [A] striking point often overlooked by contemporary interpretivists [who most often focus their attack on 'substantive due process'] is that the demise of substantive due process must constitutionally free the federal government to engage in explicit racial discrimination. There is no textual warrant for reading into the due process clause of the fifth amendment any of the prohibitions directed against the states by the equal protection clause [see Ch. 6, fn. a to Introductory Note].

* * *

"All of the 'fundamental interests' that trigger 'strict scrutiny' under the equal protection clause would have to be discarded, if the interpretive model were to control constitutional adjudication. [If] the values implicit in the equal protection clause are limited only to those that its framers intended at the time

g. "But," maintains Monaghan, *Commentary* (panel discussion), 56 N.Y.U.L.Rev. 525, 526 (1981), "the Constitution doesn't contain generalities. The due process clause and the ninth amendment in my judgment are judge-made and commentator-made generalities. Take the phrase 'due process of law.' If there was ever a phrase that had a fixed, certain meaning when it was introduced in the Constitution and adopted in 1868, it was that phrase. It was the judges who transformed it into a general license to review the substance of legislation. * * * Let's assume that the Constitution contains some generalities like freedom of speech and let's assume that you are going to need a Hercules to interpret such provisions. Even if that Hercules has to rely on some external political theory, which can't be fairly related or thought to underlie the constitutional text, at least the first amendment is a stopping point: it limits the subjects about which judges ought to be concerned. But take the question of abortion. There's nothing in the constitutional text or in its history to 'constitutionalize.' Nor is the theory that would authorize review containable."

of enactment, the clause clearly does not speak to questions of eligibility for the franchise or of legislative apportionment.

"[I]t should be clear that an extraordinarily radical purge of established constitutional doctrine would be required if we candidly and consistently applied the pure interpretive model. Surely that makes out at least a prima facie practical case against the model. Conservatives ought to be cautious about adopting any abstract premise which requires so drastic a change in accepted practice, and liberals presumably will be dismayed by the prospect of any major diminution in the courts' authority to protect basic human rights."[h]

* * *

11. *"Consensus" or "conventional morality" and "deeply embedded" values.* Consider Wellington, *Common Law Rules and Constitutional Double Standards; Some Notes on Adjudication,* 83 Yale L.J. 221, 299, 311 (1973): "My claim has been that the plaintiff's interest [in *Roe*] is protected under the Fourteenth Amendment by reference to the people: that the meaning of liberty in that Amendment and its weight in the context of the Texas abortion statute depends, in the first instance, upon its weight in conventional morality. [The] Court's task is to ascertain the weight of the principle in conventional morality and to convert the moral principle into a legal one by connecting it with the body of constitutional law."

Because of the rapidity of social change that renders exceedingly difficult any meaningful conclusions about "conventional morality," does Dean Wellington's view put the Court "at terrible risk that it will misperceive the near future"? Support in conventional morality may be a *necessary* condition for substantive due process activism on behalf of unenumerated rights, but is it a *sufficient* condition? Lupu, *Untangling the Strands of the Fourteenth Amendment,* 77 Mich.L.Rev. 981, 1037–1041 (1979), thinks not. He contends that proper sources for judicial discovery of fundamental libertarian values outside the constitutional text and structure—but "the only proper sources"—are "those which demonstrate that the values are 'deeply embedded' within American society," id. at 985, "*values treasured by both past and present, values behind which the society and its legal system have unmistakably thrown their weight.*"

But consider JOHN ELY, *Democracy and Distrust,* 63–64, 67–69 (1980): "The idea that society's 'widely shared values' should give content to the Constitution's open-ended provisions [turns] out to be at the core of most 'fundamental values' positions. * * * Consensus or conventional morality is postulated as something 'out there' that can be discovered. And in theory it is not undemocratic. Quite to the contrary, it is billed by [Dean] Wellington as a 'reference to the people.' [But] there is a growing literature that argues that in fact there is no consensus to be discovered (and to the extent that one may seem to exist, that is likely to reflect only the domination of some groups by others). [Even if we assume that] there *is* a consensus lurking out there that contradicts the judgment of our elected representatives, there would still remain the point, sufficient in itself, that that consensus is not reliably discoverable, at least not by courts.

"[B]y viewing society's values through one's own spectacles [one] can convince oneself that some invocable consensus supports almost any position a

h. For sharp disagreement, see Berger, *Government by Judiciary* 388–90, 411–13 (1977). See also Berger, *The Scope of Judicial Review: An Ongoing Debate,* 6 Hast.Con.L.Q. 527 (1979); Lusky, *"Government by Judiciary": What Price Legitimacy?* 6 Hast.Con.L.Q. 403 (1979). Compare Professor Grey's views in the article quoted above with his more recent views, *The Constitution as Scripture* (1984), fn. a supra.

civilized person might want to see supported. [But] as between courts and legislatures, it is clear that the latter are better situated to reflect consensus. Sophisticated commentary never tires of reminding us that legislatures are only imperfectly democratic. [B]ut that isn't going to make courts more democratic than legislatures.

* * *

"[There] are two possible reasons one might look to consensus to give content to the Constitution's open-ended provisions. One *might* say one was seeking to protect the rights of the majority by ensuring that legislation truly reflect popular values. If that were the purpose, however, the legislative process would plainly be better suited to it than the judicial. This leaves the other possible reason for the reference, to protect the rights of individuals and minority groups against the actions of the majority. [But] it makes no sense to employ the value judgments of the majority as the vehicle for protecting minorities from the value judgments of the majority."

Consider, however, Lupu, supra, at 1042–43: "[W]hat is the Constitution itself, if not a collection of '[enduring] *value judgments of the majority,*' interpreted and applied by the courts so as to be 'the vehicle for protecting minorities from the [momentary] value judgments of the majority'? [The] 'value judgments of the majority' are not only a *sensible* source of protection of minorities; these judgments turn out, in the end, to be the *only* source of protection for minorities against the hostile passions of an occasional, transient majority.

"[Ely's] rejection of the 'value judgments of the majority' as a source of rights fails to distinguish among national, statewide, and local majorities. [If] one reads [the last sentence quoted above from *Democracy and Distrust*] his sentence runs 'it simply makes no sense to employ the value judgments of [national] majorities as the vehicle for protecting [local] minorities from the value judgments of the [local] majority.' If *that* is what Professor Ely means, then he thinks that *judicial review under any substantive provision addressed to the states* makes no sense. But we know he doesn't think that at all."

POST-*ROE* ABORTION AND BIRTH CONTROL REGULATION

1. *Spousal and parental consent.* PLANNED PARENTHOOD v. DANFORTH, 428 U.S. 52, 96 S.Ct. 2831, 49 L.Ed.2d 788 (1976), per Blackmun, J., struck down, inter alia, provisions of a post-*Roe* Missouri abortion statute requiring the spouse's consent to abortion and, in the case of an unmarried woman under 18, parental consent. (These consents were required when a woman sought an abortion during the first trimester unless a physician certified that the abortion was "necessary [to] preserve the life of the mother.")

As for "spousal consent," "the State cannot 'delegate to a spouse a veto power which the state itself is absolutely and totally prohibited from exercising during the first trimester of pregnancy.' [Even] if the State had the ability to delegate to the husband a power it itself could not exercise, [the] obvious fact is that when the wife and the husband disagree on this decision, the view of only one of the two marriage partners can prevail. Since it is the woman who physically bears the child and who is the more directly and immediately affected by the pregnancy, as between the two, the balance weighs in her favor." As for "parental consent," here, too, "the State does not have the constitutional authority to give a third party an absolute, and possibly arbitrary, veto over the decision of the physician and his patient to terminate the patient's pregnancy, regardless of the reason for withholding the consent." The Court emphasized, however, that its holding "does not suggest that every minor, regardless of age or maturity, may give effective consent for termination of her pregnancy."

White, J., joined by Burger, C.J., and Rehnquist, J., dissented, baffled how the Court could find anything in the Constitution or in the 1973 *Abortion Cases requiring* a state to "assign a greater value to a mother's decision to cut off a potential human life by abortion than to a father's decision to let it mature into a live child." Nor did he see how it followed from the fact that the mother's interest in seeking an abortion "outweighs the *State's* interest in the potential life of the fetus, that the husband's interest is also outweighed and may not be protected by the State." As for parental consent, a state "is entitled to protect the minor unmarried woman from making the decision [whether or not to obtain an abortion] in a way which is not in her own best interests, and it seeks to achieve this goal by requiring consultation and consent. * * *"

Stevens, J., joined the Court's invalidation of other provisions, but dissented on parental consent: "[The] Court seems to assume that the capacity to conceive a child and the judgment of the physician are the only constitutionally permissible yardsticks for determining whether a young woman can independently make the abortion decision. I doubt the accuracy of the Court's empirical judgment. Even if it were correct, however, as a matter of constitutional law I think a State has power to conclude otherwise and to select a chronological age as its standard." [a]

Notes and Questions

(a) *If the issue is balancing.* Consider Regan, *Rewriting Roe v. Wade,* 77 Mich.L.Rev. 1569, 1644 (1979): "[I]f the whole issue is one of balancing [as the *Roe* opinion suggests], might it not be that the state's interest, which is less than the interest of the woman or of the woman and her husband together when they are aligned, is greater than the *difference* between the interests of the woman and her husband when they are opposed? Indeed, given the weightiness of the state's interest and the similarity of the woman's interests to her husband's (especially while the Court emphasizes the 'family-planning' aspect rather than the physical burdens of pregnancy), is it not quite likely?" On Regan's approach, however, "the state can no more make the unwilling woman serve the fetus and her husband than it can make her serve the fetus alone."

(b) *Sex discrimination.* Consider Burt, *The Constitution of the Family,* 1979 Sup.Ct.Rev. 329, 394: "[T]he Court's explicit assumption that the father of the fetus is as much a stranger to it as any other community member is not plausible. The Court's apparent position that the mother always has the superior claim and interest, no matter how much the father might show that her burden in childbearing would be less than his burden in losing his child, appears to me an invidious sex discrimination. * * *"

2. *Parental or judicial consent.* BELLOTTI v. BAIRD (*Bellotti II*), 443 U.S. 622, 99 S.Ct. 3035, 61 L.Ed.2d 797 (1979), struck down a Massachusetts law which

a. Cf. *Parham v. J.R.* (1979) (pp. 520, 638 infra), rejecting the contention that *Danforth* and other cases require that the parents' decision to commit a child to a mental hospital must be subjected to exacting constitutional scrutiny, including a preadmission adversary hearing: "[*Danforth*] involved an absolute parental veto over the child's ability to obtain an abortion," but Georgia parents have no "absolute right to commit their children to state mental hospitals; the statute requires [each regional hospital superintendent] to exercise independent judgment as to the child's need for confinement."

(unlike the statute in *Danforth*) required an unmarried pregnant minor to obtain the consent of both parents for an abortion or, if parental consent was not obtained, authorization from a state judge if he concluded that abortion was in her best interest. POWELL, J., joined by Burger, C.J., and Stewart and Rehnquist, JJ.,[a] announced the judgment of the Court, concluding that if the state requires a pregnant minor to obtain one or both parents' consent to an abortion, it also must provide an "alternative procedure" (which need not be a judicial proceeding) for obtaining authorization for the abortion "ensur[ing] that [the parental consent requirement] does not in fact amount to the 'absolute, and possibly arbitrary, veto' that was found impermissible in *Danforth.*" In such a proceeding a pregnant minor is entitled to show either: (1) that she is able "to make her abortion decision, in consultation with her physician, independently of her parents' wishes"; or (2) that, even if she is not, "the desired abortion would be in her best interests." Such a proceeding must also be conducted "with anonymity and sufficient expedition to provide an effective opportunity for an abortion to be obtained."

The statute fell short "in two respects: First, it permits judicial authorization for an abortion to be withheld from a minor [the court finds] to be mature and fully competent to make this decision independently. Second, it requires parental consultation or notification in every instance, without affording the pregnant minor an opportunity to receive an independent judicial determination that she is mature enough to consent or that an abortion would be in her best interests."[b]

STEVENS, J., joined by Brennan, Marshall and Blackmun, JJ., concurred in the judgment, deeming *Danforth* controlling: "It is inherent in the right to make the abortion decision that the right may be exercised without public scrutiny and in defiance of the contrary opinion of the sovereign or other third parties. In Massachusetts, however, every minor who cannot secure the consent of both her parents—which under *Danforth* cannot be an absolute prerequisite to an abortion—is required to secure the consent of the sovereign." Moreover, "the best interest of the minor" standard "provides little real guidance to the judge, and his decision must necessarily reflect personal and societal values and mores whose enforcement upon the minor [is] fundamentally at odds with privacy interests underlying the constitutional protection afforded to her decision."[c]

A Note on Bellotti II and its Aftermath

For an illuminating case study of *Bellotti II,* see Mnookin, *In the Interest of Children* 150–264 (1985). "The result in *Bellotti,*" observes Professor Mnookin, "can perhaps be best understood as a judicially imposed compromise—a compromise of difficult philosophical, political, and policy issues. Nobody won, but nobody quite lost either. [In] essence, Justice Powell rejected the moral claims of both those who argued that a pregnant minor should have the *same* abortion rights as an adult woman and those who argued that parental involvement

a. Rehnquist, J., joined only until "this Court is willing to reconsider" *Danforth.*

b. Powell, J., explicated: "If, all things considered, the court determines that an abortion is in the minor's best interests, she is entitled to court authorization without any parental involvement. On the other hand, the court may deny the abortion request of an immature minor in the absence of parental consultation if it concludes that her best interests would be served thereby, or the court may in such a case defer decision until there is parental consultation in which the court may participate. But this is the full extent to which parental involvement may be required."

c. Only White, J., dissented.

should be required. On the level of principle, neither parents nor kids get to decide alone. The result can certainly be seen as a political compromise." Id. at 260. Continues Mnookin, id. at 262–63:

"[F]or me, [Justice Powell's plurality opinion] reflects an unwarranted confidence in the ability of judges to make sound decisions on behalf of individual pregnant minors, and to make sound policy for our society as a whole. [I]n essence, it seemed the judge was to act like a parent, with broad discretion to use his personal values to make a decision on behalf of a pregnant woman. Powell's opinion seemed a high water mark of judicial arrogance. Neither legislatures nor families are to be trusted; nor are pregnant minors and their doctors. Only the modern-day secular priest, a judge, is to be trusted with the abortion decision for young women.

"My recent examination of the actual operation of the [post-*Bellotti II* Massachusetts statute] revealed that the new judicial process does not in fact involve a careful individualized assessment, but is instead a rubber-stamp, administrative operation. [Between April 1981, when the statute first went into effect, and February 1983], [n]one of the 1,300 young women who have gone to court have been successfully refused an abortion.[a] [This finding] is perhaps not so surprising. After all, the proceedings before the judges are not contested, and the judge has no independent source of information. More fundamentally, even if the judge decides that the young woman before him is not mature, on what basis (other than moral revulsion to abortion) could he possibly decide that it is not in the best interests of an immature minor to have a first-trimester abortion? [H]ow could the judge determine that it is in the interest of a minor to give birth to a child if she is too immature even to decide to have an abortion? Indeed, if one looks only at the result for pregnant minors who go to court, the process seems an unnecessary and expensive waste of time."

3. *Parental notice.* Distinguishing *Danforth* and *Bellotti v. Baird* (1979) (*Bellotti II*), H.L. v. MATHESON, 450 U.S. 398, 101 S.Ct. 1164, 67 L.Ed.2d 388 (1981), per BURGER, C.J., upheld a Utah statute, as applied to an unemancipated minor living with and dependent upon her parents, that required a physician to "notify, if possible" the parents of a minor upon whom an abortion is to be performed. Although appellant challenged the statute as unconstitutional on its face, contending that it was "overbroad in that it can be construed to apply to all unmarried minor girls, including those who are mature and emancipated," the Court held that since appellant, a 15-year-old living with, and dependent on, her parents, had not shown that she was "mature or emancipated," she lacked standing to bring such a challenge. In a narrow ruling, the Court sustained the law as applied to appellant and members of her class:

"The Utah statute gives neither parents nor judges a veto power over the minor's abortion decision.[17] [As] applied to immature and dependent minors, the

a. Under the new statute, the judge's discretion to deny an abortion is limited. If he decides the young woman is "mature," he allows her to decide for herself. If the judge does not find the minor to be "mature," he gets to decide according to her "best interest." In about 90 percent of the cases the Supreme Court simply found the minor to be "mature." In the remaining cases the court found the abortion to be in the minor's best interest in virtually all instances. See id. at 239, 261–62. Although the requirement of judicial authorization is not leading to the denial of abortion *for those who go to court,* "the business of Massachusetts abortion clinics has significantly declined. It would appear that many girls who formerly would have secured abortions in Massachusetts are now going to other states, particularly New Hampshire." Id. at 242.

17. The main premise of the dissent seems to be that a requirement of notice to the parents is the equivalent of a requirement of parental consent. In *Bellotti II,* however, we

statute plainly serves the important considerations of family integrity and protected adolescents [identified] in *Bellotti II.* [Moreover], the statute serves a significant state interest by providing an opportunity for parents to supply essential medical and other information to a physician." The notice requirement may inhibit some minors from seeking abortions, but "the Constitution does not compel a state to fine-tune its statutes so as to encourage or facilitate abortions. To the contrary, state action 'encouraging child-birth except for the most urgent circumstances' is 'rationally related to the legitimate governmental objective of protecting potential life.' *Harris v. McRae* [infra]." [a]

Dissenting JUSTICE MARSHALL, joined by Brennan and Blackmun, JJ., contended that appellant had standing to challenge the statute in its application to all minors. He then found the statute unconstitutional: The mandatory parental notice requirement "unquestionably burdens the minor's privacy right"—"many minor women will encounter interference from their parents after the state-imposed notification" and "the threat of parental notice may cause [some] to delay past the first trimester of pregnancy after which the health risks increase significantly"—and none of the reasons offered by the State justifies the infringement on a minor woman's constitutional right to privacy "for the statute is not tailored to serve them. * * * Rather than respecting the private realm of family life, the statute invokes the criminal machinery of the State in an attempt to influence the interactions within the family."

4. *Abortion funding.* MAHER v. ROE, 432 U.S. 464, 97 S.Ct. 2376, 53 L.Ed. 2d 484 (1977) (also discussed at p. 1185 infra), per POWELL, J., sustained Connecticut's use of Medicaid funds to reimburse women for the costs of childbirth and "medically necessary" first trimester abortions (defined to include "psychiatric necessity"), but not for the costs of elective or nontherapeutic first trimester abortions.[a]

On "the central question"—"whether the regulation 'impinges upon a fundamental right explicitly or implicitly protected by the Constitution' "—the Court held that *Roe* did not establish "an unqualified 'constitutional right to an abortion,' " but only a "right protect[ing] the woman from unduly burdensome interference with her freedom to decide whether to terminate her pregnancy. It implies no limitation on the authority of a State to make a value judgment favoring childbirth over abortion, and to implement that judgment by the

expressly declined to equate notice requirements with consent requirements.

a. Powell, J., joined by Stewart, J., concurred, emphasizing that they joined the Court's opinion "on the understanding that it leaves open the question whether [the Utah statute] unconstitutionally burdens the right of a mature minor or a minor whose best interests would not be served by parental notification." For the reasons set forth in his plurality opinion in *Bellotti II* (dealing with parental *consent*), Powell maintained that "a state may not validly require notice to parents in all cases, without providing an independent decisionmaker to whom a pregnant minor can have recourse if she believes that she is mature enough to make the abortion decision independently or that notification otherwise would not be in her best interests."

Stevens, J., concurring only in the judgment, would reach the question reserved by the Court and uphold the statute as applied to *all* unmarried women who are suffering unwanted pregnancies and desire to terminate them, but may not do so because their physicians insist on complying with state law.

a. In a companion case, *Beal v. Doe,* 432 U.S. 438, 97 S.Ct. 2366, 53 L.Ed.2d 464 (1977), per Powell, J., held that the Medicaid Act does not require state funding of nontherapeutic first trimester abortions as a condition of participation in the joint federal-state program.

In another companion case, *Poelker v. Doe,* 432 U.S. 519, 97 S.Ct. 2391, 53 L.Ed.2d 528 (1977), per curiam, for the reasons set forth in *Maher,* found "no constitutional violation by the city of St. Louis in electing, as a policy choice, to provide publicly financed hospital services for childbirth without providing corresponding services for nontherapeutic abortions."

allocation of public funds. [The] State may have made childbirth a more attractive alternative, thereby influencing the woman's decision, but it has imposed no restriction on access to abortions that was not already there. The indigency that may make it difficult—and in some cases, perhaps, impossible—for some women to have abortions is neither created nor in any way affected by the [regulation.]

"Our conclusion signals no retreat from *Roe* or the cases applying it. There is a basic difference between direct state interference with a protected activity and state encouragement of an alternative activity consonant with legislative policy. * * * We think it abundantly clear that a State is not required to show a compelling interest for its policy choice to favor normal childbirth any more than a State must so justify its election to fund public but not private education."

The Court then sustained the regulation "under the less demanding test of rationality that applies in the absence of a suspect classification or the impingement of a fundamental right." It had little difficulty finding the distinction drawn between childbirth and nontherapeutic abortion " 'rationally related' to a 'constitutionally permissible' purpose." "*Roe* itself explicitly acknowledged the State's strong interest in protecting the potential life of the fetus. [The] State unquestionably has a 'strong and legitimate interest in encouraging normal childbirth' " and subsidizing the substantial and significantly increasing costs incident to childbirth is "a rational means of encouraging childbirth." [13]

BRENNAN, J., joined by Marshall and Blackmun, JJ., dissented, accusing the majority of "a distressing insensitivity to the plight of impoverished pregnant women." The "disparity in funding [clearly] operates to coerce indigent pregnant women to bear children they would not otherwise choose to have, and just as clearly, this coercion can only operate upon the poor, who are uniquely the victims of this form of financial pressure." *Roe* and its progeny held that "an area of privacy invulnerable to the State's intrusion surrounds the decision of a pregnant woman whether or not to carry her pregnancy to term. The Connecticut scheme clearly infringes upon that area of privacy."

As for *Poelker,* fn. a supra, "the fundamental right of a woman freely to choose to terminate her pregnancy has been infringed by the city of St. Louis through a deliberate policy based on opposition to elective abortions on moral grounds by city officials. [The] city policy is a significant, and in some cases insurmountable, obstacle to indigent pregnant women who cannot pay for abortions in [clinics or private hospitals].

In a second dissent, MARSHALL, J., thought it "all too obvious that the governmental actions in these cases, ostensibly taken to 'encourage' women to carry pregnancies to term, are in reality intended to impose a moral viewpoint that no State may constitutionally enforce. Since efforts to overturn [*Roe* and *Doe*] have been unsuccessful, the opponents of abortion have attempted every imaginable means to circumvent the commands of the Constitution and impose

13. Much of the rhetoric of the three dissenting opinions would be equally applicable if Connecticut had elected not to fund either abortions or childbirth. Yet none of the dissents goes so far as to argue that the Constitution *requires* such assistance for all indigent pregnant women.

[Compare Simson, *Abortion, Poverty and the Equal Protection of the Laws,* 13 Ga.L.Rev. 505, 508 (1979): "[I]f Connecticut funded neither childbirth nor abortion, poverty would not lead indigent women to prefer childbirth to abortion. Rather, since a safe abortion in the early months of pregnancy is materially cheaper than a safe childbirth, financial considerations probably would militate strongly *in favor of* abortion."]

their moral choices upon the rest of society. The present cases involve the most vicious attacks yet devised. The impact of the regulations here fall tragically upon those among us least able to help or defend themselves."

In a third dissent, BLACKMUN, J., joined by Brennan and Marshall, JJ., charged that "the Court concedes the existence of a constitutional right but denies the realization and enjoyment of that right on the ground that existence and realization are separate and distinct. [Implicit in today's holdings] is the condescension that [the indigent woman] may go elsewhere for her abortion. I find that disingenuous and alarming, almost reminiscent of: 'Let them eat cake.' "

5. *More on abortion funding; The Hyde Amendment.* Title XIX of the Social Security Act established the Medicaid program to provide federal financial assistance to states choosing to reimburse certain costs of medical treatment for needy persons. Since 1976, various versions of the so-called Hyde Amendment have limited federal funding of abortions under the Medicaid program to those necessary to save the life of the mother and certain other exceptional circumstances.[a] HARRIS v. McRAE, 448 U.S. 297, 100 S.Ct. 2671, 65 L.Ed.2d 784 (1980), per STEWART, J., determined that Title XIX does not obligate a participating state to pay for those medically necessary abortions for which Congress has withheld federal funding and then held—relying heavily on *Maher*—that the Hyde Amendment is constitutionally valid:

"The Hyde Amendment, like [the regulation upheld] in *Maher,* places no governmental obstacle in the path of a woman who chooses to terminate her pregnancy, but rather, by means of unequal subsidization of abortion and other medical services, encourages alternative activity deemed in the public interest. The present case does differ factually from *Maher* insofar as that case involved a failure to fund nontherapeutic abortions, whereas the Hyde Amendment withholds funding of certain medically necessary abortions. [But] regardless of [how] the freedom of a woman to choose to terminate her pregnancy for health reasons [is characterized], it simply does not follow that [this freedom] carries with it a constitutional entitlement to the financial resources to avail herself of the full range of protected choices. The reason why was explained in *Maher:* although government may not place obstacles in the path of a woman's exercise of her freedom of choice, it need not remove those not of its own creation. [T]he Hyde Amendment leaves an indigent woman with at least the same range of choice in deciding whether to obtain a medically necessary abortion as she would have had if Congress had chosen to subsidize no health costs at all.

"[Acceptance of appellees' argument] would mark a drastic change in our understanding of the Constitution. It cannot be that because government may not prohibit the use of contraceptives, *Griswold,* or prevent parents from sending their child to a private school, *Pierce,* government, therefore, has an affirmative constitutional obligation to assure that all persons have the financial resources to obtain contraceptives or send their children to private [schools.] [b]

a. The version of the Hyde Amendment applicable for fiscal year 1980 prohibited federal funding of abortions "except where the life of the mother would be endangered if the fetus were carried to term" or except for cases of rape or incest "when such rape or incest has been reported promptly to a law enforcement agency or public health service." But the initial version of the Hyde Amendment, which triggered the instant case, did not include the "rape or incest" exception.

b. The Court then rejected the contention that the Hyde Amendment violates the Establishment Clause because, as the argument ran, "it incorporates into law the doctrines of the Roman Catholic Church": A statute does not run afoul of the Establishment Clause "because it 'happens to coincide or harmonize

Responding to the arguments of the dissents—especially Stevens, J.'s—WHITE, J. concurring, characterized the constitutional right recognized in *Roe* as "the right to choose to undergo an abortion without coercive interference by the government. [The pregnant] woman's choice remains unfettered, the government is not attempting to use its interest in life to justify a coercive restraint, and hence in disbursing its Medicaid funds it is free to implement rationally what *Roe* recognized to be its legitimate interest in a potential life by covering the medical costs of childbirth but denying funds for abortions. Neither *Roe* [nor its progeny] invalidates this legislative preference. We decided as much in *Maher* * * *."

Four justices dissented—Brennan, Marshall and Blackmun, JJ. (the three *Maher* dissenters), and Stevens, J. who had joined the opinion of the Court in *Maher.*

STEVENS, J., maintained that the instant case presented "[a] fundamentally different question" than the one decided in *Maher:* "This case involves the pool of benefits that Congress created by enacting [Title XIX]. Individuals who satisfy two neutral criteria—financial need and medical need—are entitled to equal access to that pool. The question is whether certain persons who satisfy those criteria may be denied access to benefits solely because they must exercise the constitutional right to have an abortion in order to obtain the medical care they need. Our prior cases plainly dictate [the answer].

"Unlike these plaintiffs, [those] in *Maher* did not satisfy the neutral criterion of medical need; they sought a subsidy for nontherapeutic abortions—medical procedures which by definition they did not need. [This case] involves a special exclusion of women who, by definition, are confronted with a choice between two serious harms: serious health damage to themselves on the one hand and abortion on the other. The competing interests are the interest in maternal health and the interest in protecting potential human life. It is now part of our law that the pregnant woman's decision as to which of these conflicting interests shall prevail is entitled to constitutional protection.

"[If] a woman has a constitutional right to place a higher value on avoiding either serious harm to her own health or perhaps an abnormal childbirth [3] than on protecting potential life, the exercise of that right cannot provide the basis for the denial of a benefit to which she would otherwise be entitled. The Court's sterile equal protection analysis evades this critical though simple point. The Court focuses exclusively on the 'legitimate interest in protecting the potential

with the tenets of some or all religions,' *McGowan v. Maryland* [discussed at p. 827 fn. b infra]"; the Hyde Amendment "is as much a reflection of 'traditionalist' values toward abortion, as it is an embodiment of the views of any particular religion."

"Again draw[ing] guidance from" *Maher,* the Court also rejected the argument that the Hyde Amendment "violates the equal protection component of the Fifth Amendment": The Hyde Amendment "is not predicated on a constitutionally suspect classification. [Here,] as in *Maher,* the principal impact of [the] Amendment falls on the indigent. But that fact alone does not itself render the funding restriction constitutionally invalid, for this Court has held repeatedly that poverty, standing alone, is not a suspect classification." See generally Ch. 6, Sec. 4, III & IV. Thus, the Hyde Amendment need only satisfy the rational-basis standard of review and it does—"by encouraging childbirth except in the most urgent circumstances, [it] is rationally related to the legitimate governmental objective of protecting potential life."

3. The Court relies heavily on the premise [that] the State's legitimate interest in preserving potential life provides a sufficient justification for funding medical services that are necessarily associated with normal childbirth without also funding abortions that are not medically necessary. The *Maher* opinion repeatedly referred to the policy of favoring "normal childbirth." But this case involves a refusal to fund abortions which are medically necessary to avoid abnormal childbirth.

life of the fetus.' [*Roe*] squarely held that the States may not protect that interest when a conflict with the interest in a pregnant woman's health exists. It is thus perfectly clear that neither the Federal Government nor the States may exclude a woman from medical benefits to which she would otherwise be entitled solely to further an interest in potential life when a physician, 'in appropriate medical judgment,' certifies that an abortion is necessary 'for the preservation of the life or health of the mother.' *Roe.* The Court totally fails to explain why this reasoning is not dispositive here.[4]

"[Nor] can it be argued that the exclusion of this type of medically necessary treatment of the indigent can be justified on fiscal grounds. [For] the cost of an abortion is only a small fraction of the costs associated with childbirth. Thus, the decision to tolerate harm to indigent persons who need an abortion in order to avoid 'serious and long lasting health damage' is one that is financed by draining money out of the pool that is used to fund all other necessary medical procedures. Unlike most invidious classifications, this discrimination harms not only its direct victims but also the remainder of the class of needy persons that the pool was designed to benefit. * * *

"Having decided to alleviate some of the hardships of poverty by providing necessary medical care, the Government must use neutral criteria in distributing benefits. [It] may not create exceptions for the sole purpose of furthering a governmental interest that is constitutionally subordinate to the individual interest that the entire program was designed to protect. The Hyde amendments not only exclude financially and medically needy persons from the pool of benefits for a constitutionally insufficient reason; they also require the expenditure of millions of dollars in order to thwart the exercise of a constitutional right, thereby effectively inflicting serious and long lasting harm on impoverished women who want and need abortions for valid medical reasons. [Thus,] these amendments constitute an unjustifiable, and indeed blatant, violation of the sovereign's duty to govern impartially."

The other three dissenters wrote separately, each voicing agreement with Stevens, J.'s analysis. BRENNAN, J., joined by Marshall and Blackmun, JJ., expressed his "continuing disagreement with the Court's mischaracterization of the nature of the fundamental right recognized in *Roe* and its misconception of the manner in which that right is infringed [by] legislation withdrawing all funding for medically necessary abortions":

"The proposition for which [*Roe* and its progeny stand] is not that the State is under an affirmative obligation to ensure access to abortions for all who may desire them; it is that the State must refrain from wielding its enormous power and influence in a manner that might burden the pregnant woman's freedom to choose whether to have an abortion. * * * [W]hat the Court fails to appreciate is that it is not simply the woman's indigency that interferes with her freedom of choice, but the combination of her own poverty and the government's unequal subsidization of abortion and childbirth."

4. [In] responding to my analysis of this case, Justice White has described the constitutional right recognized in *Roe* as "the right to choose to undergo an abortion without coercive interference by the Government" or a right "only to be free from unreasonable official interference with private choice." No such language is found in the *Roe* opinion itself. Rather, that case squarely held that State interference is unreasonable if it attaches a greater importance to the interest in potential life than to the interest in protecting the mother's health. One could with equal justification describe the right protected by the First Amendment as the right to make speeches without coercive interference by the Government and then sustain a Government subsidy for all medically needy persons except those who publicly advocate a change of administration.

Although he called this case "perhaps the most dramatic illustration to date of the deficiencies in the Court's obsolete 'two-tiered' approach to the Equal Protection Clause" [see generally Ch. 6, Sec. 3, I], Marshall, J. was "unable to see how even a minimally rational legislature could conclude that the interest in fetal life outweighs the brutal effect of the Hyde Amendment on indigent women."

Notes and Questions

(a) *The logic of the abortion funding cases.* "There is," notes Tribe, *Treatise* at 1346, "a certain logic [to the abortion funding cases]: if the abortion choice is constitutionally private, why should the state be prevented from declining to make it a matter for public funding?" "But," continues Tribe, "this logic is far from inexorable":

"The government obviously has the constitutional *authority* to make abortion, like childbirth, available at no charge to the woman, either in a public facility or by public subsidy. The government's *affirmative* choice *not* to do so can fairly be characterized as a decision to enforce alienation of the woman's right to end her pregnancy, whether that alienation—or 'waiver'—was brought about voluntarily (by the woman's failure to save money for an abortion), or involuntarily (by economic circumstances beyond her control). After all, the unavailability of abortion to such a woman follows from her lack of funds only by virtue of the government's quite conscious decision to treat that medical procedure in particular as a purely private commodity available only to those who can pay the market price. The constitutionality of that decision is rendered dubious by the government's simultaneous decision to take *childbirth* procedures for the same poor woman *off* the private market: the result, as Justice Stevens put it, [dissenting in *McRae,*] is a government program that selfconsciously 'require[s] the expenditure of millions and millions of dollars in order to thwart the exercise of a constitutional right.' The state's position with respect to reproductive rights—rights it is bound to respect—is therefore neither as neutral nor as passive as a majority of the Court supposed in *Maher* and *McRae.*"

Consider, too, Estrich & Sullivan, *Abortion Politics: Writing for an Audience of One,* 138 U.Pa.L.Rev. 119, 150 (1989): "[*McRae*] involved an affirmative government decision to provide funds to poor women for childbirth, but not for abortion. Whatever position one takes on the decision to fund, it is surely different than a state policy which seeks to 'encourage childbirth' by *taxing* abortion. Even assuming that rewards may be appropriate to secure the end of childbirth, punishments should not."

(b) *Preventing constitutional caste.* Where "rights are too important to be reserved for selected privileged groups," observes Sullivan, *Unconstitutional Conditions,* 102 Harv.L.Rev. 1413, 1498–99 (1989), "conditions on benefits that affect their exercise can pose a similar danger of hierarchy. For example, conditioning welfare benefits on contribution of body organs to a public organ bank, or aid to mothers with dependent children on their service as surrogate mothers in a public program to remedy infertility, would unconstitutionally create a donor caste. This argument does not depend on either the view that such exchanges are 'coerced' by the desperation of privacy, or the view that body parts or gestational services are generally inalienable.

"A straightforward application of such equality arguments to the abortion funding cases [would] reverse the outcome. Government cannot universally criminalize abortion, nor universally burden it with heavy restrictions, at least in the first trimester. The only difference between such general bans and the selective subsidization of childbirth but not abortion for indigent women is the class affected. Dependency on government defines the class here. But what the government cannot restrict for all, it may not restrict for those over whom it has special leverage because of their dependency—especially where the displacement of private alternatives creates special responsibility. To hold otherwise would sanction a two-tier system of constitutional rights—a system of constitutional caste."

(c) *Abortion as a private privilege, not a public right.* Consider MacKinnon, *Privacy v. Equality: Beyond Roe v. Wade*, in *Feminism Unmodified* 93, 100–01 (1987): "[*Roe*] presumes that government nonintervention into the private sphere promotes a woman's freedom of choice. When the alternative is jail, there is much to be said for this argument. But the [*McRae*] result sustains the meaning of privacy in *Roe*: women are guaranteed by the public no more than what we can get in private—that is, what we can extract through our intimate associations with men. Women with privileges get rights.

"So women got abortion as a private privilege, not as a public right. We got control over reproduction that is controlled by "a man or The Man," an individual man or the doctors or the government. Abortion was not decriminalized; it was legalized. * * *

"It is not inconsistent, then, that framed as a privacy right a woman's decision to abort would have no claim on public support and would genuinely not be seen as burdened by that deprivation. Privacy conceived as a right from public intervention and disclosure is the opposite of the relief that [*McRae*] sought for welfare women. State intervention would have provided a choice women did *not* have in private. The women in [*McRae*], women whose sexual refusal has counted for particularly little, needed something to make their privacy effective. The logic of the Court's response resembles the logic by which women are supposed to consent to sex. Preclude the alternatives, then call the sole remaining option "her choice". The point is that the alternatives are precluded *prior* to the reach of the chosen legal doctrine. They are precluded by conditions of sex, race, and class—the very conditions the privacy frame not only leaves tacit but exists to *guarantee*."

(d) *On looking at the government's purpose.* Perry, *Why the Supreme Court Was Plainly Wrong in the Hyde Amendment Case,* 32 Stan.L.Rev. 1113, 1122 (1980), observes that, although *Roe* does not forbid all government actions that might have the effect of making a woman prefer childbirth to abortion (e.g., the government could decide to fund childbirth *solely* in order to increase the size of the labor force), "*Roe* does require that government take no action, including the selective withholding of Medicaid funds, predicated on the view that abortion is per se morally objectionable—just as government has an undisputed obligation (to borrow one of the Court's own examples) not to take action predicated on the view that sending one's children to a private school is morally objectionable. [This means] that the central question in *McRae* ought to have been whether the Hyde Amendment is predicated on the illicit view. [The *McRae* majority] never even addressed that crucial question." After pointing out, inter alia, that Congressman Hyde stated that the purpose of his Amendment was "not to fund abortion because it's the killing of an innocently inconvenient pre-born child," Professor Perry concludes, id. at 1126, that "[i]t strains credulity to the breaking point to suggest that those charged with defending the Hyde Amendment in court could possibly establish that the view that abortion is per se morally objectionable did not play a but-for role in passage of the Amendment."

(e) *On not looking at the government's purpose.* Consider the remarks of Professor Tribe in Choper, Kamisar & Tribe, *The Supreme Court: Trends and Developments*, 1979–80 (1981) at 286–87: "Purpose is a treacherous inquiry. It is manipulable. If someone had told Representative Hyde that he had better be careful to talk only about 'encouraging childbirth' and to say nothing nasty about women who choose abortions, I am sure he could have managed to contain himself long enough. In addition, many think it is an affront to a coordinate branch of government to make what is going on inside its head the touchstone for constitutional adjudication. And it may be an affront to the woman to hold that her life, her freedom, depends on Representative Hyde's motivations. [The] reason that the Court began looking to purpose, in cases involving race, is that the central concern of the Equal Protection Clause in the context of suspect classification has been stigma and the subjugation it reinforces. In deciding whether government is singling someone out as a member of a distinct and dominated minority, it is relevant what government *says* and even what it *means,* as well as what it has *done.* But it has never been established doctrine that, when we're talking about fundamental rights as opposed to suspect classes, 'purpose' is the start, or the core, of the inquiry. * * *

"Suppose the government studied the problem and concluded, 'Divorce is a terrible, traumatic thing. We want to discourage divorce. So we're going to give people who are considering divorces bonuses if they go to marriage counselors. We're going to pay them extra money, and we're doing it specifically to *discourage* divorce.' I do not think that somebody who believes that there is a fundamental right to sever a marriage, a right underlying *Boddie v. Connecticut* [p. 1166 infra], should feel that he is in a corner and has to say the government cannot try to discourage divorce through providing such subsidies and thereby helping people stay married. The government's purpose cannot be the touchstone in a case where (a) you can't really find out what it was; (b) they can gimmick up the record to make it look right if you make the result turn on apparent motive; and (c) it doesn't make a damn bit of difference to the individual *what* the government's purpose was. Outside the limited area where purpose is critical because we're talking about symbolism and stigma, a strong case could be made for junking the whole issue of purpose."

THE ATTACK ON *ROE*

In AKRON v. AKRON CENTER FOR REPRODUCTIVE HEALTH, 462 U.S. 416, 103 S.Ct. 2481, 76 L.Ed.2d 687 (1983), a 6–3 majority, per POWELL, J., struck down five provisions of an ordinance regulating abortions: (1) a requirement that after the first trimester all abortions be "performed in a hospital," thus preventing abortions in outpatient clinics that are not part of an acute-care, full-service hospital; (2) a prohibition of abortions on unmarried minors under 15 without consent of one of her parents or a court order; (3) a "truly informed" consent provision requiring the "attending physician" to inform his patient, inter alia, of the physical and emotional complications that may result from an abortion and the particular risks associated with her pregnancy and the abortion technique to be utilized; (4) a mandatory 24-hour waiting period after the pregnant woman signs a consent form; and (5) a requirement that physicians performing abortions "insure that the remains of the unborn child are disposed of in a humane and sanitary manner."

The Court reaffirmed that "a state's interest in health regulation becomes compelling at approximately the end of the first trimester, but [the] state's regulation may be upheld only if it is reasonably designed to further that state interest." As for (1) the second-trimester requirement, Akron's defense of it "as a reasonable health regulation [had] strong support at the time of *Roe,* [but since then] the safety of second-trimester abortions has increased dramatically. The principal reason is that the [dilation and evacuation] D & E procedure is now widely and successfully used for the second-trimester abortions.

"[A]n even more significant factor is that experience indicates that D & E may be performed safely on an outpatient basis in appropriate nonhospital facilities. The evidence is strong enough to have convinced the American Public Health Association (APHA) to abandon its prior recommendation of hospitalization for all second-trimester [abortions]. Similarly, the American College of Obstetricians and Gynecologists (ACOG) no longer suggests that all second-trimester abortions be performed in a hospital.

"[These] developments, and the professional commentary supporting them, constitute impressive evidence that—at least during the early weeks of the second trimester—D & E abortions may be performed as safely in an outpatient clinic as in a full-service hospital. [Thus,] 'present medical knowledge' convincingly undercuts Akron's justification for requiring that *all* second-trimester abortions be performed in a hospital.

"[Although] a state abortion regulation is not unconstitutional simply because it does not correspond perfectly in all cases to the asserted state interest, [the] lines drawn in a state regulation must be reasonable, and this cannot be said of [the hospitalization requirement]. By preventing the performance of D & E abortions in an appropriate nonhospital setting, Akron has imposed a heavy, and unnecessary, burden on women's access to a relatively inexpensive, otherwise accessible, and safe abortion procedure. [The hospitalization requirement] unreasonably infringes upon a woman's constitutional right to obtain an abortion."

As for (2) the parental consent requirement, "we do not think the Akron ordinance, as applied to Ohio juvenile proceedings, is reasonably susceptible of being construed to create an 'opportunity for case-by-case evaluations of the maturity of pregnant minors.' *Bellotti II.*"

As for (3) the "informed consent" provision, much of the information required, such as the provisions that the physician inform his patient of the numerous possible physical and psychological complications of abortions and inform her that "the unborn child is a human life from the moment of conception," "is designed not to inform the woman's consent but rather to persuade her to withhold it altogether. [A]n additional, and equally decisive, objection to [this provision] is its intrusion upon the discretion of the pregnant woman's physician. This provision specifies a litany of information that the physician must recite to each woman regardless of whether in his judgment the information is relevant to her personal decision. [By] insisting upon recitation of a lengthy and inflexible list of information, Akron unreasonably has placed 'obstacles in the path of the doctor upon whom [the woman is] entitled to rely for advice in connection with her decision.' *Whalen v. Roe.*"

As for (4) the mandatory 24-hour waiting provision, which increases the cost of obtaining an abortion by requiring the woman to make two separate trips to the abortion facility, "Akron has failed to demonstrate that any legitimate state interest is furthered by an arbitrary and inflexible waiting period. [I]f a woman, after appropriate counseling, is prepared to give her written informed consent and proceed with the abortion, a State may not demand that she delay the effectuation of that decision."

As for (5), the provision dealing with the disposal of fetal remains, the phrase "humane and sanitary" suggests, as the court below noted, "a possible intent to 'manifest some sort of "decent burial" of an embryo at the earliest stage of formation.' This level of uncertainty is fatal where criminal liability is imposed."

In the face of a dissenting opinion which, said the Court, "rejects the basic premise of *Roe* and its progeny," the Court stated at the outset: "[A]rguments continue to be made, [that in *Roe*] we erred in interpreting the Constitution. Nonetheless, the doctrine of stare decisis, while perhaps never entirely persuasive on a constitutional question, is a doctrine that demands respect in a society governed by the rule of law.[1] We respect it today, and reaffirm *Roe*."

Before specifically addressing the regulations at issue and concluding that all should be upheld, O'CONNOR, J., joined by White and Rehnquist, JJ., dissenting, launched a broad attack on the Court's approach and the "trimester framework adopted in *Roe*.": "[N]either sound constitutional theory nor our need to decide cases based on the application of neutral principles can accommodate an analytical framework that varies according to the 'stages' of pregnancy, where those stages, and their concomitant standards of review, differ according to the level of medical technology available when a particular challenge to state regulation occurs. The Court's analysis of the Akron regulations is inconsistent both with the methods of analysis employed in previous cases dealing with abortion, and with the Court's approach to fundamental rights in other areas.

"Our recent cases indicate that a regulation imposed on 'a lawful abortion "is not unconstitutional unless it unduly burdens the right to seek an abortion."' *Maher v. Roe* (quoting *Bellotti I*). In my view, this 'unduly burdensome' standard should be applied to the challenged regulations throughout the entire pregnancy without reference to the particular 'stage' of pregnancy involved. If the particular regulation does not 'unduly burden[ ]' the fundamental right, then our evaluation of that regulation is limited to our determination that the regulation rationally relates to a legitimate state purpose.

"[D]espite the Court's purported adherence to the trimester approach adopted in *Roe*, the lines drawn in that decision have now been 'blurred' because of what the Court accepts as technological advancement in the safety of abortion procedure. The State may no longer rely on a 'bright line' that separates permissible from impermissible regulation, and it is no longer free to consider the second trimester as a unit and weigh the risks posed by all abortion procedures throughout that trimester. * * *

"[The] *Roe* framework [is] clearly on a collision course with itself. As the medical risks of various abortion procedures decrease, the point at which the

1. There are especially compelling reasons for adhering to stare decisis in applying the principles of *Roe*. That case was considered with special care. [Since then] the Court repeatedly and consistently has accepted and applied the basic principle that a woman has a fundamental right to make the highly personal choice whether or not to terminate her pregnancy.

[I]t appears that the dissent would uphold virtually any abortion regulation under a rational-basis test. It also appears that even where heightened scrutiny is deemed appropriate, the dissent would uphold virtually any abortion-inhibiting regulation because of the State's interest in preserving potential human life. [This] analysis is wholly incompatible with the existence of the fundamental right recognized in *Roe*.

State may regulate for reasons of maternal health is moved further forward to actual childbirth. As medical science becomes better able to provide for the separate existence of the fetus, the point of viability is moved further back toward conception. Moreover, it is clear that the trimester approach violates the fundamental aspiration of judicial decision making through the application of neutral principles 'sufficiently absolute to give them roots throughout the community and continuity over significant periods of time.' Cox, *The Role of the Supreme Court in American Government* 114 (1976). The *Roe* framework is inherently tied to the state of medical technology that exists whenever particular litigation ensues. Although legislatures are better suited to make the necessary factual judgments in this area, the Court's framework forces legislatures, as a matter of constitutional law, to speculate about what constitutes 'accepted medical practice' at any given time. Without the necessary expertise or ability, courts must then pretend to act as science review boards and examine those legislative judgments. [Even] assuming that there is a fundamental right to terminate pregnancy in some situations, there is no justification in law or logic for the trimester framework adopted in *Roe* and employed by the Court today on the basis of stare decisis.

"[I agree with *Roe* that the state has legitimate and important interests in seeing that abortion is 'performed under circumstances that insure maximum safety for the patient' and in 'protecting the potentiability of life'], but in my view [these] interests are present *throughout* pregnancy. [The] fallacy inherent in the *Roe* framework is apparent: just because the State has a compelling interest in ensuring maternal safety once an abortion may be more dangerous [than] childbirth, it simply does not follow that the State has *no* interest before that point that justifies state regulation to ensure that first-trimester abortions are performed as safely as possible.

"The state interest in potential human life is likewise extant throughout pregnancy. [*Roe* held that] that interest could not become compelling until the point at which the fetus was viable. The difficulty with this analysis is clear: *potential* life is no less potential in the first weeks of pregnancy than it is at viability or afterward. At any stage in pregnancy, there is the *potential* for human life.

" '[*Roe*] did not declare an unqualified "constitutional right to an abortion," [but] protects the woman from unduly burdensome interference with her freedom to decide whether to terminate her pregnancy.' *Maher.* The Court and its individual Justices have repeatedly utilized the 'unduly burdensome' standard in abortion cases.

"[The] 'undue burden' required in the abortion cases represents the required threshold inquiry that must be conducted before this Court can require a State to justify its legislative actions under the exacting 'compelling state interest' standard. [In] determining whether the State imposes an 'undue burden,' we must keep in mind that when we are concerned with extremely sensitive issues, such as the one involved here, 'the appropriate forum for their resolution in a democracy is the legislature. * * *' "

A companion case to *Akron,* PLANNED PARENTHOOD v. ASHCROFT, 462 U.S. 476, 103 S.Ct. 2517, 76 L.Ed.2d 733 (1983), invalidated a Missouri second-trimester hospitalization requirement under the *Akron* analysis, but upheld other statutory provisions requiring the presence of a second physician during abortions performed after viability; a pathology report for each abortion performed in clinics as well as in hospitals; and that minors seeking abortion secure parental or judicial consent.

As for the second-physician requirement, POWELL, J., joined by Burger, C.J., reasoned that "[b]y giving medical attention to a fetus that is delivered alive, the second physician will assure that the State's interests are protected more fully than the first physician alone would be able to do. And given the compelling interest that the State has in preserving life, we cannot say that [the second-physician requirement] in those unusual circumstances where Missouri permits a third-trimester abortion is unconstitutional." O'CONNOR, J., joined by White and Rehnquist, JJ., concurred in the result "because the State possesses a compelling interest in protecting and preserving fetal life," but maintained that "this state interest is extant throughout pregnancy."

As for the requirement that minors secure parental consent or consent from the juvenile court for an abortion, POWELL, J., joined by Burger, C.J., concluded that, as interpreted by the Court of Appeals to mean that the juvenile court could not deny a petition "for good cause" unless it first found that the minor was not mature enough to make her own decision, the provision avoided any constitutional infirmities. "Assuming arguendo that the State cannot impose a parental veto on the decision of a minor to undergo an abortion," O'Connor, J., joined by White and Rehnquist, JJ., agreed that the parental consent provision was constitutional. "However, I believe that the provision is valid because it imposes no undue burden on any right that a minor may have to undergo an abortion."

BLACKMUN, J., joined by Brennan, Marshall and Stevens, JJ., would strike down all the challenged provisions. As for the second-physician requirement, it imposes an unjustified burden on women because "when a D & E abortion is performed, the second physician can do nothing to further the State's compelling interest in protecting life." As for the pathology-report requirement, it "is not in accord with 'generally accepted medical standards' " and "the State has not 'met its burden of demonstrating that [it] furthers important health-related concerns.' *Akron.*" [a]

Notes and Questions

1. *Should the focus of the abortion inquiry be on the state of fetal development rather than on the existing state of medical technology?* "If the legal system adheres to the reasoning of *Roe,*" warns Comment, 29 U.C.L.A.L.Rev. 1194, 1204–05 (1982), "there is no limit to the extent to which advances in

a. Another companion case to *Akron, Simopoulos v. Virginia,* 462 U.S. 506, 103 S.Ct. 2532, 76 L.Ed.2d 755 (1983), per Powell, J., upheld the conviction of a physician for performing an abortion during the second trimester of pregnancy outside of a licensed "hospital." Unlike the hospitalization requirements invalidated in *Akron* and *Ashcroft,* "the Virginia Statute and regulations do not require that second-trimester abortions be performed exclusively in full-service hospitals. [O]utpatient surgical hospitals may qualify for licensing as 'hospitals' [for this purpose]." As the Court interpreted the Virginia regulations, it saw "no reason to doubt that an adequately equipped clinic could, upon proper application, obtain an outpatient hospital license permitting the performance of second-trimester abortions. [The State's] requirement that second-trimester abortions be performed in licensed clinics is not an unreasonable means of furthering the State's compelling interest in 'protecting the woman's own health and safety.' *Roe.* O'Connor, J., joined by White and Rehnquist, JJ., concurred in the judgment, but did "not agree that the constitutional validity of the Virginia mandatory hospitalization requirement is contingent in any way on the trimester in which it is imposed. Rather, I believe that the requirement in this case is not an undue burden on the decision to undergo an abortion."

technology may diminish a woman's right to an abortion. [I]f, however, the focus is placed upon the degree of fetal development [rather than on viability], the courts can avoid the problems resulting from technological advances. The ultimate question should be at what point does the fetus become a human being." Continues the UCLA Comment (at 1207–11, 1215):

"An appropriate standard for determining the beginning of human life is when the fetal brain is developed to the point where the fetus is a thinking, conscious being. A survey of existing scientific research indicates that a fetus [reaches this stage] between twelve and thirty-two weeks [and primarily between 19 and 30 weeks] after conception.

"[If] the competing interests of the woman and society are balanced by asking at what point the fetus becomes a human being, then advances in technology will not erode the balance that is struck. In fact, [such advances will enable us] to more accurately determine when the fetus becomes a human being.

"[A] standard for determining when human life begins based on brain function [would] provide a workable and religiously neutral resolution of the competing interests of the woman and the fetus [and] also create a symmetry between the legal definitions for the beginning and end of life, thereby giving us a unified legal theory of what constitutes a human being."

2. *Is the "Roe framework," as Justice O'Connor maintains, "on a collision course with itself"?* Consider the remarks of LAURENCE TRIBE in Choper, Kamisar & Tribe, *The Supreme Court: Trends and Developments, 1982–83* (1984) at 257–58: "I think that [Justice O'Connor is] simply confused about one important aspect of the abortion decision. There are two different rationales on which the states purport to regulate abortion. One is to protect the health of the mother. As to that, it's true that medical advances make later and later abortions safe and, thereby, make it more and more difficult for the government to justify regulating even very late abortions. The other and wholly independent rationale, having absolutely nothing to do with a woman's safety or her health, is the protection of the life of the fetus. As to that, the Supreme Court [concluded] that the power of the state to coerce a woman to remain pregnant is inherently linked to the viability of the fetus. That is, it is when the fetus is not yet viable that saving its life requires coercing continued pregnancy.

"Once, of course, the fetus is viable, then a desire to protect it is no longer necessarily coincident with forcing a woman to remain, as it were, an involuntary incubator. If fetal viability is possible earlier in pregnancy as a result of medical advances, it is possible simultaneously to respect the woman's right not to be pregnant involuntarily, and the fetus' right to survive.

"The fact that medical advances may bring about a kind of brave new world of artificial placenta and artificial uteri earlier and earlier in the pregnancy simply means that regulation on the rationale of protecting the fetus, as opposed to the rationale of protecting the woman's health, may justify governmental intervention even in the first trimester to say, 'If you don't want to remain pregnant, fine. Give us the fetus, and we'll take care of it in the hospital.' Some would find that a nightmarish prospect because it would substitute technology for what ought to be a human undertaking. But that really raises an issue of a very different kind from those in the abortion case itself, and I think that Justice O'Connor is simply wrong in assuming that the two kinds of regulations are on a collision course."

THORNBURGH v. AMERICAN COLLEGE OF OBSTETRICIANS AND GYNECOLOGISTS

476 U.S. 747, 106 S.Ct. 2169, 90 L.Ed.2d 779 (1986).

JUSTICE BLACKMUN delivered the opinion of the Court. * * *

[Appellees challenged the constitutionality of various provisions of the Pennsylvania Abortion Control Act of 1982. The district court ruled that, with one exception, appellees had failed to establish a likelihood of success on the merits and thus were not entitled to preliminary injunctive relief. The Third Circuit enjoined enforcement of the entire Act, holding unconstitutional, on the basis of the intervening decisions in *Akron, Ashcroft* and *Simopoulos,* the following provisions of the Act: (1) the portions of § 3205 ("informed consent") that, with respect to the requirement that the woman give her "informed consent" to an abortion, require her, inter alia, to be informed of the name of the physician who will perform the abortion, the probable gestational age of the fetus, the "particular medical risks" of the abortion procedure to be used, the facts that there may be "unforeseeable detrimental physical and psychological effects," that medical assistance benefits may be available for prenatal care, childbirth, and neonatal care, and the availability of printed materials from the state that describe the fetus and list agencies offering alternatives to abortion; (2) § 3208 ("printed information"), requiring such printed materials to include a statement that there are agencies willing to help the mother carry her child to term and to assist her afterwards and a description of the probable anatomical and physiological characteristics of an unborn child at "two-week gestational increments"; (3) portions of § 3214 (reporting requirements), that require the physician to report, inter alia, the identity of the performing and referring physicians, information as to the woman's residence, age, race, marital status, and number of prior pregnancies, and the basis for any judgment that a medical emergency existed or for any determination of nonviability, and further provide that such reports shall not be deemed public records, but shall be available for public inspection and copying in a form that will not disclose the identity of any person filing a report; (4) § 3211(a) (determination of viability), requiring the physician, after the first trimester, to report the basis for his determination that a fetus is not viable; (5) § 3210(b) (requisite care in postviability abortions), requiring a physician performing a postviability abortion to use the abortion technique providing the best opportunity for the unborn child to be aborted alive unless it would present a "significantly greater medical risk" to the woman's life or health; and (6) § 3210(c) (second-physician provision), requiring a second physician to be present when viability is possible, such physician to take all reasonable measures to preserve the child's life and health. The U.S. Supreme Court affirmed.]

[In] the years [since] *Roe,* States and municipalities have adopted a number of measures seemingly designed to prevent a woman, with the advice of her physician, from exercising her freedom of choice. [But] the constitutional principles that led this Court to its decisions in 1973 still provide the compelling reason for recognizing the constitutional dimensions of a woman's right to decide whether to end her pregnancy. [The] States are not free, under the guise of protecting maternal health or potential life, to intimidate women into continuing pregnancies. Appellants claim that the statutory provisions before us today further legitimate compelling interests of the Commonwealth. Close analysis of those provisions, however, shows that they wholly subordinate constitutional privacy interests and concerns with maternal health in an effort to deter a woman from making a decision that, with her physician, is hers to make.

[The Court then examined various statutory provisions and found them constitutionally defective. As was true of the informational requirements in the Akron ordinance, Pennsylvania's "informed consent" and "printed information" provisions were "designed not to inform the woman's consent but rather to persuade her to withhold it altogether" and they "intrude upon the discretion of the pregnant woman's physician and thereby impose the 'undesired and uncomfortable strait jacket' with which the Court in *Danforth* was concerned." That Pennsylvania "does not, and surely would not, compel similar disclosure of every possible peril of necessary surgery or of simple vaccination, reveals the anti-abortion character of the statute and its real purpose."

[As for the reporting requirements, "a woman and her physician will necessarily be more reluctant to choose an abortion if there exists a possibility the her decision and her identity will become known publicly. * * * Identification is the obvious purpose of these extreme reporting requirements. [They] raise the specter of public exposure and harassment of women who choose to exercise their personal, intensely private, right, with their physician, to end a pregnancy. Thus, they pose an unacceptable danger of deterring the exercise of that right * * *."

[The provision concerning the standard of care for postviability abortions requires a "trade-off" between the woman's health and fetal survival, and fails to require that maternal health be the physician's paramount consideration. Finally, unlike the provision in *Ashcroft*, the requirement that a second physician be present during an abortion performed when viability is possible cannot be construed to contain an exception for those emergency situations where the health of the mother would be endangered by delay in the arrival of the second physician.]

Our cases long have recognized that the Constitution embodies a promise that a certain private sphere of individual liberty will be kept largely beyond the reach of government. That promise extends to women as well as to men. Few decisions are more personal and intimate, more properly private, or more basic to individual dignity and autonomy, than a woman's decision—with the guidance of her physician and within the limits specified in *Roe*—whether to end her pregnancy. A woman's right to make that choice freely is fundamental. Any other result, in our view, would protect inadequately a central part of the sphere of liberty that our law guarantees equally to all. * * *

JUSTICE STEVENS, concurring.

[T]he aspect of liberty at stake in this case is the freedom from unwarranted governmental intrusion into individual decisions in matters of childbearing. As Justice White explained in *Griswold*, that aspect of liberty comes to this Court with a momentum for respect that is lacking when appeal is made to liberties which derive merely from shifting economic arrangements.

[If] Justice White were correct in regarding the postconception decision of the question whether to bear a child as a relatively unimportant, second-class sort of interest, I might agree with his view that the individual should be required to conform her decision to the will of the majority. But if that decision commands the respect that is traditionally associated with the "sensitive areas of liberty" protected by the Constitution, as Justice White characterized reproductive decisions in *Griswold*, no individual should be compelled to surrender the freedom to make that decision for herself simply because her "value preferences" are not shared by the majority. In a sense, the basic question is whether the "abortion decision" should be made by the individual or by the majority "in the unrestrained imposition of its own, extraconstitutional value preferences." But surely Justice White is quite wrong in suggesting that the Court is imposing value preferences on anyone else.[6]

Justice White is also surely wrong in suggesting that the governmental interest in protecting fetal life is equally compelling during the entire period from the moment of conception until the moment of birth. Again, I recognize that a powerful theological argument can be made for that position, but I believe our jurisdiction is limited to the evaluation of secular state interests.[7] I should think it obvious that the State's interest in the protection of an embryo—even if that interest is defined as "protecting those who will be citizens"—increases progressively and dramatically as the organism's capacity to feel pain, to experience pleasure, to survive, and to react to its surroundings increases day by day. The development of a fetus—and pregnancy itself—are not static conditions, and the assertion that the government's interest is static simply ignores this reality.

Nor is it an answer to argue that life itself is not a static condition, and that "there is no nonarbitrary line separating a fetus from a child, or indeed, an adult human being." For, unless the religious view that a fetus is a "person" is adopted—a view Justice White refuses to embrace—there is a fundamental and well-recognized difference between a fetus and a human being; indeed, if there is not such a difference, the permissibility of terminating the life of a fetus could scarcely be left to the will of the state legislatures.[8] And if distinctions may be drawn between a fetus and a human being in terms of the state interest in their protection—even though the fetus represents one of "those who will be citizens"—it seems to me quite odd to argue that distinctions may not also be drawn between the state interest in protecting the freshly fertilized egg and the state interest in protecting the 9-month-gestated, fully sentient fetus on the eve of birth. Recognition of this distinction is supported not only by logic, but also by history and by our shared experiences.

Turning to Justice White's comments on *stare decisis,* he is of course correct in pointing out that the Court "has not hesitated to overrule decisions, or even whole lines of cases, where experience, scholarship, and reflection demonstrated that their fundamental premises were not to be found in the Constitution." But Justice White has not disavowed the "fundamental premises" on which the decision in *Roe* rests. He has not disavowed the Court's prior approach to the interpretation of the word "liberty" or, more narrowly, the line of cases that

6. Justice White's characterization of the governmental interest as "protecting those who will be citizens if their lives are not ended in the womb" reveals that his opinion may be influenced as much by his own value preferences as by his view about the proper allocation of decisionmaking responsibilities between the individual and the State. For if federal judges must allow the State to make the abortion decision, presumably the State is free to decide that a woman may *never* abort, may *sometimes* abort, or, as in the People's Republic of China, must *always* abort if her family is already too large. In contrast, our cases represent a consistent view that the individual is primarily responsible for reproductive decisions, whether the State seeks to prohibit reproduction, *Skinner,* or to require it, *Roe.*

7. The responsibility for nurturing the soul of the newly born, as well as the unborn, rests with individual parents, not with the State. No matter how important a sacrament such as baptism may be, a State surely could not punish a mother for refusing to baptize her child.

8. No member of this Court has ever suggested that a fetus is a "person" within the meaning of the Fourteenth Amendment.

culminated in the unequivocal holding, applied to unmarried persons and married persons alike, "that the Constitution protects individual decisions in matters of childbearing from unjustified intrusion by the State." *Carey* (White, J., concurring in pertinent part).

[In] the final analysis, the holding in *Roe* presumes that it is far better to permit some individuals to make incorrect decisions than to deny all individuals the right to make decisions that have a profound effect upon their destiny. Arguably a very primitive society would have been protected from evil by a rule against eating apples; a majority familiar with Adam's experience might favor such a rule. But the lawmakers who placed a special premium on the protection of individual liberty have recognized that certain values are more important than the will of a transient majority.

CHIEF JUSTICE BURGER, dissenting.

I agree with much of Justice White's and Justice O'Connor's dissents.

[E]very member of the *Roe* Court rejected the idea of abortion on demand. The Court's opinion today, however, plainly undermines that important principle, and I regretfully conclude that some of the concerns of the dissenting Justices in *Roe,* as well as the concerns I expressed in my separate opinion, have now been realized.

[In] discovering constitutional infirmities in state regulations of abortion that are in accord with our history and tradition, we may have lured judges into "roaming at large in the constitutional field." *Griswold* (Harlan, J., concurring). The soundness of our holdings must be tested by the decisions that purport to follow them. If *Danforth* and today's holding really mean what they seem to say, I agree we should reexamine *Roe.*

JUSTICE WHITE, with whom JUSTICE REHNQUIST joins, dissenting.

* * * I was in dissent in *Roe* and am in dissent today. * * * I continue to believe that this venture has been fundamentally misguided since its inception. I submit that even accepting *Roe,* the concerns underlying that decision by no means command or justify the results reached today. * * *

[D]ecisions that find in the Constitution principles or values that cannot fairly be read into that document usurp the people's authority, for such decisions represent choices that the people have never made and that they cannot disavow through corrective legislation. For this reason, it is essential that this Court maintain the power to restore authority to its proper possessors by correcting constitutional decisions that, on reconsideration, are found to be mistaken.

* * * *Stare decisis* did not stand in the way of the Justices who, in the late 1930s, swept away constitutional doctrines that had placed unwarranted restrictions on the power of the State and Federal Governments to enact social and economic legislation. Nor did *stare decisis* deter a different set of Justices, some fifteen years later, from rejecting the theretofore prevailing view that the Fourteenth Amendment permitted the States to maintain the system of racial segregation. *Brown v. Board of Education.* In both instances, history has been far kinder to those who departed from precedent than to those who would have blindly followed the rule of *stare decisis.* * * *

In my view, the time has come to recognize that [*Roe*] "departs from a proper understanding" of the Constitution and to overrule it. I do not claim that the arguments in support of this proposition are new ones or that they were not considered by the Court in *Roe* or in the cases that succeeded it. But if an argument that a constitutional decision is erroneous must be novel in order to justify overruling that precedent, the Court's decisions in *Lochner* and *Plessy* would remain the law, for the doctrines announced in those decisions were nowhere more eloquently or incisively criticized than in the dissenting opinions of Justices Holmes (in *Lochner*) and Harlan (in both cases).

[A] reader of the Constitution might be surprised to find that it encompassed *Roe's* detailed rules, for the text obviously contains no references to abortion, nor, indeed, to pregnancy or reproduction generally; and, of course, it is highly doubtful that the authors of any of the provisions of the Constitution believed that they were giving protection to abortion. As its prior cases clearly show, however, this Court does not subscribe to the simplistic view that constitutional interpretation can possibly be limited to the "plain meaning" of the Constitution's text or to the subjective intention of the Framers. The Constitution is not a deed setting forth the precise metes and bounds of its subject matter; rather, it is a document announcing fundamental principles in value-laden terms that leave ample scope for the exercise of normative judgment by those charged with interpreting and applying it. In particular, the Due Process Clause of the Fourteenth Amendment [has] been read by the majority of the Court to be broad enough to provide substantive protection against state infringement of a broad range of individual interests.

In most instances, the substantive protection afforded the liberty or property of an individual by the Fourteenth Amendment is extremely limited: State action impinging on individual interests need only be rational to survive scrutiny under the Due Process Clause, and the determination of rationality is to be made with a heavy dose of deference to the policy choices of the legislature. Only "fundamental" rights are entitled to the added protection provided by strict judicial scrutiny of legislation that impinges upon them. I can certainly agree with the proposition—which I deem indisputable—that a woman's ability to choose an abortion is a species of "liberty" that is subject to the general protections of the Due Process Clause. I cannot agree, however, that this liberty is so "fundamental" that restrictions upon it call into play anything more than the most minimal judicial scrutiny.

Fundamental liberties and interests are most clearly present when the Constitution provides specific textual recognition of their existence and importance. Thus, the Court is on relatively firm ground when it deems certain of the liberties set forth in the Bill of Rights to be fundamental and therefore finds them incorporated in the Fourteenth Amendment's guarantee that no State may deprive any person of liberty without due process of law. When the Court ventures further and defines as "fundamental" liberties that are nowhere mentioned in the Constitution (or that are present only in the so-called "penumbras" of specifically enumerated rights), it must, of necessity, act with more caution, lest it open itself to the accusation that, in the name of identifying constitutional principles to which the people have consented in framing their Constitution, the Court has done nothing more than impose its own controversial choices of value upon the people.

[However] one answers the metaphysical or theological question whether the fetus is a "human being" or the legal question whether it is a "person" as that term is used in the Constitution, one must at least recognize, first, that the fetus is an entity that bears in its cells all the genetic information that characterizes a member of the species homo sapiens and distinguishes an individual member of that species from all others, and second, that there is no nonarbitrary line separating a fetus from a child or, indeed, an adult human being. Given that the continued existence and development—that is to say, the *life*—of such an entity are so directly at stake in the woman's decision whether or not to terminate her pregnancy, that decision must be recognized as sui generis, different in kind from the others that the Court has protected under the rubric of personal or family privacy and autonomy. Accordingly, the decisions cited by the Court both in *Roe* and in its opinion today as precedent for the fundamental nature of the liberty to choose abortion do not, even if all are accepted as valid, dictate the Court's classification.

If the woman's liberty to choose an abortion is fundamental, then, it is not because any of our precedents (aside from *Roe* itself) commands or justifies that result; it can only be because protection for this unique choice is itself "implicit in the concept of ordered liberty" or, perhaps, "deeply rooted in this Nation's history and tradition." It seems clear to me that it is neither. The Court's opinion in *Roe* itself convincingly refutes the notion that the abortion liberty is deeply rooted in the history or tradition of our people, as does the continuing and deep division of the people themselves over the question of abortion. As for the notion that choice in the matter of abortion is implicit in the concept of ordered liberty, it seems apparent to me that a free, egalitarian, and democratic society does not presuppose any particular rule or set of rules with respect to abortion. And again, the fact that many men and women of good will and high commitment to constitutional government place themselves on both sides of the abortion controversy strengthens my own conviction that the values animating the Constitution do not compel recognition of the abortion liberty as fundamental. In so denominating that liberty, the Court engages not in constitutional interpretation, but in the unrestrained imposition of its own, extraconstitutional value preferences.[3]

A second, equally basic error infects the Court's decision in *Roe.* The detailed set of rules governing state restrictions on abortion that the Court first articulated in *Roe* and has since refined and elaborated presupposes not only that the woman's liberty to choose an abortion is fundamental, but also that the state's countervailing interest in protecting fetal life (or, as the Court would have it, "potential human life") becomes "compelling" only at the point at which the fetus is viable. As Justice O'Connor pointed out three years ago in her dissent in *Akron,* the Court's choice of viability as the point at which the State's interest becomes compelling is entirely arbitrary.

[The] governmental interest at issue is in protecting those who will be citizens if their lives are not ended in the womb. The substantiality of this interest is in no way dependent on the probability that the fetus may be capable of surviving outside the womb at any given point in its development, as the possibility of fetal survival is contingent on the state of medical practice and technology, factors that are in essence morally and constitutionally irrelevant. The State's interest is in the fetus as an entity in itself, and the character of this

3. Justice Stevens asserts that I am "quite wrong in suggesting that the Court is imposing value preferences on anyone else" when it denominates the liberty to choose abortion as "fundamental" (in contradistinction to such other, nonfundamental liberties as the liberty to use dangerous drugs or to operate a business without governmental interference) and thereby disempowers state electoral majorities from legislating in this area. I can only respond that I cannot conceive of a definition of the phrase "imposing value preferences" that does not encompass the Court's action.

Justice Stevens also suggests that it is the legislative majority that has engaged in "the unrestrained imposition of its own, extraconstitutional value choices" when a state legislature restricts the availability of abortion. But a legislature, unlike a court, has the inherent power to do so unless its choices are constitutionally *forbidden,* which, in my view, is not the case here.

entity does not change at the point of viability under conventional medical wisdom. Accordingly, the State's interest, if compelling after viability, is equally compelling before viability.[4]

* * *

* * * Abortion is a hotly contested moral and political issue. Such issues, in our society, are to be resolved by the will of the people, either as expressed through legislation or through the general principles they have already incorporated into the Constitution they have adopted. *Roe* implies that the people have already resolved the debate by weaving into the Constitution the values and principles that answer the issue. As I have argued, I believe it is clear that the people have never—not in 1787, 1791, 1868, or at any time since—done any such thing. I would return the issue to the people by overruling *Roe*.

* * *

JUSTICE O'CONNOR, with whom JUSTICE REHNQUIST joins, dissenting.

[In affirming the Third Circuit's invalidation of various provisions of the Pennsylvania Act], the Court prematurely decides serious constitutional questions on an inadequate record * * *. There has been no trial on the merits, and appellants have had no opportunity to develop facts that might have a bearing on the constitutionality of the statute. The only question properly before the Court is whether or not a preliminary injunction should have been issued to restrain enforcement of the challenged provisions pending trial on the merits. [Our prior decisions] do not establish a likelihood that appellees would succeed on the merits of their constitutional claims sufficient to warrant overturning the District Court's denial of a preliminary injunction. Under the approach to abortion regulation outlined in my dissenting opinion in *Akron*, to which I adhere, it is even clearer that no preliminary injunction should have issued. I therefore dissent.

[The] State has compelling interests in ensuring maternal health and in protecting potential human life, and these interests exist "throughout pregnancy." Under this Court's fundamental-rights jurisprudence, judicial scrutiny of state regulation of abortion should be limited to whether the state law bears a rational relationship to legitimate purposes such as the advancement of these compelling interests, with heightened scrutiny reserved for instances in which the State has imposed an "undue burden" on the abortion decision. An undue burden will generally be found "in situations involving absolute obstacles or severe limitations on the abortion decision," not wherever a state regulation

4. Contrary to Justice Stevens' suggestion, this is no more a "theological" position than is the Court's own judgment that viability is the point at which the state interest becomes compelling. (Interestingly, Justice Stevens omits any real effort to defend this judgment.) The point is that the specific interest the Court has recognized as compelling after the point of viability—that is, the interest in protecting "potential human life"—is present as well before viability, and the point of viability seems to bear no discernible relationship to the strength of that interest. Thus, there is no basis for concluding that the essential character of the state interest becomes transformed at the point of viability.

Further, it is self-evident that neither the legislative decision to assert a state interest in fetal life before viability nor the judicial decision to recognize that interest as compelling constitutes an impermissible "religious" decision merely because it coincides with the belief of one or more religions. Certainly the fact that the prohibition of murder coincides with one of the Ten Commandments does not render a State's interest in its murder statutes less than compelling, nor are legislative and judicial decisions concerning the use of the death penalty tainted by their correspondence to varying religious views on that subject. The simple, and perhaps unfortunate, fact of the matter is that in determining whether to assert an interest in fetal life, a State cannot avoid taking a position that will correspond to some religious beliefs and contradict others. * * *

"may 'inhibit' abortions to some degree." And if a state law does interfere with the abortion decision to an extent that is unduly burdensome, so that it becomes "necessary to apply an exacting standard of review," the possibility remains that the statute will withstand the stricter scrutiny.

[The] Court today goes well beyond mere distortion of the "unduly burdensome" standard. By holding that each of the challenged provisions is facially unconstitutional as a matter of law, and that no conceivable facts appellants might offer could alter this result, the Court appears to adopt as its new test a per se rule under which any regulation touching on abortion must be invalidated if it poses "an unacceptable danger of deterring the exercise of that right." Under this prophylactic test, it seems that the mere possibility that some women will be less likely to choose to have an abortion by virtue of the presence of a particular state regulation suffices to invalidate it. Simultaneously, the Court strains to discover "the anti-abortion character of the statute," and, as Justice White points out, invents an unprecedented canon of construction under which "in cases involving abortion, a permissible reading of a statute is to be avoided at all costs." * * * I dispute not only the wisdom but the legitimacy of the Court's attempt to discredit and preempt state abortion regulation regardless of the interests it serves and the impact it has. * * *

Notes and Questions

1. *Did the Thornburgh case move beyond the standard of coerciveness?* Although state persuasion or propaganda may be tantamount to coercion, was that true of the informed-consent provision invalidated in *Thornburgh?* Is requiring the woman to know the name of the physician performing the abortion, the probable gestational age of the fetus and the possibility of unforeseeable risks any more coercive than informed-consent provisions for other medical procedures? See Note, 100 Harv.L.Rev. 200, 206–08 (1986).

2. *Arousing Roe's opponents.* Should *Thornburgh* have served as a warning to the shrinking majority of justices still supporting *Roe* not to read the abortion right too broadly lest they arouse its opponents on the Court and provide them with the resolve to overturn *Roe?* See id. at 201, 209–10.

"The antiabortion campaign to alter the complexion of the American judiciary truly bore fruit in 1989, in the landmark [*Webster* decision]. In a different setting the *Webster* case might have been routine, presenting another in a series of post-*Roe* challenges to a variety of abortion restrictions. The Missouri law includes a restriction on the performance of abortions in public institutions, even when the woman would be paying her own bill; a preamble in the statute that declares that 'the life of each human being begins at conception'; and a regulatory requirement that a number of tests of fetal viability be performed when a woman seeking an abortion is believed to be twenty weeks pregnant.

"What made the *Webster* case so critical was the change in the composition of the Supreme Court. This was to be the first public test of the positions of Justice Scalia and Justice Kennedy on the question of abortion since they had become members of the Court. While Justice Scalia had expressed scholarly opposition to *Roe* before his appointment to the Supreme Court, Justice Kennedy, though conservative, seemed more of a question mark. And, notwithstanding her dissents in previous abortion cases, Justice O'Connor had scrupulously avoided joining any opinion expressly calling for *Roe* 's reversal. The depth of her opposition to *Roe* was thus unknown.

"With only four solid votes to reaffirm *Roe,* the tenuous nature of the constitutional right to choose to terminate a pregnancy was evident to anyone who could count."

—Tribe, *Abortion: The Clash of Absolutes* 20 (1990).

WEBSTER v. REPRODUCTIVE HEALTH SERVICES

492 U.S. 490, 109 S.Ct. 3040, 106 L.Ed.2d 410 (1989).

CHIEF JUSTICE REHNQUIST announced the judgment of the Court and delivered the opinion of the Court with respect to Parts I, II–A, II–B, and II–C, and an opinion with respect to Parts II–D, and III, in which JUSTICE WHITE and JUSTICE KENNEDY join.

This appeal concerns the constitutionality of a [1986] Missouri statute regulating the performance of abortions. The United States Court of Appeals for the Eighth Circuit struck down several provisions of the statute on the ground that they violated [*Roe v. Wade*]. [We] now reverse.

I. [The challenged statute contains] 20 provisions, 5 of which are now before the Court. The first provision, or preamble, contains "findings" by the state legislature that "[t]he life of each human being begins at conception," and that "unborn children have protectable interests in life, health, and well-being." §§ 1.205.1(1), (2) (1986). The Act further requires that all Missouri laws be interpreted to provide unborn children with the same rights enjoyed by other persons, subject to the Federal Constitution and this Court's precedents. § 1.205.2. Among its other provisions, the Act requires that, prior to performing an abortion on any woman whom a physician has reason to believe is 20 or more weeks pregnant, the physician ascertain whether the fetus is viable by performing "such medical examinations and tests as are necessary to make a finding of the gestational age, weight, and lung maturity of the unborn child." § 188.029. The Act also prohibits the use of public employees and facilities to perform or assist abortions not necessary to save the mother's life, and it prohibits the use of public funds, employees, or facilities for the purpose of "encouraging or counseling" a woman to have an abortion not necessary to save her life. §§ 188.205, 188.210, 188.215.

* * *

II. Decision of this case requires us to address four sections of the Missouri Act: (a) the preamble; (b) the prohibition on the use of public facilities or employees to perform abortions; (c) the prohibition on public funding of abortion counseling; and (d) the requirement that physicians conduct viability tests prior to performing abortions. We address these seriatim.

A. [In] invalidating the preamble, the Court of Appeals relied on [this] Court's dictum that " 'a State may not adopt one theory of when life begins to justify its regulation of abortions.' " [quoting *Akron,* which cited *Roe*]. It rejected Missouri's claim that the preamble was "abortion-neutral," and "merely determine[d] when life begins in a nonabortion context, a traditional state prerogative." The court thought that "[t]he only plausible inference" from the fact that "every remaining section of the bill save one regulates the performance of abortions" was that "the state intended its abortion regulations to be understood against the backdrop of its theory of life."

[In] our view, the Court of Appeals misconceived the meaning of the *Akron* dictum, which was only that a State could not "justify" an abortion regulation otherwise invalid under *Roe* on the ground that it embodied the State's view about when life begins. Certainly the preamble does not by its terms regulate abortion or any other aspect of appellees' medical practice. The Court has emphasized that *Roe* "implies no limitation on the authority of a State to make a value judgment favoring childbirth over abortion." *Maher.* The preamble can be read simply to express that sort of value judgment.

We think the extent to which the preamble's language might be used to interpret other state statutes or regulations is something that only the courts of Missouri can definitively decide. State law has offered protections to unborn children in tort and probate law and [the preamble] can be interpreted to do no more than that. [It] will be time enough for federal courts to address the meaning of the preamble should it be applied to restrict the activities of appellees in some concrete way. Until then, this Court "is not empowered to decide * * * abstract propositions * * *." We therefore need not pass on the constitutionality of the Act's preamble.

B. Section 188.210 provides that "[i]t shall be unlawful for any public employee within the scope of his employment to perform or assist in an abortion not necessary to save the life of the mother," while § 188.215 makes it "unlawful for any public facility to be used for the purpose of performing or assisting an abortion not necessary to save the life of the mother." [We uphold these provisions.]

As we said earlier this Term in *DeShaney v. Winnebago County* [p. 1243 infra], "our cases have recognized that the Due Process Clauses generally confer no affirmative right to governmental aid, even where such aid may be necessary to secure life, liberty, or property interests of which the government itself may not deprive the individual." [As] in *Maher* and *Poelker,* the [*McRae*] Court required only a showing that Congress' authorization of "reimbursement for medically necessary services generally, but not for certain medically necessary abortions" was rationally related to the legitimate governmental goal of encouraging childbirth.

* * * Just as Congress' refusal to fund abortions in *McRae* left "an indigent woman with at least the same range of choice in deciding whether to obtain a medically necessary abortion as she would have had if Congress had chosen to subsidize no health care costs at all," Missouri's refusal to allow public employees to perform abortions in public hospitals leaves a pregnant woman with the same choices as if the State had chosen not to operate any public hospitals at all. The challenged provisions only restrict a woman's ability to obtain an abortion to the extent that she chooses to use a physician affiliated with a public hospital. This circumstance is more easily remedied, and thus considerably less burdensome, than indigency, which "may make it difficult—and in some cases, perhaps, impossible—for some women to have abortions" without public funding. *Maher.* Having held that the State's refusal to fund abortions does not violate *Roe,* it strains logic to reach a contrary result for the use of public facilities and employees. * * *

"Constitutional concerns are greatest," we said in *Maher,* "when the State attempts to impose its will by the force of law; the State's power to encourage actions deemed to be in the public interest is necessarily far broader." Nothing in the Constitution requires States to enter or remain in the business of performing abortions. Nor, as appellees suggest, do private physicians and their patients have some kind of constitutional right of access to public facilities for the performance of abortions. * * * [8]

Maher, Poelker, and *McRae* all support the view that the State need not commit any resources to facilitating abortions, even if it can turn a profit by doing so. * * *

C. The Missouri Act contains three provisions relating to "encouraging or counseling a woman to have an abortion not necessary to save her life." Section 188.205 states that no public funds can be used for this purpose; § 188.210 states that public employees cannot, within the scope of their employment, engage in public speech; and § 188.215 forbids such speech in public facilities. [The Court of Appeals] held that all three of these provisions were unconstitutionally vague, and that "the ban on using public funds, employees, and facilities to encourage or counsel a woman to have an abortion is an unacceptable infringement of the woman's fourteenth amendment right to choose an abortion after receiving the medical information necessary to exercise the right knowingly and intelligently."

Missouri has chosen only to appeal the Court of Appeals' invalidation of the public funding provision, § 188.205. * * * We accept, for purposes of decision, the State's claim that [this provision] "is not directed at the conduct of any physician or health care provider, private or public," but "is directed solely at those persons responsible for expending public funds."

Appellees contend that they are not "adversely" affected under the State's interpretation of § 188.205, and therefore that there is no longer a case or controversy before us on this question. Plaintiffs are masters of their complaints and remain so at the appellate stage of a litigation. [The] controversy over § 188.205 is now moot, because appellees' argument amounts to a decision to no longer seek a declaratory judgment that § 188.205 is unconstitutional * * *.

D. Section 188.029 of the Missouri Act provides:

> "Before a physician performs an abortion on a woman he has reason to believe is carrying an unborn child of twenty or more weeks gestational age, the physician shall first determine if the unborn child is viable by using and exercising that degree of care, skill, and proficiency commonly exercised by the ordinarily skillful, careful, and prudent physician engaged in similar practice under the same or similar conditions. In making this determination of viability, the physician shall perform or cause to be performed such medical examinations and tests as are necessary to make a finding of the gestational age, weight, and lung maturity of the unborn child and shall enter such findings and determination of viability in the medical record of the mother."

[The] Court of Appeals read § 188.029 as requiring that after 20 weeks "doctors *must* perform tests to find gestational age, fetal weight and lung maturity." The court indicated that the tests needed to determine fetal weight at 20 weeks are "unreliable and inaccurate" and would add $125 to $250 to the cost of an abortion. * * *

8. A different analysis might apply if a particular State had socialized medicine and all of its hospitals and physicians were publicly funded. This case might also be different if the State barred doctors who performed abortions in private facilities from the use of public facilities for any purpose.

We think the viability-testing provision makes sense only if the second sentence is read to require only those tests that are useful to making subsidiary findings as to viability. If we construe this provision to require a physician to perform those tests needed to make the three specified findings *in all circumstances,* including when the physician's reasonable professional judgment indicates that the tests would be irrelevant to determining viability or even dangerous to the mother and the fetus, the second sentence of § 188.029 would conflict with the first sentence's *requirement* that a physician apply his reasonable professional skill and judgment.

[The] viability-testing provision of the Missouri Act is concerned with promoting the State's interest in potential human life rather than in maternal health. Section 188.029 creates what is essentially a presumption of viability at 20 weeks, which the physician must rebut with tests indicating that the fetus is not viable prior to performing an abortion. It also directs the physician's determination as to viability by specifying consideration, if feasible, of gestational age, fetal weight, and lung capacity. The District Court found that "the medical evidence is uncontradicted that a 20–week fetus is *not* viable," and that "$23^1/_2$ to 24 weeks gestation is the earliest point in pregnancy where a reasonable possibility of viability exists." But it also found that there may be a 4–week error in estimating gestational age, which supports testing at 20 weeks.

* * *

We think that the doubt cast upon the Missouri statute by [our earlier] cases is not so much a flaw in the statute as it is a reflection of the fact that the rigid trimester analysis of the course of a pregnancy enunciated in *Roe* has resulted in subsequent cases like *Colautti* and *Akron* making constitutional law in this area a virtual Procrustean bed. Statutes specifying elements of informed consent to be provided abortion patients, for example, were invalidated if they were thought to "structur[e] [the] dialogue between the woman and her physician." *Thornburgh.* As the dissenters in *Thornburgh* pointed out, such a statute would have been sustained under any traditional standard of judicial review, or for any other surgical procedure except abortion.

Stare decisis is a cornerstone of our legal system, but it has less power in constitutional cases, where, save for constitutional amendments, this Court is the only body able to make needed changes. We have not refrained from reconsideration of a prior construction of the Constitution that has proved "unsound in principle and unworkable in practice." We think the *Roe* trimester framework falls into that category.

In the first place, the rigid *Roe* framework is hardly consistent with the notion of a Constitution cast in general terms, as ours is, and usually speaking in general principles, as ours does. The key elements of the *Roe* framework—trimesters and viability—are not found in the text of the Constitution or in any place else one would expect to find a constitutional principle. Since the bounds of the inquiry are essentially indeterminate, the result has been a web of legal rules that have become increasingly intricate, resembling a code of regulations rather than a body of constitutional doctrine.[15]

15. For example, the Court has held that a State may require that certain information be given to a woman by a physician or his assistant, *Akron,* but that it may not require that such information be furnished to her only by the physician himself. Likewise, a State may require that abortions in the second trimester be performed in clinics, *Simopoulos,* but it may not require that such abortions be performed only in hospitals. *Akron.* We do not think these distinctions are of any constitutional import in view of our abandonment of the trimester framework. The dissent's claim that the State goes too far, even under *Maher,*

[In] the second place, we do not see why the State's interest in protecting potential human life should come into existence only at the point of viability, and that there should therefore be a rigid line allowing state regulation after viability but prohibiting it before viability. * * * "[T]he State's interest, if compelling after viability, is equally compelling before viability." *Thornburgh* (White, J., dissenting); (O'Connor, J., dissenting) ("State has compelling interests in ensuring maternal health and in protecting potential human life, and these interests exist 'throughout pregnancy' ").

The tests that § 188.029 requires the physician to perform are designed to determine viability. The State here has chosen viability as the point at which its interest in potential human life must be safeguarded. [It] is true that the tests in question increase the expense of abortion, and regulate the discretion of the physician in determining the viability of the fetus. Since the tests will undoubtedly show in many cases that the fetus is not viable, the tests will have been performed for what were in fact second-trimester abortions. But we are satisfied that the requirement of these tests permissibly furthers the State's interest in protecting potential human life * * *.

The dissent takes us to task for our failure to join in a "great issues" debate as to whether the Constitution includes an "unenumerated" general right to privacy as recognized in cases such as *Griswold* and *Roe.* But *Griswold,* unlike *Roe,* did not purport to adopt a whole framework, complete with detailed rules and distinctions, to govern the cases in which the asserted liberty interest would apply. As such, it was far different from the opinion, if not the holding, of *Roe.* [That] framework sought to deal with areas of medical practice traditionally subject to state regulation, and it sought to balance once and for all by reference only to the calendar the claims of the State to protect the fetus as a form of human life against the claims of a woman to decide for herself whether or not to abort a fetus she was carrying. The experience of the Court in applying *Roe* in later cases, see n. 15, suggests to us that there is wisdom in not unnecessarily attempting to elaborate the abstract differences between a "fundamental right" to abortion, as the Court described it in *Akron,* a "limited fundamental constitutional right," which Justice Blackmun's dissent today treats *Roe* as having established, or a liberty interest protected by the Due Process Clause, which we believe it to be. The Missouri testing requirement here is reasonably designed to ensure that abortions are not performed where the fetus is viable—an end which all concede is legitimate—and that is sufficient to sustain its constitutionality.

The dissent also accuses us, inter alia, of cowardice and illegitimacy in dealing with "the most politically divisive domestic legal issue of our time." There is no doubt that our holding today will allow some governmental regulation of abortion that would have been prohibited under the language of cases such as *Colautti* and *Akron.* But the goal of constitutional adjudication is surely not to remove inexorably "politically divisive" issues from the ambit of the legislative process, whereby the people through their elected representatives deal with matters of concern to them. The goal [, rather,] is to hold true the balance between that which the Constitution puts beyond the reach of the democratic process and that which it does not. We think we have done that today. The dissent's suggestion that legislative bodies, in a Nation where more than half of our population is women, will treat our decision today as an invitation to enact

Poelker and *McRae,* by refusing to permit the use of public facilities, as defined in § 188.200, for the performance of abortions is another example of the fine distinctions endemic in the *Roe* framework.

abortion regulation reminiscent of the dark ages not only misreads our views but does scant justice to those who serve in such bodies and the people who elect them.

III. Both appellants and the United States as Amicus Curiae have urged that we overrule [*Roe*]. The facts of the present case, however, differ from those at issue in *Roe.* Here, Missouri has determined that viability is the point at which its interest in potential human life must be safeguarded. In *Roe,* on the other hand, the Texas statute criminalized the performance of *all* abortions, except when the mother's life was at stake. This case therefore affords us no occasion to revisit the holding of *Roe,* [and] we leave it undisturbed. To the extent indicated in our opinion, we would modify and narrow *Roe* and succeeding cases. [Reversed.]

JUSTICE O'CONNOR, concurring in part and concurring in the judgment.

I concur in Parts I, II–A, II–B, and II–C of the Court's opinion.

I. Nothing in the record before us or the opinions below indicates that [the] preamble to Missouri's [statute] will affect a woman's decision to have an abortion. [It] may be correct that the use of postfertilization contraceptive devices is constitutionally protected by *Griswold* and its progeny but, as with a woman's abortion decision, nothing in the record or the opinions below indicates that the preamble will affect a woman's decision to practice contraception. [Neither] is there any indication of the possibility that the preamble might be applied to prohibit the performance of *in vitro* fertilization. I agree with the Court, therefore, that all of these intimations of unconstitutionality are simply too hypothetical to support the use of declaratory judgment procedures and injunctive remedies in this case.

Similarly, it seems to me to follow directly from our previous decisions concerning [abortion funding] that appellees' facial challenge to the constitutionality of Missouri's ban on the utilization of public facilities and the participation of public employees in the performance of abortions not necessary to save the life of the mother cannot succeed. Given Missouri's definition of "public facility" as "any public institution, public facility, public equipment, or any physical asset owned, leased, or controlled by this state or any agency or political subdivisions thereof," § 188.200(2), there may be conceivable applications of the ban on the use of public facilities that would be unconstitutional. Appellees and *amici* suggest that the State could try to enforce the ban against private hospitals using public water and sewage lines, or against private hospitals leasing state-owned equipment or state land. Whether some or all of these or other applications of § 188.215 would be constitutional need not be decided here. *Maher, Poelker,* and *McRae* stand for the proposition that some quite straightforward applications of the Missouri ban on the use of public facilities for performing abortions would be constitutional and that is enough to defeat appellees' assertion that the ban is facially unconstitutional. * * *

II. In its interpretation of Missouri's "determination of viability" provision, § 188.029, the plurality has proceeded in a manner unnecessary to deciding the question at hand. I agree with the plurality that it was plain error for the Court of Appeals to interpret the second sentence of § 188.029 as meaning that "doctors *must* perform tests to find gestational age, fetal weight and lung maturity" (emphasis in original). [The] plurality is quite correct: "the viability-testing provision makes sense only if the second sentence is read to require only those tests that are useful to making subsidiary findings as to viability," and, I would add, only those examinations and tests that it would not be imprudent or careless to perform in the particular medical situation before the physician.

Unlike the plurality, I do not understand these viability testing requirements to conflict with any of the Court's past decisions concerning state regulation of abortion. Therefore, there is no necessity to accept the State's invitation to reexamine the constitutional validity of *Roe.* [When] the constitutional invalidity of a State's abortion statute actually turns on the constitutional validity of *Roe v. Wade,* there will be time enough to reexamine *Roe.* And to do so carefully.

In assessing § 188.029 it is especially important to recognize that appellees did not appeal the District Court's ruling that the first sentence of § 188.029 is constitutional. There is, accordingly, no dispute between the parties before us over the constitutionality of the "presumption of viability at 20 weeks," created by the first sentence of § 188.029. If anything might arguably conflict with the Court's previous decisions concerning the determination of viability, I would think it is the introduction of this presumption. [The] 20–week presumption of viability in the first sentence of § 188.029, it could be argued (though, I would think, unsuccessfully), restricts "the judgment of the responsible attending physician," by imposing on that physician the burden of overcoming the presumption. This presumption may be a "superimpos[ition] [of] state regulation on the medical determination of whether a particular fetus is viable," but, if so, it is a restriction on the physician's judgment that is not before us. * * *

I do not think the second sentence of § 188.029, as interpreted by the Court, imposes a degree of state regulation on the medical determination of viability that in any way conflicts with prior decisions of this Court. As the plurality recognizes, the requirement that, where not imprudent, physicians perform examinations and tests useful to making subsidiary findings to determine viability "promot[es] the State's interest in potential human life rather than in maternal health." No decision of this Court has held that the State may not directly promote its interest in potential life when viability is possible. Quite the contrary. In *Thornburgh* the Court considered a constitutional challenge to a Pennsylvania statute requiring that a second physician be present during an abortion performed "when viability is possible." [The] *Thornburgh* majority struck down the Pennsylvania statute merely because the statute had no exception for emergency situations and not because it found a constitutional difference between the State's promotion of its interest in potential life when viability is possible and when viability is certain. [All] nine Members of the *Thornburgh* Court appear to have agreed that it is not constitutionally impermissible for the State to enact regulations designed to protect the State's interest in potential life when viability is possible. That is exactly what Missouri has done in § 188.029.

* * *

Finally, and rather half-heartedly, the plurality suggests that the marginal increase in the cost of an abortion created by Missouri's viability testing provision may make § 188.029, even as interpreted, suspect under this Court's decision in *Akron,* striking down a second-trimester hospitalization requirement. I dissented [in] *Akron* because it was my view that, even apart from *Roe's* trimester framework which I continue to consider problematic, see *Thornburgh* (dissenting opinion), the *Akron* majority had distorted and misapplied its own standard for evaluating state regulation of abortion which the Court had applied with fair consistency in the past: that, previability, "a regulation imposed on a lawful abortion is not unconstitutional unless it unduly burdens the right to seek an abortion."

It is clear to me that requiring the performance of examinations and tests useful to determining whether a fetus is viable, when viability is possible, and when it would not be medically imprudent to do so, does not impose an undue burden on a woman's abortion decision. On this ground alone I would reject the suggestion that § 188.029 as interpreted is unconstitutional. More to the point, however, just as I see no conflict between § 188.029 and *Colautti* or any decision of this Court concerning a State's ability to give effect to its interest in potential life, I see no conflict between § 188.029 [and] *Akron.* The second-trimester hospitalization requirement struck down in *Akron* imposed, in the majority's view, "a heavy, and unnecessary, burden," more than doubling the cost of "women's access to a relatively inexpensive, otherwise accessible, and safe abortion procedure." By contrast, the cost of examinations and tests that could usefully and prudently be performed when a woman is 20–24 weeks pregnant to determine whether the fetus is viable would only marginally, if at all, increase the cost of an abortion.

[Moreover,] the examinations and tests required by § 188.029 are to be performed when viability is possible. This feature of § 188.029 distinguishes it from the second-trimester hospitalization requirement struck down by the *Akron* majority. As the court recognized in *Thornburgh* the State's compelling interest in potential life postviability renders its interest in determining the critical point of viability equally compelling. Under the Court's precedents, the same cannot be said for the *Akron* second-trimester hospitalization requirement. As I understand the Court's opinion in *Akron,* therefore, the plurality's suggestion today that *Akron* casts doubt on the validity of § 188.029, even as the Court has interpreted it, is without foundation and cannot provide a basis for reevaluating *Roe.* * * *

JUSTICE SCALIA, concurring in part and concurring in the judgment.

I join Parts I, II–A, II–B and II–C of the opinion of The Chief Justice. As to Part II–D, I share Justice Blackmun's view that it effectively would overrule *Roe.* I think that should be done, but would do it more explicitly.

[The] outcome of today's case will doubtless be heralded as a triumph of judicial statesmanship. It is not that, unless it is statesmanlike needlessly to prolong this Court's self-awarded sovereignty over a field where it has little proper business since the answers to most of the cruel questions posed are political and not juridical—a sovereignty which therefore quite properly, but to the great damage of the Court, makes it the object of the sort of organized public pressure that political institutions in a democracy ought to receive.

Justice O'Connor's assertion, that a " 'fundamental rule of judicial restraint' " requires us to avoid reconsidering *Roe,* cannot be taken seriously. * * * We have not disposed of this case on some statutory or procedural ground, but have decided, and could not avoid deciding, whether the Missouri statute meets [constitutional requirements]. The only choice available is whether, in deciding [that] question, we should use *Roe* as the benchmark, or something else. What is involved, therefore, is not the rule of avoiding constitutional issues where possible, but the quite separate principle that we will not " 'formulate a rule of constitutional law broader than is required by the precise facts to which it is to be applied.' " The latter is a sound general principle, but one often departed from when good reason exists. * * * I have not identified with certainty the first instance of our deciding a case on broader constitutional grounds than absolutely necessary, but it is assuredly no later than *Marbury v. Madison,* where we held that mandamus could constitutionally issue against the Secretary of State, although that was unnecessary given our holding that the law authorizing issuance of the mandamus by this Court was unconstitutional.

[It] would be wrong, in any decision, to ignore the reality that our policy not to "formulate a rule of constitutional law broader than is required by the precise facts" has a frequently applied good-cause exception. But it seems particularly perverse to convert the policy into an absolute in the present case, in order to place beyond reach the inexpressibly "broader-than-was-required-by-the-precise-facts" structure established by *Roe.*

The real question, then, is whether there are valid reasons to go beyond the most stingy possible holding today. It seems to me there are not only valid but compelling ones. * * * Alone sufficient to justify a broad holding is the fact that our retaining control, through *Roe,* of what I believe to be, and many of our citizens recognize to be, a political issue, continuously distorts the public perception of the role of this Court. We can now look forward to at least another Term with carts full of mail from the public, and streets full of demonstrators, urging us—their unelected and life-tenured judges who have been awarded those extraordinary, undemocratic characteristics precisely in order that we might follow the law despite the popular will—to follow the popular will. Indeed, I expect we can look forward to even more of that than before, given our indecisive decision today. And if these reasons for taking the unexceptional course of reaching a broader holding are not enough, then consider the nature of the constitutional question we avoid: In most cases, we do no harm by not speaking more broadly than the decision requires. Anyone affected by the conduct that the avoided holding would have prohibited will be able to challenge it himself, and have his day in court to make the argument. Not so with respect to the harm that many States believed, pre-*Roe,* and many may continue to believe, is caused by largely unrestricted abortion. That will continue to occur if the States have the constitutional power to prohibit it, and would do so, but we skillfully avoid telling them so. Perhaps those abortions cannot constitutionally be proscribed. That is surely an arguable question, the question that reconsideration of *Roe* entails. But what is not at all arguable, it seems to me, is that we should decide now and not insist that we be run into a corner before we grudgingly yield up our judgment. The only sound reason for the latter course is to prevent a change in the law—but to think that desirable begs the question to be decided.

It was an arguable question today whether § 188.029 of the Missouri law contravened this Court's understanding of *Roe,** and I would have examined *Roe*

* That question, compared with the question whether we should reconsider and reverse *Roe,* is hardly worth a footnote, but I think Justice O'Connor answers that incorrectly as well. In *Roe* we said that "the physician [has the right] to administer medical treatment according to his professional judgment up to the points where important state interests provide compelling justifications for intervention." We have subsequently made clear that it is also a matter of medical judgment when viability (one of those points) is reached. "The time when viability is achieved may vary with each pregnancy, and the determination of whether a particular fetus is viable is, and must be, a matter for the judgment of the responsible attending physician." *Danforth.* Section 188.029 conflicts with the purpose and hence the fair import of this principle because it will sometimes require a physician to perform tests that he would not otherwise have performed to determine whether a fetus is viable. It is therefore a legislative imposition on the judgment of the physician, and one that increases the cost of an abortion.

Justice O'Connor would nevertheless uphold the law because it "does not impose an undue burden on a woman's abortion decision." This conclusion is supported by the observation that the required tests impose only a marginal cost on the abortion procedure, far less of an increase than the cost-doubling hosrather than examining the contravention. Given the Court's newly contracted abstemiousness, what will it take, one must wonder, to permit us to reach that fundamental question? The result of our vote today is that we will not reconsider that prior opinion, even if most of the Justices think it is wrong, unless we have before us a statute that in fact contradicts it—and even then (under our newly discovered "no-broader-than-necessary" requirement) only minor problematical aspects of *Roe* will be reconsidered, unless one expects State legislatures to adopt provisions whose compliance with *Roe* cannot even be argued with a straight face. It thus appears that the mansion of constitutionalize abortion-law, constructed overnight in *Roe v. Wade,* must be disassembled door-jamb by door-jamb, and never entirely brought down, no matter how wrong it may be.

Of the four courses we might have chosen today—to reaffirm *Roe,* to overrule it explicitly, to overrule it sub silentio, or to avoid the question—the last is the least responsible. On the question of the constitutionality of § 188.029, I concur in the judgment of the Court and strongly dissent from the manner in which it has been reached.

JUSTICE BLACKMUN, with whom JUSTICE BRENNAN and JUSTICE MARSHALL join, concurring in part and dissenting in part.

Today, *Roe v. Wade,* and the fundamental constitutional right of women to decide whether to terminate a pregnancy, survive but are not secure. Although the Court extricates itself from this case without making a single, even incremental, change in the law of abortion, the plurality and Justice Scalia would overrule *Roe* (the first silently, the other explicitly) and would return to the States virtually unfettered authority to control the quintessentially intimate, personal, and life-directing decision whether to carry a fetus to term. Although today, no less than yesterday, the Constitution and the decisions of this Court prohibit a State from enacting laws that inhibit women from the meaningful exercise of that right, a plurality of this Court implicitly invites every state legislature to enact more and more restrictive abortion regulations in order to provoke more and more test cases, in the hope that sometime down the line the Court will return the law of procreative freedom to the severe limitations that generally prevailed in this country before January 22, 1973. Never in my memory has a plurality announced a judgment of this Court that so foments disregard for the law and for our standing decisions.

Nor in my memory has a plurality gone about its business in such a deceptive fashion. At every level of its review, from its effort to read the real meaning out of the Missouri statute, to its intended evisceration of precedents

pitalization requirement invalidated in *Akron.* The fact that the challenged regulation is less costly than what we struck down in *Akron* tells us only that we cannot decide the present case on the basis of that earlier decision. It does not tell us whether the present requirement is an "undue burden," and I know of no basis for determining that this particular burden (or any other for that matter) is "due." One could with equal justification conclude that it is not. To avoid the question of *Roe* 's validity, with the attendant costs that this will have for the Court and for the principles of self-governance, on the basis of a standard that offers "no guide but the Court's own discretion," merely adds to the irrationality of what we do today.

Similarly irrational is the new concept that Justice O'Connor introduces into the law in order to achieve her result, the notion of a State's "interest in potential life when viability is possible." Since "viability" means the mere *possibility* (not the certainty) of survivability outside the womb, "possible viability" must mean the possibility of a possibility of survivability outside the womb. Perhaps our next opinion will expand the third trimester into the second even further, by approving state action designed to take account of "the chance of possible viability."

and its deafening silence about the constitutional protections that it would jettison, the plurality obscures the portent of its analysis. With feigned restraint, the plurality announces that its analysis leaves *Roe* "undisturbed," albeit "modif[ied] and narrow[ed]." But this disclaimer is totally meaningless. The plurality opinion is filled with winks, and nods, and knowing glances to those who would do away with *Roe* explicitly, but turns a stone face to anyone in search of what the plurality conceives as the scope of a woman's right under the Due Process Clause to terminate a pregnancy free from the coercive and brooding influence of the State. The simple truth is that *Roe* would not survive the plurality's analysis, and that the plurality provides no substitute for *Roe's* protective umbrella.

I fear for the future. I fear for the liberty and equality of the millions of women who have lived and come of age in the 16 years since *Roe* was decided. I fear for the integrity of, and public esteem for, this Court.

I dissent.

I. The plurality parades through the four challenged sections of the Missouri statute seriatim. I shall not do this, but shall relegate most of my comments as to those sections to the margin.[1] Although I disagree with the

1. Contrary to the plurality (with whom Justice O'Connor on this point joins), I do not see how the preamble, § 1.205, realistically may be construed as "abortion-neutral." It declares that "[t]he life of each human being begins at conception" and that "[u]nborn children have protectable interests in life, health, and well-being." By the preamble's specific terms, these declarations apply to all of Missouri's laws which, in turn, are to be interpreted to protect the rights of the unborn to the fullest extent possible under the Constitution of the United States and the decisions of this Court. As the Court of Appeals concluded, the Missouri Legislature "intended its abortion regulations to be understood against the backdrop of its theory of life." I note the Solicitor General's acknowledgment that this backdrop places "a burden of uncertain scope on the performance of abortion by supplying a general principle that would fill in whatever interstices may be present in existing abortion precedents."

[The] plurality (again joined by Justice O'Connor) upholds §§ 188.210 and .215 on the ground that the constitutionality of these provisions follows from our holdings in *Maher, Poelker* and *Harris v. McRae.* There were strong dissents in all those cases.

Whatever one may think of *Maher, Poelker,* and *Harris,* however, they most certainly do not control this case, where the State not only has withdrawn from the business of abortion, but has taken affirmative steps to assure that abortions are not performed by *private* physicians in *private* institutions. Specifically, by defining "public facility" as "any public institution, public facility, public equipment, or any physical asset owned, leased, or controlled by this state or any agency or political subdivision thereof," § 188.200, the Missouri statute prohibits the performance of abortions in institutions that in all pertinent respects are private, yet are located on property owned, leased, or controlled by the government. Thus, under the statute, no abortion may be performed at Truman Medical Center in Kansas City—where, in 1985, 97 percent of all Missouri hospital abortions at 16 weeks or later were performed—even though the Center is a private hospital, staffed primarily by private doctors, and administered by a private corporation: the Center is located on ground leased from a political subdivision of the State.

The sweeping scope of Missouri's "public facility" provision sharply distinguishes this case from *Maher, Poelker,* and *Harris.* * * * Missouri's public facility ban, by contrast, goes far beyond merely offering incentives in favor of childbirth (as in *Maher* and *Harris*), or a straightforward disassociation of state-owned institutions and personnel from abortion services (as in *Poelker*). Here, by defining as "public" every health-care institution with some connection to the State, no matter how attenuated, Missouri has brought to bear the full force of its economic power and control over essential facilities to discourage its citizens from exercising their constitutional rights, even where the State itself could never be understood as authorizing, supporting, or having any other positive association with the performance of an abortion. See R. Dworkin, *The Great Abortion Case,* New York Review of Books, June 29, 1989, p. 49. * * *

Indeed, Justice O'Connor appears to recognize the constitutional difficulties presented by Missouri's "public facilities" ban, and rejects respondents' "facial" challenge to the provisions on the ground that a facial chalplurality's consideration of §§ 1.205, 188.210, and 188.215, and am especially disturbed by its misapplication of our past decisions in upholding Missouri's ban on the performance of abortions at "public facilities," the plurality's discussion of these provisions is merely prologue to its consideration of the statute's viability-testing requirement, § 188.029—the only section of the Missouri statute that the plurality construes as implicating *Roe* itself. There, tucked away at the end of its opinion, the plurality suggests a radical reversal of the law of abortion; and there, primarily, I direct my attention.

In the plurality's view, the viability-testing provision imposes a burden on second-trimester abortions as a way of furthering the State's interest in protecting the potential life of the fetus. Since under the *Roe* framework, the State may not fully regulate abortion in the interest of potential life (as opposed to maternal health) until the third trimester, the plurality finds it necessary, in order to save the Missouri testing provision, to throw out *Roe's* trimester framework. In flat contradiction to *Roe,* the plurality concludes that the State's interest in potential life is compelling before viability, and upholds the testing provision because it "permissibly furthers" that state interest.

A. At the outset, I note that in its haste to limit abortion rights, the plurality compounds the errors of its analysis by needlessly reaching out to address constitutional questions that are not actually presented. The conflict between § 188.029 and *Roe's* trimester framework, which purportedly drives the plurality to reconsider our past decisions, is a contrived conflict: the product of an aggressive misreading of the viability-testing requirement and a needlessly wooden application of the *Roe* framework.

The plurality's reading of § 188.029 (also joined by Justice O'Connor) is irreconcilable with the plain language of the statute and is in derogation of this Court's settled view that " 'district courts and courts of appeals are better schooled in and more able to interpret the laws of their respective States.' " [The] statute's plain language requires the physician to undertake whatever tests are necessary to determine gestational age, weight, and lung maturity, regardless of whether these tests are necessary to a finding of viability, and regardless of whether the tests subject the pregnant woman or the fetus to additional health risks or add substantially to the cost of an abortion.[2]

Had the plurality read the statute as written, it would have had no cause to reconsider the *Roe* framework. As properly construed, the viability-testing provision does not pass constitutional muster under even a rational-basis standard, the least restrictive level of review applied by this Court. By mandating tests to determine fetal weight and lung maturity for every fetus thought to be more than 20 weeks gestational age, the statute requires physicians to undertake procedures, such as amniocentesis, that, in the situation presented, have no medical justification, impose significant additional health risks on both the pregnant woman and the fetus, and bear no rational relation to the State's interest in protecting fetal life. As written, § 188.029 is an arbitrary imposition of discomfort, risk, and expense, furthering no discernible interest except to make the procurement of an abortion as arduous and difficult as possible. Thus, were it not for the plurality's tortured effort to avoid the plain import of

lenge cannot succeed where, as here, at least some applications of the challenged law are constitutional. While I disagree with this approach, Justice O'Connor's writing explicitly leaves open the possibility that some applications of the "public facilities" ban may be unconstitutional, regardless of *Maher, Poelker,* and *Harris.* * * *

2. I consider irrefutable Justice Stevens' discussion of this interpretive point.

§ 188.029, it could have struck down the testing provision as patently irrational irrespective of the *Roe* framework.

The plurality eschews this straightforward resolution, in the hope of precipitating a constitutional crisis. Far from avoiding constitutional difficulty, the plurality attempts to engineer a dramatic retrenchment in our jurisprudence by exaggerating the conflict between its untenable construction of § 188.029 and the *Roe* trimester framework.

No one contests that under the *Roe* framework the State, in order to promote its interest in potential human life, may regulate and even proscribe non-therapeutic abortions once the fetus becomes viable. If, as the plurality appears to hold, the testing provision simply requires a physician to use appropriate and medically sound tests to determine whether the fetus is actually viable when the estimated gestational age is greater than 20 weeks (and therefore within what the District Court found to be the margin of error for viability), then I see little or no conflict with *Roe.* Nothing in *Roe,* or any of its progeny, holds that a State may not effectuate its compelling interest in the potential life of a viable fetus by seeking to ensure that no viable fetus is mistakenly aborted because of the inherent lack of precision in estimates of gestational age. [The] testing provision, as construed by the plurality is consistent with the *Roe* framework and could be upheld effortlessly under current doctrine.

* * *

B. Having set up the conflict between § 188.029 and the *Roe* trimester framework, the plurality summarily discards *Roe's* analytic core as " 'unsound in principle and unworkable in practice.' " This is so, the plurality claims, because the key elements of the framework do not appear in the text of the Constitution, because the framework more closely resembles a regulatory code than a body of constitutional doctrine, and because under the framework the State's interest in potential human life is considered compelling only after viability, when, in fact, that interest is equally compelling throughout pregnancy.

1. [The] plurality opinion is far more remarkable for the arguments that it does not advance than for those that it does. The plurality does not even mention, must less join, the true jurisprudential debate underlying this case: whether the Constitution includes an "unenumerated" general right to privacy as recognized in many of our decisions, most notably *Griswold* and *Roe,* and, more specifically, whether and to what extent such a right to privacy extends to matters of childbearing and family life, including abortion.[7] These are ques-

7. The plurality, ignoring all of the aforementioned cases except *Griswold,* responds that this case does not require consideration of the "great issues" underlying this case because *Griswold,* "unlike *Roe,* did not purport to adopt a whole framework [to] govern the cases in which the asserted liberty interest would apply." This distinction is highly ironic. [*Roe*] adopted the framework of which the plurality complains as a mechanism necessary to give effect both to the constitutional rights of the pregnant woman and to the State's significant interests in maternal health and potential life. Concededly, *Griswold* does not adopt a framework for determining the permissible scope of state regulation of contraception. The reason is simple: in *Griswold* (and *Eisenstadt*), the Court held that the challenged statute, regulating the use of medically safe contraception, did not properly serve *any* significant state interest. Accordingly, the Court had no occasion to fashion a framework to accommodate a State's interests in regulating contraception. Surely, the plurality is not suggesting that it would find *Roe* unobjectionable if the Court had forgone the framework and, as in the contraception decisions, had left the State with little or no regulatory authority. The plurality's focus on the framework is merely an excuse for avoiding the real issues embedded in this case and a mask for its hostility to the constitutional rights that *Roe* recognized.

tions of unsurpassed significance in this Court's interpretation of the Constitution, and mark the battleground upon which this case was fought. [On] these grounds, abandoned by the plurality, the Court should decide this case.

But rather than arguing that the text of the Constitution makes no mention of the right to privacy, the plurality complains that the critical elements of the *Roe* framework—trimesters and viability—do not appear in the Constitution and are, therefore, somehow inconsistent with a Constitution cast in general terms. Were this a true concern, we would have to abandon most of our constitutional jurisprudence. [The] Constitution makes no mention, for example, of the First Amendment's "actual malice" standard for proving certain libels or of the standard for determining when speech is obscene. Similarly, the Constitution makes no mention of the rational-basis test, or the specific verbal formulations of intermediate and strict scrutiny by which this Court evaluates claims under the Equal Protection Clause. The reason is simple. Like the *Roe* framework, these tests or standards are not, and do not purport to be, rights protected by the Constitution. Rather, they are judge-made methods for evaluating and measuring the strength and scope of constitutional rights or for balancing the constitutional rights of individuals against the competing interests of government.

With respect to the *Roe* framework, the general constitutional principle, indeed the fundamental constitutional right, for which it was developed is the right to privacy, a species of "liberty" protected by the Due Process Clause, which under our past decisions safeguards the right of women to exercise some control over their own role in procreation. [The] trimester framework simply defines and limits that right to privacy in the abortion context to accommodate, not destroy, a State's legitimate interest in protecting the health of pregnant women and in preserving potential human life. Fashioning such accommodations between individual rights and the legitimate interests of government, establishing benchmarks and standards with which to evaluate the competing claims of individuals and government, lies at the very heart of constitutional adjudication. To the extent that the trimester framework is useful in this enterprise, it is not only consistent with constitutional interpretation, but necessary to the wise and just exercise of this Court's paramount authority to define the scope of constitutional rights.

2. The plurality next alleges that the result of the trimester framework has "been a web of legal rules that have become increasingly intricate, resembling a code of regulations rather than a body of constitutional doctrine." Again, if this were a true and genuine concern, we would have to abandon vast areas of our constitutional jurisprudence. Are [the distinctions that have been drawn in the abortion area] any finer, or more "regulatory," than the distinctions we have often drawn in our First Amendment jurisprudence, where, for example, we have held that a "release time" program permitting public-school students to leave school grounds during school hours to receive religious instruction does not violate the Establishment Clause, even though a release-time program permitting religious instruction on school grounds does violate the Clause? Our Fourth Amendment jurisprudence recognizes factual distinctions no less intricate. * * *

3. Finally, the plurality asserts that the trimester framework cannot stand because the State's interest in potential life is compelling throughout pregnancy, not merely after viability. The opinion contains not one word of rationale for its view of the State's interest. This "it-is-so-because-we-say-so" jurisprudence con-

stitutes nothing other than an attempted exercise of brute force; reason, much less persuasion, has no place.

In answering the plurality's claim that the State's interest in the fetus is uniform and compelling throughout pregnancy, I cannot improve upon what Justice Stevens has written [quoting at length from Justice Stevens' concurring opinion in *Thornburgh,* from line 11, p. 207 of this Casebook to line 32, p. 207].

For my own part, I remain convinced, as six other Members of this Court 16 years ago were convinced, that the *Roe* framework, and the viability standard in particular, fairly, sensibly, and effectively functions to safeguard the constitutional liberties of pregnant women while recognizing and accommodating the State's interest in potential human life. The viability line reflects the biological facts and truths of fetal development; it marks that threshold moment prior to which a fetus cannot survive separate from the woman and cannot reasonably and objectively be regarded as a subject of rights or interests distinct from, or paramount to, those of the pregnant woman. At the same time, the viability standard takes account of the undeniable fact that as the fetus evolves into its postnatal form, and as it loses its dependence on the uterine environment, the State's interest in the fetus' potential human life, and in fostering a regard for human life in general, becomes compelling. As a practical matter, because viability follows "quickening"—the point at which a woman feels movement in her womb—and because viability occurs no earlier than 23 weeks gestational age, it establishes an easily applicable standard for regulating abortion while providing a pregnant woman ample time to exercise her fundamental right with her responsible physician to terminate her pregnancy.[9] [The] plurality today advances not one reasonable argument as to why our judgment in [*Roe*] was wrong and should be abandoned.

C. Having contrived an opportunity to reconsider the *Roe* framework, and then having discarded that framework, the plurality finds the testing provision unobjectionable because it "permissibly furthers the State's interest in protecting potential human life." This newly minted standard is circular and totally meaningless. Whether a challenged abortion regulation "permissibly furthers" a legitimate state interest is the *question* that courts must answer in abortion cases, not the standard for courts to apply. In keeping with the rest of its opinion, the plurality makes no attempt to explain or to justify its new standard, either in the abstract or as applied in this case. Nor could it. The "permissibly furthers" standard has no independent meaning, and consists of nothing other than what a majority of this Court may believe at any given moment in any given case. The plurality's novel test appears to be nothing more than a dressed-up version of rational-basis review, this Court's most lenient level of scrutiny. One thing is clear, however: were the plurality's "permissibly fur-

9. Notably, neither the plurality nor Justice O'Connor advance the now-familiar catchphrase criticism of the *Roe* framework that because the point of viability will recede with advances in medical technology, *Roe* "is clearly on a collision course with itself." This critique has no medical foundation. As the medical literature and the amicus briefs filed in this case conclusively demonstrate, "there is an 'anatomic threshold' for fetal viability of about 23–24 weeks gestation." Prior to that time, the crucial organs are not sufficiently mature to provide the mutually sustaining functions that are prerequisite to extrauterine survival, or viability. Moreover, "no technology exists to bridge the development gap between the three-day embryo culture and the 24th week of gestation." Nor does the medical community believe that the development of any such technology is possible in the foreseeable future. In other words, the threshold of fetal viability is, and will remain, no different from what it was at the time *Roe* was decided. Predictions to the contrary are pure science fiction. See Brief for A Group of American Law Professors as Amici Curiae 23–25.

thers" standard adopted by the Court, for all practical purposes, *Roe* would be overruled.

The "permissibly furthers" standard completely disregards the irreducible minimum of *Roe:* the Court's recognition that a woman has a limited fundamental constitutional right to decide whether to terminate a pregnancy. That right receives no meaningful recognition in the plurality's written opinion. Since, in the plurality's view, the State's interest in potential life is compelling as of the moment of conception, and is therefore served only if abortion is abolished, every hindrance to a woman's ability to obtain an abortion must be "permissible." Indeed, the more severe the hindrance, the more effectively (and permissibly) the State's interest would be furthered. A tax on abortions or a criminal prohibition would both satisfy the plurality's standard. So, for that matter, would a requirement that a pregnant woman memorize and recite today's plurality opinion before seeking an abortion.

The plurality pretends that *Roe* survives, explaining that the facts of this case differ from those in *Roe:* here, Missouri has chosen to assert its interest in potential life only at the point of viability, whereas, in *Roe,* Texas had asserted that interest from the point of conception, criminalizing all abortions, except where the life of the mother was at stake. This, of course, is a distinction without a difference. The plurality repudiates every principle for which *Roe* stands; in good conscience, it cannot possibly believe that *Roe* lies "undisturbed" merely because this case does not call upon the Court to reconsider the Texas statute, or one like it. If the Constitution permits a State to enact any statute that reasonably furthers its interest in potential life, and if that interest arises as of conception, why would the Texas statute fail to pass muster? One suspects that the plurality agrees. It is impossible to read the plurality opinion and especially its final paragraph, without recognizing its implicit invitation to every State to enact more and more restrictive abortion laws, and to assert their interest in potential life as of the moment of conception. All these laws will satisfy the plurality's non-scrutiny, until sometime, a new regime of old dissenters and new appointees will declare what the plurality intends: that *Roe* is no longer good law.[11]

D. Thus, "not with a bang, but a whimper," the plurality discards a landmark case of the last generation, and casts into darkness the hopes and visions of every woman in this country who had come to believe that the Constitution guaranteed her the right to exercise some control over her unique

11. The plurality claims that its treatment of *Roe,* and a woman's right to decide whether to terminate a pregnancy, "hold[s] true the balance between that which the Constitution puts beyond the reach of the democratic process and that which it does not." This is unadulterated nonsense. The plurality's balance matches a lead weight (the State's allegedly compelling interest in fetal life as of the moment of conception) against a feather (a "liberty interest" of the pregnant woman that the plurality barely mentions, much less describes). The plurality's balance—no balance at all—places nothing, or virtually nothing, beyond the reach of the democratic process.

Justice Scalia candidly argues that this is all for the best. I cannot agree. "The very purpose of a Bill of Rights was to withdraw certain subjects from the vicissitudes of political controversy, to place them beyond the reach of majorities and officials and to establish them as legal principles to be applied by the Courts. * * *." *West Virginia Board of Education v. Barnette,* 319 U.S. 624, 638, 63 S.Ct. 1178, 87 L.Ed. 1628 (1943). In a Nation that cherishes liberty, the ability of a woman to control the biological operation of her body and to determine with her responsible physician whether or not to carry a fetus to term, must fall within that limited sphere of individual autonomy that lies beyond the will or the power of any transient majority. This Court stands as the ultimate guarantor of that zone of privacy, regardless of the bitter disputes to which our decisions may give rise. In *Roe,* and our numerous cases reaffirming *Roe,* we did no more than discharge our constitutional duty.

ability to bear children. The plurality does so either oblivious or insensitive to the fact that millions of women, and their families, have ordered their lives around the right to reproductive choice, and that this right has become vital to the full participation of women in the economic and political walks of American life. [The] plurality would clear the way again for the State to conscript a woman's body and to force upon her a "distressful life and future." *Roe.*

The result, as we know from experience, would be that every year hundreds of thousands of women, in desperation, would defy the law, and place their health and safety in the unclean and unsympathetic hands of back-alley abortionists, or they would attempt to perform abortions upon themselves, with disastrous results. Every year, many women, especially poor and minority women, would die or suffer debilitating physical trauma, all in the name of enforced morality or religious dictates or lack of compassion, as it may be.

Of the aspirations and settled understandings of American women, of the inevitable and brutal consequences of what it is doing, the tough-approach plurality utters not a word. This silence is callous. It is also profoundly destructive of this Court as an institution. To overturn a constitutional decision is a rare and grave undertaking. To overturn a constitutional decision that secured a fundamental personal liberty to millions of persons would be unprecedented in our 200 years of constitutional history. Although the doctrine of *stare decisis* applies with somewhat diminished force in constitutional cases generally, even in ordinary constitutional cases "any departure from *stare decisis* demands special justification." [This] requirement of justification applies with unique force where, as here, the Court's abrogation of precedent would destroy people's firm belief, based on past decisions of this Court, that they possess an unabridgeable right to undertake certain conduct.

[The] doctrine of *stare decisis* "permits society to presume that bedrock principles are founded in the law rather than in the proclivities of individuals, and thereby contributes to the integrity of our constitutional system of government, both in appearance and in fact." Today's decision involves the most politically divisive domestic legal issue of our time. By refusing to explain or to justify its proposed revolutionary revision in the law of abortion, and by refusing to abide not only by our precedents, but also by our canons for reconsidering those precedents, the plurality invites charges of cowardice and illegitimacy to our door. I cannot say that these would be undeserved.

II. For today, at least, the law of abortion stands undisturbed. For today, the women of this Nation still retain the liberty to control their destinies. But the signs are evident and very ominous, and a chill wind blows. * * *

JUSTICE STEVENS, concurring in part and dissenting in part.

Having joined Part II–C of the Court's opinion, I shall not comment on § 188.205 of the Missouri statute. With respect to the challenged portions of §§ 188.210 and 188.215, I agree with Justice Blackmun that the record identifies a sufficient number of unconstitutional applications to support the Court of Appeals' judgment invalidating those provisions. The reasons why I would also affirm that court's invalidation of § 188.029, the viability testing provision, and § 1.205.1(1), (2) of the preamble, require separate explanation.

I. It seems to me that in Part II–D of its opinion, the plurality strains to place a construction on § 188.029 that enables it to conclude, "[W]e would modify and narrow *Roe* and succeeding cases." That statement is ill-advised because there is no need to modify even slightly the holdings of prior cases in er to uphold § 188.029. For the most plausible nonliteral construction, as 1 Justice Blackmun [and] Justice O'Connor have demonstrated, is constitual and entirely consistent with our precedents.

* * *

II. The Missouri statute defines "conception" as "the fertilization of the ovum of a female by a sperm of a male," even though standard medical texts equate "conception" with implantation in the uterus, occurring about six days after fertilization. Missouri's declaration therefore implies regulation not only of previability abortions, but also of common forms of contraception such as the IUD and the morning-after pill.[7] Because the preamble, read in context, threatens serious encroachments upon the liberty of the pregnant woman and the health professional, I am persuaded that these plaintiffs, appellees before us, have standing to challenge its constitutionality.

To the extent that the Missouri statute interferes with contraceptive choices, I have no doubt that it is unconstitutional under the Court's holdings in *Griswold, Eisenstadt* and *Carey* * * *.

[Justice Stevens then quotes at length from Justice Stewart's concurring opinion in *Roe,* where Justice Stewart viewed *Griswold* as one of a long line of cases "decided under the doctrine of substantive due process," and "accept[ed] it as such," and concluded that "the Court today is correct in holding that the right asserted by Jane Roe is embraced within the personal liberty protected by the Due Process Clause of the Fourteenth Amendment."][8]

One might argue that the *Griswold* holding applies to devices "preventing conception"—that is, fertilization—but not to those preventing implantation, and therefore, that *Griswold* does not protect a woman's choice to use an IUD or take a morning-after pill. There is unquestionably a theological basis for such an argument,[9] just as there was unquestionably a theological basis for the Connecticut statute that the Court invalidated in *Griswold.* Our jurisprudence, however, has consistently required a secular basis for valid legislation. Because I am not aware of any secular basis for differentiating between contraceptive procedures that are effective immediately before and those that are effective immediately after fertilization, I believe it inescapably follows that the preamble to the Missouri statute is invalid under *Griswold* and its progeny.

Indeed, I am persuaded that the absence of any secular purpose for the legislative declarations that life begins at conception and that conception occurs at fertilization makes the relevant portion of the preamble invalid under the Establishment Clause of the First Amendment to the Federal Constitution. This conclusion does not, and could not, rest on the fact that the statement happens to coincide with the tenets of certain religions or on the fact that the legislators who voted to enact it may have been motivated by religious considerations.

7. An intrauterine device, commonly called an IUD, "works primarily by preventing a fertilized egg from implanting." Other contraceptive methods that may prevent implantation include "morning-after pills," high-dose estrogen pills taken after intercourse, particularly in cases of rape, ARHP Brief 33, and the French RU 486, a pill that works "during the indeterminate period between contraception and abortion." Low-level estrogen "combined" pills—a version of the ordinary, daily ingested birth control pill—also may prevent the fertilized egg from reaching the uterine wall and implanting.

8. The contrast between Justice Stewart's careful explication that our abortion precedent flowed naturally from a stream of substantive due process cases and Justice Scalia's notion that our abortion law was "constructed overnight in *Roe v. Wade*" is remarkable.

9. Several *amici* state that the "sanctity of human life from conception and opposition to abortion are, in fact, sincere and deeply held religious beliefs" * * *.

Rather, it rests on the fact that the preamble, an unequivocal endorsement of a religious tenet of some but by no means all Christian faiths, serves no identifiable secular purpose. That fact alone compels a conclusion that the statute violates the Establishment Clause.[12]

My concern can best be explained by reference to the position on this issue that was endorsed by St. Thomas Aquinas and widely accepted by the leaders of the Roman Catholic Church for many years [the view that the soul was not present until the formation of the fetus 40 or 80 days after conception, for males and females respectively].

If the views of St. Thomas were held as widely today as they were in the Middle Ages, and if a state legislature were to enact a statute prefaced with a "finding" that female life begins 80 days after conception and male life begins 40 days after conception, I have no doubt that this Court would promptly conclude that such an endorsement of a particular religious tenent is violative of the Establishment Clause.

In my opinion the difference between that hypothetical statute and Missouri's preamble reflects nothing more than a difference in theological doctrine. The preamble to the Missouri statute endorses the theological position that there is the same secular interest in preserving the life of a fetus during the first 40 or 80 days of pregnancy as there is after viability—indeed, after the time when the fetus has become a "person" with legal rights protected by the Constitution.[13] To sustain that position as a matter of law, I believe Missouri has the burden of identifying the secular interests that differentiate the first 40 days of pregnancy from the period immediately before or after fertilization when, as *Griswold* and related cases establish, the Constitution allows the use of contraceptive procedures to prevent potential life from developing into full personhood. Focusing our attention on the first several weeks of pregnancy is especially appropriate because that is the period when the vast majority of abortions are actually performed.

As a secular matter, there is an obvious difference between the state interest in protecting the freshly fertilized egg and the state interest in protecting a 9–month–gestated, fully sentient fetus on the eve of birth. There can be no interest in protecting the newly fertilized egg from physical pain or mental anguish, because the capacity for such suffering does not yet exist; respecting a developed fetus, however, that interest is valid. In fact, if one prescinds the theological concept of ensoulment—or one accepts St. Thomas Aquinas' view that ensoulment does not occur for at least 40 days, a State has no greater secular interest in protecting the potential life of an embryo that is still "seed" than in protecting the potential life of a sperm or an unfertilized ovum.

[In] my opinion the preamble to the Missouri statute is unconstitutional for two reasons. To the extent that it has substantive impact on the freedom to use contraceptive procedures, it is inconsistent with the central holding in *Griswold.*

12. Pointing to the lack of consensus about life's onset among experts in medicine, philosophy, and theology, the *Roe* Court established that the Constitution does not permit a State to adopt a theory of life that overrides a pregnant woman's rights. [The] constitutional violation is doubly grave if, as here, the only basis for the State's "finding" is nonsecular.

13. No Member of this Court has ever questioned the holding in *Roe* that a fetus is not a "person" within the meaning of the Fourteenth Amendment. Even the dissenters in *Roe* implicitly endorsed that holding by arguing that state legislatures should decide whether to prohibit or to authorize abortions. [By] characterizing the basic question as "a political issue," Justice Scalia likewise implicitly accepts this holding.

To the extent that it merely makes "legislative findings without operative effect," as the State argues, it violates the Establishment Clause of the First Amendment. Contrary to the theological "finding" of the Missouri Legislature, a woman's constitutionally protected liberty encompasses the right to act on her own belief that—to paraphrase St. Thomas Aquinas—until a seed has acquired the powers of sensation and movement, the life of a human being has not yet begun.

Notes and Questions

1. *The significance of Webster.* Consider Estrich & Sullivan, *Abortion Politics: Writing for an Audience of One,* 138 U.Pa.L.Rev. 119–20 (1989): "As the Court construed them, *Webster*'s three particular issues fit well within previous regulations upheld by the Court. The majority was able to avoid any ruling at all on Missouri's declaration that life begins at conception by concluding that the passage merely expressed a value judgment. Restrictions on using public facilities for abortion, particularly as narrowly although perhaps inaccurately framed by the state's Attorney General, fit within the Court's precedents upholding the exclusion of public support for abortion. Finally, the state's seeming viability testing requirement at twenty weeks or more became, with a little interpretive twisting, no more than a recommendation that doctors perform such tests where medically appropriate.[a]

"Of course, if little was decided in *Webster,* a good deal was nonetheless said. The Chief Justice, writing for three members of the Court, made plain that he was ready to jettison [the] trimester approach of *Roe,* presumably finding the state's interest in potential life as compelling in the first month as the last, and leaving it to the state to balance its own interest against the woman's, subject only to some rationality review. The genius of the approach, if you can call it that, is that it effectively overrules *Roe* without ever even suggesting that a woman lacks a privacy or autonomy interest in her own body."

2. *The state's interest in protecting potential human life before viability.* "There is," observe Professors Estrich and Sullivan, id. at 146–47, "only one way to protect potential life before a fetus has the potential to survive outside the womb: forbid or discourage abortion. After viability, there are surely other ways abortion regulations can preserve an interest in potential life. For example, the state may require two doctors' presence or forbid saline procedures in late abortions to enhance survival if an attempted abortion turns into a live birth. Imposing any 'undue burdens,' or indeed any burdens at all, on a woman's right *prior* to viability in the name of preserving life, though, is to say that a woman has a right and then to take it away. By definition, her right is to control her bodily autonomy *even at the expense of potential human life.*

a. But see Tribe, *The Curvature of Constitutional Space: What Lawyers Can Learn From Modern Physics,* 103 Harv.L.Rev. 1, 16 (1989): "In *Webster,* the Supreme Court went further than it had in the abortion funding cases: *Webster* upheld a ban on *privately* financed abortions in a public facility, under a statute that defined the concept of 'public facility' broadly enough to include essentially the only hospital in a large part of the state of Missouri—a hospital that was privately owned but happened to be located in a space rented from the government."

See also Olsen, *Unraveling Compromise,* 103 Harv.L.Rev. 105, 116 (1989): "In a sense, *Webster* turns [*McRae*] upside down. [*McRae*] began from the idea that the right to abortion was a private right and concluded that deprivation of public funding was constitutional; the *Webster* plurality and Justice O'Connor began from the premise that deprivation of funding is constitutional to conclude that less burdensome restrictions on abortion—even burdens not related to funding, such as viability testing—are constitutional as well."

"Every abortion regulation, including the absolute prohibition struck down in *Roe,* can be defended by its supporters as furthering the state's interest in preserving potential human life. To acknowledge that the state interest does not itself magically 'appear' at the point of viability may comport with common sense, but that is not, after all, a fair statement of *Roe* 's holding. The question *Roe* asked and answered, here as in the case of a state's interest in maternal health, was not whether the state might have any valid interest cognizable in any setting, but rather when, if at all, the Court could consider the state interest sufficiently 'compelling' to override a woman's right to have an abortion. It was *that* question to which viability provided the answer."

3. *Compelling abortions v. prohibiting them.* Consider Dellinger & Sperling, *Abortion and the Supreme Court: The Retreat from Roe v. Wade,* 138 U.Pa. L.Rev. 83, 95 (1989): "Former Solicitor General Fried argued in *Webster* that even if it held that abortion choice is not a fundamental liberty, the Court could still strike down a compulsory abortion law as an unconstitutional seizure. The state would be 'violently taking hands on, laying hands on a woman and submitting her to an operation.' Fried's attempt to distinguish between forcing an abortion and forcing childbirth * * * is wholly inadequate. * * *

"Obviously, it would not be necessary to physically seize a woman to enforce a compulsory abortion law. The state could punish failure to undergo an abortion by after-the-fact civil or criminal fines, jail sentences, or other sanctions, including the punitive withholding of governmental benefits. In each case, the government would override a woman's decision about how to treat her pregnancy. It is simply unclear where the strong 'substantive due process protection' Fried would invoke to prevent forced abortions would find its source if the Court overturned *Roe* * * * [b]

"Attempting to improve on Fried's answer to the compelled abortion question, Kenneth Starr, the new Solicitor General, revisited the issue in his brief in *Hodgson v. Minnesota* [discussed infra]. After arguing that 'it cannot reasonably be said that the right to abortion is fundamental,' the Solicitor General proceeded nonetheless to argue that there is a fundamental liberty interest in being free from compelled abortion. He wrote: 'By contrast, a state law *mandating* abortions would present a starkly different question. [Our] nation's history and traditions establish that a competent adult may generally refuse unwanted medical intrusion. This right [would] extend to an unwanted abortion.' [But a] competent adult's decision to have an abortion in the early weeks is clearly a decision to 'refuse unwanted medical intrusion.' Compelled childbirth is a major medical event and far more dangerous than aborting an early pregnancy. Moreover, a quarter of all pregnancies end with Cesarean section, a major medical procedure."

Consider, too, Tribe, fn. a supra, at 31–32: "[What various commentators have recognized] is the profoundly flawed character of the notion that there exists a natural, pre-political and pre-legal state of things—such as [the] 'natural'

b. See also Estrich & Sullivan, supra, at 127 & fn. 30: "[F]ormer Solicitor General Fried conceded that [if the state attempted to compel abortions rather than to restrict them], liberty principles, although unenumerated, would compel the strictest review. To be sure, as Mr. Fried suggested, restrictive abortion laws do not literally involve 'laying hands on a woman.' But this distinction should make no difference: the state would plainly infringe its citizens' bodily integrity whether its agents inflicted knife wounds or its laws forbade surgery or restricted blood transfusions in cases of private knifings. Likewise, a state would surely infringe reproductive freedom by compelling abortions even if it became technologically possible to do so without 'laying hands on a woman.'"

condition of a pregnancy continuing to its conclusion despite a woman's wish to end it—and that the process of making and interpreting law has no 'effect' on that 'natural' background. But in what sense *is* it 'natural' that a woman must continue to remain pregnant, even against her will, when there is a doctor willing to perform a surgical procedure that will terminate her pregnancy? When there is a pharmaceutical firm willing to produce RU–486, which will prevent the implantation of the embryo in the wall of her placenta?[c] If [continuing a pregnancy to its conclusion] seem[s] 'natural,' is it not only by virtue of an entire background of legal arrangements—including the licensing and regulations of physicians and the control of new drugs by the FDA? This means the transmutation from biology to destiny is mediated not by an inexorable order of nature, but by a set of prior legal observations that have changed the very universe being observed."

The *Webster* case, commented Tribe, *Abortion* at 24, "was and remains an open invitation to state legislators to see just how strictly they can regulate abortion without Justice O'Connor's finding the burden on the abortion right 'undue.'" At the time Professor Tribe made this remark Justice O'Connor had never found a restriction on the abortion right "unduly burdensome" and thus constitutionally defective. But shortly thereafter she did—in HODGSON v. MINNESOTA, ___ U.S. ___, 110 S.Ct. 2926, 111 L.Ed.2d 344 (1990).

In *Hodgson,* Justice O'Connor voted to invalidate a state statutory provision (subdivision 2) requiring *both* parents of an unemancipated minor to be notified 48 hours before she underwent an abortion, unless an immediate abortion was necessary to prevent her death or she declared she was a victim of parental abuse or neglect (in which event the appropriate authorities had to be notified). Stevens, J., wrote the majority opinion on this issue, joined by Brennan, Marshall and O'Connor, JJ. But another part of the same statute (subdivision 6)—a "judicial bypass" alternative—provided that if the two-parent notice requirement were to be judicially enjoined the same notice requirement will be effective unless the pregnant woman obtained a court order authorizing the abortion. Under the bypass provision, a court may authorize an abortion without parental notice upon finding that the minor is "mature" and capable of giving informed consent or, if immature, that an abortion without notification would be in her "best interests." A different 5–4 majority—Justice O'Connor and the four justices who would have sustained the two-parent notification requirement *without* a judicial bypass (Kennedy, J., joined by Rehnquist, C.J., and White and Scalia, JJ.,) (the Kennedy group)—voted to uphold the two-parent notice requirement *combined with* a bypass. Thus *Hodgson* produced two distinct majorities and in each instance Justice O'Connor provided the crucial vote. In addition, six members of the Court—Stevens and O'Connor, JJ., and the Kennedy group—concluded that requiring a minor to wait 48 hours after notifying a *single* parent of her intention to obtain an abortion would be constitutionally permissible.

JUSTICE STEVENS wrote the opinion of the Court with respect to the two-parent notification requirement unaccompanied by the judicial bypass procedure and delivered the judgment of the Court with respect to the 48–hour waiting period. Pointing to the many adverse effects of the two-parent notification

c. For the view that the government cannot keep the "French abortion pill," RU486, out of the United States indefinitely and that "[i]n the end, this new technology is likely to render early pregnancy abortion as much a nonissue as birth control is today," see Cole, *The End of the Abortion Debate,* 138 U.Pa.L. Rev. 217, 221, 223 (1989).

requirement, especially on both the minor and the custodial parent when the parents were divorced or separated, and maintaining that the requirement "does not reasonably further any legitimate interest," Justice Stevens concluded that it did not pass constitutional muster:

"Although the Massachusetts statute reviewed in [the *Bellotti* cases] required the consent of both parents, and the Utah statute reviewed in *H.L. v. Matheson* required notice to 'the parents,' none of the opinions in any of those cases focused on the possible significance of making the consent or the notice requirement applicable to both parents instead of just one. In contrast, the arguments in these cases, as well as the extensive findings of the District Court, are directed primarily at that distinction. It is therefore appropriate to summarize these findings before addressing the constitutionality of the [statute's provisions], particularly since none of the findings has been challenged in either this Court or the Court of Appeals.

"Approximately one out of every two marriages ends in divorce. Unrebutted evidence indicates that only 50% of minors in the State of Minnesota reside with both biological parents. This conclusion is substantially corroborated by a study indicating that 9% of the minors in Minnesota live with neither parent and 33% live with only one parent.

"The District Court found—on the basis of extensive testimony at trial—that the two-parent notification requirement had particularly harmful effects on both the minor and the custodial parent when the parents were divorced or separated. Relations between the minor and absent parent were not reestablished as a result of the forced notification thereby often producing disappointment in the minor 'when an anticipated reestablishment of her relationship with the absent parent d[id] not occur.' Moreover, '[t]he reaction of the custodial parent to the requirement of forced notification is often one of anger, resentment and frustration at the intrusion of the absent parent,' and fear that notification will threaten the custody rights of the parent or otherwise promote intrafamily violence. Tragically, those fears were often realized * * *.

"[It is] clear that the requirement that *both* parents be notified, whether or not both wish to be notified or have assumed responsibility for the upbringing of the child, does not reasonably further any legitimate state interest. The usual justification for a parental consent or notification provision is that it supports the authority of a parent who is presumed to act in the minor's best interest and thereby assures that the minor's decision to terminate her pregnancy is knowing, intelligent, and deliberate. To the extent that such an interest is legitimate, it would be fully served by a requirement that the minor notify one parent who can then seek the counsel of his or her mate or any other party, when such advice and support is deemed necessary to help the child make a difficult decision. [In] many families, however, the parent notified by the child would not notify the other parent. In those cases the State has no legitimate interest in questioning one parent's judgment that notice to the other parent would not assist the minor or in presuming that the parent who has assumed parental duties is incompetent to make decisions regarding the health and welfare of the child.

"Not only does two-parent notification fail to serve any state interest with respect to functioning families, it disserves the state interest in protecting and assisting the minor with respect to dysfunctional families. The record reveals that in the thousands of dysfunctional families affected by this statute, the two-parent notice requirement proved positively harmful to the minor and her family. The testimony at trial established that this requirement, ostensibly designed for the benefit of the minor, resulted in major trauma to the child, and often to a parent as well.

"[The State] argues that, in the ideal family, the minor should make her decision only after consultation with both parents who should naturally be concerned with the child's welfare and that the State has an interest in protecting the independent right of the parents 'to determine and strive for what they believe to be best for their children.' Neither of these reasons can justify the two-parent notification requirement. The second parent may well have an interest in the minor's abortion decision, making full communication among all members of a family desirable in some cases, but such communication may not be decreed by the State. The State has no more interest in requiring all family members to talk with one another than it has in requiring certain of them to live together [citing *Moore v. East Cleveland,* p. 241 infra].

"[Nor] can any state interest in protecting a parent's interest in shaping a child's values and lifestyle overcome the liberty interests of a minor acting with the consent of a single parent or court."

Concurring JUSTICE O'CONNOR observed:

"It has been my understanding in this area that '[i]f the particular regulation does not 'unduly burden' the fundamental right, [then] our evaluation of that regulation is limited to our determination that the regulation rationally relates to a legitimate state purpose.' *Akron v. Akron Center for Reproductive Health* (O'Connor, J., dissenting); see also *Webster* (O'Connor, J., concurring). It is with that understanding that I agree with Justice Stevens' statement that the 'statute cannot be sustained if the obstacles it imposes are not reasonably related to legitimate state interests.'

"I agree with Justice Stevens that Minnesota has offered no sufficient justification for its interference with the family's decisionmaking processes created by subdivision 2—two-parent notification. Subdivision 2 is the most stringent notification statute in the country.

"[The] Minnesota exception to notification for minors who are victims of neglect or abuse is, in reality, a means of notifying the parents. As Justice Stevens points out, to avail herself of the neglect or abuse exception, the minor must report the abuse. A report requires the welfare agency to immediately 'conduct an assessment.' If the agency interviews the victim, it must notify the parent of the fact of the interview; if the parent is the subject of an investigation, he has a right of access to the record of the investigation. [The] combination of the abused minor's reluctance to report sexual or physical abuse with the likelihood that invoking the abuse exception for the purpose of avoiding notice will result in notice, makes the abuse exception less than effectual.

"Minnesota's two-parent notice requirement is all the more unreasonable when one considers that only half of the minors in the State of Minnesota reside with both biological parents. A third live with only one parent. Given its broad sweep and its failure to serve the purposes asserted by the State in too many cases, I join the Court's striking of subdivision 2."

JUSTICE KENNEDY, joined by Rehnquist C.J., and White and Scalia, JJ., dissented on this issue:

"[A] State pursues a legitimate end under the Constitution when it attempts to foster and preserve the parent-child relation by giving all parents the opportunity to participate in the care and nurture of their children. We have held that parents have a liberty interest, protected by the Constitution, in having a reasonable opportunity to develop close relations with their children. [A] State may seek to protect and facilitate the parent-child bond on the assumption that parents will act in their child's best interests. * * *

* * *

"Minnesota has done no more than act upon the common-sense proposition that, in assisting their daughter in deciding whether to have an abortion, parents can best fulfill their roles if they have the same information about their own child's medical condition and medical choices as the child's doctor does; and that to deny parents this knowledge is to risk, or perpetuate, estrangement or alienation from the child when she is in the greatest need of parental guidance and support. The Court does the State, and our constitutional tradition, sad disservice by impugning the legitimacy of these elemental objectives.

"[In] applying the standards established in our prior decisions to the case at hand, 'we must keep in mind that when we are concerned with extremely sensitive issues, such as the one involved here, the appropriate forum for their resolution in a democracy is the legislature.' We should not forget that 'legislatures are ultimate guardians of the liberties and welfare of the people in quite as great a degree as the courts.' The Minnesota Legislature, like the legislatures of many States, has found it necessary to address the issue of parental notice in its statutory laws. In my view it has acted in a permissible manner. * * *

"I acknowledge that in some cases notifying both parents will not produce desirable results * * *. [But the Court] need not decide today [whether] the Constitution permits a State to require that a physician notify both biological parents before performing an abortion on any minor, for the simple reason that Minnesota has not enacted such a law." [The dissent then discussed various exceptions in the statute designed to ensure that the notice requirements do not apply if they pose a serious threat to the minor's health or welfare.]

Because Justice O'Connor agreed with the "Kennedy group" that the constitutional objection to the two parent notification requirement is removed by the judicial bypass—"the interference with the internal operation of the family required by subdivision 2," she said, "simply does not exist where the minor can avoid notifying one or both parents by use of the bypass procedure"—JUSTICE KENNEDY, joined by the Chief Justice and White and Scalia, JJ., wrote the principal opinion upholding the constitutionality of subdivision 6:

"In providing for the bypass, Minnesota has done nothing other than attempt to fit its legislation into the framework that we have supplied in our previous cases. The simple fact is [that] *Bellotti II* stands for the proposition that a two-parent consent law is constitutional if it provides for a sufficient judicial bypass alternative, and it requires us to sustain the statute before us here. [Although] eight Members of the [*Bellotti II*] Court concluded that the statute was unconstitutional, five indicated that they would uphold a two-parent consent statute with an adequate judicial bypass.

"[If] a judicial bypass is mandated by the Constitution at all, it must be because a general consent rule is unreasonable in at least some of its applications, and the bypass is necessary to save the statute. No reason can be given for refusing to apply a similar analysis to the less demanding case of a notice statute. It follows that a similar result should obtain: a law that requires notice to one or both parents is constitutional with a bypass."

JUSTICE MARSHALL, joined by Brennan and Blackmun, JJ., dissented from the judgment of the Court that the judicial bypass option renders the parental notice and 48–hour delay requirements constitutional:

"The bypass procedure cannot save [the parental notification and 48–hour delay] requirements because the bypass itself is unconstitutional both on its face and as applied. At the very least, this scheme substantially burdens a woman's right to privacy without advancing a compelling state interest. More significantly, in some instances it usurps a young woman's control over her own body by giving either a parent or a court the power effectively to veto her decision to have an abortion.

"[A] substantial proportion of pregnant minors voluntarily consult with a parent regardless of the existence of a notification requirement. [But] for those young women who would choose not to inform their parents, the burden is evident: the notification requirement destroys their right to avoid disclosure of a deeply personal matter.

"A notification requirement can also have severe physical and psychological effects on a young woman. First, forced notification of one parent, like forced notification of both parents, can be extremely traumatic for a young woman, depending on the nature of her relationship with her parents. The disclosure of a daughter's intention to have an abortion often leads to a family crisis, characterized by severe parental anger and rejection. * * * Second, the prospect of having to notify a parent causes many young women to delay their abortions, thereby increasing the health risks of the procedure.

"[In] addition, a notification requirement compels many minors seeking an abortion to travel to a State without such a requirement to avoid notifying a parent. Other women may resort to the horrors of self-abortion or illegal abortion rather than tell a parent. Still others would forgo an abortion entirely and carry the fetus to term, subjecting themselves to the much greater health risks of pregnancy and childbirth and to the physical, psychological, and financial hardships of unwanted motherhood. Clearly, then, requiring notification of one parent significantly burdens a young woman's right to terminate her pregnancy.

"[Because] the parental notification and delay requirements burden a young woman's right freely to decide whether to terminate her pregnancy, the State must show that these requirements are justified by a compelling state interest and are closely tailored to further that interest. [T]he strictures here are not closely tailored to further the State's asserted goal. * * *

"Even if I did not believe that a judicial bypass procedure was facially unconstitutional, the experience of Minnesota's procedure in operation demonstrates that the bypass provision before us cannot save the parental notification and delay requirements. This Court has addressed judicial bypass procedures only in the context of facial challenges. The Court has never considered the actual burdens a particular bypass provision imposes on a woman's right to choose an abortion. Such consideration establishes that, even if judges authorized every abortion sought by petitioning minors,[a] Minnesota's judicial bypass is far too burdensome to remedy an otherwise unconstitutional statute.

a. Of 3,573 judicial bypass petitions filed in Minnesota courts during a period of four and a half years, all but 15 were granted. Recall Professor Mnookin's characterization of the utilization of the post-*Bellotti II* Massachusetts statute (see p. 191 supra)—"a rubber-stamp, administrative operation."

"[The two-parent notice requirement with a judicial bypass alternative] forces a young woman in an already dire situation to choose between two fundamentally unacceptable alternatives: notifying a possibly dictatorial or even abusive parent and justifying her profoundly personal decision in an intimidating judicial proceeding to a blackrobed stranger. For such a woman, this dilemma is more likely to result in trauma and pain than in an informed and voluntary decision." [b]

In a separate opinion JUSTICE SCALIA, who dissented from the Court's invalidation of the two-parent notice requirement but concurred in the Court's judgment that any constitutional objection to that requirement is removed by the judicial bypass option provided by the statute, made some general observations:

"As I understand the various opinions today: One Justice holds that two-parent notification is unconstitutional (at least in the present circumstances) without judicial bypass, but constitutional with bypass [O'Connor, J.]; four Justices would hold that two-parent notification is constitutional with or without bypass [the Kennedy group]; four Justices would hold that two-parent notification is unconstitutional with or without bypass, though the four apply two different standards [Stevens, J., and Marshall, J., joined by Brennan and Blackmun, JJ.]; six Justices hold that one-parent notification with bypass is constitutional, though for two different sets of reasons * * *; and three Justices would hold that one-parent notification with bypass is unconstitutional [Blackmun, J., joined by Brennan and Marshall, JJ., dissenting in the companion case of *Ohio v. Akron Center for Reproductive Health*]. One will search in vain the document we are supposed to be construing for text that provides the basis for the argument over these distinctions; and will find in our society's tradition regarding abortion no hint that the distinctions are constitutionally relevant, much less any indication how a constitutional argument about them ought to be resolved. The random and unpredictable results of our consequently unchanneled individual views make it increasingly evident, Term after Term, that the tools for this job are not to be found in the lawyer's—and hence not in the judge's—workbox. I continue to dissent from this enterprise of devising an Abortion Code, and from the illusion that we have authority to do so." [c]

b. In a separate opinion, Stevens, J., also maintained that the two-parent notice requirement was not saved by the judicial bypass option:

"[A] rule requiring consent or notification of both parents is not reasonably related to the state interest in giving the pregnant minor the benefit of parental advice. [T]he fact that one-parent consent is the virtually uniform rule for any other activity which affects the minor's health, safety or welfare emphasizes the aberrant quality of the two-parent notice requirement.

"A judicial bypass that is designed to handle exceptions from a reasonable general rule, and thereby preserve the constitutionality of that rule, is quite different from a requirement that a minor—or a minor and one of her parents—must apply to a court for permission to avoid the application of a rule that is not reasonably related to legitimate state goals. [T]he requirement that the bypass procedure must be invoked when the minor and one parent agree that the other parent should not be notified represents [an] unjustified governmental intrusion into the family's decisional process."

c. In *Ohio v. Akron Center for Reproductive Health,* ___ U.S. ___, 110 S.Ct. 2972, 111 L.Ed.2d 405 (1990), a companion case to *Hodgson,* a 6–3 majority rejected a facial challenge to a state law that made it a criminal offense for a physician or other person to perform an abortion on an unemancipated minor absent notice to one of the minor's parents or a court order authorizing the minor to consent. (Under the bypass procedure, a minor, who is appointed a lawyer to represent her, must establish by "clear and convincing evidence" *either* that she is mature enough to decide the matter for herself *or* that one of her parents has engaged in a pattern of physical or sexual abuse *or* that notice is not otherwise in her best interest.)

FAMILY LIVING ARRANGEMENTS, PARENTAL RIGHTS, AND THE "RIGHT TO MARRY"

As illustrated by WHALEN v. ROE (1977), p. 87 supra (sustaining a New York law that doctors disclose the names of persons obtaining certain drugs for storage in a central computer file), those attacking legislation can often cast their challenge in terms of an invasion of a constitutionally protected "zone of privacy." But the Court upheld the legislation as "a reasonable exercise of New York's broad police powers," holding that the program did not require extraordinary justification because it "does not, on its face, pose a sufficiently grievous threat" to either the "privacy" interest "in avoiding disclosure of personal matters" [a] or the "privacy" interest "in independence in making certain kinds of important decisions [e.g., abortion, marriage]." The cases discussed below deal with the latter "privacy" interest.

---

1. *Zoning; choice of household companions; "extended family" relationships.* Relying on earlier decisions sustaining local zoning regulations, BELLE TERRE v. BORAAS, 416 U.S. 1, 94 S.Ct. 1536, 39 L.Ed.2d 797 (1974), per DOUGLAS, J., upheld a village ordinance restricting land use to one-family dwellings (defining "family" to mean not more than two unrelated persons living together as a single housekeeping unit, and expressly excluding from the term lodging, boarding, fraternity or multiple-dwelling houses). Appellees, who had leased their houses to six unrelated college students, challenged the ordinance, inter alia, on the ground that it "trenches on the newcomers' rights of privacy."

Justice Kennedy announced the judgment of the Court and delivered the opinion of the Court with respect to the first four parts (in which Rehnquist, C.J., and White, Stevens, O'Connor and Scalia, JJ. joined) and an opinion with respect to Part V—consisting of a brief, general statement about the appropriateness of legislation such as Ohio's—in which Justices Stevens and O'Connor declined to join.

In upholding the judicial bypass procedure, Kennedy, J., noted that although the Court had required bypass procedures for parental *consent* statutes it had not decided whether parental *notice* laws must also contain such procedures. The Court left the question open because Ohio's bypass procedures met the requirements identified for parental consent statutes in prior cases such as *Danforth* and *Bellotti II.* (However, in *Hodgson,* decided the same day as the Ohio case, dissenting Justice Kennedy, joined by the Chief Justice and White and Scalia, JJ., maintained that the difference between notice and consent is "apparent"—unlike parental *consent* laws, a parental *notice* requirement does not allow any third party to make the minor's decision for her or to prevent her from obtaining an abortion—and thus a parental notice requirement *without* a judicial bypass is constitutional.)

Dissenting Justice Blackmun, joined by Brennan and Marshall, JJ., spelled out why he thought various aspects of Ohio's judicial bypass system were constitutionally defective. He called the challenged provisions of the Ohio statute "merely 'poorly disguised elements of discouragement for the abortion decision.' "

a. The Court, however, specifically did *not* decide "any question which might be presented by the unwarranted disclosure of accumulated private data—whether intentional or unintentional—or by a system that did not contain [adequate] security provisions."

See also *Paul v. Davis,* per Rehnquist, J., Sec. 5, I infra, holding that police disclosure of a person's shoplifting arrest did not violate his right of privacy: "His claim is based not upon any challenge to the State's ability to restrict his freedom of action in a sphere contended to be 'private,' but instead on a claim that the State may not publicize a record of an official act such as an arrest. None of our substantive privacy decisions hold this or anything like this and we decline to enlarge them in this manner." Brennan, J., joined by Marshall, J., observed that "a host of state and federal courts, relying on both privacy notions and the presumption of innocence, have begun to develop a line of cases holding that there are substantive limits on the power of the Government to disseminate unresolved arrest records outside the law enforcement [system]. I fear that after today's decision, these nascent doctrines will never have the opportunity for full growth and analysis."

The Court disagreed: "We deal with economic and social legislation where legislatures have historically drawn lines which we respect [if the law] bears 'a rational relationship to a [permissible] state objective.'" "[B]oarding houses, fraternity houses, and the like present urban problems. [The] police power is not confined to elimination of filth, stench, and unhealthy places."

MARSHALL, J., dissented: The ordinance burdened "fundamental rights of association and privacy," and thus required extraordinary justification, not a mere showing that the ordinance "bears a rational relationship to the accomplishment of legitimate governmental objectives." He viewed "the right to 'establish a home'" as an "essential part" of fourteenth amendment liberty and maintained that "the choice of household companions"—which "involves deeply personal considerations as to the kind and quality of intimate relationships within the home"—"surely falls within the right to privacy protected by the Constitution." The state's purposes "could be as effectively achieved by means of an ordinance that did not discriminate on the basis of constitutionally protected choices of life style." [b]

Distinguishing *Belle Terre* as involving an ordinance "affect[ing] only *unrelated* individuals," MOORE v. EAST CLEVELAND, 431 U.S. 494, 97 S.Ct. 1932, 52 L.Ed.2d 531 (1977), invalidated a housing ordinance that limited occupancy to single families, but defined "family" so as to forbid appellant from having her two grandsons live with her. (It did not permit living arrangements if, as in this case, the grandchildren were cousins rather than brothers.) [a] POWELL, J., announcing the Court's judgment and joined by Brennan, Marshall, and Blackmun, JJ., struck down the ordinance on substantive due process grounds:

"[O]n its face [the ordinance] selects certain categories of relatives who may live together and declares that others may not. [When] a city undertakes such intrusive regulation of the family [the] usual judicial deference to the legislature is inappropriate. 'This Court has long recognized that freedom of personal choice in matters of marriage and family life is one of the liberties protected by [due process].' Of course the family is not beyond regulation. But when the government intrudes on choices concerning family living arrangements, this Court must examine carefully the importance of the governmental interests advanced and the extent to which they are served by the challenged regulation [referring to Harlan, J.'s dissent in *Poe v. Ullman*]." "[T]hus examined, this ordinance cannot survive." [3] Although the city's goals—preventing overcrowding, minimizing congestion and avoiding financial strain on its school system—were "legitimate," the ordinance served them "marginally at best."

"[T]he history of the *Lochner* [era] counsels caution and restraint [but] it does [not] require what the city urges here: cutting off any family rights at the first convenient, if arbitrary boundary—the boundary of the nuclear family. * * * Appropriate limits on substantive due process come not from drawing arbitrary lines but rather from careful 'respect for the teachings of history [and] solid recognition of the basic values that underlie our society.' *Griswold*

b. Compare Marshall, J.'s views in *Belle Terre* with the Court's discussion of "freedom of intimate association" in *Roberts v. United States Jaycees,* p. 752 infra. See also the Court's discussion of "the freedom to enter into and carry on certain intimate of private relationships" in *Board of Directors of Rotary International v. Rotary Club of Duarte,* p. 757 infra.

a. The second grandson came to live with his grandmother after the death of his mother.

3. Appellant also claims that the ordinance contravenes the Equal Protection Clause, but it is not necessary for us to reach that contention.

(Harlan, J., concurring). Our decisions teach that the Constitution protects the sanctity of the family precisely because the institution of the family is deeply rooted in this Nation's history and tradition. [Ours] is by no means a tradition limited to respect for [the] nuclear family. The tradition of uncles, aunts, cousins, and especially grandparents sharing a household along with parents and children [especially in times of adversity] has roots equally venerable and equally deserving of constitutional recognition. [In *Pierce,* the Constitution prevented a state from] 'standardiz[ing] its children by forcing them to accept instruction from public teachers only.' By the same token the Constitution prevents East Cleveland from standardizing its children—and its adults—by forcing all to live in certain narrowly defined family patterns." [b]

STEWART, J., joined by Rehnquist, J., dissented, rejecting the argument that "the importance of the 'extended family' in American society" renders appellant's "decision to share her residence with her grandsons," like the decisions involved in bearing and raising children, "an aspect of 'family life' " entitled to substantive constitutional protection. To equate appellant's interest in sharing her residence with some of her relatives "with the fundamental decisions to marry and to bear children," he maintained, "is to extend the limited substantive contours of the Due Process Clause beyond recognition." He thought the challenged "family" definition "rationally designed to carry out the legitimate governmental purposes identified in *Belle Terre.*" A different line "could hardly be drawn that would not sooner or later become the target of a challenge like the appellant's," such as "the hard case of an orphaned niece or nephew."

Nor could he understand why "the traditional importance of the extended family in America" need imply "that the residents of East Cleveland are constitutionally prevented from following what Justice Brennan calls the 'pattern' of 'white suburbia,' even though that choice may reflect 'cultural myopia.' In point of fact, East Cleveland is a predominantly Negro community, with a Negro City Manager and City Commission." [c]

White, J., dissenting, voiced disbelief "that the interest in residing with more than one set of grandchildren is one that calls for any kind of heightened

b. Brennan, J., joined by Marshall, J., concurred, characterizing the ordinance as "senseless," "arbitrary" and "eccentric" and as reflecting "cultural myopia" and "a distressing insensitivity toward the economic and emotional needs of a very large part of our society." He called the "extended family" "virtually a means of survival" for many poor and black families. [The] 'nuclear family' is the pattern so often found in much of white suburbia," but "the Constitution cannot * * * tolerate the imposition by government upon the rest of us of white suburbia's preference in patterns of family living." But see dissenting Justice Stewart's response, infra.

Stevens, J., concurring, thought this "unprecedented ordinance" unconstitutional even under the "limited standard of review of zoning decisions": "The city has failed totally to explain the need for a rule which would allow a homeowner to have two grandchildren live with her if they are brothers, but not if they are cousins. Since the ordinance has not been shown to have any 'substantial relation to [East Cleveland's] public health, safety, morals or general welfare' [and] since it cuts so deeply into a fundamental right normally associated with the ownership of residential property—that of an owner to decide who may reside on his or her property—it must fall [as] a taking of property without due process and without just compensation."

c. "[I]n assessing [appellant's] claim that the ordinance is 'arbitrary' and 'irrational,' " Stewart, J., considered a provision permitting her to request a variance "particularly persuasive evidence to the contrary. [The] variance procedure, a traditional part of American land-use law, bends the straight lines of East Cleveland's ordinance, shaping their contours to respond more flexibly to the hard cases that are the inevitable byproduct of legislative linedrawing."

Burger, C.J., dissented on the ground that appellant should have pursued the "plainly adequate administrative remedy" of seeking a variance, thus finding it "unnecessary to reach the difficult constitutional issue."

protection under the Due Process Clause. [The] present claim is hardly one of which it could be said that 'neither liberty nor justice would exist if [it] were sacrificed.' *Palko.*"

He maintained that Powell, J.'s approach—construing the Due Process Clause to protect from all but "quite important" state interests any right "that in his estimate is deeply rooted in the country's traditions"—"suggests a far too expansive charter for this Court. [What] the deeply rooted traditions of the country are is arguable; which of them deserve [due process protection] is even more debatable. The suggested view would broaden enormously the horizons of the Clause." [d]

Notes and Questions

(a) *The elusiveness of the search for sources of fundamental rights. Moore v. East Cleveland,* maintains Grano, *Judicial Review and a Written Constitution in a Democratic Society,* 28 Wayne L.Rev. 1, 25–27 (1981), "demonstrates both how elusive the search for sources of fundamental rights can be and how unsatisfying the Court's attempts at demonstration necessarily are. Justice Powell's plurality opinion concluded that 'the Constitution protects the sanctity of the family precisely because the institution of the family is deeply rooted in the Nation's history and tradition.' Societies do change, however, and cognizant of this, the Court could not have intended to become constitutionally committed to every practice rooted in our history and tradition. In particular, progress toward racial and sexual equality depends upon success in freeing ourselves from the yoke of history and tradition. Moreover, by implication, Justice Powell's opinion suggested that the result would have been different had an unrelated neighbor taken charge of Mrs. Moore's grandson, [but did not explain] why history and tradition would not protect a neighbor's decision to do what Mrs. Moore did. Nor did he explain why, if it would not, history and tradition should be determinative. [Justice White's dissent], while accepting noninterpretivism with caution, rejected Justice Powell's history and tradition test for defining fundamental rights. [T]he issue that prompted [the Powell-White] exchange is intractable: freed from the need to use the written Constitution as a source of judgment, noninterpretivist judges may select any source that is personally appealing." [a]

(b) *Should Moore have been decided on "naked substantive due process grounds"? Moore*'s choice of rationale, comments Lupu, *Untangling the Strands of the Fourteenth Amendment,* 77 Mich.L.Rev. 981, 1017 (1979), "reversed a pattern that had endured for four decades: it was the first decision since the 1937 revolution to invalidate a statute on naked substantive due process grounds when equal protection grounds seemed readily available. [*Griswold* and *Roe*] had not presented such alternatives; in both cases, the complained-of prohibition swept broadly across the state's entire population, and thus offered no classification readily subject to equal protection attack. In *Moore,* by contrast, the 'family' definition in the ordinance seemed perfect for invalidation as an arbitrary [classification]. The plurality opinion stood at least thirty years of conven-

d. "[A]n approach grounded in history," replied Justice Powell [fn. 12], "imposes limits on the judiciary that are more meaningful than any based on [White, J.'s] abstract formula taken from *Palko.*"

a. But see Sedler, *The Legitimacy Debate in Constitutional Adjudication,* 44 Ohio St. L.J. 93, 111–13 (1983) (neither White, J., who alluded to the legitimacy question in *Moore,* nor any other Justice on the Court "has ever disputed that it was legitimate for the Court to have imputed a substantive meaning to the due process clause").

tional wisdom on its head by adopting a substantive due process theory and proclaiming in a one-sentence footnote that the due process holding rendered it unnecessary for the Court to reach the equal protection claims."

If *Moore* had invalidated the ordinance on equal protection grounds, observes Lupu, at 1019, it might have suggested "the permissibility of other, less arbitrary definitions of 'family.' Instead, *Moore* holds that families, defined by blood and marriage relations, cannot be carved up unless such limitations are critically necessary to achieve substantial zoning objectives." [b]

(c) *Was the purpose of the ordinance quite straightforward?* How significant is it that "East Cleveland is a predominantly Negro community, with a Negro City Manager and City Commissioner"? Consider Burt, *The Constitution of the Family,* 1979 Sup.Ct.Rev. 329, 389: "The plurality viewed the ordinance as directed against [over-crowding, minimizing traffic and the like, but] did not consider that the purpose of the ordinance was quite straightforward: to exclude from a middle-class, predominantly black community, that saw itself as socially and economically upwardly mobile, other black families most characteristic of lower-class ghetto life. Perhaps the Court did not see this purpose or, if it did, considered this an 'illegitimate goal,' though in other cases the Court had been exceedingly solicitous of white middle-class communities' attempts to preserve a common social identity—'zones,' as the Court had put the matter three years earlier [in *Belle Terre*]—'where family values, youth values, and the blessings of the quiet seclusion and clean air make the area a sanctuary for people.' [Although Brennan, J., had dissented in *Belle Terre*], I find in his characterization of the East Cleveland ordinance as 'senseless' and 'eccentric,' precisely what he alleges in it: 'a depressing insensitivity toward the economic and emotional needs' of the current majority of residents in East Cleveland."

(d) *Was Moore a dispute about the meaning of "family"?* Which way does it cut that the East Cleveland ordinance was "unusual" or even "eccentric"? Was victory for Mrs. Moore "total defeat" for the other city residents, but victory for them "not total defeat for her, except insofar as she wished to remain in their community while transferring its membership to her taste"? Consider *Burt,* supra, at 391: "[T]he very oddity of the East Cleveland ordinance suggests that Mrs. Moore is not alone in her opposition to it, that the city residents are more the vulnerable, isolated dissenters than she in the broader society, that they more than she deserve special judicial solicitude as a 'discrete and insular minority.' The Court in *Moore* myopically saw the case as a dispute between 'a family' and 'the state' rather than as a dispute among citizens about the meaning of 'family.' "

(e) *The blood relationship of the parties.* The *Moore* plurality emphasized the blood relationship of the parties. Should this factor be regarded as decisive? Consider Tribe, *Treatise* at 1420: "If a city or town may require that every home be occupied by a single 'family' consisting entirely of persons related by blood or marriage, it would be difficult to respond to the argument that the same city or town may also decide what a 'family' is: If longtime friends can be excluded by ordinance, why not second cousins? And if second cousins, why not certain grandchildren?" Should governmental interference with *any* "enduring relationships" be invalidated unless compellingly justified? See id. Could a town prohibit unmarried people or homosexuals from living together? Compare

b. But see Gerety, *Doing Without Privacy,* 42 Ohio St.L.J. 143, 156–59 (1981) (*Moore* demonstrates need for "privacy" rationale and inadequacy of "pure equal protection theory of individual rights").

Karst, *The Freedom of Intimate Association,* 89 Yale L.J. 624, 686–89 (1980) with Hafen, *The Constitutional Status of Marriage, Kinship, and Sexual Privacy,* 81 Mich.L.Rev. 463, 487, 559 (1983).

2. *Adoption and rights of the natural father.* QUILLOIN v. WALCOTT, 434 U.S. 246, 98 S.Ct. 549, 54 L.Ed.2d 511 (1978): Under Georgia law, if the natural father has not "legitimated" his offspring (appellant had not sought to do so during the 11 years between the child's birth and the adoption petition), only the mother's consent is required for the adoption of the illegitimate child. When the child was 11, the mother consented to his adoption by her husband with whom she and her son were living. Appellant attempted to block the adoption, but did not seek custody or object to the child's continuing to live with his mother and stepfather. On the basis of various findings (e.g., appellant had provided support only on an irregular basis, the child himself expressed a desire to be adopted by his stepfather who was found to be fit to adopt the child), the trial court concluded that the adoption would be in the "best interests of the child."

A unanimous Court, per MARSHALL, J., affirmed: "We have recognized on numerous occasions that the relationship between parent and child is constitutionally protected, e.g. *Wisconsin v. Yoder* [discussed at pp. 891–92, 900 infra]; *Stanley v. Illinois* [p. 1193 infra] [and] [w]e have little doubt that the Due Process Clause would be offended '[i]f a State were to attempt to force the breakup of a natural family, over the objection of the parents and their children, without some showing of unfitness and for the sole reason that to do so was thought to be in the children's best interests.' *Smith v. Organization of Foster Families,* 431 U.S. 816, 862, 97 S.Ct. 2094, 53 L.Ed.2d 14 (1977) (Stewart, J., concurring). But this is not a case [where] the unwed father had, or sought [custody, or where] the proposed adoption would place the child with a new set of parents with whom the child had never before lived. Rather, the result of the adoption in this case is to give full recognition to a family unit already in existence, a result desired by all concerned, except appellant. [Under these circumstances it suffices that the state found] that the adoption, and denial of legitimation, was in the 'best interests of the child.' "

3. *Right to marry.* ZABLOCKI v. REDHAIL, 434 U.S. 374, 98 S.Ct. 673, 54 L.Ed.2d 618 (1978): A Wisconsin law forbade marriage by any resident with minor children not in his custody whom he is under court order to support, unless he proves compliance with the support obligation and that the children "are not then and are not likely thereafter to become public charges." Appellee and the woman he desired to marry were expecting a child, but he was denied a marriage license because he had not satisfied his support obligations to his illegitimate child who had been a public charge since birth. In the course of striking down the marriage prohibition under the "fundamental rights" branch of equal protection doctrine (see Ch. 6, Sec. 4)—which Stewart, J., concurring, called, "in a case like [this] no more than substantive due process by another name"—the Court, per MARSHALL, J., had a good deal to say about "the right to marry":

"Since our past decisions make clear that the right to marry is of fundamental importance, and since the classification at issue here significantly interferes with the exercise of that right, we believe that 'critical examination' of the state's interests advanced in support of the classification is required. [Cases] subsequent to *Griswold* and *Loving v. Virginia* (1967) [p. 966 infra, invalidating state miscegenation laws] have routinely categorized the decision to marry as among the personal decisions protected by the right of privacy. [It] is not surprising that the decision to marry has been placed on the same level of importance as decisions relating to procreation, childbirth, child rearing, and family relationships [for] it would make little sense to recognize a right of privacy with respect to other matters of family life and not with respect to the decision to enter the relationship that is the foundation of the family in our society. The woman whom appellee desired to marry had a fundamental right to seek an abortion of their expected child or to bring the child into life to suffer [the] disabilities that the status of illegitimacy brings. Surely, a decision to marry and raise the child in a traditional family setting must receive equivalent protection. And, if appellee's right to procreate means anything at all, it must imply some right to enter the only relationship in which [the state] allows sexual relations legally to take place.

"By reaffirming the fundamental character of the right to marry, we do not mean to suggest that every state regulation which relates in any way to the incidents of or prerequisites for marriage must be subjected to rigorous scrutiny. [R]easonable regulations that do not significantly interfere with decisions to enter into the marital relationships may legitimately be imposed. See *Califano v. Jobst,* 434 U.S. 47, 98 S.Ct. 95, 54 L.Ed.2d 228 (1977), n. 12 infra." However, because the statute prevents any Wisconsin resident in the affected class from marrying anywhere without a court order, some in the affected class, like appellee, "are absolutely prevented from ever getting married," for "they either lack the financial means to meet their support obligations or cannot prove that their children will not become public charges"; and because "many others [will] be sufficiently burdened by having to [satisfy the statute's requirements] that they will in effect be coerced into foregoing their right to marry," this statute "clearly does interfere directly and substantially with the right to marry.[12]

"When a statutory classification significantly interferes with the exercise of a fundamental right, it cannot be upheld unless it is supported by sufficiently important state interests and is closely tailored to effectuate only those interests. [Assuming that the state interests said to be served by the statute—furnishing an opportunity to counsel the applicant as to the need to fulfill his prior support obligations, and protecting the welfare of the out-of-custody children—] are legitimate and substantial interests, [since] the means selected by the State for achieving these interests unnecessarily impinge on the right to marry, the statute cannot be sustained.

"[The counseling interest] obviously cannot support the withholding of court permission to marry once counseling is completed. [As for the argument that the statute provides incentive for the applicant to make support payments to his children], with respect to [those] unable to meet the statutory requirements, the statute merely prevents the applicant from getting married, without delivering any money at all into the hands of the [children]. More importantly, [the] State

12. The directness and substantiality of the interference with the freedom to marry distinguish the instant case from *Jobst.* In *Jobst* [applying the "rationality" standard of review] we upheld sections of the Social Security Act providing, inter alia, for termination of a dependent child's benefits upon marriage to an individual not entitled to benefits under the Act. As the opinion for the Court expressly noted, the rule terminating benefits upon marriage was not "an attempt to interfere with the individual's freedom to make a decision as important as marriage." The Social Security provisions placed no direct legal obstacle in the path of persons desiring to get married, [and] there was no evidence that the laws significantly discouraged, let alone made "practically impossible," any marriages. Indeed, the provisions had not deterred the individual who challenged the statute from getting married, even though he and his wife were both disabled. * * *

already has numerous other means for exacting compliance with support obligations, means that are at least as effective as the instant statute's and yet do not impinge upon the right to marry [such as wage assignments, civil contempt proceedings and criminal penalties]."

As for the suggestion that the statute protects the ability of marriage applicants to meet prior support obligations by preventing the applicants from incurring new ones, the statute is "grossly underinclusive" since it in no way limits other new financial commitments and "substantially overinclusive as well," for the new spouse may actually improve the applicant's financial situation. "[P]reventing the marriage may only result in [new] children being born out of wedlock, as in fact occurred in appellee's case. Since the support obligation is the same whether the child is born in or out of wedlock, the net result of preventing the marriage is simply more illegitimate children." [a]

STEWART, J., concurred: "I do not agree with the Court that there is a 'right to marry' in the constitutional sense. [A] State may not only 'significantly interfere with decisions to enter into the marriage relationship,' but may in many circumstances absolutely prohibit it. Surely, for example, a State may legitimately say that no one can marry his or her sibling, that no one can marry who is not at least 14 years old, that no one can marry without first passing an examination for venereal disease, or that no one can marry who has a living husband or wife. But, just as surely, in regulating the intimate human relationship of marriage, there is a limit beyond which a State may not constitutionally go.

"[S]ome people simply cannot afford to meet the statute's financial requirements. To deny these people permission to marry penalizes them for failing to do that which they cannot do. Insofar as it applies to indigents, the state law is an irrational means of achieving these objectives of the State. As directed against either the indigent or the delinquent parent, the law is substantially more rational if viewed as a means of assuring the financial viability of future marriages. [But] the State's legitimate concern with the financial soundness of prospective marriages must stop short of telling people they may not marry because they are too poor or because they might persist in their financial irresponsibility. The invasion of constitutionally protected liberty and the chance of erroneous prediction are simply too great. A legislative judgment so alien to our traditions and so offensive to our shared notions of fairness offends the Due Process Clause of the Fourteenth Amendment.

"[E]qual protection doctrine has become the Court's chief instrument for invalidating state laws. Yet, in a case like this one, the doctrine is no more than substantive due process by another name. [T]he effect of the Court's decision in this case is not to require Wisconsin to draw its legislative classifications with greater precision or to afford similar treatment to similarly situated persons. Rather, the message of the Court's opinion is that Wisconsin may not use its control over marriage to achieve the objectives of the state statute. Such restrictions on basic governmental power are at the heart of substantive due process. The Court is understandably reluctant to rely on substantive due process. But to embrace the essence of that doctrine under the guise of equal protection serves no purpose but obfuscation."

POWELL, J., concurred in the judgment, but wrote separately "because the majority's rationale sweeps too broadly in an area which traditionally has been

a. Burger, C.J., joined the Court's opinion and briefly concurred.

subject to state regulation": "The Court apparently would subject all state regulation which 'directly and substantially' interferes with the decision to marry in a traditional family setting to 'critical examination' or 'compelling state interest' analysis. Presumably, 'reasonable regulations that do not significantly interfere with decisions to enter into the marital relationship may legitimately be imposed.' The Court does not present, however, any principled means for distinguishing between the two types of regulations. Since state regulation in this area typically takes the form of a prerequisite or barrier to marriage or divorce, the degree of 'direct' interference with the decision to marry or to divorce is unlikely to provide either guidance for state legislatures or a basis for judicial oversight.

"[State] regulation has included bans on incest, bigamy, and homosexuality, as well as various preconditions to marriage, such as blood tests. Likewise, a showing of fault on the part of one of the partners traditionally has been a prerequisite to the dissolution of an unsuccessful union. A 'compelling state purpose' inquiry would cast doubt on the network of restrictions that the States have fashioned to govern marriage and divorce.

"State power over domestic relations is not without constitutional limits. The Due Process Clause requires a showing of justification 'when the government intrudes on choices concerning family living arrangements' in a manner which is contrary to deeply rooted traditions, *Moore v. East Cleveland,* [and it also limits] the extent to which the State may monopolize the process of ordering certain human relationships while excluding the truly indigent from that process. *Boddie v. Connecticut* [p. 1166 infra]. Furthermore, under the Equal Protection Clause, the means chosen by the State in this case must bear 'a fair and substantial relation' to the object of the legislation [citing *Reed v. Reed* and his concurring opinion in *Craig v. Boren,* both in Ch. 6, Sec. 3, II.].

"The Wisconsin measure in this case does not pass muster under either due process or equal protection standards. [As for the state's 'collection device' justification, [t]o the extent this restriction applies to persons who are able to make the required payments but simply wish to shirk their moral and legal obligation, the Constitution interposes no bar to this additional collection mechanism. The vice inheres not in the collection concept, but in the failure to make provision for those without the means to comply with child-support obligations. [As for the state interest in preserving 'the ability of marriage applicants to support their prior issue by preventing them from incurring new obligations'], [the law is] so grossly underinclusive with respect to this objective, given the many ways that additional financial obligations may be incurred by the applicant quite apart from a contemplated marriage, that the classification 'does not bear a fair and substantial relation to the object of the legislation.' *Craig* (Powell, J., concurring)."

STEVENS, J., concurred on the ground that the challenged statute reflected a judgment that "persons who have demonstrated an inability to support their offspring should not be permitted to marry and [to have] additional children" and that "that sort of reasoning cannot justify this deliberate discrimination against the poor": "Under this statute, a person's economic status may determine his eligibility to enter into a lawful marriage. A noncustodial parent whose children are 'public charges' may not marry even if he has met his court-ordered obligations. Thus, within the class of parents who have fulfilled their court-ordered obligations, the rich may marry and the poor may not. This type of statutory discrimination is, I believe, totally unprecedented, as well as inconsistent with our tradition of administering justice equally to the rich and to the [poor.]" [b]

Notes and Questions

(a) Consider Lupu, supra, at 1072: "[If *Zablocki*] had assessed the Wisconsin statute by analogy to the libertarian principles governing free expression, it would have discovered a significant threat to preferred liberty: the delegation to judges of power to authorize the marriage under the highly discretionary standard 'that such children [are] not likely thereafter to become public charges.' Once the liberty to marry is recognized as fundamental, doctrines requiring clear and imminent danger to legitimate state interests and confining the discretion to make that determination should play as critical a role as they traditionally do in speech cases."

(b) In response to the district court's invalidation of the statute at issue in *Zablocki,* Wisconsin enacted a replacement statute limited to *previously married persons* who had incurred support obligations and who now intended to marry, establishing a *rebuttable presumption* that the remarriage of a person with support obligations for children not in custody would substantially affect the children's welfare and, finally, providing that the applicant who submits proof that "for reasonable cause" he was unable to meet support obligations may remarry. Under *Zablocki,* would this replacement statute (subsequently repealed) pass constitutional muster? See Note, 1979 Wis.L.Rev. 682.

(c) "*Significant interference.*" Is the key to a clear application of *Zablocki* "the identification of what constitutes a significant interference with the right to marry"? Does the Court's reconciliation of *Zablocki* and *Jobst* provide much guidance on this point? See Note, *The Constitution and the Family,* 93 Harv.L. Rev. 1156, 1251–55 (1980): "[*Zablocki*] explicitly identifies directness as important to the determination of significance. [A] direct interference makes the state an actual participant in the decision to marry, [i.e.], represents a determination by the state that an individual should not be permitted to marry unless he meets some condition prior to marriage. An indirect interference, on the other hand, weighs the choice by imposing certain consequences upon marriage but leaves the ultimate choice with the individual. It is consistent with the concept of a free society to let the individual determine whether he can meet the burdens of marriage rather than, as in [*Zablocki*], to have the state decide whether the burdens of marriage will make it too difficult to manage problems like meeting child support payments."

4. *Civil commitment of children by their parents.* In rejecting the argument that only a formal hearing prior to parents' commitment of their minor children to a mental institution could adequately protect a child's rights, *Parham v. J.R.* (1979), per Burger, C.J. (a case treated more fully in the "procedural due process" section, infra), applied "the traditional presumption that the parents act in the best interests of the child." That some parents may act against the interests of the child some times "is hardly a reason to discard wholesale those pages of human experience that teach that parents generally do act in the child's best interests."

b. Rehnquist, J., dissented, "view[ing] this legislative judgment in the light of the traditional presumption of validity [, just as] the traditional standard of review was applied in *Jobst,* despite the claim that the statute there in question burdened [the] right to marry." He concluded that the challenged statute, "despite its imperfections, is sufficiently rational to satisfy the demands of the Fourteenth Amendment."

Is *Parham,* like *Planned Parenthood v. Danforth,* p. 188 supra, a situation in which the parents cannot be relied on to speak for the child's interests? Consider Note, 93 Harv.L.Rev. 89, 94 (1979): "[The *Danforth* Court] ruled that parents cannot prevent their daughters from having abortions [, reasoning] that the existence of the pregnancy itself fractured the family unit too severely to suggest that parental authority should be upheld to preserve the family structure. This reasoning is clearly applicable to a situation in which parents seek to remove a child from the family." Cf. Burt, supra, at 336; Garvey, *Children and the Idea of Liberty,* 68 Ky.L.J. 809, 832–33 (1979–80).

MICHAEL H. v. GERALD D.

491 U.S. 110, 109 S.Ct. 2333, 105 L.Ed.2d 91 (1989).

JUSTICE SCALIA announced the judgment of the Court and delivered an opinion in which the CHIEF JUSTICE joins, and in all but footnote 6 of which JUSTICE O'CONNOR and JUSTICE KENNEDY join.

[Claiming to be the father of Victoria, the child of Carole D. and Gerald D., a married couple, Michael H. brought an action in California to establish his paternity and visitation rights. Although Gerald was listed as the father on the birth certificate and has always claimed the child as her father, blood tests showed a 98.07% probability that Michael, with whom the mother had had an adulterous affair, was the father. During the first three years of the child's life, she and her mother resided at times with Michael, who held the child out as his own. During this time, mother and child also resided at times with another man and with Gerald.

[Under California law, a child born to a married woman living with her husband, who is neither impotent nor sterile, is presumed to be a child of the marriage, a presumption that may be rebutted only in very limited circumstances. Relying on this presumption, the California courts rejected Michael's claims. The U.S. Supreme Court affirmed.]

Michael contends as a matter of substantive due process that because he has established a parental relationship with Victoria, protection of Gerald's and Carole's marital union is an insufficient state interest to support termination of that relationship. This argument is, of course, predicated on the assertion that Michael has a constitutionally protected liberty interest in his relationship with Victoria.

[In] an attempt to limit and guide interpretation of the [Due Process] Clause, we have insisted not merely that the interest denominated as a "liberty" be "fundamental" (a concept that, in isolation, is hard to objectify), but also that it be an interest traditionally protected by our society.[2] As we have put it, the Due Process Clause affords only those protections "so rooted in the traditions and conscience of our people as to be ranked as fundamental." * * *

This insistence that the asserted liberty interest be rooted in history and tradition is evident, as elsewhere, in our cases according constitutional protec-

2. We do not understand what Justice Brennan has in mind by an interest "that society traditionally has thought important * * * without protecting it." The protection need not take the form of an explicit constitutional provision or statutory guarantee, but it must at least exclude (all that is necessary to decide the present case) a societal tradition of enacting laws *denying* the interest. Nor do we understand why our practice of limiting the Due Process Clause to traditionally protected interests turns the clause "into a redundancy." Its purpose is to prevent future generations from lightly casting aside important traditional values—not to enable this Court to invent new ones.

tion to certain parental rights. Michael [reads] *Stanley v. Illinois* [p. 1193 infra, invalidating an irrebuttable statutory presumption that unwed fathers are unfit parents, and such subsequent cases as *Quilloin v. Walcott*], as establishing that a liberty interest is created by biological fatherhood plus an established parental relationship—factors that exist in the present case as well. [As] we view [these cases], they rest not upon such isolated factors but upon the historic respect—indeed, sanctity would not be too strong a term—traditionally accorded to the relationships that develop within the unitary family.

[Thus,] the legal issue in the present case reduces to whether the relationship between persons in the situation of Michael and Victoria has been treated as a protected family unit under the historic practices of our society, or whether on any other basis it has been accorded special protection. We think it impossible to find that it has. In fact, quite to the contrary, our traditions have protected the marital family (Gerald, Carole, and the child they acknowledge to be theirs) against the sort of claim Michael asserts.[4]

* * *

We have found nothing in the older sources, nor in the older cases, addressing specifically the power of the natural father to assert parental rights over a child born into a woman's existing marriage with another man. Since it is Michael's burden to establish that such a power (at least where the natural father has established a relationship with the child) is so deeply embedded within our traditions as to be a fundamental right, the lack of evidence alone might defeat his case. But the evidence shows that even in modern times [the] ability of a person in Michael's position to claim paternity has not been generally acknowledged.

[What] Michael asserts here is a right to have himself declared the natural father *and thereby to obtain parental prerogatives.* What he must establish, therefore, is not that our society has traditionally allowed a natural father in his circumstances to establish paternity, but that it has traditionally accorded such a father parental rights, or at least has not traditionally denied them. [What] counts is whether the States in fact award substantive parental rights to the natural father of a child conceived within and born into an extant marital union that wishes to embrace the child. We are not aware of a single case, old or new, that has done so. This is not the stuff of which fundamental rights qualifying as liberty interests are made.[6] * * *

4. Justice Brennan insists that in determining whether a liberty interest exists we must look at Michael's relationship with Victoria in isolation, without reference to the circumstance that Victoria's mother was married to someone else when the child was conceived, and that that woman and her husband wish to raise the child as their own. We cannot imagine what compels this strange procedure of looking at the act which is assertedly the subject of a liberty interest in isolation from its effect upon other people—rather like inquiring whether there is a liberty interest in firing a gun where the case at hand happens to involve its discharge into another person's body. The logic of Justice Brennan's position leads to the conclusion that if Michael had begotten Victoria by rape, that fact would in no way affect his possession of a liberty interest in his relationship with her.

6. Justice Brennan criticizes our methodology in using historical traditions specifically relating to the rights of an adulterous natural father, rather than inquiring more generally "whether parenthood is an interest that historically has received our attention and protection." There seems to us no basis for the contention that this methodology is "nove[l]." For example, in *Bowers v. Hardwick* [p. 257 infra], we noted that at the time the Fourteenth Amendment was ratified all but 5 of the 37 States had criminal sodomy laws, that all 50 of the States had such laws prior to 1961, and that 24 States and the District of Columbia continued to have them; and we concluded from that record, regarding that very specific aspect of sexual conduct, that "to claim that a right to engage in such conduct is 'deeply rooted in this Nation's history and tradition' or 'implicit in the concept of ordered

JUSTICE O'CONNOR, with whom JUSTICE KENNEDY joins, concurring in part.

I concur in all but footnote 6 of Justice Scalia's opinion. This footnote sketches a mode of historical analysis to be used when identifying liberty interests protected by the Due Process Clause of the Fourteenth Amendment that may be somewhat inconsistent with our past decisions in this area. See *Griswold; Eisenstadt.* On occasion the Court has characterized relevant traditions protecting asserted rights at levels of generality that might not be "the most specific level" available. See *Loving v. Virginia* [p. 966 infra, invalidating state antimiscegenation laws]; *Turner v. Safley,* 482 U.S. 78, 107 S.Ct. 2254, 96 L.Ed.2d 64 (1987) [where, relying on *Zablocki,* a unanimous Court struck down a prison regulation permitting inmates to marry only when there were "compelling reasons" to do so]. I would not foreclose the unanticipated by the prior imposition of a single mode of historical analysis. *Poe v. Ullman* (Harlan, J., dissenting).[a]

JUSTICE BRENNAN, with whom JUSTICE MARSHALL and JUSTICE BLACKMUN join, dissenting. * * *

Once we recognized that the "liberty" protected by the Due Process Clause of the Fourteenth Amendment encompasses more than freedom from bodily restraint, today's plurality opinion emphasizes, the concept was cut loose from one natural limitation on its meaning. This innovation paved the way, so the plurality hints, for judges to substitute their own preferences for those of elected officials. Dissatisfied with this supposedly unbridled and uncertain state of affairs, the plurality casts about for another limitation on the concept of liberty.

It finds this limitation in "tradition." Apparently oblivious to the fact that this concept can be as malleable and as elusive as "liberty" itself, the plurality pretends that tradition places a discernible border around the Constitution. The

liberty' is, at best, facetious." In *Roe* we spent about a fifth of our opinion negating the proposition that there was a longstanding tradition of laws proscribing abortion.

We do not understand why, having rejected our focus upon the societal tradition regarding the natural father's rights vis-à-vis a child whose mother is married to another man, Justice Brennan would choose to focus instead upon "parenthood." Why should the relevant category not be even more general—perhaps "family relationships"; or "personal relationships"; or even "emotional attachments in general"? Though the dissent has no basis for the level of generality it would select, we do: We refer to the most specific level at which a relevant tradition protecting, or denying protection to, the asserted right can be identified. If, for example, there were no societal tradition, either way, regarding the rights of the natural father of a child adulterously conceived, we would have to consult, and (if possible) reason from, the traditions regarding natural fathers in general. But there is such a more specific tradition, and it unqualifiedly denies protection to such a parent.

[Because] general traditions provide such imprecise guidance, they permit judges to dictate rather than discern the society's views. The need, if arbitrary decision-making is to be avoided, to adopt the most specific tradition as the point of reference—or at least to announce, as Justice Brennan declines to do, some other criterion for selecting among the innumerable relevant traditions that could be consulted—is well enough exemplified by the fact that in the present case Justice Brennan's opinion and Justice O'Connor's opinion, which disapproves this footnote, *both* appeal to tradition, but on the basis of the tradition they select reach opposite results. Although assuredly having the virtue (if it be that) of leaving judges free to decide as they think best when the unanticipated occurs, a rule of law that binds neither by text nor by any particular, identifiable tradition, is no rule of law at all. * * *

a. Justice Stevens, who concurred in the judgment, "would not foreclose the possibility that a constitutionally protected relationship between a natural father and his child might exist in a case like this. Indeed, I am willing to assume for the purpose of deciding this case that Michael's relationship with Victoria is strong enough to give him a constitutional right to try to convince a trial judge that Victoria's best interest would be served by granting him visitation rights. I am satisfied, however, that the California statute, as applied in this case, gave him that opportunity."

pretense is seductive; it would be comforting to believe that a search for "tradition" involves nothing more idiosyncratic or complicated than poring through dusty volumes on American history. Yet, as Justice White observed in his dissent in *Moore v. East Cleveland:* "What the deeply rooted traditions of the country are is arguable." [Because] reasonable people can disagree about the content of particular traditions, and because they can disagree even about which traditions are relevant to the definition of "liberty," the plurality has not found the objective boundary that it seeks.

Even if we could agree, moreover, on the content and significance of particular traditions, we still would be forced to identify the point at which a tradition becomes firm enough to be relevant to our definition of liberty and the moment at which it becomes too obsolete to be relevant any longer. The plurality supplies no objective means by which we might make these determinations. * * *

It is not that tradition has been irrelevant to our prior decisions. Throughout our decisionmaking in this important area runs the theme that certain interests and practices—freedom from physical restraint, marriage, childbearing, childrearing, and others—form the core of our definition of "liberty." Our solicitude for these interests is partly the result of the fact that the Due Process Clause would seem an empty promise if it did not protect them, and partly the result of the historical and traditional importance of these interests in our society. In deciding cases arising under the Due Process Clause, therefore, we have considered whether the concrete limitation under consideration impermissibly impinges upon one of these more generalized interests.

Today's plurality, however, does not ask whether parenthood is an interest that historically has received our attention and protection; the answer to that question is too clear for dispute. Instead, the plurality asks whether the specific variety of parenthood under consideration—a natural father's relationship with a child whose mother is married to another man—has enjoyed such protection.

If we had looked to tradition with such specificity in past cases, many a decision would have reached a different result. Surely the use of contraceptives by unmarried couples, *Eisenstadt;* or even by married couples, *Griswold;* the freedom from corporal punishment in schools, *Ingraham v. Wright* [p. 354 fn. e infra], [and] even the right to raise one's natural but illegitimate children, *Stanley v. Illinois,* were not "interest[s] traditionally protected by our society" at the time of their consideration by this Court.

[The] plurality's interpretive method is more than novel; it is misguided. It ignores the good reasons for limiting the role of "tradition" in interpreting the Constitution's deliberately capacious language. In the plurality's constitutional universe, we may not take notice of the fact that the original reasons for the conclusive presumption of paternity are out of place in a world in which blood tests can prove virtually beyond a shadow of a doubt who sired a particular child and in which the fact of illegitimacy no longer plays the burdensome and stigmatizing role it once did. [By] describing the decisive question as whether Michael and Victoria's interest is one that has been "traditionally *protected by* our society" (emphasis added), rather than one that society traditionally has thought important (with or without protecting it), and by suggesting that our sole function is to "*discern* the society's views," n. 6 (emphasis added), the plurality acts as if the only purpose of the Due Process Clause is to confirm the importance of interests already protected by a majority of the States. Transforming the protection afforded by the Due Process Clause into a redundancy mocks those who, with care and purpose, wrote the Fourteenth Amendment.

In construing the Fourteenth Amendment to offer shelter only to those interests specifically protected by historical practice, moreover, the plurality ignores the kind of society in which our Constitution exists. We are not an assimilative, homogeneous society, but a facilitative, pluralistic one, in which we must be willing to abide someone else's unfamiliar or even repellant practice because the same tolerant impulse protects our own idiosyncracies. Even if we can agree, therefore, that "family" and "parenthood" are part of the good life, it is absurd to assume that we can agree on the content of those terms and destructive to pretend that we do. In a community such as ours, "liberty" must include the freedom not to conform. The plurality today squashes this freedom by requiring specific approval from history before protecting anything in the name of liberty.

The document that the plurality construes today is unfamiliar to me. It is not the living charter that I have taken to be our Constitution; it is instead a stagnant, archaic, hidebound document steeped in the prejudices and superstitions of a time long past. *This* Constitution does not recognize that times change, does not see that sometimes a practice or rule outlives its foundations. I cannot accept an interpretive method that does such violence to the character that I am bound by oath to uphold. * * *

* * *

DETERMINING THE APPROPRIATE LEVEL OF GENERALITY IN DEFINING RIGHTS; USING TRADITION AS A SUBSTITUTE FOR VALUE CHOICES: CRITICISM OF JUSTICE SCALIA'S APPROACH

1. *Looking to "tradition."* Does "looking to tradition" for guidance in defining fundamental rights involve great risk? Are legally cognizable "traditions" likely to "mirror majoritan, middle-class conventions"? Are historical traditions susceptible to as much manipulation—or even greater manipulation—than are legal precedents? What if it could be demonstrated unequivocally that public flogging and handbranding were widely accepted forms of punishment in 1791? How does one know when to *reject* an historical pattern or understanding? See Tribe & Dorf, *Levels of Generality in the Definition of Rights,* 57 U.Chi. L.Rev. 1057, 1087, 1090 (1990).

2. *What is "tradition"? Does tradition ever speak with one voice?* How, asks J. M. BALKIN, *Tradition, Betrayal, and the Politics of Deconstruction,* 11 Cardozo L.Rev. 1613, 1617 (1990), do we determine tradition's "boundaries or entailments, and what is its normative status?" Continues Professor Balkin at 1617–18:

"If there is a tradition of protecting marital privacy, but not a more specific tradition protecting marital purchase of contraceptives, how do we know whether the latter situation is nevertheless subsumed under the former for purposes of constitutionally protected liberty? Might one not conclude instead that the *real* historical tradition was protection of marital privacy in the home, so that the purchase of contraceptives in the open marketplace could be regulated or even proscribed consistent with the tradition? Would this not be more consistent with the experiences of Margaret Sanger and her followers, who publicly advocated birth control in the early twentieth century, and were met with incredible resistance? Again, if sexual harassment directed toward women in the workplace and respect for marital privacy are both traditions, but only one is worth protecting, how do we tell the difference? If back alley abortions are a tradition in response to the 'traditional' prohibition on abortion in America, does this make abortion (in or out of a back alley) a tradition worth protecting and sustaining? In short, what normative status should be assigned to a set of values given the fact that many people have held these values at one point or another in our nation's history?

"[W]hat is most troubling about Justice Scalia's call for respecting the most specific tradition available is that our most specific historical traditions may often be opposed to our more general commitments to liberty or equality. Curiously, then, different parts of the American tradition may conflict with each other. And indeed, this is one of the untidy facts of historical experience. The fourteenth amendment's abstract commitment to racial equality was accompanied by simultaneous acceptance of segregated public schools in the District of Columbia and acquiescence in antimiscegenation laws. The establishment clause and the principle of separation of church and state have coexisted with presidential proclamations of national days of prayer, official congressional chaplains, and national Christmas trees. Traditions do not exist as integrated wholes. They are a motley collection of principles and counterprinciples, standing for one thing when viewed narrowly and standing for another when viewed more generally. Tradition never speaks with one voice, although, to be sure, persons of particular predelictions may hear only one."

3. *In formulating the rights at stake, what information does one "abstract away"?* "What," ask LAURENCE TRIBE & MICHAEL DORF, note 1 supra, at 1090, "precisely is the 'most specific level at which a relevant tradition' exists?" They continue, id. at 1092–93:

" * * * Justice Scalia's formulation of the rights at stake [in *Michael H.*] as the rights of "the natural father of a child adulterously conceived" [is] already a considerable abstraction. He has abstracted away lots of information that virtually everybody would agree is irrelevant. But he has also abstracted away some information that many people would see as quite relevant. The natural father in *Michael H.* had a longstanding, albeit adulterous and sporadic, relationship with the mother of his child. He also had fairly extensive, if sporadic, contact with his child. Surely this information is more significant than the plaintiff's race or age. A more specific formulation of the issue than Justice Scalia gives us would be: *what are the rights of the natural father of a child conceived in an adulterous but longstanding relationship, where the father has played a major, if sporadic, role in the child's early development?*

"It is unlikely that any tradition addresses this very question at this precise level of specificity. Thus, we are left with the problem of specifying the *next* most specific tradition. [Do] we abstract away the father's relationship with his child and her mother, as Justice Scalia does? Or do we instead abstract away the fact that the relationship with the mother was an adulterous one, as Justice Brennan does? If we do the latter, then we will find ourselves consulting traditions regarding natural fathers who play major roles in their children's development. This sounds an awful lot like 'traditions regarding natural fathers in general,' which Justice Scalia regarded as less specific than his formulation of the problem. By starting from an even *more* specific description of the case than did Justice Scalia, we have seen that he had no greater justification for abstracting away the father-child relationship than Justice Brennan had for abstracting away the adultery."

4. *Are Justices Brennan and Scalia both traditionalists of the first order?* "Justice Scalia," maintains Balkin, note 2 supra, at 1624, "uses tradition as a substitute for value choices—as a sort of congealed or immanent source of values, for which the Justices are not responsible. Their responsibility only arises if they deviate from its commands." Yet—

"Justice Brennan makes an identical argument about precedent—that Justice Scalia is constrained by his institutional role to obey the Court's past decisions, and that he is lawless, or inserting his own values into the Constitution, if he fails to do this. Just as Justice Scalia asks us to look to the narrowest and most specific traditions of our culture, Justice Brennan demands of Justice Scalia that he follow the most specific holding available—the precedents closest to the case at hand—as the appropriate source of authority.[47] Thus, while Scalia takes a broad view of precedent and a narrow view of tradition, Brennan does precisely the opposite, with predictably opposite results.

"[We] might marvel at Brennan's manipulation of the concept of tradition, as he miraculously discovers that the traditions protected by the Constitution—adultery, homosexuality, and fornication—are precisely those traditions to which majoritarian society objects the most. The general description of society's traditions proves the undoing of their most specific manifestations. It is tradition used against itself. Perhaps if Justice Brennan is right, the Constitution never fails to protect tradition, no matter what the Supreme Court decides.

"In this way, both Justices Brennan and Scalia prove to be traditionalists of the first order. Justice Scalia seeks to enforce his view of 'tradition,' establishing the hegemony of his vision of culture, thus betraying other values and other traditions in the process. But Justice Brennan is equally a betrayer. For he seeks to use a general concept of tradition to subvert tradition, thus betraying it. If Scalia's use of tradition is a betrayal, Brennan's use of tradition against itself is a betrayal of a betrayal. And in so doing Brennan attempts to elevate a countertradition—which rejects Justice Scalia's views of socially appropriate behavior—to constitutional importance."

5. *Justice Scalia's footnote 4 approach: incorporating the state's interest into an asserted liberty.* Although footnote 6 to Justice Scalia's plurality opinion in *Michael H.* has generated much comment, worthy of attention, too, is footnote 4—criticizing the Court's practice of first deciding whether a liberty is fundamental and then asking whether a government practice restricting that liberty can be justified. Consider Tribe & Dorf, supra, at 1096–97:

"When we automatically incorporate the factors that provide the state's possible justification for its regulation into the initial definition of a liberty, the fundamental nature of that liberty nearly vanishes. Unless the state's interest is facially absurd, when it is suitably incorporated into an asserted liberty it will render that liberty so specific as to seem insupportable, or at least radically disconnected from precedent. At a minimum, the privacy right protected in *Roe* becomes the implausible 'right' to destroy a living fetus. If one takes footnote 4

47. Thus, according to Justice Brennan, the proper question to ask is "whether the specific parent-child relationship under consideration is close enough to the interests that we already have protected to be deemed an aspect of 'liberty' as well." He argues that previous cases have held that "although an unwed father's biological link to his child does not, in and of itself, guarantee him a constitutional stake in his relationship with that child, such a link combined with a substantial parent-child relationship will do so." The issue in each case is whether the biological father "act[s] as a father toward his children." Interestingly, Justice Brennan's doctrinal definition of fatherhood is parasitic on the traditional role of the father in the unitary family.

to its logical limit in the interpretation of *enumerated* rights, then the free speech right protected in *New York Times Co. v. Sullivan* [p. 424 infra] becomes the dubious 'right' to libel a public official and the right to an exclusionary remedy protected in *Mapp v. Ohio* [p. 136 supra] becomes the counter-intuitive 'right' of a criminal to suppress the truth. To state these cases this way is to decide them in the government's favor. Anyone is free to argue that each of these cases was wrongly decided. But arguments to this effect must explain why the state interest overcomes the liberty interest. Under Justice Scalia's footnote 4 approach, by contrast, the state interest obliterates, without explanation and at the outset, any trace of the individual liberty at stake."

WHAT SHALL WE CALL THIS SEGMENT—THE RIGHT TO ENGAGE IN HOMOSEXUAL SODOMY? ADULT, CONSENSUAL SEXUAL CONDUCT IN THE HOME? THE AUTONOMY OF PRIVATE SEXUAL CHOICES? SEXUAL EXPRESSION AND CONTROL OF ONE'S BODY? UNCONVENTIONAL SEXUAL LIFESTYLES? THE RIGHT TO CONTROL ONE'S INTIMATE ASSOCIATIONS? THE RIGHT TO BE LET ALONE?

BOWERS v. HARDWICK

478 U.S. 186, 106 S.Ct. 2841, 92 L.Ed.2d 140 (1986).

JUSTICE WHITE delivered the opinion of the Court.

In August 1982, respondent was charged with violating the Georgia statute criminalizing sodomy [1] by committing that act with another adult male in the bedroom of respondent's home. After a preliminary hearing, the District Attorney decided not to present the matter to the grand jury unless further evidence developed.

Respondent then brought suit in the Federal District Court, challenging the constitutionality of the statute insofar as it criminalized consensual sodomy.[2] He asserted that he was a practicing homosexual, that the Georgia statute, as administered by the defendants, placed him in imminent danger of arrest, and that the statute [violated the Constitution]. The District Court granted the defendant's motion to dismiss for failure to state a claim. [The U.S. Court of Appeals for the Eleventh Circuit reversed, holding] that the Georgia statute violated respondent's fundamental rights because his homosexual activity is a

1. Ga.Code Ann. § 16–6–2 (1984) provides, in pertinent part, as follows:

"(a) A person commits the offense of sodomy when he performs or submits to any sexual act involving the sex organs of one person and the mouth or anus of [another].

"(b) A person convicted of the offense of sodomy shall be punished by imprisonment for not less than one nor more than 20 [years]."

2. John and Mary Doe were also plaintiffs in the action. They alleged that they wished to engage in sexual activity proscribed by § 16–6–2 in the privacy of their home, and that they had been "chilled and deterred" from engaging in such activity by both the existence of the statute and Hardwick's arrest. The District Court held, however, that because they had neither sustained, nor were in immediate danger of sustaining, any direct injury from the enforcement of the statute, they did not have proper standing to maintain the action. The Court of Appeals affirmed the District Court's judgment dismissing the Does' claim for lack of standing, and the Does do not challenge that holding in this Court.

The only claim properly before the Court, therefore, is Hardwick's challenge to the Georgia statute as applied to consensual homosexual sodomy. We express no opinion on the constitutionality of the Georgia statute as applied to other acts of sodomy.

private and intimate association that is beyond the reach of state regulation by reason of the Ninth Amendment and the Due Process Clause * * *. We agree with the State that the Court of Appeals erred, and hence we reverse its judgment.

This case does not require a judgment on whether laws against sodomy between consenting adults in general, or between homosexuals in particular, are wise or desirable. [T]he issue presented is whether the Federal Constitution confers a fundamental right upon homosexuals to engage in sodomy and hence invalidates the laws of the many States that still make such conduct illegal and have done so for a very long time. The case also calls for some judgment about the limits of the Court's role in carrying out its constitutional mandate.

We first register our disagreement with the Court of Appeals [that] the Court's prior cases have construed the Constitution to confer a right of privacy that extends to homosexual sodomy and for all intents and purposes have decided this case. [We] think it evident that none of the rights announced in [such cases as *Skinner, Griswold* and *Roe*] bears any resemblance to the claimed constitutional right of homosexuals to engage in acts of sodomy that is asserted in this case. No connection between family, marriage, or procreation on the one hand and homosexual activity on the other has been [demonstrated]. Moreover, any claim that these cases nevertheless stand for the proposition that any kind of private sexual conduct between consenting adults is constitutionally insulated from state proscription is unsupportable. * * *

Precedent aside, however, respondent would have us announce [a] fundamental right to engage in homosexual sodomy. This we are quite unwilling to do. * * *

Striving to assure itself and the public that announcing rights not readily identifiable in the Constitution's text involves much more than the imposition of the Justices' own choice of values on the States and the Federal Government, the Court has sought to identify the nature of the rights qualifying for heightened judicial protection. In *Palko* it was said that this category includes those fundamental liberties that are "implicit in the concept of ordered liberty," such that "neither liberty nor justice would exist if [they] were sacrificed." A different description of fundamental liberties appeared in *Moore v. East Cleveland* (opinion of Powell, J.), where they are characterized as those liberties that are "deeply rooted in this Nation's history and tradition."

It is obvious to us that neither of these formulations would extend a fundamental right to homosexuals to engage in acts of consensual sodomy. Proscriptions against that conduct have ancient roots. Sodomy was a criminal offense at common law and was forbidden by the laws of the original thirteen States when they ratified the Bill of Rights. In 1868, when the Fourteenth Amendment was ratified, all but 5 of the 37 States in the Union had criminal sodomy laws. In fact, until 1961, all 50 States outlawed sodomy, and today, 24 States and the District of Columbia continue to provide criminal penalties for sodomy performed in private and between consenting adults. Against this background, to claim that a right to engage in such conduct is "deeply rooted in this Nation's history and tradition" or "implicit in the concept of ordered liberty" is, at best, facetious.

Nor are we inclined to take a more expansive view of our authority to discover new fundamental rights imbedded in the Due Process Clause. The Court is most vulnerable and comes nearest to illegitimacy when it deals with judge-made constitutional law having little or no cognizable roots in the language or design of the Constitution. That this is so was painfully demonstrated by the face-off between the Executive and the Court in the 1930's, which resulted in the repudiation of much of the substantive gloss that the Court had placed on the Due Process Clause of the Fifth and Fourteenth Amendments. There should be, therefore, great resistance to expand the substantive reach of those Clauses, particularly if it requires redefining the category of rights deemed to be fundamental. Otherwise, the Judiciary necessarily takes to itself further authority to govern the country without express constitutional authority. The claimed right pressed on us today falls far short of overcoming this resistance.

Respondent, however, asserts that the result should be different where the homosexual conduct occurs in the privacy of the home. He relies on *Stanley v. Georgia,* where the Court held that the First Amendment prevents conviction for possessing and reading obscene material in the privacy of [one's home].

Stanley did protect conduct that would not have been protected outside the home, and it partially prevented the enforcement of state obscenity laws; but the decision was firmly grounded in the First Amendment. The right pressed upon us here has no similar support in the text of the Constitution, and it does not qualify for recognition under the prevailing principles for construing the Fourteenth Amendment. Its limits are also difficult to discern. Plainly enough, otherwise illegal conduct is not always immunized whenever it occurs in the home. Victimless crimes, such as the possession and use of illegal drugs do not escape the law where they are committed at home. *Stanley* itself recognized that its holding offered no protection for the possession in the home of drugs, firearms, or stolen goods. And if respondent's submission is limited to the voluntary sexual conduct between consenting adults, it would be difficult, except by fiat, to limit the claimed right to homosexual conduct while leaving exposed to prosecution adultery, incest, and other sexual crimes even though they are committed in the home. We are unwilling to start down that road.

Even if the conduct at issue here is not a fundamental right, respondent asserts that there must be a rational basis for the law and that there is none in this case other than the presumed belief of a majority of the electorate in Georgia that homosexual sodomy is immoral and unacceptable. This is said to be an inadequate rationale to support the law. The law, however, is constantly based on notions of morality, and if all laws representing essentially moral choices are to be invalidated under the Due Process Clause, the courts will be very busy indeed. Even respondent makes no such claim, but insists that majority sentiments about the morality of homosexuality should be declared inadequate. We do not agree, and are unpersuaded that the sodomy laws of some 25 States should be invalidated on this basis.[8] [Reversed.]

CHIEF JUSTICE BURGER, concurring.

I join the Court's opinion, but I write separately to underscore my view that in constitutional terms there is no such thing as a fundamental right to commit homosexual sodomy. [To] hold that the act of homosexual sodomy is somehow protected as a fundamental right would be to cast aside millennia of moral teaching.

This is essentially not a question of personal "preferences" but rather of the legislative authority of the State. I find nothing in the Constitution depriving a State of power to enact the statute challenged here.

8. Respondent does not defend the judgment below based on the Ninth Amendment, the Equal Protection Clause or the Eighth Amendment.

JUSTICE POWELL, concurring.

I join the opinion of the Court. I agree with the Court that there is no fundamental right—i.e., no substantive right under the Due Process Clause—such as that claimed by respondent, and found to exist by the Court of Appeals. This is not to suggest, however, that respondent may not be protected by the Eighth Amendment of the Constitution. The Georgia statute at issue in this case authorizes a court to imprison a person for up to 20 years for a single private, consensual act of sodomy. In my view, a prison sentence for such conduct—certainly a sentence of long duration—would create a serious Eighth Amendment issue. Under the Georgia statute a single act of sodomy, even in the private setting of a home, is a felony comparable in terms of the possible sentence imposed to serious felonies such as aggravated battery, first degree arson, and robbery.

In this case, however, respondent has not been tried, much less convicted and sentenced.[2] Moreover, respondent has not raised the Eighth Amendment issue below. For these reasons this constitutional argument is not before us.

JUSTICE BLACKMUN, with whom JUSTICE BRENNAN, JUSTICE MARSHALL, and JUSTICE STEVENS join, dissenting.

This case is no more about "a fundamental right to engage in homosexual sodomy," as the Court purports to declare, than *Stanley* was about a fundamental right to watch obscene movies, or *Katz v. United States,* 389 U.S. 347, 88 S.Ct. 507, 19 L.Ed.2d 576 (1967), was about a fundamental right to place interstate bets from a telephone booth.[a] Rather, this case is about "the most comprehensive of rights and the right most valued by civilized men," namely, "the right to be let alone." *Olmstead v. United States,* 277 U.S. 438, 478, 48 S.Ct. 564, 572, 72 L.Ed. 944 (1928) (Brandeis, J., dissenting).

The statute at issue denies individuals the right to decide for themselves whether to engage in particular forms of private, consensual sexual activity. [T]he fact that the moral judgments expressed by statutes like § 16–6–2 may be "natural and familiar [should not] conclude our judgment upon the question whether statutes embodying them conflict with the Constitution of the United States." *Roe,* quoting *Lochner* (Holmes, J., dissenting). [We] must analyze respondent's claim in the light of the values that underlie the constitutional right to privacy. If that right means anything, it means that, before Georgia can prosecute its citizens for making choices about the most intimate aspects of their lives, it must do more than assert that the choice they have made is an " 'abominable crime not fit to be named among Christians.' " * * *

[T]he Court's almost obsessive focus on homosexual activity is particularly hard to justify in light of the broad language Georgia has used. Unlike the

2. It was conceded at oral argument that, prior to the complaint against respondent Hardwick, there had been no reported decision involving prosecution for private homosexual sodomy under this Statute for several decades. Moreover, the State has declined to present the criminal charge against Hardwick to a grand jury, and this is a suit for declaratory judgment brought by respondents challenging the validity of the statute. The history of nonenforcement suggests the moribund character today of laws criminalizing this type of private, consensual conduct. Some 26 states have repealed similar statutes. But the constitutional validity of the Georgia statute was put in issue by respondents, and for the reasons stated by the Court, I cannot say that conduct condemned for hundreds of years has now become a fundamental right.

a. *Katz* held that electronic surveillance of defendant violated the privacy upon which he justifiably relied when using a telephone booth and thus constituted a "search and seizure" within the meaning of the Fourth Amendment, even though the challenged surveillance technique involved no physical penetration of the phone booth from which defendant placed his calls.

Court, the Georgia Legislature has not proceeded on the assumption that homosexuals are so different from other citizens that their lives may be controlled in a way that would not be tolerated if it limited the choices of those other citizens. Rather, Georgia has provided that "[a] person commits the offense of sodomy when he performs or submits to any sexual act involving the sex organs of one person and the mouth or anus of another." The sex or status of the persons who engage in the act is irrelevant as a matter of state law. In fact, to the extent I can discern a legislative purpose for Georgia's 1968 enactment, that purpose seems to have been to broaden the coverage of the law to reach heterosexual as well as homosexual activity. I therefore see no basis for the Court's decision to treat this case as an "as applied" challenge to § 16–6–2, see n. 2, or for Georgia's attempt, both in its brief and at oral argument, to defend § 16–6–2 solely on the grounds that it prohibits homosexual activity. Michael Hardwick's standing may rest in significant part on Georgia's apparent willingness to enforce against homosexuals a law it seems not to have any desire to enforce against heterosexuals. But his claim that § 16–6–2 involves an unconstitutional intrusion into his privacy and his right of intimate association does not depend in any way on his sexual orientation. * * *

"Our cases long have recognized that the Constitution embodies a promise that a certain private sphere of individual liberty will be kept largely beyond the reach of government." *Thornburgh.* In construing the right to privacy, the Court has proceeded along two somewhat distinct, albeit complementary, lines. First, it has recognized a privacy interest with reference to certain *decisions* that are properly for the individual to make. E.g., *Roe, Pierce.* Second, it has recognized a privacy interest with reference to certain *places* without regard for the particular activities in which the individuals who occupy them are engaged. The case before us implicates both the decisional and the spatial aspects of the right to privacy.

The Court concludes today that none of our prior cases dealing with various decisions that individuals are entitled to make free of governmental interference "bears any resemblance to the claimed constitutional right of homosexuals to engage in acts of sodomy that is asserted in this case." While it is true that these cases may be characterized by their connection to protection of the family, the Court's conclusion that they extend no further than this boundary ignores the warning in *Moore* (plurality opinion), against "clos[ing] our eyes to the basic reasons why certain rights associated with the family have been accorded shelter under the Fourteenth Amendment's Due Process Clause." We protect those rights not because they contribute, in some direct and material way, to the general public welfare, but because they form so central a part of an individual's life. "[T]he concept of privacy embodies the 'moral fact that a person belongs to himself and not others nor to society as a whole.'" *Thornburgh* (Stevens, J., concurring). * * *

Only the most willful blindness could obscure the fact that sexual intimacy is "a sensitive, key relationship of human existence, central to family life, community welfare, and the development of human personality." The fact that individuals define themselves in a significant way through their intimate sexual relationships with others suggests, in a Nation as diverse as ours, that there may be many "right" ways of conducting those relationships, and that much of the richness of a relationship will come from the freedom an individual has to *choose* the form and nature of these intensely personal bonds. See Karst, *The Freedom of Intimate Association,* 89 Yale L.J. 624, 637 (1980).

In a variety of circumstances we have recognized that a necessary corollary of giving individuals freedom to choose how to conduct their lives is acceptance of the fact that different individuals will make different choices. [The] Court claims that its decision today merely refuses to recognize a fundamental right to engage in homosexual sodomy; what the Court really has refused to recognize is the fundamental interest all individuals have in controlling the nature of their intimate associations with others.

The behavior for which Hardwick faces prosecution occurred in his own home, a place to which the Fourth Amendment attaches special significance. The Court's treatment of this aspect of the case is symptomatic of its overall refusal to consider the broad principles that have informed our treatment of privacy in specific cases. Just as the right to privacy is more than the mere aggregation of a number of entitlements to engage in specific behavior, so too, protecting the physical integrity of the home is more than merely a means of protecting specific activities that often take place there. * * *

The Court's interpretation of the pivotal case of *Stanley v. Georgia* is entirely unconvincing. *Stanley* held that Georgia's undoubted power to punish the public distribution of constitutionally unprotected, obscene material did not permit the State to punish the private possession of such material. According to the majority here, *Stanley* relied entirely on the First Amendment, and thus, it is claimed, sheds no light on cases not involving printed materials. But that is not what *Stanley* said. Rather, the *Stanley* Court anchored its holding in the Fourth Amendment's special protection for the individual in his home.

[The] central place that *Stanley* gives Justice Brandeis' dissent in *Olmstead,* a case raising *no* First Amendment claim, shows that *Stanley* rested as much on the Court's understanding of the Fourth Amendment as it did on the First. * * * "The right of the people to be secure in [their] houses," expressly guaranteed by the Fourth Amendment, is perhaps the most "textual" of the various constitutional provisions that inform our understanding of the right to privacy, and thus I cannot agree with the Court's statement that "[t]he right pressed upon us here has [no] support in the text of the Constitution." Indeed, the right of an individual to conduct intimate relationships in the intimacy of his or her own home seems to me to be the heart of the Constitution's protection of privacy.

The Court's failure to comprehend the magnitude of the liberty interests at stake in this case leads it to slight the question whether [petitioner] has justified Georgia's infringement on these interests. I believe that neither of the two general justifications for § 16–6–2 that petitioner has advanced warrants dismissing respondent's challenge for failure to state a claim.

First, petitioner asserts that the acts made criminal by the statute may have serious adverse consequences for "the general public health and welfare," such as spreading communicable diseases or fostering other criminal activity. [Nothing in the record] provides any justification for finding the activity forbidden by § 16–6–2 to be physically dangerous, either to the persons engaged in it or to others.[4]

4. Although I do not think it necessary to decide today issues that are not even remotely before us, it does seem to me that a court could find simple, analytically sound distinctions between certain private, consensual sexual conduct, on the one hand, and adultery and incest (the only two vaguely specific "sexual crimes" to which the majority points), on the other. For example, marriage, in addition to its spiritual aspects, is a civil contract that entitles the contracting parties to a variety of governmentally provided benefits. A State might define the contractual commitment necessary to become eligible for these benefits to

The core of petitioner's defense of § 16–6–2, however, is that respondent and others who engage in the conduct prohibited by § 16–6–2 interfere with Georgia's exercise of the " 'right of the Nation and of the States to maintain a decent society,' " *Paris Adult Theatre.* Essentially, petitioner argues, and the Court agrees, that the fact that the acts described in § 16–6–2 "for hundreds of years, if not thousands, have been uniformly condemned as immoral" is a sufficient reason to permit a State to ban them today.

I cannot agree that either the length of time a majority has held its convictions or the passions with which it defends them can withdraw legislation from this Court's scrutiny. See, e.g., *Roe; Loving; Brown v. Board of Education.*[5] [It] is precisely because the issue raised by this case touches the heart of what makes individuals what they are that we should be especially sensitive to the rights of those whose choices upset the majority.

The assertion that "traditional Judeo–Christian values proscribe" the conduct involved cannot provide an adequate justification for § 16–6–2. That certain, but by no means all, religious groups condemn the behavior at issue gives the State no license to impose their judgments on the entire citizenry. The legitimacy of secular legislation depends instead on whether the State can advance some justification for its law beyond its conformity to religious doctrine. A State can no more punish private behavior because of religious intolerance than it can punish such behavior because of racial animus. * * *

Nor can § 16–6–2 be justified as a "morally neutral" exercise of Georgia's power to "protect the public environment," *Paris Adult Theatre.* * * * Petitioner and the Court fail to see the difference between laws that protect public sensibilities and those that enforce private morality. Statutes banning public sexual activity are entirely consistent with protecting the individual's liberty interest in decisions concerning sexual relations: the same recognition that those decisions are intensely private which justifies protecting them from governmental interference can justify protecting individuals from unwilling exposure to the sexual activities of others. But the mere fact that intimate behavior may be punished when it takes place in public cannot dictate how States can regulate intimate behavior that occurs in intimate places.[7]

include a commitment of fidelity and then punish individuals for breaching that contract. Moreover, a State might conclude that adultery is likely to injure third persons, in particular, spouses and children of persons who engage in extramarital affairs. With respect to incest, a court might well agree with respondent that the nature of familial relationships renders true consent to incestuous activity sufficiently problematical that a blanket prohibition of such activity is warranted. Notably, the Court makes no effort to explain why it has chosen to group private, consensual homosexual activity with adultery and incest rather than with private, consensual heterosexual activity by unmarried persons or, indeed, with oral or anal sex within marriage.

5. The parallel between *Loving* [which invalidated a Virginia antimiscegenation law] and this case is almost uncanny. There, too, the State relied on a religious justification for its law. [There], too, defenders of the challenged statute relied heavily on the fact that when the Fourteenth Amendment was ratified, most of the States had similar prohibitions. There, too, at the time the case came before the Court, many of the States still had criminal statutes concerning the conduct at issue. [Yet] the Court held, not only that the individious racism of Virginia's law violated the Equal Protection Clause, but also that the law deprived the Lovings of due process by denying them the "freedom of choice to marry" that had "long been recognized as one of the vital personal rights essential to the orderly pursuit of happiness by free men."

7. At oral argument a suggestion appeared that, while the Fourth Amendment's special protection of the home might prevent the State from enforcing § 16–6–2 against individuals who engage in consensual sexual activity there, that protection would not make the statute invalid. The suggestion misses the point entirely. If the law is not invalid, then the police *can* invade the home to enforce it, provided, of course, that they obtain a determination of probable cause from a neutral magistrate. One of the reasons for the

This case involves no real interference with the rights of others, for the mere knowledge that other individuals do not adhere to one's value system cannot be a legally cognizable interest, let alone an interest that can justify invading the houses, hearts, and minds of citizens who choose to live their lives differently. * * *

JUSTICE STEVENS, with whom JUSTICE BRENNAN and JUSTICE MARSHALL join, dissenting.

Like the statute that is challenged in this case, the rationale of the Court's opinion applies equally to the prohibited conduct regardless of whether the parties who engage in it are married or unmarried, or are of the same or different sexes.[2] Sodomy was condemned as an odious and sinful type of behavior during the formative period of the common law. That condemnation was equally damning for heterosexual and homosexual sodomy. Moreover, it provided no special exemption for married couples. The license to cohabit and to produce legitimate offspring simply did not include any permission to engage in sexual conduct that was considered a "crime against nature."

The history of the Georgia statute before us clearly reveals this traditional prohibition of heterosexual, as well as homosexual, sodomy. Indeed, at one point in the 20th century, Georgia's law was construed to permit certain sexual conduct between homosexual women even though such conduct was prohibited between heterosexuals. The history of the statutes cited by the majority as proof for the proposition that sodomy is not constitutionally protected similarly reveals a prohibition on heterosexual, as well as homosexual, sodomy.

Because the Georgia statute expresses the traditional view that sodomy is an immoral kind of conduct regardless of the identity of the persons who engage in it, I believe that a proper analysis of its constitutionality requires consideration of two questions: First, may a State totally prohibit the described conduct by means of a neutral law applying without exception to all persons subject to its jurisdiction? If not, may the State save the statute by announcing that it will only enforce the law against homosexuals? The two questions merit separate discussion.

Our prior cases make two propositions abundantly clear. First, the fact that the governing majority in a State has traditionally viewed a particular practice as immoral is not a sufficient reason for upholding a law prohibiting the practice; neither history nor tradition could save a law prohibiting miscegenation from constitutional attack.[9] Second, individual decisions by married persons, concerning the intimacies of their physical relationship, even when not intended to produce offspring, are a form of "liberty" protected by the Due Process Clause of the Fourteenth Amendment. *Griswold.* Moreover, this pro-

Court's holding in *Griswold* was precisely the possibility, and repugnancy, of permitting searches to obtain evidence regarding the use of contraceptives. Permitting the kinds of searches that might be necessary to obtain evidence of the sexual activity banned by § 16–6–2 seems no less intrusive, or repugnant.

2. The Court states that the "issue presented is whether the Federal Constitution confers a fundamental right upon homosexuals to engage in sodomy and hence invalidates the laws of the many States that still make such conduct illegal and have done so for a very long time." In reality, however, it is the indiscriminate prohibition of sodomy, heterosexual as well as homosexual, that has been present "for a very long time." Moreover, the reasoning the Court employs would provide the same support for the statute as it is written as it does for the statute as it is narrowly construed by the Court.

9. See *Loving.* Interestingly, miscegenation was once treated as a crime similar to sodomy.

tection extends to intimate choices by unmarried as well as married persons. *Carey; Eisenstadt.* * * *

Society has every right to encourage its individual members to follow particular traditions in expressing affection for one another and in gratifying their personal desires. It, of course, may prohibit an individual from imposing his will on another to satisfy his own selfish interests. It also may prevent an individual from interfering with, or violating, a legally sanctioned and protected relationship, such as marriage. And it may explain the relative advantages and disadvantages of different forms of intimate expression. But when individual married couples are isolated from observation by others, the way in which they voluntarily choose to conduct their intimate relations is a matter for them—not the State—to decide.[10] The essential "liberty" that animated the development of the law in cases like *Griswold, Eisenstadt,* and *Carey* surely embraces the right to engage in nonreproductive, sexual conduct that others may consider offensive or immoral.

Paradoxical as it may seem, our prior cases thus establish that a State may not prohibit sodomy within "the sacred precincts of marital bedrooms," *Griswold,* or, indeed, between unmarried heterosexual adults. *Eisenstadt.* [If] the Georgia statute cannot be enforced as it is written—if the conduct it seeks to prohibit is a protected form of liberty for the vast majority of Georgia's citizens—the State must assume the burden of justifying a selective application of its law. Either the persons to whom Georgia seeks to apply its statute do not have the same interest in "liberty" that others have, or there must be a reason why the State may be permitted to apply a generally applicable law to certain persons that it does not apply to others.

The first possibility is plainly unacceptable. Although the meaning of the principle that "all men are created equal" is not always clear, it surely must mean that every free citizen has the same interest in "liberty" that the members of the majority share. From the standpoint of the individual, the homosexual and the heterosexual have the same interest in deciding how he will live his own life, and, more narrowly, how he will conduct himself in his personal and voluntary associations with his companions. State intrusion into the private conduct of either is equally burdensome.

The second possibility is similarly unacceptable. A policy of selective application must be supported by a neutral and legitimate interest—something more substantial than a habitual dislike for, or ignorance about, the disfavored group. Neither the State nor the Court has identified any such interest in this case. The Court has posited as a justification for the Georgia statute "the presumed belief of a majority of the electorate in Georgia that homosexual sodomy is immoral and unacceptable." But the Georgia electorate has expressed no such belief—instead, its representatives enacted a law that presumably reflects the belief that *all sodomy* is immoral and unacceptable. Unless the Court is prepared to conclude that such a law is constitutional, it may not rely on the work product of the Georgia Legislature to support its holding. For the Georgia statute does not single out homosexuals as a separate class meriting special disfavored treatment.

Nor, indeed, does the Georgia prosecutor even believe that all homosexuals who violate this statute should be punished. This conclusion is evident from the

10. Indeed, the Georgia Attorney General concedes that Georgia's statute would be unconstitutional if applied to a married couple. * * * Significantly, Georgia passed the current statute three years after the Court's decison in *Griswold.*

fact that the respondent in this very case has formally acknowledged in his complaint and in court that he has engaged, and intends to continue to engage, in the prohibited conduct, yet the State has elected not to process criminal charges against him. As Justice Powell points out, moreover, Georgia's prohibition on private, consensual sodomy has not been enforced for decades. The record of nonenforcement, in this case and in the last several decades, belies the Attorney General's representations about the importance of the State's selective application of its generally applicable law.

Both the Georgia statute and the Georgia prosecutor thus completely fail to provide the Court with any support for the conclusion that homosexual sodomy, *simpliciter,* is considered unacceptable conduct in that State, and that the burden of justifying a selective application of the generally applicable law has been met.

The Court orders the dismissal of respondent's complaint even though the State's statute prohibits all sodomy; even though that prohibition is concededly unconstitutional with respect to heterosexuals; and even though the State's post hoc explanations for selective application are belied by the State's own actions. At the very least, I think it clear at this early stage of the litigation that respondent has alleged a constitutional claim sufficient to withstand a motion to dismiss. * * *

CRITICISM OF *BOWERS v. HARDWICK*

1. *Homosexuality as an aspect of identity demanding respect,* Consider Michelman, *Law's Republic,* 97 Yale L.J. 1493, 1532–33 (1988):

"All the components of the republican constitutional argument for an opposite result in *Bowers v. Hardwick* are now before us. The argument construes Hardwick's complaint as, in essence, one of unjustified denial of due citizenship (or is it due foundership?) by reason of denial of liberty, and specifically of that aspect of liberty we have come to know as privacy; its text is section 1 of the Fourteenth Amendment. The argument accepts without question Georgia's explanation of the meaning and purpose of its challenged law: the meaning is to brand and punish as criminal the engagement by homosexual partners, but not heterosexual partners, in certain forms of sexual intimacy, and the purpose is to give expression and effect to a legislative majority's moral rejection of homosexual life.

"Such a purpose is deeply suspect under the modern republican commitment to social plurality. In the circumstances of contemporary society, homosexuality has come to signify not just a certain sort of inclination that 'anyone' might feel, but a more personally constitutive and distinctive way, or ways, of being.[164] Homosexuality has come to be experienced, claimed, socially reflected and—if ambiguously—confirmed as an aspect of identity demanding respect.[165] What is more, by its very emergence as an aspect of ways of living and not just an inclination or taste, homosexuality challenges established orders.[166]

"It seems very likely that among the effects of a law like Georgia's on persons for whom homosexuality is an aspect of identity is denial or impairment of their citizenship, in the broad sense which I have suggested is appropriate to

164. See Law, *Homosexuality and the Social Meaning of Gender,* 1988 Wisc.L.Rev. 1, 15, 24–26; Richards, *Constitutional Legitimacy and Constitutional Privacy,* 61 N.Y.U.L. Rev. 800, 854 (1986); Note, 98 Harv.L.Rev. 1285, 1304–05 (1985).

165. See Law, supra, 20–31.

166. [See Law at 24, 31–32].

modern republican constitutionalism: that of admission to full and effective participation in the various arenas of public life.[167] It has this effect, in the first place, as a public expression endorsing and reinforcing majoritarian denigration and suppression of homosexual identity.[168] It also—and for my purposes more interestingly—denies citizenship by violating privacy."

2. *Reflecting the popular morality of the majority.* *Hardwick,* observes Note, 100 Harv.L.Rev. 210, 219 (1986), "reflects the Court's new-found willingness to allow states to intrude into the private lives of their citizens and to justify such intrusions solely on the basis that they reflect the popular morality of the majority. This approach ignores two fundamental principles embodied in the Bill of Rights: that of limited government and that of preservation of the rights of minorities against majority action. * * * Given that all law, as Justice White himself observed, 'is constantly based on notions of morality,' to allow a state to justify its laws solely on this ground is to suggest that all laws have a constitutionally unobjectionable basis. The Court should have forced Georgia to offer for its legislation an independent rational basis, something more than the moral choice of a majority."

But cf. Bork, *The Tempting of America* 123, 125–26 (1990): "The dissent makes a point of the fact that Hardwick's behavior was not physically dangerous to those engaged in it or to others and refers to 'victimless' activity. That, as we have reason to know, is not true. But, in any event, physical danger does not exhaust the categories of harms society may seek to prevent by legislation, and no activity that society thinks immoral is victimless. Knowledge that an activity is taking place is a harm to those who find it profoundly immoral. That statement will be taken as repressive by many, but only because they really do not disapprove of the conduct involved in *Bowers.* If the sexual conduct involved was bestiality, they might agree that it could be prohibited by law, although the only objection to it is moral.

"[T]he dissenting opinion also made the elementary error of confusing its power to override legislated morality when that morality conflicts with the Constitution and its power to override legislated morality when that morality conflicts with nothing in the Constitution but only with the judge's preferences. * * * Judges who vigorously deny elected representatives the right to base law on morality simultaneously claim for themselves the right to create constitutional law on the basis of morality, their morality. There being nothing in the Constitution prohibiting morality, the only opposition to it rests upon a moral view. The *Bowers* dissent said as much when it stated as a 'moral fact' that a person belongs to himself and not to others or to society. Moral relativism, is after all, one moral position. But the imposition of moral relativism upon legislatures by judges is not, strictly speaking, moral relativism in itself. It is more accurately described as the belief that the only valid and trustworthy morality is the judges'."

3. *More on the level of generality in defining rights.* Did the *Hardwick* Court define the claim of liberty at the wrong level of generality? Yes, maintains Professor Tribe (who, as he notes, argued the case for Hardwick in the Supreme Court). Observes Tribe, *Treatise* at 1427–28:

"Obviously, the history of homosexuality has been largely a history of opprobrium; indeed, it would not be implausible to find on this basis that

167. *Cf.* Karst, *Paths to Belonging: The Constitution and Cultural Identity,* 64 N.C.L. Rev. 303 (1986) (developing similar conception of constitutional citizenship rights for members of ethnoculturally identifiable groups).

168. [See Law at 4, 6–8.]

homosexuals constitute a discrete and insular minority entitled to heightened protection under the equal protection clause. Yet when the Court uses the history of violent disapproval of the behavior that forms part of the very definition of homosexuality as the basis for denying homosexuals' claim to protection, it effectively inverts the equal protection axiom of heightened judicial solicitude for despised groups and their characteristic activities and uses that inverted principle to bootstrap antipathy toward homosexuality into a tautological rationale for continuing to criminalize homosexuality. Therefore, in asking whether an alleged right forms part of a traditional liberty, it is crucial to define the liberty at a high enough level of generality to permit unconventional variants to claim protection along with mainstream versions of protected conduct. The proper question, as the dissent in *Hardwick* recognized, is not whether oral sex as such has long enjoyed a special place in the pantheon of constitutional rights, but whether private, consensual, adult sexual acts partake of traditionally revered liberties of intimate association and individual autonomy.

"Once the inquiry is shifted from the particular proscribed acts—and the group of people who engage in them—to the claim of liberty that must be balanced against the state's assertion of power, it becomes clear that a proscription on private acts of sodomy should not survive."

But consider Bork, supra, at 203–04: "Tribe [thinks that a] constitutional right to homosexual conduct within the home [is] part of a broader right to sexual intimacies between consenting adults. * * * 'The Court's error in *Hardwick* [, states Tribe,] 'was that it used the wrong level of generality to conceptualize the plaintiff's claim of liberty to test its pedigree.' How, one might ask, are we to know what level of generality is appropriate? [Tribe's answer] is entirely result-oriented. The Court [, he tells us,] must choose the level of generality at which it states 'traditional liberty' at any level that results in a constitutional right for unconventional behavior. This bypasses the question of whether the Constitution contains protection for any sexual conduct or whether that is left to the moral sense of the people. It also fails to come to grips with the central question[:] How can any individual, professor, judge, or moral philosopher tell us convincingly that, regardless of law or our own moral sense, certain forms of unconventional behavior must be allowed? There is no apparent reason why the Court should manipulate the level of generality to protect unconventional sexual behavior any more than liberty should be taken at a high enough level of abstraction to protect kleptomania. Tribe has more sympathy for one than for the other, but that hardly rises to the level of a constitutional principle." [a]

4. *Drawing guidance from the text itself; Hardwick, Roe, and the "right" to use a sperm bank.* "The basic choice," maintain Tribe and Dorf, fn. a supra, at 1107 "—and neither the Constitution's text nor its structure nor its history can make it for us—is between emphasizing the 'conservative' functions of both the liberty and equality clauses (as well as others), and emphasizing their potential as generators of critique and change." They continue, id. at 1107–08:

"We must justify the choice extratextually, but we may and should then implement it in ways that draw as much guidance as possible from the text itself. Justice Harlan exemplified such a program in his [*Poe v. Ullman*] dissent, in which he opted for a moderately conservative orientation toward generaliza-

a. For a partial response to Judge Bork, see Tribe & Dorf, *Levels of Generality in the Definitions of Rights,* 57 U.Chi.L.Rev. 1057, 1099–1100 (1990).

tion (one considerably less tradition-conserving than Justice Scalia's, however) and sought unifying structures for specified rights in an intermediate level of generality, drawing heavily upon textual points of reference.

"In the *Hardwick* context, if one is willing to generalize much at all, the Constitution's text—in the First Amendment's protection of peaceful assembly and in the Fourth Amendment's protection of the home—points toward generalizing in the direction of intimate personal association in the privacy of the home rather than generalizing in the direction of, let us say, freedom of choice in matters of procreation. It is for this reason that *Hardwick* seems to us so egregiously wrong; that *Roe* seems a closer and more difficult case; that a supposed 'fundamental right' to use a sperm bank would represent a particularly bold leap; and that a 'right' to enforce a surrogacy contract against a woman who has changed her mind and wishes to keep her gestational child entails a leap across a constitutionally unbridgeable void."

MORE ON PRIVACY AND AUTONOMY

1. *Personal appearance and lifestyles.* KELLEY v. JOHNSON, 425 U.S. 238, 96 S.Ct. 1440, 47 L.Ed.2d 708 (1976), per REHNQUIST, J., held that regulations directed at the style and length of male police officers' hair, sideburns and mustaches, and prohibiting beards and goatees except for medical reasons, violated no " 'liberty' interest protected by the Fourteenth Amendment": "The 'liberty' interest claimed [here] is distinguishable from [those] protected in *Roe, Eisenstadt* [and] *Griswold,* [which] involved a substantial claim of infringement on the individual's freedom of choice with respect to certain basic matters of procreation, marriage, and family life."

Assuming that "the citizenry at large has some sort of 'liberty' interest within the Fourteenth Amendment in matters of personal appearance," this assumption is insufficient to topple the regulation, for respondent has sought constitutional protection "as an employee of the county and, more particularly, as a policeman. [T]he county has chosen a mode of organization which it undoubtedly deems the most efficient in enabling its police to carry out the duties assigned to them under state and local law. Such a choice necessarily gives weight to the overall need for discipline, esprit de corps, and uniformity.

"The promotion of safety of persons and property is unquestionably at the core of the State's police [power]. Choice of organization, dress and equipment for law enforcement personnel is a decision entitled to the same sort of presumption of legislative validity as are state choices designed to promote other aims within the cognizance of the State's police power. [Thus] the question is not [whether] the State can 'establish' a 'genuine public need' for the specific regulation [but] whether respondent can demonstrate that there is no rational connection between the regulation, based as it is on petitioner's method of organizing its police force, and the promotion of safety of persons and property.

"[The courts are not] in a position to weigh the policy arguments in favor of and against a rule regulating hairstyles as a part of regulations governing a uniformed civilian service. The constitutional issue [is whether the] determination that such regulations should be enacted is so irrational that it may be branded 'arbitrary,' and therefore a deprivation of respondent's 'liberty' interest in freedom to choose his own hairstyle. *Williamson v. Lee Optical Co.* [p. 935 infra]. The overwhelming majority of state and local police of the present day are uniformed. This fact itself testifies to the recognition by those who direct those operations, and by the people of the States and localities who directly or indirectly choose such persons, that similarity in appearance of police officers is desirable. This choice may be based on a desire to make police officers readily recognizable to the members of the public, or a desire for the esprit de corps which such similarity is felt to inculcate within the police force itself. Either one is a sufficiently rational justification for" the regulations.[a]

MARSHALL, J., joined by Brennan, J., dissented: "An individual's personal appearance may reflect, sustain, and nourish his personality and may well be used as a means of expressing his attitude and lifestyle.[2] In taking control over a citizen's personal appearance, the Government forces him to sacrifice substantial elements of his integrity and identity as well. To say that the liberty guarantee of the Fourteenth Amendment does not encompass matters of personal appearance would be fundamentally inconsistent with the values of privacy, self-identity, autonomy, and personal integrity that I have always assumed the Constitution was designed to protect [referring, e.g., to *Roe* and *Griswold*].[b]

"[While] fully accepting the aims of 'identifiability' and maintenance of esprit de corps, I find no rational relationship between the challenged regulation and these goals. As for the first justification offered by the Court, I simply do not see how requiring policemen to maintain hair of under a certain length could rationally be argued to contribute to making them identifiable to the public as policemen. [As] for the Court's second justification, the fact that it is the President of the Patrolmen's Benevolent Association, in his official capacity, who has challenged the regulation here would seem to indicate that the regulation would if anything, decrease rather than increase the police force's esprit de corps.[6] And even if one accepted the argument that substantial similarity in appearance would increase a force's esprit de corps, I simply do not understand how implementation of this regulation could be expected to create any increment in similarity of appearance among members of a uniformed police force. While the regulation prohibits hair below the ears or the collar and limits the length of sideburns, it allows the maintenance of any type of hair style, other than a pony tail. Thus, as long as their hair does not go below their collars, two police officers, with an 'Afro' hair style and the other with a crew cut could both be in full compliance with the regulation.[7] * * *[8]"

a. Powell, J., joined the Court's opinion, but underscored that, unlike the dissenters, he found "no negative implications in the opinion with respect to a liberty interest within the Fourteenth Amendment as to matters of personal appearance."

2. While the parties did not address any First Amendment issues in any detail in this Court, governmental regulation of a citizen's personal appearance may in some circumstances not only deprive him of liberty under the Fourteenth Amendment but violate his First Amendment rights as well. *Tinker v. Des Moines School District* [p. 673 infra].

b. See also Wilkinson & White, [*Constitutional Protection for Personal Lifestyles*, 62 Corn.L.Rev. 562, 605 (1977): "Appearance, like speech, is a chief medium of self-expression that involves important choices about how we wish to project ourselves and be perceived by others. To link appearance with privacy and speech values is not, of course, to require similar constitutional treatment. It does imply, however, that we deal with a substantive constitutional liberty."

6. Nor, to say the least, is the esprit de corps argument bolstered by the fact that the International Brotherhood of Police Officers, a 25,000 member union representing uniformed police officers, has filed a brief as amicus curiae arguing that the challenged regulation is unconstitutional.

7. The regulation itself eschews what would appear to be a less intrusive means of achieving similarity in the hair length of on-duty officers. According to the regulation, a policeman cannot comply with the hair length requirements by wearing a wig with hair of the proper length while on duty. The regulation prohibits the wearing of wigs or hair pieces "on duty in uniform except for cosmetic reasons to cover natural baldness or physical disfiguration." Thus, while the regulation in terms applies to grooming standards of policemen while on duty, the hair length provision

8. See note 8 on page 271.

2. *The substantive due process rights of involuntarily-committed mentally retarded persons.* In YOUNGBERG v. ROMEO, 457 U.S. 307, 102 S.Ct. 2452, 73 L.Ed.2d 28 (1982), the Court considered for the first time the substantive due process rights of involuntarily-committed mentally retarded persons. On his mother's petition, Romeo, a profoundly retarded 33-year-old was involuntarily committed to a Pennsylvania state institution (Pennhurst). Subsequently, concerned about injuries Romeo had suffered at Pennhurst, his mother filed a federal action against institution officials claiming that her son had constitutional rights to (1) safe conditions of confinement, (2) freedom from bodily restraint, and (3) "a constitutional right to minimally adequate habilitation," i.e., minimal training and development of needed skills. (In light of his severe retardation, however, respondent conceded that no amount of training would make his release possible.) The Court, per POWELL, J., pointed out that respondent's first two claims "involve liberty interests recognized by prior decisions of this Court, interests that involuntary commitment proceedings do not extinguish," but found respondent's remaining claim "more troubling":

"On the basis of the record before us, it is quite uncertain whether respondent seeks any 'habilitation' or training unrelated to [his constitutionally protected liberty interest in] safety and freedom from bodily restraints. [If,] as seems the case, respondent seeks only training related to safety and freedom from restraints, this case does not present the difficult question whether a mentally retarded person, involuntarily committed to a state institution, has some general constitutional right to training per se, even when no type or amount of training would lead to freedom. [On the basis of the record], we conclude that respondent's liberty interests require the State to provide minimally adequate or reasonable training to ensure safety and freedom from undue restraint. [W]e need go no further in this case.

"[But the question] is not simply whether a liberty interest has been infringed but whether the extent or nature of the restraint or lack of absolute safety is such as to violate due process. In determining whether a substantive right protected by the Due Process Clause has been violated, it is necessary to balance 'the liberty of the individual' and 'the demands of an organized society.' "

The Court then considered "the proper standard for determining whether a State adequately has protected the rights of the involuntarily-committed mentally retarded." It agreed with the concurring judge below "that 'the Constitution only requires that the courts make certain that professional judgment was in fact exercised. It is not appropriate for the courts to specify which of several professionally acceptable choices should have been made.' Persons who have been involuntarily committed are entitled to more considerate treatment [than] criminals whose conditions of confinement are designed to punish. At the same time, the standard is lower than [a] 'compelling' or 'substantial' necessity [test for justifying restraints] that would place an undue burden on the administration of [state institutions] and also would restrict unnecessarily the exercise of professional judgment as to the needs of residents.

effectively controls both on-duty and off-duty appearance.

[Why did the *Kelley* majority see no need to respond to the dissent's point that simply requiring a police officer to wear an appropriate wig while on duty would serve all of the county's articulated interests? See Tribe, *Treatise* at 1387 n. 26.]

8. Because, to my mind, the challenged regulation fails to pass even a minimal degree of scrutiny, there is no need to determine whether, given the nature of the interests involved and the degree to which they are affected, the application of a more heightened scrutiny would be appropriate.

"[In] determining what is 'reasonable'—in this and in any case presenting a claim for training by a state—we emphasize that courts must show deference to the judgment exercised by a qualified professional. [The] decision, if made by a professional, is presumptively valid; liability may be imposed only when the decision by the professional is such a substantial departure from accepted professional judgment, practice or standards as to demonstrate that the person responsible actually did not base the decision on such a judgment.[a] In an action for damages against a professional in his individual capacity, however, the professional will not be liable if he was unable to satisfy his normal professional standards because of budgetary constraints; in such a situation, good-faith immunity would bar liability."

BLACKMUN, J., joined by Brennan and O'Connor, JJ., joined the Court's opinion, but concurred separately to clarify why, because of the uncertainty in the record, "that opinion properly leaves open two difficult and important questions." Unlike Burger, C.J., who considered the issue "frivolous," Blackmun, J., believed that whether Pennsylvania could accept respondent for "care and treatment" and then constitutionally refuse to provide him any "treatment," as that term is defined by state law, would, if properly before the Court, present "a serious issue." As for the second difficult question left open—whether respondent had an "independent constitutional claim [to] that 'habilitation' or training necessary to *preserve* those basic self-care skills he possessed when he first entered Pennhurst"—he believed that "it would be consistent with the Court's reasoning today to include within the 'minimally adequate training required by the Constitution' such training as is reasonably necessary to prevent a person's pre-existing self-care skills from *deteriorating* because of his commitment" and he viewed such deterioration "because of the State's unreasonable refusal to provide him training [a] loss of liberty quite distinct from—and as serious as—the loss of safety and freedom from unreasonable restraints."

BURGER, C.J., concurring, agreed with much of the Court's opinion, but "would hold flatly that respondent has no constitutional right to training, or 'habilitation,' per se." He agreed that "some amount of self-care instruction may be necessary to avoid unreasonable infringement of a mentally-retarded person's interests in safety and freedom from restraint"; but he thought it "clear" that "the Constitution does not otherwise place an affirmative duty on the State to provide any particular kind of training or habilitation—even such as might be encompassed under the essentially standardless rubric 'minimally adequate training,' to which the Court refers." Since respondent had asserted "a right to 'minimally adequate' habilitation '[q]uite apart from its relationship to decent care,'" unlike the Court he saw "no way to avoid the issue."[b]

THE "RIGHT TO DIE"

CRUZAN v. DIRECTOR, MISSOURI DEP'T. OF HEALTH

___ U.S. ___, 110 S.Ct. 2841, 111 L.Ed.2d 224 (1990).

CHIEF JUSTICE REHNQUIST delivered the opinion of the Court.

[The case arose as follows: Since 1983, when, at the age of 25, she suffered severe injuries during an automobile accident, petitioner Nancy Beth Cruzan has

a. Does this place "a seemingly insurmountable burden" on plaintiff mental patients? See Note, 96 Harv.L.Rev. 77, 85 (1982).

b. Consider, too, *DeShaney v. Winnebago County*, p. 1243 infra.

been in a persistent vegetative state, a condition in which a person exhibits motor reflexes, but evinces no indications of significant cognitive function. (Some 10,000 persons are being maintained in a persistent vegetative state (PVS) in the United States and the number is expected to increase significantly in the near future.) Although the trial court found that Nancy is "oblivious to her environment except for reflective responses to sound and perhaps painful stimuli," medical experts testified that if her life support were not removed she could be kept alive another 30 years.

[Nancy is able to breathe on her own, but for a number of years she has received all her nutrition and fluids through a gastrostomy tube (a feeding and hydration tube inserted into her stomach). About a month after the accident, when Nancy was unconscious, surgeons implanted the feeding tube with the consent of Nancy's then husband. This step was taken in order to ease feeding and improve chances of possible recovery. When it became apparent that Nancy had virtually no chance of regaining her cognitive faculties, co-petitioners Lester and Joyce Cruzan, Nancy's parents and co-guardians, sought to discontinue the tubal feeding. They were rebuffed by officials of the Missouri state hospital, where Nancy is a patient.

[Nancy's parents then sought a court order directing the removal of the feeding tube. The trial court so ordered, maintaining that a person in Nancy's condition had a fundamental right to refuse or to direct removal of her life support and that no state interest outweighed Nancy's "right to liberty."

[Before lapsing into her present condition, Nancy had neither executed a living will nor designated anyone to make health-care decisions for her in the event she became incompetent. But when still a vibrant person Nancy had once remarked that she did not want to live "as a vegetable." In another conversation, she had stated that if she couldn't do things for herself "even halfway, let alone not at all," she "wouldn't want to live that way." The trial court concluded that such evidence "suggests that given her present condition [Nancy] would not wish to continue on with her nutrition and hydration."

[The Missouri Supreme Court reversed (4–3). The majority considered Nancy's remarks so remote, general and casual as to be "unreliable for the purposes of establishing her intent." For a guardian to exercise whatever right an incompetent patient may have to be free of life support, ruled the court, the patient must have complied with "the formalities required under Missouri's living will statutes" or there must be "clear and convincing, inherently reliable evidence" of her wishes. Such evidence, concluded the court, was lacking in this case. The U.S. Supreme Court affirmed.]

As [various state] cases demonstrate, the common-law doctrine of informed consent is viewed as generally encompassing the right of a competent individual to refuse medical treatment. Beyond that, these decisions demonstrate both similarity and diversity in their approach to decision of what all agree is a perplexing question with unusually strong moral and ethical overtones. State courts have available to them for decision a number of sources—state constitutions, statutes, and common law—which are not available to us. In this Court, the question is simply and starkly whether the United States Constitution prohibits Missouri from choosing the rule of decision which it did.

[The] Fourteenth Amendment provides that no State shall "deprive any person of life, liberty, or property, without due process of law." The principle that a competent person has a constitutionally protected liberty interest in refusing unwanted medical treatment may be inferred from our prior decisions.

In *Jacobson v. Massachusetts,* 197 U.S. 11, 25 S.Ct. 358, 49 L.Ed. 643 (1905), for instance, the Court balanced an individual's liberty interest in declining an unwanted smallpox vaccine against the State's interest in preventing disease.

[Just] this Term, in the course of holding that a State's procedures for administering antipsychotic medication to prisoners were sufficient to satisfy due process concerns, we recognized that prisoners possess "a significant liberty interest in avoiding the unwanted administration of [such] drugs under the Due Process Clause." *Washington v. Harper,* 494 U.S. 210, 110 S.Ct. 1028, 108 L.Ed. 2d 178 (1990).

[But] determining that a person has a "liberty interest" under the Due Process Clause does not end the inquiry;[7] "whether respondent's constitutional rights have been violated must be determined by balancing his liberty interests against the relevant state interests." *Youngberg v. Romeo.*

Petitioners insist that under the general holdings of our cases, the forced administration of life-sustaining medical treatment, and even of artificially-delivered food and water essential to life, would implicate a competent persons' liberty interest. Although we think the logic of the cases discussed above would embrace such a liberty interest, the dramatic consequences involved in refusal of such treatment would inform the inquiry as to whether the deprivation of that interest is constitutionally permissible. But for purposes of this case, we assume that the United States Constitution would grant a competent person a constitutionally protected right to refuse lifesaving hydration and nutrition.

Petitioners go on to assert that an incompetent person should possess the same right in this respect as is possessed by a competent person. They rely primarily on our decisions in *Parham v. J.R.* and *Youngberg v. Romeo.*

[The] difficulty with petitioners' claim is that in a sense it begs the question: an incompetent person is not able to make an informed and voluntary choice to exercise a hypothetical right to refuse treatment or any other right. Such a "right" must be exercised for her, if at all, by some sort of surrogate. Here, Missouri has in effect recognized that under certain circumstances a surrogate may act for the patient in electing to have hydration and nutrition withdrawn in such a way as to cause death, but it has established a procedural safeguard to assure that the action of the surrogate conforms as best it may to the wishes expressed by the patient while competent. Missouri requires that evidence of the incompetent's wishes as to the withdrawal of treatment be proved by clear and convincing evidence. The question, then, is whether the United States Constitution forbids the establishment of this procedural requirement by the State. We hold that it does not.

Whether or not Missouri's clear and convincing evidence requirement comports with the United States Constitution depends in part on what interests the State may properly seek to protect in this situation. Missouri relies on its interest in the protection and preservation of human life, and there can be no gainsaying this interest. As a general matter, the States—indeed, all civilized nations—demonstrate their commitment to life by treating homicide as serious crime. Moreover, the majority of States in this country have laws imposing criminal penalties on one who assists another to commit suicide. We do not

7. Although many state courts have held that a right to refuse treatment is encompassed by a generalized constitutional right of privacy, we have never so held. We believe this issue is more properly analyzed in terms of a Fourteenth Amendment liberty interest. See *Bowers v. Hardwick.*

think a State is required to remain neutral in the face of an informed and voluntary decision by a physically-able adult to starve to death.

But in the context presented here, a State has more particular interests at stake. The choice between life and death is a deeply personal decision of obvious and overwhelming finality. We believe Missouri may legitimately seek to safeguard the personal element of this choice through the imposition of heightened evidentiary requirements. It cannot be disputed that the Due Process Clause protects an interest in life as well as an interest in refusing life-sustaining medical treatment. Not all incompetent patients will have loved ones available to serve as surrogate decisionmakers. And even where family members are present, "[t]here will, of course, be some unfortunate situations in which family members will not act to protect a patient." A State is entitled to guard against potential abuses in such situations. Similarly, a State is entitled to consider that a judicial proceeding to make a determination regarding an incompetent's wishes may very well not be an adversarial one, with the added guarantee of accurate factfinding that the adversary process brings with it. Finally, we think a State may properly decline to make judgments about the "quality" of life that a particular individual may enjoy, and simply assert an unqualified interest in the preservation of human life to be weighed against the constitutionally protected interests of the individual.

In our view, Missouri has permissibly sought to advance these interests through the adoption of a "clear and convincing" standard of proof to govern such proceedings. "The function of a standard of proof, as that concept is embodied in the Due Process Clause and in the realm of factfinding, is to 'instruct the factfinder concerning the degree of confidence our society thinks he should have in the correctness of factual conclusions for a particular type of adjudication.' " * * *

We think it self-evident that the interests at stake in the instant proceedings are more substantial, both on an individual and societal level, than those involved in a run-of-the-mine civil dispute. But not only does the standard of proof reflect the importance of a particular adjudication, it also serves as "a societal judgment about how the risk of error should be distributed between the litigants." The more stringent the burden of proof a party must bear, the more that party bears the risk of an erroneous decision. We believe that Missouri may permissibly place an increased risk of an erroneous decision on those seeking to terminate an incompetent individual's life-sustaining treatment. An erroneous decision not to terminate results in a maintenance of the status quo; the possibility of subsequent developments such as advancements in medical science, the discovery of new evidence regarding the patient's intent, changes in the law, or simply the unexpected death of the patient despite the administration of life-sustaining treatment, at least create the potential that a wrong decision will eventually be corrected or its impact mitigated. An erroneous decision to withdraw life-sustaining treatment, however, is not susceptible of correction.

[In] sum, we conclude that a State may apply a clear and convincing evidence standard in proceedings where a guardian seeks to discontinue nutrition and hydration of a person diagnosed to be in a persistent vegetative state.

[The] Supreme Court of Missouri held that in this case the testimony adduced at trial did not amount to clear and convincing proof of the patient's desire to have hydration and nutrition withdrawn. In so doing, it reversed a decision of the Missouri trial court which had found that the evidence "suggest[ed]" Nancy Cruzan would not have desired to continue such measures, but which had not adopted the standard of "clear and convincing evidence" enunciated by the Supreme Court. The testimony adduced at trial consisted primarily of Nancy Cruzan's statements made to a housemate about a year before her accident that she would not want to live should she face life as a "vegetable," and other observations to the same effect. The observations did not deal in terms with withdrawal of medical treatment or of hydration and nutrition. We cannot say that the Supreme Court of Missouri committed constitutional error in reaching the conclusion that it did.[11]

Petitioners alternatively contend that Missouri must accept the "substituted judgment" of close family members even in the absence of substantial proof that their views reflect the views of the patient. They rely primarily upon our decisions in *Michael H. v. Gerald D.* and *Parham v. J.R.* But we do not think these cases support their claim. In *Michael H.,* we upheld the constitutionality of California's favored treatment of traditional family relationships; such a holding may not be turned around into a constitutional requirement that a State must recognize the primacy of those relationships in a situation like this. And in *Parham,* where the patient was a minor, we also upheld the constitutionality of a state scheme in which parents made certain decisions for mentally ill minors. Here again petitioners would seek to turn a decision which allowed a State to rely on family decisionmaking into a constitutional requirement that the State recognize such decisionmaking. But constitutional law does not work that way.

No doubt is engendered by anything in this record but that Nancy Cruzan's mother and father are loving and caring parents. If the State were required by the United States Constitution to repose a right of "substituted judgment" with anyone, the Cruzans would surely qualify. But we do not think the Due Process Clause requires the State to repose judgment on these matters with anyone but the patient herself. Close family members may have a strong feeling—a feeling not at all ignoble or unworthy, but not entirely disinterested, either—that they do not wish to witness the continuation of the life of a loved one which they regard as hopeless, meaningless, and even degrading. But there is no automatic assurance that the view of close family members will necessarily be the same as the patient's would have been had she been confronted with the prospect of her situation while competent. All of the reasons previously discussed for allowing Missouri to require clear and convincing evidence of the patient's wishes lead us to conclude that the State may choose to defer only to those wishes, rather than confide the decision to close family members.[12]

JUSTICE O'CONNOR, concurring.

I agree that a protected liberty interest in refusing unwanted medical treatment may be inferred from our prior decisions and that the refusal of

11. The clear and convincing standard of proof has been variously defined in this context as "proof sufficient to persuade the trier of fact that the patient held a firm and settled commitment to the termination of life supports under the circumstances like those presented" and as evidence which "produces in the mind of the trier of fact a firm belief or conviction as to the truth of the allegations sought to be established, evidence so clear, direct and weighty and convincing as to enable [the factfinder] to come to a clear conviction, without hesitancy, of the truth of the precise facts in issue." * * *

12. We are not faced in this case with the question of whether a State might be required to defer to the decision of a surrogate if competent and probative evidence established that the patient herself had expressed a desire that the decision to terminate life-sustaining treatment be made for her by that individual. * * *

artificially delivered food and water is encompassed within that liberty interest. I write separately to clarify why I believe this to be so.

As the Court notes, the liberty interest in refusing medical treatment flows from decisions involving the State's invasions into the body. Because our notions of liberty are inextricably entwined with our idea of physical freedom and self-determination, the Court has often deemed state incursions into the body repugnant to the interests protected by the Due Process Clause. [The] State's imposition of medical treatment on an unwilling competent adult necessarily involves some form of restraint and intrusion. A seriously ill or dying patient whose wishes are not honored may feel a captive of the machinery required for life-sustaining measures or other medical interventions. Such forced treatment may burden that individual's liberty interests as much as any state coercion.

[The] State's artificial provision of nutrition and hydration implicates identical concerns. Artificial feeding cannot readily be distinguished from other forms of medical treatment. [A] gastrostomy tube (as was used to provide food and water to Nancy Cruzan) or jejunostomy tube must be surgically implanted into the stomach or small intestine. Requiring a competent adult to endure such procedures against her will burdens the patient's liberty, dignity, and freedom to determine the course of her own treatment. Accordingly, the liberty guaranteed by the Due Process Clause must protect, if it protects anything, an individual's deeply personal decision to reject medical treatment, including the artificial delivery of food and water.

I also write separately to emphasize that the Court does not today decide the issue whether a State must also give effect to the decisions of a surrogate decisionmaker. In my view, such a duty may well be constitutionally required to protect the patient's liberty interest in refusing medical treatment. Few individuals provide explicit oral or written instructions regarding their intent to refuse medical treatment should they become incompetent. States which decline to consider any evidence other than such instructions may frequently fail to honor a patient's intent. Such failures might be avoided if the State considered an equally probative source of evidence: the patient's appointment of a proxy to make health care decisions on her behalf. Delegating the authority to make medical decisions to a family member or friend is becoming a common method of planning for the future. * * *

Today's decision, holding only that the Constitution permits a State to require clear and convincing evidence of Nancy Cruzan's desire to have artificial hydration and nutrition withdrawn, does not preclude a future determination that the Constitution requires the States to implement the decisions of a patient's duly appointed surrogate. Nor does it prevent States from developing other approaches for protecting an incompetent individual's liberty interest in refusing medical treatment. [N]o national consensus has yet emerged on the best solution for this difficult and sensitive problem. Today we decide only that one State's practice does not violate the Constitution * * *.

JUSTICE SCALIA, concurring.

The various opinions in this case portray quite clearly the difficult, indeed agonizing, questions that are presented by the constantly increasing power of science to keep the human body alive for longer than any reasonable person would want to inhabit it. The States have begun to grapple with these problems through legislation. I am concerned, from the tenor of today's opinions, that we are poised to confuse that enterprise as successfully as we have confused the enterprise of legislating concerning abortion—requiring it to be conducted against a background of federal constitutional imperatives that are unknown because they are being newly crafted from Term to Term. That would be a great misfortune.

While I agree with the Court's analysis today, and therefore join in its opinion, I would have preferred that we announce, clearly and promptly, that the federal courts have no business in this field; that American law has always accorded the State the power to prevent, by force if necessary, suicide—including suicide by refusing to take appropriate measures necessary to preserve one's life; that the point at which life becomes "worthless," and the point at which the means necessary to preserve it become "extraordinary" or "inappropriate," are neither set forth in the Constitution nor known to the nine Justices of this Court any better than they are known to nine people picked at random from the Kansas City telephone directory; and hence, that even when it *is* demonstrated by clear and convincing evidence that a patient no longer wishes certain measures to be taken to preserve her life, it is up to the citizens of Missouri to decide, through their elected representatives, whether that wish will be honored. It is quite impossible (because the Constitution says nothing about the matter) that those citizens will decide upon a line less lawful than the one we would choose; and it is unlikely (because we know no more about "life-and-death" than they do) that they will decide upon a line less reasonable.

The text of the Due Process Clause does not protect individuals against deprivations of liberty *simpliciter.* It protects them against deprivations of liberty "without due process of law." To determine that such a deprivation would not occur if Nancy Cruzan were forced to take nourishment against her will, it is unnecessary to reopen the historically recurrent debate over whether "due process" includes substantive restrictions. It is at least true that no "substantive due process" claim can be maintained unless the claimant demonstrates that the State has deprived him of a right historically and traditionally protected against State interference. *Michael H.* (plurality opinion); *Hardwick.* [That] cannot possibly be established here.

At common law in England, a suicide—defined as one who "deliberately puts an end to his own existence, or commits any unlawful malicious act, the consequence of which is his own death"—was criminally liable. [And] most States that did not explicitly prohibit assisted suicide in 1868 recognized, when the issue arose in the 50 years following the Fourteenth Amendment's ratification, that assisted and (in some cases) attempted suicide were unlawful. Thus, "there is no significant support for the claim that a right to suicide is so rooted in our tradition that it may be deemed 'fundamental' or 'implicit in the concept of ordered liberty.' "

Petitioners rely on three distinctions to separate Nancy Cruzan's case from ordinary suicide: (1) that she is permanently incapacitated and in pain; (2) that she would bring on her death not by any affirmative act but by merely declining treatment that provides nourishment; and (3) that preventing her from effectuating her presumed wish to die requires violation of her bodily integrity. None of these suffices. Suicide was not excused even when committed "to avoid those ills which [persons] had not the fortitude to endure."

[The] second asserted distinction [relies] on the dichotomy between action and inaction. Suicide, it is said, consists of an affirmative act to end one's life; refusing treatment is not an affirmative act "causing" death, but merely a passive acceptance of the natural process of dying. I readily acknowledge that the distinction between action and inaction has some bearing upon the legislative judgment of what ought to be prevented as suicide—though even there it would seem to me unreasonable to draw the line precisely between action and inaction, rather than between various forms of inaction.

[But] to return to the principal point for present purposes: the irrelevance of the action-inaction distinction. Starving oneself to death is no different from putting a gun to one's temple as far as the common-law definition of suicide is concerned; the cause of death in both cases is the suicide's conscious decision to "pu[t] an end to his own existence." Of course the common law rejected the action-inaction distinction in other contexts involving the taking of human life as well. In the prosecution of a parent for the starvation death of her infant, it was no defense that the infant's death was "caused" by no action of the parent but by the natural process of starvation, or by the infant's natural inability to provide for itself. A physician, moreover, could be criminally liable for failure to provide care that could have extended the patient's life, even if death was immediately caused by the underlying disease that the physician failed to treat.

[The] third asserted basis of distinction—that frustrating Nancy Cruzan's wish to die in the present case requires interference with her bodily integrity—is likewise inadequate, because such interference is impermissible only if one begs the question whether her refusal to undergo the treatment on her own is suicide. It has always been lawful not only for the State, but even for private citizens, to interfere with bodily integrity to prevent a felony. That general rule has of course been applied to suicide. [It] is not even reasonable, much less required by the Constitution, to maintain that although the State has the right to prevent a person from slashing his wrists it does not have the power to apply physical force to prevent him from doing so, nor the power, should he succeed, to apply, coercively if necessary, medical measures to stop the flow of blood.

[The] dissents of Justices Brennan and Stevens make a plausible case for our intervention here only by embracing—the latter explicitly and the former by implication—a political principle that the States are free to adopt, but that is demonstrably not imposed by the Constitution. [I]nsofar as balancing the relative interests of the State and the individual is concerned, there is nothing distinctive about accepting death through the refusal of "medical treatment," as opposed to accepting it through the refusal of food, or through the failure to shut off the engine and get out of the car after parking in one's garage after work. [Justice] Brennan's position ultimately rests upon the proposition that it is none of the State's business if a person wants to commit suicide. Justice Stevens is explicit on the point: "Choices about death touch the core of liberty. [N]ot much may be said with confidence about death unless it is said from faith, and that alone is reason enough to protect the freedom to conform choices about death to individual conscience." This is a view that some societies have held, and that our States are free to adopt if they wish. But it is not a view imposed by our constitutional traditions, in which the power of the State to prohibit suicide is unquestionable.

What I have said above is not meant to suggest that I would think it desirable, if we were sure that Nancy Cruzan wanted to die, to keep her alive by the means at issue here. I assert only that the Constitution has nothing to say about the subject. To raise up a constitutional right here we would have to create out of nothing (for it exists neither in text nor tradition) some constitutional principle whereby, although the State may insist that an individual come in out of the cold and eat food, it may not insist that he take medicine; and although it may pump his stomach empty of poison he has ingested, it may not fill his stomach with food he has failed to ingest. Are there, then, no reasonable and humane limits that ought not to be exceeded in requiring an individual to preserve his own life? There obviously are, but they are not set forth in the Due Process Clause. What assures us that those limits will not be exceeded is the same constitutional guarantee that is the source of most of our protection—what protects us, for example, from being assessed a tax of 100% of our income above the subsistence level, from being forbidden to drive cars, or from being required to send our children to school for 10 hours a day, none of which horribles is categorically prohibited by the Constitution. Our salvation is the Equal Protection Clause, which requires the democratic majority to accept for themselves and their loved ones what they impose on you and me. This Court need not, and has no authority to, inject itself into every field of human activity where irrationality and oppression may theoretically occur, and if it tries to do so it will destroy itself.

JUSTICE BRENNAN, with whom JUSTICE MARSHALL and JUSTICE BLACKMUN join, dissenting.

[Because] I believe that Nancy Cruzan has a fundamental right to be free of unwanted artificial nutrition and hydration, which right is not outweighed by any interests of the State, and because I find that the improperly biased procedural obstacles imposed by the Missouri Supreme Court impermissibly burden that right, I respectfully dissent. Nancy Cruzan is entitled to choose to die with dignity.

[The] starting point for our legal analysis must be whether a competent person has a constitutional right to avoid unwanted medical care. Earlier this Term, this Court held that the Due Process Clause of the Fourteenth Amendment confers a significant liberty interest in avoiding unwanted medical treatment. *Washington v. Harper.* Today, the Court concedes that our prior decisions "support the recognition of a general liberty interest in refusing medical treatment." The Court, however, avoids discussing either the measure of that liberty interest or its application by assuming, for purposes of this case only, that a competent person has a constitutionally protected liberty interest in being free of unwanted artificial nutrition and hydration. Justice O'Connor's opinion is less parsimonious. She openly affirms that "the Court has often deemed state incursions into the body repugnant to the interests protected by the Due Process Clause," that there is a liberty interest in avoiding unwanted medical treatment and that it encompasses the right to be free of "artificially delivered food and water."

But if a competent person has a liberty interest to be free of unwanted medical treatment, as both the majority and Justice O'Connor concede, it must be fundamental.

[The] right to be free from medical attention without consent, to determine what shall be done with one's own body, *is* deeply rooted in this Nation's traditions, as the majority acknowledges. [Thus,] freedom from unwanted medical attention is unquestionably among those principles "so rooted in the traditions and conscience of our people as to be ranked as fundamental." * * *

No material distinction can be drawn between the treatment to which Nancy Cruzan continues to be subject—artificial nutrition and hydration—and any other medical treatment. The artificial delivery of nutrition and hydration is undoubtedly medical treatment.

[Nor] does the fact that Nancy Cruzan is now incompetent deprive her of her fundamental rights. See *Youngberg v. Romeo* (holding that severely retarded man's liberty interests in safety, freedom from bodily restraint and reasonable training survive involuntary commitment); *Parham v. J.R.* (recognizing a child's substantial liberty interest in not being confined unnecessarily for medical treatment). [As] the majority recognizes, the question is not whether an incompetent has constitutional rights, but how such rights may be exercised.

[The] right to be free from unwanted medical attention is a right to evaluate the potential benefit of treatment and its possible consequences according to one's own values and to make a personal decision whether to subject oneself to the intrusion. For a patient like Nancy Cruzan, the sole benefit of medical treatment is being kept metabolically alive. Neither artificial nutrition nor any other form of medical treatment available today can cure or in any way ameliorate her condition. Irreversibly vegetative patients are devoid of thought, emotion and sensation; they are permanently and completely unconscious.

[Although] the right to be free of unwanted medical intervention, like other constitutionally protected interests, may not be absolute, no State interest could outweigh the rights of an individual in Nancy Cruzan's position. Whatever a State's possible interests in mandating life-support treatment under other circumstances, there is no good to be obtained here by Missouri's insistence that Nancy Cruzan remain on life-support systems if it is indeed her wish not to do so. Missouri does not claim, nor could it, that society as a whole will be benefited by Nancy's receiving medical treatment. No third party's situation will be improved and no harm to others will be averted.[13]

The only state interest asserted here is a general interest in the preservation of life.[14] But the State has no legitimate general interest in someone's life, completely abstracted from the interest of the person living that life, that could outweigh the person's choice to avoid medical treatment. [Thus,] the State's general interest in life must accede to Nancy Cruzan's particularized and intense interest in self-determination in her choice of medical treatment. There is simply nothing legitimately within the State's purview to be gained by superseding her decision.

Moreover, there may be considerable danger that Missouri's rule of decision would impair rather than serve any interest the State does have in sustaining life. Current medical practice recommends use of heroic measures if there is a scintilla of a chance that the patient will recover, on the assumption that the measures will be discontinued should the patient improve. When the Presi-

13. Were such interests at stake, however, I would find that the Due Process Clause places limits on what invasive medical procedures could be forced on an unwilling comatose patient in pursuit of the interests of a third party. If Missouri were correct that its interests outweigh Nancy's interest in avoiding medical procedures as long as she is free of pain and physical discomfort, it is not apparent why a State could not choose to remove one of her kidneys without consent on the ground that society would be better off if the recipient of that kidney were saved from renal poisoning. Nancy cannot feel surgical pain. Nor would removal of one kidney be expected to shorten her life expectancy. * * * Indeed, why could the State not perform medical experiments on her body, experiments that might save countless lives, and would cause her no greater burden than she already bears by being fed through the gastrostomy tube? This would be too brave a new world for me and, I submit, for our Constitution.

14. The Missouri Supreme Court reviewed the state interests that had been identified by other courts as potentially relevant—prevention of homicide and suicide, protection of interests of innocent third parties, maintenance of the ethical integrity of the medical profession, and preservation of life—and concluded that: "In this case, only the state's interest in the preservation of life is implicated."

dent's Commission in 1982 approved the withdrawal of life support equipment from irreversibly vegetative patients, it explained that "[a]n even more troubling wrong occurs when a treatment that might save life or improve health is not started because the health care personnel are afraid that they will find it very difficult to stop the treatment if, as is fairly likely, it proves to be of little benefit and greatly burdens the patient."

This is not to say that the State has no legitimate interests to assert here. As the majority recognizes, Missouri has a *parens patriae* interest in providing Nancy Cruzan, now incompetent, with as accurate as possible a determination of how she would exercise her rights under these circumstances. Second, if and when it is determined that Nancy Cruzan would want to continue treatment, the State may legitimately assert an interest in providing that treatment. But *until* Nancy's wishes have been determined, the only state interest that may be asserted is an interest in safeguarding the accuracy of that determination.

Accuracy, therefore, must be our touchstone. Missouri may constitutionally impose only those procedural requirements that serve to enhance the accuracy of a determination of Nancy Cruzan's wishes or are at least consistent with an accurate determination. The Missouri "safeguard" that the Court upholds today does not meet that standard. The determination needed in this context is whether the incompetent person would choose to live in a persistent vegetative state on life-support or to avoid this medical treatment. Missouri's rule of decision imposes a markedly asymmetrical evidentiary burden. Only evidence of specific statements of treatment choice made by the patient when competent is admissible to support a finding that the patient, now in a persistent vegetative state, would wish to avoid further medical treatment. Moreover, this evidence must be clear and convincing. No proof is required to support a finding that the incompetent person would wish to continue treatment.

[The] majority claims that the allocation of the risk of error is justified because it is more important not to terminate life-support for someone who would wish it continued than to honor the wishes of someone who would not. An erroneous decision to terminate life-support is irrevocable, says the majority, while an erroneous decision not to terminate "results in a maintenance of the status quo." [17] But, from the point of view of the patient, an erroneous decision in either direction is irrevocable. An erroneous decision to terminate artificial nutrition and hydration, to be sure, will lead to failure of that last remnant of physiological life, the brain stem, and result in complete brain death. An erroneous decision not to terminate life-support, however, robs a patient of the very qualities protected by the right to avoid unwanted medical treatment. His own degraded existence is perpetuated; his family's suffering is protracted; the memory he leaves behind becomes more and more distorted.

[Even] more than its heightened evidentiary standard, the Missouri court's categorical exclusion of relevant evidence dispenses with any semblence of accurate factfinding. The court adverted to no evidence supporting its decision, but held that no clear and convincing, inherently reliable evidence had been presented to show that Nancy would want to avoid further treatment. In doing so, the court failed to consider statements Nancy had made to family members and a close friend. The court also failed to consider testimony from Nancy's

17. The majority's definition of the "status quo," of course, begs the question. Artificial delivery of nutrition and hydration represents the "status quo" only if the State has chosen to permit doctors and hospitals to keep a patient on life-support systems over the protests of his family or guardian. The "status quo" absent that state interference would be the natural result of his accident or illness (and the family's decision). * * *

mother and sister that they were certain that Nancy would want to discontinue artificial nutrition and hydration, even after the court found that Nancy's family was loving and without malignant motive. * * *

Too few people execute living wills or equivalently formal directives for such an evidentiary rule to ensure adequately that the wishes of incompetent persons will be honored. While it might be a wise social policy to encourage people to furnish such instructions, no general conclusion about a patient's choice can be drawn from the absence of formalities. The probability of becoming irreversibly vegetative is so low that many people may not feel an urgency to marshal formal evidence of their preferences. Some may not wish to dwell on their own physical deterioration and mortality. Even someone with a resolute determination to avoid life-support under circumstances such as Nancy's would still need to know that such things as living wills exist and how to execute one. Often legal help would be necessary, especially given the majority's apparent willingness to permit States to insist that a person's wishes are not truly known unless the particular medical treatment is specified.

[The] testimony of close friends and family members, on the other hand, may often be the best evidence available of what the patient's choice would be. It is they with whom the patient most likely will have discussed such questions and they who know the patient best. [The] Missouri court's decision to ignore this whole category of testimony is also at odds with the practices of other States.

The Missouri court's disdain for Nancy's statements in serious conversations not long before her accident, for the opinions of Nancy's family and friends as to her values, beliefs and certain choice, and even for the opinion of an outside objective factfinder appointed by the State evinces a disdain for Nancy Cruzan's own right to choose. The rules by which an incompetent person's wishes are determined must represent every effort to determine those wishes. The rule that the Missouri court adopted and that this Court upholds, however, skews the result away from a determination that as accurately as possible reflects the individual's own preferences and beliefs. It is a rule that transforms human beings into passive subjects of medical technology.

[The] majority justifies its position by arguing that, while close family members may have a strong feeling about the question, "there is no automatic assurance that the view of close family members will necessarily be the same as the patient's would have been had she been confronted with the prospect of her situation while competent." I cannot quarrel with this observation. But it leads only to another question: Is there any reason to suppose that a State is *more* likely to make the choice that the patient would have made than someone who knew the patient intimately? To ask this is to answer it.

[A] State's inability to discern an incompetent patient's choice still need not mean that a State is rendered powerless to protect that choice. But I would find that the Due Process Clause prohibits a State from doing more than that. A State may ensure that the person who makes the decision on the patient's behalf is the one whom the patient himself would have selected to make that choice for him. And a State may exclude from consideration anyone having improper motives. But a State generally must either repose the choice with the person whom the patient himself would most likely have chosen as proxy or leave the decision to the patient's family.

[The] new medical technology can reclaim those who would have been irretrievably lost a few decades ago and restore them to active lives. For Nancy Cruzan, it failed, and for others with wasting incurable disease it may be doomed to failure. In these unfortunate situations, the bodies and preferences and memories of the victims do not escheat to the State; nor does our Constitution permit the State or any other government to commandeer them. No singularity of feeling exists upon which such a government might confidently rely as *parens patriae.*

[Yet] Missouri and this Court have displaced Nancy's own assessment of the processes associated with dying. They have discarded evidence of her will, ignored her values, and deprived her of the right to a decision as closely approximating her own choice as humanly possible. They have done so disingenuously in her name, and openly in Missouri's own. * * *

JUSTICE STEVENS, dissenting.

[The Court] permits the State's abstract, undifferentiated interest in the preservation of life to overwhelm the best interests of Nancy Beth Cruzan, interests which would, according to an undisputed finding, be served by allowing her guardian to exercise her constitutional right to discontinue medical treatment. [Because] he believed he had a duty to do so, the independent guardian ad litem appealed the trial court's order to the Missouri Supreme Court. In that appeal, however, the guardian advised the court that he did not disagree with the trial court's decision. Specifically, he endorsed the critical finding that "it was in Nancy Cruzan's best interests to have the tube feeding discontinued."

That important conclusion thus was not disputed by the litigants. One might reasonably suppose that it would be dispositive: if Nancy Cruzan has no interest in continued treatment, and if she has a liberty interest in being free from unwanted treatment, and if the cessation of treatment would have no adverse impact on third parties, and if no reason exists to doubt the good faith of Nancy's parents, then what possible basis could the State have for insisting upon continued medical treatment? Yet, instead of questioning or endorsing the trial court's conclusions about Nancy Cruzan's interests, the State Supreme Court largely ignored them.

* * * Choices about death touch the core of liberty. Our duty, and the concomitant freedom, to come to terms with the conditions of our own mortality are undoubtedly "so rooted in the traditions and conscience of our people as to be ranked as fundamental," and indeed are essential incidents of the unalienable rights to life and liberty endowed us by our Creator.

The more precise constitutional significance of death is difficult to describe; not much may be said with confidence about death unless it is said from faith, and that alone is reason enough to protect the freedom to conform choices about death to individual conscience. We may also, however, justly assume that death is not life's simple opposite, or its necessary terminus, but rather its completion.

[These] considerations cast into stark relief the injustice, and unconstitutionality, of Missouri's treatment of Nancy Beth Cruzan. Nancy Cruzan's death, when it comes, cannot be an historic act of heroism; it will inevitably be the consequence of her tragic accident. But Nancy Cruzan's interest in life, no less than that of any other person, includes an interest in how she will be thought of after her death by those whose opinions mattered to her. There can be no doubt that her life made her dear to her family, and to others. How she dies will affect how that life is remembered. The trial court's order authorizing Nancy's parents to cease their daughter's treatment would have permitted the family that cares for Nancy to bring to a close her tragedy and her death. Missouri's objection to that order subordinates Nancy's body, her family, and the lasting significance of her life to the State's own interests. The decision we review thereby interferes with constitutional interests of the highest order.

To be constitutionally permissible, Missouri's intrusion upon these fundamental liberties must, at a minimum, bear a reasonable relationship to a legitimate state end. Missouri asserts that its policy is related to a state interest in the protection of life. In my view, however, it is an effort to define life, rather than to protect it, that is the heart of Missouri's policy. Missouri insists, without regard to Nancy Cruzan's own interests, upon equating her life with the biological persistence of her bodily functions. Nancy Cruzan, it must be remembered, is not now simply incompetent. She is in a persistent vegetative state, and has been so for seven years. The trial court found, and no party contested, that Nancy has no possibility of recovery and no consciousness.

It seems to me that the Court errs insofar as it characterizes this case as involving "judgments about the 'quality' of life that a particular individual may enjoy." Nancy Cruzan is obviously "*alive*" in a physiological sense. But for patients like Nancy Cruzan, who have no consciousness and no chance of recovery, there is a serious question as to whether the mere persistence of their bodies is "*life*" as that word is commonly understood, or as it is used in both the Constitution and the Declaration of Independence. The State's unflagging determination to perpetuate Nancy Cruzan's physical existence is comprehensible only as an effort to define life's meaning, not as an attempt to preserve its sanctity.

This much should be clear from the oddity of Missouri's definition alone. Life, particularly human life, is not commonly thought of as a merely physiological condition or function. Its sanctity is often thought to derive from the impossibility of any such reduction. [A]bsent some theological abstraction, the idea of life is not conceived separately from the idea of a living person. Yet, it is by precisely such a separation that Missouri asserts an interest in Nancy Cruzan's life in opposition to Nancy Cruzan's own interests. The resulting definition is uncommon indeed.

[In] short, there is no reasonable ground for believing that Nancy Beth Cruzan has any *personal* interest in the perpetuation of what the State has decided is her life. As I have already suggested, it would be possible to hypothesize such an interest on the basis of theological or philosophical conjecture. But even to posit such a basis for the State's action is to condemn it. It is not within the province of secular government to circumscribe the liberties of the people by regulations designed wholly for the purpose of establishing a sectarian definition of life. See *Webster* (Stevens, J., dissenting).

My disagreement with the Court is thus unrelated to its endorsement of the clear and convincing standard of proof for cases of this kind. Indeed, I agree that the controlling facts must be established with unmistakable clarity. The critical question, however, is not how to prove the controlling facts but rather what proven facts should be controlling. In my view, the constitutional answer is clear: the best interests of the individual, especially when buttressed by the interests of all related third parties, must prevail over any general state policy that simply ignores those interests. Indeed, the only apparent secular basis for the State's interest in life is the policy's persuasive impact upon people other than Nancy and her family. * * *

Only because Missouri has arrogated to itself the power to define life, and only because the Court permits this usurpation, are Nancy Cruzan's life and liberty put into disquieting conflict. If Nancy Cruzan's life were defined by reference to her own interests, so that her life expired when her biological existence ceased serving *any* of her own interests, then her constitutionally protected interest in freedom from unwanted treatment would not come into conflict with her constitutionally protected interest in life. Conversely, if there were *any* evidence that Nancy Cruzan herself defined life to encompass every form of biological persistence by a human being, so that the continuation of treatment would serve Nancy's own liberty, then once again there would be no conflict between life and liberty. The opposition of life and liberty in this case are thus not the result of Nancy Cruzan's tragic accident, but are instead the artificial consequence of Missouri's effort, and this Court's willingness, to abstract Nancy Cruzan's life from Nancy Cruzan's person.

Both this Court's majority and the state court's majority express great deference to the policy choice made by the state legislature. That deference is, in my view, based upon a severe error in the Court's constitutional logic. The Court believes that the liberty interest claimed here on behalf of Nancy Cruzan is peculiarly problematic because "an incompetent person is not able to make an informed and voluntary choice to exercise a hypothetical right to refuse treatment or any other right." The impossibility of such an exercise affords the State, according to the Court, some discretion to interpose "a procedural requirement" that effectively compels the continuation of Nancy Cruzan's treatment.

There is, however, nothing "hypothetical" about Nancy Cruzan's constitutionally protected interest in freedom from unwanted treatment, and the difficulties involved in ascertaining what her interests are do not in any way justify the State's decision to oppose her interests with its own. As this case comes to us, the crucial question—and the question addressed by the Court—is not what Nancy Cruzan's interests are, but whether the State must give effect to them.

[T]he Court's deference seems ultimately to derive from the premise that chronically incompetent persons have no constitutionally cognizable interests at all, and so are not persons within the meaning of the Constitution. Deference of this sort is patently unconstitutional. It is also dangerous in ways that may not be immediately apparent. Today the State of Missouri has announced its intent to spend several hundred thousand dollars in preserving the life of Nancy Beth Cruzan in order to vindicate its general policy favoring the preservation of human life. Tomorrow, another State equally eager to champion an interest in the "quality of life" might favor a policy designed to ensure quick and comfortable deaths by denying treatment to categories of marginally hopeless cases. If the State in fact has an interest in defining life, and if the State's policy with respect to the termination of life-sustaining treatment commands deference from the judiciary, it is unclear how any resulting conflict between the best interests of the individual and the general policy of the State would be resolved. I believe the Constitution requires that the individual's vital interest in liberty should prevail over the general policy in that case, just as in this.

That a contrary result is readily imaginable under the majority's theory makes manifest that this Court cannot defer to any State policy that drives a theoretical wedge between a person's life, on the one hand, and that person's liberty or happiness, on the other. The consequence of such a theory is to deny the personhood of those whose lives are defined by the State's interests rather than their own. This consequence may be acceptable in theology or in speculative philosophy, but it is radically inconsistent with the foundation of all legitimate government. Our Constitution presupposes a respect for the personhood of every individual, and nowhere is strict adherence to that principle more essential than in the Judicial Branch.

[The] Cruzan family's continuing concern provides a concrete reminder that Nancy Cruzan's interests did not disappear with her vitality or her consciousness. However commendable may be the State's interest in human life, it cannot pursue that interest by appropriating Nancy Cruzan's life as a symbol for its own purposes. Lives do not exist in abstraction from persons, and to pretend otherwise is not to honor but to desecrate the State's responsibility for protecting life. A State that seeks to demonstrate its commitment to life may do so by aiding those who are actively struggling for life and health. In this endeavor, unfortunately, no State can lack for opportunities: there can be no need to make an example of tragic cases like that of Nancy Cruzan.

REFLECTIONS ON *CRUZAN* AND THE *"RIGHT TO DIE"*

1. *The death of Nancy Cruzan.* Two months after the Supreme Court's decision in the *Cruzan* case, Nancy's parents asked the state probate court for a second hearing. At this new hearing, three of Nancy's former co-workers recalled conversations in which she said she never would want to live "like a vegetable" on medical machines. See N.Y. Times, Nov. 2, 1990, p. A12. Since the State of Missouri withdrew from the case and Nancy's court-appointed guardian sought to disconnect the feeding tube, see N.Y. Times, Dec. 7, 1990, p. A12, all remaining parties agreed that artificial nutrition and hydration should cease. A week later, the probate judge ruled that there was "clear evidence" that the "intent" of Nancy, "if mentally able, would be to terminate her nutrition and hydration" and that there was "no evidence of substance" to the contrary. He then authorized the cessation of nutrition and hydration. See N.Y. Times, Dec. 15, 1990, p. 1. Twelve days later, and nearly eight years after she had lost consciousness and a feeding tube had first been implanted in her stomach, Nancy Cruzan died. Did the probate court take the "substituted judgment" seriously or did it really apply an objective test? Cf. Baron, note 3 infra.

2. *Is the "right to die" a right to a preferable state of being—death over vegetative "life"?* No, answers ROBIN WEST, *Taking Freedom Seriously,* 104 Harv.L.Rev. 43, 99 (1990), the "right to die" is "rather merely one of many rights to have one's subjective desires respected." She continues, id. at 99–100:

"The right stems from the desire, not the preferability of the state of death over vegetative life. Because insular, subjective desires have no objective logic or 'preference order' and hence are utterly idiosyncratic, that subjective desire is presumptively unknowable and unknown unless expressed. Given the assumptions of liberal legalism, there is no more reason to assume an individual would prefer death over vegetation than to assume that he would prefer Catholicism to Judaism, republicanism to pluralism, or vanilla to chocolate. It is hardly inconsistent with the antipaternalism central to liberal legalism to claim that whether an individual would 'want' to be kept alive in a vegetative state cannot be presumed but can only be garnered from the individual's objectively manifested desires.

"Not surprisingly, then, the powerful liberal dissents in *Cruzan* were hampered by their reluctance to challenge the liberal legalist antipaternalistic assumption behind the plurality's limitation on the 'right to die.' Justice Brennan's dissent in particular seemed to embrace the antipaternalistic assumption that 'each man is a master of his own body' and that each individual thus possesses the power to reject medical treatment, even as he arrived at the unavoidably paternalistic conclusion that persons in a vegetative state, facing 'an ignoble and steeped in decay,' would find such a state 'abhorrent' and accordingly have a right to have that hypothetical desire to die a 'quiet, proud death' respected. Justice Brennan seems untroubled by the resulting tension in his argument."

But cf. Cantor, *The Permanently Unconscious Patient, Non-Feeding and Euthanasia,* 15 Am.J.L. & Med. 381, 388 (1989) "The author asserts that an incompetent patent has a right to be treated with human dignity, and that human dignity includes implementation of a decision that the clear majority of persons would want implemented given the circumstances facing the now incompetent person."[a]

3. *What upsets critics of the Cruzan case? What really drives death decisions in PVS cases?* "If Missouri's approach burdens individual liberty interests," observes CHARLES BARON, *On Taking Substituted Judgment Seriously,* Hastings Center Rep., Sept.-Oct., 1990, at 7–8, "so does that of every other state that employs substituted judgment for PVS cases. By requiring clear and convincing evidence of substituted judgment, Missouri prevents death decisions for some persons who are in PVS. But so do those states [that] do not allow death decisions where there is *no* evidence for substituted judgment, or where the patient's family has not reached a death decision for the patient. What reason is there for thinking that Missouri's procedural safeguards that cause many PVS patients to be continued on life support are unconstitutionally burdensome but those of other states are not?"

"What upsets critics of *Cruzan,*" maintains Professor Baron, "is that Missouri has taken the substituted judgment test seriously. What actually drives death decisions in PVS cases is an objective test based on the convergence of 'best interests' and economic criteria. [But] the extreme discomfort of making death decisions for other people and our fear of the slippery slope * * * leads us to pretend that we are merely complying (however reluctantly) with the wishes of the patient. The result in most states is mere lip service to substituted judgment: Almost any evidence is deemed sufficient to establish a preference for death over PVS. Or families are empowered to express patient preferences for death—with few questions asked." Adds Baron: "What everyone *ought* to be upset about is that virtually all our states (including Missouri) have not adopted rules that openly and honestly apply the objective criteria really driving death decisions in PVS cases."

4. *If there is a constitutional "right to die," does it embrace "active euthanasia"?* Is there a constitutional "right to die"? If a state law requires life-sustaining treatment despite "clear and convincing" evidence that the patient would not want such treatment, would it be struck down? In such a case, might there be "as many as eight votes" for "the unenumerated constitutional

a. One might, suggests Professor Cantor, id. at 417, "draw the line defining a degrading status for incompetent patients (who have not previously expressed their treatment preferences) at permanent unconsciousness." "A possible safeguard against abuse of handicapped populations," he notes, id. at 421–22, "would be to confine the notions of indignity discussed here to previously competent and active individuals. The keystone of the elements of indignity [discussed earlier in the article] is the drastic reduction in capacity affecting a person who was accustomed to an independent, vigorous lifestyle. * * * [T]he notions of indignity, degradation and humane medical handling are extremely problematic in the context of the never-competent patient. We certainly cannot say that the level of deterioration which would make continued medical intervention degrading and inhumane for a previously competent patient would do the same for a never-competent patient."

right to die"? See Tribe & Dorf, *Levels of Generality in the Definition of Rights,* 57 U.Chi.L.Rev. 1057, 1093 (1990). If there is such a right, what is its nature and scope? Consider Kamisar, *Right to Die, or License to Kill?,* Legal Times, Nov. 13, 1989, p. 26: "What if there is clear and convincing evidence that [if she ever becomes a PVS case] the patient would prefer to die quickly by lethal injection, rather than slowly by starvation and dehydration? If a person has a constitutional right to die, why doesn't she have the right to choose what she regards as the most 'humane' or 'dignified' way to die?"

Is it a sufficient objection to a claimed right to "active euthanasia" that (a) It is "intrinsically immoral"? (b) "The prevailing ethos in American society is that we 'take life' only in extraordinary circumstances," such as war, capital punishment and self-defense and active euthanasia might have an adverse impact "on the 'tone' of society, or on the sense of security of citizens"? (c) "[M]ost American physicians, even those vigorously supporting termination of medical intervention in some circumstances, seem to regard active euthanasia as outside the physician's proper role"? Or that (d) Active euthanasia would work "such a radical alteration in the legal framework surrounding terminally ill patients" that it "ought not to be instituted unless it is absolutely essential" and "there has been no showing that the current framework—as it is evolving in light of modern technology—is so inadequate or inhumane that active euthanasia has become essential"? See Cantor, note 2 supra, at 427–35. See also Wolf, *Holding the Line on Euthanasia,* Hastings Center Rep., Jan.-Feb. 1989, at 13.

But consider Mayo, *Constitutionalizing the "Right to Die,"* 49 Md.L.Rev. 103, 139–40 (1990) noting that "[i]f there is a dominant position with respect to these terms, it is that passive euthanasia may be ethically and legally permissible under certain circumstances, while active euthanasia is not," but adding: "[H]owever a strong riptide of dissent runs just below the seemingly placid surface of this general agreement." Moreover, id. at 144, "the history of our activities and beliefs concerning the ethics of death and dying is a history of lost distinctions of former significance."

5. *Justice Scalia's reliance on the analogy to suicide.* Consider Note, 104 Harv.L.Rev. 257, 262 (1990): "The distinction between an affirmative act to assist suicide and a failure to provide medical assistance to a patient who refuses it is significantly more marked than Justice Scalia suggested. As the majority and Justice Brennan recognized, the common law right to refuse medical treatment has long existed alongside anti-suicide laws. Acting outside the purview of the legal system, doctors have traditionally withheld certain treatments that would delay death on the grounds that the treatment was unnecessarily painful, that it would not improve the patient's condition, or that it was against the patient's wishes. Further, courts have explicitly rejected the notion that terminating treatment constitutes homicide and have held that the right to refuse treatment exists even if the consequence of refusal is death. Thus, even under Justice Scalia's narrow historical test [referring to fn. 6 of the plurality opinion in *Michael H.*], a competent person has a liberty interest in refusing life-sustaining medical treatment. Justice Scalia's zeal for avoiding the entire 'right to die' area led him to evaluate the interest with a history not specifically applicable to the facts of *Cruzan.*"

State courts have rejected the notion that terminating life-sustaining treatment constitutes homicide, but almost all the cases to this effect have been decided in the last fifteen or twenty years. How long does it take to build up a "tradition"? In identifying the "relevant tradition" (fn. 6 to *Michael H.*), should one take into account, as the Harvard Note does, medical practices "*outside* the purview of the legal system" (emphasis added)? Reconsider the remarks of Professor Balkin, set forth in the Notes & Questions following *Michael H.*

6. *More on the level of generality in defining rights or liberty interests. In Cruzan, did Chief Justice Rehnquist break away from Justice Scalia?*

(a) *The feeding tube vs. other forms of life support.* As recently as 1980, the idea that fluids and nutriment might be withdrawn from a comatose patient "was a notion that would have been repudiated, if not condemned, by most health professionals" and regarded by them as "morally and psychologically objectionable, legally problematic, and medically wrong." Siegler & Weisbard, *Against the Emerging Stream: Should Fluids and Nutritional Support Be Discontinued?,* 145 Archives of Internal Med. 129 (1985). But our way of thinking about this matter changed dramatically in the 1980s. The President's Commission for the Study of Ethical Problems in Medicine, the American Medical Association, a Hastings Center report on the termination of life-sustaining treatment, and various other medical/legal groups, as well as several state supreme courts, rejected any distinction between the artificial delivery of food and water and other forms of life support.

On the eve of *Cruzan,* however, the issue was still a matter of considerable dispute. A number of commentators maintained that the distinction should be preserved for various reasons: Nutrition and hydration are basic care, not medical treatment; denial of such care poses a serious threat to the doctor-patient relationship; and permitting withdrawal of artificial nutrition and hydration undermines the psychological distinction between "killing" and "letting die." See Kamisar, note 4 supra; Mayo, note 4 supra, at 134–36. Moreover, nearly half of the forty states that have adopted living will statutes (including Missouri) "specifically exclude artificial nutrition and hydration from the category of life-sustaining treatment that may be refused." Francis, *The Evanescence of Living Wills,* 27 J.Contemp.L. 27, 33–34 (1988). See also Zinberg, *Decisions for the Dying,* 13 Vt.L.Rev. 445, 458–90 (1989).

(b) *How significant is it that the patient is neither "dying" nor "terminally ill"?* Although some state courts have recently rejected this restriction (at least for PVS patients), living will statutes generally provide that the directive only becomes operative when its maker becomes "terminally ill" and about half the states, including Missouri, define this term to mean an irreversible condition that will produce death in a short time *despite* or *regardless* of medical intervention. See Cantor, supra, at 405–06; Francis, supra, at 35; Gelfand, *Living Will Statutes: The First Decade,* 1987 Wisc.L.Rev. 737, 741–42. Under this definition, at the time her case was decided, Nancy Cruzan was neither "dying" nor "terminally ill." If artificial nutrition and hydration were not withdrawn, she could have remained alive for many years. The Missouri Supreme Court seemed to give a good deal of weight to this feature of the *Cruzan* case; it was included in the court's articulation of the "issue presented," see 760 S.W.2d at 410, and it was mentioned or discussed five more times in the majority opinion. See id. at 411, 412, 419, 422, 424.

(c) *How might Chief Justice Rehnquist have been expected to frame the issue presented in Cruzan?* Chief Justice Rehnquist joined Justice Scalia's plurality opinion in *Michael H.,* including fn. 6. In light of this, and the discussion in (a) and (b) above, would one have expected, or at least not have been surprised, if the Chief Justice had defined the right or liberty interest at issue in *Cruzan* something as follows: "Is the liberty (or right) of an incompetent patient *who is neither dying nor terminally ill,* as those terms are commonly defined, to refuse *lifesaving artificial hydration and nutrition* deeply rooted in the Nation's history and tradition?"

Did the Chief Justice assign any particular significance to the fact that the lifesaving measure involved in the *Cruzan* case was artificial feeding? Did he give any weight to the fact that Nancy Cruzan was neither "dying" nor "terminally ill," as those terms are defined by Missouri and many other states? [b] At any point, did he expressly discuss the level of generality at which the liberty interest in *Cruzan* should be defined (and why)? [c]

To what extent does Chief Justice Rehnquist's opinion in *Cruzan* mark a break with the plurality's approach in *Michael H.*, especially fn. 6? With Justice White's opinion of the Court in *Bowers v. Hardwick*?

7. *The "right to die" and the abortion cases.* "There is no inconsistency, or even irony," comments Mayo, note 4 supra, at 124–25 (writing on the eve of *Cruzan*), "between the Court's extension of constitutional protections to a patient's choice of medical treatment to end the biological existence of a fetus, on the one hand, and the conclusion that the same privacy right does not extend necessarily to the decision to terminate an incompetent patient's life-sustaining treatment. The Court in *Roe* declined to hold that a fetus is a 'person,' and it consistently has adhered to that [view]. The only relevant person in the Court's abortion analysis is the pregnant woman, whose life and health, not death, the Court has sought to protect by keeping the process of choice as private as possible. [It] would strain the Court's language and logic [in *Roe* and its progeny] to divorce the element of abortion from these cases and find a generalized right to make significant medical decisions."

But consider Tribe, *Abortion* at 231: "[M]uch like arguments over abortion, right-to-die disputes may, in the end, pit the value of preserving life against the value of avoiding grotesque technological intrusions. At bottom there is a similarity between the state's decision to lay hands on the intimate and delicate matter of life's reproduction and the state's decision to have the last word on the personal and subtle matter of life's termination. A woman's right to decide if and how to give birth thus shares a common root with the right to avoid the demeaning tangle of state-mandated technology that has become death's least human face. Thus, it may be that the right-to-life impulse and the pro-choice impulse may yet find common cause—in the desire to avoid government manipulation of technologies to save or preserve life, but only at the expense of sacrificing what we sense to be most natural."

b. Consider Kamisar, *The "Right to Die": Green Lights and Yellow Lights,* Law Quadrangle Notes, Fall, 1990, pp. 3, 5: "I venture to say that in some future case the Court will make plain what I think is implicit in *Cruzan:* A patient's 'right to die' cannot be denied solely on the ground that she is neither 'dying' nor 'terminally ill'—no more than it can be denied solely for the reason that the life support involved is a feeding tube rather than a respirator."

c. The Chief Justice might have said, for example, that even under the narrow approach he and Justice Scalia took in *Michael H.*, "the liberty interest at issue is properly defined at the level of generality of medical treatment, not medical sustenance * * * because that is 'the most specific level at which a relevant tradition protecting, or denying protection to, the asserted right can be identified.' Because the technology by which food and water may be routinely provided by means other than oral intake is of relatively recent origin, no societal tradition exists either permitting or prohibiting individuals to deny themselves medically provided nutrition and hydration." *Developments in the Law—Medical Technology and the Law,* 103 Harvard L.Rev. 1520, 1662 n. 142 (1990). But see Note 6(a) supra.

8. *Inconsistent views of families: can Cruzan and Ohio v. Akron Center be harmonized?* In the *Cruzan* case, Chief Justice Rehnquist's opinion noted "family members will not act to protect a patient" and that "there is no automatic assurance that the view of close family members will necessarily be the same as the patient's would have been." But Chief Justice Rehnquist joined Justice Kennedy's lead opinion in *Ohio v. Akron Center,* p. 239 fn. c supra, where the majority deemed it fair for a state to assume that "in most instances, the family will strive to give a lonely or even terrified minor advice that is both compassionate and mature." Consider MARTHA MINOW, *The Role of Families in Medical Decisions,* 1991 Utah L.Rev. 1, 8–11:

"In the context of medical treatment for an incompetent patient, the Court imagines the circumstances under which family members will not be available or will not act in the patient's interests. Yet in the context of the minor's abortion decision, the Court envisions a compassionate and helpful family. Another point of contrast concerns the significance given to specific evidence compared with asserted generalizations. The actual evidence of a caring family—with no suggested conflict of interest—made no difference in *Cruzan* because the Court could imagine other less caring families. [In] *Akron Center,* in contrast, the Court treats the generalization about families as the important fact. The Court simultaneously treats as irrelevant the possibility of exceptions to what the Court assumes will be 'most cases' of parental guidance and understanding. This assumption is all the more noteworthy as a choice, rather than simply the state of affairs, in light of the evidence proffered in the case about the number of minors who confront parental abuse and neglect, and who face further risks if their parent learns about the minor's pregnancy.

"[The] dissenting views in *Cruzan* and *Akron Center* reconfirm the inconsistency I have noted in the majority opinions; indeed, we seem to have something like a musical round. The majority in *Cruzan* emphasizes the danger that some families may not act in concert with the incompetent patient's wishes or even in violation of that person's interests; the *Akron Center* dissent does the same, and stresses the danger that some parents may actually threaten abuse of a minor upon discovering her pregnancy. Others may be unable to provide compassionate and mature advice. The majority in *Akron Center* emphasized instead the 'good' families—assumed to be most families—who will provide warmth and helpful assistance to the pregnant minor who has sought help from a doctor. And the dissents in *Cruzan* speculate that family members may know more about the patient and care more about her than anyone else. The inconsistency is complete: the majorities and the dissents have simply swapped places in the two cases when it comes to expressing attitudes and assumptions about the families' participation in the medical decisions at issue."

9. *More on Cruzan and Akron Center: was the Court wrong in both cases?* Yes, concludes Professor Minow, id. at 23–24:

"[P]erhaps I too am inconsistent. I argue for deference to families in one case and individual automony in the other; I just disagree with the Supreme Court's judgment about which case is which. More specifically: I think that families should be entrusted to make treatment decisions on behalf of a comatose or incompetent relative absent a specific showing of their conflicting interests because the alternative of a state decision-maker is not presumptively better. At the same time, I think that the dangers of parental abuse and punishment faced by a pregnant minor are real enough to deny states the power to require parental involvement in a minor's abortion decision. I wonder why the only alternative to parental involvement is a judicial hearing. I wonder why we don't simply trust the minor herself.

"* * * I'm certainly consistent in disliking judicial involvement in either instance. But more to the point, I think that the specific comparison of alternatives in each setting really matters, and really differs. [A] minor *is* different from a comatose patient—different because the minor has a present desire that can indeed be expressed. And the abortion decision is different than the decision to terminate medical treatment for a comatose patient."

10. *Does (should) "family privacy" include the "right" to terminate a close relative's life support? Would recognition of such a right constitute "piggybacking" the family's claim on the patient's right of self-determination?* Consider JOHN ROBERTSON, *Cruzan: No Rights Violated,* Hastings Center Rep., Sept.-Oct. 1990, at 8, 9:

"One could argue that an incompetent patient has a right to have a proxy decide for the patient on the basis of her previous values. But that claim cannot be based on the comatose patient's current interests (there are none), nor on a past exercise of autonomy, for no directive against treatment has issued. Surely there is no constitutional right to be treated 'like one once was' now that one is so radically different.

"The claim in *Cruzan* thus becomes the family's right to decide the matter because of the impact of continued treatment on their own, not Nancy's interests. Does family privacy, recognized by the Court to include decisions about having children and how they are reared, include the right to terminate medical treatment that is not harming (or helping) their daughter? Parents have never had the right to deny their children medical care that the state deems necessary. [The] Supreme Court should not expand family privacy when harm to the comatose ward from the disputed treatment does not exist. * * * Treating Nancy over her parents' objections may be unwise, but it does not follow that anyone's constitutional rights are thereby violated."

Consider, too, IRA ELLMAN, *Cruzan v. Harmon and the Dangerous Claim that Others Can Exercise An Incapacitated Patient's Right to Die,* 29 Jurimetrics 389, 393–94 (1989): "From the premise that Nancy retains her right to decide [the Cruzans] proceed to the conclusion that others can exercise that right on her behalf. But any constitutional rule protecting each individual's right to make her own medical decisions emerges from a principle of self-determination—or autonomy—and can therefore protect only an individual's right to make decisions about her own treatment. A guardian's or family member's judgment is not entitled to the special deference arising from the autonomy principle, for it is a judgment that one person makes about another, not a judgment that the patient makes about herself.

"We may well wish, as a matter of sound policy, to ensure that the views of close family members have great weight in making treatment decisions for the incapacitated. We may even wish to make their views dispositive. But we cannot base that policy on the autonomy principle. Since the autonomy principle is foundational to any constitutional claim that individuals may decide for themselves whether to accept or refuse life-sustaining treatment, the constitutional claim fails in this case. The family's claim to decide cannot be piggybacked on Nancy's autonomy. * * *

"Where nature has deprived the patient of the capacity to exercise a right, the Constitution cannot restore it. To say that the Constitution protects the right of others to exercise Nancy's right for her will not do where, as here, the right in question is a right *to make a choice.* It stands on the same footing as a claim that Nancy Cruzan's right to vote can be exercised by her family. A right to choose for oneself can be vindicated only if the individual herself makes the choice. A constitutional right arising from our core belief in individual autonomy cannot possibly be exercised by a stand-in appointed by the state. Where the patient has become incapacitated, and has left no instructions, the character of the decision about her treatment necessarily changes."

SECTION 3. THE RIGHT TO TRAVEL

Introduction

"The 'right to travel' from state to state has been a favorite of both the Warren and Burger Courts. The Constitution makes no mention of any such right. By now we know that cannot be determinative, but we are entitled to some sort of explanation of why the right is appropriately attributable. In recent years the Court has been almost smug in its refusal to provide one." [a]

—Ely, *Democracy and Distrust* 177 (1980).

Dissenting in *Shapiro v. Thompson* (1969) (discussed at p. 1150 infra), Harlan, J., observed: "Opinions of the Court and of individual Justices have suggested four provisions of the Constitution as possible sources of a right to travel enforceable against the federal or state governments: the Commerce Clause; the Privileges and Immunities Clause of Art. IV, § 2; the Privileges and Immunities Clause of the Fourteenth Amendment; and the Due Process Clause of the Fifth Amendment." (He concluded that "the right to travel interstate is a 'fundamental' right which, for present purposes, should be regarded as having its source in [the fifth amendment due process clause].") Other possible sources for the constitutional right to travel are the equal protection clause, the "penumbra" of the first amendment, the ninth amendment and "the nature of the federal union." [b] One recent constitutional law text discusses the right to travel in its "equal protection" chapter,[c] another treats the subject primarily in a chapter on "rights of privacy and personhood." [d]

APTHEKER v. SECRETARY OF STATE, 378 U.S. 500, 84 S.Ct. 1659, 12 L.Ed.2d 992 (1964), concerned an attack by top-ranking leaders of the Communist Party on § 6 of the Subversive Activities Control Act of 1950, which denied passports to members of an organization "with knowledge or notice" that it was required to register as "a Communist organization." The Court, per GOLDBERG,

a. At this point Professor Ely refers to language in *Shapiro v. Thompson* and *United States v. Guest,* both quoted infra. See also Note, 40 U.M.K.C.L.Rev. 66, 77 (1971): "In some situations, the Court has refused to pinpoint the source of the protection it is giving to free travel, in effect saying: 'We know the right to travel is protected by the Constitution and we don't need to say where.' "

b. See generally Lupu, *Untangling the Strands of the Fourteenth Amendment,* 77 Mich.L.Rev. 981, 993, 1031, 1060–64 (1979); Notes, 22 U.C.L.A.L.Rev. 1129, 1140–45 (1975); 40 U.M.K.C.L.Rev. 66, 67–77, 93–95 (1971); 55 Neb.L.Rev. 117–22, 132 (1975) and authorities collected therein.

c. Nowak, Rotunda & Young, *Constitutional Law* 802–16 (2d ed.1983).

d. Tribe, *American Constitutional Law* 896–97, 953–58 (1978).

J., struck down § 6 as "unconstitutional on its face" because it "too broadly and indiscriminately restricts the right to travel and thereby abridges the liberty guaranteed by the Fifth Amendment." It pointed to the dictum in *Kent v. Dulles,* 357 U.S. 116, 78 S.Ct. 1113, 2 L.Ed.2d 1204 (1958), that "The right to travel is a part of the 'liberty' of which the citizen cannot be deprived without [fifth amendment due process]. Freedom of movement across frontiers in either direction, and inside frontiers as well, was a part of our heritage. Travel abroad, like travel within the country [is] basic in our scheme of values." "Since freedom of association is itself guaranteed in the First Amendment, restrictions imposed upon the right to travel cannot be dismissed by asserting that the right to travel could be fully exercised if the individual would first yield up his membership in a given association." [a]

As for the government's argument that § 6 should be held constitutional as applied to "the top-ranking Party leaders involved here," such a "construction" would require "substantial rewriting" of the statute and would "inject an element of vagueness into the statute's scope," a course neither proper nor desirable "in dealing with a section which so severely curtails personal liberty." Since "freedom of travel is a constitutional liberty closely related to rights of free speech and association, [appellants] should not be required to assume the burden of demonstrating that Congress could not have written a statute constitutionally prohibiting their travel."

DOUGLAS, J., joined the Court's opinion, adding that "the right to move freely from State to State is a privilege and immunity of national citizenship." "Absent war, I see no way to keep a citizen from traveling within or without the country [unless] he has been convicted of a crime [or] there is probable cause for issuing a warrant [to arrest him]. Freedom of movement [is] the very essence of our free society, setting us apart. Like the right of assembly and the right of association, it often makes all other rights meaningful—knowing, studying, arguing, exploring, conversing, observing and even thinking." [b]

ZEMEL v. RUSK, 381 U.S. 1, 85 S.Ct. 1271, 14 L.Ed.2d 179 (1965), concerned refusal to issue passports to United States citizens for travel to Cuba "unless specifically endorsed [by] the Secretary of State." Appellant sought a passport "to satisfy my curiosity about the state of affairs in Cuba and to make me a better informed citizen." The Court, per WARREN, C.J., affirmed denial of the request: "The requirements of due process are a function not only of the extent of the governmental restriction imposed, but also of the extent of the necessity for the restriction. [The] United States and other members of the Organization of American States have determined that travel between Cuba and the other countries of the Western Hemisphere is an important element in the spreading of subversion. [In light of this factor and others], the Secretary has justifiably concluded that travel to Cuba by American citizens might involve the Nation in dangerous international incidents, and that the Constitution does not require him to validate passports for such travel.

a. *Kent* invalidated State Department regulations denying passports to Communists on the ground they exceeded the congressional grant of authority, thus avoiding the constitutional question.

b. Clark, J., joined by Harlan and White, JJ., dissented, maintaining that the Due Process Clause does not prohibit "reasonable regulation" of the right to travel abroad and that Congress had "a rational basis" for denying passports to members of the Communist Party.

"The right to travel *within* the United States is of course also constitutionally protected. But that freedom does not mean that areas ravaged by flood, fire or pestilence cannot be quarantined when it can be demonstrated that unlimited travel to the area would directly and materially interfere with the safety and welfare of the area or the Nation as a whole. So it is with international travel. [That the challenged restriction] is supported by the weightiest considerations of national security is perhaps best pointed up by recalling that the Cuban Missile crisis of October 1962 preceded the filing of appellant's complaint by less than two months."

DOUGLAS, J., joined by Goldberg, J., dissented: "[T]here are areas [such as those stricken by pestilence or war] to which Congress can [prohibit] travel. [But] the only so-called danger present here is the Communist regime in Cuba. The world, however, is filled with Communist thought [and] if we are to know them and understand them, we must mingle with [them]. Restrictions on the right to travel in times of peace should be so particularized that a First Amendment right is not precluded unless some clear countervailing national interest stands in the way of its assertion." [a]

HAIG v. AGEE, 453 U.S. 280, 101 S.Ct. 2766, 69 L.Ed.2d 640 (1981) (other aspects of which are discussed at p. 624 infra), arose as follows: Agee, a former CIA employee then residing in West Germany, announced and engaged in a campaign to expose undercover CIA agents stationed abroad and "to drive them out of the countries where they are operating." In carrying out his campaign he travelled in various countries. On several occasions, his public identifications of alleged CIA agents in foreign countries were "followed by episodes of violence against the persons and organizations." Because of Agee's activities, his passport was revoked on the basis of a 1966 regulation authorizing passport revocation when the Secretary of State determines that an American citizen's activities abroad "are causing or likely to cause serious damage to the national security or the foreign policy of the United States." [a] After holding that the Passport Act of 1926 authorized the revocation of Agee's passport pursuant to the policy announced by the challenged regulation, such policy being " 'sufficiently substan-

a. Compare *Zemel* with *Regan v. Wald,* 468 U.S. 222, 104 S.Ct. 3026, 82 L.Ed.2d 171 (1984). In 1982, in order to "reduce Cuba's hard currency earnings from travel by U.S. persons to and from Cuba," a treasury regulation was amended to restrict travel-related economic transactions. Respondents, American citizens who wanted to travel to Cuba, challenged the amendment on both statutory and constitutional grounds. After devoting most of its opinion to a discussion of why the regulation was authorized by Congress, a 5–4 majority, per Rehnquist, J., rejected the constitutional challenge:

"We see no reason to differentiate between the travel restrictions imposed by the President in the present case and the passport restrictions imposed by the Secretary of State in *Zemel.* Both have the practical effect of preventing travel to Cuba by most American citizens, and both are justified by weighty concerns of foreign policy. Respondents apparently feel that only a Cuban missile crisis in the offing will make area restrictions on international travel constitutional. [The] holding in *Zemel,* however, was not tied to the Court's independent foreign policy analysis, [but] merely an example of [our] classical deference to the political branches in matters of foreign policy."

Blackmun, J., joined by Brennan, Marshall and Powell, JJ., dissented, maintaining that the restrictions on travel-related expenditures in Cuba were not authorized by Congress.

a. As a condition for his employment by the CIA, Agee contracted not to make any public statements about Agency matters, either during or after the term of his employment by the Agency, "without specific approval by the Agency." In a separate action brought by the government to enforce Agee's agreement, a federal district court held that "Agee has shown a flagrant disregard for the requirements of the Secrecy Agreement."

tial and consistent' to compel the conclusion that Congress has approved it," [b] a 7–2 majority, per BURGER, C.J., rejected Agee's contention that the revocation violated, inter alia, his "right to travel," stressing the distinction between interstate and international travel:

"Revocation of a passport undeniably curtails travel, but the freedom to travel abroad with a 'letter of introduction' in the form of a passport issued by the sovereign is subordinate to national security and foreign policy considerations; as such, it is subject to reasonable governmental regulation. The Court

b. Relying on *Kent v. Dulles,* Agee argued that "the only way the Executive can establish implicit congressional approval is by proof of longstanding and consistent *enforcement* of the claimed power: that is by showing that many passports were revoked on national security and foreign policy grounds." The Court disagreed, pointing out that there were few occasions to call the Secretary's authority into play: "The exercise of a power emerges only in relation to a factual situation, and the continued validity of the power is not diluted simply because there is no need to use it. [Although] a pattern of actual enforcement is one indicator of Executive policy, it suffices that the Executive has 'openly asserted' the power at issue. *Kent* is not to the contrary. [In that case, the] Court had serious doubts as to whether there was in reality any definite policy in which Congress could have acquiesced."

Relying on language in *Kent* that "illegal conduct" and problems of allegiance were "the only [grounds] which it could fairly be argued were adopted by Congress in light of prior administrative practice," Agee also contended that "this enumeration was exclusive and is controlling here." Again the Court disagreed: "The *Kent* Court had no occasion to consider whether the Executive had the power to revoke the passport of an individual whose *conduct* is damaging the national security and foreign policy of the United States. *Kent* involved denials of passports solely on the basis of political beliefs entitled to First Amendment protection. [As *Aptheker* illustrates, the] protections accorded beliefs standing alone is very different from the protection accorded conduct. [But] [b]eliefs and speech are only part of Agee's 'campaign to fight the United States CIA.' In that sense, this case contrasts markedly with the facts in *Kent* and *Aptheker.* No presumptions, rebuttable or otherwise, are involved, for Agee's conduct in foreign countries presents a serious danger to the national security."

Blackmun, J., concurring, "would have preferred to have the Court disavow forthrightly the aspects of *Zemel* and *Kent* that may suggest that evidence of a longstanding Executive policy or construction in this area is not probative of the issue of congressional authorization. Nonetheless, believing this is what the Court in effect has done," he joined the Court's opinion.

Brennan, J., joined by Marshall, J., dissenting, read *Kent* as "stat[ing] that any infringement of [the 'right to travel'] can only 'be pursuant to the lawmaking functions of the Congress,' and that delegations to the Executive Branch that curtail that liberty must be construed narrowly. Because the Passport Act of 1926—the same statute at issue here—did not expressly authorize the denial of passports to alleged Communists, the Court examined cases of actual passport refusals [to] determine whether 'it could be fairly argued' that the category of passport refusals was 'adopted by Congress in light of prior administrative practice.' The Court was unable to find such prior administrative practice, and therefore held that the regulation was unauthorized."

"[C]learly neither *Zemel* nor *Kent* holds," protested the dissenters, "that a longstanding Executive *policy* or *construction* is sufficient proof that Congress has implicitly authorized the Secretary's action. The cases hold that an administrative *practice* must be demonstrated; in fact *Kent* unequivocally states that mere *construction* by the Executive—no matter how longstanding and consistent—is *not* sufficient. [Not] only does the Court ignore the *Kent-Zemel* requirement that Executive discretion be supported by a consistent administrative practice, but it also relies on the very Executive construction and policy deemed irrelevant in *Kent.*

"[The] point that *Kent* and *Zemel* make, and that today's opinion should make, is that the Executive authority to revoke passports touches an area fraught with important constitutional rights, and that the Court should therefore 'construe narrowly all delegated powers that curtail or dilute them.' *Kent.* The presumption is that Congress must expressly delegate authority to the Secretary to deny or revoke passports for foreign policy or national security reasons before he may exercise such authority. To overcome the presumption against an implied delegation, the Government must show 'an administrative practice sufficiently substantial and consistent.' *Zemel.* Only in this way can the Court satisfy itself that Congress has implicitly approved such exercise of authority by the Secretary."

has made it plain that the *freedom* to travel outside the United States must be distinguished from the *right* to travel within the United States. This was underscored in *Califano v. Aznavorian.* 439 U.S. 170, 99 S.Ct. 471, 58 L.Ed.2d 435 (1978).[c]

"It is 'obvious and unarguable' that no governmental interest is more compelling than the security of the Nation. Protection of the foreign policy of the United States is a governmental interest of great importance, since foreign policy and national security considerations cannot neatly be compartmentalized. [Not] only has Agee jeopardized the security of the United States, but he has endangered the interests of countries other than the United States—thereby creating serious problems for American foreign relations and foreign policy. Restricting Agee's foreign travel, although perhaps not certain to prevent all of Agee's harmful activities, is the only avenue open to the Government to limit these activities.[60]"

BRENNAN, J., joined by Marshall, J., dissenting, devoted most of his opinion to the argument that the regulation under which Agee's passport had been revoked was "invalid as an unlawful exercise of authority by the Secretary [of State] under the Passport Act of 1926." [d] He then cited *Agee* as "a prime example of the adage that 'bad facts make bad law.'" "Agee is hardly a model representative of our Nation, [but] just as the Constitution protects both popular and unpopular speech, it likewise protects both popular and unpopular travelers." [e]

Notes and Questions

1. *The shift from Kent to Agee.* Consider Farber, *National Security, The Right to Travel, and the Court,* 1981 Sup.Ct.Rev. 263, 285–87: "[*Agee*] represents a major shift from previous travel cases such as *Kent* [which] laid heavy stress on the importance of the right to travel and took a correspondingly grudging approach to discretionary travel controls. *Agee,* on the other hand, distinguishes the *right* to travel within the United States from the mere *freedom* to travel outside the United States. It takes a correspondingly generous view of executive discretion. For three reasons, the *Kent* approach is preferable, even ignoring the matter of stare decisis.

"First is the importance of the right to travel itself. [One] important aspect of international travel is its relation to freedom of speech. Without the right to travel, criticism of foreign policy is greatly impeded. [Second,] *Kent* 's grudging attitude toward executive discretion is amply supported by history. [The] *Agee*

c. In upholding a provision of the Social Security Act denying certain benefits for any month during all of which the recipient is outside the United States, the *Aznovorian* Court, per Stewart, J., rejected the view that international travel, no less than interstate travel, is "a basic constitutional right." In light of the "crucial distinction between the *freedom* to travel internationally and the *right* of interstate travel" (emphasis added), a statute "said to infringe the freedom to travel abroad is not to be judged by the same standard applied to laws that penalize the right of interstate travel, such as durational residency requirements imposed by the States [referring to the cases discussed at pp. 1150–61 infra]." See generally Note, 19 Va.J.Int'l L. 707 (1979).

60. Agee argues that the Government should be limited to an injunction ordering him to comply with his secrecy agreement [see fn. a]. This argument ignores the governmental interests at stake. As Agee concedes, such an injunction would not be enforceable outside of the United States.

d. See fn. b. supra.

e. Although the dissenters did not specifically address Agee's contention that the challenged regulation violated his right to travel, they did comment briefly on "the Court's whirlwind treatment" of Agee's first amendment claims.

Court seems to have assumed that the discretion to control travel had only been exercised on a principled basis. Too many counterexamples exist to allow reliance on this assumption. The third reason for preferring *Kent* to *Agee* is that *Kent* aligns more closely with congressional intent. Since *Kent*, Congress has strongly supported the principle of freedom of travel. Despite urgent pleas from [President Eisenhower], Congress refused to supply the statutory power held lacking in *Kent*. * * * Twenty years later, Congress abolished the other major elements of the Cold War program of travel control [area restrictions and a penalty for travel without a passport]. In sum, not only the holding but also the underlying policies of *Kent* have received congressional endorsement. This is of critical importance, because both *Kent* and *Agee* proceed from the premise that the President's power flows from Congress. Indeed, even if the President did have some inherent power in the area, that power would be greatly diminished by Congressional disapproval."

2. *The right to travel intrastate.* Is *intrastate* travel entitled to as much protection as travel across state lines? See *King v. New Rochelle Municipal Housing Auth.*, 442 F.2d 646 (2d Cir.1971) (it "would be meaningless to describe the right to travel between states as a fundamental precept of personal liberty and not to acknowledge a correlative constitutional right to travel within a state"). See also Tribe, *Treatise* at 1380; Note, 22 U.C.L.A.L.Rev. 1129, 1145–46 (1975). But see Comment, 55 Neb.L.Rev. 117, 128–29 (1975) ("intrastate travel is not a fundamental right" and statutes limiting such travel will be upheld on "reasonable basis" test).

3. *Zoning ordinances.* The "one-family dwellings" zoning ordinance upheld in *Belle Terre*, Sec. 2 supra, was challenged, inter alia, on the ground that "it interferes with the right to migrate to and settle within a State." The Court, per Douglas, J., made short shrift of this contention, noting that the ordinance "is not aimed at transients." Professor Tribe, supra, at 1381, agrees that "qualitative as opposed to quantitative restraints on how a jurisdiction's land may be developed or used should [be] immune to challenge on right-to-travel grounds so long as they do not discriminate against new residents." At some point, however, "local laws making towns and municipalities homogeneous enclaves might cumulatively lead to a society in which migration from one jurisdiction to another, as a practical matter, becomes extremely difficult. If a showing is made that persons must in effect choose between changing their way of life and staying put, a right-to-travel challenge should succeed. Cf. *Aptheker.*" Id. at n. 19. See generally Notes, 39 U.Chi.L.Rev. 612 (1972); 12 Harv.J.Leg. 244 (1975); 84 Yale L.J. 1564 (1975).

4. *A rationale for the right to travel.* Consider Ely, *Democracy and Distrust* 178–79 (1980): "The right at issue in the modern cases [is] not simply a right to travel to or through a state but rather a right to move there—the right, if you will, to relocate. [To] a large extent America was founded by persons escaping from environments they found oppressive. Mobility was quite free during the colonial period, and '[a]s a result, most colonials who dissented from their own community's conception of right and justice could move without great difficulty to a more congenial community.' And of course the symbolism, and indeed the reality, of 'the frontier' took much of its sustenance from the notion that a person should have the option of pulling up stakes and starting over elsewhere. [I think this tradition] points us in the right direction, one that associates the right to relocate not with the idea that it is some kind of handmaiden of majoritarian democracy but, quite to the contrary, with the notion that one

should have an option of escaping an incompatible majority. [A dissenting member of a community] should have the option of exiting and relocating in a community whose values he or she finds more compatible. [S]ome differences remain [among the states]—relating perhaps most pertinently to the extent to which deviance of various sorts is tolerated or represented by law or enforcement policy, and indeed to the scope of such government services as education and welfare. [I]t's an old idea, dating back at least as far as Rousseau's 'droit d'emigration': it's just that the Court hasn't fixed on it. That is unfortunate, since it provides something the Court hasn't, a rationale for the right to travel it in fact has established."

See also Tribe at 1383–84: "[C]lose surveillance and control of travel in both its senses [as an aspect of expression or education and as a means of changing one's residence and starting life anew] has always been a central technique of the totalitarian state, but centuries of experience should suffice to mark as especially suspect any governmental measure designed to prevent the emigration of those dissatisfied with the existing order, or the immigration of those who might alter the status quo. Just as government should be forbidden to expel the citizen who has become a source of unrest, so it cannot be permitted to imprison the citizen who seeks freedom in another land."

SECTION 4. THE DEATH PENALTY AND RELATED PROBLEMS: CRUEL AND UNUSUAL PUNISHMENT

Introduction

"The question of capital punishment has been the subject of endless discussion and will probably never be settled so long as men believe in punishment. [The] reasons why it cannot be settled are plain. There is first of all no agreement as to the objects of punishment. Next there is no way to determine the results of punishment. [Moreover,] questions of this sort, or perhaps of any sort, are not settled by reason; they are settled by prejudices and sentiments or by emotion. When they are settled they do not stay settled, for the emotions change as new stimuli are applied to the machine."

—Clarence Darrow, *Crime, Its Cause and Treatment* 166 (1922).

At the time he made it, Darrow's prediction that the question of capital punishment "will probably never be settled" appeared well-founded. That the issue might ever be settled as a matter of constitutional law seemed almost inconceivable. The Court had already specifically sanctioned death by firing squad and by electrocution. Indeed, 25 years after Darrow's remarks, *Louisiana ex rel. Francis v. Resweber,* 329 U.S. 459, 67 S.Ct. 374, 91 L.Ed. 422 (1947), sustained what the dissenters called the horror of "death by installments." (After a first attempt to electrocute petitioner had failed because of mechanical difficulties, the state strapped him in the electric chair a second time and threw the switch again.) And in the 1950s the Court twice upheld the execution of men whose sanity was in doubt, leaving the question to the judgment of a governor and a warden. See Kamisar, *The Reincarnation of the Death Penalty: Is it Possible?* Student Lawyer, May 1973, pp. 22–23.

In *Trop v. Dulles,* 356 U.S. 86, 78 S.Ct. 590, 2 L.Ed.2d 630 (1958), speaking for four justices, (Brennan, J., had found the "expatriation" provision invalid on other grounds), Warren, C.J., deemed deprivation of a native-born American's citizenship because of wartime desertion from the army—leaving him "stateless"—a "fate forbidden by the principle of civilized treatment guaranteed by the Eighth Amendment," but was quick to add: "[W]hatever the arguments may be against the [death penalty, it] has been employed throughout our history, and, in a day when it is still widely accepted, it cannot be said to violate the constitutional concept of cruelty." As late as 1968, a close student of the problem, observed: "[N]ot a single death penalty statute, not a single statutorily imposed mode of execution, not a single attempted execution has ever been held by any court to be 'cruel and unusual punishment' under any state or federal constitution. Nothing less than a mighty counterthrust would appear to be required to alter the direction of these decisions." Bedau, *The Courts, the Constitution, and Capital Punishment,* 1968 Utah L.Rev. 201.

In the 1960s the NAACP Legal Defense and Educational Fund, Inc. (LDF), led by Professor Anthony Amsterdam, did launch a major constitutional assault on the death penalty. Convinced that "each year the United States went without executions, the more hollow would ring claims that the American people could not do without them" and that "the longer death-row inmates waited, the greater their numbers, the more difficult it would be for the courts to permit the first execution," the LDF developed a "moratorium strategy," creating "a death-row logjam." Meltsner, *Cruel and Unusual: The Supreme Court and Capital Punishment* 107 (1973).

Largely as a result of LDF efforts in blocking all executions on every conceivable legal ground, when the Court handed down *Furman,* infra, in 1972, there had not been a single execution in five years.

Actually, the number of executions had started to decline as early as the 1940s and had dropped dramatically in the 1960s, several years before the LDF had successfully developed its moratorium strategy. After peaking in the 1930s (152 per year during this decade, and reaching an all-time high of 199 executions in 1935), the annual rate of executions averaged 128 in the 1940s and 72 in the 1950s. There were only 21 executions in 1963, 15 in 1964 and a mere seven in 1965. (In the 1930–50 period, executions had averaged more than ten *a month*). See D. Baldus, G. Woodworth & C. Pulaski, *Equal Justice and the Death Penalty* 9 (1990); Greenberg, *Capital Punishment as a System,* 91 Yale L.J. 908, 924–25 (1982); Kamisar, supra.

If, as appeared to be the case, the Court was reluctant to enter into the hotly contested capital punishment debate, yet equally hesitant to "legitimate" the punishment, the preferable way to proceed would seem to have been to continue to chip away at the procedural administration of the death penalty rather than launch a more frontal assault as the Court did (or most thought it did at the time) in *Furman.* Thus, LDF lawyers suffered a serious set-back in 1971 when the Court "refused an invitation to abolish capital punishment piecemeal." Meltsner, supra, at 244–45. *McGautha v. California* and *Crampton v. Ohio,* 402 U.S. 183, 91 S.Ct. 1454, 28 L.Ed.2d 711 (1971), rejected (1) petitioners' common claim that permitting the jury to impose the death penalty without any governing standards violated due process and (2) the Ohio petitioner's contention that allowing the jury to impose the death penalty in the same proceeding and verdict which determines the issue of guilt "creates an intolerable tension" between one's constitutional right not to be compelled to be a witness against himself on the issue of guilt and his constitutional right to be heard on the issue of punishment, a tension which can be avoided by a bifurcated trial, such as that required by California and five other states.[a]

In rejecting the contention that the states had to develop and articulate criteria under which convicted felons should be chosen to live and die, a 6–3 majority (including Stewart and White, JJ., whose votes would be pivotal in *Furman*) observed, per Harlan, J.:

"To identify before the fact those characteristics of criminal homicides and their perpetrators which call for the death penalty, and to express those characteristics in language which can be fairly understood and applied by the sentencing authority, appear to be tasks which are beyond present human ability. * * * In light of history, experience, and the present limitations of human knowledge, we find it quite impossible to say that committing to the untrammeled discretion of the jury the power to pronounce life or death in capital cases is offensive to anything in the Constitution. The States are entitled to assume that jurors confronted with the truly awesome responsibility of decreeing death for a fellow human will act with due regard for the consequences of their decision and will consider a variety of factors * * *. For a court to attempt to catalog the appropriate factors in this elusive area could inhibit rather than expand the scope of consideration, for no list of circumstances would ever be really complete." [b]

Consider Weisberg, *Deregulating Death,* 1983 Sup.Ct.Rev. 305, 313: "In the end, Harlan concludes [in *McGautha*] that, morally and intellectually, the Court has nothing to teach the states about capital punishment. One can of course dispute the truth of Harlan's central insight—that we cannot write a law of capital punishment in conventional legal language. Even if one accepts that truth, one can reject Harlan's inference from it—that the Court must leave the issue to the states. Indeed what follows *McGautha* is a struggle over both the truth and the significance of Harlan's assertion."

I. IS THE DEATH PENALTY ALWAYS—OR EVER—"CRUEL AND UNUSUAL"?

FURMAN v. GEORGIA, 408 U.S. 238, 92 S.Ct. 2726, 33 L.Ed.2d 346 (1972), considered the death sentence in three cases (all involving black defendants), two dealing with a murderer and rapist in Georgia, the third a rapist in Texas.[c] (Each had been sentenced to death after trial by jury. Under the applicable state statutes, the judge or jury had discretion to impose the death penalty.) Also at stake, however, were the lives of almost 600 condemned persons who had "piled up" in "death rows" throughout the land in recent years. Striking down the laws of 39 states [d] and various federal statutory provisions, a 5–4 majority,

a. To what extent did the Court reject *McGautha* and *Crampton* in subsequent decisions?

b. Brennan, J., joined by Douglas and Marshall, JJ., dissenting, refused to "believe that the legislatures of the 50 states are so devoid of wisdom and the power of rational thought that they are unable to face the problem of capital punishment directly, and to determine for themselves the criteria under which convicted felons should be chosen to live or die." He maintained that such procedures may take a variety of forms, e.g., requiring the decision to rest upon the presence or absence of specific factors, or directing the decision-maker's attention to the basic policy determinations underlying the death penalty statute.

c. Since 1930, murder and rape had accounted for nearly 99% of total executions and murder alone for about 87%. But various jurisdictions also permitted capital punishment for other crimes, e.g., kidnapping, treason, espionage, aircraft piracy.

d. Forty states authorized capital punishment for a variety of crimes, but since Rhode per curiam, held that "the imposition and carrying out" of the death penalty under the current arbitrarily and randomly administered system constitutes "cruel and unusual" punishment in violation of the eighth and fourteenth amendments. Each of the justices wrote a separate concurring or dissenting opinion explaining his reasons for invalidating or upholding the death penalty. (The nine opinions totalled 230 pages in the official reports.) *Furman* has been called "not so much a case as a badly orchestrated opera, with nine characters taking turns to offer their own arias." Weisberg, *Deregulating Death,* 1983 Sup. Ct.Rev. 305, 315.

The pivotal opinions of Stewart and White, JJ., left open the question whether *any* system of capital punishment, as opposed to the presently capriciously administered one, would be unconstitutional. A third member of the majority, Douglas, J., also reserved for another day whether a nondiscriminatorily operated mandatory death penalty would be constitutional.

STEWART, J.: "If we were reviewing death sentences imposed under [laws making death the mandatory punishment for every person convicted of engaging in certain designated criminal conduct] we would be faced with the need to decide whether capital punishment is unconstitutional for all crimes and under all circumstances. We would need to decide whether a legislature—state or federal—could constitutionally determine that certain criminal conduct is so atrocious that society's interest in deterrence and retribution wholly outweighs any considerations of reform or rehabilitation of the perpetrator, and that, despite the inconclusive empirical evidence, only the automatic penalty of death will provide maximum deterrence.

"On that score I would say only that I cannot agree that retribution is a constitutionally impermissible ingredient in the imposition of punishment. The instinct for retribution is part of the nature of man, and channeling that instinct in the administration of criminal justice serves an important purpose in promoting the stability of a society governed by law. When people begin to believe that organized society is unwilling or unable to impose upon criminal offenders the punishment they 'deserve,' then there are sown the seeds of anarchy—of self-help, vigilante justice, and lynch law.

"The constitutionality of capital punishment in the abstract is not, however, before us in these cases. For the Georgia and Texas legislatures have not provided that the death penalty shall be imposed upon all those who are found guilty of forcible rape [or] murder. In a word, neither State has made a legislative determination that forcible rape and murder can be deterred only by imposing the penalty of death upon all who perpetrate those offenses. As [concurring] Justice White so tellingly puts it, the 'legislative will is not frustrated if the penalty is never imposed.'

"Instead, the death sentences now before us are the product of a legal system that brings them, I believe, within the very core of the Eighth Amendment's guarantee against cruel and unusual punishments, a guarantee applicable against the States through the Fourteenth Amendment. In the first place, it is clear that these sentences are 'cruel' in the sense that they excessively go beyond, not in degree but in kind, the punishments that the state legislatures have determined to be necessary. In the second place, it is equally clear that these sentences are 'unusual' in the sense that the penalty of death is infre-

Island's only capital statute, murder by a life term prisoner, carried a mandatory death sentence, it was not invalidated by the instant case.

quently imposed for murder, and that its imposition for rape is extraordinarily rare. But I do not rest my conclusion upon these two propositions alone.

"These death sentences are cruel and unusual in the same way that being struck by lightning is cruel and unusual. For, of all the people convicted of rapes and murders in 1967 and 1968, many just as reprehensible as these, the petitioners are among a capriciously selected random handful upon whom the sentence of death has in fact been imposed. My concurring Brothers have demonstrated that, if any basis can be discerned for the selection of these few to be sentenced to die, it is the constitutionally impermissible basis of race. But racial discrimination has not been proved, and I put it to one side. I simply conclude that the Eighth and Fourteenth Amendments cannot tolerate the inflicting of a sentence of death under legal systems that permit this unique penalty to be so wantonly and so freakishly imposed."

WHITE, J.: "The imposition and execution of the death penalty are obviously cruel in the dictionary sense. But the penalty has not been considered cruel and unusual punishment in the constitutional sense because it was thought justified by the social ends it was deemed to serve. At the moment that it ceases realistically to further these purposes, however, the emerging question is whether its imposition in such circumstances would violate the Eighth Amendment. It is my view that it would, for its imposition would then be the pointless and needless extinction of life with only marginal contributions to any discernible social or public purposes. A penalty with such negligible returns to the State would be patently excessive and cruel and unusual punishment violative of the Eighth Amendment.

"It is also my judgment that this point has been reached with respect to capital punishment as it is presently administered under the statutes involved in these cases. [A]s the statutes before us are now administered, the penalty is so infrequently imposed that the threat of execution is too attenuated to be of substantial service to criminal justice.

" * * * I must arrive at judgment; and I can do no more than state a conclusion based on 10 years of almost daily exposure to the facts and circumstances of hundreds and hundreds of federal and state criminal cases involving crimes for which death is the authorized penalty. [T]he death penalty is exacted with great infrequency even for the most atrocious crimes [and] there is no meaningful basis for distinguishing the few cases in which it is imposed from the many cases in which it is not.[e] The short of it is that the policy of vesting sentencing authority primarily in juries—a decision largely motivated by the desire to mitigate the harshness of the law and to bring community judgment to bear on the sentence as well as guilt or innocence—has so effectively achieved its aims that capital punishment within the confines of the statutes now before us has for all practical purposes run its course.

e. But consider Vance, *The Death Penalty after Furman,* 48 Notre Dame Law. 850, 858 (1973): "Actually there is a fairly universal consensus on which cases should receive the harshest penalties. [It] is only in the bizarre murder, the killing for hire or during another serious crime, and a few other isolated instances that the people of this country want to see the death penalty applied. [Any prosecutor] (as well as any judge or defense attorney) can listen to a set of facts and tell you whether it is a death penalty case. [T]here *should* be very few death penalty sentences. Only a very few cases warrant this extreme measure. It takes two essential [ingredients]: (1) overwhelming proof [of] guilt and (2) an extremely aggravated fact situation. What is so surprising is Justice White's and Justice Stewart's conclusion that there is something highly improper in so few people receiving the death penalty."

"[P]ast and present legislative judgment with respect to the death penalty loses much of its force when viewed in light of the recurring practice of delegating sentencing authority to the jury and the fact that a jury, in its own discretion and without violating its trust or any statutory policy, may refuse to impose the death penalty no matter what the circumstances of the crime. Legislative 'policy' is thus necessarily defined not by what is legislatively authorized but by what juries and judges do in exercising the discretion so regularly conferred upon them. In my judgment what was done in these cases violated the Eighth Amendment."

DOUGLAS, J.: "The words 'cruel and unusual' certainly include penalties that are barbaric. But the words, at least when read in light of the English proscription against selective and irregular use of penalties, suggest that it is 'cruel and unusual' to apply the death penalty—or any other penalty—selectively to minorities whose numbers are few, who are outcasts of society, and who are unpopular, but whom society is willing to see suffer though it would not countenance general application of the same penalty across the board. * * *

"[T]hese discretionary statutes are unconstitutional in their operation. They are pregnant with discrimination and discrimination is an ingredient not compatible with the idea of equal protection of the laws that is implicit in the ban on 'cruel and unusual' punishments."

As BRENNAN, J., perceived the question, there are four principles "recognized in our cases and inherent in" the eighth amendment prohibition "sufficient to permit a judicial determination whether a challenged punishment" "does not comport with human dignity" and therefore is "cruel and unusual": (1) "a punishment must not be so severe as to be degrading to the dignity of human beings"; (2) the government "must not arbitrarily inflict a severe punishment"; (3) "a severe punishment must not be unacceptable to contemporary society"; and (4) "a severe punishment must not be excessive," i.e., "unnecessary." Applying the first and "primary" principle, Brennan, J., concluded that capital punishment "involves by its very nature a denial of the executed person's humanity" and, in comparison to all other punishments today, "is uniquely degrading to human dignity." He "would not hesitate to hold, on that ground alone, that death is today a 'cruel and unusual punishment,' *were it not that death is a punishment of longstanding usage and acceptance in this country.*" [Emphasis added.] He then turned to a discussion of the other three principles and, relying heavily upon the fact that today the death sentence is inflicted very rarely and most arbitrarily, concluded that the death penalty is inconsistent with these other principles as well. * * * "The function of these principles is to enable a court to determine whether a punishment comports with human dignity. Death, quite simply, does not."

MARSHALL, J.'s "historical foray" led to the question "whether American society has reached a point where abolition is not dependent on a successful grass roots movement in particular jurisdictions, but is demanded by the Eighth Amendment." He concluded that the death penalty constitutes "cruel and unusual" punishment on two independent grounds: (1) "it is excessive and serves no valid legislative purpose," i.e., it is not a more effective deterrent than life imprisonment; (2) "it is abhorrent to currently existing moral values."

As for the first ground: "Punishment for the sake of retribution" is "not permissible under the Eighth Amendment. [At] times a cry is heard that morality requires vengeance to evidence society's abhorrence of the act. But the Eighth Amendment is our insulation from our baser selves. The cruel and unusual language limits the avenues through which vengeance can be channeled.[f] Were this not so, the language would be empty and a return to the rack and other tortures would be possible in a given case." Nor, "in light of the massive amount of evidence before us, [showing no correlation between the rate of murder or other capital crimes and the presence or absence of the death penalty, can capital punishment] be justified on the basis of its deterrent effect."

As for the second independent ground: Although recent opinion polls indicate that Americans are about equally divided on the question of capital punishment, "whether or not a punishment is cruel or unusual depends, not on whether its mere mention 'shocks the conscience and sense of justice of the people,' but on whether people who were fully informed as to the purposes of the penalty and its liabilities would find the penalty shocking, unjust and unacceptable." Marshall, J., then concluded that *if* the average citizen possessed "knowledge of all the facts presently available" (for example, that death is no more effective a deterrent than life imprisonment; "convicted murderers are rarely executed"; "no attempt is made in the sentencing process to ferret out likely recidivists for execution"; the punishment "is imposed discriminatorily against certain identifiable classes of people"; "innocent people have been executed";) "the average citizen *would,* in my opinion, find [capital punishment] shocking to his conscience and sense of justice. [Emphasis added.][g] For this reason alone capital punishment cannot stand."

There were four separate dissenting opinions. BURGER, C.J., warned that "it is essential to our role as a court that we not seize upon the enigmatic character of the [eighth amendment] guarantee as an invitation to enact our personal predilictions into law." As for the argument that the death penalty was "excessive" or "unnecessary," he found "no authority suggesting that the Eighth Amendment was intended to purge the law of its retributive elements" nor any basis for prohibiting "all punishments the States are unable to prove necessary to deter crime."

"Real change," maintained the Chief Justice, "could clearly be brought about [by legislatures responding to today's ruling if they] provided mandatory death sentences in such a way as to deny juries the opportunity to bring in a verdict on a lesser charge; under such a system, the death sentence could only be avoided by a verdict of acquittal. If this is the only alternative that the legislatures can safely pursue under today's ruling, I would have preferred that the Court opt for total abolition. * * *

f. But consider Polsby, *The Death of Capital Punishment,* 1972 Sup.Ct.Rev. 1, 37, 39–40: "The confusion between the proposition that the death penalty deters and the proposition that it is appropriate is a fairly stable feature of retentionist argument. [I submit] that the declaration that the death penalty is a superior deterrent to serious crime, in spite of evidence to the contrary, amounts to nothing more than the expression of a value preference that, whether the penalty is a superior deterrent or not, it ought to be used. A priori, I can find nothing wrong with this value preference. It may be flinty and stern, but it does not seem to me necessarily barbaric, that someone might believe that certain criminals ought to be put to death, the inhuman brutality of their crimes being so great as to outrun all possibility of forgiveness or amends. But if the argument is to rest upon straight moralistic dogma [why] should it dress itself up in the guise of a utilitarian argument instead? [One] answer may be that retentionists would be ashamed to admit to having such values. If so, surely it is relevant to a judgment whether death is a cruel and unusual punishment." Cf. Black, *Capital Punishment: The Inevitability of Caprice and Mistake* 23–28 (1974).

g. Is this a valid means of ascertaining whether "popular sentiment" or "the average citizen" abhors capital punishment? Or does Marshall, J.'s approach represent excessive speculation or inappropriate "elitism" about moral judgment? Compare Kamisar, supra, at 48, and Polsby, supra, at 23–24 with Radin, *The Jurisprudence of Death,* 126 U.Pa.L.Rev. 989, 1040–42 (1978).

* * *

"Quite apart from the limitations of the Eighth Amendment itself, the preference for legislative action is justified by the inability of the courts to participate in the debate at the level where the controversy is focused. The case against capital punishment is not the product of legal dialectic but rests primarily on factual claims, the truth of which cannot be tested by conventional judicial processes."

BLACKMUN, J., filed a separate dissent, "personally rejoicing" at the Court's result, but unable to accept it "as a matter of history, of law, or of constitutional pronouncement."

In a third dissent, POWELL, J., called the Court's ruling "the very sort of judgment that the legislative branch is competent to make and for which the judiciary is ill-equipped." He maintained that "the sweeping judicial action undertaken today reflects a basic lack of faith and confidence in the democratic process."

In a fourth dissent, REHNQUIST, J., concluded that the majority's ruling "significantly lack[ed]" the "humility" and "deference to legislative judgment" with which the task of judging constitutional cases must be approached; indeed, "it is not an act of judgment, but rather an act of will."

Notes and Questions

1. Of *"life" and "limb."* Consider L. Levy, *Against the Law* 396 (1974): "To argue as a matter of public morality or policy that the state should not take a life as a penalty for crime is an appropriate task for legislation. The responsible [Supreme Court justice] has a different task. In this case the text of the Constitution itself seemed confining, indeed, seemed to erect an insuperable barricade against acceptance of the abolitionist position. The [Eighth Amendment prohibition] appears in the same Bill of Rights that clearly sanctions the death penalty. The Fifth Amendment begins with a guarantee [that] '[n]o person shall be held to answer for a *capital,* or otherwise infamous crime, unless * * *.' The same amendment [also provides]: 'nor shall any person be subject for the same offense to be twice put in jeopardy of *life* or limb' [nor] 'be deprived of *life,* liberty, or property without due process * * *.' In 1868 the Fourteenth Amendment made an identical due-process clause applicable to the [states]. Thus, the Constitution itself in four places recognizes and permits capital punishment, a penalty that was common when the Fifth, Eighth and Fourteenth Amendments were adopted." See also R. Berger, *Death Penalties: The Supreme Court's Obstacle Course* 43–50 (1982). But cf. Levy, supra, at 402: "[Brennan, J.,] relegated to one of his footnotes a stunning retort to the dissenters who so heavily stressed the fact that the language of the Fifth Amendment authorized the death penalty. One of its clauses prohibited placing any person in double jeopardy of life 'or limb,' [but] Brennan asserted correctly that no one now contends that the reference to jeopardy of limb 'provides a perpetual constitutional sanction for such corporal punishments as branding and earcropping, which were common punishments when the Bill of Rights was adopted' [n. 28]. Not one of the four dissenters took note of the point; it was irrefutable."

2. *McGautha and Furman.* Why didn't Stewart and White JJ., take the route offered a year earlier by *McGautha* rather than the broader avenue presented in *Furman?* Was it because, in *Furman,* they were free of a powerful force which had operated on them the previous year—the restraining influence of that great "judge's judge"—Harlan, J.? Was it because they did not them-

selves know until the "moment of decision" that they *would* vote to strike down the death penalty? Was it because, after struggling for years to avoid meeting the issue head-on, when they finally had to do so they simply could not bring themselves to authorize "pulling the switch"—even if they had to go off on grounds which seem quite inconsistent with their previous position in *McGautha?*

3. *The "analytic" and "normative" approaches of the Furman majority.* Daniel Polsby has called "the Douglas-Stewart-White approach to the Eighth Amendment 'analytic' to distinguish it from the 'normative' approach of Brennan and Marshall." He observes, Polsby, fn. f supra at 24–25: "[The analytic approach's chief virtue is at the same time its chief vice: it avoids the core normative question whether the 'evolving standards of decency that mark the progress of a maturing society' have now risen high enough to wash the death penalty away. [W]hatever the analytic approach gains in avoiding subjective and impressionistic sallies into the shadow world of language, it also fails to meet Mr. Justice Brennan's implicit objection that the Eighth Amendment—whatever it means—must mean something, and, indeed, must mean something different from the other provisions of the Constitution. The arguments of Justices Douglas, Stewart, and White seem rather intent on avoiding, if possible, that core question. Rather, they prefer to emphasize the use of the Eighth Amendment as a tool for testing whether the penalty of death is evenhandedly applied. Why they should have done this is obscure in view of the fact that existing doctrines of equal protection (which was the emphasis of the Douglas opinion) or due process of law should have furnished more than adequate ground for striking down the death penalty, once the factual premises which these three Justices proffer (relating to the arbitrariness or irrationality of the penalty's use, or in Douglas's case, to its use on despised or dispossessed minorities) are accepted.[h] To view the Eighth Amendment in those terms deprives it of a dimension which is latent in almost all of the previous [decisions]—as an independently potent moral force which is at the disposal of the least dangerous branch of government and which may be used to make the most dangerous branch a little less so."

GREGG v. GEORGIA, 428 U.S. 153, 96 S.Ct. 2909, 49 L.Ed.2d 859 (1976), upheld the constitutionality of Georgia's post-*Furman* capital-sentencing procedures, rejecting the basic contention that "the punishment of death always, regardless of the enormity of the offense or the procedure followed in imposing the sentence, is cruel and unusual punishment in violation of the Constitution." STEWART, POWELL and STEVENS, JJ., who announced the judgment of the Court and filed an opinion delivered by Justice Stewart, concluded that "the concerns expressed in *Furman* that the penalty of death not be imposed in an arbitrary or capricious manner can be met by a carefully drafted statute that ensures that the sentencing authority is given adequate information and guidance. As a general proposition these concerns are best met by a system [such as Georgia's] that provides for a bifurcated proceeding at which the sentencing authority is apprised of the information relevant to the imposition of sentence and provided with standards to guide its use of the information."

h. But in *Furman* and companion cases certiorari was granted limited to the following question: "Does the imposition and carrying out of the death penalty in [these cases] constitute cruel and unusual punishment in violation of the Eighth and Fourteenth Amendments?"

Unlike the procedures before the Court in *Furman*, the new Georgia sentencing procedures "focus the jury's attention on the particularized nature of the crime and the particularized characteristics of the individual defendant. While the jury is permitted to consider any aggravating or mitigating circumstances,[a] it must find and identify at least one [of 10 statutory aggravating circumstances [b] beyond a reasonable doubt] before it may impose a penalty of death. In this way the jury's discretion is channelled. No longer can a jury wantonly and freakishly impose the death sentence; it is always circumscribed by the legislative guidelines. In addition, the review function of the Supreme Court of Georgia [which is required to review every death sentence to determine, inter alia, whether it was imposed under the influence of passion or prejudice and whether it is 'excessive or disproportionate to the penalty imposed in similar cases, considering both the crime and the defendant'] affords additional assurance that the concerns that prompted our decision in *Furman* are not present to any significant degree in the Georgia procedure applied here."

At the guilt stage (or guilt trial) of Georgia's bifurcated procedure, the jury found petitioner guilty of two counts of armed robbery and two counts of murder. At the sentencing stage, which took place before the same jury, the judge instructed the jury that it would not be authorized to consider the death penalty unless it first found beyond a reasonable doubt one of these statutorily defined "aggravating circumstances": (1) that murder was committed while the offender was engaged in the commission of "another capital felony," to-wit armed robbery; (2) the offender committed murder "for the purpose of receiving money"; (3) the murder was "outrageously or wantonly vile [in] that it [involved] depravity of the mind." Finding the first two "aggravating circumstances," the jury returned verdicts of death on each count. The Georgia Supreme Court affirmed the convictions. After reviewing the record and comparing the evidence and sentences in similar cases, the court upheld the death sentences for the murders, but vacated the armed robbery sentences on the ground, inter alia, that the death penalty had rarely been imposed in Georgia for that crime. In rejecting petitioner's claim that his death sentence under the Georgia statute constituted "cruel and unusual" punishment, the plurality observed:

"[A]n assessment of contemporary values concerning the infliction of a challenged sanction is relevant to the application of the Eighth Amendment, [but] our cases also make clear that public perceptions of standards of decency with respect to criminal sanctions are not conclusive. A penalty also must accord with 'the dignity of man,' which is the 'basic concept underlying the Eighth Amendment.' *Trop* (plurality opinion). This means, at least, that the punishment not be 'excessive.' When a form of punishment in the abstract [is challenged], the inquiry into 'excessiveness' has two aspects. First, the punish-

a. The plurality pointed out that the jury is not *required* to find any mitigating circumstance in order to make a recommendation of mercy that is binding on the court, "but it must find a *statutory* aggravating circumstance before recommending a sentence of death."

b. Georgia authorized the death penalty for six categories of crime: murder, kidnapping under certain circumstances, rape, treason and aircraft hijacking. The statutory aggravating circumstances for murder include "a prior record of conviction for a capital offense" or "a substantial history of serious assaultive criminal convictions"; commission of the crime against a police officer or fireman while performing his official duties; commission of the crime while engaged in certain other felonies; or commission of an "outrageously or wantonly vile, horrible or inhuman" murder (§ (b)(7)). *Godfrey v. Georgia*, 446 U.S. 420, 100 S.Ct. 1759, 64 L.Ed.2d 398 (1980), held that the Georgia courts had "adopted such a broad and vague construction" of the § (b)(7) aggravating circumstance as to violate the eighth and fourteenth amendments. But cf. *Walton v. Arizona*, infra.

ment must not involve the unnecessary and wanton infliction of pain. Second, the punishment must not be grossly out of proportion to the severity of the crime.

"[I]n assessing a punishment selected by a democratically elected legislature against the constitutional measure, we presume its validity. We may not require the legislature to select the least severe penalty possible so long as the penalty selected is not cruelly inhumane or disproportionate to the crime involved. And a heavy burden rests on those who would attack the judgment of the representatives of the people.

"[Petitioners renew the argument made in *Furman* that 'standards of decency' have evolved to the point where capital punishment no longer can be tolerated, a view accepted only by Justices Brennan and Marshall four years ago], but developments [since] *Furman* have undercut substantially the assumptions upon which [this] argument rested. [It] is now evident that a large proportion of American society continues to regard [capital punishment] as an appropriate and necessary criminal sanction.

"The most marked indication of society's endorsement of the death penalty for murder is the legislative response to *Furman.* The legislatures of at least 35 States have enacted new statutes that provide for the death penalty for at least some crimes that result in the death of another person.[c] And the Congress of the United States, in 1974, enacted a statute providing the death penalty for aircraft piracy that results in death.

"[The] jury also is a significant and reliable objective index of contemporary values because it is so directly involved. [It] may be true that evolving standards have influenced juries in recent decades to be more discriminating in imposing the sentence of death. But the relative infrequency of jury verdicts imposing the death sentence does not indicate rejection of capital punishment per se. Rather, [it] may well reflect the humane feeling that this most irrevocable of sanctions should be reserved for a small number of extreme cases.

"[H]owever, the Eighth Amendment demands more than that a challenged punishment be acceptable to contemporary society. The Court also must ask whether is comports with the basic concept of human dignity at the core of the Amendment. *Trop* (plurality opinion). * * *

"The death penalty is said to serve two principal social purposes: retribution and deterrence of capital crimes by prospective offenders.

"In part, capital punishment is an expression of society's moral outrage at particularly offensive conduct. This function [is] essential in an ordered society that asks its citizens to rely on legal processes rather than self-help to vindicate their wrongs. 'The instinct for retribution is part of the nature of man, and channeling that instinct in the administration of criminal justice serves an important purpose in promoting the stability of a society governed by law. * * *'

c. But consider Zimring & Hawkins, *Capital Punishment and the Eighth Amendment: Furman and Gregg in Retrospect*, 18 U.C.Davis L.Rev., 927, 950 (1985): The "legislative extravaganza" of post-*Furman* death penalty statutes "is reminiscent of the 'pouring panic of capital statutes' which was a feature of the history of the criminal law in eighteenth-century England. Whatever the social psychology of that development may have been, the post-*Furman* reaction in America would probably be best characterized as a typical frustration-aggression response. Like parallel incidents in school prayer and pornography, legislative backlash was entirely to be expected by anyone familiar with the history of judicial invalidation in this country."

For a useful summary of the post-*Furman* statutes, see Gillers, *Deciding Who Dies*, 129 U.Pa.L.Rev. 1, 13, 101–10 (1980).

"[The] value of capital punishment as a deterrent of crime is a complex factual issue the resolution of which properly rests with the legislatures, which can evaluate the results of statistical studies in terms of their own local conditions and with a flexibility of approach that is not available to the courts. Indeed, many of the post-*Furman* statutes reflect just such a responsible effort to define those crimes and those criminals for which capital punishment is most probably an effective deterrent.

"In sum, we cannot say that the judgment of the Georgia legislature that capital punishment may be necessary in some cases is clearly wrong. Considerations of federalism, as well as respect for the ability of a legislature to evaluate, in terms of its particular state the moral consensus concerning the death penalty and its social utility as a sanction, require us to conclude, in the absence of more convincing evidence, that the infliction of death as a punishment for murder is not without justification and thus is not unconstitutionally severe.

"[Petitioner contends] that the changes in the Georgia sentencing procedures are only cosmetic, [focusing] on the opportunities for discretionary action that are inherent in the processing of any murder case under Georgia law. He notes that the state prosecutor has unfettered authority to select those persons whom he wishes to prosecute for a capital offense and to plea bargain with them. Further, at the trial the jury may choose to convict a defendant of a lesser included offense rather than find him guilty of a crime punishable by death, even if the evidence would support a capital verdict. And finally, a defendant who is convicted and sentenced to die may have his sentence commuted by the Governor of the State and the Georgia Board of Pardons and Paroles.[d]

"The existence of these discretionary stages is not determinative of the issues before us. [*Furman*] dealt with the decision to impose the death sentence on a specific individual who had been convicted of a capital offense. Nothing in any of our cases suggests that the decision to afford an individual defendant mercy violates the Constitution. *Furman* held only that, in order to minimize the risk that the death penalty would be imposed on a capriciously selected group of offenders, the decision to impose it had to be guided by standards so that the sentencing authority would focus on the particularized circumstances of the crime and the defendant.[50] "

WHITE, J., joined by Burger, C.J., and Rehnquist, J., concurred in the judgment: "Petitioner's argument that there is an unconstitutional amount of discretion in the system which separates those suspects who receive the death penalty from those who receive life imprisonment, a lesser penalty, or are

d. For a forceful statement of the view that the post-*Furman* statutes do not effectively restrict jury discretion by any real standards and that capital sentencing statutes "never will"—"no society is going to kill everybody who meets certain present verbal requirements"—see Black, *Capital Punishment: The Inevitability of Caprice and Mistake* 67–68 (1974).

50. The petitioner's argument is nothing more than a veiled contention that *Furman* indirectly outlawed capital punishment by placing totally unrealistic conditions on its use. In order to repair the alleged defects pointed to by the petitioner, it would be necessary to require that prosecuting authorities charge a capital offense whenever arguably there had been a capital murder and that they refuse to plea bargain with the defendant. If a jury refused to convict even though the evidence supported the charge, its verdict would have to be reversed and a verdict of guilty entered or a new trial ordered, since the discretionary act of jury nullification would not be permitted. Finally, acts of executive clemency would have to be prohibited. Such a system, of course, would be totally alien to our notions of criminal justice.

Moreover, it would be unconstitutional. Such a system in many respects would have the vices of the mandatory death penalty statutes we hold unconstitutional today in *Woodson* and *Stanislaus Roberts* [infra].

acquitted or never charged, seems to be in final analysis an indictment of our entire system of justice. Petitioner has argued, in effect, that no matter how effective the death penalty may be as a punishment, government, created and run as it must be by humans, is inevitably incompetent to administer it. This cannot be accepted as a proposition of constitutional law. [I] decline to interfere with the manner in which Georgia has chosen to enforce [the death penalty] on what is simply an assertion of lack of faith in the ability of the system of justice to operate in a fundamentally fair manner." [e]

BRENNAN, J., dissented: "In *Furman,* I read 'evolving standards of decency' as requiring focus upon the essence of the death penalty itself and not primarily or solely upon the procedures under which the determination to inflict the penalty upon a particular person was made. [That] continues to be my view."

MARSHALL, J., also dissented: "The two purposes that sustain the death penalty as nonexcessive in the Court's view are general deterrence and retribution. [The] evidence I reviewed in *Furman* remains convincing, in my view, that 'capital punishment is not necessary as a deterrent to crime in our society.' The justification for the death penalty must be found elsewhere.

"[The plurality's view of the important purpose served by 'channeling' 'the instinct for retribution' in the administration of criminal justice] is wholly inadequate to justify the death penalty. [It] simply defies belief to suggest that the death penalty is necessary to prevent the American people from taking the law into their own hands.

"[The contention] that the expression of moral outrage through the imposition of the death penalty serves to reinforce basic moral values [also] provides no support for the death penalty. It is inconceivable that any individual concerned about conforming his conduct to what society says is 'right' would fail to realize that murder is 'wrong' if the penalty were simply life imprisonment. * * *

"There remains for consideration, however, what might be termed the purely retributive justification for the death penalty—that the death penalty is appropriate, not because of its beneficial effect on society, but because the taking of the murderer's life is itself morally good. Some of the language of the plurality's opinion appears positively to embrace this notion of retribution for its own sake as a justification for capital punishment.

"[T]hat society's judgment that the murderer 'deserves' death must be respected not simply because the preservation of order requires it, but because it is appropriate that society make the judgment and carry it out [is a notion] fundamentally at odds with the Eighth Amendment. The mere fact that the community demands the murderer's life in return for the evil he has done cannot sustain the death penalty, for as the plurality reminds us, 'the Eighth Amendment demands more than that a challenged punishment be acceptable to contemporary society.' [Under appropriate Eighth Amendment] standards, the taking of life 'because the wrong-doer deserves it' surely must fall, for such a punishment has as its very basis the total denial of the wrong-doer's dignity and worth."

e. Blackmun, J., concurred in the judgment, referring solely to his dissenting opinion in *Furman.*

Notes and Questions

1. *The Texas statute upheld in Jurek.* In companion cases to *Gregg,* dividing the same way, the Court upheld the constitutionality of two other state capital-sentencing procedures which, it concluded, essentially resembled the Georgia system. *Proffitt v. Florida,* 428 U.S. 242, 96 S.Ct. 2960, 49 L.Ed.2d 913 (1976); *Jurek v. Texas,* 428 U.S. 262, 96 S.Ct. 2950, 49 L.Ed.2d 929 (1976). For forceful criticism of *Jurek* and for the view that the Texas statute is "much worse than either the Georgia or the Florida statutes, bad as they are," see Black, *Due Process for Death,* 26 Cath.U.L.Rev. 1, 2 (1976). See also 90 Harv.L. Rev. 71–75 (1976).

2. *Gregg, Jurek* and *Proffitt* reached the question reserved in *Furman*—"the constitutionality of capital punishment in the abstract"—and upheld it. But consider Black, *Reflections on Opposing the Penalty of Death,* 10 St. Mary's L.J. 1, 7 (1978): "[T]he *only* question that actually confronts us [is] whether it is right to kill such people as are chosen by our system as it stands. [I]t doesn't really make any difference at all what I think about the abstract rightness of capital punishment. There exists no abstract capital punishment." See also Amsterdam, *Capital Punishment,* in Bedau, *The Death Penalty in America* 346, 349–51 (3rd ed. 1982); Black, *The Death Penalty Now,* 51 Tul.L.Rev. 429, 445 (1977).

3. *Public endorsement of the death penalty.* "The critical holding in *Gregg,*" observe S. Gross & R. Mauro, *Death & Discrimination: Racial Disparaties in Capital Sentencing* 216 (1990), "was not the endorsement of 'guided discretion' but the decision that the use of the death penalty is consistent with 'contemporary values' and 'public attitude[s]' toward crime, and therefore that it is not constitutionally 'cruel and unusual.' By 1976 the evidence of public endorsement of the death penalty was undeniable." In 1972, when *Furman* was decided, 57 percent of a national sample favored the death penalty for murder. In 1976, when Gregg was decided, support for the death penalty had increased to 65 percent. A decade later, the level of support was between 70–75 percent. See id. at 255 n. 14. See also Bedau, "The Half Empty Glass" (1988), in *A Punishment in Search of a Crime* 255, 229 (Gray & Stanley ed. 1989), noting the high level of support for the death penalty "all across the board, academics, non-academics, men, women, white, non-white, college-educated, not college-educated. [The] incoming college freshmen support the death penalty by about three to one, which is extraordinary. Historically, [it] was the young who, by and large, were opposed to capital punishment. Not now."

4. *The continuing reluctance to impose the death penalty in all death-eligible cases.* "[O]ne obstacle to eliminating excessive or discriminatory death sentences under the post-*Furman* statutes," note D. Baldus, G. Woodworth & C. Pulaski, *Equal Justice and the Death Penalty* 413–14 (1990), "is the continuing reluctance of prosecutors and juries to favor imposition of death sentences in all death-eligible cases. Not only is this reluctance contrary to the Supreme Court's expectations when it decided *Gregg,* but there is no practical remedy for this inaction. No one involved in the criminal-justice process is going to argue that the Eighth Amendment requires the more frequent imposition of death sentences. The fact remains, however, that when only a few of the many defendants convicted of capital murder actually receive death sentences the ability of the selection process to operate rationally and consistently in each case undergoes substantial strain."

5. *How much "guidance" does the Georgia statute provide?* Consider Weisberg, *Deregulating Death,* 1983 Sup.Ct.Rev. 305, 322, 375: "In the end * * * all the rhetoric about 'guidance' and 'channeling' interwoven through [the *Gregg* plurality's] summary of the statute amounts to little more than judicial sighs of relief over how Georgia has allowed the Court to escape gracefully from the responsibility it posed for itself in *Furman.* One can say little with certainty about *Gregg* except that it makes a great many things constitutionally significant, but makes nothing either constitutionally necessary or clearly constitutionally sufficient. * * * Weighing and balancing legally defined factors may be useful in helping the jury frame the issue, but the penalty decision is ultimately irreducible to legal terms. With enhanced rules of murder liability and aggravating circumstances about the defendant's crime and criminal record, the law perhaps can sensibly screen out those defendants who do not deserve to die. But that leaves no legal theory about which defendants *do* deserve to die." See also Ely, *Democracy and Distrust* 175–76 (1980); Kaplan, *Administering Capital Punishment,* 36 U.Fla.L.Rev. 177, 188–89 (1984). Does the system of capital punishment upheld in *Gregg* even screen out those who do *not* deserve to die? Consider W. White, *Life in the Balance* 30 (1984): Although in theory requiring the sentencer to find an aggravating circumstance potentially reduces the number of capital defendants subject to arbitrary action, "[u]nder most [post-*Furman*] statutes [the] aggravating circumstances taken together are so broad that almost any traditional first-degree murder case could be found to include at least one of them." See also Bentele, *The Death Penalty in Georgia: Still Arbitrary,* 62 Wash.U.L.Q. 573, 581 (1985) (at least one of Georgia's ten statutory aggravating circumstances "occurs in the great majority of murder cases").

6. *Assuming that evidence whether the death penalty is a better deterrent than life imprisonment is "inconclusive," what follows?* Consider Amsterdam, supra, at 355: "*Because* the [Supreme Court deemed the evidence] inconclusive, [it] held that the Constitution did not forbid judgment either way. But if the evidence is inconclusive, is it *your* judgment that we should conclusively kill people on a factual theory that the evidence does not conclusively sustain?" But see Ernest van den Haag in van den Haag & Conrad, *The Death Penalty: A Debate* 69 (1983).

7. *Whatever the answer when the issue is one of legislative policy, once a state enacts a death penalty statute, is it plain who has the "burden of proof"?* The *Gregg* plurality thought so. It "presumed" the "validity" of the challenged statute, put "a heavy burden [on] those who would attack the judgment of the representatives of the people" and framed the issue in terms of whether the Georgia legislature's judgment was "clearly wrong." But see Radin, *The Jurisprudence of Death,* 126 U.Pa.L.Rev. 989, 1029–30, 1064 & n. 280 (1978): "The conjunction of the factors of irrevocability, enormity and fundamental right peculiar to the death penalty demands a searching analysis with no initial presumptions in favor of the past. The death penalty should be subject to strict scrutiny for cruelty. [If] we as a society are seriously divided on whether a fundamental interest may be invaded by the government under certain circumstances, it is morally wrong to behave as if there existed a moral consensus that justified invading that interest. [*Roe v. Wade*] recognized that in a conflict between fundamental rights of individuals and the interests of the state, questions of the validity of a moral theory concerning which there exists no consensus should be resolved against the state."

8. *"Mercy."* Consider Black, note 1 supra, at 12: "[T]he question posed is not whether [as the *Gregg* plurality put it] 'the decision to afford an individual

defendant mercy violates the Constitution,' [but] whether a 'legal system' which regularly, and in great numbers, runs the death question through a gauntlet of decisions in no way even formally standard-bound, so that, at the end of the process, no one can say why some were selected and others were not selected for death, rises to due process. That is not a trivial question and it cannot [be] answered by calling it, [as Justice White does, concurring in *Gregg*], 'in final analysis an indictment of our entire system of justice.' If it is that, it is an indictment pleading to which would present some difficulty, for it is hard to find informed persons today who think very well of our 'entire system' of criminal justice. But death is unique, and the procedures we must use, having no better, in our entire system of justice—and that is really the kindest thing one can say of that system—may still not be good enough for the death choice. The Court has not really focused on and answered that question—in reason, I mean, and not by fiat." See also Radin, note 7 supra, at 1024.

But consider van den Haag, *Refuting Reiman and Nathanson,* 14 Philosophy & Public Affairs 165, 173–74 (1985): "If we grant that some (even all) murderers of blacks,[a] or, some (even all) white and rich murderers, escape the death penalty, how does that reduce the guilt of murderers of whites, or of black and poor murderers, so that they should be spared execution too? Guilt is personal. No murderer becomes less guilty, or less deserving of punishment, because another murderer was punished leniently, or escaped punishment altogether. We should try our best to bring every murderer to justice. But if one got away with murder wherein is that a reason to let anyone else get away? A group of murderers does not become less deserving of punishment because another equally guilty group is not punished, or punished less. We can punish only a very small proportion of all criminals. Unavoidably they are selected accidentally. We should reduce this accidentality as much as possible but we cannot eliminate it."

II. MANDATORY DEATH SENTENCES; REQUIRING CONSTRAINTS ON THE SENTENCER'S DISCRETION TO IMPOSE THE DEATH PENALTY vs. FORBIDDING RESTRICTIONS ON THE SENTENCER'S DISCRETION TO BE MERCIFUL

1. Unlike Georgia, Florida and Texas, whose post-*Furman* capital-sentencing procedures were designed to guide and to channel sentencing authority, 10 states responded to *Furman* by replacing discretionary jury sentencing in capital cases with *mandatory death penalties.* These mandatory death statutes were invalidated in WOODSON v. NORTH CAROLINA, 428 U.S. 280, 96 S.Ct. 2978, 49 L.Ed.2d 944 (1976) and ROBERTS (STANISLAUS) v. LOUISIANA, 428 U.S. 325, 96 S.Ct. 3001, 49 L.Ed.2d 974 (1976), both decided the same day as *Gregg.* As occurred in *Gregg,* in both *Woodson* and *Roberts* JUSTICES STEWART, POWELL and STEVENS announced the judgment of the Court. (In each case, for the reasons stated in their *Gregg* dissents, Justices Brennan and Marshall concurred in the result.) The history of mandatory death penalty laws in this country, observed the *Woodson* plurality, reveals that the practice "has been rejected as unduly harsh and unworkably rigid." Post–*Furman* enactments were dismissed as merely "attempts [to] retain the death penalty in a form consistent with the Constitution, rather than a renewed social acceptance of mandatory death sentencing."

a. See the Baldus study, discussed in *McCloskey v. Kemp* infra.

"A separate deficiency" of the North Carolina statute was its failure to respond adequately to "*Furman's* rejection of unbridled jury discretion in the imposition of capital sentences." In light of the widespread and persistent jury resistance to mandatory death penalties—and the high probability that many juries, despite their oaths, would exercise discretion in deciding which murderers "shall live and which shall die" under these "mandatory" statutes—North Carolina had not remedied "the problem of unguided and unchecked jury discretion" that was "central to the limited holding in *Furman,*" but "simply papered over" it. Not only does North Carolina's mandatory death penalty statute provide "no standards to guide the jury in its inevitable exercise" of discretion, but "there is no way under [state law] for the judiciary to check arbitrary and capricious exercise of that power through a review of death sentences. Instead of rationalizing the sentencing process, a mandatory scheme may well exacerbate the problem identified in *Furman* by resting the penalty determination on the particular jury's willingness to act lawlessly."

Another constitutional shortcoming of the statute was "its failure to allow the particularized consideration of relevant aspects of the character and record of each convicted defendant before the imposition upon him of a sentence of death. [D]eath is a punishment different from all other sanctions in kind rather than degree. A process that accords no significance to relevant facets of the character and record of the individual offender or the circumstances of the particular offense excludes from consideration in fixing the ultimate punishment of death the possibility of compassionate or mitigating factors stemming from the diverse frailties of humankind. It treats all persons convicted of a designated offense not as uniquely individual human beings, but as members of a faceless, undifferentiated mass to be subjected to the blind infliction of the penalty of death." [a]

a. The *Woodson* Court reserved judgment on the constitutionality of a mandatory death penalty statute "limited to an extremely narrow category of homicide, such as murder by a prisoner serving a life sentence." A decade later, in *Sumner v. Shuman,* 483 U.S. 66, 107 S.Ct. 2716, 97 L.Ed.2d 56 (1987), a 6–3 majority, per Blackmun, J., held that "a departure from the individualized capital-sentencing doctrine is not justified" even in such a case:

"Not only do the two elements that are incorporated in the [now-repealed Nevada statute, (a) that defendant had been convicted of murder while in prison, and (b) that he had been convicted of an earlier crime which yielded a sentence of life imprisonment without possibility of parole,] serve as incomplete indicators of the circumstances surrounding the murder and of the defendant's criminal record, but they say nothing of the 'circumstances such as the youth of the offender, [the] influence of drugs, alcohol, or extreme emotional disturbance, and even the existence of circumstances which the offender reasonably believed provided a moral justification for his conduct.' * * *

"The force of the deterrent argument for the mandatory statute is weakened considerably by the fact that every prison system in the country is currently operating without the threat of a mandatory death penalty for life-term inmates."

As for the State's retribution interests, "there are other sanctions less severe than execution that can be imposed even on a life-term inmate. [His] confinement can be limited further, such as through a transfer to a more restrictive custody or correctional facility or deprivation of privileges of work or socialization. In any event, even the retribution interests of the State cannot be characterized according to a category of offense because '[s]ociety's legitimate desire for retribution is less strong with respect to a defendant who played a minor role in the murder for which he was convicted.' Although a sentencing authority may decide that a sanction less than death is not appropriate in a particular case, the fundamental respect for humanity underlying the Eighth Amendment requires that the defendant be able to present any relevant mitigating evidence that could justify a lesser sentence."

Dissenting Justice White, joined by Rehnquist, C.J., and Scalia, J., maintained that "the Constitution does not bar a state legislature from determining, in this limited class of cases, that, as a matter of law, no amount of mitigating evidence could ever be sufficient to outweigh the aggravating factors that charac-

Dissenting, REHNQUIST, J., rejected the view that the 10 post-*Furman* mandatory death statutes merely represented "a wrong-headed reading [of] *Furman.* While those States may be presumed to have preferred their prior systems reposing sentencing discretion in juries or judges, they indisputably preferred mandatory capital punishment to no capital punishment at all. Their willingness to enact statutes providing that penalty is utterly inconsistent with the notion that they regarded mandatory capital sentencing as beyond 'evolving standards of decency.'" [b]

Dissenting in *Roberts* (which invalidated a Louisiana mandatory death sentence statute the *Woodson* plurality deemed fatally similar to North Carolina's), WHITE, J., joined by Burger, C.J., and Blackmun and Rehnquist, JJ., maintained: "As the plurality now interprets the Eighth Amendment, the Louisiana and North Carolina statutes are infirm because the jury is deprived of all discretion once it finds the defendant guilty. Yet in the next breath it invalidates these statutes because they are said to invite or allow too much discretion: despite their instructions, when they feel that defendants do not deserve to die, juries will so often and systematically disobey their instructions and find the defendant not guilty or guilty of a noncapital offense that the statute fails to satisfy the standards of *Furman.* If it is truly the case that Louisiana juries will exercise *too much* discretion—and I do not agree that it is—then it seems strange indeed that the statute is also invalidated because it purports to give the jury *too little* discretion by making the death penalty mandatory. Furthermore, if there is danger of freakish and too infrequent imposition of capital punishment under a mandatory system such as Louisiana's, there is very little ground for believing that juries will be any more faithful to their instructions under the Georgia and Florida systems where the opportunity is much, much greater for juries to practice their own brand of unbridled discretion."

2. *Gregg and the "mandatory death" cases.* Are *Gregg* and *Woodson* and *Roberts,* handed down the same day, reconcilable? The *Woodson* plurality points out that "instead of rationalizing the sentencing process, a mandatory scheme may well exacerbate the problem identified in *Furman* by resting the penalty determination on the particular jury's willingness to act lawlessly." But are not "these lawless juries, whose lawlessness will taint and bend a mandatory system," the very same juries who are supposed "to follow with patient care the intricacies of the Georgia and Florida statutes [upheld the same day in *Gregg* and *Proffitt*], and the unfathomed mysteries of the Texas statute [upheld the same day in *Jurek*], and base these answers on nothing but sound discretion guided by law"? See Black, *Due Process for Death,* 26 Cath.U.L.Rev. 1, 10 (1976); Black, *The Death Penalty Now,* 51 Tul.L.Rev. 429, 441 (1977). See also Bedau, *Are Mandatory Capital Statutes Unconstitutional?,* in *The Courts, the Constitution, and Capital Punishment* 106 (1977).

3. LOCKETT v. OHIO, 438 U.S. 586, 98 S.Ct. 2954, 57 L.Ed.2d 973 (1978), struck down a post-*Furman* statute that required the trial judge, once a verdict of aggravated murder with specifications had been returned, to impose the death sentence unless he found one of three narrowly defined mitigating circumstances present. A four-justice plurality, BURGER, C.J., joined by Stewart, Powell and

terize a first-degree murder committed by one who is already incarcerated for committing a previous murder and serving a life sentence."

b. White, J., joined by Burger, C.J., and Rehnquist, J., also dissented, rejecting the Court's analysis for the reasons stated in his dissent in *Roberts,* infra. Blackmun, J., also dissented in *Woodson* for the reasons stated in his *Furman* dissent. All four *Woodson* dissenters also dissented in *Roberts.*

Stevens, JJ., concluded that "the sentencer, in all but the rarest kind of capital case, [must] not be precluded from considering *as a mitigating factor,* any aspect of a defendant's character or record and any of the circumstances of the offense that the defendant proffers as a basis for a sentence less than death. [The] nonavailability of corrective or modifying mechanisms with respect to an executed capital sentence underscores the need for individualized consideration as a constitutional requirement in imposing the death sentence." Dissenting Justice REHNQUIST protested: "By encouraging defendants in capital cases, and presumably sentencing judges and juries, to take into consideration anything under the sun as a 'mitigating circumstance,' it will not guide sentencing discretion but will totally unleash it."

4. EDDINGS v. OKLAHOMA, 455 U.S. 104, 102 S.Ct. 869, 71 L.Ed.2d 1 (1982), underscored the Court's commitment to the principle that *all* mitigating evidence must be considered by the sentencer. The defense offered in mitigation the fact that the defendant, who was 16 at the term of the murder, had a history of beatings by a brutal father and a serious emotional disturbance. Although the state statute permitted consideration of *any* mitigating circumstances, the trial judge refused to consider, as a matter of law, either defendant's emotional disturbance or the circumstances of his unhappy upbringing. The state appellate court found the excluded evidence irrelevant because it did not tend to provide a legal excuse from criminal responsibility. A 5–4 majority, per POWELL, J., vacated the death sentence:

"[T]he rule in *Lockett* [reflects] the law's effort to develop a system of capital punishment at once consistent and principled but also humane and sensible to the uniqueness of the individual. [By] holding that the sentencer in capital cases must be permitted to consider any relevant mitigating factor, the rule in *Lockett* recognizes that a consistency produced by ignoring individual differences is a false consistency. * * * Just as the State may not by statute preclude the sentencer from considering any mitigating factor, neither may the sentencer refuse to consider, *as a matter of law,* any relevant mitigating evidence. [The] sentencer, and [the state appellate court] on review, may determine the weight to be given relevant mitigating evidence. But they may not give it no weight by excluding such evidence from their consideration."

5. *Exacerbating the disparity in capital defendant's representation.* The sentencer need only consider and, of course, *can* only consider the mitigating evidence that is *introduced.* And the quantity and quality of the mitigating evidence presented turns largely on the skill, dedication, resourcefulness and funding of the capital defendant's attorney. See *Special Project: The Constitutionality of the Death Penalty in New Jersey,* 15 Rutgers L.J. 261, 293–94 (1984). Thus, although the penalty trial affords an able defense lawyer the opportunity to present an enormous amount of material "personalizing" and "humanizing" the capital defendant, "it also exacerbates the disparity in capital defendants' representation at trial, which, in turn, may be expected to exacerbate the death penalty's uneven application." W. White, *The Death Penalty in the Eighties* 69 (1987).

JUSTICE SCALIA—CONCURRING IN WALTON v. ARIZONA

___ U.S. ___, 110 S.Ct. 3047, 111 L.Ed.2d 511 (1990).

[Defendant Walton was convicted of first-degree murder and sentenced in a separate proceeding before the judge, as required by Arizona law. Under that law the judge determines the existence of aggravating and mitigating circumstances and "shall impose" a death sentence if she finds one or more statutory aggravating circumstances present and that there are no mitigating circumstances "sufficiently substantial to call for leniency." Walton offered in mitigation testimony from a psychiatrist that he had a long history of substance abuse which impaired his judgment and that he might have been sexually abused as a child. After finding two aggravating circumstances—the murder was for pecuniary gain (robbery) and committed "in an especially heinous, cruel or deprived manner"—and concluding that there was no mitigating factor sufficiently substantial to call for leniency—the judge sentenced Walton to death. The state supreme court affirmed. Defendant argued, in effect, that (a) the broad phrasing of the "especially heinous, cruel or deprived manner" aggravating factor violated *Furman* because it permitted the sentencer too much discretion to impose the death sentence and that (b) other aspects of the state law violated *Woodson* and *Lockett* because they unduly restricted the sentencer's discretion to be merciful.

[Writing for a 5–4 majority, WHITE, J. (joined by Rehnquist, C.J., and O'Connor, Scalia and Kennedy, JJ.,), rejected the *Furman* claim. Similarly worded "especially heinous" aggravating factors had been invalidated in *Maynard v. Cartwright,* 486 U.S. 356, 108 S.Ct. 1853, 100 L.Ed.2d 372 (1988) and *Godfrey v. Georgia,* 446 U.S. 420, 100 S.Ct. 1759, 64 L.Ed.2d 398 (1980), but in those cases the defendant had been sentenced to death by a jury and the jury had either been instructed only in the bare terms of the relevant statutory language or in terms nearly as vague. But trial judges are presumed to know the law and the construction given the statutory language by the state supreme court—"cruelty" being defined as involving the infliction of mental anguish or physical abuse before the victim's death and "depravity" being defined as involving the relishing of the murder or indifference to the victim's suffering—"is constitutionally sufficient because it gives meaningful guidance to the sentencer."

[Writing for a four-justice plurality (Justice Scalia did not join this part of the opinion), Justice White also rejected Walton's *Woodson—Lockett* arguments: A state may impose on defendant the burden of establishing, by a preponderance of evidence, the existence of mitigating circumstances sufficiently substantial to call for leniency so long as, as here, the procedure does not lessen the state's burden to prove every element of the offense charged and the existence of aggravating circumstances. Nor is a state law "impermissibly 'mandatory'" within the meaning of *Woodson* when, as here, it does not automatically impose death upon conviction for certain types of murder.]

JUSTICE SCALIA, concurring in part and concurring in the judgment.

Today a petitioner before this Court says that a State sentencing court (1) had unconstitutionally *broad* discretion to sentence him to death instead of imprisonment, *and* (2) had unconstitutionally *narrow* discretion to sentence him to imprisonment instead of death. An observer unacquainted with our death penalty jurisprudence (and in the habit of thinking logically) would probably say these positions cannot both be right. The ultimate choice in capital sentencing, he would point out, is a unitary one—the choice between death and imprisonment. One cannot have discretion whether to select the one yet lack discretion whether to select the other. Our imaginary observer would then be surprised to discover that, under this Court's Eighth Amendment jurisprudence of the past 15 years, petitioner would have a strong chance of winning on *both* of these antagonistic claims, simultaneously—as evidenced by the facts that four Members of this Court think he should win on both. [But] that just shows that our jurisprudence and logic have long since parted ways. I write separately to say that, and explain why, I will no longer seek to apply one of the two incompatible branches of that jurisprudence.

[The] critical opinions [in *Furman*], in light of the subsequent development of our jurisprudence, were those of Justices Stewart and White. They focused on the infrequency and seeming randomness with which, under the discretionary state systems, the death penalty was imposed. [They] went out of the way to say that capital punishment was not in itself a cruel and unusual punishment, and that a mandatory system of capital sentencing, in which everyone convicted of a particular crime received that punishment, would "present quite different issues." * * *

Since [*Gregg* and the other 1976 cases], we have routinely read *Furman* as standing for the proposition that "channelling and limiting [the] sentencer's discretion in imposing the death penalty" is a "fundamental constitutional requirement" and have insisted that States furnish the sentencer with " 'clear and objective standards' that provide 'specific and detailed guidance,' and that 'make rationally reviewable the process for imposing a sentence of death.' " * * * Shortly after introducing our doctrine *requiring* constraints on the sentencer's discretion to "impose" the death penalty, the Court began developing a doctrine *forbidding* constraints on the sentencer's discretion to "*decline* to impose" it. This second doctrine—counterdoctrine would be a better word—has completely exploded whatever coherence the notion of "guided discretion" once had.

[The decisions in *Woodson, Lockett, Eddings* and *Sumner*], of course, had no basis in *Furman.* One might have supposed that curtailing or eliminating discretion in the sentencing of capital defendants was not only consistent with *Furman,* but positively required by it—as many of the States, of course, *did* suppose. But in *Woodson* and *Lockett,* it emerged that uniform treatment of offenders guilty of the same capital crime was not only not *required* by the Eighth Amendment, but was all but *prohibited.*

[As] elaborated in the years since, the *Woodson–Lockett* principle has prevented States from imposing all but the most minimal constraints on the sentencer's discretion to decide that an offender eligible for the death penalty should nonetheless not receive it. [It] would misdescribe the sweep of this principle to say that "all mitigating evidence" must be considered by the sentencer. That would assume some objective criterion of what is mitigating, which is precisely what we have forbidden. Our cases proudly announce that the Constitution effectively prohibits the States from excluding from the sentencing decision *any* aspect of a defendant's character or record, or *any* circumstance surrounding the crime: that the defendant had a poor and deprived childhood, or that he had a rich and spoiled childhood; that he had a great love for the victim's race, or that he had a pathological hatred for the victim's race; that he has limited mental capacity, or that he has a brilliant mind which can make a great contribution to society; that he was kind to his mother, or that he despised his mother. *Whatever* evidence bearing on the crime or the criminal the defense wishes to introduce as rendering the defendant less deserving of the death penalty must be admitted into evidence and considered by the sentencer.

[To] acknowledge that "there perhaps is an inherent tension" between this line of cases and the line stemming from *Furman* is rather like saying that there was perhaps an inherent tension between the Allies and the Axis Powers in

World War II. [They] cannot be reconciled. * * * *

[The] Court has attempted to explain the contradiction by saying that the two requirements serve different functions: the first serves to "narrow" according to rational criteria the class of offenders eligible for the death penalty, while the second guarantees that each offender who is death-eligible is not actually sentenced to death without "an individualized assessment of the appropriateness of the death penalty." [But] it is not "individualized assessment" that is the issue here. No one asserts that the Constitution permits condemnation *en masse.* The issue is whether, in the process of the individualized sentencing determination, the society may specify which factors are relevant, and which are not—whether it may insist upon a rational scheme in which all sentencers making the individualized determinations apply the same standard. That is *precisely* the issue that was involved in *Furman,* no more and no less. Having held, in *Furman,* that the aggravating factors to be sought in the individualized determination must be specified in advance, we are able to refer to the defendants who will qualify under those factors as a "class of death eligibles"—from among whom those actually to receive death will be selected on the basis of unspecified mitigating factors. But if we had held in Lockett that the *mitigating* factors to be sought in the individualized determination must be specified in advance, we would equally have been able to refer to the defendants who will qualify under those factors as a "class of mercy eligibles"—from among whom those actually to receive mercy will be selected on the basis of unspecified aggravating factors. In other words, classification *versus* individuation does not *explain* the opposite treatment of aggravating and mitigating factors; it is merely one way of *describing the result* of that opposite treatment. What is involved here is merely setting standards for individualized determinations, and the question remains why the Constitution demands that the aggravating standards and mitigating standards be accorded opposite treatment. It is impossible to understand why. Since the individualized determination is a unitary one (does this defendant deserve death for this crime?) once one says each sentencer must be able to answer "no" for whatever reason it deems morally sufficient (and indeed, for whatever reason any one of 12 jurors deems morally sufficient), it becomes impossible to claim that the Constitution requires consistency and rationality among sentencing determinations to be preserved by strictly limiting the reasons for which each sentencer can say "yes."

* [Dissenting] Justice Stevens contends that the purpose of *Furman* is merely to narrow the group of crimes (to which the sentencer's unconstrained discretion is then applied) to some undefined point near the "tip of the pyramid" of murder—the base of that pyramid consisting of all murders, and the apex consisting of a particular type crime of murder defined in minute detail. There is, however, no hint in our *Furman* jurisprudence of an attempt to determine what constitutes the critical line below the "tip of the pyramid," and to assess whether *either* the elements of the crime are alone sufficient to bring the statute above that line (in which case no aggravating factors whatever need be specified) *or* whether the aggravating factors are sufficient for that purpose. I read the cases (and the States, in enacting their post-*Furman* statutes, have certainly read them) as requiring aggravating factors to be specified *whenever* the sentencer is given discretion. It is a means of confining the sentencers' discretion—giving them something specific to look for rather than leaving them to wander at large among all aggravating circumstances. That produces a consistency of result which is unachievable—no matter how narrowly the crime is defined—if they are left to take into account any aggravating factor at all. * * * We have never allowed sentencers to be given complete discretion without a requisite finding of aggravating factors. If and when the Court redefines *Furman* to permit the latter, and to require an assessment (I cannot imagine on what basis) that a sufficiently narrow level of the "pyramid" of murder has been reached, I shall be prepared to reconsider my evaluation of *Woodson* and *Lockett.*

[In] a jurisprudence containing the contradictory commands that discretion to impose the death penalty must be limited but discretion not to impose the death penalty must be virtually unconstrained, a vast number of procedures support a plausible claim in one direction or the other. Conscientious counsel are obliged to make those claims, and conscientious judges to consider them. There has thus arisen, in capital cases, a permanent flood-tide of stay applications and petitions for certiorari to review adverse judgments at each round of direct and collateral review, alleging novel defects in sentencing procedure arising out of some permutation of either *Furman* or *Lockett.* * * * Small wonder, then, that the statistics show a capital punishment system that has been approved, in many States, by the democratic vote of the people, that has theoretically been approved as constitutional by this Court, but that seems unable to function except as a parody of swift or even timely justice. As of May 1990 there were 2,327 convicted murderers on death row; only 123 have been executed since our 1972 *Furman* decision. Those executions that have been carried out have occurred an average of eight years after the commission of the capital crime.

In my view, it is time for us to reexamine our efforts in this area and to measure them against the text of the constitutional provision on which they are purportedly based. * * *

Our decision in *Furman* was arguably supported by [the text of the Eighth Amendment]. I am therefore willing to adhere to the precedent established by our *Furman* line of cases, and to hold that when a State adopts capital punishment for a given crime but does not make it mandatory, the Eighth Amendment bars it from giving the sentencer unfettered discretion to select the recipients, but requires it to establish in advance, and convey to the sentencer, a governing standard.

[The] *Woodson–Lockett* line of cases is another matter. [T]hat bears no relation whatever to the text of the Eighth Amendment. The mandatory imposition of death—without sentencing discretion—for a crime which States have traditionally punished with death cannot possibly violate the Eighth Amendment, because it will not be "cruel" (neither absolutely nor for the particular crime) and it will not be "unusual" (neither in the sense of being a type of penalty that is not traditional nor in the sense of being rarely or "freakishly" imposed).

[I cannot adhere to *Woodson* and *Lockett*] because of the doctrine of *stare decisis*. [My problem] is not that *Woodson* and *Lockett* are wrong, but that [they] are rationally irreconcilable with *Furman.* * * * *Stare decisis* cannot command the impossible. Since I cannot possibly be guided by what seem to me incompatible principles, I must reject the one that is plainly in error.

* * * Accordingly, I will not, in this case or in the future, vote to uphold an Eighth Amendment claim that the sentencer's discretion has been unlawfully restricted. * * *

[In a brief dissent, JUSTICE BRENNAN, joined by Marshall, J., maintained that Justice Scalia had misdescribed and apparently misunderstood the Court's death penalty doctrine: "The *Lockett* and *Furman* principles speak to different concerns underlying our notion of civilized punishment; the *Lockett* rule flows primarily from the [Eighth] Amendment's core concern for human dignity, whereas the *Furman* principle reflects the understanding that the Amendment commands that punishment not be meted out in a wholly arbitrary and irrational manner."

[In a separate dissent, JUSTICE BLACKMUN, joined by Brennan, Marshall and Stevens, JJ., contended that the challenged statute violated both *Furman* and the *Woodson–Lockett* principle: "The statute defines a wide range of relevant mitigating evidence—evidence with some degree of persuasiveness which has not been proved by a preponderance—that *cannot* be given effect by the capital sentencer," thus violating *Lockett.* Moreover the statute mandates that death is to be deemed the appropriate penalty unless the defendant satisfies the burden of proving mitigating circumstances "sufficiently substantial to call for leniency," thereby establishing a mechanical "presumption of death" in violation of *Woodson.* As for *Furman,* the state supreme court's construction of the "especially heinous" aggravating circumstance could not possibly have served to guide or channel the trial judge's discretion because the state cases, "like the bare words of the statute, provided 'no principled way to distinguish this case' from other homicides where capital sentences were not imposed."

[In a third dissent, JUSTICE STEVENS contended that the Sixth Amendment requires a jury determination of facts that must be established before the death penalty can be imposed. He also maintained that, contrary to the opinion of Justice Scalia, the *Woodson–Lockett* line of cases could be reconciled with the central holding of *Furman:* The size of the class of convicted persons eligible for the death penalty may be narrowed to reduce sufficiently the risk that race and other irrelevant factors affect the determination of who shall die and who shall not die, "even if a jury is then given complete discretion to show mercy when evaluating the individual characteristics of the few individuals who have been found death eligible." According to Justice Stevens, "Justice Scalia ignores the difference between the base of [a pyramid containing all homicide cases] and its apex. A rule that forbids unguided discretion at the base is completely consistent with one that requires discretion at the apex. After narrowing the class of cases to those at the tip of the pyramid, it is then appropriate to allow the sentencer discretion to show mercy based on individual mitigating circumstances in the cases that remain"].

Notes and Questions

1. *Antisympathy instructions.* Consider SAFFLE v. PARKS, 494 U.S. 484, 110 S.Ct. 1257, 108 L.Ed.2d 415 (1990). Parks was convicted of capital murder. At the sentencing phase, his lawyer argued that the jury should consider his deprived background. In a sentencing instruction, the judge advised the jury that in considering the mitigating evidence proffered by Parks, "you must avoid any influence of sympathy, sentiment, passion, prejudice, or other arbitrary factor when imposing sentence." Parks was sentenced to death; his conviction and death sentence became final in 1983. He sought federal habeas relief, arguing that the antisympathy instruction violated the Eighth Amendment because it in effect told the jury to disregard the mitigating evidence he had presented.

A 5–4 majority, per KENNEDY, J., held that Parks was not entitled to federal habeas corpus because he was urging a "new rule" that could neither be announced nor applied on collateral review. Parks argued that he was not seeking a "new rule"; the challenged instruction ran afoul of *Lockett* and *Eddings,* both decided before his conviction became final, because jurors who react sympathetically to mitigating evidence may interpret the instruction as preventing them from considering that evidence altogether. The Court disagreed:

"[Parks'] argument misapprehends the distinction between allowing the jury to consider mitigating evidence and guiding their consideration. It is no doubt constitutionally permissible, if not constitutionally required, for the State to insist that 'the individualized assessment of the death penalty [be] a moral inquiry into the culpability of the defendant, and not an emotional response to the mitigating evidence.' [It] would be very difficult to reconcile a rule allowing the fate of a defendant to turn on the vagaries of particular jurors' emotional sensitivities with our longstanding recognition that, above all, capital sentencing must be reliable, accurate, and nonarbitrary. At the very least, nothing in *Lockett* and *Eddings* prevents the State from attempting to ensure reliability and nonarbitrariness by requiring that the jury consider and give effect to the defendant's mitigating evidence in the form of a 'reasoned *moral* response' rather than an emotional one. The State must not cut off full and fair consideration of mitigating evidence; but it need not grant the jury the choice to make the sentencing decision according to its own whims or caprice."

Dissenting JUSTICE BRENNAN, joined by Marshall, Blackmun and Stevens, JJ., maintained that the majority had "mischaracterize[d]" Parks' claim: "[He] concedes the State's contention that a decision to impose the death penalty must reflect a 'reasoned moral response' to the defendant's culpability. What he argues is [that] because much of the mitigating evidence relevant to his culpability also evoked sympathy, a juror who reacted sympathetically to the evidence would have believed that he was not entitled to consider that evidence *at all*—not even for its 'moral' weight. * * * Until today, the Court consistently has vacated a death sentence [when] there was any ambiguity about whether the sentencer actually considered mitigating evidence."

2. *Appealing to the sentencer's emotions.* Compare *Saffle v. Parks* with W. White, *The Death Penalty in the Eighties* 82–83, 86 (1987): "In arguing to save the life of a capital defendant, the great defense attorneys have successfully appealed to the emotions of the sentencer. For example, Clarence Darrow's famous argument asking the judge to spare the lives of Loeb and Leopold was said to be so moving that at its conclusion, 'Darrow, the judge, and many in the audience were crying.' [In presenting argument at the penalty trial], counsel should not be precluded from using any kind of eloquence that will arouse the sentencer's feelings. Under *Lockett,* the sentencer is required to act for the community in deciding whether the defendant should be executed or spared. To do so, the sentencer must rely on more than logic, and in seeking to persuade the sentencer to exercise mercy, defense counsel should be permitted to appeal to the sentencer's feelings as well as its cognitive faculties."

III. OTHER CONSTITUTIONAL CHALLENGES TO CAPITAL (AND LIFE) SENTENCES

A. "GROSSLY DISPROPORTIONATE" PUNISHMENT

COKER v. GEORGIA, 433 U.S. 584, 97 S.Ct. 2861, 53 L.Ed.2d 982 (1977): While serving life terms for murder, rape and kidnapping (all capital felonies) and another sentence for aggravated assault, petitioner escaped and raped and abducted an adult woman (after robbing and tying up her husband). After his conviction for rape and other offenses, petitioner was sentenced to death when the jury found two of the statutory aggravating circumstances present: the rape was (i) by a person with a prior capital felony conviction and (ii) in the course of another capital felony, armed robbery of the husband. (The jury was instructed that even if aggravating circumstances were present, the death penalty need not be imposed if it found they were outweighed by mitigating circumstances.) The Court invalidated the death sentence. The principal opinion was written by WHITE, J., joined by Stewart, Blackmun and Stevens, JJ.,[a] who concluded that death is a "grossly disproportionate and excessive punishment" for raping an adult woman and therefore forbidden by the Eighth Amendment:

"At no time in the last 50 years has a majority of the States authorized death as a punishment for rape [and] none of the [34] States that had not previously authorized death for rape [changed its position after *Furman*]. Of the 16 States in which rape had been a capital offense only three provided for rape of an adult woman in their [post-*Furman*] statutes—Georgia, North Carolina, and Louisiana. In the latter two States, the death penalty was mandatory and those laws were invalidated by *Woodson* and *Stanislaus Roberts.* [Louisiana and North Carolina then] reenacted the death penalty for murder but not for rape. [Thus,] Georgia is the sole [American] jurisdiction [that presently] authorizes a sentence of death when the rape victim is an adult woman.[b] [Moreover, in] the vast majority of [rape] cases, at least nine out of 10, [Georgia juries] have not imposed the death sentence. * * *

"Rape is without doubt deserving of serious punishment; but in terms of moral depravity and of the injury to the person and to the public, it does not compare with murder, which does involve the unjustified taking of human life. [Rape] does not include the death or even the serious injury to [another]. Life is over for the [murder victim]; for the rape victim, life may not be nearly so happy as it was, but it is not over and normally is not beyond repair. We have the abiding conviction that the death penalty, which 'is unique in its severity and revocability,' is an excessive penalty for the rapist who, as such, does not take human life.

"This does not end the matter; for under Georgia law, death may not be imposed [unless] the jury finds one of the statutory aggravating circumstances and then elects to impose that sentence. [But neither of the aggravating circumstances found in the present case], nor both of them together, change our conclusion that [Coker's sentence] is a disproportionate punishment for rape. [Coker's prior capital felony convictions] do not change the fact that the instant crime being punished is a rape not involving the taking of life."

BURGER, C.J., joined by Rehnquist, J., dissenting, protested that the Court's holding prevents the imposition of "any effective punishment upon Coker for his latest rape" and "bars Georgia from guaranteeing its citizens that they will suffer no further attacks from this habitual rapist.[c]

"* * * Whatever one's view may be as to the State's constitutional power to impose the death penalty upon a rapist who stands before a court convicted for the first time, this case reveals a chronic rapist whose continuing danger to

a. Brennan and Marshall, JJ., concurred in the judgment. Powell, J., also concurred in the judgment that "ordinarily death is a disproportionate punishment for the crime of raping an adult woman, [i.e., when, as here,] there is no indication that petitioner's offense was committed with excessive brutality or that the victim sustained serious or lasting injury."

b. The Court noted that two other jurisdictions, Florida and Mississippi, provide capital punishment when the rape victim is a child. Tennessee had also authorized the death penalty in some circumstances when the victim was a child, but its statute had been invalidated because the death penalty was mandatory.

c. In 1971 Coker raped and murdered a young woman. Less than 8 months later, he kidnapped, raped and severely beat a 16-year-old woman, leaving her for dead in a wooded area. In 1974, he escaped from the state prison and promptly raped another 16-year-old, for which the death sentence under review was imposed.

the community is abundantly clear. [T]he Eighth Amendment does not prevent the State from taking an individual's 'well-demonstrated propensity for life-endangering behavior' [d] into account in devising punitive measures which will prevent inflicting further harm upon innocent victims.

"[I]t is myopic to base sweeping constitutional principles upon the narrow experience of the past five years. [L]egislatures were left in serious doubt [by *Furman*] as to whether this Court would sustain *any* statute imposing death as a criminal sanction. Failure of more States to enact statutes imposing death for rape of an adult woman may thus reflect hasty legislative compromise occasioned by time pressures following *Furman,* a desire to wait on the experience of those States which did enact such statutes, or simply an accurate forecast of today's holding."

Notes and Questions

1. Was the question raised by *Coker* whether the eighth amendment prohibits the death penalty for rape or whether the death penalty is "so irrational as to offend due process, an issue that exists quite independently [of] the eighth amendment"? See Packer, fn. d supra at 1074.

2. After *Coker,* would the Court sustain the death penalty for treason? Would the absence of a death "directly traceable" to the treasonous activity render the death penalty disproportionate to the crime or would treason be viewed as "a crime against masses of people [causing] more aggregate harm than a single murder"? See 91 Harv.L.Rev. 124, 128 (1977). See also Note, 78 Colum. L.Rev. 1714, 1729 (1979) (discussion of death penalty for hijacking).

3. Was it (should it have been) crucial that only three post-*Furman* statutes made rape a capital offense? The Court gave little weight to legislative enactments in *Roe v. Wade,* which invalidated a Texas abortion statute despite the fact that most states had enacted similar laws. Isn't "[a] defendant's right to life [at] least as fundamental as the mother's right of privacy"? See 91 Harv.L.Rev. 124 n. 127 (1977).

4. None of the opinions in *Coker* makes any mention of the "racial factor" in the administration of the death penalty for rape. Should the Court have explicitly discussed this factor? Despite the Court's silence on this matter, to what extent was it nevertheless influenced by it? Bedau, *The Death Penalty in America* 188 (3d ed. 1982), calls rape "the most dramatic type of case in which we can see how the racist heritage of our society made the death penalty fall with disproportionate and unfair frequency on nonwhite offenders. [T]he best explanation for the pattern of death sentences for rape in the South [a] is the race of the (black) offender and of the (white) victim." The mid-1960's constitutional assault on the death penalty "began with a campaign to eliminate the discriminatory application of the death penalty for rape. Between 1930 and the present, of the 455 persons executed for rape, 405 were black and two were members of other minorities. Almost 90% of those executed were black men convicted for the rape of white women." Greenberg, *Capital Punishment as a System,* 91 Yale

d. At this point, the dissent is quoting from Packer, *Making the Punishment Fit the Crime,* 77 Harv.L.Rev. 1071, 1080 (1964): "A well-demonstrated propensity for life-endangering behavior is thought to provide a more solid basis for infliction of the most severe measures of incapacitation than does the fortuity of a single homicidal incident."

a. Since 1930, all of the executions for rape were in southern or border states or the District of Columbia. In ten of these states and the District of Columbia, 137 blacks were executed for rape since 1930, but only five whites. See Wolfgang & Riedel, *Race, Judicial Discretion, and the Death Penalty,* 407 Annals 119 (1973).

L.J. 908, 912 (1982). See also Meltsner, *Cruel and Unusual* 75–77 (1973); Wolfgang & Reidel, fn. a supra.

5. "*Accomplice murder*". (a) Consider ENMUND v. FLORIDA, 458 U.S. 782, 102 S.Ct. 3368, 73 L.Ed.2d 1140 (1982). While his codefendants went to a farmhouse to rob an elderly couple, Enmund remained in a nearby parked car, waiting to help the robbers escape. When one of the victims resisted, Enmund's codefendants killed both. Under state law, this made Enmund a constructive aider and abettor and hence a principal in the murder upon whom the death penalty could be imposed. After looking to "the historical development of the punishment at issue, legislative judgments, international opinion, and the sentencing decisions juries have made," a 5–4 majority, per WHITE, J., concluded that the Eighth Amendment barred the imposition of the death penalty on "one such as Enmund [who] does not himself kill, attempt to kill, or intend that a killing take place or that lethal force will be employed. [As] was said of the crime of rape in *Coker,* [the] death penalty, which is 'unique in its severity and irrevocability,' is an excessive penalty for the robber who, as such, does not take human life."

(b) Under the rubric of "proportionality," did the *Enmund* Court try to use its eighth amendment powers to prod some reform in state homicide law? See Weisberg, *Regulating Death,* 1983 Sup.Ct.Rev. 305, 334. Is it easy to distinguish *Enmund* from a felony-murder case in which a defendant is sentenced to death after *accidentally* killing the victim during the perpetration of a felony? See Weisberg, supra, at 334 n. 119; W. White, *Life in the Balance* 93–95 (1984); Note, 73 J.Crim.L. & C. 1553 (1982).

(c) Distinguishing *Enmund,* a 5–4 majority held in TISON v. ARIZONA, 481 U.S. 137, 107 S.Ct. 1676, 95 L.Ed.2d 127 (1987), that the Eighth Amendment proportionality requirement does not bar the death penalty in the case of a defendant who neither intended to kill the victim nor inflicted the fatal wounds, but whose participation in the felony resulting in murder "is major and whose mental state is one of reckless indifference to the value of human life." Petitioner brothers planned and effected the prison escape of their father and another convicted murderer. After leaving the prison, petitioners helped to abduct, detain and rob a family of four. They then watched their father and the other convict murder the members of that family. Although both petitioners maintained that they were surprised by the shooting, neither made any effort to help the victims. Petitioners were convicted of capital murder and sentenced to death on the basis of a state felony-murder rule providing that a killing occurring during the perpetration of robbery or kidnapping is capital murder and that each participant in the kidnapping or robbery is legally responsible for the acts of his accomplices. Observed the Court, per O'CONNOR, J.:

"A narrow focus on the question of whether or not a given defendant 'intended to kill' [is] a highly unsatisfactory means of definitively distinguishing the most culpable and dangerous of murderers. [T]he reckless disregard for human life implicit in knowingly engaging in criminal activities known to carry a grave risk of death represents a highly culpable mental state, [one] that may be taken into account in making a capital sentencing judgment when that conduct causes its natural, though also not inevitable, lethal result.

"The petitioners' own personal involvement in the crimes was not minor, [but] 'substantial.' Far from merely sitting in a car away from the actual scene of the murders acting as the getaway driver to a robbery, each petitioner was actively involved in every element of the kidnapping-robbery and was physically present during the entire sequence of criminal activity culminating in the murder of [the] family and the subsequent flight."

Dissenting JUSTICE BRENNAN, joined by Marshall, Blackmun and Stevens, JJ., maintained that the Court's decision could not be reconciled with *Enmund:*

"Like Enmund, the Tisons have been sentenced to death for the intentional acts of others which the Tisons did not expect, which were not essential to the felony, and over which they had no control. Unlike Enmund, however, the Tisons will be the first individuals in over 30 years to be executed for such behavior. * * *

"So rarely does any State (let alone any Western country other than our own) ever execute a person who neither killed nor intended to kill that 'these death sentences are cruel and unusual in the same way that being struck by lightning is cruel and unusual.' This case thus demonstrates, as *Furman* also did, that we have yet to achieve a system capable of 'distinguishing the few cases in which the [death penalty] is imposed from the many cases in which it is not.' "

6. *Life sentences disproportionate to the severity of the crime.* (a) When convicted of a third nonviolent property-related felony, Rummel received a mandatory life sentence pursuant to Texas's recidivist statute. He contended that his life sentence was so disproportionate to the crimes he had committed as to constitute cruel and unusual punishment. A 5–4 majority, per Rehnquist, J., disagreed, *Rummel v. Estelle,* 445 U.S. 263, 100 S.Ct. 1133, 63 L.Ed.2d 382 (1980). The majority stressed the "unique nature of the death penalty for purposes of Eighth Amendment analysis," the wide range of punishments for similar offenses, the highly subjective character of legislatively mandated terms of imprisonment, and the desirability, in a federal system, of giving the states a wide latitude of judgment in these matters. The majority also noted that it could not ignore the possibility that Rummel would not actually be imprisoned for life; indeed, he might become eligible for parole in as little as 12 years.

(b) Three years later, however, a 5–4 majority (consisting of the four *Rummel* dissenters, Powell, J., joined by Brennan, Marshall and Stevens, JJ., plus Blackmun, J.) did find a life sentence without the possibility of parole violative of the Eighth Amendment. SOLEM v. HELM, 463 U.S. 277, 103 S.Ct. 3001, 77 L.Ed.2d 637 (1983). When Helm was convicted of a seventh nonviolent felony he was sentenced to life without the possibility of parole pursuant to a South Dakota recidivist statute that may be invoked when a defendant has three of more prior felony convictions. The Governor refused to commute Helm's sentence to a fixed term of years so that he would be eligible for parole when he had served three-fourths of his reduced sentence. The Court held, per POWELL, J., that Helm's sentence was "significantly disproportionate to his crime" and thus prohibited by the Eighth Amendment:

"The constitutional principle of proportionality has been recognized in this Court for almost a century. [The Court then referred to *Weems v. United States,* 217 U.S. 349, 30 S.Ct. 544, 54 L.Ed.2d 793 (1910) [a] and to *Robinson v. California,*

a. In *Weems,* a public official, working in the Philippine Islands at a time when they were subject to the jurisdiction of the United States, was convicted of falsifying a public record. The sentence imposed, under a provision of the Spanish Penal Code still in force, was the punishment known as "cadena temporal"—a minimum term of 12 years' imprisonment at hard labor while chained at ankle and wrist, together with harsh "accessory" penalties (such as loss of parental and property rights and surveillance for life upon release).

Over the dissent of Holmes and White, JJ., the Court struck down Weems' sentence under the eighth amendment. But consider Packer, *Making the Punishment Fit the Crime,* 77 Harv.L.Rev. 1071, 1075–76 (1964): "It was

370 U.S. 660, 82 S.Ct. 1417, 8 L.Ed.2d 758 (1962), finding, as the Court characterized the case, a 90-day sentence "excessive for the crime of being 'addicted to the use of narcotics.' "] Most recently, the Court has applied the principle of proportionality to hold capital punishment excessive in certain circumstances [referring to *Enmund* and *Coker*].

"It is true that the 'penalty of death differs from all other forms of capital punishment, not in degree, but in kind.' [This] does not mean, however, that proportionality is entirely inapplicable in noncapital cases. [N]o penalty is per se constitutional. As the Court noted in *Robinson,* a single day in prison may be unconstitutional in some circumstances.

"[A] court's proportionality analysis under the Eighth Amendment should be guided by objective criteria, including (i) the gravity of the offense and the harshness of the penalty; (ii) the sentences imposed on other criminals in the same jurisdiction; and (iii) the sentences imposed for commission of the same crime in other jurisdictions."

Applying this criteria, all of Helms's offenses were relatively minor and none involved violence or the threat of it; since South Dakota does not have capital punishment, Helms's sentence was "the most severe punishment that the State could have imposed on any criminal for any crime"; and "it appears that Helm was treated more severely than he would have been in any other State." [b]

BURGER, C.J., joined by White, Rehnquist and O'Connor, JJ., dissented, finding the Court's decision inconsistent with the approach taken in *Rummel.* "By asserting the power to review sentences of imprisonment for excessiveness," protested the dissenters, "the Court launches into uncharted and unchartable waters. Today it holds that a sentence of life imprisonment, without the possibility of parole, is excessive punishment for a seventh allegedly 'nonviolent' felony. How about the eighth 'nonviolent' felony. The ninth? The twelfth? Suppose one offense was a simple assault? Or selling liquor to a minor? Or statutory rape? Or pricefixing? The permutations are endless and the Court's opinion is bankrupt of realistic guiding principles."

(c) In an age when the death penalty is imposed rarely and barbaric physical punishments have been rejected, would limiting proportionality review to cases involving such punishments have rendered the Eighth Amendment "nearly obsolete"? See Note, 97 Harv.L.Rev. 127, 135 (1983). Did the *Helm* majority embrace a philosophy discordant with a utilitarian view of punishment? Applied to the concept of "excessive punishment," do retributivist and utilitarian analyses yield conflicting results? See Note, 26 Ariz.L.Rev. 871, 873, 883 (1984). Does *Rummel* still apply to those cases that do not involve a life sentence without the possibility of parole?

plainly not the length of [Weems'] imprisonment alone, considered in relation to the gravity of the offense, that determined [the Court's] result. Rather, it was the combination of an excessive but conventional mode of punishment with a good deal of laid-on unpleasantness offensive for its novelty as well as its severity that supported the characterization of Weems' punishment as cruel and unusual. The case is much closer to the conventional view that cruel and unusual punishment is a matter of mode not proportion than it is usually thought to be. Whether mode or proportion or both, the case is in the eighth amendment tradition. It speaks to the issue of decency, not rationality." See also Meltsner, *Cruel and Unusual* 173–75 (1973).

b. Helm could have received a life sentence without parole under only one other State's recidivist statute, Nevada's, but apparently no person whose prior offenses were so minor actually has received the maximum penalty in that state.

B. EXECUTION OF JUVENILES

1. In THOMPSON v. OKLAHOMA, 487 U.S. 815, 108 S.Ct. 2687, 101 L.Ed. 2d 702 (1988), a 5–3 majority (Kennedy, J., not participating) ruled that the Eighth and Fourteenth Amendments prohibit the execution of a person who was under 16 years of age at the time of his or her offense. The principal opinion was written by STEVENS, J., joined by Brennan, Marshall, and Blackmun, JJ., whose review of relevant legislative enactments [a] and jury determinations [b]—"indicators of contemporary standards of decency"—led to the conclusion that "the imposition of the death penalty on a 15–year–old offender is now generally abhorrent to the conscience of the community."

Retribution and deterrence of capital crimes are said to be the two principal purposes of the death penalty. "Given the lesser culpability of the juvenile offender, [his or her] capacity for growth, and society's fiduciary obligations to its children, [the retributive purpose] is simply inapplicable to the execution of a 15–year–old offender." The deterrence rationale "is equally unacceptable." For "[t]he likelihood that the teenage offender has made the kind of cost-benefit analysis that attaches any weight to the possibilities of execution is so remote as to be virtually nonexistent. And even if one posits such a cold-blooded calculation by a 15–year–old, it is fanciful to believe that he would be deterred by the knowledge that a small number of persons his age have been executed during the 20th century."

Thus, the four-Justice plurality was "not persuaded that the imposition of the death penalty for offenses committed by persons under 16 years of age has made, or can be expected to make, any measurable contribution to the goals that capital punishment is intended to achieve. It is, therefore, 'nothing more than the purposeless and needless imposition of pain and suffering,' *Coker,* and thus an unconstitutional punishment."

JUSTICE O'CONNOR, whose vote was pivotal, concurred in the judgment:

"Although I believe that a national consensus forbidding the execution of any person for a crime committed before the age of 16 very likely does exist, I am reluctant to adopt this conclusion as a matter of constitutional law without better evidence than we now possess. Because I conclude that the sentence in this case can and should be set aside on narrower grounds than those adopted by the plurality, and because the grounds on which I rest should allow us to face the more general question when better evidence is available, I concur only in the judgment of the Court. * * *

"Oklahoma has enacted a statute that authorizes capital punishment for murder without setting any minimum age at which the commission of murder may lead to the imposition of that penalty. The State has also, but quite

a. Nineteen of the 37 States that authorize capital punishment do not explicitly set any minimum age. "When we confine our attention to the 18 States that have expressly established a minimum age in their death-penalty statutes, we find that all of them require that the defendant have attained at least the age of 16 at the time of the capital offense." Moreover, observed Justice Stevens, "[t]he conclusion that it would offend civilized standards of decency to execute a person who was less than 16 years old at the time of his or her offense is consistent with the views that have been expressed by professional organizations [such as the American Bar Association and the American Law Institute], by other nations that share our Anglo–American heritage, and by the leading members of the Western European community."

b. Of the 1,393 persons sentenced to death for willful homicide during the years 1982–86, only five, including petitioner in this case, were less than 16 years old at the time of the offense. No execution of a person under 16 has taken place since 1948.

separately, provided that 15–year–old murder defendants may be treated as adults in some circumstances. Because it proceeded in this manner, there is a considerable risk that the Oklahoma legislature either did not realize that its actions would have the effect of rendering 15–year–old defendants death-eligible or did not give the question the serious consideration that would have been reflected in the explicit choice of some minimum age for death-eligibility. Were it clear that no national consensus forbids the imposition of capital punishment for crimes committed before the age of 16, the implicit nature of the Oklahoma legislature's decision would not be constitutionally problematic. In the peculiar circumstances we face today, however, the Oklahoma statutes have presented this Court with a result that is of very dubious constitutionality, and they have done so without the earmarks of careful consideration that we have required for other kinds of decisions leading to the death penalty. In this unique situation, I am prepared to conclude that petitioner and others who were below the age of 16 at the time of their offense may not be executed under the authority of a capital punishment statute that specifies no minimum age at which the commission of a capital crime can lead to the offender's execution."

Dissenting JUSTICE SCALIA, joined by Rehnquist, C.J., and White, J., emphasized that the question presented was not whether an automatic death penalty could be applied to individuals younger than 16 when they commit certain crimes or whether such individuals can be deprived of the benefit of a rebuttable presumption that he or she is not responsible enough to be punished as an adult, but "whether there is a national consensus that no criminal so much as one day under 16, after individualized consideration of his circumstances, including the overcoming of a presumption that he should not be tried as an adult, can possibly be deemed mature and responsible enough to be punished with death for any crime." He saw "no plausible basis for answering [this] question in the affirmative." The plurality had focused on the 18 States establishing a minimum age for capital punishment. But the dissent failed to see why an accurate analysis would not include the 19 States that have determined that no minimum age for capital punishment is appropriate, "leaving that to be governed by their general rules for the age at which juveniles can be criminally responsible."

Nor were the dissenters impressed with Justice O'Connor's approach. As they understood her separate concurrence, "it agrees (1) that we have no constitutional authority to set aside this death penalty unless we can find it contrary to a firm national consensus that persons younger than 16 at the time of their crime cannot be executed, and (2) that we cannot make such a finding. It does not, however, reach the seemingly inevitable conclusion that (3) we therefore have no constitutional authority to set aside this death penalty."

The concurrence, maintained the dissenters, "hoists on to the deck of our Eighth Amendment jurisprudence the loose cannon of a brand new principle. If the concurrence's view were adopted, henceforth a finding of national consensus would no longer be required to invalidate state action in the area of capital punishment. All that would be needed is uncertainty regarding the existence of a national consensus, whereupon various protective requirements could be imposed, even to the point of specifying the process of legislation. If 15–year–olds must be explicitly named in capital statutes, why not those of extremely low intelligence, or those over 75, or any number of other appealing groups as to which the existence of a national consensus regarding capital punishment may be in doubt for the same reason the concurrence finds it in doubt here, *viz.*, because they are not specifically named in the capital statutes?"

2. A year later, however, in the consolidated cases of STANFORD v. KENTUCKY and WILKINS v. MISSOURI, 492 U.S. 361, 109 S.Ct. 2969, 106 L.Ed.2d 306 (1989), "discern[ing] neither an historical nor a modern societal consensus forbidding the imposition of capital punishment on any person who murders at 16 or 17 years of age," a 5–4 majority, per SCALIA, J., held that such punishment does not violate the Eighth Amendment:

" '[F]irst' among the 'objective indicia that reflect the public attitude toward a given sanction' are statutes passed by society's elected representatives. Of the 37 states whose laws permit capital punishment, 15 decline to impose it upon 16–year–old offenders and 12 decline to impose it on 17–year–old offenders. This does not establish the degree of national consensus this Court has previously thought sufficient to label a particular punishment cruel and unusual. [Even if there were no national consensus in *favor* of capital punishment for 16– or 17–year–olds, it] is not the burden of Kentucky and Missouri [to] establish a national consensus approving what their citizens have voted to do; rather, it is the 'heavy burden' of petitioners to establish a national consensus *against* it. As far as the most reliable indication of consensus is concerned—the pattern of enacted laws—petitioners have failed to carry that burden."

"Together," concluded dissenting JUSTICE BRENNAN, joined by Marshall, Blackmun and Stevens, JJ., "the rejection of the death penalty for juveniles by a majority of the States [including those jurisdictions in which capital punishment is not authorized at all], the rarity of the sentence for juveniles, both as an absolute and a comparative matter, the decisions of respected organizations in relevant fields [such as the American Bar Association, the American Law Institute and the National Council of Juvenile and Family Court Judges] that this punishment is unacceptable, and its rejection generally throughout the world, provide to my mind a strong grounding for the view that it is not constitutionally tolerable that certain states persist in authorizing the execution of adolescent offenders. It is unnecessary, however, to rest a view that the Eighth Amendment prohibits the execution of minors solely upon a judgment as to the meaning to be attached to the evidence of contemporary values outlined above, for [such execution] fails to satisfy two well-established and independent Eighth Amendment requirements—that a punishment not be disproportionate, and that it made a contribution to acceptable goals of punishment."

C. ADMINISTERING THE DEATH PENALTY IN A RACIALLY DISCRIMINATORY MANNER

McCLESKEY v. KEMP

481 U.S. 279, 107 S.Ct. 1756, 95 L.Ed.2d 262 (1987).

JUSTICE POWELL delivered the opinion of the Court.

[Petitioner, a black man, was convicted in a Georgia trial court of armed robbery and the murder of a white police officer in the course of the robbery and sentenced to death. He sought federal habeas corpus relief, contending that the Georgia capital sentencing process was administered in a racially discriminatory manner in violation of the Eighth Amendment and the Equal Protection Clause of the Fourteenth Amendment.[a] In support of his claim, petitioner proffered a

a. For discussion of the portion of Justice Powell's opinion for the Court rejecting petitioner's equal protection claim, see p. 972 infra.

statistical study by David Baldus, Charles Pulaski and George Woodworth (the Baldus study).

[This study examined over 2,000 murder cases that occurred in Georgia during the 1970s and concluded that, even after taking account of many nonracial variables, defendants charged with killing white victims were 4.3 times as likely to receive a death sentence as those charged with killing blacks. Moreover, according to this study, black defendants were 1.1 times as likely to receive a death sentence as other defendants. Thus, the study indicates that black defendants, such as petitioner, who kill whites have the greatest likelihood of being sentenced to death.

[The federal district court ruled that the Baldus study "failed to contribute anything of value" to petitioner's claim and denied relief. The U.S. Court of Appeals for the Eleventh Circuit assumed that the Baldus study "showed that systematic and substantial disparities existed in the penalties imposed upon homicide victims in Georgia based on race of the homicide victim, that the disparities existed at a less substantial rate in death sentencing based on race of defendants and that [these factors] were at work in [the county in which petitioner was tried]." Even assuming the validity of the study, however, the Court of Appeals found the statistics "insufficient to demonstrate discriminatory intent or unconstitutional discrimination in the Fourteenth Amendment context [and] insufficient to show irrationality, arbitrariness and capriciousness under any kind of Eighth Amendment analysis." Thus, it affirmed the district court's denial of habeas corpus relief.]

[McCleskey argues, inter alia,] that the Baldus study demonstrates that the Georgia capital sentencing system violates the Eighth Amendment.[b] * * *

[O]ur decisions since *Furman* have identified a constitutionally permissible range of discretion in imposing the death penalty. First, there is a required threshold below which the death penalty cannot be imposed. In this context, the State must establish rational criteria that narrow the decisionmaker's judgment as to whether the circumstances of a particular defendant's case meet the threshold. Moreover, a societal consensus that the death penalty is disproportionate to a particular offense prevents a State from imposing the death penalty for that offense. Second, States cannot limit the sentencer's consideration of any relevant circumstance that could cause it to decline to impose the penalty. In this respect, the State cannot channel the sentencer's discretion, but must allow it to consider any relevant information offered by the defendant.

In light of our precedents under the Eighth Amendment, McCleskey cannot argue successfully that his sentence is "disproportionate to the crime in the traditional sense." He does not deny that he committed a murder in the course of a planned robbery, a crime for which this Court has determined that the death penalty constitutionally may be imposed. [He argues, rather,] that the sentence in his case is disproportionate to the sentences in other murder cases.

On the one hand, he cannot base a constitutional claim on an argument that his case differs from other cases in which defendants *did* receive the death

b. The Court noted [fn. 7]: "As did the Court of Appeals, we assume the [Baldus] study is valid statistically without reviewing the factual findings of the District Court. Our assumption that the Baldus study is statistically valid does not include the assumption that the study shows that racial considerations actually enter into any sentencing decisions in Georgia. Even a sophisticated multiple regression analysis such as the Baldus study can only demonstrate a *risk* that the factor of race entered into some capital sentencing decisions and a necessarily lesser risk that race entered into any particular sentencing decision."

penalty. On automatic appeal, the Georgia Supreme Court found that McCleskey's death sentence was not disproportionate to other death sentences imposed in the State. [Moreover,] where the statutory procedures adequately channel the sentencer's discretion, such proportionality review is not constitutionally required.

On the other hand, absent a showing that the Georgia capital punishment system operates in an arbitrary and capricious manner, McCleskey cannot prove a constitutional violation by demonstrating that other defendants who may be similarly situated did *not* receive the death penalty. In *Gregg,* the Court confronted the argument that "the opportunities for discretionary action that are inherent in the processing of any murder case under Georgia law," specifically the opportunities for discretionary leniency, rendered the capital sentences imposed arbitrary and capricious. We rejected this contention. * * *

Because McCleskey's sentence was imposed under Georgia sentencing procedures that focus discretion "on the particularized nature of the crime and the particularized characteristics of the individual defendant," we lawfully may presume that McCleskey's death sentence was not "wantonly and freakishly" imposed and thus that the sentence is not disproportionate within any recognized meaning under the Eighth Amendment.

Although our decision in *Gregg* as to the facial validity of the Georgia capital punishment statute appears to foreclose McCleskey's disproportionality argument, he further contends that the Georgia capital punishment system is arbitrary and capricious in *application,* and therefore his sentence is excessive, because racial considerations may influence capital sentencing decisions in Georgia. We now address this claim.

To evaluate McCleskey's challenge, we must examine exactly what the Baldus study may show. Even Professor Baldus does not contend that his statistics *prove* that race enters into any capital sentencing decisions or that race was a factor in McCleskey's particular case. Statistics at most may show only a likelihood that a particular factor entered into some decisions. There is, of course, some risk of racial prejudice influencing a jury's decision in a criminal case. There are similar risks that other kinds of prejudice will influence other criminal trials. The question "is at what point that risk becomes constitutionally unacceptable." McCleskey asks us to accept the likelihood allegedly shown by the Baldus study as the constitutional measure of an unacceptable risk of racial prejudice influencing capital sentencing decisions. This we decline to do.

[At] most, the Baldus study indicates a discrepancy that appears to correlate with race. Apparent disparities in sentencing are an inevitable part of our criminal justice system. The discrepancy indicated by the Baldus study is "a far cry from the major systemic defects identified in *Furman.*" [O]ur consistent rule has been that constitutional guarantees are met when "the mode [for determining guilt or punishment] itself has been surrounded with safeguards to make it as fair as possible." Where the discretion that is fundamental to our criminal process is involved, we decline to assume that what is unexplained is invidious. In light of the safeguards designed to minimize racial bias in the process, the fundamental value of jury trial in our criminal justice system, and the benefits that discretion provides to criminal defendants, we hold that the Baldus study does not demonstrate a constitutionally significant risk of racial bias affecting the Georgia capital-sentencing process.[37]

37. * * * We have held that discretion in a capital punishment system is necessary to satisfy the Constitution. *Woodson.* Yet, the dissent now claims that the "discretion af-

Two additional concerns inform our decision in this case. First, McCleskey's claim, taken to its logical conclusion, throws into serious question the principles that underlie our entire criminal justice system. The Eighth Amendment is not limited in application to capital punishment, but applies to all penalties. Thus, if we accepted McCleskey's claim that racial bias has impermissibly tainted the capital sentencing decision, we could soon be faced with similar claims as to other types of penalty. Moreover, the claim that his sentence rests on the irrelevant factor of race easily could be extended to apply to claims based on unexplained discrepancies that correlate to membership in other minority groups, and even to gender. Similarly, since McCleskey's claim relates to the race of his victim, other claims could apply with equally logical force to statistical disparities that correlate with the race or sex of other actors in the criminal justice system, such as defense attorneys, or judges. Also, there is no logical reason that such a claim need be limited to racial or sexual bias. If arbitrary and capricious punishment is the touchstone under the Eighth Amendment, such a claim could—at least in theory—be based upon any arbitrary variable, such as the defendant's facial characteristics, or the physical attractiveness of the defendant or the victim, that some statistical study indicates may be influential in jury decisionmaking. As these examples illustrate, there is no limiting principle to the type of challenge brought by McCleskey.[45] The Consti-

forded prosecutors and jurors in the Georgia capital sentencing system" violates the Constitution by creating "opportunities for racial considerations to influence criminal proceedings." The dissent contends that in Georgia "[n]o guidelines govern prosecutorial decisions [and] that Georgia provides juries with no list of aggravating and mitigating factors, nor any standard for balancing them against one another." Prosecutorial decisions necessarily involve both judgmental and factual decisions that vary from case to case. Thus, it is difficult to imagine guidelines that would produce the predictability sought by the dissent without sacrificing the discretion essential to a humane and fair system of criminal justice. Indeed, the dissent suggests no such guidelines for prosecutorial discretion.

[The] dissent repeatedly emphasizes the need for "a uniquely high degree of rationality in imposing the death penalty." Again, no suggestion is made as to how greater "rationality" could be achieved under any type of statute that authorizes capital punishment. The *Gregg*-type statute imposes unprecedented safeguards in the special context of capital punishment. These include: (i) a bifurcated sentencing proceeding; (ii) the threshold requirement of one or more aggravating circumstances; and (iii) mandatory state Supreme Court review. All of these are administered pursuant to this Court's decisions interpreting the limits of the Eighth Amendment on the imposition of the death penalty, and all are subject to ultimate review by this Court. These ensure a degree of care in the imposition of the sentence of death that can be described only as unique. Given these safeguards already inherent in the imposition and review of capital sentences, the dissent's call for greater rationality is no less than a claim that a capital-punishment system cannot be administered in accord with the Constitution. As we reiterate, the requirement of heightened rationality in the imposition of capital punishment does not "plac[e] totally unrealistic conditions on its use." *Gregg.*

45. Justice Stevens, who would not overrule *Gregg,* suggests in his dissent that the infirmities alleged by McCleskey could be remedied by narrowing the class of death-eligible defendants to categories identified by the Baldus study where "prosecutors consistently seek, and juries consistently impose, the death penalty without regard to the race of the victim or the race of the offender." This proposed solution is unconvincing. First, "consistently" is a relative term, and narrowing the category of death-eligible defendants would simply shift the borderline between those defendants who received the death penalty and those who did not. A borderline area would continue to exist and vary in its boundaries. Moreover, because the discrepancy between borderline cases would be difficult to explain, the system would likely remain open to challenge on the basis that the lack of explanation rendered the sentencing decisions unconstitutionally arbitrary.

Second, even assuming that a category with theoretically consistent results could be identified, it is difficult to imagine how Justice Stevens' proposal would or could operate on a case-by-case basis. Whenever a victim is white and the defendant is a member of a different race, what steps would a prosecutor be required to take—in addition to weighing the customary prosecutorial considerations—before concluding in the particular case that he lawfully could prosecute? * * *

tution does not require that a State eliminate any demonstrable disparity that correlates with a potentially irrelevant factor in order to operate a criminal justice system that includes capital punishment. * * *

Second, McCleskey's arguments are best presented to the legislative bodies. It is not the responsibility—or indeed even the right—of this Court to determine the appropriate punishment for particular crimes. * * * Despite McCleskey's wide ranging arguments that basically challenge the validity of capital punishment in our multi-racial society, the only question before us is whether in his case, the law of Georgia was properly applied. We agree with the [courts below] that this was carefully and correctly done in this case. * * *

JUSTICE BRENNAN, with whom JUSTICE MARSHALL joins, and with whom JUSTICE BLACKMUN and JUSTICE STEVENS join in all but Part I, dissenting. * * *

II. At some point in this case, Warren McCleskey doubtless asked his lawyer whether a jury was likely to sentence him to die. A candid reply to this question would have been disturbing. First, counsel would have to tell McCleskey that few of the details of the crime or of McCleskey's past criminal conduct were more important than the fact that his victim was white. Furthermore, counsel would feel bound to tell McCleskey that defendants charged with killing white victims in Georgia are 4.3 times as likely to be sentenced to death as defendants charged with killing blacks. [The] story could be told in a variety of ways, but McCleskey could not fail to grasp its essential narrative line: there was a significant chance that race would play a prominent role in determining if he lived or died.

[The Court] finds no fault in a system in which lawyers must tell their clients that race casts a large shadow on the capital sentencing process. [It] arrives at this conclusion by stating that the Baldus study cannot "prove that race enters into any capital sentencing decisions or that race was a factor in McCleskey's particular case." [The likelihood that race influenced some decisions], holds the Court, is insufficient to establish a constitutional violation. The Court reaches this conclusion by placing four factors on the scales opposite McCleskey's evidence: the desire to encourage sentencing discretion, the existence of "statutory safeguards" in the Georgia scheme, the fear of encouraging widespread challenges to other sentencing decisions, and the limits of the judicial role. The Court's evaluation of the significance of petitioner's evidence is fundamentally at odds with our consistent concern for rationality in capital sentencing, and the considerations that the majority invokes to discount that evidence cannot justify ignoring its force.

III. It is important to emphasize at the outset that the Court's observation that McCleskey cannot prove the influence of race on any particular sentencing decision is irrelevant in evaluating his Eighth Amendment claim. Since *Furman,* the Court has been concerned with the *risk* of the imposition of an arbitrary sentence, rather than the proven fact of one. * * * This emphasis on risk acknowledges the difficulty of divining the jury's motivation in an individual case. In addition, it reflects the fact that concern for arbitrariness focuses on the rationality of the system as a whole, and that a system that features a significant probability that sentencing decisions are influenced by impermissible considerations cannot be regarded as rational.[1]

1. Once we can identify a pattern of arbitrary sentencing outcomes, we can say that a defendant runs a risk of being sentenced arbitrarily. It is thus immaterial whether the operation of an impermissible influence such as race is intentional. While the Equal Protection Clause forbids racial discrimination, and intent may be critical in a successful

[The] Court assumes the statistical validity of the Baldus study, and acknowledges that McCleskey has demonstrated a risk that racial prejudice plays a role in capital sentencing in Georgia. Nonetheless, it finds the probability of prejudice insufficient to create constitutional concern. Close analysis of the Baldus study, however, in light of both statistical principles and human experience, reveals that the risk that race influenced McCleskey's sentence is intolerable by any imaginable standard. * * *

McCleskey's statistics have particular force because most of them are the product of sophisticated multiple-regression analysis. Such analysis is designed precisely to identify patterns in the aggregate, even though we may not be able to reconstitute with certainty any individual decision that goes to make up that pattern.

[The] statistical evidence in this case thus relentlessly documents the risk that McCleskey's sentence was influenced by racial considerations. This evidence shows that there is a better than even chance in Georgia that race will influence the decision to impose the death penalty: a majority of defendants in white-victim crimes would not have been sentenced to die if their victims had been black. [In] determining the guilt of a defendant, a state must prove its case beyond a reasonable doubt. That is, we refuse to convict if the chance of error is simply less likely than not. Surely, we should not be willing to take a person's life if the chance that his death sentence was irrationally imposed is *more* likely than not. In light of the gravity of the interest at stake, petitioner's statistics on their face are a powerful demonstration of the type of risk that our Eighth Amendment jurisprudence has consistently condemned.

Evaluation of McCleskey's evidence cannot rest solely on the numbers themselves. We must also ask whether the conclusion suggested by those numbers is consonant with our understanding of history and human experience. Georgia's legacy of a race-conscious criminal justice system, as well as this Court's own recognition of the persistent danger that racial attitudes may affect criminal proceedings, indicate that McCleskey's claim is not a fanciful product of mere statistical artifice. * * *

History and its continuing legacy * * * buttress the probative force of McCleskey's statistics. Formal dual criminal laws may no longer be in effect, and intentional discrimination may no longer be prominent. Nonetheless, as we acknowledged in *Turner v. Murray,* 476 U.S. 28, 106 S.Ct. 1683, 90 L.Ed.2d 27 (1986), "subtle, less consciously held racial attitudes" continue to be of concern, and the Georgia system gives such attitudes considerable room to operate. The conclusions drawn from McCleskey's statistical evidence are therefore consistent with the lessons of social experience. * * *

IV. The Court cites four reasons for shrinking from the implications of McCleskey's evidence: the desirability of discretion for actors in the criminal-justice system, the existence of statutory safeguards against abuse of that discretion, the potential consequences for broader challenges to criminal sentencing, and an understanding of the contours of the judicial role. While these

claim under that provision, the Eighth Amendment has its own distinct focus: whether punishment comports with social standards of rationality and decency. It may be, as in this case, that on occasion an influence that makes punishment arbitrary is also proscribed under another constitutional provision. That does not mean, however, that the standard for determining an Eighth Amendment violation is superseded by the standard for determining a violation under this other provision. Thus, the fact that McCleskey presents a viable Equal Protection claim does not require that he demonstrate intentional racial discrimination to establish his Eighth Amendment claim.

concerns underscore the need for sober deliberation, they do not justify rejecting evidence as convincing as McCleskey has presented.

[The Court] also declines to find McCleskey's evidence sufficient in view of "the safeguards designed to minimize racial bias in the [capital sentencing] process." [It] is clear that *Gregg* bestowed no permanent approval on the Georgia system. It simply held that the State's statutory safeguards were assumed sufficient to channel discretion without evidence otherwise.

[The] challenge to the Georgia system is not speculative or theoretical; it is empirical. As a result, the Court cannot rely on the statutory safeguards in discounting McCleskey's evidence, for it is the very effectiveness of those safeguards that such evidence calls into question.

[In] fairness, the Court's fear that McCleskey's claim is an invitation to descend a slippery slope also rests on the realization that any humanly imposed system of penalties will exhibit some imperfection. Yet to reject McCleskey's powerful evidence on this basis is to ignore both the qualitatively different character of the death penalty and the particular repugnance of racial discrimination, considerations which may properly be taken into account in determining whether various punishments are "cruel and unusual." Furthermore, it fails to take account of the unprecedented refinement and strength of the Baldus study.

[The] Court also maintains that accepting McCleskey's claim would pose a threat to all sentencing because of the prospect that a correlation might be demonstrated between sentencing outcomes and other personal characteristics. Again, such a view is indifferent to the considerations that enter into a determination of whether punishment is "cruel and unusual." Race is a consideration whose influence is expressly consistently proscribed. We have expressed a moral commitment, as embodied in our fundamental law, that this specific characteristic should not be the basis for allotting burdens and benefits. * * *

Certainly, a factor that we would regard as morally irrelevant, such as hair color, at least theoretically could be associated with sentencing results to such an extent that we would regard as arbitrary a system in which that factor played a significant role. [However,] the evaluation of evidence suggesting such a correlation must be informed not merely by statistics, but by history and experience. One could hardly contend that this nation has on the basis of hair color inflicted upon persons deprivation comparable to that imposed on the basis of race. Recognition of this fact would necessarily influence the evaluation of data suggesting the influence of hair color on sentencing, and would require evidence of statistical correlation even more powerful than that presented by the Baldus study.

[Finally,] the Court justifies its rejection of McCleskey's claim by cautioning against usurpation of the legislatures' role in devising and monitoring criminal punishment. [The] judiciary's role in this society counts for little if the use of governmental power to extinguish life does not elicit close scrutiny. [The Court] fulfills, rather than disrupts, the scheme of separation of powers by closely scrutinizing the imposition of the death penalty, for no decision of a society is more deserving of the "sober second thought." * * * [c]

c. In a separate dissent, Justice Blackmun, with whom Marshall and Stevens, JJ., joined and with whom Brennan, J., joined in all but Part IV–B (maintaining that acceptance of petitioner's claim would not eliminate capital punishment in Georgia because "in extremely aggravated murders the risk of discriminatory enforcement of the death penalty is minimized"), concluded that if one assumes that the data presented by petitioner is valid, "as we must in light of the Court of Appeals' assumption, there exists in the Georgia capi-

Notes and Questions

1. *The end of doubts?* Consider Burt, *Disorder in the Court: The Death Penalty and the Constitution,* 85 Mich.L.Rev. 1741 (1987): "For twenty years, the Court has struggled to determine the constitutional status of capital punishment. Broadly speaking, there have been three distinct phases in this effort: the first, beginning in 1968, when the Court announced substantial doubts about the constitutional validity of the death penalty; the second, beginning in 1976, when the Court attempted to appease those doubts by rationalizing and routinizing the administration of the penalty; and the third, beginning in 1983 and culminating [in] *McClesky,* when the Court proclaimed the end of its doubts and correspondingly signalled its intention to turn away from any continuing scrutiny of the enterprise."

2. *The reluctance to "find" racial discrimination.* According to R. Kennedy, *McCleskey v. Kemp: Race, Capital Punishment and the Supreme Court,* 101 Harv.L.Rev. 1388, 1418 (1988), the *McClesky* majority manifested a "lack of concern for the feelings of blacks," an attitude that may be related to the Court's "very keen concern for the sensitivities of those—mainly whites—subject to being labeled 'racist.'" Continues Professor Kennedy:

"One of the great achievements of social reform in American history has involved the stigmatization of overt racial prejudice. But this triumph in principle has produced an unforseen consequence in application: it is precisely the sense that racial discrimination is a terrible evil that inhibits the Justices from 'finding' it in all but the clearest circumstances. Perhaps they assume that conduct so horrible must be plainly observable. Or perhaps their sense of the shamefulness of racism is so intense that they find it difficult to burden an official or agency with the moral opprobrium that the 'racist' label connotes without absolutely positive proof of culpability."

3. *Discretion, arbitrariness and discrimination.* Although the information on discrimination and on arbitrariness was much sketchier in 1972 than in 1988, "to the extent that [comparisons] can be made, they certainly show no marked

tal-sentencing scheme a risk of racially based discrimination that is so acute that it violates the Eighth Amendment." But the great bulk of Justice Blackmun's opinion was devoted to a discussion of why he believed the Georgia capital punishment system violates the Equal Protection Clause. See p. 972 infra.

In a third dissenting opinion, Justice Stevens, joined by Blackmun, J., maintained that the studies supporting McCleskey's claim "demonstrate a strong probability that [his] sentencing jury * * * was influenced by the fact that McCleskey is black and his victim was white, and that [the jury's sense that a defendant has lost his moral entitlement to live] would not have been generated if he had killed a member of his own race. This sort of disparity is constitutionally intolerable."

Justice Stevens called the majority's evident fear "that the acceptance of McCleskey's claim would sound the death knell for capital punishment in Georgia unfounded": "One of the lessons of the Baldus study is that there exist certain categories of extremely serious crimes for which prosecutors consistently seek, and juries consistently impose, the death penalty without regard to the race of the victim or the race of the offender. If Georgia were to narrow the class of death-eligible defendants to those categories, the danger of arbitrary and discriminatory imposition of the death penalty would be significantly decreased, if not eradicated."

Although Justice Stevens would reverse, he believed that further proceedings were needed to determine whether McCleskey's death sentence should be set aside: "First, the Court of Appeals must decide whether the Baldus study is valid. I am persuaded that it is, but orderly procedure requires that the Court of Appeals address this issue before we actually decide the question. Second, it is necessary for the District Court to determine whether the particular facts of McCleskey's crime and his background place this case within the range of cases that present an unacceptable risk that race played a decisive role in McCleskey's sentencing."

improvement. The courts' determined assertions that the pre-*Furman* problems have been solved must be seen as statements of faith rather than fact, or perhaps as wishful thinking, since the evidence, if it shows anything, shows remarkable constancy rather than change." S. Gross & R. Mauro, *Death & Discrimination: Racial Disparities in Capital Sentencing* 200 (1989).[a] "In the last analysis," conclude Gross & Mauro, id. at 224, "the discretion that is so highly praised in *McClesky* is the power to threaten to kill thousands but to do it only to dozens.[b] Whatever else might be said for the use of death as a punishment, one lesson is clear from experience: this is a power that we cannot exercise fairly and without discrimination."

SECTION 5. PROCEDURAL DUE PROCESS IN NON-CRIMINAL CASES [a]

I. DEPRIVATION OF "LIBERTY" AND "PROPERTY" INTERESTS [b]

"When a litigant is adversely affected entirely as a predictable consequence of procedural grossness and not as a consequence of ulterior design by government (or by its agents) to utilize constitutionally impermissible substantive standards, he is in serious difficulty. The essence of his complaint is to the felt unfairness of procedural grossness itself—that it builds in such a large margin of probable mistake as itself to be intolerable in a humane society. [But] *unlike* his freedom [of expression and religion] (sheltered by the first amendment), and *unlike* his entitlement to privacy (sheltered by the fourth and fifth amendments), [the litigant] cannot anchor a claim to freedom from procedural grossness per se in any clause of the Constitution.

"He cannot rely upon the equal protection clause, for we are here dealing with situations in which all similarly situated persons are uniformly subject to the same degree of procedural grossness * * *. Nor can one say (as doubtless is one's first impulse) that the individual's entitlement to 'due' process is obviously anchored in the very clauses sheltering due process. The difficulty is that such reasoning (ironically akin to the reasoning that created the right-

a. See also D. Baldus, G. Woodworth & C. Pulaski, *Equal Justice and the Death Penalty* 398 (1990).

b. "[I]n spite of the broad theoretical support for capital punishment reflected in public-opinion polls and in numerous death-sentencing statutes," observes Baldus, Woodworth & Pulaski, fn. a supra, at 411, "in practice, support for the death penalty has been and continues to be quite limited. * * * This country now appears to have a de facto national quota of 250 to 300 death sentences annually, which symbolizes its commitment to the value of life. At the same time, however, the widespread exercise of leniency by prosecutors and juries in the vast majority of death-eligible cases reflects the nation's unwillingness to take the lives of even our most culpable criminals on a wholesale basis."

"Rare as post-*Furman* death sentences have been," point out Gross & Mauro, supra, at 199, "they are far more common than executions. [T]here were only 98 executions from *Furman* [1972] through May 1, 1988. In the same period, approximately 3500 people were sentenced to death and over 2000 are now on death row. The total number of executions may be somewhat misleading, since reasonably regular executions began only in late 1983. There were 21 executions in 1984, 18 in 1985, 18 in 1986, and 25 in 1987. But even if this rate were to increase sharply to fifty or seventy executions a year, those executed would remain the exceptions among those sentenced to death and a tiny minority of those convicted of homicide."

a. The creditors' remedies cases are briefly considered in *Flagg Bros. v. Brooks*, p. 1255 infra.

b. See also *DeShaney v. Winnebago County Dep't of Social Servs.*, p. 1243 infra.

privilege distinction) must imagine a clause *which in fact is not there.* It imagines that the fourteenth amendment (or the same phrase in the fifth amendment) provides something like this: 'No State [shall] deprive any person of life, liberty, property, or of due process of law, without due process of law * * *.' Alternatively, it imagines that the next clause of the fourteenth amendment provides something like this '[Nor shall any State] deny to any person [either] due process of law or the equal protection of the laws.'

"[But as the amendments] read in fact, due process is not itself a protected entitlement. [It] stands in relation to ['life, liberty, [and] property'] not as an equivalent constitutionally established entitlement, but only as a condition to be observed insofar as the state may move to imperil one of the named [interests]. [P]rocedural due process appears never to be anything more than a kind of 'constitutional condition.' It is evidently not a free standing human interest."

—Van Alstyne, *Cracks in "The New Property": Adjudicative Due Process in the Administrative State,* 62 Corn.L.Rev. 445, 450–52 (1977).[c]

---

1. According to most commentators, the "procedural due process revolution" began with GOLDBERG v. KELLY, 397 U.S. 254, 90 S.Ct. 1011, 25 L.Ed.2d 287 (1970), holding that due process requires that welfare recipients be afforded an evidentiary hearing *prior* to the termination of benefits. As pointed out in Simon, fn. c supra, at 150, *Goldberg* "did not in fact present the issue of whether welfare benefits were within the 'life, liberty or property' protected by the due process clauses, because [the Social Services Commissioner] conceded that 'the protections of the due process clause apply.'[a] Nevertheless, [the Court] ad-

c. But Professor Van Alstyne goes on to say, id. at 487, that "it is plausible [to] treat *freedom from arbitrary adjudicative procedures* as a substantive element of one's liberty"—"a freedom whose abridgement government must sustain the burden of justifying, even as it must do when it seeks to subordinate other freedoms, such as those of speech and privacy"—"that the protected essences of personal freedom include a freedom from fundamentally unfair modes of governmental action, an immunity (if you will) from procedural arbitrariness." But see Simon, *Liberty and Property in the Supreme Court: A Defense of Roth and Perry,* 71 Calif.L.Rev. 146, 186 (1983). See also Smolla, *The Reemergency of the Right-Privilege Distinction in Constitutional Law,* 35 Stan.L.Rev. 69, 85–86 (1982); Williams, *Liberty and Property: The Problem of Government Benefit,* 12 J.Legal Stud. 3, 17–19 (1983).

Compare Van Alstyne, supra, with Ely, *Democracy and Distrust* 19 (1980), maintaining that the phrase "life, liberty or property" used to be, and ought to be, "read as a unit and given an open-ended, functional interpretation," meaning that the government cannot "*seriously hurt* you without due process of law" (emphasis added). But consider Terrell, *"Property," "Due Process," and the Distinction Between Definition and Theory in Legal Analysis,* 70 Geo.L.J. 861, 899–900 (1982): "[I]f the phrase seriously hurt [has] discoverable substance, then its content necessarily would develop [judicially] in the same manner that the substance of 'life, liberty, or property' has developed. [The] analysis would raise the same sort of questions previously raised about property: what is the definition of 'seriously hurt'? [And] why do we use this phrase rather than one which is more restrictive, such as 'extremely seriously hurt,' or less restrictive, such as 'slightly hurt'? That is, what is the justificatory theory for Ely's substitute phrase?

"This analysis indicates that Ely's objection to the Court's treatment of 'life, liberty, or property' is based on an apparent belief that the Court should not engage in a definitional exercise at all. In effect, he argues that the purpose of the due process clause is to protect citizens from government arbitrariness, and, therefore, that these terms should relate solely to that justification. [Ely] recognizes by his use of the phrase seriously hurt the need for a trigger mechanism that must precede any due process inquiry. Yet if arbitrariness is the evil to avoid, why have any preliminary obstacle to judicial scrutiny, much less the one he has rather casually identified?"

a. "[W]hile there were three dissents in *Goldberg* respecting the *fullness* of the procedure that government would be required to observe before terminating an allegedly ineligible welfare recipient, no one (not even the government itself, as Justice Brennan obdressed this issue [suggesting] that whether the right to continue receiving a government benefit was within the protection of the due process clause turned upon the importance of the benefit to the individual." Thus, the Court, per BRENNAN, J., observed:

"[Welfare] benefits are a matter of statutory entitlement for persons qualified to receive them.[b] Their termination involves state action that adjudicates important rights. The constitutional challenge cannot be answered by an argument that public assistance benefits are 'a "privilege" and not a "right."' Relevant constitutional restraints apply as much to the withdrawal of public assistance benefits as to disqualification for unemployment compensation or to denial of a tax exemption or to discharge from public employment. The extent to which procedural due process must be afforded the recipient is influenced by the extent to which he may be 'condemned to suffer grievous loss,' and depends upon whether the recipient's interest in avoiding the loss outweighs the governmental interest in summary adjudication."

2. As observed in Monaghan, *Of "Liberty" and "Property,"* 62 Corn.L.Rev. 401, 407 (1977), BELL v. BURSON, 402 U.S. 535, 91 S.Ct. 1586, 29 L.Ed.2d 90 (1971), "represented the high-water mark of [the] approach [that] whether an interest deserved due process clause process protection involved a simple pragmatic assessment of its 'importance' to the individual." The Court, per BRENNAN, J., invalidated a Georgia statute providing that the vehicle registration and driver's license of an uninsured motorist involved in an accident shall be suspended unless he posts security to cover the damages claimed by agreed parties in accident reports: "[Although a state could bar] the issuance of licenses to all motorists who did not carry liability insurance [or] post security, [o]nce licenses are issued, as in petitioner's case [a clergyman whose ministry requires him to cover three rural communities by car], their continued possession may become *essential* in the pursuit of a livelihood. Suspension of issued licenses thus involves state action that adjudicates *important interests* of the licensees. In such cases the licenses are not to be taken away without that procedural due process required by the Fourteenth Amendment." (Emphasis added.)

Bell "could have said that the license was sufficient to qualify as 'property,' or that a suspension of an individual's freedom to drive was a restriction on his 'liberty.' The Court said neither; the importance of the interest alone sufficed, and 'importance' was determined as a matter of federal, not state, law." Monaghan 407–08.

3. But "*Bell's* latitudinarian approach to 'liberty' and 'property,'" Monaghan 408, did not prevail. Stressing that before deciding what form of hearing is required by procedural due process the Court must "determine whether due process requirements apply in the first place," i.e., whether one has been deprived of "liberty" or "property"—and in doing so "we must look not to the 'weight' but to the nature of the interest at stake"—BOARD OF REGENTS v. ROTH, 408 U.S. 564, 92 S.Ct. 2701, 33 L.Ed.2d 548 (1972), per STEWART, J., for the first time, rejected a procedural due process claim because it implicated

served) dissented from the proposition that the due process clause was applicable to the case." Van Alstyne 456.

b. At this point, the Court noted [fn. 8] that "[i]t may be more realistic today to regard welfare entitlements as more like 'property' than a 'gratuity,'" citing Reich, *The New Property,* 73 Yale L.J. 733 (1964), and quoting extensively from Reich, *Individual Rights and Social Welfare: The Emerging Social Issues,* 74 Yale L.J. 1245 (1965). In these articles Professor Reich maintained that public employment, welfare assistance, franchises, licenses and other forms of governmental largess should be given the kind of protection afforded traditional property rights.

neither "liberty" nor "property." Hired by Wisconsin State University for a fixed term of one year, and given no tenure rights to continued employment, Roth had been informed that he would not be rehired for the next academic year. The Court rejected his contention that the University's failure to give him any reason for its decision or any opportunity to challenge it at any sort of hearing violated procedural due process: "The requirements of procedural due process apply only to the deprivation of interests encompassed within the Fourteenth Amendment's protection of liberty and property. [T]he range of interests protected by procedural due process is not infinite.

"[The] State, in declining to rehire [Roth], did not make any charge against him that might seriously damage his standing and associations in his community [e.g., accuse him of dishonesty or immorality,][a] [nor] impose on him a stigma or other disability that foreclosed his freedom to take advantage of other employment opportunities. [It did not, for example, bar him] from all other public employment in State universities.[b] [O]n the record before us,[c] all that clearly appears is that [Roth] was not rehired for one year at one University. It stretches the concept too far to suggest that [one] is deprived of 'liberty' when he simply is not rehired in one job but remains as free as before to seek another.

"[As for 'property' interests protected by procedural due process, to] have a property interest in a benefit, [one] must have more than a unilateral expectation of it. He must, instead, have a legitimate claim of entitlement to [it]. Property interests, of course, are not created by the Constitution, [but by, and] defined by existing rules or understandings that stem from an independent source such as state law—rules or understandings that secure certain benefits and that support claims of entitlement to those benefits. [But the terms of Roth's employment] specifically provided that [his] employment was to terminate on June 30. They did not provide for contract renewal absent 'sufficient cause.' Indeed, they made no provision for renewal whatsoever.[d] [Thus, although Roth]

a. "Had it done so," noted the Court, "this would be a different case. For '[w]here a person's good name, reputation, honor, or integrity is at stake because of what the government is doing to him, notice and an opportunity to be heard are essential.' *Wisconsin v. Constantineau,* 400 U.S. 433, 91 S.Ct. 507, 27 L.Ed.2d 515 (1971)." *Constantineau* (Burger, C.J., and Black and Blackmun, JJ., dissenting on procedural grounds), invalidated on due process grounds a state law providing that when, by "excessive drinking," one produces certain conditions or exhibits certain traits (e.g., exposing himself or family "to want" or becoming "dangerous to the peace"), designated officials may—without notice or hearing to the person involved—post a notice in all retail liquor stores that sales or gifts of liquor to him are forbidden for one year. But cf. *Paul v. Davis* (1976), infra.

b. "Had it done so," noted the Court, "this, again, would be a different case."

c. Roth had also alleged that non-renewal of his contract was based on his exercise of his right to freedom of speech, but this allegation was not before the Court. *Perry v. Sindermann,* 408 U.S. 593, 92 S.Ct. 2694, 33 L.Ed.2d 570 (1972), a companion case, made clear that the lack of a public employee's "right" to reemployment "is immaterial to his free speech claim." For "even though a person has no 'right' to a valuable governmental benefit and even though the government may deny him the benefit for any number of reasons, there are some reasons upon which the government may not act. It may not deny a benefit to a person on a basis that infringes his constitutionally protected interests—especially, his interest in freedom of speech."

d. But *Sindermann,* fn. c supra, involving another state college teacher serving on a year-to-year basis whose appointment had not been renewed and who had not received a hearing, per Stewart, J., held that a "lack of a contractual or tenure right to re-employment, taken alone," does not defeat one's claim that nonrenewal of his contract violated procedural due process. Sindermann had ten years service and had alleged, but not been permitted to prove, that the college had a de facto tenure program and that he had tenure under that program. He must, ruled the Court, be given an opportunity to prove the legitimacy of his claim of entitlement to continued employment absent "sufficient cause" "in light of 'the policies and practices of the institution.'" (Roth, on the other hand, had failed to estabsurely had an abstract concern in being rehired, [he lacked] a *property* interest sufficient to require the University [to] give him a hearing when [declining] to renew his contract of employment." [e]

4. *"The bitter with the sweet."* ARNETT v. KENNEDY, 416 U.S. 134, 94 S.Ct. 1633, 40 L.Ed.2d 15 (1974): Kennedy, a nonprobationary federal civil service employee in a regional OEO office, was removed by the Regional Director for allegedly publicly accusing the Director of bribery "in reckless disregard" of the facts. The relevant statutes provided, inter alia, that, prior to removal the employee had a right to reply to the charges orally and in writing and to submit affidavits to the official authorized to remove him (the Regional Director).[a] Instead of responding to the charges against him in a proceeding to be conducted and decided by the very person he had allegedly slandered, and who had filed the complaint against him, Kennedy instituted a federal suit, asserting that the discharge procedures denied him procedural due process because they failed to provide for a trial-type hearing before an impartial agency official prior to removal. The Court, with no majority opinion, held that the procedures satisfied due process.

The plurality opinion was by REHNQUIST, J., joined by Burger, C.J., and Stewart, J., but (as pointed out by White, J. joined by three other justices, dissenting in *Bishop v. Wood,* infra) the two justices who concurred in *Arnett,* as well as the four who dissented on this issue, rejected the plurality's analysis. As described by Van Alstyne, supra, at 462, according to Rehnquist, J., it was unnecessary to reach step two and "decide whether submitting Mr. Kennedy's fate to the judgment of his accuser was incompatible with [due process] because a close examination of Mr. Kennedy's property interest made it clear that *nothing* was in fact being taken from him to which he had *any* legally recognizable entitlement. In short, he failed at step one." Observed Rehnquist, J.:

"[A]ppellee did have a statutory expectancy that he not be removed other than for 'such cause as will promote the efficiency of the service.' But the very section of the statute [granting him that right] expressly provided also for the procedure by which 'cause' was to be determined, and expressly omitted the procedural guarantees [appellee claims]. [W]here the grant of a substantive right is inextricably intertwined with the limitations on the procedures which are to be employed in determining that right, a litigant in the position of appellee must take the bitter with the sweet. [Here] the property interest [in] employment was itself conditioned by procedural limitations [accompanying] the grant of that interest."

As for appellee's contention that the charges on which his dismissal was based "in effect accused [him] of dishonesty, and that therefore a hearing was required before he could be deprived of this element of his 'liberty' ": "Since the

lish "anything approaching a 'common law' of re-employment.")

e. Dissenting, Marshall, J., maintained that "every citizen who applies for a government job is entitled to it unless the government can establish some reason for denying the employment. This is the 'property' right [that] is protected by the Fourteenth Amendment and that cannot be denied 'without due process of law.' And it is also liberty—liberty to work—which is the 'very essence of the personal freedom and opportunity' secured by the Fourteenth Amendment."

Dissenting, Brennan, J., joined by Douglas, J., agreed with Marshall, J., that Roth had been denied due process when his contract had not been renewed without being informed of the reasons or given a chance to respond. Powell, J., did not participate.

a. The employee may also appeal an adverse decision to a reviewing authority within the agency. Only on appeal is he entitled to an evidentiary trial-type hearing, but if reinstated on appeal he receives full back pay.

purpose of [such a hearing] is to provide the person 'an opportunity to clear his name,' a hearing afforded by administrative appeal procedures after the actual dismissal is a sufficient compliance with [due process requirements]."

POWELL, J., joined by Blackmun, J., concurred in the result, but criticized the plurality's approach: "[The Rehnquist analysis] would lead directly to the conclusion that whatever the nature of [one's] statutorily created property interest, deprivation of that interest could be accomplished without notice or a hearing at any time. This view misconceives the origin of the right to procedural due process. That right is conferred not by legislative grace, but by constitutional guarantee. While the legislature may elect not to confer a property interest in federal employment, it may not constitutionally authorize the deprivation of such an interest, once conferred, without appropriate procedural safeguards." [b]

But after "weighing" the government's interest against the affected employee's,[c] Powell concluded that "a prior evidentiary hearing" was not required before removal. "The Government's interest in being able to act expeditiously to remove an unsatisfactory employee is substantial" and, since he would be reinstated and awarded back pay if he prevailed on the merits, Kennedy's "actual injury" would consist only of "a temporary interruption of his income during the interim." Thus, the challenged statutes and regulations "comport with due process by providing a reasonable accommodation of the competing interests." [d]

Notes and Questions

(a) *Circumventing Goldberg.* "The only difference" between *Arnett* and *Goldberg,* comments D. Shapiro, *Mr. Justice Rehnquist: A Preliminary View,* 90 Harv.L.Rev. 293, 324 (1976), "is that [in *Goldberg*] the statutes and regulations governing eligibility were not 'inextricably intertwined' with [those] providing for post-termination but not pre-termination hearings. Thus, under Justice Rehnquist's approach all the legislature would have to do to circumvent [*Goldberg*] would be to place the procedural limitations (which presumably could deny *any* opportunity to be heard at any time) in the same statutory section with the substantive provisions on eligibility. Surely, as six members of the Court seemed to agree, the effect would be to turn what looked like a landmark constitutional decision into the flimsiest of trivia."

(b) *Did Powell miss Rehnquist's point?* Consider Van Alstyne at 464–65: In *Arnett,* Powell, J., "fully recognized the devastating effect of the Rehnquist

b. This passage was quoted with approval by the Court in *Vitek v. Jones* (1980), *Logan v. Zimmerman Brush Co.* (1982), and *Cleveland Board of Education v. Loudermill* (1985), all discussed infra.

c. For a more extensive articulation of Powell, J.'s "balancing process," see his opinion for the Court in *Mathews v. Eldridge,* Part II infra.

d. White, J., concurring in part and dissenting in part, rejected the Rehnquist plurality's analysis and largely agreed with Powell, J.'s constitutional analysis. (Consider his opinion for the Court in *Vitek v. Jones,* infra). Although he found the pretermination procedures involved in *Arnett* generally adequate, White, J., would affirm the lower court's judgment, ordering reinstatement and backpay, "due to the failure to provide an impartial hearing officer at the pretermination hearing"—a right he maintained that the challenged statute, although silent on the matter, should be construed as requiring in this case.

Dissenting, Marshall, J., joined by Douglas and Brennan, JJ., rejected the plurality's analysis on grounds similar to Powell's, but as Marshall "balanced" the interests involved (stressing the long delay in the processing of adverse personnel actions), Kennedy was entitled to "an evidentiary hearing before an impartial decision-maker prior to dismissal."

treatment of the new property, [but] seemed to miss Rehnquist's point in his own reply." Recall that Powell, J., stated that the legislature "may not constitutionally authorize the deprivation of [a property interest in employment], *once conferred,* without appropriate safeguards" (emphasis added). Comments Van Alstyne: "But to speak of '[a property] interest, *once conferred,*' plainly begs the question Justice Rehnquist had raised: What 'interest' *was* 'conferred'? Show us a title or a jot of 'interest' actually 'conferred' by the legislature apart from the interest Kennedy held—the interest exactly bounded, as Rehnquist said, by the procedural provisions of the only source giving it any substance at all."

(c) *Must a government employee always "take the bitter with the sweet"?* "It is clear," comments Van Alstyne at 462, that he "need *not* [if] the bitter is a substantive restriction forbidden to government by the Constitution (which applies, of course, even when the government is operating as an employer), whether the bitter requires one to abstain from insisting upon one's first amendment rights or to relinquish one's rights to due process."

5. BISHOP v. WOOD, 426 U.S. 341, 96 S.Ct. 2074, 48 L.Ed.2d 684 (1976), per STEVENS, J., held—over the protest of the dissenters that the majority was adopting an analysis rejected by six members of the Court in *Arnett*—that the dismissal of a city policeman implicated neither the "property" or "liberty" interests protected by due process. The City Manager of Marion, North Carolina, terminated petitioner's employment as a policeman without affording him a hearing to determine the sufficiency of the cause for his dismissal. Petitioner brought suit, contending that since he was classified as a "permanent employee" he had a constitutional right to a pretermination hearing.[a] During pretrial discovery he was informed that he had been discharged for insubordination, "causing low morale," and "conduct unsuited to an officer."

"[T]he sufficiency of the claim of entitlement," observed the Court, "must be decided by reference to state law. The [state supreme court] has held that an enforceable expectation of continued [state employment] can exist only if the employer, by statute or contract, has actually granted some form of guarantee. Whether [this is so] can be determined only by an examination of the particular statute or ordinance in question. * * * Based on his understanding of state law, [the federal district court] concluded that petitioner 'held his position at the will and pleasure of the city.' [As the ordinance was thus construed], the City Manager's determination of the adequacy of the grounds for discharge is not subject to judicial review; the employee is merely given certain procedural rights which the District Court found not to have been violated in this case. The District Court's reading of the ordinance is tenable; it derives some support from a [state supreme court decision]; and it was accepted by [the] Fourth Circuit. These reasons are sufficient to foreclose our independent examination of the state law issue. Under [this view], petitioner's discharge did not deprive him of a property interest protected by the Fourteenth Amendment.[b]

a. The relevant provision of the city ordinance provided:

"*Dismissal.* A permanent employee whose work is not satisfactory over a period of time shall be notified in what way his work is deficient and what he must do if his work is to be satisfactory. If a permanent employee fails to perform work up to the standard of the classification held, or continues to be negligent, inefficient, or unfit to perform his duties, he may be dismissed by the City Manager. Any discharged employee shall be given written notice of his discharge setting forth the effective date and reasons for his discharge if he shall request such a notice."

b. In *Arnett*, noted Stevens, J., "the Court concluded that because the employee could only be discharged for cause, he had a property interest which was entitled to constitutional protection. In this case, a holding that as a matter of state law the employee 'held his position at the will and pleasure of the city'

"Petitioner's claim that he has been deprived of liberty has two components. He contends that the reasons given for his discharge are so serious as to constitute a stigma that may severely damage his reputation in the community; in addition, he claims that those reasons were false.[c] * * *

"In *Roth,* we recognized that the nonretention of an untenured college teacher might make him somewhat less attractive to other employers, but nevertheless concluded that it would stretch the concept too far 'to suggest that a person is deprived of "liberty" when he simply is not retained in one position but remains as free as before to seek another.' This same conclusion applies to the discharge of a public employee whose position is terminable at the will of the employer when [prior to his instituting a law suit] there is no public disclosure of the reasons for the discharge.

"[Even if the reasons given for petitioner's discharge were false], the reasons stated to him in private had no different impact on his reputation than if they had been true. And the answers to his interrogatories, whether true or false, did not cause the discharge. The truth or falsity of the City Manager's statement determines whether or not his decision to discharge the petitioner was correct or prudent, but neither enhances nor diminishes petitioner's claim that his constitutionally protected interest in liberty has been impaired.[13] A contrary evaluation of his contention would enable every discharged employee to assert a constitutional claim merely by alleging that his former supervisor made a mistake.

"The federal court is not the appropriate forum in which to review the multitude of personnel decisions that are made daily by public agencies.[14] [In] the absence of any claim that the public employer was motivated by a desire to curtail or to penalize the exercise of an employee's constitutionally protected rights, we must presume that official action was regular and, if erroneous, can best be corrected in other ways. The Due Process Clause of the Fourteenth Amendment is not a guarantee against incorrect or ill-advised personnel decisions." [d]

necessarily establishes that he had *no* property interest."

c. Since the District Court granted summary judgment against petitioner, noted the Court, "we [must] assume that his discharge was a mistake and based on incorrect information."

13. Indeed, the impact on petitioner's constitutionally protected interest in liberty is no greater even if we assume that the City Manager deliberately lied. Such fact might conceivably provide the basis for a state law claim, the validity of which would be entirely unaffected by our analysis of the federal constitutional question.

14. [U]nless we were to adopt Justice Brennan's remarkably innovative suggestion that we develop a federal common law of property rights, or his equally far reaching view that almost every discharge implicates a constitutionally protected liberty interest, the ultimate control of state personnel relationships is, and will remain, with the States; they may grant or withhold tenure at their unfettered discretion. In this case, whether we accept or reject the construction of the ordinance adopted by the two lower courts, the power to change or clarify that ordinance will remain in the hands of the City Council of the city of Marion.

[But see Rabin, *Job Security and Due Process: Monitoring Discretion Through a Reasons Requirement,* 44 U.Chi.L.Rev. 60, 72 (1976) "[*Bishop's* reference to] 'Justice Brennan's remarkably innovative suggestion that we develop a federal common law of property' [goes] to the heart of the matter. For if the cases beginning with *Goldberg* were not developing 'a federal common law of property rights' it is impossible to comprehend the decisions. One would have thought that the dialogue sparked by Justice Rehnquist in *Arnett* made that clear."]

d. Smolla, first fn. c supra, 88–89, points to this "profoundly honest passage" as providing "the best insights into the motivations that underlie the Court's adoption of the entitlement doctrine."

BRENNAN, J., joined by Marshall, J., dissented: "Petitioner was discharged as a policeman on the grounds of insubordination, 'causing low morale,' and 'conduct unsuited to an officer.' It is difficult to imagine a greater 'badge of infamy' that could be imposed on one following petitioner's calling; in a profession in which prospective employees are invariably investigated, petitioner's job prospects will be severely constricted by the governmental action in this case. [Yet the Court holds] that a State may tell an employee that he is being fired for some nonderogatory reason, and then turn around and inform prospective employers that [he] was in fact discharged for a stigmatizing reason that will effectively preclude future employment.

"The Court purports to limit its holding to situations in which there is 'no public disclosure of the reasons for the discharge,' but in this case the stigmatizing reasons have been disclosed, and there is no reason to believe that respondents will not convey these actual reasons to petitioner's prospective employers. [The stigma was not imposed until after petitioner brought suit, but] the 'claim' does not arise until the State has officially branded petitioner in some way, and the purpose of the due process hearing is to accord him an opportunity to clear his [name].

"[T]he strained reading of the local ordinance, which the Court deems to be 'tenable,' cannot be dispositive of the existence vel non of petitioner's 'property' interest. There is certainly a federal dimension to the definition of 'property' in the Federal Constitution [and] at least before a state law is definitively construed as not securing a 'property' interest, the relevant inquiry is whether it was objectively reasonable for the employee to believe he could rely on continued employment.[4] [At] a minimum, this would require in this case an analysis of the common practices utilized and the expectations generated by respondents, and the manner in which the local ordinance would reasonably be read by respondents' employees.[5] "

White, J., joined by Brennan, Marshall and Blackmun, JJ., also dissented: "The majority's holding that petitioner had no property interest in his job in spite of the unequivocal language in the city ordinance that he may be dismissed only for certain kinds of cause rests, then, on the fact that state law provides no *procedures* for assuring that the City Manager dismiss him only for cause. The right to his job apparently given by the first two sentences of the ordinance is thus redefined, according to the majority, by the procedures provided for in the third sentence and as redefined is infringed only if the procedures are not followed.

"This is precisely the reasoning which was embraced by only three and expressly rejected by six Members of this Court in [*Kennedy*]. [The] ordinance

4. By holding that States have "unfettered discretion" in defining "property" for purposes of the Due Process Clause, [the] Court is, as my Brother White argues, effectively adopting the analysis rejected by a majority of the Court in *Arnett.* More basically, the Court's approach is a resurrection of the discredited rights/privileges distinction, for a State may now avoid all due process safeguards attendant upon the loss of even the necessities of life, cf. *Goldberg,* merely by labeling them as not constituting "property."

5. For example, petitioner was hired for a "probationary" period of six months, after which he became a "permanent" employee. No reason appears on the record for this distinction, other than the logical assumption, confirmed by a reasonable reading of the local ordinance, that after completion of the former period, an employee may only be discharged for "cause." As to respondents' personnel practices, it is important to note that in a department which currently employs 17 persons, petitioner's was the only discharge, for cause or otherwise, during the period of over three years from the time of his hiring until the time of pretrial discovery.

plainly grants petitioner a right to his job unless there is cause to fire him. Having granted him such a right it is the Federal Constitution,[3] not state law, which determines the process to be applied in connection with any state decision to deprive him of it." [e]

Notes and Questions

(a) Consider Van Alstyne at 468–69: "[According to the Court], Bishop, as a 'permanent employee,' had even less fourteenth amendment property than had Roth, probationary employee at Oshkosh, Wisconsin. Roth had the enforceable assurance of at least the one year of assistant professor status (which he had completed) before encountering the hazard of nonrenewal. Although unknown to him, Bishop as a 'permanent employee' literally had no job *even from day to day,* but was dependent upon the non-happening of an event (receipt of notice of dismissal from the City Manager) as a condition precedent to vest affirmatively in him each day's entitlement to his status."

(b) Does *Roth* leave the courts a role that would allow them to decide for themselves whether interests defined by the state are fourteenth amendment "property"? Compare Monaghan 440 with Simon, first fn. c supra at 182–83.

(c) *Is there a degree of circularity to the Bishop dissent?* "If the Court were to focus on real expectations and the role a government job actually plays in someone's life," observes Tribe, *American Constitutional Law* 698–99 (2d ed. 1988) "then it would have to move well beyond the positivist framework it first adopted in *Bishop.* Yet the [*Bishop* dissenters do] not offer a practical alternative. [They] attempt to find a statutory entitlement to a job as a policeman. But there is a degree of circularity to their argument that there may have been 'reasonable expectations' in *Bishop* that justified a finding of a property interest: it is questionable whether a person can truly be said to 'justifiably rely' on continued employment where the person's contract or statute expressly indicates either that the employment can be terminated without cause, or that cause is theoretically required but no hearing is to be allowed. This circle can be broken only by an assertion of substantive values or norms in the name of the Constitution—norms as to what an employee, for example, is *entitled* to expect *whatever* the contract or statute may say. Indeed, breaking the circle would require an acceptance of the proposition that due process is not merely a means to the end of implementing the state's own substantive rules and allocations but

3. The majority intimates in [fn. b] that the views of the three plurality Justices in *Arnett* were rejected because the other six Justices disagreed on the question of how the federal *statute* involved in that case should be construed. This is incorrect. All Justices agreed on the meaning of the statute. [I]t was the constitutional significance of the statute on which the six disagreed with the plurality.

Similarly, here, I do not disagree with the majority or the courts below on the meaning of the state law. If I did, I might be inclined to defer to the judgments of the two lower courts. The state law says that petitioner may be dismissed by the City Manager only for certain kinds of cause and then provides that he will receive notice and an explanation, but no hearing and no review. I agree that as a matter of state law petitioner has no remedy no matter how arbitrarily or erroneously the City Manager has acted. This is what the lower courts say the statute means. I differ with those courts and the majority only with respect to the constitutional significance of an unambiguous state law. A majority of the Justices in *Arnett* stood on the proposition that the Constitution requires procedures *not* required by state law when the state conditions dismissal on "cause."

e. In a third dissent, Blackmun, J., joined by Brennan, J., maintained that the Marion ordinance "contains a 'for cause' standard for dismissal and [thus] creates a proper expectation of privacy of continued employment so long as [the employee] performs his work satisfactorily. At this point, the Federal Constitution steps in and requires that appropriate procedures be followed before the employee may be deprived of his property interest."

either a means to some very different and larger purpose, or—as in the intrinsic approach to procedural safeguards—an end in itself."

(d) Since the civil service bureaucracy has great potential for adversely affecting constitutional rights and civil service tenure would help free lower level bureaucrats from political control, should civil service employment be recognized as constitutionally protected? Compare Tushnet, *The Newer Property: Suggestions for the Revival of Substantive Due Process,* 1975 Sup.Ct.Rev. 261, 284 with Van Alstyne at 482–87.

(e) *Public employment, welfare benefits, and the "government as monopolist" theory.* Consider Terrell, first fn. c supra, at 864–65, 902–04, 907–08, "propos[ing] a threshold inquiry for determining whether a particular government entitlement should be considered a protected property interest under the due process clause[,] [the] 'government as monopolist' theory. [W]hen government acts as a 'monopolist' [then] the due process constraint is properly applied to balance the power of government over the individual's life. When the individual is not forced to deal with government, however, but chooses to do so freely and voluntarily, the constitutional protection of due process is misplaced. In this case, the 'market' created by existing alternatives to the government's offer already has established the balance between government and the individual. * * *

"Based on this factor of individual choice, cases involving government employment—such as *Roth, Bishop,* and *Arnett*—and potentially other contractual relations would seem to fall generally into the permissible arbitrariness, not the due process, set. Government is rarely a monopolist in these contractual situations, as either the only available employer or the only supplier or purchaser of a particular item. [O]nce an individual voluntarily accepts a job that has less than full due process protections for termination, then the individual has indeed taken 'the bitter with the sweet' and should not be able to base a cause of action on the inadequacy of these protections. * * * Welfare benefits cases, like professional licenses cases, should fall in the due process set, just as the Court concluded in *Goldberg.* [M]ost welfare recipients would appear to have no viable alternative to which they could turn for subsistence. Consequently, their position is probably best seen as one of forced association automatically attended by some degree of procedural protection."

6. *Reading "liberty" narrowly.* PAUL v. DAVIS, 424 U.S. 693, 96 S.Ct. 1155, 47 L.Ed.2d 405 (1976), arose as follows: After respondent Davis had been arrested on a shoplifting charge, petitioner police officials circulated a "flyer" to 800 merchants in the Louisville, Ky. area designating him an "active shoplifter." When the shoplifting charge was dismissed, Davis brought a § 1983 action alleging that the police officials' action under color of law had deprived him of his constitutional rights, by inhibiting him from entering business establishments and by impairing his employment opportunities. A 5–3 majority, per REHNQUIST, J., was unimpressed:

"[R]espondent's complaint would appear to state a classical claim for defamation actionable in the courts of virtually every State, [but he] brought his action [not] in the state courts of Kentucky, but in a [federal court]. [He contends that since petitioners are government officials] his action is thereby transmuted into one for deprivation by the State of rights secured under the Fourteenth Amendment. [It] is hard to perceive any logical stopping place to [respondent's] line of reasoning. [His] construction would seem almost necessarily to result in every legally cognizable injury which may have been inflicted by a state official acting under 'color of law' establishing a violation of the Fourteenth Amendment. [But our cases do] not establish the proposition that reputation alone, apart from some more tangible interests such as employment, is either 'liberty' or 'property' by itself sufficient to invoke the procedural protection of the Due Process Clause." Thus, no inquiry had to be made as to whether the police officials had followed adequate procedures before issuing the flyers.

The Court distinguished *Constantineau,* fn. a in *Bell v. Burson,* supra, as dependent on the fact that posting the person's name in liquor stores as a chronic drinker "deprived [him] of a right previously held under state law—the right [to] obtain liquor in common with the rest of the citizenry"—and thus "significantly altered his status as a matter of state law. [I]t was that alteration of legal status which, combined with the injury resulting from the defamation, justified the invocation of procedural safeguards." Interests "comprehended within the meaning of either 'liberty' or 'property' as meant in the Due Process Clause attain this constitutional status by virtue of the fact that they have been initially recognized and protected by state law,[5] and we have repeatedly ruled that the procedural guarantees of the Fourteenth Amendment apply whenever the State seeks to remove or significantly alter that status. [But] the interest in reputation alone which respondent seeks to vindicate [is] quite different from the 'liberty' or 'property' recognized in [such decisions as *Bell v. Burson*]. [Although the interest in reputation is protected by the state by virtue of its tort law], any harm or injury to that interest, even where as here inflicted by an officer of the State, does not result in a deprivation of any 'liberty' or 'property' recognized by state or federal law, nor has it worked any change of respondent's status as theretofore recognized under the State's laws."

BRENNAN, J., joined by White and Marshall, JJ., dissented: "The Court today holds that public officials, acting in their official capacities as law enforcers, may on their own initiative and without trial constitutionally condemn innocent individuals as criminals and thereby brand them with one of the most stigmatizing and debilitating labels in our society. If there are no constitutional restraints on such oppressive behavior, the safeguards constitutionally accorded an accused in a criminal trial are rendered a sham, and no individual can feel secure that he will not be arbitrarily singled out for similar *ex parte* punishment by those primarily charged with fair enforcement of the law.

"[There] is no attempt by the Court to analyze the question as one of reconciliation of constitutionally protected personal rights and the exigencies of law enforcement. [Rather,] the Court by mere fiat and with no analysis wholly excludes personal interest in reputation from the ambit of 'life, liberty, or property' under the Fifth and Fourteenth Amendments, thus rendering due process concerns *never* applicable to the official stigmatization, however arbitrary, of an individual. The logical and disturbing corollary of this holding is that no due process infirmities would inhere in a statute constituting a commission to conduct *ex parte* trials of individuals, so long as the only official judgment pronounced was limited to the public condemnation and branding of a person as a Communist, a traitor, an 'active murderer,' a homosexual, or any other mark that 'merely' carries social approbrium. The potential of today's decision is frightening for a free people."

5. There are other interests, of course, protected not by virtue of their recognition by the law of a particular State, but because they are guaranteed in one of the provisions of the Bill of Rights which has been "incorporated" into the Fourteenth Amendment. Section 1983 makes a deprivation of such rights actionable independently of state law.

Despite the majority's efforts to distinguish them, cases such as *Roth, Constantineau* [a] and *Goss v. Lopez,*[b] maintained Brennan, J., "are cogent authority that a person's interest in his good name and reputation falls within the broad term 'liberty' and clearly require that the government afford procedural protections before infringing that name and reputation by branding a person as a criminal. [It] is inexplicable how the Court can say that a person's status is 'altered' when the State suspends him from school, revokes his driver's license, fires him from a job, or denies him the right to purchase a drink of alcohol, but is in no way 'altered' when it officially pins upon him the brand of a criminal." [c]

Notes and Questions

(a) *"An unsettling conception of liberty."* Consider Monaghan at 424–27: "[I]t is an unsettling conception of 'liberty' that protects an individual against state interference with his access to liquor but not with his reputation in the community. * * * Defamation is a serious assault upon an individual's sense of 'self-identity,' and has from ancient times been viewed as 'psychic mayhem.' Accordingly, the Court's conclusion that such an assault implicates no constitutionally protected interest stands wholly at odds with our ethical, political, and constitutional assumption about the worth of each individual."

(b) *A defense of the result in, but not the reasoning of, Paul v. Davis.* Consider RODNEY SMOLLA, fn. a supra, at 841–47: "The critics of *Paul* have never explained satisfactorily how a section 1983 action is in any substantive law sense an improvement on the law of libel. [A § 1983] action shifts the substantive focus of the lawsuit away from the two issues that have always been at the core of libel actions: the truth or falsity of the defamatory language, and the conduct of the defendant in publishing it. * * * Substantive law aside, the critics of *Paul* have also failed to build a convincing case for construing the fourteenth amendment as mandating an alternate federal forum for what are essentially defamation actions. [Rehnquist, J.,] might have argued, as he would eventually come to argue, that there is no need to treat deprivations of interests in liberty or property as matters of federal concern as long as the state has an adequate system in place to compensate victims of those deprivations.[d] This

a. For the view that "the heart of the complaint" in *Constantineau* was "defamation, not restriction of access to liquor," see Monaghan at 431. See also id. at 423–24; Mashaw, *Due Process in the Administrative State* 95 (1985); D. Shapiro, *Mr. Justice Rehnquist: A Preliminary View,* 90 Harv.L.Rev. 293, 326 (1976); Smolla, *The Displacement of Federal Due Process Claims by State Tort Remedies,* 1982 U.Ill.L.F. 831, 839–40, 845.

b. *Goss v. Lopez,* 419 U.S. 565, 95 S.Ct. 729, 42 L.Ed.2d 725 (1975) (also discussed in Part II infra), held that students suspended from public high schools for up to ten days were entitled to procedural protections against unfair suspensions. The *Goss* Court, per White, J., pointed out that state law had established a "property interest" in educational benefits, but also recognized "the liberty interest in reputation" implicated by suspensions: "The Due Process Clause also forbids arbitrary deprivations of liberty. 'Where a person's good name, reputation, honor, or integrity is at stake because of what the government is doing to him,' the minimal requirements of the Clause must be satisfied. *Constantineau.* [If] sustained and recorded, [the charges of misconduct] could seriously damage the students' standing with their fellow pupils and their teachers as well as interfere with later opportunities for higher education and employment. * * * Neither the property interest in educational benefits temporarily denied nor the liberty interest in reputation, which is also implicated, is so insubstantial that suspensions may constitutionally be imposed by any procedure the school chooses, no matter how arbitrary."

c. Stevens, J., did not participate, but a year later, dissenting in *Ingraham v. Wright,* discussed in fn. e infra, he suggested that *Paul* "may have been correctly decided on an incorrect rationale." See the extract from his opinion in fn. e.

d. Consider Justice Rehnquist's opinion for the Court in Parratt v. Taylor, 451 U.S. 527, 101 S.Ct. 1908, 68 L.Ed.2d 420 (1981). Al-reasoning would not have denied that reputation was a sufficiently substantial interest to deserve characterization as property or liberty; such a position would merely have held that the interest in reputation was not deprived 'without due process of law' as long as the state courts remain ready, willing and able to provide 'due process' in the form of post-deprivation compensation.

"[In *Constantineau*] the Wisconsin posting statute may very well have preempted the normal remedies of the common law by authorizing the very posting

though the state had a torts claim procedure which provided a remedy for tortious losses at the hands of the state, respondent, a state prisoner, brought a § 1983 action against prison officials, alleging that they had negligently lost certain hobby materials he had ordered by mail, thus depriving him of property without due process of law. The Court thought it plain that the prison officials had acted under color of state law; the lost materials constituted "property"; and that the alleged loss, although negligently caused, amounted to a "deprivation." But standing alone, "these three elements do not establish a violation of the Fourteenth Amendment. Nothing in that Amendment protects against all deprivations of life, liberty, or property by the State. [The Amendment] protects only against deprivations 'without due process of law.'" The Court then addressed the question whether "the tort remedies which Nebraska provides as a means of redress for property deprivations satisfy the requirements of procedural due process" and concluded that they did:

"There is no contention [that] it was practicable for the State to provide a predeprivation hearing. [The State] has provided respondent with the means by which he can receive redress for the deprivation. [Through its] torts claims procedure the State hears and pays claims of prisoners housed in its penal institutions. This procedure was in existence at the time of the loss here in question but respondent did not use it. [Although] the state remedies may not provide the respondent with all the relief which may have been available if he could have proceeded under § 1983, [they] are sufficient to satisfy the requirements of due process."

Noting that citation to *Paul* is prominent in *Parratt,* Smolla comments, id. at 843, that "the Supreme Court, in looking back at *Paul,* seems to have revised history to place *Paul* within the post-deprivation due process framework," but that "concept—the idea that state tort remedies were all the process due Mr. Davis—was not the rationale used by Justice Rehnquist [and] the rationale that he did use has evoked an endless chain of muddled conundrums."

Parratt was extended to intentional deprivations of property in *Hudson v. Palmer,* 468 U.S. 517, 104 S.Ct. 3194, 82 L.Ed.2d 393 (1984). Respondent, an inmate in a Virginia prison, brought a § 1983 action against a prison official, alleging that the latter had engaged in an unreasonable "shakedown" search of respondent's locker and cell and that during the search, in violation of respondent's right to due process, had intentionally destroyed some of respondent's noncontraband personal property. The Court, per Burger, C.J., viewed the reasoning of *Parratt* applicable to intentional deprivation of property:

"The State can no more anticipate and control in advance the random and unauthorized intentional conduct of its employees than it can anticipate similar negligent conduct. [If] negligent deprivations of property do not violate [due process] because predeprivation process is impracticable, it follows that intentional deprivations do not [either] [provided that] adequate state postdeprivation remedies are available." Because Virginia did furnish such an adequate remedy, "even if petitioner intentionally destroyed respondent's personal property during the challenged shakedown search, the destruction did not violate the Fourteenth Amendment."

But see Tribe, supra, at 727–29: "[T]he magnitude of the [*Hudson*] opinion's apparent leap beyond *Parratt* seems unwarranted. It is one thing to say that no deprivation of life, liberty, or property without due process of law has occurred simply because a state agent negligently injures someone in the course of carrying out his official duties—as the Court was later to hold in *Daniels v. Williams* [474 U.S. 327, 106 S.Ct. 662, 88 L.Ed.2d 662 (1986)] and *Davidson v. Cannon* [474 U.S. 344, 106 S.Ct. 668, 88 L.Ed.2d 677 (1986)]. It is quite another thing to suggest that even an intentional abuse of state authority cannot inflict any constitutional injury unless and until the state has failed to provide redress. * * * Certainly a police officer's deliberate and unauthorized decision to inflict a severe beating on someone he has just arrested, or indeed to destroy such a person's property, rather than to await the usual processes of trial and sentencing, constitutes a violation of procedural due process complete when it occurs, regardless of the avenues of redress available under state law. Dirty Harry violated the Constitution even if the state made it possible for his victims to sue him. Any contrary intimation in the needlessly broad language of *Hudson* ought to be regarded as dictum, and should be reconsidered when a suitable case presents itself."

procedure used by the police chief against Mrs. Constantineau, in all likelihood immunizing the police chief from the 'common law process' to which the police chiefs in Kentucky were still subject. [The] constitutional fault in Wisconsin's posting statute was thus systemic. It is precisely in cases in which the state enacts a regime that allows the state to visit substantial harm on its citizens without traditional recourse to the courts for compensation that federal constitutional law *should* be activated to override that system and 'superimpose a font of tort law' on the deficient state.

"[Rehnquist, J.,] could have finished off Davis' claim by simply pointing out that Davis continued to enjoy precisely the right and status that he always had under Kentucky law: the right to sue the police chiefs in a common law action for damages. Such a finish would have built upon the truism of modern legal thought that 'reputation' is not a right with Platonic *a priori* existence, but rather a collection of remedial and procedural devices that the state guarantees it will make available to permit one wrongfully deprived of reputation to seek redress. If Kentucky had taken away from Davis his common law tort cause of action, *then* it would have extinguished 'a right or status previously recognized by state law.' But Kentucky did not.

"[As] much as Paul's language and logic were muddled and misleading, [its] result was sound. The result, however, was not justified by the reason Justice Rehnquist gave—that Kentucky law did not extend its protection to Mr. Davis' reputation—but by precisely the opposite fact: because Kentucky law *did* protect Davis, Kentucky did nothing to violate the due process clause." [e]

7. (a) *In some situations, at least, a litigant need not "take the bitter with the sweet."* A Nebraska law, § 83–180(1), provides that if a designated physician finds that a prisoner "suffers from a mental disease or defect" that cannot be

e. Professor Smolla then turns to *Ingraham v. Wright*, 430 U.S. 651, 97 S.Ct. 1401, 51 L.Ed.2d 711 (1977) (also discussed in Part II infra), a case finding that the "paddling" of students as a means of maintaining discipline in the public schools "implicates a constitutionally protected liberty interest," but concluding that the Due Process Clause does not require notice and hearing prior to imposition of corporal punishment as that practice is authorized and limited by the common law—the state's traditional common-law constraints and remedies "are fully adequate to afford due process." Comments Smolla at 847–48:

"As was true in *Paul*, in *Ingraham* state law had in place a remedial scheme that provided redress for the harm that was alleged to form the basis of the due process violation. The Court in *Ingraham* avoided the confusion of *Paul*, however, by steering clear of the notion that the existence of state tort law remedies somehow automatically displaced the due process clause. Instead [*Ingraham*] conceded the logical point that *Paul* had irrationally and stubbornly seemed to deny, recognizing that at a threshold level, common law protection and constitutional protection could be duplicative. [U]nlike the reputational interest at issue in *Paul*, an interest without independent federal content, the liberty interest in *Ingraham* was undeniably 'constitutional'—the right to be free of physical restraint and punishment, *Ingraham* thus made it clear that state common law remedies could serve as an adequate surrogate for due process safeguards even when 'hard core' constitutional interests in property or liberty were at stake."

Dissenting in *Ingraham*, Stevens, J. (who did not participate in *Paul*), observed: "When only an invasion of a property interest is involved, there is a greater likelihood that a damage award will make a person completely whole than when an invasion of the individual's interest in freedom from bodily restraint and punishment has occurred. In the property context, therefore, frequently a postdeprivation state remedy may be all the process that the Fourteenth Amendment requires. It may also be true—although I do not express an opinion on the point—that an adequate state remedy for defamation may satisfy the due process requirement when a State has impaired an individual's interest in his reputation. [Thus,] *Paul* may have been correctly decided on an incorrect rationale. Perhaps the Court will one day agree with Justice Brennan's appraisal of the importance of the constitutional interest at stake in [*Paul*] and nevertheless conclude that an adequate state remedy may prevent every state inflicted injury to a person's reputation from violating 42 U.S.C. § 1983."

properly treated in prison the Director of Correctional Services may transfer a prisoner to a mental hospital. Jones maintained that a prisoner is entitled to certain procedural protections, including notice, an adversary hearing and provision of counsel, before he is transferred to a state mental hospital for treatment. The Court agreed, VITEK v. JONES, 445 U.S. 480, 100 S.Ct. 1254, 63 L.Ed.2d 552 (1980), per WHITE, J. The involuntary transfer of a state prisoner to a mental hospital implicates a constitutionally protected "liberty interest" and once a state grants prisoners such an interest "due process protections are necessary 'to insure that the state-created right is not arbitrarily abrogated' "—these protections "being a matter of federal law, they are not diminished by the fact that the State may have specified its own procedures that it may deem adequate for determining the preconditions to adverse official action":

"We have repeatedly held that state statutes may create liberty interests that are entitled to the procedural protections of the Due Process Clause of the Fourteenth Amendment. There is no 'constitutional or inherent right' to parole, *Greenholtz v. Nebraska Penal Inmates,* 442 U.S. 1, 7, 99 S.Ct. 2100, 2103, 60 L.Ed. 2d 668 (1979),[a] but once a State grants a prisoner the conditional liberty properly dependent on the observance of special parole restrictions, due process protections attach to the decision to revoke parole. *Morrissey v. Brewer,* 408 U.S. 471, 92 S.Ct. 2593, 33 L.Ed.2d 484 (1972). The same is true of the revocation of probation. *Gagnon v. Scarpelli,* 411 U.S. 778, 93 S.Ct. 1756, 36 L.Ed.2d 656 (1973). In *Wolff v. McDonnell,* 418 U.S. 539, 94 S.Ct. 2963, 41 L.Ed.2d 935 (1974), we held that a state-created right to good-time credits, which could be forfeited only for serious misbehavior, constituted a liberty interest protected by the Due Process Clause.

"[In] *Meachum v. Fano,* 427 U.S. 215, 96 S.Ct. 2532, 49 L.Ed.2d 451 (1976), and *Montanye v. Haymes,* 427 U.S. 236, 96 S.Ct. 2543, 49 L.Ed.2d 466 (1976), we held that the transfer of a prisoner from one prison to another does not infringe a protected liberty interest. But in those cases transfers were discretionary with the prison authorities, and in neither case did the prisoner possess any right or justifiable expectation that he would not be transferred except for misbehavior or upon the occurrence of other specified events.[b]

a. The *Greenholtz* Court observed, per Burger, C.J., that "there is no constitutional right of a convicted person to be conditionally released before the expiration of a valid sentence. The natural desire of an individual to be released is indistinguishable from the initial resistance to being confined. But the conviction, with all its procedural safeguards, has extinguished that liberty right: 'Given a valid conviction, the criminal defendant has been constitutionally deprived of his liberty.' " But "[w]e can accept respondents' view that the expectancy of release provided by this statute is entitled to some measure of constitutional protection. However, we emphasize that this statute has unique structure and language and thus whether any other state statute provides a protectible entitlement must be decided on a case-by-case basis." Consider also Professor Nowak's criticism of *Greenholtz,* p. 372 infra.

Cf. *Connecticut Bd. of Pardons v. Dumschat,* 452 U.S. 458, 101 S.Ct. 2460, 69 L.Ed.2d 158 (1981), per Burger, C.J., rejecting the argument that "the fact that the Connecticut Board of Pardons has granted approximately three-fourths of the applications for commutation of life sentences creates a constitutional 'liberty interest' or 'entitlement' in life-term inmates so as to require that Board to explain its reasons for denial of an application for commutation."

b. The *Meachum* Court, per Rehnquist, J., rejected the contention that "*any* change in the conditions of confinement having a substantial adverse impact on the prisoner involved" invokes due process protections, maintaining instead that the original valid conviction and imprisonment decision "sufficiently extinguished the defendant's liberty interest to empower the State to confine him in *any* of its prisons." The *Meachum,* Court, observes Tribe at 694, "was wary of subjecting to 'judicial review a wide spectrum of discretionary actions that traditionally have been the business of prison administrations rather than of federal courts.' "

"[The] 'objective expectation, firmly fixed in state law and official penal complex practice,' that a prisoner would not be transferred unless he suffered from a mental disease or defect that could not be adequately treated in the prison, gave Jones a liberty interest that entitled him to the benefits of appropriate procedures in connection with determining the conditions that warranted his transfer to a mental hospital. [Appellants] maintain that any state-created liberty interest that Jones had was completely satisfied once a [designated physician] made the findings required by § 83–180(1) and that Jones was not entitled to any procedural protections.[6] But if the State grants a prisoner a right or expectation that adverse action will not be taken against him except upon the occurrence of specified behavior, 'the determination of whether such behavior has occurred becomes critical, and the minimum requirements of procedural due process appropriate for the circumstances must be observed.' *Wolff.* These minimum requirements being a matter of federal law, they are not diminished by the fact that the State may have specified its own procedures that it may deem adequate for determining the preconditions to adverse official action. [The state's] reliance on the opinion of a designated physician [for] determining whether the conditions warranting a transfer exist neither removes the prisoner's interest from due process protection nor answers the question of what process is due under the Constitution."

(b) *Recognizing a protected 'liberty interest' independently of state law.* The *Vitek* Court went on to hold that "independently of § 83–180(1), the transfer of a prisoner from a prison to a mental hospital must be accompanied by appropriate procedural protections":

"[F]or the ordinary citizen, commitment to a mental hospital produces 'a massive curtailment of liberty' [and thus] 'requires due process protection.' The loss of liberty produced by an involuntary commitment is more than a loss of freedom from confinement. It is indisputable that commitment to a mental hospital 'can engender adverse social consequences to the individual' and that '[w]hether we label this phenomena "stigma" [or] something else [it can occur and it] can have a very significant impact on the individual.' * * * Compelled treatment in the form of mandatory behavior modification programs, [to which] Jones was exposed in this case was a proper factor to be weighed * * *.

"Were an ordinary citizen to be subjected involuntarily to these consequences, it is undeniable that protected liberty interests would be unconstitutionally infringed absent compliance with the procedures required by the Due Process Clause. We conclude that a convicted felon also is entitled to the benefit of procedures appropriate in the circumstances before he is found to have a

See also *Olim v. Wakinekona,* 461 U.S. 238, 103 S.Ct. 1741, 75 L.Ed.2d 813 (1983), per Blackmun, J., ruling that the transfer of a state prisoner from Hawaii to a maximum security facility in California "does not deprive an inmate of any liberty interest protected by the Due Process Clause in and of itself". Cf. *Hewitt v. Helms,* 459 U.S. 460, 103 S.Ct. 864, 74 L.Ed.2d 675 (1983) (transfer of inmate from general prison population to administrative segregation implicates no liberty interest "independently protected by the Due Process Clause").

6. A majority of the Justices rejected an indentical position in *Arnett* [referring to the separate opinions of White, Marshall and Powell, JJ., and then quoting extensively from Powell, J.'s concurring opinion].

[But consider Terrell, supra, at 935 n. 378: "[T]he government as monopolist theory explains far more satisfactorily [than the *Vitek* Court did] the Court's reluctance to let a state designate its own procedures in prison situations. In the prison context, a state is obviously in the position of absolute monopolist, whereas it is not such a monopolist concerning employment. Thus, this theory satisfactorily explains both the conclusion reached by the plurality in *Arnett,* permitting the state to narrow the definition of a job, and the conclusion in *Vitek,* limiting the state's ability to transfer prisoners to mental institutions."]

mental disease and transferred to a mental hospital. [A] criminal conviction and sentence of imprisonment extinguish an individual's right to freedom from confinement for the term of his sentence, but they do not authorize the State to classify him as mentally ill and to subject him to involuntary psychiatric treatment without affording him additional due process protections." [c]

8. (a) *A state is not free to employ such procedures as it pleases for adjudicating a claim it need not have created.* In LOGAN v. ZIMMERMAN BRUSH CO., 455 U.S. 422, 102 S.Ct. 1148, 71 L.Ed.2d 265 (1982), appellant filed a charge with the Illinois Employment Practices Commission, alleging that his employment had been lawfully terminated because of his physical handicap. This triggered the Commission's statutory obligation to convene a fact-finding conference within 120 days, but, apparently through inadvertence, the conference was scheduled five days *after* expiration of the statutory period. The state court held that the failure to convene a conference within 120 days deprived the Commission of jurisdiction to consider appellant's claim under the Illinois Fair Employment Practices Act (FEPA). The Court, per BLACKMUN, J., reversed, deeming appellant's FEPA claim "a species of property" protected by fourteenth amendment due process and holding that the state scheme had deprived appellant of his property right.

The Court pointed out that its recent cases had emphasized that "[t]he hallmark of property [is] an individual entitlement grounded in state law, which cannot be removed except 'for cause.' [And] an FEPA claim, which presumably can be surrendered for value, is at least as substantial as the right to an education labeled as property in *Goss v. Lopez.* Certainly, it would require a remarkable reading of a 'broad and majestic term' to conclude that a horse trainer's license is a protected property interest under the Fourteenth Amendment, while a state-created right to redress discrimination is not."

"Because the entitlement arises from statute, the [state supreme court] reasoned, it was the legislature's prerogative to establish the 'procedures to be followed upon a charge.' [This analysis] misunderstands the nature of the Constitution's due process guarantee. [B]ecause 'minimum [procedural] requirements [are] a matter of federal law, they are not diminished by the fact that the State may have specified its own procedures that it may deem adequate for determining the preconditions to adverse official action.' *Vitek.* Indeed, any other conclusion would allow the State to destroy at will virtually any state-created property interest. The Court has considered and rejected such an approach [quoting from that portion of the *Vitek* opinion quoting with approval from Powell, J.'s concurring opinion in *Arnett*].

"Of course, the State remains free to create substantive defenses or immunities for use in adjudication—or to eliminate its statutorily created causes of action altogether—just as it can amend or terminate its welfare or employment programs [or adjust benefit levels]. [But the 120-day limitation] is a procedural

c. Cf. *Washington v. Harper,* 494 U.S. 210, 110 S.Ct. 1028, 108 L.Ed.2d 178 (1990) (also discussed in Part II infra). The Court recognized that a state prisoner had a "significant liberty interest," protected by the Due Process Clause, in avoiding the forced administration of antipsychotic drugs. Thus, such treatment could be refused unless certain preconditions were met and procedural safeguards were established to ensure that the prisoners' interests were taken into account. But the Court went on to hold that the state's administrative hearing procedures (an unconsenting prisoner was entitled to a hearing before a committee of medical professionals) satisfied procedural due process; a judicial hearing is not a prerequisite for the involuntary treatment of prison inmates.

limitation on the claimant's ability to assert his rights, not a substantive element of the FEPA claim."

(b) *Why can't a state "enfeeble" any entitlement it creates?* Consider Easterbrook, *Substance and Due Process,* 1982 Sup.Ct.Rev. 85–86, 109–110, 120: "The process a legislature describes for vindicating the entitlements that it creates is a way of indicating how effective its plan should be. The more process it affords, the more the legislature values the entitlements and thus is willing to sacrifice to avoid mistakes. A court that protects the legislative power to define substantive entitlements ought to give it control of process as well.

"[The] Court's justification for specifying process once the statute has specified substance is that 'any other conclusion would allow the State to destroy at will virtually any state-created property interest.' This would be a good argument if the Court could explain why a state may not destroy the interest it creates, at least prospectively. But the Court has never so argued. Under the Court's decisions legislatures are free to enact precatory statutes, statutes that contain no rules of decision, retroactive statutes, statutes that lack any methods of enforcement, statutes creating absolute immunities, and otherwise to have vacuous 'entitlements.' To use some invented numbers, if states may elect ten percent reliability in enforcement (the amount of adherence to a precatory statute), why can they not elect ninety percent (the amount obtained from rudimentary procedures)? Why, in other words, is the expedient of enfeebling a statutory entitlement by providing 'deficient' procedures out of bounds? The Court's cases contain no answers to this question because they are not consistent. There is no single view that could be respected in the name of stare decisis.

"[Illinois] need not have created any right to be free of discrimination because of handicap or given the right of any particular dimensions. That being so, [Illinois] also should have been allowed to employ such procedure as it pleased for adjudicating (or not adjudicating) Logan's claim.[105] "

(c) *Why wasn't Logan's right to sue the Commission in tort for its negligence in losing his claim sufficient to satisfy due process?* The Zimmerman Brush Company had another argument in support of the Illinois Supreme Court's decision. As described in Smolla, p. 352 fn. a supra, at 860, the Company argued that even if Logan possessed an "entitlement" under Illinois law "no federal due process violation existed, because Logan could sue the Commission for damages under the Illinois Court of Claims Act for having negligently destroyed his 'property'—his [FEPA cause of action]. Logan in effect had an action for 'malpractice' against the Commission, just as he would have had an action against his own attorney if the attorney had negligently caused Logan's claim to lapse. Under the reasoning in *Parratt v. Taylor* [p. 352 fn. d supra], the Company argued, the state had not deprived Logan of property without due process since the state's own tort remedies were adequate to make Logan whole." This argument, responded the Court, "misses *Parratt's* point":

"In *Parratt,* the Court emphasized that it was dealing with 'a tortious loss [of] property as a result of a random and unauthorized act by a state employee [rather than] some established procedure.' Here, in contrast, it is the state system itself that destroys a complainant's property interest, by operation of law, whenever the Commission fails to convene a timely conference—whether the

105. [As] the Supreme Court of Illinois saw things, the statute (effectively) allowed Logan's claim to be distinguished for no reason at all. Thus the statute gave Logan no property right. *Bishop.* The Court never told us why it was disregarding the state court's construction of the state's statute.

Commission's action is taken through negligence, maliciousness, or otherwise. *Parratt* was not designed to reach such a situation. Unlike the complainant in *Parratt,* Logan is challenging not the Commission's error, but the 'established state procedure' that destroys his entitlement without according him proper procedural safeguards.

"In any event, the Court's decisions suggest that, absent 'the necessity of quick action by the State or the impracticality of providing any predeprivation process,' a post-deprivation hearing here would be constitutionally inadequate. *Parratt.* [That] is particularly true where, as here, the State's only post-termination process comes in the form of an independent tort action.[10] Seeking redress through a tort suit is apt to be a lengthy and speculative process, which in a situation such as this one will never make the complainant entirely whole: the Illinois Court of Claims Act does not provide for reinstatement [and] even a successful suit will not vindicate entirely Logan's right to be free from discriminatory treatment."

(d) *The post-deprivation due process doctrine: reconciling Zimmerman Brush and Parratt.* The relationship between *Zimmerman Brush* and *Parratt,* observes Smolla at 861–62, "parallels the relationship that arguably existed between *Constantineau* and *Paul.* Random and unauthorized harm caused by the state, for which the state itself provides a remedy, does not implicate the Constitution. But when the state consciously enacts a system that places its imprimatur on arbitrary conduct, whether it be through a bizarre posting statute or a capricious administrative structure for handling handicap discrimination, federal court intervention under the due process clause is warranted."

9. *"[I]t is settled that the 'bitter with the sweet' approach misconceives the [due process] guarantee."* CLEVELAND BOARD OF EDUCATION v. LOUDERMILL, 470 U.S. 532, 105 S.Ct. 1487, 84 L.Ed.2d 494 (1985): Under Ohio law, respondents Loudermill and Donnelly were "classified civil servants" who could be discharged only for cause. Loudermill, a security guard, was dismissed because of dishonesty in filling out his employment application. He was not afforded an opportunity to respond to the dishonesty charge or to challenge the dismissal.[a] Donnelly was fired as a bus mechanic because he had failed an eye examination. He appealed to the Civil Service Commission, which ordered him reinstated without pay. "The statute plainly supports the conclusion [that] respondents possessed property rights in continued employment," but petitioners contended that "the property right is defined by, and conditioned on, the legislature's choice of procedures for its deprivation. [Petitioners stress] that in addition to specifying the grounds for termination, the statute sets out procedures by which termination may take place [and that these procedures were followed]. [Therefore,] '[t]o require additional procedures would in effect expand

10. In *Ingraham v. Wright* [p. 354 fn. e supra] the Court concluded that state tort remedies provided adequate process for students subjected to corporal punishment in school, [but it] emphasized that the state scheme "preserved what 'has always been the law of the land,' " [and] that adding additional safeguards would be unduly burdensome. Here neither of those rationales is available. Terminating potentially meritorious claims in a random manner is hardly a practice in line with our common-law traditions. And the State's abandonment of the challenged practice [after the inception of the present litigation] makes it difficult to argue that requiring a determination on the merits will impose undue burdens on the state administrative process.

a. On his 1979 job application, Loudermill stated that he had never been convicted of a felony. Eleven months later it was discovered that he had been convicted of grand larceny in 1968. Loudermill maintained that he had thought his larceny conviction was for a misdemeanor rather than a felony.

the scope of the property interest itself.' " The Court, per WHITE, J., rejected this approach:

"[Petitioners' argument] has its genesis in the plurality opinion in *Arnett.* [This approach] garnered three votes in *Arnett,* but was specifically rejected by the other six Justices. [I]n light of [*Vitek* and *Zimmerman Brush*], it is settled that the 'bitter with the sweet' approach misconceives the [due process] guarantee. If a clearer holding is needed, we provide it today. The point is straightforward: the Due Process Clause provides that certain substantive rights—life, liberty, and property—cannot be deprived except pursuant to constitutionally adequate procedures. The categories of substance and procedure are distinct. Were the rule otherwise, the Clause would be reduced to a mere tautology. 'Property' cannot be defined by the procedures provided for its deprivation any more than can life or liberty. The right to due process 'is conferred, not by legislative grace, but by constitutional guarantee. While the legislature may elect not to confer a property interest in [public] employment, it may not constitutionally authorize the deprivation of such an interest, once conferred, without appropriate procedural safeguards.' *Arnett* (Powell, J., [concurring opinion]); see id. (White, J., [concurring in part]). [O]nce it is determined that the Due Process Clause applies, 'the question remains what process is due.' The answer is not to be found in the Ohio statute." [b]

REHNQUIST, J., the sole Justice to dissent on this issue, maintained that the Fourteenth Amendment "does not support the conclusion that Ohio's effort to confer a limited form of tenure upon respondents resulted in the creation of a 'property right' in their employment":

"Here, as in *Arnett,* '[t]he employee's statutorily defined right is not a guarantee against removal without cause in the abstract, but such a guarantee as enforced by the procedures which [the Ohio legislature] has designated for the determination of cause' (opinion of Rehnquist, J.). [We] ought to recognize the totality of the State's definition of the property right in question, and not merely seize upon one of several paragraphs in a unitary statute to proclaim that in that paragraph the State has inexorably conferred upon a civil service employee something which it is powerless to qualify in the next paragraph of the statute. [While] it does not impose a federal definition of property, the Court departs from the full breadth of the holding in *Roth* by its selective choice from among the sentences the Ohio legislature chooses to use in establishing and qualifying a right."

10. *A hard look at Loudermill's substance-procedure distinction.* Did the *Loudermill* majority provide a convincing basis for its rejection of Justice Rehnquist's position? Can procedural problems, as the majority seemed to think, be neatly separated from substantive choices? See Tribe at 709–12. If the state is free to define and limit underlying substantive entitlements, why shouldn't it be equally free to define the procedure that goes with each entitlement? If substantive restrictions on entitlements can be adopted which have the effect of limiting procedural rights, why can't the government take the "intermediate course of limiting public benefits and opportunities in an explicitly procedural way"? See id. at 711. "Ultimately," concludes Professor Tribe, id. at 713, "the clarity of the demarcation the Court declared in *Loudermill* between the

b. The Court then held that respondents were not entitled to a "full adversarial hearing prior to adverse governmental action. [A]ll the process that is due is provided by a pretermination opportunity to respond, coupled with [a full post-termination hearing] as provided by the Ohio statute." This aspect of *Loudermill* is treated in Part II infra.

rights-conferring function and the process-prescribing function is illusory; the Court must eventually move toward more deference on matters of procedure or less deference on matters of substance. Since the former course would leave the due process clause with little content in the modern state, where so much has come to depend on relationships with government, the latter seems preferable, certainly in relationships created to meet the needs of the individuals involved, and probably also in relationships created to meet the needs of others."

II. WHAT KIND OF HEARING—AND WHEN?

GOLDBERG v. KELLY, 397 U.S. 254, 90 S.Ct. 1011, 25 L.Ed.2d 287 (1970), per BRENNAN, J. (Burger, C.J., and Black and Stewart, JJ., dissenting) held that due process requires an evidentiary hearing prior to termination of welfare benefits, stressing the "crucial factor [that] termination of aid pending resolution of a controversy over eligibility may deprive an *eligible* recipient of the very means by which to live while he waits. Since he lacks independent resources, his situation becomes immediately desperate. His need to concentrate upon [survival], in turn, adversely affects his ability to seek redress from the welfare bureaucracy." The hearing "need not take the form of a judicial or quasi-judicial trial," but a recipient must have "timely and adequate notice detailing the reasons for a proposed termination, and an effective opportunity to defend by confronting any adverse witnesses and by presenting his own arguments and evidence orally." The Court declined to "say that counsel must be provided" but the recipient must be allowed to retain counsel.

Consider JERRY MASHAW, *Due Process in the Administrative State* 35–36 (1985): "[T]he underprotectionist critic may claim that the due process revolution has stopped short of its essential goals: building legal security and democratic control into the administrative state. Legal security for the welfare claimant, for example, would at a minimum require that the hearing right be oriented to the issues that produce erroneous deprivations and that the recipient class has the necessary resources to make use of hearings to protect its interests. Yet neither condition seems to obtain. A careful study of errors suggests that they occur at least as often through misinterpretation of policy as through mistakes on questions of fact. The *Goldberg* decision limits due process hearings to facts. Moreover, welfare recipients generally lack the human or material resources to make use of the hearings *Goldberg* provided. Except for an occasional flurry of political activism expressed through appeals requests, hearings have been utilized about as infrequently after *Goldberg* as before.

"This sort of criticism may be pressed further to suggest that the hearing technique—the demand for individualized and detailed attention through quasi-judicial process—simply misses the point of the welfare state. The problem has become one of mass, not individual, justice. Legal security for the class of welfare claimants lies, not in hearings, but in good management. Unless due process, therefore, comes to terms with administration, becomes systems—rather than case-oriented, it will be irrelevant.

"The underprotectionist case goes further. *Goldberg*'s hearing rights extend only to the protection of what can be termed 'positive entitlements,' substantive interests already enjoying common law or statutory legal significance. Due process hearings are thus only an addition to the legal security of existing rights. They provide no access to the administrative forums in which rights are being created and no opportunity to avoid the application of general rules on the basis of individual circumstances. *Goldberg*'s hearing rights thus leave untouched the contemporary concern with (1) the remoteness of administrative policy making from immediate participation by affected interests and (2) the unfairness and irrationality that seem to attend bureaucratic implementation of general rules." [a]

MATHEWS v. ELDRIDGE, 424 U.S. 319, 96 S.Ct. 893, 47 L.Ed.2d 18 (1976), per POWELL, J., held that although Social Security disability benefits constitute "a statutorily created 'property' interest protected by the Fifth Amendment," due process does not require a *Goldberg*-type hearing prior to their termination on the ground that "the worker is no longer disabled": "In recent years this Court increasingly has had occasion to consider the extent to which due process requires an evidentiary hearing prior to the deprivation of some type of property interest even if such a hearing is provided thereafter. In only one case, *Goldberg,* has the Court held that a hearing closely approximating a judicial trial is necessary. [For example,] *Bell v. Burson* [held] that due process required only that the prerevocation hearing involve a probable-cause determination as to the fault of the licensee, noting that the hearing 'need not take the form of a full adjudication of the question of liability.' [O]ur prior decisions indicate that identification of the specific dictates of due process generally requires consideration of three distinct factors: First, the private interest that will be affected by the official action; second, the risk of an erroneous deprivation of such interest through the procedures used, and the probable value, if any, of additional or substitute procedural safeguards; and finally, the government's interest, including the function involved and the fiscal and administrative burdens that the additional or substitute procedural requirement would entail." [a]

a. At this point, Professor Mashaw turns to *O'Bannon v. Town Court Nursing Center,* 447 U.S. 773, 100 S.Ct. 2467, 65 L.Ed.2d 506 (1980), per Stevens, J., holding that, because nursing home residents had no government-established entitlement to continued residence at a particular home, they had no right to a hearing before the government decertified the home as provider of services at government expenses under Medicare and Medicaid agreements. Decertification would force the patients to seek care elsewhere and would probably mean that they would be separated from each and might mean that they would have to relocate away from their friends and families. But, responded the Court, Medicaid provisions only give recipients "the right to choose among a range of *qualified* providers, without government interference, [not the right] to enter an unqualified home and demand a hearing to certify it, nor [the right] to continue to receive benefits for care in a home that has been decertified. [A]lthough the regulations do protect patients by limiting the circumstances under which a *home* may transfer or discharge a Medicaid recipient, they do not purport to limit the Government's right to make a transfer necessary by decertifying a facility. [Whatever rights the patients may have against the nursing home] for failing to maintain its status[,] enforcement by [state and federal agencies] of their valid regulations did not directly affect their legal rights or deprive them of any constitutionally protected interest in life, liberty or property."

Blackmun, J., concurred, but found the Court's analysis "simplistic and unsatisfactory." He did not find the distinction between "direct" and "indirect" losses helpful and, in any event, had "great difficulty concluding that the patients' loss of their home should be characterized as 'indirect and incidental.'" For extensive criticism of *O'Bannon,* see Mashaw, supra, at 36–41; Tribe, supra, at 766–67; Terrell, supra, at 927–35.

a. The Court subsequently utilized the factors set forth in *Eldridge* in analyzing *Ingraham v. Wright* (corporal punishment in public schools) and *Parham v. J.R.* (parents' commitment of minor children), both discussed in the notes following this case. The *Eldridge* "balancing approach" was also utilized in, e.g., *Dixon v. Love,* 431 U.S. 105, 97 S.Ct. 1723, 52 L.Ed.2d 172 (1977) (Blackmun, J.) (no prior evidentiary hearing required for driver license revocation pursuant to regulation mandating such revocation if license had been suspended three times within 10 years for conviction of traffic violations); *Memphis Light, Gas & Water Division v. Craft,* 436 U.S. 1, 98 S.Ct. 1554, 56 L.Ed.2d 30 (1978) (Powell, J.) (municipal utility must provide its customers with some administrative procedure for entertaining complaints before cutting off services); *Mackey v. Montrym,* 443 U.S. 1, 99 S.Ct. 2612,

First, in contrast to *Goldberg*, "eligibility for disability benefits [is] not based upon financial need." Rather, such benefits are "wholly unrelated to the worker's income or support from many other sources, such as earnings of other family members, workmen's compensation awards, tort claims awards, savings, [insurance, pensions and public assistance.]" Thus, "there is less reason here than in *Goldberg* to depart from the ordinary principle, established by our decisions, that something less than an evidentiary hearing is sufficient prior to adverse administrative action."

Second, "the potential value of an evidentiary hearing, or even oral presentation to the decisionmaker, is substantially less in this context than in *Goldberg*." Here, "a medical assessment of the worker's physical or mental condition is required. This is a more sharply focused and easily documented decision than the typical determination of welfare entitlement [where] a wide variety of information may be deemed relevant, and issues of witness credibility and veracity often are critical to the decision-making process." Further, "the information critical [in the disability case] usually is derived from medical sources, [which are likely] to communicate more effectively through written documents than are welfare recipients or the lay witnesses supporting their cause."

Third, as to the "additional cost in terms of money and administrative burden" if pretermination hearings were required, "at some point the benefit of an additional safeguard to the individual affected by the administrative action and to society in terms of increased assurance that the action is just, may be outweighed by the cost. Significantly, the cost of protecting those whom the preliminary administrative process has identified as likely to be found undeserving may in the end come out of the pockets of the deserving since resources available for any particular program of social welfare are not unlimited."

Finally, "in assessing what process is due in this case, substantial weight must be given to the good-faith judgments of the individuals charged by Congress with the administration of the social welfare system that the procedures they have provided assure fair consideration of the entitlement claims of individuals." [b]

The *Eldridge* approach, observes Mashaw, *The Supreme Court's Due Process Calculus for Administrative Adjudication in Mathews v. Eldridge*, 44 U.Chi.L. Rev. 28, 39 (1976), "is subjective and impressionistic. [The Court] assumes that disability recipients are less dependent on income support than welfare recipi-

61 L.Ed.2d 321 (1979) (Burger, C.J.) (license of driver lawfully arrested for drunk driving may be suspended for 90 days without prior hearing for refusing to take breath-analysis test so long as immediate post-suspension hearing is available; *Little v. Streater*, 452 U.S. 1, 101 S.Ct. 2202, 68 L.Ed.2d 627 (1981) (Burger, C.J.) (state's refusal to pay cost of blood grouping test for indigent defendant in paternity action, a proceeding with " 'quasi-criminal' overtones," denies him "meaningful opportunity to be heard" and thus violates procedural due process); *Walters v. National Association of Radiation Survivors*, 473 U.S. 305, 105 S.Ct. 3180, 87 L.Ed.2d 220 (1985) (Rehnquist, J.) (federal statute limiting to $10 the fee that may be paid an attorney or agent representing one seeking benefits from Veterans Administration (VA) for service-connected death or disability does not violate procedural due process; since benefits are not granted on basis of need, they are more like social security benefits involved in *Eldridge* than welfare benefits involved in *Goldberg*; elimination of fee limitation "would bid fair to complicate a proceeding which Congress wished to keep as simple as possible").

b. Brennan, J., joined by Marshall, J., dissented: "[I]n the present case, it is indicated that because disability benefits were terminated there was a foreclosure upon the Eldridge home and the family's furniture was repossessed, forcing Eldridge, his wife and children to sleep in one bed. [It] is also no argument that a worker, who has been placed in the untenable position of having been denied disability benefits, may still seek other forms of public assistance." Stevens, J., did not participate.

ents. This assumption is buttressed only by the notion that welfare is for the needy and disability insurance is for prior taxpayers. [But], any number of circumstances might make a terminated welfare recipient's plight less desperate than that of his disabled SSA counterpart,[42] or vice versa." Mashaw finds several of the *Eldridge* conclusions questionable, especially that it was dealing with an essentially medical determination. Id. at 40. "The *Goldberg* decision's approach to prescribing due process—specification of the attributes of adjudicatory hearings by analogy to judicial trial—makes the Court resemble an administrative engineer with an outdated professional education. It is at once intrusive and ineffectual. Retreating from this stance, [*Eldridge*] relies on the administrator's good faith—an equally troublesome posture in a political system that depends heavily on judicial review for the protection of countermajoritarian values." Id. at 58.

Consider, too, Tribe at 718: "[The *Eldridge*] Court's unwillingness to consider values beyond accuracy of result in the context of a utilitarian balancing test when deciding what process is due, and the Court's grant of a strong presumption of constitutionality to statutory procedural provisions, amount to a serious abdication of traditional notions of judicial responsibility under the due process clauses. Like many other provisions of the Constitution, the due process requirement represented a decision on the part of the Framers to safeguard certain rights and values, those considered fundamental in a free society and yet unusually vulnerable to the risk of denial by the majority. Adequate protection of such 'core' concerns cannot be afforded by 'balancing' the general interests of the majority against those of the individual. [Moreover, there] is no reason to believe that the judiciary would be better suited to that task of utilitarian comparison than the legislature even if it were called for."

---

1. *"Educational due process" cases.* (a) GOSS v. LOPEZ, 419 U.S. 565, 95 S.Ct. 729, 42 L.Ed.2d 725 (1975) (also discussed at p. 352 fn. b supra), per WHITE, J., held that "as a general rule," before a student is given a temporary suspension (ten days or less) from public school, due process requires "that the student be given oral or written notice of the charges against him and, if he denies them, an explanation of the evidence the authorities have and an opportunity to present his side of the story": "[T]otal exclusion from the educational process for more than a trivial period, and certainly if the suspension is for 10 days, is a serious event in the life of the suspended child. [T]he State is constrained to recognize a student's legitimate entitlement to a public education as a property interest which is protected by the Due Process Clause and which may not be taken away for misconduct without adherence to the minimum procedures required by that clause. [Due process] also forbids arbitrary deprivations of liberty. [Many] charges could seriously damage the students' standing with their fellow pupils and their teachers as well as interfere with later opportunities for higher education and employment."

POWELL, J., joined by Burger, C.J., and Blackmun and Rehnquist, JJ., dissented: "Whether *any* procedural protections are due" turns on the extent to which one will be "condemned to suffer *grievous* loss," [but] the record in this

42. The terminated [welfare] recipient may have access to home or general relief depending upon his residence, whereas the disability claimant in a different state or locality may not. The disability claimant may be totally dependent for his livelihood on the disability payments, whereas the welfare recipient who is terminated may have been receiving a small AFDC payment to supplement inadequate family earnings.

case reflects no educational injury to appellees. Each completed the semester in which the suspension occurred and performed at least as well as he or she had in previous years. [Few] rulings would interfere more extensively in the daily functioning of schools than subjecting routine discipline to the formalities and judicial oversight of due process." [a]

(b) But cf. INGRAHAM v. WRIGHT, 430 U.S. 651, 97 S.Ct. 1401, 51 L.Ed.2d 711 (1977) (also discussed at p. 354 fn. e supra), per Powell, J., holding that disciplinary corporal punishment in public school "implicates a constitutionally protected liberty interest," but that procedural due process does not require notice and an opportunity to be heard prior to imposition of that punishment as it is authorized and limited by Florida common law: "Were it not for the common-law privilege permitting teachers to inflict reasonable corporal punishment [and] the availability of the traditional remedies for abuse, the case for requiring advance procedural safeguards would be strong indeed. [But the disciplinarian] must exercise prudence and restraint. [And if] the punishment inflicted is later found to have been excessive [the] school authorities inflicting it may be held liable in damages to the child and, if malice is shown, they may be subject to criminal penalties.

"[Moreover,] because paddlings are usually inflicted in response to conduct directly observed by teachers in their presence, the risk that a child will be paddled without cause is typically insignificant. In the ordinary case, a disciplinary paddling neither threatens seriously to violate any substantive rights nor condemns the child 'to suffer grievous loss of any kind.'

"[T]he low incidence of abuse, and the availability of established judicial remedies in the event of abuse, distinguish this case from *Goss*. [The] subsequent [proceedings] available in this case may be viewed as affording substantially greater protection to the child than the informal conference mandated by *Goss*. [E]ven if the need for advance procedural safeguards were clear, the question would remain whether the incremental benefit could justify the [cost.] 'At some point the benefit of an additional safeguard [may] be outweighed by the cost.' *Eldridge*. We think that point has been reached in this case."

WHITE, J., joined by Brennan, Marshall and Stevens, JJ., dissented: "[The common law] tort action is utterly inadequate to protect against erroneous infliction of punishment for two reasons. First, under Florida law [the] student has no remedy at all for punishment imposed on the basis of mistaken facts, at least as long as the punishment was reasonable from the point of view of the disciplinarian, uninformed by any prior hearing. [Second], [the] lawsuit occurs after the punishment has been finally imposed. The infliction of physical pain is final and irreparable; it cannot be undone in a subsequent proceeding." [b]

a. Compare *Goss* with *Bethel School Dist. v. Fraser* (1986) (discussed in more detail at pp. 679–80 infra). Fraser, a high school senior, was suspended for two days for making a sexually suggestive speech at a school-sponsored assembly. The Court, per Burger, C.J., rejected Fraser's contention that his suspension violated due process because he had no way of knowing that his speech would subject him to disciplinary sanctions: "Given the school's need to be able to impose disciplinary sanctions for a wide range of unanticipated conduct disruptive of the educational process, the school disciplinary rules need not be as detailed as a criminal code which imposes criminal sanctions. Cf. *Arnett*. Two days' suspension from school does not rise to the level of a penal sanction calling for the full panoply of procedural due process protections applicable to a criminal prosecution. Cf. *Goss*. The school disciplinary rule proscribing 'obscene' language and the prespeech admonition of teachers gave adequate warning to Fraser that his lewd speech could subject him to sanctions."

b. Compare *Ingraham* and *Parratt* (p. 352 fn. d supra) with *Zimmerman Brush* (p. 357 supra).

(c) *Criticism of Ingraham.* "Government's interests in punishing guilty students first and asking questions about guilt later," maintain Alexander & Horton, *Ingraham v. Wright: A Primer for Cruel and Unusual Jurisprudence,* 52 S.Cal.L.Rev. 1305, 1384–85 (1979), "surely pale in significance when compared to the interests of innocent students in avoiding punishment.[282] Usually no emergency is averted by instantaneous corporal punishment.[283] The costs—monetary and otherwise—of providing pre-punishment hearings for the guilty are more than justified by the savings to the innocent. Finally, the burden imposed on the innocent in bringing post-deprivation actions is undoubtedly heavier than the burden imposed on government by a requirement of pre-punishment hearings. [In] none of the cases [upholding] a post-deprivation hearing was there both the strong likelihood of irreparable injury and the absence of a compelling justification for prompt action precluding a prior hearing."

"In other cases in which a post-deprivation hearing has been held adequate," emphasizes Rosenberg, *Ingraham v. Wright: The Supreme Court's Whipping Boy,* 78 Colum.L.Rev. 75, 91 (1978), "the interest involved was 'property' rather than 'liberty.' [Where] a liberty interest is invoked, the injured person is considerably less likely to be made whole by a belated award of damages. Particularly is this true in the case of corporal punishment, where the liberty interest is freedom from 'infliction of appreciable physical pain.'" Professor Rosenberg continues, id. at 93–94:

"To [the] very real barriers impairing vindication of the child's rights [by bringing a tort action][c] must be added not only the defense of sovereign immunity available to school boards, and the possible defense of good faith mistake available to teachers, but also the inadequacy of money damages as a means of repairing physical and psychological injury deliberately inflicted on a child.

"[The *Ingraham* Court] refused to attempt to distinguish between trivial and severe corporal punishment, while at the same time invoking [the] existence of common law and statutory restraints against *unreasonable* corporal punishment. In effect, the majority was asking the nation's school teachers to make the sorts of decisions about reasonableness that, if erroneous, could lead to tort liability, while at the same time acknowledging its own inability (or unwillingness) to make such judgments."

(d) *In defense of Ingraham.* "Tort law," observes Smolla, *The Displacement of Federal Due Process Claims by State Tort Remedies,* 1982 U.Ill.L.Rev. 831, 850–51, "has always awarded money for the taking of interests without any objectively discernable value—millions of dollars are awarded for lost reputation, for emotional distress, and for pain and suffering. [A] substantial damage award against a school teacher for excessive corporal punishment is easily conceivable, particularly in communities in which a consensus against such conduct prevails. It is not at all obvious that the threat of such awards is any less a deterrent to

282. [*Ingraham*] is an easy case in this respect, considering that a more reparable student interest (freedom from 10-day suspension) outweighed similar government interests in *Goss.*"

283. In that respect, corporal punishment differs from temporary suspensions, without pre-deprivation hearings, which may avert dangers to persons and property.

c. Rosenberg notes, e.g., that it may prove difficult to secure an attorney willing to accept a case of this sort; completion of state court actions may take years, during which time "the child's memory of the controverted events may dim"; the formality of a jury trial is "considerably less conducive to articulate testimony by the public than an informal pre-punishment hearing would be"; and that a teacher is more likely to be believed than his or her ex-pupil. See id. at 92–93.

misconduct than internal administrative hearings, in which teachers who know the administrative ropes may often be able to prevail in proceedings stacked against students.

"[Professor Rosenberg's point] that the Supreme Court preferred to allow school teachers to make decisions about the reasonableness of discipline that the Court felt unable or unwilling to make is correct, but the Court's reticence is grounds for criticism only if one first assumes that federal court judges are or should be better qualified than school teachers to make such judgments. * * * Local school boards can always alter punishment policies and procedures, and they are accountable through the political process if parents or students are displeased. As long as a state keeps its courts open to police abuses there is enough 'due process of law' available to guarantee balance against excess.

"[*Ingraham*] did not totally eliminate federal concern with paddling—a due process violation could still exist if a state were to disable its own courts in their policing of local practices—but it placed federal law in a back-up role. *Ingraham* is in this sense consistent with the Court's general movement in procedural due process cases, toward initial deference to local prerogative in setting procedural norms when the substantive interests at stake are heavily imbued with localized values."

(e) BOARD OF CURATORS v. HOROWITZ, 435 U.S. 78, 98 S.Ct. 948, 55 L.Ed.2d 124 (1978), per REHNQUIST, J., "decline[d] to ignore the historic judgment of educators [and] formalize the academic dismissal process by requiring a hearing." Because of dissatisfaction with her clinical performance and personal hygiene, and after notice from and discussion with the dean of the medical school, a state medical school student was put on probation. After continued dissatisfaction with her work, and pursuant to a faculty-student council recommendation (supported by the dean and the provost), she was dismissed from school in her final year. Assuming but not deciding that there was "a liberty interest" in pursuing a medical career, "respondent has been awarded at least as much due process as the Fourteenth Amendment requires." The Court underscored the distinction between "academic evaluations of a student" and "disciplinary determinations," contrasting the instant case with *Goss,* where "[t]he requirement of a hearing [could] 'provide a meaningful hedge against erroneous action.' The decision to dismiss respondent, by comparison, rested on the academic judgment of school officials," a judgment "by its nature more subjective and evaluative than the typical factual questions presented in the average disciplinary decision."

2. "*Family due process.*" (a) Balancing the three factors set forth in *Eldridge,* PARHAM v. J.R., 442 U.S. 584, 99 S.Ct. 2493, 61 L.Ed.2d 101 (1979) (also discussed at p. 189 fn. a and p. 249 supra), per BURGER, C.J., held that a preadmission adversary hearing is not required when parents (or a state agency acting in loco parentis) seek to commit their minor children to a mental institution—so long as the commitment is approved by an "independent medical judgment." The Court "assume[d] that a child has a protectible interest not only in being free of unnecessary bodily restraints but also in not being labelled erroneously" as "mentally ill," but concluded that "our precedents permit the parents to retain a substantial, if not the dominant, role in the decision, absent a finding of neglect or abuse, and that the traditional presumption that the parents act in the best interests of the child should apply. [But the] child's rights and the nature of the commitment decision are such that parents cannot

always have absolute and unreviewable discretion [to institutionalize their child]. [They] retain plenary authority [to do so], subject to a physician's independent examination and medical judgment." In the course of a wide-ranging opinion the Court observed:

"That some parents 'may at times be acting against the interests of their children' [is reason] for caution, [but] hardly a reason to discard wholesale those pages of human experience that teach that parents generally do act in the child's best interests. The statist notion that governmental power should supersede parental authority in *all* cases because *some* parents abuse and neglect children is repugnant to American tradition.

"[Appellees] urge that [the] liberty interest of the child and the likelihood of parental abuse require us to hold that the parents' decision to have a child admitted to a mental hospital must be subjected to an exacting constitutional scrutiny, including a formal adversary, pre-admission hearing. [This argument] sweeps too broadly. Simply because the decision of a parent is not agreeable to a child or because it involves risks does not automatically transfer the power to make that decision from the parents to [the] state. The same characterizations can be made for a tonsillectomy, appendectomy, or other medical procedure. Most children, even in adolescence, simply are not able to make sound judgments concerning many decisions, including their need for medical care or treatment. Parents can and must make those judgments.

"[Appellees] place particular reliance on *Planned Parenthood v. Danforth* [Sec. 2 supra], arguing that its holding indicates how little deference to parents is appropriate when the child is exercising a constitutional right. [But that case] involved an absolute parental veto over the child's ability to obtain an abortion. Parents in Georgia in no sense have an absolute right to commit their children to state mental hospitals; the statute requires [each regional hospital superintendent] to exercise independent judgment as to the child's need for confinement.

"[W]hat process is constitutionally due cannot be divorced from the nature of the ultimate decision that is being made. [Here,] the questions are essentially medical in character. [W]e recently stated in *Addington v. Texas,* 439 U.S. 908, 99 S.Ct. 276, 58 L.Ed.2d 254 (1979),[a] that the determination of 'whether a person is mentally ill turns on the *meaning* of the facts which must be interpreted by expert psychiatrists and psychologists.' [We reject] the notion that the shortcomings of specialists can always be avoided by shifting the decision [to] an untrained judge or administrative hearing officer after a judicial-type hearing. Even after a hearing, the nonspecialist decisionmaker must make a medical-psychiatric decision. Common human experience and scholarly opinions suggest that the supposed protections of an adversary proceeding to determine the appropriateness of medical decisions for the commitment and treatment of mental and emotional illness may well be more illusory than real. * * *

a. *Addington* held that one's interest in the outcome of a civil commitment proceeding is so important that due process requires the state to justify confinement by "clear and convincing" evidence, rather than the normal "preponderance of the evidence" standard. Consider Note, 93 Harv.L.Rev. 89, 98 (1979): "It is difficult to reconcile *Parham* with *Addington.* [In] insisting on a strict standard of proof [*Addington*] assumed that an individual could not be confined without an adversary hearing. In *Parham,* by contrast, the Court allowed minors to be institutionalized with fewer procedural standards than is required for the termination of welfare benefits. The presumption that parents or state agencies will act in a child's best interests is too tenuous a rationale to justify the denial of an adversary hearing."

" '[P]rocedural due process rules are shaped by the risk of error inherent in the truthfinding process as applied to the generality of cases, not the rare exceptions.' *Eldridge.* In general, we are satisfied that an independent medical decision-making process, [followed] by additional periodic review of a child's condition, will protect children who should not be admitted; we do not believe the risks of error in that process would be significantly reduced by a more formal, judicial-type hearing."

Concurring and dissenting in part, BRENNAN, J., joined by Marshall and Stevens, JJ., agreed that the parent-child relationship "militate[s] in favor of postponement of formal commitment proceedings and against mandatory adversary preconfinement commitment hearings." But "[w]hile the question of the frequency of postadmission review hearings may properly be deferred, the right to at least one post-admission hearing can and should be affirmed now." "This case is governed by the rule of *Danforth.* The right to be free from wrongful incarceration, physical intrusion, and stigmatization has significance for the individual surely as great as the right to an abortion. [Indeed,] *Danforth* involved only a potential dispute between parent and child, whereas here a break in family autonomy has actually resulted in the parents' decision to surrender custody of their child to a state mental institution. [A] child who has been ousted from his family has even greater need for an independent advocate." [b]

(b) *Parental prerogatives and governmental intrusions: Parham and Ingraham compared.* Consider Burt, *The Constitution of the Family,* 1979 Sup.Ct.Rev. 329, 332–33: "The Court spoke in *Parham* as if it were upholding parental prerogatives against governmental intrusions. [But the parents in that case] were not seeking to resist governmental power over their children; they were invoking that power by attempting to confine their children in state psychiatric institutions.

"This paean to parental prerogatives would have had greater relevance if state officials had sought to impose behavioral controls on children against their parent's wishes. The Court did consider a case two years earlier that directly implicated that question. School officials had administered corporal punishment to children. [In *Ingraham,* the] Court majority, composed of the same conservative nucleus as in *Parham* [but here joined by Stewart, J., with White, J., dissenting], ruled that school officials were free to disregard parental objections to this form of behavior control of their children. Justice Powell [said this] for the Court: 'Although the early cases viewed the authority of the teacher as deriving from the parents, [this concept] has been replaced by the view [that] the State itself may impose such corporal punishment as is reasonably necessary for the proper education of the child and for the maintenance of group discipline.' So much for the American tradition—paraded in *Parham* as well as 'the early cases'—that 'governmental power should [not] supersede parental authority.' "

(c) *"The subtleties and nuances of psychiatric diagnoses": Parham and Vitek compared.* The *Parham* Court, observes Mashaw, *Due Process in the Administrative State* 111 (1985), did not believe that a minor need be given a hearing prior to commitment to a mental institution, "apparently in substantial part because a hearing could provide little additional protection from error * * *. Yet, somehow, when in *Vitek* [p. 355 supra] the question was whether a prisoner should have a hearing prior to being transferred to a mental hospital, the

b. See also Note, 93 Harv.L.Rev. 89, 94 (1979).

suggestion that psychiatric judgment was involved elicited the following judicial response: 'The medical nature of the [inquiry] does not justify dispensing with due process requirements. *It is precisely the subtleties and nuances of psychiatric diagnoses that justify the requirement of adversary hearings.*'" [Emphasis added by Mashaw.] See also Garvey, *Children and the Idea of Liberty*, 68 Ky. L.J. 809, 826–30 (1979–80).

(d) *Parental status termination proceedings.* LASSITER v. DEPARTMENT OF SOCIAL SERVICES, 452 U.S. 18, 101 S.Ct. 2153, 68 L.Ed.2d 640 (1981), per STEWART, J., rejected the view that due process requires the appointment of counsel in every parental status termination proceeding involving indigent parents and left the appointment of counsel in such proceedings to be determined by the state courts on a case-by-case basis: "The pre-eminent generalization that emerges from this Court's precedents on an indigent's right to appointed counsel is that such a right has been recognized to exist only where the litigant may lose his physical liberty if he loses the litigation. * * * Significantly, as a litigant's interest in personal liberty diminishes, so does his right to appointed counsel. [Thus, *Gagnon v. Scarpelli,* 411 U.S. 778, 93 S.Ct. 1756, 36 L.Ed.2d 656 (1973),] declined to hold that indigent probationers have, per se, a right to counsel at revocation hearings, and instead left the decision whether counsel should be appointed to be made on a case-by-case basis."

The Court then held that in the circumstances of this case the trial judge did not deny Ms. Lassiter due process when he failed to appoint counsel for her: "[The] case presented no specially troublesome points of law, either procedural or substantive. While hearsay evidence was no doubt admitted, and while Ms. Lassiter no doubt left incomplete her defense that the Department had not adequately assisted her in rekindling her interest in her son, the weight of the evidence that she had few sparks of such an interest was sufficiently great that the presence of counsel for [her] could not have made a determinative difference." [c]

BLACKMUN, J., joined by Brennan and Marshall, JJ., dissented: "In this case, the State's aim is not simply to influence the parent-child relationship but to *extinguish* it. A termination of parental rights is both total and irrevocable. [It] is hardly surprising that this forced dissolution of the parent-child relationship has been recognized as a punitive sanction by courts, Congress, and commentators.

"[Faced] with a formal accusatory adjudication, with an adversary—the State—that commands great investigative and prosecutorial resources, with standards that involve ill-defined notions of fault and adequate parenting, and with the inevitable tendency of a court to apply subjective values or to defer to the State's 'expertise,' the defendant parent plainly is outstripped if he or she is without the assistance of 'the guiding hand of counsel.' When the parent is indigent, lacking in education, and easily intimidated by figures of authority, the imbalance may well become insuperable. [W]here as here, the threatened loss of liberty is severe and absolute, the State's role is so clearly adversarial and punitive, and the cost involved is relatively slight, there is no sound basis for refusing to recognize the right to counsel as a requisite of due process in a proceeding initiated by the State to terminate parental rights." [d]

c. Burger, C.J., who joined the Court's opinion, also added, in a brief concurrence responding to the dissenters, that the purpose of the parental status termination proceeding "was not 'punitive'" but "*protective* of the child's best interests."

d. The dissent then examined the termination hearing in considerable detail and, "[i]n

STEVENS, J., also dissented: "[T]he Court appears to treat this case as though it merely involved the deprivation of an interest in property that is less worthy of protection than a person's liberty. * * * Meeting the Court on its own terms, Justice Blackmun demonstrates that the *Eldridge* analysis requires the appointment of counsel in this type of case. I agree [but] would take one further step.

"In my opinion the reasons supporting the conclusion that [due process] entitle the defendant in a criminal case to representation by counsel apply with equal force to a case of this kind. The issue is one of fundamental fairness, not of weighing the pecuniary costs against the societal benefits. Accordingly, even if the costs to the State were not relatively insignificant but rather were just as great as the costs of providing prosecutors, judges, and defense counsel to ensure the fairness of criminal proceedings, I would reach the same result in this category of cases. For the value of protecting our liberty from deprivation by the State without due process of law is priceless." [e]

Compare *Lassiter* with SANTOSKY v. KRAMER, 455 U.S. 745, 102 S.Ct. 1388, 71 L.Ed.2d 599 (1982). Under New York law, the state may terminate, over parental objection, the rights of parents in their natural child upon a finding that the child is "permanently neglected," a finding that need be supported only by a "fair preponderance of the evidence." Because "the private interest affected is commanding; the risk of error from using a preponderance standard is substantial; and the countervailing government interest favoring that standard is comparatively slight," a 5–4 majority, per BLACKMUN, J., held that a "fair preponderance of the evidence" standard in such proceedings violates due process. Thus, before a state may terminate permanently the rights of parents in their natural child, it must support its allegations by at least "clear and convincing evidence." Such a standard "strikes a fair balance" between the parents' rights and the State's concerns and only such a standard "adequately conveys to the factfinder the level of subjective certainty [about] factual conclusions necessary to satisfy due process. [Unlike] a constitutional requirement of hearings or court-appointed counsel, a stricter standard of proof [than 'preponderance'] would reduce factual error without imposing substantial fiscal burdens upon the State."

Given the flexibility of the due process principle, dissenting JUSTICE REHNQUIST, joined by Burger, C.J., and White and O'Connor, JJ., thought it "obvious that a proper due process inquiry cannot be made by focusing upon one narrow provision of the challenged statutory scheme. [Courts] must examine *all* procedural protections offered by the State, and must assess the *cumulative* effect of such safeguards." The dissent then pointed to the "host of procedural protections" the state had "placed around parental rights and interests." In addition to the basic fairness of the statutory scheme, "the standard of proof chosen by New York clearly reflects a constitutionally permissible balance of the interests at stake in this case. [When] the interests of the child and the State in a stable, nurturing homelife are balanced against the interests of the parents in the rearing of their child, it cannot be said that either set of interests is so clearly

light of the unpursued avenues of defense, and of the experience petitioner underwent at this hearing," found "virtually incredible" the Court's conclusion that the termination proceeding was fundamentally fair.

e. For the view that the *Lassiter* Court forgot the teaching of *Gideon*—a reviewing court *cannot* conclude that "the case presented no specially troublesome points of law" on the basis of a record made *without* the assistance of counsel—see Kamisar, *Gideon v. Wainwright A Quarter–Century Later,* 10 Pace L.Rev. 343, 354–55 (1990).

paramount as to require that the risk of error be allocated to one side or the other."

3. "*Open analysis of the values at stake.*" Consider Nowak, *Foreword—Due Process Methodology in the Postincorporation World,* 70 J.Crim.L. & C. 397, 403 (1979): "Although one may disagree with the results in [cases such as *Parham,* which employed the *Eldridge* 'balancing test,'] the Court's open analysis of the values at stake [and] its attempt to accommodate the competing values of liberty and efficient administrative procedures certainly is preferable to the masking of such decisions through vaguely worded opinions or formalistic interpretations of constitutional provisions. [By contrast], in *Greenholtz v. Nebraska Prison Inmates* (1979) [p. 355 fn. a supra], [holding] that inmates of penal institutions were not entitled to due process protection in decisionmaking processes related to their possible release on parole, a majority of the Justices totally failed to analyze the basic due process question. [*Greenholtz,* per Burger, C.J., found] no liberty interest meriting protection by the due process clause at issue in these proceedings. The four Justices [Brennan, Marshall, Powell and Stevens] who dissented, at least in part, found that the individual prisoners had a liberty interest at stake [and thus] struggled openly with the problem of determining what, if any, procedural safeguards should be given to [them]. Even if one agreed with the majority's conclusion[,] [it is] easier to accept the separate opinion of Justice Powell, [recognizing] that inmates had an interest worthy of protection by the due process clause [but finding] that the need of efficiently processing inmate files outweighed the interest in freedom preceding the expiration of a properly imposed sentence. [Powell, J.'s] balancing approach is more satisfying than the majority's simple assertion that the possibility of parole is no more than a hope—'a hope which is not protected by due process.' By failing to adopt the Powell approach it was possible to avoid questions of fairness and value identification even in due process decisions."

4. *Separating the "property" or "liberty" issue from that of "what process is due."* While recent cases "fall short of providing the full inventory of procedural safeguards required by *Goldberg,*" observes ROBERT RABIN, *Job Security and Due Process: Monitoring Administrative Discretion Through A Reasons Requirement,* 44 U.Chi.L.Rev. 60, 74–79 (1976), they proceed from the same basic assumption about the relationship between property interests and procedural due process: at a minimum, procedural due process contemplates some kind of a hearing—an opportunity to join issue, through the presentation of evidence to a decision maker who is then obliged to reach a reasoned determination on the basis of the submissions. Underlying this conception is the vital interest in promoting an accurate decision, in assuring that facts have been correctly established and properly characterized in conformity with the applicable legal [standard.]

"By equating procedural due process with a value that seems to require a right to some kind of a hearing, the Court has correspondingly been driven to set too high a threshold when arriving at an initial determination of whether a property interest exists. In theory, of course, the inquiry into whether a form of government largess creates a property interest can, as the Court and commentators [and, in a way, the editors of this casebook] suggest, be neatly separated from the question of 'what process is due.' In practice, however, whether an entitlement is established or not is determined with an eye to the minimum procedural requirements that would follow as a consequence of a decision in favor of the recipient's claim. A threshold perception of security of interest focuses both on the existence of a 'property' interest and the procedural safeguards attendant upon its recognition. [The] result, as *Roth* and *Bishop* illustrate, is that when the state equivocates about job security, a court cognizant of the high costs of a hearing requirement in terms of administrative efficiency is likely to be reluctant to recognize a property interest. The court then ends up affording no procedural protection at all, even though the employee in such a case may be on a tenure track or even in a 'permanent' position.

"In what way is a threshold linked to the right to some kind of hearing too high? First, because preoccupation with a hearing has diverted attention from the fact that a significant measure of respect can be afforded the interest in accuracy with a more modest procedural safeguard that does not have the same consequences for administrative efficiency. Second, because excessive attention to the hearing safeguard has concealed the existence of an independent interest—what I will refer to as the interest in an adequate explanation—which has a compelling claim for protection through a more limited due process safeguard.

"Fundamental to the concept of procedural due process is the right to a reasoned explanation of government conduct that is contrary to the expectations the government has created by conferring a special status upon an individual. [It] is crucial that this value be seen as distinct from the concern about administrative accuracy—the interest in correcting wrong decisions. Obviously, the two are related[, but] I would insist that the respect for individual autonomy that is at the foundation of procedural due process imposes a distinct obligation upon the government to explain fully its adverse status decision. * * *

"Procedural due process can be viewed as a layered approach aimed at accomplishing a fundamental objective—protection against arbitrary conduct by the state. One could view the [various rights] [a] as various layers intended to provide increasingly effective insulation from arbitrariness: each layer adds something to the defensive capacity to ward off an arbitrary effort to destroy a status relationship. In some cases—a job security case involving a first amendment claim, for example—the balance struck between the individual values to be protected and the costs of administration weighs so heavily in favor of the individual claimant that a many-layered approach, some form of 'evidentiary hearing,' seems clearly required. But as we respond to less exigent claims by peeling away the layers of protection—indeed as we strip away any semblance of a 'hearing'—it is essential that we retain the core safeguard against arbitrariness, the right to receive a meaningful explanation of what is being done to the individual."

a. For factors—"roughly in order of priority"—that have been considered to be elements of a fair hearing, see Friendly, *"Some Kind of Hearing,"* 123 U.Pa.L.Rev. 1267, 1279–95 (1975): (1) "an unbiased tribunal" (but recall *Arnett v. Kennedy*); (2) "notice of the proposed action and the grounds asserted for it"; (3) "an opportunity to present reasons why the proposed action should not be taken"; (4), (5) and (6) "the right to call witnesses, to know the evidence against one, and to have decision based only on the evidence presented"; (7) "counsel"; (8) and (9), "the making of a record and a statement of reasons"; (10) "public attendance"; and (11) "judicial review."

Chapter 4

FREEDOM OF EXPRESSION AND ASSOCIATION

SECTION 1. WHAT SPEECH IS NOT PROTECTED?

The first amendment provides that "Congress shall make no law * * * abridging the freedom of speech, or of the press." Some have stressed that no law means NO LAW. For example, Black, J., dissenting in *Konigsberg v. State Bar,* 366 U.S. 36, 81 S.Ct. 997, 6 L.Ed.2d 105 (1961) argued that the "First Amendment's unequivocal command * * * shows that the men who drafted our Bill of Rights did all the 'balancing' that was to be done in this field."

Laws forbidding speech, however, are commonplace. Laws against perjury, blackmail, and fraud prohibit speech.[a] So does much of the law of contracts. Black, J., himself conceded that speech pursued as an integral part of criminal conduct was beyond first amendment protection. Indeed no one contends that citizens are free to say anything, anywhere, at any time. As Holmes, J., observed, citizens are not free to yell "fire" falsely in a crowded theater.

The spectre of a man crying fire falsely in the theater, however, has plagued first amendment theory. The task is to formulate principles that separate the protected from the unprotected. But speech interacts with too many other values in too many complicated ways to expect that a single formula will prove productive.

Are advocates of illegal action, pornographers selling magazines, or publishers of defamation like that person in the theater or are they engaged in freedom of speech? Do citizens have a right to speak on government property? Which property? Is there a right of access to the print or broadcast media? Can government force private owners to grant access for speakers? Does the first amendment offer protection for the wealthy, powerful corporations, and media conglomerates against government attempts to assure greater equality in the intellectual marketplace? Can government demand information about private political associations or reporters' confidential sources without first amendment limits? Does the first amendment require government to produce information it might otherwise withhold?

The Court has approached questions such as these without much attention to the language or history[b] of the first amendment and without a commitment

a. But see fn. b in *Roth v. United States,* p. 457 infra.

b. See, e.g., Perry, *The Constitution, The Courts, and Human Rights,* 63–64 (1982). For a variety of views about the history surrounding the adoption of the first amendment, com-to any general theory.[c] Rather it has sought to develop principles on a case-by-case basis and has produced a complex and conflicting body of constitutional precedent. Many of the basic principles were developed in a line of cases involving the advocacy of illegal action.[d]

I. ADVOCACY OF ILLEGAL ACTION

A. EMERGING PRINCIPLES

SCHENCK v. UNITED STATES, 249 U.S. 47, 39 S.Ct. 247, 63 L.Ed. 470 (1919): Defendants were convicted of a conspiracy to violate the 1917 Espionage Act by causing and attempting to cause insubordination in the armed forces of the United States, and obstruction of the recruiting and enlistment service of the United States, when at war with Germany, by printing and circulating to men accepted for military service approximately fifteen thousand copies of the document described in the opinion. In affirming, HOLMES, J., said for a unanimous Court: "The document in question upon its first printed side recited the first section of the Thirteenth Amendment, said that the idea embodied in it was violated by the conscription act and that a conscript is little better than a convict. In impassioned language it intimated that conscription was despotism in its worst form and a monstrous wrong against humanity in the interest of Wall Street's chosen few. It said, 'Do not submit to intimidation,' but in form at least confined itself to peaceful measures such as a petition for the repeal of the act. The other and later printed side of the sheet was headed 'Assert Your Rights.' It stated reasons for alleging that any one violated the Constitution when he refused to recognize 'your right to assert your opposition to the draft,' and went on, 'If you do not assert and support your rights, you are helping to deny or disparage rights which it is the solemn duty of all citizens and residents of the United States to retain.' It described the arguments on the other side as coming from cunning politicians and a mercenary capitalist press, and even silent consent to the conscription law as helping to support an infamous conspiracy. It denied the power to send our citizens away to foreign shores to shoot up the people of other lands, and added that words could not express the

pare Levy, *Legacy of Suppression* (1960) with Levy, *Emergence of a Free Press* (1985); Levy, *The Legacy Reexamined,* 37 Stan.L.Rev. 767 (1985); Levy, *On the Origins of the Free Press Clause,* 32 U.C.L.A.L.Rev. 177 (1984) and Anastaplo, *Book Review,* 39 N.Y.U.L.Rev. 735 (1964); Anderson, *The Origins of the Press Clause,* 30 U.C.L.A.L.Rev. 455 (1983); Hamburger, *The Development of the Law of Seditious Libel and the Control of the Press,* 37 Stan.L.Rev. 661 (1985); Mayton, *Seditious Libel and the Lost Guarantee of a Freedom of Expression,* 84 Colum.L.Rev. 91 (1984); Mayton, *From a Legacy of Suppression to the 'Metaphor of the Fourth Estate,'* 39 Stan. L.Rev. 139 (1986); Rabban, *The Ahistorical Historian: Leonard Levy on Freedom of Expression in Early American History,* 37 Stan.L. Rev. 795 (1985).

For an ambitious attempt to marry history, philosophy, and the first amendment, see Richards, *A Theory of Free Speech,* 34 UCLA L.Rev. 1837 (1987).

c. On the difficulties involved in developing general theory, see Alexander & Horton, *The Impossibility of a Free Speech Principle,* 78 Nw.U.L.Rev. 1319 (1983); Farber & Frickey, *Practical Reason and the First Amendment,* 34 UCLA L.Rev. 1615 (1987); Shiffrin, *The First Amendment and Economic Regulation: Away From a General Theory of the First Amendment,* 78 Nw.U.L.Rev. 1212 (1983); Tribe, *Toward A Metatheory of Free Speech,* 10 Sw.U.L.Rev. 237 (1978).

d. For discussion of the case law preceding *Schenck v. United States,* infra, see Gibson, *The Supreme Court and Freedom of Expression from 1791 to 1917,* 55 Fordham L.Rev. 263 (1986); Rabban, *The First Amendment in Its Forgotten Years,* 90 Yale L.J. 514 (1981). A general history of free speech and suppression is much needed. For useful commentary see Chafee, *Free Speech in the United States* (1941); Whipple, *The Story of Civil Liberty in the United States* (1927); Kairys, *Freedom of Speech* in The Politics of Law 160 (Kairys ed. 1982).

condemnation such coldblooded ruthlessness deserves, &c., &c., winding up, 'You must do your share to maintain, support and uphold the rights of the people of this country.' Of course the document would not have been sent unless it had been intended to have some effect, and we do not see what effect it could be expected to have upon persons subject to the draft except to influence them to obstruct the carrying of it out. The defendants do not deny that the jury might find against them on this point.

"But it is said, suppose that that was the tendency of this circular, it is protected by the First Amendment to the Constitution. [We] admit that in many places and in ordinary times the defendants in saying all that was said in the circular would have been within their constitutional rights. But the character of every act depends upon the circumstances in which it is done. The most stringent protection of free speech would not protect a man in falsely shouting fire in a theatre and causing a panic. [The] question in every case is whether the words used are used in such circumstances and are of such a nature as to create a clear and present danger that they will bring about the substantive evils that Congress has a right to prevent. It is a question of proximity and degree.[a] When a nation is at war many things that might be said in time of peace are such a hindrance to its effort that their utterance will not be endured so long as men fight and that no Court could regard them as protected by any constitutional right. It seems to be admitted that if an actual obstruction of the recruiting service were proved, liability for words that produced that effect might be enforced. The statute of 1917 punishes conspiracies to obstruct as well as actual obstruction. If the act, (speaking, or circulating a paper), its tendency and the intent with which it is done are the same, we perceive no ground for saying that success alone warrants making the act a crime."[b]

DEBS v. UNITED STATES, 249 U.S. 211, 39 S.Ct. 252, 63 L.Ed. 566 (1919): Defendant was convicted of violating the Espionage Act for obstructing and attempting to obstruct the recruiting service and for causing and attempting to cause insubordination and disloyalty in the armed services. He was given a ten-year prison sentence on each count, to run concurrently. His criminal conduct consisted of giving the anti-war speech described in the opinion at the state

a. Although Schenck was convicted for violating a conspiracy statute, Holmes appears to have used the occasion to import the law of criminal attempts into the freedom of expression area. "In *Schenck,* 'clear and present danger,' 'a question of proximity and degree' bridged the gap between the defendant's acts of publication and the [prohibited interferences with the war.] This connection was strikingly similar to the Holmesian analysis of the requirement of 'dangerous proximity to success' [quoting from an earlier Holmes opinion] that, in the law of attempts, bridges the gap between the defendant's acts and the completed crime. In either context, innocuous efforts are to be ignored." Rogat, *Mr. Justice Holmes: Some Modern Views—The Judge as Spectator,* 31 U.Chi.L.Rev. 213, 215 (1964). See also Chafee, *Free Speech in the United States* 81–82 (1941); Shapiro, *Freedom of Speech* 55–58 (1966). But see Holmes, J., dissenting in *Abrams* infra, and fn. b below.

b. See also *Frohwerk v. United States,* 249 U.S. 204, 39 S.Ct. 249, 63 L.Ed. 561 (1919), where a unanimous Court, per Holmes, J., sustained a conviction for conspiracy to obstruct recruiting in violation of the Espionage Act, by means of a dozen newspaper articles praising the spirit and strength of the German nation, criticizing the decision to send American troops to France, maintaining that the government was giving false and hypocritical reasons for its course of action and implying that "the guilt of those who voted the unnatural sacrifice" is greater than the wrong of those who seek to escape by resistance: "[*Schenck* decided] that a person may be convicted of a conspiracy to obstruct recruiting by words of persuasion. [S]o far as the language of the articles goes there is not much to choose between expressions to be found in them and those before us in *Schenck.*"

convention of the Socialist Party of Ohio, held at a park in Canton, Ohio, on a June 16, 1918 Sunday afternoon before a general audience of 1,200 persons. At the time of the speech, defendant was a national political figure.[a] In affirming, HOLMES, J., observed for a unanimous Court:

"The main theme of the speech was socialism, its growth, and a prophecy of its ultimate success. With that we have nothing to do, but if a part or the manifest intent of the more general utterances was to encourage those present to obstruct the recruiting service and if in passages such encouragement was directly given, the immunity of the general theme may not be enough to protect the speech. [Defendant had come to the park directly from a nearby jail, where he had visited three socialists imprisoned for obstructing the recruiting service. He expressed sympathy and admiration for these persons and others convicted of similar offenses, and then] said that the master class has always declared the war and the subject class has always fought the battles—that the subject class has had nothing to gain and all to lose, including their lives; [and that] 'You have your lives to lose; you certainly ought to have the right to declare war if you consider a war necessary.' [He next said of a woman serving a ten-year sentence for obstructing the recruiting service] that she had said no more than the speaker had said that afternoon; that if she was guilty so was [he].

"There followed personal experiences and illustrations of the growth of socialism, a glorification of minorities, and a prophecy of the success of [socialism], with the interjection that 'you need to know that you are fit for something better than slavery and cannon fodder.' [Defendant's] final exhortation [was] 'Don't worry about the charge of treason to your masters; but be concerned about the treason that involves yourselves.' The defendant addressed the jury himself, and while contending that his speech did not warrant the charges said 'I have been accused of obstructing the war. I admit it. Gentlemen, I abhor war. I would oppose the war if I stood alone.' The statement was not necessary to warrant the jury in finding that one purpose of the speech, whether incidental or not does not matter, was to oppose not only war in general but this war, and that the opposition was so expressed that its natural and intended effect would be to obstruct recruiting. If that was intended and if, in all the circumstances, that would be its probable effect, it would not be protected by reason of its being part of a general program and expressions of a general and conscientious belief.

"[Defendant's constitutional objections] based upon the First Amendment [were] disposed of in *Schenck.*

"[T]he admission in evidence of the record of the conviction [of various persons he mentioned in his speech was proper] to show what he was talking about, to explain the true import of his expression of sympathy and to throw light on the intent of the address. [Properly admitted, too, was an 'Anti-war Proclamation and Program' adopted the previous year, coupled with testimony that shortly before his speech defendant had stated that he approved it]. Its first recommendation was, 'continuous, active, and public opposition to the war, through demonstrations, mass petitions, and all other means within our power.' Evidence that the defendant accepted this view and this declaration of his duties at the time that he made his speech is evidence that if in that speech he used

a. Debs had run for the Presidency on the Socialist ticket for the fourth time in 1912. At the 1920 election, while in prison, Debs ran again and received over 900,000 votes as the Socialist candidate, a significant portion of all votes cast in that election. Consider Kalven, *Ernst Freund and the First Amendment Tradition,* 40 U.Chi.L.Rev. 235, 237 (1973): "To put the case in modern context, it is somewhat as though George McGovern had been sent to prison for his criticism of the [Vietnam] war."

words tending to obstruct the recruiting service he meant that they should have that effect. [T]he jury were most carefully instructed that they could not find the defendant guilty for advocacy of any of his opinions unless the words used had as their natural tendency and reasonably probable effect to obstruct the recruiting service [and] unless the defendant had the specific intent to do so in his mind."

Notes and Questions

1. *The Man in the Theater.* Consider Kalven, *A Worthy Tradition* 133–34 (1988): "*Schenck*—and perhaps even Holmes himself—are best remembered for the example of the man 'falsely shouting fire' in a crowded theater. Judge Hand said in *Masses* that 'words are not only the keys of persuasion, but the triggers of action.' Justice Holmes makes the same point by means of the 'fire' example, an image which was to catch the fancy of the culture. But the example has long seemed to me trivial and misleading. It is as if the only conceivable controversy over speech policy were with an adversary who asserts that *all* use of words is absolutely immunized under the First Amendment. The 'fire' example then triumphantly impeaches this massive major premise. Beyond that, it adds nothing to our understanding. If the point were that *only* speech which is a comparable 'trigger of action' could be regulated, the example might prove a stirring way of drawing the line at incitement, but it is abundantly clear that Justice Holmes is not comparing Schenck's leaflet to the shouting of 'fire.' Moreover, because the example is so wholly apolitical, it lacks the requisite complexity for dealing with any serious speech problem likely to confront the legal system. The man shouting 'fire' does not offer premises resembling those underlying radical political rhetoric—premises that constitute criticism of government."

2. *Reflections.* (a) Consider Kalven, *Ernst Freund and the First Amendment Tradition,* 40 U.Chi.L.Rev. 235, 236–38 (1973): "It has been customary to lavish care and attention on the *Schenck* case, [but *Debs,* argued well before *Schenck* was handed down and decided just one week later,] represented the first effort by Justice Holmes to apply what he had worked out about freedom of speech in *Schenck.* The start of the law of the first amendment is not *Schenck;* it is *Schenck* and *Debs* read together. [Deb's speech] fell into the genre of bitter criticism of government and government policy, sometimes called seditious libel; freedom of such criticism from government marks, we have come to understand, 'the central meaning of the First Amendment' [*New York Times v. Sullivan,* p. 424 infra]. During the Vietnam War thousands of utterances strictly comparable in bitterness and sharpness of criticism, if not in literacy, were made; it was pretty much taken for granted they were beyond the reach of government.[b] [*Debs*] raises serious questions as to what the first amendment, and more especially, what the clear and present danger formula can possibly have meant at the time. [Holmes] does not comment on the fact difference between [*Schenck* and *Debs*]: the defendant in *Schenck* had sent his leaflets directly to men who awaited draft call whereas [Debs] was addressing a general audience at a public meeting. Holmes offers no discussion of the sense in which Debs's speech presented a clear and present danger. [In fact, *Debs*] did not move [Holmes] to discuss free speech at all; his brief opinion is occupied with two points about admissibility of [evidence]. It was for Holmes a routine criminal appeal."

b. Compare *Debs* with *Bond v. Floyd,* p. 415 infra.

(b) Consider Freund, *The Debs Case and Freedom of Speech,* The New Republic, May 3, 1919, p. 13, reprinted in 40 U.Chi.L.Rev. 239, 240–41 (1973): "[*Debs*] illustrates most clearly the arbitrariness of the whole idea of implied provocation. A violent, if you please, a seditious speech is made; a docile jury finds a design to obstruct recruiting, and the finding is conclusive because the court does not consider it inconsistent with possibility. What are the intrinsic probabilities? An experienced speaker like Debs knows the effect of words. He must have known that while he might keep alive and even create disaffection, his power to create actual obstruction to a compulsory draft was practically nil, and he could hardly have intended what he could not hope to achieve; in fact it is difficult to conceive of a form of obstruction that can be opposed to a compulsory draft. [Yet] Holmes would make us believe that the relation of the speech to obstruction is like that of the shout of Fire! in a crowded theatre to the resulting panic! Surely implied provocation in connection with political offenses is an unsafe doctrine if it has to be made plausible by a parallel so manifestly inappropriate."

3. *"Breathing space" for free speech under the Espionage Act.* Consider Chafee, *Free Speech in the United States* 50–51 (1941): "[With a few exceptions, notably Judge Learned Hand's opinion in *Masses,* infra, the lower federal courts] allowed conviction [under the Espionage Act] for any words which had an indirect effect to discourage recruiting and the war spirit [so long as] the intention to discourage existed. [Moreover, the] requirement of intention became a mere form since it could be inferred from the existence of the indirect injurious effect. [T]he words of the Espionage Act of 1917 bear slight resemblance to the Sedition Law of 1798, but the judicial construction is much the same, except that under the Sedition Law truth was a defense."

Consider Ernst Freund's criticism of *Debs,* supra at 240–41: "To know what you may do and what you may not do, and how far you may go in criticism, is the first condition of political liberty; to be permitted to agitate at your own peril, subject to a jury's guessing at motive, tendency and possible effect, makes the right of free speech a precarious gift. [For] arbitrary executive, [the Espionage Act] practically substitutes arbitrary, judicial power; since a jury's findings, within the limits of a conceivable psychological nexus between words and deeds, are beyond scrutiny and control; and while the jury may have been a protection against governmental power when the government was a thing apart from the people, its checking function fails where government policies are supported by majority opinion."

Holmes, J.'s response, in private correspondence, see Ginsburg, *Afterword,* 40 U.Chi.L.Rev. 243, 245 (1973), to Professor Freund's objection, in his article on *Debs,* to a jury "guessing at motive, tendency and possible effect" was that this could be said about "pretty much the whole body of the law, which for thirty years I have made my brethren smile by insisting to be everywhere a matter of degree." Holmes recalled the comment he made in a case involving a criminal prosecution under the Sherman Act that "the law is full of instances where a man's fate depends on his estimating rightly, that is, as the jury subsequently estimates it, some matter of degree. If his judgment is wrong, not only may he incur a fine or [prison term, but] the penalty of death."

4. MASSES PUBLISHING CO. v. PATTEN, 244 Fed. 535 (S.D.N.Y.1917): The Postmaster of New York advised plaintiff that an issue of his monthly revolutionary journal, *The Masses,* would be denied the mails under the Espionage Act since it tended to encourage the enemies of the United States and to

hamper the government in its conduct of the war. The Postmaster subsequently specified as objectionable several cartoons entitled, e.g., "Conscription," "Making the World Safe for Capitalism"; several articles admiring the "sacrifice" of conscientious objectors and a poem praising two persons imprisoned for conspiracy to resist the draft. Plaintiff sought a preliminary injunction against the postmaster from excluding its magazine from the mails. LEARNED HAND, D.J., granted relief:

"[The postmaster maintains] that to arouse discontent and disaffection among the people with the prosecution of the war and with the draft tends to promote a mutinous and insubordinate temper among the troops. This [is] true; men who become satisfied that they are engaged in an enterprise dictated by the unconscionable selfishness of the rich, and effectuated by a tyrannous disregard for the will of those who must suffer and die, will be more prone to insubordination than those who have faith in the cause and acquiesce in the means. Yet to interpret the word 'cause' [in the statutory language forbidding one to 'willfully cause' insubordination in the armed forces] so broadly would [necessarily involve] the suppression of all hostile criticism, and of all opinion except what encouraged and supported the existing policies, or which fell within the range of temperate argument. It would contradict the normal assumption of democratic government that the suppression of hostile criticism does not turn upon the justice of its substance or the decency and propriety of its temper. Assuming that the power to repress such opinion may rest in Congress in the throes of a struggle for the very existence of the state, its exercise is so contrary to the use and wont of our people that only the clearest expression of such a power justifies the conclusion that it was intended.

"The defendant's position, therefore, in so far as it involves the suppression of the free utterance of abuse and criticism of the existing law, or of the policies of the war, is not, in my judgment, supported by the language of the statute. Yet there has always been a recognized limit to such expressions, incident indeed to the existence of any compulsive power of the state itself. One may not counsel or advise others to violate the law as it stands. Words are not only the keys of persuasion, but the triggers of action, and those which have no purport but to counsel the violation of law cannot by any latitude of interpretation be a part of that public opinion which is the final source of government in a democratic state. [To] counsel or advise a man to an act is to urge upon him either that it is his interest or his duty to do it. While, of course, this may be accomplished as well by indirection as expressly, since words carry the meaning that they impart, the definition is exhaustive, I think, and I shall use it. Political agitation, by the passions it arouses or the convictions it engenders, may in fact stimulate men to the violation of law. Detestation of existing policies is easily transformed into forcible resistance of the authority which puts them in execution, and it would be folly to disregard the causal relation between the two. Yet to assimilate agitation, legitimate as such, with direct incitement to violent resistance, is to disregard the tolerance of all methods of political agitation which in normal times is a safeguard of free government. The distinction is not a scholastic subterfuge, but a hard-bought acquisition in the fight for freedom, and the purpose to disregard it must be evident when the power exists. If one stops short of urging upon others that it is their duty or their interest to resist the law, it seems to me one should not be held to have attempted to cause its violation. If that be not the test, I can see no escape from the conclusion that under this section every political agitation which can be shown to be apt to create a seditious temper is illegal. I am confident that by such language Congress had no such revolutionary purpose in view.

"It seems to me, however, quite plain that none of the language and none of the cartoons in this paper can be thought directly to counsel or advise insubordination or mutiny, without a violation of their meaning quite beyond any tolerable understanding. I come, therefore to the [provision of the Act forbidding] any one from willfully obstructing [recruiting or enlistment]. I am not prepared to assent to the plaintiff's position that this only refers to acts other than words, nor that the act thus defined must be shown to have been successful. One may obstruct without preventing, and the mere obstruction is an injury to the service; for it throws impediments in its way. Here again, however, since the question is of the expression of opinion, I construe the sentence, so far as it restrains public utterance, [as] limited to the direct advocacy of resistance to the recruiting and enlistment service. If so, the inquiry is narrowed to the question whether any of the challenged matter may be said to advocate resistance to the draft, taking the meaning of the words with the utmost latitude which they can bear.

"As to the cartoons it seems to me quite clear that they do not fall within such a test. [T]he most that can be said [is that they] may breed such animosity to the draft as will promote resistance and strengthen the determination of those disposed to be recalcitrant. There is no intimation that, however, hateful the draft may be, one is in duty bound to resist it, certainly none that such resistance is to one's interest. I cannot, therefore, even with the limitations which surround the power of the court, assent to the assertion that any of the cartoons violate the act.

"[As for the text], it is plain enough that the [magazine] has the fullest sympathy for [those who resist the draft or obstruct recruiting], that it admires their courage, and that it presumptively approves their conduct. [Moreover,] these passages, it must be remembered, occur in a magazine which attacks with the utmost violence the draft and the war. That such comments have a tendency to arouse emulation in others is clear enough, but that they counsel others to follow these examples is not so plain. Literally at least they do not, and while, as I have said, the words are to be taken, not literally, but according to their full import, the literal meaning is the starting point for interpretation. One may admire and approve the course of a hero without feeling any duty to follow him. There is not the least implied intimation in these words that others are under a duty to follow. The most that can be said is that, if others do follow, they will get the same admiration and the same approval. Now, there is surely an appreciable distance between esteem and emulation; and unless there is here some advocacy of such emulation, I cannot see how the passages can be said to fall within the [law.] Surely, if the draft had not excepted Quakers, it would be too strong a doctrine to say that any who openly admire their fortitude or even approved their conduct was willfully obstructing the draft.

"When the question is of a statute constituting a crime, it seems to me that there should be more definite evidence of the act. The question before me is quite the same as what would arise upon a motion to dismiss an indictment at the close of the proof: Could any reasonable man say, not that the indirect result of the language might be to arouse a seditious disposition, for that would not be enough, but that the language directly advocated resistance to the draft? I cannot think that upon such language any verdict would stand." [c]

What result if the Court had applied the *Masses* test in *Schenck* or *Debs*? In *Abrams* or *Gitlow,* infra?

JUSTICE HOLMES—DISSENTING IN ABRAMS v. UNITED STATES

250 U.S. 616, 624, 40 S.Ct. 17, 20, 63 L.Ed. 1173, 1178 (1919).

[In the summer of 1918, the United States sent a small body of marines to Siberia. Although the defendants maintained a strong socialist opposition to "German militarism," they opposed the "capitalist" invasion of Russia, and characterized it as an attempt to crush the Russian Revolution. Shortly thereafter, they printed two leaflets and distributed several thousand copies in New York City. Many of the copies were thrown from a window where one defendant was employed; others were passed around at radical meetings. Both leaflets supported Russia against the United States; one called upon workers to unite in a general strike. There was no evidence that workers responded to the call.

[The Court upheld the defendants' convictions for conspiring to violate two provisions of the 1918 amendments to the Espionage Act. One count prohibited language intended to "incite, provoke and encourage resistance to the United States"; the other punished those who urged curtailment of war production. As the Court interpreted the statute, an intent to interfere with efforts against a *declared* war was a necessary element of both offenses. Since the United States had not declared war upon Russia, "the main task of the government was to establish an [*intention*] *to interfere with the war with Germany.*" Chafee, supra, at 115. The Court found intent on the principle that "Men must be held to have intended, and to be accountable for, the effects which their acts were likely to produce. Even if their primary purpose and intent was to aid the cause of the Russian Revolution, the plan of action which they adopted necessarily involved, before it could be realized, defeat of the war program of the United States * * *."

[HOLMES, J., dissented in an opinion with which Brandeis, J., concurred:]

[I] am aware of course that the word "intent" as vaguely used in ordinary legal discussion means no more than knowledge at the time of the act that the consequences said to be intended will ensue. [But,] when words are used exactly, a deed is not done with intent to produce a consequence unless that consequence is the aim of the deed. It may be obvious, and obvious to the actor, that the consequence will follow, and he may be liable for it even if he regrets it, but he does not do the act with intent to produce it unless the aim to produce it is the proximate motive of the specific act although there may be some deeper motive behind.

It seems to me that this statute must be taken to use its words in a strict and accurate sense. They would be absurd in any other. A patriot might think that we were wasting money on aeroplanes, or making more cannon of a certain kind than we needed, and might advocate curtailment with success, yet even if it

c. In reversing, 246 Fed. 24 (C.C.A. N.Y.1917), the Second Circuit observed: "If the natural and probable effect of what is said is to encourage resistance to a law, and the words are used in an endeavor to persuade to resistance, it is immaterial that the duty to resist is not mentioned, or the interest of the person addressed in resistance is not suggested. That one may willfully obstruct the enlistment service, without advising in direct language against enlistments, and without stating that to refrain from enlistment is a duty or in one's interest, seems to us too plain for controversy."

turned out that the curtailment hindered and was thought by other minds to have been obviously likely to hinder the United States in the prosecution of the war, no one would hold such conduct a crime. * * *

I never have seen any reason to doubt that the questions of law that alone were before this Court in the cases of *Schenck, Frohwerk* and *Debs* were rightly decided. I do not doubt for a moment that by the same reasoning that would justify punishing persuasion to murder, the United States constitutionally may punish speech that produces or is intended to produce a clear and imminent danger that it will bring about forthwith certain substantive evils that the United States constitutionally may seek to prevent. The power undoubtedly is greater in time of war than in time of peace because war opens dangers that do not exist at other times.

But as against dangers peculiar to war, as against others, the principle of the right to free speech is always the same. It is only the present danger of immediate evil or an intent to bring it about that warrants Congress in setting a limit to the expression of opinion where private rights are not concerned. Congress certainly cannot forbid all effort to change the mind of the country. Now nobody can suppose that the surreptitious publishing of a silly leaflet by an unknown man, without more, would present any immediate danger that its opinions would hinder the success of the government arms or have any appreciable tendency to do so.[a] Publishing those opinions for the very purpose of obstructing, however, might indicate a greater danger and at any rate would have the quality of an attempt.[b] * * *

a. See also Chafee, supra, at 140: "The maximum sentence available against a formidable pro-German plot [20 years] was meted out [for] the silly, futile circulars of five obscure and isolated young aliens, misguided by their loyalty to their endangered country and ideals, who hatched their wild scheme in a garret, and carried it out in a cellar." But cf. Wigmore, *Abrams v. U.S.: Freedom of Speech and Freedom of Thuggery in War-Time and Peace-Time,* 14 Ill.L.Rev. 539, 549–50 (1920): "[The *Abrams* dissent] is dallying with the facts and the law. None know better than judges that what is lawful for one is lawful for a thousand others. If these five men could, without the law's restraint, urge munition workers to a general strike and armed violences then others could lawfully do so; and a thousand disaffected undesirables, aliens and natives alike, were ready and waiting to do so. Though this circular was 'surreptitious,' the next ones need not be so. If such urgings were lawful, every munitions factory in the country could be stopped by them. The relative amount of harm that one criminal act can effect is no measure of its criminality, and no measure of the danger of its criminality. To put forward such a palliation is merely to reveal more clearly the indifference to the whole crisis. [At a time] when the fate of the civilized world hung in the balance, how could the Minority Opinion interpret law and conduct in such a way as to let loose men who were doing their hardest to paralyze the supreme war efforts of our country?"

b. Would it, if, under the circumstances, the defendant had no reasonable prospect of success? If his efforts were utterly ineffectual? Is bad intention or purpose, without more, an attempt? Or even everything done in furtherance of that bad intention? Or is unlawful "intention" or "purpose" merely one factor in determining whether defendant's conduct comes dangerously near success or stamps the actor as sufficiently dangerous? Cf. Holmes, *The Common Law* 65–66, 68–69 (1881): "Intent to commit a crime is not itself criminal. [Moreover], the law does not punish every act which is done with the intent to bring about a crime. [We] have seen what amounts to an attempt to burn a haystack [lighting a match with intent to start fire to a haystack]; but it was said in the same case, that, if the defendant had gone no further than to buy a box of matches for the purpose, he would not have been liable. [Relevant considerations are] the nearness of the danger, the greatness of the harm and the degree of apprehension felt." See also Holmes, C.J., in *Commonwealth v. Peaslee,* 177 Mass. 267, 59 N.E. 55 (1901) ("if the preparation comes very near to the accomplishment of the act, the intent to complete it renders the crime so probable" that the conduct will constitute an attempt); Holmes, J., dissenting in *Hyde v. United States,* 225 U.S. 347, 387, 32 S.Ct. 793, 56 L.Ed. 1114 (1912) (preliminary acts become an attempt when "so near to the result [completed crime] that if coupled with an intent to produce that result, the danger is very great"). See generally Chafee, supra, at 46–47; Linde,

I do not see how anyone can find the intent required by the statute in any of the defendants' words. The leaflet advocating a general strike is the only one that affords even a foundation for the charge, and [its only object] is to help Russia and stop American intervention there against the popular government—not to impede the United States in the war that it was carrying on. * * *

In this case sentences of twenty years imprisonment have been imposed for the publishing of two leaflets that I believe the defendants had as much right to publish as the Government has to publish the Constitution of the United States now vainly invoked by them. [E]ven if what I think the necessary intent were shown; the most nominal punishment seems to me all that possibly could be inflicted, unless the defendants are to be made to suffer not for what the indictment alleges but for the creed that they avow—[which,] although made the subject of examination at the trial, no one has a right even to consider in dealing with the charges before the Court.

Persecution for the expression of opinions seems to me perfectly logical. If you have no doubt of your premises or your power and want a certain result with all your heart you naturally express your wishes in law and sweep away all opposition. To allow opposition by speech seems to indicate that you think the speech impotent, as when a man says that he has squared the circle, or that you do not care whole-heartedly for the result, or that you doubt either your power or your premises. But when men have realized that time has upset many fighting faiths, they may come to believe even more than they believe the very foundations of their own conduct that the ultimate good desired is better reached by free trade in ideas—that the best test of truth is the power of the thought to get itself accepted in the competition of the market, and that truth is the only ground upon which their wishes safely can be carried out.[c] That at any rate is the theory of our Constitution. It is an experiment, as all life is an experiment. Every year if not every day we have to wager our salvation upon some prophecy based upon imperfect knowledge. While that experiment is part of our system I think that we should be eternally vigilant against attempts to check the expression of opinions that we loathe and believe to be fraught with death, unless they so imminently threaten immediate interference with the lawful and pressing purposes of the law that an immediate check is required to save the country. [Only] the emergency that makes it immediately dangerous to leave the correction of evil counsels to time warrants making any exception to the sweeping command, "Congress shall make no law * * * abridging the freedom of speech." Of course I am speaking only of expressions of opinion and exhortations, which were all that were uttered [here].[d]

"Clear and Present Danger" Reexamined, 22 Stan.L.Rev. 1163, 1168–69, 1183–86 (1970); Shapiro, *Freedom of Speech* 55–58 (1966).

c. But see Wigmore, fn. a supra, at 550–51: "This apotheosis of Truth, however, shows a blindness to the deadly fact that meantime the 'power of the thought' of these circulars might 'get itself accepted in the competition of the market,' by munitions workers, so as to lose the war; in which case, the academic victory which Truth, 'the ultimate good,' might later secure in the market, would be too 'ultimate' to have any practical value for a defeated America. [To] weigh in juxtaposition the dastardly sentiments of these circulars and the great theme of world-justice for which [we were fighting], and then to assume the sacred cause of Truth as equally involved in both, is to misuse high ideals. This [dissenting opinion, if it had commanded a majority], would have ended by our letting soldiers die helpless in France, through our anxiety to protect the distribution of a leaflet whose sole purpose was to cut off the soldiers' munitions and supplies. How would this have advanced the cause of Truth?"

d. For illuminating discussion of *Abrams* and the period of which it is a part, see Polenberg, *Fighting Faiths* (1987).

Notes and Questions

1. *"Marketplace of ideas."* (a) Contrast Holmes' statement of the "marketplace of ideas" argument with John Milton's statement in *Areopagitica:* "And though all the winds of doctrine were let loose to play upon the earth, so Truth be in the field, we do injuriously by licensing and prohibiting to misdoubt her strength. Let her and Falsehood grapple; who ever knew Truth put to the worse, in a free and open encounter?" Holmes claims that the competition of the market is the best test of truth; Milton maintains that truth will emerge in a free and open encounter. How would one verify either hypothesis?

Is the "marketplace of ideas" a "free and open encounter"? Consider Lindblom, *Politics and Markets* 207 (1977): "Early, persuasive, unconscious conditioning—[to] believe in the fundamental politico-economic institutions of one's society is ubiquitous in every society. These institutions come to be taken for granted. Many people grow up to regard them not as institutions to be tested but as standards against which the correctness of new policies and institutions can be tested. When that happens, as is common, processes of critical judgment are short-circuited." Consider also Tribe, *American Constitutional Law* 786 (2d Ed.1988): "Especially when the wealthy have more access to the most potent media of communication than the poor, how sure can we be that 'free trade in ideas' is likely to generate truth?"

For a specific example, see Shiffrin, *The First Amendment and Economic Regulation: Away From A General Theory of the First Amendment,* 78 Nw.U.L. Rev. 1212, 1281 (1983): "Living in a society in which children and adults are daily confronted with multiple communications that ask them to purchase products inevitably places emphasis on materialistic values. The authors of the individual messages may not intend that general emphasis, but the whole is greater than the sum of the parts. [Advertisers] spend some sixty billion dollars per year. [Those] who would oppose the materialist message must combat forces that have a massive economic advantage. Any confidence that we will know what is truth by seeing what emerges from such combat is ill placed."

Do the different market failure considerations offered by Lindblom, Tribe, and Shiffrin add up to a rebuttal of the marketplace argument? Consider *Nimmer on Freedom of Speech* 1–12 (1984): "If acceptance of an idea in the competition of the market is not the 'best test' [what] is the alternative? It can only be acceptance of an idea by some individual or group narrower than that of the public at large. Thus, the alternative to competition in the market must be some form of elitism. It seems hardly necessary to enlarge on the dangers of that path." Is elitism the only alternative to the marketplace perspective? Is elitism always wrong?

(b) Evaluate the following hypothetical commentary: "Liberals have favored government intervention in the economic marketplace but pressed for laissez-faire in the intellectual marketplace. Conservatives have done the reverse. Liberals and conservatives have one thing in common: inconsistent positions."

(c) Does the marketplace argument overvalue truth? Consider Schauer, *Free Speech: A Philosophical Enquiry* 23 (1982). Government may seek to suppress opinions "because their expression is thought to impair the authority of a lawful and effective government, interfere with the administration of justice (such as publication of a defendant's criminal record in advance of a jury trial), cause offence, invade someone's privacy, or cause a decrease in public order. When these are the motives for suppression, the possibility of losing some truth is relevant but hardly dispositive. [In such circumstances] the argument from truth [is] not wholly to the point." Is Holmes persuasive when he maintains that before we can suppress opinion we must wait until "an immediate check is required to save the country"?

(d) Does the marketplace argument threaten first amendment values? Consider Ingber, *The Marketplace of Ideas: A Legitimizing Myth,* 1984 Duke L.J. 1, 4–5 "[C]ourts that invoke the marketplace model of the first amendment justify free expression because of the aggregate benefits to society, and not because an individual speaker receives a particular benefit. Courts that focus their concern on the audience rather than the speaker relegate free expression to an instrumental value, a means toward some other goal, rather than a value unto itself. Once free expression is viewed solely as an instrumental value, however, it is easier to allow government regulation of speech if society as a whole 'benefits' from a regulated system of expression."

(e) Does the marketplace argument slight other important free speech values? Consider Wolff, *The Poverty of Liberalism* 18 (1968) "[I]t is not to assist the advance of knowledge that free debate is needed. Rather, it is in order to guarantee that every legitimate interest shall make itself known and felt in the political [process]. Justice, not truth, is the ideal served by liberty of speech." Compare Chevigny, *Philosophy of Language and Free Expression,* 55 N.Y.U.L. Rev. 157 (1980); Leitner, *Liberalism, Separation and Speech,* 1985 Wis.L.Rev. 79, 89–90 & 103–04. The standard starting place for discussion of free speech values continues to be Emerson, *The System of Freedom of Expression* 6–9 (1970).

(f) Would an emphasis on dissent be preferable to an emphasis on the marketplace metaphor? Consider Shiffrin, *The First Amendment, Democracy, and Romance* (1990): "[A] commitment to sponsoring dissent does not require a belief that what emerges in the 'market' is usually right or that the 'market' is the best test of truth. Quite the contrary, the commitment to sponsor dissent assumes that societal pressures to conform are strong and that incentives to keep quiet are often great. If the marketplace metaphor encourages the view that an invisible hand or voluntaristic arrangements have guided us patiently, but slowly, to Burkean harmony, the commitment to sponsoring dissent encourages us to believe that the cozy arrangements of the status quo have settled on something less than the true or the just. If the marketplace metaphor encourages the view that conventions, habits, and traditions have emerged as our best sense of the truth from the rigorous testing ground of the marketplace of ideas, the commitment to sponsoring dissent encourages the view that conventions, habits, and traditions are compromises open to challenge. If the marketplace metaphor counsels us that the market's version of truth is more worthy of trust than any that the government might dictate, a commitment to sponsoring dissent counsels us to be suspicious of both. If the marketplace metaphor encourages a sloppy form of relativism (whatever has emerged in the marketplace is right for now), the commitment to sponsoring dissent emphasizes that truth is not decided in public opinion polls."

(g) For a powerful critique of marketplace models, see Baker, *Human Liberty and Freedom of Speech* 6–24, 37–46 (1989). For qualified defenses, see Greenawalt, *Free Speech Justifications,* 89 Colum.L.Rev. 119, 130–41, 153–54 (1989); Schauer, *Language, Truth, and the First Amendment,* 64 Va.L.Rev. 263 (1978). For commentary on metaphors in general and the marketplace metaphor in particular, see Winter, *Transcendental Nonsense, Metaphoric Reasoning, and the Cognitive Stakes for Law,* 137 U.Pa.L.Rev. 1105 (1989).

2. Why did *Abrams,* but not *Debs,* stir Holmes to speak seriously and eloquently about freedom of speech? One suggestion is that "Holmes was biding his time until the Court should have before it a conviction so clearly wrong as to let him speak out his deepest thoughts about the First Amendment" and that "the opportunity [came] eight months after Debs went to prison, in *Abrams,*" Chafee, supra, at 86. See generally Bogen, *The Free Speech Metamorphosis of Mr. Justice Holmes*, 11 Hof.L.Rev. 97 (1982). For the view that the criticism of *Debs* in both the Ernst Freund article and in Learned Hand's correspondence with Holmes may have contributed to a marked change in Holmes' thinking about the first amendment between *Debs* and *Abrams,* see Ginsburg, *Afterword,* 40 U.Chi.L.Rev. 243 (1973). The literature on Holmes' first amendment views and their connection to his larger world view is substantial. See, e.g., Rogat & O'Fallon, *Mr. Justice Holmes: A Dissenting Opinion—The Speech Cases,* 36 Stan. L.Rev. 1349 (1984); Rabban, *The Emergence of Modern First Amendment Doctrine,* 50 U.Chi.L.Rev. 1205 (1983). For further analysis of the Holmes-Hand correspondence, see Gunther, *Learned Hand and the Origins of Modern First Amendment Doctrine: Some Fragments of History,* 27 Stan.L.Rev. 719 (1975).

B. STATE SEDITION LAWS

The second main group of cases in the initial development of first amendment doctrine involved state "sedition laws" of two basic types: criminal anarchy laws, typified by the New York statute in *Gitlow,* infra, and criminal syndicalism laws similar to the California statute in *Whitney,* infra. Most states enacted anarchy and syndicalism statutes between 1917 and 1921, in response to World War I and the fear of Bolshevism that developed in its wake, but the first modern sedition law was passed by New York in 1902, soon after the assassination of President McKinley. The law, which prohibited not only actual or attempted assassinations or conspiracies to assassinate, but advocacy of anarchy as well, lay idle for nearly twenty years, until the *Gitlow* prosecution.

GITLOW v. NEW YORK, 268 U.S. 652, 45 S.Ct. 625, 69 L.Ed. 1138 (1925): Defendant was a member of the Left Wing Section of the Socialist Party and a member of its National Council, which adopted a "Left Wing Manifesto," condemning the dominant "moderate Socialism" for its recognition of the necessity of the democratic parliamentary state; advocating the necessity of accomplishing the "Communist Revolution" by a militant and "revolutionary Socialism" based on "the class struggle"; and urging the development of mass political strikes for the destruction of the parliamentary state. Defendant arranged for printing and distributing, through the mails and otherwise, 16,000 copies of the Manifesto in the Left Wing's official organ, The Revolutionary Age. There was no evidence of any effect from the publication and circulation of the Manifesto.

In sustaining a conviction under the New York "criminal anarchy" statutes, prohibiting the "advocacy, advising or teaching the duty, necessity or propriety of overthrowing or overturning organized government by force or violence" and the publication or distribution of such matter, the majority, per SANFORD, J., stated that for present purposes we may and do assume [a] that first amendment freedoms of expression "are among the fundamental personal rights and 'liber-

a. Although *Gitlow* is often cited for the proposition that first amendment freedoms apply to restrict state conduct, its language is dictum. Some would say the first case so holding is *Fiske v. Kansas,* 274 U.S. 380, 47 S.Ct. 655, 71 L.Ed. 1108 (1927) (no evidence to support criminal syndicalism conviction) even though no reference to the first amendment appears in the opinion. See Chafee at 352. Perhaps the honor belongs to *Near v. Minnesota* (1931), p. 600 infra.

ties' protected by the due process clause of the Fourteenth Amendment from impairment by the States," but ruled:

"By enacting the present statute the State has determined, through its legislative body, that utterances advocating the overthrow of organized government by force, violence and unlawful means, are so inimical to the general welfare and involve such danger of substantive evil that they may be penalized in the exercise of its police power. That determination must be given great weight. Every presumption is to be indulged in favor of the validity of the statute. And the case is to be considered 'in the light of the principle that the State is primarily the judge of regulations required in the interest of public safety and welfare'; and that its police 'statutes may only be declared unconstitutional where they are arbitrary or unreasonable attempts to exercise authority vested in the State in the public interest.' That utterances inciting to the overthrow of organized government by unlawful means, present a sufficient danger of substantive evil to bring their punishment within the range of legislative discretion, is clear. Such utterances, by their very nature, involve danger to the public peace and to the security of the State. They threaten breaches of the peace and ultimate revolution. And the immediate danger is none the less real and substantial, because the effect of a given utterance cannot be accurately foreseen. The State cannot reasonably be required to measure the danger from every such utterance in the nice balance of a jeweler's scale. A single revolutionary spark may kindle a fire that, smoldering for a time, may burst into a sweeping and destructive conflagration. It cannot be said that the State is acting arbitrarily or unreasonably when in the exercise of its judgment as to the measures necessary to protect the public peace and safety, it seeks to extinguish the spark without waiting until it has enkindled the flame or blazed into the conflagration. It cannot reasonably be required to defer the adoption of measures for its own peace and safety until the revolutionary utterances lead to actual disturbances of the public peace or imminent and immediate danger of its own destruction; but it may, in the exercise of its judgment, suppress the threatened danger in its incipiency.

"[It] is clear that the question in [this case] is entirely different from that involved in those cases where the statute merely prohibits certain acts involving the danger of substantive evil, without any reference to language itself, and it is sought to apply its provisions to language used by the defendant for the purpose of bringing about the prohibited results. There, if it be contended that the statute cannot be applied to the language used by the defendant because of its protection by the freedom of speech or press, it must necessarily be found, as an original question, without any previous determination by the legislative body, whether the specific language used involved such likelihood of bringing about the substantive evil as to deprive it of the constitutional protection. In such cases it has been held that the general provisions of the statute may be constitutionally applied to the specific utterance of the defendant if its natural tendency and probable effect was to bring about the substantive evil which the legislative body might prevent. *Schenck; Debs.* And the general statement in the *Schenck* case that the 'question in every case is whether the words are used in such circumstances and are of such a nature as to create a clear and present danger that they will bring about the substantive evils,' [was] manifestly intended, as shown by the context, to apply only in cases of this class, and has no application to those like the present, where the legislative body itself has previously determined the danger of substantive evil arising from utterances of a specified character."

HOLMES, J., joined by Brandeis, J., dissented: "The general principle of free speech, it seems to me, must be taken to be included in the Fourteenth Amendment, in view of the scope that has been given to the word 'liberty' as there used, although perhaps it may be accepted with a somewhat larger latitude of interpretation than is allowed to Congress by the sweeping language that governs or ought to govern the laws of the United States. If I am right then I think that the criterion sanctioned by the full Court in *Schenck* applies. [It] is true that in my opinion this criterion was departed from in *Abrams,* but the convictions that I expressed in that case are too deep for it to be possible for me as yet to believe that it [has] settled the law. If what I think the correct test is applied it is manifest that there was no present danger of an attempt to overthrow the government by force on the part of the admittedly small minority who shared the defendant's views. It is said that this manifesto was more than a theory, that it was an incitement. Every idea is an incitement. It offers itself for belief and if believed it is acted on unless some other belief outweighs it or some failure of energy stifles the movement at its birth. The only difference between the expression of an opinion and an incitement in the narrower sense is the speaker's enthusiasm for the result. Eloquence may set fire to reason. But whatever may be thought of the redundant discourse before us it had no chance of starting a present conflagration.[b] If in the long run the beliefs expressed in proletarian dictatorship are destined to be accepted by the dominant forces of the community, the only meaning of free speech is that they should be given their chance and have their way.[c]

"If the publication of this document had been laid as an attempt to induce an uprising against government at once and not at some indefinite time in the future it would have presented a different question. The object would have been one with which the law might deal, subject to the doubt whether there was any danger that the publication could produce any result, or in other words, whether it was not futile and too remote from possible consequences. But the indictment alleges the publication and nothing more."

Notes and Questions

1. *What if in the long run the belief in genocide is destined to be accepted?* Consider Bickel, *The Morality of Consent* 72 (1975): "[Although, in *Gitlow,* he

b. Consider Kalven, *A Worthy Tradition* 156 (1988): "This famous passage points up the ironies in tradition building. The basic problem of finding an accommodation between speech too close to action and censorship too close to criticism might, we have argued, have been tolerably solved by settling on 'incitement' as the key term. It is a term which came easily to the mind of Learned Hand. But for Holmes it does not resonate as it did for Hand. It strikes his ear as a loose, expansible term. At an inopportune moment in the history of free speech the great master of the common law turns poet: 'Every idea is an incitement.' There is of course a sense in which this is true and in which it is a 'scholastic subterfuge' to pretend that speech can be arrayed in firm categories. But the defendants' proposed instruction had offered a sense in which it was not true, in which incitement required advocacy of some definite and immediate acts of force. The weakness of the prosecution's case was not that the defendants' radicalism was not dangerous; it was that their manifesto was not concrete enough to be an incitement.

"Justice Holmes's dissent in *Gitlow,* like his *Abrams* peroration, is extraordinary prose to find in a judicial opinion, and I suspect it has contributed beyond measure to the charisma of the First Amendment. But it also carries the disturbing suggestion that the defendants' speech is to be protected precisely because it is harmless and unimportant. It smacks, as will the later protections of Jehovah's Witnesses, of a luxury civil liberty."

c. But see Posner, *Free Speech in an Economic Perspective,* 20 Suff.L.Rev. 1, 7 (1986): "If those beliefs are destined to prevail, free speech is irrelevant. Holmes is not describing a competitive market in ideas but a natural monopoly."

saw no clear and present danger, Holmes] did admit that all ideas carried the seed of future dangers as well as benefits. His answer was this: 'If in the long run the beliefs expressed in proletarian dictatorships are destined to be accepted [, the] only meaning of free speech [—*the only*—] is that they should be given their chance and have their way.' If in the long run the belief, let us say, in genocide is destined to be accepted [, the] only meaning of free speech is that it should be given its chance and have its way. Do we believe that? Do we accept it?" But consider Wellington, *On Freedom of Expression,* 88 Yale L.J. 1105, 1142 (1979): "The state cannot prevent advocacy [of genocide] on the ground that individuals will come to believe this false doctrine. But when there is a clear and present danger of action, the state must have the power to stop advocacy. [It] remains unfortunately imaginable that genocide could be implemented in a secular democracy: the state—including the courts—could be captured by a coalition of sick and evil minorities. But I do not believe that more restrictive control of expression would prevent such a catastrophe: unlike his cruelty, man's laws do have effective limits."

2. The statute in *Schenck* was not aimed directly at expression, but at conduct, i.e., certain actual or attempted interferences with the war effort. Thus, an analysis in terms of proximity between the words and the conduct prohibited (by a concededly valid law) seemed useful. But in *Gitlow* (and in *Dennis,* p. 397 infra) the statute was directed expressly against *advocacy* of a certain doctrine. Once the legislature *designates the point at which words became unlawful,* how helpful is the clear and present danger test? Is the question still how close words come to achieving certain consequences? In *Gitlow,* did Holmes "evade" the difficulty of applying an unmodified *Schenck* test to a different kind of problem? See Rogat, *Mr. Justice Holmes: Some Modern Views—The Judge as Spectator,* 31 U.Chi.L.Rev. 213, 217 (1964). See also Berns, *Freedom, Virtue and the First Amendment* 63 (Gateway ed. 1965); Linde, *"Clear and Present Danger" Reexamined,* 22 Stan.L.Rev. 1163, 1169–79 (1970).

3. Consider Linde, supra, at 1171: "Since New York's law itself defined the prohibited speech, the [*Gitlow*] Court could choose among three positions. It could (1) accept this legislative judgment of the harmful potential of the proscribed words, subject to conventional judicial review; (2) independently scrutinize the facts to see whether a 'danger,' as stated in *Schenck,* justified suppression of the particular expression; or (3) hold that by legislating directly against the words rather than the effects, the lawmaker had gone beyond the leeway left to trial and proof by the holding in *Schenck* and had made a law forbidden by the first amendment." Which course did the *Gitlow* majority choose? The dissenters? Which position should the Court have chosen?

Cases such as *Whitney,* infra, raise questions not only about freedom of speech, but also about the right of assembly. In turn, *Whitney* raises the issue of the existence and scope of a right not mentioned in the first amendment: freedom of association. Freedom of association is explored in Sec. 9 infra. Several of the cases which follow are primarily characterized as speech cases because the assemblies or associations at issue were designed for the purpose of organizing future speech activity.

WHITNEY v. CALIFORNIA

274 U.S. 357, 47 S.Ct. 641, 71 L.Ed. 1095 (1927).

JUSTICE SANFORD delivered the opinion of the Court.

[Charlotte Anita Whitney was convicted of violating the 1919 Criminal Syndicalism Act of California whose pertinent provisions were]:

"Section 1. The term 'criminal syndicalism' as used in this act is hereby defined as any doctrine or precept advocating, teaching or aiding and abetting the commission of crime, sabotage (which word is hereby defined as meaning willful and malicious physical damage or injury to physical property), or unlawful acts of force and violence or unlawful methods of terrorism as a means of accomplishing a change in industrial ownership or control, or effecting any political change.

"Sec. 2. Any person who: * * * 4. Organizes or assists in organizing, or is or knowingly becomes a member of, any organization, society, group or assemblage of persons organized or assembled to advocate, teach or aid and abet criminal syndicalism; * * *

"Is guilty of a felony and punishable by imprisonment."

The first count of the information, on which the conviction was had, charged that on or about November 28, 1919, in Alameda County, the defendant, in violation of the Criminal Syndicalism Act, "did then and there unlawfully, willfully, wrongfully, deliberately and feloniously organize and assist in organizing, and was, is, and knowingly became a member of [a group] organized and assembled to advocate, teach, aid and abet criminal syndicalism." * * *

1. While it is not denied that the evidence warranted the jury in finding that the defendant became a member of and assisted in organizing the Communist Labor Party of California, and that this was organized to advocate, teach, aid or abet criminal syndicalism as defined by the Act, it is urged that the Act, as here construed and applied, deprived the defendant of her liberty without due process of law. [Defendant's] argument is, in effect, that the character of the state organization could not be forecast when she attended the convention; that she had no purpose of helping to create an instrument of terrorism and violence; that she "took part in formulating and presenting to the convention a resolution which, if adopted, would have committed the new organization to a legitimate policy of political reform by the use of the ballot"; that it was not until after the majority of the convention turned out to be "contrary minded, and other less temperate policies prevailed" that the convention could have taken on the character of criminal syndicalism; and that as this was done over her protest, her mere presence in the convention, however violent the opinions expressed therein, could not thereby become a crime. This contention [is in effect] an effort to review the weight of the evidence for the purpose of showing that the defendant did not join and assist in organizing the Communist Labor Party of California with a knowledge of its unlawful character and purpose. This question, which is foreclosed by the verdict of the jury, [is] one of fact merely which is not open to review in this Court, involving as it does no constitutional question whatever. * * *

[That a state] may punish those who abuse [freedom of speech] by utterances inimical to the public welfare, tending to incite to crime, disturb the public peace, or endanger the foundations of organized government and threaten its overthrow by unlawful means, is not open to question. [*Gitlow*].

The essence of the offense denounced by the Act is the combining with others in an association for the accomplishment of the desired ends through the advocacy and use of criminal and unlawful methods. It partakes of the nature of a criminal conspiracy. That such united and joint action involves even greater danger to the public peace and security than the isolated utterances and acts of individuals is clear. We cannot hold that, as here applied, the Act is an unreasonable or arbitrary exercise of the police power of the State, unwarrantably infringing any right of free speech, assembly or association, or that those persons are protected from punishment by the due process clause who abuse such rights by joining and furthering an organization thus menacing the peace and welfare of the State. * * *

Affirmed.

JUSTICE BRANDEIS (concurring.) * * *

The felony which the statute created is a crime very unlike the old felony of conspiracy or the old misdemeanor of unlawful assembly. The mere act of assisting in forming a society for teaching syndicalism, of becoming a member of it, or assembling with others for that purpose is given the dynamic quality of crime. There is guilt although the society may not contemplate immediate promulgation of the doctrine. Thus the accused is to be punished, not for attempt, incitement or conspiracy, but for a step in preparation, which, if it threatens the public order at all, does so only remotely. The novelty in the prohibition introduced is that the statute aims, not at the practice of criminal syndicalism, nor even directly at the preaching of it, but at association with those who propose to preach it.

Despite arguments to the contrary which had seemed to me persuasive, it is settled that the due process clause of the Fourteenth Amendment applies to matters of substantive law as well as to matters of procedure. Thus all fundamental rights comprised within the term liberty are protected by the federal Constitution from invasion by the states. The right of free speech, the right to teach and the right of assembly are, of course, fundamental rights. These may not be denied or abridged. But, although the rights of free speech and assembly are fundamental, they are not in their nature absolute. Their exercise is subject to restriction, if the particular restriction proposed is required in order to protect the state from destruction or from serious injury, political, economic or moral. That the necessity which is essential to a valid restriction does not exist unless speech would produce, or is intended to produce,[a] a clear and imminent danger of some substantive evil which the state constitutionally may seek to prevent has been settled. See *Schenck*.

[The] Legislature must obviously decide, in the first instance, whether a danger exists which calls for a particular protective measure. But where a statute is valid only in case certain conditions exist, the enactment of the statute cannot alone establish the facts which are essential to its validity. Prohibitory legislation has repeatedly been held invalid, because unnecessary, where the denial of liberty involved was that of engaging in a particular business. The powers of the courts to strike down an offending law are no less when the

a. Unless speech would produce, *or* is intended to produce? Unless speech *would produce* a clear and imminent danger, although the harm produced was neither advocated nor intended by the speaker? Unless the speaker *intended* to produce a clear and imminent danger, even under extrinsic conditions of actual harmlessness? Compare *Brandenburg v. Ohio,* p. 416 infra. See generally Linde, supra, at 1168–69, 1181, 1185.

interests involved are not property rights, but the fundamental personal rights of free speech and assembly.

This Court has not yet fixed the standard by which to determine when a danger shall be deemed clear; how remote the danger may be and yet be deemed present; and what degree of evil shall be deemed sufficiently substantial to justify resort to abridgment of free speech and assembly as the means of protection. To reach sound conclusions on these matters, we must bear in mind why a state is, ordinarily, denied the power to prohibit dissemination of social, economic and political doctrine which a vast majority of its citizens believes to be false and fraught with evil consequence.

Those who won our independence believed that the final end of the state was to make men free to develop their faculties, and that in its government the deliberative forces should prevail over the arbitrary. They valued liberty both as an end and as a means. They believed liberty to be the secret of happiness and courage to be the secret of liberty. They believed that freedom to think as you will and to speak as you think are means indispensable to the discovery and spread of political truth; [b] that without free speech and assembly discussion would be futile; that with them, discussion affords ordinarily adequate protection against the dissemination of noxious doctrine; [c] that the greatest menace to freedom is an inert people; that public discussion is a political duty; and that this should be a fundamental principle of the American government. They recognized the risks to which all human institutions are subject. But they knew that order cannot be secured merely through fear of punishment for its infraction; that it is hazardous to discourage thought, hope and imagination; that fear breeds repression; that repression breeds hate; that hate menaces stable government; that the path of safety lies in the opportunity to discuss freely supposed grievances and proposed remedies; and that the fitting remedy for evil counsels is good ones. Believing in the power of reason as applied through public discussion, they eschewed silence coerced by law—the argument of force in its worst form. Recognizing the occasional tyrannies of governing majorities, they amended the Constitution so that free speech and assembly should be guaranteed.

Fear of serious injury cannot alone justify suppression of free speech and assembly. Men feared witches and burnt women. It is the function of speech to free men from the bondage of irrational fears. To justify suppression of free speech there must be reasonable ground to fear that serious evil will result if free speech is practiced. There must be reasonable ground to believe that the

b. Consider Blasi, *The First Amendment and the Ideal of Civic Courage,* 29 Wm. & Mary L.Rev. 653, 673–74 (1988): "This is as close as Brandeis gets to the claim that unregulated discussion yields truth. Notice that, in contrast to Holmes, Brandeis never tells us what is 'the best test of truth.' He never employs the metaphor of the marketplace. He speaks only of 'political truth,' and he uses the phrase 'means indispensable' to link activities described in highly personal terms—'think as you will,' 'speak as you think'—with the collective social goal of 'political truth.' I think his emphasis in this passage is on the attitudes and atmosphere that must prevail if the ideals of self-government and happiness through courage are to be realized. Brandeis is sketching a good society here, but not, I think, an all-conquering dialectic."

c. Consider Blasi, supra, at 674–75: "It is noteworthy that Brandeis never speaks of noxious doctrine being refuted or eliminated or defeated. He talks of societal self-protection and the fitting remedy. He warns us not to underestimate the value of discussion, education, good counsels. To me, his point is that noxious doctrine is most likely to flourish when its opponents lack the personal qualities of wisdom, creativity, and confidence. And those qualities, he suggests, are best developed by discussion and education, not by lazy and impatient reliance on the coercive authority of the state."

danger apprehended is imminent. There must be reasonable ground to believe that the evil to be prevented is a serious one.[d] Every denunciation of existing law tends in some measure to increase the probability that there will be violation of it. Condonation of a breach enhances the probability. Expressions of approval add to the probability. Propagation of the criminal state of mind by teaching syndicalism increases it. Advocacy of lawbreaking heightens it still further. But even advocacy of violation, however reprehensible morally, is not a justification for denying free speech where the advocacy falls short of incitement and there is nothing to indicate that the advocacy would be immediately acted on. The wide difference between advocacy and incitement, between preparation and attempt, between assembling and conspiracy, must be borne in mind. In order to support a finding of clear and present danger it must be shown either that immediate serious violence was to be expected or was advocated,[e] or that the past conduct furnished reason to believe that such advocacy was then contemplated.

Those who won our independence by revolution were not cowards. They did not fear political change. They did not exalt order at the cost of liberty. To courageous, self-reliant men, with confidence in the power of free and fearless reasoning applied through the processes of popular government, no danger flowing from speech can be deemed clear and present, unless the incidence of the evil apprehended is so imminent that it may befall before there is opportunity for full discussion. If there be time to expose through discussion the falsehood and fallacies, to avert the evil by the processes of education, the remedy to be applied is more speech, not enforced silence. Only an emergency can justify repression. Such must be the rule if authority is to be reconciled with freedom. Such, in my opinion, is the command of the Constitution. It is therefore always open to Americans to challenge a law abridging free speech and assembly by showing that there was no emergency justifying it.

Moreover, even imminent danger cannot justify resort to prohibition of these functions essential to effective democracy, unless the evil apprehended is relatively serious. Prohibition of free speech and assembly is a measure so stringent that it would be inappropriate as the means for averting a relatively trivial harm to society. A police measure may be unconstitutional merely because the remedy, although effective as means of protection, is unduly harsh or oppressive. Thus, a state might, in the exercise of its police power, make any trespass upon the land of another a crime, regardless of the results or of the intent or purpose of the trespasser. It might, also, punish an attempt, a conspiracy, or an incitement to commit the trespass. But it is hardly conceivable that this court would hold constitutional a statute which punished as a felony the mere voluntary assembly with a society formed to teach that pedestrians had the moral right to cross uninclosed, unposted, waste lands and to advocate their doing so, even if there was imminent danger that advocacy would lead to a trespass. The fact that speech is likely to result in some violence or in destruction of property is not enough to justify its suppression. There must be the probability of serious injury to the State.[f] Among free men, the deterrents

d. Does this suffice, regardless of the intent of the speaker? Regardless of the nature of the words he uses?

e. What if violence is advocated, but the advocacy is utterly ineffectual? What if the speaker neither desires nor advocates violence, but, under the circumstances the speech nevertheless is "expected" to produce violence?

f. But see Bork, *Neutral Principles and Some First Amendment Problems,* 47 Ind.L.J. 1, 34 (1971): "It is difficult to see how a constitutional court could properly draw the distinction proposed. Brandeis offered no ordinarily to be applied to prevent crime are education and punishment for violations of the law, not abridgement of the rights of free speech and assembly.

* * * Whenever the fundamental rights of free speech and assembly are alleged to have been invaded, it must remain open to a defendant to present the issue whether there actually did exist at the time a clear danger, whether the danger, if any, was imminent, and whether the evil apprehended was one so substantial as to justify the stringent restriction interposed by the Legislature. The legislative declaration, like the fact that the statute was passed and was sustained by the highest court of the State, creates merely a rebuttable presumption that these conditions have been satisfied.

Whether in 1919, when Miss Whitney did the things complained of, there was in California such clear and present danger of serious evil, might have been made the important issue in the case. She might have required that the issue be determined either by the court or the jury. She claimed below that the statute as applied to her violated the federal Constitution; but she did not claim that it was void because there was no clear and present danger of serious evil, nor did she request that the existence of these conditions of a valid measure thus restricting the rights of free speech and assembly be passed upon by the court or a jury. On the other hand, there was evidence on which the court or jury might have found that such danger existed. I am unable to assent to the suggestion in the opinion of the court that assembling with a political party, formed to advocate the desirability of a proletarian revolution by mass action at some date necessarily far in the future, is not a right within the protection of the Fourteenth Amendment. In the present case, however, there was other testimony which tended to establish the existence of a conspiracy, on the part of members of the International Workers of the World, to commit present serious crimes, and likewise to show that such a conspiracy would be furthered by the activity of the society of which Miss Whitney was a member. Under these circumstances the judgment of the State court cannot be disturbed. * * *

JUSTICE HOLMES joins in this opinion.

Notes and Questions

1. "*They valued liberty both as an end and as a means.*" Should recognition of the value of liberty[g] as an end augment the marketplace perspective or replace it? Compare Baker, *Scope of the First Amendment Freedom of Speech,* 25 U.C.L.A.L.Rev. 964 (1978) (liberty theory should replace marketplace theory) with Redish, *The Value of Free Speech,* 130 U.Pa.L.Rev. 591 (1982) (self-realization should be regarded as the first amendment's exclusive value) and Shiffrin, *The First Amendment and Economic Regulation: Away From a General Theory of the First Amendment,* 78 Nw.U.L.Rev. 1212 (1983) (many values including liberty and self-realization underpin the first amendment; single valued orientations are reductionist). But see Schauer, *Must Speech Be Special,* 78 Nw.U.L. Rev. 1284 (1983) (neither liberty nor self-realization should play *any* role in first amendment theory).

analysis to show that advocacy of law violation merited protection by the Court. Worse, the criterion he advanced is the importance, in the judge's eye, of the law whose violation is urged."

g. For discussion of the value of autonomy and its connection to the problem of advocacy of illegal action, compare Scanlon, *A Theory of Freedom of Expression,* 1 Philosophy & Pub. Aff. 204 (1972) with Scanlon, *Freedom of Expression and Categories of Expression,* 40 U.Pitt.L.Rev. 519 (1979).

2. *Brandeis and Republicanism.* Consider Lahav, *Holmes and Brandeis: Libertarian and Republican Justifications for Free Speech,* 4 J.L. & Pol. 451, 460–461 (1987): "[I]n his *Whitney* concurrence, Brandeis tells us, that in the American polity, 'the deliberative forces should prevail over the arbitrary,' that 'public discussion is a political duty,' and that 'the occasional tyranny of governing majorities' should be thwarted. This is radically different from the notion that individuals are free to remain aloof from politics if they so choose (a notion espoused by Holmes), and from the principle of the separation of the state from society. Implied here is the notion of civic virtue—the duty to participate in politics, the importance of deliberation, and the notion that the end of the state is not neutrality but active assistance in providing conditions of freedom which in turn are the 'secret of happiness.' One may even speculate that Brandeis, the progressive leader, believed that the final end of the state was the happiness of mankind.

"These ingredients of the Brandeis position in *Whitney* resonate with republican theory. The theory rests on two central themes: the idea of civic virtue and the idea that the end of politics (or the state) is the common good, which in turn is more than the sum of individual wills. Thus, the state is not separated from society, but rather is committed to the public good, and to a substantive notion of public morality. The members of society are not individuals encased in their autonomous zones, but rather social beings who recognize that they are an integral part of the society. This organic sense of belonging implicitly rejects the notion of combat zones. The republic and its citizens care for the welfare of all. Correctly understood, Brandeis' concurrence in *Whitney* is more than a justification from self-fulfillment or from self-rule. It is a justification from civic virtue." [h]

3. *Scope of the opinions.* Did Brandeis, J., simply reaffirm the clear and present danger test? Significantly clarify it? Significantly change it? Did Sanford, J., modify the position he had taken in *Gitlow*? Did he at least make it plain in *Whitney* that some state sedition convictions may be set aside under the first and fourteenth amendments? See Chafee, supra, at 351.

4. Ten years after *Whitney, De Jonge v. Oregon,* 299 U.S. 353, 57 S.Ct. 255, 81 L.Ed. 278 (1937) held that mere participation in a meeting called by the Communist party could not be made a crime. The right of peaceable assembly was declared to be "cognate to those of free speech and free press and is equally fundamental."

C. COMMUNISM AND ILLEGAL ADVOCACY

Kent Greenawalt has well described the pattern of decisions for much of the period between *Whitney* and *Dennis* infra: "[T]he clear and present danger formula emerged as the applicable standard not only for the kinds of issues with respect to which it originated but also for a wide variety of other First Amendment problems. If the Court was not always very clear about the relevance of that formula to those different problems, its use of the test, and its employment of ancillary doctrines, did evince a growing disposition to protect expression." *Speech and Crime,* 1980 Am.B.Found.Res.J. 645, 706. By 1951, however, anti-communist sentiment was a powerful theme in American politics. The Soviet Union had detonated a nuclear weapon; communists had firm control of the

h. For further background comparing the views of Brandeis and Holmes, JJ., see Blasi, fn. b supra; Cover, *The Left, The Right and the First Amendment: 1919–28,* 40 Md.L.Rev. 349 (1981).

Chinese mainland; the Korean War had reached a stalemate; Alger Hiss had been convicted of perjury in congressional testimony concerning alleged spying activities for the Soviet Union while he was a State Department official; and Senator Joseph McCarthy of Wisconsin had created a national sensation by accusations that many "card carrying Communists" held important State Department jobs. In this context, the top leaders of the American Communist Party asked the Court to reverse their criminal conspiracy convictions.

DENNIS v. UNITED STATES

341 U.S. 494, 71 S.Ct. 857, 95 L.Ed. 1137 (1951).

CHIEF JUSTICE VINSON announced the judgment of the Court and an opinion in which JUSTICE REED, JUSTICE BURTON and JUSTICE MINTON join.

Petitioners were indicted in July, 1948, for violation of the conspiracy provisions of the Smith Act during the period of April, 1945, to July, 1948. * * * A verdict of guilty as to all the petitioners was [affirmed by the Second Circuit]. We granted certiorari, limited to the following two questions: (1) Whether either § 2 or § 3 of the Smith Act, inherently or as construed and applied in the instant case, violates the First Amendment and other provisions of the Bill of Rights; (2) whether either § 2 or § 3 of the Act, inherently or as construed and applied in the instant case, violates the First and Fifth Amendments, because of indefiniteness.

Sections 2 and 3 of the Smith Act provide as follows:

"Sec. 2.

"(a) It shall be unlawful for any person—

"(1) to knowingly or willfully advocate, abet, advise, or teach the duty, necessity, desirability, or propriety of overthrowing or destroying any government in the United States by force or violence, or by the assassination of any officer of any such government; * * *

"Sec. 3. It shall be unlawful for any person to attempt to commit, or to conspire to commit, any of the acts prohibited by the provisions [of] this title."

The indictment charged the petitioners with wilfully and knowingly conspiring (1) to organize as the Communist Party of the United States of America a society, group and assembly of persons who teach and advocate the overthrow and destruction of the Government of the United States by force and violence, and (2) knowingly and wilfully to advocate and teach the duty and necessity of overthrowing and destroying the Government of the United States by force and violence. The indictment further alleged that § 2 of the Smith Act proscribes these acts and that any conspiracy to take such action is a violation of § 3 of the Act.

The trial of the case extended over nine months, six of which were devoted to the taking of evidence, resulting in a record of 16,000 pages. Our limited grant of the writ of certiorari has removed from our consideration any question as to the sufficiency of the evidence to support the jury's determination that petitioners are guilty of the offense charged. Whether on this record petitioners did in fact advocate the overthrow of the Government by force and violence is not before us, and we must base any discussion of this point upon the conclusions stated in the opinion of the Court of Appeals, which treated the issue in great detail [and] held that the record supports the following broad conclusions: [that] the Communist Party is a highly disciplined organization, adept at infiltration into strategic positions, use of aliases, and double-meaning language; that the Party is rigidly controlled; that Communists, unlike other political parties, tolerate no dissension from the policy laid down by the guiding [forces]; that the literature of the Party and the statements and activities of its leaders, petitioners here, advocate, and the general goal of the Party was, during the period in question, to achieve a successful overthrow of the existing order by force and violence. * * *

The obvious purpose of the statute is to protect existing Government, not from change by peaceable, lawful and constitutional means, but from change by violence, revolution and terrorism. That it is within the *power* of the Congress to protect the Government of the United States from armed rebellion is a proposition which requires little discussion. Whatever theoretical merit there may be to the argument that there is a "right" to rebellion against dictatorial governments is without force where the existing structure of the government provides for peaceful and orderly change. We reject any principle of governmental helplessness in the face of preparation for revolution, which principle, carried to its logical conclusion, must lead to anarchy. No one could conceive that it is not within the power of Congress to prohibit acts intended to overthrow the Government by force and violence. The question with which we are concerned here is not whether Congress has such *power,* but whether the *means* which it has employed conflict with the First and Fifth Amendments to the Constitution.

One of the bases for the contention that the means which Congress has employed are invalid takes the form of an attack on the face of the statute on the grounds that by its terms it prohibits academic discussion of the merits of Marxism-Leninism, that it stifles ideas and is contrary to all concepts of a free speech and a free press. [This] is a federal statute which we must interpret as well as judge. Herein lies the fallacy of reliance upon the manner in which this Court has treated judgments of state courts. Where the statute as construed by the state court transgressed the First Amendment, we could not but invalidate the judgments of conviction.

The very language of the Smith Act negates the interpretation which petitioners would have us impose on that Act. It is directed at advocacy, not discussion. Thus, the trial judge properly charged the jury that they could not convict if they found that petitioners did "no more than pursue peaceful studies and discussions or teaching and advocacy in the realm of ideas." * * * Congress did not intend to eradicate the free discussion of political theories, to destroy the traditional rights of Americans to discuss and evaluate ideas without fear of governmental sanction. * * *

But although the statute is not directed at the hypothetical cases which petitioners have conjured, its application in this case has resulted in convictions for the teaching and advocacy of the overthrow of the Government by force and violence, which, even though coupled with the intent to accomplish that overthrow, contains an element of speech. For this reason, we must pay special heed to the demands of the First Amendment marking out the boundaries of speech.

[T]he basis of the First Amendment is the hypothesis that speech can rebut speech, propaganda will answer propaganda, free debate of ideas will result in the wisest governmental policies. [An] analysis of the leading cases in this Court which have involved direct limitations on speech, however, will demonstrate that both the majority of the Court and the dissenters in particular cases have recognized that this is not an unlimited, unqualified right, but that the societal value of speech must, on occasion, be subordinated to other values and considerations. * * *

Although no case subsequent to *Whitney* and *Gitlow* has expressly overruled the majority opinions in those cases, there is little doubt that subsequent opinions have inclined toward the Holmes-Brandeis rationale. * * *

In this case we are squarely presented with the application of the "clear and present danger" test, and must decide what that phrase imports.[a] We first note that many of the cases in which this Court has reversed convictions by use of this or similar tests have been based on the fact that the interest which the State was attempting to protect was itself too insubstantial to warrant restriction of speech. * * * Overthrow of the Government by force and violence is certainly a substantial enough interest for the Government to limit speech. Indeed, this is the ultimate value of any society, for if a society cannot protect its very structure from armed internal attack, it must follow that no subordinate value can be protected. If, then, this interest may be protected, the literal problem which is presented is what has been meant by the use of the phrase "clear and present danger" of the utterances bringing about the evil within the power of Congress to punish.

Obviously, the words cannot mean that before the Government may act, it must wait until the putsch is about to be executed, the plans have been laid and the signal is awaited. If Government is aware that a group aiming at its overthrow is attempting to indoctrinate its members and to commit them to a course whereby they will strike when the leaders feel the circumstances permit, action by the Government is required. The argument that there is no need for Government to concern itself, for Government is strong, it possesses ample powers to put down a rebellion, it may defeat the revolution with ease needs no answer. For that is not the question. Certainly an attempt to overthrow the Government by force, even though doomed from the outset because of inadequate numbers or power of the revolutionists, is a sufficient evil for Congress to prevent. The damage which such attempts create both physically and politically to a nation makes it impossible to measure the validity in terms of the probability of success, or the immediacy of a successful attempt. In the instant case the trial judge charged the jury that they could not convict unless they found that petitioners intended to overthrow the Government "as speedily as circumstances would permit." This does not mean, and could not properly mean, that they would not strike until there was certainty of success. What was meant was that the revolutionists would strike when they thought the time was ripe. We must therefore reject the contention that success or probability of success is the criterion.

The situation with which Justices Holmes and Brandeis were concerned in *Gitlow* was a comparatively isolated event, bearing little relation in their minds to any substantial threat to the safety of the community. [They] were not confronted with any situation comparable to the instant one—the development of an apparatus designed and dedicated to the overthrow of the Government, in the context of world crisis after crisis.

Chief Judge Learned Hand, writing for the majority below, interpreted the phrase as follows: "In each case [courts] must ask whether the gravity of the

a. Consider Kalven, *A Worthy Tradition* 190–91 (1988): "The [Vinson opinion] acknowledges clear and present danger as the constitutional measure of free speech, but in the process, to meet the political exigencies of the case, it officially adjusts the test, giving it the kiss of death."

'evil,' discounted by its improbability, justifies such invasion of free speech as is necessary to avoid the danger." We adopt this statement of the rule. As articulated by Chief Judge Hand, it is as succinct and inclusive as any other we might devise at this time. * * *

Likewise, we are in accord with the court below, which affirmed the trial court's finding that the requisite danger existed. The mere fact that from the period 1945 to 1948 petitioners' activities did not result in an attempt to overthrow the Government by force and violence is of course no answer to the fact that there was a group that was ready to make the attempt. The formation by petitioners of such a highly organized conspiracy, with rigidly disciplined members subject to call when the leaders, these petitioners, felt that the time had come for action, coupled with the inflammable nature of world conditions, similar uprisings in other countries, and the touch-and-go nature of our relations with countries with whom petitioners were in the very least ideologically attuned, convince us that their convictions were justified on this score. And this analysis disposes of the contention that a conspiracy to advocate, as distinguished from the advocacy itself, cannot be constitutionally restrained, because it comprises only the preparation. It is the existence of the conspiracy which creates the danger. * * *

Although we have concluded that the finding that there was a sufficient danger to warrant the application of the statute was justified on the merits, there remains the problem of whether the trial judge's treatment of the issue was correct. He charged the jury, in relevant part, as follows:

"In further construction and interpretation of the statute I charge you that it is not the abstract doctrine of overthrowing or destroying organized government by unlawful means which is denounced by this law, but the teaching and advocacy of action for the accomplishment of that purpose, by language reasonably and ordinarily calculated to incite persons to such action. Accordingly, you cannot find the defendants or any of them guilty of the crime charged unless you are satisfied beyond a reasonable doubt that they conspired to organize a society, group and assembly of persons who teach and advocate the overthrow or destruction of the Government of the United States by force and violence and to advocate and teach the duty and necessity of overthrowing or destroying the Government of the United States by force and violence, with the intent that such teaching and advocacy be of a rule or principle of action and by language reasonably and ordinarily calculated to incite persons to such action, all with the intent to cause the overthrow or destruction of the Government of the United States by force and violence as speedily as circumstances would permit. * * *

"If you are satisfied that the evidence establishes beyond a reasonable doubt that the defendants, or any of them, are guilty of a violation of the statute, as I have interpreted it to you, I find as matter of law that there is sufficient danger of a substantive evil that the Congress has a right to prevent to justify the application of the statute under the First Amendment of the Constitution. This is matter of law about which you have no concern. * * *"

It is thus clear that he reserved the question of the existence of the danger for his own determination, and the question becomes whether the issue is of such a nature that it should have been submitted to the jury.

[When] facts are found that establish the violation of a statute, the protection against conviction afforded by the First Amendment is a matter of law. The doctrine that there must be a clear and present danger of a substantive evil that Congress has a right to prevent is a judicial rule to be applied as a matter of law by the courts. The guilt is established by proof of facts. Whether the First Amendment protects the activity which constitutes the violation of the statute must depend upon a judicial determination of the scope of the First Amendment applied to the circumstances of the case.

[In] *Schenck* this Court itself examined the record to find whether the requisite danger appeared, and the issue was not submitted to a jury. And in every later case in which the Court has measured the validity of a statute by the "clear and present danger" test, that determination has been by the court, the question of the danger not being submitted to the jury. * * * Petitioners intended to overthrow the Government of the United States as speedily as the circumstances would permit. Their conspiracy to organize the Communist Party and to teach and advocate the overthrow of the Government of the United States by force and violence created a "clear and present danger" of an attempt to overthrow the Government by force and violence. They were properly and constitutionally convicted * * *.

Affirmed.

JUSTICE CLARK took no part in the consideration or decision of this case.

JUSTICE FRANKFURTER, concurring in affirmance of the judgment.

[The] demands of free speech in a democratic society as well as the interest in national security are better served by candid and informed weighing of the competing interests, within the confines of the judicial process, than by announcing dogmas too inflexible for the non-Euclidian problems to be solved.

But how are competing interests to be assessed? Since they are not subject to quantitative ascertainment, the issue necessarily resolves itself into asking, who is to make the adjustment?—who is to balance the relevant factors and ascertain which interest is in the circumstances to prevail? Full responsibility for the choice cannot be given to the courts. Courts are not representative bodies. They are not designed to be a good reflex of a democratic society. Their judgment is best informed, and therefore most dependable, within narrow limits. Their essential quality is detachment, founded on independence. History teaches that the independence of the judiciary is jeopardized when courts become embroiled in the passions of the day and assume primary responsibility in choosing between competing political, economic and social pressures.

Primary responsibility for adjusting the interests which compete in the situation before us of necessity belongs to the Congress. [We] are to set aside the judgment of those whose duty it is to legislate only if there is no reasonable basis for [it]. Free-speech cases are not an exception to the principle that we are not legislators, that direct policy-making is not our province. How best to reconcile competing interests is the business of legislatures, and the balance they strike is a judgment not to be displaced by ours, but to be respected unless outside the pale of fair judgment. [A] survey of the relevant decisions indicates that the results which we have reached are on the whole those that would ensue from careful weighing of conflicting interests. The complex issues presented by regulation of speech in public places by picketing, and by legislation prohibiting advocacy of crime have been resolved by scrutiny of many factors besides the imminence and gravity of the evil threatened. The matter has been well summarized by a reflective student of the Court's work. "The truth is that the clear-and-present-danger test is an oversimplified judgment unless it takes account also of a number of other factors: the relative seriousness of the danger in comparison with the value of the occasion for speech or political activity; the availability of more moderate controls than those which the state has imposed; and perhaps the specific intent with which the speech or activity is launched. No matter how rapidly we utter the phrase 'clear and present danger,' or how closely we hyphenate the words, they are not a substitute for the weighing of values. They tend to convey a delusion of certitude when what is most certain is the complexity of the strands in the web of freedoms which the judge must disentangle." Freund, *On Understanding the Supreme Court* 27–28 [1949]. * * *

To make validity of legislation depend on judicial reading of events still in the womb of time—a forecast, that is, of the outcome of forces at best appreciated only with knowledge of the topmost secrets of nations—is to charge the judiciary with duties beyond its equipment. * * *

Even when moving strictly within the limits of constitutional adjudication, judges are concerned with issues that may be said to involve vital finalities. The too easy transition from disapproval of what is undesirable to condemnation as unconstitutional, has led some of the wisest judges to question the wisdom of our scheme in lodging such authority in courts. But it is relevant to remind that in sustaining the power of Congress in a case like this nothing irrevocable is done. The democratic process at all events is not impaired or restricted. Power and responsibility remain with the people and immediately with their representation. All the Court says is that Congress was not forbidden by the Constitution to pass this enactment and that a prosecution under it may be brought against a conspiracy such as the one before us. * * *

JUSTICE JACKSON, concurring.

[E]ither by accident or design, the Communist strategem outwits the anti-anarchist pattern of statute aimed against "overthrow by force and violence" if qualified by the doctrine that only "clear and present danger" of accomplishing that result will sustain the prosecution.

The "clear and present danger" test was an innovation by Mr. Justice Holmes in the *Schenck* case, reiterated and refined by him and Mr. Justice Brandeis in later cases, all arising before the era of World War II revealed the subtlety and efficacy of modernized revolutionary techniques used by totalitarian parties. In those cases, they were faced with convictions under so-called criminal syndicalism statutes aimed at anarchists but which, loosely construed, had been applied to punish socialism, pacifism, and left-wing ideologies, the charges often resting on farfetched inferences which, if true, would establish only technical or trivial violations. They proposed "clear and present danger" as a test for the sufficiency of evidence in particular cases.

I would save it, unmodified, for application as a "rule of reason" in the kind of case for which it was devised. When the issue is criminality of a hotheaded speech on a street corner, or circulation of a few incendiary pamphlets, or parading by some zealots behind a red flag, or refusal of a handful of school children to salute our flag, it is not beyond the capacity of the judicial process to gather, comprehend, and weigh the necessary materials for decision whether it is a clear and present danger of substantive evil or a harmless letting off of steam. It is not a prophecy, for the danger in such cases has matured by the time of trial or it was never present. The test applies and has meaning where a conviction is sought to be based on a speech or writing which does not directly or explicitly advocate a crime but to which such tendency is sought to be attributed by construction or by implication from external circumstances. The formula in such cases favors freedoms that are vital to our society, and, even if sometimes applied too generously, the consequences cannot be grave. But its recent expansion has extended, in particular to Communists, unprecedented immunities. Unless we are to hold our Government captive in a judge-made verbal trap, we must approach the problem of a well-organized, nation-wide conspiracy, such as I have described, as realistically as our predecessors faced the trivialities that were being prosecuted until they were checked with a rule of reason.

I think reason is lacking for applying that test to this case.

If we must decide that this Act and its application are constitutional only if we are convinced that petitioner's conduct creates a "clear and present danger" of violent overthrow, we must appraise imponderables, including international and national phenomena which baffle the best informed foreign offices and our most experienced politicians. We would have to foresee and predict the effectiveness of Communist propaganda, opportunities for infiltration, whether, and when, a time will come that they consider propitious for action, and whether and how fast our existing government will deteriorate. And we would have to speculate as to whether an approaching Communist coup would not be anticipated by a nationalistic fascist movement. No doctrine can be sound whose application requires us to make a prophecy of that sort in the guise of a legal decision. The judicial process simply is not adequate to a trial of such far-flung issues. The answers given would reflect our own political predilections and nothing more.

The authors of the clear and present danger test never applied it to a case like this, nor would I. If applied as it is proposed here, it means that the Communist plotting is protected during its period of incubation; its preliminary stages of organization and preparation are immune from the law; the Government can move only after imminent action is manifest, when it would, of course, be too late.

The highest degree of constitutional protection is due to the individual acting without conspiracy. But even an individual cannot claim that the Constitution protects him in advocating or teaching overthrow of government by force or violence. I should suppose no one would doubt that Congress has power to make such attempted overthrow a crime. But the contention is that one has the constitutional right to work up a public desire and will to do what it is a crime to attempt. I think direct incitement by speech or writing can be made a crime, and I think there can be a conviction without also proving that the odds favored its success by 99 to 1, or some other extremely high ratio. * * *

What really is under review here is a conviction of conspiracy, after a trial for conspiracy, on an indictment charging conspiracy, brought under a statute outlawing conspiracy. With due respect to my colleagues, they seem to me to discuss anything under the sun except the law of conspiracy. * * *

The Constitution does not make conspiracy a civil right. [Although] I consider criminal conspiracy a dragnet device capable of perversion into an instrument of injustice in the hands of a partisan or complacent judiciary, it has an established place in our system of law, and no reason appears for applying it only to concerted action claimed to disturb interstate commerce and withholding it from those claimed to undermine our whole Government. * * *

I do not suggest that Congress could punish conspiracy to advocate something, the doing of which it may not punish. Advocacy or exposition of the doctrine of communal property ownership, or any political philosophy unassociated with advocacy of its imposition by force or seizure of government by unlawful means could not be reached through conspiracy prosecution. But it is not forbidden to put down force or violence, it is not forbidden to punish its teaching or advocacy, and the end being punishable, there is no doubt of the power to punish conspiracy for the purpose. * * *

JUSTICE BLACK, dissenting. * * *

So long as this Court exercises the power of judicial review of legislation, I cannot agree that the First Amendment permits us to sustain laws suppressing freedom of speech and press on the basis of Congress' or our own notions of mere "reasonableness." Such a doctrine waters down the First Amendment so that it amounts to little more than an admonition to Congress. The Amendment as so construed is not likely to protect any but those "safe" or orthodox views which rarely need its protection. I must also express my objection to the holding because, as Mr. Justice Douglas' dissent shows, it sanctions the determination of a crucial issue of fact by the judge rather than by the jury. * * *

Public opinion being what it now is, few will protest the conviction of these Communist petitioners. There is hope, however, that in calmer times, when present pressures, passions and fears subside, this or some later Court will restore the First Amendment liberties to the high preferred place where they belong in a free society.

JUSTICE DOUGLAS, dissenting.

If this were a case where those who claimed protection under the First Amendment were teaching the techniques of sabotage, the assassination of the President, the filching of documents from public files, the planting of bombs, the art of street warfare, and the like, I would have no doubts. The freedom to speak is not absolute; the teaching of methods of terror and other seditious conduct should be beyond the pale along with obscenity and immorality. This case was argued as if those were the facts. The argument imported much seditious conduct into the record. That is easy and it has popular appeal, for the activities of Communists in plotting and scheming against the free world are common knowledge. But the fact is that no such evidence was introduced at the trial. There is a statute which makes a seditious conspiracy unlawful. Petitioners, however, were not charged with a "conspiracy to overthrow" the Government. They were charged with a conspiracy to form a party and groups and assemblies of people who teach and advocate the overthrow of our Government by force or violence and with a conspiracy to advocate and teach its overthrow by force and violence. It may well be that indoctrination in the techniques of terror to destroy the Government would be indictable under either statute. But the teaching which is condemned here is of a different character.

So far as the present record is concerned, what petitioners did was to organize people to teach and themselves teach the Marxist-Leninist doctrine contained chiefly in four books: *Foundations of Leninism* by Stalin (1924); *The Communist Manifesto* by Marx and Engels (1848); *State and Revolution* by Lenin (1917); *History of the Communist Party of the Soviet Union* (B.) (1939).

Those books are to Soviet Communism what *Mein Kampf* was to Nazism. If they are understood, the ugliness of Communism is revealed, its deceit and cunning are exposed, the nature of its activities becomes apparent, and the chances of its success less likely. That is not, of course, the reason why petitioners chose these books for their classrooms. They are fervent Communists to whom these volumes are gospel. They preached the creed with the hope that some day it would be acted upon.

The opinion of the Court does not outlaw these texts nor condemn them to the fire, as the Communists do literature offensive to their creed. But if the books themselves are not outlawed, if they can lawfully remain on library shelves, by what reasoning does their use in a classroom become a crime? It would not be a crime under the Act to introduce these books to a class, though that would be teaching what the creed of violent overthrow of the Government is. The Act, as construed, requires the element of intent—that those who teach the creed believe in it. The crime then depends not on what is taught but on who the teacher is. That is to make freedom of speech turn not on *what is said,* but on the *intent* with which it is said. Once we start down that road we enter territory dangerous to the liberties of every citizen. * * *

The vice of treating speech as the equivalent of overt acts of a treasonable or seditious character is emphasized by a concurring opinion, which by invoking the law of conspiracy makes speech do service for deeds which are dangerous to society. [N]ever until today has anyone seriously thought that the ancient law of conspiracy could constitutionally be used to turn speech into seditious conduct. Yet that is precisely what is suggested. I repeat that we deal here with speech alone, not with speech *plus* acts of sabotage or unlawful conduct. Not a single seditious act is charged in the indictment. To make a lawful speech unlawful because two men conceive it is to raise the law of conspiracy to appalling proportions. * * *

There comes a time when even speech loses its constitutional immunity. Speech innocuous one year may at another time fan such destructive flames that it must be halted in the interests of the safety of the Republic. That is the meaning of the clear and present danger test. When conditions are so critical that there will be no time to avoid the evil that the speech threatens, it is time to call a halt. Otherwise, free speech which is the strength of the Nation will be the cause of its destruction.

Yet free speech is the rule, not the exception. The restraint to be constitutional must be based on more than fear, on more than passionate opposition against the speech, on more than a revolted dislike for its contents. There must be some immediate injury to society that is likely if speech is allowed. * * *

I had assumed that the question of the clear and present danger, being so critical an issue in the case, would be a matter for submission to the jury. [The] Court, I think, errs when it treats the question as one of law.

Yet, whether the question is one for the Court or the jury, there should be evidence of record on the issue. This record, however, contains no evidence whatsoever showing that the acts charged viz., the teaching of the Soviet theory of revolution with the hope that it will be realized, have created any clear and present danger to the Nation. The Court, however, rules to the contrary. [The majority] might as well say that the speech of petitioners is outlawed because Soviet Russia and her Red Army are a threat to world peace.

The nature of Communism as a force on the world scene would, of course, be relevant to the issue of clear and present danger of petitioners' advocacy within the United States. But the primary consideration is the strength and tactical position of petitioners and their converts in this country. On that there is no evidence in the record. If we are to take judicial notice of the threat of Communists within the nation, it should not be difficult to conclude that *as a political party* they are of little consequence. Communists in this country have never made a respectable or serious showing in any election. I would doubt that there is a village, let alone a city or county or state, which the Communists could carry. Communism in the world scene is no bogeyman; but Communism as a political faction or party in this country plainly is. Communism has been so thoroughly exposed in this country that it has been crippled as a political force. Free speech has destroyed it as an effective political party. It is inconceivable that those who went up and down this country preaching the doctrine of revolution which petitioners espouse would have any success. In days of trouble and confusion, when bread lines were long, when the unemployed walked the streets, when people were starving, the advocates of a short-cut by revolution might have a chance to gain adherents. But today there are no such conditions. The country is not in despair; the people know Soviet Communism; the doctrine of Soviet revolution is exposed in all of its ugliness and the American people want none of it.

[Unless] and until extreme and necessitous circumstances are shown our aim should be to keep speech unfettered and to allow the processes of law to be invoked only when the provocateurs among us move from speech to action. * * * [b]

Notes and Questions

1. What was the "substantive evil" in the *Dennis* case, the danger of which was sufficiently "clear and present" to warrant the application of the rule as originally formulated by Holmes and Brandeis? A *successful* revolution? An *attempted* revolution, however futile such an attempt might be? A *conspiracy* to plan the overthrow of the government by force and violence? A "conspiracy *to advocate*" such overthrow? See Gorfinkel & Mack, *Dennis v. United States and the Clear and Present Danger Rule,* 39 Calif.L.Rev. 475, 496–501 (1951); Nathanson, *The Communist Trial and the Clear-and-Present-Danger Test,* 63 Harv.L. Rev. 1167, 1168, 1173–75 (1950). Suppose it were established in *Dennis* that the odds were 99–1 against the Communists attempting an overthrow of the Government until 1961? 1971? Same result?

2. *Suppression of "totalitarian movements".* Consider Auerbach, *The Communist Control Act of 1954,* 23 U.Chi.L.Rev. 173, 188–89 (1956): "[I]n suppressing totalitarian movements a democratic society is not acting to protect the status quo, but the very same interests which freedom of speech itself seeks to secure—the possibility of peaceful progress under freedom. That suppression may sometimes have to be the means of securing and enlarging freedom is a paradox which is not unknown in other areas of the law of modern democratic states. The basic 'postulate,' therefore, which should 'limit and control' the First Amendment is that it is part of the framework for a constitutional democracy and should, therefore, not be used to curb the power of Congress to exclude from the political struggle those groups which, if victorious, would crush democracy and impose totalitarianism. Whether in any particular case and at any particular time, Congress should suppress a totalitarian movement should be regarded as a matter of wisdom for its sole determination. But a democracy should claim

b. Eighteen years later, concurring in *Brandenburg,* p. 416 infra, Douglas, J., declared: "I see no place in the regime of the First Amendment for any 'clear and present danger' test whether strict and tight as some would make it or free-wheeling as the Court in *Dennis* rephrased it. When one reads the opinions closely and sees when and how the 'clear and present danger' test has been applied, great misgivings are aroused. First, the threats were often loud but always puny and made serious only by judges so wedded to the status quo that critical analysis made them nervous. Second, the test was so twisted and perverted in *Dennis* as to make the trial of those teachers of Marxism an all-out political trial which was part and parcel of the cold war that has eroded substantial parts of the First Amendment."

the moral and constitutional right to suppress these movements whenever it deems it advisable to do so." See also Bork, *Neutral Principles and Some First Amendment Problems,* 47 Ind.L.J. 1, 30–33 (1971).

3. *Seditious conspiracy.* Consider Shapiro, *Freedom of Speech* 63–64 (1966): "Brandeis had demanded no restriction while there was still time to call the police. The trouble in [*Dennis*] was that the police had been called but hadn't found any evidence of wrong-doing. The prosecution was instituted under the advocacy provisions because there was not sufficient evidence to meet the normal requirements of the criminal law of sedition. Thus, paradoxically, the defendants were convicted in an area where they were protected by the supposedly rigorous demands of the First Amendment *precisely because* they could not be convicted in an area under the routine protections of criminal law."

4. *Deference to legislative judgment.* Consider Linde, *"Clear and Present Danger" Reexamined,* 22 Stan.L.Rev. 1163, 1176–78 (1970): "The Smith Act in 1940 wrote into federal law almost the exact terms of the New York Criminal Anarchy Act sustained in *Gitlow.* New York had enacted that law in 1902, soon after the assassination of [President McKinley]. Between the occupation of Czechoslovakia and the Ribbentrap-Molotov pact of 1939, the House of Representatives was working on a bill [H.R. 5138] whose provenance was the fear of anarchist agitation in 1900 and the hatred of alien radicalism in 1919. It became law in 1940. * * *

"What was the legislative judgment that would deserve deference for its assessment of the danger from revolutionary speech? [A] member of the 76th Congress presumably might stand up in 1940 and demand to know whether H.R. 5138 [violated the first amendment]. Constitutional law, in its original function antecedent to judicial review, owes him an answer. The Congressman's decision must be constitutionally right or wrong, in that place and at that time—not only a prosecutor's, a jury's, or a judge's decisions at the time of a later trial.

"The answer the Congressman would get in 1940, of course, would be that in 1925 the Supreme Court had held that the New York legislature could reasonably have believed in 1902 that advocacy of violent overthrow of government was too dangerous to be permitted. [That theory] simply accepts a lawmaker's judgment of danger intrinsic in the content of such advocacy, quite independent of any extrinsic conditions. This answer would not pretend to anticipate in 1940 the external dangers in an atomic age that were invoked to sustain the act in 1951, nor would it need to. [I]s the answer Holmes and Brandeis would give the member of the 76th Congress more satisfactory—that it all depended on the circumstances; that the constitutionality of H.R. 5138 could be determined only in the context of future eventualities of clear and present danger which he might now be unable to foresee; that the danger which would justify his law to suppress revolutionary speech and organization might shift from indigenous rampages to foreign military menaces and back again so that the bill presently before him for enactment might well be unconstitutional now but might be constitutional in the light of diverse events in 1945, in 1948, in 1951, in 1957, and in 1961, perhaps not in 1966, but again in 1968?"

In 1954, Senator McCarthy was censured by the United States Senate for acting contrary to its ethics and impairing its dignity. In 1957, when the convictions of the "second string" communist leaders reached the Supreme Court in *Yates,* McCarthy had died, and so had McCarthyism. Although strong anti-communist sentiment persisted, the political atmosphere in *Yates'* 1957 was profoundly different from that of *Dennis'* 1951.

YATES v. UNITED STATES, 354 U.S. 298, 77 S.Ct. 1064, 1 L.Ed.2d 1356 (1957), reversed the convictions of 14 "second-string" Communist Party officials for conspiring, in violation of §§ 2(a)(1) and (3) of the Smith Act, (1) to advocate and teach the duty and necessity of overthrowing the federal government by force and violence, and (2) to organize, as the Communist Party of the United States, a group who so advocate and teach, all with the intent of causing the overthrow of the government by force and violence as speedily as circumstances would permit.

The trial judge, as the Court described it, "regarded as immaterial, and intended to withdraw from the jury's consideration, any issue as to the character of the advocacy in terms of its capacity to stir listeners to forcible action," by instructing the jury: "The kind of advocacy and teaching which is charged and upon which your verdict must be reached is not merely a desirability but a necessity that the Government of the United States be overthrown and destroyed by force and violence and not merely a propriety but a duty to overthrow [by] force and violence." Both the petitioners and the Government had submitted proposed instructions "which would have required the jury to find that the proscribed advocacy was not of a mere abstract doctrine of forcible overthrow, but of action to that end, by the use of language reasonably and ordinarily calculated to incite persons to such action," but the trial court had rejected these instructions on the basis of *Dennis*.

The Court was "thus faced with the question whether the Smith Act prohibits advocacy and teaching of forcible overthrow, as an abstract principle, divorced from any effort to instigate action to that end, so long as such advocacy or teaching is engaged in with evil intent." In holding that it did not, the Court, per HARLAN, J., avoided resolution of the issue "in terms of constitutional compulsion" [a] and construed the Smith Act—in light of the legislative history showing "beyond all question that Congress was aware of the distinction between the advocacy or teaching of abstract doctrine and the advocacy or teaching of action, and that it did not intend to disregard it"—as "aimed at the advocacy and teaching of concrete action for the forcible overthrow of the Government, and not of principles divorced from action":

"The Government's reliance on this Court's decision in *Dennis* is misplaced. The jury instructions which were refused here were given there, and were referred to by this Court as requiring 'the jury to find the facts *essential* to establish the substantive crime.' (Emphasis added). It is true that at one point in the late Chief Justice's opinion it is stated that the Smith Act 'is directed at advocacy, not discussion,' but it is clear that the reference was to advocacy of action, not ideas, for in the very next sentence the opinion emphasizes that the jury was properly instructed that there could be no conviction for 'advocacy in the realm of ideas.' * * *

"In failing to distinguish between advocacy of forcible overthrow as an abstract doctrine and advocacy of action to that end, the District Court appears to have been led astray by the holding in *Dennis* that advocacy of violent action to be taken at some future time was enough. [T]he District Court apparently thought that *Dennis* obliterated the traditional dividing line between advocacy of abstract doctrine and advocacy of action.

a. But see *Brandenburg*, Part D infra.

"This misconceives the situation confronting the Court in *Dennis* and what was held there. Although the jury's verdict, interpreted in light of the trial court's instructions, did not justify the conclusion that the defendants' advocacy was directed at, or created any danger of, immediate overthrow, it did establish that the advocacy was aimed at building up a seditious group and maintaining it in readiness for action at a propitious time. [The] essence of the *Dennis* holding was that indoctrination of a group in preparation for future violent action, as well as exhortation to immediate action, by advocacy found to be directed to 'action for the accomplishment' of forcible overthrow, to violence as 'a rule or principle of action,' and employing 'language of incitement,' is not constitutionally protected when the group is of sufficient size and cohesiveness, is sufficiently oriented towards action, and other circumstances are such as reasonably to justify apprehension that action will occur. This is quite a different thing from the view of the District Court here that mere doctrinal justification of forcible overthrow, if engaged in with the intent to accomplish overthrow, is punishable per se under the Smith Act. That sort of advocacy, even though uttered with the hope that it may ultimately lead to violent revolution, is too remote from concrete action to be regarded as the kind of indoctrination preparatory to action which was condemned in *Dennis*.

"[*Dennis* was] not concerned with a conspiracy to engage at some future time in seditious advocacy, but rather with a conspiracy to advocate presently the taking of forcible action in the future. It was action, not advocacy, that was to be postponed until 'circumstances' would 'permit.' * * *

"In light of the foregoing we are unable to regard the District Court's charge upon this aspect of the case as adequate. [T]he trial court's statement that the proscribed advocacy must include the 'urging,' 'necessity,' and 'duty' of forcible overthrow, and not merely its 'desirability' and 'propriety,' may not be regarded as a sufficient substitute for charging that the Smith Act reaches only advocacy of action for the overthrow of government by force and violence. The essential distinction is that those to whom the advocacy is addressed must be urged to *do* something, now or in the future, rather than merely to *believe* in something. * * *

"We recognize that distinctions between advocacy or teaching of abstract doctrines, with evil intent, and that which is directed to stirring people to action, are often subtle and difficult to grasp, for in a broad sense, as Mr. Justice Holmes said in his dissenting opinion in *Gitlow*: 'Every idea is an incitement.' But the very subtlety of these distinctions required the most clear and explicit instructions with reference to them, for they concerned an issue which went to the very heart of the charges against these petitioners. The need for precise and understandable instructions on this issue is further emphasized by the equivocal character of the evidence in this [record]. Instances of speech that could be considered to amount to 'advocacy of action' are so few and far between as to be almost completely overshadowed by the hundreds of instances in the record in which overthrow, if mentioned at all, occurs in the course of doctrinal disputation so remote from action as to be almost wholly lacking in probative value. Vague references to 'revolutionary' or 'militant' action of an unspecified character, which are found in the evidence, might in addition be given too great weight by the jury in the absence of more precise instructions. Particularly in light of this record, we must regard the trial court's charge in this respect as furnishing wholly inadequate guidance to the jury on this central point in the case."

On the basis of its interpretation of the Smith Act, the Court ordered an acquittal of five of the 14 petitioners,[b] finding "no adequate evidence in the record" to sustain their convictions on retrial.[c]

BLACK, J., joined by Douglas, J., dissented in part, maintaining, as they had in *Dennis,* that the Smith Act provisions on which the prosecutions were based violated the first amendment and that therefore acquittal should have been directed for all 14 petitioners.

CLARK, J., dissented: "*Dennis* merely held that a charge was sufficient where it requires a finding that 'the Party advocates the theory that there is a duty and necessity to overthrow the Government by force and violence [as] a program for winning adherents and as a policy to be translated into action' as soon as the circumstances permit [concurring opinion of Frankfurter, J.]." Thus, "the trial judge charged in essence all that was required under the *Dennis* opinion." He also maintained that instead of freeing five of the petitioners "solely on the *facts*"—which he regarded an unprecedented usurpation of the jury's function—the Court should have afforded the Government an opportunity, on remand, to present its evidence against petitioners "under the new theories announced by the Court for Smith Act prosecutions." [d]

Notes and Questions

1. *Dennis and Yates compared.* (a) On what did *Yates* focus: whether a *conspiracy* itself presents a "clear and present" danger or whether the *speech* of the conspirators does? On what did *Dennis* focus? Did *Yates* attach the same significance as did *Dennis* to membership in the Communist Party, as either an indication of intent or proof of membership in a conspiracy? To what extent does the fact that the *Yates* petitioners were not first-string leaders of the Party account for the result?

(b) Is it understandable that the *Yates* trial judge was "misled" by language in Vinson, C.J.'s *Dennis* opinion into thinking that punishment of the advocacy of abstract doctrine was permissible under the first amendment? Consider Greenawalt, *Speech and Crime,* 1980 Am.B.Found.Res.J. 645, 720 n. 279: "In defense of the trial court's instruction, it might be said that if someone is told he has a duty to participate in the forcible overthrow of the government, that signifies that he should perform illegal actions when the time arises. If all the Supreme Court opinion demanded is an explicit urging that listeners perform illegal actions at some future time, it is hard to distinguish that from what is clearly implied in advocacy of the ' "duty" of forcible overthrow.' But Justice Harlan may have meant that the advocacy must be more closely linked with action, either in the sense of recommending specific action or in the sense of being more positively directed to producing action among listeners."

2. *Advocating "doctrine" and advocating "action."* Consider Gellhorn, *American Rights* 80–81 (1960): "[O]ne can recognize a qualitative distinction between a speaker who expresses the opinion before a student audience that all law professors are scoundrels whose students should band together to beat them

b. None of the remaining nine petitioners were ever tried again. Upon remand, the government requested dismissal of the indictments, explaining that a "comprehensive review [establishes] that we cannot satisfy the evidentiary requirements laid down by" the Court in *Yates.* See Mollan, *Smith Act Prosecutions: The Effect of the Dennis and Yates Decisions,* 26 U.Pitt.L.Rev. 705, 732 (1965).

c. The type of evidence which led the Court to order the acquittal of the five petitioners and the kind of evidence which caused it to deny directed acquittals as to the nine others are summarized in *Scales* infra.

d. Brennan and Whittaker, JJ., took no part. Burton, J.'s concurrence is omitted.

within an inch of their lives, and a second speaker who, taking up that theme, urges the audience to obtain baseball bats, meet behind the law faculty building at three o'clock next Thursday afternoon, and join him in attacking any professor who can then be found. The first speaker, in [the *Yates*] view, should not be prosecuted; the second has stepped over the line between advocating a belief and advocating an illegal action." Cf. Hand, *The Bill of Rights* 59–60 (1958).

3. *Clear and present danger test.* After *Yates,* was a call for concrete, forcible action even in the unspecified future still "unprotected speech" and participation in a group calling for such action still "unprotected association"? Did the constitutional criteria developed by Harlan, J.'s majority opinions in *Yates* and *Scales* and *Noto,* infra, concern the advocate's intent and the content of his advocacy or the probability of its success? See Linde, *"Clear and Present Danger" Reexamined,* 22 Stan.L.Rev. 1163, 1166 (1970). To what extent is Harlan, J.'s analysis similar to Judge Hand's in *Masses,* supra?

Does *Yates* scrap the clear-and-present standard or establish a special category within that standard? When a subversive group is involved, may evidence of the "presentness of its organizational effectiveness" be substituted for the presentness of the danger? See Shapiro, *Freedom of Speech* 66, 71 (1966).

In an effort to avoid the demanding evidentiary requirements of *Yates*, the government began prosecuting communists under the "membership clause" of the Smith Act, 18 U.S.C.A. § 2385. After *Scales* and *Noto*, infra, the government abandoned Smith Act prosecutions altogether.

SCALES v. UNITED STATES, 367 U.S. 203, 81 S.Ct. 1469, 6 L.Ed.2d 782 (1961) affirmed the conviction of the Chairman of the North and South Carolina Districts of the Communist Party under the "membership clause" of the Smith Act, 18 U.S.C.A. § 2385, described by the Court, per HARLAN, J., as making a felony "the acquisition or holding of knowing membership in any organization which advocates the overthrow of the [federal] Government by force or violence." [1] The trial judge had instructed the jury that, as the Supreme Court described it, "in order to convict it must find [that] (1) the Communist Party advocated the violent overthrow of the Government, in the sense of 'present advocacy of action' to accomplish that end as soon as circumstances were propitious; and (2) petitioner was an 'active' member of the Party, and not merely 'a nominal, passive * * *' member, with knowledge of the Party's illegal advocacy and a specific intent to bring about violent overthrow 'as speedily as circumstances would permit.' "

The Court held that "the membership clause permissibly bears the construction put upon it below" and as thus construed neither "imputes guilt to an individual merely on the basis of his associations and sympathies" in violation of due process nor infringes First Amendment freedoms:

1. Section 2385 (whose membership clause we place in italics) reads: "Whoever organizes or helps or attempts to organize any society, group, or assembly of persons who teach, advocate, or encourage the overthrow or destruction of any such government by force or violence; *or becomes or is a member of,* or affiliates with, *any such society, group, or assembly of persons, knowing the purposes thereof—*

"Shall be fined not more than $20,000 or imprisoned not more than twenty years, or both, and shall be ineligible for employment by the United States or any department or agency thereof, for the five years next following his conviction. * * *"

"It was settled in *Dennis* that the advocacy with which we are here concerned is not constitutionally protected speech, and it was further established that a combination to promote such advocacy, albeit under the aegis of what purports to be a political party, is not such association as is protected by the First Amendment. We can discern no reason why membership, when it constitutes a purposeful form of complicity in a group engaging in this same forbidden advocacy, should receive any greater degree of protection from the guarantees of that Amendment.

"The [membership] clause does not make criminal all association with an organization, which has been shown to engage in illegal advocacy. There must be clear proof that a defendant 'specifically intend[s] to accomplish [the aims of the organization] by resort to violence.' *Noto* [this Part infra]. Thus the member for whom the organization is a vehicle for the advancement of legitimate aims and policies does not fall within the ban of the statute: he lacks the requisite specific intent 'to bring about the overthrow of the government as speedily as circumstances would permit.' Such a person may be foolish, deluded, or perhaps merely optimistic, but he is not by this statute made a criminal."

The Court also rejected the contention "that the evidence was insufficient to establish that the Communist Party was engaged in present advocacy of violent overthrow of the Government in the sense required by the Smith Act": "[T]he evidentiary question here is controlled in large part by *Yates* [which] rested on the view (not articulated in the opinion, though perhaps it should have been) that the Smith Act offenses, involving as they do subtler elements than are present in most other crimes, call for strict standards in assessing the adequacy of the proof needed to make out a case of illegal advocacy. This premise is as applicable to prosecutions under the membership clause of the Smith Act as it is to conspiracy prosecutions under that statute as we had in *Yates*. [*Yates*] indicates what type of evidence is needed to permit a jury to find that (a) there was 'advocacy of action' and (b) the Party was responsible for such advocacy.

"First, *Yates* makes clear what type of evidence is not *in itself* sufficient to show illegal advocacy. This category includes evidence of the following: the teaching of Marxism-Leninism and the connected use of Marxist 'classics' as textbooks; the official general resolutions and pronouncements of the Party at past conventions; dissemination of the Party's general literature, including the standard outlines on Marxism; the Party's history and organizational structure; the secrecy of meetings and the clandestine nature of the Party generally; statements by officials evidencing sympathy for and alliance with the U.S.S.R. It was the predominance of evidence of this type which led the Court to order the acquittal of several *Yates* [defendants].

"Second, *Yates* also indicates what kind of evidence is sufficient. There the Court pointed to two series of events which justified the denial of directed acquittals as to nine of the *Yates* defendants. The Court noted that with respect to seven of the defendants, meetings in San Francisco might be considered to be 'the systematic teaching and advocacy of illegal action which is condemned by the statute.' In those meetings, a small group of members were not only taught that violent revolution was inevitable, but they were also taught techniques for achieving that end. [T]he Court [also] referred to certain activities in the Los Angeles area 'which might be considered to amount to "advocacy of action"' and with which two *Yates* defendants were linked. Here again, the participants did not stop with teaching of the inevitability of eventual revolution, but went on to explain techniques, both legal and illegal, to be employed in preparation for or in connection with the revolution. [Viewed] together, these events described in *Yates* indicate at least two patterns of evidence sufficient to show illegal advocacy: (a) the teaching of forceful overthrow, accompanied by directions as to the type of illegal action which must be taken when the time for the revolution is reached; and (b) the teaching of forceful overthrow, accompanied by a contemporary, though legal, course of conduct clearly undertaken for the specific purpose of rendering effective the later illegal activity which is advocated."

After examining the *Scales* record, the Court concluded "this evidence sufficed to make a case for the jury on the issue of illegal Party advocacy. *Dennis* and *Yates* have definitely laid at rest any doubt that present advocacy of *future* action for violent overthrow satisfies statutory and constitutional requirements equally with advocacy of *immediate* action to that end. Hence this record cannot be considered deficient because it contains no evidence of advocacy for immediate overthrow. [T]he evidence amply showed that Party leaders were continuously preaching during the indictment period the inevitability of eventual forcible overthrow [and] the jury, under instructions which fully satisfied the requirements of *Yates*,[27] was entitled to infer from this systematic preaching [that] the doctrine of violent revolution [was] put forward as a guide to future action * * *; in short that 'advocacy of action' was engaged in." And "such advocacy was sufficiently broadly based to permit its attribution to the Party."

DOUGLAS, J., dissented: "When we allow petitioner to be sentenced to prison for six years for being a 'member' of the Communist Party, we make a sharp break with traditional concepts of First Amendment [rights]. Even the Alien and Sedition Laws—shameful reminders of an early chapter in intolerance—never went so far as we go today. They were aimed at conspiracy and advocacy of insurrection and at the publication of 'false, scandalous and malicious' writing against the Government. [There] is here no charge of conspiracy, no charge of any overt act to overthrow the Government by force and violence, no charge of any other criminal act. The charge is being a 'member' of the Communist Party, 'well-knowing' that it advocated the overthrow of the Government by force and violence, 'said defendant intending to bring about such overthrow by force and

27. The trial court charged: "Moreover, the teaching in the abstract or teaching objectively, that is, teaching, discussing, explaining, or expounding what is meant by the aim or purpose of any author, group, or society of overthrowing the Government by force and violence is not criminal. * * *

"However, if the Party went further, and with the intention of overthrowing the Government by force and violence, it taught, or advocated a rule or principle of action which both, one, called on its members to take forcible and concrete action at some advantageous time thereafter to overthrow the Government by force and violence, and, two, expressed that call in such written or oral words as would reasonably and ordinarily be calculated to incite its members to take concrete and forcible action for such overthrow; then, if the Communist Party did that, the Party became such a society or group, as was outlawed by the Smith Act.

"To be criminal the teaching or advocacy, or the call to action just described need not be for immediate action, that is, for action today, tomorrow, next month, or next year. It is criminal, nonetheless, if the action is to be at an unnamed time in the future, to be fixed by the circumstances or on signal from the Party.

"It is criminal if it is a call upon the members to be ready, or to stand in readiness for action, or for a summons to action at a favorable, or opportune time in the future, or as speedily as circumstances will permit, provided always that the urging of such readiness be by words which would reasonably and ordinarily be calculated to spur a person to ready himself for, and to take action towards, the overthrow of the Government. But those to whom the advocacy or urging is addressed must be urged to do something now or in the future, rather than merely to believe in something. In other words, the advocacy must be of concrete action, and not merely a belief in abstract doctrine. However, the immediate concrete action urged should be intended to lead towards the forcible overthrow, and be so understood by those to whom the advocacy is addressed."

violence as speedily as circumstances would permit.' That falls far short of a charge of conspiracy. Conspiracy rests not in intention alone but in an agreement with one or more others to promote an unlawful project. * * *

"The case is not saved by showing that petitioner was an active member. None of the activity constitutes a crime. [Scales] recruited new members into the Party, and promoted the advanced education of selected young Party members in the theory of communism to be undertaken at secret schools. He was a director of one such school [at which] students were told (by someone else) that one of the Party's weaknesses was in failing to place people in key industrial positions. One witness told of a meeting arranged by Scales at which the staff of the school urged him to remain in his position in an industrial plant rather than return to college. In Scales' presence, students at the school were once shown how to kill a person with a pencil, a device which, it was said, might come in handy on a picket line. Other evidence showed Scales [at different times to have said or distributed literature which said] that the Party line was that the Negroes in the South and the working classes should be used to foment a violent revolution; that a Communist government could not be voted into power in this country because the Government controlled communication media, newspapers, the military, and the educational system, and that force was the only way to achieve the revolution; [that] the revolution would come within a generation; that it would be easier in the United States than in Russia to effectuate the revolution because of assistance and advice from Russian Communists. * * *

"Not one single illegal act is charged to petitioner. That is why the essence of the crime covered by the indictment is merely belief—belief in the proletarian revolution, belief in Communist creed."

BLACK, J., dissented primarily for the reasons of Douglas and Brennan, JJ. He also maintained that although the Court had suggested in other cases in which it had applied the "balancing test," that it was justified "because no direct abridgment of First Amendment freedoms was involved," in the instant case "petitioner is being sent to jail for the express reason that he has associated with people who have entertained unlawful ideas and said unlawful things, and that of course is a *direct* abridgment of his freedoms of speech and assembly * * *. Nevertheless, [the] Court relies upon its prior decisions to the effect that the Government has power to abridge speech and assembly if its interest in doing so is sufficient to outweigh the interest in protecting these First Amendment freedoms. This, I think, demonstrates the unlimited breadth and danger of the 'balancing test' as it is currently being employed by a majority of this Court." [a]

In another Smith Act "membership clause" case, the same day as *Scales*, NOTO v. UNITED STATES, 367 U.S. 290, 81 S.Ct. 1517, 6 L.Ed.2d 836 (1961), per HARLAN, J., reversed the conviction of a communist worker in upstate New York, finding that the record "bears much of the infirmity that we found in the *Yates* record, and requires us to conclude that the evidence of illegal Party advocacy was insufficient to support this conviction." There was much evidence of "the Party's teaching of abstract doctrine that revolution is an inevitable product of the 'proletarian' effort to achieve communism in a capitalistic society," but testimony of evidence which supported an inference of " 'advocacy of action' to accomplish that end" was "sparse indeed" and "lacked the compelling quality

a. Brennan, J., joined by Warren, C.J., and Douglas, J., dissented on the ground that subsequent legislation had superseded the membership provision of the Smith Act.

which in *Scales* was supplied by the petitioner's utterances and systematic course of conduct as a high Party official."

Notes and Questions

1. See Shapiro, *Freedom of Speech* 119 (1966) for the view that when Congress had prohibited "membership" in organizations advocating the forcible overthrow of the government, it plainly had *not* meant "active" membership with "specific intent" and "the acrobatic display of statutory interpretation necessary to have made it mean all that simply demonstrated again the paradox of modest Justices who cannot bring themselves to challenge Congress, but yet cannot completely escape the feeling that they owe some independent duty to the Constitution."

2. Could Scales have been convicted under the advocacy or conspiracy to advocate clauses of the Smith Act? Could any really "active" Party member probably be? Without sufficient proof to satisfy *Yates*, can the government prove "membership" of the sort required for conviction in *Scales* and *Noto*? As a practical matter, did the Court eliminate the membership clause of the Smith Act as a separate means of prosecuting Communist Party members? See Shapiro, supra, at 120; 75 Harv.L.Rev. 116–17 (1961).

3. *Spock.* Dr. Spock, Rev. Coffin and others were convicted of conspiring to counsel and abet Selective Service registrants to refuse to have their draft cards in their possession and to disobey other duties imposed by the Selective Service Act of 1967. Spock signed a document entitled "A Call to Resist Illegitimate Authority," which "had 'a double aspect: in part it was a denunciation of governmental policy [in Vietnam] and, in part, it involved a public call to resist the duties imposed by the [Selective Service] Act.' " Several weeks later, Spock attended a demonstration in Washington, D.C., where an unsuccessful attempt was made to present collected draft cards to the Attorney General. *United States v. Spock,* 416 F.2d 165 (1st Cir.1969), per ALDRICH, J., ruled that Spock should have been acquitted: "[Spock] was one of the drafters of the Call, but this does not evidence the necessary intent to adhere to its illegal aspects. [H]is speech was limited to condemnation of the war and the draft, and lacked any words or content of counselling. The jury could not find proscribed advocacy from the mere fact [that] he hoped the frequent stating of his views might give young men 'courage to take active steps in draft resistance.' This is a natural consequence of vigorous speech. Similarly, Spock's actions lacked the clear character necessary to imply specific intent under the First Amendment standard. [H]e was at the Washington demonstration, [but took] no part in its planning. [His statements at this demonstration did not extend] beyond the general anti-war, anti-draft remarks he had made before. His attendance is as consistent with a desire to repeat this speech as it is to aid a violation of the law. The dissent would fault us for drawing such distinctions, but it forgets the teaching of [*Bond v. Floyd* [b]] that expressing one's views in broad areas is not foreclosed by knowledge of the consequences, and the important lesson of *Noto, Scales* and *Yates* that one may belong to a group, knowing of its illegal aspects, and still not be found to adhere thereto."

b. *Bond v. Floyd,* 385 U.S. 116, 87 S.Ct. 339, 17 L.Ed.2d 235 (1966) found ambiguity in expressions of support for those unwilling to respond to the draft that earlier opinions would have characterized as clear advocacy of illegal action. As Thomas Emerson puts it "the distance traversed [from *Schenck* and *Debs* to *Bond*] is quite apparent." *Freedom of Expression in Wartime,* 116 U.Pa.L.Rev. 975, 988 (1968).

D. A MODERN "RESTATEMENT"

BRANDENBURG v. OHIO

395 U.S. 444, 89 S.Ct. 1827, 23 L.Ed.2d 430 (1969).

PER CURIAM.

The appellant, a leader of a Ku Klux Klan group, was convicted under [a 1919] Ohio Criminal Syndicalism statute of "advocat[ing] the duty, necessity, or propriety of crime, sabotage, violence, or unlawful methods of terrorism as a means of accomplishing industrial or political reform" and of "voluntarily assembl[ing] with any society, group or assemblage of persons formed to teach or advocate the doctrines of criminal syndicalism." He was fined $1,000 and sentenced to one to 10 years' imprisonment. * * *

The record shows that a man, identified at trial as the appellant, telephoned an announcer-reporter on the staff of a Cincinnati television station and invited him to come to a Ku Klux Klan "rally" to be held at a farm in Hamilton County. With the cooperation of the organizers, the reporter and a cameraman attended the meeting and filmed the events. Portions of the films were later broadcast on the local station and on a national network.

The prosecution's case rested on the films and on testimony identifying the appellant as the person who communicated with the reporter and who spoke at the rally. The State also introduced into evidence several articles appearing in the film, including a pistol, a rifle, a shotgun, ammunition, a Bible, and a red hood worn by the speaker in the films.

One film showed 12 hooded figures, some of whom carried firearms. They were gathered around a large wooden cross, which they burned. No one was present other than the participants and the newsmen who made the film. Most of the words uttered during the scene were incomprehensible when the film was projected, but scattered phrases could be understood that were derogatory of Negroes and, in one instance, of Jews. Another scene on the same film showed the appellant, in Klan regalia, making a speech. The speech, in full, was as follows:

"This is an organizers' meeting. We have had quite a few members here today which are—we have hundreds, hundreds of members throughout the State of Ohio. I can quote from a newspaper clipping from the Columbus Ohio Dispatch, five weeks ago Sunday morning. The Klan has more members in the State of Ohio than does any other organization. We're not a revengent organization, but if our President, our Congress, our Supreme Court, continues to suppress the white, Caucasian race, it's possible that there might have to be some revengence taken.

"We are marching on Congress July the Fourth, four hundred thousand strong. From there we are dividing into two groups, one group to march on St. Augustine, Florida, the other group to march into Mississippi. Thank you."

The second film showed six hooded figures one of whom, later identified as the appellant, repeated a speech very similar to that recorded on the first film. The reference to the possibility of "revengence" was omitted, and one sentence was added: "Personally, I believe the nigger should be returned to Africa, the Jew returned to Israel." Though some of the figures in the films carried weapons, the speaker did not.

[*Whitney*] sustained the constitutionality of California's Criminal Syndicalism Act, the text of which is quite similar to that of the laws of Ohio. The Court upheld the statute on the ground that, without more, "advocating" violent means to effect political and economic change involves such danger to the security of the State that the State may outlaw it. But *Whitney* has been thoroughly discredited by later decisions [such as *Dennis* which] have fashioned the principle that the constitutional guarantees of free speech and free press do not permit a State to forbid or proscribe advocacy of the use of force or of law violation except where such advocacy is directed to inciting or producing imminent lawless action and is likely to incite or produce such action.[2] As we said in *Noto*, "the mere abstract teaching [of] the moral propriety or even moral necessity for a resort to force and violence, is not the same as preparing a group for violent action and steeling it to such action." See also *Bond v. Floyd*. A statute which fails to draw this distinction impermissibly intrudes upon the freedoms guaranteed by the First and Fourteenth Amendments. It sweeps within its condemnation speech which our Constitution has immunized from governmental control. Cf. *Yates* * * *.

Measured by this test, Ohio's Criminal Syndicalism Act cannot be sustained. The Act punishes persons who "advocate or teach the duty, necessity, or propriety" of violence "as a means of accomplishing industrial or political reform"; or who publish or circulate or display any book or paper containing such advocacy; or who "justify" the commission of violent acts "with intent to exemplify, spread or advocate the propriety of the doctrines of criminal syndicalism"; or [who] "voluntarily assemble" with a group formed "to teach or advocate the doctrines of criminal syndicalism." Neither the indictment nor the trial judge's instructions to the jury in any way refined the statute's bald definition of the crime in terms of mere advocacy not distinguished from incitement to imminent lawless action.[3]

Accordingly, we are here confronted with a statute which, by its own words and as applied, purports to punish mere advocacy and to forbid, on pain of criminal punishment, assembly with others merely to advocate the described type of action.[4] Such a statute falls within the condemnation of the First and Fourteenth Amendments. The contrary teaching of *Whitney* cannot be supported, and that decision is therefore overruled.

Reversed.

JUSTICE BLACK, concurring.

I agree with the views expressed by Mr. Justice Douglas in his concurring opinion in this case that the "clear and present danger" doctrine should have no

2. It was on the theory that the Smith Act embodied such a principle and that it had been applied only in conformity with it that this Court sustained the Act's constitutionality. That this was the basis for *Dennis* was emphasized in *Yates*, in which the Court overturned convictions for advocacy of the forcible overthrow of the Government under the Smith Act, because the trial judge's instructions had allowed conviction for mere advocacy, unrelated to its tendency to produce forcible action.

3. The first count of the indictment charged that appellant "did unlawfully by word of mouth advocate the necessity, or propriety of crime, violence, or unlawful methods of terrorism as a means of accomplishing political reform * * *." The second count charged that appellant "did unlawfully voluntarily assemble with a group or assemblage of persons formed to advocate the doctrines of criminal syndicalism * * *." The trial judge's charge merely followed the language of the indictment. * * *

4. Statutes affecting the right of assembly, like those touching on freedom of speech, must observe the established distinctions between mere advocacy and incitement to lawless action * * *.

place in the interpretation of the First Amendment. I join the Court's opinion, which, as I understand it, simply cites *Dennis*, but does not indicate any agreement on the Court's part with the "clear and present danger" doctrine on which *Dennis* purported to rely.

JUSTICE DOUGLAS, concurring.

While I join the opinion of the Court, I desire to enter a caveat.

[Whether] the war power—the greatest leveler of them all—is adequate to sustain [the "clear and present danger"] doctrine is debatable. The dissents in *Abrams* [and other cases] show how easily "clear and present danger" is manipulated to crush what Brandeis called "the fundamental right of free men to strive for better conditions through new legislation and new institutions" by argument and discourse even in time of war. Though I doubt if the "clear and present danger" test is congenial to the First Amendment in time of a declared war, I am certain it is not reconcilable with the First Amendment in days of peace. * * *

Mr. Justice Holmes, though never formally abandoning the "clear and present danger" test, moved closer to the First Amendment ideal when he said in dissent in *Gitlow* [quoting the passage beginning, "Every idea is an incitement."] We have never been faithful to the philosophy of that dissent.

"[In *Dennis,* we distorted] the "clear and present danger" test beyond recognition. [I] see no place in the regime of the First Amendment for any "clear and present danger" test whether strict and tight as some would make it or free-wheeling as the Court in *Dennis* rephrased it.

Notes and Questions

1. What pre-*Brandenburg* decisions, if any, "have fashioned the principle" that advocacy may not be prohibited "except [where] directed to inciting or producing *imminent* lawless action *and* * * * *likely* to incite or produce such action"? (Emphasis added.) Did *Dennis, Yates* and *Scales* take pains to *deny* that the unlawful action advocated need be "imminent" or that the advocacy must be "likely" to produce the forbidden action? See Linde, *"Clear and Present Danger" Reexamined,* 22 Stan.L.Rev. 1163, 1166–67, 1183–86 (1970).

2. Does *Brandenburg* adopt the *Masses* incitement test as a major part of the required showing? Consider Gunther, *Learned Hand and the Origins of Modern First Amendment Doctrine: Some Fragments of History,*" 27 Stan.L.Rev. 719, 754–55 (1975): "An incitement-nonincitement distinction had only fragmentary and ambiguous antecedents in the pre-*Brandenburg* era; it was *Brandenburg* that really 'established' it; and, it was essentially an establishment of the legacy of Learned Hand. [Under] *Brandenburg,* probability of harm is no longer the central criterion for speech limitations. The inciting language of the speaker—the Hand focus on 'objective' words—is the major consideration. And punishment of the harmless inciter is prevented by the *Schenck*-derived requirement of a likelihood of dangerous consequences." (citing *Brandenburg*'s note 4.) But see Shiffrin, *Defamatory Non-Media Speech and First Amendment Methodology,* 25 U.C.L.A.L.Rev. 915, 947 n. 206 (1978): "Several leading commentators assume that *Brandenburg* adopts an incitement requirement. [The] conclusion is apparently based on this line from *Brandenburg*: 'Neither the indictment nor the trial judge's instructions to the jury in any way refined the statute's bald definition of the crime in terms of mere advocacy, not distinguished from incitement to imminent lawless action' [also citing note 4]. The difficulty with

attaching significance to this ambiguous statement is that the term 'incitement' is used in the alternative in the Court's statement of its test. Thus, advocacy of imminent lawless action is protected unless it is directed to inciting *or* producing imminent lawless action and is likely to incite *or* produce imminent lawless action. Thus, even assuming that the use of the word incitement refers to express use of language, as opposed to the nature of results (an interpretation which is strained in light of the Court's wording of the test), incitement is not necessary to divorce the speech from first amendment protection. It is enough that the speech is directed to producing imminent lawless action and is likely to produce such action."

If one wants to argue that *Brandenburg* adopted *Masses*, is there anything to be made of the phrase "directed to" in the *Brandenburg* test? Alternatively, did *Yates* adopt the *Masses* test? If so, does its favorable citation in *Brandenburg* constitute an adoption of the *Masses* test?

3. The *Brandenburg* "inciting or producing imminent lawless action" standard was the basis for reversal of a disorderly conduct conviction in HESS v. INDIANA, 414 U.S. 105, 94 S.Ct. 326, 38 L.Ed.2d 303 (1973) (per curiam). After antiwar demonstrators on the Indiana University campus had blocked a public street, police moved them to the curbs on either side. As an officer passed him, appellant stated loudly, "We'll take the fucking street later (or again)," which led to his disorderly conduct conviction. His statement, observed the Court, "was not addressed to any person or group in particular" and "his tone, although loud, was no louder than that of the other people in the area. [At] best, [the] statement could be taken as counsel for present moderation; at worst, it amounted to nothing more than advocacy of illegal action at some indefinite future time." This was insufficient, under *Brandenburg,* to punish appellant's words, as the State had, on the ground that they had a "tendency to produce violence." It could not be said that appellant "was advocating, in the normal sense, any action" and there was "no evidence" that "his words were intended to produce, and likely to produce, *imminent* disorder."

REHNQUIST, J., joined by Burger, C.J., and Blackmun, J., dissented: "The simple explanation for the result in this case is that the majority has interpreted the evidence differently from the courts below." The dissenters quarrelled with the Court's conclusion that appellant's advocacy "was not directed towards inciting imminent action. [T]here are surely possible constructions of the statement which would encompass more or less immediate and continuing action against the police. They should not be rejected out of hand because of an unexplained preference for other acceptable alternatives." [a]

a. See also *NAACP v. Claiborne Hardware Co.,* 458 U.S. 886, 102 S.Ct. 3409, 73 L.Ed.2d 1215 (1982). The Court stated that the remarks of Charles Evers "might have been understood" as inviting violence, but stated that when "such appeals do not incite lawless action, they must be regarded as protected speech." If violent action had followed his remarks, a "substantial question" of liability would have been raised. The Court also observed, however, that the defendant might be held criminally liable for the acts of others if the speeches could be taken as evidence that the defendant gave "other specific instructions to carry out violent acts or threats." Compare *Watts v. United States,* 394 U.S. 705, 89 S.Ct. 1399, 22 L.Ed.2d 664 (1969) (statute prohibiting knowing and wilful threat of bodily harm upon the President is constitutional on its face) (dictum); *Rankin v. McPherson* (clerical employee's private expression of desire that Presidential assassination attempt be successful is insufficient justification for dismissal even in a law enforcement agency). For commentary on threats and the first amendment, compare Justice Linde's opinion in *State v. Robertson,* 293 Or. 402, 649 P.2d 569 (1982) with Greenawalt, *Criminal Coercion and Freedom of Speech,* 78 Nw.U.L.Rev. 1081 (1984).

4. Does *Yates* survive *Brandenburg*'s emphasis on *imminent* lawless action? Consider Kalven, *A Worthy Tradition* 234 (1988): "It is [possible] that [*Brandenburg*] has preserved the group/individual distinction. Under such an approach the *Yates* incitement-to-future-action standard would apply to group speech and the *Brandenburg* incitement-to-immediate-action standard would apply to the individual speaker." Is light shed on the question by *Communist Party of Indiana v. Whitcomb,* 414 U.S. 441, 94 S.Ct. 656, 38 L.Ed.2d 635 (1974), invalidating an Indiana statute denying a political party or its candidates access to the ballot unless the party files an affidavit that it "does not advocate the overthrow of local, state or national government by force or violence"? The Court, per Brennan J., maintained that the required oath (which had been interpreted to include advocacy of abstract doctrine) violated the principle of *Brandenburg* and stated that the principle applied not only to attempted denials of public employment, bar licensing, and tax exemption, but also to ballot access denials. The flaw with the state's position was that it furnished access to the ballot "not because the Party urges others 'to *do* something now *or in the future* [but] merely to believe in something,' [*Yates*]" (Second emphasis added).

What happened to the "imminent lawless action" requirement? Does the *Whitcomb* language clarify *Brandenburg*? Modify it?

5. Does *Brandenburg* apply to the advocacy of trivial crimes? Suppose the advocacy of trespass across a lawn? What result under *Brandenburg*? What result under *Dennis*? Is *Dennis* potentially more speech protective than *Brandenburg*?

6. Does *Brandenburg* apply to solicitation of crime in private or non-ideological contexts? Consider Shiffrin, note 3 supra, at 950: "How different it might be if the factual context were to involve advocacy of murder in a non-socio-political context. One suspects that little rhetoric about the marketplace of ideas or other first amendment values would be employed and that the serious and explicit advocacy of murder in a concrete way would suffice to divorce the speech from first amendment protection even in the absence of a specific showing of likelihood." Would it matter if it were not explicit or not concrete? For trenchant analysis of the issues raised by the shift in context from public to private or in subject matter from ideological to non-ideological, see Greenawalt, *Speech and Crime,* 1980 Am.B.Found.Res.J. 645.

7. Should the line of cases from *Schenck* to *Brandenburg* fuel cynicism about the binding force of legal doctrine and about the willingness or capacity of the judiciary to protect dissent? [b] To what extent does the focus on Supreme Court cases exaggerate the frailty of legal doctrine? [c]

b. In fashioning first amendment doctrine, should the overriding objective be at "all times [to] equip the first amendment to do maximum service in those historical periods when intolerance of unorthodox ideas is most prevalent and when governments are most able and most likely to stifle dissent systematically"? Should the first amendment "be targeted for the worst of times"? What impact would such a perspective have on the general development of first amendment doctrine? See Blasi, *The Pathological Perspective and the First Amendment,* 85 Colum.L.Rev. 449 (1985).

c. For a comprehensive review and critical analysis of the problems and policies raised by advocacy of illegal action, see Greenawalt, note 7 supra. See generally Greenawalt, *Speech, Crime, and the Uses of Language* (1989); Kalven, *A Worthy Tradition* (1987).

II. REPUTATION AND PRIVACY

In an important article, Harry Kalven coined the phrase "two level theory." Kalven, *The Metaphysics of the Law of Obscenity,* 1960 Sup.Ct.Rev. 1, 11. As he described it, *Beauharnais,* infra, and other cases employed a first amendment methodology that classified speech at two levels. Some speech—libel, obscenity, "fighting words"—was thought to be so bereft of social utility as to be beneath first amendment protection. At the second level, speech of constitutional value was thought to be protected unless it presented a clear and present danger of a substantive evil.

In considering libel and privacy, we will witness the collapse of "two level theory." The purpose is not a detailed examination of libel and privacy law. Our interests include the initial exclusion of defamation from first amendment protection, the themes and methods contributing to the erosion of that exclusion, and the articulation of basic first amendment values having implications and applications beyond defamation and the right to privacy.

A. GROUP LIBEL

BEAUHARNAIS v. ILLINOIS, 343 U.S. 250, 72 S.Ct. 725, 96 L.Ed. 919 (1952), per FRANKFURTER, J., sustained a statute prohibiting exhibition in any public place of any publication portraying "depravity, criminality, unchastity, or lack of virtue of a class of citizens, of any race, color, creed or religion [which exposes such citizens] to contempt, derision or obloquy or which is productive of breach of the peace or riots." The Court affirmed a conviction for organizing the distribution of a leaflet which petitioned the Mayor and City Council of Chicago "to halt the further encroachment, harassment and invasion of white people, their property, neighborhoods and persons by the Negro"; called for "one million self respecting white people in Chicago to unite"; and warned that if "the need to prevent the white race from becoming mongrelized by the Negro will not unite us, then the [aggressions], rapes, robberies, knives, guns, and marijuana of the Negro, surely will.":

"Today every American jurisdiction [punishes] libels directed at individuals. '[There] are certain well-defined and narrowly limited classes of speech, the prevention and punishment of which have never been thought to raise any constitutional problem. These include the lewd and obscene, the profane, the libelous, and the insulting or "fighting" words—those which by their very utterance inflict injury or tend to incite to an immediate breach of the peace. It has been well observed that such utterances are no essential part of any exposition of ideas, and are of such slight social value as a step to truth that any benefit that may be derived from them is clearly outweighed by the social interest in order and morality. "Resort to epithets or personal abuse is not in any proper sense communication of information or opinion safeguarded by the Constitution, and its punishment as a criminal act would raise no question under that instrument." *Cantwell v. Connecticut.' Such were the views of a unanimous Court in Chaplinsky v. New Hampshire.*[6]

"No one will gainsay that it is libelous falsely to charge another with being a rapist, robber, carrier of knives and guns, and user of marijuana. The [question is whether the fourteenth amendment] prevents a State from punishing such

6. In all but five States, the constitutional guarantee of free speech to every person is explicitly qualified by holding him "responsible for the abuse of that right." * * *

libels—as criminal libel has been defined, limited and constitutionally recognized time out of mind—directed at designated collectivities and flagrantly disseminated. [I]f an utterance directed at an individual may be the object of criminal sanctions, we cannot deny to a State power to punish the same utterance directed at a defined group, unless we can say that this is a wilful and purposeless restriction unrelated to the peace and well-being of the State.

"Illinois did not have to look beyond her own borders to await the tragic experience of the last three decades to conclude that wilful purveyors of falsehood concerning racial and religious groups promote strife and tend powerfully to obstruct the manifold adjustments required for free, orderly life in a metropolitan, polyglot community. From the murder of the abolitionist Lovejoy in 1837 to the Cicero riots of 1951, Illinois has been the scene of exacerbated tension between races, often flaring into violence and destruction. In many of these outbreaks, utterances of the character here in question, so the Illinois legislature could conclude, played a significant [part.]

"In the face of this history and its frequent obligato of extreme racial and religious propaganda, we would deny experience to say that the Illinois legislature was without reason in seeking ways to curb false or malicious defamation of racial and religious groups, made in public places and by means calculated to have a powerful emotional impact on those to whom it was presented.

"[It would] be arrant dogmatism, quite outside the scope of our authority [for] us to deny that the Illinois Legislature may warrantably believe that a man's job and his educational opportunities and the dignity accorded him may depend as much on the reputation of the racial and religious group to which he willynilly belongs, as on his own merits. This being so, we are precluded from saying that speech concededly punishable when immediately directed at individuals cannot be outlawed if directed at groups with whose position and esteem in society the affiliated individual may be inextricably involved. * * * [18]

"As to the defense of truth, Illinois in common with many States requires a showing not only that the utterance state the facts, but also that the publication be made 'with good motives and for justifiable ends'. Both elements are necessary if the defense is to prevail. [The] teaching of a century and a half of criminal libel prosecutions in this country would go by the board if we were to hold that Illinois was not within her rights in making this combined requirement. Assuming that defendant's offer of proof directed to a part of the defense was adequate, it did not satisfy the entire requirement which Illinois could exact."

The Court ruled that the trial court properly declined to require the jury to find a "clear and present danger": "Libelous utterances not being within the area of constitutionally protected speech, it is unnecessary, either for us or for the State courts, to consider the issues behind the phrase 'clear and present danger.' Certainly no one would contend that obscene speech, for example, may be punished only upon a showing of such circumstances. Libel, as we have seen, is in the same class."

BLACK, J., joined by Douglas, J., dissented: "[The Court] acts on the bland assumption that the First Amendment is wholly irrelevant. [Today's] case degrades First Amendment freedoms to the 'rational basis' level. [We] are

18. [If] a statute sought to outlaw libels of political parties, quite different problems not now before us would be raised. For one thing, the whole doctrine of fair comment as indispensable to the democratic political process would come into play. Political parties, like public men, are, as it were, public property.

cautioned that state legislatures must be left free to 'experiment' and to make legislative judgments. [State] experimentation in curbing freedom of expression is startling and frightening doctrine in a country dedicated to self-government by its people.

"[As] 'constitutionally recognized,' [criminal libel] has provided for punishment of false, malicious, scurrilous charges against individuals, not against huge groups. This limited scope of the law of criminal libel is of no small importance. It has confined state punishment of speech and expression to the narrowest of areas involving nothing more than private feuds. Every expansion of the law of criminal libel so as to punish discussion of matters of public concern means a corresponding invasion of the area dedicated to free expression by the First Amendment.

"[If] there be minority groups who hail this holding as their victory, they might consider the possible relevancy of this ancient remark: 'Another such victory and I am undone.' "

REED, J., joined by Douglas, J., dissenting, argued that the statute was unconstitutionally vague: "These words—'virtue,' 'derision,' and 'obloquy'—have neither general nor special meanings well enough known to apprise those within their reach as to limitations on speech. Philosophers and poets, thinkers of high and low degree from every age and race have sought to expound the meaning of virtue. * * * Are the tests of the Puritan or the Cavalier to be applied, those of the city or the farm, the Christian or non-Christian, the old or the young?"

DOUGLAS, J., dissented: "Hitler and his Nazis showed how evil a conspiracy could be which was aimed at destroying a race by exposing it to contempt, derision, and obloquy. I would be willing to concede that such conduct directed at a race or group in this country could be made an indictable offense. For such a project would be more than the exercise of free speech. [It] would be free speech plus.

"I would also be willing to concede that even without the element of conspiracy there might be times and occasions when the legislative or executive branch might call a halt to inflammatory talk, such as the shouting of 'fire' in a school or a theatre.

"My view is that if in any case other public interests are to override the plain command of the First Amendment, the peril of speech must be clear and present, leaving no room for argument, raising no doubts as to the necessity of curbing speech in order to prevent disaster."

JACKSON, J., dissenting, argued that the fourteenth amendment does not incorporate the first, as such, but permits the states more latitude than the Congress. He concluded, however, that due process required the trier of fact to evaluate the evidence as to the truth and good faith of the speaker and the clarity and presence of the danger. He was unwilling to assume danger from the tendency of the words and felt that the trial court had precluded the defendant's efforts to show truth and good motives.

Notes and Questions

1. *The right to petition.* Should it make a difference that the leaflet was in the form of a petition to the mayor and city council? Does the right of the people "to petition the Government for a redress of grievances" add anything of substance to Beauharnais' other first amendment arguments? Consider Kalven, *The Negro and the First Amendment* 40 (1965): "If it would make a difference

whether the petition was genuine and not just a trick of form, can the Court penetrate the form and appraise the true motivation or must it, as it does with congressional committees accept the official motivation?" [a]

2. *Equality and freedom of speech.* Consider the following hypothetical commentary: "Group libel statutes pose uniquely difficult issues for they involve a clash between two constitutional commitments: the principle of equality and the principle of free speech. They force us to decide what we want to express as a nation: Do we want a powerful symbol of our belief in uninhibited debate or do we want to be the kind of nation that will not tolerate the public calumny of religious, ethnic, and racial groups?" Compare Beth, *Group Libel and Free Speech,* 39 Minn.L.Rev. 167, 180–81 (1955).

3. *Tolerance and freedom of speech.* Should the first amendment be a means of institutionalizing a national commitment to the value of tolerance? By tolerating the intolerable, would we carve out one area of social interaction for extraordinary self-restraint and thereby develop [b] and demonstrate a vital social capacity? See generally Bollinger, *The Tolerant Society: Freedom of Speech and Extremist Speech in America* (1986); Bollinger, *Free Speech and Intellectual Values,* 92 Yale L.J. 438 (1983); Bollinger, *Book Review,* 80 Mich.L.Rev. 617 (1982).

4. *Libel, group libel, and seditious libel.* Consider Kalven, supra, at 15, 16 and 50–51: Seditious libel "is the doctrine that criticism of government officials and policy may be viewed as defamation of government and may be punished as a serious crime. [On] my view, the absence of seditious libel as a crime is the true pragmatic test of freedom of speech. This I would argue is what freedom of speech is about. [The] most revealing aspect of the opinions, and particularly that of Justice Frankfurter, is the absence of any sense of the proximity of the case before them to seditious libel. The case presents almost a perfect instance of that competition among analogies which Edward Levi has emphasized as the essential circumstance of legal reasoning. In the middle we have group libel and Justice Frankfurter's urging its many resemblances to individual libel. [If] the Court's speech theory had been more grounded, as it seems to me it should be, on the relevance of the concept of seditious libel and less on the analogy to the law of attempts found in the slogan 'clear and present danger,' it is difficult to believe that either the debate or the result in *Beauharnais* would have been the same."

B. PUBLIC OFFICIALS AND SEDITIOUS LIBEL

NEW YORK TIMES CO. v. SULLIVAN

376 U.S. 255, 84 S.Ct. 710, 11 L.Ed.2d 686 (1964).

JUSTICE BRENNAN delivered the opinion of the Court.

[Sullivan, the Montgomery, Ala. police commissioner, sued the New York Times and four black Alabama clergymen for alleged libelous statements in a paid, full-page fund-raising advertisement signed by a "Committee to defend Martin Luther King and the struggle for freedom in the South." The advertisement stated that "truckloads of police armed with shotguns and tear-gas ringed Alabama State College Campus" in Montgomery, and that "the Southern viola-

a. See *McDonald v. Smith,* 472 U.S. 479, 105 S.Ct. 2787, 86 L.Ed.2d 384 (1985) (denying any special first amendment status for the Petition Clause).

b. For skepticism about the capacity of courts to achieve any substantial impact in promoting tolerance, see Nagel, *Constitutional Cultures* 27–59 (1989).

tors [have] bombed [Dr. King's] home, assaulted his person [and] arrested him seven times." In several respects the statements were untrue. Several witnesses testified that they understood the statements to refer to Sullivan because he supervised Montgomery police. Sullivan proved he did not participate in the events described. He offered no proof of pecuniary loss.[3] Pursuant to Alabama law, the trial court submitted the libel issue to the jury, giving general and punitive damages instructions. It returned a $500,000 verdict for Sullivan against all of the defendants.] We hold that the rule of law applied by the Alabama courts is constitutionally deficient for failure to provide the safeguards for freedom of speech and of the press that are required by the First and Fourteenth Amendments in a libel action brought by a public official against critics of his official conduct.[4] We further hold that under the proper safeguards the evidence presented in this case is constitutionally insufficient to support the judgment for respondent.

I. [The] publication here [communicated] information, expressed opinion, recited grievances, protested claimed abuses, and sought financial support on behalf of a movement whose existence and objectives are matters of the highest public interest and concern. That the Times was paid for publishing the advertisement is as immaterial in this connection as is the fact that newspapers and books are sold. *Smith v. California.* Any other conclusion would discourage newspapers from carrying "editorial advertisements" of this type, and so might shut off an important outlet for the promulgation of information and ideas by persons who do not themselves have access to publishing facilities.

II. Under Alabama law [once] "libel per se" has been established, the defendant has no defense as to stated facts unless he can persuade the jury that they were true in all their particulars. [His] privilege of "fair comment" for expressions of opinion depends on the truth of the facts upon which the comment is based. [Unless] he can discharge the burden of proving truth, general damages are presumed, and may be awarded without proof of pecuniary injury.

[Respondent] relies heavily, as did the Alabama courts, on statements of this Court to the effect that the Constitution does not protect libelous publications. Those statements do not foreclose our inquiry here. None of the cases sustained the use of libel laws to impose sanctions upon expression critical of the official conduct of public officials. [L]ibel can claim no talismanic immunity from constitutional limitations. It must be measured by standards that satisfy the First Amendment.

The First Amendment, said Judge Learned Hand, "presupposes that right conclusions are more likely to be gathered out of a multitude of tongues, than

3. Approximately 394 copies of the edition of the Times containing the advertisement were circulated in Alabama. Of these, about 35 copies were distributed in Montgomery County. The total circulation of the Times for that day was approximately 650,000 copies.

4. [The] Times contends that the assumption of jurisdiction over its corporate person by the Alabama courts overreaches the territorial limits of the Due Process Clause. The latter claim is foreclosed from our review by the ruling of the Alabama courts that the Times entered a general appearance in the action and thus waived its jurisdictional objection. * * *

[Since *New York Times* the Court has upheld expansive personal jurisdiction against media defendants. *Calder v. Jones*, 465 U.S. 783, 104 S.Ct. 1482, 79 L.Ed.2d 804 (1984); *Keeton v. Hustler*, 465 U.S. 770, 104 S.Ct. 1473, 79 L.Ed.2d 790 (1984). *Calder* rejected the suggestion that first amendment concerns enter into jurisdictional analysis. It feared complicating the inquiry and argued that because first amendment concerns are taken into account in limiting the substantive law of defamation, "to reintroduce those concerns at the jurisdictional stage would be a form of double counting."]

through any kind of authoritative selection. To many this is, and always will be, folly; but we have staked upon it our all." [Thus] we consider this case against the background of a profound national commitment to the principle that debate on public issues should be uninhibited, robust, and wide-open, and that it may well include vehement, caustic, and sometimes unpleasantly sharp attacks on government and public officials. The present advertisement, as an expression of grievance and protest on one of the major public issues of our time, would seem clearly to qualify for the constitutional protection. The question is whether it forfeits that protection by the falsity of some of its factual statements and by its alleged defamation of respondent.

Authoritative interpretations of the First Amendment guarantees have consistently refused to recognize an exception for any test of truth—whether administered by judges, juries, or administrative officials—and especially not one that puts the burden of proving truth on the speaker. [E]rroneous statement is inevitable in free debate, and [it] must be protected if the freedoms of expression are to have the "breathing space" that they "need [to] survive."

[Injury] to official reputation affords no more warrant for repressing speech that would otherwise be free than does factual error. Where judicial officers are involved, this Court has held that concern for the dignity and reputation of the courts does not justify the punishment as criminal contempt of criticism of the judge or his decision. This is true even though the utterance contains "half-truths" and "misinformation." Such repression can be justified, if at all, only by a clear and present danger of the obstruction of justice. If judges are to be treated as "men of fortitude, able to thrive in a hardy climate," surely the same must be true of other government officials, such as elected city commissioners. Criticism of their official conduct does not lose its constitutional protection merely because it is effective criticism and hence diminishes their official reputations.

If neither factual error nor defamatory content suffices to remove the constitutional shield from criticism of official conduct, the combination of the two elements is no less inadequate. This is the lesson to be drawn from the great controversy over the Sedition Act of 1798, 1 Stat. 596, which first crystallized a national awareness of the central meaning of the First Amendment. [Although] the Sedition Act was never tested in this Court, the attack upon its validity has carried the day in the court of history. Fines levied in its prosecution were repaid by Act of Congress on the ground that it was unconstitutional. * * * Jefferson, as President, pardoned those who had been convicted and sentenced under the Act and remitted their fines. [Its] invalidity [has] also been assumed by Justices of this Court. [These] views reflect a broad consensus that the Act, because of the restraint it imposed upon criticism of government and public officials, was inconsistent with the First Amendment. * * *

What a State may not constitutionally bring about by means of a criminal statute is likewise beyond the reach of its civil law of libel. The fear of damage awards under a rule such as that invoked by the Alabama courts here may be markedly more inhibiting than the fear of prosecution under a criminal statute. [The] judgment awarded in this case—without the need for any proof of actual pecuniary loss—was one thousand times greater than the maximum fine provided by the Alabama criminal [libel law], and one hundred times greater than that provided by the Sedition Act. And since there is no double-jeopardy limitation applicable to civil lawsuits, this is not the only judgment that may be awarded against petitioners for the same publication.[18] Whether or not a newspaper can survive a succession of such judgments, the pall of fear and timidity imposed upon those who would give voice to public criticism is an atmosphere in which the First Amendment freedoms cannot [survive].

The state rule of law is not saved by its allowance of the defense of truth. A defense for erroneous statements honestly made is no less essential here than was the requirement of proof of guilty knowledge which, in *Smith v. California,* we held indispensable to a valid conviction of a bookseller for possessing obscene writings for [sale].

A rule compelling the critic of official conduct to guarantee the truth of all his factual assertions—and to do so on pain of libel judgments virtually unlimited in amount—leads to a comparable "self-censorship." Allowance of the defense of truth, with the burden of proving it on the defendant, does not mean that only false speech will be deterred.[19] [Under] such a rule, would-be critics of official conduct may be deterred from voicing their criticism, even though it is believed to be true and even though it is in fact true, because of doubt whether it can be proved in court or fear of the expense of having to do so. They tend to make only statements which "steer far wider of the unlawful zone." The rule thus dampens the vigor and limits the variety of public [debate].

The constitutional guarantees require, we think, a federal rule that prohibits a public official from recovering damages for a defamatory falsehood relating to his official conduct unless he proves that the statement was made with "actual malice"—that is, with knowledge that it was false or with reckless disregard of whether it was false or [not].

Such a privilege for criticism of official conduct is appropriately analogous to the protection accorded a public official when *he* is sued for libel by a private citizen. In *Barr v. Matteo,* 360 U.S. 564, 575, 79 S.Ct. 1335, 1341, 3 L.Ed.2d 1434 (1959), this Court held the utterance of a federal official to be absolutely privileged if made "within the outer perimeter" of his duties. The States accord the same immunity to statements of their highest officers, although some differentiate their lesser officials and qualify the privilege they enjoy. But all hold that all officials are protected unless actual malice can be proved. The reason for the official privilege is said to be that the threat of damage suits would otherwise "inhibit the fearless, vigorous, and effective administration of policies of government" and "dampen the ardor of all but the most resolute, or the most irresponsible, in the unflinching discharge of their duties." *Barr.* Analogous considerations support the privilege for the citizen-critic of government. It is as much his duty to criticize as it is the official's duty to administer. [It] would give public servants an unjustified preference over the public they serve, if critics of official conduct did not have a fair equivalent of the immunity granted to the officials themselves. We conclude that such a privilege is required by the First and Fourteenth Amendments.[23]

18. The Times states that four other libel suits based on the advertisement have been filed against it by [others]; that another $500,000 verdict has been awarded in [one]; and that the damages sought in the other three total $2,000,000.

19. Even a false statement may be deemed to make a valuable contribution to the public debate, since it brings about "the clearer perception and livelier impression of truth, produced by its collision with error." Mill, *On Liberty* 15 (1955).

23. We have no occasion here to determine how far down into the lower ranks of government employees the "public official" designation would extend for purposes of this rule, or otherwise to specify categories of persons who would or would not be included. [Nor] need we here determine the boundaries of the "official conduct" concept. * * *

III. [W]e consider that the proof presented to show actual malice lacks the convincing clarity [a] which the constitutional standard demands, and hence that it would not constitutionally sustain the judgment for respondent under the proper rule of law. [T]here is evidence that the Times published the advertisement without checking its accuracy against the news stories in the Times' own files. The mere presence of the stories in the files does [not] establish that the Times "knew" the advertisement was false, since the state of mind required for actual malice would have to be brought home to the persons in the Times' organization having responsibility for the publication of the advertisement. With respect to the failure of those persons to make the check, the record shows that they relied upon their knowledge of the good reputation of many [whose] names were listed as sponsors of the advertisement, and upon the letter from A. Philip Randolph, known to them as a responsible individual, certifying that the use of the names was authorized. There was testimony that the persons handling the advertisement saw nothing in it that would render it unacceptable under the Times' policy of rejecting advertisements containing "attacks of a personal character"; their failure to reject it on this ground was not unreasonable. We think the evidence against the Times supports at most a finding of negligence in failing to discover the misstatements, and is constitutionally insufficient to show the recklessness that is required for a finding of actual malice.

[T]he evidence was constitutionally defective in another respect: [b] it was incapable of supporting the jury's finding that the allegedly libelous statements were made "of and concerning" respondent. [On this point, the Supreme Court of Alabama] based its ruling on the proposition that: "[The] average person knows that municipal agents, such as police and firemen, and others, are under the control and direction of the city governing body, and more particularly under the direction and control of a single commissioner. In measuring the performance or deficiencies of such groups, praise or criticism is usually attached to the official in complete control of the body."

This proposition has disquieting implications for criticism of governmental conduct. [It would transmute] criticism of government, however impersonal it may seem on its face, into personal criticism, and hence potential libel, of the officials of whom the government is composed. [Raising] as it does the possibility that a good-faith critic of government will be penalized for his criticism, the proposition relied on by the Alabama courts strikes at the very center of the constitutionally protected area of free expression. We hold that such a proposition may not constitutionally be utilized to establish that an otherwise impersonal attack on governmental operations was a libel of an official responsible for those operations. Since it was relied on exclusively here, and there was no other evidence to connect the statements with respondent, the evidence was constitutionally insufficient to support a finding that the statements referred to respon-

a. Compare *Bose Corp. v. Consumers Union*, 466 U.S. 485, 104 S.Ct. 1949, 80 L.Ed. 2d 502 (1984) (appellate courts "must exercise independent judgment and determine whether the record establishes actual malice with convincing clarity."). Accord *Harte–Hanks Communications, Inc. v. Connaughton*, 491 U.S. 657, 109 S.Ct. 2678, 105 L.Ed.2d 562 (1989). See also *Anderson v. Liberty Lobby, Inc.*, 477 U.S. 242, 106 S.Ct. 2505, 91 L.Ed.2d 202 (1986) (same standard at summary judgment). Should independent appellate judgment be required in all first amendment cases? All constitutional cases? For broadranging commentary, see Monaghan, *Constitutional Fact Review*, 85 Colum.L.Rev. 229 (1985).

b. Implicitly, the Court left open the possibility of a new trial with new evidence. For discussion of the Court's internal debate on the question, see B. Schwartz, *Super Chief* 531–41 (1983).

dent. * * *[c]

JUSTICE BLACK, with whom JUSTICE DOUGLAS joins (concurring).

* * * "Malice," even as defined by the Court, is an elusive, abstract concept, hard to prove and hard to disprove. The requirement that malice be proved provides at best an evanescent protection for the right critically to discuss public affairs and certainly does not measure up to the sturdy safeguard embodied in the First Amendment. Unlike the Court, therefore, I vote to reverse exclusively on the ground that the Times and the individual defendants had an absolute, unconditional constitutional right to publish in the Times advertisement their criticisms of the Montgomery agencies and [officials].

The half-million-dollar verdict [gives] dramatic proof [that] state libel laws threaten the very existence of an American press virile enough to publish unpopular views on public affairs and bold enough to criticize the conduct of public officials. [B]riefs before us show that in Alabama there are now pending eleven libel suits by local and state officials against the Times seeking $5,600,000, and five such suits against the Columbia Broadcasting System seeking $1,700,000. Moreover, this technique for harassing and punishing a free press—now that it has been shown to be possible—is by no means limited to cases with racial overtones; it can be used in other fields where public feelings may make local as well as out-of-state newspapers easy prey for libel verdict seekers.

In my opinion the Federal Constitution has dealt with this deadly danger to the press in the only way possible without leaving the press open to destruction—by granting the press an absolute immunity for criticism of the way public officials do their public duty.

[This] Nation, I suspect, can live in peace without libel suits based on public discussions of public affairs and public officials. But I doubt that a country can live in freedom where its people can be made to suffer physically or financially for criticizing their government, its actions, or its officials. * * *[d]

Professor Kalven observed that the Court in *New York Times* was moving toward "the theory of free speech that Alexander Meiklejohn has been offering us for some fifteen years now." Kalven, *The New York Times Case: A Note On "The Central Meaning of the First Amendment,"* 1964 Sup.Ct.Rev. 191, 221. Indeed Kalven reported Meiklejohn's view that the case was " 'an occasion for dancing in the streets.' " Id. at 221 n. 125. Consider the following excerpts from Meiklejohn's most significant work and Zechariah Chafee's pointed response.

c. For a similar ruling that impersonal criticism of a government operation cannot be the basis for defamation "of and concerning" the supervisor of the operation, see *Rosenblatt v. Baer,* 383 U.S. 75, 86 S.Ct. 669, 15 L.Ed.2d 597 (1966): "[T]antamount to a demand for recovery based on libel of government."

d. Goldberg, J., joined by Douglas, J., concurring, also asserted for "the citizen and [the] press an absolute unconditional privilege to criticize official conduct," but maintained that the imposition of liability for "[p]urely private defamation" did not abridge the first amendment because it had "little to do with the political ends of a self-governing society." For background on the *New York Times* case, see Smolla, *Suing The Press* 26–52 (1986).

ALEXANDER MEIKLEJOHN—FREE SPEECH AND ITS RELATION TO SELF-GOVERNMENT

3, 26–27, 93–94, 89–91 (1948), reprinted in Meiklejohn, *Political Freedom* 9, 27–28, 79–80, 75–77 (1960).

We Americans think of ourselves as politically free. We believe in self-government. If men are to be governed, we say, then that governing must be done, not by others, but by themselves. So far, therefore, as our own affairs are concerned, we refuse to submit to alien control. That refusal, if need be, we will carry to the point of rebellion, of revolution. And if other men, within the jurisdiction of our laws, are denied their right to political freedom, we will, in the same spirit, rise to their defense. Governments, we insist, derive their just powers from the consent of the governed. If that consent be lacking, governments have no just powers.

[The] principle of the freedom of speech springs from the necessities of the program of self-government. It is not a Law of Nature or of Reason in the abstract. It is a deduction from the basic American agreement that public issues shall be decided by universal suffrage.

If, then, on any occasion in the United States it is allowable to say that the Constitution is a good document it is equally allowable, in that situation, to say that the Constitution is a bad document. If a public building may be used in which to say, in time of war, that the war is justified, then the same building may be used in which to say that it is not justified. If it be publicly argued that conscription for armed service is moral and necessary, it may likewise be publicly argued that it is immoral and unnecessary. If it may be said that American political institutions are superior to those of England or Russia or Germany, it may, with equal freedom, be said that those of England or Russia or Germany are superior to ours. These conflicting views may be expressed, must be expressed, not because they are valid, but because they are relevant. If they are responsibly entertained by anyone, we, the voters, need to hear them. When a question of policy is "before the house," free men choose to meet it not with their eyes shut, but with their eyes open. To be afraid of ideas, any idea, is to be unfit for self-government. Any such suppression of ideas about the common good, the First Amendment condemns with its absolute disapproval. The freedom of ideas shall not be abridged. * * *

If, however, as our argument has tried to show, the principle of the freedom of speech is derived, not from some supposed "Natural Right," but from the necessities of self-government by universal suffrage, there follows at once a very large limitation of the scope of the principle. The guarantee given by the First Amendment is not, then, assured to all speaking. It is assured only to speech which bears, directly or indirectly, upon issues with which voters have to deal—only, therefore, to the consideration of matters of public interest. Private speech, or private interest in speech, on the other hand, has no claim whatever to the protection of the First Amendment. If men are engaged, as we so commonly are, in argument, or inquiry, or advocacy, or incitement which is directed toward our private interests, private privileges, private possessions, we are, of course, entitled to "due process" protection of those activities. But the First Amendment has no concern over such protection. * * *

Here, then, are the charges which I would bring against the "clear and present danger" theory. They are all, it is clear, differing forms of the basic accusation that the compact of self-government has been ignored or repudiated.

First, the theory denies or obscures the fact that free citizens have two distinct sets of civil liberties. As the makers of the laws, they have duties and responsibilities which require an absolute freedom. As the subjects of the laws, they have possessions and rights, to which belongs a relative freedom.

Second, the theory fails to keep clear the distinction between the constitutional status of discussions of public policy and the corresponding status of discussions of private policy.

Third, the theory fails to recognize that, under the Constitution, the freedom of advocacy or incitement to action *by the government* may never be abridged. It is only advocacy or incitement to action by individuals or nonpolitical groups which is open to regulation.

Fourth, the theory regards the freedom of speech as a mere device which is to be abandoned when dangers threaten the public welfare. On the contrary, it is the very presence of those dangers which makes it imperative that, in the midst of our fears, we remember and observe a principle upon whose integrity rests the entire structure of government by consent of the governed.

Fifth, the Supreme Court, by adopting a theory which annuls the First Amendment, has struck a disastrous blow at our national education. It has denied the belief that men can, by processes of free public discussion, govern themselves. * * *

The unabridged freedom of public discussion is the rock on which our government stands. With that foundation beneath us, we shall not flinch in the face of any clear and present—or, even, terrific—danger.

ZECHARIAH CHAFEE, JR.—BOOK REVIEW

62 Harv.L.Rev. 891, 894–901 (1949).

[M]y main objection to Mr. Meiklejohn's book [is that he] places virtually all his argument against current proposals for suppression on a constitutional position which is extremely dubious. Whereas the supporters of these measures are genuinely worried by the dangers of Communism, he refuses to argue that these dangers are actually small. Instead, his constitutional position obliges him to argue that these dangers are irrelevant. No matter how terrible and immediate the dangers may be, he keeps saying, the First Amendment will not let Congress or anybody else in the Government try to deal with Communists who have not yet committed unlawful [acts.]

Mr. Meiklejohn's basic proposition is that there are two distinct kinds of freedom of speech, protected by quite different clauses of the Constitution. Freedom of speech on matters affecting self-government is protected by the First Amendment and is not open to restrictions by the Government. [By] contrast, private discussion is open to restrictions because it is protected by [fifth amendment due process].

The truth is, I think, that the framers had no very clear idea as to what they meant by "the freedom of speech or of the press," but we can say three things with reasonable assurance. First, these politicians, lawyers, scholars, churchgoers and philosophers, scientists, agriculturalists, and wide readers used the phrase to embrace the whole realm of thought. Second, they intended the First Amendment to give all the protection they desired, and had no idea of supplementing it by the Fifth Amendment. Finally, the freedom which Congress was forbidden to abridge was not, for them, some absolute concept which had never existed on earth. It was the freedom which they believed they already had—what they had wanted before the Revolution and had acquired through independence. In thinking about it, they took for granted the limitations which had been customarily applied in the day-to-day work of colonial courts. Now, they were setting up a new federal government of great potential strength, and (as in the rest of Bill of Rights) they were determined to make sure that it would not take away the freedoms which they then enjoyed in their thirteen sovereign states.

Still, the First Amendment has the power of growing to meet new needs. As Marshall said, it is a *Constitution* which we are interpreting. Although in 1791 the Amendment did not mean what Mr. Meiklejohn says, perhaps it ought to mean that now. But the Supreme Court is unlikely to think so in any foreseeable future. The author condemns the clear and present danger test as "a peculiarly inept and unsuccessful attempt to formulate an exception" to the constitutional protection of public discussion, but he does not realize how unworkable his own views would prove when applied in litigation.

In the first place, although it may be possible to draw a fairly bright line between speech which is completely immune and action which may be punished, some speech on public questions is so hateful that the Court would be very reluctant to protect it from statutory penalties. We are not dealing with a philosopher who can write what he pleases, but with at least five men who are asked to block legislators and prosecutors. The history of the Court Plan in 1937 shows how sure judges have to be of their ground to do that. Take a few examples. A newspaper charges the mayor with taking bribes. Ezra Pound broadcasts from an Italian radio station that our participation in the war is an abominable mistake. A speaker during a very bad food shortage tells a hungry mass of voters that the rationing board is so incompetent and corrupt that the best way to avoid starvation is to demand the immediate death of its members, unless they are ready to resign. Plainly few judges can grant constitutional protection to such speeches.

Even the author begins to hedge. Although his main insistence is on immunity for all speech connected with self-government, as my examples surely are, occasionally he concedes that "repressive action by the government is imperative for the sake of the general welfare," e.g., against libelous assertions, slander, words inciting men to crime, sedition, and treason by words. Here he is diving into very deep water. Once you push punishment beyond action into the realm of language, then you have to say pretty plainly how far back the law should go. You must enable future judges and jurymen to know where to stop. That is just what Holmes did when he drew his line at clear and present danger and the author gives us no substitute test for distinguishing between good public speech and bad public speech. He never faces the problem of Mark Anthony's Oration—discussion which is calculated to produce unlawful acts without ever mentioning them.

At times he hints that the line depends on the falsity of the assertions or the bad motives of the speakers. In the mayor's case, it is no answer to say that false charges are outside the Constitution; the issue is whether a jury shall be permitted to find them false even if they are in fact true. Moreover, in such charges a good deal of truth which might be useful to the voters is frequently mixed with some falsehood, so that the possibility of a damage action often keeps genuine information away from voters. And the low character of speakers and writers does not necessarily prevent them from uttering wholesome truths about politics. Witness the Essays of Francis Bacon. Mr. Meiklejohn has a special dislike for paid "lobbyists for special interests." But if discussing public questions with money in sight is outside the First Amendment, how about speeches by aspirants to a $75,000 job in Washington or editorials in newspapers or books on Free Speech? Dr. Johnson declared that any man who writes except for money is a fool. In short, the trouble with the bad-motive test is that courts and juries would apply it only to the exponents of unpopular views. If what is said happens to be our way, the speaker is as welcome as an ex-revolutionist to the Un-American Committee.

The most serious weakness in Mr. Meiklejohn's argument is that it rests on his supposed boundary between public speech and private speech. That line is extremely blurred. Take the novel *Strange Fruit*, which was lately suppressed in Massachusetts. It did not discuss any question then before the voters, but it dealt thoughtfully with many problems of the relations between whites and Negroes, a matter of great national concern. Was this under the First Amendment or the Fifth? [The] truth is that there are public aspects to practically every subject. [The] author recognizes this when he says that the First Amendment is directed against "mutilation of the thinking process of the community." [This] attitude, however, offers such a wide area for the First Amendment that very little is left for his private speech under the Fifth Amendment. For example, if books and plays are public speech, how can they be penalized for gross obscenity or libels?

On the other hand, if private speech does include scholarship (as the author suggests) and also art and literature, it is shocking to deprive these vital matters of the protection of the inspiring words of the First Amendment. The individual interest in freedom of speech, which Socrates voiced when he said that he would rather die than stop talking, is too precious to be left altogether to the vague words of the due process clause. Valuable as self-government is, it is in itself only a small part of our lives. That a philosopher should subordinate all other activities to it is indeed surprising.

[Even] if Holmes had agreed with Mr. Meiklejohn's view of the First Amendment, his insistence on such absolutism would not have persuaded a single colleague, and scores of men would have gone to prison who have been speaking freely for three decades. After all, a judge who is trying to establish a doctrine which the Supreme Court will promulgate as law cannot write like a solitary philosopher. He has to convince at least four men in a specific group and convince them very soon. The true alternative to Holmes' view of the First Amendment was not at all the perfect immunity for public discussion which Mr. Meiklejohn desires. It was no immunity at all in the face of legislation. Any danger, any tendency in speech to produce bad acts, no matter how remote, would suffice to validate a repressive statute, and the only hope for speakers and writers would lie in being tried by liberal jurymen. * * * Holmes worked out a formula which would invalidate a great deal of suppression, and won for it the solid authority of a unanimous Court. Afterwards, again and again, when his test was misapplied by the majority, Holmes restated his position in ringing words which, with the help of Brandeis and Hughes, eventually inspired the whole Court.

Notes and Questions

1. To what extent does *New York Times* incorporate Meiklejohn's perspective?[a] What is the "central meaning" of the first amendment?

2. *New York Times, definitional balancing, and the two-level theory of the first amendment.* By holding that some libel was within the protection of the first amendment, did the Court dismantle its two-level theory? See Kalven, supra, at 217–218. Or did the Court merely rearrange its conception of what was protected and what was not?

Does *Garrison v. Louisiana,* 379 U.S. 64, 85 S.Ct. 209, 13 L.Ed.2d 125 (1964) shed light on the question? The Court stated: "Calculated falsehood falls into that class of utterances '[of] such slight social value as a step to truth that any benefit that may be derived from them is clearly outweighed by the social interest in order and morality.' *Chaplinsky.*"

Could the judicial process here fairly be called *definitional* classification—defining which categories of libel are to be viewed as "speech" within the first amendment, and which are not? Consider Nimmer, *The Right to Speak from Times to Time, First Amendment Theory Applied to Libel and Misapplied to Privacy,* 56 Calif.L.Rev. 935, 942–43 (1968): "[*New York Times*] points the way to the employment of the balancing process on the definitional rather than the litigation or ad hoc level, [that is,] balancing not for the purpose of determining which litigant deserves to prevail in the particular case, but only for the purpose of defining which forms of speech are to be regarded as 'speech' within the meaning of the first amendment. [By] in effect holding that knowingly and recklessly false speech was not 'speech' within the meaning of the first amendment, the Court must have implicitly (since no explicit explanation was offered) referred to certain competing policy considerations. This is surely a kind of balancing, but it is just as surely not ad hoc balancing."[b]

a. For elaboration and modification of Meiklejohn's views, see Meiklejohn, *The First Amendment Is an Absolute,* 1961 Sup.Ct.Rev. 245. For commentary, see Bollinger, *Free Speech and Intellectual Values,* 92 Yale L.J. 438 (1983); Kalven, p. 429 supra. For work proceeding from a politically based interpretation of the first amendment, see Anastaplo, *The Constitutionalist* (1971); BeVier, *The First Amendment and Political Speech: An Inquiry Into the Substance and Limits of Principle,* 30 Stan.L.Rev. 299 (1978); Bloustein, *The First Amendment and Privacy: The Supreme Court Justice and the Philosopher,* 28 Rutg.L.Rev. 41 (1974); Bork, *Neutral Principles and Some First Amendment Problems,* 47 Ind.L.J. 1 (1971). See also Brennan, *The Supreme Court and the Meiklejohn Interpretation of the First Amendment,* 79 Harv.L.Rev. 1 (1965).

b. The literature about balancing is voluminous. Compare, e.g., Frantz, *The First Amendment in the Balance,* 71 Yale L.J. 1424 (1962); Frantz, *Is the First Amendment Law?—A Reply to Professor Mendelson,* 51 Calif.L. Rev. 729 (1963) with Mendelson, *On the Meaning of the First Amendment: Absolutes in the Balance,* 50 Calif.L.Rev. 821 (1962); Mendelson, *The First Amendment and the Judicial Process: A Reply to Mr. Frantz,* 17 Vand.L. Rev. 479 (1984). For recent criticism of balancing, see Aleinikoff, *Constitutional Law in the Age of Balancing,* 96 Yale L.J. 943 (1987); Nagel, *Constitutional Cultures* (1989); Nagel, *Rationalism in Constitutional Law,* 4 Const. Comm. 9 (1987); Nagel, *The Formulaic Constitution,* 84 Mich.L.Rev. 165 (1985). For a philosophical attack on cost benefit analysis, see Tribe, *Policy Science: Analysis or Ideology?,* 2 Phil. & Pub.Aff. 66 (1972); Tribe, *Technology Assessment and the Fourth Discontinuity: The Limits of Instrumental Rationality,* 46 So.Cal. L.Rev. 617 (1973). For philosophical defenses of balancing, see Schlag, *An Attack on Categorical Approaches to Freedom of Speech,* 30 U.C.L.A.L.Rev. 671 (1983); Shiffrin, *Liberalism, Radicalism, and Legal Scholarship,* 30 U.C.L.A.L.Rev. 1103 (1983) (both resisting any necessary connection between balancing and instrumentalism or cost-benefit analysis). For more doctrinally focused analysis, compare, e.g., Emerson, *First Amendment Doctrine and the Burger Court,* 68 Calif.L.Rev. 422 (1980); Tribe, *Constitutional Calculus: Equal Justice or Economic Efficiency?,* 98 Harv.L.Rev. 592 (1985) with Schauer, *Categories and the First Amendment: A Play in Three Acts,* 34 Vand.L.

3. *The scope of New York Times.* Professor Kalven argued that given the Court's conception of freedom of speech, its holding could not be confined: "the invitation to follow a dialectic progression from public official to government policy to public policy to matters in the public domain, like art, seems * * * overwhelming." Kalven, supra, at 221.

(a) *Public officials. New York Times,* fn. 23 left open "how far down into the lower ranks of governmental employees" the rule would extend, and *Rosenblatt v. Baer,* 383 U.S. 75, 86 S.Ct. 669, 15 L.Ed.2d 597 (1966) suggested the rule might apply to the supervisor of a publicly owned ski resort, saying it applies to those who "appear to the public to [have] substantial responsibility for or control over the conduct of government affairs." Should criticism of the official conduct of *very* high ranking government officials (e.g., the President, the Secretary of State, a general commanding troops in war) be given greater protection than that afforded in *New York Times*?

(b) *Private conduct of public officials and candidates. Garrison,* extended *New York Times* to "anything which might touch on an official's fitness for office," even if the defamation did not concern official conduct in office. Invoking that standard, *Monitor Patriot Co. v. Roy,* 401 U.S. 265, 91 S.Ct. 621, 28 L.Ed. 2d 35 (1971) applied *New York Times* to a news column describing a candidate for public office as a "former small-time bootlegger."

(c) *Public figures.* In CURTIS PUB. CO. v. BUTTS and ASSOCIATED PRESS v. WALKER, 388 U.S. 130, 87 S.Ct. 1975, 18 L.Ed.2d 1094 (1967), HARLAN, J., contended that because public figures were not subject to the restraints of the political process, any criticism of them was not akin to seditious libel and was, therefore, a step removed from the central meaning of the first amendment. Nonetheless, he argued that public figure actions should not be left entirely to the vagaries of state defamation law and would have required that public figures show "highly unreasonable conduct constituting an extreme departure from the standards of investigation and reporting ordinarily adhered to by responsible publishers" as a prerequisite to recovery. In response, WARREN, C.J., argued that the inapplicability of the restraints of the political process to public figures underscored the importance for uninhibited debate about their activities since "public opinion may be the only instrument by which society can attempt to influence their conduct." He observed that increasingly "the distinctions between governmental and private sectors are blurred," that public figures, like public officials, "often play an influential role in ordering society," and as a class have a ready access to the mass media "both to influence policy and to counter criticism of their views and activities." He accordingly concluded that the *New York Times* rule should be extended to public figures. Four other justices in *Butts* and *Walker* were willing to go at least as far as Warren, C.J., and subsequent cases have settled on the position that public figures must meet the *New York Times* requirements in order to recover in a defamation action. The critical issues are how to define the concept of public figure and how to apply it in practice. See *Gertz,* infra.

(d) *Private plaintiffs and public issues.* Without deciding whether any first amendment protection should extend to matters not of general or public interest, a plurality led by BRENNAN, J., joined by Burger, C.J., and Blackmun, J., argued in ROSENBLOOM v. METROMEDIA, INC., 403 U.S. 29, 91 S.Ct. 1811, 29 L.Ed.

Rev. 265 (1981); Shiffrin, *The First Amendment and Economic Regulation: Away From a General Theory of the First Amendment,* 78 Nw.U.L.Rev. 1212 (1983); Van Alstyne, *A Graphic Review of the Free Speech Clause,* 70 Calif.L.Rev. 107 (1982).

2d 296 (1971), that the *New York Times* rule should be extended to defamatory statements involving matters of public or general interest "without regard to whether the persons involved are famous or anonymous." Black, J., would have gone further, opining that the first amendment "does not permit the recovery of libel judgments against the news media even when statements are broadcast with knowledge they are false," and Douglas, J., shared Black, J.'s approach (at least with respect to matters of public interest, although he did not participate in *Rosenbloom.*) White, J., felt that the *New York Times* rule should apply to reporting on the official actions of public servants and to reporting on those involved in or affected by their official action. That principle was broad enough to cover Rosenbloom, a distributor of nudist magazines who had been arrested by the Philadelphia police for distributing obscene materials. The defamatory broadcast wrongly assumed his guilt. Dissenting, Harlan, Stewart and Marshall, JJ., counselled an approach similar to that taken in *Gertz,* infra.

After *Rosenbloom* the lower courts rather uniformly followed the approach taken by the plurality. By 1974, however, the composition of the Court had changed and so had the minds of some of the justices.

C. PRIVATE INDIVIDUALS AND PUBLIC FIGURES

GERTZ v. ROBERT WELCH, INC.

418 U.S. 323, 94 S.Ct. 2997, 41 L.Ed.2d 789 (1974).

Justice Powell delivered the opinion of the Court.

[Respondent published *American Opinion,* a monthly outlet for the John Birch Society. It published an article falsely stating that Gertz, a lawyer, was the "architect" in a "communist frameup" of a policeman convicted of murdering a youth whose family Gertz represented in resultant civil proceedings, and that Gertz had a "criminal record" and had been an officer in a named "Communist-fronter" organization that advocated violent seizure of our government. In Gertz' libel action there was evidence that *Opinion* 's managing editor did not know the statements were false and had relied on the reputation of the article's author and prior experience with the accuracy of his articles. After a $50,000 verdict for Gertz, the trial court entered judgment n.o.v., concluding that the *New York Times* rule applied to any discussion of a "public issue." The court of appeals affirmed, ruling that the publisher did not have the requisite "awareness of probable falsity." The Court held that *New York Times* did not apply to defamation of private individuals, but remanded for a new trial "because the jury was allowed to impose liability without fault [and] to presume damages without proof of injury."]

II. The principal issue in this case is whether a newspaper or broadcaster that publishes defamatory falsehoods about an individual who is neither a public official nor a public figure may claim a constitutional privilege against liability for the injury inflicted by those statements. * * *

In his opinion for the plurality in *Rosenbloom,* Mr. Justice Brennan took the *Times* privilege one step further [than *Butts* and *Walker*]. He concluded that its protection should extend to defamatory falsehoods relating to private persons if the statements concerned matters of general or public interest. He abjured the suggested distinction between public officials and public figures on the one hand and private individuals on the other. He focused instead on society's interest in learning about certain issues: "If a matter is a subject of public or general interest, it cannot suddenly become less so merely because a private individual is involved or because in some sense the individual did not choose to become involved." Thus, under the plurality opinion, a private citizen involuntarily associated with a matter of general interest has no recourse for injury to his reputation unless he can satisfy the demanding requirements of the *Times* [test].

III. [Under] the First Amendment there is no such thing as a false idea. However pernicious an opinion may seem, we depend for its correction not on the conscience of the judges and juries but on the competition of other ideas.[a] But there is no constitutional value in false statements of fact. Neither the intentional lie nor the careless error materially advances society's interest in "uninhibited, robust, and wide-open" debate on public issues. * * *

Although the erroneous statement of fact is not worthy of constitutional protection, it is nevertheless inevitable in free debate. [P]unishment of error runs the risk of inducing a cautious and restrictive exercise of the constitutionally guaranteed freedoms of speech and press. [The] First Amendment requires that we protect some falsehood in order to protect speech that matters.

The need to avoid self-censorship by the news media is, however, not the only societal value at issue. [The] legitimate state interest underlying the law of libel is the compensation of individuals for the harm inflicted on them by defamatory falsehoods. We would not lightly require the State to abandon this purpose, for, as Mr. Justice Stewart has reminded us, the individual's right to the protection of his own good name "reflects no more than our basic concept of the essential dignity and worth of every human being—a concept at the root of any decent system of ordered liberty. * * *" *Rosenblatt.*[b]

Some tension necessarily exists between the need for a vigorous and uninhibited press and the legitimate interest in redressing wrongful injury. [In] our continuing effort to define the proper accommodation between these competing concerns, we have been especially anxious to assure to the freedoms of speech and press that "breathing space" essential to their fruitful exercise. To that end this Court has extended a measure of strategic protection to defamatory falsehood.

The *New York Times* standard defines the level of constitutional protection appropriate to the context of defamation of [public figures and those who hold governmental office]. Plainly many deserving plaintiffs, including some intentionally subjected to injury, will be unable to surmount the barrier of the *New York Times* test. [For] the reasons stated below, we conclude that the state interest in compensating injury to the reputation of private individuals requires that a different rule should obtain with respect to them.

[W]e have no difficulty in distinguishing among defamation plaintiffs. The first remedy of any victim of defamation is self-help—using available opportuni-

a. For many years the lower courts took this language seriously and deemed opinion to be absolutely protected (see, e.g., *Ollman v. Evans,* 750 F.2d 970 (D.C.Cir.1984)), but *Milkovich v. Lorain Journal Co.,* ___ U.S. ___, 110 S.Ct. 2695, 111 L.Ed.2d 1 (1990), per Rehnquist, C.J., ultimately denied that there is any "wholesale defamation exception for anything that might be labelled 'opinion.' "

b. Justice Stewart continued: "The protection of private personality, like the protection of life itself, is left primarily to the individual States under the Ninth and Tenth Amendments. But this does not mean that the right is entitled to any less recognition by this Court as a basic of our constitutional system." Consider Post, *The Social Foundations of Defamation Law,* 74 Calif.L.Rev. 691, 708 (1986): "[I]t is not immediately clear how reputation, which is social and public, and which resides in the 'common or general estimate of person,' can possibly affect the 'essential dignity' of a person's 'private personality.' The gulf that appears to separate reputation from dignity can be spanned only if defamation law contains an implicit theory of the relationship between the private and public aspects of the self."

ties to contradict the lie or correct the error and thereby to minimize its adverse impact on reputation. Public officials and public figures usually enjoy significantly greater access to the channels of effective communication and hence have a more realistic opportunity to counteract false statements than private individuals normally enjoy.[9] Private individuals are therefore more vulnerable to injury, and the state interest in protecting them is correspondingly greater.

More important than the likelihood that private individuals will lack effective opportunities for rebuttal, there is a compelling normative consideration underlying the distinction between public and private defamation plaintiffs. An individual who decides to seek governmental office must accept certain necessary consequences of that involvement in public affairs. He runs the risk of closer public scrutiny than might otherwise be the case. [Those] classed as public figures stand in a similar [position.]

Even if the foregoing generalities do not obtain in every instance, the communications media are entitled to act on the assumption that public officials and public figures have voluntarily exposed themselves to increased risk of injury from defamatory falsehoods concerning them. No such assumption is justified with respect to a private individual. He has not accepted public office nor assumed an "influential role in ordering society." *Butts.* He has relinquished no part of his interest in the protection of his own good name, and consequently he has a more compelling call on the courts for redress of injury inflicted by defamatory falsehood. Thus, private individuals are not only more vulnerable to injury than public officials and public figures; they are also more deserving of recovery.

For these reasons we conclude that the States should retain substantial latitude in their efforts to enforce a legal remedy for defamatory falsehood injurious to the reputation of a private individual. The extension of the *Times* test proposed by the *Rosenbloom* plurality would abridge this legitimate state interest to a degree that we find unacceptable. And it would occasion the additional difficulty of forcing state and federal judges to decide on an ad hoc basis which publications address issues of "general or public interest" and which do not—to determine, in the words of Mr. Justice Marshall, "what information is relevant to self-government." *Rosenbloom.* We doubt the wisdom of committing this task to the conscience of judges. [The] "public or general interest" test for determining the applicability of the *Times* standard to private defamation actions inadequately serves both of the competing values at stake. On the one hand, a private individual whose reputation is injured by defamatory falsehood that does concern an issue of public or general interest has no recourse unless he can meet the rigorous requirements of *Times.* This is true despite the factors that distinguish the state interest in compensating private individuals from the analogous interest involved in the context of public persons. On the other hand,

9. Of course, an opportunity for rebuttal seldom suffices to undo harm of defamatory falsehood. Indeed, the law of defamation is rooted in our experience that the truth rarely catches up with a lie. But the fact that the self-help remedy of rebuttal, standing alone, is inadequate to its task does not mean that it is irrelevant to our inquiry. [Consider Shiffrin, *Defamatory Non-Media Speech and First Amendment Methodology,* 25 U.C.L.A.L.Rev. 915, 952–53 (1978): "[F]ootnote nine, has seemingly left the first amendment in a peculiar spot. *Gertz* holds that the first amendment offers some protection for defamatory utterances presumably so that our Constitution can continue 'to preserve an uninhibited marketplace of ideas in which truth will ultimately prevail. * * *' And yet the Court recognizes that 'an opportunity for rebuttal seldom suffices to undo [the] harm of defamatory falsehood,' i.e., truth does not emerge in the marketplace of ideas. Is the Court trapped in an obvious contradiction?"]

a publisher or broadcaster of a defamatory error which a court deems unrelated to an issue of public or general interest may be held liable in damages even if it took every reasonable precaution to ensure the accuracy of its assertions. And liability may far exceed compensation for any actual injury to the plaintiff, for the jury may be permitted to presume damages without proof of loss and even to award punitive damages.

We hold that, so long as they do not impose liability without fault, the States may define for themselves the appropriate standard of liability for a publisher or broadcaster of defamatory falsehood injurious to a private individual. This approach provides a more equitable boundary between the competing concerns involved here. It recognizes the strength of the legitimate state interest in compensating private individuals for wrongful injury to reputation, yet shields the press and broadcast media from the rigors of strict liability for defamation. At least this conclusion obtains where, as here, the substance of the defamatory statement "makes substantial danger to reputation apparent." *Butts.* This phrase places in perspective the conclusion we announce today. Our inquiry would involve considerations somewhat different from those discussed above if a State purported to condition civil liability on a factual misstatement whose content did not warn a reasonably prudent editor or broadcaster of its defamatory potential. Cf. *Time, Inc. v. Hill* [Part D infra]. Such a case is not now before us, and we intimate no view as to its proper resolution.

IV. [T]he strong and legitimate state interest in compensating private individuals for injury to reputation [extends] no further than compensation for actual injury. For the reasons stated below, we hold that the States may not permit recovery of presumed or punitive damages, at least when liability is not based on a showing of knowledge of falsity or reckless disregard for the truth.

The common law of defamation is an oddity of tort [law]. Juries may award substantial sums as compensation for supposed damage to reputation without any proof that such harm actually occurred. [This] unnecessarily compounds the potential of any system of liability for defamatory falsehood to inhibit the vigorous exercise of First Amendment freedoms [and] invites juries to punish unpopular opinion rather than to compensate individuals for injury sustained by the publication of a false fact. More to the point, the States have no substantial interest in securing for plaintiffs such as this petitioner gratuitous awards of money damages far in excess of any actual injury.

We would not, of course, invalidate state law simply because we doubt its wisdom, but here we are attempting to reconcile state law with a competing interest grounded in the constitutional command of the First Amendment. It is therefore appropriate to require that state remedies for defamatory falsehood reach no farther than is necessary to protect the legitimate interest involved. It is necessary to restrict defamation plaintiffs who do not prove knowledge of falsity or reckless disregard for the truth to compensation for actual injury. We need not define "actual injury," as trial courts have wide experience in framing appropriate jury instructions in tort action. Suffice it to say that actual injury is not limited to out-of-pocket loss. Indeed, the more customary types of actual harm inflicted by defamatory falsehood include impairment of reputation and standing in the community, personal humiliation, and mental anguish and suffering. Of course, juries must be limited by appropriate instructions, and all awards must be supported by competent evidence concerning the injury, although there need be no evidence which assigns an actual dollar value to the injury.

We also find no justification for allowing awards of punitive damages against publishers and broadcasters held liable under state-defined standards of liability for defamation. In most jurisdictions jury discretion over the amounts awarded is limited only by the gentle rule that they not be excessive. Consequently, juries assess punitive damages in wholly unpredictable amounts bearing no necessary relation to the actual harm caused. And they remain free to use their discretion selectively to punish expressions of unpopular views. [J]ury discretion to award punitive damages unnecessarily exacerbates the danger of media self-censorship; [punitive] damages are wholly irrelevant to the state interest that justifies a negligence standard for private defamation actions. They are not compensation for injury. Instead, they are private fines levied by civil juries to punish reprehensible conduct and to deter its future occurrence. In short, the private defamation plaintiff who establishes liability under a less demanding standard than that stated by *Times* may recover only such damages as are sufficient to compensate him for actual injury.[c]

V. Notwithstanding our refusal to extend the *New York Times* privilege to defamation of private individuals, respondent contends that we should affirm the judgment below on the ground that petitioner is [a] public figure. [That] designation may rest on either of two alternative bases. In some instances an individual may achieve such pervasive fame or notoriety that he becomes a public figure for all purposes and in all contexts. More commonly, an individual voluntarily injects himself or is drawn into a particular public controversy and thereby becomes a public figure for a limited range of issues. In either case such persons assume special prominence in the resolution of public questions.

Petitioner has long been active in community and professional affairs. He has served as an officer of local civic groups and of various professional organizations, and he has published several books and articles on legal subjects. Although petitioner was consequently well known in some circles, he had achieved no general fame or notoriety in the community. None of the prospective jurors called at the trial had ever heard of petitioner prior to this litigation, and respondent offered no proof that this response was atypical of the local population. We would not lightly assume that a citizen's participation in community and professional affairs rendered him a public figure for all purposes. Absent clear evidence of general fame or notoriety in the community, and pervasive involvement in the affairs of society, an individual should not be deemed a public personality for all aspects of his life. It is preferable to reduce the public-figure question to a more meaningful context by looking to the nature and extent of an individual's participation in the particular controversy giving rise to the defamation.

In this context it is plain that petitioner was not a public figure. He played a minimal role at the coroner's inquest, and his participation related solely to his representation of a private client. He took no part in the criminal prosecution of Officer Nuccio. Moreover, he never discussed either the criminal or civil litigation with the press and was never quoted as having done so. He plainly did not thrust himself into the vortex of this public issue, nor did he engage the public's attention in an attempt to influence its outcome. We are persuaded that the trial court did not err in refusing to characterize petitioner as a public figure for the purpose of this litigation.

c. On remand, Gertz was awarded $100,000 in compensatory damages and $300,000 in punitive damages. In the prior trial, he had been awarded only $50,000 in damages.

We therefore conclude that the *New York Times* standard is inapplicable to this case and that the trial court erred in entering judgment for respondent. Because the jury was allowed to impose liability without fault and was permitted to presume damages without proof of injury, a new trial is necessary.[d]

JUSTICE BRENNAN, dissenting.

[While the Court's] arguments are forcefully and eloquently presented, I cannot accept them for the reasons I stated in *Rosenbloom:* "The *New York Times* standard was applied to libel of a public official or public figure to give effect to the Amendment's function to encourage ventilation of public issues, not because the public official has any less interest in protecting his reputation than an individual in private life. [In] the vast majority of libels involving public officials or public figures, the ability to respond through the media will depend on the same complex factor on which the ability of a private individual depends: the unpredictable event of the media's continuing interest in the story. Thus the unproved, and highly improbable, generalization that an as yet [not fully defined] class of 'public figures' involved in matters of public concern will be better able to respond through the media than private individuals also involved in such matters seems too insubstantial a reed on which to rest a constitutional distinction."

[Adoption], by many States, of a reasonable care standard in cases where private individuals are involved in matters of public interest—the probable result of today's decision—[will] lead to self-censorship since publishers will be required carefully to weigh a myriad of uncertain factors before publication. The reasonable care standard is "elusive," *Time, Inc. v. Hill;* it saddles the press with "the intolerable burden of guessing how a jury might assess the reasonableness of steps taken by it to verify the accuracy of every reference to a name, picture or portrait." Ibid. Under a reasonable care regime, publishers and broadcasters will have to make pre-publication judgments about juror assessment of such diverse considerations as the size, operating procedures, and financial condition of the newsgathering system, as well as the relative costs and benefits of instituting less frequent and more costly reporting at a higher level of accuracy. [And] most hazardous, the flexibility which inheres in the reasonable care standard will create the danger that a jury will convert it into "an instrument for the suppression of those 'vehement, caustic, and sometimes unpleasantly sharp attacks,' [which] must be protected if the guarantees of the First and Fourteenth Amendments are to prevail." *Monitor Patriot Co.*

[A] jury's latitude to impose liability for want of due care poses a far greater threat of suppressing unpopular views than does a possible recovery of presumed or punitive damages. Moreover, the Court's broad-ranging examples of "actual

d. Blackmun, J., concurred: "[Although I joined Brennan, J.'s plurality opinion in *Rosenbloom,* from which the Court's opinion in the present case departs, I join] the Court's opinion and its judgment for two reasons:

"1. By removing the spectres of presumed and punitive damages in the absence of *Times* malice, the Court eliminates significant and powerful motives for self-censorship that otherwise are present in the traditional libel action. By so doing, the Court leaves what should prove to be sufficient and adequate breathing space for a vigorous press. What the Court has done, I believe, will have little, if any, practical effect on the functioning of responsible journalism.

"2. The Court was sadly fractionated in *Rosenbloom.* A result of that kind inevitably leads to uncertainty. I feel that it is of profound importance for the Court to come to rest in the defamation area and to have a clearly defined majority position that eliminates the unsureness engendered by *Rosenbloom's* diversity. If my vote were not needed to create a majority, I would adhere to my prior view. A definitive ruling, however, is paramount."

injury" [allow] a jury bent on punishing expression of unpopular views a formidable weapon for doing so. [E]ven a limitation of recovery to "actual injury"—however much it reduces the size or frequency of recoveries—will not provide the necessary elbow room for First Amendment expression. "[The] very possibility of having to engage in litigation, an expensive and protracted process, is threat enough to cause discussion and debate to 'steer far wider of the unlawful zone' thereby keeping protected discussion from public cognizance. * * *" *Rosenbloom.*

[I] reject the argument that my *Rosenbloom* view improperly commits to judges the task of determining what is and what is not an issue of "general or public interest."[3] I noted in *Rosenbloom* that performance of this task would not always be easy. But surely the courts, the ultimate arbiters of all disputes concerning clashes of constitutional values, would only be performing one of their traditional functions in undertaking this duty. [The] public interest is necessarily broad; any residual self-censorship that may result from the uncertain contours of the "general or public interest" concept should be of far less concern to publishers and broadcasters than that occasioned by state laws imposing liability for negligent falsehood. * * *[e]

JUSTICE WHITE, dissenting.

[T]he Court, in a few printed pages, has federalized major aspects of libel law by declaring unconstitutional in important respects the prevailing defamation law in all or most of the 50 States. * * *

I. [These] radical changes in the law and severe invasions of the prerogatives of the States [should] at least be shown to be required by the First Amendment or necessitated by our present circumstances. Neither has been [demonstrated.]

The central meaning of *New York Times,* and for me the First Amendment as it relates to libel laws, is that seditious libel—criticism of government and

3. The Court, taking a novel step, would not limit application of First Amendment protection to private libels involving issues of general or public interest, but would forbid the States from imposing liability without fault in any case where the substance of the defamatory statement made substantial danger to reputation apparent. As in *Rosenbloom,* I would leave open the question of what constitutional standard, if any, applies when defamatory falsehoods are published or broadcast concerning either a private or public person's activities not within the scope of the general or public interest.

Parenthetically, my Brother White argues that the Court's view and mine will prevent a plaintiff—unable to demonstrate some degree of fault—from vindicating his reputation by securing a judgment that the publication was false. This argument overlooks the possible enactment of statutes, not requiring proof of fault, which provide for an action for retraction or for publication of a court's determination of falsity if the plaintiff is able to demonstrate that false statements have been published concerning his activities. Although it may be that questions could be raised concerning the constitutionality of such statutes, certainly nothing I have said today (and, as I read the Court's opinion, nothing said there) should be read to imply that a private plaintiff, unable to prove fault, must inevitably be denied the opportunity to secure a judgment upon the truth or falsity of statements published about him.

e. Douglas, J., dissented, objecting to "continued recognition of the possibility of state libel suits for public discussion of public issues" as diluting first amendment protection. He added: "Since this case involves a discussion of public affairs, I need not decide at this point whether the First Amendment prohibits all libel actions. 'An unconditional right to say what one pleases about public affairs is what I consider to be *the minimum guarantee* of the First Amendment.' *New York Times* (Black, J., concurring) (emphasis added). But 'public affairs' includes a great deal more than merely political affairs. Matters of science, economics, business, art, literature, etc., are all matters of interest to the general public. Indeed, any matter of sufficient general interest to prompt media coverage may be said to be a public affair. Certainly police killings, 'Communist conspiracies,' and the like qualify."

public officials—falls beyond the police power of the State. In a democratic society such as ours, the citizen has the privilege of criticizing his government and its officials. But neither *New York Times* nor its progeny suggest that the First Amendment intended in all circumstances to deprive the private citizen of his historic recourse to redress published falsehoods damaging to reputation or that, contrary to history and precedent, the amendment should now be so interpreted. Simply put, the First Amendment did not confer a "license to defame the citizen." Douglas, *The Right of the People* 38 (1958).

[T]he law has heretofore put the risk of falsehood on the publisher where the victim is a private citizen and no grounds of special privilege are invoked. The Court would now shift this risk to the victim, even though he has done nothing to invite the calumny, is wholly innocent of fault, and is helpless to avoid his injury. I doubt that jurisprudential resistance to liability without fault is sufficient ground for employing the First Amendment to revolutionize the law of libel, and in my view, that body of legal rules poses no realistic threat to the press and its service to the public. The press today is vigorous and robust. To me, it is quite incredible to suggest that threats of libel suits from private citizens are causing the press to refrain from publishing the truth. I know of no hard facts to support that proposition, and the Court furnishes none.

[I]f the Court's principal concern is to protect the communications industry from large libel judgments, it would appear that its new requirements with respect to general and punitive damages would be ample protection. Why it also feels compelled to escalate the threshold standard of liability I cannot fathom, particularly when this will eliminate in many instances the plaintiff's possibility of securing a judicial determination that the damaging publication was indeed false, whether or not he is entitled to recover money damages. [I] find it unacceptable to distribute the risk in this manner and force the wholly innocent victim to bear the injury; for, as between the two, the defamer is the only culpable party. It is he who circulated a falsehood that he was not required to publish. * * * [f]

V. [I] fail to see how the quality or quantity of public debate will be promoted by further emasculation of state libel laws for the benefit of the news media.[41] If anything, this trend may provoke a new and radical imbalance in the communications process. Cf. Barron, *Access to the Press—A New First Amendment Right,* 80 Harv.L.Rev. 1641, 1657 (1967). It is not at all inconceivable that virtually unrestrained defamatory remarks about private citizens will discourage them from speaking out and concerning themselves with social problems. This would turn the First Amendment on its head. * * * [g]

f. White, J., also argued strongly against the Court's rulings on actual and punitive damages.

41. Cf. Pedrick, *Freedom of the Press and the Law of Libel: The Modern Revised Translation,* 49 Cornell L.Q. 581, 601–02 (1964): "A great many forces in our society operate to determine the extent to which men are free in fact to express their ideas. Whether there is a privilege for good faith defamatory misstatements on matters of public concern or whether there is strict liability for such statements may not greatly affect the course of public discussion. How different has life been in those states which heretofore followed the majority rule imposing strict liability for misstatements of fact defaming public figures from life in the minority states where the good faith privilege held sway?"

g. Burger, C.J., also dissented: "I am frank to say I do not know the parameters of a 'negligence' doctrine as applied to the news media. [I] would prefer to allow this area of law to continue to evolve as it has up to now with respect to private citizens rather then embark on a new doctrinal theory which has no jurisprudential ancestry. [I would remand] for reinstatement of the verdict of the jury and the entry of an appropriate judgment on that verdict."

Notes and Questions

1. *Gertz and Meiklejohn.* By affording some constitutional protection to all media defamatory speech whether or not it relates to public issues, does the Court squarely reject the Meiklejohn theory of the first amendment? Consider Shiffrin, *Defamatory Non-Media Speech and First Amendment Methodology,* 25 U.C.L.A.L.Rev. 915, 929 (1978): "It may be that the Court has refused to adopt the Meiklejohn 'public issues' test not because it believes that private speech (i.e., speech unrelated to public issues) is as important as public speech but rather because it doubts its ability to distinguish unerringly between the two. [B]y placing all defamatory media speech within the scope of the first amendment, the Court may believe it has protected relatively little non-public speech. On the other hand, [putting aside comments about public officials and public figures], the Court may fear that if *Gertz* were extended to non-media speech, the result would be to protect much speech having nothing to do with public issues, while safeguarding relatively little that does." [h] For consideration of the distinction between public and private speech and of the media non-media distinction, see *Greenmoss,* p. 592 infra. See also *Philadelphia Newspapers, Inc. v. Hepps,* 475 U.S. 767, 106 S.Ct. 1558, 89 L.Ed.2d 783 (1986) (private figure plaintiff has burden of showing falsity at least when issue is of "public concern" and leaving open the question of what standards apply to non-media defendants).

2. *Public figures.* TIME, INC. v. FIRESTONE, 424 U.S. 448, 96 S.Ct. 958, 47 L.Ed.2d 154 (1976), per REHNQUIST, J., declared that persons who have not assumed a role of especial prominence in the affairs of society are not public figures unless they have " 'thrust themselves to the forefront of particular public controversies in order to influence the resolution of the issues involved.' " It held that a divorce proceeding involving one of America's wealthiest industrial families and containing testimony concerning the extramarital sexual activities of the parties did not involve a "public controversy," "even though the marital difficulties of extremely wealthy individuals may be of interest to some portion of the reading public." Nor was the filing of a divorce suit, or the holding of press conferences ("to satisfy inquiring reporters") thought to be freely publicizing the issues in order to influence their outcome. Recall *Gertz* doubted the wisdom of forcing judges to determine on an ad hoc basis what is and is not of "general or public interest." Is there a basis for distinguishing a public figure test requiring judges to determine on an ad hoc basis what is or is not a "public controversy"?

What does it mean to assume a role of especial prominence in the affairs of society? If Elmer Gertz, a prominent Illinois attorney, does not qualify, does Johnny Carson? Julia Child? Mr. Rogers? If so, is the slide from public officials to television chefs and personalities too precipitous because the latter "have little, if any effect, on questions of politics, public policy, or the organiza-

h. For the claim that speech on private matters deserves as much protection as speech on public matters, see id. at 938–42. For discussion of the different meanings of public and private speech, see Schauer, *"Private" Speech and the "Private" Forum: Givhan v. Western Line School District,* 1979 Sup.Ct.Rev. 217. For additional commentary on the question of whether *Gertz* should extend to non-media defendants see, e.g., Hill, *Defamation and Privacy Under the First Amendment,* 76 Colum.L.Rev. 1205 (1976); Lange, *The Speech and Press Clauses,* 23 U.C.L.A.L.Rev. 77 (1975); Nimmer, *Is Freedom of the Press a Redundancy: What Does It Add to Freedom of Speech?,* 26 Hast.L.J. 639 (1975); Van Alstyne, Comment: *The Hazards to the Press of Claiming a "Preferred Position,"* 28 Hast.L.J. 761 (1977); Note, *Mediaocracy and Mistrust: Extending New York Times Defamation Protection to Nonmedia Defendants,* 95 Harv.L.Rev. 1876 (1982).

tion and determination of societal affairs"? See Schauer, *Public Figures,* 25 Wm. & Mary L.Rev. 905 (1984). For replies, see Ashdown, *Of Public Figures and Public Interest—The Libel Law Conundrum,* id. at 937; Daniels, *Public Figures Revisited,* id. at 957. Does a narrow definition of public figures discriminate in favor of orthodox media and discourage attempts "to illuminate previously unexposed aspects of society." Does the negligence concept itself threaten to discriminate "against media or outlets whose philosophies and methods deviate from those of the mainstream"? See generally Anderson, *Libel and Press Self-Censorship,* 53 Tex.L.Rev. 422, 453, 455 (1975).

3. *"There is no constitutional value in false statements of fact."* Consider Shiffrin, supra at 954: "This is dangerous doctrine. It begins with the presumption that false speech is unprotected and looks to determine if other factors are present which necessitate protection nonetheless. This begs the basic first amendment question: When can government perceptions of truth or falsity be imposed upon the individual? Moreover, it demeans the interests of self-expression and cathartic release. In the final analysis, however, the *Gertz* formulation may make no difference. By recognizing that some false speech must be protected in order to prevent true speech from being driven out of the marketplace, *Gertz* arrives at the same results which would be reached if it were assumed that speech is protected whether true or false unless other important interests predominate. Nonetheless, starting points can influence [decisions]." See also Schauer, *Categories and the First Amendment: A Play in Three Acts,* 34 Vand.L.Rev. 265, 280–81 (1981).

4. *Taking reputation too seriously?* Consider Smolla, *Suing the Press* 257 (1986): "[I]f we take the libel suit too seriously, we are in danger of raising our collective cultural sensitivity to reputation to unhealthy levels. We are in danger of surrendering a wonderful part of our national identity—our strapping, scrambling, free-wheeling individualism, in danger of becoming less American, less robust, wild-eyed, pluralistic and free, and more decorous, image-conscious, and narcissistic. The media is itself partly to blame for this direction, and it would be dangerous to release it totally from the important check and balance that the libel laws provide. But in the United States, the balance that must be struck between reputation and expression should never be tilted too far against expression, for the right to defiantly, robustly, and irreverently speak one's mind just because it is one's mind is quintessentially what it means to be an American." [i]

i. For historical perspective on the social messages communicated by defamation law, see Rosenberg, *Protecting the Best Men* (1986). For valuable material on how the *Gertz* rules work in practice, see Bezanson, Cranberg & Soloski, *Libel Law and the Press: Myth and Reality* (1987); Kaufman, *Libel 1980–85: Promises and Realities,* 90 Dick.L.Rev. 545 (1985); Franklin, *Suing Media for Libel: A Litigation Study,* 1981 Am.B.Found.Res.J. 795; Franklin, *Winners and Losers and Why: A Study of Defamation Litigation,* 1980 Am.B. Found.Res.J. 455. For commentary suggesting reforms, see Annenberg Washington Program, *Libel Law* (1988). See also Bezanson, *The Libel Tort Today,* 45 Wash. & Lee L.Rev. 535 (1988); Epstein, *Was New York Times v. Sullivan Wrong?,* 53 U.Chi.L.Rev. 782 (1986); Fein, *New York Times v. Sullivan: An Obstacle to Enlightened Public Discourse and Government Responsiveness to the People* (1984); Franklin, *Public Officials and Libel: In Defense of New York Times Co. v. Sullivan,* 5 Cardozo Arts & Ent.L.J. 51 (1986); Franklin, *Constitutional Libel Law: The Role of Content,* 34 UCLA L.Rev. 1657 (1987); Franklin, *A Declaratory Judgment Alternative to Current Libel Law,* 74 Calif.L.Rev. 809 (1986); Ingber, *Defamation: A Conflict Between Reason and Decency,* 65 Va.L.Rev. 785 (1979); Leval, *The No–Money, No–Fault Libel Suit: Keeping Sullivan in Its Proper Place,* 101 Harv.L.Rev. 1287 (1988); Levine, *Book Review,* 56 G.W. U.L.Rev. 246 (1987); Lewis, *New York Times v. Sullivan Reconsidered: Time to Return to "The Central Meaning of the First Amendment,"* 83 Colum.L.Rev. 603 (1983); Smolla, *Let the Author Beware: The Rejuvenation of*

D. FALSE LIGHT PRIVACY

TIME, INC. v. HILL, 385 U.S. 374, 87 S.Ct. 534, 17 L.Ed.2d 456 (1967), applied the *New York Times* knowing and reckless falsity standard to a right of privacy action for publishing an erroneous but not defamatory report about private individuals involved in an incident of public interest. In 1952 the Hill family was the subject of national news coverage when held hostage in its home for 19 hours by three escaped convicts who treated the family courteously with no violence. This incident formed part of the basis for a novel, later made into a play, which involved violence against the hostage family. In 1955 *Life* published a picture story that showed the play's cast reenacting scenes from the play in the former Hill home. According to *Life,* the play "inspired by the [Hill] family's experience" "is a heartstopping account of how a family arose to heroism in a crisis." Hill secured a $30,000 judgment for compensatory damages against the publisher under the New York Right to Privacy statute, which, as interpreted, made truth a complete defense to actions based on "newsworthy people or events" but gave a right of action to one whose name or picture was the subject of an article containing "material and substantial falsification." The Court, per BRENNAN, J., reversed, holding that "the constitutional protections for speech and press preclude the application of the New York statute to redress false reports of matters of public interest in the absence of proof that the defendant published the report with knowledge of its falsity or in reckless disregard of the truth," and that the instructions did not adequately advise the jury that a verdict for Hill required a finding of knowing or reckless falsity:

"The guarantees for speech and press are not the preserve of political expression or comment upon public affairs, essential as those are to healthy government. One need only pick up any newspaper or magazine to comprehend the vast range of published matter which exposes persons to public view, both private citizens and public officials. Exposure of the self to others in varying degrees is a concomitant of life in a civilized community. The risk of this exposure is an essential incident of life in a society which places a primary value on freedom of speech and press. [We] have no doubt that the subject of the *Life* article, the opening of a new play linked to an actual incident, is a matter of public interest. 'The line between the informing and the entertaining is too elusive for the protection of [freedom of the press.]' Erroneous statement is no less inevitable in such case than in the case of comment upon public affairs, and in both, if innocent or merely negligent, '[it] must be protected if the freedoms of expression are to have the "breathing space" that they "need [to] survive".' [*New York Times.*] We create a grave risk of serious impairment of the indispensable service of a free press in a free society if we saddle the press with the impossible burden of verifying to a certainty the facts associated in news articles with a person's name, picture or portrait, particularly as related to non-defamatory matter. Even negligence would be a most elusive standard, especially when the content of the speech itself affords no warning of prospective harm to another through falsity. A negligence test would place on the press the intolerable burden of guessing how a jury might assess the reasonableness of steps taken by it to verify the accuracy of every reference to a name, picture or [portrait].

the American Law of Libel, 132 U.Pa.L.Rev. 1 (1983).

"We find applicable here the standard of knowing or reckless falsehood not through blind application of *New York Times,* relating solely to libel actions by public officials, but only upon consideration of the factors which arise in the particular context of the application of the New York statute in cases involving private individuals."

BLACK, J., joined by Douglas, J., concurred in reversal on the grounds stated in the Brennan opinion "in order for the Court to be able at this time to agree on an opinion in this important case based on the prevailing constitutional doctrine expressed in *New York Times,*" but reaffirmed their belief that the "malicious," "reckless disregard of the truth" and "knowing and reckless falsity" exceptions were impermissible "abridgments" of freedom of expression. Douglas, J., also filed a separate concurrence, deeming it "irrelevant to talk of any right of privacy in this context. Here a private person is catapulted into the news by events over which he had no control. He and his activities are then in the public domain as fully as the matters at issue in *New York Times.* Such privacy as a person normally has ceases when his life has ceased to be private."

HARLAN, J., concurring in part and dissenting in part, would have made the test of liability negligence, rather than the *New York Times* "reckless falsity": "It would be unreasonable to assume that Mr. Hill could find a forum for making a successful refutation of the *Life* material or that the public's interest in it would be sufficient for the truth to win out by comparison as it might in that area of discussion central to a free society. Thus the state interest in encouraging careful checking and preparation of published material is far stronger than in *Times.* The dangers of unchallengeable untruth are far too well documented to be summarily dismissed.

"Second, there is a vast difference in the state interest in protecting individuals like Mr. Hill from irresponsibly prepared publicity and the state interest in similar protection for a public official. In *Times* we acknowledged public officials to be a breed from whom hardiness to exposure to charges, innuendos, and criticisms might be demanded and who voluntarily assumed the risk of such things by entry into the public arena. But Mr. Hill came to public attention through an unfortunate circumstance not of his making rather than his voluntary actions and he can in no sense be considered to have 'waived' any protection the State might justifiably afford him from irresponsible publicity. Not being inured to the vicissitudes of journalistic scrutiny such an individual is more easily injured and his means of self-defense are more limited. The public is less likely to view with normal skepticism what is written about him because it is not accustomed to seeing his name in the press and expects only a disinterested report.

"The coincidence of these factors in this situation leads me to the view that a State should be free to hold the press to a duty of making a reasonable investigation of the underlying facts and limiting itself to 'fair comment' on the materials so gathered. Theoretically, of course, such a rule might slightly limit press discussion of matters touching individuals like Mr. Hill. But, from a pragmatic standpoint, until now the press, at least in New York, labored under the more exacting handicap of the existing New York privacy law and has certainly remained robust. Other professional activity of great social value is carried on under a duty of reasonable care and there is no reason to suspect the press would be less hardy than medical practitioners or attorneys." [a]

a. Fortas, J., joined by Warren, C.J., and Clark, J., dissented, because "the jury instructions, although [not] a textbook model, satisfied [the *New York Times*] standard."

Notes and Questions

1. Compare ZACCHINI v. SCRIPPS–HOWARD BROADCASTING CO, 433 U.S. 562, 97 S.Ct. 2849, 53 L.Ed.2d 965 (1977): Zacchini performed as a "human cannonball," being shot from a cannon into a net some 200 feet away. Without Zacchini's permission to film or broadcast his act, Scripps-Howard obtained and broadcast the tape of his "shot" on the news. The Ohio Supreme Court held the telecast was protected under *Time, Inc. v. Hill* as a newsworthy event. The Court, per WHITE, J., reversed. *Hill* was distinguishable because Zacchini's claim was based not on privacy or reputation but "in protecting the proprietary interest," an interest "closely analogous to the goals of patent and copyright law." Unlike *Hill,* the issue was not whether Zacchini's act would be available to the public: "[T]he only question is who gets to do the publishing." [b]

2. Does *Hill* survive *Gertz?* Consider the following statement: "In *Hill* and *Gertz* the same class of plaintiffs have to meet different constitutional standards in order to recover. Only the name of the tort has changed. This makes no sense." Is the state interest significantly different in *Gertz* than in *Hill*? Should it matter whether the statement at issue would appear innocuous to a reasonable editor? Offensive? See Zimmerman, *False Light Invasion of Privacy: The Light that Failed,* 64 N.Y.U.L.Rev. 364 (1989).

3. *False news.* Should injury to any particular person be a prerequisite to state regulation of false publications? Consider *Keeton v. Hustler Magazine, Inc.,* 465 U.S. 770, 104 S.Ct. 1473, 79 L.Ed.2d 790 (1984): "False statements of fact harm both the subject of the falsehood *and* the readers of the statement. New Hampshire may rightly employ its libel laws to discourage the deception of its citizens." Could New Hampshire make it a criminal offense to publish false statements with knowledge of their falsity without any requirement of injury to any particular person? See Zimmerman, supra.

E. EMOTIONAL DISTRESS

HUSTLER MAGAZINE v. FALWELL, 485 U.S. 46, 108 S.Ct. 876, 99 L.Ed.2d 41 (1988), per REHNQUIST, C.J., held that public figures and public officials offended by a mass media parody could not recover for the tort of intentional infliction of emotional distress without a showing of *New York Times* malice. Parodying a series of liquor advertisements in which celebrities speak about their "first time" the editors of *Hustler* chose plaintiff Jerry Falwell (a nationally famous minister, host of a nationally syndicated television show, and founder of the Moral Majority political organization) "as the featured celebrity and drafted an alleged 'interview' with him in which he states that his 'first time' was during a drunken incestuous rendezvous with his mother in an outhouse. The *Hustler* parody portrays [Falwell] and his mother [a] 'as drunk and immoral,' and suggests that [Falwell] is a hypocrite who preaches only when he is drunk. In small print at the bottom of the page, the ad contains the disclaimer, 'ad parody—not to be taken seriously.' The magazine's table of contents also lists the ad as 'Fiction; Ad and Personality Parody.' * * *

b. Powell, J., joined by Brennan and Marshall, JJ., dissented, observing that there was no showing that the broadcast was a "subterfuge or cover for private or commercial exploitation." Stevens, J., dissented on procedural grounds.

a. Falwell's mother was not a plaintiff. What result if she were?

"This case presents us with a novel question involving First Amendment limitations upon a State's authority to protect its citizens from the intentional infliction of emotional distress.[3] We must decide whether a public figure may recover damages for emotional harm caused by the publication of an ad parody offensive to him, and doubtless gross and repugnant in the eyes of most. [Falwell] would have us find that a State's interest in protecting public figures from emotional distress is sufficient to deny First Amendment protection to speech that is patently offensive and is intended to inflict emotional injury, even when that speech could not reasonably have been interpreted as stating actual facts about the public figure involved. * * *

"In [Falwell's] view, [so] long as the utterance was intended to inflict emotional distress, was outrageous, and did in fact inflict serious emotional distress, it is of no constitutional import whether the statement was a fact or an opinion, or whether it was true or false. It is the intent to cause injury that is the gravamen of the tort, and the State's interest in preventing emotional harm simply outweighs whatever interest a speaker may have in speech of this type.

"Generally speaking the law does not regard the intent to inflict emotional distress as one which should receive much solicitude, and it is quite understandable that most if not all jurisdictions have chosen to make it civilly culpable where the conduct in question is sufficiently 'outrageous.' But in the world of debate about public affairs, many things done with motives that are less than admirable are protected by the First Amendment. '[Debate] on public issues will not be uninhibited if the speaker must run the risk that it will be proved in court that he spoke out of hatred; even if he did speak out of hatred, utterances honestly believed contribute to the free interchange of ideas and the ascertainment of truth.' *Garrison.* Thus while such a bad motive may be deemed controlling for purposes of tort liability in other areas of the law, we think the First Amendment prohibits such a result in the area of public debate about public figures.

"Were we to hold otherwise, there can be little doubt that political cartoonists and satirists would be subjected to damage awards without any showing that their work falsely defamed its subject. * * *

"[Falwell] contends, however, that the caricature in question here was so 'outrageous' as to distinguish it from more traditional political cartoons. There is no doubt that the caricature of [Falwell] and his mother published in Hustler is at best a distant cousin of [traditional] political cartoons * * * and a rather poor relation at that. If it were possible by laying down a principled standard to separate the one from the other, public discourse would probably suffer little or no harm. But we doubt that there is any such standard, and we are quite sure that the pejorative description 'outrageous' does not supply one. 'Outrageousness' in the area of political and social discourse has an inherent subjectiveness about it which would allow a jury to impose liability on the basis of the jurors' tastes or views, or perhaps on the basis of their dislike of a particular expression.

"We conclude that public figures and public officials may not recover for the tort of intentional infliction of emotional distress by reason of publications such as the one here at issue without showing in addition that the publication contains a false statement of fact which was made with 'actual malice,' i.e., with

3. Under Virginia law, in an action for intentional infliction of emotional distress a plaintiff must show that the defendant's conduct (1) is intentional or reckless; (2) offends generally accepted standards of decency or morality; (3) is causally connected with the plaintiff's emotional distress; and (4) caused emotional distress that was severe.

knowledge that the statement was false or with reckless disregard as to whether or not it was true." [b]

Notes and Questions

1. Does the rationale sweep beyond the holding? If debate on public issues should be uninhibited and if speakers filled with hatred have a place in that debate, why is the holding confined to suits brought by public officials and public figures? Is the holding likely to follow a "dialectic progression" from public official and public figure to all matters in the public domain? Should it? Is that far enough? Should the holding encompass all media speech? All non-media speech? Consider Smolla, *Emotional Distress and the First Amendment,* 20 Ariz. St.L.J. 423, 427 (1988): "The intellectual challenge posed by Falwell's suit is not how to construct a convincing rationale for rejecting his claim, but rather how to articulate limits on that rationale that will permit suits for emotional distress inflicted through speech in other contexts to survive." See generally Smolla, *Jerry Falwell v. Larry Flynt: The First Amendment on Trial* (1988).

2. Is the problem with the outrageousness standard less its subjectivity than its enabling "a single community to use the authority of the state to confine speech within its own notions of propriety." Does *Falwell* exhibit a need to respect a "marketplace of communities?" Can we respect that marketplace without "blunt[ing the] rules of civility that define the essence of reason and dignity within community life?" See Post, *The Constitutional Concept of Public Discourse,* 103 Harv.L.Rev. 601, 632, 643 (1990).

3. Is there any distinction to be made between persons and trademarks? The Second Circuit permitted an injunction to issue against exhibition of the film *Debbie Does Dallas* on the ground that it infringed on the trademarked uniform of the Dallas Cowboys Cheerleaders. *Dallas Cowboys Cheerleaders, Inc. v. Pussycat Cinema, Ltd.* 604 F.2d 200 (2d Cir.1979). The movie involves women performing sexual services for a fee so they can go to Dallas to become "Texas Cowgirls." Consistent with *Falwell?* Consider Kravitz, *Trademarks, Speech, and the Gay Olympics Case,* 69 B.U.L.Rev. 131 (1989): "If Rev. Jerry Falwell cannot succeed on a cause of action against an advertising parody suggesting he had a sexual encounter with his mother while drunk in an outhouse, why should an inanimate trademark enjoy greater protection against similar slurs? If Falwell cannot recover, surely Campari, whose trademark was also parodied in the fake ad, should not. [Broadly] interpreted, the holding in *Dallas Cowboys Cheerleaders* suggests that Ford Motor Company might enjoin the distribution of a book or a film that portrayed teenagers having sex in the back of a Ford car." See also Denicola, *Trademarks as Speech,* 1982 Wisc.L.Rev. 158.

F. DISCLOSURE OF PRIVATE FACTS

FLORIDA STAR v. B.J.F.

491 U.S. 524, 109 S.Ct. 2603, 105 L.Ed.2d 443 (1989).

JUSTICE MARSHALL delivered the opinion of the Court.

Florida Stat. § 794.03 (1987) makes it unlawful to "print, publish, or broadcast * * * in any instrument of mass communication" the name of the victim of a sexual offense. Pursuant to this statute, appellant The Florida Star was

b. White, J., concurred, but stated that *New York Times* was irrelevant because of the jury's finding that the parody contained no assertion of fact. Kennedy, J., took no part.

found civilly liable for publishing the name of a rape victim which it had obtained from a publicly released police report. The issue presented here is whether this result comports with the First Amendment. We hold that it does not. * * *

[B.J.F.] testified that she had suffered emotional distress from the publication of her name. She stated that she had heard about the article from fellow workers and acquaintances; that her mother had received several threatening phone calls from a man who stated that he would rape B.J.F. again; and that these events had forced B.J.F. to change her phone number and residence, to seek police protection, and to obtain mental health counseling. * * *

The jury awarded B.J.F. $75,000 in compensatory damages and $25,000 in punitive damages. * * *

[We do not] accept appellant's invitation to hold broadly that truthful publication may never be punished consistent with the First Amendment. Our cases have carefully eschewed reaching this ultimate question, mindful that the future may bring scenarios which prudence counsels our not resolving anticipatorily. See, e.g., *Near v. Minnesota,* [Section 4, I, B] (hypothesizing "publication of the sailing dates of transports or the number and location of troops"); see also *Garrison v. Louisiana* (endorsing absolute defense of truth "where discussion of public affairs is concerned," but leaving unsettled the constitutional implications of truthfulness "in the discrete area of purely private libels"). Indeed, in [*Cox Broadcasting v. Cohn,* 420 U.S. 469, 95 S.Ct. 1029, 43 L.Ed.2d 328 (1975)], we pointedly refused to answer even the less sweeping question "whether truthful publications may ever be subjected to civil or criminal liability" for invading "an area of privacy" defined by the State. [We] continue to believe that the sensitivity and significance of the interests presented in clashes between First Amendment and privacy rights counsel relying on limited principles that sweep no more broadly than the appropriate context of the instant case.

In our view, this case is appropriately analyzed with reference to such a limited First Amendment principle. It is the one, in fact, which we articulated in *Smith v. Daily Mail Pub. Co.,* [Section 5, I] in our synthesis of prior cases involving attempts to punish truthful publication: "[I]f a newspaper lawfully obtains truthful information about a matter of public significance then state officials may not constitutionally punish publication of the information, absent a need to further a state interest of the highest order." * * *

Applied to the instant case, the *Daily Mail* principle clearly commands reversal. The first inquiry is whether the newspaper "lawfully obtain[ed] truthful information about a matter of public significance." It is undisputed that the news article describing the assault on B.J.F. was accurate. In addition, appellant lawfully obtained B.J.F.'s name. Appellee's argument to the contrary is based on the fact that under Florida law, police reports which reveal the identity of the victim of a sexual offense are not among the matters of "public record" which the public, by law, is entitled to inspect. But the fact that state officials are not required to disclose such reports does not make it unlawful for a newspaper to receive them when furnished by the government. Nor does the fact that the Department apparently failed to fulfill its obligation under § 794.03 not to "cause or allow to be * * * published" the name of a sexual offense victim make the newspaper's ensuing receipt of this information unlawful. Even assuming the Constitution permitted a State to proscribe *receipt* of information, Florida has not taken this step. It is, clear, furthermore, that the news article concerned "a matter of public significance[.]" That is, the article generally, as opposed to the specific identity contained within it, involved a matter of paramount public import: the commission, and investigation, of a violent crime which had been reported to authorities.

The second inquiry is whether imposing liability on appellant pursuant to § 794.03 serves "a need to further a state interest of the highest order." Appellee argues that a rule punishing publication furthers three closely related interests: the privacy of victims of sexual offenses; the physical safety of such victims, who may be targeted for retaliation if their names become known to their assailants; and the goal of encouraging victims of such crimes to report these offenses without fear of exposure.

At a time in which we are daily reminded of the tragic reality of rape, it is undeniable that these are highly significant interests, a fact underscored by the Florida Legislature's explicit attempt to protect these interests by enacting a criminal statute prohibiting much dissemination of victim identities. We accordingly do not rule out the possibility that, in a proper case, imposing civil sanctions for publication of the name of a rape victim might be so overwhelmingly necessary to advance these interests as to satisfy the *Daily Mail* standard. For three independent reasons, however, imposing liability for publication under the circumstances of this case is too precipitous a means of advancing these interests to convince us that there is a "need" within the meaning of the *Daily Mail* formulation for Florida to take this extreme step.

First is the manner in which appellant obtained the identifying information in question. [B.J.F.'s] identity would never have come to light were it not for the erroneous, if inadvertent, inclusion by the Department of her full name in an incident report made available in a press room open to the public. Florida's policy against disclosure of rape victims' identities, reflected in § 794.03, was undercut by the Department's failure to abide by this policy. Where, as here, the government has failed to police itself in disseminating information, it is clear [that] the imposition of damages against the press for its subsequent publication can hardly be said to be a narrowly tailored means of safeguarding anonymity.

That appellant gained access to the information in question through a government news release makes it especially likely that, if liability were to be imposed, self-censorship would result. Reliance on a news release is a paradigmatically "routine newspaper reporting techniqu[e]." The government's issuance of such a release, without qualification, can only convey to recipients that the government considered dissemination lawful, and indeed expected the recipients to disseminate the information further. Had appellant merely reproduced the news release prepared and released by the Department, imposing civil damages would surely violate the First Amendment. The fact that appellant converted the police report into a news story by adding the linguistic connecting tissue necessary to transform the report's facts into full sentences cannot change this result.

A second problem with Florida's imposition of liability for publication is the broad sweep of the negligence *per se* standard applied under the civil cause of action implied from § 794.03. Unlike claims based on the common law tort of invasion of privacy, civil actions based on § 794.03 require no case-by-case findings that the disclosure of a fact about a person's private life was one that a reasonable person would find highly offensive. On the contrary, under the *per se* theory of negligence adopted by the courts below, liability follows automatically from publication. This is so regardless of whether the identity of the victim is already known throughout the community; whether the victim has voluntarily called public attention to the offense; or whether the identity of the victim has otherwise become a reasonable subject of public concern—because, perhaps, questions have arisen whether the victim fabricated an assault by a particular person. Nor is there a scienter requirement of any kind under § 794.03, engendering the perverse result that truthful publications challenged pursuant to this cause of action are less protected by the First Amendment than even the least protected defamatory falsehoods: those involving purely private figures, where liability is evaluated under a standard, usually applied by a jury, of ordinary negligence. See *Gertz.* * * *

Third, and finally, the facial underinclusiveness of § 794.03 raises serious doubts about whether Florida is, in fact, serving, with this statute, the significant interests which appellee invokes in support of affirmance. Section 794.03 prohibits the publication of identifying information only if this information appears in an "instrument of mass communication," a term the statute does not define. Section 794.03 does not prohibit the spread by other means of the identities of victims of sexual offenses. An individual who maliciously spreads word of the identity of a rape victim is thus not covered, despite the fact that the communication of such information to persons who live near, or work with, the victim may have consequences equally devastating as the exposure of her name to large numbers of strangers.

When a State attempts the extraordinary measure of punishing truthful publication in the name of privacy, it must demonstrate its commitment to advancing this interest by applying its prohibition evenhandedly, to the small-time disseminator as well as the media giant. Where important First Amendment interests are at stake, the mass scope of disclosure is not an acceptable surrogate for injury. Without more careful and inclusive precautions against alternative forms of dissemination, we cannot conclude that Florida's selective ban on publication by the mass media satisfactorily accomplishes its stated purpose.

Our holding today is limited. We do not hold that truthful publication is automatically constitutionally protected, or that there is no zone of personal privacy within which the State may protect the individual from intrusion by the press, or even that a State may never punish publication of the name of a victim of a sexual offense. We hold only that where a newspaper publishes truthful information which it has lawfully obtained, punishment may lawfully be imposed, if at all, only when narrowly tailored to a state interest of the highest order, and that no such interest is satisfactorily served by imposing liability under § 794.03 to appellant under the facts of this case. * * *

JUSTICE SCALIA, concurring in part and concurring in the judgment.

I think it sufficient to decide this case to rely upon the third ground set forth in the Court's opinion: that a law cannot be regarded as protecting an interest "of the highest order" and thus as justifying a restriction upon truthful speech, when it leaves appreciable damage to that supposedly vital interest unprohibited. In the present case, I would anticipate that the rape victim's discomfort at the dissemination of news of her misfortune among friends and acquaintances would be at least as great as her discomfort at its publication by the media to people to whom she is only a name. Yet the law in question does not prohibit the former in either oral or written form. Nor is it at all clear, as I think it must be to validate this statute, that Florida's general privacy law would prohibit such gossip. Nor, finally, is it credible that the interest meant to be served by the statute is the protection of the victim against a rapist still at large—an interest that arguably would extend only to mass publication. There would be little reason to limit a statute with that objective to rape alone; or to extend it to all rapes, whether or not the felon has been apprehended and confined. In any case, the instructions here did not require the jury to find that the rapist was at large.

This law has every appearance of a prohibition that society is prepared to impose upon the press but not upon itself. Such a prohibition does not protect an interest "of the highest order." For that reason, I agree that the judgment of the court below must be reversed.

JUSTICE WHITE, with whom THE CHIEF JUSTICE and JUSTICE O'CONNOR join, dissenting.

"Short of homicide, [rape] is the 'ultimate violation of self.'" *Coker v. Georgia,* [433 U.S. 584, 97 S.Ct. 2861, 53 L.Ed.2d 982 (1977)] (opinion of White, J.). For B.J.F., however, the violation she suffered at a rapist's knife-point marked only the beginning of her ordeal. A week later, while her assailant was still at large, an account of this assault—identifying by name B.J.F. as the victim—was published by The Florida Star. As a result, B.J.F. received harassing phone calls, required mental health counseling, was forced to move from her home, and was even threatened with being raped again. Yet today, the Court holds that a jury award of $75,000 to compensate B.J.F. for the harm she suffered due to the Star's negligence is at odds with the First Amendment. I do not accept this result.

[T]he three "independent reasons" the Court cites for reversing the judgment for B.J.F. [do not] support its result.

The first of these reasons [is] the fact "appellant gained access to [B.J.F.'s name] through a government news release." "The government's issuance of such a release, without qualification, can only convey to recipients that the government considered dissemination lawful," the Court suggests. [But the] "release" of information provided by the government was not, as the Court says, "without qualification." As the Star's own reporter conceded at trial, the crime incident report that inadvertently included B.J.F.'s name was posted in a room that contained signs making it clear that the names of rape victims were not matters of public record, and were not to be published. The Star's reporter indicated that she understood that she "[was not] allowed to take down that information" (i.e., B.J.F.'s name) and that she "[was] not supposed to take the information from the police department." Thus, by her own admission the posting of the incident report did not convey to the Star's reporter the idea that "the government considered dissemination lawful"; the Court's suggestion to the contrary is inapt. * * *

Unfortunately, as this case illustrates, mistakes happen: even when States take measures to "avoid" disclosure, sometimes rape victim's names are found out. As I see it, it is not too much to ask the press, in instances such as this, to respect simple standards of decency and refrain from publishing a victim's name, address, and/or phone number.

Second, the Court complains that appellant was judged here under too strict a liability standard. The Court contends that a newspaper might be found liable under the Florida courts' negligence *per se* theory without regard to a newspaper's scienter or degree of fault. The short answer to this complaint is that whatever merit the Court's argument might have, it is wholly inapposite here, where the jury found that appellant acted with "reckless indifference towards the rights of others," a standard far higher than the *Gertz* standard the Court urges as a constitutional minimum today. B.J.F. proved the Star's negligence at trial—and, actually, far more than simple negligence; the Court's concerns about damages resting on a strict liability or mere causation basis are irrelevant to the validity of the judgment for appellee.

But even taking the Court's concerns in the abstract, they miss the mark. Permitting liability under a negligence *per se* theory does not mean that defendants will be held liable without a showing of negligence, but rather, that the standard of care has been set by the legislature, instead of the courts. The Court says that negligence *per se* permits a plaintiff to hold a defendant liable without a showing that the disclosure was "of a fact about a person's private life [that] a reasonable person would find highly offensive." But the point here is that the legislature—reflecting popular sentiment—has determined that disclosure of the fact that a person was raped is categorically a revelation that reasonable people find offensive. And as for the Court's suggestion that the Florida courts' theory permits liability without regard for whether the victim's identity is already known, or whether she herself has made it known—these are facts that would surely enter into the calculation of damages in such a case. In any event, none of these mitigating factors was present here; whatever the force of these arguments generally, they do not justify the Court's ruling against B.J.F. in this case.

Third, the Court faults the Florida criminal statute for being underinclusive: § 794.03 covers disclosure of rape victim's names in "instrument[s] of mass communication," but not other means of distribution, the Court observes. But our cases which have struck down laws that limit or burden the press due to their underinclusiveness have involved situations where a legislature has singled out one segment of the news media or press for adverse treatment. Here, the Florida law evenhandedly covers all "instrument[s] of mass communication" no matter their form, media, content, nature or purpose. It excludes neighborhood gossips because presumably the Florida Legislature has determined that neighborhood gossips do not pose the danger and intrusion to rape victims that "instrument[s] of mass communication" do. Simply put: Florida wanted to prevent the widespread distribution of rape victim's names, and therefore enacted a statute tailored almost as precisely as possible to achieving that end. * * *

At issue in this case is whether there is any information about people, which—though true—may not be published in the press. By holding that only "a state interest of the highest order" permits the State to penalize the publication of truthful information, and by holding that protecting a rape victim's right to privacy is not among those state interests of the highest order, the Court accepts appellant's invitation to obliterate one of the most note-worthy legal inventions of the 20th-Century: the tort of the publication of private facts. W. Prosser, J. Wade, & V. Schwartz, *Torts* 951–952 (8th ed. 1988). Even if the Court's opinion does not say as much today, such obliteration will follow inevitably from the Court's conclusion here. * * *

I do not suggest that the Court's decision today is radical departure from a previously charted course. The Court's ruling has been foreshadowed. In *Time, Inc. v. Hill,* we observed that—after a brief period early in this century where Brandeis' view was ascendant—the trend in "modern" jurisprudence has been to eclipse an individual's right to maintain private any truthful information that the press wished to publish. More recently, in *Cox Broadcasting,* we acknowledged the possibility that the First Amendment may prevent a State from ever subjecting the publication of truthful but private information to civil liability. Today, we hit the bottom of the slippery slope.

I would find a place to draw the line higher on the hillside: a spot high enough to protect B.J.F.'s desire for privacy and peace-of-mind in the wake of a horrible personal tragedy. There is no public interest in publishing the names, addresses, and phone numbers of persons who are the victims of crime—and no public interest in immunizing the press from liability in the rare cases where a State's efforts to protect a victim's privacy have failed. Consequently, I respectfully dissent.[5]

III. OBSCENITY

A. THE SEARCH FOR A RATIONALE

Roth v. United States, infra, contains the Court's first extended discussion of the constitutionality of obscenity laws. The Court's opinion was framed by briefs that proceeded from sharply different visions of first amendment law. Roth argued that no speech including obscenity could be prohibited without meeting the clear and present danger test, that a danger of lustful thoughts was not the type of evil with which a legislature could be legitimately concerned, and that no danger of anti-social conduct had been shown. On the other hand, the government urged the Court to adopt a balancing test that prominently featured a consideration of the value of the speech involved. The government tendered an illustrative hierarchy of nineteen speech categories with political, religious, economic, and scientific speech at the top; entertainment, music, and humor in the middle; and libel, obscenity, profanity, and commercial pornography at the bottom.

ROTH v. UNITED STATES

ALBERTS v. CALIFORNIA

354 U.S. 476, 77 S.Ct. 1304, 1 L.Ed.2d 1498 (1957).

JUSTICE BRENNAN delivered the opinion of the Court. [Roth and Alberts were convicted of violating the federal and California obscenity laws respectively. The issues raised were whether the statutes, "*on their faces and in a vacuum,* violated the freedom of expression and definiteness requirements of the Constitution." [a]]

The dispositive question is whether obscenity is utterance within the area of protected speech and press.[8] Although this is the first time the question has been squarely presented to this Court [expressions] found in numerous opinions indicate that this Court has always assumed that obscenity is not protected by the freedoms of speech and press.

The guaranties of freedom of expression in effect in 10 of the 14 States which by 1792 had ratified the Constitution, gave no absolute protection for

5. The Court does not address the distinct constitutional questions raised by the award of punitive damages in this case. Consequently, I do not do so either. That award is more troublesome than the compensatory award discussed above. Cf. Note, *Punitive Damages and Libel Law,* 98 Harv.L.Rev. 847 (1985).

a. See Lockhart & McClure, *Censorship of Obscenity: The Developing Constitutional Standards,* 45 Minn.L.Rev. 5, 13 (1960).

8. No issue is presented in either case concerning the obscenity of the material involved.

every utterance. Thirteen of the 14 States provided for the prosecution of libel, and all of those States made either blasphemy or profanity, or both, statutory crimes. As early as 1712, Massachusetts made it criminal to publish "any filthy, obscene, or profane song, pamphlet, libel or mock sermon" in imitation or mimicking of religious services. * * *

In light of this history, it is apparent that the unconditional phrasing of the First Amendment was not intended to protect every utterance. This phrasing did not prevent this Court from concluding that libelous utterances are not within the area of constitutionally protected speech. *Beauharnais.* At the time of the adoption of the First Amendment, obscenity law was not as fully developed as libel law, but there is sufficiently contemporaneous evidence to show that obscenity, too, was outside the protection intended for speech and press.[b]

The protection given speech and press was fashioned to assure unfettered interchange of ideas for the bringing about of political and social changes desired by the people. [All] ideas having even the slightest redeeming social importance—unorthodox ideas, controversial ideas, even ideas hateful to the prevailing climate of opinion—have the full protection of the guaranties, unless excludable because they encroach upon the limited area of more important interests. But implicit in the history of the First Amendment is the rejection of obscenity as utterly without redeeming social importance. This rejection for that reason is mirrored in the universal judgment that obscenity should be restrained, reflected in the international agreement of over 50 nations, in the obscenity laws of all of the 48 States, and in the 20 obscenity laws enacted by the Congress from 1842 to 1956. This is the same judgment expressed by this Court in *Chaplinsky* [p. 485 infra]: "There are certain well-defined and narrowly limited classes of speech, the prevention and punishment of which have never been thought to raise any Constitutional problem. *These include the lewd and obscene. [It] has been well observed that such utterances are no essential part of any exposition of ideas, and are of such slight social value as a step to truth that any benefit that may be derived from them is clearly outweighed by the social interest in order and morality.*" (Emphasis added [by Court].)

We hold that obscenity is not within the area of constitutionally protected speech or press.

It is strenuously urged that these obscenity statutes offend the constitutional guaranties because they punish incitation to impure sexual *thoughts,* not shown to be related to any overt antisocial conduct which is or may be incited in the persons stimulated to such *thoughts.* [It] is insisted that the constitutional guaranties are violated because convictions may be had without proof either that obscene material will perceptibly create a clear and present danger of antisocial

b. The Court here cited three state court decisions (1808 to 1821) recognizing as a common law offense the distribution or display of obscene or indecent materials, and four state statutes aimed at similar conduct (1800 to 1842). For the contention that obscenity is not "speech" within the meaning of the first amendment (let alone, not *protected* speech), see Schauer, *Free Speech: A Philosophical Enquiry* 181–84 (1982) (a sex aid, not speech). See generally Schauer, *Speech and "Speech"—Obscenity and "Obscenity": An Exercise in the Interpretation of Constitutional Language,* 67 Geo.L.J. 899 (1979). But see Alexander & Horton, *The Impossibility of a Free Speech Principle,* 78 Nw.U.L.Rev. 1319, 1331–34 (1984). Compare Greenawalt, *Criminal Coercion and Freedom of Speech,* 78 Nw.U.L.Rev. 1081 (1984) (discussing the question of whether all ordinary language should be included within the scope of the first amendment, even if much is ultimately unprotected, and contending that some ordinary language should be wholly outside the scope of the first amendment); Greenawalt, *Speech, Crime and the Uses of Language.* But see Haiman, *Comments on Kent Greenawalt's Criminal Coercion and Freedom of Speech,* 78 Nw.U.L.Rev. 1125 (1983).

conduct, or will probably induce its recipients to such conduct. But, in light of our holding that obscenity is not protected speech, the complete answer to this argument is in the holding of this Court in *Beauharnais:* "Libelous utterances not being within the area of constitutionally protected speech, it is unnecessary, either for us or for the State courts, to consider the issues behind the phrase 'clear and present danger.' Certainly no one would contend that obscene speech, for example, may be punished only upon a showing of such circumstances. * * *"

However, sex and obscenity are not synonymous. Obscene material is material which deals with sex in a manner appealing to prurient interest.[20] The portrayal of sex, e.g., in art, literature and scientific works, is not itself sufficient reason to deny material the constitutional protection of freedom of speech and press. Sex, a great and mysterious motive force in human life, has indisputably been a subject of absorbing interest to mankind through the ages; it is one of the vital problems of human interest and public [concern].

The fundamental freedoms of speech and press have contributed greatly to the development and well-being of our free society and are indispensable to its continued growth. [It] is therefore vital that the standards for judging obscenity safeguard the protection of freedom of speech and press for material which does not treat sex in a manner appealing to prurient interest.

The early leading standard of obscenity allowed material to be judged merely by the effect of an isolated excerpt upon particularly susceptible persons. *Regina v. Hicklin,* [1868] L.R. 3 Q.B. 360. Some American courts adopted this standard but later decisions have rejected it and substituted this test: whether to the average person, applying contemporary community standards, the dominant theme of the material taken as a whole appeals to prurient interest. The *Hicklin* test, judging obscenity by the effect of isolated passages upon the most susceptible persons, might well encompass material legitimately treating with sex, and so it must be rejected as unconstitutionally restrictive of the freedoms of speech and press. On the other hand, the substituted standard provides safeguards adequate to withstand the charge of constitutional infirmity. Both trial courts below sufficiently followed the proper standard. Both courts used the proper definition of obscenity.[c]

20. I.e., material having a tendency to excite lustful thoughts. *Webster's New International Dictionary* (Unabridged, 2d ed., 1949) defines *prurient,* in pertinent part, as follows:

"Itching; longing; uneasy with desire or longing; of persons, having itching, morbid, or lascivious longings; of desire, curiosity, or propensity, lewd * * *."

We perceive no significant difference between the meaning of obscenity developed in the case law and the definition of the A.L.I., *Model Penal Code,* § 207.10(2) (Tent. Draft No. 6, 1957), viz.: "[A] thing is obscene if, considered as a whole, its predominant appeal is to prurient interest, i.e. a shameful or morbid interest in nudity, sex, or excretion, and if it goes substantially beyond customary limits of candor in description or representation of such [matters]." See Comment, id. at 10, and the discussion at page 29 et seq.

c. The opinion quoted with apparent approval from the trial court's instruction in *Roth:* "[The] test is not whether it would arouse sexual desires or sexual impure thoughts in those comprising a particular segment of the community, the young, the immature or the highly prudish or would leave another segment, the scientific or highly educated or the so-called worldly-wise and sophisticated indifferent and unmoved. [The] test in each case is the effect of the book, picture or publication considered as a whole, not upon any particular class, but upon all those whom it is likely to reach. In other words, you determine its impact upon the average person in the community. The books, pictures and circulars must be judged as a whole, in their entire context, and you are not to consider detached or separate portions in reaching a conclusion. You judge the circulars, pictures and publications which have been put in evidence by present-day standards of the community. You may ask yourselves does it offend the common conscience of the community by present-day standards."

[It] is argued that the statutes do not provide reasonably ascertainable standards of guilt and therefore violate the constitutional requirements of due process. *Winters v. New York,* 333 U.S. 507, 68 S.Ct. 665, 92 L.Ed. 840 (1948). The federal obscenity statute makes punishable the mailing of material that is "obscene, lewd, lascivious, or filthy [or] other publication of an indecent character." The California statute makes punishable, inter alia, the keeping for sale or advertising material that is "obscene or indecent." The thrust of the argument is that these words are not sufficiently precise because they do not mean the same thing to all people, all the time, everywhere. Many decisions have recognized that these terms of obscenity statutes are not precise. This Court, however, has consistently held that lack of precision is not itself offensive to the requirements of due process. "[T]he Constitution does not require impossible standards"; all that is required is that the language "conveys sufficiently definite warning as to the proscribed conduct when measured by common understanding and [practices.]" * * *

In summary, then, we hold that these statutes, applied according to the proper standard for judging obscenity, do not offend constitutional safeguards against convictions based upon protected material, or fail to give men in acting adequate notice of what is prohibited. * * *

Affirmed.

CHIEF JUSTICE WARREN, concurring in the result.

[It] is not the book that is on trial; it is a person. The conduct of the defendant is the central issue, not the obscenity of a book or picture. The nature of the materials is, of course, relevant as an attribute of the defendant's conduct. [The] defendants in both these cases were engaged in the business of purveying textual or graphic matter openly advertised to appeal to the erotic interest of their customers. They were plainly engaged in the commercial exploitation of the morbid and shameful craving for materials with prurient effect. * * *

JUSTICE HARLAN, concurring in the result in [*Alberts*], and dissenting in [*Roth*].

I. [The] Court seems to assume that "obscenity" is a peculiar genus of "speech and press," which is as distinct, recognizable, and classifiable as poison ivy is among other plants. On this basis the *constitutional* question before us simply becomes, as the Court says, whether "obscenity," as an abstraction, is protected by the First and Fourteenth Amendments, and the question whether a *particular* book may be suppressed becomes a mere matter of classification, of "fact," to be entrusted to a fact-finder and insulated from independent constitutional judgment. But surely the problem cannot be solved in such a generalized fashion. Every communication has an individuality and "value" of its own. The suppression of a particular writing or other tangible form of expression is, therefore, an *individual* matter, and in the nature of things every such suppression raises an individual constitutional problem, in which a reviewing court must determine for *itself* whether the attacked expression is suppressable within constitutional [standards].

I do not think that reviewing courts can escape this responsibility by saying that the trier of the facts, be it a jury or a judge, has labeled the questioned matter as "obscene," for, if "obscenity" is to be suppressed, the question whether a particular work is of that character involves not really an issue of fact but a question of constitutional *judgment* of the most sensitive and delicate kind. Many juries might find that Joyce's "Ulysses" or Bocaccio's "Decameron" was obscene, and yet the conviction of a defendant for selling either book would raise, for me, the gravest constitutional problems, for no such verdict could convince me, without more, that these books are "utterly without redeeming social importance." [I] am very much afraid that the broad manner in which the Court has decided these cases will tend to obscure the peculiar responsibilities resting on state and federal courts in this field and encourage them to rely on easy labeling and jury verdicts as a substitute for facing up to the tough individual problems of constitutional judgment involved in every obscenity case.

[In] California the book must have a "tendency to deprave or corrupt its readers"; under the federal statute it must tend "to stir sexual impulses and lead to sexually impure thoughts." [T]he Court compounds confusion when it superimposes on these two statutory definitions a third, drawn from the American Law Institute's *Model Penal Code,* Tentative Draft No. 6: "A thing is obscene if, considered as a whole, its predominant appeal is to prurient interest." The bland assurance that this definition is the same as the ones with which we deal flies in the face of the authors' express rejection of the "deprave and corrupt" and "sexual thoughts" tests.[d] [T]he Court merely assimilates the various tests into one indiscriminate potpourri. * * *

II. I concur in [*Alberts*]. [T]he [California] legislature has made the judgment that printed words *can* "deprave or corrupt" the reader—that words can incite to anti-social or immoral action. [It] is well known, of course, that the validity of this assumption is a matter of dispute among critics, sociologists, psychiatrists, and penologists. [I]t is not our function to decide this question. That function belongs to the state legislature. [I]t is not irrational, in our present state of knowledge, to consider that pornography can induce a type of sexual conduct which a State may deem obnoxious to the moral fabric of [society].

Furthermore, even assuming that pornography cannot be deemed ever to cause, in an immediate sense, criminal sexual conduct, other interests within the proper cognizance of the States may be protected by the prohibition placed on such materials. The State can reasonably draw the inference that over a long period of time the indiscriminate dissemination of materials, the essential character of which is to degrade sex, will have an eroding effect on moral standards. And the State has a legitimate interest in protecting the privacy of the home against invasion of unsolicited obscenity.

[I] concur in the judgment because, upon an independent perusal of the material involved, and in light of the considerations discussed above, I cannot say that its suppression would so interfere with the communication of "ideas" in any proper sense of that term that it would offend the Due Process Clause.[e]

d. The opinion quoted the explanation in the Tentative Draft: "Obscenity [in the Tentative Draft] is defined in terms of material which appeals predominantly to prurient interest in sexual matters and which goes beyond customary freedom of expression in these matters. We reject the prevailing test of tendency to arouse lustful thoughts or desires because it is unrealistically broad for a society that plainly tolerates a great deal of erotic interest in literature, advertising, and art, and because regulation of thought or desire, unconnected with overt misbehavior, raises the most acute constitutional as well as practical difficulties. We likewise reject the common definition of obscene as that which 'tends to corrupt or debase.' If this means anything different from tendency to arouse lustful thought and desire, it suggests that change of character or actual misbehavior follows from contact with obscenity. Evidence of such consequences is lacking. [On] the other hand, 'appeal to prurient interest' refers to qualities of the material itself: the capacity to attract individuals eager for a forbidden look."

e. Harlan, J., dissented in *Roth.* He would have limited federal power to reach only "what the Government has termed as 'hard-core' pornography." He stressed both the ab-

JUSTICE DOUGLAS, with whom JUSTICE BLACK concurs, dissenting.

When we sustain these convictions, we make the legality of a publication turn on the purity of thought which a book or tract instills in the mind of the reader. I do not think we can approve that standard and be faithful to the command of the First Amendment * * *.

The tests by which these convictions were obtained require only the arousing of sexual thoughts. Yet the arousing of sexual thoughts and desires happens every day in normal life in dozens of ways. Nearly 30 years ago a questionnaire sent to college and normal school women graduates asked what things were most stimulating sexually. Of 409 replies, 9 said "music"; 18 said "pictures"; 29 said "dancing"; 40 said "drama"; 95 said "books"; and 218 said "man." Alpert, *Judicial Censorship of Obscene Literature,* 52 Harv.L.Rev. 40, 73 (1938).

The test of obscenity the Court endorses today gives the censor free range over a vast domain. To allow the State to step in and punish mere speech or publication that the judge or the jury thinks has an *undesirable* impact on thoughts but that is not shown to be a part of unlawful action is drastically to curtail the First Amendment. As recently stated by two of our outstanding authorities on obscenity, "The danger of influencing a change in the current moral standards of the community, or of shocking or offending readers, or of stimulating sex thoughts or desires apart from objective conduct, can never justify the losses to society that result from interference with literary freedom." Lockhart & McClure, *Literature, The Law of Obscenity, and the Constitution,* 38 Minn.L.Rev. 295, 387 (1954).

If we were certain that impurity of sexual thoughts impelled to action, we would be on less dangerous ground in punishing the distributors of this sex literature. But it is by no means clear that obscene literature, as so defined, is a significant factor in influencing substantial deviations from the community standards. [The] absence of dependable information on the effect of obscene literature on human conduct should make us wary. It should put us on the side of protecting society's interest in literature, except and unless it can be said that the particular publication has an impact on action that the government can [control.]

Any test that turns on what is offensive to the community's standards is too loose, too capricious, too destructive of freedom of expression to be squared with the First Amendment. Under that test, juries can censor, suppress, and punish what they don't like, provided the matter relates to "sexual impurity" or has a tendency "to excite lustful thoughts." This is community censorship in one of its worst forms. It creates a regime where in the battle between the literati and the Philistines, the Philistines are certain to win. If experience in this teaches anything, it is that "censorship of obscenity has almost always been both irrational and indiscriminate." Lockhart & McClure at 371.

* * *

I do not think that the problem can be resolved by the Court's statement that "obscenity is not expression protected by the First Amendment." With the exception of *Beauharnais* none of our cases has resolved problems of free speech and free press by placing any form of expression beyond the pale of the absolute prohibition of the First Amendment. Unlike the law of libel, wrongfully relied on in *Beauharnais*, there is no special historical evidence that literature dealing with sex was intended to be treated in a special manner by those who drafted the

sence of federal "power over sexual morality" and the danger to free expression of a "blanket ban over the Nation" on such books as *Lady Chatterley's Lover.*

First Amendment. [I] reject too the implication that problems of freedom of speech and of the press are to be resolved by weighing against the values of free expression, the judgment of the Court that a particular form of that expression has "no redeeming social importance." * * *

I would give the broad sweep of the First Amendment full support. I have the same confidence in the ability of our people to reject noxious literature as I have in their capacity to sort out the true from the false in theology, economics, politics, or any other field.

Notes and Questions

1. *Non-obscene advocacy of "sexual immorality."* Two years after *Roth,* KINGSLEY INTERN. PICTURES CORP. v. REGENTS, 360 U.S. 684, 79 S.Ct. 1362, 3 L.Ed.2d 1512 (1959), per STEWART, J., underlined the distinction between obscenity and non-obscene "portrayal of sex" in art and literature. *Kingsley* held invalid New York's denial of a license to exhibit the film *Lady Chatterley's Lover* pursuant to a statute requiring such denial when a film "portrays acts of sexual immorality [as] desirable, acceptable or proper patterns of behavior":

"The Court of Appeals unanimously and explicitly rejected any notion that the film is obscene [but] found that the picture as a whole 'alluringly portrays adultery as proper behavior.' [What] New York has done, [is] to prevent the exhibition of a motion picture because that picture advocates an idea—that adultery under certain circumstances may be proper behavior. Yet the First Amendment's basic guarantee is of freedom to advocate ideas. The State, quite simply, has thus struck at the very heart of constitutionally protected liberty.

"[T]he guarantee is not confined to the expression of ideas that are conventional or shared by a majority. It protects advocacy of the opinion that adultery may sometimes be proper, no less than advocacy of socialism or the single tax. And in the realm of ideas it protects expression which is eloquent no less than that which is unconvincing. Advocacy of conduct proscribed by law is not, as Mr. Justice Brandeis long ago pointed out, 'a justification for denying free speech where the advocacy falls short of incitement and there is nothing to indicate that the advocacy would be immediately acted on.' *Whitney.*" [f]

2. *Ideas and the first amendment.* Consider Kalven, *The Metaphysics of the Law of Obscenity,* 1960 Sup.Ct.Rev. 1, 15–16: "The classic defense of John Stuart Mill and the modern defense of Alexander Meiklejohn do not help much when the question is why the novel, the poem, the painting, the drama, or the piece of sculpture falls within the protection of the First Amendment. Nor do the famous opinions of Hand, Holmes, and Brandeis. [The] people do not need novels or dramas or paintings or poems because they will be called upon to vote. Art and belles-lettres do not deal in such ideas—at least not good art or belles-lettres—and it makes little sense here to talk [of] whether there is still time for counter-speech.

f. While joining the opinion, Black and Douglas, JJ., also stated that prior censorship of motion pictures violates the first amendment. See discussion of this issue in Sec. 4, II infra. Harlan, J., joined by Frankfurter and Whittaker, JJ., concurred in the result. While "granting that abstract public discussion [of] adultery, unaccompanied by obscene portrayal or actual incitement [may] not constitutionally be proscribed," they concluded that the New York Court of Appeals had found the film obscene, but on viewing the film they concluded it was not obscene. Clark, J., concurred in the result because the statutory standard was too vague.

[B]eauty has constitutional status too, [and] the life of the imagination is as important to the human adult as the life of the intellect. I do not think that the Court would find it difficult to protect Shakespeare, even though it is hard to enumerate the important ideas in the plays and poems. I am only suggesting that Mr. Justice Brennan might not have found it so easy to dismiss obscenity because it lacked socially useful ideas if he had recognized that as to this point, at least, obscenity is in the same position as all art and literature." See generally Nahmod, *Artistic Expression and Aesthetic Theory: The Beautiful, The Sublime and The First Amendment,* 1987 Wisc.L.Rev. 221.

3. *The moral rationale for prohibition.* Consider Clor, *Obscenity and Public Morality* 41–43 (1969): *Roth* "rejected the government's formula for the decision of obscenity cases, a formula which would have involved it in judgments concerning the importance of public morality and the role of government, as well as judgments concerning the effects of obscenity and the relative value of different forms of speech. The Court preferred to decide the case on the narrow and negative grounds that obscenity is without redeeming social importance. [W]hile the idea of redeeming social importance can be valuable as a definition of what should be protected, it cannot serve as a defense of regulation. Justices Harlan and Douglas can be answered only by a course of reasoning which provides some grounds for government activity in the area of morality, showing that the ends are legitimate and important, which provides some justification for the claims of community conscience, and which explores, more thoroughly than does the Court, the character of the 'thoughts' with which the law is here concerned."

The Court does assert that any value of obscenity as a step to truth is "outweighed by the social interest in order and morality.'" But consider Richards, *Free Speech and Obscenity Law: Toward A Moral Theory of the First Amendment,* 123 U.Pa.L.Rev. 45, 81 (1974): "[P]ornography can be seen as the unique medium of a vision of sexuality * * * a view of sensual delight in the erotic celebration of the body, a concept of easy freedom without consequences, a fantasy of timelessly repetitive indulgence. In opposition to the Victorian view that narrowly defines proper sexual function in a rigid way that is analogous to ideas of excremental regularity and moderation, pornography builds a model of plastic variety and joyful excess in sexuality. In opposition to the sorrowing Catholic dismissal of sexuality as an unfortunate and spiritually superficial concomitant of propagation, pornography affords the alternative idea of the independent status of sexuality as a profound and shattering ecstasy." [g]

Even if these characterizations were somewhat overwrought with respect to Roth's publications (e.g., *Wild Passion* and *Wanton By Night*) what of the view that individuals should be able to decide what they want to read and make moral decisions for themselves? Consider John Stuart Mill's statement of the harm principle in *On Liberty:* "[T]he only purpose for which power can be rightfully

g. For the view that pornography can best be defended as a form of anti-social dissent, consider Gey, *The Apologetics of Suppression,* 86 Mich.L.Rev. 1564, 1630 (1988): "Porn exposes a rot in the framework of society, and the great popularity of porn makes the burghers uneasily suspicious that the surface rot may evidence a more deeply rooted degeneration of their moral and political primacy. Thus, the imperative to suppress pornography reveals a much deeper and more insidious insecurity than the moralists will ever acknowledge." Cf. West, *The Feminist–Conservative Anti–Pornography Alliance and the 1986 Attorney General's Commission on Pornography Report,* 1987 Am.B.Found.Res.J. 681, 686–99 (discussing victimizing and liberating aspects of pornography from the perspectives of women while contending that women's experience of pornography, albeit diverse, is different from that of men).

exercised over any member of a civilized community, against his will is to prevent harm to others."

Does the liberal view overestimate human rational capacity and underestimate the importance of the state in promoting a virtuous citizenry? See generally Clor, supra. Do liberals fail to appreciate the morally corrosive effects of obscenity? Consider the following observation: "Obscenity emphasizes the base animality of our nature, reduces the spirituality of humanity to mere bodily functions, and debases civilization by transforming the private into the public." Consider Kristol, *Reflections of a Neoconservative* 45, 47 (1983): "Bearbaiting and cockfighting are prohibited only in part out of compassion for the suffering animals; the main reason they were abolished was because it was felt that they debased and brutalized the citizenry who flocked to witness such spectacles. And the question we face with regard to pornography and obscenity is whether [they] can or will brutalize and debase our citizenry. We are, after all, not dealing with one passing incident—one book, or one play, or one movie. We are dealing with a general tendency that is suffusing our entire culture. [W]hen men and women make love, as we say, they prefer to be alone—because it is only when you are alone that you can make love, as distinct from merely copulating in an animal and casual way. And that, too, is why those who are voyeurs, if they are not irredeemably sick, also feel ashamed at what they are witnessing. When sex is a public spectacle, a human relationship has been debased into a mere animal connection." See also Clor, supra; Berns, *Pornography vs. Democracy: The Case for Censorship,* 22 Pub.Int. 13 (1971).

4. *Feminism and pornography.* Does the Court's cryptic recitation of the interests in order and morality obscure the implications of pornography for women in a male-dominated culture? Consider Brownmiller, *Against Our Will: Men, Women & Rape* 442–43, 444 (1976): Pornography is a "systematized commercially successful propaganda machine" encouraging males to get a "sense of power from viewing females as anonymous, panting playthings, adult toys, dehumanized objects to be used, abused, broken and discarded." See also MacKinnon, *Not a Moral Issue,* 2 Yale L. & Pol.Rev. 321, 327 (1984): "[T]he liberal defense of pornography as human sexual liberation, as de-repression—whether by feminists, lawyers, or neo-Freudians—is a defense not only of force and sexual terrorism, but of the subordination of women. Sexual liberation in the liberal sense frees male sexual aggression in the feminist sense. What in the liberal view looks like love and romance looks a lot like hatred and torture to the feminist. Pleasure and eroticism become violation. Desire appears as lust for dominance and submission."

5. *The impact of obscenity on anti-social conduct.* After citing the conclusion of the U.S. Commission on Obscenity and Pornography that " 'empirical research has found no evidence to date that exposure to explicit sexual materials plays a significant role in the causation of delinquent or criminal behaviour among youth or adults,' " the British Committee on Obscenity and Film Censorship concluded: "It is still possible to say [that] there does not appear to be any strong evidence that exposure to sexually explicit material triggers off anti-social sexual behaviour. [T]his is consistent with what we learned from the clinical experience of those experienced medical witnesses we consulted." Williams, Chair, *Report of the Committee on Obscenity and Film Censorship* § 6.16, at 66 (1979). Subsequent studies claimed to strongly "link exposure to pornographic material among men to an increase in the acceptance of violence against women." Malamuth & Billings, *Why Pornography? Models of Functions and*

Effects, 34 J. of Comm. 117, 129 (1984). The 1986 *Report of the Attorney General's Commission on Pornography* concluded that "substantial exposure" to "sexually violent material" or "non-violent materials depicting degradation, domination, or humiliation" "bears some causal relationship to the level of sexual violence, sexual coercion, or unwanted sexual aggression in the population so exposed." For commentary from diverse perspectives, see *Symposium on the 1986 Commission on Pornography,* 1987 Am.B.Found.Res.J. 641; Richards, *Pornography Commissions and the First Amendment,* 39 Me.L.Rev. 275 (1987). For analysis of much of the research, see *Pornography & Sexual Aggression* (Malamuth & Donnerstein eds. 1984).

STANLEY v. GEORGIA, 394 U.S. 557, 89 S.Ct. 1243, 22 L.Ed.2d 542 (1969), per MARSHALL, J., reversed a conviction for knowing "possession of obscene matter," based on three reels of obscene films found in Stanley's home when police entered under a search warrant for other purposes: "[*Roth*] and the cases following it discerned [an] 'important interest' in the regulation of commercial distribution of obscene material. That holding cannot foreclose an examination of the constitutional implications of a statute forbidding mere private possession of such material. [The constitutional] right to receive information and ideas, regardless of their social worth [*Winters*] is fundamental to our free society. Moreover, in the context of this case—a prosecution for mere possession of printed or filmed matter in the privacy of a person's own home—that right takes on an added dimension. For also fundamental is the right to be free, except in very limited circumstances, from unwanted governmental intrusions into one's privacy.

" 'The makers of our Constitution undertook to secure conditions favorable to the pursuit of happiness. They recognized the significance of man's spiritual nature, of his feelings and of his intellect. [They] sought to protect Americans in their beliefs, their thoughts, their emotions and their sensations. They conferred, as against the government, the right to be let alone—the most comprehensive of rights and the right most valued by civilized man.' *Olmstead v. United States,* 277 U.S. 438, 48 S.Ct. 564, 72 L.Ed. 944 (1928) (Brandeis, J., dissenting). * * *

"These are the rights that appellant is asserting in the case before us. He is asserting the right to read or observe what he pleases—the right to satisfy his intellectual and emotional needs in the privacy of his own home. He is asserting the right to be free from state inquiry into the contents of his library. Georgia contends that appellant does not have these rights, that there are certain types of materials that the individual may not read or even possess. [W]e think that mere categorization of these films as 'obscene' is insufficient justification for such a drastic invasion of personal liberties guaranteed by the First and Fourteenth Amendments. Whatever may be the justifications for other statutes regulating obscenity, we do not think they reach into the privacy of one's own home. If the First Amendment means anything, it means that a State has no business telling a man, sitting alone in his own house, what books he may read or what films he may watch. Our whole constitutional heritage rebels at the thought of giving government the power to control men's minds.

"[I]n the face of these traditional notions of individual liberty, Georgia asserts the right to protect the individual's mind from the effects of obscenity. We are not certain that this argument amounts to anything more than the assertion that the State has the right to control the moral content of a person's thoughts.[8] To some, this may be a noble purpose, but it is wholly inconsistent with the philosophy of the First Amendment. [*Kingsley Pictures.*] Nor is it relevant that obscenity in general, or the particular films before the Court, are arguably devoid of any ideological content. The line between the transmission of ideas and mere entertainment is much too elusive for this Court to draw, if indeed such a line can be drawn at all. [*Winters*]. Whatever the power of the state to control public dissemination of ideas inimical to the public morality, it cannot constitutionally premise legislation on the desirability of controlling a person's private thoughts.

"[Georgia] asserts that exposure to obscenity may lead to deviant sexual behavior or crimes of sexual violence. There appears to be little empirical basis for that assertion. But more importantly, if the State is only concerned about literature inducing antisocial conduct, we believe that in the context of private consumption of ideas and information we should adhere to the view that '[a]mong free men, the deterrents ordinarily to be applied to prevent crime are education and punishment for violations of the [law].' *Whitney* (Brandeis, J., concurring). See Emerson, *Toward a General Theory of the First Amendment,* 72 Yale L.J. 877, 938 (1963). Given the present state of knowledge, the State may no more prohibit mere possession of obscenity on the ground that it may lead to antisocial conduct than it may prohibit possession of chemistry books on the ground that they may lead to the manufacture of homemade spirits.

"It is true that in *Roth* this Court rejected the necessity of proving that exposure to obscene material would create a clear and present danger of antisocial conduct or would probably induce its recipients to such conduct. But that case dealt with public distribution of obscene materials and such distribution is subject to different objections. For example, there is always the danger that obscene material might fall into the hands of children, see *Ginsberg,* or that it might intrude upon the sensibilities or privacy of the general public. No such dangers are present in this [case.]

"We hold that the First and Fourteenth Amendments prohibit making mere private possession of obscene material a crime. *Roth* and the cases following that decision are not impaired by today's holding. As we have said, the States retain broad power to regulate obscenity; that power simply does not extend to mere possession by the individual in the privacy of his own home." [a]

Notes and Questions

1. *Obscenity and the first amendment.* Is *Stanley* consistent with the constitutional theory of *Roth?* Can the first amendment rationally be viewed as applicable to *private use* but not to *public distribution* of obscenity? Cf. Katz, *Privacy and Pornography,* 1969 Sup.Ct.Rev. 203, 210–11. Might the definitional two-level approach reconcile *Stanley* with *Roth?*

8. "Communities believe, and act on the belief, that obscenity is immoral, is wrong for the individual, and has no place in a decent society. They believe, too, that adults as well as children are corruptible in morals and character, and that obscenity is a source of corruption that should be eliminated. Obscenity is not suppressed primarily for the protection of others. Much of it is suppressed for the purity of the community and for the salvation and welfare of the 'consumer.' Obscenity, at bottom, is not crime. Obscenity is sin." Henkin, *Morals and the Constitution: The Sin of Obscenity,* 63 Col.L.Rev. 391, 395 (1963).

a. Black, J., concurred separately. Stewart, J., joined by Brennan and White, JJ., concurred in the result on search and seizure grounds.

2. *Implications of Stanley.* Could *Stanley*'s recognition of a first amendment right to "receive" and use obscene matter in the home fairly be viewed as implying a right to purchase it from commercial suppliers, or to import it for personal use, or to view it in a theater limited to consenting adults?

PARIS ADULT THEATRE I v. SLATON

413 U.S. 49, 93 S.Ct. 2628, 37 L.Ed.2d 446 (1973).

[The entrance to Paris Adult Theatres I & II was conventional and inoffensive without any pictures. Signs read: "Adult Theatre—You must be 21 and able to prove it. If viewing the nude body offends you, Please Do Not Enter." The District Attorney, nonetheless, had brought an action to enjoin the showing of two films that the Georgia Supreme Court described as "hard core pornography" leaving "little to the imagination." The Georgia Supreme Court assumed that the adult theaters in question barred minors and gave a full warning to the general public of the nature of the films involved, but held that the showing of the films was not constitutionally protected.]

CHIEF JUSTICE BURGER delivered the opinion of the Court.

[We] categorically disapprove the theory [that] obscene, pornographic films acquire constitutional immunity from state regulation simply because they are exhibited for consenting adults only. [Although we have] recognized the high importance of the state interest in regulating the exposure of obscene materials to juveniles and unconsenting adults, this Court has never declared these to be the only legitimate state interests permitting regulation of obscene material.

[W]e hold that there are legitimate state interests at stake in stemming the tide of commercialized obscenity, even assuming it is feasible to enforce effective safeguards against exposure to juveniles and to the passerby.[7] [These] include the interest of the public in the quality of life and the total community environment, the tone of commerce in the great city centers, and, possibly, the public safety itself. The Hill-Link Minority Report of the Commission on Obscenity and Pornography indicates that there is at least an arguable correlation between obscene material and crime. Quite apart from sex crimes, however, there remains one problem of large proportions aptly described by Professor Bickel: "It concerns the tone of the society, the mode, or to use terms that have perhaps greater currency, the style and quality of life, now and in the future. A man may be entitled to read an obscene book in his room, or expose himself indecently there. [We] should protect his privacy. But if he demands a right to obtain the books and pictures he wants in the market, and to foregather in public places—discreet, if you will, but accessible to all—with others who share his tastes, *then to grant him his right is to affect the world about the rest of us, and to impinge on other privacies.* Even supposing that each of us can, if he wishes, effectively avert the eye and stop the ear (which, in truth, we cannot),

7. It is conceivable that an "adult" theatre can—if it really insists—prevent the exposure of its obscene wares to juveniles. An "adult" bookstore, dealing in obscene books, magazines, and pictures, cannot realistically make this claim. The Hill-Link Minority Report of the Commission on Obscenity and Pornography emphasizes evidence (the Abelson National Survey of Youth and Adults) that, although most pornography may be bought by elders, "the heavy users and most highly exposed people to pornography are adolescent females (among women) and adolescent and young males (among men)." *The Report of the Commission on Obscenity* 401 (1970). The legitimate interest in preventing exposure of juveniles to obscene materials cannot be fully served by simply barring juveniles from the immediate physical premises of "adult" bookstores, when there is a flourishing "outside business" in these materials.

what is commonly read and seen and heard and done intrudes upon us all, want it or not." 22 *The Public Interest* 25, 25–26 (Winter, 1971). (Emphasis supplied.) [T]here is a "right of the Nation and of the States to maintain a decent [society]," *Jacobellis* (Warren, C.J., dissenting).

But, it is argued, there is no scientific data which conclusively demonstrates that exposure to obscene materials adversely affects men and women or their society. It is urged [that], absent such a demonstration, any kind of state regulation is "impermissible." We reject this argument. It is not for us to resolve empirical uncertainties underlying state legislation, save in the exceptional case where that legislation plainly impinges upon rights protected by the Constitution itself. [Although] there is no conclusive proof of a connection between antisocial behavior and obscene material, the legislature of Georgia could quite reasonably determine that such a connection does or might exist. In deciding *Roth,* this Court implicitly accepted that a legislature could legitimately act on such a conclusion to protect "*the social interest in order and morality.*"

From the beginning of civilized societies, legislators and judges have acted on various unprovable assumptions. Such assumptions underlie much lawful state regulation of commercial and business affairs. The same is true of the federal securities, antitrust laws and a host of other federal regulations. [Likewise], when legislatures and administrators act to protect the physical environment from pollution and to preserve our resources of forests, streams and parks, they must act on such imponderables as the impact of a new highway near or through an existing park or wilderness area. [The] fact that a congressional directive reflects unprovable assumptions about what is good for the people, including imponderable aesthetic assumptions, is not a sufficient reason to find that statute unconstitutional.

If we accept the unprovable assumption that a complete education requires certain books, and the well nigh universal belief that good books, plays, and art lift the spirit, improve the mind, enrich the human personality and develop character, can we then say that a state legislature may not act on the corollary assumption that commerce in obscene books,[a] or public exhibitions focused on obscene conduct, have a tendency to exert a corrupting and debasing impact leading to antisocial behavior? [The] sum of experience, including that of the past two decades, affords an ample basis for legislatures to conclude that a sensitive, key relationship of human existence, central to family life, community welfare, and the development of human personality, can be debased and distorted by crass commercial exploitation of sex. Nothing in the Constitution prohibits a State from reaching such a conclusion and acting on it legislatively simply because there is no conclusive evidence or empirical data.

[Nothing] in this Court's decisions intimates that there is any "fundamental" privacy right "implicit in the concept of ordered liberty" to watch obscene

a. The only case after *Roth* in which the Court upheld a conviction based upon books was in *Mishkin* [p. 474 infra] and most, if not all, of those books were illustrated. *Kaplan v. California,* 413 U.S. 115, 93 S.Ct. 2680, 37 L.Ed.2d 492 (1973) held that books without pictures can be legally obscene "in the sense of being unprotected by the First Amendment." It observed that books are "passed hand to hand, and we can take note of the tendency of widely circulated books of this category to reach the impressionable young and have a continuing impact. A State could reasonably regard the 'hard core' conduct described by *Suite 69* as capable of encouraging or causing antisocial behavior, especially in its impact on young people." Is *Kaplan*'s explanation in tension with *Butler v. Michigan* [p. 473 infra]? Why should the obscenity standard focus on the average adult if the underlying worry is that books will fall in the hands of children?

movies in places of public accommodation. [W]e have declined to equate the privacy of the home relied on in *Stanley* with a "zone" of "privacy" that follows a distributor or a consumer of obscene materials wherever he goes.[b]

[W]e reject the claim that Georgia is here attempting to control the minds or thoughts of those who patronize theatres. Preventing unlimited display or distribution of obscene material, which by definition lacks any serious literary, artistic, political, or scientific value as communication, is distinct from a control of reason and the intellect. Cf. Finnis, *"Reason and Passion": The Constitutional Dialectic of Free Speech and Obscenity,* 116 U.Pa.L.Rev. 222, 229–230, 241–243 (1967).

[Finally], petitioners argue that conduct which directly involves "consenting adults" only has, for that sole reason, a special claim to constitutional protection. Our Constitution establishes a broad range of conditions on the exercise of power by the States, but for us to say that our Constitution incorporates the proposition that conduct involving consenting adults only is always beyond state regulation,[14] is a step we are unable to take.[15] [The] issue in this context goes beyond whether someone, or even the majority, considers the conduct depicted as "wrong" or "sinful." The States have the power to make a morally neutral judgment that public exhibition of obscene material, or commerce in such material, has a tendency to injure the community as a whole, to endanger the public safety, or to jeopardize, in Mr. Chief Justice Warren's words, the States' "right [to] maintain a decent society." *Jacobellis* (dissenting). * * *

JUSTICE BRENNAN, with whom JUSTICE STEWART and JUSTICE MARSHALL join, dissenting.

[I] am convinced that the approach initiated 15 years ago in *Roth* and culminating in the Court's decision today, cannot bring stability to this area of the law without jeopardizing fundamental First Amendment values, and I have concluded that the time has come to make a significant departure from that [approach.]

[The] decision of the Georgia Supreme Court rested squarely on its conclusion that the State could constitutionally suppress these films even if they were displayed only to persons over the age of 21 who were aware of the nature of

b. In a series of cases, the Court limited *Stanley* to its facts. It held that *Stanley* did not protect the mailing of obscene material to consenting adults, *United States v. Reidel,* 402 U.S. 351, 91 S.Ct. 1410, 28 L.Ed.2d 813 (1971) or the transporting or importing of obscene materials for private use, *United States v. Orito,* 413 U.S. 139, 93 S.Ct. 2674, 37 L.Ed.2d 513 (1973) (transporting); *United States v. 12 200–Ft. Reels,* 413 U.S. 123, 93 S.Ct. 2665, 37 L.Ed.2d 500 (1973) (importing). Dissenting in *Reels,* Douglas, J., argued that *Stanley* rights could legally be realized "only if one wrote or designed a tract in his attic and printed or processed it in his basement, so as to be able to read it in his study." Do these decisions take the first amendment out of *Stanley*? Are they justified by the rationale in *Paris Adult Theatre*? For example, does importation for personal use intrude "upon us all"? Affect the total community environment?

For the declaration that *Stanley's* "privacy of the home" principle is "firmly grounded" in the first amendment while resisting the principle's expansion to protect consensual adult homosexual sodomy in the home, see *Bowers v. Hardwick.* But see Blackmun, J., joined by Brennan, Marshall, and Stevens, JJ., dissenting in *Bowers* ("*Stanley* rested as much on the Court's understanding of the Fourth Amendment as it did on the First").

14. Cf. Mill, *On Liberty* 13 (1955).

15. The state statute books are replete with constitutionally unchallenged laws against prostitution, suicide, voluntary self-mutilation, brutalizing "bare fist" prize fights, and duels, although these crimes may only directly involve "consenting adults." Statutes making bigamy a crime surely cut into an individual's freedom to associate, but few today seriously claim such statutes violate the First Amendment or any other constitutional provision.

their contents and who had consented to viewing them. [I] am convinced of the invalidity of that conclusion [and] would therefore vacate the [judgment]. I have no occasion to consider the extent of State power to regulate the distribution of sexually oriented materials to juveniles or to unconsenting [adults.] [*Stanley*] reflected our emerging view that the state interests in protecting children and in protecting unconsenting adults may stand on a different footing from the other asserted state interests. It may well be, as one commentator has argued, that "exposure to [erotic material] is for some persons an intense emotional experience. A communication of this nature, imposed upon a person contrary to his wishes, has all the characteristics of a physical assault * * *. [And it] constitutes an invasion of his [privacy]." [24] [But] whatever the strength of the state interests in protecting juveniles and unconsenting adults from exposure to sexually oriented materials, those interests cannot be asserted in defense of the holding of the Georgia Supreme Court, [which] assumed for the purposes of its decision that the films in issue were exhibited only to persons over the age of 21 who viewed them willingly and with prior knowledge of the nature of their contents. [The] justification for the suppression must be found, therefore, in some independent interest in regulating the reading and viewing habits of consenting [adults].

In *Stanley* we pointed out that "[t]here appears to be little empirical basis for" the assertion that "exposure to obscene materials may lead to deviant sexual behavior or crimes of sexual violence." In any event, we added that "if the State is only concerned about printed or filmed materials inducing antisocial conduct, we believe that in the context of private consumption of ideas and information we should adhere to the view that '[a]mong free men, the deterrents ordinarily to be applied to prevent crime are education and punishment for violations of the [law].' "

Moreover, in *Stanley* we rejected as "wholly inconsistent with the philosophy of the First Amendment," the notion that there is a legitimate state concern in the "control [of] the moral content of a person's thoughts." [The] traditional description of state police power does embrace the regulation of morals as well as the health, safety, and general welfare of the citizenry. [But] the State's interest in regulating morality by suppressing obscenity, while often asserted, remains essentially unfocused and ill-defined. And, since the attempt to curtail unprotected speech necessarily spills over into the area of protected speech, the effort to serve this speculative interest through the suppression of obscene material must tread heavily on rights protected by the First Amendment. * * * [27]

In short, while I cannot say that the interests of the State—apart from the question of juveniles and unconsenting adults—are trivial or nonexistent, I am compelled to conclude that these interests cannot justify the substantial damage to constitutional rights and to this Nation's judicial machinery that inevitably results from state efforts to bar the distribution even of unprotected material to consenting adults.[c]

MR. JUSTICE DOUGLAS, dissenting. * * *

"Obscenity" at most is the expression of offensive ideas. There are regimes in the world where ideas "offensive" to the majority (or at least to those who

24. Emerson, *The System of Freedom of Expression* 496 (1970).

27. See Henkin, *Morals and the Constitution: The Sin of Obscenity,* 63 Col.L.Rev. 391, 395 (1963).

c. For the portion of Brennan, J.'s dissent addressing the difficulties of formulating an acceptable constitutional standard, see *Miller v. California,* infra.

control the majority) are suppressed. There life proceeds at a monotonous pace. Most of us would find that world offensive. One of the most offensive experiences in my life was a visit to a nation where bookstalls were filled only with books on mathematics and books on religion.

I am sure I would find offensive most of the books and movies charged with being obscene. But in a life that has not been short, I have yet to be trapped into seeing or reading something that would offend me. I never read or see the materials coming to the Court under charges of "obscenity," because I have thought the First Amendment made it unconstitutional for me to act as a censor. * * *

B. A REVISED STANDARD

MILLER v. CALIFORNIA

413 U.S. 15, 93 S.Ct. 2607, 37 L.Ed.2d 419 (1973).

CHIEF JUSTICE BURGER delivered the opinion of the Court. [The Court remanded, "for proceedings not inconsistent" with the opinion's obscenity standard, Miller's conviction under California's obscenity law for mass mailing of unsolicited pictorial advertising brochures depicting men and women in a variety of group sexual activities.]

This is one of a group of "obscenity-pornography" cases being reviewed by the Court in a re-examination of standards enunciated in earlier cases involving what Mr. Justice Harlan called "the intractable obscenity problem." [I]n this context [a] [we] are called on to define the standards which must be used to identify obscene material that a State may [regulate].

[Nine years after *Roth v. United States*], in *Memoirs v. Massachusetts,* 383 U.S. 413, 86 S.Ct. 975, 16 L.Ed.2d 1 (1966), the Court veered sharply away from the Roth concept and, with only three Justices in the plurality opinion, articulated a new test of obscenity. The plurality held that under the Roth definition "as elaborated in subsequent cases, three elements must coalesce: it must be established that (a) the dominant theme of the material taken as a whole appeals to a prurient interest in sex; (b) the material is patently offensive because it affronts contemporary community standards relating to the description or representation of sexual matters; and (c) the material is utterly without redeeming social value." * * *

While *Roth* presumed "obscenity" to be "utterly without redeeming social importance," *Memoirs* required that to prove obscenity it must be affirmatively established that the material is "*utterly* without redeeming social value."

Thus, even as they repeated the words of *Roth,* the *Memoirs* plurality produced a drastically altered test that called on the prosecution to prove a negative, i.e., that the material was "*utterly* without redeeming social value"—a burden virtually impossible to discharge under our criminal standards of proof. [Apart] from the initial formulation in *Roth,* no majority of the Court has at any given time been able to agree on a standard to determine what constitutes obscene, pornographic material subject to regulation under the States' police power. See, e.g., *Redrup v. New York,* 386 U.S. 767, 87 S.Ct. 1414, 18 L.Ed.2d 515

a. The "context" was that in *Miller* "sexually explicit materials have been thrust by aggressive sales action upon unwilling recipients." But nothing in *Miller* limited the revised standard to that context, and the companion case, *Paris Adult Theatre,* applied the same standard to dissemination limited to consenting adults.

(1967).[3] This is not remarkable, for in the area of freedom of speech and press the courts must always remain sensitive to any infringement on genuinely serious literary, artistic, political, or scientific expression. * * *

II. This much has been categorically settled by the Court, that obscene material is unprotected by the First Amendment. [We] acknowledge, however, the inherent dangers of undertaking to regulate any form of expression. State statutes designed to regulate obscene materials must be carefully limited. As a result, we now confine the permissible scope of such regulation to works which depict or describe sexual conduct. That conduct must be specifically defined by the applicable state law, as written or authoritatively construed.[6] A state offense must also be limited to works which, taken as a whole, appeal to the prurient interest in sex, which portray sexual conduct in a patently offensive way, and which, taken as a whole, do not have serious literary, artistic, political, or scientific value.

The basic guidelines for the trier of fact must be: (a) whether "the average person, applying contemporary community standards" would find that the work, taken as a whole, appeals to the prurient interest, (b) whether the work depicts or describes, in a patently offensive way, sexual conduct specifically defined by the applicable state law, and (c) whether the work, taken as a whole, lacks serious literary, artistic, political, or scientific value. We do not adopt as a constitutional standard the "*utterly* without redeeming social value" test of *Memoirs;* that concept has never commanded the adherence of more than three Justices at one time.[7] If a state law that regulates obscene material is thus limited, as written or construed, the First Amendment values applicable to the States [are] adequately protected by the ultimate power of appellate courts to conduct an independent review of constitutional claims when necessary.

We emphasize that it is not our function to propose regulatory schemes for the States. [It] is possible, however, to give a few plain examples of what a state statute could define for regulation under the second part (b) of the standard announced in this opinion, supra:

(a) Patently offensive representations or descriptions of ultimate sexual acts, normal or perverted, actual or simulated.

3. In the absence of a majority view, this Court was compelled to embark on the practice of summarily reversing convictions for the dissemination of materials that at least five members of the Court, applying their separate tests, found to be protected by the First Amendment. *Redrup.* [Beyond] the necessity of circumstances, however, no justification has ever been offered in support of the *Redrup* "policy." The *Redrup* procedure has cast us in the role of an unreviewable board of censorship for the 50 States, subjectively judging each piece of material brought before us.

6. See, e.g., Oregon Laws 1971, c. 743, Art. 29, §§ 255–262, and Hawaii Penal Code, Tit. 37, §§ 1210–1216, 1972 Hawaii Session Laws, pp. 126–129, Act 9, Pt. II, as examples of state laws directed at depiction of defined physical conduct, as opposed to expression. [We] do not hold, as Mr. Justice Brennan intimates, that all States other than Oregon must now enact new obscenity statutes. Other existing state statutes, as construed heretofore or hereafter, may well be adequate.

7. "[We] also reject, as a constitutional standard, the ambiguous concept of 'social importance'." [*Hamling v. United States*, 418 U.S. 87, 94 S.Ct. 2887, 41 L.Ed.2d 590 (1974) upheld a conviction in which the jury had been instructed to find that the material was "utterly without redeeming social value." Defendant argued that the latter phrase was unconstitutionally vague and cited *Miller.* The Court rejected the vagueness challenge: "[O]ur opinion in *Miller* plainly indicates that we rejected the '[social] value' formulation, not because it was so vague as to deprive criminal defendants of adequate notice, but instead because it represented a departure from [*Roth*], and because in calling on the prosecution to 'prove a negative,' it imposed a '[prosecutorial] burden virtually impossible to discharge' and which was not constitutionally required."]

(b) Patently offensive representations or descriptions of masturbation, excretory functions, and lewd exhibition of the genitals.[b]

Sex and nudity may not be exploited without limit by films or pictures exhibited or sold in places of public accommodation any more than live sex and nudity can be exhibited or sold without limit in such public places.[8] At a minimum, prurient,[c] patently offensive depiction or description of sexual conduct must have serious literary, artistic, political, or scientific value to merit First Amendment protection. For example, medical books for the education of physicians and related personnel necessarily use graphic illustrations and descriptions of human anatomy. In resolving the inevitably sensitive questions of fact and law, we must continue to rely on the jury system, accompanied by the safeguards that judges, rules of evidence, presumption of innocence and other protective features [provide].

Mr. Justice Brennan [has] abandoned his former positions and now maintains that no formulation of this Court, the Congress, or the States can adequately distinguish obscene material unprotected by the First Amendment from protected expression, *Paris Adult Theatre I v. Slaton* (Brennan, J., dissenting). Paradoxically, Mr. Justice Brennan indicates that suppression of unprotected obscene material is permissible to avoid exposure to unconsenting adults, as in this case, and to juveniles, although he gives no indication of how the division between protected and nonprotected materials may be drawn with greater precision for these purposes than for regulation of commercial exposure to consenting adults only. Nor does he indicate where in the Constitution he finds the authority to distinguish between a willing "adult" one month past the state law age of majority and a willing "juvenile" one month younger.[d]

b. *Jenkins v. Georgia,* 418 U.S. 153, 94 S.Ct. 2750, 41 L.Ed.2d 642 (1974) held the film *Carnal Knowledge* not obscene because it did not " 'depict or describe patently offensive "hard core" sexual conduct' " as required by *Miller:* "[While there] are scenes in which sexual conduct including 'ultimate sexual acts' is to be understood to be taking place, the camera does not focus on the bodies of the actors at such times. There is no exhibition whatever of the actors' genitals, lewd or otherwise, during these scenes. There are occasional scenes of nudity, but nudity alone is not enough to make material legally obscene under the *Miller* standards." *Ward v. Illinois,* 431 U.S. 767, 97 S.Ct. 2085, 52 L.Ed.2d 738 (1977) held that it was not necessary for the legislature or the courts to provide an "exhaustive list of the sexual conduct [the] description of which may be held obscene." It is enough that a state adopt *Miller's* explanatory examples. Stevens, J., joined by Brennan, Stewart and Marshall, JJ., dissented: "[I]f the statute need only describe the 'kinds' of proscribed sexual conduct, it adds no protection to what the Constitution itself creates. [The] specificity requirement as described in *Miller* held out the promise of a principled effort to respond to [the vagueness] argument. By abandoning that effort today, the Court withdraws the cornerstone of the *Miller* [structure]."

8. Although we are not presented here with the problem of regulating lewd public conduct itself, the States have greater power to regulate nonverbal, physical conduct than to suppress depictions or descriptions of the same behavior. * * *

c. *Brockett v. Spokane Arcades, Inc.,* 472 U.S. 491, 105 S.Ct. 2794, 86 L.Ed.2d 394 (1985) held that appeals to prurient interest could not be taken to include appeals to "normal" interests in sex. Only appeals to a "shameful or morbid interest in sex" are prurient. Although the Court was resolute in its position that appeals to "good, old fashioned, healthy" interests in sex were constitutionally protected, it did not further specify how "normal" sex was to be distinguished from the "shameful" or "morbid."

d. The suggestion that the same book may be obscene in some contexts but not in others has been endorsed in several different contexts. *Butler v. Michigan,* 352 U.S. 380, 77 S.Ct. 524, 1 L.Ed.2d 412 (1957) held that the state could not ban sales to the general public of material unsuitable for children: "The State insists that [by] quarantining the general reading public against books not too rugged for grown men and women in order to shield juvenile innocence, it is exercising its power to promote the general welfare. Surely, this is to burn the house to roast the pig. [The] incidence of this enactment is to reduce the adult population of Michigan to reading only

Under the holdings announced today, no one will be subject to prosecution for the sale or exposure of obscene materials unless these materials depict or describe patently offensive "hard core" sexual conduct specifically defined by the regulating state law, as written or construed. We are satisfied that these specific prerequisites will provide fair notice to a dealer in such materials that his public and commercial activities may bring prosecution. If the inability to define regulated materials with ultimate, god-like precision altogether removes the power of the States or the Congress to regulate, then "hard core" pornography may be exposed without limit to the juvenile, the passerby, and the consenting adult alike, as indeed, Mr. Justice Douglas contends.

[N]o amount of "fatigue" should lead us to adopt a convenient "institutional" rationale—an absolutist, "anything goes" view of the First Amendment—because it will lighten our burdens. [Nor] should we remedy "tension between state and federal courts" by arbitrarily depriving the States of a power reserved to them under the Constitution, a power which they have enjoyed and exercised continuously from before the adoption of the First Amendment to this day. See *Roth.* "Our duty admits of no 'substitute for facing up to the tough individual problems of constitutional judgment involved in every obscenity case.' " *Jacobellis* (opinion of Brennan, J.).

III. Under a national Constitution, fundamental First Amendment limitations on the powers of the States do not vary from community to community, but this does not mean that there are, or should or can be, fixed, uniform national standards of precisely what appeals to the "prurient interest" or is "patently offensive." These are essentially questions of fact, and our nation is simply too big and too diverse for this Court to reasonably expect that such standards could be articulated for all 50 States in a single formulation, even assuming the prerequisite consensus exists. When triers of fact are asked to decide whether "the average person, applying contemporary community standards" would consider certain materials "prurient," it would be unrealistic to require that the answer be based on some abstract formulation. The adversary system, with lay jurors as the usual ultimate factfinders in criminal prosecutions, has historically permitted triers-of-fact to draw on the standards of their community, guided always by limiting instructions on the law. To require a State to structure obscenity proceedings around evidence of a *national* "community standard" would be an exercise in [futility].

We conclude that neither the State's alleged failure to offer evidence of "national standards," nor the trial court's charge that the jury consider state community standards, were constitutional errors. Nothing in the First Amendment requires that a jury must consider hypothetical and unascertainable "national standards" when attempting to determine whether certain materials are obscene as a matter of [fact].

what is fit for children." *Ginsberg v. New York,* 390 U.S. 629, 88 S.Ct. 1274, 20 L.Ed.2d 195 (1968), however, held that the state could bar the distribution to children of books that were suitable for adults, the Court recognizing it was adopting a "variable" concept of obscenity. See also *Ginzburg v. United States,* 383 U.S. 463, 86 S.Ct. 942, 16 L.Ed.2d 31 (1966) ("pandering" method of marketing supports obscenity conviction even though the materials might not otherwise have been considered obscene); *Mishkin v. New York,* 383 U.S. 502, 86 S.Ct. 958, 16 L.Ed.2d 56 (1966) (material designed for and primarily disseminated to deviant sexual group can meet prurient appeal requirement even if the material lacks appeal to an average member of the general public; appeal is to be tested with reference to the sexual interests of the intended and probable recipient group).

The variable obscenity approach had previously been advocated and elaborated by Lockhart and McClure, *Censorship of Obscenity: The Developing Constitutional Standards,* 45 Minn.L.Rev. 5, 77 (1960).

It is neither realistic nor constitutionally sound to read the First Amendment as requiring that the people of Maine or Mississippi accept public depiction of conduct found tolerable in Las Vegas, or New York City. People in different States vary in their tastes and attitudes, and this diversity is not to be strangled by the absolutism of imposed uniformity. As the Court made clear in *Mishkin,* the primary concern with requiring a jury to apply the standard of "the average person, applying contemporary community standards" is to be certain that, so far as material is not aimed at a deviant group, it will be judged by its impact on an average person, rather than a particularly susceptible or sensitive person—or indeed a totally insensitive one.[e] [We] hold the requirement that the jury evaluate the materials with reference to "contemporary standards of the State of California" serves this protective purpose and is constitutionally adequate.[f]

* * *

In sum we (a) reaffirm the *Roth* holding that obscene material is not protected by the First Amendment, (b) hold that such material can be regulated by the States, subject to the specific safeguards enunciated above, without a showing that the material is "*utterly* without redeeming social value," and (c) hold that obscenity is to be determined by applying "contemporary community standards," not "national standards." * * *

JUSTICE DOUGLAS, dissenting. * * *

My contention is that until a civil proceeding has placed a tract beyond the pale, no criminal prosecution should be sustained. For no more vivid illustration of vague and uncertain laws could be designed than those we have fashioned. [If] a specific book [or] motion picture has in a civil proceeding been condemned as obscene and review of that finding has been completed, and thereafter a person publishes [or] displays that particular book or film, then a vague law has been made specific. There would remain the underlying question whether the First Amendment allows an implied exception in the case of obscenity. I do not think it does and my views on the issue have been stated over and again. But at least a criminal prosecution brought at that juncture would not violate the time-honored void-for-vagueness test.[8]

e. *Pinkus v. United States,* 436 U.S. 293, 98 S.Ct. 1808, 56 L.Ed.2d 293 (1978) upheld a jury instruction stating "you are to judge these materials by the standard of the hypothetical average person in the community, but in determining this average standard you must include the *sensitive and the insensitive,* in other words, [everyone] in the community." On the other hand, in the absence of evidence that "children were the intended recipients" or that defendant "had reason to know children were likely to receive the materials," it was considered erroneous to instruct the jury that children were part of the relevant community. *Butler.* When the evidence would support such a charge, the Court stated that prurient appeal to deviant sexual groups could be substituted for appeal to the average person; moreover, the jury was entitled to take pandering into account. *Ginzburg.*

f. *Jenkins,* fn. b supra, stated that a judge may instruct a jury to apply "contemporary community standards" without any further specification. Alternatively, the state may choose "to define the standards in more precise geographic terms, as was done by California in *Miller.*" *Hamling v. United States,* fn. 7 supra, interpreted a federal obscenity statute to make the relevant community the one from which the jury was drawn. The judge's instruction to consider the "community standards of the 'nation as a whole' delineated a wider geographical area than would be warranted by [*Miller*]" or the Court's construction of the statute, but the error was regarded as harmless under the circumstances. See also *Sable Communications v. FCC* ("dial-a-porn" company bears burden of complying with congressional obscenity ban despite diverse local community standards). After these decisions, what advice should lawyers give to publishers who distribute in national markets?

8. The Commission on Obscenity and Pornography has advocated such a procedure. [See] *Report of the Commission on Obscenity and Pornography* 70–71 (1970).

No such protective procedure has been designed by California in this case. Obscenity—which even we cannot define with precision—is a hodge-podge. To send men to jail for violating standards they cannot understand, construe, and apply is a monstrous thing to do in a Nation dedicated to fair trials and due process. * * *

JUSTICE BRENNAN, with whom JUSTICE STEWART and JUSTICE MARSHALL join, dissenting.

In my dissent in *Paris Adult Theatre,* decided this date, I noted that I had no occasion to consider the extent of state power to regulate the distribution of sexually oriented material to juveniles or the offensive exposure of such material to unconsenting adults. [I] need not now decide whether a statute might be drawn to impose, within the requirements of the First Amendment, criminal penalties for the precise conduct at issue here. For it is clear that under my dissent in *Paris Adult Theatre,* the statute under which the prosecution was brought is unconstitutionally overbroad, and therefore invalid on its face. * * *

[In his *Paris Adult Theatre* dissent, Justice Brennan, joined by Stewart and Marshall, JJ., argued that the state interests in regulating obscenity were not strong enough to justify the degree of vagueness. He criticized not only the Court's standard in *Miller,* but also a range of alternatives:]

II. [The] essence of our problem [is] that we have been unable to provide "sensitive tools" to separate obscenity from other sexually oriented but constitutionally protected speech, so that efforts to suppress the former do not spill over into the suppression of the latter. [The dissent traced the Court's experience with *Roth* and its progeny.]

III. Our experience with the *Roth* approach has certainly taught us that the outright suppression of obscenity cannot be reconciled with the fundamental principles of the First and Fourteenth Amendments. For we have failed to formulate a standard that sharply distinguishes protected from unprotected speech, and out of necessity, we have resorted to the *Redrup* approach, which resolves cases as between the parties, but offers only the most obscure guidance to legislation, adjudication by other courts, and primary conduct. [T]he vagueness problem would be largely of our own creation if it stemmed primarily from our failure to reach a consensus on any one standard. But after 15 years of experimentation and debate I am reluctantly forced to the conclusion that none of the available formulas, including the one announced today, can reduce the vagueness to a tolerable level while at the same time striking an acceptable balance between the protections of the First and Fourteenth Amendments, on the one hand, and on the other the asserted state interest in regulating the dissemination of certain sexually oriented materials. Any effort to draw a constitutionally acceptable boundary on state power must resort to such indefinite concepts as "prurient interest," "patent offensiveness," "serious literary value," and the like. The meaning of these concepts necessarily varies with the experience, outlook, and even idiosyncracies of the person defining them. Although we have assumed that obscenity does exist and that we "know it when [we] see it," *Jacobellis* (Stewart, J., concurring), we are manifestly unable to describe it in advance except by reference to concepts so elusive that they fail to distinguish clearly between protected and unprotected speech.

[Added to the inherent vagueness of standards] is the further complication that the obscenity of any particular item may depend upon nuances of presentation and the context of its dissemination. See *Ginzburg.* [N]o one definition, no matter how precisely or narrowly drawn, can possibly suffice for all situations, or carve out fully suppressable expression from all media without also creating a substantial risk of encroachment upon the guarantees of the Due Process Clause and the First Amendment.

[The] resulting level of uncertainty is utterly intolerable, not alone because it makes "[b]ookselling [a] hazardous profession," *Ginsberg* (Fortas, J., dissenting), but as well because it invites arbitrary and erratic enforcement of the law. [We] have indicated that "stricter standards of permissible statutory vagueness may be applied to a statute having a potentially inhibiting effect on speech; a man may the less be required to act at his peril here, because the free dissemination of ideas may be the loser." * * *

The problems of fair notice and chilling protected speech are very grave standing alone. But [a] vague statute in this area creates a third [set] of problems. These [concern] the institutional stress that inevitably results where the line separating protected from unprotected speech is excessively vague. [Almost] every obscenity case presents a constitutional question of exceptional difficulty. [As] a result of our failure to define standards with predictable application to any given piece of material, there is no probability of regularity in obscenity decisions by state and lower federal courts. [O]ne cannot say with certainty that material is obscene until at least five members of this Court, applying inevitably obscure standards, have pronounced it [so].

We have managed the burden of deciding scores of obscenity cases by relying on per curiam reversals or denials of certiorari—a practice which conceals the rationale of decision and gives at least the appearance of arbitrary action by this Court. More important, [the] practice effectively censors protected expression by leaving lower court determinations of obscenity intact even though the status of the allegedly obscene material is entirely unsettled until final review here. In addition, the uncertainty of the standards creates a continuing source of tension between state and federal [courts].

The severe problems arising from the lack of fair notice, from the chill on protected expression, and from the stress imposed on the state and federal judicial machinery persuade me that a significant change in direction is urgently required. I turn, therefore, to the alternatives that are now open.

IV. 1. The approach requiring the smallest deviation from our present course would be to draw a new line between protected and unprotected speech, still permitting the States to suppress all material on the unprotected side of the line. In my view, clarity cannot be obtained pursuant to this approach except by drawing a line that resolves all doubts in favor of state power and against the guarantees of the First Amendment. We could hold, for example, that any depiction or description of human sexual organs, irrespective of the manner or purpose of the portrayal, is outside the protection of the First Amendment and therefore open to suppression by the States. That formula would, no doubt, offer much fairer notice [and] give rise to a substantial probability of regularity in most judicial determinations under the standard. But such a standard would be appallingly overbroad, permitting the suppression of a vast range of literary, scientific, and artistic masterpieces. Neither the First Amendment nor any free community could possibly tolerate such a standard.

2. [T]he Court today recognizes that a prohibition against any depiction or description of human sexual organs could not be reconciled with the guarantees of the First Amendment. But the Court [adopts] a restatement of the *Roth-Memoirs* definition of obscenity [that] permits suppression if the government can

prove that the materials lack "*serious* literary, artistic, political or scientific value." [In] *Roth* we held that certain expression is obscene, and thus outside the protection of the First Amendment, precisely *because* it lacks even the slightest redeeming social value. [The] Court's approach necessarily assumes that some works will be deemed obscene—even though they clearly have *some* social value—because the State was able to prove that the value, measured by some unspecified standard, was not sufficiently "serious" to warrant constitutional protection. That result [is] nothing less than a rejection of the fundamental First Amendment premises and rationale of the *Roth* opinion and an invitation to widespread suppression of sexually oriented speech. Before today, the protections of the First Amendment have never been thought limited to expressions of *serious* literary or political value. *Gooding v. Wilson; Cohen v. California; Terminiello v. Chicago* [Part V infra].

[T]he Court's approach [can] have no ameliorative impact on the cluster of problems that grow out of the vagueness of our current standards. Indeed, even the Court makes no argument that the reformulation will provide fairer notice to booksellers, theatre owners, and the reading and viewing public. Nor does the Court contend that the approach will provide clearer guidance to law enforcement officials or reduce the chill on protected expression [or] mitigate [the] institutional [problems].

Of course, the Court's restated *Roth* test does limit the definition of obscenity to depictions of physical conduct and explicit sexual acts. And that limitation may seem, at first glance, a welcome and clarifying addition to the *Roth-Memoirs* formula. But just as the agreement in *Roth* on an abstract definition of obscenity gave little hint of the extreme difficulty that was to follow in attempting to apply that definition to specific material, the mere formulation of a "physical conduct" test is no assurance that it can be applied with any greater facility. [The] Court surely demonstrates little sensitivity to our own institutional problems, much less the other vagueness-related difficulties, in establishing a system that requires us to consider whether a description of human genitals is sufficiently "lewd" to deprive it of constitutional protection; whether a sexual act is "ultimate"; whether the conduct depicted in materials before us fits within one of the categories of conduct whose depiction the state or federal governments have attempted to suppress; and a host of equally pointless inquiries. * * *

If the application of the "physical conduct" test to pictorial material is fraught with difficulty, its application to textual material carries the potential for extraordinary abuse. Surely we have passed the point where the mere written description of sexual conduct is deprived of First Amendment protection. Yet the test offers no guidance to us, or anyone else, in determining which written descriptions of sexual conduct are protected, and which are not.

Ultimately, the reformulation must fail because it still leaves in this Court the responsibility of determining in each case whether the materials are protected by the First Amendment. * * *

3. I have also considered the possibility of reducing our own role, and the role of appellate courts generally, in determining whether particular matter is obscene. Thus, [we] might adopt the position that where a lower federal or state court has conscientiously applied the constitutional standard, its finding of obscenity will be no more vulnerable to reversal by this Court than any finding of fact. [E]ven if the Constitution would permit us to refrain from judging for ourselves the alleged obscenity of particular materials, that approach would

solve at best only a small part of our problem. For while it would mitigate the institutional stress, [it] would neither offer nor produce any cure for the other vices of vagueness. Far from providing a clearer guide to permissible primary conduct, the approach would inevitably lead to even greater uncertainty and the consequent due process problems of fair notice. And the approach would expose much protected, sexually oriented expression to the vagaries of jury determinations. Plainly, the institutional gain would be more than offset by the unprecedented infringement of First Amendment rights.

4. Finally, I have considered the view, urged so forcefully since 1957 by our Brothers Black and Douglas, that the First Amendment bars the suppression of any sexually oriented expression. That position would effect a sharp reduction, although perhaps not a total elimination, of the uncertainty that surrounds our current approach. Nevertheless, I am convinced that it would achieve that desirable goal only by stripping the States of power to an extent that cannot be justified by the commands of the Constitution, at least so long as there is available an alternative approach that strikes a better balance between the guarantee of free expression and the States' legitimate interests.

[I] would hold, therefore, that at least in the absence of distribution to juveniles or obtrusive exposure to unconsenting adults, the First and Fourteenth Amendments prohibit the state and federal governments from attempting wholly to suppress sexually oriented materials on the basis of their allegedly "obscene" contents.[g] Nothing in this approach precludes those governments from taking action to serve what may be strong and legitimate interests through regulation of the manner of distribution of sexually oriented material.

VI. [I] do not pretend to have found a complete and infallible [answer]. Difficult questions must still be faced, notably in the areas of distribution to juveniles and offensive exposure to unconsenting adults. Whatever the extent of state power to regulate in those areas,[29] it should be clear that the view I espouse today would introduce a large measure of clarity to this troubled area, would reduce the institutional pressure on this Court and the rest of the State and Federal judiciary, and would guarantee fuller freedom of expression while leaving room for the protection of legitimate governmental interests. * * *

Notes and Questions

1. *Serious value.* Consider Clor, *Obscenity and the First Amendment: Round Three,* 7 Loy.L.A.L.Rev. 207, 210, 218 (1974): "The *Miller* decision abandons the requirement that a censorable work must be '*utterly* without redeeming social value' and substitutes the rule of 'serious value'—literary, artistic, political, or scientific. This is the most important innovation in the law of obscenity introduced by these decisions. [Serious] literature is to be protected regardless of majority opinions about prurience and offensiveness. *This* is the national principle which is not subject to variation from community to community. If it is to perform this function, the rule will have to be elaborated and the meaning of 'serious value' articulated in some measure. This is the most important item on the legal agenda."

g. For the portion of Brennan, J.'s dissent addressing the strength and legitimacy of the state interests, see *Paris Adult Theatre,* supra.

29. The Court erroneously states, *Miller,* that the author of this opinion "indicates that suppression of unprotected obscene material is permissible to avoid exposure to unconsenting adults [and] to juveniles * * *." I defer expression of my views as to the scope of state power in these areas until cases squarely presenting these questions are before the Court.

(a) *An independent factor?* Under *Miller* would material found to have "serious artistic value" be entitled to first amendment protection regardless of how offensive or prurient? Must each factor in the *Miller* guidelines be independently satisfied, as in *Memoirs? Should* that be so? Would or should that preclude the degree of offensiveness or prurient appeal from affecting the conclusion on the value factor?

(b) *"Serious."* Do you find any guidance for determining when a first amendment value in material depicting sexual conduct is sufficiently "serious" to preclude finding it obscene? Does *Pope v. Illinois,* 481 U.S. 497, 107 S.Ct. 1918, 95 L.Ed.2d 439 (1987) assist?: "The proper inquiry is not whether an ordinary member of any given community would find serious literary, artistic, political, or scientific value[,] but whether a reasonable person would find such value in the material taken as a whole."

(c) *Scope of protected values.* Could the Court consistent with the first amendment exclude serious educational value from those that preclude a finding of obscenity? Serious entertainment value? Could the guidelines be interpreted to include such values? What might explain their omission?

2. *Vagueness and scienter.* Is the *Miller* test intolerably vague? Are there any alternatives that could mitigate the problem? Consider Lockhart, *Escape from the Chill of Uncertainty: Explicit Sex and the First Amendment,* 9 Ga.L. Rev. 533, 563 (1975): "[E]ither legislative action, or constitutional adjudication, could establish as a defense to a criminal obscenity prosecution that the defendant *reasonably believed* that the material involved was not obscene, that is, was constitutionally protected. [Material] that would support such a court or jury finding is not the kind that requires or justifies quick action by the police and prosecutor. The public interest in preventing distribution of borderline material that can reasonably be believed not obscene is not so pressing as to require immediate criminal sanctions and can adequately be protected by a declaratory judgment or injunction action to establish the obscenity of the material."

Smith v. California, 361 U.S. 147, 80 S.Ct. 215, 4 L.Ed.2d 205 (1959) invalidated an ordinance that dispensed with any requirement that a seller of an obscene book have knowledge of its contents, but did not decide what sort of mental element was needed to prosecute. *Hamling v. United States,* supra, stated that it was constitutionally sufficient to show that a distributor of an advertising collage of pictures of sexual acts "had knowledge of the contents of the materials [and] that he knew the character and nature of the materials." Would it be consistent with *Hamling* to afford constitutional protection to a distributor who reasonably believed the material disseminated was not obscene? See Lockhart, supra, at 568.

C. VAGUENESS AND OVERBREADTH: AN OVERVIEW

In *Paris Adult Theatre,* Brennan, J., dissents on the ground that the obscenity statute is unconstitutionally vague. He envisions the possibility that an obscenity statute might overcome his vagueness objection if it were tailored to combat distribution to unconsenting adults or to children. In *Miller,* the materials were in fact distributed to unconsenting adults. There Brennan, J., does not reach the vagueness question but objects on the ground that the statute is overbroad,—i.e., it is not confined to the protection of unconsenting adults and children, but also prohibits distribution of obscene materials to consenting adults. In Brennan, J.'s view, even if the particular conduct at issue in *Miller* might be constitutionally prohibited by a narrower statute, it cannot be reached under a statute that sweeps so much protected speech within its terms.

The doctrines of "vagueness" and "overbreadth" referred to in Brennan, J.'s dissents are deeply embedded in first amendment jurisprudence. At first glance, the doctrines appear discrete. A statute that prohibits the use of the words "kill" and "President" in the same sentence may not be vague, but it is certainly overbroad even though some sentences using those words may be unprotected. Conversely, a vague statute may not be overbroad; it may not pertain to first amendment freedoms at all, or it may clearly be intended to exclude all protected speech from its prohibition but use vague language to accomplish that purpose.

Ordinarily, however, the problems of "vagueness" and "overbreadth" are closely related; indeed the two concepts often merge. Consider, for example, an actual and a hypothetical "red flag" ban. A statute prohibiting anyone from "publicly display[ing] a red flag [or] device of any color or form whatever [as] a sign, symbol or emblem of opposition to organized government" was held fatally vague in *Stromberg v. California,* 283 U.S. 359, 51 S.Ct. 532, 75 L.Ed. 1117 (1931). The statute purported to be less than a total ban, but how much less was ambiguous and uncertain. The "opposition to organized government" language was vague because it might (or might not) be read as banning constitutionally protected red flag displays, e.g., those flown as an expression of peaceful and orderly opposition to the political party currently in power by members of another political party. But a hypothetical "absolute ban" on red flag displays, for any reason or under any circumstances, although *superficially* clear, would presumably also be struck down—for "overbreadth." The same may be said for a hypothetical statute "absolutely banning" picketing or parades—or the sale of literature containing any description of human sexual organs, regardless of the manner or purpose of the portrayal, the dominant theme of the material, the primary audience to which it is sold, or the social, literary, scientific or artistic value of the work.

The *language* of these hypothetical bans may not be vague, but if the language literally covers a variety of constitutionally protected activities, it *cannot be read literally.* Thus, the clarity of the language "is delusive, since it will have to be recast in order to separate the constitutional from the unconstitutional applications. If it is read as applicable only where constitutionally so, the reading uncovers the vagueness that is latent in its terms" and the problem of an "overbroad" law can emerge as "a special case of the problem of vagueness." See Freund, *The Supreme Court of the United States* 67–68 (1961). In other words, one may regard the aforementioned "overbroad" hypothetical statutes as no less vague and indefinite than laws whose very language forbids the public display of a red flag "except where one is constitutionally entitled to display it" or bans picketing "unless, under the circumstances, such conduct is constitutionally protected" or bars literature containing descriptions of human sexual organs "except where such descriptions do not constitute sufficient cause to deny the material the constitutional protection of freedom of speech and press."

Of course, statutes may be interpreted in ways that will avoid vagueness or overbreadth difficulties. See, e.g., *Scales v. United States,* p. 411 supra. It is established doctrine, for example, that an attack based either upon vagueness or overbreadth will be unsuccessful in federal court if the statute in question is "readily subject to a narrowing construction by the state courts." *Young v. American Mini-Theatres, Inc.; Erznoznik v. Jacksonville,* Sec. 3, A infra. Moreover, "[f]or the purpose of determining whether a state statute is too vague and indefinite to constitute valid legislation [the Court takes] 'the statute as though it read precisely as the highest court of the State has interpreted it.'" *Wainwright v. Stone,* 414 U.S. 21, 94 S.Ct. 190, 38 L.Ed.2d 179 (1973). Under this policy, a litigant can be prosecuted successfully for violating a statute that by its terms appears vague or overbroad but is interpreted by the state court in the same prosecution to mean something clearer or narrower than its literal language would dictate. *Cox v. New Hampshire,* p. 643 infra. The harshness of this doctrine is mitigated somewhat by the fact that "unexpected" or "unforeseeable" judicial constructions in such contexts violate due process. See *Marks v. United States,* 430 U.S. 188, 97 S.Ct. 990, 51 L.Ed.2d 260 (1977).[a]

Somewhat more complicated is the issue of when general attacks on a statute are permitted. Plainly litigants may argue that statutes are vague as to their own conduct or that their own speech is protected. In other words, litigants are always free to argue that a statute is invalid "as applied" to their own conduct. The dispute concerns when litigants can attack a statute without reference to their own conduct, an attack sometimes called "on its face."

A separate question is: when should such attacks result in partial or total invalidation of a statute? The terminology here has become as confused as the issues. In the past, the Court has frequently referred to facial attacks on statutes in a way that embraces attempts at either partial or total invalidation. In some recent opinions, however, including those quoted below, it uses the term "facial attack" or "on its face" to refer only to arguments seeking total invalidation of a statute.

Terminology aside, one of the recurrent questions has been the extent to which litigants may argue that a statute is unconstitutionally overbroad even though their own conduct would not otherwise be constitutionally protected. This is often characterized as a standing issue. Ordinarily litigants do not have standing to raise the rights of others. See Ch. 9, Sec. 1, II, B. But, it has been argued that "[u]nder 'conventional' standing principles, a litigant has always had the right to be judged in accordance with a constitutionally valid rule of law." Monaghan, *Overbreadth,* 1981 S.Ct.Rev. 1, 3. On this view, if a statute is unconstitutionally overbroad, it is not a valid rule of law, and any defendant prosecuted under the statute has standing to raise the overbreadth issue.[b] However the issue may be characterized, White, J., has contended for many years that a litigant whose own conduct is unprotected should not prevail on an overbreadth challenge without a showing that the statute's overbreadth is "real and substantial." After much litigation, White, J., has finally prevailed. The "substantial" overbreadth doctrine now burdens all litigants who argue that a statute should be declared overbroad when their own conduct is unprotected.[c] *Brockett v. Spokane Arcades, Inc.; New York v. Ferber,* p. 497 infra.

a. For commentary on overbreadth with special focus on the implications of the doctrine mentioned in this paragraph, see Fallon, *Making Sense of Overbreadth,* 100 Yale L.J. 853 (1991).

b. For more recent elaboration, see Monaghan, *Third Party Standing,* 84 Colum.L. Rev. 277 (1984). See also Sedler, *The Assertion of Constitutional Jus Tertii: A Substantive Approach,* 70 Calif.L.Rev. 1308, 1327 (1982) ("It may be the potential chilling effect upon others' expression that makes the statute invalid, but the litigant has his own right not to be subject to the operation of an invalid statute.").

c. For commentary on the concept of "substantial" overbreadth, see Redish, *The Warren Court, The Burger Court and the First Amendment Overbreadth Doctrine,* 78 Nw.U.L.Rev. 1031, 1056–69 (1983).

Less clear are the circumstances in which a litigant whose conduct *is* protected can go beyond a claim that the statute is unconstitutional "as applied." Again, litigants are always free to argue that their own conduct is protected. Moreover, the Court has stated that "[t]here is no reason to limit challenges to case-by-case 'as applied' challenges when the statute [in] all its applications falls short of constitutional demands." [d] *Maryland v. Joseph H. Munson Co.,* 467 U.S. 947, 104 S.Ct. 2839, 81 L.Ed.2d 786 (1984). How far beyond this the Court will go is unclear. In *Brockett v. Spokane Arcades, Inc.,* p. 473 supra, it referred to the "normal rule that partial, rather than facial invalidation" of statutes is to be preferred and observed that: "[A]n individual whose own speech or expressive conduct may validly be prohibited or sanctioned is permitted to challenge a statute on its face because it also threatens others not before the court—those who desire to engage in legally protected expression but who may refrain from doing so rather than risk prosecution or undertake to have the law declared partially invalid. If the overbreadth is 'substantial,' the law may not be enforced against anyone, including the party before the court, until it is narrowed to reach only unprotected activity, whether by legislative action or by judicial construction or partial invalidation.

"It is otherwise where the parties challenging the statute are those who desire to engage in protected speech that the overbroad statute purports to punish, or who seek to publish both protected and unprotected material. There is then no want of a proper party to challenge the statute, no concern that an attack on the statute will be unduly delayed or protected speech discouraged. The statute may forthwith be declared invalid to the extent that it reaches too far, but otherwise left intact." [e]

Brockett takes the view that it must give standing to the otherwise unprotected to raise an overbreadth challenge, in order to secure the rights of those whose speech should be protected. But it sees no purpose in giving standing to the protected in order to secure rights for those whose speech should not be protected. This position is not without its ironies. In some circumstances, a litigant whose speech is unprotected will be in a better position than one whose speech is protected, at least if the litigant's goal is completely to stop enforcement of a statute.

Finally, what of the cases when it is uncertain whether the litigant's speech is protected? Should courts consider as applied attacks before proceeding to overbreadth attacks? *Board of Trustees v. Fox,* p. 583 infra, declared it "not the usual judicial practice" and "generally undesirable" to proceed to an overbreadth challenge without first determining whether the statute would be valid as applied.[f] Yet the Court has frequently (see, e.g., pp. 495–96 infra (fighting words cases); *Board of Airport Commissioners v. Jews for Jesus, Inc.,* p. 650 infra)

d. There is a terminological dispute here. Compare *Los Angeles City Council v. Taxpayers For Vincent,* p. 656 infra (such challenges are not overbreadth challenges) with *Munson,* supra (such challenges are properly called overbreadth challenges).

e. After the Court has declared that the statute is invalid to the extent it reaches too far, the remaining portion of the statute will be examined to determine whether that portion is severable. That is, it could well be the intent of the legislature that the statute stands or falls as a single package. To invalidate a part, then, could be to invalidate the whole. Alternatively, the legislature may have intended to salvage whatever it might. The question of severability is regarded as one of legislative intent, but, at least with respect to federal legislation, courts will presume that severability was intended. See, e.g., *Regan v. Time, Inc.,* 468 U.S. 641, 104 S.Ct. 3262, 82 L.Ed.2d 487 (1984). The question of whether a provision of a state statute is severable is one of state law.

f. The case arose in the federal courts, and the Court might be less likely to remand to a state court for an as applied determination, but the Court did not address that distinction.

declared statutes overbroad without an as applied determination. The Court has yet systematically to detail the considerations relevant to separating the "usual" judicial practice from the unusual.

The issues with respect to vagueness challenges are similar. It remains possible, however, that the Court will resolve them in ways different from the approaches it has fashioned in the law of overbreadth. White, J., clearly would pursue a different course. He has suggested that vagueness challenges should be confined to "as applied" attacks unless a statute is vague in all of its applications. Accordingly, if a statute clearly proscribes the conduct of a particular defendant, to allow that defendant to challenge a statute for vagueness is in his view "to confound vagueness and overbreadth." *Kolender v. Lawson,* 461 U.S. 352, 103 S.Ct. 1855, 75 L.Ed.2d 903 (1983) (White, J., dissenting). In response, the Court has stated that a facial attack upon a statute need not depend upon a showing of vagueness in all of a statute's applications: "[W]e permit a facial challenge if a law reaches 'a substantial amount of constitutionally protected conduct,'" *Kolender,* supra. Moreover, the Court has previously allowed litigants to raise the vagueness issue "even though there is no uncertainty about the impact of the ordinances on their own rights." *Young.* But see, e.g., *Broadrick v. Oklahoma,* p. 499 infra, in which White, J., writing for the Court suggests that standing to raise the vagueness argument should not be permitted in this situation.

Much less clear are the circumstances in which litigants whose conduct is *not* clearly covered by a statute can go beyond an "as applied" attack.[g] One approach would be to apply the same rule to all litigants, e.g., allowing total invalidation of statutes upon a showing of a "substantial" vagueness. In *Kolender,* the Court made no determination whether the statute involved was vague as to the defendant's own conduct; arguably, the opinion implied that it made no difference. Another approach would analogize to the approach suggested in *Brockett* for overbreadth challenges. Thus, a court might refrain from total invalidation of a statute and confine itself to striking the vague part insofar as the vague part seems to cover protected speech, leaving the balance of the statute intact. *Kolender* itself recites that the Court has "traditionally regarded vagueness and overbreadth as logically related and similar doctrines," but the Court's attitudes toward vagueness remain unclear. The questions of what standards should govern challenges to statutes that go beyond the facts before the Court, who should be able to raise the challenges, and under what circumstances continue to divide the Court.[h]

g. Conceivably, it could make a difference whether the litigants in this class of those "not clearly covered" have engaged in protected or unprotected conduct.

h. For commentary on vagueness and overbreadth, see, e.g., *Nimmer on Freedom of Speech,* 4-147—4-162 (1984); Alexander, *Is There an Overbreadth Doctrine?,* 22 San Diego L.Rev. 541 (1985); Amsterdam, *The Void-For-Vagueness Doctrine in the Supreme Court,* 109 U.Pa.L.Rev. 67 (1960); Bogen, *First Amendment Ancillary Doctrines,* 37 Md.L.Rev. 679, 705–26 (1978); Monaghan, supra; Redish, supra; Note, *The First Amendment Overbreadth Doctrine,* 83 Harv.L.Rev. 844 (1970). On the relationship between the overbreadth doctrine and the less drastic means test, see fn. b in *Central Hudson Gas & Elec. Corp. v. Public Serv. Comm'n,* p. 580 infra.

IV. "FIGHTING WORDS," OFFENSIVE WORDS AND HOSTILE AUDIENCES

A. FIGHTING WORDS

CHAPLINSKY v. NEW HAMPSHIRE, 315 U.S. 568, 62 S.Ct. 766, 86 L.Ed. 1031 (1942): In the course of proselytizing on the streets, appellant, a Jehovah's Witness, denounced organized religion. Despite the city marshal's warning to "go slow" because his listeners were upset with his attacks on religion, appellant continued and a disturbance occurred. At this point, a police officer led appellant toward the police station, without arresting him. While enroute, appellant again encountered the city marshal who had previously admonished him. Appellant then said to the marshal (he claimed, but the marshal denied, in response to the marshal's cursing him): "You are a God damned racketeer" and "a damned Fascist and the whole government of Rochester are Fascists or agents of Fascists." He was convicted of violating a state statute forbidding anyone to address "any offensive, derisive or annoying word to any other person who is lawfully in any [public place] [or] call[ing] him by any offensive or derisive name." The Court, per MURPHY, J., upheld the conviction:

"There are certain well-defined and narrowly limited classes of speech, the prevention and punishment of which have never been thought to raise any Constitutional problem.[a] These include the lewd and obscene, the profane, the libelous, and the insulting or 'fighting' words—those which by their very utterance inflict injury or tend to incite an immediate breach of the peace. [S]uch utterances are no essential part of any exposition of ideas, and are of such slight social value as a step to truth that any benefit that may be derived from them is clearly outweighed by the social interest in order and morality. * * *

"On the authority of its earlier decisions, the state court declared that the statute's purpose was to preserve the public peace, no words being 'forbidden except such as have a direct tendency to cause acts of violence by the person to whom, individually, the remark is addressed'. It was further said: 'The word "offensive" is not to be defined in terms of what a particular addressee thinks. [The] test is what men of common intelligence would understand would be words likely to cause an average addressee to fight. [The] English language has a number of words and expressions which by general consent are "fighting words" when said without a disarming smile. [Such] words, as ordinary men know, are likely to cause a fight. So are threatening, profane or obscene revilings.

a. See Haiman, *How Much of Our Speech is Free?*, The Civ.Lib.Rev., Winter, 1975, pp. 111, 123: "[T]his discrimination between two classes of speech made its first U.S. Supreme Court appearance in *Cantwell v. Connecticut* (1940) [p. 1160 infra]." Jehovah's Witnesses had been convicted of religious solicitation without a permit and of breach of the peace. The Court set aside both convictions. It invalidated the permit system for "religious" solicitation, because it permitted the licensing official to determine what causes were "religious," thus allowing a "censorship of religion." In setting aside the breach of peace conviction, because the offense covered much protected conduct and left "too wide a discretion in its application," the Court, per Roberts, J., noted: "One may, however, be guilty of [breach of the peace] if he commits acts or makes statements likely to provoke violence and disturbance of good order. [I]n practically all [such decisions to this effect], the provocative language [held to constitute] a breach of the peace consisted of profane, indecent or abusive remarks directed to the person of the hearer. *Resort to epithets or personal abuse is not in any proper sense communication of information or opinion safeguarded by the Constitution,* and its punishment as a criminal act [under a narrowly drawn statute] would raise no question under that instrument." (Emphasis added). For commentary, see Post, *Cultural Heterogeneity and Law*, 76 Calif.L.Rev. 297 (1988).

Derisive and annoying words can be taken as coming within the purview of the statute as heretofore interpreted only when they have this characteristic of plainly tending to excite the addressee to a breach of the peace. [The] statute, as construed, does no more than prohibit the face-to-face words plainly likely to cause a breach of the peace by the addressee, words whose speaking constitute a breach of the peace by the speaker—including "classical fighting words", words in current use less "classical" but equally likely to cause violence, and other disorderly words, including profanity, obscenity and threats.'

"[A] statute punishing verbal acts, carefully drawn so as not unduly to impair liberty of expression, is not too vague for a criminal law. * * *[8]

"Nor can we say that the application of the statute to the facts disclosed by the record substantially or unreasonably impinges upon the privilege of free speech. Argument is unnecessary to demonstrate that the appellations 'damn racketeer' and 'damn Fascist' are epithets likely to provoke the average person to retaliation, and thereby cause a breach of the peace.

"The refusal of the state court to admit evidence of provocation and evidence bearing on the truth or falsity of the utterances is open to no Constitutional objection. Whether the facts sought to be proved by such evidence constitute a defense to the charge or may be shown in mitigation are questions for the state court to determine. Our function is fulfilled by a determination that the challenged statute, on its face and as applied, does not contravene the Fourteenth Amendment."

Notes and Questions

1. *Fighting words and free speech values.* (a) *Self realization.* Does speech have to step toward truth to be of first amendment value? Consider Redish, *The Value of Free Speech,* 130 U.Pa.L.Rev. 591, 626 (1982): "Why not view Chaplinsky's comments as a personal catharsis, as a means to vent his frustration at a system he deemed—whether rightly or wrongly—to be oppressive? Is it not a mark of individuality to be able to cry out at a society viewed as crushing the individual? Under this analysis, so-called 'fighting words' represent a significant means of self-realization, whether or not they can be considered a means of attaining some elusive 'truth.'"

(b) *Fighting words and truth.* Are fighting words always false? Should truth be a defense? Always?

(c) *Fighting words and self-government.* Was Chaplinsky's statement *something other than* the expression of an idea? Did he wish to inform the marshal of his opinion of him and did he do so "in a way which was not only unquestionably clear, [but] all too clear"? Loewy, *Punishing Flag Desecrators,* 49 N.C.L.Rev. 48, 82 (1970). How significant is it that Chaplinsky's remarks were not made in the context of a public debate or discussion of political or social issues? Taking into account the events preceding Chaplinsky's remarks, and that the addressee was "an important representative of the Rochester city government," may Chaplinsky's epithets be viewed as "a sharply-expressed form of political protest against indifferent or biased police services in the enforcement of his right to free speech"? Rutzick, *Offensive Language and the Evolution of First Amend-*

8. [Even] if the interpretative gloss placed on the statute by the court below be disregarded, the statute had been previously construed as intended to preserve the public peace by punishing conduct, the direct tendency of which was to provoke the person against whom it was directed to acts of violence.

Appellant need not therefore have been a prophet to understand what the statute condemned.

ment Protection, 9 Harv.Civ.Rts.—Civ.Lib.L.Rev. 1 (1974). If the speech is directed at a police officer or other official in his representative capacity, is "the real target the government"? See id.

2. *The social interest in order and morality.* What was the social interest in this case? (a) *The likelihood and immediacy of violent retaliation?* Should the Court have considered whether a *law enforcement officer* so reviled would have been provoked to retaliate? Whatever is assumed about the reaction of an average citizen to offensive words, may it be assumed that police are "trained to remain calm in the face of citizen anger such as that expressed by Chaplinsky"? Rutzick, supra, at 10. See also Powell, J., concurring in *Lewis v. New Orleans;* Note, 53 B.U.L.Rev. 834, 847 (1973).

(b) *The highly personal nature of the insult, delivered face to face?* Was the marshal "verbally slapped in the face"? May the *Chaplinsky* statute be viewed as "a special type of assault statute"? See Loewy, supra, at 83–84. See also Emerson, *The System of Freedom of Expression* 337–38 (1970). To what extent should the tort of intentional infliction of emotional distress raise constitutional problems? Compare Haiman, *Speech and Law in a Free Society* 148–56 (1981) with Downs, *Skokie Revisited: Hate Group Speech and the First Amendment,* 60 Not.D.Law. 629, 673–85 (1985). See generally Greenawalt, *Speech, Crime, and the Uses of Language* 143–48 (1989) (discussing personal insults).

B. HOSTILE AUDIENCES

TERMINIELLO v. CHICAGO, 337 U.S. 1, 69 S.Ct. 894, 93 L.Ed. 1131 (1949): Petitioner "vigorously, if not viciously" criticized various political and racial groups and condemned "a surging, howling mob" gathered in protest outside the auditorium in which he spoke. He called his adversaries "slimy scum," "snakes," "bedbugs," and the like. Those inside the hall could hear those on the outside yell, "Fascists, Hitlers!" The crowd outside tried to tear the clothes off those who entered. About 28 windows were broken; stink bombs were thrown. But in charging the jury, the trial court defined "breach of the peace" to include speech which "stirs the public to anger, *invites dispute,* [or] brings about a condition of unrest (emphasis added)." A 5–4 majority, per DOUGLAS, J., struck down the breach of peace ordinance as thus construed: "[A] function of free speech under our system of government is to invite dispute. It may indeed best serve its high purpose when it induces a condition of unrest, creates dissatisfaction with conditions as they are, or even stirs people to anger. [That] is why freedom of speech, though not absolute, *Chaplinsky,* is nevertheless protected against censorship or punishment, unless shown likely to produce a clear and present danger of a serious substantive evil that rises far above public inconvenience, annoyance, or unrest."

FEINER v. NEW YORK, 340 U.S. 315, 71 S.Ct. 303, 95 L.Ed. 295 (1951): Petitioner made a speech on a street corner in a predominantly black residential section of Syracuse, N.Y. A crowd of 75 to 80 persons, black and white, gathered around him, and several pedestrians had to go into the highway in order to pass by. A few minutes after he started, two police officers arrived and observed the rest of the meeting. In the course of his speech, publicizing a meeting of the Young Progressives of America to be held that evening in a local hotel and protesting the revocation of a permit to hold the meeting in a public school auditorium, petitioner referred to the President as a "bum," to the American

Legion as "a Nazi Gestapo," and to the Mayor of Syracuse as a "champagne-sipping bum" who "does not speak for the Negro people." He also indicated in an excited manner: "The Negroes don't have equal rights; they should rise up in arms and fight for them."

These statements "stirred up a little excitement." One man indicated that if the police did not get that "S . . . O . . . B . . ." off the stand, he would do so himself. There was not yet a disturbance, but according to police testimony "angry muttering and pushing." In the words of the arresting officer whose testimony was accepted by the trial judge, he "stepped in to prevent it from resulting in a fight." After disregarding two requests to stop speaking, petitioner was arrested and convicted for disorderly conduct. The Court, per VINSON, C.J., affirmed: "The language of *Cantwell* is appropriate here. '[Nobody would] suggest that the principle of freedom of speech sanctions incitement to riot or that religious liberty connotes the privilege to exhort others to physical attack upon those belonging to another sect. When clear and present danger of riot, disorder, interference with traffic upon the public street or other immediate threat to public safety, peace, or order, appears, the power of the State to prevent or punish is obvious.'

"[It] is one thing to say that the police cannot be used as an instrument for the suppression of unpopular views, and another to say that, when as here the speaker passes the bounds of argument or persuasion and undertakes incitement to riot, they are powerless to prevent a breach of the peace. Nor in this case can we condemn the considered judgment of three New York courts approving the means which the police, faced with a crisis, used in the exercise of their power and duty to preserve peace and order."

BLACK, J., dissented: "The Court's opinion apparently rests on this reasoning: The policeman, under the circumstances detailed, could reasonably conclude that serious fighting or even riot was imminent; therefore he could stop petitioner's speech to prevent a breach of peace; accordingly, it was 'disorderly conduct' for petitioner to continue speaking in disobedience of the officer's request. As to the existence of a dangerous situation on the street corner, it seems far-fetched to suggest that the 'facts' show any imminent threat of riot or uncontrollable disorder. It is neither unusual nor unexpected that some people at public street meetings mutter, mill about, push, shove, or disagree, even violently, with the speaker. Indeed, it is rare where controversial topics are discussed that an outdoor crowd does not do some or all of these things. Nor does one isolated threat to assault the speaker forebode disorder. Especially should the danger be discounted where, as here, the person threatening was a man whose wife and two small children accompanied him and who, so far as the record shows, was never close enough to petitioner to carry out the threat.

"Moreover, assuming that the 'facts' did indicate a critical situation, I reject the implication of the Court's opinion that the police had no obligation to protect petitioner's constitutional right to talk. The police of course have power to prevent breaches of the peace. But if, in the name of preserving order, they ever can interfere with a lawful public speaker, they first must make all reasonable efforts to protect him. Here the policemen did not even pretend to try to protect petitioner. According to the officers' testimony, the crowd was restless but there is no showing of any attempt to quiet it; pedestrians were forced to walk into the street, but there was no effort to clear a path on the sidewalk; one person threatened to assault petitioner but the officers did nothing to discourage this when even a word might have sufficed. Their duty was to protect petitioner's right to talk, even to the extent of arresting the man who threatened to interfere. Instead, they shirked that duty and acted only to suppress the right to speak.

"Finally, I cannot agree with the Court's statement that petitioner's disregard of the policeman's unexplained request amounted to such 'deliberate defiance' as would justify an arrest or conviction for disorderly conduct. On the contrary, I think that the policeman's action was a 'deliberate defiance' of ordinary official duty as well as of the constitutional right of free speech. For at least where time allows, courtesy and explanation of commands are basic elements of good official conduct in a democratic society. Here petitioner was 'asked' then 'told' then 'commanded' to stop speaking, but a man making a lawful address is certainly not required to be silent merely because an officer directs it.[a] Petitioner was entitled to know why he should cease doing a lawful act. Not once was he told."

DOUGLAS, J., joined by Minton, J., dissented: "A speaker may not, of course, incite a riot any more than he may incite a breach of the peace by the use of 'fighting words'. But this record shows no such extremes. It shows an unsympathetic audience and the threat of one man to haul the speaker from the stage. It is against that kind of threat that speakers need police protection. If they do not receive it and instead the police throw their weight on the side of those who would break up the meetings, the police become the new censors of speech. Police censorship has all the vices of the censorship from city halls which we have repeatedly struck down."

Notes and Questions

1. Should *Feiner* have used an objective test? Consider Barnum, *Freedom of Assembly and the Hostile Audience in Anglo–American Law,* 29 Am.J.Comp.L. 59, 73–75 (1981): "The argument that some nonpersonal insults should be punishable because they are inherently likely to provoke violent reaction is essentially an extension of the reasoning [in] *Chaplinsky.* [T]he public utterance of such insults could be punished, even though the actual audience to which they are addressed would not be likely, for whatever reasons, to react with violence. [I]t is essential for the law to attempt to distinguish between messages which are sufficiently threatening, abusive, or insulting in content to be inherently likely to provoke a breach of the peace and those which are not, and the police must be prepared to intervene in some situations by arresting demonstrators and in others by controlling or arresting the members of a hostile audience."

2. What was the subject of disagreement in *Feiner*? (1) The standard for police interruption of a speech when danger of violence exists and the speaker intends to create disorder rather than to communicate ideas? (2) The standard when such danger exists, but the speaker only desires to communicate ideas? (3) Whether the danger of disorder and violence *was* plain and imminent? (4) Whether the speaker *did* intend to create disorder and violence?

May *Feiner* be limited to the proposition that when a speaker "incites to riot"—but only then—police may stop him without bothering to keep his audience in check? Cf. *Sellers v. Johnson,* 163 F.2d 877 (8th Cir.1947), cert. denied, 332 U.S. 851, 68 S.Ct. 356, 92 L.Ed. 421 (1948). See Stewart, *Public Speech and*

a. Compare *Houston v. Hill,* p. 496 infra (ordinance forbidding speech that in any manner interrupts a police officer in the performance of duties is overbroad).

Public Order in Britain and the United States, 13 Vand.L.Rev. 625, 632–33 (1960).

Should the speech *always* be prohibitable when the speaker intends to create disorder, rather than communicate ideas? Should the speech be prohibitable *only* under these circumstances? Should a speech *ever* be prohibitable because listeners arrive or will arrive, as they would have in *Sellers,* with a preconceived intent to create disturbance? Is the only really difficult problem in this area posed when *neither* the speaker *nor* the audience which gathers intends to create disorder, but the audience becomes *genuinely* aroused, honestly—whether or not justifiably—enraged? Here, should the police protect the speechmaking to the fullest extent possible? If they are firmly told they must before they can arrest the speaker, what is the likelihood that adequate preventive steps will be taken? See Gellhorn, *American Rights* 55–62 (1960); Note, 49 Colum.L.Rev. 1118, 1123–24 (1949).

3. *Edwards v. South Carolina,* 372 U.S. 229, 83 S.Ct. 680, 9 L.Ed.2d 697 (1963) reversed a breach of the peace conviction of civil rights demonstrators who refused to disperse within 15 minutes of a police command. The Court maintained that the 200 to 300 onlookers did not threaten violence and that the police protection was ample. It described the situation as a "far cry from [*Feiner*]." Clark, J., dissenting, pointed to the racially charged atmosphere ("200 youthful Negro demonstrators were being aroused to a 'fever pitch' before a crowd of some 300 people who undoubtedly were hostile.") and concluded that city officials in good faith believed that disorder and violence were imminent. Did *Edwards* miss a golden opportunity to clarify *Feiner*? What if the crowd had been pushing, shoving and pressing more closely around the demonstrators in *Edwards*? Would the case still be a "far cry" from *Feiner* because the demonstrators had not "passed the bounds of argument or persuasion and undertaken incitement to riot"?

4. In the advocacy of illegal action context, the fear of violence arises from audience cooperation with the speaker. In the hostile audience context, the fear of violence arises from audience conflict with the speaker. How do the elements set out in *Brandenburg* relate to those implied in *Feiner*? How should they relate? Should the standard for "fighting words" cases be different from the "hostile audience" cases?

5. Should police be able to prosecute or silence disruptive audiences? Heckling audiences? In what contexts? See generally *In re Kay,* 1 Cal.3d 930, 83 Cal.Rptr. 686, 464 P.2d 142 (1970).

C. OFFENSIVE WORDS

COHEN v. CALIFORNIA

403 U.S. 15, 91 S.Ct. 1780, 29 L.Ed.2d 284 (1971).

JUSTICE HARLAN delivered the opinion of the Court.

[Defendant was convicted of violating that part of a general California disturbing-the-peace statute which prohibits "maliciously and willfully disturb[ing] the peace or quiet of any neighborhood or person" by "offensive conduct." He had worn a jacket bearing the plainly visible words "Fuck the Draft" in a Los Angeles courthouse corridor, where women and children were present. He testified that he did so as a means of informing the public of the depth of his feelings against the Vietnam War and the draft. He did not engage in, nor threaten, any violence, nor was anyone who saw him violently aroused. Nor was there any evidence that he uttered any sound prior to his arrest. In affirming, the California Court of Appeal construed "offensive conduct" to mean "behavior which has a tendency to provoke *others* to acts of violence or to in turn disturb the peace" and held that the state had proved this element because it was "reasonably foreseeable" that defendant's conduct "might cause others to rise up to commit a violent act against [him] or attempt to forceably remove his jacket."]

In order to lay hands on the precise issue which this case involves, it is useful first to canvass various matters which this record does *not* present.

The conviction quite clearly rests upon the asserted offensiveness of the *words* Cohen used to convey his message to the public. The only "conduct" which the State sought to punish is the fact of communication. Thus, we deal here with a conviction resting solely upon "speech," not upon any separately identifiable conduct which allegedly was intended by Cohen to be perceived by others as expressive of particular views but which, on its face, does not necessarily convey any message and hence arguably could be regulated without effectively repressing Cohen's ability to express himself. Cf. *United States v. O'Brien.* Further, the State certainly lacks power to punish Cohen for the underlying content of the message the inscription conveyed. At least so long as there is no showing of an intent to incite disobedience to or disruption of the draft, Cohen could not, consistently with the First and Fourteenth Amendments, be punished for asserting the evident position on the inutility or immorality of the draft his jacket reflected. *Yates.*

Appellant's conviction, then, rests squarely upon his exercise [of] "freedom of speech" [and] can be justified, if at all, only as a valid regulation of the manner in which he exercised that freedom, not as a permissible prohibition on the substantive message it conveys. This does not end the inquiry, of course, for the First and Fourteenth Amendments have never been thought to give absolute protection to every individual to speak whenever or wherever he pleases, or to use any form of address in any circumstances that he chooses. In this vein, too, however, we think it important to note that several issues typically associated with such problems are not presented here.

In the first place, Cohen was tried under a statute applicable throughout the entire State. Any attempt to support this conviction on the ground that the statute seeks to preserve an appropriately decorous atmosphere in the courthouse where Cohen was arrested must fail in the absence of any language in the statute that would have put appellant on notice that certain kinds of otherwise permissible speech or conduct would nevertheless, under California law, not be tolerated in certain places. No fair reading of the phrase "offensive conduct" can be said sufficiently to inform the ordinary person that distinctions between certain locations are thereby created.[3]

In the second place, as it comes to us, this case cannot be said to fall within those relatively few categories of instances where prior decisions have established the power of government to deal more comprehensively with certain forms of individual expression simply upon a showing that such a form was employed.

3. It is illuminating to note what transpired when Cohen entered a courtroom in the building. He removed his jacket and stood with it folded over his arm. Meanwhile, a policeman sent the presiding judge a note suggesting that Cohen be held in contempt of court. The judge declined to do so and Cohen was arrested by the officer only after he emerged from the courtroom.

This is not, for example, an obscenity case. Whatever else may be necessary to give rise to the States' broader power to prohibit obscene expression, such expression must be, in some significant way, erotic. *Roth.* It cannot plausibly be maintained that this vulgar allusion to the Selective Service System would conjure up such psychic stimulation in anyone likely to be confronted with Cohen's crudely defaced jacket.

This Court has also held that the States are free to ban the simple use, without a demonstration of additional justifying circumstances, of so-called "fighting words," those personally abusive epithets which, when addressed to the ordinary citizen, are, as a matter of common knowledge, inherently likely to provoke violent reaction. *Chaplinsky.* While the four-letter word displayed by Cohen in relation to the draft is not uncommonly employed in a personally provocative fashion, in this instance it was clearly not "directed to the person of the hearer." No individual actually or likely to be present could reasonably have regarded the words on appellant's jacket as a direct personal insult. Nor do we have here an instance of the exercise of the State's police power to prevent a speaker from intentionally provoking a given group to hostile reaction. Cf. *Feiner; Terminiello.* There is, as noted above, no showing that anyone who saw Cohen was in fact violently aroused or that appellant intended such a result.

[T]he mere presumed presence of unwitting listeners or viewers does not serve automatically to justify curtailing all speech capable of giving offense. While this Court has recognized that government may properly act in many situations to prohibit intrusion into the privacy of the home of unwelcome views and ideas which cannot be totally banned from the public dialogue, we have at the same time consistently stressed that "we are often 'captives' outside the sanctuary of the home and subject to objectionable speech." The ability of government, consonant with the Constitution, to shut off discourse solely to protect others from hearing it is, in other words, dependent upon a showing that substantial privacy interests are being invaded in an essentially intolerable manner. Any broader view of this authority would effectively empower a majority to silence dissidents simply as a matter of personal predilections.

[Given] the subtlety and complexity of the factors involved if Cohen's "speech" was otherwise entitled to constitutional protection, we do not think the fact that some unwilling "listeners" in a public building may have been briefly exposed to it can serve to justify this breach of the peace conviction where, as here, there was no evidence that persons powerless to avoid appellant's conduct did in fact object to it, and where [unlike another portion of the same statute barring the use of "vulgar, profane or indecent language within [the] hearing of women or children, in a loud and boisterous manner"], the [challenged statutory provision] evinces no concern [with] the special plight of the captive auditor, but, instead, indiscriminately sweeps within its prohibitions all "offensive conduct" that disturbs "any neighborhood or person."

Against this background, the issue flushed by this case stands out in bold relief. It is whether California can excise, as "offensive conduct," one particular scurrilous epithet from the public discourse, either upon the theory of the court below that its use is inherently likely to cause violent reaction or upon a more general assertion that the States, acting as guardians of public morality, may properly remove this offensive word from the public vocabulary.

The rationale of the California court is plainly untenable. At most it reflects an "undifferentiated fear or apprehension of disturbance [which] is not enough to overcome the right to freedom of expression." *Tinker* [p. 673 infra].

We have been shown no evidence that substantial numbers of citizens are standing ready to strike out physically at whoever may assault their sensibilities with execrations like that uttered by Cohen. There may be some persons about with such lawless and violent proclivities, but that is an insufficient base upon which to erect, consistently with constitutional values, a governmental power to force persons who wish to ventilate their dissident views into avoiding particular forms of expression. The argument amounts to little more than the self-defeating proposition that to avoid physical censorship of one who has not sought to provoke such a response by a hypothetical coterie of the violent and lawless, the States may more appropriately effectuate that censorship themselves.

Admittedly, it is not so obvious that the First and Fourteenth Amendments must be taken to disable the States from punishing public utterance of this unseemly expletive in order to maintain what they regard as a suitable level of discourse within the body politic. We think, however, that examination and reflection will reveal the shortcomings of a contrary viewpoint.

[The] constitutional right of free expression is powerful medicine in a society as diverse and populous as ours. It is designed and intended to remove governmental restraints from the arena of public discussion, putting the decision as to what views shall be voiced largely into the hands of each of us, in the hope that use of such freedom will ultimately produce a more capable citizenry and more perfect polity and in the belief that no other approach would comport with the premise of individual dignity and choice upon which our political system rests.

To many, the immediate consequence of this freedom may often appear to be only verbal tumult, discord, and even offensive utterance. These are, however, within established limits, in truth necessary side effects of the broader enduring values which the process of open debate permits us to achieve. That the air may at times seem filled with verbal cacophony is, in this sense not a sign of weakness but of strength. We cannot lose sight of the fact that, in what otherwise might seem a trifling and annoying instance of individual distasteful abuse of a privilege, these fundamental societal values are truly implicated. * * *

Against this perception of the constitutional policies involved, we discern certain more particularized considerations that peculiarly call for reversal of this conviction. First, the principle contended for by the State seems inherently boundless. How is one to distinguish this from any other offensive word? Surely the State has no right to cleanse public debate to the point where it is grammatically palatable to the most squeamish among us. Yet no readily ascertainable general principle exists for stopping short of that result were we to affirm the judgment below. For, while the particular four-letter word being litigated here is perhaps more distasteful than most others of its genre, it is nevertheless often true that one man's vulgarity is another's lyric. Indeed, we think it is largely because governmental officials cannot make principled distinctions in this area that the Constitution leaves matters of taste and style so largely to the individual.

Additionally, we cannot overlook the fact, because it is well illustrated by the episode involved here, that much linguistic expression serves a dual communicative function: it conveys not only ideas capable of relatively precise, detached explication, but otherwise inexpressible emotions as well. In fact, words are often chosen as much for their emotive as their cognitive force. We cannot sanction the view that the Constitution, while solicitous of the cognitive content of individual speech, has little or no regard for that emotive function which, practically speaking, may often be the more important element of the overall message sought to be communicated. * * *

Finally, and in the same vein, we cannot indulge the facile assumption that one can forbid particular words without also running a substantial risk of suppressing ideas in the process. Indeed, governments might soon seize upon the censorship of particular words as a convenient guise for banning the expression of unpopular views. We have been able [to] discern little social benefit that might result from running the risk of opening the door to such grave results.

It is, in sum, our judgment that, absent a more particularized and compelling reason for its actions, the State may not, consistently with the First and Fourteenth Amendments, make the simple public display here involved of this single four-letter expletive a criminal offense. * * *

[BLACKMUN, J., joined by Burger, C.J., and Black, J., dissented for two reasons: (1) "Cohen's absurd and immature antic [was] mainly conduct and little speech" and the case falls "well within the sphere of *Chaplinsky* "; (2) although it declined to review the state court of appeals' decision in *Cohen,* the California Supreme Court subsequently narrowly construed the breach-of-the-peace statute in another case and *Cohen* should be remanded to the California Court of Appeal in the light of this subsequent construction. White, J., concurred with the dissent on the latter ground.]

Notes and Questions

1. For criticism of *Cohen,* see Bickel, *The Morality of Consent* 72 (1975) (Cohen's speech "constitutes an assault" and this sort of speech "may create [an] environment [in which] actions that were not possible before become possible"); Cox, *The Role of the Supreme Court in American Government* 47–48 (1976) (state has interest in "level at which public discourse is conducted"; state should not have to "allow exhibitionists and [others] trading upon our lower prurient interests to inflict themselves upon the public consciousness and dull its sensibilities"). For a defense (but what not a few would consider a narrow reading) of *Cohen,* see Farber, *Civilizing Public Discourse: An Essay on Professor Bickel, Justice Harlan, and the Enduring Significance of Cohen v. California,* 1980 Duke L.J. 283. See also Ely, *Democracy and Distrust* 114 (1980); Tribe, *American Constitutional Law* 787–88, 851–52, 916–17, 953–54 (2d Ed.1988). For an overview of Harlan, J.'s approach to the first amendment, see Farber & Nowak, *Justice Harlan and the First Amendment,* 2 Const.Comm. 425 (1985).

2. To what extent, if at all, and in what ways, if any, does *Cohen* restrict the "fighting words" doctrine? Consider Arkes, *Civility and the Restriction of Speech: Rediscovering the Defamation of Groups,* 1974 Sup.Ct.Rev. 281, 316: *Cohen* turned "the presumptions in *Chaplinsky* around: instead of presuming that profane or defamatory speech was beneath constitutional protection, he presumed that the speech was protected and that the burden of proof lay with those who would restrict it." If "one man's vulgarity is another's lyric," how are discriminations to be made in the "fighting words" area? See Rutzick, p. 486 supra, at 20.

3. Was the flaw in the *Chaplinsky* formulation that "[i]ts paradigm was a debating society, a sedate assembly of speakers who calmly discussed the issues of the day and became ultimately persuaded by the logic of one of the competing

positions"? That it viewed "emotion" as never entering the debate, "for emotion had nothing to do with 'truth' "? See Rutzick 18. Once it is conceded that "the offensiveness of language used in a political protest often measures the intensity of interest in the outcome of a governmental decision," does "protection for the use of offensive language [become] not a luxury but a necessity in a democratic society"? See id. at 19.

4. Does the "use of elaborate explanations and high sounding principles to resolve" cases like *Cohen* erect "obstacles to an enhanced public appreciation of free speech?" Does systematic judicial protection of "seemingly silly, unsavory, or dangerous activities" ultimately undermine public support for the idea of free speech? See Nagel, *Constitutional Cultures* 47 (1989).

5. What does *Cohen* decide? Consider Cohen, *A Look Back at Cohen v. California,* 34 UCLA L.Rev. 1595, 1602–03 (1987): "Unless it is overruled or dishonestly distinguished, *[Cohen]* has settled the proposition that a criminal statute is unconstitutional if it punishes all public use of profanity without reference to details such as the nature of the location and the audience. The opinion, however, left much to be decided about government controls on the use of profanity based on considerations of time, place, and manner. To what extent can profanity be punished because of the nature of the audience, the nature of the occasion on which it is uttered or displayed, or the manner of its utterance or display."

6. A series of cases in the early 1970s reversed convictions involving abusive language. *Gooding v. Wilson,* 405 U.S. 518, 92 S.Ct. 1103, 31 L.Ed.2d 408 (1972), invalidated a Georgia ordinance primarily because it had been previously applied to "utterances where there was no likelihood that the person addressed would make an immediate violent utterance." *Lewis v. New Orleans,* 415 U.S. 130, 94 S.Ct. 970, 39 L.Ed.2d 214 (1974), ruled that vulgar or offensive speech was protected under the first amendment. Because the statute punished "opprobrious language," it was deemed by the Court to embrace words that do not " 'by their very utterance inflict injury or tend to invite an immediate breach of the peace.' "

Although *Gooding* seemed to require a danger of immediate violence, *Lewis* recited that infliction of injury was sufficient. Dissenting in both cases, Burger, C.J., and Blackmun and Rehnquist, JJ., complained that the majority invoked vagueness and overbreadth analysis "indiscriminately without regard to the nature of the speech in question, the possible effect the statute or ordinance has upon such speech, the importance of the speech in relation to the exposition of ideas, or the purported or asserted community interest in preventing that speech." The dissenters focused upon the facts of the cases (e.g., Gooding to a police officer: "White son of a bitch, I'll kill you," "You son of a bitch, I'll choke you to death," and "You son of a bitch, if you ever put your hands on me again, I'll cut you to pieces."). They complained that the majority had relegated the facts to "footnote status, conveniently distant and in less disturbing focus." In *Gooding, Lewis,* and the other cases, Powell, J., insisted upon the importance of context in decisionmaking. Dissenting in *Rosenfeld v. New Jersey,* 408 U.S. 901, 92 S.Ct. 2479, 33 L.Ed.2d 321 (1972), he suggested that *Chaplinsky* be extended to the "wilful use of scurrilous language calculated to offend the sensibilities of an unwilling audience"; concurring in *Lewis,* he maintained that allowing prosecutions for offensive language directed at police officers invited law enforcement abuse. Finally, he suggested in *Rosenfeld* that whatever the scope of the "fighting words" doctrine, overbreadth analysis was inappropriate in such cases.

He doubted that such statutes deter others from exercising first amendment rights.[a]

Without questioning the power of states or municipalities to proscribe fighting words, or the failure to disperse in response to a valid police order, or the physical obstruction of an officer's investigation, or disorderly conduct, HOUSTON v. HILL, 482 U.S. 451, 107 S.Ct. 2502, 96 L.Ed.2d 398 (1987), per BRENNAN, J., invalidated as overbroad a Houston ordinance forbidding speech that in any manner interrupts a police officer in the performance of his or her duties: "The ordinance's plain language is admittedly violated scores of times daily, [yet] only some individuals—those chosen by the police in their unguided discretion—are arrested." [b]

POWELL, J., concurring in part and dissenting in part, argued that if the state were to construe the ordinance to require proof of intent to interfere with an officer's duties, overbreadth and vagueness difficulties might be overcome. In order to narrow the focus of the constitutional question, he would have certified that state law question to the appropriate Texas court.[c] Bowing to the court's determination to consider the ordinance without such a narrowing construction, he concluded that the ordinance was unconstitutionally vague.[d]

V. SHOULD NEW CATEGORIES BE CREATED?

Suppose a legislature were to outlaw speech whose dominant theme appeals to a morbid interest in violence, that is patently offensive to contemporary community standards, and that lacks serious literary, artistic, political or scientific value. Constitutional? One approach would be to contend that speech is protected unless it falls into already established categorical exceptions to first amendment protection. Another would be to argue by analogy, e.g., if obscenity is beneath first amendment protection, this speech should (or should not) be beneath such protection. Similarly, one could argue that exceptions to first amendment protection has been fashioned by resort to a balancing methodology and that balancing the relevant interests is the right approach. Alternatively, one could proceed from a particular substantive vision of the first amendment, such as the Meiklejohn view. Which approach has been applied by the Court? [a]

a. For commentary on Powell, J.'s approach, see Gunther, *In Search of Judicial Quality on a Changing Court: The Case of Justice Powell,* 24 Stan.L.Rev. 1001, 1029–35 (1972).

b. Blackmun, J., concurring, joined the Court's opinion, but reaffirmed his view that *Gooding* and *Lewis* were wrongly decided.

c. O'Connor, J., and Rehnquist, C.J., joined this portion of Powell, J.'s opinion.

d. Scalia, J., joined with Powell, J., on the vagueness issue and on some procedural issues, but thought the ordinance was properly before the Court. Rehnquist, C.J., dissenting, stated that he did not agree that the ordinance "in the absence of an authoritative construction by the Texas courts, is unconstitutional."

a. For commentary on the Court's methodology, see Redish, *Freedom of Expression: A Critical Analysis* (1984); Shiffrin, *The First Amendment, Democracy, and Romance* (1990); Van Alstyne, *Interpretations of the First Amendment* (1984); Van Alstyne, *A Graphic Review of the Free Speech Clause,* 70 Calif.L. Rev. 107 (1982); Aleinikoff, *Constitutional Law in the Age of Balancing,* 96 Yale L.J. 943 (1987); Fallon, *A Constructivist Coherence Theory of Constitutional Interpretation,* 100 Harv.L.Rev. 1189, 1228 n.191 (1987); Farber, *Content Regulation and the First Amendment: A Revisionist View,* 68 Geo.L.J. 727 (1980); Schauer, *Mrs. Palsgraf and the First Amendment,* 47 Wash.& Lee L.Rev. 161 (1990); Schauer, *The Second–Best First Amendment,* 31 Wm.& M.L.Rev. 1 (1989); Schauer, *Categories and the First Amendment: A Play in Three Acts,* 34 Vand.L.Rev. 265 (1981); Schlag, *Rules and Standards,* 33 U.C.L.A.L.Rev. 379 (1985); Stone, *Content Regulation and the First Amendment,* 25 Wm.& Mary L.Rev. 189 (1983); Stone, *Content–Neutral Restrictions,* 54 U.Chi.L.Rev. 46 (1987).

New York v. Ferber, infra, is interesting because it involves the question of whether to create a new category.

A. HARM TO CHILDREN AND THE OVERBREADTH DOCTRINE

NEW YORK v. FERBER, 458 U.S. 747, 102 S.Ct. 3348, 73 L.Ed.2d 1113 (1982), per WHITE, J., upheld conviction of a seller of films depicting young boys masturbating, under N.Y.Penal Law § 263.15, for "promoting [a] a sexual performance," defined as "any performance [which] includes sexual conduct [b] by a child" under 16. The Court addressed the "single question": " 'To prevent the abuse of children who are made to engage in sexual conduct for commercial purposes, could the New York State Legislature, consistent with the First Amendment, prohibit the dissemination of material which shows children engaged in sexual conduct, regardless of whether such material is obscene?' [c] * * *

"The *Miller* standard, like its predecessors, was an accommodation between the state's interests in protecting the 'sensibilities of unwilling recipients' from exposure to pornographic material and the dangers of censorship inherent in unabashedly content-based laws. Like obscenity statutes, laws directed at the dissemination of child pornography run the risk of suppressing protected expression by allowing the hand of the censor to become unduly heavy. For the following reasons, however, we are persuaded that the States are entitled to greater leeway in the regulation of pornographic depictions of children.

"First. [The] prevention of sexual exploitation and abuse of children constitutes a government objective of surpassing importance. The legislative findings accompanying passage of the New York laws reflect this concern. * * *

"We shall not second-guess this legislative judgment. Respondent has not intimated that we do so. Suffice it to say that virtually all of the States and the United States have passed legislation proscribing the production of or otherwise combatting 'child pornography.' The legislative judgment, as well as the judgment found in the relevant literature, is that the use of children as subjects of pornographic materials is harmful to the physiological, emotional, and mental health of the child. That judgment, we think, easily passes muster under the First Amendment.

"Second. The distribution of photographs and films depicting sexual activity by juveniles is intrinsically related to the sexual abuse of children in at least two ways. First, the materials produced are a permanent record of the children's participation and the harm to the child is exacerbated by their circulation. Second, the distribution network for child pornography must be closed if the production of material which requires the sexual exploitation of children is to be effectively controlled. Indeed, there is no serious contention that the

a. "Promote" was defined to include all aspects of production, distribution, exhibition and sale.

b. Sec. 263.3 defined "sexual conduct" as "actual or simulated sexual intercourse, deviate sexual intercourse, sexual bestiality, masturbation, sado-masochistic abuse, or lewd exhibition of the genitals."

c. The opinion gave the background for such legislation: "In recent years, the exploitive use of children in the production of pornography has become a serious national problem. The federal government and forty-seven States have sought to combat the problem with statutes specifically directed at the production of child pornography. At least half of such statutes do not require that the materials produced be legally obscene. Thirty-five States and the United States Congress have also passed legislation prohibiting the distribution of such materials; twenty States prohibit the distribution of material depicting children engaged in sexual conduct without requiring that the material be legally obscene. New York is one of the twenty."

legislature was unjustified in believing that it is difficult, if not impossible, to halt the exploitation of children by pursuing only those who produce the photographs and movies. While the production of pornographic materials is a low-profile, clandestine industry, the need to market the resulting products requires a visible apparatus of distribution. The most expeditious if not the only practical method of law enforcement may be to dry up the market for this material by imposing severe criminal penalties on persons selling, advertising, or otherwise promoting the product. Thirty-five States and Congress have concluded that restraints on the distribution of pornographic materials are required in order to effectively combat the problem, and there is a body of literature and testimony to support these legislative conclusions.

"[The] *Miller* standard, like all general definitions of what may be banned as obscene, does not reflect the State's particular and more compelling interest in prosecuting those who promote the sexual exploitation of children. Thus, the question under the *Miller* test of whether a work, taken as a whole, appeals to the prurient interest of the average person bears no connection to the issue of whether a child has been physically or psychologically harmed in the production of the work. Similarly, a sexual explicit depiction need not be 'patently offensive' in order to have required the sexual exploitation of a child for its production. In addition, a work which, taken on the whole, contains serious literary, artistic, political, or scientific value may nevertheless embody the hardest core of child pornography. 'It is irrelevant to the child [who has been abused] whether or not the material [has] a literary, artistic, political, or social value.' We therefore cannot conclude that the *Miller* standard is a satisfactory solution to the child pornography problem.

"Third. The advertising and selling of child pornography provides an economic motive for and is thus an integral part of the production of such materials, an activity illegal throughout the nation. 'It rarely has been suggested that the constitutional freedom for speech and press extends its immunity to speech or writing used as an integral part of conduct in violation of a valid criminal statute.' * * *

"Fourth. The value of permitting live performances and photographic reproductions of children engaged in lewd sexual conduct is exceedingly modest, if not de minimis. We consider it unlikely that visual depictions of children performing sexual acts or lewdly exhibiting their genitals would often constitute an important and necessary part of a literary performance or scientific or educational work. As the trial court in this case observed, if it were necessary for literary or artistic value, a person over the statutory age who perhaps looked younger could be utilized. * * *

"Fifth. Recognizing and classifying child pornography as a category of material outside the protection of the First Amendment is not incompatible with our earlier decisions. 'The question whether speech is, or is not protected by the First Amendment often depends on the content of the speech.' *Young v. American Mini Theatres, Inc.* [p. 556 infra]. '[I]t is the content of an utterance that determines whether it is a protected epithet or [an] unprotected "fighting comment"'. Leaving aside the special considerations when public officials are the target, *New York Times Co. v. Sullivan,* a libelous publication is not protected by the Constitution. *Beauharnais.* [It] is not rare that a content-based classification of speech has been accepted because it may be appropriately generalized that within the confines of the given classification, the evil to be restricted so overwhelmingly outweighs the expressive interests, if any, at stake, that no process of case-by-case adjudication is required. When a definable class of material, such as that covered by § 263.15, bears so heavily and pervasively on the welfare of children engaged in its production, we think the balance of competing interests is clearly struck and that it is permissible to consider these materials as without the protection of the First Amendment.

"There are, of course, limits on the category of child pornography which, like obscenity, is unprotected by the First Amendment. As with all legislation in this sensitive area, the conduct to be prohibited must be adequately defined by the applicable state law, as written or authoritatively construed. Here the nature of the harm to be combatted requires that the state offense be limited to works that *visually* depict sexual conduct by children below a specified age. The category of 'sexual conduct' proscribed must also be suitably limited and described.

"The test for child pornography is separate from the obscenity standard enunciated in *Miller*, but may be compared to it for purpose of clarity. The *Miller* formulation is adjusted in the following respects: A trier of fact need not find that the material appeals to the prurient interest of the average person; it is not required that sexual conduct portrayed be done so in a patently offensive manner; and the material at issue need not be considered as a whole. We note that the distribution of descriptions or other depictions of sexual conduct, not otherwise obscene, which do not involve live performance or photographic or other visual reproduction of live performances, retains First Amendment protection. As with obscenity laws, criminal responsibility may not be imposed without some element of scienter on the part of the defendant. * * *

"It remains to address the claim that the New York statute is unconstitutionally overbroad because it would forbid the distribution of material with serious literary, scientific, or educational value or material which does not threaten the harms sought to be combated by the State. * * *

"The traditional rule is that a person to whom a statute may constitutionally be applied may not challenge that statute on the ground that it may conceivably be applied unconstitutionally to others in situations not before the Court. *Broadrick v. Oklahoma,* 413 U.S. 601, 93 S.Ct. 2908, 37 L.Ed.2d 830 (1973). In *Broadrick,* we recognized that this rule reflects two cardinal principles of our constitutional order: the personal nature of constitutional rights and prudential limitations on constitutional adjudication.[20] [By] focusing on the factual situation before us, and similar cases necessary for development of a constitutional rule,[21] we face 'flesh-and-blood' legal problems with data 'relevant and adequate to an informed judgment.' This practice also fulfills a valuable institutional purpose: it allows state courts the opportunity to construe a law to avoid constitutional infirmities.

"What has come to be known as the First Amendment overbreadth doctrine is one of the few exceptions to this principle and must be justified by weighty countervailing policies. The doctrine is predicated on the sensitive nature of protected expression: persons whose expression is constitutionally protected may

20. In addition to prudential restraints, the traditional rule is grounded in Art. III limits on the jurisdiction of federal courts to actual cases and controversies. * * *

21. Overbreadth challenges are only one type of facial attack. A person whose activity may be constitutionally regulated nevertheless may argue that the statute under which he is convicted or regulated is invalid on its face. See, e.g., *Terminiello.* See generally Monaghan, *Overbreadth,* 1981 S.Ct.Rev. 1, 10–14.

well refrain from exercising their rights for fear of criminal sanctions by a statute susceptible of application to protected expression. * * *

"In *Broadrick,* we explained [that]: '[T]he plain import of our cases is, at the very least, that facial overbreadth adjudication is an exception to our traditional rules of practice and that its function, a limited one at the outset, attenuates as the otherwise unprotected behavior that it forbids the State to sanction moves from "pure speech" toward conduct and that conduct—even if expressive—falls within the scope of otherwise valid criminal laws that reflect legitimate state interests in maintaining comprehensive controls over harmful, constitutionally unprotected conduct. * * *'

"[*Broadrick*] examined a regulation involving restrictions on political campaign activity, an area not considered 'pure speech,' and thus it was unnecessary to consider the proper overbreadth test when a law arguably reaches traditional forms of expression such as books and films. As we intimated in *Broadrick,* the requirement of substantial overbreadth extended 'at the very least' to cases involving conduct plus speech. This case, which poses the question squarely, convinces us that the rationale of *Broadrick* is sound and should be applied in the present context involving the harmful employment of children to make sexually explicit materials for distribution.

"The premise that a law should not be invalidated for overbreadth unless it reaches a substantial number of impermissible applications is hardly novel. On most occasions involving facial invalidation, the Court has stressed the embracing sweep of the statute over protected expression.[26] Indeed, Justice Brennan observed in his dissenting opinion in *Broadrick*: 'We have never held that a statute should be held invalid on its face merely because it is possible to conceive of a single impermissible application, and in that sense a requirement of substantial overbreadth is already implicit in the doctrine.'

"The requirement of substantial overbreadth is directly derived from the purpose and nature of the doctrine. While a sweeping statute, or one incapable of limitation, has the potential to repeatedly chill the exercise of expressive activity by many individuals, the extent of deterrence of protected speech can be expected to decrease with the declining reach of the regulation. This observation appears equally applicable to the publication of books and films as it is to activities, such as picketing or participation in election campaigns, which have previously been categorized as involving conduct plus speech. We see no appreciable difference between the position of a publisher or bookseller in doubt as to the reach of New York's child pornography law and the situation faced by the Oklahoma state employees with respect to the State's restriction on partisan political activity.[d] * * *

"Applying these principles, we hold that § 263.15 is not substantially overbroad. We consider this the paradigmatic case of a state statute whose legitimate reach dwarfs its arguably impermissible applications. [While] the reach of

26. In *Gooding v. Wilson,* the Court's invalidation of a Georgia statute making it a misdemeanor to use " 'opprobrious words or abusive language, tending to cause a breach of the peace' " followed from state judicial decisions indicating that "merely to speak words offensive to some who hear them" could constitute a "breach of the peace." * * *

d. *Brockett v. Spokane Arcades, Inc.,* stated: "The Court of Appeals erred in holding that the *Broadrick* substantial overbreadth requirement is inapplicable where pure speech rather than conduct is at issue. *Ferber* specifically held to the contrary." For commentary on the overbreadth discussion in *Broadrick* and *Ferber,* see Redish, *The Warren Court, The Burger Court and the First Amendment Overbreadth Doctrine,* 78 Nw.U.L.Rev. 1031, 1056–69 (1983).

the statute is directed at the hard core of child pornography, the Court of Appeals was understandably concerned that some protected expression, ranging from medical textbooks to pictorials in the National Geographic would fall prey to the statute. How often, if ever, it may be necessary to employ children to engage in conduct clearly within the reach of § 263.15 in order to produce educational, medical, or artistic works cannot be known with certainty. Yet we seriously doubt, and it has not been suggested, that these arguably impermissible applications of the statute amount to more than a tiny fraction of the materials within the statute's reach." [e]

Notes and Questions

1. Consider Schauer, *Codifying the First Amendment: New York v. Ferber,* 1982 Sup.Ct.Rev. 285, 295: The new category created in *Ferber* "bears little resemblance to the category of obscenity delineated by *Miller.* The Court in *Ferber* explicitly held that child pornography need not appeal to the prurient interest, need not be patently offensive, and need not be based on a consideration of the material as a whole. This last aspect is most important, because it means that the presence of some serious literary, artistic, political, or scientific matter will not constitutionally redeem material containing depictions of sexual conduct by children. The Court referred to the foregoing factors in terms of having 'adjusted' the *Miller* test, but that is like saying a butterfly is an adjusted camel." What precisely is the new category created in *Ferber*?

2. What test or standard of review did the Court use to determine whether the speech should be protected? For general discussion, see Schauer, supra. Did it apply a different test or a standard of review when it formulated its rules in *Gertz*? Are tests or standards of review needed in these contexts? Desirable? Consider Shiffrin, *The First Amendment and Economic Regulation: Away From a General Theory of the First Amendment,* 78 Nw.U.L.Rev. 1212, 1268 (1983): "The complex set of rules produced in *Gertz,* right or wrong, resulted from an

e. Brennan, J., joined by Marshall, J., agreed "with much of what is said in the Court's opinion. [This] special and compelling interest (in protecting the well-being of the State's youth), and the particular vulnerability of children, afford the State the leeway to regulate pornographic material, the promotion of which is harmful to children, even though the State does not have such leeway when it seeks only to protect consenting adults from exposure to such materials. * * * I also agree with the Court that the 'tiny fraction' of material of serious artistic, scientific or educational value that could conceivably fall within the reach of the statute is insufficient to justify striking the statute on grounds of overbreadth." But the concurrence stated that application of the statute to such materials as "do have serious artistic, scientific or medical value would violate the First Amendment."

On that issue O'Connor, J., wrote a short concurrence: "Although I join the Court's opinion, I write separately to stress that the Court does not hold that New York must except 'material with serious literary, scientific or educational value' from its statute. The Court merely holds that, even if the First Amendment shelters such material, New York's current statute is not sufficiently overbroad to support respondent's facial attack. The compelling interests identified in today's opinion suggest that the Constitution might in fact permit New York to ban knowing distribution of works depicting minors engaged in explicit sexual conduct, regardless of the social value of the depictions. For example, a 12-year-old child photographed while masturbating surely suffers the same psychological harm whether the community labels the photograph 'edifying' or 'tasteless.' The audience's appreciation of the depiction is simply irrelevant to New York's asserted interest in protecting children from psychological, emotional, and mental harm."

Stevens, J., also concurred in the judgment in a short opinion that noted his conclusion that the films in the case were not entitled to first amendment protection, and his view that overbreadth analysis should be avoided by waiting until the hypothetical case actually arises.

Blackmun, J., concurred in the result without opinion.

appreciation that the protection of truth was important but that the protection of reputation also was important. The Court wisely avoided discussion of levels of scrutiny because any resort to such abstractions would have constitutionalized reductionism." Is "constitutionalized reductionism" desirable because it protects speech and provides guidance to the lower courts?

3. *Overbreadth without a chilling effect?* Massachusetts prohibited adults from posing or exhibiting nude children for purposes of photographs, publications, or pictures, moving or otherwise. Bona fide scientific or medical purposes were excepted as were educational or cultural purposes for a bona fide school, museum, or library. Douglas Oakes was prosecuted for taking 10 color photographs of his 14–year–old stepdaughter in a state of nudity covered by the statute. The Massachusetts Supreme Judicial Court declared the statute overbroad. After certiorari was granted in MASSACHUSETTS v. OAKES, 491 U.S. 576, 109 S.Ct. 2633, 105 L.Ed.2d 493 (1989), Massachusetts added a "lascivious intent" requirement to the statute and eliminated the exemptions. O'CONNOR, J., joined by Rehnquist, C.J., and White and Kennedy, JJ., accordingly refused to entertain the overbreadth challenge and voted to remand the case for determination of the statute's constitutionality as applied: "Because it has been repealed, the former version of [the Massachusetts law] cannot chill protected speech."

SCALIA, J., joined by Blackmun, Brennan, Marshall, and Stevens, JJ., disagreed:[a] "It seems to me strange judicial theory that a conviction initially invalid can be resuscitated by postconviction alteration of the statute under which it was obtained. [Even as a policy matter, the] overbreadth doctrine serves to protect constitutionally legitimate speech not merely *ex post,* that is, after the offending statute is enacted, but also *ex ante,* that is, when the legislature is contemplating what sort of statute to enact. If the promulgation of overbroad laws affecting speech was cost free[,] if *no* conviction of constitutionally proscribable conduct would be lost, so long as the offending statute was narrowed before the final appeal—then legislatures would have significantly reduced incentive to stay within constitutional bounds in the first place. [More] fundamentally, however, [it] seems to me that we are only free to pursue policy objectives through the modes of action traditionally followed by the courts and by the law. [I] have heard of a voidable contract, but never of a voidable law. The notion is bizarre."

4. *How substantial is substantial overbreadth?* Five justices addressed the overbreadth question in *Oakes,* supra, but the substantive issue was not resolved. BRENNAN, J., joined by Marshall and Stevens, JJ., objected that the statute would make it criminal for parents "to photograph their infant children or toddlers in the bath or romping naked on the beach." More generally, he argued that the first amendment "blocks the prohibition of nude posing by minors in connection with the production of works of art not depicting lewd behavior. * * * Many of the world's great artists—Degas, Renoir, Donatello, to name but a few—have worked from models under 18 years of age, and many acclaimed photographs have included nude or partially clad minors."

a. Although these five justices agreed that the overbreadth challenge should be entertained, they divided on the merits of the challenge. Scalia, J., joined by Blackmun, J., found no merit in the overbreadth claim (see note 4 infra) and voted to reverse and to remand for determination of the statute's constitutionality as applied. The three remaining justices (see note 4 infra) agreed with the overbreadth challenge and voted to affirm the judgment below. O'Connor, J.'s opinion, therefore, became the plurality opinion, and the Court's judgment was to vacate the judgment below and to remand. In the end, six justices voted against the overbreadth challenge: four because it was moot; two because it did not meet the requirement of substantial overbreadth.

SCALIA, J., joined by Blackmun, J., disagreed: "[G]iven the known extent of the kiddie-porn industry[,] I would estimate that the legitimate scope [of the statute] vastly exceeds the illegitimate. * * * Even assuming that proscribing artistic depictions of preadolescent genitals and postadolescent breasts is impermissible,[2] the body of material that would be covered is, as far as I am aware, insignificant compared with the lawful scope of the statute. That leaves the family photos. [Assuming] that it is unconstitutional (as opposed to merely foolish) to prohibit such photography, I do not think it so common as to make the statute *substantially* overbroad. [My] perception differs, for example, from Justice Brennan's belief that there is an 'abundance of baby and child photographs taken every day' depicting genitals."

Subject to exceptions [a] Ohio prohibited the possession of material showing a minor in a state of nudity. Clyde Osborne was convicted for possessing photographs of a nude male adolescent in a variety of sexually explicit poses.[b] The photographs were secured in his home pursuant to a valid search warrant. On appeal the Ohio Supreme Court narrowed the statute to apply only to depictions of nudity involving a lewd exhibition or a graphic focus on the genitals.

OSBORNE v. OHIO, ___ U.S. ___, 110 S.Ct. 1691, 109 L.Ed.2d 98 (1990), per White, J., upheld the statute as construed and remanded for a showing that the photographs possessed by the defendant met the elements fashioned by the Ohio Supreme Court.

WHITE, J., first distinguished *Stanley v. Georgia*: "In *Stanley,* we struck down a Georgia law outlawing the private possession of obscene material. We recognized that the statute impinged upon Stanley's right to receive information in the privacy of his home, and we found Georgia's justifications for its law inadequate.[3]

"*Stanley* should not be read too broadly. We have previously noted that *Stanley* was a narrow holding and, since the decision in that case, the value of permitting child pornography has been characterized as 'exceedingly modest, if not *de minimis.*' *New York v. Ferber.* But assuming, for the sake of argument, that Osborne has a First Amendment interest in viewing and possessing child pornography, we nonetheless find this case distinct from *Stanley* because the interests underlying child pornography prohibitions far exceed the interests justifying the Georgia law at issue in *Stanley.* * * *

"In *Stanley,* Georgia primarily sought to proscribe the private possession of obscenity because it was concerned that obscenity would poison the minds of its viewers. [The] difference here is obvious: the State does not rely on a paternalistic interest in regulating Osborne's mind. Rather, Ohio has [acted] in order to

2. [Most] adults, I expect, would not hire themselves out as nude models, whatever the intention of the photographer or artist, and however unerotic the pose. There is no cause to think children are less sensitive. It is not unreasonable, therefore, for a State to regard parents' using (or permitting the use) of their children as nude models, or other adults' use of consenting minors, as a form of child exploitation.

a. Ohio excepted material possessed for "bona fide" purposes (e.g., artistic or scientific) or that showed the possessor's child or ward or where the possessor knew that the parents or guardians had consented in writing to the photography and to the manner in which it had been transferred.

b. Two of the photographs focused on the anus of the boy, one with a plastic object apparently inserted; another on his erect penis with an electric object in his hand.

3. We have since indicated that our decision in *Stanley* was "firmly grounded in the First Amendment." *Bowers v. Hardwick.*

protect the victims of child pornography; it hopes to destroy a market for the exploitative use of children. * * *

"Osborne contends that the State should use other measures, besides penalizing possession, to dry up the child pornography market. Osborne points out that in *Stanley* we rejected Georgia's argument that its prohibition on obscenity possession was a necessary incident to its proscription on obscenity distribution. This holding, however, must be viewed in light of the weak interests asserted by the State in that case. *Stanley* itself emphasized that we did not 'mean to express any opinion on statutes making criminal possession of other types of printed, filmed, or recorded materials. * * * In such cases, compelling reasons may exist for overriding the right of the individual to possess those materials.' [5]

"Given the importance of the State's interest in protecting the victims of child pornography, we cannot fault Ohio for attempting to stamp out this vice at all levels in the distribution chain. * * *

"Osborne contends that it was impermissible for the Ohio Supreme Court to apply its [narrowed] construction of the statute when evaluating his overbreadth claim.[c] Our cases, however, have long held that a statute as construed 'may be applied to conduct occurring prior to the construction, provided such application affords fair warning to the defendan[t].' [12] [That] Osborne's photographs of adolescent boys in sexually explicit situations constitute child pornography hardly needs elaboration. Therefore, although [Ohio's statute] as written may have been imprecise at its fringes, someone in Osborne's position would not be surprised to learn that his possession of the four photographs at issue in this case constituted a crime. * * *

"Finally, despite Osborne's contention to the contrary, we do not believe that *Massachusetts v. Oakes,* supports his theory of this case.

"[F]ive of the *Oakes* Justices feared that if we allowed a legislature to correct its mistakes without paying for them (beyond the inconvenience of passing a new law), we would decrease the legislature's incentive to draft a narrowly tailored law in the first place.

"Legislators who know they can cure their own mistakes by amendment without significant cost may not be as careful to avoid drafting overbroad statutes as they might otherwise be. But a similar effect will not be likely if a judicial construction of a statute to eliminate overbreadth is allowed to be applied in the case before the Court. This is so primarily because the legisla-

5. [T]he *Stanley* Court cited illicit possession of defense information as an example of the type of offense for which compelling state interests might justify a ban on possession. *Stanley,* however, did not suggest that this crime exhausted the entire category of proscribable offenses.

c. Given the statutory limitations and exceptions (see fn. a supra), the Court expressed doubt that the statute was substantially overbroad even without the Ohio Supreme Court's limiting construction although it conceded that the statute by its terms seemed to criminalize some constitutionally protected conduct.

12. This principle, of course, accords with the rationale underlying overbreadth challenges. We normally do not allow a defendant to challenge a law as it is applied to others. In the First Amendment context, however, we have said that "[b]ecause of the sensitive nature of constitutionally protected expression, we have not required that all those subject to overbroad regulations risk prosecution to test their rights. For free expression—of transcendent value to all society, and not merely to those exercising their rights—might be the loser." But once a statute is authoritatively construed, there is no longer any danger that protected speech will be deterred and therefore no longer any reason to entertain the defendant's challenge to the statute on its face.

tures cannot be sure that the statute, when examined by a court, will be saved by a narrowing construction rather than invalidated for overbreadth. In the latter event, there could be no convictions under that law even of those whose own conduct is unprotected by the First Amendment. Even if construed to obviate overbreadth, applying the statute to pending cases might be barred by the Due Process Clause. Thus, careless drafting cannot be considered to be cost free based on the power of the courts to eliminate overbreadth by statutory construction. * * *

"To conclude, although we find Osborne's First Amendment arguments unpersuasive, we reverse his conviction and remand for a new trial in order to ensure that Osborne's conviction stemmed from a finding that the State had proved each of the elements of the Ohio statute." [d]

BRENNAN, J., joined by Marshall, J., and Stevens, J., dissented: "As written, the Ohio statute is plainly overbroad.[2] * * *

"Wary of the statute's use of the 'nudity' standard, the Ohio Supreme Court construed § 2907.323(A)(3) to apply only 'where such nudity constitutes a lewd exhibition or involves a graphic focus on the genitals.' The 'lewd exhibition' and 'graphic focus' tests not only fail to cure the overbreadth of the statute, but they also create a new problem of vagueness. * * *

"The Ohio law is distinguishable [from *Ferber*] for several reasons. First, the New York statute did not criminalize materials with a '*graphic focus*' on the genitals, and, as discussed further below, Ohio's 'graphic focus' test is impermissibly capacious. Even setting aside the 'graphic focus' element, the Ohio Supreme Court's narrowing construction is still overbroad because it focuses on 'lewd exhibitions of *nudity*' rather than 'lewd exhibitions of *the genitals*' in the context of *sexual conduct,* as in the New York statute at issue in *Ferber.*[e] Ohio law defines 'nudity' to include depictions of pubic areas, buttocks, the female breast, and covered male genitals 'in a discernibly turgid state,' *as well as* depictions of the genitals. On its face, then, the Ohio law is much broader than New York's. * * *

d. Defendant's attorney did not ask for a scienter instruction (even though Ohio law generally provides for a scienter requirement in criminal cases) and the Court stated that Osborne could be precluded from raising the question on remand. But Osborne did raise the overbreadth issue and was, therefore, entitled to dispute the application of the statute, as construed, to the photographs in his possession even though Osborne's attorney had not specifically objected to the jury instructions.

Blackmun, J., concurring, agreed with the dissent's position that due process entitled the defendant to instructions on "lewd exhibition" and "graphic focus" without regard to whether an objection had been lodged at trial.

2. The Court hints that § 2907.323's exemptions and "proper purposes" provisions might save it from being overbroad. I disagree. The enumerated "proper purposes" (*e.g.,* a "bona fide artistic, medical, scientific, educational * * * or other proper purpose") are simultaneously too vague and too narrow. What is an acceptable "artistic" purpose? Would erotic art along the lines of Robert Mapplethorpe's qualify? What is a valid "scientific" or "educational" purpose? What about sex manuals? What is a permissible "other proper purpose"? What about photos taken for one purpose and recirculated for other, more prurient purposes? The "proper purposes" standard appears to create problems analogous to those this Court has encountered in describing the "redeeming social importance" of obscenity.

At the same time, however, Ohio's list of "proper purposes" is too limited; it excludes such obviously permissible uses as the commercial distribution of fashion photographs or the simple exchange of pictures among family and friends. Thus, a neighbor or grandparent who receives a photograph of an unclothed toddler might be subject to criminal sanctions.

e. The Court read the Ohio Court's opinion to refer to the lewd exhibition of the genitals rather than the lewd exhibition of nudity, but maintained that the distinction was not important anyway.

"Indeed, the broad definition of nudity in the Ohio statutory scheme means that 'child pornography' could include any photograph depicting a 'lewd exhibition' of even a small portion of a minor's buttocks or any part of the female breast below the nipple. Pictures of topless bathers at a Mediterranean beach, of teenagers in revealing dresses, and even of toddlers romping unclothed, all might be prohibited.[5]

"It might be objected that many of these depictions of nudity do not amount to 'lewd exhibitions.' But in the absence of *any* authoritative definition of that phrase by the Ohio Supreme Court, we cannot predict which ones. * * *

"The Ohio Supreme Court, moreover, did not specify the perspective from which 'lewdness' is to be determined. A 'reasonable' person's view of 'lewdness'? A reasonable pedophile's? An 'average' person applying contemporary local community standards? Statewide standards? Nationwide standards? In sum, the addition of a 'lewd exhibition' standard does not narrow adequately the statute's reach. If anything, it creates a new problem of vagueness, affording the public little notice of the statute's ambit and providing an avenue for 'policemen, prosecutors, and juries to pursue their personal predilections.'[12] Given the important First Amendment interests at issue, the vague, broad sweep of the 'lewd exhibition' language means that it cannot cure [the overbreadth problem].

"The Ohio Supreme Court also added a 'graphic focus' element to the nudity definition. This phrase, a stranger to obscenity regulation, suffers from the same vagueness difficulty as 'lewd exhibition.' Although the Ohio Supreme Court failed to elaborate what a 'graphic focus' might be, the test appears to involve nothing more than a subjective estimation of the centrality or prominence of the genitals in a picture or other representation. Not only is this factor dependent on the perspective and idiosyncrasies of the observer, it also is unconnected to whether the material at issue merits constitutional protection. Simple nudity, no matter how prominent or 'graphic,' is within the bounds of the First Amendment. Michelangelo's 'David' might be said to have a 'graphic focus' on the genitals, for it plainly portrays them in a manner unavoidable to even a casual observer. Similarly, a painting of a partially clad girl could be said to involve a 'graphic focus,' depending on the picture's lighting and emphasis, as could the depictions of nude children on the friezes that adorn our Courtroom. Even a photograph of a child running naked on the beach or playing in the bathtub might run afoul of the law, depending on the focus and camera angle.

"In sum, the 'lewd exhibition' and 'graphic focus' tests are too vague to serve as any workable limit. Because the statute, even as construed authoritatively by the Ohio Supreme Court, is impermissibly overbroad, I would hold that appellant cannot be retried under it.

"Even if the statute was not overbroad, our decision in *Stanley v. Georgia* forbids the criminalization of appellant's private possession in his home of the materials at issue. [Appellant] was convicted for possessing four photographs of

5. [A] well-known commercial advertisement for a suntan lotion shows a dog pulling down the bottom half of a young girl's bikini, revealing a stark contrast between her suntanned back and pale buttocks. That this advertisement might be illegal in Ohio is an absurd yet altogether too conceivable conclusion under the language of the [statute.]

12. The danger of discriminatory enforcement assumes particular importance of the context of the instant case, which involves child pornography with male homosexual overtones. Sadly, evidence indicates that the overwhelming majority of arrests for violations of "lewdness" laws involve male homosexuals.

nude minors, seized from a desk drawer in the bedroom of his house during a search executed pursuant to a warrant. Appellant testified that he had been given the pictures in his home by a friend. There was no evidence that the photographs had been produced commercially or distributed. All were kept in an album that appellant had assembled for his personal use and had possessed privately for several years.

"In these circumstances, the Court's focus on *Ferber* rather than *Stanley* is misplaced. [*Ferber*] did nothing more than place child pornography on the same level of First Amendment protection as *obscene* adult pornography, meaning that its production and distribution could be proscribed. The distinction established in *Stanley* between *what* materials may be regulated and *how* they may be regulated still stands. * * *

"At bottom, the Court today is so disquieted by the possible exploitation of children in the *production* of the pornography that it is willing to tolerate the imposition of criminal penalties for simple *possession.* While I share the majority's concerns, I do not believe that it has struck the proper balance between the First Amendment and the State's interests, especially in light of the other means available to Ohio to protect children from exploitation and the State's failure to demonstrate a causal link between a ban on possession of child pornography and a decrease in its production. * * *

"When speech is eloquent and the ideas expressed lofty, it is easy to find restrictions on them invalid. But were the First Amendment limited to such discourse, our freedom would be sterile indeed. Mr. Osborne's pictures may be distasteful, but the Constitution guarantees both his right to possess them privately and his right to avoid punishment under an overbroad law. I respectfully dissent."

B. HARM TO WOMEN: FEMINISM AND PORNOGRAPHY

Catharine MacKinnon and Andrea Dworkin have drafted an anti-pornography ordinance that has been considered in a number of jurisdictions.[a]

PROPOSED LOS ANGELES COUNTY ANTI-PORNOGRAPHY CIVIL RIGHTS LAW

Section 1. Statement of Policy

Pornography is sex discrimination. It exists in the County of Los Angeles, posing a substantial threat to the health, safety, welfare and equality of citizens in the community. Existing state and federal laws are inadequate to solve these problems in the County of Los Angeles.

Section 2. Findings

Pornography is a systematic practice of exploitation and subordination based on sex which differentially harms women. The harm of pornography includes dehumanization, sexual exploitation, forced sex, forced prostitution, physical injury, and social and sexual terrorism and inferiority presented as entertainment. The bigotry and contempt pornography promotes, with the acts of

a. The ordinance was first considered in Minneapolis. For political, rhetorical, and sociological discussion, see Brest & Vandenberg, *Politics, Feminism, and the Constitution: The Anti-Pornography Movement in Minneapolis,* 39 Stan.L.Rev. 607 (1987). Different versions of the ordinance were passed in Indianapolis, Indiana (see *Hudnut,* p. 784 infra) and Bellingham, Washington (see Baldwin, *Pornography and the Traffic in Women,* 1 Yale J.L. & Fem. 111 (1989)). Both versions were declared unconstitutional.

aggression it fosters, diminish opportunities for equality of rights in employment, education, property, public accommodations and public services; create public and private harassment, persecution and denigration; promote injury and degradation such as rape, battery, child sexual abuse, and prostitution and inhibit just enforcement of laws against these acts; contribute significantly to restricting women in particular from full exercise of citizenship and participation in public life, including in neighborhoods; damage relations between the sexes; and undermine women's equal exercise of rights to speech and action guaranteed to all citizens under the Constitutions and laws of the United States, the State of California and the County of Los Angeles.

Section 3. Definitions

1. *Pornography* is the graphic sexually explicit subordination of women through pictures and/or words that also includes one or more of the following: (i) women are presented dehumanized as sexual objects, things or commodities; or (ii) women are presented as sexual objects who enjoy pain or humiliation; or (iii) women are presented as sexual objects who experience sexual pleasure in being raped; or (iv) women are presented as sexual objects tied up or cut up or mutilated or bruised or physically hurt; or (v) women are presented in postures of sexual submission, servility, or display; or (vi) women's body parts—including but not limited to vaginas, breasts, or buttocks—are exhibited such that women are reduced to those parts; or (vii) women are presented as whores by nature; or (viii) women are presented as being penetrated by objects or animals; or (ix) women are presented in scenarios of degradation, injury, torture, shown as filthy or inferior, bleeding, bruised or hurt in a context that makes these conditions sexual.

2. The use of men, children, or transsexuals in the place of women in (1) above is also pornography for purposes of this law.

Section 4. Unlawful Practices

1. *Coercion into pornography*: It shall be sex discrimination to coerce, intimidate, or fraudulently induce (hereafter, "coerce") any person, including transsexual, into performing for pornography, which injury may date from any appearance or sale of any product(s) of such performance(s). The maker(s), seller(s), exhibitor(s) and/or distributor(s) of said pornography may be sued, including for an injunction to eliminate the product(s) of the performance(s) from the public view.

Proof of one or more of the following facts or conditions shall not, without more, negate a finding of coercion:

(i) that the person is a woman; or

(ii) that the person is or has been a prostitute; or

(iii) that the person has attained the age of majority; or

(iv) that the person is connected by blood or marriage to anyone involved in or related to the making of the pornography; or

(v) that the person has previously had, or been thought to have had, sexual relations with anyone, including anyone involved in or related to the making of the pornography; or

(vi) that the person has previously posed for sexually explicit pictures with or for anyone, including anyone involved in or related to the making of the pornography at issue; or

(vii) that anyone else, including a spouse or other relative, has given permission on the person's behalf; or

(viii) that the person actually consented to a use of the performance that is changed into pornography; or

(ix) that the person knew that the purpose of the acts or events in question was to make pornography; or

(x) that the person showed no resistance or appeared to cooperate actively in the photographic sessions or in the events that produced the pornography; or

(xi) that the person signed a contract, or made statements affirming a willingness to cooperate in the production of pornography; or

(xii) that no physical force, threats, or weapons were used in the making of the pornography; or

(xiii) that the person was paid or otherwise compensated.

2. *Trafficking in pornography:* It shall be sex discrimination to produce, sell, exhibit, or distribute pornography, including through private clubs.

(i) City, state, and federally funded public libraries or private and public university and college libraries in which pornography is available for study, including on open shelves but excluding special display presentations, shall not be construed to be trafficking in pornography.

(ii) Isolated passages or isolated parts shall not be actionable under this section.

(iii) Any woman has a claim hereunder as a woman acting against the subordination of women. Any man, child, or transsexual who alleges injury by pornography in the way women are injured by it also has a claim.

3. *Forcing pornography on a person:* It shall be sex discrimination to force pornography on a person, including child or transsexual, in any place of employment, education, home, or public place. Only the perpetrator of the force and/or institution responsible for the force may be sued.

4. *Assault or physical attack due to pornography:* It shall be sex discrimination to assault, physically attack or injure any person, including child or transsexual, in a way that is directly caused by specific pornography. The perpetrator of the assault or attack may be sued. The maker(s), distributor(s), seller(s), and/or exhibitor(s) may also be sued, including for an injunction against the specific pornography's further exhibition, distribution or sale.

Section 5. Defenses

1. It shall not be a defense that the defendant in an action under this law did not know or intend that the materials were pornography or sex discrimination.

2. No damages or compensation for losses shall be recoverable under Sec. 4(2) or other than against the perpetrator of the assault or attack in Sec. 4(4) unless the defendant knew or had reason to know that the materials were pornography.

3. In actions under Sec. 4(2) or other than against the perpetrator of the assault or attack in Sec. 4(4), no damages or compensation for losses shall be recoverable against maker(s) for pornography made, against distributor(s) for pornography distributed, against seller(s) for pornography sold, or against exhibitor(s) for pornography exhibited, prior to the effective date of this law.

Section 6. Enforcement

a. Civil Action: Any person, or their estate, aggrieved by violations of this law may enforce its provisions by means of a civil action. No criminal penalties shall attach for any violation of the provisions of this law. Relief for violations of this law, except as expressly restricted or precluded herein, may include compensatory and punitive damages and reasonable attorney's fees, costs and disbursements.

b. Injunction: Any person who violates this law may be enjoined except that:

(i) In actions under Sec. 4(2), and other than against the perpetrator of the assault or attack under Sec. 4(4), no temporary or permanent injunction shall issue prior to a final judicial determination that the challenged activities constitute a violation of this law.

(ii) No temporary or permanent injunction shall extend beyond such material(s) that, having been described with reasonable specificity by the injunction, have been determined to be validly proscribed under this law.

Section 7. Severability

Should any part(s) of this law be found legally invalid, the remaining part(s) remain valid. A judicial declaration that any part(s) of this law cannot be applied validly in a particular manner or to a particular case or category of cases shall not affect the validity of that part(s) as otherwise applied, unless such other application would clearly frustrate the intent of the Board of Supervisors in adopting this law.

Section 8. Limitation of Action

Actions under this law must be filed within one year of the alleged discriminatory acts.

Notes and Questions

1. *Relationship between obscenity and pornography.* Consider Andrea Dworkin, *Against the Male Flood: Censorship, Pornography, and Equality,* 8 Harv. Women's L.J. 1, 8–9 (1985): "What is at stake in obscenity law is always erection: under what conditions, in what circumstances, how, by whom, by what materials men want it produced in themselves. Men have made this public policy. Why they want to regulate their own erections through law is a question of endless interest and importance to feminists. * * *

"The insult pornography offers, invariably, to sex is accomplished in the active subordination of women: the creation of a sexual dynamic in which the putting-down of women, the suppression of women, and ultimately the brutalization of women, *is* what sex is taken to be. Obscenity in law, and in what it does socially, is erection. Law recognizes the act in this. Pornography, however, is a broader, more comprehensive act, because it crushes a whole class of people through violence and subjugation: and sex is the vehicle that does the crushing. The penis is not the test, as it is in obscenity. Instead, the status of women is the issue. Erection is implicated in the subordinating, but who it reaches and how are the pressing legal and social questions. Pornography, unlike obscenity, is a discrete, identifiable system of sexual exploitation that hurts women as a class by creating inequality and abuse."

Consider MacKinnon, *Pornography, Civil Rights, and Speech,* 20 Harv.Civ. Rts.-Civ.Lib.L.Rev. 1, 50–52 & 16–17 (1985): "To reach the magnitude of this problem on the scale it exists, our law makes trafficking in pornography—production, sale, exhibition, or distribution—actionable. Under the obscenity rubric, much legal and psychological scholarship has centered on a search for the elusive link between pornography defined as obscenity and harm. They have looked high and low—in the mind of the male consumer, in society or in its 'moral fabric,' in correlations between variations in levels of anti-social acts and liberalization of obscenity laws. The only harm they have found has been one they have attributed to 'the social interests in order and morality.' Until recently, no one looked very persistently for harm to women, particularly harm to women through men. The rather obvious fact that the sexes *relate* has been overlooked in the inquiry into the male consumer and his mind. The pornography doesn't just drop out of the sky, go into his head and stop there. Specifically, men rape, batter, prostitute, molest, and sexually harass women. Under conditions of inequality, they also hire, fire, promote, and grade women, decide how much or whether or not we are worth paying and for what, define and approve and disapprove of women in ways that count, that determine our lives.

"In pornography, there it is, in one place, all of the abuses that women had to struggle so long even to begin to articulate, all the *unspeakable* abuse: the rape, the battery, the sexual harassment, the prostitution, and the sexual abuse of children. Only in the pornography it is called something else: sex, sex, sex, sex, and sex, respectively. Pornography sexualizes rape, battery, sexual harassment, prostitution, and child sexual abuse; it thereby celebrates, promotes, authorizes, and legitimizes them. More generally, it eroticizes the dominance and submission that is the dynamic common to them all. It makes hierarchy sexy and calls that 'the truth about sex' or just a mirror of reality." See generally Dworkin, *Pornography: Men Possessing Women* (1981). MacKinnon, *Toward a Feminist Theory of the State* 195–214 (1989); MacKinnon, *Feminism Unmodified* 127–228 (1987).

2. *The trafficking section.* Is the trafficking section constitutional under *Miller?* Consider the following hypothetical commentary: "The Dworkin-MacKinnon proposal focuses on a narrower class of material than *Miller* because it excludes erotic materials that do not involve subordination. That class of material upon which it does focus appeals to prurient interest because it is graphic and sexually explicit. Moreover, the eroticization of dominance in the ways specified in the ordinance is so patently offensive to community standards that it can be said as a matter of law that this class of materials lacks *serious* literary, artistic, political, or scientific value as a matter of law." Do you agree?

Is there a good analogy to *Beauharnais?* To *Ferber?* Did more or less harm exist in *Gertz? Miller? Ferber?* Was there more or less of a threat to first amendment values in *Gertz? Miller? Ferber?* Should this be accepted as a new category? Consider, Kaminer, *Pornography and the First Amendment: Prior Restraints and Private Action,* 239, 245 in *Take Back the Night: Women on Pornography* (Lederer ed. 1980): "The Women's Movement is a civil rights movement, and we should appreciate the importance of individual freedom of choice and the danger of turning popular sentiment into law in areas affecting individual privacy.

"Legislative or judicial control of pornography is simply not possible without breaking down the legal principles and procedures that are essential to our own right to speak and, ultimately, our freedom to control our own lives. We must continue to organize against pornography and the degradation and abuse of women, but we must not ask the government to take up our struggle for us. The power it will assume to do so will be far more dangerous to us all than the 'power' of pornography." [b]

3. *The pornography definition.* Is the proposed definition too vague? Is it more or less vague than the terminology employed in *Miller?* Is there a core of clear meaning? How would you revise it to clarify its meaning? Is the definition overbroad? What revisions, if any, would you suggest to narrow its scope?

Consider Emerson, *Pornography and the First Amendment: A Reply to Professor MacKinnon,* 3 Yale L. & Pol. Rev. 130, 131–32 (1985): "The sweep of the Indianapolis Ordinance is breathtaking. It would subject to governmental ban virtually all depictions of rape, verbal or pictorial, and a substantial proportion of other presentations of sexual encounters. More specifically, it would outlaw such works of literature as the *Arabian Nights,* John Cleland's *Fanny Hill,* Henry Miller's *Tropic of Cancer,* William Faulkner's *Sanctuary,* and Norman Mailer's *Ancient Evenings,* to name but a few. The ban would extend from Greek mythology and Shakespeare to the millions of copies of 'romance novels' now being sold in the supermarkets. It would embrace much of the world's art, from ancient carvings to Picasso, well-known films too numerous to mention, and a large amount of commercial advertising.

"The scope of the Indianapolis Ordinance is not accidental. Nor could it be limited by more precise drafting without defeating the purpose of its authors. As Professor MacKinnon emphasizes, male domination has deep, pervasive and ancient roots in our society, so it is not surprising that our literature, art, entertainment and commerical practices are permeated by attitudes and behavior that create and reflect the inferior status of women. If the answer to the problem, as Professor MacKinnon describes it, is government suppression of sexual expression that contributes to female subordination, then the net of restraint has to be cast on a nearly limitless scale. Even narrowing the proscribed area to depictions of sexual activities involving violence would outlaw a large segment of the world's literature and art."

b. Compare Hunter & Law, *Brief Amici Curiae of Feminist Anti-Censorship Taskforce* (on appeal in *Hudnut,* below), 21 U.Mich.J.L. Ref. 69, 109 & 129–30 (1987–88). The ordinance conceivably "would require the judiciary to impose its views of correct sexuality on a diverse community. The inevitable result would be to disapprove those images that are least conventional and privilege those that are closest to majoritarian beliefs about proper sexuality. [Moreover] [b]y defining sexually explicit images of women as subordinating and degrading to them, the ordinance reinforces the stereotypical view that 'good' women do not seek and enjoy sex. [Finally], the ordinance perpetuates a stereotype of women as helpless victims, incapable of consent, and in need of protection."

For collections of feminist perspectives, see *Take Back the Night,* supra; Burstyn, ed., *Women Against Censorship* (1985); Snitow, Stansell & Thompson, etc., *Powers of Desire* 419–67 (1983). For a variety of views (including feminist views), see Rhode, *Justice and Gender,* 263–73 (1989); Tushnet, *Red, White, and Blue* 293–312 (1988); Downs, *The Attorney General's Commission and the New Politics of Pornography,* 1987 Am.B.Found.Res.J. 641; Gey, *The Apologetics of Suppression,* 86 Mich.L.Rev. 1564 (1988); Hoffman, *Feminism, Pornography, and the Law,* 133 U.Pa.L.Rev. 497 (1985); Post, *Cultural Heterogeneity and the Law,* 76 Calif.L.Rev. 297 (1988); Richards, *Pornography Commissions and the First Amendment,* 39 Me.L.Rev. 275 (1987); Schauer, *Causation Theory and the Causes of Sexual Violence,* 1987 Am.B.Found.Res.J. 737; Sherry, *An Essay Concerning Toleration,* 71 Minn. L.Rev. 963 (1987); Stone, *Anti-Pornography Legislation as Viewpoint-Discrimination,* 9 Harv.J.Pub.Pol'y 461 (1986); Strossen, *The Convergence of Feminist and Civil Liberties Principles in the Pornography Debate,* 62 N.Y. U.L.Rev. 201 (1987); Sunstein, *Pornography and the First Amendment,* 1986 Duke L.J. 589; West, *The Feminist-Conservative Anti-Pornography Alliance and the 1986 Attorney General's Commission on Pornography Report,* 1987 Am.B.Found.Res.J. 681; Note, *Violent Pornography and the Obscenity Doctrine,* 75 Geo.L.J. 1475 (1987); Note, *Anti-Pornography Laws and First Amendment Values,* 98 Harv. L.Rev. 460 (1984). See also *American Booksellers Ass'n v. Hudnut,* 771 F.2d 323 (7th Cir.1985) (declaring Indianapolis ordinance unconstitutional).

Is the proposed ordinance susceptible to a narrower construction than that offered by Professor Emerson?

4. *The coercion into pornography section.* Is this part of the proposed ordinance a straightforward application of *Ferber?* Is the conception of coercion constitutional? What was the conception in *Ferber?* If modifications are needed, what should they be?

5. *The assault provision.* Should the maker of a pornographic work be responsible for assaults prompted by the work? Should the maker of non-pornographic works be responsible for imitative assaults. In *Olivia N. v. NBC,* 126 Cal.App.3d 488, 178 Cal.Rptr. 888 (1981), the victim of a sexual assault allegedly imitating a sexual assault in NBC's "Born Innocent" sued the network. Olivia N. claimed that NBC negligently exposed her to serious risk because it knew or should have known that someone would imitate the act portrayed in the movie. Suppose Olivia N. could show that NBC had been advised that such an assault was likely if the movie were shown? Should a court analogize to cases like *Gertz?* The California court ruled that Olivia N. could not prevail unless she met the *Brandenburg* standard.[c]

The Indianapolis version of the anti-pornography civil rights ordinance was struck down in AMERICAN BOOKSELLERS ASS'N, INC. v. HUDNUT, 771 F.2d 323 (7th Cir.1985), affirmed, 475 U.S. 1001, 106 S.Ct. 1172, 89 L.Ed.2d 291 (1986). The Seventh Circuit, per EASTERBROOK, J., ruled that the definition of pornography infected the entire ordinance (including provisions against trafficking, coercion into pornography, forcing pornography on a person, and assault or physical attack due to pornography) because it impermissibly discriminated on the basis of point of view: "Indianapolis enacted an ordinance defining 'pornography' as a practice that discriminates against women. * * *

" 'Pornography' under the ordinance is 'the graphic sexually explicit subordination of women, whether in pictures or in words, that also includes one or more of the following: (1) Women are presented as sexual objects who enjoy pain or humiliation; or (2) Women are presented as sexual objects who experience sexual pleasure in being raped; or (3) Women are presented as sexual objects tied up or cut up or mutilated or bruised or physically hurt, or as dismembered or truncated or fragmented or severed into body parts; or (4) Women are presented as being penetrated by objects or animals; or (5) Women are presented in scenarios of degradation, injury, abasement, torture, shown as filthy or inferior, bleeding, bruised, or hurt in a context that makes these conditions sexual; or (6) Women are presented as sexual objects for domination, conquest, violation, exploitation, possession, or use, or through postures or positions of servility or submission or display.'

"The statute provides that the 'use of men, children, or transsexuals in the place of women in paragraphs (1) through (6) above shall also constitute pornography under this section.' The ordinance as passed in April 1984 defined 'sexually explicit' to mean actual or simulated intercourse or the uncovered exhibition of the genitals, buttocks or anus. An amendment in June 1984 deleted this provision, leaving the term undefined.

"The Indianapolis ordinance does not refer to the prurient interest, to offensiveness, or to the standards of the community. It demands attention to

c. For relevant commentary, see Balkin, *The Rhetoric of Responsibility,* 76 Va.L.Rev. 197 (1990); Schauer, *Mrs. Palsgraf and the First Amendment,* 47 Wash. & Lee L.Rev. 161 (1990).

particular depictions, not to the work judged as a whole. It is irrelevant under the ordinance whether the work has literary, artistic, political, or scientific value. The City and many amici point to these omissions as virtues. They maintain that pornography influences attitudes, and the statute is a way to alter the socialization of men and women rather than to vindicate community standards of offensiveness. And as one of the principal drafters of the ordinance has asserted, 'if a woman is subjected, why should it matter that the work has other value?' MacKinnon, *Pornography, Civil Rights, and Speech,* 20 Harv.Civ.Rts.—Civ.Lib.L.Rev. 1, 21 (1985).

"Civil rights groups and feminists have entered this case as amici on both sides. Those supporting the ordinance say that it will play an important role in reducing the tendency of men to view women as sexual objects, a tendency that leads to both unacceptable attitudes and discrimination in the workplace and violence away from it. Those opposing the ordinance point out that much radical feminist literature is explicit and depicts women in ways forbidden by the ordinance and that the ordinance would reopen old battles. It is unclear how Indianapolis would treat works from James Joyce's *Ulysses* to Homer's *Iliad;* both depict women as submissive objects for conquest and domination.

"We do not try to balance the arguments for and against an ordinance such as this. The ordinance discriminates on the ground of the content of the speech. Speech treating women in the approved way—in sexual encounters 'premised on equality' (MacKinnon, supra, at 22)—is lawful no matter how sexually explicit. Speech treating women in the disapproved way—as submissive in matters sexual or as enjoying humiliation—is unlawful no matter how significant the literary, artistic, or political qualities of the work taken as a whole. The state may not ordain preferred viewpoints in this way. The Constitution forbids the state to declare one perspective right and silence opponents. * * *

" 'If there is any fixed star in our constitutional constellation, it is that no official, high or petty, can prescribe what shall be orthodox in politics, nationalism, religion, or other matters of opinion or force citizens to confess by word or act their faith therein.' *West Virginia State Bd. of Educ. v. Barnette.* Under the First Amendment the government must leave to the people the evaluation of ideas. Bald or subtle, an idea is as powerful as the audience allows it to be. A belief may be pernicious—the beliefs of Nazis led to the death of millions, those of the Klan to the repression of millions. A pernicious belief may prevail. Totalitarian governments today rule much of the planet, practicing suppression of billions and spreading dogma that may enslave others. One of the things that separates our society from theirs is our absolute right to propagate opinions that the government finds wrong or even hateful. * * *

"Under the ordinance graphic sexually explicit speech is 'pornography' or not depending on the perspective the author adopts. Speech that 'subordinates' women and also, for example, presents women as enjoying pain, humiliation, or rape, or even simply presents women in 'positions of servility or submission or display' is forbidden, no matter how great the literary or political value of the work taken as a whole. Speech that portrays women in positions of equality is lawful, no matter how graphic the sexual content. This is thought control. It establishes an 'approved' view of women, of how they may react to sexual encounters, of how the sexes may relate to each other. Those who espouse the approved view may use sexual images; those who do not, may not.

"Indianapolis justifies the ordinance on the ground that pornography affects thoughts. Men who see women depicted as subordinate are more likely to treat them so. Pornography is an aspect of dominance.[1] It does not persuade people so much as change them. It works by socializing, by establishing the expected and the permissible. In this view pornography is not an idea; pornography is the injury.

"There is much to this perspective. Beliefs are also facts. People often act in accordance with the images and patterns they find around them. People raised in a religion tend to accept the tenets of that religion, often without independent examination. People taught from birth that black people are fit only for slavery rarely rebelled against that creed; beliefs coupled with the self-interest of the masters established a social structure that inflicted great harm while enduring for centuries. Words and images act at the level of the subconscious before they persuade at the level of the conscious. Even the truth has little chance unless a statement fits within the framework of beliefs that may never have been subjected to rational study.

"Therefore we accept the premises of this legislation. Depictions of subordination tend to perpetuate subordination. The subordinate status of women in turn leads to affront and lower pay at work, insult and injury at home, battery and rape on the streets.[2] In the language of the legislature, '[p]ornography is central in creating and maintaining sex as a basis of discrimination. Pornography is a systematic practice of exploitation and subordination based on sex which differentially harms women. The bigotry and contempt it produces, with the acts of aggression it fosters, harm women's opportunities for equality and rights [of all kinds].'

"Yet this simply demonstrates the power of pornography as speech. All of these unhappy effects depend on mental intermediation. Pornography affects how people see the world, their fellows, and social relations. If pornography is

1. "Pornography constructs what a woman is in terms of its view of what men want sexually. * * * Pornography's world of equality is a harmonious and balanced place. Men and women are perfectly complementary and perfectly bipolar. [All] the ways men love to take and violate women, women love to be taken and violated. [What] pornography *does* goes beyond its content: It eroticizes hierarchy, it sexualizes inequality. It makes dominance and submission sex. Inequality is its central dynamic; the illusion of freedom coming together with the reality of force is central to its working. [P]ornography is neither harmless fantasy nor a corrupt and confused misrepresentation of an otherwise neutral and healthy sexual situation. It institutionalizes the sexuality of male supremacy, fusing the erotization of dominance and submission with the social construction of male and female. * * * Men treat women as who they see women as being. Pornography constructs who that is. Men's power over women means that the way men see women defines who women can be. Pornography [is] a sexual reality." MacKinnon, supra, at 17–18 (note omitted, emphasis in original). See also Dworkin, *Pornography: Men Possessing Women* (1981). A national commission in Canada recently adopted a similar rationale for controlling pornography. Special Commission on Pornography and Prostitution, 1 *Pornography and Prostitution in Canada* 49–59 (1985).

2. MacKinnon's article collects empirical work that supports this proposition. The social science studies are very difficult to interpret, however, and they conflict. Because much of the effect of speech comes through a process of socialization, it is difficult to measure incremental benefits and injuries caused by particular speech. Several psychologists have found, for example, that those who see violent, sexually explicit films tend to have more violent thoughts. But how often does this lead to actual violence? National commissions on obscenity here, in the United Kingdom, and in Canada have found that it is not possible to demonstrate a direct link between obscenity and rape or exhibitionism. The several opinions in *Miller v. California* discuss the U.S. commission. See also *Report of the Committee on Obscenity and Film Censorship* 61–95 (Home Office, Her Majesty's Stationery Office, 1979); 1 *Pornography and Prostitution in Canada* 71–73, 95–103. In saying that we accept the finding that pornography as the ordinance defines it leads to unhappy consequences, we mean only that there is evidence to this effect, that this evidence is consistent with much human experience, and that as judges we must accept the legislative resolution of such disputed empirical questions.

what pornography does, so is other speech. Hitler's orations affected how some Germans saw Jews. Communism is a world view, not simply a *Manifesto* by Marx and Engels or a set of speeches. Efforts to suppress communist speech in the United States were based on the belief that the public acceptability of such ideas would increase the likelihood of totalitarian government. [Many] people believe that the existence of television, apart from the content of specific programs, leads to intellectual laziness, to a penchant for violence, to many other ills. The Alien and Sedition Acts passed during the administration of John Adams rested on a sincerely held belief that disrespect for the government leads to social collapse and revolution—a belief with support in the history of many nations. Most governments of the world act on this empirical regularity, suppressing critical speech. In the United States, however, the strength of the support for this belief is irrelevant. Seditious libel is protected speech unless the danger is not only grave but also imminent. See *New York Times v. Sullivan;* cf. *Brandenburg v. Ohio.*

"Racial bigotry, anti-semitism, violence on television, reporters' biases—these and many more influence the culture and shape our socialization. None is directly answerable by more speech, unless that speech too finds its place in the popular culture. Yet all is protected as speech, however insidious. Any other answer leaves the government in control of all of the institutions of culture, the great censor and director of which thoughts are good for us.

"Sexual responses often are unthinking responses, and the association of sexual arousal with the subordination of women therefore may have a substantial effect. But almost all cultural stimuli provoke unconscious responses. Religious ceremonies condition their participants. Teachers convey messages by selecting what not to cover; the implicit message about what is off limits or unthinkable may be more powerful than the messages for which they present rational argument. Television scripts contain unarticulated assumptions. People may be conditioned in subtle ways. If the fact that speech plays a role in a process of conditioning were enough to permit governmental regulation, that would be the end of freedom of speech. * * *

"Much of Indianapolis's argument rests on the belief that when speech is 'unanswerable,' and the metaphor that there is a 'marketplace of ideas' does not apply, the First Amendment does not apply either. The metaphor is honored; Milton's *Aeropagitica* and John Stewart Mill's *On Liberty* defend freedom of speech on the ground that the truth will prevail, and many of the most important cases under the First Amendment recite this position. The Framers undoubtedly believed it. As a general matter it is true. But the Constitution does not make the dominance of truth a necessary condition of freedom of speech. To say that it does would be to confuse an outcome of free speech with a necessary condition for the application of the amendment.

"A power to limit speech on the ground that truth has not yet prevailed and is not likely to prevail implies the power to declare truth. At some point the government must be able to say (as Indianapolis has said): 'We know what the truth is, yet a free exchange of speech has not driven out falsity, so that we must now prohibit falsity.' If the government may declare the truth, why wait for the failure of speech? Under the First Amendment, however, there is no such thing as a false idea, *Gertz v. Robert Welch, Inc.,* so the government may not restrict speech on the ground that in a free exchange truth is not yet dominant. * * *

"We come, finally, to the argument that pornography is 'low value' speech, that it is enough like obscenity that Indianapolis may prohibit it. Some cases hold that speech far removed from politics and other subjects at the core of the

Framers' concerns may be subjected to special regulation. E.g., *FCC v. Pacifica Foundation; Young v. American Mini Theatres, Inc.* (plurality opinion); *Chaplinsky v. New Hampshire.* These cases do not sustain statutes that select among viewpoints, however. In *Pacifica* the FCC sought to keep vile language off the air during certain times. The Court held that it may; but the Court would not have sustained a regulation prohibiting scatological descriptions of Republicans but not scatological descriptions of Democrats, or any other form of selection among viewpoints.

"At all events, pornography is not low value speech within the meaning of these cases. Indianapolis seeks to prohibit certain speech because it believes this speech influences social relations and politics on a grand scale, that it controls attitudes at home and in the legislature. This precludes a characterization of the speech as low value. True, pornography and obscenity have sex in common. But Indianapolis left out of its definition any reference to literary, artistic, political, or scientific value. The ordinance applies to graphic sexually explicit subordination in works great and small.[3] The Court sometimes balances the value of speech against the costs of its restriction, but it does this by category of speech and not by the content of particular works. See Ely, *Flag Desecration: A Case Study in the Roles of Categorization and Balancing in First Amendment Analysis,* 88 Harv.L.Rev. 1482 (1975); Stone, *Restrictions of Speech Because of its Content: The Strange Case of Subject–Matter Restrictions,* 46 U.Chi.L.Rev. 81 (1978). Indianapolis has created an approved point of view and so loses the support of these cases.

"Any rationale we could imagine in support of this ordinance could not be limited to sex discrimination. Free speech has been on balance an ally of those seeking change. Governments that want stasis start by restricting speech. Culture is a powerful force of continuity; Indianapolis paints pornography as a part of the culture of power. Change in any complex system ultimately depends on the ability of outsiders to challenge accepted views and the reigning institutions. Without a strong guarantee of freedom of speech, there is no effective right to challenge what is." [a]

Notes and Questions

1. In response to the last paragraph, supra, Professor Michelman observes: "[I]t is a fair and obvious question why preservation of 'effective right[s] to challenge what is' does not require protection of a 'freedom of speech' more broadly conceived to protect social critics—'outsiders,' in Judge Easterbrook's

3. Indianapolis briefly argues that *Beauharnais v. Illinois,* which allowed a state to penalize "group libel," supports the ordinance. In *Collin v. Smith,* we concluded that cases such as *New York Times v. Sullivan* had so washed away the foundations of *Beauharnais* that it could not be considered authoritative. If we are wrong in this, however, the case still does not support the ordinance. It is not clear that depicting women as subordinate in sexually explicit ways, even combined with a depiction of pleasure in rape, would fit within the definition of a group libel. The well received film *Swept Away* used explicit sex, plus taking pleasure in rape, to make a political statement, not to defame. Work must be an insult or slur for its own sake to come within the ambit of *Beauharnais,* and a work need not be scurrilous at all to be pornography under the ordinance.

a. The balance of the opinion suggested ways that parts of the ordinance might be salvaged, if redrafted. It suggested, for example, that the city might forbid coerced participation in any film or in "any film containing explicit sex." If the latter were adopted, would it make a difference if the section applied to persons coerced into participation in such films without regard to whether they were forced into explicit sex scenes? Swygert, J., concurring, joined part of Easterbrook, J.'s opinion for the court, but objected both to the "questionable and broad assertions regarding how human behavior can be conditioned" and to the "advisory" opinion on how parts of the ordinance might be redrafted.

phrase—against suppression by nongovernmental as well as by governmental power. It is a fair and obvious question why the assertion that '[g]overnments that want stasis start by restricting speech' does not apply equally to the nongovernmental agencies of power in society. It is a fair and obvious question why our society's openness to challenge does not need protection against repressive private as well as public action." *Conceptions of Democracy in American Constitutional Argument: The Case of Pornography Regulation,* 56 Tenn.L.Rev. 291 (1989), citing MacKinnon, *Feminism Unmodified* 155–58 (1987).

2. *Free speech and silence.* Consider MacKinnon, *Toward a Feminist Theory of the State* 206 (1989): "That pornography chills women's expression is difficult to demonstrate empirically because silence is not eloquent. Yet on no more of the same kind of evidence, the argument that suppressing pornography might chill legitimate speech has supported its protection. [T]he law of the First Amendment comprehends that freedom of expression, in the abstract, is a system but fails to comprehend that sexism (and racism), in the concrete, are also systems."

3. "*We do not try to balance* * * *." Does the existence of point of view discrimination preclude balancing under existing law? Consider MacKinnon, supra at 213: In *Hudnut,* "[o]bscenity law, which is based on nothing but value judgments about morality, was presented as the standard for constitutional point-of-viewlessness. The Court saw legal intervention against acts (most of which are already crimes) as 'point of view' discrimination without doubting the constitutionality of state intervention against obscenity, which has no connection with acts and is expressly defined on the basis of point of view about sex. [When] is a point of view not a point of view? When it is yours * * *. In the epistemologically hermetic doublethink of the male point of view, prohibiting advances toward sex equality under law is state neutrality."

4. Does pornography as defined by Indianapolis (or some part of that category) implicate such little first amendment value as to foreclose constitutional protection? How should such value be assessed? Consider Sunstein, *Pornography and the First Amendment,* 1986 Duke Law Journal 603–04: "First, the speech must be far afield from the central concern of the first amendment, which, broadly speaking, is effective popular control of public affairs. Speech that concerns governmental processes is entitled to the highest level of protection; speech that has little or nothing to do with public affairs may be accorded less protection. Second, a distinction is drawn between cognitive and noncognitive aspects of speech. Speech that has purely noncognitive appeal will be entitled to less constitutional protection.[b] Third, the purpose of the speaker is relevant: if the speaker is seeking to communicate a message, he will be treated more favorably than if he is not. Fourth, the various classes of low-value speech reflect judgments that in certain areas, government is unlikely to be acting for constitutionally impermissible reasons or producing constitutionally troublesome harms."

How do Sunstein's factors apply to the Indianapolis ordinance?

To what extent is it desirable to consider the value of speech in forging a balance? Compare, e.g., Redish, *The Value of Free Speech,* 130 U.Pa.L.Rev. 591, 596–611 (1982) and Alexander, *Low Value Speech,* 83 Nw.U.L.Rev. 547 (1989) with Sunstein, *Low Value Speech Revisited,* 83 Nw.U.L.Rev. 555 (1989). Reconsider the question after completing Section 3.

b. For debate about this factor compare Chevigny, *Pornography and Cognition,* 1989 Duke L.J. 420 with Sunstein, *The First Amendment and Cognition,* 1989 Duke L.J. 433. See also Karst, *Boundaries and Reasons: Freedom of Expression and the Subordination of Groups,* 1990 U.Ill.L.Rev. 95.

C. RACIST SPEECH REVISITED: THE NAZIS

"*What do you want to sell in the marketplace? What idea? The idea of murder?*"

Erna Gans, a concentration camp survivor and active leader in the Skokie B'nai B'rith.[a]

COLLIN v. SMITH, 578 F.2d 1197 (7th Cir.1978), cert. denied, 439 U.S. 916, 99 S.Ct. 291, 58 L.Ed.2d 264 (1978), per PELL, J., struck down a Village of Skokie *"Racial Slur" Ordinance,* making it a misdemeanor to disseminate any material (defined to include "public display of markings and clothing of symbolic significance") promoting and inciting racial or religious hatred. The Village would apparently apply this ordinance to the display of swastikas and military uniforms by the NSPA, a "Nazi organization" which planned to peacefully demonstrate for some 20–30 minutes in front of the Skokie Village Hall.

Although there was some evidence that some individuals "might have difficulty restraining their reactions to the Nazi demonstration," the Village "does not rely on a fear of responsive violence to justify the ordinance, and does not even suggest that there will be any physical violence if the march is held. This confession takes the case out of the scope of *Brandenburg* and *Feiner.* [It] also eliminates any argument based on the fighting words doctrine of *Chaplinsky,* [which] applied only to words with a direct tendency to cause violence by the persons to whom, individually, the words were addressed."

The court rejected, inter alia, the argument that the Nazi march, with its display of swastikas and uniforms, "will create a substantive evil that it has a right to prohibit: the infliction of psychic trauma on resident holocaust survivors [some 5,000] and other Jewish residents. [The] problem with engrafting an exception on the First Amendment for such situations is that they are indistinguishable in principle from speech that 'invite[s] dispute [or] induces a condition of unrest [or] even stirs people to anger,' *Terminiello.* Yet these are among the 'high purposes' of the First Amendment. [Where,] as here, a crime is made of a silent march, attended only by symbols and not by extrinsic conduct offensive in itself, we think the words of *Street v. New York* are very much on point: '[A]ny shock effect [must] be attributed to the content of the ideas expressed. [P]ublic expression of ideas may not be prohibited merely because the ideas are themselves offensive to some of their hearers.' "

Nor was the court impressed with the argument that the proposed march was "not speech, [but] rather an invasion, intensely menacing no matter how peacefully conducted" (most of Skokie's residents are Jewish): "There *need be* no captive audience, as Village residents may, if they wish, simply avoid the Village Hall for thirty minutes on a Sunday afternoon, which no doubt would be their normal course of conduct on a day when the Village Hall was not open in the regular course of business. Absent such intrusion or captivity, there is no justifiable substantial privacy interest to save [the ordinance], when it attempts, by fiat, to declare the entire Village, at all times, a privacy zone that may be sanitized from the offensiveness of Nazi ideology and symbols."[b]

a. Quoted in Friendly & Elliot, *The Constitution: That Delicate Balance* 83 (1984).

b. See also *Skokie v. National Socialist Party,* 69 Ill.2d 605, 14 Ill.Dec. 890, 373 N.E.2d 21 (1978). For commentary relating the Skokie issue to regulation of pornography, and of commercial speech, for the purpose of asking whether there are general principles of freedom of expression and whether freedom of expression should be category-dependent, see Scanlon, *Freedom of Expression and Categories of Expression,* 40 U.Pitt.L.Rev. 519 (1979). For assessment of the complicated connection between Skokie and equality values especially

Notes and Questions

1. Is *Beauharnais,* p. 421 supra, still "good law"?

2. *Abstraction and the first amendment.* Consider Schauer, *Harry Kalven and the Perils of Particularism,* 56 U.Chi.L.Rev. 397, 408 (1989): "[O]ne sees in the *Skokie* litigation an available distinction between Nazis and others, an equally available distinction between speech designed to persuade and speech designed to assault, and a decision made by the people rather than a decision designed to interfere with the people's wishes. If doctrinal development under the free speech clause were merely an instance of common law decision making, one might expect to see some or all of these factors treated as relevant, and new distinctions developed in order to make relevant those factors, such as the ones just enumerated, that had been suppressed by previous formulations. Yet we know that this is not what happened. The particular events were abstracted in numerous ways. Nazis became political speakers, a suburban community populated by Holocaust survivors became a public forum, and popularly inspired restrictions became governmental censorship. The resolution of the controversy, therefore, stands not as a monument to the ever-more-sensitive development of common law doctrine, but instead as an embodiment of the way in which the First Amendment operates precisely by the entrenchment of categories whose breadth prevents the consideration of some number of relevant factors, and prevents the free speech decision maker from 'thinking small.'"

3. *Toleration and the Nazis.* Consider Bollinger, *Book Review,* 80 Mich.L. Rev. 617, 631 (1982) (reviewing Neier, *Defending My Enemy: American Nazis, The Skokie Case, and the Risks of Freedom* (1979)): "The value of any act is dependent upon the reasons behind it, and in free speech, as in any other area, getting the reasons straight is of first importance. One can understand [a] choice to protect the free speech activities of Nazis, but not because people should value their message in the slightest or believe it should be seriously entertained, not because a commitment to self-government or rationality logically demands that such ideas be presented for consideration, not because of a simple hope *qua* conviction that anti-Nazi sentiment will win in the end, not because the anti-Nazi belief will be stimulated by open confrontation and argument with the Nazi belief, not because a line could not be drawn that would exclude this ideology without inevitably encroaching on ideas that one likes—not for any of these reasons nor others related to them that are a part of the traditional baggage of the free speech argumentation; but rather because the danger of intolerance toward ideas is so pervasive an issue in our social lives, the process of mastering a capacity for tolerance so difficult, that it makes sense somewhere in the system to attempt to confront that problem and exercise more self-restraint than may be otherwise required. We should be, in short, more concerned with addressing through the act of tolerance the potential problems of intolerance than with valuing the act of speech itself.

"On this basis, then, tolerance becomes not merely a futile attempt at shoring up the legal barricades, a response devoid of intrinsic value and meaning, but instead a symbolic act indicating an awareness of the risks and dangers of intolerance and a commitment to developing a certain attitude toward the ideas and beliefs of others. At least a part of this attitude is a willingness to

in light of the rest of first amendment law, see Tribe, *Constitutional Choices* 219–20 (1985). Compare Downs, *Skokie Revisited: Hate Group Speech and the First Amendment,* 60 Not.D.Law. 629 (1985). More generally, see Kretzmer, *Freedom of Speech and Racism,* 8 Cardozo L.Rev. 445 (1987).

recognize the existence of ideas within society that we might otherwise prefer to ignore, and to see the risks involved in succumbing to the wish to refuse to acknowledge their existence. Self-knowledge may be the best defense available against the ideas that we hate."

For rich elaboration of this perspective, see Bollinger, *The Tolerant Society: Freedom of Speech and Extremist Speech in America* (1986).

4. Should (does) the first amendment bar an action for intentional infliction of emotional distress for face-to-face racial insults? [c] Is it enough that the words in question inflict injury or must the victim show that the words were likely to promote a fight? Suppose a crowd of whites gathers to taunt a young black child on the way to a previously all white school? Suppose short of using violence, they do everything they can to harm the child? Is it the case that "no government that would call itself a decent government would fail to intervene [and] disperse the crowd" and that "the rights of the crowd [cannot] really stand on the same plane" as the child on the way to school? See Arkes, *Civility and the Restriction of Speech: Rediscovering the Defamation of Groups,* 1974 Sup.Ct. Rev. 281, 310–11. Should the first amendment bar state criminal or civil actions precisely tailored to punish racial insults? Insults directed against the handicapped? For the case in favor of a tort action against racial insults, see Delgado, *Words That Wound: A Tort Action for Racial Insults, Epithets, and Name-Calling,* 17 Harv.Civ.Rts.–Civ.Lib.L.Rev. 133 (1982). For a spirited exchange, see Heins, *Banning Words: A Comment on "Words that Wound,"* 18 Har.Civ.Rts.–Civ.Lib.L.Rev. 585 (1983) and *Professor Delgado Replies,* Id. at 593.

5. Consider Downs, *Nazis in Skokie* 147 (1985): "[N]either Cohen nor Beauharnais intentionally directed his speech to definite targets, so their speech acts were less assaultive than the speech acts of Collin[.] Had Beauharnais passed his leaflets out in front of black homes or given them directly to blacks in similar settings, the very nature of his speech act would have been transformed from a racialist plea into an act of intimidation."

6. Is one person's "racialist's plea" another person's act of intimidation? Are these responses patterned? Consider Matsuda, *Public Response to Racist Speech: Considering the Victim's Story,* 87 Mich.L.Rev. 2320, 2326–27 (1989): "[I] am forced to ask why the world looks so different to me from how it looks to many of the civil libertarians whom I consider my allies. [In] advocating legal restriction of hate speech, I have found my most sympathetic audience in people who identify with target groups, while I have encountered incredulity, skepticism, and even hostility from others.

"This split in reaction is also evident in case studies of hate speech. The typical reaction of target-group members to an incident of racist propaganda is alarm and immediate calls for redress. The typical reaction of non-target-group members is to consider the incidents isolated pranks,[d] the product of sick-but-harmless minds. This is in part a defensive reaction: a refusal to believe that real people, people just like us, are racists. This disassociation leads logically to

c. On the relationship between discriminatory speech and the tort of intentional infliction of emotional distress, see Love, *Discriminatory Speech and the Tort of Intentional Infliction of Emotional Distress,* 47 Wash. & Lee L.Rev. 123 (1990).

d. For discussion of the extent and character of the harm, see Matsuda, supra; Lawrence, infra; Delgado, *Campus Antiracism Rules Constitutional Narratives in Collision,* 85 Nw.U.L.Rev. 343, 384 (1991) ("The ubiquity and incessancy of harmful racial depiction are [the] source of its virulence. Like water dripping on sandstone, it is a pervasive harm which only the most hardy can resist. Yet the prevailing first amendment paradigm predisposes us to treat racist speech as individual harm, as though we only had to evaluate the effect of a single drop of water.").

the claim that there is no institutional or state responsibility to respond to the incident.[e] It is not the kind of real and pervasive threat that requires the state's power to quell."

See also Lawrence, *If He Hollers Let Him Go: Regulating Racist Speech on Campus,* 1990 Duke L.J. 431, 474–75: "If one asks why we always begin by asking whether we can afford to fight racism rather than asking whether we can afford not to, or if one asks why my colleagues who oppose all regulation of racist speech do not feel the burden is theirs (to justify a reading of the first amendment that requires sacrificing rights guaranteed under the equal protection clause), then one sees an example of how unconscious racism operates in the marketplace of ideas. * * * [O]ur unconscious racism causes us (even those of us who are the direct victims of racism) to view the first amendment as the 'regular' amendment—an amendment that works for all people—and the equal protection clause and racial equality as a special interest-amendment important to groups that are less valued."

7. Consider Karst, *Boundaries and Reasons: Freedom of Expression and the Subordination of Groups,* 1990 U.Ill.L.Rev. 95, 140–41: "Group libel and pornography each respond to a sense of inadequacy, but the two types of hate literature are circulated differently. Where the defamation of racial or religious groups is driven by the felt inadequacies of its distributors, today's pornography is largely driven by the inadequacies of its consumers, with most distributors simply profiting from that demand and seeking to increase it. In neither case will elimination of the literature cause the underlying sense of inadequacy to disappear. Anxious hatemongers, thwarted in purveying their racist leaflets, can find plenty of other ways to express their fear and hate, as the Ku Klux Klan and the Nazis have made clear. And anxious men, thwarted in the consumption of pornography, can find substitute symbols of sexual objectification not just in magazine ads or on television but in every woman they see."

8. Consider Stanford University's definition of harassment by personal vilification: "Speech or other expression constitutes harassment by personal vilification if it a) is intended to insult or stigmatize an individual or a small number of individuals on the basis of their sex, race, color, handicap, religion, sexual orientation, or national and ethnic origin; and b) is addressed directly to the individual or individuals whom it insults or stigmatizes; and c) makes use of insulting or 'fighting words' or non-verbal symbols." Does this go too far? See Strossen, *Regulating Racist Speech on Campus: A Modest Proposal?* 1990 Duke L.J. 484. Does it not go far enough? See Lawrence, supra at 450 n. 82: "I supported a proposal which would have been broader in scope by prohibiting speech of this nature in all common areas, excepting organized rallies and speeches. It would have been narrower in its protection in that it would not have protected persons who were vilified on the basis of their membership in dominant majority groups." Compare Matsuda, supra at 2357, arguing that speech with a message of racial inferiority, that is directed against a historically oppressed group, and that is persecutorial, hateful, and degrading should be outlawed.[f]

e. For the argument that the best interpretation of *Brown v. State Board of Education requires* government to respond, see Lawrence, infra. For response, see Strossen, infra.

f. For other relevant literature, see, e.g., p. 424 supra; Williams, *The Alchemy of Race and Rights* (1991); Grano, *Free Speech v. The University of Michigan,* Academic Questions 7 (Spring 1990); Greenawalt, *Insults and Epithets: Are They Protected Speech?,* 42 Rutgers L.Rev. 287 (1990); Grey, *Civil Rights v. Civil Liberties: The Case of Discriminatory Verbal Harassment,* Soc.Phil.&Pol'y 81 (Spring 1991); Post, *Racist Speech, Democracy, and the First Amendment,* 32 Wm.&Mary L.Rev. 267 (1991); Smolla, *Rethinking First Amendment Assump-*

SECTION 2. DISTINGUISHING BETWEEN CONTENT REGULATION AND MANNER REGULATION: UNCONVENTIONAL FORMS OF COMMUNICATION

Special first amendment questions are often said to arise by regulation of the time, place, and manner of speech as opposed to regulation of its content. But the two types of regulation are not mutually exclusive. It is possible to regulate time, place, manner, and content in the same regulation. For example, in *Linmark,* p. 575 infra, the township outlawed signs (but not leaflets) advertising a house for sale (but not other advertisements or other messages) on front lawns (but not other places).

Further, the terms, manner and content are strongly contested concepts. Indeed, an issue recurring in this section is whether the regulations in question are of manner or content. To the extent this section is about manner regulation, it is not exhaustive—much comes later. Most of the cases in this section involve unconventional forms of expression. Speakers claim protection for burning draft cards, wearing armbands, mutilating flags, nude dancing, wearing long hair. Fact patterns such as these fix renewed attention on the question of how "speech" should be defined. It may be a nice question as to whether obscenity is not speech within the first amendment lexicon, whether it is such speech but has been balanced into an unprotected state, or whether it is not *freedom* of speech or *the* freedom of speech.[a] But assassinating a public figure, even to send a message, raises no first amendment problem. Robbing a bank does not raise a free speech issue. What does? How do we decide?

The fact patterns in this section also invite scrutiny of other issues that appear in succeeding sections. Should it make a difference if the state's interest in regulating speech is unrelated to what is being said? Suppose the state's concern arises from the non-communicative impact of the speech act—from its manner. Should that distinction make a constitutional difference, and, if so, how much? These questions become more complicated because in context it is often difficult to determine what the state interest is and sometimes difficult to determine whether there is a meaningful distinction between what is said and how it is said.

Even when the distinction between the manner of the speech and the content of the speech is clear, further doctrinal complications abound. Sometimes the regulation considered by the Court is described as one regulating the "time, place, or manner" of speech, and the Court employs the "time, place, or manner test" which is itself differently phrased in different cases. On other occasions the regulation is described as having an "incidental" impact on freedom of speech, and the Court turns to a different test. These different tests are sometimes described by the Court as functional equivalents. Should there be different tests? In what circumstances?[b]

Finally, in this and succeeding sections the question arises of the extent to which freedom of speech should require special sensitivity to the methods and communications needs of the less powerful.

tions About Racist and Sexist Speech, 47 Wash.&Lee L.Rev. 171 (1990).

a. See fn. b in *Roth,* p. 457 supra.

b. See generally Williams, *Content Discrimination and the First Amendment,* 139 U.Pa.L.Rev. 201 (1991).

UNITED STATES v. O'BRIEN

391 U.S. 367, 88 S.Ct. 1673, 20 L.Ed.2d 672 (1968).

CHIEF JUSTICE WARREN delivered the opinion of the Court.

On the morning of March 31, 1966, David Paul O'Brien and three companions burned their Selective Service registration certificates on the steps of the South Boston Courthouse. A sizable crowd, including several [FBI agents] witnessed the event. Immediately after the burning, members of the crowd began attacking O'Brien [and he was ushered to safety by an FBI agent.] O'Brien stated to FBI agents that he had burned his registration certificate because of his beliefs, knowing that he was violating federal law.

[For this act, O'Brien was convicted in federal court.] He [told] the jury that he burned the certificate publicly to influence others to adopt his antiwar beliefs, as he put it, "so that other people would reevaluate their positions with Selective Service, with the armed forces, and reevaluate their place in the culture of today, to hopefully consider my position."

The indictment upon which he was tried charged that he "wilfully and knowingly did mutilate, destroy, and change by burning [his] Registration Certificate; in violation of [§ 462(b)(3) of the Universal Military Training and Service Act of 1948], amended by Congress in 1965 (adding the words italicized below), so that at the time O'Brien burned his certificate an offense was committed by any person, "who forges, alters, *knowingly destroys, knowingly mutilates,* or in any manner changes any such certificate * * *." (Italics supplied.)

[On appeal, the] First Circuit held the 1965 Amendment unconstitutional as a law abridging freedom of speech. At the time the Amendment was enacted, a regulation of the Selective Service System required registrants to keep their registration certificates in their "personal possession at all times." Wilful violations of regulations promulgated pursuant to the Universal Military Training and Service Act were made criminal by statute. The Court of Appeals, therefore, was of the opinion that conduct punishable under the 1965 Amendment was already punishable under the nonpossession regulation, and consequently that the Amendment served no valid purpose; further, that in light of the prior regulation, the Amendment must have been "directed at public as distinguished from private destruction." On this basis, the Court concluded that the 1965 Amendment ran afoul of the First Amendment by singling out persons engaged in protests for special treatment. * * *

When a male reaches the age of 18, he is required by the Universal Military Training and Service Act to register with a local draft board. He is assigned a Selective Service number, and within five days he is issued a registration certificate. Subsequently, and based on a questionnaire completed by the registrant, he is assigned a classification denoting his eligibility for induction, and "[a]s soon as practicable" thereafter he is issued a Notice of Classification. * * *

Both the registration and classification certificates bear notices that the registrant must notify his local board in writing of every change in address, physical condition, and occupational, marital, family, dependency, and military status, and of any other fact which might change his classification. Both also contain a notice that the registrant's Selective Service number should appear on all communications to his local board.

[The 1965] Amendment does not distinguish between public and private destruction, and it does not punish only destruction engaged in for the purpose of expressing views.[a] A law prohibiting destruction of Selective Service certificates no more abridges free speech on its face than a motor vehicle law prohibiting the destruction of drivers' licenses, or a tax law prohibiting the destruction of books and records.

O'Brien nonetheless argues [first] that the 1965 Amendment is unconstitutional [as] applied to him because his act of burning his registration certificate was protected "symbolic speech" within the First Amendment. [He claims that] the First Amendment guarantees include all modes of "communication of ideas by conduct," and that his conduct is within this definition because he did it in "demonstration against the war and against the draft."

We cannot accept the view that an apparently limitless variety of conduct can be labelled "speech" whenever the person engaging in the conduct intends thereby to express an idea. However, even on the assumption that the alleged communicative element in O'Brien's conduct is sufficient to bring into play the First Amendment, it does not necessarily follow that the destruction of a registration certificate is constitutionally protected activity. This Court has held that when "speech" and "nonspeech" elements are combined in the same course of conduct, a sufficiently important governmental interest in regulating the nonspeech element can justify incidental limitations on First Amendment freedoms. To characterize the quality of the governmental interest which must appear, the Court has employed a variety of descriptive terms: compelling; substantial; subordinating; paramount; cogent; strong. [W]e think it clear that a government regulation is sufficiently justified if it is within the constitutional power of the government; if it furthers an important or substantial governmental interest; if the governmental interest is unrelated to the suppression of free expression;[b] and if the incidental restriction on alleged First Amendment freedom is no greater than is essential to the furtherance of that interest. We find that the 1965 Amendment meets all of these requirements, and consequently that O'Brien can be constitutionally convicted for violating it. [Pursuant to its power to classify and conscript manpower for military service], Congress may establish a system of registration for individuals liable for training and service, and may require such individuals within reason to cooperate in the registration system. The issuance of certificates indicating the registration and eligibility classification of individuals is a legitimate and substantial administrative aid in the functioning of this system. And legislation to insure the continuing availability of issued certificates serves a legitimate and substantial purpose in the system's administration.

[O'Brien] essentially adopts the position that [Selective Service] certificates are so many pieces of paper designed to notify registrants of their registration or classification, to be retained or tossed in the wastebasket according to the convenience or taste of the registrant. Once the registrant has received notifica-

a. But compare Chief Judge Aldrich below, 376 F.2d at 541: "We would be closing our eyes in the light of the prior law if we did not see on the face of the amendment that it was precisely directed at public as distinguished from private destruction. [In] singling out persons engaging in protest for special treatment the amendment strikes at the very core of what the First Amendment protects."

b. For the contention that the many tests formulated by the Court are best regarded as prophylactic rules designed to assure that the forbidden purpose of suppressing ideas does not underlie government acts, see Bogen, *Balancing Freedom of Speech,* 38 Md.L.Rev. 387 (1979); Bogen, *The Supreme Court's Interpretation of the Guarantee of Freedom of Speech,* 35 Md.L.Rev. 555 (1976). See generally Bogen, *Bulwark of Liberty: The Court and the First Amendment* (1984).

tion, according to this view, there is no reason for him to retain the certificates. [However, the registration and classification certificates serve] purposes in addition to initial notification. Many of these purposes would be defeated by the certificates' destruction or mutilation. Among these are [simplifying verification of the registration and classification of suspected delinquents, evidence of availability for induction in the event of emergency, ease of communication between registrants and local boards, continually reminding registrants of the need to notify local boards of changes in status].

The many functions performed by Selective Service certificates establish beyond doubt that Congress has a legitimate and substantial interest in preventing their wanton and unrestrained destruction and assuring their continuing availability by punishing people who knowingly and wilfully destroy or mutilate them. And we are unpersuaded that the pre-existence of the nonpossession regulations in any way negates this interest.

In the absence of a question as to multiple punishment, it has never been suggested that there is anything improper in Congress providing alternative statutory avenues of prosecution to assure the effective protection of one and the same interest. Here, the pre-existing avenue of prosecution was not even statutory. Regulations may be modified or revoked from time to time by administrative discretion. Certainly, the Congress may change or supplement a regulation.

[The] gravamen of the offense defined by the statute is the deliberate rendering of certificates unavailable for the various purposes which they may serve. Whether registrants keep their certificates in their personal possession at all times, as required by the regulations, is of no particular concern under the 1965 Amendment, as long as they do not mutilate or destroy the certificates so as to render them unavailable. [The 1965 amendment] is concerned with abuses involving *any* issued Selective Service certificates, not only with the registrant's own certificates. The knowing destruction or mutilation of someone else's certificates would therefore violate the statute but not the nonpossession regulations.

We think it apparent that the continuing availability to each registrant of his Selective Service certificates substantially furthers the smooth and proper functioning of the system that Congress has established to raise armies. * * *

It is equally clear that the 1965 Amendment specifically protects this substantial governmental interest. We perceive no alternative means that would more precisely and narrowly assure the continuing availability of issued Selective Service certificates than a law which prohibits their wilful mutilation or destruction. The 1965 Amendment prohibits such conduct and does nothing more. [The] governmental interest and the scope of the 1965 Amendment are limited to preventing a harm to the smooth and efficient functioning of the Selective Service System. When O'Brien deliberately rendered unavailable his registration certificate, he wilfully frustrated this governmental interest. For this noncommunicative impact of his conduct, and for nothing else, he was convicted.

The case at bar is therefore unlike one where the alleged governmental interest in regulating conduct arises in some measure because the communication allegedly integral to the conduct is itself thought to be harmful [distinguishing *Stromberg,* p. 481 supra].

[B]ecause of the Government's substantial interest in assuring the continuing availability of issued Selective Service certificates, because amended § 462(b) is an appropriately narrow means of protecting this interest and condemns only the independent noncommunicative impact of conduct within its reach, and because the noncommunicative impact of O'Brien's act of burning his registration certificate frustrated the Government's interest, a sufficient governmental interest has been shown to justify O'Brien's conviction.

O'Brien finally argues that the 1965 Amendment is unconstitutional as enacted because what he calls the "purpose" of Congress was "to suppress freedom of speech." We reject this argument because under settled principles the purpose of Congress, as O'Brien uses that term, is not a basis for declaring this legislation unconstitutional.

It is a familiar principle of constitutional law that this Court will not strike down an otherwise constitutional statute on the basis of an alleged illicit legislative motive.[c]

[I]f we were to examine legislative purpose in the instant case, we would be obliged to consider not only [the statements of the three members of Congress who addressed themselves to the amendment, all viewing draft-card burning as a brazen display of unpatriotism] but also the more authoritative reports of the Senate and House Armed Services Committees. [B]oth reports make clear a concern with the "defiant" destruction of so-called "draft cards" and with "open" encouragement to others to destroy their cards, [but they] also indicate that this concern stemmed from an apprehension that unrestrained destruction of cards would disrupt the smooth functioning of the Selective Service System. * * *

Reversed.[d]

JUSTICE HARLAN concurring. * * *

I wish to make explicit my understanding that [the Court's analysis] does not foreclose consideration of First Amendment claims in those rare instances when an "incidental" restriction upon expression, imposed by a regulation which furthers an "important or substantial" governmental interest and satisfies the Court's other criteria, in practice has the effect of entirely preventing a "speaker" from reaching a significant audience with whom he could not otherwise lawfully communicate. This is not such a case, since O'Brien manifestly could have conveyed his message in many ways other than by burning his draft card.

JUSTICE DOUGLAS, dissenting.

[Douglas, J., thought that "the underlying and basic problem in this case" was the constitutionality of a draft "in the absence of a declaration of war" and that the case should be put down for reargument on this question. The following Term, concurring in *Brandenburg,* he criticized *O'Brien* on the merits. After recalling that the Court had rejected O'Brien's first amendment argument on the ground that "legislation to insure the continuing availability of issued certificates serves a legitimate and substantial purpose in the [selective service] system's administration," he commented: "But O'Brien was not prosecuted for not having his draft card available when asked for by a federal agent. He was indicted, tried, and convicted for burning the card. And this Court's affirmance [was not] consistent with the First Amendment." He observed, more generally in *Brandenburg:*

["Action is often a method of expression and within the protection of the First Amendment. Suppose one tears up his own copy of the Constitution in eloquent protest to a decision of this Court. May he be indicted? Suppose one

c. See generally Ch. 6, Sec. 2, III.

d. Marshall, J., took no part.

rips his own Bible to shreds to celebrate his departure from one 'faith' and his embrace of atheism. May he be indicted? * * *

["The act of praying often involves body posture and movement as well as utterances. It is nonetheless protected by the Free Exercise Clause. Picketing [is] 'free speech plus.' [Therefore], it can be regulated when it comes to the 'plus' or 'action' side of the protest. It can be regulated as to the number of pickets and the place and hours, because traffic and other community problems would otherwise suffer. But none of these considerations are implicated in the symbolic protest of the Vietnam war in the burning of a draft card."]

Notes and Questions

1. *Expression v. action.* What of the Court's rejection of the idea that conduct is speech "whenever the person engaging in the conduct intends thereby to express an idea." Was it right to question whether O'Brien's conduct was speech? What was it about O'Brien's conduct that made the Court doubt that it was speech? What if O'Brien had burned a copy of the Constitution? Consider Emerson, *The System of Freedom of Expression* 80 & 84 (1970): "To some extent expression and action are always mingled; most conduct includes elements of both. Even the clearest manifestations of expression involve some action, as in the case of holding a meeting, publishing a newspaper, or merely talking. At the other extreme, a political assassination includes a substantial mixture of expression. The guiding principle must be to determine which element is predominant in the conduct under consideration. Is expression the major element and the action only secondary? Or is the action the essence and the expression incidental? The answer, to a great extent, must be based on a common-sense reaction, made in light of the functions and operations of a system of freedom of expression. * * *

"The burning of a draft card is, of course, conduct that involves both communication and physical acts. Yet it seems quite clear that the predominant element in such conduct is expression (opposition to the draft) rather than action (destruction of a piece of cardboard). The registrant is not concerned with secret or inadvertent burning of his draft card, involving no communication with other persons. The main feature, for him, is the public nature of the burning, through which he expresses to the community his ideas and feelings about the war and the draft."

Compare Ely, *Flag Desecration: A Case Study in the Roles of Categorization and Balancing in First Amendment Analysis,* 88 Harv.L.Rev. 1482, 1495 (1975): "[B]urning a draft card to express opposition to the draft is an undifferentiated whole, 100% action and 100% expression. It involves no conduct that is not at the same time communication, and no communication that does not result from conduct. Attempts to determine which element 'predominates' will therefore inevitably degenerate into question-begging judgments about whether the activity should be protected.

"The *O'Brien* Court thus quite wisely dropped the 'speech-conduct' distinction as quickly as it had picked it up." [e]

e. But, as Dean Ely recognizes, the Court picked it up again in *Cohen*: "[W]e deal here with a conviction resting solely upon 'speech', cf. *Stromberg,* not upon any separately identifiable conduct which allegedly was intended by Cohen to be perceived by others as expressive of particular views but which, on its face, does not necessarily convey any message and hence arguably could be regulated without effectively repressing Cohen's ability to express himself. Cf. *O'Brien.*"

Consider, too, Baker, *Scope of the First Amendment Freedom of Speech,* 25 U.C.L.A.L.Rev. 964, 1010–12 (1978): "[S]ince both verbal and nonverbal conduct advances first amendment values, the purpose of the [expression-action] distinction is unclear. Moreover, only an extremely crabbed reading of other clauses of the first amendment will be consistent with implementing an expression-action dichotomy. If religion plays a significant role in one's life, its *free exercise* normally will require doing or abstaining from certain conduct. And people typically assemble and associate to multiply their power in order to do something. Nevertheless, even if his 'expression-action' dichotomy is not very helpful, Emerson consistently makes very perceptive analyses of concrete situations; and these analyses frequently appear to make a different distinction: whether or not the conduct is, or is intended to be, coercive or physically injurious to another. All Emerson's examples of unprotected conduct, 'action,' involve coercion or injury to or physical interference with another or damage to physical property. * * *

"Expressive political protests sometimes involve acts of physical obstruction like lying down in front of troop trains, blocking traffic in a city, or pouring blood over files. Emerson argues that these must be considered 'action,' [but] [n]either the physical activity nor the motives of the actor distinguish these 'action' cases from draft card burning, which Emerson characterizes as expression. Rather, Emerson classifies the first examples of civil disobedience 'action' because the '[c]ivil disobedience attempts to achieve results through a kind of *coercion or pressure* * * *.' However, [draft-card burning], unlike failing to carry a draft card [which presumably 'interferes' or 'obstructs' the working of the selective service system], does not involve coercing or directly injuring or physically obstructing any person or government activity. This fact apparently explains why Emerson concludes that the expression element clearly predominates in draft card burning." [f] See generally Baker, *Human Liberty and Freedom of Speech* 70–91 (1989).

2. *Nature of the state interest and first amendment methodology.* Melville Nimmer, *The Meaning of Symbolic Speech under the First Amendment,* 21 U.C.L.A.L.Rev. 29 (1973), followed by John Hart Ely, note 1 supra, and Laurence Tribe, infra, has proposed that the crucial starting point for first amendment methodology is and should be the nature of the state interest.[g] As Ely puts it, at 1497: "The critical question would therefore seem to be whether the harm that the state is seeking to avert is one that grows out of the fact that the defendant is communicating, and more particularly out of the way people can be expected to react to his message, or rather would arise even if the defendant's conduct had no communicative significance whatever."

For one view of the difference that the distinction makes, see Tribe, *American Constitutional Law* 791–92 (2d ed. 1988): "The Supreme Court has evolved two distinct approaches to the resolution of first amendment claims; the two correspond to the two ways in which government may 'abridge' speech. If a government regulation is aimed at the communicative impact of an act, analysis should proceed along what we will call *track one.* On that track, a regulation is unconstitutional unless government shows that the message being suppressed poses a 'clear and present danger,' constitutes a defamatory falsehood, or otherwise falls on the unprotected side of one of the lines the Court has drawn to

f. For discussion of Professor Baker's approach and refinement of the expression-action dichotomy, see Emerson, *First Amendment Doctrine and the Burger Court,* 68 Calif. L.Rev. 422, 474–80 (1980).

g. The distinction is a major organizing principle in *Nimmer on Freedom of Speech* (1984).

distinguish those expressive acts privileged by the first amendment from those open to government regulation with only minimal due process scrutiny. If a government regulation is aimed at the noncommunicative impact of an act, its analysis proceeds on what we will call *track two.* On that track, a regulation is constitutional, even as applied to expressive conduct, so long as it does not unduly constrict the flow of information and ideas. On track two, the 'balance' between the values of freedom of expression and the government's regulatory interests is struck on a case-by-case basis, guided by whatever unifying principles may be articulated."

Professor Nimmer, in distinguishing between anti-speech interests (track one) and non-speech interests (track two), would apply definitional balancing (with a presumption in favor of speech) to the former and the *O'Brien* test to the latter. Dean Ely would prevent all regulations on track one except for speech that falls "within a few clearly and narrowly defined catagories." Ely, *Democracy and Distrust* 110 (1980) (emphasis deleted). On track two, Ely insists that balancing is desirable and unavoidable. Ely, note 1 supra, at 1496–1502.

(a) *Normative value of the distinction.* Is balancing unavoidable on either track? How does one decide what the categories should be without balancing? Does the metaphor of balancing wrongly imply that all values are reduced to a single measure and imply non-existent quantitative capacities? Is the distinction between the tracks important enough to require rules on track one, even if ad hoc procedures are allowable on track two?

Is the distinction between the two tracks at least strong enough to justify a rebuttable presumption that regulation on track one is invalid, but regulation on track two is not? Consider a regulation governing express warranties in commercial advertising. Is much of contract law on track one? Consider "a nationwide ban on *all* posters (intended to conserve paper)." Isn't that on track two? Do these examples suggest that too much emphasis is being placed on a single factor? See Farber, *Content Regulation and the First Amendment: A Revisionist View,* 68 Geo.U.L.Rev. 727, 746–47 (1980).[h]

(b) *Application to O'Brien.* Consider Ely, note 1 supra, at 1498–99: "The interests upon which the government relied were interests, having mainly to do with the preservation of selective service records, that would have been equally threatened had O'Brien's destruction of his draft card totally lacked communicative significance—had he, for example, used it to start a campfire for a solitary cookout or dropped it in his garbage disposal for a lark. (The law prohibited all knowing destructions, public or private)."

Compare Nimmer, note 2 supra, at 41—contending that the *O'Brien* statute was "overnarrow": "[An overnarrow statute] may be said to create a conclusive presumption that in fact the state interest which the statute serves is an anti- rather than a non-speech interest. If the state interest asserted in *O'Brien* were truly the non-speech interest of assuring availability of draft cards, why did Congress choose not to prohibit any knowing conduct which leads to unavailability, rather than limiting the scope of the statute to those instances in which the proscribed conduct carries with it a speech component hostile to governmental policy? The obvious inference to be drawn is that in fact the Congress was completely indifferent to the 'availability' objective, and was concerned only with an interest which the *O'Brien* opinion states is impermissible—an interest in the

h. See generally Redish, *The Content Distinction in First Amendment Analysis,* 34 Stan.L.Rev. 113 (1981). See notes after *Chicago Police Dept. v. Mosley,* p. 644 infra.

suppression of free expression." [i]

(c) *Descriptive value of the distinction.* Does the distinction between the two tracks fully explain the Court's approach in *O'Brien*? Suppose again that an assassin truthfully claims that his or her killing was intended to and did communicate an idea? The assassin's first amendment claim would not prevail, but would it fail because the *O'Brien* test was not met or because no first amendment problem was implicated at all? Is a speech/conduct distinction a necessary prerequisite to the application of the *O'Brien* test? [j]

How different is the *O'Brien* test from the methods used to make decisions on track one? Is the *O'Brien* test as phrased potentially more speech protective than its application in the principal case would suggest? More speech protective than tests sometimes used on track one? Does the application in *O'Brien* offer "little more than the minimal rational-basis test applied in economic due process cases"? See Werhan, *The O'Briening of First Amendment Methodology,* 19 Ariz. St.L.J. 635, 641 (1987): "There is no speech side to the Court's balance. [T]he absence of true balancing within the *O'Brien* methodology can be traced to the origins of the *O'Brien* test. [Having] avoided deciding whether O'Brien's act was protected expression, the Court hardly was in a position to take the next step of incorporating expressive interests into its balance." Id. at 641–42.

3. Does *O'Brien* shortchange the value of dissent? Consider Shiffrin, *The First Amendment, Democracy, and Romance* 5–6, 81 (1990): "If an organizing symbol makes sense in first amendment jurisprudence, it is not the image of a content-neutral government; it is not a town hall meeting or even a robust marketplace of ideas; still less is it liberty, equality, self-realization, respect, dignity, autonomy, or even tolerance. If the first amendment is to have an organizing symbol, let it be an Emersonian [k] symbol, let it be the image of the dissenter. A major purpose of the first amendment [is] to protect the romantics—those who would break out of classical forms: the dissenters, the unorthodox, the outcasts. [That] Emersonian ideal of freedom of speech has deep roots in the nation's culture, but it has been subtly denigrated in recent first amendment theory and seriously abused in practice.

"[N]either the town hall metaphor nor the marketplace of ideas metaphor[, for example,] is quite apt as a symbol for why *O'Brien* is a first amendment horror story. Town hall meetings can function without the burning of draft cards. And it is hard to claim that truth was kept from the marketplace of ideas. *O'Brien* is one of those not infrequent cases where government prosecutions assist the dissemination of the dissenter's message. Yet, *O'Brien* is perhaps the ultimate first amendment insult. O'Brien is jailed because the authorities find his manner of expression unpatriotic, threatening, and offensive. When he complains that his freedom of speech has been abridged, the authorities deny that he has spoken."

4. *Scope of O'Brien.* Should the *O'Brien* test be confined to unconventional forms of communication? Would a distinction of this type be defensible? See Ely, note 1 supra, at 1489: "The distinction is its own objection." See also Alfange, *Free Speech and Symbolic Conduct: The Draft-Card Burning Case,* 1968 Sup.Ct.Rev. 1, 23–24; Velvel, *Freedom of Speech and the Draft Card Burning*

i. On the inadequacy of the *O'Brien* methodology to serve as a proxy for problematic motivation, see Bollinger, *The Tolerant Society* 206–12 (1986). On its inadequacy as an organizing principle for first amendment doctrine, see Shiffrin, Note 3 infra, ch. 1.

j. For commentary on the difficulties in defining speech, see Alexander & Horton, *The Impossibility of a Free Speech Principle,* 78 Nw.U.L.Rev. 1319 (1984).

k. See generally *Ralph Waldo Emerson: Essays and Lectures* (J. Porte ed.1983).

Cases, 16 U.Kan.L.Rev. 149, 153 (1968); Henkin, *On Drawing Lines,* 82 Harv.L. Rev. 63, 79 (1968).

TEXAS v. JOHNSON

491 U.S. 397, 109 S.Ct. 2533, 105 L.Ed.2d 342 (1989).

JUSTICE BRENNAN delivered the opinion of the Court.

After publicly burning an American flag as a means of political protest, Gregory Lee Johnson was convicted of desecrating a flag in violation of Texas law. This case presents the question whether his conviction is consistent with the First Amendment. We hold that it is not.

I

While the Republican National Convention was taking place in Dallas in 1984, respondent Johnson participated in a political demonstration dubbed the "Republican War Chest Tour." As explained in literature distributed by the demonstrators and in speeches made by them, the purpose of this event was to protest the policies of the Reagan administration and of certain Dallas-based corporations. The demonstrators marched through the Dallas streets, chanting political slogans and stopping at several corporate locations to stage "die-ins" intended to dramatize the consequences of nuclear war. On several occasions they spray-painted the walls of buildings and overturned potted plants, but Johnson himself took no part in such activities. He did, however, accept an American flag handed to him by a fellow protestor who had taken it from a flag pole outside one of the targeted buildings.

The demonstration ended in front of Dallas City Hall, where Johnson unfurled the American flag, doused it with kerosene, and set it on fire. While the flag burned, the protestors chanted, "America, the red, white, and blue, we spit on you." After the demonstrators dispersed, a witness to the flag-burning collected the flag's remains and buried them in his backyard. No one was physically injured or threatened with injury, though several witnesses testified that they had been seriously offended by the flag-burning.

Of the approximately 100 demonstrators, Johnson alone was charged with a crime. The only criminal offense with which he was charged was the desecration of a venerated object in violation of Tex.Penal Code Ann. § 42.09(a)(3) (1989).[1] * * *

II

Johnson was convicted of flag desecration for burning the flag rather than for uttering insulting words.[2] This fact somewhat complicates our consideration

1. Tex.Penal Code Ann. § 42.09 (1989) provides in full: "§ 42.09. Desecration of Venerated Object

"(a) A person commits an offense if he intentionally or knowingly desecrates:

"(1) a public monument;

"(2) a place of worship or burial; or

"(3) a state or national flag.

"(b) For purposes of this section, 'desecrate' means deface, damage, or otherwise physically mistreat in a way that the actor knows will seriously offend one or more persons likely to observe or discover his action.

"(c) An offense under this section is a Class A misdemeanor."

2. Because the prosecutor's closing argument observed that Johnson had led the protestors in chants denouncing the flag while it burned, Johnson suggests that he may have been convicted for uttering critical words rather than for burning the flag. He relies on *Street v. New York* [394 U.S. 576, 89 S.Ct. 1354, 22 L.Ed.2d 572 (1969)] in which we reversed a conviction obtained under a New York statute that prohibited publicly defying or casting contempt on the flag "either by words or act" because we were persuaded that the defendant may have been convicted for his words alone. Unlike the law we faced in

of his conviction under the First Amendment. We must first determine whether Johnson's burning of the flag constituted expressive conduct, permitting him to invoke the First Amendment in challenging his conviction. If his conduct was expressive, we next decide whether the State's regulation is related to the suppression of free expression. *O'Brien.* If the State's regulation is not related to expression, then the less stringent standard we announced in *O'Brien* for regulations of noncommunicative conduct controls. If it is, then we are outside of *O'Brien*'s test, and we must ask whether this interest justifies Johnson's conviction under a more demanding standard.[3] A third possibility is that the State's asserted interest is simply not implicated on these facts, and in that event the interest drops out of the picture. * * *

In deciding whether particular conduct possesses sufficient communicative elements to bring the First Amendment into play, we have asked whether "[a]n intent to convey a particularized message was present, and [whether] the likelihood was great that the message would be understood by those who viewed it." [*Spence v. Washington,* 418 U.S. 405, 94 S.Ct. 2727, 41 L.Ed.2d 842 (1974)].

We have not automatically concluded, however, that any action taken with respect to our flag is expressive. Instead, in characterizing such action for First Amendment purposes, we have considered the context in which it occurred. In *Spence,* for example, we emphasized that Spence's taping of a peace sign to his flag was "roughly simultaneous with and concededly triggered by the Cambodian incursion and the Kent State tragedy." The State of Washington had conceded, in fact, that Spence's conduct was a form of communication, and we stated that "the State's concession is inevitable on this record."

Street, however, the Texas flag-desecration statute does not on its face permit conviction for remarks critical of the flag, as Johnson himself admits. Nor was the jury in this case told that it could convict Johnson of flag desecration if it found only that he had uttered words critical of the flag and its referents.

Johnson emphasizes, though, that the jury was instructed—according to Texas' law of parties—that " 'a person is criminally responsible for an offense committed by the conduct of another if acting with intent to promote or assist the commission of the offense, he solicits, encourages, directs, aids, or attempts to aid the other person to commit the offense.' " The State offered this instruction because Johnson's defense was that he was not the person who had burned the flag. Johnson did not object to this instruction at trial, and although he challenged it on direct appeal, he did so only on the ground that there was insufficient evidence to support it. It is only in this Court that Johnson has argued that the law-of-parties instruction might have led the jury to convict him for his words alone. Even if we were to find that this argument is properly raised here, however, we would conclude that it has no merit in these circumstances. The instruction would not have permitted a conviction merely for the pejorative nature of Johnson's words, and those words themselves did not encourage the burning of the flag as the instruction seems to require. Given the additional fact that "the bulk of the State's argument was premised on Johnson's culpability as a sole actor," we find it too unlikely that the jury convicted Johnson on the basis of this alternative theory to consider reversing his conviction on this ground.

3. Although Johnson has raised a facial challenge to Texas' flag-desecration statute, we choose to resolve this case on the basis of his claim that the statute as applied to him violates the First Amendment. Section 42.09 regulates only physical conduct with respect to the flag, not the written or spoken word, and although one violates the statute only if one "knows" that one's physical treatment of the flag "will seriously offend one or more persons likely to observe or discover his action," this fact does not necessarily mean that the statute applies only to *expressive* conduct protected by the First Amendment. A tired person might, for example, drag a flag through the mud, knowing that this conduct is likely to offend others, and yet have no thought of expressing any idea; neither the language nor the Texas courts' interpretations of the statute precludes the possibility that such a person would be prosecuted for flag desecration. Because the prosecution of a person who had not engaged in expressive conduct would pose a different case, and because we are capable of disposing of this case on narrower grounds, we address only Johnson's claim that § 42.09 as applied to political expression like his violates the First Amendment.

The State of Texas conceded for purposes of its oral argument in this case that Johnson's conduct was expressive conduct and this concession seems to us as prudent as was Washington's in *Spence*. * * *

III

In order to decide whether *O'Brien* 's test applies here * * * we must decide whether Texas has asserted an interest in support of Johnson's conviction that is unrelated to the suppression of expression. [The] State offers two separate interests to justify this conviction: preventing breaches of the peace, and preserving the flag as a symbol of nationhood and national unity. We hold that the first interest is not implicated on this record and that the second is related to the suppression of expression.

A

Texas claims that its interest in preventing breaches of the peace justifies Johnson's conviction for flag desecration.[4] However, no disturbance of the peace actually occurred or threatened to occur because of Johnson's burning of the flag. [The] only evidence offered by the State at trial to show the reaction to Johnson's actions was the testimony of several persons who had been seriously offended by the flag-burning.

The State's position, therefore, amounts to a claim that an audience that takes serious offense at particular expression is necessarily likely to disturb the peace and that the expression may be prohibited on this basis. [W]e have not permitted the Government to assume that every expression of a provocative idea will incite a riot, but have instead required careful consideration of the actual circumstances surrounding such expression, asking whether the expression "is directed to inciting or producing imminent lawless action and is likely to incite or produce such action." *Brandenburg.* To accept Texas' arguments that it need only demonstrate "the potential for a breach of the peace," and that every flag-burning necessarily possesses that potential, would be to eviscerate our holding in *Brandenburg.* This we decline to do.

Nor does Johnson's expressive conduct fall within that small class of "fighting words" that are "likely to provoke the average person to retaliation, and thereby cause a breach of the peace." *Chaplinsky.* No reasonable onlooker would have regarded Johnson's generalized expression of dissatisfaction with the policies of the Federal Government as a direct personal insult or an invitation to exchange fisticuffs.

We thus conclude that the State's interest in maintaining order is not implicated on these facts. * * *

B

The State also asserts an interest in preserving the flag as a symbol of nationhood and national unity. [The] State, apparently, is concerned that such conduct will lead people to believe either that the flag does not stand for nationhood and national unity, but instead reflects other, less positive concepts,

4. Relying on our decision in *Boos v. Barry,* [p. 535 infra,] Johnson argues that this state interest is related to the suppression of free expression within the meaning of *O'Brien.* He reasons that the violent reaction to flag-burning feared by Texas would be the result of the message conveyed by them, and that this fact connects the State's interest to the suppression of expression. This view has found some favor in the lower courts. Johnson's theory may overread *Boos* insofar as it suggests that a desire to prevent a violent audience reaction is "related to expression" in the same way that a desire to prevent an audience from being offended is "related to expression." Because we find that the State's interest in preventing breaches of the peace is not implicated on these facts, however, we need not venture further into this area.

or that the concepts reflected in the flag do not in fact exist, that is, we do not enjoy unity as a Nation. These concerns blossom only when a person's treatment of the flag communicates some message, and thus are related "to the suppression of free expression" within the meaning of *O'Brien.* We are thus outside of *O'Brien* 's test altogether.

IV

It remains to consider whether the State's interest in preserving the flag as a symbol of nationhood and national unity justifies Johnson's conviction. [If Johnson] had burned the flag as a means of disposing of it because it was dirty or torn, he would not have been convicted of flag desecration under this Texas law: federal law designates burning as the preferred means of disposing of a flag "when it is in such condition that it is no longer a fitting emblem for display," 36 U.S.C. § 176(k), and Texas has no quarrel with this means of disposal. The Texas law is thus not aimed at protecting the physical integrity of the flag in all circumstances, but is designed instead to protect it only against impairments that would cause serious offense to others.[6] Texas concedes as much: "Section 42.09(b) reaches only those severe acts of physical abuse of the flag carried out in a way likely to be offensive. The statute mandates intentional or knowing abuse, that is, the kind of mistreatment that is not innocent, but rather is intentionally designed to seriously offend other individuals."

Whether Johnson's treatment of the flag violated Texas law thus depended on the likely communicative impact of his expressive conduct. Our decision in *Boos v. Barry* [485 U.S. 312, 108 S.Ct. 1157, 99 L.Ed.2d 333 (1988)] tells us that this restriction on Johnson's expression is content-based. In *Boos,* we considered the constitutionality of a law prohibiting "the display of any sign within 50 feet of a foreign embassy if that sign tends to bring that foreign government into 'public odium' or 'public disrepute.' " Rejecting the argument that the law was content-neutral because it was justified by "our international law obligation to shield diplomats from speech that offends their dignity," we held that "[t]he emotive impact of speech on its audience is not a 'secondary effect' " unrelated to the content of the expression itself.

According to the principles announced in *Boos,* Johnson's political expression was restricted because of the content of the message he conveyed. We must therefore subject the State's asserted interest in preserving the special symbolic character of the flag to "the most exacting scrutiny." *Boos v. Barry.*[8] * * *

According to Texas, if one physically treats the flag in a way that would tend to cast doubt on either the idea that nationhood and national unity are the flag's referents or that national unity actually exists, the message conveyed thereby is a harmful one and therefore may be prohibited.

6. *Cf. Smith v. Goguen* [415 U.S. 566, 94 S.Ct. 1242, 39 L.Ed.2d 605 (1974)] (Blackmun, J., dissenting) (emphasizing that lower court appeared to have construed state statute so as to protect physical integrity of the flag in all circumstances); *id.* (Rehnquist, J., dissenting) (same). [In *Goguen,* Blackmun, J., argued that "Goguen's punishment was constitutionally permissible for harming the physical integrity of the flag by wearing it affixed to the seat of his pants" and emphasized that such punishment would not be for "speech—a communicative element."].

8. Our inquiry is, of course, bounded by the particular facts of this case and by the statute under which Johnson was convicted. There was no evidence that Johnson himself stole the flag he burned, nor did the prosecution or the arguments urged in support of it depend on the theory that the flag was stolen. Thus, our analysis does not rely on the way in which the flag was acquired, and nothing in our opinion should be taken to suggest that one is free to steal a flag so long as one later uses it to communicate an idea. We also emphasize that Johnson was prosecuted *only* for flag desecration—not for trespass, disorderly conduct, or arson.

If there is a bedrock principle underlying the First Amendment, it is that the Government may not prohibit the expression of an idea simply because society finds the idea itself offensive or disagreeable. [We] have not recognized an exception to this principle even where our flag has been involved. [We] never before have held that the Government may ensure that a symbol be used to express only one view of that symbol or its referents. Indeed, in *Schacht v. United States* [398 U.S. 58, 90 S.Ct. 1555, 26 L.Ed.2d 44 (1970)] we invalidated a federal statute permitting an actor portraying a member of one of our armed forces to " 'wear the uniform of that armed force if the portrayal does not tend to discredit that armed force.' " This proviso, we held, "which leaves Americans free to praise the war in Vietnam but can send persons like Schacht to prison for opposing it, cannot survive in a country which has the First Amendment."

We perceive no basis on which to hold that the principle underlying our decision in *Schacht* does not apply to this case. To conclude that the Government may permit designated symbols to be used to communicate only a limited set of messages would be to enter territory having no discernible or defensible boundaries. Could the Government, on this theory, prohibit the burning of state flags? Of copies of the Presidential seal? Of the Constitution? In evaluating these choices under the First Amendment, how would we decide which symbols were sufficiently special to warrant this unique status? To do so, we would be forced to consult our own political preferences, and impose them on the citizenry, in the very way that the First Amendment forbids us to do.

There is, moreover, no indication—either in the text of the Constitution or in our cases interpreting it—that a separate judicial category exists for the American flag alone. Indeed, we would not be surprised to learn that the persons who framed our Constitution and wrote the Amendment that we now construe were not known for their reverence for the Union Jack. The First Amendment does not guarantee that other concepts virtually sacred to our Nation as a whole—such as the principle that discrimination on the basis of race is odious and destructive—will go unquestioned in the marketplace of ideas. See *Brandenburg.* We decline, therefore, to create for the flag an exception to the joust of principles protected by the First Amendment.

It is not the State's ends, but its means, to which we object. It cannot be gainsaid that there is a special place reserved for the flag in this Nation, and thus we do not doubt that the Government has a legitimate interest in making efforts to "preserv[e] the national flag as an unalloyed symbol of our country." We reject the suggestion, urged at oral argument by counsel for Johnson, that the Government lacks "any state interest whatsoever" in regulating the manner in which the flag may be displayed. Congress has, for example, enacted precatory regulations describing the proper treatment of the flag, see 36 U.S.C. §§ 173–177, and we cast no doubt on the legitimacy of its interest in making such recommendations. To say that the Government has an interest in encouraging proper treatment of the flag, however, is not to say that it may criminally punish a person for burning a flag as a means of political protest. "National unity as an end which officials may foster by persuasion and example is not in question. The problem is whether under our Constitution compulsion as here employed is a permissible means for its achievement."

We are fortified in today's conclusion by our conviction that forbidding criminal punishment for conduct such as Johnson's will not endanger the special role played by our flag or the feelings it inspires. To paraphrase Justice Holmes, we submit that nobody can suppose that this one gesture of an unknown man will change our Nation's attitude towards its flag. See *Abrams* (Holmes, J., dissenting). Indeed, Texas' argument that the burning of an American flag " 'is an act having a high likelihood to cause a breach of the peace,' " and its statute's implicit assumption that physical mistreatment of the flag will lead to "serious offense," tend to confirm that the flag's special role is not in danger; if it were, no one would riot or take offense because a flag had been burned.

We are tempted to say, in fact, that the flag's deservedly cherished place in our community will be strengthened, not weakened, by our holding today. Our decision is a reaffirmation of the principles of freedom and inclusiveness that the flag best reflects, and of the conviction that our toleration of criticism such as Johnson's is a sign and source of our strength. Indeed, one of the proudest images of our flag, the one immortalized in our own national anthem, is of the bombardment it survived at Fort McHenry. It is the Nation's resilience, not its rigidity, that Texas sees reflected in the flag—and it is that resilience that we reassert today.

The way to preserve the flag's special role is not to punish those who feel differently about these matters. It is to persuade them that they are wrong. [And,] precisely because it is our flag that is involved, one's response to the flag-burner may exploit the uniquely persuasive power of the flag itself. We can imagine no more appropriate response to burning a flag than waving one's own, no better way to counter a flag-burner's message than by saluting the flag that burns, no surer means of preserving the dignity even of the flag that burned than by—as one witness here did—according its remains a respectful burial. We do not consecrate the flag by punishing its desecration, for in doing so we dilute the freedom that this cherished emblem represents. * * *

JUSTICE KENNEDY, concurring.

I write not to qualify the words Justice Brennan chooses so well, for he says with power all that is necessary to explain our ruling. I join his opinion without reservation, but with a keen sense that this case, like others before us from time to time, exacts its personal toll. * * *

Our colleagues in dissent advance powerful arguments why respondent may be convicted for his expression, reminding us that among those who will be dismayed by our holding will be some who have had the singular honor of carrying the flag in battle. And I agree that the flag holds a lonely place of honor in an age when absolutes are distrusted and simple truths are burdened by unneeded apologetics.

With all respect to those views, I do not believe the Constitution gives us the right to rule as the dissenting members of the Court urge, however painful this judgment is to announce. Though symbols often are what we ourselves make of them, the flag is constant in expressing beliefs Americans share, beliefs in law and peace and that freedom which sustains the human spirit. The case here today forces recognition of the costs to which those beliefs commit us. It is poignant but fundamental that the flag protects those who hold it in contempt.

For all the record shows, this respondent was not a philosopher and perhaps did not even possess the ability to comprehend how repellent his statements must be to the Republic itself. But whether or not he could appreciate the enormity of the offense he gave, the fact remains that his acts were speech, in both the technical and the fundamental meaning of the Constitution. So I agree with the Court that he must go free.

CHIEF JUSTICE REHNQUIST, with whom JUSTICE WHITE and JUSTICE O'CONNOR join, dissenting.

In holding this Texas statute unconstitutional, the Court ignores Justice Holmes' familiar aphorism that "a page of history is worth a volume of logic." *New York Trust Co. v. Eisner,* 256 U.S. 345, 41 S.Ct. 506, 65 L.Ed. 963 (1921). For more than 200 years, the American flag has occupied a unique position as the symbol of our Nation, a uniqueness that justifies a governmental prohibition against flag burning in the way respondent Johnson did here. * * * [a]

The American flag, then, throughout more than 200 years of our history, has come to be the visible symbol embodying our Nation. It does not represent the views of any particular political party, and it does not represent any particular political philosophy. The flag is not simply another "idea" or "point of view" competing for recognition in the marketplace of ideas. Millions and millions of Americans regard it with an almost mystical reverence regardless of what sort of social, political, or philosophical beliefs they may have. I cannot agree that the First Amendment invalidates the Act of Congress, and the laws of 48 of the 50 States, which make criminal the public burning of the flag.

More than 80 years ago in *Halter v. Nebraska* [205 U.S. 34, 27 S.Ct. 419, 51 L.Ed. 696 (1907)], this Court upheld the constitutionality of a Nebraska statute that forbade the use of representations of the American flag for advertising purposes upon articles of merchandise. The Court there said: "For that flag every true American has not simply an appreciation but a deep affection. * * * Hence, it has often occurred that insults to a flag have been the cause of war, and indignities put upon it, in the presence of those who revere it, have often been resented and sometimes punished on the spot."

Only two Terms ago, in *San Francisco Arts & Athletics, Inc. v. United States Olympic Committee,* [483 U.S. 522, 107 S.Ct. 2971, 97 L.Ed.2d 427 (1987)], the Court held that Congress could grant exclusive use of the word "Olympic" to the United States Olympic Committee. The Court thought that this "restrictio[n] on expressive speech properly [was] characterized as incidental to the primary congressional purpose of encouraging and rewarding the USOC's activities." As the Court stated, "when a word [or symbol] acquires value 'as the result of organization and the expenditure of labor, skill, and money' by an entity, that entity constitutionally may obtain a limited property right in the word [or symbol]." Surely Congress or the States may recognize a similar interest in the flag.[b]

But the Court insists that the Texas statute prohibiting the public burning of the American flag infringes on respondent Johnson's freedom of expression. Such freedom, of course, is not absolute. [T]he public burning of the American flag by Johnson was no essential part of any exposition of ideas, and at the same time it had a tendency to incite a breach of the peace. Johnson was free to make any verbal denunciation of the flag that he wished; indeed, he was free to burn

a. Rehnquist, C.J., proceeded for some pages to invoke a legacy of prose, poetry, and law in honor of flags in general and the American flag in particular both in peace and in war, quoting poetry from, among others, Ralph Waldo Emerson and John Greenleaf Whittier. Emerson's poem referred to the Union Jack, but he did not always speak so warmly of the American flag. After passage of the Fugitive Slave Law Emerson wrote, "We sneak about with the infamy of crime in the streets, & cowardice in ourselves and frankly once for all the Union is sunk, the flag is hateful, and shall be hissed." *Emerson in His Journals* 421 (J. Porte ed. 1982).

b. In response, Brennan, J., observed that *Halter* was decided "nearly twenty years" before the first amendment was applied to the states and "[m]ore important" that *Halter* involved "purely commercial rather than political speech." Similarly, he stated that the authorization "to prohibit certain commercial and promotional uses of the word 'Olympic' [does not] even begin to tell us whether the Government may criminally punish physical conduct towards the flag engaged in as a means of political protest."

the flag in private. He could publicly burn other symbols of the Government or effigies of political leaders. He did lead a march through the streets of Dallas, and conducted a rally in front of the Dallas City Hall. He engaged in a "die-in" to protest nuclear weapons. He shouted out various slogans during the march, including: "Reagan, Mondale which will it be? Either one means World War III"; "Ronald Reagan, killer of the hour, Perfect example of U.S. power"; and "red, white and blue, we spit on you, you stand for plunder, you will go under." For none of these acts was he arrested or prosecuted; it was only when he proceeded to burn publicly an American flag stolen from its rightful owner that he violated the Texas statute. * * * As with "fighting words," so with flag burning, for purposes of the First Amendment: It is "no essential part of any exposition of ideas, and [is] of such slight social value as a step to truth that any benefit that may be derived from [it] is clearly outweighed" by the public interest in avoiding a probable breach of the peace. * * *

The result of the Texas statute is obviously to deny one in Johnson's frame of mind one of many means of "symbolic speech." Far from being a case of "one picture being worth a thousand words," flag burning is the equivalent of an inarticulate grunt or roar that, it seems fair to say, is most likely to be indulged in not to express any particular idea, but to antagonize others. [The] Texas statute deprived Johnson of only one rather inarticulate symbolic form of protest—a form of protest that was profoundly offensive to many—and left him with a full panoply of other symbols and every conceivable form of verbal expression to express his deep disapproval of national policy. Thus, in no way can it be said that Texas is punishing him because his hearers—or any other group of people—were profoundly opposed to the message that he sought to convey. Such opposition is no proper basis for restricting speech or expression under the First Amendment. It was Johnson's use of this particular symbol, and not the idea that he sought to convey by it or by his many other expressions, for which he was punished. * * *

The uniquely deep awe and respect for our flag felt by virtually all of us are bundled off under the rubric of "designated symbols," that the First Amendment prohibits the government from "establishing." But the government has not "established" this feeling; 200 years of history have done that. The government is simply recognizing as a fact the profound regard for the American flag created by that history when it enacts statutes prohibiting the disrespectful public burning of the flag.

The Court concludes its opinion with a regrettably patronizing civics lecture, presumably addressed to the Members of both Houses of Congress, the members of the 48 state legislatures that enacted prohibitions against flag burning, and the troops fighting under that flag in Vietnam who objected to its being burned: "The way to preserve the flag's special role is not to punish those who feel differently about these matters. It is to persuade them that they are wrong." The Court's role as the final expositor of the Constitution is well established, but its role as a platonic guardian admonishing those responsible to public opinion as if they were truant school children has no similar place in our system of government. The cry of "no taxation without representation" animated those who revolted against the English Crown to found our Nation—the idea that those who submitted to government should have some say as to what kind of laws would be passed. Surely one of the high purposes of a democratic society is to legislate against conduct that is regarded as evil and profoundly offensive to the majority of people—whether it be murder, embezzlement, pollution, or flag burning. * * *

Uncritical extension of constitutional protection to the burning of the flag risks the frustration of the very purpose for which organized governments are instituted. The Court decides that the American flag is just another symbol, about which not only must opinions pro and con be tolerated, but for which the most minimal public respect may not be enjoined. The government may conscript men into the Armed Forces where they must fight and perhaps die for the flag, but the government may not prohibit the public burning of the banner under which they fight. I would uphold the Texas statute as applied in this case.[2]

JUSTICE STEVENS, dissenting. * * *

Even if flag burning could be considered just another species of symbolic speech under the logical application of the rules that the Court has developed in its interpretation of the First Amendment in other contexts, this case has an intangible dimension that makes those rules inapplicable.

A country's flag is a symbol of more than "nationhood and national unity." [T]he American flag * * * is more than a proud symbol of the courage, the determination, and the gifts of nature that transformed 13 fledgling Colonies into a world power. It is a symbol of freedom, of equal opportunity, of religious tolerance, and of goodwill for other peoples who share our aspirations. The symbol carries its message to dissidents both at home and abroad who may have no interest at all in our national unity or survival.

The value of the flag as a symbol cannot be measured. Even so, I have no doubt that the interest in preserving that value for the future is both significant and legitimate. Conceivably that value will be enhanced by the Court's conclusion that our national commitment to free expression is so strong that even the United States as ultimate guarantor of that freedom is without power to prohibit the desecration of its unique symbol. But I am unpersuaded. The creation of a federal right to post bulletin boards and graffiti on the Washington Monument might enlarge the market for free expression, but at a cost I would not pay. Similarly, in my considered judgment, sanctioning the public desecration of the flag will tarnish its value—both for those who cherish the ideas for which it waves and for those who desire to don the robes of martyrdom by burning it. That tarnish is not justified by the trivial burden on free expression occasioned by requiring that an available, alternative mode of expression—including uttering words critical of the flag be employed.

It is appropriate to emphasize certain propositions that are not implicated by this case. [The] statute does not compel any conduct or any profession of respect for any idea or any symbol. [Nor] does the statute violate "the government's paramount obligation of neutrality in its regulation of protected communication." The content of respondent's message has no relevance whatsoever to the case. The concept of "desecration" does not turn on the substance of the message the actor intends to convey, but rather on whether those who view the act will take serious offense. Accordingly, one intending to convey a message of respect for the flag by burning it in a public square might nonetheless be guilty of desecration if he knows that others—perhaps simply because they misperceive

2. In holding that the Texas statute as applied to Johnson violates the First Amendment, the Court does not consider Johnson's claims that the statute is unconstitutionally vague or overbroad. I think those claims are without merit. [By] defining "desecrate" as "deface," "damage" or otherwise "physically mistreat" in a manner that the actor knows will "seriously offend" others, § 42.09 only prohibits flagrant acts of physical abuse and destruction of the flag of the sort at issue here—soaking a flag with lighter fluid and igniting it in public—and not any of the examples of improper flag etiquette cited in Respondent's brief.

the intended message—will be seriously offended. Indeed, even if the actor knows that all possible witnesses will understand that he intends to send a message of respect, he might still be guilty of desecration if he also knows that this understanding does not lessen the offense taken by some of those witnesses. The case has nothing to do with "disagreeable ideas." It involves disagreeable conduct that, in my opinion, diminishes the value of an important national asset.

The Court is therefore quite wrong in blandly asserting that respondent "was prosecuted for his expression of dissatisfaction with the policies of this country, expression situated at the core of our First Amendment values." Respondent was prosecuted because of the method he chose to express his dissatisfaction with those policies. Had he chosen to spray paint—or perhaps convey with a motion picture projector—his message of dissatisfaction on the facade of the Lincoln Memorial, there would be no question about the power of the Government to prohibit his means of expression. The prohibition would be supported by the legitimate interest in preserving the quality of an important national asset. Though the asset at stake in this case is intangible, given its unique value, the same interest supports a prohibition on the desecration of the American flag.*

The ideas of liberty and equality have been an irresistible force in motivating leaders like Patrick Henry, Susan B. Anthony, and Abraham Lincoln, schoolteachers like Nathan Hale and Booker T. Washington, the Philippine Scouts who fought at Bataan, and the soldiers who scaled the bluff at Omaha Beach. If those ideas are worth fighting for—and our history demonstrates that they are—it cannot be true that the flag that uniquely symbolizes their power is not itself worthy of protection from unnecessary desecration.

I respectfully dissent.

Notes and Questions

1. *Was Johnson convicted for his speech?* Johnson defended at trial on the ground that he did *not* burn the flag. Two witnesses, who had been observers of the march for the American Civil Liberties Union, testified that Johnson did not burn the flag. One witness, a police officer, testified that he saw Johnson set the flag on fire. The jury was instructed (over Johnson's objection) that Johnson could be convicted *either* if he burned the flag himself or if he encouraged the flag burning (the "law of the parties" rule). In closing argument the prosecutor argued both theories to the jury. In particular, the prosecutor said: "[I]f you look at this evidence from start to finish, the participating in the beginning, the literature, the shirt [Johnson wore a shirt bearing the name of the Revolutionary Communist Youth Brigade], who he is, the chanting, the yelling, the megaphone, the encouragement * * * being there, wanting this to happen, there is no

* The Court suggested that a prohibition against flag desecration is not content-neutral because this form of symbolic speech is only used by persons who are critical of the flag or the ideas it represents. In making this suggestion the Court does not pause to consider the far-reaching consequences of its introduction of disparate impact analysis into our First Amendment jurisprudence. It seems obvious that a prohibition against the desecration of a gravesite is content-neutral even if it denies some protesters the right to make a symbolic statement by extinguishing the flame in Arlington Cemetery where John F. Kennedy is buried while permitting others to salute the flame by bowing their heads. Few would doubt that a protester who extinguishes the flame has desecrated the gravesite, regardless of whether he prefaces that act with a speech explaining that his purpose is to express deep admiration or unmitigated scorn for the late President. Likewise, few would claim that the protester who bows his head has desecrated the gravesite, even if he makes clear that his purpose is to show disrespect. In such a case, as in a flag burning case, the prohibition against desecration has absolutely nothing to do with the content of the message that the symbolic speech is intended to convey.

question he encouraged it all. He's guilty as sin as far as the law of parties is concerned."

Is Brennan, J., on solid ground in fn. 2 when he finds it unlikely that Johnson was convicted on the encouragement theory? Did the Court need to reach the flagburning issue? Was it wise to do so?

2. *The flag's "physical integrity."* Brennan, J., observes that the Texas law is "not aimed at protecting the physical integrity of the flag in all circumstances. * * *" What if it were? [c]

In response to *Johnson,* Congress passed the Flag Protection Act of 1989 which attached criminal penalties to the knowing mutilation, defacement, burning, maintaining on the floor or ground, or trampling upon any flag of the United States.

UNITED STATES v. EICHMAN, ___ U.S. ___, 110 S.Ct. 2404, 110 L.Ed.2d 287 (1990), per BRENNAN, J., invalidated the statute: "Although the Flag Protection Act contains no explicit content-based limitation on the scope of prohibited conduct, it is nevertheless clear that the Government's asserted *interest* is 'related "to the suppression of free expression"' and concerned with the content of such expression. The Government's interest in protecting the 'physical integrity' of a privately owned flag rests upon a perceived need to preserve the flag's status as a symbol of our Nation and certain national ideals. But the mere destruction or disfigurement of a particular physical manifestation of the symbol, without more, does not diminish or otherwise affect the symbol itself in any way. For example, the secret destruction of a flag in one's own basement would not threaten the flag's recognized meaning. Rather, the Government's desire to preserve the flag as a symbol for certain national ideals is implicated 'only when a person's treatment of the flag communicates [a] message' to others that is inconsistent with those ideals."

STEVENS, J., joined by Rehnquist, C.J., White and O'Connor, JJ., dissenting, argued that the government's "legitimate interest in protecting the symbolic value of the American flag" outweighed the free speech interest. In describing the flag's symbolic value he stated that the flag "inspires and motivates the average citizen to make personal sacrifices in order to achieve societal goals of overriding importance; at all times, it serves as a reminder of the paramount importance of pursuing the ideals that characterize our society. * * * [T]he communicative value of a well-placed bomb in the Capital does not entitle it to the protection of the First Amendment. Burning a flag is not, of course, equivalent to burning a public building. Assuming that the protester is burning his own flag, it causes no physical harm to other persons or to their property. The impact is purely symbolic, and it is apparent that some thoughtful persons believe that impact far from depreciating the value of the symbol, will actually decrease its meaning. I most respectfully disagree." [d]

c. For commentary concerning the extent to which a focus on physical integrity can be separated from a concern with content, see Greenawalt, *O'er the Land of the Free: Flag Burning as Speech,* 37 UCLA L.Rev. 925 (1990); Michelman, *Saving Old Glory: On Constitutional Iconography,* 42 Stan.L.Rev. 1337 (1990); Stone, *Flag Burning and the Constitution,* 75 Ia.L.Rev. 111 (1989); Tushnet, *The Flag–Burning Episode: An Essay on the Constitution,* 61 U.Col.L.Rev. 39 (1990).

d. But see Loewy, *The Flag–Burning Case: Freedom of Speech When We Need It Most,* 68 N.C.L.Rev. 165, 174 (1989): "Perhaps the ultimate irony is that *Johnson* has done more to preserve the flag as a symbol of liberty than any prior decision, while the decision's detractors would allow real desecration of the flag by making it a symbol of political oppression." Compare West, *Foreword: Taking Freedom Seriously,* 104 Harv.L.Rev. 43, 97–98 (1990) (the militaristic patriotism associated with the flag menaces dissent); see also Greenawalt, fn. c supra.

3. Prior to adopting the Flag Protection Act, the Senate by a vote of 97–3 had passed a resolution expressing "profound disappointment with the [*Johnson*] decision." The House had approved a similar resolution by a vote of 411–5, and President Bush had proposed a constitutional amendment to overrule *Johnson.* Opponents of the amendment argued that a carefully drawn statute might (or would) be upheld by the Court. Suppose you were a member of the House or Senate at that time. Suppose you supported *Johnson* but believed that the statute might be held constitutional, even though you did not think it should be. Suppose you also believed that if a statute were not passed an amendment would.[e]

Consider this exchange during hearings of the House Subcommittee on Civil and Constitutional Rights on *Statutory and Constitutional Responses to the Supreme Court Decision in Texas v. Johnson* (1989): Former Solicitor General Charles Fried: "My good friends and colleagues, Rex Lee and Laurence Tribe, have testified that a statute might be drawn that would pass constitutional muster. [I] hope and urge and pray that we will not act—that no statute be passed and of course that the Constitution not be amended. In short, I believe that *Johnson* is right [in] principle." * * *

Representative Schroeder: "I thought your testimony was eloquent. I think in a purist world, that is where we should go. But [we] are not talking about a purist world. We are talking about a very political world." * * *

Mr. Fried: "There are times when you earn your rather inadequate salary by just doing the right thing, and where you seem to agree with me is that the right thing to do is to do neither one of these. * * * It is called leadership."

Representative Schroeder: "It is called leadership. * * * But I guess what I am saying is if we can't stop a stampede on an amendment without something, isn't it better to try to save the Bill of Rights and the Constitution?"

Community for Creative Non–Violence (CCNV) sought to conduct a winter-time demonstration near the White House in Lafayette Park and the Mall to dramatize the plight of the homeless. The National Park Service authorized the erection of two symbolic tent cities for purposes of the demonstration, but denied CCNV's request that demonstrators be permitted to sleep in the tents. National Park Service regulations permit camping (the "use of park land for living accommodation purposes such as sleeping activities") in National Parks only in campgrounds designated for that purpose.

CLARK v. COMMUNITY FOR CREATIVE NON–VIOLENCE, 468 U.S. 288, 104 S.Ct. 3065, 82 L.Ed.2d 221 (1984), per WHITE, J., rejected CCNV's claim that the regulations could not be constitutionally applied against its demonstration: "We need not differ with the view of the Court of Appeals that overnight sleeping in connection with the demonstration is expressive conduct protected to some extent by the First Amendment.[5] We assume for present purposes, but do

e. For commentary, see Michelman, fn. c supra.

5. We reject the suggestion of the plurality below, however, that the burden on the demonstrators is limited to "the advancement of a plausible contention" that their conduct is expressive. Although it is common to place the burden upon the Government to justify impingements on First Amendment interests, it is the obligation of the person desiring to engage in assertedly expressive conduct to demonstrate that the First Amendment even applies. To hold otherwise would be to create a rule that all conduct is presumptively expressive. In the absence of a showing that such a rule is necessary to protect vital First Amendment interests, we decline to deviate from the general rule that one seeking relief bears the burden of demonstrating that he is entitled to it.

not decide, that such is the case, cf. *O'Brien,* but this assumption only begins the inquiry. Expression, whether oral or written or symbolized by conduct, is subject to reasonable time, place, or manner restrictions. We have often noted that restrictions of this kind are valid provided that they are justified without reference to the content of the regulated speech, that they are narrowly tailored to serve a significant governmental interest, and that they leave open ample alternative channels for communication of the information.

"It is also true that a message may be delivered by conduct that is intended to be communicative and that, in context, would reasonably be understood by the viewer to be communicative. Symbolic expression of this kind may be forbidden or regulated if the conduct itself may constitutionally be regulated, if the regulation is narrowly drawn to further a substantial governmental interest, and if the interest is unrelated to the suppression of free speech. O'Brien.

"[That] sleeping, like the symbolic tents themselves, may be expressive and part of the message delivered by the demonstration does not make the ban any less a limitation on the manner of demonstrating, for reasonable time, place, or manner regulations normally have the purpose and direct effect of limiting expression but are nevertheless valid. Neither does the fact that sleeping, *arguendo,* may be expressive conduct, rather than oral or written expression, render the sleeping prohibition any less a time, place, or manner regulation. To the contrary, the Park Service neither attempts to ban sleeping generally nor to ban it everywhere in the parks. It has established areas for camping and forbids it elsewhere, including Lafayette Park and the Mall. Considered as such, we have very little trouble concluding that the Park Service may prohibit overnight sleeping in the parks involved here.

"The requirement that the regulation be content-neutral is clearly satisfied. The courts below accepted that view, and it is not disputed here that the prohibition on camping, and on sleeping specifically, is content-neutral and is not being applied because of disagreement with the message presented.[a] Neither was the regulation faulted, nor could it be, on the ground that without overnight sleeping the plight of the homeless could not be communicated in other ways. The regulation otherwise left the demonstration intact, with its symbolic city, signs, and the presence of those who were willing to take their turns in a day-and-night vigil. Respondents do not suggest that there was, or is, any barrier to delivering to the media, or to the public by other means, the intended message concerning the plight of the homeless.

"It is also apparent to us that the regulation narrowly focuses on the Government's substantial interest in maintaining the parks in the heart of our Capital in an attractive and intact condition, readily available to the millions of people who wish to see and enjoy them by their presence. To permit camping—using these areas as living accommodations—would be totally inimical to these purposes, as would be readily understood by those who have frequented the National Parks across the country and observed the unfortunate consequences of the activities of those who refuse to confine their camping to designated areas.

"It is urged by [CCNV], and the Court of Appeals was of this view, that if the symbolic city of tents was to be permitted and if the demonstrators did not intend to cook, dig, or engage in aspects of camping other than sleeping, the incremental benefit to the parks could not justify the ban on sleeping, which was

a. Marshall, J., dissenting, observed that CCNV had held a demonstration the previous winter in which it set up nine tents and slept in Lafayette Park. The D.C. Circuit held that the regulations did not preclude such a demonstration. According to Marshall, J., "The regulations at issue in this case were passed in direct response" to that holding.

here an expressive activity said to enhance the message concerning the plight of the poor and homeless. We cannot agree. In the first place, we seriously doubt that the First Amendment requires the Park Service to permit a demonstration in Lafayette Park and the Mall involving a 24–hour vigil and the erection of tents to accommodate 150 people. Furthermore, although we have assumed for present purposes that the sleeping banned in this case would have an expressive element, it is evident that its major value to this demonstration would be facilitative. Without a permit to sleep, it would be difficult to get the poor and homeless to participate or to be present at all.[b] This much is apparent from the permit application filed by respondents: 'Without the incentive of sleeping space or a hot meal, the homeless would not come to the site.' The sleeping ban, if enforced, would thus effectively limit the nature, extent, and duration of the demonstration and to that extent ease the pressure on the parks.

"Beyond this, however, it is evident from our cases that the validity of this regulation need not be judged solely by reference to the demonstration at hand.[c] Absent the prohibition on sleeping, there would be other groups who would demand permission to deliver an asserted message by camping in Lafayette Park. Some of them would surely have as credible a claim in this regard as does CCNV, and the denial of permits to still others would present difficult problems for the Park Service. With the prohibition, however, as is evident in the case before us, at least some around-the-clock demonstrations lasting for days on end will not materialize, others will be limited in size and duration, and the purposes of the regulation will thus be materially served. Perhaps these purposes would be more effectively and not so clumsily achieved by preventing tents and 24–hour vigils entirely in the core areas. But the Park Service's decision to permit nonsleeping demonstrations does not, in our view, impugn the camping prohibition as a valuable, but perhaps imperfect, protection to the parks. If the Government has a legitimate interest in ensuring that the National Parks are adequately protected, which we think it has, and if the parks would be more exposed to harm without the sleeping prohibition than with it, the ban is safe from invalidation under the First Amendment as a reasonable regulation of the manner in which a demonstration may be carried out. * * *

"Contrary to the conclusion of the Court of Appeals, the foregoing analysis demonstrates that the Park Service regulation is sustainable under the four-factor standard of *United States v. O'Brien,* for validating a regulation of expressive conduct, which, in the last analysis is little, if any, different from the standard applied to time, place, or manner restrictions.[8] No one contends that aside from its impact on speech a rule against camping or overnight sleeping in

b. What if it were the exclusive value? For discussion, see Francione, *Experimentation and the Marketplace Theory of the First Amendment,* 136 U.Pa.L.Rev. 417 (1987).

c. For debate about this point and its implications, compare Easterbrook, *Foreword: The Court and the Economic System,* 98 Harv. L.Rev. 4, 19–21 (1984) with Tribe, *Constitutional Calculus: Equal Justice or Economic Efficiency?* 98 Harv.L.Rev. 592, 599–603 (1985) and Easterbrook, *Method, Result, and Authority: A Reply,* 98 Harv.L.Rev. 622, 626 (1985).

8. Reasonable time, place, or manner restrictions are valid even though they directly limit oral or written expression. It would be odd to insist on a higher standard for limitations aimed at regulable conduct and having only an incidental impact on speech. Thus, if the time, place, or manner restriction on expressive sleeping, if that is what is involved in this case, sufficiently and narrowly serves a substantial enough governmental interest to escape First Amendment condemnation, it is untenable to invalidate it under *O'Brien* on the ground that the governmental interest is insufficient to warrant the intrusion on First Amendment concerns or that there is an inadequate nexus between the regulation and the interest sought to be served. We note that only recently, in a case dealing with the regulation of signs, the Court framed the issue under *O'Brien* and then based a crucial part of its analysis on the time, place, or manner cases.

public parks is beyond the constitutional power of the Government to enforce. And for the reasons we have discussed above, there is a substantial Government interest in conserving park property, an interest that is plainly served by, and requires for its implementation, measures such as the proscription of sleeping that are designed to limit the wear and tear on park properties. That interest is unrelated to suppression of expression.

"We are unmoved by the Court of Appeals' view that the challenged regulation is unnecessary, and hence invalid, because there are less speech-restrictive alternatives that could have satisfied the Government interest in preserving park lands. * * * The Court of Appeals' suggestions that the Park Service minimize the possible injury by reducing the size, duration, or frequency of demonstrations would still curtail the total allowable expression in which demonstrators could engage, whether by sleeping or otherwise, and these suggestions represent no more than a disagreement with the Park Service over how much protection the core parks require or how an acceptable level of preservation is to be attained. We do not believe, however, that either *United States v. O'Brien* or the time, place, or manner decisions assign to the judiciary the authority to replace the Park Service as the manager of the Nation's parks or endow the judiciary with the competence to judge how much protection of park lands is wise and how that level of conservation is to be [attained.]"

BURGER, C.J., concurred "fully in the Court's opinion," but added: "[CCNV's] attempt at camping in the park is a form of 'picketing'; it is conduct, not speech. [It] trivializes the First Amendment to seek to use it as a shield in the manner asserted here."

MARSHALL, J., joined by Brennan, J., dissented: "The majority assumes, without deciding, that the respondents' conduct is entitled to constitutional protection. The problem with this assumption is that the Court thereby avoids examining closely the reality of respondents' planned expression. The majority's approach denatures respondents' asserted right and thus makes all too easy identification of a Government interest sufficient to warrant its abridgment.

"[Missing] from the majority's description is any inkling that Lafayette Park and the Mall have served as the sites for some of the most rousing political demonstrations in the Nation's history.[2] [The] primary purpose for making *sleep* an integral part of the demonstration was 'to re-enact the central reality of homelessness' and to impress upon public consciousness, in as dramatic a way as possible, that homelessness is a widespread problem, often ignored, that confronts its victims with life-threatening deprivations. As one of the homeless men seeking to demonstrate explained: 'Sleeping in Lafayette Park or on the Mall, for me, is to show people that conditions are so poor for the homeless and poor in this city that we would actually sleep *outside* in the winter to get the point across.' * * * Here respondents clearly intended to protest the reality of homelessness by sleeping outdoors in the winter in the near vicinity of the magisterial residence of the President of the United States. In addition to accentuating the political character of their protest by their choice of location and mode of communication, respondents also intended to underline the meaning of their protest by giving their demonstration satirical names. Respondents planned to name the demonstration on the Mall 'Congressional Village,' and the demonstration in Lafayette Park, 'Reaganville II.'

2. At oral argument, the Government informed the Court "that on any given day there will be an average of three or so demonstrations going on" in the Mall–Lafayette Park area. Respondents accurately describe Lafayette Park "as the American analogue to 'Speaker's Corner' in Hyde Park."

"Nor can there be any doubt that in the surrounding circumstances the likelihood was great that the political significance of sleeping in the parks would be understood by those who viewed it. Certainly the news media understood the significance of respondents' proposed activity; newspapers and magazines from around the Nation reported their previous sleep-in and their planned [display].

"Although sleep in the context of this case is symbolic speech protected by the First Amendment, it is nonetheless subject to reasonable time, place, and manner restrictions. I agree with the standard enunciated by the majority.[6] I conclude, however, that the regulations at issue in this case, as applied to respondents, fail to satisfy this [standard].

"[T]here are no substantial Government interests advanced by the Government's regulations as applied to respondents. All that the Court's decision advances are the prerogatives of a bureaucracy that over the years has shown an implacable hostility toward citizens' exercise of First Amendment [rights].

"The disposition of this case impels me to make two additional observations. First, in this case, as in some others involving time, place, and manner restrictions, the Court has dramatically lowered its scrutiny of governmental regulations once it has determined that such regulations are content-neutral.[d] The result has been the creation of a two-tiered approach to First Amendment cases: while regulations that turn on the content of the expression are subjected to a strict form of judicial review, regulations that are aimed at matters other than expression receive only a minimal level of scrutiny. The minimal scrutiny prong of this two-tiered approach has led to an unfortunate diminution of First Amendment protection. By narrowly limiting its concern to whether a given regulation creates a content-based distinction, the Court has seemingly overlooked the fact that content-neutral restrictions are also capable of unnecessarily restricting protected expressive activity.[13] * * * The Court [has] transformed the ban against content distinctions from a floor that offers all persons at least equal liberty under the First Amendment into a ceiling that restricts persons to the protection of First Amendment equality—but nothing more.[14] The consistent imposition of silence upon all may fulfill the dictates of an evenhanded content-neutrality. But it offends our 'profound national commitment to the principle that debate on public issues should be uninhibited, robust, and wide-open'. *New York Times Co. v. Sullivan.*

"Second, the disposition of this case reveals a mistaken assumption regarding the motives and behavior of Government officials who create and administer content-neutral regulations. The Court's salutary skepticism of governmental decisionmaking in First Amendment matters suddenly dissipates once it deter-

6. I also agree with the majority that no substantial difference distinguishes the test applicable to time, place, and manner restrictions and the test articulated in *O'Brien.*

d. In support of Marshall, J.'s contention, see generally Lee, *Lonely Pamphleteers, Little People, and the Supreme Court,* 54 G.W.U.L. Rev. 757 (1986).

13. See Redish, *The Content Distinction in First Amendment Analysis,* 34 Stan.L.Rev. 113 (1981).

14. Furthermore, a content-neutral regulation does not necessarily fall with random or equal force upon different groups or different points of view. A content-neutral regulation that restricts an inexpensive mode of communication will fall most heavily upon relatively poor speakers and to points of view that such speakers typically espouse. [See Lee, fn. d supra.] This sort of latent inequality is very much in evidence in this case, for respondents lack the financial means necessary to buy access to more conventional modes of persuasion.

A disquieting feature about the disposition of this case is that it lends credence to the charge that judicial administration of the First Amendment, in conjunction with a social order marked by large disparities of wealth and other sources of power, tends systematically to discriminate against efforts by the relatively disadvantaged to convey their political ideas. * * *

mines that a restriction is not content-based. The Court evidently assumes that the balance struck by officials is deserving of deference so long as it does not appear to be tainted by content discrimination. What the Court fails to recognize is that public officials have strong incentives to overregulate even in the absence of an intent to censor particular views. This incentive stems from the fact that of the two groups whose interests officials must accommodate—on the one hand, the interests of the general public and, on the other, the interests of those who seek to use a particular forum for First Amendment activity—the political power of the former is likely to be far greater than that of the latter.[16] "

Notes and Questions

1. Consider Tushnet, *Character as Argument,* 14 Law and Social Inquiry 539, 549 (1989) (reviewing Kalven, *A Worthy Tradition*): "[W]hen political dissidence is in a sense validated by tradition it can lose its political effect. When dissidents use traditional forms of protest, they may be met by [a] kind of indifference—not the considered rejection of their protests but rather resigned acceptance of their actions as the kind of thing we have to put up with every now and then. To capture the attention of a public accustomed to dignified protest, and able to screen it from consciousness, dissidents may have to adopt novel forms of protest, such as sleeping in a national park overnight to draw attention to the disgrace of a national policy that deprives many people of decent shelter. Yet, precisely because their protests take a novel form, they may not be covered by the worthy tradition that Kalven honors. In this sense the dynamics of protest may make the protection of free speech what Kalven tellingly calls a 'luxury civil liberty,' a civil liberty to be enjoyed when nothing of consequence turns on protecting speech and to be abandoned when it really matters."

2. Should the Court have decided whether sleeping in the park in these circumstances was a form of expression entitled to some degree of first amendment protection? Should all forms of expression receive some level of first amendment protection?

(a) *Terrorism.* Would a political assassination be unprotected expression because it is not within the scope of the first amendment or because the government interests outweigh the expressive values. Does it matter?

(b) *The absence of "ideas."* Is the presence of an "idea" a necessary condition for expression to come within the first amendment's scope? Should nude dancing be excluded from the first amendment's scope because it is not intended to communicate ideas? Should protection for paintings depend upon whether "ideas" are expressed? See *Schad v. Mount Ephraim,* p. 561 infra: "[N]ude dancing is not without its First Amendment protections from official regulation." Should hair styles be afforded first amendment protection? Are hair styles distinguishable from nude dancing on the ground that the latter is a form of expressive entertainment? If so, should video games be afforded first amendment protection? See Note, *The First Amendment Side Effects of Curing Pac–Man Fever,* 84 Colum.L.Rev. 744 (1984). But see Schauer, *Free Speech and the Demise of the Soapbox* Book Review, 84 Colum.L.Rev. 558, 565 (1984) ("Maybe there is something I am missing, but the first amendment importance of the messages from an automatic teller to the bank's central computer completely escapes me, as does the first amendment importance of the mutual exchange of electronic and visual symbols between me and the Pac–Man machine.").

16. See Goldberger, *Judicial Scrutiny in Public Forum Cases: Misplaced Trust in the Judgment of Public Officials,* 32 Buffalo L.Rev. 175, 208 (1983).

3. The "time, place, or manner" test set out in *Clark* is differently stated in different cases. For example, *United States Postal Service v. Council of Greenburgh Civic. Associations,* 453 U.S. 114, 101 S.Ct. 2676, 69 L.Ed.2d 517 (1981), speaks of "adequate" as opposed to "ample" alternative channels of communication, and *City of Renton v. Playtime Theatres, Inc.,* p. 561 infra, transcends the difference by requiring that the restriction not "unreasonably limit" alternative channels of communication. Beyond these differences, a number of cases state that the regulation must serve a significant government interest without stating that it must be "narrowly tailored" to serve a significant government interest. See e.g., *Heffron v. International Soc. For Krishna Consciousness,* p. 643 infra. But see *Ward v. Rock Against Racism,* p. 643 infra (reaffirming and defining narrowly tailored requirement).

4. Assuming sleeping in the *Clark* context implicates first amendment values, what test should apply? Consider Shiffrin, *The First Amendment, Democracy, and Romance* 186–187 fn. 122 (1990): "An interesting puzzle for those schooled [in] casuistry (for example litigants and judges in the lower courts) [has been] to wonder how the time, place, and manner test differed from the *O'Brien* test and to determine which test applied when. Only one prepared to learn that the Emperor had no clothes would have summoned the temerity to ask *why* these different sets of tests had developed in the first place. To be sure, if the concern is with a regulation's "incidental" impact on free speech, it makes sense to inquire whether means less restrictive of free speech are available. So too, if a place restriction on free speech is in question, it makes sense to wonder about alternative possibilities for communication. Nonetheless, if a place restriction limits speech, it would also make sense to inquire whether the state objectives could be achieved by means less restrictive of speech. Similarly, depending on what the "incidental" restriction might be, it could make sense to consider alternative channels of, or possibilities for, communication as one means of evaluating the severity of the restriction."

Given the different factors stated by the two tests, is it reasonable for the Court to assert that they are "little, if any, different." Is the phrasing of a test less important than its application? Consider Stone, *Content–Neutral Restrictions,* 54 U.Chi.L.Rev. 46, 52 (1987): "The test of a test is not its formulation, but its application. Despite the apparent differences among formulations [referring among others to the *O'Brien* test and a variation of the time, place, and manner test], the result [is] the same—the Court upholds the challenged restriction." See also Schauer, *Cuban Cigars, Cuban Books, and the Problem of Incidental Restrictions on Communications,* 26 Wm. & Mary L.Rev. 779, 788 (1985).

But cf. Shiffrin, supra at 187 n. 122, 34–35: "This is a plausible reading of the small number of Supreme Court cases that have applied these tests, but Stone's conclusion has nothing to do with the law as it has functioned in the lower courts. Not only have restrictions been struck down under both of the tests, but the lower courts have frequently struggled with the Court's meanderings in an attempt to figure out which test to apply, sometimes with the view that determining which test or version of the test to apply might matter.

"[Standards] of review are a way of trying to generalize the requirements of justification in particular classes of cases. One difficulty with the technique is that the strength of state interests and the impact on speech values interact in too many complicated ways to make the prospects for standards of review realistic. After all, the only occasion for their use is in circumstances where the categories of regulation at issue are too unmanageable to have given rise to rules. Thus, it is understandable that standards of review in the first amendment area quickly deteriorate (or ripen—depending on your perspective) into general balancing tests.

"Ultimately, the standards of review are overconfident or cynical. If they are designed with the view that they state the factors to be weighed with appreciation for the needs of diverse situations, they reveal a stunning naivete about the complexities of social reality. If they are designed to mask the subjective aspects of first amendment decisionmaking, by providing a 'test' that makes an ad hoc process *appear* determinative, they mask cynicism."

New York Public Health law authorizes the forced closure of a building for one year if it has been used for the purpose of "lewdness, assignation or prostitution." Pursuant to this statute, a civil complaint alleged that prostitution solicitation and sexual activities by patrons were occurring on the premises of an adult bookstore all within the observation of the proprietor. Accordingly, the complaint called for the closure of the building for one year. There was no claim that any books in the store were obscene. The New York Court of Appeals held that the closure remedy violated the first amendment because it was broader than necessary to achieve the restriction against illicit sexual activities. It reasoned that an injunction against the alleged sexual conduct could further the state interest without infringing on first amendment values.

ARCARA v. CLOUD BOOKS, INC., 478 U.S. 697, 106 S.Ct. 3172, 92 L.Ed.2d 568 (1986), per BURGER, C.J., reversed, holding that the closure remedy did not violate the first amendment; indeed, that the closure remedy did not require any first amendment scrutiny: "This Court has applied First Amendment scrutiny to a statute regulating conduct which has the incidental effect of burdening the expression of a particular political opinion. *United States v. O'Brien.* * * *

"We have also applied First Amendment scrutiny to some statutes which, although directed at activity with no expressive component, impose a disproportionate burden upon those engaged in protected First Amendment activities. In *Minneapolis Star & Tribune v. Minnesota Commissioner of Revenue,* 460 U.S. 575, 103 S.Ct. 1365, 75 L.Ed.2d 295 (1983), we struck down a tax imposed on the sale of large quantities of newsprint and ink because the tax had the effect of singling out newspapers to shoulder its burden. We imposed a greater burden of justification on the State even though the tax was imposed upon a nonexpressive activity, since the burden of the tax inevitably fell disproportionately—in fact, almost exclusively—upon the shoulders of newspapers exercising the constitutionally protected freedom of the press. Even while striking down the tax in *Minneapolis Star,* we emphasized: 'Clearly, the First Amendment does not prohibit all regulation of the press. It is beyond dispute that the States and the Federal Government can subject newspapers to generally applicable economic regulations without creating constitutional problems.'

"The New York Court of Appeals held that the *O'Brien* test for permissible governmental regulation was applicable to this case because the closure order sought by petitioner would also impose an incidental burden upon respondents' bookselling activities. That court ignored a crucial distinction between the circumstances presented in *O'Brien* and the circumstances of this case: unlike the symbolic draft card burning in *O'Brien,* the sexual activity carried on in this case manifests absolutely no element of protected expression.[a] In *Paris Adult Theatre,* we underscored the fallacy of seeking to use the First Amendment as a cloak for obviously unlawful public sexual conduct by the diaphanous device of

a. In an earlier section of the opinion, Burger, C.J., stated that, "petitioners in *O'Brien* had, as respondents here do not, at least the semblence of expressive activity in their claim that the otherwise unlawful burning of a draft card was to 'carry a message' of the actor's opposition to the draft."

attributing protected expressive attributes to that conduct. First Amendment values may not be invoked by merely linking the words 'sex' and 'books.'

"Nor does the distinction drawn by the New York Public Health Law inevitably single out bookstores or others engaged in First Amendment protected activities for the imposition of its burden, as did the tax struck down in *Minneapolis Star.* As we noted in *Minneapolis Star,* neither the press nor booksellers may claim special protection from governmental regulations of general applicability simply by virtue of their First Amendment protected activities. If the city imposed closure penalties for demonstrated Fire Code violations or health hazards from inadequate sewage treatment, the First Amendment would not aid the owner of premises who had knowingly allowed such violations to persist. * * *

"It is true that the closure order in this case would require respondents to move their bookselling business to another location. Yet we have not traditionally subjected every criminal and civil sanction imposed through legal process to 'least restrictive means' scrutiny simply because each particular remedy will have some effect on the First Amendment activities of those subject to sanction. Rather, we have subjected such restrictions to scrutiny only where it was conduct with a significant expressive element that drew the legal remedy in the first place, as in *O'Brien,* or where a statute based on a nonexpressive activity has the inevitable effect of singling out those engaged in expressive activity, as in *Minneapolis Star.* This case involves neither situation, and we conclude the First Amendment is not implicated by the enforcement of a public health regulation of general application against the physical premises in which respondents happen to sell books.[4] " [b]

O'CONNOR, J., joined by Stevens, J., concurred: "I agree that the Court of Appeals erred in applying a First Amendment standard of review where, as here, the government is regulating neither speech nor an incidental, non-expressive effect of speech. Any other conclusion would lead to the absurd result that any government action that had some conceivable speech-inhibiting consequences, such as the arrest of a newscaster for a traffic violation, would require analysis under the First Amendment. If, however, a city were to use a nuisance statute as a pretext for closing down a book store because it sold indecent books or because of the perceived secondary effects of having a purveyor of such books in the neighborhood, the case would clearly implicate First Amendment concerns and require analysis under the appropriate First Amendment standard of review. Because there is no suggestion in the record or opinion below of such pretextual use of the New York nuisance provision in this case, I concur in the Court's opinion and judgment."

4. Respondents assert that closure of their premises is sought as a pretext for suppression of First Amendment protected expression. However, there is no suggestion on the record before us that the closure of respondents' bookstore was sought under the public health nuisance statute as a pretext for the suppression of First Amendment protected material. Were respondents able to establish the existence of such a speech suppressive motivation or policy on the part of the District Attorney, they might have a claim of selective prosecution. Respondents in this case made no such assertion before the trial court.

b. On remand, the New York Court of Appeals held that, in the absence of a showing that the state had chosen a course no broader than necessary to accomplish its purpose, any forced closure of the bookstore would unduly impair the bookseller's rights of free expression under the New York State constitution. From New York's perspective, the question is not "who is aimed at but who is hit." See *People ex rel. Arcara v. Cloud Books, Inc.,* 68 N.Y.2d 553, 510 N.Y.S.2d 844, 503 N.E.2d 492 (1986).

BLACKMUN, J., joined by Brennan and Marshall, JJ., dissented: "Despite the obvious role that commercial bookstores play in facilitating free expression, the Court today concludes that a closure order would raise no First Amendment concerns, apparently because it would be triggered, not by respondents' sale of books, but by the nonexpressive conduct of patrons. But the First Amendment, made applicable to the States by the Fourteenth Amendment, protects against all laws 'abridging the freedom of speech'—not just those specifically directed at expressive activity. Until today, this Court has never suggested that a State may suppress speech as much as it likes, without justification, so long as it does so through generally applicable regulations that have 'nothing to do with any expressive conduct.' * * *

"At some point, of course, the impact of state regulation on First Amendment rights become so attenuated that it is easily outweighed by the state interest. But when a State directly and substantially impairs First Amendment activities, such as by shutting down a bookstore, I believe that the State must show, at a minimum, that it has chosen the least restrictive means of pursuing its legitimate objectives. The closure of a bookstore can no more be compared to a traffic arrest of a reporter than the closure of a church could be compared to the traffic arrest of its clergyman.

"A State has a legitimate interest in forbidding sexual acts committed in public, including a bookstore. An obvious method of eliminating such acts is to arrest the patron committing them. But the statute in issue does not provide for that. Instead, it imposes absolute liability on the bookstore simply because the activity occurs on the premises. And the penalty—a mandatory 1-year closure—imposes an unnecessary burden on speech. Of course 'linking the words "sex" and "books"' is not enough to extend First Amendment protection to illegal sexual activity, but neither should it suffice to remove First Amendment protection from books situated near the site of such activity. The State's purpose in stopping public lewdness cannot justify such a substantial infringement of First Amendment rights. * * *

"Petitioner has not demonstrated that a less restrictive remedy would be inadequate to abate the nuisance. The Court improperly attempts to shift to the bookseller the responsibility for finding an alternative site. But surely the Court would not uphold a city ordinance banning all public debate on the theory that the residents could move somewhere else. [Because] the statute is not narrowly tailored to further the asserted governmental interest, it is unconstitutional as applied to respondents."

Notes and Questions

1. Should the state's closing of a bookstore *always* trigger heightened judicial scrutiny? Is the first amendment really "not implicated" in *Arcara?* Should fire code regulations trigger first amendment scrutiny? Consider, Comment, *Padlock Orders and Nuisance Laws,* 51 Albany L.Rev. 1007, 1026–27 (1987): "Closure penalties for fire code violations or health hazards from inadequate sewage treatment were offered as examples of generally applicable regulations which could constitutionally be applied to bookstores where the owner 'had knowingly allowed such violations to persist.' Few would argue with this conclusion. These generally applicable regulations would be within the state's constitutional power, would further a substantial governmental interest unrelated to the suppression of free expression, and the incidental restriction on first amendment freedoms, where the owner knowingly allowed the violations to

persist, would be no greater than is essential to further the state's interest. Concluding that the *O'Brien* test is satisfied, however, does not support the conclusion that the test does not apply."

2. *Negative theory.* Should the scope of the first amendment be confined to instances in which government may have acted in a biased way? Consider Cass, *Commercial Speech, Constitutionalism, Collective Choice,* 56 U.Cin.L.Rev. 1317, 1352 (1988): "The root concern for first amendment prohibitions on abridgement of speech and press freedom is official bias. There is widespread agreement that limitation of official bias is the principal aim of the first amendment, historically and as amplified over the past half-century by the courts." See generally Cass, *The Perils of Positive Thinking: Constitutional Interpretation and Negative First Amendment Theory,* 34 UCLA L.Rev. 1405 (1987) (emphasizing official self interest and, to a lesser extent, intolerance as the principal motives of concern).

Professor Schauer has also attempted a justification for freedom of speech not based on any positive aspects of speech, but based on the premise that governments are "less capable of regulating speech than they are of regulating other forms of conduct." F. Schauer, *Free Speech: A Philosophical Enquiry* 81 (1982). See also Schauer, *Must Speech Be Special?,* 78 Nw.U.L.Rev. 1284 (1983). He suggests that bias, self-interest, and a general urge to suppress that with which one disagrees are significant reasons for this incapability. See *Free Speech,* supra, at 80–86. As he interprets the first amendment, therefore, its "focus * * * is on the motivations of the government." Schauer, *Cuban Cigars, Cuban Books, and the Problem of Incidental Restrictions on Communications,* 26 Wm. & Mary L.Rev. 779, 780 (1985).

Is negative theory consistent with what the Court has *said* about free speech? With the doctrine it has produced? Consider, e.g., *Arcara. O'Brien.* The defamation line of cases. Compare Schauer, *Cuban Cigars,* supra with Shiffrin, *The First Amendment, Democracy, and Romance* (1990). Is the content-based/content-neutral distinction founded exclusively on a concern with government motive? See generally Stone, *Content Regulation and the First Amendment,* 25 Wm. & Mary L.Rev. 189 (1983) (arguing that the basis for the distinction is more complicated). Does an emphasis on motive or content unreasonably downplay the notion that the *effect* of government conduct on the quantity or quality of speech is of independent first amendment value? See generally Redish, *The Content Distinction in First Amendment Analysis,* 34 Stan. L.Rev. 113 (1981).

3. Could *Arcara's* failure to find the first amendment implicated be justified without resort to negative theory or motive theory? Consider Tribe, *Amer. Constitutional Law* 978–79 n. 2 (2d ed. 1988): "[W]hen *neither* the law, *nor* the act triggering its enforcement has any significant first amendment dimension, the fact that the law *incidentally* operates to restrict first amendment activity, and that some alternative state measure might offer a less restrictive means of pursuing the state's legitimate objectives, should not serve to condemn what the state has done as unconstitutional." Why not?

SECTION 3. IS SOME PROTECTED SPEECH LESS EQUAL THAN OTHER PROTECTED SPEECH?

I. NEAR OBSCENE SPEECH

ERZNOZNIK v. JACKSONVILLE, 422 U.S. 205, 95 S.Ct. 2268, 45 L.Ed.2d 125 (1975), per POWELL, J., held invalid on its face an ordinance that prohibited drive-in theaters from showing films containing nudity ("bare buttocks, * * * female bare breasts, or human bare pubic areas") when visible from a public street or public place: "Appellee concedes that its ordinance sweeps far beyond the permissible restraints on obscenity, and thus applies to films that are protected by the First Amendment. [Its] primary argument is that it may protect its citizens against unwilling exposure to materials that may be offensive. Jacksonville's ordinance, however, does not protect citizens from all movies that might offend; rather it singles out films containing nudity, presumably because the lawmakers considered them especially offensive to passersby. * * *

"The plain, if at times disquieting, truth is that in our pluralistic society, constantly proliferating new and ingenious forms of expression, 'we are inescapably captive audiences for many purposes.' Much that we encounter offends our esthetic, if not our political and moral, sensibilities. Nevertheless, the Constitution does not permit the government to decide which types of otherwise protected speech are sufficiently offensive to require protection for the unwilling listener or viewer. Rather,[6] the burden normally falls upon the viewer to 'avoid further bombardment of [his] sensibilities simply by averting [his] eyes.' *Cohen v. California.* The Jacksonville ordinance discriminates among movies solely on the basis of content.[7] Its effect is to deter drive-in theaters from showing movies containing any nudity, however innocent or even educational.[8] This discrimina-

6. It has also been suggested that government may proscribe, by a properly framed law, "the willful use of scurrilous language calculated to offend the sensibilities of an unwilling audience." *Rosenfeld* (Powell, J., dissenting). [In] the present case, however, appellant is not trying to reach, much less shock, unwilling viewers. Appellant manages a commercial enterprise which depends for its success on *paying* customers, not on freeloading passersby. Presumably, where economically feasible, the screen of a drive-in theater will be shielded from those who do not pay.

7. Scenes of nudity in a movie, like pictures of nude persons in a book, must be considered as a part of the whole work. In this respect such nudity is distinguishable from the kind of public nudity traditionally subject to indecent exposure laws.

The Chief Justice's dissent, in response to this point, states that "[u]nlike persons reading books, passersby cannot consider fragments of drive-in movies as a part of the 'whole work' for the simple reason that they see but do not *hear* the [performance]." (emphasis in original). At issue here, however, is not the viewing rights of unwilling viewers but rather the rights of those who operate drive-in theatres and the public that attends these establishments. The effect of the Jacksonville ordinance is to increase the cost of showing films containing nudity. See n. 8, infra. In certain circumstances theatres will avoid showing these movies rather than incur the additional costs. As a result persons who want to see such films at drive-ins will be unable to do so. It is in this regard that a motion picture must be considered as a whole, and not as isolated fragments or scenes of nudity.

[The Chief Justice's response to fn. 7 also stated: "[T]hose persons who legitimately desire to consider the 'work as a whole' are not foreclosed from doing so. The record shows that the film from which appellant's prosecution arose was exhibited in several indoor theaters in the Jacksonville area. And the owner of a drive-in movie theater is not prevented from exhibiting nonobscene films involving nudity so long as he effectively shields the screen from public view. Thus, regardless of whether the ordinance involved here can be loosely described as regulating the content of a certain type of display, it is not a restriction of any 'message.' The First Amendment interests involved in this case are trivial at best."]

8. Such a deterrent, although it might not result in total suppression of these movies, is a restraint on free expression. The record does

tion cannot be justified as a means of preventing significant intrusions on privacy. The ordinance seeks only to keep these films from being seen from public streets and places where the offended viewer readily can avert his eyes. In short, the screen of a drive-in theater is not 'so obtrusive as to make it impossible for an unwilling individual to avoid exposure to it.' *Redrup.* Thus, we conclude that the limited privacy interest of persons on the public streets cannot justify this censorship of otherwise protected speech on the basis of its [content].

"In this case, assuming the ordinance is aimed at prohibiting youths from viewing the films, the restriction is broader than permissible. The ordinance is not directed against sexually explicit nudity, nor is it otherwise limited. Rather, [it] would bar a film containing a picture of a baby's buttocks, the nude body of a war victim, or scenes from a culture in which nudity is indigenous. The ordinance also might prohibit newsreel scenes of the opening of an art exhibit as well as shots of bathers on a beach. Clearly all nudity cannot be deemed obscene even as to minors. See *Ginsberg.* Nor can such a broad restriction be justified by any other governmental interest pertaining to minors. Speech that is neither obscene as to youths nor subject to some other legitimate proscription cannot be suppressed solely to protect the young from ideas or images that a legislative body thinks unsuitable for them." [a]

BURGER, C.J., joined by Rehnquist, J., dissented: "[T]he conclusion that only a limited interest of persons on the public streets is at stake here can be supported only if one completely ignores the unique visual medium to which the Jacksonville ordinance is directed. Whatever validity the notion that passersby may protect their sensibilities by averting their eyes may have when applied to words printed on an individual's jacket, see *Cohen,* [it] distorts reality to apply that notion to the outsize screen of a drive-in movie [theater].

"[The] screen of a drive-in movie theater is a unique type of eye-catching display that can be highly intrusive and distracting. Public authorities have a legitimate interest in regulating such displays under the police power; for example, even though traffic safety may not have been the only target of the ordinance in issue here, I think it not unreasonable for lawmakers to believe that public nudity on a giant screen, visible at night to hundreds of drivers of automobiles, may have a tendency to divert attention from their task and cause accidents." [b]

not indicate how much it would cost to block public view of appellant's theater. Such costs generally will vary with circumstances. In one case the expense was estimated at approximately a quarter million dollars. See *Olympic Drive-In Theatre, Inc. v. Pagedale,* 441 S.W.2d 5, 8 (Mo.1969).

a. The Court also rejected the argument that the ordinance was aimed at traffic regulation: "[The] ordinance applies to movie screens visible from public places as well as public streets, thus indicating that it is not a traffic regulation. But even if this were the purpose [it] would be invalid" because "strikingly underinclusive" in "singling out [even] the most fleeting and innocent glimpses of nudity," which violated both the equal protection clause and the first amendment by discriminating on the basis of content without justification, since "other scenes in the customary screen diet, ranging from soap opera to violence, would be [no] less distracting to the passing motorist."

b. White, J., also dissented. Douglas, J., concurred.

YOUNG v. AMERICAN MINI THEATRES, INC.

427 U.S. 50, 96 S.Ct. 2440, 49 L.Ed.2d 310 (1976).

JUSTICE STEVENS delivered the opinion of the Court.*

[Detroit "Anti-Skid Row" ordinances prohibited "adult motion picture theaters" and "adult book stores" within 1,000 feet of any two other "regulated uses," which included such theaters and book stores, liquor stores, pool halls, pawnshops, and the like. The ordinances defined "adult motion picture theater" as one "presenting material distinguished or characterized by an emphasis on matter depicting, describing or relating to 'Specified Sexual Activities' [a] or 'Specified Anatomical Areas' " [b] and "adult book store" in substantially the same terms. The Court upheld the ordinances, reversing a decision in a federal declaratory judgment action by two theater owners wishing regularly to exhibit "adult" motion pictures.]

I. [R]espondents claim that the ordinances are too vague [because] they cannot determine how much of the ["specified"] activity may be permissible before the exhibition is "characterized by an emphasis" on such matter. [We] find it unnecessary to consider the validity of [this argument. Both] theaters propose to offer adult fare on a regular basis. [Therefore], the element of vagueness in these ordinances has not affected these respondents. * * *

Because the ordinances affect communication protected by the First Amendment, respondents argue that they may raise the vagueness issue even though there is no uncertainty about the impact of the ordinances on their own rights. On several occasions we have determined that a defendant whose own speech was unprotected had standing to challenge the constitutionality of a statute which purported to prohibit protected speech, or even speech arguably protected. *Broadrick*. The exception is justified by the overriding importance of maintaining a free and open market for the interchange of ideas. Nevertheless, if the statute's deterrent effect of legitimate expression is not "both real and substantial" and if the statute is "readily subject to a narrowing construction by the state courts" the litigant is not permitted to assert the rights of third parties.

We are not persuaded that the Detroit Zoning Ordinances will have a significant deterrent effect on the exhibition of films protected by the First Amendment. [T]he only vagueness in the ordinances relates to the amount of sexually explicit activity that may be portrayed before the material can be said to be "characterized by an emphasis" on such matter. For most films the question will be readily answerable; to the extent that an area of doubt exists, we see no reason why the statute is not "readily subject to a narrowing construction by the state courts." Since there is surely a less vital interest in

* Part III of this opinion is joined only by The Chief Justice, Mr. Justice White, and Mr. Justice Rehnquist.

a. "Specified Sexual Activities" were defined thus:

"1. Human Genitals in a state of sexual stimulation or arousal;

"2. Acts of human masturbation, sexual intercourse or sodomy;

"3. Fondling or other erotic touching of human genitals, pubic region, buttock or female breast."

b. "Specified Anatomical Areas" were defined thus:

"1. Less than completely and opaquely covered: (a) human genitals, pubic region, (b) buttock, and (c) female breast below a point immediately above the top of the areola, and

"2. Human male genitals in a discernibly turgid state, even if completely and opaquely covered."

the uninhibited exhibition of material that is on the border line between pornography and artistic expression than in the free dissemination of ideas of social and political significance,[c] and since the limited amount of uncertainty in the statute is easily susceptible of a narrowing construction, we think this is an inappropriate case in which to adjudicate the hypothetical claims of persons not before the Court. * * *

III. [T]he use of streets and parks for the free expression of views on national affairs may not be conditioned upon the sovereign's agreement with what a speaker may intend to say. [If] picketing in the vicinity of a school is to be allowed to express the point of view of labor, that means of expression in that place must be allowed for other points of view as well. As we said in [*Chicago Police Dep't v. Mosley*]. "The central problem with Chicago's ordinance is that it describes permissible picketing in terms of its subject matter. [A]bove all else, the First Amendment means that government has no power to restrict expression because of its message, its ideas, its subject matter, or its content. [Any] restriction on expressive activity because of its content would completely undercut the 'profound national commitment to the principle that debate on public issues should be uninhibited, robust, and wide-open.' [*New York Times*]. Selective exclusions from a public forum may not be based on content alone, and may not be justified by reference to content alone."

This statement, and others to the same effect, read literally and without regard for the facts of the case in which it was made, would absolutely preclude any regulation of expressive activity predicated in whole or in part on the content of the communication. But we learned long ago that broad statements of principle, no matter how correct in the context in which they are made, are sometimes qualified by contrary decisions before the absolute limit of the stated principle is reached. When we review this Court's actual adjudications in the First Amendment area, we find this to have been the case with the stated principle that there may be no restriction whatever on expressive activity because of its content. * * *

The question whether speech is, or is not, protected by the First Amendment often depends on the content of the speech. Thus, the line between permissible advocacy and impermissible incitation to crime or violence depends, not merely on the setting in which the speech occurs, but also on exactly what the speaker had to say. Similarly, it is the content of the utterance that determines whether it is a protected epithet or an unprotected "fighting comment." * * *

Even within the area of protected speech, a difference in content may require a different governmental response. [*New York Times*] held that a public official may not recover damages from a critic of his official conduct without proof of "malice" as specially defined in that opinion. Implicit in the opinion is the assumption that if the content of the newspaper article had been different—that is, if its subject matter had not been a public official—a lesser standard of proof would have been adequate. [We] have recently held that the First

c. But see Hunter & Law, p. 512 supra, at 119–20: "[S]exual speech is political. One core insight of modern feminism is that the personal is political. The question of who does the dishes and rocks the cradle affects both the nature of the home and the composition of the legislature. The dynamics of intimate relations are likewise political, both to the individuals involved and by their multiplied effects to the wider society. To argue [that] sexually explicit speech is less important than other categories of discourse reinforces the conceptual structures that have identified women's concerns with relationships and intimacy as less significant and valuable precisely because those concerns are falsely regarded as having no bearing on the structure of social and political life."

Amendment affords some protection to commercial speech. [The] measure of [protection] to commercial speech will surely be governed largely by the content of the communication.[32] * * *

More directly in point are opinions dealing with the question whether the First Amendment prohibits the state and federal governments from wholly suppressing sexually oriented materials on the basis of their "obscene character." In *Ginsberg,* the Court upheld a conviction for selling to a minor magazines which were concededly not "obscene" if shown to adults. Indeed, the Members of the Court who would accord the greatest protection to such materials have repeatedly indicated that the State could prohibit the distribution or exhibition of such materials to juveniles and unconsenting adults. Surely the First Amendment does not foreclose such a prohibition; yet it is equally clear that any such prohibition must rest squarely on an appraisal of the content of material otherwise within a constitutionally protected area.

Such a line may be drawn on the basis of content without violating the Government's paramount obligation of neutrality in its regulation of protected communication. For the regulation of the places where sexually explicit films may be exhibited is unaffected by whatever social, political, or philosophical message the film may be intended to communicate; whether the motion picture ridicules or characterizes one point of view or another, the effect of the ordinances is exactly the same.

Moreover, even though we recognize that the First Amendment will not tolerate the total suppression of erotic materials that have some arguably artistic value, it is manifest that society's interest in protecting this type of expression is of a wholly different, and lesser, magnitude than the interest in untrammeled political debate that inspired Voltaire's immortal comment.[d] Whether political oratory or philosophical discussion moves us to applaud or to despise what is said, every school-child can understand why our duty to defend the right to speak remains the same. But few of us would march our sons and daughters off to war to preserve the citizen's right to see "Specified Sexual Activities" exhibited in the theaters of our choice. Even though the First Amendment protects communication in this area from total suppression, we hold that the State may legitimately use the content of these materials as the basis for placing them in a different classification from other motion pictures.

The remaining question is whether the line drawn by these ordinances is justified by the city's interest in preserving the character of its neighborhoods. [The] record discloses a factual basis for the Common Council's conclusion that this kind of restriction will have the desired effect.[34] It is not our function to appraise the wisdom of its decision to require adult theaters to be separated rather than concentrated in the same areas. In either event, the city's interest in attempting to preserve the quality of urban life is one that must be accorded

32. As Mr. Justice Stewart pointed out in *Virginia Pharmacy,* the "differences between commercial price and product advertising [and] ideological communication" permits regulation of the former that the First Amendment would not tolerate with respect to the latter (concurring opinion).

d. The opinion had earlier quoted Voltaire: "I disapprove of what you say, but I will defend to the death your right to say it."

34. The City Council's determination was that a concentration of "adult" movie theaters causes the area to deteriorate and become a focus of crime, effects which are not attributable to theaters showing other types of films. It is this secondary effect which this zoning ordinance attempts to avoid, not the dissemination of "offensive" speech. In contrast, in *Erznoznik,* the justifications offered by the city rested primarily on the city's interest in protecting its citizens from exposure to unwanted, "offensive" speech. * * *

high respect. Moreover, the city must be allowed a reasonable opportunity to experiment with solutions to admittedly serious problems.

Since what is ultimately at stake is nothing more than a limitation on the place where adult films may be exhibited,[35] even though the determination of whether a particular film fits that characterization turns on the nature of its content, we conclude that the city's interest in the present and future character of its neighborhoods adequately supports its classification of motion pictures. * * *

JUSTICE POWELL, concurring in the judgment and portions of the opinion.

Although I agree with much of what is said in the plurality opinion, [my] approach to the resolution of this case is sufficiently different to prompt me to write separately.[1] I view the case as presenting an example of innovative land-use regulation, implicating First Amendment concerns only incidentally and to a limited extent. * * *

In this case, there is no indication that the application of the Anti-Skid Row Ordinance to adult theaters has the effect of suppressing production of or, to any significant degree, restricting access to adult movies. Nortown concededly will not be able to exhibit adult movies at its present location, and the ordinance limits the potential location of the proposed Pussy Cat. The constraints of the ordinance with respect to location may indeed create economic loss for some who are engaged in this business. But in this respect they are affected no differently than any other commercial enterprise that suffers economic detriment as a result of land-use regulation. The cases are legion that sustained zoning against claims of serious economic damage.

The inquiry for First Amendment purposes is not concerned with economic impact; rather, it looks only to the effect of this ordinance upon freedom of expression. This prompts essentially two inquiries: (i) does the ordinance impose any content limitation on the creators of adult movies or their ability to make them available to whom they desire, and (ii) does it restrict in any significant way the viewing of these movies by those who desire to see them? On the record in this case, these inquiries must be answered in the negative. At most the impact of the ordinance on these interests is incidental and minimal.[2] Detroit has silenced no message, has invoked no censorship, and has imposed no limitation upon those who wish to view them. The ordinance is addressed only to the places at which this type of expression may be presented, a restriction that does not interfere with content. Nor is there any significant overall curtailment of adult movie presentations, or the opportunity for a message to reach an audience. On the basis of the District Court's finding, it appears that if a sufficient market exists to support them the number of adult movie theaters in Detroit will remain approximately the same, free to purvey the same message.

35. The situation would be quite different if the ordinance had the effect of suppressing, or greatly restricting access to, lawful speech. Here, however, the District Court specifically found that "[t]he Ordinances do not affect the operation of existing establishments but only the location of new ones. There are myriad locations in the City of Detroit which must be over 1000 feet from existing regulated establishments. This burden on First Amendment rights is slight." * * *

1. I do not think we need reach, nor am I inclined to agree with, the holding in Part III (and supporting discussion) that nonobscene, erotic materials may be treated differently under First Amendment principles from other forms of protected expression. I do not consider the conclusions in Part I of the opinion to depend on distinctions between protected speech.

2. The communication involved here is not a kind in which the content or effectiveness of the message depends in some measure upon where or how it is conveyed. * * *

To be sure some prospective patrons may be inconvenienced by this dispersal. But other patrons, depending upon where they live or work, may find it more convenient to view an adult movie when adult theaters are not concentrated in a particular section of the city.

In these circumstances, it is appropriate to analyze the permissibility of Detroit's action under the four-part test of *United States v. O'Brien*. Under that test, a governmental regulation is sufficiently justified, despite its incidental impact upon First Amendment interests, "if it is within the constitutional power of the Government; if it furthers an important government interest; if the government interest is unrelated to the suppression of free expression; and if the incidental restriction [on] First Amendment freedoms is no greater than is essential to the furtherance of that interest." [Powell, J., concluded that the Detroit ordinance satisfied the *O'Brien* test.]

JUSTICE STEWART, with whom JUSTICE BRENNAN, JUSTICE MARSHALL and JUSTICE BLACKMUN join, dissenting.

[This case involves] the constitutional permissibility of selective interference with protected speech whose content is thought to produce distasteful effects. It is elementary that a prime function of the First Amendment is to guard against just such interference. By refusing to invalidate Detroit's ordinance the Court rides roughshod over cardinal principles of First Amendment law, which require that time, place and manner regulations that affect protected expression be content-neutral except in the limited context of a captive or juvenile audience. In place of these principles the Court invokes a concept wholly alien to the First Amendment. Since "few of us would march our sons and daughters off to war to preserve the citizen's right to see 'Specified Sexual Activities' exhibited in the theaters of our choice," the Court implies that these films are not entitled to the full protection of the Constitution. This stands "Voltaire's immortal comment," on its head. For if the guarantees of the First Amendment were reserved for expression that more than a "few of us" would take up arms to defend, then the right of free expression would be defined and circumscribed by current popular opinion. The guarantees of the Bill of Rights were designed to protect against precisely such majoritarian limitations on individual liberty.

The fact that the "offensive" speech here may not address "important" topics—"ideas of social and political significance," in the Court's terminology—does not mean that it is less worthy of constitutional protection. "Wholly neutral futilities [come] under the protection of free speech as fully as do Keats' poems or Donne's sermons." *Winters* (Frankfurter, J., dissenting), accord, *Cohen v. California*. Moreover, in the absence of a judicial determination of obscenity, it is by no means clear that the speech is not "important" even on the Court's terms [*Roth; Kingsley Pictures*].

I can only interpret today's decision as an aberration. The Court is undoubtedly sympathetic, as am I, to the well-intentioned efforts of Detroit to "clean up" its streets and prevent the proliferation of "skid rows." But it is in those instances where protected speech grates most unpleasantly against the sensibilities that judicial vigilance must be at its [height].

The factual parallels between [*Erznoznik* and this case] are striking. There, as here, the ordinance did not forbid altogether the "distasteful" expression but merely required an alteration in the physical setting of the forum. There, as here, the city's principal asserted interest was in minimizing the "undesirable" effects of speech having a particular content. [And] the particular content of the restricted speech at issue in *Erznoznik* precisely parallels the content restricted in [Detroit's] definition of "Specified Anatomical Areas." * * *

The Court must never forget that the consequences of rigorously enforcing the guarantees of the First Amendment are frequently unpleasant. Much speech that seems to be of little or no value will enter the marketplace of ideas, threatening the quality of our social discourse and, more generally, the serenity of our lives. But that is the price to be paid for constitutional freedom. * * * [e]

Notes and Questions

1. *A hierarchy of protected speech.* Stevens, J., contends that as a matter of law some "protected" speech is less worthy than other protected speech. The dissenters and Powell, J., reject that view. Which approach is more likely to preserve first amendment values? Would treating all protected speech equally invite a dilution of the force of the first amendment with respect to the speech that "really" matters? Is the process of allowing judges to pick and choose between types of protected speech too dangerous? Would it be dangerous to protect political speech more than sexually explicit speech? Is sexually explicit speech non-political? If the plaintiff's approach were accepted, would the Court ultimately "rank speech in all its myriad forms, in order of its perceived importance," with new rankings being "created and old ones rejected depending on the Court's view of the worthiness of the speech at issue"? Goldman, *A Doctrine of Worthier Speech: Young v. American Mini Theatres, Inc.,* 21 St. Louis U.L.J. 281, 300–01 (1977).

2. *The exhibitor's free expression.* Did Powell, J., assume that the "first amendment rights [involved] in *Young* were primarily vested in creator and audience"? Note, 42 Mo.L.Rev. 461, 468 (1977); Note, 28 Case W.Res.L.Rev. 456, 482 (1978). Does the plurality opinion and its fn. 35 reflect similar lack of concern for exhibitor's interests? How would a record be built to distinguish *Young* from a similar ordinance in another city?

3. *Exclusionary zoning. Schad v. Mt. Ephraim,* 452 U.S. 61, 101 S.Ct. 2176, 68 L.Ed.2d 671 (1981) invalidated a Borough ordinance that permitted adult theaters and bookstores, but excluded live entertainment from its commercial zone. Even as applied to nude dancing, the Court found that the ordinance was not narrowly drawn to serve a sufficiently substantial state interest.[f] The Court observed that there was no evidence to show that the entertainment at issue was available in reasonably nearby areas. What if it were? Suppose the Borough banned adult theaters and bookstores, but could show they were available nearby?

RENTON v. PLAYTIME THEATRES, INC., 475 U.S. 41, 106 S.Ct. 925, 89 L.Ed.2d 29 (1986), per REHNQUIST, J., upheld a zoning ordinance that prohibited

e. Blackmun, J., joined by the other three dissenters, also filed a dissent that protested the rejection of the vagueness argument, concluding on this issue: "As to the third reason, that 'adult' material is simply entitled to less protection, it certainly explains the lapse in applying settled vagueness principles, as indeed it explains this whole case. In joining Mr. Justice Stewart I have joined his forthright rejection of the notion that First Amendment protection is diminished for 'erotic materials' that only a 'few of us' see the need to protect."

f. But cf. *Newport v. Iacobucci,* 479 U.S. 92, 107 S.Ct. 383, 93 L.Ed.2d 334 (1986) (upholding ordinance prohibiting nude or nearly nude dancing in establishments serving liquor).

adult motion picture theaters from locating within 1,000 feet of any residential zone, church, park, or school. The effect was to exclude such theaters from approximately 94% of the land in the city. Of the remaining 520 acres, a substantial part was occupied by a sewage disposal and treatment plant, a horse racing track and environs, a warehouse and manufacturing facilities, a Mobil Oil tank farm, and a fully-developed shopping center: "[T]he resolution of this case is largely dictated by our decision in *Young.*[a] There, although five Members of the Court did not agree on a single rationale for the decision, we held that the city of Detroit's zoning ordinance, which prohibited locating an adult theater within 1,000 feet of any two other 'regulated uses' or within 500 feet of any residential zone, did not violate the First and Fourteenth Amendments. The Renton ordinance, like the one in *Young,* does not ban adult theaters altogether, but merely provides that such theaters may not be located within 1,000 feet of any residential zone, single- or multiple-family dwelling, church, park, or school. The ordinance is therefore properly analyzed as a form of time, place, and manner regulation.

"Describing the ordinance as a time, place, and manner regulation is, of course, only the first step in our inquiry. This Court has long held that regulations enacted for the purpose of restraining speech on the basis of its content presumptively violate the First Amendment. See *Chicago Police Dept. v. Mosley,* [p. 915 infra].[b] On the other hand, so-called 'content-neutral' time, place, and manner regulations are acceptable so long as they are designed to serve a substantial governmental interest and do not unreasonably limit alternative avenues of communication.[c]

"At first glance, the Renton ordinance, like the ordinance in *Young,* does not appear to fit neatly into either the 'content-based' or the 'content-neutral' category. To be sure, the ordinance treats theaters that specialize in adult films differently from other kinds of theaters. Nevertheless, [the] City Council's '*predominate* concerns' were with the secondary effects of adult theaters, and not with the content of adult films themselves. * * *

"[This] finding as to 'predominate' intent is more than adequate to establish that the city's pursuit of its zoning interests here was unrelated to the suppression of free expression.[d] The ordinance by its terms is designed to prevent

a. But cf. Note, *Motivation Analysis in Light of Renton,* 87 Colum.L.Rev. 344, 348–49 (1987): "Had the Court applied the rationale of [the *Mini Theatres* plurality], however, it could have applied the balancing test without scrutinizing government motivation or labelling the ordinance content-neutral."

b. *Mosley* involved an ordinance that banned picketing near a school building except the "peaceful picketing of any school involved in a labor dispute." The Court stated: "The regulation '[slips] from the neutrality of time, place, and circumstance into a concern about content.' This is never permitted."

c. Compare the statement of the time, place, and manner test in *Clark,* p. 544 supra. For commentary, see Day, *The Hybridization of the Content–Neutral Standards for the Free Speech Clause,* 19 Ariz.St.L.J. 195 (1987).

d. The court of appeals had held that a finding of predominate intent was inadequate, and would have remanded for the district court to determine whether a "motivating factor" to restrict the exercise of first amendment rights was present. In response, the Court interpreted the court of appeals opinion to require the invalidation of the ordinance if such a motive were found to be present "apparently no matter how small a part this motivating factor may have played in the City Council's decision." This view of the law, the Court continued, "was rejected in *United States v. O'Brien:* 'It is a familiar principle of constitutional law that this Court will not strike down an otherwise constitutional statute on the basis of an alleged illicit legislative motive. [What] motivates one legislator to make a speech about a statute is not necessarily what motivates scores of others to enact it, and the stakes are sufficiently high for us to eschew guesswork.' "

crime, protect the city's retail trade, maintain property values,[e] and generally 'protec[t] and preserv[e] the quality of [the city's] neighborhoods, commercial districts, and the quality of urban life,' not to suppress the expression of unpopular views. As Justice Powell observed in *Young,* '[i]f [the city] had been concerned with restricting the message purveyed by adult theaters, it would have tried to close them or restrict their number rather than circumscribe their choice as to location.'

"In short, the [ordinance] does not contravene the fundamental principle that underlies our concern about 'content-based' speech regulations: that 'government may not grant the use of a forum to people whose views it finds acceptable, but deny use to those wishing to express less favored or more controversial views.' *Mosley.*

"It was with this understanding in mind that, in *Young,* a majority of this Court decided that at least with respect to businesses that purvey sexually explicit materials,[2] zoning ordinances designed to combat the undesirable secondary effects of such businesses are to be reviewed under the standards applicable to 'content-neutral' time, place, and manner regulations.

"The appropriate inquiry in this case, then, is whether the Renton ordinance is designed to serve a substantial governmental interest and allows for reasonable alternative avenues of communication."

After concluding that the ordinance was designed to serve substantial government interests, the Court ruled that the Renton ordinance allowed "for reasonable alternative avenues of communication": "[W]e note that the ordinance leaves some 520 acres, or more than five percent of the entire land area of Renton, open to use as adult theater sites. [Respondents] argue, however, that some of the land in question is already occupied by existing businesses, that 'practically none' of the undeveloped land is currently for sale or lease, and that in general there are no 'commercially viable' adult theater sites within the 520 acres left open by the Renton ordinance. The Court of Appeals accepted these arguments, concluded that the 520 acres was not truly 'available' land, and therefore held that the Renton ordinance 'would result in a substantial restriction' on speech.

"We disagree with both the reasoning and the conclusion of the Court of Appeals. That respondents must fend for themselves in the real estate market, on an equal footing with other prospective purchasers and lessees, does not give rise to a First Amendment violation. And although we have cautioned against the enactment of zoning regulations that have 'the effect of suppressing, or greatly restricting access to, lawful speech,' *Young,* fn. 35 (plurality opinion), we have never suggested that the First Amendment compels the Government to ensure that adult theaters, or any other kinds of speech-related businesses for that matter, will be able to obtain sites at bargain prices. [T]he First Amendment requires only that Renton refrain from effectively denying respondents a reasonable opportunity to open and operate an adult theater within the city, and the ordinance before us easily meets this requirement. * * *[4]" [f]

e. For support, see Clarke, *Freedom of Speech and the Problems of the Lawful Harmful Public Reaction,* 20 Akron L.Rev. 187 (1986).

2. See *Young* (plurality opinion) ("[I]t is manifest that society's interest in protecting this type of expression is of a wholly different, and lesser, magnitude than the interest in untrammeled political debate * * *.").

4. [We] reject respondents' "vagueness" argument for the same reasons that led us to reject a similar challenge in *Young.* There, the Detroit ordinance applied to theaters

f. See note f on page 564.

BRENNAN, J., joined by Marshall, J., dissented: "The fact that adult movie theaters may cause harmful 'secondary' land use effects may arguably give Renton a compelling reason to regulate such establishments; it does not mean, however, that such regulations are content-neutral. * * *

"The ordinance discriminates on its face against certain forms of speech based on content. Movie theaters specializing in 'adult motion pictures' may not be located within 1,000 feet of any residential zone, single- or multiple-family dwelling, church, park, or school. Other motion picture theaters, and other forms of 'adult entertainment,' such as bars, massage parlors, and adult bookstores, are not subject to the same restrictions. This selective treatment strongly suggests that Renton was interested not in controlling the 'secondary effects' associated with adult businesses, but in discriminating against adult theaters based on the content of the films they exhibit. [Moreover,] many of the City Council's 'findings' do not relate to legitimate land use concerns. As the Court of Appeals observed, '[b]oth the magistrate and the district court recognized that many of the stated reasons for the ordinance were no more than expressions of dislike for the subject matter.' [3] That some residents may be offended by the *content* of the films shown at adult movie theaters cannot form the basis for state regulation of speech. See *Terminiello v. Chicago.*

"Some of the 'findings' [do] relate to supposed 'secondary effects' associated with adult movie theaters [4] [but they were added by the City Council only after this law suit was filed and the Court should not] accept these post-hoc statements at face value. [As] the Court of Appeals concluded, '[t]he record presented by Renton to support its asserted interest in enacting the zoning ordinance is very thin.' [5] * * * [7]

"used to present material distinguished or characterized by an emphasis on [sexually explicit matter]." We held that "even if there may be some uncertainty about the effect of the ordinances on other litigants, they are unquestionably applicable to these respondents." We also held that the Detroit ordinance created no "significant deterrent effect" that might justify invocation of the First Amendment "overbreadth" doctrine.

f. Blackmun, J., concurred in the result without opinion.

3. For example, "finding" number 2 states that "[l]ocation of adult entertainment land uses on the main commercial thoroughfares of the City gives an impression of legitimacy to, and causes a loss of sensitivity to the adverse effect of pornography upon children, established family relations, respect for marital relationship and for the sanctity of marriage relations of others, and the concept of nonaggressive, consensual sexual relations."

"Finding" number 6 states that "[l]ocation of adult land uses in close proximity to residential uses, churches, parks, and other public facilities, and schools, will cause a degradation of the community standard of morality. Pornographic material has a degrading effect upon the relationship between spouses."

4. For example, "finding" number 12 states that "[l]ocation of adult entertainment land uses in proximity to residential uses, churches, parks and other public facilities, and schools, may lead to increased levels of criminal activities, including prostitution, rape, incest and assaults in the vicinity of such adult entertainment land uses."

5. As part of the amendment passed after this lawsuit commenced, the City Council added a statement that it had intended to rely on the Washington Supreme Court's opinion in *Northend Cinema, Inc. v. Seattle,* 90 Wash.2d 709, 585 P.2d 1153 (1978), cert. denied, 441 U.S. 946, 99 S.Ct. 2166, 60 L.Ed.2d 1048 (1979), which upheld Seattle's zoning regulations against constitutional attack. Again, despite the suspicious coincidental timing of the amendment, the Court holds that "Renton was entitled to rely [on] the 'detailed findings' summarized in [the] *Northend Cinema* opinion." In *Northend Cinema,* the court noted that "[t]he record is replete with testimony regarding the effects of adult movie theater locations on residential neighborhoods." The opinion however, does not explain the evidence it purports to summarize, and provided no basis for determining whether Seattle's experience is relevant to Renton's.

7. As one commentator has noted: "[A]nyone with any knowledge of human nature should naturally assume that the decision to adopt almost any content-based restriction might have been affected by an antipathy on the part of at least some legislators to the ideas or information being suppressed. The

"Even assuming that the ordinance should be treated like a content-neutral time, place, and manner restriction, I would still find it unconstitutional. [T]he ordinance is invalid because it does not provide for reasonable alternative avenues of communication.[g] The District Court found that the ordinance left 520 acres in Renton available for adult theater sites, an area comprising about five percent of the city. However, the Court of Appeals found that because much of this land was already occupied, '[l]imiting adult theater uses to these areas is a substantial restriction on speech.' Many 'available' sites are also largely unsuited for use by movie theaters. [T]hese facts serve to distinguish this case from *Young,* where there was no indication that the Detroit zoning ordinance seriously limited the locations available for adult businesses. See *Young,* fn. 35 (plurality opinion) ('The situation would be quite different if the ordinance had the effect of * * * greatly restricting access to, lawful speech').

"Despite the evidence in the record, the Court reasons that the fact 'that respondents must fend for themselves in the real estate market, on an equal footing with other prospective purchasers and lessees, does not give rise to a First Amendment violation.' However, respondents are not on equal footing with other prospective purchasers and lessees, but must conduct business under severe restrictions not imposed upon other establishments. The Court also argues that the First Amendment does not compel 'the government to ensure that adult theatres, or any other kinds of speech-related businesses for that matter, will be able to obtain sites at bargain prices.' However, respondents do not ask Renton to guarantee low-price sites for their businesses, but seek, only a reasonable opportunity to operate adult theaters in the city. By denying them this opportunity, Renton can effectively ban a form of protected speech from its borders. The ordinance 'greatly restrict[s] access to, lawful speech,' *Young* (plurality opinion), and is plainly unconstitutional."

Notes and Questions

1. Does *Renton*—see fn. 2—endorse a hierarchy of categories among types of protected speech? Consider Tribe, *American Constitutional Law* 939 n. 66 (2d ed. 1988): "[I]t is doubtful that Renton can fairly be read as endorsing the concept of a hierarchy of intermediate categories, because the case turned on the majority's characterization of the restriction as content-neutral, and the issue of the relative importance of the speech involved, was, strictly speaking, irrelevant." But cf. Prygoski, *Low Value Speech: From Young to Fraser,* 32 St. Louis Univ.L.J. 317, 345 (1987) (despite the content-neutral language, "antipathy toward the kind of expression involved" swayed the case).

2. Was the ordinance fairly characterized as content-neutral? Is the focus on "secondary effects" convincing? Consider Stone, *Content–Neutral Restrictions,* 54 U.Chi.L.Rev. 46, 115–117 (1987): "[T]he ordinance in *Renton* was not defended in terms of its communicative impact—at least in the sense that the city's concerns did not implicate either of the constitutionally disfavored justifications ordinarily associated with communicative impact. But the Court had never before *Renton* suggested that the absence of a constitutionally disfavored

logical assumption, in other words, is not that there is not improper motivation but, rather, because legislators are only human, that there is a substantial risk that an impermissible consideration has in fact colored the deliberative process." Stone, *Restrictions on Speech Because of its Content: The Peculiar Case of Subject–Matter Restrictions,* 46 U.Chi.L.Rev. 81, 106 (1978).

g. Brennan, J., argued that the ordinance also failed as an acceptable time, place, and manner restriction because it was not narrowly tailored to serve a significant governmental interest.

justification is in itself a justification for treating an expressly content-based restriction as if it were content-neutral. To the contrary, with the single exception of *Renton,* the Court in such circumstances has always invoked the stringent standards of content-based review.

"[I]n *New York v. Ferber* [, for example], the Court treated as content-based a law prohibiting 'child pornography,' even though the government defended the law not in terms of communicative impact, but on the ground that the law was necessary to protect children who participate in 'sexual performances.' * * *

"[I]f taken seriously, and extended to other contexts, the Court's transmogrification in *Renton* of an expressly content-based restriction into one that is content-neutral threatens to undermine the very foundation of the content-based/content-neutral distinction. This would in turn erode the coherence and predictability of first amendment doctrine. One can only hope that this aspect of *Renton* is soon forgotten."

But cf. Farber & Frickey, *The Jurisprudence of Public Choice,* 65 Texas L.Rev. 873 (1987): "*[Renton]* appears to adopt the view that the government generally may take into account the content of speech when channeling speech, but may only rarely consider content when the purpose is censorship. We believe that in doing so *Renton* merely states explicitly what was implicit in a long line of prior cases."

Are subject matter restrictions as a class less problematic than other forms of content discrimination in that they often do not discriminate on the basis of point of view? Should *Renton's* secondary effects emphasis be limited to subject-matter-based restrictions? See Note, *The Content Distinction in Free Speech Analysis After Renton,* 102 Harv.L.Rev. 1904 (1989). Even if some subject matter restrictions are less problematic, is the Renton ordinance neutral as to point of view? Consider Stone, *Restrictions of Speech Because of its Content: The Peculiar Case of Subject–Matter Restrictions,* 46 U.Chi.L.Rev. 81, 111–12 (1978): "[T]he speech suppressed by restrictions such as those involved in [cases like *Erznoznik* and *Young*] will almost invariably carry an implicit, if not explicit, message in favor of more relaxed sexual mores. Such restrictions, in other words, have a potent viewpoint-differential impact. [I]n our society, the very presence of sexual explicitness in speech seems ideologically significant, without regard to whatever other messages might be intended. To treat such restrictions as viewpoint-neutral seems simply to ignore reality. Finally, [a] large percentage of citizens apparently feel threatened by nonobscene, sexually-explicit speech and believe it to be morally reprehensible. If it were not for the Court's relatively narrow construction of the obscenity concept, much of this speech would undoubtedly be banned outright. Thus, any restriction along these lines will carry an extraordinarily high risk that its enactment was tainted by this fundamentally illegitimate consideration. Such restrictions, although superficially viewpoint-neutral, pose a uniquely compelling case for content-based scrutiny." Are feminist or neo-conservative objections to near obscene speech both "fundamentally illegitimate." Should all content-based scrutiny be the same? Does *Renton* reconstruct the Court's "narrow construction of the obscenity concept?"

Is the concept of viewpoint neutrality itself problematic? Consider Sunstein, *Pornography and the First Amendment,* 1986 Duke L.J. 589, 615: "One does not 'see' a viewpoint-based restriction when the harms invoked in defense of a regulation are obvious and so widely supported by social consensus that they allay any concern about impermissible government motivation. Whether a classification is viewpoint-based thus ultimately turns on the viewpoint of the decisionmaker." See generally MacKinnon, *Feminism, Marxism, Method, and the State,* 7 Signs 515, 535–36 (1981).

3. *Renton's* "secondary effects" notion was revisited by several justices in *BOOS v. BARRY,* p. 535 supra. A District of Columbia ordinance banned the display of any sign within 500 feet of a foreign embassy that would tend to bring the embassy into "public odium" or "public disrepute." O'CONNOR, J., joined by Stevens and Scalia, JJ., distinguished *Renton:* "Respondents and the United States do not point to the 'secondary effects' of picket signs in front of embassies. They do not point to congestion, to interference with ingress or egress, to visual clutter, or to the need to protect the security of embassies. Rather, they rely on the need to protect the dignity of foreign diplomatic personnel by shielding them from speech that is critical of their governments. This justification focuses *only* on the content of the speech and the direct impact that speech has on its listeners. The emotive impact of speech on its audience is not a 'secondary effect.' Because the display clause regulates speech due to its potential primary impact, we conclude it must be considered content-based." [h]

BRENNAN, J., joined by Marshall, J., agreed with the conclusion that the ordinance was content-based, but objected to O'Connor, J.'s "assumption that the *Renton* analysis applies not only outside the context of businesses purveying sexually explicit materials but even to political speech." [i]

II. COMMERCIAL SPEECH

VIRGINIA STATE BOARD OF PHARMACY v. VIRGINIA CITIZENS CONSUMER COUNCIL, INC.

425 U.S. 748, 96 S.Ct. 1817, 48 L.Ed.2d 346 (1976).

JUSTICE BLACKMUN delivered the opinion of the Court.

[The Court held invalid a Virginia statute that made advertising the prices of prescription drugs "unprofessional conduct," subjecting pharmacists to license suspension or revocation. Prescription drug prices strikingly varied within the same locality, in Virginia and nationally, sometimes by several hundred percent. Such drugs were dispensed exclusively by licensed pharmacists but 95% were prepared by manufacturers, not compounded by the pharmacists.]

h. In an earlier passage O'Connor, J., responded to the argument that the ordinance was not content-based on the theory that the government was not selecting between viewpoints. The argument was instead that "the permissible message on a picket sign is determined solely by the policies of a foreign government. We reject this contention, although we agree the provision is not viewpoint-based. The display clause determines which viewpoint is acceptable in a neutral fashion by looking to the policies of foreign governments. While this prevents the display clause from being directly viewpoint-based, a label with potential First Amendment ramifications of its own, it does not render the statute content-neutral. Rather, we have held that a regulation that 'does not favor either side of a political controversy' is nonetheless impermissible because the 'First Amendment's hostility to content-based regulation extends . . . to prohibition of public discussion of an entire topic.' Here the government has determined that an entire category of speech—signs or displays critical of foreign governments—is not to be permitted."

i. Rehnquist, J., joined by White and Blackmun, JJ., voted to uphold the ordinance on the basis of Bork, J.'s opinion below in *Finzer v. Barry,* 798 F.2d 1450 (D.C.Cir.1986). Bork, J., stated that the need to adhere to principles of international law might constitute a secondary effect under *Renton* but was not "entirely sure" whether *Renton* alone could dictate that result and did not resolve the issue. Id. at 1469–70 n. 15. For a review of secondary effects doctrine see Prygoski, The Supreme Court's "Secondary Effects" Analysis in Free Speech Cases, 6 Cooley L.Rev. 1 (1989).

[Appellants] contend that the advertisement of prescription drug prices is outside the protection of the First Amendment because it is "commercial speech." There can be no question that in past decisions the Court has given some indication that commercial speech is unprotected.[a]

Last Term, in *Bigelow v. Virginia,* 421 U.S. 809, 95 S.Ct. 2222, 44 L.Ed.2d 600 (1975), the notion of unprotected "commercial speech" all but passed from the scene. We reversed a conviction for violation of a Virginia statute that made the circulation of any publication to encourage or promote the processing of an abortion in Virginia a misdemeanor. The defendant had published in his newspaper the availability of abortions in New York. The advertisement in question, in addition to announcing that abortions were legal in New York, offered the services of a referral agency in that State. [We] concluded that "the Virginia courts erred in their assumptions that advertising, as such, was entitled to no First Amendment protection," and we observed that the "relationship of speech to the marketplace of products or of services does not make it valueless in the marketplace of ideas."

Some fragment of hope for the continuing validity of a "commercial speech" exception arguably might have persisted because of the subject matter of the advertisement in *Bigelow.* We noted that in announcing the availability of legal abortions in New York, the advertisement "did more than simply propose a commercial transaction. It contained factual material of clear 'public interest.' " And, of course, the advertisement related to activity with which, at least in some respects, the State could not interfere. See *Roe v. Wade.* Indeed, we observed: "We need not decide in this case the precise extent to which the First Amendment permits regulation of advertising that is related to activities the State may legitimately regulate or even prohibit."

Here, [the] question whether there is a First Amendment exception for "commercial speech" is squarely before us. Our pharmacist does not wish to editorialize on any subject, cultural, philosophical, or political. He does not wish to report any particularly newsworthy fact, or to make generalized observations even about commercial matters. The "idea" he wishes to communicate is simply this: "I will sell you the X prescription drug at the Y price." Our question, then, is whether this communication is wholly outside the protection of the First Amendment.

V. [Speech] does not lose its First Amendment protection because money is spent to project it, as in a paid advertisement of one form or another. *New York Times Co. v. Sullivan.* Speech likewise is protected even though it is carried in a form that is "sold" for profit. *Smith v. California.* [Our] question is whether speech which does "no more than propose a commercial transaction," is so removed from any "exposition of ideas," and from "truth, science, morality, and arts in general, in its diffusion of liberal sentiments on the administration of Government", *Roth,* that it lacks all protection. Our answer is that it is not.

Focusing first on the individual parties to the transaction that is proposed in the commercial advertisement, we may assume that the advertiser's interest is a purely economic one. That hardly disqualifies him for protection under the First Amendment. The interests of the contestants in a labor dispute are

a. Starting with *Valentine v. Chrestensen,* 316 U.S. 52, 62 S.Ct. 920, 86 L.Ed. 1262 (1942), the opinion summarized the decisions and dicta that gave such "indication." Long after *Chrestensen,* strong arguments against a first amendment exception for commercial speech had appeared. See Redish, *The First Amendment in the Market Place,* 39 Geo.Wash.L.Rev. 420 (1971); Note, 50 Ore.L.Rev. 177 (1971); cf. Note, 78 Harv.L.Rev. 1191 (1965).

primarily economic, but it has long been settled that both the employee and the employer are protected by the First Amendment when they express themselves on the merits of the dispute in order to influence its outcome. * * * [17]

As to the particular consumer's interest in the free flow of commercial information, that interest may be as keen, if not keener by far, than his interest in the day's most urgent political debate.[b] Appellees' case in this respect is a convincing one. Those whom the suppression of prescription drug price information hits the hardest are the poor, the sick, and particularly the aged. A disproportionate amount of their income tends to be spent on prescription drugs; yet they are the least able to learn, by shopping from pharmacist to pharmacist, where their scarce dollars are best spent. When drug prices vary as strikingly as they do, information as to who is charging what becomes more than a convenience. It could mean the alleviation of physical pain or the enjoyment of basic necessities.

Generalizing, society also may have a strong interest in the free flow of commercial information. Even an individual advertisement, though entirely "commercial," may be of general public interest. The facts of decided cases furnish illustrations: advertisements stating that referral services for legal abortions are available, *Bigelow;* that a manufacturer of artificial furs promotes his product as an alternative to the extinction by his competitors of fur-bearing mammals, see *Fur Information & Fashion Council, Inc. v. E.F. Timme & Son,* 364 F.Supp. 16 (SDNY 1973); and that a domestic producer advertises his product as an alternative to imports that tend to deprive American residents of their jobs, cf. *Chicago Joint Board v. Chicago Tribune Co.,* 435 F.2d 470 (CA7 1970), cert. denied, 402 U.S. 973 (1971). Obviously, not all commercial messages contain the same or even a very great public interest element. There are few to which such an element, however, could not be added. Our pharmacist, for example, could cast himself as a commentator on store-to-store disparities in drug prices, giving his own and those of a competitor as proof. We see little point in requiring him to do so, and little difference if he does not.

Moreover, there is another consideration that suggests that no line between publicly "interesting" or "important" commercial advertising and the opposite kind could ever be drawn. Advertising, however tasteless and excessive it sometimes may seem, is nonetheless dissemination of information as to who is producing and selling what product, for what reason, and at what price. So long as we preserve a predominantly free enterprise economy, the allocation of our resources in large measure will be made through numerous private economic decisions. It is a matter of public interest that those decisions, in the aggregate, be intelligent and well informed. To this end, the free flow of commercial

17. The speech of labor disputants, of course, is subject to a number of restrictions. The Court stated in *NLRB v. Gissel Packing Co.,* 395 U.S., at 618, 89 S.Ct., at 1942, 23 L.Ed. 2d, at 581 (1969), for example, that an employer's threats of retaliation for the labor actions of his employees are "without the protection of the First Amendment." The constitutionality of restrictions upon speech in the special context of labor disputes is not before us here. We express no views on that complex subject, and advert to cases in the labor field only to note that in some circumstances speech of an entirely private and economic character enjoys the protection of the First Amendment. [For the contention that labor speech receives less protection than commercial speech, see Pope, *The Three-Systems Ladder of First Amendment Values: Two Rungs and a Black Hole,* 11 Hast.Con.L.Q. 189 (1984)].

b. Consider Tushnet, *Red, White, and Blue* 290 (1988): "The listener's interest in receiving information, a private interest, thus prevails over a more republican vision of politics, in which political discussion is, at least on the level of public norms, 'keener by far' than private interest."

information is indispensable. And if it is indispensable to the proper allocation of resources in a free enterprise system, it is also indispensable to the formation of intelligent opinions as to how that system ought to be regulated or altered. Therefore, even if the First Amendment were thought to be primarily an instrument to enlighten public decisionmaking in a democracy, we could not say that the free flow of information does not serve that goal.

Arrayed against these substantial individual and societal interests are a number of justifications for the advertising ban. These have to do principally with maintaining a high degree of professionalism on the part of licensed pharmacists. [Price] advertising, it is argued, will place in jeopardy the pharmacist's expertise and, with it, the customer's health. It is claimed that the aggressive price competition that will result from unlimited advertising will make it impossible for the pharmacist to supply professional services in the compounding, handling, and dispensing of prescription drugs. Such services are time-consuming and expensive; if competitors who economize by eliminating them are permitted to advertise their resulting lower prices, the more painstaking and conscientious pharmacist will be forced either to follow suit or to go out of business. [It] is further claimed that advertising will lead people to shop for their prescription drugs among the various pharmacists who offer the lowest prices, and the loss of stable pharmacist-customer relationships will make individual [attention] impossible. Finally, it is argued that damage will be done to the professional image of the pharmacist. This image, that of a skilled and specialized craftsman, attracts talent to the profession and reinforces the better habits of those who are in [it].

The strength of these proffered justifications is greatly undermined by the fact that high professional standards, to a substantial extent, are guaranteed by the close regulation to which pharmacists in Virginia are subject. [At] the same time, we cannot discount the Board's justifications entirely. The Court regarded justifications of this type sufficient to sustain the advertising bans challenged on due process and equal protection [grounds].[c]

The challenge now made, however, is based on the First Amendment. This casts the Board's justifications in a different light, for on close inspection it is seen that the State's protectiveness of its citizens rests in large measure on the advantages of their being kept in ignorance. The advertising ban does not directly affect professional standards one way or the other. It affects them only through the reactions it is assumed people will have to the free flow of drug price information. There is no claim that the advertising ban in any way prevents the cutting of corners by the pharmacist who is so inclined. That pharmacist is likely to cut corners in any event. The only effect the advertising ban has on him is to insulate him from price competition and to open the way for him to make a substantial, and perhaps even excessive, profit in addition to providing an inferior service. The more painstaking pharmacist is also protected but, again, it is a protection based in large part on public ignorance.

It appears to be feared that if the pharmacist who wishes to provide low cost, and assertedly low quality, services is permitted to advertise, he will be taken up on his offer by too many unwitting customers. They will choose the low-cost, low-quality service and drive the "professional" pharmacist out of business. [They] will go from one pharmacist to another, following the discount, and

c. The Court referred here to cases upholding bans on advertising prices for eyeglass frames and optometrist and dental services.

destroy the pharmacist-customer relationship. They will lose respect for the profession because it advertises. All this is not in their best interests, and all this can be avoided if they are not permitted to know who is charging what.

[A]n alternative to this highly paternalistic [d] approach [is] to assume that this information is not in itself harmful, that people will perceive their own best interests if only they are well enough informed, and that the best means to that end is to open the channels of communication rather than to close them. If they are truly open, nothing prevents the "professional" pharmacist from marketing his own assertedly superior product, and contrasting it with that of the low-cost, high-volume prescription drug retailer. But the choice among these alternative approaches is not ours to make or the Virginia General Assembly's. It is precisely this kind of choice, between the dangers of suppressing information, and the dangers of its misuse if it is freely available, that the First Amendment makes for [us].

VI. In concluding that commercial speech, like other varieties, is protected, we of course do not hold that it can never be regulated in any way. Some forms of commercial speech regulation are surely permissible. We mention a few. [There] is no claim, for example, that the prohibition on prescription drug price advertising is a mere time, place, and manner restriction. We have often approved restrictions of that kind provided that they are justified without reference to the content of the regulated speech, that they serve a significant governmental interest, and that in so doing they leave open ample alternative channels for communication of the information. Whatever may be the proper bounds of time, place, and manner restrictions on commercial speech, they are plainly exceeded by this Virginia statute, which singles out speech of a particular content and seeks to prevent its dissemination completely.

Nor is there any claim that prescription drug price advertisements are forbidden because they are false or misleading in any way. Untruthful speech, commercial or otherwise, has never been protected for its own sake. *Gertz.* Obviously much commercial speech is not provably false, or even wholly false, but only deceptive or misleading. We foresee no obstacle to a State's dealing effectively with this problem.[24] The First Amendment, as we construe it today,

d. Consider Schauer, *The Role of the People in First Amendment Theory,* 74 Calif.L. Rev. 761, 788 (1986): "We ought to recognize that popular control over nonpolitical speech may in some circumstances be a bad idea and address directly just why this is so. Perhaps it is time to face up to the paternalism of the first amendment, and maybe much of the rest of the Constitution as well." Is the Court's anti-paternalism paternalistic? For the contention that the Virginia price advertising ban was not paternalistic, see Lowenstein, *"Too Much Puff": Persuasion, Paternalism, and Commercial Speech,* 56 U.Cin.L.Rev. 1205, 1238 (1988).

24. [C]ommonsense differences between speech that does "no more than propose a commercial transaction," *Pittsburgh Press,* and other varieties [suggest] that a different degree of protection is necessary to insure that the flow of truthful and legitimate commercial information is unimpaired. The truth of commercial speech, for example, may be more easily verifiable by its disseminator than, let us say, news reporting or political commentary, in that ordinarily the advertiser seeks to disseminate information about a specific product or service that he himself provides and presumably knows more about than anyone else. Also, commercial speech may be more durable than other kinds. Since advertising is the sine qua non of commercial profits, there is little likelihood of its being chilled by proper regulation and foregone entirely.

Attributes such as these, the greater objectivity and hardiness of commercial speech, may make it less necessary to tolerate inaccurate statements for fear of silencing the speaker. They may also make it appropriate to require that a commercial message appear in such a form, or include such additional information, warnings and disclaimers, as are necessary to prevent its being deceptive. They may also make inapplicable the prohibition on prior restraints. Compare *New York Times Co. v. United States* [p. 616 infra] with *Donaldson v. Read Magazine,* 333 U.S. 178, 68 S.Ct. 591, 92 L.Ed. 628 (1948).

does not prohibit the State from insuring that the stream of commercial information flows cleanly as well as freely.

Also, there is no claim that the transactions proposed in the forbidden advertisements are themselves illegal in any way. Finally, the special problems of the electronic broadcast media are likewise not in this case.

What is at issue is whether a State may completely suppress the dissemination of concededly truthful information about entirely lawful activity, fearful of that information's effect upon its disseminators and its recipients. Reserving other questions,[25] we conclude that the answer to this one is in the [negative].

JUSTICE STEWART, concurring.[e]

[I] write separately to explain why I think today's decision does not preclude [governmental regulation of false or deceptive advertising]. The Court has on several occasions addressed the problems posed by false statements of fact in libel cases. [Factual] errors are inevitable in free debate, and the imposition of liability for [such errors] can "dampe[n] the vigor and limi[t] the variety of public debate" by inducing "self-censorship." [In] contrast to the press, which must often attempt to assemble the true facts from sketchy and sometimes conflicting sources under the pressure of publication deadlines, the commercial advertiser generally knows the product or service he seeks to sell and is in a position to verify the accuracy of his factual representations before he disseminates them. The advertiser's access to the truth about his product and its price substantially eliminates any danger that governmental regulation of false or misleading price or product advertising will chill accurate and nondeceptive commercial [expression].

Since the factual claims contained in commercial price or product advertisements relate to tangible goods or services, they may be tested empirically and corrected to reflect the truth without in any manner jeopardizing the free dissemination of thought. Indeed, the elimination of false and deceptive claims serves to promote the one facet of commercial price and product advertising that warrants First Amendment protection—its contribution to the flow of accurate and reliable information relevant to public and private decisionmaking.

JUSTICE REHNQUIST, dissenting.

[Under] the Court's opinion the way will be open not only for dissemination of price information but for active promotion of prescription drugs, liquor, cigarettes and other products the use of which it has previously been thought desirable to discourage. Now, however, such promotion is protected by the First Amendment so long as it is not misleading or does not promote an illegal product or [enterprise].

The Court speaks of the consumer's interest in the free flow of commercial information. [This] should presumptively be the concern of the Virginia Legislature, which sits to balance [this] and other claims in the process of making laws such as the one here under attack. The Court speaks of the importance in a

25. We stress that we have considered in this case the regulation of commercial advertising by pharmacists. Although we express no opinion as to other professions, the distinctions, historical and functional, between professions, may require consideration of quite different factors. Physicians and lawyers, for example, do not dispense standardized products; they render professional *services* of almost infinite variety and nature, with the consequent enhanced possibility for confusion and deception if they were to undertake certain kinds of advertising.

e. Burger, C.J., separately concurring, stressed the reservation in fn. 25 of the opinion with respect to advertising by attorneys and physicians. Stevens, J., took no part.

"predominantly free enterprise economy" of intelligent and well-informed decisions as to allocation of resources. While there is again much to be said for the Court's observation as a matter of desirable public policy, there is certainly nothing in the United States Constitution which requires the Virginia Legislature to hew to the teachings of Adam Smith in its legislative decisions regulating the pharmacy profession. E.g., *Nebbia v. New York; Olsen v. Nebraska* [Ch. 2, Sec. 3].

[There] are undoubted difficulties with an effort to draw a bright line between "commercial speech" on the one hand and "protected speech" on the other, and the Court does better to face up to these difficulties than to attempt to hide them under labels. In this case, however, the Court has unfortunately substituted for the wavering line previously thought to exist between commercial speech and protected speech a no more satisfactory line of its own—that between "truthful" commercial speech, on the one hand, and that which is "false and misleading" on the other. The difficulty with this line is not that it wavers, but on the contrary that it is simply too Procrustean to take into account the congeries of factors which I believe could, quite consistently with the First and Fourteenth Amendments, properly influence a legislative decision with respect to commercial advertising.

[S]uch a line simply makes no allowance whatever for what appears to have been a considered legislative judgment in most States that while prescription drugs are a necessary and vital part of medical care and treatment, there are sufficient dangers attending their widespread use that they simply may not be promoted in the same manner as hair creams, deodorants, and toothpaste. The very real dangers that general advertising for such drugs might create in terms of encouraging, even though not sanctioning, illicit use of them by individuals for whom they have not been prescribed, or by generating patient pressure upon physicians to prescribe them are simply not dealt with in the Court's [opinion].

Notes and Questions

1. As compared to political decisionmaking, is commercial advertising "neither more nor less significant than a host of other market activities that legislatures concededly may regulate."? Is there an "absence of any principled distinction between commercial soliciting and other aspects of economic activity"? Has economic due process been "resurrected, clothed in the ill-fitting garb of the first amendment"? See Jackson & Jeffries, *Commercial Speech: Economic Due Process and the First Amendment,* 65 Va.L.Rev. 1, 18 and 30 (1979). Why may government "be paternalistic regarding the purchase of goods but may not be paternalistic regarding information about those goods"? Alexander, *Speech in the Local Marketplace: Implications of Virginia State Board of Pharmacy v. Virginia Citizens Consumer Council, Inc. for Local Regulatory Power,* 14 San Diego L.Rev. 357, 376 (1977).

2. Footnote 24 suggests that *deceptive* commercial speech may be regulated in ways that would be barred if the speech were political. Sound distinction?

(a) *"Commonsense" differences between commercial speech and other speech.* (1) *Verifiability.* Consider Farber, *Commercial Speech and First Amendment Theory,* 74 Nw.U.L.Rev. 372, 385–86 (1979): "[C]ommercial speech is not necessarily more verifiable than other speech. There may well be uncertainty about some quality of a product, such as the health effect of eggs * * *. On the other hand, political speech is often quite verifiable by the speaker. A political candidate knows the truth about his own past and his present intentions, yet misrepresentations on these subjects are immune from state regulation." (2) *Durability.* Consider Redish, *The Value of Free Speech,* 130 U.Pa.L.Rev. 591, 633 (1982): "[I]t is also incorrect to distinguish commercial from political expression on the ground that the former is somehow hardier because of the inherent profit motive. It could just as easily be said that we need not fear that commercial magazines and newspapers will cease publication for fear of governmental regulation, because they are in business for profit. Of course, the proper response to this contention is that our concern is not *whether* they will publish, but *what* they will publish: fear of regulation might deter them from dealing with controversial subjects." But see Cass, *Commercial Speech, Constitutionalism, Collective Choice,* 56 U.Cin.L.Rev. 1317, 1368–73 (1988).

(b) *Commercial speech and self-expression.* Is commercial speech distinguishable from political speech because it is unrelated to self-expression? Consider Baker, *Commercial Speech: A Problem in the Theory of Freedom,* 62 Iowa L.Rev. 1, 17 (1976): In commercial speech, the dissemination of the profit motive "breaks the connection between speech and any vision, or attitude, or value of the individual or group engaged in advocacy. Thus the content and form of commercial speech cannot be attributed to individual value allegiances." See generally Baker, *Human Liberty and Freedom of Speech* chs. 3, 9, 10 (1989). For criticism, see, e.g., Schlag, *An Attack on Categorical Approaches to Freedom of Speech,* 30 U.C.L.A.L.Rev. 671, 710–21 (1983); Shiffrin, *The First Amendment and Economic Regulation: Away From A General Theory of the First Amendment,* 78 Nw.U.L.Rev. 1212 (1983). Even if commercial speech is divorced from self expression (or dignity), should it merit substantial protection, nonetheless. See Estreicher, *Securities Regulation and the First Amendment,* 24 Ga.L.Rev. 223 (1990); Neuborne, *The First Amendment and Government Regulation of Capital Markets,* 55 Brooklyn L.Rev. 5 (1989).

(c) *Contract approach to commercial speech.* Is commercial advertising distinguishable from other forms of speech because of the state interest in regulating contracts? Consider Farber, supra, at 389: "[C]ommercial speech is [more] akin to conduct than are other forms of speech. The unique aspect of commercial speech is that it is a prelude to, and therefore becomes integrated into, a contract, the essence of which is the presence of a promise. Because a promise is an undertaking to ensure that a certain state of affairs takes place, promises obviously have a closer connection with conduct than with self-expression. Second, this approach focuses on the distinctive and powerful state interests implicated by the process of contract formation. In a fundamentally market economy, the government understandably is given particular deference in its enforcement of contractual expectations. Indeed, the Constitution itself gives special protection to contractual expectations in the contract clause. Finally, this approach connects a rather nebulous area of first amendment law with the commonplaces of contract law of which every lawyer has knowledge. Obviously, the technicalities of contract law, with its doctrines of privity, consideration, and the like, should not be blindly translated into first amendment jurisprudence. The basic doctrines of contract law, however, provide a helpful guide in considering commercial speech problems." For discussion, see Alexander & Farber, *Commercial Speech and First Amendment Theory: A Critical Exchange,* 75 Nw.U.L.Rev. 307 (1980).

(d) *Error costs.* Is commercial speech distinguishable because the risks of error are less? Consider Cass, supra at 1360: "[T]he inquiry can be framed as asking four questions: (1) will officials err less systematically or less often in regulation of commercial speech than in regulation of other speech?; (2) will officials err less systematically or less often in regulation of commerce than in regulation of speech?; (3) will the consequences of errors in regulation of one sort of activity generally be less significant than the consequences of errors in the other?; and (4) will the process costs associated with error correction be lower in respect of one activity than the other?" On the risks of error, see generally Cass, supra; McChesney, *A Positive Regulatory Theory of the First Amendment,* 20 Conn.L.Rev. 335 (1988). See also Coase, *Advertising and Free Speech,* 6 J.Legal Stud. 1 (1977); Posner, *Free Speech in an Economic Perspective,* 20 Suffolk U.L.Rev. 1 (1986); Scanlon, *Freedom of Expression and Categories of Expression,* 40 U.Pitt.L.Rev. 519 (1979).

3. *Limits on regulation of deceptive advertising. Bates v. State Bar,* 433 U.S. 350, 97 S.Ct. 2691, 53 L.Ed.2d 810 (1977), struck down an Arizona Supreme Court rule against a lawyer "publicizing himself" through advertising. It rejected the claim that attorney price advertising was inherently misleading, but left open the "peculiar problems" associated with advertising claims regarding the quality of legal services.[f] Could a lawyer truthfully advertise that he or she has (1) tried twice as many personal injury cases as any other lawyer in the country? (2) averaged $10,000 more in recoveries per case than any other lawyer in the county? (3) graduated from Harvard Law School in the upper 10% of the class? (4) received "the best legal education this country offers"? Should an advertisement be protected if it is "sufficiently factual to be subject to verification" even if "implications of quality might be drawn from it"? See Canby and Gellhorn, *Physician Advertising: The First Amendment and the Sherman Act,* 1978 Duke L.J. 543, 560–62. Should the Court have deferred to the judgment of the State Bar of Arizona? If not, should it defer to the SEC when it regulates the advertising of securities? The FTC when it regulates automobile advertising? The Virginia Board of Pharmacy when it regulates quality advertising by pharmacists? For deferential treatment of a state ban on the use of tradenames by optometrists, see *Friedman v. Rogers,* 440 U.S. 1, 99 S.Ct. 887, 59 L.Ed.2d 100 (1979).

4. *Truth and commercial advertising.* Should Mercedes Benz be able to truthfully advertise that Frank Sinatra drives its car without getting Sinatra's permission? See Liebeler, *A Property Rights Approach to Judicial Decision Making,* 4 Cato J. 783, 802–03 (1985); Shiffrin, supra note 2, at 1257–58 n. 275; Felcher & Rubin, *Privacy, Publicity, and the Portrayal of Real People by the Media,* 88 Yale L.J. 1577 (1979); Treece, *Commercial Exploitation of Names, Likenesses, and Personal Histories,* 51 Tex.L.Rev. 637 (1973). Should the state be able to prevent homeowners from posting "for sale" signs in order to prevent panic selling in order to maintain an integrated neighborhood? See *Linmark Associates, Inc. v. Willingboro,* 431 U.S. 85, 97 S.Ct. 1614, 52 L.Ed.2d 155 (1977). May a state regulate the content of contraceptive advertising in order to

f. *Zauderer v. Office of Disciplinary Counsel,* p. 733 infra, held that a state may not discipline attorneys who solicit legal business through newspaper advertisements containing "truthful and nondeceptive information and advice regarding the legal rights of potential clients" or for the advertising use of "accurate and nondeceptive" illustrations. Zauderer had placed illustrated ads in 36 Ohio newspapers publicizing his availability to represent women who had suffered injuries from use of a contraceptive device known as the Dalkon Shield Intrauterine Device. In the ad Zauderer stated that he had represented other women in Dalkon Shield litigation. The Court observed that accurate statements of fact cannot be proscribed "merely because it is possible that some readers will infer that he has some expertise in those areas." But it continued to "leave open the possibility that States may prevent attorneys from making non-verifiable claims regarding the quality of their services. *Bates.*"

minimize its offensive character? Cf. *Carey v. Population Services Int'l.* (total ban on contraceptive advertising unconstitutional).

OHRALIK v. OHIO STATE BAR ASS'N, 436 U.S. 447, 98 S.Ct. 1912, 56 L.Ed.2d 444 (1978) upheld the indefinite suspension of an attorney for violating the anti-solicitation provisions of the Ohio Code of Professional Responsibility. Those provisions generally do not allow lawyers to recommend themselves to anyone who has not sought "their advice regarding employment of a lawyer." Albert Ohralik had approached two young accident victims to solicit employment—Carol McClintock in a hospital room where she lay in traction and Wanda Lou Holbert on the day she came home from the hospital. He employed a concealed tape recorder with Holbert, apparently to insure he would have evidence of her assent to his representation. The next day, when Holbert's mother informed Ohralik that she and her daughter did not want to have appellant represent them, he insisted that the daughter had entered into a binding agreement. McClintock also discharged Ohralik, and Ohralik sued her for breach of contract. The Court ruled, per POWELL, J., that a state may forbid in-person solicitation of clients by lawyers for pecuniary gain:

"Expression concerning purely commercial transactions has come within the ambit of the Amendment's protection only recently. In rejecting the notion that such speech is wholly outside the protection of the First Amendment, *Virginia Pharmacy,* we were careful not to hold that it is wholly undifferentiable from other forms of speech.

"We have not discarded the common sense distinction between speech proposing a commercial transaction, which occurs in an area traditionally subject to government regulation, and other varieties of speech. To require a parity of constitutional protection for commercial and noncommercial speech alike could invite dilution, simply by a leveling process, of the force of the Amendment's guarantee with respect to the latter kind of speech. Rather than subject the First Amendment to such a devitalization, we instead have afforded commercial speech a limited measure of protection, commensurate with its subordinate position in the scale of First Amendment values, while allowing modes of regulation that might be impermissible in the realm of noncommercial expression.

"Moreover, 'it has never been deemed an abridgment of freedom of speech or press to make a course of conduct illegal merely because the conduct was in part initiated, evidenced, or carried out by means of language, either spoken, written, or printed.' *Giboney v. Empire Storage & Ice Co.,* 336 U.S. 490, 502, 69 S.Ct. 684, 691, 93 L.Ed. 834 (1949). Numerous examples could be cited of communications that are regulated without offending the First Amendment, such as the exchange of information about securities, *SEC v. Texas Gulf Sulphur Co.,* 401 F.2d 833 (CA2 1968), cert. denied, 394 U.S. 976, 89 S.Ct. 1454, 22 L.Ed.2d 756 (1969), corporate proxy statements, *Mills v. Electric Auto-Lite Co.,* 396 U.S. 375, 90 S.Ct. 616, 24 L.Ed.2d 593 (1970), the exchange of price and production information among competitors, *American Column & Lumber Co. v. United States,* 257 U.S. 377, 42 S.Ct. 114, 66 L.Ed. 284 (1921), and employers' threats of retaliation for the labor activities of employees, *NLRB v. Gissel Packing Co.,* 395 U.S. 575, 618, 89 S.Ct. 1918, 1942, 23 L.Ed.2d 547 (1969). Each of these examples illustrates that the State does not lose its power to regulate commercial activity deemed harmful to the public whenever speech is a component of that activity. Neither

Virginia Pharmacy nor *Bates* purported to cast doubt on the permissibility of these kinds of commercial regulation.

"In-person solicitation by a lawyer of remunerative employment is a business transaction in which speech is an essential but subordinate component. While this does not remove the speech from the protection of the First Amendment, as was held in *Bates* and *Virginia Pharmacy,* it lowers the level of appropriate judicial scrutiny. [A] lawyer's procurement of remunerative employment is a subject only marginally affected with First Amendment concerns. It falls within the State's proper sphere of economic and professional regulation. While entitled to some constitutional protection, appellant's conduct is subject to regulation in furtherance of important state [interests].

" 'The interest of the States in regulating lawyers is especially great since lawyers are essential to the primary function of administering justice and have historically been officers of the courts' [and] act 'as trusted agents of their clients and as assistants to the court in search of a just solution to disputes.'

"[The] substantive evils of solicitation have been stated over the years in sweeping terms: stirring up litigation, assertion of fraudulent claims, debasing the legal profession, and potential harm to the solicited client in the form of overreaching, overcharging, underrepresentation, and misrepresentation." In providing information about the availability and terms of proposed legal services "in-person solicitation serves much the same function as the advertisement at issue in *Bates.* But there are significant differences as well. Unlike a public advertisement, which simply provides information and leaves the recipient free to act upon it or not, in-person solicitation may exert pressure and often demands an immediate response, without providing an opportunity for comparison or reflection. The aim and effect of in-person solicitation may be to provide a one-sided presentation and to encourage speedy and perhaps uninformed decisionmaking; there is no opportunity for intervention or counter-education by agencies of the Bar, supervisory authorities, or persons close to the solicited individual. The admonition that 'the fitting remedy for evil counsels is good ones' is of little value when the circumstances provide no opportunity for any remedy at all. In-person solicitation is as likely as not to discourage persons needing counsel from engaging in a critical comparison of the 'availability, nature, and prices' of legal services; it actually may disserve the individual and societal interest, identified in *Bates,* in facilitating 'informed and reliable decisionmaking.'

"[Appellant's argument that none of the evils of solicitation was found in his case] misconceives the nature of the State's interest. The rules prohibiting solicitation are prophylactic measures whose objective is the prevention of harm before it occurs.[a] The rules were applied in this case to discipline a lawyer for soliciting employment for pecuniary gain under circumstances likely to result in the adverse consequences the State seeks to avert. In such a situation, which is inherently conducive to overreaching and other forms of misconduct, the State has a strong interest in adopting and enforcing rules of conduct designed to protect the public from harmful solicitation by lawyers whom it has [licensed].

"The efficacy of the State's effort to prevent such harm to prospective clients would be substantially diminished if, having proved a solicitation in circumstances like those of this case, the State were required in addition to prove actual injury. Unlike the advertising in *Bates,* in-person solicitation is not visible or

a. But see McChesney, *Commercial Speech in the Professions,* 134 U.Pa.L.Rev. 45 (1985) (anti-solicitation provisions may be motivated by anti-competitive considerations).

otherwise open to public scrutiny. Often there is no witness other than the lawyer and the lay person whom he has solicited, rendering it difficult or impossible to obtain reliable proof of what actually took place. This would be especially true if the lay person were so distressed at the time of the solicitation that he or she could not recall specific details at a later date. If appellant's view were sustained, in-person solicitation would be virtually immune to effective oversight and regulation by the State or by the legal profession, in contravention of the State's strong interest in regulating members of the Bar in an effective, objective, and self-enforcing manner. It therefore is not unreasonable, or violative of the Constitution, for a State to respond with what in effect is a prophylactic rule." [b]

Notes and Questions

1. *Companion case.* IN RE PRIMUS, 436 U.S. 412, 98 S.Ct. 1893, 56 L.Ed. 2d 417 (1978), per POWELL, J., held that a state could not constitutionally discipline an ACLU "cooperating lawyer" who, after advising a gathering of allegedly illegally sterilized women of their rights, initiated further contact with one of the women by writing her a letter informing her of the ACLU's willingness to provide free legal representation for women in her situation and of the organization's desire to file a lawsuit on her behalf. "South Carolina's action in punishing appellant for soliciting a prospective litigant by mail, on behalf of ACLU, must withstand the 'exacting scrutiny applicable to limitations on core First Amendment rights.' [Where] political expression or association is at issue, this Court has not tolerated the degree of imprecision that often characterizes government regulation of the conduct of commercial affairs. The approach we adopt today in *Ohralik* that the State may proscribe in-person solicitation for pecuniary gain under circumstances likely to result in adverse consequences, cannot be applied to appellant's activity on behalf of the ACLU. Although a showing of potential danger may suffice in the former context, appellant may not be disciplined unless her activity in fact involved the type of misconduct at which South Carolina's broad prohibition is said to be directed. The record does not support appellee's contention that undue influence, overreaching, misrepresentation, or invasion of privacy actually occurred in this case."

2. *A hierarchy of protected speech.* Consider Shiffrin, supra, at 1218 & 1220–21 (1983). In *Virginia Pharmacy,* "the Court never admitted that commercial speech was less valuable than political speech. The 'commonsense differences' had nothing to do with value. [Although] Justice Blackmun labored to defend the asserted equal relationship between commercial speech and political speech for the *Virginia Pharmacy* majority, Justice Powell in *Ohralik* was content to lead the Court to an opposite position without explanation. In so doing, Justice Powell steered the Court to accept a hierarchy of protected speech for the first time, despite his own stated opposition [in *Young*] to creating any such hierarchy." Does the concern that the protection of non-commercial speech would be subject to dilution if it were placed on a par with commercial speech presuppose an unexplained difference between the two types of speech? See id. at 1221 n. 59. For discussion of the dilution argument, see Marshall, *The Dilution of the First Amendment and the Equality of Ideas,* 38 Case W.Res.L. Rev. 566 (1988).

b. Marshall and Rehnquist, JJ., each separately concurred in the judgment. Brennan, J., did not participate.

3. *Billboards and speech hierarchy.* Seven justices in METROMEDIA, INC. v. SAN DIEGO, 453 U.S. 490, 101 S.Ct. 2882, 69 L.Ed.2d 800 (1981) stated that San Diego could ban commercial billboards without banning non-commercial billboards and that it could permit on-site commercial billboards while prohibiting off-site commercial billboards.

Nonetheless, the ordinance before the Court was struck down. WHITE, J., joined by Stewart, Marshall, and Powell, JJ., found it defective first, because it discriminated against non-commercial speech (permitting commercial signs on business sites while prohibiting non-commercial signs) and second, because it discriminated between types of non-commercial speech (making exceptions for signs involving governmental functions, time/weather/news public service signs, and temporary political campaign signs).

BRENNAN, J., joined by Blackmun, J., concurring, found the ordinance defective because it was the functional equivalent of a total ban that had not been adequately justified. He also argued that government agencies should not be permitted to make ad hoc determinations as to what speech was commercial.

In separate opinions Stevens, Rehnquist, JJ., and Burger, C.J., argued in favor of the constitutionality of bans on billboards and further maintained that San Diego should be able to distinguish between commercial and non-commercial billboards, between types of commercial speech, and, to some extent, between types of non-commercial speech so long as there was no point-of-view discrimination.

4. The plurality in *Metromedia* stated that, "We deal here with the law of billboards." Can (should) the following be distinguished?

(a) In *Martin v. Struthers,* 319 U.S. 141, 63 S.Ct. 862, 87 L.Ed. 1313 (1943), a city forbade knocking on the door or ringing the doorbell of a resident in order to deliver handbills (in an industrial community where many worked night shifts and slept during the day). In striking down the ordinance, the Court, per Black, J., pointed out that the city's objectives could be achieved by means of a law making it an offense for any person to ring the doorbell of a householder who has "appropriately indicated that he is unwilling to be disturbed. This or any similar regulation leaves the decision as to whether distributors of literature may lawfully call at a home where it belongs—with the homeowner himself." By contrast, *Breard v. Alexandria,* 341 U.S. 622, 71 S.Ct. 920, 95 L.Ed. 1233 (1951) upheld an ordinance forbidding the practice of going door to door to solicit orders for the sale of goods. The commercial element was said to distinguish *Martin.* Does *Breard* survive *Virginia Pharmacy?* Does (should) *Metromedia* settle the issue? What if, as in *Breard,* the solicitor is selling subscriptions for magazines?

(b) Compare *Schneider,* p. 641 infra (prohibition against leaflet distribution on streets unconstitutional) with *Valentine,* p. 568 supra (prohibition against distribution of commercial leaflets upheld). Does (should) the *holding* of *Valentine* survive *Virginia Pharmacy?* Does *Metromedia* settle the issue? [c]

---

c. For relevant commentary on the normative issues, see Baker, *Commercial Speech: A Problem in the Theory of Freedom,* 62 Iowa L.Rev. 1 (1976); Redish, *The First Amendment in the Marketplace: Commercial Speech and the Values of Free Expression,* 39 Geo.Wash.L. Rev. 429 (1971); Redish, *The Value of Free Speech,* 130 U.Pa.L.Rev. 591 (1982); Shiffrin, *The First Amendment and Economic Regulation: Away From a General Theory of the First Amendment,* 78 Nw.U.L.Rev. 1212, 1220, 1276–82 (1983).

CENTRAL HUDSON GAS & ELEC. CORP. v. PUBLIC SERVICE COM'N, 447 U.S. 557, 100 S.Ct. 2343, 65 L.Ed.2d 341 (1980), per POWELL, J., invalidated a Commission regulation that, in an effort to conserve power, prohibited promotional advertising by an electric utility except for encouraging shifts of consumption from peak demand times: "The Commission's order restricts only commercial speech, that is, expression related solely to the economic interests of the speaker and its audience. [In] commercial speech cases, [a] four-part analysis has developed. At the outset, we must determine whether the expression is protected by the First Amendment. For commercial speech to come within that provision, it at least must concern lawful activity [a] and not be misleading. Next, we ask whether the asserted governmental interest is substantial. If both inquiries yield positive answers, we must determine whether the regulation directly advances the governmental interest asserted, and whether it is not more extensive than is necessary to serve that interest.[b]

"[T]he State's interest in energy conservation is directly advanced by the Commission order at issue here. There is an immediate connection between advertising and the demand for electricity. [Thus], we find a direct link between the state interest in conservation and the Commission's order.

"[T]he critical inquiry [is] whether the Commission's complete suppression of speech ordinarily protected by the First Amendment is no more extensive than necessary to further the State's interest in energy conservation. The Commission's order reaches all promotional advertising, regardless of the impact of the touted service on overall energy use. But the energy conservation rationale, as important as it is, cannot justify suppressing information about electric devices or services that would cause no net increase in total energy use. In addition, no showing has been made that a more limited restriction on the content of promotional advertising would not serve adequately the State's interests.

"Appellant insists that but for the ban, it would advertise products and services that use energy efficiently. These include the 'heat pump,' which both parties acknowledge to be a major improvement in electric heating, and the use of electric heat as a 'back-up' to solar and other heat sources. Although the Commission has questioned the efficiency of electric heating before this Court, neither the Commission's Policy Statement nor its order denying rehearing made findings on this issue. In the absence of authoritative findings to the contrary, we must credit as within the realm of possibility the claim that electric heat can be an efficient alternative in some circumstances.

"The Commission's order prevents appellant from promoting electric services that would reduce energy use by diverting demand from less efficient sources, or that would consume roughly the same amount of energy as do alternative sources. In neither situation would the utility's advertising endan-

a. *Pittsburgh Press Co. v. Human Relations Comm'n,* p. 610 infra, upheld an order forbidding publication of sex-designated help-wanted columns as a forbidden "aid" to prohibited sex discrimination in employment: "Discrimination in employment is *illegal* commercial activity under the ordinance. We have no doubt that a newspaper constitutionally could be forbidden to publish a want-ad proposing a sale of narcotics or soliciting prostitutes."

b. In an earlier footnote, the Court emphasized that this requirement was "not an application of the 'overbreadth' doctrine. The latter theory permits the invalidation of regulations on First Amendment grounds even when the litigant challenging the regulation has engaged in no constitutionally protected activity. [In] this case, the Commission's prohibition acts directly against the promotional activities of Central Hudson, and to the extent the limitations are unnecessary to serve the state's interest, they are invalid." For a different perspective on the overbreadth doctrine, see Redish, *The Warren Court, The Burger Court and the First Amendment Overbreadth Doctrine,* 78 Nw.U.L.Rev. 1031 (1983).

ger conservation or mislead the public. To the extent that the Commission's order suppresses speech that in no way impairs the State's interest in energy conservation, the Commission's order violates the First and Fourteenth Amendments and must be invalidated.

"The Commission also has not demonstrated that its interest in conservation cannot be protected adequately by more limited regulation of appellant's commercial expression. To further its policy of conservation, the Commission could attempt to restrict the format and content of Central Hudson's advertising. It might, for example, require that the advertisements include information about the relative efficiency and expense of the offered service, both under current conditions and for the foreseeable future.[13] In the absence of a showing that more limited speech regulation would be ineffective, we cannot approve the complete suppression of Central Hudson's advertising."

BLACKMUN, J., joined by Brennan, J., concurring in the judgment, saw in the Court's "four-part analysis" approval of "an intermediate level of scrutiny" whenever a restraint on commercial speech " 'directly advance[s]' a 'substantial' governmental interest and is 'not more extensive than is necessary to serve that interest.' I agree with the Court that this level of intermediate scrutiny is appropriate for a restraint on commercial speech designed to protect consumers from misleading or coercive speech, or a regulation related to the time, place, or manner of commercial speech. I do not agree, however, that the Court's four-part test is the proper one to be applied when a State seeks to suppress information about a product in order to manipulate a private economic decision that the State cannot or has not regulated or outlawed directly. * * *

"I seriously doubt whether suppression of information concerning the availability and price of a legally offered product is ever a permissible way for the State to 'dampen' demand for or use of the product. Even though 'commercial' speech is involved, such a regulatory measure strikes at the heart of the First Amendment. This is because it is a covert attempt by the State to manipulate the choices of its citizens, not by persuasion or direct regulation, but by depriving the public of the information needed to make a free choice. As the Court recognizes, the State's policy choices are insulated from the visibility and scrutiny that direct regulation would entail and the conduct of citizens is molded by the information that government chooses to give [them].

"It appears that the Court would permit the State to ban all direct advertising of air conditioning, assuming that a more limited restriction on such advertising would not effectively deter the public from cooling its homes. In my view, our cases do not support this type of suppression. If a governmental unit believes that use or over-use of air conditioning is a serious problem, it must attack that problem directly, by prohibiting air conditioning or regulating thermostat levels."

STEVENS, J., joined by Brennan, J., also concurred: "Because 'commercial speech' is afforded less constitutional protection than other forms of speech, it is important that the commercial speech concept not be defined too broadly lest speech deserving of greater constitutional protection be inadvertently suppressed. The issue in this case is whether New York's prohibition on the

13. The Commission also might consider a system of previewing advertising campaigns to insure that they will not defeat conservation policy. It has instituted such a program for approving "informational" advertising under the Policy Statement challenged in this case. We have observed that commercial speech is such a sturdy brand of expression that traditional prior restraint doctrine may not apply to it. *Virginia Pharmacy.* * * *

promotion of the use of electricity through advertising is a ban on nothing but commercial [speech].

"This case involves a governmental regulation that completely bans promotional advertising by an electric utility. This ban encompasses a great deal more than mere proposals to engage in certain kinds of commercial transactions. It prohibits all advocacy of the immediate or future use of electricity. It curtails expression by an informed and interested group of persons of their point of view on questions relating to the production and consumption of electrical energy—questions frequently discussed and debated by our political leaders. For example, an electric company's advocacy of the use of electric heat for environmental reasons, as opposed to wood-burning stoves, would seem to fall squarely within New York's promotional advertising ban and also within the bounds of maximum First Amendment protection. The breadth of the ban thus exceeds the boundaries of the commercial speech concept, however that concept may be defined.

"The justification for the regulation is nothing more than the expressed fear that the audience may find the utility's message persuasive. Without the aid of any coercion, deception, or misinformation, truthful communication may persuade some citizens to consume more electricity than they otherwise would. I assume that such a consequence would be undesirable and that government may therefore prohibit and punish the unnecessary or excessive use of electricity. But if the perceived harm associated with greater electrical usage is not sufficiently serious to justify direct regulation, surely it does not constitute the kind of clear and present danger that can justify the suppression of [speech].

"In sum, I concur in the result because I do not consider this to be a 'commercial speech' case. Accordingly, I see no need to decide whether the Court's four-part analysis adequately protects commercial speech—as properly defined—in the face of a blanket ban of the sort involved in this case."

REHNQUIST, J., dissented in a long opinion, summarized in his introduction: "The Court's analysis in my view is wrong in several respects. Initially, I disagree with the Court's conclusion that the speech of a state-created monopoly, which is the subject of a comprehensive regulatory scheme, is entitled to protection under the First Amendment. I also think that the Court errs here in failing to recognize that the state law is most accurately viewed as an economic regulation and that the speech involved (if it falls within the scope of the First Amendment at all) occupies a significantly more subordinate position in the hierarchy of First Amendment values than the Court gives it today. Finally, the Court in reaching its decision improperly substitutes its own judgment for that of the State in deciding how a proper ban on promotional advertising should be drafted. With regard to this latter point, the Court adopts as its final part of a four-part test a 'no more extensive than necessary' analysis that will unduly impair a state legislature's ability to adopt legislation reasonably designed to promote interests that have always been rightly thought to be of great importance to the State."

In commenting on the Court's four part test, Rehnquist, J., stated: "The [test] elevates the protection accorded commercial speech that falls within the scope of the First Amendment to a level that is virtually indistinguishable from that of noncommercial speech. I think the Court in so doing has effectively accomplished the 'devitalization' of the First Amendment that it counseled against in *Ohralik*. I think it has also by labeling economic regulation of business conduct as a restraint on 'free speech' gone far to resurrect the discredited doctrine of cases such as *Lochner.* New York's order here is in my view more akin to an economic regulation to which virtually complete deference should be accorded by this Court.

"I doubt there would be any question as to the constitutionality of New York's conservation effort if the Public Service Commission had chosen to raise the price of electricity, to condition its sale on specified terms, or to restrict its production. In terms of constitutional values, I think that such controls are virtually indistinguishable from the State's ban on promotional advertising."

Notes and Questions

1. *The four part test.* Is Rehnquist, J., correct in stating that the Court's test "elevates the protection of commercial speech to a level that is virtually indistinguishable from that of noncommercial speech"? Is it possible to state "the" test that has been applied to noncommercial speech?

2. *Paternalism and Central Hudson.* Consider Blasi, *The Pathological Perspective and the First Amendment,* 85 Colum.L.Rev. 449, 487 (1985): "[T]he claim of the regulators in the drug and lawyer advertising cases was that consumers would be influenced by the advertising to act against their own self-interest; in the promotional advertising case, the fear was that consumers would act against the public interest in pursuit of their own short range self-interest. The rationale in the first type of case is more paternalistic because it necessarily assumes that listeners cannot evaluate the message even when they have every incentive to try to do so. The rationale in the promotional advertising case is consistent with respect for the message-screening capacities of listeners; what the rationale doubts is the capacity of listeners to behave as public-spirited citizens when prompted to act selfishly by sophisticated advertising techniques."

3. In what sense was the speech in *Central Hudson* solely in the economic interests of speaker and audience? [c] Should the Court decide on an ad hoc basis which advertisements have political impact and which do not? In addressing this question, *Central Hudson,* noted that any product could be tied to public concerns and that since companies are otherwise free to speak about public issues,[d] "there is no reason for providing similar protection when such statements are made only in the context of commercial transactions." Compare *Bolger v. Youngs Drug Products Corp.,* 463 U.S. 60, 103 S.Ct. 2875, 77 L.Ed.2d 469 (1983) ("advertisers should not be permitted to immunize false or misleading product information from government regulation simply by including references to public issues"); *Board of Trustees v. Fox,* 492 U.S. 469, 109 S.Ct. 3028, 106 L.Ed.2d 388 (1989) (housewares sales presentations are commercial speech even though they provide information on matters of financial responsibility and how to run an efficient home). If a cigarette company buys space in the *New York Times* to print a deceptive message about health and cigarettes, under what circumstances would the communication be properly characterized as commercial speech? Consider Tribe, *Constitutional Choices* 218 (1985): "The distinction between commercial and noncommercial speech [exemplifies] a propensity for pigeonholing as a method for deciding First Amendment questions. Such a method masks the essentially political nature of the underlying issues by pretending to cabin judicial discretion within the limits established by the category itself." Does this sort of pigeonholing "pars[e] First Amendment

c. Is this category intended to be larger than the category of proposing a commercial transaction? Consider the question in connection with *Greenmoss,* p. 592 infra.

d. See Sec. 10 infra.

doctrine too fine"? Does it "endange[r] the pigeon?" See id.[e]

Puerto Rico permits advertising for several forms of gambling, including horse racing, cockfighting, and the lottery. Advertising of casino gambling, however, is subject to a complicated body of regulations enforced by the Tourism Company of Puerto Rico (a public company with regulatory powers). These regulations allow casino advertising designed to attract tourists; they prohibit casino advertising aimed at Puerto Rican residents. For example, casino advertising is permitted when distributed in airports or on docks where cruise ships arrive and is permitted in media that primarily reach tourists rather than residents, e.g., *The New York Times,* trade magazines, even advertisements on network television (that reaches Puerto Rico via cable). Advertising of the hotels containing the casinos is permitted in the local Puerto Rican media "when the trade name of the hotel is used even though it may contain a reference to the casino provided that the word casino is never used alone nor specified." But advertisements designed to attract residents of Puerto Rico to the casinos are expressly prohibited.

POSADAS DE PUERTO RICO ASSOCIATES v. TOURISM COMPANY, 478 U.S. 328, 106 S.Ct. 2968, 92 L.Ed.2d 266 (1986), per REHNQUIST, J., upheld the advertising restrictions: "The particular kind of commercial speech at issue here, namely, advertising of casino gambling aimed at the residents of Puerto Rico, concerns a lawful activity and is not misleading or fraudulent, at least in the abstract. We must therefore proceed to the three remaining steps of the *Central Hudson* analysis in order to determine whether Puerto Rico's advertising restrictions run afoul of the First Amendment. The first of these three steps involves an assessment of the strength of the government's interest in restricting the speech. The interest at stake in this case, as determined by the Superior Court, is the reduction of demand for casino gambling by the residents of Puerto Rico. Appellant acknowledged the existence of this interest in [a] letter to the Tourism Company. ('The legislators wanted the tourists to flock to the casinos to gamble, but not our own people'). The Tourism Company's brief before this Court explains the legislature's belief that '[e]xcessive casino gambling among local residents—[would] produce serious harmful effects on the health, safety and welfare of the Puerto Rican citizens, such as the disruption of moral and cultural patterns, the increase in local crime, the fostering of prostitution, the development of corruption, and the infiltration of organized crime.' These are some of the very same concerns, of course, that have motivated the vast majority of the 50 States to prohibit casino gambling. We have no difficulty in concluding that the Puerto Rico Legislature's interest in the health, safety, and welfare of its citizens constitutes a 'substantial' governmental interest. Cf. *Renton.*

"The last two steps of the *Central Hudson* analysis basically involve a consideration of the 'fit' between the legislature's ends and the means chosen to accomplish those ends. Step three asks the question whether the challenged restrictions on commercial speech 'directly advance' the government's asserted interest. In the instant case, the answer to this question is clearly 'yes.' The Puerto Rico Legislature obviously believed, when it enacted the advertising restrictions at issue here, that advertising of casino gambling aimed at the residents of Puerto Rico would serve to increase the demand for the product

e. On the definitional difficulties, see Kozinski & Banner, *Who's Afraid of Commercial Speech?,* 76 Va.L.Rev. 627 (1990).

advertised. We think the legislature's belief is a reasonable one, and the fact that appellant has chosen to litigate this case all the way to this Court indicates that appellant shares the legislature's view. See *Central Hudson* ('There is an immediate connection between advertising and demand for electricity. Central Hudson would not contest the advertising ban unless it believed that promotion would increase its sales').

"Appellant argues, however, that the challenged advertising restrictions are underinclusive because other kinds of gambling such as horse racing, cockfighting, and the lottery may be advertised to the residents of Puerto Rico. Appellant's argument is misplaced for two reasons. First, whether other kinds of gambling are advertised in Puerto Rico or not, the restrictions on advertising of casino gambling 'directly advance' the legislature's interest in reducing demand for games of chance. Second, the legislature's interest, as previously identified, is not necessarily to reduce demand for all games of chance, but to reduce demand for casino gambling. According to the Superior Court, horse racing, cockfighting, 'picas,' or small games of chance at fiestas, and the lottery 'have been traditionally part of the Puerto Rican's roots,' so that 'the legislator could have been more flexible than in authorizing more sophisticated games which are not so widely sponsored by the people.' In other words, the legislature felt that for Puerto Ricans the risks associated with casino gambling were significantly greater than those associated with the more traditional kinds of gambling in Puerto Rico. In our view, the legislature's separate classification of casino gambling, for purposes of the advertising ban, satisfies the third step of the *Central Hudson* analysis.

"We also think it clear beyond peradventure that the challenged statute and regulations satisfy the fourth and last step of the *Central Hudson* analysis, namely, whether the restrictions on commercial speech are no more extensive than necessary to serve the government's interest. The narrowing constructions of the advertising restrictions announced by the Superior Court ensure that the restrictions will not affect advertising of casino gambling aimed at tourists, but will apply only to such advertising when aimed at the residents of Puerto Rico. Appellant contends, however, that the First Amendment requires the Puerto Rico Legislature to reduce demand for casino gambling among the residents of Puerto Rico not by suppressing commercial speech that might *encourage* such gambling, but by promulgating additional speech designed to *discourage* it. We reject this contention. We think it is up to the legislature to decide whether or not such a 'counterspeech' policy would be as effective in reducing the demand for casino gambling as a restriction on advertising. The legislature could conclude, as it apparently did here, that residents of Puerto Rico are already aware of the risks of casino gambling, yet would nevertheless be induced by widespread advertising to engage in such potentially harmful conduct.

"In short, we conclude that the statute and regulations at issue in this case, as construed by the Superior Court, pass muster under each prong of the *Central Hudson* test. We therefore hold that the Supreme Court of Puerto Rico properly rejected appellant's First Amendment claim.[9]

9. It should be apparent from our discussion of the First Amendment issue, and particularly the third and fourth prongs of the *Central Hudson* test, that appellant can fare no better under the equal protection guarantee of the Constitution. Cf. *Renton.* If there is a sufficient "fit" between the legislature's means and ends to satisfy the concerns of the First Amendment, the same "fit" is surely adequate under the applicable "rational basis" equal protection analysis.

Justice Stevens, in dissent, asserts the additional equal protection claim, not raised by appellant either below or in this Court, that

"Appellant argues, however, that the challenged advertising restrictions are constitutionally defective under our decisions in *Carey* and *Bigelow.* In *Carey,* this Court struck down a ban on any 'advertisement or display' of contraceptives, and in *Bigelow,* we reversed a criminal conviction based on the advertisement of an abortion clinic. We think appellant's argument ignores a crucial distinction between the *Carey* and *Bigelow* decisions and the instant case. In *Carey* and *Bigelow,* the underlying conduct that was the subject of the advertising restrictions was constitutionally protected and could not have been prohibited by the State. Here, on the other hand, the Puerto Rico Legislature surely could have prohibited casino gambling by the residents of Puerto Rico altogether. In our view, the greater power to completely ban casino gambling necessarily includes the lesser power to ban advertising of casino gambling, and *Carey* and *Bigelow* are hence inapposite.

"Appellant also makes the related argument that, having chosen to legalize casino gambling for residents of Puerto Rico, the First Amendment prohibits the legislature from using restrictions on advertising to accomplish its goal of reducing demand for such gambling. We disagree. In our view, appellant has the argument backwards. As we noted in the preceding paragraph, it is precisely *because* the government could have enacted a wholesale prohibition of the underlying conduct that it is permissible for the government to take the less intrusive step of allowing the conduct, but reducing the demand through restrictions on advertising. It would surely be a Pyrrhic victory for casino owners such as appellant to gain recognition of a First Amendment right to advertise their casinos to the residents of Puerto Rico, only to thereby force the legislature into banning casino gambling by residents altogether. It would just as surely be a strange constitutional doctrine which would concede to the legislature the authority to totally ban a product or activity, but deny to the legislature the authority to forbid the stimulation of demand for the product or activity through advertising on behalf of those who would profit from such increased demand. Legislative regulation of products or activities deemed harmful, such as cigarettes, alcoholic beverages, and prostitution, has varied from outright prohibition on the one hand, see, e.g., Cal.Penal Code (prohibiting soliciting or engaging in act of prostitution), to legalization of the product or activity with restrictions on stimulation of its demand on the other hand, see e.g., Nev.Rev.Stat. (authorizing licensing of houses of prostitution except in counties with more than 250,000 population), (prohibiting advertising of houses of prostitution '[i]n any public theater, on the public streets of any city or town, or on any public highway,' or 'in [a] place of business'). To rule out the latter, intermediate kind of response would require more than we find in the First Amendment.[11]"

the Puerto Rico statute and regulations impermissibly discriminate between different kinds of publications. Justice Stevens misunderstands the nature of the Superior Court's limiting construction of the statute and regulations. According to the Superior Court, "[i]f the object of [an] advertisement is the tourist, it passes legal scrutiny." It is clear from the court's opinion that this basic test applies *regardless of whether the advertisement appears in a local or non-local publication.* Of course, the likelihood that a casino advertisement appearing in *The New York Times* will be primarily addressed to tourists, and not Puerto Rico residents, is far greater than would be the case for a similar advertisement appearing in the *San Juan Star.* But it is simply the demographics of the two newspapers' readerships, and not any form of "discrimination" on the part of the Puerto Rico Legislature or the Superior Court, which produces this result.

11. Justice Stevens claims that the Superior Court's narrowing construction creates an impermissible "prior restraint" on protected speech, because that court required the submission of certain casino advertising to appellee for its prior approval. This argument was not raised by appellant, either below or in this Court, and we therefore express no view on the constitutionality of the particular portion

BRENNAN, J., joined by Marshall and Blackmun, JJ., dissented: "[W]hile the First Amendment ordinarily prohibits regulation of speech based on the content of the communicated message, the government may regulate the content of commercial speech in order to prevent the dissemination of information that is false, deceptive, or misleading, see *Zauderer; Friedman; Ohralik,* or that proposes an illegal transaction, see *Pittsburgh Press.* We have, however, consistently invalidated restrictions designed to deprive consumers of accurate information about products and services legally offered for sale.

"[N]o differences between commercial and other kinds of speech justify protecting commercial speech less extensively where, as here, the government seeks to manipulate private behavior by depriving citizens of truthful information concerning lawful activities. [Accordingly,] I believe that where the government seeks to suppress the dissemination of nonmisleading commercial speech relating to legal activities, for fear that recipients will act on the information provided, such regulation should be subject to strict judicial scrutiny.

"The Court, rather than applying strict scrutiny, evaluates Puerto Rico's advertising ban under the relaxed standards normally used to test government regulation of commercial speech. Even under these standards, however, I do not believe that Puerto Rico constitutionally may suppress all casino advertising directed to its residents. [Neither] the statute on its face nor the legislative history indicates that the Puerto Rico Legislature thought that serious harm would result if residents were allowed to engage in casino gambling;[2] indeed, the available evidence suggests exactly the opposite. Puerto Rico has legalized gambling casinos, and permits its residents to patronize them. Thus, the Puerto Rico legislature has determined that permitting residents to engage in casino gambling will not produce the 'serious harmful effects' that have led a majority of States to ban such activity. Residents of Puerto Rico are also permitted to engage in a variety of other gambling activities—including horse racing, 'picas', dog racing, cockfighting, and the Puerto Rico lottery—all of which are allowed to advertise freely to residents.[3] Indeed, it is surely not far-fetched to suppose that the legislature chose to restrict casino advertising not because of the 'evils' of casino gambling, but because it preferred that Puerto Ricans spend their gambling dollars on the Puerto Rico lottery. In any event, in light of the legislature's determination that serious harm will *not* result if residents are permitted and *encouraged* to gamble, I do not see how Puerto Rico's interest in discourag-

of the Superior Court's narrowing construction cited by Justice Stevens.

2. The Act's Statement of Motives says only that: "The purpose of this Act is to contribute to the development of tourism by means of the authorization of certain games of chance—[and] by the establishment of regulations for and the strict surveillance of said games by the government, in order to ensure for tourists the best possible safeguards, while at the same time opening for the Treasurer of Puerto Rico an additional source of income." There is no suggestion that discouraging residents from patronizing gambling casinos would further Puerto Rico's interests in developing tourism, ensuring safeguards for tourists, or producing additional revenue.

3. The Court seeks to justify Puerto Rico's selective prohibition of casino advertising by asserting that "the legislature felt that for Puerto Ricans the risks associated with casino gambling were significantly greater than those associated with the more traditional kinds of gambling in Puerto Rico." Nothing in the record suggests that the legislature believed this to be the case. Appellee has failed to show that casino gambling presents risks different from those associated with other gambling activities, such that Puerto Rico might, consistently with the First Amendment, choose to suppress only casino advertising directed to its residents. For this reason, I believe that Puerto Rico's selective advertising ban also violates appellant's rights under the Equal Protection Clause. In rejecting appellant's equal protection claim, the Court erroneously uses a "rational basis" analysis, thereby ignoring the important First Amendment interests implicated by this case.

ing its residents from engaging in casino gambling can be characterized as 'substantial,' even if the legislature had actually asserted such an interest which, of course, it has not.

"The Court nevertheless sustains Puerto Rico's advertising ban because the legislature *could* have determined that casino gambling would seriously harm the health, safety, and welfare of the Puerto Rican citizens.[4] This reasoning is contrary to this Court's long established First Amendment jurisprudence. When the government seeks to place restrictions upon commercial speech, a court may not, as the Court implies today, simply speculate about valid reasons that the government might have for enacting such restrictions. [A]ppellees have failed to show that a substantial government interest supports Puerto Rico's ban on protected expression.

"[E]ven assuming that an advertising ban would effectively reduce residents' patronage of gambling casinos,[5] it is not clear how it would directly advance Puerto Rico's interest in controlling the 'serious harmful effects' the Court associates with casino gambling. In particular, it is unclear whether banning casino advertising aimed at residents would affect local crime, prostitution, the development of corruption, or the infiltration of organized crime. Because Puerto Rico actively promotes its casinos to tourists, these problems are likely to persist whether or not residents are also encouraged to gamble. Absent some showing that a ban on advertising aimed only at residents will directly advance Puerto Rico's interest in controlling the harmful effects allegedly associated with casino gambling, Puerto Rico may not constitutionally restrict protected expression in that way.

"Finally, appellee has failed to show that Puerto Rico's interest in controlling the harmful effects allegedly associated with casino gambling 'cannot be protected adequately by more limited regulation of appellant's commercial expression.' *Central Hudson.* Rather than suppressing constitutionally protected expression, Puerto Rico could seek directly to address the specific harms thought to be associated with casino gambling. Thus, Puerto Rico could continue carefully to monitor casino operations to guard against 'the development of corruption, and the infiltration of organized crime.' It could vigorously enforce its criminal statutes to combat 'the increase in local crime [and] the fostering of prostitution.' It could establish limits on the level of permissible betting, or promulgate additional speech designed to discourage casino gambling among residents, in order to avoid the 'disruption of moral and cultural patterns,' that

4. The Court reasons that because Puerto Rico could legitimately decide to prohibit casino gambling entirely, it may also take the "less intrusive step" of legalizing casino gambling but restricting speech. According to the Court, it would "surely be a strange constitutional doctrine which would concede to the legislature the authority to totally ban [casino gambling] but deny to the legislature the authority to forbid the stimulation of demand for [casino gambling]" by banning advertising. I do not agree that a ban on casino advertising is "less intrusive" than an outright prohibition of such activity. A majority of States have chosen not to legalize casino gambling, and we have never suggested that this might be unconstitutional. However, having decided to legalize casino gambling, Puerto Rico's decision to ban truthful speech concerning entirely lawful activity raises serious First Amendment problems. Thus, the "constitutional doctrine" which bans Puerto Rico from banning advertisements concerning lawful casino gambling is not so strange a restraint—it is called the First Amendment.

5. Unlike the Court, I do not read the fact that appellant has chosen to litigate the case here necessarily to indicate the appellant itself believes that Puerto Rico residents would respond to casino advertising. In light of appellee's arbitrary and capricious application of § 8, appellant could justifiably have believed that, notwithstanding the Superior Court's "narrowing" construction, its First Amendment rights could be safeguarded effectively only if the Act was invalidated on its face.

might result if residents were to engage in excessive casino gambling. Such measures would directly address the problems appellee associates with casino gambling, while avoiding the First Amendment problems raised where the government seeks to ban constitutionally protected speech.

"[I]t is incumbent upon the government to *prove* that more limited means are not sufficient to protect its interests, and for a *court* to decide whether or not the government has sustained this burden. See *Central Hudson.* In this case, nothing suggests that the Puerto Rico Legislature ever considered the efficacy of measures other than suppressing protected expression. More importantly, there has been no showing that alternative measures would inadequately safeguard the Commonwealth's interest in controlling the harmful effects allegedly associated with casino gambling. Under these circumstances, Puerto Rico's ban on advertising clearly violates the First Amendment.[6]"

STEVENS, J., joined by Marshall and Blackmun, JJ., also dissented: "The Court concludes that 'the greater power to completely ban casino gambling necessarily includes the lesser power to ban advertising of casino gambling.' Whether a State may ban all advertising of an activity that it permits but could prohibit—such as gambling, prostitution, or the consumption of marijuana or liquor—is an elegant question of constitutional law. It is not, however, appropriate to address that question in this case because Puerto Rico's rather bizarre restraints on speech are so plainly forbidden by the First Amendment. * * *

"With respect to the publisher, in stark, unabashed language, the Superior Court's construction favors certain identifiable publications and disfavors others. If the publication (or medium) is from outside Puerto Rico, it is very favored indeed. [If] the publication is native to Puerto Rico, however—the *San Juan Star,* for instance—it is subject to a far more rigid system of restraints and controls regarding the manner in which a certain form of speech (casino ads) may be carried in its pages. Unless the Court is prepared to uphold an Illinois regulation of speech that subjects *The New York Times* to one standard and *The Chicago Tribune* to another, I do not understand why it is willing to uphold a Puerto Rico regulation that applies one standard to *The New York Times* and another to the *San Juan Star.*

"With respect to the audience, the newly construed regulations plainly discriminate in terms of the intended listener or reader. [The] regulation thus poses what might be viewed as a reverse Privileges and Immunities problem: Puerto Rico's residents are singled out for disfavored treatment in comparison to all other Americans. But nothing so fancy is required to recognize the obvious First Amendment problem in this kind of audience discrimination. I cannot imagine that this Court would uphold an Illinois regulation that forbade advertising 'addressed' to Illinois residents while allowing the same advertiser to communicate his message to visitors and commuters; we should be no more willing to uphold a Puerto Rico regulation that forbids advertising 'addressed' to Puerto Rico residents.

"With respect to the message, the regulations now take one word of the English language—'casino'—and give it a special opprobrium. Use of that suspicious six letter word is permitted only 'where the trade name of the hotel is

6. The Court seeks to buttress its holding by noting that some States have regulated other "harmful" products, such as cigarettes, alcoholic beverages, and legalized prostitution, by restricting advertising. While I believe that Puerto Rico may not prohibit all casino advertising directed to its residents, I reserve judgment as to the constitutionality of the variety of advertising restrictions adopted by other jurisdictions.

used even though it may contain a reference to the casino.' The regulations explicitly include an important provision—'that the word casino is never used alone nor specified.' (The meaning of 'specified'—perhaps italicization, or boldface or all capital letters—is presumably left to subsequent case-by-case adjudication). Singling out the use of a particular word for official sanctions raises grave First Amendment concerns, and Puerto Rico has utterly failed to justify the disfavor in which that particular six-letter word is held. * * *

"The general proposition advanced by the majority today—that a State may prohibit the advertising of permitted conduct if it may prohibit the conduct altogether—bears little resemblance to the grotesquely flawed regulation of speech advanced by Puerto Rico in this case.[2] The First Amendment surely does not permit Puerto Rico's frank discrimination among publications, audiences, and words. Nor should sanctions for speech be as unpredictable and haphazardous as the role of dice in a casino."

Notes and Questions

1. *The greater includes the lesser.* Consider, Abrams, *Commercial Free Speech in the Marketplace of Ideas,* 41 Rutgers L.Rev. 737, 739 (1989): Justice Rehnquist's opinion said that "because casino gambling could be banned, it therefore followed that the advertising of it could be banned. That is, simply and totally, an inversion of first amendment theory. Usually we say [that] we control speech last, not first; that we control conduct first, not last. [Usually] we say to legislatures: bite the bullet. If you really care enough, [do] something about the *thing* that you are concerned about. That thing is not speech, it is people engaging in casino gambling." Consider Rotunda, *The Constitutional Future of the Bill of Rights,* 65 N.C.L.Rev. 917 (1987): "What about [*Central Hudson*]? No one has a constitutional right to waste electricity. New York, in *Central Hudson,* could have simply banned the use of all electric hair dryers, or all energy inefficient heat pumps, or all electric toothbrushes. Yet *Central Hudson* teaches us that New York could not [prohibit] advertising that promotes the wasteful (but lawful) use of electricity. If New York cannot constitutionally dampen New Yorkers' demand for electricity by prohibiting promotional advertising, [why] can Puerto Rico dampen Puerto Rican demand for casino advertising by prohibiting promotional advertising?" Is the *Posadas* dictum consistent with *Virginia Pharmacy?*[a]

2. Does *Posadas* adopt a "vice" or "morals" exception to *Central Hudson?* See Epstein, *Foreword: Unconstitutional Conditions, State Power, and the Limits of Consent,* 102 Harv.L.Rev. 5, 67 (1988). But cf. Kurland, *Posadas de Puerto Rico v. Tourism Company,* 1986 Sup.Ct.Rev. 1, 15: "Perhaps *Posadas* was intended to further a new moral code, which tolerates government restraint not only on speech that is conducive to illegal behavior but also on speech that may lead to immoral though legal conduct. The difficulty here is that we know or can find out, more or less, what has been made illegal. We cannot know what

2. Moreover, the Court has relied on an inappropriate major premise. The fact that Puerto Rico might prohibit all casino gambling does not necessarily mean that it could prohibit residents from patronizing casinos that are open to tourists. Even under the Court's reasoning, discriminatory censorship cannot be justified as a less restrictive form of economic regulation unless discriminatory regulation is itself permissible.

a. For criticism of the "greater includes the lesser" argument, see Garvey, *The Power and the Duties of Government,* 26 San Diego L. Rev. 209, 215–19 (1989); Kreimer, *Allocational Sanctions: The Problem of Negative Rights in a Positive State,* 132 U.Pa.L.Rev. 1293, 1304–14 (1984).

the courts will determine to be immoral until they tell us. Is gambling immoral? Only casino gambling? Is wine drinking immoral? When do purchases of luxuries become immoral? Doing any business with South Africa, Libya, Syria? If immorality is to be the guide to legitimating censorship, we have entered on a long and rocky road indeed."

3. Is the presence or absence of informational content in commercial advertising a key factor? Consider Lowenstein, *"Too Much Puff": Persuasion, Paternalism, and Commercial Speech,* 56 U.Cin.L.Rev. 1205, 1230 & 1236 (1988): "If we are to understand the commercial speech doctrine in practice, it is of great significance to recognize that the Court has struck down every restriction of purely or predominantly informational advertising to come before it, whereas all or nearly all (depending on how one classifies *Central Hudson*) restrictions of noninformational commercial speech have been upheld. [Given] the strong interest of the state in discouraging cigarette smoking, [for example,] it may be that a ban even on [purely] informational [cigarette] advertising would be or ought to be upheld. Nevertheless, the case for allowing the prohibition of such advertising is not as strong as the case for prohibiting the overwhelming majority of cigarette advertising, which seeks to induce smoking by associating a brand of cigarettes with some desirable activity or by other manipulative means. As in *Posadas,* the Court might uphold the statute knowing that in almost all its applications it will apply to noninformational advertising. Alternatively, and this would be more likely if the party challenging the statute were one who wished to run purely informational advertisements, the Court might uphold the statute as a general matter, but rule it unconstitutional as applied to informational advertising. At this point, the distinction between informational and noninformational advertising would have to become an explicit part of the Court's doctrine, and the Court would be forced to work out some refinements." [b]

4. *Less restrictive alternatives? Central Hudson* insisted that the Commission "demonstrat[e] that its interest in conservation cannot be protected adequately by more limited regulation of appellant's commercial expression." Moreover, it listed a number of alternatives the Commission might consider. *Posadas* settled for the conclusion that the legislature "could" conclude as it "apparently did" that a suggested alternative would be ineffective. Should the legislature have been forced to demonstrate that the suggested alternative would be ineffective?

BOARD OF TRUSTEES v. FOX, p. 583 supra, per SCALIA, J., held that the *Central Hudson* test does not require government to foreclose the possibility of all less restrictive alternatives. It is enough if the fit between means and ends is "reasonable." It need not be "perfect." Like time, place, and manner regulations, however, the relationship between means and end must be "narrowly tailored to achieve the desired objective." Under that standard, as interpreted (see p. 915 infra), government may not " 'burden substantially more speech than is necessary to further the government's legitimate interest,' " [c] but need not foreclose "all conceivable alternatives." Scalia, J., argued that to have a more

b. For a sampling of views concerning a ban on tobacco advertising, see, e.g., Arbogast, *A Proposal to Regulate the Manner of Tobacco Advertising,* 11 J. Health Pol., Pol'y & L. 393 (1986); Blasi & Monaghan, *The First Amendment and Cigarette Advertising,* 256 J.A.M.A. 502 (1986); Blasi & Monaghan, *Posadas and the Prohibition of Cigarette Advertising,* 2 Tobacco Prod.Lit.Rep. 4.38 (1987); Kurland, supra; Lowenstein, supra; Richards, *Clearing the Air About Cigarettes: Will Advertisers' Rights Go Up in Smoke,* 19 Pac.L.J. 1 (1987); Comment, *First Amendment Values and the Constitutional Protection of Tobacco Advertising,* 82 N.W.U.L.Rev. 145 (1987).

c. Quoting *Ward v. Rock Against Racism,* p. 643 infra.

demanding test in commercial speech than that used for time, place, and manner regulations would be inappropriate because time, place, and manner regulations can apply to political speech.[d]

III. PRIVATE SPEECH

Before studying *Dun & Bradstreet,* below, review *Gertz,* p. 436 supra.

Dun & Bradstreet, Inc., a credit reporting agency, falsely and negligently reported to five of its subscribers that Greenmoss Builders, Inc. had filed a petition for bankruptcy and also negligently misrepresented Greenmoss' assets and liabilities. In the ensuing defamation action, Greenmoss recovered $50,000 in compensatory damages and $300,000 in punitive damages. Dun & Bradstreet argued that, under *Gertz,* its first amendment rights had been violated because presumed and punitive damages had been imposed without instructions requiring a showing of *New York Times* malice. Greenmoss argued that the *Gertz* protections did not extend to non-media defendants and, in any event, did not extend to commercial speech. DUN & BRADSTREET, INC. v. GREENMOSS BUILDERS, INC., 472 U.S. 749, 105 S.Ct. 2939, 86 L.Ed.2d 593 (1985), rejected Dun & Bradstreet's contention, but there was no opinion of the Court. The common theme of the five justices siding with Greenmoss was that the first amendment places less value on "private" speech than upon "public" speech.

POWELL, J., joined by Rehnquist and O'Connor, JJ., noted that the Vermont Supreme Court below had held "as a matter of federal constitutional law" that "the media protections outlined in *Gertz* are inapplicable to nonmedia defamation actions." In affirming, Powell, J., stated that his reasons were "different from those relied upon by the Vermont Supreme Court": "Like every other case in which this Court has found constitutional limits to state defamation laws, *Gertz* involved expression on a matter of undoubted public concern. * * *

"We have never considered whether the *Gertz* balance obtains when the defamatory statements involve no issue of public concern. To make this determination, we must employ the approach approved in *Gertz* and balance the State's interest in compensating private individuals for injury to their reputation against the First Amendment interest in protecting this type of expression. This state interest is identical to the one weighed in *Gertz.* * * *

"The First Amendment interest, on the other hand, is less important than the one weighed in *Gertz.* We have long recognized that not all speech is of equal First Amendment importance.[5] It is speech on 'matters of public concern'

d. Blackmun, J., joined by Brennan and Marshall, JJ., dissenting, did not reach this issue.

5. This Court on many occasions has recognized that certain kinds of speech are less central to the interests of the First Amendment than others. Obscene speech and "fighting words" long have been accorded no protection. *Roth; Chaplinsky.* In the area of protected speech, the most prominent example of reduced protection for certain kinds of speech concerns commercial speech. Such speech, we have noted, occupies a "subordinate position in the scale of First Amendment values." *Ohralik.* * * *

Other areas of the law provide further examples. In *Ohralik* we noted that there are "[n]umerous examples [of] communications that are regulated without offending the First Amendment, such as the exchange of information about securities, * * * corporate proxy statements, [the] exchange of price and production information among competitors, [and] employers' threats of retaliation for the labor activities of employees." Yet similar regulation of political speech is subject to the most rigorous scrutiny. Likewise, while the power of the State to license lawyers, psychiatrists, and public school teachers—all of whom speak for a living—is unquestioned, this Court has held that a law requiring licensing of union organizers is unconstitutional under the First Amendment. *Thomas v. Collins*; see also *Rosenbloom v. Metromedia* (opinion of Brennan, J.) ("the determinant whether the First that is 'at the heart of the First Amendment's protection.' [In] contrast, speech on matters of purely private concern is of less First Amendment concern. As a number of state courts, including the court below, have recognized, the role of the Constitution in regulating state libel law is far more limited when the concerns that activated *New York Times* and *Gertz* are absent.[6] In such a case, '[t]here is no threat to the free and robust debate of public issues; there is no potential interference with a meaningful dialogue of ideas concerning self-government; and there is no threat of liability causing a reaction of self-censorship by the press. The facts of the present case are wholly without the First Amendment concerns with which the Supreme Court of the United States has been struggling.' *Harley-Davidson Motorsports, Inc. v. Markley,* 279 Or. 361, 366, 568 P.2d 1359, 1363 (1977).

"While such speech is not totally unprotected by the First Amendment, see *Connick,* its protections are less stringent. [In] light of the reduced constitutional value of speech involving no matters of public concern, we hold that the state interest adequately supports awards of presumed and punitive damages—even absent a showing of 'actual malice.'[7]

"The only remaining issue is whether petitioner's credit report involved a matter of public concern. In a related context, we have held that '[w]hether [speech] addresses a matter of public concern must be determined by [the expression's] content, form, and context [as] revealed by the whole record.' *Connick v. Myers* [p. 741 infra]. These factors indicate that petitioner's credit report concerns no public issue.[8] It was speech solely in the individual interest of the speaker and its specific business audience. Cf. *Central Hudson.* This particular interest warrants no special protection when—as in this case—the speech is wholly false and clearly damaging to the victim's business reputation. Moreover, since the credit report was made available to only five subscribers, who, under the terms of the subscription agreement, could not disseminate it further, it cannot be said that the report involves any 'strong interest in the free flow of commercial information.' *Virginia Pharmacy.* There is simply no credible argument that this type of credit reporting requires special protection to

Amendment applies to state libel actions is whether the utterance involved concerns an issue of public or general concern").

6. As one commentator has remarked with respect to "the case of a commercial supplier of credit information that defames a person applying for credit"—the case before us today—"If the first amendment requirements outlined in *Gertz* apply, there is something clearly wrong with the first amendment or with *Gertz.*" Shiffrin, *The First Amendment and Economic Regulation: Away From a General Theory of the First Amendment,* 78 Nw.L. Rev. 1212, 1268 (1983).

7. The dissent, purporting to apply the same balancing test that we do today, concludes that even speech on purely private matters is entitled to the protections of *Gertz.*

* * *

The dissent's "balance" [would] lead to the protection of all libels—no matter how attenuated their constitutional interest. If the dissent were the law, a woman of impeccable character who was branded a "whore" by a jealous neighbor would have no effective recourse unless she could prove "actual malice" by clear and convincing evidence. This is not malice in the ordinary sense, but in the more demanding sense of *New York Times.* The dissent would, in effect, constitutionalize the entire common law of libel.

8. The dissent suggests that our holding today leaves all credit reporting subject to reduced First Amendment protection. This is incorrect. The protection to be accorded a particular credit report depends on whether the report's "content, form, and context" indicate that it concerns a public matter. We also do not hold, as the dissent suggests we do, that the report is subject to reduced constitutional protection because it constitutes economic or commercial speech. We discuss such speech, along with advertising, only to show how many of the same concerns that argue in favor of reduced constitutional protection in those areas apply here as well.

ensure that 'debate on public issues [will] be uninhibited, robust, and wide-open.' *New York Times.*

"In addition, the speech here, like advertising, is hardy and unlikely to be deterred by incidental state regulation. See *Virginia Pharmacy.* It is solely motivated by the desire for profit, which, we have noted, is a force less likely to be deterred than others. Arguably, the reporting here was also more objectively verifiable than speech deserving of greater protection. In any case, the market provides a powerful incentive to a credit reporting agency to be accurate, since false credit reporting is of no use to creditors. Thus, any incremental 'chilling' effect of libel suits would be of decreased significance.

"We conclude that permitting recovery of presumed and punitive damages in defamation cases absent a showing of 'actual malice' does not violate the First Amendment when the defamatory statements do not involve matters of public concern."

Although expressing the view that *Gertz* should be overruled and that the *New York Times* malice definition should be reconsidered, BURGER, C.J., concurring, stated that: "The single question before the Court today is whether *Gertz* applies to this case. The plurality opinion holds that *Gertz* does not apply because, unlike the challenged expression in *Gertz,* the alleged defamatory expression in this case does not relate to a matter of public concern. I agree that *Gertz* is limited to circumstances in which the alleged defamatory expression concerns a matter of general public importance, and that the expression in question here relates to a matter of essentially private concern. I therefore agree with the plurality opinion to the extent that it holds that *Gertz* is inapplicable in this case for the two reasons indicated. No more is needed to dispose of the present case."

WHITE, J., who had dissented in *Gertz,* was prepared to overrule that case or to limit it, but he disagreed with Powell, J.'s, suggestion that the plurality's resolution of the case was faithful to *Gertz:*

"It is interesting that Justice Powell declines to follow the *Gertz* approach in this case. I had thought that the decision in *Gertz* was intended to reach cases that involve any false statements of fact injurious to reputation, whether the statement is made privately or publicly and whether or not it implicates a matter of public importance. Justice Powell, however, distinguishes *Gertz* as a case that involved a matter of public concern, an element absent here. Wisely, in my view, Justice Powell does not rest his application of a different rule here on a distinction drawn between media and non-media defendants. On that issue, I agree with Justice Brennan that the First Amendment gives no more protection to the press in defamation suits than it does to others exercising their freedom of speech. None of our cases affords such a distinction; to the contrary, the Court has rejected it at every turn. It should be rejected again, particularly in this context, since it makes no sense to give the most protection to those publishers who reach the most readers and therefore pollute the channels of communication with the most misinformation and do the most damage to private reputation. If *Gertz* is to be distinguished from this case, on the ground that it applies only where the allegedly false publication deals with a matter of general or public importance, then where the false publication does not deal with such a matter, the common-law rules would apply whether the defendant is a member of the media or other public disseminator or a non-media individual publishing privately. Although Justice Powell speaks only of the inapplicability of the *Gertz* rule with respect to presumed and punitive damages, it must be that the

Gertz requirement of some kind of fault on the part of the defendant is also inapplicable in cases such as this. * * *

"The question before us is whether *Gertz* is to be applied in this case. For either of two reasons, I believe that it should not. First, I am unreconciled to the *Gertz* holding and believe that it should be overruled. Second, as Justice Powell indicates, the defamatory publication in this case does not deal with a matter of public importance."

BRENNAN, J., joined by Marshall, Blackmun and Stevens, JJ., dissented:

"This case involves a difficult question of the proper application of *Gertz* to credit reporting—a type of speech at some remove from that which first gave rise to explicit First Amendment restrictions on state defamation law—and has produced a diversity of considered opinions, none of which speaks for the Court. Justice Powell's plurality opinion affirming the judgment below would not apply the *Gertz* limitations on presumed and punitive damages [because] the speech involved a subject of purely private concern and was circulated to an extremely limited audience. * * * Justice White also would affirm; he would not apply *Gertz* to this case on the ground that the subject matter of the publication does not deal with a matter of general or public importance. The Chief Justice apparently agrees with Justice White. The four who join this opinion would reverse the judgment of the Vermont Supreme Court. We believe that, although protection of the type of expression at issue is admittedly not the 'central meaning of the First Amendment,' *Gertz* makes clear that the First Amendment nonetheless requires restraints on presumed and punitive damage awards for this expression. * * *

"[Respondent urged that *Gertz* be restricted] to cases in which the defendant is a 'media' entity. Such a distinction is irreconcilable with the fundamental First Amendment principle that '[t]he inherent worth [of] speech in terms of its capacity for informing the public does not depend upon the identity of its source, whether corporation, association, union, or individual.' *First National Bank v. Bellotti* [p. 789 infra]. First Amendment difficulties lurk in the definitional questions such an approach would generate. And the distinction would likely be born an anachronism.[7] Perhaps most importantly, the argument that *Gertz* should be limited to the media misapprehends our cases. We protect the press to ensure the vitality of First Amendment guarantees. This solicitude implies no endorsement of the principle that speakers other than the press deserve lesser First Amendment protection. * * *

"The free speech guarantee gives each citizen an equal right to self-expression and to participation in self-government. [Accordingly,] at least six Members of this Court (the four who join this opinion and Justice White and The Chief Justice) agree today that, in the context of defamation law, the rights of the institutional media are no greater and no less than those enjoyed by other individuals or organizations engaged in the same activities.[10] * * *

"Purporting to 'employ the approach approved in *Gertz*,' Justice Powell balances the state interest in protecting private reputation against the First Amendment interest in protecting expression on matters not of public

7. Owing to transformations in the technological and economic structure of the communications industry, there has been an increasing convergence of what might be labeled "media" and "nonmedia."

10. Justice Powell's opinion does not expressly reject the media/nonmedia distinction, but does expressly decline to apply that distinction to resolve this case.

concern.[11]

"The five Members of the Court voting to affirm the damage award in this case have provided almost no guidance as to what constitutes a protected 'matter of public concern.' Justice White offers nothing at all, but his opinion does indicate that the distinction turns on solely the subject matter of the expression and not on the extent or conditions of dissemination of that expression. Justice Powell adumbrates a rationale that would appear to focus primarily on subject matter.[12] The opinion relies on the fact that the speech at issue was 'solely in the individual interest of the speaker and its *business* audience.' Analogizing explicitly to advertising, the opinion also states that credit reporting is 'hardy' and 'solely motivated by the desire for profit.' These two strains of analysis suggest that Justice Powell is excluding the subject matter of credit reports from 'matters of public concern' because the speech is predominantly in the realm of matters of economic concern."

Brennan, J., pointed to precedents (particularly labor cases) protecting speech on economic matters and argued that, "the breadth of this protection evinces recognition that freedom of expression is not only essential to check tyranny and foster self-government but also intrinsic to individual liberty and dignity and instrumental in society's search for truth."

Moreover, he emphasized the importance of credit reporting: "The credit reporting of Dun & Bradstreet falls within any reasonable definition of 'public concern' consistent with our precedents. Justice Powell's reliance on the fact that Dun & Bradstreet publishes credit reports 'for profit' is wholly unwarranted. Time and again we have made clear that speech loses none of its constitutional protection 'even though it is carried in a form that is "sold" for profit.' *Virginia Pharmacy*. More importantly, an announcement of the bankruptcy of a local company is information of potentially great concern to residents of the community where the company is [located]. And knowledge about solvency and the effect and prevalence of bankruptcy certainly would inform citizen opinions about questions of economic regulation. It is difficult to suggest that a bankruptcy is not a subject matter of public concern when federal law requires invocation of judicial mechanisms to effectuate it and makes the fact of the bankruptcy a matter of public record. * * *

"Even if the subject matter of credit reporting were properly considered—in the terms of Justice White and Justice Powell—as purely a matter of private

11. One searches *Gertz* in vain for a single word to support the proposition that limits on presumed and punitive damages obtained only when speech involved matters of public concern. *Gertz* could not have been grounded in such a premise. Distrust of placing in the courts the power to decide what speech was of public concern was precisely the rationale *Gertz* offered for rejecting the *Rosenbloom* plurality approach. * * *

12. Justice Powell also appears to rely in part on the fact that communication was limited and confidential. Given that his analysis also relies on the subject matter of the credit report, it is difficult to decipher exactly what role the nature and extent of dissemination plays in Justice Powell's analysis. But because the subject matter of the expression at issue is properly understood as a matter of public concern, it may well be that this element of confidentiality is crucial to the outcome as far as Justice Powell's opinion is concerned. In other words, it may be that Justice Powell thinks this particular expression could not contribute to public welfare because the public generally does not receive it. This factor does not suffice to save the analysis. See n. 18 infra.

[In fn. 18, Brennan, J., indicated that, "Dun & Bradstreet doubtless provides thousands of credit reports to thousands of subscribers who receive the information pursuant to the same strictures imposed on the recipients in this case. As a systemic matter, therefore, today's decision diminishes the free flow of information because Dun & Bradstreet will generally be made more reticent in providing information to all its subscribers."]

discourse, this speech would fall well within the range of valuable expression for which the First Amendment demands protection. Much expression that does not directly involve public issues receives significant protection. Our cases do permit some diminution in the degree of protection afforded one category of speech about economic or commercial matters. 'Commercial speech'—defined as advertisements that 'do no more than propose a commercial transaction'—may be more closely regulated than other types of speech. [Credit] reporting is not 'commercial speech' as this Court has defined the term.

"[In] *every* case in which we have permitted more extensive state regulation on the basis of a commercial speech rationale—the speech being regulated was pure advertising—an offer to buy or sell goods and services or encouraging such buying and selling. Credit reports are not commercial advertisements for a good or service or a proposal to buy or sell such a product. We have been extremely chary about extending the 'commercial speech' doctrine beyond this narrowly circumscribed category of advertising because often vitally important speech will be uttered to advance economic interests and because the profit motive making such speech hardy dissipates rapidly when the speech is not advertising." [a]

Finally, Brennan, J., argued that even if credit reports were characterized as commercial speech, "unrestrained" presumed and punitive damages would violate the commercial speech requirement that "the regulatory means chosen be narrowly tailored so as to avoid any unnecessary chilling of protected expression. [Accordingly,] Greenmoss Builders should be permitted to recover for any actual damage it can show resulted from Dun & Bradstreet's negligently false credit report, but should be required to show actual malice to receive presumed or punitive damages."

Notes and Questions

1. Which of the following are "private" according to the opinions of Powell, J., Burger, C.J., and White, J.? (a) a report in the *Wall Street Journal* that Greenmoss has gone bankrupt; (b) a confidential report by Dun & Bradstreet to a bank that a famous politician has poor credit. Would the answer be different if the subject of the report were an actor? (c) a statement in the campus newspaper or by one student to another that a law professor is an alcoholic. Would it make a difference if the law professor was being considered for a Supreme Court appointment?

Consider the relationship between the public/private focus of the *Greenmoss* decision and the "public controversy" aspect of the public figure definition. If the speech does not relate to a "public" controversy, can it be "public" within the terms of *Greenmoss*? See Smolla, *Law of Defamation* 3–15 (1986). Reconsider *Time, Inc. v. Firestone*, p. 444 supra.[b]

a. Brennan, J., cited *Consolidated Edison*, p. 790 infra, which invalidated a regulation that prohibited a utility company from inserting its views on "controversial issues of public policy" into its monthly electrical bill mailings. The mailing that prompted the regulation advocated nuclear power.

b. For discussion of the different meanings of public and private speech, see Schauer, *"Private" Speech and the "Private" Forum: Givhan v. Western Line School District*, 1979 Sup.Ct.Rev. 217. Compare Perry, *Freedom of Expression: An Essay on Theory and Doctrine*, 78 Nw.U.L.Rev. 1137 (1983) (denying any meaningful distinction between personal and political decisions). See generally Symposium, *The Public/Private Distinction*, 130 U.Pa. L.Rev. 1289 (1982); Lieberwitz, *Freedom of Speech in Public Sector Employment: The Deconstitutionalization of the Public Sector Workplace*, 19 U.C.Davis L.Rev. 597 (1986); Massaro, *Significant Silences: Freedom of Speech in the Public Sector Workplace*, 61 S.Cal.L.Rev. 1, 68–76 (1987). For commentary on the question of whether *Gertz* should ex-

Finally, does it matter why the D & B subscribers received the information about Greenmoss? Suppose, for investment or insurance purposes, the subscribers had asked for reports on all aspects of the construction industry in Vermont? Compare *Lowe v. SEC,* p. 611 infra.

2. Should the focus of the decision have been commercial speech instead of private speech? Would an expansion of the commercial speech definition have been preferable to the promotion of ad hoc decisionmaking about the nature of "private" speech? Consider Shiffrin, *The First Amendment and Economic Regulation: Away From A General Theory of the First Amendment,* 78 Nw.U.L.Rev. 1212, 1269 n. 327 (1983): "[D]rawing lines based on underlying first amendment values is a far cry from sending out the judiciary on a general ad hoc expedition to separate matters of general public interest from matters that are not. A commitment to segregate certain commercial speech from *Gertz* protection is not a commitment to general ad hoc determinations."

3. According to Powell, J., in fn. 5, are the *Ohralik* examples, i.e., exchange of information about securities, corporate proxy statements and the like, examples of protected speech subject to regulation? In what sense, are those examples of communication protected? What is the significance of Powell, J.'s suggestion that they are something other than commercial speech? [c] Where do those examples fit into Brennan, J.'s view of the first amendment? For general discussion, see Shiffrin, note 2 supra; Wolfson, *The First Amendment and the SEC,* 20 Conn.L.Rev. 265 (1988). See also Comment, *A Political Speech Exception to the Regulation of Proxy Solicitations,* 86 Colum.L.Rev. 1453 (1986).

SECTION 4. PRIOR RESTRAINTS

Prior restraint is a technical term in first amendment law. A criminal statute prohibiting all advocacy of violent action would *restrain* speech and would have been enacted *prior* to any restrained communication. The statute would be overbroad, but it would not be a prior restraint. A prior restraint refers only to closely related, distinctive methods of regulating expression that are said to have in common their own peculiar set of evils and problems, in addition to those that accompany most any governmental interference with free expression. "The issue is not whether the government may impose a particular restriction of substance in an area of public expression, such as forbidding obscenity in newspapers, but whether it may do so by a particular method, such as advance screening of newspaper copy. In other words, restrictions which could be validly imposed when enforced by subsequent punishment are, nevertheless, forbidden if attempted by prior restraint." Emerson, *The Doctrine of Prior Restraint,* 20 Law and Contemp.Prob. 648 (1955).

The classic prior restraints were the English licensing laws which required a license in advance to print any material or to import or to sell any book.[a] One of the questions raised in this chapter concerns the types of government conduct beyond the classic licensing laws that should be characterized as prior restraints. Another concerns the question of when government licensing of speech, press, or assembly should be countenanced. Perhaps, most important, the Section ex-

tend to non-media defendants see e.g. sources cited in note 1 after *Gertz,* p. 444 supra.

c. Consider *Board of Trustees v. Fox,* (dictum stating that attorneys or tutors dispensing advice for a fee do not engage in commercial speech and strongly suggesting that regulations prohibiting such speech in college dormitories may be unconstitutional).

a. For a persuasive chronicling of the abuses in a modern licensing system, see generally Powe, *American Broadcasting and the First Amendment* (1987).

plores the circumstances in which otherwise protected speech may be restrained on an ad hoc basis.

I. FOUNDATION CASES

A. LICENSING

LOVELL v. GRIFFIN, 303 U.S. 444, 58 S.Ct. 666, 82 L.Ed. 949 (1938), per HUGHES, C.J., invalidated an ordinance prohibiting the distribution of handbooks, advertising or literature within the city of Griffin, Georgia without obtaining written permission of the City Manager: "[T]he ordinance is invalid on its face. Whatever the motive which induced its adoption, its character is such that it strikes at the very foundation of the freedom of the press by subjecting it to license and censorship. The struggle for the freedom of the press was primarily directed against the power of the licensor. It was against that power that John Milton directed his assault by his 'Appeal for the Liberty of Unlicensed Printing.' And the liberty of the press became initially a right to publish '*without* a license what formerly could be published only *with* one.' While this freedom from previous restraint upon publication cannot be regarded as exhausting the guaranty of liberty, the prevention of that restraint was a leading purpose in the adoption of the constitutional provision. Legislation of the type of the ordinance in question would restore the system of license and censorship in its baldest form.

"The liberty of the press is not confined to newspapers and periodicals. It necessarily embraces pamphlets and leaflets. These indeed have been historic weapons in the defense of liberty, as the pamphlets of Thomas Paine and others in our own history abundantly attest. The press in its historic connotation comprehends every sort of publication which affords a vehicle of information and opinion. * * *

"The ordinance cannot be saved because it relates to distribution and not to publication. 'Liberty of circulating is as essential to that freedom as liberty of publishing; indeed, without the circulation, the publication would be of little value.' *Ex parte Jackson,* 96 U.S. (6 Otto) 727, 733, 24 L.Ed. 877 (1877).

"[As] the ordinance is void on its face, it was not necessary for appellant to seek a permit under it. She was entitled to contest its validity in answer to the charge against her." [a]

Notes and Questions

1. *First amendment procedure.* Notice that Lovell would get the benefit of the prior restraint doctrine even if the material she distributed was obscene or otherwise unprotected. In that respect, the prior restraint doctrine is similar to the doctrines of overbreadth and vagueness. For particular concerns that underlie the prior restraint doctrine, consider Emerson, *The System of Freedom of Expression* 506 (1970): "A system of prior restraint is in many ways more inhibiting than a system of subsequent punishment: It is likely to bring under government scrutiny a far wider range of expression; it shuts off communication before it takes place; suppression by a stroke of the pen is more likely to be applied than suppression through a criminal process; the procedures do not require attention to the safeguards of the criminal process; the system allows less opportunity for public appraisal and criticism; the dynamics of the system

a. Cardozo, J., took no part.

drive toward excesses, as the history of all censorship shows." [b]

2. *Scope and character of the doctrine.* What is the vice of the licensing scheme in *Lovell*? Is the concern that like vague statutes it affords undue discretion and potential for abuse? Is the real concern the uncontrolled power of the licensor to deny licenses? Suppose licenses were automatically issued to anyone who applied?

To what extent should the prior restraint doctrine apply to non-press activities? To a licensing ordinance that otherwise forbids soliciting membership in organizations that exact fees of their members? See *Staub v. Baxley,* 355 U.S. 313, 78 S.Ct. 277, 2 L.Ed.2d 302 (1958) (yes). To a licensing ordinance that otherwise prohibits attempts to secure contributions for charitable or religious causes? See *Cantwell v. Connecticut,* 310 U.S. 296, 60 S.Ct. 900, 84 L.Ed. 1213 (1940) (yes).

Should the prior restraint doctrine apply to all aspects of newspaper circulation? See *Lakewood v. Plain Dealer Publishing Co.,* 486 U.S. 750, 108 S.Ct. 2138, 100 L.Ed.2d 771 (1988) (invalidating ordinance granting Mayor power to grant or deny annual permits to place newsracks on public property).[c]

Suppose, in the above cases, that the authority of the licensor were confined by narrow, objective, and definite standards or that licenses were automatically issued to anyone who applied. *Hynes v. Mayor,* 425 U.S. 610, 96 S.Ct. 1755, 48 L.Ed.2d 243 (1976), per Burger, C.J., stated in dictum that a municipality could regulate house to house soliciting by requiring advance notice to the police department in order to protect its citizens from crime and undue annoyance: "A narrowly drawn ordinance, that does not vest in municipal officials the undefined power to determine what messages residents will hear, may serve these important interests without running afoul of the First Amendment." But cf. *Thomas v. Collins,* 323 U.S. 516, 65 S.Ct. 315, 89 L.Ed. 430 (1945) (registration requirement for paid union organizers invalid prior restraint); *Talley v. California,* 362 U.S. 60, 80 S.Ct. 536, 4 L.Ed.2d 559 (1960) (ban on anonymous handbills "void on its face," noting that the "obnoxious press licensing law of England, which was also enforced on the Colonies was due in part to the knowledge that exposure of the names of printers, writers and distributors would lessen the circulation of literature critical of the government").

B. INJUNCTIONS

NEAR v. MINNESOTA

283 U.S. 697, 51 S.Ct. 625, 75 L.Ed. 1357 (1931).

CHIEF JUSTICE HUGHES delivered the opinion of the Court.

[The *Saturday Press* published articles charging that through graft and incompetence named public officials failed to expose and punish gangsters responsible for gambling, bootlegging, and racketeering in Minneapolis. It demanded a special grand jury and special prosecutor to deal with the situation

b. But see Posner, *Free Speech in an Economic Perspective,* 20 Suff.L.Rev. 1, 13 (1986): "The conventional arguments for why censorship is worse than criminal punishment are little better than plausible (though I think there is at least one good argument)" [observing that speech ordinarily does not produce sufficient damage to justify sifting through massive materials].

c. White, J., joined by Stevens and O'Connor, JJ., dissenting, contended that *Lovell* should apply only if the newspaper had a constitutional right to place newsracks on public sidewalks. Otherwise, the newspaper should be required to show that a denial was based on improper reasons.

and to investigate an alleged attempt to assassinate one of its publishers. Under a statute that authorized abatement of a "malicious, scandalous and defamatory newspaper" the state secured, and its supreme court affirmed, a court order that "abated" the Press and perpetually enjoined the defendants from publishing or circulating "any publication whatsoever which is a malicious, scandalous or defamatory newspaper." The order did not restrain the defendants from operating a newspaper "in harmony with the general welfare."]

The object of the statute is not punishment, in the ordinary sense, but suppression of the offending newspaper. [In] the case of public officers, it is the reiteration of charges of official misconduct, and the fact that the newspaper [is] principally devoted to that purpose, that exposes it to suppression. [T]he operation and effect of the statute [is] that public authorities may bring the owner or publisher of a newspaper or periodical before a judge upon a charge of conducting a business of publishing scandalous and defamatory matter—in particular that the matter consists of charges against public officers of official dereliction—and, unless the owner or publisher is able and disposed to bring competent evidence to satisfy the judge that the charges are true and are published with good motives and for justifiable ends, his newspaper or periodical is suppressed and further publication is made punishable as a contempt. This is of the essence of censorship.

The question is whether a statute authorizing such proceedings [is] consistent with the conception of the liberty of the press as historically conceived and guaranteed. [I]t has been generally, if not universally, considered that it is the chief purpose of the guaranty to prevent previous restraints upon publication. The struggle in England, directed against the legislative power of the licenser, resulted in renunciation of the censorship of the press. The liberty deemed to be established was thus described by Blackstone: "The liberty of the press is indeed essential to the nature of a free state; but this consists in laying no *previous* restraints upon publications, and not in freedom from censure for criminal matter when published. Every freeman has an undoubted right to lay what sentiments he pleases before the public; to forbid this, is to destroy the freedom of the press; but if he publishes what is improper, mischievous or illegal, he must take the consequence of his own temerity." [The] criticism upon Blackstone's statement has not been because immunity from previous restraint upon publication has not been regarded as deserving of special emphasis, but chiefly because that immunity cannot be deemed to exhaust the conception of the liberty guaranteed by State and Federal Constitutions.

[T]he protection even as to previous restraint is not absolutely unlimited. But the limitation has been recognized only in exceptional cases. [N]o one would question but that a government might prevent actual obstruction to its recruiting service or the publication of the sailing dates of transports or the number and location of troops. On similar grounds, the primary requirements of decency may be enforced against obscene publications. The security of the community life may be protected against incitements to acts of violence and the overthrow by force of orderly [government].[a] * * *

The fact that for approximately one hundred and fifty years there has been almost an entire absence of attempts to impose previous restraints upon publica-

a. For critical commentary on the concessions in *Near,* see Linde, *Courts and Censorship,* 66 Minn.L.Rev. 171 (1981); Smith, *Prior Restraint: Original Intentions and Modern Interpretations,* 28 Wm. & M.Rev. 439, 462 (1987).

tions relating to the malfeasance of public officers is significant of the deep-seated conviction that such restraints would violate constitutional right. Public officers, whose character and conduct remain open to debate and free discussion in the press, find their remedies for false accusations in actions under libel laws providing for redress and punishment, and not in proceedings to restrain the publication of newspapers and periodicals. [The] fact that the liberty of the press may be abused by miscreant purveyors of scandal does not make any the less necessary the immunity of the press from previous restraint in dealing with official misconduct. Subsequent punishment for such abuses as may exist is the appropriate remedy, consistent with constitutional [privilege].

The statute in question cannot be justified by reason of the fact that the publisher is permitted to show, before injunction issues, that the matter published is true and is published with good motives and for justifiable ends. If such a statute, authorizing suppression and injunction on such a basis, is constitutionally valid, it would be equally permissible for the Legislature to provide that at any time the publisher of any newspaper could be brought before a court, or even an administrative officer (as the constitutional protection may not be regarded as resting on mere procedural details), and required to produce proof of the truth of his publication, or of what he intended to publish and of his motives, or stand enjoined. If this can be done, the Legislature may provide machinery for determining in the complete exercise of its discretion what are justifiable ends and restrain publication accordingly. And it would be but a step to a complete system of censorship.

[For] these reasons we hold the statute, so far as it authorized the proceedings in this action, [to] be an infringement of the liberty of the press guaranteed by the Fourteenth Amendment. * * *

JUSTICE BUTLER (dissenting).

[T]he *previous restraints* referred to by [Blackstone] subjected the press to the arbitrary will of an administrative officer. [The] Minnesota statute does not operate as a *previous* restraint on publication within the proper meaning of that phrase. It does not authorize administrative control in advance such as was formerly exercised by the licensers and censors, but prescribes a remedy to be enforced by a suit in equity. In this case [t]he business and publications unquestionably constitute an abuse of the right of free press. [A]s stated by the state Supreme Court [they] threaten morals, peace, and good order. [The] restraint authorized is only in respect of continuing to do what has been duly adjudged to constitute a nuisance. [It] is fanciful to suggest similarity between the granting or enforcement of the decree authorized by this statute to prevent *further* publication of malicious, scandalous, and defamatory articles and the *previous restraint* upon the press by licensers as referred to by Blackstone and described in the history of the times to which he alludes. * * *

It is well known, as found by the state supreme court, that existing libel laws are inadequate effectively to suppress evils resulting from the kind of business and publications that are shown in this case. The doctrine [of this decision] exposes the peace and good order of every community and the business and private affairs of every individual to the constant and protracted false and malicious assaults of any insolvent publisher who may have purpose and sufficient capacity to contrive and put into effect a scheme or program for oppression, blackmail or extortion. * * *

JUSTICE VAN DEVANTER, JUSTICE MCREYNOLDS, and JUSTICE SUTHERLAND concur in this opinion.[b]

Notes and Questions

1. *Near and seditious libel: a misuse of prior restraint? Near* was decided three decades before *New York Times v. Sullivan.* Should the Court have looked to the substance of the regulation rather than its form? Consider Jeffries, *Rethinking Prior Restraint,* 92 Yale L.J. 409, 416–17 (1983): "In truth, *Near* involved nothing more or less than a repackaged version of the law of seditious libel, and this the majority rightly refused to countenance. Hence, there was pressure, so typical of this doctrine, to cram the law into the disfavored category of prior restraint, even though it in fact functioned very differently from a scheme of official licensing. Here there was no license and no censor, no ex parte determination of what was prohibited, and no suppression of publication based on speculation about what somebody might say. Here the decision to suppress was made by a judge (not a bureaucrat), after adversarial (not ex parte) proceedings, to determine the legal character of what had been (and not what might be) published. The only aspect of prior restraint was the incidental fact that the defendants were commanded not to repeat that which they were proved to have done.

"[I]f *Near* reached the right result, does it really matter that it gave the wrong reason? The answer, I think, is that it does matter, at least that it has come to matter as *Near* has become a prominent feature of the First Amendment landscape—a landmark, as the case is so often called, from which we chart our course to future decisions. [T]he Court has yet to explain (at least in terms that I understand) what it is about an injunction that justifies this independent rule of constitutional disfavor."

Should a court be able to enjoin the continued distribution of material it has finally adjudicated to be unprotected defamation under existing law? Suppose it enjoins the publication of any material that does not comply with the mandates of *New York Times* and *Gertz*?

2. *The collateral bar rule.* Does the collateral bar rule shed light on the relationship between prior restraints and injunctions? That rule insists "that a court order must be obeyed until it is set aside, and that persons subject to the order who disobey it may not defend against the ensuing charge of criminal contempt on the ground that the order was erroneous or even unconstitutional." Barnett, *The Puzzle of Prior Restraint,* 29 Stan.L.Rev. 539, 552 (1977). WALKER v. BIRMINGHAM, 388 U.S. 307, 87 S.Ct. 1824, 18 L.Ed.2d 1210 (1967) upheld the rule against a first amendment challenge in affirming the contempt conviction of defendants for violating an ex parte injunction issued by an Alabama court enjoining them from engaging in street parades without a municipal permit issued pursuant to the city's parade ordinance. The Court, per STEWART, J., (Warren, C.J., Brennan, Douglas, and Fortas, JJ., dissenting) held that because the petitioners neither moved to dissolve the injunction nor sought to comply with the city's parade ordinance, their claim that the injunction and ordinance were unconstitutional[c] did not need to be considered: "This Court

b. For background on the *Near* case, see Friendly, *Minnesota Rag* (1981); Murphy, *Near v. Minnesota in the Context of Historical Developments,* 66 Minn.L.Rev. 95, 133–60 (1981).

c. Indeed, the ordinance in question was declared unconstitutional two years later. *Shuttlesworth v. Birmingham,* 394 U.S. 147, 89 S.Ct. 935, 22 L.Ed.2d 162 (1969) (ordinance conferring unbridled discretion to prohibit cannot hold that the petitioners were constitutionally free to ignore all the procedures of the law and carry their battle to the streets. [R]espect for judicial process is a small price to pay for the civilizing hand of law, which alone can give abiding meaning to constitutional freedom." Although *Walker* suggested that its holding might be different if the court issuing the injunction lacked jurisdiction or if the injunction were "transparently invalid or had only a frivolous pretense to validity," it held that Alabama's invocation of the collateral bar rule was not itself unconstitutional.

Cf. *Poulos v. New Hampshire,* 345 U.S. 395, 73 S.Ct. 760, 97 L.Ed. 1105 (1953) (claim of arbitrary refusal to issue license for open air meeting need not be entertained when a licensing statute is considered to be valid on its face in circumstance where speaker fails to seek direct judicial relief and proceeds without a license).[d] Does *Poulos* pose considerable danger to first amendment interests because the low visibility of the administrative decision permits easy abridgement of free expression? See Monaghan, *First Amendment "Due Process,"* 83 Harv.L.Rev. 518, 543 (1970). Do *Lovell, Walker,* and *Poulos* fit easily together? Consider Blasi, *Prior Restraints on Demonstrations,* 68 Mich.L.Rev. 1482, 1555 (1970): "A refuses to apply for a permit; he undertakes a march that could have been prohibited in the first place; he is prosecuted for parading without a permit under a statute that is defective for overbreadth. B applies for a permit; he is rudely rebuffed by a city official in clear violation of the state permit statute (which is not invalid on its face); he marches anyway in a manner that would be protected by the first amendment, he is prosecuted for parading without a permit. C applies for a permit; he is rudely rebuffed; he notifies city officials that he will march anyway; the officials obtain an injunction against the march; the injunction is overbroad and is also based on a state statute that is overbroad; C marches in a manner ordinarily within his constitutional rights; he is prosecuted for contempt. Under the law as it now stands, A wins, but B and C lose!"

3. *The commentators, injunctions, and prior restraint.* Should the link between prior restraint doctrine and injunctions depend upon the collateral bar rule? Does the analogy between licensing systems and injunctions hold only in that event? See Fiss, *The Civil Rights Injunction* 30, 69–74 (1978); Barnett, note 2 supra, at 553–54. Should the prior restraint doctrine be wholly inapplicable to injunctions so long as "expedited appellate review allows an immediate opportunity to test the validity of an injunction against speech and only so long as that opportunity is genuinely effective to allow timely publication should the injunction ultimately be adjudged invalid"? Jeffries, note 1 supra, at 433.[e] Indeed should the whole concept of prior restraint be abandoned? Consider id. at 433–34: "In the context of administrative preclearance, talking of prior restraint is unhelpful, though not inapt. A more informative frame of reference would be overbreadth, the doctrine that explicitly identifies why preclearance is specially objectionable. In the context of injunctions, however, the traditional doctrine of prior restraint is not merely unhelpful, but positively misleading. It focuses on

any parade or demonstration is unconstitutional prior restraint).

d. For consideration of when licensing statutes for assemblies are valid, see *Cox v. New Hampshire,* p. 643 infra.

e. For the argument that regulation by injunction is generally more speech protective than regulation via subsequent punishment, see Mayton, *Toward A Theory of First Amendment Process: Injunctions of Speech, Subsequent Punishment, and the Costs of the Prior Restraint Doctrine,* 67 Corn.L.Rev. 245 (1982). For the contention that this should count in favor of subsequent punishment in many contexts, see Redish, *The Proper Role of the Prior Restraint Doctrine in First Amendment Theory,* 70 Va.L.Rev. 53, 92–93 (1984).

a constitutionally inconsequential consideration of form and diverts attention away from the critical substantive issues of First Amendment coverage. The result is a two-pronged danger. On the one hand, vindication of First Amendment freedoms in the name of prior restraint may exaggerate the legitimate reach of official competence to suppress by subsequent punishment. On the other hand, insistence on special disfavor for prior restraints outside the realm of substantive protection under the First Amendment may deny to the government an appropriate choice of means to vindicate legitimate interests. In my view, neither risk is justified by any compelling reason to continue prior restraint as a doctrinally independent category of contemporary First Amendment analysis." [f]

For a nuanced argument that the prior restraint doctrine should apply to injunctions even in those jurisdictions that reject the applicability of the collateral bar rule to first amendment arguments, see Blasi, *Toward a Theory of Prior Restraint: The Central Linkage,* 66 Minn.L.Rev. 11 (1981). Except in particular contexts, Professor Blasi does not claim that the chilling effect of injunctions on speech is more severe than those associated with criminal laws and civil liability rules. He does argue that unlike criminal laws and civil liability rules, regulation of speech by licensing and injunctions requires abstract and unduly speculative adjudication, stimulates overuse by regulatory agents, can to some extent distort the way in which audiences perceive the message at issue, and unreasonably implies that the activity of disseminating controversial communications is "a threat to, rather than an integral feature of, the social order." Id. at 85. He argues that many of these factors are aggravated if the collateral bar rule applies and that other undesirable features are added. For example, speakers are forced to reveal planned details about their communication. He concludes that the "concept of prior restraint is coherent at the core." Id. at 93.[g]

II. PRIOR RESTRAINTS, OBSCENITY, AND COMMERCIAL SPEECH

KINGSLEY BOOKS, INC. v. BROWN, 354 U.S. 436, 77 S.Ct. 1325, 1 L.Ed.2d 1469 (1957), per FRANKFURTER, J., upheld a state court decree, issued pursuant to a New York statute, enjoining the publisher from further distribution of 14 booklets the state court found obscene. On appeal to the Supreme Court the publisher challenged only the prior restraint, not the obscenity finding: "The phrase 'prior restraint' is not a self-wielding sword. Nor can it serve as a talismatic test. The duty of closer analysis and critical judgment in applying the thought behind the phrase has thus been authoritatively put by one who brings weighty learning to his support of constitutionally protected liberties: 'What is needed,' writes Professor Paul A. Freund, 'is a pragmatic assessment of its operation in the particular circumstances. The generalization that prior restraint is particularly obnoxious in civil liberties cases must yield to more particularistic analysis.' *The Supreme Court and Civil Liberties,* 4 Vand.L.Rev. 533, 539.

"Wherein does § 22–a differ in its effective operation from the type of statute upheld in *Alberts,* [p. 456 supra]? One would be bold to assert that the in

f. See also Scordato, *Distinction Without a Difference,* 68 N.C.L.Rev. 1 (1989) (generally agreeing with Jeffries but arguing that a small part of prior restraint doctrine should be salvaged).

g. For detailed criticism of Blasi's position, all in defense of a different core, see Redish, fn. e supra, at 59–75.

terrorem effect of [criminal] statutes less restrains booksellers in the period before the law strikes than does § 22–a. Instead of requiring the bookseller to dread that the offer for sale of a book may, without prior warning, subject him to a criminal prosecution with the hazard of imprisonment, the civil procedure assures him that such consequences cannot follow unless he ignores a court order specifically directed to him for a prompt and carefully circumscribed determination of the issue of obscenity. Until then, he may keep the book for sale and sell it on his own judgment rather than steer 'nervously among the treacherous shoals.' [a]

"Criminal enforcement and the proceeding under § 22–a interfere with a book's solicitation of the public precisely at the same stage. In each situation the law moves after publication; the book need not in either case have yet passed into the hands of the public. [H]ere as a matter of fact copies of the booklets whose distribution was enjoined had been on sale for several weeks when process was served. In each case the bookseller is put on notice by the complaint that sale of the publication charged with obscenity in the period before trial may subject him to penal consequences. In the one case he may suffer fine and imprisonment for violation of the criminal statute, in the other, for disobedience of the temporary injunction. The bookseller may of course stand his ground and confidently believe that in any judicial proceeding the book could not be condemned as obscene, but both modes of procedure provide an effective deterrent against distribution prior to adjudication of the book's content—the threat of subsequent penalization.[2]"

The Court pointed out that in both criminal misdemeanor prosecutions and injunction proceedings a jury could be called as a matter of discretion, but that defendant did not request a jury trial and did not attack the statute for its failure to require a jury.

"Nor are the consequences of a judicial condemnation for obscenity under § 22–a more restrictive of freedom of expression than the result of conviction for a misdemeanor. In *Alberts,* the defendant was fined $500, sentenced to sixty days in prison, and put on probation for two years on condition that he not violate the obscenity statute. Not only was he completely separated from society for two months but he was also seriously restrained from trafficking in all obscene publications for a considerable time. Appellants, on the other hand, were enjoined from displaying for sale or distributing only the particular booklets theretofore published and adjudged to be obscene. Thus, the restraint upon appellants as merchants in obscenity was narrower than that imposed on *Alberts.*

"Section 22–a's provision for the seizure and destruction of the instruments of ascertained wrongdoing expresses resort to a legal remedy sanctioned by the long history of Anglo-American law. See Holmes, *The Common Law,* 24–26.

"[It] only remains to say that the difference between *Near* and this case is glaring in fact. The two cases are no less glaringly different when judged by the appropriate criteria of constitutional law. Minnesota empowered its courts to

a. In fact, § 22–a did not require a civil adjudication before criminal prosecution, as intimated by the opinion. The feasibility of such a requirement is considered in Lockhart, *Escape from the Chill of Uncertainty,* 9 Ga.L. Rev. 533, 569–86 (1975).

2. This comparison of remedies takes note of the fact that we do not have before us a case where, although the issue of obscenity is ultimately decided in favor of the bookseller, the State nevertheless attempts to punish him for disobedience of the interim injunction. For all we know, New York may impliedly condition the temporary injunction so as not to subject the bookseller to a charge of contempt if he prevails on the issue of obscenity.

enjoin the dissemination of future issues of a publication because its past issues had been found offensive. In the language of Mr. Chief Justice Hughes, 'This is of the essence of censorship.' As such, it was enough to condemn the statute wholly apart from the fact that the proceeding in *Near* involved not obscenity but matters deemed to be derogatory to a public officer. Unlike *Near,* § 22–a is concerned solely with obscenity and, as authoritatively construed, it studiously withholds restraint upon matters not already published and not yet found to be offensive." [b]

TIMES FILM CORP. v. CHICAGO

365 U.S. 43, 81 S.Ct. 391, 5 L.Ed.2d 403 (1961).

JUSTICE CLARK delivered the opinion of the Court.

Petitioner challenges on constitutional grounds the validity on its face of that portion of § 155–4 [1] of the Municipal Code of the City of Chicago which requires submission of all motion pictures for examination prior to their public exhibition. Petitioner is a New York corporation owning the exclusive right to publicly exhibit in Chicago the film known as "Don Juan." It applied for a permit, as Chicago's ordinance required, and tendered the license fee but refused to submit the film for examination. The appropriate city official refused to issue the permit and his order was made final on appeal to the Mayor. The sole ground for denial was petitioner's refusal to submit the film for examination as required. Petitioner then brought this suit seeking injunctive relief ordering the issuance of the permit without submission of the [film] * * *. Its sole ground is that the provision of the ordinance requiring submission of the film constitutes, on its face, a prior restraint [2] * * * [Admittedly,] the challenged section of the ordinance imposes a previous restraint, and the broad justiciable issue is therefore present as to whether the ambit of constitutional protection includes complete and absolute freedom to exhibit, at least once, any and every kind of motion picture. It is that question alone which we decide.

[T]here is not a word in the record as to the nature and content of "Don Juan." We are left entirely in the dark in this regard, as were the city officials and the other reviewing courts. Petitioner claims that the nature of the film is irrelevant, and that even if this film contains the basest type of pornography, or incitement to riot, or forceful overthrow of orderly government, it may nonethe-

b. Warren, C.J., dissented, objecting that the New York law "places the book on trial" without any consideration of its "manner of use." Black and Douglas, JJ., dissented, objecting to a state-wide decree depriving the publisher of separate trials in different communities, and to substituting "punishment by contempt for punishment by jury trial." Brennan, J., dissenting, contended that a jury trial is required to apply properly the *Roth* standard for obscenity.

1. The portion of the section here under attack is as follows: "Such permit shall be granted only after the motion picture film for which said permit is requested has been produced at the office of the commissioner of police for examination or [censorship]."

2. That portion of § 155–4 of the Code providing standards is as follows: "If a picture or series of pictures, for the showing or exhibition of which an application for a permit is made, is immoral or obscene, or portrays, depravity, criminality, or lack of virtue of a class of citizens of any race, color, creed, or religion and exposes them to contempt, derision, or obloquy, or tends to produce a breach of the peace or riots, or purports to represent any hanging, lynching, or burning of a human being, it shall be the duty of the commissioner of police to refuse such permit; otherwise it shall be his duty to grant such permit.

"In case the commissioner of police shall refuse to grant a permit as hereinbefore provided, the applicant for the same may appeal to the mayor. Such appeal shall be presented in the same manner as the original application to the commissioner of police. The action of the mayor on any application for a permit shall be final." * * *

less be shown without prior submission for examination. The challenge here is to the censor's basic authority; it does not go to any statutory standards employed by the censor or procedural requirements as to the submission of the film. * * *

Petitioner would have us hold that the public exhibition of motion pictures must be allowed under any circumstances. The State's sole remedy, it says, is the invocation of criminal process under the Illinois pornography statute and then only after a transgression. But this position [is] founded upon the claim of absolute privilege against prior restraint under the First Amendment—a claim without sanction in our cases. To illustrate its fallacy, we need only point to one of the "exceptional cases" which Chief Justice Hughes enumerated in *Near,* namely, "the primary requirements of decency [that] may be enforced against obscene publications." Moreover, we later held specifically "that obscenity is not within the area of constitutionally protected speech or press." *Roth.* Chicago emphasizes here its duty to protect its people against the dangers of obscenity in the public exhibition of motion pictures. To this argument petitioner's only answer is that regardless of the capacity for, or extent of, such an evil, previous restraint cannot be justified. With this we cannot agree. We recognized in [*Joseph Burstyn, Inc. v. Wilson,* 343 U.S. 495, 72 S.Ct. 777, 96 L.Ed. 1098 (1952)] that "capacity for evil [may] be relevant in determining the permissible scope of community control," and that motion pictures were not "necessarily subject to the precise rules governing any other particular method of expression. Each method," we said, "tends to present its own peculiar problems." [It] is not for this Court to limit the State in its selection of the remedy it deems most effective to cope with such a problem, absent, of course, a showing of unreasonable strictures on individual liberty resulting from its application in particular circumstances. * * *

As to what may be decided when a concrete case involving a specific standard provided by this ordinance is presented, we intimate no opinion. [At] this time we say no more than this—that we are dealing only with motion pictures and, even as to them, only in the context of the broadside attack presented on this record.

Affirmed.

CHIEF JUSTICE WARREN, with whom JUSTICE BLACK, JUSTICE DOUGLAS and JUSTICE BRENNAN join, dissenting.

I cannot agree either with the conclusion reached by the Court or with the reasons advanced for its support. To me, this case clearly presents the question of our approval of unlimited censorship of motion pictures before exhibition through a system of administrative licensing. Moreover, the decision presents a real danger of eventual censorship for every form of communication, be it newspapers, journals, books, magazines, television, radio or public speeches. The Court purports to leave these questions for another day, but I am aware of no constitutional principle which permits us to hold that the communication of ideas through one medium may be censored while other media are immune. Of course each medium presents its own peculiar problems, but they are not of the kind which would authorize the censorship of one form of communication and not others. * * *

I hesitate to disagree with the Court's formulation of the issue before us, but, with all deference, I must insist that the question presented in this case is *not* whether a motion picture exhibitor has a constitutionally protected, "complete and absolute freedom to exhibit, at least once, any and every kind of motion picture." [The] question here presented is whether the City of Chicago—or, for that matter, any city, any State or the Federal Government—may require all motion picture exhibitors to submit all films to a police chief, mayor or other administrative official, for licensing and censorship prior to public exhibition within the jurisdiction.

[In *Near*,] the Court recognized that the First Amendment's rejection of prior censorship through licensing and previous restraint is an inherent and basic principle of freedom of speech and press. Now, the Court strays from that principle; it strikes down that tenet without requiring any demonstration that this is an "exceptional case," whatever that might be, and without any indication that Chicago has sustained the "heavy burden" which was supposed to have been placed upon it. Clearly, this is neither an exceptional case nor has Chicago sustained *any* burden. * * *

The booklets enjoined from distribution in *Kingsley* were concededly obscene. There is no indication that this is true of the moving picture here. This was treated as a particularly crucial distinction. Thus, the Court has suggested that, in times of national emergency, the Government might impose a prior restraint upon "the publication of the sailing dates of transports or the number and location of troops." *Near*. But, surely this is not to suggest that the Government might require that all newspapers be submitted to a censor in order to assist it in preventing such information from reaching print. Yet in this case the Court gives its blessing to the censorship of all motion pictures in order to prevent the exhibition of those it feels to be constitutionally unprotected.

[E]ven if the impact of the motion picture is greater than that of some other media, that fact constitutes no basis for the argument that motion pictures should be subject to greater suppression. This is the traditional argument made in the censor's behalf; this is the argument advanced against newspapers at the time of the invention of the printing press. The argument was ultimately rejected in England, and has consistently been held to be contrary to our Constitution.[a] No compelling reason has been predicated for accepting the contention now. * * *[b]

Notes and Questions

1. Should the producers of *Bambi* be forced to submit their film to show it in a particular city? Should they be forced to pay a license fee? Suppose hundreds of cities adopted the Chicago system? If films must be submitted before exhibition, can a city constitutionally require that books be submitted before distribution? What are the "peculiar problems" associated with films?

2. *Procedural safeguards.* FREEDMAN v. MARYLAND, 380 U.S. 51, 85 S.Ct. 734, 13 L.Ed.2d 649 (1965), per Brennan, J., set out procedural safeguards designed to reduce the dangers associated with prior restraints of films. It required that the procedure must "assure a prompt final judicial decision, to minimize the deterrent effect of an interim and possibly erroneous denial of a license," that the censor must promptly institute the proceedings, that the burden of proof to show that the speech in question is unprotected must rest on the censor, and that the proceedings be adversarial. The *Freedman* standards

a. For the contention that the argument has in fact received a warm reception in the twentieth century, see Lively, *Fear and the Media: A First Amendment Horror Show*, 69 Minn.L.Rev. 1071 (1985).

b. Douglas, J., joined by Warren, C.J., and Black, J., dissenting, elaborated on the evils connected with systems of censorship.

have been applied in other contexts. *Blount v. Rizzi,* 400 U.S. 410, 91 S.Ct. 423, 27 L.Ed.2d 498 (1971) (postal stop orders of obscene materials); *United States v. Thirty-Seven Photographs,* 402 U.S. 363, 91 S.Ct. 1400, 28 L.Ed.2d 822 (1971) (customs seizure of obscene materials); *Southeastern Promotions Ltd. v. Conrad,* 420 U.S. 546, 95 S.Ct. 1239, 43 L.Ed.2d 448 (1975) (denial of permit to use municipal theater for the musical, Hair); *Carroll v. President and Commissioners,* 393 U.S. 175, 89 S.Ct. 347, 21 L.Ed.2d 325 (1968) (10 day restraining order against particular rallies or meetings invalid because *ex parte*). But cf. *FW/PBS, Inc. v. Dallas,* 493 U.S. 215, 110 S.Ct. 596, 107 L.Ed.2d 603 (1990) (suggesting that partial application of *Freedman* standards (dispensing with burden of going to court and burden of proof, but retaining assurance of timely decisionmaking by licensor and prompt judicial review) to ordinance licensing sexually oriented businesses ostensibly without regard to content of films or books would be appropriate). Should the collateral bar rule apply to *Carroll*? Do the *Freedman* standards make the *Times Film* decision palatable?[c] For thorough discussion of the procedural issues, see Monaghan, *First Amendment "Due Process,"* 83 Harv.L.Rev. 518 (1970).

3. *Enjoining habitual use of premises to exhibit obscene films.* Could a state authorize state courts to "abate" the "nuisance" of "habitual use [of premises for] commercial exhibition of obscene" films by enjoining future exhibition of any obscene films at the theater, once a finding of such habitual use is made, based on two or more convictions under the obscenity laws? Cf. *Vance v. Universal Amusement Co.,* 445 U.S. 308, 100 S.Ct. 1156, 63 L.Ed.2d 413 (1980).

4. *Comparing obscenity and commercial speech.* To combat deception, could commercial advertising be constitutionally subjected to a *Times Film* regime? Would such a scheme be permissible for advertising via some media, but not others? Reconsider fn. 24 in *Virginia Pharmacy,* p. 571 supra. Should the prohibition on prior restraints be inapplicable to injunctions against commercial advertising? Should *Freedman* standards be required? Should injunctions be permitted against a newspaper that carries unprotected advertising in addition to the advertiser? PITTSBURGH PRESS CO. v. PITTSBURGH COMM'N ON HUMAN RELATIONS, 413 U.S. 376, 93 S.Ct. 2553, 37 L.Ed.2d 669 (1973), per Powell, J., upheld an order forbidding Pittsburgh Press to carry sex-designated "help wanted" ads, except for exempt jobs: "As described by Blackstone, the protection against prior restraint at common law barred only a system of administrative censorship. [While] the Court boldly stepped beyond this narrow doctrine in *Near* [it] has never held that all injunctions are impermissible. See *Lorain Journal Co. v. United States,* 342 U.S. 143, 72 S.Ct. 181, 96 L.Ed. 162 (1951).[d] The special vice of a prior restraint is that communication will be suppressed, either directly or by inducing excessive caution in the speaker, before an adequate determination that it is unprotected by the First Amendment.

"The present order does not endanger arguably protected speech. Because the order is based on a continuing course of repetitive conduct, this is not a case in which the Court is asked to speculate as to the effect of publication. Moreover, the order is clear and sweeps no more broadly than necessary. And

c. For the contention that *Freedman* procedures fail to address the main concern of the prior restraint doctrine, see Redish, *The Proper Role of the Prior Restraint Doctrine in First Amendment Theory,* 70 Va.L.Rev. 53, 75–89 (1984).

d. *Lorain* upheld a Sherman Act injunction restraining a newspaper from seeking to monopolize commerce by refusing to carry advertising from merchants who advertised through a competing radio station.

because no interim relief was granted, the order will not have gone into effect until it was finally determined that the actions of Pittsburgh Press were unprotected."

STEWART, J., joined by Douglas, J., dissented: Putting to one side "the question of governmental power to prevent publication of information that would clearly imperil the military defense of our Nation," "no government agency can tell a newspaper in advance what it can print and what it cannot." [e]

5. *Informal prior restraints.* BANTAM BOOKS, INC. v. SULLIVAN, 372 U.S. 58, 83 S.Ct. 631, 9 L.Ed.2d 584 (1963), per BRENNAN, J., (Harlan, J. dissenting) held unconstitutional the activities of a government commission that would identify "objectionable" books (some admittedly not obscene), notify the distributor in writing, inform the distributor of the Commission's duty to recommend obscenity prosecutions to the Attorney General and that the Commission's list of objectionable books was distributed to local police departments. The Commission thanked distributors in advance for their "cooperation," and a police officer usually visited the distributor to learn what action had been taken. In characterizing these practices as a system of prior administrative restraints, rather than mere legal advice, the Court observed that it did not mean to foreclose private consultation between law enforcement officers and distributors so long as such consultations were "genuinely undertaken with the purpose of aiding the distributor to comply" with the laws and avoid prosecution. What if the Commission circulated its list to distributors, police and prosecutors without mentioning prosecution? What if the prosecutor circulates a list of sixty books he or she regards as obscene and subject to prosecution?

III. LICENSING "PROFESSIONALS": A DICHOTOMY BETWEEN SPEECH AND PRESS?

LOWE v. SEC, 472 U.S. 181, 105 S.Ct. 2557, 86 L.Ed.2d 130 (1985): The Investment Advisors Act of 1940 provides for injunctions and criminal penalties against anyone using the mails in conjunction with the advisory business who is not registered with the SEC or otherwise exempt from registration. An investment advisor includes "any person who, for compensation, engages in the business of advising others, either directly or through publications or writings, as to the value of securities or as to the advisability of investing in, purchasing, or selling securities, or who, for compensation and as part of a regular business, issues or promulgates analyses or reports concerning securities; but does not include [the] publisher of any bona fide newspaper, news magazine or business or financial publication of general and regular [circulation]." The SEC sought an injunction against Lowe and his affiliated businesses primarily alleging that Lowe's registration with the SEC had been properly revoked because of various fraudulent activities,[a] and that by publishing investment newsletters, Lowe was using the mails as an investment advisor. The SEC did not claim that any information in the newsletters had been false or materially misleading or that Lowe had yet profited from the advice tendered. The SEC did contend that Lowe's prior criminal conduct showed his "total lack of fitness" to remain in an occupation with "numerous opportunities for dishonesty and self-dealing." Lowe

e. Blackmun, J., dissented "for substantially the reasons stated by" Stewart, J. Burger, C.J., dissenting, argued that the majority had mischaracterized the character and interim effect of the Commission's order.

a. For example, during the period that he was giving personal investment advice, Lowe had been convicted of misappropriating funds of a client, tampering with evidence to cover up fraud of a client, and stealing from a bank.

admitted that his registration had been properly revoked, but denied that his newsletters were covered by the act and argued that, in any event, they were protected against registration and restraint under the first amendment.

The Court, per STEVENS, J., denied that Lowe's publication of financial newsletters made him an investment advisor under the act. The Court's interpretation was strongly influenced by first amendment considerations. It stated that Congress was "undoubtedly aware of two major First Amendment [cases] decided before the enactment of the Act." Citing *Near* and *Lovell*, the Court pointed to the maxim that "It is always appropriate to assume that our elected representatives, like other citizens, know the law." The doctrine against prior restraints and the notion that freedom of the press includes everything from distributing leaflets to mass circulation of magazines was said to support a "broad reading" of the exclusion for bona fide publishers of regular and general circulation:

"The exclusion itself uses extremely broad language that encompasses any newspaper, business publication, or financial publication provided that two conditions are met. The publication must be 'bona fide,' and it must be 'of regular and general circulation.' Neither of these conditions is defined, but the two qualifications precisely differentiate 'hit and run tipsters' and 'touts' from genuine publishers. Presumably a 'bona fide' publication would be genuine in the sense that it would contain disinterested commentary and analysis as opposed to promotional material disseminated by a 'tout.' Moreover, publications with a 'general and regular' circulation would not include 'people who send out bulletins from time to time on the advisability of buying and selling stocks' or 'hit and run tipsters.' Because the content of petitioners' newsletters was completely disinterested, and because they were offered [b] to the general public on a regular schedule, they are described by the plain language of the [exclusion].

"The dangers of fraud, deception, or overreaching that motivated the enactment of the statute are present in personalized communications but are not replicated in publications that are advertised and sold in an open market.[57] To the extent that the chart service contains factual information about past transactions and market trends, and the newsletters contain commentary on general market conditions, there can be no doubt about the protected character of the communications,[58] a matter that concerned Congress when the exclusion was drafted. The content of the publications and the audience to which they are directed in this case reveal the specific limits of the exclusion. As long as the communications between petitioners and their subscribers remain entirely impersonal and do not develop into the kind of fiduciary, person-to-person relationships that were discussed at length in the legislative history of the Act and that are characteristic of investment adviser-client relationships, we believe the

b. Lowe's newsletters in fact did not appear according to schedule. White, J., concurring, remarked: "As is evident from the Court's conclusion that petitioner's publications meet the regularity requirement, the Court's construction of the requirement adopts the view of our major law reviews on the issue of regular publication: good intentions are enough."

57. Cf. *Ohralik*. It is significant that the Commission has not established that petitioners have had authority over the funds of subscribers; that petitioners have been delegated decisionmaking authority to handle subscribers' portfolios or accounts; or that there have been individualized, investment-related interactions between petitioners and subscribers.

58. Moreover, because we have squarely held that the expression of opinion about a commercial product such as a loudspeaker is protected by the First Amendment, *Bose Corp.*, it is difficult to see why the expression of an opinion about a marketable security should not also be protected.

publications are, at least presumptively, within the exclusion and thus not subject to registration under the Act." [c]

WHITE, J., joined by Burger, C.J., and Rehnquist, J., concurring, argued that the Court's statutory interpretation was "improvident" and "based on a thinly disguised conviction" that the Act was unconstitutional as applied to prohibit publication by unregistered advisors: "Indeed the Court tips its hand when it discusses [*Lovell*] and *Near.* [While] purporting not to decide the question, the Court bases its statutory holding in large measure on the assumption that Congress already knew the answer to it when the statute was enacted. The Court thus attributes to the 76th Congress a clairvoyance the Solicitor General and the Second Circuit apparently lack—that is, the ability to predict our constitutional holdings 45 years in advance of our declining to reach them."

Finding it necessary to reach the constitutional question, White, J., argued that an injunction against Lowe's publications would violate the first amendment: "The power of government to regulate the professions is not lost whenever the practice of a profession entails speech. The underlying principle was expressed by the Court in *Giboney v. Empire Storage & Ice Co.,* [336 U.S. 490, 69 S.Ct. 684, 93 L.Ed. 834 (1949)]: 'it has never been deemed an abridgment of freedom of speech or press to make a course of conduct illegal merely because the conduct was in part initiated, evidenced, or carried out by means of language, either spoken, written, or printed.'

"Perhaps the most obvious example of a 'speaking profession' that is subject to governmental licensing is the legal profession. Although a lawyer's work is almost entirely devoted to the sort of communicative acts that, viewed in isolation, fall within the First Amendment's protection, we have never doubted that '[a] State can require high standards of qualification, such as good moral character or proficiency in its law, before it admits an applicant to the [bar].' [To] protect investors, the Government insists, it may require that investment advisers, like lawyers, evince the qualities of truth-speaking, honor, discretion, and fiduciary responsibility.

"But the principle that the government may restrict entry into professions and vocations through licensing schemes has never been extended to encompass the licensing of speech per se or of the press. At some point, a measure is no longer a regulation of a profession but a regulation of speech or of the press; beyond that point, the statute must survive the level of scrutiny demanded by the First Amendment.

"[It] is for us, then, to find some principle by which to answer the question whether the Investment Advisers Act as applied to petitioner operates as a regulation of speech or of professional conduct.

"This is a problem Justice Jackson wrestled with in his concurring opinion in *Thomas v. Collins.* His words are instructive: '[A] rough distinction always exists, I think, which is more shortly illustrated than explained. A state may forbid one without its license to practice law as a vocation, but I think it could not stop an unlicensed person from making a speech about the rights of man or the rights of labor, or any other kind of right, including recommending that his hearers organize to support his views. Likewise, the state may prohibit the pursuit of medicine as an occupation without its license, but I do not think it could make it a crime publicly or privately to speak urging persons to follow or reject any school of medical thought. So the state to an extent not necessary

c. Powell, J., took no part.

now to determine may regulate one who makes a business or a livelihood of soliciting funds or memberships for unions. But I do not think it can prohibit one, even if he is a salaried labor leader, from making an address to a public meeting of workmen, telling them their rights as he sees them and urging them to unite in general or to join a specific union.'

"Justice Jackson concluded that the distinguishing factor was whether the speech in any particular case was 'associat[ed] [with] some other factor which the state may regulate so as to bring the whole within its official control.' If 'in a particular case the association or characterization is a proven and valid one,' he concluded, the regulation may stand.

"These ideas help to locate the point where regulation of a profession leaves off and prohibitions on speech begin. One who takes the affairs of a client personally in hand and purports to exercise judgment on behalf of the client in the light of the client's individual needs and circumstances is properly viewed as engaging in the practice of a profession. Just as offer and acceptance are communications incidental to the regulable transaction called a contract, the professional's speech is incidental to the conduct of the profession. [Where] the personal nexus between professional and client does not exist, and a speaker does not purport to be exercising judgment on behalf of any particular individual with whose circumstances he is directly acquainted, government regulation ceases to function as legitimate regulation of professional practice with only incidental impact on speech; it becomes regulation of speaking or publishing as such, subject to the First Amendment's [command].

"I do not believe it is necessary to the resolution of this case to determine whether petitioner's newsletters contain fully protected speech or commercial speech. [E]ven where mere 'commercial speech' is concerned, the First Amendment permits restraints on speech only when they are narrowly tailored to advance a legitimate governmental interest. The interest here is certainly legitimate: the Government wants to prevent investors from falling into the hands of scoundrels and swindlers. The means chosen, however, is extreme. [Our] commercial speech cases have consistently rejected the proposition that such drastic prohibitions on speech may be justified by a mere possibility that the prohibited speech will be fraudulent. See *Zauderer; Bates.* * * *

"I emphasize the narrowness of the constitutional basis on which I would decide this case. I see no infirmity in defining the term 'investment adviser' to include a publisher like petitioner, and I would by no means foreclose the application of, for example, the Act's antifraud or reporting provisions to investment advisers (registered or unregistered) who offer their advice through publications. Nor do I intend to suggest that it is unconstitutional to invoke the Act's provisions for injunctive relief and criminal penalties against unregistered persons who, for compensation, offer personal investment advice to individual clients. I would hold only that the Act may not constitutionally be applied to prevent persons who are unregistered (including persons whose registration has been denied or revoked) from offering impersonal investment advice through publications such as the newsletters published by petitioner."

Notes and Questions

1. Is White, J.'s speech/profession dichotomy persuasive? Should the existence of a "profession" justify prior restraints?

2. Does White, J., suggest an element of special privilege for the press? Consider Shiffrin, *The First Amendment and Economic Regulation: Away From a General Theory of the First Amendment,* 78 Nw.U.L.Rev. 1212, 1276 (1983): "The doctrine of prior restraint may have been designed to put the press on an equal footing. People could speak or write without a license and that ought not to change merely because they used a printing press. Yet we now license a good deal of speech (for example, of lawyers), and those licenses are clearly prior restraints. So we have turned the law upside down. To speak you sometimes need a license; to use the press you almost never do. A doctrine designed to create equality for the press has evolved into one that gives it a special place."

3. If lawyers, psychiatrists, and investment advisors can be licensed, what about fortune tellers? Union organizers? Journalists?

4. Does *Lowe* threaten the "foundations of SEC financial disclosure regulation [and cast] a pall on the validity of government regulation of the professions." See generally Wolfson, *The First Amendment and the SEC,* 20 Conn.L. Rev. 265 (1988) (arguing that much securities and professional regulation violates the first amendment). See also Estreicher, *Securities Regulation and the First Amendment,* 24 Ga.L.Rev. 223 (1990) (arguing against restrictions of securities' advertising). For general commentary, see Symposium, *The First Amendment and Federal Securities Regulation,* 20 Conn.L.Rev. 261 (1988).

RILEY v. NATIONAL FEDERATION OF THE BLIND, 487 U.S. 781, 108 S.Ct. 2667, 101 L.Ed.2d 669 (1988), per BRENNAN, J., invalidated a scheme for licensing professional fundraisers who were soliciting on behalf of charitable organizations: "[North Carolina's] provision requires professional fundraisers to await a determination regarding their license application before engaging in solicitation, while volunteer fundraisers, or those employed by the charity, may solicit immediately upon submitting an application. [It] is well settled that a speaker's rights are not lost merely because compensation is received; a speaker is no less a speaker because he or she is paid to speak. [Generally,] speakers need not obtain a license to speak. However, that rule is not absolute. For example, states may impose valid time, place, or manner restrictions. North Carolina seeks to come within the exception by alleging a heightened interest in regulating those who solicit money. Even assuming that the State's interest does justify requiring fundraisers to obtain a license before soliciting, such a regulation must provide that the licensor 'will, within a specified brief period, either issue a license or go to court.' *Freedman.* That requirement is not met here * * *. The statute on its face does not purport to require when a determination must be made, nor is there an administrative regulation or interpretation doing so."

REHNQUIST, C.J., joined by O'Connor, J., dissented: "It simply is not true that [fundraisers] are prevented from engaging in any protected speech on their own behalf by the State's licensing requirements; the requirements only restrict their ability to engage in the profession of 'solicitation' without a license. We do not view bar admission requirements as invalid because they restrict a prospective lawyer's 'right' to be hired as an advocate by a client. So in this case we should not subject to strict scrutiny the State's attempt to license a business—professional fundraising—some of whose members might reasonably be thought to pose a risk of fraudulent activity." [a]

IV. PRIOR RESTRAINTS AND NATIONAL SECURITY

NEW YORK TIMES CO. v. UNITED STATES [THE PENTAGON PAPERS CASE]

403 U.S. 713, 91 S.Ct. 2140, 29 L.Ed.2d 822 (1971).

PER CURIAM.

We granted certiorari in these cases in which the United States seeks to enjoin the *New York Times* and the *Washington Post* from publishing the contents of a classified study entitled "History of U.S. Decision-Making Process on Viet Nam Policy." [a]

"Any system of prior restraints of expression comes to this Court bearing a heavy presumption against its constitutional validity." *Bantam Books;* see also *Near.* The Government "thus carries a heavy burden of showing justification for the enforcement of such a restraint." [The district court in the *Times* case and both lower federal courts] in the *Post* case held that the Government had not met that burden. We agree. [T]he stays entered [by this Court five days previously] are vacated. * * *

JUSTICE BLACK, with whom JUSTICE DOUGLAS joins, concurring.

I adhere to the view that the Government's case against the *Post* should have been dismissed and that the injunction against the *Times* should have been vacated without oral argument when the cases were first presented to this Court. I believe that every moment's continuance of the injunctions against these newspapers amounts to a flagrant, indefensible, and continuing violation of the First Amendment. Furthermore, after oral arguments, I agree [with] the reasons stated by my Brothers Douglas and Brennan. In my view it is unfortunate that some of my Brethren are apparently willing to hold that the publication of news may sometimes be enjoined. Such a holding would make a shambles of the First Amendment.

[F]or the first time in the 182 years since the founding of the Republic, the federal courts are asked to hold that the First Amendment does not mean what it says, but rather means that the Government can halt the publication of current news of vital importance to the people of this country.

* * *

The Government does not even attempt to rely on any act of Congress. Instead it makes the bold and dangerously far-reaching contention that the courts should take it upon themselves to "make" a law abridging freedom of the press in the name of equity, presidential power and national security, even when the representatives of the people in Congress have adhered to the command of the First Amendment and refused to make such a law. To find that the President has "inherent power" to halt the publication of news by resort to the courts would wipe out the First Amendment and destroy the fundamental liberty and security of the very people the Government hopes to make "secure." [The]

a. Stevens, J., also dissented from the Court's treatment of the licensing issue. For other aspects of the case, see p. 733 infra.

a. On June 12–14, 1971 the *New York Times* and on June 18 the *Washington Post* published portions of this "top secret" Pentagon study. Government actions seeking temporary restraining orders and injunctions progressed through two district courts and two courts of appeals between June 15–23. After a June 26 argument, ten Supreme Court opinions were issued on June 30, 1971.

word "security" is a broad, vague generality whose contours should not be invoked to abrogate the fundamental law embodied in the First Amendment. * * *

JUSTICE DOUGLAS, with whom JUSTICE BLACK joins, concurring.

While I join the opinion of the Court I believe it necessary to express my views more fully.

[The First Amendment leaves] no room for governmental [b] restraint on the press.

There is, moreover, no statute barring the publication by the press of the material which the *Times* and *Post* seek to use. * * *

These disclosures may have a serious impact. But that is no basis for sanctioning a previous restraint on the press * * *.

The dominant purpose of the First Amendment was to prohibit the widespread practice of governmental suppression of embarrassing information. [A] debate of large proportions goes on in the Nation over our posture in Vietnam. That debate antedated the disclosure of the contents of the present documents. The latter are highly relevant to the debate in progress.

Secrecy in government is fundamentally anti-democratic, perpetuating bureaucratic errors. Open debate and discussion of public issues are vital to our national health. * * *

The stays in these cases that have been in effect for more than a week constitute a flouting of the principles of the First Amendment as interpreted in *Near.*

JUSTICE BRENNAN, concurring.

I write separately [to] emphasize what should be apparent: that our judgment in the present cases may not be taken to indicate the propriety, in the future, of issuing temporary stays and restraining orders to block the publication of material sought to be suppressed by the Government. So far as I can determine, never before has the United States sought to enjoin a newspaper from publishing information in its possession. * * *

The entire thrust of the Government's claim throughout these cases has been that publication of the material sought to be enjoined "could," or "might," or "may" prejudice the national interest in various ways. But the First Amendment tolerates absolutely no prior judicial restraints of the press predicated upon surmise or conjecture that untoward consequences may result.* Our cases, it is true, have indicated that there is a single, extremely narrow class of cases in which the First Amendment's ban on prior judicial restraint may be overriden. Our cases have thus far indicated that such cases may arise only when the Nation "is at war," [*Schenck*]. Even if the present world situation were assumed to be tantamount to a time of war, or if the power of presently available armaments would justify even in peacetime the suppression of information that would set in motion a nuclear holocaust, in neither of these actions has the

b. But see Denbeaux, *The First Word of the First Amendment,* 80 Nw.U.L.Rev. 1156 (1986).

* *Freedman* and similar cases regarding temporary restraints of allegedly obscene materials are not in point. For those cases rest upon the proposition that "obscenity is not protected by the freedoms of speech and press." *Roth.* Here there is no question but that the material sought to be suppressed is within the protection of the First Amendment; the only question is whether, notwithstanding that fact, its publication may be enjoined for a time because of the presence of an overwhelming national interest. * * *

Government presented or even alleged that publication of items from or based upon the material at issue would cause the happening of an event of that nature. [Thus,] only governmental allegation and proof that publication must inevitably, directly and immediately cause the occurrence of an event kindred to imperiling the safety of a transport already at sea can support even the issuance of an interim restraining order. In no event may mere conclusions be sufficient: for if the Executive Branch seeks judicial aid in preventing publication, it must inevitably submit the basis upon which that aid is sought to scrutiny by the judiciary. And therefore, every restraint issued in this case, whatever its form, has violated the First Amendment—and not less so because that restraint was justified as necessary to afford the courts an opportunity to examine the claim more thoroughly. Unless and until the Government has clearly made out its case, the First Amendment commands that no injunction may issue.

JUSTICE STEWART, with whom JUSTICE WHITE joins, concurring.

[I]n the cases before us we are asked neither to construe specific regulations nor to apply specific laws. [We] are asked, quite simply, to prevent the publication by two newspapers of material that the Executive Branch insists should not, in the national interest, be published. I am convinced that the Executive is correct with respect to some of the documents involved. But I cannot say that disclosure of any of them will surely result in direct, immediate, and irreparable damage to our Nation or its people. That being so, there can under the First Amendment be but one judicial resolution of the issues before us. I join the judgments of the Court.

JUSTICE WHITE, with whom JUSTICE STEWART joins, concurring.

I concur in today's judgments, but only because of the concededly extraordinary protection against prior restraints enjoyed by the press under our constitutional system. I do not say that in no circumstances would the First Amendment permit an injunction against publishing information about government plans or operations. Nor, after examining the materials the Government characterizes as the most sensitive and destructive, can I deny that revelation of these documents will do substantial damage to public interests. Indeed, I am confident that their disclosure will have that result. But I nevertheless agree that the United States has not satisfied the very heavy burden which it must meet to warrant an injunction against publication in these cases, at least in the absence of express and appropriately limited congressional authorization for prior restraints in circumstances such as these.

The Government's position is simply stated: The responsibility of the Executive for the conduct of the foreign affairs and for the security of the Nation is so basic that the President is entitled to an injunction against publication of a newspaper story whenever he can convince a court that the information to be revealed threatens "grave and irreparable" injury to the public interest; and the injunction should issue whether or not the material to be published is classified, whether or not publication would be lawful under relevant criminal statutes enacted by Congress and regardless of the circumstances by which the newspaper came into possession of the information.

At least in the absence of legislation by Congress, based on its own investigations and findings, I am quite unable to agree that the inherent powers of the Executive and the courts reach so far as to authorize remedies having such sweeping potential for inhibiting publications by the press. [To] sustain the Government in these cases would start the courts down a long and hazardous road that I am not willing to travel at least without congressional guidance and direction.

* * * Prior restraints require an unusually heavy justification under the First Amendment; but failure by the Government to justify prior restraints does not measure its constitutional entitlement to a conviction for criminal publication. That the Government mistakenly chose to proceed by injunction does not mean that it could not successfully proceed in another way.

* * * Congress has addressed itself to the problems of protecting the security of the country and the national defense from unauthorized disclosure of potentially damaging information. It has not, however, authorized the injunctive remedy against threatened publication. It has apparently been satisfied to rely on criminal sanctions and their deterrent effect on the responsible as well as the irresponsible press. * * *

JUSTICE HARLAN, with whom THE CHIEF JUSTICE and JUSTICE BLACKMUN join, dissenting. * * *

With all respect, I consider that the Court has been almost irresponsibly feverish in dealing with these cases.

Both [the] Second Circuit and [the] District of Columbia Circuit rendered judgment on June 23. [This] Court's order setting a hearing before us on June 26 at 11 a.m., a course which I joined only to avoid the possibility of even more peremptory action by the Court, was issued less than 24 hours before. The record in the *Post* case was filed with the Clerk shortly before 1 p.m. on June 25; the record in the *Times* case did not arrive until 7 or 8 o'clock that same night. The briefs of the parties were received less than two hours before argument on June 26.

This frenzied train of events took place in the name of the presumption against prior restraints created by the First Amendment. Due regard for the extraordinarily important and difficult questions involved in these litigations should have led the Court to shun such a precipitate timetable. In order to decide the merits of these cases properly, some or all of the following questions should have been faced: * * *

2. Whether the First Amendment permits the federal courts to enjoin publication of stories which would present a serious threat to national security. See *Near* (dictum). * * *

4. Whether the unauthorized disclosure of any of these particular documents would seriously impair the national security.

5. What weight should be given to the opinion of high officers in the Executive Branch of the Government with respect to [question 4]. * * *

7. Whether the threatened harm to the national security or the Government's possessory interest in the documents justifies the issuance of an injunction against publication in light of—

a. The strong First Amendment policy against prior restraints on publication; b. The doctrine against enjoining conduct in violation of criminal statutes; and c. The extent to which the materials at issue have apparently already been otherwise disseminated.

These are difficult questions of fact, of law, and of judgment; the potential consequences of erroneous decision are enormous. The time which has been available to us, to the lower courts, and to the parties has been wholly inadequate for giving these cases the kind of consideration they deserve. It is a reflection on the stability of the judicial process that these great issues—as important as any that have arisen during my time on the Court—should have been decided under the pressures engendered by the torrent of publicity that has attended these litigations from their inception.

Forced as I am to reach the merits of these cases, I dissent from the opinion and judgments of the Court. Within the severe limitations imposed by the time constraints under which I have been required to operate, I can only state my reasons in telescoped form, even though in different circumstances I would have felt constrained to deal with the cases in the fuller sweep indicated above.

[It] is plain to me that the scope of the judicial function in passing upon the activities of the Executive Branch of the Government in the field of foreign affairs is very narrowly restricted. This view is, I think, dictated by the concept of separation of powers upon which our constitutional system [rests.] I agree that, in performance of its duty to protect the values of the First Amendment against political pressures, the judiciary must review the initial Executive determination to the point of satisfying itself that the subject matter of the dispute does lie within the proper compass of the President's foreign relations power. Constitutional considerations forbid "a complete abandonment of judicial control." Moreover, the judiciary may properly insist that the determination that disclosure of the subject matter would irreparably impair the national security be made by the head of the Executive Department concerned—here the Secretary of State or the Secretary of Defense—after actual personal consideration by that officer.[c] This safeguard is required in the analogous area of executive claims of privilege for secrets of state.

But in my judgment the judiciary may not properly go beyond these two inquiries and redetermine for itself the probable impact of disclosure on the national security. "[T]he very nature of executive decisions as to foreign policy is political, not judicial. Such decisions are wholly confided by our Constitution to the political departments of the government, Executive and Legislative. They are delicate, complex, and involve large elements of prophecy. They are and should be undertaken only by those directly responsible to the people whose welfare they advance or imperil. They are decisions of a kind for which the judiciary has neither aptitude, facilities nor responsibility and which has long been held to belong in the domain of political power not subject to judicial intrusion or inquiry." *Chicago & S. Air Lines v. Waterman S.S. Corp.* (Jackson, J.), 333 U.S. 103, 68 S.Ct. 431, 92 L.Ed. 568 (1948).

Even if there is some room for the judiciary to override the executive determination, it is plain that the scope of review must be exceedingly narrow. I can see no indication in the opinions of either the District Court or the Court of Appeals in the *Post* litigation that the conclusions of the Executive were given even the deference owing to an administrative agency, much less that owing to a co-equal branch of the Government operating within the field of its constitutional prerogative. * * *

c. Consider Godofsky & Rogatnick, *Prior Restraints: The Pentagon Papers Case Revisited,* 18 Cum.L.Rev. 527, 536–37 (1988): "Ironically, Justice Harlan's view of the Constitution might, ultimately, have presented more problems for the Government than those of most of the other Justices. Realistically, how often can the Secretary of State or Secretary of Defense devote 'actual personal consideration' to the question of whether material about to be published should be suppressed? And of what does 'actual personal consideration' consist? Must the Secretary himself read the documents? Is it sufficient 'consideration' by a Cabinet officer to act on the advice of his subordinates? If so, is not the 'actual personal consideration' test substantially meaningless? Could a Cabinet officer be required to testify as to the basis for his decision in order to test his 'bona fides'?"

Pending further hearings in each case conducted under the appropriate ground rules, I would continue the restraints on publication. I cannot believe that the doctrine prohibiting prior restraints reaches to the point of preventing courts from maintaining the status quo long enough to act responsibly in matters of such national importance as those involved here.

JUSTICE BLACKMUN, dissenting.

[The First Amendment] is only one part of an entire Constitution. Article II of the great document vests in the Executive Branch primary power over the conduct of foreign affairs and places in that branch the responsibility for the Nation's safety. Each provision of the Constitution is important, and I cannot subscribe to a doctrine of unlimited absolutism for the First Amendment at the cost of downgrading other provisions. First Amendment absolutism has never commanded a majority of this Court. What is needed here is a weighing, upon properly developed standards, of the broad right of the press to print and of the very narrow right of the Government to prevent. Such standards are not yet developed. The parties here are in disagreement as to what those standards should be. But even the newspapers concede that there are situations where restraint is in order and is constitutional. Mr. Justice Holmes gave us a suggestion when he said in *Schenck,* "It is a question of proximity and degree. When a nation is at war many things that might be said in time of peace are such a hindrance to its effort that their utterance will not be endured so long as men fight and that no Court could regard them as protected by any constitutional right."

I therefore would remand these cases to be developed expeditiously, of course, but on a schedule permitting the orderly presentation of evidence from both sides [and] with the preparation of briefs, oral argument and court opinions of a quality better than has been seen to this point. [T]hese cases and the issues involved and the courts, including this one, deserve better than has been produced thus far. * * * [d]

Notes and Questions

1. *What did the case decide?* Do you agree that "the case [did] not make any law at all, good or bad"? That on the question "whether injunctions against the press are permissible, it is clear that [the case] can supply no precedent?" See Junger, *Down Memory Lane: The Case of the Pentagon Papers,* 23 Case W.Res.L.Rev. 3, 4–5 (1971). Or do you find in several concurring opinions a discernible standard that must be satisfied before a majority of the Court would permit an injunction against the press on national security grounds? Cf. 85 Harv.L.Rev. 199, 205–06 (1971). Do you find guidance as to the outcome if Congress were to authorize an injunction in narrow terms to protect national security? Cf. id. at 204–05. Might it fairly be said that this is a separation of powers decision, like the *Steel Seizure* case, as well as a first amendment decision? See Junger, supra, at 19.

d. Marshall, J., concurring, did not deal with first amendment issues but only with separation of powers—the government's attempt to secure through the Court injunctive relief that Congress had refused to authorize.

Burger, C.J., dissenting, complained that because of "unseemly haste," "we do not know the facts of this case. [W]e literally do not know what we are acting on." He expressed no views on the merits, apart from his joinder in Harlan, J.'s opinion, and a statement that he would have continued the temporary restraints in effect while returning the cases to the lower courts for more thorough exploration of the facts and issues.

2. *Injunctions against publishing specific material.* Is the special policy against prior restraints, as distinct from use of criminal sanctions, appropriately applied to a specific injunction against publishing identified material? Or should the policy against prior restraints, when applied to court injunctions after a hearing, be limited to broad orders against forbidden types of publications, as in *Near?* To what extent are the evils that underlie the general policy against prior restraints applicable to the specific injunction sought in *Pentagon Papers?* Cf. 85 Harv.L.Rev. at 207–08 (1971).

3. *"De facto" prior restraint.* One difficulty with viewing the prior restraint doctrine as "simply creat[ing] a 'presumption' against the validity of the restraint" (Emerson's characterization of the current approach) rather than as "a prohibition on all restraints subject to certain categorical exceptions," observes Emerson, *First Amendment Doctrine and the Burger Court,* 68 Calif.L.Rev. 422, 457–58 (1980), is that "the requirement of ad hoc scrutiny of prior restraints is itself likely to result in a 'de facto' prior restraint." Pointing to Brennan, J.'s comment in *Pentagon Papers* that "every restraint issued in this case [has] violated the First Amendment—and not less so because that restraint was justified as necessary to afford the courts an opportunity to examine the claim more thoroughly," Emerson notes that "[t]his is exactly what happened when the government sought to enjoin *The Progressive* magazine from publishing an article on the manufacture of the hydrogen bomb. The Supreme Court refused to order an expedited appeal from the [federal district court] injunction against publication [and, although the case was ultimately dismissed by the Seventh Circuit,] *The Progressive* remained under effective prior restraint for nearly seven months."

Compare *Near* and *Pentagon Papers* with UNITED STATES v. PROGRESSIVE, INC., 467 F.Supp. 990 (W.D.Wis.1979) (preliminary injunction issued Mar. 28, 1979), request for writ of mandamus denied sub nom. *Morland v. Sprecher,* 443 U.S. 709, 99 S.Ct. 3086, 61 L.Ed.2d 860 (1979), case dismissed, Nos. 79–1428, 79–1664 (7th Cir. Oct. 1, 1979).[e] *The Progressive* planned to publish an article entitled, "The H-Bomb Secret—How We Got It, Why We're Telling It," maintaining that the article would contribute to informed opinion about nuclear weapons and demonstrate the inadequacies of a system of secrecy and classification. Although the government conceded that at least some of the information contained in the article was "in the public domain" or had been "declassified," it argued that "national security" permitted it to censor information originating in the public domain "if when drawn together, synthesized and collated, such information acquires the character of presenting immediate, direct and irreparable harm to the interests of the United States." The Secretary of State stated that publication would increase thermonuclear proliferation and that this would "irreparably impair the national security of the United States." The Secretary of Defense maintained that dissemination of the Morland article would lead to a substantial increase in the risk of thermonuclear proliferation and to use or threats that would "adversely affect the national security of the United States."

Although recognizing that this constituted "the first instance of prior restraint against a publication in this fashion in the [nation's history]," the district court enjoined defendants, pending final resolution of the litigation, from publishing or otherwise disclosing any information designated by the government as "restricted data" within the meaning of The Atomic Energy Act of 1954:

e. The government's action against *The Progressive* was abandoned after information similar to that it sought to enjoin was published elsewhere.

"What is involved here is information dealing with the most destructive weapon in the history of mankind, information of sufficient destructive potential to nullify the right to free speech and to endanger the right to life itself. [Faced] with a stark choice between upholding the right to continued life and the right to freedom of the press, most jurists would have no difficulty in opting for the chance to continue to breathe and function as they work to achieve perfect freedom of expression.

"[A] mistake in ruling against *The Progressive* will seriously infringe cherished First Amendment rights. [A] mistake in ruling against the United States could pave the way for thermonuclear annihilation for us all. In that event, our right to life is extinguished and the right to publish becomes moot.

"[W]ar by foot soldiers has been replaced in large part by machines and bombs. No longer need there be any advance warning or any preparation time before a nuclear war could be commenced. [In light of these factors] publication of the technical information on the hydrogen bomb contained in the article is analogous to publication of troop movements or locations in time of war and falls within the extremely narrow exception to the rule against prior restraint [recognized in *Near*].[f]

"The government has met its burden under § 2274 of The Atomic Energy Act [which authorizes injunctive relief against one who would communicate or disclose restricted data 'with reason to believe such data will be utilized to injure the United States or to secure an advantage to any foreign nation.'] [I]t has also met the test enunciated by two Justices in *Pentagon Papers,* namely grave, direct, immediate and irreparable harm to the United States."

The court distinguished *Pentagon Papers* as follows: "[T]he study involved [there] contained historical data relating to events some three to twenty years previously. Secondly, the Supreme Court agreed with the lower court that no cogent reasons were advanced by the government as to why the article affected national security except that publication might cause some embarrassment to the United States. A final and most vital difference between these two cases is the fact that a specific statute is involved here [§ 2274 of The Atomic Energy Act]."

4. *CIA secrecy agreement.* The Central Intelligence Agency requires employees to sign a "secrecy agreement" as a condition of employment, an agreement committing the employee not to reveal classified information nor to publish any information obtained during the course of employment without prior approval of the Agency. In SNEPP v. UNITED STATES, 444 U.S. 507, 100 S.Ct. 763, 62 L.Ed.2d 704 (1980), Snepp had published a book called *Decent Interval* about certain CIA activities in South Vietnam based on his experiences as an agency employee without seeking prepublication review. At least for purposes of the litigation, the government conceded that Snepp's book divulged no confidential information. The Court, per curiam (Stevens, J., joined by Brennan and Marshall, JJ., dissenting) held that Snepp's failure to submit the book was a breach of trust and the government was entitled to a constructive trust on the proceeds of the book: "[E]ven in the absence of an express agreement, the CIA could have acted to protect substantial government interests by imposing reason-

f. One of the reasons the court gave for finding that the objected-to technical portions of the article fell within the *Near* exception was that it was "unconvinced that suppression of [these portions] would in any plausible fashion impede the defendants in their laudable crusade to stimulate public knowledge of nuclear armament and bring about enlightened debate on national policy questions." Should this have been a factor in the decision to issue the preliminary injunction?

able restrictions on employee activities that in other contexts might be protected by the First Amendment. The Government has a compelling interest in protecting both the secrecy of information important to our national security and the appearance of confidentiality so essential to the effective operation of our foreign intelligence service." [g] When employees or past employees do submit publications for clearance, should *Freedman* standards apply? Can former CIA employees be required to submit all public speeches relating to their former employment for clearance? Are extemporaneous remarks permitted? To what extent can secrecy agreements be required of public employees outside the national security area? [h]

SECTION 5. FAIR ADMINISTRATION OF JUSTICE AND THE FIRST AMENDMENT AS SWORD

This section poses two connected problems. The first implicates familiar themes, albeit in a different context. The government seeks to deter or punish speech it regards as threatening to the fair administration of justice, but the speech at issue falls into no recognized category of unprotected speech. Thus, the courts must consider whether absolute protection is called for, or, alternatively, whether new categories or ad hoc determinations are appropriate, and whether prior restraints are permissible.

A second problem is unique. Government seeks not to punish speech, but to administer justice in private. It refuses to let the public or press witness its handling of prisoners, or its conduct of trial or pre-trial proceedings. The question is whether the first amendment can serve as a sword allowing citizen-critics to gather information. Assuming it can, what are its limits within the justice system? Does a right of access reach beyond the justice system?

Finally, a recurring issue concerns the role of the press. If the press cannot be prevented from speaking about trials, can prosecutors, defense attorneys, litigants and potential witnesses be prevented from speaking to the press? Is this one problem or many problems? Does the first amendment require that the press be granted access not afforded the public? Does the first amendment permit differential access? If so, what are the limits on how government defines the press?

I. JUSTICE AND THE FIRST AMENDMENT AS SHIELD

In a number of cases, defendants have asserted that their rights to a fair trial have been abridged by newspaper publicity. SHEPPARD v. MAXWELL, 384 U.S. 333, 86 S.Ct. 1507, 16 L.Ed.2d 600 (1966) is probably the most notorious

g. Compare *Haig v. Agee,* 453 U.S. 280, 101 S.Ct. 2766, 69 L.Ed.2d 640 (1981), stating that "repeated disclosures of intelligence operations and names of intelligence personnel" for the "purpose of obstructing intelligence operations and the recruiting of intelligence personnel" are "clearly not protected by the Constitution." What if the publisher of the information merely has "reason to believe that such activities would impair or impede the foreign intelligence activities of the United States"? See 50 U.S.C.A. § 421.

h. For discussion of *Snepp,* see Cheh, *Judicial Supervision of Executive Secrecy,* 69 Corn. L.Rev. 690 (1984); Easterbrook, *Insider Trading, Secret Agents, Evidentiary Privileges, and the Production of Information,* 1981 Sup.Ct. Rev. 309, 339–53; Godofsky & Rogatnick, *Prior Restraints: The Pentagon Papers Case Revisited,* fn. c supra, at 543–54 (1988); Koffler & Gershman, *The New Seditious Libel,* 69 Corn.L.Rev. 816 (1984); Medow, *The First Amendment and the Secrecy State: Snepp v. United States,* 130 U.Pa.L.Rev. 775 (1982). For a thorough exploration of the occasions in which secrecy has been preferred over public knowledge, see DuVal, *The Occasions of Secrecy,* 47 U.Pitt.L.Rev. 579 (1986).

"trial by newspaper" case. The Court, per CLARK, J., (Black, J. dissenting) agreed with the "finding" of the Ohio Supreme Court that the atmosphere of defendant's murder trial was that of a " 'Roman holiday' for the news media." The courtroom was jammed with reporters. And in the corridors outside the courtroom, "a host of photographers and television personnel" photographed witnesses, counsel and jurors as they entered and left the courtroom. Throughout the trial, there was a deluge of publicity, much of which contained information never presented at trial, yet the jurors were not sequestered until the trial was over and they had begun their deliberations.

The Court placed the primary blame on the trial judge. He could "easily" have prevented "the carnival atmosphere of the trial" since "the courtroom and courthouse premises" were subject to his control. For example, he should have provided privacy for the jury, insulated witnesses from the media, instead of allowing them to be interviewed at will, and "made some effort to control the release of leads, information, and gossip to the press by police officers, witnesses, and the counsel for both sides." No one "coming under the jurisdiction of the court should be permitted to frustrate its function."

The Court recognized that "there is nothing that proscribes the press from reporting events that transpire in the courtroom. But where there is a reasonable likelihood that prejudicial news prior to trial will prevent a fair trial, the judge should continue the case until the threat abates, or transfer it to another county not so permeated with publicity. In addition, sequestration of the jury was something the judge should have raised sua sponte with counsel. If publicity during the proceedings threatens the fairness of the trial, a new trial should be ordered. But we must remember that reversals are but palliatives; the cure lies in those remedial measures that will prevent the prejudice at its inception."

The Court, however, reiterated its extreme reluctance "to place any direct limitations on the freedom traditionally exercised by the news media for '[w]hat transpires in the courtroom is public property.' " The press "does not simply publish information about trials but guards against the miscarriage of justice by subjecting the police, prosecutors, and judicial processes to extensive public scrutiny and criticism."

In anticipation of the trial of Simants for a mass murder which had attracted widespread news coverage, the county court prohibited everyone in attendance from, inter alia, releasing or authorizing for publication "any testimony given or evidence adduced." Simants' preliminary hearing (open to the public) was held the same day, subject to the restrictive order. Simants was bound over for trial. Respondent Nebraska state trial judge then entered an order which, as modified by the state supreme court, restrained the press and broadcasting media from reporting any confessions or incriminating statements made by Simants to law enforcement officers or third parties, except members of the press, and from reporting other facts "strongly implicative" of the defendant. The order expired when the jury was impaneled. NEBRASKA PRESS ASS'N v. STUART, 427 U.S. 539, 96 S.Ct. 2791, 49 L.Ed.2d 683 (1976), per BURGER, C.J., struck down the state court order: "To the extent that the order prohibited the reporting of evidence adduced at the open preliminary hearing, it plainly violated settled principles: 'There is nothing that proscribes the press from reporting events that transpire in the courtroom.' *Sheppard.*" [a] To the extent that the order prohibited publication "based on information gained from other sources, [the] heavy burden imposed as a condition to securing a prior restraint was not met." The portion of the order regarding "implicative" information was also "too vague and too broad" to survive scrutiny of restraints on first amendment rights.

"[P]retrial publicity—even pervasive, adverse publicity—does not inevitably lead to an unfair trial. The capacity of the jury eventually impaneled to decide the case fairly is influenced by the tone and extent of the publicity, which is in part, and often in large part, shaped by what attorneys, police and other officials do to precipitate news coverage. [T]he measures a judge takes or fails to take to mitigate the effects of pretrial publicity—the measures described in *Sheppard*—may well determine whether the defendant receives a trial consistent [with] due process.

"[The] Court has interpreted [first amendment] guarantees to afford special protection against orders that prohibit the publication or broadcast of particular information or commentary—orders that impose [a] 'prior' restraint on speech. None of our decided cases on prior restraint involved restrictive orders entered to protect a defendant's right to a fair and impartial jury, but [they] have a common thread relevant to this case. * * *

"The thread running through [*Near* and *Pentagon Papers*], is that prior restraints on speech and publication are the most serious and the least tolerable infringement on First Amendment rights. A criminal penalty or a judgment in a defamation case is subject to the whole panoply of protections afforded by deferring the impact of the judgment until all avenues of appellate review have been exhausted. [But] a prior restraint [has] an immediate and irreversible sanction. If it can be said that a threat of criminal or civil sanctions after publication 'chills' speech, prior restraint 'freezes' it at least for the time.

"[I]f the authors of [the first and sixth amendments], fully aware of the potential conflicts between them, were unwilling or unable to resolve the issue by assigning to one priority over the other, it is not for us to rewrite the Constitution by undertaking what they declined. [Yet] it is nonetheless clear that the barriers to prior restraint remain high unless we are to abandon what the Court has said for nearly a quarter of our national existence and implied throughout all of [it.]

"We turn now to the record in this case to determine whether, as Learned Hand put it, 'the gravity of the "evil," discounted by its improbability, justifies such invasion of free speech as is necessary to avoid the danger,' *Dennis* [2d Cir.], aff'd. To do so, we must examine the evidence before the trial judge when the order was entered to determine (a) the nature and extent of pretrial news coverage; (b) whether other measures would be likely to mitigate the effects of unrestrained pretrial publicity; (c) how effectively a restraining order would operate to prevent the threatened danger. The precise terms of the restraining order are also important. We must then consider whether the record supports the entry of a prior restraint on publication, one of the most extraordinary remedies known to our jurisprudence."

As to (a), although the trial judge was justified in concluding there would be extensive pretrial publicity concerning this case, he "found only 'a clear and

a. The Court added, however, that the county court "could not know that closure of the preliminary hearing was an alternative open to it until the Nebraska Supreme Court so construed state law."

present danger that pretrial publicity *could* impinge upon the defendant's right to a fair trial.' [Emphasis added by the Court]. His conclusion as to the impact of such publicity on prospective jurors was of necessity speculative, dealing as he was with factors unknown and unknowable."

As to (b), "there is no finding that alternative means [e.g., change of venue, postponement of trial to allow public attention to subside, searching questions of prospective jurors] would not have protected Simants' rights, and the Nebraska Supreme Court did no more than imply that such measures might not be adequate. Moreover, the record is lacking in evidence to support such a finding."

As to (c), in view of such practical problems as the limited territorial jurisdiction of the trial court issuing the order, the difficulties of predicting what information "will in fact undermine the impartiality of jurors," the problem of drafting an order that will "effectively keep prejudicial information from prospective jurors," and that the events "took place in a community of only 850 people"—throughout which, "it is reasonable to assume," rumors that "could well be more damaging than reasonably accurate news accounts" would "travel swiftly by word of mouth"—"it is far from clear that prior restraint on publication would have protected Simants' rights."

"[It] is significant that when this Court has reversed a state conviction because of prejudicial publicity, it has carefully noted that some course of action short of prior restraint would have made a critical difference. However difficult it may be, we need not rule out the possibility of showing the kind of threat to fair trial rights that would possess the requisite degree of certainty to justify restraint. [We] reaffirm that the guarantees of freedom of expression are not an absolute prohibition under all circumstances, but the barriers to prior restraint remain high and the presumption against its use continues intact. We hold that, with respect to the order entered in this case [the] heavy burden imposed as a condition to securing a prior restraint was not [met]."

BRENNAN, J., joined by Stewart and Marshall, JJ., concurring, would hold that "resort to prior restraints on the freedom of the press is a constitutionally impermissible method for enforcing [the right to a fair trial by a jury]; judges have at their disposal a broad spectrum of devices for ensuring that fundamental fairness is accorded the accused without necessitating so drastic an incursion on the equally fundamental and salutary constitutional mandate that discussion of public affairs in a free society cannot depend on the preliminary grace of judicial censors": "* * * Settled case law concerning the impropriety and constitutional invalidity of prior restraints on the press compels the conclusion that there can be no prohibition on the publication by the press of any information pertaining to pending judicial proceedings or the operation of the criminal justice system, no matter how shabby the means by which the information is obtained.[15] This does not imply, however, any subordination of Sixth Amendment rights, for an accused's right to a fair trial may be adequately assured through methods that do not infringe First Amendment values.

"[The narrow national security exception mentioned in *Near* and *Pentagon Papers*] does not mean, as the Nebraska Supreme Court assumed, that prior restraints can be justified on an ad hoc balancing approach that concludes that

15. Of course, even if the press cannot be enjoined from reporting certain information, that does not necessarily immunize it from civil liability for libel or invasion of privacy or from criminal liability for transgressions of general criminal laws during the course of obtaining that information.

the 'presumption' must be overcome in light of some perceived 'justification.' Rather, this language refers to the fact that, as a matter of procedural safeguards and burden of proof, prior restraints even within a recognized exception to the rule against prior restraints will be extremely difficult to justify; but as an initial matter, the purpose for which a prior restraint is sought to be imposed 'must fit within one of the narrowly defined exceptions to the prohibition against prior restraints.' Indeed, two Justices in [*Pentagon Papers*] apparently controverted the existence of even a limited 'military security' exception to the rule against prior restraints on the publication of otherwise protected material. (Black, J., concurring); (Douglas, J., concurring). And a majority of the other Justices who expressed their views on the merits made it clear that they would take cognizance only of a 'single, extremely narrow class of cases in which the First Amendment's ban on prior judicial restraint may be overridden.' (Brennan, J., concurring). * * *

"The only exception that has thus far been recognized even in dictum to the blanket prohibition against prior restraints against publication of material which would otherwise be constitutionally shielded was the 'military security' situation addressed in [*Pentagon Papers*]. But unlike the virtually certain, direct, and immediate harm required for such a restraint [the] harm to a fair trial that might otherwise eventuate from publications which are suppressed pursuant to orders such as that under review must inherently remain speculative."

Although they joined the Court's opinion, White and Powell, JJ., also filed brief concurrences. WHITE, J., expressed "grave doubts" that these types of restrictive orders "would ever be justifiable." POWELL, J., "emphasize[d] the unique burden" resting upon one who "undertakes to show the necessity for prior restraint on pretrial publicity." In his judgment, a prior restraint "requires a showing that (i) there is a clear threat to the fairness of trial, (ii) such a threat is posed by the actual publicity to be restrained, and (iii) no less restrictive alternatives are available. Notwithstanding such a showing, a restraint may not issue unless it also is shown that previous publicity or publicity from unrestrained sources will not render the restraint inefficacious. [A]ny restraint must comply with the standards of specificity always required in the First Amendment context."

STEVENS, J., concurred in the judgment. He agreed with Brennan, J., that the "judiciary is capable of protecting the defendant's right to a fair trial without enjoining the press from publishing information in the public domain, and that it may not do so." But he reserved judgment, until further argument, on "[w]hether the same absolute protection would apply no matter how shabby or illegal the means by which the information is obtained, no matter how serious an intrusion on privacy might be involved, no matter how demonstrably false the information might be, no matter how prejudicial it might be to the interests of innocent persons, and no matter how perverse the motivation for publishing it." He indicated that "if ever required to face the issue squarely" he "may well accept [Brennan, J.'s] ultimate conclusion." [b]

b. For background on *Nebraska Press,* see Friendly & Elliot, *The Constitution: That Delicate Balance* 148–58 (1984).

Notes and Questions

1. *Why the prior restraint reliance?* Does "the reasoning used by all of the justices premised solely on the traditional aversion to prior restraints, insufficiently" protect the press? Sack, *Principle and Nebraska Press Association v. Stuart,* 29 Stan.L.Rev. 411, 411 (1977). Would the *Nebraska Press* order have been "equally objectionable" if "framed as a statutory sanction punishing publication after it had occurred"? Id. at 415. See also Barnett, *The Puzzle of Prior Restraint,* 29 Stan.L.Rev. 539, 542–44, 560 (1977).

2. *Why the Dennis citation?* Consider Schmidt, *Nebraska Press Association: An Expansion of Freedom and Contraction of Theory,* 29 Stan.L.Rev. 431, 459–60 (1977): Burger, C.J.'s reliance on *Dennis* "is remarkable, almost unbelievable, because that test is both an exceedingly odd means of determining the validity of a prior restraint and a controversial and recently neglected technique of first amendment adjudication. [If] the [*Dennis*] test is the right one for prior restraints, what tests should govern a subsequent punishment case resting on legislation?" See also Barnett, note 1 supra, at 542–44. Burger, C.J.'s citation to *Dennis* should be read in conjunction with dictum in his majority opinion in *Landmark Communications, Inc. v. Virginia,* note 6 infra. There he questioned reliance upon the clear and present danger standard but observed: "Properly applied, the test requires a court to make its own inquiry into the imminence and magnitude of the danger said to flow from the particular utterance and then to balance the character of the evil, as well as its likelihood, against the need for free and unfettered expression. The possibility that other measures will serve the State's interests should also be weighed."

3. *Future press restraints.* Was *Nebraska Press* a strong case for restraint? Is it "difficult to believe that any other case will provide an exception to the rule against prior restraints in fair trial/free press cases"? Goodale, *The Press Ungagged: The Practical Effect on Gag Order Litigation of Nebraska Press Association v. Stuart,* 29 Stan.L.Rev. 497, 504 (1977). If so, does the dispute between the justices over the right standard make a difference? Does the collateral bar rule shed light on that question? See id. at 511–12; Barnett, note 1 supra, at 553–58. Should the collateral bar rule apply in this situation?

4. *Application to non-press defendants.* Should *Nebraska Press* standards apply to court orders preventing prosecutors, witnesses, potential witnesses, jurors, defendants, or defense attorneys from talking to the press about the case? Should different standards apply to each category—e.g., do defendants and defense attorneys deserve as much protection as the press? See Freedman & Starwood, *Prior Restraints on Freedom of Expression by Defendants and Defense Attorneys: Ratio Decidendi v. Obiter Dictum,* 29 Stan.L.Rev. 607 (1977); Comment, *First Amendment Protection of Criminal Defense Attorneys' Extrajudicial [Statements],* 8 Whittier L.Rev. 1021 (1987).

5. *Obstructing justice.* A series of cases have held that the first amendment greatly restricts contempt sanctions against persons whose comments on pending cases were alleged to have created a danger of obstruction of the judicial process. "Such repression can be justified, if at all, only by a clear and present danger of the obstruction of justice." *New York Times Co. v. Sullivan.* In *Bridges v. California,* 314 U.S. 252, 62 S.Ct. 190, 86 L.Ed. 192 (1941), union leader Bridges had caused publication or acquiesced in publication of a telegram threatening a strike if an "outrageous" California state decision involving Bridges' dock workers were enforced. The Court reversed Bridges' contempt

citation. Consider Tribe, *American Constitutional Law* 624 (1978): "If Bridges' threat to cripple the economy of the entire West Coast did not present danger enough, the lesson of the case must be that almost nothing said outside the courtroom is punishable as contempt." [c]

Would it make a difference if a petit jury were impaneled? Suppose Bridges published an open letter to petit jurors? What if copies were sent by Bridges to each juror? Cf. *Wood v. Georgia,* 370 U.S. 375, 82 S.Ct. 1364, 8 L.Ed.2d 569 (1962) (open letter to press and grand jury—contempt citation reversed). But cf. *Cox v. Louisiana,* p. 648 infra (statute forbidding parades near courthouse with intent to interfere with administration of justice upheld): ("[W]e deal not with the contempt power [but] a statute narrowly drawn to punish" not a pure form of speech but expression mixed with conduct "that infringes a substantial state interest in protecting the judicial process.").

6. *Confidentiality and privacy.* A series of cases has rebuffed state efforts to protect confidentiality or privacy by prohibiting publication. *Cox Broadcasting Corp. v. Cohn* (state could not impose liability for public dissemination of the name of rape victim derived from public court documents); *Oklahoma Pub. Co. v. District Court,* 430 U.S. 308, 97 S.Ct. 1045, 51 L.Ed.2d 355 (1977) (pretrial order enjoining press from publishing name or picture of 11-year-old boy accused of murder invalid when reporters had been lawfully present at a prior public hearing and had photographed him en route from the courthouse); *Landmark Communications, Inc. v. Virginia,* 435 U.S. 829, 98 S.Ct. 1535, 56 L.Ed.2d 1 (1978) (statute making it a crime to publish information about particular confidential proceedings invalid as applied to non-participant in the proceedings, at least when the information had been lawfully acquired); *Smith v. Daily Mail Pub. Co.,* 443 U.S. 97, 99 S.Ct. 2667, 61 L.Ed.2d 399 (1979) (statute making it a crime for newspapers (but not broadcasters) to publish the name of any youth charged as a juvenile offender invalid as applied to information lawfully acquired from private sources). But cf. *Seattle Times Co. v. Rhinehart,* 467 U.S. 20, 104 S.Ct. 2199, 81 L.Ed.2d 17 (1984) (order enjoining newspaper from disseminating information acquired as a litigant in pretrial discovery valid so long as order is entered on a showing of good cause and does not restrict the dissemination of the information if gained from other sources).

II. JUSTICE AND THE FIRST AMENDMENT AS SWORD

By 1978, no Supreme Court holding contradicted Burger, C.J.'s contention for the plurality in *Houchins v. KQED, Inc.,* 438 U.S. 1, 98 S.Ct. 2588, 57 L.Ed.2d 553 (1978) that, "neither the First Amendment nor the Fourteenth Amendment mandates a right of access to government information or sources of information within the government's control." Or as Stewart, J., put it in an often-quoted statement, "The Constitution itself is neither a Freedom of Information Act nor an Official Secrets Act." "*Or of the Press,*" 26 Hast.L.J. 631, 636 (1975). *Richmond Newspapers,* infra, constitutes the Court's first break with its past denials of first amendment rights to information within governmental control.

c. Compare Rieger, *Lawyers' Criticism of Judges: Is Freedom of Speech A Figure of Speech?,* 2 Const.Comm. 69 (1985).

RICHMOND NEWSPAPERS, INC. v. VIRGINIA

448 U.S. 555, 100 S.Ct. 2814, 65 L.Ed.2d 973 (1980).

[At the commencement of his fourth trial on a murder charge (his first conviction having been reversed and two subsequent retrials having ended in mistrials), defendant moved, without objection by the prosecutor or two reporters present, that the trial be closed to the public—defense counsel stating that he did not "want any information being shuffled back and forth when we have a recess as [to] who testified to what." The trial judge granted the motion, stating that "the statute gives me that power specifically." He presumably referred to Virginia Code § 19.2–266, providing that in all criminal trials "the court may, in its discretion, exclude [any] persons whose presence would impair the conduct of a fair trial, provided that the [defendant's right] to a public trial shall not be violated." Later the same day the trial court granted appellants' request for a hearing on a motion to vacate the closure order. At the closed hearing, appellants observed that prior to the entry of its closure order the court had failed to make any evidentiary findings or to consider any other, less drastic measures to ensure a fair trial. Defendant stated that he "didn't want information to leak out," be published by the media, perhaps inaccurately, and then be seen by the jurors. Noting inter alia that "having people in the Courtroom is distracting to the jury" and that if "the rights of the defendant are infringed in any way [and if his closure motion] doesn't completely override all rights of everyone else, then I'm inclined to go along with" the defendant, the court denied the motion to vacate the closure order. Defendant was subsequently found not guilty.]

CHIEF JUSTICE BURGER announced the judgment of the Court and delivered an opinion in which JUSTICE WHITE and JUSTICE STEVENS joined.

[T]he precise issue presented here has not previously been before this Court for decision. [*Gannett Co. v. DePasquale,* 443 U.S. 368, 99 S.Ct. 2898, 61 L.Ed.2d 608 (1979)] was not required to decide whether a right of access to *trials,* as distinguished from hearings on *pre*trial motions, was constitutionally guaranteed. The Court held that the Sixth Amendment's guarantee to the accused of a public trial gave neither the public nor the press an enforceable right of access to a *pre*trial suppression hearing. One concurring opinion specifically emphasized that "a hearing on a motion before trial to suppress evidence is not a *trial.*" (Burger, C.J., concurring). Moreover, the Court did not decide whether the First and Fourteenth Amendments guarantee a right of the public to attend trials; nor did the dissenting opinion reach this issue. [H]ere for the first time the Court is asked to decide whether a criminal trial itself may be closed to the public upon the unopposed request of a defendant, without any demonstration that closure is required to protect the defendant's superior right to a fair trial, or that some other overriding consideration requires closure.

[T]he historical evidence demonstrates conclusively that at the time when our organic laws were adopted, criminal trials both here and in England had long been presumptively open [, thus giving] assurance that the proceedings were conducted fairly to all concerned, [and] discourag[ing] perjury, the misconduct of participants, and decisions based on secret bias or partiality. [Moreover, the] early history of open trials in part reflects the widespread acknowledgment [that] public trials had significant therapeutic value. [When] a shocking crime occurs, a community reaction of outrage and public protest often follows.

Thereafter the open processes of justice serve an important prophylactic purpose, providing an outlet for community concern, hostility, and emotion.

[The] crucial prophylactic aspects of the administration of justice cannot function in the dark; no community catharsis can occur if justice is "done in a corner [or] in any covert manner." [To] work effectively, it is important that society's criminal process "satisfy the appearance of justice," and the appearance of justice can best be provided by allowing people to observe it.

[From] this unbroken, uncontradicted history, supported by reasons as valid today as in centuries past, we are bound to conclude that a presumption of openness inheres in the very nature of a criminal trial under our system of criminal justice. [Nevertheless,] the State presses its contention that neither the Constitution nor the Bill of Rights contains any provision which by its terms guarantees to the public the right to attend criminal trials. Standing alone, this is correct, but there remains the question whether, absent an explicit provision, the Constitution affords protection against exclusion of the public from criminal trials.

[The] expressly guaranteed [first amendment] freedoms share a common core purpose of assuring freedom of communication on matters relating to the functioning of government. Plainly it would be difficult to single out any aspect of government of higher concern and importance to the people than the manner in which criminal trials are conducted * * *.

The Bill of Rights was enacted against the backdrop of the long history of trials being presumptively open. [In] guaranteeing freedoms such as those of speech and press, the First Amendment can be read as protecting the right of everyone to attend trials so as to give meaning to those explicit guarantees. * * * Free speech carries with it some freedom to listen. "In a variety of contexts this Court has referred to a First Amendment right to 'receive information and ideas.'" *Kleindienst v. Mandel,* 408 U.S. 753, 762, 92 S.Ct. 2576, 2581, 33 L.Ed.2d 683 (1972).[a] What this means in the context of trials is that the First Amendment guarantees of speech and press, standing alone, prohibit government from summarily closing courtroom doors which had long been open to the public at the time that amendment was adopted.

[It] is not crucial whether we describe this right to attend criminal trials to hear, see, and communicate observations concerning them as a "right of access," cf. *Gannett* (Powell, J., concurring); *Saxbe v. Washington Post Co.,* 417 U.S. 843, 94 S.Ct. 2811, 41 L.Ed.2d 514 (1974); *Pell v. Procunier,* 417 U.S. 817, 94 S.Ct. 2800, 41 L.Ed.2d 495 (1974),[11] or a "right to gather information," for we have recognized that "without some protection for seeking out the news, freedom of the press could be eviscerated." *Branzburg v. Hayes,* [p. 763 infra]. The explicit, guaranteed rights to speak and to publish concerning what takes place at a trial would lose much meaning if access to observe the trial could, as it was here, be foreclosed arbitrarily.

a. *Mandel* held that the Executive had plenary power to exclude a Belgium journalist from the country, at least so long as it operated on the basis of a facially legitimate and bona fide reason for exclusion. Although the Court decided ultimately not to balance the government's particular justification against the first amendment interest, it recognized that those who sought personal communication with the excluded alien did have a first amendment interest at stake. The Court apparently assumed that the excluded speaker had no rights at stake, and none were asserted on his behalf.

11. *Procunier* and *Saxbe* are distinguishable in the sense that they were concerned with penal institutions which, by definition, are not "open" or public places. * * * See also *Greer v. Spock* (military bases) [p. 650 infra].

The right of access to places traditionally open to the public, as criminal trials have long been, may be seen as assured by the amalgam of the First Amendment guarantees of speech and press; and their affinity to the right of assembly is not without relevance. From the outset, the right of assembly was regarded not only as an independent right but also as a catalyst to augment the free exercise of the other First Amendment rights with which it was deliberately linked by the draftsmen. * * * Subject to the traditional time, place, and manner restrictions, streets, sidewalks, and parks are places traditionally open, where First Amendment rights may be exercised [see generally Sec. 6 infra]; a trial courtroom also is a public place where the people generally—and representatives of the media—have a right to be present, and where their presence historically has been thought to enhance the integrity and quality of what takes place.

* * * Notwithstanding the appropriate caution against reading into the Constitution rights not explicitly defined, the Court has acknowledged that certain unarticulated rights are implicit in enumerated guarantees [referring, inter alia, to the rights of association and of privacy and the right to travel. See generally Ch. 3, Secs. 2 & 3]. [T]hese important but unarticulated rights [have] been found to share constitutional protection in common with explicit guarantees. The concerns expressed by Madison and others have thus been [resolved].[b]

We hold that the right to attend criminal trials [17] is implicit in the guarantees of the First Amendment; without the freedom to attend such trials, which people have exercised for centuries, important aspects of freedom of speech and "of the press could be eviscerated." *Branzburg.*

[In the present case,] the trial court made no findings to support closure; no inquiry was made as to whether alternative solutions would have met the need to ensure fairness; there was no recognition of any right under the Constitution for the public or press to attend the trial. In contrast to the pretrial proceeding dealt with in *Gannett,* there exist in the context of the trial itself various tested alternatives to satisfy the constitutional demands of fairness. [For example, there was nothing] to indicate that sequestration of the jurors would not have guarded against their being subjected to any improper information.[c] * * * Absent an overriding interest articulated in findings, the trial of a criminal case must be open to the public. * * *

Reversed.[d]

JUSTICE BRENNAN, with whom JUSTICE MARSHALL joins, concurring in the judgment.

[*Gannett*] held that the Sixth Amendment right to a public trial was personal to the accused, conferring no right of access to pretrial proceedings that is separately enforceable by the public or the press. [This case] raises the

b. The Chief Justice noted "the perceived need" of the Constitution's draftsmen "for some sort of constitutional 'saving clause' [which] would serve to foreclose application to the Bill of Rights of the maxim that the affirmation of particular rights implies a negation of those not expressly defined. Madison's efforts, culminating in the Ninth Amendment, served to allay the fears of those who were concerned that expressing certain guarantees could be read as excluding others."

17. Whether the public has a right to attend [civil trials is] not raised by this case, but we note that historically both civil and criminal trials have been presumptively open.

c. Once the jurors are selected, when, if ever, will their sequestration *not* be a satisfactory alternative to closure?

d. Powell, J., took no part. In *Gannett,* he took the position that a first amendment right of access applied to courtroom proceedings, albeit subject to overriding when justice so demanded or when confidentiality was necessary.

question whether the First Amendment, of its own force and as applied to the States through the Fourteenth Amendment, secures the public an independent right of access to trial proceedings. Because I believe that [it does secure] such a public right of access, I agree [that], without more, agreement of the trial judge and the parties cannot constitutionally close a trial to the public.[1]

While freedom of expression is made inviolate by the First Amendment, and with only rare and stringent exceptions, may not be suppressed, the First Amendment has not been viewed by the Court in all settings as providing an equally categorical assurance of the correlative freedom of access to information.[2] Yet the Court has not ruled out a public access component to the First Amendment in every circumstance. Read with care and in context, our decisions must therefore be understood as holding only that any privilege of access to governmental information is subject to a degree of restraint dictated by the nature of the information and countervailing interests in security or confidentiality. [Cases such as *Houchins, Saxbe* and *Pell*] neither comprehensively nor absolutely deny that public access to information may at times be implied by the First Amendment and the principles which animate it.

The Court's approach in right of access cases simply reflects the special nature of a claim of First Amendment right to gather information. Customarily, First Amendment guarantees are interposed to protect communication between speaker and listener. When so employed against prior restraints, free speech protections are almost insurmountable. See generally Brennan, *Address,* 32 Rutg.L.Rev. 173, 176 (1979). But the First Amendment embodies more than a commitment to free expression and communicative interchange for their own sakes; it has a *structural* role to play in securing and fostering our republican system of self-government. Implicit in this structural role is not only "the principle that debate on public issues should be uninhibited, robust, and wide-open," but the antecedent assumption that valuable public debate—as well as other civic behavior—must be informed. The structural model links the First Amendment to that process of communication necessary for a democracy to survive, and thus entails solicitude not only for communication itself, but for the indispensable conditions of meaningful communication.

[A]n assertion of the prerogative to gather information must [be] assayed by considering the information sought and the opposing interests invaded. This judicial task is as much a matter of sensitivity to practical necessities as it is of abstract reasoning. But at least two helpful principles may be sketched. First, the case for a right of access has special force when drawn from an enduring and vital tradition of public entree to particular proceedings or information. Such a tradition commands respect in part because the Constitution carries the gloss of history. More importantly, a tradition of accessibility implies the favorable

1. Of course, the Sixth Amendment remains the source of the *accused's* own right to insist upon public judicial proceedings. *Gannett.*

That the Sixth Amendment explicitly establishes a public trial right does not impliedly foreclose the derivation of such a right from other provisions of the Constitution. The Constitution was not framed as a work of carpentry, in which all joints must fit snugly without overlapping. * * *

2. A conceptually separate, yet related, question is whether the media should enjoy greater access rights than the general public. But no such contention is at stake here. Since the media's right of access is at least equal to that of the general public, this case is resolved by a decision that the state statute unconstitutionally restricts public access to trials. As a practical matter, however, the institutional press is the likely, and fitting, chief beneficiary of a right of access because it serves as the "agent" of interested citizens, and funnels information about trials to a large number of individuals.

judgment of experience. Second, the value of access must be measured in specifics. Analysis is not advanced by rhetorical statements that all information bears upon public issues; what is crucial in individual cases is whether access to a particular government process is important in terms of that very process.

[This Court has] persistently defended the public character of the trial process. *In re Oliver,* 333 U.S. 257, 68 S.Ct. 499, 92 L.Ed. 682 (1948), established that [fourteenth amendment due process] forbids closed criminal trials [and] acknowledged that open trials are indispensable to First Amendment political and religious freedoms.

By the same token, a special solicitude for the public character of judicial proceedings is evident in the Court's rulings upholding the right to report about the administration of justice. While these decisions are impelled by the classic protections afforded by the First Amendment to pure communication, they are also bottomed upon a keen appreciation of the structural interest served in opening the judicial system to public inspection. So, in upholding a privilege for reporting truthful information about judicial misconduct proceedings, *Landmark* emphasized that public scrutiny of the operation of a judicial disciplinary body implicates a major purpose of the First Amendment—"discussion of governmental affairs." Again, *Nebraska Press* noted that the traditional guarantee against prior restraint "should have particular force as applied to reporting of criminal proceedings." And *Cox Broadcasting* instructed that "[w]ith respect to judicial proceedings in particular, the function of the press serves to guarantee the fairness of trials and to bring to bear the beneficial effects of public scrutiny upon the administration of justice."

* * * Open trials play a fundamental role in furthering the efforts of our judicial system to assure the criminal defendant a fair and accurate adjudication of guilt or innocence. But, as a feature of our governing system of justice, the trial process serves other, broadly political, interests, and public access advances these objectives as well. To that extent, trial access possesses specific structural significance.

[For] a civilization founded upon principles of ordered liberty to survive and flourish, its members must share the conviction that they are governed equitably. That necessity * * * mandates a system of justice that demonstrates the fairness of the law to our citizens. One major function of the trial is to make that demonstration.

Secrecy is profoundly inimical to this demonstrative [purpose]. Public access is essential, therefore, if trial adjudication is to achieve the objective of maintaining public confidence in the administration of justice. But the trial [also] plays a pivotal role in the entire judicial process, and, by extension, in our form of government. Under our system, judges are not mere umpires, but, in their own sphere, lawmakers—a coordinate branch of *government.* [Thus], so far as the trial is the mechanism for judicial factfinding, as well as the initial forum for legal decisionmaking, it is a genuine governmental proceeding.

[More] importantly, public access to trials acts as an important check, akin in purpose to the other checks and balances that infuse our system of government. "The knowledge that every criminal trial is subject to contemporaneous review in the forum of public opinion is an effective restraint on possible abuse of judicial power," *Oliver*—an abuse that, in many cases, would have ramifications beyond the impact upon the parties before the court. * * *

Popular attendance at trials, in sum, substantially furthers the particular public purposes of that critical judicial proceeding. In that sense, public access is an indispensable element of the trial process itself. Trial access, therefore, assumes structural importance in our "government of laws."

As previously noted, resolution of First Amendment public access claims in individual cases must be strongly influenced by the weight of historical practice and by an assessment of the specific structural value of public access in the circumstances. With regard to the case at hand, our ingrained tradition of public trials and the importance of public access to the broader purposes of the trial process, tip the balance strongly toward the rule that trials be open.[23] What countervailing interests might be sufficiently compelling to reverse this presumption of openness need not concern us now,[24] for the statute at stake here authorizes trial closures at the unfettered discretion of the judge and parties.[25] [Thus it] violates the First and Fourteenth Amendments * * *.

JUSTICE STEWART, concurring in the judgment.

Whatever the ultimate answer [may] be with respect to pretrial suppression hearings in criminal cases, the First and Fourteenth Amendments clearly give the press and the public a right of access to trials themselves, civil as well as criminal. * * *

In conspicuous contrast to a military base, *Greer v. Spock*; a jail, *Adderley v. Florida* [p. 649 infra]; or a prison, *Pell,* a trial courtroom is a public place. Even more than city streets, sidewalks, and parks as areas of traditional First Amendment activity, a trial courtroom is a place where representatives of the press and of the public are not only free to be, but where their presence serves to assure the integrity of what goes on.

But this does not mean that the First Amendment right of members of the public and representatives of the press to attend civil and criminal trials is absolute. Just as a legislature may impose reasonable time, place and manner restrictions upon the exercise of First Amendment freedoms, so may a trial judge impose reasonable limitations upon the unrestricted occupation of a courtroom by representatives of the press and members of the public. Moreover, [there] may be occasions when not all who wish to attend a trial may do so.[3] And while there exist many alternative ways to satisfy the constitutional demands of a fair trial, those demands may also sometimes justify limitations upon the unrestricted presence of spectators in the courtroom.[5]

23. The presumption of public trials is, of course, not at all incompatible with reasonable restrictions imposed upon courtroom behavior in the interests of decorum. Thus, when engaging in interchanges at the bench, the trial judge is not required to allow public or press intrusion upon the huddle. Nor does this opinion intimate that judges are restricted in their ability to conduct conferences in chambers, inasmuch as such conferences are distinct from trial proceedings.

24. For example, national security concerns about confidentiality may sometimes warrant closures during sensitive portions of trial proceedings, such as testimony about state secrets.

25. Significantly, closing a trial lacks even the justification for barring the door to pretrial hearings: the necessity of preventing dissemination of suppressible prejudicial evidence to the public before the jury pool has become, in a practical sense, finite and subject to sequestration.

3. In such situations, representatives of the press must be assured access, *Houchins* (concurring opinion).

5. This is not to say that only constitutional considerations can justify such restrictions. The preservation of trade secrets, for example, might justify the exclusion of the public from at least some segments of a civil trial. And the sensibilities of a youthful prosecution witness, for example, might justify similar exclusion in a criminal trial for rape, so long as the defendant's Sixth Amendment right to a public trial were not impaired.

Since in the present case the trial judge appears to have given no recognition to the right [of] the press and [the] public to be present at [the] murder trial over which he was presiding, the judgment under review must be reversed. * * *

JUSTICE WHITE, concurring.

This case would have been unnecessary had *Gannett* construed the Sixth Amendment to forbid excluding the public from criminal proceedings except in narrowly defined circumstances. But the Court there rejected the submission of four of us to this effect, thus requiring that the First Amendment issue involved here be addressed. On this issue, I concur in the opinion of the Chief Justice.

JUSTICE BLACKMUN, concurring in the judgment.

My opinion and vote in partial dissent [in] *Gannett* compels my vote to reverse the judgment. [It] is gratifying [to] see the Court now looking to and relying upon legal history in determining the fundamental public character of the criminal trial. * * *

The Court's ultimate ruling in *Gannett,* with such clarification as is provided by the opinions in this case today, apparently is now to the effect that there is no *Sixth* Amendment right on the part of the public—or the press—to an open hearing on a motion to suppress. I, of course, continue to believe that *Gannett* was in error, both in its interpretation of the Sixth Amendment generally, and in its application to the suppression hearing, for I remain convinced that the right to a public trial is to be found where the Constitution explicitly placed it—in the Sixth Amendment.

[But] with the Sixth Amendment set to one side in this case, I am driven to conclude, as a secondary position, that the First Amendment must provide some measure of protection for public access to the trial. The opinion in partial dissent in *Gannett* explained that the public has an intense need and a deserved right to know about the administration of justice in general; about the prosecution of local crimes in particular; about the conduct of the judge, the prosecutor, defense counsel, police officers, other public servants, and all the actors in the judicial arena; and about the trial itself. It is clear and obvious to me, on the approach the Court has chosen to take, that, by closing this criminal trial, the trial judge abridged these First Amendment interests of the public. * * *

JUSTICE STEVENS, concurring.

This is a watershed case. Until today the Court has accorded virtually absolute protection to the dissemination of information or ideas, but never before has it squarely held that the acquisition of newsworthy matter is entitled to any constitutional protection whatsoever. An additional word of emphasis is therefore appropriate.

Twice before, the Court has implied that any governmental restriction on access to information, no matter how severe and no matter how unjustified, would be constitutionally acceptable so long as it did not single out the press for special disabilities not applicable to the public at large. In a dissent joined by [Brennan and Marshall, JJ.] in *Saxbe,* Justice Powell unequivocally rejected [that conclusion.] And in *Houchins,* I explained at length why [Brennan, Powell, JJ.] and I were convinced that "[a]n official prison policy of concealing * * * knowledge from the public by arbitrarily cutting off the flow of information at its source abridges [first amendment freedoms]." Since [Marshall and Blackmun, JJ.] were unable to participate in that case, a majority of the Court neither accepted nor rejected that conclusion or the contrary conclusion expressed in the prevailing opinions. Today, however, for the first time, the Court unequivocally holds that an arbitrary interference with access to important information is an abridgment of the freedoms of speech and of the press protected by the First Amendment.

It is somewhat ironic that the Court should find more reason to recognize a right of access today than it did in *Houchins*. For *Houchins* involved the plight of a segment of society least able to protect itself, an attack on a longstanding policy of concealment, and an absence of any legitimate justification for abridging public access to information about how government operates. In this case we are protecting the interests of the most powerful voices in the community, we are concerned with an almost unique exception to an established tradition of openness in the conduct of criminal trials, and it is likely that the closure order was motivated by the judge's desire to protect the individual defendant from the burden of a fourth criminal trial.[2]

In any event, for the reasons stated [in] my *Houchins* opinion, as well as those stated by the Chief Justice today, I agree that the First Amendment protects the public and the press from abridgment of their rights of access to information about the operation of their government, including the Judicial Branch; given the total absence of any record justification for the closure order entered in this case, that order violated the First Amendment * * *.

JUSTICE REHNQUIST, dissenting.

[I] do not believe that [anything in the Constitution] require[s] that a State's reasons for denying public access to a trial, where both [the prosecution and defense] have consented to [a court-approved closure order], are subject to any additional constitutional review at our hands.

[The] issue here is not whether the "right" to freedom of the press * * * overrides the defendant's "right" to a fair trial, [but] whether any provision in the Constitution may fairly be read to prohibit what the [trial court] did in this case. Being unable to find any such prohibition in the First, Sixth, Ninth, or any other Amendments to [the] Constitution, or in the Constitution itself, I dissent.

Notes and Questions

1. *Beyond the justice system.* May (should) "public access to information about how government operates" (to use Stevens, J.'s phrase) be denied, as the Chief Justice suggests, simply on the ground that the place at issue has not been *traditionally* open to the public (recall how the Chief Justice distinguishes penal institutions from criminal trials) or should the government also have to advance, as Stevens, J., suggests, "legitimate justification" for "abridging" public access? Compare the controversy over whether "the right to a public forum" should turn on whether the place at issue has *historically* been dedicated to the exercise of first amendment rights or on whether the manner of expression is *basically incompatible* with the normal activity of the place at a particular time. See generally the materials on the Public Forum: New Forums, Sec. 6, II infra. See

2. Neither that likely motivation nor facts showing the risk that a fifth trial would have been necessary without closure of the fourth are disclosed in this record, however. The absence of any articulated reason for the closure order is a sufficient basis for distinguishing this case from *Gannett*. The decision today is in no way inconsistent with the perfectly unambiguous holding in *Gannett* that the rights guaranteed by the Sixth Amendment are rights that may be asserted by the accused rather than members of the general public. * * *

also Note, *The First Amendment Right to Gather State-Held Information,* 89 Yale L.J. 923, 933–39 (1979). Consider, too, Blasi, *The Checking Value in First Amendment Theory,* 1977 Am.B.Found.Res.J. 521, 609–10: "[U]nder the checking value, the interest of the press (and ultimately the public) in learning certain information relevant to the abuse of official power would sometimes take precedence over perfectly legitimate and substantial government interests such as efficiency and confidentiality. Thus, the First Amendment may require that journalists have access as a general matter to some records, such as certain financial documents, which anyone investigating common abuses of the public trust would routinely want to inspect, even though the granting of such access would undoubtedly entail some costs and risks. Also, the balance might be tilted even more in the direction of access if a journalist could demonstrate that there are reasonable grounds to believe that certain records contain evidence of misconduct by public officials."

But cf. Kamisar, *Right of Access to Information Generated or Controlled by the Government: Richmond Newspapers Examined and Gannett Revisited* in Choper, Kamisar & Tribe, The Supreme Court: Trends and Developments, 1979–80 145, 166 (1981): "I am sure I am not alone when I say that these law review commentaries go quite far. But *someday* the views they advance may be the law of the land. In the meantime, however, many more battles will have to be fought. *Someday* we may look back on *Richmond Newspapers* as the '*Powell v. Alabama*' of the right of access to government-controlled information—but it was a long, hard road from *Powell* to *Gideon.*" [e]

2. *Within the justice system.* How far does (should) *Richmond Newspapers* extend within the justice system? To criminal pre-trial proceedings? [f] How is a trial defined? Should it extend to conferences in chambers or at the bench? To grand jury hearings? To civil trials? To depositions? To records of any or all of the above? Should it apply outside judicial proceedings? Should wardens be permitted to completely preclude access by the public and press to prisons? To executions? What if the prisoner wants to close the execution? For wide-ranging discussion of these and related questions, see Choper, Kamisar, and Tribe, note 1 supra, at 145–206 (Professor Tribe was winning counsel in *Richmond Newspapers*). See also Fenner & Koley, *Access to Judicial Proceedings: To Richmond Newspapers and Beyond,* 16 Harv.Civ.Rts-Civ.Lib.L.Rev. 415 (1981).

3. *Closing trials.* After *Richmond Newspapers,* what showing should suffice to justify closure of a criminal trial? See *Globe Newspaper Co. v. Superior Court,* 457 U.S. 596, 102 S.Ct. 2613, 73 L.Ed.2d 248 (1982) (routine exclusion of press and public during testimony of minor victim of sex offense unconstitutional); *Press-Enterprise Co. v. Superior Court,* 464 U.S. 501, 104 S.Ct. 819, 78 L.Ed.2d 629 (1984) (extending *Richmond Newspapers* to voir dire examination of jurors). To overcome either the first amendment or the sixth amendment right to a public trial, the Court has required that the party seeking to close the proceedings "must advance an overriding interest that is likely to be prejudiced, the closure must be no broader than necessary to protect that interest, the trial

e. For endorsements of generous access, see Haiman, *Speech and Law in a Free Society* 108–14, 368–97 (1981); Yudof, *When Government Speaks* 246–55 (1983); Emerson, *Legal Foundations of the Right to Know,* 1976 Wash. U.L.Q. 1, 14–17; Lewis, *A Public Right to Know about Public Institutions: The First Amendment as Sword,* 1980 Sup.Ct.Rev. 1. But see Bevier, *An Informed Public, an Informing Press: The Search for a Constitutional Principle,* 68 Calif.L.Rev. 482 (1980).

f. See *Press–Enterprise Co. v. Superior Court,* 478 U.S. 1, 106 S.Ct. 2735, 92 L.Ed.2d 1 (1986) ("California preliminary hearings are sufficiently like a trial" to implicate *Richmond Newspapers'* "qualified First Amendment right of access").

court must consider reasonable alternatives to closing the proceeding, and it must make findings adequate to support the closure." *Waller v. Georgia,* 467 U.S. 39, 104 S.Ct. 2210, 81 L.Ed.2d 31 (1984).

4. *Special access rights for the press.* Is a press section in public trials required when the seating capacity would be exhausted by the public? Is a press section permitted? What limits attach to government determinations of who shall get press passes? See, e.g., *Sherrill v. Knight,* 569 F.2d 124 (D.C.Cir.1977) (denial of White House press pass infringes upon first amendment guarantees in the absence of adequate process); *Borreca v. Fasi,* 369 F.Supp. 906 (D.Haw.1974) (preliminary injunction against denial of access of a reporter to Mayor's press conferences justified when basis for exclusion is allegedly "inaccurate" and "irresponsible" reporting); *Los Angeles Free Press, Inc. v. Los Angeles,* 9 Cal.App. 3d 448, 88 Cal.Rptr. 605 (1970) (exclusion of weekly newspaper from scenes of disaster and police press conferences upheld when newspaper did not report police and fire events "with some regularity"). When access is required, may the press be prevented from taking notes? Is the right to bring tape recorders into public trials protected under *Richmond Newspapers?* What about "unobtrusive" television cameras? Consider Ares, *Chandler v. Florida: Television, Criminal Trials, and Due Process,* 1981 Sup.Ct.Rev. 157, 174: "Television in the courtroom expands public access to public institutions both qualitatively, because of its immediacy, and quantitatively, because of its reach. It is reported that a majority of Americans acquire their news primarily from television rather than from newspapers. To exclude the most important source of information about the working of courts without some compelling reason cannot be squared with the First Amendment." Cf. *Chandler v. Florida,* 449 U.S. 560, 101 S.Ct. 802, 66 L.Ed.2d 740 (1981) (subject to certain safeguards a state may *permit* electronic media and still photography coverage of public criminal proceedings over the objection of the accused).

Does *Chandler's* holding demean the interest in fair trials? Consider Griswold, *The Standards of the Legal Profession: Canon 35 Should Not Be Surrendered,* 48 A.B.A.J. 615, 617 (1962): "The presence of cameras and television [has] an inhibiting effect on some people, and an exhilarating effect on others. In either event, there would be distortion, and an inevitable interference with the administration of justice. With all the improved techniques in the world, the introduction of radio and television to the courtroom will surely and naturally convert it into a stage for those who can act, and into a place of additional burden for those who cannot." Do these objections apply with the same force to appellate proceedings?[g] Consider Kamisar, *Chandler v. Florida: What Can Be Said for a "Right of Access" to Televise Judicial Proceedings?* in Choper, Kamisar, & Tribe, The Supreme Court: Trends and Developments 1980–81, at 149, 168 (1982): "At the present time, no federal court allows TV coverage. *The place to begin* may well be the place that is likely to be the last holdout—the United States Supreme Court."

SECTION 6. GOVERNMENT PROPERTY AND THE PUBLIC FORUM[a]

The case law treating the question of when persons can speak on public property has come to be known as public forum doctrine. But "[t]he public

g. See Ares, supra, at 189–90.

a. For treatment of the related question whether, and if so under what circumstances, there is a first amendment right of access to forum saga began, and very nearly ended," Stone, *Fora Americana: Speech in Public Places,* 1974 Sup.Ct.Rev. 233, 236, with an effort by Holmes, J., then on the Supreme Judicial Court of Massachusetts, "to solve a difficult first amendment problem by simplistic resort to a common-law concept," Blasi, *Prior Restraints on Demonstrations,* 68 Mich.L.Rev. 1482, 1484 (1970). For holding religious meetings on the Boston Common, a preacher was convicted under an ordinance prohibiting "any public address" upon publicly-owned property without a permit from the mayor. In upholding the permit ordinance Holmes, J., observed: "For the legislature absolutely or conditionally to forbid public speaking in a highway or public park is no more an infringement of rights of a member of the public than for the owner of a private house to forbid it in the house." *Massachusetts v. Davis,* 162 Mass. 510, 511, 39 N.E. 113, 113 (1895). On appeal, a unanimous Supreme Court adopted the Holmes position, 167 U.S. 43, 17 S.Ct. 731, 42 L.Ed. 71 (1897): "[T]he right to absolutely exclude all right to use [public property], necessarily includes the authority to determine under what circumstances such use may be availed of, as the greater power contains the lesser."

This view survived until *Hague v. CIO,* 307 U.S. 496, 59 S.Ct. 954, 83 L.Ed. 1423 (1939), which rejected Jersey City's claim that its ordinance requiring a permit for an open air meeting was justified by the "plenary power" rationale of *Davis.* In rejecting the implications of the *Davis* dictum, Roberts, J., in a plurality opinion, uttered a famous "counter dictum," which has played a central role in the evolution of public forum theory: "Wherever the title of streets and parks may rest, they have immemorially been held in trust for the use of the public and, time out of mind, have been used for purposes of assembly, communicating thoughts between citizens, and discussing public questions. Such use of the streets and public places has, from ancient times, been a part of the privileges, immunities, rights, and liberties of citizens. [This privilege of a citizen] is not absolute, but relative, and must be exercised in subordination to the general comfort and convenience, and in consonance with peace and good order; but it must not, in the guise of regulation, be abridged or denied." Eight months later, the *Hague* dictum was given impressive content by Roberts, J., for the Court, in *Schneider* infra.

I. FOUNDATION CASES

A. MANDATORY ACCESS

SCHNEIDER v. IRVINGTON, 308 U.S. 147, 60 S.Ct. 146, 84 L.Ed. 155 (1939), per ROBERTS, J., invalidated several ordinances prohibiting leafleting on public streets or other public places: "Municipal authorities, as trustees for the public, have the duty to keep their communities' streets open and available for movement of people and property, the primary purpose to which the streets are dedicated. So long as legislation to this end does not abridge the constitutional liberty of one rightfully upon the street to impart information through speech or the distribution of literature, it may lawfully regulate the conduct of those using the streets. For example, a person could not exercise this liberty by taking his stand in the middle of a crowded street, contrary to traffic regulations, and maintain his position to the stoppage of all traffic; a group of distributors could not insist upon a constitutional right to form a cordon across the street and to

privately-owned facilities, such as shopping centers, see *Marsh v. Alabama,* p. 1207 infra; *Hudgens v. NLRB,* p. 1479 infra; *PruneYard Shopping Center v. Robins,* p. 730 infra.

allow no pedestrian to pass who did not accept a tendered leaflet; nor does the guarantee of freedom of speech or of the press deprive a municipality of power to enact regulations against throwing literature broadcast in the streets. Prohibition of such conduct would not abridge the constitutional liberty since such activity bears no necessary relationship to the freedom to speak, write, print or distribute information or opinion. * * *

"In *Lovell* this court held void an ordinance which forbade the distribution by hand or otherwise of literature of any kind without written permission from the city manager. [Similarly] in *Hague v. C.I.O.*, an ordinance was held void on its face because it provided for previous administrative censorship of the exercise of the right of speech and assembly in appropriate public places.

"The [ordinances] under review do not purport to license distribution but all of them absolutely prohibit it in the streets and, one of them, in other public places as well.

"The motive of the legislation under attack in Numbers 13, 18 and 29 is held by the courts below to be the prevention of littering of the streets and, although the alleged offenders were not charged with themselves scattering paper in the streets, their convictions were sustained upon the theory that distribution by them encouraged or resulted in such littering. We are of opinion that the purpose to keep the streets clean and of good appearance is insufficient to justify an ordinance which prohibits a person rightfully on a public street from handing literature to one willing to receive it. Any burden imposed upon the city authorities in cleaning and caring for the streets as an indirect consequence of such distribution results from the constitutional protection of the freedom of speech and press. This constitutional protection does not deprive a city of all power to prevent street littering. There are obvious methods of preventing littering. Amongst these is the punishment of those who actually throw papers on the streets.

"It is suggested that [the] ordinances are valid because their operation is limited to streets and alleys and leaves persons free to distribute printed matter in other public places. But, as we have said, the streets are natural and proper places for the dissemination of information and opinion; and one is not to have the exercise of his liberty of expression in appropriate places abridged on the plea that it may be exercised in some other place."

MCREYNOLDS, J., "is of opinion that the judgment in each case should be affirmed."

Notes and Questions

1. *Leaflets and the streets as public forum.* Consider Kalven, *The Concept of the Public Forum: Cox v. Louisiana,* 1965 S.Ct.Rev. 1, 18 & 21: "Leaflet distribution in public places in a city is a method of communication that carries as an inextricable and expected consequence substantial littering of the streets, which the city has an obligation to keep clean. It is also a method of communication of some annoyance to a majority of people so addressed; that its impact on its audience is very high is doubtful. Yet the constitutional balance in *Schneider* was struck emphatically in favor of keeping the public forum open for this mode of communication.

"[The] operative theory of the Court, at least for the leaflet situation, is that, although it is a method of communication that interferes with the public use of the streets, the right to the streets as a public forum is such that leaflet distribution cannot be prohibited and can be regulated only for weighty reasons."

2. *Litter prevention as a substantial interest.* Does the interest in distributing leaflets always outweigh the interest in preventing littering? Suppose helicopters regularly dropped tons of leaflets on the town of Irvington?

3. *Beyond leaflets.* COX v. NEW HAMPSHIRE, 312 U.S. 569, 61 S.Ct. 762, 85 L.Ed. 1049 (1941), per HUGHES, C.J., upheld convictions of sixty-eight Jehovah's Witnesses for parading without a permit. They had marched in four or five groups (with perhaps twenty others) along the sidewalk in single file carrying signs and handing out leaflets: "[T]he state court considered and defined the duty of the licensing authority and the rights of the appellants to a license for their parade, with regard only to consideration of time, place and manner so as to conserve the public convenience." The licensing procedure was said to "afford opportunity for proper policing" and " 'to prevent confusion by overlapping parades, [to] secure convenient use of the streets by other travelers, and to minimize the risk of disorder.' " A municipality "undoubtedly" has "authority to control the use of its public streets for parades or processions." But see Baker, *Unreasoned Reasonableness: Mandatory Parade Permits and Time, Place, and Manner Regulations,* 78 Nw.U.L.Rev. 937, 992 (1984): Approximately 26,000 people walked on the same sidewalks during the same hour the defendants in *Cox* "marched." "This single difference in what [the defendants] did—'marching in formation,' which they did for expressive purposes and which presumably is an 'assembly' that the first amendment protects—turned out to have crucial significance. This sole difference, engaging in first amendment protected conduct, made them guilty of a criminal offense. [Surely] something is wrong with this result."

4. *Charging for use of public forum.* *Cox* said there was nothing "contrary to the Constitution" in the exaction of a fee " 'incident to the administration of the [licensing] Act and to the maintenance of public order in the matter licensed.' " Could leafleters be charged for the costs of cleaning up litter? Controversial speakers for the expense of police protection? See generally Goldberger, *A Reconsideration of Cox v. New Hampshire: Can Demonstrators Be Required to Pay the Costs of Using America's Public Forums?,* 62 Tex.L.Rev. 403 (1983); Blasi, *Demonstrations,* supra at 1527–32.

5. *Reasonable time, place, and manner regulations.* As *Cox* reveals, a right of access to a public forum does not guarantee immunity from reasonable time, place, and manner regulations. In *Heffron v. International Soc. for Krishna Consciousness,* 452 U.S. 640, 101 S.Ct. 2559, 69 L.Ed.2d 298 (1981), for example, the Court, per White, J., upheld a state fair rule prohibiting the distribution of printed material or the solicitation of funds except from a duly licensed booth on the fairgrounds. The Court noted that consideration of a forum's special attributes is relevant to the determination of reasonableness, and the test of reasonableness is whether the restrictions "are justified without reference to the content of the regulated speech, that they serve a significant governmental interest, and that in doing so they leave open ample alternative channels for communication of the information" [a]

WARD v. ROCK AGAINST RACISM, 491 U.S. 781, 109 S.Ct. 2746, 105 L.Ed. 2d 661 (1989), per KENNEDY, J., observes that "[E]ven in a public forum the government may impose reasonable restrictions on the time, place, or manner of

a. Brennan, J., joined by Marshall and Stevens, JJ., dissented in part as did Blackmun, J., in a separate opinion. Their dispute was not with the Court's test, but its application.

protected speech, provided the restrictions 'are justified without reference to the content of the regulated speech, that they are narrowly tailored to serve a significant governmental interest, and that they leave open ample alternative channels for communication of the information.' " The case reasserts that the *O'Brien* test is little different from the time, place, and manner test, and then states: "Lest any confusion on the point remain, we reaffirm today that a regulation of the time, place, or manner of protected speech must be narrowly tailored to serve the government's legitimate content-neutral interests but that it need not be the least-restrictive or least-intrusive means of doing so. Rather, the requirement of narrow tailoring is satisfied 'so long as [the] regulation promotes a substantial government interest that would be achieved less effectively absent the regulation.' To be sure, this standard does not mean that a time, place, or manner regulation may burden substantially more speech than is necessary to further the government's legitimate interests. Government may not regulate expression in such a manner that a substantial portion of the burden on speech does not serve to advance its goals." [7] Marshall, J., dissenting, joined by Brennan and Stevens, JJ., complains of the Court's "serious distortion of the narrowly tailoring requirement" and states that the Court's rejection of the less restrictive alternative test relies on "language in a few opinions * * * taken out of context."

Should the time, place, and manner test be different from the *O'Brien* test? Is there any difference between those tests and the approach employed in *Schneider*?

B. EQUAL ACCESS

CHICAGO POLICE DEPT. v. MOSLEY, 408 U.S. 92, 92 S.Ct. 2286, 33 L.Ed. 2d 212 (1972), invalidated an ordinance banning all picketing within 150 feet of a school building while the school is in session and one half-hour before and afterwards, except "the peaceful picketing of any school involved in a labor dispute."

The suit was brought by a federal postal employee who, for seven months prior to enactment of the ordinance, had frequently picketed a high school in Chicago. "During school hours and usually by himself, Mosley would walk the public sidewalk adjoining the school, carrying a sign that read: 'Jones High School practices black discrimination. Jones High School has a black quota.' His lonely crusade was always peaceful, orderly, and [quiet]." The Court, per MARSHALL, J., viewed the ordinance as drawing "an impermissible distinction between labor picketing and other peaceful picketing": "The central problem with Chicago's ordinance is that it describes permissible picketing in terms of its subject matter. Peaceful picketing on the subject of a school's labor-management dispute is permitted, but all other peaceful picketing is prohibited. The operative distinction is the message on a picket sign. But, above all else, the First Amendment means that government has no power to restrict expression because of its message, its ideas, its subject matter, or its content.

"[U]nder the Equal Protection Clause, not to mention the First Amendment itself,[a] government may not grant the use of a forum to people whose

7. A ban on handbilling, of course, would suppress a great quantity of speech that does not cause the evils that it seeks to eliminate, whether they be fraud, crime, litter, traffic congestion, or noise. For that reason, a complete ban on handbilling would be substantially broader than necessary to achieve the interests justifying it.

a. *Consolidated Edison Co. v. Public Service Comm'n*, p. 789 infra, abandoned equal views it finds acceptable, but deny use to those wishing to express less favored or more controversial views. And it may not select which issues are worth discussing or debating in public facilities. There is an 'equality of status in the field of ideas,' and government must afford all points of view an equal opportunity to be heard. Once a forum is opened up to assembly or speaking by some groups, government may not prohibit others from assembling or speaking on the basis of what they intend to say. Selective exclusions from a public forum may not be based on content alone, and may not be justified by reference to content alone.

"[Not] all picketing must always be allowed. We have continually recognized that reasonable 'time, place and manner' regulations of picketing may be necessary to further significant governmental interests. Similarly, under an equal protection analysis, there may be sufficient regulatory interests justifying selective exclusions or distinctions among picketers. [But] [b]ecause picketing plainly involves expressive conduct within the protection of the First Amendment, discriminations among picketers must be tailored to serve a substantial governmental interest. In this case, the ordinance itself describes impermissible picketing not in terms of time, place and manner, but in terms of subject matter. The regulation 'thus slip[s] from the neutrality of time, place and circumstance into a concern about content.' This is never permitted. * * *

"Although preventing school disruption is a city's legitimate concern, Chicago itself has determined that peaceful labor picketing during school hours is not an undue interference with school. Therefore, under the Equal Protection clause, Chicago may not maintain that other picketing disrupts the school unless that picketing is clearly more disruptive than the picketing Chicago already permits. If peaceful labor picketing is permitted, there is no justification for prohibiting all nonlabor picketing, both peaceful and nonpeaceful. 'Peaceful' labor picketing, however the term 'peaceful' is defined, is obviously no less disruptive than 'peaceful' nonlabor picketing. But Chicago's ordinance permits the former and prohibits the latter.

"[We also] reject the city's argument that, although it permits peaceful labor picketing, it may prohibit all nonlabor picketing because, as a class, nonlabor picketing is more prone to produce violence than labor picketing. Predictions about imminent disruption from picketing involve judgments appropriately made on an individualized basis, not by means of broad classifications, especially those based on subject matter. Freedom of expression, and its intersection with the guarantee of equal protection, would rest on a soft foundation indeed if government could distinguish among picketers on such a wholesale and categorical basis. '[I]n our system, undifferentiated fear or apprehension of disturbance is not enough to overcome the right to freedom of expression.' *Tinker*. Some labor picketing is peaceful, some disorderly; the same is true for picketing on other themes. No labor picketing could be more peaceful or less prone to violence than Mosley's solitary vigil. In seeking to restrict nonlabor picketing which is clearly more disruptive than peaceful labor picketing, Chicago may not prohibit all nonlabor picketing at the school forum." [b]

protection and cited *Mosley* as a first amendment case: "The First Amendment's hostility to content-based regulation extends not only to restrictions on particular viewpoints, but also to prohibition of public discussion of an entire topic." But see, e.g., *Minnesota State Board v. Knight,* 465 U.S. 271, 104 S.Ct. 1058, 79 L.Ed.2d 299 (1984) (stating that *Mosley* is an equal protection case).

b. Burger, C.J., joined the Court's opinion, but also concurred. Blackmun and Rehnquist, JJ., concurred in the result.

Notes and Questions

1. Consider Karst, *Equality as a Central Principle in the First Amendment,* 43 U.Chi.L.Rev. 20, 28 (1975): "*Mosley* is a landmark first amendment decision. It makes two principal points: (1) the essence of the first amendment is its denial to government of the power to determine which messages shall be heard and which suppressed * * *. (2) Any 'time, place and manner' restriction that selectively excludes speakers from a public forum must survive careful judicial scrutiny to ensure that the exclusion is the minimum necessary to further a significant government interest. Taken together, these statements declare a principle of major importance. The Court has explicitly adopted the principle of equal liberty of expression. [The] principle requires courts to start from the assumption that all speakers and all points of view are entitled to a hearing, and permits deviation from this basic assumption only upon a showing of substantial necessity."

2. What if the *Mosley* ordinance had not excepted labor picketing, but had banned *all* picketing within 150 feet of a school during school hours? Consider Karst 37–38: "The burden of this restriction would fall most heavily on those who have something to communicate to the school [population]. Student picketers presenting a grievance against a principal, or striking custodians with a message growing out of a labor dispute, would be affected more seriously by this ostensibly content-neutral ordinance than would, say the proponents of a candidate for Governor [who could just as effectively carry their message elsewhere]. This differential impact amounts to de facto content discrimination, presumptively invalid under the first amendment equality principle.

"[The city faces] an apparent dilemma. [If it] bars all picketing within a certain area, it will effectively discriminate against those groups that can communicate to their audience only by picketing within that area. But if the city adjusts its ordinance to this differential impact, as by providing a student-picketing or labor-picketing exemption, [it runs] afoul of *Mosley* itself. The city can avoid the dilemma by amending the ordinance to ban not all picketing but only noisy picketing." [c]

3. Does equality fully explain the special concern with content regulation? Consider Stone, *Content Regulation and the First Amendment,* 25 Wm. & Mary L.Rev. 189, 207 (1983): "The problem, quite simply, is that restrictions on expression are rife with 'inequalities,' many of which have nothing whatever to do with content. The ordinance at issue in *Mosley,* for example, restricted picketing near schools, but left unrestricted picketing near hospitals, libraries, courthouses, and private homes. The ordinance at issue in *Erznoznik* restricted drive-in theaters that are visible from a public street, but did not restrict billboards. [Whatever] the effect of these content-neutral inequalities on first amendment analysis, they are not scrutinized in the same way as content-based inequalities. Not all inequalities, in other words, are equal. And although the concern with equality may support the content-based/content-neutral distinction, it does not in itself have much explanatory power."

Is the concern with content discrimination explainable because of concerns about communicative impact, distortion of public debate, or government motivation? See generally Stone, supra. See also sources cited in notes 1 & 2 after

c. As Professor Karst notes, such an ordinance was upheld in *Grayned v. Rockford,* Part II infra, the companion case to *Mosley.*

O'Brien, Sec. 4 supra and Cass, *First Amendment Access to Government Facilities,* 65 Va.L.Rev. 1287, 1323–25 (1979); Stephan, *The First Amendment and Content Discrimination,* 68 Va.L.Rev. 203 (1982); Stone, *Restrictions of Speech Because of its Content: The Peculiar Case of Subject-Matter Restrictions,* 46 U.Chi.L.Rev. 81 (1978).

4. An Illinois statute prohibited picketing residences or dwellings—except when the dwelling is "used as a place of business," or is "a place of employment involved in a labor dispute or the place of holding a meeting [on] premises commonly used to discuss subjects of general public interest," or when a "person is picketing his own [dwelling]. Can a conviction for picketing the Mayor of Chicago's home be upheld? Is *Mosley* distinguishable? See *Carey v. Brown,* 447 U.S. 455, 100 S.Ct. 2286, 65 L.Ed.2d 263 (1980).

II. NEW FORUMS

Are first amendment rights on government property confined to streets and parks? "[W]hat about other publicly owned property, ranging from the grounds surrounding a public building, to the inside of a welfare office, publicly run bus, or library, to a legislative gallery?" Stone, *Fora Americana,* supra, at 245. Compare the approaches in *Grayned* and *Perry* infra.

GRAYNED v. ROCKFORD, 408 U.S. 104, 92 S.Ct. 2294, 33 L.Ed.2d 222 (1972): Appellant and some 200 others participated in a demonstration about 100 feet from a high school building, protesting the principal's failure to act on black students' grievances. They were convicted, inter alia, of violating an "anti-noise" ordinance providing: "[N]o person, while on public or private grounds adjacent to any [school] building in which [a class] is in session, shall willfully make or assist in the making of any noise or diversion which disturbs or tends to disturb the peace or good order of such school session." An 8–1 majority, per MARSHALL, J., upheld the ordinance against vagueness and overbreadth objections.

As for the vagueness claim, it was clear to the Court that "the ordinance as a whole" prohibits "deliberately noisy or diversionary activity which disrupts or is about to disrupt normal school activities." In light of Illinois cases construing similar ordinances, "only actual or imminent interference with the 'peace or good order' of the school" is prohibited. At issue is not "a vague, general 'breach of the peace' ordinance, but a specific statute for the school context, where the prohibited disturbances are easily measured by their impact on the normal activities of the school. Given this 'particular context,' the ordinance gives 'fair notice to whom it is directed.' [Rockford's] anti-noise ordinance does not permit punishment for the expression of an unpopular point of view, and it contains no broad invitation to subjective or discriminatory enforcement."

As for the overbreadth claim: "[G]overnment has no power to restrict [expressive] activity because of its message [but] reasonable 'time, place and manner' regulations may be necessary to further significant governmental interests, and are permitted. For example, two parades cannot march on the same street simultaneously, and government may allow only one. *Cox v. New Hampshire.* A demonstration or parade on a large street during rush hour might put an intolerable burden on the essential flow of traffic, and for that reason could be prohibited. If overamplified loudspeakers assault the citizenry, government may turn them down.

"The nature of a place, 'the pattern of its normal activities, dictates the kinds of regulations of time, place, and manner that are reasonable.' Although a silent vigil may not unduly interfere with a public library, *Brown v. Louisiana,* 383 U.S. 131, 86 S.Ct. 719, 15 L.Ed.2d 637 (1966) [a] making a speech in the reading room almost certainly would. That same speech should be perfectly appropriate in a park. The crucial question is whether the manner of expression is basically incompatible with the normal activity of a particular place at a particular time. Our cases make clear that in assessing the reasonableness of regulation, we must weigh heavily the fact that communication is involved; the regulation must be narrowly tailored to further the State's legitimate interest. 'Access to [the streets, sidewalks, parks, and other similar public places] for the purpose of exercising [First Amendment rights] cannot constitutionally be denied broadly * * *.' Free expression 'must not, in the guise of regulation, be abridged or denied.'

"In light of these general principles, we do not think that Rockford's ordinance is an unconstitutional regulation of activity around a school. [Just] as *Tinker* [p. 673 infra] made clear that school property may not be declared off-limits for expressive activity by students, we think it clear that the public sidewalk adjacent to school grounds may not be declared off-limits for expressive activity by members of the public. But in each case, expressive activity may be prohibited if it 'materially disrupts classwork or involves substantial disorder or invasion of the rights of others.' * * *

"Rockford's anti-noise ordinance [is] narrowly tailored to further Rockford's compelling interest in having an undisrupted school session conducive to the students' learning, and does not unnecessarily interfere with First Amendment rights. Far from having an impermissibly broad prophylactic ordinance, Rockford punishes only conduct which disrupts or is about to disrupt normal school activities. That decision is made, as it should be, on an individualized basis, given the particular fact situation. Peaceful picketing which does not interfere with the ordinary functioning of the school is permitted. And the ordinance gives no license to punish anyone because of what he is saying.

"We recognize that the ordinance prohibits some picketing which is neither violent nor physically obstructive. Noisy demonstrations which disrupt or are incompatible with normal school activities are obviously within the ordinance's reach. Such expressive conduct may be constitutionally protected at other places or other times, but next to a school, while classes are in session, it may be prohibited. The anti-noise ordinance imposes no such restriction on expressive activity before or after the school session, while the student/faculty 'audience' enters and leaves the school.

"In *Cox v. Louisiana,* 379 U.S. 559, 85 S.Ct. 476, 13 L.Ed.2d 487 (1965), this Court indicated that, because of the special nature of the place, persons could be constitutionally prohibited from picketing 'in or near' a courthouse 'with the intent of interfering with, obstructing, or impeding the administration of jus-

a. In *Brown,* only three justices (Fortas, J., joined by Warren and Douglas, JJ.) held there was a constitutional right to conduct a silent demonstration in the library. Brennan, J., found the statute involved to be overbroad and thus found it unnecessary to decide whether the actual conduct was constitutionally protected. White, J., concluded that the demonstrators had been unconstitutionally punished because of their race. Black, J., dissenting joined by Clark, Harlan, and Stewart, JJ., insisted that the first amendment "does not guarantee to any person the right to use someone else's property, even that owned by government and dedicated to other purposes, as a stage to express dissident ideas."

tice.' [b] [Similarly], Rockford's modest restriction on some peaceful picketing represents a considered and specific legislative judgment that some kinds of expressive activity should be restricted at a particular time and place, here in order to protect the schools. Such a reasonable regulation is not inconsistent with the First and Fourteenth Amendments.[49] The anti-noise ordinance is not invalid on its face." [c]

A collective bargaining agreement between the board of education and Perry Education Association (PEA), the duly elected exclusive bargaining representative of the school district's teachers, granted PEA access to the interschool mail system and teacher mailboxes in the district, access rights not available to any rival union such as Perry Local Educators' Association (PLEA). (Prior to the 1978 collective bargaining agreement, PLEA had had equal access to the school mailboxes and delivery system). PLEA maintained that PEA's exclusive access to these facilities violated the first amendment and equal protection. PERRY EDUC. ASS'N v. PERRY LOCAL EDUCATORS' ASS'N, 460 U.S. 37, 103 S.Ct. 948, 74 L.Ed.2d 794 (1983), per WHITE, J., rejected both contentions: "The existence of a right of access to public property and the standard by which limitations upon such a right must be evaluated differ depending on the character of the property at issue.

"In places which by long tradition or by government fiat have been devoted to assembly and debate, the rights of the state to limit expressive activity are sharply circumscribed. At one end of the spectrum are streets and parks which 'have immemorially been held in trust for the use of the public, and, time out of mind, have been used for purposes of assembly, communicating thoughts between citizens, and discussing public questions.' *Hague.* In these quintessential public forums, the government may not prohibit all communicative activity. For the state to enforce a content-based exclusion it must show that its regulation is necessary to serve a compelling state interest and that it is narrowly drawn to achieve that end. The state may also enforce regulations of the time, place, and manner of expression which are content-neutral, are narrowly tai-

b. But cf. *United States v. Grace,* 461 U.S. 171, 103 S.Ct. 1702, 75 L.Ed.2d 736 (1983) (invalidating statute prohibiting all leafleting and picketing on sidewalk adjoining Supreme Court).

49. Cf. *Adderley v. Florida,* 385 U.S. 39, 87 S.Ct. 242, 17 L.Ed.2d 149 (1966). In *Adderley* the Court held that demonstrators could be barred from jailhouse grounds not ordinarily open to the public, at least where the demonstration obstructed the jail driveway and interfered with the functioning of the jail. [But see Post, *Between Governance and Management: The History and Theory of the Public Forum,* 34 UCLA L.Rev. 1713, 1731 n. 64 (1987): "In fact *Adderley* had contained no showing that the student demonstration had actually 'interfered' with the functioning of the jail."] In *Tinker,* we noted that "a school is not like a hospital or a jail enclosure."

[In *Adderly,* Black J. (over the dissent of Douglas, J., joined by Warren, C.J., Brennan, and Fortas, JJ.), opposed the premise that "people who want to propagandize protests or views have a constitutional right to do so whenever and however and whereever they please." He observed broadly that the state no less than a private property owner had power "to control the use of its own property for its own lawful nondiscriminatory purpose." But see Post, supra, at 1798: "It is simply self-contradictory, however, to claim for the government the prerogatives of a sphere of personal privacy, because the government cannot intelligibly claim that it should be 'let alone' from its own processes."]

c. Blackmun, J., concurred in the result. Douglas, J., dissented, maintaining that there was no violence, or boisterous conduct. "[T]he disruptive force loosened at this school was an issue dealing with race—an issue that is preeminently one for solution by First Amendment means. That is all that was done here; and the entire picketing [was] done in the best First Amendment tradition."

lored to serve a significant government interest, and leave open ample alternative channels of communication. *Grayned; Schneider.*

"A second category consists of public property which the state has opened for use by the public as a place for expressive activity. The Constitution forbids a state to enforce certain exclusions from a forum generally open to the public even if it was not required to create the forum in the first place. * * * [7] Although a state is not required to indefinitely retain the open character of the facility, as long as it does so it is bound by the same standards as apply in a traditional public forum. Reasonable time, place and manner regulations are permissible, and a content-based prohibition must be narrowly drawn to effectuate a compelling state interest.

"Public property which is not by tradition or designation a forum for public communication is governed by different standards. [In] addition to time, place, and manner regulations, the state may reserve the forum for its intended purposes, communicative or otherwise, as long as the regulation on speech is reasonable [a] and not an effort to suppress expression merely because public officials oppose the speaker's view.[b]

"The school mail facilities at issue here fall within this third category. [But PLEA contends] that the school mail facilities have become a 'limited public forum' from which it may not be excluded because of the periodic use of the system by private non-school connected groups, and PLEA's own unrestricted access to the system prior to PEA's certification as exclusive representative.

"Neither of these arguments is persuasive. The use of the internal school mail by groups not affiliated with the schools is no doubt a relevant consideration. If by policy or by practice the Perry School District has opened its mail system for indiscriminate use by the general public, then PLEA could justifiably argue a public forum has been created. This, however, is not the case. As the case comes before us, there is no indication in the record that the school mailboxes and interschool delivery system are open for use by the general public. Permission to use the system to communicate with teachers must be secured from the individual building principal. There is [no evidence] that this permission has been granted as a matter of course to all who seek to distribute material. We can only conclude that the schools do allow some outside organizations such as the YMCA, Cub Scouts, and other civic and church organizations to use the facilities. This type of selective access does not transform government property into a public forum. In *Greer v. Spock,* 424 U.S. 828, 96 S.Ct. 1211, 47 L.Ed.2d 505 (1976),[c] the fact that other civilian speaker and entertainers had sometimes been invited to appear at Fort Dix did not convert the military base into a public forum. * * *

"Moreover, even if we assume that by granting access to the Cub Scouts, YMCAs, and parochial schools, the school district has created a 'limited' public

7. A public forum may be created for a limited purpose such as use by certain groups, e.g., *Widmar v. Vincent* [p. 842 infra] (student groups), or for the discussion of certain subjects, e.g., *City of Madison Joint School District v. Wisconsin Employ. Relat. Comm'n,* 429 U.S. 167, 97 S.Ct. 421, 50 L.Ed.2d 376 (1976) (school board business).

a. See *Board of Airport Commissioners v. Jews for Jesus, Inc.,* 482 U.S. 569, 107 S.Ct. 2568, 96 L.Ed.2d 500 (1987) (resolution banning all "First Amendment activities" in airport unconstitutionally overbroad whether or not airport is public forum).

b. Can speakers be excluded from the Oval Room of the White House "merely because public officials oppose the speaker's view"?

c. *Greer* held that a military base commander could constitutionally preclude a presidential candidate from speaking or distributing leaflets on a military base even though members of the public were free to visit the base.

forum, the constitutional right of access would in any event extend only to other entities of similar character. * * *

"[According to the Court of Appeals], the access policy adopted by the Perry schools favors a particular viewpoint, that of the PEA, on labor relations, and consequently must be strictly scrutinized regardless of whether a public forum is involved. There is, however, no indication that the school board intended to discourage one viewpoint and advance another. We believe it is more accurate to characterize the access policy as based on the *status* of the respective unions rather than their views. Implicit in the concept of the nonpublic forum is the right to make distinctions in access on the basis of subject matter and speaker identity. These distinctions may be impermissible in a public forum but are inherent and inescapable in the process of limiting a nonpublic forum to activities compatible with the intended purpose of the property. The touchstone for evaluating these distinctions is whether they are reasonable in light of the purpose which the forum at issue serves.

"The differential access provided PEA and PLEA is reasonable because it is wholly consistent with the district's legitimate interest in 'preserv[ing] the property [for] the use to which it is lawfully dedicated.' Use of school mail facilities enables PEA to perform effectively its obligations as exclusive representative of *all* Perry Township teachers. Conversely, PLEA does not have any official responsibility in connection with the school district and need not be entitled to the same rights of access to school mailboxes. [W]hen government property is not dedicated to open communication the government may—without further justification—restrict use to those who participate in the forum's official business. * * *

"Finally, the reasonableness of the limitations on PLEA's access to the school mail system is also supported by the substantial alternative channels that remain open for union-teacher communication to take place. These means range from bulletin boards to meeting facilities to the United States mail. During election periods, PLEA is assured of equal access to all modes of communication. There is no showing here that PLEA's ability to communicate with teachers is seriously impinged by the restricted access to the internal mail system. The variety and type of alternative modes of access present here compare favorably with those in other nonpublic forum cases where we have upheld restrictions on access. See, e.g. *Greer* (servicemen free to attend political rallies off-base).

"The Court of Appeals also held that the differential access provided the rival unions constituted impermissible content discrimination in violation of the Equal Protection Clause of the Fourteenth Amendment. We have rejected this contention when cast as a First Amendment argument, and it fares no better in equal protection garb. [Because] PLEA did not have a First Amendment or other right of access to the interschool mail system [the] decision to grant such privileges to the PEA need not be tested by the strict scrutiny applied when government action impinges upon a fundamental right protected by the Constitution. The school district's policy need only rationally further a legitimate state purpose. That purpose is clearly found in the special responsibilities of an exclusive bargaining representative.

"[PLEA's reliance on *Mosley* and *Carey* is misplaced. [The] key to those decisions [was] the presence of a public forum. In a public forum, by definition, all parties have a constitutional right of access and the state must demonstrate compelling reasons for restricting access to a single class of speakers, a single viewpoint, or a single subject.

"When speakers and subjects are similarly situated, the state may not pick and choose. Conversely on government property that has not been made a public forum, not all speech is equally situated, and the state may draw distinctions which relate to the special purpose for which the property is used. As we have explained above, for a school mail facility, the difference in status between the exclusive bargaining representative and its rival is such a distinction."

BRENNAN, J., joined by Marshall, Powell, and Stevens, JJ., dissented: "Based on a finding that the interschool mail system is not a 'public forum,' the Court states that the respondents have no right of access to the system, and that the school board is free 'to make distinctions in access on the basis of subject matter and speaker identity,' if the distinctions are 'reasonable in light of the purpose which the forum at issue serves.'

"[The] Court fundamentally misperceives the essence of [PLEA's claims]. This case does not involve an 'absolute access' claim. It involves an 'equal access' claim. As such it does not turn on whether the internal school mail system is a 'public forum.' In focusing on the public forum issue, the Court disregards the First Amendment's central proscription against censorship, in the form of viewpoint discrimination, in any forum, public or nonpublic. [Generally], the concept of content neutrality prohibits the government from choosing the subjects that are appropriate for public discussion. The content neutrality cases frequently refer to the prohibition against viewpoint discrimination and both concepts have their roots in the First Amendment's bar against censorship. But unlike the viewpoint discrimination concept, which is used to strike down government restrictions on speech by particular speakers, the content neutrality principle is invoked when the government has imposed restrictions on speech related to an entire subject area. The content neutrality principle can be seen as an outgrowth of the core First Amendment prohibition against viewpoint discrimination. See generally, Stone, *Restrictions of Speech Because of its Content: The Peculiar Case of Subject-Matter Restrictions,* 46 U.Chi.L.Rev. 81 (1978). * * *

"Once the government permits discussion of certain subject matter, it may not impose restrictions that discriminate among viewpoints on those subjects whether a nonpublic forum is involved or not.[5] This prohibition is implicit in the *Mosley* line of cases, in *Tinker,* and in those cases in which we have approved content-based restrictions on access to government property that is not a public forum.[d]

"[The] Court responds to the allegation of viewpoint discrimination by suggesting that there is no indication that the board intended to discriminate and that the exclusive access policy is based on the parties' status rather than on their views. In this case, for the reasons discussed below, the intent to discriminate can be inferred from the effect of the policy, which is to deny an effective

5. This is not to suggest that a government may not close a nonpublic forum altogether or limit access to the forum to those involved in the "official business" of the agency. Restrictions of this type are consistent with the government's right "to preserve the property under its control for the use to which it is lawfully dedicated."

d. Brennan, J., characterized *Greer* as involving an unusual nonpublic forum where the speech had been determined to be incompatible with the forum. He agreed that *Greer* and other cases authorized the exclusion of some subjects from such forums, but argued that the exclusions had been viewpoint neutral.

channel of communication to the respondents, and from other facts in the case. In addition, the petitioner's status has nothing to do with whether viewpoint discrimination in fact has occurred. If anything, the petitioner's status is relevant to the question of whether the exclusive access policy can be justified, not to whether the board has discriminated among viewpoints.

"Addressing the question of viewpoint discrimination directly, free of the Court's irrelevant public forum analysis, it is clear that the exclusive access policy discriminates on the basis of viewpoint. The Court of Appeals found that 'the access policy * * * favors a particular viewpoint on labor relations in the Perry schools * * *: the teachers inevitably will receive from [the petitioner] self-laudatory descriptions of its activities on their behalf and will be denied the critical perspective offered by [the respondents].' This assessment of the effect of the policy is eminently reasonable. Moreover, certain other factors strongly suggest that the policy discriminates among viewpoints.

"On a practical level, the only reason for the petitioner to seek an exclusive access policy is to deny its rivals access to an effective channel of communication. No other group is explicitly denied access to the mail system. In fact, as the Court points out, many other groups have been granted access to the system. Apparently, access is denied to the respondents because of the likelihood of their expressing points of view different from the petitioner's on a range of subjects. The very argument the petitioner advances in support of the policy, the need to preserve labor peace, also indicates that the access policy is not viewpoint-neutral. * * *

"The petitioner attempts to justify the exclusive access provision based on its status as the exclusive bargaining representative for the teachers and on the state's interest in efficient communication between collective bargaining representatives and the members of the unit. The petitioner's status and the state's interest in efficient communication are important considerations. They are not sufficient, however, to sustain the exclusive access policy.

"[But] the exclusive access policy is both 'overinclusive and underinclusive' as a means of serving the state's interest in the efficient discharge of the petitioner's legal duties to the teachers. The policy is overinclusive because it does not strictly limit the petitioner's use of the mail system to performance of its special legal duties and underinclusive because the board permits outside organizations with no special duties to the teachers, or to the students, to use the system. The Court of Appeals also suggested that even if the board had attempted to tailor the policy more carefully by denying outside groups access to the system and by expressly limiting the petitioner's use of the system to messages relating to its official duties, 'the fit would still be questionable, for it might be difficult—both in practice and in principle—effectively to separate "necessary" communications from propaganda.' * * *

"Putting aside the difficulties with the fit between this policy and the asserted interests, the Court of Appeals properly pointed out that the policy is invalid 'because it furthers no discernible state interest.' While the board may have a legitimate interest in granting the petitioner access to the system, it has no legitimate interest in making that access exclusive by denying access to the respondents. * * *

"Although the state's interest in preserving labor peace in the schools in order to prevent disruption is unquestionably substantial, merely articulating the interest is not enough to sustain the exclusive access policy in this case. There must be some showing that the asserted interest is advanced by the policy.

In the absence of such a showing, the exclusive access policy must fall.[13]"

Notes and Questions

1. *The first amendment and geography.* Consider Farber & Nowak, *The Misleading Nature of Public Forum Analysis: Content and Context in First Amendment Adjudication,* 70 Va.L.Rev. 1219, 1234–35 (1984): "Classification of public places as various types of forums has only confused judicial opinions by diverting attention from the real first amendment issues involved in the cases. Like the fourth amendment, the first amendment protects people, not places. Constitutional protection should depend not on labeling the speaker's physical location but on the first amendment values and governmental interests involved in the case. Of course, governmental interests are often tied to the nature of the place. [To] this extent, the public forum doctrine is a useful heuristic [device]. But when the heuristic device becomes the exclusive method of analysis, only confusion and mistakes can result." Compare Post, *Between Governance and Management: The History and Theory of the Public Forum,* 34 UCLA L.Rev. 1713, 1777 (1987): "*Grayned*'s 'incompatibility' test takes into account only the specific harm incident to a plaintiff's proposed speech; it does not recognize the generic damage to managerial authority flowing from the very process of independent judicial review of institutional decisionmaking. [The] Court's present focus 'on the character of the property at issue' is a theoretical dead end, because there is no satisfactory theory connecting the classification of government property with the exercise of first amendment rights. But there is great potential for a rich and principled jurisprudence if the Court were to focus instead on the relationship between judicial review and the functioning of institutional authority."

2. *"Public."* See Post, supra at 1800: "The concept of the 'public' in public forum doctrine [is] extraordinarily complex. In part it refers to government facilitation of symbolic interaction. This facilitation, however, must be of a particular kind. If it is oriented toward the achievement of particular purposes or goals, the government's intervention will be perceived as creating a nonpublic forum like a courtroom or a university. The facilitation must instead be passive enough to be appropriated and used by purely private purposes. This points toward a conclusion whose irony should not be missed: in the end the public realm created by public forum doctrine is nothing other than a governmentally protected space for the achievement of private ordering. The irony, of course, has a final twist, for in a democracy like our own private ordering is the very stuff of public will."

3. *Footnote 7 forums.* What is the relationship between the Court's second category of property and fn. 7? Is the discretion to create forums limited? Is it necessary to show that restrictions on such forums are necessary to achieve a compelling state interest? If a restriction (to certain speakers or subjects) is challenged, can the restrictions be used to show that that the property is not a

13. The Court also cites the availability of alternative channels of communication in support of the "reasonableness" of the exclusive access policy. In a detailed discussion, the Court of Appeals properly concluded that the other channels of communication available to the respondents were "not nearly as effective as the internal mail system." In addition, the Court apparently disregards the principle that "one is not to have the exercise of his liberty of expression in appropriate places abridged on the plea that it may be exercised in some other place." *Schneider.* In this case, the existence of inferior alternative channels of communication does not affect the conclusion that the petitioner has failed to justify the viewpoint-discriminatory exclusive access policy.

public forum of the second category? Is this inadmissible circularity? See Tribe, *Equality as a First Amendment Theme: The "Government—as—Private Actor" Exception* in Choper, Kamisar & Tribe, The Supreme Court: Trends and Developments 1982–1983, at 221, 226 (1984); Post, supra at 1752–56.[d] In any event, does fn. 7 create a fourth category of property without setting guiding standards? Are the *Perry* mailboxes fn. 7 forums?

LEHMAN v. SHAKER HEIGHTS, 418 U.S. 298, 94 S.Ct. 2714, 41 L.Ed.2d 770 (1974) held that a public transit system could sell commercial advertising space for cards on its vehicles while refusing to sell space for "political" or "public issue" advertising. BLACKMUN, J., joined by Burger, C.J., White and Rehnquist, JJ., ruled the bus cards not to be a public forum and found the city's decision reasonable because it minimized "chances of abuse, the appearance of favoritism, and the risk of imposing upon a captive audience."

DOUGLAS, J., concurring, maintained that political messages and commercial messages were both offensive and intrusive to captive audiences, noted that the commercial advertising policy was not before the Court, and voted to deny a right to spread a political message to a captive audience.

BRENNAN, J., joined by Stewart, Marshall, and Powell, JJ., dissenting, observed that the "city's solicitous regard for 'captive riders' [has] a hollow ring in the present case where [it] has opened its rapid transit system as a forum for communication."

Is *Lehman* a fn. 7 forum?

4. *Alternative channels.* Does consideration of alternative channels of communication violate *Schneider's* observation that "one is not to have the exercise of his liberty of expression in appropriate places abridged on the plea that it may be exercised in some other place?" For discussion emphasizing the importance of considering alternative channels of communications and the methods for doing so, see generally Cass, *First Amendment Access to Government Facilities,* 65 Va.L.Rev. 1287 (1979).

5. For commentary on speaker-based restrictions, see Stone, *Content Regulation and the First Amendment,* 25 Wm. & Mary L.Rev. 189, 244–51 (1983).

Los Angeles prohibits posting signs on public property (e.g., sidewalks, crosswalks, street lamp posts, hydrants, or traffic signs). A group ("Taxpayers") contracted with a company to post cardboard campaign signs ("Roland Vincent—City Council") on the cross-arms supporting utility poles. Taxpayers argued that

d. Compare Blackmun, J., dissenting in *Cornelius v. NAACP Legal Defense and Educational Fund, Inc.,* 473 U.S. 788, 105 S.Ct. 3439, 87 L.Ed.2d 567 (1985): "If the Government does not create a limited public forum unless it intends to provide an 'open forum' for expressive activity, and if the exclusion of some speakers is evidence that the Government did not intend to create such a forum, no speaker challenging denial of access will ever be able to prove that the forum is a limited public forum. The very fact that the Government denied access to the speaker indicates that the Government did not intend to provide an open forum for expressive activity, and [that] fact alone would demonstrate that the forum is not a limited public forum." In *Cornelius,* a 4–3 majority, per O'Connor, J., determined that "government does not create a public forum by inaction or by permitting limited discourse, but only by intentionally opening a non-traditional forum for public discourse." Observing that the Court will look to the policy and practice of the government, the nature of the property and its compatibility with expressive activity in discerning intent, O'Connor, J., insisted that "we will not find that a public forum has been created in the face of clear evidence of a contrary intent, nor will we infer that the Government intended to create a public forum when the nature of the property is inconsistent with expressive activity."

the ordinance was unconstitutional at least as applied to the placing of signs on the cross-arms of utility poles.[a] LOS ANGELES CITY COUNCIL v. TAXPAYERS FOR VINCENT, 466 U.S. 789, 104 S.Ct. 2118, 80 L.Ed.2d 772 (1984), per STEVENS, J., upheld the ordinance: "[T]he First Amendment forbids the government from regulating speech in ways that favor some viewpoints or ideas at the expense of others. That general rule has no application to this case. For there is not even a hint of bias or censorship in [this] ordinance.

"In *O'Brien,* the Court set forth the appropriate framework for reviewing a viewpoint neutral regulation of this kind: [b] '[A] government regulation is sufficiently justified if it is within the constitutional power of the Government; if it furthers an important or substantial governmental interest; if the governmental interest is unrelated to the suppression of free expression; and if the incidental restriction on alleged First Amendment freedoms is no greater than is essential to the furtherance of that interest.'

"In this case, [Taxpayers does] not dispute that it is within the constitutional power of the City to attempt to improve its appearance, or that this interest is basically unrelated to the suppression of ideas. Therefore the critical inquiries are whether that interest is sufficiently substantial to justify the effect of the ordinance on appellees' expression, and whether that effect is no greater than necessary to accomplish the City's purpose.[c]

"In *Kovacs v. Cooper,* [336 U.S. 77, 69 S.Ct. 448, 93 L.Ed. 513 (1949)], the Court rejected the notion that a city is powerless to protect its citizens from unwanted exposure to certain methods of expression which may legitimately be deemed a public nuisance. In upholding an ordinance that prohibited loud and raucous sound trucks, the Court held that the state had a substantial interest in protecting its citizens from unwelcome noise.[24] * * *

"*Metromedia* [, *Inc. v. San Diego*, p. 579 supra] considered the city's interest in avoiding visual clutter, and seven Justices explicitly concluded that this interest was sufficient to justify a prohibition of billboards.[d] [The] problem addressed by this ordinance—the visual assault on the citizens of Los Angeles presented by an accumulation of signs posted on public property—constitutes a significant substantive evil within the City's power to prohibit. * * *

"We turn to the question whether the scope of the restriction on appellees' expressive activity is substantially broader than necessary to protect the City's interest in eliminating visual clutter.[e] The incidental restriction on expression which results from the City's attempt to accomplish such a purpose is considered justified as a reasonable regulation of the time, place, or manner of expression if it is narrowly tailored to serve that interest. [By] banning these signs, the City

a. Taxpayers also argued that the ordinance was overbroad and should be declared invalid on its face. The Court concluded that Taxpayers had failed to demonstrate "a realistic danger that the ordinance [would] significantly compromise recognized First Amendment protections of individuals not before the Court." It, therefore, refused to entertain an overbreadth challenge.

b. Is the Court suggesting that the *O'Brien* test is the appropriate framework for all viewpoint neutral regulations or just for regulations "of this kind"? What "kind" of ordinance is this? How is it different from other kinds of viewpoint neutral regulations?

c. Is this the same as the *O'Brien* test?

24. Justice Reed wrote: "The unwilling listener is not like the passer-by who may be offered a pamphlet in the street but may not be made to take it. In his home or on the street he is practically helpless to escape this interference with his privacy by loud speakers except through the protection of the municipality." * * *

d. But compare fn. 20 of the plurality opinion in *Metromedia*: "Because a total prohibition of outdoor advertising is not before us, we do not indicate whether such a ban would be consistent with the First Amendment."

e. Does this depart from the *O'Brien* test?

did no more than eliminate the exact source of the evil it sought to remedy. [The] ordinance curtails no more speech than is necessary to accomplish its purpose.[f]

"The Court of Appeals accepted the argument that a prohibition against the use of unattractive signs cannot be justified on esthetic grounds if it fails to apply to all equally unattractive signs wherever they might be located. A comparable argument was categorically rejected in *Metromedia.* In that case it was argued that the city could not simultaneously permit billboards to be used for on-site advertising and also justify the prohibition against offsite advertising on esthetic grounds, since both types of advertising were equally unattractive. The Court held, however, that the city could reasonably conclude that the esthetic interest was outweighed by the countervailing interest in one kind of advertising even though it was not outweighed by the other. So here, the validity of the esthetic interest in the elimination of signs on public property is not compromised by failing to extend the ban to private property. The private citizen's interest in controlling the use of his own property justifies the disparate treatment. Moreover, by not extending the ban to all locations, a significant opportunity to communicate by means of temporary signs is preserved, and private property owners' esthetic concerns will keep the posting of signs on their property within reasonable bounds. Even if some visual blight remains, a partial, content-neutral ban may nevertheless enhance the City's appearance.

"Furthermore, there is no finding that in any area where appellees seek to place signs, there are already so many signs posted on adjacent private property that the elimination of appellees' signs would have an inconsequential effect on the esthetic values with which the City is concerned. There is simply no predicate in the findings of the District Court for the conclusion that the prohibition against the posting of appellees' signs fails to advance the City's esthetic interest.[g]

"While the First Amendment does not guarantee the right to employ every conceivable method of communication at all times and in all places, a restriction on expressive activity may be invalid if the remaining modes of communication are inadequate.[h] * * * [Notwithstanding] appellees' general assertions in their brief concerning the utility of political posters, nothing in the findings indicates that the posting of political posters on public property is a uniquely valuable or important mode of communication, or that appellees' ability to communicate effectively is threatened by ever-increasing restrictions on expression.[30]

f. The Court distinguished *Schneider,* p. 641 supra by observing that an anti-littering statute would have been a less restrictive alternative in that case. Does this trivialize *Schneider*? Consider Stone, *O.T. 1983 and the Era of Aggressive Majoritarianism: A Court in Transition,* 19 Ga.L.Rev. 15, 21 (1984): "The Court understood in *Schneider* that not everyone can afford a newspaper or television campaign. In *Vincent,* the Court gave short shrift to this central first amendment insight." See generally Tribe, *Constitutional Calculus: Equal Justice or Economic Efficiency*?, 98 Harv.L.Rev. 592, 601–03 (1985); Werhan, *The O'Briening of Free Speech Methodology,* 19 Ariz.St.L.J. 635, 650–58 (1987).

g. How much advancement is required under the *O'Brien* test?

h. Does this modify the *O'Brien* test?

30. Although the Court has shown special solicitude for forms of expression that are much less expensive than feasible alternatives and hence may be important to a large segment of the citizenry, see, e.g., *Martin v. Struthers* [p. 579 supra] ("Door to door distribution of circulars is essential to the poorly financed causes of little people."), this solicitude has practical boundaries, see, e.g., *Kovacs v. Cooper* ("That more people may be more easily and cheaply reached by sound trucks [is] not enough to call forth constitutional protection for what those charged with public welfare reasonably think is a nuisance when easy means of publicity are open."). * * *

"Appellees suggest that the public property covered by the ordinance is either itself a 'public forum' for First Amendment purposes, or at least should be treated in the same respect as the 'public forum' in which the property is located. [But they] fail to demonstrate the existence of a traditional right of access respecting such items as utility poles for purposes of their communication comparable to that recognized for public streets and parks.[i] * * *

"Lampposts can of course be used as signposts, but the mere fact that government property can be used as a vehicle for communication does not mean that the Constitution requires such uses to be permitted. Public property which is not by tradition or designation a forum for public communication may be reserved by the state 'for its intended purposes, communicative or otherwise, as long as the regulation on speech is reasonable and not an effort to suppress expression merely because public officials oppose the speaker's view.' *Perry.* Given our analysis of the legitimate interest served by the ordinance, its viewpoint neutrality, and the availability of alternative channels of communication, the ordinance is certainly constitutional as applied to appellees under this standard.[32]

"[We] hold that on this record [the city] interests are sufficiently substantial to justify this content neutral, impartially administered prohibition against the posting of appellees' temporary signs on public property and that such an application of the ordinance does not create an unacceptable threat to the 'profound national commitment to the principle that debate on public issues should be uninhibited, robust, and wide-open.' *New York Times Co. v. Sullivan.*"

BRENNAN, J., joined by Marshall and Blackmun, JJ., dissented because "Los Angeles' total ban sweeps so broadly and trenches so completely on appellees' use of an important medium of political expression" and because "the Court's lenient approach towards the restriction of speech for reasons of aesthetics threatens seriously to undermine the protections of the First Amendment":

"The Court finds that the City's 'interest is sufficiently substantial to justify the restrictive effect of the ordinance on appellees' expression' and that the effect of the ordinance on speech is 'no greater than necessary to accomplish the City's purpose.' These are the right questions [but] Los Angeles has not shown that its interest in eliminating 'visual clutter' justifies its restriction of appellees' ability to communicate with the local electorate. * * *

"In deciding [the] First Amendment question, the critical importance of the posting of signs as a means of communication must not be overlooked. Use of this medium of communication is particularly valuable in part because it entails

i. Compare *United States v. Kokinda,* ___ U.S. ___, 110 S.Ct. 3115, 111 L.Ed.2d 571 (1990) (plurality argues that particular sidewalk outside post office is not the kind of sidewalk that is a traditional public forum).

32. Just as it is not dispositive to label the posting of signs on public property as a discrete medium of expression, it is also of limited utility in the context of this case to focus on whether the tangible property itself should be deemed a public forum. Generally an analysis of whether property is a public forum provides a workable analytical tool. However, "the analytical line between a regulation of the 'time, place, and manner' in which First Amendment rights may be exercised in a traditional public forum, and the question of whether a particular piece of personal or real property owned or controlled by the government is in fact a 'public forum' may blur at the edges," *United States Postal Service v. Greenburgh Civic Ass'n,* 453 U.S. 114, 132, 101 S.Ct. 2676, 2686, 69 L.Ed.2d 517 (1981), and this is particularly true in cases falling between the paradigms of government property interests essentially mirroring analogous private interests and those clearly held in trust, either by tradition or recent convention, for the use of citizens at large.

a relatively small expense in reaching a wide audience, allows flexibility in accommodating various formats, typographies, and graphics, and conveys its message in a manner that is easily read and understood by its reader or viewer. There may be alternative channels of communication, but the prevalence of a large number of signs in Los Angeles is a strong indication that, for many speakers, those alternatives are far less satisfactory.

"Nevertheless, the City of Los Angeles asserts that ample alternative avenues of communication are available. The City notes that, although the posting of signs on public property is prohibited, the posting of signs on private property and the distribution of handbills are not. But there is no showing that either of these alternatives would serve appellees' needs nearly as well as would the posting of signs on public property. First, there is no proof that a sufficient number of private parties would allow the posting of signs on their property. Indeed, common sense suggests the contrary at least in some instances. * * *

"Similarly, the adequacy of distributing handbills is dubious, despite certain advantages of handbills over signs. Particularly when the message to be carried is best expressed by a few words or a graphic image, a message on a sign will typically reach far more people than one on a handbill. The message on a posted sign remains to be seen by passersby as long as it is posted, while a handbill is typically read by a single reader and discarded. Thus, not only must handbills be printed in large quantity, but many hours must be spent distributing them. The average cost of communicating by handbill is therefore likely to be far higher than the average cost of communicating by poster. For that reason, signs posted on public property are doubtless 'essential to the poorly financed causes of little people,' and their prohibition constitutes a total ban on an important medium of communication. Cf. Stone, *Fora Americana: Speech in Public Places,* 1974 Sup.Ct.Rev. 233, 257. Because the City has completely banned the use of this particular medium of communication, and because, given the circumstances, there are no equivalent alternative media that provide an adequate substitute, the Court must examine with particular care the justifications that the City proffers for its ban. * * *

"The fundamental problem in this kind of case [is] the unavoidable subjectivity of aesthetic judgments—the fact that 'beauty is in the eye of the beholder.' As a consequence of this subjectivity, laws defended on aesthetic grounds raise problems for judicial review that are not presented by laws defended on more objective grounds—such as national security, public health, or public safety. In practice, therefore, the inherent subjectivity of aesthetic judgments makes it all too easy for the government to fashion its justification for a law in a manner that impairs the ability of a reviewing court meaningfully to make the required inquiries. * * *

"For example, in evaluating the ordinance before us in this case, the City might be pursuing either of two objectives, motivated by two very different judgments. One objective might be the elimination of 'visual clutter.' [A] second objective might simply be the elimination of the messages typically carried by the signs.[5] In that case, the aesthetic judgment would be that the signs' messages are themselves displeasing. The first objective is lawful, of course, but the second is not. Yet the City might easily mask the second

5. The fact that a ban on temporary signs applies to all signs does not necessarily imply content-neutrality. Because particular media are often used disproportionately for certain types of messages, a restriction that is content-neutral on its face may, in fact, be content-hostile. Cf. Stone, supra.

objective by asserting the first and declaring that signs constitute visual clutter. In short, we must avoid unquestioned acceptance of the City's bare declaration of an aesthetic objective lest we fail in our duty to prevent unlawful trespasses upon First Amendment protections.

"A total ban on an important medium of communication may be upheld only if the government proves that the ban (1) furthers a substantial government objective, and (2) constitutes the least speech-restrictive means of achieving that objective. Here too, however, meaningful judicial application of these standards is seriously frustrated.

"[The] possibility of interdependence between means and ends in the development of policies to promote aesthetics poses a major obstacle to judicial review of the availability of alternative means that are less restrictive of speech. Indeed, when a court reviews a restriction of speech imposed in order to promote an aesthetic objective, there is a significant possibility that the court will be able to do little more than pay lip service to the First Amendment inquiry into the availability of less restrictive alternatives. The means may fit the ends only because the ends were defined with the means in mind. In this case, for example, the City has expressed an aesthetic judgment that signs on public property constitute visual clutter throughout the City and that its objective is to eliminate visual clutter. We are then asked to determine whether that objective could have been achieved with less restriction of speech. But to ask the question is to highlight the circularity of the inquiry. Since the goal, at least as currently expressed, is essentially to eliminate all signs, the only available means of achieving that goal is to eliminate all signs.

"The ease with which means can be equated with aesthetic ends only confirms the importance of close judicial scrutiny of the substantiality of such ends. In this case, for example, it is essential that the Court assess the City's ban on signs by evaluating whether the City has a substantial interest in eliminating the visual clutter caused by *all* posted signs *throughout* the City—as distinguished from an interest in banning signs in some areas or in preventing densely packed signs. If, in fact, either of the latter two objectives constitute the substantial interest underlying this ordinance, they could be achieved by means far less restrictive of speech than a total ban on signs, and the ban, therefore, would be invalid.

"Regrettably, the Court's analysis is seriously inadequate. Because the Court has failed to develop a reliable means of gauging the nature or depth of the City's commitment to pursuing the goal of eradicating 'visual clutter,' it simply approves the ordinance with only the most cursory degree of judicial oversight. [W]here a total ban is imposed on a particularly valuable method of communication, a court should require the government to provide tangible proof of the legitimacy and substantiality of its aesthetic objective. Justifications for such restrictions articulated by the government should be critically examined to determine whether the government has committed itself to addressing the identified aesthetic problem. * * *

"This does not mean that a government must address all aesthetic problems at one time or that a government should hesitate to pursue aesthetic objectives. What it does mean, however, is that when such an objective is pursued, it may not be pursued solely at the expense of First Amendment freedoms, nor may it be pursued by arbitrarily discriminating against a form of speech that has the same aesthetic characteristics as other forms of speech that are also present in the community.

"Accordingly, in order for Los Angeles to succeed in defending its total ban on the posting of signs, the City would have to demonstrate that it is pursuing its goal of eliminating visual clutter in a serious and comprehensive manner. Most importantly, the City would have to show that it is pursuing its goal through programs other than its ban on signs, that at least some of those programs address the visual clutter problem through means that do not entail the restriction of speech, and that the programs parallel the ban in their stringency, geographical scope, and aesthetic focus. In this case, however, [there] is no indication that the City has addressed its visual clutter problem in any way other than by prohibiting the posting of signs—throughout the City and without regard to the density of their presence."

Notes and Questions

1. Why does the Court turn to the *O'Brien* test? [j] Does *Vincent* suggest that *O'Brien* should replace the *Perry* standards? Complement them? To what extent does *Vincent* suggest that the *O'Brien* test should apply to all viewpoint neutral regulations? Is there a general point to be drawn from *Vincent*? Or do we deal here with the law of cross-arms supporting utility poles?

2. The Court states that *O'Brien* supplies the appropriate framework, yet seems to deviate from its literal terms at various points in the opinion. Are those constructive modifications of the *O'Brien* test?

3. In reciting the facts, the Court observes that "among the 1,207 signs removed from public property during that week, 48 were identified as 'Roland Vincent' signs. Most of the other signs identified in that report were apparently commercial in character." Should the Court take the predominance of commercial signs into account? The insubstantial development of the messages involved? Do these factors minimize the force of Professor Stone's suggestion, fn. f, that *Vincent* is insensitive to the equality values at stake? In any event, does *Vincent's* appreciation of aesthetic values outstrip the facts? Is a utility pole more beautiful without a sign? Does it make aesthetic sense to allow signs everywhere on business property except on the utility poles?

III. THE PUBLIC FORUM AND THE PRIVATE RESIDENCE

On a number of occasions between April 20, 1985 and May 20, 1985, Sandra Schultz, together with groups ranging from ten to more than forty, marched with anti-abortion pickets for one to one and a half hours on the street outside a doctor's home in Brookfield, Wisconsin. In response, the Town Board passed an ordinance prohibiting picketing "before or about" any residence. Schultz filed suit challenging the ordinance on its face.

FRISBY v. SCHULTZ, 487 U.S. 474, 108 S.Ct. 2495, 101 L.Ed.2d 420 (1988), per O'CONNOR, J., interpreted the ordinance to apply only to "focused picketing [a] taking place solely in front of [and directed at] a particular residence," not to "general marching through residential neighborhoods, or even walking a route in front of an entire block of houses." So construed,[b] the Court upheld the

j. For commentary on the relationship between the *O'Brien* test and the tests ordinarily employed in the public forum line of cases, see *Nimmer on Freedom of Speech* 4–67 to 4–81 (1984).

a. The Court understood picketing to embrace posting or marching at a particular place—whether or not a sign was carried.

b. The lower courts understood the ordinance to ban all picketing in residential areas. The Court adopted a narrowing construction "in order to avoid constitutional difficulties."

ordinance: "The antipicketing ordinance operates at the core of the First Amendment by prohibiting appellees from engaging in picketing on an issue of public concern. [Moreover,] a public street does not lose its status as a traditional public forum simply because it runs through a residential neighborhood. [The] residential character of those streets may well inform the application of the relevant test, but it does not lead to a different test; the antipicketing ordinance must be judged against the stringent standards we have established for restrictions on speech in traditional public fora * * *."

The Court ruled that the ordinance was content neutral and proceeded to inquire whether it was narrowly tailored to serve a significant government interest while leaving open ample alternative channels of communication:

"As appellants explain, the limited nature of the prohibition makes it virtually self-evident that ample alternatives remain: 'Protestors have not been barred from the residential neighborhoods. They may enter such neighborhoods, alone or in groups, even marching. * * * They may go door-to-door to proselytize their views. They may distribute literature in this manner * * * or through the mails. They may contact residents by telephone, short of harassment.'

"We readily agree that the ordinance preserves ample alternative channels of communication and thus move on to inquire whether the ordinance serves a significant government interest. '[The] State's interest in protecting the well-being, tranquility, and privacy of the home is certainly of the highest order in a free and civilized society.' *Carey v. Brown.* [One] important aspect of residential privacy is protection of the unwilling listener. Although in many locations, we expect individuals simply to avoid speech they do not want to hear, cf. *Erznoznik, Cohen,* the home is different. [I]ndividuals are not required to welcome unwanted speech into their own homes and [the] government may protect this freedom.

"This principle is reflected even in prior decisions in which we have invalidated complete bans on expressive activity, including bans operating in residential areas. See, e.g., *Schneider* (handbilling); *Martin v. Struthers* (door-to-door solicitation). In all such cases, we have been careful to acknowledge that unwilling listeners may be protected when within their own homes. In *Schneider,* for example, in striking down a complete ban on handbilling, we spoke of a right to distribute literature only 'to one willing to receive it.' Similarly, when we invalidated a ban on door-to-door solicitation in *Martin,* we did so on the basis that the 'home owner could protect himself from such intrusion by an appropriate sign "that he is unwilling to be disturbed."' [There] simply is no right to force speech into the home of an unwilling listener.

"It remains to be considered, however, whether the Brookfield ordinance is narrowly tailored to protect only unwilling recipients of the communications. A statute is narrowly tailored if it targets and eliminates no more than the exact source of the 'evil' it seeks to remedy. [The] type of focused picketing prohibited by the Brookfield ordinance is fundamentally different from more generally directed means of communication that may not be completely banned in residential areas. [In] such cases 'the flow of information [is not] into * * * household[s], but to the public.' *Organization for a Better Austin v. Keefe,* 402 U.S. 415, 91 S.Ct. 1575, 29 L.Ed.2d 1 (1971).[c] Here, in contrast, the picketing is

c. *Keefe* involved the distribution of leaflets alleging that a real estate broker was involved in racial "blockbusting" and "panic peddling." The leaflets were distributed at a shopping center, at the broker's church, and at the doors of his neighbors. The Court, per narrowly directed at the household, not the public. The type of picketers banned by the Brookfield ordinance generally do not seek to disseminate a message to the general public, but to intrude upon the targeted resident, and to do so in an especially offensive way. Moreover, even if some such picketers have a broader communicative purpose, their activity nonetheless inherently and offensively intrudes on residential privacy. * * *

"In this case, for example, appellees subjected the doctor and his family to the presence of a relatively large group of protestors on their doorstep in an attempt to force the doctor to cease performing abortions. But the actual size of the group is irrelevant; even a solitary picket can invade residential privacy. See *Carey* (Rehnquist, J., dissenting) ('Whether * * * alone or accompanied by others * * * there are few of us that would feel comfortable knowing that a stranger lurks outside our home'). The offensive and disturbing nature of the form of the communication banned by the Brookfield ordinance thus can scarcely be questioned.

"The First Amendment permits the government to prohibit offensive speech as intrusive when the 'captive' audience cannot avoid the objectionable speech. The target of the focused picketing banned by the Brookfield ordinance is just such a 'captive.' The resident is figuratively, and perhaps literally, trapped within the home, and because of the unique and subtle impact of such picketing is left with no ready means of avoiding the unwanted speech. Thus, the 'evil' of targeted residential picketing, 'the very presence of an unwelcome visitor at the home' is 'created by the medium of expression itself.' Accordingly, the Brookfield ordinance's complete ban of that particular medium of expression is narrowly tailored.

"Of course, this case presents only a facial challenge to the ordinance. Particular hypothetical applications of the ordinance—to, for example, a particular resident's use of his or her home as a place of business or public meeting, or to picketers present at a particular home by invitation of the resident—may present somewhat different questions. [S]ince our First Amendment analysis is grounded in protection of the unwilling residential listener, the constitutionality of applying the ordinance to such hypotheticals remains open to question. These are, however, questions we need not address today in order to dispose of appellees' facial challenge." [d]

BRENNAN, J., joined by Marshall, J., dissented: "Without question there are many aspects of residential picketing that, if unregulated, might easily become intrusive or unduly coercive. Indeed, some of these aspects are illustrated by this very case. As the District Court found, before the ordinance took effect up to 40 sign-carrying, slogan-shouting protesters regularly converged on Dr. Victoria's home and, in addition to protesting, warned young children not to go near the house because Dr. Victoria was a 'baby killer.' Further, the throng repeatedly trespassed onto the Victoria's property and at least once blocked the exits to their home. Surely it is within the government's power to enact regulations as

Burger, C.J., stated: "The claim that the expressions were intended to exercise a coercive impact on [the broker] does not remove them from the reach of the First Amendment." Nor were the places of distribution deemed problematic.

d. White, J., concurring, was unsure about the scope of the ordinance. He would sustain the ordinance as applied to the picketing at issue in this case and deny a facial challenge for the present. He stated that the ordinance would be unconstitutional on its face if it were ultimately construed to prohibit all picketing in residential neighborhoods, but not if it were confined to picketing before a single residence. Nonetheless, he suggested that single residence picketing by small groups might be constitutionally protected in some circumstances.

necessary to prevent such intrusive and coercive abuses. Thus, for example, the government could constitutionally regulate the number of residential picketers, the hours during which a residential picket may take place, or the noise level of such a picket. In short, substantial regulation is permitted to neutralize the intrusive or unduly coercive aspects of picketing around the home. But to say that picketing may be substantially regulated is not to say that it may be prohibited in its entirety. Once size, time, volume, and the like have been controlled to ensure that the picket is no longer intrusive or coercive, only the speech itself remains, conveyed perhaps by a lone, silent individual, walking back and forth with a sign. Such speech, which no longer implicates the heightened government interest in residential privacy, is nevertheless banned by the Brookfield law. Therefore, the ordinance is not narrowly tailored.

"[The Court] conjures up images of a 'lurking' stranger, secreting himself or herself outside a residence like a thief in the night, threatening physical harm. This hardly seems an apt depiction of a solitary picket, especially at midafternoon, whose presence is objectionable because it is notorious. Contrary to the Court's declaration in this regard, it seems far more likely that a picketer who truly desires only to harass those inside a particular residence will find that goal unachievable in the face of a narrowly tailored ordinance substantially limiting, for example, the size, time, and volume of the protest. If, on the other hand, the picketer intends to communicate generally, a carefully crafted ordinance will allow him or her to do so without intruding upon or unduly harassing the resident. Consequently, the discomfort to which the Court must refer is merely that of knowing there is a person outside who disagrees with someone inside. This may indeed be uncomfortable, but it does not implicate the Town's interest in residential privacy and therefore does not warrant silencing speech." [e]

STEVENS, J., also dissented: " 'GET WELL CHARLIE—OUR TEAM NEEDS YOU.'

"In Brookfield, Wisconsin, it is unlawful for a fifth grader to carry such a sign in front of a residence for the period of time necessary to convey its friendly message to its intended audience. * * *

"My hunch is that the town will probably not enforce its ban against friendly, innocuous, or even brief unfriendly picketing, and that the Court may be right in concluding that its legitimate sweep makes its overbreadth insubstantial. But there are two countervailing considerations that are persuasive to me. The scope of the ordinance gives the town officials far too much discretion in making enforcement decisions; while we sit by and await further developments, potential picketers must act at their peril. Second, it is a simple matter for the town to amend its ordinance and to limit the ban to conduct that unreasonably interferes with the privacy of the home and does not serve a reasonable communicative purpose."

SECTION 7. GOVERNMENT SUPPORT OF SPEECH

Public forum doctrine recognizes that government is obligated to permit some of its property to be used for communicative purposes without content discrimination, but public forum doctrine also allows other government property to be restricted to some speakers or for talk about selected subjects. See *Greer*;

e. Like White, J., Brennan, J., was suspicious of the Court's single residence construction of the ordinance, but he accepted it for purposes of the dissent.

Perry. In short, in some circumstances government can provide resources for some speech while denying support for other speech. Indeed, government is a significant actor in the marketplace of ideas. Sometimes the government speaks as government; sometimes it subsidizes speech without purporting to claim that the resulting message is its own. It supports speech in many ways: official government messages; statements of public officials at publicly subsidized press conferences; artistic, scientific, or political subsidies, even the classroom communications of public school teachers.

If content distinctions are suspect when government acts as censor, they are the norm when government speaks or otherwise subsidizes speech. Government makes editorial judgments; it decides that some content is appropriate for the occasion and other content is not. The public museum curator makes content decisions in selecting exhibits; the librarian in selecting books; the public board in selecting recipients for research grants; the public official in composing press releases.

The line between support for speech and censorship of speech is not always bright, however. In any event, the Constitution limits the choices government may make in supporting speech. For example, government support of religious speech is limited under the establishment clause. See Ch. 9. This section explores the extent to which the speech clause or constitutional conceptions of equality should limit government discretion in supporting speech.

I. SUBSIDIES AND TAX EXPENDITURES

REGAN v. TAXATION WITH REPRESENTATION OF WASHINGTON

461 U.S. 540, 103 S.Ct. 1997, 76 L.Ed.2d 129 (1983).

JUSTICE REHNQUIST delivered the opinion of the Court.

[Section 501(c) of the Internal Revenue Code affords tax exempt status to various nonprofit organizations. Section 501(c)(19) affords a tax exemption to veterans' organizations. Moreover, contributions to veterans' organizations are treated by the IRS as deductible (up to 20% of adjusted gross income) even if the veterans organizations engage in substantial lobbying activity at state or federal levels. Section 501(c)(3) grants exempt status to various groups commonly called "charitable" organizations that are "organized and operated exclusively for religious, charitable, scientific [or] educational purposes * * * no substantial part of the activities of which is carrying on propaganda, or otherwise attempting to influence legislation [and] which does not participate in, or intervene in (including the publishing or distributing of statements), any political campaign on behalf of any candidate for public office." Section 501(c)(4) grants exempt status to groups organized for the purposes identified in 501(c)(3) (and for some other purposes) regardless of the amount of lobbying or political activity. Contributions made to groups meeting 501(c)(3) standards are deductible (up to 50% of adjusted gross income); contributions to 501(c)(4) groups are not deductible.

[Taxpayers for Representation of Washington ("TWR"), a group organized to represent the taxpayer's public interest in Washington was denied 501(c)(3) status because of its lobbying activities. It argued that affording tax deductible contributions to the substantial lobbying activities of veterans while denying such benefits to charitable organizations involved in similar activities was unconstitutional discrimination. The District of Columbia Court of Appeals agreed with TWR:[a] "If veterans' organizations and organizations such as Taxation lobby on different sides of the same questions, Congress has chosen to favor one lobbyist on a particular issue over another. If veterans' organizations and [charitable] organizations lobby on entirely distinct matters, Congress has ensured that greater attention will be devoted to some causes than others."

[It concluded that, "[A] First Amendment concern must inform the equal protection analysis in this case. Courts must scrutinize with special care any act of Congress that facilitates the speech of one speaker over another, even when legislation is enacted in the dry, classification-ridden context of the Internal Revenue Code. By subsidizing the lobbying activities of veterans' organizations while failing to subsidize the lobbying of [TWR] and other charitable groups, Congress has violated the equal protection guarantees of the Constitution. * * *

["The First Amendment occupies a preferred place in our scheme of government. This does not mean, however, that its application in a legal dispute is always simple. The lines will seem clearer when Congress directly prohibits a particular group from speaking in a particular place, and more confused when Congress subsidizes First Amendment expression unevenly through the intricacies of the Internal Revenue Code. Nevertheless, the principle remains the same."

[The Supreme Court reversed:] * * *

Both tax exemptions and tax-deductibility are a form of subsidy[b] that is administered through the tax system. A tax exemption has much the same effect as a cash grant to the organization of the amount of tax it would have to pay on its income. Deductible contributions are similar to cash grants of the amount of a portion of the individual's contributions.[5] The system Congress has enacted provides this kind of subsidy to non profit civic welfare organizations generally, and an additional subsidy to those charitable organizations that do not engage in substantial lobbying. In short, Congress chose not to subsidize lobbying as extensively as it chose to subsidize other activities that non profit organizations undertake to promote the public welfare.

It appears that TWR could still qualify for a tax exemption under § 501(c)(4). It also appears that TWR can obtain tax-deductible contributions for its nonlobbying activity by returning to the dual structure it used in the past, with a § 501(c)(3) organization for nonlobbying activities and a § 501(c)(4) organization for lobbying. TWR would, of course, have to ensure that the § 501(c)(3) organization did not subsidize the § 501(c)(4) organization; otherwise, public funds might be spent on an activity Congress chose not to subsidize.

TWR contends that Congress' decision not to subsidize its lobbying violates the First Amendment. It claims, relying on *Speiser v. Randall,* 357 U.S. 513, 78 S.Ct. 1332, 2 L.Ed.2d 1460 (1958), that the prohibition against substantial

a. *Taxation With Representation of Washington v. Regan,* 676 F.2d 715, (D.C.Cir.1982).

b. The IRS accepted "the analogy between tax exemptions and direct government subsidies" for purposes of the case (676 F.2d at 725 n. 19), but the question of what should be characterized as a subsidy is much debated in tax circles. Compare e.g., Bittker & Kaufman, *Taxes and Civil Rights: "Constitutionalizing" the Internal Revenue Code,* 82 Yale L.J. 51, 63–68 (1972) with Surrey & McDaniel, *The Tax Expenditure Concept and the Budget Reform Act of 1974,* 17 B.C. Indust. & Comm.L. Rev. 679 (1976).

5. In stating that exemptions and deductions, on one hand, are like cash subsidies, on the other, we of course do not mean to assert that they are in all respects identical. See, e.g., *Walz v. Tax Commission* [p. 846 infra].

lobbying by § 501(c)(3) organizations imposes an "unconstitutional condition" on the receipt of tax-deductible contributions. In *Speiser,* California established a rule requiring anyone who sought to take advantage of a property tax exemption to sign a declaration stating that he did not advocate the forcible overthrow of the Government of the United States. This Court stated that "[t]o deny an exemption to claimants who engage in certain forms of speech is in effect to penalize them for such speech."

TWR is certainly correct when it states that we have held that the government may not deny a benefit to a person because he exercises a constitutional right. See *Perry v. Sindermann,* p. 730 infra. But TWR is just as certainly incorrect when it claims that this case fits the *Speiser–Perry* model. The Code does not deny TWR the right to receive deductible contributions to support its nonlobbying activity, nor does it deny TWR any independent benefit on account of its intention to lobby. Congress has merely refused to pay for the lobbying out of public moneys. This Court has never held that Congress must grant a benefit such as TWR claims here to a person who wishes to exercise a constitutional right.

[The] case would be different if Congress were to discriminate invidiously in its subsidies in such a way as to " 'aim[ ] at the suppression of dangerous ideas.' " But the veterans' organizations that qualify under § 501(c)(19) are entitled to receive tax-deductible contributions regardless of the content of any speech they may use, including lobbying. We find no indication that the statute was intended to suppress any ideas or any demonstration that it has had that effect. The sections of the Internal Revenue Code here at issue do not employ any suspect classification. The distinction between veterans' organizations and other charitable organizations is not at all like distinctions based on race or national origin.

The Court of Appeals nonetheless held that "strict scrutiny" is required because the statute "*affect[s]* First Amendment rights on a discriminatory basis." Its opinion suggests that strict scrutiny applies whenever Congress subsidizes some speech, but not all speech. This is not the law. Congress could, for example, grant funds to an organization dedicated to combatting teenage drug abuse, but condition the grant by providing that none of the money received from Congress should be used to lobby state legislatures. [S]uch a statute would be valid. Congress might also enact a statute providing public money for an organization dedicated to combatting teenage alcohol abuse, and impose no condition against using funds obtained from Congress for lobbying. The existence of the second statute would not make the first statute subject to strict scrutiny. * * *

These are scarcely novel principles. We have held [that] a legislature's decision not to subsidize the exercise of a fundamental right does not infringe the right, and thus is not subject to strict scrutiny. *Buckley v. Valeo,* [p. 1048 infra] upheld a statute that provides federal funds for candidates for public office who enter primary campaigns, but does not provide funds for candidates who do not run in party primaries. We rejected First Amendment and equal protection challenges to this provision without applying strict scrutiny.[c]

c. In *Buckley,* Rehnquist, J., dissenting, complained that the scheme for public funding of Presidential candidates "enshrined the Republican and Democratic Parties in a permanently preferred position, and has established requirements for funding minor-party and independent candidates to which the two major parties are not subject. [B]ecause of the First Amendment overtones of the appellants' Fifth Amendment equal protection claim, something more than a merely rational basis for the difference in treatment must be

The reasoning [is] simple: "although government may not place obstacles in the path of a [person's] exercise [of] freedom of [speech], it need not remove those not of its own creation." * * * Congress—not TWR or this Court—has the authority to determine whether the advantage the public would receive from additional lobbying by charities is worth the money the public would pay to subsidize that lobbying, and other disadvantages that might accompany that lobbying. It appears that Congress was concerned that exempt organizations might use tax-deductible contributions to lobby to promote the private interests of their members.[d] It is not irrational for Congress to decide that tax exempt charities such as TWR should not further benefit at the expense of taxpayers at large by obtaining a further subsidy for lobbying.

It is also not irrational for Congress to decide that, even though it will not subsidize substantial lobbying by charities generally, it will subsidize lobbying by veterans' organizations. Veterans have "been obliged to drop their own affairs and take up the burdens of the nation," "subjecting themselves to the mental and physical hazards as well as the economic and family detriments which are peculiar to military service and which do not exist in normal civil life." Our country has a long standing policy of compensating veterans for their past contributions by providing them with numerous advantages.[e] This policy has "always been deemed to be legitimate."[f] * * *

Notes and Questions

1. Consider Sullivan, *Unconstitutional Conditions,* 102 Harv.L.Rev. 1413, 1436, 1441 (1989). "[T]he characterization of a condition as a 'penalty' or as a 'nonsubsidy' depends on the baseline from which one measures. [As] in the abortion funding cases, [none] of the *Taxation With Representation* opinions explained why the Court assumed a baseline of no subsidy for lobbying activities (in which case there is tautologically no penalty), rather than subsidy for all nonprofit activities (in which case the exclusion of the lobbying strand of those activities resembles a penalty). Nor did the opinions seriously discuss the potential deterrent effect on the lobbying activities of nonprofit organizations.

"In contrast to *Taxation With Representation,* the Court in *FCC v. League of Women Voters* invalidated a condition denying federal public broadcasting funds to stations that engage in editorializing. Treating this condition as flatly coercive, the majority repeatedly referred to it as a 'ban' or 'restriction' rather than an offer to the stations to choose between entirely private funding and a federal subsidy. Justice Rehnquist, in a biting dissent, depicted it as just such an offer. To the dissenters, 'Congress simply ha[d] decided not to subsidize stations which engage in [editorializing].' In light of such divisions, the Court's current penalty/nonsubsidy distinction seems no more helpful than its other attempts to use coercion as the ordering principle of

shown, as the Court apparently recognizes." *Buckley* found the funding scheme to be "in furtherance of *sufficiently important* government interests and has not unfairly or unnecessarily burdened the political opportunity of any party or candidate." (Emphasis added).

d. Does this concern apply equally to veterans' organizations? See Note, *Charitable Lobbying Restraints and Tax Exempt Organizations: Old Problems, New Directions?,* 1984 Utah L.Rev. 337, 357–59 (1984).

e. Is it a sufficient response to note that veterans can be rewarded in many ways that do not tread on first amendment equality values?

f. Blackmun, J., joined by Brennan and Marshall, JJ., joined the opinion, but concurred to emphasize the importance of the tax code being administered in a manner that did not discourage lobbying by TWR or other groups.

unconstitutional conditions doctrine." [g]

2. The Court observes that veterans' organizations receive tax benefits "regardless of the content of any speech they may use." Is this disingenuous because the content of veterans' organizations' speech is predictable? Could the Congress give money to Republican party organizations "regardless of the content of any speech they may use." What if Congress said it was benefiting veterans' organizations in part because Congress thought such organizations were delivering a message that deserved to be heard? Does it matter that favorable tax treatment assists veterans' lobbying at local, state, and federal levels? Could Congress withdraw favorable tax treatment from some veterans' organizations on the ground that their lobbying was not "worth the money"? Could Congress benefit charitable organizations, but not the veterans? Some charitable organizations, but not others? Could Congress give favorable tax treatment to lobbying of the Moral Majority, but no other group? [h]

3. Was TWR the wrong plaintiff? Was its claim weak because it failed to show viewpoint discrimination? Should a group whose primary purpose conflicts with that of veterans' groups be granted relief? See Note, *The Tax Code's Differential Treatment of Lobbying Under Section 501(c)(3): A Proposed First Amendment Analysis,* 66 Va.L.Rev. 1513 (1980).

4. If TWR had prevailed, what would have been the appropriate remedy? Denial of the veterans' benefit? Extension of the veterans' benefit to all charitable organizations?

5. Treasury regulations provide that a charitable organization whose primary purpose is education may retain its § 501(c)(3) status even if it advocates a particular position or viewpoint "so long as it presents a sufficiently full and fair exposition of the pertinent facts as to permit an individual or the public to form an independent opinion or conclusion." Treas.Reg. § 1.501(c)(3)–1(d)(3)(i) (1959). Should tax benefits depend upon IRS determinations of "fairness" and its identification of "pertinent" facts? Compare *Big Mama Rag, Inc. v. United States,* 631 F.2d 1030 (D.C.Cir.1980) with *National Alliance v. United States,* 710 F.2d 868 (D.C.Cir.1983).

6. Suppose that nothing in the tax law bars veterans' organizations from using tax deductible contributions for participation in political campaigns on behalf of candidates for public office. Is this more troublesome than the lobbying benefits? Suppose instead of supporting the political speech of others, government itself enters the political fray. Should a city government be able to buy media time to speak on behalf of candidates? To influence the outcome of initiative campaigns? [i]

---

g. On the penalty/subsidy distinction, see Tribe, *American Constitutional Law* 781–84 (2d ed. 1988); Kreimer, *Allocational Sanctions: The Problem of Negative Rights in a Positive State,* 132 U.Pa.L.Rev. 1293, 1351–78 (1984); McConnell, *Unconstitutional Conditions: Unrecognized Implications for the Establishment Clause,* 26 San Diego L.Rev. 255, 261–63 (1989); Sullivan, *Unconstitutional Conditions and the Distribution of Liberty,* 26 San Diego L.Rev. 367 (1989). See also Seidman, *Reflections on Context and the Constitution,* 73 Minn.L.Rev. 73 (1988).

h. For general criticism of the tax code's treatment of charitable organizations, see Clark, *The Limitation on Political Activities: A Discordant Note in the Law of Charities,* 46 Va.L.Rev. 439 (1960); Garrett, *Federal Tax Limitations on Political Activities of Public Interest and Educational Organizations,* 59 Geo.L.J. 561 (1971); Troyer, *Charities, Law-Making, and the Constitution: The Validity of the Restrictions on Influencing Legislation,* 31 N.Y.U.Inst. on Fed. Tax'n 1415 (1973).

i. For relevant commentary, see Yudof, *When Government Speaks: Politics, Law, and Government Expression in America* (1983);

ARKANSAS WRITERS' PROJECT, INC. v. RAGLAND, 481 U.S. 221, 107 S.Ct. 1722, 95 L.Ed.2d 209 (1987), per MARSHALL, J., held that "a state sales tax scheme that taxes general interest magazines, but exempts newspaper and religious, professional, trade, and sports journals violates the First Amendment's guarantee of freedom of the press": "Our cases clearly establish that a discriminatory tax on the press burdens rights protected by the First Amendment.[3] See *Minneapolis Star & Tribune v. Minnesota Commissioner of Revenue* [p. 550 supra]; *Grosjean v. American Press Co.* [297 U.S. 233, 56 S.Ct. 444, 80 L.Ed. 660 (1936)]. In *Minneapolis Star,* the discrimination took two distinct forms. First, in contrast to generally applicable economic regulations to which the press can legitimately be subject, the Minnesota use tax treated the press differently from other enterprises. Second, the tax targeted a small group of newspapers. This was due to the fact that the first $100,000 of paper and ink were exempt from the tax; thus 'only a handful of publishers pay any tax at all, and even fewer pay any significant amount of tax.'

"Both types of discrimination can be established even where, as here, there is no evidence of an improper censorial motive. [On] the facts of this case, the fundamental question is not whether the tax singles out the press as a whole,[a] but whether it targets a small group within the press. While we indicated in *Minneapolis Star* that a genuinely nondiscriminatory tax on the receipts of newspapers would be constitutionally permissible, the Arkansas sales tax cannot be characterized as nondiscriminatory, because it is not evenly applied to all magazines. [Because] the Arkansas sales tax scheme treats some magazines less favorably than others, it suffers from the second type of discrimination identified in *Minneapolis Star.*

"Indeed, this case involves a more disturbing use of selective taxation than *Minneapolis Star,* because the basis on which Arkansas differentiates between magazines is particularly repugnant to First Amendment principles: a magazine's tax status depends entirely on its *content.* [If] articles in *Arkansas Times* were uniformly devoted to religion or sports, the magazine would be exempt from the sales tax. [In] order to determine whether a magazine is subject to sales tax, Arkansas' 'enforcement authorities must necessarily examine the content of the message that is conveyed * * *.' *FCC v. League of Women Voters of California.* Such official scrutiny of the content of publications as the basis for imposing a tax is entirely incompatible with the First Amendment's guarantee of freedom of the press. * * *

Delgado, *The Language of the Arms Race,* 64 B.U.L.Rev. 961 (1984); Emerson, *The Affirmative Side of the First Amendment,* 15 Ga.L. Rev. 795 (1981); Kamenshine, *The First Amendment's Implied Political Establishment Clause,* 67 Calif.L.Rev. 1104 (1979); Shiffrin; *Government Speech,* 27 U.C.L.A.L.Rev. 565 (1980); Schauer, *Book Review,* 35 Stan.L.Rev. 373 (1983); Yudof, *When Governments Speak: Toward A Theory of Government Expression and the First Amendment,* 57 Tex.L.Rev. 863 (1979); Ziegler, *Government Speech and the Constitution: The Limits of Official Partisanship,* 21 B.C.L.Rev. 578 (1980); Note, *The Constitutionality of Municipal Advocacy in Statewide Referendum Campaigns,* 93 Harv.L.Rev. 535 (1980).

3. Appellant's First Amendment claims are obviously intertwined with interests arising under the Equal Protection Clause. See *Mosley.* However, since Arkansas' sales-tax system directly implicates freedom of the press, we analyze it primarily in First Amendment terms. See *Minneapolis Star.*

a. Consider Barron, Book Review, 54 G.W. U.L.Rev. 434, 448 (1986): "The Newspaper Preservation Act is specific federal legislation directed to the press [15 U.S.C.A. § 1801–04 (1982)]. It conveys to the press a benefit [—] immunity from the antitrust laws if competing newspapers pool or share advertising and printing resources [in cases of economic distress]. Should we conclude that special benefits can be extended to the press but that special burdens cannot be imposed on them? [*Minneapolis Star*] appears to reject that distinction. But [the] opinion does not cite the Newspaper Preservation Act."

"The Commissioner [suggests] that the exemption of religious, professional, trade and sports journals was intended to encourage 'fledgling' publishers, who have only limited audiences and therefore do not have access to the same volume of advertising revenues as general interest magazines such as *Arkansas Times.* Even assuming that an interest in encouraging fledgling publications might be a compelling one, we do not find the [exemption] narrowly tailored to achieve that end. To the contrary, the exemption is both overinclusive and underinclusive. The types of magazines enumerated [are] exempt, regardless of whether they are 'fledgling;' even the most lucrative and well-established religious, professional, trade and sports journals do not pay sales tax. By contrast, struggling general interest magazines and struggling specialty magazines on subjects other than those specified [are] ineligible for favorable tax treatment.

"[Because] we hold today that the State's selective application of its sales tax to magazines is unconstitutional and therefore invalid, our ruling eliminates the differential treatment of newspapers and magazines. Accordingly, we need not decide whether a distinction between different types of periodicals presents an additional basis for invalidating the sales tax, as applied to the press." [b]

SCALIA, J., joined by Rehnquist, C.J., dissented: * * *

"The reason that denial of participation in a tax exemption or other subsidy scheme does not necessarily 'infringe' a fundamental right is that—unlike direct restriction or prohibition—such a denial does not, as a general rule, have any significant coercive effect. It may, of course, be manipulated so as to do so, in which case the courts will be available to provide relief. But that is not remotely the case here. It is implausible that the 4% sales tax, generally applicable to all sales in the State with the few enumerated exceptions, was meant to inhibit, or had the effect of inhibiting, this appellant's publication.

"Perhaps a more stringent, prophylactic rule is appropriate, and can consistently be applied, when the subsidy pertains to the expression of a particular viewpoint on a matter of political concern—a tax exemption, for example, that is expressly available only to publications that take a particular point of view on a controversial issue of foreign policy. [There] is no need, however, and it is realistically quite impossible, to extend to all speech the same degree of protection against exclusion from a subsidy that one might think appropriate for opposing shades of political expression.

"By seeking to do so, the majority casts doubt upon a wide variety of tax preferences and subsidies that draw distinctions based upon subject-matter. The U.S. Postal Service, for example, grants a special bulk rate to written material disseminated by certain nonprofit organizations—religious, educational, scientific, philanthropic, agricultural, labor, veterans', and fraternal organizations. See Domestic Mail Manual § 623 (1985). Must this preference be justified by a 'compelling governmental need' because a nonprofit organization devoted to some other purpose—dissemination of information about boxing, for example—does not receive the special rate? The Kennedy Center, which is subsidized by the Federal Government in the amount of up to $23 million per year, see 20 U.S.C. § 76n(a), is authorized by statute to 'present classical and contemporary music, opera, drama, dance, and poetry.' § 76j. Is this subsidy subject to strict scrutiny because other kinds of expressive activity, such as learned lectures and political speeches, are excluded? Are government research grant programs or the funding activities of the Corporation for Public Broadcasting, see 47 U.S.C.

b. Stevens, J., concurred in part and concurred in the judgment.

§ 396(g)(2), subject to strict scrutiny because they provide money for the study or exposition of some subjects but not others?

"Because there is no principled basis to distinguish the subsidization of speech in these areas—which we would surely uphold—from the subsidization that we strike down here, our decision today places the granting or denial of protection within our own idiosyncratic discretion. In my view, that threatens First Amendment rights infinitely more than the tax exemption at issue." [c]

Notes and Questions

1. Is the Court's dictum approving a non-discriminatory tax on the receipts of newspapers unproblematic? *GROSJEAN v. AMERICAN PRESS CO.*, p. 670 supra, per SUTHERLAND, J., invalidated a 2% gross receipts tax on any publication that included paid advertisements and that circulated more than 20,000 copies per week. The Court invoked a long history of opposition to "taxes on knowledge," observing that "the revolution really began when, in 1765, [England] sent stamps for newspaper duties to the American colonies." [d] The Court denied that owners of newspapers were entitled to be immune from any of the "ordinary forms of taxation" but did not specify what "ordinary" might include. The tax at issue, however, was not "an ordinary form of tax, but one single in kind, with a long history of hostile misuse against the freedom of press." Since the adoption of the Constitution, however, the Court's research unearthed no instance of a state imposing any tax "like the one in question."

In addition, the Court found the form of the tax (tied to the amount of circulation) suspicious enough to conclude that it was enacted with the purpose of penalizing a selected group of newspapers.

Should a sales tax applied to all commodities including newspapers be upheld as an "ordinary form" of taxation or should it be struck down as a "tax on knowledge"?

2. Assuming taxes on the press are not uniquely unconstitutional, should a special tax on the press be acceptable when it *favors* the press and does not discriminate among members of the press? *Minneapolis Star,* [p. 550 supra], expressed reluctance to approve any such scheme because "special treatment threatens the press not only with the current *differential* treatment, but also with the possibility of subsequent differentially more *burdensome* treatment." Consider Bezanson, *Political Agnosticism, Editorial Freedom, and Government Neutrality Toward the Press,* 72 Iowa L.Rev. 1359, 1373–74 (1987): "If a different form [of taxation] was not necessary, its use would present the risk, if not the likelihood, that the affected [news]papers would have to direct their energies to their political self-interest. They could not seek shelter against political change in the broader majoritarian process. * * * [A] differential tax on the press, although broadly applied to all elements of the press, may at some level pose a risk of financial dependence of the press on government, just as the English [taxes] in the eighteenth century were calculated to ensure obedience of the press through subsidy, special privileges, and bribes."

c. For a response to Scalia, J., see Sobel, *First Amendment Standards for Government Subsidies of Artistic and Cultural Expression,* 41 Vand.L.Rev. 517 (1988).

d. As Professor Tribe observes, times change: "[W]hile the Framers fought a war precipitated in part by the Stamp Act, today's telephone bills are subject to a special federal tax." Tribe, *American Constitutional Law* 1004 (2d ed. 1988).

3. Is *Ragland* consistent with *TRW?* See Epstein, *Foreward, Unconstitutional Conditions, State Power, and the Limits of Consent,* 102 Harv.L.Rev. 4, 76–79 (1988). For a variety of views bearing on the general problem of subsidies, see Tribe, *American Constitutional Law* 781–84 (2nd ed., 1988); Epstein, supra; Kreimer, *Allocational Sanctions: The Problem of Negative Rights in a Positive State,* 132 U.Pa.L.Rev. 1293 (1984); Shiffrin, *Government Speech,* 27 UCLA L.Rev. 565 (1980); Sullivan, supra.

II. GOVERNMENT AS EDUCATOR AND EDITOR

TINKER v. DES MOINES SCHOOL DISTRICT

393 U.S. 503, 89 S.Ct. 733, 21 L.Ed.2d 731 (1969).

JUSTICE FORTAS delivered the opinion of the Court.

[Petitioners, two high school students and one junior high student, wore black armbands to school to publicize their objections to the Vietnam conflict and their advocacy of a truce. They refused to remove the armbands when asked to do so. In accordance with a ban on armbands which the city's school principals had adopted two days before in anticipation of such a protest, petitioners were sent home and suspended from school until they would return without the armbands. They sought a federal injunction restraining school officials from disciplining them, but the lower federal courts upheld the constitutionality of the school authorities' action on the ground that it was reasonable in order to prevent a disturbance which might result from the wearing of the armbands.]

[T]he wearing of armbands in the circumstances of this case was entirely divorced from actually or potentially disruptive conduct by those participating in it. It was closely akin to "pure speech" which, we have repeatedly held, is entitled to comprehensive protection under the First Amendment. * * *

First Amendment rights, applied in light of the special characteristics of the school environment, are available to teachers and students. It can hardly be argued that either students or teachers shed their constitutional rights to freedom of speech or expression at the schoolhouse gate. This has been the unmistakable holding of this Court for almost 50 years. In *Meyer v. Nebraska* [1923] [discussed in *Griswold v. Connecticut,* p. 143 supra], this Court [held that fourteenth amendment due process] prevents States from forbidding the teaching of a foreign language to young students. Statutes to this effect, the Court held, unconstitutionally interfere with the liberty of teacher, student, and parent. * * *

The problem presented by the present case does not relate to regulation of the length of skirts or the type of clothing, to hair style or deportment. [It] does not concern aggressive, disruptive action or even group demonstrations. Our problem involves direct, primary First Amendment rights akin to "pure speech."

The school officials banned and sought to punish petitioners for a silent, passive, expression of opinion, unaccompanied by any disorder or disturbance on the part of petitioners. There is here no evidence whatever of petitioners' interference, actual or nascent, with the school's work or of collision with the rights of other students to be secure and to be let alone. Accordingly, this case does not concern speech or action that intrudes upon the work of the school or the rights of other students.

Only a few of the 18,000 students in the school system wore the black armbands. Only five students were suspended for wearing them. There is no indication that the work of the school or any class was disrupted. Outside the classrooms, a few students made hostile remarks to the children wearing armbands, but there were no threats or acts of violence on school premises.

[I]n our system, undifferentiated fear or apprehension of disturbance [the District Court's basis for sustaining the school authorities' action] is not enough to overcome the right to freedom of expression. Any departure from absolute regimentation may cause trouble. Any variation from the majority's opinion may inspire fear. Any words spoken, in class, in the lunchroom or on the campus, that deviates from the views of another person, may start an argument or cause a disturbance. But our Constitution says we must take this risk [and] our history says that it is this sort of hazardous freedom—this kind of openness—that is the basis of our national strength and of the independence and vigor of Americans who grow up and live in this relatively permissive, often disputatious society.

In order for the State in the person of school officials to justify prohibition of a particular expression of opinion, it must be able to show that its action was caused by something more than a mere desire to avoid the discomfort and unpleasantness that always accompany an unpopular viewpoint. Certainly where there is no finding and no showing that the exercise of the forbidden right would "materially and substantially interfere with the requirements of appropriate discipline in the operation of the school," the prohibition cannot be sustained.

In the present case, the District Court made no such finding, and our independent examination of the record fails to yield evidence that the school authorities had reason to anticipate that the wearing of the armbands would substantially interfere with the work of the school or impinge upon the rights of other students. Even an official memorandum prepared after the suspension that listed the reasons for the ban on wearing the armbands made no reference to the anticipation of such disruption.[3]

On the contrary, the action of the school authorities appears to have been based upon an urgent wish to avoid the controversy which might result from the expression, even by the silent symbol of armbands, of opposition to this Nation's part in the conflagration in Vietnam. * * *

It is also relevant that the school authorities did not purport to prohibit the wearing of all symbols of political or controversial significance. The record shows that students in some of the schools wore buttons relating to national political campaigns, and some even wore the Iron Cross, traditionally a symbol of nazism. The order prohibiting the wearing of armbands did not extend to these. Instead, a particular symbol—black armbands worn to exhibit opposition to this Nation's involvement in Vietnam—was singled out for prohibition. Clearly, the

3. The only suggestions of fear of disorder in the report are these: "A former student of one of our high schools was killed in Viet Nam. Some of his friends are still in school and it was felt that if any kind of a demonstration existed, it might evolve into something which would be difficult to control.

"Students at one of the high schools were heard to say they would wear arm bands of other colors if the black bands prevailed."

Moreover, the testimony of school authorities at trial indicates that it was not fear of disruption that motivated the regulation prohibiting the armbands; the regulation was directed against "the principle of the demonstration" itself. School authorities simply felt that "the schools are no place for demonstrations," and if the students "didn't like the way our elected officials were handling things, it should be handled with the ballot box and not in the halls of our public schools."

prohibition of expression of one particular opinion, at least without evidence that it is necessary to avoid material and substantial interference with school work or discipline, is not constitutionally permissible.[a]

In our system, state-operated schools may not be enclaves of totalitarianism. School officials do not possess absolute authority over their students. Students in school as well as out of school are "persons" under our Constitution. They are possessed of fundamental rights which the State must respect, just as they themselves must respect their obligations to the State. In our system, students may not be regarded as closed-circuit recipients of only that which the State chooses to communicate. They may not be confined to the expression of those sentiments that are officially approved. In the absence of a specific showing of constitutionally valid reasons to regulate their speech, students are entitled to freedom of expression of their views.

[The principle of prior cases underscoring the importance of diversity and exchange of ideas in the schools,] is not confined to the supervised and ordained discussion which takes place in the classroom. The principal use to which the schools are dedicated is to accommodate students during prescribed hours for the purpose of certain types of activities. Among those activities is personal intercommunication among the students.[6] This is not only an inevitable part of the process of attending school. It is also an important part of the educational process.

A student's rights therefore, do not embrace merely the classroom hours. When he is in the cafeteria, or on the playing field, or on the campus during the authorized hours, he may express his opinions, even on controversial subjects like the conflict in Vietnam, if he does so "[without] materially and substantially interfering [with] appropriate discipline in the operation of the school" and without colliding with the rights of others. *Burnside.* But conduct by the student, in class or out of it, which for any reason—whether it stems from time, place, or type of behavior—materially disrupts classwork or involves substantial disorder or invasion of the rights of others is, of course, not immunized by the [first amendment].

We properly read [the first amendment] to permit reasonable regulation of speech-connected activities in carefully restricted circumstances. But we do not

a. Cf. *Guzick v. Drebus,* 305 F.Supp. 472 (N.D.Ohio 1969), upholding "a long-standing and consistently-applied rule prohibiting the wearing of buttons and other insignia on school grounds during school hours unless these are related to a school-sponsored activity" as "reasonably related to the prevention of the distractions and disruptive and violent conduct" at a racially tense high school; although the button in the instant case did not convey an inflammatory message, the blanket prohibition avoids a situation "in which inflammatory and often insulting buttons would be worn"; a policy permitting certain buttons and excluding others would be "unworkable" in the context of the particular school and "would very likely lead to disruption itself"; a selective policy could not "practically be enforced, for it would require the school authorities to patrol the halls and classes in search of offending buttons"; moreover, such a policy would "necessarily involve the school administration in the controversies" at the school, destroy its "image of complete neutrality," "undermine the structure of discipline" and "materially and substantially affect the educational process"; and any attempt to enforce such a selective policy "would likely entangle the school authorities in the First Amendment prohibition against prior restraints on free speech."

6. In *Hammond v. South Carolina State College,* 272 F.Supp. 947 (D.C.D.S.C.1967). District Judge Hemphill had before him a case involving a meeting on campus of 300 students to express their views on school practices. He pointed out that a school is not like a hospital or a jail enclosure. It is a public place and its dedication to specific uses does not imply that the constitutional rights of persons entitled to be there are to be gauged as if the premises were purely private property.

confine the permissible exercise of First Amendment rights to a telephone booth or the four corners of a pamphlet, or to supervised and ordained discussion in a school classroom.[b] * * * Reversed and remanded.

JUSTICE STEWART, concurring.[c]

Although I agree with much of what is said in the Court's opinion, and with its judgment in this case, I cannot share the Court's uncritical assumption that, school discipline aside, the First Amendment rights of children are co-extensive with those of adults. Indeed, I had thought the Court decided otherwise just last Term in *Ginsberg v. New York* [p. 474 supra.] I continue to hold the view I expressed in that case: "[A] State may permissibly determine that, at least in some precisely delineated areas, a child—like someone in a captive audience—is not possessed of that full capacity for individual choice which is the presupposition of First Amendment guarantees." (concurring opinion). * * *

JUSTICE BLACK, dissenting. * * *

Assuming that the Court is correct in holding that the conduct of wearing armbands for the purpose of conveying political ideas is protected by the First Amendment [the] crucial remaining questions are whether students and teachers may use the schools at their whim as a platform for the exercise of free speech—"symbolic" or "pure"—and whether the Courts will allocate to themselves the function of deciding how the pupils' school day will be spent. * * *

While the record does not show that any of these armband students shouted, used profane language, or were violent in any manner, detailed testimony by some of them shows their armbands caused comments, warnings by other students, the poking of fun at them, and a warning by an older football player that other, nonprotesting students had better let them alone. There is also evidence that the professor of mathematics had his lesson period practically "wrecked" chiefly by disputes with Beth Tinker, who wore her armband for her "demonstration." Even a casual reading of the record shows that this armband did divert students' minds from their regular lessons, and that talk, comments, etc., made John Tinker "self-conscious" in attending school with his armband. While the absence of obscene or boisterous and loud disorder perhaps justifies the Court's statement that the few armband students did not actually "disrupt" the classwork, I think the record overwhelmingly shows that the armbands did exactly what the elected school officials and principals foresaw it would, that is, took the students' minds off their classwork and diverted them to thoughts about the highly emotional subject of the Vietnam war.

[E]ven if the record were silent as to protests against the Vietnam war distracting students from their assigned class work, members of this Court, like all other citizens, know, without being told, that the disputes over the wisdom of the Vietnam war have disrupted and divided this country as few other issues ever have. Of course students, like other people, cannot concentrate on lesser issues when black armbands are being ostentatiously displayed in their presence to call attention to the wounded and dead of the war, some of the wounded and the dead being their friends and neighbors. It was, of course, to distract the attention of other students that some students insisted up to the very point of their own suspension from school that they were determined to sit in school with their symbolic armbands. * * *

b. See also Yudof, *When Governments Speak: Toward a Theory of Government Expression and the First Amendment,* 57 Tex.L. Rev. 863, 884–85 (1979).

c. White, J., also briefly concurred.

JUSTICE HARLAN, dissenting.

I certainly agree that state public school authorities in the discharge of their responsibilities are not wholly exempt from the requirements of the Fourteenth Amendment respecting the freedoms of expression and association. At the same time I am reluctant to believe that there is any disagreement between the majority and myself on the proposition that school officials should be accorded the widest authority in maintaining discipline and good order in their institutions. To translate that proposition into a workable constitutional rule, I would, in cases like this, cast upon those complaining the burden of showing that a particular school measure was motivated by other than legitimate school concerns—for example, a desire to prohibit the expression of an unpopular point of view, while permitting expression of the dominant opinion.

Finding nothing in this record which impugns the good faith of respondents in promulgating the arm band regulation, I would affirm the judgment below.

Notes and Questions

1. Should the government's interest in education trump the school child's interest in speaking in the classroom? Are the two interests compatible in this case? May students be prohibited from voicing their opinions of the Vietnam War in the middle of a math class? If so, why can't they be prevented from expressing their views on the same issue in the same class by means of "symbolic speech"? Cf. Nahmod, *Beyond Tinker: The High School as an Educational Public Forum,* 5 Harv.Civ.Rts. & Civ.Lib.L.Rev. 278 (1970).

2. Could school authorities adopt a regulation forbidding *teachers* to wear black armbands in the classroom? Or prohibiting teachers from wearing *all* symbols of political or controversial significance in the classroom or anywhere on school property? Are students a "captive" group? Do the views of a teacher occupying a position of authority carry much more influence with a student than would those of students inter sese? Consider *James v. Board of Educ.,* 461 F.2d 566 (2d Cir.1972), holding that school officials violated a high school teacher's constitutional rights by discharging him because he had worn a black armband in class in symbolic protest of the Vietnam War. But the court stressed that "the armband did not disrupt classroom activities [nor] have any influence on any students and did not engender protest from any student, teacher or parent." What if it had? By implication, did the court confirm the potency of the "heckler's veto"? See Note, 39 Brook.L.Rev. 918 (1973). Same result if appellant had been a 3rd grade teacher rather than an 11th grade teacher? See Shiffrin, *Government Speech,* 27 U.C.L.A.L.Rev. 565, 647–53 (1980).

HAZELWOOD SCHOOL DISTRICT v. KUHLMEIER

484 U.S. 260, 108 S.Ct. 562, 98 L.Ed.2d 592 (1988).

JUSTICE WHITE delivered the opinion of the Court.

This case concerns the extent to which educators may exercise editorial control over the contents of a high school newspaper produced as part of the school's journalism curriculum.

I

Petitioners are the Hazelwood School District in St. Louis County, Missouri; various school officials; Robert Eugene Reynolds, the principal of Hazelwood East High School, and Howard Emerson, a teacher in the school district.

Respondents are three former Hazelwood East students who were staff members of Spectrum, the school newspaper. They contend that school officials violated their First Amendment rights by deleting two pages of articles from the May 13, 1983, issue of Spectrum.

Spectrum was written and edited by the Journalism II class at Hazelwood East. The newspaper was published every three weeks or so during the 1982–1983 school year. More than 4,500 copies of the newspaper were distributed during that year to students, school personnel, and members of the community.

The Board of Education allocated funds from its annual budget for the printing of Spectrum. [The] Journalism II course was taught by Robert Stergos for most of the 1982–1983 academic year. Stergos left Hazelwood East to take a job in private industry on April 29, 1983, when the May 13 edition of Spectrum was nearing completion, and petitioner Emerson took his place as newspaper adviser for the remaining weeks of the term.

The practice at Hazelwood East during the spring 1983 semester was for the journalism teacher to submit page proofs of each Spectrum issue to Principal Reynolds for his review prior to publication. On May 10, Emerson delivered the proofs of the May 13 edition to Reynolds, who objected to two of the articles scheduled to appear in that edition. One of the stories described three Hazelwood East students' experiences with pregnancy; the other discussed the impact of divorce on students at the school.

Reynolds was concerned that, although the pregnancy story used false names "to keep the identity of these girls a secret," the pregnant students still might be identifiable from the text. He also believed that the article's references to sexual activity and birth control were inappropriate for some of the younger students at the school. In addition, Reynolds was concerned that a student identified by name in the divorce story had complained that her father "wasn't spending enough time with my mom, my sister and I" prior to the divorce, "was always out of town on business or out late playing cards with the guys," and "always argued about everything" with her mother. Reynolds believed that the student's parents should have been given an opportunity to respond to these remarks or to consent to their publication. He was unaware that Emerson had deleted the student's name from the final version of the article.

Reynolds believed that there was no time to make the necessary changes in the stories before the scheduled press run and that the newspaper would not appear before the end of the school year if printing were delayed to any significant extent. He concluded that his only options under the circumstances were to publish a four-page newspaper instead of the planned six-page newspaper, eliminating the two pages on which the offending stories appeared, or to publish no newspaper at all. Accordingly, he directed Emerson to withhold from publication the two pages containing the stories on pregnancy and divorce.[1] He informed his superiors of the decision, and they concurred. * * *

II

Students in the public schools do not "shed their constitutional rights to freedom of speech or expression at the schoolhouse gate." *Tinker.* They cannot

1. The two pages deleted from the newspaper also contained articles on teenage marriage, runaways, and juvenile delinquents, as well as a general article on teenage pregnancy. Reynolds testified that he had no objection to these articles and that they were deleted only because they appeared on the same pages as the two objectionable articles.

be punished merely for expressing their personal views on the school premises—whether "in the cafeteria, or on the playing field, or on the campus during the authorized hours"—unless school authorities have reason to believe that such expression will "substantially interfere with the work of the school or impinge upon the rights of other students." *Tinker.*

We have nonetheless recognized that the First Amendment rights of students in the public schools "are not automatically coextensive with the rights of adults in other settings," *Bethel School District No. 403 v. Fraser,* 478 U.S. 675, 106 S.Ct. 3159, 92 L.Ed.2d 549 (1986), and must be "applied in light of the special characteristics of the school environment." *Tinker.* A school need not tolerate student speech that is inconsistent with its "basic educational mission," *Fraser,* even though the government could not censor similar speech outside the school. Accordingly, we held in *Fraser* that a student could be disciplined for having delivered a speech that was "sexually explicit" but not legally obscene at an official school assembly, because the school was entitled to "disassociate itself" from the speech in a manner that would demonstrate to others that such vulgarity is "wholly inconsistent with the 'fundamental values' of public school education." We thus recognized that "[t]he determination of what manner of speech in the classroom or in school assembly is inappropriate properly rests with the school board," rather than with the federal courts. It is in this context that respondents' First Amendment claims must be considered.

A

We deal first with the question whether Spectrum may appropriately be characterized as a forum for public expression. * * * [T]he evidence relied upon by the Court of Appeals fails to demonstrate the "clear intent to create a public forum," *Cornelius,* that existed in cases in which we found public forums to have been created. School [officials] "reserve[d] the forum for its intended purpos[e]," *Perry,* as a supervised learning experience for journalism students. Accordingly, school officials were entitled to regulate the contents of Spectrum in any reasonable manner. It is this standard, rather than our decision in *Tinker,* that governs this case.

B

The question whether the First Amendment requires a school to tolerate particular student speech—the question that we addressed in *Tinker*—is different from the question whether the First Amendment requires a school affirmatively to promote particular student speech. The former question addresses educators' ability to silence a student's personal expression that happens to occur on the school premises. The latter question concerns educators' authority over school-sponsored publications, theatrical productions, and other expressive activities that students, parents, and members of the public might reasonably perceive to bear the imprimatur of the school. These activities may fairly be characterized as part of the school curriculum, whether or not they occur in a traditional classroom setting, so long as they are supervised by faculty members and designed to impart particular knowledge or skills to student participants and audiences.

[A] school may in its capacity as publisher of a school newspaper or producer of a school play "disassociate itself," *Fraser,* not only from speech that would "substantially interfere with [its] work * * * or impinge upon the rights of other students," *Tinker,* but also from speech that is, for example, ungrammatical, poorly written, inadequately researched, biased or prejudiced, vulgar or profane, or unsuitable for immature audiences.[4] A school must be able to set high standards for the student speech that is disseminated under its auspices—standards that may be higher than those demanded by some newspaper publishers or theatrical producers in the "real" world—and may refuse to disseminate student speech that does not meet those standards. [Otherwise,] the schools would be unduly constrained from fulfilling their role as "a principal instrument in awakening the child to cultural values, in preparing him for later professional training, and in helping him to adjust normally to his environment." *Brown v. Board of Education.*

Accordingly, we conclude that the standard articulated in *Tinker* for determining when a school may punish student expression need not also be the standard for determining when a school may refuse to lend its name and resources to the dissemination of student expression. Instead, we hold that educators do not offend the First Amendment by exercising editorial control over the style and content of student speech in school-sponsored expressive activities so long as their actions are reasonably related to legitimate pedagogical concerns.[7] * * *[a]

JUSTICE BRENNAN, with whom JUSTICE MARSHALL and JUSTICE BLACKMUN join, dissenting. * * *

The Court is certainly correct that the First Amendment permits educators "to assure that participants learn whatever lessons the activity is designed to teach. * * *" That is, however, the essence of the *Tinker* test, not an excuse to abandon it. Under *Tinker,* school officials may censor only such student speech as would "materially disrup[t]" a legitimate curricular function. Manifestly, student speech is more likely to disrupt a curricular function when it arises in the context of a curricular activity—one that "is designed to teach" something—than when it arises in the context of a noncurricular activity. Thus, under *Tinker,* the school may constitutionally punish the budding political orator if he disrupts calculus class but not if he holds his tongue for the cafeteria. That is not because some more stringent standard applies in the curricular context. (After all, this Court applied the same standard whether the Tinkers wore their armbands to the "classroom" or the "cafeteria.") It is because student speech in the noncurricular context is less likely to disrupt materially any legitimate pedagogical purpose.

4. The dissent perceives no difference between the First Amendment analysis applied in *Tinker* and that applied in *Fraser.* We disagree. The decision in *Fraser* rested on the "vulgar," "lewd," and "plainly offensive" character of a speech delivered at an official school assembly rather than on any propensity of the speech to "materially disrupt[ ] classwork or involve[ ] substantial disorder or invasion of the rights of others." Indeed, the *Fraser* Court cited as "especially relevant" a portion of Justice Black's dissenting opinion in *Tinker* "disclaim[ing] any purpose * * * to hold that the Federal Constitution compels the teachers, parents and elected school officials to surrender control of the American public school system to public school students." Of course, Justice Black's observations are equally relevant to the instant case.

7. A number of lower federal courts have similarly recognized that educators' decisions with regard to the content of school sponsored newspapers, dramatic productions, and other expressive activities are entitled to substantial deference. We need not now decide whether the same degree of deference is appropriate with respect to school-sponsored expressive activities at the college and university level.

a. White, J., concluded that Principal Reynolds acted reasonably in requiring deletion of the pages from the newspaper. In addition to concerns about privacy and failure to contact persons discussed in the stories, White, J., found that it was "not unreasonable for the principal to have concluded that [frank talk about sexual histories, albeit not graphic, with comments about use or nonuse of birth control] was inappropriate in a school-sponsored publication distributed to 14-year-old freshmen and presumably taken home to be read by students' even younger brothers and sisters."

I fully agree with the Court that the First Amendment should afford an educator the prerogative not to sponsor the publication of a newspaper article that is "ungrammatical, poorly written, inadequately researched, biased or prejudiced," or that falls short of the "high standards [for] student speech that is disseminated under [the school's] auspices * * *." But we need not abandon *Tinker* to reach that conclusion; we need only apply it. The enumerated criteria reflect the skills that the curricular newspaper "is designed to teach." The educator may, under *Tinker*, constitutionally "censor" poor grammar, writing, or research because to reward such expression would "materially disrup[t]" the newspaper's curricular purpose. * * *

The Court relies on bits of testimony to portray the principal's conduct as a pedagogical lesson to Journalism II students who "had not sufficiently mastered those portions of [the] curriculum that pertained to the treatment of controversial issues and personal attacks, the need to protect the privacy of individuals [and] 'the legal, moral, and ethical restrictions imposed upon journalists * * *.'" In that regard, the Court attempts to justify censorship of the article on teenage pregnancy on the basis of the principal's judgment that (1) "the [pregnant] students' anonymity was not adequately protected," despite the article's use of aliases; and (2) the judgment "that the article was not sufficiently sensitive to the privacy interests of the students' boyfriends and parents * * *." Similarly, the Court finds in the principal's decision to censor the divorce article a journalistic lesson that the author should have given the father of one student an "opportunity to defend himself" against her charge that (in the Court's words) he "chose 'playing cards with the guys' over home and family * * *."

But the principal never consulted the students before censoring their work. [T]hey learned of the deletions when the paper was released. [Further,] he explained the deletions only in the broadest of generalities. In one meeting called at the behest of seven protesting Spectrum staff members (presumably a fraction of the full class), he characterized the articles as " 'too sensitive' for 'our immature audience of readers,' " and in a later meeting he deemed them simply "inappropriate, personal, sensitive and unsuitable for the newspaper." The Court's supposition that the principal intended (or the protesters understood) those generalities as a lesson on the nuances of journalistic responsibility is utterly incredible. If he did, a fact that neither the District Court nor the Court of Appeals found, the lesson was lost on all but the psychic Spectrum staffer.

The Court's second excuse for deviating from precedent is the school's interest in shielding an impressionable high school audience from material whose substance is "unsuitable for immature audiences." [*Tinker*] teaches us that the state educator's undeniable, and undeniably vital, mandate to inculcate moral and political values is not a general warrant to act as "thought police" stifling discussion of all but state-approved topics and advocacy of all but the official position.

[The] mere fact of school sponsorship does not, as the Court suggests, license such thought control in the high school, whether through school suppression of disfavored viewpoints or through official assessment of topic sensitivity. [Moreover, the] State's prerogative to dissolve the student newspaper entirely (or to limit its subject matter) no more entitles it to dictate which viewpoints students may express on its pages, than the State's prerogative to close down the schoolhouse entitles it to prohibit the nondisruptive expression of antiwar sentiment within its gates.

Official censorship of student speech on the ground that it addresses "potentially sensitive topics" is, for related reasons, equally impermissible. I would not begrudge an educator the authority to limit the substantive scope of a school-sponsored publication to a certain, objectively definable topic, such as literary criticism, school sports, or an overview of the school year. Unlike those determinate limitations, "potential topic sensitivity" is a vaporous nonstandard [that] invites manipulation to achieve ends that cannot permissibly be achieved through blatant viewpoint discrimination and chills student speech to which school officials might not object. * * * [b]

Notes and Questions

1. Consider Hafen, *Hazelwood School District and the Role of First Amendment Institutions,* 1988 Duke L.J. 685, 701, 704–05: "[T]he question whether authoritarian or anti-authoritarian approaches will best develop the minds and expressive powers of children is more a matter of educational philosophy and practice than of constitutional law. For that reason alone, first amendment theories applied by courts largely on the basis of anti-authoritarian assumptions are at best a clumsy and limited means of ensuring optimal educational development, whether the goal is an understanding of democratic values or a mastery of basic intellectual skills. Thus, one of *Hazelwood's* major contributions is its reaffirmation of schools' institutional role—and their accountability to the public for fulfilling it responsibly—in nurturing the underlying values of the first amendment. * * *

"The first amendment must [protect] not only individual writers, but newspapers; not only religious persons, but churches; not only individual students and teachers, but schools. These 'intellectual and moral associations' form a crucial part of the constitutional structure, for they help teach the peculiar and sometimes paradoxical blend of liberty and duty that sustains both individual freedom and the entire culture from one generation to the next."

2. *Fraser* involved a speech on behalf of a candidate in a student election at an official school assembly. Was that speech "school-sponsored?" Or is the Court suggesting in fn. 4 that *Tinker's* standard is inadequate even for non-school-sponsored speech?

3. *A narrow holding?* Consider Abrams & Goodman, *End of an Era? The Decline of Student Press [Rights],* 1988 Duke L.J. 706, 728: "*Kuhlmeier* is limited by its own terms to secondary-school-sponsored publications that are not public forums for student expression. [Publications] at institutions of higher education and independent (or forum) publications in secondary schools retain, for the time being, extensive first amendment protections." See also Buss, *School Newspapers, Public Forum, and the First Amendment,* 74 Iowa L.Rev. 505 (1989).

4. Consider Minow & Spellman, *Passion For Justice,* 10 Cardozo L.Rev. 37, 69 (1988): "The majority does not acknowledge the power it is exercising in the act of deferring to the 'reasonable' judgments of the [principal:] the power to signal to school officials all around the country, that it is all right to err on the side of eliminating student speech, it is all right to indulge your paternalistic attitudes toward the students; you do not need to guard against your own discomfort with what students want to discuss, for the 'rights' really lie within your own judgment about what they need." See also id. at 68 n. 108: "The

b. Brennan, J. further argued that the material deleted was not conceivably tortious and that less restrictive alternatives, such as more precise deletions, were readily available.

dissent is acutely sensitive to the impact of censorship on students, but less attentive to the impact of judicial review on the school officials. Although equal attention to competing sides may make a decision more difficult, refraining from seeing the power of competing arguments itself may lead to tragic blindness."

BOARD OF EDUCATION v. PICO, 457 U.S. 853, 102 S.Ct. 2799, 73 L.Ed.2d 435 (1982): Several members of the Island Trees Board of Education attended a conference sponsored by Parents of New York United (PONYU), a politically conservative organization. At the conference these board members obtained lists of books they described as "objectionable" and "improper fare for school students." On ascertaining that its school libraries contained eleven of the books,[a] the Board informally directed, over the objection of the school superintendent, that the books be delivered to the Board's offices so that Board members could read them. The Board justified its action by characterizing the listed books as "anti-American, anti-Christian, anti-Semitic, and just plain filthy" and concluding that it had a "duty" and a "moral obligation" "to protect the children in our school from this moral danger as surely as from physical and medical dangers." The Board then appointed a parent-teacher "Book Review Committee" to recommend to the board which books should be retained. The Committee recommended that only two books be removed and a third be available to students only with parental approval. But the Board, without giving any reasons, decided that nine books should be removed and that another should be made available subject to parental approval. Respondent students then brought an action for declaratory and injunctive relief under 42 U.S.C. § 1983, contending that the Board's actions had violated their first amendment rights. The district court granted summary judgment for the Board, stating that the Board had "restricted access only to certain books which [it] believed to be, in essence, vulgar." A 2–1 majority of the Second Circuit reversed. One member of the majority concluded that at least at the summary judgment stage, the Board had not offered sufficient justification for its action. A second member of the majority "viewed the case as turning on the contested factual issue of whether [the Board's] removal decision was motivated by a justifiable desire to remove books containing vulgarities and sexual explicitness, or rather by an impermissible desire to suppress ideas." The Supreme Court (5–4) upheld reversal of the summary dismissal of the suit, but there was no opinion of the Court. BRENNAN, J., announced the judgment of the Court in an opinion joined by Marshall and Stevens, JJ., and in part by Blackmun, J.: "We emphasize at the outset the limited nature of the substantive question presented by the case before us. [T]his case [does] not involve textbooks, or indeed any books that Island Trees students would be required to read. Respondents do not seek in this Court to impose limitations upon their school Board's discretion to prescribe the curricula of the Island Trees schools. On the contrary, the only books at issue in this case

a. As the plurality opinion noted: "The nine [listed] books in the High School library were: *Slaughter House Five*, by Kurt Vonnegut, Jr.; *The Naked Ape*, by Desmond Morris; *Down These Mean Streets*, by Piri Thomas; *Best Short Stories of Negro Writers*, edited by Langston Hughes; *Go Ask Alice*, of anonymous authorship; *Laughing Boy*, by Oliver LaFarge; *Black Boy*, by Richard Wright; *A Hero Ain't Nothin' But A Sandwich*, by Alice Childress; and *Soul On Ice*, by Eldridge Cleaver. The [listed] book in the Junior High School library was *A Reader for Writers*, edited by Jerome Archer. Still another listed book, *The Fixer*, by Bernard Malamud, was found to be included in the curriculum of a twelfth grade literature course."

The Board subsequently decided that only *Laughing Boy* should be returned to the library without restriction, and that *Black Boy* should be made available subject to parental approval.

are *library* books, books that by their nature are optional rather than required reading. [Furthermore,] even as to library books, the action before us does not involve the *acquisition* of books. Respondents have not sought to compel their school Board to add to the school library shelves any books that students desire to read. Rather, the only action challenged in this case is the *removal* from school libraries of books originally placed there by the school authorities, or without objection from them.

"[We] think that the First Amendment rights of students may be directly and sharply implicated by the removal of books from the shelves of a school library. * * * [W]e have held that in a variety of contexts 'the Constitution protects the right to receive information and ideas.' *Stanley v. Georgia.* [W]e do not deny that local school boards have a substantial legitimate role to play in the determination of school library content. [But] that discretion may not be exercised in a narrowly partisan or political manner. If a Democratic school board, motivated by party affiliation, ordered the removal of all books written by or in favor of Republicans, few would doubt that the order violated the constitutional rights of the students denied access to those books. The same conclusion would surely apply if an all-white school board, motivated by racial animus, decided to remove all books authored by blacks or advocating racial equality and integration. Our Constitution does not permit the official suppression of *ideas.* Thus whether petitioners' removal of books from their school libraries denied respondents their First Amendment rights depends upon the motivation behind petitioners' actions. If petitioners *intended* by their removal decision to deny respondents access to ideas with which petitioners disagreed, and if this intent was the decisive factor in petitioners' decision,[22] then petitioners have exercised their discretion in violation of the Constitution. * * * On the other hand, respondents implicitly concede that an unconstitutional motivation would *not* be demonstrated if it were shown that petitioners had decided to remove the books at issue because those books were pervasively vulgar. And again, respondents concede that if it were demonstrated that the removal decision was based solely upon the 'educational suitability' of the books in question, then their removal would be 'perfectly permissible.' In other words, in respondents' view such motivations if decisive of petitioners' actions, would not carry the danger of an official suppression of ideas, and thus would not violate respondents' First Amendment rights.

"[This] would be a very different case if the record demonstrated that petitioners had employed established, regular, and facially unbiased procedures for the review of controversial materials. But [respondents'] allegations and some of the evidentiary materials presented below do not rule out the possibility that petitioners' removal procedures were highly irregular and ad hoc—the antithesis of those procedures that might tend to allay suspicions regarding petitioners' motivations.

"Construing these claims, affidavit statements, and other evidentiary materials in a manner favorable to respondents, we cannot conclude that petitioners were 'entitled to a judgment as a matter of law.' The evidence plainly does not foreclose the possibility that petitioners' decision to remove the books rested decisively upon disagreement with constitutionally protected ideas in those books, or upon a desire on petitioners' part to impose upon the students of the

22. By "decisive factor" we mean a "substantial factor" in the absence of which the opposite decision would have been reached.

Island Trees High School and Junior High School a political orthodoxy to which petitioners and their constituents adhered." [b]

In the view of BLACKMUN, J., concurring, "the principle involved here is both narrower and more basic than 'the right to receive information' identified by the plurality. I do not suggest that the State has any affirmative obligation to provide students with information or ideas, something that may well be associated with a 'right to receive.' And I do not believe, as the plurality suggests, that the right at issue here is somehow associated with the peculiar nature of the school library; if schools may be used to inculcate ideas, surely libraries may play a role in that process. Instead, I suggest that certain forms of state discrimination *between* ideas are improper. In particular, our precedents command the conclusion that the State may not act to deny access to an idea simply because state officials disapprove of that idea for partisan or political [reasons].[2]

"[S]chool officials may seek to instill certain values 'by persuasion and example,' or by choice of emphasis. That sort of positive educational action, however, is the converse of an intentional attempt to shield students from certain ideas that officials find politically distasteful. Arguing that the majority in the community rejects the ideas involved, does not refute this principle: 'The very purpose of a Bill of Rights was to withdraw certain subjects from the vicissitudes of political controversy, to place them beyond the reach of majorities and officials * * *.' *Barnette.*"

WHITE, J., who concurred in the judgment, noted that although the District Court found that the books were removed because the school board believed them "to be, in essence, vulgar," both Court of Appeals judges in the majority concluded that there was a material issue of fact that precluded summary judgment for petitioners. As White, J., understood it, "[t]he unresolved factual issue [is] the reason or reasons underlying the school board's removal of the books" and he was "not inclined to disagree with the Court of Appeals on such a fact-bound issue. [The] Court seems compelled to go further and issue a dissertation on the extent to which the First Amendment limits the discretion of the school board to remove books from the school library. I see no necessity for doing so at this point. When findings of fact and conclusions of law are made by the District Court, that may end the case."

BURGER, C.J., joined by Powell, Rehnquist, and O'Connor, JJ., dissented:

"[The] plurality concludes that under the Constitution school boards cannot choose to retain or dispense with books if their discretion is exercised in a 'narrowly partisan or political manner.' The plurality concedes that permissible factors are whether the books are 'pervasively vulgar' or educationally unsuitable. 'Educational suitability,' however, is a standardless phrase. This conclusion will undoubtedly be drawn in many—if not most—instances because of the decisionmaker's content-based judgment that the ideas contained in the book or the idea expressed from the author's method of communication are inappropriate for teenage pupils. * * *

b. For criticism of Brennan, J.'s opinion, see Lee, *The Supreme Court and the Right to Receive Expression,* 1987 Sup.Ct.Rev. 303, 323–27.

2. In effect, my view presents the obverse of the plurality's analysis: while the plurality focuses on the failure to provide information, I find crucial the State's decision to single out an idea for disapproval and then deny access to it.

"Further, there is no guidance whatsoever as to what constitutes 'political' factors. [V]irtually all educational decisions necessarily involve 'political' determinations.

"What the plurality views as valid reasons for removing a book at their core involve partisan judgments. Ultimately the federal courts will be the judge of whether the motivation for book removal was 'valid' or 'reasonable.' Undoubtedly the validity of many book removals will ultimately turn on a judge's evaluation of the books. Discretion must be used, and the appropriate body to exercise that discretion is the local elected school board, not judges."

POWELL, J., also dissented: "In different contexts and in different times, the destruction of written materials has been the symbol of despotism and intolerance. But the removal of nine vulgar or racist books from a high school library by a concerned local school board does not raise this specter. For me, today's decision symbolizes a debilitating encroachment upon the institutions of a free people." [c]

REHNQUIST, J., joined by Burger, C.J., and Powell, J., "disagree[d] with Justice Brennan's opinion because it is largely hypothetical in character, failing to take account of the facts as admitted by the parties [and] because it is analytically unsound and internally inconsistent": "I can cheerfully concede [that a Democratic school board could not, for political reasons, remove all books by or in favor of Republicans, and that an all-white school board, motivated by racial animus, could not remove all books authored by blacks or advocating racial equality], but as in so many other cases the extreme examples are seldom the ones that arise in the real world of constitutional litigation. In *this case* the facts taken most favorably to respondents suggest that nothing of this sort happened. The nine books removed undoubtedly did contain 'ideas,' but in the light of the excerpts from them found in the dissenting opinion [in the court below], it is apparent that eight of them contained demonstrable amounts of vulgarity and profanity and the ninth contained nothing that could be considered partisan or political. [R]espondents admitted as much. Petitioners did not, for the reasons stated hereafter, run afoul of the First and Fourteenth Amendments by removing these particular books from the library in the manner in which they did. I would save for another day—feeling quite confident that that day will not arrive—the extreme examples posed in Justice Brennan's opinion.

"Considerable light is shed on the correct resolution of the constitutional question in this case by examining the role played by petitioners. Had petitioners been the members of a town council, I suppose all would agree that, absent a good deal more than is present in this record, they could not have prohibited the sale of these books by private booksellers within the municipality. But we have also recognized that the government may act in other capacities than as sovereign, and when it does the First Amendment may speak with a different voice * * *. By the same token, expressive conduct which may not be prohibited by the State as sovereign may be proscribed by the State as property owner [quoting from *Adderley*, p. 649 supra].

"With these differentiated roles of government in mind, it is helpful to assess the role of government as educator, as compared with the role of government as sovereign. When it acts as an educator, at least at the elementary and secondary school level, the government is engaged in inculcating social

c. Powell, J., appended a summary of excerpts from the books at issue collected in the opinion of Judge Mansfield dissenting below.

values and knowledge in relatively impressionable young people. Obviously there are innumerable decisions to be made as to what courses should be taught, what books should be purchased, or what teachers should be employed. In every one of these areas the members of a school board will act on the basis of their own personal or moral values, will attempt to mirror those of the community, or will abdicate the making of such decisions to so-called 'experts.' [In] the very course of administering the many-faceted operations of a school district, the mere decision to purchase some books will necessarily preclude the possibility of purchasing others. The decision to teach a particular subject may preclude the possibility of teaching another subject. A decision to replace a teacher because of ineffectiveness may by implication be seen as a disparagement of the subject matter taught. In each of these instances, however, the book or the exposure to the subject matter may be acquired elsewhere. The managers of the school district are not proscribing it as to the citizenry in general, but are simply determining that it will not be included in the curriculum or school library. In short, actions by the government as educator do not raise the same First Amendment concerns as actions by the government as sovereign. * * *

"Education consists of the selective presentation and explanation of ideas. The effective acquisition of knowledge depends upon an orderly exposure to relevant information. Nowhere is this more true than in elementary and secondary schools, where, unlike the broad-ranging inquiry available to university students, the courses taught are those thought most relevant to the young students' individual development. Of necessity, elementary and secondary educators must separate the relevant from the irrelevant, the appropriate from the inappropriate. Determining what information *not* to present to the students is often as important as identifying relevant material. This winnowing process necessarily leaves much information to be discovered by students at another time or in another place, and is fundamentally inconsistent with any constitutionally required eclecticism in public education.

"[Unlike] university or public libraries, elementary and secondary school libraries are not designed for free-wheeling inquiry; they are tailored, as the public school curriculum is tailored, to the teaching of basic skills and ideas. Thus, Justice Brennan cannot rely upon the nature of school libraries to escape the fact that the First Amendment right to receive information simply has no application to the one public institution which, by its very nature, is a place for the selective conveyance of ideas."

In a brief separate dissent, O'CONNOR, J., observed: "If the school board can set the curriculum, select teachers, and determine initially what books to purchase for the school library, it surely can decide which books to discontinue or remove from the school library so long as it does not also interfere with the right of students to read the material and to discuss it. As Justice Rehnquist persuasively argues, the plurality's analysis overlooks the fact that in this case the government is acting in its special role as educator.

"I do not personally agree with the board's action with respect to some of the books in question here, but it is not the function of the courts to make the decisions that have been properly relegated to the elected members of school boards. It is the school board that must determine educational suitability, and it has done so in this case. I therefore join the Chief Justice's dissent."

Notes & Question

1. Consider Yudof, *Library Book Selection and Public Schools: The Quest for the Archimedean Point,* 59 Ind.L.J. 527, 530 (1984): The critical questions in *Pico* are "who will control socialization of the young, what are the values to which they will be socialized, and how will cultural grounding and critical reflection be accommodated." On the latter point, see Mendelson, *The Habermas-Gadamer Debate,* New German Critique 18 (1979). See also Unger, *Knowledge and Politics* (1975); Cornell, *Toward a Modern/Postmodern Reconstruction of Ethics,* 133 U.Pa.L.Rev. 291 (1985).[d]

2. Should librarians have a first amendment right to select and retain books against the objections of a school board? Against a city council in a non-school context? See O'Neil, *Libraries, Librarians and First Amendment Freedoms,* 4 Hum.Rts. 295 (1975); O'Neil, *Libraries, Liberties and the First Amendment,* 42 U.Cin.L.Rev. 209 (1973). Should elementary school teachers have a first amendment right to resist interference with their teaching by "politically" motivated administrators or school boards? At secondary levels? Should student newspapers have a first amendment right to resist ad hoc intervention by administrators? See Canby, *The First Amendment and the State as Editor: Implications for Public Broadcasting,* 52 Tex.L.Rev. 1123 (1974). What of an approach that allows (requires?) administrators to set policies and procedures but prohibits ad hoc intervention?

3. Every Justice recognizes that some content discrimination is permitted in selecting books and making curricular decisions. The line between a public forum and a facility subject to the government's editorial discretion, however, may be hard to draw. SOUTHEASTERN PROMOTIONS, LTD. v. CONRAD, 420 U.S. 546, 95 S.Ct. 1239, 43 L.Ed.2d 448 (1975), reacting to reports that the musical *Hair* included nudity and was obscene, a publicly-appointed board denied *Hair's* producers a permit to use a theater dedicated for "cultural advancement and for clean, healthful, entertainment which will make for the upbuilding of a better citizenship." The Court, per BLACKMUN, J., held that the theater was a public forum "designed for and dedicated to expressive activities" and that the board's procedures amounted to a prior restraint in violation of *Freedman* requirements, p. 880 supra. One of the dissenters, REHNQUIST, J., asked: "May a municipal theater devote an entire season to Shakespeare, or is it required to book any potential producer on a first come, first served basis? [T]he Court's opinion [seems] to give no constitutionally permissible role in the way of

d. For a range of views on the scope and propriety of government promotion of particular values, see sources collected in fn. i after *Regan* supra. See also Dworkin, *A Matter of Principle* 181–204, 221–33 (1985); Tussman, *Government and the Mind* (1977); Diamond, *The First Amendment and Public Schools: The Case Against Judicial Intervention,* 59 Tex.L.Rev. 477 (1981); Garvey, *Children and the First Amendment,* 57 Tex.L.Rev. 321 (1979); Goldstein, *The Asserted Constitutional Right of Public School Teachers to Determine What They Teach,* 124 U.Pa.L.Rev. 1293 (1976); Gottlieb, *In The Name of Patriotism: The Constitutionality of "Bending" History in Public Secondary Schools,* 62 N.Y.U.L.Rev. 497 (1987); Moskowitz, *The Making of the Moral Child: Legal Implications of Values Education,* 6 Pepp.L.Rev. 105 (1978); Nahmod, *Controversy in the Classroom: The High School Teacher and Freedom of Expression,* 39 Geo.Wash.L.Rev. 1032 (1971); van Geel, *The Search for Constitutional Limits on Governmental Authority to Inculcate Youth,* 62 Tex. L.Rev. 197 (1983); Note, *Education and the Court: The Supreme Court's Educational Ideology,* 40 Vand.L.Rev. 939 (1987); Note, *The Promise of Pico: A New Definition of Orthodoxy,* 97 Yale L.J. 1805 (1988); Note, *State Indoctrination and the Protection of Non-State Voices in the Schools: Justifying a Prohibition of School Library Censorship,* 35 Stan.L.Rev. 497 (1983).

selection to the municipal authorities." For commentary, see Karst, *Public Enterprise and the Public Forum: A Comment on Southeastern Promotions, Ltd. v. Conrad,* 37 Ohio St.L.J. 247 (1976); Shiffrin, fn. i after *Regan,* supra, at 581–88; Comment, *Access to State-Owned Communications Media—The Public Forum Doctrine,* 26 U.C.L.A.L.Rev. 1410, 1440–44 (1979).

4. Blackmun, J., states in fn. 2 that the crucial point is the state's decision to "single out an idea for disapproval and then deny access to it." Suppose the government does not deny access to speech but officially denounces it. Constitutional? [e]

LAMONT v. POSTMASTER GENERAL, 381 U.S. 301, 85 S.Ct. 1493, 14 L.Ed.2d 398 (1965), per DOUGLAS, J., invalidated a federal statute permitting delivery of "communist political propaganda" only if the addressee specifically requested in writing that it be delivered: "We rest on the narrow ground that the addressee in order to receive his mail must request in writing that it be delivered. [The] addressee carries an affirmative obligation which we do not think the Government may impose on him. This requirement is almost certain to have a deterrent effect, especially as respects those who have sensitive positions. [Public] officials, like school teachers who have no tenure, might think they would invite disaster if they read what the Federal Government says contains the seeds of treason. Apart from them, any addressee is likely to feel some inhibition in sending for literature which federal officials have condemned as 'communist political propaganda.'"

MEESE v. KEENE, 481 U.S. 465, 107 S.Ct. 1862, 95 L.Ed.2d 415 (1987), per STEVENS, J., held that the government could label a film as "political propaganda" without violating the first amendment: "The Foreign Agents Registration Act [uses] the term 'political propaganda,' [f] [to] identify those expressive materials that must comply with the Act's registration, filing, and disclosure requirements." The government had identified three Canadian films as "political propaganda." Because Keene was not a foreign agent, he was not subject to the Act's requirements, but he maintained that he should be free to exhibit the three films without being considered an exhibitor of governmentally designated "propaganda." Without otherwise reaching the Act's requirements, the Court rejected

e. Consider Professor Lawrence's suggestion that segregation's "*only* purpose is to label or define blacks as inferior." Lawrence, "*'One More River to Cross'—Recognizing the Real Injury in Brown,*" *in* Shades of Brown 49, 50 (Bell ed. 1980). See also Lawrence, *If He Hollers Let Him Go: Regulating Racist Speech on Campus,* 1990 Duke L.J. 431. When should governmental denunciation of persons or groups be considered a violation of the first amendment?

f. The Act defines political propaganda to include: "* * * any oral, visual, graphic, written, pictorial, or other communication or expression by any person (1) which is reasonably adapted to, or which the person disseminating the same believes will, or which he intends to, prevail upon, indoctrinate, convert, induce, or in any other way influence a recipient or any section of the public within the United States with reference to the political or public interests, policies, or relations of a government or a foreign country or a foreign political party or with reference to the foreign policies of the United States or promote in the United States racial, religious, or social dissensions, or (2) which advocates, advises, instigates, or promotes any racial, social, political, or religious disorder, civil riot, or other conflict involving the use of force or violence in any other American republic or the overthrow of any government or political subdivision of any other American republic by any means involving the use of force or violence." 22 U.S.C. § 611(j).

Stevens, J., commented, "As defined in the Act, the term political propaganda includes misleading advocacy. [But] it also includes advocacy materials that are completely accurate and merit the closest attention and the highest respect. Standard reference works include both broad, neutral definitions of the word 'propaganda' that are consistent with the way the word is defined in this statute, and also the narrower, pejorative definition."

Keene's claim: "The District Court [found] that the basic purpose of the statute as a whole was 'to inform recipients of advocacy materials produced by or under the aegis of a foreign government of the source of such materials' [and] that it could not be gainsaid that this kind of disclosure serves rather than disserves the First Amendment. The statute itself neither prohibits nor censors the dissemination of advocacy materials by agents of foreign principals. [T]he term 'political propaganda' does nothing to place regulated expressive materials 'beyond the pale of legitimate discourse.' [g] [To] the contrary, Congress simply required the disseminators of such material to make additional disclosures that would better enable the public to evaluate the import of the propaganda. The statute does not prohibit appellee from advising his audience that the films have not been officially censured in any way. Disseminators of propaganda may go beyond the disclosures required by statute and add any further information they think germane to the public's viewing of the materials. By compelling some disclosure of information and permitting more, the Act's approach recognizes that the best remedy for misleading or inaccurate speech contained within materials subject to the Act is fair, truthful, and accurate speech. * * *

"[The argument that the District Court accepted rests not on what the statute actually says, requires, or prohibits, but rather upon a potential misunderstanding of its effect.] Ironically, it is the injunction entered by the District Court that withholds information from the public. The suppressed information is the fact that the films fall within the category of materials that Congress has judged to be 'political propaganda'. A similar paternalistic strategy of protecting the public from information was followed by the Virginia Assembly, which enacted a ban on the advertising of prescription drug prices by pharmacists. See *Virginia Pharmacy.*

"We have no occasion here to decide the permissible scope of Congress' 'right to speak'; we simply view this particular choice of language, statutorily defined in a neutral and evenhanded manner, as one that no constitutional provision prohibits the Congress from making. [If] the term 'political propaganda' is construed consistently with the neutral definition contained in the text of the statute itself, the constitutional concerns voiced by the District Court completely disappear." [h]

g. The Court distinguished *Lamont v. Postmaster General* stating that the physical detention of mail, not its mere designation as "communist political propaganda" was the offending element of the statutory scheme. By contrast, the Court argued that the Foreign Agents Registration Act posed no obstacle to Keene's access to the materials.

In response, Blackmun, J., dissenting, observed that the "communist political propaganda [detained in *Lamont*] and delivered only upon the addressee's request was defined by reference to the same 'neutral' definition of 'political propaganda' in the Act that is at issue here. Yet the Court examined the effects of the statutory requirements and had no trouble concluding that the need to request delivery of mail classified as 'communist political propaganda' was almost certain to have a deterrent effect upon debate."

h. Scalia, J., took no part. In *Block v. Meese,* 793 F.2d 1303 (D.C.Cir.1986), however, then Circuit Judge Scalia ruled on the issue. "[E]ven if classification as 'propaganda' constituted an expression of official government disapproval of the ideas in question, neither precedent nor reason would justify us in finding such an expression *in itself* unlawful. [W]e know of no case in which the first amendment has been held to be implicated by governmental action consisting of no more than governmental criticism of the speech's content. [A] rule excluding official praise or criticism of ideas would lead to the strange conclusion that it is permissible for the government to prohibit racial discrimination, but not to criticize racial bias; to criminalize polygamy, but not to praise the monogamous family; to make war on Hitler's Germany, but not to denounce Nazism. [The] line of permissibility [falls] not between criticism of ideas in general and criticism of the ideas contained in specific books or expressed by specific persons; but between the disparagement of ideas general or specific and the suppression of ideas through the exercise or threat of state power. If the latter is rigorously prescribed, see *Bantam Books,* the former can hold no terror."

BLACKMUN, J., joined by Brennan and Marshall, JJ., dissented: "The Court likens the injunction issued by the District Court to the state ban on advertising prices of prescription drugs struck down in *Virginia Pharmacy*. But there is a significant difference between the 'paternalistic strategy of protecting the public from information,' by way of a *ban* on information and a prohibition of the government disparagement at issue in this case. [Under] the District Court's ruling, opponents of the viewpoint expressed by the [film] remained completely free to point out [its] foreign [source]. The difference was that dialogue on the value of the films and the viewpoints they express could occur in an atmosphere free of the constraint imposed by government condemnation. It is the Government's classification of those films as 'political propaganda' that is paternalistic. For that government action does more than simply provide additional information. It places the power of the Federal Government, with its authority, presumed neutrality, and assumed access to all the facts, behind an appellation *designed* to reduce the effectiveness of the speech in the eyes of the public."

SECTION 8. BROADCAST REGULATION AND ACCESS TO THE MASS MEDIA

The mass media are not invariably the most effective means of communication. For example, the right to place messages on utility poles concerning a lost dog may be more important than access to a radio or a television station. In some circumstances, picketing outside a school or placing leaflets in teachers' mailboxes may be the most effective communications medium. Nonetheless, the law regulating access to the mass media is of vital societal importance. This section considers first, cases in which government seeks to force newspapers and broadcasters to grant access; second, in *CBS v. DNC*, infra, a claim that the first amendment requires government to afford access for excluded groups to the broadcast media; third, a case in which government seeks to encourage diverse programming by promoting diversity among broadcast licensees; finally, cases in which government commands broadcasters not to carry particular programming at particular times or not to editorialize. A persistent theme is that broadcasting is "special," but whether it is, why it is, and what difference it should make are matters of considerable debate. Beyond this, attitudes about the most effective channel of communication raise questions about our commitment to and understanding of first amendment principles. If the assumption that broadcasting is special is a masquerade, why the masquerade?

I. ACCESS TO THE MASS MEDIA

MIAMI HERALD PUB. CO. v. TORNILLO, 418 U.S. 241, 94 S.Ct. 2831, 41 L.Ed.2d 730 (1974), per BURGER, C.J., unanimously struck down a Florida "right of reply" statute, which required any newspaper that "assails" the personal character or official record of a candidate in any election to print, on demand, free of cost, any reply the candidate may make to the charges, in as conspicuous a place and the same kind of type, provided the reply takes up no more space than the charges. The opinion carefully explained the aim of the statute to "ensure that a wide variety of views reach the public" even though "chains of newspapers, national newspapers, national wire and news services, and one-newspaper towns, are the dominant features of a press that has become noncompetitive and enormously powerful and influential in its capacity to manipulate popular opinion and change the course of events," placing "in a few hands the power to inform the American people and shape public opinion." [a] Nonetheless, the Court concluded that to require the printing of a reply violated the first amendment: "Compelling editors or publishers to publish that which ' "reason" tells them should not be published' is what is at issue in this case. The Florida statute operates as a command in the same sense as a statute or regulation forbidding appellant from publishing specified matter. [The] Florida statute exacts a penalty on the basis of the content of a newspaper. The first phase of the penalty resulting from the compelled printing of a reply is exacted in terms of the cost in printing and composing time and materials and in taking up space that could be devoted to other material the newspaper may have preferred to print. It is correct, as appellee contends, that a newspaper is not subject to the finite technological limitations of time that confront a broadcaster but it is not correct to say that, as an economic reality, a newspaper can proceed to infinite expansion of its column space to accommodate the replies that a government agency determines or a statute commands the readers should have available.

"Faced with the penalties that would accrue to any newspaper that published news or commentary arguably within the reach of the right of access statute, editors might well conclude that the safe course is to avoid controversy and that, under the operation of the Florida statute, political and electoral coverage would be blunted or reduced. Government enforced right of access inescapably 'dampens the vigor and limits the variety of public debate,' *New York Times*.

"Even if a newspaper would face no additional costs to comply with a compulsory access law and would not be forced to forego publication of news or opinion by the inclusion of a reply, the Florida statute fails to clear the barriers of the First Amendment because of its intrusion into the function of editors. A newspaper is more than a passive receptacle or conduit for news, comment, and advertising. The choice of material to go into a newspaper, and the decisions made as to limitations on the size of the paper, and content, and treatment of public issues and public officials—whether fair or unfair—constitutes the exercise of editorial control and judgment. It has yet to be demonstrated how governmental regulation of this crucial process can be exercised consistent with First Amendment guarantees of a free press as they have evolved to this time." [b]

---

a. The opinion developed these views at greater length, citing "generally" Barron, *Access to the Press—A New First Amendment Right,* 80 Harv.L.Rev. 1641 (1967); Lange, *The Role of the Access Doctrine in the Regulation of the Mass Media: A Critical Review and Assessment,* 52 N.C.L.Rev. 1, 8–9 (1973). For historical background and a spirited criticism of the statute, see Powe, *Tornillo,* 1987 *Sup.Ct. Rev.* 345.

b. Brennan, J., joined by Rehnquist, J., joined the Court's opinion in a short statement to express the understanding that the opinion "implies no view upon the constitutionality of 'retraction' statutes affording plaintiffs able to prove defamatory falsehoods a statutory action to require publication of a retraction."

White, J., concurred. After agreeing that "prior compulsion by government in matters going to the very nerve center of a newspaper—the decision as to what copy will or will not be included in any given edition—collides with the First Amendment," he returned to his attack on *Gertz,* decided the same day: "Reaffirming the rule that the press cannot be forced to print an answer to a personal attack made by it [throws] into stark relief the consequences of the new balance forged by the Court in the companion case also announced today. *Gertz* goes far toward eviscerating the effectiveness of the ordinary libel action, which has long been the only potent response available to the private citizen libeled by the press. [To] me it is a near absurdity to so deprecate individual dignity, as the Court does in *Gertz,* and to leave the people at the complete mercy of the press, at least in this stage of our history when the press, as the majority in this case so well documents, is steadily becoming more powerful and much less likely to be deterred by threats of libel suits."

The Federal Communications Commission for many years imposed on radio and television broadcasters the "fairness doctrine"—requiring that stations (1) devote a reasonable percentage of broadcast time to discussion of public issues and (2) assure fair coverage for each side.[c] At issue in RED LION BROADCASTING CO. v. FCC, 395 U.S. 367, 89 S.Ct. 1794, 23 L.Ed.2d 371 (1969), were the application of the fairness doctrine to a particular broadcast[d] and two specific access regulations promulgated under the doctrine: (1) the "political editorial" rule, requiring that when a broadcaster, in an editorial, "endorses or opposes" a political candidate, it must notify the candidate opposed, or the rivals of the candidate supported, and afford them a "reasonable opportunity" to respond; (2) the "personal attack" rule, requiring that "when, during the presentation of views on a controversial issue of public importance, an attack is made on the honesty, character [or] integrity [of] an identified person or group," the person or group attacked must be given notice, a transcript of the attack, and an opportunity to respond.[e] "[I]n view of [the] scarcity of broadcast frequencies, the Government's role in allocating those frequencies, and the legitimate claims of those unable without government assistance to gain access to those frequencies for expression of their views," a 7–0 majority, per WHITE, J., upheld both access regulations:[f]

"[The broadcasters] contention is that the First Amendment protects their desire to use their allotted frequencies continuously to broadcast whatever they choose, and to exclude whomever they choose from ever using that frequency. No man may be prevented from saying or publishing what he thinks, or from refusing in his speech or other utterances to give equal weight to the views of his opponents. This right, they say, applies equally to broadcasters.

"Although broadcasting is clearly a medium affected by a First Amendment interest, differences in the characteristics of new media justify differences in the First Amendment standards applied to [them]. Just as the Government may limit the use of sound-amplifying equipment potentially so noisy that it drowns out civilized private speech, so may the Government limit the use of broadcast equipment. The right of free speech of a broadcaster, the user of a sound truck, or any other individual does not embrace a right to snuff out the free speech of [others].

"Where there are substantially more individuals who want to broadcast than there are frequencies to allocate, it is idle to posit an unabridgeable First Amendment right to broadcast comparable to the right of every individual to speak, write, or publish. [It] would be strange if the First Amendment, aimed at protecting and furthering communications, prevented the Government from

c. For helpful background on the origins, justification and administration of the fairness doctrine, see Barrow, *The Fairness Doctrine: A Double Standard for Electronic and Print Media,* 26 Hast.L.J. 659 (1975); Schmidt, *Freedom of the Press vs. Public Access* 157–98 (1976).

d. *Red Lion* grew out of a series of radio broadcasts by fundamentalist preacher Billy James Hargis, who had attacked Fred J. Cook, author of an article attacking Hargis and "hate clubs of the air." When Cook heard about the broadcast, he demanded that the station give him an opportunity to reply. Cook refused to pay for his "reply time" and the FCC ordered the station to give Cook the opportunity to reply whether or not he would pay for it. The Supreme Court upheld the order of free reply time. See Schmidt, fn. c supra, at 161–63.

e. Excepted were "personal attacks [by] legally qualified candidates [on] other such candidates" and "bona fide newscasts, bona fide news interviews, and on-the-spot coverage of a bona fide news event."

f. Surprisingly, none of the justices joining White, J.'s opinion felt the need to make additional remarks, but Douglas, J., who did not participate in *Red Lion,* expressed his disagreement with it in the *CBS* case, infra.

making radio communication possible by requiring licenses to broadcast and by limiting the number of licenses so as not to overcrowd the spectrum. * * *

"By the same token, as far as the First Amendment is concerned those who are licensed stand no better than those to whom licenses are refused. A license permits broadcasting, but the licensee has no constitutional right [to] monopolize a radio frequency to the exclusion of his fellow citizens. There is nothing in the First Amendment which prevents the Government from requiring a licensee to share his frequency with others and to conduct himself as a proxy or fiduciary with obligations to present those views and voices which are representative of his community and which would otherwise, by necessity, be barred from the airwaves.

"[The] people as a whole retain their interest in free speech by radio and their collective right to have the medium function consistently with the ends and purposes of the First Amendment. It is the right of the viewers and listeners, not the right of the broadcasters, which is paramount. [It] is the purpose of the First Amendment to preserve an uninhibited marketplace of ideas in which truth will ultimately prevail, rather than to countenance monopolization of that market, whether it be by the Government itself or a private licensee. [It] is the right of the public to receive suitable access to social, political, esthetic, moral, and other ideas and experiences which is crucial [here.]

"In terms of constitutional principle, and as enforced sharing of a scarce resource, the personal attack and political editorial rules are indistinguishable from the equal-time provision of § 315 [of the Communications Act], a specific enactment of Congress requiring [that stations allot equal time to qualified candidates for public office] and to which the fairness doctrine and these constituent regulations are important complements. [Nor] can we say that it is inconsistent with the First Amendment goal of producing an informed public capable of conducting its own affairs to require a broadcaster to permit answers to personal attacks occurring in the course of discussing controversial issues, or to require that the political opponents of those endorsed by the station be given a chance to communicate with the public. Otherwise, station owners and a few networks would have unfettered power to make time available only to the highest bidders, to communicate only their own views on public issues, people and candidates, and to permit on the air only those with whom they agreed. There is no sanctuary in the First Amendment for unlimited private censorship operating in a medium not open to all.

"[It is contended] that if political editorials or personal attacks will trigger an obligation in broadcasters to afford the opportunity for expression to speakers who need not pay for time and whose views are unpalatable to the licensees, then broadcasters will be irresistibly forced to self-censorship and their coverage of controversial public issues will be eliminated or at least rendered wholly ineffective. Such a result would indeed be a serious matter, [but] that possibility is at best speculative. [If these doctrines turn out to have this effect], there will be time enough to reconsider the constitutional implications. The fairness doctrine in the past has had no such overall effect. That this will occur now seems unlikely, however, since if present licensees should suddenly prove timorous, the Commission is not powerless to insist that they give adequate and fair attention to public issues. It does not violate the First Amendment to treat licensees given the privilege of using scarce radio frequencies as proxies for the entire community, obligated to give suitable time and attention to matters of great public concern. To condition the granting or renewal of licenses on a willingness to present representative community views on controversial issues is consistent with the ends and purposes of those constitutional provisions forbidding the abridgment of freedom of speech and freedom of the press." [g]

Notes and Questions

1. *Tension between Miami Herald and Red Lion.* Consider Bollinger, *Freedom of the Press and Public Access: Toward a Theory of Partial Regulation of the Mass Media,* 75 Mich.L.Rev. 1, 4–6, 10–12 (1976): "What seems so remarkable about the unanimous *Miami Herald* opinion is the complete absence of any reference to the Court's unanimous decision five years earlier in *Red Lion* [, upholding] the so-called personal attack rule, [which] is almost identical in substance to the Florida statute declared unconstitutional in *Miami Herald.* That omission, however, is no more surprising than the absence of any discussion in *Red Lion* of the cases in which the Court expressed great concern about the risks attending government regulation of the print media.

"[The] scarcity rationale [articulated in *Red Lion* does not] explain why what appears to be a similar phenomenon of natural monopolization within the newspaper industry does not constitute an equally appropriate occasion for access regulation. A difference in the cause of concentration—the exhaustion of a physical element necessary for communication in broadcasting as contrasted with the economic constraints on the number of possible competitors in the print media—would seem far less relevant from a first amendment standpoint than the fact of concentration itself.

"[Instead] of exploring the relevance for the print media of the new principle developed in broadcasting, the Court merely reiterated the opposing, more traditional, principle that the government cannot tell editors what to publish. It thus created a paradox, leaving the new principle unscathed while preserving tradition."

2. *The absence of balancing in Miami Herald.* Did *Miami Herald* present a confrontation between the rights of speech and press? "Nowhere does [*Miami Herald*] explicitly acknowledge [such a confrontation], but implicit recognition of the speech interest," observes Nimmer, *Is Freedom of the Press a Redundancy? What Does it Add to Freedom of Speech?,* 26 Hast.L.J. 639, 645, 657 (1975), "may be found in the Court's reference to the access advocates' argument that, given the present semimonopolistic posture of the press, speech can be effective and therefore free only if enhanced by devices such as a right of reply statute. The Court in accepting the press clause argument in effect necessarily found it to be superior to any competing speech clause claims. [But] the issue cannot be resolved merely by noting, as did [*Miami Herald*], that a right of reply statute 'constitutes the [state] exercise of editorial control and judgment.' This is but

g. The Court noted that it "need not deal with the argument that even if there is no longer a technological scarcity of frequencies limiting the number of broadcasters, there nevertheless is an economic scarcity in the sense that the Commission could or does limit entry to the broadcasting market on economic grounds and license no more stations than the market will support. Hence, it is said, the fairness doctrine or its equivalent is essential to satisfy the claims of those excluded and of the public generally. A related argument, which we also put side, is that quite apart from scarcity of frequencies, technological or economic, Congress does not abridge freedom of speech or press by legislation directly or indirectly multiplying the voices and views presented to the public through time sharing, fairness doctrines, or other devices which limit or dissipate the power of those who sit astride the channels of communication with the general public." For background and discussion of *Red Lion,* see Friendly, *The Good Guys, The Bad Guys and the First Amendment* (1975).

one half of the equation. [*Miami Herald*] ignored the strong conflicting claims of 'speech.' Perhaps on balance the press should still prevail, but those who doubt the efficacy of such a result are hardly persuaded by an approach that apparently fails to recognize that any balancing of speech and press rights is required." [h]

3. *Scope of Miami Herald.* Consider Schmidt, supra, note c, at 233–35: "From the perspective of First Amendment law generally, *Miami Herald* would be a stark and unexplained deviation if one were to read the decision as creating absolute prohibitions on access obligations.[i] [The] fact the Court offers no discussion as to why First Amendment rules respecting access should be absolute, while all other rules emanating from that Amendment are relative, suggests that the principle of *Miami Herald* probably is destined for uncharted qualifications and exceptions." But see Powe, *Tornillo,* 1987 Sup.Ct.Rev. 345, 391, 390: "Quite frankly I do not believe that a twenty page Supreme Court opinion meeting all the standards of craft (all considerations are ventilated fully and the opinion be of publishable quality for a good legal journal) can as effectively protect the right of press autonomy as the blunt rejection in *Tornillo.*

"Chief Justice Burger's failure to engage, so annoying to Schmidt and other commentators, is in fact a great strength of the opinion."

Would a statute requiring nondiscriminatory access to the classified ads section of a newspaper pass muster under *Miami Herald?* A requirement that legal notices be published?

4. *Absolute editorial autonomy—some of the time.* Is it ironic that *Gertz,* p. 707 supra was decided the same day as *Miami Herald?* Which poses a greater threat to editorial autonomy—a negligence standard in defamation cases or the guaranteed access contemplated by the Florida statute? Whose autonomy is important—the editors or the owners? May government protect editors from ad hoc intervention by corporate owners? See generally Baker, *Human Liberty and Freedom of Speech* 225–71 (1989).

5. *The threat to editorial autonomy in Red Lion.* Consider Schmidt, fn. c supra, at 166: *Red Lion* "left broadcaster autonomy almost entirely at the mercy of the FCC." See also Van Alstyne, *The Möbius Strip of the First Amendment: Perspectives on Red Lion,* 29 S.C.L.Rev. 539, 571 (1978): "Indeed, if one continues to be troubled by *Red Lion,* I think it is not because one takes lightly the difficulty of forum allocation in a society of scarce resources. Rather, it is because one believes that the technique of the fairness doctrine in particular may represent a very trivial egalitarian gain and a major first amendment loss; that a twist has been given to the equal protection idea by a device the principal effect of which is merely to level down the most vivid and versatile forum we have, to flatten it out and to render it a mere commercial mirror of each community. What may have been lost is a willingness to risk the partisanship of licensees as catalysts and as active advocates with a freedom to exhort, a

h. Does *Miami Herald* demonstrate, as Professor Nimmer believes, at 644–46, that free speech and press can be distinct, even conflicting interests? A. Lewis, *A Preferred Position for Journalism?,* 7 Hof.L.Rev. 595, 603 (1979), thinks not: "[T]he vice of the [Florida right of reply] law lay in the compulsion to publish; and I think the result would be no different if the case involved a compulsion to speak. If a state statute required any candidate who spoke falsely about another to make a corrective speech, would it survive challenge under the first amendment?"

i. "Even in the area of 'the central freedom of the First Amendment,' which is criticism of the governmental acts of public officials," recalls Professor Schmidt, fn. c supra, at 232, "there is no absolute protection for expression."

freedom that dares to exclaim 'Fuck the draft,' and not be made to yield by government at once to add, 'but on the other hand there is also the view, held by many.' "

6. *The best of both worlds.* "[T]he critical difference between what the Court was asked to do in *Red Lion* and what it was asked to do in *Miami Herald,*" maintains Professor Bollinger note 1 supra, at 27, "involved choosing between a partial regulatory system and a universal one. Viewed from that perspective, the Court reached the correct result in both cases." Continues Bollinger at 27, 32–33, 36–37: "[T]here are good first amendment reasons for being both receptive to and wary of access regulation. This dual nature of access legislation suggests the need to limit carefully the intrusiveness of the regulation in order safely to enjoy its remedial benefits. Thus, a proper judicial response is one that will permit the legislature to provide the public with access *somewhere* within the mass media, but not throughout the press. The Court should not, and need not, be forced into an all-or-nothing position on this matter; there is nothing in the first amendment that forbids having the best of both worlds."

For a powerful critique of the regulated world, see Powe, *American Broadcasting and the First Amendment* (1987). For a powerful critique of the unregulated world, see Ingber, *The First Amendment in Modern Garb,* 56 G.W.U.L.Rev. 187 (1987).

7. *Cable television.* Can government require cable operators to grant an access channel for the public, for the government, and for educational institutions? Which is the better analogy: *Red Lion* or *Miami Herald?*

Need government lease space or otherwise afford access to utility poles under its control (and grant rights of way) to all competing cable companies? Is the appropriate analogy to *Schneider? Perry? Vincent? Red Lion? Miami Herald?*

LOS ANGELES v. PREFERRED COMMUNICATIONS, INC., 476 U.S. 488, 106 S.Ct. 2034, 90 L.Ed.2d 480 (1986), per REHNQUIST, J., upheld the refusal to dismiss a complaint brought by a cable company demanding access to a city's utility poles and resisting access channels: "Cable television partakes of some of the aspects of speech and the communication of ideas as do the traditional enterprises of newspapers and [book publishers]. Respondent's proposed activities would seem to implicate First Amendment interests as do the activities of wireless broadcasters, which were found to fall within the ambit of the First Amendment in [*Red Lion*]. Of course, ['Even] protected speech is not equally permissible in all places and at all times.' *Cornelius.* Moreover, where speech and conduct are joined in a single course of action, the First Amendment values must be balanced against competing societal interests. See, e.g., *Vincent; O'Brien.*"

The Court postponed fuller discussion of any cable rights until a factual record had been developed.[j]

---

j. For cogent discussion of the technology and the first amendment issues involved, see Brenner, *Cable Television and the Freedom of Expression,* 1988 Duke L.J. 329. See also Powe, supra, at 216–47; Saylor, *Municipal Ripoff: The Unconstitutionality of Cable Television Franchise Fees and Access Support Payments,* 35 Cath.U.L.Rev. 671 (1986); Pool, *Technologies of Freedom* 151–88 (1983); Price, *Taming Red Lion: The First Amendment and Structural Approaches to Media Regulation,* 31 Fed.Comm.L.J. 215 (1979); Comment, *Access to Cable Television: A Critique of the Affirmative Duty Theory of the First Amendment,* 70 Calif.L.Rev. 1393 (1982). For discussion of other technologies, see Special Issue, *Videotex,* 36 Fed.Comm.L.J. 119 (1984).

"Like many equal protection issues," observes Karst, p. 646 supra, at 45, "the media-access problem should be approached from two separate constitutional directions. First, what does the Constitution *compel* government to do in the way of equalizing? Second, what does the Constitution *permit* government to do in equalizing by statute?" *Red Lion* and *Miami Herald* presented the second question; the first is raised by COLUMBIA BROADCASTING SYSTEM, INC. v. DEMOCRATIC NAT. COMMITTEE, 412 U.S. 94, 93 S.Ct. 2080, 36 L.Ed.2d 772 (1973) (*CBS*): The FCC rejected the claims of Business Executives' Move for Vietnam Peace (BEM) and the Democratic National Committee (DNC) that "responsible" individuals and groups are entitled to purchase advertising time to comment on public issues, even though the broadcaster has complied with the fairness doctrine. The District of Columbia Circuit held that "a flat ban on paid public issue announcements" violates the first amendment "at least when other sorts of paid announcements are accepted," and remanded to the FCC to develop "reasonable procedures and regulations determining which and how many 'editorial advertisements' will be put on the air." The Supreme Court, per BURGER, C.J., reversed, holding that neither the "public interest" standard of the Communications Act (which draws heavily from the first amendment) nor the first amendment itself—assuming that refusal to accept such advertising constituted "governmental action" for first amendment purposes[a]—requires broadcasters to accept paid editorial announcements. As pointed out in Blasi, *The Checking Value in First Amendment Theory*, 1977 Am.B.Found.Res.J. 521, 613–14 although the Chief Justice "built to some extent" on *Red Lion*, his opinion "evinced a most important change of emphasis. For whereas Justice White based his argument in *Red Lion* on the premise that broadcasters are mere 'proxies' or 'fiduciaries' for the general public, the Chief Justice's opinion [in *CBS*] invoked a concept of 'journalistic independence' or 'journalistic discretion,' the essence of which is that broadcasters do indeed have special First Amendment interests which have to be considered in the constitutional calculus."

Observed the Chief Justice: "[From various provisions of the Communications Act of 1934] it seems clear that Congress intended to permit private broadcasting to develop with the widest journalistic freedom consistent with its public obligations. Only when the interests of the public are found to outweigh the private journalistic interests of the broadcasters will government power be asserted within the framework of the Act. License renewal proceedings, in which the listening public can be heard, are a principal means of such regulation.

"[W]ith the advent of radio a half century ago, Congress was faced with a fundamental choice between total Government ownership and control of the new medium—the choice of most other countries—or some other alternative. Long before the impact and potential of the medium was realized, Congress opted for a system of private broadcasters licensed and regulated by Government. The legislative history suggests that this choice was influenced not only by traditional attitudes toward private enterprise, but by a desire to maintain for licensees, so far as consistent with necessary regulation, a traditional journalistic [role.]

a. Burger, C.J., joined by Stewart and Rehnquist, JJ., concluded that a broadcast licensee's refusal to accept an advertisement was not "governmental action" for first amendment purposes. Although White, Blackmun and Powell, JJ., concurred in other parts of the Chief Justice's opinion, they did not decide this question for, *assuming* governmental action, they found that the challenged ban did not violate the first amendment. Douglas, J., who concurred in the result, assumed *no* governmental action. Dissenting, Brennan, J., joined by Marshall, J., found that the challenged ban did constitute "governmental action."

"The regulatory scheme evolved slowly, but very early the licensee's role developed in terms of a 'public trustee' charged with the duty of fairly and impartially informing the public audience. In this structure the Commission acts in essence as an 'overseer,' but the initial and primary responsibility for fairness, balance, and objectivity rests with the licensee. This role of the Government as an overseer and ultimate arbiter and guardian of the public interest and the role of the licensee as a journalistic 'free agent' call for a delicate balancing of competing interests. The maintenance of this balance for more than 40 years has called on both the regulators and the licensees to walk a 'tightrope' to preserve the First Amendment values written into the Radio Act and its successor, the Communications Act.

"The tensions inherent in such a regulatory structure emerge more clearly when we compare a private newspaper with a broadcast licensee. The power of a privately owned newspaper to advance its own political, social, and economic views is bounded by only two factors: first, the acceptance of a sufficient number of readers—and hence advertisers—to assure financial success; and, second, the journalistic integrity of its editors and publishers. A broadcast licensee has a large measure of journalistic freedom but not as large as that exercised by a newspaper. A licensee must balance what it might prefer to do as a private entrepreneur with what it is required to do as a 'public trustee.' To perform its statutory duties, the Commission must oversee without censoring. This suggests something of the difficulty and delicacy of administering the Communications Act—a function calling for flexibility and the capacity to adjust and readjust the regulatory mechanism to meet changing problems and needs.

"The licensee policy challenged in this case is intimately related to the journalistic role of a licensee for which it has been given initial and primary responsibility by Congress. The licensee's policy against accepting editorial advertising cannot be examined as an abstract proposition, but must be viewed in the context of its journalistic role. It does not help to press on us the idea that editorial ads are 'like' commercial ads, for the licensee's policy against editorial spot ads is expressly based on a journalistic judgment that 10- to 60-second spot announcements are ill-suited to intelligible and intelligent treatment of public issues; the broadcaster has chosen to provide a balanced treatment of controversial questions in a more comprehensive form. Obviously, the licensee's evaluation is based on its own journalistic judgment of priorities and newsworthiness.

"Moreover, the Commission has not fostered the licensee policy challenged here; it has simply declined to command particular action because it fell within the area of journalistic discretion. [The] Commission's reasoning, consistent with nearly 40 years of precedent, is that so long as a licensee meets its 'public trustee' obligation to provide balanced coverage of issues and events, it has broad discretion to decide how that obligation will be met. We do not reach the question whether the First Amendment or the Act can be read to preclude the Commission from determining that in some situations the public interest requires licensees to re-examine their policies with respect to editorial advertisements.[b] The Commission has not yet made such a determination; it has, for the

b. *Columbia Broadcasting System, Inc. v. FCC,* 453 U.S. 367, 101 S.Ct. 2813, 69 L.Ed.2d 706 (1981) upheld FCC administration of a statutory provision guaranteeing "reasonable" access to the airwaves for federal election candidates. The Court, per Burger, C.J., observed that "the Court has never approved a *general* right of access to the media. *Miami Herald; CBS v. DNC.* Nor do we do so today." But it found that the limited right of access "properly balances the First Amendment rights of federal candidates, the public, present at least, found the policy to be within the sphere of journalistic discretion which Congress has left with the licensee.

"[I]t must constantly be kept in mind that the interest of the public is our foremost concern. With broadcasting, where the available means of communication are limited in both space and time, [Meiklejohn's admonition] that '[w]hat is essential is not that everyone shall speak, but that everything worth saying shall be said' is peculiarly appropriate.

"[Congress] has time and again rejected various legislative attempts that would have mandated a variety of forms of individual access. [It] has chosen to leave such questions with the Commission, to which it has given the flexibility to experiment with new ideas as changing conditions require. In this case, the Commission has decided that on balance the undesirable effects of the right of access urged by respondents would outweigh the asserted [benefits.]

"The Commission was justified in concluding that the public interest in providing access to the marketplace of 'ideas and experiences' would scarcely be served by a system so heavily weighted in favor of the financially affluent, or those with access to wealth. Even under a first-come-first-served system [the] views of the affluent could well prevail over those of others, since they would have it within their power to purchase time more frequently. Moreover, there is the substantial danger [that] the time allotted for editorial advertising could be monopolized by those of one political persuasion.

"These problems would not necessarily be solved by applying the Fairness Doctrine, including the *Cullman* doctrine [requiring broadcasters to provide free time for the presentation of opposing views if a paid sponsor is unavailable], to editorial advertising. If broadcasters were required to provide time, free when necessary, for the discussion of the various shades of opinion on the issue discussed in the advertisement, the affluent could still determine in large part the issues to be discussed. Thus, the very premise of the Court of Appeals' holding—that a right of access is necessary to allow individuals and groups the opportunity for self-initiated speech—would have little meaning to those who could not afford to purchase time in the first instance.

"If the Fairness Doctrine were applied to editorial advertising, there is also the substantial danger that the effective operation of that doctrine would be jeopardized. To minimize financial hardship and to comply fully with its public responsibilities a broadcaster might well be forced to make regular programming time available to those holding a view different from that expressed in an editorial advertisement. [The] result would be a further erosion of the journalistic discretion of broadcasters in the coverage of public issues, and a transfer of control over the treatment of public issues from the licensees who are accountable for broadcast performance to private individuals who are not. The public interest would no longer be 'paramount' but rather subordinate to private whim especially since, under the Court of Appeals' decision, a broadcaster would be largely precluded from rejecting editorial advertisements that dealt with matters trivial or insignificant or already fairly covered by the broadcaster. If the Fairness Doctrine and the *Cullman* doctrine were suspended to alleviate these problems, as respondents suggest might be appropriate, the question arises whether we would have abandoned more than we have gained. Under such a

and broadcasters." White, J., joined by Rehnquist and Stevens, JJ., dissented on statutory grounds. For criticism, see Polsby, *Candidate Access to the Air: The Uncertain Future of Broadcaster Discretion,* 1981 Sup.Ct.Rev. 223.

regime the congressional objective of balanced coverage of public issues would be seriously threatened.

"Nor can we accept the Court of Appeals' view that every potential speaker is 'the best judge' of what the listening public ought to hear or indeed the best judge of the merits of his or her views. All journalistic tradition and experience is to the contrary. For better or worse, editing is what editors are for; and editing is selection and choice of material. That editors—newspaper or broadcast—can and do abuse this power is beyond doubt, but that is not reason to deny the discretion Congress provided. Calculated risks of abuse are taken in order to preserve higher values. The presence of these risks is nothing new; the authors of the Bill of Rights accepted the reality that these risks were evils for which there was no acceptable remedy other than a spirit of moderation and a sense of responsibility—and civility—on the part of those who exercise the guaranteed freedoms of expression.

"It was reasonable for Congress to conclude that the public interest in being informed requires periodic accountability on the part of those who are entrusted with the use of broadcast frequencies, scarce as they are. In the delicate balancing historically followed in the regulation of broadcasting Congress and the Commission could appropriately conclude that the allocation of journalistic priorities should be concentrated in the licensee rather than diffused among many. This policy gives the public some assurance that the broadcaster will be answerable if he fails to meet their legitimate needs. No such accountability attaches to the private individual, whose only qualifications for using the broadcast facility may be abundant funds and a point of view. To agree that debate on public issues should be 'robust, and wide-open' does not mean that we should exchange 'public trustee' broadcasting, with all its limitations, for a system of self-appointed editorial commentators.

"[T]he risk of an enlargement of Government control over the content of broadcast discussion of public issues [is] inherent in the Court of Appeals' remand requiring regulations and procedures to sort out requests to be heard—a process involving the very editing that licensees now perform as to regular programming. [Under] a constitutionally commanded and government supervised right-of-access system urged by respondents and mandated by the Court of Appeals, the Commission would be required to oversee far more of the day-to-day operations of broadcasters' conduct, deciding such questions as whether a particular individual or group has had sufficient opportunity to present its viewpoint and whether a particular viewpoint has already been sufficiently aired. Regimenting broadcasters is too radical a therapy for the ailment respondents complain of. * * *

"The Commission is also entitled to take into account the reality that in a very real sense listeners and viewers constitute a 'captive audience.' [It] is no answer to say that because we tolerate pervasive commercial advertisement [we] can also live with its political counterparts.

"The rationale for the Court of Appeals' decision imposing a constitutional right of access on the broadcast media was that the licensee impermissibly discriminates by accepting commercial advertisements while refusing editorial advertisements. The court relied on [lower court cases] holding that state-supported school newspapers and public transit companies were forbidden by the First Amendment from excluding controversial editorial advertisements in favor of commercial advertisements.[c] The court also attempted to analogize this case to some of our decisions holding that States may not constitutionally ban certain protected speech while at the same time permitting other speech in public areas [citing e.g., *Grayned* and *Mosley,* Sec. 6 supra].

"These decisions provide little guidance, however, in resolving the question whether the First Amendment required the Commission to mandate a private right of access to the broadcast media. In none of those cases did the forum sought for expression have an affirmative and independent statutory obligation to provide full and fair coverage of public issues, such as Congress has imposed on all broadcast licensees. In short, there is no 'discrimination' against controversial speech present in this case. The question here is not whether there is to be discussion of controversial issues of public importance on the broadcast media, but rather who shall determine what issues are to be discussed by whom, and when."

DOUGLAS, J., concurred in the result, but "for quite different reasons." Because the Court did not decide whether a broadcast licensee is "a federal agency within the context of this case," he assumed that it was not. He "fail[ed] to see," then "how constitutionally we can treat TV and the radio differently than we treat newspapers":

"I did not participate in [*Red Lion* and] would not support it. The Fairness Doctrine has no place in our First Amendment regime. It puts the head of the camel inside the tent and enables administration after administration to toy with TV or radio in order to serve its sordid or its benevolent ends. [The uniqueness of radio and TV] is due to engineering and technical problems. But the press in a realistic sense is likewise not available to all. [T]he daily newspapers now established are unique in the sense that it would be virtually impossible for a competitor to enter the field due to the financial exigencies of this era. The result is that in practical terms the newspapers and magazines, like the TV and radio, are available only to a select few. [That] may argue for a redefinition of the responsibilities of the press in First Amendment terms. But I do not think it gives us carte blanche to design systems of supervision and control nor empower [the government to] make 'some' laws 'abridging' freedom of the press. * * *

"Licenses are, of course, restricted in time and while, in my view, Congress has the power to make each license limited to a fixed term and nonreviewable, there is no power to deny renewals for editorial or ideological reasons [for] the First Amendment gives no preference to one school of thought over the others.

"The Court in today's decision by endorsing the Fairness Doctrine sanctions a federal saddle on broadcast licensees that is agreeable to the traditions of nations that never have known freedom of press and that is tolerable in countries that do not have a written constitution containing prohibitions as absolute as those in the First Amendment."[d]

BRENNAN, J., joined by Marshall, J., dissented, viewing "the *absolute* ban on the sale of air time for the discussion of controversial issues" as "governmental action"[e] violating the first amendment: "As a practical matter, the Court's reliance on the Fairness Doctrine as an 'adequate' alternative to editorial advertising seriously overestimates the ability—or willingness—of broadcasters

c. But see *Lehman v. Shaker Heights*, p. 926 supra.

d. Noting that his views "closely approach those expressed by Mr. Justice Douglas," Stewart, J., also concurred.

e. See fn. a supra and p. 1217 infra.

to expose the public to the 'widest possible dissemination of information from diverse and antagonistic sources.' [Indeed,] in light of the strong interest of broadcasters in maximizing their audience, and therefore their profits, it seems almost naive to expect the majority of broadcasters to produce the variety and controversiality of material necessary to reflect a full spectrum of viewpoints. Stated simply, angry customers are not good customers and, in the commercial world of mass communications, it is simply 'bad business' to espouse—or even to allow others to espouse—the heterodox or the controversial. As a result, even under the Fairness Doctrine, broadcasters generally tend to permit only established—or at least moderated—views to enter the broadcast world's 'marketplace of ideas.' [24]

"Moreover, the Court's reliance on the Fairness Doctrine as the *sole* means of informing the public seriously misconceives and underestimates the public's interest in receiving ideas and information directly from the advocates of those ideas without the interposition of journalistic middlemen. Under the Fairness Doctrine, broadcasters decide what issues are 'important,' how 'fully' to cover them, and what format, time and style of coverage are 'appropriate.' The retention of such *absolute* control in the hands of a few government licensees is inimical to the First Amendment, for vigorous, free debate can be attained only when members of the public have at least *some* opportunity to take the initiative and editorial control into their own hands.

"[S]tanding alone, [the Fairness Doctrine] simply cannot eliminate the need for a further, complementary airing of controversial views through the limited availability of editorial advertising. Indeed, the availability of at least *some* opportunity for editorial advertising is imperative if we are ever to attain the 'free and general discussion of public matters [that] seems absolutely essential to prepare the people for an intelligent exercise of their rights as citizens.'

"Moreover, a proper balancing of the competing First Amendment interests at stake in this controversy must consider, not only the interests of broadcasters and of the listening and viewing public, but also the independent First Amendment interest of groups and individuals in effective self-expression. [I]n a time of apparently growing anonymity of the individual in our society, it is imperative that we take special care to preserve the vital First Amendment interest in assuring 'self-fulfillment [of expression] for each individual.' For our citizens may now find greater than ever the need to express their own views directly to the public, rather than through a governmentally appointed surrogate, if they are to feel that they can achieve at least some measure of control over their own destinies.

"[F]reedom of speech does not exist in the abstract. [It] can flourish only if it is allowed to operate in an effective forum—whether it be a public park, a schoolroom, a town meeting hall, a soapbox, or a radio and television frequency. For in the absence of an effective means of communication, the right to speak would ring hollow indeed. And, in recognition of these principles, we have consistently held that the First Amendment embodies not only the abstract right to be free from censorship, but also the right of an individual to utilize an appropriate and effective medium for the expression of his views.

"[W]ith the assistance of the Federal Government, the broadcast industry has become what is potentially the most efficient and effective 'marketplace of ideas' ever devised. [Thus], although 'full and free discussion' of ideas may have

24. [Citing many secondary sources to support this statement.]

been a reality in the heyday of political pamphleteering, modern technological developments in the field of communications have made the soapbox orator and the leafleteer virtually obsolete. And, in light of the current dominance of the electronic media as the most effective means of reaching the public, any policy that *absolutely* denies citizens access to the airwaves necessarily renders even the concept of 'full and free discussion' practically meaningless.

"[T]he challenged ban can be upheld only if it is determined that such editorial advertising would unjustifiably impair the broadcaster's assertedly overriding interest in exercising *absolute* control over 'his' frequency. Such an analysis, however, hardly reflects the delicate balancing of interests that this sensitive question demands. Indeed, this 'absolutist' approach wholly disregards the competing First Amendment rights of all 'nonbroadcaster' citizens, ignores the teachings of our recent decision in *Red Lion,* and is not supported by the historical purposes underlying broadcast regulation in this Nation. [T]here is simply no overriding First Amendment interest of broadcasters that can justify the *absolute* exclusion of virtually all of our citizens from the most effective 'marketplace of ideas' ever devised.

"[T]his case deals *only* with the allocation of *advertising* time—airtime that broadcasters regularly relinquish to others without the retention of significant editorial control. Thus, we are concerned here not with the speech of broadcasters themselves but, rather, with their 'right' to decide which *other* individuals will be given an opportunity to speak in a forum that has already been opened to the public.

"Viewed in this context, the *absolute* ban on editorial advertising seems particularly offensive because, although broadcasters refuse to sell any airtime whatever to groups or individuals wishing to speak out on controversial issues of public importance, they make such airtime readily available to those 'commercial' advertisers who seek to peddle their goods and services to the public. [Yet an] individual seeking to discuss war, peace, pollution, or the suffering of the poor is denied this right to speak. Instead, he is compelled to rely on the beneficence of a corporate 'trustee' appointed by the Government to argue his case for him.

"It has been long recognized, however, that although access to public forums may be subjected to reasonable 'time, place, and manner' regulations, '[s]elective exclusions from a public forum, may not be based on *content* alone.' *Mosley* (emphasis added). Here, of course, the differential treatment accorded 'commercial' and 'controversial' speech clearly violates that principle. Moreover, and not without some irony, the favored treatment given 'commercial' speech under the existing scheme clearly reverses traditional First Amendment priorities. For it has generally been understood that 'commercial' speech enjoys *less* First Amendment protection than speech directed at the discussion of controversial issues of public importance."

Notes and Questions

1. *Confronting scarcity.* Consider Tribe, *American Constitutional Law* 1005 (2d ed.1988): "*CBS* took a step away from *Red Lion* by its treatment of broadcasters as part of the 'press' with an important editorial function to perform rather than as analogous to the postal or telephone systems, but *CBS* was firmly in the *Red Lion* tradition when it refused to consider the possibility that either the technologically scarce radio and television channels, or the finite time available on such channels, might be allocated much as economically scarce

newspaper opportunities are allocated: by a combination of market mechanisms and chance rather than by government design coupled with broadcaster autonomy."

Suppose the government sold the airwaves to the highest bidder and allowed subsequent exchange according to property and contract law. Consider Note, *Reconciling Red Lion and Tornillo: A Consistent Theory of Media Regulation,* 28 Stan.L.Rev. 563, 583 (1976): "This regulatory strategy would remove the government from direct determination of the particular individuals who are allowed to broadcast, leaving this decision to market forces, and would avoid the need for specific behavioral commands and sanctions now necessary to secure compliance by broadcasters with the various obligations imposed by the public interest standard. [Under] strict scrutiny, then, the existence of this clearly identifiable less restrictive alternative indicates that the Communications Act is unconstitutional."

But see Van Alstyne, p. 696 supra, at 563: "Congress may indeed be free to 'sell off' the airwaves, and it may be wholly feasible to allocate most currently established broadcast signals by competitive bidding that, when done, may well produce private licensees operating truly without subsidy. But only a singularly insensitive observer would believe that this choice is not implicitly also a highly speech-restrictive choice by Congress. It is fully as speech-restrictive as though, in the case of land, government were to withdraw from *all* ownership and all subsidized maintenance of all land, including parks, auditoriums, and streets and to remain in the field exclusively as a policeman to enforce the proprietary decisions of all private landowners." [f]

Should it be constitutional for the government to exercise "ownership" over the entire broadcast spectrum? See Spitzer, *The Constitutionality of Licensing Broadcasters,* 64 N.Y.U.L.Rev. 990 (1989); Shiffrin, *Government Speech,* 27 UCLA L.Rev. 565, 587 n. 122, 644–45 (1980).

2. *The "fairness" doctrine criticized.* The Court's assumption that the fairness doctrine works tolerably well has been roasted by the commentators. See, e.g., Rowan, *Broadcast Fairness: Doctrine, Practice, Prospects* (1984); Simmons, *The Fairness Doctrine and the Media* (1978); Johnson & Dystel, *A Day in the Life: The Federal Communications Commission,* 82 Yale L.J. 1575 (1973). Consider Krattenmaker & Powe, *The Fairness Doctrine Today: A Constitutional Curiosity and an Impossible Dream,* 1985 Duke L.J. 151, 175: "If the doctrine is to be taken seriously then suspected violations lurk everywhere and the FCC should undertake continuous oversight of the industry. If the FCC will not—or cannot—do that, then the doctrine must be toothless except for the randomly-selected few who are surprised to feel its bite after the fact." For a vigorous defense of the fairness doctrine, see Ferris & Kirkland, *Fairness—The Broadcaster's Hippocratic Oath,* 34 Cath.U.L.Rev. 605 (1985).

3. *The fairness doctrine repealed.* The FCC concluded a 15 month administrative proceeding with an official denunciation of the fairness doctrine, pointing in particular to the marked increase in the information services marketplace since *Red Lion* and the effects of the doctrine in application. FCC, [*General*] *Fairness Doctrine Obligations of Broadcast Licensees,* 102 F.C.C.2d 143 (1985). *Syracuse Peace Council,* 2 FCC Rcd 5043 (1987) held that "under the constitutional standard established by *Red Lion* and its progeny, the fairness doctrine contravenes the First Amendment and its enforcement is no longer in the public

f. For detailed criticism of the scarcity argument, see Spitzer, *Controlling the Content of Print and Broadcast,* 58 S.Cal.L.Rev. 1349 (1985).

interest." [g]

4. *The worst of both worlds.* Evaluate the following hypothetical commentary: "*CBS v. DNC* allows government to grant virtually exclusive control over American's most valuable communication medium to corporations who regard it as their mission to 'deliver' audiences to advertisers. The system gives us the worst of both worlds: the world of profit-seeking—without a free market; the world of regulation—without planning." For discussion of alternatives, see Cass, *Revolution in the Wasteland* (1981); Owen, *Economics and Freedom of Expression: Media Structure and the First Amendment* (1975); Firestone & Jacklin, *Deregulation and the Pursuit of Fairness* in Telecommunications Policy and the Citizen 107 (Haight ed. 1979); Nader & Riley, *Oh Say Can You See: A Broadcast Network for the Audience,* 5 J.L. & Pol. 1 (1988). Owen, *Structural Approaches to the Problem of Television Network Economic Dominance,* 1979 Duke L.J. 191.

5. Do access proposals miss the central problem? Is television at the heart of an "amusement-centered culture" that substitutes images and sound bites for serious public discourse while encouraging a privatized nonengaged citizenry? Consider Collins and Scover, *The First Amendment in an Age of Paratroopers,* 68 Tex.L.Rev. 1087, 1088–89 (1990): "With entertainment as the paradigm for most public discourse, traditional first amendment values—which stress civic restraint and serious dialogue—are overshadowed. Given these core values and the anticensorial direction of first amendment theory, is there anything that could (or should) be done to thwart, rather than to feed, an amusement-centered culture?

"In attempting to answer this question, we confront a paradox: by saving itself, the first amendment destroys itself. On the one hand, to preserve its anticensorial ideals, the first amendment must protect both the old and new media cultures. Accordingly, it must constrain most governmental controls over expression, including those over the commercial use of electronic media. On the other hand, if the first amendment's protections do not differentiate between the old and new media cultures, the modern obsession with self-amusement will trivialize public discourse and undermine the traditional aim of the first amendment." [h]

METRO BROADCASTING v. FCC, ___ U.S. ___, 110 S.Ct. 2997, 111 L.Ed.2d 445 (1990), per BRENNAN, J., reaffirmed the government's power to regulate the airwaves in the context of upholding minority ownership policies designed to effectuate more diverse programming: "We have long recognized that '[b]ecause of the scarcity of [electromagnetic] frequencies, the Government is permitted to put restraints on licensees in favor of others whose views should be expressed on this unique medium.' *Red Lion.* The Government's role in distributing the limited number of broadcast licenses is not merely that of a 'traffic officer;' rather, it is axiomatic that broadcasting may be regulated in light of the rights of the viewing and listening audience and that 'the widest possible dissemination of information from diverse and antagonistic sources is essential to the welfare

g. *Syracuse Peace Council v. FCC,* 867 F.2d 654 (D.C.Cir.1989) affirmed the FCC's determination that the fairness doctrine no longer serves the public interest without reaching constitutional issues. On June 20, 1987 President Reagan had vetoed congressional legislation designed to preserve the fairness doctrine on the ground that the legislation was unconstitutional.

h. For discussion of the Collins–Skover paradox by Max Lerner, David M. O'Brien, Martin Redish, Edward Rubin, Herbert Schiller, and Mark Tushnet, see Colloquy: *The First Amendment and the Paratroopers Paradox,* 68 Texas L.Rev. 1087 (1990).

of the public.' Safeguarding the public's right to receive a diversity of views and information over the airwaves is [consistent] with 'the ends and purposes of the First Amendment' * * *.

"The benefits of such diversity are not limited to the members of minority groups who gain access to the broadcasting industry by virtue of the ownership policies; rather, the benefits redound to all members of the viewing and listening audience. [W]e conclude that the interest in enhancing broadcast diversity is, at the very least, an important governmental objective and is therefore a sufficient basis for the Commission's minority ownership policies. Just as a 'diverse student body' contributing to a 'robust exchange of ideas' is a 'constitutionally permissible goal' on which a race-conscious university admissions program may be predicated, *Bakke* (opinion of Powell, J.), the diversity of views and information on the airwaves serves important First Amendment values."

O'CONNOR, J., joined by Rehnquist, C.J., Scalia and Kennedy, JJ., dissenting, also recognized and reaffirmed governmental power to regulate broadcasting: "The Court has recognized an interest in obtaining diverse broadcasting viewpoints as a legitimate basis for the FCC, acting pursuant to its 'public interest' statutory mandate, to adopt limited measures to increase the number of competing licensees and to encourage licensees to present varied views on issues of public concern. See, e.g., *Red Lion.* We have also concluded that [such] measures do not run afoul of the First Amendment's usual prohibition of Government regulation of the marketplace of ideas, in part because first amendment concerns support limited but inevitable Government regulation of the peculiarly constrained broadcasting spectrum. See, e.g., *Red Lion.* But the conclusion that measures adopted to further the interest in diversity of broadcasting viewpoints are neither beyond the FCC's statutory authority nor contrary to the First Amendment hardly establishes the interest as important for equal protection purposes.

"The FCC's extension of the asserted interest in diversity of views in this case presents, at the very least, an unsettled First Amendment issue. The FCC has concluded that the American broadcasting public receives the incorrect mix of ideas and claims to have adopted the challenged policies to supplement programming content with a particular set of views. Although we have approved limited measures designed to increase information and views generally, the Court has never upheld a broadcasting measure designed to amplify a distinct set of views or the views of a particular class of speakers. [Even] if an interest is determined to be legitimate in one context, it does not suddenly become important enough to justify distinctions based on race."

II. BROADCASTING AND CONTENT REGULATION: BEYOND THE FAIRNESS DOCTRINE

A. INDECENT SPEECH

FCC v. PACIFICA FOUNDATION

438 U.S. 726, 98 S.Ct. 3026, 57 L.Ed.2d 1073 (1978).

[JUSTICE STEVENS delivered the opinion of the Court (Parts I, II, III, and IV–C) and an opinion in which CHIEF JUSTICE BURGER and JUSTICE REHNQUIST joined (Parts IV–A and IV–B).

[In an early afternoon weekday broadcast in October 1973, respondent's New York radio station aired a 12-minute selection called "Filthy Words," from a comedy album by a satiric humorist, George Carlin. The monologue, which had evoked frequent laughter from a live theater audience before whom it had originally been delivered, began by referring to Carlin's thought about the seven words you can't say on the public airwaves, "the ones you definitely wouldn't say ever." He then listed the words ("shit," "piss," "fuck," "motherfucker," "cocksucker," "cunt," and "tits"), "the ones that will curve your spine, grow hair on your hands and (laughter) maybe, even bring us, God help us, peace without honor (laughter) um, and a bourbon (laughter)," and repeated them over and over in a variety of colloquialisms. The monologue was played as part of the station's regular program, which was devoted that day to contemporary attitudes toward the use of language. Immediately prior to the broadcast of the Carlin monologue, listeners were advised that it included sensitive language which some might regard as offensive. Those who might be offended were advised to change the station and return in fifteen minutes.

[The FCC received a complaint from a man in New York stating that while driving in his car with his young son he had heard the broadcast of the Carlin monologue. In response, the FCC issued a Declaratory Order granting the complaint and holding that Pacifica "could have been the subject of administrative sanctions," but that this order would only be "associated with the station's license file, and in the event that subsequent complaints are received, the Commission will then decide whether it should utilize any of the available sanctions it has been granted by Congress."] [a]

The Commission characterized the language used in the Carlin monologue as "patently offensive," though not necessarily obscene, and expressed the opinion that it should be regulated by principles analogous to those found in the law of nuisance where the "law generally speaks to *channeling* behavior more than actually prohibiting it. [T]he concept of 'indecent' is intimately connected with the exposure of children to language that describes, in terms patently offensive as measured by contemporary community standards for the broadcast medium, sexual or excretory activities and organs, at times of the day when there is a reasonable risk that children may be in the audience." [5]

Applying these considerations to the language used in the monologue as broadcast by respondent, the Commission concluded that certain words depicted sexual and excretory activities in a patently offensive manner, noted that they "were broadcast at a time when children were undoubtedly in the audience (i.e., in the early afternoon)," and that the prerecorded language, with these offensive words "repeated over and over," was "deliberately broadcast." In summary, the Commission stated: "We therefore hold that the language as broadcast was indecent and prohibited by 18 U.S.C. 1464 [forbidding the use of "any obscene, indecent or profane language" by means of radio communications.]" [The Commission subsequently clarified its opinion, pointing out] that it "never intended to place an absolute prohibition on the broadcast of this type of language, but rather sought to channel it to times of day when children most likely would not be exposed to it." * * *

IV.[b] Pacifica makes two constitutional attacks on the Commission's order. First, it argues that the Commission's construction of the statutory language

a. The FCC's action is placed in the context of other similar actions in Powe, *American Broadcasting and the First Amendment* 162–90 (1987).

5. Thus, the Commission suggested, if an offensive broadcast had literary, artistic, political or scientific value, and were preceded by warnings, it might not be indecent in the late evening, but would be so during the day, when children are in the audience.

b. Parts I, II, and III of the opinion are omitted.

broadly encompasses so much constitutionally protected speech that reversal is required even if Pacifica's broadcast of the "Filthy Words" monologue is not itself protected by the First Amendment. Second, Pacifica argues that inasmuch as the recording is not obscene, the Constitution forbids any abridgment of the right to broadcast it on the radio.

A. The first argument fails because our review is limited to the question whether the Commission has the authority to proscribe this particular broadcast. As the Commission itself emphasized, its order was "issued in a specific factual context." That approach is appropriate for courts as well as the Commission when regulation of indecency is at stake, for indecency is largely a function of context—it cannot be adequately judged in the abstract.

The approach is also consistent with *Red Lion.* In that case the Court rejected an argument that the Commission's regulations defining the fairness doctrine were so vague that they would inevitably abridge the broadcasters' freedom of speech. * * *

It is true that the Commission's order may lead some broadcasters to censor themselves. At most, however, the Commission's definition of indecency will deter only the broadcasting of patently offensive references to excretory and sexual organs and activities.[18] While some of these references may be protected, they surely lie at the periphery of First Amendment concern. The danger dismissed so summarily in *Red Lion,* in contrast, was that broadcasters would respond to the vagueness of the regulations by refusing to present programs dealing with important social and political controversies. Invalidating any rule on the basis of its hypothetical application to situations not before the Court is "strong medicine" to be applied "sparingly and only as a last resort." *Broadrick* [p. 770 supra]. We decline to administer that medicine to preserve the vigor of patently offensive sexual and excretory speech.

B. When the issue is narrowed to the facts of this case, the question is whether the First Amendment denies government any power to restrict the public broadcast of indecent language in any circumstances. For if the government has any such power, this was an appropriate occasion for its exercise.

The words of the Carlin monologue are unquestionably "speech" within the meaning of the First Amendment. It is equally clear that the Commission's objections to the broadcast were based in part on its content. The order must therefore fall if, as Pacifica argues, the First Amendment prohibits all governmental regulation that depends on the content of speech. Our past cases demonstrate, however, that no such absolute rule is mandated * * *.

The question in this case is whether a broadcast of patently offensive words dealing with sex and excretion may be regulated because of its content.[20] Obscene materials have been denied the protection of the First Amendment because their content is so offensive to contemporary moral standards. *Roth.* But the fact that society may find speech offensive is not a sufficient reason for suppressing it. Indeed, if it is the speaker's opinion that gives offense, that consequence is a reason for according it constitutional protection. For it is a central tenet of the First Amendment that the government must remain neutral

18. A requirement that indecent language be avoided will have its primary effect on the form, rather than the content, of serious communication. There are few, if any, thoughts that cannot be expressed by the use of less offensive language.

20. Although neither Justice Powell nor Justice Brennan directly confronts this question, both have answered it affirmatively, the latter explicitly, at fn. 3, infra, and the former implicitly by concurring in a judgment that could not otherwise stand.

in the marketplace of ideas. If there were any reason to believe that the Commission's characterization of the Carlin monologue as offensive could be traced to its political content—or even to the fact that it satirized contemporary attitudes about four letter words[22]—First Amendment protection might be required. But that is simply not this case. These words offend for the same reasons that obscenity offends. Their place in the hierarchy of First Amendment values was aptly sketched by Mr. Justice Murphy when he said, "such utterances are no essential part of any exposition of ideas, and are of such slight social value as a step to truth that any benefit that may be derived from them is clearly outweighed by the social interest in order and morality." *Chaplinsky.*

Although these words ordinarily lack literary, political, or scientific value, they are not entirely outside the protection of the First Amendment. Some uses of even the most offensive words are unquestionably protected. Indeed, we may assume, arguendo, that this monologue would be protected in other contexts. Nonetheless, the constitutional protection accorded to a communication containing such patently offensive sexual and excretory language need not be the same in every context. It is a characteristic of speech such as this that both its capacity to offend and its "social value," to use Mr. Justice Murphy's term, vary with the circumstances. Words that are commonplace in one setting are shocking in another. To paraphrase Mr. Justice Harlan, one occasion's lyric is another's vulgarity. Cf. *Cohen v. California.*[25]

In this case it is undisputed that the content of Pacifica's broadcast was "vulgar," "offensive," and "shocking." Because content of that character is not entitled to absolute constitutional protection under all circumstances, we must consider its context in order to determine whether the Commission's action was constitutionally permissible.

C. We have long recognized that each medium of expression presents special First Amendment problems. And of all forms of communication, it is broadcasting that has received the most limited First Amendment [protection.]

The reasons for these distinctions are complex, but two have relevance to the present case. First, the broadcast media have established a uniquely pervasive presence in the lives of all Americans. Patently offensive, indecent material presented over the airwaves confronts the citizen, not only in public, but also in the privacy of the home, where the individual's right to be let alone plainly outweighs the First Amendment rights of an intruder. *Rowan.* Because the broadcast audience is constantly tuning in and out, prior warnings cannot completely protect the listener or viewer from unexpected program content. To

22. The monologue does present a point of view; it attempts to show that the words it uses are "harmless" and that our attitudes toward them are "essentially silly." The Commission objects, not to this point of view, but to the way in which it is expressed. The belief that these words are harmless does not necessarily confer a First Amendment privilege to use them while proselytizing just as the conviction that obscenity is harmless does not license one to communicate that conviction by the indiscriminate distribution of an obscene leaflet.

25. The importance of context is illustrated by the *Cohen* case. [So] far as the evidence showed no one in the courthouse was offended by [Cohen's jacket.]

In holding that criminal sanctions could not be imposed on Cohen for his political statement in a public place, the Court rejected the argument that his speech would offend unwilling viewers; it noted that "there was no evidence that persons powerless to avoid [his] conduct did in fact object to it." In contrast, in this case the Commission was responding to a listener's strenuous complaint, and Pacifica does not question its determination that this afternoon broadcast was likely to offend listeners. It should be noted that the Commission imposed a far more moderate penalty on Pacifica than the state court imposed on Cohen. Even the strongest civil penalty at the Commission's command does not include criminal prosecution.

say that one may avoid further offense by turning off the radio when he hears indecent language is like saying that the remedy for an assault is to run away after the first blow. One may hang up on an indecent phone call, but that option does not give the caller a constitutional immunity or avoid a harm that has already taken place.[27]

Second, broadcasting is uniquely accessible to children, even those too young to read. Although Cohen's written message might have been incomprehensible to a first grader, Pacifica's broadcast could have enlarged a child's vocabulary in an instant. Other forms of offensive expression may be withheld from the young without restricting the expression at its source. Bookstores and motion picture theaters, for example, may be prohibited from making indecent material available to children. We held in *Ginsberg* [p. 474 supra] that the government's interest in the "well being of its youth" and in supporting "parents' claim to authority in their own household" justified the regulation of otherwise protected expression.[28] The ease with which children may obtain access to broadcast material, coupled with the concerns recognized in *Ginsberg,* amply justify special treatment of indecent broadcasting.

It is appropriate, in conclusion, to emphasize the narrowness of our holding. This case does not involve a two-way radio conversation between a cab driver and a dispatcher, or a telecast of an Elizabethan comedy. We have not decided that an occasional expletive in either setting would justify any sanction or, indeed, that this broadcast would justify a criminal prosecution. The Commission's decision rested entirely on a nuisance rationale under which context is all-important. The concept requires consideration of a host of variables. The time of day was emphasized by the Commission. The content of the program in which the language is used will also affect the composition of the audience, and differences between radio, television, and perhaps closed-circuit transmissions, may also be relevant. As Mr. Justice Sutherland wrote, a "nuisance may be merely a right thing in the wrong place—like a pig in the parlor instead of the barnyard." We simply hold that when the Commission finds that a pig has entered the parlor, the exercise of its regulatory power does not depend on proof that the pig is obscene.

[R]eversed.

JUSTICE POWELL, with whom JUSTICE BLACKMUN joins, concurring.

[The] Court today reviews only the Commission's holding that Carlin's monologue was indecent "as broadcast" at two o'clock in the afternoon, and not the broad sweep of the Commission's opinion. In addition to being consistent with our settled practice of not deciding constitutional issues unnecessarily, this narrow focus also is conducive to the orderly development of this relatively new and difficult area of law, in the first instance by the Commission, and then by the reviewing courts. * * *

[T]he language employed is, to most people, vulgar and offensive. It was chosen specifically for this quality, and it was repeated over and over as a sort of

27. Outside the home, the balance between the offensive speaker and the unwilling audience may sometimes tip in favor of the speaker, requiring the offended listener to turn away. See *Erznoznik.* * * *

28. The Commission's action does not by any means reduce adults to hearing only what is fit for children. Cf. *Butler v. Michigan* [p. 744 supra]. Adults who feel the need may purchase tapes and records or go to theatres and nightclubs to hear these words. In fact, the Commission has not unequivocally closed even broadcasting to speech of this sort; whether broadcast audiences in the late evening contain so few children that playing this monologue would be permissible is an issue neither the Commission nor this Court has decided.

verbal shock treatment. The Commission did not err in characterizing the narrow category of language used here as "patently offensive" to most people regardless of age.

The issue, however, is whether the Commission may impose civil sanctions on a licensee radio station for broadcasting the monologue at two o'clock in the afternoon. The Commission's primary concern was to prevent the broadcast from reaching the ears of unsupervised children who were likely to be in the audience at that hour. In essence, the Commission sought to "channel" the monologue to hours when the fewest unsupervised children would be exposed to it. In my view, this consideration provides strong support for the Commission's holding.

[The] Commission properly held that the speech from which society may attempt to shield its children is not limited to that which appeals to the youthful prurient interest. The language involved in this case is as potentially degrading and harmful to children as representations of many erotic acts.

In most instances, the dissemination of this kind of speech to children may be limited without also limiting willing adults' access to it. Sellers of printed and recorded matter and exhibitors of motion pictures and live performances may be required to shut their doors to children, but such a requirement has no effect on adults' access. See *Ginsberg.* The difficulty is that such a physical separation of the audience cannot be accomplished in the broadcast media. During most of the broadcast hours, both adults and unsupervised children are likely to be in the broadcast audience, and the broadcaster cannot reach willing adults without also reaching children. This, as the Court emphasizes, is one of the distinctions between the broadcast and other media to which we often have adverted as justifying a different treatment of the broadcast media for First Amendment purposes. In my view, the Commission was entitled to give substantial weight to this difference in reaching its decision in this case.

[Another difference] is that broadcasting—unlike most other forms of communication—comes directly into the home, the one place where people ordinarily have the right not to be assaulted by uninvited and offensive sights and sounds. *Erznoznik; Cohen; Rowan.* Although the First Amendment may require unwilling adults to absorb the first blow of offensive but protected speech when they are in public before they turn away, see, e.g., *Erznoznik,* but cf. *Rosenfeld* (Powell, J., dissenting), a different order of values obtains in the home. "That we are often 'captives' outside the sanctuary of the home and subject to objectionable speech and other sound does not mean we must be captives everywhere." *Rowan.* The Commission also was entitled to give this factor appropriate weight in the circumstances of the instant case. This is not to say, however, that the Commission has an unrestricted license to decide what speech, protected in other media, may be banned from the airwaves in order to protect unwilling adults from momentary exposure to it in their homes.[2] * * *

The Commission's holding does not prevent willing adults from purchasing Carlin's record, from attending his performances, or, indeed, from reading the transcript reprinted as an appendix to the Court's opinion. On its face, it does not prevent respondent from broadcasting the monologue during late evening

2. It is true that the radio listener quickly may tune out speech that is offensive to him. In addition, broadcasters may preface potentially offensive programs with warnings. But such warnings do not help the unsuspecting listener who tunes in at the middle of a program. In this respect, too, broadcasting appears to differ from books and records, which may carry warnings on their faces, and from motion pictures and live performances, which may carry warnings on their marquees.

hours when fewer children are likely to be in the audience, nor from broadcasting discussions of the contemporary use of language at any time during the day. The Commission's holding, and certainly the Court's holding today, does not speak to cases involving the isolated use of a potentially offensive word in the course of a radio broadcast, as distinguished from the verbal shock treatment administered by respondent here. In short, I agree that on the facts of this case, the Commission's order did not violate respondent's First Amendment rights.

As the foregoing demonstrates, my views are generally in accord with what is said in Part IV(C) of opinion. I therefore join that portion of his opinion. I do not join Part IV(B), however, because I do not subscribe to the theory that the Justices of this Court are free generally to decide on the basis of its content which speech protected by the First Amendment is most "valuable" and hence deserving of the most protection, and which is less "valuable" and hence deserving of less protection.[3] In my view, the result in this case does not turn on whether Carlin's monologue, viewed as a whole, or the words that comprise it, have more or less "value" than a candidate's campaign speech. This is a judgment for each person to make, not one for the judges to impose upon him.[4]

The result turns instead on the unique characteristics of the broadcast media, combined with society's right to protect its children from speech generally agreed to be inappropriate for their years, and with the interest of unwilling adults in not being assaulted by such offensive speech in their homes. Moreover, I doubt whether today's decision will prevent any adult who wishes to receive Carlin's message in Carlin's own words from doing so, and from making for himself a value judgment as to the merit of the message and words. These are the grounds upon which I join the judgment of the Court as to Part IV.

JUSTICE BRENNAN, with whom JUSTICE MARSHALL joins, dissenting.

[For] the second time in two years, see *Young v. American Mini Theatres* [p. 827 supra], the Court refuses to embrace the notion, completely antithetical to basic First Amendment values, that the degree of protection the First Amendment affords protected speech varies with the social value ascribed to that speech by five Members of this Court. See opinion of Justice Powell. Moreover, [all] Members of the Court agree that [the monologue] does not fall within one of the categories of speech, such as "fighting words," or obscenity, that is totally without First Amendment protection. [Yet] despite the Court's refusal to create a sliding scale of First Amendment protection calibrated to this Court's perception of the worth of a communication's content, and despite our unanimous agreement that the Carlin monologue is protected speech, a majority of the Court[1] nevertheless finds that, on the facts of this case, the FCC is not

3. The Court has, however, created a limited exception to this rule in order to bring commercial speech within the protection of the First Amendment. See *Ohralik*.

4. For much the same reason, I also do not join Part IV(A). I had not thought that the application vel non of overbreadth analysis should depend on the Court's judgment as to the value of the protected speech that might be deterred. Except in the context of commercial speech, see *Bates*, it has not in the past. See, e.g., *Lewis v. New Orleans; Gooding*.

As Justice Stevens points out, however, the Commission's order was limited to the facts of this case; "it did not purport to engage in formal rulemaking or in the promulgation of any regulations." In addition, since the Commission may be expected to proceed cautiously, as it has in the past, I do not foresee an undue "chilling" effect on broadcasters' exercise of their rights. I agree, therefore, that respondent's overbreadth challenge is meritless.

1. Where I refer without differentiation to the actions of "the Court," my reference is to this majority, which consists of my Brothers Powell and Stevens and those Members of the Court joining their separate opinions.

constitutionally barred from imposing sanctions on Pacifica for its airing of the Carlin monologue. This majority apparently believes that the FCC's disapproval of Pacifica's afternoon broadcast of Carlin's "Dirty Words" recording is a permissible time, place, and manner regulation. [The opinions of both Stevens and Powell, JJ.,] rely principally on two factors in reaching this conclusion: (1) the capacity of a radio broadcast to intrude into the unwilling listener's home, and (2) the presence of children in the listening audience. Dispassionate analysis, removed from individual notions as to what is proper and what is not, starkly reveals that these justifications, whether individually or together, simply do not support even the professedly moderate degree of governmental homogenization of radio communications—if, indeed, such homogenization can ever be moderate given the pre-eminent status of the right of free speech in our constitutional scheme—that the Court today permits.

[A]n individual's actions in switching on and listening to communications transmitted over the public airways and directed to the public at-large do not implicate fundamental privacy interests, even when engaged in within the home. Instead, because the radio is undeniably a public medium, these actions are more properly viewed as a decision to take part, if only as a listener, in an ongoing public discourse. Although an individual's decision to allow public radio communications into his home undoubtedly does not abrogate all of his privacy interests, the residual privacy interests he retains vis-à-vis the communication he voluntarily admits into his home are surely no greater than those of the people present in the corridor of the Los Angeles courthouse in *Cohen* who bore witness to the words "Fuck the Draft" emblazoned across Cohen's jacket. Their privacy interests were held insufficient to justify punishing Cohen for his offensive communication.

Even if an individual who voluntarily opens his home to radio communications retains privacy interests of sufficient moment to justify a ban on protected speech if those interests are "invaded in an essentially intolerable manner," *Cohen,* the very fact that those interests are threatened only by a radio broadcast precludes any intolerable invasion of privacy; for unlike other intrusive modes of communication, such as sound trucks, "[t]he radio can be turned off"—and with a minimum of effort. As Judge Bazelon aptly observed below, "having elected to receive public airwaves, the scanner who stumbles onto an offensive program is in the same position as the unsuspected passers-by in *Cohen* and *Erznoznik;* he can avert his attention by changing channels or turning off the set." Whatever the minimal discomfort suffered by a listener who inadvertently tunes into a program he finds offensive during the brief interval before he can simply extend his arm and switch stations or flick the "off" button, it is surely worth the candle to preserve the broadcaster's right to send, and the right of those interested to receive, a message entitled to full First Amendment protection. To reach a contrary balance, as does the Court, is clearly, to follow Justice Stevens' reliance on animal metaphors, "to burn the house to roast the pig."

The Court's balance, of necessity, fails to accord proper weight to the interests of listeners who wish to hear broadcasts the FCC deems offensive. It permits majoritarian tastes completely to preclude a protected message from entering the homes of a receptive, unoffended minority. No decision of this Court supports such a result. Where the individuals comprising the offended majority may freely choose to reject the material being offered, we have never found their privacy interests of such moment to warrant the suppression of speech on privacy grounds. [In] *Rowan,* the Court upheld a statute, permitting householders to require that mail advertisers stop sending them lewd or offensive materials and remove their names from mailing lists. Unlike the situation here, householders who wished to receive the sender's communications were not prevented from doing so. Equally important, the determination of offensiveness vel non under the statute involved in *Rowan* was completely within the hands of the individual householder; no governmental evaluation of the worth of the mail's content stood between the mailer and the householder. In contrast, the visage of the censor is all too discernable here.

[Although] the government unquestionably has a special interest in the well-being of children and consequently "can adopt more stringent controls on communicative materials available to youths than on those available to adults," *Erznoznik*, the Court has accounted for this societal interest by adopting a "variable obscenity" standard that permits the prurient appeal of material available to children to be assessed in terms of the sexual interests of minors. *Ginsberg*. [But] we have made it abundantly clear that "under any test of obscenity as to minors [to] be obscene 'such expression must be, in some significant way, erotic.' "

Because the Carlin monologue is obviously not an erotic appeal to the prurient interests of children, the Court, for the first time, allows the government to prevent minors from gaining access to materials that are not obscene, and are therefore protected, as to them.[2] It thus ignores our recent admonition that "[s]peech that is neither obscene as to youths nor subject to some other legitimate proscription cannot be suppressed solely to protect the young from ideas or images that a legislative body thinks unsuitable for them." *Erznoznik*.[3] The Court's refusal to follow its own pronouncements is especially lamentable since it has the anomalous subsidiary effect, at least in the radio context at issue here, of making completely unavailable to adults material which may not constitutionally be kept even from children. This result violates in spades the principle of *Butler v. Michigan*. [Powell, J.'s opinion] acknowledges that there lurks in today's decision a potential for " 'reduc[ing] the adult population [to] [hearing] only what is fit for children,' " but expresses faith that the FCC will vigilantly prevent this potential from ever becoming a reality. I am far less certain than [he] that such faith in the Commission is warranted; and even if I shared it, I could not so easily shirk the responsibility assumed by each Member of this Court jealously to guard against encroachments on First Amendment freedoms.

[T]he opinions of Justices Powell and Stevens both stress the time-honored right of a parent to raise his child as he sees fit—a right this Court has consistently been vigilant to protect. Yet this principle supports a result directly contrary to that reached by the Court. *Yoder* and *Pierce*, [Ch. 5, Sec. 2,

2. Even if the monologue appealed to the prurient interest of minors, it would not be obscene as to them unless, as to them, "the work, taken as a whole, lacks serious literary, artistic, political, or scientific value." *Miller*.

3. It may be that a narrowly drawn regulation prohibiting the use of offensive language on broadcasts directed specifically at younger children constitutes one of the "other legitimate proscription[s]" alluded to in *Erznoznik*. This is so both because of the difficulties inherent in adapting the *Miller* formulation to communications received by young children, and because such children are "not possessed of that full capacity for individual choice which is the presupposition of the First Amendment guarantees." *Ginsberg*. (Stewart, J., concurring). I doubt, as my Brother Stevens suggests, that such a limited regulation amounts to a regulation of speech based on its content, since, by hypothesis, the only persons at whom the regulated communication is directed are incapable of evaluating its content. To the extent that such a regulation is viewed as a regulation based on content, it marks the outermost limits to which content regulation is permissible.

I], hold that parents, *not* the government, have the right to make certain decisions regarding the upbringing of their children. As surprising as it may be to individual Members of this Court, some parents may actually find Mr. Carlin's unabashed attitude towards the seven "dirty words" healthy, and deem it desirable to expose their children to the manner in which Mr. Carlin defuses the taboo surrounding the words. Such parents may constitute a minority of the American public, but the absence of great numbers willing to exercise the right to raise their children in this fashion does not alter the right's nature or its existence. Only the Court's regrettable decision does that.[4]

As demonstrated above, neither of the factors relied on by both [Justices Powell and Stevens]—the intrusive nature of radio and the presence of children in the listening audience—can, when taken on its own terms, support the FCC's disapproval of the Carlin monologue. These two asserted justifications are further plagued by a common failing: the lack of principled limits on their use as a basis for FCC censorship. No such limits come readily to mind, and neither of the opinions comprising the Court serve to clarify the extent to which the FCC may assert the privacy and children-in-the-audience rationales as justification for expunging from the airways protected communications the Commission finds offensive. Taken to their logical extreme, these rationales would support the cleansing of public radio of any "four-letter words" whatsoever, regardless of their context. The rationales could justify the banning from radio of a myriad of literary works, novels, poems, and plays by the likes of Shakespeare, Joyce, Hemingway, Ben Jonson, Henry Fielding, Robert Burns, and Chaucer; they could support the suppression of a good deal of political speech, such as the Nixon tapes; and they could even provide the basis for imposing sanctions for the broadcast of certain portions of the Bible.

In order to dispel the spectre of the possibility of so unpalatable a degree of censorship, and to defuse Pacifica's overbreadth challenge, the FCC insists that it desires only the authority to reprimand a broadcaster on facts analogous to those present in this case. [Justices Powell and Stevens] take the FCC at its word, and consequently do no more than permit the Commission to censor the afternoon broadcast of the "sort of verbal shock treatment," opinion of Justice Powell, involved here. To insure that the FCC's regulation of protected speech does not exceed these bounds, my Brother Powell is content to rely upon the judgment of the Commission while my Brother Stevens deems it prudent to rely on this Court's ability accurately to assess the worth of various kinds of speech.[6] For my own part, even accepting that this case is limited to its facts,[7] I would place

4. The opinions of my Brothers Powell and Stevens rightly refrain from relying on the notion of "spectrum scarcity" to support their result. As Chief Judge Bazelon noted below, "although scarcity has justified *increasing* the diversity of speakers and speech, it has never been held to justify censorship." See *Red Lion.*

6. Although ultimately dependent upon the outcome of review in this Court, the approach taken by my Brother Stevens would not appear to tolerate the FCC's suppression of any speech, such as political speech, falling within the core area of First Amendment concern. The same, however, cannot be said of the approach taken by my Brother Powell, which, on its face, permits the Commission to censor even political speech if it is sufficiently offensive to community standards. A result more contrary to rudimentary First Amendment principles is difficult to imagine.

7. Having insisted that it seeks to impose sanctions on radio communications only in the limited circumstances present here, I believe that the FCC is estopped from using either this decision or its own orders in this case, as a basis for imposing sanctions on any public radio broadcast other than one aired during the daytime or early evening and containing the relentless repetition, for longer than a brief interval, of "language that describes, in terms patently offensive as measured by contemporary community standards for the broadcast medium, sexual or excretory activities and organs." For surely broadcasters are not now on notice that the Commission desires

the responsibility and the right to weed worthless and offensive communications from the public airways where it belongs and where, until today, it resided: in a public free to choose those communications worthy of its attention from a marketplace unsullied by the censor's hand. * * *

My Brother Stevens, in reaching a result apologetically described as narrow, takes comfort in his observation that "[a] requirement that indecent language be avoided will have its primary effect on the form, rather than the content, of serious communication," and finds solace in his conviction that "[t]here are few, if any, thoughts that cannot be expressed by the use of less offensive language." The idea that the content of a message and its potential impact on any who might receive it can be divorced from the words that are the vehicle for its expression is transparently fallacious. A given word may have a unique capacity to capsule an idea, evoke an emotion, or conjure up an image. Indeed, for those of us who place an appropriately high value on our cherished First Amendment rights, the word "censor" is such a word. Mr. Justice Harlan, speaking for the Court, recognized the truism that a speaker's choice of words cannot surgically be separated from the ideas he desires to express when he warned that "we cannot indulge the facile assumption that one can forbid particular words without also running a substantial risk of suppressing ideas in the process." *Cohen.* Moreover, even if an alternative phrasing may communicate a speaker's abstract ideas as effectively as those words he is forbidden to use, it is doubtful that the sterilized message will convey the emotion that is an essential part of so many communications. This, too, was apparent to Mr. Justice Harlan and the Court in *Cohen.*

[Stevens, J.] also finds relevant to his First Amendment analysis the fact that "[a]dults who feel the need may purchase tapes and records or go to theatres and nightclubs to hear [the tabooed] words." [Powell, J.,] agrees. [The] opinions of my Brethren display both a sad insensitivity to the fact that these alternatives involve the expenditure of money, time, and effort that many of those wishing to hear Mr. Carlin's message may not be able to afford, and a naive innocence of the reality that in many cases, the medium may well be the message.

The Court apparently believes that the FCC's actions here can be analogized to the zoning ordinances upheld in *American Mini Theatres.* For two reasons, it is wrong. First, the zoning ordinances found to pass constitutional muster [had] valid goals other than the channeling of protected speech. No such goals are present here. Second, and crucial to the opinions of my Brothers Powell and Stevens in *American Mini Theatres*—opinions, which, as they do in this case, supply the bare five-person majority of the Court—the ordinances did not restrict the access of distributors or exhibitors to the market or impair the viewing public's access to the regulated material. Again, this is not the situation [here.]

It is quite evident that I find the Court's attempt to unstitch the warp and woof of First Amendment law in an effort to reshape its fabric to cover the patently wrong result the Court reaches in this case dangerous as well as lamentable. Yet there runs throughout the opinions of my Brothers Powell and Stevens another vein I find equally disturbing: a depressing inability to appreciate that in our land of cultural pluralism, there are many who think, act, and

to regulate any offensive broadcast other than the type of "verbal shock treatment" condemned here, or even this "shock treatment" type of offensive broadcast during the late evening.

talk differently from the Members of this Court, and who do not share their fragile sensibilities. It is only an acute ethnocentric myopia that enables the Court to approve the censorship of communications solely because of the words they [contain.]

Today's decision will thus have its greatest impact on broadcasters desiring to reach, and listening audiences comprised of, persons who do not share the Court's view as to which words or expressions are acceptable and who, for a variety of reasons, including a conscious desire to flout majoritarian conventions, express themselves using words that may be regarded as offensive by those from different socio-economic backgrounds.[8] In this context, the Court's decision may be seen for what, in the broader perspective, it really is: another of the dominant culture's inevitable efforts to force those groups who do not share its mores to conform to its way of thinking, acting, and speaking. * * *[c]

Notes and Questions

1. *Implications for broadcasting.* Consider Krattenmaker & Powe, *Televised Violence: First Amendment Principles and Social Science Theory,* 64 Va.L. Rev. 1123, 1228 (1978): *Pacifica* "marks the first time any theory other than scarcity has received the official imprimatur of the Court. [S]carcity could not have authorized the result in *Pacifica* because regardless of whether one thinks the incredible abundance of radio stations in the United States (and especially in New York City) is insufficient, scarcity supports adding voices not banning them." What is the significance of the Court's comment that "the broadcast media have established a uniquely pervasive presence in the lives of all Americans"? Consider Brenner, *Censoring the Airwaves: The Supreme Court's Pacifica Decision* in Free But Regulated: Conflicting Traditions in Media Law 175, 177 & 79 (1982): "[N]ewspapers, drive-in movies, direct mail advertisements and imprinted T-shirts are media that have also 'established a uniquely pervasive presence' in our lives, in and out of [home]. Offhand comments about broadcasting enjoying 'the most limited' First Amendment protection—What of comic books? Playing cards? Chinese cookie fortunes?—are not simply harmless baffle; they constitute Delphic pronouncements made at a watershed period in the development of electronic media." See also Powe, supra fn. a, at 210–11.

Is the Court suggesting that the broadcast media are uniquely powerful? If so, should that factor cut for or against government regulation? See Powe, supra, at 211–15; Powe, "*Or of the [Broadcast] Press,*" 55 Tex.L.Rev. 39, 58–62 (1976). Does *Pacifica* support regulation of sex and violence on television, of "offensive" commercials, of advertising directed toward children? See generally Spitzer, *Seven Dirty Words and Six Other Stories* (1986) (criticizing *Pacifica*'s distinctions between print and broadcast).

2. *Cohen and Pacifica.* Consider Tribe, *American Constitutional Law* 66 n. 51 (1979 Supp.): "In order to make *Cohen* illustrate his theme that context is everything, Justice Stevens reinterprets *Cohen,* casting it in the mold of a

8. Under the approach taken by my Brother Powell, the availability of broadcasts *about* groups whose members comprise such audiences might also be affected. Both news broadcasts about activities involving these groups and public affairs broadcasts about their concerns are apt to contain interviews, statements, or remarks by group leaders and members which may contain offensive language to an extent my Brother Powell finds unacceptable.

c. Stewart, J., joined by Brennan, White, and Marshall, JJ., dissenting maintained that the Commission lacked statutory authority to issue its order and did not reach the constitutional question.

'fighting words' case [referring to fn. 25]. [But in] *Cohen* what was clear to Harlan was that California did not arrest [petitioner] to preserve the peace [but] to cleanse public debate of offensive language, something Harlan was certain the state could not safely be entrusted to do. Justice Stevens cannot reasonably claim that his opinion has been misread if one concludes that his position is essentially California's claim against Cohen, albeit limited to the airwaves."

But Farber, *Civilizing Public Disclosure: An Essay on Professor Bickel, Justice Harlan, and the Enduring Significance of Cohen v. California,* 1980 Duke L.J. 283, 294, maintains that *Cohen* has "little relevance" to *Pacifica*: The FCC's justifications for regulating speech in *Pacifica* "turned on the context of the midafternoon broadcast, whereas Justice Harlan found that none of the possible context-related justifications were properly presented in *Cohen.* Instead, the issue [Harlan] did find to be properly presented—and therefore the only issue he decided—was whether the state, acting as a paternalistic guardian of public morality, could ban the use of certain words in *all* contexts. Because *Pacifica* dealt with context and *Cohen* dealt only with content, *Cohen* contributes little to the issue presented in *Pacifica.*"

3. Consider Shiffrin, *The First Amendment, Democracy, and Romance* 80 (1990): "Most people with any first amendment bones in their bodies are troubled by *[Pacifica]*. But the nub of the first amendment insult has little to do with self-government or with the marketplace of ideas. The concern does not flow from a worry that voters will be deprived of valuable information. Concern that the truth about vulgar language might not emerge in the marketplace of ideas may be well placed, but is not a sufficient concern to explain the widespread outrage against the decision. Again, the decision is an affront to a notion of content neutrality, but there are many of those. The *Pacifica* case produces heat precisely because Carlin's speech is considered by many to be precisely what the first amendment is *supposed* to protect. Carlin is attacking conventions; assaulting the prescribed orthodoxy; mocking the stuffed shirts; Carlin *is* the prototypical dissenter.

"It matters not at all whether the target of his invective is society at large or a public official. The outrage is that the stuffed shirts are in a position to silence Carlin, or at least in a position to keep him from 'offending' the mass audience."

4. "The strangest thing about the Court's decision in *Pacifica,*" comments Tribe, *American Constitutional Law* 937 (2d ed. 1988), "was that no one could suppose that children were listening to the radio station at 2 o'clock in the afternoon. WBAI [is] listener-supported, carries no ads, does not play 'top forty' records, and directs its programming at a distinctly adult, left-to-radical, upper-middle class audience. [S]tudies show that virtually no children listen to any radio station whatsoever at that time on a weekday for the reason that most children are then in school." [d]

5. *Telephonic "indecency" compared.* SABLE COMMUNICATIONS v. FCC, 492 U.S. 115, 109 S.Ct. 2829, 106 L.Ed.2d 93 (1989), per White, J., invalidated a congressional ban on "indecent" interstate commercial telephone messages, i.e., "dial-a-porn." [e] The Court thought *Pacifica* was "readily distinguishable from

d. One citizen complained that he heard the broadcast while driving with his son in the car. Professor Powe reports that the complaining citizen was John R. Douglas, a member of the national planning board of Morality in Media, that his son was 15 years old, and that the complaint was filed six weeks after the broadcast. Powe, supra, at 186.

e. The Court upheld a ban on "obscene" interstate commercial telephonic messages. See p. 475 supra. Scalia, J., concurring, not-this case, most obviously because it did not involve a total ban on broadcasting indecent material. [Second,] there is no 'captive audience' problem here; callers will generally not be unwilling listeners. [Third,] the congressional record contains no legislative findings that would justify us in concluding that there is no constitutionally acceptable less restrictive means, short of a total ban, to achieve the Government's interest in protecting minors."

B. "PUBLIC" BROADCASTERS AND EDITORIALS

FCC v. LEAGUE OF WOMEN VOTERS, 468 U.S. 364, 104 S.Ct. 3106, 82 L.Ed.2d 278 (1984): The Public Broadcasting Act of 1967 (Act), a keystone of Congress' program to sponsor independent sources of broadcast programming as an alternative to commercial broadcasting, established the Corporation for Public Broadcasting (CPB), a nonprofit corporation authorized to disburse federal funds to noncommercial TV and radio stations in support of station operations and educational programming. Section 399 of the Act forbids any noncommercial educational station that receives a grant from the CPB to "engage in editorializing." Appellees (Pacifica Foundation, a nonprofit corporation that owns and operates several stations that receive grants from the CPB; the League of Women Voters of California; and a Congressman who regularly listened to and viewed public broadcasting) challenged the constitutionality of § 399.[a] The federal district court granted summary judgment for appellees. A 5–4 majority, per BRENNAN, J. agreed, concluding that "the specific interests sought to be advanced by § 399's ban on editorializing are either not sufficiently substantial or are not served in a sufficiently limited manner to justify the substantial abridgement of important journalistic freedoms which the First Amendment jealously protects": "Section 399 plainly operates to restrict the expression of editorial opinion on matters of public importance, and, as we have repeatedly explained, communication of this kind is entitled to the most exacting degree of First Amendment protection. Were a similar ban on editorializing applied to newspapers and magazines, we would not hesitate to strike it down as violative of the First Amendment. But, as the Government correctly notes, because broadcast regulation involves unique considerations, our cases have not followed precisely the same approach that we have applied to other media and have never gone so far as to demand that such regulations serve 'compelling' governmental interests. * * *[11] * * *[13].

ed: "[W]hile we hold the Constitution prevents Congress from banning indecent speech in this fashion, we do not hold that the Constitution requires public utilities to carry it." Brennan, J., joined by Marshall and Stevens, JJ., concurred on the indecency issue and dissented on the obscenity issue.

a. The plaintiffs did not challenge and the Court did not reach a provision of 399 which prevents noncommercial stations from supporting or opposing political candidates whether or not they receive federal funds.

11. [The] prevailing rationale for broadcast regulation based on spectrum scarcity has come under increasing criticism in recent years. Critics, including the incumbent Chairman of the FCC, charge that with the advent of cable and satellite television technology, communities now have access to such a wide variety of stations that the scarcity doctrine is obsolete. See, *e.g.,* Fowler & Brenner, *A Marketplace Approach to Broadcast Regulation,* 60 Tex.L.Rev. 207, 221–226 (1982). We are not prepared, however, to reconsider our long-standing approach without some signal from Congress or the FCC that technological developments have advanced so far that some revision of the system of broadcast regulation may be required. [For a few "signals," see Note 3, p. 705 supra.]

13. [*Pacifica*] is consistent with the approach taken in our other broadcast cases. There, the Court focused on certain physical characteristics of broadcasting—specifically, that the medium's uniquely pervasive presence renders impossible any prior warning for those listeners who may be offended by indecent language, and, second, that the case with which children may gain access to the medium, especially during daytime hours, creates a

"[A]lthough the broadcasting industry plainly operates under restraints not imposed upon other media, the thrust of these restrictions has generally been to secure the public's First Amendment interest in receiving a balanced presentation of views on diverse matters of public concern. As a result of these restrictions, of course, the absolute freedom to advocate one's own positions without also presenting opposing viewpoints—a freedom enjoyed, for example, by newspaper publishers and soapbox orators—is denied to broadcasters. But, as our cases attest, these restrictions have been upheld only when we were satisfied that the restriction is narrowly tailored to further a substantial governmental interest, such as ensuring adequate and balanced coverage of public issues.

"[Before] assessing the government's proffered justifications for the statute, however, two central features of the ban against editorializing must be examined, since they help to illuminate the importance of the First Amendment interests at stake in this case.

"First, the restriction imposed by § 399 is specifically directed at a form of speech—namely, the expression of editorial opinion—that lies at the heart of First Amendment protection. In construing the reach of the statute, the FCC has explained that 'although the use of noncommercial educational broadcast facilities by licensees, their management or those speaking on their behalf for the propagation of the licensee's own views on public issues is not permitted, such prohibition should not be construed to inhibit any *other* presentations on controversial issues of public importance.' (emphasis added). The Commission's interpretation of § 399 simply highlights the fact that what the statute forecloses is the expression of editorial opinion on 'controversial issues of public importance.' As we recently reiterated in *NAACP v. Claiborne Hardware Co.*, 'expression on public issues "has always rested on the highest rung of the hierarchy of First Amendment values."'

"[T]he special place of the editorial in our First Amendment jurisprudence simply reflects the fact that the press, of which the broadcasting industry is indisputably a part, carries out a historic, dual responsibility in our society of reporting information and of bringing critical judgment to bear on public affairs. [Because] § 399 appears to restrict precisely that form of speech which the Framers of the Bill of Rights were most anxious to protect—speech that is 'indispensable to the discovery and spread of political truth'—we must be especially careful in weighing the interests that are asserted in support of this restriction and in assessing the precision with which the ban is crafted.

"Second, the scope of § 399's ban is defined solely on the basis of the content of the suppressed speech. A wide variety of non-editorial speech 'by licensees, their management or those speaking on their behalf,' is plainly not prohibited by § 399. Examples of such permissible forms of speech include daily announcements of the station's program schedule or over-the-air appeals for contributions from listeners. Consequently, in order to determine whether a particular statement by station management constitutes an 'editorial' proscribed by § 399,

substantial risk that they may be exposed to such offensive expression without parental supervision. The governmental interest in reduction of those risks through Commission regulation of the timing and character of such "indecent broadcasting" was thought sufficiently substantial to outweigh the broadcaster's First Amendment interest in controlling the presentation of its programming. In this case, by contrast, we are faced not with indecent expression, but rather with expression that is at the core of First Amendment protections, and no claim is made by the Government that the expression of editorial opinion by noncommercial stations will create a substantial "nuisance" of the kind addressed in *Pacifica.*

enforcement authorities must necessarily examine the content of the message that is conveyed to determine whether the views expressed concern 'controversial issues of public importance.'

"[Section 399] singles out noncommercial broadcasters and denies them the right to address their chosen audience on matters of public importance. Thus, in enacting § 399 Congress appears to have sought, in much the same way that the New York Public Service Commission had attempted through the regulation of utility company bill inserts struck down in *Consolidated Edison* [p. 790 infra], to limit discussion of controversial topics and thus to shape the agenda for public debate. Since, as we observed in *Consolidated Edison,* '[t]he First Amendment's hostility to content-based regulation extends not only to restrictions on particular viewpoints, but also to prohibition of an entire topic,' we must be particularly wary in assessing § 399 to determine whether it reflects an impermissible attempt 'to allow the government [to] control [the] search for political truth.'

"In seeking to defend the prohibition on editorializing imposed by § 399, the Government urges that the statute was aimed at preventing two principal threats to the overall success of [the Act]. According to this argument, the ban was necessary, first, to protect noncommercial educational broadcasting stations from being coerced, as a result of federal financing, into becoming vehicles for government propagandizing or the objects of governmental influence; and, second, to keep these stations from becoming convenient targets for capture by private interest groups wishing to express their own partisan viewpoints. [The ban is said to] safeguard the public's right to a balanced presentation of public issues through the prevention of either governmental or private bias * * *.

"[A]n examination of both the overall legislative scheme established by the 1967 Act and the character of public broadcasting demonstrates that the interest asserted by the Government is not substantially advanced by § 399. First, to the extent that federal financial support creates a risk that stations will lose their independence through the bewitching power of governmental largesse, the elaborate structure established by the Act already operates to insulate local stations from governmental interference. Congress not only mandated that the new Corporation for Public Broadcasting would have a private, bipartisan structure, but also imposed a variety of important limitations on its powers. The Corporation was prohibited from owning or operating any station, it was required to adhere strictly to a standard of 'objectivity and balance' in disbursing federal funds to local stations, and it was prohibited from contributing to or otherwise supporting any candidate for office.

"The Act also established a second layer of protections which serve to protect the stations from governmental coercion and interference. Thus, in addition to requiring the Corporation to operate so as to 'assure the maximum freedom [of local stations] from interference with or control of program content or other activities,' the Act expressly forbids 'any department, agency, officer, or employee of the United States [from] exercis[ing] any direction, supervision, or control over educational television or radio broadcasting, or over the Corporation or any of its [grantees].' Subsequent amendments to the Act have confirmed Congress' commitment to the principle that because local stations are the 'bedrock of the system,' their independence from governmental interference and control must be fully guaranteed.

"[T]he manifest imprecision of the ban imposed by § 399 reveals that its proscription is not sufficiently tailored to the harms it seeks to prevent to justify its substantial interference with broadcasters' speech. Section 399 includes within its grip a potentially infinite variety of speech, most of which would not be related in any way to governmental affairs, political candidacies or elections. Indeed, the breadth of editorial commentary is as wide as human imagination permits. But the Government never explains how, say, an editorial by local station management urging improvements in a town's parks or museums will so infuriate Congress or other Federal officials that the future of public broadcasting will be imperiled unless such editorials are suppressed. Nor is it explained how the suppression of editorials alone serves to reduce the risk of governmental retaliation and interference when it is clear that station management is fully able to broadcast controversial views so long as such views are not labelled as its own. * * *

"Finally, the public's interest in preventing public broadcasting stations from becoming forums for lopsided presentations of narrow partisan positions is already secured by a variety of other regulatory means that intrude far less drastically upon the 'journalistic freedom' of noncommercial broadcasters. *CBS v. DNC.* The requirements of the FCC's fairness doctrine, for instance, which apply to commercial and noncommercial stations alike, ensure that such editorializing would maintain a reasonably balanced and fair presentation of controversial issues. Thus, even if the management of a non-commercial educational station were inclined to seek to further only its own partisan views when editorializing, it simply could not do so. * * *[b]

REHNQUIST, J., joined by Burger, C.J., and White, J., dissented: "All but three paragraphs of the Court's lengthy opinion in this case are devoted to the development of a scenario in which the government appears as the 'Big Bad Wolf,' and appellee Pacifica as 'Little Red Riding Hood.' In the Court's scenario the Big Bad Wolf cruelly forbids Little Red Riding Hood from taking to her grandmother some of the food that she is carrying in her basket. Only three paragraphs are used to delineate a truer picture of the litigants, wherein it appears that some of the food in the basket was given to Little Red Riding Hood by the Big Bad Wolf himself, and that the Big Bad Wolf had told Little Red Riding Hood in advance that if she accepted his food she would have to abide by his conditions. Congress in enacting § 399 of the Public Broadcasting Act has simply determined that public funds shall not be used to subsidize noncommercial, educational broadcasting stations which engage in 'editorializing' or which support or oppose any political candidate. I do not believe that anything in the First Amendment [prevents] Congress from choosing to spend public monies in that manner. Perhaps a more appropriate analogy than that of Little Red Riding Hood and the Big Bad Wolf is that of Faust and Mephistopheles; Pacifica, well aware of § 399's condition on its receipt of public money, nonetheless accepted the public money and now seeks to avoid the conditions which Congress legitimately has attached to receipt of that funding. * * *

"The Court's three-paragraph discussion of why § 399, repeatedly reexamined and retained by Congress, violates the First Amendment is to me utterly

b. The Court also held that § 399 cannot be justified on the basis of Congress' spending power as simply determining that Congress will not subsidize public broadcasting station editorials. It deemed the government's reliance on *Regan v. Taxation With Representation*, p. 665 supra, misplaced. Here, "unlike the situation faced by the charitable organization in *Taxation With Representation*, a noncommercial educational station that receives only 1% of its overall income from CPB grants is barred absolutely from all editorializing. Therefore, in contrast to the appellee in *Taxation With Representation*, such a station is not able to segregate its activities according to the source of its funding. The station has no way of limiting the use of its Federal funds to all non-editorializing activities, and, more importantly, it is barred from using even wholly private funds to finance its editorial activity."

unpersuasive. Congress has rationally determined that the bulk of the taxpayers whose monies provide the funds for grants by the CPB would prefer not to see the management of local educational stations promulgate its own private views on the air at taxpayer expense. Accordingly Congress simply has decided not to subsidize stations which engage in that activity. * * *

"The Court seems to believe that Congress actually subsidizes editorializing only if a station uses federal money specifically to cover the expenses that the Court believes can be isolated as editorializing expenses. But to me the Court's approach ignores economic reality. CPB's unrestricted grants are used for salaries, training, equipment, promotion, etc.—financial expenditures which benefit all aspects of a station's programming, including management's editorials. Given the impossibility of compartmentalizing programming expenses in any meaningful way, it seems clear to me that the only effective means for preventing the use of public monies to subsidize the airing of management's views is for Congress to ban a subsidized station from all on-the-air editorializing. Under the Court's view, if Congress decided to withhold a 100% subsidy from a station which editorializes, that decision would be constitutional under the principle affirmed in our *Taxation With Representation* decision. Surely on these facts, the distinction between the government's power to withhold a 100% subsidy, on the one hand, and the 20–30% subsidy involved here, on the other hand, is simply trivialization.

"This is not to say that the government may attach *any* condition to its largess; it is only to say that when the government is simply exercising its power to allocate its own public funds, we need only find that the condition imposed has a rational relationship to Congress' purpose in providing the subsidy and that it is not primarily 'aimed at the suppression of dangerous ideas.' In this case Congress' prohibition is directly related to its purpose in providing subsidies for public broadcasting, and it is plainly rational for Congress to have determined that taxpayer monies should not be used to subsidize management's views or to pay for management's exercise of partisan politics. [Furthermore,] Congress' prohibition is strictly neutral. In no sense can it be said that Congress has prohibited only editorial views of one particular ideological bent. Nor has it prevented public stations from airing programs, documentaries, interviews, etc. dealing with controversial subjects, so long as management itself does not expressly endorse a particular viewpoint. And Congress has not prevented station management from communicating its own views on those subjects through any medium other than subsidized public broadcasting. * * *

"I find this case entirely different from the so-called 'unconstitutional condition' cases, wherein the Court has stated that the government 'may not deny a benefit to a person on a basis that infringes his constitutionally protected interests—especially his interest in freedom of speech.' *Perry v. Sindermann*, 408 U.S. 593, 92 S.Ct. 2694, 33 L.Ed.2d 570 (1972). In those cases the suppressed speech was not content-neutral in the same sense as here, and in those cases, there is at best only a strained argument that the legislative purpose of the condition imposed was to avoid *subsidizing* the prohibited speech. *Speiser v. Randall* [p. 995 infra] is illustrative of the difference. In that case California's decision to deny its property tax exemption to veterans who would not declare that they would not work to overthrow the government was plainly directed at suppressing what California regarded as speech of a dangerous content. And the condition imposed was so unrelated to the benefit to be conferred that it is difficult to argue that California's property tax exemption actually subsidized the dangerous speech.

"Here, in my view, Congress has rationally concluded that the bulk of taxpayers whose monies provide the funds for grants by the CPB would prefer not to see the management of public stations engage in editorializing or the endorsing or opposing of political candidates. Because Congress' decision to enact § 399 is a rational exercise of its spending powers and strictly neutral, I would hold that nothing in the First Amendment makes it unconstitutional." [b]

In a separate dissent, STEVENS, J., protested: "By enacting the statutory provision that the Court invalidates today, a sophisticated group of legislators expressed a concern about the potential impact of government funds on pervasive and powerful organs of mass communication. One need not have heard the raucous voice of Adolph Hitler over Radio Berlin to appreciate the importance of that concern. * * *

The quality of the interest in maintaining government neutrality in the free market of ideas—of avoiding subtle forms of censorship and propaganda—outweigh the impact on expression that results from this statute. Indeed, by simply terminating or reducing funding, Congress could curtail much more expression with no risk whatever of a constitutional transgression.

"[T]he fact that editorial opinion has traditionally been an important kind of speech, is [not] sufficient to identify the character or the significance of the statute's impact on speech. Three additional points are relevant. First, the statute does not prohibit Pacifica from expressing its opinion through any avenue except the radio stations for which it receives federal financial support. It eliminates the subsidized channel of communication as a forum for Pacifica itself, and thereby deprives Pacifica of an advantage it would otherwise have over other speakers, but it does not exclude Pacifica from the marketplace for ideas. Second, the statute does not curtail the expression of opinion by individual commentators who participate in Pacifica's programs. The only comment that is prohibited is a statement that Pacifica agrees or disagrees with the opinions that others may express on its programs. Third, and of greatest significance for me, the statutory restriction is completely neutral in its operation—it prohibits all editorials without any distinction being drawn concerning the subject matter or the point of view that might be expressed.

"The statute does not violate the fundamental principle that the citizen's right to speak may not be conditioned upon the sovereign's agreement with what the speaker intends to say. On the contrary, the statute was enacted in order to protect that very principle—to avoid the risk that some speakers will be rewarded or penalized for saying things that appeal to—or are offensive to—the sovereign.[7] The interests the statute is designed to protect are interests that underlie the First Amendment itself.

b. White, J., filed a brief dissenting opinion.

7. It is ironic indeed that the majority states that it must be particularly wary in assessing § 399 "to determine whether it reflects an impermissible attempt 'to allow the Government [to] control [the] search for political truth' ", given that the very object of § 399 is to prevent the Government from controlling the search for political truth.

Moreover, the statute will also protect the listener's interest in not having his tax payments used to finance the advocacy of causes he opposes. The majority gives extremely short shrift to the Government's interest in minimizing the use of taxpayer monies to promote private views with which the taxpayers may disagree. The Court briefly observes that the taxpayers do not have a constitutionally protected right to enjoin such expenditures and then leaps to the conclusion that given the fact that the funding scheme itself is not unconstitutional, this interest cannot be used to support the statute at issue here. The conclusion manifestly does not follow from the premise, and this interest is plainly legitimate and significant.

"In my judgment the interest in keeping the Federal Government out of the propaganda arena is of overriding importance. That interest is of special importance in the field of electronic communication, not only because that medium is so powerful and persuasive, but also because it is the one form of communication that is licensed by the Federal Government. When the Government already has great potential power over the electronic media, it is surely legitimate to enact statutory safeguards to make sure that it does not cross the threshold that separates neutral regulation from the subsidy of partisan opinion.

"The Court does not question the validity of the basic interests served by § 399. Instead, it suggests that the statute does not substantially serve those interests because [the Act] operates in many other respects to insulate local stations from governmental interference. In my view, that is an indication of nothing more than the strength of the governmental interest involved here—Congress enacted many safeguards because the evil to be avoided was so grave. Organs of official propaganda are antithetical to this nation's heritage and Congress understandably acted with great caution in this area. It is no answer to say that the other statutory provisions 'substantially reduce the risk of government interference with the editorial judgments of the local stations without restricting the stations' ability to speak out on matters of public concern.' The other safeguards protect the stations from interference with judgments that they will necessarily make in selecting programming, but those judgments are relatively amorphous. No safeguard is foolproof; and the fact that funds are dispensed according to largely 'objective' criteria certainly is no guarantee. Individuals must always make judgments in allocating funds, and pressure can be exerted in subtle ways as well as through outright fund-cutoffs.

"Members of Congress, not members of the Judiciary, live in the world of politics. When they conclude that there is a real danger of political considerations influencing the dispensing of this money and that this provision is necessary to insulate grantees from political pressures in addition to the other safeguards, that judgment is entitled to our respect."

Notes and Questions

1. *The public/private distinction.* Is there a justification for permitting editorials by commercial broadcasters—but not by noncommercial broadcasters? Public broadcasters are given dollar grants and free, but restricted use of the airwaves (no commercials); commercial broadcasters are given free use of the airwaves and the right to charge advertisers for access. Which is the greater subsidy? It is wrong to characterize commercial broadcasters as unsubsidized and "private" argues Shiffrin, *Book Review,* 96 Harv.L.Rev. 1745, 1753–54 (1983): Commercial broadcasters "after all, are given an in-kind subsidy (relatively unrestricted use of the governmentally controlled airwaves) that is vastly greater than the puny amounts given to public broadcasters; and they are licensed by the government as trustees to manage public resources. Moreover, the government has substantially influenced the content of messages on the 'private' stations. Television in America was organized by government as an enterprise financed by commercial [advertisers]. The result of such government structuring is a society in which people are taught in their homes, through a government subsidized medium, to be acquisitive consumers. [There] may be a case for considering 'private' broadcasters nongovernmental for purposes of state action doctrine, but probing government participation in the formulation of basic values requires rethinking the public-private distinction."

2. Can Congress constitutionally prohibit public broadcasters from endorsing candidates? Commercial broadcasters? Organizations receiving tax deductible contributions? See Sec. 6, I (supra); Sec. 10 infra.

3. How is the Court's test related to the test in *Central Hudson,* p. 580 supra; in *Vincent,* p. 656 supra? Is the Court's test justified by anything in *Red Lion, CBS,* or *Pacifica*? Is the Court's refusal in fn. 11 to reconsider the scarcity rationale an "abdication of its constitutional responsibility." Consider Note, 98 Harv.L.Rev. 205, 216: "If it chooses to recognize that physical scarcity is now no more than a myth, the Court will find itself in possession of a valuable opportunity to adapt constitutional law to economic reality. The special status of broadcasting might then be seen not as an aberration, but as the foundation of a first amendment theory that addresses the economic phenomenon of a modern communications industry that excludes most Americans from the public debate on which democracy depends."

SECTION 9. THE RIGHT NOT TO SPEAK, THE RIGHT TO ASSOCIATE, AND THE RIGHT NOT TO ASSOCIATE

NAACP v. Alabama ex rel. Patterson, 357 U.S. 449, 78 S.Ct. 1163, 2 L.Ed.2d 1488 (1958), per Harlan, J., held that the first amendment barred Alabama from compelling production of NAACP membership lists. The opinion used the phrase freedom of association repeatedly, "elevat[ing] freedom of association to an independent right, possessing an equal status with the other rights specifically enumerated in the first amendment." Emerson, *Freedom of Association and Freedom of Expression,* 74 Yale L.J. 1, 2 (1964).

From the materials on advocacy of illegal action (Sec. 1, I supra) onward, it has been evident that individuals have rights to join with others for expressive purposes. This section explores other aspects of the freedom to associate and its corollary, the freedom not to associate. First, we explore cases which the Court bases on a right not to speak, but might better be understood as establishing a right not to be associated with particular ideas. Second, we explore aspects of free association in the employment context—in particular the claims of employees not to be associated with a political party, or a union or its policies. Those claims are to some extent derived from the cases establishing a right not to be associated with particular ideas. Third, instead of persons resisting forced membership in a group, we confront a group resisting members.

Finally, freedom of association is used to resist government mandated disclosure. There is no general right not to speak. Every day witnesses are subpoenaed to testify against their will. But the first amendment affords a particularized right not to speak when forced disclosure would jeopardize important associational rights. One of the questions of the final part is whether press relationships with confidential sources are uniquely protected associations. That issue carries beyond the subject of the section and back to the question of whether the Constitution contemplates a special role for the institutional press.

I. THE RIGHT NOT TO BE ASSOCIATED WITH PARTICULAR IDEAS

"If there is any fixed star in our constitutional constellation, it is that no official, high or petty, can prescribe what shall be

> *orthodox in politics, nationalism, religion, or other matter of opinion or force citizens to confess by word or act their faith therein."*

West Virginia State Bd. of Educ. v. Barnette, p. 890 infra (Jackson, J.) (upholding right of public school students to refuse to salute flag).

New Hampshire required that noncommercial vehicles bear license plates embossed with the state motto, "Live Free or Die." "Refus[ing] to be coerced by the State into advertising a slogan which I find morally, ethically, religiously and politically abhorrent," appellee, a Jehovah's Witness, covered up the motto on his license plate, a misdemeanor under state law. After being convicted several times of violating the misdemeanor statute, appellee sought federal injunctive and declaratory relief. WOOLEY v. MAYNARD, 430 U.S. 705, 97 S.Ct. 1428, 51 L.Ed.2d 752 (1977), per BURGER, C.J., held that requiring appellee to display the motto on his license plates violated his first amendment right to "refrain from speaking":

"[T]he freedom of thought protected by the First Amendment [includes] both the right to speak freely and the right to refrain from speaking at all. See *Barnette.* The right to speak and the right to refrain from speaking are complementary components of the broader concept of 'individual freedom of mind.' This is illustrated [by] *Miami Herald Publishing Co. v. Tornillo,* where we held unconstitutional a Florida statute placing an affirmative duty upon newspapers to publish the replies of political candidates whom they had criticized.

"* * * Compelling the affirmative act of a flag salute [the situation in *Barnette*] involved a more serious infringement upon personal liberties than the passive act of carrying the state motto on a license plate, but the difference is essentially one of degree. Here, as in *Barnette,* we are faced with a state measure which forces an individual as part of his daily life—indeed constantly while his automobile is in public view—to be an instrument for fostering public adherence to an ideological point of view he finds unacceptable. In doing so, the State 'invades the sphere of intellect and spirit which it is the purpose of the First Amendment [to] reserve from all official control.' *Barnette.*

"New Hampshire's statute in effect requires that appellees use their private property as a 'mobile billboard' for the State's ideological message—or suffer a penalty, as Maynard already has. [The] fact that most individuals agree with the thrust of [the] motto is not the test; most Americans also find the flag salute acceptable. The First Amendment protects the right of individuals to hold a point of view different from the majority and to refuse to foster, in the way New Hampshire commands, an idea they find morally objectionable."

The Court next considered whether "the State's countervailing interest" was "sufficiently compelling" to justify appellees to display the motto on their license plates. The two interests claimed by the state were (1) facilitating the identification of state license plates from those of similar colors of other states and (2) promoting "appreciation of history, state pride, [and] individualism." As to (1), the record revealed that these state license plates were readily distinguishable from others without reference to the state motto and, in any event, the state's purpose could be achieved by "less drastic means," i.e., by alternative methods less restrictive of first amendment freedoms. As to (2), where the State's interest is to communicate an "official view" as to history and state pride or to disseminate any other "ideology," "such interest cannot outweigh an individual's First Amendment right to avoid becoming the courier for such message."

REHNQUIST, J., joined by Blackmun, J., dissented, not only agreeing with what he called "the Court's implicit recognition that there is no protected 'symbolic speech' in this case," but maintaining that "that conclusion goes far to undermine the Court's ultimate holding that there is an element of protected expression here. The State has not forced appellees to 'say' anything; and it has not forced them to communicate ideas with nonverbal actions reasonably likened to 'speech,' such as wearing a lapel button promoting a political candidate or waving a flag as a symbolic gesture.[a] The State has simply required that *all* noncommercial automobiles bear license tags with the state motto. [Appellees] have not been forced to affirm or reject that motto; they are simply required by the State [to] carry a state auto license tag for identification and registration purposes. [The] issue, unconfronted by the Court, is whether appellees, in displaying, as they are required to do, state license tags, the format of which is known to all as having been prescribed by the State, would be considered to be advocating political or ideological views.

"[H]aving recognized the rather obvious differences between [*Barnette* and this case], the Court does not explain why the same result should obtain. The Court suggests that the test is whether the individual is forced 'to be an instrument for fostering public adherence to an ideological point of view he finds unacceptable,' [but] these are merely conclusory words. [For] example, were New Hampshire to erect a multitude of billboards, each proclaiming 'Live Free or Die,' and tax all citizens for the cost of erection and maintenance, clearly the message would be 'fostered' by the individual citizen-taxpayers and just as clearly those individuals would be 'instruments' in that communication. Certainly, however, that case would not fall within the ambit of *Barnette.* In that case, as in this case, there is no *affirmation* of belief. For First Amendment principles to be implicated, the State must place the citizen in the position of either appearing to, or actually, 'asserting as true' the message. This was the focus of *Barnette,* and clearly distinguishes this case from that one."[b]

Notes and Questions

1. *Compelled expression vs. symbolic speech.* In *Wooley,* the lower court had held that by covering up the state motto on their automobile license plate, appellees were engaging in "symbolic speech," inferring the requisite intent to communicate from the use of reflective red tape to mask the motto—which not only called attention to the obscuring of the motto, but also conveyed disagreement with it. But the Supreme Court found it unnecessary to pass judgment on this issue, finding "more appropriate grounds" to affirm the judgment. It did, however, note that the symbolic speech claim was "substantially undermined" by a request for plates without the motto. Were appellees engaged in symbolic speech? If they were not, was *Wooley* correctly decided? Does the answer turn on whether *the state* was engaging in "speech"? Consider Note, 1977 Utah L.Rev. 797, 805–07: "While an objective approach is perhaps useful in finding 'symbolic speech,' [it] becomes suspect when applied to finding 'compelled expression.' [Utilizing] an objective test to find compelled expression defeats [one of

a. Does *compelled* expression have to be understood by others to be "speech" or does it suffice that the Maynards *subjectively believed* that they were being forced to make an expression? See note 1 following this case.

b. White, J., joined by Blackmun and Rehnquist, JJ., dissented on procedural grounds.

the goals of the first amendment], for it forces an individual to express a view not his own. This situation clearly invades 'the sphere [which] it is the purpose of the First Amendment [to] reserve from all official control.' *Barnette.*

"Care must be exercised, however, to distinguish compelled symbolic expression from compelled acts which have no expressive conduct [e.g., compelling one to place a license plate on his car or number on his house]. To make this distinction, an objective test is correctly applied first to ascertain if the [government] intended to communicate [a] message. If it did, then a subjective test is properly applied to determine if the individual citizen was compelled to communicate that message. '[E]xpression' is a prerequisite of 'compelled expression,' and 'expression,' if symbolic in nature, is properly found by using an objective test. Expression that is compelled, however, must be found subjectively if the guarantees of the first amendment are to have any real significance. In [*Wooley*], there can be little doubt that the state intended to communicate a message. [Thus], the majority properly applied a subjective test to find that such expression had been compelled in violation of the Maynards' first amendment rights."

2. Consider Tribe, *The Curvature of Constitutional Space: What Lawyers Can Learn From Modern Physics,* 103 Harv.L.Rev. 1, 22 (1989): "[T]he very existence of the challenged New Hampshire Law in a sense *protected* free speech rights. For it was well known that people had no choice about whether the state motto was to appear on their license plates. [Ironically], by requiring the state to give people the option whether or not to have its motto displayed on their license plates, the *Wooley* Court forced people into a symbolic expression. [An] adequate constitutional analysis cannot ignore the impact on social meaning of the Court's own action."

3. *Compelling citizens through taxes.* The *Wooley* majority, notes Tribe, *American Constitutional Law* 807–08 n. 8 (2d ed. 1988), "silently accepted Justice Rehnquist's assertion that citizens of New Hampshire could be compelled through their taxes to pay for the cost of erecting and maintaining billboards proclaiming 'Live Free or Die.'" Should the majority have done so? Consider Tribe, supra: "Any notion that the very relation of taxpayer to government makes the refund argument inherently inapt seems refuted by positing a hypothetical instance in which, say, half the state budget [is spent] broadcasting 'Live Free or Die' across the countryside. In such a case, even assuming that this allocation of public resources does not itself violate the first and fourteenth amendments, the Supreme Court should probably conclude that the broadcast cannot constitutionally be financed with the involuntary contributions of persons who disagree with the message."

4. *Use of private property as a forum for the speech of others.* Appellees sought to enjoin a shopping center from denying them access to the center's central courtyard in order to solicit signatures from passersby for petitions opposing a U.N. resolution. The California Supreme Court held they were entitled to conduct their activity at the center, construing the state constitution to protect "speech and petitioning, reasonably exercised, in shopping centers, even [when] privately owned." PRUNEYARD SHOPPING CENTER v. ROBINS, 447 U.S. 74, 100 S.Ct. 2035, 64 L.Ed.2d 741 (1980) per REHNQUIST, J., affirmed, rejecting, inter alia, the argument, based on *Wooley,* that "a State may not constitutionally require an individual to participate in the dissemination of an ideological message by displaying it on his private property [so] that it be observed and read by the public": "[In *Wooley*] the government itself prescribed

the message, required it to be displayed openly on appellee's personal property that was used 'as part of his daily life,' and refused to permit him [to] cover up the motto even though the Court found that the display of the motto served no important state interest. Here, by contrast, there are a number of distinguishing factors. Most important, [the center] is not limited to the personal use of appellants, [but is] a business establishment that is open to the public to come and go as they please. The views expressed by members of the public in passing out pamphlets or seeking signatures for a petition thus will not likely be identified with those of the owner. Second, no specific message is dictated by the State to be displayed on appellants' property. There consequently is no danger of government discrimination for or against a particular message. Finally, [it appears] appellants can expressly disavow any connection with the message by simply posting signs in the area where the speakers or handbillers stand."

The Court also found appellants' reliance on *Barnette* and *Tornillo* misplaced: Unlike *Barnette,* appellants "are not [being] compelled to affirm their belief in any governmentally prescribed position or view, and they are free to publicly dissociate themselves from the views of the speakers or handbillers. [*Tornillo*] rests on the principle that the State cannot tell a newspaper what it must print. [There was also a danger in *Tornillo* that the invalidated statute requiring a newspaper to publish a political candidate's reply to previously published criticism would deter] editors from publishing controversial political [statements]. Thus, the statute was found to be an 'intrusion into the function of editors.' These concerns obviously are not present here."

POWELL, J., joined by White, J., concurring in part and in the judgment, agreed that "the owner of this shopping center has failed to establish a cognizable First Amendment claim," but maintained that "state action that transforms privately owned property into a forum for the expression of the public's views could raise serious First Amendment questions": "I do not believe that the result in *Wooley* would have changed had [the state] directed its citizens to place the slogan 'Live Free or Die' in their shop windows rather than on their automobiles. [The *Wooley* principle] on its face protects a person who refuses to allow use of his property as a market place for the ideas of others. [One] who has merely invited the public onto his property for commercial purposes cannot fairly be said to have relinquished his right 'to decline to be an instrument for fostering public adherence to an ideological point of view he finds unacceptable.' *Wooley.*

"[E]ven when [as here] no particular message is mandated by the State, First Amendment interests are affected by state action that forces a property owner to admit third-party speakers. [A] right of access [may be] no less intrusive than speech compelled by the State itself. For example, a law requiring that a newspaper permit others to use its columns imposes an unacceptable burden upon the newspaper's First Amendment right to select material for publication. *Tornillo.*

"[If] a state law mandated public access to the bulletin board of a freestanding store [or] small shopping center [or allowed soliciting or pamphleteering in the entrance area of a store] customers might well conclude that the messages reflect the view of the proprietor. [He] either could permit his customers to receive a mistaken impression [or] disavow the messages. Should he take the first course, he effectively has been compelled to affirm someone else's belief. Should he choose the second, he has been forced to speak when he would prefer to remain silent. In short, he has lost control over his freedom to speak or not to speak on certain issues. The mere fact that he is free to dissociate himself from the views expressed on his property cannot restore his 'right to refrain from speaking at all.' *Wooley.*

"A property owner may also be faced with speakers who wish to use his premises as a platform for views that he finds morally repugnant [, for example, a] minority-owned business confronted with leafleteers from the American Nazi Party or the Ku Klux Klan, [or] a church-operated enterprise asked to host demonstrations in favor of abortion. [The] strong emotions evoked by speech in such situations may virtually compel the proprietor to respond.

"The pressure to respond is particularly apparent [in the above cases, but] an owner who strongly objects to some of the causes to which the state-imposed right of access would extend may oppose ideological activities 'of *any* sort' that are not related to the purposes for which he has invited the public onto his property. See *Abood.* To require the owner to specify the particular ideas he finds objectionable enough to compel a response would force him to relinquish his 'freedom to maintain his own beliefs without public disclosure.' *Abood.* Thus, the right to control one's own speech may be burdened impermissibly even when listeners will not assume that the messages expressed on private property are those of the owner.

"[On this record] I cannot say that customers of this vast center [occupying several city blocks and containing more than 65 shops] would be likely to assume that appellees' limited speech activity expressed the views of [the center]. [Moreover, appellants] have not alleged that they object to [appellees' views, nor asserted] that some groups who reasonably might be expected to speak at [the center] will express views that are so objectionable as to require a response even when listeners will not mistake their source. [Thus,] I join the judgment of the Court, [but] I do not interpret our decision today as a blanket approval for state efforts to transform privately owned commercial property into public forums." [c]

5. *Economic pressure to engage in political activity.* NAACP v. CLAIBORNE HARDWARE CO., 458 U.S. 886, 102 S.Ct. 3409, 73 L.Ed.2d 1215 (1982): The NAACP had organized a consumer boycott whose principal objective was, according to the lower court, "to force the white merchants [to] bring pressure upon [the government] to grant defendants' demands or, in the alternative, to suffer economic ruin." Mississippi characterized the boycott as a tortious and malicious interference with the plaintiffs' businesses. The Court, per STEVENS, J., held that the NAACP boycott was immune from state prohibition: Although labor boycotts organized for economic ends had long been subject to prohibition, "speech to protest racial discrimination" was "essential political speech lying at the core of the First Amendment" and was therefore distinguishable. Is the boycott protected association? Are there association rights on the other side? Does the state have a legitimate interest in protecting merchants from being forced to support political change they would otherwise oppose? Cf. *NLRB v. Retail Store Employees Union,* 447 U.S. 607, 100 S.Ct. 2372, 65 L.Ed.2d 377 (1980) (ban on labor picketing encouraging consumer boycott of neutral employer upheld). Are the white merchants neutral? [d] For commentary, compare Harper, *The Consumer's Emerging Right to Boycott: NAACP v. Claiborne Hardware and Its Implications for American Labor Law,* 93 Yale L.J. 409 (1984) with

c. For commentary, see Levinson, *Freedom of Speech and the Right of Access to Private Property Under State Constitutional Law* in Developments in State Constitutional Law 51 (McGraw ed. 1985).

d. Stevens, J., also argued in *Claiborne* that the boycott was protected as a right to petition the government. Are the white merchants the government?

Schwarzschild & Alexander, *Consumer Boycotts and Freedom of Association: Comment on a Recently Proposed Theory,* 22 San Diego L.Rev. 555 (1985).

6. *Orthodoxy and commercial advertising.* ZAUDERER v. OFFICE OF DISCIPLINARY COUNSEL, 471 U.S. 626, 105 S.Ct. 2265, 85 L.Ed.2d 652 (1985), per WHITE, J., upheld an Ohio requirement that an attorney advertising availability on a contingency basis must disclose in the ad that the clients would have to pay costs if their lawsuits should prove unsuccessful whenever that is the proposed financial arrangement: "[T]he interests at stake in this case are not of the same order as those discussed in *Wooley, Tornillo,* and *Barnette.* Ohio has not attempted to 'prescribe what shall be orthodox in politics, nationalism, religion, or other matters of opinion or force citizens to confess by word or act their faith therein.' The State has attempted only to prescribe what shall be orthodox in commercial advertising, and its prescription has taken the form of a requirement that appellant include in his advertising purely factual and uncontroversial [e] information about the terms under which his services will be available. Because the extension of First Amendment protection to commercial speech is justified principally by the value to consumers of the information such speech provides, *Virginia Pharmacy,* appellant's constitutionally protected interest in *not* providing any particular factual information in his advertising is minimal. * * *

"We do not suggest that disclosure requirements do not implicate the advertiser's First Amendment rights at all. We recognize that unjustified or unduly burdensome disclosure requirements might offend the First Amendment by chilling protected commercial speech. But we hold that an advertiser's rights are adequately protected as long as disclosure requirements are reasonably related to the State's interest in preventing deception of consumers."

The Court stated that the first amendment interests "implicated by disclosure requirements are substantially weaker than those at stake when speech is factually suppressed." Accordingly it rejected any requirement that the advertisement in question be shown to be deceptive absent the disclosure or that the state meet a "least restrictive means" analysis.

BRENNAN, J., joined by Marshall, J., dissenting on this issue, conceded that the distinction between disclosure and suppression "supports some differences in analysis," but thought the Court had exaggerated the importance of the distinction: "We have noted in traditional First Amendment cases that an affirmative publication requirement 'operates as a command in the same sense as a statute or regulation forbidding [someone] to publish specified matter,' and that a compulsion to publish that which 'reason tells [one] should not be published' therefore raises substantial first amendment concerns. *Tornillo.*" Accordingly, he would have required a demonstration that the advertising was inherently likely to deceive or record evidence that the advertising was in fact deceptive, or a showing that another substantial interest was directly advanced by state

e. What if the requested disclosures are controverted? Do cigarette companies have first amendment grounds to resist forced disclosures?

Do doctors have a first amendment right to resist state mandated disclosures to patients considering abortion? Reconsider *Thornburgh v. American College of Obstetricians and Gynecologists,* p. 205 supra (state-mandated disclosures regarding abortion unconstitutionally structure the patient/physician dialogue, but no mention of first amendment).

Can professional fundraisers be required to disclose their professional status before soliciting funds? The percentage of charitable contributions that have been turned over to charity in the past 12 months? See *Riley v. National Federation of the Blind,* p. 615 supra (the former can be required, but not the latter).

action extending only as far as the interest served. Applying this standard, Brennan, J., agreed with the Court that a state may require an advertising attorney to include a costs disclaimer, but concluded that the state had provided Zauderer with inadequate notice of what he was required to include in the advertisement.

II. FREEDOM OF ASSOCIATION AND EMPLOYMENT

ELROD v. BURNS, 427 U.S. 347, 96 S.Ct. 2673, 49 L.Ed.2d 547 (1976), (Stevens, J., not participating) declared unconstitutional the dismissal of nonpolicymaking and nonconfidential state and local government employees solely on the ground that they were not affiliated with or sponsored by a particular political party. (The newly elected Democratic Sheriff of Cook County, Illinois, had sought to replace noncivil-service employees in his office, all Republicans, with members of his own party. The employees who brought suit were process servers and a juvenile court bailiff). BRENNAN, J., announced the judgment and an opinion joined by White and Marshall, JJ.: "The cost of the practice of patronage is the restraint it places on freedoms of belief and association. [The] free functioning of the electoral process also suffers. Conditioning political employment on partisan support prevents support of competing public interests. [As] government employment, state or federal, becomes more pervasive, the greater the dependence on it becomes, and therefore the greater becomes the power to starve political [opposition]. Patronage thus tips the electoral process in favor of the incumbent party.

"[P]olitical belief and association constitute the core of those activities protected by the First Amendment. "[The] Court recognized in *United Public Workers v. Mitchell,* 330 U.S. 75, 100, 67 S.Ct. 556, 569, 91 L.Ed. 754 (1947), that 'Congress may not "enact a regulation providing that no Republican, Jew or Negro shall be appointed to federal office."' This principle was reaffirmed in *Wieman v. Updegraff,* 344 U.S. 183, 73 S.Ct. 215, 97 L.Ed. 216 (1952), which held that a State could not require its employees to establish their loyalty by extracting an oath denying past affiliation with Communists. And in *Cafeteria & Restaurant Workers v. McElroy,* 367 U.S. 886, 898, 81 S.Ct. 1743, 1750, 6 L.Ed. 2d 1230 (1961), the Court recognized again that the government could not deny employment because of previous membership in a particular party.[11]

"Particularly pertinent to the constitutionality of the practice of patronage dismissals are *Keyishian v. Board of Regents,* 385 U.S. 589, 87 S.Ct. 675, 17 L.Ed. 2d 629 (1967), and *Perry v. Sindermann,* 408 U.S. 593, 92 S.Ct. 2694, 33 L.Ed.2d 570 (1972). In *Keyishian,* the Court invalidated New York statutes barring employment merely on the basis of membership in 'subversive' organizations. *Keyishian* squarely held that political association alone could not, consistently with the First Amendment, constitute an adequate ground for denying public employment.[12] In *Perry,* the Court broadly rejected the validity of limitations on

11. Protection of First Amendment interests has not been limited to invalidation of conditions on government employment requiring allegiance to a particular political party. This Court's decisions have prohibited conditions on public benefits, in the form of jobs or otherwise, which dampen the exercise generally of First Amendment rights, however slight the inducement to the individual to forsake those rights. [T]he First Amendment prohibits limiting the grant of a tax exemption to only those who affirm their loyalty to the State granting the exemption. *Speiser v. Randall,* 357 U.S. 513, 78 S.Ct. 1332, 2 L.Ed.2d 1460 (1958).

12. Thereafter, *United States v. Robel,* 389 U.S. 258, 88 S.Ct. 419, 19 L.Ed.2d 508 (1967), similarly held that mere membership in the Communist Party could not bar a person from

First Amendment rights as a condition to the receipt of a governmental benefit, stating that the government 'may not deny a benefit to a person on a basis that infringes his constitutionally protected interests—especially, his interest in freedom of speech. For if the government could deny a benefit to a person because of his constitutionally protected speech or associations, his exercise of those freedoms would in effect be penalized and inhibited. This would allow the government to "produce a result which [it] could not command directly." *Speiser v. Randall.* Such interference with constitutional rights is impermissible.' * * * [13]"

If the practice is to survive constitutional challenge, "it must further some vital government end by a means that is least restrictive of freedom of belief and association in achieving that end, and the benefit gained must outweigh the loss of constitutionally protected rights." The plurality then considered and rejected three interests offered in justification of patronage—(1) "the need to insure effective government"; (2) "the need for political loyalty of employees" to assure implementation of the new administration's policies; and (3) "the preservation of the democratic process" and the continued vitality of "party politics":

As to (1), the argument fails, inter alia, "because it is doubtful that the mere difference of political persuasion motivates poor performance; nor do we think it legitimately may be used for imputing such behavior. [At] all events, less drastic means for insuring [this interest] are available"—discharge for good cause, "such as insubordination or poor job performance, when those bases exist."

"[Moreover] the lack of any justification for patronage dismissals as a means of furthering government effectiveness and efficiency distinguishes this case from *CSC v. Letter Carriers,* 413 U.S. 548, 93 S.Ct. 2880, 37 L.Ed.2d 796 (1973), and *Mitchell.* In both of those cases, legislative restraints on political management and campaigning by public employees were upheld despite their encroachment on First Amendment rights because, inter alia, they did serve in a necessary manner to foster and protect efficient and effective government. Interestingly, the activities that were restrained by the legislation involved in those cases are characteristic of patronage practices. As the Court observed in *Mitchell,* 'The conviction that an actively partisan governmental personnel threatens good administration has deepened since [1882]. Congress recognizes danger to the service in that political rather than official effort may earn advancement and to the public in that governmental favor may be channeled through political connections.' "

employment in private defense establishments important to national security.

13. The increasingly pervasive nature of public employment provides officials with substantial power through conditioning jobs on partisan support, particularly in this time of high unemployment. Since the government however, may not seek to achieve an unlawful end either directly or indirectly, the inducement afforded by placing conditions on a benefit need not be particularly great in order to find that rights have been violated. Rights are infringed both where the government fines a person a penny for being a Republican and where it withholds the grant of a penny for the same reason.

Petitioners contend that even though the government may not provide that public employees may retain their jobs only if they become affiliated with or provide support for the in-party, respondents here have waived any objection to such requirements. The difficulty with this argument is that it completely swallows the rule. Since the qualification may not be constitutionally imposed absent an appropriate justification, to accept the waiver argument is to say that the government may do what it may not do. A finding of waiver in this case, therefore, would be contrary to our view that a partisan job qualification abridges the First Amendment.

As for the second interest, the need for political loyalty and implementation of new policies "may be adequately met" by limiting patronage dismissals to "policymaking positions." As for the third interest—one "premised on the centrality of partisan politics in the democratic process"—"we are not persuaded [that] the interdiction of patronage dismissals [will cause] the demise of party politics." Political parties existed prior to active patronage and "they have survived substantial reduction in their patronage power through the establishment of the merit system.

"Patronage dismissals thus are not the least restrictive alternative to achieving the contributions they may make to the democratic process. The process functions as well without the practice, perhaps even better, for patronage dismissals clearly also retard that practice. [U]nlike the gain to representative government provided by the Hatch Act in *Letter Carriers* and *Mitchell,* the gain to representative government provided by [the practice], if any, would be insufficient to justify its sacrifice of First Amendment rights.

"To be sure, *Letter Carriers* and *Mitchell* upheld Hatch Act restraints sacrificing political campaigning and management, activities themselves protected by the First Amendment. But in those cases it was the Court's judgment that congressional subordination of those activities was permissible to safeguard the core interests of individual belief and association. Subordination of some First Amendment activity was permissible to protect other such activity. Today, we hold that subordination of other First Amendment activity, that is, patronage dismissals, not only is permissible, but also is mandated by the First Amendment. And since patronage dismissals fall within the category of political campaigning and management, this conclusion irresistibly flows from *Mitchell* and *Letter Carriers.* For if the First Amendment did not place individual belief and association above political campaigning and management, at least in the setting of public employment, the restraints on those latter activities could not have been judged permissible in *Mitchell* and *Letter Carriers.*"

STEWART, J., joined by Blackmun, J., concurred: "This case does not require us to consider the broad contours of the so-called patronage system, with all its variations and permutations. In particular, it does not require us to consider the constitutional validity of a system that confines the hiring of some governmental employees to those of a particular political party, and I would intimate no views whatever on that question.

"The single substantive question involved in this case is whether a nonpolicymaking, nonconfidential government employee can be discharged or threatened with discharge from a job that he is satisfactorily performing upon the sole ground of his political beliefs. I agree with the plurality that he cannot. See *Perry v. Sindermann.*"

POWELL, J., joined by Burger, C.J., and Rehnquist, J., dissented: "[Here, we have] complaining employees who apparently accepted patronage jobs knowingly and willingly, while fully familiar with the 'tenure' practices long prevailing in the Sheriff's Office. Such employees have *benefited* from their political beliefs and activities; they have not been penalized for them. In these circumstances, I am inclined to [the view that they] may not be heard to challenge [the patronage system] when it comes their turn to be replaced."

Beyond waiver, he complained that the Court "unnecessarily constitutionalizes another element of American life—an element not without its faults but one which generations have accepted on balance as having merit." Powell, J., stressed the importance of political parties and their dependency upon patronage. "History and long prevailing practice across the country support the view that patronage hiring practices make a sufficiently substantial contribution to the practical functioning of our democratic system to support their relatively modest intrusion on First Amendment interests. * * *

"It is difficult to disagree with the view, as an abstract proposition, that government employment ordinarily should not be conditioned upon one's political beliefs or activities. But we deal here with a highly practical and rather fundamental element of our political system, not the theoretical abstraction of a political science seminar. [T]he plurality seriously underestimates the strength of the government interest—especially at the local level—in allowing some patronage hiring practices, and it exaggerates the perceived burden on First Amendment rights. * * *

"It is naive to think that [local political activity supporting parties is] motivated [by] some academic interest in 'democracy' or other public service impulse. For the most part, the hope of some reward generates a major portion of [such activity]. It is difficult to overestimate the contributions to our system by the major political parties, fortunately limited in number compared to the fractionalization that has made the continued existence of democratic government doubtful in some other countries. * * *

"It is against decades of experience to the contrary, then, that the plurality opinion concludes that patronage hiring practices interfere with the 'free functioning of the electoral process.' This *ad hoc* judicial judgment runs counter to the judgments of the representatives of the people in state and local governments, representatives who have chosen, in most instances, to retain some patronage practices in combination with a merit-oriented civil service. One would think that elected representatives of the people are better equipped than we to weigh the need for some continuation of patronage practices in light of the interests above identified,[9] and particularly in view of local conditions. *Letter Carriers; Mitchell.*"[a]

Notes and Questions

1. BRANTI v. FINKEL, 445 U.S. 507, 100 S.Ct. 1287, 63 L.Ed.2d 574 (1980), per STEVENS, J., applied *Elrod* to "protect an assistant public defender who is satisfactorily performing his job from discharge solely because of his political beliefs."[b] The Court rejected the argument that even if party sponsorship is an

9. The plurality might be taken to concede some promotion of the democratic process by patronage hiring practices but to conclude that in net effect such practices will reduce political debate impermissibly by affecting some employees or potential employees and thereby depriving society of the 'unfettered judgment of each citizen on matters of political concern.' In the past the Court has upheld congressional actions designed to increase the overall level of political discourse but affecting adversely the First Amendment interests of some individuals. In *Letter Carriers* we indicated specifically that the First Amendment freedoms of federal employees could be limited in an effort to further the functioning of the democratic process. I do not believe that local legislative judgments as to what will further the democratic process in light of local conditions should receive less weight than these congressional judgments. Surely that should be the case until we have a record, if one could be created, showing the fears of the plurality to be justified.

a. Burger, C.J., dissented, contending that the decision "represents a significant intrusion into the area of legislative and policy concerns."

b. The Court noted that in *Elrod,* as in the instant case, "the only practice at issue was the *dismissal* of public employees for partisan reasons" and thus there was "no occasion to address petitioner's argument that there is a compelling governmental interest in maintaining a political sponsorship system for *filling vacancies* in the public defender's office." (Emphasis added.)

unconstitutional condition for retaining low-level public employees it is a permissible requirement for an assistant public defender: "[P]arty affiliation is not necessarily relevant to every policymaking or confidential position. The coach of a state university's football team formulates policy, but no one could seriously claim that Republicans make better coaches than Democrats, or vice versa, no matter which party is in control of the state government. On the other hand, it is equally clear that the governor of a state may appropriately believe that the official duties of various assistants who help him write speeches, explain his views to the press, or communicate with the legislature cannot be performed effectively unless those persons share his political beliefs and party commitments. In sum, the ultimate inquiry is not whether the label 'policymaker' or 'confidential' fits a particular position; rather, the question is whether the hiring authority can demonstrate that party affiliation is an appropriate requirement for the effective performance of the public office involved."

The Court concluded that neither the policymaking of an assistant public defender nor the access of client's confidential information had any bearing on partisan political considerations.

2. RUTAN v. REPUBLICAN PARTY OF ILLINOIS, ___ U.S. ___, 110 S.Ct. 2729, 111 L.Ed.2d 52 (1990), per BRENNAN, J., extended *Elrod* and *Branti* not only to promotion, transfer, and recall decisions, but also to hiring decisions: "It is unnecessary here to consider whether not being hired is less burdensome than being discharged because the government is not pressed to do *either* on the basis of political affiliation." [c]

STEVENS, J., concurring, argued that "[T]he entire rationale for patronage hiring [rests] on the assumption that the patronage employee filling the government position must be paid a premium to reward him for his partisan services. * * * This defense of patronage [assumes] that governmental power and public resources—in this case employment opportunities—may appropriately be used to subsidize partisan activities [4] even when the political affiliation of the employee or the job applicant is entirely unrelated to his or her public service. The premise on which this position rests would justify the use of public funds to compensate party members for their campaign work, or conversely, a legislative

c. The opinion excepted employment decisions where party affiliation or support was an "appropriate requirement for the position involved." Illinois, according to the complaint, however, was operating a wholesale patronage system out of the governor's office that functioned broadly to limit state hiring to those supported by the Republican Party.

4. Although Justice Scalia's defense of patronage turns on the benefits of fostering the two-party system, his opinion is devoid of reference to meaningful evidence that patronage practices have played a significant role in the preservation of the two-party system. In each of the examples that he cites—"the Boss Tweeds, the Tammany Halls, the Pendergast Machines, the Byrd Machines and the Daley Machines," patronage practices were used solely to protect the power of an entrenched majority. See Laycock, *Notes on the Role of Judicial Review, the Expansion of Federal Power, and the Structure of Constitutional Rights,* 99 Yale L.J. 1711, 1722 (1990) (describing the "hopelessness of contesting elections" in Chicago's "one-party system" when "half a dozen employees of the city and of city contractors were paid with public funds to work [a precinct] for the other side"); Johnson, *Successful Reform Litigation: The Shakman Patronage Case,* 64 Chi.-Kent L.Rev. 479, 481 (1988) (the "massive Democratic patronage employment system" maintained a "noncompetitive political system" in Cook County in the 1960's).

Without repeating the Court's studied rejection of the policy arguments for patronage practices in *Elrod,* I note only that many commentators agree more with Justice Scalia's admissions of the systemic costs of patronage practices—the "financial corruption, such as salary kickbacks and partisan political activity on government-paid time," the reduced efficiency of government, and the undeniable constraint upon the expression of views by employees than with his belief that patronage is necessary to political stability and integration of powerless groups. * * *

enactment denying public employment to nonmembers of the majority party. If such legislation is unconstitutional—as it clearly would be—an equally pernicious rule promulgated by the Executive must also be invalid."

SCALIA, J., joined by Rehnquist, C.J., and Kennedy, J., and in part[d] by O'Connor, J., dissenting, argued that *Elrod* and *Branti* were wrongly decided and opposed their extension:

"As the merit principle [for government employment] has been extended and its effects increasingly felt; as the Boss Tweeds, the Tammany Halls, the Pendergast Machines, the Byrd Machines and the Daley Machines have faded into history; we find that political leaders at all levels increasingly complain of the helplessness of elected government, unprotected by 'party discipline,' before the demands of small and cohesive interest-groups.

"The choice between patronage and the merit principle—or, to be more realistic about it, the choice between the desirable mix of merit and patronage principles in widely varying federal, state, and local political contexts—is not so clear that I would be prepared, as an original matter, to chisel a single, inflexible prescription into the Constitution. * * *

"The provisions of the Bill of Rights were designed to restrain transient majorities from impairing long-recognized personal liberties. They did not create by implication novel individual rights overturning accepted political norms. Thus, when a practice not expressly prohibited by the text of the Bill of Rights bears the endorsement of a long tradition of open, wide-spread, and unchallenged use that dates back to the beginning of the Republic, we have no proper basis for striking it down.[1] Such a venerable and accepted tradition is not to be laid on the examining table and scrutinized for its conformity to some abstract principle of First–Amendment adjudication devised by this Court. To the contrary, such traditions are themselves the stuff out of which the Court's principles are to be formed. They are, in these uncertain areas, the very points of reference by which the legitimacy or illegitimacy of *other* practices are to be figured out. When it appears that the latest 'rule,' or 'three-part test,' or 'balancing test' devised by the Court has placed us on a collision course with such a landmark practice, it is the former that must be recalculated by us, and not the latter that must be abandoned by our citizens. I know of no other way to formulate a constitutional jurisprudence that reflects, as it should, the principles adhered to, over time, by the American people, rather than those favored by the personal (and necessarily shifting) philosophical dispositions of a majority of this Court.

"I will not describe at length the claim of patronage to landmark status as one of our accepted political traditions. Justice Powell discussed it in his

d. O'Connor, J., did not join the sections of Scalia, J's opinion quoted infra, but did join sections arguing that *Elrod* and *Branti* were wrongly decided.

1. The customary invocation of *Brown v. Board of Education* as demonstrating the dangerous consequences of this principle, (Stevens, J., concurring), is unsupportable. I argue for the role of tradition in giving content only to *ambiguous* constitutional text; no tradition can supersede the Constitution. In my view the Fourteenth Amendment's requirement of "equal protection of the laws," combined with the Thirteenth Amendment's abolition of the institution of black slavery, leaves no room for doubt that laws treating people differently because of their race are invalid. Moreover, even if one does not regard the Fourteenth Amendment as crystal clear on this point, a tradition of *unchallenged* validity did not exist with respect to the practice in *Brown*. To the contrary, in the 19th century the principle of "separate-but-equal" had been vigorously opposed on constitutional grounds, litigated up to this Court, and upheld only over the dissent of one of our historically most respected Justices. See *Plessy v. Ferguson* (Harlan, J., dissenting).

dissenting opinions in *Elrod* and *Branti*. Suffice it to say that patronage was, without any thought that it could be unconstitutional, a basis for government employment from the earliest days of the Republic until *Elrod*—and has continued unabated since *Elrod*, to the extent still permitted by that unfortunate decision. Given that unbroken tradition regarding the application of an ambiguous constitutional text, there was in my view no basis for holding that patronage-based dismissals violated the First Amendment—much less for holding, as the Court does today, that even patronage hiring does so.[2]" [e]

3. Might Communists be treated differently from Republican or Democrats for some confidential employment? Consider White, J., dissenting in *Robel* (cited in Brennan, J.'s *Elrod* opinion fn. 12): "[D]enying the opportunity to be employed in some defense plants is a much smaller deterrent to the exercise of associational rights than [a] criminal penalty attached solely to membership, and the Government's interest in keeping potential spies and saboteurs from defense plants is much greater than its interest [in] committing all Party members to prison." Compare Israel, *Elfbrandt v. Russell: The Demise of the Oath?*, 1966 Sup.Ct.Rev. 193, 201–07 and O'Neil, *Unconstitutional Conditions*, 54 Calif.L.Rev. 443 (1966) with Van Alstyne, *The Constitutional Rights of Employees*, 16 U.C. L.A.L.Rev. 751 (1969).

COLE v. RICHARDSON, 405 U.S. 676, 92 S.Ct. 1332, 31 L.Ed.2d 593 (1972), per BURGER, C.J. (over the dissents of Douglas, J., and Marshall, J., joined by Brennan, J.), upheld the dismissal of Richardson's employment at a state hospital for refusing to sign a loyalty oath calling in part for an affirmation that "I will oppose the overthrow of the government [by] force, violence, or by any illegal or unconstitutional method": "Since there is no constitutionally protected right to overthrow a government by force, violence, or illegal or unconstitutional means, no constitutional right is infringed by an oath to abide by the constitutional system in the future." [f] Should the first amendment permit requiring

2. Justice Stevens seeks to counteract this tradition by relying upon the supposed "unequivocal repudiation" of the right-privilege distinction. That will not do. If the right-privilege distinction was once used to explain the practice, and if that distinction is to be repudiated, then one must simply devise some other theory to explain it. The order of precedence is that a constitutional theory must be wrong if its application contradicts a clear constitutional tradition; not that a clear constitutional tradition must be wrong if it does not conform to the current constitutional theory. On Justice Stevens' view of the matter, this Court examines a historical practice, endows it with an intellectual foundation, and later, by simply undermining that foundation, relegates the constitutional tradition to the dustbin of history. That is not how constitutional adjudication works. I am not sure, in any event, that the right-privilege distinction has been as unequivocally rejected as Justice Stevens supposes. It has certainly been recognized that the fact that the government need not confer a certain benefit does not mean that it can attach any conditions whatever to the conferral of that benefit. But it remains true that certain conditions can be attached to benefits that cannot be imposed as prescriptions upon the public at large. If Justice Stevens chooses to call this something other than a right-privilege distinction, that is fine and good—but it is in any case what explains the nonpatronage restrictions upon federal employees that the Court continues to approve, and there is no reason why it cannot support patronage restrictions as well.

e. In addition to the arguments referred to in footnotes 1 and 2 of Scalia, J.'s opinion, Stevens, J., maintained in response:

"The tradition that is relevant in this case is the American commitment to examine and reexamine past and present practices against the basic principles embodied in the Constitution. The inspirational command by our President in 1961 is entirely consistent with that tradition: 'Ask not what your country can do for you—ask what you can do for your country.' This case involves a contrary command: 'Ask not what job applicants can do for the State—ask what they can do for our party.' Whatever traditional support may remain for a command of that ilk, it is plainly an illegitimate excuse for the practices rejected by the Court today."

f. Powell and Rehnquist, JJ., took no part.

public employees to oppose that which they have a right to advocate? Is *Cole* consistent with the cases cited in the plurality opinion? With *Robel*? With *Wooley*?

4. The plurality argues that its conclusion flows irresistibly from *Mitchell* and *Letter Carriers*? Were these cases rightly decided? Is a ban on active participation in political campaigns by government employees necessary (as the Court thought in *Letter Carriers*) to avoid the impression that the government practices "political justice" or to prevent the government work force from becoming a "peaceful, invincible, and perhaps corrupt political machine"? Would prohibitions against coercion (such as those commanded by *Elrod*) be sufficient? If not, is the concern about coercion relevant only to participation on behalf of incumbents? See Blasi, *The Checking Value in First Amendment Theory,* 1977 Am.B.Found.Res.J. 521, 634–35. Is it of major import that the restrictions are "not aimed at particular parties, groups or points of [view]"? *Letter Carriers.* Does an emphasis on this factor, denigrate the liberty and associational interests of government employees? See Redish, *The Content Distinction in First Amendment Analysis,* 34 Stan.L.Rev. 113 (1981). See also Note, *"Un–Hatching" Federal Employee Political Endorsements,* 134 U.Pa.L.Rev. 1497 (1986) (criticizing Hatch Act policies).

When District Attorney Connick proposed to transfer Assistant D.A. Myers to a different section of the criminal court, she strongly opposed it. Shortly thereafter, Myers prepared and distributed to the other assistants a questionnaire concerning office transfer policy, office morale, the need for a grievance committee and two questions Connick particularly objected to—the level of confidence in various supervisors and whether employees felt pressured to work in political campaigns. Connick then told Myers that she was being terminated for refusal to accept the transfer and that he considered distribution of the questionnaire an act of insubordination. Myers filed suit under 42 U.S.C. § 1983, contending that she was wrongfully discharged because she had exercised her right of free speech. The district court agreed. It found that the questionnaire was the real reason for Myers' termination, and that the state had not "clearly demonstrated" that the survey "substantially interfered" with the operation of the District Attorney's office. The Fifth Circuit affirmed. But CONNICK v. MYERS, 461 U.S. 138, 103 S.Ct. 1684, 75 L.Ed.2d 708 (1983), per WHITE, J., held that respondent's discharge did not offend the first amendment:

"For most of this century, the unchallenged dogma was that a public employee had no right to object to conditions placed upon the terms of employment—including those which restricted the exercise of constitutional rights. The classic formulation of this position was Justice Holmes', who, when sitting on the Supreme Judicial Court of Massachusetts, observed: 'A policeman may have a constitutional right to talk politics, but he has no constitutional right to be a policeman.' *McAuliffe v. Mayor,* 155 Mass. 216, 220, 29 N.E. 517, 517 (1892). For many years, Holmes' epigram expressed this Court's law. *Adler v. Bd. of Educ.,* 342 U.S. 485, 72 S.Ct. 380, 96 L.Ed. 517 (1952); *Garner v. Bd. of Pub. Works,* 341 U.S. 716, 71 S.Ct. 909, 95 L.Ed. 1317 (1951)."

The Court proceeded, however, to recount a series of cases in which it had subsequently repudiated Holmes' epigram.[a] Indeed, for some two decades it had

a. Most of the cases involved the right of public employees to associate.

become wholly impermissible to deny freedom of expression "by the denial of or placing of conditions upon a benefit or a privilege." As the Court characterized the public employee cases, they were all rooted in the rights of public employees to participate in public affairs.[b] In particular, the Court focused upon *Pickering v. Board of Educ.,* 391 U.S. 563, 88 S.Ct. 1731, 20 L.Ed.2d 811 (1968): "In *Pickering,* we stated that a public employee does not relinquish First Amendment rights to comment on matters of public interest by virtue of government employment. [The] repeated emphasis in *Pickering* on the right of a public employee 'as a citizen, in commenting upon matters of public concern,' was not accidental. This language, reiterated in all of *Pickering's* progeny, reflects both the historical evolvement of the rights of public employees, and the common sense realization that government offices could not function if every employment decision became a constitutional matter.[5] * * *

"*Pickering* [held] impermissible under the First Amendment the dismissal of a high school teacher for openly criticizing the Board of Education on its allocation of school funds between athletics and education and its methods of informing taxpayers about the need for additional revenue. Pickering's subject was a matter of legitimate public concern upon which free and open debate is vital to informed decision-making by the electorate. [Most] recently, in *Givhan v. Western Line Cons. School Dist.,* 439 U.S. 410, 99 S.Ct. 693, 58 L.Ed.2d 619 (1979), we held that First Amendment protection applies when a public employee arranges to communicate privately with his employer rather than to express his views publicly. Although the subject-matter of Mrs. Givhan's statements were not the issue before the Court, it is clear that her statements concerning the school district's allegedly racially discriminatory policies involved a matter of public concern.

"*Pickering,* its antecedents and progeny, lead us to conclude that if Myers' questionnaire cannot be fairly characterized as constituting speech on a matter of public concern, it is unnecessary for us to scrutinize the reasons for her discharge. When employee expression cannot be fairly considered as relating to any matter of political, social, or other concern to the community, government officials should enjoy wide latitude in managing their offices, without intrusive oversight by the judiciary in the name of the First Amendment. * * * We do not suggest, however, that Myers' speech, even if not touching upon a matter of public concern, is totally beyond the protection of the First Amendment. * * * [We] in no sense suggest that speech on private matters falls into one of the narrow and well-defined classes of expression which carries so little social value, such as obscenity, that the state can prohibit and punish such expression by all persons in its jurisdiction. See *Chaplinsky; Roth; Ferber.* For example, an employee's false criticism of his employer on grounds not of public concern may be cause for his discharge but would be entitled to the same protection in a libel action accorded an identical statement made by a man on the street. We hold only that when a public employee speaks not as a citizen upon matters of public concern, but instead as an employee upon matters only of personal interest, absent the most unusual circumstances, a federal court is not the appropriate forum in which to review the wisdom of a personnel decision taken

b. But see *Letter Carriers,* p. 735 supra.

5. The question of whether expression is of a kind that is of legitimate concern to the public is also the standard in determining whether a common-law action for invasion of privacy is present. See Restatement (Second) of Torts, § 652D. See also *Cox Broadcasting Co. v. Cohn* (action for invasion of privacy cannot be maintained when the subject-matter of the publicity is matter of public record); *Time, Inc. v. Hill.*

by a public agency allegedly in reaction to the employee's behavior. Our responsibility is to ensure that citizens are not deprived of fundamental rights by virtue of working for the government; this does not require a grant of immunity for employee grievances not afforded by the First Amendment to those who do not work for the state.

"Whether an employee's speech addresses a matter of public concern must be determined by the content, form, and context of a given statement, as revealed by the whole record. In this case, with but one exception, the questions posed by Myers to her coworkers do not fall under the rubric of matters of 'public concern.' We view the questions pertaining to the confidence and trust that Myers' coworkers possess in various supervisors, the level of office morale, and the need for a grievance committee as mere extensions of Myers' dispute over her transfer to another section of the criminal court. * * * Indeed, the questionnaire, if released to the public, would convey no information at all other than the fact that a single employee is upset with the status quo. [T]he focus of Myers' questions is not to evaluate the performance of the office but rather to gather ammunition for another round of controversy with her superiors. These questions reflect one employee's dissatisfaction with a transfer and an attempt to turn that displeasure into a cause celèbre.[8] * * *

"One question in Myers' questionnaire, however, does touch upon a matter of public concern. Question 11 inquires if assistant district attorneys 'ever feel pressured to work in political campaigns on behalf of office supported candidates.' [This issue] is a matter of interest to the community upon which it is essential that public employees be able to speak out freely without fear of retaliatory dismissal.

"Because one of the questions in Myers' survey touched upon a matter of public concern, and contributed to her discharge we must determine whether Connick was justified in discharging Myers. Here the District Court again erred in imposing an unduly onerous burden on the state to justify Myers' discharge. The District Court viewed the issue of whether Myers' speech was upon a matter of 'public concern' as a threshold inquiry, after which it became the government's burden to 'clearly demonstrate' that the speech involved 'substantially interfered' with official responsibilities. Yet *Pickering* unmistakably states, and respondent agrees, that the state's burden in justifying a particular discharge varies depending upon the nature of the employee's expression. Although such particularized balancing is difficult, the courts must reach the most appropriate possible balance of the competing interests. * * *

"We agree with the District Court that there is no demonstration here that the questionnaire impeded Myers' ability to perform her responsibilities. The District Court was also correct to recognize that 'it is important to the efficient and successful operation of the District Attorney's office for Assistants to maintain close working relationships with their superiors.' Connick's judgment, and apparently also that of his first assistant [who] characterized Myers' actions

8. This is not a case like *Givhan,* where an employee speaks out as a citizen on a matter of general concern, not tied to a personal employment dispute, but arranges to do so privately. Mrs. Givhan's right to protest racial discrimination—a matter inherently of public concern—is not forfeited by her choice of a private forum. Here, however, a questionnaire not otherwise of public concern does not attain that status because its subject matter could, in different circumstances, have been the topic of a communication to the public that might be of general interest. The dissent's analysis of whether discussions of office morale and discipline could be matters of public concern is beside the point—it does not answer whether *this* questionnaire is such speech.

as causing a 'mini-insurrection', was that Myers' questionnaire was an act of insubordination which interfered with working relationships. When close working relationships are essential to fulfilling public responsibilities, a wide degree of deference to the employer's judgment is appropriate. Furthermore, we do not see the necessity for an employer to allow events to unfold to the extent that the disruption of the office and the destruction of working relationships is manifest before taking action. We caution that a stronger showing may be necessary if the employee's speech more substantially involved matters of public [concern].

"Myers' questionnaire touched upon matters of public concern in only a most limited sense; her survey, in our view, is most accurately characterized as an employee grievance concerning internal office policy. The limited First Amendment interest involved here does not require that Connick tolerate action which he reasonably believed would disrupt the office, undermine his authority, and destroy close working relationships. Myers' discharge therefore did not offend the First Amendment. * * *

BRENNAN, J., joined by Marshall, Blackmun and Stevens, JJ., dissented: "It is hornbook law [that] speech about 'the manner in which government is operated or should be operated' is an essential part of the communications necessary for self-governance the protection of which was a central purpose of the First Amendment. Because the questionnaire addressed such matters and its distribution did not adversely affect the operations of the District Attorney's Office or interfere with Myers' working relationship with her fellow employees, I dissent. * * *

"The balancing test articulated in *Pickering* comes into play only when a public employee's speech implicates the government's interests as an employer. When public employees engage in expression unrelated to their employment while away from the work place, their First Amendment rights are, of course, no different from those of the general public. Thus, whether a public employee's speech addresses a matter of public concern is relevant to the constitutional inquiry only when the statements at issue—by virtue of their content or the context in which they were made—may have an adverse impact on the government's ability to perform its duties efficiently.

"The Court's decision today is flawed in three respects. First, the Court distorts the balancing analysis required under *Pickering* by suggesting that one factor, the context in which a statement is made, is to be weighed *twice*—first in determining whether an employee's speech addresses a matter of public concern and then in deciding whether the statement adversely affected the government's interest as an employer. Second, in concluding that the effect of respondent's personnel policies on employee morale and the work performance of the District Attorney's Office is not a matter of public concern, the Court impermissibly narrows the class of subjects on which public employees may speak out without fear of retaliatory dismissal. Third, the Court misapplies the *Pickering* balancing test in holding that Myers could constitutionally be dismissed for circulating a questionnaire addressed to at least one subject that *was* 'a matter of interest to the community,' in the absence of evidence that her conduct disrupted the efficient functioning of the District Attorney's Office.

"[Based] on its own narrow conception of which matters are of public concern, the Court implicitly determines that information concerning employee morale at an important government office will not inform public debate. To the contrary, the First Amendment protects the dissemination of such information so that the people, not the courts may evaluate its usefulness. The proper means to ensure that the courts are not swamped with routine employee grievances mischaracterized as First Amendment cases is not to restrict artificially the concept of 'public concern,' but to require that adequate weight be given to the public's important interests in the efficient performance of governmental functions and in preserving employee discipline and harmony sufficient to achieve that end. * * *

In the face of the District Court's finding that the circulation of the questionnaire had no disruptive effect, the Court holds that respondent may be dismissed because petitioner 'reasonably believed [the action] would disrupt the office, undermine his authority and destroy close working relationships.' Even though the District Court found that the distribution of the questionnaire did not impair Myers' working relationship with her supervisors, the Court bows to petitioner's judgment because '[w]hen close working relationships are essential to fulfilling public responsibilities, a wide degree of deference to the employer's judgment is appropriate.'

"Such extreme deference to the employer's judgment is not appropriate when public employees voice critical views concerning the operations of the agency for which they work. Although an employer's determination that an employee's statements have undermined essential working relationships must be carefully weighed in the *Pickering* balance, we must bear in mind that 'the threat of dismissal from public employment is [a] potent means of inhibiting speech.' * * *

"The Court's decision today inevitably will deter public employees from making critical statements about the manner in which government agencies are operated for fear that doing so will provoke their dismissal. As a result, the public will be deprived of valuable information with which to evaluate the performance of elected officials. Because protecting the dissemination of such information is an essential function of the First Amendment, I dissent."

Notes and Questions

1. *Holmes' epigram.* Does the Court reject Holmes' epigram with one hand and embrace it with the other? Does it to some extent hold that because there is no right to hold a government job, its retention is a revocable privilege? Consider Tribe, *Constitutional Choices* 208 (1985): "*Connick* resurrects the right-privilege doctrine for 'private' speech by government employees. By hinging protection on the distinction between public and private speech, the Court has embarked on a difficult definitional course. The stated test, which includes the 'content, form, and context' of the expression, provides little guidance. As Justice Brennan pointed out in dissent, the Court significantly narrowed the concept of a public issue in holding that criticism of governmental officials is not necessarily of public concern, but provided no clear alternative formulation. The mere fact that expression constitutes an employee grievance surely cannot be decisive, since the Court found that pressure upon employees to work on political campaigns was of public concern. Nor can the absence of partisan political concerns be determinative, since an employee grievance criticizing hiring and personnel management policies is of public concern if based upon a claim of racial discrimination. What is clear is that, at least until the precise reach of *Connick* is determined, public employees, who often possess unique information, will be discouraged from adding their voices to the debate on

government performance." [c]

2. Consider the tension between *Letter Carriers* and *Pickering* or *Connick.* Consider also the relationship between *Pickering, Connick,* and *Elrod.* Suppose a deputy sheriff is discharged for meeting with a political opponent of the incumbent sheriff. Does *Elrod* apply or *Pickering–Connick?* [d] What is the difference? For discussion, see Note, *Politics and the Non–Civil Service Public Employee: A Categorical Approach to First Amendment Protection,* 85 Colum.L. Rev. 558 (1985).

3. Does *Connick* provide less protection for the public employee than is afforded to the school child in *Tinker,* p. 673 supra? Does the public/private distinction distinguish *Tinker?* If Tinker's black arm band symbolized criticism of the school principal, would the outcome have been different?

4. After hearing of an assassination attempt on the life of the President, a clerical employee in a county constable's office remarked to a friend in the office, "If they go after him again, I hope they get him." Free speech? See *Rankin v. McPherson,* 483 U.S. 378, 107 S.Ct. 2891, 97 L.Ed.2d 315 (1987). For discussion, see Shiffrin, *The First Amendment, Democracy, and Romance* (1990); Massaro, *Significant Silences: Freedom of Speech in the Public Sector Workplace,* 61 S.Cal. L.Rev. 1, 68–76 (1987).[e]

A 1981 amendment to the Food Stamp Act provides that no family shall become eligible to participate in the program during the time that any member of the household is on strike nor shall receive any increase in food stamp allotments by virtue of decreased income of the striking member. LYNG v. UAW, 485 U.S. 360, 108 S.Ct. 1184, 99 L.Ed.2d 380 (1988), per WHITE, J., stated that associational rights included the "combination of workers together in order better to assert their lawful rights" but found no interference with such association: "[The statute] does not 'order' appellees not to associate together for the purpose of conducting a strike, or for any other purpose, and it does not 'prevent' them from associating together or burden their ability to do so in any significant manner. [I]t seems 'exceedingly unlikely' that this statute will prevent individuals from continuing to associate together in unions to promote their lawful objectives.[a] [A] 'legislature's decision not to subsidize the exercise of a fundamental right does not infringe the right.' *Regan.*" [b]

c. Much of the literature relevant to the "right-privilege" distinction is cited in Ch. 3, Sec. 5.

d. Should the standards for public teachers, professors, professionals, and non-professional employees each be controlled by *Connick?* Should academic freedom apply to "intramural" speech in ways that permit freer speech than that available to other public employees? For discussion, see Finkin, *Intramural Speech, Academic Freedom, and the First Amendment,* 66 Texas L.Rev. 1323 (1988); Yudof, *Intramural Musings on Academic Freedom,* 66 Texas L.Rev. 1351 (1988); Brest, *Protecting Academic Freedom Through the First Amendment,* 66 Texas L.Rev. 1359 (1988).

e. For discussion of *Connick,* see eg., Shiffrin, supra, Massaro, supra, Lieberwitz, *Freedom of Speech in Public Sector Employment: The Deconstitutionalization of the Public Sector Workplace,* 19 U.C.Davis L.Rev. 597 (1986); Post, *Between Governance and Management,* 34 UCLA L.Rev. 1713, 1813–16 (1987); Comment, *The Public Employee's Right of Free Speech,* 55 U.Cin.L.Rev. 449 (1986). For relevant pre-*Connick* commentary, see Schauer, *"Private" Speech and the "Private" Forum: Givhan v. Western Line School District,* 1979 Sup.Ct.Rev. 217.

a. Should a penalty for the exercise of a right be unconstitutional even if it does not inhibit the exercise of that right?

b. How does one distinguish the mere failure to subsidize from a penalty? Is participation in a strike protected association? For commentary discussing and ranging beyond *Lyng,* see Sullivan, *Unconstitutional Conditions,* 102 Harv.L.Rev. 1413, 1428–56, 1474 (1989).

MARSHALL, J., joined by Brennan and Blackmun, JJ., dissenting, saw no need to reach the First Amendment issue (although he was "unconvinced" by the Court's treatment of the issue) because, he argued, the statute failed to meet even the most deferential scrutiny. In light of a variety of statutory benefits easing management's burden in labor disputes, he concluded: "Altering the backdrop of governmental support in this one-sided and devastating way amounts to a penalty on strikers, not neutrality." [c]

In ABOOD v. DETROIT BD. OF EDUC., 431 U.S. 209, 97 S.Ct. 1782, 52 L.Ed. 2d 261 (1977), a Michigan statute permitted an "agency shop" arrangement, whereby all local governmental employees represented by a union, even though not themselves union members, must, as a condition of employment, pay to the union "service charges" equal in amount to union dues. Alleging that they were unwilling to pay union dues, that (1) they opposed public sector collective bargaining and that (2) the union was engaged in non-collective bargaining political-ideological activities which they disapproved, public school teachers challenged the validity of the agency-shop clause in a collective bargaining agreement between the Board of Education and the union. The Court, per STEWART, J., rejected plaintiffs' first contention, but sustained the second—the union's expenditure of a part of such "service charges" "to contribute to political candidates and to express political views unrelated to its duties as exclusive bargaining representative" violates the first amendment rights of non-union employees who oppose such causes.

"To compel employees financially to support their collective-bargaining representative has an impact upon their First Amendment interests. An employee may very well have ideological objections to a wide variety of activities undertaken by the union in its role as exclusive representative. His moral or religious views about the desirability of abortion may not square with the union's policy in negotiating a medical benefits plan. One individual might disagree with a union policy of negotiating limits on the right to strike, believing that to be the road to serfdom for the working class, while another might have economic or political objections to unionism itself. An employee might object to the union's wage policy because it violates guidelines designed to limit inflation, or might object to the union's seeking a clause in the collective-bargaining agreement proscribing racial discrimination. The examples could be multiplied. To be required to help finance the union as a collective-bargaining agent might well be thought, therefore, to interfere in some way with an employee's freedom to associate for the advancement of ideas, or to refrain from doing so, as he sees fit. But the judgment clearly made in [*Railway Employees' Dep't v. Hanson,* 351 U.S. 225, 76 S.Ct. 714, 100 L.Ed. 1112 (1956), upholding against first amendment challenge a union-shop clause, authorized by the Railway Labor Act (RLA), requiring financial support of the union by every member of the bargaining unit, and *International Ass'n of Machinists v. Street,* 367 U.S. 740, 81 S.Ct. 1784, 6 L.Ed.2d 1141 (1961), avoiding serious constitutional issues by construing RLA to prohibit the use of compulsory union dues for political purposes] is that such interference as exists is constitutionally justified by the legislative assessment of the important contribution of the union shop to the system of labor relations established by the Congress. '[As long as the union leadership acts] to promote

c. The government had argued that the statute was justified by the interest of governmental neutrality in private labor disputes.

the cause which justified bringing the group together, the individual cannot withdraw his financial support merely because he disagrees with the group's strategy.' *Street* (Douglas, J., concurring).

"[The] desirability of labor peace is no less important in the public sector, nor is the risk of 'free riders' any smaller. [Thus], insofar as the service charge is used to finance expenditures by the union for the purposes of collective bargaining, contract administration, and grievance adjustment, [*Hanson* and *Street*] appear to require validation of the agency-shop agreement before us."

In agreeing with plaintiffs' contention that they fall within the protection of *Elrod* and other cases guaranteeing the freedom to associate for the purpose of advancing ideas and forbidding the government to require one to relinquish first amendment rights as a condition of public employment "because they have been prohibited not from actively associating, but rather from refusing to associate," and in ruling that plaintiffs could constitutionally prevent the union's spending a part of their required service fees for political and ideological purposes unrelated to collective bargaining, the Court pointed out: "The fact that [plaintiffs] are compelled to make, rather than prohibited from making, contributions for political purposes works no less an infringement of their constitutional rights. For at the heart of the First Amendment is the notion that an individual should be free to believe as he will, and that in a free society one's beliefs should be shaped by his mind and his conscience rather than coerced by the State. See [*Elrod.*]

"These principles prohibit a State from compelling an individual [to] associate with a political party, *Elrod,* as a condition of employment. They are no less applicable to the case at bar, and they thus prohibit the [union] from requiring any [plaintiff] to contribute to the support of an ideological cause he may oppose as a condition of holding a job as a public school teacher.

"We do not hold that a union cannot constitutionally spend funds for the expression of political views, on behalf of political candidates, or towards the advancement of other ideological causes not germane to its duties as collective bargaining representative. Rather, the Constitution requires only that expenditures be financed from [charges] paid by employees who do not object to advancing those ideas and who are not coerced into doing so against their will by the threat of loss of government employment."

The Court remanded to devise an appropriate "way of preventing subsidization of ideological activity by employees who object thereto without restricting the union's ability to require every employee to contribute to the cost of collective-bargaining activities." [a]

POWELL, J., joined by Burger, C.J., and Blackmun, J., agreed that a state cannot constitutionally compel public employees to contribute to union political activities which they oppose and thus joined the Court's judgment remanding the case for further proceedings, but balked at the Court's apparent ruling "that public employees can be compelled by the State to pay full union dues to a union with which they disagree, subject only to a possible rebate or deduction if they are willing to step forward, declare their opposition to the union, and initiate a proceeding to establish that some portion of their dues has been spent on 'ideological activities unrelated to collective bargaining.' Such a sweeping

a. For procedural aspects of the implementation, see *Chicago Teachers Union v. Hudson,* 475 U.S. 292, 106 S.Ct. 1066, 89 L.Ed.2d 232 (1986).

limitation of First Amendment rights by the Court is not only unnecessary on this record; it [is] unsupported by either precedent or reason. * * *

"The Court's extensive reliance on *Hanson* and *Street* requires it to rule that there is no constitutional distinction between what the Government can require of its own employees and what it can permit private employees to do. To me the distinction is fundamental. Under the First Amendment the Government may authorize private parties to enter into voluntary agreements whose terms it could not adopt as its own.

"[The] collective-bargaining agreement to which a public agency is a party is not merely analogous to legislation; it has all of the attributes of legislation for the subjects [e.g., residency requirements for state employees] with which it deals. [The] State in this case has not merely authorized union-shop agreements between willing parties; it has negotiated and adopted such an agreement itself. [It] has undertaken to compel employees to pay full dues [to] a union as a condition of employment. Accordingly, the [Board of Education's] collective-bargaining agreement, like any other enactment of state law, is fully subject to the constraints that the Constitution imposes on coercive governmental regulation.

"[I] would make it more explicit [than has the majority] that compelling a government employee to give financial support to a union in the public sector—regardless of the use to which the union puts the contribution—impinges seriously upon interests in free speech and association protected by the First Amendment.

"In *Buckley* [we held that] limitations on political contributions 'impinge on protected associational freedoms.' [That] *Buckley* dealt with a contribution limitation requirement does not alter its importance for this case. An individual can no more be required to affiliate with a candidate by making a contribution than he can be prohibited from such affiliation. The only question after *Buckley* is whether a union in the public sector is sufficiently distinguishable from a political candidate or committee to remove the withholding of financial contributions from First Amendment protection. In my view no principled distinction exists.

"The ultimate objective of a union in the public sector, like that of a political party, is to influence public decisionmaking in accordance with the views and perceived interests of the membership. [In this sense], the public sector union is indistinguishable from the traditional political party in this country.

"[It] is possible that paramount governmental interests may be found—at least with respect to certain narrowly defined subjects of bargaining—that would support this restriction on First Amendment rights. But 'the burden is on the government to show the existence of such an interest.' *Elrod.* Because this appeal reaches this Court on a motion to dismiss, the record is barren of any demonstration by the State that excluding minority views from the processes by which governmental policy is made is necessary to serve overriding governmental objectives. * * *

"Before today it had been well established that when state law intrudes upon protected speech, the State itself must shoulder the burden of proving that its action is justified by overriding state interests. See *Elrod; Speiser v. Randall.* The Court, for the first time in a First Amendment case, simply reverses this principle. Under today's decision, a nonunion employee who would vindicate his First Amendment rights apparently must initiate a proceeding to prove that the union has allocated some portion of its budget to 'ideological activities unrelated to collective bargaining.' I would adhere to established First Amendment principles and require the State to come forward and demonstrate, as to each union expenditure for which it would exact support from minority employees, that the compelled contribution is necessary to serve overriding governmental objectives." [b]

REHNQUIST, J., concurring, noted that had he joined the *Elrod* plurality, he "would find it virtually impossible to join the Court's opinion in this case." He did not "read the Court's opinion as leaving intact the 'unfettered judgment of each citizen on matters of political concern' [*Elrod*] when it holds that Michigan [may] require an objecting member of a public employees' union to contribute to the funds necessary for the union to carry out its bargaining activities. Nor does the Court's opinion leave such a member free 'to believe as he will and to act and associate according to his beliefs' [*Elrod*]." He was "unable to see a constitutional distinction between a governmentally imposed requirement that a public employee be a Democrat or Republican or else lose his job, and a similar requirement that a public employee contribute to the collective-bargaining expenses of a labor union." [c]

Notes and Questions

1. How should the *Abood* rules apply to forced employee payments for union conventions, union newsletters, union social activities or union organizing? See *Ellis v. Brotherhood of Railway, Airline & Steamship Clerks,* 466 U.S. 435, 104 S.Ct. 1883, 80 L.Ed.2d 428 (1984). See also *Communications Workers v. Beck,* 487 U.S. 735, 108 S.Ct. 2641, 101 L.Ed.2d 634 (1988) (forced expenditures for purposes other than collective bargaining including non-germane-non-ideological activities violates National Labor Relations Act). For exploration of the issues raised by *Abood,* see Cantor, *Forced Payments to Service Institutions and Constitutional Interests in Ideological Non-Association,* 36 Rut.L.Rev. 3 (1984).

2. Does *Abood* exaggerate the first amendment interests? See generally, Gaebler, *First Amendment Protection Against Government Compelled Expression and Association,* 23 B.C.L.R. 995 (1982). If Michigan subsidized unions directly, would dissenting taxpayers have a first amendment claim? Suppose Michigan taxed those most likely to benefit from union activity, i.e., the employees? Are compelled contributions different from government taxation? See Shiffrin, *Government Speech,* 27 U.C.L.A.L.Rev. 565, 594 (1980). Suppose the union contract provided for a direct payment from the employer and that union dues were not required of employees? Would this arrangement affect the rules set out in *Abood?*

3. Although *Abood* limits the sources of funding for union speech, it does not question union rights of free speech and association. Such rights include not only the endorsement of political candidates [b] and causes, but also associational

b. Reading *Elrod* and *Abood* together, Powell, J., maintains that public employees may be forced to support a political party, but not the union which represents them in collective bargaining. For revealing commentary, see Kahn, *The Court, the Community and the Judicial Balance: The Jurisprudence of Justice Powell,* 97 Yale L.J. 1, 45–47 (1987).

c. Stevens, J., also filed a brief concurrence: "The Court's opinion does not foreclose the argument that the Union should not be permitted to exact a service fee from nonmembers without first establishing a procedure which will avoid the risk that their funds will be used, even temporarily, to finance ideological activities unrelated to collective bargaining."

b. See also *Eu v. San Francisco County Democratic Central Committee,* 489 U.S. 214, 109 S.Ct. 1013, 103 L.Ed.2d 271 (1989) (statute rights to pursue legal claims. Even as against state bar regulations, for example, unions are free to recommend attorneys to their members and to hire or engage in contracts with attorneys to represent individual union members. See *United Transportation Union v. State Bar,* 401 U.S. 576, 91 S.Ct. 1076, 28 L.Ed.2d 339 (1971): "[C]ollective activity undertaken to obtain meaningful access to the courts is a fundamental right within the protection of the First Amendment. [T]hat right would be a hollow promise if courts could deny associations of workers or others the means of enabling their members to meet the costs of legal representation."

4. Suppose the state declared the dues gathering body to be a governmental agency? California requires all attorneys to join and pay dues to the State Bar. Under California law the State Bar is a regulated state agency authorized not only to examine prospective attorneys and to recommend bar admission or discipline, but also to use compulsory dues for a broad range of lobbying and amicus curiae activities. The state believes that the input of the bar organization is valuable. It also believes that ad hoc decisionmaking about which legislation is or is not an appropriate concern of the bar is unworkable.

KELLER v. STATE BAR OF CALIFORNIA, ___ U.S. ___, 110 S.Ct. 2228, 110 L.Ed.2d 1 (1990), per REHNQUIST, C.J., unanimously held that compulsory bar dues could only be used if "reasonably incurred for the purpose of regulating the legal profession or improving the quality of the legal service available to the people of the State." Recognizing that difficult line-drawing questions could arise, the Court observed that the case presented clear ends of a spectrum:

"Compulsory dues may not be expended to endorse or advance a gun control or nuclear weapons freeze initiative; at the other end of the spectrum petitioners have no valid constitutional objection to their compulsory dues being spent for activities connected with disciplining members of the bar or proposing ethical codes for the profession. * * *

"Of course the Supreme Court of California is the final authority on the 'governmental' status of the State Bar of California for purposes of state law. But its determination that respondent is a 'government agency,' and therefore entitled to the treatment accorded a governor, a mayor or a State Tax Commission, for instance, is not binding on us when such a determination is essential to the decision of a federal question. The State Bar of California is a good deal different from most other entities that would be regarded in common parlance as 'governmental agencies.' Its principal funding comes not from appropriations made to it by the legislature, but from dues levied on its members by the Board of Governors. Only lawyers admitted to practice in the State of California are members of the State Bar, and all 122,000 lawyers admitted to practice in the State must be members. Respondent undoubtedly performs important and valuable services for the State by way of governance of the profession, but those services are essentially advisory in nature. The State Bar does not admit anyone to the practice of law, it does not finally disbar or suspend anyone, nor does it ultimately establish ethical codes of conduct. All of those functions are reserved by California law to the State Supreme Court. * * *

"The State Bar of California was created, not to participate in the general government of the State, but to provide specialized professional advice to those

forbidding official governing bodies of political parties from endorsing or opposing candidates for partisan office in primary elections violates protected speech and association rights. But see *Geary v. Renne,* 880 F.2d 1062 (9th Cir.1989) (upholding ban on such endorsements in non-partisan elections).

with the ultimate responsibility of governing the legal profession. Its members and officers are such not because they are citizens or voters, but because they are lawyers. We think that these differences between the State Bar, on the one hand, and traditional government agencies and officials, on the other hand, render unavailing respondent's argument that it is not subject to the same constitutional rule with respect to the use of compulsory dues as are labor unions representing public and private employees."

III. INTIMATE ASSOCIATION AND EXPRESSIVE ASSOCIATION

ROBERTS v. UNITED STATES JAYCEES, 468 U.S. 609, 104 S.Ct. 3244, 82 L.Ed.2d 462 (1984): Appellee U.S. Jaycees, a nonprofit national membership corporation whose objective is to pursue educational and charitable purposes that promote the growth and development of young men's civic organizations, limits regular membership to young men between the ages of 18 and 35. Associate membership is available to women and older men. An associate member may not vote or hold local or national office. Two local chapters in Minnesota violated appellee's bylaws by admitting women as regular members. When they learned that revocation of their charters was to be considered, members of both chapters filed discrimination charges with the Minnesota Department of Human Rights, alleging that the exclusion of women from full membership violated the Minnesota Human Rights Act (Act), which makes it an "unfair discriminatory practice" to deny anyone "the full and equal enjoyment of goods, services, facilities, privileges, advantages, and accommodations of a place of accommodation" because, inter alia, of sex.

Before a hearing on the state charge took place, appellee brought federal suit, alleging that requiring it to accept women as regular members would violate the male members' constitutional "freedom of association." A state hearing officer decided against appellee and the federal district court certified to the Minnesota Supreme Court the question whether appellee is "a place of public accommodation" within the meaning of the Act. With the record of the administrative hearing before it, the state supreme court answered that question in the affirmative. The U.S. Court of Appeals held that application of the Act to appellee's membership policies would violate its freedom of association.[a]

In rejecting appellee's claims,[b] the Court, per BRENNAN, J., pointed out that the Constitution protects " 'freedom of association' in two distinct senses," what might be called "freedom of intimate association" and "freedom of expressive association": "In one line of decisions, the Court has concluded that choices to enter into and maintain certain intimate human relationships must be secured against undue intrusion by the State because of the role of such relationships in safeguarding the individual freedom that is central to our constitutional scheme. In this respect, freedom of association receives protection as a fundamental element of personal liberty. In another set of decisions, the Court has recognized a right to associate for the purpose of engaging in those activities protected

a. When the state supreme court held that appellee was "a place of public accommodation" within the meaning of the Act, it suggested that, unlike appellee, the Kiwanis Club might be sufficiently "private" to be outside the scope of the Act. Appellee then amended its complaint to allege that the state court's interpretation of the Act rendered it unconstitutionally vague. The Eighth Circuit so held, but the Supreme Court reversed.

b. There was no dissent. Rehnquist, J., concurred in the judgment. O'Connor, J., joined part of the Court's opinion and concurred in the judgment. See infra. Burger, C.J., and Blackmun, J., took no part.

by the First Amendment—speech, assembly, petition for the redress of grievances, and the exercise of religion. The Constitution guarantees freedom of association of this kind as an indispensable means of preserving other individual liberties."

The freedom of intimate association was deemed important because, "certain kinds of personal bonds have played a critical role in the culture and traditions of the Nation by cultivating and transmitting shared ideals and beliefs; they thereby foster diversity and act as critical buffers between the individual and the power of the State.[c] Moreover, the constitutional shelter afforded such relationships reflects the realization that individuals draw much of their emotional enrichment from close ties with others. Protecting these relationships from unwarranted state interference therefore safeguards the ability independently to define one's identity that is central to any concept of liberty.

"The personal affiliations that exemplify these considerations [are] distinguished by such attributes as relative smallness, a high degree of selectivity in decisions to begin and maintain the affiliation, and seclusion from others in critical aspects of the relationship. As a general matter, only relationships with these sorts of qualities are likely to reflect the considerations that have led to an understanding of freedom of association as an intrinsic element of personal liberty. Conversely, an association lacking these qualities—such as a large business enterprise—seems remote from the concerns giving rise to this constitutional protection. * * *

"Between these poles, of course, lies a broad range of human relationships that may make greater or lesser claims to constitutional protection from particular incursions by the State. [We] need not mark the potentially significant points on this terrain with any precision. We note only that factors that may be relevant include size, purpose, policies, selectivity, congeniality, and other characteristics that in a particular case may be pertinent. In this case, however, several features of the Jaycees clearly place the organization outside of the category of relationships worthy of this kind of constitutional protection.

"The undisputed facts reveal that the local chapters of the Jaycees are large and basically unselective groups. * * * Apart from age and sex, neither the national organization nor the local chapters employs any criteria for judging applicants for membership, and new members are routinely recruited and admitted with no inquiry into their backgrounds. In fact, a local officer testified that he could recall no instance in which an applicant had been denied membership on any basis other than age or sex. Furthermore, despite their inability to vote, hold office, or receive certain awards, women affiliated with the Jaycees attend various meetings, participate in selected projects, and engage in many of the organization's social functions. Indeed, numerous non-members of both genders regularly participate in a substantial portion of activities central to the decision of many members to associate with one another, including many of the organization's various community programs, awards ceremonies, and recruitment meetings.

"[Thus], we conclude that the Jaycees chapters lack the distinctive characteristics that might afford constitutional protection to the decision of its mem-

c. For commentary on this aspect of association from a variety of perspectives, see McIntyre, *After Virtue* (1981); Nisbet, *The Quest For Community* (1969); Rosenblum, *Another Liberalism* (1987); Unger, *Knowledge and Politics* (1975); Frug, *The City as a Legal Concept*, 93 Harv.L.Rev. 1057 (1980); Karst, *Equality and Community: Lessons From the Civil Rights Era*, 56 Not.D.Law. 183 (1980); Sullivan, *Rainbow Republicanism*, 97 Yale L.J. 1713 (1988).

bers to exclude women. We turn therefore to consider the extent to which application of the Minnesota statute to compel the Jaycees to accept women infringes the group's freedom of expressive association. * * *

"Government actions that may unconstitutionally infringe upon [freedom of expressive association] can take a number of forms. Among other things, government may seek to impose penalties or withhold benefits from individuals because of their membership in a disfavored group; it may attempt to require disclosure of the fact of membership in a group seeking anonymity; and it may try to interfere with the internal organization or affairs of the group. By requiring the Jaycees to admit women as full voting members, the Minnesota Act works an infringement of the last type. There can be no clearer example of an intrusion into the internal structure or affairs of an association than a regulation that forces the group to accept members it does not desire. Such a regulation may impair the ability of the original members to express only those views that brought them together. Freedom of association therefore plainly presupposes a freedom not to associate. See *Abood.*

"The right to associate for expressive purposes is not, however, absolute. Infringements on that right may be justified by regulations adopted to serve compelling state interests, unrelated to the suppression of ideas, that cannot be achieved through means significantly less restrictive of associational freedoms. We are persuaded that Minnesota's compelling interest in eradicating discrimination against its female citizens justifies the impact that application of the statute to the Jaycees may have on the male members' associational freedoms.

"[I]n upholding Title II of the Civil Rights Act of 1964, which forbids race discrimination in public accommodations, we emphasized that its 'fundamental object [was] to vindicate "the deprivation of personal dignity that surely accompanies denials of equal access to public establishments."' *Heart of Atlanta Motel.* That stigmatizing injury, and the denial of equal opportunities that accompanies it, is surely felt as strongly by persons suffering discrimination on the basis of their sex as by those treated differently because of their race.

"Nor is the state interest in assuring equal access limited to the provision of purely tangible goods and services. A State enjoys broad authority to create rights of public access on behalf of its citizens. *Pruneyard.* Like many States and municipalities, Minnesota has adopted a functional definition of public accommodations that reaches various forms of public, quasi-commercial conduct. This expansive definition reflects a recognition of the changing nature of the American economy and of the importance, both to the individual and to society, of removing the barriers to economic advancement and political and social integration that have historically plagued certain disadvantaged groups, including women. * * *

"In applying the Act to the Jaycees, the State has advanced those interests through the least restrictive means of achieving its ends. Indeed, the Jaycees have failed to demonstrate that the Act imposes any serious burdens on the male members' freedom of expressive association. See *Hishon v. King & Spalding,* 467 U.S. 69, 104 S.Ct. 2229, 81 L.Ed.2d 59 (1984) (law firm 'has not shown how its ability to fulfill [protected] function[s] would be inhibited by a requirement that it consider [a woman lawyer] for partnership on her merits'). To be sure, a 'not insubstantial part' of the Jaycees' activities constitutes protected expression on political, economic, cultural, and social affairs. [There] is, however, no basis in the record for concluding that admission of women as full voting members will impede the organization's ability to engage in these protected activities or to disseminate its preferred views. The Act requires no change in the Jaycees' creed of promoting the interests of young men, and it imposes no restrictions on the organization's ability to exclude individuals with ideologies or philosophies different from those of its existing members. Moreover, the Jaycees already invite women to share the group's views and philosophy and to participate in much of its training and community activities. Accordingly, any claim that admission of women as full voting members will impair a symbolic message conveyed by the very fact that women are not permitted to vote is attenuated at best.

"[In] claiming that women might have a different attitude about such issues as the federal budget, school prayer, voting rights, and foreign relations, or that the organization's public positions would have a different effect if the group were not 'a purely young men's association,' the Jaycees rely solely on unsupported generalizations about the relative interests and perspectives of men and women. Although such generalizations may or may not have a statistical basis in fact with respect to particular positions adopted by the Jaycees, we have repeatedly condemned legal decisionmaking that relies uncritically on such assumptions. In the absence of a showing far more substantial than that attempted by the Jaycees, we decline to indulge in the sexual stereotyping that underlies appellee's contention that, by allowing women to vote, application of the Minnesota Act will change the content or impact of the organization's speech.

"In any event, even if enforcement of the Act causes some incidental abridgement of the Jaycees' protected speech, that effect is no greater than is necessary to accomplish the State's legitimate purposes. [A]cts of invidious discrimination in the distribution of publicly available goods, services, and other advantages cause unique evils that government has a compelling interest to prevent—wholly apart from the point of view such conduct may transmit. Accordingly, like violence or other types of potentially expressive activities that produce special harms distinct from their communicative impact, such practices are entitled to no constitutional protection."

O'CONNOR, J., concurring, joined the Court's opinion except for its analysis of freedom of expressive association. She maintained that "the Court has adopted a test that unadvisedly casts doubt on the power of States to pursue the profoundly important goal of ensuring nondiscriminatory access to commercial opportunities" yet "accords insufficient protection to expressive associations and places inappropriate burdens on groups claiming the protection of the First Amendment":

"The Court analyzes Minnesota's attempt to regulate the Jaycees' membership using a test that I find both over-protective of activities undeserving of constitutional shelter and under-protective of important First Amendment concerns. The Court declares that the Jaycees' right of association depends on the organization's making a 'substantial' showing that the admission of unwelcome members 'will change the message communicated by the group's speech.' I am not sure what showing the Court thinks would satisfy its requirement of proof of a membership-message connection, but whatever it means, the focus on such a connection is objectionable.

"Imposing such a requirement, especially in the context of the balancing-of-interests test articulated by the Court, raises the possibility that certain commercial associations, by engaging occasionally in certain kinds of expressive activities, might improperly gain protection for discrimination. The Court's focus raises other problems as well. [W]ould the Court's analysis of this case be different if, for example, the Jaycees membership had a steady history of opposing public issues thought (by the Court) to be favored by women? It might seem easy to conclude, in the latter case, that the admission of women to the Jaycees' ranks would affect the content of the organization's message, but I do not believe that should change the outcome of this case. Whether an association is or is not constitutionally protected in the selection of its membership should not depend on what the association says or why its members say it.

"The Court's readiness to inquire into the connection between membership and message reveals a more fundamental flaw in its analysis. The Court pursues this inquiry as part of its mechanical application of a 'compelling interest' test, under which the Court weighs the interests of the State of Minnesota in ending gender discrimination against the Jaycees' First Amendment right of association. The Court entirely neglects to establish at the threshold that the Jaycees is an association whose activities or purposes should engage the strong protections that the First Amendment extends to expressive associations.

"On the one hand, an association engaged exclusively in protected expression enjoys First Amendment protection of both the content of its message and the choice of its members. Protection of the message itself is judged by the same standards as protection of speech by an individual. Protection of the association's right to define its membership derives from the recognition that the formation of an expressive association is the creation of a voice, and the selection of members is the definition of that voice. [A] ban on specific group voices on public affairs violates the most basic guarantee of the First Amendment—that citizens, not the government, control the content of public discussion.

"On the other hand, there is only minimal constitutional protection of the freedom of *commercial* association. There are, of course, some constitutional protections of commercial speech—speech intended and used to promote a commercial transaction with the speaker. But the State is free to impose any rational regulation on the commercial transaction itself. The Constitution does not guarantee a right to choose employees, customers, suppliers, or those with whom one engages in simple commercial transactions, without restraint from the State. A shopkeeper has no constitutional right to deal only with persons of one sex.

"[A]n association should be characterized as commercial, and therefore subject to rationally related state regulation of its membership and other associational activities, when, and only when, the association's activities are not predominantly of the type protected by the First Amendment. It is only when the association is predominantly engaged in protected expression that state regulation of its membership will necessarily affect, change, dilute, or silence one collective voice that would otherwise be heard. An association must choose its market. Once it enters the marketplace of commerce in any substantial degree it loses the complete control over its membership that it would otherwise enjoy if it confined its affairs to the marketplace of ideas.

"[N]otwithstanding its protected expressive activities, [appellee] is, first and foremost, an organization that, at both the national and local levels, promotes and practices the art of solicitation and management. The organization claims that the training it offers its members gives them an advantage in business, and business firms do indeed sometimes pay the dues of individual memberships for their employees. Jaycees members hone their solicitation and management skills, under the direction and supervision of the organization, primarily through their active recruitment of new members. * * *

"Recruitment and selling are commercial activities, even when conducted for training rather than for profit. The 'not insubstantial' volume of protected Jaycees activity found by the Court of Appeals is simply not enough to preclude state regulation of the Jaycees' commercial activities. The State of Minnesota has a legitimate interest in ensuring nondiscriminatory access to the commercial opportunity presented by membership in the Jaycees. The members of the Jaycees may not claim constitutional immunity from Minnesota's anti-discrimination law by seeking to exercise their First Amendment rights through this commercial organization."

Notes and Questions

1. *Freedom of intimate association.* The reference to the freedom of intimate association is the first in the Court's history, but the notion that the concept should serve as an organizing principle is found in Karst, *Freedom of Intimate Association,* 89 Yale L.J. 624 (1980). To what extent should freedom of intimate association itself be regarded as a first amendment right? Compare Karst with Baker, *Scope of the First Amendment Freedom of Speech,* 25 U.C. L.A.L.Rev. 964 (1978) and Raggi, *An Independent Right to Freedom of Association,* 12 Harv.Civ.Rts.-Civ.Lib.L.Rev. 1 (1977).

Although the freedom of intimate association has limited relevance for the 295,000 member Jaycees, the concept "has important implications for other private associations with discriminatory membership policies." Linder, *Freedom of Association After Roberts v. United States Jaycees,* 82 Mich.L.Rev. 1878, 1885 (1984). What are (should be) the implications for golf and country clubs, fraternal societies, athletic clubs and downtown or city clubs? Consider Comment, *Discrimination in Private Social Clubs: Freedom of Association and Right to Privacy,* 1970 Duke L.J. 1181, 1222: "Whether this society is capable of free evolution to social equality seems irrelevant in light of the influence of the social club in perpetuating general racial and religious economic and social inferiority and in light of the urgent need for reversal of racial polarization. Many private social clubs have become so affected with the public interest that some regulation of their membership practices is not only a proper but also a necessary exercise of legislative power." [d] See generally Burns, *The Exclusion of Women From Influential Men's Clubs: The Inner Sanctum and the Myth of Full Equality,* 18 Harv.Civ.Rts.-Civ.Lib.L.Rev. 321 (1983). How do O'Connor and Brennan, JJ., differ on such questions. For appreciation of O'Connor, J.'s perspective, see Linder, supra. For defense of Brennan, J.'s perspective, see Note, 98 Harv.L.Rev. 195 (1984).

d. For cases following or extending *Roberts,* see *Board of Directors of Rotary International v. Rotary Club of Duarte,* 481 U.S. 537, 107 S.Ct. 1940, 95 L.Ed.2d 474 (1987); *New York State Club Ass'n v. New York,* 487 U.S. 1, 108 S.Ct. 2225, 101 L.Ed.2d 1 (1988) (upholding city ordinance against facial challenge that prohibits discrimination based on race, creed, or sex by institutions (except benevolent orders or religious corporations) with more than 400 members that provide regular meal service and receive payment from nonmembers for the furtherance of trade or business); *Dallas v. Stanglin,* 490 U.S. 19, 109 S.Ct. 1591, 104 L.Ed.2d 18 (1989) (upholding ordinance restricting admission to certain dance halls to persons between the ages of 14 and 18).

2. *Feminist perspectives.* From any feminist perspective, is *Roberts* a victory or a defeat? Note that what *Roberts* guarantees is the right of women to join an organization dedicated to promoting the interests of young men. What if a state attacked the goal of the organization as itself violative of civil rights? Could the Ku Klux Klan or the Nazis be outlawed by a civil rights statute? Reconsider *Beauharnais,* Sec. 1, II, A supra. Is the distinction between race and sex of any importance in this context? Should a distinction be made between organizations designed to promote the interests of advantaged groups and those designed to promote the interests of disadvantaged groups? Compare Ch. 6, Sec. 2, V and Ch. 6, Sec. 3, IV.

3. *Tashjian v. Republican Party of Connecticut,* 479 U.S. 208, 107 S.Ct. 544, 93 L.Ed.2d 514 (1986) held that a law prohibiting party non-members from voting in primary elections impermissibly burdened the association rights of the political party and its members.

IV. GOVERNMENT MANDATED DISCLOSURES AND FREEDOM OF ASSOCIATION

A. POLITICAL ASSOCIATION AND GOVERNMENT MANDATED DISCLOSURES

BARENBLATT v. UNITED STATES

360 U.S. 109, 79 S.Ct. 1081, 3 L.Ed.2d 1115 (1959).

JUSTICE HARLAN delivered the opinion of the Court. * * *

[In] the present case congressional efforts to learn the extent of a nation-wide, indeed world-wide, problem have brought one of its investigating committees into the field of education. Of course, broadly viewed, inquiries cannot be made into the teaching that is pursued in any of our educational institutions. When academic teaching-freedom and its corollary learning-freedom, so essential to the well-being of the Nation, are claimed, this Court will always be on the alert against intrusion by Congress into this constitutionally protected domain. But this does not mean that the Congress is precluded from interrogating a witness merely because he is a teacher. An educational institution is not a constitutional sanctuary from inquiry into matters that may otherwise be within the constitutional legislative domain merely for the reason that inquiry is made of someone within its walls. * * *

We here review petitioner's conviction under 2 U.S.C. § 192 for contempt of Congress, arising from his refusal to answer certain questions put to him by a Subcommittee of the House Committee on Un-American Activities during the course of an inquiry concerning alleged Communist infiltration into the field of education. * * *

Pursuant to a subpoena, and accompanied by counsel, petitioner on June 28, 1954, appeared as a witness before this congressional Subcommittee. After answering a few preliminary questions and testifying that he had been a graduate student and teaching fellow at the University of Michigan from 1947 to 1950 and an instructor in psychology at Vassar College from 1950 to shortly before his appearance before the Subcommittee, petitioner objected generally to the right of the Subcommittee to inquire into his "political" and "religious" beliefs or any "other personal and private affairs" or "associational activities," upon grounds set forth in a previously prepared memorandum which he was allowed to file with the Subcommittee.[2] Thereafter petitioner specifically declined to answer [the following questions]:

"Are you now a member of the Communist Party? (Count One.)

"Have you ever been a member of the Communist Party? (Count Two.) * * *

"Were you ever a member of the Haldane Club of the Communist Party while at the University of Michigan? (Count Four.) * * *"

In each instance the grounds of refusal were those set forth in the prepared statement. Petitioner expressly disclaimed reliance upon "the Fifth Amendment." [Upon conviction under all counts in a federal court, petitioner was sentenced to 6 months imprisonment.]

Undeniably, the First Amendment in some circumstances protects an individual from being compelled to disclose his associational relationships. However, the protections of the First Amendment, unlike a proper claim of the privilege against self-incrimination under the Fifth Amendment, do not afford a witness the right to resist inquiry in all circumstances. Where First Amendment rights are asserted to bar governmental interrogation resolution of the issue always involves a balancing by the courts of the competing private and public interests at stake in the particular circumstances shown. * * *

The first question is whether this investigation was related to a valid legislative purpose, for Congress may not constitutionally require an individual to disclose his political relationships or other private affairs except in relation to such a purpose.

That Congress has wide power to legislate in the field of Communist activity in this Country, and to conduct appropriate investigations in aid thereof, is hardly debatable. The existence of such power has never been questioned by this Court, and it is sufficient to say, without particularization, that Congress has enacted or considered in this field a wide range of legislative measures, not a few of which have stemmed from recommendations of the very Committee whose actions have been drawn in question here. In the last analysis this power rests on the right of self-preservation, "the ultimate value of any society," *Dennis*. Justification for its exercise in turn rests on the long and widely accepted view that the tenets of the Communist Party include the ultimate overthrow of the Government of the United States by force and violence, a view which has been given formal expression by the Congress.

We think that investigatory power in this domain is not to be denied Congress solely because the field of education is involved. [Indeed] we do not understand petitioner here to suggest that Congress in no circumstances may inquire into Communist activity in the field of education. Rather, his position is in effect that this particular investigation was aimed not at the revolutionary aspects but at the theoretical classroom discussion of communism.

In our opinion this position rests on a too constricted view of the nature of the investigatory process, and is not supported by a fair assessment of the record before us. An investigation of advocacy of or preparation for overthrow certainly embraces the right to identify a witness as a member of the Communist Party

2. In the words of the panel of the Court of Appeals which first heard the case this memorandum "can best be described as a lengthy legal brief attacking the jurisdiction of the committee to ask appellant any questions or to conduct any inquiry at all, based on the First, Ninth and Tenth Amendments, the prohibition against bills of attainder, and the doctrine of separation of powers."

and to inquire into the various manifestations of the Party's tenets. The strict requirements of a prosecution under the Smith Act are not the measure of the permissible scope of a congressional investigation into "overthrow," for of necessity the investigatory process must proceed step by step. Nor can it fairly be concluded that this investigation was directed at controlling what is being taught at our universities rather than at overthrow. The statement of the Subcommittee Chairman at the opening of the investigation evinces no such intention,[31] and so far as this record reveals nothing thereafter transpired which would justify our holding that the thrust of the investigation later changed. [C]ertainly the conclusion would not be justified that the questioning of petitioner would have exceeded permissible bounds had he not shut off the Subcommittee at the threshold.

Nor can we accept the further contention that this investigation should not be deemed to have been in furtherance of a legislative purpose because the true objective of the Committee and of the Congress was purely "exposure." So long as Congress acts in pursuance of its constitutional power, the judiciary lacks authority to intervene on the basis of the motives which spurred the exercise of that power. [Having] scrutinized this record we cannot say that the unanimous panel of the Court of Appeals which first considered this case was wrong in concluding that "the primary purposes of the inquiry were in aid of legislative processes." * * *

Finally, the record is barren of other factors which in themselves might sometimes lead to the conclusion that the individual interests at stake were not subordinate to those of the state. There is no indication in this record that the Subcommittee was attempting to pillory witnesses. Nor did petitioner's appearance as a witness follow from indiscriminate dragnet procedures, lacking in probable cause for belief that he possessed information which might be helpful to the Subcommittee. And the relevancy of the questions put to him by the Subcommittee is not open to doubt.

We conclude that the balance between the individual and the governmental interests here at stake must be struck in favor of the latter, and that therefore the provisions of the First Amendment have not been offended. * * *

Affirmed.

JUSTICE BLACK, with whom THE CHIEF JUSTICE, and JUSTICE DOUGLAS concur, dissenting. * * *

I do not agree that laws directly abridging First Amendment freedoms can be justified by a congressional or judicial balancing process. There are, of course, cases [such as those involving the right of a city to control its streets] suggesting that a law which primarily regulates conduct but which might also

31. The following are excerpts from that statement: "[In] opening this hearing, it is well to make clear to you and others just what the nature of this investigation is.

"From time to time, the committee has investigated Communists and Communist activities within the entertainment, newspaper, and labor fields, and also within the professions and the Government. In no instance has the work of the committee taken on the character of an investigation of entertainment organizations, newspapers, labor unions, the professions, or the Government, as such, and it is not now the purpose of this committee to investigate education or educational institutions, as [such.]

"The Committee is equally concerned with the opportunities that the Communist Party has to wield its influence upon members of the teaching profession and students through Communists who are members of the teaching profession. Therefore, the objective of this investigation is to ascertain the character, extent and objects of Communist Party activities when such activities are carried on by members of the teaching profession who are subject to the directives and discipline of the Communist Party." * * *

indirectly affect speech can be upheld if the effect on speech is minor in relation to the need for control of the conduct. With these cases I agree. [But they do not] even remotely suggest that a law directly aimed at curtailing speech and political persuasion could be saved through a balancing process. * * *

But even assuming what I cannot assume, that some balancing is proper in this case, I feel that the Court after stating the test ignores it completely. At most it balances the right of the Government to preserve itself, against Barenblatt's right to refrain from revealing Communist affiliations. Such a balance, however, mistakes the factors to be weighed. In the first place, it completely leaves out the real interest in Barenblatt's silence, the interest of the people as a whole in being able to join organizations, advocate causes and make political "mistakes" without later being subjected to governmental penalties for having dared to think for themselves. It is this right, the right to err politically, which keeps us strong as a Nation. [It] is these interests of society, rather than Barenblatt's own right to silence, which I think the Court should put on the balance against the demands of the Government, if any balancing process is to be tolerated. Instead they are not mentioned, while on the other side the demands of the Government are vastly overstated and called "self preservation." [Such an approach] reduces "balancing" to a mere play on words and is completely inconsistent with the rules this Court has previously given for applying a "balancing test," where it is proper. * * *

Finally, I think Barenblatt's conviction violates the Constitution because the chief aim, purpose and practice of the House Un-American Activities Committee, as disclosed by its many reports, is to try witnesses and punish them because they are or have been Communists or because they refuse to admit or deny Communist affiliations. The punishment imposed is generally punishment by humiliation and public shame. [T]he proof that the Un-American Activities Committee is here undertaking a purely judicial function is [overwhelming].

It is the protection from arbitrary punishments through the right to a judicial trial with all these safeguards which over the years has distinguished America from lands where drum-head courts and other similar "tribunals" deprive the weak and the unorthodox of life, liberty and property without due process of law. It is this same right which is denied to Barenblatt, because the Court today fails to see what is here for all to see—that exposure and punishment is the aim of this Committee and the reason for its existence. To deny this aim is to ignore the Committee's own claims and the reports it has issued ever since it was established. * * *

Ultimately all the questions in this case really boil down to one—whether we as a people will try fearfully and futilely to preserve democracy by adopting totalitarian methods, or whether in accordance with our traditions and our Constitution we will have the confidence and courage to be free.

[Brennan, J., dissenting, expressed his "complete agreement with my Brother Black that no purpose for the investigation of Barenblatt is revealed by the record except exposure purely for the sake of exposure. This is not a purpose to which Barenblatt's rights under the First Amendment can validly be subordinated."]

Notes and Questions

1. *Compelling testimony vs. investigating.* Is the power of Congress to *compel testimony* in aid of legislation as broad as its power to *investigate* for this

purpose. *Ought* it be? When Congress calls a hostile witness, is it concerned with this person's appraisal of the general problem or his advice? What does it contribute to legislative insight, how does it aid the consideration of general legislation, to call a witness who wishes to *conceal* some thing about his individual case or that of his friends? To "inventory the Communists in the United States one at a time"? Kalven, *Mr. Alexander Meiklejohn and the Barenblatt Opinion,* 27 U.Chi.L.Rev. 315, 327 (1960).

2. *"Balancing".* (a) In "balancing the interests," did *Barenblatt* adequately consider and weigh the *alternative methods* for achieving the investigative purpose? Did it consider the necessity of gathering the information sought by the Subcommittee in the particular way it attempted to obtain it from Barenblatt: by forcing him to disclose or deny Communist affiliation at a *public* hearing? See Kauper, *Civil Liberties and the Constitution* 121 (1962).

(b) What *are* the "interests" on either side that the Court must "balance"? Whatever they are, on what basis can a judge compare them qualitatively without some independent standard to which they can be referred? Does the "balancing process" make it more—or less—difficult for judges to rest on their predispositions? See Frantz, *The First Amendment in the Balance,* 71 Yale L.J. 1424 (1962).

3. *Fifth vs. first amendments. Barenblatt* points out that "the protections of the First Amendment, unlike a proper claim of the privilege against self-incrimination [do] not afford a witness the right to resist inquiry in all circumstances. Where First Amendment rights are asserted [the] issue *always* involves a balancing by the courts of the competing private and public interests at stake." (Emphasis added.) Why, when confronted by the same national danger must the fifth amendment always prevail over the care for national security, but the first amendment give way to it? Should the interest of a citizen, and of the nation, in freedom of speech and association be entitled to less weight than the interest of a private individual in his safety from self-incrimination? See Meiklejohn, *The Balancing of Self-Preservation Against Political Freedom,* 49 Calif.L.Rev. 4, 6–7 (1961).

4. *The "Equality Principle."* Although disclosure cases do not follow a uniform course, the Court has manifested more concern about the impact of disclosure on private associations than is exhibited in *Barenblatt.* It has been especially protective of the NAACP. Consider Karst, *Equality as a Central Principle in the First Amendment,* 43 U.Chi.L.Rev. 20, 42–43 (1975): "In the late 1950s, when the civil rights movement was gathering momentum in the South, public disclosure of one's membership in the NAACP typically was followed by annoyances [and] often by more tangible reprisals like being fired. In a series of cases, the Court held that [government] could not constitutionally insist on such disclosure, either by the NAACP itself [a] or by individual members.[b]

a. *Gibson v. Florida Leg. Investig. Comm.,* 372 U.S. 539, 83 S.Ct. 889, 9 L.Ed.2d 929 (1963), per Goldberg, J., reversed a Florida Supreme Court holding that the custodian of NAACP records could be compelled to bring membership lists to legislative hearings so that he could be forced to refer to them in determining whether individuals suspected as being communists were NAACP members. This could not be required said the Court without a substantial relation between the NAACP and "conduct in which the State may have a compelling regulatory concern." Because no substantial relation was shown, compelling the NAACP to disclose its membership presented "a question wholly different from compelling the Communist Party to disclose its own membership." Harlan, J., joined by Clark, Stewart, and White, JJ., dissenting, complained that the Court had required "an investigating agency to prove in advance the very things it is trying to find out."

b. *Shelton v. Tucker,* 364 U.S. 479, 81 S.Ct. 247, 5 L.Ed.2d 231 (1960) held that teachers

"The governments' demands for information in these cases usually were presented for ostensibly neutral purposes. [The] Court, solemnly going along with the gag, took these asserted justifications at face value but concluded nonetheless that the required disclosures unconstitutionally invaded first amendment rights of political association.

"[The] Court's concern in these cases grows out of the first amendment's equality principle. If all the school teachers in Arkansas were to disclose their respective memberships in organizations, it is a safe bet that most Rotarians and Job's Daughters would not be greeted with heavy breathing when they answered the phone at night. The private harassment that concerned the Court was reserved for those associated with an unpopular challenge to the local orthodoxy. The point here is not simply that first amendment liberties normally matter most to underdogs; it is also that these decisions parallel one type of solution to the 'state action' problem that historically has plagued efforts to use the equal protection clause to protect individuals against private racial discrimination. In the disclosure cases, the state is seen as 'encouraging' private discrimination against those who espouse ideas with a particular content, even though the encouragement is embodied in a formally neutral law."

5. *Election disclosure requirements.* BROWN v. SOCIALIST WORKERS, 459 U.S. 87, 103 S.Ct. 416, 74 L.Ed.2d 250 (1982), per MARSHALL, J., held that an Ohio statute requiring every political party to report the names and addresses of campaign contributors and recipients of campaign disbursements could not be applied to the Socialist Workers Party. Citing *Buckley v. Valeo*, p. 777 infra, the Court held that the " 'evidence offered [by a minor party] need show only a reasonable probability that the compelled disclosure [of] names will subject them to threats, harassment, or reprisals from either Government officials or private parties.' " Consider Stone & Marshall, *Brown v. Socialist Workers: Inequality As A Command of the First Amendment*, 1983 Sup.Ct.Rev. 583, 592: "[I]n *Brown* the Court expressly exempted particular political parties from an otherwise content-neutral regulation for reasons directly related to the content of their expression. [The] constitutionally compelled exemption substitutes a content-based law for one that is content neutral. It stands the presumption in favor of 'content neutrality' on its head." Is the decision, nonetheless, consistent with first amendment values? See Stone & Marshall, supra.

B. REPORTER'S PRIVILEGE

BRANZBURG v. HAYES

408 U.S. 665, 92 S.Ct. 2646, 33 L.Ed.2d 626 (1972).

JUSTICE WHITE delivered the opinion of the Court.

[Branzburg, a Kentucky reporter, wrote articles describing his observations of local hashish-making and other drug violations. He refused to testify before a grand jury regarding his information. The state courts rejected his claim of a first amendment privilege.

could not be required as a condition of employment to list all of the organizations they had belonged to or contributed to during the preceding five years. Professor Karst suggests that Barenblatt should have received the same hospitality. But what standard should govern? Should the Court endorse a general right not to speak? A right not to speak about political associations? Suppose, after a wave of racially motivated bombings, the leader of a white racist organization is called before a grand jury and asked to reveal the group's membership. What standard should govern?

[Pappas, a Massachusetts TV newsman-photographer, was allowed to enter and remain inside a Black Panther headquarters on condition he disclose nothing. When an anticipated police raid did not occur, he wrote no story. Summoned before a local grand jury, he refused to answer any questions about what had occurred inside the Panther headquarters or to identify those he had observed. The state courts denied his claim of a first amendment privilege.

[Caldwell, a N.Y. Times reporter covering the Black Panthers, was summoned to appear before a federal grand jury investigating Panther activities. A federal court issued a protective order providing that although he had to divulge information given him "for publication," he could withhold "confidential" information "developed or maintained by him as a professional journalist." Maintaining that absent a specific need for his testimony he should be excused from attending the grand jury altogether, Caldwell disregarded the order and was held in contempt. The Ninth Circuit reversed, holding that absent "compelling reasons" Caldwell could refuse even to attend the grand jury, because of the potential impact of such an appearance on the flow of news to the public.]

[Petitioners' first amendment claims] may be simply put: that to gather news it is often necessary to agree either not to identify [sources] or to publish only part of the facts revealed, or both; that if the reporter is nevertheless forced to reveal these confidences to a grand jury, the source so identified and other confidential sources of other reporters will be measurably deterred from furnishing publishable information, all to the detriment of the free flow of information protected by the First Amendment. Although petitioners do not claim an absolute privilege [they] assert that the reporter should not be forced either to appear or to testify before a grand jury or at trial until and unless sufficient grounds are shown for believing that the reporter possesses information relevant to a crime the grand jury is investigating, that the information the reporter has is unavailable from other sources, and that the need for the information is sufficiently compelling to override the claimed invasion of First Amendment interests occasioned by the disclosure. [The] heart of the claim is that the burden on news gathering resulting from compelling reporters to disclose confidential information outweighs any public interest in obtaining the information.

[We agree] that news gathering [qualifies] for First Amendment protection; without some protection for seeking out the news, freedom of the press could be eviscerated. But this case involves no intrusions upon speech [and no] command that the press publish what it prefers to withhold. [N]o penalty, civil or criminal, related to the content of published material is at issue here. The use of confidential sources by the press is not forbidden or restricted; reporters remain free to seek news from any source by means within the law. No attempt is made to require the press to publish its sources of information or indiscriminately to disclose them on request.

The sole issue before us is the obligation of reporters to respond to grand jury subpoenas as other citizens do and to answer questions relevant to an investigation into the commission of crime. The claim is, [that] reporters are exempt from [the average citizen's] obligations because if forced to respond to subpoenas and identify their sources or disclose other confidences, their informants will refuse or be reluctant to furnish newsworthy information in the future.

[T]he First Amendment does not guarantee the press a constitutional right of special access to information not available to the public generally. [Although] news gathering may be hampered, the press is regularly excluded from grand jury proceedings, our own conferences, the meetings of other official bodies gathered in executive session, and the meetings of private organizations. Newsmen have no constitutional right of access to the scenes of crime or disaster when the general public is excluded, and they may be prohibited from attending or publishing information about trials if such restrictions are necessary to assure a defendant a fair trial before an impartial tribunal. [It] is thus not surprising that the great weight of authority is that newsmen are not exempt from the normal duty of appearing before a grand jury and answering questions relevant to a criminal investigation.

[Because] its task is to inquire into the existence of possible criminal conduct and to return only well-founded indictments, [the grand jury's] investigative powers are necessarily broad. [T]he long standing principle that "the public has a right to every man's evidence," except for those persons protected by a constitutional, common law, or statutory privilege, is particularly applicable to grand jury proceedings.

A [minority] of States have provided newsmen a statutory privilege of varying breadth, [but] none has been provided by federal statute. [We decline to create one] by interpreting the First Amendment to grant newsmen a testimonial privilege that other citizens do not enjoy. [On] the records now before us, we perceive no basis for holding that the public interest in law enforcement and in ensuring effective grand jury proceedings is insufficient to override the consequential, but uncertain, burden on news gathering which is said to result from insisting that reporters, like other citizens, respond to relevant questions put to them in the course of a valid grand jury investigation or criminal trial.

This conclusion [does not] threaten the vast bulk of confidential relationships between reporters and their sources. Grand juries address themselves to the issues of whether crimes have been committed and who committed them. Only where news sources themselves are implicated in crime or possess information relevant to the grand jury's task need they or the reporter be concerned about grand jury subpoenas. Nothing before us indicates that a large number or percentage of *all* confidential news sources fall into either category and would in any way be deterred by [our holding].

It would be frivolous to assert—and no one does in these cases—that the First Amendment, in the interest of securing news or otherwise, confers a license on either the reporter or his news sources to violate otherwise valid criminal laws. [W]e cannot seriously entertain the notion that the First Amendment protects a newsman's agreement to conceal the criminal conduct of his source, or evidence thereof, on the theory that it is better to write about crime than to do something about [it.]

There remain those situations where a source is not engaged in criminal conduct but has information suggesting illegal conduct by others. [But] we remain unclear how often and to what extent informers are actually deterred from furnishing information when newsmen are forced to testify before a grand jury. The available data indicates that some newsmen rely a great deal on confidential sources and that some informants are particularly sensitive to the threat of exposure and may be silenced if it is held by this Court that, ordinarily, newsmen must testify pursuant to subpoenas, but the evidence fails to demonstrate that [our holding would cause] a significant constriction of the flow of news to the public * * *. Estimates of the inhibiting effect of such subpoenas on the willingness of informants to make disclosures to newsmen are widely divergent and to a great extent speculative. It would be difficult to canvass the views of the informants themselves; surveys of reporters on this topic are chiefly opinions of predicted informant behavior and must be viewed in the light of the professional self-interest of the interviewees.[33] Reliance by the press on confidential informants does not mean that all such sources will in fact dry up because of the later possible appearance of the newsman before a grand jury. The reporter may never be called and if he objects to testifying, the prosecution may not insist. Also, the relationship of many informants to the press is a symbiotic one which is unlikely to be greatly inhibited by the threat of subpoena: quite often, such informants are members of a minority political or cultural group which relies heavily on the media to propagate its views, publicize its aims, and magnify its exposure to the public. * * *

Accepting the fact, however, that an undetermined number of informants not themselves implicated in crime will nevertheless, for whatever reason, refuse to talk to newsmen if they fear identification by a reporter in an official investigation, we cannot accept the argument that the public interest in possible future news about crime from undisclosed, unverified sources must take precedence over the public interest in pursuing and prosecuting those crimes reported to the press by informants and in thus deterring the commission of such crimes in the future.

[C]oncealment of crime and agreements to do so are not looked upon with favor. Such conduct deserves no encomium, and we decline now to afford it First Amendment [protection].

[T]he common law recognized no [reporter's] privilege, and the constitutional argument was not even asserted until 1958. From the beginning of our country the press has operated without constitutional protection for press informants, and the press has [flourished.]

The argument for [a] constitutional privilege rests heavily on those cases holding that the infringement of protected First Amendment rights must be no broader than necessary to achieve a permissible governmental purpose. We do not deal, however, with a governmental institution that has abused its proper function, as a legislative committee does when it "expose[s] for the sake of exposure." [Nor is there any] attempt here by the grand juries to invade protected First Amendment rights by forcing wholesale disclosure of names and organizational affiliations for a purpose which is not germane to the determination of whether crime has been committed, and the characteristic secrecy of grand jury proceedings is a further protection against the undue invasion of such rights. * * *

[The] requirements of those cases which hold that a State's interest must be "compelling" or "paramount" to justify even an indirect burden on First Amendment rights, are also met here. [If] the test is that the Government "convincingly show a substantial relation between the information sought and a subject of overriding and compelling state interest," *Gibson,* it is quite apparent (1) that the State has the necessary interest in extirpating the traffic in illegal drugs, in forestalling assassination attempts on the President, and in preventing the

33. In his *Press Subpoenas: An Empirical and Legal Analysis* 6–12 (1971), Prof. Blasi discusses these methodological problems. [His] survey found that slightly more than half of the 975 reporters questioned said that they relied on regular confidential sources for at least 10% of their stories. Of this group of reporters, only 8% were able to say with some certainty that their professional functioning had been adversely affected by the threat of subpoena; another 11% were not certain whether or not they had been adversely affected. [See also Blasi, *The Newsman's Privilege: An Empirical Study,* 70 Mich.L.Rev. 229 (1971).]

community from being disrupted by violent disorders endangering both persons and property; and (2) that, based on the stories Branzburg and Caldwell wrote and Pappas' admitted conduct, the grand jury called these reporters as they would others—because it was likely that they could supply information to help the Government determine whether illegal conduct had occurred and, if it had, whether there was sufficient evidence to return an indictment.

Similar considerations dispose of the reporters' claims that preliminary to requiring their grand jury appearance, the State must show that a crime has been committed and that they possess relevant information not available from other sources, for only the grand jury itself can make this determination. [A] grand jury investigation "is not fully carried out until every available clue has been run down and all witnesses examined in every proper way to find if a crime has been committed." * * *

[The] privilege claimed here is conditional, not absolute; given the suggested preliminary showings and compelling need, the reporter would be required to testify. [If] newsmen's confidential sources are as sensitive as they are claimed to be, the prospect of being unmasked whenever a judge determines the situation justifies it is hardly a satisfactory solution to the problem. For them, it would appear that only an absolute privilege would suffice.

We are unwilling to embark the judiciary on a long and difficult journey to such an uncertain destination. The administration of a constitutional newsman's privilege would present practical and conceptual difficulties of a high order. Sooner or later, it would be necessary to define those categories of newsmen who qualified for the privilege, a questionable procedure in light of the traditional doctrine that liberty of the press is the right of the lonely pamphleteer who uses carbon paper or a mimeograph just as much as of the large metropolitan publisher who utilizes the latest photocomposition methods. [The] informative function asserted by representatives of the organized press in the present cases is also performed by lecturers, political pollsters, novelists, academic researchers, and dramatists. Almost any author may quite accurately assert that he is contributing to the flow of information to the public, that he relies on confidential sources of information, and that these sources will be silenced if he is forced to make disclosures before a grand jury.

In each instance where a reporter is subpoenaed to testify, the courts would also be embroiled in preliminary factual and legal determinations with respect to whether the proper predicate had been laid for the reporters' appearance. [I]n the end, by considering whether enforcement of a particular law served a "compelling" governmental interest, the courts would be inextricably involved in distinguishing between the value of enforcing different criminal laws. By requiring testimony from a reporter in investigations involving some crimes but not in others, they would be making a value judgment which a legislature had declined to [make.]

At the federal level, Congress has freedom to determine whether a statutory newsman's privilege is necessary and desirable and to fashion standards and rules as narrow or broad as deemed necessary [and], equally important, to refashion those rules as experience from time to time may dictate. There is also merit in leaving state legislatures free, within First Amendment limits, to fashion their own standards in light of the conditions and problems with respect to the relations between law enforcement officials and press in their own [areas].

In addition, there is much force in the pragmatic view that the press has at its disposal powerful mechanisms of communication and is far from helpless to protect itself from harassment or substantial harm. Furthermore, if what the newsmen urged in these cases is true—that law enforcement cannot hope to gain and may suffer from subpoenaing newsmen before grand juries—prosecutors will be loath to risk so much for so little. Thus, at the federal level the Attorney General has already fashioned a set of rules for federal officials in connection with subpoenaing members of the press to testify before grand juries or at criminal trials.[a] These rules are a major step in the direction petitioners desire to move. They may prove wholly sufficient to resolve the bulk of disagreements and controversies between press and federal officials.

[G]rand jury investigations if instituted or conducted other than in good faith, would pose wholly different issues for resolution under the First Amendment. Official harassment of the press undertaken not for purposes of law enforcement but to disrupt a reporter's relationship with his news sources would have no justification. Grand juries are subject to judicial control and subpoenas to motions to quash. We do not expect courts will forget that grand juries must operate within the limits of the First Amendment as well as the Fifth.

We turn, therefore, to the disposition of the cases before us. [*Caldwell*] must be reversed. If there is no First Amendment privilege to refuse to answer the relevant and material questions asked during a good-faith grand jury investigation, then it is a fortiori true that there is no privilege to refuse to appear before such a grand jury until the Government demonstrates some "compelling need" for a newsman's testimony. [*Branzburg*] must be affirmed. Here, petitioner refused to answer questions that directly related to criminal conduct which he had observed and written about. [If] what petitioner wrote was true, he had direct information to provide the grand jury concerning the commission of serious crimes. [In *Pappas,* we] affirm [and] hold that petitioner must appear before the grand jury to answer the questions put to him, subject, of course, to the supervision of the presiding judge as to "the propriety, purposes, and scope of the grand jury inquiry and the pertinence of the probable testimony."

JUSTICE POWELL, concurring in the opinion of the Court.

I add this brief statement to emphasize what seems to me to be the limited nature of the Court's holding. The Court does not hold that newsmen, subpoenaed to testify before a grand jury, are without constitutional rights with respect to the gathering of news or in safeguarding their sources. [As] indicated in the concluding portion of the opinion, the Court states that no harassment of newsmen will be tolerated. If a newsman believes that the grand jury investigation is not being conducted in good faith he is not without remedy. Indeed, if the newsman is called upon to give information bearing only a remote and tenuous relationship to the subject of the investigation, or if he has some other reason to believe that his testimony implicates confidential source relationships without a legitimate need of law enforcement, he will have access to the Court on a motion to quash and an appropriate protective order may be entered. The asserted claim to privilege should be judged on its facts by the striking of a proper balance between freedom of the press and the obligation of all citizens to give relevant testimony with respect to criminal conduct. The balance of these vital constitutional and societal interests on a case-by-case basis accords with the tried

a. The "Guidelines for Subpoenas to the News Media," noted the Court, recognize that "compulsory process in some circumstances may have a limiting effect on the exercise of First Amendment rights" and provide, inter alia, that that factor "must [be] weight[ed]" in every case against the public interest to be served in administering justice.

and traditional way of adjudicating such questions.*

In short, the courts will be available to newsmen under circumstances where legitimate First Amendment interests require protection.

JUSTICE DOUGLAS, dissenting. * * *

It is my view that there is no "compelling need" that can be shown [by the Government] which qualifies the reporter's immunity from appearing or testifying before a grand jury, unless the reporter himself is implicated in a crime. His immunity in my view is therefore quite complete, for absent his involvement in a crime, the First Amendment protects him against an appearance before a grand jury and if he is involved in a crime, the Fifth Amendment stands as a barrier. Since in my view there is no area of inquiry not protected by a privilege, the reporter need not appear for the futile purpose of invoking one to each [question.]

Two principles which follow from [Alexander Meiklejohn's] understanding of the First Amendment are at stake here. One is that the people, the ultimate governors, must have absolute freedom of and therefore privacy of their individual opinions and beliefs regardless of how suspect or strange they may appear to others. Ancillary to that principle is the conclusion that an individual must also have absolute privacy over whatever information he may generate in the course of testing his opinions and beliefs. In this regard, Caldwell's status as a reporter is less relevant than is his status as a student who affirmatively pursued empirical research to enlarge his own intellectual viewpoint. The second principle is that effective self-government cannot succeed unless the people are immersed in a steady, robust, unimpeded, and uncensored flow of opinion and reporting which are continuously subjected to critique, rebuttal, and re-examination. In this respect, Caldwell's status as a newsgatherer and an integral part of that process becomes critical. * * *

Sooner or later any test which provides less than blanket protection to beliefs and associations will be twisted and relaxed so as to provide virtually no protection at all. [A] compelling interest test may prove as pliable as did the clear and present danger test. Perceptions of the worth of state objectives will change with the composition of the Court and with the intensity of the politics of the [times.]

JUSTICE STEWART, with whom JUSTICE BRENNAN and JUSTICE MARSHALL join, dissenting.

The Court's crabbed view of the First Amendment reflects a disturbing insensitivity to the critical role of an independent press in our society. [While] Mr. Justice Powell's enigmatic concurring opinion gives some hope of a more flexible view in the future, the Court in these cases holds that a newsman has no First Amendment right to protect his sources when called before a grand jury.

* It is to be remembered that Caldwell asserts a constitutional privilege not even to appear before the grand jury unless a court decides that the government has made a showing that meets the three preconditions specified in [Stewart, J.'s dissent]. To be sure, this would require a "balancing" of interests by the Court, but under circumstances and constraints significantly different from the balancing that will be appropriate under the Court's decision. The newsman witness, like all other witnesses, will have to appear; he will not be in a position to litigate at the threshold the State's very authority to subpoena him. Moreover, absent the constitutional preconditions that [the dissent] would impose as heavy burdens of proof to be carried by the State, the court—when called upon to protect a newsman from improper or prejudicial questioning—would be free to balance the competing interests on their merits in the particular case. The new constitutional rule endorsed by [the dissent] would, as a practical matter, defeat such a fair balancing and the essential societal interest in the detection and prosecution of crime would be heavily subordinated.

The Court thus invites state and federal authorities to undermine the historic independence of the press by attempting to annex the journalistic profession as an investigative arm of government. Not only will this decision impair performance of the press' constitutionally protected functions, but it will, I am convinced, in the long run, harm rather than help the administration of justice.

[As] private and public aggregations of power burgeon in size and the pressures for conformity necessarily mount, there is obviously a continuing need for an independent press to disseminate a robust variety of information and opinion through reportage, investigation and criticism, if we are to preserve our constitutional tradition of maximizing freedom of choice by encouraging diversity of expression. * * *

A corollary of the right to publish must be the right to gather news. [This right] implies, in turn, a right to a confidential relationship between a reporter and his source. This proposition follows as a matter of simple logic once three factual predicates are recognized: (1) newsmen require informants to gather news; (2) confidentiality—the promise or understanding that names or certain aspects of communications will be kept off-the-record—is essential to the creation and maintenance of a news-gathering relationship with informants; and (3) the existence of an unbridled subpoena power—the absence of a constitutional right protecting, in *any* way, a confidential relationship from compulsory process—will either deter sources from divulging information or deter reporters from gathering and publishing information. * * *

After today's decision, the potential informant can never be sure that his identity or off-the-record communications will not subsequently be revealed through the compelled testimony of a newsman. A public spirited person inside government, who is not implicated in any crime, will now be fearful of revealing corruption or other governmental wrong-doing, because he will now know he can subsequently be identified by use of compulsory process. The potential source must, therefore, choose between risking exposure by giving information or avoiding the risk by remaining silent.

The reporter must speculate about whether contact with a controversial source or publication of controversial material will lead to a subpoena. In the event of a subpoena, under today's decision, the newsman will know that he must choose between being punished for contempt if he refuses to testify, or violating his profession's ethics [10] and impairing his resourcefulness as a reporter if he discloses confidential information. * * *

The impairment of the flow of news cannot, of course, be proven with scientific precision, as the Court seems to demand. [But] we have never before demanded that First Amendment rights rest on elaborate empirical studies demonstrating beyond any conceivable doubt that deterrent effects exist; we have never before required proof of the exact number of people potentially affected by governmental action, who would actually be dissuaded from engaging in First Amendment activity.

Rather, on the basis of common sense and available information, we have asked, often implicitly, (1) whether there was a rational connection between the cause (the governmental action) and the effect (the deterrence or impairment of First Amendment activity) and (2) whether the effect would occur with some regularity, i.e., would not be de minimus. And, in making this determination,

10. The American Newspaper Guild has adopted the following rule as part of the newsman's code of ethics: "Newspaper men shall refuse to reveal confidences or disclose sources of confidential information in court or before other judicial or investigative bodies."

we have shown a special solicitude towards the "indispensable liberties" protected by the First Amendment, *NAACP v. Alabama*, for "freedoms such as these are protected not only against heavy-handed frontal attack, but also from being stifled by more subtle government interference." Once this threshold inquiry has been satisfied, we have then examined the competing interests in determining whether there is an unconstitutional infringement of First Amendment freedoms. * * *

We cannot await an unequivocal—and therefore unattainable—imprimatur from empirical studies. We can and must accept the evidence developed in the record, and elsewhere, that overwhelmingly supports the premise that deterrence will occur with regularity in important types of newsgathering relationships. Thus, we cannot escape the conclusion that when neither the reporter nor his source can rely on the shield of confidentiality against unrestrained use of the grand jury's subpoena power, valuable information will not be published and the public dialogue will inevitably be impoverished.

[W]hen an investigation impinges on First Amendment rights, the government must not only show that the inquiry is of "compelling and overriding importance" but it must also "convincingly" demonstrate that the investigation is "substantially related" to the information sought. Governmental officials must, therefore, demonstrate that the information sought is *clearly* relevant to a *precisely* defined subject of governmental inquiry. They must demonstrate that it is reasonable to think the witness in question has that information. And they must show that there is not any means of obtaining the information less destructive of First Amendment liberties. * * *

I believe the safeguards developed in our decisions involving governmental investigations must apply to the grand jury inquiries in these cases. Surely the function of the grand jury to aid in the enforcement of the law is no more important than the function of the legislature, and its committees, to make the law. [T]he vices of vagueness and overbreadth which legislative investigations may manifest are also exhibited by grand jury inquiries, since grand jury investigations are not limited in scope to specific criminal acts.

[Thus,] when a reporter is asked to appear before a grand jury and reveal confidences, I would hold that the government must (1) show that there is probable cause to believe that the newsman has information which is clearly relevant to a specific probable violation of law; (2) demonstrate that the information sought cannot be obtained by alternative means less destructive of First Amendment rights; and (3) demonstrate a compelling and overriding interest in the information. * * *

The crux of the Court's rejection of any newsman's privilege is its observation that only "where news sources themselves are implicated in crime or possess information *relevant* to the grand jury's task need they or the reporter be concerned about grand jury subpoenas." (emphasis supplied). But this is a most misleading construct. [G]iven the grand jury's extraordinarily broad investigative powers and the weak standards of relevance and materiality that apply during such inquiries, reporters, if they have no testimonial privilege, will be called to give information about informants who have neither committed crimes nor have information about crime. It is to avoid deterrence of such sources and thus to prevent needless injury to First Amendment values that I think the government must be required to show probable cause that the newsman has information which is clearly relevant to a specific probable violation of criminal law. * * *

Both the "probable cause" and "alternative means" requirements [would] serve the vital function of mediating between the public interest in the administration of justice and the constitutional protection of the full flow of information. These requirements would avoid a direct conflict between these competing concerns, and they would generally provide adequate protection for newsmen.[35] No doubt the courts would be required to make some delicate judgments in working out this accommodation. But that, after all, is the function of courts of law. Better such judgments, however difficult, than the simplistic and stultifying absolutism adopted by the Court in denying any force to the First Amendment in these cases.[36]

[I]n the name of advancing the administration of justice, the Court's decision, I think, will only impair the achievement of that goal. People entrusted with law enforcement responsibility, no less than private citizens, need general information relating to controversial social problems. [W]hen a grand jury may exercise an unbridled subpoena power, and sources involved in sensitive matters become fearful of disclosing information, the newsman will not only cease to be a useful grand jury witness; he will cease to investigate and publish information about issues of public import.

[In Stewart, J.'s view, the Ninth Circuit correctly ruled that in the circumstances of the case, Caldwell need not divulge confidential information and, moreover, that in this case Caldwell had established that "his very appearance [before] the grand jury would jeopardize his relationship with his sources, leading to a severance of the news gathering relationship and impairment of the flow of news to the public." But because "only in very rare circumstances would a confidential relationship between a reporter and his source be so sensitive [as to preclude] his mere appearance before the grand jury," Stewart, J., would confine "*this* aspect of the *Caldwell* judgment [to] its own facts." Thus, he would affirm in *Caldwell* and remand the other cases for further proceedings not inconsistent with his views.]

Notes and Questions

1. *The role of the press.* Consider Blasi, *The Checking Value in First Amendment Theory,* 1977 Am.B.Found.Res.J. 521, 593: The White, J., opinion "characterized the press as a private-interest group rather than an institution with a central function to perform in the constitutional system of checks and balances [and] labeled the source relationships that the reporters sought to maintain 'a private system of informers operated by the press to report on criminal conduct' [cautioning] that this system would be 'unaccountable to the public' were a reporter's privilege to be recognized." In contrast to White, J.'s perspective, consider the remarks of Stewart, J., in a much-discussed address, "*Or of the Press,*" 26 Hast.L.J. 631, 634 (1975): "In setting up the three branches of the Federal Government, the Founders deliberately created an internally competitive[b] system. [The] primary purpose[c] of [the Free Press Clause] was a

35. We need not, therefore, reach the question of whether government's interest in these cases is "overriding and compelling." I do not, however, believe, as the Court does, that *all* grand jury investigations automatically would override the newsman's testimonial privilege.

36. The disclaimers in Mr. Justice Powell's concurring opinion leave room for the hope that in some future case the Court may take a less absolute position in this area.

b. For commentary on how the "cozy connections" between press and government demonstrate that the relationship is often more cooperative than adversarial, see Soifer, *Freedom of the Press in the United States* in

c. See note c on page 773.

similar one: to create a fourth institution outside the Government as an additional check on the three official branches." [d] Proceeding from variations of this fourth estate view of the press, most commentators endorse a reporter's privilege. See, e.g., Baker, *Press Rights and Government Power to Structure the Press,* 34 U.Miami L.Rev. 819, 858 (1980) (absolute protection). But see Bezanson, *The New Free Press Guarantee,* 63 Va.L.Rev. 731, 759–62 (1977) (press clause prevents special governmental assistance for press). Claims for an independent press-clause, however, need not interpret the press clause along fourth estate lines, see *Nimmer on Freedom of Speech* 2–104—2–129 (1984).[e]

2. Whatever role is assigned to the press, are press relationships with confidential sources not entitled to at least the same protections afforded to civil rights groups and minority parties? Does *Branzburg* exhibit insensitivity to free speech values? Consider Blasi, note 1 supra, at 593: Two of the journalists before the Court "were covering the Black Panther Party, [which] claimed to be the victim of an official nationwide policy of persecution and extermination. Yet the White opinion made no reference to the speech value of news about possible official misbehavior obtained from persons against whom abuses of power may have been directed. Instead, Justice White spoke only of the criminal activities of the sources themselves and their peers, and denigrated the speech value at stake as that in 'possible future news about crime from undisclosed, unverified sources.' "

3. *Evaluating Powell, J.'s concurrence.* Did five justices—or only four—hold that grand juries may pursue their goals by any means short of bad faith? May one conclude that the information sought bears "only a remote and tenuous relationship to the subject of investigation" on grounds falling short of demonstrating "bad faith"? Does Powell, J.'s suggested test—the privilege claim "should be judged on its facts by [balancing the] vital constitutional and societal interests on a case-by-case basis"—resemble Stewart, J.'s dissenting approach more than White, J.'s? Extrajudicially, Stewart, J., has referred to *Branzburg* as a case which rejected claims for a journalist's privilege "by a vote of 5–4, or, considering Mr. Justice Powell's concurring opinion, perhaps by a vote of 4½–4½." Stewart, *"Or of the Press,"* 26 Hast.L.J. 631, 635 (1975). The majority of

Press Law in Modern Democracies 79, 108–110 (Lahav, ed., 1985).

c. For spirited debate about the historical evidence, compare Anderson, *The Origins of the Press Clause,* 30 U.C.L.A.L.Rev. 455 (1983) with Levy, *On the Origins of the Free Press Clause,* 32 U.C.L.A.L.Rev. 177 (1984). See generally Levy, *Emergence of a Free Press* (1985).

d. For Brennan, J.'s views, see *Address,* 32 Rutg.L.Rev. 173 (1979).

e. For criticism of the notion of an independent press clause, see Lange, *The Speech and Press Clauses,* 23 U.C.L.A.L.Rev. 77 (1975); Lewis, *A Preferred Position for Journalism?,* 7 Hof.L.Rev. 595 (1979); Van Alstyne, *The First Amendment and the Free Press: A Comment on Some New Trends and Some Old Theories,* 9 Hof.L.Rev. 1 (1980); Van Alstyne, *The Hazards to the Press of Claiming a "Preferred Position",* 28 Hast.L.J. 761 (1977). But see Abrams, *The Press is Different: Reflections on Justice Stewart and the Autonomous Press,* 7 Hof.L.Rev. 563 (1979). For an effort to transcend the issues involved, see generally Sack, *Reflections on the Wrong Question: Special Constitutional Privilege for the Institutional Press,* 7 Hof.L.Rev. 629 (1979). Finally, for commentary on the "tension between journalism as the political, sometimes partisan fourth estate and journalism as a profession" purporting to operate as a "neutral and objective medium," see Lahav, *An Outline for a General Theory of Press Law in Democracy* in Press Law in Modern Democracies 339, 352–54 (Lahav ed. 1985). See also Bollinger, *The Press and the Public Interest: An Essay on the Relationship Between Social Behavior and the Language of First Amendment Theory,* 82 Mich.L.Rev. 1447, 1457 (1984) (commenting generally on the pitfalls connected with justifying a free press by arguing that it serves the public interest: "More than most groups (compare lawyers, for example) the press is in conflict over its relationship to the world on which it regularly reports.").

courts applying *Branzburg* have concluded that Powell, J.'s opinion read together with the dissents affords the basis for a qualified privilege. Among the issues litigated are whether the privilege should be confined to journalists (or extended e.g. to academics) and the related question of how to define journalists and whether the privilege belongs to the source, the reporter, or both. For an exhaustive survey, see Goodale, Moodhe & Imes, *Reporter's Privilege Cases* in Communications Law 1984, at 339 (1984).

The Court's most recent expression on the subject unanimously refuses, at least in the absence of bad faith, to extend a qualified first amendment privilege to "confidential" tenure files and, in dictum, confines *Branzburg* to the recognition that the " 'bad faith' exercise of grand jury powers might raise First Amendment concerns." *University of Pennsylvania v. EEOC,* 493 U.S. 182, 110 S.Ct. 577, 107 L.Ed.2d 571 (1990) (gender discrimination claim). For relevant commentary, see Byrne, *Academic Freedom: A "Special Concern of the First Amendment,"* 99 Yale L.J. 251 (1989).

4. *Other contexts.* Does *Branzburg's* emphasis on the grand jury's special role in the American criminal justice system warrant different treatment of the journalist's privilege when a prosecutor seeks disclosure? See Murasky, *The Journalist's Privilege: Branzburg and Its Aftermath,* 52 Tex.L.Rev. 829, 885 (1974). Are the interests of civil litigants in compelling disclosure of a journalist's confidences significantly weaker than those of criminal litigants? Should there be an absolute journalist's privilege in civil discovery proceedings? See id. at 898–903. What if the journalist is a party to the litigation?

5. *State "shield laws" and a criminal defendant's right to compulsory process.* As of 1984, 26 states had enacted "shield" laws. Some protect only journalists' sources; some (including New Jersey) protect undisclosed information obtained in the course of a journalist's professional activities as well as sources. See Goodale, Moodhe & Imes, note 3 supra.

In re Farber, 78 N.J. 259, 394 A.2d 330 (1978), cert. denied, 439 U.S. 997, 99 S.Ct. 598, 58 L.Ed.2d 670 (1978): *New York Times* investigative reporter Myron Farber wrote a series of articles claiming that an unidentified "Doctor X" had caused the death of several patients by poisoning. This led to the indictment and eventual prosecution of Dr. Jascalevich for murder. (He was ultimately acquitted.) In response to the defendant's request, the trial court demanded the disclosure of Farber's sources and the production of his interview notes and other information for his in camera inspection. Relying on the first amendment and the state shield law, Farber refused to comply with the subpoenas. After White, J., and then Marshall, J., had denied stays, each deeming it unlikely that four justices would grant certiorari at this stage of the case, Farber was jailed for civil contempt and the *Times* heavily fined.

The state supreme court (5–2) upheld civil and criminal convictions of the *Times* and Farber. Under the circumstances, it ruled, the first amendment did not protect Farber against disclosure. Nor did the New Jersey shield law, for Farber's statutory rights had to yield to Dr. Jascalevich's sixth amendment right "to have compulsory process for obtaining witnesses in his favor." [e]

---

e. For an exhaustive analysis of the case, see Note, 32 Rutg.L.Rev. 545 (1979). The case is also discussed at length by *New York Times* columnist Anthony Lewis, *A Preferred Position for Journalism?*, 7 Hof.L.Rev. 595, 610–18 (1979). See also Nowak, Rotunda & Young, *Constitutional Law* 912–13 (2d ed. 1983); Tribe, *American Constitutional Law* 975 n. 35 (2d ed. 1988).

ZURCHER v. STANFORD DAILY, 436 U.S. 547, 98 S.Ct. 1970, 56 L.Ed.2d 525 (1978), again declined to afford the press special protection—dividing very much as in *Branzburg.*[a] A student newspaper that had published articles and photographs of a clash between demonstrators and police brought this federal action, claiming that a search of its offices for film and pictures showing events at the scene of the police-demonstrators clash (the newspaper was not involved in the unlawful acts) had violated its first and fourth amendment rights. A 5–3 majority, per WHITE, J., held that the fourth amendment does not prevent the government from issuing a search warrant (based on reasonable cause to believe that the "things" to be searched for are located on the property) simply because the owner or possessor of the place to be searched is not reasonably suspected of criminal involvement. The Court also rejected the argument that "whatever may be true of third-party searches generally, where the third party is a newspaper, there are additional [first amendment factors justifying] a nearly per se rule forbidding the search warrant and permitting only the subpoena duces tecum. The general submission is that searches of newspaper offices for evidence of crime reasonably believed to be on the premises will seriously threaten the ability of the press to gather, analyze, and disseminate news.

"[Although] [a]ware of the long struggle between Crown and press and desiring to curb unjustified official intrusions, [the Framers] did not forbid warrants where the press was involved, did not require special showing that subpoenas would be impractical, and did not insist that the owner of the place to be searched, if connected with the press, must be shown to be implicated in the offense being investigated. Further, the prior cases do no more than insist that the courts apply the warrant requirements with particular exactitude when First Amendment interests would be endangered by the search. [N]o more than this is required where the warrant requested is for the seizure of criminal evidence reasonably believed to be on the premises occupied by a newspaper. Properly administered, the preconditions for a warrant—probable cause, specificity [as to] place [and] things to be seized and overall reasonableness—should afford [the press] sufficient protection * * *.

"[R]espondents and amici have pointed to only a very few instances [since] 1971 involving [newspaper office searches]. This reality hardly suggests abuse, and if abuse occurs, there will be time enough to deal with it. Furthermore, the press [is] not easily intimidated—nor should it be."

POWELL, J., concurring, rejected Stewart, J.'s dissenting view that the press is entitled to "a special procedure, not available to others," when the government requires evidence in its possession, but added: "This is not to say [that a warrant] sufficient to support the search of an apartment or an automobile would be reasonable in supporting the search of a newspaper office. [While] there is no justification for the establishment of a separate Fourth Amendment procedure for the press, a magistrate asked to issue a warrant for the search of press offices can and should take cognizance of the independent values protected by the First Amendment—such as those highlighted by [Stewart, J., dissent-

a. In both cases, White, J., joined by Burger, C.J., Blackmun, Powell and Rehnquist, JJ., delivered the opinion of the Court and in both cases the "fifth vote"—Powell, J.,—also wrote a separate opinion which seemed to meet the concerns of the dissent part way. In both cases Stewart, J., dissented, maintaining that the Court's holding would seriously impair "newsgathering." Stevens, J., who had replaced Douglas, J., also dissented in *Zurcher,* as had Douglas in *Branzburg.* Brennan, J., who had joined Stewart, J.'s dissent in *Branzburg,* did not participate in *Zurcher.*

ing]—when he weighs such factors." [b]

STEWART, joined by Marshall, J., dissented: "A search warrant allows police officers to ransack the files of a newspaper, reading each and every document until they have found the one named in the warrant, while a subpoena would permit the newspaper itself to produce only the specific documents requested. A search, unlike a subpoena, will therefore lead to the needless exposure of confidential information completely unrelated to the purpose of the investigation. The knowledge that police officers can make an unannounced raid on a newsroom is thus bound to have a deterrent effect on the availability of confidential news sources. [The result] will be a diminishing flow of potentially important information to the public.

"[Here, unlike *Branzburg,* the newspaper does] not claim that any of the evidence sought was privileged [, but] only that a subpoena would have served equally well to produce that evidence. Thus, we are not concerned with the principle, central to *Branzburg,* that '"the public [has] a right to everyman's evidence,"' but only with whether any significant social interest would be impaired if the police were generally required to obtain evidence from the press by means of a subpoena rather than a search. * * *

"Perhaps as a matter of abstract policy a newspaper office should receive no more protection from unannounced police searches than, say, the office of a doctor or the office of a bank. But we are here to uphold a Constitution. And our Constitution does not explicitly protect the practice of medicine or the business of banking from all abridgement by government. It does explicitly protect the freedom of the press." [c]

Notes and Questions

1. The distinctions between search and subpoena are underscored in Tribe, *American Constitutional Law* 973 (2d ed. 1988): "When a subpoena is served on a newspaper, it has the opportunity to assert constitutional and statutory rights [such as 'shield laws,' enacted in many states, protecting reporters from divulging information given them in confidence] to keep certain materials confidential. Such protection is circumvented when officials can proceed *ex parte,* by search warrant. And the risk of abuse may be greatest exactly when the press plays its most vital and creative role in our political system, the role of watchdog on official corruption and abuse. Officials who find themselves the targets [of] media investigations may well be tempted to conduct searches to find out precisely what various journalists have discovered, and to retaliate against reporters who have unearthed and reported official wrongdoing."

2. The difficulty in identifying suspects at the early stages of a criminal investigation, relied on by the *Zurcher* majority, does not, maintains Note, 92 Harv.L.Rev. 206–07 (1978), "require that the court refuse to adopt a special rule for those *classes* of witnesses who are so unlikely to destroy evidence as to deserve special protection from third party searches. [One reasonable approach] would be a narrow rule favoring the use of the subpoena only when the material is sought from neutral observers who possess evidence specifically because of the nature of their work, such as journalists, doctors, lawyers and accountants.

b. Powell, J., noted that his *Branzburg* concurrence may "properly be read as supporting the view expressed in the text above, and in the Court's [*Zurcher*] opinion," that under the warrant requirement "the magistrate should consider the values of a free press as well as the societal interest in enforcing the criminal laws."

c. Stevens, J., dissented on the general fourth amendment issue.

Such parties are relatively easy to identify and are extremely unlikely to be either culpable or sympathetic to those who are culpable." [d]

SECTION 10. WEALTH AND THE POLITICAL PROCESS: CONCERNS FOR EQUALITY

The idea of equality has loomed large throughout this chapter. Some feel it should be a central concern of the first amendment. See Tribe, *Constitutional Choices* 188–220 (1985); Karst, *Equality as a Central Principle in the First Amendment,* 43 U.Chi.L.Rev. 20 (1975). Equality has been championed by those who seek access to government property and to media facilities. It has been invoked in support of content regulation and against it. This section considers government efforts to prevent the domination of the political process by wealthy individuals and business corporations. In the end, it would be appropriate to reconsider the arguments for and against a marketplace conception of the first amendment, to ask whether the Court's interpretations overall (e.g., taking the public forum materials, the media materials, and the election materials together) have adequately considered the interest in equality, and to inquire generally about the relationship between liberty and equality in the constitutional scheme.

BUCKLEY v. VALEO

424 U.S. 1, 96 S.Ct. 612, 46 L.Ed.2d 659 (1976).

PER CURIAM.

[In this portion of a lengthy opinion dealing with the validity of the Federal Election Campaign Act of 1971, as amended in 1974, the Court considers those parts of the Act limiting *contributions* to a candidate for federal office (all sustained), and those parts limiting *expenditures* in support of such candidacy (all held invalid).[a]]

A. *General Principles.* The Act's contribution and expenditure limitations operate in an area of the most fundamental First Amendment activities. Discussion of public issues and debate on the qualifications of candidates are integral to the operation of the system of government established by our Constitution.

[Appellees] contend that what the Act regulates is conduct, and that its effect on speech and association is incidental at most. Appellants respond that contributions and expenditures are at the very core of political speech, and that the Act's limitations thus constitute restraints on First Amendment liberty that are both gross and [direct.]

We cannot share the view [that] the present Act's contribution and expenditure limitations are comparable to the restrictions on conduct upheld in *O'Brien* [p. 847 supra]. The expenditure of money simply cannot be equated with such conduct as destruction of a draft card. Some forms of communication made possible by the giving and spending of money involve speech alone, some involve conduct primarily, and some involve a combination of the two. Yet this Court has never suggested that the dependence of a communication on the expenditure

d. For discussion of executive and legislative response to *Zurcher,* see Goodale, Moodhe, and Imes, note 3 supra after *Branzburg,* at 375–77. In particular, see The Privacy Protection Act of 1980, 42 U.S.C. §§ 2000aa–2000aa–12 (limiting the impact of *Zurcher* on the media).

a. Other aspects of *Buckley* are briefly considered in Sec. 7, I supra (public funding); Sec. 9, IV supra (disclosure).

of money operates itself to introduce a non-speech element or to reduce the exacting scrutiny required by the First Amendment. * * *

Even if the categorization of the expenditure of money as conduct were accepted, the limitations challenged here would not meet the *O'Brien* test because the governmental interests advanced in support of the Act involve "suppressing communication." The interests served by the Act include restricting the voices of people and interest groups who have money to spend and reducing the overall scope of federal election campaigns. [Unlike] *O'Brien,* where [the] interest in the preservation of draft cards was wholly unrelated to their use as a means of communication, it is beyond dispute that the interest in regulating the alleged "conduct" of giving or spending money "arises in some measure because the communication allegedly integral to the conduct is itself thought to be harmful."

Nor can the Act's contribution and expenditure limitations be sustained, as some of the parties suggest, by reference to the constitutional principles reflected in such decisions as *Cox v. Louisiana, Adderley,* and *Kovacs,* [Secs. 7, II and 8 supra]. [The] critical difference between this case and those time, place and manner cases is that the present Act's contribution and expenditure limitations impose direct quantity restrictions on political communication and association by persons, groups, candidates and political parties in addition to any reasonable time, place, and manner regulations otherwise imposed.

A restriction on the amount of money a person or group can spend on political communication during a campaign necessarily reduces the quantity of expression by restricting the number of issues discussed, the depth of their exploration, and the size of the audience reached. This is because virtually every means of communicating ideas in today's mass society requires the expenditure of [money].

The expenditure limitations contained in the Act represent substantial rather than merely theoretical restraints on the quantity and diversity of political speech. The $1,000 ceiling on spending "relative to a clearly identified candidate," 18 U.S.C. § 608(e)(1), would appear to exclude all citizens and groups except candidates, political parties and the institutional press from any significant use of the most effective modes of communication.[20] * * *

By contrast with a limitation upon expenditures for political expression, a limitation [on] the amount of money a person may give to a candidate or campaign organization [involves] little direct restraint on his political communication, for it permits the symbolic expression of support evidenced by a contribution but does not in any way infringe the contributor's freedom to discuss candidates and issues. While contributions may result in political expression if spent by a candidate or an association to present views to the voters, the transformation of contributions into political debate involves speech by someone other than the contributor.

[There] is no indication [that] the contribution limitations imposed by the Act would have any dramatic adverse effect on the funding of campaigns and political associations.[23] The overall effect of the Act's contribution ceilings is

20. The record indicates that, as of January 1, 1975, one full-page advertisement in a daily edition of a certain metropolitan newspaper costs $6,971.04—almost seven times the annual limit on expenditures "relative to" a particular candidate imposed on the vast majority of individual citizens and associations by § 608(e)(1).

23. Statistical findings agreed to by the parties reveal that approximately 5.1% of the $73,483,613 raised by the 1161 candidates for Congress in 1974 was obtained in amounts in merely to require candidates and political committees to raise funds from a greater number of persons and to compel people who would otherwise contribute amounts greater than the statutory limits to expend such funds on direct political expression, rather than to reduce the total amount of money potentially available to promote political expression. * * *

In sum, although the Act's contribution and expenditure limitations both implicate fundamental First Amendment interests, its expenditure ceilings impose significantly more severe restrictions on protected freedoms of political expression and association than do its limitations on financial contributions.

B. *Contribution Limitations.* [Section] 608(b) provides, with certain limited exceptions, that "no person shall make contributions to any candidate with respect to any election for Federal office which, in the aggregate, exceeds $1,000."[b] * * *

Appellants contend that the $1,000 contribution ceiling unjustifiably burdens First Amendment freedoms, employs overbroad dollar limits, and discriminates against candidates opposing incumbent officeholders and against minor-party candidates in violation of the Fifth Amendment.

[In] view of the fundamental nature of the right to associate, governmental "action which may have the effect of curtailing the freedom to associate is subject to the closest scrutiny." Yet, it is clear that "[n]either the right to associate nor the right to participate in political activities is absolute." *Letter Carriers* [p. 1006 supra]. Even a " 'significant interference' with protected rights of political association" may be sustained if the State demonstrates a sufficiently important interest and employs means closely drawn to avoid unnecessary abridgment of associational freedoms. * * *

It is unnecessary to look beyond the Act's primary purpose—to limit the actuality and appearance of corruption resulting from large individual financial contributions—in order to find a constitutionally sufficient justification for the $1,000 contribution limitation. [The] increasing importance of the communications media and sophisticated mass mailing and polling operations to effective campaigning make the raising of large sums of money an ever more essential ingredient of an effective candidacy. To the extent that large contributions are given to secure political quid pro quos from current and potential office holders, the integrity of our system of representative democracy is undermined. Although the scope of such pernicious practices can never be reliably ascertained, the deeply disturbing examples surfacing after the 1972 election demonstrate that the problem is not an illusory one.

Of almost equal concern as the danger of actual quid pro quo arrangements is the impact of the appearance of corruption stemming from public awareness of the opportunities for abuse inherent in a regime of large individual financial contributions. In *Letter Carriers,* the Court found that the danger to "fair and effective government" posed by partisan political conduct on the part of federal

excess of $1,000. In 1974, two major-party senatorial candidates, Ramsey Clark and Senator Charles Mathias, Jr., operated large-scale campaigns on contributions raised under a voluntarily imposed $100 contribution limitation.

b. As defined, "person" includes "an individual, partnership, committee, association, corporation or any other organization or group." The limitation applies to: (1) anything of value, such as gifts, loans, advances, and promises to give, (2) contributions made direct to the candidate or to an intermediary, or a committee authorized by the candidate, (3) the aggregate amounts contributed to the candidate for each election, treating primaries, run-off elections and general elections separately and all Presidential primaries within a single calendar year as one election.

employees charged with administering the law was a sufficiently important concern to justify broad restrictions on the employees' right of partisan political association. Here, as there, Congress could legitimately conclude that the avoidance of the appearance of improper influence "is also critical [if] confidence in the system of representative Government is not to be eroded to a disastrous extent." [29]

Appellants contend that the contribution limitations must be invalidated because bribery laws and narrowly-drawn disclosure requirements constitute a less restrictive means of dealing with "proven and suspected quid pro quo arrangements." But laws [against] bribes deal with only the most blatant and specific attempts of those with money to influence governmental action. [And] Congress was surely entitled to conclude that disclosure was only a partial measure, and that contribution ceilings were a necessary legislative concomitant to deal with the reality or appearance of corruption inherent in a system permitting unlimited financial contributions, even when the identities of the contributors and the amounts of their contributions are fully disclosed.

The Act's $1,000 contribution limitation focuses precisely on the problem of large campaign contributions—the narrow aspect of political association where the actuality and potential for corruption have been identified—while leaving persons free to engage in independent political expression, to associate actively through volunteering their services. [The] Act's contribution limitations [do] not undermine to any material degree the potential for robust and effective discussion of candidates and campaign [issues].

We find that, under the rigorous standard of review established by our prior decisions, the weighty interests served by restricting the size of financial contributions to political candidates are sufficient to justify the limited effect upon First Amendment freedoms caused by the $1,000 contribution ceiling.[c]

C. *Expenditure Limitations.* [1.] Section 608(e)(1) provides that "[n]o person may make any expenditure [relative] to a clearly identified candidate during a calendar year which, when added to all other expenditures made by such person during the year advocating the election or defeat of such candidate, exceeds $1,000." [Its] plain effect [is] to prohibit all individuals, who are neither candidates nor owners of institutional press facilities, and all groups, except political parties and campaign organizations, from voicing their views "relative

29. Although the Court in *Letter Carriers* found that this interest was constitutionally sufficient to justify legislation prohibiting federal employees from engaging in certain partisan political activities, it was careful to emphasize that the limitations did not restrict an employee's right to express his views on political issues and candidates.

c. The Court rejected the challenges that the $1,000 limit was overbroad because (1) most large contributors do not seek improper influence over a candidate, and (2) much more than $1,000 would still not be enough to influence improperly a candidate or office holder. With respect to (1), "Congress was justified in concluding that the interest in safeguarding against the appearance of impropriety requires that the opportunity for abuse inherent in the process of raising large monetary contributions be eliminated." With respect to (2), "As the Court of Appeals observed, '[a] court has no scalpel to probe, whether, say, a $2,000 ceiling might not serve as well as $1,000.' Such distinctions in degree become significant only when they can be said to amount to differences in kind."

The Court also rejected as without support in the record the claims that the contribution limitations worked invidious discrimination between incumbents and challengers to whom the same limitations applied.

The Court then upheld (1) exclusion from the $1,000 limit of the value of unpaid volunteer services and of certain expenses paid by the volunteer up to a maximum of $500; (2) the higher limit of $5,000 for contributions to a candidate by established, registered political committees with at least 50 contributing supporters and fielding at least five candidates for federal office; and (3) the $25,000 limit on total contributions to all candidates by one person in one calendar year.

to a clearly identified candidate" through means that entail aggregate expenditures of more than $1,000 during a calendar year. The provision, for example, would make it a federal criminal offense for a person or association to place a single one-quarter page advertisement "relative to a clearly identified candidate" in a major metropolitan newspaper.

[Although] "expenditure," "clearly identified," and "candidate" are defined in the Act, there is no definition clarifying what expenditures are "relative to" a candidate. [But the "when" clause in § 608(e)(1)] clearly permits, if indeed it does not require, the phrase "relative to" a candidate to be read to mean "advocating the election or defeat of" a candidate.

But while such a construction of § 608(e)(1) refocuses the vagueness question, [it hardly] eliminates the problem of unconstitutional vagueness altogether. For the distinction between discussion of issues and candidates and advocacy of election or defeat of candidates may often dissolve in practical application. Candidates, especially incumbents, are intimately tied to public issues involving legislative proposals and governmental actions. Not only do candidates campaign on the basis of their positions on various public issues, but campaigns themselves generate issues of public interest.

[Constitutionally deficient uncertainty which "compels the speaker to hedge and trim"] can be avoided only by reading § 608(e)(1) as limited to communications that include explicit words of advocacy of election or defeat of a candidate, much as the definition of "clearly identified" in § 608(e)(2) requires that an explicit and unambiguous reference to the candidate appear as part of the communication. This is the reading of the provision suggested by the non-governmental appellees in arguing that "[f]unds spent to propagate one's views on issues without expressly calling for a candidate's election or defeat are thus not covered." We agree that in order to preserve the provision against invalidation on vagueness grounds, § 608(e)(1) must be construed to apply only to expenditures for communications that in express terms advocate the election or defeat of a clearly identified candidate for federal office.

We turn then to the basic First Amendment question—whether § 608(e)(1), even as thus narrowly and explicitly construed, impermissibly burdens the constitutional right of free expression. * * *

We find that the governmental interest in preventing corruption and the appearance of corruption is inadequate to justify § 608(e)(1)'s ceiling on independent expenditures. First, assuming arguendo that large independent expenditures pose the same dangers of actual or apparent quid pro quo arrangements as do large contributions, § 608(e)(1) does not provide an answer that sufficiently relates to the elimination of those dangers. Unlike the contribution limitations' total ban on the giving of large amounts of money to candidates, § 608(e)(1) prevents only some large expenditures. So long as persons and groups eschew expenditures that in express terms advocate the election or defeat of a clearly identified candidate, they are free to spend as much as they want to promote the candidate and his views. The exacting interpretation of the statutory language necessary to avoid unconstitutional vagueness thus undermines the limitation's effectiveness as a loophole-closing provision by facilitating circumvention by those seeking to exert improper influence upon a candidate or office-holder. It would naively underestimate the ingenuity and resourcefulness of persons and groups desiring to buy influence to believe that they would have much difficulty devising expenditures that skirted the restriction on express advocacy of election or defeat but nevertheless benefited the candidate's campaign. * * *

Second, [the] independent advocacy restricted by the provision does not presently appear to pose dangers of real or apparent corruption comparable to those identified with large campaign contributions. The parties defending § 608(e)(1) contend that it is necessary to prevent would-be contributors from avoiding the contribution limitations by the simple expedient of paying directly for media advertisements or for other portions of the candidate's campaign activities. [Section] 608(b)'s contribution ceilings rather than § 608(e)(1)'s independent expenditure limitation prevent attempts to circumvent the Act through prearranged or coordinated expenditures amounting to disguised contributions.[53] By contrast, § 608(e)(1) limits expenditures for express advocacy of candidates made totally independently of the candidate and his campaign. [The] absence of prearrangement and coordination of an expenditure with the candidate or his agent not only undermines the value of the expenditure to the candidate, but also alleviates the danger that expenditures will be given as a quid pro quo for improper commitments from the candidate. Rather than preventing circumvention of the contribution limitations, § 608(e)(1) severely restricts all independent advocacy despite its substantially diminished potential for abuse.

While the independent expenditure ceiling thus fails to serve any substantial governmental interest in stemming the reality or appearance of corruption in the electoral process, it heavily burdens core First Amendment expression. [Advocacy] of the election or defeat of candidates for federal office is no less entitled to protection under the First Amendment than the discussion of political policy generally or advocacy of the passage or defeat of legislation.

It is argued, however, that the ancillary governmental interest in equalizing the relative ability of individuals and groups to influence the outcome of elections serves to justify the limitation on express advocacy of the election or defeat of candidates imposed by § 608(e)(1)'s expenditure ceiling. But the concept that government may restrict the speech of some elements of our society in order to enhance the relative voice of others [d] is wholly foreign to the First Amendment, which was designed "to secure 'the widest possible dissemination of information from diverse and antagonistic sources,'" and "'to assure unfettered interchange of ideas for the bringing about of political and social changes desired by the people.'" *New York Times Co. v. Sullivan.* The First Amendment's protection against governmental abridgement of free expression cannot properly be made to depend on a person's financial ability to engage in public discussion.[55]

53. Section 608(e)(1) does not apply to expenditures "on behalf of a candidate within the meaning of" § 608(2)(B). That section provides that expenditures "authorized or requested by the candidate, an authorized committee of the candidate, or an agent of the candidate" are to be treated as expenditures of the candidate and contributions by the person or group making the expenditure. [In] view of [the] legislative history and the purposes of the Act, we find that the "authorized or requested" standard of the Act operates to treat all expenditures placed in cooperation with or with the consent of a candidate, his agents, or an authorized committee of the candidate as contributions subject to the limitations set forth in § 608(b).

d. The lower court characterized the issue somewhat differently. Can "the wealthy few [claim] a constitutional guarantee to a stronger political voice than the unwealthy many because they are able to give and spend more money, and because the amounts they give and spend cannot be limited"? 519 F.2d 821, 841 (D.C.Cir.1975).

55. Neither the voting rights cases [Ch. 10, Sec. 4, I, A] nor the Court's decision upholding the FCC's fairness doctrine [p. 693 supra] lends support to appellees' position that the First Amendment permits Congress to abridge the rights of some persons to engage in political expression in order to enhance the relative voice of other segments of our [society].

[*Mills*] *v. Alabama,* 384 U.S. 214, 86 S.Ct. 1434, 16 L.Ed.2d 484 (1966), held that legislative restrictions on advocacy of the election or defeat of political candidates are wholly at odds with the guarantees of the First Amendment. [Yet] the prohibition on election day editorials invalidated in *Mills* is clearly a lesser intrusion on constitutional freedom than a $1,000 limitation on the amount of money any person or association can spend *during an entire election year* in advocating the election or defeat of a candidate for public office.

For the reasons stated, we conclude that § 608(e)(1)'s independent expenditure limitation is unconstitutional under the First Amendment.

2. [The] Act also sets limits on expenditures by a candidate "from his personal funds, or the personal funds of his immediate family, in connection with his campaigns during any calendar year." § 608(a)(1).[e]

The ceiling on personal expenditures by candidates on their own behalf [imposes] a substantial restraint on the ability of persons to engage in protected First Amendment expression. The candidate, no less than any other person, has a First Amendment right to engage in the discussion of public issues and vigorously and tirelessly to advocate his own election and the election of other candidates. Indeed, it is of particular importance that candidates have the unfettered opportunity to make their views known so that the electorate may intelligently evaluate the candidates' personal qualities and their positions on vital public issues before choosing among them on election day. [Section] 608(a)'s ceiling on personal expenditures by a candidate in furtherance of his own candidacy thus clearly and directly interferes with constitutionally protected freedoms.

The primary governmental interest served by the Act—the prevention of actual and apparent corruption of the political process—does not support the limitation on the candidate's expenditure of his own personal funds. [Indeed], the use of personal funds reduces the candidate's dependence on outside contributions and thereby counteracts the coercive pressures and attendant risks of abuse to which the Act's contribution limitations are directed.

The ancillary interest in equalizing the relative financial resources of candidates competing for elective office, therefore, provides the sole relevant rationale for Section 608(a)'s expenditure ceiling. That interest is clearly not sufficient to justify the provision's infringement of fundamental First Amendment rights. First, the limitation may fail to promote financial equality among candidates. [Indeed], a candidate's personal wealth may impede his [fundraising efforts]. Second, and more fundamentally, the First Amendment simply cannot tolerate § 608(a)'s restriction upon the freedom of a candidate to speak without legislative limit on behalf of his own candidacy. We therefore hold that § 608(a)'s restrictions on a candidate's personal expenditures is unconstitutional.

3. [Section] 608(c) of the Act places limitations on overall campaign expenditures by candidates [seeking] election to federal office. [For Presidential candidates the ceiling is $10,000,000 in seeking nomination and $20,000,000 in the general election campaign; for House of Representatives candidates it is $70,000 for each campaign—primary and general; for candidates for Senator the ceiling depends on the size of the voting age population.]

No governmental interest that has been suggested is sufficient to justify [these restrictions] on the quantity of political expression. [The] interest in

e. $50,000 for Presidential or Vice Presidential candidates; $35,000 for Senate candidates; $25,000 for most candidates for the House of Representatives.

alleviating the corrupting influence of large contributions is served by the Act's contribution limitations and disclosure provisions rather than by § 608(c)'s campaign expenditure ceilings. [There] is no indication that the substantial criminal penalties for violating the contribution ceilings combined with the political repercussion of such violations will be insufficient to police the contribution provisions. Extensive reporting, auditing, and disclosure requirements applicable to both contributions and expenditures by political campaigns are designed to facilitate the detection of illegal contributions. * * *

The interest in equalizing the financial resources of candidates competing for federal office is no more convincing a justification for restricting the scope of federal election campaigns. Given the limitation on the size of outside contributions, the financial resources available to a candidate's campaign, like the number of volunteers recruited, will normally vary with the size and intensity of the candidate's support. There is nothing invidious, improper, or unhealthy in permitting such funds to be spent to carry the candidate's message to the electorate. Moreover, the equalization of permissible campaign expenditures might serve not to equalize the opportunities of all candidates but to handicap a candidate who lacked substantial name recognition or exposure of his views before the start of the campaign.

The campaign expenditure ceilings appear to be designed primarily to serve the governmental interests in reducing the allegedly skyrocketing costs of political campaigns. [But the] First Amendment denies government the power to determine that spending to promote one's political views is wasteful, excessive, or unwise. In the free society ordained by our Constitution it is not the government but the people individually as citizens and candidates and collectively as associations and political committees who must retain control over the quantity and range of debate on public issues in a political campaign.

For these reasons we hold that § 608(c) is constitutionally invalid. * * *

CHIEF JUSTICE BURGER, concurring in part and dissenting in part.

[I] agree fully with that part of the Court's opinion that holds unconstitutional the limitations the Act puts on campaign expenditures. [Yet] when it approves similarly stringent limitations on contributions, the Court ignores the reasons it finds so persuasive in the context of expenditures. For me contributions and expenditures are two sides of the same First Amendment coin.

[Limiting] contributions, as a practical matter, will limit expenditures and will put an effective ceiling on the amount of political activity and debate that the Government will permit to take place.[5]

The Court attempts to separate the two communicative aspects of political contributions—the "moral" support that the gift itself conveys, which the Court suggests is the same whether the gift is of $10 or $10,000,[6] and the fact that

5. The Court notes that 94.9% of the funds raised by congressional candidates in 1974 came in contributions of less than $1,000, n. 27, and suggests that the effect of the contribution limitations will be minimal. This logic ignores the disproportionate influence large contributions may have when they are made early in a campaign; "seed money" can be essential, and the inability to obtain it may effectively end some candidacies before they begin. Appellants have excerpted from the record data on nine campaigns to which large, initial contributions were critical. Campaigns such as these will be much harder, and perhaps impossible, to mount under the Act.

6. Whatever the effect of the limitation, it is clearly arbitrary—Congress has imposed the same ceiling on contributions to a New York or California senatorial campaign that it has put on House races in Alaska or Wyoming. Both the strength of support conveyed by the gift of $1,000 *and* the gift's potential for corruptly influencing the recipient will vary enormously from place to place. * * *

money translates into communication. The Court dismisses the effect of the limitations on the second aspect of contributions: "[T]he transformation of contributions into political debate involves speech by someone other than the contributor." On this premise—that contribution limitations restrict only the speech of "someone other than the contributor"—rests the Court's justification for treating contributions differently from expenditures. The premise is demonstrably flawed; the contribution limitations will, in specific instances, limit exactly the same political activity that the expenditure ceilings limit, and at least one of the "expenditure" limitations the Court finds objectionable operates precisely like the "contribution" limitations.[8]

The Court's attempt to distinguish the communication inherent in political *contributions* from the speech aspects of political *expenditures* simply will not wash. We do little but engage in word games unless we recognize that people—candidates and contributors—spend money on political activity because they wish to communicate ideas, and their constitutional interest in doing so is precisely the same whether they or someone else utter the words.

[T]he restrictions are hardly incidental in their effect upon particular campaigns. Judges are ill-equipped to gauge the precise impact of legislation, but a law that impinges upon First Amendment rights requires us to make the attempt. It is not simply speculation to think that the limitations on contributions will foreclose some candidacies.[9] The limitations will also alter the nature of some electoral contests drastically.[10]

[In] striking down the limitations on campaign expenditures, the Court relies in part on its conclusion that other means—namely, disclosure and contribution ceilings—will adequately serve the statute's aim. It is not clear why the same analysis is not also appropriate in weighing the need for contribution ceilings in addition to disclosure requirements. Congress may well be entitled to conclude that disclosure was a "partial measure," but I had not thought until today that Congress could enact its conclusions in the First Amendment area into laws immune from the most searching review by this Court. * * *[f]

JUSTICE WHITE, concurring in part and dissenting in part. * * *

I [agree] with the Court's judgment upholding the limitations on contributions. I dissent [from] the Court's view that the expenditure limitations [violate] the First Amendment. [This] case depends on whether the nonspeech interests of the Federal Government in regulating the use of money in political campaigns

8. The Court treats the Act's provisions limiting a candidate's spending from his *personal resources* as *expenditure* limits, as indeed the Act characterizes them, and holds them unconstitutional. As Mr. Justice Marshall points out, infra, by the Court's logic these provisions could as easily be treated as limits on *contributions,* since they limit what the candidate can give to his own campaign.

9. Candidates who must raise large initial contributions in order to appeal for more funds to a broader audience will be handicapped. See n. 5, supra. It is not enough to say that the contribution ceilings "merely require candidates [to] raise funds from a greater number of persons," where the limitations will effectively prevent candidates without substantial personal resources from doing just that.

10. Under the Court's holding, candidates with personal fortunes will be free to contribute to their own campaigns as much as they like, since the Court chooses to view the Act's provisions in this regard as unconstitutional "expenditure" limitations rather than "contribution" limitations. See n. 8, supra.

f. Blackmun, J., also dissented separately from that part of the Court's opinion upholding the Act's restrictions on campaign contributions, unpersuaded that "a principled constitutional distinction" could be made between the contribution and expenditure limitations involved.

are sufficiently urgent to justify the incidental effects that the limitations visit upon the First Amendment interests of candidates and their supporters.

[The Court] accepts the congressional judgment that the evils of unlimited contributions are sufficiently threatening to warrant restriction regardless of the impact of the limits on the contributor's opportunity for effective speech and in turn on the total volume of the candidate's political communications by reason of his inability to accept large sums from those willing to give.

The congressional judgment, which I would also accept, was that other steps must be taken to counter the corrosive effects of money in federal election campaigns. One of these steps is § 608(e), which [limits] what a contributor may independently spend in support or denigration of one running for federal office. Congress was plainly of the view that these expenditures also have corruptive potential; but the Court strikes down the provision, strangely enough claiming more insight as to what may improperly influence candidates than is possessed by the majority of Congress that passed this Bill and the President who signed it. Those supporting the Bill undeniably included many seasoned professionals who have been deeply involved in elective processes and who have viewed them at close range over many years.

It would make little sense to me, and apparently made none to Congress, to limit the amounts an individual may give to a candidate or spend with his approval but fail to limit the amounts that could be spent on his behalf. Yet the Court permits the former while striking down the latter limitation. [I] would take the word of those who know—that limiting independent expenditures is essential to prevent transparent and widespread evasion of the contribution limits. * * *

The Court also rejects Congress' judgment manifested in § 608(c) that the federal interest in limiting total campaign expenditures by individual candidates justifies the incidental effect on their opportunity for effective political speech. I disagree both with the Court's assessment of the impact on speech and with its narrow view of the values the limitations will serve.

[M]oney is not always equivalent to or used for speech, even in the context of political campaigns. [There are] many expensive campaign activities that are not themselves communicative or remotely related to speech. Furthermore, campaigns differ among themselves. Some seem to spend much less money than others and yet communicate as much or more than those supported by enormous bureaucracies with unlimited financing. The record before us no more supports the conclusion that the communicative efforts of congressional and Presidential candidates will be crippled by the expenditure limitations than it supports the contrary. The judgment of Congress was that reasonably effective campaigns could be conducted within the limits established by the Act and that the communicative efforts of these campaigns would not seriously suffer. In this posture of the case, there is no sound basis for invalidating the expenditure limitations, so long as the purposes they serve are legitimate and sufficiently substantial, which in my view they are.

[E]xpenditure ceilings reinforce the contribution limits and help eradicate the hazard of corruption. [Without] limits on total expenditures, campaign costs will inevitably and endlessly escalate. Pressure to raise funds will constantly build and with it the temptation to resort in "emergencies" to those sources of large sums, who, history shows, are sufficiently confident of not being caught to risk flouting contribution [limits.]

The ceiling on candidate expenditures represents the considered judgment of Congress that elections are to be decided among candidates none of whom has overpowering advantage by reason of a huge campaign war chest. At least so long as the ceiling placed upon the candidates is not plainly too low, elections are not to turn on the difference in the amounts of money that candidates have to spend. This seems an acceptable purpose and the means chosen a common sense way to achieve [it.]

I also disagree with the Court's judgment that § 608(a), which limits the amount of money that a candidate or his family may spend on his campaign, violates the Constitution. Although it is true that this provision does not promote any interest in preventing the corruption of candidates, the provision does, nevertheless, serve salutary purposes related to the integrity of federal campaigns. By limiting the importance of personal wealth, § 608(a) helps to assure that only individuals with a modicum of support from others will be viable candidates. This in turn would tend to discourage any notion that the outcome of elections is primarily a function of money. Similarly, § 608(a) tends to equalize access to the political arena, encouraging the less wealthy, unable to bankroll their own campaigns, to run for political office.[g]

Notes and Questions

1. *Expenditure limitations.* Is it "foreign" to the first amendment to curb the spending of the wealthy in an effort to preserve the integrity of the elections process? Would it have been "foreign" to first amendment doctrine to engage in some type of balancing? Does the Court's expenditure ruling denigrate the interest in equality? See, e.g., Tribe, *Constitutional Choices* 193–94 (1985); Nicholson, *Buckley v. Valeo: The Constitutionality of the Federal Election Campaign Act Amendments of 1974,* 1977 Wis.L.Rev. 323, 336; Wright, *Money and the Pollution of Politics: Is the First Amendment an Obstacle to Political Equality?,* 82 Colum.L.Rev. 609 (1982). Even if the concept of political equity is a "legitimizing myth," is *Buckley* flawed because it underestimates the necessity of promoting political leadership that is autonomous and independent of pluralistic forces? Is government autonomy necessary for minimally adequate regulation of the economy? See Blum, *The Divisible First Amendment: A Critical Functionalist Approach to Freedom of Speech and Electoral Campaign Spending,* 58 N.Y.U.L.Rev. 1273, 1369–78 (1983). Alternatively, would it be better to solve the wealth problem by redistribution (and control of corporate power), while holding fast to a strong liberty principle? See Baker, *Realizing Self-Realization: Corporate Political Expenditures and Redish's The Value of Free Speech,* 130 U.Pa.L. Rev. 646, 652 (1982); Baker, *Scope of the First Amendment Freedom of Speech,* 25 U.C.L.A.L.Rev. 964, 983–90 (1978).

g. Marshall, J., dissented from that part of the Court's opinion invalidating the limitation on the amount a candidate or his family may spend on his campaign. He considered "the interest in promoting the reality and appearance of equal access to the political arena" sufficient to justify the limitation: "[T]he wealthy candidate's immediate access to a substantial personal fortune may give him an initial advantage that his less wealthy opponent can never overcome. [With the option of large contributions removed by § 608(b)], the less wealthy candidate is without the means to match the large initial expenditures of money of which the wealthy candidate is capable. In short, the limitations on contributions put a premium on a candidate's personal wealth. "[Section 608(a) then] emerges not simply as a device to reduce the natural advantage of the wealthy candidate, but as a provision providing some symmetry to a regulatory scheme that otherwise enhances the natural advantage of the wealthy."

For background on the *Buckley* case, see Friendly & Elliot, *The Constitution: That Delicate Balance* 91–107 (1984).

2. To what extent are campaign finance laws likely to advance equality values?[h] Aren't they most likely to benefit incumbents? See Epstein, *Modern Republicanism—Or the Flight From Substance,* 97 Yale L.J. 1633, 1643–45 (1988); Macey, *The Missing Element in the Republican Revival,* 97 Yale L.J. 1673, 1680–81 (1988). Consider this hypothetical response: "The system has always been stacked in favor of incumbents. Campaign finance legislation might free incumbents from the need to rely on interest group funding and could improve not only the quality of representation, but also the substantive fairness of legislation." Is increased legislative autonomy desirable? Compare Sunstein, *Beyond the Republican Revival,* 97 Yale L.J. 1539 (1988) with Fitts, *Look Before You Leap,* 97 Yale L.J. 1651 (1988); Fitts, *The Vices of Virtue,* 136 U.Pa.L.Rev. 1567 (1988).

3. *Varying scrutiny.* (a) Did *Buckley* apply less exacting scrutiny to impairment of associational freedoms by contribution limits than to impairment of free expression by expenditure limits? Cf. 90 Harv.L.Rev. 178–79 (1976). "Granted that freedom of association is merely ancillary to speech, a means of amplifying and effectuating communication but logically secondary to speech," is this also "true of expenditures of money in aid of speech"? See Polsby, *Buckley v. Valeo: The Special Nature of Political Speech,* 1976 Sup.Ct.Rev. 1, 22. Can a lesser degree of scrutiny be justified for contributions? Or were the differing results based on the Court's perceiving a greater threat to first amendment interests in the expenditure limits and less risk of corruption and undue influence in unlimited independent expenditures? Cf. Nicholson, note 1 supra, at 340–45. Does the opinion indicate why greater deference was paid to congressional judgment on review of the contribution limits than on review of the expenditure limits? Cf. Note, 76 Colum.L.Rev. 852, 862 (1976). For a defense of strict scrutiny across the board, see BeVier, *Money and Politics: A Perspective on the First Amendment and Campaign Finance Reform,* 73 Calif.L. Rev. 1045 (1985).

(b) *The O'Brien analogy.* May the Court's rejection of the less-exacting *O'Brien* standard on the ground that the expenditure of money did not introduce a non-speech element fairly be criticized for asking the wrong question: whether "*pure speech* can be regulated where there is some incidental effect on *money,*" rather than whether "the use of *money* can be regulated, by analogy to such conduct as draft-card burning, where there is an undoubted incidental effect on *speech*"? See Wright, *Politics and the Constitution: Is Money Speech?,* 85 Yale L.J. 1001, 1007 (1976). But compare Balkin, *Some Realism About Pluralism: Legal Realist Approaches to the First Amendment,* 1990 Duke L.J. 375, 414: "I suspect that the slogan 'money is not speech' is attractive because it appeals to a certain humanistic vision—that there is something quite different between the situation of a lone individual expressing her views and the purchase of hired mouths using hired expressions created by hired minds to saturate the airwaves with ideological drivel. Yet in one sense, this humanistic vision really turns upon a set of unstated egalitarian assumptions about economic and social power. Certainly we would have no objection to a person with a speech impediment hiring someone to do her talking for her; that is because we think that, under

h. Consider Brest, *Further Beyond the Republican Revival,* 97 Yale L.J. 1623, 1627 (1988): " 'Those who are better off participate more, and by participating more they exercise more influence on government officials.' Unequal resources produce unequal influence in determining which issues get on the political [agenda]. Campaign finance regulations barely begin to remedy the systematic ways in which inequalities of wealth distort the political process."

these circumstances, it is fair for such a person to boost her communicative powers. Modern political campaigns seem a far cry from this example because of the massive amounts of economic power expended to get the message across. I think we should isolate the egalitarian assumptions implicit in the 'money is not speech' position and put them to their best use—the justification of campaign finance reforms on the ground that gross inequalities of economic power destroy the integrity of the political process.

"My conclusion, then, is that campaign finance reforms may be constitutional not because money is not speech, but because in a very important sense it is. The government is responsible for inequalities in access to the means of communication because it has created the system of property rights that makes such inequalities possible. Therefore, it is not only wrong but also incoherent for opponents of campaign finance reform to contend that the government should not regulate access to the political process. Government already regulates access to the political process—the first amendment simply demands that it do so fairly."

4. *Federal funding and expenditure limitations.* A separate section of the *Buckley* opinion seemed to approve expenditure limitations imposed upon candidates who accept federal funding: "[A]cceptance of federal funding entails voluntary acceptance of an expenditure ceiling." The existence of federal funding for a candidate has not, however, served to justify limitations on expenditures by groups who work on behalf of, but independently of, the candidate. FEC v. NATIONAL CONSERVATIVE POLITICAL ACTION COMMITTEE, 470 U.S. 480, 105 S.Ct. 1459, 84 L.Ed.2d 455 (1985), per REHNQUIST, J., invalidated a provision making it a political offense for such groups to expend more than $1000 to further the nomination or election of a candidate receiving federal financing. The Court argued that *Buckley* protected the freedom of association of "large numbers of individuals of modest means" to join together and amplify their voices.[i] The Court stressed that the case involved expenditures, not contributions within the meaning of *Buckley;* that the provision was not directed to the size of the contributions the organizations received, and was not confined to corporations.

In dissent, WHITE, J., noted his continuing objection to the distinction between contributions and expenditures, and Marshall, J., a new convert to that position, separately dissented on the same ground. Even assuming *Buckley* was correctly decided, White, J., argued that contributors to political committees were not engaging in speech to any greater extent than those who contribute directly to political campaigns: only the donee had changed. Moreover, he worried, as had Congress, that candidates would "go around hat in hand, begging for money from Washington-based special interest groups, political action committees whose sole purpose for existing is to seek a quid pro quo. [The] candidate may be forced to please the spenders rather than the voters, and the two groups are not identical."[j]

FIRST NAT. BANK v. BELLOTTI, 435 U.S. 765, 98 S.Ct. 1407, 55 L.Ed.2d 707 (1978), per POWELL, J., held invalid under the first and fourteenth amendments a Massachusetts criminal statute prohibiting banks or business corpora-

i. One defendant had received an average of $75 from 101,000 people during 1979–80; another, an average of $25 from approximately 100,000 people.

j. For discussion of the character evoked by the opinions of Rehnquist, J., and White, J., see Frug, *Argument as Character,* 40 Stan. L.Rev. 869, 896–921 (1988).

tions from making contributions or expenditures to influence "the vote on any question submitted to the voters, other than one materially affecting any of the property, business or assets of the corporation," defined to exclude from the exception questions "concerning the taxation of the income, property or transactions of individuals":

"The speech proposed by appellants is at the heart of the First Amendment's protection. [If] the speakers here were not corporations, no one would suggest that the state could silence their proposed speech. It is the type of speech indispensable to decisionmaking in a democracy, and this is no less true because the speech comes from a corporation rather than an individual. The inherent worth of the speech in terms of its capacity for informing the public does not depend upon the identity of its source, whether corporation, association, union or individual.

"The court below nevertheless held that corporate speech is protected by the First Amendment only when it pertains directly to the corporation's business interests. In deciding whether this novel and restrictive gloss on the First Amendment comports with the Constitution and the precedents of this Court, we need not survey the outer boundaries of the Amendment's protection of corporate speech, or address the abstract question whether corporations have the full measure of rights that individuals enjoy under the First Amendment.[13] The question in this case, simply put, is whether the corporate identity of the speaker deprives this proposed speech of what otherwise would be its clear entitlement to protection. We turn now to that question.

"[A]ppellee suggests that First Amendment rights generally have been afforded only to corporations engaged in the communications business or through which individuals express themselves. [But] the Court's decisions involving corporations in the business of communication or entertainment are based not only on the role of the First Amendment in fostering individual self-expression but also on its role in affording the public access to discussion, debate, and the dissemination of information and ideas. See *Red Lion*; *Stanley v. Georgia*; *Time, Inc. v. Hill.*

"[We] find no support in the First or Fourteenth Amendments, or in the decisions of this Court, for the proposition that speech that otherwise would be within the protection of the First Amendment loses that protection simply because its source is a corporation that cannot prove, to the satisfaction of a court, a material effect on its business or property. The 'materially affecting' requirement is not an identification of the boundaries of corporate speech etched by the Constitution itself. Rather, it amounts to an impermissible legislative prohibition of speech based on the identity of the interests that spokesmen may represent in public debate over controversial issues and a requirement that the speaker have a sufficiently great interest in the subject to justify communication.

13. Nor is there any occasion to consider in this case whether, under different circumstances, a justification for a restriction on speech that would be inadequate as applied to individuals might suffice to sustain the same restriction as applied to corporations, unions, or like entities.

[*Consolidated Edison Co. v. Public Serv. Comm'n,* 447 U.S. 530, 100 S.Ct. 2326, 65 L.Ed. 2d 319 (1980) held that neither Consolidated Edison's corporate status, nor its status as a government regulated monopoly precluded it from asserting a first amendment right to insert controversial messages in its billing envelopes. Citing *Bellotti,* the Court stressed that the worth of speech does not depend upon its source.]

"[In] the realm of protected speech, the legislature is constitutionally disqualified from dictating the subjects about which persons may speak and the speakers who may address a public issue. *Chicago Police Dep't v. Mosley.* If a legislature may direct business corporations to 'stick to business,' it also may limit other corporations—religious, charitable, or civic—to their respective 'business' when addressing the public. Such power in government to channel the expression of views is unacceptable under the First Amendment. Especially where, as here, the legislature's suppression of speech suggests an attempt to give one side of a debatable public question an advantage in expressing its views to the people, the First Amendment is plainly offended. * * *

"The constitutionality of § 8's prohibition of the 'exposition of ideas' by corporations turns on whether it can survive the exacting scrutiny necessitated by a state-imposed restriction of freedom of speech. Especially where, as here, a prohibition is directed at speech itself,[23] and the speech is intimately related to the process of governing, 'the State may prevail only upon showing a subordinating interest which is compelling.' *Bates v. Little Rock,* 361 U.S. 516, 80 S.Ct. 412, 4 L.Ed.2d 480 (1960).

"Preserving the integrity of the electoral process, preventing corruption, and 'sustain[ing] the active, alert responsibility of the individual citizen in a democracy for the wise conduct of government' are interests of the highest importance. *Buckley.* Preservation of the individual citizen's confidence in government is equally important.

"[Appellee's arguments] that these interests are endangered by corporate participation in discussion of a referendum [issue] hinge upon the assumption that such participation would exert an undue influence on the outcome of a referendum vote, and—in the end—destroy the confidence of the people in the democratic process and the integrity of government. According to appellee, corporations are wealthy and powerful and their views may drown out other points of view. If appellee's arguments were supported by record or legislative findings that corporate advocacy threatened imminently to undermine democratic processes, thereby denigrating rather than serving First Amendment interests,[a] these arguments would merit our consideration.[b] Cf. *Red Lion.* But there has been no showing that the relative voice of corporations has been overwhelming or even significant in influencing referenda in Massachusetts, or that there has been any threat to the confidence of the citizenry in government.

23. It is too late to suggest "that the dependence of a communication on the expenditure of money operates itself to introduce a nonspeech element or to reduce the exacting scrutiny required by the First Amendment." *Buckley.* Furthermore, § 8 is an "attempt directly to control speech [rather than] to protect, from an evil shown to be grave, some interest clearly within the sphere of governmental concern." *Speiser.* Compare *O'Brien.*

a. Legislatures wishing to support such findings need not look far. See, e.g., Lowenstein, *Campaign Spending and Ballot Propositions: Recent Experience, Public Choice Theory and the First Amendment,* 29 U.C.L.A. L.Rev. 505 (1982); Schockley, *Direct Democracy, Campaign Finance, and the Courts: Can Corruption, Undue Influence, and Declining Voter Confidence Be Found?,* 39 U.Miami L.Rev. 377 (1985). For additional information and commentary, see Cox, *Constitutional Issues in the Regulation of the Financing of Election Campaigns,* 31 Clev.St.L.Rev. 395 (1982); Symposium, *Political Action Committees and Campaign Finance,* 22 Ariz.L.Rev. 351 (1981); Symposium, *Campaign Finance Reform,* 10 Hast.Con.L.Q. 463 (1983).

b. "[I]f *Tornillo* and *Buckley* slammed the door on excessive power arguments, [*Bellotti*] opened a window. [The] Court did not pause, however, to explain why factors found in *Buckley* and *Tornillo* to be foreign to the first amendment would have 'merited consideration' in *Bellotti.*" Shiffrin, *Government Speech,* 27 U.C.L.A. L.Rev. 565, 598–99 (1980).

"[Referenda] are held on issues, not candidates for public office. The risk of corruption perceived in cases involving candidate elections simply is not present [c] in a popular vote on a public issue.[26] To be sure, corporate advertising may influence the outcome of the vote; this would be its purpose. But the fact that advocacy may persuade the electorate is hardly a reason to suppress [it.] We noted only recently that 'the concept that government may restrict the speech of some elements of our society in order to enhance the relative voice of others is wholly foreign to the First Amendment.' *Buckley.* Moreover, the people in our democracy are entrusted with the responsibility for judging and evaluating the relative merits of conflicting arguments.[31] They may consider, in making their judgment, the source and credibility of the advocate. But if there be any danger that the people cannot evaluate the information and arguments advanced by appellants, it is a danger contemplated by the Framers of the First Amendment."

The Court rejected the argument that § 8 was justified by the interest in preventing use of corporate resources to advance views with which some shareholders disagreed. In this respect the statute was under-inclusive in not forbidding "the expenditure of corporate funds on any public issue until it becomes the subject of a referendum, though the displeasure of disapproving shareholders is unlikely to be any less. The fact that a particular kind of ballot question has been singled out for special treatment undermines the likelihood of a genuine state interest in protecting shareholders. It suggests instead that the legislature may have been concerned with silencing corporations on a particular subject. Indeed, appellee has conceded that 'the legislative and judicial history of the statute indicates [that] the second crime was "tailor-made" to prohibit corporate campaign contributions to oppose a graduated income tax amendment.'

"[The] over-inclusiveness of the statute is demonstrated by the fact that § 8 would prohibit a corporation from supporting or opposing a referendum proposal even if its shareholders unanimously authorized the contribution or expenditure. Ultimately shareholders may decide, through the procedures of corporate democ-

c. *Citizens Against Rent Control v. Berkeley,* 454 U.S. 290, 102 S.Ct. 434, 70 L.Ed.2d 492 (1981) (White, J., dissenting) struck down a city ordinance placing a $250 limitation on contributions to committees formed to support or oppose ballot measures submitted to popular vote. The Court, per Burger, C.J., observed that the case did not involve an ordinance confined to contributions by corporations and that the case involved ballot measures, not candidate elections. Rehnquist, J., concurring noted the presence of a corporate petitioner, but emphasized that the ordinance was not aimed only at corporations. In separate concurrences Marshall, J., and Blackmun, J., joined by O'Connor, J., noted that the record did not contain the kind of evidence that would warrant consideration under *Bellotti.* For commentary, see Tribe, Constitutional Choices 195–97 (1985); Lowenstein, fn. a supra, at 584–602; Nicholson, *The Constitutionality of Contribution Limitations in Ballot Measure Elections,* 9 Ecol.L.Q. 683 (1981).

26. [Appellants] do not challenge the constitutionality of laws prohibiting or limiting corporate contributions to political candidates or committees, or other means of influencing candidate elections. About half of these laws, including the Federal Corrupt Practices Act, by their terms do not apply to referendum votes. [The] overriding concern behind the enactment of statutes such as the Federal Corrupt Practices Act was the problem of corruption of elected representatives through the creation of political debts. [The] case before us presents no comparable problem, and our consideration of a corporation's right to speak on issues of general public interest implies no comparable right in the quite different context of participation in a political campaign for election to public office. Congress might well be able to demonstrate the existence of a danger of real or apparent corruption in independent expenditures by corporations to influence candidate elections. Cf. *Buckley.*

31. Government is forbidden to assume the task of ultimate judgment, lest the people lose their ability to govern themselves. The First Amendment rejects the "highly paternalistic" approach of statutes like § 8 which restrict what the people may hear. *Virginia Pharmacy.*

racy, whether their corporation should engage in debate on public issues.[34]"

BURGER, C.J., who joined the Court's opinion, concurred: "A disquieting aspect of Massachusetts' position is that it may carry the risk of impinging on the First Amendment rights of those who employ the corporate form—as most do—to carry on the business of mass communications, particularly the large media conglomerates. This is so because of the difficulty, and perhaps impossibility, of distinguishing, either as a matter of fact or constitutional law, media corporations from corporations such as appellants.

"Making traditional use of the corporate form, some media enterprises have amassed vast wealth and power and conduct many activities, some directly related—and some not—to their publishing and broadcasting activities. See *Miami Herald.* Today, a corporation might own the dominant newspaper in one or more large metropolitan centers, television and radio stations in those same centers and others, a newspaper chain, news magazines with nationwide circulation, national or worldwide wire news services, and substantial interests in book publishing and distribution enterprises. Corporate ownership may extend, vertically, to pulp mills and pulp timberlands to insure an adequate, continuing supply of newsprint and to trucking and steamship lines for the purpose of transporting the newsprint to the presses. Such activities would be logical economic auxiliaries to a publishing conglomerate. Ownership also may extend beyond to business activities unrelated to the task of publishing newspapers and magazines or broadcasting radio and television programs. Obviously, such far-reaching ownership would not be possible without the state-provided corporate form and its 'special rules relating to such matters as limited liability, perpetual life, and the accumulation, distribution, and taxation of assets'. (White, J., dissenting).

"In terms of 'unfair advantage in the political process' and 'corporate domination of the electoral process,' it could be argued that such media conglomerates as I describe pose a much more realistic threat to valid interests than do appellants and similar entities not regularly concerned with shaping popular opinion on public issues. See *Miami Herald.*

34. [White, J.'s] repeatedly expressed concern for corporate shareholders who may be "coerced" into supporting "causes with which they disagree" apparently is not shared by appellants' shareholders. Not a single shareholder has joined appellee in defending the Massachusetts statute, or so far as the record shows, has interposed any objection to the right asserted by the corporations to make the proscribed expenditures.

The dissent of Mr. Justice White relies heavily on *Abood v. Detroit Bd. of Educ.* and *International Assn. of Machinists v. Street,* [Sec. 9, II supra]. These decisions involved the First Amendment rights of employees in closed or agency shops not to be compelled, as a condition of employment, to support with financial contributions the political activities of other union members with which the dissenters disagreed.

Street and *Abood* are irrelevant to the question presented in this case. In those cases employees were required, either by state law or by agreement between the employer and the union, to pay dues or a "service fee" to the exclusive bargaining representative. To the extent that these funds were used by the union in furtherance of political goals, unrelated to collective bargaining, they were held to be unconstitutional because they compelled the dissenting union member "to furnish contributions of money for the propagation of opinions which he disbelieves."

The critical distinction here is that no shareholder has been "compelled" to contribute anything. Apart from the fact, noted by the dissent, that compulsion by the State is wholly absent, the [shareholder] invests in a corporation of his own volition and is [free to withdraw his investment at any time and for any reason.] A more relevant analogy, therefore, is to the situation where an employee voluntarily joins a union, or an individual voluntarily joins an association, and later finds himself in disagreement with its stance on a political issue. * * *

"In terms of Massachusetts' other concern, the interests of minority shareholders, I perceive no basis for saying that the managers and directors of the media conglomerates are more or less sensitive to the views and desires of minority shareholders than are corporate officers generally. Nor can it be said, even if relevant to First Amendment analysis—which it is not—that the former are more virtuous, wise, or restrained in the exercise of corporate power than are the latter. Thus, no factual distinction has been identified as yet that would justify government restraints on the right of appellants to express their views without, at the same time, opening the door to similar restraints on media conglomerates with their vastly greater influence."

WHITE, J., joined by Brennan and Marshall, JJ., dissented, stressing two arguments: (1) The statute was designed to protect first amendment rights by "preventing institutions which have been permitted to amass wealth as a result of special advantages extended by the State for certain economic purposes from using that wealth to acquire an unfair advantage in the political process, especially where, as here, the issue involved has no material connection with the business of the corporation. The State need not permit its own creation to consume it. Massachusetts could permissibly conclude that not to impose limits upon the political activities of corporations would have placed it in a position of departing from neutrality and indirectly assisting the propagation of corporate views because of the advantages its laws give to the corporate acquisition of funds to finance such activities. Such expenditures may be viewed as seriously threatening the role of the First Amendment as a guarantor of a free marketplace of ideas.

"[This] Nation has for many years recognized the need for measures designed to prevent corporate domination of the political process. The Corrupt Practices Act, first enacted in 1907, has consistently barred corporate contributions in connection with federal elections. This Court has repeatedly recognized that one of the principal purposes of this prohibition is 'to avoid the deleterious influences on federal elections resulting from the use of money by those who exercise control over large aggregations of capital.' *United States v. United Auto. Workers,* 352 U.S. 567, 585, 77 S.Ct. 529, 538, 1 L.Ed.2d 563 (1957). Although this Court has never adjudicated the constitutionality of the Act, there is no suggestion in its cases construing it that this purpose is in any sense illegitimate or deserving of other than the utmost respect; indeed, the thrust of its opinions, until today, has been to the contrary."

(2) The Massachusetts law advances the "overriding interest [of] assuring that shareholders are not compelled to support and financially further beliefs with which they disagree, where [the issue] does not materially affect the business, property, or other affairs of the corporation.[12] [The law] protects the very freedoms that this Court has held to be guaranteed by the First Amendment. [Last Term, in *Abood,* we] held that, a State may not, even indirectly, require an individual to contribute to the support of an ideological cause he may oppose as a condition of [employment].

"Presumably, unlike [*Street* and *Abood,*] the use of funds invested by shareholders with opposing views by Massachusetts corporations in connection with referenda or elections would not constitute state action and, consequently, not violate the First Amendment. Until now, however, the States have always

12. This, of course, is an interest that was not present in *Buckley,* and would not justify limitations upon the activities of associations, corporate or otherwise, formed for the express purpose of advancing a political or social cause.

been free to adopt measures designed to further rights protected by the Constitution even when not compelled to do so."

REHNQUIST, J., dissenting, argued that "the Fourteenth Amendment does not require a State to endow a business corporation with the power of political speech": "A State grants to a business corporation the blessings of potentially perpetual life and limited liability to enhance its efficiency as an economic entity. It might reasonably be concluded that those properties, so beneficial in the economic sphere, pose special dangers in the political sphere. [T]he States might reasonably fear that the corporation would use its economic power to obtain further benefits beyond those already bestowed. I would think that any particular form of organization upon which the State confers special privileges or immunities different from those of natural persons would be subject to like regulation, whether the organization is a labor union, a partnership, a trade association, or a corporation." [d]

Notes and Questions

1. *Protecting the privileged.* (a) Consider Tushnet, *An Essay on Rights,* 62 Tex.L.Rev. 1363, 1387 (1984): "The first amendment has replaced the due process clause as the primary guarantor of the privileged. Indeed, it protects the privileged more perniciously than the due process clause ever did. Even in its heyday the due process clause stood in the way only of specific legislation designed to reduce the benefits of privilege. Today, in contrast, the first amendment stands as a general obstruction to all progressive legislative efforts. To protect their positions of privilege, the wealthy can make prudent investments either in political action or, more conventionally, in factories or stocks. But since the demise of substantive due process, their investments in factories and stocks can be regulated by legislatures. Under *Buckley* and *Bellotti,* however, their investments in politics—or politicians—cannot be regulated significantly. Needless to say, careful investment in politics may prevent effective regulation of traditional investments." See also Tushnet, *Corporations and Free Speech* in The Politics of Law 253 (Kairys ed. 1982).[e]

Compare Levinson, *Book Review,* 83 Mich.L.Rev. 939, 945 (1985): "Overtly, justifying restriction of campaign spending by reference to the idea of fair access to the public forum may seem content neutral. However, it is worth considering to what extent we in fact support such restrictions because of tacit assumptions about the contents of the views held by the rich, who would obviously feel most of the burden of the restrictions. If both political views and the propensity to spend money on politics were distributed randomly among the entire populace, it is hard to see why anyone would be very excited about the whole issue of campaign finance."

Does Levinson's observation shortchange participatory values? Consider Sunstein, *Beyond the Republican Revival,* 97 Yale L.J. 1539, 1577 (1988): "[R]epublican understandings would point toward large reforms of the electoral

d. Rehnquist, J., suggested that when the state creates a corporation such as a newspaper, "it necessarily assumes that the corporation is entitled to the liberty of the press essential to the conduct of its business." But a newspaper has "no greater right than any other corporation" to contribute money to political campaigns although its right to endorse a candidate in its editorial columns would be fully protected.

e. For discussion on a broad range of issues concerning the relationship between speech values and property values in Burger Court decisions, see Dorsen & Gara, *Free Speech, Property, and the Burger Court: Old Values, New Balances,* 1982 Sup.Ct.Rev. 195.

process in an effort to improve political deliberation and to promote political equality and citizenship."

(b) Colorado made it a felony to pay persons to circulate initiative or referendum petitions. The purposes of the provision were to assure that a ballot measure had a sufficiently broad base of popular support to warrant its placement on the ballot and to eliminate an incentive to produce fraudulent signatures. Constitutional? See *Meyer v. Grant,* 486 U.S. 414, 108 S.Ct. 1886, 100 L.Ed.2d 425 (1988) (invalidating statute). For criticism, see Lowenstein & Stern, *The First Amendment and Paid Initiative Petition Circulators: A Dissenting View and a Proposal,* 17 Hastings Con.L.Q. 175 (1989).

2. *Distinguishing media corporations.* Consider Nicholson, *The Constitutionality of the Federal Restrictions on Corporate and Union Campaign Contributions and Expenditures,* 65 Corn.L.Rev. 945, 959 (1980): "A solution may be to focus on the distinction between media activities and other activities. A diversified corporation, partially involved in the media, would be entitled to full first amendment protection for its media-related operations. Under this approach, a newspaper would not lose its first amendment rights because it purchased a pulp mill, but it could not extend these rights to its pulp mill operations. An oil company that purchased a newspaper would not gain first amendment rights for its oil operations, but it would be able to assert these first amendment rights in the operation of its newspaper. The problem is not, to paraphrase Chief Justice Burger, the impracticability of making a distinction, but rather the difficulty of finding a theory that will justify a distinction."

Can self-expression serve as a distinguishing factor? See id. at 959–60. Is there more freedom "to choose and create the content of the delivered speech in the communications industry than in other industries"? Does the communication industry "display less allegiance to the profit motive than other industries"? Does it matter that the communications industry's product is speech? Can a fourth estate theory distinguish the press? On that premise, is there no reason to expand the definition of the press to include business corporations? See generally Baker, *Human Liberty and Freedom of Speech,* Chs. 10, 11 (1989); Baker, *Commercial Speech: A Problem in the Theory of Freedom,* 62 Iowa L.Rev. 1, 25–40 (1976); Baker, *Press Rights and Government Power to Structure the Press,* 34 U.Miami L.Rev. 819, 822–36 (1980).

3. *Protecting shareholders.* After *Bellotti,* could government "authorize management to make some kinds of corporate speech, such as commercial speech, but not others, such as political or noncommercial speech, without the approval or express consent of stockholders"? See generally Brudney, *Business Corporations and Stockholders' Rights Under the First Amendment,* 91 Yale L.J. 235 (1981).

4. *Protecting associational rights.* Should the Court have considered the possibly "stronger argument: corporate political expression should be protected as the speech and associational activity of the individual owners"? Cf. Note, 92 Harv.L.Rev. 163, 165–66 (1978). Does this argument slight the extent to which the state has altered political influence by creating corporations and conferring advantages upon them? See Patton & Bartlett, *Corporate "Persons" and Freedom of Speech: The Political Impact of Legal Mythology,* 1981 Wis.L.Rev. 494. Does the association argument also assume too much about the connection between the owners' views and the corporation's speech? See Baker, *Commercial Speech,* note 2 supra and Brudney note 3 supra.

5. *Protecting listeners.* Is *Bellotti* justifiable because of listeners' rights? See Redish, *Self-Realization, Democracy, and Freedom of Expression: A Reply to Professor Baker,* 130 U.Pa.L.Rev. 678–79 (1982). But see Note, *Statutory Limitations on Corporate Spending in Ballot Measure Campaigns: The Case for Constitutionality,* 36 Hast.L.J. 433 (1985) (legal and market limitations on corporate speech inherently negate its value for listeners). Reconsider the arguments for and against the marketplace of ideas argument, Sec. 1, I supra.

6. *Aftermath of fn. 26.* 2 U.S.C.A. § 441(b) prohibits corporations or unions from making contributions or expenditures in connection with federal elections, but allows corporations and unions to establish and pay the expenses of segregated funds to be used for political purposes during federal elections. It prohibits corporations from soliciting contributions from persons other than its "stockholders and their families and its executive or administrative personnel and their families." In lieu of shareholders, corporations without capital stock are permitted to solicit contributions for such a fund from their "members." FEC v. NATIONAL RIGHT TO WORK COMMITTEE, 459 U.S. 197, 103 S.Ct. 552, 74 L.Ed.2d 364 (1982), per REHNQUIST, J., characterized these provisions as sufficiently tailored to prevent corruption or its appearance and to protect corporate contributors as to negate any judgment that restriction on associational interests was "undue." The National Right to Work Committee is an advocacy group organized as a nonprofit corporation without capital stock. It conceded that it was required to set up a segregated fund under § 441(b) but argued that it was entitled to solicit contributions from anyone that had previously responded to any of its prior mass mailings. The Court unanimously held that this conception of membership would render the statutory corporation "meaningless." Without requiring any evidentiary showing, the Court stated that the interest in avoiding corruption or its appearance justified "treating unions, corporations, and similar organizations differently from individuals."

FEC v. National Conservative Political Action Comm., p. 789 supra, per REHNQUIST, J., characterized *National Right to Work Comm.* as proceeding from the premise that "in return for the special advantages that the State confers on the corporate form, individuals acting jointly through corporations forgo some of the rights they have as individuals." But, citing *Bellotti's* fn. 26, he suggested that the question of whether a corporation could constitutionally be restricted in making independent expenditures to influence elections for public office was still open. Should advocacy groups organized in corporate form be treated like business corporations?

Michigan law prohibits corporations, profit or nonprofit, from making contributions to candidates or independent expenditures on behalf of or opposed to candidates. The law entitles such corporations, however, to solicit contributions for allowable expenditures from a segregated fund. The Michigan State Chamber of Commerce, a nonprofit corporation with more than 8,000 members, (three quarters of whom are profit corporations) challenged the prohibition on independent expenditures. It sought to place a newspaper advertisement in support of a Congressional candidate and argued that Michigan's prohibition of such corporate ads was unconstitutional.

AUSTIN v. MICHIGAN STATE CHAMBER OF COMMERCE, 494 U.S. 652, 110 S.Ct. 1391, 108 L.Ed.2d 652 (1990), per MARSHALL, J., upheld the scheme as applied to the Chamber of Commerce and its proposed advertisement: "[T]he political advantage of corporations is unfair because '[t]he resources in the treasury of a business corporation * * * are not an indication of popular support for the corporation's political ideas. They reflect instead the economically motivated decisions of investors and customers. The availability of these resources may make a corporation a formidable political presence, even though the power of the corporation may be no reflection of the power of its ideas.' *FEC v. Massachusett's Citizens for Life, Inc.,* 479 U.S. 238, 107 S.Ct. 616, 93 L.Ed.2d 539 (1986). [MCFL]

* * *

"The Chamber argues that this concern about corporate domination of the political process is insufficient to justify restrictions on independent expenditures. Although this Court has distinguished these expenditures from direct contributions in the context of federal laws regulating individual donors, it has also recognized that a legislature might demonstrate a danger of real or apparent corruption posed by such expenditures when made by corporations to influence candidate elections, *Bellotti,* n. 26. Regardless of whether this danger of 'financial *quid pro quo*' corruption may be sufficient to justify a restriction on independent expenditures, Michigan's regulation aims at a different type of corruption in the political arena: the corrosive and distorting effects of immense aggregations of wealth that are accumulated with the help of the corporate form and that have little or no correlation to the public's support for the corporation's political ideas. The Act does not attempt 'to equalize the relative influence of speakers on elections'; rather, it ensures that expenditures reflect actual public support for the political ideas espoused by corporations. We emphasize that the mere fact that corporations may accumulate large amounts of wealth is not the justification for [the statute]; rather, the unique state-conferred corporate structure that facilitates the amassing of large treasuries warrants the limit on independent expenditures. Corporate wealth can unfairly influence elections when it is deployed in the form of independent expenditures, just as it can when it assumes the guise of political contributions. We therefore hold that the State has articulated a sufficiently compelling rationale to support its restriction on independent expenditures by corporations.

"We next turn to the question whether the Act is sufficiently narrowly tailored to achieve its goal. We find that the Act is precisely targeted to eliminate the distortion caused by corporate spending while also allowing corporations to express their political views. [T]he Act does not impose an *absolute* ban on all forms of corporate political spending but permits corporations to make independent political expenditures through separate segregated funds. Because persons contributing to such funds understand that their money will be used solely for political purposes, the speech generated accurately reflects contributors' support for the corporation's political views.

"The Chamber argues that [the statute] is substantially overinclusive, because it includes within its scope closely held corporations that do not possess vast reservoirs of capital. [Although] some closely held corporations, just as some publicly held ones, may not have accumulated significant amounts of wealth, they receive from the State the special benefits conferred by the corporate structure and present the potential for distorting the political process. This potential for distortion justifies § 54(1)'s general applicability to all corporations. The section therefore is not substantially overbroad.

"The Chamber contends that even if the Campaign Finance Act is constitutional with respect to for-profit corporations, it nonetheless cannot be applied to a nonprofit ideological corporation like a chamber of commerce. [The Chamber relied on *MCFL,* supra, per Brennan, J., which held that 2 U.S.C. § 441b prohibiting corporations from using their treasury funds for the purpose of influencing any election for public office was unconstitutional as applied to the expenditures of a nonprofit, nonstock corporation. Specifically, MCFL an anti-abortion organization had printed and distributed some 100,000 "newsletters" advocating the election of a number of candidates. Rehnquist, C.J., joined by White, Blackmun, and Stevens, JJ., dissenting, argued that organizations opting for a corporate form could be barred from using treasury funds for election purposes.] [a] In *MCFL,* we held that the nonprofit organization there had 'features more akin to voluntary political associations than business firms, and therefore should not have to bear burdens on independent spending solely because of [its] incorporated status.' In reaching that conclusion, we enumerated three characteristics of the corporation that were 'essential' to our holding. Because the Chamber does not share these crucial features, the Constitution does not require that it be exempted from the generally applicable provisions of [the statute].

"The first characteristic of Massachusetts Citizens for Life, Inc., that distinguished it from ordinary business corporations was that the organization 'was formed for the express purpose of promoting political ideas, and cannot engage in business activities.' [*MCFL* 's] narrow political focus thus 'ensure[d] that [its] political resources reflect[ed] political support.'

"In contrast, the Chamber's bylaws set forth more varied purposes, several of which are not inherently political. For instance, the Chamber compiles and disseminates information relating to social, civic, and economic conditions, trains and educates its members, and promotes ethical business practices. Unlike *MCFL*'s, the Chamber's educational activities are not expressly tied to political goals; many of its seminars, conventions, and publications are politically neutral and focus on business and economic issues. The Chamber's President and Chief Executive Officer stated that one of the corporation's main purposes is to provide 'service to [its] membership that includes everything from group insurance to educational seminars, and * * * litigation activities on behalf of the business community.' The Chamber's nonpolitical activities therefore suffice to distinguish it from *MCFL* in the context of this characteristic.

"We described the second feature of *MCFL* as the absence of 'shareholders or other persons affiliated so as to have a claim on its assets or earnings. This ensures that persons connected with the organization will have no economic disincentive for disassociating with it if they disagree with its political activity.' Although the Chamber also lacks shareholders, many of its members may be similarly reluctant to withdraw as members even if they disagree with the Chamber's political expression, because they wish to benefit from the Chamber's nonpolitical programs and to establish contacts with other members of the business community. The Chamber's political agenda is sufficiently distinct from its educational and outreach programs that members who disagree with the former may continue to pay dues to participate in the latter. * * * [2]

a. For commentary on *MCFL,* see Seidman, *Reflections on Context and the Constitution,* 73 Minn.L.Rev. 73, 80–84 (1988).

2. A requirement that the Chamber disclose the nature and extent of its political activities, see *post* (Kennedy, J., dissenting), would not eliminate the possible distortion of the political process inherent in independent expenditures from general corporate funds. Given the significant incentive for members to continue their financial support for the Chamber in spite of their disagreement with its political agenda, disclosure will not ensure that the funds in the Chamber's treasury correspond to members' support for its ideas.

"The final characteristic upon which we relied in *MCFL* was the organization's independence from the influence of business corporations. On this score, the Chamber differs most greatly from the Massachusetts organization. *MCFL* was not established by, and had a policy of not accepting contributions from, business corporations. Thus it could not 'serv[e] as [a] condui[t] for the type of direct spending that creates a threat to the political marketplace.' In striking contrast, more than three-quarters of the Chamber's members are business corporations, whose political contributions and expenditures can constitutionally be regulated by the State. As we read the Act, a corporation's payments into the Chamber's general treasury would not be considered payments to influence an election, so they would not be 'contributions' or 'expenditures' and would not be subject to the Act's limitations. Business corporations therefore could circumvent the Act's restrictions by funneling money through the Chamber's general treasury.[3] Because the Chamber accepts money from for-profit corporations, it could, absent application of § 54(1), serve as a conduit for corporate political spending. In sum, the Chamber does not possess the features that would compel the State to exempt it from restrictions on independent political expenditures.

"The Chamber also attacks § 54(1) as underinclusive because it does not regulate the independent expenditures of unincorporated labor unions.[4] Whereas unincorporated unions, and indeed individuals, may be able to amass large treasuries, they do so without the significant state-conferred advantages of the corporate structure; corporations are 'by far the most prominent example of entities that enjoy legal advantages enhancing their ability to accumulate wealth.' The desire to counterbalance those advantages unique to the corporate form is the State's compelling interest in this case; thus, excluding from the statute's coverage unincorporated entities that also have the capacity to accumulate wealth 'does not undermine its justification for regulating corporations.'

"Moreover, labor unions differ from corporations in that union members who disagree with a union's political activities need not give up full membership in the organization to avoid supporting its political activities. [As] a result, the funds available for a union's political activities more accurately reflects members' support for the organization's political views than does a corporation's general treasury. * * *

"Because we hold that [Michigan's statute] does not violate the First Amendment, we must address the Chamber's contention that the provision infringes its rights under the Fourteenth Amendment. The Chamber argues that the statute treats similarly situated entities unequally. Specifically, it contends that the State should also restrict the independent expenditures of [corporations] engaged in the media business. * * * [5]

"Although all corporations enjoy the same state-conferred benefits inherent in the corporate form, media corporations differ significantly from other corporations in that their resources are devoted to the collection of information and its dissemination to the public. We have consistently recognized the unique role

3. A nonprofit corporation's segregated fund, on the other hand, apparently cannot receive contributions from corporations. * * *

4. The Federal Election Campaign Act restricts the independent expenditures of labor organizations as well as those of corporations. 2 U.S.C. § 441b(a).

5. The Federal Election Campaign Act contains a similar exemption that excludes from the definition of expenditure "any news story, commentary, or editorial distributed through the facilities of any broadcasting station, newspaper, magazine, or other periodical publication, unless such facilities are owned or controlled by any political party, political committee, or candidate." 2 U.S.C. § 431(9)(B)(i).

that the press plays in 'informing and educating the public, offering criticism, and providing a forum for discussion and debate.' *Bellotti.* See also *Mills v. Alabama* ('[T]he press serves and was designed to serve as a powerful antidote to any abuses of power by governmental officials and as a constitutionally chosen means for keeping officials elected by the people responsible to all the people whom they were selected to serve'). [The] media exception ensures that the Act does not hinder or prevent the institutional press from reporting on and publishing editorials about newsworthy events. Cf. 15 U.S.C. §§ 1801–1804 (enacting a limited exemption from the antitrust laws for newspapers in part because of the recognition of the special role of the press). A valid distinction thus exists between corporations that are part of the media industry and other corporations that are not involved in the regular business of imparting news to the public. Although the press' unique societal role may not entitle the press to greater protection under the Constitution, it does provide a compelling reason for the State to exempt media corporations from the scope of political expenditure limitations. We therefore hold that the Act does not violate the Equal Protection Clause.

"Michigan identified as a serious danger the significant possibility that corporate political expenditures will undermine the integrity of the political process, and it has implemented a narrowly tailored solution to that problem. By requiring corporations to make all independent political expenditures through a separate fund made up of money solicited expressly for political purposes, the Michigan Campaign Finance Act reduces the threat that huge corporate treasuries amassed with the aid of favorable state laws will be used to influence unfairly the outcome of elections. The Michigan Chamber of Commerce does not exhibit the characteristics identified in *MCFL* that would require the State to exempt it from generally applicable restrictions on independent corporate expenditures."

BRENNAN, J., joined the Court's opinion, but referring to himself as "one of the 'Orwellian' 'censors' derided by the dissents and as the author of [*MCFL*]," also concurred to express his views: "The Michigan law at issue is not an across-the-board prohibition on political participation by corporations or even a complete ban on corporate political expenditures. Rather, the statute merely requires those corporations wishing to make independent expenditures in support of candidates to do so through segregated funds or political action committees (PACs) rather than directly from their corporate treasuries. * * *

"In evaluating the First Amendment challenge in *MCFL* we 'acknowledge[d] the legitimacy of Congress' concern that organizations that amass great wealth in the economic marketplace not gain unfair advantage in the political marketplace.' Specifically, we noted that '*[d]irect corporate spending* on political activity raises the prospect that resources amassed in the economic marketplace may be used to provide an unfair advantage in the political marketplace,' because '[t]he resources in the treasury of a business corporation * * * are not an indication of popular support for the corporation's political ideas.' Instead, these resources reflect 'the economically motivated decisions of investors and customers.' A stockholder might oppose the use of corporate funds drawn from the general treasury—which represents, after all, *his* money—in support of a particular political candidate. The requirement that corporate independent expenditures be financed through a segregated fund or political action committee expressly established to engage in campaign spending is designed to avert this danger. * * *

"The PAC requirement may be unconstitutional as applied to some corporations because they do not present the dangers at which expenditure limitations are aimed. Indeed, we determined that Massachusetts Citizens for Life—the antiabortion advocacy organization at issue in *MCFL*—fell into this category.[3]

"[Justice] Kennedy, by repeatedly using the qualifier 'nonprofit' throughout his opinion, appears to concede that the Michigan law legitimately may be applied to for-profit business corporations, or at least that the Court's rationale might 'suffice to justify restricting political speech by for-profit corporations.' If that is so, Justice Kennedy's failure to sustain the statute as applied in this case is perplexing, because the Chamber, unlike other nonprofits such as *MCFL,* is clearly a conduit for corporations barred from making independent expenditures directly.[4] * * *

* * *

"The Michigan law is concededly 'underinclusive' insofar as it does not ban other types of political expenditures to which a dissenting Chamber member or corporate shareholder might object. The particular provision at issue prohibits corporations from using treasury funds only for making independent expenditures in support of or in opposition to any candidate in state elections. A corporation remains free, for example, to use general treasury funds to support an initiative proposal in a state referendum. See *Bellotti.*

"I do not find this underinclusiveness fatal, for several reasons.[8] First, as the dissents recognize, discussions on candidate elections lie 'at the heart of

3. Justice Kennedy is mistaken when he suggests that by upholding the as-applied challenge in *MCFL* and rejecting it here, we are embarking on "value-laden, content-based speech suppression that permits some nonprofit corporate groups but not others to engage in political speech." The mere fact that some as-applied challenges succeed while others fail does not create a system of "speech suppression." Whether an organization presents the threat at which the campaign finance laws are aimed has to do with the particular characteristics of the organization at issue and not with the content of its speech. Of course, if a correlation between the two factors could be shown to exist, a group would be free to mount a First Amendment challenge on that basis. * * *

4. According to Justice Kennedy's dissent, the majority holds that "it is now a felony in Michigan for the Sierra Club, or the American Civil Liberties Union" to make independent expenditures. This characterization is inaccurate. Not only are those groups not part of the proceeding before us, but the dissent has overlooked the central lesson of *MCFL* that the First Amendment may require exemptions, on an as-applied basis, from expenditure restrictions. If a nonprofit corporation is formed with the express purpose of promoting political ideas, is not composed of members who face an economic incentive for disassociating with it, and does not accept contributions from business corporations or labor unions, then it would be governed by our *MCFL* holding.

8. Justice Scalia also maintains that protection of dissenting shareholders cannot qualify as a valid state interest because shareholders purchase their stock on the understanding that the corporation will use their money for any profitmaking purpose, including support for political candidates with whom the shareholders may not agree. We have already rejected this argument in the context of labor unions. See *Abood.* Rather than assuming that an employee accepts as "the deal," that the union will use his dues for any purpose that will advance the interests of the bargaining unit, including political contributions and expenditures, we have determined that "the authority to impose dues and fees [is] restricted at least to the 'extent of denying the unions the right, over the employee's objection, to use his money to support political causes which he opposes,' even though Congress was well aware that *unions had historically expended funds in the support of political candidates and issues.*" *Ellis v. Railway Clerks* [p. 750 supra].

Given the extensive state regulation of corporations, shareholder expectations are always a function of *state law.* It is circular to say, as does Justice Scalia, that *if* a State did not protect shareholders, they would have no expectation of being protected, and therefore that the State has no legitimate interest in protecting them. [I] believe it entirely proper for a State to decide to promote the ability of investors to purchase stock in corporations without fear that their money will be used to support candidates with whom they do not agree.

political debate.' But just as speech interests are at their zenith in this area, so too are the interests of unwilling Chamber members and corporate shareholders forced to subsidize that speech. The State's decision to focus on this especially sensitive context is a justifiable one. Second, in light of our decisions in *First National Bank of Boston v. Bellotti, Consolidated Edison Co. v. Public Service Comm'n of New York,* and related cases, a State cannot prohibit corporations from making many other types of political expenditures. One purpose of the underinclusiveness inquiry is to ensure that the proffered state interest actually underlies the law. But to the extent that the Michigan statute is 'underinclusive' only because it does not regulate corporate expenditures in referenda or other corporate expression (besides merely commercial speech), this reflects the requirements of our decisions rather than the lack of an important state interest on the part of Michigan in regulating expenditures in *candidate* elections. In this sense, the Michigan law is not 'underinclusive' at all. Finally, the provision in Michigan corporate law authorizing shareholder actions against corporate waste might serve as a remedy for other types of political expenditures that have no legitimate connection to the corporation's business.

"For these reasons, I concur in the Court's opinion."

STEVENS, J., joined in the Court's opinion and concurred: "In my opinion the distinction between individual expenditures and individual contributions that the Court identified in *Buckley v. Valeo,* should have little, if any, weight in reviewing corporate participation in candidate elections. In that context, I believe the danger of either the fact, or the appearance, of *quid pro quo* relationships provides an adequate justification for state regulation of both expenditures and contributions. Moreover, as we recognized in *First National Bank of Boston v. Bellotti,* there is a vast difference between lobbying and debating public issues on the one hand, and political campaigns for election to public office on the other."

SCALIA, J., dissented: "'Attention all citizens. To assure the fairness of elections by preventing disproportionate expression of the views of any single powerful group, your Government has decided that the following associations of persons shall be prohibited from speaking or writing in support of any candidate: ________'. In permitting Michigan to make private corporations the first object of this Orwellian announcement, the Court today endorses the principle that too much speech is an evil that the democratic majority can proscribe. I dissent because that principle is contrary to our case law and incompatible with the absolutely central truth of the First Amendment: that government cannot be trusted to assure, through censorship, the 'fairness' of political debate.

"The Court's opinion says that political speech of corporations can be regulated because '[s]tate law grants [them] special advantages' and because this 'unique state-conferred corporate structure * * * facilitates the amassing of large treasuries.' This analysis seeks to create one good argument by combining two bad ones. Those individuals who form that type of voluntary association known as a corporation are, to be sure, given special advantages—notably, the immunization of their personal fortunes from liability for the actions of the association—that the State is under no obligation to confer. But so are other associations and private individuals given all sorts of special advantages that the State need not confer, ranging from tax breaks to contract awards to public employment to outright cash subsidies. It is rudimentary that the State cannot exact as the price of those special advantages the forfeiture of First Amendment rights. The categorical suspension of the right of any person, or of any association of persons, to speak out on political matters must be justified by a compelling state need. Which is why the Court puts forward its second bad argument, the fact that corporations 'amas[s] large treasuries.' But that alone is also not sufficient justification for the suppression of political speech, unless one thinks it would be lawful to prohibit men and women whose net worth is above a certain figure from endorsing political candidates. Neither of these two flawed arguments is improved by combining them * * *.

"The Court's extensive reliance upon the fact that the objects of this speech restriction, corporations, receive 'special advantages' is in stark contrast to our opinion issued just six years ago in *FCC v. League of Women Voters of California,* [p. 991 supra]. In that decision, striking down a congressionally imposed ban upon editorializing by noncommercial broadcasting stations that receive federal funds, the *only* respect in which we considered the receipt of that 'special advantage' relevant was in determining whether the speech limitation could be justified under Congress' spending power, as a means of assuring that the subsidy was devoted only to the purposes Congress intended, which did not include political editorializing. We held it could not be justified on that basis, since 'a noncommercial educational station that receives only 1% of its overall income from [federal] grants is barred absolutely from all editorializing. * * * The station has no way of limiting the use of its federal funds to all noneditorializing activities, and, more importantly, it is barred from using even wholly private funds to finance its editorial activity.' Of course the same is true here, even assuming that tax exemptions and other benefits accorded to incorporated associations constitute an exercise of the spending power. It is not just that portion of the corporation's assets attributable to the gratuitously conferred 'special advantages' that is prohibited from being used for political endorsements, but *all* of the corporation's assets. I am at a loss to explain the vast difference between the treatment of the present case and *League of Women Voters.* Commercial corporations may not have a public *persona* as sympathetic as that of public broadcasters, but they are no less entitled to this Court's concern.[a]

"As for the second part of the Court's argumentation, the fact that corporations (or at least some of them) possess 'massive wealth': Certain uses of 'massive wealth' in the electoral process—whether or not the wealth is the result of 'special advantages' conferred by the State—pose a substantial risk of corruption which constitutes a compelling need for the regulation of speech. Such a risk plainly exists when the wealth is given directly to the political candidate, to be used under his direction and control. * * *

"The contention that prohibiting overt advocacy for or against a political candidate satisfies a 'compelling need' to avoid 'corruption' is easily dismissed. As we said in *Buckley,* '[i]t would naively underestimate the ingenuity and resourcefulness of persons and groups desiring to buy influence to believe that they would have much difficulty devising expenditures that skirted the restriction on express advocacy of election or defeat but nevertheless benefited the candidate's campaign.' Independent advocacy, moreover, unlike contributions, 'may well provide little assistance to the candidate's campaign and indeed may prove counterproductive,' thus reducing the danger that it will be exchanged 'as a *quid pro quo* for improper commitments from the candidate.' The latter point

a. Scalia, J., also argued that *Buckley v. Valeo* had decided the question of independent corporate political expenditures. He observed that *Buckley* had included corporate plaintiffs. Those plaintiffs apparently were the New York Civil Liberties Union, Inc. and Human Events, Inc. Can *Buckley* be distinguished?

seems even more plainly true with respect to corporate advocates than it is with respect to individuals. I expect I could count on the fingers of one hand the candidates who would generally welcome, much less negotiate for, a formal endorsement by AT & T or General Motors. The advocacy of such entities that have 'amassed great wealth' will be effective only to the extent that it brings to the people's attention *ideas* which—despite the invariably self-interested and probably uncongenial source—strike them as true.

"The Court does not try to defend the proposition that independent advocacy poses a substantial risk of political 'corruption,' as English-speakers understand that term. Rather, it asserts that that concept (which it defines as ' "financial *quid pro quo*" corruption,' is really just a narrow subspecies of a hitherto unrecognized genus of political corruption. 'Michigan's regulation,' we are told, 'aims at a different type of corruption in the political arena: the corrosive and distorting effects of immense aggregations of wealth that are accumulated with the help of the corporate form and that have little or no correlation to the public's support for the corporation's political ideas.' Under this mode of analysis, virtually anything the Court deems politically undesirable can be turned into political corruption—by simply describing its effects as politically 'corrosive,' which is close enough to 'corruptive' to qualify. It is sad to think that the First Amendment will ultimately be brought down not by brute force but by poetic metaphor.

"The Court's opinion ultimately rests upon that proposition whose violation constitutes the New Corruption: expenditures must 'reflect actual public support for the political ideas espoused.' This illiberal free-speech principle of 'one man, one minute' was proposed and soundly rejected in *Buckley*. * * * But it can be said that I have not accurately quoted today's decision. It does not endorse the proposition that government may ensure that expenditures 'reflect actual public support for the political ideas espoused,' but only the more limited proposition that government may ensure that expenditures 'reflect actual public support for the political ideas espoused *by corporations*.' The limitation is of course entirely irrational. Why is it perfectly all right if advocacy by an individual billionaire is out of proportion with 'actual public support' for his positions? There is no explanation, except the effort I described at the outset of this discussion to make one valid proposition out of two invalid ones: When the vessel labeled 'corruption' begins to founder under weight too great to be logically sustained, the argumentation jumps to the good ship 'special privilege'; and when that in turn begins to go down, it returns to 'corruption.' Thus hopping back and forth between the two, the argumentation may survive but makes no headway towards port, where its conclusion waits in vain.

"Justice Brennan's concurrence would have us believe that the prohibition adopted by Michigan and approved by the Court is a paternalistic measure to protect the corporate shareholder of America. [But] such solicitude is a most implausible explanation for the Michigan statute, inasmuch as it permits corporations to take as many ideological and political positions as they please, so long as they are not 'in assistance of, or in opposition to, the nomination or election of a candidate.' That is indeed the Court's sole basis for distinguishing *First National Bank of Boston v. Bellotti,* which invalidated restriction of a corporation's general political speech. The Michigan law appears to be designed, in other words, neither to protect shareholders, nor even (impermissibly) to 'balance' general political debate, but to protect political candidates. Given the degree of political sophistication that ought to attend the exercise of our constitutional responsibilities, it is regrettable that this should come as a surprise.

"But even if the object of the prohibition could plausibly be portrayed as the protection of shareholders (which the Court's opinion, at least, does not even assert), that would not suffice as a 'compelling need' to support this blatant restriction upon core political speech. A person becomes a member of that form of association known as a for-profit corporation in order to pursue economic objectives, *i.e.,* to make money. Some corporate charters may specify the line of commerce to which the company is limited, but even that can be amended by shareholder vote. Thus, in joining such an association, the shareholder knows that management may take any action that is ultimately in accord with what the majority (or a specified supermajority) of the shareholders wishes, so long as that action is designed to make a profit. That is the deal. The corporate actions to which the shareholder exposes himself, therefore, include many things that he may find politically or ideologically uncongenial: investment in South Africa, operation of an abortion clinic, publication of a pornographic magazine, or even publication of a newspaper that adopts absurd political views and makes catastrophic political endorsements. His only protections against such assaults upon his ideological commitments are (1) his ability to persuade a majority (or the requisite minority) of his fellow shareholders that the action should not be taken, and ultimately (2) his ability to sell his stock. (The latter course, by the way, does not ordinarily involve the severe psychic trauma or economic disaster that Justice Brennan's opinion suggests.) It seems to me entirely fanciful, in other words, to suggest that the Michigan statute makes any significant contribution towards insulating the exclusively profit-motivated shareholder from the rude world of politics and ideology.

"But even if that were not fanciful, it would be fanciful to think, as Justice Brennan's opinion assumes, that there is any difference between for-profit and not-for-profit corporations insofar as the need for protection of the individual member's ideological psyche is concerned. Would it be any more upsetting to a shareholder of General Motors that it endorsed the election of Henry Wallace (to stay comfortably in the past) than it would be to a member of the American Civil Liberties Union that it endorsed the election of George Wallace? I should think much less so. Yet in the one case as in the other, the only protection against association-induced trauma is the will of the majority and, in the last analysis, withdrawal from membership. * * *

"Finally, a few words are in order concerning the Court's approval of the Michigan law's exception for 'media corporations.' This is all right, we are told, because of 'the unique role that the press plays in "informing and educating the public, offering criticism, and providing a forum for discussion and debate."' But if one believes in the Court's rationale of 'compelling state need' to prevent amassed corporate wealth from skewing the political debate, surely that 'unique role' of the press does not give Michigan justification for *excluding* media corporations from coverage, but provides especially strong reason to *include* them. Amassed corporate wealth that regularly sits astride the ordinary channels of information is much more likely to produce the New Corruption (too much of one point of view) than amassed corporate wealth that is generally busy making money elsewhere. Such media corporations not only have vastly greater power to perpetrate the evil of overinforming, they also have vastly greater opportunity. General Motors, after all, will risk a stockholder suit if it makes a political endorsement that is not plausibly tied to its ability to make money for its shareholders. But media corporations make money *by* making political commentary, including endorsements. For them, unlike any other corporations, the whole world of politics and ideology is fair game. Yet the Court tells us that it is reasonable to *exclude* media corporations, rather than target them specially.

"Members of the institutional press, despite the Court's approval of their illogical exemption from the Michigan law, will find little reason for comfort in today's decision. The theory of New Corruption it espouses is a dagger at their throat. The Court today holds merely that media corporations *may* be excluded from the Michigan law, not that they *must* be. * * * One must hope, I suppose, that Michigan will continue to provide this generous and voluntary exemption. * * *

"Because today's decision is inconsistent with unrepudiated legal judgments of our Court, but even more because it is incompatible with the unrepealable political wisdom of our First Amendment, I dissent."

KENNEDY, J., joined by O'Connor and Scalia, JJ., dissented: "With the imprimatur of this Court, it is now a felony in Michigan for the Sierra Club, or the American Civil Liberties Union, or the Michigan State Chamber of Commerce, to advise the public how a candidate voted on issues of urgent concern to their members. In both practice and theory, the prohibition aims at the heart of political debate. * * *

"First, the Act prohibits corporations from speaking on a particular subject, the subject of candidate elections. It is a basic precept that the State may not confine speech to certain subjects. Content-based restrictions are the essence of censorial power.

"Second, the Act discriminates on the basis of the speaker's identity. Under the Michigan law, any person or group other than a corporation may engage in political debate over candidate elections; but corporations, even nonprofit corporations that have unique views of vital importance to the electorate, must remain mute. Our precedents condemn this censorship. See *Bellotti; Mosley.*

"[By] using distinctions based upon both the speech and the speaker, the Act engages in the rawest form of censorship: the State censors what a particular segment of the political community might say with regard to candidates who stand for election. * * *

"The second censorship scheme validated by today's holding is the one imposed by the Court. [Those] who thought that the First Amendment exists to protect all points of view in candidate elections will be disillusioned by the Court's opinion today; for that protection is given only to a preferred class of nonprofit corporate speakers: small, single issue nonprofit corporations that pass the Court's own vague test for determining who are the favored participants in the electoral process. There can be no doubt that if a State were to enact a statute empowering an administrative board to determine which corporations could place candidate advertisements in newspapers and which could not, with authority to enforce the guidelines the Court adopts today to distinguish between the Massachusetts Citizens for Life and the Michigan Chamber of Commerce, the statute would be held unconstitutional. The First Amendment does not permit courts to exercise speech suppression authority denied to legislatures. * * *

"The Act does not meet our standards for laws that burden fundamental rights. * * *

"The majority almost admits that, in the case of independent expenditures, the danger of a political *quid pro quo* is insufficient to justify a restriction of this kind. Since the specter of corruption, which had been 'the only legitimate and compelling government interes[t] thus far identified for restricting campaign finances' is missing in this case, the majority invents a new interest: combatting the 'corrosive and distorting effects of immense aggregations of wealth' accumulated in corporate form without shareholder or public support. The majority styles this novel interest as simply a different kind of corruption, but has no support for its assertion. While it is questionable whether such imprecision would suffice to justify restricting political speech by for-profit corporations, it is certain that it does not apply to nonprofit entities. * * *

"With regard to nonprofit corporations in particular, there is no reason to assume that the corporate form has an intrinsic flaw that makes it corrupt, or that all corporations possess great wealth, or that all corporations can buy more media coverage for their views than can individuals or other groups. * * *

"The Court purports to distinguish *MCFL* on the ground that the nonprofit corporation permitted to speak in that case received no funds from profit-making corporations. It is undisputed that the Michigan Chamber of Commerce is itself a nonprofit corporation. The crucial difference, it is said, is that the Chamber receives corporate contributions. But this distinction rests on the fallacy that the source of the speaker's funds is somehow relevant to the speaker's right of expression or society's interest in hearing what the speaker has to say. [Many] persons can trace their funds to corporations, if not in the form of donations, than in the form of dividends, interest, or salary. That does not provide a basis to deprive such individuals or associations of their First Amendment freedoms. The more narrow alternative of recordkeeping and funding disclosure is available. A wooden rule prohibiting independent expenditures by nonprofit corporations that receive funds from business corporations invites discriminatory distinctions. The principled approach is to acknowledge that where political speech is concerned, freedom to speak extends to all nonprofit corporations, not the special favorites of a majority of this Court.

"The majority concludes that the Michigan Act is narrowly tailored. First, it seeks support in the availability of political action committees (PAC's) as an alternative to direct speech. * * *

"The secondhand endorsement structure required by the Michigan state law debases the value of the voice of nonprofit corporate speakers. The public is not interested in what a PAC says; it does care what the group itself says, so that the group itself can be given credit or blame for the candidates it has endorsed or opposed. PAC's suffer from a poor public image. An advertisement for which a nonprofit group takes direct responsibility, in all likelihood, will have more credibility and generate less distrust than one funded by a PAC. PAC's are interim, ad hoc organizations with little continuity or responsibility. The respected organizations affected by this case have a continuity, a stability and an influence that makes it critical for their members and the public at large to evaluate their official policies to determine whether the organization has earned credibility over a period of time. If a particular organization supports a candidate who injures its cause or offends its ideals, the organization itself, not some intermediary committee, ought to take the blame. It is a sad irony that the group before us wishes to assume that responsibility but the action of the State, endorsed by this Court, does not allow it to do so.

"The diffusion of the corporate message produced by the PAC requirement also ensures a lack of fit between the statute's ends and its means. If the concern is that nonprofit corporate speech distorts the political process, it would seem that injecting the confusion of a PAC as an intermediary, albeit one controlled and directed by the corporation, further diffuses responsibility. Even if there were any possibility of corruption by allowing the Michigan Chamber of Commerce to finance the proposed advertisement supporting a candidate, it makes no sense to argue that such a possibility would be eliminated by requiring the disclaimer at the bottom to read 'Paid for by the Michigan Chamber of Commerce PAC' rather than 'Paid for by the Michigan Chamber of Commerce.'

"The majority relies on the state interest in protecting members from the use of nonprofit corporate funds to support candidates whom they may oppose. We should reject this interest as insufficient to save the Act here, just as we rejected the argument in *Bellotti.*

"The Court takes refuge in the argument that some members or contributors to nonprofit corporations may find their own views distorted by the organization, and cites our holding in *Abood. Abood* does not apply here, as the disincentives to dissociate are not comparable. One need not become a member of the Michigan Chamber of Commerce or the Sierra Club in order to earn a living. To the extent that members disagree with a nonprofit corporation's policies, they can seek change from within, withhold financial support, cease to associate with the group, or form a rival group of their own. Allowing government to use the excuse of protecting shareholder rights to stifle the speech of private, voluntary organizations undermines the First Amendment. * * *

"An independent ground for invalidating this statute is the blanket exemption for media corporations. It is beyond peradventure that the media could not be prohibited from speaking about candidate qualifications. The First Amendment would not tolerate a law prohibiting a newspaper or television network from spending on political comment because it operates through a corporation. See *Mills v. Alabama.* As Justice Brennan, joined by a majority of the Court in *Dun & Bradstreet, Inc. v. Greenmoss Builders, Inc.,* stated 'the rights of the institutional media are no greater and no less than those enjoyed by other individuals or organizations engaged in the same activities.' The argument relied on by the majority, that media corporations are in the business of communicating and other corporations are not, is unsatisfying. All corporations communicate with the public to some degree, whether it is their business or not; and communication is of particular importance for nonprofit corporations.

"The web of corporate ownership that links media and nonmedia corporations is difficult to untangle for the purpose of any meaningful distinction. Newspapers, television networks, and other media may be owned by parent corporations with multiple business interests. Nothing in the statutory scheme prohibits a business corporate parent from directing its newspaper to support or oppose a particular candidate. The Act not only permits that discretion or control, but makes it a crime for a public-interest nonprofit corporation to bring to light such activity if to do so infers candidate support or opposition. I can find no permissible basis under the First Amendment for the States to make this unsupported distinction among corporate speakers. * * *

"The Court's hostility to the corporate form used by the speaker in this case and its assertion that corporate wealth is the evil to be regulated is far too imprecise to justify the most severe restriction on political speech ever sanctioned by this Court."

PACIFIC GAS & ELECTRIC CO. v. PUBLIC UTILITIES COM'N

475 U.S. 1, 106 S.Ct. 903, 89 L.Ed.2d 1 (1986).

JUSTICE POWELL announced the judgment of the Court and delivered an opinion in which the CHIEF JUSTICE, JUSTICE BRENNAN, and JUSTICE O'CONNOR joined.

The question in this case is whether the California Public Utilities Commission may require a privately owned utility company to include in its billing envelopes speech of a third party with which the utility disagrees.

For the past 62 years, appellant Pacific Gas and Electric Company has distributed a newsletter in its monthly billing envelope. Appellant's newsletter, called *Progress,* reaches over three million customers. It has included political editorials, feature stories on matters of public interest, tips on energy conservation, and straightforward information about utility services and bills.[1]

In 1980, appellee Toward Utility Rate Normalization (TURN), an intervenor in a ratemaking proceeding before California's Public Utilities Commission, another appellee, urged the Commission to forbid appellant to use the billing envelopes to distribute political editorials, on the ground that the appellant's customers should not bear the expense of appellant's own political speech. The Commission decided that the envelope space that appellant had used to disseminate *Progress* is the property of the ratepayers.[3] This "extra space" was defined as "the space remaining in the billing envelope, after inclusion of the monthly bill and any required legal notices, for inclusion of other materials up to such total envelope weight as would not result in any additional postage cost."

In an effort to apportion this "extra space" between appellant and its customers, the Commission permitted TURN to use the "extra space" four times a year for the next two years. During these months, appellant may use any space not used by TURN and it may include additional materials if it pays any extra postage. [T]he Commission determined that ratepayers would benefit from permitting TURN to use the extra space in the billing envelopes to raise funds and to communicate with ratepayers: "Our goal [is] to change the present system to one which uses the extra space more efficiently for the ratepayers' benefit. It is reasonable to assume that the ratepayers will benefit more from exposure to a variety of views than they will from only that of PG & E." The Commission concluded that appellant could have no interest in excluding TURN's message from the billing envelope since appellant does not own the space that message would fill. The Commission placed no limitations on what TURN or appellant could say in the envelope, except that TURN is required to state that its messages are not those of appellant. The Commission reserved the

1. For example, the December 1984 issue of *Progress* included a story on appellant's "automatic payment" and "balanced payment" plans, an article instructing ratepayers on how to weatherstrip their homes, recipes for holiday dishes, and a feature on appellant's efforts to help bald eagles in the Pit River area of California. * * *

3. The Commission summarized its reasoning as follows: "[E]nvelope and postage costs and any other costs of mailing bills are a necessary part of providing utility service to the customer. [However,] due to the nature of postal rates * * * extra space exists in these billing envelopes. * * * Mindful that the extra space is an artifact generated with ratepayer funds, and is not an intended or necessary item of rate base, and that the only alternative treatment would unjustly enrich PG & E and simultaneously deprive the ratepayers of the value of that space, we concluded that the extra space in the billing envelope 'is properly considered as ratepayer property.'"

right to grant other groups access to the envelopes in the future.[5] * * *

Compelled access like that ordered in this case both penalizes the expression of particular points of view and forces speakers to alter their speech to conform with an agenda they do not set. These impermissible effects are not remedied by the Commission's definition of the relevant property rights.

This Court has previously considered the question whether compelling a private corporation to provide a forum for views other than its own may infringe the corporation's freedom of speech. *Miami Herald Publishing Co. v. Tornillo;* see also *PruneYard Shopping Center v. Robins.* [[6]]

The concerns that caused us to invalidate the compelled access rule in *Tornillo* apply to appellant as well as to the institutional press.[7] See *First National Bank of Boston v. Bellotti.* Cf. *Lovell v. Griffin.* Just as the state is not free to "tell a newspaper in advance what it can print and what it cannot," *Pittsburgh Press,* the State is not free either to restrict appellant's speech to certain topics or views or to force appellant to respond to views that others may hold. Under *Tornillo* a forced access rule that would accomplish these purposes indirectly is similarly forbidden.

[*PruneYard*] is not to the contrary. [This] Court held that [a] shopping center did not have a constitutionally protected right to exclude [pamphleteers] from the area open to the public at large. Notably absent from *PruneYard* was any concern that access to this area might affect the shopping center owner's exercise of his own right to speak: the owner did not even allege that he objected to the content of the pamphlets; nor was the access right content-based. *PruneYard* thus does not undercut the proposition that forced associations that burden protected speech are impermissible.[8]

The Commission's order is inconsistent with these principles. The order does not simply award access to the public at large; rather, it discriminates on the basis of the viewpoints of the selected speakers. Two of the acknowledged purposes of the access order are to offer the public a greater variety of views in

5. The Commission has already *denied* access to at least one group based on the content of its speech. The Commission denied the application of a taxpayer group—the "Committee of More than One Million Taxpayers to Save Proposition 13"—on the ground that that group neither wished to participate in Commission proceedings nor alleged that its use of the billing envelope space would improve consumer participation in those proceedings. The record does not reveal whether any other groups have sought access to the billing envelopes.

6. This Court has sustained a limited government-enforced right of access to broadcast media. *Red Lion Broadcasting Co. v. FCC.* Cf. *Columbia Broadcasting System, Inc. v. Democratic National Committee.* Appellant's billing envelopes do not, however, present the same constraints that justify the result in *Red Lion:* "[A] broadcaster communicates through use of a scarce, publicly owned resource. No person can broadcast without a license, whereas all persons are free to send correspondence to private homes through the mails." *Consolidated Edison Co. v. Public Service Comm'n of N.Y.*

7. Unlike the right-of-reply statute at issue in *Tornillo,* the Commission's order does not require appellant to place TURN's message in appellant's newsletter. Instead, the Commission ordered appellant to place TURN's message in appellant's envelope four months out of the year. Like the Miami Herald, however, appellant is still required to carry speech with which it disagreed, and might well feel compelled to reply or limit its own speech in response to TURN's.

The Court's opinion in *Tornillo* emphasizes that the right-of-reply statute impermissibly deterred protected speech. In the last paragraph of the opinion, the Court concluded that an *independent* ground for invalidating the statute was its effect on editors' allocation of scarce newspaper space. That discussion in no way suggested that the State was free otherwise to burden the newspaper's speech as long as the actual paper on which the newspaper was printed was not invaded.

8. In addition, the relevant forum in *PruneYard* was the open area of the shopping center into which the general public was invited. This area was, almost by definition, peculiarly public in nature. * * *

appellant's billing envelope, and to assist groups (such as TURN) that challenge appellant in the Commission's ratemaking proceedings in raising funds. Access to the envelopes thus is not content-neutral. [Access] is limited to persons or groups—such as TURN—who disagree with appellant's views as expressed in *Progress* and who oppose appellant in Commission proceedings.

Such one-sidedness impermissibly burdens appellant's own expression. *Tornillo* illustrates the point. Access to the newspaper in that case was content-based in two senses: (i) it was triggered by a particular category of newspaper speech, and (ii) it was awarded only to those who disagreed with the newspaper's views. The Commission's order is not, in *Tornillo*'s words, a "content-based penalty" in the first sense, because TURN's access to appellant's envelopes is not conditioned on any particular expression by appellant. But because access is awarded only to those who disagree with appellant's views and who are hostile to appellant's interests, appellant must contend with the fact that whenever it speaks out on a given issue, it may be forced—at TURN's discretion—to help disseminate hostile views. Appellant "might well conclude" that, under these circumstances, "the safe course is to avoid controversy," thereby reducing the free flow of information and ideas that the First Amendment seeks to promote.

Appellant does not, of course, have the right to be free from vigorous debate. But it *does* have the right to be free from government restrictions that abridge its own rights in order to "enhance the relative voice" of its opponents. *Buckley v. Valeo.* The Commission's order requires *appellant* to assist in disseminating *TURN's* views; it does not equally constrain both sides of the debate about utility regulation.[10] This kind of favoritism goes well beyond the fundamentally content-neutral subsidies that we sustained in *Buckley* and in *Regan v. Taxation With Representation.* See *Buckley* (sustaining funding of general election campaign expenses of major party candidates); *Regan* (sustaining tax deduction for contributors to veterans' organizations). Unlike these permissible government subsidies of speech, the Commission's order identifies a favored speaker "based on the identity of the interests that [the speaker] may represent," *Bellotti,* and forces the speaker's opponent—not the taxpaying public—to assist in disseminating the speaker's message. Such a requirement necessarily burdens the expression of the disfavored speaker.

The Commission's access order also impermissibly requires appellant to associate with speech with which appellant may disagree.[11] * * *.[12] [Espe-

10. Justice Stevens analogizes this aspect of the Commission's order to Securities and Exchange Commission regulations that require management to transmit proposals of minority shareholders in shareholder mailings. The analogy is inappropriate. The regulations Justice Stevens cites differ from the Commission's order in two important ways. First, they allocate shareholder property between management and certain groups of shareholders. Management has no interest in corporate property except such interest as derives from the shareholders; therefore, regulations that limit management's ability to exclude some shareholders' views from corporate communications do not infringe corporate First Amendment rights. Second, the regulations govern speech by a corporation *to itself.* *Bellotti* and *Consolidated Edison* establish that the Constitution protects corporations' right to speak to the public based on the informational value of corporate speech. Rules that define how corporations govern themselves do not limit the range of information that the corporation may contribute to the public debate. The Commission's order, by contrast, burdens appellant's right freely to speak to the public at large.

11. The presence of a disclaimer on TURN's messages does not suffice to eliminate the impermissible pressure on appellant to respond to TURN's speech. The disclaimer serves only to avoid giving readers the mistaken impression that TURN's words are really those of appellant. It does nothing to reduce the risk that appellant will be forced to respond when there is strong disagreement with the substance of TURN's message.

12. The Commission's order is thus readily distinguishable from orders requiring appel-

cially] since TURN has been given access in part to create a multiplicity of views in the envelopes, there can be little doubt that appellant will feel compelled to respond to arguments and allegations made by TURN in its messages to appellant's customers.

That kind of forced response is antithetical to the free discussion that the First Amendment seeks to foster. For corporations as for individuals, the choice to speak includes within it the choice of what not to say. [Were] the government freely able to compel corporate speakers to propound political messages with which they disagree, this protection would be empty, for the government could require speakers to affirm in one breath that which they deny in the next. * * *

The Commission has emphasized that appellant's customers own the "extra space" in the billing envelopes. * * *

The Commission expressly declined to hold that under California law appellant's customers own the entire billing envelopes and everything contained therein. [The] envelopes themselves, the bills, and *Progress* all remain appellant's property. The Commission's access order thus clearly requires appellant to use *its* property as a vehicle for spreading a message with which it disagrees. In *Wooley,* we held that New Hampshire could not require two citizens to display a slogan on their license plates and thereby "use their private property as a 'mobile billboard' for the State's ideological message." The "private property" that was used to spread the unwelcome message was the automobile, not the license plates. Similarly, the Commission's order requires appellant to use its property—the billing envelopes—to distribute the message of another. This is so whoever is deemed to own the "extra space."

A different conclusion would necessarily imply that our decision in *Tornillo* rested on the Miami Herald's ownership of the space that would have been used to print candidate replies. Nothing in *Tornillo* suggests that the result would have been different had the Florida Supreme Court decided that the newspaper space needed to print candidates' replies was the property of the newspaper's readers, or had the court ordered the Miami Herald to distribute inserts owned and prepared by the candidates together with its newspapers. The constitutional difficulty with the right-of-reply statute was that it required the newspaper to disseminate a message with which the newspaper disagreed. This difficulty did not depend on whether the particular paper on which the replies were printed belonged to the newspaper or to the candidate.

Appellees' argument suffers from the same constitutional defect. The Commission's order forces appellant to disseminate TURN's speech in envelopes that appellant owns and that bear appellant's return address. Such forced association with potentially hostile views burdens the expression of views different from TURN's and risks forcing appellant to speak where it would prefer to remain silent. Those effects do not depend on who "owns" the "extra space." [15]

lant to carry various legal notices, such as notices of upcoming Commission proceedings or of changes in the way rates are calculated. The State, of course, has substantial leeway in determining appropriate information disclosure requirements for business corporations. See *Zauderer*. Nothing in *Zauderer* suggests, however, that the State is equally free to require corporations to carry the messages of third parties, where the messages themselves are biased against or are expressly contrary to the corporation's views.

15. * * * "Extra space" exists not only in billing envelopes but also on billboards, bulletin boards, and sides of buildings and motor vehicles. Under the Commission's reasoning, a State could force business proprietors of such items to use the space for the dissemination of speech the proprietor opposes. At least where access to such fora is

* * * [a]

JUSTICE BLACKMUN took no part in the consideration or decision of this case.

CHIEF JUSTICE BURGER, concurring.

I join Justice Powell's opinion, but think we need not go beyond the authority of *Wooley* to decide this case. I would not go beyond the central question presented by this case, which is the infringement of Pacific's right to be free from forced association with views with which it disagrees. I would also rely on that part of *Tornillo* holding that a forced right of reply violates a newspaper's right to be free from forced dissemination of views it would not voluntarily disseminate, just as we held that Maynard must be free from being forced by the State to disseminate views with which he disagreed. To compel Pacific to mail messages for others cannot be distinguished from compelling it to carry the messages of others on its trucks, its buildings, or other property used in the conduct of its business. For purposes of this case, those properties cannot be distinguished from property like the mailing envelopes acquired by Pacific from its income and resources.

JUSTICE MARSHALL, concurring in the judgment.

* * * Two significant differences between the State's grant of access in this case and the grant of access in *PruneYard* lead me to find a constitutional barrier here that I did not find in the earlier case.

The first difference is the degree of intrusiveness of the permitted access.

[In] the present case [appellant] has never opened up its billing envelope to the use of the public.[1] Appellant has not abandoned its right to exclude others from its property to the degree that the shopping center owner had done in *PruneYard.* Were appellant to use its billing envelope as a sort of community billboard, regularly carrying the messages of third parties, its desire to exclude a particular speaker would be deserving of lesser solicitude. As matters stand, however, appellant has issued no invitation to the general public to use its billing envelope, for speech or for any other purpose.[2] Moreover, the shopping

granted on the basis of the speakers' viewpoints, the public's ownership of the "extra space" does not nullify the First Amendment rights of the owner of the property from which that space derives.

a. Powell, J., denied that the Commission's order was a narrowly tailored means of serving a compelling state interest. He observed that the state interest in effective ratemaking proceedings and the state interest in making a variety of views available to the customers could be advanced by means that did not burden the utility company's expression. The lack of content neutrality was further said to undercut any contention that the Commission's order furthered the interest in making a variety of views available and also disposed of the suggestion that the Commission's order was a valid time, place, or manner regulation.

1. The State seizes upon appellant's status as a regulated monopoly in order to argue that the inclusion of postage and other billing costs in the utility's rate base demonstrates that these items "belong" to the public, which has paid for them. However, a consumer who purchases food in a grocery store is "paying" for the store's rent, heat, electricity, wages, etc., but no one would seriously argue that the consumer thereby acquires a property interest in the store. That the utility passes on its overhead costs to ratepayers at a rate fixed by law rather than the market cannot affect the utility's ownership of its property, nor its right to use that property for expressive purposes, see *Consolidated Edison Co. v. Public Service Comm'n.* The State could have concluded that the public interest would be best served by state ownership of utilities. Having chosen to keep utilities in private hands, however, the State may not arbitrarily appropriate property for the use of third parties by stating that the public has "paid" for the property by paying utility bills.

I hasten to add that nothing in this opinion nor, as I understand it, the plurality's opinion, addresses the issue whether the State may exclude the cost of mailing *Progress* from petitioner's rate base. Indeed, appellant concedes that the State may force its shareholders to bear those costs.

2. The State also argues that it frequently requires appellant to carry messages concern-center in *PruneYard* bore a strong resemblance to the streets and parks that are traditional public forums. People routinely gathered there, at the owner's invitation, and engaged in a wide variety of activities. Adding speech to the list of those activities did not in any great way change the complexion of the property. The same is not true in this case.

The second difference between this case and *PruneYard* is that the State has chosen to give TURN a right to speak at the expense of appellant's ability to use the property in question as a forum for the exercise of its own First Amendment rights. While the shopping center owner in *PruneYard* wished to be free of unwanted expression, he nowhere alleged that his own expression was hindered in the slightest. In contrast, the present case involves a forum of inherently limited scope. By appropriating, four times a year, the space in appellant's envelope that appellant would otherwise use for its own speech, the State has necessarily curtailed petitioner's use of its own forum. The regulation in this case, therefore, goes beyond a mere infringement of appellant's desire to remain silent.

While the interference with appellant's speech is, concededly, very slight, the State's justification—the subsidization of another speaker chosen by the State—is insufficient to sustain even that minor burden. We have held that the State may use its own resources for subsidization, *Regan v. Taxation With Representation,* but that interest, standing alone, cannot justify interference with the speech of others. See *Buckley; Bellotti.*

[In] the present case, the State has redefined a property right in the extra space in appellant's billing envelope in such a way as to achieve a result—burdening the speech of one party in order to enhance the speech of another—that the First Amendment disallows. In doing so, moreover, it has sanctioned an intrusion onto appellant's property that exceeds the slight incursion permitted in *PruneYard.* Under these circumstances, I believe that the State has crossed the boundary between constitutionally permissible and impermissible redefinitions of private property. * * *

JUSTICE REHNQUIST, with whom JUSTICE WHITE and JUSTICE STEVENS join as to Part I, dissenting. * * *

I. This Court established in *Bellotti* that the First Amendment prohibits the Government from *directly* suppressing the affirmative speech of corporations. A newspaper publishing corporation's right to express itself freely is also implicated by governmental action that penalizes speech, see *Tornillo,* because the deterrent effect of a penalty is very much like direct suppression. Our cases cannot be squared, however, with the view that the First Amendment prohibits governmental action that only *indirectly* and *remotely* affects a speaker's contribution to the overall mix of information available to society. * * *

Of course, the First Amendment does prohibit governmental action affecting the mix of information available to the public if the effect of the action approximates that of direct content-based suppression of speech. [*Tornillo*] held that a governmentally imposed "penalty" for the exercise of protected speech is

ing utility ratemaking and the rights of utility consumers. These messages, however, do not include political speech, and are directly relevant to commercial transactions between the ratepayer and the utility. The State's interest in requiring appellant to carry such messages is therefore particularly compelling. Somewhat analogously, the State could not argue that, because it may demand access for the State's agents to a private home to monitor compliance with health or safety regulations, it may also grant access to third parties for nongovernmental purposes.

sufficiently like direct suppression to trigger heightened First Amendment scrutiny. * * *

Although the plurality draws its deterrence rationale from *Tornillo,* it does not even attempt to characterize the right of access as a "penalty"; indeed, such a Procrustean effort would be doomed to failure. Instead, the plurality stretches *Tornillo* to stand for the general proposition that the First Amendment prohibits any regulation that deters a corporation from engaging in some expressive behavior. But the deterrent effect of any statute is an empirical question of degree. When the potential deterrent effect of a particular state law is remote and speculative, the law simply is not subject to heightened First Amendment scrutiny. The plurality does not adequately explain how the potential deterrent effect of the right of access here is sufficiently immediate and direct to warrant strict scrutiny. While a statutory penalty, like the right of reply statute in *Tornillo,* may sufficiently deter speech to trigger such heightened First Amendment scrutiny, the right of access here will not have such an effect on PG & E's incentives to speak.

The record does not support the inference that PUC issued its order to penalize PG & E because of the content of its inserts or because PG & E included the inserts in its billing envelopes in the first place. The order does not prevent PG & E from using the billing envelopes in the future to distribute inserts whenever it wishes. Nor does its vitality depend on whether PG & E includes inserts in any future billing envelopes. Moreover, the central reason for the access order—to provide for an effective ratepayer voice—would not vary in importance if PG & E had never distributed the inserts or ceased distributing them tomorrow. The most that can be said about the connection between the inserts and the order is that the existence of the inserts quite probably brought to TURN's attention the possibility of requesting access.

Nor does the access order create any cognizable risk of deterring PG & E from expressing its views in the most candid fashion. Unlike the reply statute in *Tornillo,* which conditioned access upon discrete instances of certain expression, the right of access here bears no relationship to PG & E's future conduct. PG & E cannot prevent the access by remaining silent or avoiding discussion of controversial subjects. The plurality suggests, however, that the possibility of minimizing the undesirable content of TURN's speech may induce PG & E to adopt a strategy of avoiding certain topics in hopes that TURN will not think to address them on its own. But this is an extremely implausible prediction. The success of such a strategy would depend on any group given access being little more than a reactive organization. TURN or any other group eventually given access will likely address the controversial subjects in spite of PG & E's silence. I therefore believe that PG & E will have no incentive to adopt the conservative strategy. Accordingly, the right of access should not be held to trigger heightened First Amendment scrutiny on the ground that it somehow might deter PG & E's right to speak.

II. The plurality argues, however, that the right of access also implicates PG & E's right not to speak or to associate with the speech of others, thereby triggering heightened scrutiny. [There is a] fundamental flaw with the plurality's analysis. This Court has recognized that natural persons enjoy negative free speech rights because of their interest in self-expression; an individual's right not to speak or to associate with the speech of others is a component of the broader constitutional interest of natural persons in freedom of conscience. *Barnette; Wooley.* * * *

In *Tornillo,* the Court extended negative free speech rights to newspapers without much discussion. The Court stated that the right of reply statute not only deterred affirmative speech, but it "fail[ed] to clear the barriers of the First Amendment because of its intrusion into the function of editors." The Court explained that interference with "the exercise of editorial control and judgment" creates a peril for the liberty of the press like government control over "what is to go into a newspaper." The Court did not elaborate further on the justification for its holding.

Extension of the individual freedom of conscience decisions to business corporations strains the rationale of those cases beyond the breaking point. To ascribe to such artificial entities an "intellect" or "mind" for freedom of conscience purposes is to confuse metaphor with reality. Corporations generally have not played the historic role of newspapers as conveyers of individual ideas and opinion. In extending positive free speech rights to corporations, this Court drew a distinction between the First Amendment rights of corporations and those of natural persons. It recognized that corporate free speech rights do not arise because corporations, like individuals, have any interest in self-expression. It held instead that such rights are recognized as an instrumental means of furthering the First Amendment purpose of fostering a broad forum of information to facilitate self-government.

The interest in remaining isolated from the expressive activity of others, and in declining to communicate at all, is for the most part divorced from this "broad public forum" purpose of the First Amendment. The right of access here constitutes an effort to facilitate and enlarge public discussion; it therefore furthers rather than abridges First Amendment values. See *Harper & Row.* [B]ecause the interest on which the constitutional protection of corporate speech rests is the societal interest in receiving information and ideas, the constitutional interest of a corporation in not permitting the presentation of other distinct views clearly identified as those of the speaker is *de minimis.* This is especially true in the case of PG & E, which is after all a regulated public utility. Any claim it may have had to a sphere of corporate autonomy was largely surrendered to extensive regulatory authority when it was granted legal monopoly status. * * *

JUSTICE STEVENS, dissenting. * * *

The narrow question we must address is whether a state public utility commission may require the fund-raising solicitation of a consumer advocacy group to be carried in a utility billing envelope. Since the utility concedes that *it* has no right to use the extra space in the billing envelope for its own newsletter, the question is limited to whether the Commission's requirement that it be the courier for the message of a third party violates the First Amendment. In my view, this requirement differs little from regulations applied daily to a variety of commercial communications that have rarely been challenged—and to my knowledge never invalidated—on First Amendment grounds. * * * [b]

I assume that the plurality would not object to a utility commission rule dictating the format of the bill, even as to required warnings and the type size of

b. Stevens, J., next argued that TURN had been given only a limited editorial license to explain its program, to describe pending and anticipated PG & E applications likely to have a significant effect on customers' rates and services, and to invite financial support for TURN's advocacy before the Commission. He denied that TURN had been granted the "postal equivalent of a soap box in the park."

various provisos and disclaimers.[3] Such regulation is not too different from that applicable [under federal regulations] to credit card bills, loan forms, and media advertising. I assume also the plurality would permit the Commission to require the utility to disseminate legal notices of public hearings and ratemaking proceedings written by it.[5] These compelled statements differ little from mandating disclosure of information in the bill itself, as the plurality recognizes.

Given that the Commission can require the utility to make certain statements and to carry the Commission's own messages to its customers, it seems but a small step to acknowledge that the Commission can also require the utility to act as the conduit for a public interest group's message that bears a close relationship to the purpose of the billing envelope.[7] An analogue to this requirement appears in securities law: the Securities and Exchange Commission requires the incumbent board of directors to transmit proposals of dissident shareholders which it opposes.[8] Presumably the plurality does not doubt the constitutionality of the SEC's requirement under the First Amendment, and yet—although the analogy is far from perfect—it performs the same function as the Commission's rule by making accessible the relevant audience, whether it be shareholders investing in the corporation or consumers served by the utility, to individuals or groups with demonstrable interests in reaching that audience for certain limited and approved purposes.

If the California Public Utility Commission had taken over company buildings and vehicles for propaganda purposes, or even engaged in viewpoint discrimination among speakers desirous of sending messages via the billing envelope, I would be concerned. But nothing in this case presents problems even remotely

3. Since 1919 the predecessor to the California Public Utility Commission ordered that each electric bill reprint the regulations "regarding payment of bills, disputed bills and discontinuance of service." Other States have similar requirements.

5. At various times the Commission has required that inserts be placed in billing envelopes to "explai[n] the reasons behind [a] gas rate increase," and to "describe the components of utility costs." See *Pacific Gas & Electric Co.*, 7 P.U.C.2d 349, 518 (1981) ("By March 1, 1982, PG & E shall mail to all its customers a bill insert which describes the components of the utility's costs. The complete bill insert to be sent is given in Appendix G of this decision. Its size and form shall be approved by the Executive Director in writing prior to inclusion with any customer's bill.").

California has also enacted legislation requiring that utilities notify their customers of rate increases. These notices, which by statute must be included in utility bill envelopes, "shall state the amount of the proposed increase expressed in both dollar and percentage terms, a brief statement of the reasons the increase is required or sought, and the mailing address of commission to which any customer inquiries relative to the proposed increase [may] be directed." Other states likewise require certain service-related communications to be carried in a utility company's billing envelope.

7. Because TURN's purpose is to solicit funds to fight utility rate increases, the success of its appeal bears directly on the size of the bill which, after all, the billing envelope contains.

8. This regulation cannot be justified on the basis of the commercial character of the communication, because the Rule can and has been used to propagate purely political proposals. See, e.g., *Medical Committee for Human Rights v. SEC*, 432 F.2d 659, 662 (1970) (shareholder proposal to stop sale of napalm in part because of use in Vietnam), vacated as moot, 401 U.S. 973, 91 S.Ct. 1191, 28 L.Ed.2d 322 (1971).

Even if the SEC Rule were justified largely on the basis of the commercial character of the communication, that justification is not irrelevant in this case. The messages that the utility disseminates in its newsletter are unquestionably intended to advance the corporation's commercial interests and its objections to the public interest groups messages are based on their potentially adverse impact on the utility's ability to obtain rate increases. These commercial factors do not justify an abridgment of the utility's constitutionally protected right to communicate in *its* newsletter, but they do provide a legitimate and an adequate justification for the Commission's action in giving TURN access to the same audience that receives the utility's newsletter.

resembling or portending the ones just mentioned. Although the plurality's holding may wisely forestall serious constitutional problems that are likely to arise in the future, I am not convinced that the order under review today has crossed the threshold of unconstitutionality. * * *

Chapter 5

FREEDOM OF RELIGION

This chapter concerns the "religion clauses" of the first amendment, commonly known as the "establishment clause" (forbidding laws "respecting an establishment of religion") and the "free exercise clause" (forbidding laws "prohibiting the free exercise thereof"). It is difficult to explore either clause in isolation from the other. The extent to which the clauses interact may be illustrated by the matter of public financial aid to parochial schools, the subject of a number of cases that follow: On the one hand, does such aid violate the establishment clause? On the other hand, does a state's failure to provide such aid violate the free exercise clause? Another example of the potential conflict between the clauses—also considered in the materials below—is whether, on the one hand, a state's exemption of church buildings from property taxes contravenes the establishment clause or whether, on the other hand, a state's taxing these buildings contravenes the free exercise clause.

Despite this interrelationship of the two clauses, Sec. 1 deals almost exclusively with the establishment clause. Sec. 2, I then considers conventional problems under the free exercise clause. Sec. 2, II examines the complex issues of defining "religion" for purposes of the first amendment and determining the bona fides of an asserted "religious" belief—both matters usually presumed in the cases decided by the Supreme Court and the former never specifically addressed by a majority of the justices. Finally, issues under each clause having been explored in some detail, Sec. 3 discusses problems presented by government action that attempts to accommodate the seemingly opposing demands of the two religion clauses.

SECTION 1. ESTABLISHMENT CLAUSE

Prior to 1947, only two decisions concerning the establishment clause produced any significant consideration by the Court. *Bradfield v. Roberts,* 175 U.S. 291, 20 S.Ct. 121, 44 L.Ed. 168 (1899) upheld federal appropriations to a hospital in the District of Columbia, operated by the Catholic Church, for ward construction and care of indigent patients. *Quick Bear v. Leupp,* 210 U.S. 50, 28 S.Ct. 690, 52 L.Ed. 954 (1908) upheld federal disbursement of funds, held in trust for the Sioux Indians, to Catholic schools designated by the Sioux for payment of tuition costs. Since 1947, however, a substantial number of cases have dealt with the meaning of the establishment clause. The major areas of controversy have concerned public financial assistance to church-related institutions (mainly parochial schools) and religious practices in the public schools. During the 1980s, several decisions have involved government action that publicly acknowledges religion.[a]

---

a. For discussion of the various "articulated justifications for the special constitutional place of religion" by the Justices, see Smith, *The Special Place of Religion in the Constitution,* 1983 Sup.Ct.Rev. 83.

EVERSON v. BOARD OF EDUC., 330 U.S. 1, 67 S.Ct. 504, 91 L.Ed. 711 (1947): A New Jersey township reimbursed parents for the cost of sending their children "on regular buses operated by the public transportation system," to and from schools, including nonprofit private and parochial schools. The Court, per BLACK, J., rejected a municipal taxpayer's contention that payment for Catholic parochial school students violated the establishment clause, observing that the religion clauses of the first amendment, "as made applicable to the states by the Fourteenth," "reflected in the minds of early Americans a vivid mental picture of conditions and practices which they fervently wished to stamp out in order to preserve liberty for themselves and for their posterity."

The Court detailed the history of religious persecution in Europe "before and contemporaneous with the colonization of America" and the "repetition of many of the old world practices" in the colonies—emphasizing the compulsion "to pay tithes and taxes to support government-sponsored churches whose ministers preached inflammatory sermons designed to strengthen and consolidate the established faith by generating a burning hatred against dissenters." The abhorrence of these practices "reached its dramatic climax in Virginia in 1785–86" when "Madison wrote his great Memorial and Remonstrance" against renewal of "Virginia's tax levy for support of the established church" and the Virginia Assembly "enacted the famous 'Virginia Bill for Religious Liberty' originally written by Thomas Jefferson. [T]he provisions of the First Amendment, in the drafting and adoption of which Madison and Jefferson played such leading roles, had the same objective and were intended to provide the same protection against governmental intrusion on religious liberty as the Virginia statute. [The] interrelationship of these complementary clauses was well summarized [in] *Watson v. Jones,* 13 Wall. 679, 730, 20 L.Ed. 666: 'The structure of our government has, for the preservation of civil liberty, rescued the temporal institutions from religious interference. On the other hand, it has secured religious liberty from the invasions of the civil authority.'

"The 'establishment of religion' clause of the First Amendment means at least this: Neither a state nor the Federal Government can set up a church. Neither can pass laws which aid one religion, aid all religions, or prefer one religion over another. Neither can force nor influence a person to go to or to remain away from church against his will or force him to profess a belief or disbelief in any religion. No person can be punished for entertaining or professing religious beliefs or disbeliefs, for church attendance or non-attendance. No tax in any amount, large or small can be levied to support any religious activities or institutions, whatever they may be called, or whatever form they may adopt to teach or practice religion. Neither a state nor the Federal Government can, openly or secretly, participate in the affairs of any religious organizations or groups and vice versa. In the words of Jefferson, the clause against establishment of religion by law was intended to erect 'a wall of separation between Church and State.'

"We must [not invalidate the New Jersey statute] if it is within the state's constitutional power even though it approaches the verge of that power. New Jersey cannot consistently with the 'establishment of religion' clause of the First Amendment contribute tax-raised funds to the support of an institution which teaches the tenets and faith of any church. On the other hand, other language of the amendment commands that New Jersey cannot hamper its citizens in the free exercise of their own religion. Consequently, it cannot exclude individual Catholics, Lutherans, Mohammedans, Baptists, Jews, Methodists, Non-believers,

Presbyterians, or the members of any other faith, *because of their faith, or lack of it,* from receiving the benefits of public welfare legislation. While we do not mean to intimate that a state could not provide transportation only to children attending public schools, we must be careful, in protecting the citizens of New Jersey against state-established churches, to be sure that we do not inadvertently prohibit New Jersey from extending its general State law benefits to all its citizens without regard to their religious belief."

Noting that "the New Jersey legislature has decided that a public purpose will be served" by having children "ride in public buses to and from schools rather than run the risk of traffic and other hazards incident to walking or 'hitchhiking,'" the Court conceded "that children are helped to get to church schools. There is even a possibility that some of the children might not be sent to the church schools if the parents were compelled to pay their children's bus fares out of their own pockets when transportation to a public school would have been paid for by the State. [But] state-paid policemen, detailed to protect children going to and from church schools from the very real hazards of traffic, would serve much the same [purpose]. Similarly, parents might be reluctant to permit their children to attend schools which the state had cut off from such general government services as ordinary police and fire protection, connections for sewage disposal, public highways and sidewalks. Of course, cutting off church schools from these services, so separate and so indisputably marked off from the religious function, would make it far more difficult for the schools to operate. But such is obviously not the purpose of the First Amendment. That Amendment requires the state to be a neutral in its relations with groups of religious believers and non-believers; it does not require the state to be their adversary. State power is no more to be used so as to handicap religions, than it is to favor them.

"This Court had said that parents may, in the discharge of their duty under state compulsory education laws, send their children to a religious rather than a public school if the school meets the secular educational requirements which the state has power to impose. See *Pierce v. Society of Sisters,* [p. 144 supra]. It appears that these parochial schools meet New Jersey's requirements. The State contributes no money to the schools. It does not support them. Its legislation, as applied, does no more than provide a general program to help parents get their children, regardless of their religion, safely and expeditiously to and from accredited schools.

"The First Amendment has erected a wall between church and state. That wall must be kept high and impregnable. We could not approve the slightest breach. New Jersey has not breached it here."

RUTLEDGE, J., joined by Frankfurter, Jackson and Burton, JJ., filed the principal dissent, arguing that the statute aided children "in a substantial way to get the very thing which they are sent to the particular school to secure, namely, religious training and teaching. * * * Commingling the religious with the secular teaching does not divest the whole of its religious permeation and emphasis or make them of minor part, if proportion were material. Indeed, on any other view, the constitutional prohibition always could be brought to naught by adding a modicum of the secular. [Transportation] cost is as much a part of the total expense, except at times in amount, as the cost of textbooks, of school lunches, of athletic equipment, of writing and other [materials]. Payment of transportation is [no] less essential to education, whether religious or secular, than payment for tuitions, for teachers' salaries, for buildings, equipment and necessary materials. [No] rational line can be drawn between payment for such larger, but not more necessary, items and payment for transportation. [Now], as in Madison's time, not the amount but the principle of assessment is wrong.

"But we are told that the New Jersey statute is valid [because] the appropriation is for a public, not a private purpose, namely, the promotion of education, and the majority accept this idea in the conclusion that all we have here is 'public welfare legislation.' If that is true and the Amendment's force can be thus destroyed, what has been said becomes all the more pertinent. For then there could be no possible objection to more extensive support of religious education by New Jersey.

" * * * Public money devoted to payment of religious costs, educational or other, brings the quest for more. It brings too the struggle of sect against sect for the larger share or for any. Here one by numbers alone will benefit most, there another. That is precisely the history of societies which have had an established religion and dissident groups. It is the very thing Jefferson and Madison experienced and sought to guard against, whether in its blunt or in its more screened forms. The end of such strife cannot be other than to destroy the cherished liberty. The dominating group will achieve the dominant benefit; or all will embroil the state in their dissensions. * * *

"No one conscious of religious values can be unsympathetic toward the burden which our constitutional separation puts on parents who desire religious instruction mixed with secular for their children. They pay taxes for others' children's education, at the same time the added cost of instruction for their own. [But] discrimination in the legal sense does not exist. The child attending the religious school has the same right as any other to attend the public school. But he forgoes exercising it because the same guaranty which assures his freedom forbids the public school or any agency of the state to give or aid him in securing the religious instruction he seeks. * * *

"Nor is the case comparable to one of furnishing fire or police protection, or access to public highways. These things are matters of common right, part of the general need for safety. Certainly the fire department must not stand idly by while the church burns."

I. RELIGION AND PUBLIC SCHOOLS

The Court did not again confront the subject of aid to parochial schools until 1968. These decisions are considered in Part II infra. During the intervening two decades, however, the Court was presented with other problems—the most prominent concerning religious influence in the public schools—that enabled it to further develop the establishment clause rationale begun in *Everson.*

WALLACE v. JAFFREE

472 U.S. 38, 105 S.Ct. 2479, 86 L.Ed.2d 29 (1985).

Justice Stevens delivered the opinion of the Court.

[In 1978, Alabama enacted § 16–1–20 authorizing a one-minute period of silence in all public schools "for meditation"; in 1981, it enacted § 16–1–20.1 authorizing a period of silence "for meditation or voluntary prayer." Appellees] have not questioned the holding that § 16–1–20 is valid. Thus, the narrow question for decision [concerns § 16–1–20.1].

Appellee [filed] a complaint on behalf of three of his minor children; two of them were second-grade students and the third was then in kindergarten. [T]he District Court dismissed appellees' challenge [based] on its conclusion that the Establishment Clause did not bar the States from establishing a religion.

The Court of Appeals [reversed, noting] that this Court had considered and had rejected the historical arguments that the District Court found persuasive * * *.

As is plain from its text, the First Amendment was adopted to curtail the power of Congress to interfere with the individual's freedom to believe, to worship, and to express himself in accordance with the dictates of his own conscience. [W]hen the Constitution was amended to prohibit any State from depriving any person of liberty without due process of law, that Amendment imposed the same substantive limitations on the States' power to legislate that the First Amendment had always imposed on the Congress' power. This Court has confirmed and endorsed this elementary proposition of law time and time again.[a]

a. *Application of the establishment clause to the states.* Is nonestablishment as "implicit in the concept of ordered liberty" as the freedoms of speech, press, religious exercise, and assembly? See *Palko v. Connecticut,* p. 120 supra. Is it "fundamental to the American scheme"? See *Duncan v. Louisiana,* p. 125 supra.

Brennan, J., has stated: "It has been suggested, with some support in history, that absorption of the First Amendment's ban against congressional legislation 'respecting an establishment of religion' is conceptually impossible because the Framers meant the Establishment Clause also to foreclose any attempt by Congress to disestablish the existing official state churches. [But] the last of the formal state establishments was dissolved more than three decades before the Fourteenth Amendment was ratified, and thus the problem of protecting official state churches from federal encroachments could hardly have been any concern of those who framed the post-Civil War Amendments. [T]he Fourteenth Amendment created a panoply of new federal rights for the protection of citizens of the various States. And among those rights was freedom from such state governmental involvement in the affairs of religion as the Establishment Clause had originally foreclosed on the part of Congress.

"It has also been suggested that the 'liberty' guaranteed by the Fourteenth Amendment logically cannot absorb the Establishment Clause because that clause is not one of the provisions of the Bill of Rights which in terms protects a 'freedom' of the individual. The fallacy in this contention, I think, is that it underestimates the role of the Establishment Clause as a coguarantor, with the Free Exercise Clause, of religious liberty. * * *

"Finally, it has been contended that absorption of the Establishment Clause is precluded by the absence of any intention on the part of the Framers of the Fourteenth Amendment to circumscribe the residual powers of the States to aid religious activities and institutions in ways which fell short of formal establishments. That argument relies in part upon the express terms of the abortive Blaine Amendment—proposed several years after the adoption of the Fourteenth Amendment—which would have added to the First Amendment a provision that '[n]o state shall make any law respecting an establishment of religion.' Such a restriction would have been superfluous, it is said, if the Fourteenth Amendment had already made the Establishment Clause binding upon the States.

"The argument proves too much, for the Fourteenth Amendment's protection of the free exercise of religion can hardly be questioned; yet the Blaine Amendment would also have added an explicit protection against state laws abridging that liberty." *School Dist. v. Schempp,* Part I infra (concurring opinion).

Consider Howe, *The Constitutional Question,* in Religion and the Free Society 49, 55 (1958): "The Court did not seem to be aware of the fact that some legislative enactments respecting an establishment of religion affect most remotely, if at all, the personal rights of religious liberty. [If the Court] reexamined its own interpretations of history [it might allow] the states to take such action in aid of religion as does not appreciably affect the religious or other constitutional rights of individuals * * *."

Compare Choper, *The Establishment Clause and Aid to Parochial Schools,* 56 Calif.L.Rev. 260, 274–75 (1968): "[Howe] assumes that while the fourteenth amendment prevents infringements of liberty which 'significantly affect' the individual, the first amendment forbids abridgements which do not do so. [A] central design of the establishment clause was that it [prevent] government generally from coercing religious belief and specifically from

[T]he individual's freedom to choose his own creed is the counterpart of his right to refrain from accepting the creed established by the majority. At one time it was thought that this right merely proscribed the preference of one Christian sect over another, but would not require equal respect for the conscience of the infidel, the atheist, or the adherent of a non-Christian faith such as Islam or Judaism. But when the underlying principle has been examined in the crucible of litigation, the Court has unambiguously concluded that the individual freedom of conscience protected by the First Amendment embraces the right to select any religious faith or none at all.[37] This conclusion derives support not only from the interest in respecting the individual's freedom of conscience, but also from the conviction that religious beliefs worthy of respect are the product of free and voluntary choice by the faithful, and from recognition of the fact that the political interest in forestalling intolerance extends beyond intolerance among Christian sects—or even intolerance among "religions"—to encompass intolerance of the disbeliever and the uncertain. * * *

When the Court has been called upon to construe the breadth of the Establishment Clause, it has examined the criteria developed over a period of many years. Thus, in *Lemon v. Kurtzman,* 403 U.S. 602, 612–613, 91 S.Ct. 2105, 2111, 29 L.Ed.2d 745 (1971), we wrote: "* * * Three such tests may be gleaned from our cases. First, the statute must have a secular legislative purpose; second, its principal or primary effect must be one that neither advances nor inhibits religion,[b] finally, the statute must not foster 'an excessive government entanglement with religion.'" It is the first of these three criteria that is most plainly implicated by this case. As the District Court correctly recognized, no consideration of the second or third criteria is necessary if a statute does not have a clearly secular purpose. For even though a statute that is motivated in part by a religious purpose may satisfy the first criterion, the First Amendment requires that a statute must be invalidated if it is entirely motivated by a purpose to advance religion.

In applying the purpose test, it is appropriate to ask "whether government's actual purpose is to endorse or disapprove of religion."[42] In this case, the

compulsorily taxing individuals for strictly religious purposes. If nonsecular federal action involves either of these consequences, [it] has 'significantly' affected individual freedom. Thus, if such state action involves either, it has seemingly violated the fourteenth amendment by 'significantly' affecting personal liberty. However, if federal action involves neither consequence, then [the] establishment clause itself—as a matter of constitutional construction—has probably not been breached." See also Note, *Toward a Uniform Valuation of the Religion Guarantees,* 80 Yale L.J. 77 (1970).

37. [See] *Torcaso v. Watkins,* [Sec. 2, II infra] ("We repeat and again reaffirm that neither a State nor the Federal Government can constitutionally force a person 'to profess a belief or disbelief in any religion.' Neither can constitutionally pass laws or impose requirements which aid all religions as against non-believers, and neither can aid those religions based on a belief in the existence of God as against those religions founded on different beliefs").

b. Compare Laycock, *Towards a General Theory of the Religion Clauses: The Case of Church Labor Relations and the Right to Church Autonomy,* 81 Colum.L.Rev. 1373, 1381, 1384 (1981): "The 'inhibits' language is at odds with the constitutional text and with the Court's own statements of the origins and purposes of the [establishment] clause. Government support for religion is an element of every establishment claim, just as a burden or restriction on religion is an element of every free exercise claim. Regulation that burdens religion, enacted because of the government's general interest in regulation, is simply not establishment."

42. *Lynch v. Donnelly,* [Part III infra] (O'Connor, J., concurring) ("The purpose prong of the *Lemon* test asks whether government's actual purpose is to endorse or disapprove of religion. The effect prong asks whether, irrespective of government's actual purpose, the practice under review in fact conveys a message of endorsement or disapproval. An affirmative answer to either quesanswer to that question is dispositive. * * *

The sponsor of the bill that became § 16–1–20.1, Senator Donald Holmes, inserted into the legislative record—apparently without dissent—a statement indicating that the legislation was an "effort to return voluntary prayer" to the public schools. Later Senator Holmes confirmed this purpose before the District Court. In response to the question whether he had any purpose for the legislation other than returning voluntary prayer to public schools, he stated: "No, I did not have no other purpose in mind." [44] The State did not present evidence of *any* secular purpose.[45] * * *

The legislative intent to return prayer to the public schools is, of course, quite different from merely protecting every student's right to engage in voluntary prayer during an appropriate moment of silence during the schoolday. The 1978 statute already protected that right, containing nothing that prevented any student from engaging in voluntary prayer during a silent minute of meditation. [The] legislature enacted § 16–1–20.1, despite the existence of § 16–1–20 for the sole purpose of expressing the State's endorsement of prayer activities for one minute at the beginning of each schoolday. The addition of "or voluntary prayer" indicates that the State intended to characterize prayer as a favored practice. Such an endorsement is not consistent with the established principle that the government must pursue a course of complete neutrality toward religion.

The importance of that principle does not permit us to treat this as an inconsequential case involving nothing more than a few words of symbolic speech on behalf of the political majority.[51] For whenever the State itself speaks

tion should render the challenged practice invalid").

44. The District Court and the Court of Appeals agreed that the purpose of § 16–1–20.1 was "an effort on the part of the State of Alabama to encourage a religious activity." The evidence presented to the District Court elaborated on the express admission of the Governor of Alabama (then Fob James) that the enactment of § 16–1–20.1 was intended to "clarify [the State's] intent to have prayer as part of the daily classroom activity," and that the "expressed legislative purpose in enacting Section 16–1–20.1 (1981) was to 'return voluntary prayer to public schools.' "

45. Appellant Governor George C. Wallace now argues that § 16–1–20.1 "is best understood as a permissible accommodation of religion" and that viewed even in terms of the *Lemon* test, the "statute conforms to acceptable constitutional criteria." These arguments seem to be based on the theory that the free exercise of religion of some of the State's citizens was burdened before the statute was enacted. The United States, appearing as amicus curiae in support of the appellants, candidly acknowledges that "it is unlikely that in most contexts a strong Free Exercise claim could be made that time for personal prayer must be set aside during the school day." There is no basis for the suggestion that § 16–1–20.1 "is a means for accommodating the religious and meditative needs of students without in any way diminishing the school's own neutrality or secular atmosphere." In this case, it is undisputed that at the time of the enactment of § 16–1–20.1 there was no governmental practice impeding students from silently praying for one minute at the beginning of each schoolday; thus, there was no need to "accommodate" or to exempt individuals from any general governmental requirement because of the dictates of our cases interpreting the Free Exercise Clause. * * *

51. As this Court stated in *Engel v. Vitale,* [infra]: "The Establishment Clause, unlike the Free Exercise Clause, does not depend upon any showing of direct governmental compulsion and is violated by the enactment of laws which establish an official religion whether those laws operate directly to coerce nonobserving individuals or not." Moreover, this Court has noted that "[w]hen the power, prestige and financial support of government is placed behind a particular religious belief, the indirect coercive pressure upon religious minorities to conform to the prevailing officially approved religion is plain." Id. This comment has special force in the public-school context where attendance is mandatory. Justice Frankfurter acknowledged this reality in *McCollum v. Board of Education,* [note 1(a) infra] (concurring opinion): "That a child is offered an alternative may reduce the constraint; it does not eliminate the operation of influence by the school in matters sacred to conscience and outside the school's domain.

on a religious subject, one of the questions that we must ask is "whether the government intends to convey a message of endorsement or disapproval of religion." * * *

The judgment of the Court of Appeals is affirmed.

JUSTICE O'CONNOR concurring in the judgment.

* * * Although a distinct jurisprudence has enveloped each of [the Religion] Clauses, their common purpose is to secure religious liberty. On these principles the Court has been and remains unanimous. * * * I do believe, however, that the standards announced in *Lemon* should be reexamined and refined in order to make them more useful in achieving the underlying purpose of the First Amendment. [O]ur goal should be "to frame a principle for constitutional adjudication that is not only grounded in the history and language of the first amendment, but one that is also capable of consistent application to the relevant problems." Choper, *Religion in the Public Schools: A Proposed Constitutional Standard,* 47 Minn.L.Rev. 329, 332–333 (1963). Last Term, I proposed a refinement of the *Lemon* test with this goal in mind. *Lynch v. Donnelly* (concurring opinion).

The *Lynch* concurrence suggested that the religious liberty protected by the Establishment Clause is infringed when the government makes adherence to religion relevant to a person's standing in the political community. Direct government action endorsing religion or a particular religious practice is invalid under this approach because it "sends a message to nonadherents that they are outsiders, not full members of the political community, and an accompanying message to adherents that they are insiders, favored members of the political community." * * *

The endorsement test is useful because of the analytic content it gives to the *Lemon*-mandated inquiry into legislative purpose and effect. In this country, church and state must necessarily operate within the same community. Because of this coexistence, it is inevitable that the secular interests of government and the religious interests of various sects and their adherents will frequently intersect, conflict, and combine. A statute that ostensibly promotes a secular interest often has an incidental or even a primary effect of helping or hindering a sectarian belief. Chaos would ensue if every such statute were invalid under the Establishment Clause. For example, the State could not criminalize murder for fear that it would thereby promote the Biblical command against killing.[b] The task for the Court is to sort out those statutes and government practices

The law of imitation operates, and non-conformity is not an outstanding characteristic of children." * * *

b. On this analysis, *McGowan v. Maryland,* 366 U.S. 420, 81 S.Ct. 1101, 6 L.Ed.2d 393 (1961), per Warren, C.J., held that the "present purpose and effect" of Maryland's Sunday Closing Laws were not religious and did not violate the establishment clause. Although "the original laws which dealt with Sunday labor were motivated by religious forces," the Court showed that secular emphases in language and interpretation have come about, that recent "legislation was supported by labor groups and trade associations," and that "secular justifications have been advanced for making Sunday a day of rest, a day when people may recover from the labors of the week just passed and may physically and mentally prepare for the week's work to come. [It] would seem unrealistic for enforcement purposes and perhaps detrimental to the general welfare to require a State to choose a common day of rest other than that which most persons would select of their own accord."

Douglas, J., dissented: "No matter how much is written, no matter what is said," Sunday is a Christian holiday. "There is an 'establishment' of religion in the constitutional sense if any practice of any religious group has the sanction of law behind it."

whose purpose and effect go against the grain of religious liberty protected by the First Amendment.

The endorsement test does not preclude government from acknowledging religion or from taking religion into account in making law and policy. It does preclude government from conveying or attempting to convey a message that religion or a particular religious belief is favored or preferred. Such an endorsement infringes the religious liberty of the nonadherent, for "[w]hen the power, prestige and financial support of government is placed behind a particular religious belief, the indirect coercive pressure upon religious minorities to conform to the prevailing officially approved religion is plain." *Engel.* * * *

Twenty-five states permit or require public school teachers to have students observe a moment of silence in their classrooms. A few statutes provide that the moment of silence is for the purpose of meditation alone. The typical statute, however, calls for a moment of silence at the beginning of the schoolday during which students may meditate, pray, or reflect on the activities of the day. * * * Relying on this Court's decisions disapproving vocal prayer and Bible reading in the public schools, see *Abington School District v. Schempp,* 374 U.S. 203, 83 S.Ct. 1560, 10 L.Ed.2d 844 (1963); *Engel v. Vitale,* 370 U.S. 421, 82 S.Ct. 1261, 8 L.Ed.2d 601 (1962), the courts that have struck down the moment of silence statutes generally conclude that their purpose and effect are to encourage prayer in public schools.

The *Engel* and *Abington* decisions are not dispositive on the constitutionality of moment of silence laws. In those cases, public school teachers and students led their classes in devotional exercises. In *Engel,* a New York statute required teachers to lead their classes in a vocal prayer.[c] The Court concluded that "it is no part of the business of government to compose official prayers for any group of the American people to recite as part of a religious program carried on by the government." [d] In *Abington,* the Court addressed Pennsylvania and Maryland statutes that authorized morning Bible readings in public schools.[e] The Court reviewed the purpose and effect of the statutes, concluded that they required religious exercises, and therefore found them to violate the Establishment Clause. Under all of these statutes, a student who did not share the religious beliefs expressed in the course of the exercise was left with the choice of participating, thereby compromising the nonadherent's beliefs, or withdrawing, thereby calling attention to his or her nonconformity. The decisions acknowledged the coercion implicit under the statutory schemes, see *Engel,*[f] but they expressly turned only on the fact that the government was sponsoring a manifestly religious exercise.[g]

c. The prayer, composed by the N.Y. Board of Regents, provided: "Almighty God, we acknowledge our dependence upon Thee, and we beg Thy blessings upon us, our parents, our teachers and our country."

d. Stewart, J., dissented. Frankfurter and White, JJ., did not participate.

e. The reading of the Bible, without comment, was followed by recitation of the Lord's Prayer. In Pennsylvania, various students read passages they selected from any version of the Bible. Plaintiff father testified that "specific religious doctrines purveyed by a literal reading of the Bible" were contrary to the family's Unitarian religious beliefs; one expert testified that "portions of the New Testament were offensive to Jewish tradition" and, if "read without explanation, they could [be] psychologically harmful to the child and had caused a divisive force within the social media of the school"; a defense expert testified "that the Bible [was] non-sectarian within the Christian faiths."

Stewart, J., dissented.

f. See fn. 51 in the Court's opinion, supra.

g. *Engel* distinguished "the fact that school children and others are officially encouraged to express love for our country by reciting historical documents such as the Declaration of Independence which contain references to the Deity or by singing officially

A state-sponsored moment of silence in the public schools is different from state-sponsored vocal prayer or Bible reading. First, a moment of silence is not inherently religious. Silence, unlike prayer or Bible reading, need not be associated with a religious exercise. Second, a pupil who participates in a moment of silence need not compromise his or her beliefs. During a moment of silence, a student who objects to prayer is left to his or her own thoughts, and is not compelled to listen to the prayers or thoughts of others. [It] is difficult to discern a serious threat to religious liberty from a room of silent, thoughtful schoolchildren.

By mandating a moment of silence, a State does not necessarily endorse any activity that might occur during the period. Even if a statute specifies that a student may choose to pray silently during a quiet moment, the State has not thereby encouraged prayer over other specified alternatives. Nonetheless, it is also possible that a moment of silence statute, either as drafted or as actually implemented, could effectively favor the child who prays over the child who does not. For example, the message of endorsement would seem inescapable if the teacher exhorts children to use the designated time to pray. Similarly, the fact of the statute or its legislative history may clearly establish that it seeks to encourage or promote voluntary prayer over other alternatives, rather than merely provide a quiet moment that may be dedicated to prayer by those so inclined. The crucial question is whether the State has conveyed or attempted to convey the message that children should use the moment of silence for prayer.[2] This question cannot be answered in the abstract, but instead requires courts to examine the history, language, and administration of a particular statute to determine whether it operates as an endorsement of religion.

Before reviewing Alabama's moment of silence law to determine whether it endorses prayer, some general observations on the proper scope of the inquiry are in order. First, the inquiry into the purpose of the legislature in enacting a moment of silence law should be deferential and limited. In determining whether the government intends a moment of silence statute to convey a message of endorsement or disapproval of religion, a court has no license to psychoanalyze the legislators. If a legislature expresses a plausible secular purpose for a moment of silence statute in either the text or the legislative history, or if the statute disclaims an intent to encourage prayer over alternatives during a moment of silence, then courts should generally defer to that stated intent. It is particularly troublesome to denigrate an expressed secular purpose due to postenactment testimony by particular legislators or by interested persons who witnessed the drafting of the statute.[h] Even if the text and official history of a statute express no secular purpose, the statute should be held

espoused anthems which include the composer's professions of faith in a Supreme Being, or with the fact that there are many manifestations in our public life of belief in God. Such patriotic or ceremonial occasions bear no true resemblance to the unquestioned religious exercise that the State of New York has sponsored in this instance."

2. Appellants argue that *Zorach v. Clauson,* [note 1(b) infra,] suggests there is no constitutional infirmity in a State's encouraging a child to pray during a moment of silence. [There] the Court stated that "[w]hen the state encourages religious instruction—*[by] adjusting the schedule of public events to sectarian needs,* it follows the best of our traditions." When the State provides a moment of silence during which prayer may occur at the election of the student, it can be said to be adjusting the schedule of public events to sectarian needs. But when the State also encourages the student to pray during a moment of silence, it converts an otherwise inoffensive moment of silence into an effort by the majority to use the machinery of the State to encourage the minority to participate in a religious exercise.

h. For further discussion of this point, see Burger, C.J.'s opinion infra.

to have an improper purpose only if it is beyond purview that endorsement of religion or a religious belief "was and is the law's reason for existence." *Epperson v. Arkansas,* [note 3(b) infra]. Since there is arguably a secular pedagogical value to a moment of silence in public schools, courts should find an improper purpose behind such a statute only if the statute on its face, in its official legislative history, or in its interpretation by a responsible administrative agency suggests it has the primary purpose of endorsing prayer.

[It] is not a trivial matter [to] require that the legislature manifest a secular purpose and omit all sectarian endorsements from its laws. That requirement is precisely tailored to the Establishment Clause's purpose of assuring that government not intentionally endorse religion or a religious practice. It is of course possible that a legislature will enunciate a sham secular purpose for a statute. I have little doubt that our courts are capable of distinguishing a sham secular purpose from a sincere one, or that the *Lemon* inquiry into the effect of an enactment would help decide those close cases where the validity of an expressed secular purpose is in doubt. * * *

Second, the *Lynch* concurrence suggested that the effect of a moment of silence law is not entirely a question of [fact]. The relevant issue is whether an objective observer, acquainted with the text, legislative history, and implementation of the statute, would perceive it as a state endorsement of prayer in public schools. A moment of silence law that is clearly drafted and implemented so as to permit prayer, meditation, and reflection within the prescribed period, without endorsing one alternative over the others, should pass this test.

The analysis above suggests that moment of silence laws in many States should pass Establishment Clause scrutiny because they do not favor the child who chooses to pray during a moment of silence over the child who chooses to meditate or reflect. § 16–1–20.1 does not stand on the same footing. However deferentially one examines its text and legislative history, however objectively one views the message attempted to be conveyed to the public, the conclusion is unavoidable that the purpose of the statute is to endorse prayer in public [schools.][5] * * *[i]

CHIEF JUSTICE BURGER dissenting.

[For] decades our opinions have stated that hostility toward any religion or toward all religions is as much forbidden by the Constitution as is an official establishment of religion. The Alabama Legislature has no more "endorsed" religion than a state or the Congress does when it provides for legislative chaplains, or than this Court does when it opens each session with an invocation to God. Today's decision recalls the observations of Justice Goldberg: "[U]ntutored devotion to the concept of neutrality can lead to invocation or approval of results which partake not simply of that noninterference and noninvolvement with the religious which the Constitution commands, but of a brooding and pervasive dedication to the secular and a passive, or even active, hostility to the religious. Such results are not only not compelled by the

5. The Chief Justice suggests that one consequence of the Court's emphasis on the difference between § 16–1–20.1 and its predecessor statute might be to render the Pledge of Allegiance unconstitutional because Congress amended it in 1954 to add the words "under God". I disagree. In my view, the words "under God" in the Pledge serve as an acknowledgement of religion with "the legitimate secular purposes of solemnizing public occasions, [and] expressing confidence in the future." *Lynch* (concurring opinion).

i. Powell, J., who was the fifth justice to join the Court's opinion, also separately concurred, agreeing "fully with Justice O'Connor's assertion that some moment-of-silence statutes may be constitutional, a suggestion set forth in the Court's opinion as well."

Constitution, but, it seems to me, are prohibited by it." *Schempp* (concurring opinion). * * *

Curiously, the opinions do not mention that *all* of the sponsor's statements relied upon—including the statement "inserted" into the Senate Journal—were made *after* the legislature had passed the statute; indeed, the testimony that the Court finds critical was given well over a year after the statute was enacted. As even the appellees concede, there is not a shred of evidence that the legislature as a whole shared the sponsor's motive or that a majority in either house was even aware of the sponsor's view of the bill when it was passed. The sole relevance of the sponsor's statements, therefore, is that they reflect the personal, subjective motives of a single legislator. No case in the 195–year history of this Court supports the disconcerting idea that post-enactment statements by individual legislators are relevant in determining the constitutionality of legislation.

Even if an individual legislator's after-the-fact statements could rationally be considered relevant, all of the opinions fail to mention that the sponsor also testified that one of his purposes in drafting and sponsoring the moment-of-silence bill was to clear up a widespread misunderstanding that a schoolchild is legally *prohibited* from engaging in silent, individual prayer once he steps inside a public school building. That testimony is at least as important as the statements the Court relies upon, and surely that testimony manifests a permissible purpose. * * *

The several preceding opinions conclude that the principal difference between § 16–1–20.1 and its predecessor statute proves that the sole purpose behind the inclusion of the phrase "or voluntary prayer" in § 16–1–20.1 was to endorse and promote prayer. This reasoning is simply a subtle way of focusing exclusively on the religious component of the statute rather than examining the statute as a whole. Such logic—if it can be called that—would lead the Court to hold, for example, that a state may enact a statute that provides reimbursement for bus transportation to the parents of all schoolchildren, but may not *add* parents of parochial school students to an existing program providing reimbursement for parents of public school students. Congress amended the statutory Pledge of Allegiance 31 years ago to add the words "under God." Do the several opinions in support of the judgment today render the Pledge unconstitutional? [3]

[The] statute does not remotely threaten religious liberty; it affirmatively furthers the values of religious freedom and tolerance that the Establishment Clause was designed to protect. Without pressuring those who do not wish to pray, the statute simply creates an opportunity to think, to plan, or to pray if one wishes—as Congress does by providing chaplains and chapels. [The] statute also provides a meaningful opportunity for schoolchildren to appreciate the absolute constitutional right of each individual to worship and believe as the individual wishes. The statute "endorses" only the view that the religious

3. The House Report on the legislation amending the Pledge states that the purpose of the amendment was to affirm the principle that "our people and our Government [are dependent] upon the moral directions of the Creator." If this is simply "acknowledgement," not "endorsement," of religion, (O'Connor, J., concurring in the judgment), the distinction is far too infinitesimal for me to grasp.

[Compare Fordham, *The Implications of the Supreme Court Decisions Dealing with Religious Practices in the Public Schools,* 6 J. of Chur. & St. 44, 56 (1964): "In view of the patriotic element here, one may suggest that the likelihood of indirect compulsion is much greater than in the simple prayer case. Here the individual dissenter is made to stand out as one unwilling to engage in a patriotic act and recital. Does this not overbalance the countervailing consideration that the prime purpose is promotion of patriotism and the religious element is secondary?"]

observances of others should be tolerated and where possible, accommodated. If the government may not accommodate religious needs when it does so in a wholly neutral and noncoercive manner, the "benevolent neutrality" that we have long considered the correct constitutional standard will quickly translate into the "callous indifference" that the Court has consistently held the Establishment Clause does not require. * * *

JUSTICE REHNQUIST, dissenting. * * *

It is impossible to build sound constitutional doctrine upon a mistaken understanding of constitutional history, but unfortunately the Establishment Clause has been expressly freighted with Jefferson's misleading [wall of separation] metaphor for nearly 40 years. * * * James Madison was undoubtedly the most important architect among the Members of the House of the Amendments which became the Bill of Rights. [H]e saw the Amendment as designed to prohibit the establishment of a national religion, and perhaps to prevent discrimination among sects. He did not see it as requiring neutrality on the part of government between religion and irreligion. Thus the Court's opinion in *Everson*—while correct in bracketing Madison and Jefferson together in their exertions in their home State leading to the enactment of the Virginia Statute of Religious Liberty—is totally incorrect in suggesting that Madison carried these views onto the floor of the United States House of Representatives when he proposed the language which would ultimately become the Bill of Rights. * * *

None of the other Members of Congress who spoke during the August 15th debate expressed the slightest indication that they thought the language before them from the Select Committee, or the evil to be aimed at, would require that the Government be absolutely neutral as between religion and irreligion. The evil to be aimed at, so far as those who spoke were concerned, appears to have been the establishment of a national church, and perhaps the preference of one religious sect over another; but it was definitely not concerned about whether the Government might aid all religions evenhandedly. * * *

The actions of the First Congress, which reenacted the Northwest Ordinance for the governance of the Northwest Territory in 1789, confirm the view that Congress did not mean that the Government should be neutral between religion and irreligion. [The] Northwest Ordinance [provides] that "[r]eligion, morality, and knowledge, being necessary to good government and the happiness of mankind, schools and the means of education shall forever be encouraged."

[I]n the 38 years since Everson our Establishment Clause cases have been neither principled nor unified. [The "purpose and effect" tests] have the same historical deficiencies as the wall concept itself: they are in no way based on either the language or intent of the drafters.

The secular purpose prong has proven mercurial in application because it has never been fully defined, and we have never fully stated how the test is to operate. If the purpose prong is intended to void those aids to sectarian institutions accompanied by a stated legislative purpose to aid religion, the prong will condemn nothing so long as the legislature utters a secular purpose and says nothing about aiding religion. Thus the constitutionality of a statute may depend upon what the legislators put into the legislative history and, more importantly, what they leave out. * * *

However, if the purpose prong is aimed to void all statutes enacted with the intent to aid sectarian institutions, whether stated or not, then most statutes providing any aid, such as textbooks or bus rides for sectarian school children, will fail because one of the purposes behind every statute, whether stated or not, is to aid the target of its largesse. * * *

If a constitutional theory has no basis in the history of the amendment it seeks to interpret, is difficult to apply and yields unprincipled results, I see little use in it. [It] would come as much of a shock to those who drafted the Bill of Rights as it will to a large number of thoughtful Americans today to learn that the Constitution, as construed by the majority, prohibits the Alabama Legislature from "endorsing" prayer. George Washington himself, at the request of the very Congress which passed the Bill of Rights, proclaimed a day of "public thanksgiving and prayer, to be observed by acknowledging with grateful hearts the many and signal favors of Almighty God." History must judge whether it was the Father of his Country in 1789, or a majority of the Court today, which has strayed from the meaning of the Establishment Clause. * * * [j]

Notes and Questions

1. *Released time.* (a) McCOLLUM v. BOARD OF EDUC., 333 U.S. 203, 68 S.Ct. 461, 92 L.Ed. 649 (1948), per BLACK, J., held that a Champaign, Illinois public school released time program violated the establishment clause. Privately employed religious teachers held weekly classes, on public school premises, in their respective religions, for students whose parents signed request cards, while non-attending students pursued secular studies in other parts of the building. "Here not only are the state's tax-supported public school buildings used for the dissemination of religious doctrines. The State also affords sectarian groups an invaluable aid in that it helps to provide pupils for their religious classes through use of the state's compulsory public school machinery." [a]

(b) ZORACH v. CLAUSON, 343 U.S. 306, 72 S.Ct. 679, 96 L.Ed. 954 (1952), per DOUGLAS, J., upheld a New York City released time program in which the religious classes were held in church buildings: "[This] program involves neither religious instruction in public school classrooms nor the expenditure of public funds. All costs, including the application blanks, are paid by the religious organizations. The case is therefore unlike *McCollum.*

"[The] nullification of this law would have wide and profound effects. A Catholic student applies to his teacher for permission to leave the school during hours on a Holy Day of Obligation to attend a mass. A Jewish student asks his teacher for permission to be excused for Yom Kippur. A Protestant wants the afternoon off for a family baptismal ceremony. In each case the teacher requires parental consent in writing. In each case the teacher, in order to make sure the student is not a truant, goes further and requires a report from the priest, the rabbi, or the minister. The teacher in other words cooperates in a religious program to the extent of making it possible for her students to participate in it. Whether she does it occasionally for a few students, regularly for one, or pursuant to a systematized program designed to further the religious needs of all the students does not alter the character of the act.

"We are a religious people whose institutions presuppose a Supreme Being. We guarantee the freedom to worship as one chooses. [When] the state encour-

j. White, J., also dissented, "for the most part agreeing with the opinion of [Burger, C.J.]," and, noting that in light of Rehnquist, J.'s "explication of the history of the religion clauses, [it] would be quite understandable if we undertook to reassess our cases dealing with these clauses, particularly [the] Establishment Clause."

a. Frankfurter and Jackson, JJ., each filed concurrences. Reed, J., dissented.

ages religious instruction or cooperates with religious authorities by adjusting the schedule of public events to sectarian needs, [it] respects the religious nature of our people and accommodates the public service to their spiritual needs. To hold that it may not would be to find in the Constitution a requirement that the government show a callous indifference to religious groups. That would be preferring those who believe in no religion over those who do believe. [The] problem, like many problems in constitutional law, is one of degree."

JACKSON, J., dissented: "If public education were taking so much of the pupils' time as to injure the public or the students' welfare by encroaching upon their religious opportunity, simply shortening everyone's school day would facilitate voluntary and optional attendance at Church classes. But that suggestion is rejected upon the ground that if they are made free many students will not go to the Church. [Here] schooling is more or less suspended during the 'released time' so the nonreligious attendants will not forge ahead of the churchgoing absentees. But it serves as a temporary jail for a pupil who will not go to Church. It takes more subtlety of mind than I possess to deny that this is governmental constraint in support of religion." [b]

(c) *Cost.* Can *Zorach* be reconciled with *McCollum* on the ground that the *McCollum* plan involved a significantly greater cost to the public? Brennan, J., has distinguished the cases "not [because] of the difference in public expenditures involved. True, the *McCollum* program involved the regular use of school facilities, classrooms, heat and light and time from the regular school day—even though the actual incremental cost may have been negligible. [But the] deeper difference was that the *McCollum* program placed the religious instructor in the public school classroom in precisely the position of authority held by the regular teachers of secular subjects, while the *Zorach* program did not. The *McCollum* program, in lending to the support of sectarian instruction all the authority of the governmentally operated public school system, brought government and religion into that proximity which the Establishment Clause forbids." *Schempp* (concurring opinion).

(d) *Coercion.* *Zorach* found "no evidence [that] the system involves the use of coercion to get public school students into religious classrooms. [If] it were established that any one or more teachers were using their office to persuade or force students to take the religious instruction, a wholly different case would be presented.[7]" Would the *Zorach* plan be inherently coercive, and therefore unconstitutional, if it were shown that most children found religious instruction more appealing than remaining in the public schools? Even if the alternative for those remaining was secular instruction with academic credit? If so, would it be permissible to excuse children from classes to enable them to attend special religious services of their faith? Would the first amendment forbid attendance at parochial schools, as an alternative to public schools, on the ground that this was simply one hundred per cent released time?

Under this analysis, would a program of "dismissed time" (all children released early permitting those who so wish to attend religious schools) be

b. Black and Frankfurter, JJ., also filed separate dissents.

For a description of the interaction of the justices in fashioning the *Everson, McCollum* and *Zorach* opinions, see Note, *The "Released Time" Cases Revisited: A Study of Group Decisionmaking by the Supreme Court,* 83 Yale L.J. 1202 (1974).

7. [The] only allegation in the complaint that bears on the issue is that the operation of the program "has resulted and inevitably results in the exercise of pressure and coercion upon parents and children to secure attendance by the children for religious instruction." But this charge does not even implicate the school authorities. * * *

unconstitutional? Would "dismissed time" be nonetheless invalid if it could be shown that the purpose for the early school closing was to facilitate religious education? Or is this merely an accommodation "adjusting the schedule of public events to sectarian needs"?

What of the argument that the *Zorach* program is inherently coercive, and therefore unconstitutional, because, as Frankfurter, J., contended in *McCollum,* "the law of imitation operates" placing "an obvious pressure upon children to attend" religious classes? Under this analysis, what result in the case of excusing students to attend a religious service? In the case of parochial schools? In the case of "dismissed time"? Do you agree with Jackson, J.'s assertion in *McCollum* that "it may be doubted whether the Constitution [protects] one from the embarrassment that always attends nonconformity, whether in religion, politics, behavior or dress"?

(e) *Use of public property.* Is the use of public school classrooms for religious purposes during nonschool hours distinguishable from *McCollum?* Consider Tribe, *American Constitutional Law* 1175 (2d ed. 1988): "Religious instructors will no longer stand in 'the position of authority held by the regular teachers,' because the activities lie outside the mandatory school day. Although coercion is conceivable, it is not inherent, as it probably is with official school prayer; students who do not want to take part in the religious activities may take part in other activities or leave the campus. No symbolic mingling of church and state functions takes place, so long as access to the campus is entirely independent of the religious or other content of the meetings. Thus, the state neither lends power to religion, nor borrows legitimacy from religion. Permitting a religious group to use school facilities during non-school hours, accordingly, conveys no message of endorsement."

2. *School prayer and the relevance of coercion.* (a) Should *Engel* and *Schempp* (and *McCollum*) have been explicitly based on "the coercion implicit under the statutory schemes"? Consider Stewart, J., dissenting in *Schempp:* "[T]he duty laid upon government in connection with religious exercises in the public schools is that of refraining from so structuring the school environment as to put any kind of pressure on a child to participate in those exercises; it is not that of providing an atmosphere in which children are kept scrupulously insulated from any awareness that some of their fellows may want to open the school day with prayer, or of the fact that there exist in our pluralistic society differences of religious belief.[c] [A] law which provided for religious exercises during the school day and which contained no excusal provision would obviously

c. Consider Griswold, *Absolute is in the Dark—A Discussion of the Approach of the Supreme Court to Constitutional Questions,* 8 Utah L.Rev. 167, 177, (1963): "When the prayer is recited, if [a] child or his parents feel that he cannot participate, he may stand or sit, in respectful attention, while the other children take part in the ceremony. Or he may leave the room. It is said that this is bad, because it sets him apart from other children. It is even said that there is an element of compulsion in this. [But] is this the way it should be looked at? The child of a nonconforming or minority group is, to be sure, different in his beliefs. That is what it means to be a member of a minority. Is it not desirable, and educational, for him to learn and observe this, in the atmosphere of the school—not so much that he is different, as that other children are different from him? And is it not desirable that, at the same time, he experiences and learns the fact that his difference is tolerated and accepted? No compulsion is put upon him. He need not participate. But he, too, has the opportunity to be tolerant. He allows the majority of the group to follow their own tradition, perhaps coming to understand and to respect what they feel is significant to them." See also Sutherland, *Establishment According to Engel,* 76 Harv.L. Rev. 25 (1962); Kurland, *The Regents' Prayer Case: "Full of Sound and Fury, Signifying * * *,"* 1962 Sup.Ct.Rev. 1.

be unconstitutionally coercive upon those who did not wish to participate. And even under a law containing an excusal provision, if the exercises were held during the school day, and no equally desirable alternative were provided by the school authorities, the likelihood that children might be under at least some psychological compulsion to participate would be great. [Here,] the record shows no more than a subjective prophecy by a parent of what he thought would happen if a request were made to be excused from participation in the exercises under the amended statute. [It] is conceivable that these school boards, or even all school boards, might eventually find it impossible to administer a system of religious exercises during school hours in such a way as to meet this constitutional standard—in such a way as completely to free from any kind of official coercion those who do not affirmatively want to participate.[8] But I think we must not assume that school boards so lack the qualities of inventiveness and good will as to make impossible the achievement of that goal."

What evidence of coercion does Stewart, J. require? That the objectors first ask to be excused from participation and then show that social pressures were brought to bear on them? Would this force an objector to surrender his rights in order to vindicate them? Or would Stewart, J., accept the testimony of social scientists that the program was coercive? Could this be judicially noticed? Cf. *Brown v. Board of Educ.*, p. 958 infra. Or would he require a showing that these particular objectors were coerced? Were likely to be coerced? If so, is this a desirable test?

Consider Brown, *Quis Custodiet Ipsos Custodes?—The School Prayer Cases,* 1963 Sup.Ct.Rev. 1, 30–31: "Submitting the question of coercion to a jury will be objected to because: (1) it will produce non-uniform results; and (2) it will make constitutional rights turn upon what is by definition a sampling of the majority. In the context of these cases, the objections are not overwhelming. If the constitutional 'right' is not regarded in purely abstract and doctrinaire fashion, but is dependent upon the fact of an ascertainable and objectionable degree of coercion, that fact will not be uniform under all circumstances and for all persons. To insist upon uniformity of result is only another way to eliminate the question of standing. Giving a jury an opportunity to intervene on at least one aspect of a problem delicately balanced in its general aspects as well as in its individual impact appears a not inappropriate solution."

(b) *Establishment vs. free exercise.* Consider Kauper, *Prayer, Public Schools and the Supreme Court,* 61 Mich.L.Rev. 1031, 1065–66 (1963): "[I]mmature and impressionable children are susceptible to a pressure to conform and to participate in the expression of religious beliefs that carry the sanction and compulsion of the state's authority. [A] decision resting on the narrower ground of freedom of religion or of conscience, explaining why the considerations advanced in support of the prayer were outweighed by the rights of the objectors, and why under the circumstances the feature of voluntary participation did not sufficiently protect the interests of objectors, would have been much more satisfactory."

Would this analysis permit prayer in an elementary school where every child was willing to participate? In *any* high school? Consider Pollak, *Public Prayers in Public Schools,* 77 Harv.L.Rev. 62, 70 (1963): "[T]o have pitched the decision [on the free exercise clause] would presumably have meant that the

8. For example, if the [record] contained proof (rather than mere prophecy) that the timing of morning announcements by the school was such as to handicap children who did not want to listen to the Bible reading, or that the excusal provision was so administered as to carry any overtones of social inferiority, then impermissible coercion would clearly exist.

prayer programs were constitutionally unobjectionable unless and until challenged, and, therefore, that school boards would have been under no discernible legal obligation, as assuredly they now are, to suspend ongoing prayer programs on their own initiative. [Indeed,] the hypothetical schoolchild plaintiff, whose free exercise rights would thus be enforced, would have to be a child with the gumption not only to disassociate himself from the prayer program but to prefer litigation to the relatively expeditious exit procedure contemplated by the excusal proviso."

3. *Secular purpose.* Several decisions, in addition to *Jaffree,* have invalidated public school practices because their "purpose" has been found to be "religious":

(a) STONE v. GRAHAM, 449 U.S. 39, 101 S.Ct. 192, 66 L.Ed.2d 199 (1980), per curiam held that a Kentucky statute—requiring "the posting of a copy of the Ten Commandments, purchased with private contributions, on the wall of each public classroom in the State," with the notation at the bottom that "The secular application of the Ten Commandments is clearly seen in its adoption as the fundamental legal code of Western Civilization and the Common Law of the United States"—had "no secular legislative purpose": "The Ten Commandments is undeniably a sacred text in the Jewish and Christian faiths, and no legislative recitation of a supposed secular purpose can blind us to that [fact]. Posting of religious texts on the wall serves [no] educational function. If the posted copies of the Ten Commandments are to have any effect at all, it will be to induce the school children to read, meditate upon, perhaps to venerate and obey, the Commandments. However desirable this might be as a matter of private devotion, it is not a permissible state objective under the Establishment Clause."

Rehnquist, J., dissented: "The Court's summary rejection of a secular purpose articulated by the legislature and confirmed by the state court is without precedent in Establishment Clause jurisprudence. [This] Court has recognized that 'religion has been closely identified with our history and government,' *Schempp,* and that 'the history of man is inseparable from the history of religion,' *Engel.* Kentucky has decided to make students aware of this fact by demonstrating the secular impact of the Ten Commandments." [b]

(b) EPPERSON v. ARKANSAS, 393 U.S. 97, 89 S.Ct. 266, 21 L.Ed.2d 228 (1968), per Fortas, J., held that an "anti-evolution" statute, forbidding teachers in public schools "to teach the theory or doctrine that mankind ascended or descended from a lower order of animals," violated "the First Amendment's prohibition of laws respecting an establishment of religion or prohibiting the free exercise thereof": "Arkansas' law selects from the body of knowledge a particular segment which it proscribes for the sole reason that it is deemed to conflict with a particular religious doctrine." Citing newspaper advertisements and letters supporting adoption of the statute in 1928, the Court found it "clear that fundamentalist sectarian conviction was and is the law's reason for existence. Its antecedent, Tennessee's 'monkey law,' candidly stated" a religious purpose. "Perhaps the sensational publicity attendant upon the *Scopes* trial induced Arkansas to adopt less explicit language [but] there is no doubt that the motivation for the law was the same * * *. Arkansas' law cannot be defended as an act of religious neutrality. Arkansas did not seek to excise from the curricula of its schools and universities all discussion of the origin of man."

b. Stewart, J., also dissented. Burger, C.J., and Blackmun, J., dissented from not giving the case plenary consideration.

BLACK, J., concurring on the ground of "vagueness," found the first amendment questions "troublesome": "Since there is no indication that the literal Biblical doctrine of the origin of man is included in the curriculum of Arkansas schools, does not the removal of the subject of evolution leave the State in a neutral position toward these supposedly competing religious and anti-religious doctrines? [It] is plain that a state law prohibiting all teaching of human development or biology is constitutionally quite different from a law that compels a teacher to teach as true only one theory of a given doctrine. It would be difficult to make a First Amendment case out of a state law eliminating the subject of higher mathematics, or astronomy, or biology from its curriculum. [T]here is no reason I can imagine why a State is without power to withdraw from its curriculum any subject deemed too emotional and controversial for its public schools." [c]

(c) EDWARDS v. AGUILLARD, 482 U.S. 578, 107 S.Ct. 2573, 96 L.Ed.2d 510 (1987), per BRENNAN, J., held that a Louisiana statute, which forebade "the teaching of the theory of evolution in public schools unless accompanied by instruction in 'creation science,'" had "no clear secular purpose": "True, the Act's stated purpose is to protect academic freedom. [While] the Court is normally deferential to a State's articulation of a secular purpose, it is required that the statement of such purpose be sincere and not a sham. See *Jaffree; Stone v. Graham; Schempp.* [It] is clear from the legislative history that the purpose [was] to narrow the science curriculum. [It] is equally clear that requiring schools to teach creation science with evolution does not advance academic freedom. The Act does not grant teachers a flexibility that they did not already possess to supplement the present science curriculum with the presentation of theories, besides evolution, about the origin of life. [While] requiring that curriculum guides be developed for creation science, the Act says nothing of comparable guides for evolution. [The] Act forbids school boards to discriminate against anyone who 'chooses to be a creation-scientist' or to teach 'creationism,' but fails to protect those who choose to teach evolution or any other non-creation science theory, or who refuse to teach creation science.

"If the Louisiana legislature's purpose was solely to maximize the comprehensiveness and effectiveness of science instruction, it would have encouraged the teaching of all scientific theories about the origins of humankind. But [the] legislative history documents that the Act's primary purpose was to change the science curriculum of public schools in order to provide persuasive advantage to a particular religious doctrine that rejects the factual basis of evolution in its entirety [and that] embodies the religious belief that a supernatural creator was responsible for the creation of humankind. * * *

"We do not imply that a legislature could never require that scientific critiques of prevailing scientific theories be taught. [T]eaching a variety of scientific theories about the origins of humankind to school children might be validly done with the clear secular intent of enhancing the effectiveness of science instruction. But because the primary purpose of the Creationism Act is to endorse a particular religious doctrine, the Act furthers religion in violation of the Establishment Clause." [a]

c. Harlan, J., concurred in the Court's "establishment of religion" rationale. Stewart, J., concurred on the ground of vagueness.

a. Powell, J., joined by O'Connor, J., joined the Court's opinion but wrote separately "to emphasize that nothing in the Court's opinion diminishes the traditionally broad discretion accorded state and local school officials in the selection of the public school curriculum." White, J., concurred only in the judgment, with which he agreed "unless [we] are to reconsider the Court's decisions interpreting the Establishment Clause."

SCALIA, J., joined by Rehnquist, C.J., dissented: "Even if I agreed with the questionable premise that legislation can be invalidated under the Establishment Clause on the basis of its motivation alone, without regard to its effects, I would still find no justification for today's decision. [The] Louisiana Legislature explicitly set forth its secular purpose ('protecting academic freedom') [which] meant: *students'* freedom from *indoctrination.* The legislature wanted to ensure that students would be free to decide for themselves how life began, based upon a fair and balanced presentation of the scientific evidence. [The] legislature did not care *whether* the topic of origins was taught; it simply wished to ensure that *when* the topic was taught, students would receive 'all of the evidence.' * * *

"If one adopts the obviously intended meaning of the statutory terms 'academic freedom,' there is no basis whatever for concluding that the purpose they express is a 'sham.' To the contrary, the Act pursues that purpose plainly and consistently. It requires that, whenever the subject of origins is covered, evolution be 'taught as a theory, rather than as proven scientific fact' and that scientific evidence inconsistent with the theory of evolution (viz., 'creation science') be taught as well. Living up to its title of '*Balanced Treatment* for Creation–Science and Evolution–Science Act,' it treats the teaching of creation the same way. It does *not* mandate instruction in creation science; *forbids* teachers to present creation science 'as proven scientific fact'; and *bans* the teaching of creation science unless the theory [is] 'discredit[ed] at every turn' with the teaching of evolution. It surpasses understanding how the Court can see in this a purpose 'to restructure the science curriculum to conform with a particular religious viewpoint,' 'to provide a persuasive advantage to a particular religious doctrine,' 'to promote the theory of creation science which embodies a particular religious tenet,' and 'to endorse a particular religious doctrine.'

"[The] Louisiana legislators had been told repeatedly that creation scientists were scorned by most educators and scientists, who themselves had an almost religious faith in evolution. It is hardly surprising, then, that in seeking to achieve a balanced, 'nonindoctrinating' curriculum, the legislators protected from discrimination only those teachers whom they thought were *suffering* from discrimination. [The] two provisions respecting the development of curriculum guides are also consistent with 'academic freedom' as the Louisiana Legislature understood the term. [In] light of the unavailability of works on creation science suitable for classroom use (a fact appellees concede) and the existence of ample materials on evolution, it was entirely reasonable for the Legislature to conclude that science teachers attempting to implement the Act would need a curriculum guide on creation science, but not on evolution. [Thus,] the provisions of the Act of so much concern to the Court *support* the conclusion that the Legislature acted to advance 'academic freedom.' * * *

"It is undoubtedly true that what prompted the Legislature to direct its attention to the misrepresentation of evolution in the schools (rather than the inaccurate presentation of other topics) was its awareness of the tension between evolution and the religious beliefs of many children. But even appellees concede that a valid secular purpose is not rendered impermissible simply because its pursuit is prompted by concern for religious sensitivities. [I] am astonished by the Court's unprecedented readiness to [disbelieve] the secular purpose set forth in the Act [and to conclude] that it is a sham enacted to conceal the legislators' violation of their oaths of office. [I] can only attribute [this] to an intellectual predisposition [and] an instinctive reaction that any governmentally imposed requirements bearing upon the teaching of evolution must be a manifestation of

Christian fundamentalist repression. In this case, however, it seems to me the Court's position is the repressive one. The people of Louisiana, including those who are Christian fundamentalists, are quite entitled, as a secular matter, to have whatever scientific evidence there may be against evolution presented in their schools, just as Mr. Scopes was entitled to present whatever scientific evidence there was for it. Perhaps what the Louisiana Legislature has done is unconstitutional because there *is* no such evidence, and the scheme they have established will amount to no more than a presentation of the Book of Genesis. But we cannot say that on the evidence before us in this summary judgment context, which includes ample uncontradicted testimony that 'creation science' is a body of scientific knowledge rather than revealed belief.[b] *Infinitely less* can we say (or should we say) that the scientific evidence for evolution is so conclusive that no one could be gullible enough to believe that there is any real scientific evidence to the contrary, so that the legislation's stated purpose must be a lie. Yet that illiberal judgment, that *Scopes*-in-reverse, is ultimately the basis on which the Court's facile rejection of the Louisiana Legislature's purpose must rest. * * *

"I have to this point assumed the validity of the *Lemon* 'purpose' test. In fact, however, I think [it] is 'a constitutional theory [that] has no basis in the history of the amendment it seeks to interpret, is difficult to apply and yields unprincipled results.' *Jaffree* (Rehnquist, J., dissenting).

"Our cases interpreting and applying the purpose test have made such a maze of the Establishment Clause that even the most conscientious governmental officials can only guess what motives will be held unconstitutional. We have said essentially the following: Government may not act with the purpose of advancing religion, except when forced to do so by the Free Exercise Clause (which is now and then); or when eliminating existing governmental hostility to religion (which exists sometimes); or even when merely accommodating governmentally uninhibited religious practices, except that at some point (it is unclear where) intentional accommodation results in the fostering of religion, which is of course unconstitutional.

"[D]iscerning the subjective motivation of those enacting the statute is, to be honest, almost always an impossible task. The number of possible motivations, to begin with, is not binary, or indeed even finite. In the present case, for example, a particular legislator need not have voted for the Act either because he wanted to foster religion or because he wanted to improve education. He may have thought the bill would provide jobs for his district, or may have wanted to make amends with a faction of his party he had alienated on another vote, or he may have been a close friend of the bill's sponsor, or he may have been repaying a favor he owed the Majority Leader, or he may have hoped the Governor would appreciate his vote and make a fundraising appearance for him, or he may have been pressured to vote for a bill he disliked by a wealthy contributor or by a flood of constituent mail, or he may have been seeking favorable publicity, or he may have been reluctant to hurt the feelings of a loyal staff member who worked on the bill, or he may have been settling an old score with a legislator who opposed the bill, or he may have been mad at his wife who opposed the bill, or he may have been intoxicated and utterly *un*motivated when

b. "The only evidence in the record [defining] 'creation science' is found in five affidavits filed by appellants. In those affidavits, two scientists, a philosopher, a theologian, and an educator, all of whom claim extensive knowledge of creation science, swear that it is essentially a collection of scientific data supporting the theory that the physical universe and life within it appeared suddenly and have not changed substantially since appearing."

the vote was called, or he may have accidentally voted 'yes' instead of 'no,' or, of course, he may have had (and very likely did have) a combination of some of the above and many other motivations. To look for *the sole purpose* of even a single legislator is probably to look for something that does not exist."

(d) Is it meaningful to distinguish between *secular* vs. *religious* purposes? Consider Johnson, *Concepts and Compromise in First Amendment Religious Doctrine,* 72 Calif.L.Rev. 817, 827 (1984): "[There is great difficulty] making sense out of the crucial distinction between *religious* purpose or effect and *secular* purpose or effect. Governments usually act out of secular motives, even when they are directly aiding a particular religious sect. An atheistic ruler might well create an established church because he thinks it a useful way of raising money, or of ensuring that the clergy do not preach seditious doctrines. In democratic societies, elected officials have an excellent secular reason to accommodate (or at least to avoid offending) groups and individuals who are religious, as well as groups and individuals who are not. They wish to be re-elected, and they do not want important groups to feel that the community does not honor their values."

(e) If the "purpose" of government action is found to be "religious," *should* that alone be enough to invalidate it under the establishment clause? If so, what result in *Zorach?* For a public school "dismissed time" program implemented to facilitate religious education? [d] Consider Tribe, supra, at 1211: "The secular purpose requirement, partly because of its sketchy parameters, could raise two particularly important conceptual problems in application. First, it might be used to strike down laws whose effects are utterly secular. A legislature might, for example, vote to increase welfare benefits because individual legislators feel religiously compelled to do so. So too, when a legislature passes a neutral moment-of-silence statute, many legislators may hope that students will use the time for prayer. However improper these purposes may be, it is hard to see a meaningful establishment clause problem so long as the statute's effects are completely secular. A visible religious purpose may independently convey a message of endorsement or exclusion, but such a message, standing alone, should rarely if ever suffice to transform a secular action into an establishment clause violation. A religious message may be conveyed by the legislative debates concerning a bill, but the same result is possible from debates that lead to no legislation; it can hardly be said that the debates themselves establish a religion."

Compare Redlich, *Separation of Church and State: The Burger Court's Tortuous Journey,* 60 Not.D.L.Rev. 1094, 1136 (1985): "When the state encourages silent prayer, it endorses a practice that is unacceptable to those whose faith requires that they pray only in a place of worship, or before some religious symbol. Some faiths may forbid praying with members of another faith, or with the opposite sex; some require believers to stand, or face a certain direction, or sit down, or wear certain apparel, or be led by ordained spiritual leaders—the variables reflect the infinite capacity of the human spirit to worship God in different ways. Any state expression of preference for prayer, whether vocal or silent, destroys the neutral position of the [state]. All prescribed moments of silence are highly suspect."

d. For use of this test to invalidate the "religiously motivated" Utah firing squad, see Gardner, *Illicit Legislative Motivation as a Sufficient Condition for Unconstitutionality Under the Establishment Clause,* 1979 Wash. U.L.Q. 435.

Contrast Choper, *The Religion Clauses of the First Amendment: Reconciling the Conflict,* 41 U.Pitt.L.Rev. 673, 686–87 (1980): "[I]t is only when religious purpose is coupled with threatened impairment of religious freedom that government action should be held to violate the Establishment Clause. [Conceding] that the [*Epperson*] statute had a solely religious purpose, [there] was no evidence that religious beliefs were either coerced, compromised or influenced. That is, it was not shown, nor do I believe that it could be persuasively argued, that the anti-evolution law either (1) induced children of fundamentalist religions to accept the biblical theory of creation, or (2) conditioned other children for conversion to fundamentalism. [Thus,] the accommodation for religion in [*Epperson*] should have survived the Establishment Clause challenge."

Similarly, "I would find that the creation science law had a religious purpose * * * to placate those religious fundamentalists whose beliefs rejected the Darwinian theory of evolution. But, under my approach, so long as the theory of creation science is taught in an objective rather than a prosyletyzing fashion, it does not seem to me to pose a danger to religious liberty [and] should not be held to violate the Establishment Clause." Choper, *Church, State and the Supreme Court: Current Controversy,* 29 Ariz.L.Rev. 551, 557 (1987).

4. *Purpose, primary effect, and equal access.* BOARD OF EDUC. v. MERGENS, ___ U.S. ___, 110 S.Ct. 2356, 110 L.Ed.2d 191 (1990), interpreted the Equal Access Act, passed by Congress in 1984, to apply to public secondary schools that (a) receive federal financial assistance, and (b) give official recognition to noncurriculum related student groups (e.g., chess club and scuba diving club in contrast to Latin club and math club) in such ways as allowing them to meet on school premises during noninstructional time. The Act prohibited these schools from denying equal access to, or otherwise discriminating against, student groups "on the basis of the religious, political, philosophical, or other content of the speech at [their] meetings." O'CONNOR, J., joined by Rehnquist, C.J., and White and Blackmun, JJ., held that the establishment clause did not forbid Westside High School from including within its thirty recognized student groups a Christian club "to read and discuss the Bible, to have fellowship and to pray together": "In *Widmar v. Vincent,* 454 U.S. 263, 102 S.Ct. 269, 70 L.Ed.2d 440 (1981), we applied the three-part *Lemon* test to hold that an 'equal access' policy, at the university level, does not violate the Establishment Clause. We concluded that 'an open-forum policy, including nondiscrimination against religious speech, would have a secular purpose,' and would in fact *avoid* entanglement with religion. See id. ("[T]he University would risk greater 'entanglement' by attempting to enforce its exclusion of 'religious worship' and 'religious speech' "). We also found that although incidental benefits accrued to religious groups who used university facilities, this result did not amount to an establishment of religion. First, we stated that a university's forum does not 'confer any imprimatur of state approval on religious sects or practices.' Indeed, the message is one of neutrality rather than endorsement; if a State refused to let religious groups use facilities open to others, then it would demonstrate not neutrality but hostility toward religion. Second, we noted that '[t]he [University's] provision of benefits to [a] broad spectrum of groups'—both nonreligious and religious speakers—was 'an important index of secular effect.'

"We think the logic of *Widmar* applies with equal force to the Equal Access [Act.] Congress' avowed purpose—to prevent discrimination against religious and other types of speech—is undeniably secular. Even if some legislators were motivated by a conviction that religious speech in particular was valuable and worthy of protection, that alone would not invalidate the Act, because what is relevant is the legislative *purpose* of the statute, not the possibly religious *motives* of the legislators who enacted the law. Because the Act on its face grants equal access to both secular and religious speech, we think it clear that the Act's purpose was not to 'endorse or disapprove of religion,' *Jaffree* (O'Connor, J., concurring).

"Petitioners' principal contention is that the Act has the primary effect of advancing religion. Specifically, petitioners urge that, because the student religious meetings are held under school aegis, and because the state's compulsory attendance laws bring the students together (and thereby provide a ready-made audience for student evangelists), an objective observer in the position of a secondary school student will perceive official school support for such religious meetings.

"We disagree. First, [there] is a crucial difference between *government* speech endorsing religion, which the Establishment Clause forbids, and *private* speech endorsing religion, which the Free Speech and Free Exercise Clauses protect. We think that secondary school students are mature enough and are likely to understand that a school does not endorse or support student speech that it merely permits on a nondiscriminatory basis. * * *

"Second, we note that the Act expressly limits participation by school officials at meetings of student religious groups, and that any such meetings must be held during 'noninstructional time.' The Act therefore avoids the problems of 'the students' emulation of teachers as role models' and 'mandatory attendance requirements,' *Aguillard;* see also *McCollum.* To be sure, the possibility of *student* peer pressure remains, but there is little if any risk of official state endorsement or coercion where no formal classroom activities are involved and no school officials actively participate. Moreover, petitioners' fear of a mistaken inference of endorsement is largely self-imposed, because the school itself has control over any impressions it gives its students. * * *

"Third, the broad spectrum of officially recognized student clubs at Westside, and the fact that Westside students are free to initiate and organize additional student clubs counteract any possible message of official endorsement of or preference for religion or a particular religious belief."

KENNEDY, J., joined by Scalia, J., concurred, emphasizing his disagreement with the plurality's "endorsement test" developed more fully in *Allegheny County v. ACLU,* Part III infra: "I should think it inevitable that a public high school 'endorses' a religious club, in a common-sense use of the term, if the club happens to be one of many activities that the school permits students to choose in order to further the development of their intellect and character in an extracurricular setting. But no constitutional violation occurs if the school's action is based upon a recognition of the fact that membership in a religious club is one of many permissible ways for a student to further his or her own personal enrichment. The inquiry with respect to coercion must be whether the government imposes pressure upon a student to participate in a religious activity. This inquiry, of course, must be undertaken with sensitivity to the special circumstances that exist in a secondary school where the line between voluntary and coerced participation may be difficult to draw. No such coercion, however, has been shown to exist as a necessary result of this statute, either on its face or as respondents seek to invoke it on the facts of this case."

MARSHALL, J., joined by Brennan, J., concurred "to emphasize the steps Westside must take to avoid appearing to endorse the Christian Club's goals":

"[A]lthough a school may permissibly encourage its students to become well-rounded as student-athletes, student-musicians, and student-tutors, the Constitution forbids schools to encourage students to become well-rounded as student-worshippers. [To] the extent a school tolerates speech by a wide range of ideological clubs, students cannot reasonably understand the school to endorse all of the groups' divergent and contradictory views. But if the religion club is the sole advocacy-oriented group in the forum, or one of a very limited number, and the school continues to promote its student-club program as instrumental to citizenship, then the school's failure to disassociate itself from the religious activity will reasonably be understood as an endorsement of that activity. [The] State has structured an environment in which students holding mainstream views may be able to coerce adherents of minority religions to attend club meetings or to adhere to club beliefs. Thus, the State cannot disclaim its responsibility for those resulting pressures.

" * * * Westside must do more than merely prohibit faculty members from actively participating in the Christian Club's meetings. It must fully disassociate itself from the Club's religious speech and avoid appearing to sponsor or endorse the Club's goals. It could, for example, entirely discontinue encouraging student participation in clubs and clarify that the clubs are not instrumentally related to the school's overall mission. Or, if the school sought to continue its general endorsement of those student clubs that did not engage in controversial speech, it could do so if it also affirmatively disclaimed any endorsement of the Christian Club."

STEVENS, J., dissented: "Under the Court's interpretation of the Act, Congress has imposed a difficult choice on public high schools receiving federal financial assistance. If such a school continues to allow students to participate in such familiar and innocuous activities as a school chess or scuba diving club, it must also allow religious groups to make use of school facilities. [The] Act, as construed by the majority, comes perilously close to an outright command to allow organized prayer, and perhaps the kind of religious ceremonies involved in *Widmar,* on school premises." [a]

5. *Military chaplains.* In rejecting the argument that Bible reading and prayer exercises in public schools furthered "the majority's right to free exercise of religion," *Schempp* did "not pass upon a situation such as military service, where the Government regulates the temporal and geographic environment of individuals to a point that, unless it permits voluntary religious services to be conducted with the use of government facilities, military personnel would be unable to engage in the practice of their faiths." Might it be that, while free exercise considerations may justify government provision for opportunity to worship, the establishment clause nonetheless bars a government subsidized ministry? "Could the governmental interest be satisfied merely by allowing free time for the serviceman to seek non-military worship or by merely giving the religious orders the right to come into the military environment, at their own expense, to provide the opportunity for worship?" Figinski, *Military Chaplains—A Constitutionally Permissible Accommodation Between Church and State,* 24 Md.L.Rev. 377, 409 (1964). Or might it be "that the Government need

a. May elementary or secondary schools permit their facilities to be used for instruction by religious groups if they also permit instruction by outside teachers of art, music, crafts, dance, etc. (cf. *McCollum*)? May they post the Ten Commandments if they also post the symbols of other civic or charitable groups (cf. *Stone*)? See Laycock, *Equal Access and Moments of Silence: The Equal Status of Religious Speech by Private Speakers,* 81 Nw.U.L. Rev. 1, 33–35 (1986).

not necessarily provide chapels and chaplains to those of its armed personnel who are *not* cut off from civilian church facilities"? Herrmann, *Some Considerations on the Constitutionality of the United States Military Chaplaincy,* 14 Am. U.L.Rev. 24, 34 (1964). Consider Figinski, supra: "To allow merely free-time and off-post worship, even where available, would allow the serviceman seeking worship to be flung far and wide, making emergency re-call to duty more difficult and troublesome. Moreover, this means could conceivably place an unforeseen burden on civilian areas of worship that might be resented by the civilians, and increase the possibility of military-civilian friction. Furthermore, in overseas areas the language barrier to effective worship would be considerable. The alternative means of relying on the religious orders of the United States to provide, at their own expense, chaplains is less easily put aside. Three objections can be made. First, if the orders failed to provide chaplains, the military man would be left without effective opportunity for worship. Second, the availability of services would not be as readily available. One can easily conceive of a death situation where the distance the civilian clergyman would need to travel would render his service all but unattainable. The problems of civilian chaplains would be magnified in areas where hostilities were being carried on. Third, if the chaplain were not an officer, the military would not have control over his non-religious life to the extent that it could assure a suitable (in the sense of a non-debt ridden, or even non-subversive) ministry."

6. *Public school secularism. Schempp* emphasized that "it might well be said that one's education is not complete without a study of comparative religion or the history of religion and its relationship to the advancement of civilization. It certainly may be said that the Bible is worthy of study for its literary and historic qualities. Nothing we have said here indicates that such study of the Bible or of religion, when presented objectively as part of a secular program of education, may not be [effected]." Consider Manning, *The Douglas Concept of God in Government,* 39 Wash.L.Rev. 47, 63 (1964): "[I]f we forbid the teaching of recognized religions in our public schools and forbid a prayer which simply acknowledges the existence of God and at the same time permit—as, indeed, we must—the teaching of some code of ethical conduct, some system of value norms, does not the system which the school then sponsors become the system of Secular Humanism or simply secular humanism? Do we not then prefer, in public education, one religion, Secular Humanism, over other religions which are founded upon a belief in the existence of God?" Compare Kauper, *Schempp and Sherbert: Studies in Neutrality and Accommodation,* 1963 Relig. & Pub.Or. 3, 23: "[I]n the interest of neutrality as between theistic and humanistic religions, the public schools must carefully avoid any program of indoctrination in ultimate values." May it be argued in response that, simply because the religion of Secular Humanism "adopts" as its own a moral or ideological tenet that is also a publicly accepted behavioral standard, this does not make it a "religious" tenet under the establishment clause for the purpose of its being taught in the public schools? See note 4, Sec. 2, II infra. If government requires that public employees be of "good moral character," is this a "religious test" for public office?

Contrast Stewart, J., dissenting in *Schempp:* "It might also be argued that parents who want their children exposed to religious influences can adequately fulfill that wish off school property and outside school time. [But] a compulsory state educational system so structures a child's life that if religious exercises are held to be an impermissible activity in schools, [this] is seen, not as the realization of state neutrality, but rather as the establishment of a religion of secularism, or at the least, as government support of the beliefs of those who think that religious exercises should be conducted only in private."

II. FINANCIAL AID TO RELIGION

The issue of aid to parochial schools first arose again after *Everson* in BOARD OF EDUC. v. ALLEN, 392 U.S. 236, 88 S.Ct. 1923, 20 L.Ed.2d 1060 (1968). The Court, per WHITE, J., held that New York's lending state-approved secular textbooks to all secondary school children did not violate the establishment clause. The New York law, like that in *Everson,* had "a secular legislative purpose and a primary effect that neither advances nor inhibits religion." [a]

The next important establishment clause decision, WALZ v. TAX COM'N, 397 U.S. 664, 90 S.Ct. 1409, 25 L.Ed.2d 697 (1970), per BURGER, C.J., upheld state tax exemption for "real or personal property used exclusively for religious, educational or charitable purposes": "The legislative purpose of a property tax exemption is neither the advancement nor the inhibition of religion; it is neither sponsorship nor hostility. New York, in common with the other States, has determined that certain entities that exist in a harmonious relationship to the community at large, and that foster its 'moral or mental improvement,' should not be inhibited in their activities by property taxation or the hazard of loss of those properties for nonpayment of taxes. It [has] granted exemption to all houses of religious worship within a broad class of property owned by nonprofit, quasi-public corporations which include hospitals, libraries, playgrounds, scientific, professional, historical and patriotic groups. * * *

"We find it unnecessary to justify the tax exemption on the social welfare services or 'good works' that some churches perform for parishioners and others—family counselling, aid to the elderly and the infirm, and to children. [To] give emphasis to so variable an aspect of the work of religious bodies would introduce an element of governmental evaluation and standards as to the worth of particular social welfare programs, thus producing a kind of continuing day-to-day relationship which the policy of neutrality seeks to minimize. * * *

" * * * We must also be sure that the end result—the effect—is not an excessive government entanglement with religion. The test is inescapably one of degree. * * * Elimination of exemption would tend to expand the involvement of government by giving rise to tax valuation of church property, tax liens, tax foreclosures, and the direct confrontations and conflicts that follow in the train of those legal processes.

"Granting tax exemptions to churches necessarily operates to afford an indirect economic benefit and also gives rise to some, but yet a lesser, involvement than taxing [them]. Obviously a direct money subsidy would be a relationship pregnant with involvement and, as with most governmental grant programs, could encompass sustained and detailed administrative relationships for enforcement of statutory or administrative standards, but that is not this case. * * *

"It is obviously correct that no one acquires a vested or protected right in violation of the Constitution by long [use]. Yet an unbroken practice of according the exemption to churches [is] not something to be lightly cast aside."

a. Black, Douglas and Fortas, JJ., dissented. See also Note, *Sectarian Books, The Supreme Court and the Establishment Clause,* 79 Yale L.J. 111 (1969).

BRENNAN, J., concurred: "Tax exemptions and general subsidies [both] provide economic assistance, [but a] subsidy involves the direct transfer of public monies to the subsidized enterprise and uses resources exacted from taxpayers as a whole. An exemption, on the other hand, involves no such transfer.[a] It assists the exempted enterprise only passively." [b]

DOUGLAS, J., dissented: "If history be our guide, then tax exemption of church property in this country is indeed highly suspect, as it arose in the early days when the church was an agency of the state. [The] financial support rendered here is to the church, the place of worship. A tax exemption is a subsidy."

Notes and Questions

1. *Secular purpose.* Does *Walz* abandon the "secular purpose" prerequisite of the "test" relied on in *Allen?* Consider Duval, *The Constitutionality of State Aid to Nonpublic Elementary and Secondary Schools,* 1970 U.Ill.L.F. 342, 349: "The emphasis in *Walz* is not on whether legislation is intended to promote and in fact does promote purely secular ends. Rather the question is whether either the purpose or effect is to advance or inhibit religion. Thus under *Walz* but not *Allen* if neither the purpose nor effect is to advance or inhibit religion, it is immaterial whether the legislation serves a secular objective." Thus viewed, is *Walz* a direct descendant of *Zorach?*

2. *Direct subsidies vs. tax exemption.* Consider Van Alstyne, *Constitutional Separation of Church and State: The Quest for a Coherent Position,* 57 Am.Pol. Sci.Rev. 865, 881 (1963): "To finance expanding government services, [taxes] may gradually divert an increasing fraction of total personal income, necessarily leaving proportionately less money in the private sector to each person to spend according to his individual choice, in support of religion or other undertakings. To the extent that the tax revenues thus collected may not be spent by government to support religious enterprises, but must be used exclusively for secular purposes, the net effect, arguably, is to reduce the relative supply of funds available to religion." Does this warrant tax exemption for "religion"? Does it "warrant the judicial junking of the establishment clause"? Id. Is it "equally arguable that government fiscal activity, far from reducing disposable personal income, actually increases it"? Id. See also A. Schwartz, *The Nonestablishment Principle: A Reply to Professor Giannella,* 81 Harv.L.Rev. 1465, 1469–70 (1968).

3. *"Excessive government entanglement" in ecclesiastical disputes.* (a) In JONES v. WOLF, 443 U.S. 595, 99 S.Ct. 3020, 61 L.Ed.2d 775 (1979), a majority of the Vineville Presbyterian Church of Macon, Ga. voted to separate from the Presbyterian Church in the United States (PCUS). A commission of PCUS, acting pursuant to the PCUS constitution (called the Book of Church Order), declared the Vineville minority to be "the true congregation." The minority sued to establish its right to the local church property. The Supreme Court of Georgia applied "the 'neutral principles of law' method for resolving church property disputes. The court examined the deeds to the properties, the state statutes dealing with implied trusts, and the Book of Church Order, to determine whether there was any basis for a trust in favor of the general church. Finding nothing that would give rise to a trust in any of these documents, the court

a. What of the fact that exemption for churches augments the tax bills of others? See generally Bittker, *Churches, Taxes and The Constitution,* 78 Yale L.J. 1285 (1969).

b. Harlan, J., also concurred.

awarded the property on the basis of legal title, which was in the local church, or in the names of trustees for the local church. [Without] further analysis or elaboration, [it] further decreed that the local congregation was represented by the majority faction, respondents herein."

The Court, per BLACKMUN, J., stated the established principle that "the First Amendment prohibits civil courts from resolving church property disputes on the basis of religious doctrine and practice. *Presbyterian Church v. Hull Church,* 393 U.S. 440, 89 S.Ct. 601, 21 L.Ed.2d 658 (1969). As a corollary to this commandment, the Amendment requires that civil courts defer to the resolution of issues of religious doctrine or polity by the highest court of a hierarchical church organization. *Serbian Orthodox Diocese v. Milivojevich,* 426 U.S. 696, 96 S.Ct. 2372, 49 L.Ed.2d 151 (1976) [a] Subject to these limitations, however, * * * 'a State may adopt *any* of various approaches for settling church property disputes so long as it involves no consideration of doctrinal matters, whether the ritual and liturgy of worship or the tenets of faith.' *Maryland & Va. Eldership v. Sharpsburg Church,* 396 U.S. 367, 90 S.Ct. 499, 24 L.Ed.2d 582 (1970) (Brennan, J., concurring) (emphasis in original).

"[W]e think the 'neutral principles of law' approach is consistent with the foregoing constitutional principles. [It] relies extensively on objective, well-established concepts of trust and property law familiar to lawyers and judges. It thereby promises to free civil courts completely from entanglement in questions of religious doctrine, polity, and practice. Furthermore, the neutral principles analysis [affords] flexibility in ordering private rights and obligations to reflect the intentions of the parties. Through appropriate reversionary clauses and trust provisions, religious societies can specify what is to happen to church property in the event of a particular contingency, or what religious body will determine the ownership in the event of a schism or doctrinal controversy. In this manner, a religious organization can ensure that a dispute over the ownership of church property will be resolved in accord with the desires of the members.

"[The] neutral principles method [does require] a civil court to examine certain religious documents, such as a church constitution, for language of trust in favor of the general church. In undertaking such an examination, a civil court must take special care to scrutinize the document in purely secular terms, and not to rely on religious precepts in determining whether the document indicates that the parties have intended to create a trust. In addition, there may be cases where the deed, the corporate charter, or the constitution of the general church incorporates religious concepts in the provisions relating to the ownership of property. If in such a case the interpretation of the instruments of ownership would require the civil court to resolve a religious controversy, then

a. *Serbian,* per Brennan, J., reversed a state court decision that the Mother Church's removal of respondent as bishop of the American–Canadian diocese was "procedurally and substantively defective under the internal regulations of the Mother Church and were therefore arbitrary and invalid": "[W]hether or not there is room for 'marginal civil court review' under the narrow rubrics of 'fraud' or 'collusion' when church tribunals act in bad faith for secular purposes, no 'arbitrariness' exception—in the sense of an inquiry whether the decisions of the highest ecclesiastical tribunal of a hierarchical church complied with church laws and regulations—is consistent with the constitutional mandate that civil courts are bound to accept the decisions of the highest judicatories of a religious organization of hierarchical polity on matters of discipline, faith, internal organization, or ecclesiastical rule, custom or law. [I]t is the essence of religious faith that ecclesiastical decisions are reached and are to be accepted as matters of faith whether or not rational or measurable by objective criteria."

Rehnquist and Stevens, JJ., dissented. See 1977 Utah L.Rev. 138.

the court must defer to the resolution of the doctrinal issue by the authoritative ecclesiastical body. *Serbian.*"

The Court vacated the judgment, however, since "the grounds for the decision that respondents represent the Vineville church remain unarticulated": "If in fact Georgia has adopted a presumptive rule of majority representation, defeasible upon a showing that the identity of the local church is to be determined by some other means, we think this would be consistent with [the] First Amendment. Majority rule is generally employed in the governance of religious societies. Furthermore, the majority faction generally can be identified without resolving any question of religious doctrine or polity. [Most] importantly, any rule of majority representation can always be overcome, under the neutral principles approach, either by providing, in the corporate charter or the constitution of the general church, that the identity of the local church is to be established in some other way, or by providing that the church property is held in trust for the general church and those who remain loyal to it. Indeed, the State may adopt any method of overcoming the majoritarian presumption, so long as the use of that method does not impair free exercise rights or entangle the civil courts in matters of religious controversy.

"[But] there are at least some indications that under Georgia law the process of identifying the faction that represents the Vineville church [must] be determined according to terms of the Book of Church Order * * *. Such a determination, however, would appear to require a civil court to pass on questions of religious doctrine, and to usurp the function of the commission appointed by the Presbytery * * *. Therefore, if Georgia law provides that the identity of the Vineville church is to be determined according to the 'laws and regulations' of the PCUS, then the First Amendment requires that the Georgia courts give deference to the presbyterial commission's determination of that church's identity."

POWELL, J., joined by Burger, C.J., and Stewart and White, JJ., dissented, finding that the neutral principles "approach inevitably will increase the involvement of civil courts in church controversies": "Until today, [the] first question presented in a case involving an intrachurch dispute over church property was where within the religious association the rules of polity, accepted by its members before the schism, had placed ultimate authority over the use of the church property. The courts, in answering this question have recognized two broad categories of church government. One is congregational, in which authority over questions of church doctrine, practice, and administration rests entirely in the local congregation or some body within it. In disputes over the control and use of the property of such a church, the civil courts enforce the authoritative resolution of the controversy within the local church itself. *Watson v. Jones,* 80 U.S. 679, 20 L.Ed. 666 (1871). The second is hierarchical, in which the local church is but an integral and subordinate part of a larger church and is under the authority of the general church. Since the decisions of the local congregation are subject to review by the tribunals of the church hierarchy, this Court has held that the civil courts must give effect to the duly made decisions of the highest body within the hierarchy that has considered the dispute. [By] doing so, the [civil] court avoids two equally unacceptable departures from the genuine neutrality mandated by the First Amendment. First, it refrains from direct review and revision of decisions of the church on matters of religious doctrine and practice that underlie the church's determination of intrachurch controversies, including those that relate to control of church property.[b] Equally important, by recognizing the authoritative resolution reached within the religious association, the civil court avoids interfering indirectly with the religious governance of those who have formed the association and submitted themselves to its authority." [c]

(b) *Scope of the decision.* After *Jones v. Wolf,* what results in the following situations: (i) A donor who made a bequest "to the First Methodist Church" seeks return of the money because subsequently a majority of the church's members decided to affiliate with another denomination. Suppose the bequest had been "to the First Methodist Church so long as it does not substantially deviate from existing doctrine"? (ii) A state statute makes it a crime for sellers to falsely represent food to be "kosher." See Note, 71 Mich.L.Rev. 1641 (1973).

(c) *Proposed approach.* "The solution most of the time is to honor internal church agreements, just as a court would honor the internal agreements of a secular organization. Only when doctrinal decisions [d] or the imposition of external policies are involved [e] need a court refrain from deciding a dispute. This approach serves both organizational autonomy and the other interests of the church and its members, while preserving the religious neutrality demanded by the first amendment." Ellman, *Driven from the Tribunal: Judicial Resolution of Internal Church Disputes,* 69 Calif.L.Rev. 1378, 1444 (1981).[f]

Since 1970, the Court has decided a large number of cases concerning financial aid to church-related educational programs. Several indirectly related decisions, invoking various themes from *Walz,* have played a significant role.

TEXAS MONTHLY, INC. v. BULLOCK, 489 U.S. 1, 109 S.Ct. 890, 103 L.Ed. 2d 1 (1989), held violative of the establishment clause a Texas sales tax exemption for "periodicals that are published or distributed by a religious faith and

b. In response, the Court pointed out that, under the dissent's approach, "civil courts would always be required to examine the polity and administration of a church to determine which unit of government has ultimate control over church property. In some cases, this task would not prove to be difficult. But in others, the locus of control would be ambiguous, and 'a careful examination of the constitutions of the general and local church, as well as other relevant documents, [would] be necessary to ascertain the form of governance adopted by the members of the religious association.' In such cases, the suggested rule would appear to require 'a searching and therefore impermissible inquiry into church polity.' *Serbian.* The neutral principles approach, in contrast, obviates entirely the need for an analysis or examination of ecclesiastical polity or doctrine in settling church property disputes."

c. In response, the Court contended that "the neutral principles approach cannot be said to 'inhibit' the free exercise of religion, any more than do other neutral provisions of state law governing the manner in which churches own property, hire employees, or purchase goods. Under the neutral principles approach, the outcome of a church property dispute is not foreordained. At any time before the dispute erupts, the parties can ensure, if they so desire, that the faction loyal to the hierarchical church will retain the church property" by using reversionary clauses, trust provisions, etc.

d. "Few [cases] present the problem of governmental determination of religious doctrine. [More] common are a second group of cases in which the court is asked to determine which religious doctrine the embattled parties agreed to follow. This kind of question is very different and need not present the first amendment difficulties inherent in the first group of cases." Id. at 1414.

e. "[T]he application of judge-made rules of procedural fairness in associational governance, and the use of charitable trust rules of charitable assets [are issues that] present the potential for courts to impose government-created policies on religious organizations [rather than rules seeking to fulfill the parties' intentions]." Id. at 1421.

f. For the view that "freedom of church groups" should be preferred to "freedom of individual members," and therefore the rule of "deference" to church decisions should prevail over the "neutral principles" approach, see Garvey, *Churches and the Free Exercise of Religion,* 4 Notre D.J.L.Eth & Pub.Pol. 567 (1990).

that consist wholly of writings promulgating the teaching of the faith and books that consist wholly of writings sacred to a religious faith." BRENNAN, J., joined by Marshall and Stevens, JJ., reasoned that *Walz* and *Widmar,* Part I supra, "emphasized that the benefits derived by religious organizations flowed to a large number of nonreligious groups as well": "However, when government directs a subsidy exclusively to religious organizations that is not required by the Free Exercise Clause and that either burdens nonbeneficiaries markedly or cannot reasonably be seen as removing a significant state-imposed deterrent to the free exercise of religion, as Texas has done, it 'provide[s] unjustifiable awards of assistance to religious organizations' and cannot but 'conve[y] a message of endorsement' to slighted members of the community. This is particularly true where, as here, the subsidy is targeted at writings that *promulgate* the teachings of religious faiths. It is difficult to view Texas' narrow exemption as anything but state sponsorship of religious belief [which] lacks a secular objective."

BLACKMUN, J., joined by O'Connor, J., concurred: "[A] tax exemption *limited* to the sale of religious literature * * * offends our most basic understanding of what the Establishment Clause is all about." [a]

SCALIA, J., joined by Rehnquist, C.J., and Kennedy, J., pointing out that "at least 45 state [tax] codes contain exemptions for religious groups without analogous exemptions for other types of nonprofit institutions," dissented: *Walz* "is utterly dispositive" and Brennan, J.'s distinction of *Walz* "is not a plausible reading of the opinion. [*Walz*] is just one of a long line of cases in which we have recognized that the government may (and sometimes must) accommodate religious practices and that it may do so without violating the Establishment Clause." [b]

MUELLER v. ALLEN

463 U.S. 388, 103 S.Ct. 3062, 77 L.Ed.2d 721 (1983).

JUSTICE REHNQUIST delivered the opinion of the Court.

Minnesota allows taxpayers, in computing their state income tax, to deduct certain expenses incurred in providing for the education of their children.[1] [A]bout 820.000 students attended [Minnesota's public] school system in the most recent school year. During the same year, approximately 91,000 elementary and secondary students attended some 500 privately supported schools located in Minnesota, and about 95% of these students attended schools considering themselves to be sectarian. * * *

a. White, J., concurred on the ground that the law "discriminates on the basis of the content of publications [and] is plainly forbidden by the Press Clause of the First Amendment [under] *Arkansas Writer's Project v. Ragland,*" 941 supra.

b. Scalia, J.'s reasoning continues at p. 927 infra, where the case is also discussed.

1. Minn.Stat. § 290.09(22) (1982) permits a taxpayer to deduct from his or her computation of gross income the following: "[The] amount he has paid to others, not to exceed $500 for each dependent in grades K to 6 and $700 for each dependent in grades 7 to 12, for tuition, textbooks and transportation of each dependent in attending an elementary or secondary school [wherein] a resident of this state may legally fulfill the state's compulsory attendance laws, which is not operated for profit, and which adheres to the provisions of the Civil Rights Act of 1964 * * *. As used in this subdivision, 'textbooks' shall mean and include books and other instructional materials and equipment used in elementary and secondary schools in teaching only those subjects legally and commonly taught in public elementary and secondary schools in this state and shall not include instructional books and materials used in the teaching of religious tenets, doctrines or worship * * *."

Today's case is no exception to our oft-repeated statement that the Establishment Clause presents especially difficult questions of interpretation and application. [It] is not at all easy [to] apply this Court's various decisions construing the Clause to governmental programs of financial assistance to sectarian schools and the parents of children attending those schools. Indeed, in many of these decisions "we have expressly or implicitly acknowledged that we can only dimly perceive the lines of demarcation in this extraordinarily sensitive area of constitutional law." *Lemon.* [a]

One fixed principle in this field is our consistent rejection of the argument that "any program which in some manner aids an institution with a religious affiliation" violates the Establishment Clause. For example, it is now well established that a State may reimburse parents for expenses incurred in transporting their children to school, *Everson,* and that it may loan secular textbooks to all schoolchildren within the State, *Allen.* [But] our decisions also have struck down arrangements resembling, in many respects, these forms of assistance. See, e.g., *Lemon; Levitt v. Committee for Pub. Educ.,* 413 U.S. 472, 93 S.Ct. 2814, 37 L.Ed.2d 736 (1973); *Meek v. Pittenger,* 421 U.S. 349, 95 S.Ct. 1753, 44 L.Ed.2d 217 (1975); *Wolman v. Walter,* 433 U.S. 229, 237–238, 97 S.Ct. 2593, 2599–2600, 53 L.Ed.2d 714 (1977).[3] Petitioners place particular reliance on our decision in *Committee for Pub. Educ. v. Nyquist,* 413 U.S. 756, 93 S.Ct. 2955, 37 L.Ed.2d 948 (1973), where we held invalid a New York [statute] granting thinly disguised "tax benefits," actually amounting to tuition grants, to the parents of children attending private schools. As explained below, we conclude that § 290.09(22) bears less resemblance to the arrangement struck down in *Nyquist* than it does to assistance programs upheld in our prior [decisions].

Little time need be spent on the question of whether the Minnesota tax deduction has a secular purpose. Under our prior decisions, governmental assistance programs have consistently survived this inquiry even when they have run afoul of other aspects of the *Lemon* framework. This reflects, at least in part, our reluctance to attribute unconstitutional motives to the states, particularly when a plausible secular purpose for the state's program may be discerned from the face of the statute.

A state's decision to defray the cost of educational expenses incurred by parents—regardless of the type of schools their children attend—evidences a purpose that is both secular and understandable. An educated populace is essential to the political and economic health of any community, and a state's efforts to assist parents in meeting the rising cost of educational expenses plainly serves this secular purpose of ensuring that the state's citizenry is well-educated. Similarly, Minnesota, like other states, could conclude that there is a strong

a. *Committee for Pub. Educ. v. Regan,* 444 U.S. 646, 100 S.Ct. 840, 63 L.Ed.2d 94 (1980), per White, J., observed that the "decisions have tended to avoid categorical imperatives and absolutist approaches at either end of the range of possible outcomes. This course sacrifices clarity and predictability for flexibility * * *." For the view "that application of the Court's three-prong test has generated ad hoc judgments which are incapable of being reconciled on any principled basis," see Choper, *The Religion Clauses of the First Amendment,* 41 U.Pitt.L.Rev. 673, 680–81 (1980).

3. In *Lemon,* the Court concluded that the State's reimbursement of nonpublic schools for the cost of teachers' salaries, textbooks, and instructional materials, and its payment of a salary supplement to teachers in nonpublic schools, resulted in excessive entanglement of church and state. In *Levitt,* we struck down on Establishment Clause grounds a state program reimbursing nonpublic schools for the cost of teacher-prepared examinations. Finally, in *Meek* and *Wolman,* we held unconstitutional a direct loan of instructional materials to nonpublic schools, while upholding the loan of textbooks to individual students.

public interest in assuring the continued financial health of private schools, both sectarian and non-sectarian. By educating a substantial number of students such schools relieve public schools of a correspondingly great burden—to the benefit of all taxpayers. In addition, private schools may serve as a benchmark for public schools * * *.

We turn therefore to the more difficult but related question whether the Minnesota statute has "the primary effect of advancing the sectarian aims of the non-public schools." In concluding that it does not, we find several features of the Minnesota tax deduction particularly significant. First, an essential feature of Minnesota's arrangement is the fact that § 290.09(22) is only one among many deductions—such as those for medical expenses and charitable contributions [b]—available under the Minnesota tax laws.[5] Our decisions consistently have recognized that [the] legislature's judgment that a deduction for educational expenses fairly equalizes the tax burden of its citizens and encourages desirable expenditures for educational purposes is entitled to substantial deference.[6]

Other characteristics of § 290.09(22) argue equally strongly for the provision's constitutionality. Most importantly, the deduction is available for educational expenses incurred by *all* parents, including those whose children attend public schools and those whose children attend non-sectarian private schools or sectarian private schools. Just as in *Widmar,* [so] here: "the provision of benefits to so broad a spectrum of groups is an important index of secular effect."

In this respect, as well as others, this case is vitally different from the scheme struck down in *Nyquist.* There, public assistance amounting to tuition grants, was provided only to parents of children in *nonpublic* schools. This fact had considerable bearing on our decision striking down the New York statute at

b. Compare Choper, *The Establishment Clause and Aid to Parochial Schools—An Update,* 75 Calif.L.Rev. 5, 8 (1987): "This [is] no different than saying that an appropriation to build a new Lutheran church in St. Paul would be only one of many appropriations by the Minnesota legislature. It follows from Justice Rehnquist's reasoning that since Minnesota appropriates money for the University of Minnesota and for all kinds of other things, an appropriation to build a Lutheran church should be treated just like one of many appropriations. But the establishment clause is plainly meant to prohibit some things, even though they are much like other things, if they involve religion."

5. Deductions for charitable contributions, allowed by Minnesota law, include contributions to religious institutions, and exemptions from property tax for property used for charitable purposes under Minnesota law include property used for wholly religious purposes. In each case, it may be that religious institutions benefit very substantially from the allowance of such deductions. The Court's holding in *Walz* indicates, however, that this does not require the conclusion that such provisions of a state's tax law violate the Establishment Clause.

6. Our decision in *Nyquist* is not to the contrary on this point. We expressed considerable doubt there that the "tax benefits" provided by New York law properly could be regarded as parts of a genuine system of tax laws. Plainly, the outright grants to low-income parents ["of $50 to $100 per child (but no more than 50% of tuition actually paid)"] did not take the form of ordinary tax benefits. As to the benefits provided to middle-income parents, the Court said: "The amount of the deduction is unrelated to the amount of money actually expended by any parent on tuition, but is calculated on the basis of a formula contained in the statute. The formula is apparently the product of a legislative attempt to assure that each family would receive a carefully estimated net benefit, and that the tax benefit would be comparable to, and compatible with, the tuition grant for lower income families." Indeed, the question whether a program having the elements of a "genuine tax deduction" would be constitutionally acceptable was expressly reserved in *Nyquist.* While the economic consequences of the program in *Nyquist* and that in this case may be difficult to distinguish, we have recognized on other occasions that "the form of the [state's assistance to parochial schools must be examined] for the light that it casts on the substance." The fact that the Minnesota plan embodies a "genuine tax deduction" is thus of some relevance, especially given the traditional rule of deference accorded legislative classifications in tax statutes.

issue; we explicitly distinguished both *Allen* and *Everson* on the grounds that "In both cases the class of beneficiaries included *all* schoolchildren, those in public as well as those in private schools." Moreover, we intimated that "public assistance (e.g., scholarships) made available generally without regard to the sectarian-nonsectarian or public-nonpublic nature of the institution benefited," might not offend the Establishment Clause. We think the tax deduction adopted by Minnesota is more similar to this latter type of program than it is to the arrangement struck down in *Nyquist*. * * *

We also agree with the Court of Appeals that, by channeling whatever assistance it may provide to parochial schools through individual parents, Minnesota has reduced the Establishment Clause objections to which its action is subject. It is true, of course, that financial assistance provided to parents ultimately has an economic effect comparable to that of aid given directly to the schools attended by their children. It is also true, however, that under Minnesota's arrangement public funds become available only as a result of numerous, private choices of individual parents of school-age children. [It] is noteworthy that all but one of our recent cases invalidating state aid to parochial schools have involved the direct transmission of assistance from the state to the schools themselves. The exception, of course, was *Nyquist,* which, as discussed previously is distinguishable from this case on other grounds. Where, as here, aid to parochial schools is available only as a result of decisions of individual parents no "imprimatur of State approval," *Widmar,* can be deemed to have been conferred on any particular religion, or on religion generally.

[The] Establishment Clause of course extends beyond prohibition of a state church or payment of state funds to one or more churches. We do not think, however, that its prohibition extends to the type of tax deduction established by Minnesota. The historic purposes of the clause simply do not encompass the sort of attenuated financial benefit, ultimately controlled by the private choices of individual parents, that eventually flows to parochial schools from the neutrally available tax benefit at issue in this case.

Petitioners argue that, notwithstanding the facial neutrality of § 290.09(22), [most] parents of public school children incur no tuition expenses, and that other expenses deductible under § 290.09(22) are negligible in value; moreover, they claim that 96% of the children in private schools in 1978–1979 attended religiously-affiliated institutions. Because of all this, they reason, the bulk of deductions taken under § 290.09(22) will be claimed by parents of children in sectarian schools. Respondents reply that petitioners have failed to consider the impact of deductions for items such as transportation, summer school tuition, tuition paid by parents whose children attended schools outside the school districts in which they resided, rental or purchase costs for a variety of equipment, and tuition for certain types of instruction not ordinarily provided in public schools.

We need not consider these contentions in detail. We would be loath to adopt a rule grounding the constitutionality of a facially neutral law on annual reports reciting the extent to which various classes of private citizens claimed benefits under the law. Such an approach would scarcely provide the certainty that this field stands in need of, nor can we perceive principled standards by which such statistical evidence might be evaluated. Moreover, the fact that private persons fail in a particular year to claim the tax relief to which they are entitled—under a facially neutral statute—should be of little importance in determining the constitutionality of the statute permitting such relief.

Finally, [if] parents of children in private schools choose to take especial advantage of the relief provided by § 290.09(22), it is no doubt due to the fact that they bear a particularly great financial burden in educating their children. More fundamentally, whatever unequal effect may be attributed to the statutory classification can fairly be regarded as a rough return for the benefits, discussed above, provided to the state and all taxpayers by parents sending their children to parochial schools. In the light of all this, we believe it wiser to decline to engage in the type of empirical inquiry into those persons benefited by state law which petitioners urge. * * *

Turning to the third part of the *Lemon* inquiry, we have no difficulty in concluding that the Minnesota statute does not "excessively entangle" the state in religion.[c] [T]hat state officials must determine whether particular textbooks qualify for a deduction [does] not differ substantially from making the types of decisions approved in [*Allen*].[11]

Affirmed.

JUSTICE MARSHALL, with whom JUSTICE BRENNAN, JUSTICE BLACKMUN and JUSTICE STEVENS join, dissenting.

[§ 290.09(22)] has a direct and immediate effect of advancing religion. [Although it] allows a deduction for the tuition expenses of children attending public schools, Minnesota public schools [may] assess tuition charges only for students accepted from outside the district. In the 1978–1979 school year, only 79 public school students fell into this category. * * *

As we recognized in *Nyquist,* direct government subsidization of parochial school tuition is impermissible because "the effect of the aid is unmistakably to provide desired financial support for nonpublic, sectarian institutions." "[A]id to

c. In *Lemon,* "comprehensive, discriminating, and continuing state surveillance will inevitably be required [under statutory restrictions] to ensure [that] subsidized teachers do not inculcate religion. [Unlike] a book, a teacher cannot be inspected once so as to determine the extent and intent of his or her personal beliefs and subjective acceptance of the limitations imposed by the First Amendment. These prophylactic contacts will involve excessive and enduring entanglement between state and church."

11. No party to this litigation has urged that the Minnesota plan is invalid because it runs afoul of the rather elusive inquiry, subsumed under the third part of the *Lemon* test, whether the Minnesota statute partakes of the "divisive political potential" condemned in *Lemon.* [Since] this aspect of the "entanglement" inquiry originated with *Lemon,* and the Court's opinion there took pains to distinguish both *Everson* and *Allen,* the Court in *Lemon* must have been referring to a phenomenon which, although present in that case, would have been absent in the two cases it distinguished.

The Court's language in *Lemon* respecting political divisiveness was made in the context of Pennsylvania and Rhode Island statutes which provided for either direct payments of, or reimbursement of, a proportion of teachers' salaries in parochial schools. We think, in the light of the treatment of the point in later cases discussed above, the language must be regarded as confined to cases where direct financial subsidies are paid to parochial schools or to teachers in parochial schools.

[Subsequent reliance on this point in *Lynch v. Donnelly,* discussed in Part III infra, produced the following response by the same dissenters as in *Mueller:*

"The suggestion in *Mueller,* n. 11, relied upon by the Court today, that inquiry into potential political divisiveness is unnecessary absent direct subsidies to church-sponsored schools or colleges, derives from a distorted reading of our prior cases. Simply because the Court in *Lemon*—a case involving such subsidies—inquired into potential divisiveness while distinguishing *Everson* and *Allen*—cases not involving such subsidies—does not provide any authority for the proposition that the Court in *Lemon* meant to confine the divisiveness inquiry only to cases factually identical to *Lemon* itself. Indeed, in *Walz,* the Court considered the question of divisiveness in the context of state tax exemptions to all religious institutions. I agree, however, with Justice O'Connor's helpful suggestion that while political divisiveness is 'an evil addressed by the Establishment Clause,' the ultimate inquiry must always focus on 'the character of the government activity that might cause such divisiveness.' "]

the educational function of [parochial schools] necessarily results in aid to the sectarian enterprise as a whole" because "[t]he very purpose of those schools is to provide an integrated secular and religious education." For this reason, aid to sectarian schools must be restricted to ensure that it may not be used to further the religious mission of those schools. While "services such as police and fire protection, sewage disposal, highways, and sidewalks," may be provided to parochial schools in common with other institutions, because this type of assistance is clearly "marked off from the religious function" of those schools, unrestricted financial assistance, such as grants for the maintenance and construction of parochial schools, may not be provided. * * *

Indirect assistance in the form of financial aid to parents for tuition payments is similarly impermissible because it is not "subject [to] restrictions" which "guarantee the separation between secular and religious educational functions [and] ensure that State financial aid supports only the former." *Lemon.* [As] was true of the law struck down in *Nyquist,* "it is precisely the function of [Minnesota's] law to provide assistance to private schools, the great majority of which are sectarian. By reimbursing parents for a portion of their tuition bill, the State seeks to relieve their financial burdens sufficiently to assure that they continue to have the option to send their children to religion-oriented schools. And while the other purposes for that aid—to perpetuate a pluralistic educational environment and to protect the fiscal integrity of overburdened public schools—are certainly unexceptional, the effect of the aid is unmistakably to provide desired financial support for nonpublic, sectarian institutions."

That parents receive a reduction of their tax liability, rather than a direct reimbursement, is of no greater significance here than it was in *Nyquist.* "[F]or purposes of determining whether such aid has the effect of advancing religion," it makes no difference whether the qualifying "parent receives an actual cash payment [or] is allowed to reduce [the] sum he would otherwise be obliged to pay over to the State." It is equally irrelevant whether a reduction in taxes takes the form of a tax "credit," a tax "modification," or a tax "deduction." What is of controlling significance is not the form but the "substantive impact" of the financial aid. * * *

The majority first attempts to distinguish *Nyquist* on the ground that Minnesota makes all parents eligible to deduct up to $500 or $700 for each dependent, whereas the New York law allowed a deduction only for parents whose children attended nonpublic schools. Although Minnesota taxpayers who send their children to local public schools may not deduct tuition expenses because they incur none, they may deduct other expenses, such as the cost of gym clothes, pencils, and notebooks, which are shared by all parents of school-age children. * * *

That the Minnesota statute makes some small benefit available to all parents cannot alter the fact that the most substantial benefit provided by the statute is available only to those parents who send their children to schools that charge tuition.[2] Of the total number of taxpayers who are eligible for the

2. Even if the Minnesota statute allowed parents of public school students to deduct expenses that were likely to be equivalent to the tuition expenses of private school students, it would still be unconstitutional. Insofar as the Minnesota statute provides a deduction for parochial school tuition, it provides a benefit to parochial schools that furthers the religious mission of those schools. *Nyquist* makes clear that the State may not provide any financial assistance to parochial schools unless that assistance is limited to secular uses.

tuition deduction, approximately 96% send their children to religious schools. [In] *Nyquist* we unequivocally rejected any suggestion that, in determining the effect of a tax statute, this Court should look exclusively to what the statute on its face purports to do and ignore the actual operation of the challenged provision. In determining the effect of the New York statute, we emphasized [that] "tax reductions authorized by this law flow primarily to the parents of children attending sectarian, nonpublic schools." Similarly, in *Sloan v. Lemon,* 413 U.S. 825, 93 S.Ct. 2982, 37 L.Ed.2d 939 (1973), we considered important to our "consider[ation of] the new law's effect [that] 'more than 90% of the children attending nonpublic schools in the Commonwealth of Pennsylvania are enrolled in schools that are controlled by religious institutions or that have the purpose of propagating and promoting religious faith.'"

* * * Financial assistance for tuition payments has a consequence that "is quite unlike the sort of 'indirect' and 'incidental' benefits that flowed to sectarian schools from programs aiding *all* parents by supplying bus transportation and secular textbooks for their children. *Such benefits were carefully restricted to the purely secular side of church-affiliated institutions* and provided no special aid for those who had chosen to support religious schools. Yet such aid approached the 'verge' of the constitutionally impermissible." *Sloan* (emphasis added in part). As previously noted, the Minnesota tuition tax deduction is not available to *all* parents, but only to parents whose children attend schools that charge tuition, which are comprised almost entirely of sectarian schools. More importantly, the assistance that flows to parochial schools as a result of the tax benefit is not restricted, and cannot be restricted, to the secular functions of those schools.

In my view, Minnesota's tax deduction for the cost of textbooks and other instructional materials is also constitutionally infirm. * * *

The instructional materials which are subsidized by the Minnesota tax deduction plainly may be used to inculcate religious values and belief. In *Meek,* we held that even the use of "wholly neutral, secular instructional material and equipment" by church-related schools contributes to religious instruction because " '[t]he secular education those schools provide goes hand in hand with the religious mission that is the only reason for the schools' existence.' " In *Wolman,* we concluded that precisely the same impermissible effect results when the instructional materials are loaned to the pupil or his parent, rather than directly to the schools. We stated that "it would exalt form over substance if this distinction were found to justify a result different from that in *Meek.*" It follows that a tax deduction to offset the cost of purchasing instructional materials for use in sectarian schools, like a loan of such materials to parents, "necessarily results in aid to the sectarian school enterprise as a whole" and is therefore a "substantial advancement of religious activity" that "constitutes an impermissible establishment of religion."

There is no reason to treat Minnesota's tax deduction for textbooks any differently. Secular textbooks, like other secular instructional materials, contribute to the religious mission of the parochial schools that use those books. [D]istinguishing secular instructional materials and secular textbooks is simply untenable, and is inconsistent with many of our more recent decisions concerning state aid to parochial schools. * * * [6]

6. For similar reasons, I would hold that the deduction for transportation expenses is constitutional only insofar as it relates to the costs of traveling between home and school. See *Wolman* (reimbursement of nonpublic schools for field trip transportation impermis-

[For] the first time, the Court has upheld financial support for religious schools without any reason at all to assume that the support will be restricted to the secular functions of those schools and will not be used to support religious instruction. This result is flatly at odds with the fundamental principle that [the] Court stated in *Everson* and has often repeated, see, e.g., *Meek; Nyquist,* "No tax in any amount, large or small, can be levied to support any religious activities or institutions, whatever they may be called, or whatever form they may adopt to teach or practice religion."

GRAND RAPIDS SCHOOL DIST. v. BALL

473 U.S. 373, 105 S.Ct. 3216, 87 L.Ed.2d 267 (1985).

JUSTICE BRENNAN delivered the opinion of the Court.

[In 1976, the school district adopted two publicly financed programs held on parochial school premises. Under the Shared Time Program, "remedial" and "enrichment" courses in mathematics and reading, and courses in art, music and physical education were taught during the regular school day by public school teachers; supplies, material and equipment were provided at public expense. Under the Community Education Program, classes for children and adults—in subjects such as "Arts and Crafts, Home Economics, Spanish, Gymnastics, Yearbook Production, Christmas Arts and Crafts, Drama, Newspaper, Humanities, Chess, Model Building, and Nature Appreciation"—were taught at the end of the regular school day. Both programs were conducted in parochial school classrooms which were "leased" by the school district and which had to be free of any religious symbols; during the programs, a posted sign stated that it was a "public school classroom." No attempt was made in either program "to monitor [the] courses for religious content."]

Since *Everson,* [we] have often grappled with the problem of state aid to nonpublic, religious schools. In all of these cases, our goal has been to give meaning to the sparse language and broad purposes of the [Establishment] Clause, while not unduly infringing on the ability of the States to provide for [the] education of schoolchildren. [But] our cases have consistently recognized that even such a praiseworthy, secular purpose cannot validate government aid to parochial schools when the aid has the effect of promoting a single religion or religion generally or when the aid unduly entangles the government in matters religious. * * *

As has often been true in school aid cases, there is no dispute [that] the purpose of the Community Education and Shared Time programs was "manifestly secular." We [go] on to consider whether the primary or principal effect of the challenged programs is to advance or inhibit religion.

[Of] the 41 private schools where these "part-time public schools" have operated, 40 are identifiably religious schools. [The] District Court found "[that] the religious institutions receiving instructional services from the public schools are sectarian in the sense that a substantial portion of their functions are subsumed in the religious mission." [6] [Thus, the programs] may impermissibly

sibly fosters religion because the nonpublic schools control the timing, frequency, and destination of the trips, which, for sectarian schools, are an integral part of the sectarian education). * * *

6. [Many] of the schools in this case include prayer and attendance at religious services as a part of their curriculum, are run by churches or other organizations whose members must subscribe to particular religious tenets, have faculties and student bodies composed largely of adherents of the particular denomination, and give preference in attendance to children belonging to the denomination.

advance religion in three different ways. * * *

(1) [In] *Meek,* the Court invalidated a statute providing for the loan of state-paid professional staff—including teachers—to nonpublic schools to provide remedial and accelerated instruction, guidance counseling and testing, and other services on the premises of the nonpublic schools. Such a program, if not subjected to a "comprehensive, discriminating, and continuing state surveillance," *Lemon,* would entail an unacceptable risk that the state-sponsored instructional personnel would "advance the religious mission of the church-related schools in which they serve." Even though the teachers were paid by the State, "[t]he potential for impermissible fostering of religion under these circumstances, although somewhat reduced, is nonetheless present." * * *

The programs before us today share the defect that we identified in *Meek.* With respect to the Community Education Program, the District Court found that "virtually every Community Education course conducted on facilities leased from nonpublic schools has an instructor otherwise employed full time by the same nonpublic school." These instructors, many of whom no doubt teach in the religious schools precisely because they are adherents of the controlling denomination and want to serve their religious community zealously, are expected during the regular school day to inculcate their students with the tenets and beliefs of their particular religious faiths. Yet the premise of the program is that those instructors can put aside their religious convictions and engage in entirely secular Community Education instruction as soon as the school day is over. [T]here is a substantial risk that, overtly or subtly, the religious message they are expected to convey during the regular school day will infuse the supposedly secular classes they teach after school. The danger arises "not because the public employee [is] likely deliberately to subvert his task to the service of religion, but rather because the pressures of the environment might alter his behavior from its normal course." *Wolman.* * * *

The Shared Time program [poses] a substantial risk of state-sponsored indoctrination. The most important difference between the programs is that most of the instructors in the Shared Time program are full-time teachers hired by the public schools [although] "[a] significant portion" of the Shared Time instructors previously worked in the religious schools.[7] [They] are teaching academic subjects in religious schools in courses virtually indistinguishable from the other courses offered during the regular religious-school day [and] may well subtly (or overtly) conform their instruction to the environment in which they teach, while students will perceive the instruction provided in the context of the dominantly religious message of the institution, thus reinforcing the indoctrinating effect. [Unlike] types of aid that the Court has upheld, such as state-created standardized tests, *Regan,* or diagnostic services, *Wolman,* there is a "substantial risk" that programs operating in this environment would "be used for religious educational purposes."

[T]hat respondents adduced no evidence of specific incidents of religious indoctrination in this case [is] not dispositive. When conducting a supposedly secular class in the pervasively sectarian environment of a religious school, a teacher may knowingly or unwillingly tailor the content of the course to fit the school's announced goals. If so, there is no reason to believe that this kind of ideological influence would be detected or [reported]. After spending the balance

7. Approximately 10 percent of the Shared Time instructors were previously employed by the religious schools, and many of these were reassigned back to the school at which they had previously taught.

of their school day in classes heavily influenced by a religious perspective, [the students] would have little motivation or ability to discern improper ideological content that may creep into a Shared Time or Community Education course. Neither their parents nor the parochial schools would have cause to complain if the effect of the publicly-supported instruction were to advance the schools' sectarian mission. And the public school system itself has no incentive to detect or report any specific incidents of improper state-sponsored indoctrination. * * *

(2) Our cases have recognized that the Establishment Clause guards against more than direct, state-funded efforts to indoctrinate youngsters in specific religious beliefs. [A]n important concern of the effects test is whether the symbolic union of church and state effected by the challenged governmental action is sufficiently likely to be perceived by adherents of the controlling denominations as an endorsement, and by the nonadherents as a disapproval, of their individual religious choices. [The] symbolism of a union between church and state is most likely to influence children of tender years, whose experience is limited and whose beliefs consequently are the function of environment as much as of free and voluntary choice.[10] Consequently, even the student who notices the "public school" sign temporarily posted would have before him a powerful symbol of state endorsement and encouragement of the religious beliefs taught in the same class at some other time during the day. * * *

(3) [With] but one exception, our [cases] have struck down attempts by States to make payments out of public tax dollars directly to primary or secondary religious educational institutions. See, e.g., *Nyquist* (reimbursement for maintenance and repair expenses); *Levitt* (reimbursement for teacher-prepared tests); *Lemon* (salary supplements for nonpublic school teachers). But see *Regan* (permitting public subsidy for certain routinized recordkeeping and testing services performed by nonpublic schools but required by state law).

Aside from cash payments, the Court has distinguished between two categories of programs in which public funds are used to finance secular activities that religious schools would otherwise fund from their own resources. In the first category, the Court has noted ["that] not every law that confers an 'indirect,' 'remote,' or 'incidental' benefit upon religious institutions is, for that reason alone, constitutionally invalid." In such "indirect" aid cases, the government has used primarily secular means to accomplish a primarily secular end, and no "primary effect" of advancing religion has thus been found. [See *Allen; Everson.*]

In the second category of cases, the Court has relied on the Establishment Clause prohibition of forms of aid that provide "direct and substantial advancement of the sectarian enterprise." In such "direct aid" cases, the government, although acting for a secular purpose, has done so by directly supporting a religious institution. Under this rationale, the Court has struck down state schemes providing for tuition grants and tax benefits for parents whose children attend religious school, see *Sloan; Nyquist,* and programs providing for "loan" of instructional materials to be used in religious schools, see *Wolman; Meek.* In *Sloan* and *Nyquist,* the aid was formally given to parents and not directly to the religious schools, while in *Wolman* and *Meek,* the aid was in-kind assistance rather than the direct contribution of public funds. Nonetheless, these differ-

10. Compare *Meek* (invalidating program providing for state-funded remedial services on religious-school premises) with *Wolman* (upholding program providing for similar services at neutral sites off the premises of the religious school).

ences in form were insufficient to save programs whose effect was indistinguishable from that of a direct subsidy to the religious school.

Thus, the Court has never accepted the mere possibility of subsidization, as the above cases demonstrate, as sufficient to invalidate an aid program. On the other hand, this effect is not wholly unimportant for Establishment Clause purposes. If it were, the public schools could gradually take on themselves the entire responsibility for teaching secular subjects on religious school premises. The question in each case must be whether the effect of the proffered aid is "direct and substantial," or indirect and incidental. "The problem, like many problems in constitutional law, is one of degree." *Zorach.* [Cf.] *Wolman* (upholding provision of diagnostic services, which were "general welfare services for children that may be provided by the State regardless of the incidental benefit that accrues to church-related schools.") * * *

Petitioners claim that the aid here, like the textbooks in *Allen,* flows primarily to the students, not to the religious schools.[13] Of course, all aid to religious schools ultimately "flows to" the students, and petitioners' argument if accepted would validate all forms of nonideological aid to religious schools, including those explicitly rejected in our prior cases. Yet in *Meek,* we held unconstitutional the loan of instructional materials to religious schools and in *Wolman,* we rejected the fiction that a similar program could be saved by masking it as aid to individual students. It follows a fortiori that the aid here, which includes not only instructional materials but also the provision of instructional services by teachers in the parochial school building, "inescapably [has] the primary effect of providing a direct and substantial advancement of the sectarian enterprise." * * *

Petitioners also argue that this "subsidy" effect is not significant in this case, because the Community Education and Shared Time programs supplemented the curriculum with courses not previously offered in the religious schools and not required by school rule or state regulation. [But first,] there is no way of knowing whether the religious schools would have offered some or all of these courses if the public school system had not offered them first. The distinction between courses that "supplement" and those that "supplant" the regular curriculum is therefore not nearly as clear as petitioners allege. Second, although the precise courses offered in these programs may have been new to the participating religious schools, their general subject matter—reading, math, etc.—was surely a part of the curriculum in the past, and the concerns of the Establishment Clause may thus be triggered despite the "supplemental" nature of the courses. Third, and most important, petitioners' argument would permit the public schools gradually to take over the entire secular curriculum of the religious school, for the latter could surely discontinue existing courses so that they might be replaced a year or two later by a Community Education or Shared Time course with the same content. The average religious school student, for instance, now spends 10 percent of the school day in Shared Time classes. But there is no principled basis on which this Court can impose a limit on the percentage of the religious-school day that can be subsidized by the public school. To let the genie out of the bottle in this case would be to permit ever larger segments of the religious school curriculum to be turned over to the public school system, thus violating the cardinal principle that the State may not in effect become the prime supporter of the religious school system. * * *

13. [Unlike] *Mueller,* the aid provided here is unmediated by the tax code and the "numerous, private choices of individual parents of school-age children."

Nonpublic schools have played an important role in the development of American education, and we have long recognized that parents and their children have the right to choose between public schools and available sectarian alternatives. As The Chief Justice noted in *Lemon:* "[N]othing we have said can be construed to disparage the role of church-related elementary and secondary schools in our national life. Their contribution has been and is enormous." But the Establishment Clause "rest[s] on the belief that a union of government and religion tends to destroy government and to degrade religion." *Engel.* * * *

[AGUILAR v. FELTON, 473 U.S. 402, 105 S.Ct. 3232, 87 L.Ed.2d 290 (1985), a companion case, involved Title I of a federal plan—for "educationally deprived children from low-income families"—similar to the *Grand Rapids* Shared Time Program. Since 1966, New York City paid federal funds to public employees (teachers, guidance counselors, psychologists and social workers) for "remedial" courses and "guidance" services provided in parochial school classrooms (the "vast majority" of which were Catholic)[8] which had to be "clear [of] all religious symbols." Unlike Grand Rapids, New York "adopted a system for monitoring the religious content" of the classes. The Court, per BRENNAN, J., relying on the "administrative surveillance" aspect of *Lemon,* held that "the supervisory system * * * inevitably results in the excessive entanglement of church and state, an Establishment Clause concern distinct from that addressed by the effects doctrine. Even where state aid to parochial institutions does not have the primary effect of advancing religion, the provision of such aid may nonetheless violate the Establishment Clause owing to the nature of the interaction of church and state in the administration of that aid. * * *

["In *Roemer v. Maryland Public Works Board,* 426 U.S. 736, 96 S.Ct. 2337, 49 L.Ed.2d (1976), the Court sustained state programs of aid to religiously affiliated institutions of higher learning. The State allowed the grants to be used for any non-sectarian purpose. The Court upheld the grants on the ground that the institutions were not 'pervasively sectarian,' and therefore a system of supervision was unnecessary to ensure that the grants were not being used to effect a religious end. In so holding, the Court identified 'what is crucial to a nonentangling aid program: the ability of the State to identify and subsidize separate secular functions carried out at the school, without on-the-site inspections being necessary to prevent diversion of the funds to sectarian purposes.' Similarly, in *Tilton v. Richardson,* 403 U.S. 672, 91 S.Ct. 2091, 29 L.Ed.2d 790 (1971), the Court upheld one-time grants to sectarian institutions because ongoing supervision was not required. See also *Hunt v. McNair,* 413 U.S. 734, 93 S.Ct. 2863, 37 L.Ed.2d 923 (1973).

["As the Court of Appeals recognized, the elementary and secondary schools here are far different from the colleges at issue in *Roemer, Hunt,* and *Tilton.* Unlike the colleges, which were found not to be 'pervasively sectarian,' many of the schools involved in this case are the same sectarian schools which had 'as a substantial purpose the inculcation of religious values' in *Nyquist.*"][a]

8. Appellants suggest that the degree of sectarianism differs from school to school. This has little bearing on our analysis. As Judge Friendly, writing for the court below, noted: "It may well be that the degree of sectarianism in Catholic schools in, for example, black neighborhoods, with considerable proportions of non-Catholic pupils and teachers, is relatively low; by the same token, in other schools it may be relatively high. [Yet] enforcement of the Establishment Clause does not rest on means or medians. [It] would be simply incredible [that] all, or almost all, New York City's parochial schools receiving Title I aid [have] abandoned 'the religious mission that is the only reason for the schools' existence."

a. *Tilton* added: "There are generally significant differences between the religious aspects of church-related institutions of higher

JUSTICE POWELL concurring [in] the Court's opinions * * *.

I agree with the Court that [the] Establishment Clause is violated because there is too great a risk of government entanglement in the administration of the religious schools [and] is compounded by the additional risk of political divisiveness stemming from the aid to religion at issue here. I do not suggest that at this point in our history [the] plans could result in the establishment of a state religion. There likewise is small chance that these programs would result in significant religious or denominational control over our democratic processes. Nonetheless, there remains a considerable risk of continuing political strife over the propriety of direct aid to religious schools and the proper allocation of limited governmental resources.[b] * * *

learning and parochial elementary and secondary schools. The 'affirmative, if not dominant, policy' of the instruction in pre-college church-schools is 'to assure future adherents to a particular faith by having control of their total education at an early age.' There is substance to the contention that college students are less impressionable and less susceptible to religious indoctrination. [Further], by their very nature, college and postgraduate courses tend to limit the opportunities for sectarian influence by virtue of their own internal disciplines. Many church-related colleges and universities are characterized by a high degree of academic freedom and seek to evoke free and critical responses from their students."

Compare Giannella, *Lemon and Tilton: The Bitter and the Sweet of Church–State Entanglement,* 1971 Sup.Ct.Rev. 147, 175: "The Court's point is probably well taken that religion is more central to the activities of parochial schools than to those of most church-related colleges. But it is highly questionable to conclude that the risk of sectarian instruction creeping into a parochial school's physical education course is greater than the risk of a similar entry into a college history course."

Brennan, J., concurred in *Lemon* but dissented in *Tilton:* "[A] sectarian university is the equivalent in the realm of higher education of the Catholic elementary schools in Rhode Island; it is an educational institution in which the propagation and advancement of a particular religion is a primary function of the institution. [It] is not that religion 'permeates' the secular education that is provided. Rather, it is that the secular education is provided within the environment of religion; the institution is dedicated to two goals, secular education *and* religious instruction. When aid flows directly to the institution, both functions benefit."

White, J., concurred in *Tilton* but dissented in *Lemon:* "The Court strikes down the Rhode Island statute on its face [accepting] the model for the Catholic elementary and secondary schools that it rejected for the Catholic universities or colleges in [*Tilton.* It] strikes down this Rhode Island statute based primarily on its own model and its own suppositions and unsupported views of what is likely to happen in Rhode Island parochial school [classrooms]."

b. *Lemon* amplified the point: "In a community where such a large number of pupils are served by church-related schools, it can be assumed that state assistance will entail considerable political activity [by partisans and opponents]. Candidates will be forced to declare and voters to choose. It would be unrealistic to ignore the fact that many people confronted with issues of this kind will find their votes aligned with their faith.

"Ordinarily political debate and division, however vigorous or even partisan, are normal and healthy manifestations of our democratic system of government, but political division along religious lines was one of the principal evils against which the First Amendment was intended to protect. Freund, *Public Aid to Parochial Schools,* 82 Harv.L.Rev. 1680, 1692 (1969)."

Compare A. Schwartz, *No Imposition of Religion: The Establishment Clause Value,* 77 Yale L.J. 692, 711 (1968): "If avoidance of strife were an independent [establishment clause] value, no legislation could be adopted on any subject which aroused strong and divided [religious] feelings." See Choper, *The Establishment Clause and Aid to Parochial Schools,* 56 Calif.L.Rev. 260, 273 (1968): "Nor would a denial of aid to parochial schools largely diminish the extent of religious political activity. In fact, it 'might lead to greater political ruptures caused by the alienation of segments of the religious community.' Those who send their children to parochial schools might intensify opposition to increased governmental aid to public education." Contrast Valente & Stanmeyer, *Public Aid to Parochial Schools—A Reply to Professor Freund,* 59 Geo. L.J. 59, 70 n. 46 (1970): "[O]ne's assessment of the accuracy of the views of Professors Freund, Schwartz, and Choper as to likely political repercussions is itself a political judgment and not judicial, and [the] weighing of political reactions is a function of legislatures and not of courts." See also Ripple, *The Entanglement Test of the Religion Clauses—A Ten Year Assessment,* 27 U.C.L.A.L.Rev. 1195 (1980). For the view that the historical evi-

I recognize the difficult dilemma in which governments are placed by the interaction of the "effects" and entanglement prongs of the *Lemon* test. Our decisions require governments extending aid to parochial schools to tread an extremely narrow line between being certain that the "principal or primary effect" of the aid is not to advance religion, and avoiding excessive entanglement.[c] Nonetheless, the Court has never foreclosed the possibility that some types of aid to parochial schools could be valid under the Establishment Clause [citing *Mueller, Allen* and *Everson,* where] the assistance programs made funds available equally to public and nonpublic schools without entanglement. [If,] for example, Congress could fashion a program of evenhanded financial assistance to both public and private schools that could be administered, without governmental supervision in the private schools, so as to prevent the diversion of the aid from secular purposes, we would be presented with a different question. * * *

JUSTICE O'CONNOR, concurring [and] dissenting in part [in *Grand Rapids* and], with whom JUSTICE REHNQUIST joins as to Parts II and III, dissenting [in *Aguilar*].

For the reasons stated [in respect to New York's program, below,] I dissent from the Court's holding that the Grand Rapids Shared Time Program impermissibly advances religion. [But] Community Education courses in the parochial schools are overwhelmingly taught by instructors who are current full-time employees of the parochial school. [In] addition, the supervisors of the Community Education program in the parochial schools are by and large the principals of the very schools where the classes are offered. When full-time parochial school teachers receive public funds to teach secular courses to their parochial school students under parochial school supervision, I agree that the program has the perceived and actual effect of advancing the religious aims of the church-related schools. * * *

I. [By contrast, in New York], in 19 years there has never been a single incident in which a Title I instructor "subtly or overtly" attempted to "indoctrinate the students in particular religious tenets at public expense."

Common sense suggests a plausible explanation for this unblemished record. New York City's public Title I instructors are professional educators who can and do follow instructions not to inculcate religion in their classes. They are unlikely to be influenced by the sectarian nature of the parochial schools where they teach, not only because they are carefully supervised by public officials, but also because the vast majority of them visit several different schools each week and are not of the same religion as their parochial students. In light of the ample record, an objective observer of the implementation of the Title I program

dence shows "that it is misguided to interpret the first amendment as prohibiting legislative consideration of an issue affecting religion on the ground that the very act of consideration will spawn impermissible religious division," see Schotten, *The Establishment Clause and Excessive Governmental–Religious Entanglement: The Constitutional Status of Aid to Nonpublic Elementary and Secondary Schools,* 15 Wake For.L.Rev. 207, 225 (1979).

c. White, J., dissenting in *Lemon,* accused the Court of "creat[ing] an insoluble paradox for the State and the parochial schools. The State cannot finance secular instruction if it permits religion to be taught in the same classroom; but if it exacts a promise that religion not be so taught—a promise the school and its teachers are quite willing and on this record able to give—and enforces it, it is then entangled in the 'no entangelement' aspect of the Court's Establishment Clause jurisprudence."

Rehnquist, J., dissenting in *Aguilar,* accused the Court of "tak[ing] advantage of the 'Catch–22' paradox of its own creation whereby aid must be supervised to ensure no entanglement but the supervision itself is held to cause an entanglement."

in New York would hardly view it as endorsing the tenets of the participating parochial schools. * * *

The only type of impermissible effect that arguably could carry over from the *Grand Rapids* decision to this litigation, then, is the effect of subsidizing "the religious functions of the parochial schools by taking over a substantial portion of their responsibility for teaching secular subjects." That effect is tenuous, however, in light of the statutory directive that Title I funds may be used only to provide services that otherwise would not be available to the participating students. * * *

Even if we were to assume that Title I remedial classes in New York may have duplicated to some extent instruction parochial schools would have offered in the absence of Title I, the Court's delineation of this third type of effect proscribed by the Establishment Clause would be seriously flawed. Our Establishment Clause decisions have not barred remedial assistance to parochial school children, but rather remedial assistance *on the premises of the parochial school.* Under *Wolman,* the New York City classes prohibited by the Court today would have survived Establishment Clause scrutiny if they had been offered in a neutral setting off the property of the private school. Yet it is difficult to understand why a remedial reading class offered on parochial school premises is any more likely to supplant the secular course offerings of the parochial school than the same class offered in a portable classroom next door to the school. * * *

II. Recognizing the weakness of any claim of an improper purpose or effect, the Court today relies entirely on the entanglement prong of *Lemon* to invalidate the New York City Title I program [which] I acknowledge, finds support in some of this Court's precedents. * * *

I would accord these decisions the appropriate deference commanded by the doctrine of stare decisis [but] experience has demonstrated that the analysis [is] flawed. [It] is not intuitively obvious that a dedicated public school teacher will tend to disobey instructions and commence proselytizing students at public expense merely because the classroom is within a parochial school. [Given] that not a single incident of religious indoctrination has been identified as occurring in the thousands of classes offered in Grand Rapids and New York over the past two decades, it is time to acknowledge that the risk [is] greatly exaggerated.

Just as the risk that public schoolteachers in parochial classrooms will inculcate religion has been exaggerated, so has the degree of supervision required to manage that risk. In [New York, public] officials have prepared careful instructions warning public schoolteachers of their exclusively secular mission, and have required Title I teachers to study and observe them. Under the rules, Title I teachers are not accountable to parochial or private school officials; they have sole responsibility for selecting the students who participate in their class, must administer their own tests for determining eligibility, cannot engage in team teaching or cooperative activities with parochial school teachers, must make sure that all materials and equipment they use are not otherwise used by the parochial school, and must not participate in religious activities in the schools or introduce any religious matter into their teaching. To ensure compliance with the rules, a field supervisor and a program coordinator, who are full-time public school employees, make unannounced visits to each teacher's classroom at least once a month. [This] does not differ significantly from the supervision any public schoolteacher receives, regardless of the location of the classroom. Justice Powell suggests that the required supervision is extensive because the State must be *certain* that public schoolteachers do not inculcate religion. That reasoning would require us to close our public schools, for there is always some chance that a public schoolteacher will bring religion into the classroom, regardless of its location. Even if I remained confident of the usefulness of entanglement as an Establishment Clause test, I would conclude that New York's efforts [have] been adequate and have not caused excessive institutional entanglement of church and state.

The Court's reliance on the potential for political divisiveness as evidence of undue entanglement is also unpersuasive. There is little record support for the proposition that New York's admirable Title I program has ignited any controversy other than this litigation. [M]any of the inconsistencies in our Establishment Clause decisions can be ascribed to our insistence that parochial aid programs with a valid purpose and effect may still be invalid by virtue of undue entanglement. For example, we permit a State to pay for bus transportation to a parochial school, *Everson,* but preclude States from providing buses for parochial school field trips, on the theory such trips involve excessive state supervision of the parochial officials who lead them. *Wolman.* To a great extent, the anomalous results in our Establishment Clause cases are "attributable to [the] 'entanglement' prong." Choper, *The Religion Clauses of the First Amendment: Reconciling the Conflict,* 41 U.Pitt.L.Rev. 673, 681 (1980).

[S]tate efforts to ensure that public resources are used only for nonsectarian ends should not in themselves serve to invalidate an otherwise valid statute. The State requires sectarian organizations to cooperate on a whole range of matters without thereby advancing religion or giving the impression that the government endorses religion. *Wallace v. Jaffree* (dissenting opinion of Rehnquist, J.) (noting that State educational agencies impose myriad curriculum, attendance, certification, fire, and safety regulations on sectarian schools). If a statute lacks a purpose or effect of advancing or endorsing religion, I would not invalidate it merely because it requires some ongoing cooperation between church and state or some state supervision to ensure that state funds do not advance religion.

III. Today's ruling does not spell the end of the Title I program of remedial education for disadvantaged children. [The] only disadvantaged children who lose under the Court's holding are those in cities where it is not economically and logistically feasible to provide public facilities for remedial education adjacent to the parochial school. But [this] includes more than 20,000 New York City schoolchildren and uncounted others elsewhere in the country.

For these children, the Court's decision is tragic. The Court deprives them of a program that offers a meaningful chance at success in life, and it does so on the untenable theory that public schoolteachers (most of whom are of different faiths than their students) are likely to start teaching religion merely because they have walked across the threshold of a parochial school. * * * [d]

Notes and Questions

1. *Primary effect.* In *Tilton,* Douglas, J., joined by Black and Marshall, JJ., dissenting, argued that "religion pervades" parochial schools, which "operate on one budget" and "money not spent for one purpose becomes available for other purposes." If so, does bus transportation or secular textbooks for parochial

d. The opinions of Burger, C.J., dissenting in *Aguilar,* of White, J., dissenting in *Grand Rapids* and *Aguilar* on the basis of his views in *Lemon,* and of Rehnquist, J., dissenting on the basis of his dissent in *Wallace v. Jaffree,* Part I supra, are omitted.

school students "have a primary effect that advances religion"? If so, would this forbid stationing traffic police near parochial schools? Having the fire department put out fires in them? Furnishing sidewalks in front of them? If the public did not provide parochial schools with sidewalks and police and fire protection, would the schools have to include these items in their budgets? If so, does the public's supplying them "release" funds? May a public library lend books to parochial school students in which readings have been assigned by their teacher? Suppose it were shown that these books were "in fact instrumental in the teaching of religion"?

Consider Tribe, *American Constitutional Law* 1221 (2d ed. 1988): "Another reason that religious colleges are treated differently from parochial schools is the *public's* view of the aid programs. Aid for secular programs in all colleges, including those with church affiliation, is generally perceived as assistance to non-religious activities. But the moment aid is sent to a parochial school as such, it is widely seen as aid to religion. The number of dollars released for religious purposes may be identical; the symbolism is not."

2. *Broad spectrum of beneficiary groups.* (a) *Vouchers.* After *Mueller,* would an "education voucher" plan pass muster if the vouchers were given to *all* parents for use in *any* school?

WITTERS v. WASHINGTON DEP'T OF SERVICES, 474 U.S. 481, 106 S.Ct. 748, 88 L.Ed.2d 846 (1986), per MARSHALL, J.—focusing on the "effect" prong of the *Lemon* test—unanimously upheld "assistance under a state vocational rehabilitation assistance program to a blind person studying at a Christian college and seeking to become a pastor, missionary, or youth director": Assistance "is paid directly to the student, who transmits it to the educational institution of his or her choice. Any aid [that] ultimately flows to religious institutions does so only as a result of the genuinely independent and private choices of aid recipients. Washington's program is 'made available generally without regard to the sectarian-nonsectarian, or public-nonpublic nature of the institution benefitted,' and is in no way skewed towards religion. [Further], nothing in the record indicates that [any] significant portion of the aid expended under the Washington program as a whole will end up flowing to religious education. [No] evidence has been presented indicating that any other person has ever sought to finance religious education or activity pursuant to the State's program." [a]

POWELL, J., joined by Burger, C.J., and Rehnquist, J., concurred "to emphasize that *Mueller* strongly supports the result": "state programs that are wholly neutral in offering educational assistance to a class defined without reference to religion do not violate the second part of the *Lemon* test, because any aid to religion results from the private choices of individual beneficiaries." O'Connor, J., concurred, specifically subscribing to this statement. White, J., concurred "with respect to the relevance of *Mueller,*" as stated by Powell, J.[b]

(b) *Social welfare programs.* BOWEN v. KENDRICK, 487 U.S. 589, 108 S.Ct. 2562, 101 L.Ed.2d 520 (1988), per REHNQUIST, C.J., held that the Adolescent

a. On remand, the state court held that the aid in this case would violate the Washington constitution's provision that "no public money [shall] be appropriated for [any] religious instruction." *Witters v. State Department for the Blind,* 112 Wash.2d 363, 771 P.2d 1119, cert. denied, ___ U.S. ___ (1989).

b. Consider Choper, p. 853 supra, at 13: "These five Justices (who comprised the majority in *Mueller*) clearly described a situation that includes vouchers: the aid goes to all parents who have children in schools—public, private, and parochial; if the vouchers are cashed at parochial schools, that is the product of private choice. Thus, vouchers are now valid." To what extent is *Witters* limited by the fact that it involves higher education?

Family Life Act (AFLA)—which grants funds to a variety of public and private agencies (including religious organizations) to provide counseling for prevention of adolescent sexual relations and care for pregnant adolescents and adolescent parents—did not, on its face, violate the establishment clause:

"AFLA was motivated primarily, if not entirely, by a legitimate secular purpose—the elimination or reduction of social and economic problems caused by teenage sexuality, pregnancy, and parenthood. [Although] two of its stated purposes are to 'promote self discipline and other prudent approaches to the problem of adolescent premarital sexual relations,' and to 'promote adoption as an alternative,' [this] approach is not inherently religious, although it may coincide with the approach taken by certain religions."

As for the role of religious organizations, "when, as Congress found, 'prevention of adolescent sexual activity depends primarily upon developing strong family values and close family ties,' it seems quite sensible for Congress to recognize that religious organizations can influence values and can have some influence on family life, including parents' relations with their adolescent children. To the extent that this Congressional recognition has any effect of advancing religion, the effect is at most 'incidental and remote.' * * *

"[T]his Court has never held that religious institutions are disabled by the First Amendment from participating in publicly sponsored social welfare programs [*Bradfield v. Roberts,* and] nothing on the face of the AFLA indicates that a significant proportion of the federal funds will be disbursed to 'pervasively sectarian' institutions. Indeed, the contention that there is a substantial risk of such institutions receiving direct aid is undercut by the AFLA's facially neutral grant requirements, the wide spectrum of public and private organizations which are capable of meeting the AFLA's requirements, and the fact that, of the eligible religious institutions, many will not deserve the label of 'pervasively sectarian.' [As] in *Tilton* and *Roemer,* we do not think the possibility that AFLA grants may go to religious institutions that can be considered 'pervasively sectarian' is sufficient to conclude that no grants whatsoever can be given under the statute to religious organizations. We think that the District Court was wrong in concluding otherwise [and in presuming] that religiously affiliated AFLA grantees are not capable of carrying out their functions under the AFLA in a lawful, secular manner. * * *

"Here, [there] is no reason to assume that the religious organizations which may receive grants are 'pervasively sectarian' in the same sense as the Court has held parochial schools to be. There is accordingly no reason to fear that the less intensive monitoring involved here will cause the Government to intrude unduly in the day-to-day operation of the religiously affiliated AFLA grantees. Unquestionably, the Secretary will review the programs set up and run by the AFLA grantees, and undoubtedly this will involve a review of, for example, the educational materials that a grantee proposes to use. The Secretary may also wish to have government employees visit the clinics or offices where AFLA programs are being carried out to see whether they are in fact being administered in accordance with statutory and constitutional requirements. But in our view, this type of grant monitoring does not amount to 'excessive entanglement,' at least in the context of a statute authorizing grants to religiously affiliated organizations that are not necessarily 'pervasively sectarian.' [c]

c. Consider McConnell, *Political and Religious Disestablishment,* 1986 B.Y.U.L.Rev. 405, 422–23: "[An] argument for treating parochial school aid with more exacting scrutiny rests on the assumption that education involves religious indoctrination but other social

"[I]t will be open to appellees on remand to show that AFLA aid is flowing to grantees that can be considered 'pervasively sectarian' religious institutions, such as we have held parochial schools to be.[d] The District Court should also consider on remand whether in particular cases AFLA aid has been used to fund 'specifically religious activit(ies) in an otherwise substantially secular setting,' [for example], whether the Secretary has permitted AFLA grantees to use materials that have an explicitly religious content or are designed to inculcate the views of a particular religious faith."

O'CONNOR, J., who joined the Court's opinion, concurred: "Using religious organizations to advance the secular goals of the AFLA, without thereby permitting religious indoctrination, is inevitably more difficult than in other projects, such as ministering to the poor and the sick. I nonetheless agree with the Court that the partnership between governmental and religious institutions contemplated by the AFLA need not result in constitutional violations, despite an undeniably greater risk than is present in cooperative undertakings that involve less sensitive objectives."

KENNEDY, J., joined by Scalia, J., joined the Court's opinion, adding that "where, as in this case, a statute provides that the benefits of a program are to be distributed in a neutral fashion to religious and non-religious applicants alike, and the program withstands a facial challenge, it is not unconstitutional as applied solely by reason of the religious character of a specific recipient. The question in an as-applied challenge is not whether the entity is of a religious character, but how it spends its grant."[e]

BLACKMUN, J., joined by Brennan, Marshall and Stevens, JJ., dissented: "The majority's holding that the AFLA is not unconstitutional on its face marks a sharp departure from our precedents. While aid programs providing nonmonetary, verifiably secular aid have been upheld notwithstanding the indirect effect they might have on the allocation of an institution's own funds for religious activities, see, e.g., *Allen; Everson,* direct cash subsidies have always required much closer scrutiny into the expected and potential uses of the funds, and much greater guarantees that the funds would not be used inconsistently with the Establishment Clause. [Here, for example, the] teaching materials that may be purchased, developed, or disseminated with AFLA funding are in no way restricted to those already selected and approved for use in secular contexts.

"Notwithstanding the fact that government funds are paying for religious organizations to teach and counsel impressionable adolescents on a highly sensitive subject of considerable religious significance, often on the premises of a church or parochial school and without any effort to remove religious symbols from the sites, the majority concludes that the AFLA is not facially invalid. The

welfare functions do not. However, many, if not most, churches understand their ministry to physical needs as integrally related to their mission of spreading the gospel. Who can doubt that the Salvation Army puts a message into each cup of coffee? Indeed, to the extent that parochial schools are selected predominantly by persons who are already members of the schools' religious group, while most social welfare programs are targeted to the public at large, proselytizing is more likely in the latter than the former."

d. For the view that the Court's "categorical distinction" in the parochial schools cases between elementary/secondary and colleges/universities,—which "allows general rules of law to have a conclusive effect on institutions not in the litigation, and thus has the virtue of providing a bright-line rule,"—"will be of little assistance [in] the social services context," see Note, *Government Aid to Religious Social Services Providers: The Supreme Court's "Pervasively Sectarian" Standard,* 75 Va.L.Rev. 1077 (1989).

e. Are *Grand Rapids* and *Aguilar* still "good law"?

majority acknowledges the constitutional proscription on government-sponsored religious indoctrination but, on the basis of little more than an indefensible assumption that AFLA recipients are not pervasively sectarian and consequently are presumed likely to comply with statutory and constitutional mandates, dismisses as insubstantial the risk that indoctrination will enter counseling. [Whereas] there may be secular values promoted by the AFLA, including the encouragement of adoption and premarital chastity and the discouragement of abortion, it can hardly be doubted that when promoted in theological terms by religious figures, those values take on a religious nature. Not surprisingly, the record is replete with observations to that effect. It should be undeniable by now that religious dogma may not be employed by government even to accomplish laudable secular purposes such as 'the promotion of moral values, the contradiction to the materialistic trends of our times, the perpetuation of our institutions and the teaching of literature.' *Schempp.*

"[O]ur cases do not require a plaintiff to demonstrate that a government action *necessarily* promotes religion, but simply that it creates such a substantial risk. [After] such further proceedings as are now to be deemed appropriate, and after the District Court enters findings of fact on the basis of the testimony and documents entered into evidence, it may well decide, as I would today, that the AFLA as a whole indeed has been unconstitutionally applied."

(c) *Political divisiveness.* To what extent does a "broad spectrum" of beneficiary groups affect this criterion? Consider Note, *The Constitutionality of Tax Relief for Parents of Children Attending Public and Nonpublic Schools,* 67 Minn. L.Rev. 793, 820–21 (1983): "Legislation that primarily aids sectarian education disrupts political equality and promotes rivalry among religious sects by favoring those groups that emphasize private primary and secondary education. [In] contrast, aid which broadly benefits secular as well as sectarian groups is less likely to generate interfaith rivalries or imbalances of power. Even if only some sects receive aid directly, members of other faiths will probably benefit as members of the broader legislative class. Because particular religious groups will not be perceived as the primary beneficiaries of state aid, competition among sects for government funds will also be reduced." For further consideration of "political divisiveness," see *Lynch v. Donnelly,* Part III infra.

3. *Delegation of government power.* LARKIN v. GRENDEL'S DEN, INC., 454 U.S. 116, 103 S.Ct. 505, 74 L.Ed.2d 297 (1982), per BURGER, C.J., held that a Massachusetts law (§ 16C), giving churches and schools the power "to veto applications for liquor licenses within a five hundred foot radius of the church or school, violates the Establishment Clause": "[T]here can be little doubt about the power of a state to regulate the environment in the vicinity of schools, churches, hospitals and the like by exercise of reasonable zoning laws. [But] § 16C is not simply a legislative exercise of zoning power [because it] delegates * * * discretionary governmental powers [to] religious bodies.[b]

"[The] valid secular objectives [of protecting] spiritual, cultural, and educational centers from the 'hurly-burly' associated with liquor outlets [can] be readily accomplished by other means—either through an absolute legislative ban on liquor outlets within reasonable prescribed distances from churches, schools, hospitals and like institutions, or by ensuring a hearing for the views of affected institutions at licensing proceedings * * *. [But the] churches' power under the statute is standardless [and] may therefore be used by churches [for]

b. Does the "delegation" to church-related schools of the authority to satisfy state requirements for elementary and secondary education violate the establishment clause?

explicitly religious goals, for example, favoring liquor licenses for members of that congregation or adherents of that faith. [In] addition, the mere appearance of a joint exercise of legislative authority by Church and State provides a significant symbolic benefit to religion in the minds of some by reason of the power conferred. It does not strain our prior holdings to say that the statute can be seen as having a 'primary' and 'principal' effect of advancing religion. [Finally, § 16C] enmeshes churches in the processes of government and creates the danger of 'political fragmentation and divisiveness along religious lines.' "

REHNQUIST, J., dissented: A "flat ban [on] the grant of an alcoholic beverages license to any establishment located within 500 feet of a church or a [school], which the majority concedes is valid, is more protective of churches and more restrictive of liquor sales than the present § 16C. * * * Nothing in the Court's opinion persuades me why the more rigid prohibition would be constitutional, but the more flexible not. [It] does not sponsor or subsidize any religious group or activity. It does not encourage, much less compel, anyone to participate in religious activities or to support religious institutions. To say that it 'advances' religion is to strain at the meaning of the word. [If] a church were to seek to advance the interests of its members [by favoring them for licenses], there would be an occasion to determine whether it had violated any right of an unsuccessful applicant for a liquor license. But our ability to discern a risk of such abuse does not render § 16C violative of the Establishment Clause."

4. *"Excessive entanglement."* (a) Does this forbid application of the National Labor Relations Act's collective bargaining requirements to lay teachers employed by parochial schools? See *NLRB v. Catholic Bishop,* 440 U.S. 490, 99 S.Ct. 1313, 59 L.Ed.2d 533 (1979) (constitutional issue avoided by statutory construction).

(b) Even if classroom surveillance in church-related colleges is not needed to assure a primary secular effect, does the Court's focus on each college's profile itself fail the "entanglement" test? See Kauper, *Public Aid for Parochial Schools and Church Colleges,* 13 Ariz.L.Rev. 567, 593 (1971). Does this type of "entanglement" also invalidate *Zorach*-type programs which authorize released time only for "religious instruction or devotional exercises"? For further consideration, see note 2, Sec. 2, II infra.

5. *Burden of proof.* Of what significance is the question of who—state or recipient—has the burden of proof in respect to each of the establishment clause criteria articulated in the decisions? In fact, to whom was the burden of proof assigned? Is the constitutionality of the programs invalidated still open on a showing that religion no more "permeates the secular education" in primary and secondary parochial schools than it does in church-related colleges?

6. *"Shared time."* Would a state "dual enrollment" plan, allowing parochial school students to take selected courses in the public schools, pass muster? Consider 85 Harv.L.Rev. 178 (1971): "[The] plan would have no impermissible effect, for public school teachers in public school buildings are unlikely to advance religion. However, the legislative purpose behind such a plan would be suspect: the obvious motive for releasing students for part of the day is to preserve the ability of their parents to give them religion-tinged instruction. In addition, such a plan might produce considerable conflict between public and parochial school authorities. If parochial school pupils were educated together with full-time public school pupils, accommodation of the scheduling needs of both systems could be quite difficult. Moreover, parochial school authorities might try to influence the content of the public school [courses]. Finally, since

parochial schools would be the only beneficiaries of such legislation any modification of it would precipitate political controversy along religious lines." But see Haskell, *The Prospects for Public Aid to Parochial Schools,* 56 Minn.L.Rev. 159 (1971).

7. *Other approaches.* Commentators have proposed various "tests" to measure the validity of public aid to church-related schools. In evaluating those that follow, what results would they produce in the decided cases?

(a) Gordon, *The Unconstitutionality of Public Aid to Parochial Schools,* in The Wall Between Church and State 73, 92 (Oaks ed. 1963): "The [test] is whether it is the church (or church institution) or the state that performs or controls the performance of the services paid for by the state. [It] is reasonable to assume that services performed or controlled by a religious institution could and would be used to further the religious objectives of that institution, whereas services performed or controlled by a public body would be secular in purpose and form." What result in *Everson* if the buses were rented by the parochial school? What about lunches preceded by prayers in the parochial school cafeteria?

(b) Choper, *The Establishment Clause and Aid to Parochial Schools,* 56 Calif.L.Rev. 260, 265–66 (1968): "[G]overnmental financial aid may be extended directly or indirectly to support parochial schools [so] long as such aid does not exceed the value of the secular educational service rendered by the school." [c] Would such aid have "a secular legislative purpose and a primary effect that neither advances nor inhibits religion"? Compare Hammett, *The Homogenized Wall,* 53 A.B.A.J. 929, 932–33 (1967): "If the net effect of the financial aid is to increase proportionally the influence of both the church and the state, so that their influence relative to each other remains at the same original ratio, the 'primary' effect on religion has been neutral." [d] Contrast Sugarman, *New Perspectives on "Aid" to Private School Users,* in Nonpublic School Aid 64, 66 (West ed. 1976): "Even if the [effect] principle were limited to cases in which there was (or the legislature knew there would be) a *large* beneficial impact on religion, it would intolerably inhibit secular government action. For example, perhaps building roads and running public transportation on Sunday may be shown to have large beneficial impacts on religion. [For] me the concerns underlying the Establishment clause could be satisfied with an affirmative answer to this hypothetical question: Would the legislature have acted as it did were there no interdependency with religion involved? If so, then I think it would be fair to say that there is no subsidy of religion, that the religious benefits are constitutionally permitted side effects." [e]

c. For further analysis, see McConnell & Posner, *An Economic Approach to Issues of Religious Freedom,* 56 U.Chi.L.Rev. 1 (1989); Note, *The Supreme Court, Effect Inquiry, and Aid to Parochial Education,* 37 Stan.L.Rev. 219 (1984).

d. See also Valente, *Aid to Church Related Education—New Directions Without Dogma,* 55 Va.L.Rev. 579 (1969); Legal Dep't, NCWC, *The Constitutionality of the Inclusion of Church-Related Schools in Federal Aid to Education,* 50 Geo.L.J. 397 (1961).

e. Problems under the free exercise clause raised by the exclusion of parochial schools from public aid programs are considered in note 2, p. 893 infra.

III. OFFICIAL ACKNOWLEDGMENT OF RELIGION

ALLEGHENY COUNTY v. ACLU

492 U.S. 573, 109 S.Ct. 3086, 106 L.Ed.2d 472 (1989).

JUSTICE BLACKMUN announced the judgment of the Court and delivered the opinion of the Court with respect to Parts III–A, IV, and V, an opinion with respect to Parts I and II, in which JUSTICE O'CONNOR and JUSTICE STEVENS join, an opinion with respect to Part III–B, in which JUSTICE STEVENS joins, and an opinion with respect to Part VI.

This litigation concerns the constitutionality of two recurring holiday displays located on public property in downtown Pittsburgh. The first is a crèche placed on the Grand Staircase of the Allegheny County Courthouse. The second is a Chanukah menorah placed just outside the City–County Building, next to a Christmas tree and a sign saluting liberty. The Court of Appeals for the Third Circuit ruled that each display violates the Establishment Clause [because] each has the impermissible effect of endorsing religion. We agree that the crèche display has that unconstitutional effect but reverse the Court of Appeals' judgment regarding the menorah display.

I.A. [The] crèche [is] a visual representation of the scene in the manger in Bethlehem shortly after the birth of Jesus, as described in the Gospels of Luke and Matthew. The crèche includes figures of the infant Jesus, Mary, Joseph, farm animals, shepherds, and wise men, all placed in or before a wooden representation of a manger, which has at its crest an angel bearing a banner that proclaims "Gloria in Excelsis Deo!" [5]

[III.A.] Although "the myriad, subtle ways in which Establishment Clause values can be eroded," are not susceptible to a single verbal formulation, this Court has attempted to encapsulate the essential precepts of the Establishment Clause. Thus, in *Everson,* the Court gave this often-repeated summary [stating the third ¶ on p. 1092]. In *Lemon,* the Court sought to refine these principles by focusing on three "tests" for determining whether a government practice violates the Establishment Clause. [Our] subsequent decisions further have refined the definition of governmental action that unconstitutionally advances religion. In recent years, we have paid particularly close attention to whether the challenged governmental practice either has the purpose or effect of "endorsing" religion, a concern that has long had a place in our Establishment Clause jurisprudence. See *Engel.* * * *

Of course, the word "endorsement" is not self-defining. Rather, it derives its meaning from other words that this Court has found useful over the years in interpreting the Establishment Clause.[a] [Whether] the key word is "endorsement," "favoritism," or "promotion," the essential principle remains the same. The Establishment Clause, at the very least, prohibits government from appearing to take a position on questions of religious belief or from "making adherence to a religion relevant in any way to a person's standing in the political community." *Lynch v. Donnelly,* 465 U.S. 668, 687, 104 S.Ct. 1355, 1386, 79 L.Ed.2d 604 (1984) (O'Connor, J., concurring).

5. [It] is unlikely that an observer standing at the bottom of the Grand Staircase would be able to read the text of the angel's banner from that distance, but might be able to do so from a closer vantage point.

a. For further discussion, see note 2(b) infra.

B. [In *Lynch,*] we considered whether the city of Pawtucket, R.I., had violated the Establishment Clause by including a crèche in its annual Christmas display, located in a private park within the downtown shopping district.[b] By a 5–4 decision in that difficult case, the Court upheld inclusion of the crèche in the Pawtucket display, holding, inter alia, that the inclusion of the crèche did not have the impermissible effect of advancing or promoting religion.[45]

The rationale [contains] two strands, neither of which provides guidance for decision in subsequent cases. First, the opinion states that the inclusion of the crèche in the display was "no more an advancement or endorsement of religion" than other "endorsements" this Court has approved in the past—but the opinion offers no discernible measure for distinguishing between permissible and impermissible endorsements. Second, the opinion observes that any benefit the government's display of the crèche gave to religion was no more than "indirect, remote, and incidental"—without saying how or why.

Although Justice O'Connor joined the majority opinion in *Lynch,* she wrote a concurrence [that] provides a sound analytical framework for evaluating governmental use of religious symbols.

First and foremost, the concurrence [recognizes] any endorsement of religion as "invalid," because it "sends a message to nonadherents that they are outsiders, not full members of the political community, and an accompanying message to adherents that they are insiders, favored members of the political community."

Second, the concurrence articulates a method for determining whether the government's use of an object with religious meaning has the effect of endorsing religion. The effect of the display depends upon the message that the government's practice communicates: the question is "what viewers may fairly understand to be the purpose of the display." That inquiry, of necessity, turns upon the context in which the contested object appears: "a typical museum setting, though not neutralizing the religious content of a religious painting, negates any message of endorsement of that content." * * *[46]

b. "[Ten years ago], when [the] crèche was acquired, it cost the City $1365; it now is valued at $200. The erection and dismantling of the crèche costs the City about $20 per year; nominal expenses are incurred in lighting the crèche. No money has been expended on its maintenance for the past 10 years."

45. There is no need here to review the applications in *Lynch* of the "purpose" and "entanglement" elements of the *Lemon* inquiry, since in the present action the Court of Appeals did not consider these issues.

[See note 1 infra for discussion of "secular purpose" in *Lynch.* In respect to "administrative entanglement," *Lynch* found "no evidence of contact with church authorities concerning the content or design of the exhibit prior to or since Pawtucket's purchase of the crèche. [In] many respects the display requires far less ongoing, day-to-day interaction between church and state than religious paintings in public galleries." As for "political divisiveness," see fn. 11 in *Mueller,* Part II supra.]

46. The difference in approach between the *Lynch* majority and the concurrence is especially evident in each opinion's treatment of *Marsh v. Chambers,* 463 U.S. 783, 103 S.Ct. 3330, 77 L.Ed.2d 1019 (1983). In that case, the Court sustained the practice of legislative prayer based on its unique history: Congress authorized the payment of legislative chaplains during the same week that it reached final agreement on the language of the Bill of Rights. The *Lynch* majority employed *Marsh* comparatively: to forbid the use of the crèche, "while the Congress and legislatures open sessions with prayers by paid chaplains, would be a stilted overreaction contrary to our history and to our holdings."

The concurrence, in contrast, harmonized a result in *Marsh* with the endorsement principle in a rigorous way, explaining that legislative prayer (like the invocation that commences each session of this Court) is a form of acknowledgment of religion that "serve[s], in the only wa[y] reasonably possible in our culture, the legitimate secular purposes of solemnizing public occasions, expressing confidence in the future, and encouraging the recognition of what is worthy of appreciation in society." * * *

The concurrence applied this mode of analysis to the Pawtucket crèche, seen in the context of that city's holiday celebration as a whole. In addition to the crèche the city's display contained: a Santa Claus House with a live Santa distributing candy, reindeer pulling Santa's sleigh; a live 40–foot Christmas tree strung with lights; statues of carolers in old-fashioned dress; candy-striped poles; a "talking" wishing well; a large banner proclaiming "SEASONS GREETINGS"; a miniature "village" with several houses and a church, and various "cut-out" figures, including those of a clown, a dancing elephant, a robot, and a teddy bear. The concurrence concluded that both because the crèche is "a traditional symbol" of Christmas, a holiday with strong secular elements, and because the crèche was "displayed along with purely secular symbols," the crèche's setting "changes what viewers may fairly understand to be the purpose of the display and "negates any message of endorsement" of "the Christian beliefs represented by the crèche."

The four *Lynch* dissenters agreed with the concurrence that the controlling question was "whether Pawtucket ha[d] run afoul of the Establishment Clause by endorsing religion through its display of the crèche." The dissenters also agreed with the general proposition that the context in which the government uses a religious symbol is relevant for determining the answer to that question. They simply reached a different answer: the dissenters concluded that the other elements of the Pawtucket display did not negate the endorsement of Christian faith caused by the presence of the crèche. They viewed the inclusion of the crèche in the city's overall display as placing "the government's imprimatur of approval on the particular religious beliefs exemplified by the crèche." Thus, they stated: "The effect on minority religious groups, as well as on those who may reject all religion, is to convey the message that their views are not similarly worthy of public recognition nor entitled to public support."

Thus, despite divergence at the bottom line, the five Justices in concurrence and dissent in *Lynch* agreed upon the relevant constitutional principles [which] are sound, and have been adopted by the Court in subsequent cases. [*Grand Rapids*.]

IV. We turn first to the county's crèche display. There is no doubt, of course, that the crèche itself is capable of communicating a religious message. Indeed, the crèche in this lawsuit uses words, as well as the picture of the nativity scene, to make its religious meaning unmistakably clear. "Glory to God in the Highest!" says the angel in the crèche—Glory to God because of the birth of Jesus. [Here,] unlike *Lynch*, nothing in the context of the display detracts from the crèche's religious message. [The] floral decoration surrounding the crèche [serves] only to draw one's attention to the message inside the frame. [Furthermore,] the crèche sits on the Grand Staircase, the "main" and "most beautiful part" of the building that is the seat of county government. No viewer could reasonably think that it occupies this location without the support and approval of the government.[50] * * *

In sum, *Lynch* teaches that government may celebrate Christmas in some manner and form, but not in a way that endorses Christian doctrine. Here,

50. The Grand Staircase does not appear to be the kind of location in which all were free to place their displays for weeks at a time, so that the presence of the crèche in that location for over six weeks would then not serve to associate the government with the crèche. [In] this respect, the crèche here does not raise the kind of "public forum" issue, cf. *Widmar*, presented by the crèche in *McCreary v. Stone*, 739 F.2d 716 (CA2 1984), aff'd by an equally divided Court sub nom. *Board of Trustees of Scarsdale v. McCreary*, 471 U.S. 83 (1985) (private crèche in public park).

Allegheny County has transgressed this line. It has chosen to celebrate Christmas in a way that has the effect of endorsing a patently Christian message: Glory to God for the birth of Jesus Christ. * * *

V. Justice Kennedy and the three Justices who join him would find the display of the crèche consistent with the Establishment Clause. [The] reasons for deciding otherwise are so far-reaching in their implications that they require a response in some depth:

A. In *Marsh,* the Court relied specifically on the fact that Congress authorized legislative prayer at the same time that it produced the Bill of Rights.[c] Justice Kennedy, however, argues that *Marsh* legitimates all "practices with no greater potential for an establishment of religion" than those "accepted traditions dating back to the Founding." Otherwise, the Justice asserts, such practices as our national motto ("In God We Trust") and our Pledge of Allegiance (with the phrase "under God," added in 1954) are in danger of invalidity.

Our previous opinions have considered in dicta the motto and the pledge, characterizing them as consistent with the proposition that government may not communicate an endorsement of religious belief. We need not return to the subject of "ceremonial deism," see n. 46, supra, because there is an obvious distinction between crèche displays and references to God in the motto and the pledge. However history may affect the constitutionality of nonsectarian references to religion by the government,[52] history cannot legitimate practices that demonstrate the government's allegiance to a particular sect or creed. [The] history of this Nation, it is perhaps sad to say, contains numerous examples of official acts that endorsed Christianity specifically. Some of these examples date back to the Founding of the Republic,[54] but this heritage of official discrimination against non-Christians has no place in the jurisprudence of the Establishment Clause. * * *

[B. Perhaps] the only real distinction between Justice Kennedy's "proselytization" test and the Court's "endorsement" inquiry is a burden of "unmistakable" clarity that Justice Kennedy apparently would require of government favoritism for specific sects in order to hold the favoritism in violation of the Establishment Clause. The question whether a particular practice "would place

c. *Marsh* also pointed, inter alia, to the practice in the colonies (including Virginia after adopting its Declaration of Rights which has been "considered the precursor of both the Free Exercise and Establishment Clauses"), to the opening invocations in federal courts (including the Supreme Court), and to the Continental Congress and First Congress: "[T]he practice of opening sessions with prayer has continued without interruption ever since that early session of Congress. It has also been followed consistently in most of the states."

Brennan, Marshall and Stevens, JJ. dissented.

Of what relevance is it that, subsequently, "Madison acknowledged that he had been quite mistaken in approving—as a member of the House, in 1789—bills for the payment of congressional chaplains"? Van Alstyne, *Trends in the Supreme Court: Mr. Jefferson's Crumbling Wall,* 1984 Duke L.J. 770, 776.

52. It is worth noting that just because *Marsh* sustained the validity of legislative prayer, it does not necessarily follow that practices like proclaiming a National Day of Prayer are constitutional. Legislative prayer does not urge citizens to engage in religious practices, and on that basis could well be distinguishable from an exhortation from government to the people that they engage in religious conduct. But, as this practice is not before us, we express no judgment about its constitutionality.

54. In 1776, for instance, Maryland adopted a "Declaration of Rights" that allowed its Legislature to impose a tax "for the support of the Christian religion" and a requirement that all state officials declare "a belief in the Christian religion." Efforts made in 1797 to remove these discriminations against non-Christians were unsuccessful. ([See] the explicitly Christian proclamation of President John Adams, who urged all Americans to seek God's grace "through the Redeemer of the world" and "by His Holy Spirit").

the government's weight behind an obvious effort to proselytize for a particular religion," is much the same as whether the practice demonstrates the government's support, promotion, or "endorsement" of the particular creed of a particular sect—except to the extent that it requires an "obvious" allegiance between the government and the sect.

Our cases, however, impose no such burden on demonstrating that the government has favored a particular sect or creed. On the contrary, we have expressly required "strict scrutiny" of practices suggesting "a denominational preference," *Larson v. Valente,* [Sec. 3 infra]. Thus, when all is said and done, Justice Kennedy's effort to abandon the "endorsement" inquiry in favor of his "proselytization" test seems nothing more than an attempt to lower considerably the level of scrutiny in Establishment Clause cases. * * *

C. Although Justice Kennedy repeatedly accuses the Court of harboring a "latent hostility" or "callous indifference" toward religion, nothing could be further from the truth. [The] government does not discriminate against any citizen on the basis of the citizen's religious faith if the government is secular in its functions and operations. On the contrary, the Constitution mandates that the government remain secular, rather than affiliating itself with religious beliefs or institutions, precisely in order to avoid discriminating among citizens on the basis of their religious faiths.

A secular state, it must be remembered, is not the same as an atheistic or antireligious state. A secular state establishes neither atheism nor religion as its official creed. * * * [59]

VI. The display of the Chanukah menorah in front of the City–County Building may well present a closer [issue. The] relevant question for Establishment Clause purposes is whether the combined display of the tree, the sign, and the menorah has the effect of endorsing both Christian and Jewish faiths, or rather simply recognizes that both Christmas and Chanukah are part of the same winter-holiday season, which has attained a secular status in our society. Of the two interpretations of this particular display, the latter seems far more plausible and is also in line with *Lynch.*[64]

The Christmas tree, unlike the menorah, is not itself a religious symbol. [Indeed,] a 40–foot Christmas tree was one of the objects that validated the crèche in *Lynch.* The widely accepted view of the Christmas tree as the preeminent secular symbol of the Christmas holiday season serves to emphasize the secular component of the message communicated by other elements of an accompanying holiday display, including the Chanukah menorah.[66]

59. In his attempt to legitimate the display of the crèche on the Grand Staircase, Justice Kennedy repeatedly characterizes it as an "accommodation" of religion. But an accommodation of religion, in order to be permitted under the Establishment Clause, must lift "an identifiable burden *on the exercise of religion.*" *Corporation of Presiding Bishop v. Amos,* [Sec. 3 infra]. Prohibiting the display of a crèche at this location [does] not impose a burden on the practice of Christianity (except to the extent some Christian sect seeks to be an officially approved religion), and therefore permitting the display is not an "accommodation" of religion in the conventional sense.

["Accomodation" of religion and the relationship between the establishment and free exercise clauses is considered in detail in Sec. 3 infra.]

64. [The] conclusion that Pittsburgh's combined Christmas–Chanukah display cannot be interpreted as endorsing Judaism alone does not mean, however, that it is implausible, as a general matter, for a city like Pittsburgh to endorse a minority faith. The display of a menorah alone might well have that effect.

66. Although the Christmas tree represents the secular celebration of Christmas, its very association with Christmas (a holiday with religious dimensions) makes it conceivable that the tree might be seen as represent-

The tree, moreover, is clearly the predominant element in the city's display. The 45–foot tree occupies the central position [in] the City–County Building; the 18–foot menorah is positioned to one side. Given this configuration, it is much more sensible to interpret the meaning of the menorah in light of the tree, rather than vice versa. In the shadow of the tree, the menorah is readily understood as simply a recognition that Christmas is not the only traditional way of observing the winter-holiday season. * * *

Although the city has used a symbol with religious meaning as its representation of Chanukah, this is not a case in which the city has reasonable alternatives that are less religious in nature. [Where] the government's secular message can be conveyed by two symbols, only one of which carries religious meaning, an observer reasonably might infer from the fact that the government has chosen to use the religious symbol that the government means to promote religious faith. See *Schempp* (Brennan, J., concurring) (Establishment Clause forbids use of religious means to serve secular ends when secular means suffice).[67] But where, as here, no such choice has been made, this inference of endorsement is not present.[68]

The Mayor's sign further diminishes the possibility that the tree and the menorah will be interpreted as a dual endorsement of Christianity and Judaism. The sign states that during the holiday season the city salutes liberty. Moreover, the sign draws upon the theme of light, common to both Chanukah and Christmas as winter festivals, and links that theme with this Nation's legacy of freedom, which allows an American to celebrate the holiday season in whatever way he wishes, religiously or otherwise. * * *

Given all these considerations, it is not "sufficiently likely" that residents of Pittsburgh will perceive the combined display of the tree, the sign, and the menorah as an "endorsement" or "disapproval [of] their individual religious choices." *Grand Rapids.* While an adjudication of the display's effect must take into account the perspective of one who is neither Christian nor Jewish, as well as of those who adhere to either of these religions, the constitutionality of its effect must also be judged according to the standard of a "reasonable observer." See Tribe, *American Constitutional Law* 1296 (2d ed. 1988) (challenged government practices should be judged "from the perspective of a 'reasonable non-adherent' ").[d] When measured against this standard, the menorah need not be excluded from this particular display.[69]

ing Christian religion when displayed next to an object associated with Jewish religion. For this reason, I agree with Justice Brennan and Justice Stevens that one must ask whether the tree and the menorah together endorse the *religious* beliefs of Christians and Jews. For the reasons stated in the text, however, I conclude the city's overall display does not have this impermissible effect.

67. Contrary to the assertions of Justice O'Connor and Justice Kennedy, I have not suggested here that the government's failure to use an available secular alternative *necessarily* results in an Establishment Clause violation. Rather, it suffices to say that the availability or unavailability of secular alternatives is an obvious *factor* to be considered in deciding whether the government's use of a religious symbol amounts to an endorsement of religious faith.

68. In *Lynch,* in contrast, there was no need for Pawtucket to include a crèche in order to convey a secular message about Christmas. (Blackmun, J., dissenting). [In] displaying the menorah next to the tree, the city has demonstrated no preference for the *religious* celebration of the holiday season. This conclusion, however, would be untenable had the city substituted a crèche for its Christmas tree or if the city had failed to substitute for the menorah an alternative, more secular, representation of Chanukah.

d. For further discussion, see note 2(a) infra.

69. This is not to say that the combined display of a Christmas tree and a menorah is constitutional wherever it may be located on government property. For example, when located in a public school, such a display might raise additional constitutional considerations.

The conclusion here that, in this particular context, the menorah's display does not have an effect of endorsing religious faith does not foreclose the possibility that the display of the menorah might violate either the "purpose" or "entanglement" prong of the *Lemon* analysis. These issues were not addressed by the Court of Appeals and may be considered by that court on remand.
* * *

JUSTICE KENNEDY, with whom THE CHIEF JUSTICE, JUSTICE WHITE, and JUSTICE SCALIA join, concurring in the judgment in part and dissenting in part. * * *

I. In keeping with the usual fashion of recent years, the majority applies the *Lemon* test to judge the constitutionality of the holiday displays here in question. I am content for present purposes to remain within the *Lemon* framework, but do not wish to be seen as advocating, let alone adopting, that test as our primary guide in this difficult area. Persuasive criticism of *Lemon* has emerged. See *Aguillard* (Scalia, J., dissenting); *Aguilar v. Felton* (O'Connor, J., dissenting); *Jaffree* (Rehnquist, J., dissenting); *Roemer* (White, J., concurring in judgment). Our cases often question its utility in providing concrete answers to Establishment Clause questions, calling it but a "helpful signpos[t]" or "guidelin[e]", to assist our deliberations rather than a comprehensive test. *Mueller;* See *Lynch* ("we have repeatedly emphasized our unwillingness to be confined to any single test or criterion in this sensitive area").[e] Substantial revision of our Establishment Clause doctrine may be in order; but it is unnecessary to undertake that task today, for even the *Lemon* test, when applied with proper sensitivity to our traditions and our caselaw, supports the conclusion that both the crèche and the menorah are permissible displays in the context of the holiday season. * * *

Rather than requiring government to avoid any action that acknowledges or aids religion, the Establishment Clause permits government some latitude in recognizing and accommodating the central role religion plays in our society. *Lynch; Walz.* Any approach less sensitive to our heritage would border on latent hostility toward religion, as it would require government in all its multifaceted roles to acknowledge only the secular, to the exclusion and so to the detriment of the religious. A categorical approach would install federal courts as jealous guardians of an absolute "wall of separation," sending a clear message of disapproval. In this century, as the modern administrative state expands to touch the lives of its citizens in such diverse ways and redirects their financial choices through programs of its own, it is difficult to maintain the fiction that requiring government to avoid all assistance to religion can in fairness be viewed as serving the goal of neutrality. * * *

The ability of the organized community to recognize and accommodate religion in a society with a pervasive public sector requires diligent observance of the border between accommodation and establishment. Our cases disclose two limiting principles: government may not coerce anyone to support or participate in any religion or its exercise; and it may not, in the guise of avoiding hostility or callous indifference, give direct benefits to religion in such a degree that it in

e. In *Marsh,* Brennan, J., joined by Marshall, J. dissenting, noting that "the Court makes no pretense of subjecting Nebraska's practice of legislative prayer to any of the formal 'tests' that have traditionally structured our inquiry under the Establishment Clause": "I have no doubt that, if any group of law students were asked to apply the principles of *Lemon* to the question of legislative prayer, they would nearly unanimously find the practice to be unconstitutional. [W]e are faced here with the regularized practice of conducting official prayers, on behalf of the entire legislature, as part of the order of business constituting the formal opening of every single session of the legislative term."

fact "establishes a [state] religion or religious faith, or tends to do so." *Lynch.* These two principles, while distinct, are not unrelated, for it would be difficult indeed to establish a religion without some measure of more or less subtle coercion, be it in the form of taxation to supply the substantial benefits that would sustain a state-established faith, direct compulsion to observance, or governmental exhortation to religiosity that amounts in fact to proselytizing.

[The] freedom to worship as one pleases without government interference or oppression is the great object of both the Establishment and the Free Exercise Clauses. Barring all attempts to aid religion through government coercion goes far toward attainment of this object. [S]ome of our recent cases reject the view that coercion is the sole touchstone of an Establishment Clause violation. See *Engel* (dictum) (rejecting, without citation of authority, proposition that coercion is required to demonstrate an Establishment Clause violation); *Schempp; Nyquist.* That may be true if by "coercion" is meant *direct* coercion in the classic sense of an establishment of religion that the Framers knew. But coercion need not be a direct tax in aid of religion or a test oath. Symbolic recognition or accommodation of religious faith may violate the Clause in an extreme case.[1] I doubt not, for example, that the Clause forbids a city to permit the permanent erection of a large Latin cross on the roof of city hall. This is not because government speech about religion is per se suspect, as the majority would have it, but because such an obtrusive year-round religious display would place the government's weight behind an obvious effort to proselytize on behalf of a particular religion. Cf. *Friedman v. Board of Comm'rs,* 781 F.2d 777 (CA10 1985) (Latin cross on official county seal); *American Civil Liberties Union v. Rabun County Chamber of Commerce, Inc.,* 698 F.2d 1098 (CA11 1983) (cross erected in public park); *Lowe v. Eugene,* 254 Or. 518, 463 P.2d 360 (1969) (same). Speech may coerce in some circumstances, but this does not justify a ban on all government recognition of religion. As Chief Justice Burger wrote for the Court in *Walz:* "[W]e will not tolerate either governmentally established religion or governmental interference with religion. Short of those expressly proscribed governmental acts there is room for play in the joints productive of a benevolent neutrality which will permit religious exercise to exist without sponsorship and without interference." * * * Absent coercion, the risk of infringement of religious liberty by passive or symbolic accommodation is minimal. [In] determining whether there exists an establishment, or a tendency toward one, we refer to the other types of church-state contacts that have existed unchallenged throughout our history, or that have been found permissible in our caselaw [discussing *Lynch* and *Marsh*].

II. These principles are not difficult to apply to the facts of the case before us. In permitting the displays on government property of the menorah and the crèche, the city and county sought to do no more than "celebrate the season," and to acknowledge, along with many of their citizens, the historical background and the religious as well as secular nature of the Chanukah and Christmas holidays. * * *

If government is to participate in its citizens' celebration of a holiday that contains both a secular and a religious component, enforced recognition of only

1. [O]ur cases have held only that *direct* coercion need not always be shown to establish an Establishment Clause violation. The prayer invalidated in *Engel* was unquestionably coercive in an indirect manner, as the *Engel* Court itself recognized * * *. [*Marsh* noted that "here, the individual claiming injury by the practice is an adult, presumably not readily susceptible to 'religious indoctrination,' see *Tilton,* or peer pressure, compare *Schempp* (Brennan, J., concurring)."]

the secular aspect would signify the callous indifference toward religious faith that our cases and traditions do not require; for by commemorating the holiday only as it is celebrated by nonadherents, the government would be refusing to acknowledge the plain fact, and the historical reality, that many of its citizens celebrate its religious aspects as well. [The] Religion Clauses do not require government to acknowledge these holidays or their religious component; but our strong tradition of government accommodation and acknowledgment permits government to do so.

There is no suggestion here that the government's power to coerce has been used to further the interests of Christianity or Judaism in any way. No one was compelled to observe or participate in any religious ceremony or activity. Neither the city nor the county contributed significant amounts of tax money to serve the cause of one religious faith. The crèche and the menorah are purely passive symbols of religious holidays. Passersby who disagree with the message conveyed by these displays are free to ignore them, or even to turn their backs, just as they are free to do when they disagree with any other form of government speech.

There is no realistic risk that the crèche or the menorah represent an effort to proselytize or are otherwise the first step down the road to an establishment of religion.[3] [If] Congress and the state legislatures do not run afoul of the Establishment Clause when they begin each day with a state-sponsored prayer for divine guidance offered by a chaplain whose salary is paid at government expense, I cannot comprehend how a menorah or a crèche, displayed in the limited context of the holiday season, can be invalid. [Crucial] to the Court's conclusion [in *Lynch*] was not the number, prominence, or type of secular items contained in the holiday display but the simple fact that, when displayed by government during the Christmas season, a crèche presents no realistic danger of moving government down the forbidden road toward an establishment of religion. Whether the crèche be surrounded by poinsettias, talking wishing wells, or carolers, the conclusion remains the same, for the relevant context is not the items in the display itself but the season as a whole. * * *

[III.] Even if *Lynch* did not control, I would not commit this Court to the test applied by the majority today. The notion that cases arising under the Establishment Clause should be decided by an inquiry into whether a " 'reasonable observer' " may " 'fairly understand' " government action to " 'sen[d] a message to nonadherents that they are outsiders, not full members of the political community,' " is a recent, and in my view most unwelcome, addition to our tangled Establishment Clause jurisprudence. * * *

[A.] *Marsh* stands for the proposition, not that specific practices common in 1791 are an exception to the otherwise broad sweep of the Establishment Clause, but rather that the meaning of the Clause is to be determined by reference to historical practices and understandings.[7] Whatever test we choose to apply

3. One can imagine a case in which the use of passive symbols to acknowledge religious holidays could present this danger. For example, if a city chose to recognize, through religious displays, every significant Christian holiday while ignoring the holidays of all other faiths, the argument that the city was simply recognizing certain holidays celebrated by its citizens without establishing an official faith or applying pressure to obtain adherents would be much more difficult to maintain. On the facts of this case, no such unmistakable and continual preference for one faith has been demonstrated or alleged.

7. Contrary to the majority's discussion, the relevant historical practices are those conducted by governmental units which were subject to the constraints of the Establishment Clause. Acts of "official discrimination against non-Christians" perpetrated in the eighteenth and nineteenth centuries by States and municipalities are of course irrelevant to this inquiry, but the practices of past Congresses and Presidents are highly informative.

must permit not only legitimate practices two centuries old but also any other practices with no greater potential for an establishment of religion. * * *

If the endorsement test, applied without artificial exceptions for historical practice, reached results consistent with history, my objections to it would have less force. But, as I understand that test, the touchstone of an Establishment Clause violation is whether nonadherents would be made to feel like "outsiders" by government recognition or accommodation of religion. Few of our traditional practices recognizing the part religion plays in our society can withstand scrutiny under a faithful application of this formula.

Some examples suffice to make plain my concerns. Since the Founding of our Republic, American Presidents have issued Thanksgiving Proclamations establishing a national day of celebration and prayer. The first such proclamation was issued by President Washington at the request of the First Congress [and] the forthrightly religious nature of these proclamations has not waned with the years. President Franklin D. Roosevelt went so far as to "suggest a nationwide reading of the Holy Scriptures during the period from Thanksgiving Day to Christmas" so that "we may bear more earnest witness to our gratitude to Almighty God." It requires little imagination to conclude that these proclamations would cause nonadherents to feel excluded, yet they have been a part of our national heritage from the beginning.[9]

The Executive has not been the only Branch of our Government to recognize the central role of religion in our society. The fact that this Court opens its sessions with the request that "God save the United States and this honorable Court" has been noted elsewhere. The Legislature has gone much further, not only employing legislative chaplains, but also setting aside a special prayer room in the Capitol for use by Members of the House and Senate. The room is decorated with a large stained glass panel that depicts President Washington kneeling in prayer; around him is etched the first verse of the 16th Psalm: "Preserve me, O God, for in Thee do I put my trust." * * * Congress has directed the President to "set aside and proclaim a suitable day each year [as] a National Day of Prayer, on which the people of the United States may turn to God in prayer and meditation at churches, in groups, and as individuals." [Also] by statute, the Pledge of Allegiance to the Flag describes the United States as "one Nation under God." To be sure, no one is obligated to recite this phrase, see *West Virginia State Bd. of Educ. v. Barnette,* [Sec. 2, I infra] but it borders on sophistry to suggest that the " 'reasonable' " atheist would not feel less than a " 'full membe[r] of the political community' " every time his fellow Americans recited, as part of their expression of patriotism and love for country, a phrase he believed to be false. Likewise, our national motto, "In God we trust," which is prominently engraved in the wall above the Speaker's dias in the Chamber of the House of Representatives and is reproduced on every coin minted and every dollar printed by the Federal Government, must have the same effect.

If the intent of the Establishment Clause is to protect individuals from mere feelings of exclusion, then legislative prayer cannot escape invalidation. It has been argued that "[these] government acknowledgments of religion serve, in the only ways reasonably possible in our culture, the legitimate secular purposes of solemnizing public occasions, expressing confidence in the future, and encouraging the recognition of what is worthy of appreciation in society." *Lynch*

9. Similarly, our presidential inaugurations have traditionally opened with a request for divine blessing. * * *

(O'Connor, J., concurring). I fail to see why prayer is the only way to convey these messages; appeals to patriotism, moments of silence, and any number of other approaches would be as effective, were the only purposes at issue the ones described by the *Lynch* concurrence. Nor is it clear to me why "encouraging the recognition of what is worthy of appreciation in society" can be characterized as a purely secular purpose, if it can be achieved only through religious prayer. No doubt prayer is "worthy of appreciation," but that is most assuredly not because it is secular. Even accepting the secular-solemnization explanation at face value, moreover, it seems incredible to suggest that the average observer of legislative prayer who either believes in no religion or whose faith rejects the concept of God would not receive the clear message that his faith is out of step with the political norm.[10]

[B.] If there be such a person as the "reasonable observer," I am quite certain that he or she will take away a salient message from our holding in this case: the Supreme Court of the United States has concluded that the First Amendment creates classes of religions based on the relative numbers of their adherents. Those religions enjoying the largest following must be consigned to the status of least-favored faiths so as to avoid any possible risk of offending members of minority religions. I would be the first to admit that many questions arising under the Establishment Clause do not admit of easy answers, but whatever the Clause requires, it is not the result reached by the Court today.

[IV.] The case before us is admittedly a troubling one. It must be conceded that, however neutral the purpose of the city and county, the eager proselytizer may seek to use these symbols for his own ends. The urge to use them to teach or to taunt is always present. It is also true that some devout adherents of Judaism or Christianity may be as offended by the holiday display as are nonbelievers, if not more so. To place these religious symbols in a common hallway or sidewalk, where they may be ignored or even insulted, must be distasteful to many who cherish their meaning.

For these reasons, I might have voted against installation of these particular displays were I a local legislative official. But [the] principles of the Establishment Clause and our Nation's historic traditions of diversity and pluralism allow communities to make reasonable judgments respecting the accommodation or acknowledgment of holidays with both cultural and religious aspects. No constitutional violation occurs when they do so by displaying a symbol of the holiday's religious origins. * * *

JUSTICE O'CONNOR with whom JUSTICE BRENNAN and JUSTICE STEVENS join as to Part II, concurring in part and concurring in the judgment. * * *

II. In his separate opinion, Justice Kennedy asserts that the endorsement test "is flawed in its fundamentals and unworkable in practice." * * *

10. If the majority's test were to be applied logically, it would lead to the elimination of all nonsecular Christmas caroling in public buildings or, presumably, anywhere on public property. It is difficult to argue that lyrics like "Good Christian men, rejoice," "Joy to the world! the Savior reigns," "This, this is Christ the King," "Christ, by highest heav'n adored," and "Come and behold Him, Born the King of angels," have acquired such a secular nature that nonadherents would not feel "left out" by a government-sponsored or approved program that included these carols. We do not think for a moment that the Court will ban such carol programs, however. Like Thanksgiving Proclamations, the reference to God in the Pledge of Allegiance, and invocations to God in sessions of Congress and of this Court, they constitute practices that the Court will not proscribe, but that the Court's reasoning today does not explain.

An Establishment Clause standard that prohibits only "coercive" practices or overt efforts at government proselytization, but fails to take account of the numerous more subtle ways that government can show favoritism to particular beliefs or convey a message of disapproval to others, would not, in my view, adequately protect the religious liberty or respect the religious diversity of the members of our pluralistic political community. Thus, this Court has never relied on coercion alone as the touchstone of Establishment Clause analysis. To require a showing of coercion, even indirect coercion, as an essential element of an Establishment Clause violation would make the Free Exercise Clause a redundancy. [Moreover,] as even Justice Kennedy recognizes, any Establishment Clause test limited to "*direct* coercion" clearly would fail to account for forms of "[s]ymbolic recognition or accommodation of religious faith" that may violate the Establishment Clause.

[To] be sure, the endorsement test depends on a sensitivity to the unique circumstances and context of a particular challenged practice and, like any test that is sensitive to context, it may not always yield results with unanimous agreement at the margins. But that is true of many standards in constitutional law, and even the modified coercion test offered by Justice Kennedy involves judgment and hard choices at the margin. He admits as much by acknowledging that the permanent display of a Latin cross at city hall would violate the Establishment Clause, as would the display of symbols of Christian holidays alone. Would the display of a Latin cross for six months have such an unconstitutional effect, or the display of the symbols of most Christian holidays and one Jewish holiday? Would the Christmas-time display of a crèche inside a courtroom be "coercive" if subpoenaed witnesses had no opportunity to "turn their backs" and walk away? Would displaying a crèche in front of a public school violate the Establishment Clause under Justice Kennedy's test? * * *

Justice Kennedy submits that the endorsement test is inconsistent with our precedents and traditions because, in his words, if it were "applied without artificial exceptions for historical practice," it would invalidate many traditional practices recognizing the role of religion in our society. This criticism shortchanges both the endorsement test itself and my explanation of the reason why certain longstanding government acknowledgments of religion do not, under that test, convey a message of endorsement. Practices such as legislative prayers or opening Court sessions with "God save the United States and this honorable Court," serve the secular purposes of "solemnizing public occasions," and "expressing confidence in the future," *Lynch* (concurring opinion). These examples of ceremonial deism [f] do not survive Establishment Clause scrutiny simply by virtue of their historical longevity alone. Historical acceptance of a practice does not in itself validate that practice under the Establishment Clause if the practice violates the values protected by that Clause, just as historical acceptance of racial or gender based discrimination does not immunize such practices from scrutiny under the 14th Amendment.[g] [On] the contrary, the "history and

f. Brennan, J., joined by Marshall, Blackmun and Stevens, JJ., dissenting in *Lynch* "suggest[ed] that such practices as the designation of 'In God We Trust' as our national motto, or the references to God contained in the Pledge of Allegiance can best be understood [as] a form of 'ceremonial deism,' protected from Establishment Clause scrutiny chiefly because they have lost through rote repetition any significant religious content."

g. In contending that "specific historical practice should [not] override [the] clear constitutional imperative," Brennan, J., joined by Marshall, J., dissenting in *Marsh,* noted that "the sort of historical argument made by the Court should be advanced with some hesitation in light of certain other skeletons in the congressional closet. See, e.g., An Act for the Punishment of certain Crimes against the United States (1790) (enacted by the First ubiquity" of a practice is relevant because it provides part of the context in which a reasonable observer evaluates whether a challenged governmental practice conveys a message of endorsement of religion. [Thus,] the celebration of Thanksgiving as a public holiday, despite its religious origins, is now generally understood as a celebration of patriotic values rather than particular religious beliefs.[h] * * *

III. For reasons which differ somewhat from those set forth in Part VI of Justice Blackmun's opinion, I also conclude that the city of Pittsburgh's combined holiday display of a Chanukah menorah, a Christmas tree, and a sign saluting liberty does not have the effect of conveying an endorsement of religion. [My] conclusion does not depend on whether or not the city had "a more secular alternative symbol" of Chanukah, just as the Court's decision in *Lynch* clearly did not turn on whether the city of Pawtucket could have conveyed its tribute to the Christmas holiday season by using a "less religious" alternative to the crèche symbol in its display of traditional holiday symbols. See *Lynch* ("Justice Brennan argues that the city's objectives could have been achieved without including the crèche in the display. True or not, that is irrelevant. The question is whether the display of the crèche violates the Establishment Clause"). In my view, Justice Blackmun's new rule that an inference of endorsement arises every time government uses a symbol with religious meaning if a "more secular alternative" is available, is too blunt an instrument for Establishment Clause analysis, which depends on sensitivity to the context and circumstances presented by each case. * * *

JUSTICE BRENNAN, with whom JUSTICE MARSHALL and JUSTICE STEVENS join, concurring in part and dissenting in part.

* * * I continue to believe that the display of an object that "retains a specifically Christian [or other] religious meaning," is incompatible with the separation of church and state demanded by our Constitution. I therefore agree with the Court that Allegheny County's display of a crèche at the county courthouse signals an endorsement of the Christian faith in violation of the Establishment Clause, and join Parts III–A, IV, and V of the Court's opinion. I cannot agree, however, [with] the decision as to the menorah [which] rests on three premises: the Christmas tree is a secular symbol; Chanukah is a holiday with secular dimensions, symbolized by the menorah; and the government may promote pluralism by sponsoring or condoning displays having strong religious associations on its property. None of these is sound.

[I.] Even though the tree alone may be deemed predominantly secular, it can hardly be so characterized when placed next to such a forthrightly religious symbol. Consider a poster featuring a star of David, a statue of Buddha, a Christmas tree, a mosque, and a drawing of Krishna. There can be no doubt

Congress and requiring that persons convicted of certain theft offenses 'be publicly whipped, not exceeding thirty-nine stripes'); Act of July 23, 1866 (reaffirming the racial segregation of the public schools in the District of Columbia; enacted exactly one week after Congress proposed Fourteenth Amendment to the States)."

Brennan, J., concurring in *Schempp,* further observed that "today the Nation is far more heterogeneous religiously, including as it does substantial minorities not only of Catholics and Jews but as well of those who worship according to no version of the Bible and those who worship no God at all. In the face of such profound changes, practices which may have been objectionable to no one in the time of Jefferson and Madison may today be highly offensive to many persons, the deeply devout and the non-believers alike. [Thus], our use of the history of their time must limit itself to broad purposes, not specific practices."

h. Brennan, J.'s dissent in *Lynch,* supra, expressed a similar view.

that, when found in such company, the tree serves as an unabashedly religious symbol. * * *

[II.] The menorah is indisputably a religious symbol, used ritually in a celebration that has deep religious significance. That, in my view, is all that need be said. Whatever secular practices the holiday of Chanukah has taken on in its contemporary observance are beside the point. * * * Pittsburgh's secularization of an inherently religious symbol, aided and abetted here by Justice Blackmun's opinion, recalls the effort in *Lynch* to render the crèche a secular symbol. As I said then: "To suggest, as the Court does, that such a symbol is merely 'traditional' and therefore no different from Santa's house or reindeer is not only offensive to those for whom the crèche has profound significance, but insulting to those who insist for religious or personal reasons that the story of Christ is in no sense a part of 'history' nor an unavoidable element of our national 'heritage.'" * * *

III. Justice Blackmun, in his acceptance of the city's message of "diversity," and, even more so, Justice O'Connor, in her approval of the "message of pluralism and freedom to choose one's own beliefs," appear to believe that, where seasonal displays are concerned, more is better. Whereas a display might be constitutionally problematic if it showcased the holiday of just one religion, those problems vaporize as soon as more than one religion is included. I know of no principle under the Establishment Clause, however, that permits us to conclude that governmental promotion of religion is acceptable so long as one religion is not favored. We have, on the contrary, interpreted that Clause to require neutrality, not just among religions, but between religion and nonreligion.

Nor do I discern the theory under which the government is permitted to appropriate particular holidays and religious objects to its own use in celebrating "pluralism." The message of the sign announcing a "Salute to Liberty" is not religious, but patriotic; the government's use of religion to promote its own cause is undoubtedly offensive to those whose religious beliefs are not bound up with their attitude toward the Nation.

The uncritical acceptance of a message of religious pluralism also ignores the extent to which even that message may offend. Many religious faiths are hostile to each other, and indeed, refuse even to participate in ecumenical services designed to demonstrate the very pluralism Justices Blackmun and O'Connor extol. * * *

JUSTICE STEVENS, with whom JUSTICE BRENNAN and JUSTICE MARSHALL join, concurring in part and dissenting in part. * * *

Treatment of a symbol of a particular tradition demonstrates one's attitude toward that tradition. Thus the prominent display of religious symbols on government property falls within the compass of the First Amendment, even though interference with personal choices about supporting a church, by means of governmental tithing, was the primary concern in 1791. Whether the vice in such a display is characterized as "coercion," or "endorsement," or merely as state action with the purpose and effect of providing support for specific faiths, it is common ground that this symbolic governmental speech "respecting an establishment of religion" may violate the Constitution.

In my opinion the Establishment Clause should be construed to create a strong presumption against the display of religious symbols on public property. There is always a risk that such symbols will offend nonmembers of the faith being advertised as well as adherents who consider the particular advertisement disrespectful. [Even] though "[p]assersby who disagree with the message conveyed by these displays are free to ignore them, or even turn their backs," displays of this kind inevitably have a greater tendency to emphasize sincere and deeply felt differences among individuals than to achieve an ecumenical goal. The Establishment Clause does not allow public bodies to foment such disagreement.

Application of a strong presumption against the public use of religious symbols scarcely will "require a relentless extirpation of all contact between government and religion," (Kennedy, J., concurring and dissenting), for it will prohibit a display only when its message, evaluated in the context in which it is presented, is nonsecular. For example, a carving of Moses holding the Ten Commandments, if that is the only adornment on a courtroom wall, conveys an equivocal message, perhaps of respect for Judaism, for religion in general, or for law. The addition of carvings depicting Confucius and Mohammed may honor religion, or particular religions, to an extent that the First Amendment does not tolerate any more than it does "the permanent erection of a large Latin cross on the roof of city hall." Placement of secular figures such as Caesar Augustus, William Blackstone, Napoleon Bonaparte, and John Marshall alongside these three religious leaders, however, signals respect not for great proselytizers but for great lawgivers. It would be absurd to exclude such a fitting message from a courtroom,[13] as it would to exclude religious paintings by Italian Renaissance masters from a public museum.[i] Far from "border[ing] on latent hostility toward religion," this careful consideration of context gives due regard to religious and nonreligious members of our society. * * *

Notes and Questions

1. *Secular purpose. Lynch* found that "Pawtucket has *a* secular purpose for its display": "The City [has] principally taken note of a significant historical religious event long celebrated in the Western World. The crèche in the display depicts the historical origins of this traditional event long recognized as a National Holiday. [Were] the test that the government must have 'exclusively secular' objectives, much of the conduct and legislation this Court has approved in the past would have been invalidated."

Brennan, J.'s dissent in *Lynch,* reasoned: "When government decides to recognize Christmas day as a public holiday, it does no more than accommodate the calendar of public activities to the plain fact that many Americans will expect on that day to spend time visiting with their families, attending religious services, and perhaps enjoying some respite from preholiday activities. [If] public officials go further and participate in the *secular* celebration of Christmas—by, for example, decorating public places with such secular images as wreaths, garlands or Santa Claus figures—they move closer to the limits of their constitutional power but nevertheless remain within the boundaries set by the Establishment Clause. But when those officials participate in or appear to endorse the distinctively religious elements of this otherwise secular event, they encroach upon First Amendment freedoms. [The] Court seems to assume that

13. All these leaders, of course, appear in friezes on the walls of our courtroom.

i. As an example of government "reference to our religious heritage," *Lynch* noted that "the National Gallery in Washington, maintained with Government support, for example, has long exhibited masterpieces with religious messages, notably the Last Supper, and paintings depicting the Birth of Christ, the Crucifixion, and the Resurrection, among many others with explicit Christian themes and messages."

forbidding Pawtucket from displaying a crèche would be tantamount to forbidding a state college from including the Bible or Milton's Paradise Lost in a course on English literature. But in those cases the religiously-inspired materials are being considered solely as literature. [The] same may be said of a course devoted to the study of art; when the course turns to Gothic architecture, the emphasis is not on the religious beliefs which the cathedrals exalt, but rather upon the 'aesthetic consequences of [such religious] thought.' In this case, by contrast, the crèche plays no comparable secular role. [It] would be another matter if the crèche were displayed in a museum setting, in the company of other religiously-inspired artifacts, as an example, among many, of the symbolic representation of religious myths. In that setting, we would have objective guarantees that the crèche could not suggest that a particular faith had been singled out for public favor and recognition."

Does the dissent's approach require that government have "exclusively secular" objectives? If so, is this inconsistent with the Court's subsequent opinion in *Wallace* (joined by all the *Lynch* dissenters) that "a statute that is motivated in part by a religious purpose may satisfy the first [*Lemon*] criterion."

2. *O'Connor, J.'s approach.* (a) *"Reasonable observer."* Consider Marshall, *"We Know It When We See It," The Supreme Court and Establishment,* 59 So.Cal. L.Rev. 495, 537 (1986): "Is the objective observer (or average person) a religious person, an agnostic, a separationist, a person sharing the predominate religious sensibility of the community, or one holding a minority view? Is there any 'correct' perception?" Compare Note, *Religion and the State,* 100 Harv.L.Rev. 1606, 1648 (1987): "[If the test] is governed by the perspective of the majority, it will be inadequately sensitive to the impact of government actions on religious minorities, thereby in effect basing the protection of religious minorities on the judgment of the very majority that is accused of infringing the minority's religious autonomy. If the establishment clause is to prohibit government from sending the message to religious minorities or nonadherents that the state favors certain beliefs and that as nonadherents they are not fully members of the political community, its application must turn on the message received *by the minority or nonadherent.*"

(b) *"Endorsement:"* Is "the concept [the] source of serious and seemingly irreconcilable ambiguities"? Smith, *Symbols, Perceptions, and Doctrinal Illusions: Establishment Neutrality and the "No Endorsement" Test,* 86 Mich.L.Rev. 266, 283, 301–03, 310–12 (1987): "[E]vidence of the test's indeterminate character appears in [Loewy, *Rethinking Government Neutrality Towards Religion Under the Establishment Clause: The Untapped Potential of Justice O'Connor's Insight,* 64 N.C.L.Rev. 1049 (1986).] Loewy likes the 'no endorsement' test. In applying that test to particular controversies, however, he concludes that Pawtucket's sponsorship of a nativity scene violated the establishment clause, that Alabama's 'moment of silence' law probably did *not* violate the clause, and that ceremonial invocations of deity, such as those occurring in the Pledge of Allegiance or the opening of a Supreme Court session, *do* violate the "no endorsement" test. In each instance, Justice O'Connor would disagree. [From] the Continental Congress [139] through the framing of the Bill of Rights [140] and on down to the present

139. [The] Continental Congress "sprinkled its proceedings liberally with the mention of God, Jesus Christ, the Christian religion, and many other religious references."

140. Shortly after approving the Bill of Rights, which of course included the establishment clause, the first Congress resolved to observe a day of thanksgiving and prayer in appreciation of "the many signal favors of Almighty God."

day, government and government officials—including Presidents [not] to mention the Supreme Court itself [141]—have frequently expressed approval of religion and religious ideas. Such history [at] least demonstrates that many Americans, including some of our early eminent statesmen, have *believed* such approval was proper. That fact alone is sufficient to show that the 'no endorsement' principle is controversial, not easily self-evident. * * * Religious diversity in this country is rich enough to ensure that *any* governmental policy in an area that potentially concerns religion will probably alienate some people. If public institutions employ religious symbols, persons who do not adhere to the predominant religion may feel like 'outsiders.' But if religious symbols are banned from such contexts, some religious people will feel that their most central values and concerns—and thus, in an important sense, they themselves—have been excluded from a public culture devoted purely to secular concerns. [We] might conclude, however, that any alienation felt by such groups, although perfectly sincere, should be disregarded because their dissatisfaction actually results not from particular governmental actions but rather from the very meaning of the establishment clause."

See also 103 Harv.L.Rev. 235 (1989): "A separationist could argue that governmental acknowledgment and accommodation of religion, as a form of implicit approval, constitutes endorsement. At the other end of the spectrum, one could argue that there is no endorsement of religion absent an 'endorsement of truthfulness' of a religion or religious belief."

SECTION 2. FREE EXERCISE CLAUSE AND RELATED PROBLEMS

I. CONFLICT WITH STATE REGULATION

The most common problem that has arisen respecting free exercise of religion has involved a government regulation, whose purpose is nonreligious, that either makes illegal (or otherwise burdens) conduct that is dictated by some religious belief, or requires (or otherwise encourages) conduct that is forbidden by some religious belief. REYNOLDS v. UNITED STATES, 98 U.S. 145, 25 L.Ed. 244 (1879), the first major decision on the free exercise clause, upheld a federal law making polygamy illegal as applied to a Mormon whose religious duty was to practice polygamy: "Congress was deprived of all legislative power over mere opinion, but was left free to reach actions which were in violation of social duties or subversive of good order." CANTWELL v. CONNECTICUT, 310 U.S. 296, 60 S.Ct. 900, 84 L.Ed. 1213 (1940), reemphasized this distinction between religious opinion or belief, on the one hand, and action taken because of religion, on the other, although the Court spoke more solicitously about the latter: "The [Constitution] forestalls compulsion by law of the acceptance of any creed or the practice of any form of worship. Freedom of conscience and freedom to adhere to such religious organization or form of worship as the individual may choose cannot be restricted by law. [Free exercise] embraces two concepts,—freedom to believe and freedom to act. The first is absolute but, in the nature of things, the second cannot be. [The] freedom to act must have appropriate definition to preserve the enforcement of that protection [although]

141. See, e.g., *Zorach* ("We are a religious people whose institutions presuppose a Supreme Being."); *Church of the Holy Trinity v. United States,* 143 U.S. 457, 471, 12 S.Ct. 511, 516, 36 L.Ed. 226 (1892) (asserting that "this is a Christian nation").

the power to regulate must be so exercised as not, in attaining a permissible end, unduly to infringe the protected freedom."

Beginning with *Cantwell*—which first held that the fourteenth amendment made the free exercise guarantee applicable to the states—a number of cases invalidated application of state laws to conduct undertaken pursuant to religious beliefs. Like *Cantwell,* these decisions, a number of which are set forth in Ch. 1,[a] rested in whole or in part on the freedom of expression protections of the first and fourteenth amendments. Similarly, WEST VIRGINIA STATE BD. OF EDUC. v. BARNETTE, 319 U.S. 624, 63 S.Ct. 1178, 87 L.Ed. 1628 (1943),[b] held that compelling a flag salute by public school children whose religious scruples forbade it violated the first amendment: "[The] freedoms of speech and of press, of assembly, and of worship [are] susceptible of restriction only to prevent grave and immediate danger to interests which the state may lawfully protect. [The] freedom asserted by these appellees does not bring them into collision with rights asserted by any other individual. It is such conflicts which most frequently require intervention of the State to determine where the rights of one end and those of another begin. [T]he compulsory flag salute and pledge requires *affirmation of a belief* and an *attitude of mind.* [If] there is any fixed star in our constitutional constellation, it is that no official, high or petty, can prescribe what shall be orthodox in politics, nationalism or other matters of opinion or force citizens to confess by word or act their faith therein."

It was not until 1963, in *Sherbert v. Verner* (discussed below), that the Court held conduct protected by the free exercise clause alone.

HOBBIE v. UNEMPLOYMENT APPEALS COM'N

480 U.S. 136, 107 S.Ct. 1046, 94 L.Ed.2d 190 (1987).

JUSTICE BRENNAN delivered the opinion of the Court.

Appellant's employer discharged her when she refused to work certain scheduled hours because of sincerely-held religious convictions adopted after beginning employment. * * * Under our precedents, the [Florida] Appeals Commission's disqualification of appellant from receipt of [unemployment compensation] benefits violates the Free Exercise Clause of the First Amendment, applicable to the States through the Fourteenth Amendment. *Sherbert v. Verner,* 374 U.S. 398, 83 S.Ct. 1790, 10 L.Ed.2d 965 (1963); *Thomas v. Review Board,* 450 U.S. 707, 101 S.Ct. 1425, 67 L.Ed.2d 624 (1981). In *Sherbert* we considered South Carolina's denial of unemployment compensation benefits to a Sabbatarian who, like Hobbie, refused to work on Saturdays. The Court held that the State's disqualification of Sherbert "force[d] her to choose between following the precepts of her religion and forfeiting benefits, on the one hand, and abandoning one of the precepts of her religion in order to accept work, on the other hand. Governmental imposition of such a choice puts the same kind of burden upon the free exercise of religion as would a fine imposed against [her] for her Saturday worship." * * *

In *Thomas,* [a] Jehovah's Witness, held religious beliefs that forbade his participation in the production of armaments. He was forced to leave his job when the employer closed his department and transferred him to a division that

a. E.g., *Schneider v. Irvington,* p. 641 supra; *Lovell v. Griffin,* p. 599 supra. See also *Marsh v. Alabama,* p. 1207 infra.

b. Overruling *Minersville School Dist. v. Gobitis,* 310 U.S. 586, 60 S.Ct. 1010, 84 L.Ed. 1375 (1940).

fabricated turrets for tanks. Indiana then denied Thomas unemployment compensation benefits. * * *

We see no meaningful distinction among the situations of Sherbert, Thomas, and Hobbie. We again affirm, as stated in *Thomas:* "Where the state conditions receipt of an important benefit upon conduct proscribed by a religious faith, *or where it denies such a benefit because of conduct mandated by religious belief, thereby putting substantial pressure on an adherent to modify his behavior and to violate his beliefs,* a burden upon religion exists. While the compulsion may be indirect, the infringement upon free exercise is nonetheless substantial." (emphasis added).

Both *Sherbert* and *Thomas* held that such infringements must be subjected to strict scrutiny and could be justified only by proof by the State of a compelling interest. The Appeals Commission does not seriously contend that its denial of benefits can withstand strict scrutiny; [a] rather it urges that we hold that its justification should be determined under the less rigorous standard articulated in Chief Justice Burger's opinion in *Bowen v. Roy:* "the Government meets its burden when it demonstrates that a challenged requirement for governmental benefits, neutral and uniform in its application, is a reasonable means of promoting a legitimate public interest." [b] 476 U.S. 693, 707–08, 106 S.Ct. 2147, 2156, 90 L.Ed.2d 735 (1986). Five Justices expressly rejected this argument in *Roy.* See (Blackmun, J., concurring in part); (O'Connor, J., concurring in part and dissenting in part, joined by Brennan and Marshall, JJ.); (White, J., dissenting). We reject the argument again today. As Justice O'Connor pointed out in *Roy,* "[s]uch a test has no basis in precedent and relegates a serious First Amendment value to the barest level of minimal scrutiny that the Equal Protection Clause already provides." See also *Wisconsin v. Yoder,* 406 U.S. 205, 215, 92 S.Ct. 1526, 1533, 32 L.Ed.2d 15 (1972) ("[O]nly those interests of the highest order and those not otherwise served can overbalance legitimate claims to the free exercise of religion").[7] * * *

The Appeals Commission also attempts to distinguish this case by arguing that [in] *Sherbert* and *Thomas,* the employees held their respective religious beliefs at the time of hire; subsequent changes in the conditions of employment

a. In *Sherbert,* the state "suggest[ed] no more than a possibility that the filing of fraudulent claims by unscrupulous claimants feigning religious objections to Saturday work [might] dilute the unemployment compensation fund [but] there is no proof whatever to warrant such fears of malingering or deceit [and] it is highly doubtful whether such evidence would be sufficient to warrant a substantial infringement of religious liberties. For [it] would plainly be incumbent upon the [state] to demonstrate that no alternative forms of regulation would combat such abuses without infringing First Amendment rights."

b. Burger, C.J., joined by Powell and Rehnquist, JJ., prefaced this statement in *Roy* as follows: "[G]overnment regulation that indirectly and incidentally calls for a choice between securing a governmental benefit and adherence to religious beliefs is wholly different from government [action] that criminalizes religiously inspired activity or inescapably compels conduct that some find objectionable for religious reasons. Although the denial of governmental benefits over religious objection can raise serious Free Exercise problems, these two very different forms of government action are not governed by the same constitutional standard. * * * Absent proof of an intent to discriminate against particular religious beliefs or against religion in general, the Government meets its burden [etc.]"

7. In *Roy* [the parents of a two year old girl (named Little Bird of the Snow), for whom a social security number had been assigned at birth, contended that federal requirements—that recipients of AFDC and Food Stamps must submit their social security numbers, which shall be used by the government to prevent welfare fraud—violated their Native American religious beliefs. Five justices—O'Connor, Brennan, Marshall, Blackmun and White, JJ.—found that *Sherbert* and *Thomas* sustained the parents' claim.]

[Another issue in *Roy* is discussed in *Lyng,* note 5(d) infra.]

made *by the employer* caused the conflict between work and belief. In this case, Hobbie's beliefs changed during the course of her employment, creating a conflict between job and faith that had not previously existed. * * *

In effect, the Appeals Commission asks us to single out the religious convert for different, less favorable treatment than that given an individual whose adherence to his or her faith precedes employment. We decline to do so. * * *

Finally, we reject the Appeals Commission's argument that the awarding of benefits to Hobbie would violate the Establishment Clause. This Court has long recognized that the government may (and sometimes must) accommodate religious practices and that it may do so without violating the Establishment Clause.[10] See e.g., *Yoder* (judicial exemption of Amish children from compulsory attendance at high school); *Walz* (tax exemption for churches). * * *

Reversed.[c]

CHIEF JUSTICE REHNQUIST, dissenting.

I adhere to the views I stated in dissent in *Thomas* [where Rehnquist, J., stated:

["As to the proper interpretation of the Free Exercise Clause, I would accept the decision of *Braunfeld v. Brown,* 366 U.S. 599, 81 S.Ct. 1144, 6 L.Ed.2d 563 (1961), and the dissent in *Sherbert.* In *Braunfeld,* we held that Sunday closing laws do not violate the First Amendment rights of Sabbatarians. Chief Justice Warren explained that the statute did not make unlawful any religious practices of appellants; it simply made the practice of their religious beliefs more expensive. We concluded that '[t]o strike down, without the most critical scrutiny, legislation which imposes only an indirect burden on the exercise of religion, i.e. legislation which does not make unlawful the religious practice itself, would radically restrict the operating latitude of the legislature.'[d] Likewise in this case, it cannot be said that the State discriminated against Thomas on the basis of his religious beliefs or that he was denied benefits *because* he was a Jehovah's Witness.[1] Where, as here, a State has enacted a general statute, the purpose and effect of which is to advance the State's secular goals, the Free Exercise Clause does not in my view require the State to conform that statute to the dictates of religious conscience of any group. As Justice Harlan recognized

10. In the unemployment benefits context, the majorities *and* those dissenting have concluded that, were a state voluntarily to provide benefits to individuals in Hobbie's situation, such an accommodation would not violate the Establishment Clause. See *Thomas* (Rehnquist, J., dissenting); *Sherbert,* (Harlan, J., dissenting).

[The conflict between the establishment and free exercise clauses is considered in note 4, Sec. 3 infra.]

c. The opinions of Powell and Stevens, JJ., concurring in the judgment, are omitted.

d. *Braunfeld* continued: "Statutes which tax income and limit the amount which may be deducted for religious contributions impose an indirect economic burden on the observance of the religion of the citizen whose religion requires him to donate a greater amount to his church; statutes which require the courts to be closed on Saturday and Sunday impose a similar indirect burden on the observance of the religion of the trial lawyer whose religion requires him to rest on a weekday. The list of legislation of this nature is nearly limitless."

Query: If a statute makes a religious practice unlawful but the maximum penalty is a fine, does this impose a "direct" or "indirect" burden?

1. [In] this case, the Indiana Supreme Court *has* construed the State's unemployment statute to make every personal subjective reason for leaving a job a basis for disqualification. [Because] Thomas left his job for a personal reason, the State of Indiana should not be prohibited from disqualifying him from receiving benefits.

in his dissent in *Sherbert*: 'Those situations in which the Constitution may require special treatment on account of religion [are] few and far between.' "]

Notes and Questions

1. *Scope of decisions.* After *Sherbert, Thomas* and *Hobbie,* may a state deny unemployment benefits (a) to member of a pacifist religion who agreed to produce tanks as a condition of employment and who was fired for subsequently refusing to do so because of religious beliefs, see *Oregon Dep't of Human Resources v. Smith,* 485 U.S. 660, 108 S.Ct. 1444, 99 L.Ed.2d 753 (1988); (b) to a Sabbatarian who is dismissed from a job in the post office for refusal to work on Saturday because to grant an exemption would require paying overtime to another employee? [e] May (c) a state deny worker's compensation to the widow of an employee who, after being injured at work, died because of his refusal on religious grounds to accept a blood transfusion?

2. *Aid to parochial schools.* (a) Is the Court's conclusion, that denial of financial benefits to parochial schools does not infringe the free exercise rights of attending children, consistent with *Sherbert, Thomas* and *Hobbie*? After *Everson,* could a student bus transportation program exclude children who attend parochial schools? See *Luetkemeyer v. Kaufmann,* 419 U.S. 888, 95 S.Ct. 167, 42 L.Ed.2d 134 (1974). If some religions impose a duty on parents to send children to religious schools, may these parents argue that, since they must pay public school taxes, the state's failure to support parochial as well as public schools and thus defray their parochial school tuition costs imposes a serious financial burden on their exercise of religion? That "if the state gives financial assistance only to the school where education is deliberately divorced from religion [this is] preferential treatment of irreligion"? See Drinan, *The Constitutionality of Public Aid to Parochial Schools,* in The Wall Between Church and State 55, 68 (Oaks ed. 1963). That, "conditioning the availability of benefits upon their willingness to violate a cardinal principle of their religious faith effectively penalizes the free exercise of their constitutional liberties" (*Sherbert*); that there is no "compelling state interest to justify the substantial infringement of their First Amendment rights"? May these parents further argue that their position is stronger than *Sherbert, Thomas* and *Hobbie* because the purpose of granting an exemption in that case was *solely* to aid religion whereas there is a wholly nonreligious purpose in giving aid to all nonpublic schools—improving the quality of the secular education?

Consider Kauper, *Religion and the Constitution* 36–37 (1964): "If the public policy of the state is to limit the use of educational funds to schools under public control, this involves no discrimination except the distinction between schools under public and those under private control—a distinction well recognized in our law. But if public funds are made available for all educational institutions whether public or private except those that are under the control of a religious body, it is indeed hard to avoid the conclusion that the religious factor is being used as a ground for disqualification from public benefits." Compare 25 U.Pitt. L.Rev. 713 (1964): "If the state in *Sherbert could not deny* compensation to one refusing work for religious reasons how could the state in *Everson* deny transportation reimbursement to students who choose for religious reasons to attend a

e. See also *TWA v. Hardison,* 432 U.S. 63, 97 S.Ct. 2264, 53 L.Ed.2d 113 (1977), interpreting the Civil Rights Act prohibition against religious discrimination in employment as permitting dismissal of a Sabbatarian if accommodating his work schedule would require "more than a de minimis cost" by the employer. Brennan and Marshall, JJ., dissented.

parochial rather than public school? Suppose that the statute in *Everson* had dictated that all those attending nonpublic schools should not obtain free transportation, except that those students who attended religious schools because of the dictates of their religion also should qualify for fare reimbursement. It is submitted that under the rationale of *Sherbert* such a statute would be constitutional." But see the dictum in *Sloan v. Lemon,* p. 857 supra: "[V]alid aid to nonpublic, nonsectarian schools would provide no lever for aid to their sectarian counterparts."

3. *Other forms of government largesse.* If a state fluoridates drinking water, must it supply nonfluoridated water to persons whose religion forbids such "medicinal aids"? If a state gives financial support to various voluntary and eleemosynary institutions, does *Sherbert* require it to give such support to churches? Consider Tribe, *American Constitutional Law* 1274 (2d ed. 1988): "Presumably the government could provide subsidized loans to beef producers without facing a colorable free exercise claim brought by people whose religion requires them to raise and eat only vegetables; or provide tax benefits to medical or military professionals without facing a claim brought by people whose religious tenets forbid such work. But the principles underlying [the distinctions between these policies and that in *Sherbert, Thomas* and *Hobbie*] resist ready definition."

4. *Discrimination against religion.* McDANIEL v. PATY, 435 U.S. 618, 98 S.Ct. 1322, 55 L.Ed.2d 593 (1978)—an unusual case because it involved a law that singled out religion[f]—invalidated Tennessee provisions disqualifying clergy from being legislators. BURGER, C.J., joined by Powell, Rehnquist and Stevens, JJ., characterized the disqualification as "directed primarily at status, acts and conduct" rather than at "belief." Relying on the "delicate balancing" required by *Sherbert,* they found the restriction violative of free exercise: "The essence of the rationale underlying the Tennessee restriction on ministers is that if elected to public office they will necessarily exercise their powers and influence to promote the interests of one sect or thwart the interests of another thus pitting one against the others, contrary to the antiestablishment principle with its command of neutrality. [But] American experience provides no persuasive support for the fear that clergymen in public office will be less careful of antiestablishment interests or less faithful to their oaths of civil office than their unordained counterparts."[g]

BRENNAN, J., joined by Marshall, J., concurred: "The characterization of the exclusion as one burdening appellant's 'career or calling' and not religious belief cannot withstand analysis. [T]o bar from political office persons regarded as deeply committed to religious participation because of that participation—participation itself not regarded as harmful by the State and which therefore must be conceded to be protected"—is "absolutely prohibited" by the free exercise clause.[h] Further, "the State's goal of preventing sectarian bickering and strife may not be accomplished by regulating religious speech and political association."[i]

f. See also *Torcaso v. Watkins,* Part II infra.

g. Compare Marty, *Of Darters and Schools and Clergymen: The Religion Clauses Worse Confounded,* 1978 Sup.Ct.Rev. 171, 183: "[I]n issues having to do with everything from homosexuality to the Equal Rights Amendment to abortion to pornography, lay and especially clerical leadership in many denominations has been more aggressive, always with an eye to having one's own sect prevail in the legislative and judicial arenas."

h. Stewart, J., concurred separately, essentially on this ground.

i. White, J., concurred, on equal protection grounds, pointing to cases (Ch. 6, Sec. 4, I.C infra) requiring "States to provide substantial justification for any requirement that prevents a class of citizens from gaining ballot access." Blackmun, J., did not participate.

5. *Additional rejections of free exercise claims.* (a) *Taxation.* (i) JIMMY SWAGGART MINISTRIES v. BOARD OF EQUAL., 493 U.S. 378, 110 S.Ct. 688, 107 L.Ed.2d 796 (1990), per O'CONNOR, J., unanimously held that the free exercise clause does not prohibit imposing a generally applicable sales and use tax to the sale of religious materials by a religious organization. The Court distinguished *Murdock v. Pennsylvania,* 319 U.S. 105, 63 S.Ct. 870, 87 L.Ed. 1292 (1943) and *Follett v. McCormick,* 321 U.S. 573, 64 S.Ct. 717, 88 L.Ed. 938 (1944), which had invalidated license taxes for sellers as applied to Jehovah's Witnesses who went from house to house selling religious pamphlets, because of the "particular nature of the challenged taxes—flat license taxes that operated as a prior restraint on the exercise of religious liberty": "As the Court made clear in *Hernandez v. Commissioner* [Sec. 3 infra], holding that the Government's disallowance of a tax deduction for religious 'auditing' and 'training' services did not violate [free exercise], to the extent that imposition of a generally applicable tax merely decreases the amount of money appellant has to spend on its religious activities, any such burden is not constitutionally significant. * * *

"Finally, because appellant's religious beliefs do not forbid payment of the sales and use tax, appellant's reliance on *Sherbert* and its progeny is misplaced. [Although] it is of course possible to imagine that a more onerous tax, even if generally applicable, might effectively choke off an adherent's religious practices, cf. *Murdock* (the burden of a flat tax could render itinerant evangelism 'crushed and closed out by the sheer weight of the toll or tribute which is exacted town by town'), we face no such situation in this case."

(ii) UNITED STATES v. LEE, 455 U.S. 252, 102 S.Ct. 1051, 71 L.Ed.2d 127 (1982), per BURGER, C.J., held that the free exercise clause does not require an exemption for members of the Old Order Amish from payment of social security taxes even though "both payment and receipt of social security benefits is forbidden by the Amish faith": "The state may justify a limitation on religious liberty by showing that it is essential to accomplish an overriding governmental interest [and] mandatory participation is indispensable to the fiscal vitality of the social security system. [To] maintain an organized society that guarantees religious freedom to a great variety of faiths requires that some religious practices yield to the common good. [The] tax system could not function if denominations were allowed to challenge the tax system because tax payments were spent in a manner that violates their religious belief. * * * [12]"

STEVENS, J., concurred in the judgment: "As a matter of fiscal policy, an enlarged exemption probably would benefit the social security system because the nonpayment of these taxes by the Amish would be more than offset by the elimination of their right to collect benefits.[c] * * * Nonetheless, I agree with the Court's conclusion that the difficulties associated with processing other claims to tax exemption on religious grounds justify a rejection of this claim.[2]"

12. We note that here the statute compels contributions to the system by way of taxes; it does not compel anyone to accept benefits. Indeed, it would be possible for an Amish member, upon qualifying for social security benefits, to receive and pass them along to an Amish fund having parallel objectives. It is not for us to speculate whether this would ease or mitigate the perceived sin of participation.

c. Stevens, J., found the distinction between this case and *Yoder* "unconvincing because precisely the same religious interest is implicated in both cases and Wisconsin's interest in requiring its children to attend school until they reach the age of 16 is surely not inferior to the federal interest in collecting these social security taxes."

2. In my opinion, the principal reason for adopting a strong presumption against such claims is not a matter of administrative convenience. It is the overriding interest in keeping the government—whether it be the legislature or the courts—out of the business of

(b) *Conscription.* (i) GILLETTE v. UNITED STATES, 401 U.S. 437, 91 S.Ct. 828, 28 L.Ed.2d 168 (1971), per MARSHALL, J., held that the free exercise clause does not forbid Congress from "conscripting persons who oppose a particular war on grounds of conscience and religion. * * * [23]": "The conscription laws [are] not designed to interfere with any religious ritual or practice, and do not work a penalty against any theological position. The incidental burdens felt by persons in petitioners' position are strictly justified by substantial governmental interests that relate directly to the very impacts questioned. And more broadly, of course, there is the Government's interest in procuring the manpower necessary for military purposes * * *."

DOUGLAS, J., dissented: "[M]y choice is the dicta of Chief Justice Hughes who, dissenting in *Macintosh,* spoke for Holmes, Brandeis, and Stone: '[Among] the most eminent statesmen here and abroad have been those who condemned the action of their country in entering into wars they thought to be unjustified. [If] the mere holding of religious or conscientious scruples against all wars should not disqualify a citizen from holding office in this country, or an applicant otherwise qualified from being admitted to citizenship, there would seem to be no reason why a reservation of religious or conscientious objection to participation in wars believed to be unjust should constitute such a disqualification.' " [d]

(ii) In JOHNSON v. ROBISON, 415 U.S. 361, 94 S.Ct. 1160, 39 L.Ed.2d 389 (1974), a federal statute granted educational benefits for veterans who served on active duty but disqualified conscientious objectors who performed alternate civilian service. The Court, per BRENNAN, J., found a "rational basis" for the classification and thus no violation of equal protection: The "disruption caused by military service is quantitatively greater" because "the military veteran remains subject to [a Reserve] obligation after release from active duty" whereas a conscientious objector is only "obligated to work for two years." The disruptions are also "qualitatively different. Military veterans suffer a far greater loss of personal freedom during their service careers." The "classification also bears

evaluating the relative merits of differing religious claims. The risk that governmental approval of some and disapproval of others will be perceived as favoring one religion over another is an important risk the Establishment Clause was designed to preclude.

23. We are not faced with the question whether the Free Exercise Clause itself would require exemption of any class other than objectors to particular wars. * * * We note that the Court has previously suggested that relief for conscientious objectors is not mandated by the Constitution. See *Hamilton v. Regents; United States v. Macintosh,* 283 U.S. at 623–24, 51 S.Ct. at 574–75, 75 L.Ed. 1302 (1931).

d. Did *Gillette* discard the "alternative means" approach found in *Sherbert?* Consider Tribe, *American Constitutional Law* 1266 (2d ed. 1988): "In light of the relative ease with which the conscientious-objector exemption has been administered throughout our history without placing a noticeable burden on the country's military manpower needs, a court might well require a concrete showing of threat to such needs in order to justify abolition of the exemption. The use of conscientious objectors—even selective conscientious objectors—in paramedical or other non-military roles could meet both the personnel argument and the morale argument well enough to constitute a required alternative under *Sherbert.*"

Or is such "evaluation of alternatives" a task that "inevitably involves judgments about costs and policy objectives that are customarily left to legislatures"? 85 Harv.L.Rev. 184–85 (1971).

See generally Macgill, *Selective Conscientious Objection: Divine Will and Legislative Grace,* 54 Va.L.Rev. 1355 (1968); Hochstadt, *The Right to Exemption from Military Service of a Conscientious Objector to a Particular War,* 3 Harv.Civ.Rts.–Civ.Lib.L.Rev. 1 (1967).

For the view that the Court "has shown little enthusiasm for strict review in post-*Sherbert* and *Yoder* decisions," see Kamenshine, *Scrapping Strict Review in Free Exercise Cases,* 4 Const.Comm. 147 (1987).

a rational relationship" to the objective of "enhancing and making more attractive" military service.

Further, the statute "involves only an incidental burden upon appellee's free exercise of religion—if, indeed, any burden exists at all.[19] [T]he Government's substantial interest in raising and supporting armies is of 'a kind and weight' clearly sufficient to sustain the challenged legislation, for the burden upon appellee's free exercise [is] not nearly of the same order or magnitude as" in *Gillette.*

DOUGLAS, J., dissented: "Full benefits are available to occupants of safe desk jobs and the thousands of veterans who performed civilian type duties at home and for whom the 'rigors' of the war were far from 'totally disruptive.'" [Unlike] *Gillette,* this classification is not "religiously neutral" but "excludes only those [with] religious-based objections to war"—and "the only government interest here is the financial one of denying these appellees educational benefits."

(c) *Tax exemption.* BOB JONES UNIV. v. UNITED STATES, 461 U.S. 574, 103 S.Ct. 2017, 76 L.Ed.2d 157 (1983), per BURGER, C.J., held that IRS denial of tax exempt status to private schools that practice racial discrimination on the basis of sincerely held religious beliefs does not violate the free exercise clause: "[T]he Government has a fundamental, overriding interest in eradicating racial discrimination in education [which] substantially outweighs whatever burden denial of tax benefits places on petitioners' exercise of their religious beliefs. The interests asserted by petitioners cannot be accommodated with that compelling governmental interest, see *Lee;* and no 'less restrictive means' are available to achieve the governmental interest." [e] Rehnquist, J., agreeing with the Court's free exercise analysis, dissented on the ground that Congress had not authorized the IRS denial of tax exemption.[f]

(d) *Internal government affairs.* LYNG v. NORTHWEST INDIAN CEMETERY PROTECTIVE ASS'N, 485 U.S. 439, 108 S.Ct. 1319, 99 L.Ed.2d 534 (1988), per O'CONNOR, J., held the federal government's building a road and allowing timber harvesting in a national forest did not violate the free exercise rights of American Indian tribes even though this would "virtually destroy the Indians' ability to practice their religion" because it would irreparably damage "sacred areas which are an integral and necessary part of [their] belief systems": "In *Bowen v. Roy,* we considered a challenge to a federal statute that required the States to use Social Security numbers in administering certain welfare programs. Two applicants for benefits under these programs contended that their religious beliefs prevented them from acceding to the use of a Social Security number for their two-year-old daughter because the use of a numerical identifier

19. * * * Congress has bestowed relative benefits upon conscientious objectors by permitting them to perform their alternate service obligation as civilians. Thus, Congress' decision to grant educational benefits to military servicemen might arguably be viewed as an attempt to equalize the burdens of military service and civilian alternate service, rather than an effort [to] place a relative burden upon a conscientious objector's free exercise of religion.

e. For a contrary view, see Laycock, *Tax Exemptions for Racially Discriminatory Religious Schools,* 60 Tex.L.Rev. 259 (1982); Freed & Polsby, *Race, Religion, and Public Policy: Bob Jones University v. United States,* 1983 Sup.Ct.Rev. 1, 20–30.

f. Four justices also rejected the claim that Nebraska's denial of a driver's license to a person whose sincerely held religious beliefs—pursuant to the Second Commandment prohibition of "graven images"—forbade her to be photographed, violated the free exercise clause. *Quaring v. Peterson,* 728 F.2d 1121 (8th Cir.1984) (free exercise violation), affirmed by an equally divided Court, 472 U.S. 478, 105 S.Ct. 3492, 86 L.Ed.2d 383 (1985).

would '"rob the spirit" of [their] daughter and prevent her from attaining greater spiritual power.' [The] Court rejected this kind of challenge in *Roy:* 'The Free Exercise Clause simply cannot be understood to require the Government to conduct its own internal affairs in ways that comport with the religious beliefs of particular citizens. Just as the Government may not insist that [the Roys] engage in any set form of religious observance, so [they] may not demand that the Government join in their chosen religious practices by refraining from using a number to identify their daughter. [The] Free Exercise Clause affords an individual protection from certain forms of governmental compulsion; it does not afford an individual a right to dictate the conduct of the Government's internal procedures.'

"The building of a road or the harvesting of timber on publicly owned land cannot meaningfully be distinguished from the use of a Social Security number in *Roy.* In both cases, the challenged government action would interfere significantly with private persons' ability to pursue spiritual fulfillment according to their own religious beliefs. In neither case, however, would the affected individuals be coerced by the Government's action into violating their religious beliefs; nor would either governmental action penalize religious activity by denying any person an equal share of the rights, benefits, and privileges enjoyed by other citizens.

"[However] much we might wish that it were otherwise, government simply could not operate if it were required to satisfy every citizen's religious needs and desires. A broad range of government activities—from social welfare programs to foreign aid to conservation projects—will always be considered essential to the spiritual well-being of some citizens, often on the basis of sincerely held religious beliefs. Others will find the very same activities deeply offensive, and perhaps incompatible with their own search for spiritual fulfillment and with the tenets of their religion. The First Amendment must apply to all citizens alike, and it can give to none of them a veto over public programs that do not prohibit the free exercise of religion. * * *

"[The] dissent now offers to distinguish [*Roy*] by saying that the Government was acting there 'in a purely internal manner,' whereas land-use decisions 'are likely to have substantial external effects.' [But robbing] the spirit of a child, and preventing her from attaining greater spiritual power, is both a 'substantial external effect' and one that is remarkably similar to the injury claimed by respondents in the case before us today." [a]

BRENNAN, J., joined by Marshall and Blackmun, JJ., dissented: "The Court does not for a moment suggest that the interests served by the G–O road are in any way compelling, or that they outweigh the destructive effect construction of the road will have on respondents' religious practices. [Indeed,] the Government's proposed activities will restrain religious practice to a far greater degree here than in any of the cases cited by the Court today. None of the religious adherents in *Hobbie, Thomas,* and *Sherbert,* for example, claimed or could have claimed that the denial of unemployment benefits rendered the practice of their religions impossible; at most, the challenged laws made those practices more expensive. Here, in stark contrast, respondents have claimed—and proved—that the desecration of the high country will prevent religious leaders from attaining the religious power or medicine indispensable to the success of virtual-

a. *Nature of remedy.* Is there a difference between the remedy needed to satisfy the free exercise claim in *Roy* and that in *Lyng?* If so, what about the required remedy in the other instances in which the Court has sustained the free exercise claim?

ly all their rituals and ceremonies. [T]oday's ruling sacrifices a religion at least as old as the Nation itself, along with the spiritual well-being of its approximately 5,000 adherents, so that the Forest Service can build a six-mile segment of road that two lower courts found had only the most marginal and speculative utility, both to the Government itself and to the private lumber interests that might conceivably use it." Kennedy, J., did not participate.

EMPLOYMENT DIVISION v. SMITH

___ U.S. ___, 110 S.Ct. 1595, 108 L.Ed.2d 876 (1990).

JUSTICE SCALIA delivered the opinion of the Court. * * *

Respondents Alfred Smith and Galen Black were fired from their jobs with a private drug rehabilitation organization because they ingested peyote for sacramental purposes at a ceremony of the Native American Church, of which both are members. When respondents applied to petitioner Employment Division for unemployment compensation, they were determined to be ineligible for benefits because they had been discharged for work-related "misconduct". [We believe] that "if a State has prohibited through its criminal laws certain kinds of religiously motivated conduct without violating the First Amendment, it certainly follows that it may impose the lesser burden of denying unemployment compensation benefits to persons who engage in that conduct." * * *

[The] free exercise of religion means, first and foremost, the right to believe and profess whatever religious doctrine one desires. Thus, the First Amendment obviously excludes all "governmental regulation of religious *beliefs* as such." The government may not compel affirmation of religious belief, see *Torcaso v. Watkins,* [Part II infra], punish the expression of religious doctrines it believes to be false, *United States v. Ballard,* [Part II infra], impose special disabilities on the basis of religious views or religious status, see *McDaniel v. Paty;* cf. *Larson v. Valente,* [Sec. 3 infra] or lend its power to one or the other side in controversies over religious authority or dogma, see *Presbyterian Church v. Hull Church,* [Sec. 1, II supra.]

But the "exercise of religion" often involves not only belief and profession but the performance of (or abstention from) physical acts: assembling with others for a worship service, participating in sacramental use of bread and wine, proselytizing, abstaining from certain foods or certain modes of transportation. It would be true, we think (though no case of ours has involved the point), that a state would be "prohibiting the free exercise [of religion]" if it sought to ban such acts or abstentions only when they are engaged in for religious reasons, or only because of the religious belief that they display. It would doubtless be unconstitutional, for example, to ban the casting of "statues that are to be used for worship purposes," or to prohibit bowing down before a golden calf.

Respondents in the present case, however, seek to carry the meaning of "prohibiting the free exercise [of religion]" one large step further. They contend that their religious motivation for using peyote places them beyond the reach of a criminal law that is not specifically directed at their religious practice, and that is concededly constitutional as applied to those who use the drug for other reasons. [As] a textual matter, we do not think the words must be given that meaning. It is no more necessary to regard the collection of a general tax, for example, as "prohibiting the free exercise [of religion]" by those citizens who believe support of organized government to be sinful, than it is to regard the same tax as "abridging the freedom [of] the press" of those publishing companies that must pay the tax as a condition of staying in business. It is a permissible reading of the text, in the one case as in the other, to say that if prohibiting the exercise of religion (or burdening the activity of printing) is not the object of the tax but merely the incidental effect of a generally applicable and otherwise valid provision, the First Amendment has not been offended. Compare *Citizen Publishing Co. v. United States,* 394 U.S. 131, 89 S.Ct. 927, 22 L.Ed.2d 148 (1969) (upholding application of antitrust laws to press), with *Grosjean v. American Press Co.*, [p. 670 supra] (striking down license tax applied only to newspapers with weekly circulation above a specified level); see generally *Minneapolis Star & Tribune Co. v. Minnesota Commissioner of Revenue* [p. 550 supra].

Our decisions reveal that the latter reading is the correct one. We have never held that an individual's religious beliefs excuse him from compliance with an otherwise valid law prohibiting conduct that the State is free to regulate. [In] *Prince v. Massachusetts,* 321 U.S. 158, 64 S.Ct. 438, 88 L.Ed. 645 (1944), we held that a mother could be prosecuted under the child labor laws for using her children to dispense literature in the streets, her religious motivation notwithstanding. [The opinion also discusses *Braunfeld, Gillette,* and *Lee.*]

The only decisions in which we have held that the First Amendment bars application of a neutral, generally applicable law to religiously motivated action have involved not the Free Exercise Clause alone, but the Free Exercise Clause in conjunction with other constitutional protections, such as freedom of speech and of the press, see *Cantwell* (invalidating a licensing system for religious and charitable solicitations under which the administrator had discretion to deny a license to any cause he deemed nonreligious); *Murdock* (invalidating a flat tax on solicitation as applied to the dissemination of religious ideas); *Follett* (same), or the right of parents, acknowledged in *Pierce v. Society of Sisters* [Sec. 1 supra] to direct the education of their children, see *Yoder,* (invalidating compulsory school-attendance laws as applied to Amish parents who refused on religious grounds to send their children to school).[1] Some of our cases prohibiting compelled expression, decided exclusively upon free speech grounds, have also involved freedom of religion, cf. *Wooley v. Maynard* [p. 728 supra] (invalidating compelled display of a license plate slogan that offended individual religious beliefs); *Barnette.* And it is easy to envision a case in which a challenge on freedom of association grounds would likewise be reinforced by Free Exercise Clause concerns. Cf. *Roberts v. United States Jaycees* [p. 752 supra] ("An individual's freedom to speak, to worship, and to petition the government for the redress of grievances could not be vigorously protected from interference by the State [if] a correlative freedom to engage in group effort toward those ends were not also guaranteed."). * * *

Respondents argue that even though exemption from generally applicable criminal laws need not automatically be extended to religiously motivated actors, at least the claim for a religious exemption must be evaluated under the balancing test set forth in *Sherbert.* Under the *Sherbert* test, governmental actions that substantially burden a religious practice must be justified by a compelling governmental interest. [We] have never invalidated any governmental action on the basis of the *Sherbert* test except the denial of unemployment

1. [*Yoder*] said that "the Court's holding in *Pierce* stands as a charter of the rights of parents to direct the religious upbringing of their children. And, when the interests of parenthood are combined with a free exercise claim of the nature revealed by this record, more than merely a 'reasonable relation to some purpose within the competency of the State' is required to sustain the validity of the State's requirement under the First Amendment."

compensation. Although we have sometimes purported to apply the *Sherbert* test in contexts other than that, we have always found the test satisfied, see *Lee, Gillette.* In recent years we have abstained from applying the *Sherbert* test (outside the unemployment compensation field) at all [discussing *Roy* and *Lyng*]. In *Goldman v. Weinberger,* 475 U.S. 503, 106 S.Ct. 1310, 89 L.Ed.2d 478 (1986), we rejected application of the *Sherbert* test to military dress regulations that forbade the wearing of yarmulkes. In *O'Lone v. Shabazz,* 482 U.S. 342, 107 S.Ct. 2400, 96 L.Ed.2d 282 (1987), we sustained, without mentioning the *Sherbert* test, a prison's refusal to excuse inmates from work requirements to attend worship services.

Even if we were inclined to breathe into *Sherbert* some life beyond the unemployment compensation field, we would not apply it to require exemptions from a generally applicable criminal law. The *Sherbert* test, it must be recalled, was developed in a context that lent itself to individualized governmental assessment of the reasons for the relevant conduct. As a plurality of the Court noted in *Roy,* a distinctive feature of unemployment compensation programs is that their eligibility criteria invite consideration of the particular circumstances behind an applicant's unemployment. [As] the plurality pointed out in *Roy,* our decisions in the unemployment cases stand for the proposition that where the State has in place a system of individual exemptions, it may not refuse to extend that system to cases of "religious hardship" without compelling reason.

Whether or not the decisions are that limited, they at least have nothing to do with an across-the-board criminal prohibition on a particular form of conduct. [We] conclude today that the sounder approach, and the approach in accord with the vast majority of our precedents, is to hold the test inapplicable to such challenges. [To] make an individual's obligation to obey such a law contingent upon the law's coincidence with his religious beliefs, except where the State's interest is "compelling"—permitting him, by virtue of his beliefs, "to become a law unto himself," *Reynolds*—contradicts both constitutional tradition and common sense.[2]

The "compelling government interest" requirement seems benign, because it is familiar from other fields. But using it as the standard that must be met before the government may accord different treatment on the basis of race, see [p. 969 infra], or before the government may regulate the content of speech, is not remotely comparable to using it for the purpose asserted here. What it produces in those other fields—equality of treatment, and an unrestricted flow of contending speech—are constitutional norms; what it would produce here—a private right to ignore generally applicable laws—is a constitutional anomaly.[3]

2. Justice O'Connor seeks to distinguish *Lyng* and *Roy* on the ground that those cases involved the government's conduct of "its own internal affairs." [But] it is hard to see any reason in principle or practicality why the government should have to tailor its health and safety laws to conform to the diversity of religious belief, but should not have to tailor its management of public lands, *Lyng,* or its administration of welfare programs, *Roy.*

3. [Just] as we subject to the most exacting scrutiny laws that make classifications based on race or on the content of speech, so too we strictly scrutinize governmental classifications based on religion, see *McDaniel;* see also *Torcaso.* But we have held that race-neutral laws that have the *effect* of disproprotionately disadvantaging a particular racial group do not thereby become subject to compelling-interest analysis under the Equal Protection Clause, see *Washington v. Davis* [p. 973 infra] (police employment examination); and we have held that generally applicable laws unconcerned with regulating speech that have the *effect* of interfering with speech do not thereby become subject to compelling-interest analysis under the First Amendment, see *Citizen Publishing Co. v. United States* (antitrust laws). Our conclusion that generally applicable, religion-neutral laws that have the effect of burdening a particular religious practice need not be justified by a compelling governmental inter-

Nor is it possible to limit the impact of respondents' proposal by requiring a "compelling state interest" only when the conduct prohibited is "central" to the individual's religion. It is no more appropriate for judges to determine the "centrality" of religious beliefs before applying a "compelling interest" test in the free exercise field, than it would be for them to determine the "importance" of ideas before applying the "compelling interest" test in the free speech field. What principle of law or logic can be brought to bear to contradict a believer's assertion that a particular act is "central" to his personal faith? [I]n many different contexts, we have warned that courts must not presume to determine the place of a particular belief in a religion or the plausibility of a religious claim. See, e.g., *Thomas* [Part II infra]; *Jones v. Wolf,* [Sec. 1, II supra]; *Ballard.*[4]

If the "compelling interest" test is to be applied at all, then, it must be applied across the board, to all actions thought to be religiously commanded. Moreover, if "compelling interest" really means what it says (and watering it down here would subvert its rigor in the other fields where it is applied), many laws will not meet the test. Any society adopting such a system would be courting anarchy, but that danger increases in direct proportion to the society's diversity of religious beliefs, and its determination to coerce or suppress none of them. Precisely because "we are a cosmopolitan nation made up of people of almost every conceivable religious preference," and precisely because we value and protect that religious divergence, we cannot afford the luxury of deeming *presumptively invalid,* as applied to the religious objector, every regulation of conduct that does not protect an interest of the highest order. The rule respondents favor would open the prospect of constitutionally required religious exemptions from civic obligations of almost every conceivable kind—ranging from compulsory military service, see, e.g., *Gillette,* to the payment of taxes, see, e.g., *Lee,* to health and safety regulation such as manslaughter and child neglect laws, see, *e.g., Funkhouser v. State,* 763 P.2d 695 (Okla.Crim.App.1988), compulsory vaccination laws, see, *e.g., Cude v. State,* 237 Ark. 927, 377 S.W.2d 816 (1964), drug laws, see, *e.g., Olsen v. Drug Enforcement Administration,* 878 F.2d 1458 (D.C.Cir.1989), and traffic laws, see *Cox v. New Hampshire,* [p. 643 supra], to social welfare legislation such as minimum wage laws, see *Susan and Tony Alamo Foundation v. Secretary of Labor,* 471 U.S. 290, 105 S.Ct. 1953, 85 L.Ed.2d 278 (1985), child labor laws, see *Prince;* animal cruelty laws, see, e.g., *Church of the Lukumi Babalu Aye Inc. v. Hialeah,* 723 F.Supp. 1467 (S.D.Fla.1989); environmental protection laws, see *United States v. Little,* 638 F.Supp. 337 (Mont. 1986), and laws providing for equality of opportunity for the races, see e.g., *Bob Jones University.* The First Amendment's protection of religious liberty does not require this.[5]

est is the only approach compatible with these precedents.

4. [In] any case, dispensing with a "centrality" inquiry is utterly unworkable. It would require, for example, the same degree of "compelling state interest" to impede the practice of throwing rice at church weddings as to impede the practice of getting married in church. There is no way out of the difficulty that, if general laws are to be subjected to a "religious practice" exception, *both* the importance of the law at issue *and* the centrality of the practice at issue must reasonably be considered. * * *

5. Justice O'Connor contends that the "parade of horribles" in the text only "demonstrates [that] courts have been quite capable of strik[ing] sensible balances between religious liberty and competing state interests." But the cases we cite have struck "sensible balances" only because they have all applied the general laws, despite the claims for religious exemption. In any event, Justice O'Connor mistakes the purpose of our parade: it is not to suggest that courts would necessarily permit harmful exemptions from these laws (though they might), but to suggest that courts would constantly be in the business of determining whether the "severe impact" of var-

[A] number of States have made an exception to their drug laws for sacramental peyote use. But to say that a nondiscriminatory religious-practice exemption is permitted, or even that it is desirable, is not to say that it is constitutionally required, and that the appropriate occasions for its creation can be discerned by the courts. It may fairly be said that leaving accommodation to the political process will place at a relative disadvantage those religious practices that are not widely engaged in; but that unavoidable consequence of democratic government must be preferred to a system in which each conscience is a law unto itself or in which judges weigh the social importance of all laws against the centrality of all religious beliefs. * * *

JUSTICE O'CONNOR, with whom JUSTICE BRENNAN, JUSTICE MARSHALL, and JUSTICE BLACKMUN join as to [Part II], concurring in the judgment. * * *

II. The Court [today] interprets the [Free Exercise] Clause to permit the government to prohibit, without justification, conduct mandated by an individual's religious beliefs, so long as that prohibition is generally applicable. But a law that prohibits certain conduct—conduct that happens to be an act of worship for someone—manifestly does prohibit that person's free exercise of his religion. [Moreover,] that person is barred from freely exercising his religion regardless of whether the law prohibits the conduct only when engaged in for religious reasons, only by members of that religion, or by all persons.

[If] the First Amendment is to have any vitality, it ought not be construed to cover only the extreme and hypothetical situation in which a State directly targets a religious practice. As we have noted in a slightly different context, " '[s]uch a test has no basis in precedent and relegates a serious First Amendment value to the barest level of minimum scrutiny that the Equal Protection Clause already provides.' " *Hobbie.*

To say that a person's right to free exercise has been burdened, of course, does not mean that he has an absolute right to engage in the conduct. Under our established First Amendment jurisprudence, we [have] respected both the First Amendment's express textual mandate and the governmental interest in regulation of conduct by requiring the Government to justify any substantial burden on religiously motivated conduct by a compelling state interest and by means narrowly tailored to achieve that interest. * * *

The Court attempts to support its narrow reading of the Clause by claiming that "[w]e have never held that an individual's religious beliefs excuse him from compliance with an otherwise valid law prohibiting conduct that the State is free to regulate." But [in] *Yoder* we expressly rejected the interpretation the Court now adopts: "[T]o agree that religiously grounded conduct must often be subject to the broad police power of the State is not to deny that there are areas of conduct protected by the Free Exercise Clause of the First Amendment and thus beyond the power of the State to control, *even under regulations of general applicability.* [A] regulation neutral on its face may, in its application, nonetheless offend the constitutional requirement for government neutrality if it unduly burdens the free exercise of religion."

The Court endeavors to escape from our decisions in *Cantwell* and *Yoder* by labeling them "hybrid" decisions but there is no denying that both cases

ious laws on religious practice (to use Justice Blackmun's terminology) or the "constitutiona[l] significan[ce]" of the "burden on the particular plaintiffs" (to use Justice O'Connor's terminology) suffices to permit us to confer an exemption. It is a parade of horribles because it is horrible to contemplate that federal judges will regularly balance against the importance of general laws the significance of religious practice.

expressly relied on the Free Exercise Clause and that we have consistently regarded those cases as part of the mainstream of our free exercise jurisprudence. Moreover, in each of the other cases cited by the Court to support its categorical rule, we rejected the particular constitutional claims before us only after carefully weighing the competing interests. [That] we rejected the free exercise claims in those cases hardly calls into question the applicability of First Amendment doctrine * * *. [I]t is surely unusual to judge the vitality of a constitutional doctrine by looking to the win-loss record of the plaintiffs who happen to come before us.

[W]e have never distinguished between cases in which a State conditions receipt of a benefit on conduct prohibited by religious beliefs and cases in which a State affirmatively prohibits such conduct. The *Sherbert* compelling interest test applies in both kinds of cases. [A] neutral criminal law prohibiting conduct that a State may legitimately regulate is, if anything, *more* burdensome than a neutral civil statute placing legitimate conditions on the award of a state benefit.

[Even] if, as an empirical matter, a government's criminal laws might usually serve a compelling interest in health, safety, or public order, the First Amendment at least requires a case-by-case determination of the question, sensitive to the facts of each particular claim. Given the range of conduct that a State might legitimately make criminal, we cannot assume, merely because a law carries criminal sanctions and is generally applicable, that the First Amendment *never* requires the State to grant a limited exemption for religiously motivated conduct.

Moreover, we have not "rejected" or "declined to apply" the compelling interest test in our recent cases. See, e.g., *Hobbie* (rejecting Chief Justice Burger's suggestion in *Roy,* that free exercise claims be assessed under a less rigorous "reasonable means" standard). The cases cited by the Court signal no retreat from our consistent adherence to the compelling interest test. In both *Roy* and *Lyng,* for example, we expressly distinguished *Sherbert* on the ground that the First Amendment does not "require the Government *itself* to behave in ways that the individual believes will further his or her spiritual development. [The] Free Exercise Clause simply cannot be understood to require the Government to conduct its own internal affairs in ways that comport with the religious beliefs of particular citizens." This distinction makes sense because "the Free Exercise Clause is written in terms of what the government cannot do to the individual, not in terms of what the individual can exact from the government." *Sherbert* (Douglas, J., concerning).[a] Because the case sub judice, like the other cases in which we have applied *Sherbert,* plainly falls into the former category, I would apply those established precedents to the facts of this case.

Similarly, the other cases cited by the Court for the proposition that we have rejected application of the *Sherbert* test outside the unemployment compensation field are distinguishable because they arose in the narrow, specialized contexts in which we have not traditionally required the government to justify a burden on religious conduct by articulating a compelling interest. See *Goldman v. Weinberger* ("Our review of military regulations challenged on First Amendment

a. For the view that the *Lyng* approach, which "seems to involve neither social science nor theology" is attractive to the Court because it functions to "reduce the number of claims that must be afforded the searching inquiry demanded by the free exercise clause" and to permit the Court to avoid resolving the difficult issues of "cognizability of the asserted burden, the sincerity of the claimant, and religiosity of the claim," see Lupu, *Where Rights Begin: The Problem of Burdens on The Free Exercise of Religion,* 102 Harv.L.Rev. 933 (1989).

grounds is far more deferential than constitutional review of similar laws or regulations designed for civilian society"); *O'Lone v. Shabazz* ("[P]rison regulations alleged to infringe constitutional rights are judged under a 'reasonableness' test less restrictive than that ordinarily applied to alleged infringements of fundamental constitutional rights"). That we did not apply the compelling interest test in these cases says nothing about whether the test should continue to apply in paradigm free exercise cases such as the one presented here.[b]

[We have] recognized that the Free Exercise Clause protects values distinct from those protected by the Equal Protection Clause. See *Hobbie.* As the language of the Clause itself makes clear, an individual's free exercise of religion is a preferred constitutional activity. A law that makes criminal such an activity therefore triggers constitutional concern—and heightened judicial scrutiny—even if it does not target the particular religious conduct at issue. Our free speech cases similarly recognize that neutral regulations that affect free speech values are subject to a balancing, rather than categorical, approach. See, e.g., *United States v. O'Brien,* [p. 524 supra]; *Renton v. Playtime Theatres, Inc.,* [p. 561 supra]; cf. *Anderson v. Celebrezze,* [p. 1146 infra] (generally applicable laws may impinge on free association concerns). * * *

Finally, the Court today suggests that the disfavoring of minority religions is an "unavoidable consequence" under our system of government and that accommodation of such religions must be left to the political process. In my view, however, the First Amendment was enacted precisely to protect the rights of those whose religious practices are not shared by the majority and may be viewed with hostility. The history of our free exercise doctrine amply demonstrates the harsh impact majoritarian rule has had on unpopular or emerging religious groups such as the Jehovah's Witnesses and the Amish.[c] [The] compelling interest test reflects the First Amendment's mandate of preserving religious liberty to the fullest extent possible in a pluralistic society. For the Court to deem this command a "luxury," is to denigrate "[t]he very purpose of a Bill of Rights."

III. The Court's holding today not only misreads settled First Amendment precedent; it appears to be unnecessary to this case. I would reach the same result applying our established free exercise jurisprudence.

There is no dispute that Oregon's criminal prohibition of peyote places a severe burden on the ability of respondents to freely exercise their religion. Peyote is a sacrament of the Native American Church and is regarded as vital to respondents' ability to practice their religion. * * *

b. See also McConnell, *Free Exercise Revisionism and the Smith Decision,* 57 U.Chi.L. Rev. 1109, 1127 (1990): "The Court also failed to point out that in [*Roy*], five Justices expressed the view that adherents to a traditional Abenaki religion under which computer-generated numbers are deemed to rob the individual's spirit of its power were entitled to an exemption from the requirement that welfare recipients provide a social security number on their application. This did not become a holding of the Court because one of the five Justices supporting the result concluded that this aspect of the case had become moot."

c. See also Laycock, *Formal, Substantive, and Disaggregated Neutrality Toward Religion,* 39 De Paul L.Rev. 993, 1016 (1990): "Of course, inadvertence can interact with hostility, or with an insensitivity that borders on hostility. Consider what might happen when Frances Quaring [see fn.f supra] writes her legislator. She may get a sympathetic response and a legislated exemption. But her legislator may find it so impossible to empathize with her belief that he never seriously considers whether an exemption would be workable. Even if he empathizes, the legislative calendar is crowded, and the original statute having been enacted, all the burdens of legislative inertia now work against an exemption."

There is also no dispute that Oregon has a significant interest in enforcing laws that control the possession and use of controlled substances by its citizens. [Indeed,] under federal law (incorporated by Oregon law in relevant part), peyote is specifically regulated as a Schedule I controlled substance, which means that Congress has found that it has a high potential for abuse, that there is no currently accepted medical use, and that there is a lack of accepted safety for use of the drug under medical supervision. In light of our recent decisions holding that the governmental interests in the collection of income tax, *Hernandez,* a comprehensive social security system, see *Lee,* and military conscription, see *Gillette,* are compelling, respondents do not seriously dispute that Oregon has a compelling interest in prohibiting the possession of peyote by its citizens.

Thus, the critical question in this case is whether exempting respondents from the State's general criminal prohibition "will unduly interfere with fulfillment of the governmental interest." *Lee.* Although the question is close, I would conclude that uniform application of Oregon's criminal prohibition is "essential to accomplish," *Lee,* its overriding interest in preventing the physical harm caused by the use of a Schedule I controlled substance. Oregon's criminal prohibition represents that State's judgment that the possession and use of controlled substances, even by only one person, is inherently harmful and dangerous. Because the health effects caused by the use of controlled substances exist regardless of the motivation of the user, the use of such substances, even for religious purposes, violates the very purpose of the laws that prohibit them. Moreover, in view of the societal interest in preventing trafficking in controlled substances, uniform application of the criminal prohibition at issue is essential to the effectiveness of Oregon's stated interest in preventing any possession of peyote. * * *

Respondents contend that any incompatibility is belied by the fact that the Federal Government and several States provide exemptions for the religious use of peyote. But other governments may surely choose to grant an exemption without Oregon, with its specific asserted interest in uniform application of its drug laws, being *required* to do so by the First Amendment. Respondents also note that the sacramental use of peyote is central to the tenets of the Native American Church, but I agree with the Court, that because "[i]t is not within the judicial ken to question the centrality of particular beliefs or practices to a faith," our determination of the constitutionality of Oregon's general criminal prohibition cannot, and should not, turn on the centrality of the particular religious practice at issue. This does not mean, of course, that courts may not make factual findings as to whether a claimant holds a sincerely held religious belief that conflicts with, and thus is burdened by, the challenged law. The distinction between questions of centrality and questions of sincerity and burden is admittedly fine, but it is one that is an established part of our free exercise doctrine * * *.

JUSTICE BLACKMUN, with whom JUSTICE BRENNAN and JUSTICE MARSHALL join, dissenting.

This Court over the years painstakingly has developed a consistent and exacting standard to test the constitutionality of a state statute that burdens the free exercise of religion. Such a statute may stand only if the law in general, and the State's refusal to allow a religious exemption in particular, are justified by a compelling interest that cannot be served by less restrictive means.

In weighing respondents' clear interest in the free exercise of their religion against Oregon's asserted interest in enforcing its drug laws, it is important to articulate in precise terms the state interest involved. It is not the State's broad interest in fighting the critical "war on drugs" that must be weighed against respondents' claim, but the State's narrow interest in refusing to make an exception for the religious, ceremonial use of peyote. [The] State cannot plausibly assert that unbending application of a criminal prohibition is essential to fulfill any compelling interest, if it does not, in fact, attempt to enforce that prohibition. * * * Oregon has never sought to prosecute respondents, and does not claim that it has made significant enforcement efforts against other religious users of peyote.[3] The State's asserted interest thus amounts only to the symbolic preservation of an unenforced prohibition. * * *

Similarly, this Court's prior decisions have not allowed a government to rely on mere speculation about potential harms, but have demanded evidentiary support for a refusal to allow a religious exception. [In] this case, the State's justification for refusing to recognize an exception to its criminal laws for religious peyote use is entirely speculative.

The State [offers] no evidence that the religious use of peyote has ever harmed anyone.[4] The factual findings of other courts cast doubt on the State's assumption that religious use of peyote is harmful. See *State v. Whittingham,* 19 Ariz.App. 27, 30, 504 P.2d 950, 953 (1973) ("the State failed to prove that the quantities of peyote used in the sacraments of the Native American Church are sufficiently harmful to the health and welfare of the participants so as to permit a legitimate intrusion under the State's police power"); *People v. Woody,* 61 Cal. 2d 716, 722–723, 40 Cal.Rptr. 69, 74, 394 P.2d 813, 818 (1964) ("as the Attorney General [admits,] the opinion of scientists and other experts is 'that peyote [works] no permanent deleterious injury to the Indian' ").

The fact that peyote is classified as a Schedule I controlled substance does not, by itself, show that any and all uses of peyote, in any circumstance, are inherently harmful and dangerous. The Federal Government, which created the classifications of unlawful drugs from which Oregon's drug laws are derived, apparently does not find peyote so dangerous as to preclude an exemption for religious use.[5] Moreover, other Schedule I drugs have lawful uses. See *Olsen v. Drug Enforcement Admin.* (medical and research uses of marijuana).

The carefully circumscribed ritual context in which respondents used peyote is far removed from the irresponsible and unrestricted recreational use of unlawful drugs.[6] * * * [7]

3. The only reported case in which the State of Oregon has sought to prosecute a person for religious peyote use is *State v. Soto,* 21 Ore.App. 794, 537 P.2d 142 (1975).

4. This dearth of evidence is not surprising, since the State never asserted this health and safety interest before the Oregon courts; thus, there was no opportunity for factfinding concerning the alleged dangers of peyote use. What has now become the State's principal argument for its view that the criminal prohibition is enforceable against religious use of peyote rests on no evidentiary foundation at all.

5. [Moreover,] 23 States, including many that have significant Native American populations, have statutory or judicially crafted exemptions in their drug laws for religious use of peyote.

6. In this respect, respondents' use of peyote seems closely analogous to the sacramental use of wine by the Roman Catholic Church. During Prohibition, the Federal Government exempted such use of wine from its general ban on possession and use of alcohol. However compelling the Government's then general interest in prohibiting the use of alcohol may have been, it could not plausibly have asserted an interest sufficiently compelling to outweigh Catholics' right to take communion.

7. The use of peyote is, to some degree, self-limiting. The peyote plant is extremely bitter, and eating it is an unpleasant experience, which would tend to discourage casual or recreational use.

Moreover, just as in *Yoder,* the values and interests of those seeking a religious exemption in this case are congruent, to a great degree, with those the State seeks to promote through its drug laws. See *Yoder* (since the Amish accept formal schooling up to 8th grade, and then provide "ideal" vocational education, State's interest in enforcing its law against the Amish is "less substantial than [for] children generally"). Not only does the Church's doctrine forbid nonreligious use of peyote; it also generally advocates self-reliance, familial responsibility, and abstinence from alcohol. There is considerable evidence that the spiritual and social support provided by the Church has been effective in combatting the tragic effects of alcoholism on the Native American population. * * *

The State also seeks to support its refusal to make an exception for religious use of peyote by invoking its interest in abolishing drug trafficking. There is, however, practically no illegal traffic in peyote. Also, the availability of peyote for religious use, even if Oregon were to allow an exemption from its criminal laws, would still be strictly controlled by federal regulations, see 21 U.S.C. §§ 821–823 (registration requirements for distribution of controlled substances); and by the State of Texas, the only State in which peyote grows in significant quantities. Peyote simply is not a popular drug; its distribution for use in religious rituals has nothing to do with the vast and violent traffic in illegal narcotics that plagues this country.

Finally, the State argues that, [if] it grants an exemption for religious peyote use, a flood of other claims to religious exemptions will follow. It would then be placed in a dilemma, it says, between allowing a patchwork of exemptions that would hinder its law enforcement efforts, and risking a violation of the Establishment Clause by arbitrarily limiting its religious exemptions. [This] Court, however, consistently has rejected similar arguments in past free exercise cases, and it should do so here as well. [And almost] half the States, and the Federal Government, have maintained an exemption for religious peyote use for many years, and apparently have not found themselves overwhelmed by claims to other religious exemptions.[8] Allowing an exemption for religious peyote use would not necessarily oblige the State to grant a similar exemption to other religious groups. The unusual circumstances that make the religious use of peyote compatible with the State's interests in health and safety and in preventing drug trafficking would not apply to other religious claims. Some religions, for example, might not restrict drug use to a limited ceremonial context, as does the Native American Church. See, e.g., *Olsen* ("the Ethiopian Zion Coptic Church [teaches] that marijuana is properly smoked 'continually all day' "). Some religious claims involve drugs such as marijuana and heroin, in which there is significant illegal traffic, with its attendant greed and violence, so that it would be difficult to grant a religious exemption without seriously compromising law enforcement efforts.[9] That the State might grant an exemption for religious peyote use, but deny other religious claims arising in different circumstances, would not violate the Establishment Clause. Though the State must treat all religions equally, and not favor one over another, this obligation is fulfilled by

8. Over the years, various sects have raised free exercise claims regarding drug use. In no reported case, except those involving claims of religious peyote use, has the claimant prevailed.

9. Thus, this case is distinguishable from *Lee,* in which the Court concluded that there was "no principled way" to distinguish other exemption claims, and the "tax system could not function if denominations were allowed to challenge the tax system because tax payments were spent in a manner that violates their religious belief."

the uniform application of the "compelling interest" *test* to all free exercise claims, not by reaching uniform *results* as to all claims. * * *

Finally, although I agree with Justice O'Connor that courts should refrain from delving into questions of whether, as a matter of religious doctrine, a particular practice is "central" to the religion, I do not think this means that the courts must turn a blind eye to the severe impact of a State's restrictions on the adherents of a minority religion.

Respondents believe, and their sincerity has *never* been at issue, that the peyote plant embodies their deity, and eating it is an act of worship and communion. Without peyote, they could not enact the essential ritual of their religion. [This] potentially devastating impact must be viewed in light of the federal policy—reached in reaction to many years of religious persecution and intolerance—of protecting the religious freedom of Native Americans. See American Indian Religious Freedom Act. * * *

Notes and Questions

1. *"Generally applicable" regulations, "neutrality," and the religion clauses.* Are the positions of the Justices comprising both the majority and dissent in *Smith* consistent with their positions in other religion cases? Consider Laycock, *The Remnants of Free Exercise,* 1990 Sup.Ct.Rev. ___, ___: "Four Justices [O'Connor, J., joined by Brennan, Marshall and Blackmun, JJ.] found religion-blindness undeniably neutral in the context of taxation [in *Swaggart*], but oppressive in the context of regulation [in *Smith*]. *Swaggart's* claim that formally neutral taxation 'neither advances nor inhibits religion' invokes the language of the cases on government payments to church-sponsored schools, but it is inconsistent with the substance of those cases. When government pays money to church-sponsored schools, the Court says the benefit advances religion; it is irrelevant that government spends comparable sums on secular schools. But when government takes money from churches, the 'burden is not constitutionally significant,' and it is dispositive that government takes comparable sums from secular taxpayers."

2. *Balancing process.* Of what significance is it that all the decisions sustaining free exercise claims against government regulations of conduct (*Sherbert—Thomas—Hobbie, Yoder* and *Roy*) involved religious refusal to engage in conduct required by government rather than religiously dictated action forbidden by the state? What should be the results in respect to the religiously mandated *inaction* in the following: (a) Citing for contempt person who refuses to serve on jury. See *In re Jenison,* 265 Minn. 96, 120 N.W.2d 515 (1963), vacated, 375 U.S. 14, 84 S.Ct. 63, 11 L.Ed.2d 39 (1963), reversed, 267 Minn. 136, 125 N.W.2d 588 (1963); (b) Statute requiring smallpox vaccination applied to person whose religion forbids medicinal aids. See *Jacobson v. Massachusetts,* 197 U.S. 11, 25 S.Ct. 358, 49 L.Ed. 643 (1905); (c) Court order of blood transfusion, to save life of pregnant mother and child, for woman of Jehovah's Witness faith which obligates adherents to "abstain from blood." Suppose the woman were not pregnant but had infant children? See *Application of Georgetown College, Inc.,* 331 F.2d 1000 (D.C.Cir.1964), cert. denied, 377 U.S. 978, 84 S.Ct. 1883, 12 L.Ed.2d 746 (1964). Suppose the woman were neither pregnant nor had any children? Suppose there were only a slight chance that the transfusion would save the life? That the woman is a brilliant scientist whose work is vital to national security? Suppose the transfusion is thought necessary not to preserve life but to bring back to good health?

3. *Willingness of others.* In the case of *action* due to religious beliefs, should a distinction be drawn between action that is requested by the people affected and action that is imposed on others? Should the conviction of a religious Spiritualist for fortune telling be sustained despite the fact that fortunes were told only upon request? If not, how do you distinguish the polygamy cases?[a]

II. UNUSUAL RELIGIOUS BELIEFS AND PRACTICES

1. In UNITED STATES v. BALLARD, 322 U.S. 78, 64 S.Ct. 882, 88 L.Ed. 1148 (1944), defendant was indicted for mail fraud. He had solicited funds for the "I Am" movement, asserting, inter alia, that he had been selected as a divine messenger, had the divine power of healing incurable diseases, and had talked with Jesus and would transmit these conversations to mankind. The Court, per DOUGLAS, J., held that the first amendment barred submitting to the jury the question of whether these religious beliefs were true: "Men may believe what they cannot prove. * * * Religious experiences which are as real as life to some may be incomprehensible to others. [The] miracles of the New Testament, the Divinity of Christ, life after death, the power of prayer are deep in the religious convictions of many. If one could be sent to jail because a jury in a hostile environment found those teachings false, little indeed would be left of religious freedom."

(a) Should the prosecution be permitted to prove that, irrespective of whether the incidents described by defendant happened, he did not honestly believe that they had? If so, may the prosecution introduce evidence that the incidents did not in fact happen and that therefore defendant could not honestly believe that they did? Should this line of proof be permitted in the prosecution of an official of the Catholic church for soliciting funds to construct a shrine commemorating the Miracle of Fatima in 1930?

(b) Is it relevant that in *Ballard* the alleged divine revelation was made to defendant himself? Would it be material if the experiences had allegedly occurred at a definite time and place? Many Biblical happenings are so identified. Could the prosecution introduce evidence that Ballard was not physically present at the alleged place at the alleged time? If Protestant, Catholic or Jewish clergy were prosecuted and there was overwhelming scientific evidence disputing the Biblical doctrine, what would the jury be likely to find as to the honesty of the beliefs? Should the first amendment permit people to obtain money in the name of religion by knowingly making false statements? See Tribe, *American Constitutional Law* 1243–47 (2d ed. 1988).

(c) Should the prosecution be able to prove that defendant had stated on many occasions that he believed none of his representations but that by saying that he did he was amassing great wealth? Suppose it can be shown that a priest or rabbi is *somewhat* skeptical as to the truth of certain Biblical occurrences? See Noonan, *How Sincere Do You Have to Be to Be Religious,* 1988 U.Ill. L.Rev. 713. Could Ballard be convicted on the ground that fraudulent procure-

a. For earlier reviews of the cases and refined "balancing" approaches, see Dodge, *The Free Exercise of Religion: A Sociological Approach,* 67 Mich.L.Rev. 679 (1969); Giannella, *Religious Liberty, Nonestablishment, and Doctrinal Development—Part I. The Religious Liberty Guarantee,* 80 Harv.L.Rev. 1381–1423 (1967); Rodes, *Sub Deo et Lege: A Study of Free Exercise,* 4 Relig. & Pub.Or. 3 (1968); Clark, *Guidelines for the Free Exercise Clause,* 83 Harv.L.Rev. 327 (1969); Marcus, *The Forum of Conscience: Applying Standards Under the Free Exercise Clause,* 1973 Duke L.J. 1217.

ment of money, just like polygamy, is conduct which may be constitutionally prohibited even if done in the name of religion?

2. *What is "religion"?* May the Court determine that asserted religious beliefs and practices do not constitute a valid religion? Consider Weiss, *Privilege, Posture and Protection—"Religion" in the Law,* 73 Yale L.J. 593, 604 (1964): "[A]ny definition of religion would seem to violate religious freedom in that it would dictate to religions, present and future, what they must [be]. Furthermore, an attempt to define religion, even for purposes of increasing freedom for religions, would run afoul of the 'establishment' clause as excluding some religions, or even as establishing a notion respecting religion."

Is it relevant that the beliefs of a group do not include the existence of God? TORCASO v. WATKINS, per BLACK, J., 367 U.S. 488, 81 S.Ct. 1680, 6 L.Ed.2d 982 (1961), invalidating a Maryland provision requiring a declaration of belief in the existence of God as a test for public office, stated: "Neither [a state nor the federal government can] impose requirements which aid all religions as against nonbelievers, and neither can aid those religions based on a belief in the existence of God as against those religions founded on different beliefs." The Court noted that "among religions in this country which do not teach what would generally be considered a belief in the existence of God are Buddhism, Taoism, Ethical Culture, Secular Humanism and others."

What if the Communist Party claimed religious status? Consider Kauper, *Religion and the Constitution* 31 (1964): "What makes secular humanism a religion? Is it because it is an ideology or system of belief that attempts to furnish a rationale of life? But if any ideology, creed, or philosophy respecting man and society is a religion, then must not democracy, fascism, and communism also qualify as religions? It is not uncommon to refer to these as secular or quasi religions, for some find in these systems an adequate explanation of the meaning and purpose of life and the source of values that command faith and devotion. Certainly in the case of communism, with its discipline, its cultus, its sense of community, and its obligation to duties owing to the system, the resemblance to religion in the conventional sense is [clear]."

May a single person establish his or her own religion? Consider Konvitz, *Religious Liberty and Conscience* 84 (1968): "[Many religions] had their origin in a 'private and personal' religious experience. Mohammed did not take over an on-going, established religion; the history of Islam records the names of his first three converts. John Wesley is given credit as the founder of Methodism. Mrs. Mary Baker Eddy was the founder of the Christian Science church. Menno Simons organized a division of Anabaptists that in due course became the sect known as the Mennonites. Jacob Ammon broke away from the Mennonites and founded the sect known as the Amish."

How important is it that the group has regular weekly services? Designated leaders who conduct these services? Ceremonies for naming, marrying and burying members? Does the first amendment extend only to those groups that conform to the "conventional" concept of religion? Consider Cox (Harvard Divinity School), N.Y. Times 25 (Feb. 16, 1977): "[C]ourts [often] turn to some vague 'man-in-the-street' idea of what 'religion' should be. [But] a man-in-the-street approach would surely have ruled out early Christianity, which seemed both subversive and atheistic to the religious Romans of the day. The truth is that one man's 'bizarre cult' is another's true path to salvation, and the Bill of Rights was designed to safeguard minorities from the man-on-the-street's uncertain capacity for tolerance. The new challenge to our pluralism often comes from Oriental religious movements, because their views of religion differ so fundamentally from ours." To what extent should a group's "brainwashing," mental coercion techniques affect its constitutional status as a "religion"? Compare Delgado, *Religious Totalism: Gentle and Ungentle Persuasion Under the First Amendment,* 51 So.Cal.L.Rev. 1 (1977) with Note, *Conservatorship and Religious Cults: Divining A Theory of Free Exercise,* 53 N.Y.U.L.Rev. 1247 (1978).

Suppose that a group has certain characteristics of "traditional" religions, such as a holy book, ministers, houses of worship, prescribed prayers, a strict moral code, a belief in the hereafter and an appeal to faith, but also has announced social and economic tenets? (Methodism developed originally out of social concerns.) Consider Note, *Toward a Constitutional Definition of Religion,* 91 Harv.L.Rev. 1056, 1069 (1978): "[A] spokesman for the new 'liberation theology' within Catholicism argues that true religion is to be found in liberation 'as the creation of a new social consciousness and as a social appropriation not only of the means of production, but also of the political processes.' The church, he says, seeks 'the abolition of the exploitation of man by man.' The views of these and other significant Christian theologians coalesce around one important theme: the Christian church will find itself only by discarding what until now has been perceived to be religious and by immersing itself in the secular world." Does the first amendment encompass any philosophical, moral or social doctrine espoused by some group in the name of religion?

UNITED STATES v. SEEGER, 380 U.S. 163, 85 S.Ct. 850, 13 L.Ed.2d 733 (1965), interpreted § 6(j) of the Universal Military Training and Service Act, which exempted from combat any person "who, by reason of religious training and belief, is conscientiously opposed to participation in war in any form. Religious training and belief in this connection means an individual's belief in a relation to a Supreme Being involving duties superior to those arising from any human relation, but does not include essentially political, sociological or philosophical views or a merely personal moral code."[a] The Court, per CLARK, J., avoided constitutional questions and upheld claims for exemption of three conscientious objectors. One declared "that he preferred to leave the question as to his belief in a Supreme Being open, [and] that his was a 'belief in and devotion to goodness and virtue for their own sakes, and a religious faith in a purely ethical creed.'" Another said "that he felt it a violation of his moral code to take human life and that he considered this belief superior to his obligation to the state. As to whether his conviction was religious, he quoted with approval Reverend John Haynes Holmes' definition of religion as 'the consciousness of some power manifest in nature which helps man in the ordering of his life in harmony with its demands * * *; it is man thinking his highest, feeling his deepest, and living his best.' The source of his conviction he attributed to reading and meditation 'in our democratic American culture, with its values derived from the western religious and philosophical tradition.' As to his belief in a Supreme Being, Peter stated that he supposed 'you could call that a belief in the Supreme Being or God. These just do not happen to be the words I use.'"

The Court "concluded that Congress, in using the expression 'Supreme Being' rather than the designation 'God,' was merely clarifying the meaning of religious training and belief so as to embrace all religions and to exclude

a. The statute was subsequently amended to omit the "belief in a Supreme Being" element.

essentially political, sociological, or philosophical views [and that] the test of belief 'in a relation to a Supreme Being' is whether a given belief that is sincere and meaningful occupies a place in the life of its possessor parallel to that filled by the orthodox belief in God of one who clearly qualifies for the exemption.[b] [No] party claims to be an atheist * * *. We do not deal with or intimate any decision on that situation in these cases. [The] use by Congress of the words 'merely personal' seems to us to restrict the exception to a moral code which [is] in no way related to a Supreme Being. [Congress did] not distinguish between externally and internally derived beliefs. Such a determination [would] prove impossible as a practical matter."

In WELSH v. UNITED STATES, 398 U.S. 333, 90 S.Ct. 1792, 26 L.Ed.2d 308 (1970), petitioner, in his application for exemption, "struck the word 'religious' entirely and later characterized his beliefs as having been formed 'by reading in the fields of history and sociology.'" BLACK, J., joined by Douglas, Brennan and Marshall, JJ., held that, under *Seeger,* "if an individual deeply and sincerely holds beliefs which are purely ethical or moral in source and content but that nevertheless impose upon him a duty of conscience to refrain from participating in any war at any time, those beliefs certainly occupy in the life of that individual 'a place parallel to that filled [by] God' in traditionally religious persons." "Although [Welsh] originally characterized his beliefs as nonreligious, he later upon reflection wrote a long and thoughtful letter to his Appeal Board in which he declared that his beliefs were 'certainly religious in the ethical sense of that word.' * * * § 6(j)'s exclusion of those persons with 'essentially political, sociological, or philosophical views or a merely personal moral code' should [not] be read to exclude those who hold strong beliefs about our domestic and foreign affairs or even those whose conscientious objection to participation in all wars is founded to a substantial extent upon considerations of public policy. The two groups of registrants which obviously do fall within these exclusions from the exemption are those whose beliefs are not deeply held and those whose objection to war does not rest at all upon moral, ethical, or religious principle but instead rests solely upon considerations of policy, pragmatism, or expediency." [c]

3. *What is "religious belief"?* (a) Of what significance is it that the practice is an "age-old form" of religious conduct (see *Murdock*)? Is a "cardinal principle" of the asserted religious faith (see *Sherbert*)? Consider Laycock, fn. b in *Jaffree,* Sec. 1, I supra, at 1390–91: "Many activities that obviously are exercises of religion are not required by conscience or doctrine. Singing in the church choir and saying the Roman Catholic rosary are two common examples. Any activity engaged in by a church as a body is an exercise of religion. [Indeed,] many would say that an emphasis on rules and obligations misconceives the essential nature of some religions." Compare Giannella, fn. a, Part I supra, at 1427–28: "[Use of hallucinogenics] should be denied the status of religious claims

b. Consider Note, 91 Harv.L.Rev. at 1065 n. 37: "[*Seeger*] left several important questions unanswered: What does it mean to say that a principle occupies a place parallel to that of a traditional deity? Must that principle explain the existence of the cosmos, of humankind? Need it be the source of moral precepts, punishing infractions in this life or the next?"

c. In separate opinions, Harlan, J., and White, J., (joined by Burger, C.J., and Stewart, J.) dissented on the issue of statutory construction. For their views on the constitutional issue, see Sec. 4 infra.

See generally Note, *Defining Religion,* 32 U.Chi.L.Rev. 533 (1965); Note, *The Sacred and the Profane: A First Amendment Definition of Religion,* 61 Tex.L.Rev. 139 (1982). For criticism of "sincerity," see Comment, *The Legal Relationship of Conscience to Religion: Refusals to Bear Arms,* 38 U.Chi.L.Rev. 583 (1971).

[because] denial [does] not create problems for the individual's conscience similar to those created by traditionally religious claims to freedom of worship. Personal alienation from one's Maker, frustration of one's ultimate mission in life, and violation of the religious person's integrity are all at stake when the right to worship is threatened. Although the seeker of new psychological worlds may feel equally frustrated when deprived of his gropings for a higher reality, there is not the same sense of acute loss—the loss of the Be-all and End-all of life. [A] different problem presents itself when an individual who does not believe in a supernatural or personal God asserts conscientious objection to certain conduct because of its injurious effects on his fellow man. [T]his ethical belief may be held with such a degree of intensity that its violation occasions the same interior revulsion and anguish as does violation of the law of God to the pious." Under this approach, on what evidence should these factual questions be determined? Suppose a drug-use defendant claims "that its use was essential to attain a unique level of spiritual consciousness [and] compared the effect of depriving him of marihuana with that of forbidding a Catholic to celebrate the Mass"? Finer, *Psychedelics and Religious Freedom,* 19 Hastings L.J. 667, 692 (1968).

For the view that "belief [in] 'extratemporal consequences'—whether the effects of actions taken pursuant or contrary to the dictates of a person's beliefs extend in some meaningful way beyond his lifetime—is a sensible and desirable criterion (albeit plainly far short of ideal) for determining when the free exercise clause should trigger judicial consideration of whether an exemption from general government regulations of conduct is constitutionally required," see Choper, *Defining "Religion" in the First Amendment,* 1982 U.Ill.L.Rev. 579, 599, 603–04: [d] "It may be persuasively argued that *all* beliefs that invoke a transcendent reality—and especially those that provide their adherents with glimpses of meaning and truth that make them so important and so uncompromisable—should be encompassed by the special constitutional protection granted 'religion' by the free exercise clause. [In] many ways, however, transcendental explanations of worldly realities are essentially no different [than] conventional exegeses for temporal outcomes that are based on such 'rational' disciplines as economics, political science, sociology, or psychology, or even such 'hard' sciences [as] physics. When justifying competing government policies on such varied matters as social welfare, the economy, and military and foreign affairs, there is at bedrock only a gossamer line between 'rational' and 'supernatural' causation—the former really being little more capable of 'scientific proof' than the latter. [Therefore, government's] plenary authority to regulate the worldly affairs of society [should] not be restricted because of the nature of the causes, which are all basically unverifiable, that different groups believe will produce consequences that the state seeks to achieve."

For the view that this approach "does not promise to yield sound results for many free exercise cases," see Greenawalt, *Religion as a Concept in Constitutional Law,* 72 Calif.L.Rev. 753, 763, 815 (1984): "No specification of essential conditions will capture all and only the beliefs, practices, and organizations that are regarded as religious in modern culture and should be treated as such under the Constitution. [Rather, determining] whether questionable beliefs, practices, and organizations are religious by seeing how closely they resemble what is

d. For criticism of this view, see Ingber, *Religion or Ideology: A Needed Clarification of the Religion Clauses,* 41 Stan.L.Rev. 233, 274–77 (1989); Note, *Religion and Morality Legislation: A Reexamination of Establishment Clause Analysis,* 59 N.Y.U.L.Rev. 301, 346–52 (1984); Note, *Defining "Religion" in the First Amendment: A Functional Approach,* 74 Corn.L.Rev. 532 (1989).

undeniably religious is a method that has been implicitly used by courts in difficult borderline cases [and] is consonant with Supreme Court decisions." See also Freeman, *The Misguided Search for the Constitutional Definition of "Religion,"* 71 Geo.L.J. 1519 (1983).

(b) *Judicial role.* In THOMAS v. REVIEW BD., Part I supra, petitioner testified that, although his religious convictions forbade him to manufacture weapons, "he could, in good conscience, engage indirectly in the production, [for] example, as an employee of a raw material supplier or of a roll foundry." The Indiana Supreme Court, viewing petitioner's positions as inconsistent, ruled that "Thomas had made a merely 'personal philosophical choice rather than a religious choice.'" The Court, per BURGER, C.J. reversed: "The determination of what is a 'religious' belief or practice is more often than not a difficult and delicate task, [but] resolution of that question is not to turn upon a judicial perception of the particular belief or practice in question; religious beliefs need not be acceptable, logical, consistent, or comprehensible to others in order to merit First Amendment protection.

" * * * Thomas drew a line and it is not for us to say that the line he drew was an unreasonable one. Courts should not undertake to dissect religious beliefs because the believer admits that he is 'struggling' with his position or because his beliefs are not articulated with the clarity and precision that a more sophisticated person might employ.

"The Indiana court also appears to have given significant weight to the fact that another Jehovah's Witness had no scruples about working on tank turrets; for that other Witness, at least, such work was 'scripturally' acceptable. Intrafaith differences of that kind are not uncommon among followers of a particular creed, and the judicial process is singularly ill equipped to resolve such differences in relation to the Religion Clauses. [The] narrow function of a reviewing court in this context is to determine whether there was an appropriate finding that petitioner terminated his work because of an honest conviction that such work was forbidden by his religion."

4. *Variable definition.* (a) May "religion" be defined differently for purposes of the establishment clause than the free exercise clause? Consider Galanter, *Religious Freedom in the United States: A Turning Point?* 1966 Wis. L.Rev. 217, 266–67: "[For purposes of the establishment clause, the] effect and purpose of government action are not to be assessed by the religious sensibilities of the person who is complaining of the alleged establishment. It must be essentially religious in some widely shared public understanding. [But, for the free exercise clause, the] claimants' view of religion controls the characterization of their objection as a religious one." Does this analysis solve the dilemma of Manning, note 5, after *Wallace v. Jaffree,* supra, at 66: "If religion need not be predicated on a belief in God or even in a god and if it may not be tested by the common consensus of what reasonable men would reasonably call religion, if it is so private that—so long as it does not inflict injury on society—it is immured from governmental interference and from judicial inquiry, [might] not a group of gymnasts proclaiming on their trampolines that physical culture is their religion be engaged in a religious exercise? And if Congress, in a particular Olympic year, appropriated funds to subsidize their calisthenics would this not [be] an establishment of religion?" See generally Note, *Transcendental Meditation and the Meaning of Religion Under the Establishment Clause,* 62 Minn.L.Rev. 887 (1978).

(b) May a group be considered a religion for the purpose of prosecution for fraudulent solicitation but not a religion for the purposes of statutory tax exemption or draft exemption? May government test the sincerity of asserted religious beliefs in one instance but not the other? See Nowak, Rotunda & Young, *Constitutional Law* 1088 (3d ed. 1986).

SECTION 3. PREFERENCE AMONG RELIGIONS

LARSON v. VALENTE, 456 U.S. 228, 102 S.Ct. 1673, 72 L.Ed.2d 33 (1982), involved a challenge by the Unification Church ("Moonies") to "a Minnesota statute, imposing certain registration and reporting requirements upon only those religious organizations that solicit more than fifty per cent of their funds from nonmembers." The Court, per BRENNAN, J., noting that "the clearest command of the Establishment Clause is that one religious denomination cannot be officially preferred over another, [*Everson*]," and that the "constitutional prohibition of denominational preferences is inextricably connected with the continuing vitality of the Free Exercise Clause," held that the statute violated the establishment clause because it did not survive "strict scrutiny." [a] Assuming that the state's "valid secular purpose [in] protecting its citizens from abusive practices in the solicitation of funds for charity" is "compelling," the state "failed to demonstrate that the fifty per cent rule [is] 'closely fitted' " to furthering that interest. Moreover, the statute failed the third *Lemon* "test": "The fifty per cent [rule] effects the *selective* legislative imposition of burdens and advantages upon particular denominations. The 'risk of politicizing religion' that inheres in such legislation is obvious, and indeed is confirmed by the provision's legislative history [which] demonstrates that the provision was drafted with the explicit intention of including particular religious denominations and excluding others."

WHITE, J., joined by Rehnquist, J., dissented,[b] disagreeing with the Court's view "that the rule on its face represents an explicit and deliberate preference for some religious beliefs over others": "The rule [names] no churches or denominations that are entitled to or denied the exemption. [Some] religions will qualify and some will not, but this depends on the source of their contribu-

a. The Court rejected the argument that the statute was merely "a law based upon secular criteria which may not identically affect all religious organizations." This "is not simply a facially neutral statute, the provisions of which happen to have a 'disparate impact' upon different religious organizations. On the contrary [it] makes explicit and deliberate distinctions between different religious organizations [and] effectively distinguishes between 'well-established churches' that have 'achieved strong but not total financial support from their members,' on the one hand, and 'churches which are new and lacking in a constituency, or, which, as a matter of policy, may favor public solicitation over general reliance on financial support from members,' on the other hand."

The Court found *Gillette v. United States,* Sec. 2, I supra, "readily distinguishable": "In that case, we rejected an Establishment Clause attack upon § 6(j) of the Military Selective Service Act of 1967, which afforded 'conscientious objector' status to any person who, 'by reason of religious training and belief,' was 'conscientiously opposed to participation in war in any form * * *.' Section 6(j) 'focused on individual conscientious belief, not on sectarian affiliation.' Under § 6(j), conscientious objector status was available on an equal basis to both the Quaker and the Roman Catholic, despite the distinction drawn by the latter's church between 'just' and 'unjust' wars. As we noted in *Gillette,* the 'critical weakness of petitioners' establishment claim' arose 'from the fact that § 6(j), on its face, simply [did] not discriminate on the basis of religious affiliation.' In contrast, the statute challenged in the case before us focuses precisely and solely upon religious organizations."

b. Rehnquist, J., joined by Burger, C.J. and White and O'Connor, JJ., also dissented on the ground that appellee Unification Church had no standing.

tions, not on their brand of religion. [The Court's assertion] that the limitation might burden the less well-organized denominations [is contrary to the state's claim] that both categories include not only well-established, but also not so well-established organizations. The Court appears to concede that the Minnesota law at issue does not constitute an establishment of religion merely because it has a disparate impact. An intentional preference must be expressed. To find that intention on the face of the provision at issue here seems to me to be patently wrong." [c] Further, "I cannot join the Court's easy rejection of the state's submission that a valid secular purpose justifies basing the exemption on the percentage of external funding." Finally, there is arguably "a more evident secular reason for exempting religious organizations who rely on their members to a great extent than there is to exempt all religious organizations; [the latter] could be said to prefer religious organizations over non-religious organizations and hence amount to an establishment of religion."

Notes and Questions

1. *The Gillette rationale.* (a) Should the existence of a "neutral, secular justification" justify government preference—de jure or de facto—among religions? Consider Greenawalt, *All or Nothing at All: The Defeat of Selective Conscientious Objection,* 1971 Sup.Ct.Rev. 31, 71: "If a sociological survey indicated that Protestants generally work harder than Catholics, the government might simplify its hiring problems by interviewing only Protestants. If the doctors of Catholic hospitals were determined to be on the average more qualified than those at Lutheran hospitals, aid might be limited to the Catholic hospitals. It is, of course, inconceivable that such legislation would be passed and its unconstitutionality is [apparent]." How significant was the Court's observation that the *Gillette* law "attempts to accommodate free exercise values"?

(b) Was the Draft Act of 1917, which exempted only conscientious objectors affiliated with some "well-recognized religious sect" whose principles forbade participation in war, also valid under the *Gillette* rationale? Consider 48 Minn.L. Rev. 776–77 (1964): "Since pacifism often arises from religious beliefs, a workable method for ascertaining sincerity may have to be couched in terms of those beliefs. Such a test should be permissible, even though it may theoretically 'prefer' some sincere conscientious objectors over others, if it reasonably advances the [statute's] purpose by aiding local draft boards in administering the act. For example, since membership in an organized pacifist sect may be better evidence of sincerity than the mere assertion of pacificist beliefs, a requirement to that effect should be permissible." See also Comment, 64 Colum.L.Rev. 938 (1964).

2. *The Larson rationale.* (a) Consider Choper, *The Free Exercise Clause: A Structural Overview and An Appraisal of Recent Developments,* 27 Wm. & M.L. Rev. 943, 958–61 (1986): "*Larson* should be seen as a free exercise clause decision parading in an establishment clause disguise. [The] major thrust of the Court's opinion [used] classic free exercise clause analysis, [holding] that discrimination among religions must survive strict scrutiny. [The] major disagreement between the majority and dissent concerned whether this law discriminated among religions or simply was a neutral law with a disparate impact on different religious groups. [But even if] the Minnesota statute did not specifically give preference to some religions over others, it did expressly deal with the subject of religion, and it

c. *Gillette* held that there was no religious "gerrymander" if there was "a neutral, secular basis for the lines government has drawn."

resulted in favoring some and disfavoring others. In my view, it should have been as vulnerable—that is, subject to the same level of scrutiny—as a general, neutral law that says nothing about religion but that happens to have an adverse impact on some faiths, like the Wisconsin compulsory education law at issue in *Yoder.* The problem is that when the Court has invoked the establishment clause, it has applied a much more lenient test to laws that expressly deal with religion and subject some faiths to discriminatory treatment than it has applied under the free exercise clause to general, neutral laws that come into conflict with religious beliefs. [*Gillette*] ruled that as long as Congress had a "valid secular reason" for the law, that law could survive an establishment clause challenge. [If] that were all that the Court had required in *Larson* [it] would have had no problem upholding the Minnesota [statute]. In reality, I believe that the Selective Service Act survived strict scrutiny in *Gillette* [because of the] powerful government interest in raising an army and the difficulties in administering a draft exemption based on "just war" beliefs. [In] sum, the doctrine in *Gillette,* that a valid secular basis for de facto religious discrimination is enough to sustain it under the establishment clause, plainly supports Justice White's dissent in *Larson.* The *Gillette* doctrine, however, effectively has been abandoned, and rightly so. Laws that explicitly deal with the subject of religion, and result in a preference of some religions over others, fall into a separate category of government action that ought to be treated under the free exercise clause. Although *Larson* did not purport to analyze the statute in that case under the free exercise clause, it explicitly employed a rationale that does."

(b) HERNANDEZ v. COMMISSIONER, 490 U.S. 680, 109 S.Ct. 2136, 104 L.Ed.2d 766 (1989), per MARSHALL, J., found no violation of the establishment clause in not permitting federal taxpayers to deduct as "charitable contributions" payments to the Church of Scientology for "auditing" and "training" sessions. A central tenet of the Church requires "fixed donations" for these sessions to study the faith's tenets and to increase spiritual awareness. The proceeds are the Church's primary source of income:

Unlike *Larson,* IRS disallowance for payments made "with some expectation of a quid pro quo in terms of goods or services [makes] no 'explicit and deliberate distinctions between different religious organizations,' applying instead to all religious entities. [It] may be that a consequence of the quid pro quo orientation of the 'contribution or gift' requirement is to impose a disparate burden on those charitable and religious groups that rely on sales of commodities or services as a means of fund-raising, relative to those groups that raise funds primarily by soliciting unilateral donations. But a statute primarily having a secular effect does not violate the Establishment Clause merely because it 'happens to coincide or harmonize with the tenets of some or all religions.' *McGowan.*"

Because of the absence of "a proper factual record," the Court did not consider the contention of O'CONNOR, J., joined by Scalia, J., dissenting, that "at least some of the fixed payments which the IRS has treated as charitable deductions [are as much a 'quid pro quo exchange'] as the payments [here]": "In exchange for their payment of pew rents, Christians receive particular seats during worship services. Similarly, in some synagogues attendance at the worship services for Jewish High Holy Days is often predicated upon the purchase of a general admission ticket or a reserved seat ticket. Religious honors such as publicly reading from Scripture are purchased or auctioned periodically in some synagogues of Jews from Morocco and Syria. Mormons must tithe ten percent of their income as a necessary but not sufficient condition to obtaining a 'temple recommend,' i.e., the right to be admitted into the temple. A Mass stipend—a fixed payment given to a Catholic priest, in consideration of which he is obliged to apply the fruits of the Mass for the intention of the donor—has similar overtones of exchange. [Thus, the case] involves the differential application of a standard based on constitutionally impermissible differences drawn by the Government among religions." Brennan and Kennedy, JJ., did not participate.

3. *Preference for "religious" objectors.* Is Congress' limitation of draft exemption to "religious" conscientious objectors valid? Consider Mansfield, *Conscientious Objection—1964 Term,* 1965 Relig. & Pub.Or. 3, 76: "[T]here are really no convincing reasons why the religious objector should be exempt and not the non-religious conscientious objector. [T]he religious objector's opposition rests on somewhat more fundamental grounds [and] makes reference to realities that can more easily be described as spiritual. But the non-religious conscientious objector's opposition does rest on basic propositions about the nature of reality and the significance of human existence; this is what distinguishes it from objection that is not even conscientious. Even if the non-religious conscientious objector does not subscribe to the answers nor perceive the vision of the religious objector, he does at least address himself to questions that are nearly as fundamental, and it is in respect to the dialogue within this general area of fundamental issues that government should take care not to prefer one answer over another." See D. Cohen & Greenspan, *Conscientious Objection, Democratic Theory, and the Constitution,* 29 U.Pitt.L.Rev. 389, 403 (1968): "Nothing is more repugnant to a sense of fairness than the rejection of the claim of a conscientious objector because he does not believe in a transcendent reality. If his belief were coupled with a belief that the sun controlled man's destiny, communicating it through sun-spots, his exemption would be immediately granted. This places a premium upon madness and is a celebration of cranks and utopians. The concerned citizen, whose belief is intelligible and commends itself more to our understanding is turned away because he did not indulge in fantastic flights of imagination." Does the "religious" exemption result in more or less government "entanglement" with religion than an exemption for *all* conscientious objectors?

SECTION 4. CONFLICT BETWEEN THE CLAUSES

The decision in *Employment Division v. Smith* appears to have relieved some of the tension that had existed between the doctrines that the Court had developed under the establishment and free exercise clauses. But substantial questions remain, e.g., do (a) the decisions in *Sherbert (Thomas, Hobbie), Yoder* and *Roy,* and (b) statutes such as exemptions for Sabbatarians from Sunday Closing Laws and draft exemptions for religious conscientious objectors violate the establishment clause because they impermissibly aid religion?

CORPORATION OF THE PRESIDING BISHOP OF THE CHURCH OF JESUS CHRIST OF LATTER-DAY SAINTS v. AMOS

483 U.S. 327, 107 S.Ct. 2862, 97 L.Ed.2d 273 (1987).

JUSTICE WHITE delivered the opinion of the Court.

Section 702 of the Civil Rights Act of 1964 exempts religious organizations from Title VII's prohibition against discrimination in employment on the basis of religion. * * *

The Deseret Gymnasium (Gymnasium) in Salt Lake City, Utah, is a nonprofit facility, open to the public, run by [an] unincorporated religious association sometimes called the Mormon or LDS Church.

Appellee Mayson worked at the Gymnasium for some 16 years as an assistant building engineer and then building engineer. He was discharged in 1981 because he failed to qualify for a temple recommend, that is, a certificate that he is a member of the Church and eligible to attend its temples.

Mayson [contended] that if construed to allow religious employers to discriminate on religious grounds in hiring for nonreligious jobs, § 702 violates the Establishment Clause. * * *

"This Court has long recognized that the government may (and sometimes must) accommodate religious practices and that it may do so without violating the Establishment Clause." It is well established, too, that "[t]he limits of permissible state accommodation to religion are by no means co-extensive with the noninterference mandated by the Free Exercise Clause." *Walz.*[a] [At] some point, accommodation may devolve into "an unlawful fostering of religion," but this is not such a case, in our view. * * *

Lemon requires first that the law at issue serve a "secular legislative purpose." This does not mean that the law's purpose must be unrelated to religion * * *. Rather, *Lemon*'s "purpose" requirement aims at preventing the relevant governmental decisionmaker—in this case, Congress—from abandoning neutrality and acting with the intent of promoting a particular point of view in religious matters.

Under the *Lemon* analysis, it is a permissible legislative purpose to alleviate significant governmental interference with the ability of religious organizations to define and carry out their religious missions.[b] Appellees argue that there is no such purpose here because § 702 provided adequate protection for religious employers prior to the 1972 amendment, when it exempted only the religious activities of such employers from the statutory ban on religious discrimination. We may assume for the sake of argument that the pre-1972 exemption was adequate in the sense that the Free Exercise Clause required no more. Nonetheless, it is a significant burden on a religious organization to require it, on pain of substantial liability, to predict which of its activities a secular court will consider religious. The line is hardly a bright one, and an organization might understandably be concerned that a judge would not understand its religious tenets

a. Consider McConnell, *Accommodation of Religion,* 1985 Sup.Ct.Rev. 1, 34: "[S]ome government employees may view attendance at religious services on a holy day a sacred duty; they could make out a plausible free exercise case if the government refused them leave. Others may view attendance at services as no more than a spiritually wholesome activity; their free exercise claim would be much weaker. It is not unreasonable for the government to disregard these distinctions—to implement a general policy permitting leave for employees on the holy days of their faith. There seems little reason to confine the government to the exacting standards appropriate to courts when they exercise their function of judicial review. Religious liberty is not enhanced by a rule confining government accommodations to the minimum compelled under the Constitution."

b. See also Katz, *Note on the Constitutionality of Shared Time,* 1964 Relig. & Pub.Or. 85, 88: "It is no violation of neutrality for the government to express its concern for religious freedom by measures which merely neutralize what would otherwise be restrictive effects of government action. Provision for voluntary worship in the armed forces is constitutional, not because government policy may properly favor religion, but because the government is not required to exercise its military powers in a manner restrictive of religious freedom. Affirmative government action to maintain religious freedom in these instances serves the secular purpose of promoting a constitutional right, the free exercise of religion."

and sense of mission. Fear of potential liability might affect the way an organization carried out what it understood to be its religious mission. * * *

The second requirement under *Lemon* is that the law in question have "a principal or primary effect [that] neither advances nor inhibits religion." Undoubtedly, religious organizations are better able now to advance their purposes than they were prior to the 1972 amendment to § 702. But religious groups have been better able to advance their purposes on account of many laws that have passed constitutional muster: for example, the property tax exemption at issue in *Walz,* or the loans of school books to school children, including parochial school students, upheld in *Allen.* A law is not unconstitutional simply because it *allows* churches to advance religion, which is their very purpose. For a law to have forbidden "effects" under *Lemon,* it must be fair to say that the *government itself* has advanced religion through its own activities and influence. [Moreover,] we find no persuasive evidence in the record before us that the Church's ability to propagate its religious doctrine through the Gymnasium is any greater now than it was prior to the passage of the Civil Rights Act in 1964. In such circumstances, we do not see how any advancement of religion achieved by the Gymnasium can be fairly attributed to the Government, as opposed to the Church.[15]

We find unpersuasive the District Court's reliance on the fact that § 702 singles out religious entities for a benefit. [The Court] has never indicated that statutes that give special consideration to religious groups are per se invalid. That would run contrary to the teaching of our cases that there is ample room for accommodation of religion under the Establishment Clause. Where, as here, government acts with the proper purpose of lifting a regulation that burdens the exercise of religion, we see no reason to require that the exemption come packaged with benefits to secular entities. * * * *Larson* indicates that laws discriminating *among* religions are subject to strict scrutiny, and that laws "affording a uniform benefit to *all* religions" should be analyzed under *Lemon.* In a case such as this, where a statute is neutral on its face and motivated by a permissible purpose of limiting governmental interference with the exercise of religion, we see no justification for applying strict scrutiny to a statute that passes the *Lemon* test. [A]s applied to the nonprofit activities of religious employers, § 702 is rationally related to the legitimate purpose of alleviating significant governmental interference with the ability of religious organizations to define and carry out their religious missions. * * *

The judgment of the District Court is reversed * * *.

JUSTICE BRENNAN, with whom JUSTICE MARSHALL joins, concurring in the judgment.

[Any] exemption from Title VII's proscription on religious discrimination [says] that a person may be put to the choice of either conforming to certain religious tenets or losing a job opportunity, a promotion, or, as in this case, employment itself. The potential for coercion created by such a provision is in serious tension with our commitment to individual freedom of conscience in matters of religious belief.

At the same time, religious organizations have an interest in autonomy in ordering their internal affairs * * *. Determining that certain activities are in furtherance of an organization's religious mission, and that only those

15. Undoubtedly, Mayson's freedom of choice in religious matters was impinged upon, but it was the Church [and] not the Government, who put him to the choice of changing his religious practices or losing his [job.]

committed to that mission should conduct them, is thus a means by which a religious community defines itself. Solicitude for a church's ability to do so reflects the idea that furtherance of the autonomy of religious organizations often furthers individual religious freedom as well. * * *

This rationale suggests that, ideally, religious organizations should be able to discriminate on the basis of religion *only* with respect to religious activities [because] the infringement on religious liberty that results from conditioning performance of *secular* activity upon religious belief cannot be defended as necessary for the community's self-definition. Furthermore, the authorization of discrimination in such circumstances is not an accommodation that simply enables a church to gain members by the normal means of prescribing the terms of membership for those who seek to participate in furthering the mission of the community. Rather, it puts at the disposal of religion the added advantages of economic leverage in the secular realm. * * *

What makes the application of a religious-secular distinction difficult is that the character of an activity is not self-evident. As a result, determining whether an activity is religious or secular requires a searching case-by-case analysis. This results in considerable ongoing government entanglement in religious affairs. Furthermore, this prospect of government intrusion raises concern that a religious organization may be chilled in its Free Exercise activity. While a church may regard the conduct of certain functions as integral to its mission, a court may disagree. A religious organization therefore would have an incentive to characterize as religious only those activities about which there likely would be no dispute, even if it genuinely believed that religious commitment was important in performing other tasks as well. As a result, the community's process of self-definition would be shaped in part by the prospects of litigation. * * *

The risk of chilling religious organizations is most likely to arise with respect to *nonprofit* activities. The fact that an operation is not organized as a profit-making commercial enterprise makes colorable a claim that it is not purely secular in orientation. * * *

Sensitivity to individual religious freedom dictates that religious discrimination be permitted only with respect to employment in religious activities. Concern for the autonomy of religious organizations demands that we avoid the entanglement and the chill on religious expression that a case-by-case determination would produce. We cannot escape the fact that these aims are in tension. Because of the nature of nonprofit activities, I believe that a categorical exemption for such enterprises appropriately balances these competing concerns. * * *

JUSTICE BLACKMUN, concurring in the judgment.

Essentially for the reasons set forth in Justice O'Connor's opinion, * * * I too, concur in the judgment of the Court. * * *

JUSTICE O'CONNOR, concurring in the judgment. * * *

In *Wallace v. Jaffree,* I noted a tension in the Court's use of the *Lemon* test to evaluate an Establishment Clause challenge to government efforts to accommodate the free exercise of religion: "On the one hand, a rigid application of the *Lemon* test would invalidate legislation exempting religious observers from generally applicable government obligations. By definition, such legislation has a religious purpose and effect in promoting the free exercise of religion.[c] On the other hand, judicial deference to all legislation that purports to facilitate the free exercise of religion would completely vitiate the Establishment Clause. Any statute pertaining to religion can be viewed as an 'accommodation' of free exercise rights." [d]

In my view, the opinion for the Court leans toward the second of the two unacceptable options described [above.] Almost any government benefit to religion could be recharacterized as simply "allowing" a religion to better advance itself, unless perhaps it involved actual proselytization by government agents. In nearly every case of a government benefit to religion, the religious mission would not be advanced if the religion did not take advantage of the benefit; even a direct financial subsidy to a religious organization would not advance religion if for some reason the organization failed to make any use of the [funds.]

The necessary first step in evaluating an Establishment Clause challenge to a government action lifting from religious organizations a generally applicable regulatory burden is to recognize that such government action *does* have the effect of advancing religion. The necessary second step is to separate those benefits to religion that constitutionally accommodate the free exercise of religion from those that provide unjustifiable awards of assistance to religious organizations. As I have suggested in earlier opinions, the inquiry framed by the *Lemon* test should be "whether government's purpose is to endorse religion and whether the statute actually conveys a message of endorsement." To ascertain whether the statute conveys a message of endorsement, the relevant issue is how it would be perceived by an objective observer, acquainted with the text, legislative history, and implementation of the statute.[e] [This] case involves a government decision to lift from a nonprofit activity of a religious organization

c. In her *Jaffree* concurrence, O'Connor, J., added: "Indeed, the statute at issue in *Lemon* [can] be viewed as an accommodation of the religious beliefs of parents who choose to send their children to religious schools."

In this connection, consider Kurland, *Religion and the Law* 112 (1962): "The [free exercise and establishment] clauses should be read as stating a single precept: that government cannot utilize religion as a standard for action or inaction because these clauses, read together as they should be, prohibit classification in terms of religion either to confer a benefit or to impose a burden." For thoughtful comment, see Kauper, *Book Review,* 41 Texas L.Rev. 467 (1963); Pfeffer, *Religion–Blind Government,* 15 Stan.L.Rev. 389 (1963); Mansfield, *Book Review,* 52 Calif.L.Rev. 212 (1964).

Similarly, for the view that the free exercise clause should generally only guarantee "equality of treatment for those who act out of sincere religious belief" and should afford special protection only for acts of "worship," as defined, see Fernandez, *The Free Exercise of Religion,* 36 So.Calif.L.Rev. 546 (1963). For the view that free exercise claims should be treated "no differently than free expression claims," see Marshall, *Solving the Free Exercise Dilemma: Free Exercise as Expression,* 67 Minn.L.Rev. 545 (1983).

d. In *Jaffree,* O'Connor, J. added: "It [is] difficult to square any notion of 'complete neutrality' with the mandate of the Free Exercise Clause that government must sometimes exempt a religious observer from an otherwise generally applicable obligation. A government that confers a benefit on an explicitly religious basis is not neutral toward religion. The solution [lies] in identifying workable limits to the Government's license to promote the free exercise of religion. [O]ne can plausibly assert that government pursues free exercise clause values when it lifts a government-imposed burden on the free exercise of religion. If a statute falls within this category, then the standard Establishment Clause test should be modified accordingly. [T]he Court should simply acknowledge that the religious purpose of such a statute is legitimated by the Free Exercise Clause."

e. In *Jaffree,* O'Connor, J., added: "[C]ourts should assume that the 'objective observer,' is acquainted with the Free Exercise Clause and the values it promotes. Thus individual perceptions, or resentment that a religious observer is exempted from a particular government requirement, would be entitled to little weight if the Free Exercise Clause strongly supported the exemption."

the burden of demonstrating that the particular nonprofit activity is religious as well as the burden of refraining from discriminating on the basis of religion. Because there is a probability that a nonprofit activity of a religious organization will itself be involved in the organization's religious mission, in my view the objective observer should perceive the government action as an accommodation of the exercise of religion rather than as a government endorsement of religion.

* * * While I express no opinion on the issue, I emphasize that under the holding of the Court, and under my view of the appropriate Establishment Clause analysis, the question of the constitutionality of the § 702 exemption as applied to for-profit activities of religious organizations remains open.

Notes and Questions

1. *Draft exemption.* Did the statute in *Gillette,* exempting only "religious" conscientious objectors, impermissibly prefer religion over nonreligion? In WELSH v. UNITED STATES, Sec. 2, II supra, four justices addressed the issue. WHITE, J., joined by Burger, C.J., and Stewart, J., found it valid: "First, § 6(j) may represent a purely practical judgment that religious objectors, however admirable, would be of no more use in combat than many others unqualified for military service. [On] this basis, the exemption has neither the primary purpose nor the effect of furthering religion. * * *

"Second, Congress may have [believed that] to deny the exemption would violate the Free Exercise Clause or at least raise grave problems in this respect. True, this Court has more than once stated its unwillingness to construe the First Amendment, standing alone, as requiring draft exemptions for religious believers. [But] just as in *Katzenbach v. Morgan,* [p. 1272 infra], where we accepted the judgment of Congress as to what legislation was appropriate to enforce the Equal Protection Clause of the Fourteenth Amendment, here we should respect congressional judgment accommodating the Free Exercise Clause and the power to raise armies. This involves no surrender of the Court's function as ultimate arbiter in disputes over interpretation of the Constitution. But it was enough in *Katzenbach* 'to perceive a basis upon which the Congress might resolve the conflict as it did' * * *.

"[If] it is 'favoritism' and not 'neutrality' to exempt religious believers from the draft, is it 'neutrality' and not 'inhibition' of religion to compel religious believers to fight * * *? It cannot be ignored that the First Amendment itself contains a religious classification [and the free exercise clause] protects conduct as well as religious belief and speech. [It] was not suggested [in *Braunfeld*] that the Sunday closing laws in 21 States exempting Sabbatarians and others violated the Establishment Clause because no provision was made for others who claimed nonreligious reasons for not working on some particular day of the week. Nor was it intimated in *Zorach* that the no-establishment holding might be infirm because only those pursuing religious studies for designated periods were released from the public school routine; neither was it hinted that a public school's refusal to institute a released time program would violate the Free Exercise Clause. The Court in *Sherbert* construed the Free Exercise Clause to require special treatment for Sabbatarians under the State's unemployment compensation law. But the State could deal specially with Sabbatarians whether the Free Exercise Clause required it or not * * *." [a]

a. See generally Donnici, *Governmental Encouragement of Religious Ideology: A Study of the Current Conscientious Objector Exemption from Military Service,* 13 J.Pub.L. 16, 43 (1964).

HARLAN, J., disagreed, believing that "having chosen to exempt, [Congress] cannot draw the line between theistic or nontheistic religious beliefs on the one hand and secular beliefs on the other. [I]t must encompass the class of individuals it purports to exclude, those whose beliefs emanate from a purely moral, ethical, or philosophical source.[9] The common denominator must be the intensity of moral conviction with which a belief is [held]. *Everson, McGowan* and *Allen,* all sustained legislation on the premise that it was neutral in its application and thus did not constitute an establishment, notwithstanding the fact that it may have assisted religious groups by giving them the same benefits accorded to nonreligious groups.[12] To the extent that *Zorach* and *Sherbert* stand for the proposition that the Government may (*Zorach*), or must (*Sherbert*), shape its secular programs to accommodate the beliefs and tenets of religious groups, I think these cases unsound.[13]"

2. *Unemployment compensation.* (a) Did the Court's decisions in *Sherbert, Thomas* and *Hobbie* impermissibly prefer religion? In THOMAS v. REVIEW BD., Sec. 2 supra, REHNQUIST, J., dissented, finding the result "inconsistent with many of our prior Establishment Clause cases" [2]. "If Indiana were to legislate what the Court today requires—an unemployment compensation law which permitted benefits to be granted to those persons who quit their jobs for religious reasons—the statute would 'plainly' violate the Establishment Clause as interpreted in such cases as *Lemon* and *Nyquist.* First, [the] proviso would clearly serve only a religious purpose. It would grant financial benefits for the sole purpose of accommodating religious beliefs. Second, there can be little doubt that the primary effect of the proviso would be to 'advance' religion by facilitating the exercise of religious belief. Third, any statute including such a proviso would surely 'entangle' the State in religion far more than the mere grant of tax exemptions, as in *Walz,* or the award of tuition grants and tax credits, as in *Nyquist.* By granting financial benefits to persons solely on the basis of their

9. * * * I suggested [in *Sherbert*] that a State could constitutionally create exceptions to its program to accommodate religious scruples. [But] any such exception in order to satisfy the Establishment Clause [would] have to be sufficiently broad so as to be religiously neutral. This would require creating an exception for anyone who, as a matter of conscience, could not comply with the statute. * * *

12. [I] fail to see how [§ 6(j)] has "any substantial legislative purpose" apart from honoring the conscience of individuals who oppose war on only religious grounds. * * *

13. [At] the very least the Constitution requires that the State not excuse students early for the purpose of receiving religious instruction when it does not offer to nonreligious students the opportunity to use school hours for spiritual or ethical instruction of a nonreligious nature. Moreover, whether a released-time program cast in terms of improving "conscience" to the exclusion of artistic or cultural pursuits, would be "neutral" and consistent with the requirement of "voluntarism," is by no means an easy question. * * *

2. To the extent *Sherbert* was correctly decided, it might be argued that cases such as *McCollum, Engel, Schempp, Lemon,* and *Nyquist* were wrongly decided. The "aid" rendered to religion in these latter cases may not be significantly different, in kind or degree, than the "aid" afforded Mrs. Sherbert or Thomas. For example, if the State in *Sherbert* could not deny compensation to one refusing work for religious reasons, it might be argued that a State may not deny reimbursement to students who choose for religious reasons to attend parochial schools. The argument would be that although a State need not allocate any funds to education, once it has done so, it may not require any person to sacrifice his religious beliefs in order to obtain an equal education. There can be little doubt that to the extent secular education provides answers to important moral questions without reference to religion or teaches that there are no answers, a person in one sense sacrifices his religious belief by attending secular schools. And even if such "aid" were not constitutionally compelled by the Free Exercise Clause, Justice Harlan may well be right in *Sherbert* when he finds sufficient flexibility in the Establishment Clause to permit the States to voluntarily choose to grant such benefits to individuals.

religious beliefs, the State must necessarily inquire whether the claimant's belief is 'religious' and whether it is sincerely held. [Just] as I think that Justice Harlan in *Sherbert* correctly stated the proper approach to free exercise questions, I believe that Justice Stewart, dissenting in *Schempp,* accurately stated the reach of the Establishment Clause [as] limited to 'government support of proselytizing activities of religious sects by throwing the weight of secular authorities behind the dissemination of religious tenets.' See *McCollum* (Reed, J., dissenting) (impermissible aid is only 'purposeful assistance directly to the church itself or to some religious [group] performing ecclesiastical functions'). Conversely, governmental assistance which does not have the effect of 'inducing' religious belief, but instead merely 'accommodates' or implements an independent religious choice does not impermissibly involve the government in religious choices and therefore does not violate the Establishment [Clause]. I would think that in this case, as in *Sherbert,* had the state voluntarily chosen to pay unemployment compensation benefits to persons who left their jobs for religious reasons, such aid would be constitutionally permissible because it redounds directly to the benefit of the individual."

(b) *Accommodation vs. inducement vs. imposition vs. coercion.* Consider A. Schwartz, *No Imposition of Religion: The Establishment Clause Value,* 77 Yale L.J. 692, 693, 723, 728 (1968): "[T]he dilemma [between the religion clauses] results from an unnecessarily broad reading of the establishment clause; that clause should be read to prohibit only aid which has as its motive or substantial effect the imposition of religious belief or practice * * *. Conversely, aid which does not have the effect of inducing religious belief, but merely accommodates or implements an individual religious choice, does not increase the danger of religion and [does] not violate the no-imposition standard. * * * Exemption of Mrs. Sherbert [represents] a judgment that the exercise of Seventh-day Adventism is more worthy than bowling on Saturdays, but the exemption has no significant effect and arguably no effect at all upon whether someone becomes a Seventh-day Adventist. Similarly, the Sabbatarian exemption from Sunday closing laws does not induce one to become a Jew; draft exemption to conscientious objectors does not normally induce one to become a Quaker; closing the public schools on all religious holidays or on every Wednesday at 2 P.M. does not induce the adoption of religion; and compulsory Sunday closing, while implementing an independent desire to attend church services, has no substantial effect upon the creation of such desire. The availability of preferential aid to religious exercise may, to be sure, induce false claims of religious belief, but the establishment clause is not concerned with false claims of belief, only with induced belief." Does this distinguish *McCollum, Engel* and *Schempp* from *Sherbert?* Do you agree with all of the *factual* assumptions made? Under this analysis, what result in *Epperson?* What of a small governmental payment to all persons who would lose salary because they have to be absent from their jobs in order to attend religious services? Would the state's failure to provide Mrs. Sherbert with unemployment compensation be the same as its not having on-premises released time and school prayer in that all of these actions simply "make the practice of religious beliefs more expensive"?

Compare Choper, *The Religion Clauses of the First Amendment: Reconciling the Conflict,* 41 U.Pitt.L.Rev. 673, 691, 697–700 (1980): "My proposal for resolving the conflict between the two Religion Clauses seeks to implement their historically and contemporarily acknowledged common goal: to safeguard religious liberty. [I]t is only when an accommodation would jeopardize religious liberty—when it would coerce, compromise, or influence religious choice—that it would fail. [For example, in *Yoder,* unless] it could be shown that relieving the Amish [would] tend to coerce, compromise, or influence religious choice—and it is extremely doubtful that it could—the exemption was permissible under the Establishment Clause. In contrast, in *Sherbert,* [the] exemption results in impairment of religious liberty because compulsorily raised tax funds must be used to subsidize Mrs. Sherbert's exercise of religion.[b] [In the draft exemption cases], professing a personal 'religion' (as opposed to 'essentially political, sociological or philosophical considerations') was enough to gain the enormous advantage of avoiding combat duty. [D]raftees seeking exemption would have to formulate a statement of personal doctrine that would pass muster. This endeavor would involve deep and careful thought, and perhaps reading in philosophy and religion. Some undoubtedly would be persuaded by what they read. Moreover, the theory of 'cognitive dissonance'—which posits that to avoid madness we tend to become what we hold ourselves to be and what others believe us to be—also suggests that some initially fraudulent claims of belief in a personal religion would develop into true belief. Thus, a draft exemption for religious objectors threatens values of religious freedom by encouraging the adoption of religious beliefs by those who seek to qualify for the benefit."

(c) *Breadth of exemption.* In TEXAS MONTHLY, INC. v. BULLOCK, Sec. 1, II supra, SCALIA, J., joined by Rehnquist, C.J., and Kennedy, J., charged that according to Brennan, J.'s plurality opinion, "no law is constitutional whose 'benefits [are] confined to religious organizations,' except, of course, those laws that are unconstitutional *unless* they contain benefits confined to religious organizations. [But] 'the limits of permissible state accommodation to religion are by no means co-extensive with the noninterference mandated by the Free Exercise Clause.' Breadth of coverage is essential to constitutionality whenever a law's benefiting of religious activity is sought to be defended not specifically (or not exclusively) as an intentional and reasonable accommodation of religion, but as merely the incidental consequence of seeking to benefit *all* activity that achieves a particular secular goal. But that is a different rationale—more commonly invoked than accommodation of religion but, as our cases show, not preclusive of it. Where accommodation of religion is the justification, by definition religion is being singled out." Finally, "the proper lesson to be drawn from" the fact that the free exercise clause may not require the Texas sales tax exemption and "that *Murdock* and *Follett* are narrowly distinguishable" is that "if the exemption comes so close to being a constitutionally required accommodation, there is no doubt that it is at least a permissible one." [c]

BRENNAN, J., joined by Marshall and Stevens, JJ., responded: "Contrary to the dissent's claims, we in no way suggest that *all* benefits conferred exclusively upon religious groups or upon individuals on account of their religious beliefs are forbidden by the Establishment Clause unless they are mandated by the Free Exercise Clause. Our decisions in *Zorach* and *Amos* offer two examples. Similarly, if the Air Force provided a sufficiently broad exemption from its dress

b. See also Choper, *The Free Exercise Clause,* 27 Wm. & M.L.Rev. 943, 951 n. 25 (1986): "Under Justice Rehnquist's [and Professor Schwartz's] rationale, if a municipally-owned bus company wanted to waive the fare to take people to churches, it could do so. According to Justice Rehnquist, the waiver would not 'induce' religion, but would simply 'accommodate' a religious choice that already had been made. That may be true, but the waiver also would result in what the religion clauses protect against—the use of tax funds for exclusively religious purposes."

c. Why didn't Texas' exemption violate the establishment clause test articulated by Kennedy, J. (joined by Rehnquist, C.J., and White and Scalia, JJ.) in *Allegheny County v. ACLU,* Sec. I, III supra, because it gave "direct benefits to religion" and involved "subtle coercion [in] the form of taxation"?

requirements for servicemen whose religious faiths commanded them to wear certain headgear or other attire, see *Goldman v. Weinberger,* that exemption presumably would not be invalid under the Establishment Clause even though this Court has not found it to be required by the Free Exercise Clause.

"All of these cases, however, involve legislative exemptions that did not or would not impose substantial burdens on nonbeneficiaries while allowing others to act according to their religious beliefs, or that were designed to alleviate government intrusions that might significantly deter adherents of a particular faith from conduct protected by the Free Exercise Clause. New York City's decision to release students from public schools so that they might obtain religious instruction elsewhere, which we upheld in *Zorach,* was found not to coerce students who wished to remain behind to alter their religious beliefs, nor did it impose monetary costs on their parents or other taxpayers who opposed or were indifferent to the religious instruction given to students who were released. The hypothetical Air Force uniform exemption also would not place a monetary burden on those required to conform to the dress code or subject them to any appreciable privation. And the application of Title VII's exemption for religious organizations that we approved in *Amos* though it had some adverse effect on those holding or seeking employment with those organizations (if not on taxpayers generally), prevented potentially serious encroachments on protected religious freedoms.

"Texas' tax exemption, by contrast, does not remove a demonstrated and possible grave imposition on religious activity sheltered by the Free Exercise Clause. Moreover, it burdens nonbeneficiaries by increasing their tax bills by whatever amount is needed to offset the benefit bestowed on subscribers to religious publications."

3. *Sabbath observance.* THORNTON v. CALDOR, INC., 472 U.S. 703, 105 S.Ct. 2914, 86 L.Ed.2d 557 (1985), per BURGER, C.J., held that a Connecticut law—which provided "that those who observe a Sabbath any day of the week as a matter of religious conviction must be relieved of the duty to work on that day, no matter what burden or inconvenience this imposes on the employer or fellow workers"—"has a primary effect that impermissibly advances a particular religious practice" and thus violates the establishment clause: "The statute arms Sabbath observers with an absolute and unqualified right not to work on whatever day they designate as their Sabbath [and thus] goes beyond having an incidental or remote effect of advancing religion."[d]

O'CONNOR, J., joined by Marshall, J., concurred, distinguishing "the religious accommodation provisions of Title VII of the Civil Rights Act [which] require private employers to reasonably accommodate the religious practices of employees unless to do so would cause undue hardship to the employer's business": "In my view, a statute outlawing employment discrimination based on race, color, religion, sex or national origin has the valid secular purpose of assuring employment opportunity to all groups in our pluralistic society. Since Title VII calls for reasonable rather than absolute accommodation and extends that requirement to all religious beliefs and practices rather than protecting only the

d. Rehnquist, J., dissented without opinion.

Consider Epstein, *Religious Liberty in the Welfare State,* 31 Wm.& M.L.Rev. 375, 406 (1990): "[It would plainly unconstitutional] if the state offered to pay a small sum out of public funds to the employer to defray the additional costs it had to bear to keep the religious worker on its payroll. [If] a public subsidy of religious workers is not acceptable under the establishment clause, then a public mandate of a private subsidy is unacceptable as well."

Sabbath observance, I believe an objective observer would perceive it as an anti-discrimination law rather than an endorsement of religion or a particular religious practice."

Was the purpose or effect of the *Caldor* statute any different than that of the *Amos* statute or the Court's decisions in *Sherbert, Thomas, Hobbie, Roy* and *Yoder? Amos* distinguished *Caldor* on the ground that in *Amos,* "appellee was not legally obligated to take the steps necessary to qualify for a temple recommend, and his discharge was not required by statute."

For purposes of the establishment clause, of what significance is the fact that the *Caldor* statute grants "an absolute and unqualified right not to work" rather than a Title VII-like exemption?

Does the *Caldor* statute "promote" and "endorse" a particular "religion" or "religious belief" or "religious practice" any moreso than the Court's decisions in *Sherbert, Thomas, Hobbie, Yoder* and *Roy,* or than the statutory exemptions from the draft or Sunday Closing Laws? Do all these exemptions simply "accommodate" religion? *Hobbie* distinguished *Caldor* as follows: "Florida's provision of unemployment benefits to religious observers does not single out a particular class of such persons for favorable treatment and thereby have the effect of implicitly endorsing a particular religious belief. Rather, the provision of unemployment benefits generally available within the State to religious observers who must leave their employment due to an irreconcilable conflict between the demands of work and conscience neutrally accommodates religious beliefs and practices, without endorsement."

4. *School prayer.* In *Jaffree,* O'Connor, J., applied her "solution" to Alabama's moment of silence law: "No law prevents a student who is so inclined from praying silently in public schools. [Of] course, the State might argue that § 16–1–20.1 protects not silent prayer, but rather group silent prayer under State sponsorship. Phrased in these terms, the burden lifted by the statute is not one imposed by the State of Alabama, but by the Establishment Clause as interpreted in *Engel* and *Schempp.* In my view, it is beyond the authority of the State of Alabama to remove burdens imposed by the Constitution itself."

5. *Reconciling the conflict.* Assuming the validity of the distinction between *McCollum, Engel, Schempp* and *Jafree* on the one hand, and the programs such as that in *Amos* and exemption from the draft etc. on the other, are the above approaches nonetheless undesirable because they result not merely in protection of free exercise (or neutrality or accommodation) but in relieving persons with certain religious beliefs of significant burdens from which many other persons strongly desire to be exempted? That, in this sense, there is "preference" for minority religions and "discrimination" against the other persons because of their religion or lack of it? Should free exercise exemptions "be allowed only if the petitioner agrees to the imposition of some alternative duty or burden"? Note, 91 Harv.L.Rev. at 1082. Consider Galanter, note 4, Sec. 2, II supra, at 290–91: "[In *Sherbert*] it was clear that the state was already solicitous of the scruples of Sunday worshippers, though not of Saturday ones. In such a case, it is easy to appreciate that the exception [required by the decision] is restorative or equalizing. It puts the minority in the same position that the majority enjoys. [But] can it be said that the kind of disparity found in *Sherbert* between the treatment of majority and minority is a unique or unusual thing? Whatever seriously interferes with majority religious beliefs and practices is unlikely to become a legal requirement—for example, work on Sunday or Christmas. And whatever the majority considers necessary for its religious

practice is quite unlikely to be prohibited by law. And whatever the majority finds religiously objectionable is unlikely to become a legal requirement—for example, medical practices which substantial groups find abhorrent, like contraception, sterilization, euthanasia, or abortion. Exceptions then, give to minorities what majorities have by virtue of suffrage and representative government. The question is not whether the state may prefer these minorities, but whether it may counterbalance the natural advantages of majorities."

Chapter 6

EQUAL PROTECTION

Virtually no legislation applies universally and treats all persons equally; all laws classify (or "discriminate") by imposing special burdens (or granting exemptions from such burdens) or by conferring special benefits on some people and not others. Under what circumstances do such laws violate the fourteenth amendment's command that no state shall "deny to any person within its jurisdiction the equal protection of the laws"? [a]

Despite the fact that the language of the equal protection clause is not confined to racial discrimination, the *Slaughter-House Cases,* p. 72 supra (the first decision interpreting the Civil War amendments), "doubt[ed] very much whether any action of a state not directed by way of discrimination against the negroes as a class, or on account of their race, will ever be held to come within the purview of this provision." Sec. 2 will concern the "strict scrutiny" given to racial (and ethnic) classifications which the Court has deemed to be "suspect." Sec. 3 will consider the extension of a nondeferential standard of review to government action that disadvantages several other discrete groups. At least as early as 1897, however, the Court invoked the equal protection clause to invalidate a commonplace economic regulation that obligated railroad defendants (but not others) to pay the attorneys' fees of successful plaintiffs. The Court acknowledged that "as a general proposition, [it] is undeniably true [that] it is not within the scope of the Fourteenth Amendment to withhold from States the power of classification." But "it must appear" that a classification is "based upon some reasonable ground—some difference which bears a just and proper relation to the attempted classification—and is not a mere arbitrary selection." *Gulf, C. & S. F. Ry. v. Ellis,* 165 U.S. 150, 17 S.Ct. 255, 41 L.Ed. 666 (1897).[b]

a. By its terms, the equal protection clause does not apply to the federal government. A series of decisions, however, has held that the fifth amendment's due process clause—although not containing the language of equal protection—forbids "unjustifiable" discrimination (*Bolling v. Sharpe,* Sec. 2, II infra) and that—except under special circumstances (see Sec. 3, I infra: "Alienage")—the "approach to Fifth Amendment equal protection claims has always been precisely the same as to equal protection claims under the Fourteenth Amendment" (*Weinberger v. Wiesenfeld,* Sec. 3, IV infra).

In 1976, *Hampton v. Wong,* Sec. 3, I infra, advanced a different approach. It stated that "when a federal rule is applicable to only a limited territory, such as the District of Columbia, or an insular possession, and when there is no special national interest involved, the Due Process Clause has been construed as having the same significance as the Equal Protection Clause," but suggested a different standard for "a federal rule having a nationwide impact." Subsequent decisions, however, have continued to treat equal protection claims against the federal government under the fifth amendment in the same way as equal protection claims against the states under the fourteenth amendment, even though the challenged federal rule had "nationwide impact." See generally Karst, *The Fifth Amendment's Guarantee of Equal Protection,* 55 N.C.L.Rev. 541 (1977).

b. For an even earlier invocation of the equal protection clause to invalidate a classifi-

Sec. 1 deals with this "traditional approach" under the equal protection clause to general economic and social welfare regulations, as distinguished from either "suspect" or "quasi-suspect" classifications (Secs. 2–3) or laws that affect what have come to be known as "fundamental rights" (Sec. 4).

SECTION 1. TRADITIONAL APPROACH

As observed in Ch. 2, Sec. 1, III, the due process clause was the usual provision used by the Court in the first third of this century to overturn a great many economic and social welfare regulations. But despite Holmes, J.'s reference during this period to the equal protection clause as "the usual last resort of constitutional arguments,"[a] the Court held that approximately twenty such state and local laws violated equal protection.[b] In doing so, the Court employed the deferential standard of judicial review called for by the "traditional approach" which granted a state "a broad discretion in classification in the exercise of its power of regulation" and interposed the "constitutional guaranty of equal protection" only "against discriminations that are entirely arbitrary."[c]

But fuller articulations of the standard of review often appeared to vary significantly. LINDSLEY v. NATURAL CARBONIC GAS CO., 220 U.S. 61, 31 S.Ct. 337, 55 L.Ed. 369 (1911), illustrates an extremely deferential formulation: "1. The equal protection clause [does] not take from the state the power to classify in the adoption of police laws, but admits of the exercise of a wide scope of discretion in that regard, and avoids what is done only when it is without any reasonable basis and therefore is purely arbitrary. 2. A classification having some reasonable basis does not offend against that clause merely because it is not made with mathematical nicety, or because in practice it results in some inequality. 3. When the classification in such a law is called in question, if any state of facts reasonably can be conceived that would sustain it, the existence of that state of facts at the time the law was enacted must be assumed. 4. One who assails the classification in such a law must carry the burden of showing that it does not rest upon any reasonable basis, but is essentially arbitrary."[d] In contrast, ROYSTER GUANO CO. v. VIRGINIA, 253 U.S. 412, 40 S.Ct. 560, 64 L.Ed. 989 (1920), suggests a more active judicial role: "[T]he classification must be reasonable, not arbitrary, and must rest upon some ground of difference having a fair and substantial relation to the object of the legislation, so that all persons similarly circumstanced shall be treated alike."

The materials that follow concern the Court's use of the "traditional approach" under equal protection to economic and social welfare regulations since the late 1930s when it abandoned active substantive due process review of such legislation.

cation of transportation rates, see *Reagan v. Farmers' Loan & Trust Co.,* 154 U.S. 362, 14 S.Ct. 1047, 38 L.Ed. 1014 (1894). For an informative review of the Court's earliest use of the equal protection clause, see 2 Dorsen, Bender, Neuborne & Law, *Political and Civil Rights in the United States* 57–58 (Law School ed., 4th ed. 1979).

a. *Buck v. Bell,* 274 U.S. 200, 47 S.Ct. 584, 71 L.Ed. 1000 (1927).

b. 2 Dorsen et al., supra, at 336.

c. *Smith v. Cahoon,* 283 U.S. 553, 51 S.Ct. 582, 75 L.Ed. 1264 (1931).

d. For more recent reliance on this language, see *McGowan v. Maryland,* 366 U.S. 420, 81 S.Ct. 1101, 6 L.Ed.2d 393 (1961), per Warren, C.J., unanimously rejecting an equal protection challenge to state laws requiring stores to be closed on Sunday but containing numerous exemptions.

RAILWAY EXPRESS AGENCY v. NEW YORK

336 U.S. 106, 69 S.Ct. 463, 93 L.Ed. 533 (1949).

JUSTICE DOUGLAS delivered the opinion of the Court.

[T]he Traffic Regulations of the City of New York [provide]: "No person shall operate [on] any street an advertising vehicle; [except for] business notices upon business delivery vehicles, so long as such vehicles are engaged in the usual business [of] the owner and not used merely or mainly for advertising."

Appellant [operates] about 1,900 trucks in New York City and sells the space on the exterior sides of these trucks for advertising [for] the most part unconnected with its own business. It was convicted * * *.

The court [below] concluded that advertising on [vehicles] constitutes a distraction to vehicle drivers and to pedestrians alike and therefore affects the safety of the public in the use of the streets. We do not sit to weigh evidence on the due process issue in order to determine whether the regulation is sound or appropriate; nor is it our function to pass judgment on its wisdom. See *Olsen v. Nebraska* [p. 86 supra]. We would be trespassing on one of the most intensely local and specialized of all municipal problems if we held that this regulation had no relation to the traffic problem of New York City. It is the judgment of the local authorities that it does have such a relation. And nothing has been advanced which shows that to be palpably false.

The question of equal protection of the laws is pressed more strenuously on us. [It] is said, for example, that one of appellant's trucks carrying the advertisement of a commercial house would not cause any greater distraction of pedestrians and vehicle drivers than if the commercial house carried the same advertisement on its own truck. Yet the regulation allows the latter to do what the former is forbidden from doing. It is therefore contended that the classification which the regulation makes has no relation to the traffic problem since a violation turns not on what kind of advertisements are carried on trucks but on whose trucks they are carried.

That, however, is a superficial way of analyzing the [problem]. The local authorities may well have concluded that those who advertised their own wares on their trucks do not present the same traffic problem in view of the nature or extent of the advertising which they use. * * *

We cannot say that that judgment is not an allowable one. Yet if it is, the classification has relation to the purpose for which it is made and does not contain the kind of discrimination against which the Equal Protection Clause affords protection. It is by such practical considerations based on experience rather than by theoretical inconsistencies that the question of equal protection is to be answered. And the fact that New York City sees fit to eliminate from traffic this kind of distraction but does not touch what may be even greater ones in a different category, such as the vivid displays on Times Square, is immaterial. It is no requirement of equal protection that all evils of the same genus be eradicated or none at all. * * *

Affirmed.

JUSTICE RUTLEDGE acquiesces in the Court's opinion and judgment, dubitante on the question of equal protection of the laws.

JUSTICE JACKSON, concurring. * * *

The burden should rest heavily upon one who would persuade us to use the due process clause to strike down a substantive [law]. Even its provident use against municipal regulations frequently disables all government—state, municipal and federal—from dealing with the conduct in question because the requirement of due process is also applicable to State and Federal Governments. * * *

Invocation of the equal protection clause, on the other hand, does not disable any governmental body from dealing with the subject at hand. It merely means that the prohibition or regulation must have a broader impact. I regard it as a salutary doctrine that cities, states and the Federal Government must exercise their powers so as not to discriminate between their inhabitants except upon some reasonable differentiation fairly related to the object of regulation. [T]here is no more effective practical guaranty against arbitrary and unreasonable government than to require that the principles of law which officials would impose upon a minority must be imposed generally. Conversely, nothing opens the door to arbitrary action so effectively as to allow those officials to pick and choose only a few to whom they will apply legislation and thus to escape the political retribution that might be visited upon them if larger numbers were affected. Courts can take no better measure to assure that laws will be just than to require that laws be equal in operation. * * *

In this case, if the City of New York should assume that display of any advertising on vehicles tends and intends to distract the attention of persons using the highways and to increase the dangers of its traffic, I should think it fully within its constitutional powers to forbid it all. [Instead], however, the City seeks to reduce the hazard only by saying that while some may, others may not exhibit such appeals. The same display, for example, advertising cigarettes, which this appellant is forbidden to carry on its trucks, may be carried on the trucks of a cigarette dealer. [The] courts of New York have declared that the sole nature and purpose of the regulation before us is to reduce traffic hazards. There is not even a pretense here that the traffic hazard created by the advertising which is forbidden is in any manner or degree more hazardous than that which is permitted. * * *

* * * I do not think differences of treatment under law should be approved on classification because of differences unrelated to the legislative purpose. The equal protection clause ceases to assure either equality or protection if it is avoided by any conceivable difference that can be pointed out between those bound and those left free. This Court has often announced the principle that the differentiation must have an appropriate relation to the object of the [legislation].

The question in my mind comes to this. Where individuals contribute to an evil or danger in the same way and to the same degree, may those who do so for hire be prohibited, while those who do so for their own commercial ends but not for hire be allowed to continue? I think the answer has to be that the hireling may be put in a class by himself and may be dealt with differently than those who act on their own. But this is not merely because such a discrimination will enable the lawmaker to diminish the evil. That might be done by many classifications, which I should think wholly unsustainable. It is rather because there is a real difference between doing in self-interest and doing for hire, so that it is one thing to tolerate action from those who act on their own and it is another thing to permit the same action to be promoted for a price. [Of] course this appellant did not hold itself out to carry or display everybody's advertising, and its rental of space on the sides of its trucks was only incidental to the main business which brought its trucks into the streets. But it is not difficult to see that, in a day of extravagant advertising more or less subsidized by tax deduction, the rental of truck space could become an obnoxious enterprise. [I]n view of the control I would concede to cities to protect citizens in quiet and orderly use for their proper purposes of the highways and public places, I think the judgment below must be affirmed.

NEW ORLEANS v. DUKES

427 U.S. 297, 96 S.Ct. 2513, 49 L.Ed.2d 511 (1976).

PER CURIAM.

[A 1972 New Orleans ordinance banned all pushcart food vendors in the French Quarter ("Vieux Carre") except those who had continuously operated there for eight or more years. Two vendors had done so for twenty or more years and qualified under the "grandfather clause." Appellee, who had operated a pushcart for only two years, attacked the ordinance.]

* * * Stating expressly [that] *Morey v. Doud,* 354 U.S. 457, 77 S.Ct. 1344, 1 L.Ed.2d 1485 (1957),[a] was "our chief guide in resolving this case," the Court of Appeals focused on the "exclusionary character" of the ordinance and its concomitant "creation of a protected monopoly for the favored class member." [Thus,] the ordinance was declared violative of [equal protection].

When local economic regulation is challenged solely as violating the Equal Protection Clause, this Court consistently defers to legislative determinations as to the desirability of particular statutory discriminations. Unless a classification trammels fundamental personal rights or is drawn upon inherently suspect distinctions such as race, religion, or alienage, our decisions presume the constitutionality of the statutory discriminations and require only that the classification challenged be rationally related to a legitimate state interest. States are accorded wide latitude in the regulation of their local economies under their police powers, and rational distinctions may be made with substantially less than mathematical exactitude. Legislatures may implement their program step by step in such economic areas, adopting regulations that only partially ameliorate a perceived evil and deferring complete elimination of the evil to future regulations. See, e.g., *Williamson v. Lee Optical Co.*[b] In short, the judiciary may not sit as a superlegislature to judge the wisdom or desirability of legislative policy determinations made in areas that neither affect fundamental rights nor proceed along suspect lines; in the local economic sphere, it is only the invidious discrimination, the wholly arbitrary act, which cannot stand consistently with the Fourteenth Amendment. See, e.g., *Ferguson v. Skrupa.*[5]

a. *Morey* held that an Illinois statute that comprehensively regulated companies that sold money orders, but exempted American Express Co. by name, violated equal protection.

b. In *Lee Optical,* p. 87 supra, the statute generally prohibiting the fitting of eyeglasses without a prescription exempted businesses that sold ready-to-wear glasses. The Court found no violation of equal protection: "Evils in the same field may be of different dimensions and proportions, requiring different remedies. Or so the legislature may think. Or the reform may take one step at a time, addressing itself to the phase of the problem which seems most acute to the legislative mind. The legislature may select one phase of one field and apply a remedy there, neglecting the others. [For] all this record shows, the ready-to-wear branch of this business may not loom large in Oklahoma or may present problems of regulation distinct from the other branch."

5. *Ferguson* [p. 87 supra] presented an analogous situation. There, a Kansas statute excepted lawyers from the prohibition of a statute making it a misdemeanor for any person to engage in the business of debt adjusting. We held that the exception of lawyers was not a denial of [equal protection].

[New Orleans'] classification rationally furthers the purpose which [the] city had identified as its objective in enacting the provision, that is, as a means "to preserve the appearance and custom valued by the Quarter's residents and attractive to tourists." The legitimacy of that objective is obvious. The City Council plainly could further that objective by making the reasoned judgment that street peddlers and hawkers tend to interfere with the charm and beauty of an historic area [and] that to ensure the economic vitality of that area, such businesses should be substantially curtailed in the Vieux Carre, if not totally banned.

It is suggested that the "grandfather provision" [was] a totally arbitrary and irrational method of achieving the city's purpose. But rather than proceeding by the immediate and absolute abolition of all pushcart food vendors, the city could rationally [decide] that newer businesses were less likely to have built up substantial reliance interests in continued operation in the Vieux Carre and that the two vendors who qualified under the "grandfather clause" [had] themselves become part of the distinctive character and charm that distinguishes the Vieux Carre. We cannot say that these judgments so lack rationality that they constitute a constitutionally impermissible denial of equal protection.

Nevertheless, [the] Court of Appeals held that even though the exemption of the two vendors was rationally related to legitimate city interests on the basis of facts extant when the ordinance was amended, the "grandfather clause" still could not stand because "the hypothesis that a present eight year veteran of the pushcart hot dog market in the Vieux Carre will continue to operate in a manner more consistent with the traditions of the Quarter than would any other operator is without foundation." Actually, the reliance on the statute's potential irrationality in *Morey,* as the dissenters in that case correctly pointed out, (Frankfurter, J., joined by Harlan, J., dissenting), was a needlessly intrusive judicial infringement on the State's legislative powers, and we have concluded that the equal protection analysis employed in that opinion should no longer be followed. *Morey* was the only case in the last half century to invalidate a wholly economic regulation solely on equal protection grounds, and we are now satisfied that the decision was erroneous. * * *

Reversed.

JUSTICE MARSHALL concurs in the judgment.

JUSTICE STEVENS took no part in [the] case.

Notes and Questions

1. *Legislative purpose.* Of what relevance in *Railway Express* was it that the state courts "declared that the sole purpose" of the law "is to reduce traffic hazards"? Would it be more accurate (and realistic) to describe the purpose as being "to promote public safety slightly by reducing the number of distractions on the sides of moving vehicles to the extent this is feasible without jeopardizing the economic well-being of those merchants who advertise on their own trucks," Note, *Legislative Purpose, Rationality and Equal Protection,* 82 Yale L.J. 123, 144 (1972)—a purpose to which the classification unquestionably was "rationally related"? Is it not true that many government programs "involve goals that reflect an accommodation of various purposes which are determined by subtle or blatant policy trade-offs"? Id. That often "the legislature is simply a 'market-like arena' in which individuals and special interest groups trade with each other through representatives to further their own private ends"? Bice, *Rationality Analysis in Constitutional Law,* 65 Minn.L.Rev. 1, 19 (1980).

Are such legislative purposes (or goals) "legitimate"? "Constitutionally permissible"? Consider Tussman & tenBroek, *The Equal Protection of the Laws,* 37 Calif.L.Rev. 341, 350 (1949): "[T]he requirement that laws be equal rests upon a theory of legislation quite distinct from that of pressure groups—a theory which puts forward some conception of a 'general good' as the 'legitimate public purpose' at which legislation must aim, and according to which the triumph of private or group pressure marks the corruption of the legislative process." Compare Posner, *The DeFunis Case and the Constitutionality of Preferential Treatment of Racial Minorities,* 1974 Sup.Ct.Rev. 1, 27: "[A] vast part of the output of the governmental process would be seen to consist of discrimination, in the sense of an effort to redistribute wealth (in one form or another) from one group in the community to another, founded on the superior ability of one group to manipulate the political process rather than on any principle of justice or efficiency. Yet it would be odd, indeed, to condemn as unconstitutional the most characteristic product of a democratic (perhaps of any) political system."

The legislative history of state and local legislation is often unrecorded and not readily available. Should the Court "assess the rationality of the [classification] in terms of the *state's* purposes, rather than hypothesizing conceivable justifications on its own initiative"? Gunther, *In Search of Evolving Doctrine on a Changing Court: A Model for a Newer Equal Protection,* 86 Harv.L.Rev. 1, 44–46 (1972): "If the Court were to require an articulation of purpose from an authoritative state source"—"a state court's or attorney general's office description of purpose should be acceptable"—"rather than hypothesizing one on its own, there would at least be indirect pressure on the legislature to state its own reasons for selecting particular means and classifications [and thus] improve the quality of the political process [by] encouraging a fuller airing in the political arena of the grounds for legislative action." Is improving the political process a proper function of the judiciary? Compare Tribe, *Toward a Model of Roles in the Due Process of Life and Law,* 87 Harv.L.Rev. 1, 6 n. 28 (1973): "A mismatch between means and ends, when the only ends examined are those argued in a law's defense by an executive officer, may indicate no more than that the officer did not advance the right ends in the law's defense. That his oversight or deliberate choice should be allowed thereby to frustrate the past efforts of his jurisdiction's legislature seems strange." See also Greenawalt, *The Unresolved Problems of Reverse Discrimination,* 67 Calif.L.Rev. 87, 107 (1979): "If it is enough that a lawyer defending the classification state a purpose, then, since lawyers can be almost as imaginative as judges and are likely to suggest many purposes in complex and controversial cases, the requirement of articulated purpose is unlikely often to be crucial." See generally Ely, *Democracy and Distrust* 125–31 (1980).

2. *"One step at a time."* (a) Does the Court's permitting legislatures to "implement their program step by step" immunize "pressure group" lawmaking from equal protection attack? Should it? Consider Note, *Equal Protection,* 82 Harv.L.Rev. 1065, 1085 (1969): "To require that the state remedy all aspects of a particular mischief or none at all might preclude a state from undertaking any program of correction until its resources were adequate to deal with the entire problem. Second, in some instances, the state may not be convinced that a particular policy is a wise one, or it may prove impossible to marshal a legislative majority in favor of extending the policy's coverage any further. Thus, to demand application of the policy to all whom it might logically

encompass, would severely restrict the state's opportunities to experiment." [a]

(b) Does the Court's "step by step" approach, combined with its "minimum rationality" requirement for legislative classifications as reflected in *Railway Express* and *Dukes,* mean that "unless a classification trammels fundamental personal rights or is drawn upon inherently suspect distinctions," it will never be held to violate equal protection? May a law that was rationally related to the purpose that caused its enactment subsequently become irrational because of a change of factual circumstances? If so, suppose a present purpose (not even conceivable by the enacting legislature) now rationally supports the law? See generally Linde, *Due Process of Lawmaking,* 55 Neb.L.Rev. 197, 215–22 (1976); Bice, note 1 supra, at 33–45.

3. *Underinclusion.* (a) Does the "step by step" approach, which permits "underinclusive" legislation [b]—allowing "officials to pick and choose only a few to whom they will apply legislation and thus to escape the political retribution that might be visited upon them if larger numbers were affected"—promote "arbitrary and unreasonable government"? Is it inconsistent with the *Carolene Products* concern, Ch. 1, Sec. 1, for "prejudice against discrete and insular minorities"? When "politically disadvantaged minorities are affected," should "the legislative judgment [be] more critically regarded, for such disadvantaged groups wield less influence in legislative councils than their proportion in the population would seem to warrant" and thus "it might be argued that the legislative decisions do not represent a proper majoritarian choice"? Note, 82 Harv.L.Rev. at 1125.

Consider Choper, *Judicial Review and the National Political Process* 75–77 (1980): "Majoritarians should have scant difficulty [with] the Court's assistance of persons who are not represented in the political process *at all*—best illustrated by aliens [or] minority racial groups who were illegally disenfranchised in certain parts of the nation. But the matter becomes painfully more complicated [when] the judicially favored minority is one that, although fully enfranchised in accordance with its numbers, is nonetheless characterized as being 'politically impotent,' 'not adequately represented,' 'discrete and insular,' or the like. The initial complexity arises because almost all, if not all, groups and interests in the American political process are 'minorities.' Thus, each time any group loses any political battle in which it has an interest—and some group always does—it may lay claim to the label of 'political weakness' or 'submerged and beaten minority.' [It] is true that some minorities, because of their sophistication and combined arithmetical and financial strength, are more influential than others on most political issues; and that some groups with modest numbers may win powerful surrogates who give them forceful representation. Similarly, there are some minorities who are less effective than others on most legislative matters because of their geographic isolation, the general inexcitability or unpopularity of their ideas, their relative inarticulateness, their lack of numbers and resources, or because they are viewed with such resentment, distaste, or hatred that they can neither join working coalitions nor prevent hostile action. But there are many disparate groups who may legitimately claim to meet some or all of these varied criteria for judicial solicitude. Thus, the Court may have to be as sympathetic to

a. If the legislature's "step by step" justification is based on (i) "presently inadequate resources" or (ii) a "desire to experiment," should the Court uphold the classification "only for the specific period that corresponds to the nature of the legislature's timebound objective"? Note, *Reforming the One Step at a Time Justification in Equal Protection Cases,* 90 Yale L.J. 1777, 1784 (1981).

b. For the classic discussion of various types of legislative classifications, see Tussman & tenBroek, note 1 supra.

the pleas of apartment dwellers in Iowa, tobacco farmers in Massachusetts, debt adjustors in Kansas, oil well producers in New York, and cedar tree owners in Virginia as it is to the complaints of Jehovah's Witnesses in Rhode Island, communists in New Hampshire, progressives in Ohio, Asian-Americans in California, and blacks in Mississippi—all these illustrations assuming a given temporal span, presumably also to be determined by the Court." See also REHNQUIST, J., dissenting in *Sugarman v. Dougall* and *In re Griffiths,* Sec. 3, I infra, which held state discriminations against aliens subject to "strict scrutiny": "Our society, consisting of over 200 million individuals of multitudinous origins, customs, tongues, beliefs, and cultures is, to say the least, diverse. It would hardly take extraordinary ingenuity for a lawyer to find 'insular and discrete' minorities at every turn of the road. Yet, unless the Court can precisely define and constitutionally justify both the terms and analysis it uses, [the] Court can choose a 'minority' it 'feels' deserves 'solicitude' and thereafter prohibit the States from classifying that 'minority' differently from the 'majority.' I cannot find [any] constitutional authority for such a 'ward of the Court' approach to equal protection." See also Sandalow, *The Distrust of Politics,* 56 N.Y.U.L.Rev. 446, 466–67 (1981): "Corporations also do not vote, but those who argue that aliens should be accorded [special protection] do not frequently complain that corporations should also receive that protection because they lack political influence. Any attempt to appraise the inner workings of the political process must, as the illustration of the corporation suggests, examine the entire process to ascertain the extent of a group's influence. [But] what measure have we, other than an evaluation of outcomes [—i.e., the desirability of the substantive policies enacted by the legislature]?"

(b) To what extent is the objection to underinclusive classifications limited to laws that impose "burdens" (e.g., *Railway Express*) rather than confer "benefits" (e.g., *Dukes*)? Were the "burdened" groups in the cases discussed in this Sec.—*Railway Express, Dukes, Morey, Lee Optical, Ferguson*—"politically disadvantaged minorities"? Compare *New York City Transit Auth. v. Beazer,* infra (burden on methadone users).

4. *Overinclusion.* Many laws, based on a plausible (often persuasive) judgment that many or most persons within the classification pose the problem sought to be remedied, subject the entire class to the regulation even though not every person within the class may pose the problem. For example, in *Ferguson,* the law was not only underinclusive in permitting only lawyers to be debt adjusters, but was also overinclusive in that there were surely *some* nonlawyers who would not engage in abusive debt adjusting. A common justification for overinclusive laws is avoidance of the administrative cost and chance of error in making individualized determinations for each person within the class.

Should the Court be more deferential to overinclusiveness because it "poses less danger than underinclusiveness, at least from the viewpoint of political accountability, for overinclusiveness does not ordinarily exempt potentially powerful opponents from a law's reach"? Tribe, *American Constitutional Law* 1049 (2d ed. 1988). Or is overinclusion "less tolerable than underinclusion, for while the latter fails to impose the burden on some who should logically bear it, the former actually does impose the burden on some who do not belong in the class"? Note, 82 Harv.L.Rev. at 1086.[c]

---

c. For the view that the Court should use a "legitimacy principle" in determining equal protection claims—which "requires simply that in enacting classifications legislators

The post 1930s cases considered to this point almost all invoke the extremely deferential "minimum rationality" standard of review. This approach has been used often in recent years in rejecting equal protection challenges to economic and social welfare legislation.[d] Several such decisions, in which the challengers unsuccessfully sought to have the classifications characterized as being "suspect" or involving "fundamental rights" (and thus subject to "strict scrutiny"), are considered in Sec. 4 infra. In some situations, however, although employing the traditional "rational basis" standard, the Court has held laws violative of equal protection.[e]

Furthermore, the Court has periodically articulated the "traditional" standard in a way that suggests a more active judicial examination of the challenged classification. For example, JOHNSON v. ROBISON, p. 896 supra, per BRENNAN, J., upheld a federal statute granting educational benefits to military veterans but not to conscientious objectors who performed alternate civilian service under the "rational basis" standard, but stated the *Royster Guano* formulation that the classification "must rest upon some ground of difference having a fair and substantial relation to the object of the legislation," and then devoted several pages to considering the justification.[f]

NEW YORK CITY TRANSIT AUTH. v. BEAZER, 440 U.S. 568, 99 S.Ct. 1355, 59 L.Ed.2d 587 (1979), per STEVENS, J., upheld the exclusion of all methadone users from any Transit Authority (TA) employment. It reversed the federal district court's conclusion that, because about 75% of "patients who have been on methadone maintenance for at least a year are free from illicit drug use" and because the exclusion applied to non-safety sensitive jobs, it had "no rational relation to the demands of the job to be performed": "[A]ny special rule short of total exclusion that TA might adopt is likely to be less precise—and will assuredly be more costly—than the one that it currently enforces. If eligibility is marked at any intermediate point—whether after one year of treatment or later—the classification will inevitably discriminate between employees or applicants equally or almost equally apt to achieve full recovery. [By] contrast, the 'no drugs' policy now enforced by TA is supported by the legitimate inference that as long as a treatment program (or other drug use) continues, a degree of uncertainty persists. * * *

"[T]he District Court's conclusion was that TA's rule is broader than necessary to exclude those methadone users who are not actually qualified to work for TA. We may assume [that] it is probably unwise for a large employer like TA to rely on a general rule instead of individualized consideration of every job applicant. But these assumptions concern matters of personnel policy that do not implicate the principle safeguarded by the Equal Protection Clause. As the District Court recognized, the special classification created by TA's rule serves

must: (1) avoid palpably inaccurate factual judgments; (2) not act discriminatorily, classifying persons, for example, in ways that offend the individualist ethic; and (3) be sensitive to the need for some proportion between the advantages of avoiding individualized determinations and the costs of abridging certain important interests"—see Perry, *Constitutional "Fairness": Notes on Equal Protection and Due Process,* 63 Va.L.Rev. 383 (1977).

d. For citations, see Nowak, Rotunda & Young, *Constitutional Law* 535–36 (3d ed. 1986).

e. See, e.g., *Eisenstadt v. Baird* (1972), p. 154 supra; *United States Dep't of Agriculture v. Moreno* (1973), Sec. 4, IV infra; *Baxstrom v. Herold,* 383 U.S. 107, 86 S.Ct. 760, 15 L.Ed.2d 620 (1966) (extensive procedural rights prior to civil commitment except for persons who are ending a prison term); *Logan v. Zimmerman Brush Co.,* infra.

f. See also *Reed v. Reed* (1971), Sec. 3, II infra, per Burger, C.J., using this formulation in holding a law that discriminated against women violative of equal protection.

the general objectives of safety and efficiency. Moreover, the exclusionary line challenged by respondents [does] not circumscribe a class of persons characterized by some unpopular trait or affiliation, it does not create or reflect any special likelihood of bias on the part of the ruling majority. Under these circumstances, it is of no constitutional significance that the degree of rationality is not as great with respect to certain ill-defined subparts of the classification as it is with respect to the classification as a whole." [a]

WHITE, J., joined by Marshall, J., dissented: Both courts below "found that those who have been maintained on methadone for at least a year and who are free from the use of illicit drugs and alcohol can easily be identified through normal personnel procedures and, for a great many jobs, are as employable as and present no more risk than applicants from the general population. [On] the facts as found [one] can reach the Court's result only if [equal protection] imposes no real constraint at all in this situation. * * *

"Of course, the District Court's order permitting total exclusion of all methadone users maintained for less than one year, whether successfully or not, would still exclude some employables and would to this extent be overinclusive. [But although] many of those who have not been successfully maintained for a year are employable, as a class they, unlike the protected group, are not as employable as the general population. Thus, even assuming the bad risks could be identified, serving the end of employability would require unusual efforts to determine those more likely to revert. But that legitimate secondary goal is not fulfilled by excluding the protected [class]. Accordingly, the rule's classification of successfully maintained persons as dispositively different from the general population is left without any justification and, with its irrationality and invidiousness thus uncovered, must fall before the Equal Protection Clause.[15] " [b]

a. See also *Vance v. Bradley*, 440 U.S. 93, 99 S.Ct. 939, 59 L.Ed.2d 171 (1979), per White, J., (sustaining mandatory retirement at age 60 for federal Foreign Service personnel), conceding that the classification was "to some extent both under-and over-inclusive" but holding that "perfection is by no means required. [In] an equal protection case of this type, [those] challenging the legislative judgment must convince the court that the legislative facts on which the classification is apparently based could not reasonably be conceived to be true by the governmental decisionmaker."

Minnesota v. Clover Leaf Creamery Co., 449 U.S. 456, 101 S.Ct. 715, 66 L.Ed.2d 659 (1981), per Brennan, J., relied on this language in unanimously rejecting an equal protection challenge to economic legislation.

15. I have difficulty also with the Court's easy conclusion that the challenged rule was "[q]uite plainly" not motivated "by any special animus against a specific group of persons." Heroin addiction is a special problem of the poor, and the addict population is composed largely of racial minorities that the Court has previously recognized as politically powerless and historical subjects of majoritarian neglect. Persons on methadone maintenance have few interests in common with members of the majority, and thus are unlikely to have their interests protected, or even considered, in governmental decisionmaking. Indeed, petitioners stipulated that "[o]ne of the reasons for [the] drug policy is the fact that [petitioners] feel[ ] an adverse public reaction would result if it were generally known that [petitioners] employed persons with a prior history of drug abuse, including persons participating in methadone maintenance programs." It is hard for me to reconcile that stipulation of animus against former addicts with our past holdings that "a bare [desire] to harm a politically unpopular group cannot constitute a *legitimate* governmental interest." *U.S. Dept. of Agriculture v. Moreno.* On the other hand, the afflictions to which petitioners are more sympathetic, such as alcoholism and mental illness, are shared by both white and black, rich and poor.

Some weight should also be given to the history of the rule. Petitioners admit that it was not the result of a reasoned policy decision and stipulated that they had never studied the ability of those on methadone maintenance to perform petitioners' jobs. Petitioners are not directly accountable to the public, are not the type of official body that normally makes legislative judgments of fact such as those relied upon by the majority today, and are by nature more concerned with business efficiency than with other public policies for which they have no direct responsibili-

b. See note b on page 942.

UNITED STATES R.R. RETIREMENT BD. v. FRITZ

449 U.S. 166, 101 S.Ct. 453, 66 L.Ed.2d 368 (1980).

JUSTICE REHNQUIST delivered the opinion of the Court.

The United States District Court [held violative of the "equal protection component of the Fifth Amendment" § 231b(h)] of the Railroad Retirement Act of 1974. [Under the] Act's predecessor statute, a person who worked for both railroad and nonrailroad employers and who qualified for railroad retirement benefits and social security benefits received retirement benefits under both systems and an accompanying "windfall" benefit. [Congress] determined to place the system on a "sound financial basis" by eliminating future accruals of those benefits. Congress also enacted various transitional provisions [which] expressly preserved windfall benefits for some classes of employees.

* * * First, those employees who lacked the requisite 10 years of railroad employment to qualify for railroad retirement benefits as of January 1, 1975, the changeover date, would have their retirement benefits computed under the new system and would not receive any windfall benefit. Second, those individuals already retired and already receiving dual benefits [would] continue to receive a windfall benefit. Third, those employees who had qualified for both railroad and social security benefits as of the changeover date, but who had not yet retired as of that date (and thus were not yet receiving dual benefits), were entitled to windfall benefits if they had (1) performed some railroad service in 1974 or (2) had a "current connection" with the railroad industry as of December 31, 1974,[6] or (3) completed 25 years of railroad service as of December 31, 1974. * * *

Thus, an individual who, as of the changeover date, was unretired and had 11 years of railroad employment and sufficient nonrailroad employment to qualify for social security benefits is eligible for the full windfall amount if he worked for the railroad in 1974 or had a current connection with the railroad as of December 31, 1974, or his later retirement date. But an unretired individual with 24 years of railroad service and sufficient nonrailroad service to qualify for social security benefits is not eligible for a full windfall amount unless he worked for the railroad in 1974, or had a current connection with the railroad as of December 31, 1974 or his later retirement date. * * *

The District Court agreed with appellees that a differentiation based solely on whether an employee was "active" in the railroad business as of 1974 was not "rationally related" to the congressional purposes of insuring the solvency of the railroad retirement system and protecting vested benefits. We disagree and reverse.

The initial issue [is] the appropriate standard of judicial review to be applied when social and economic legislation enacted by Congress is challenged. [B]ecause the distinctions drawn in § 231b(h) do not burden fundamental constitutional rights or create "suspect" classifications, such as race or national origin, we may put cases involving judicial review of such claims to one side.

ty. Both the State and City of New York, which do exhibit those democratic characteristics, hire persons in methadone programs for similar jobs.

These factors together strongly point to a conclusion of invidious discrimination. * * *

b. White, J., joined by Brennan, J., also dissented on statutory grounds. Powell, J.'s separate concurrence is omitted.

6. The term "current connection" is defined [to] mean, in general, employment in the railroad industry in 12 of the preceding 30 calendar months.

Despite the narrowness of the issue, this Court in earlier cases has not been altogether consistent in its pronouncements in this area [contrasting the language in *National Carbonic Gas* and *Royster Guano,* set forth supra].

In more recent years, however, the Court in cases involving social and economic benefits has consistently refused to invalidate on equal protection grounds legislation which it simply deemed unwise or unartfully drawn.

Thus in *Dandridge v. Williams,* [Sec. 4, IV infra], the Court [stated] "The problems of government are practical ones and may justify, if they do not require, rough accommodations—illogical, it may be, and unscientific.' [The rational basis standard] is true to the principle that the Fourteenth Amendment gives the federal courts no power to impose upon the States their views of what constitutes wise economic or social policy." Of like tenor are *Vance v. Bradley* and *New Orleans v. Dukes.* * * *

Applying those principles to this case, the plain language of § 231b(h) marks the beginning and end of our inquiry.[10] There Congress determined that some of those who in the past received full windfall benefits would not continue to do so. Because Congress could have eliminated windfall benefits for all classes of employees, it is not constitutionally impermissible for Congress to have drawn lines between groups of employees for the purpose of phasing out those benefits. *Dukes.*

The only remaining question is whether Congress achieved its purpose in a patently arbitrary or irrational way. [Congress] could properly conclude that persons who had actually acquired statutory entitlement to windfall benefits while still employed in the railroad industry had a greater equitable claim to those benefits than the members of appellees' class who were no longer in railroad employment when they became eligible for dual benefits. [Furthermore,] Congress could assume that those who had a current connection with the railroad industry when the Act was passed in 1974, or who returned to the industry before their retirement, were more likely than those who had left the industry prior to 1974 and who never returned, to be among the class of persons who pursue careers in the railroad industry, the class for whom the Railroad Retirement Act was designed.

Where, as here, there are plausible reasons for Congress' action, our inquiry is at an end. It is, of course, "constitutionally irrelevant whether this reasoning in fact underlay the legislative decision," because this Court has never insisted that a legislative body articulate its reasons for enacting a statute. This is particularly true where the legislature must necessarily engage in a process of line drawing. The "task of classifying persons for [benefits] inevitably requires that some persons who have an almost equally strong claim to favorite treatment be placed on different sides of the line," *Mathews v. Diaz,* [Sec. 3, I infra], and the fact the line might have been drawn differently at some points is a matter for legislative, rather than judicial consideration.

10. This opinion and Justice Brennan's dissent cite a number of equal protection [cases]. The most arrogant legal scholar would not claim that all of these cases applied a uniform or consistent test under the Equal Protection Clause. [But] like our predecessors and our successors, we are obliged to apply the equal protection component of the Fifth Amendment as we believe the Constitution requires and in so doing we have no hesitation in asserting, contrary to the dissent, that where social or economic regulations are involved *Dandridge* [and] this case, state the proper application of the test. The comments in the dissenting opinion about the proper cases for which to look for the correct statement of the equal protection rational basis standard, and about which cases limit earlier cases, are just that: comments in a dissenting opinion.

Finally, we disagree with the District Court's conclusion that Congress was unaware of what it accomplished or that it was misled by the groups that appeared before it. If this test were applied literally to every member of any legislature that ever voted on a law, there would be very few laws which would survive it. The language of the statute is clear, and we have historically assumed that Congress intended what it enacted. To be sure, appellees lost a political battle in which they had a strong interest, but this is neither the first nor the last time that such a result will occur in the legislative forum. * * *

JUSTICE STEVENS, concurring in the judgment.

In my opinion Justice Brennan's criticism of the Court's approach to this case merits a more thoughtful response than that contained in footnote 10. [When] Congress deprives a small class of persons of vested [rights,] I believe the Constitution requires something more than merely a "conceivable" or a "plausible" explanation for the unequal treatment.

I do not, however, share Justice Brennan's conclusion that every statutory classification must further an objective that can be confidently identified as the "actual purpose" of the legislature. Actual purpose is sometimes unknown. Moreover, undue emphasis on actual motivation may result in identically worded statutes being held valid in one State and invalid in a neighboring State. I therefore believe that we must discover a correlation between the classification and either the actual purpose of the statute or a legitimate purpose that we may reasonably presume to have motivated an impartial legislature. If the adverse impact on the disfavored class is an apparent aim of the legislature, its impartiality would be suspect. If, however, the adverse impact may reasonably be viewed as an acceptable cost of achieving a larger goal, an impartial lawmaker could rationally decide that that cost should be incurred.

In this case, however, we need not look beyond the actual purpose of the legislature. As is often true, this legislation is the product of multiple and somewhat inconsistent purposes that led to certain compromises. One purpose was to eliminate in the future the benefit that is described by the Court as a "windfall benefit" and by Justice Brennan as an "earned dual benefit." That aim was incident to the broader objective of protecting the solvency of the entire railroad retirement program. Two purposes that conflicted somewhat with this broad objective were the purposes of preserving those benefits that had already vested and of increasing the level of payments to beneficiaries whose rights were not otherwise to be changed. As Justice Brennan emphasizes, Congress originally intended to protect *all* vested benefits, but it ultimately sacrificed some benefits in the interest of achieving other objectives.

[The] congressional purpose to eliminate dual benefits is unquestionably legitimate; that legitimacy is not undermined by the adjustment in the level of remaining benefits in response to inflation in the economy. [Further], some hardship—in the form of frustrated long-term expectations—must inevitably result from any reduction in vested benefits. Arguably, therefore, Congress had a duty—and surely it had the right to decide—to eliminate no more vested benefits than necessary to achieve its fiscal purpose. Having made that decision, any distinction it chose within the class of vested beneficiaries would involve a difference of degree rather than a difference in entitlement. I am satisfied that a distinction based upon currency of railroad employment represents an impartial method of identifying that sort of difference. Because retirement plans frequently provide greater benefits for recent retirees than for those who retired years ago—and thus give a greater reward for recent service than for past service of equal duration—the basis for the statutory discrimination is supported by relevant precedent. It follows, in my judgment, that the timing of the employees' railroad service is a "reasonable basis" for the classification as that term is used in *National Carbonic Gas* and *Dandridge,* as well as a "ground of difference having a fair and substantial relation to the object of the legislation," as those words are used in *Royster Guano.* * * *

JUSTICE BRENNAN, with whom JUSTICE MARSHALL joins, dissenting.

[T]he legal standard applicable to this case is the "rational basis" test. [The] Court today purports to apply this standard, but [fails] to scrutinize the challenged classification in the manner established by our governing precedents. I suggest that the mode of analysis employed by the Court in this case virtually immunizes social and economic legislative classifications from judicial review.

[Perhaps] the clearest statement of this Court's present approach to "rational basis" scrutiny may be found in *Johnson v. Robison,* [where] eight Members of this Court agreed [to the *Royster Guano* formulation]. The enactments of Congress are entitled to a presumption of constitutionality, and the burden rests on those challenging a legislative classification to demonstrate that it does not bear the "fair and substantial relation to the object of the legislation" required under the Constitution.

Nonetheless, the rational basis standard "is not a toothless one," *Mathews v. Lucas,* [Sec. 3, III infra]. When faced with a challenge to a legislative classification under the rational basis test, the court should ask, first, what the purposes of the statute are, and second, whether the classification is rationally related to achievement of those purposes.

The purposes of the Railroad Retirement Act of 1974 are clear, because Congress has commendably stated them in the House and Senate reports accompanying the Act. A section of the reports is entitled "Principal Purpose of the Bill." It notes generally that "[t]he bill provides for a complete restructuring of the Railroad Retirement Act of 1937, and will place it on a sound financial basis," and then states: "Persons who already have vested rights under both the Railroad Retirement and the Social Security systems will in the future be permitted to receive benefits computed under both systems just as is true under existing law." [3] Moreover, Congress explained that this purpose was based on considerations of fairness and the legitimate expectations of the retirees. [The] classification at issue here, which deprives some retirees of vested dual benefits that they had earned prior to 1974, directly conflicts with Congress' stated purpose. As such, the classification is not only rationally unrelated to the congressional purpose; it is inimical to it.

The Court today avoids the conclusion that § 231b(h) must be invalidated by deviating in three ways from traditional rational basis analysis. * * *

A. The Court states that "the plain language of § 231b(h) marks the beginning and end of our inquiry." [Since] the Act deprives appellees of their vested earned dual benefits, the Court apparently assumes that Congress must have *intended* that result. But by presuming purpose from result, the Court reduces analysis to tautology. It may always be said that Congress intended to do what it in fact did. If that were the extent of our analysis, we would find every statute, no matter how arbitrary or irrational, perfectly tailored to achieve

3. Several pages later, the reports again make clear that persons with vested rights to earned dual benefits would retain [them]. Only in technical discussions and in the section-by-section analyses do the reports reflect the actual consequences of the Act on the appellee class. * * *

its purpose. But equal protection scrutiny under the rational basis test requires the courts first to deduce the independent objectives of the statute, usually from statements of purpose and other evidence in the statute and legislative history, and second to analyze whether the challenged classification rationally furthers achievement of those objectives. The Court's tautological approach will not suffice.

B. The Court analyzes the rationality of § 231b(h) in terms of a justification suggested by Government attorneys, but never adopted by Congress. [But] this Court has frequently recognized that the actual purposes of Congress, rather than the post hoc justifications offered by Government attorneys, must be the primary basis for analysis under the rational basis test. [For example], in *San Antonio Independent School District v. Rodriguez* [Sec. 4, IV infra], this Court stated that a challenged classification will pass muster under "rational basis" scrutiny only if it "rationally furthers some legitimate, *articulated* state purpose," (emphasis added), and in *Massachusetts Board of Retirement v. Murgia* [Sec. 3, I infra], we stated that such a classification will be sustained only if it "rationally furthers the purpose *identified by the State.*" (Emphasis added.) * * *

The Court argues that Congress chose to discriminate against appellees for reasons of equity, [but, as] I have shown, Congress expressed the view that it would be inequitable to deprive any retirees of any portion of the benefits they had been promised and that they had earned under prior law. The Court is unable to cite even one statement in the legislative history by a Representative or Senator that makes the equitable judgment it imputes to Congress. In the entire legislative history of the Act, the only persons to state that the equities justified eliminating appellees' earned dual benefits were representatives of railroad management and labor, whose self-serving interest in bringing about this result destroys any basis for attaching weight to their statements. [They] were not appointed by public officials, nor did they represent the interests of the appellee class, who were no longer active railroaders or union members.

[L]abor representatives demanded that benefits be increased for their current members, the cost to be offset by divesting the appellee class of a portion of the benefits they had earned under prior law. [In] fact, the [management and labor representatives] and Railroad Retirement Board members who testified at congressional hearings perpetuated the inaccurate impression that all retirees with earned vested dual benefits under prior law would retain their benefits unchanged. * * *

Of course, a misstatement or several misstatements by witnesses before Congress would not ordinarily lead us to conclude that Congress misapprehended what it was doing. In this instance, however, where complex legislation was drafted by outside parties and Congress relied on them to explain it, where the misstatements are frequent and unrebutted, and where no Member of Congress can be found to have stated the effect of the classification correctly, we are entitled to suspect that Congress may have been misled. As the District Court found: "At no time during the hearings did Congress even give a hint that it understood that the bill by its language eliminated an earned benefit of plaintiff's class."

Therefore, I do not think that this classification was rationally related to an *actual* governmental purpose.

C. The third way in which the Court has deviated from the principles of rational basis scrutiny is its failure to analyze whether the challenged classification is genuinely related to the purpose identified by the Court. Having suggested that "equitable considerations" underlay the challenged classification—in direct contradiction to Congress' evaluation of those considerations, and in the face of evidence that the classification was the product of private negotiation by interested parties, inadequately examined and understood by Congress—the Court proceeds to accept that suggestion without further [analysis.]

In my view, the following considerations are of greatest relevance to the equities of this case: (1) contribution to the system; (2) reasonable expectation and reliance; (3) need; and (4) character of service to the railroad industry. With respect to each of these considerations, I would conclude that appellees have as great an equitable claim to their earned dual benefits as do their more favored coworkers, who remain entitled to their earned dual benefits under § 231b(h).

[Because] the Court is willing to accept a tautological analysis of congressional purpose, an assertion of "equitable" considerations contrary to the expressed judgment of Congress, and a classification patently unrelated to achievement of the identified purpose, it succeeds in effectuating neither equity nor congressional intent. * * *

Notes and Questions

1. *"Actual purpose."* Does *Fritz* put to rest—at least for a majority of the Court—the issue of "actual" vs. "hypothetically conceivable" legislative purpose? Within three months after *Fritz,* SCHWEIKER v. WILSON, 450 U.S. 221, 101 S.Ct. 1074, 67 L.Ed.2d 186 (1981), per BLACKMUN, J., upheld Congress' denial of SSI "comfort allowances" to needy aged, blind and disabled persons confined in public institutions unless the institutions received federal Medicaid funds: "[T]he pertinent inquiry is whether the [classification] advances legitimate legislative goals in a rational fashion. The Court has said that, although this rational basis standard is 'not a toothless one,' *Mathews v. Lucas,* it does not allow us to substitute our personal notions of good public [policy].[a] We believe that the decision to incorporate the Medicaid eligibility standards into the SSI scheme must be considered Congress' deliberate, considered choice." It "is rationally related to the legitimate legislative desire to avoid spending federal resources on behalf of individuals whose care and treatment are being fully provided for by state and local government units" and "may be said to implement a congressional policy choice to provide supplemental financial assistance for only those residents of public institutions who already receive significant federal support in the form of Medicaid coverage."

POWELL, J., joined by Brennan, Marshall and Stevens, JJ., dissented: "In my view, the Court should receive with some skepticism post hoc hypotheses about legislative purpose, unsupported by the legislative history. When no indication of legislative purpose appears other than the current position of the Secretary, the Court should require that the classification bear a 'fair and substantial relation' to the asserted purpose. See *Royster Guano.*"[b]

a. See also *Schweiker v. Hogan,* 457 U.S. 569, 102 S.Ct. 2597, 73 L.Ed.2d 227 (1982) (unanimous opinion, per Stevens, J., applying "rationality" test to Medicaid benefits discrimination despite the fact that it "may be inequitable or unwise").

b. For the view that if "rationality is to be a meaningful standard of review, the court must conceive of its task as identifying the legislature's *probable* goals based on the available evidence," see Bice, note 1 after *Dukes,* at 30.

2. *"Means/end fit."* To what extent should the Court employ a "strengthened 'rational' scrutiny" by requiring "that legislative means must substantially further legislative ends"? Gunther, note 1 after *Dukes,* supra: "Examination of means in light of asserted state purposes would directly promote public consideration of the benefits assertedly sought by the proposed legislation; indirectly, it would stimulate fuller political examination, in relation to those benefits, of the costs that would be incurred if the proposed means were adopted."

Compare REHNQUIST, J., dissenting in *Trimble v. Gordon,* Sec. 3, III infra, which held that an Illinois statute, forbidding illegitimate children to inherit from their fathers by intestate succession, violated equal protection: "[Judicial review of means/end fit] requires a conscious second-guessing of legislative judgment in an area where this Court has no special expertise whatever. [In] most cases, [the] 'fit' will involve a greater or lesser degree of imperfection. Then the Court asks itself how much 'imperfection' between means and ends is permissible? In making this judgment it must throw into the judicial hopper the whole range of factors which were first thrown into the legislative hopper. What alternatives were reasonably available? What reasons are there for the legislature to accomplish this 'purpose' in the way it did? What obstacles stood in the way of other solutions?

"[Without] any antecedent constitutional mandate, we have created on the premises of the Equal Protection Clause a school for legislators, whereby opinions of this Court are written to instruct them in a better understanding of how to accomplish their ordinary legislative tasks. [Since] Illinois' distinction is not mindless and patently irrational, I would [affirm]."[c]

3. *"Irrationality."* (a) In LOGAN v. ZIMMERMAN BRUSH CO. (1982), p. ___ supra, for the first time in 25 years, a majority of the justices employed "the lowest level of permissible equal protection scrutiny" and found a violation of equal protection. Appellant filed an employment discrimination complaint before an Illinois Commission which inadvertently scheduled the hearing at a date after the statutory time period expired. The state court held that this deprived the Commission of jurisdiction and terminated appellant's claim. BLACKMUN, J., joined by Brennan, Marshall and O'Connor, JJ., found this discrimination against those who did not get a hearing to be "patently irrational in light of [the law's] stated purpose": "I cannot agree that terminating a claim that the State itself has misscheduled is a rational way of expediting the resolution of disputes. [The] state's rationale must be something more than the exercise of a strained imagination; while the connection between means and ends need not be precise, it, at the least, must have some objective basis. That is not so here." POWELL, J., joined by Rehnquist, J., concurred as to "this unusual classification": "As appellants possessed no power to convene hearings, it is unfair and irrational to punish them for the Commission's failure to do so."[d]

c. For the view that the "rationality" requirement does—and should—function as a balance of costs, benefits, and alternatives as well as the legitimacy of legislative purpose and the closeness of fit between means and ends, see Bennett, *"Mere" Rationality in Constitutional Law: Judicial Review and Democratic Theory,* 67 Calif.L.Rev. 1049 (1979). But see Barrett, *The Rational Basis Standard for Equal Protection Review of Ordinary Legislative Classifications,* 68 Ky.L.J. 845 (1980).

d. See also *G.D. Searle & Co. v. Cohn,* 455 U.S. 404, 102 S.Ct. 1137, 71 L.Ed.2d 250 (1982), for a dissent by Stevens, J., finding no "rational basis" for a statutory classification.

See also *Bowen v. Owens,* 476 U.S. 340, 106 S.Ct. 1881, 90 L.Ed.2d 316 (1986), for a dissent by Blackmun, J., finding no "rational basis" for a Social Security Act classification. Marshall and Brennan, JJ., also dissented on the ground that Congress had no "actual purpose" "for drawing this line other than its desire to

(b) ALLEGHENY PITTSBURGH COAL CO. v. COUNTY COM'N, 488 U.S. 336, 109 S.Ct. 633, 102 L.Ed.2d 688 (1989), per REHNQUIST, C.J., unanimously found an equal protection violation when a West Virginia county tax assessor "valued petitioners' real property on the basis of its recent purchase price, but made only minor modifications in the assessments of land which had not been recently sold," resulting in the fact that "petitioners' property has been assessed at roughly 8 to 35 times more than comparable neighboring property, and these discrepancies have continued for more than 10 years with little change." The Court, noting that it was not passing on a scheme like California's that deliberately reassessed the value of property only when it was transferred, held that the county assessor's practice was not "rationally related" to West Virginia's rule "that all property of the kind held by petitioners shall be taxed at a rate uniform throughout the state according to its estimated market value." [e]

4. *Legislative role.* Is the "traditional"—"rational basis"—"minimum rationality" approach premised "on the propriety of unelected federal judges' displacing the judgments of elected state officials, or upon the competence of federal courts to prescribe workable standards of state conduct and devise measures to enforce them"? See Sager, *Fair Measure: The Legal Status of Underenforced Constitutional Norms,* 91 Harv.L.Rev. 1212, 1217 (1978). If either, of what relevance is the "traditional" approach to state and local legislators? State judges? Congress? Consider id. at 1218–21: "Institutional rather than analytical reasons appear to have prompted the broad exclusion of state tax and regulatory measures from the reach of the equal protection construct fashioned by the federal judiciary. This is what creates the disparity between this construct and a true conception of equal protection, and thus substantiates the claim that equal protection is an underenforced constitutional norm. [C]onstitutional norms which are underenforced by the federal judiciary should be understood to be legally valid to their full conceptual limits, and federal judicial decisions which stop short of these limits should be understood as delineating only the boundaries of the federal courts' role in enforcing the norm: By 'legally valid,' I mean that the unenforced margins of underenforced norms should have the full status of positive law which we generally accord to the norms of our Constitution, save only that the federal judiciary will not enforce these margins. Thus, the legal powers or legal obligations of government officials which are subtended in the unenforced margins of underenforced constitutional norms are to be understood to remain in full force." For further consideration, see *Katzenbach v. Morgan,* p. 1272 infra, and notes thereafter.[f]

find a point of compromise between the two Houses."

See also *Lyng v. Intern. Union,* 485 U.S. 360, 108 S.Ct. 1184, 99 L.Ed.2d 380 (1988), for a dissent by Marshall, J., joined by Brennan and Blackmun, JJ., finding that Congress' denial of food stamps to persons who meet the low income test because they are on strike "cannot survive even rational basis scrutiny"; *Bankers Life & Casualty Co. v. Crenshaw,* 486 U.S. 71, 108 S.Ct. 1645, 100 L.Ed.2d 62 (1988), for a dissent by Blackmun, J., finding that a statutory classification was not "reasonably related" to the asserted state interests and was thus "arbitrary and irrational."

e. For the view that *Allegheny* "revived a doctrine that had lain dormant for fifty years," see Glennon, *Taxation and Equal Protection,* 58 Geo.Wash.L.Rev. 261, 290 (1990): "The systematic and intentional undervaluation test [is] at war both with rational basis review and with the broad latitude given states in creating tax schemes. [In] every instance that [the] Court [has] found that a tax scheme violated rational basis equal protection, [the] opinion was either poorly reasoned or over the dissents of Justices of great stature." Accord, Cohen, *State Law in Equality Clothing,* 38 U.C.L.A.L.Rev. 87 (1990).

f. For the view that the Court should defer to a *state court's* "factual conclusions" that a state law's classification "was not rationally related to a legitimate state purpose," see Stevens, J., dissenting in *Minnesota v. Clover Leaf Creamery Co.*

SECTION 2. RACE AND ETHNIC ANCESTRY

I. DISCRIMINATION AGAINST RACIAL AND ETHNIC MINORITIES

The "evil to be remedied" by the equal protection clause, declared the *Slaughter-House Cases,* was "the existence of laws in the States where the newly emancipated negroes resided, which discriminated with gross injustice and hardship against them as a class." STRAUDER v. WEST VIRGINIA, 100 U.S. 303, 25 L.Ed. 664 (1880)—the first post-Civil War racial discrimination case to reach the Court—per STRONG, J., invalidating the state murder conviction of a black on the ground that state law forbade blacks from serving on grand or petit juries,[a] observed that "the true spirit and meaning" of the Civil War amendments was "securing to a race recently emancipated [the] enjoyment of all the civil rights that under the law are enjoyed by [whites]. What is [equal protection but] that all persons, whether colored or white, shall stand equal before the laws of the States, and, in regard to the colored race, for whose protection the amendment was primarily designed, that no discrimination shall be made against them by law because of their color? The words of the amendment [contain] a positive immunity or right, most valuable to the colored race,—the right to exemption from unfriendly legislation against them distinctively as colored,—exemption from legal discriminations, implying inferiority in civil society, lessening the security of their enjoyment of the rights which others enjoy, and discriminations which are steps towards reducing them to the condition of a subject race.

"That the West Virginia statute respecting juries [is] such a discrimination ought not to be doubted. [And if] in those States where the colored people constitute a majority of the entire population a law should be enacted excluding all white men from jury service, [we] apprehend no one would be heard to claim that it would not be a denial to white men of the equal protection of the laws.[b] Nor if a law should be passed excluding all naturalized Celtic Irishmen, would there be any doubt of its inconsistency with the spirit of the amendment. * * *

"We do not say that within the limits from which it is not excluded by the amendment a State may not prescribe the qualifications of its jurors, and in so doing make discriminations. It may confine the selection to males, to freeholders, to citizens, to persons within certain ages, or to persons having educational qualifications. We do not believe the Fourteenth Amendment was ever intended to prohibit this. Looking at its history, it is clear it had no such purpose. Its aim was against discrimination because of race or color."

a. The Court emphasized that the question was *not* whether a black defendant "has a right to a grand or a petit jury composed in whole or in part of persons of his own race or color, but [whether] all persons of his race or color may be excluded by law solely because of their race or color."

The Court has adhered to *Strauder's* requirement of systematic exclusion. See note 1 following *Yick Wo v. Hopkins,* Sec. III infra. But it has permitted criminal defendants who are not themselves members of the excluded group to challenge the jury's composition on the ground that it violates the defendant's sixth amendment right to a jury "selected from a fair cross section of the community." See, e.g., *Peters v. Kiff,* 407 U.S. 493, 92 S.Ct. 2163, 33 L.Ed.2d 83 (1972) (white challenging exclusion of blacks); *Duren v. Missouri,* 439 U.S. 357, 99 S.Ct. 664, 58 L.Ed.2d 579 (1979) (man challenging exclusion of women).

b. The issue of discrimination against the majority race—that of "favorable," "reverse," or "benign" discrimination—is considered in Part V infra.

Thus, as stated in *Brown v. Board of Education,* Part II infra, "in the first cases in this Court construing the Fourteenth Amendment, decided shortly after its adoption, the Court interpreted it as proscribing all state-imposed discriminations against the Negro race." Subsequent decisions extended this proscription to state discrimination against persons because of their national origin, such as those of Chinese or Mexican ancestry.[c]

KOREMATSU v. UNITED STATES

323 U.S. 214, 65 S.Ct. 193, 89 L.Ed. 194 (1944).

JUSTICE BLACK delivered the opinion of the Court.

The petitioner, an American citizen of Japanese descent, was convicted in a federal district court for remaining in San Leandro, California, a "Military Area," contrary to Civilian Exclusion Order No. 34 of the Commanding General of the Western Command, U.S. Army, which directed that after May 9, 1942, all persons of Japanese ancestry should be excluded from that area. No question was raised as to petitioner's loyalty to the United States. * * *

[A]ll legal restrictions which curtail the civil rights of a single racial group are immediately suspect. That is not to say that all such restrictions are unconstitutional. It is to say that courts must subject them to the most rigid scrutiny. Pressing public necessity may sometimes justify the existence of such restrictions; racial antagonism never can. * * *

Exclusion Order No. 34 [was] one of a number of military orders [and a] curfew order, [also] promulgated pursuant to Executive Order 9066, subjected all persons of Japanese ancestry in prescribed West Coast military areas to remain in their residences from 8 p.m. to 6 a.m. [In] *Hirabayashi v. United States,* 320 U.S. 81, 63 S.Ct. 1365, 87 L.Ed. 1774 (1943), we sustained a conviction [for] violation of the curfew order [as] an exercise of the power [to] take steps necessary to prevent espionage and sabotage in an area threatened by Japanese attack.

In the light of the principles we announced in the *Hirabayashi* case, we are unable to conclude that it was beyond the war power of Congress and the Executive to exclude those of Japanese ancestry from the West Coast war area at the time they [did]. Nothing short of apprehension by the proper military authorities of the gravest imminent danger to the public safety can constitutionally justify either. But exclusion from a threatened area, no less than curfew, has a definite and close relationship to the prevention of espionage and sabotage. The military authorities, charged with the primary responsibility of defending our shores, concluded that curfew provided inadequate protection and ordered exclusion [in] accordance with Congressional authority * * *.

Here, as in *Hirabayashi,* "we cannot reject as unfounded the judgment of the military authorities and of Congress that there were disloyal members of that population, whose number and strength could not be precisely and quickly ascertained. We cannot say that the war-making branches of the Government did not have ground for believing that in a critical hour such persons could not readily be isolated and separately dealt with, and constituted a menace to the national defense and safety, which demanded that prompt and adequate measures be taken to guard against it."

c. *Yick Wo v. Hopkins* (1886), Sec. III infra; *Hernandez v. Texas,* 347 U.S. 475, 74 S.Ct. 667, 98 L.Ed. 866 (1954).

[This] answers the contention that the exclusion was in the nature of group punishment based on antagonism to those of Japanese origin. That there were members of the group who retained loyalties to Japan has been confirmed by investigations made subsequent to the exclusion. Approximately five thousand American citizens of Japanese ancestry refused to swear unqualified allegiance to the United States [and] several thousand evacuees requested repatriation to Japan.

[H]ardships are part of war, and war is an aggregation of hardships. [E]xclusion of large groups of citizens from their homes, except under circumstances of direst emergency and peril, is inconsistent with our basic governmental institutions. But when under conditions of modern warfare our shores are threatened by hostile forces, the power to protect must be commensurate with the threatened danger. * * *

It is said that we are dealing here with the case of imprisonment of a citizen in a concentration camp solely because of his ancestry, without evidence or inquiry concerning his loyalty and good disposition towards the United States. [But] we are dealing specifically with nothing but an exclusion order. To cast this case into outlines of racial prejudice, without reference to the real military dangers which were presented, merely confuses the issue. Korematsu was not excluded from the Military Area because of hostility to him or his race. He was excluded because we are at war with the Japanese Empire, because the properly constituted military authorities feared an invasion of our West Coast and felt constrained to take proper security measures, because they decided that the military urgency of the situation demanded that all citizens of Japanese ancestry be segregated from the West Coast temporarily, and finally, because Congress, reposing its confidence in this time of war in our military leaders—as inevitably it must—determined that they should have the power to do just this. There was evidence of disloyalty on the part of some, the military authorities considered that the need for action was great, and time was short. We cannot—by availing ourselves of the calm perspective of hindsight—now say that at that time these actions were unjustified.[a]

Affirmed.

JUSTICE FRANKFURTER [who joined the Court's opinion], concurring.

[To] find that the Constitution does not forbid the military measures now complained of does not carry with it approval of that which Congress and the Executive did. That is their business, not ours.

JUSTICE MURPHY, dissenting.

[In] adjudging the military action taken in light of the then apparent dangers, [it] is necessary only that the action have some reasonable relation to the removal of the dangers of invasion, sabotage and espionage. But the exclusion, either temporarily or permanently, of all persons with Japanese blood in their veins [must] rely for its reasonableness upon the assumption that *all* persons of Japanese ancestry may have a dangerous tendency to commit sabotage and espionage and [it] is difficult to believe that reason, logic or experience

a. Consider, Simon, *Racially Prejudiced Governmental Actions: A Motivation Theory of the Constitutional Ban Against Racial Discrimination,* 15 San Diego L.Rev. 1041, 1074 (1978): "The Japanese exclusion cases [are] most troubling not because the Court found that the challenged rules would have been promulgated even apart from prejudice, but because it refused seriously to consider whether maintaining the exclusionary system and continuing its enforcement as of the time the cases reached the Court could be explained on grounds other than racial prejudice."

could be marshalled in support of such an assumption. [The] reasons appear, instead, to be largely an accumulation of much of the misinformation, half-truths and insinuations that for years have been directed against Japanese Americans by people with racial and economic prejudices—the same people who have been among the foremost advocates of the evacuation. A military judgment based upon such racial and sociological considerations is not entitled to the great weight ordinarily given the judgments based upon strictly military considerations. Especially is this so when every charge relative to race, religion, culture, geographical location, and legal and economic status has been substantially discredited by independent studies made by experts in these matters. * * *

Moreover, there was no adequate proof that the FBI and the military and naval intelligence services did not have the espionage and sabotage situation well in hand during this long period. Nor is there any denial of the fact that not one person of Japanese ancestry was accused or convicted of espionage or sabotage after Pearl Harbor while they were still free, a fact which is some evidence of the loyalty of the vast majority of these individuals and of the effectiveness of the established methods of combatting these evils. It seems incredible that under these circumstances it would have been impossible to hold loyalty hearings for the mere 112,000 persons involved—or at least for the 70,000 American citizens—especially when a large part of this number represented children and elderly men and women. Any inconvenience that may have accompanied an attempt to conform to procedural due process cannot be said to justify violations of constitutional [rights].

JUSTICE JACKSON, dissenting.

Korematsu was born on our soil, of parents born in Japan. [Had] Korematsu been one of four—the others being, say, a German alien enemy, an Italian alien enemy, and a citizen of American-born ancestors, convicted of treason but out on parole—only Korematsu's presence would have violated the order. The difference between their innocence and his crime would result, not from anything he did, said, or thought, different than they, but only in that he was born of different racial stock.

Now, if any fundamental assumption underlies our system, it is that guilt is personal and not inheritable. [If] Congress in peace-time legislation should enact such a criminal law, I should suppose this Court would refuse to enforce it.

But [it] would be impracticable and dangerous idealism to expect or insist that each specific military command in an area of probable operations will conform to conventional tests of constitutionality. When an area is so beset that it must be put under military control at all, the paramount consideration is that its measures be successful, rather than legal. * * * I cannot say, from any evidence before me, that the orders of General DeWitt were not reasonably expedient military precautions, nor could I say that they were. But even if they were permissible military procedures, I deny that it follows that they are constitutional. If, as the Court holds, it does follow, then we may as well say that any military order will be constitutional and have done with it.[b]

b. Compare Warren, C.J., *The Bill of Rights and the Military,* 37 N.Y.U.L.Rev. 181, 192–93 (1962): "[*Hirabayashi* and *Korematsu*] demonstrate dramatically that there are some circumstances in which the Court will, in effect, conclude that it is simply not in a position to reject descriptions by the Executive of the degree of military necessity. Thus, in a case like *Hirabayashi,* only the Executive is qualified to determine whether, for example, an invasion is imminent. In such a situation, where time is of the essence, if the Court is to deny the asserted right of the military authorities, it must be on the theory that the

The limitation under which courts always will labor in examining the necessity for a military order are illustrated by this case. How does the Court know that these orders have a reasonable basis in necessity? No evidence whatever on that subject has been taken by this or any other court. There is sharp controversy as to the credibility of the DeWitt report. So the Court, having no real evidence before it, has no choice but to accept General DeWitt's own unsworn, self-serving statement, untested by any cross-examination, that what he did was reasonable. And thus it will always be when courts try to look into the reasonableness of a military order. * * *

[A] judicial construction of the due process clause that will sustain this order is a far more subtle blow to liberty than the promulgation of the order itself. A military order, however unconstitutional, is not apt to last longer than the military emergency. [But] once a judicial opinion rationalizes [the] Constitution to show that the Constitution sanctions such an order, the Court for all time has validated the principle of racial discrimination in criminal procedure and of transplanting American citizens. The principle then lies about like a loaded weapon ready for the hand of any authority that can bring forward a plausible claim of an urgent need. * * *

My duties as a justice as I see them do not require me to make a military judgment as to whether General DeWitt's evacuation and detention program was a reasonable military necessity. I do not suggest that the courts should have attempted to interfere with the Army in carrying out its task. But I do not think they may be asked to execute a military expedient that has no place in law under the Constitution. I would reverse the judgment and discharge the prisoner.[c]

Notes and Questions

1. *Standard of review. Hirabayashi* and *Korematsu* have been the last instances in which the Court has failed to invalidate intentional (or "de jure") government discrimination against a racial or ethnic minority.[d] In 1967, the Court observed that laws imposing "invidious racial discriminations" bear a "very heavy burden of justification" and "if they are ever to be upheld, they must be shown to be necessary to the accomplishment of some permissible state objective"; they are unlike statutes "involving no racial discrimination" where "the Court has merely asked whether there is any rational foundation for the discriminations, and has deferred to the wisdom of the state legislatures." [e]

2. *"Rigid scrutiny" and "special traits."* (a) Should state discrimination against a racial minority ever be upheld? Consider Douglas, J., *We the Judges* 399 (1956): "Experience shows that liquor has a devastating effect on the North

claimed justification, though factually unassailable, is insufficient. [S]uch cases would be extraordinary indeed. [To] put it another way, the fact that the Court rules in a case like *Hirabayashi* that a given program is constitutional, does not necessarily answer the question whether, in a broader sense, it actually is."

c. The dissenting opinion of Roberts, J., is omitted. The Japanese evacuation and *Korematsu* have been the subject of extensive criticism. See, e.g., Girdner & Loftis, *The Great Betrayal* (1969); Grodzins, *Americans Betrayed* (1949); Rostow, *The Japanese American Cases—A Disaster,* in The Sovereign Prerogative 193 (1962).

d. On the same day as *Korematsu, Ex parte Endo,* 323 U.S. 283, 65 S.Ct. 208, 89 L.Ed. 243 (1944), per Douglas, J., held that Executive Order 9066 did not authorize the continued detention of concededly loyal persons of Japanese ancestry: "This Court [has] favored that interpretation of legislation which gives it the greater chance of surviving the test of constitutionality."

e. *Loving v. Virginia,* Part II infra. For discussion of "refinements" of the "test," see note 1 after *Loving.*

American Indian and Eskimo. It is, therefore, commonly provided [that] no liquor should be sold to those races. Other regulations based on race may likewise be justified by reason of the special traits of those races [and] what at first blush may seem to be an invidious discrimination may on analysis be found to have plausible grounds justifying it." [f]

May a state require that all blacks undergo a blood test for sickle cell anemia? Suppose that "studies have indicated that seven to nine percent of the American Black population carries the sickle cell trait, while 0.3 percent suffer from the disease" and that "the incidence of sickle cell anemia in the White population is negligible"? Note, *Constitutional and Practical Considerations in Mandatory Sickle Cell Anemia Testing,* 7 U.C.D.L.Rev. 509, 519 (1974). Should it make a difference if the state, rather than the individual, pays for the blood test? May "overinclusive" racial laws be distinguished on the basis of the severity of the burden imposed? Compare *Hirabayashi, Korematsu* and *Endo.*

(b) Is a law providing "that anyone whose skin is darker than a certain shade (either attached as an exhibit or defined in terms of albedo or reflecting power) is negligent for walking on a road at night without wearing some light-colored item of clothing" distinguishable from the other situations referred to above? See Kaplan, *Equal Justice in an Unequal World: Equality for the Negro—The Problem of Special Treatment,* 61 Nw.U.L.Rev. 363, 383 (1966).

(c) May the federal government consider racial (religious) differences in assigning personnel to official American posts in foreign countries?

II. SEGREGATION AND OTHER CLASSIFICATIONS

Part I involved laws that imposed burdens on racial and ethnic minorities. This section concerns laws that segregate or otherwise classify on a racial basis but, at least in a literal sense, treat all races identically. The principal question is whether (and, if so, why) such laws should be subject to the same "rigid" or "strict" standard of review.

PLESSY v. FERGUSON

163 U.S. 537, 16 S.Ct. 1138, 41 L.Ed. 256 (1896).

JUSTICE BROWN delivered the opinion of the Court.

[An 1890 Louisiana law required that railway passenger cars have "equal but separate accommodations for the white, and colored races." Plessy, alleging that he "was seven-eights Caucasian and one-eighth African blood; that the mixture of colored blood was not discernible in him; and that he was entitled to every right [of] the white race," was arrested for refusing to vacate a seat in a coach for whites.]

That it does not conflict with the thirteenth amendment [is] too clear for argument. Slavery implies involuntary servitude,—a state of bondage * * *. This amendment [was] regarded by the statesmen of that day as insufficient to protect the colored race from certain laws [imposing] onerous disabilities and burdens, and curtailing their rights in the pursuit of life, liberty, and property to such an extent that their freedom was of little value; [and] the fourteenth amendment was devised to meet this exigency. * * *

f. For discussion of federal laws that specially classify members of American Indian tribes, see Tribe, *American Constitutional Law* 1467–74 (2d ed. 1988); *Morton v. Mancari,* 417 U.S. 535, 94 S.Ct. 2474, 41 L.Ed.2d 290 (1974), upholding a hiring preference for qualified Indians in the Bureau of Indian Affairs of the Department of the Interior.

The object of the amendment was undoubtedly to enforce the absolute equality of the two races before the law, but, in the nature of things, it could not have been intended to abolish distinctions based upon color, or to enforce social, as distinguished from political, equality, or a commingling of the two races upon terms unsatisfactory to either. [Laws] requiring their separation, in places where they are liable to be brought into contact [have] been generally, if not universally, recognized as within the competency of the state legislatures in the exercise of their police power. The most common instance of this is connected with the establishment of separate schools for white and colored children, which have been [upheld] even by courts of states where the political rights of the colored race have been longest and most earnestly enforced [citing cases from Mass., Ohio, Mo., Cal., La., N.Y., Ind. and Ky.].

Laws forbidding the intermarriage of the two races may be said in a technical sense to interfere with the freedom of contract, and yet have been universally recognized as within the police power of the state. [S]tatutes for the separation of the two races upon public conveyances were held to be constitutional in [federal decisions and cases from Pa., Mich., Ill., Tenn. and N.Y. It is suggested] that the same argument that will justify the state legislature in requiring railways to provide separate accommodations for the two races will also authorize them to require separate cars to be provided for people whose hair is of a certain color, or who are aliens, or who belong to certain nationalities, or to enact laws requiring colored people to walk upon one side of the street, and white people upon the other, or requiring white men's houses to be painted white, and colored men's black, or their vehicles or business signs to be of different colors, upon the theory that one side of the street is as good as the other, or that a house or vehicle of one color is as good as one of another color. The reply to all this is that every exercise of the police power must be reasonable, and extend only to such laws as are enacted in good faith for the promotion of the public good, and not for the annoyance or oppression of a particular class. [In] determining the question of reasonableness, [the state] is at liberty to act with reference to the established usages, customs, and traditions of the people, and with a view to the promotion of their comfort, and the preservation of the public peace and good order. Gauged by this standard, we cannot say [this law] is unreasonable, or more obnoxious to the fourteenth amendment than the [acts] requiring separate schools for colored children in the District of Columbia, the constitutionality of which does not seem to have been questioned or the corresponding acts of state legislatures.[a]

We consider the underlying fallacy of the plaintiff's argument to consist in the assumption that the enforced separation of the two races stamps the colored race with a badge of inferiority. If this be so, it is not by reason of anything found in the act, but solely because the colored race chooses to put that construction upon it. [The] argument also assumes that social prejudices may be overcome by legislation, and that equal rights cannot be secured to the negro except by an enforced commingling of the two races. We cannot accept this proposition. If the two races are to meet upon terms of social equality, it must be the result [of] voluntary consent of individuals. * * * Legislation is powerless to eradicate racial instincts, or to abolish distinctions based upon

a. Compare Harris, *The Constitution, Education, and Segregation,* 29 Temp.L.Q. 409, 413 (1956): "[T]he dictum [that] reasonableness is to be construed with reference to established usages, customs and traditions of the people [wholly] ignores the fact that it was to prevent these customs and traditions from being enacted into law that the fourteenth amendment was adopted."

physical differences, and the attempt to do so can only result in accentuating the difficulties of the present situation. * * *

Affirmed.

JUSTICE BREWER did [not] participate in the decision of this case.

JUSTICE HARLAN dissenting.

[No] legislative body or judicial tribunal may have regard to the race of citizens when the civil rights of those citizens are involved. * * *

It was said in argument that the statute of Louisiana does not discriminate against either race, but prescribes a rule applicable alike to white and colored citizens. But [e]very one knows that [it] had its origin in the purpose, not so much to exclude white persons from railroad cars occupied by blacks, as to exclude colored people from coaches occupied by or assigned to white persons. [The] fundamental objection, therefore, to the statute, is that it interferes with the personal freedom of citizens.[b] * * *

The white race deems itself to be the dominant race in this country. And so it is, in prestige, in achievements, in education, in wealth, and in power. So, I doubt not, it will continue to be for all time, if it remains true to its great heritage, and holds fast to the principles of constitutional liberty. But in view of the constitution, in the eye of the law, there is in this country no superior, dominant, ruling class of citizens. There is no caste here. Our constitution is color-blind * * *.

In my opinion, the judgment this day rendered will, in time, prove to be quite as pernicious as the decision made by this tribunal in the *Dred Scott Case* [that] the descendants of Africans who were imported into this country, and sold as slaves, were not included nor intended to be included under the word "citizens" in the constitution; [that,] at the time of the adoption of the constitution, they were "considered as a subordinate and inferior class of beings, who had been subjugated by the dominant race, and, whether emancipated or not, yet remained subject to their authority, and had no rights or privileges but such as those who held the power and the government might choose to grant them." 19 How. 393, 404. The recent amendments of the constitution, it was supposed, had eradicated these principles from our institutions. [What] can more certainly arouse race hate, what more certainly create and perpetuate a feeling of distrust between these races, than state enactments which, in fact, proceed on the ground that colored citizens are so inferior and degraded that they cannot be allowed to sit in public coaches occupied by white citizens? [The] thin disguise of "equal" accommodations for passengers in railroad coaches will not mislead any one, nor atone for the wrong this day done. * * *

I do not deem it necessary to review the decisions of state courts to which reference was made in argument. Some [are] inapplicable, because rendered prior to the adoption of the last amendments of the [constitution]. Others were made at a time [when] race prejudice was, practically, the supreme law of the

b. See Frank & Munro, *The Original Understanding of "Equal Protection of the Laws,"* 1972 Wash.U.L.Q. 421, 455: "We believe that the equal protection clause, in the eyes of its contemporaries, froze into constitutional law the existing common law obligation of transportation companies to take all comers and to eliminate any possibility of their segregation. Congress decided so often in this period that color classifications were not permissible for purposes of transportation that it is difficult to understand how equal protection could possibly be given another meaning." For a discussion of "civil" rights in the fourteenth amendment's history, see Bickel, *The Original Understanding and the Segregation Decision,* 69 Harv.L.Rev. 1 (1955). Compare Berger, *Government By Judiciary: The Transformation of the Fourteenth Amendment* (1977).

land. Those decisions cannot be guides in the era introduced by the recent amendments of the supreme law, which established universal civil freedom * * *.[c]

BROWN v. BOARD OF EDUCATION

347 U.S. 483, 74 S.Ct. 686, 98 L.Ed. 873 (1954).

CHIEF JUSTICE WARREN delivered the opinion of the Court.

These cases come to us from the States of Kansas, South Carolina, Virginia, and Delaware. * * *

In each of the cases, minors of the Negro race [seek] the aid of the courts in obtaining admission to the public schools of their community on a nonsegregated basis. [In] each of the cases other than the Delaware case, a three-judge federal district court denied relief to the plaintiffs on the so-called "separate but equal" doctrine announced by this Court in [*Plessy*]. In the Delaware case, the Supreme Court of Delaware adhered to that doctrine, but ordered that the plaintiffs be admitted to the white schools because of their superiority to the Negro schools.

* * * Argument was heard in the 1952 Term, and reargument was heard this Term on certain questions propounded by the Court.

Reargument was largely devoted to the circumstances surrounding the adoption of the Fourteenth Amendment in 1868. It covered exhaustively consideration of the Amendment in Congress, ratification by the states, then existing practices in racial segregation, and the views of proponents and opponents of the Amendment. This discussion and our own investigation convince us that, although these sources cast some light, it is not enough to resolve the problem with which we are faced. At best, they are inconclusive. The most avid proponents of the post-War Amendments undoubtedly intended them to remove all legal distinctions among "all persons born or naturalized in the United States." Their opponents, just as certainly, were antagonistic to both the letter and the spirit of the Amendments and wished them to have the most limited effect. What others in Congress and the state legislatures had in mind cannot be determined with any degree of certainty.

An additional reason for the inconclusive nature of the Amendment's history, with respect to segregated schools, is the status of public education at that time. In the South, the movement toward free common schools, supported by general taxation, had not yet taken hold. Education of white children was largely in the hands of private groups. Education of Negroes was almost nonexistent, and practically all of the race were illiterate. In fact, any education of Negroes was forbidden by law in some states. Today, in contrast, many Negroes have achieved outstanding success in the arts and sciences as well as in the business and professional world. It is true that public school education at the time of the Amendment had advanced further in the North, but the effect of the Amendment on Northern States was generally ignored in the congressional debates. Even in the North, the conditions of public education did not approximate those existing today. The curriculum was usually rudimentary; ungraded schools were common in rural areas; the school term was but three months a year in many states; and compulsory school attendance was virtually unknown.

c. For discussion of *Plessy* and its background, see Oberst, *The Strange Career of Plessy v. Ferguson*, 15 Ariz.L.Rev. 389 (1973).

As a consequence, it is not surprising that there should be so little in the history of the Fourteenth Amendment relating to its intended effect on public education.

In the first cases in this Court construing the Fourteenth Amendment, decided shortly after its adoption, the Court interpreted it as proscribing all state-imposed discriminations against the Negro race.[5] The doctrine of "separate but equal" did not make its appearance in this Court until 1896 in *Plessy*, involving not education but transportation. [In] this Court, there have been six cases involving the "separate but equal" doctrine in the field of public education. In *Cumming v. Board of Education*, 175 U.S. 528, 20 S.Ct. 197, 44 L.Ed. 262, and *Gong Lum v. Rice*, 275 U.S. 78, 48 S.Ct. 91, 72 L.Ed. 172, the validity of the doctrine itself was not challenged.[8] In more recent cases, all on the graduate school level, inequality was found in that specific benefits enjoyed by white students were denied to Negro students of the same educational qualifications. *Missouri ex rel. Gaines v. Canada*, 305 U.S. 337, 59 S.Ct. 232, 83 L.Ed. 208[a]; *Sipuel v. Oklahoma*, 332 U.S. 631, 68 S.Ct. 299, 92 L.Ed. 247; *Sweatt v. Painter*, 339 U.S. 629, 70 S.Ct. 848, 94 L.Ed. 1114[b]; *McLaurin v. Oklahoma State Regents*, 339 U.S. 637, 70 S.Ct. 851, 94 L.Ed. 1149.[c] In none of these cases was it necessary to re-examine the doctrine to grant relief to the Negro plaintiff. And in *Sweatt*, the Court expressly reserved decision on the question whether *Plessy* should be held inapplicable to public education.

In the instant cases, that question is directly presented. [T]here are findings below that the Negro and white schools involved have been equalized, or are being equalized, with respect to buildings, curricula, qualifications and salaries of teachers, and other "tangible" factors. Our decision, therefore, cannot turn on merely a comparison of these tangible factors in the Negro and white schools

5. *Slaughter-House Cases; Strauder* * * *. See also *Virginia v. Rives*, 1879, 100 U.S. 313, 318, 25 L.Ed. 667; *Ex parte Virginia*, 1879, 100 U.S. 339, 344–345, 25 L.Ed. 676. [See generally Brief for the Committee of Law Teachers Against Segregation in Legal Education, *Segregation and the Equal Protection Clause*, 34 Minn.L.Rev. 289 (1950).]

8. In *Cumming*, Negro taxpayers sought an injunction requiring the defendant school board to discontinue the operation of a high school for white children until the board resumed operation of a high school for Negro children. Similarly, in *Gong Lum*, the plaintiff, a child of Chinese descent, contended only that state authorities had misapplied the doctrine by classifying him with Negro children and requiring him to attend a Negro school.

a. *Gaines*, in 1938, invalidated the refusal to admit blacks to the University of Missouri School of Law, despite the state's offer to pay petitioner's tuition at an out-of-state law school pending establishment of a state law school for blacks.

b. *Sweatt*, in 1950, required admission of blacks to the University of Texas Law School despite the recent establishment of a state law school for blacks: "In terms of number of the faculty, variety of courses and opportunity for specialization, size of the student body, scope of the library, availability of law review and similar activities, the University of Texas Law School is superior. What is more important, the University of Texas Law School possesses to a far greater degree those qualities which are incapable of objective measurement but which make for greatness in a law school. Such qualities, to name but a few, include reputation of the faculty, experience of the administration, position and influence of the alumni, standing in the community, traditions and prestige. [Moreover, the law school] cannot be effective in isolation from the individuals and institutions with which the law interacts. Few students and no one who has practiced law would choose to study in an academic vacuum, removed from the interplay of ideas and the exchange of views with which the law is concerned. The law school to which Texas is willing to admit petitioner excludes from its student body members of the racial groups which number 85% of the population of the State and include most of the lawyers, witnesses, jurors, judges and other officials with whom petitioner will inevitably be dealing when he becomes a member of the Texas Bar."

c. *McLaurin*, in 1950, held violative of equal protection requirements that black graduate students at the University of Oklahoma sit at separate desks adjoining the classrooms and separate tables outside the library reading room, and eat at separate times in the school cafeteria.

involved in each of the cases. We must look instead to the effect of segregation itself on public education.

In approaching this problem, we cannot turn the clock back to 1868 when the Amendment was adopted, or even to 1896 when *Plessy* was written. We must consider public education in the light of its full development and its present place in American life throughout the Nation. Only in this way can it be determined if segregation in public schools deprives these plaintiffs of the equal protection of the laws.

Today, education is perhaps the most important function of state and local governments. Compulsory school attendance laws and the great expenditures for education both demonstrate our recognition of the importance of education to our democratic society. It is required in the performance of our most basic public responsibilities, even service in the armed forces. It is the very foundation of good citizenship. Today it is a principal instrument in awakening the child to cultural values, in preparing him for later professional training, and in helping him to adjust normally to his environment. In these days, it is doubtful that any child may reasonably be expected to succeed in life if he is denied the opportunity of an education. Such an opportunity, where the state has undertaken to provide it, is a right which must be made available to all on equal terms.

We come then to the question presented: Does segregation of children in public schools solely on the basis of race, even though the physical facilities and other "tangible" factors may be equal, deprive the children of the minority group of equal educational opportunities? We believe that it does.

In *Sweatt,* in finding that a segregated law school for Negroes could not provide them equal educational opportunities, this Court relied in large part on "those qualities which are incapable of objective measurement but which make for greatness in a law school." In *McLaurin,* the Court, in requiring that a Negro admitted to a white graduate school be treated like all other students, again resorted to intangible considerations: "[his] ability to study, to engage in discussions and exchange views with other students, and in general, to learn his profession." Such considerations apply with added force to children in grade and high schools. To separate them from others of similar age and qualifications solely because of their race generates a feeling of inferiority as to their status in the community that may affect their hearts and minds in a way unlikely ever to be undone. The effect of this separation on their educational opportunities was well stated by a finding in the Kansas case by a court which nevertheless felt compelled to rule against the Negro plaintiffs: "Segregation of white and colored children in public schools has a detrimental effect upon the colored children. The impact is greater when it has the sanction of the law; for the policy of separating the races is usually interpreted as denoting the inferiority of the Negro group. A sense of inferiority affects the motivation of a child to learn. Segregation with the sanction of law, therefore, has a tendency to [retard] the educational and mental development of Negro children and to deprive them of some of the benefits they would receive in a racial[ly] integrated school system." [10] Whatever may have been the extent of psychological knowl-

10. A similar finding was made in the Delaware case: "I conclude from the testimony that in our Delaware society, State-imposed segregation in education itself results in the Negro children, as a class, receiving educational opportunities which are substantially inferior to those available to white children otherwise similarly situated."

edge at the time of *Plessy*, this finding is amply supported by modern authority.[11] Any language in *Plessy* contrary to this finding is rejected.

We conclude that in the field of public education the doctrine of "separate but equal" has no place. Separate educational facilities are inherently unequal. Therefore, we hold that the plaintiffs and others similarly situated for whom the actions have been brought are, by reason of the segregation complained of, deprived of [equal protection].

Because these are class actions, because of the wide applicability of this decision, and because of the great variety of local conditions, the formulation of decrees in these cases presents problems of considerable complexity. On reargument, the consideration of appropriate relief was necessarily subordinated to the primary question—the constitutionality of segregation in public education. We have now announced that such segregation is a denial of the equal protection of the laws. In order that we may have the full assistance of the parties in formulating decrees, the cases will be restored to the docket, and the parties are requested to present further argument on Questions 4 and 5 previously propounded by the Court for the reargument this Term.[13] The Attorney General of the United States is again invited to participate. The Attorney General of the states requiring or permitting segregation in public education will also be permitted to appear * * *.

Notes and Questions

1. *The Court's rationale.* What was the specific basis for the decision?

(a) *Social science materials.* At trial in several of the cases, psychiatrists and social scientists testified as to the harmful effects of state-imposed segregation on black children. On appeal, appellants filed a statement to this effect by 32 sociologists, anthropologists, psychologists, and psychiatrists who worked in the area of American race relations—reprinted in 37 Minn.L.Rev. 427 (1953).

Was the decision based on this information? Is this desirable? Should *Brown* be modified or overruled if new social science data reaches different

11. Clark, *Effect of Prejudice and Discrimination on Personality Development* (Midcentury White House Conference on Children and Youth, 1950); Witmer and Kotinsky, *Personality in the Making* (1952), c. VI; Deutscher and Chein, *The Psychological Effects of Enforced Segregation: A Survey of Social Science Opinion*, 26 J.Psychol. 259 (1948); Chein, *What are the Psychological Effects of Segregation Under Conditions of Equal Facilities?*, 3 Int.J. Opinion and Attitude Res. 229 (1949); Brameld, *Educational Costs in Discrimination and National Welfare* (MacIver, ed., 1949), 44–48; Frazier, *The Negro in the United States* (1949), 674–681. And, see generally Myrdal, *An American Dilemma* (1962).

13. "4. Assuming it is decided that segregation in public schools violates the Fourteenth Amendment

"(a) would a decree necessarily follow providing that, within the limits set by normal geographic school districting, Negro children should forthwith be admitted to schools of their choice, or

"(b) may this Court, in the exercise of its equity powers, permit an effective gradual adjustment to be brought about from existing segregated systems to a system not based on color distinctions?

"5. On the assumption on which questions 4(a) and (b) are based, and assuming further that this Court will exercise its equity powers to the end described in question 4(b),

"(a) should this Court formulate detailed decrees in these cases;

"(b) if so, what specific issues should the decrees reach;

"(c) should this Court appoint a special master to hear evidence with a view to recommending specific terms for such decrees;

"(d) should this Court remand to the courts of first instance with directions to frame decrees in these cases, and if so what general directions should the decrees of this Court include and what procedures should the courts of first instance follow in arriving at the specific terms of more detailed decrees?"

conclusions? [d] Consider Cahn, *Jurisprudence,* 30 N.Y.U.L.Rev. 150, 157–58, 167 (1955): "[S]ince the behavioral sciences are so very young, imprecise, and changeful, their findings have an uncertain expectancy of life. Today's sanguine asseveration may be cancelled by tomorrow's new revelation—or new technical fad. It is one thing to use the current scientific findings, however ephemeral they may be, in order to ascertain whether the legislature has acted reasonably in adopting some scheme of social or economic regulation; deference here is shown not so much to the findings as to the legislature. It would be quite another thing to have our fundamental rights rise, fall, or change along with the latest fashions of psychological literature."

(b) Does *Brown* rest on a finding that "in terms of the most familiar and universally accepted standards of right and wrong [racial] segregation under government auspices inevitably inflicts humiliation, [and] official humiliation of innocent, law-abiding citizens is psychologically injurious and morally evil"? Cahn, supra, at 159. If so, where are such "universally accepted standards" found? See Dworkin, *Social Sciences and Constitutional Rights—The Consequences of Uncertainty,* 6 J.L. & Ed. 3 (1977).

(c) *Historical considerations.* (i) Would it have been better for the Court to rely upon the original purpose of the fourteenth amendment as stated in *Strauder:* to grant blacks "the right to exemption from unfriendly legislation against them as distinctively colored"? If so, how should *Plessy* have been treated? Was the *Brown* Court in 1954 a better judge of fourteenth amendment intent than the *Plessy* Court in 1896? Than the *Strauder* Court in 1879?

(ii) Apart from the specific intentions of the framers and ratifiers of the fourteenth amendment in respect to school segregation,[e] of what significance is the fact that "every one of the twenty-six states that had any substantial racial differences among its people either approved the operation of segregated schools already in existence or subsequently established such schools by action of the same law-making body which considered the Fourteenth Amendment"? *Declaration of Constitutional Principles Issued by 19 Senators and 77 Representatives of the Congress,* N.Y. Times, p. 19, col. 2, March 12, 1956. What justified the Court's consideration of "public education in the light of its full development and its present place in American life throughout the Nation"? Consider Bickel, *The Original Understanding and the Segregation Decision,* 69 Harv.L.Rev. 1, 59 (1955): "If the fourteenth amendment were a statute, a court might very well hold [that] it was foreclosed from applying it to segregation in public schools. [But] we are dealing with a constitutional amendment, not a statute. The tradition of a broadly worded organic law not frequently or lightly amended was well-established by 1866, and [it] cannot be assumed that [anyone] expected or wished the future role of the Constitution in the scheme of American government to differ from the past. Should not the search for congressional purpose

d. For extensive discussion and comprehensive listing of the substantial and controversial research and literature on the subject, see Symposia, *School Desegregation: Lessons of the First Twenty-Five Years,* 42 Law & Contemp.Prob., nos. 3–4 (1978). In particular, see Yudof, *School Desegregation: Legal Realism, Reasoned Elaboration, and Social Science Research in the Supreme Court,* 42 Law & Contemp.Prob. 57, 61 nn. 26–27 (no. 4, 1978). See also Goodman, *De Facto School Segregation: A Constitutional and Empirical Analysis,* 60 Calif.L.Rev. 275 (1972).

e. For the view that the framers did not intend to prohibit it, see Berger, *Government by Judiciary* 117–33 (1977); Perry, *The Constitution, the Courts, and Human Rights* 66–69 (1982). Compare Dimond, *Strict Construction and Judicial Review of Racial Discrimination Under the Equal Protection Clause,* 80 Mich.L. Rev. 462 (1982); Grano, *Judicial Review and a Written Constitution in a Democratic Society,* 28 Wayne L.Rev. 1, 67–72 (1981).

therefore, properly be twofold? One inquiry should be directed at the congressional understanding of the immediate effect of the enactment on conditions then present. Another should aim to discover what if any thought was given to the long-range effect, under future circumstances, of provisions necessarily intended for permanence."

2. *"Neutral principles."* Consider Wechsler, *Toward Neutral Principles of Constitutional Law,* 73 Harv.L.Rev. 1, 34 (1959): "[A]ssuming equal facilities, the question posed by state-enforced segregation is not one of discrimination at all. Its human and its constitutional dimensions lie [in] the denial by the state of freedom to associate, a denial that impinges in the same way on any groups or races that may be involved. [But] if the freedom of association is denied by segregation, integration forces an association upon those for whom it is unpleasant or repugnant. [W]here the state must practically choose between denying the association to those individuals who wish it or imposing it on those who would avoid it, is there a basis in neutral principles for holding that the Constitution demands that the claims for association should prevail?"

In reply, consider the following from a "draft opinion" of *Brown* by Pollak, *Racial Discrimination and Judicial Integrity: A Reply to Professor Wechsler,* 108 U.Pa.L.Rev. 1, 27, 29–30 (1959): "[W]e start from the base point that in the United States 'all legal restrictions which curtail the civil rights of a single racial group are immediately suspect.' *Korematsu.* [T]here is special need for 'a searching judicial inquiry into the legislative judgment in situations where prejudice against discrete and insular minorities may tend to curtail the operation of those political processes ordinarily to be relied on to protect minorities.' See *United States v. Carolene Products,* n. 4 [p. 18 supra]. We could not, therefore, sustain the reasonableness of these racial distinctions and the absence of harm said to flow from them, unless we were prepared to say that no factual case can be made the other way. [To] the extent that implementation of this decision forces racial mingling on school children against their will, [this] consequence follows because the community through its political processes has [chosen] compulsory education. [The resulting] coerced association [cannot] be said to emanate from this Court or from the Constitution. In any event, parents sufficiently disturbed at the prospect of having their children educated in democratic fashion in company with their peers are presumably entitled to fulfill their educational responsibilities in other ways."

See also C. Black, *The Lawfulness of the Segregation Decisions,* 69 Yale L.J. 421, 429 (1960): "The fourteenth amendment [forbids] disadvantaging the Negro race by law. It was surely anticipated that the following of this directive would entail some disagreeableness for some white southerners. [When] the directive of equality cannot be followed without displeasing the white, then something that can be called a 'freedom' of the white must be impaired. If the fourteenth amendment commands equality, and if segregation violates equality, then the status of the reciprocal 'freedom' is automatically settled." [f]

3. *Extent of the decision.* (a) Did *Brown* bar all forms of state-imposed racial segregation? Or did it apply only to public schools? For comment immediately after *Brown,* consider Kauper, *Segregation in Public Education,* 52

f. For the view that "the decision in *Brown* to break with the Court's long-held position on [segregation] cannot be understood without some consideration of the decision's value to whites [in] policymaking positions able to see the economic and political advances at home and abroad that would follow abandonment of segregation," see Bell, *Brown v. Board of Education and the Interest-Convergence Dilemma,* 93 Harv.L.Rev. 518 (1980). For amplification, see Dudziak, *Desegregation as a Cold War Imperative,* 41 Stan.L.Rev. 61 (1988).

Mich.L.Rev. 1137, 1154–55 (1954): "[*Brown*] placed emphasis upon the intangible factors that make the *Plessy* doctrine inapplicable to public schools. Education is an experience and not simply an enjoyment of physical facilities. But with respect to common carrier and public recreational facilities, the emphasis is upon the enjoyment of the physical facilities and services so that it is more nearly possible to speak of equality of enjoyment within the pattern of segregation." Compare McKay, *Segregation and Public Recreation,* 40 Va.L.Rev. 697, 724 (1954): "[T]here appears to be no reason to believe that the sense of inferiority engendered by segregation in recreation is any less than in education." See Pollak, supra, at 29: "[W]here facilities are voluntary the community's asserted need to ordain segregation seems even less weighty [for] those for whom racial mingling is obnoxious are under no obligation to attend."

(b) After *Brown,* the Court, by means of rather summary per curiam decisions, citing *Brown,* consistently held invalid state imposed racial segregation in other public facilities—e.g., golf courses, parks, playgrounds.[g]

4. *Segregation by the federal government.* BOLLING v. SHARPE, 347 U.S. 497, 74 S.Ct. 693, 98 L.Ed. 884 (1954), per WARREN, C.J., held—on the same day as *Brown*—that public school segregation in the District of Columbia "constitutes an arbitrary deprivation [of] liberty in violation of the Due Process Clause" of the fifth amendment: "The Fifth Amendment [does] not contain an equal protection clause as does the Fourteenth Amendment which applies only to the states. But the concepts of equal protection and due process, both stemming from our American ideal of fairness, are not mutually exclusive. The 'equal protection of the laws' is a more explicit safeguard of prohibited unfairness than 'due process of law,' and, therefore, we do not imply that the two are always interchangeable phrases. But, as this Court has recognized, discrimination may be so unjustifiable as to be violative of due process.

"Classifications based solely upon race must be scrutinized with particular care, since they are contrary to our traditions and hence constitutionally suspect. ["Liberty"] extends to the full range of conduct which the individual is free to pursue, and it cannot be restricted except for a proper governmental objective. Segregation in public education is not reasonably related to any proper governmental objective * * *.

"In view of our decision that the Constitution prohibits the states from maintaining racially segregated public schools, it would be unthinkable that the same Constitution would impose a lesser duty on the Federal Government."

BROWN v. BOARD OF EDUCATION

349 U.S. 294, 75 S.Ct. 753, 99 L.Ed. 1083 (1955).

CHIEF JUSTICE WARREN delivered the opinion of the Court.

These cases were decided on May 17, 1954. [There] remains for consideration the manner in which relief is to be accorded. * * *

Full implementation of these constitutional principles may require solution of varied local school problems. School authorities have the primary responsibility for elucidating, assessing, and solving [them]; courts will have to consider whether the action of school authorities constitutes good faith implementation of the governing constitutional principles. Because of their proximity to local conditions and the possible need for further hearings, the courts which originally

g. For a detailed listing of these and lower court decisions, see Lockhart, Kamisar & Choper, *Constitutional Law: Cases—Comments—Questions* 1206 (3d ed. 1970).

heard these cases can best perform this judicial appraisal. Accordingly, we believe it appropriate to remand the cases to those courts.

In fashioning and effectuating the decrees, the courts will be guided by equitable principles. Traditionally, equity has been characterized by a practical flexibility in shaping its remedies and by a facility for adjusting and reconciling public and private needs. [A]t stake is the personal interest of the plaintiffs in admission to public schools as soon as practicable on a nondiscriminatory basis. To effectuate this interest may call for elimination of a variety of obstacles in making the transition to school systems operated in accordance with the constitutional principles set forth in our May 17, 1954, decision. Courts of equity may properly take into account the public interest in the elimination of such obstacles in a systematic and effective manner. But it should go without saying that the vitality of these constitutional principles cannot be allowed to yield simply because of disagreement with them.

While giving weight to these public and private considerations, the courts will require that the defendants make a prompt and reasonable start toward full compliance with our May 17, 1954, ruling. Once such a start has been made, the courts may find that additional time is necessary to carry out the ruling in an effective manner. The burden rests upon the defendants to establish that such time is necessary in the public interest and is consistent with good faith compliance at the earliest practicable date. To that end, the courts may consider problems related to administration, arising from the physical condition of the school plant, the school transportation system, personnel, revision of school districts and attendance areas into compact units to achieve a system of determining admission to the public schools on a nonracial basis, and revision of local laws and regulations which may be necessary in solving the foregoing problems. They will also consider the adequacy of any plans the defendants may propose to meet these problems and to effectuate a transition to a racially nondiscriminatory school system. During this period of transition, the courts will retain jurisdiction of these cases.

The [cases are remanded] to take such proceedings and enter such orders and decrees consistent with this opinion as are necessary and proper to admit to public schools on a racially nondiscriminatory basis with all deliberate speed the parties to these cases. * * *

Notes and Questions

1. *"Individual" vs. "race" rights.* Was the decree consistent with *Brown I?* Since plaintiffs had only a limited number of years of school remaining, did postponement of relief partially or totally destroy the very rights the decree was intended to enforce? Does the "deliberate speed" formula assume that "Negroes (unlike whites) possess rights as a race rather than as individuals, so that a particular Negro can rightly be delayed in the enjoyment of his established rights if progress is being made in improving the legal status of Negroes generally"? Lusky, *The Stereotype: Hard Core of Racism,* 13 Buf.L.Rev. 450, 457 (1963). See also Carter, *The Warren Court and Desegregation,* 67 Mich.L.Rev. 237, 243 (1968). To what extent may the "deliberate speed" decree "have served the interests of blacks even while it accommodated the opposition of whites"? Gewirtz, *Remedies and Resistance,* 92 Yale L.J. 585, 609–28 (1983).

2. *"Deliberate speed" and the slow pace of desegregation.* What of Black, J.'s view that this formula "delayed the process of outlawing segregation" and that it would have been preferable to treat *Brown* "as an ordinary law suit and

force that judgment on the counties it affected that minute"? Transcript, *Justice Black and the Bill of Rights,* CBS News Special, Dec. 3, 1968. Should the Court have relied on social science data that "prompt, decisive action on the part of recognized authorities usually results in less anxiety and less resistance in cases where the public is opposed to the action than does a more hesitant and gradual procedure"? Clark, *Introduction to Argument: The Complete Oral Argument in Brown, 1952–55,* xxxiii (Friedman ed. 1969). Compare Graglia, *The Brown Cases Revisited: Where Are They Now?,* 1 Benchmark 23, 27 (Mar.–Apr. 1984): "There can be little doubt that if the Court had ordered the end of segregation in 1954 or 1955 the result would have been the closing of public schools in much of the South, about which the Court could have done nothing. The principal impact would have been on poor blacks, and *Brown* could have come to be seen as a blunder and symbol of judicial impotence." [a]

3. *Responsibility of local officials.* Was it wise to give *local* school authorities and *local* federal judges "primary responsibility" for effectuating desegregation? To permit "practical flexibility"? Were local school officials "most prone to resent and resist the changes ordered by the Court, and to look upon the newly enunciated constitutional doctrine as a personal repudiation"? Carter, supra, at 245. Were the district courts the sector of the federal judiciary most exposed to community pressures and least willing and able to challenge local mores? See Lusky, *Racial Discrimination and the Federal Law: A Problem in Nullification,* 63 Colum.L.Rev. 1163 (1963). Was it wise to have the lower federal courts judge compliance under such broad standards as "good faith" and "public interest"? See Carter, *Equal Educational Opportunities for Negroes—Abstraction or Reality,* 1968 U.Ill.L.F. 160, 177–80.[b]

LOVING v. VIRGINIA

388 U.S. 1, 87 S.Ct. 1817, 18 L.Ed.2d 1010 (1967).

CHIEF JUSTICE WARREN delivered the opinion of the Court.

This case presents a constitutional question never addressed by this Court: whether a statutory scheme adopted by Virginia to prevent marriages between persons solely on the basis of racial classifications violates [the] Fourteenth Amendment. [Appellants, a black woman and white man, were married in the District of Columbia, returned to reside in Virginia, and were convicted under the state antimiscegenation statute.]

Virginia is now one of 16 States which prohibit and punish marriages on the basis of racial classifications.[5] * * *

In upholding the constitutionality of these provisions [the] state court concluded that the State's legitimate purposes were "to preserve the racial integrity of its citizens," and to prevent "the corruption of blood," "a mongrel breed of citizens," and "the obliteration of racial pride," obviously an endorsement of the doctrine of White Supremacy. [T]he State [argues] that the meaning of the Equal Protection Clause, as illuminated by the statements of the Framers,

a. See also Bickel, *The Decade of School Desegregation: Progress and Prospects,* 64 Colum.L.Rev. 193, 201–02 (1964); Kaplan, *Comment on School Desegregation,* 64 Colum. L.Rev. 223, 224–26 (1964).

For a fascinating description of the Court's internal decisionmaking process in the segregation cases, see Hutchinson, *Unanimity and Desegregation: Decisionmaking in the Supreme Court, 1948–1958,* 68 Geo.L.J. 1 (1979).

b. The developments in implementing *Brown* are considered in Part IV infra.

5. [Over] the past 15 years, 14 States have repealed laws outlawing interracial marriages * * *.

is only that state penal laws containing an interracial element as part of the definition of the offense must apply equally to whites and Negroes in the sense that members of each race are punished to the same degree. * * *

Because we reject the notion that the mere "equal application" of a statute containing racial classifications is enough to remove the classifications from the Fourteenth Amendment's proscription of all invidious racial discriminations, we do not accept the State's contention that these statutes should be upheld if there is any possible basis for concluding that they serve a rational purpose. [Here], we deal with statutes containing racial classifications, and the fact of equal application does not immunize the statute from the very heavy burden of justification which the Fourteenth Amendment has traditionally required of state statutes drawn according to race.

The State argues that statements in the Thirty-ninth Congress about the time of the passage of the Fourteenth Amendment indicate that the Framers did not intend the Amendment to make unconstitutional state miscegenation laws. Many of the statements [have] some relevance to the intention of Congress in submitting the Fourteenth Amendment, [but] it must be understood that they pertained to the passage of specific statutes and not to the broader, organic purpose of a constitutional amendment. As for the various statements directly concerning the Fourteenth Amendment, we have said in connection with a related problem, that although these historical sources "cast some light" they are not sufficient to resolve the problem; "[a]t best, they are inconclusive." *Brown.* We have rejected the proposition that the debates in the Thirty-ninth Congress or in the state legislatures which ratified the Fourteenth Amendment supported the theory [that equal protection] is satisfied by penal laws defining offenses based on racial classifications so long as white and Negro participants in the offense were similarly punished. *McLaughlin v. Florida,* 379 U.S. 184, 85 S.Ct. 283, 13 L.Ed.2d 222 (1964).[a]

The State finds support for its "equal application" theory [in] *Pace v. Alabama,* 106 U.S. 583, 1 S.Ct. 637, 27 L.Ed. 207 (1883). In that case, the Court upheld a conviction under an Alabama statute forbidding adultery or fornication between a white person and a Negro which imposed a greater penalty than that of a statute proscribing similar conduct by members of the same race. The Court reasoned that the statute could not be said to discriminate against Negroes because the punishment for each participant in the offense was the same. However, as recently as the 1964 Term, in rejecting the reasoning of that case, we stated "*Pace* represents a limited view of the Equal Protection Clause which has not withstood analysis in the subsequent decisions of this Court." *McLaughlin.* [The] clear and central purpose of the Fourteenth Amendment was to eliminate all official state sources of invidious racial discrimination in the States. [At] the very least, the Equal Protection Clause demands that racial classifications, especially suspect in criminal statutes, be subjected to the "most rigid scrutiny," and, if they are ever to be upheld, they must be shown to be necessary to the accomplishment of some permissible state objective, independent of the racial discrimination which it was the object of the Fourteenth Amendment to eliminate.[b] Indeed, two [justices] have already stated that they

a. *McLaughlin* invalidated a statute making interracial cohabitation a crime.

b. *McLaughlin* also stated that racial classifications were " 'in most circumstances irrelevant' to any constitutionally acceptable legislative purpose." Harlan, J., concurring, added that "necessity, not mere reasonable relationship, is the proper test"; this "test which developed to protect free speech against state infringement should be equally applicable in a case involving state racial discrimina-

"cannot conceive of a valid legislative purpose [which] makes the color of a person's skin the test of whether his conduct is a criminal offense." *McLaughlin* (Stewart, J., joined by Douglas, J., concurring).

There is patently no legitimate overriding purpose independent of invidious racial discrimination which justifies this classification. The fact that Virginia only prohibits interracial marriages involving white persons demonstrates that the racial classifications must stand on their own justification, as measures designed to maintain White Supremacy.[11] We have consistently denied the constitutionality of measures which restrict the rights of citizens on account of race. There can be no doubt that restricting the freedom to marry solely because of racial classifications violates the central meaning of the Equal Protection Clause.

These statutes also deprive the Lovings of liberty without [due process].

Marriage is one of the "basic civil rights of man," fundamental to our very existence and survival. *Skinner v. Oklahoma* [p. 141 supra]. To deny this fundamental freedom on so unsupportable a basis as the racial classifications embodied in these statutes [surely denies due process].

Reversed.

JUSTICE STEWART, concurring.

I have previously expressed the belief that "it is simply not possible for a state law to be valid under our Constitution which makes the criminality of an act depend upon the race of the actor." *McLaughlin* (concurring opinion). Because I adhere to that belief, I concur in the judgment of the Court.

Notes and Questions

1. *Standard of review.* Is the constitutional test for laws that *classify* by race or ethnicity different from that for laws that *discriminate* against racial or ethnic minorities? Does *Loving* require only that the state purpose be "permissible" in contrast to *Korematsu's* requirement of "pressing public necessity"? Compare *In re Griffiths,* Sec. 3, I infra: "In order to justify the use of a suspect classification, a State must show that its purpose or interest is both constitutionally permissible[8] and substantial,[9] and that its use of the classification is 'necessary to the accomplishment' of its purpose or the safeguarding of its interest."

2. *Racial information.* ANDERSON v. MARTIN, 375 U.S. 399, 84 S.Ct. 454, 11 L.Ed.2d 430 (1964), held violative of equal protection a statute requiring that the race of candidates for elective office be on the ballot: "The vice lies [in] the placing of the power of the State behind a racial classification that induces

tion—prohibition of which lies at the very heart of the Fourteenth Amendment."

11. [While] Virginia prohibits whites from marrying any nonwhite (subject to the exception for the descendants of Pocahontas), Negroes, Orientals and any other racial class may intermarry without statutory interference. Appellants contend that this distinction renders Virginia's miscegenation statutes arbitrary and unreasonable even assuming the constitutional validity of an official purpose to preserve "racial integrity." We need not reach this contention because we find the racial classifications in these statutes repugnant to the Fourteenth Amendment, even assuming an evenhanded state purpose to protect the "integrity" of all races.

8. Discrimination or segregation for its own sake is not, of course, a constitutionally permissible purpose.

9. The state interest required has been characterized as "overriding," *Loving,* "compelling," *Graham v. Richardson* [Sec. 3, II infra], "important," *Dunn v. Blumstein,* [Sec. 4, II infra], or "substantial," ibid. We attribute no particular significance to these variations in diction.

racial prejudice at the polls." Should the result turn on whether a black candidate is likely to receive more or less votes because of race being designated? On whether the statute contributes to a more informed electorate? See Comments, 15 Stan.L.Rev. 339 (1963); 111 U.Pa.L.Rev. 827 (1963). May a state collect racial statistics within school districts to effectuate a policy of integration? May a national census include racial information? May a state, for statistical purposes, require designation of the parties' race on every divorce decree? See *Tancil v. Woolls,* 379 U.S. 19, 85 S.Ct. 157, 13 L.Ed.2d 91 (1964).

3. *Family issues.* PALMORE v. SIDOTI, 466 U.S. 429, 104 S.Ct. 1879, 80 L.Ed.2d 421 (1984), per BURGER, C.J., held that Florida's denial of child custody to a white mother because her new husband was black violated equal protection: "There is a risk that a child living with a step-parent of a different race may be subject to a variety of pressures and stresses not present if the child were living with parents of the same racial or ethnic origin. [But the] effects of racial prejudice, however real, cannot justify a racial classification removing an infant child from the custody of its natural mother found to be an appropriate person to have such custody."[c]

4. *Law enforcement issues.* May a police department assign all black officers to black residential areas and all white officers to white residential areas? May it *ever* consider race in determining assignment? May prison officials take racial tensions among prisoners into account in maintaining security, discipline, or good order? Cf. *Lee v. Washington,* 390 U.S. 333, 88 S.Ct. 994, 19 L.Ed.2d 1212 (1968).

III. DE JURE VS. DE FACTO DISCRIMINATION

Part I involved laws that explicitly discriminated against racial and ethnic minorities. But intentional (or "de jure") discrimination may exist even though the law in question is racially "neutral" on its face: the law may be deliberately administered in a discriminatory way; or a law, although neutral in its language and applied in accordance with its terms, may have been enacted with a purpose (or motive) to disadvantage a "suspect" class. This section concerns these additional types of "de jure" discrimination as well as government action that is racially neutral in its terms, administration, and purpose but which has a discriminatory effect or impact ("de facto" discrimination).

YICK WO v. HOPKINS

118 U.S. 356, 6 S.Ct. 1064, 30 L.Ed. 220 (1886).

JUSTICE MATTHEWS delivered the opinion of the Court.

[A San Francisco ordinance made it unlawful to operate a laundry without the consent of the board of supervisors except in a brick or stone building. Yick Wo, a Chinese alien who had operated a laundry for 22 years, had certificates from the health and fire authorities, but was refused consent by the board. It was admitted that "there were about 320 laundries in the city [and] about 240 were owned [by] subjects of China, and of the whole number, viz., 320, about 310 were constructed of wood"; that "petitioner, and more than 150 of his countrymen, have been arrested" for violating the ordinance "while those who are not

c. What result if the new husband seeks to adopt the child and the natural father objects solely because of racial prejudice? See Note, *Race as a Factor in Custody and Adoption Disputes,* 71 Corn.L.Rev. 209 (1985).

subjects of China, and who are conducting 80 odd laundries under similar conditions, are left unmolested."]

[T]he facts shown establish an administration directed so exclusively against a particular class of persons as to warrant and require the conclusion that, whatever may have been the intent of the ordinances as adopted, they are applied [with] a mind so unequal and oppressive as to amount to a practical denial by the State of [equal protection]. Though the law itself be fair on its face and impartial in appearance, yet, if it is applied and administered by public authority with an evil eye and an unequal hand, so as practically to make unjust and illegal discriminations between persons in similar circumstances, material to their rights, the denial of equal justice is still within the prohibition of the Constitution. [The] fact of this discrimination is admitted. No reason for it is shown, and the conclusion cannot be resisted that no reason for it exists except hostility to [Yick Wo's] race and nationality * * *.

Notes and Questions

1. *Proving intentional discrimination.* (a) *Jury selection.* In CASTANEDA v. PARTIDA, 430 U.S. 482, 97 S.Ct. 1272, 51 L.Ed.2d 498 (1977), respondent challenged the grand jury that indicted him in 1972. He showed that, although 79% of the county's population had Spanish surnames, the average percentage of Spanish-surnamed grand jurors between 1962–72 was 39%. In 1972, 52.5% of persons on the grand jury list had Spanish surnames as did 50% of those on respondent's grand jury list. The Court, per BLACKMUN, J., held that respondent had established a prima facie case of discrimination against Mexican-Americans: [a]

"While the earlier cases involved absolute exclusion of an identifiable group, later cases established the principle that substantial underrepresentation of the group constitutes a constitutional violation as well, if it results from purposeful discrimination. [T]he degree of underrepresentation must be proved, by comparing the proportion of the group in the total population to the proportion called to serve as grand jurors, over a significant period of time.[13] [A] selection procedure that is susceptible of abuse or is not racially neutral supports the presumption of discrimination raised by the statistical showing.[b] Once the defendant has shown substantial underrepresentation of his group, he has made out a prima facie case of discriminatory purpose, and the burden then shifts to the State to rebut that case."

Should the state's proof that a majority of the jury commissioners were Mexican-American rebut the prima facie case? A majority of elected officials in the county? See *Castaneda.*[c]

a. Burger, C.J., and Stewart, Powell and Rehnquist, JJ., dissented.

13. [If] a disparity is sufficiently large, then it is unlikely that it is due solely to chance or accident, and, in the absence of evidence to the contrary, one must conclude that racial or other class-related factors entered into the selection process.

b. The Court observed that, "as in *Alexander v. Louisiana,* 405 U.S. 625, 92 S.Ct. 1221, 31 L.Ed.2d 536 (1972), the selection procedure [here] is not racially neutral with respect to Mexican-Americans; Spanish surnames are just as easily identifiable as race was from the questionnaires in *Alexander* or the notations and card colors in *Whitus v. Georgia,* 385 U.S. 545, 87 S.Ct. 643, 17 L.Ed.2d 599 (1967)."

c. See generally Finkelstein, *The Application of Statistical Decision Theory to the Jury Discrimination Cases,* 80 Harv.L.Rev. 338 (1966); Comment, *The Civil Petitioner's Right to Representative Grand Juries and a Statistical Method of Showing Discrimination in Jury Selection Cases Generally,* 20 U.C.L.A.L.Rev. 581 (1973).

(b) *Executive appointments.* In MAYOR OF PHILA. v. EDUCATIONAL EQUALITY LEAGUE, 415 U.S. 605, 94 S.Ct. 1323, 39 L.Ed.2d 630 (1974), respondents contended that in 1971 the mayor had racially discriminated in appointments to the city's Nominating Panel for school board members. Under the city charter, the Panel had thirteen persons—four appointed from the citizenry at large and the others being the highest-ranking officers of nine city-wide organizations (e.g., labor union council, commerce group, parent-teacher association, etc.). Approximately "34% of the population of Philadelphia and approximately 60% of the students attending the city's various schools were Negroes" but "the 1971 Panel had 11 whites and two Negroes."

The Court, per POWELL, J., held the proof "too fragmentary and speculative" to establish "a prima facie case of racial discrimination." The statistics were "simplistic percentage comparisons [in] the context of this case"; because of the designated qualifications for Panel members, it could not "be assumed that all citizens are fungible for purposes of determining whether members of a particular class have been unlawfully excluded." [d]

2. *Criminal enforcement.* (a) May a black prosecuted for violating a gambling ordinance defend on the ground that the law is enforced only against blacks? May the police justify their conduct on the ground that, since *most* gambling was believed to be taking place in black residential areas, *all* the "gambling squad" was assigned there? Is this different from a state justifying its exclusion of *all* blacks from jury service because *most* did not possess adequate educational qualifications? See generally Johnson, *Race and the Decision to Detain a Suspect,* 93 Yale L.J. 214 (1983).

(b) Is *Yick Wo* distinguishable from the gambling hypothetical because, in *Yick Wo,* "*no* reason for [the discrimination was] shown" and "*no* reason for it exists except hostility to the race"? Is *Yick Wo* distinguishable because defendant operated a lawful business while, in the gambling situation, upholding the equal protection defense permits a "criminal" to go free? [e]

3. *Peremptory challenge.* BATSON v. KENTUCKY, 476 U.S. 79, 106 S.Ct. 1712, 90 L.Ed.2d 69 (1986), per POWELL, J.—declining to follow *Swain v. Alabama,* 380 U.S. 202, 85 S.Ct. 824, 13 L.Ed.2d 759 (1965)—held that, using the same "combination of factors" as in cases like *Castaneda,* "a defendant may establish a prima facie case of purposeful discrimination in selection of the petit jury solely on evidence concerning the prosecutor's exercise of peremptory challenges at the defendant's trial. [Then], the burden shifts to the State to come forward with a neutral explanation for challenging black jurors. [T]he prosecution's explanation need not rise to the level justifying exercise of a challenge for cause. [B]ut the prosecutor may not rebut the defendant's prima facie case of discrimination by stating merely that he challenged jurors of the defendant's race on the assumption—or his intuitive judgment—that they would be partial to the defendant because of their shared race, [because the] core guarantee of equal protection, ensuring citizens that their State will not discriminate on account of race, would be meaningless" if this were permitted.

REHNQUIST, J., joined by Burger, C.J., dissented: "[T]here is simply nothing 'unequal' about the State using its peremptory challenges to strike blacks from the jury in cases involving black defendants, so long as such challenges are also

d. White, J., joined by Douglas, Brennan and Marshall, JJ., dissented.

e. See generally Tieger, *Police Discretion and Discriminatory Enforcement,* 1971 Duke L.J. 717; Givelber, *The Application of Equal Protection Principles to Selective Enforcement of the Criminal Law,* 1971 U.Ill.L.F. 88.

used to exclude whites in cases involving white defendants, Hispanics in cases involving Hispanic defendants, Asians in cases involving Asian defendants, and so on. This case-specific use of peremptory challenges by the State does not single out blacks, or members of any other race for that matter, for discriminatory treatment."

4. *Capital sentencing.* McCLESKEY v. KEMP, whose facts are set forth in detail at p. 332 supra, per POWELL, J., rejected petitioner's claim "that the Baldus study compels an inference that his sentence rests on purposeful discrimination." Unlike the jury selection cases, where "the factors that may be considered are limited, usually by state [statute], each particular decision to impose the death penalty is made by a [jury] unique in its composition, and the Constitution requires that its decision rest on consideration of innumerable factors that vary according to the characteristics of the individual defendant and the facts of the particular capital offense." Further, unlike the jury selection context, "here, the State has no practical opportunity to rebut the Baldus study" because "policy considerations" (1) "dictate that jurors [not] be called [to] testify to the motives and influences that led to their verdict" and (2) "suggest the impropriety of our requiring prosecutors to defend their decisions to seek death penalties, often years after they were made." [17] Finally, implementation of laws against murder, which are "at the heart of the State's criminal justice system, [requires] discretionary judgments. [W]e would demand exceptionally clear proof before we would infer that the discretion has been abused."

BLACKMUN, J., joined by Brennan, Marshall and Stevens, JJ., dissented, reviewing parts of the Baldus study in detail: "I concentrate on the decisions within the prosecutor's office through which the State decided to seek the death penalty and, in particular, the point at which the State proceeded to the penalty phase after conviction. This is a step at which the evidence of the effect of the racial factors was especially strong" and not adequately rebutted by the state.

"I agree [as] to the difficulty of examining the jury's decisionmaking process [but not with the] Court's refusal to require that the prosecutor provide an explanation for his actions * * *. Prosecutors undoubtedly need adequate discretion to allocate the resources of their offices and to fulfill their responsibilities to the public in deciding how best to enforce the law, but this does not place them beyond the constraints imposed on state action under the Fourteenth Amendment. Cf. *Ex parte Virginia.*"

WASHINGTON v. DAVIS

426 U.S. 229, 96 S.Ct. 2040, 48 L.Ed.2d 597 (1976).

JUSTICE WHITE delivered the opinion of the Court.

This case involves the validity of a qualifying test administered to applicants for positions as police officers in the District of Columbia. [T]he police recruit was required to satisfy certain physical and character standards, to be a high school graduate or its equivalent and to receive a grade of at least 40 out of 80 on "Test 21," which is "an examination that is used generally throughout the federal service," which "was developed by the Civil Service Commission, not the Police Department," and which was "designed to test verbal ability, vocabulary, reading and comprehension."

17. Requiring a prosecutor to rebut a study that analyzes the past conduct of scores of prosecutors is quite different from requiring a prosecutor to rebut a contemporaneous challenge to his own acts. See *Batson.*

[The] District Court rejected the assertion that Test 21 was culturally slanted to favor whites and was "satisfied that the undisputable facts prove the test to be reasonably and directly related to the requirements of the police recruit training program and that it is neither so designed nor operates to discriminate against otherwise qualified blacks." [The Court of Appeals held] that lack of discriminatory intent in designing and administering Test 21 was irrelevant; the critical fact was rather [that] four times as many [blacks] failed the test than did whites. This disproportionate impact [was] held sufficient to establish a constitutional violation, absent proof by petitioners that the test was an adequate measure of job performance in addition to being an indicator of probable success in the training program, a burden which the court ruled petitioners had failed to discharge. * * *

The central purpose of the Equal Protection Clause [is] the prevention of official conduct discriminating on the basis of race. [But] our cases have not embraced the proposition that a law or other official act, without regard to whether it reflects a racially discriminatory purpose, is unconstitutional *solely* because it has a racially disproportionate impact.

Almost 100 years ago, *Strauder* established that the exclusion of Negroes from grand and petit juries in criminal proceedings violated the Equal Protection Clause, but the fact that a particular jury or a series of juries does not statistically reflect the racial composition of the community does not in itself make out an invidious discrimination forbidden by the Clause. "A purpose to discriminate must be present which may be proven by systematic exclusion of eligible jurymen of the prescribed race or by an unequal application of the law to such an extent as to show intentional discrimination." * * *

The school desegregation cases have also adhered to the basic equal protection principle that the invidious quality of a law claimed to be racially discriminatory must ultimately be traced to a racially discriminatory purpose. That there are both predominantly black and predominantly white schools in a community is not alone violative of the Equal Protection Clause. The essential element ["differentiating] between de jure segregation and so-called de facto segregation [is] *purpose* or *intent* to segregate." *Keyes v. School Dist.,* [Part IV infra].

This is not to say that the necessary discriminatory racial purpose must be express or appear on the face of the statute, or that a law's disproportionate impact is irrelevant. [A] statute, otherwise neutral on its face, must not be applied so as invidiously to discriminate on the basis of race. *Yick Wo.* It is also clear from the cases dealing with racial discrimination in the selection of juries that [a] prima facie case of discriminatory purpose may be proved [by] the absence of Negroes on a particular jury combined with the failure of the jury commissioners to be informed of eligible Negro jurors in a community, or with racially non-neutral selection procedures. With a prima facie case made out, "the burden of proof shifts to the State to rebut the presumption of unconstitutional action by showing that permissible racially neutral selection criteria and procedures have produced the monochromatic result."

Necessarily, an invidious discriminatory purpose may often be inferred from the totality of the relevant facts, including [that] the law bears more heavily on one race than another. It is also not infrequently true that the discriminatory impact—in the jury cases for example, the total or seriously disproportionate exclusion of Negroes from jury venires—may for all practical purposes demonstrate unconstitutionality because in various circumstances the discrimination is very difficult to explain on nonracial grounds. Nevertheless, we have not held that a law, neutral on its face and serving ends otherwise within the power of government to pursue, is invalid under the Equal Protection Clause simply because it may affect a greater proportion of one race than of another. Disproportionate impact [s]tanding alone [does] not trigger the rule that racial classifications are to be subjected to the strictest scrutiny and are justifiable only by the weightiest of considerations.

There are some indications to the contrary in our cases. In *Palmer v. Thompson,* 403 U.S. 217, 91 S.Ct. 1940, 29 L.Ed.2d 438 (1971), the city of Jackson, Miss., following a court decree to this effect, desegregated all of its public facilities save five swimming pools which [were] closed by ordinance pursuant to a determination by the city council that closure was necessary to preserve peace and order and that integrated pools could not be economically operated. [T]his Court rejected the argument that [the] otherwise seemingly permissible ends served by the ordinance could be impeached by demonstrating that racially invidious motivations had prompted the city council's action. [W]hatever dicta the opinion may contain, the decision did not involve, much less invalidate, a statute or ordinance having neutral purposes but disproportionate racial consequences.[11]

[Test 21] seeks to ascertain whether those who take it have acquired a particular level of verbal skill; and it is untenable that the Constitution prevents the government from seeking modestly to upgrade the communicative abilities of its employees rather than to be satisfied with some lower level of competence, particularly where the job requires special ability to communicate orally and in writing. Respondents, as Negroes, could no more successfully claim that the test denied them equal protection than could white applicants who also failed. The conclusion would not be different in the face of proof that more Negroes than whites had been disqualified by Test 21. * * *

Nor on the facts of the case before us would the disproportionate impact of Test 21 warrant the conclusion that it is a purposeful device to discriminate against Negroes * * *. [T]he test is neutral on its face and rationally may be said to serve a purpose the government is constitutionally empowered to pursue. Even agreeing with the District Court that the differential racial effect of Test 21 called for further inquiry, we think the District Court correctly held that the affirmative efforts of the Metropolitan Police Department to recruit black officers, the changing racial composition of the recruit classes and of the force in general, and the relationship of the test to the training program negated any inference that the Department discriminated on the basis of race * * *.

Under Title VII [of the Civil Rights Act of 1964], Congress provided that when hiring and promotion practices disqualifying substantially disproportionate numbers of blacks are challenged, discriminatory purpose need not be proved, and that it is an insufficient response to demonstrate some rational basis for the challenged practices. It is necessary, in addition, that they be "validated" in terms of job performance * * *. However this process proceeds, it involves a more probing judicial review of, and less deference to, the seemingly reasonable acts of administrators and executives than is appropriate under the Constitution

11. To the extent that *Palmer* suggests a generally applicable proposition that legislative purpose is irrelevant in constitutional adjudication, our prior cases—as indicated in the text—are to the contrary; and very shortly after *Palmer,* all Members of the Court majority in that case [joined] *Lemon v. Kurtzman,* [stating that] the validity of public aid to church-related schools includes close inquiry into the purpose of the challenged statute.

where special racial impact, without discriminatory purpose, is claimed. We are not disposed to adopt this more rigorous standard for the purposes of applying the Fifth and the Fourteenth Amendments in cases such as this.[a]

A rule that a statute designed to serve neutral ends is nevertheless invalid, absent compelling justification, if in practice it benefits or burdens one race more than another would be far-reaching and would raise serious questions about, and perhaps invalidate, a whole range of tax, welfare, public service, regulatory, and licensing statutes that may be more burdensome to the poor and to the average black than to the more affluent white.[14]

Given that rule, such consequences would perhaps be likely to follow. However, in our view, extension of the rule beyond those areas where it is already applicable by reason of statute, such as in the field of public employment, should await legislative prescription. * * *[b]

JUSTICE STEVENS [who joined the Court's opinion] concurring. * * *

The requirement of purposeful discrimination is a common thread running through the cases summarized [by the Court. But] in each of these contexts, the burden of proving a prima facie case may well involve differing evidentiary considerations. The extent of deference that one pays to the trial court's determination of the factual issue, and indeed, the extent to which one characterizes the intent issue as a question of fact or a question of law, will vary in different contexts.

Frequently the most probative evidence of intent will be objective evidence of what actually happened rather than evidence describing the subjective state of mind of the actor. For normally the actor is presumed to have intended the natural consequences of his deeds. This is particularly true in the case of governmental action which is frequently the product of compromise, of collective decisionmaking, and of mixed motivation. It is unrealistic, on the one hand, to require the victim of alleged discrimination to uncover the actual subjective intent of the decisionmaker or conversely, to invalidate otherwise legitimate action simply because an improper motive affected the deliberation of a participant in the decisional process. A law conscripting clerics should not be invalidated because an atheist voted for it.

My point [is] to suggest that the line between discriminatory purpose and discriminatory impact is not nearly as bright, and perhaps not quite as critical, as the reader of the Court's opinion might assume. I agree [that] a constitution-

a. For materials on the different types of claims that may arise under Title VII and other statutes and the techniques of proof to show a prima facie violation, see Eisenberg, *Civil Rights Legislation* (2d ed. 1987).

14. Goodman, *De Facto School Segregation: A Constitutional and Empirical Analysis*, 60 Calif.L.Rev. 275, 300 (1972), suggests that disproportionate-impact analysis might invalidate "tests and qualifications for voting, draft deferment, public employment, jury service, and other government-conferred [benefits]; [s]ales taxes, bail schedules, utility rates, bridge tolls, license fees, and other state-imposed charges." It has also been argued that minimum wage and usury laws as well as professional licensing requirements would require major modifications in light of the unequal-impact rule. Silverman, *Equal Protection, Economic Legislation, and Racial Discrimination*, 25 Vand.L.Rev. 1183 (1972). * * *

b. The Court also found no violation of the relevant statutory provisions. Stewart, J., joined only the constitutional aspects of the Court's opinion. Brennan, J., joined by Marshall, J., did not address the constitutional questions but dissented on statutory grounds.

For detailed criticism of this decision, as well as many others, for enshrining the "perpetrator perspective" of racial discrimination and ignoring the "victim perspective," see Freeman, *Legitimizing Racial Discrimination Through Antidiscrimination Law: A Critical Review of Supreme Court Doctrine*, 62 Minn.L. Rev. 1049 (1978).

al issue does not arise every time some disproportionate impact is shown. On the other hand, when the disproportion is as dramatic as in *Gomillion v. Lightfoot,* 364 U.S. 339, 81 S.Ct. 125, 5 L.Ed.2d 110 (1960)[c] or *Yick Wo,* it really does not matter whether the standard is phrased in terms of purpose or effect. Therefore, although I accept the statement of the general rule in the Court's opinion, I am not yet prepared to indicate how that standard should be applied in the many cases which have formulated the governing standard in different language. * * *

There are two reasons why I am convinced that the challenge to Test 21 is insufficient. First, the test serves the neutral and legitimate purpose of requiring all applicants to meet a uniform minimum standard of literacy. Reading ability is manifestly relevant to the police function, there is no evidence that the required passing grade was set at an arbitrarily high level, and there is sufficient disparity among high schools and high school graduates to justify the use of a separate uniform test. Second, the same test is used throughout the federal service. The applicants for employment in the District of Columbia Police Department represent such a small fraction of the total number of persons who have taken the test that their experience is of minimal probative value in assessing the neutrality of the test itself. That evidence, without more, is not sufficient to overcome the presumption that a test which is this widely used by the Federal Government is in fact neutral in its effect as well as its "purpose" as that term is used in constitutional adjudication. * * *

ARLINGTON HEIGHTS v. METROPOLITAN HOUSING DEV. CORP., 429 U.S. 252, 97 S.Ct. 555, 50 L.Ed.2d 450 (1977), per POWELL, J.—holding that petitioner Village's refusal to rezone land from single-family (R–3) to multiple-family (R–5), so as to permit respondent MHDC's construction of racially integrated housing, did not violate equal protection—amplified *Davis:*

"*Davis* does not require a plaintiff to prove that the challenged action rested solely on racially discriminatory purposes. Rarely can it be said that a legislature or administrative body operating under a broad mandate made a decision motivated solely by a single concern, or even that a particular purpose was the 'dominant' or 'primary' one. In fact, it is because legislators and administrators are properly concerned with balancing numerous competing considerations that courts refrain from reviewing the merits of their decisions, absent a showing of arbitrariness or irrationality. But racial discrimination is not just another competing consideration. When there is proof that a discriminatory purpose has been a motivating factor in the decision, this judicial deference is no longer justified.[12]

c. In *Gomillion,* an Alabama statute changed the Tuskegee city boundaries from a square to a 28 sided figure, allegedly removing "all save only four or five of its 400 Negro voters while not removing a single white voter or resident." The Court held that the complaint "amply alleges a claim of racial discrimination" in violation of the fifteenth amendment. "If these allegations upon a trial remained uncontradicted or unqualified, the conclusion would be irresistible, tantamount for all practical purposes to a mathematical demonstration, that the legislation is solely concerned with segregating white and colored voters by fencing Negro citizens out of town so as to deprive them of their pre-existing municipal vote."

12. For a scholarly discussion of legislative motivation, see Brest, *Palmer v. Thompson: An Approach to The Problem of Unconstitutional Motive,* 1971 Sup.Ct. 95, 116–118. [Compare Ely, *Legislative and Administrative Motivation in Constitutional Law,* 79 Yale L.J. 1205 (1970).]

"Determining whether invidious discriminatory purpose was a motivating factor demands a sensitive inquiry into such circumstantial and direct evidence of intent as may be available. The impact of the official action [may] provide an important starting point. Sometimes a clear pattern, unexplainable on grounds other than race, emerges from the effect of the state action even when the governing legislation appears neutral on its face. *Yick Wo; Guinn v. United States,* 238 U.S. 347, 35 S.Ct. 926, 59 L.Ed. 1340 (1915); *Lane v. Wilson,* 307 U.S. 268, 59 S.Ct. 872, 83 L.Ed. 1281 (1939); [a] *Gomillion.* The evidentiary inquiry is then relatively easy.[13] But such cases are rare. Absent a pattern as stark as that in *Gomillion* or *Yick Wo,* impact alone is not determinative,[14] and the Court must look to other evidence.[15]

"The historical background of the decision is one evidentiary source, particularly if it reveals a series of official actions taken for invidious purposes. See *Lane.* The specific sequence of events leading up to the challenged decision also may shed some light on the decision-maker's purposes. *Reitman v. Mulkey.* For example, if the property involved here always had been zoned R–5 but suddenly was changed to R–3 when the town learned of MHDC's plans to erect integrated housing, we would have a far different case. Departures from the normal procedural sequence also might afford evidence that improper purposes are playing a role. Substantive departures too may be relevant, particularly if the factors usually considered important by the decisionmaker strongly favor a decision contrary to the one reached.

"The legislative or administrative history may be highly relevant, especially where there are contemporary statements by members of the decisionmaking body, minutes of its meetings, or reports. In some extraordinary instances the members might be called to the stand at trial to testify concerning the purpose of the official action, although even then such testimony frequently will be barred by privilege. See *Tenney v. Brandhove,* 341 U.S. 367, 71 S.Ct. 783, 95 L.Ed. 1019 (1951).[18]

"[This] summary identifies, without purporting to be exhaustive, subjects of proper inquiry in determining whether racially discriminatory intent existed."

Both courts below found that the rezoning denial was not racially motivated.

a. *Guinn* held that Oklahoma's literacy test for voting violated the fifteenth amendment because its "grandfather clause" effectively exempted whites. Oklahoma then immediately enacted a new law providing that all persons who previously voted were qualified for life but that all others must register within a twelve day period or be permanently disenfranchised. *Lane* held that this new law violated the fifteenth amendment.

13. Several of our jury selection cases fall into this category. Because of the nature of the jury selection task, however, we have permitted a finding of constitutional violation even when the statistical pattern does not approach the extremes of *Yick Wo* or *Gomillion.*

[For the view that the Court has used the allocation of burden of proof in respect to discriminatory purpose or intent to obscure its own "balancing of competing individual and public interests" and its own "making many of the ultimate value choices implicit in equal protection," see Ortiz, *The Myth of Intent in Equal Protection,* 41 Stan.L.Rev. 1105 (1989).]

14. This is not to say that a consistent pattern of official racial discrimination is a necessary predicate to a violation of [equal protection]. A single invidiously discriminatory governmental act—in the exercise of the zoning power as elsewhere—would not necessarily be immunized by the absence of such discrimination in the making of other comparable decisions.

15. In many instances, to recognize the limited probative value of disproportionate impact is merely to acknowledge the "heterogeneity" of the nation's population.

18. This Court has recognized, ever since *Fletcher v. Peck,* that judicial inquiries into legislative or executive motivation represent a substantial intrusion into the workings of other branches of government. Placing a decisionmaker on the stand is therefore "usually to be avoided."

"We also have reviewed the evidence. The impact of the Village's decision does arguably bear more heavily on racial minorities. [But] there is little about the sequence of events leading up to the decision that would spark suspicion. The area [has] been zoned R–3 since 1959, the year when Arlington Heights first adopted a zoning map. Single-family homes surround the 80-acre site, and the Village is undeniably committed to single-family homes as its dominant residential land use. The rezoning request progressed according to the usual procedures. * * *

"The statements by the Plan Commission and Village Board members, as reflected in the official minutes, focused almost exclusively on the zoning aspects of the MHDC petition, and the zoning factors on which they relied are not novel criteria in the Village's rezoning decisions. * * * MHDC called one member of the Village Board to the stand at trial. Nothing in her testimony supports an inference of invidious purpose.

"In sum, [r]espondents simply failed to carry their burden of proving that discriminatory purpose was a motivating factor in the Village's decision.[21] This conclusion ends the constitutional inquiry." [b]

PERSONNEL ADMINISTRATOR v. FEENEY, 442 U.S. 256, 99 S.Ct. 2282, 60 L.Ed.2d 870 (1979), per STEWART, J.,—relying on *Davis* and *Arlington Heights*—upheld Massachusetts' "absolute lifetime preference to veterans" for state civil service positions, even though "the preference operates overwhelmingly to the advantage of males" [a]: "When a statute gender-neutral on its face is challenged on the ground that its effects upon women are disproportionably adverse, a two-fold inquiry [is] appropriate. The first question is whether the statutory classification is indeed neutral * * *. If the classification itself, covert or overt, is not based upon gender, the second question is whether the adverse effect reflects invidious gender-based discrimination. In this second inquiry, impact provides an 'important starting point,' *Arlington Heights,* but purposeful discrimination is 'the condition that offends the Constitution.'"

As to the first question, "The District Court [found] first, that ch. 31 serves legitimate and worthy purposes; second, that the absolute preference was not established for the purpose of discriminating against women. [Thus,] the distinction between veterans and nonveterans drawn by ch. 31 is not a pretext for gender discrimination. * * *

21. Proof that the decision by the Village was motivated in part by a racially discriminatory purpose would not necessarily have required invalidation of the challenged decision. Such proof would, however, have shifted to the Village the burden of establishing that the same decision would have resulted even had the impermissible purpose not been considered. If this were established, the complaining party in a case of this kind no longer fairly could attribute the injury complained of to improper consideration of a discriminatory purpose.

b. The Court remanded for further consideration of respondents' claims under the Fair Housing Act. Marshall, J., joined by Brennan, J., concurred in the Court's substantive discussion but, along with White, J., would have remanded "this entire case [for] further proceedings consistent with *Davis.*" Stevens, J., did not participate.

On remand, the court of appeals held that proof of a discriminatory purpose was not required to find a violation of the Fair Housing Act. 558 F.2d 1283 (7th Cir.1977), cert. denied, 434 U.S. 1025 (1978).

a. Sex discrimination is considered in Sec. 3, II infra. Although such discrimination has not been held to be "suspect," it has been held to be subject to special judicial scrutiny and the Court's approach to the "purpose" vs. "impact" issue has been similar to cases involving discrimination against racial or ethnic minorities.

"If the impact of this statute could not be plausibly explained on a neutral ground, impact itself would signal that the real classification made by the law was in fact not neutral. But there can be but one answer to the question whether this veteran preference excludes significant numbers of women from preferred state jobs because they are women or because they are nonveterans. [T]his is not a law that can plausibly be explained only as a gender-based classification. Indeed, it is not a law that can rationally be explained on that ground. Veteran status is not uniquely male. Although few women benefit from the preference, the nonveteran class is not substantially all-female. To the contrary, significant numbers of nonveterans are men, and all nonveterans—male as well as female—are placed at a disadvantage. Too many men are affected by ch. 31 to permit the inference that the statute is but a pretext for preferring men over women. * * *

"The dispositive question, then, is whether the appellee has shown that a gender-based discriminatory purpose has, at least in some measure, shaped [ch. 31. Her] contention that this veterans' preference is 'inherently non-neutral' or 'gender-biased' presumes that the State, by favoring veterans, intentionally incorporated into its public employment policies the panoply of sex-based and assertedly discriminatory federal laws that have prevented all but a handful of women from becoming veterans. There are two serious difficulties with this argument. First, it is wholly at odds with the District Court's central finding that Massachusetts has not offered a preference to veterans for the purpose of discriminating against women. Second, it cannot be reconciled with the assumption made by both the appellee and the District Court that a more limited hiring preference for veterans could be sustained. Taken together, these difficulties are fatal.

"To the extent that the status of veteran is one that few women have been enabled to achieve, every hiring preference for veterans, however modest or extreme, is inherently gender-biased. If Massachusetts by offering such a preference can be said intentionally to have incorporated into its state employment policies the historical gender-based federal military personnel practices, the degree of the preference would or should make no constitutional difference. Invidious discrimination does not become less so because the discrimination accomplished is of a lesser magnitude.[23] Discriminatory intent is simply not amenable to calibration. It either is a factor that has influenced the legislative choice or it is not. The District Court's conclusion that the absolute veterans' preference was not originally enacted or subsequently reaffirmed for the purpose of giving an advantage to males as such necessarily compels the conclusion that the State intended nothing more than to prefer 'veterans.' * * *

"To be sure, this case is unusual in that it involves a law that by design is not neutral. [As] opposed to the written test at issue in *Davis*, it does not purport to define a job related characteristic. To the contrary, it confers upon a specifically described group—perceived to be particularly deserving—a competitive head start. But the District Court found, and the appellee has not disputed, that this legislative choice was legitimate. [Thus, it] must be analyzed as is any other neutral law that casts a greater burden upon women as a group than upon men as a group. The enlistment policies of the armed services may well have

23. This is not to say that the degree of impact is irrelevant to the question of intent. But it is to say that a more modest preference, while it might well lessen impact and, as the State argues, might lessen the effectiveness of the statute in helping veterans, would not be any more or less "neutral" in the constitutional sense.

discriminated on the basis of sex. But the history of discrimination against women in the military is not on trial in this case.

"The appellee's ultimate argument rests upon the presumption, common to the criminal and civil law, that a person intends the natural and foreseeable consequences of his voluntary actions. * * *

" 'Discriminatory purpose,' however, implies more than intent as volition or intent as awareness of consequences. It implies that the decisionmaker, in this case a state legislature, selected or reaffirmed a particular course of action at least in part 'because of,' not merely 'in spite of,' its adverse effects upon an identifiable group.[25] Yet nothing in the record demonstrates that this preference for veterans was originally devised or subsequently re-enacted because it would accomplish the collateral goal of keeping women in a stereotypic and predefined place in the Massachusetts Civil Service."

STEVENS, J., joined by White, J., concurred in the Court's opinion, adding: "If a classification is not overtly based on gender, I am inclined to believe the question whether it is covertly gender-based is the same as the question whether its adverse effects reflect invidious gender-based discrimination. However the question is phrased, for me the answer is largely provided by the fact that the number of males disadvantaged by Massachusetts' Veterans Preference (1,867,000) is sufficiently large—and sufficiently close to the number of disadvantaged females (2,954,000)—to refute the claim that the rule was intended to benefit males as a class over females as a class."

MARSHALL, J., joined by Brennan, J., dissented: "In my judgment, [ch. 31] evinces purposeful gender-based discrimination. * * *

"That a legislature seeks to advantage one group does not, as a matter of logic or of common sense, exclude the possibility that it also intends to disadvantage another. Individuals in general and lawmakers in particular frequently act for a variety of reasons. [S]ince reliable evidence of subjective intentions is seldom obtainable, resort to inference based on objective factors is generally unavoidable. To discern the purposes underlying facially neutral policies, this Court has therefore considered the degree, inevitability, and foreseeability of any disproportionate impact as well as the alternatives reasonably available.

"[T]he impact of the Massachusetts statute on women is undisputed. Any veteran with a passing grade on the civil service exam must be placed ahead of a nonveteran, regardless of their respective scores. [Because] less than 2% of the women in Massachusetts are veterans, the absolute preference formula has rendered desirable state civil service employment an almost exclusively male prerogative. [Where] the foreseeable impact of a facially neutral policy is so disproportionate, the burden should rest on the State to establish that sex-based considerations played no part in the choice of the particular legislative scheme.

"Clearly, that burden was not sustained here. The legislative history of the statute reflects the Commonwealth's patent appreciation of the impact the preference system would have on women, and an equally evident desire to

25. This is not to say that the inevitability or foreseeability of consequences of a neutral rule has no bearing upon the existence of discriminatory intent. Certainly, when the adverse consequences of a law upon an identifiable group are as inevitable as the gender-based consequences of ch. 31, a strong inference that the adverse effects were desired can reasonably be drawn. But in this inquiry—made as it is under the Constitution—an inference is a working tool, not a synonym for proof. When as here, the impact is essentially an unavoidable consequence of a legislative policy that has in itself always been deemed to be legitimate, and when, as here, the statutory history and all of the available evidence affirmatively demonstrate the opposite, the inference simply fails to ripen into proof.

mitigate that impact only with respect to certain traditionally female occupations. Until 1971, the statute [and] regulations exempted from operation of the preference any job requisitions 'especially calling for women.' In practice, this exemption, coupled with the absolute preference for veterans, has created a gender-based civil service hierarchy, with women occupying low grade clerical and secretarial jobs and men holding more responsible and remunerative positions.

"[Such] a statutory scheme both reflects and perpetuates precisely the kind of archaic assumptions about women's roles which we have previously held invalid [citing cases in Sec. 3, II infra]. Particularly when viewed against the range of less discriminatory alternatives available to assist veterans,[2] Massachusetts's choice of a formula that so severely restricts public employment opportunities for women cannot reasonably be thought gender-neutral. The Court's conclusion to the contrary—that 'nothing in the record' evinces a 'collateral goal of keeping women in a stereotypic and predefined place in the Massachusetts Civil Service'—displays a singularly myopic view of the facts established below.[3] "

MOBILE v. BOLDEN, Sec. 4, I, A infra, involved the question of whether a fifteenth amendment violation requires "discriminatory purpose." STEWART, J., joined by Burger, C.J., and Powell and Rehnquist, JJ., relying on *Guinn, Lane* and *Gomillion,* found that it did. WHITE, J., appeared to avoid explicitly addressing the question, finding that the election scheme at issue had a discriminatory purpose. BLACKMUN, J., "assuming that proof of intent is a prerequisite," agreed with White, J.'s finding. STEVENS, J., did not directly address the question, but disagreed with Stewart, J.'s "reach[ing] out to decide [it]."

MARSHALL, J., dissented: "*Davis* required a showing of discriminatory purpose to support racial discrimination claims largely because it feared that a standard based solely on disproportionate impact would unduly interfere with the far-ranging governmental distribution of constitutional gratuities [citing *Davis'* text at fn. 14]. Underlying the Court's decision was a determination that, since the Constitution does not entitle any person to such governmental benefits, courts should accord discretion to those officials who decide how the government shall allocate its scarce resources. * * *

"Such judicial deference to official decisionmaking has no place under the Fifteenth Amendment. Section 1 of that Amendment differs from the Fourteenth Amendment's prohibition on racial discrimination in two crucial respects: it explicitly recognizes the right to vote free of hindrances related to race, and it sweeps no further. In my view, these distinctions justify the conclusion that proof of racially discriminatory impact should be sufficient to support a claim under the Fifteenth Amendment. The right to vote is of such fundamental importance in the constitutional scheme that the Fifteenth Amendment's command that it shall not be 'abridged' on account of race must be interpreted as

2. Only four States afford a preference comparable in [scope]. Other States and the Federal Government grant point or tie-breaking preferences that do not foreclose opportunities for women.

3. Although it is relevant that the preference statute also disadvantages a substantial group of men, it is equally pertinent that 47% of Massachusetts men over 18 are veterans, as compared to 0.8% of Massachusetts women. Given this disparity, and the indicia of intent noted supra, the absolute number of men denied preference cannot be dispositive, especially since they have not faced the barriers to achieving veteran status confronted by women.

providing that the votes of citizens of all races shall be of substantially equal weight. Furthermore, a disproportionate-impact test under the Fifteenth Amendment would not lead to constant judicial intrusion into the process of official decisionmaking. Rather, the standard would reach only those decisions having a discriminatory effect upon the minority's vote. The Fifteenth Amendment cannot tolerate that kind of decision, even if made in good faith, because the Amendment grants racial minorities the full enjoyment of the right to vote, not simply protection against the unfairness of intentional vote dilution along racial lines.[32]

"In addition, it is beyond dispute that a standard based solely upon the motives of official decisionmakers creates significant problems of proof [and] creates the risk that officials will be able to adopt policies that are the products of discriminatory intent so long as they sufficiently mask their motives through the use of subtlety and illusion. [That] risk becomes intolerable [when] the precious right to vote protected by the Fifteenth Amendment is concerned."[a]

In MEMPHIS v. GREENE, 451 U.S. 100, 101 S.Ct. 1584, 67 L.Ed.2d 769 (1981), the city—at the behest of citizens of Hein Park, a white residential community within Memphis—closed a street, West Drive, that traversed Hein Park and was used mainly by blacks who lived in an adjacent area. The Court, per STEVENS, J., agreeing that "the adverse impact on blacks was greater than on whites," found no violation of 42 U.S.C.A. § 1982 [p. 1265 infra] or the thirteenth amendment: "[T]he critical facts established by the record are these: The city's decision to close West Drive was motivated by its interest in protecting the safety and tranquility of a residential neighborhood. The procedures followed in making the decision were fair and were not affected by any racial or other impermissible factors. The city has conferred a benefit on certain white property owners but there is no reason to believe that it would refuse to confer a comparable benefit on black property owners. The closing has not affected the value of property owned by black citizens, but it has caused some slight inconvenience to black motorists.

"[T]he record discloses no racially discriminatory motive on the part of the City Council [and] a review of the justification for the official action challenged in this case demonstrates that its disparate impact on black citizens could not [be] fairly characterized as a badge or incident of slavery.

"[To] decide the narrow constitutional question presented by this record we need not speculate about the sort of impact on a racial group that might be prohibited by the Amendment itself. We merely hold that the impact of the closing of West Drive on nonresidents of Hein Park [does] not reflect a violation of the Thirteenth Amendment."

MARSHALL, J., joined by Brennan and Blackmun, JJ., dissented: "I [do] not mean to imply that all municipal decisions that affect Negroes adversely and benefit whites are prohibited by the Thirteenth Amendment. I would, however,

32. Even if a municipal policy is shown to dilute the right to vote, however, the policy will not be struck down if the city shows that it serves highly important local interests and is closely tailored to effectuate only those interests.

a. In a brief opinion, Brennan, J., agreed with Marshall, J.'s conclusion.

For an opinion of the Court per White, J.—joined by Burger, C.J., and Brennan, Marshall, Blackmun and O'Connor, JJ.—even more strongly suggesting that a fifteenth amendment violation requires a "discriminatory purpose," see *Rogers v. Lodge,* Sec. 4, I, A infra.

insist that the government carry a heavy burden of justification before I would sustain against Thirteenth Amendment challenge conduct as egregious as erection of a barrier to prevent predominantly-Negro traffic from entering a historically all-white neighborhood. [I] do not believe that the city has discharged that burden in this case, and for that reason I would hold that the erection of the barrier at the end of West Drive amounts to a badge or incident of slavery forbidden by the Thirteenth Amendment."

Notes and Questions

1. *The "discriminatory purpose" requirement.* (a) Should "racially disproportionate impact" alone trigger special judicial scrutiny? Consider Tribe, *American Constitutional Law* 1516–20 (2d ed. 1988): "The goal of the equal protection clause is not to stamp out impure thoughts, but to guarantee a full measure of human dignity for all. [Beyond] the purposeful, affirmative adoption or use of rules that disadvantage [them,] minorities can also be injured when the government is 'only' indifferent to their suffering or 'merely' blind to how prior official discrimination contributed to it and how current official acts will perpetuate it. [S]trict judicial scrutiny [should be used] for those government acts that, given their history, context, source, and effect, seem most likely not only to perpetuate subordination but also to reflect a tradition of hostility toward an historically subjugated group, or a pattern of blindness or indifference to the interests of that group." Compare Bennett, *"Mere" Rationality in Constitutional Law: Judicial Review and Democratic Theory,* 67 Calif.L.Rev. 1049, 1076 (1979): "If members of racial minorities statistically obtain benefits and suffer detriments as one or another piece of legislation is passed without attention to its racial impact, they are obtaining, not being deprived of, equal protection of the laws. To forbid all legislation that disadvantages them would give them the gains from political bargaining without the losses. This would be so regardless of the degree of the racially disproportionate impact or the importance of the interest affected."

To what extent "must equal protection doctrine address the unconscious racism that underlies much of the racially disproportionate impact of governmental policy"? Lawrence, *The Id, the Ego, and Equal Protection: Reckoning with Unconscious Racism,* 39 Stan.L.Rev. 317, 355 (1987). Consider id. at 364–65: "What does it mean [in *Memphis v. Greene*] to construct a barrier between all-white and all-black sections of Memphis? In a city where just twenty years ago such barriers were built down the middle of rest rooms and restaurants with signs on them that read 'white' and 'colored' won't there be a considerable consensus as to whether the barrier speaks in racial terms? [The] meaning says that the peace and quiet of a white neighborhood has been weighed against the stigmatization of blacks. The decision to build a barrier issues the statement that white tranquility is more important than black pride. * * *

"At the opposite end of the spectrum is a hypothetical increase in the municipal railway fare [or] an increase in the sales tax, the fee for obtaining a driver's license, or the cost of a building permit. These are all cases where the impact on blacks in a particular instance may be greater than it is on whites. They are also cases where some stigma may attach to those who are excluded by the governmental action. But we are likely to think of the in-group and out-group in economic rather than racial terms. These actions do not contribute directly to the system of beliefs that labels blacks as inferior. Where the culture as a whole does not think of an action in racial terms, it is also unlikely that unconscious attitudes about race influenced the governmental decisionmaker."

Is there a "discriminatory purpose" if it is determined that the challenged law would not have been passed "if its racial impact had been reversed, i.e., if the disparate impact had been on whites rather than on blacks"? Schnapper, *Two Categories of Discriminatory Intent,* 17 Harv.Civ.Rts.—Civ.Lib.L.Rev. 31, 51 (1982). Consider id. at 55–56: "The central issue [in *Feeney*] is whether Massachusetts would have adopted in 1896 a veterans' preference [that would have excluded 98% of all male applicants] or would have amended its statutes successively in 1919, 1943, 1949, and 1968 to assure such preferential treatment for new generations of predominantly female veterans. The all too familiar history of discrimination on the basis of sex in this country renders implausible the suggestion * * *." [a]

Contrast Perry, *The Disproportionate Impact Theory of Racial Discrimination,* 125 U.Pa.L.Rev. 540, 559–60 (1977): "Laws employing a racial criterion of selection are inherently more dangerous than laws involving no racial criterion. The former, unlike the latter, directly encourage racialism [and] are usually difficult if not impossible to justify on legitimate grounds. By contrast, laws having a disproportionate racial impact are quite easy to explain on legitimate grounds because such laws serve a legitimate function in addition to the function of racial selection. Accordingly, the standard of review [should be] more rigorous than that required by the rational relationship test but less rigorous than that required by the strict scrutiny test. [In] determining whether a disproportionate disadvantage is justified, a court would weigh several factors: (1) the degree of disproportion in the impact; (2) the private interest disadvantaged; (3) the efficiency of the challenged law in achieving its objective and the availability of alternative means having a less disproportionate impact; and (4) the government objective sought to be advanced." [b]

(b) *First amendment freedoms.* In cases holding "neutral" laws that had an adverse impact on speech or association to violate the first amendment—such as *In re Primus*—in which the Court required a "compelling state interest" or "more than merely a 'reasonable relation to some purpose within the competency of the state,'" did the Court find that the challenged state programs had a "discriminatory purpose"? If not, how is the disproportionate racial impact situation distinguishable? See Silard, *Toward Nationwide School Desegregation: A "Compelling State Interest" Test of Racial Concentration in Public Education,* 51 N.C.L.Rev. 675 (1973). Consider Perry, supra, at 556: "The first amendment protects values and interests believed indispensable to the democratic functioning of the political process. Government is charged with the duty, under the first amendment, of safeguarding those values and interests [by] acting solicitously toward them as well as by refraining from deliberately abridging them. The equal protection clause serves principally as a brake on the lamentable tendency of the majority race wilfully to oppress or exploit racial minorities, and in this regard it prohibits, absent compelling justification, the use of race as a

a. For detailed development of this approach, see also Strauss, *Discriminatory Intent and the Taming of Brown,* 56 U.Chi.L.Rev. 935 (1989).

b. For a similar "balancing approach," see Eisenberg, *Disproportionate Impact and Illicit Motive: Theories of Constitutional Adjudication,* 52 N.Y.U.L.Rev. 36 (1977).

For the view that "serious scrutiny is preferable to ad hoc balancing," see Binion, *Intent and Equal Protection: A Reconsideration,* 1983 Sup.Ct.Rev. 397—comprehensively criticizing the "discriminatory purpose" requirement as developed and applied in the cases.

criterion of selection. Traditionally, however, it has not been thought wrong—unfortunate, perhaps, but not wrong—that an individual or group is incidentally burdened by a law serving the public good. [Thus], with respect to racial discrimination equal protection doctrine has focused almost exclusively on *wilful* oppression or exploitation of minorities by the majority. This focus is especially understandable in light of what historically has been this society's severest moral affliction, racial animus." [c]

(c) *Burden of proof.* Who does (should) have the burden of proving a "discriminatory purpose"? What does (should) a challenger have to prove to shift the burden to the state "to rebut the presumption of unconstitutional action"? Consider Simon, fn. a in *Korematsu,* at 1111: "[A] showing of significant disproportionate disadvantage to a racial minority group, *without more,* gives rise to an inference that the action may have been taken or at least maintained or continued with knowledge that such groups would be relatively disadvantaged. [I]t raises a possibility sufficient to oblige the government to come forward with a credible explanation showing that the action was (or would have been) taken quite apart from prejudice. Depending upon the type of governmental action at issue, discharging this burden will often be easy for the government, but sometimes it will be difficult or impossible. In all cases, however, the government should be required to show more than that the action has some racially innocent 'conceivable basis in fact' because, as anyone familiar with this standard is aware, it can result in the validation of actions on the basis of explanations that are virtually incredible." Compare Karst, *The Costs of Motive-Centered Inquiry,* 15 San Diego L.Rev. 1163, 1165 (1978): "Because an individual's behavior results from the interaction of a multitude of motives, and because racial attitudes often operate at the margin of consciousness, in any given case there almost certainly will be an opportunity for a government official to argue that his action was prompted by racially neutral considerations. When that argument is made, should we not expect the judge to give the official the benefit of the moral doubt? When the governmental action is the product of a group decision, will not that tendency toward generosity be heightened? The first objection to a motive-centered doctrine of racial discrimination, then, is that it places a 'very heavy burden' of persuasion on the wrong side of the dispute, to the severe detriment of the constitutional protection of racial equality." See generally Blumstein, *Defining and Proving Race Discrimination: Perspectives on the Purpose vs. Results Approach from the Voting Rights Act,* 69 Va.L.Rev. 633 (1983).

2. *Prior state discrimination.* (a) Should there be special judicial scrutiny if the disproportionate racial impact of a law, whose purpose is racially neutral, is produced (influenced) by prior intentional state discrimination? See *Lane v. Wilson,* fn. a in *Arlington Heights.* Suppose a state requires that all applicants furnish recommendations from alumni and that there are no black alumni because the university admitted no blacks in the past? Suppose a state hires teachers wholly on the basis of merit and racial segregation in schools has rendered the quality of education of black teachers inferior to that of whites? Would (should) there have been special judicial scrutiny in *Feeney* if the disproportionate impact had been produced (influenced) by prior intentional discrimination by Massachusetts rather than military personnel practices of the federal government? If so, why should Massachusetts' "incorporation" of intentional

c. As to whether "discriminatory purpose" is required in respect to laws that allegedly violate equal protection because they affect "fundamental rights," see *Mobile v. Bolden,* Sec. 4, I, A infra.

discrimination by another government agency make a "constitutional difference"?

(b) Does the "prior discrimination" factor provide a limiting principle that ameliorates *Davis'* concern about the "far-reaching" consequences of "disproportionate-impact analysis"? Consider Perry, supra, at 557–58: "When disadvantage is suffered not merely as a consequence of a law, but [also] *as a consequence of prior governmental action that was constitutionally (and ethically) offensive,* it cannot be maintained that the disadvantage is ethically inoffensive. The disadvantage, in such a circumstance, is the fruit of prior government misdeeds and, accordingly, should bear a heavier burden of justification than that required of a truly neutral disadvantage. [The] failure of American society to outlaw racial discrimination—at least those instances of discrimination (in schooling, housing, and employment) most destructive to the social position of blacks—was hardly better, as a moral matter, than the discrimination itself. In terms of moral responsibility this failure, which endured for too long, amounted to complicity. Laws having a disproportionate racial impact burden blacks *because* of their especially disadvantaged position in American society. A failure to require government to take account of that especially disadvantaged social position by selecting and fine-tuning laws to avoid the unnecessary or thoughtless aggravation of the situation would effectively ignore American society's responsibility for that social position. Furthermore, the failure would compound the responsibility."

Compare Fiss, *Groups and the Equal Protection Clause,* 5 Phil. & Pub.Afrs. 107, 145 (1976): "A true inquiry into past discrimination [requires] the courts to construct causal connections that span significant periods of time, periods greater than those permitted under any general statute of limitations (a common device used to prevent the judiciary from undertaking inquiries where the evidence is likely to be stale, fragmentary, and generally unreliable). The difficulties of these backward-looking inquiries are compounded because the court must invariably deal with aggregate behavior, not just a single transaction; it must determine the causal explanation for the residential patterns of an entire community, or the skill levels of all the black applicants." See also Schnapper, *Perpetuation of Past Discrimination,* 96 Harv.L.Rev. 828 (1983); Brest, *In Defense of the Antidiscrimination Principle,* 90 Harv.L.Rev. 1, 42 (1976).

3. *Consequences of "discriminatory purpose."* If it is found that a law "was motivated by a racially discriminatory purpose," should the state be permitted to prove "that the same decision would have resulted had the impermissible purpose not been considered"? *Arlington Heights,* fn. 21. May a state defend a statute that discriminates on its face by proving that the same effect would have resulted even if the legislature had never taken race into account? Or should the Court invalidate a racially motivated law and "remand to the legislature for a reconsideration [on] the basis of purely legitimate factors"? Schwemm, *From Washington to Arlington Heights and Beyond: Discriminatory Purpose in Equal Protection Litigation,* 1977 U.Ill.L.F. 961, 1020. Would the latter course be futile "because the legislature could immediately pass an identical statute for valid reasons"? Eisenberg, supra, at 116. Consider id.: "[I]t is absurd to assume that all legislators would completely ignore a court holding that the legislature used constitutionally impermissible criteria in initially passing a statute. Some legislators, after being informed that they initially acted unconstitutionally, may refuse to vote for reenactment. Furthermore, if a statute is invalidated on judicial review, the legislature often will decline or fail to consider a new law.

In many situations, therefore, judicial action on the basis of motive results in an effective, not a futile, invalidation." If there is a remand and the law is reenacted, should there be a presumption "that the decisionmaker continues to entertain the motives that led to the original decision (and to its invalidation)"? Brest, fn. 12 in *Arlington Heights,* at 125–26.

IV. REMEDYING SEGREGATION

Although there was prompt compliance with *Brown* in the District of Columbia and some of the border states, the initial response in the deep south was one of "massive resistance"—exemplified by the Governor's use of the Arkansas national guard in 1957 to prevent desegregation in Little Rock and Virginia's 1956 legislation closing any racially mixed public schools. See generally McKay, *"With All Deliberate Speed": Legislative Reaction and Judicial Development 1956–1957,* 43 Va.L.Rev. 1205 (1957).

COOPER v. AARON, 358 U.S. 1, 78 S.Ct. 1401, 3 L.Ed.2d 5 (1958), the first decision to follow the remands in *Brown,* involved the Little Rock school board's request to stay an integration plan that had been in operation at Central High School during the 1957–58 school year, but only after federal troops had been sent by the President to protect black students from "extreme public hostility" engendered largely by the Governor's and Legislature's opposition. The opinion, unprecedented in that it was signed by all nine justices (including those appointed since *Brown*), "unanimously reaffirmed" *Brown.* The Court agreed that "the educational progress of all the students [will] continue to suffer if the conditions which prevailed last year are permitted to continue," but denied the request for delay: "The constitutional rights of [black children] are not to be sacrificed or yielded to the violence and disorder which have followed upon the actions of the Governor and Legislature." The difficulties, created by state action, "can also be brought under control by state action." *Brown* "can neither be nullified openly and directly by state legislators or state executive or judicial officers, nor nullified indirectly by them through evasive schemes." [a]

GRIFFIN v. COUNTY SCHOOL BD., 377 U.S. 218, 84 S.Ct. 1226, 12 L.Ed.2d 256 (1964): In 1959, Prince Edward County, Va. closed its public schools rather than comply with a desegregation order. Private schools, supported by state and local tuition grants and tax credits, were operated for whites. The Court, per Black, J., held the closing to deny blacks equal protection: States have "wide discretion in deciding whether laws shall operate statewide or shall operate only in certain counties [but] Prince Edward's public schools were closed and private schools operated in their place with state and county assistance, for one reason [only]. Whatever nonracial grounds might support a State's allowing a county to abandon public schools, the object must be a constitutional one, and grounds of race and opposition to desegregation do not qualify as constitutional." [b]

---

a. Who determines whether public hostility may "be brought under control by state action"? May it ever be found that the hostility is so great that it is uncontrollable? Of what relevance is the financial cost to the state? Suppose the state, although *able,* is *unwilling* to quiet the hostility? See generally Gewirtz, *Remedies and Resistance,* 92 Yale L.J. 585 (1983).

b. The Court affirmed the district court's order enjoining public financial aid to the private schools and held (Clark and Harlan, JJ. disagreeing) that "the District Court [may]

In the late 1950s, some states sought to comply with *Brown* by simply permitting students to apply for transfer to another school. Procedures were complex and time-consuming; standards were vague, making it difficult to show that denials were due to race. See Note, *The Federal Courts and Integration of Southern Schools: Troubled Status of the Pupil Placement Act,* 62 Colum.L.Rev. 1448 (1962). By the early 1960s, most federal courts refused to accept these "tokenism" plans. See Bickel, *The Decade of School Desegregation: Progress and Prospects,* 64 Colum.L.Rev. 193 (1964). *Goss v. Bd. of Educ.,* 373 U.S. 683, 83 S.Ct. 1405, 10 L.Ed.2d 632 (1963), invalidated a provision permitting students, assigned to school zones on a neutral basis, to transfer if the student was in a racial minority: "It is readily apparent that the transfer system proposed lends itself to perpetuation of segregation." Similarly, by 1961, most federal courts rejected "grade-a-year" desegregation plans. See 64 Mich.L.Rev. 341 (1965). *Rogers v. Paul,* 382 U.S. 198, 86 S.Ct. 358, 15 L.Ed.2d 265 (1965), ordered "immediate transfer" of petitioning students who still attended segregated schools because, under the grade-a-year plan, their grade had not been covered. Finally, *Alexander v. Holmes Cty. Bd. of Educ.,* 396 U.S. 19, 90 S.Ct. 29, 24 L.Ed. 2d 19 (1969), ordered denial of "all motions for additional time" and made clear that "the obligation of every school district is to terminate dual school systems at once and to operate now and hereafter only unitary schools."

GREEN v. COUNTY SCHOOL BD., 391 U.S. 430, 88 S.Ct. 1689, 20 L.Ed.2d 716 (1968): The population of New Kent County in rural Virginia was about half black. Although there was no residential segregation, its two combined elementary and high schools, previously segregated by law, remained wholly segregated in fact until 1964. In 1965, the board adopted a "freedom-of-choice" plan to remain eligible for federal financial aid under federal guidelines.[c] After three years, no white child chose to go to the black school which 85% of the black children continued to attend. School buses traveled "overlapping routes throughout the county to transport pupils to and from the two schools."

A unanimous Court, per BRENNAN, J., held "it is against this background that 13 years after *Brown II* commanded the abolition of dual systems we must measure the effectiveness of [respondent's plan]. School boards [then] operating

require the Supervisors to exercise the power that is theirs to levy taxes to raise funds adequate to reopen, operate, and maintain without racial discrimination a public school system [like] that operated in other counties in Virginia."

Accord, *Missouri v. Jenkins,* ___ U.S. ___, 110 S.Ct. 1651, 109 L.Ed.2d 31 (1990) ("District Court [also may] set aside state laws preventing local governments from raising funds sufficient to satisfy their constitutional obligations").

Griffin was subsequently distinguished in *Palmer v. Thompson* (1971)—involving the closing of swimming pools—discussed in *Washington v. Davis,* Part III supra.

c. The Civil Rights Act of 1964 bars federal financial assistance for any program administered in a racially discriminatory manner. Pursuant thereto, the Dep't of Health, Education and Welfare conditioned eligibility for federal aid to local school districts either on compliance with existing court desegregation orders or, in the absence of such an order, on submission of a desegregation plan consistent with HEW "guidelines." See generally Dunn, *Title VI, The Guidelines and School Desegregation in the South,* 53 Va.L.Rev. 42 (1967): Note, *The Courts, HEW, and Southern School Desegregation,* 77 Yale L.J. 321 (1967).

In the 1964–65 school year, before implementation of the guidelines, only 2.14% of black students in the eleven "southern states" attended schools in which they were not the racial majority. In 1968, the figure was reported at 20.3%. By the 1972–73 school year, it was 46.3%. Statistical Abstract of the United States 124 (1974). The comparable figure for 1972–73 in the six "border states and the District of Columbia" was 31.8%; for the 32 "northern and western states" it was 28.3%. Id.

state-compelled dual systems [were] clearly charged with the affirmative duty to take whatever steps might be necessary to convert to a unitary system in which racial discrimination would be eliminated root and branch. [It] is incumbent upon the school board to establish that its proposed plan promises meaningful and immediate progress toward disestablishing state-imposed segregation. [Where] more promising courses of action are open to the board, that may indicate a lack of good faith; and at the least it places a heavy burden upon the board to explain its preference for an apparently less effective method. [The instant] plan has operated simply to burden children and their parents with a responsibility which *Brown II* placed squarely on the School Board. The Board must be required to formulate a new plan and, in light of other courses which appear open to the Board, such as zoning, [or consolidating the two schools, one serving grades 1–7, the other, grades 8–12,] fashion steps which promise realistically to convert promptly to a system without a 'white' school and a 'Negro' school, but just schools." [d]

SWANN v. CHARLOTTE–MECKLENBURG BD. OF EDUC.

402 U.S. 1, 91 S.Ct. 1267, 28 L.Ed.2d 554 (1971).

CHIEF JUSTICE BURGER delivered the opinion of the Court.

[This case concerned desegregation of the Charlotte, N.C. metropolitan area school district, which had had a statutorily mandated dual system. A companion case involved Mobile, Ala. The history included the district court's rejection in 1969 of three plans submitted by respondent board of education; its acceptance of a plan prepared at its request by "an expert in education administration"; modification of the district court decree by the court of appeals; and the district court's subsequent rejection of a plan prepared by HEW and its conclusion that either the education expert's plan or a new plan submitted by a minority of the school board was "reasonable and acceptable."]

The problems encountered by the [lower federal courts] make plain that we should now try to amplify guidelines, however incomplete and imperfect, for the assistance of school authorities and courts. [Elimination of dual school systems] has been rendered more difficult by changes since 1954 in the structure and patterns of communities, the growth of student population, movement of families, and other changes, some of which had marked impact on school planning, sometimes neutralizing or negating remedial action before it was fully implemented. Rural areas accustomed for half a century to the consolidated school systems implemented by bus transportation could make adjustments more readily than metropolitan areas with dense and shifting population, numerous schools, congested and complex traffic patterns. * * *

If school authorities fail in their affirmative obligations ["to eliminate from the public schools all vestiges of state-imposed segregation"] judicial authority may be invoked. Once a right and a violation have been shown, the scope of a district court's equitable powers to remedy past wrongs is broad, for breadth and flexibility are inherent in equitable remedies. [The] task is to correct, by a balancing of the individual and collective interests, the condition that offends the Constitution. [But] it is important to remember that judicial powers may be exercised only on the basis of a constitutional violation. * * *

d. See also *Monroe v. Bd. of Comm'rs,* 391 U.S. 450, 88 S.Ct. 1700, 20 L.Ed.2d 733 (1968) (school board's rezoning to create racially mixed schools, but permitting "free-transfer" which resulted in "resegregation" when whites and blacks returned to their "old" schools, did not satisfy board's burden to eliminate dual system).

School authorities are traditionally charged with broad power to formulate and implement educational policy and might well conclude, for example, that in order to prepare students to live in a pluralistic society each school should have a prescribed ratio of Negro to white students reflecting the proportion for the district as a whole. To do this as an educational policy is within the broad discretionary powers of school authorities; absent a finding of a constitutional violation, however, that would not be within the authority of a federal court. * * *

The school authorities argue that the equity powers of federal district courts have been limited by Title IV of the Civil Rights Act of 1964, 42 U.S.C.A. [§ 2000c–6, which states]: "nothing herein shall empower any official or court of the United States to issue any order seeking to achieve a racial balance in any school by requiring the transportation of pupils [or] otherwise enlarge the existing power of the court to insure compliance with constitutional standards."[a]

* * * § 2000c–6 is in terms designed to foreclose any interpretation of the Act as expanding the *existing* powers of federal courts to enforce the Equal Protection Clause. There is no suggestion of an intention to restrict those powers or withdraw from courts their historic equitable remedial powers. The legislative history of Title IV indicates that Congress was concerned that the Act might be read as creating a right of action under the Fourteenth Amendment in the situation of so-called "de facto segregation," where racial imbalance exists in the schools but with no showing that this was brought about by discriminatory action of state authorities. * * *

The central issue in this case is that of student assignment, and there are essentially four problem areas: * * *

(1) *Racial Balances or Racial Quotas.* [I]t is urged that the District Court has imposed a racial balance requirement of 71%–29% on individual schools, [reflecting] the pupil constituency of the system. If we were to read the holding of the District Court to require, as a matter of substantive constitutional right, any particular degree of racial balance or mixing, that approach would be disapproved [for the] constitutional command to desegregate schools does not mean that every school in every community must always reflect the racial composition of the school system as a whole.

[But] the use made of mathematical ratios was no more than a starting point in the process of shaping a [remedy]. As we said in *Green,* a school authority's remedial plan or a district court's remedial decree is to be judged by its effectiveness. Awareness of the racial composition of the whole school system is likely to be a useful starting point in shaping a remedy to correct past constitutional violations. In sum, the very limited use made of mathematical ratios was within the equitable remedial discretion of the District Court.[b]

a. Congress enacted a series of similar provisions during the 1970s. For example, the Education Amendments Act of 1974 required that federal courts and agencies give priority to nonbusing remedies, but also provided "that the provisions of this title are not intended to modify or diminish the authority of the courts of the United States to enforce fully the fifth and fourteenth amendments."

b. Cf. Rehnquist, J., joined by Burger, C.J., and Powell, J., dissenting from denial of certiorari in *Cleveland Bd. of Educ. v. Reed,* 445 U.S. 935, 100 S.Ct. 1329, 63 L.Ed. 2d 770 (1980), in which the district court's remedy required that "every grade in every school [have] a ratio of black and white students in approximate proportion to the systemwide ratio."

(2) *One-Race Schools.* The record in this case reveals the familiar phenomenon that in metropolitan areas minority groups are often found concentrated in one part of the city. In some circumstances certain schools may remain all or largely of one race until new schools can be provided or neighborhood patterns change. [T]he existence of some small number of one-race, or virtually one-race schools within a district is not in and of itself the mark of a system which still practices segregation by law. [But] the burden upon the school authorities will be to satisfy the court that their racial composition is not the result of present or past discriminatory action on their part.

An optional majority-to-minority transfer provision [is] an indispensable remedy for those students willing to transfer to other schools in order to lessen the impact on them of the state-imposed stigma of segregation. [S]uch a transfer arrangement must grant the transferring student free transportation and space must be made available in the school to which he desires to move. * * *

(3) *Remedial Altering of Attendance Zones.* [O]ne of the principal tools employed by school planners and by courts to break up the dual school system has been a frank—and sometimes drastic—gerrymandering of school districts and attendance zones. An additional step was pairing, "clustering," or "grouping" of schools with attendance assignments made deliberately to accomplish the transfer of Negro students out of formerly segregated Negro schools and transfer of white students to formerly all-Negro schools. More often than not, these zones are neither compact nor contiguous; indeed they may be on opposite ends of the city. As an interim corrective measure, this cannot be said to be beyond the broad remedial powers of a court.

Absent a constitutional violation there would be no basis for judicially ordering assignment of students on a racial basis. All things being equal, with no history of discrimination, it might well be desirable to assign pupils to schools nearest their homes. But all things are not equal in a system that has been deliberately constructed and maintained to enforce racial segregation. The remedy for such segregation may be administratively awkward, inconvenient and even bizarre in some situations and may impose burdens on some; but [this] cannot be avoided in the interim period when remedial adjustments are being made to eliminate the dual school systems.

No fixed or even substantially fixed guidelines can be established as to how far a court can go, but it must be recognized that there are limits. The objective is to dismantle the dual school system. "Racially neutral" assignment plans [may] fail to counteract the continuing effects of past school segregation resulting from discriminatory location of school sites or distortion of school size in order to achieve or maintain an artificial racial separation. When school authorities present a district court with a "loaded game board," affirmative action in the form of remedial altering of attendance zones is proper to achieve truly non-discriminatory assignments. [W]e must of necessity rely to a large extent, as this Court has for more than 16 years, on the informed judgment of the district courts in the first instance and on courts of appeals. * * *

(4) *Transportation of Students.* [No] rigid guidelines as to student transportation can be given for application to the infinite variety of problems presented in thousands of situations. Bus transportation has been an integral part of the public education system for [years]. Eighteen million of the nation's public school children, approximately 39%, were transported to their schools by bus in 1969–1970 in all parts of the country.

The importance of bus transportation as a normal and accepted tool of educational policy is readily discernible in this and the companion case.[11] * * *

The decree provided that [trips] for elementary school pupils average about seven miles and the District Court found that they would take "not over 35 minutes at the most." [12] This system compares favorably with the transportation plan previously operated in Charlotte under which each day 23,600 students on all grade levels were transported an average of 15 miles one way for an average trip requiring over an hour. In these circumstances, we find no basis for holding that the local school authorities may not be required to employ bus transportation as one tool of school desegregation. Desegregation plans cannot be limited to the walk-in school.

An objection to transportation of students may have validity when the time or distance of travel is so great as to risk either the health of the children or significantly impinge on the educational process. District courts must weigh the soundness of any transportation plan in light of what is said in subdivisions (1), (2), and (3) above. [L]imits on time of travel will vary with many factors, but probably with none more than the age of the students. The reconciliation of competing values in a desegregation case is, of course, a difficult task with many sensitive facets but fundamentally no more so than remedial measures courts of equity have traditionally employed. * * *

At some point, these school authorities and others like them should have achieved full compliance with this Court's decision in *Brown I.* * * *

It does not follow that the communities served by such systems will remain demographically stable, for in a growing, mobile society, few will do so. Neither school authorities nor district courts are constitutionally required to make year-by-year adjustments of the racial composition of student bodies once the affirmative duty to desegregate has been accomplished and racial discrimination through official action is eliminated from the system. This does not mean that federal courts are without power to deal with future problems; but in the absence of a showing that either the school authorities or some other agency of the State has deliberately attempted to fix or alter demographic patterns to affect the racial composition of the schools, further intervention by a district court should not be necessary. * * * [c]

Notes and Questions

1. *Scope of duty.* Do *Green* and *Swann* require school boards that had de jure segregated systems to take "*whatever* steps might be necessary" for "meaningful and immediate progress toward disestablishing state-imposed segregation" (*Green*)? Or need they only adopt plans that are "reasonable, *feasible* and

11. During 1967–1968, for example, the Mobile board used 207 buses to transport 22,094 students daily for an average round trip of 31 miles. During 1966–1967, 7,116 students in the metropolitan area were bused daily. In Charlotte-Mecklenburg [m]ore elementary school children than high school children were to be bused, and four- and five-year-olds travel the longest routes in the system.

12. The District Court found that the school system would have to employ 138 more buses than it had previously operated. But 105 of those buses were already available and the others could easily be obtained. Additionally, it should be noted that North Carolina requires provision of transportation for all students who are assigned to schools more than one and one-half miles from their homes.

c. In a companion case, *North Carolina State Bd. of Educ. v. Swann,* 402 U.S. 43, 91 S.Ct. 1284, 28 L.Ed.2d 586 (1971), the Court held that an Anti-Busing Law, enacted during the instant litigation—barring (1) pupil assignment on the basis of race or to create a racial balance or ratio in the schools, and (2) busing for such purposes—contravened the doctrine "that all reasonable methods be available to formulate an effective remedy."

workable" (*Swann*)? Who determines what is "feasible"? Consider Goodman, *Racial Imbalance in the Oakland Public Schools: A Legal Analysis* 69 (1966): "Whether a particular course of action is 'feasible' depends largely upon which elements of the situation are assumed to be fixed and unalterable and which are regarded as freely variable. If, for example, one accepts as a 'given' the basic validity of the neighborhood school concept and the existing facilities and financial resources of the school district, the range of 'feasible' desegregation measures is apt to be rather limited. Drop these assumptions and the range of feasibilities becomes broader. Assume, finally, that money is no obstacle, and that proximity to schools can be dismissed as a mere matter of 'convenience,' and nearly *everything* becomes feasible. [Black] children could be bused to predominantly white schools without regard to space limitations, and those schools placed on double sessions pending the construction of new facilities." Compare Kaplan, *Segregation Litigation and the Schools—Part II: The General Northern Problem,* 58 Nw.U.L.Rev. 157, 183 (1963): "How can the courts weigh the value of a 30 per cent increase in integration against a requirement that students cross a dangerous traffic artery or walk five extra blocks? How could the courts weigh the achievement of integration through busing children against the greater cost and a somewhat larger class size?" Do courts often make judgments of this nature in constitutional litigation? See Fiss, *The Charlotte-Mecklenburg Case—Its Significance for Northern School Desegregation,* 38 U.Chi.L.Rev. 697, 702 (1971): "[Under *Swann,*] if there is a conflict between integration and other values, integration will generally prevail. [In the *Mobile* case, the] Court rejected a desegregation plan that allowed some all-black schools to remain [whose elimination] required assigning students across a major highway that divided the metropolitan area. [The] Court remanded because 'inadequate consideration was given to the possible use of bus transportation and split zoning.' "

2. *Resegregation.* (a) In PASADENA CITY BD. OF EDUC. v. SPANGLER, 427 U.S. 424, 96 S.Ct. 2697, 49 L.Ed.2d 599 (1976), a court ordered plan to remedy de jure segregation resulted in no racially imbalanced schools in 1970. But this lasted only one year; by 1974, five of the district's 32 schools were over half black. The Court, per REHNQUIST, J., reversed the district judge's order "to require annual readjustment of attendance zones so that there would not be a majority of any minority in any Pasadena public school": "[The] quite normal pattern of human migration resulted in some changes in the demographics of Pasadena's residential patterns, with resultant shifts in the racial makeup of some of the schools. [But] these shifts were not attributed to any segregative actions on the part of the defendants. [H]aving once implemented a racially neutral attendance pattern in order to remedy the perceived constitutional violations on the part of the defendants, the District Court had fully performed its function of providing the appropriate remedy for previous racially discriminatory attendance patterns." [d]

d. The Court thought "it important to note [that] this case does not involve [a] plan embodying specific revisions of the attendance zones for particular schools, as well as provisions for later appraisal of whether such discrete individual modifications had achieved the 'unitary system' required by *Brown I.*"

Marshall, J., joined by Brennan, J., dissented on the ground that a "unitary system" had not been established. Stevens, J., did not participate.

Consider Gewirtz, *Choice in the Transition: School Desegration and the Corrective Ideal,* 86 Colum.L.Rev. 728, 753 (1986): "[R]equiring integration for a period of time is a plausible precondition to having an untainted post-violation choice plan. [To] be untainted, choices must be made from among schools that are not racially identified; the segregated ar-

(b) When the "duty to desegregate has been accomplished" by rezoning etc., may students be assigned to classrooms within the schools (or reassigned among schools) on the basis of "standardized ability and achievement tests" if this tends to result in resegregation? See generally Kirp, *Schools as Sorters: The Constitutional and Policy Implications of Student Classification,* 121 U.Pa.L.Rev. 706 (1973).

(c) OKLAHOMA CITY BD. OF EDUC. v. DOWELL, ___ U.S. ___, 111 S.Ct. 630, 112 L.Ed.2d 715 (1991): Eight years after a federal court finding that "unitariness had been achieved," the school board adopted a new neighborhood assignment plan (SRP). Its asserted purpose was to alleviate greater busing burdens on young black children caused by demographic changes and to increase parental involvement. This resulted in about half the schools becoming primarily uniracial. The Court, per REHNQUIST, C.J., held that a desegregation decree should be dissolved if the board has "complied in good faith [since] it was entered" and "the vestiges of past discrimination have been eliminated to the extent practicable." In doing so, "the District Court should look not only at student assignments, but 'to every facet of school operations—faculty, staff, transportation, extra-curricular activities and facilities.' *Green.* [If] the Board was entitled to have the decree terminated, [the] District Court should then evaluate the Board's decision to implement the SRP under appropriate equal protection principles. See *Washington v. Davis, Arlington Heights.*" [e]

KEYES v. SCHOOL DIST., 413 U.S. 189, 93 S.Ct. 2686, 37 L.Ed.2d 548 (1973), was the first case of segregation that had never been statutorily mandated. The district court found that the Denver school board—by school construction, gerrymandering attendance zones, and excessive use of mobile classroom units—"had engaged over almost a decade after 1960 in an unconstitutional policy of deliberate racial segregation with respect to the Park Hill schools," and ordered their desegregation. However, although the "core city schools" were also segregated in fact, the district court found that the school board had no segregative policy as to them and declined to order their desegregation.

The Court, per BRENNAN, J., reversed, first holding that since, in the southwest, Negroes and Hispanos "suffer identical discrimination in treatment when compared with the treatment afforded Anglo[s,] schools with a combined predominance of Negroes and Hispanos [should be] included in the category of 'segregated' schools." It then held that "where plaintiffs prove that the school authorities have carried out a systematic program of segregation affecting a substantial portion of the students, schools, teachers and facilities [it] is only common sense to conclude that there exists a predicate for a finding of the existence of a dual school system" because "racially inspired school board actions have an impact beyond the particular schools that are the subjects of those actions. This is not to say, of course, that there can never be a case in which the geographical structure of or the natural boundaries within a school district may have the effect of dividing the district into separate, identifiable and unrelated

rangements must be actually disestablished and attendance patterns transformed. Indeed, in order for the racial identity of the schools to be transformed, integration will have to be maintained for a period of time sufficient to change public perceptions and understandings."

e. Marshall, J., joined by Blackmun and Stevens, JJ., dissented: "I believe a desegregation decree cannot be lifted so long as conditions likely to inflict the stigmatic injury condemned in *Brown I* persist and there remain feasible methods of eliminating such conditions." Souter, J., did not participate.

units. Such a determination is essentially a question of fact to be resolved by the trial court [but] such cases must be rare."

Finally, emphasizing "that the differentiating factor between de jure segregation and so-called de facto segregation [is] *purpose* or *intent* to segregate," it held "that a finding of intentionally segregative school board actions in a meaningful portion of a school system [creates] a prima facie case of unlawful segregative design on the part of school authorities, and shifts to those authorities the burden of proving that other segregated schools within the system are not also the result of intentionally segregative actions. This is true even if it is determined that different areas of the school district should be viewed independently of each [other].[a] In discharging that burden, it is not enough, of course, that the school authorities rely upon some allegedly logical, racially neutral explanation for their actions. Their burden is to adduce proof sufficient to support a finding that segregative intent was not among the factors that motivated their actions." Further, "if the actions of school authorities were to any degree motivated by segregative intent and the segregation resulting from those actions continues to exist, the fact of remoteness in time certainly does not make those actions any less 'intentional.'

"This is not to say, however, that the prima facie case may not be met by evidence supporting a finding that a lesser degree of segregated schooling in the core city area would not have resulted even if the Board had not acted as it [did]. Intentional school segregation in the past may have been a factor in creating a natural environment for the growth of further segregation. Thus, if respondent School Board cannot disprove segregative intent, it can rebut the prima facie case only by showing that its past segregative acts did not create or contribute to the current segregated condition of the core city schools."

Respondent invoked "its 'neighborhood school policy' as explaining racial and ethnic concentrations within the core city schools. [But] the mere assertion of such a policy is not dispositive where, as in this case, the school authorities have been found to have practiced de jure segregation * * *."[b]

POWELL, J., filed a lengthy separate opinion: "In imposing on metropolitan southern school districts an affirmative duty, entailing large-scale transportation of pupils, to eliminate segregation in the schools, the Court required these districts to alleviate conditions which in large part did *not* result from historic, state-imposed de jure segregation. Rather, the familiar root cause of segregated schools in *all* the biracial metropolitan areas of our country is essentially the same: one of segregated residential and migratory patterns the impact of which on the racial composition of the schools was often perpetuated and rarely ameliorated by action of public school authorities. This is a national, not a southern phenomenon. And it is largely unrelated to whether a particular State had or did not have segregative school laws. * * *[c]

a. What constitutes a "substantial" or "meaningful portion" of a school system? Consider Comment, *Unlocking the Northern Schoolhouse Doors,* 9 Harv.Civ.Rts.—Civ.Lib. L.Rev. 124, 150 (1974): "Park Hill is a neighborhood of eight schools educating less than thirty-eight percent of Denver's black students and less than ten percent of all pupils in the district. [Thus], a decree compelling extensive desegregation will almost invariably flow from a finding of localized de jure practices." Does "a finding of intentionally segregative school board actions" for all elementary schools "create a prima facie case of unlawful segregative design" for all secondary schools?

b. Burger, C.J., concurred in the result. Douglas, J., joined the Court's opinion but stated "that there [is] no difference between de facto and de jure segregation." White, J., did not participate.

c. Powell, J., quoted from Goodman, *De Facto School Segregation: A Constitutional and Empirical Analysis,* 60 Calif.L.Rev. 275, 297 (1972): "Ohio discarded [legally mandated

"I would hold [that] where segregated public schools exist within a school district to a substantial degree, there is a prima facie case that the duly constituted public authorities [are] sufficiently responsible to impose upon them a nationally applicable burden to demonstrate they nevertheless are operating a genuinely integrated school system. [This] does not mean—and indeed could not mean in view of the residential patterns of most of our major metropolitan areas—that *every school* must in fact be an integrated unit." [d]

REHNQUIST, J., dissented: "[I]t would be a quite unprecedented application of principles of equitable relief to determine that if the gerrymandering of one attendance zone were proven, particular racial mixtures could be required by a federal district court for every school in the district. [U]nless the Equal Protection Clause [be] held to embody a principle of 'taint,' [such] a result can only be described as the product of judicial fiat. * * *

"The drastic extension of *Brown* which *Green* represented was barely, if at all, explicated in the latter opinion. To require that a genuinely 'dual' system be disestablished, in the sense that the assignment to a child of a particular school is not made to depend on his race, is one thing. To require that school boards affirmatively undertake to achieve racial mixing in schools where such mixing is not achieved in sufficient degree by neutrally drawn boundary lines is quite obviously something else."

COLUMBUS BOARD OF EDUC. v. PENICK

443 U.S. 449, 99 S.Ct. 2941, 61 L.Ed.2d 666 (1979).

JUSTICE WHITE delivered the opinion of the Court.

The public schools of Columbus, Ohio, are highly segregated by race. In 1976, over 32% of the 96,000 students in the system were black. About 70% of all students attended schools that were at least 80% black or 80% white. Half of the 172 schools were 90% black or 90% white. * * *

segregation] in 1887, Indiana in 1949, [New York in 1938, New Mexico and Wyoming in 1954 (85 Harv.L.Rev. 85 n. 72 (1971))]. [T]here is no reason to suppose that 1954 is a universally appropriate dividing line between de jure segregation that may safely be assumed to have spent itself and that which may not. For many remedial purposes, adoption of an arbitrary but easily administrable cutoff point might not be objectionable. But in a situation such as school desegregation, where both the rights asserted and the remedial burdens imposed are of such magnitude, and where the resulting sectional discrimination is passionately resented, it is surely questionable whether such arbitrariness is either politically or morally acceptable."

Consider also Karst, *Not One Law at Rome and Another at Athens: The Fourteenth Amendment in Nationwide Application,* 1972 Wash.U.L.Q. 383, 388–89: "If the decisions of a southern school board concerning school location and school sizes can be said to have contributed to racial segregation among residential areas, then with far greater force it can be argued that official state action in northern and western cities has produced residential segregation. Until 1948, racially restrictive covenants in deeds were regularly enforced by state courts; governmental action has often located public housing [as] to intensify residential segregation; and, in a variety of ways, the federal government's programs of subsidy and loan guarantees have explicitly encouraged racial segregation in private housing."

d. Powell, J., further argued that "transportation orders should be applied with special caution to any proposal as disruptive of family life and interests—and ultimately of education itself—as extensive transportation of elementary age children solely for desegregation purposes. As a minimum, this Court should not require school boards to engage in the unnecessary transportation away from their neighborhoods of elementary age children."

Compare 85 Harv.L.Rev. 80 (1971): "[The] critical stages in children's social and educational development are the earliest elementary school years, and if segregation does indeed do educational or social damage, early segregation may do harm that later integration cannot heal."

We have discovered no reason [to] disturb the judgment of the Court of Appeals, based on the findings and conclusions of the District Court, that the Board's conduct at the time of trial [in 1975] and before not only was animated by an unconstitutional, segregative purpose, but also had current, segregative impact that was sufficiently systemwide to warrant the [systemwide] remedy ordered by the District Court. * * *

First, [t]he Board insists that, since segregated schooling was not commanded by state law ["at least since 1888,"] and since not all schools were wholly black or wholly white in 1954, the District Court was not warranted in finding a dual system. But the District Court found that the "Columbus Public Schools were *officially* segregated by race in 1954"; and in any event, there is no reason to question the finding that as the "direct result of cognitive acts or omissions" the Board maintained "an enclave of separate, black schools on the near east side of Columbus." Proof of purposeful and effective maintenance of a body of separate black schools in a substantial part of the system itself is prima facie proof of a dual school system and supports a finding to this effect absent sufficient contrary proof by the Board, which was not forthcoming in this case. *Keyes.*

Second, both courts below declared that since the decision in *Brown II,* the Columbus Board has been under a continuous constitutional obligation to disestablish its dual school system. [Each] failure or refusal to fulfill this affirmative duty continues the violation of the Fourteenth Amendment. *United States v. Scotland Neck Bd. of Educ.,* 407 U.S. 484, 92 S.Ct. 2214, 33 L.Ed.2d 75 (1972) (creation of a new school district in a city that had operated a dual school system but was not yet the subject of court-ordered desegregation).[a] * * * Whatever the Board's current purpose with respect to racially separate education might be, it knowingly continued its failure to eliminate the consequences of its past intentionally segregative policies. * * *

Third, the District Court [also] found that in the intervening years there had been a series of Board actions and practices that could not "reasonably be explained without reference to racial concerns," and that "intentionally aggravated, rather than alleviated," racial separation in the schools. These matters included the general practice of assigning black teachers only to those schools with substantial black student populations, a practice that was terminated only in 1974[;] the intentionally segregative use of optional attendance zones,[8] discontiguous attendance areas,[9] and boundary changes; [10] and the selection of sites for new school construction that had the foreseeable and anticipated effect of

a. In *Scotland Neck,* the school officials defended their action as "necessary to avoid 'white flight' [but this cannot] be accepted as a reason for achieving anything less than complete uprooting" of the dual system. For critical analysis, see Note, *White Flight as a Factor in Desegregation Analysis: A Judicial Recognition of Reality,* 66 Va.L.Rev. 961 (1980). For the view that the Court's "rejection of the white flight argument should not be understood as an absolute principle," see Gewirtz, *Remedies and Resistance,* 92 Yale L.J. 585, 628–65 (1983).

8. Despite petitioners' avowedly strong preference for neighborhood schools, in times of residential racial transition the Board created optional attendance zones to allow white students to avoid predominantly black schools, which were often closer to the homes of the white pupils. * * *

9. This technique was applied when neighborhood schools would have tended to desegregate the involved schools. In the 1960s, a group of white students were bused past their neighborhood school to a "whiter" school. The District Court could "discern no other explanation than a racial one for the existence of the Moler discontiguous attendance area for the period 1963 through 1969." * * *

10. Gerrymandering of boundary lines also continued after 1954. * * *

maintaining the racial separation of the schools.[11] * * *

[It] is urged that the courts below failed to heed the requirements of *Keyes, Washington v. Davis,* and *Arlington Heights,* that a plaintiff seeking to make out an equal protection violation on the basis of racial discrimination must show purpose. [But] the District Court correctly noted that actions having foreseeable and anticipated disparate impact are relevant evidence to prove the ultimate fact, forbidden purpose.[b] * * *

It is also urged that the District Court and the Court of Appeals failed to observe the requirements [of] *Dayton Bd. of Educ. v. Brinkman (Dayton I),* 433 U.S. 406, 97 S.Ct. 2766, 53 L.Ed.2d 851 (1977), which reiterated the accepted rule that the remedy imposed by a court of equity should be commensurate with the violation ascertained, and held that the remedy for the violations that had then been established in that case should be aimed at rectifying the "incremental segregative effect" of the discriminatory acts identified. In *Dayton I,* only a few apparently isolated discriminatory practices had been found; yet a systemwide remedy had been imposed without proof of a systemwide impact.[c] Here, however, the District Court [and the Court of Appeals] repeatedly emphasized that it had found purposefully segregative practices with current, systemwide impact.[15] * * *

Affirmed.[d]

JUSTICE REHNQUIST, with whom JUSTICE POWELL joins, dissenting.

The school desegregation remedy imposed [is] as complete and dramatic a displacement of local authority by the federal judiciary as is possible in our federal system [—] 42,000 of the system's 96,000 students are reassigned to new schools. There are like reassignment of teachers, staff, and administrators, reorganization of the grade structure of virtually every elementary school in the system, the closing of 33 schools, and the additional transportation of 37,000 students. * * *

Today the Court affirms [in] opinions so Delphic that lower courts will be hard pressed to fathom their implications for school desegregation litigation. I can only offer two suggestions. The first is that the Court, possibly chastened by the complexity and emotion that accompanies school desegregation cases, wishes to relegate the determination of a violation of [equal protection] in any plan of pupil assignment, and the formulation of a remedy for its violation, to the judgment of a single District Judge. * * * "Discriminatory purpose" and

11. The District Court found that, of the 103 schools built by the Board between 1950 and 1975, 87 opened with racially identifiable student bodies and 71 remained that way at the time of trial. This result was reasonably foreseeable under the circumstances in light of the sites selected, and the Board was often specifically warned that it was, without apparent justification, choosing sites that would maintain or further segregation. * * *

b. For criticism of the Court's "subjective intent" approach and a supporting rationale for *Oliver's* "institutional segregative intent" test, see Note, *Reading the Mind of the School Board: Segregative Intent and the De Facto/De Jure Distinction,* 86 Yale L.J. 317 (1976).

c. *Dayton I,* per Rehnquist, J., also observed: "The finding [that many Dayton] schools are either predominantly white or predominantly black"—"standing by itself, is not a violation of the Fourteenth Amendment in the absence of a showing that this condition resulted from intentionally segregative actions on the part of the Board. *Davis.*"

15. Mr. Justice Rehnquist's dissent erroneously states that we have "reliev[ed] school desegregation plaintiffs from any showing of a causal nexus between intentional segregative actions and the conditions they seek to remedy." [But both courts below] found that the Board's purposefully discriminatory conduct and policies had current, systemwide impact—an essential predicate, as both courts recognized, for a systemwide remedy. * * *

d. The concurring opinions of Burger, C.J., and Stewart, J., and the dissenting opinion of Powell, J., are omitted.

"systemwide violation" are to be treated as talismanic phrases which once invoked, warrant only the most superficial scrutiny by appellate courts.

Such an [approach] holds out the disturbing prospect of very different remedies being imposed on similar school systems because of the predilections of individual judges and their good faith but incongruent efforts to make sense of this Court's confused pronouncements today. * * *

[Alternatively, the] Court suggests a radical new approach to desegregation cases in systems without a history of statutorily mandated separation of the races: if a district court concludes—employing what in honesty must be characterized as an irrebuttable presumption—that there was a "dual" school system at the time of *Brown I,* it must find post-1954 constitutional violations in a school board's failure to take every affirmative step to integrate the system. Put differently, *racial imbalance* at the time the complaint is filed is sufficient to support a systemwide, racial balance school busing remedy if the district court can find *some* evidence of discriminatory purpose prior to 1954, without any inquiry into the causal relationship between those pre-1954 violations and current segregation in the school system.

[As] a matter of history, 1954 makes no more sense as a benchmark—indeed it makes *less* sense—than 1968, 1971 or 1973. Perhaps the [last] year has the most to commend it, if one insists on a benchmark, because in *Keyes* this Court first confronted the problem of school segregation in the context of systems without a history of statutorily mandated separation of the races. * * *

Causality plays a central role in *Keyes* [which] held that before the burden of production shifts to the school board, the plaintiffs must prove "that the school authorities have carried out a systematic program of segregation *affecting a substantial portion of the students, schools, teachers and facilities within the school system.*" The Court recognized that a trial court might find "that [at] some point in time the relationship between past segregative acts and present segregation may become so attenuated as to be incapable of supporting a finding of de jure segregation warranting judicial intervention." The relevance of past acts of the school board was to depend on whether "segregation resulting from those actions continues to exist." That inquiry is not central under the approach approved by the Court today. Henceforth, the question is apparently whether pre-1954 acts contributed in some unspecified manner to segregated conditions that existed in 1954. If the answer is yes, then the only question is whether the school board has exploited all integrative opportunities that presented themselves in the subsequent 25 years. If not, a systemwide remedy is in order, despite the plaintiff's failure to demonstrate a link between those past acts and current racial imbalance.

The Court's use of the term "affirmative duty" implies that integration be the pre-eminent—indeed, the controlling—educational consideration in school board decisionmaking. It takes precedence over other legitimate educational objectives subject to some vague feasibility limitation. * * *

This unprecedented "affirmative duty" superstructure sits atop a weak foundation—the existence of a "dual" school system in 1954. This finding was predicated on the presence of four predominantly black elementary schools and one predominantly black junior high school on the "near east side of Columbus," a then and now black residential area. The Columbus School Board at that time employed, as it does now, a neighborhood school policy. The specific Board actions that the District Court cited were racial assignment of teachers and gerrymandering along part of the border between two school districts.

[V]iolations with respect to five schools, only three of which exist today, occurring over 30 years ago are the key premise for a systemwide racial balance remedy involving 172 schools—most of which did not exist in 1950.

[O]bjective evidence [of segregative intent] must be carefully analyzed for it may otherwise reduce the "discriminatory purpose" requirement to a "discriminatory impact" test by another name. [In] a school system with racially imbalanced schools, *every* school board action regarding construction, pupil assignment, transportation, annexation and temporary facilities will promote integration, aggravate segregation or maintain segregation. Foreseeability follows from the obviousness of that proposition. Such a tight noose on school board decisionmaking will invariably move government of a school system [to] the courthouse. * * *

Once a showing is made that the District Court believes satisfies the *Keyes* requirement of purposeful discrimination in a substantial part of the school system, the school board will almost invariably rely on its neighborhood school policy and residential segregation to show that it is not responsible for the existence of certain predominantly black and white schools in other parts of the school system. [Here] the District Court relied on a general proposition that "there is often a substantial reciprocal effect between the color of the school and the color of the neighborhood it serves" to block any inquiry into whether racially identifiable schools were the product of racially identifiable neighborhoods or whether past discriminatory acts bore a "but for" relationship to current segregative conditions. [But] as the District Court recognized, other factors play an important role in determining segregated residential patterns. [Yet] today the School Board is called to task for all the forces beyond their control that shaped residential segregation in Columbus. There is thus no room for *Keyes* or *Swann* rebuttal either with respect to the school system today or that of 30 years ago. * * *

DAYTON BOARD OF EDUC. v. BRINKMAN (DAYTON II)

443 U.S. 526, 99 S.Ct. 2971, 61 L.Ed.2d 720 (1979).

JUSTICE WHITE delivered the opinion of the Court.

[The] public schools of Dayton are highly segregated. [In 1972, when] the complaint was filed, 43% of the students in the Dayton system were black, but 51 of the 69 schools in the system were virtually all-white or all-black. * * *

The District Court's judgment that the Board had violated the Fourteenth Amendment was affirmed by the Court of Appeals; but after twice being reversed on the ground that the prescribed remedy was inadequate to eliminate all vestiges of state-imposed segregation, the District Court ordered the Board [to] assure that each school in the system would roughly reflect the systemwide ratio of black and white students. The Court of Appeals then affirmed.

We reversed [in *Dayton I*, and the District Court then dismissed] the complaint [because] plaintiffs had failed to prove that acts of intentional segregation over 20 years old had any current incremental segregative effects [6] [and that] plaintiffs had failed to show either discriminatory purpose or segregative

6. The District Court observed that "[m]any of these practices, if they existed today, would violate the Equal Protection Clause." The court identified certain Board policies as being "among" such practices: until at least 1934, black elementary students were kept separate from white students; until approximately 1950 high school athletics were deliberately segregated [and] black students at one high school were ordered or induced to sit at the rear of classrooms and suffered other indignities.

effect, or both, with respect to the challenged practices and policies of the [Board].[7]

The Court of Appeals reversed [and] held that, "at the time of *Brown I*, defendants were intentionally operating a dual school [system]" and that the "finding of the District Court to the contrary is clearly erroneous." On the record before us, we perceive no basis for petitioners' challenge to this holding of the Court of Appeals.[8] * * *

Part of the affirmative duty imposed by our cases [is] the obligation not to take any action that would impede the process of disestablishing the dual system and its effects. [T]he measure of the post-*Brown* conduct of a school board under an unsatisfied duty to liquidate a dual system is the effectiveness, not the purpose, of the actions in decreasing or increasing the segregation caused by the dual system. *Emporia*. As was clearly established in *Keyes* and *Swann*, the Board had to do more than abandon its prior discriminatory purpose. The Board has had an affirmative responsibility to see that pupil assignment policies and school construction and abandonment practices "are not used and do not serve to perpetuate or re-establish the dual school system," *Columbus*, and the Board has a "'heavy burden'" of showing that actions that increased or continued the effects of the dual system serve important and legitimate ends.

[The] Court of Appeals held that far from performing its constitutional duty, the Board had engaged in "post-1954 actions which actually have exacerbated the racial separation existing at the time of *Brown I*." The court reversed as

7. Reviewing the faculty assignment and hiring practices, the District Court found that until at least 1951 the Board's policies had been intentionally segregative. But in that year the Board instituted a policy of "dynamic gradualism" and "by 1969 all traces of segregation were virtually eliminated." [T]he court ruled that plaintiffs had not established that past discrimination in faculty assignments had an incremental segregative effect.

Similarly, the court ruled that the plaintiff children had not shown that the Board's use of attendance zones and transfers denied equal protection. In certain instances, segregative intent had not been satisfactorily demonstrated. [In] other instances, current segregative effect had not been proved. Though another high school, Dunbar, had been created and maintained until 1962 as a citywide black high school, the District Court found that because of the increasing black population in that area Dunbar would have been virtually all black by 1960 anyway. And though until the early 1950's black orphans had been bused past nearby white schools to all-black schools, this "arguably" discriminatory conduct had not been shown by "objective proof" to have any continued segregative effect.

The court also looked to school construction and siting practices. Although 22 of 24 new schools, 78 of 95 additions, and 26 of 26 portable schools built or utilized by the Board between 1950 and 1972 opened virtually all black or all white, and though many of the accompanying decisions appeared to be so without any rationale as to be "haphazard," the District Court found that the plaintiffs had not shown purposeful segregation. The court also refused to investigate whether the Board had any legitimate grounds for the failure to close some schools and consolidate others when enrollment declined in recent years. Though such a course would have decreased racial separation and saved money, the court found no evidence of discriminatory purpose in those facts. Nor did the court see any hint of impermissible purpose in the Board's decisions in the 1940's to supply school services for legally segregated housing projects and to rent elementary school space in such projects.

Finally, the court held that the Board's rescission of its earlier resolutions ["recognizing its responsibility to eradicate racial separation in the public schools"] was not violative of the Fourteenth Amendment since, in light of the court's finding that the current segregation had no unconstitutional origin, the Board had no constitutional obligation to adopt the resolutions in the first place.

8. We have no quarrel with our Brother Stewart's general conclusion [joined by Burger, C.J.] that there is great value in appellate courts showing deference to the fact-finding of local trial judges. The clearly erroneous standard serves that purpose well. [The] Court of Appeals performed its unavoidable duty in this case and concluded that the District Court had erred. [W]e see no reason on the record before us to upset the judgment of the Court of Appeals in this respect.

clearly erroneous the District Court's finding that intentional faculty segregation had ended in 1951; the Court of Appeals found that it had effectively continued into the 1970's.[11] This was a systemwide practice and strong evidence that the Board was continuing its efforts to segregate students. [Furthermore,] the Court of Appeals held that since 1954 the Board had used some "optional attendance zones for racially discriminatory [purposes]." The District Court's finding to the contrary was clearly erroneous. At the very least, the use of such zones amounted to a perpetuation of the existing dual school system. Likewise, the Board failed in its duty [by] its pattern of school construction and site selection, recited by the District Court, see n. 7 * * *. We see no reason to disturb these factual determinations, which conclusively show the breach of duty found by the Court of Appeals. * * *

Affirmed.

JUSTICE REHNQUIST, with whom JUSTICE POWELL joins, dissenting [in *Dayton II*].

[The] District Judge in *Dayton* did not employ a post-1954 "affirmative duty" test. Violations he did identify were found not to have any causal relationship to existing conditions of segregation in the Dayton school system. He did not employ a foreseeability test for intent, hold the school system responsible for residential segregation, or impugn the neighborhood school policy, as an explanation for some existing one race schools. In short, the Dayton and Columbus district judges had completely different ideas of what the law required.[e] [And] I have no doubt that the Court of Appeals' heavy-handed approach in this case is to some degree explained by the perceived inequity of imposing a systemwide racial-balance remedy on Columbus while finding no violation in Dayton. The simple meting out of equal remedies, however, is [not] "equal justice under law." * * *

Notes and Questions

1. *Scope of the decisions.* (a) Do *Keyes, Columbus* and *Dayton II* "sweep away the distinction between de facto and de jure segregation"? In a district that presently has substantial racial imbalance in its schools, but that had no statutorily mandated segregation in 1954, if plaintiffs fail to prove "intentionally segregative school board actions in a meaningful portion of the school system" (*Keyes*), does the school board have an "affirmative duty" to desegregate? Do "*Columbus* and *Dayton II* leave open the possibility that if a school board

11. Under the policy of "dynamic gradualism" instituted in 1951, see n. 7, black teachers were assigned to white or mixed schools when the surrounding communities were ready to accept black teachers, and white teachers who agreed were assigned to black schools. By 1969 each school in the system had at least one black teacher. The District Court apparently did not think the post-1951 policy was purposeful discrimination. We think the Court of Appeals was completely justified in finding that conclusion to be clearly erroneous on the undisputed facts. As late as the 1968–1969 school year, the Board assigned 72% of all black teachers to schools that were 90% or more black, and only 9% of white teachers to such schools. And faculty segregation disappeared completely only after efforts of the Department of HEW under Title VI of the Civil Rights Act of 1964.

e. For a detailed review of the *Keyes* litigation, criticizing the district judge's findings of deliberate segregation and concluding that "perhaps nothing emerges more clearly [than] the fact of the almost totally unrestrained freedom of choice district judges possess in 'desegregation' litigation," see Graglia, *Disaster By Decree* 162–99 (1976): "If this one judge had found—as he should have and as the federal judges in New Jersey did find in *Spencer v. Kugler,* 404 U.S. 1027, 92 S.Ct. 707, 30 L.Ed.2d 723 (1972)—that the racial imbalance in the schools was not the result of racial discrimination by school officials, the travail of Denver would have been at an end. Never in our history has the fate of so many people so importantly depended on the whim of a single, unelected, lifetime official."

operated a dual system prior to 1954, but abandoned its segregative policies before *Brown I* was decided, it might not be subject to an affirmative duty to desegregate"? 93 Harv.L.Rev. 126 n. 58 (1979). In these circumstances, must the school board prove that the segregation that existed in 1954 (or that exists today) was not "caused" by its earlier intentionally segregative actions? If so, is the presumption of causality "irrebuttable" (Rehnquist, J.)? Is the task of overcoming the presumption "virtually impossible"? "Extraordinarily difficult"? See Choper, Kamisar & Tribe, *The Supreme Court: Trends and Developments, 1978–1979,* 253–54 (1979). What is the relevance of *Pasadena?* Consider Kitch, *The Return of Color-Consciousness to the Constitution: Weber, Dayton, and Columbus,* 1979 Sup.Ct.Rev. 1, 14: "The emphasis in *Columbus* and *Dayton II* on the 'continuing constitutional duty' to desegregate, if taken literally, would mean that the school systems must be perpetually operated in a way that eliminates identifiable black schools each school year. [*Pasadena*] can be distinguished on the ground that the district court had not found that the school system operated a dual school system in 1954, and hence was not under what the Court calls the continuing constitutional duty to desegregate."

(b) In *Keyes,* if plaintiffs make out "a prima facie case of unlawful segregative design on the part of school authorities," is the scope of the burden imposed on the school board "of proving that other segregated schools within the system are not also the result of intentionally segregative actions" consistent with the approach of *Arlington Heights* fn. 21? See Choper, Kamisar & Tribe, supra, at 241. Is the subject of intentional school segregation distinguishable from other forms of intentional racial discrimination?

(c) If, apart from school location and assignment policies, many "other factors play an important role in determining segregated residential patterns" (Rehnquist, J.), do *Keyes, Columbus* and *Dayton II* answer a question left open in *Swann:* if plaintiffs prove "that school segregation is a consequence of other types of state action [see Karst, fn. c. in *Keyes*], without any discriminatory action by the school authorities, is there a constitutional violation requiring remedial action"? See generally Comment, *School Desegregation After Swann: A Theory of Government Responsibility,* 39 U.Chi.L.Rev. 421 (1972).

2. *"De facto" school segregation.* (a) Contrary to *Dayton I,* in the absence of any "intentionally segregative actions" on the part of any state agency, *should* the fact that many schools in a district "are either predominantly white or predominantly black" "standing by itself" violate equal protection? For an early view, see Fiss, *Racial Imbalance in the Public Schools: The Constitutional Concepts,* 78 Harv.L.Rev. 564 (1965).

(b) *Effect on students.* Consider Note, *Racial Imbalance in the Public Schools: Constitutional Dimensions and Judicial Response,* 18 Vand.L.Rev. 1290, 1295–96 (1965): "Fiss points out 'that students in such schools are also deprived of the intellectual stimulation that comes from the exchange of ideas and the development of personal relationships in a racially and socially heterogeneous context.' [Because *Brown*] found that 'to separate [blacks] from others of similar age and qualifications solely because of their race generates a feeling of inferiority,' proponents of racial balance in the schools argue analogously that racial imbalance also breeds inferiority. [A] more damaging aspect of racial imbalance relates to [a] corollary goal of education [which is] 'to induct the young person systematically into the culture and society to which he is an heir and in which he should be a partner.' The Supreme Court recognized [this] in *Brown.* [It] seems clear that regardless of the cause of the separation of the races the isolation of a minority race will prevent the achievement of this educational goal."[f] Compare Kaplan, note 1 after *Swann,* at 174: "[V]irtually every bit of the sociological evidence of harm presented [in *Brown*] involved compulsory segregation based overtly on race in the social setting of the South where school segregation was merely one facet of the general exclusion of the Negro from the dominant life of the community. It is by no means obvious that harm will automatically follow where the segregation is of the de facto variety, occurring in the Northern setting, and is not purposively based on race." Consider Yudof, *Equal Educational Opportunity and the Courts,* 51 Tex.L.Rev. 411, 436 (1973): "One study of the psychological impact of segregation on black children has found that the black child's self-concept is inversely related to the proportion of white students in the school; the whiter his school the lower the black child rated himself. Other studies have reached the opposite conclusion. Studies of the relationship between personality development and segregation are similarly conflicting. [Moreover,] available studies are inconclusive as to whether integration in fact accelerates academic achievement. Further complicating the evidence are the many additional variables that may alter the effect of integration or segregation: the degree of interracial hostility, the percentage of black students in relation to the school population, the socio-economic makeup of the student body, the existence of ability grouping, and the attitudes of parents, teachers, and administrators." See also Goodman, fn. c. in *Keyes,* at 400–435 for an intensive review of various studies, concluding that "the influence of biracial schooling upon the achievement of black students is highly *uncertain.*" Compare Liebman, *Implementing Brown in the Nineties: Political Reconstruction, Liberal Recollection, and Litigatively Enforced Legislative Reform,* 76 Va.L.Rev. 349, 356–57 (1990), reviewing studies in the 1980s which conclude that "northern desegregation has a substantial positive effect on black students' achievement," and that "more certain is desegregation's positive impact on dropout, teenage pregnancy, and delinquency rates; on the likelihood that blacks will attend and succeed at college (particularly four-year colleges), secure employment in predominantly white job settings, and live in integrated neighborhoods as adults; and on the salary levels blacks attain in the labor market."

(c) *Constitutional "values" and judicial interpretation.* Consider Goodman, note 1(b) after *Swann,* at 21–23: "[T]here is a *moral* difference of the first importance between a law which discriminates against citizens solely on the ground of race and one which, though based on racially neutral criteria, operates to the detriment of a minority group.[g] [A] second important difference between

f. See also *D. Strauss, Discriminatory Intent and the Taming of Brown,* 56 U.Chi.L. Rev. 935, 962 (1989): "[T]he argument that conscious or obvious discrimination is especially debilitating is an argument about the effects of government actions, not about the intent or process that produced them. If this argument is correct, what follows is that any action that has the same effects as obvious discrimination—the same insulting, stigmatizing, or subordinating effects—should also be unconstitutional. [T]here is no reason to believe that the class of actions with those effects is limited to overt and covert racial classifications. Depending on how the crucial psychological effect is defined, race-neutral measures that leave blacks in an inferior position may be equally harmful."

g. Compare Goodman, note (b) supra, at 319: "Is there really a decisive moral difference between the state of mind that produces de facto segregation and that which produced de jure segregation? Those who advocate the neighborhood school may not want segregation, but they well know their policy begets it; either they see no harm or they deem the harm an acceptable cost. On the other hand, if de facto segregation is rarely inadvertent, de jure segregation is not always malevolent. Many an avowed segregationist genuinely believes his policy benefits all, black and white alike, offering them a classroom free from racial friction."

legislation requiring, and legislation merely resulting in, racial segregation is the absence in the former case of any legitimate State interest which might countervail the harm inflicted on Negro children. [The] only rationale for segregation which has even a semblance of plausibility is that it helps to avoid needless friction between the races and thus preserves tranquility both in the classroom and in the larger society. In the long run, however, by creating barriers to normal intergroup relations and arousing the resentment and frustration of the minority group, segregation probably does more to defeat than to promote racial peace. And even were this not so, it still could not be said that segregation is a necessary means to that end, for there are many other ways of dealing with the problem of racial conflict. [This] is not the case with de facto segregation. Here the psychological injury suffered by Negro children results from the use of otherwise legitimate means (geographical districting criteria) to accomplish an otherwise legitimate end (the neighborhood school) which could not be accomplished in any other way."

Even if de jure and de facto segregation are distinguishable, should the school board at least be required "to take reasonable steps—as opposed to all possible steps [as with de jure segregation]—to eliminate" de facto segregation? Fiss, note 1 after *Swann,* at 706. Consider Kaplan, note b supra, at 180: "It is hard [to] argue that the cause of mixing Negro and white children, taken as it must be from the vague words of the equal protection clause, deserves the same standing as the right of free expression which not only is founded in the explicit wording of the first amendment, but also is at the very basis of any free [society]. Integration may be an important value [but] it is hard to argue that it is more fundamental than the right of the state to provide for the health, safety, and education of its children."

Does *Washington v. Davis* plainly reject the view that "other values" should be disregarded in "the cause of racial integration"? Consider Goodman, note b supra, at 306: "[If] it is true that de facto, like de jure segregation, generates feelings of racial inferiority in black school children, the injury is one they incur distinctively as blacks, solely on account of their race. A white child similarly situated would not be similarly affected. In that sense, the neighborhood school policy can be said to inflict a 'racially specific' harm, a harm differing in kind from that inflicted by [the] examples of state action [in fn. 14 of *Davis*] that hurt more blacks than whites, but hurt the individual black no more than his white counterpart."

At the least, contrary to fn. 9 in *Dayton II,* should "the foreseeability of segregative consequences" make out "a prima facie case of purposeful racial discrimination" on the part of the school board and shift the burden to it to prove nonsegregative intent? [h]

3. *Interdistrict remedies.* (a) *Schools.* In MILLIKEN v. BRADLEY, 418 U.S. 717, 94 S.Ct. 3112, 41 L.Ed.2d 1069 (1974), the district court found that various actions of the Detroit Board of Education, the State Board of Education and the Michigan legislature (e.g., barring use of state funds for busing), produced de jure segregation in Detroit; that, because of the city's racial composition, desegregation plans limited to Detroit "would accentuate the racial identifiability of the district as a Black school system, and would not accomplish desegregation." Thus, the district judge ordered a plan encompassing 53 neighboring suburban school districts (in Oakland and Macomb counties). The Court,

h. The constitutional issues presented when school boards *voluntarily* undertake to remedy de facto segregation are considered in Part V infra.

per BURGER, C.J.,—emphasizing that, apart from one "isolated instance affecting two of the school districts," the record "contains evidence of de jure segregated conditions only in" Detroit—reversed, stating the issue as "whether a federal court may impose a multidistrict [remedy] absent any finding that the other included school districts have failed to operate unitary school systems within their districts, [that] the boundary lines of any affected school district were established with the purpose of fostering racial segregation [, that] the included districts committed acts which effected segregation within the other districts, and absent a meaningful opportunity for the included neighboring school districts to [be] heard on the propriety of a multidistrict remedy or on the question of constitutional violations by those neighboring districts":

"The controlling principle [is] that the scope of the remedy is determined by the nature and extent of the constitutional violation. *Swann.* [Before] imposing a cross-district remedy, it must first be shown that there has been a constitutional violation within one district that produces a significant segregative effect in [another][a]. The constitutional right of the Negro respondents residing in Detroit is to attend a unitary school system in that district."[b]

The courts below assumed "that the Detroit schools could not be truly desegregated—in their view of what constituted desegregation—unless the racial composition of the student body of each school substantially reflected the racial composition of the population of the metropolitan area as a whole. [But this is contrary to] the clear import of" *Swann.*

WHITE, J., joined by Douglas, Brennan and Marshall, JJ., dissented: "[The district] court's express finding was [that] 'desegregation within the area described is physically easier and more practicable and feasible, than desegregation efforts limited [to] Detroit.' The Court of Appeals [concluded] that an interdistrict remedy 'is supported by the status of school districts under Michigan law and by the historical control exercised over local school districts by the legislature of Michigan and by State agencies and officials.' Obviously, whatever difficulties there might be, they are surmountable; for the Court itself concedes that had there been sufficient evidence of an interdistrict violation, the District Court could have fashioned a single remedy for the districts implicated * * *.

"I am even more mystified how the Court can ignore the legal reality that the constitutional violations, even if occurring locally, were committed by governmental entities for which the State is responsible and that it is the State that must respond to the command of the Fourteenth Amendment. [T]here is no acceptable reason for permitting the party responsible for the constitutional violation to contain the remedial powers of the federal court within administrative boundaries over which the transgressor itself has plenary power."

MARSHALL, J., joined by Douglas, Brennan, and White, JJ., dissented: "Ironically purporting to base its result on the principle that the scope of the remedy

a. Is this allocation of the burden of proof consistent with *Keyes?* Are there reasons for a presumption of segregative intent or effect in a *Keyes*-type situation but not in a *Milliken*-type one?

For a listing of subsequent cases imposing interdistrict remedies, see Note, *Interdistrict Remedies for Segregated Schools,* 79 Colum.L. Rev. 1168 n. 5 (1979). See generally Sedler, *The Profound Impact of Milliken v. Bradley,* 33 Wayne L.Rev. 1693 (1987); Sedler, *Metropolitan Desegregation in the Wake of Milliken—On Losing Big Battles and Winning Small Wars: The View Largely from Within,* 1975 Wash.U.L.Q. 535.

b. For the view that this states an improperly narrow perception of the constitutional right at issue, see Amaker, *Milliken v. Bradley: The Meaning of the Constitution in School Desegregation Cases,* 2 Hast.Con.L.Q. 349 (1975); Lawrence, *Segregation "Misunderstood": The Milliken Decision Revisited,* 12 U.S.F.L.Rev. 15 (1977).

[should] be determined by the nature and the extent of the constitutional violation, the Court's answer is to provide no remedy at all [thus] guaranteeing that Negro children in Detroit will receive the same separate and inherently unequal education in the future as they have been unconstitutionally afforded in the past. * * *

"The State's creation, through de jure acts of segregation, of a growing core of all-Negro schools inevitably acted as a magnet to attract Negroes to the areas served by such schools [and] helped drive whites to other areas of the city or to the suburbs. [Having] created a system where whites and Negroes were intentionally kept apart so that they could not become accustomed to learning together, the State is responsible for the fact that many whites will react to the dismantling of that segregated system by attempting to flee to the suburbs." [c]

(b) *Housing.* In HILLS v. GAUTREAUX, 425 U.S. 284, 96 S.Ct. 1538, 47 L.Ed.2d 792 (1976), the district court found that the federal Dep't of Housing (HUD) and the Chicago Housing Authority (CHA) had racially segregated public housing projects in Chicago. The Court, per STEWART, J., held that "nothing in [*Milliken*] suggests a per se rule that federal courts lack authority to order parties found to have violated the Constitution to undertake remedial efforts beyond the municipal boundaries of the city where the violation occurred. [The] proposed remedy in *Milliken* was impermissible because of the limits on the federal judicial power to interfere with the operation of state political entities that were not implicated in unconstitutional conduct. Here, [a] judicial order directing relief beyond the boundary lines of Chicago will not necessarily entail coercion of uninvolved governmental units, because [both] CHA and HUD have the authority to operate outside the Chicago city limits.[14]

"[In] contrast to the desegregation order in [*Milliken*], a metropolitan relief order directed to HUD would not consolidate or in any way restructure local governmental units. The remedial decree would neither force suburban governments to submit public housing proposals to HUD nor displace the rights and powers accorded local government entities under federal or state housing statutes or existing land use laws. The order would have the same effect on the suburban governments as a discretionary decision by HUD to use its statutory powers to provide the respondents with alternatives to the racially segregated Chicago public housing system created by CHA and HUD." [a]

(c) *Other remedies.* In MILLIKEN v. BRADLEY (MILLIKEN II), 433 U.S. 267, 97 S.Ct. 2749, 53 L.Ed.2d 745 (1977), the district court, on remand, fashioned a new decree which required (in addition to a pupil assignment plan for the Detroit school system) a number of "educational components"—including remedial reading and revised testing and counseling programs for pupils, and a training program for teachers. The state, which was ordered to pay for part of these programs, appealed. The Court, per BURGER, C.J., affirmed: "[T]he District

c. Douglas, J., also filed a brief dissent. For evidence that it is doubtful whether metropolitan school desegregation remedies will produce integration without a permanent "ongoing system of student-quota reassignment," see Wolf, *Northern School Desegregation and Residential Choice,* 1977 Sup.Ct.Rev. 63.

14. [Although] the state officials in *Milliken* had the authority to operate across school district lines, the exercise of that authority [would] have eliminated numerous independent school districts or at least have displaced important powers granted those uninvolved governmental entities under state law.

a. Marshall, J., joined by Brennan and White, JJ., joined the Court's opinion "except insofar as it appears to reaffirm [*Milliken*]."

Is *Gautreaux* faithful to the principle that "the scope of the remedy is determined by the nature and extent of the constitutional violation"? See Kanner, *From Denver to Dayton: The Development of a Theory of Equal Protection Remedies,* 72 Nw.U.L.Rev. 382 (1977).

Court found that [the] educational components [were] necessary to restore the victims of discriminatory conduct to the position they would have enjoyed in terms of education had these four components been provided in a nondiscriminatory manner in a school system free from pervasive de jure racial segregation. [D]iscriminatory student assignment policies can themselves manifest and breed other inequalities built into a dual system founded on racial discrimination." [b]

4. *Beyond schools.* BAZEMORE v. FRIDAY, 478 U.S. 385, 106 S.Ct. 3000, 92 L.Ed.2d 315 (1986), per WHITE, J., held that *Green's* "affirmative duty to desegregate" has "no application" to the 4–H and Homemaker Clubs (which had been deliberately segregated until 1965) operated by the North Carolina Agricultural Extension Service, despite the fact that a majority of the clubs remained uniracial in 1980: "Even if the Service in effect assigned blacks and whites to separate clubs prior to 1965, it did not do so after that time. While school children must go to school, there is no compulsion to join 4–H or Homemaker Clubs, and while School Boards customarily have the power to create school attendance areas and otherwise designate the school that particular students may attend, there is no statutory or regulatory authority to deny a young person the right to join any Club he or she wishes to join."

BRENNAN, J., joined by Marshall, Blackmun and Stevens, JJ., dissented: "Nothing in our earlier cases suggests that the State's obligation to desegregate is confined only to those activities in which members of the public are compelled to participate."

V. AFFIRMATIVE ACTION AND "BENIGN" DISCRIMINATION

Swann ruled that state officials may—and, in some circumstances, seemingly must—use racial criteria to remedy unconstitutional segregation. This section concerns voluntary government action that employs racial/ethnic criteria or favors members of racial/ethnic minorities in order to remedy (a) unlawful discrimination other than segregation, or (b) racial/ethnic inequality that occurs in the absence of a judicial finding of illegal discrimination.

The first case in the second category was *DeFunis v. Odegaard,* 416 U.S. 312, 94 S.Ct. 1704, 40 L.Ed.2d 164 (1974) involving the University of Washington Law School's preferential admissions program for members of designated racial and ethnic minorities. Unlike *Swann,* the challenged government action in *DeFunis* had not been adopted to remedy prior deliberate discrimination by the state or its law school, but rather as an effort to increase the number of law students from minority groups. The Court held that the case was moot. Only Douglas, J., addressed the merits, finding that a law school's use of an explicit racial classification violated equal protection.

Although there was no opinion for the Court, Burger, C.J., alone dissented from the ruling in *United Jewish Organizations v. Carey,* 430 U.S. 144, 97 S.Ct. 996, 51 L.Ed.2d 229 (1977), upholding a New York districting plan that overtly used racial criteria in order to create a larger number of state legislative

b. For the view that "providing unequal and inadequate school resources and excluding black parents from meaningful participation in school policymaking are at least as damaging to black children as enforced separation," see Bell, *Serving Two Masters: Integration Ideals and Client Interests in School Desegregation Litigation,* 85 Yale L.J. 470 (1976).

For decisions concerning the validity of state aid to private schools that racially discriminate, see *Norwood v. Harrison* and *Gilmore v. Montgomery.*

districts containing nonwhite majorities. As in *DeFunis,* there had never been a finding that the state had engaged in deliberate discrimination against racial minorities with respect to voting. New York had, however, been required to undertake the challenged action because certain counties were subject to § 5 of the Voting Rights Act, thus permitting an inference that the state legislation was based on congressional presumption that the counties had engaged in deliberate racial discrimination. In addition, White, J., joined by Rehnquist and Stevens, JJ., pointed out that the plan "represented no racial slur or stigma with respect to whites or any other race [and] did not minimize or unfairly cancel out white voting strength. [It] left white majorities in approximately 70% of the [districts] which had a county-wide population that was 65% white. Thus, even if voting in the county occurred strictly according to race, whites would not be underrepresented relative to their share of the population."

Thus, prior to the next major case, *Regents of Univ. of California v. Bakke,* infra, there had only been two dissenting votes against the constitutional permissibility of remedial racial classifications. See generally Choper, *Continued Uncertainty as to the Constitutionality of Remedial Racial Classifications: Identifying the Pieces of the Puzzle,* 72 Ia.L.Rev. 255 (1978).

REGENTS OF UNIV. OF CALIFORNIA v. BAKKE

438 U.S. 265, 98 S.Ct. 2733, 57 L.Ed.2d 750 (1978).

JUSTICE POWELL announced the judgment of the Court.

This case presents a challenge to the special admissions program of the petitioner, the Medical School of the University of California at Davis * * *.

For the reasons stated in the following opinion, I believe that so much of the judgment of the California court as holds petitioner's special admissions program unlawful and directs that respondent be admitted to the Medical School must be affirmed. For the reasons expressed in a separate opinion, my Brothers The Chief Justice, Mr. Justice Stewart, Mr. Justice Rehnquist, and Mr. Justice Stevens concur in this judgment.

I also conclude [that] the portion of the court's judgment enjoining petitioner from according any consideration to race in its admissions process must be reversed. For reasons expressed in separate opinions, my Brothers Mr. Justice Brennan, Mr. Justice White, Mr. Justice Marshall, and Mr. Justice Blackmun concur in this judgment. * * *

I.† The special admissions program operated with a separate [admissions] committee. [On] the 1973 application form, candidates were asked to indicate whether they wished to be considered as "economically and/or educationally disadvantaged" applicants; on the 1974 form the question was whether they wished to be considered as members of a "minority group," which the Medical School apparently viewed as "Blacks," "Chicanos," "Asians," and "American Indians." [About] one-fifth of the total number of special applicants were invited for interviews in 1973 and 1974 [and] the special committee assigned each [a] score [and] presented its top choices to the general admissions committee. The latter did not rate or compare the special candidates against the general applicants, but could reject recommended special candidates for failure to meet course requirements or other specific deficiencies. The special commit-

† Mr. Justice Brennan, Mr. Justice White, Mr. Justice Marshall, and Mr. Justice Blackmun join Parts I and V–C of this opinion. Mr. Justice White also joins Part III–A of this opinion.

tee continued to recommend special applicants until a number prescribed by faculty vote were admitted. [I]n 1973 and 1974, when the class size had doubled to 100, the prescribed number of special admissions also doubled, to 16. [Although] disadvantaged whites applied to the special program in large numbers, none received an offer of admission through that process. Indeed, in 1974, at least, the special committee explicitly considered only "disadvantaged" special applicants who were members of one of the designated minority groups.

Allan Bakke is a white male who applied [in] 1973 and 1974 [and was rejected in both years]. In both years, applicants were admitted under the special program with grade point averages [and] Medical College Admissions Test scores significantly lower than Bakke's. * * *

II. [Powell, J., found that Title VI of the Civil Rights Act of 1964—which provides that "No person in the United States shall, on the ground of race, color, or national origin, be excluded from participation in, be denied the benefits of, or be subjected to, discrimination under any program or activity receiving Federal financial assistance"—proscribes "only those racial classifications that would violate the Equal Protection Clause or the Fifth Amendment."]

III. A. [T]he parties fight a sharp preliminary action over the proper characterization of the special admissions program. Petitioner prefers to view it as establishing a "goal" of minority representation in the medical school. Respondent, echoing the courts below, labels it a racial quota.

This semantic distinction is beside the [point]. To the extent that there existed a pool of at least minimally qualified minority applicants to fill the 16 special admissions seats, white applicants could compete only for 84 seats in the entering class, rather than the 100 open to minority applicants. Whether this limitation is described as a quota or a goal, it is a line drawn on the basis of race and ethnic status.

[P]etitioner argues that the court below erred in applying strict scrutiny to the special admissions programs because white males, such as respondent, are not a "discrete and insular minority" requiring extraordinary protection from the majoritarian political process. *Carolene Products Co.,* n. 4. [These] characteristics may be relevant in deciding whether or not to add new types of classifications to the list of "suspect" categories or whether a particular classification survives close examination. Racial and ethnic classifications, however, are subject to stringent examination without regard to these additional characteristics. [*Hirabayashi; Korematsu*]

B. This perception of racial and ethnic distinctions is rooted in our Nation's constitutional and demographic history. The Court's initial view of the Fourteenth Amendment was that its "one pervading purpose" was "the freedom of the slave race * * *." *Slaughter-House Cases.* [During] the dormancy of the Equal Protection Clause, the United States had become a nation of minorities. Each had to struggle—and to some extent struggles still—to overcome the prejudices not of a monolithic majority, but of a "majority" composed of various minority groups of whom it was said—perhaps unfairly in many cases—that a shared characteristic was a willingness to disadvantage other groups. As the Nation filled with the stock of many lands, the reach of the Clause was gradually extended to all ethnic groups seeking protection from official discrimination. * * *

Petitioner urges us to adopt for the first time a more restrictive view [and] hold that discrimination against members of the white "majority" cannot be suspect if its purpose can be characterized as "benign."[34] [But it] is far too late to argue that the guarantee of equal protection to *all* persons permits the recognition of special wards entitled to a degree of protection greater than that accorded others. * * *

Once the artificial line of a "two-class theory" of the Fourteenth Amendment is put aside, the difficulties entailed in varying the level of judicial review according to a perceived "preferred" status of a particular racial or ethnic minority are intractable. The concepts of "majority" and "minority" necessarily reflect temporary arrangements and political judgments. As observed above, the white "majority" itself is composed of various minority groups, most of which can lay claim to a history of prior discrimination at the hands of the state and private individuals. Not all of these groups can receive preferential treatment and corresponding judicial tolerance of distinctions drawn in terms of race and nationality, for then the only "majority" left would be a new minority of White Anglo-Saxon Protestants. There is no principled basis for deciding which groups would merit "heightened judicial solicitude" and which would not.[36] Courts would be asked to evaluate the extent of the prejudice and consequent harm suffered by various minority groups. Those whose societal injury is thought to exceed some arbitrary level of tolerability then would be entitled to preferential classifications at the expense of individuals belonging to other groups. Those classifications would be free from exacting judicial scrutiny. As these prefer-

34. In the view of Mr. Justice Brennan, Mr. Justice White, Mr. Justice Marshall, and Mr. Justice Blackmun, the pliable notion of "stigma" is the crucial element in analyzing racial classifications. The Equal Protection Clause is not framed in terms of "stigma." Certainly the word has no clearly defined constitutional meaning. It reflects a subjective judgment that is standardless. *All* state-imposed classifications that rearrange burdens and benefits on the basis of race are likely to be viewed with deep resentment by the individuals burdened. The denial to innocent persons of equal rights and opportunities may outrage those so deprived and therefore may be perceived as invidious. These individuals are likely to find little comfort in the notion that the deprivation they are asked to endure is merely the price of membership in the dominant majority and that its imposition is inspired by the supposedly benign purpose of aiding others. One should not lightly dismiss the inherent unfairness of, and the perception of mistreatment that accompanies, a system of allocating benefits and privileges on the basis of skin color and ethnic origin. Moreover, Mr. Justice Brennan, Mr. Justice White, Mr. Justice Marshall, and Mr. Justice Blackmun offer no principle for deciding whether preferential classifications reflect a benign remedial purpose or a malevolent stigmatic classification, since they are willing in this case to accept mere post hoc declarations by an isolated state entity—a medical school faculty—unadorned by particularized findings of past discrimination, to establish such a remedial purpose.

36. [M]y Brothers Brennan, White, Marshall, and Blackmun [would] require as a justification for a program such as petitioner's, only two findings: (i) that there has been some form of discrimination against the preferred minority groups "by society at large" (it being conceded that petitioner had no history of discrimination), and (ii) that "there is reason to believe" that the disparate impact sought to be rectified by the program is the "product" of such discrimination * * *.

The breadth of this hypothesis is unprecedented in our constitutional system. The first step is easily taken. No one denies the regrettable fact that there has been societal discrimination in this country against various racial and ethnic groups. The second step, however, involves a speculative leap: but for this discrimination by society at large, Bakke "would have failed to qualify for admission" because Negro applicants—nothing is said about Asians—would have made better scores. Not one word in the record supports this conclusion, and the plurality offers no standard for courts to use in applying such a presumption of causation to other racial or ethnic classifications. This failure is a grave one, since if it may be concluded *on this record* that each of the minority groups preferred by the petitioner's special program is entitled to the benefit of the presumption, it would seem difficult to determine that any of the dozens of minority groups that have suffered "societal discrimination" cannot also claim it, in any area of social intercourse.

ences began to have their desired effect, and the consequences of past discrimination were undone, new judicial rankings would be necessary. The kind of variable sociological and political analysis necessary to produce such rankings simply does not lie within the judicial competence—even if they otherwise were politically feasible and socially desirable.

Moreover, there are serious problems of justice connected with the idea of preference itself. First, it may not always be clear that a so-called preference is in fact benign. Courts may be asked to validate burdens imposed upon individual members of particular groups in order to advance the group's general interest. Nothing in the Constitution supports the notion that individuals may be asked to suffer otherwise impermissible burdens in order to enhance the societal standing of their ethnic groups. Second, preferential programs may only reinforce common stereotypes holding that certain groups are unable to achieve success without special protection based on a factor having no relationship to individual worth. Third, there is a measure of inequity in forcing innocent persons in respondent's position to bear the burdens of redressing grievances not of their making.

By hitching the meaning of the Equal Protection Clause to these transitory considerations, we would be holding [that] judicial scrutiny of classifications touching on racial and ethnic background may vary with the ebb and flow of political forces. Disparate constitutional tolerance of such classifications well may serve to exacerbate racial and ethnic antagonisms. [Also,] the mutability of a constitutional principle, based upon shifting political and social judgments, undermines the chances for consistent application of the Constitution from one generation to the next, a critical feature of its coherent interpretation. * * *

If it is the individual who is entitled to judicial protection against classifications based upon his racial or ethnic background because such distinctions impinge upon personal rights, rather than the individual only because of his membership in a particular group, then constitutional standards may be applied consistently. Political judgments regarding the necessity for the particular classification may be weighed in the constitutional balance, *Korematsu,* but the standard of justification will remain constant. This is as it should be, since those political judgments are the product of rough compromise struck by contending groups within the democratic process. When they touch upon an individual's race or ethnic background, he is entitled to a judicial determination that the burden he is asked to bear on that basis is precisely tailored to serve a compelling governmental interest. * * *

C. Petitioner contends that on several occasions this Court has approved preferential classifications without applying the most exacting scrutiny. * * *

The school desegregation cases are inapposite. Each involved remedies for clearly determined constitutional violations.[39] [Here,] there was no judicial

39. [In] *Offermann v. Nitkowski,* 378 F.2d 22 (CA2 1967) [and] *Springfield School Committee v. Barksdale,* 348 F.2d 261 (CA1 1965) [courts] did approve voluntary districting designed to eliminate discriminatory attendance patterns. In neither, however, was there any showing that the school board planned extensive pupil transportation that might threaten liberty or privacy interests. Nor were white students deprived of an equal opportunity for education.

Respondent's position is wholly dissimilar to that of a pupil bused from his neighborhood school to a comparable school in another neighborhood in compliance with a desegregation decree. Petitioner did not arrange for respondent to attend a different medical school in order to desegregate Davis Medical School; instead, it denied him admission and may have deprived him altogether of a medical education.

determination of constitutional violation as a predicate for [a] remedial classification.

The employment discrimination cases also do not advance petitioner's cause. For example, in *Franks v. Bowman Transportation Co.,* 424 U.S. 747, 96 S.Ct. 1251, 47 L.Ed.2d 444 (1975), we approved a retroactive award of seniority to a class of Negro truck drivers who had been the victims of discrimination—not just by society at large, but by the respondent in that case. While this relief imposed some burdens on other employees, it was held necessary " 'to make [the victims] whole for injuries suffered on account of unlawful employment discrimination.' " [But] we have never approved preferential classifications in the absence of proven constitutional or statutory violations.[41] * * *

In this case, [there] has been no determination by the legislature or a responsible administrative agency that the University engaged in a discriminatory practice requiring remedial efforts. Moreover, the operation of petitioner's special admissions [program] prefers the designated minority groups at the expense of other individuals who are totally foreclosed from competition for the 16 special admissions seats in every medical school class. [When] a classification denies an individual opportunities or benefits enjoyed by others solely because of his race or ethnic background, it must be regarded as suspect.

IV. [The] special admissions program purports to serve the purposes of: (i) "reducing the historic deficit of traditionally disfavored minorities in medical schools and the medical profession," (ii) countering the effects of societal discrimination; (iii) increasing the number of physicians who will practice in communities currently underserved; and (iv) obtaining the educational benefits that flow from an ethnically diverse student body. It is necessary to decide which, if any, of these purposes is substantial enough to support the use of a suspect classification.

A. If petitioner's purpose is to assure within its student body some specified percentage of a particular group merely because of its race or ethnic origin, such a preferential purpose must be rejected not as insubstantial but as facially invalid. Preferring members of any one group for no reason other than race or ethnic origin is discrimination for its own sake. This the Constitution forbids. E.g., *Loving.*

B. The State certainly has a legitimate and substantial interest in ameliorating, or eliminating where feasible, the disabling effects of identified discrimination. [That] goal [is] far more focused than the remedying of the effects of "societal discrimination," an amorphous concept of injury that may be ageless in its reach into the past.

We have never approved a classification that aids persons perceived as members of relatively victimized groups at the expense of other innocent individuals in the absence of judicial, legislative, or administrative findings of constitutional or statutory violations. After such findings[,] the governmental

41. This case does not call into question congressionally authorized administrative actions, such as consent decrees under Title VII or approval of reapportionment plans under § 5 of the Voting Rights Act of 1965. In such cases, there has been detailed legislative consideration of the various indicia of previous constitutional or statutory violations, e.g., *South Carolina v. Katzenbach,* and particular administrative bodies have been charged with monitoring various activities in order to detect such violations and formulate appropriate remedies.

Furthermore, we are not here presented with an occasion to review legislation by Congress pursuant to its powers under § 2 of the Thirteenth Amendment and § 5 of the Fourteenth Amendment to remedy the effects of prior discrimination. *Katzenbach v. Morgan; Jones v. Alfred H. Mayer Co.*

interest in preferring members of the injured groups at the expense of others is substantial, since the legal rights of the victims must be vindicated. In such a case, the extent of the injury and the consequent remedy will have been judicially, legislatively, or administratively defined. Also, the remedial action usually remains subject to continuing oversight to assure that it will work the least harm possible to other innocent persons competing for the benefit. Without such findings of constitutional or statutory violations,[44] it cannot be said that the government has any greater interest in helping one individual than in refraining from harming another. Thus, the government has no compelling justification for inflicting such harm.

Petitioner does not purport to have made, and is in no position to make, such findings. Its broad mission is education, not the formulation of any legislative policy or the adjudication of particular claims of illegality. For reasons similar to those stated in Part III of this opinion, isolated segments of our vast governmental structures are not competent to make those decisions, at least in the absence of legislative mandates and legislatively determined criteria. Cf. *Hampton v. Wong* [Sec. 3, I infra]. Compare n. 41, supra. Before relying upon these sorts of findings in establishing a racial classification, a governmental body must have the authority and capability to establish, in the record, that the classification is responsive to identified discrimination. See, e.g., *Califano v. Webster; Califano v. Goldfarb* [p. 1355]. Lacking this capability, petitioner has not carried its burden of justification on this issue.

Hence, the purpose of helping certain groups whom the faculty of the Davis Medical School perceived as victims of "societal discrimination" does not justify a classification that imposes diadvantages upon persons like respondent, who bear no responsibility for whatever harm the beneficiaries of the special admissions program are thought to have suffered. To hold otherwise would be to convert a remedy heretofore reserved for violations of legal rights into a privilege that all institutions throughout the Nation could grant at their pleasure to whatever groups are perceived as victims of societal discrimination. That is a step we have never approved.

C. Petitioner identifies, as another purpose of its program, improving the delivery of health care services to communities currently underserved. It may be assumed that in some situations a State's interest in facilitating the health care of its citizens is sufficiently compelling to support the use of a suspect

44. Mr. Justice Brennan, Mr. Justice White, Mr. Justice Marshall, and Mr. Justice Blackmun misconceive the scope of this Court's holdings under Title VII when they suggest that "disparate impact" alone is sufficient to establish a violation of that statute and, by analogy, other civil rights measures. [This] was made quite clear in the seminal decision in this area, *Griggs v. Duke Power Co.,* 401 U.S. 424, 91 S.Ct. 849, 28 L.Ed.2d 158 (1971): "*Discriminatory preference* for any group, minority or majority, is precisely and only what Congress has proscribed. What is required by Congress is the removal of *artificial, arbitrary, and unnecessary barriers* to employment when the barriers operate invidiously to discriminate on the basis of racial or other impermissible classification." Thus, disparate impact is a basis for relief under Title VII only if the practice in question is not founded on "business necessity," or lacks "a manifest relationship to the employment in question." Nothing *in this record*—as opposed to some of the general literature cited by Mr. Justice Brennan, Mr. Justice White, Mr. Justice Marshall, and Mr. Justice Blackmun—even remotely suggests that the disparate impact of the general admissions program at Davis Medical School [is] without educational justification.

Moreover, the presumption in *Griggs*—that disparate impact without any showing of business justification established the existence of discrimination in violation of the statute—was based on legislative determinations, wholly absent here, that past discrimination had handicapped various minority groups to such an extent that disparate impact could be traced to identifiable instances of past discrimination * * *.

classification. But there is virtually no evidence in the record indicating that petitioner's special admissions program is either needed or geared to promote that goal. The court below addressed this failure of proof: "The University concedes it cannot asure that minority doctors who entered under the program, all of whom express an 'interest' in participating in a disadvantaged community, will actually do so. It may be correct to assume that some of them will carry out this intention, and that it is more likely they will practice in minority communities than the average white doctor. Nevertheless, there are more precise and reliable [ways]. An applicant of whatever race who has demonstrated his concern for disadvantaged minorities in the past and who declares that practice in such a community is his primary professional goal would be more likely to contribute to alleviation of the medical shortage than one who is chosen entirely on the basis of race and disadvantage. * * *"

D. The fourth goal asserted by petitioner is the attainment of a diverse student body. * * * Academic freedom, though not a specifically enumerated constitutional right, long has been viewed as a special concern of the First Amendment. [Thus,] in arguing that its universities must be accorded the right to select those students who will contribute the most to the "robust exchange of ideas," petitioner invokes a countervailing constitutional interest, [and] must be viewed as seeking to achieve a goal that is of paramount importance in the fulfillment of its mission. * * *

Ethnic diversity, however, is only one element in a range of factors a university properly may consider in attaining the goal of a heterogeneous student body. Although a university must have wide discretion in making the sensitive judgments as to who should be admitted, constitutional limitations protecting individual rights may not be disregarded. [As] the interest of diversity is compelling in the context of a university's admissions program, the question remains whether the program's racial classification is necessary to promote this interest.

V. A. [P]etitioner's argument that this is the only effective means of serving the interest of diversity is seriously flawed. [The] diversity that furthers a compelling state interest encompasses a far broader array of qualifications and characteristics of which racial or ethnic origin is but a single though important element. Petitioner's special admissions program, focused *solely* on ethnic diversity, would hinder rather than further attainment of genuine diversity.

Nor would the state interest in genuine diversity be served by expanding petitioner's two-track system into a multitrack program with a prescribed number of seats set aside for each identifiable category of applicants. Indeed, it is inconceivable that a university would thus pursue the logic of petitioner's two-track program to the illogical end of insulating each category of applicants with certain desired qualifications from competition with all other applicants.

The experience of other university admissions programs, which take race into account in achieving the educational diversity valued by the First Amendment, demonstrates that the assignment of a fixed number of places to a minority group is not a necessary means toward that end. An illuminating example is found in the Harvard College program:

"In recent years Harvard College has expanded the concept of diversity to include students from disadvantaged economic, racial and ethnic groups. [When] the Committee on Admissions reviews the large middle group of applicants who are 'admissible' and deemed capable of doing good work in their courses, the race of an applicant may tip the balance in his favor just as geographic origin or a life spent on a farm may tip the balance in other candidates' cases. * * *

"In Harvard College admissions the Committee has not set target-quotas for the number of blacks, or of musicians, football players, physicists or Californians to be admitted in a given year [a] [but that awareness of the necessity of including more than a token number of black students means] that in choosing among thousands of applicants who are not only 'admissible' academically but have other strong qualities, the Committee, with a number of criteria in mind, pays some attention to distribution among many types and categories of students." Brief for Columbia University, Harvard University, Stanford University, and the University of Pennsylvania, as amici curiae.

In such an admissions program, race or ethnic background may be deemed a "plus" in a particular applicant's file, yet it does not insulate the individual from comparison with all [others]. The file of a particular black applicant may be examined for his potential contribution to diversity without the factor of race being decisive when compared, for example, with that of an applicant identified as an Italian-American if the latter is thought to exhibit qualities more likely to promote beneficial educational pluralism. Such qualities could include exceptional personal talents, unique work or service experience, leadership potential, maturity, demonstrated compassion, a history of overcoming disadvantage, ability to communicate with the poor, or other qualifications deemed important. * * *

This kind of program treats each applicant as an individual in the admissions process. The applicant who loses out [to] another candidate receiving a "plus" on the basis of ethnic background will not have been foreclosed from all consideration [simply] because he was not the right color or had the wrong surname. It would mean only that his combined qualifications, which may have included similar nonobjective factors, did not outweigh those of the other applicant. His qualifications would have been weighed fairly and competitively and he would have no basis to complain of unequal treatment under the Fourteenth Amendment.

It has been suggested that an admissions program which considers race only as one factor is simply a subtle and more sophisticated—but no less effective—means of according racial preference than the Davis program. A facial intent to discriminate, however, is evident [in] this case. No such facial infirmity exists in an admissions program where race or ethnic background is simply one element—to be weighed fairly against other elements—in the selection process. "A boundary line," as Mr. Justice Frankfurter remarked in another connection, "is none the worse for being narrow." And a Court would not assume that a university, professing to employ a facially nondiscriminatory admissions policy,

a. The portion of this paragraph of the Harvard program—omitted by Powell, J., in his opinion but reprinted in full in an appendix to the opinion—is as follows: "At the same time the Committee is aware that if Harvard College is to provide a truly heterogeneous environment that reflects the rich diversity of the United States, it cannot be provided without some attention to numbers. It would not make sense, for example, to have 10 or 20 students out of 1,100 whose homes are west of the Mississippi. Comparably 10 or 20 black students could not begin to bring to their classmates and to each other the variety of points of view, backgrounds and experiences of blacks in the United States. Their small numbers might also create a sense of isolation [and] thus make it more difficult for them to develop and achieve their potential. Consequently, when making its decisions, the Committee on Admissions is aware that there is some relationship between numbers and achieving the benefits to be derived from a diverse student body, and between numbers and providing a reasonable environment for those students admitted."

would operate it as a cover for the functional equivalent of a quota system. In short, good faith would be presumed in the absence of a showing to the contrary in the manner permitted by our cases. See, e.g., *Arlington Heights; Washington v. Davis.*[53]

B. [W]hen a State's distribution of benefits or imposition of burdens hinges on the color of a person's skin or ancestry, that individual is entitled to a demonstration that the challenged classification is necessary to promote a substantial state interest. Petitioner has failed to carry this burden. For this reason, that portion of the California court's judgment holding petitioner's special admissions program invalid under the Fourteenth Amendment must be affirmed.

C. In enjoining petitioner from ever considering the race of any applicant, however, the courts below failed to recognize that the State has a substantial interest that legitimately may be served by a properly devised admissions program involving the competitive consideration of race and ethnic origin. For this reason, so much of the California court's judgment as enjoins petitioner from any consideration of the race of any applicant must be reversed.

VI. With respect to respondent's entitlement to an injunction directing his admission to the Medical School, petitioner has conceded that it could not carry its burden of proving that, but for the existence of its unlawful special admissions program, respondent still would not have been admitted. Hence, respondent is entitled to the injunction, and that portion of the judgment must be affirmed.

Opinion of JUSTICE BRENNAN, JUSTICE WHITE, JUSTICE MARSHALL, and JUSTICE BLACKMUN, concurring in the judgment in part and dissenting.

[The] difficulty of this issue [has] resulted in many opinions, no single one speaking for the Court. But [this] must not mask the central meaning of today's opinions: Government may take race into account when it acts not to demean or insult any racial group, but to remedy disadvantages cast on minorities by past racial prejudice, at least when appropriate findings have been made by judicial, legislative, or administrative bodies with competence to act in this area. * * *

We agree with Mr. Justice Powell that, as applied to the case before us, Title VI goes no further in prohibiting the use of race than the Equal Protection [Clause].[b] Since we conclude that the [Davis program] is constitutional, we would reverse the judgment below in all respects. Mr. Justice Powell agrees that some uses of race in university admissions are permissible and, therefore, he joins with us to make five votes reversing the judgment below insofar as it prohibits the University from establishing race-conscious programs in the future.[1]

53. [There] also are strong policy reasons that correspond to the constitutional distinction between petitioner's preference program and one that assures a measure of competition among all applicants. Petitioner's program will be viewed as inherently unfair by the public generally as well as by [applicants]. Fairness in individual competition for opportunities, especially those provided by the State, is a widely cherished American ethic. Indeed, in a broader sense, an underlying assumption of the rule of law is the worthiness of a system of justice based on fairness to the individual. As Mr. Justice Frankfurther declared in another connection, "[j]ustice must satisfy the appearance of justice."

b. The separate opinion of White, J.—that Title VI does not provide for a private cause of action—is omitted.

1. We also agree [that] a plan like the "Harvard" plan is constitutional [at] least so long as the use of race to achieve an integrated student body is necessitated by the lingering effects of past discrimination.

I. [C]laims that law must be "color-blind" or that the datum of race is no longer relevant to public policy must be seen as aspiration rather than as description of reality. This is not to denigrate aspiration; for reality rebukes us that race has too often been used by those who would stigmatize and oppress minorities. Yet we cannot [let] color blindness become myopia which masks the reality that many "created equal" have been treated within our lifetimes as inferior both by the law and by their fellow citizens. * * *

III. A. [Our] cases have always implied that an "overriding statutory purpose," *McLaughlin v. Florida,* could be found that would justify racial classifications. See, e.g., *Loving; Korematsu.* [W]e turn [to] articulating what our role should be in reviewing state action that expressly classifies by race.

B. [A] government practice or statute which [contains] "suspect classficiations" is to be subjected to "strict scrutiny" * * *. [But] whites as a class [do not] have any of the "traditional indicia of suspectness: the class is not saddled with such disabilities, or subjected to such a history of purposeful unequal treatment, or relegated to such a position of political powerlessness as to commend extraordinary protection from the majoritarian political process."

Moreover, [this] is not a case where racial classifications are "irrelevant and therefore prohibited." *Hirabayashi.* Nor has anyone suggested that the University's purposes contravene the cardinal principle that racial classifications that stigmatize—because they are drawn on the presumption that one race is inferior to another or because they put the weight of government behind racial hatred and separatism—are invalid without more. See *Yick Wo.* * * *

On the other hand, the fact that this case does not fit neatly into our prior analytic framework for race cases does not mean that it should be analyzed by applying the very loose rational-basis [standard]. "[T]he mere recitation of a benign, compensatory purpose is not an automatic shield which protects against any inquiry into the actual purposes underlying a statutory scheme." *Califano v. Webster,* [Sec. 3, III infra]. Instead, a number of considerations—developed in gender discrimination cases but which carry even more force when applied to racial classifications—lead us to conclude that racial classifications designed to further remedial purposes "must serve important governmental objectives and must be substantially related to achievement of those objectives." *Craig v. Boren,* [Sec. 3, III infra].

First, race, like, "gender-based classifications too often [has] been inexcusably utilized to stereotype and stigmatize politically powerless segments of society." While a carefully tailored statute designed to remedy past discrimination could avoid these vices, see *Califano v. Webster,* we nonetheless have recognized that the line between honest and thoughtful appraisal of the effects of past discrimination and paternalistic stereotyping is not so clear and that a statute based on the latter is patently capable of stigmatizing all women with a badge of inferiority. State programs designed ostensibly to ameliorate the effects of past racial discrimination obviously create the same hazard of stigma, since they may promote racial separatism and reinforce the views of those who believe that members of racial minorities are inherently incapable of succeeding on their own.

Second, race, like gender and illegitimacy, is an immutable characteristic which its possessors are powerless to escape or set aside. While a classification is not per se invalid because [of this], it is nevertheless true that such divisions are contrary to our deep belief that "legal burdens should bear some relationship to individual responsibility or wrongdoing," and that advancement sanctioned, sponsored, or approved by the State should ideally be based on individual merit or achievement, or at the least on factors within the control of an individual.

Because this principle is so deeply rooted it might be supposed that it would be considered in the legislative process and weighed against the benefits of programs preferring individuals because of their race. But [t]he "natural consequence of our governing processes [may well be] that the most 'discrete and insular' of whites [will] be called upon to bear the immediate, direct costs of benign discrimination." [Thus] our review under the Fourteenth Amendment should be strict—not " 'strict' in theory and fatal in fact," because it is stigma that causes fatality—but strict and searching nonetheless.

IV. Davis' articulated purpose of remedying the effects of past societal discrimination is, under our cases, sufficiently important to justify the use of race-conscious admissions programs where there is a sound basis for concluding that minority underrepresentation is substantial and chronic, and that the handicap of past discrimination is impeding access of minorities to the medical school.

A. At least since *Green v. County School Bd.,* [a] public body which has itself been adjudged to have engaged in racial discrimination cannot bring itself into compliance with the Equal Protection Clause simply by ending its unlawful acts and adopting a neutral stance. Three years later, *Swann* [held] that courts could enter desegregation orders which assigned students and faculty by reference to race, and that local school boards could *voluntarily* adopt desegregation plans which made express reference to race if this was necessary to remedy the effects of past discrimination. Moreover, we stated that school boards, even in the absence of a judicial finding of past discrimination, could voluntarily adopt plans which assigned students with the end of creating racial pluralism by establishing fixed ratios of black and white students in each school. *Swann.* * * *

Thus, our cases under Title VII [have] held that, in order to achieve minority participation in previously segregated areas of public life, Congress may require or authorize preferential treatment for those likely disadvantaged by societal racial discrimination. Such legislation has been sustained even without a requirement of findings of intentional racial discrimination by those required or authorized to accord preferential treatment, or a case-by-case determination that those to be benefited suffered from racial discrimination.[41] These decisions compel the conclusion that States also may adopt race-conscious programs designed to overcome substantial, chronic minority underrepresentation where there is reason to believe that the evil addressed is a product of past racial discrimination.[42] * * *

41. Our cases cannot be distinguished by suggesting, as our Brother Powell does, that in none of them was anyone deprived of "the relevant benefit." Our school cases have deprived whites of the neighborhood school of their choice; our Title VII cases have deprived nondiscriminating employees of their settled seniority expectations; and *UJO* deprived the Hassidim of bloc voting strength. Each of these injuries was constitutionally cognizable as is respondent's here.

42. We do not understand Mr. Justice Powell to disagree that providing a remedy for past racial prejudice can constitute a compelling purpose sufficient to meet strict scrutiny. Yet, because petitioner is a university, he would not allow it to exercise such power in the absence of "judicial, legislative, or administrative findings of constitutional or statutory violations." While we agree that reversal in this case would follow a fortiori had Davis been guilty of invidious racial discrimination or if a federal statute mandated that universities refrain from applying any admissions policy that had a disparate and unjustified racial impact, we do not think it of constitutional significance that Davis has not been so adjudged.

B. * * * Davis had a sound basis for believing that the problem of underrepresentation of minorities was substantial and chronic and that the problem was attributable to handicaps imposed on minority applicants by past and present racial discrimination. Until at least 1973, the practice of medicine in this country [was] largely the prerogative of whites. * * *

Moreover, Davis had very good reason to believe that the national pattern of underrepresentation of minorities in medicine would be perpetuated if it retained a single admissions standard. For example, the entering classes in 1968 and 1969, [when] such a standard was used, included only one Chicano and two Negroes out of 100 admitees. Nor is there any relief from this pattern of underrepresentation in the statistics for the regular admissions program in later years.

Davis clearly could conclude that the serious and persistent underrepresentation [is] the result of handicaps under which minority applicants labor as a consequence of a background of deliberate, purposeful discrimination against minorities in education and in society generally, as well as in the medical profession. From the inception of our national life, Negroes have been subjected to unique legal [disabilities]. The generation of minority students applying to Davis Medical School since it opened in 1968—most of whom were born before or about the time *Brown I* was decided—clearly have been victims of this discrimination. Judicial decrees recognizing discrimination in public education in California testify to the fact of widespread discrimination suffered by California-born minority applicants; many minority group members living in California, moreover, were born and reared in school districts in southern States segregated by law. [T]he conclusion is inescapable that applicants to medical school must be few indeed who endured the effects of de jure segregation, the resistance to *Brown I,* or the equally debilitating pervasive private discrimination fostered by our long history of official discrimination, cf. *Reitman v. Mulkey,* and yet come to the starting line with an education equal to whites. * * *

C. The second prong of our test—whether the Davis program stigmatizes any discrete group or individual and whether race is reasonably used in light of the program's objectives—is clearly satisfied by the Davis program. * * *

Unlike discrimination against racial minorities, the use of racial preferences for remedial purposes does not inflict a pervasive injury upon individual whites in the sense that wherever they go or whatever they do there is a significant likelihood that they will be treated as second-class citizens because of their color. This distinction does not mean that the exclusion of a white resulting from the

Generally, the manner in which a State chooses to delegate governmental functions is for it to decide. California, by constitutional provision, has chosen to place authority over the operation of the University of California in the Board of Regents [who] have been vested with full legislative (including policymaking), administrative, and adjudicative powers. [W]e, unlike our Brother Powell, find nothing in the Equal Protection Clause that requires us to depart from established principle by limiting the scope of power the Regents may exercise more narrowly than the powers that may constitutionally be wielded by the Assembly.

Because the Regents can exercise plenary legislative and administrative power, it elevates form over substance to insist that Davis could not use race-conscious remedial programs until it had been adjudged in violation of the Constitution or an antidiscrimination statute. For, if the Equal Protection Clause required such a violation as a predicate, the Regents could simply have promulgated a regulation prohibiting disparate treatment not justified by the need to admit only qualified students, and could have declared Davis to have been in violation of such a regulation on the basis of the exclusionary effect of the admissions policy applied during the first two years of its operation.

preferential use of race is not sufficiently serious to require justification; but it does mean that the injury inflicted by such a policy is not distinguishable from disadvantages caused by a wide range of government actions, none of which has ever been thought impermissible for that reason alone.

In addition, there is simply no evidence that the Davis program discriminates intentionally or unintentionally against any minority group which it purports to benefit. The program does not establish a quota in the invidious sense of a ceiling on the number of minority applicants to be admitted. Nor can the program reasonably be regarded as stigmatizing the program's beneficiaries or their race as inferior. The Davis program does not simply advance less qualified applicants; rather, it compensates applicants, whom it is uncontested are fully qualified to study medicine, for educational disadvantage which it was reasonable to conclude was a product of state-fostered discrimination. Once admitted, these students must satisfy the same degree [requirements]; they are taught by the same faculty in the same classes; and their performance is evaluated by the same standards by which regularly admitted students are judged. Under these circumstances, their performance and degrees must be regarded equally with the regularly admitted students with whom they compete for standing. Since minority graduates cannot justifiably be regarded as less well qualified than nonminority graduates by virtue of the special admissions program, there is no reasonable basis to conclude that [they] would be stigmatized as inferior by the existence of such programs.[c]

D. We disagree with the lower courts' conclusion that the Davis program's use of race was unreasonable in light of its objectives. First, as petitioner argues, there are no practical means by which it could achieve its ends in the foreseeable future without the use of race-conscious measures. With respect to any factor (such as poverty or family educational background) that may be used as a substitute for race as an indicator of past discrimination, whites greatly outnumber racial minorities simply because whites make up a far larger percentage of the total population and therefore far outnumber minorities in absolute terms at every socio-economic level. * * *

Second, [the] program does not simply equate minority status with disadvantage. Rather, Davis considers [each] applicant's personal history to determine whether he or she has likely been disadvantaged by racial discrimination. * * *

E. Finally, Davis' special admissions program cannot be said to violate the Constitution simply because it has set aside a predetermined number of places for qualified minority applicants rather than using minority status as a positive factor to be considered in evaluating the applications of disadvantaged minority applicants. For purposes of constitutional adjudication, there is no difference

c. But see Nagel, *Equal Treatment and Compensatory Discrimination,* 2 Phil. & Pub. Afrs. 348, 362 (1973): "Not only does [a racially preferential policy] inevitably produce resentment in the better qualified who are passed over [but] it also allows those in the discriminated-against group who would in fact have failed to gain a desired position in any case on the basis of their qualifications to feel that they may have lost out to someone less [qualified]. Similarly, such a practice cannot do much for the self-esteem of those who know they have benefited from it, and it may threaten the self-esteem of those in the favored group who would in fact have gained their positions even in the absence of the discriminatory policy, but who cannot be sure that they are not among its beneficiaries." Compare O'Neil, *Racial Preference and Higher Education: The Larger Context,* 60 Va.L.Rev. 925, 941 (1974): "[I]t would be perverse if a court were to strike down on this ground a program which had been sought and extensively utilized by minority applicants themselves. Such a judgment would imply a dangerously gratuitous concern about the welfare of minority groups."

between the two approaches. In any admissions program which accords special consideration to disadvantaged racial minorities, a determination of the degree of preference to be given is unavoidable, and any given preference that results in the exclusion of a white candidate is no more or less constitutionally acceptable than a program such as that at Davis. Furthermore, the extent of the preference inevitably depends on how many minority applicants the particular school is seeking to admit in any particular year so long as the number of qualified minority applicants exceeds that number. There is no sensible, and certainly no constitutional, distinction between, for example, adding a set number of points to the admissions rating of disadvantaged minority applicants as an expression of the preference with the expectation that this will result in the admission of an approximately determined number of qualified minority applicants and setting a fixed number of places for such applicants as was done here.[63]

[That] the Harvard approach does not also make public the extent of the preference and the precise workings of the system while the Davis program employs a specific, openly stated number, does not condemn the [latter]. It may be that the Harvard plan is more acceptable to the public than is the Davis "quota." If it is, any State [is] free to adopt it in preference to a less acceptable alternative, just as it is generally free [to] abjure granting any racial preferences in its admissions program. But there is no basis for preferring a particular preference program simply because in achieving the same goals that [Davis] is pursuing, it proceeds in a manner that is not immediately apparent to the public.[d] * * *

JUSTICE MARSHALL.

[I]t must be remembered that, during most of the past 200 years, the Constitution as interpreted by this Court did not prohibit the most ingenious and pervasive forms of discrimination against the Negro. Now, when a State acts to remedy the effects of that legacy of discrimination, I cannot believe that this same Constitution stands as a barrier. * * *

63. The excluded white applicant, despite Mr. Justice Powell's contention to the contrary, receives no more or less "individualized consideration" under our approach than under his. [For the view that "public choice theory" "directly supports" this position, see Spitzer, *Multicriteria Choice Processes: An Application of Public Choice Theory to Bakke, the FCC and the Courts,* 88 Yale L.J. 717 (1979).]

d. Consider Perry, *Modern Equal Protection: A Conceptualization and Appraisal,* 79 Colum.L.Rev. 1023, 1048 (1979): "One reason for subjecting any preferential program disadvantaging white persons [to] a heavier burden of justification is that such a program inevitably foments racial resentment and thereby strains the effort to gain wider acceptance for the principle of the moral equality of the races. Therefore, it makes sense to insist, as Powell did, that any preferential program be designed to accomplish its objective in a manner that causes as little resentment as possible." See also Mishkin, *The Uses of Ambivalence: Reflections on the Supreme Court and the Constitutionality of Affirmative Action,* 131 U.Pa.L.Rev. 907, 928 (1983): "The description of race as simply 'another factor' among a lot of others considered in seeking diversity tends to minimize the sense that minority students are separate and different and the recipients of special dispensations. [These] perceptions [can] facilitate or hamper the development of relationships among individuals and groups; they can advance or retard the educational process for all—including, particularly, minority students whose self-image is most crucially involved." Compare Blasi, *Bakke as Precedent: Does Mr. Justice Powell Have a Theory?* 67 Calif.L.Rev. 21, 60 (1979): "[I]t is almost always a bad thing for constitutional standards to be based on the purported perceptions of the populace regarding what is fair or rational rather than on well-considered and explicitly defended arguments respecting fairness and rationality. It is too easy to manufacture a 'general belief' or a 'widespread feeling.' [Second], if admissions programs are to be evaluated not on the basis of what they really entail but instead in terms of how they are generally perceived, educational institutions can only regard the constitutional standard as a legitimation of subterfuge and hypocrisy."

The position of the Negro today in America is the tragic but inevitable consequence of centuries of unequal treatment. Measured by any benchmark of comfort or achievement, meaningful equality remains a distant dream for the Negro [—comparing Negro and white statistics on life expectancy, infant mortality, median income, poverty, unemployment, and percentages in professions].

In light of the sorry history of discrimination and its devastating impact on the lives of Negroes, bringing the Negro into the mainstream of American life should be a state interest of the highest order. To fail to do so is to ensure that America will forever remain a divided society. * * *

Since the Congress that considered and rejected the objections to the 1866 Freedmen's Bureau Act concerning special relief to Negroes also proposed the Fourteenth Amendment, it is inconceivable that the Fourteenth Amendment was intended to prohibit all race-conscious relief measures.[e] [T]o hold that it barred state action to remedy the effects [of] discrimination [would] pervert the intent of the framers by substituting abstract equality for the genuine equality the amendment was intended to achieve.

[H]ad the Court [held in *Plessy*] that the Equal Protection Clause forbids differences in treatment based on race, we would not be faced with this dilemma in 1978. We must remember, however, that the principle that the "Constitution is color-blind" appeared only in the opinion of the lone dissenter. [F]or the next 60 years, from *Plessy* to *Brown,* ours was a Nation where, *by law,* an individual could be given "special" treatment based on the color of his skin. * * *

I fear that we have come full circle. After the Civil War our government started several "affirmative action" programs. This Court in the *Civil Rights Cases,* and *Plessy* destroyed the movement toward complete equality. For almost a century no action was taken, and this nonaction was with the tacit approval of the courts. Then we had *Brown* and the Civil Rights Acts of Congress, followed by numerous affirmative action programs. *Now,* we have this Court again stepping in, this time to stop affirmative action programs of the type used by the University of California.

JUSTICE BLACKMUN. * * *

I yield to no one in my earnest hope that the time will come when an "affirmative action" program is unnecessary and is, in truth, only a relic of the past. I would hope that we could reach this stage within a decade at the most. But the story of *Brown,* decided almost a quarter of a century ago, suggests that that hope is a slim one. At some time, however, beyond any period of what some would claim is only transitional inequality, the United States must and will reach a stage of maturity where action along this line is no longer necessary. Then persons will be regarded as persons, and discrimination of the type we address today will be an ugly feature of history that is instructive but that is behind us. * * *

e. Consider Pollak, *"Mr. Chief Justice; May It Please the Court:",* in Constitutional Government in America 247, 252 (Collins ed. 1980): "[T]he Freedmen's Bureau [authorized] a large remedial apparatus for the education and economic advancement [of] the freedmen. What could more clearly show that the fourteenth amendment, far from precluding remedial programs particularly designed to assist those groups battered by American history, was expected to be implemented in just such ways?" Compare Graglia, *Racially Discriminatory Admission to Public Institutions of Higher Education,* in Constitutional Government in America, 255, 263 (Collins ed. 1980): "[T]his argument proves too much. It is equally clear that the fourteenth amendment was not intended to prohibit school segregation either."

It is somewhat ironic to have us so deeply disturbed over a program where race is an element of consciousness, and yet to be aware of the fact, as we are, that institutions of higher learning, albeit more on the undergraduate than the graduate level, have given conceded preferences up to a point to those possessed of athletic skills, to the children of alumni, to the affluent who may bestow their largess on the institutions, and to those having connections with celebrities, the famous, and the powerful. * * *

[That] the Fourteenth Amendment has expanded beyond its original 1868 conception [does] not mean for me, however, that the Fourteenth Amendment has broken away from its moorings and its original intended purposes. [In] order to get beyond racism, we must first take account of race. There is no other way. And in order to treat some persons equally, we must treat them differently. We cannot—we dare not—let the Equal Protection Clause perpetrate racial supremacy.

* * * Today, again, we are expounding a *Constitution.* The same principles that governed McCulloch's case in 1819 govern Bakke's case in 1978. There can be no other answer.

JUSTICE STEVENS, with whom THE CHIEF JUSTICE, JUSTICE STEWART, and JUSTICE REHNQUIST join, concurring in the judgment in part and dissenting in part.[1]

[Bakke] challenged petitioner's special admissions program [and the] California Supreme Court upheld his challenge and ordered him admitted. If the state court was correct in its view that the University's special program was illegal, and that Bakke was therefore unlawfully excluded from the medical school because of his race, we should affirm its judgment, regardless of our views about the legality of admissions programs that are not now before the Court.

[Stevens, J., then construed the state court opinion as containing no "outstanding injunction forbidding any consideration of racial criteria in processing applications."] It is therefore perfectly clear that the question whether race can ever be used as a factor in an admissions decision is not an issue in this case, and that discussion of that issue is inappropriate.

[Stevens, J., then interpreted Title VI as prohibiting "the exclusion of *any* individual from a federally funded program 'on the ground of race.' "] It is therefore our duty to affirm the judgment ordering Bakke admitted * * *.

RICHMOND v. J.A. CROSON CO.

488 U.S. 469, 109 S.Ct. 706, 102 L.Ed.2d 854 (1989).

JUSTICE O'CONNOR announced the judgment of the Court and delivered the opinion of the Court with respect to Parts I, III–B, and IV, an opinion with respect to Part II, in which THE CHIEF JUSTICE and JUSTICE WHITE join, and an opinion with respect to Parts III–A and V, in which THE CHIEF JUSTICE, JUSTICE WHITE and JUSTICE KENNEDY join. * * *

I. On April 11, 1983, the Richmond City Council adopted the Minority Business Utilization Plan (the Plan). The Plan required prime contractors to whom the city awarded construction contracts to subcontract at least 30% of the dollar amount of the contract to one or more Minority Business Enterprises (MBEs) [defined] as "[a] business at least fifty-one (51) percent of which is owned

1. Four Members of the Court have undertaken to announce the legal and constitutional effect of this Court's judgment. See opinion of Justices Brennan, White, Marshall, and Blackmun. [But] only a majority can speak for the Court or determine what is the "central meaning" of any judgment of the Court.

and controlled [by] minority group members." "Minority group members" were defined as "[c]itizens of the United States who are Blacks, Spanish-speaking, Orientals, Indians, Eskimos, or Aleuts." [The] Plan declared that it was "remedial" in nature, and enacted "for the purpose of promoting wider participation by minority business enterprises in the construction of public projects." The Plan expired on June 30, 1988, and was in effect for approximately five years.

The Plan authorized the Director of the Department of General Services to promulgate rules which "shall allow waivers in those individual situations where a contractor can prove to the satisfaction of the director that the requirements herein cannot be achieved." * * *

The Plan was adopted by the Richmond City Council after a public hearing. Seven members of the public spoke to the merits of the ordinance: five were in opposition, two in favor. Proponents of the set-aside provision relied on a study which indicated that, while the general population of Richmond was 50% black, only .67% of the city's prime construction contracts had been awarded to minority businesses in the 5–year period from 1978 to 1983. It was also established that a variety of contractors' associations, whose representatives appeared in opposition to the ordinance, had virtually no minority businesses within their membership. * * *

There was no direct evidence of race discrimination on the part of the city in letting contracts or any evidence that the city's prime contractors had discriminated against minority-owned subcontractors. * * * Representatives of various contractors' associations questioned whether there were enough MBEs in the Richmond area to satisfy the 30% set-aside requirement. Mr. Murphy noted that only 4.7% of all construction firms in the United States were minority owned and that 41% of these were located in California, New York, Illinois, Florida, and Hawaii. He predicted that the ordinance would thus lead to a windfall for the few minority firms in Richmond. Council person Gillespie indicated his concern that many local labor jobs, held by both blacks and whites, would be lost because the ordinance put no geographic limit on the MBEs eligible for the 30% set-aside. Some of the representatives of the local contractors organizations indicated that they did not discriminate on the basis of race and were in fact actively seeking out minority members. * * *

[The case was brought by a contractor whose low bid on a city project was not accepted because of failure to comply with the Plan's requirements. A] divided panel of the Court of Appeals struck down the Richmond set-aside program as violating both prongs of strict scrutiny under the Equal Protection Clause * * *.

II. [In *Fullilove v. Klutznick,* 448 U.S. 448, 100 S.Ct. 2756, 65 L.Ed.2d 902 (1980)], we upheld the minority set-aside contained in § 103(f)(2) of the Public Works Employment Act of 1977 (the Act) against a challenge based on the equal protection component of the Due Process Clause. The Act authorized a four billion dollar appropriation for federal grants to state and local governments for use in public works projects [and] contained the following requirement: "Except to the extent the Secretary determines otherwise, no grant shall be made under this Act [unless] the applicant gives satisfactory assurance to the Secretary that at least 10 per centum of the amount of each grant shall be expended for minority business enterprises." MBEs were defined as businesses effectively controlled by "citizens of the United States who are Negroes, Spanish-speaking, Orientals, Indians, Eskimos, and Aleuts."

The principal opinion in *Fullilove,* written by Chief Justice Burger, did not employ "strict scrutiny" or any other traditional standard of equal protection review. The Chief Justice noted at the outset that although racial classifications call for close examination, the Court was at the same time, "bound to approach [its] task with appropriate deference to the Congress" [and that] Congress could mandate state and local government compliance with the set-aside program under its § 5 power to enforce the Fourteenth Amendment (citing *Katzenbach v. Morgan*).

The Chief Justice next turned to the constraints on Congress' power to employ race-conscious remedial relief. His opinion stressed two factors in upholding the MBE set-aside. First was the unique remedial powers of Congress under § 5 of the Fourteenth Amendment: "[It] is fundamental that *in no organ of government, state or federal, does there repose a more comprehensive remedial power than in the Congress,* expressly charged by the Constitution with competence and authority to enforce equal protection guarantees." (Emphasis added).

[In] reviewing the legislative history behind the Act, the principal opinion focused on the evidence before Congress that a nationwide history of past discrimination had reduced minority participation in federal construction grants. The Chief Justice also noted that Congress drew on its experience under § 8(a) of the Small Business Act of 1953, which had extended aid to minority businesses. The Chief Justice concluded that "Congress had abundant historical basis from which it could conclude that traditional procurement practices, when applied to minority businesses, could perpetuate the effects of prior discrimination."

The second factor emphasized by the principal opinion in *Fullilove* was the flexible nature of the 10% set-aside. Two "congressional assumptions" underlay the MBE program: first, that the effects of past discrimination had impaired the competitive position of minority businesses, and second, that "adjustment for the effects of past discrimination" would assure that at least 10% of the funds from the federal grant program would flow to minority businesses. The Chief Justice noted that both of these "assumptions" could be "rebutted" by a grantee seeking a waiver of the 10% requirement. Thus a waiver could be sought where minority businesses were not available to fill the 10% requirement or, more importantly, where an MBE attempted "to exploit the remedial aspects of the program by charging an unreasonable price, i.e., a price not attributable to the present effects of prior discrimination." The Chief Justice indicated that without this fine tuning to remedial purpose, the statute would not have "pass[ed] muster."

In his concurring opinion, Justice Powell relied on the legislative history adduced by the principal opinion in finding that "Congress reasonably concluded that private and governmental discrimination had contributed to the negligible percentage of public contracts awarded minority contractors." Justice Powell also found that the means chosen by Congress, particularly in light of the flexible waiver provisions, were "reasonably necessary" to address the problem identified. Justice Powell made it clear that other governmental entities might have to show more than Congress before undertaking race-conscious [measures].[a]

a. Burger, C.J.'s opinion was joined by White and Powell, JJ. Powell, J., also concurred separately. Marshall, J., joined by Brennan and Blackmun, JJ., concurred. Stevens, J., dissented for reasons discussed below. Stewart, J., joined by Rehnquist, J., dissented on the ground that, generally, "under our Constitution, the government may never act to the detriment of a person solely because of that person's race," and that "a judicial decree that imposes burdens on the basis of race can be upheld only where its sole purpose is to eradicate the actual effects of illegal race discrimination." For a similar statement of their views, see *Minnick v. California Dept. of Correction,* 452 U.S. 105, 101 S.Ct. 2211, 68 L.Ed.2d 706 (1981).

Appellant and its supporting amici rely heavily on *Fullilove* for the proposition that a city council, like Congress, need not make specific findings of discrimination to engage in race-conscious relief. Thus, appellant argues "[i]t would be a perversion of federalism to hold that the federal government has a compelling interest in remedying the effects of racial discrimination in its own public works program, but a city government does not."

What appellant ignores is that Congress, unlike any State or political subdivision, has a specific constitutional mandate to enforce the dictates of the Fourteenth Amendment. The power to "enforce" may at times also include the power to define situations which *Congress* determines threaten principles of equality and to adopt prophylactic rules to deal with those situations. See *Katzenbach v. Morgan.* See also *South Carolina v. Katzenbach* (similar interpretation of congressional power under § 2 of the Fifteenth Amendment). The Civil War Amendments themselves worked a dramatic change in the balance between congressional and state power over matters of race. Speaking of the Thirteenth and Fourteenth Amendments in *Ex parte Virginia,* the Court stated: "They were intended to be, what they really are, limitations of the powers of the States and enlargements of the power of Congress."

[It seems clear] however, that a state or local subdivision (if delegated the authority from the State) has the authority to eradicate the effects of private discrimination within its own legislative jurisdiction. This authority must, of course, be exercised within the constraints of § 1 of the Fourteenth Amendment. [As] a matter of state law, the city of Richmond has legislative authority over its procurement policies, and can use its spending powers to remedy private discrimination, if it identifies that discrimination with the particularity required by the Fourteenth Amendment. * * *

Thus, if the city could show that it had essentially become a "passive participant" in a system of racial exclusion practiced by elements of the local construction industry, we think it clear that the city could take affirmative steps to dismantle such a system. It is beyond dispute that any public entity, state or federal, has a compelling interest in assuring that public dollars, drawn from the tax contributions of all citizens, do not serve to finance the evil of private prejudice. Cf. *Norwood v. Harrison.*

III. A. [The] Richmond Plan denies certain citizens the opportunity to compete for a fixed percentage of public contracts based solely upon their race. To whatever racial group these citizens belong, their "personal rights" to be treated with equal dignity and respect are implicated by a rigid rule erecting race as the sole criterion in an aspect of public decisionmaking.

Absent searching judicial inquiry into the justification for such race-based measures, there is simply no way of determining what classifications are "benign" or "remedial" and what classifications are in fact motivated by illegitimate notions of racial inferiority or simple racial politics. Indeed, the purpose of strict scrutiny is to "smoke out" illegitimate uses of race by assuring that the legislative body is pursuing a goal important enough to warrant use of a highly suspect tool. The test also ensures that the means chosen "fit" this compelling goal so closely that there is little or no possibility that the motive for the classification was illegitimate racial prejudice or stereotype.

Classifications based on race carry a danger of stigmatic harm. Unless they are strictly reserved for remedial settings, they may in fact promote notions of racial inferiority and lead to a politics of racial hostility. We thus reaffirm the view expressed by the plurality in *Wygant v. Jackson Bd. of Educ.,* 476 U.S. 267,

106 S.Ct. 1842, 90 L.Ed.2d 260 (1986), that the standard of review under the Equal Protection Clause is not dependent on the race of those burdened or benefited by a particular classification. * * *

Even were we to accept a reading of the guarantee of equal protection under which the level of scrutiny varies according to the ability of different groups to defend their interests in the representative process, heightened scrutiny would still be appropriate in the circumstances of this case. One of the central arguments for applying a less exacting standard to "benign" racial classifications is that such measures essentially involve a choice made by dominant racial groups to disadvantage themselves. If one aspect of the judiciary's role under the Equal Protection Clause is to protect "discrete and insular minorities" from majoritarian prejudice or indifference, see *Carolene Products Co.,* n. 4, some maintain that these concerns are not implicated when the "white majority" places burdens upon itself. See Ely, *Democracy and Distrust* 170 (1980).

In this case, blacks comprise approximately 50% of the population of the city of Richmond. Five of the nine seats on the City Council are held by blacks. The concern that a political majority will more easily act to the disadvantage of a minority based on unwarranted assumptions or incomplete facts would seem to militate for, not against, the application of heightened judicial scrutiny in this case. * * * [b]

In *Bakke,* the Court confronted a racial quota employed by the University of California at Davis Medical School. Five Members of the Court determined that none of [the] interests [put forward] could justify a plan that completely eliminated nonminorities from consideration for a specified percentage of opportunities (Powell, J.) (addressing constitutionality of Davis plan); (Stevens, J., Burger, C.J., Stewart, and Rehnquist, JJ. concurring and dissenting) (addressing only legality of Davis admissions plan under Title VI of the Civil Rights Act of 1964).

Justice Powell's opinion applied heightened scrutiny under the Equal Protection Clause to the racial classification at issue. His opinion [contrasted] the "focused" goal of remedying "wrongs worked by specific instances of racial discrimination" with "the remedying of the effects of 'societal discrimination,' an amorphous concept of injury that may be ageless in its reach into the past." He indicated that for the governmental interest in remedying past discrimination to be triggered "judicial, legislative, or administrative findings of constitutional or statutory violations" must be made. Only then does the Government have a compelling interest in favoring one race over another.

In *Wygant,* four Members of the Court applied heightened scrutiny to a race-based system of employee layoffs. Justice Powell, writing for the plurality,

b. Compare Rosenfeld, *Decoding Richmond: Affirmative Action and the Elusive Meaning of Constitutional Equality,* 87 Mich. L.Rev. 1729, 1774 (1989): "Even assuming that all majority decisions favoring the majority should be considered suspect, [it] does not follow that a decision backed by the one half of the population that is favored by it should likewise be considered suspect. Indeed, so long as all members of society have a voice, one half of the population cannot, consistent with the premises underlying the *Carolene* approach, use the majoritarian process to subjugate the other half. Furthermore, although there may be a majority of blacks on the City Council, the fact that there is no black majority in Richmond should serve as a powerful incentive for black Council members not to act with disregard for the interests of one half of their constituents. In any event, the Richmond City Council's decision to adopt the Plan was not made strictly along racial lines. One white councilmember voted with the majority and another abstained. [Thus], the Plan would have gone through even if one of the black councilmembers had been replaced by a white member who would have voted against the Plan."

again drew the distinction between "societal discrimination" which is an inadequate basis for race-conscious classifications, and the type of identified discrimination that can support and define the scope of race-based relief. The challenged classification in that case tied the layoff of minority teachers to the percentage of minority students enrolled in the school district. The lower courts had upheld the scheme, based on the theory that minority students were in need of "role models" to alleviate the effects of prior discrimination in society. This Court reversed, with a plurality of four Justices reiterating the view expressed by Justice Powell in *Bakke* that "[s]ocietal discrimination, without more, is too amorphous a basis for imposing a racially classified remedy."

The role model theory employed by the lower courts failed for two reasons. First, the statistical disparity between students and teachers had no probative value in demonstrating the kind of prior discrimination in hiring or promotion that would justify race-based relief. Second, because the role model theory had no relation to some basis for believing a constitutional or statutory violation had occurred, it could be used to "justify" race-based decisionmaking essentially limitless in scope and duration.

B. [The] District Court found the city council's "findings sufficient to ensure that, in adopting the Plan, it was remedying the present effects of past discrimination in the *construction industry*." Like the "role model" theory employed in *Wygant,* a generalized assertion that there has been past discrimination in an entire industry provides no guidance for a legislative body to determine the precise scope of the injury it seeks to remedy. It "has no logical stopping point." *Wygant.* "Relief" for such an ill-defined wrong could extend until the percentage of public contracts awarded to MBEs in Richmond mirrored the percentage of minorities in the population as a whole.

Appellant argues that it is attempting to remedy various forms of past discrimination that are alleged to be responsible for the small number of minority businesses in the local contracting industry. Among these the city cites the exclusion of blacks from skilled construction trade unions and training programs. This past discrimination has prevented them "from following the traditional path from laborer to entrepreneur." The city also lists a host of nonracial factors which would seem to face a member of any racial group attempting to establish a new business enterprise, such as deficiencies in working capital, inability to meet bonding requirements, unfamiliarity with bidding procedures, and disability caused by an inadequate track record.

While there is no doubt that the sorry history of both private and public discrimination in this country has contributed to a lack of opportunities for black entrepreneurs, this observation, standing alone, cannot justify a rigid racial quota in the awarding of public contracts in Richmond, Virginia. Like the claim that discrimination in primary and secondary schooling justifies a rigid racial preference in medical school admissions, an amorphous claim that there has been past discrimination in a particular industry cannot justify the use of an unyielding racial quota.

It is sheer speculation how many minority firms there would be in Richmond absent past societal discrimination, just as it was sheer speculation how many minority medical students would have been admitted to the medical school at Davis absent past discrimination in educational opportunities.[c] Defining

c. For criticism of the "notion [that] discrimination must be the decisive explanation of intergroup differences," see Sowell, *Weber and Bakke, and the Presuppositions of "Affirmative Action,"* 26 Wayne L.Rev. 1309 (1980).

these sorts of injuries as "identified discrimination" would give local governments license to create a patchwork of racial preferences based on statistical generalizations about any particular field of endeavor.

These defects are readily apparent in this case. The 30% quota cannot in any realistic sense be tied to any injury suffered by anyone. The District Court relied upon five predicate "facts" [discussed below] in reaching its conclusion that there was an adequate basis for the 30% quota * * *.

None of these "findings," singly or together, provide the city of Richmond with a "strong basis in evidence for its conclusion that remedial action was necessary." *Wygant.* There is nothing approaching a prima facie case of a constitutional or statutory violation by *anyone* in the Richmond construction industry.

The District Court accorded great weight to the fact that the city council designated the Plan as "remedial." But the mere recitation of a "benign" or legitimate purpose for a racial classification, is entitled to little or no weight. Racial classifications are suspect, and that means that simple legislative assurances of good intention cannot suffice.

The District Court also relied on the highly conclusionary statement of a proponent of the Plan that there was racial discrimination in the construction industry "in this area, and the State, and around the nation." It also noted that the city manager had related his view that racial discrimination still plagued the construction industry in his home city of Pittsburgh. These statements are of little probative value in establishing identified discrimination in the Richmond construction industry. The fact-finding process of legislative bodies is generally entitled to a presumption of regularity and deferential review by the judiciary. But when a legislative body chooses to employ a suspect classification, it cannot rest upon a generalized assertion as to the classification's relevance to its goals.

[Reliance] on the disparity between the number of prime contracts awarded to minority firms and the minority population of the city of Richmond is similarly misplaced. * * *

In the employment context, we have recognized that for certain entry level positions or positions requiring minimal training, statistical comparisons of the racial composition of an employer's workforce to the racial composition of the relevant population may be probative of a pattern of discrimination. See *Teamsters v. United States,* 431 U.S. 324, 337–338, 97 S.Ct. 1843, 1855–1856, 52 L.Ed.2d 396 (1977) (statistical comparison between minority truck drivers and relevant population probative of discriminatory exclusion). But where special qualifications are necessary, the relevant statistical pool for purposes of demonstrating discriminatory exclusion must be the number of minorities qualified to undertake the particular task. *School Dist. v. United States,* 433 U.S. 299, 308, 97 S.Ct. 2736, 2741, 53 L.Ed.2d 768 (1977), *Johnson v. Transportation Agency,* 480 U.S. 616, 651–652, 107 S.Ct. 1442, 1462, 91 L.Ed.2d 615 (1987) (O'Connor, J., concurring).[d]

d. Consider Neuborne, *Observations on Weber,* 54 N.Y.U.L.Rev. 546, 547 (1979): "In most settings, [we] do not allocate goods on the basis of an open-ended search for excellence. Rather, we seek a guarantee of a respectable level of competence, and, once that guarantee is present, we use criteria unrelated to competence—such as seniority, first-come first-served, personality, appearance, acquaintanceship, or hunch—to break ties. [But] where desirable positions are allocated on the basis of an open-ended search for excellence, race should never be permitted to effect the substitution of a less qualified candidate for the most qualified candidate. Such a substitution [would] frustrate legitimate expectations which are generally the result of strenuous individual preparation. Moreover, the socie-

In this case, the city does not even know how many MBEs in the relevant market are qualified to undertake prime or subcontracting work in public construction projects. Nor does the city know what percentage of total city construction dollars minority firms now receive as subcontractors on prime contracts let by the city.

To a large extent, the set-aside of subcontracting dollars seems to rest on the unsupported assumption that white prime contractors simply will not hire minority firms.[3] Indeed, there is evidence in this record that overall minority participation in city contracts in Richmond is seven to eight percent, and that minority contractor participation in Community Block Development Grant *construction* projects is 17% to 22%. Without any information on minority participation in subcontracting, it is quite simply impossible to evaluate overall minority representation in the city's construction expenditures.

The city and the District Court also relied on evidence that MBE membership in local contractors' associations was extremely low. Again, standing alone this evidence is not probative of any discrimination in the local construction industry. There are numerous explanations for this dearth of minority participation, including past societal discrimination in education and economic opportunities as well as both black and white career and entrepreneurial choices. [The] mere fact that black membership in these trade organizations is low, standing alone, cannot establish a prima facie case of discrimination.

For low minority membership in these associations to be relevant, the city would have to link it to the number of local MBEs eligible for membership. If the statistical disparity between eligible MBEs and MBE membership were great enough, an inference of discriminatory exclusion could arise. In such a case, the city would have a compelling interest in preventing its tax dollars from assisting these organizations in maintaining a racially segregated construction market.

Finally, the city and the District Court relied on Congress' finding in connection with the set-aside approved in *Fullilove* that there had been nationwide discrimination in the construction industry. The probative value of these findings for demonstrating the existence of discrimination in Richmond is extremely limited. By its inclusion of a waiver procedure in the national program addressed in *Fullilove,* Congress explicitly recognized that the scope of the problem would vary from market area to market area. * * *

In sum, none of the evidence presented by the city points to any identified discrimination in the Richmond construction industry. We, therefore, hold that

tal loss [would] be substantial." Compare Edwards, *The Future of Affirmative Action in Employment,* 44 Wash. & Lee L.Rev. 763, 779–81 (1987): "[I]t is unclear how one should determine the number of minorities or women in a relevant labor market who 'possess the relevant qualifications' to be the assistant manager of a supermarket, to give but one example. The range of possible qualifications for this type of position is so broad that any effort to quantify the number of minorities or women who possess them may be little more than an exercise in futility. [Thus], the burden of producing refined statistical evidence reasonably should rest on the party who seeks their introduction—the nonminority or male employees in this instance."

3. Since 1975 the city of Richmond has had an ordinance on the books prohibiting both discrimination in the award of public contracts and employment discrimination by public contractors. The city points to no evidence that its prime contractors have been violating the ordinance in either their employment or subcontracting practices. The complete silence of the record concerning enforcement of the city's own anti-discrimination ordinance flies in the face of the dissent's vision of a "tight-knit industry" which has prevented blacks from obtaining the experience necessary to participate in construction contracting.

the city has failed to demonstrate a compelling interest in apportioning public contracting opportunities on the basis of race. * * *

The foregoing analysis applies only to the inclusion of blacks within the Richmond set-aside program. There is *absolutely no evidence* of past discrimination against Spanish-speaking, Oriental, Indian, Eskimo, or Aleut persons in any aspect of the Richmond construction industry. * * *

If a 30% set-aside was "narrowly tailored" to compensate black contractors for past discrimination, one may legitimately ask why they are forced to share this "remedial relief" with an Aleut citizen who moves to Richmond tomorrow? The gross overinclusiveness of Richmond's racial preference strongly impugns the city's claim of remedial motivation.

IV. As noted by the court below, it is almost impossible to assess whether the Richmond Plan is narrowly tailored to remedy prior discrimination since it is not linked to identified discrimination in any way. We limit ourselves to two observations in this regard.

First, there does not appear to have been any consideration of the use of race-neutral means to increase minority business participation in city contracting. Many of the barriers to minority participation in the construction industry relied upon by the city to justify a racial classification appear to be race neutral. If MBEs disproportionately lack capital or cannot meet bonding requirements, a race-neutral program of city financing for small firms would, a fortiori, lead to greater minority participation. The principal opinion in *Fullilove* found that Congress had carefully examined and rejected race-neutral alternatives before enacting the MBE set-aside.

Second, the 30% quota cannot be said to be narrowly tailored to any goal, except perhaps outright racial balancing. It rests upon the "completely unrealistic" assumption that minorities will choose a particular trade in lockstep proportion to their representation in the local population.

Since the city must already consider bids and waivers on a case-by-case basis, it is difficult to see the need for a rigid numerical quota. As noted above, the congressional scheme upheld in *Fullilove* allowed for a waiver of the set-aside provision where an MBE's higher price was not attributable to the effects of past discrimination. Based upon proper findings, such programs are less problematic from an equal protection standpoint because they treat all candidates individually, rather than making the color of an applicant's skin the sole relevant consideration. Unlike the program upheld in *Fullilove,* the Richmond Plan's waiver system focuses solely on the availability of MBEs; there is no inquiry into whether or not the particular MBE seeking a racial preference has suffered from the effects of past discrimination by the city or prime contractors.

Given the existence of an individualized procedure, the city's only interest in maintaining a quota system rather than investigating the need for remedial action in particular cases would seem to be simple administrative convenience. But the interest in avoiding the bureaucratic effort necessary to tailor remedial relief to those who truly have suffered the effects of prior discrimination cannot justify a rigid line drawn on the basis of a suspect classification. Under Richmond's scheme, a successful black, Hispanic, or Oriental entrepreneur from anywhere in the country enjoys an absolute preference over other citizens based solely on their race. We think it obvious that such a program is not narrowly tailored to remedy the effects of prior discrimination.

V. Nothing we say today precludes a state or local entity from taking action to rectify the effects of identified discrimination within its jurisdiction. If the city of Richmond had evidence before it that nonminority contractors were systematically excluding minority businesses from subcontracting opportunities it could take action to end the discriminatory exclusion. Where there is a significant statistical disparity between the number of qualified minority contractors willing and able to perform a particular service and the number of such contractors actually engaged by the locality or the locality's prime contractors, an inference of discriminatory exclusion could arise. Under such circumstances, the city could act to dismantle the closed business system by taking appropriate measures against those who discriminate on the basis of race or other illegitimate criteria. In the extreme case, some form of narrowly tailored racial preference might be necessary to break down patterns of deliberate exclusion. * * *

Proper findings in this regard are necessary to define both the scope of the injury and the extent of the remedy necessary to cure its effects. Such findings also serve to assure all citizens that the deviation from the norm of equal treatment of all racial and ethnic groups is a temporary matter, a measure taken in the service of the goal of equality itself. Absent such findings, there is a danger that a racial classification is merely the product of unthinking stereotypes or a form of racial politics. * * * [e]

Affirmed.

JUSTICE STEVENS, concurring in part and concurring in the judgment. * * * I believe the Constitution requires us to evaluate our policy decisions—including those that govern the relationships among different racial and ethnic groups—primarily by studying their probable impact on the future. I therefore do not agree with the premise that seems to underlie today's decision, as well as the decision in *Wygant,* that a governmental decision that rests on a racial classification is never permissible except as a remedy for a past wrong.[1] I do, however, agree with the Court's explanation of why the Richmond ordinance cannot be justified as a remedy for past discrimination, and therefore join Parts I, III–B, and IV of its opinion. I write separately to emphasize three aspects of the case that are of special importance to me.

e. For debate concerning the scope of the *Croson* decision, compare Joint Statement, *Constitutional Scholars' Statement on Affirmative Action After City of Richmond v. J. A. Croson Co.,* 98 Yale L.J. 1711 (1989) with Fried, *Affirmative Action After City of Richmond v. J. A. Croson Co.: A Response to the Scholars' Statement,* 99 Yale L.J. 155 (1989) and Comment, *Scholars Reply to Professor Fried,* 99 Yale L.J. 163 (1989). Does the Court substitute "adjectival dismissiveness" and "rhetorical devices" for analysis of "richly textured facts?" See Williams, *The Obliging Shell: An Informal Essay on Formal Equal Opportunity,* 87 Mich.L.Rev. 2128 (1989).

1. In my view the Court's approach to this case gives unwarranted deference to race-based legislative action that purports to serve a purely remedial goal, and overlooks the potential value of race-based determinations that may serve other valid purposes. With regard to the former point—as I explained at some length in *Fullilove*—I am not prepared to assume that even a more narrowly tailored set-aside program supported by stronger findings would be constitutionally justified. Unless the legislature can identify both the particular victims and the particular perpetrators of past discrimination, which is precisely what a court does when it makes findings of fact and conclusions of law, a *remedial* justification for race-based legislation will almost certainly sweep too broadly. With regard to the latter point: I think it unfortunate that the Court in neither *Wygant* nor this case seems prepared to acknowledge that some race-based policy decisions may serve a legitimate public purpose. I agree, of course, that race is so seldom relevant to legislative decisions on how best to foster the public good that legitimate justifications for race-based legislation will usually not be available. But unlike the Court, I would not totally discount the legitimacy of race-based decisions that may produce tangible and fully justified future benefits.

First, the city makes no claim that the public interest in the efficient performance of its construction contracts will be served by granting a preference to minority-business enterprises. This case is therefore completely unlike *Wygant,* in which I thought it quite obvious that the School Board had reasonably concluded that an integrated faculty could provide educational benefits to the entire student body that could not be provided by an all-white, or nearly all-white faculty. [In] the case of public contracting, however, if we disregard the past, there is not even an arguable basis for suggesting that the race of a subcontractor or general contractor should have any relevance to his or her access to the market.

Second, this litigation involves an attempt by a legislative body, rather than a court, to fashion a remedy for a past wrong. Legislatures are primarily policy-making bodies that promulgate rules to govern future conduct. [It] is the judicial system, rather than the legislative process, that is best equipped to identify past wrongdoers and to fashion remedies that will create the conditions that presumably would have existed had no wrong been committed.[f] * * *

Third, instead of engaging in a debate over the proper standard of review to apply in affirmative-action litigation, I believe it is more constructive to try to identify the characteristics of the advantaged and disadvantaged classes that may justify their disparate treatment. In this case that approach convinces me [that] the Richmond City Council has merely engaged in the type of stereotypical analysis that is a hallmark of violations of the Equal Protection Clause. * * *

The justification for the ordinance is the fact that in the past white contractors—and presumably other white citizens in Richmond—have discriminated against black contractors. The class of persons benefited by the ordinance is not, however, limited to victims of such discrimination—it encompasses persons who have never been in business in Richmond as well as minority contractors who may have been guilty of discriminating against members of other minority [groups.] Ironically, minority firms that have survived in the competitive struggle, rather than those that have perished, are most likely to benefit from an ordinance of this kind.

The ordinance is equally vulnerable because of its failure to identify the characteristics of the disadvantaged class of white contractors that justify the disparate treatment. That [class] presumably includes some who have been guilty of unlawful discrimination, some who practiced discrimination before it was forbidden by law, and some who have never discriminated against anyone on the basis of race. Imposing a common burden on such a disparate class merely because each member of the class is of the same race stems from reliance on a stereotype rather than fact or reason.[9] * * *

f. In *Fullilove* and *Wygant,* Stevens, J., also emphasized that "a race-based classification does impose a special obligation to scrutinize any governmental decisionmaking process that [draws] distinctions between citizens on the basis of their race. [For] just as procedural safeguards are necessary to guarantee impartial decisionmaking in the judicial process, so they can play a vital part in preserving the impartial character of the legislative process."

9. There is, of course, another possibility that should not be overlooked. The ordinance might be nothing more than a form of patronage. But racial patronage, like a racial gerrymander, is no more defensible than political patronage or a political gerrymander. But unlike the Court, I would not totally discount the legitimacy of race-based decisions that may produce tangible and fully justified future benefits. [For amplification, see Sullivan, *Sins of Discrimination: Last Term's Affirmative Action Cases,* 100 Harv.L.Rev. 78 (1986)].

JUSTICE KENNEDY, concurring in part and concurring in the judgment.

I join all but Part II of Justice O'Connor's opinion * * *.

[The] process by which a law that is an equal protection violation when enacted by a State becomes transformed to an equal protection guarantee when enacted by Congress poses a difficult proposition for me; but as it is not before us, any reconsideration of that issue must await some further case. * * *

The moral imperative of racial neutrality is the driving force of the Equal Protection Clause. Justice Scalia's opinion underscores that proposition, quite properly in my view. The rule suggested in his opinion, which would strike down all preferences which are not necessary remedies to victims of unlawful discrimination, would serve important structural goals, as it would eliminate the necessity for courts to pass upon each racial preference that is enacted. Structural protections may be necessities if moral imperatives are to be obeyed. His opinion would make it crystal clear to the political branches, at least those of the States, that legislation must be based on criteria other than race.

Nevertheless, given that a rule of automatic invalidity for racial preferences in almost every case would be a significant break with our precedents that require a case-by-case test, I am not convinced we need adopt it at this point. [My] reasons [are] as follows. First, I am confident that, in application, the strict scrutiny standard will operate in a manner generally consistent with the imperative of race neutrality, because it forbids the use even of narrowly drawn racial classifications except as a last resort. Second, the rule against race-conscious remedies is already less than an absolute one, for that relief may be the only adequate remedy after a judicial determination that a State or its instrumentality has violated the Equal Protection Clause. I note, in this connection, that evidence which would support a judicial finding of intentional discrimination may suffice also to justify remedial legislative action, for it diminishes the constitutional responsibilities of the political branches to say they must wait to act until ordered to do so by a court. Third, the strict scrutiny rule is consistent with our precedents, as Justice O'Connor's opinion demonstrates. * * *

JUSTICE SCALIA, concurring in the judgment.

I agree with much of the Court's opinion, and, in particular, with its conclusion that strict scrutiny must be applied to all governmental classification by race, whether or not its asserted purpose is "remedial" or "benign." I do not agree, however, with the Court's dicta suggesting that, despite the Fourteenth Amendment, state and local governments may in some circumstances discriminate on the basis of race in order (in a broad sense) "to ameliorate the effects of past discrimination." The benign purpose of compensating for social disadvantages, whether they have been acquired by reason of prior discrimination or otherwise, can no more be pursued by the illegitimate means of racial discrimination than can other assertedly benign purposes we have repeatedly rejected. See, e.g., [*Wygant*]. At least where state or local action is at issue, only a social emergency rising to the level of imminent danger to life and limb—for example, a prison race riot, requiring temporary segregation of inmates, cf. *Lee v. Washington*—can justify an exception to the principle embodied in the Fourteenth Amendment that "[o]ur Constitution is color-blind, and neither knows nor tolerates classes among citizens," *Plessy* (Harlan, J., dissenting) * * *.

A sound distinction between federal and state (or local) action based on race rests not only upon the substance of the Civil War Amendments, but upon social reality and governmental theory. It is a simple fact that what Justice Stewart described in *Fullilove* as "the dispassionate objectivity [and] the flexibility that are needed to mold a race-conscious remedy around the single objective of eliminating the effects of past or present discrimination"—political qualities already to be doubted in a national legislature—are substantially less likely to exist at the state or local level. The struggle for racial justice has historically been a struggle by the national society against oppression in the individual States. [What] the record shows, in other words, is that racial discrimination against any group finds a more ready expression at the state and local than at the federal level. To the children of the Founding Fathers, this should come as no surprise. An acute awareness of the heightened danger of oppression from political factions in small, rather than large, political units dates to the very beginning of our national history. See Wood, The Creation of the American Republic, 1776–1787, pp. 499–506 (1969).

In my view there is only one circumstance in which the States may act *by race* to "undo the effects of past discrimination": where that is necessary to eliminate their own maintenance of a system of unlawful racial classification. [This] distinction explains our school desegregation cases, in which we have made plain that States and localities sometimes have an obligation to adopt race-conscious remedies. While there is no doubt that those cases have taken into account the continuing "effects" of previously mandated racial school assignment, we have held those effects to justify a race-conscious remedy only because we have concluded, in that context, that they perpetuate a "dual school system." We have stressed each school district's constitutional "*duty to dismantle* its dual system," and have found that "[e]ach instance of a failure or refusal to fulfill this affirmative duty *continues the violation* of the Fourteenth Amendment." *Columbus.*

Our analysis in *Bazemore v. Friday,* reflected our unwillingness to conclude, outside the context of school assignment, that the continuing effects of prior discrimination can be equated with state maintenance of a discriminatory system. * * *

I agree with the Court's dictum that a fundamental distinction must be drawn between the effects of "societal" discrimination and the effects of "identified" discrimination, and that the situation would be different if Richmond's plan were "tailored" to identify those particular bidders who "suffered from the effects of past discrimination by the city or prime contractors." In my view, however, the reason that would make a difference is not, as the Court states, that it would justify race-conscious action but rather that it would enable race-neutral remediation. Nothing prevents Richmond from according a contracting preference to identified victims of discrimination. While most of the beneficiaries might be black, neither the beneficiaries nor those disadvantaged by the preference would be identified *on the basis of their race.* In other words, far from justifying racial classification, identification of actual victims of discrimination makes it less supportable than ever, because more obviously unneeded. * * *

It is plainly true that in our society blacks have suffered discrimination immeasurably greater than any directed at other racial groups. But those who believe that racial preferences can help to "even the score" display, and reinforce, a manner of thinking by race that was the source of the injustice and that will, if it endures within our society, be the source of more injustice still. The relevant proposition is not that it was blacks, or Jews, or Irish who were discriminated against, but that it was individual men and women, "created equal," who were discriminated against. And the relevant resolve is that that should never happen again. Racial preferences appear to "even the score" (in some small degree) only if one embraces the proposition that our society is appropriately viewed as divided into races, making it right that an injustice rendered in the past to a black man should be compensated for by discriminating against a white. Nothing is worth that embrace. Since blacks have been disproportionately disadvantaged by racial discrimination, any race-neutral remedial program aimed at the disadvantaged *as such* will have a disproportionately beneficial impact on blacks. Only such a program, and not one that operates on the basis of race, is in accord with the letter and the spirit of our Constitution. * * *

JUSTICE MARSHALL, with whom JUSTICE BRENNAN and JUSTICE BLACKMUN join, dissenting. * * *

My view has long been that race-conscious classifications designed to further remedial goals "must serve important governmental objectives and must be substantially related to achievement of those objectives" in order to withstand constitutional scrutiny. Analyzed in terms of this two-prong standard, Richmond's set-aside, like the federal program on which it was modeled, is "plainly constitutional." *Fullilove* (Marshall, J., concurring in judgment).

Turning first to the governmental interest inquiry, Richmond has two powerful interests in setting aside a portion of public contracting funds for minority-owned enterprises. The first is the city's interest in eradicating the effects of past racial discrimination. * * *

Richmond has a second compelling interest in setting aside, where possible, a portion of its contracting dollars. [When] government channels all its contracting funds to a white-dominated community of established contractors whose racial homogeneity is the product of private discrimination, it does more than place its imprimatur on the practices which forged and which continue to define that community. It also provides a measurable boost to those economic entities that have thrived within it, while denying important economic benefits to those entities which, but for prior discrimination, might well be better qualified to receive valuable government contracts. In my view, the interest in ensuring that the government does not reflect and reinforce prior private discrimination in dispensing public contracts is every bit as strong as the interest in eliminating private discrimination—an interest which this Court has repeatedly deemed compelling. See, e.g., *Roberts v. United States Jaycees*; *Bob Jones University v. United States*; *Runyon v. McCrary*.

The remaining question with respect to the "governmental interest" prong of equal protection analysis is whether Richmond has proffered satisfactory proof of past racial discrimination to support its twin interests in remediation and in governmental nonperpetuation. * * * Richmond acted against a backdrop of congressional and Executive Branch studies which demonstrated with such force the nationwide pervasiveness of prior discrimination that Congress presumed that " 'present economic inequities' " in construction contracting resulted from " 'past discriminatory systems.' " The city's local evidence confirmed that Richmond's construction industry did not deviate from this pernicious national pattern. The fact that just .67% of public construction expenditures over the previous fives years had gone to minority-owned prime contractors, despite the city's racially mixed population, strongly suggests that construction contracting in the area was rife with "present economic inequities." To the extent this enormous disparity did not itself demonstrate that discrimination had occurred, the descriptive testimony of Richmond's elected and appointed leaders drew the necessary link between the pitifully small presence of minorities in construction contracting and past exclusionary practices. That *no one* who testified challenged this depiction of widespread racial discrimination in area construction contracting lent significant weight to these accounts. The fact that area trade associations had virtually no minority members dramatized the extent of present inequities and suggested the lasting power of past discriminatory systems. In sum, to suggest that the facts on which Richmond has relied do not provide a sound basis for its finding of past racial discrimination simply blinks credibility.

Richmond's reliance on localized, industry-specific findings is a far cry from the reliance on generalized "societal discrimination" which the majority decries as a basis for remedial action. But [the] majority also takes the disingenuous approach of disaggregating Richmond's local evidence, attacking it piecemeal, and thereby concluding that no *single* piece of evidence adduced by the city, "standing alone," suffices to prove past discrimination. But items of evidence do not, of course, "stan[d] alone" or exist in alien juxtaposition; they necessarily work together, reinforcing or contradicting each other.

In any event, the majority's criticisms of individual items of Richmond's evidence rest on flimsy foundations. The majority states, for example, that reliance on the disparity between the share of city contracts awarded to minority firms (.67%) and the minority population of Richmond (approximately 50%) is "misplaced." * * * First, considering how miniscule the share of Richmond public construction contracting dollars received by minority-owned businesses is, it is hardly unreasonable to conclude that this case involves a "gross statistical disparit[y]." There are roughly equal numbers of minorities and nonminorities in Richmond—yet minority-owned businesses receive *one-seventy-fifth* the public contracting funds that other businesses receive.

Second, and more fundamentally, where the issue is not present discrimination but rather whether *past* discrimination has resulted in the *continuing exclusion* of minorities from an historically tight-knit industry, a contrast between population and work force is entirely appropriate to help gauge the degree of the exclusion. *Johnson v. Transportation Agency,* Justice O'Connor specifically observed that, when it is alleged that discrimination has prevented blacks from "obtaining th[e] experience" needed to qualify for a position, the "relevant comparison" is not to the percentage of blacks in the pool of qualified candidates, but to "the total percentage of blacks in the labor force." This contrast is especially illuminating in cases like this, where a main avenue of introduction into the work force—here, membership in the trade associations whose members presumably train apprentices and help them procure subcontracting assignments—is itself grossly dominated by nonminorities. The majority's assertion that the city "does not even know how many MBE's in the relevant market are qualified," is thus entirely beside the point. [The Plan] is designed precisely to ease minority contractors into the industry.

The majority's perfunctory dismissal of the testimony of Richmond's appointed and elected leaders is also deeply disturbing [and] does violence to the very principles of comity within our federal system which this Court has long championed. Local officials, by virtue of their proximity to, and their expertise with, local affairs, are exceptionally well-qualified to make determinations of public good "within their respective spheres of authority." * * *

Had the majority paused for a moment on the facts of the Richmond experience, it would have discovered that the city's leadership is deeply familiar with what racial discrimination is. The members of the Richmond City Council have spent long years witnessing multifarious acts of discrimination, including, but not limited to, the deliberate diminution of black residents' voting rights, resistance to school desegregation, and publicly sanctioned housing discrimination. Numerous decisions of federal courts chronicle this disgraceful recent history. * * *

When the legislatures and leaders of cities with histories of pervasive discrimination testify that past discrimination has infected one of their industries, armchair cynicism like that exercised by the majority has no [place.] Disbelief is particularly inappropriate here in light of the fact that appellee Croson, which had the burden of proving unconstitutionality at trial, *Wygant,* has *at no point* come forward with *any* direct evidence that the City Council's motives were anything other than sincere.[9]

Finally, I vehemently disagree with the majority's dismissal of the congressional and Executive Branch findings noted in *Fullilove* as having "extremely limited" probative value in this case. [In] thus requiring that Richmond's local evidence be severed from the context in which it was prepared, the majority would require cities seeking to eradicate the effects of past discrimination within their borders to reinvent the evidentiary wheel and engage in unnecessarily duplicative, costly, and time-consuming factfinding.

No principle of federalism or of federal power, however, forbids a state or local government from drawing upon a nationally relevant historical record prepared by the Federal Government.[10] Of course, Richmond could have built an even more compendious record of past discrimination, one including additional stark statistics and additional individual accounts of past discrimination. But nothing in the Fourteenth Amendment imposes such onerous documentary obligations upon States and localities once the reality of past discrimination is apparent.

In my judgment, Richmond's set-aside plan also comports with the second prong of the equal protection inquiry, for it is substantially related to the interests it seeks to serve in remedying past discrimination and in ensuring that municipal contract procurement does not perpetuate that discrimination. The most striking aspect of the city's ordinance is the similarity it bears to the

9. Compare *Fullilove* (Stevens, J., dissenting) (noting statements of sponsors of federal set-aside that measure was designed to give their constituents "a piece of the action").

10. Although the majority sharply criticizes Richmond for using data which it did not itself develop, it is noteworthy that the federal set-aside program upheld in *Fullilove* was adopted as a floor amendment "without any congressional hearings or investigation whatsoever." Tribe, *American Constitutional Law* 345 (2d ed. 1988). The principal opinion in *Fullilove* justified the set-aside by relying heavily on the aforementioned studies by agencies like the Small Business Administration and on legislative reports prepared in connection with prior, failed legislation. See *Fullilove* (opinion of Burger, C.J.) ("Although the Act recites no preambulary 'findings' on the subject, we are satisfied that Congress had abundant historical basis from which it could conclude that traditional procurement practices, when applied to minority businesses, could perpetuate the effects of prior discrimination"); see also (Stevens, J., dissenting) (noting "perfunctory" consideration accorded the set-aside provision); Days, *Fullilove,* 96 Yale L.J. 453, 465 (1987) (citation omitted) ("One can only marvel at the fact that the minority set-aside provision was enacted into law without hearings or committee reports, and with only token opposition").

[For further discussion of the limited factual record before Congress in *Fullilove,* see Choper, *The Constitutionality of Affirmative Action: Views from the Supreme Court,* 70 Ky. L.J. 1, 12–14 (1981–82).]

"appropriately limited" federal set-aside provision upheld in *Fullilove.* Like the federal provision, Richmond's is limited to five years in duration, and was not renewed when it came up for reconsideration in 1988. Like the federal provision, Richmond's contains a waiver provision freeing from its subcontracting requirements those nonminority firms that demonstrate that they cannot comply with its provisions. Like the federal provision, Richmond's has a minimal impact on innocent third parties. While the measure affects 30% of *public* contracting dollars, that translates to only 3% of overall Richmond area contracting.

Finally, like the federal provision, Richmond's does not interfere with any vested right of a contractor to a particular contract; instead it operates entirely prospectively. Richmond's initiative affects only future economic arrangements and imposes only a diffuse burden on nonminority competitors—here, businesses owned or controlled by nonminorities which seek subcontracting work on public construction projects. The plurality in *Wygant* emphasized the importance of this not disrupting the settled and legitimate expectations of innocent parties. "While hiring goals impose a diffuse burden, often foreclosing only one of several opportunities, layoffs impose the entire burden of achieving racial equality on particular individuals, often resulting in serious disruption of their lives. That burden is too intrusive." *Wygant;* [g] see *Steelworkers v. Weber,* 443 U.S., at 208, 99 S.Ct., at 2730, 61 L.Ed.2d 480 (1979).

[The] majority takes issue, however, with two aspects of Richmond's tailoring: the city's refusal to explore the use of race-neutral measures to increase minority business participation in contracting, and the selection of a 30% set-aside figure. The majority's first criticism is flawed in two respects. First, the majority overlooks the fact that since 1975, Richmond has barred both discrimination by the city in awarding public contracts and discrimination by public contractors. The virtual absence of minority businesses from the city's contracting rolls, indicated by the fact that such businesses have received less than 1% of public contracting dollars, strongly suggests that this ban has not succeeded in redressing the impact of past discrimination or in preventing city contract procurement from reinforcing racial homogeneity. Second, the majority's suggestion that Richmond should have first undertaken such race-neutral measures as a program of city financing for small firms ignores the fact that such measures, while theoretically appealing, have been discredited by Congress as ineffectual in eradicating the effects of past discrimination in this very industry. For this reason, this Court in *Fullilove* refused to fault Congress for not undertaking race-neutral measures as precursors to its race-conscious set-aside. The Equal Protection Clause does not require Richmond to retrace Congress' steps when Congress has found that those steps lead nowhere. * * *

As for Richmond's 30% target, the majority states that this figure "cannot be said to be narrowly tailored to any goal, except perhaps outright racial balancing." The majority ignores two important facts. First, the set-aside measure affects only 3% of overall city contracting; thus, any imprecision in tailoring has far less impact than the majority suggests. But more important,

g. Stevens, J., dissenting in *Wygant,* disagreed: "[Powell, J.] seems to assume that a teacher who has been working for a few years suffers a greater harm when he is laid off than the harm suffered by an unemployed teacher who is refused a job for which he is qualified. In either event, the adverse decision forecloses "only one of several opportunities" that may be available to the disappointed teacher. Moreover, the distinction is artificial, for the layoff provision at issue in this case was included as part of the terms of the *hiring* of minority and other teachers under the collective-bargaining agreement."

the majority ignores the fact that Richmond's 30% figure was patterned directly on the *Fullilove* precedent. Congress' 10% figure fell "roughly halfway between the present percentage of minority contractors and the percentage of minority group members in the Nation." The Richmond City Council's 30% figure similarly falls roughly halfway between the present percentage of Richmond-based minority contractors (almost zero) and the percentage of minorities in Richmond (50%). In faulting Richmond for not presenting a different explanation for its choice of a set-aside figure, the majority honors *Fullilove* only in the breach. * * *

Today, for the first time, a majority of this Court has adopted strict scrutiny as its standard of Equal Protection Clause review of race-conscious remedial measures. This is an unwelcome development. * * *

I am also troubled by the majority's assertion that, even if it did not believe generally in strict scrutiny of race-based remedial measures, "the circumstances of this case" require this Court to look upon the Richmond City Council's measure with the strictest scrutiny. The sole such circumstance which the majority cites, however, is the fact [that] "blacks comprise approximately 50% of the population of the city of Richmond" and that "[f]ive of the nine seats on the City Council are held by blacks."

While I agree that the numerical and political supremacy of a given racial group is a factor bearing upon the level of scrutiny to be applied, this Court has never held that numerical inferiority, standing alone, makes a racial group "suspect" and thus entitled to strict scrutiny review. Rather, we have identified *other* "traditional indicia of suspectness": whether a group has been "saddled with such disabilities, or subjected to such a history of purposeful unequal treatment, or relegated to such a position of political powerlessness as to command extraordinary protection from the majoritarian political process."

It cannot seriously be suggested that nonminorities in Richmond have any "history of purposeful unequal treatment." Nor is there any indication that they have any of the disabilities that have characteristically afflicted those groups this Court has deemed suspect. Indeed, the numerical and political dominance of nonminorities within the State of Virginia and the Nation as a whole provide an enormous political check against the "simple racial politics" at the municipal level which the majority fears. If the majority really believes that groups like Richmond's nonminorities, which comprise approximately half the population but which are outnumbered even marginally in political fora, are deserving of suspect class status for these reasons alone, this Court's decisions denying suspect status to women and to persons with below-average incomes stand on extremely shaky ground.

In my view, the "circumstances of this case," underscore the importance of *not* subjecting to a strict scrutiny straitjacket the increasing number of cities which have recently come under minority leadership and are eager to rectify, or at least prevent the perpetuation of, past racial discrimination. In many cases, these cities will be the ones with the most in the way of prior discrimination to rectify. * * *

Richmond's own recent political history underscores the facile nature of the majority's assumption that elected officials' voting decisions are based on the color of their skins. In recent years, white and black councilmembers in Richmond have increasingly joined hands on controversial matters. When the Richmond City Council elected a black man Mayor in 1982, for example, his victory was won with the support of the City Council's four white members. The vote on the set-aside plan a year later also was not purely along racial lines. Of the four white councilmembers, one voted for the measure and another abstained. The majority's view that remedial measures undertaken by municipalities with black leadership must face a stiffer test of Equal Protection Clause scrutiny than remedial measures undertaken by municipalities with white leadership implies a lack of political maturity on the part of this Nation's elected minority officials that is totally unwarranted. Such insulting judgments have no place in constitutional jurisprudence.

Today's decision, finally, is particularly noteworthy for the daunting standard it imposes upon States and localities contemplating the use of race-conscious measures to eradicate the present effects of prior discrimination and prevent its perpetuation. * * *

Nothing in the Constitution or in the prior decisions of this Court supports limiting state authority to confront the effects of past discrimination to those situations in which a prima facie case of a constitutional or statutory violation can be made out. By its very terms, the majority's standard effectively cedes control of a large component of the content of that constitutional provision to Congress and to state legislatures. If an antecedent Virginia or Richmond law had defined as unlawful the award to nonminorities of an overwhelming share of a city's contracting dollars, for example, Richmond's subsequent set-aside initiative would then satisfy the majority's standard. But without such a law, the initiative might not withstand constitutional scrutiny. The meaning of "equal protection of the laws" thus turns on the happenstance of whether a State or local body has previously defined illegal discrimination. Indeed, given that racially discriminatory cities may be the ones least likely to have tough, antidiscrimination laws on their books, the majority's constitutional incorporation of state and local statutes has the perverse effect of inhibiting those States or localities with the worst records of official racism from taking remedial action.

Similar flaws would inhere in the majority's standard even if it incorporated only federal anti-discrimination statutes. If Congress tomorrow dramatically expanded Title VII of the Civil Rights Act of 1964—or alternatively, if it repealed that legislation altogether—the meaning of equal protection would change precipitously along with it. Whatever the Framers of the Fourteenth Amendment had in mind in 1868, it certainly was not that the content of their Amendment would turn on the amendments to or the evolving interpretations of a federal statute passed nearly a century later.[12]

12. Although the majority purports to "adher[e] to the standard of review employed in *Wygant,*" the "prima facie case" standard it adopts marks an implicit rejection of the more generally framed "strong basis in evidence" test endorsed by the *Wygant* plurality, and the similar "firm basis" test endorsed by Justice O'Connor in her separate concurrence in that case. Under those tests, proving a prima facie violation of Title VII would appear to have been but one means of adducing sufficient proof to satisfy Equal Protection Clause analysis. See *Johnson v. Transportation Agency* (plurality opinion) (criticizing suggestion that race-conscious relief be conditioned on showing of a prima facie Title VII violation).

[In] *Wygant,* a majority of this Court rejected as unduly inhibiting and constitutionally unsupported a requirement that a municipality demonstrate that its remedial plan is designed only to benefit specific victims of discrimination. Justice O'Connor noted the Court's general agreement that a "remedial purpose need not be accompanied by contemporaneous findings of actual discrimination to be accepted as legitimate as long as the public actor has a firm basis for believing that remedial action is required [O'Connor, J. stressed that a requirement of such findings "would severely undermine public employers' incentive to meet voluntarily their civil rights obligations."] [A] plan need not be limited to the remedying of specific instances of identified discrimination for it to be deemed sufficiently 'narrowly tailored,' or 'substantially related,' to the correction of prior discrimination by the state actor." [Given] that just three Terms ago this Court rejected the "specific

To the degree that this parsimonious standard is grounded on a view that either § 1 or § 5 of the Fourteenth Amendment substantially disempowered States and localities from remedying past racial discrimination, the majority is seriously mistaken. * * *

The fact is that Congress' concern in passing the Reconstruction Amendments, and particularly their congressional authorization provisions, was that States would *not* adequately respond to racial violence or discrimination against newly freed slaves. To interpret any aspect of these Amendments as proscribing state remedial responses to these very problems turns the Amendments on their heads. * * *

Notes and Questions

1. *Prior illegality vs. societal discrimination.* Should benign race-conscious government action be restricted to remedying "the effects of identified discrimination within its jurisdiction"? Consider Greenawalt, *The Unresolved Problems of Reverse Discrimination,* 67 Calif.L.Rev. 87, 127 (1979): "[G]iven the lingering effects of discrimination against earlier generations, given people's inevitable advancement through stages of life, and given the tremendous geographic mobility in the United States, people whose opportunities are unequal because of earlier discrimination will typically not have been affected by any discrimination by the organization from which they now seek a job or other benefit. It is not sensible to demand as a matter of constitutional law that that organization itself have discriminated before racial preferences are permissible." See also O'Neil, *Racial Preference and Higher Education: The Larger Context,* 60 Va.L.Rev. 925, 930 (1974): "If previous discrimination were essential to the remedial use of race, only those states that once maintained dual higher educational systems would today be allowed to adopt preferential programs. [At] its limits, such an argument would distinguish within states between institutions that once discriminated and those that never did so. Thus the University of Texas at Austin, where racially exclusionary admission policies were once held unconstitutional, could now admit preferentially, while the newer campuses [could] not do so."

Does *Croson* permit a state or local lawmaking body to take these points into account in exercising its "authority to eradicate the effects of private discrimination within its own legislative jurisdiction"? Or do these points go to "remedying the effects of societal discrimination"?

2. *Compelling interests.* Are there any government interests beyond "remedying identified discrimination" that will (should) survive strict scrutiny?

(a) *Education.* In *Bakke,* Powell, J., stated that a public university could have a race-conscious admissions program because it had a "compelling" interest in an ethnically "diverse student body" that would contribute to a "robust exchange of ideas": "Academic freedom, though not a specifically enumerated

victims" idea as untenable, [I] take the majority's standard of "identified discrimination" merely to require some quantum of proof of discrimination within a given jurisdiction that exceeds the proof which Richmond has put forth here.

[See also Hazard, *Permissive Affirmative Action for the Benefit of Blacks,* 1987 U.Ill.L. Rev. 379, 399–400: "The function of the 'finding' by a responsible agency [is] to establish the fact of discrimination for the benefit of another audience and decisionmaker, i.e., the ordinary citizenry. Pronouncing the fact that discrimination existed serves to educate the public that racism persists and is itself a significant act. It is also an important link in justifying the marginal preferment of blacks. Without an independent 'finding' by someone outside the courts, the ordinary citizenry would perceive the courts as granting remedial preferments in situations where no discrimination is apparent. The 'finding' also politically commits the agency involved to the remedial program, and thus more widely distributes the economic and political burdens which the program entails."]

constitutional right, long has been viewed as a special concern of the First Amendment.[h] Consider McCormack, *Race and Politics in the Supreme Court: Bakke to Basics,* 1979 Utah L.Rev. 491, 530: "Most educators would agree that some element of diversity in a student body is healthy, but few would assert that this factor is the primary motivation behind minority preferences. [Thus], one problem with this approach is that it is simply not the most honest statement of the objective of the programs. [Further,] it is hard to believe that racial classifications disfavoring racial or ethnic minorities could be justified by a school's claim of academic freedom. This justification would be considered ludicrous if advanced as a basis for preferring members of the white majority. These considerations rob the principle of the very neutrality that Justice Powell was seeking elsewhere in the opinion and suggest the instability of the rationale." See also Van Alstyne, *A Preliminary Report on the Bakke Case,* 64 AAUP Bull. 286, 294 (1978): "[Suspect] classifications [must] survive 'the most exacting judicial scrutiny.' [Yet], in the dispensation the Powell opinion provides to higher education, the purpose to be served, as important as educators may deem it to be, is at best a purpose to furnish a better learning environment for all of the students—a purpose not exactly overwhelming or even nationally compelling."

Does Powell, J.'s point lead to the further conclusion "that there is a strong societal interest in [the] equal participation of blacks [whenever] a 'black [can] bring something that a white person cannot offer,'" and that this extends to *all* "institutions of government, the 'power professions' [such] as law and medicine, [and] the economic system"? Sedler, *Racial Preference and the Constitution: The Societal Interest in the Equal Participation Objective,* 26 Wayne L.Rev. 1227 (1980).

(b) *Defacto segregation.* In addition to *Swann's* dictum—that "school authorities might well conclude that in order to prepare students to live in a pluralistic society each school should have a prescribed ratio of Negro to white students reflecting the proportion for the district as a whole"—is there a compelling interest for school officials to voluntarily act on a racial basis to alleviate de facto school segregation? May a school board, to cure racial imbalance, permit only minority students to transfer?

(c) "*Benign quotas.*" Suppose that state law limited the number of blacks in a public housing project to that percentage—say 35%—which, if exceeded, would likely cause white persons to leave, thus frustrating integration? Is there a compelling interest because the purpose is to *avoid* segregation? If so, how about "public subsidies such as bonuses to landlords whose apartments enjoy a mixed occupancy, grants to Negroes to enable them to rent apartments or purchase homes in residential areas that would otherwise be beyond their means, or payments to induce white families to move or to stay in integrated neighborhoods"? Bittker, *The Case of the Checker-Board Ordinance: An Experiment in Race Relations,* 71 Yale L.J. 1387, 1411 (1962). Of what significance is the fact that some blacks—those denied entrance because the quota is already

h. In *Wygant,* O'Connor, J., subscribing to the view that "racial classification must be subject to 'strict scrutiny,'" added: "although its precise contours are uncertain, a state interest in the promotion of racial diversity has been found sufficiently 'compelling,' at least in the context of higher education, to support the use of racial considerations in furthering that interest. And certainly nothing the Court has said today necessarily forecloses the possibility that the Court will find other governmental interests which have been relied upon in the lower courts but which have not been passed on here to be sufficiently 'important' or 'compelling' to sustain the use of affirmative action policies."

Why was a "diverse student body" in *Bakke* compelling, but not the need for "role models" in *Wygant?*

filled—are being "discriminated" against because of their race? See generally Ackerman, *Integration for Subsidized Housing and the Question of Racial Occupancy Controls,* 26 Stand.L.Rev. 245 (1974); Note, *Benign Steering and Benign Quotas: The Validity of Race-Conscious Government Policies to Promote Residential Integration,* 93 Harv.L.Rev. 938 (1980).

Consider Rice, *The Legality of De Facto Segregation,* 10 Cath.Law. 309, 320 (1964): "[The benign quota] implies that the presence of [whites] automatically raises the quality of a [housing area] and that a preponderance of [blacks] automatically lowers [it]. [T]his is as much a denial of the Negro's equality under the law as are the indefensible but less sophisticated racial barriers in the South." Compare Gegan, *De Jure Integration in Education,* 11 Cath.Law. 4, 14 (1965): "Legislation designed to integrate racial minorities into the mainstream of society carries no connotation of inferiority not also present in any legislation enacted to assist a socially or economically disadvantaged class. And I know of no responsible person who would argue today that welfare or other anti-poverty legislation bespeaks a judgment that the recipient is an inferior being."

(d) *Lawyers and physicians.* Is there a compelling interest in more minority lawyers and physicians in order to improve delivery of legal and medical services? Consider Graglia p. 1023 supra, at 259–60: "It [is] said that some members of non-white groups would prefer to be served by professionals of the same group. [This is a preference] that we can accept in the interest of honoring individual choice, even the choice to racially discriminate, but not one that we should encourage or take extraordinary steps to satisfy. [T]he law should take the position that the individual's race is irrelevant, in the hope that the educative effect of law will help make this so even where it is not so already. [If] we are concerned [with] increasing the availability of professional services to the poor, that concern can be met simply, directly, and appropriately by subsidizing such services by payments to the poor or to those who serve them." Compare Sandalow, *Minority Preferences in Law School Admissions,* in id. 277, 282: "The ability to 'speak the language' of the client, to understand his perception of his problem, and to deal with others in the community on his behalf are qualities essential to being a 'good lawyer.' These qualifications are more likely to be found among lawyers who share the client's racial or ethnic identity, at least to the extent that the client's life is bound up in a community defined in these terms."

3. *"Burdens" on "innocent individuals."* In *Bakke,* Powell, J., found that "helping certain groups whom the faculty of the Davis Medical School perceived as victims of 'societal discrimination' does not justify a classification that imposes disadvantages upon persons like respondent, who bear no responsibility for whatever harm the beneficiaries of the special admissions program are thought to have suffered." Subsequent decisions have also "emphasized the importance of not disrupting the settled and legitimate expectations of innocent parties." Thus, in distinguishing between hiring goals and layoffs, the *Wygant* plurality observed: "The 'school admission' cases, which involve the same basic concepts as cases involving hiring goals, illustrate this principle. For example, in *DeFunis,* while petitioner's complaint alleged that he had been denied admission to the University of Washington Law School because of his race, he also had been accepted at the Oregon, Idaho, Gonzaga, and Willamette Law Schools. The injury to DeFunis was not of the same kind or degree as the injury that he would have suffered had he been removed from law school in his third year. Even this analogy may not rise to the level of harm suffered by a union member who is laid off."

(a) To what extent *can* affirmative action programs diminish or avoid these harms. Should race-based hiring goals be restricted to employers who have themselves engaged in illegal discrimination? Consider Sullivan, *Sins of Dis-*

crimination, 100 Harv.L.Rev. 78, 94 (1986): "Making an employer or union atone for *its* past discrimination would all be very well, [but] that is not what affirmative action does. For it is not the errant management that 'pays' for affirmative action, but 'innocent' white workers. [Nor] are employees or the rank and file responsible for the ongoing racial wrongs that might be committed by their management or union leadership. Therefore, limiting affirmative action to employers or unions guilty of discrimination is not limiting it far enough; it must not harm guiltless white workers." Is the "answer" to require the "guilty" employers to pay money damages to the "guiltless white worker"? Might a government employer's "burdening vested employment rights of white workers amount to a taking for a public purpose and thus require just compensation"? Tribe, *America Constitutional Law* 1536 (2d ed. 1988). Compare McCormack, p. 1044 supra, at 536: "Traditional tort theories assume that as between two innocent persons, a loss should stay where it has fallen unless there is some reason to shift its burden to another. In employment contexts, compensation can be made by requiring the employer to pay both innocents, but education operates with limited resources—seats in a class—and often results in a zero sum game." See also Comment, *Beyond Strict Scrutiny: The Limits of Congressional Power to Use Racial Classifications,* 74 Nw.U.L.Rev. 617, 633 (1979): "[In *Milliken II,*] the court-ordered expenditure of public funds to assist black students in overcoming the effects of past discrimination clearly had the effect of reducing the funds available for general educational purposes. Therefore, white students, who were not themselves responsible for the historic discrimination, were saddled with the burden of the program, since there was a reduction in funds available for general use."

(b) How great a role *should* this factor play? Consider D. Strauss, *The Myth of Colorblindness,* 1986 Sup.Ct.Rev. 99, 131: "[T]here is unquestionably an undertone in the affirmative action debate that affirmative action is different from nondiscrimination because affirmative action causes innocent people to suffer. The assertion that there is a difference is incorrect. Prohibiting discrimination also causes, and has caused, innocent people to suffer [pointing to *Brown* and *Palmore v. Sidolti*]. And so far as I am aware, no one has justified the suffering of these victims of nondiscrimination in a way that would not also justify the suffering of victims of affirmative action." See also Bryden, *On Race and Diversity,* 6 Const.Comm. 383, 419 (1989): "I don't regard it as a fatal objection that affirmative action entails sacrificing some innocent white people. It's a high cost, but not necessarily too high. Not as high as all the suffering blacks had to endure while we forced them to wait for the opportune times to abolish slavery and segregation. The answer to the question of whether justice can trump utility is that it depends on how much utility and how much injustice. For me, the question is whether the benefits of affirmative action outweigh the harms to people like Bakke." [i] Compare Tribe, supra at 1536–37: "[I]nterpreting equal protection to require a balancing of hardships imposed on white workers by affirmative action plans against benefits derived from such plans itself invites social engineering of the very sort that the Court so often condemns. Distinguishing between otherwise justified affirmative action plans on the basis of the degree of sacrifice they extract from equally innocent white workers unnecessa-

i. See also H. Schwartz, *The 1986 and 1987 Affirmative Action Cases: It's All Over But the Shouting,* 86 Mich.L.Rev. 524, 551 (1987): "Can one seriously equate a preference intended to remedy centuries of discrimination—even if only 'societal discrimination' the existence of which all concede—with the brutality inflicted on blacks and other minorities by racist laws and practices? The preference may take away some benefits from some white men, but none of them is being beaten, lynched, denied work, forced to take the dirtiest jobs, or stigmatized as an inferior being."

rily confounds takings and equal-protection analyses and subordinates the achievement of racial justice to whatever pattern of economic distribution our discriminatory past happens to have produced."

(c) To what extent should this issue be affected "when the 'white majority' places burdens upon itself"? Consider Sandalow, *Racial Preferences in Higher Education: Political Responsibility and the Judicial Role,* 42 U.Chi.L.Rev. 653, 694–99 (1975): "[This] analysis [is] troublesome on several grounds. First, in American politics majorities [typically] are coalitions of minorities which have varying [interests]. Resolution of the dispute depends upon which of the minorities is more successful in forging an alliance with those groups which are less immediately affected. The issue whether state schools ought to adopt preferential admissions policies is no exception. The immediate beneficiaries of these policies are the minorities which receive preferential treatment. But there is no reason to suppose that the costs of such policies are borne equally by sub-groups within the white population. To the extent that they are not, the discrimination—though nominally against a majority—is in reality against those subgroups. * * * Universities have adopted preferential admissions policies without legislative sanction. The precise issue [is] not whether such policies are valid when adopted by a broadly representative, politically responsible legislature, but whether they are valid when adopted by a university [and] whether in determining the validity of state action that trenches upon constitutional values, the courts ought to consider whether the judgment under review is that of the legislature or of an agency that is less representative of the public and lacking direct political responsibility. [O]nly by ignoring all that we know about legislative behavior could it be supposed that a legislature's failure to limit the power of such bodies is equivalent to affirmative legislative approval of their decisions." See also Greenawalt, *Judicial Scrutiny of "Benign" Racial Preference in Law School Admissions,* 75 Colum.L.R. 559, 573–74 (1975); "We may safely suppose that the faculty of most state law schools is almost entirely white, but we may not assume that most faculty members will identify more with marginal white applicants than with black applicants. As most law teachers have done very well academically [they] may have trouble identifying themselves with marginal applicants. [M]any intellectuals may actually find it easier to identify with the plight of the 'oppressed' than the problems of the 'Philistine' middle and lower middle classes, from whom many marginal white applicants may come. Furthermore, two things that are in the obvious and immediate interest of faculty members and administrators are campus peace and a minimum of administrative burdens. Without doubt, some university programs for blacks [have] been adopted after considerable pressure that threatened or actually resulted in disruption. And a straight preferential policy applicable to all members of a minority group is likely to demand much less faculty or administrative time than careful examination of individual applications. Thus, it would be a mistake for judges to suppose that since most law school teachers and educational administrators are white they will not employ preferential policies ill-advisedly."

METRO BROADCASTING CO. v. FCC, ___ U.S. ___, 110 S.Ct. 2997, 111 L.Ed.2d 445 (1990), per BRENNAN, J., upheld minority preference policies of the Federal Communications Commission. The policies provided that minority ownership would be considered a plus in the consideration of mutually exclusive applications for stations and they allowed potential minority owners to acquire licenses by sale and transfer under conditions not available to nonminorities.

"It is of overriding significance in these cases that the FCC's minority ownership programs have been specifically approved—indeed, mandated—by

Congress. In *Fullilove,* [we] explained that deference was appropriate in light of Congress' institutional competence as the national legislature (opinion of Burger, C.J.); (Powell, J., concurring), as well as Congress' powers under the Commerce Clause (opinion of Burger, C.J.); (Powell, J., concurring), the Spending Clause (opinion of Burger, C.J.), and the Civil War Amendments (opinion of Burger, C.J.); (Powell, J., concurring).[11] [We] hold that benign race-conscious measures mandated by Congress—even if those measures are not 'remedial' in the sense of being designed to compensate victims of past governmental or societal discrimination—are constitutionally permissible to the extent that they serve important governmental objectives within the power of Congress and are substantially related to achievement of those objectives.

"Our decision last Term [in] Croson reaffirmed the lesson of Fullilove that race-conscious classifications adopted by Congress to address racial and ethnic discrimination are subject to a different standard than such classifications prescribed by state and local governments. * * *

"We hold that the FCC minority ownership policies pass muster under the test we announce today. [The interest] in enhancing broadcast diversity is, at the very least, an important governmental objective and is therefore a sufficient basis for the Commission's minority ownership policies. Just as a 'diverse student body' contributing to a " 'robust exchange of ideas' " is a "constitutionally permissible goal" on which a race-conscious university admissions program may be predicated, Bakke, (opinion of Powell, J.), the diversity of views and information on the airwaves serves important First Amendment values." [a]

O'CONNOR, J., joined by Rehnquist, C.J., Scalia and Kennedy, JJ., dissented: "The Constitution's guarantee of equal protection binds the Federal Government as it does the States, and no lower level of scrutiny applies to the Federal Government's use of race classifications. In *Bolling v. Sharpe,* [the] Court held [that]: "[I]t would be unthinkable that the same Constitution would impose a lesser duty on the Federal Government." * * *

"Congress has considerable latitude, presenting special concerns for judicial review, when it exercises its "unique remedial powers [under] § 5 of the Fourteenth Amendment," see *Croson,* but this case does not implicate those powers.

11. Justice O'Connor's suggestion that the deference to Congress described in *Fullilove* rested entirely on Congress' powers under § 5 of the Fourteenth Amendment is simply incorrect. The Chief Justice expressly noted that in enacting the provision at issue, "Congress employed an amalgam of its specifically delegated powers."

a. Brennan, J.'s opinion also concluded that the minority ownership policies were substantially related to the achievement of the government's interest, that they were not based on impermissible stereotyping, and that they did not impose impermissible burdens on nonminorities. Stevens, J., joined the opinion and wrote a separate concurring opinion.

In support of the majority opinion, consider, Aleinikoff, *A Case for Race-Consciousness,* 91 Colum.L.Rev. 101, 131 (1991): "[C]olorblindness sacrifices much of the cultural critique that race-consciousness can provide. If the task is to subject dominant views to scrutiny and challenge through the investigation and acceptance of nondominant perspectives, then it would appear sensible to permit decisionmakers to adopt facilitative programs that necessarily take notice of race. *Metro Broadcasting* is an important case in this respect. The FFC policies [both] support minority cultural self-definition and provide a means for penetrating mainstream culture." See generally Williams, *Metro Broadcasting, Inc. v. FCC: Regrouping in Singular Times,* 104 Harv.L.Rev. 525, 536–37 (1990): "[D]isrespectful exclusivities [signal] the most visible sites of oppression in any society. Participation in ownership of anything, but most particularly of broadcasting stations or other tools of mass communication, is the gateway to our greatest power as Americans. * * * The property of the communications industry is all about the production of ideas, images, and cultural representations, but it also selectively silences even as it creates. Like all artistic expression, it is a crafting process of production and negation, in the same way that a painting may involve choices to include yellow and blue while leaving out red and green."

Section 5 empowers Congress to act respecting the States, and of course this case concerns only the administration of federal programs by federal officials. * * *

"The Court asserts that *Fullilove* supports its novel application of intermediate scrutiny to "benign" race conscious measures adopted by Congress. Three reasons defeat this claim. First, *Fullilove* concerned an exercise of Congress' powers under § 5 of the Fourteenth Amendment. * * * *Croson* resolved any doubt that might remain regarding this [point.] *Croson* indicated that the decision in *Fullilove* turned on 'the unique remedial powers of Congress under § 5,' and that the latitude afforded Congress in identifying and redressing past discrimination rested on § 5's 'specific constitutional mandate to enforce the dictates of the Fourteenth Amendment.' * * *

"Second, *Fullilove* applies at most only to congressional measures that seek to remedy identified past discrimination. The Court upheld the challenged measures in *Fullilove* only because Congress had identified discrimination that had particularly affected the construction industry and had carefully constructed corresponding remedial measures. See *Fullilove* (opinion of Burger, C.J.); (opinion of Powell, J.). [The] FCC and Congress are clearly not acting for any remedial purpose, and the Court today expressly extends its standard to racial classifications that are not remedial in any sense.[b]

"Finally, even if *Fullilove* applied outside a remedial exercise of Congress' § 5 power, it would not support today's adoption of the intermediate standard of [review]. Although the Court correctly observes that a majority did not apply strict scrutiny, six Members of the Court rejected intermediate scrutiny in favor of some more stringent form of review." [c]

Notes and Questions

1. *Scope of permissible remedy for identified discrimination.* (a) SHEET METAL WORKERS' v. EEOC, 478 U.S. 421, 106 S.Ct. 3019, 92 L.Ed.2d 344 (1986): In 1975, a federal district court, having found that petitioner union had discriminated against nonwhites in violation of Title VII of the Civil Rights Act of 1964, ordered a 29% nonwhite membership goal (based on the percentage of nonwhites in the labor pool) to be achieved by 1981. In both 1982 and 1983, the district court held the union in contempt for "egregious noncompliance" with the various remedial orders over the years. It also amended the nonwhite membership goal to 29.23%, to be met by 1987.

Brennan, J., joined by Marshall, Stevens and Blackmun, JJ., first held that "where * * * an employer or union has engaged in particularly longstanding or egregious discrimination, * * * requiring recalcitrant employers or unions to hire and to admit qualified minorities roughly in proportion to the number of qualified minorities in the work force may be the only effective way to ensure the full enjoyment of the rights protected by Title VII.[d] [W]hile Congress

b. For the view that the FCC's preference "is primarily a remedial measure clothed in the garb of diversity," see Devins, *Metro Broadcasting, Inc. v. FCC: Requiem for a Heavyweight,* 69 Tex.L.Rev. 125 (1990).

c. O'Connor, J.'s opinion also concluded that the FCC's policy could not withstand even an intermediate form of scrutiny. Kennedy, J., joined by Scalia, J., also filed a separate dissenting opinion. For sustained attack on the notion that Congressional action should distinguish cases such as *Croson,* see Fried, *Metro Broadcasting, Inc. v. FCC: Two Concepts of Equality,* 104 Harv.L.Rev. 107 (1990).

d. Brennan, J.'s opinion subsequently emphasized that the membership goal did not establish an "inflexible racial quota": "The record shows that the District Court has been willing to accommodate *legitimate* reasons for petitioner's failure to comply with court orders, and we have no reason to expect that this will change in the future."

opposed the use of quotas or preferences merely to maintain racial balance, it gave no intimation as to whether such measures would be acceptable as *remedies* for Title VII violations." [e]

Second, as for equal protection, "we conclude that the relief ordered in this case passes even the most rigorous test—it is narrowly tailored to further the Government's compelling interest in remedying past discrimination. [T]he District Court considered the efficacy of alternative remedies, and concluded that, in light of petitioners' long record of resistance to official efforts to end their discriminatory practices, stronger measures were necessary. The court devised the temporary membership goal [for] remedying past discrimination. More importantly, the District Court's orders will have only a marginal impact on the interests of white workers. [T]he District Court's orders did not disadvantage *existing* union members. While white applicants for union membership may be denied certain benefits available to their nonwhite counterparts, the court's orders do not stand as an absolute bar to the admission of such individuals; again, a majority of those entering the union after entry of the court's orders have been white."

Powell, J., concurred in the judgment, relying on five factors to conclude that the "remedy is 'narrowly tailored' to the goal of eradicating the discrimination engaged in by petitioners."

(b) UNITED STATES v. PARADISE, 480 U.S. 149, 107 S.Ct. 1053, 94 L.Ed. 2d 203 (1987): In 1972, a federal district court found that the Alabama Department of Public Safety had intentionally excluded all blacks from employment as state troopers during its entire 37 year history. The court enjoined the Department, inter alia, from engaging in any promotional practices "for the purpose or with the effect of discriminating against any employee [on] the ground of race or color." During the next eleven years, the court issued a series of further orders dealing with "attempts by the Department to delay or frustrate compliance." This included a consent decree in 1979—when "out of 232 state troopers at the rank of corporal or above, there is still not one black"—by which "the Department agreed to develop within one year [a] promotion procedure with little or no adverse impact on blacks." In 1983, "confronted with the Department's failure to develop promotion procedures" and with only four black corporals out of 66 and no blacks at any higher ranks, "the District Court ordered the promotion of one black trooper for each white trooper elevated in rank, as long as qualified black candidates were available, until the Department implemented an acceptable promotion procedure." * * *

BRENNAN, J., joined by Marshall, Blackmun and Powell, JJ., found "that the relief ordered survives even strict scrutiny analysis." In response to the contention "that the Department was found guilty only of discrimination in hiring, and not in its promotional practices," the plurality held that "the race-conscious relief at issue here is justified by a compelling interest in remedying the

e. Powell, J., concurred in this result "in cases [such as this] involving particularly egregious conduct." White, J., "general[ly] agreed," but dissented because he interpreted the district court's remedy in this case as establishing "not just a minority membership goal but also a strict racial quota that the union was required to attain. We have not heretofore approved this kind of racially discriminatory hiring practice, and I would not do so now." O'Connor, J., agreed with White, J.'s latter point as a matter of statutory interpretation. Rehnquist, J., joined by Burger, C.J., also dissented.

discrimination. [It] is also supported by the societal interest in compliance with the judgments of federal courts." * * *

In addition, the plurality found "that the one-for-one promotion requirement was narrowly tailored to serve its several purposes," * * * stressing that "it was *necessary* [in order] to eliminate the effects of the Department's 'long term, open, and pervasive' discrimination" without further delay.

"The requirement may be waived if no qualified black candidates are available. The Department has, for example, been permitted to promote only white troopers to the ranks of lieutenant and captain since no black troopers have qualified for those positions. Further, it applies only when the Department needs to make promotions. Thus, if external forces, such as budget cuts, necessitate a promotion freeze, the Department will not be required to make gratuitous promotions to remain in compliance with the court's order.

"Most significantly, [the] requirement endures only until the Department comes up with a procedure that does not have [an] adverse impact, demonstrating that it is not a disguised means to achieve racial balance. [When] the District Court imposed the provision, the judge expressed the hope that its use would be 'a one-time occurrence.' [Four months later, the Department] submitted procedures for promotions to corporal and sergeant, and the court has consequently suspended application of the promotional order with respect to those ranks. * * *

"The Government suggests that the one-for-one requirement [bears] no relationship to the 25% minority labor pool relevant here. This argument ignores that the 50% figure is not itself the goal; rather it represents the speed at which the goal of 25% will be achieved. [T]he District Court, with its first-hand experience of the parties and the potential for resistance, imposed the requirement that it determined would compensate for past delay and prevent future recalcitrance, while not unduly burdening the interests [of] white applicants for promotion. It was used only once at the rank of corporal and may not be utilized at all in the upper ranks. Nor has the court imposed an 'absolute bar' to white advancement. *Sheet Metal Workers.* In the one instance in which the quota was employed, 50% of those elevated were white.

"[Because] the one-for-one requirement is so limited in scope and duration, it only postpones the promotions of qualified whites. Consequently, like a hiring goal, it 'impose[s] a diffuse burden, * * * foreclosing only one of several opportunities.' *Wygant.* * * *

"Finally, the basic limitation, that black troopers promoted must be qualified, remains. Qualified white candidates simply have to compete with qualified black candidates. To be sure, should the District Court's promotion requirement be applied, black applicants would receive some advantage. But this situation is only temporary, and is subject to amelioration by the action of the Department itself.

"Accordingly, the one-for-one promotion requirement imposed in this case does not disproportionately harm the interests, or unnecessarily trammel the rights, of innocent individuals.

"In determining whether this order was 'narrowly tailored,' we must acknowledge the respect owed a District Court's judgment that specified relief is essential to cure a violation of the Fourteenth Amendment. [Nor] have we in all situations 'required remedial plans to be limited to the least restrictive means of implementation. We have recognized that the choice of remedies to redress racial discrimination is "a balancing process left, within appropriate constitutional or statutory limits, to the sound discretion of the trial court."' *Fullilove* (Powell, J., concurring)."

STEVENS, J., concurred in the judgment: "A party who has been found guilty of repeated and persistent violations of the law bears the burden of demonstrating that the chancellor's efforts to fashion effective relief exceed the bounds of 'reasonableness.' The burden of proof in a case like this is precisely the opposite of that in cases such as *Wygant* and *Fullilove,* which did not involve any proven violations of law. In such cases the governmental decisionmaker who would make race-conscious decisions must overcome a strong presumption against them. No such burden rests on a federal district judge who has found that the governmental unit before him is guilty of racially discriminatory conduct that violates the Constitution."

O'CONNOR, J., joined by Rehnquist, C.J., and Scalia, J., although agreeing that "the Federal Government has a compelling interest in remedying past and present discrimination by the Department," dissented "because the Court adopts a standardless view of 'narrowly tailored' far less stringent than that required by strict scrutiny."

In the dissent's view, "the order at issue [clearly had] one purpose only—to compel the Department to develop a promotion procedure that would not have an adverse impact on blacks. [The] District Court had available several alternatives that would have achieved full compliance with the consent decrees without trammelling on the rights of nonminority troopers. The court, for example, could have appointed a trustee to develop a promotion procedure that would satisfy the terms of the consent decrees. [Or it] could have found the recalcitrant Department in contempt of court, and imposed stiff fines or other penalties for the contempt. [What] is most disturbing [is] that the District Court imposed the promotion quota *without consideration of any of the available alternatives.* [If this] can survive strict scrutiny as narrowly tailored, the requirement that a racial classification be 'narrowly tailored' for a compelling governmental purpose has lost most of its meaning. * * *

"Moreover, even if the one-for-one quota had the purpose of eradicating the effects of the Department's delay, [it] far exceeded the percentage of blacks in the trooper force, and there is no evidence in the record that such an extreme quota was [necessary]. The Court attempts to defend this one-for-one promotion quota as merely affecting the speed by which the Department attains the goal of 25% black representation in the upper ranks. Such a justification, however, necessarily eviscerates any notion of 'narrowly tailored' because it has no stopping point; even a 100% quota could be defended on the ground that it merely 'determined how quickly the Department progressed toward' some ultimate goal."

WHITE, J., "agreeing with much of" O'Connor, J.'s opinion, found "it evident that the District Court exceeded its equitable powers in devising a remedy in this case." [f]

2. *Repealing remedies for de facto segregation.* (a) In WASHINGTON v. SEATTLE SCHOOL DIST., 458 U.S. 457, 102 S.Ct. 3187, 73 L.Ed.2d 896 (1982), shortly after appellee implemented a mandatory busing plan to reduce de facto school segregation, the Washington electorate adopted Initiative 350, providing—

f. In light of Kennedy, J.'s views in *Croson* and *Metro Broadcasting,* do the remedies upheld in *Sheet Metal Workers* and *Paradise* survive his replacing Powell, J.?

with a number of broad exceptions—that "no school board [shall] directly or indirectly require any student to attend a school other than the school which is geographically nearest or next nearest the student's place of residence." The Court, per BLACKMUN, J.—relying on *Hunter v. Erickson,* 393 U.S. 385, 89 S.Ct. 557, 21 L.Ed.2d 616 (1969)[g]—held this violated equal protection: "[T]he political majority may generally restructure the political process to place obstacles in the path of everyone seeking to secure the benefits of governmental action. But a different analysis is required when the State allocates governmental power nonneutrally, by explicitly using the *racial* nature of a decision to determine the decisionmaking process. State action of this kind, [*Hunter*] said, 'places *special* burdens on racial minorities within the governmental process,' (emphasis added), thereby 'making it *more* difficult for certain racial and religious minorities [than for other members of the community] to achieve legislation that is in their interest.' (emphasis added) (Harlan, J., concurring). * * *

"[D]espite its facial neutrality there is little doubt that the initiative was effectively drawn for racial purposes. [T]he District Court found that the text [was] carefully tailored to interfere only with desegregative busing.[b] [It] in fact allows school districts to bus their students 'for most, if not all,' of the nonintegrative purposes required by their educational policies.[6] [It] is true [that] the proponents of mandatory integration cannot be classified by race: Negroes and whites may be counted among both the supporters and the opponents of Initiative 350. And it should be equally clear that white as well as Negro children benefit from exposure to 'ethnic and racial diversity in the classroom.' [But] desegregation of the public schools, like the Akron open housing ordinance, at bottom inures primarily to the benefit of the minority, and is designed for that purpose. [Given] the racial focus of Initiative 350, this suffices to trigger application of the *Hunter* doctrine.

"We are also satisfied that the practical effect of Initiative 350 is to work a reallocation of power of the kind condemned in *Hunter.* The initiative removes the authority to address a racial problem—and only a racial problem—from the existing decisionmaking body, in such a way as to burden minority interests. Those favoring the elimination of de facto school segregation now must seek relief from the state legislature, or from the statewide electorate. Yet authority over all other student assignment decisions, as well as over most other areas of educational policy, remains vested in the local school board. [As] in *Hunter,* then, the community's political mechanisms are modified to place effective decisionmaking authority over a racial issue at a different level of government.[17] * * *[23] * * *

g. In *Hunter,* after the Akron, Ohio city council enacted a fair housing ordinance, the voters amended the city charter to prevent "any ordinance dealing with racial, religious, or ancestral discrimination without the approval of a majority of the voters." The Court, per White, J., held this "explicitly racial classification" whose "impact falls on the minority" violative of equal protection. Black, J., dissented.

b. "The initiative envisioned busing for racial purposes in only one circumstance: it did not purport to 'prevent any court of competent jurisdiction from adjudicating constitutional issues relating to the public schools.' "

6. At the beginning of the 1978–1979 academic year, approximately 300,000 of the 769,040 students enrolled in Washington's public schools were bused to school. Ninety-five percent of these students were transported for reasons unrelated to race.

17. [While] Justice Powell [finds] it crucial that the proponents of integrated schools remain free to use Washington's initiative system to further their ends, that was true in *Hunter* as well * * *.

23. [W]hat we find objectionable about Initiative 350 is the comparative burden it imposes on minority participation in the political process—that is, the racial nature of the way in which it structures the *process* of decision-

"To be sure, 'the simple repeal or modification of desegregation or antidiscrimination laws, without more, never has been viewed as embodying a presumptively invalid racial classification.' *Crawford v. Los Angeles Bd. of Educ.* [infra].

"Initiative 350, however, works something more than the 'mere repeal' of a desegregation law by the political entity that created it. It burdens all future attempts to integrate Washington schools [by] lodging decisionmaking authority over the question at a new and remote level of government. Indeed, the initiative, like the charter amendment at issue in *Hunter,* has its most pernicious effect on integration programs that do '*not* arouse extraordinary controversy.' In such situations the initiative makes the enactment of racially beneficial legislation difficult, though the particular program involved might not have inspired opposition had it been promulgated through the usual legislative processes used for comparable legislation.[27] [And] when the State's allocation of power places unusual burdens on the ability of racial groups to enact legislation specifically designed to overcome the 'special condition' of prejudice, the governmental action seriously 'curtail[s] the operation of those political processes ordinarily to be relied upon to protect minorities.' *Carolene Products,* n. 4. In a most direct sense, this implicates the judiciary's special role in safeguarding the interests of those groups that are 'relegated to such a position of political powerlessness as to command extraordinary protection from the majoritarian political process.' *Rodriguez.*"

POWELL, J., joined by Burger, C.J., and Rehnquist and O'Connor, JJ., dissented: "[I]n the absence of a prior constitutional violation, the States are under no constitutional duty to adopt integration programs in their schools, and certainly [not] to establish a regime of mandatory busing.[6] Nor does the Federal Constitution require that particular decisions concerning the schools or any other matter be made on the local as opposed to the State level. * * *

"The issue here arises only because the Seattle School District [chose] to adopt race specific school assignments with extensive busing. It is not questioned that the District itself, at any time thereafter, could [have] cancelled its integration program without violating the Federal Constitution. Yet this Court holds that neither the legislature nor the people [of] Washington could alter what the District had decided. [It] is a strange notion [that] local governmental bodies can forever preempt the ability of a State—the sovereign power—to address a matter of compelling concern to the State. * * *

"This is certainly not a case where a State [has] established a racially discriminatory requirement. Initiative 350 [is] neutral on its face, and racially neutral as public policy. Children of all races benefit from neighborhood

making. It is evident, then, that the horribles paraded by the dissent, n. 14—which have nothing to do with the ability of minorities to participate in the process of self-government—are entirely unrelated to this case. It is equally clear [that] the State remains free to vest all decisionmaking power in state officials, or to remove authority from local school boards in a race-neutral manner.

27. That phenomenon is graphically demonstrated by the circumstances of this litigation. The long-standing desegregation programs in Pasco and Tacoma, as well as the Seattle middle school integration plan, have functioned for years without creating undue controversy. Yet they have been swept away [by] Initiative 350. As a practical matter, it seems most unlikely that proponents of desegregative busing in smaller communities such as Tacoma or Pasco will be able to obtain the statewide support now needed to permit them to desegregate the schools in their communities.

6. [Indeed], in the absence of a finding of segregation by the School District, mandatory busing on the basis of race raises constitutional difficulties of its own. Extensive pupil transportation may threaten liberty or privacy interests. See *Bakke* (opinion of Powell, J.) * * *.

[schools].[9] * * *

"Nothing in *Hunter* supports the Court's extraordinary invasion into the State's distribution of authority. [Initiative 350] simply does not place unique political obstacles in the way of racial minorities. In this case, unlike in *Hunter*, the political system has *not* been redrawn or altered. The authority of the State over the public school system, acting through Initiative or the legislature, is plenary. Thus, the State's political system is not altered when it adopts for the first time a policy, concededly within the area of its authority, for the regulation of local school districts. And certainly racial minorities are not uniquely or comparatively burdened by the State's adoption of a policy that would be lawful if adopted by any School District in the State.[13] * * *[14]."

(b) In CRAWFORD v. LOS ANGELES BD. OF EDUC., 458 U.S. 527, 102 S.Ct. 3211, 73 L.Ed.2d 948 (1982), after the state courts had ordered substantial busing to remedy de facto school segregation which the state courts had found violative of the state constitution, the California electorate amended the state constitution by adopting Proposition I, providing that "state courts shall not order mandatory pupil assignment or transportation unless a federal court would do so to remedy a violation of the Equal Protection Clause." The Court,

9. [The] people of the State legitimately could decide that unlimited mandatory busing places too great a burden on the liberty and privacy interests of families and students of all races. It might decide that the reassignment of students to distant schools, on the basis of race, was too great a departure from the ideal of racial neutrality in State action. And, in light of the experience with mandatory busing in other cities, the State might conclude that such a program ultimately would lead to greater racial imbalance in the schools.

[See also Sunstein, *Public Values, Private Interests, and the Equal Protection Clause,* 1982 Sup.Ct.Rev. 127, 149, 157–58: "A classification [that] singles out a racial problem for special and disadvantageous treatment is peculiarly likely to be supported by invidious justifications. Like the heightened scrutiny applied to facial racial classifications, heightened scrutiny in *Hunter* is justified by a suspicion that improper justifications are at work. [But] arguments against busing are less likely to be animated by racial bias than are arguments against legislation preventing discrimination in housing. *Seattle* might therefore have been treated differently from *Hunter* on the ground that invidious motives may well not have been at work."]

13. The Court repeatedly states that the effect of Initiative 350 is "to redraw decision-making authority over racial matters—*and only over racial matters*—in such a way as to place *comparative* burdens on minorities." But the decision by the State to exercise its authority over the schools and over racial matters in the schools does not place a comparative burden on racial minorities. In [*Hunter,*] "fair housing legislation *alone* was subject to an automatic referendum requirement." By contrast, Initiative 350 merely places mandatory busing among the much larger group of matters—covering race relations, administration of the schools, and a variety of other matters—addressed at the State level. Racial minorities, if indeed they are burdened by Initiative 350, are not *comparatively* burdened. In this respect, they are in the same position as any other group of persons who are disadvantaged by regulations drawn at the State level.

14. The Court's decision intrudes deeply into normal State decisionmaking. Under its holding the people [apparently] are forever barred from developing a different policy on mandatory busing where a School District previously has adopted one of its own. This principle would not seem limited to the question of mandatory busing. Thus, if the admissions committee of a State law school developed an affirmative action plan that came under fire, the Court apparently would find it unconstitutional for any higher authority to intervene unless that authority traditionally dictated admissions policies. As a constitutional matter, the Dean of the Law School, the faculty of the University as a whole, the University President, the Chancellor of the University System, and the Board of Regents might be powerless to intervene despite their greater authority under State law.

After today's decision it is unclear whether the State may set policy in any area of race relations where a local governmental body arguably has done "more" than the Fourteenth Amendment requires. If local employment or benefits are distributed on a racial basis to the benefit of racial minorities, the State apparently may not thereafter ever intervene. Indeed, under the Court's theory one must wonder whether [even] the Federal Government could assert its superior authority to regulate in these areas.

per POWELL, J., found no violation of equal protection, "rejecting the contention that once a State chooses to do 'more' than the Fourteenth Amendment requires, it may never recede. [E]ven after Proposition I, the California Constitution still imposes a greater duty of desegregation than does the Federal Constitution. The state courts of California continue to have an obligation under state law to order segregated school districts to use voluntary desegregation techniques, whether or not there has been a finding of intentional segregation. The school districts themselves retain a state law obligation to take reasonably feasible steps to desegregate, and they remain free to adopt reassignment and busing plans to effectuate desegregation.[12]

" * * * Proposition I does not embody a racial classification. It neither says nor implies that persons are to be treated differently on account of their race. [The] benefit it seeks to confer—neighborhood schooling—is made available regardless of race in the discretion of school boards. Indeed, even if Proposition I had a racially discriminatory effect, in view of the demographic mix of the District it is not clear which race or races would be affected the most or in what way.[16] * * *

"Were we to hold that the mere repeal of race related legislation is unconstitutional, we would limit seriously the authority of States to deal with the problems of our heterogeneous population. States would be committed irrevocably to legislation that has proven unsuccessful or even harmful in practice. And certainly the purposes of the Fourteenth Amendment would not be advanced by an interpretation that discouraged the States from providing greater protection to racial minorities. [Moreover], we would not interpret the Fourteenth Amendment to require the people of a State to adhere to a judicial construction of their State Constitution when that Constitution itself vests final authority in the people. * * *

"*Hunter* involved more than a 'mere repeal' of the fair housing ordinance: persons seeking anti-discrimination housing laws—presumptively racial minorities—were 'singled out for mandatory referendums while no other [group] face[d] that obstacle.' By contrast, [Proposition I] is less than a 'repeal' of the California Equal Protection Clause. As noted above, after Proposition I, the State Constitution still places upon school boards a greater duty to desegregate than does the Fourteenth Amendment.

"Nor can it be said that Proposition I distorts the political process for racial reasons or that it allocates governmental or judicial power on the basis of a discriminatory principle. [The] remedies available for violation of the antitrust laws, for example, are different than those available for violation of the Civil Rights Acts. Yet a 'dual court system'—one for the racial majority and one for the racial minority—is not established simply because civil rights remedies are different from those available in other areas. * * * [28]

* * *

12. In this respect this case differs from the situation presented in *Seattle*.

16. In the Los Angeles school district, white students are now the racial minority. [I]n Los Angeles County, racial minorities, including those of Spanish origin, constitute the majority of the population.

28. Similarly, a "dual constitution" is not established when the State chooses to go beyond the requirements of the Federal Constitution in some areas but not others. Nor is a "dual executive branch" created when an agency is given enforcement powers in one area but not in another. Cf. *Brown v. Califano*, 627 F.2d 1221 (D.C.Cir.1980) (upholding federal legislation prohibiting a federal executive agency, but not local school officials or federal courts, from requiring busing).

[Compare Note, *The Constitutionality of Excluding Desegregation from the Legal Services Program*, 84 Colum.L.Rev. 1630 (1984).]

"The California Court of Appeal also rejected petitioners' claim that Proposition I, if facially valid, was nonetheless unconstitutional because enacted with a discriminatory purpose. The court reasoned that the purposes of the Proposition were well stated in the Proposition itself. Voters may have been motivated by any of these purposes, chief among them the educational benefits of neighborhood schooling. [It] characterized petitioners' claim of discriminatory intent on the part of millions of voters as but 'pure speculation.' [Here, as in *Reitman v. Mulkey,*] involving the circumstances of passage and the potential impact of a Proposition adopted at a state-wide election, we see no reason to differ with the conclusions of the state appellate court."

BLACKMUN, J., joined by Brennan, J., although joining the Court's opinion, concurred "to address [the] critical distinctions between this case [and] *Seattle*": "State courts do not create the rights they enforce; those rights originate elsewhere—in the state legislature, in the State's political subdivisions, or in the state constitution itself. When one of those rights is repealed, and therefore is rendered unenforceable in the courts, that action hardly can be said to restructure the State's decisionmaking mechanism. While the California electorate may have made it more difficult to achieve desegregation when it enacted Proposition I, [it] did so not by working a structural change in the political *process* so much as by simply repealing the right to invoke a judicial busing remedy. Indeed, ruling for petitioners on a *Hunter* theory seemingly would mean that statutory affirmative action or antidiscrimination programs never could be repealed, for a repeal of the enactment would mean that enforcement authority previously lodged in the state courts was being removed by another political entity.

"In short, the people of California—the same 'entity' that put in place the state constitution, and created the enforceable obligation to desegregate—have made the desegregation obligation judicially unenforceable. The 'political process or the decisionmaking mechanism used to *address* racially conscious legislation' has not been 'singled out for peculiar and disadvantageous treatment,' *Seattle,* for those political mechanisms that create and repeal the rights ultimately enforced by the courts were left entirely unaffected by Proposition I."

MARSHALL, J., dissented: "I fail to see how a fundamental redefinition of the governmental decisionmaking structure with respect to the same racial issue can be unconstitutional when the state seeks to remove the authority from local school boards, yet constitutional when the state attempts to achieve the same result by limiting the power of its [courts]. Despite Proposition I's apparent neutrality, it is 'beyond reasonable dispute,' *Seattle,* and the majority today concedes, that 'court ordered busing in *excess* of that required by [equal protection] prompted the initiation and probably the adoption of Proposition I.' * * *

"Nor can there be any doubt that Proposition I works a substantial reallocation of state power. [After its adoption], the only method of enforcing against a recalcitrant school board the state constitutional duty to eliminate racial isolation is to petition either the state legislature or the electorate as a whole. Clearly, the rules of the game have been significantly changed for those attempting to vindicate this state constitutional right. [It] is equally clear [that] Proposition I is not a 'mere repeal.' [I]n *Seattle, Hunter,* and *Reitman,* the three times that this Court has explicitly rejected the argument that a proposed change constituted a 'mere repeal' of an existing policy, the alleged rescission was accomplished by a governmental entity other than the entity that had taken the initial action, and resulted in a drastic alteration of the substantive effect of existing policy. This case falls squarely within this latter category.

"* * * Proposition I, by denying full access to the only branch of government that has been willing to address this issue meaningfully, is far worse for those seeking to vindicate the plainly unpopular cause of racial integration in the public schools than a simple reallocation of an often unavailable and unresponsive legislative process.[h]"

SECTION 3. SPECIAL SCRUTINY FOR OTHER CLASSIFICATIONS

In view of the history and announced purposes of the equal protection clause (see *Slaughter-House Cases,* Sec. 1 supra and *Strauder,* Sec. 2, I supra), are there any classes other than racial and ethnic minorities against whom discrimination should be held "suspect"—or at least subject to judicial scrutiny greater than the "minimum rationality" requirement of the "traditional approach"? Consider Bickel, *The Original Understanding and the Segregation Decision,* 69 Harv.L. Rev. 1, 60 (1955): "[T]he fourteenth amendment, on its face, deals not only with racial discrimination * * *. This cannot have been accidental, since the alternative considered [did] apply only to racial discrimination. Everyone's immediate preoccupation in the 39th Congress [was], of course, with hardships being visited on the colored race. Yet the fact that the proposed constitutional amendment was couched in more general terms could not have escaped those who voted for it."

If there are other classifications that should be subject to special scrutiny, by what criteria should they be identified?

I. ALIENAGE

Up to the late 1940s, the Court found a "special public interest"[a] in rejecting almost all challenges to state discriminations against aliens respecting such activities as land ownership, *Terrace v. Thompson,* 263 U.S. 197, 44 S.Ct. 15, 68 L.Ed. 255 (1923); killing wild game, *Patsone v. Pennsylvania,* 232 U.S. 138, 34 S.Ct. 281, 58 L.Ed. 539 (1914); operating poolhalls, *Clarke v. Deckebach,* 274 U.S. 392, 47 S.Ct. 630, 71 L.Ed. 1115 (1927); and working on public construction projects, *Crane v. New York,* 239 U.S. 195, 36 S.Ct. 85, 60 L.Ed. 218 (1915).[b] But *Takahashi v. Fish & Game Com'n,* 334 U.S. 410, 68 S.Ct. 1138, 92 L.Ed. 1478 (1948), relying on both Congress' "broad constitutional powers in determining what aliens shall be admitted to the United States" and the fourteenth amendment's "general policy" of "equality," invalidated California's denial of licenses

h. See also Choper, *The Repeal of Remedies for De Facto School Segregation,* in Choper, Kamisar & Tribe, *The Supreme Court: Trends and Developments 1981–82* 44 (1983). "It seems to me that, if anything, it was harder for the people of California to achieve a busing remedy after Proposition I than it was for the people of Washington after Initiative 350. That is to say—and I believe our current history demonstrates the validity of this—the easiest place to get busing to remedy de facto school segregation, certainly in California, was in the courts. Proposition I removed the courts' ability to do that. It is true that the California school districts still had this power. But I think that people who want to get a busing remedy for de facto school segregation are probably better off in Washington, even though they must go to the legislature, than they are in California, where they must go to the Los Angeles Board of Education."

a. *Truax v. Raich,* 239 U.S. 33, 36 S.Ct. 7, 60 L.Ed. 131 (1915).

b. *Truax,* however, invalidated Arizona's forbidding employers of five or more persons from hiring over 20% aliens.

for commercial fishing in coastal waters to aliens lawfully residing in the state.[c] Finally, *Graham v. Richardson,* 403 U.S. 365, 91 S.Ct. 1848, 29 L.Ed.2d 534 (1971), reasoning that "aliens as a class are a prime example of a 'discrete and insular minority'" and ruling that "classifications based on alienage [are] inherently suspect and subject to close judicial scrutiny," held that state laws denying welfare benefits to aliens violate equal protection.

Section 53 of New York's Civil Service Law required citizenship as a condition of public employment for those positions subject to competitive examination. SUGARMAN v. DOUGALL, 413 U.S. 634, 93 S.Ct. 2842, 37 L.Ed.2d 853 (1973), per BLACKMUN, J., held that section 53 unconstitutionally discriminated against aliens: "It is established, of course that an alien is entitled to the shelter of the Equal Protection Clause. [In] *Graham v. Richardson* [403 U.S. 365, 91 S.Ct. 1848, 29 L.Ed.2d 534 (1971)], we observed that aliens as a class 'are a prime example of a "discrete and insular" minority (see *United States v. Carolene Products Co.* [fn. 4, p. 18 supra]),' [a] and that classifications based on alienage are 'subject to close judicial scrutiny.'

"Applying this standard to New York's purpose in confining civil servants in the competitive class to those persons who have no ties of citizenship elsewhere, § 53 does not withstand the necessary close scrutiny. We recognize a State's interest in establishing its own form of government, and in limiting participation in that government to those who are within 'the basic conception of a political community.' We recognize, too, the State's broad power to define its political community. But in seeking to achieve this substantial purpose, with discrimination against aliens, the means the State employs must be precisely drawn in light of the acknowledged purpose.

"Section 53 is neither narrowly confined nor precise in its application. Its imposed ineligibility may apply to the 'sanitation man, class B,' to the typist, and to the office worker, as well as to the person who directly participates in the formulation and execution of important state policy. The citizenship restriction sweeps indiscriminately. Viewing the entire constitutional and statutory framework in the light of the State's asserted interest, the great breadth of the requirement is even more evident. Sections 35 and 41 of the Civil Service Law, relating generally to persons holding elective and high appointive offices, contain no citizenship restrictions. Indeed, even § 53 permits an alien to hold a classified civil service position under certain circumstances. In view of the breadth and imprecision of § 53 in the context of the State's interest, we conclude that the statute does not withstand close judicial scrutiny. * * *

"While we rule that § 53 is unconstitutional, we do not hold that, on the basis of an individualized determination, an alien may not be refused, or discharged from, public employment, even on the basis of noncitizenship, if the

c. See also *Oyama v. California,* 332 U.S. 633, 68 S.Ct. 269, 92 L.Ed. 249 (1948) (statutory presumption—that land conveyed to citizen, but paid for by alien ineligible to own land, was held for the benefit of the alien—violates equal protection).

a. How significant should it be that legislation discriminates against a "discrete and insular" minority? How are such groups to be identified? See note 3(a) after *New Orleans v. Dukes,* Sec. 1 supra. Consider Goodman, *De Facto School Segregation: A Constitutional and Empirical Analysis,* 60 Cal.L.Rev. 275, 313 (1972): "[If] there are groups that have no voice or visibility [it] is by no means clear that the urban black is among them. Numerically, blacks approach a majority in many large cities and are an increasingly formidable voting bloc in most. Numbers aside, they speak with a voice ever more audible [through] civil rights organizations and ad hoc community [groups]. Seldom have their demands been totally ignored. See generally Ackerman, *Beyond Carolene Products,* 98 Harv.L.Rev. 713 (1985) (arguing that the discrete and insular character of groups is a poor proxy for their political power).

refusal to hire, or the discharge, rests on legitimate state interests that relate to qualifications for a particular position or to the characteristics of the employee. We hold only that a flat ban on the employment of aliens in positions that have little, if any, relation to a State's legitimate interest, cannot withstand scrutiny under the Fourteenth Amendment.

"Neither do we hold that a State may not, in an appropriately defined class of positions, require citizenship as a qualification for office. [Such] power inheres in the State by virtue of its obligation, already noted above, 'to preserve the basic conception of a political community.' And this power and responsibility of the State applies, not only to the qualifications of voters, but also to persons holding state elective or important nonelective executive, legislative, and judicial positions, for officers who participate directly in the formulation, execution, or review of broad public policy perform functions that go to the heart of representative government."[b]

REHNQUIST, J., dissenting in *Sugarman* and *Griffiths* stated: "The Court, by holding in these cases and in *Graham v. Richardson,* that a citizen-alien classification is 'suspect' in the eyes of our Constitution, fails to mention, let alone rationalize, the fact that the Constitution itself recognizes a basic difference between citizens and aliens. That distinction is constitutionally important in no less than 11 instances in a political document noted for its brevity.

"[Not] only do the numerous classifications on the basis of citizenship that are set forth in the Constitution curb against both the analysis used and the results reached by the Court in these cases; the very Amendment which the Court reads to prohibit classifications based on citizenship establishes the very distinction which the Court now condemns as 'suspect.'

"[In] constitutionally defining who is a citizen of the United States, Congress obviously thought it was doing something, and something important. Citizenship meant something, a status in and relationship with a society which is continuing and more basic than mere presence or residence. The language of that Amendment carefully distinguishes between 'persons' who, whether by birth or naturalization, had achieved a certain status, and 'persons' in general. That a 'citizen' was considered by Congress to be a rationally distinct subclass of all 'persons' is obvious from the language of the Amendment. * * *

"On the 'authority' of [footnote 4], which only four Members of the Court in *Carolene Products* joined, the Court in *Graham* merely stated that 'classifications based on alienage * * * are inherently suspect' because '[a]liens as a class are a prime example of a "discrete and insular" minority * * * for whom such heightened judicial solicitude is appropriate.'

"As Mr. Justice Frankfurter so aptly observed: 'A footnote hardly seems to be an appropriate way of announcing a new constitutional doctrine, and the *Carolene* footnote did not purport to announce any new doctrine * * *.' *Kovacs v. Cooper* [336 U.S. 77, 69 S.Ct. 448, 93 L.Ed.2d 513 (1949)]. * * * The mere recitation of the words 'insular and discrete minority' is hardly a *constitutional* reason for prohibiting state legislative classifications such as are involved here * * *.

b. The same day as *Sugarman, In re Griffiths,* 413 U.S. 717, 93 S.Ct. 2851, 37 L.Ed.2d 910 (1973), per Powell, J., invalidated Connecticut's attempt to totally exclude resident aliens from practicing law: "[T]he status of holding a license to practice law [does not] place one so close to the core of the political process as to make him a formulator of government policy." Burger, C.J., and Rehnquist, J., dissented in *Griffiths.*

"Our society, consisting of over 200 million individuals of multitudinous origins, customs, tongues, beliefs, and cultures is, to say the least, diverse. It would hardly take extraordinary ingenuity for a lawyer to find 'insular and discrete' minorities at every turn in the road. Yet, unless the Court can precisely define and constitutionally justify both the terms and analysis it uses, these decisions today stand for the proposition that the Court can choose a 'minority' it 'feels' deserves 'solicitude' and thereafter prohibit the States from classifying that 'minority' differently from the 'majority.' I cannot find, and the Court does not cite, any constitutional authority for such a 'ward of the Court' approach to equal protection."

AMBACH v. NORWICK

441 U.S. 68, 99 S.Ct. 1589, 60 L.Ed.2d 49 (1979).

JUSTICE POWELL delivered the opinion of the Court.

This case presents the question whether a State, consistently with the Equal Protection Clause, may refuse to employ as elementary and secondary school teachers aliens who are eligible for United States citizenship but who refuse to seek naturalization. * * *

[*Graham*] *v. Richardson* [for] the first time treated classifications based on alienage as "inherently suspect and subject to close judicial scrutiny." Applying *Graham,* this Court has held invalid statutes that prevented aliens from entering a State's classified civil service, *Sugarman v. Dougall,* practicing law, *In re Griffiths,* working as an engineer, *Examining Bd. v. de Otero,* 426 U.S. 572, 96 S.Ct. 2264, 49 L.Ed.2d 65 (1976), and receiving state educational benefits, *Nyquist v. Mauclet,* 432 U.S. 1, 97 S.Ct. 2120, 53 L.Ed.2d 63 (1977).[a] * * *

In *Sugarman,* we recognized that a State could, "in an appropriately defined class of positions, require citizenship as a qualification for office." We went on to observe: "Such power inheres in the State by virtue of its obligation ['to] preserve the basic conception of a political community.' [T]his power and responsibility of the State applies, not only to the qualifications of voters, but also to persons holding state elective or important nonelective executive, legislative, and judicial positions, for officers who participate directly in the formulation, execution, or review of broad public policy perform functions that go to the heart of representative government." The exclusion of aliens from such governmental positions would not invite as demanding scrutiny from this Court.

Applying the rational basis standard, we held last Term that New York could exclude aliens from the ranks of its police force. *Foley v. Connelie,* 435 U.S. 291, 98 S.Ct. 1067, 55 L.Ed.2d 287 (1978). Because the police function fulfilled "a most fundamental obligation of government to its constituency" and by necessity cloaked policemen with substantial discretionary powers, we viewed the police force as being one of those appropriately defined classes of positions for which a citizenship requirement could be imposed.[b] * * *

a. Burger, C.J., one of four dissenters in *Mauclet* (see note 1 infra), argued that "the prior cases upon which the Court purports to rely involved statutes which prohibited aliens from engaging in certain occupations or professions, thereby impairing their ability to earn a livelihood. [The] only other case striking down a classification on the basis of alienage, *Graham,* involved the denial of *welfare* benefits essential to sustain [life. In] my view, [w]here a fundamental personal interest is not at stake—and higher education is hardly that—the State must be free to exercise its largesse in any reasonable manner."

b. *Cabell v. Chavez-Salido,* 454 U.S. 432, 102 S.Ct. 735, 70 L.Ed.2d 677 (1982) extended *Folie* to probation officers. Marshall, J., joined by Brennan, Marshall, and Stevens, JJ., dissented in *Folie.* Blackmun, J., joined by

The rule for governmental functions, which is an exception to the general standard applicable to classifications based on alienage, rests on important principles inherent in the Constitution. The distinction between citizens and aliens, though ordinarily irrelevant to private activity, [denotes] an association with the polity which, in a democratic republic, exercises the powers of governance. The form of this association is important: an oath of allegiance or similar ceremony cannot substitute for the unequivocal legal bond citizenship represents. It is because of this special significance of citizenship that governmental entities, when exercising the functions of government, have wider latitude in limiting the participation of noncitizens.

In determining whether, for purposes of equal protection analysis, teaching in public schools constitutes a governmental function, we look to the role of public education and to the degree of responsibility and discretion teachers possess in fulfilling that role. Each of these considerations supports the conclusion that public school teachers may be regarded as performing a task "that go[es] to the heart of representative government." [6]

Public education, like the police function, "fulfills a most fundamental obligation of government to its constituency." *Foley*. The importance of public schools in the preparation of individuals for participation as citizens, and in the preservation of the values on which our society rests, long has been recognized by our decisions [*Brown I*].[8] [In] shaping the students' experience to achieve educational goals, teachers by necessity have wide discretion over the way the course material is communicated to students. [Further], a teacher serves as a role model for his students, exerting a subtle but important influence over their perceptions and values. Thus, [a] teacher has an opportunity to influence the attitudes of students toward government, the political process, and a citizen's social responsibilities. This influence is crucial to the continued good health of a democracy. * * *

As the legitimacy of the State's interest in furthering the educational goals outlined above is undoubted, it remains only to consider whether [the statute] bears a rational relationship to this interest. The restriction is carefully framed to serve its purpose, as it bars from teaching only those aliens who have demonstrated their unwillingness to obtain United States citizenship. Appellees [in] effect have chosen to classify themselves. They prefer to retain citizenship

Brennan, Marshall, and Stevens, JJ., dissented in Cabell.

6. [Rather] than consider whether public school teachers perform a significant government function, [the] dissent focuses instead on the general societal importance of primary and secondary school teachers both public and private. Thus the dissent on the one hand depreciates the importance of New York's citizenship requirement because it is not applied to private school teachers, and on the other hand argues that the role teachers perform in our society is no more significant than that filled by attorneys. This misses the point of *Foley* and *Sugarman*. New York's citizenship requirement is limited to a governmental function because it applies only to teachers employed by and acting as agents of the State. The Connecticut statute held unconstitutional in *Griffiths*, by contrast, applied to all attorneys, most of whom do not work for the government. The exclusion of aliens from access to the bar implicated the right to pursue a chosen occupation, not access to public employment. * * *

8. The curricular requirements of New York's public school system reflect some of the ways a public school system promotes the development of the understanding that is prerequisite to intelligent participation in the democratic process. [R]equired courses include classes in civics, United States and New York history, and principles of American government.

Although private schools also are bound by most of these requirements, the State has a stronger interest in ensuring that the schools it most directly controls, and for which it bears the cost, are as effective as possible in teaching these courses.

in a foreign country with the obligations it entails of primary duty and loyalty.[14] [New York has] made a judgment that citizenship should be a qualification for teaching the young of the State in the public schools, and [the statute] furthers that judgment.

Reversed.

JUSTICE BLACKMUN, with whom JUSTICE BRENNAN, JUSTICE MARSHALL, and JUSTICE STEVENS, join, dissenting.

[T]he New York classification is irrational. Is it better to employ a poor citizen-teacher than an excellent resident alien teacher? Is it preferable to have a citizen who has never seen Spain or a Latin American country teach Spanish to eighth graders and to deny that opportunity to a resident alien who may have lived for 20 years in the culture of Spain or Latin America? The State will know how to select its teachers responsibly, wholly apart from citizenship, and can do so selectively and intelligently. * * *

[Further], it is logically impossible to differentiate between this case [and *Griffiths*]. One may speak proudly of the role model of the teacher, of his ability to mold young minds, of his inculcating force as to national ideals, and of his profound influence in the impartation of our society's values. Are the attributes of an attorney any the less? He represents us in our critical courtroom controversies even when citizenship and loyalty may be questioned. He stands as an officer of every court in which he practices. He is responsible for strict adherence to the announced and implied standards of professional conduct, to the requirements of evolving ethical codes, and for honesty and integrity in his professional and personal life. [He] is an influence in legislation, in the community, and in the role model figure that the professional person enjoys. * * *

Notes and Questions

1. BERNAL v. FAINTER, 467 U.S. 216, 104 S.Ct. 2312, 81 L.Ed.2d 175 (1984), per MARSHALL, J., held that Texas could not constitutionally preclude an alien from becoming a notary public: "We emphasize here as we have in the past that the political-function exception must be narrowly construed; otherwise the exception will swallow the rule and deprecate the significance that should attach to the designation of the group as a 'discrete and insular' minority for whom heightened judicial solicitude is appropriate."[c] Was the exception narrowly construed in *Ambach? Foley? Cabell?*

2. *"Political function" exception.* Is the Court's principle—that distinguishes excluding aliens from "the process of self-government" and discriminating against aliens generally—persuasive? Is the Court's application of this principle in the cases persuasive? Consider Note, *A Dual Standard for State Discrimination Against Aliens,* 92 Harv.L.Rev. 1516, 1531–33 (1979): "Some dual standard [appears] fundamentally consistent with general equal protection doctrine interpreted in light of distinctions the Constitution makes on the basis of

14. As our cases have emphasized, resident aliens pay taxes, serve in the armed forces, and have made significant contributions to our country in private and public endeavors. No doubt [many] would make excellent public school teachers. But the legislature, having in mind the importance of education to state and local governments, may determine eligibility for the key position in discharging that function on the assumption that *generally* persons [who] have not declined the opportunity to seek United States citizenship, are better qualified than are those who have elected to remain aliens. * * *

c. Rehnquist, J., dissented.

citizenship. [But despite *Foley's*] attempt to draw an analogy to exclusion of aliens from voting and holding high office, the existence of those exclusions only underscores the need for close review of other measures disadvantaging aliens. [Since] aliens are politically powerless because of their disenfranchisement and disqualification from high office, [the] political decision to bar aliens from the police should be stringently scrutinized." Compare Rosberg, *Aliens and Equal Protection: Why Not the Right to Vote?* 75 Mich.L.Rev. 1092, 1106 (1977): "[E]xcluding [aliens] from the political process clearly requires the strictest review of all, for it is the very fact of exclusion that made the classification suspect and necessitated strict scrutiny in the first place. Put another way, the invalidation of a statute that excludes the members of a suspect class from participation in the political process is itself a way of eliminating [the] need for strict scrutiny. [Over] time the members of the class will develop the ability to protect their own interests in the legislative process, and the need for extraordinary judicial protection will then disappear."

3. *The role of the supremacy clause. Graham* also held that "an additional reason why the state statutes [in] these cases do not withstand constitutional scrutiny emerges from the area of federal-state relations. [State] laws that restrict the eligibility of aliens for [welfare] conflict [with] overriding national policies in an area constitutionally entrusted to the Federal Government. [In] *Takahashi* it was said that the States 'can neither add to nor take from the conditions lawfully imposed by Congress upon admission, naturalization and residence of aliens in the United States or the several states.' "

TOLL v. MORENO, 458 U.S. 1, 102 S.Ct. 2977, 73 L.Ed.2d 563 (1982), per BRENNAN, J., held that a University of Maryland rule—flatly denying "in-state" tuition to nonimmigrant aliens with G–4 visas (issued to employees of certain international organizations and their immediate families)—violates the supremacy clause. The Court observed that "commentators have noted [that] many of the Court's decisions concerning alienage classifications, such as *Takahashi,* are better explained in preemption than equal protection terms. See, e.g., Perry, *Modern Equal Protection: A Conceptualization and Appraisal,* 79 Colum.L.Rev. 1023, 1060–65 (1979). [Read] together, *Takahashi* and *Graham* stand for the broad principle [17] that 'state regulation not congressionally sanctioned that discriminates against aliens lawfully admitted to the country is impermissible if it imposes additional burdens not contemplated by Congress.' To be sure, when Congress has done nothing more than permit a class of aliens to enter the country temporarily, the proper application of the principle is likely to be a matter of some dispute. But [in] light of Congress' explicit decision not to bar G–4 aliens from acquiring domicile, [the Maryland rule] surely amounts to an ancillary 'burden not contemplated by Congress.' [Further, as] a result of an array of treaties, international agreements, and federal statutes, G–4 visa holders employed by [various international organizations] are relieved of federal, and in many instances, state and local taxes, on the salaries paid by the organizations. [The Maryland rule] frustrates these federal policies." [d]

17. Our cases do recognize, however, that a State, in the course of defining its political community, may, in appropriate circumstances, limit the participation of noncitizens in the States' political and governmental functions. See, e.g., *Cabell; Ambach; Foley; Sugarman.*

d. Blackmun, J., who joined the Court's opinion, concurred, vehemently denying the suggestion in Rehnquist, J.'s dissent that "decisions holding resident aliens to be a 'suspect class' no longer are good law."

REHNQUIST, J., joined by Burger, C.J., dissented: "[T]hat a state statute can be said to discriminate against aliens does not, standing alone, demonstrate that the statute is preempted. [A] state law is invalid only if there is 'such actual conflict between the two schemes of regulation that both cannot stand in the same area,' or if Congress has in some other way unambiguously declared its intention to foreclose the state law in question. [The] Court offers no evidence that Congress' intent in permitting respondents to establish 'domicile in the United States' has any bearing at all on the tuition available to them at state universities." As for tax relief, "First, the Federal Government has not barred the States from collecting taxes from many, if not most, G–4 visa holders. Second, as to those G–4 nonimmigrants who *are* immune from state income taxes by treaty, Maryland's tuition policy cannot fairly be said to conflict with those treaties in a manner requiring its preemption." [e]

4. *Federal discrimination.* (a) It has long been held that the national government has power "to exclude aliens altogether from the United States, or to prescribe the terms and conditions upon which they may come to this country." *Sing v. United States,* 158 U.S. 538, 15 S.Ct. 967, 39 L.Ed. 1082 (1895). Thus, MATHEWS v. DIAZ, 426 U.S. 67, 96 S.Ct. 1883, 48 L.Ed.2d 478 (1976), per STEVENS, J., upheld a federal statute denying Medicare benefits to aliens unless they have (1) been admitted for permanent residence and (2) resided for at least five years in the United States: Although "aliens and citizens alike, are protected by the Due Process Clause, [i]n the exercise of its broad power over naturalization and immigration, Congress regularly makes rules that would be unacceptable if applied to citizens.

"[T]he responsibility for regulating the relationship between the United States and [aliens] has been committed to the political branches of the Federal Government. Since decisions in these matters may implicate our relations with foreign powers, and since a wide variety of classifications must be defined in the light of changing political and economic circumstances, such decisions are frequently of a character more appropriate to either the Legislature or the Executive than to the Judiciary. [The] reasons that preclude judicial review of political questions also dictate a narrow standard of review of decisions made by the Congress or the President in the area of immigration and naturalization.

"Since it is obvious that Congress has no constitutional duty to provide *all aliens* with the welfare benefits provided to citizens, the party challenging the constitutionality of the particular line Congress has drawn"—"allowing benefits to some aliens but not to others"—"has the burden of advancing principled reasoning that will at once invalidate that line and yet tolerate a different line separating some aliens from others. [Since neither of the two requirements] is wholly irrational, this case essentially involves nothing more than a claim that it would have been more reasonable for Congress to select somewhat different requirements of the same kind. [But] it remains true that some line is essential, that any line must produce some harsh and apparently arbitrary consequences,

e. O'Connor, J., concurred in part and dissented in part: "I conclude that the Supremacy Clause does not prohibit the University from charging out-of-state tuition to those G–4 aliens who are exempted by federal law from federal taxes only." See Choper, *Discrimination Against Aliens,* in Choper, Kamisar & Tribe, *The Supreme Court: Trends and Developments 1981–82* 14–21 (1983) for the view that (1) *Toll*'s use of the supremacy clause was a "salutory development," but that (2) "the Court's major difficulty resulted from its going beyond its 'broad principle' and getting into the gory details of whether the Maryland regulation actually came into some direct conflict with congressional policy"; "Rehnquist, J.'s argument was fairly strong once you accept *his* premise" of what is required for preemption.

and, of greatest importance, that those who qualify under the test Congress has chosen may reasonably be presumed to have a greater affinity to the United States than those who do not."

Consider Rosberg, *The Protection of Aliens From Discriminatory Treatment By the National Government,* 1977 Sup.Ct.Rev. 275, 336–38: "[*Diaz*] refused to acknowledge the tension between two basic facts: first, the reasons for treating alienage as a suspect classification apply as forcefully to the federal government as to the states, and second, the power to determine the standards for admission of aliens must inevitably give rise to some power to regulate what aliens can and cannot do in this country. [A] condition subsequent on entry is very different from a condition precedent precisely because its impact is felt by residents of the United States, to whom the government has an obligation of fair dealing [in] compliance with the standards of the Constitution. [The Court's] repeated insistence that Congress has plenary power to act against aliens in any way it wants must be seen as an invitation to Congress to act capriciously and without significant concern for the legitimate interests of resident aliens."

(b) HAMPTON v. WONG, 426 U.S. 88, 96 S.Ct. 1895, 48 L.Ed.2d 495 (1976), per STEVENS, J., held that a federal Civil Service Commission regulation, generally barring resident aliens from civil service employment, denied "liberty without due process of law": "[T]he federal power over aliens is [not] so plenary that any agent of the National Government may arbitrarily subject all resident aliens to different substantive rules than those applied to citizens. * * *

"The rule [has] its impact on an identifiable class of persons who [are] already subject to disadvantages not shared by the remainder of the community. [The] added disadvantage resulting [from] ineligibility for employment in a major sector of the economy [is] of sufficient significance to be characterized as a deprivation of an interest in liberty. [It] follows that some judicial scrutiny of the deprivation is mandated by the Constitution. * * *

"When the Federal Government asserts an overriding national interest as justification for a discriminatory rule which would violate the Equal Protection Clause if adopted by a State, due process requires that there be a legitimate basis for presuming that the rule was actually intended to serve that interest.[f] If the agency which promulgates the rule has direct responsibility for fostering or protecting that interest, it may reasonably be presumed that the asserted interest was the actual predicate for the rule. [Or], if the rule were expressly mandated by the Congress or the President, we might presume that any interest which might rationally be served by the rule did in fact give rise to its adoption.

"[We] may assume [that] if the Congress or the President had expressly imposed the citizenship requirement, it would be justified by the national interest in providing an incentive for aliens to become naturalized, or possibly even as providing the President with an expendable token for treaty negotiating purposes; but we are not willing to presume that the Chairman of [CSC] was deliberately fostering an interest so far removed from his normal responsibilities."

The Court reviewed the history of the regulation dating to 1884, concluding that it "cannot fairly be construed to evidence either congressional [or presidential] approval or disapproval of the [rule].[46] [Thus,] our inquiry is whether the

f. See fn. a, p. 931 supra.

46. Even if this conclusion were doubtful, in view of the consequences of the rule it would be appropriate to require a much more explicit directive from either Congress or the President * * *.

national interests which the Government identifies as justifications for the Commission rule are interests on which that agency may properly rely in making a decision implicating the constitutional and social values at stake in this litigation. * * *

"The only concern of [the] Commission is the promotion of an efficient federal service. In general it is fair to assume that its goal would be best served by removing unnecessary restrictions on the eligibility of qualified applicants for employment. With only one exception, the interests [put] forth as supporting the Commission regulation at issue in this case are not matters which are properly the business of the Commission. That one exception is the administrative desirability of having one simple rule excluding all noncitizens when it is manifest that citizenship is an appropriate and legitimate requirement for some important and sensitive positions. Arguably, therefore, administrative convenience may provide a rational basis for the general rule.

"[But there] is nothing [to] indicate that the Commission actually made any considered evaluation of the relative desirability of a simple exclusionary rule on the one hand, or the value to the service of enlarging the pool of eligible employees on the other. [Of] greater significance, however, is the quality of the interest at stake. Any fair balancing of the public interest in avoiding the wholesale deprivation of employment opportunities caused by the Commission's indiscriminate policy, as opposed to what may be nothing more than a hypothetical justification, requires rejection of the argument of administrative convenience in this case." [g]

REHNQUIST, J., joined by Burger, C.J., and White and Blackmun, JJ., dissented: "The Court's opinion enunciates a novel conception of the procedural due process guaranteed by the Fifth Amendment, and from this concept proceeds to evolve a doctrine of delegation of legislative authority which seems to me to be quite contrary to the doctrine established by a long [line of] decisions. * * *

"[T]he exclusive power of Congress to prescribe the terms and conditions of entry includes the power to regulate aliens in various ways once they are here. [This] broad congressional power is in some respects subject to procedural limitations imposed by the Due Process Clause of the Fifth Amendment. If an alien * * * lawfully obtains tenured government employment, and is thereby protected against discharge except for cause, he is entitled to a hearing before being discharged. *Arnett v. Kennedy.* But neither an alien nor a citizen has any protected liberty interests in obtaining federal employment.

"[U]nder the traditional standards governing the delegation of authority the CSC was fully empowered to act in the manner in which it did in this case. [Once] it is determined that [CSC] was properly delegated the power by Congress to make decisions regarding citizenship of prospective civil servants, then the reasons for which that power was exercised are as foreclosed from judicial scrutiny as if Congress had made the decision itself. The fact that Congress has delegated a power does not provide a back door through which to attack a policy which would otherwise have been immune from attack."

g. Brennan, J., joined by Marshall, J., joined the Court's opinion "understanding that there are reserved the equal protection questions that would be raised by congressional or Presidential enactment of a bar on employment of aliens by the Federal Government."

President Ford subsequently issued such an executive order. Valid? See *Vergara v. Hampton,* 581 F.2d 1281 (7th Cir.1978), cert. denied, 441 U.S. 905, 99 S.Ct. 1993, 60 L.Ed.2d 373 (1979); *Jalil v. Campbell,* 590 F.2d 1120 (D.C.Cir.1978).

II. GENDER

A. CLAIMS BY WOMEN

Prior to 1971, the Court used the deferential "traditional approach" (see Sec. 1 supra) for classifications based on gender. The earliest case, *Bradwell v. Illinois,* 83 U.S. 130, 21 L.Ed. 442 (1873), upheld a law denying women the right to practice law—Bradley, J., concurring with Swayne and Field, JJ., explained that "the natural and proper timidity and delicacy which belongs to the female sex evidently unfits it for many of the occupations of civil life. [The] paramount destiny and mission of woman are to fulfill the noble and benign offices of wife and mother. This is the law of the Creator." *Muller v. Oregon,* 208 U.S. 412, 28 S.Ct. 324, 52 L.Ed. 551 (1908), per Brewer, J., upheld a law barring factory work by women for more than ten hours a day, reasoning that "as healthy mothers are essential to vigorous offspring, the physical well-being of a woman becomes an object of public interest and care." [a] *Goesaert v. Cleary,* 335 U.S. 464, 69 S.Ct. 198, 93 L.Ed. 163 (1948), per Frankfurter, J., upheld a law denying bartender's licenses to most women, reasoning that "the fact that women may now have achieved the virtues that men have long claimed as their prerogatives and now indulge in vices that men have long practiced, does not preclude the States from drawing a sharp line between the sexes, certainly in such matters as the regulation of the liquor traffic." Finally, *Hoyt v. Florida,* 368 U.S. 57, 82 S.Ct. 159, 7 L.Ed.2d 118 (1961), per Harlan, J., sustained a law placing women on the jury list only if they made special request, stating that "woman is still regarded as the center of home and family life." [b]

The first decision holding sex discrimination violative of equal protection, REED v. REED, 404 U.S. 71, 92 S.Ct. 251, 30 L.Ed.2d 225 (1971), per BURGER, C.J., involved a law preferring males to females when two persons were otherwise equally entitled to be the administrator of an estate: "A classification 'must be reasonable, not arbitrary, and must rest upon some ground of difference having a fair and substantial relation to the object of the [law].' *Royster Guano,* [Sec. 1 supra]. The question" is whether the classification "bears a rational relationship to a state objective that is sought to be advanced by the [law]." It was contended that the law had the reasonable "objective of reducing the workload on probate courts by eliminating one class of contests" and that the legislature might reasonably have "concluded that in general men are better qualified to act as an administrator than are women." But "to give a mandatory preference to members of either sex over members of the other, merely to accomplish the elimination of hearings on the merits, is to make the very kind of arbitrary legislative choice forbidden by [equal protection]." [c]

---

a. But see *Adkins v. Children's Hospital,* 261 U.S. 525, 43 S.Ct. 394, 67 L.Ed. 785 (1923) (minimum wages for women violates due process), overruled, *West Coast Hotel Co. v. Parrish.*

b. *Hoyt* was effectively overruled in *Taylor v. Louisiana,* 419 U.S. 522, 95 S.Ct. 692, 42 L.Ed.2d 690 (1975), holding that a similar statute, operating largely to exclude women from jury service, deprived a criminal defendant of the sixth and fourteenth amendment right to an impartial jury drawn from a fair cross section of the community: "It is untenable to suggest these days that it would be a special hardship for each and every woman to perform jury service or that society cannot spare *any* women from their present duties."

c. Consider MacKinnon, *Sexual Harassment of Working Women* 108 (1979): "It would have been considerably more rational, factually based, not arbitrary, and substantially related to the statutory purpose to presume that

This was followed by FRONTIERO v. RICHARDSON, 411 U.S. 677, 93 S.Ct. 1764, 36 L.Ed.2d 583 (1973), which held violative of equal protection a federal statute permitting males in the armed services an automatic dependency allowance for their wives but requiring servicewomen to prove that their husbands were dependent. BRENNAN, J., joined by Douglas, White and Marshall, JJ., argued that "classifications based upon sex [are] inherently suspect and must therefore be subjected to close judicial scrutiny," finding "at least implicit support for such an approach in [*Reed's*] departure from 'traditional' rational basis analysis": "[O]ur Nation has had a long and unfortunate history of sex discrimination. Traditionally, such discrimination was rationalized by an attitude of 'romantic paternalism' which, in practical effect, put women not on a pedestal, but in a cage. * * *

"As a result of notions such as these, [statutes] became laden with gross, stereotypical distinctions between the sexes and, indeed, throughout much of the 19th century the position of women in our society was, in many respects, comparable to that of blacks under the pre-Civil War slave codes. Neither slaves nor women could hold office, serve on juries, or bring suit in their own names, and married women traditionally were denied the legal capacity to hold or convey property or to serve as legal guardians of their own children.[d] And although blacks were guaranteed the right to vote in 1870, women were denied even [that] until adoption of the Nineteenth Amendment half a century later.

"It is true, of course, that the position of women in America has improved markedly in recent decades. [But] in part because of the high visibility of the sex characteristic, women still face pervasive, although at times more subtle, discrimination in our educational institutions, on the job market and, perhaps most conspicuously, in the political arena.[17]

men would be the better administrators if most women were illiterate and wholly excluded from business affairs. Yet this reasoning would reveal a society in severe need of severe prohibitions on sex discrimination."

d. See Note, *Sex Discrimination and Equal Protection: Do We Need a Constitutional Amendment?* 84 Harv.L.Rev. 1499, 1507 (1971): "Arguments justifying different treatment for the sexes on the grounds of female inferiority, need for male protection, and happiness in their assigned roles bear a striking resemblance to the half-truths surrounding the myth of the 'happy slave.'" For discussion of the dissimilarities between race and gender for these purposes, see Wasserstrom, *Racism, Sexism, and Preferential Treatment: An Approach to the Topics,* 24 U.C.L.A.L.Rev. 581 (1977); Rutherglen, *Sexual Equality in Fringe-Benefit Plans,* 65 Va.L.Rev. 199, 205–12 (1979).

17. It is true [that] when viewed in the abstract, women do not constitute a small and powerless minority. Nevertheless, in part because of past discrimination, women are vastly underrepresented in this Nation's decision-making councils. * * *

[See also Note, 84 Harv.L.Rev. at 1505 n. 48: "Political power is a difficult concept [to] define. Furthermore, many [women] are not aware of or do not care about the inequalities based on sex in the legal structure. Others may have decided that, on balance, they are benefited rather than burdened by current laws distinguishing the sexes, and thus they may oppose the principle that no such distinctions should be allowed. These considerations weaken the argument that women can protect their interests through their political power, however defined. Even if women could use their political power to protect their interests, but do not choose to do so, the minority who feel they are discriminated against still should have a right to constitutional protection."

[Compare Ely, *Democracy and Distrust* 166–69 (1980): "[I]n assessing suspiciousness it cannot be enough simply to note that a group does not function as a political bloc. [We must] see if there are systemic bars [to] access. On that score it seems important that today discussion about the appropriate 'place' of women is common among both women and men, and between the sexes as well. The very stereotypes that gave rise to laws 'protecting' women by barring them from various activities are under daily and publicized attack, and are the subject of equally spirited defense. [Given] such open discussion [the] claim that the numerical majority is being 'dominated' [is] one it has become impossible to maintain except at the most inflated rhetorical level. It also renders the broader argument self-contradictory, since to make such a claim in the

"Moreover, since sex, like race and national origin, is an immutable characteristic [the] imposition of special disabilities [would] seem to violate 'the basic concept of our system that legal burdens should bear some relationship to individual responsibility.' And what differentiates sex from such non-suspect statuses as intelligence or physical disability [is] that the sex characteristic frequently bears no relation to ability to perform or contribute to society. As a result, statutory distinctions between the sexes often have the effect of invidiously relegating the entire class of females to inferior legal status without regard to the actual capabilities of its individual members.

"[The] Government [maintains] that, as an empirical matter, wives in our society frequently are dependent upon their husbands, while husbands rarely are dependent upon their wives. Thus, the Government argues that Congress might reasonably have concluded that it would be both cheaper and easier simply conclusively to presume that wives of male members are financially dependent upon their husbands, while burdening female members with the task of establishing dependency in fact.

"The Government offers no concrete evidence, however, tending to support its view that such differential treatment in fact saves the Government any money. [And any] statutory scheme which draws a sharp line between the sexes, *solely* [for] administrative convenience [violates equal protection]."

POWELL, J., joined by Burger, C.J., and Blackmun, J., concurring, would rely "on the authority of *Reed* and reserve for the future any expansion of its rationale" because of the "Equal Rights Amendment, which if adopted will resolve [the] question." Stewart, J., concurred, "agreeing that the [statutes] work an invidious discrimination [*Reed.*]" Rehnquist, J., dissented.[e]

Notes and Questions

1. *Other discrimination against women.* May women prison guards be excluded from duty in "contact positions" in all-male prisons? See DOTHARD v. RAWLINSON, 433 U.S. 321, 97 S.Ct. 2720, 53 L.Ed.2d 786 (1977), per STEWART, J., upheld the exclusion: "In this environment of violence and disorganization, it would be an oversimplification to characterize [the exclusion of women] as an exercise in 'romantic paternalism.' [A] woman's relative ability to maintain order in a male, maximum-security, unclassified penitentiary [could be directly

context of the current debate one must at least implicitly grant the validity of the stereotype, that women are in effect mental infants who will believe anything men tell them to believe. [But] most laws classifying by sex [probably pre-date woman suffrage]: they should be invalidated. [To] put on the group affected the burden of using its recently unblocked access to get the offending laws repealed would be to place in their path an additional hurdle that the rest of us do not have to contend with in order to protect ourselves—hardly an appropriate response to the realization that they have been unfairly blocked in the past. In fact I may be wrong in supposing that because women now are in a position to protect themselves they will, that we are thus unlikely to see in the future the sort of official gender discrimination that has marked our past. But if women don't protect themselves from sex discrimination in the future, it [will be] because for one reason or another—substantive disagreement or more likely the assignment of a low priority to the issue—they don't choose to." But see Becker, *Politics, Differences and Economic Rights*, 1989 U.Chi.L.Forum 169, 180–90.]

e. See also *Stanton v. Stanton,* 421 U.S. 7, 95 S.Ct. 1373, 43 L.Ed.2d 688 (1975), per Blackmun, J., relying on *Reed,* holding that a statute requiring child support for males to age 21 but for females only to age 18 violated equal protection: To distinguish "the boy in order to assure him parental support while he attains his education and training, [is] to be self-serving: if the female is not to be supported so long as the male, she hardly can be expected to attend school as long as he does, and bringing her education to an end earlier coincides with the role-typing society has long imposed." Rehnquist, J., dissented on procedural grounds.

reduced by her womanhood. There is as basis in fact for expecting that sex offenders who have criminally assaulted women in the past would be moved to do so again if access to women were established within the prison. There would also be a real risk that other inmates, deprived of a normal heterosexual environment, would assault women guards because they were women."[f] In "high-rape" areas, may female students be subjected to an earlier curfew than males?[g]

2. *Sex-specific traits.* GEDULDIG v. AIELLO, 417 U.S. 484, 94 S.Ct. 2485, 41 L.Ed.2d 256 (1974), per STEWART, J., held that exclusion of "disability that accompanies normal pregnancy and childbirth" from California's disability insurance system "does not exclude [anyone] because of gender * * *. While it is true that only women can become pregnant, it does not follow that every legislative classification concerning pregnancy is [sex-based]. Absent a showing that distinctions involving pregnancy are mere pretexts designed to effect an invidious discrimination against the members of one sex or the other, lawmakers are constitutionally free to include or exclude pregnancy from the coverage of legislation such as this on any reasonable basis, just as with respect to any other physical condition. [The] program divides potential recipients into two groups—pregnant women and nonpregnant persons. While the first group is exclusively female, the second includes members of both sexes. The fiscal and actuarial benefits of the program thus accrue to members of both sexes.[h] [There] is no risk from which men are protected and women are not. Likewise, there is no risk from which women are protected and men are not.[21]"[i]

f. For criticism, see Littleton, *Equality and Feminist Legal Theory,* 48 U.Pitt.L.Rev. 1043, 1049–50 (1987). See also Tribe, *Constitutional Choices* 241 (1985): "That 'the sexes are not similarly situated' in such cases as *Michael M,* [p. 1075 infra] and *Dothard* would not to anyone less mesmerized by the ideal of law as a mirror of nature, be thought to *justify* a gender discrimination as noninvidious; it would instead raise the question whether such discrimination formed part of the law's systemic support for male supremacy."

g. May women employees, because women live longer, be required to make larger contributions than men to the state pension fund? See *Los Angeles, Dept. of Water & Power v. Manhart,* 435 U.S. 702, 98 S.Ct. 1370, 55 L.Ed. 2d 657 (1978) (violation of Title VII). May only women be required to wear tops while swimming? May a married woman be required to use her husband's surname to obtain a driver's license? See Comment, 38 Ohio St. L.J. 157 (1977). May a woman be required to designate her marital status to register to vote? See Karst, *"A Discrimination So Trivial": A Note on Law and the Symbolism of Women's Dependency,* 35 Ohio St.L.J. 546 (1974).

h. Query: Consider the following description of a law that forbids blacks from unaccredited law schools from becoming lawyers: "The law divides all persons who wish to become lawyers into two groups—blacks from unaccredited schools and all others. While the first group is exclusively black, the second includes members of both races."

What result under *Geduldig* if the disability program excluded only sickle-cell anemia?

How does the rule of *Washington v. Davis* bear on these questions?

21. Indeed, the [data indicated] that both the annual claim rate and the annual claim cost are greater for women than for [men.]

i. *General Electric Co. v. Gilbert,* 429 U.S. 125, 97 S.Ct. 401, 50 L.Ed.2d 343 (1976), held that Title VII's prohibition of sex discrimination did not prevent companies from excluding pregnancy from their disability plans. In response, Congress enacted the Pregnancy Discrimination Act, 42 U.S.C.A. § 2000e(k) (1978), which defined sex discrimination to include pregnancy discrimination. Some states have given maternity leave rights that go beyond that afforded to non-pregnant employees who are unable to work. Is this sex discrimination? See *California Federal Savings & Loan Ass'n v. Guerra,* 479 U.S. 272, 107 S.Ct. 683, 93 L.Ed.2d 613 (1987) (protection for physical disabilities associated with pregnancy with no similar protection for disabilities unrelated to pregnancy is consistent with antidiscrimination policy). Does a doctrine that ignores the biological differences between men and women regarding abortion, reproduction, and creation of another human being mean that "women can claim equality only insofar as they are like men"? Law, *Rethinking Sex and the Constitution,* 132 U.Pa.L.Rev. 955, 1007 (1984). See also Finley, *Transcending Equality Theory: A Way Out of the Maternity and the Workplace Debate,* 86 Colum.L.Rev.

BRENNAN, J., joined by Douglas and Marshall, JJ., dissented, finding "sex discrimination" in the state's "singling out for less favorable treatment a gender-linked disability peculiar to women [while] men receive full compensation for all disabilities suffered, including those that affect only or primarily their sex, such as prostatectomies, circumcision, hemophilia and gout." [j]

3. Consider Rhode, *Gender and Justice* 2–3 (1989): "The law's conventional approach to gender issues has focused on gender difference. American equal-protection doctrine has drawn heavily on Aristotelian traditions, which define equality as similar treatment for those similarly situated. Within this framework, sex-based discrimination remains justifiable if the sexes are different in some sense that is related to valid regulatory objectives. For example, women's distinctive reproductive capacities have served to validate a wide array of restrictions in employment, family, and educational settings. However, this difference-oriented approach has proved inadequate in both theory and practice. As a theoretical matter, it tends toward tautology. It permits different treatment for those who differ with respect to legitimate purposes but provides no standards for determining what differences are relevant and what counts as legitimate. As a practical matter, this approach has both over- and undervalued gender differences. In some instances, biology has determined destiny, while in other contexts, women's particular needs have gone unacknowledged or unaddressed. Too often courts have treated gender as a matter of immutable difference rather than as a cultural construct open to legal challenge and social change. Reliance on 'real difference' has deflected attention from the process by which differences have been attributed and from the groups that are under-represented in that process. Such an approach has often done more to reflect sex-based inequalities than to challenge them." [k] See generally MacKinnon,

1118 (1986); Littleton, *Reconstructing Sexual Equality*, 75 Calif.L.Rev. 1279, 1297–1300 (1987); Kay, *Models of Equality*, 1985 U.Ill.L. Rev. 39; Kay, *Equality and Difference: The Case of Pregnancy*, 1 Berkeley Women's L.J. 1 (1985). Is an approach based upon "special treatment" for women a "double-edged sword"? Williams, *The Equality Crisis: Some Reflections on Culture, Courts and Feminism*, 7 Women's Rts.L.Rptr. 175, 196 (1982) ("if we can't have it both ways, we need to think carefully about which way we want to have it"). Williams, *Notes From A First Generation*, 1989 U.Chi.L.Forum 99; Williams, *Equalities Riddle: Pregnancy and the Equal Treatment/Special Treatment Debate*, 13 N.Y.U.L.Rev.L. & Soc.Change 325, 351–80 (1985). Does the phrase "special treatment" presuppose a male perspective?

Consider Bartlett, *Feminist Legal Methods*, 103 Harv.L.Rev. 829, 842 (1990): "Although feminists have split over whether women have more to lose than to gain from singling out pregnancy for different, some would say 'favored,' treatment, they agree on the critical question: what are the consequences for women of specific rules or practices."

j. Is it sex discrimination to give a prison sentence to a man but probation to a woman (because she is pregnant) for the identical offense?

For invalidation of a disability for pregnant women, on constitutional grounds other than equal protection, see *Cleveland State Bd. of Educ. v. La Fleur*, Sec. 5 infra.

k. See also Karst, *Woman's Constitution*, 1984 Duke L.J. 447, 449: "Any search for the 'true' nature of women will be hindered by the imprint of the stereotype of woman on the mind of the person who is searching, whether that person be male or female. The prevailing construct of woman is larely a male product, for it is men who have held the power to define roles and institutions in our society. And the male stereotype of woman is crucially influenced by men's need to define woman in order to define themselves as men." See generally MacKinnon, *Feminism, Marxism, Method, and the State: Toward Feminist Jurisprudence*, 8 Signs 635, at 635 (1983) ("male and female are created through the erotization of dominance and submission. The man/woman difference and the dominance/submission dynamic define each other"); MacKinnon, *Feminism, Marxism, Method, and the State: An Agenda for Theory*, 7 Signs 515 (1982); On gender roles, see also De Beauvoir, *The Second Sex* (1971); Spender, *Man Made Language* (2d ed. 1985); Littleton, *Reconstructing Sexual Equality*, 75 Calif.L.Rev. 1279 (1987); Olsen, *The Family and the Market: A Study of Ideology and Legal Reform*, 96 Harv. L.Rev. 1497 (1983); Note, *Toward a Redefini-*

Feminism Unmodified ch. 2 (1987); MacKinnon, *Toward a Feminist Theory of the State* ch. 12 (1989); Minow, *Making All the Difference* (1990); Minow, *Foreword: Justice Engendered,* 101 Harv.L.Rev. 10 (1987).

Would it be better to declare that a "rule or practice is discriminatory [if] it participates in the systemic social deprivation of one sex because of sex"? Should the "only question for litigation [be] whether the policy or practice in question integrally contributes to the maintenance of an [underclass] because of gender"? See MacKinnon, *Sexual Harassment of Working Women* 117 (1979).[1]

B. CLAIMS BY MEN

CRAIG v. BOREN, 429 U.S. 190, 97 S.Ct. 451, 50 L.Ed.2d 397 (1976), per BRENNAN, J., involving a law forbidding sale of 3.2% beer to males under age 21 and to females under 18, was the first decision (a) to hold an unambiguous discrimination against males violative of equal protection, and (b) to articulate a formal standard of review: "[P]revious cases establish that classifications by gender must serve important governmental objectives and must be substantially related to achievement of those objectives. * * * Decisions following *Reed* [have] rejected administrative ease and convenience as sufficiently important objectives to justify gender-based classifications. * * *[6]

"*Reed* has also provided the underpinning for decisions that have invalidated statutes employing gender as an inaccurate proxy for other, more germane bases of classification. Hence, 'archaic and overbroad' generalizations concerning the financial position of servicewomen, *Frontiero,* and working women, *Wiesenfeld* [p. 1355 infra], could not justify use of a gender line in determining eligibility for certain governmental entitlements. Similarly increasingly outdated misconceptions concerning the role of females in the home rather than in the 'marketplace and world of ideas' were rejected as loose-fitting characterizations incapable of supporting state statutory schemes that were premised upon their accuracy. *Stanton.* In light of the weak congruence between gender and the characteristic or trait that gender purported to represent, it was necessary that the legislatures choose either to realign their substantive laws in a gender-neutral fashion, or to adopt procedures for identifying those instances where the sex-centered generalization actually comported to fact."

tion of Equality, 95 Harv.L.Rev. 487 (1981). For a general criticism of the use of naturalism in gender cases, see Tribe, *Constitutional Choices* 238–45 (1985).

1. See generally MacKinnon, *Toward A Feminist Theory of the State,* supra; MacKinnon, *Feminism Unmodified,* supra. Does feminist thought underestimate the diversity and complexity of women's experience? See Minow, *Making All the Difference,* supra at 230–39; Spellman, *Inessential Woman* (1980); Cain, *Feminist Jurisprudence: Grounding the Theories,* 4 Berkeley Womens L.J. 191 (1989); Crenshaw, *Demarginalizing the Intersection of Race and Sex: A Black Feminist Critique of Antidiscrimination Doctrine, Feminist Theory and Antiracist Politics,* 1989 U.Chi.L.Rev. 139; Harris, *Race and Essentialism in Feminist Theory* 42 Stan.L.Rev. 581 (1990); Williams, *The Obliging Shell: Some Informal Comments on Formal Equal Opportunity,* 87 Mich.L.J. 2128 (1989).

For helpful overviews of feminist thought, see Jaggar, *Feminist Politics and Human Nature* (1983); MacKinnon, *Toward a Feminist Theory of the State,* supra, ch. 3; Abrams, *Feminist Lawyering and Legal Method,* 16 Law & Social Inquiry ___ (1991); Cain, supra; Littleton, supra; West, *Jurisprudence and Gender,* 55 U.Chi.L.Rev. 1 (1988).

6. *Kahn v. Shevin,* [p. 1083 infra] and *Schlesinger v. Ballard,* [p. 1084 infra], upholding the use of gender-based classifications, rested upon the Court's perception of the laudatory purposes of those laws as remedying disadvantageous conditions suffered by women in economic and military life. Needless to say, Oklahoma does not suggest that the age-sex differential was enacted to ensure the availability of 3.2% beer for women as compensation for previous deprivations.

The Court reviewed in detail the state's "statistical evidence" concerning "age-sex differentials" in respect to "drinking and driving" and found that it "cannot support the conclusion that the gender-based distinction closely serves to achieve" the "important" objective of "enhancement of traffic safety[23]": [a]

POWELL, J., joined the Court's opinion, but with "reservations as to some of the discussion concerning the appropriate standard for equal protection analysis.*" Relying on *Reed,* he found that "this gender-based classification does not bear a fair and substantial relation to the object of the legislation."

STEVENS, J., who joined the Court's opinion, concurred: "I am inclined to believe that what has become known as the two-tiered analysis of equal protection claims [is] a method the Court has employed to explain decisions that actually apply a single standard in a reasonably consistent fashion. * * *

"In this case, the classification [is] objectionable because it is based on an accident of birth, because it is a mere remnant of the now almost universally rejected tradition of discriminating against males in this age bracket, and because, to the extent it reflects any physical difference between males and females, it is actually perverse.[4] * * *

"The classification is not totally irrational. For the evidence does indicate that there are more males than females in this age bracket who drive and also more who drink. Nevertheless, [i]t is difficult to believe that the statute was actually intended to cope with the problem of traffic safety, since it has only a minimal effect on access to a not-very-intoxicating beverage and does not prohibit its consumption. Moreover, [the] legislation imposes a restraint on one hundred percent of the males in the class allegedly because about 2% of them have probably violated one or more laws relating to the consumption of alcoholic beverages. It is unlikely that this law will have a significant deterrent effect either on that 2% or on the law-abiding 98%. But even assuming some such slight benefit, it does not seem to me that an insult to all of the young men of the State can be justified by visiting the sins of the 2% on the 98%."

REHNQUIST, J.—with whom Burger, C.J., was "in general agreement"—dissented: The Court's "elevated or 'intermediate' level scrutiny, like that invoked in cases dealing with discrimination against females, raises the question of why the statute here should be treated any differently than countless legislative classifications unrelated to sex which have been upheld under a minimum rationality standard. [There] is no suggestion [that] males in this age group are in any way peculiarly disadvantaged, subject to systematic discriminatory treatment, or otherwise in need of special solicitude from the courts. [T]here being no plausible argument that this is a discrimination against females,[2] the Court's reliance on our previous sex-discrimination cases is ill-

23. Insofar as *Goesaert v. Cleary* may be inconsistent, that decision is [disapproved].

a. Stewart, J., concurred, relying on *Reed.*

* [As] has been true of *Reed* and its progeny, our decision today will be viewed by some as a "middle-tier" approach. While I would not endorse that characterization[,] candor compels the recognition that the relatively deferential "rational basis" standard of review normally applied takes on a sharper focus when we address a gender-based [classification].

4. Because males are generally heavier than females, they have a greater capacity to consume alcohol without impairing their driving ability than do females.

2. I am not unaware of the argument [that] all discriminations between the sexes ultimately redound to the detriment of females, because they tend to reinforce "old notions" restricting the roles and opportunities of women. As a general proposition applying equally to all sex categorizations, I believe that this argument was implicitly found to carry little weight in our decisions upholding gender-based differences. See *Ballard; Kahn.* Seeing no assertion that it has founded. * * *

"The Court's [standard of review] comes out of thin air. * * * I would think we have had enough difficulty with the two standards of review which our cases have recognized—the norm of 'rational basis,' and the 'compelling state interest' required where a 'suspect classification' is involved—so as to counsel weightily against the insertion of still another 'standard' between those two. How is this Court to divine what objectives are important? How is it to determine whether a particular law is 'substantially' related to the achievement of such objective, rather than related in some other way to its achievement? Both of the phrases used are so diaphanous and elastic as to invite subjective judicial preferences or prejudices relating to particular types of legislation, masquerading as judgments whether such legislation is directed at 'important' objectives or, whether the relationship to those objectives is 'substantial' enough.

"[I]f stereotypes are as pervasive as the Court suggests, they may in turn influence the conduct of the men and women in question, and cause the young men to conform to the wild and reckless image which is their stereotype. * * * Notwithstanding the Court's critique of the statistical evidence, that evidence suggests clear differences between the drinking and driving habits of young men and women. Those differences are grounds enough for the State reasonably to conclude that young males pose by far the greater drunk driving hazard, both in terms of sheer numbers and in terms of hazard on a per-driver basis. The gender-based difference in treatment in this case is therefore not irrational."

MICHAEL M. v. SUPERIOR COURT, 450 U.S. 464, 101 S.Ct. 1200, 67 L.Ed. 2d 437 (1981), upheld a "statutory rape" law which punished the male, but not the female, party to intercourse when the female was under 18 and not the male's wife. REHNQUIST, J., joined by Burger, C.J., and Stewart and Powell, JJ., observed "that the traditional minimum rationality test takes on a somewhat 'sharper focus' when gender-based classifications are challenged. See *Craig* (Powell, J., concurring). [But] this court has consistently upheld statutes where the gender classification is not invidious, but rather realistically reflects the fact that the sexes are not similarly situated in certain circumstances. *Parham [p. 1095 infra]; Webster [p. 1085 infra]; Ballard [p. 1084 infra]; Kahn [p. 1083 infra].* As the Court has stated, a legislature may 'provide for the special problems of women.' *Wiesenfeld [p. 1084 infra].* * * *

"We are satisfied not only that the prevention of illegitimate [teenage] pregnancy is at least one of the 'purposes' of the statute, but that the State has a strong interest in preventing such pregnancy.[7]

special applicability [here], I believe it can be dismissed as an insubstantial consideration.

[See generally Sherry, *Selective Judicial Activism in the Equal Protection Context,* 73 Geo. L.J. 89 (1984).]

7. Although petitioner concedes that the State has a "compelling" interest in preventing teenage pregnancy, he contends that the "true" purpose [is] to protect the virtue and chastity of young women. As such, the statute is unjustifiable because it rests on archaic stereotypes. [Even] if the preservation of female chastity were one of the motives of the statute, and even if that motive be impermissible, petitioner's argument must fail because "[this] court will not strike down an otherwise constitutional statute on the basis of an alleged illicit legislative motive." *United States v. O'Brien.* In *Orr v. Orr,* [p. 1087 infra], for example, the Court rejected one asserted purpose as impermissible, but then considered other purposes to determine if they could justify the statute. Similarly, in *Washington v. Davis,* the Court distinguished *Palmer v. Thompson* on the grounds that the purposes of the ordinance

"Because virtually all of the significant harmful and inescapably identifiable consequences of teenage pregnancy fall on the young female, a legislature acts well within its authority when it elects to punish only the participant who, by nature, suffers few of the consequences of his conduct. It is hardly unreasonable for a legislature acting to protect minor females to exclude them from punishment. Moreover, the risk of pregnancy itself constitutes a substantial deterrence to young females. [A] criminal sanction imposed solely on males thus serves to roughly 'equalize' the deterrents on the sexes.

"[The] State persuasively contends that a gender-neutral statute would frustrate its interest in effective enforcement. Its view is that a female is surely less likely to report violations of the statute if she herself would be subject to criminal prosecution. In an area already fraught with prosecutorial difficulties, we decline to hold that the Equal Protection Clause requires a legislature to enact a statute so broad that it may well be incapable of enforcement.

"[Finally], the statute places a burden on males [not] shared by females. But we find nothing to suggest that men, because of past discrimination or peculiar disadvantages, are in need of the special solicitude of the courts.[a] Nor is this a case where the gender classification is made 'solely [for] administrative convenience,' as in *Frontiero*, or rests on [a] 'baggage of sexual stereotypes.' "[b]

BLACKMUN, J., concurred: "I [cannot] vote to strike down the California statutory rape law, for I think it is a sufficiently reasoned and constitutional effort to control the problem at its inception. [I] am persuaded that, although a minor has substantial privacy rights in intimate affairs connected with procreation, California's [efforts] to prevent teenage pregnancy are to be viewed differently from efforts to inhibit a woman from dealing with pregnancy once it has become an inevitability. * * *

"I think [it] is only fair, with respect to this particular petitioner, to point out that his partner, Sharon, appears not to have been an unwilling participant in at least the initial stages of the intimacies that took place the night of June 3, 1978.* Petitioner's and Sharon's nonacquaintance with each other before the

there were not open to impeachment by evidence that the legislature was actually motivated by an impermissible purpose.

a. Does the statute also discriminate against females? Consider Law, *Rethinking Sex and the Constitution,* 132 U.Pa.L.Rev. 955, 1001 (1984): "[U]nder the California law a young man is free to be sexual as long as he chooses a partner who is older than eighteen, while a young woman may not legally have sex with anyone, except her husband if she is married. [The decision] accepts and reinforces the sex-based stereotype that young men may legitimately engage in sexual activity and young women may not."

b. Stewart, J., also concurred, noting "that the statutory discrimination, when viewed as part of the wider scheme of California law, is not as clearcut as might at first appear. Females are not freed from criminal liability in California for engaging in sexual activity that may be harmful. It is unlawful, for example, for any person, of either sex, [to] contribute to the delinquency of anyone under 18 years of age. All persons are prohibited [from] consensual intercourse with a child under 14. [Finally,] females may be brought within the proscription of § 261.5 itself, since a female may be charged with aiding and abetting its violation. [A]pproximately 14% of the juveniles arrested for participation in acts made unlawful by § 261.5 between 1975 and 1979 were females. Moreover, an underage female who is as culpable as her male partner, or more culpable, may be prosecuted as a juvenile delinquent."

* Sharon at the preliminary hearing testified as follows: * * *

"We were drinking at the railroad tracks and we walked over to this bush and he started kissing me and stuff, and I was kissing him back, too, at first. Then, I was telling him to stop—

"Q. Yes.

"A. —and I was telling him to slow down and stop. He said, 'Okay, okay.' But then he just kept doing it. He just kept doing it and then my sister and two other guys came over to where we were and my sister said—told me to get up and come home. And then I didn't—* * *

incident: their drinking; their withdrawal from the others of the group; their foreplay, in which she willingly participated and seems to have encouraged; and the closeness of their ages (a difference of only one year and 18 days) are factors that should make this case an unattractive one to prosecute at all, and especially to prosecute as a felony, rather than as a misdemeanor. But the State has chosen to prosecute in that manner, and the facts, I reluctantly conclude, may fit the crime."

BRENNAN, J., joined by White and Marshall, JJ., dissented: "None of the three opinions upholding the California statute fairly applies the equal protection analysis this Court has so carefully developed since *Craig*. [The] plurality assumes that a gender-neutral statute would be less effective [in] deterring sexual activity because a gender-neutral statute would create significant enforcement problems. [But] a State's bare assertion [is] not enough to meet its burden of proof under *Craig*. Rather, the State must produce evidence that will persuade the Court that its assertion is true [and the] State has [not].

"The second flaw in the State's assertion is that even assuming that a gender-neutral statute would be more difficult to enforce, the State has still not shown that those enforcement problems would make such a statute less effective than a gender-based statute in deterring minor females from engaging in sexual intercourse. Common sense, however, suggests that a gender-neutral statutory rape law is potentially a *greater* deterrent of sexual activity than a gender-based law, for the simple reason that a gender-neutral law subjects both men and women to criminal sanctions and thus arguably has a deterrent effect on twice as many potential violators. Even if fewer persons were prosecuted under the gender-neutral law, as the State suggests, it would still be true that twice as many persons would be *subject* to arrest."

STEVENS, J., also dissented: "[T]hat a female confronts a greater risk of harm than a male is a reason for applying the prohibition to her—not a reason for granting her a license to use her own judgment on whether or not to assume the risk. Surely, if we examine the problem from the point of view of society's interest in preventing the risk-creating conduct from occurring at all, it is irrational to exempt 50% of the potential violators. * * *

"Finally, even if my logic is faulty and there actually is some speculative basis for treating equally guilty males and females differently, I still believe that any such speculative justification would be outweighed by the paramount inter-

"The Witness: Yeah. We was laying there and we were kissing each other, and then he asked me if I wanted to walk him over to the park; so we walked over to the park and we sat down on a bench and then he started kissing me again and we were laying on the bench. And he told me to take my pants off.

"I said, 'No,' and I was trying to get up and he hit me back down on the bench and then I just said to myself, 'Forget it,' and I let him do what he wanted to do and he took my pants off and he was telling me to put my legs around him and stuff—* * *

"Q. Did you have sexual intercourse with the defendant?

"A. Yeah. * * *

"Q. You said that he hit you?

"A. Yeah.

"Q. How did he hit you?

"A. He slugged me in the face.

"Q. With what did he slug you?

"A. His fist.

"Q. Where abouts in the face?

"A. On my chin.

"Q. As a result of that, did you have any bruises or any kind of an injury?

"A. Yeah.

"Q. What happened?

"A. I had bruises.

"The Court: Did he hit you one time or did he hit you more than once?

"The Witness: He hit me about two or three times. * * *

est in even-handed enforcement of the law. A rule that authorizes punishment of only one of two equally guilty wrongdoers violates the essence of the constitutional requirement that the sovereign must govern impartially." [c]

Notes and Questions

Facing the social facts. Consider MacKinnon, *Reflections on Sex Equality Under Law,* 100 Yale L.J. 1281, 1305 (1991): "The plurality allowed a sex difference—potential pregnancy—to render girls 'not similarly situated' and to support a sex-differential statute that divides women by age. Never mind that many of those protected cannot become pregnant and more of those not protected can, that young boys are sexually assaulted too (usually by older males), and that girls do not lose their vulnerability to sexual coercion upon turning eighteen. The dissent revealed more concern with avoiding the stereotyping attendant to the ideological message the law communicated than with changing the facts that make the stereotype largely true. In the interest of opposing facial distinctions and debunking the supposed myth of male sexual aggression, the fact that it is overwhelmingly girls who are sexually victimized by older males for reasons wholly unrelated to their capacity to become pregnant was completely obscured. The facts of social inequality, of sex aggravated by age, that could have supported particular legislative attention to the sexual assault of girls were not even considered. Underage girls form a credible disadvantaged group for equal protection purposes when the social facts of sexual assault are faced, facts which prominently feature one-sided sexual aggression by older males. It seems that in order to imagine equality, one must first be blind to inequality, and to see inequality blinds one to seeing that equality is possible."

ROSTKER v. GOLDBERG, 453 U.S. 57, 101 S.Ct. 2646, 69 L.Ed.2d 478 (1981), per REHNQUIST, J., upheld a Military Selective Service Act (MSSA) provision "authorizing the President to require the registration of males and not females": "The case arises in the context of Congress' authority over national defense and military affairs, and perhaps in no other area has the Court accorded Congress greater deference. * * *

"Not only is the scope of Congress' constitutional power in this area broad, but the lack of competence on the part of the courts is marked. * * *

"None of this is to say that Congress is free to disregard the Constitution when it acts in the area of military affairs. [B]ut the tests and limitations to be applied may differ because of the military context. We of course do not abdicate our ultimate responsibility to decide the constitutional question, but simply recognize that the Constitution itself requires such deference to congressional choice. In deciding the question before us we must be particularly careful not to substitute our judgment of what is desirable for that of Congress, or our own evaluation of evidence for a reasonable evaluation by [Congress].

"No one could deny that under the test of *Craig,* the Government's interest in raising and supporting armies is an 'important governmental interest.' Congress and its committees carefully considered and debated two alternative means of furthering that interest: the first was to register only males for potential conscription, and the other was to register both sexes. Congress chose the

c. For commentary on *Michael M.*, see Olsen, *Statutory Rape: A Feminist Critique of Rights Analysis,* 63 Tex.L.Rev. 391 (1984).

former alternative. When that decision is challenged on equal protection grounds, the question a court must decide is not which alternative it would have chosen, [but] whether that chosen by Congress denies equal protection of the laws. * * *

"This case is quite different from several of the gender-based discrimination cases we have considered in [that] Congress did not act 'unthinkingly' or 'reflexively and not for any considered reason.' The question of registering women for the draft not only received considerable national attention and was the subject of wide-ranging public debate, but also was extensively considered by Congress in hearings, floor debate, and in committee. [This] clearly establishes that the decision to exempt women from registration was not the 'accidental byproduct of a traditional way of thinking about women.' * * *

"Congress determined that any future draft, which would be facilitated by the registration scheme, would be characterized by a need for combat troops. [Since] women are [statutorily] excluded from combat, Congress concluded that they would not be needed in the event of a draft, and therefore decided not to register them. [The] exemption of women from registration is not only sufficiently but closely related to Congress' purpose in authorizing registration. See *Michael M.; Craig; Reed.* [As] was the case in *Ballard,* 'the gender classification is not invidious, but rather realistically reflects the fact that the sexes are not similarly situated' in this case. *Michael M.* The Constitution requires that Congress treat similarly situated persons similarly, not that it engage in gestures of superficial equality.

"In holding the MSSA constitutionally invalid the District Court relied heavily on the President's decision to seek authority to register women and the testimony of members of the Executive Branch and the military in support of that decision. As stated by the Administration's witnesses before Congress, however, the President's 'decision to ask for authority to register women is based on equity.' * * * Congress was certainly entitled, in the exercise of its constitutional powers to raise and regulate armies and navies, to focus on the question of military need rather than 'equity.' * * *

"Although the military experts who testified in favor of registering women uniformly opposed the actual drafting of women, there was testimony that in the event of a draft of 650,000 the military could absorb some 80,000 female inductees [to] fill noncombat positions, freeing men to go to the front. In relying on this testimony, [the] District Court palpably exceeded its authority when it ignored Congress' considered response to this line of reasoning.

"In the first place, assuming that a small number of women could be drafted for noncombat roles, Congress simply did not consider it worth the added burdens of including women in draft and registration plans. * * *

"Congress also concluded that whatever the need for women for noncombat roles during mobilization, [it] could be met by volunteers.

"Most significantly, Congress determined that staffing noncombat positions with women during a mobilization would be positively detrimental to the important goal of military flexibility. [The] District Court was quite wrong in undertaking an independent evaluation of this evidence, rather than adopting an appropriately deferential examination of *Congress'* evaluation of that evidence."

WHITE, J., joined by Brennan, J., dissented: "I assume what has not been challenged in this case—that excluding women from combat positions does not offend the Constitution. Granting that, it is self evident that if during mobilization for war, all noncombat military positions must be filled by combat-qualified personnel available to be moved into combat positions, there would be no occasion whatsoever to have any women in the Army, whether as volunteers or inductees. The Court appears to say that Congress concluded as much and that we should accept that judgment even though the serious view of the Executive Branch, including the responsible military services, is to the contrary. * * * I perceive little, if any, indication that Congress itself concluded that every position in the military, no matter how far removed from combat, must be filled with combat-ready men. Common sense and experience in recent wars, where women volunteers were employed in substantial numbers, belie this view of reality. * * *

"I would also have little difficulty agreeing to a reversal if all the women who could serve in wartime without adversely affecting combat readiness could predictably be obtained through volunteers. In that event, [equal protection] would not require the United States to go through, and a large segment of the population to be burdened with, the expensive and essentially useless procedure of registering women. But again I cannot agree with the Court that Congress concluded or that the legislative record indicates that each of the services could rely on women volunteers to fill all the positions for which they might be eligible in the event of mobilization. On the contrary, the [record] supports the District Court's finding that the services would have to conscript at least 80,000 persons to fill positions for which combat-ready men would not be required. * * *

"The Court also submits that because the primary purpose of registration and conscription is to supply combat troops and because the great majority of noncombat positions must be filled by combat-trained men ready to be rotated into combat, the absolute number of positions for which women would be eligible is so small as to be de minimis and of no moment for equal protection purposes, especially in light of the administrative burdens involved in registering all women of suitable age. There is some sense to this; but at least on the record before us, the number of women who could be used in the military without sacrificing combat-readiness is not at all small or insubstantial, and administrative convenience has not been sufficient justification for the kind of outright gender-based discrimination involved [here]."

MARSHALL, J., joined by Brennan, J., dissented: "The Court today places its imprimatur on one of the most potent remaining public expressions of 'ancient canards about the proper role of women.' [W]e are not called upon to decide whether either men or women can be drafted at all, whether they must be drafted in equal numbers, in what order they should be drafted, or once inducted, how they are to be trained for their respective functions. In addition, this case does not involve a challenge to the statutes or policies that prohibit female members of the Armed Forces from serving in combat. It is with this understanding that I turn to the task at hand. [In] my judgment, there simply is no basis for concluding in this case that excluding women from registration is substantially related to the achievement of a concededly important governmental interest in maintaining an effective defense. * * *

"The Government does not defend the exclusion of women from registration on the ground that preventing women from serving in the military is substantially related to the effectiveness of the Armed Forces. Indeed, the successful experience of women serving in all branches of the Armed Services would belie any such claim. * * *

"The most authoritative discussion of Congress' reasons [is] contained in the report prepared by the Senate Armed Services Committee on the Fiscal Year 1981 Defense Authorization Bill. S.Rep. No. 96–826. * * *

"According to the Senate Report, '[t]he policy precluding the use of women in combat is [the] most important reason for not including women in a registration system.' [T]he Report declared: 'Registering women for assignment to combat [would] leave the actual performance of sexually mixed units as an experiment to be conducted in war with unknown risk—a risk that the committee finds militarily unwarranted and dangerous. Moreover, the committee feels that any attempt to assign women to combat positions could affect the national resolve at the time of mobilization, a time of great strain on all aspects of the Nation's resources.' [The] Court then reasons that since women are not eligible for assignment to combat, Congress' decision to exclude them from registration is not unconstitutional discrimination inasmuch as '[m]en and women, because of the combat restrictions on women, are simply not similarly situated for purposes of a draft or registration for a draft.' There is a certain logic to this reasoning, but the Court's approach is fundamentally flawed.

"In the first place, although the Court purports to apply the *Craig* test, the 'similarly situated' analysis the Court employs is in fact significantly different from the *Craig* approach. Compare *Kirchberg* (employing *Craig* test) with id. (Stewart, J., concurring) (employing 'similarly situated' analysis). The Court essentially reasons that the gender classification employed by the MSSA is constitutionally permissible because nondiscrimination is not necessary to achieve the purpose of registration to prepare for a draft of combat troops. In other words, the majority concludes that women may be excluded from registration because they will not be needed in the event of a draft.

"This analysis, however, focuses on the wrong question. The relevant inquiry under the *Craig* test is not whether a *gender-neutral* classification would substantially advance important governmental interests. Rather, the question is whether the gender-based classification is itself substantially related to the achievement of the asserted governmental interest. Thus, the Government's task in this case is to demonstrate that excluding women from registration substantially furthers the goal of preparing for a draft of combat troops. Or to put it another way, the Government must show that registering women would substantially impede its efforts to prepare for such a draft. Under our precedents, the Government cannot meet this burden without showing that a gender neutral statute would be a less effective means of attaining this end. [In] this case, the Government makes no claim that preparing for a draft of combat troops cannot be accomplished just as effectively by *registering* both men and women but *drafting* only men if only men turn out to be needed.[11] Nor can the Government argue that this alternative entails the additional cost and administrative inconvenience of registering women. This Court has repeatedly stated that [administrative convenience] is not an adequate constitutional justification under the *Craig* test.

"The fact that registering women in no way obstructs the governmental interest in preparing for a draft of combat troops points up a second flaw in the Court's analysis. The Court essentially reduces the question of the constitution-

11. Alternatively, the Government could employ a classification that is related to the statutory objective but is not based on gender, for example, combat eligibility. Under the current scheme, large subgroups of the male population who are ineligible for combat because of physical handicaps or conscientious objector status are nonetheless required to register.

ality of male-only *registration* to the validity of a hypothetical program for *conscripting* only men. [If] it could indeed be guaranteed in advance that conscription would be reimposed by Congress only in circumstances where, and in a form under which, all conscripts would have to be trained for and assigned to combat or combat rotation positions from which women are categorically excluded, then it could be argued that registration of women would be pointless.

"But of course, no such guarantee is possible. Certainly, nothing about the MSSA limits Congress to reinstituting the draft only in such circumstances. For example, Congress may decide that the All-Volunteer Armed Forces are inadequate to meet the Nation's defense needs even in times of peace and reinstitute peacetime conscription. In that event, the hypothetical draft the Court relied [on] would presumably be of little relevance * * *. The fact that registration is a first step in the conscription process does not mean that a registration law expressly discriminating between men and women may be justified by a valid conscription program which would, in retrospect, make the current discrimination appear functionally related to the program that emerged.

"But even addressing the Court's reasoning on its own terms, its analysis is flawed because the entire argument rests on a premise that is demonstrably false. As noted, the majority simply assumes that registration prepares for a draft in which *every* draftee must be available for assignment to combat. But [this] finds no support in either the testimony before Congress, or more importantly, in the findings of the Senate Report. * * * Testimony about personnel requirements in the event of a draft established that women could fill at least 80,000 of the 650,000 positions for which conscripts would be inducted. Thus, [the] statutes and policies barring women from combat do not provide a reason for distinguishing between male and female potential conscripts; the two groups are, in the majority's parlance, 'similarly situated.' As such, the combat restrictions cannot by themselves supply the constitutionally required justification for the MSSA's gender-based classification. [T]he Court asserts that 'Congress determined that staffing noncombat positions with women during a mobilization would be positively detrimental to the important goal of military flexibility.' [But] to justify the exclusion of women from registration and the draft on this ground, there must be a further showing that staffing even a limited number of noncombat positions with women would impede military flexibility. I find nothing in the Senate Report to provide any basis for the Court's representation that Congress believed this to be the case.

"The Senate Report concluded [that] drafting '*very large numbers* of women' would hinder military flexibility. [But the] testimony on this issue at the congressional hearings was that drafting a limited number of women is quite compatible with the military's need for flexibility. In concluding that the Armed Services could usefully employ at least 80,000 women conscripts out of a total of 650,000 draftees that would be needed in the event of a major European war, the Defense Department took into account both the need for rotation of combat personnel and the possibility that some support personnel might have to be sent into combat. [The] combat restrictions that would prevent a female draftee from serving in a combat or combat rotation position also apply to the 150,000–250,000 women volunteers in the Armed Services. If the presence of increasing but controlled numbers of female volunteers has not unacceptably 'divide[d] the military into two groups,' it is difficult to see how the induction of a similarly limited additional number of women could accomplish this result. [T]he Senate Report establishes that induction of a large number of men but only a limited number of women [would] be substantially relatec governmental interests. But the discussion and findings in the Se not enable the Government to carry its burden of demonstrating th excluding women from the draft by excluding them from registrat tially furthers important governmental objectives."

Notes and Questions

1. Consider Williams, *The Equality Crisis,* fn. i, p. 1072 supra, at ... JU: "As for *Rostker,* the conflicts among feminists were overtly expressed. Some of us felt it essential that we support the notion that a single-sex draft was unconstitutional; others felt that feminists should not take such a position. These latter groups explicitly contrasted the female ethic of nurturance and life-giving with a male ethic of aggression and militarism and asserted that if we argued to the Court that single-sex registration is unconstitutional we would be betraying ourselves and supporting what we find least acceptable about the male world.

"To me, this latter argument quite overtly taps qualities that the culture has ascribed to woman-as-childrearer and converts them to a normative value statement, one with which it is easy for us to sympathize. This is one of the circumstances in which the feeling that 'I want what he's got but I don't want to be what he's had to be in order to get it' comes quickly to the surface. But I also believe that the reflexive response based on these deeper cultural senses leads us to untenable positions. [To] me, *Rostker* never posed the question of whether women should be forced as men now are to fight wars, but whether we, like them, must take the responsibility for deciding whether or not to fight, whether or not to bear the cost of risking our lives, on the one hand, or resisting in the name of peace, on the other. And do we not, by insisting upon our differences at these crucial junctures, promote and reinforce the us-them dichotomy that permits the Rehnquists and the Stewarts to resolve matters of great importance and complexity by the simplistic, reflexive assertion that men and women 'are simply not similarly situated?' "

2. *Similar(?) Classifications.* Should the gender cases extend to discrimination against homosexuals? Against married persons?

C. "BENIGN"—"COMPENSATORY"—"REMEDIAL" DISCRIMINATION

KAHN v. SHEVIN, 416 U.S. 351, 94 S.Ct. 1734, 40 L.Ed.2d 189 (1974), per DOUGLAS, J., involved a property tax exemption for widows (but not widowers). Unlike *Reed,* the law is "reasonably designed to further the state policy of cushioning the financial impact of spousal loss upon the sex for whom that loss imposes a disproportionately heavy burden." Unlike *Frontiero,* the classification here is not "*solely* for administrative convenience," nor were the statutes there "in any sense designed to rectify the effects of past discrimination against women." [a]

a. Brennan, J., joined by Marshall, J., dissented: "[I]n providing special benefits for a needy segment of society long the victim of purposeful discrimination and neglect, the statute serves the compelling state interest of achieving equality for such groups." But it "is plainly overinclusive [because] the State could readily narrow the class of beneficiaries to those widows for whom the effects of past economic discrimination against women have been a practical reality."

White, J., also dissented: "It may be administratively inconvenient to make individual determinations [to] extend the exemption to needy men as well as needy women, but ad-

SCHLESINGER v. BALLARD, 419 U.S. 498, 95 S.Ct. 572, 42 L.Ed.2d 610 (1975), per STEWART, J., upheld a federal statute providing for the discharge of naval "line" officers who had not been promoted for nine years (males) or thirteen years (females): In "*Reed* and *Frontiero* the challenged classifications [were] premised on overbroad generalizations" and were sought to be justified solely on "administrative convenience." Here, because of navy restrictions on combat and sea duty for women, "Congress [may] quite rationally have believed that women line officers had less opportunity for promotion than did their male counterparts, and that a longer period of tenure for women officers would, therefore, be consistent with the goal to provide women officers with 'fair and equitable career advancement programs.' Cf. *Kahn.*" [b]

WEINBERGER v. WIESENFELD, 420 U.S. 636, 95 S.Ct. 1225, 43 L.Ed.2d 514 (1975), per BRENNAN, J., held that Social Security Act § 402(g)'s payment of benefits to the wife—but not to the husband—of a deceased wage earner with minor children violated equal protection because it "unjustifiably discriminated against women wage-earners": [c] As in *Frontiero*, an " 'archaic and overbroad' generalization [underlies] the distinction drawn by § 402(g), namely, that male [but not female] workers' earnings are vital to the support of their families." Unlike *Kahn*, "it is apparent both from the statutory scheme itself and from the legislative history of § 402(g) that Congress' purpose [was] not to provide an income to women who were, because of economic discrimination, unable to provide for themselves. Rather, § 402(g), linked as it is directly to responsibility for minor children, was intended to permit women to elect not to work and to devote themselves to the care of children. Since this purpose in no way is premised upon any special disadvantages of women, [the] gender-based distinction of § 402(g) is entirely irrational." [d]

CALIFANO v. GOLDFARB, 430 U.S. 199, 97 S.Ct. 1021, 51 L.Ed.2d 270 (1977), held that Social Security Act § 402(f)'s payment of benefits to a widow of a covered employee, but not to a widower unless he proves dependency on his deceased wife-employee, violated equal protection. Brennan, J., joined by White, Marshall and Powell, JJ., found *Wiesenfeld* "dispositive."

ministrative efficiency is not an adequate justification for discriminations based purely on sex. *Frontiero; Reed.*"

b. Brennan, J., joined by Douglas and Marshall, JJ.—and "for the most part" by White, J.—dissented: "I find quite troublesome the notion that a gender-based difference in treatment can be justified by another, broader, gender-based difference in treatment imposed directly and currently by the Navy itself." See also Kanowitz, *"Benign" Sex Discrimination: Its Troubles and Their Cure,* 31 Hast.L.J. 1379, 1407 (1980): "Nor did *Ballard* take into account another detrimental impact of the policy upon women: the easing of pressure on their superiors to promote them precisely because women officers could stay in the service two years longer than men without being promoted."

c. Against which sex did the provision discriminate? Was the discrimination in *Frontiero* against servicewomen or their male spouses? What about *Kahn?*

d. Powell, J., joined by Burger, C.J., "concur[red] generally in the opinion of the Court." Rehnquist, J., disclaiming reliance on *Frontiero,* concurred in the result because § 402(g) "does not rationally serve any valid legislative purpose, including that for which § 402(g) was obviously designed. This is so because it is irrational to distinguish between mothers and fathers when the sole question is whether a child of a deceased contributing worker should have the opportunity to receive the full-time attention of the only parent remaining to it." Douglas, J., did not participate. See generally Note, *Sex Classifications in the Social Security Benefit Structure,* 49 Ind.L.J. 181 (1973).

STEVENS, J., concurred, noting his agreement with the dissent's contentions that "the relevant discrimination in this case is against surviving male spouses, rather than against deceased female wage earners" and that "a classification which treats certain aged widows more favorably than their male counterparts is not 'invidious.'" Nonetheless, since "the history of the statute is entirely consistent with the view that Congress simply assumed that all widows should be regarded as 'dependents' in some general sense," he was "persuaded that this discrimination against a group of males is merely the accidental by-product of a traditional way of thinking about females." [e]

REHNQUIST, J., joined by Burger, C.J., and Stewart and Blackmun, JJ., dissented: "[C]ases requiring heightened levels of scrutiny for particular classifications [which] have originated [outside] the field of social insurance legislation [should] not be uncritically carried over into that field. [I]n a legislative system which distributes benefit payments among literally millions of people there are at least two characteristics which are not found in many other types of statutes. The first is that the statutory scheme will typically have been expanded by amendment over a period of years so that it is virtually impossible to say that a particular amendment fits with mathematical nicety into a carefully conceived overall plan for payment of benefits. The second is [that] 'administrative convenience' will in this area of the law bear a much more vital relation to the overall legislative plan because of congressional concern for certainty in determination of entitlement and promptness in payment of benefits." Unlike *Wiesenfeld,* "the section under attack in the instant case does not totally foreclose widowers, but simply requires from them a proof of dependency" as in *Mathews v. Lucas.*[f] Further, favoring aged widows "is scarcely an invidious discrimination. [It] in no way perpetuates the economic discrimination which has been the basis for heightened scrutiny of gender-based classifications, and is, in fact, explainable as a measure to ameliorate the characteristically depressed condition of aged widows. *Kahn.*" [g]

CALIFANO v. WEBSTER

430 U.S. 313, 97 S.Ct. 1192, 51 L.Ed.2d 360 (1977).

PER CURIAM.

[Social Security Act § 215(b)(3)'s formula—which has since been amended—afforded the chance of higher old-age benefits to female wage earners than to similarly situated males.]

To withstand scrutiny under [equal protection], "classifications by gender must serve important governmental objectives and must be substantially related

e. Stevens, J., also strongly suggested that he disagreed with *Kahn.*

f. Do the different results in *Lucas* and *Goldfarb* mean "that while both sex and illegitimacy classifications are subject to 'middle tier' scrutiny, sex classifications are viewed as more invidious [and] thus require a more substantial means-end fit"? 91 Harv.L.Rev. 186 (1977).

g. *Wengler v. Druggists Mut. Ins. Co.,* 446 U.S. 142, 100 S.Ct. 1540, 64 L.Ed.2d 107 (1980), per White, J., held that a virtually identical state workers' compensation law discriminated against women (relying on *Goldfarb, Wiesenfeld* and *Frontiero*)—and against men (relying on Stevens, J.'s concurrence in *Goldfarb*)—and thus violated equal protection. Stevens, J., concurred on the basis of his *Goldfarb* concurrence. Only Rehnquist, J., dissented.

See also *Califano v. Westcott,* 443 U.S. 76, 99 S.Ct. 2655, 61 L.Ed.2d 382 (1979), relying on *Goldfarb* and *Wiesenfeld* to unanimously hold violative of equal protection Social Security Act § 407—which "provides benefits to families whose dependent children have been deprived of parental support because of the unemployment of the father, but does not provide such benefits when the mother becomes unemployed."

to achievement of those objectives." *Craig.* Reduction of the disparity in economic condition between men and women caused by the long history of discrimination against women has been recognized as such an important governmental objective. *Ballard; Kahn.* But "the mere recitation of a benign, compensatory purpose is not an automatic shield which protects against any inquiry into the actual purposes underlying a statutory scheme." *Wiesenfeld.* Accordingly, we have rejected attempts to justify gender classifications as compensation for past discrimination against women when the classifications in fact penalized women wage earners, *Goldfarb; Wiesenfeld,* or when the statutory structure and its legislative history revealed that the classification was not enacted as compensation for past discrimination. *Goldfarb; Wiesenfeld.*

[This statute] is more analogous to those upheld in *Kahn* and *Ballard* than to those struck down in *Wiesenfeld* and *Goldfarb.* The more favorable treatment of the female wage earner enacted here was not a result of "archaic and overbroad generalizations" about women, or of "the role-typing society has long imposed" upon women such as casual assumptions that women are "the weaker sex" or are more likely to be child-rearers or dependents. Rather, "the only discernible purpose of [§ 215's more favorable treatment is] the permissible one of redressing our society's longstanding disparate treatment of women." *Goldfarb.*

The challenged statute operated directly to compensate women for past economic discrimination. Retirement benefits [are] based on past earnings. But as we have recognized, "[w]hether from overt discrimination or from the socialization process of a male-dominated culture, the job market is inhospitable to the woman seeking any but the lowest paid jobs." *Kahn.* Thus, allowing women, who as such have been unfairly hindered from earning as much as men, to eliminate additional low-earning years from the calculation of their retirement benefits works directly to remedy some part of the effect of past discrimination.[5]

[T]he legislative history is clear that the differing treatment of men and women in former § 215(b)(3) was not "the accidental byproduct of a traditional way of thinking about females," *Goldfarb* (Stevens, J., concurring in the result), but rather was deliberately enacted to compensate for particular economic disabilities suffered by women.[a]

That Congress changed its mind in 1972 and equalized the treatment of men and women does [not] constitute an admission by Congress that its previous policy was invidiously discriminatory. Congress has in recent years legislated directly upon the subject of unequal treatment of women in the job market. Congress may well have decided that "[t]hese congressional reforms [have] lessened the economic justification for the more favorable benefit computation formula in § 215(b)(3)." Moreover, elimination of the more favorable benefit computation for women wage earners, even in the remedial context, is wholly consistent with those reforms, which require equal treatment of men and women in preference to the attitudes of "romantic paternalism" that have contributed to the "long and unfortunate history of sex discrimination." *Frontiero.* * * *

Reversed.

5. Even with the advantage[,] women on the average received lower retirement benefits than men. "As of December 1972, the average monthly retirement insurance benefit for males was $179.60 and for females, $140.50."

a. See also *Heckler v. Mathews,* 465 U.S. 728, 104 S.Ct. 1387, 79 L.Ed.2d 646 (1984), unanimously upholding a "temporary revival" of the classification invalidated in *Goldfarb* "in order to protect the expectations of persons, both men and women, who had planned their retirements based on" it.

CHIEF JUSTICE BURGER, with whom JUSTICE STEWART, JUSTICE BLACKMUN, and JUSTICE REHNQUIST join, concurring in the judgment.

* * * I find it somewhat difficult to distinguish [*Goldfarb*]. I question whether certainty in the law is promoted by hinging the validity of important statutory schemes on whether five Justices view them to be more akin to the "offensive" provisions struck down in *Wiesenfeld* and *Frontiero,* or more like the "benign" provisions upheld in *Ballard* and *Kahn.* I therefore concur in the judgment [for] reasons stated by Mr. Justice Rehnquist in his dissenting opinion in *Goldfarb,* in which Mr. Justice Stewart, Mr. Justice Blackmun, and I joined.

Notes and Questions

1. Consider Tribe, *American Constitutional Law* 1568–70 (2d ed. 1988): "Male plaintiffs [in most gender benign discrimination cases] did not wish to have the preferential treatment of women terminated; rather they wished to have the preference extended to themselves. [I]n contrast to the racial context, where privileged whites cannot plausibly contend that their challenge to a racial classification benefitting disadvantaged blacks will [redound] to the benefit of blacks, men can legitimately argue that dismantling a regime of legislatively-reinforced gender roles offers the prospect for a two-way flow of enhanced liberty, opportunity and power for both sexes. Sauce for the gander may well be sauce for the goose."

2. Does a "benign," "compensatory" or "remedial" purpose justify discrimination against men? Consider Kanowitz, fn. b, p. 1084 supra: "[A] casual glance at the treatment males have received at the hands of the law solely because they are males suggests that they have paid an awesome price for other advantages they have presumably enjoyed over females in our society. Whether one talks of the male's unique obligation of compulsory military service, his primary duty for spousal and child support, his lack of the same kinds of protective labor legislation that have traditionally been enjoyed by women, or the statutory or judicial preference in child custody disputes that has long been accorded to mothers vis-à-vis fathers of minor children, sex discrimination against males in statutes and judicial decisions has been widespread and severe. * * * How many males, for example, [unable] to benefit from state laws that limited women's working hours and lifting requirements, and prescribed minimum wages for women only, had their health impaired by being forced by their employers to work excessively long hours, lift excessively heavy weights, under excessively onerous conditions, at whatever wage their employer was willing to pay? * * * How many men [were] crushed both emotionally and physically by their striving to meet their exclusive legal obligation to provide for their wives' and children's financial needs?"

3. ORR v. ORR, 440 U.S. 268, 99 S.Ct. 1102, 59 L.Ed.2d 306 (1979), considered "two legislative objectives" for an Alabama statute providing that only husbands may be required to pay alimony—(1) to "provide help for needy spouses, using sex as a proxy for need," and (2) to "compensate women for past discrimination during marriage, which assertedly has left them unprepared to fend for themselves." The Court, per Brennan, J., held this failed the *Craig* standard: "Under the statute, individualized hearings at which the parties' relative financial circumstances are considered *already* occur. There is no reason, therefore, to use sex as a proxy for need. Needy males could be helped along with needy females with little if any additional burden on the [state.] Similarly, since individualized hearings can determine which women were in

fact discriminated against vis à vis their husbands, as well as which family units defied the stereotype and left the husband dependent on the wife, Alabama's alleged compensatory purpose may be effectuated without placing burdens solely on husbands." [b]

MISSISSIPPI UNIV. FOR WOMEN v. HOGAN

458 U.S. 718, 102 S.Ct. 3331, 73 L.Ed.2d 1090 (1982).

JUSTICE O'CONNOR delivered the opinion of the Court.

[MUW, "the oldest state-supported all-female college in the United States," denied Hogan admission to its School of Nursing solely because of his sex.[a]]

* * * That this statute discriminates against males rather than against females does not exempt it from scrutiny or reduce the standard of review.[8] Our decisions also establish that the party seeking to uphold a statute that classifies individuals on the basis of their gender must carry the burden of showing an "exceedingly persuasive justification" for the classification. *Kirchberg v. Feenstra,* 450 U.S. 455, 461, 101 S.Ct. 1195, 1199, 67 L.Ed.2d 428 (1981).[b] The burden is met only by showing at least that the classification serves "important governmental objectives and that the discriminatory means employed" are "substantially related to the achievement of those objectives." [9]

Although the test [is] straightforward, it must be applied free of fixed notions concerning the roles and abilities of males and females. [Thus,] if the statutory objective is to exclude or "protect" members of one gender because they are presumed to suffer from an inherent handicap or to be innately inferior, the objective itself is illegitimate. See *Frontiero.*

If the State's objective is legitimate and important, we next determine whether the requisite direct, substantial relationship between objective and means is present. The purpose of requiring that close relationship is to assure that the validity of a classification is determined through reasoned analysis rather than through the mechanical application of traditional, often inaccurate, assumptions about the proper roles of men and women. The need for the requirement is amply revealed by reference to the broad range of statutes already invalidated by this Court, statutes that relied upon the simplistic, outdated assumption that gender could be used as a "proxy for other, more germane bases of classification," *Craig,* to establish a link between objective and classification. * * *

The State's primary justification for maintaining the single-sex admissions policy of MUW's School of Nursing is that it compensates for discrimination

b. Blackmun, J., concurred. Burger, C.J., and Powell and Rehnquist, JJ., dissented on procedural grounds to which Stevens, J.'s concurrence responded.

a. The Court declined "to address the question of whether MUW's admissions policy, as applied to males seeking admission to schools other than the School of Nursing, violates the Fourteenth Amendment."

8. Without question, MUW's admissions policy worked to Hogan's disadvantage. [Hogan] could have attended [one] of Mississippi's state-supported coeducational nursing programs [only] by driving a considerable distance from his home. * * *

b. *Kirchberg* per Marshall, J., held that a Louisiana statute giving a husband exclusive control over disposition of community property was not "substantially related to the achievement of an important governmental objective." Stewart, J., joined by Rehnquist, J., concurred in the result "since men and women were similarly situated for all relevant purposes with respect to the management and disposition of community property."

9. [Because] we conclude that the challenged statutory classification is not substantially related to an important objective, we need not decide whether classifications based upon gender are inherently suspect.

against women and, therefore, constitutes educational affirmative action. [A] state can evoke a compensatory purpose to justify an otherwise discriminatory classification only if members of the gender benefited by the classification actually suffer a disadvantage related to the classification. We considered such a situation in *Webster* [and *Ballard*].

In sharp contrast, Mississippi has made no showing that women lacked opportunities to obtain training in the field of nursing or to attain positions of leadership in that field when the MUW School of Nursing opened its door or that women currently are deprived of such opportunities. In fact, in 1970, the year before the School of Nursing's first class enrolled, women earned 94 percent of the nursing baccalaureate degrees conferred in Mississippi and 98.6 percent of the degrees earned nationwide.[14]

Rather than compensate for discriminatory barriers faced by women, MUW's [policy] tends to perpetuate the stereotyped view of nursing as an exclusively woman's job.[15] By assuring that Mississippi allots more openings in its state-supported nursing schools to women than it does to men, MUW's admissions policy lends credibility to the old view that women, not men, should become nurses, and makes the assumption that nursing is a field for women a self-fulfilling prophecy. Thus, we conclude that, although the State recited a "benign, compensatory purpose," it failed to establish that the alleged objective is the actual purpose underlying the discriminatory classification.[16]

The policy is invalid also because [the] State has made no showing that the gender-based classification is substantially and directly related to its proposed compensatory objective. To the contrary, MUW's policy of permitting men to attend classes as auditors fatally undermines its claim that women, at least those in the School of Nursing, are adversely affected by the presence of men.[17]

Affirmed.[c]

CHIEF JUSTICE BURGER, dissenting.

I agree generally with Justice Powell's dissenting opinion. I write separately, however, to emphasize that [s]ince the Court's opinion relies heavily on its finding that women have traditionally dominated the nursing profession, it suggests that a State might well be justified in maintaining, for example, the option of an all-women's business school or liberal arts program.

JUSTICE POWELL, with whom JUSTICE REHNQUIST joins, dissenting.

14. Relatively little change has taken place during the past 10 years. In 1980, women received more than 94 percent of the baccalaureate degrees conferred nationwide and constituted 96.5 percent of the registered nurses in the labor force.

15. Officials of the American Nurses Association have suggested that excluding men from the field has depressed nurses' wages. To the extent the exclusion of men has that effect, MUW's admissions policy actually penalizes the very class the State purports to benefit. Cf. *Wiesenfeld.*

16. Even were we to assume that discrimination against women affects their opportunity to obtain an education or to obtain leadership roles in nursing, the challenged policy nonetheless would be invalid, for the State has failed to establish that the legislature intended the single-sex policy to compensate for any perceived discrimination. * * *

17. Justice Powell's dissent suggests that a second objective is served by the gender-based classification in that Mississippi has elected to provide women a choice of educational environments. Since any gender-based classification provides one class a benefit or choice not available to the other class, however, that argument begs the question. The issue is not whether the benefited class profits from the classification, but whether the State's decision to confer a benefit only upon one class by means of a discriminatory classification is substantially related to achieving a legitimate and substantial goal.

c. The state's contention that Congress had authorized the MUW policy is considered at p. 1285 infra.

The Court's opinion bows deeply to conformity. Left without honor—indeed, held unconstitutional—is an element of diversity that has characterized much of American education and enriched much of American life. The Court in effect holds today that no State now may provide even a single institution of higher learning open only to women students. [The] only groups with any personal acquaintance with MUW to file amicus briefs are female students and alumnae of MUW. And they have emphatically rejected respondent's arguments. [T]he Court errs seriously by assuming [that] the equal protection standard generally applicable to sex discrimination is appropriate here. That standard was designed to free women from "archaic and overbroad generalizations." *Ballard.* In no previous case have we applied it to invalidate state efforts to *expand* women's choices. Nor are there prior sex discrimination decisions by this Court in which a male plaintiff, as in this case, had the choice of an equal benefit. * * *

By applying heightened equal protection analysis to this case,[9] the Court frustrates the liberating spirit of the Equal Protection Clause. It forbids the States from providing women with an opportunity to choose the type of university they prefer. And yet it is these women whom the Court regards as the *victims* of an illegal, stereotyped perception of the role of women in our society. The Court reasons this way in a case in which no woman has complained, and the only complainant is a man who advances no claims on behalf of anyone else. His claim [is] not that he is being denied a substantive educational opportunity, or even the right to attend an all-male or a coeducational college. It is *only* that the colleges open to him are located at inconvenient distances.

* * * I would sustain Mississippi's right to continue MUW on a rational basis analysis. But I need not apply this "lowest tier" of scrutiny. [More] than 2,000 women presently evidence their preference for MUW by having enrolled [there.] Generations of our finest minds, both among educators and students, have believed that single-sex, college-level institutions afford distinctive benefits. There are many persons, of course, who have different views. But simply because there are these differences is no reason—certainly none of constitutional dimension—to conclude that no substantial state interest is served when such a choice is made available.[17][d]

Notes and Questions

1. *Segregation.* In *Hogan,* the Court stated that it was "not faced with the question of whether States can provide 'separate but equal' undergraduate institutions for males and females. Cf. *Vorchheimer v. School Dist. of Philadelphia,* 532 F.2d 880 (3d Cir.1976), affirmed by an equally divided Court, 430 U.S.

9. Even the Court does not argue that the appropriate standard here is "strict scrutiny"—a standard that none of our "sex discrimination" cases ever has adopted. Sexual segregation in education differs from the tradition [of] "separate but equal" *racial* segregation. It was characteristic of racial segregation that segregated facilities were offered, not as alternatives to increase the choices available to blacks, but as the *sole* alternative. MUW stands in sharp contrast. Of Mississippi's eight public universities and 16 public junior colleges, only MUW considers sex as a criterion for admission. Women consequently are free to select a coeducational education environment for themselves if they so desire; their attendance of MUW is not a matter of coercion.

17. [It] is understandable that MUW might believe that it could allow men to audit courses without materially affecting its environment. MUW charges tuition but gives no academic credit for auditing. The University evidently is correct in believing that few men will choose to audit under such circumstances. This deviation from a perfect relationship between means and ends is insubstantial.

d. Blackmun, J.'s brief dissenting opinion—agreeing essentially with Powell, J.—is omitted.

703, 97 S.Ct. 1671, 51 L.Ed.2d 750 (1977) (Rehnquist, J., not participating; upholding "separate but equal" public schools for boys and girls"). May public schools have separate athletic programs for boys and girls? In all sports? See Stroud, *Sex Discrimination in High School Athletics,* 6 Ind.L.Rev. 661 (1973). May state prisons be sexually segregated? See Note, *The Sexual Segregation of American Prisons,* 82 Yale L.J. 1229 (1973). May state buildings have separate bathrooms for men and women? Of what significance is the constitutional "right of privacy"? See Ch. 3, Sec. 2. Are there reasons to distinguish between race and sex segregation in the above situations? In some, but not all? See generally Wasserstrom, fn. d supra.

2. *Equal Rights Amendment.* This proposed amendment—that "equality of rights under the law shall not be denied or abridged by the United States or by an State on account of sex"—was approved by 35 states (three less than required for ratification) at its expiration in 1982.

How would this affect the issues considered in this section? See generally B. Brown, Emerson, Falk & Freedman, *The Equal Rights Amendment: A Constitutional Basis for Equal Rights for Women,* 80 Yale L.J. 871 (1971); *Equal Rights for Women: A Symposium on the Proposed Constitutional Amendment,* 6 Harv. Civ.Rts.-Civ.Lib.L.Rev. 125 (1971).

III. ILLEGITIMACY

NEW JERSEY WELFARE RIGHTS ORG. v. CAHILL

411 U.S. 619, 93 S.Ct. 1700, 36 L.Ed.2d 543 (1973).

PER CURIAM.

This case presents the question of the constitutionality under the Equal Protection Clause of the Fourteenth Amendment of the New Jersey "Assistance to Families of the Working Poor" program that allegedly discriminates against illegitimate children in the provision of financial assistance and other services. Specifically, appellants challenge that aspect of the program that limits benefits to only those otherwise qualified families "which consist of a household composed of two adults of the opposite sex ceremonially married to each other who have at least one minor child * * * of both, the natural child of one and adopted by the other, or a child adopted by both * * *." N.J.Stat.Ann. § 44:13–3(a). Appellants do not challenge the statute's "household" requirement. Rather, they argue that although the challenged classification turns upon the marital status of the parents as well as upon the parent-child relationship, in practical effect it operates almost invariably to deny benefits to illegitimate children while granting benefits to those children who are legitimate. Although apparently conceding the correctness of this position, the [lower court] upheld the statutory scheme on the ground that it was designed "to preserve and strengthen family life." [a]

Confronted with similar arguments in the past, we have specifically declared that: "The status of illegitimacy has expressed through the ages society's condemnation of irresponsible liaisons beyond the bonds of marriage. But visiting this condemnation on the head of an infant is illogical and unjust.

a. The lower court argued that it was appropriate for the state to limit its subsidy to "legitimate families, ones where the likelihood is greater for the instillment of social norms. It is certainly a proper and a compelling state interest to refuse to subsidize a living unit which may lead to the state of anomie and which violates its laws against fornication and adultery."

Moreover, imposing disabilities on the illegitimate child is contrary to the basic concept of our system that legal burdens should bear some relationship to individual responsibility or wrongdoing. Obviously, no child is responsible for his birth and penalizing the illegitimate child is an ineffectual—as well as an unjust—way of deterring the parent." *Weber v. Aetna Casualty & Surety Co.*, 406 U.S. 164, 92 S.Ct. 1400, 31 L.Ed.2d 768 (1972). Thus, in *Weber* we held that under the Equal Protection Clause a State may not exclude illegitimate children from sharing equally with other children in the recovery of workmen's compensation benefits for the death of their parent. Similarly, in *Levy v. Louisiana*, 391 U.S. 68 (1968) 88 S.Ct. 1509, 20 L.Ed.2d 436, we held that a State may not create a right of action in favor of children for the wrongful death of a parent and exclude illegitimate children from the benefit of such a right. And only this Term, in *Gomez v. Perez*, 409 U.S. 535, 93 S.Ct. 872, 35 L.Ed.2d 56 (1973), we held that once a State posits a judicially enforceable right on behalf of children to needed support from their natural father, there is no constitutionally sufficient justification for denying such an essential right to illegitimate children.[b]

Those decisions compel the conclusion that appellants' claim of the denial of equal protection must be sustained, for there can be no doubt that the benefits extended under the challenged program are as indispensable to the health and well-being of illegitimate children as to those who are legitimate. * * *

THE CHIEF JUSTICE concurs in the result.

JUSTICE REHNQUIST, dissenting. * * *

The Court relies on *Weber v. Aetna Casualty & Surety Co.*, where a Louisiana statute that denied workmen's compensation benefits to an illegitimate child was invalidated. But the very language that the Court quotes from *Weber* shows how different this case is from that. There a disability was visited solely on an illegitimate child. Here the statute distinguishes among types of families. While the classification adopted by the New Jersey Legislature undoubtedly results in denying benefits to "families" consisting of a mother and father not ceremonially married who are living with natural children, whatever denial of benefits the classification makes is imposed equally on the parents as well as the children.

Here the New Jersey Legislature has determined that special financial assistance should be given to family units that meet the statutory definition of "working poor." It does not seem to me irrational in establishing such a special program to condition the receipt of such grants on the sort of ceremonial marriage that could quite reasonably be found to be an essential ingredient of the family unit that the New Jersey Legislature is trying to protect from dissolution due to the economic vicissitudes of modern life. The Constitution does not require that special financial assistance designed by the legislature to help poor families be extended to "communes" as well. [Here] the classification is based on a particular type of family unit, one of, if not the, core units of our social system. * * *

Notes and Questions

1. Consider Krause, *Equal Protection for the Illegitimate*, 65 Mich.L.Rev. 477, 488–89: "There has been a long history of discrimination against the

b. *Clark v. Jeter*, note 2 infra, invalidated a six year statute of limitations as applied to paternity actions required as a prerequisite for support actions. The Court pointed to "increasingly sophisticated tests for genetic markers [that] permit the exclusion of over 99% of those who might be accused of paternity."

illegitimate. The medieval church, in both its concern for the family and its aversion to illicit sex, reinforced the basic self-interest of the father, which self-interest may ultimately have been most directly responsible for the situation of the illegitimate. It was natural that men, as legislators, would have limited their accidental offsprings' claims against them, both economically and in terms of a family relationship, especially since the social status of the illegitimate mother often did not equal their own. Moreover, their legitimate wives had an interest in denying the illegitimate's claim on their husbands, since any such claim could be allowed only at the expense of the legitimate family. Against these forces have stood only the illegitimate mother and the helpless child, and thus it is not surprising that our laws are inconsiderate of the child's interests."

2. CLARK v. JETER, 486 U.S. 456, 108 S.Ct. 1910, 100 L.Ed.2d 465 (1988), per O'CONNOR, J., unanimously stated that between the "extremes of rational basis review and strict scrutiny lies a level of intermediate scrutiny, which generally has been applied to discriminatory classifications based on sex or illegitimacy. To withstand intermediate scrutiny, a statutory classification must be substantially related to an important governmental objective." [c] As Krause observes, "Between 1968 and 1983, the United States Supreme Court decided nearly thirty cases involving illegitimacy on the basis of the Equal Protection Clause of the Federal Constitution * * *. Together, these cases and uncounted state court decisions establish the principle that the nonmarital child is entitled to all but complete legal equality with the legitimate child in most substantive areas of the law." [d]

In the area of intestate succession, however, the Court has followed a wavering course.[e] *Labine v. Vincent,* 401 U.S. 532, 91 S.Ct. 1017, 28 L.Ed.2d 288 (1971), per Black, J., upheld a Louisiana law denying inheritance to a child born out of wedlock even though the father had acknowledged the child during his lifetime.[f] TRIMBLE v. GORDON, 430 U.S. 762, 97 S.Ct. 1459, 52 L.Ed.2d 31 (1977), per POWELL, J., declared unconstitutional an Illinois law that permitted marital children to recover from either intestate parent, but permitted nonmarital children to inherit from intestate mothers, not from intestate fathers.[g] Gordon had been found to be the father in a support court action prior to his death, and the Court stated that "adjudication should be equally sufficient to establish" a share in the estate. On the other hand, the Court said: "Our holding today goes only to those forms of proof which do not clearly compromise the state's interests. * * * This clearly would be the case, for example, where there is a prior adjudication or formal acknowledgement of paternity.

c. The standard has sometimes not been stated in illegitimacy cases or differently stated. See, e.g., *Mathews v. Lucas,* fn. d supra (standard of review is "not toothless"); *Califano v. Boles,* 443 U.S. 282, 99 S.Ct. 2767, 61 L.Ed.2d 541 (1979) (requiring a "close and substantial relationship to a permissible state interest"). Should the standard be stricter? Should the standard depend upon whether the person harmed by the state regulation is a child or a parent? See Note, *Equal Protection for Unmarried Parents,* 65 Ia.L.Rev. 679 (1980).

d. *Family Law* 154–55 (2d ed. 1986).

e. For other exceptions to the principle that nonmarital children win, see *Mathews v. Lucas,* 427 U.S. 495, 96 S.Ct. 2755, 49 L.Ed.2d 651 (1976) (some classes of illegitimate children required to prove dependency in order to receive social security benefits); *Fiallo v. Bell,* 430 U.S. 787, 97 S.Ct. 1473, 52 L.Ed.2d 50 (1977) (upholding federal law granting immigration preference to children of citizens (except when the children are illegitimate) and "parents" of citizens (except the natural father of a citizen who is his illegitimate child)).

f. Brennan, J., joined by Douglas, White, and Marshall, JJ., dissented finding "no rational basis for the law."

g. *Labine* was not overruled, but was declared to be "difficult to place in the pattern of this Court's equal protection cases" and its force as a precedent was said to be limited.

[W]e would have a different case if the state statute were carefully tailored to eliminate imprecise and unduly burdensome methods of establishing paternity." [h]

Finally, LALLI v. LALLI, 439 U.S. 259, 99 S.Ct. 518, 58 L.Ed.2d 503 (1978) upheld a law forbidding nonmarital children to inherit from their intestate fathers—even though there is 'convincing proof of paternity'—unless there was a judicial finding of paternity during the father's lifetime.[i]

Are *Labine* and *Lalli* consistent with the rationale in *Cahill?* Is there a convincing reason to treat intestate succession differently from the support obligations required by *Gomez v. Perez?*

3. Consider Wallach and Tenoso, *A Vindication of the Rights of Unmarried Mothers and Their Children,* 23 U.Kan.L.Rev. 23, 56 (1974): "Regardless of what the Court said, [the] fact is that *Cahill* invalidated discrimination against a *family unit,* some of whose member could be said to bear individual responsibility for the burdens imposed upon them. [Invalidation] of differential treatment of 'legitimate' and 'illegitimate' family units is a recognition that discrimination against those whose conduct is responsible for the imposition of detriments—the parents—may be as impermissible as discrimination against the innocent 'illegitimate' children." Is this because it is necessary to protect the parents in order to protect the child? See *id.*

4. *Discrimination against unmarried mothers.* GLONA v. AMERICAN GUAR. & LIAB. INS. CO., 391 U.S. 73, 88 S.Ct. 1515, 20 L.Ed.2d 441 (1968), per DOUGLAS, J., held that there was no "rational basis for assuming that if [a] mother is allowed recovery [in a wrongful death case that] the cause of illegitimacy will be served." The Court thought it "farfetched to assume that women have illegitimate children so they can be compensated in damages for their death." Consider Wallach & Tenoso, supra, at 47: "Because the statutory classification as construed in *Glona* discriminatorily affected the person responsible for the undesired conduct, [the Court could have] distinguished *Glona* on this basis and applied a rational or reasonable standard of review to validate the statute. That it did not take this approach suggests [that] what was important to the Court was not only that burdens should bear some relationship to individual responsibility, but also, regardless of social responsibility, that statutes that discriminate against unmarried mothers (parents) should be presumptively invalid." [j]

h. Burger, C.J., joined by Stewart, Blackmun, and Rehnquist, JJ., dissented.

i. Powell, J., joined by Burger, C.J., and Stewart, J., distinguished *Trimble* on the grounds that Trimble would have inherited under New York's law and that the law considered in *Trimble* swept so far as to effect "a total statutory disinheritance of children born out of wedlock who were not legitimated by the subsequent marriage of their parents." Rehnquist, J., concurred, adhering to his dissent in *Trimble.* Blackmun, J., also concurring was "unconvinced by the plurality's valiant struggle to distinguish, rather than overrule, *Trimble,*" which he would. Brennan, joined by White, Marshall, and Stevens, JJ., dissenting, saw "no reason to retreat from *Trimble.*"

j. But cf. *Califano v. Boles,* 443 U.S. 282, 99 S.Ct. 2767, 61 L.Ed.2d 541 (1979), per Rehnquist, J., upholding a provision of the Social Security Act granting "mother's benefits" to a deceased's widow or divorced wife (but not to the mother of his illegitimate child). The Court, noting that the illegitimate child received child's benefits, reasoned that the "mother's benefits" program "was not designed [for] child-care subsidies. Instead Congress sought to limit the category of beneficiaries to those who actually suffer economic dislocation upon the death of a wage earner and are likely to be confronted at that juncture with the choice between employment or the assumption of full-time child-care responsibilities. In this [light,] Congress could reasonably conclude that a woman who has never been married to the wage earner is far less

5. *Discrimination against unmarried fathers.* (a) CABAN v. MOHAMMED, 441 U.S. 380, 99 S.Ct. 1760, 60 L.Ed.2d 297 (1979), per POWELL, J., held violative of equal protection a New York statute granting the mother (but not the father) of an illegitimate child the right to veto the child's adoption: "Even if the special difficulties attendant upon locating and identifying unwed fathers at birth would justify a legislative distinction between mothers and fathers of newborns, these difficulties need not persist past infancy. When the adoption of an older child is sought, the State's interest in proceeding with adoption cases can be protected by means that do not draw such an inflexible gender-based distinction as that made in § 111. In those cases where the father never has come forward to participate in the rearing of his child, nothing in the Equal Protection Clause precludes the State from withholding from him the privilege of vetoing the adoption of that child. [But] in cases such as this, where the father has established a substantial relationship with the child and admitted his paternity, a State should have no difficulty in identifying [him.] Section 111 both excludes some loving fathers from full participation in the decision whether their children will be adopted and, at the same time, enables some alienated mothers arbitrarily to cut off the paternal rights of fathers. We conclude that this undifferentiated distinction [does] not bear a substantial relationship to the State's asserted interests."

STEVENS, J., joined by Burger, C.J., and Rehnquist, J., dissented: "[I]n the more common adoption situations, the mother [of an illegitimate child] will be the more, and often the only, responsible parent, and [a] paternal consent requirement will constitute a hindrance to the adoption process. Because this general rule is amply justified in its normal application, I would therefore require the party challenging its constitutionality to make some demonstration of unfairness in a significant number of situations before concluding that it violates [equal protection]. That the Court has found a violation without requiring such a showing can only be attributed to its own 'stereotyped reaction' to what is unquestionably, but in this case justifiably, a gender-based distinction." [f]

(b) PARHAM v. HUGHES, 441 U.S. 347, 99 S.Ct. 1742, 60 L.Ed.2d 269 (1979), upheld a law denying the father (but not the mother) of an illegitimate child the right to sue for the child's wrongful death unless he had legitimated the child. STEWART, J., joined by Burger, C.J., and Rehnquist and Stevens, JJ.,

likely to be dependent upon the wage earner at the time of his death."

Marshall, J., joined by Brennan, White and Blackmun, JJ., dissented, finding that the program, "both in purpose and effect, is a form of assistance to children," and that its discrimination against illegitimates violates equal protection.

f. Stevens, J., also explained why the Court's holding was "quite narrow": "The procedure to be followed in cases involving infants who are in the custody of their mothers—whether solely or jointly with the father—or of agencies with authority to consent to adoption, is entirely unaffected by the Court's holding or by its reasoning. In fact, as I read the Court's opinion, the statutes now in effect may be enforced as usual unless 'the adoption of older children is sought' and 'the father has established a substantial relationship with the child and admit[s] his paternity.'" Stewart, J., also dissented.

Compare *Lehr v. Robertson,* 463 U.S. 248, 103 S.Ct. 2985, 77 L.Ed.2d 614 (1983), per Stevens, J., upholding (6–3) a New York provision that denies a father, who never had any significant relationship with his illegitimate child, notice and opportunity to be heard before the child may be adopted. But see Michael H. v. Gerald D., p. 1195 infra and p. 250 supra (alleged father with significant relationship to child denied any paternal rights because mother was married to another man at time of conception and birth).

For other decisions dealing with paternal rights in respect to adoption and custody of illegitimate children, see *Stanley v. Illinois,* Sec. 5 infra, and *Quilloin v. Walcott,* p. 245 supra.

found it "clear that the Georgia statute does not invidiously discriminate against the appellant simply because he is of the male sex. The fact is that mothers and fathers of illegitimate children are not similarly situated. Under Georgia law, only a father can by voluntary unilateral action make an illegitimate child legitimate. Unlike the mother of an illegitimate [child,] the identity of the father will frequently be unknown. *Lalli.* [Georgia] has chosen to deal with this problem by allowing only fathers who have established their paternity by legitimating their children to sue for wrongful death, and we cannot say that this solution is an irrational one. [Thus] it is constitutionally irrelevant that the appellant may be able to prove paternity in another manner.

"[Since] fathers who do legitimate their children can sue for wrongful death in precisely the same circumstances as married fathers whose children were legitimate ab initio, the statutory classification does not discriminate against fathers as a class but instead distinguishes between fathers who have legitimated their children and those who have not.[9] Such a classification is quite unlike those condemned in the *Reed, Frontiero,* and *Stanton* cases which were premised upon overbroad generalizations and excluded all members of one sex even though they were similarly situated with members of the other sex."

POWELL, J., concurred because "the gender-based distinction [is] substantially related to achievement of the important state objective of avoiding difficult problems in proving paternity after the death of an illegitimate child."

WHITE, J., joined by Brennan, Marshall and Blackmun, JJ., dissented, finding a "startling circularity" in the plurality's argument: "The issue [is] whether Georgia may require unmarried fathers, but not unmarried mothers, to have pursued the statutory legitimization [procedure]. Seemingly, it is irrelevant that as a matter of state law mothers may not legitimate their children, for they are not required to do so in order to maintain a wrongful death action. That only fathers *may* resort to the legitimization process cannot dissolve the sex discrimination in *requiring* them to.[2] Under the plurality's bootstrap rationale, a State could require that women, but not men, pass a course in order to receive a taxi license, simply by limiting admission to the course to women.[3]"

IV. MENTAL RETARDATION

CLEBURNE v. CLEBURNE LIVING CENTER, INC.

473 U.S. 432, 105 S.Ct. 3249, 87 L.Ed.2d 313 (1985).

JUSTICE WHITE delivered the opinion of the Court.

A Texas city denied a special permit for the operation of a group home for the mentally retarded. [Permits under the zoning ordinance must be renewed annually and applicants must "obtain the signatures of the property owners within 200 feet of the property to be used."] It was anticipated that the

9. The ability of a father to make his child legitimate under Georgia law distinguishes this case from *Caban* [where] the father could neither change his children's status nor his own for purposes of the New York adoption statute.

2. The plurality not only fails to examine whether required resort by fathers to the legitimization procedure bears more than a rational relationship to any state interest, but also fails even to address the constitutionality of the sex discrimination in allowing fathers but not mothers to legitimate their children. It is anomalous, at least, to assert that sex discrimination in one statute is constitutionally invisible because it is tied to sex discrimination in another statute, without subjecting *either* [to] an appropriate level of scrutiny.

3. Men and women would therefore not be "similarly situated." Yet requiring a course for women but not for men is quite obviously a classification on the basis of sex.

[Featherston] home would house 13 retarded men and women, who would be under the constant supervision of CLC staff members. * * *

[The] general rule [under the Equal Protection Clause] is that legislation is presumed to be valid and will be sustained if the classification drawn by the statute is rationally related to a legitimate state interest. *Schweiker v. Wilson; United States R.R. Retirement Bd. v. Fritz; Vance v. Bradley; New Orleans v. Dukes,* [Sec. 1 supra]. When social or economic legislation is at issue, the Equal Protection Clause allows the states wide latitude, and the Constitution presumes that even improvident decisions will eventually be rectified by the democratic processes.

The general rule gives way, however, when a statute classifies by race, alienage or national origin. These factors are so seldom relevant to the achievement of any legitimate state interest that laws grounded in such considerations are deemed to reflect prejudice and antipathy—a view that those in the burdened class are not as worthy or deserving as others. For these reasons and because such discrimination is unlikely to be soon rectified by legislative means, these laws are subjected to strict scrutiny * * *.

Legislative classifications based on gender also call for a heightened standard of review. [Rather] than resting on meaningful considerations, statutes distributing benefits and burdens between the sexes in different ways very likely reflect outmoded notions of the relative capabilities of men and women. A gender classification fails unless it is substantially related to a sufficiently important governmental interest. Because illegitimacy is beyond the individual's control and bears "no relation to the individual's ability to participate in and contribute to society," official discriminations resting on that characteristic are also subject to somewhat heightened review. Those restrictions "will survive equal protection scrutiny to the extent they are substantially related to a legitimate state interest." *Mills v. Habluetzel,* 456 U.S. 91, 102 S.Ct. 1549, 71 L.Ed.2d 770 (1982).

We have declined, however, to extend heightened review to differential treatment based on [age]. The lesson of *Murgia,* [p. 1104 infra], is that where individuals in the group affected by a law have distinguishing characteristics relevant to interests the state has the authority to implement, the courts have been very reluctant, as they should be in our federal system and with our respect for the separation of powers, to closely scrutinize legislative choices as to whether, how and to what extent those interests should be pursued. In such cases, the Equal Protection Clause requires only a rational means to serve a legitimate end.

Against this background, we conclude [that] the Court of Appeals erred in holding mental retardation a quasi-suspect classification. [First, those] who are mentally retarded have a reduced ability to cope with and function in the everyday world. [T]hey range from those whose disability is not immediately evident to those who must be constantly cared for. They are thus different, immutably so, in relevant respects, and the states' interest in dealing with and providing for them is plainly a legitimate one. How this large and diversified group is to be treated under the law is a difficult and often a technical matter, very much a task for legislators guided by qualified professionals and not by the perhaps ill-informed opinions of the judiciary. Heightened scrutiny inevitably involves substantive judgments about legislative decisions, and we doubt that the predicate for such judicial oversight is present where the classification deals with mental retardation.

Second, the distinctive legislative response, both national and state, to the plight of those who are mentally retarded demonstrates not only that they have unique problems, but also that the lawmakers have been addressing their difficulties in a manner that belies a continuing antipathy or prejudice and a corresponding need for more intrusive oversight by the judiciary. Thus, the federal government has not only outlawed discrimination against the mentally retarded in federally funded programs, see § 504 of the Rehabilitation Act of 1973, 29 U.S.C. § 794, but it has also provided the retarded with the right to receive "appropriate treatment, services, and habilitation" in a setting that is "least restrictive of [their] personal liberty." Developmental Disabilities Assistance and Bill of Rights Act, 42 U.S.C. §§ 6010(1), (2). * * * Texas has similarly enacted legislation that acknowledges the special status of the mentally retarded by conferring certain rights upon them, such as "the right to live in the least restrictive setting appropriate to [their] individual needs and abilities," * * *.[11] [It] may be, as CLC contends, that legislation designed to benefit, rather than disadvantage, the retarded would generally withstand examination under a test of heightened scrutiny. The relevant inquiry, however, is whether heightened scrutiny is constitutionally mandated in the first instance. Even assuming that many of these laws could be shown to be substantially related to an important governmental purpose, merely requiring the legislature to justify its efforts in these terms may lead it to refrain from acting at all. Much recent legislation intended to benefit the retarded also assumes the need for measures that might be perceived to disadvantage them. The Education of the Handicapped Act, for example, requires an "appropriate" education, not one that is equal in all respects to the education of non-retarded children; clearly, admission to a class that exceeded the abilities of a retarded child would not be appropriate. Similarly, the Developmental Disabilities Assistance Act and the Texas act give the retarded the right to live only in the "least restrictive setting" appropriate to their abilities, implicitly assuming the need for at least some restrictions that would not be imposed on others. Especially given the wide variation in the abilities and needs of the retarded themselves, governmental bodies must have a certain amount of flexibility and freedom from judicial oversight in shaping and limiting their remedial efforts.

Third, the legislative response, which could hardly have occurred and survived without public support, negates any claim that the mentally retarded are politically powerless in the sense that they have no ability to attract the attention of the lawmakers. Any minority can be said to be powerless to assert direct control over the legislature, but if that were a criterion for higher level scrutiny by the courts, much economic and social legislation would now be suspect.

Fourth, if the large and amorphous class of the mentally retarded were deemed quasi-suspect, [it] would be difficult to find a principled way to distinguish a variety of other groups who have perhaps immutable disabilities setting them off from others, who cannot themselves mandate the desired legislative responses, and who can claim some degree of prejudice from at least part of the public at large. One need mention in this respect only the aging, the disabled, the mentally ill, and the infirm. We are reluctant to set out on that course, and we decline to do so.

11. [A] number of states have [laws] prohibiting zoning that excludes the retarded.

Doubtless, there have been and there will continue to be instances of discrimination against the retarded that are in fact invidious, and that are properly subject to judicial correction under constitutional norms. But the appropriate method of reaching such instances is [to] look to the likelihood that governmental action premised on a particular classification is valid as a general matter, not merely to the specifics of the case before us. Because mental retardation is a characteristic that the government may legitimately take into account in a wide range of decisions, and because both state and federal governments have recently committed themselves to assisting the retarded, we will not presume that any given legislative action, even one that disadvantages retarded individuals, is rooted in considerations that the Constitution will not tolerate.

Our refusal to recognize the retarded as a quasi-suspect class does not leave them entirely unprotected from invidious discrimination. To withstand equal protection review, legislation that distinguishes between the mentally retarded and others must be rationally related to a legitimate governmental purpose. This standard, we believe, affords government the latitude necessary both to pursue policies designed to assist the retarded in realizing their full potential, and to freely and efficiently engage in activities that burden the retarded in what is essentially an incidental manner. The State may not rely on a classification whose relationship to an asserted goal is so attenuated as to render the distinction arbitrary or irrational. See *Zobel v. Williams; U.S. Dep't of Agriculture v. Moreno.* Furthermore, some objectives—such as "a bare * * * desire to harm a politically unpopular group," *Moreno* —are not legitimate state interests. Beyond that, the mentally retarded, like others, have and retain their substantive constitutional rights in addition to the right to be treated equally by the law. * * *

The constitutional issue is clearly posed. The City does not require a special use permit in an R–3 zone for apartment houses, multiple dwellings, boarding and lodging houses, fraternity or sorority houses, dormitories, apartment hotels, hospitals, sanitariums, nursing homes for convalescents or the aged (other than for the insane or feeble-minded or alcoholics or drug addicts), private clubs or fraternal orders, and other specified uses. [I]n our view the record does not reveal any rational basis for believing that the Featherston home would pose any special threat to the city's legitimate interests * * *.

The District Court found that the City Council's insistence on the permit rested on several factors. First, the Council was concerned with the negative attitude of the majority of property owners located within 200 feet of the Featherston facility, as well as with the fears of elderly residents of the neighborhood. But mere negative attitudes, or fear, unsubstantiated by factors which are properly cognizable in a zoning proceeding, are not permissible bases for treating a home for the mentally retarded differently from apartment houses, multiple dwellings, and the like. * * *

Second, the Council [was] concerned that the facility was across the street from a junior high school, and it feared that the students might harass the occupants of the Featherston home. But the school itself is attended by about 30 mentally retarded students, and denying a permit based on such vague, undifferentiated fears is again permitting some portion of the community to validate what would otherwise be an equal protection violation. The other objection to the home's location was that it was located on "a five hundred year flood plain." This concern with the possibility of a flood, however, can hardly be based on a distinction between the Featherston home and, for example, nursing homes, homes for convalescents or the aged, or sanitariums or hospitals, any of which could be located on the Featherston site without obtaining a special use permit. The same may be said of another concern of the Council—doubts about the legal responsibility for actions which the mentally retarded might take. If there is no concern about legal responsibility with respect to other uses that would be permitted in the area, such as boarding and fraternity houses, it is difficult to believe that the groups of mildly or moderately mentally retarded individuals who would live at 201 Featherston would present any different or special hazard.

Fourth, the Council was concerned with the size of the home and the number of people that would occupy it. [But] there would be no restrictions on the number of people who could occupy this home as a boarding house, nursing home, family dwelling, fraternity house, or dormitory. [At] least this record does not clarify how, in this connection, the characteristics of the intended occupants of the Featherston home rationally justify denying to those occupants what would be permitted to groups occupying the same site for different purposes. Those who would live in the Featherston home are the type of individuals who, with supporting staff, satisfy federal and state standards for group housing in the community; and there is no dispute that the home would meet the federal square-footage-per-resident requirement for facilities of this type. See 42 CFR § 442.447 (1984). * * *

In the courts below the city also urged that the ordinance is aimed at avoiding concentration of population and at lessening congestion of the streets. These concerns obviously fail to explain why apartment houses, fraternity and sorority houses, hospitals and the like, may freely locate in the area without a permit. So, too, the expressed worry about fire hazards, the serenity of the neighborhood, and the avoidance of danger to other residents fail rationally to justify singling out a home such as 201 Featherston for the special use permit, yet imposing no such restrictions on the many other uses freely permitted in the neighborhood.

The short of it is that requiring the permit in this case appears to us to rest on an irrational prejudice against the mentally retarded. [Thus, the] judgment of the Court of Appeals is affirmed insofar as it invalidates the zoning ordinance as applied to the Featherston home. * * *

JUSTICE STEVENS, with whom THE CHIEF JUSTICE joins, concurring.

[O]ur cases reflect a continuum of judgmental responses to differing classifications which have been explained in opinions by terms ranging from "strict scrutiny" at one extreme to "rational basis" at the other. I have never been persuaded that these so called "standards" adequately explain the decisional process. Cases involving classifications based on alienage, illegal residency, illegitimacy, gender, age, or—as in this case—mental retardation, do not fit well into sharply defined classifications.

[It] would be utterly irrational to limit the franchise on the basis of height or weight; it is equally invalid to limit it on the basis of skin color. None of these attributes has any bearing at all on the citizen's willingness or ability to exercise that civil right. We do not need to apply a special standard, or to apply "strict scrutiny," or even "heightened scrutiny," to decide such cases.

In every equal protection case, we have to ask certain basic questions. What class is harmed by the legislation, and has it been subjected to a "tradition of disfavor" by our laws? What is the public purpose that is being served by the law? What is the characteristic of the disadvantaged class that justifies the disparate treatment? In most cases the answer to these questions will tell us whether the statute has a "rational basis." The answers will result in the virtually automatic invalidation of racial classifications and in the validation of most economic classifications, but they will provide differing results in cases involving classifications based on alienage, gender, or illegitimacy. But that is not because we apply an "intermediate standard of review" in these cases; rather it is because the characteristics of these groups are sometimes relevant and sometimes irrelevant to a valid public purpose, or, more specifically, to the purpose that the challenged laws purportedly intended to serve.

Every law that places the mentally retarded in a special class is not presumptively irrational. The differences between mentally retarded persons and those with greater mental capacity are obviously relevant to certain legislative decisions. * * *

Even so, the Court of Appeals correctly observed that through ignorance and prejudice the mentally retarded "have been subjected to a history of unfair and often grotesque mistreatment." The [record in this case] convinces me that this permit was required because of the irrational fears of neighboring property owners, rather than for the protection of the mentally retarded persons who would reside in respondent's home. * * * I cannot believe that a rational member of this disadvantaged class could ever approve of the discriminatory application of the city's ordinance in this case. * * *

JUSTICE MARSHALL, with whom JUSTICE BRENNAN and JUSTICE BLACKMUN join, concurring in the judgment in part and dissenting in part.

The Court holds [the] ordinance invalid on rational basis grounds and disclaims that anything special, in the form of heightened scrutiny, is taking place. Yet Cleburne's ordinance surely would be valid under the traditional rational basis test applicable to economic and commercial regulation. In my view, it is important to articulate, as the Court does not, the facts and principles that justify subjecting this zoning ordinance to the searching review—the heightened scrutiny—that actually leads to its invalidation. * * *

The Court, for example, concludes that legitimate concerns for fire hazards or the serenity of the neighborhood do not justify singling out respondents to bear the burdens of these concerns, for analogous permitted uses appear to pose similar threats. Yet under the traditional and most minimal version of the rational basis test, "reform may take one step at a time, addressing itself to the phase of the problem which seems most acute to the legislative mind." The "record" is said not to support the ordinance's classifications, but under the traditional standard we do not sift through the record to determine whether policy decisions are squarely supported by a firm factual foundation.

Finally, the Court further finds it "difficult to believe" that the retarded present different or special hazards than other groups. In normal circumstances, the burden is not on the legislature to convince the Court that the lines it has drawn are sensible; legislation is presumptively constitutional, and a State "is not required to resort to close distinctions or to maintain a precise, scientific uniformity with reference" to its goals. [The] same imprecision in a similar ordinance that required opticians but not optometrists to be licensed to practice, see *Williamson v. Lee Optical Co.,* [Sec. 1 supra], or that excluded new but not old businesses from parts of a community, see *Dukes,* [Sec. 1 supra], would hardly be fatal to the statutory scheme.

The refusal to acknowledge that something more than minimum rationality review is at work here is, in my view, unfortunate in at least two respects.[4] The suggestion that the traditional rational basis test allows this sort of searching inquiry creates precedent for this Court and lower courts to subject economic and commercial classifications to similar and searching "ordinary" rational basis review—a small and regrettable step back toward the days of *Lochner v. New York*. Moreover, by failing to articulate the factors that justify today's "second order" rational basis review, the Court provides no principled foundation for determining when more searching inquiry is to be invoked. Lower courts are thus left in the dark on this important question, and this Court remains unaccountable for its decisions employing, or refusing to employ, particularly searching scrutiny. * * *

I have long believed the level of scrutiny employed in an equal protection case should vary with "the constitutional and societal importance of the interest adversely affected and the recognized invidiousness of the basis upon which the particular classification is drawn." *Rodriguez* (Marshall, J., dissenting). See also *Dandridge* (Marshall, J., dissenting). When a zoning ordinance works to exclude the retarded from all residential districts in a community, these two considerations require that the ordinance be convincingly justified as substantially furthering legitimate and important purposes.

First, the interest [in] establishing group homes is substantial, [for] as deinstitutionalization has progressed, group homes have become the primary means by which retarded adults can enter life in the community. * * *

Second, the mentally retarded have been subject to a "lengthy and tragic history" of segregation and discrimination that can only be called grotesque. [The] searching scrutiny I would give to restrictions on the ability of the retarded to establish community group homes leads me to conclude that Cleburne's vague generalizations for classifying the "feeble minded" with drug addicts, alcoholics, and the insane, and excluding them where the elderly, the ill, the boarder, and the transient are allowed, are not substantial or important enough to overcome the suspicion that the ordinance rests on impermissible assumptions or outmoded and perhaps invidious stereotypes. * * *

The Court downplays the lengthy "history of purposeful unequal treatment" of the retarded by pointing to recent legislative action that is said to "beli[e] a continuing antipathy or prejudice." Building on this point, the Court similarly concludes that the retarded are not "politically powerless" and deserve no greater judicial protection than "any minority" that wins some political battles and loses others. The import of these conclusions, it seems, is that the only discrimination courts may remedy is the discrimination they alone are perspicacious enough to see. [B]ut history makes clear that constitutional principles of equality, like constitutional principles of liberty, property, and due process, evolve over [time].

It is natural that evolving standards of equality come to be embodied in legislation. When that occurs, courts should look to the fact of such change as a source of guidance on evolving principles of equality [as when the Court]

4. The two cases the Court cites in its rational basis discussion, *Zobel* and *Moreno,* expose the special nature of the rational basis test employed today. As two of only a handful of modern equal protection cases striking down legislation under what purports to be a rational basis standard, these cases must be and generally have been viewed as intermediate review decisions masquerading in rational basis language. See, e.g., Tribe, *American Constitutional Law* 1090, n. 10 (1978). (discussing *Moreno*); see also *Moreno* (Douglas, J., concurring); *Zobel* (Brennan, J., concurring).

extended heightened scrutiny to gender classifications and drew on parallel legislative developments to support that extension [*Frontiero*].

Moreover, even when judicial action *has* catalyzed legislative change, that change certainly does not eviscerate the underlying constitutional principle. The Court, for example, has never suggested that race-based classifications became any less suspect once extensive legislation had been enacted on the subject.

For the retarded, just as for Negroes and women, much has changed in recent years, but much remains the same; outdated statutes are still on the books, and irrational fears or ignorance, traceable to the prolonged social and cultural isolation of the retarded, continue to stymie recognition of the dignity and individuality of retarded people. * * *

The Court also offers a more general view of heightened [scrutiny]. First, heightened scrutiny is said to be inapplicable where *individuals* in a group have distinguishing characteristics that legislatures properly may take into account in some circumstances. Heightened scrutiny is also purportedly inappropriate when many legislative classifications affecting the *group* are likely to be [valid.]

If the Court's first principle were sound, heightened scrutiny would have to await a day when people could be cut from a cookie mold. Women are hardly alike in all their characteristics, but heightened scrutiny applies to them because legislatures can rarely use gender itself as a proxy for these other characteristics. [Similarly,] that some retarded people have reduced capacities in some areas does not justify using retardation as a proxy for reduced capacity in areas where relevant individual variations in capacity do exist.

The Court's second assertion—that the standard of review must be fixed with reference to the number of classifications to which a characteristic would validly be relevant—is similarly flawed. [Our] heightened scrutiny precedents belie the claim that a characteristic must virtually always be irrelevant to warrant heightened scrutiny. * * * Heightened but not strict scrutiny is considered appropriate in areas such as gender, illegitimacy, or alienage because the Court views the trait as relevant under some circumstances but not others. [An] inquiry into constitutional principle, not mathematics, determines whether heightened scrutiny is appropriate. Whenever evolving principles of equality, rooted in the Equal Protection Clause, require that certain classifications be viewed as *potentially* discriminatory, and when history reveals systemic unequal treatment, more searching judicial inquiry than minimum rationality becomes relevant.

Potentially discriminatory classifications exist only where some constitutional basis can be found for presuming that equal rights are required. [With] regard to economic and commercial matters, no basis for such a conclusion exists, for [t]he structure of economic and commercial life is a matter of political compromise, not constitutional principle, and no norm of equality requires that there be as many opticians as optometrists, see *Lee Optical,* or new businesses as old, see *Dukes.* * * * [24]

24. No single talisman can define those groups likely to be the target of classifications offensive to the Fourteenth Amendment and therefore warranting heightened or strict scrutiny; experience, not abstract logic, must be the primary guide. The "political powerlessness" of a group may be relevant, but that factor is neither necessary, as the gender cases demonstrate, nor sufficient, as the example of minors illustrates. [W]e see few statutes reflecting prejudice or indifference to minors, and I am not aware of any suggestion that legislation affecting them be viewed with the suspicion of heightened scrutiny. Similarly, immutability of the trait at issue may be relevant, but many immutable

In light of the scrutiny that should be applied here, Cleburne's ordinance sweeps too broadly to dispel the suspicion that it rests on a bare desire to treat the retarded as outsiders, pariahs who do not belong in the community. The Court, while disclaiming that special scrutiny is necessary or warranted, reaches the same conclusion. Rather than striking the ordinance down, however, the Court invalidates it merely as applied to respondents. I must dissent from the novel proposition that "the preferred course of adjudication" is to leave standing a legislative act resting on "irrational prejudice," thereby forcing individuals in the group discriminated against to continue to run the act's gauntlet. * * *

Notes and Questions

1. Stevens, J.: "I cannot believe that a rational member of this disadvantaged class could ever approve of the discriminatory application of the city's ordinance in this case." Consider Minow, *When Difference Has Its Home: Group Homes for the Mentally Retarded, Equal Protection and Legal Treatment of Difference,* 22 Harv.Civ.Rts.Civ.Lib.L.Rev. 111, 128 (1987): "If one assumes that people are related to each other, then assertions of difference are actually statements of relationships, since they express a comparison between the one doing the asserting and the one about whom the assertion is made. Acts of comparison, then, express and distribute power. Differences do not reside in any one person. Instead differences are comparisons drawn by some to locate themselves in relation to others. [Attributions] of difference should be sustained only if they do not express or confirm the distribution of power in ways that harm the less powerful and benefit the more powerful." Does Justice Stevens adopt this perspective? In assessing what harms or benefits the less powerful, is it possible to take their perspective? Is Justice Stevens searching for the "rational" mentally retarded person or is he independently determining what would be in the interests of the group? For consideration of these and related issues, see id.

2. *Other classifications.* MASSACHUSETTS BD. OF RETIREMENT v. MURGIA, 427 U.S. 307, 96 S.Ct. 2562, 49 L.Ed.2d 520 (1976), per curiam, upheld—"under the rational basis standard"—a law requiring uniformed state police officers to retire at age 50. After first rejecting the contention "that a right of governmental employment per se is fundamental" so as to make the legislative classification subject to "strict scrutiny" (see Sec. 4, IV infra), the

characteristics, such as height or blindness, are valid bases of governmental action and classifications under a variety of circumstances.

The political powerlessness of a group and the immutability of its defining trait are relevant insofar as they point to a social and cultural isolation that gives the majority little reason to respect or be concerned with that group's interests and needs. Statutes discriminating against the young have not been common nor need be feared because those who do vote and legislate were once themselves young, typically have children of their own, and certainly interact regularly with minors. Their social integration means that minors, unlike discrete and insular minorities, tend to be treated in legislative arenas with full concern and respect, despite their formal and complete exclusion from the electoral process.

The discreteness and insularity warranting a "more searching judicial inquiry" must therefore be viewed from a social and cultural perspective as well as a political one. To this task judges are well suited, for the lessons of history and experience are surely the best guide as to when, and with respect to what interests, society is likely to stigmatize individuals as members of an inferior caste or view them as not belonging to the community. Because prejudice spawns prejudice, and stereotypes produce limitations that confirm the stereotype on which they are based, a history of unequal treatment requires sensitivity to the prospect that its vestiges endure. In separating those groups that are discrete and insular from those that are not, as in many important legal distinctions, "a page of history is worth a volume of logic."

Court continued: "While the treatment of the aged in this Nation has not been wholly free of discrimination, such persons, unlike, say, those who have been discriminated against on the basis of race or national origin, have not experienced a 'history of purposeful unequal treatment' or been subjected to unique disabilities on the basis of stereotyped characteristics not truly indicative of their abilities. The [Massachusetts statute] cannot be said to discriminate only against the elderly. Rather, it draws the line at a certain age in middle life. But even old age does not define a 'discrete and insular' group, *Carolene Products Co.,* n. 4, in need of 'extraordinary protection from the majoritarian political process.' Instead, it marks a stage that each of us will reach if we live out our normal span. Even if the statute could be said to impose a penalty upon a class defined as the aged, it would not impose a distinction sufficiently akin to those classifications that we have found suspect to call for strict judicial scrutiny." [b]

MARSHALL, J., dissented from "the rigid two-tier model [that] still holds sway as the Court's articulated description of the equal protection test," urging the "flexible equal protection standard" developed in his earlier opinions in *Dandridge v. Williams* and *San Antonio Ind. School Dist. v. Rodriguez,* Sec. 4, IV infra—which would focus "upon the character of the classification in question, the relative importance to individuals in the class discriminated against of the governmental benefits that they do not receive, and the state interests asserted in the support of the classification": "[T]he Court is quite right in suggesting that distinctions exist between the elderly and traditional suspect classes such as [blacks]. The elderly are protected not only by certain antidiscrimination legislation, but by legislation that provides them with positive benefits not enjoyed by the public at large. Moreover, the elderly are not isolated in society, and discrimination against them is not pervasive but is centered primarily in employment. The advantage of a flexible equal protection standard, however, is that it can readily accommodate such variables. The elderly are undoubtedly discriminated against, and when legislation denies them an important benefit—employment—I conclude that to sustain the legislation the Commonwealth must show a reasonably substantial interest and a scheme reasonably closely tailored to achieving that interest." [c]

SECTION 4. "FUNDAMENTAL RIGHTS"

I. DISCRIMINATION IN RESPECT TO VOTING

A. "DILUTION" OF THE RIGHT: APPORTIONMENT

The Court's initial hesitancy to consider malapportioned legislatures—largely the product of districts drawn when the nation's rural/urban population ratio was vastly different than in mid 20th century—and its subsequent assertion of jurisdiction are presented in BAKER v. CARR, p. 31 supra.

The first full post-*Baker* opinion on the problem was GRAY v. SANDERS, 372 U.S. 368, 83 S.Ct. 801, 9 L.Ed.2d 821 (1963), invalidating the "county unit

b. See also *Vance v. Bradley,* 440 U.S. 93, 99 S.Ct. 939, 59 L.Ed.2d 171 (1979), upholding mandatory retirement at age 60 for federal Foreign Service personnel.

c. See generally Note, *Constitutional Attacks on Mandatory Retirement: A Reconsideration,* 23 U.C.L.A.L.Rev. 549 (1976).

On discriminations against children, see Tribe, *American Constitutional Law* 1077–82 (1978).

system" employed in Georgia primaries for statewide officers. The candidate receiving the highest number of votes in each county obtained "two votes for each representative to which the county is entitled in the lower House of the General Assembly," and the winner was determined on the basis of the county unit vote. Because counties were not represented in the state legislature in accordance with their population, "combination of the units from the counties having the smallest population gives counties having population of one-third of the total in the state a clear majority of county units." The Court, per DOUGLAS, J., emphasizing that the case did not involve legislative districting, held that equal protection requires that "once the geographical unit for which a representative is to be chosen is designated, all who participate in the election are to have an equal vote. [The] conception of political equality from the Declaration of Independence, to Lincoln's Gettysburg Address, to the Fifteenth, Seventeenth, and Nineteenth Amendments can mean only one thing—one person, one vote." [a]

WESBERRY v. SANDERS, 376 U.S. 1, 84 S.Ct. 526, 11 L.Ed.2d 481 (1964), per BLACK, J., struck down the Georgia congressional districting statute which accorded some districts more than twice the population of others: "[T]he command of Art. I, § 2, that Representatives be chosen 'by the People of the several States' means that as nearly as is practicable one man's vote in a congressional election is to be worth as much as another's." [b]

Notes and Questions

1. *Commitment to Congress.* Has Art. I—as argued by Harlan, J., in *Wesberry*—"conferred upon Congress exclusive authority to secure fair representation by the States" in the House of Representatives? Consider Lewis, *Legislative Apportionment and the Federal Courts,* 71 Harv.L.Rev. 1057, 1074 (1958): "[That Art. I] casts the right to equal representation in the House in terms of affirmative congressional power should not preclude judicial enforcement of the right in the absence of legislation. Such judicial action is commonplace in other areas, [e.g.,] the commerce clause, which is phrased in the most general language and entirely in terms of congressional power." Is *Wesberry* premised, sub silentio, on the commerce clause analogy? May Congress "overrule" *Wesberry* as it may a commerce clause decision?

2. *Equal representation.* What does *Wesberry* portend for the effective power of some congressional committees to "pigeon-hole" legislation? The Senate filibuster? Are these practices consistent with the principle that "one man's vote in a congressional election is to be worth as much as another's"?

a. Harlan, J., dissented. Is there a distinction between the issue in *Gray* and legislative apportionment? See 77 Harv.L.Rev. 131 (1963).

Is a state primary for selecting delegates to the national political parties' presidential nominating conventions, which awards all of the state's delegates to the candidate with the highest number of votes, valid after *Gray*? See Blumstein, *Party Reform, the Winner-Take-All Primary, and the California Delegate Challenge: The Gold Rush Revisited,* 25 Vand.L.Rev. 975 (1972).

b. Clark, J., would have remanded for consideration "against the requirements of the Equal Protection Clause." Harlan, J., would have adhered to *Colegrove* and, on the merits (joined by Stewart, J.,) dissented, finding the Court's theory "demonstrably unsound historically."

REYNOLDS v. SIMS

377 U.S. 533, 84 S.Ct. 1362, 12 L.Ed.2d 506 (1964).

CHIEF JUSTICE WARREN delivered the opinion of the Court.

[Although the Alabama constitution required the legislature to reapportion decennially on the basis of population, none had taken place since 1901. The federal district court held the existing malapportionment violative of equal protection. Under] 1960 census figures, only 25.1% of the State's total population resided in districts represented by a majority of the members of the Senate, and only 25.7% lived in counties which could elect a majority of the members of the House of Representatives. Population-variance ratios of up to about 41-to-1 existed in the Senate, and up to about 16-to-1 in the House. * * *

Gray and *Wesberry* are of course not dispositive [of] these cases involving state legislative [apportionment]. But neither are they wholly inapposite. [*Gray*] established the basic principle of equality among voters within a State, [and] *Wesberry* clearly established that the fundamental principle of representative government in this country is one of equal representation for equal numbers of people, without regard to race, sex, economic status, or place of residence within a State. Our problem, then, is to ascertain [whether] there are any constitutionally cognizable principles which would justify departures from the basic standard of equality among voters in the apportionment of seats in state legislatures.

A predominant consideration in determining whether a State's legislative apportionment scheme constitutes an invidious discrimination [is] that the rights allegedly impaired are individual and personal in nature. [Since] the right of suffrage is a fundamental matter in a free and democratic society [and] is preservative of other basic civil and political rights, any alleged infringement [must] be carefully and meticulously scrutinized. * * *

Legislators represent people, not trees or acres. Legislators are elected by voters, not farms or cities or economic interests. As long as ours is a representative form of government, [the] right to elect legislators in a free and unimpaired fashion is a bedrock of our political system. [It] is inconceivable that a state law to the effect that, in counting votes for legislators, the votes of citizens in one part of the State would be multiplied by two, five, or 10, while the votes of persons in another area would be counted only at face value, could be [constitutional]. Of course, the effect of state legislative districting schemes which give the same number of representatives to unequal numbers of constituents is identical. * * *

Logically, in a society ostensibly grounded on representative government, it would seem reasonable that a majority of the people of a State could elect a majority of that State's legislators. [T]o sanction minority control of state legislative bodies would appear to deny majority rights in a way that far surpasses any possible denial of minority rights that might otherwise be thought to result.[a] [T]he concept of equal protection has been traditionally viewed as

a. But see Bickel, *The Supreme Court and Reapportionment,* in Reapportionment in the 1970's, 57, 58–59 (Polsby ed. 1971): "[A] rigorous majoritarianism is not what our institutions rest [on]. American government [includes] a Supreme Court which wields political power and [is] not elected at all. Our government includes a Senate [in] which each state, regardless of population, has an equal vote that not even a duly enacted and ratified constitutional amendment can, without its own consent, deprive it of. Our government requiring the uniform treatment of persons standing in the same relation to the governmental action questioned or challenged. With respect to the allocation of legislative representation, all voters, as citizens of a State, stand in the same relation regardless of where they live. Any suggested criteria for the differentiation of citizens are insufficient to justify any discrimination, as to the weight of their votes, unless relevant to the permissible purposes of legislative apportionment. Since the achieving of fair and effective representation for all citizens is concededly the basic aim of legislative apportionment, we conclude that the Equal Protection Clause guarantees the opportunity for equal participation by all voters in the election of state legislators. Diluting the weight of votes because of place of residence impairs basic constitutional rights under the Fourteenth Amendment just as much as invidious discriminations based upon factors such as race, or economic status. Our constitutional system amply provides for the protection of minorities by means other than giving them majority control of state legislatures. * * *

We are told that the matter of apportioning representation in a state legislature is a complex and many-faceted one. We are advised that States can rationally consider factors other than [population]. We are admonished not to restrict the power of the States to impose differing views as to political philosophy on their citizens. We are cautioned about the dangers of entering into political thickets and mathematical quagmires. Our answer is this: a denial of constitutionally protected rights demands judicial protection; our oath and our office require no less of us. [To] the extent that a citizen's right to vote is debased, he is that much less a citizen. [A] nation once primarily rural in character becomes predominantly urban. Representation schemes once fair and equitable become archaic and outdated. But the basic principle of representative government [remains]—the weight of a citizen's vote cannot be made to depend on where he lives. Population is, of necessity, [the] controlling criterion for judgment in legislative [apportionment]. This is the clear and strong command of our Constitution's Equal Protection Clause. This is an essential part of the concept of a government of laws and not men. This is at the heart of Lincoln's vision of "government of the people, by the people, [and] for the people." * * *

We hold that, as a basic constitutional standard, the Equal Protection Clause requires that the seats in both houses of a bicameral state legislature must be apportioned on a population basis. [We] find the federal analogy inapposite and irrelevant to state legislative districting schemes. [T]he Founding Fathers clearly had no intention of establishing a pattern or model for the apportionment of seats in state legislatures when the system of representation in the Federal Congress was adopted. Demonstrative of this is the fact that the Northwest Ordinance, adopted in the same year, 1787, as the Federal Constitution, provided for the apportionment of seats in territorial legislatures solely on the basis of population.

The system of representation in the two Houses of the Federal Congress [is] based on the consideration that in establishing our type of federalism a group of formerly independent States bound themselves together under one national government. [A] compromise between the larger and smaller States on this matter averted a deadlock in the constitutional convention * * *.

includes a House of Representatives in which each state has at least one vote, even though the whole state may be (as some are) considerably smaller in population than the average congressional district."

Political subdivisions of States [never] have been considered as sovereign entities. Rather, they have been traditionally regarded as subordinate governmental instrumentalities created by the State. * * *

[The] right of a citizen to equal representation and to have his vote weighted equally with those of all other citizens in the election of members of one house of a bicameral state legislature would amount to little if States could effectively submerge the equal-population principle in the apportionment of seats in the other house. * * * Deadlock between the two bodies might result in compromise and concession on some issues. But in all too many cases the more probable result would be frustration of the majority will through minority veto in the house not apportioned on a population [basis].

We do not believe that the concept of bicameralism is rendered anachronistic and meaningless when the predominant basis of representation in the two state legislative bodies is required to be the same—population. A prime reason for bicameralism, modernly considered, is to insure mature and deliberate consideration of, and to prevent precipitate action on, proposed legislative measures. Simply because the controlling criterion for apportioning representation is required to be the same in both houses does not mean that there will be no differences in the composition and complexion of the two bodies. [The] numerical size of the two bodies could be made to differ, even significantly, and the geographical size of districts from which legislators are elected could also be made to differ. [T]he Equal Protection Clause requires that a State make an honest and good faith effort to construct districts, in both houses of its legislature, as nearly of equal population as is practicable. We realize that it is a practical impossibility to arrange legislative districts so that each one has an identical number of residents, or citizens, or voters. Mathematical exactness or precision is hardly a workable constitutional requirement.

[So] long as the divergences from a strict population standard are based on legitimate considerations incident to the effectuation of a rational state policy, some deviations from the equal-population principle are constitutionally permissible, [b]ut neither history alone, nor economic or other sorts of group interests, are permissible factors in attempting to justify disparities from population-based representation. Citizens, not history or economic interests, cast votes. Considerations of area alone provide an insufficient justification for deviations from the equal-population principle. Again, people, not land or trees or pastures, vote. Modern developments and improvements in transportation and communications make rather hollow, in the mid-1960's, most claims [for] allowing such deviations in order to insure effective representation for sparsely settled areas and to prevent legislative districts from becoming so large that the availability of access of citizens to their representatives is impaired. * * *

A consideration that appears to be of more substance [is] according political subdivisions some independent representation in at least one body of the state legislature, as long as the basic standard of equality of population among districts is maintained. [In] many States much of the legislature's activity involves the enactment of so-called local legislation, directed only to the concerns of particular political subdivisions. And a State may legitimately desire to construct districts along political subdivision lines to deter the possibilities of gerrymandering. However, permitting deviations from population-based representation does not mean that each local governmental unit or political subdivision can be given separate representation, regardless of [population].[b]

* * * Decennial reapportionment appears to be a rational approach to readjustment of legislative representation in order to take into account population shifts and growth [and] if reapportionment were accomplished with less frequency, it would assuredly be constitutionally suspect. * * *

[T]he court below acted with proper judicial restraint, after the Alabama Legislature had failed to act effectively in remedying the constitutional deficiencies in the State's legislative apportionment scheme, in ordering its own temporary reapportionment plan into effect, at a time sufficiently early to permit the holding of elections pursuant to that plan without great difficulty, and in prescribing a plan admittedly provisional in purpose so as not to usurp the primary responsibility for reapportionment which rests with the legislature.[c]

[Clark and Stewart, JJ., concurred in the result in *Reynolds,* but JUSTICE STEWART, joined by JUSTICE CLARK, dissented in two of the companion cases in an opinion sharply at odds with the *Reynolds'* rationale:] [d]

First, says the Court, it is "established that the fundamental principle of representative government in this country is one of equal representation for equal numbers of [people]." [But] this "was not the colonial system, it was not the system chosen for the national government by the Constitution, it was not the system exclusively or even predominantly practiced by the States at the time

b. Under *Reynolds,* could Colorado give [small] counties [representation] by permitting them each to have a representative in the legislature, but granting that legislator only a fractional vote determined on a population basis (or granting him a full vote but giving legislators from larger counties a more heavily weighted vote)? Consider Dixon, *Reapportionment Perspectives: What is Fair Representation?,* 51 A.B.A.J. 319, 322 (1965): "[W]eighted voting may be nullified for several reasons. One of the most important reasons would be the consideration that one man casting nineteen votes is not as effective in terms of representation as nineteen separate voices (or lobbyists). Another would be that nineteen men separately elected would provide more opportunity for expression of divergent views. [B]oth of these arguments involve going beyond the simple mathematical tenor of the Supreme Court's 'one-man, one-vote' decisions. They involve putting reapportionment in the context of the actual complexities of representation—and the difficulties in determining what is fair and effective representation." Does this objection go similarly to fractional voting? If not, should fractional voting also extend to committee voting? Assignment to committee? Compensation? What else? See generally Banzhaf, *One Man, ? Votes: Mathematical Analysis of Voting Power and Effective Representation,* 36 Geo. Wash.L.Rev. 808 (1968); Note, *Equal Representation and the Weighted Voting Alternatives,* 79 Yale L.J. 311 (1969).

c. *Travia v. Lomenzo,* 381 U.S. 431, 85 S.Ct. 1582, 14 L.Ed.2d 480 (1965), refused to stay a district court's order that New York hold a special legislative election—thus shortening the terms of legislators elected under an invalid apportionment—under a reapportionment plan enacted by the legislature but held invalid by the state court because it provided for more legislators than permitted under the state constitution.

May a court order that a convention be called to amend the state constitution apportionment provisions? Require that all plans be submitted to it for approval? Cf. *Burns v. Richardson,* 384 U.S. 73, 86 S.Ct. 1286, 16 L.Ed.2d 376 (1966). Require changing the size of the legislature? See *67th Minnesota State Senate v. Beens,* 406 U.S. 187, 92 S.Ct. 1477, 32 L.Ed.2d 1 (1972). Order that a malapportioned legislature meet only for limited purposes? See *Fortson v. Toombs,* 379 U.S. 621, 85 S.Ct. 598, 13 L.Ed.2d 527 (1965).

d. In addition to *Reynolds,* the Court invalidated apportionments in Colorado, *Lucas v. Forty-Fourth Gen. Assembly,* 377 U.S. 713, 84 S.Ct. 1459, 12 L.Ed.2d 632 (1964); Delaware, *Roman v. Sincock,* 377 U.S. 695, 84 S.Ct. 1462, 12 L.Ed.2d 620; Maryland, *Maryland Comm. for Fair Rep. v. Tawes,* 377 U.S. 656, 84 S.Ct. 1442, 12 L.Ed.2d 595; New York, *WMCA, Inc. v. Lomenzo,* 377 U.S. 633, 84 S.Ct. 1418, 12 L.Ed.2d 568 (1964); Virginia, *Davis v. Mann,* 377 U.S. 678, 84 S.Ct. 1441, 12 L.Ed.2d 609.

Stewart, J., joined by Clark, dissented in *Lucas* and *Lomenzo* in the opinion partially set out in the text infra. Stewart, J., also dissented in *Davis.* In *Lucas,* Clark, J., stated: "[I]f one house is fairly apportioned by population [then] the people should have some latitude in providing on a rational basis, for representation in the other house."

of adoption of the Fourteenth Amendment, it is not predominantly practiced by the States today." Secondly, says the Court, unless legislative districts are equal in population, voters in the more populous districts will suffer a 'debasement' amounting to a constitutional injury. [I] find it impossible to understand how or why a voter in California, for instance, either feels or is less a citizen than a voter in Nevada, simply because, despite their population disparities, each of those States is represented by two United States Senators.

[My] own understanding of the various theories of representative government is that no one theory has ever commanded unanimous [assent]. But even if it were thought that the rule announced today by the Court is, as a matter of political theory, the most desirable, [I] could not join in the fabrication of a constitutional mandate which imports and forever freezes one theory of political thought into our Constitution, and forever denies to every State any opportunity for enlightened and progressive innovation * * *.

Representative government is a process of accommodating group interests through democratic institutional arrangements. * * * Appropriate legislative apportionment, therefore, should ideally be designed to insure effective representation in the State's legislature, in cooperation with other organs of political power, of the various groups and interests making up the electorate. In practice, of course, this ideal is approximated in the particular apportionment system of any State by a realistic accommodation of the diverse and often conflicting political forces operating within the State.

[The] fact of geographic districting, the constitutional validity of which the Court does not question, carries with it an acceptance of the idea of legislative representation of regional needs and interests. Yet if geographical residence is irrelevant, as the Court suggests, and the goal is solely that of equally "weighted" votes, I do not understand why the Court's constitutional rule does not require the abolition of districts and the holding of all elections at large.

The fact is, of course, that population factors must often to some degree be subordinated in devising a legislative apportionment plan which is to achieve the important goal of ensuring a fair, effective, and balanced representation of the regional, social, and economic interests within a State. And the further fact is that throughout our history the apportionments of State Legislatures have reflected the strongly felt American tradition that the public interest is composed of many diverse interests, and that in the long run it can better be expressed by a medley of component voices than by the majority's monolithic command. [I] think the cases should be decided by application of accepted principles of constitutional adjudication under the Equal Protection Clause [and that] demands but two basic attributes of any plan of state legislative apportionment. First, it demands that, in the light of the State's own characteristics and needs, the plan must be a rational one. Secondly, it demands that the plan must be such as not to permit the systematic frustration of the will of a majority of the electorate of the State. * * *

JUSTICE HARLAN, dissenting [in all the cases decided that day.]

The Court's constitutional discussion [is] remarkable [for] its failure to address itself at all to the Fourteenth Amendment as a whole or to the legislative history of the Amendment pertinent to the matter at hand. [I] am unable to understand the Court's utter disregard of [§ 2 of the fourteenth amendment], which expressly recognizes the States' power to deny "or in any way" abridge the right of their inhabitants to vote for "the members of the [State] Legislature," and its express provision of a remedy for such denial or abridgement. The comprehensive scope of the second section and its particular reference to the state legislatures precludes the suggestion that the first section was intended to have the result reached by the [Court].

The history of the adoption of the Fourteenth Amendment provides conclusive evidence that neither those who proposed nor those who ratified the Amendment believed that the Equal Protection Clause limited the power of the States to apportion their legislatures as they saw fit. Moreover, the history demonstrates that the intention to leave this power undisturbed was deliberate and was widely believed to be essential to the adoption of the Amendment.[e] [N]ote should [also] be taken of the Fifteenth and Nineteenth Amendments. [If] constitutional amendment was the only means by which all men and, later, women, could be guaranteed the right to vote at all, even for *federal* officers, how can it be that the far less obvious right to a particular kind of apportionment of *state* legislatures—a right to which is opposed a far more plausible conflicting interest of the State than the interest which opposes the general right to vote—can be conferred by judicial construction of the Fourteenth Amendment?

[The] consequence of today's decision is that in all but the handful of States which may already satisfy the new requirements the [courts] are given blanket authority and the constitutional duty to supervise apportionment of the State Legislatures. It is difficult to imagine a more intolerable and inappropriate interference by the judiciary with the independent legislatures of the States. [No] set of standards can guide a court which has to decide how many legislative districts a State shall have, or what the shape of the districts shall be, [or] whether a State should have single-member districts or multi-member districts or some combination of both. No such standard can control the balance between keeping up with population shifts and having stable districts. In all these respects, the courts will be called upon to make particular decisions with respect to which a principle of equally populated districts will be of no assistance whatsoever. * * *

Although the Court—necessarily, as I believe—provides only generalities in elaboration of its main thesis, its opinion nevertheless fully demonstrates how far removed these problems are from fields of judicial competence. Recognizing that "indiscriminate districting" is an invitation to "partisan gerrymandering," the Court nevertheless excludes virtually every basis for the formation of electoral districts other than "indiscriminate districting." In one or another of today's opinions, the Court declares it unconstitutional for a State to give effective consideration to any of the following in establishing legislative districts: (1) history; (2) "economic or other sorts of group interests"; (3) area; (4) geographical considerations; (5) a desire "to insure effective representation for sparsely settled areas"; (6) "availability of access of citizens to their representa-

e. For refutation of Harlan, J.'s lengthy historical argument, see Van Alstyne, *The Fourteenth Amendment, The "Right" to Vote, and the Understanding of the Thirty-Ninth Congress,* 1965 Sup.Ct.Rev. 33; Goldberg, *Mr. Justice Harlan, The Uses of History, and the Congressional Globe,* 15 J.Pub.L. 181 (1966).

Consider Auerbach, *The Reapportionment Cases: One Person, One Vote—One Vote, One Value,* 1964 Sup.Ct.Rev. 1, 31–34, 77–78: "To accept Mr. Justice Harlan's view would lead to the astonishing result that—apart from the complicated and never-used remedy provided by the second section of the Fourteenth Amendment—neither the federal courts, nor Congress under the fifth section, could act to prevent a state from denying the right to vote in a state or local election to a class of citizens, otherwise qualified to vote by state law, for reasons which have nothing to do with race, color, or previous condition of servitude, but which nevertheless result in an arbitrary classification, e.g., because the citizens disfranchised are residents of a particular county or because they migrated into the state from outside the state."

tives"; (7) theories of bicameralism (except those approved by the Court); (8) occupation; (9) "an attempt to balance urban and rural power"; (10) the preference of a majority of voters in the State. So far as presently appears, the *only* factor which a State may consider, apart from numbers, is political subdivisions. But even "a clearly rational state policy" recognizing this factor is unconstitutional if "population is submerged as the controlling consideration * * *."

I know of no principle of logic or practical or theoretical politics, still less any constitutional principle, which establishes all or any of these exclusions. [L]egislators can represent their electors only by speaking for their interests—economic, social, political—many of which do reflect the place where the electors live. The Court does not establish, or indeed even attempt to make a case for the proposition that conflicting interests within a State can only be adjusted by disregarding them when voters are grouped for purposes of [representation].

[The] Constitution is not a panacea for every blot upon the public welfare, nor [does] this Court [serve] its high purpose when it exceeds its authority, even to satisfy justified impatience with the slow workings of the political [process.] [f]

Notes and Questions

1. *Results.* By mid-1968, "congressional district lines were redrawn in thirty-seven states"; "only nine states had any district with a population deviation in excess of ten per cent from the state average, while twenty-four states had no deviation as large as five per cent from the state norm"; every state legislature "had made some adjustment, and it seemed probable that more than thirty of the state legislatures satisfied any reasonable interpretation of the equal-population principle." McKay, *Reapportionment: Success Story of the Warren Court,* 67 Mich.L.Rev. 223, 229 (1968). A number of studies—as to the impact of reapportionment on state policy and the extent to which reapportioned legislatures are more likely than malapportioned ones to expend funds, be responsive to urban needs and have a competitive political system—have arrived at conflicting conclusions. For a collection and appraisal, see Bicker, *The Effects of Malapportionment in the States—A Mistrial,* in Reapportionment in the 1970's 151 (Polsby ed. 1971); Choper, *Consequences of Supreme Court Decisions Upholding Individual Constitutional Rights,* 83 Mich.L.Rev. 1, 90–94 (1984).

2. *High vote requirements.* GORDON v. LANCE, 403 U.S. 1, 91 S.Ct. 1889, 29 L.Ed.2d 273 (1971), per BURGER, C.J., upheld a West Virginia rule that forbade political subdivisions from incurring bonded indebtedness or increasing tax rates beyond designated limits without 60% approval in a referendum: "The defect [in *Gray v. Sanders* and *Cipriano v. Houma,* Part B infra] lay in the denial or dilution of voting power because of group characteristics—geographic location and property ownership—that bore no valid relation to the interest of those groups in the subject matter of the [election]. In contrast we can discern no independently identifiable group or category that favors bonded indebtedness over other forms of financing. Consequently no sector of the population may be said to be 'fenced out' from the franchise because of the way they will vote. [T]here is nothing in the language of the Constitution, our history or our cases that requires that a majority always prevail on every issue. [The] Constitution

f. A week later, the Court invalidated apportionments in nine additional states. The opinions begin at 378 U.S. 553, 84 S.Ct. 1904, 12 L.Ed.2d 1033. For thoughtful pre-*Reynolds* commentaries on apportionment standards, see Lockhart, Kamisar & Choper, *Constitutional Law: Cases—Comments—Questions* 1318 (3d. ed. 1970).

itself provides that a simple majority vote is insufficient on some issues [and] the Bill of Rights removes entire areas of legislation from the concept of majoritarian supremacy. * * *[6]"[g] Do you agree that in *Lance* "no independently identifiable group" was "fenced out"? See Wilkinson, *The Supreme Court, the Equal Protection Clause, and the Three Faces of Constitutional Equality,* 61 Va. L.Rev. 945, 972–75 (1975). After *Lance,* may a state require a 60% *legislative* vote to establish any public transit system? To enact laws affecting designated counties? Does *Lance* logically (constitutionally) extend to the situations in its fn. 6? May a state require a 60% vote to unseat any incumbent?

3. *Permissible population deviation.* The Court has permitted considerably less deviation from the one person one vote requirement for congressional districts than for state and local[h] elections. KARCHER v. DAGGETT, 462 U.S. 725, 103 S.Ct. 2653, 77 L.Ed.2d 133 (1983), per BRENNAN, J., invalidated a percentage deviation in New Jersey's congressional districts of 0.7%. But justifiable deviations were not ruled out: "Any number of consistently applied legislative policies might justify some ['minor population deviations'], including, for instance, making districts compact, respecting municipal boundaries, preserving the cores of prior districts, [preserving voting strength of racial minorities], and avoiding contests between incumbent Representatives. [The] state must, however, show with some specificity that a particular objective required the specific deviations in its plan rather than simply relying on general assertions [as here]."[i] On the other hand, GAFFNEY v. CUMMINGS, 412 U.S. 735, 93 S.Ct. 2321, 37 L.Ed.2d 298 (1973), per WHITE, J., held that a Connecticut state legislative reapportionment with a maximum deviation of 7.83% was "insignificant" and "required no justification by the state."[j]

6. We intimate no view on the constitutionality of a provision requiring unanimity or giving a veto power to a very small group. Nor do we decide whether a State [may] require extraordinary majorities for the election of public officers.

g. Harlan, J., concurred in the result. Brennan and Marshall, JJ., dissented.

h. *Avery v. Midland County,* 390 U.S. 474, 88 S.Ct. 1114, 20 L.Ed.2d 45 (1968) held that *Reynolds* applied to a county body with "general responsibility and power for local affairs" but left open the status of special purpose units of government "affecting definable groups of constituents more than other[s]." See also *Hadley v. Junior College Dist.,* 397 U.S. 50, 90 S.Ct. 791, 25 L.Ed.2d 45 (1970) (extending *Avery* to junior college district). But cf. *Sailors v. Board of Educ.,* 387 U.S. 105, 87 S.Ct. 1549, 18 L.Ed.2d 650 (1967) (constitutional to permit school boards of component districts to select school board even though component districts served unequal populations); *Dusch v. Davis,* 387 U.S. 112, 87 S.Ct. 1554, 18 L.Ed.2d 656 (1967) (constitutional for city to require in at large elections for its legislative body that some candidates come from districts varying widely in population); *Wells v. Edwards,* 409 U.S. 1095, 93 S.Ct. 904, 34 L.Ed.2d 679 (1973) (summarily affirmed provisions for election of state supreme court judges from districts established without regard to population).

In connection with *Wells,* consider Note, 47 Notre Dame Law. 316, 326–27 (1971): "Some would argue [that] the entire rationale [of] 'one man, one vote' is to achieve maximum institutional responsiveness and that by common agreement judges need not be responsive to the popular will or whim and therefore the rule has no applicability to them. [But this would] overlook the more basic concept of political equality which underlies [*Reynolds*], namely, that irrespective of the elective office involved, full and effective citizenship requires that each man's vote count the same. It should also be noted that a requirement of equal judicial districts in no way implies that the judges elected from those districts need be responsive."

i. White, J., joined by Burger, C.J., Powell and Rehnquist, JJ., dissented.

j. Brennan, J., joined by Douglas and Marshall, JJ., dissented.

White v. Regester, 412 U.S. 755, 93 S.Ct. 2332, 37 L.Ed.2d 314 (1973) (similarly divided), used the same analysis as *Gaffney* to uphold a Texas apportionment in which "the total variation between largest and smallest district" was 9.9%—although "very likely larger differences would not be tolerable without qualification."

More recently, *Brown v. Thomson,* 462 U.S. 835, 103 S.Ct. 2690, 77 L.Ed.2d 214 (1983), per Powell, J., upheld Wyoming's allocation of one

MAHAN v. HOWELL, 410 U.S. 315, 93 S.Ct. 979, 35 L.Ed.2d 320 (1973), per REHNQUIST, J., upheld Virginia's state legislative apportionment, which had a maximum percentage deviation from the ideal of "16.4%—[one] district being overrepresented by 6.8% and [another] being underrepresented by 9.6%. [T]he minimum population necessary to elect a majority of the House of Delegates was 49.29%":[k] "In *Kirkpatrick v. Preisler,* 394 U.S. 526, 89 S.Ct. 1225, 22 L.Ed.2d 519 (1969) and *Wells v. Rockefeller,* 394 U.S. 542, 89 S.Ct. 1234, 22 L.Ed.2d 535 (1969), this Court invalidated state reapportionment statutes for federal congressional districts having maximum percentage deviations of 5.97% and 13.1% respectively. [I]t was concluded that [*Wesberry's*] command 'permits only the limited population variances which are unavoidable despite a good-faith effort to achieve absolute equality, or for which justification is shown.'

"[*Reynolds* suggested] more flexibility was constitutionally permissible with respect to state legislative reapportionment than in congressional redistricting. Consideration was given to the fact [that] there is a significantly larger number of seats in state legislative bodies to be distributed within a State than Congressional seats, and that therefore it may be feasible for a State to use political subdivision lines to a greater [extent].[l] * * *

"Neither courts nor legislatures are furnished any specialized calipers which enable them to extract from the general language of the Equal Protection Clause [the] mathematical formula which establishes what range of percentage deviations are permissible, and what are not. [While] this percentage may well approach tolerable limits, we do not believe it exceeds them."

4. BURNS v. RICHARDSON, 384 U.S. 73, 86 S.Ct. 1286, 16 L.Ed.2d 376 (1966), per BRENNAN, J., upheld a Hawaii plan that used *registered voters* as the

seat in its House of Representatives to its least populous county, resulting in a maximum deviation of 89%. The Court emphasized that "appellants deliberately have limited their challenge to the alleged dilution of their voting power resulting from the one representative given to Niobrara County" rather than "the state apportionment plan as a whole."

O'Connor, J., joined by Stevens, J., expressed "the gravest doubts that a statewide legislative plan with an 85% maximum deviation would survive constitutional scrutiny despite the presence of the State's strong interest in preserving county boundaries. I join the Court's opinion on the understanding that nothing in it suggests that this Court would uphold such a scheme."

Brennan, J., joined by White, Marshall and Blackmun, JJ.,—although "stressing how extraordinarily narrow [the decision] is, and how empty of likely precedential value"—dissented.

k. *Abate* v. *Mundt,* 403 U.S. 182, 91 S.Ct. 1904, 29 L.Ed.2d 399 (1971) upheld the apportionment of Rockland County, N.Y.'s governing board. Each of the five constituent towns comprised one district and each had at least one representative. The most "underrepresented" district was by 7.1% and the most "overrepresented" by 4.8%—"a total deviation from population equality of 11.9%": "[V]iable local governments may need considerable flexibility [to] meet changing societal needs [and] a desire to preserve the integrity of political subdivisions may justify an apportionment plan which departs from numerical equality. *Reynolds.* [T]hat local legislative bodies frequently have fewer representatives than do their state and national counterparts and that some local legislative districts may have a much smaller population than do congressional and state legislative districts, lend support to the argument that slightly greater percentage deviations may be tolerable for local government [apportionment]." Would (should) the deviation permitted in *Abate* be equally precedential for Los Angeles (Cal.) County with 7,000,000 residents as for Hamilton (N.Y.) County with 4,700 residents? See Note, *Reapportionment—Nine Years into the "Revolution" and Still Struggling,* 70 Mich.L. Rev. 586 (1972).

l. See also Hobbs, *Book Review,* 16 U.C. L.A.L.Rev. 659, 682 (1969): "[C]ongressmen are assumed to represent the state as a whole as well as their district; state legislators, on the other hand, are expected to be more parochial. Therefore, there is arguably a better case on the state [level] for allowing deviation based on local communities of interest. In addition, on the state level population variations in one house can be compensated for in the other. This [is] impossible in congressional districting."

population base, which, "probably because of uneven distribution of military residents—largely unregistered," produced results significantly different than if total population figures had been used: States are not "required to include aliens, transients, short-term or temporary residents, or persons denied the vote for conviction of crime in the apportionment [base]. The decision to include or exclude any such group involves choices about the nature of representation with which we have been shown no constitutionally founded reason to interfere. [But use] of a registered voter or actual voter basis [is] susceptible to improper influences by which those in political power might be able to perpetuate underrepresentation of groups constitutionally entitled to participate in the electoral [process]. [W]e hold that the present apportionment satisfies the Equal Protection Clause only because on this record it was found to have produced a distribution of legislators not substantially different from that which would have resulted from the use of [state citizen population, which is] a permissible population base."

FORTSON v. MORRIS, 385 U.S. 231, 87 S.Ct. 446, 17 L.Ed.2d 330 (1966): In the 1966 Georgia gubernatorial election, no candidate received a majority of the popular vote. Georgia provided that in such case the Georgia legislature shall elect the governor from the two candidates receiving the highest popular vote. The Court, per BLACK, J., upheld the election: There is no federal constitutional provision "which either expressly or impliedly dictates the method a State must use to select its Governor. A method which would be valid if initially employed is equally valid when employed as an alternative."

DOUGLAS, J., joined by Warren, C.J., and Brennan and Fortas, JJ., dissented, viewing "the legislative choice" as "only a part of the popular election machinery. [A] candidate who received a minority of the popular vote might receive a clear majority of the votes cast in the legislature," thus "contrary to the principle of 'one person, one vote.' "

Scope of the decision. May a state provide that a popularly elected governor shall appoint the entire legislature? Appoint the legislator from any district in which no candidate received a majority ($^2/_3$) ($^3/_4$) of the popular vote? That all local officials shall be appointed by the legislature or some part thereof? What provision(s) of the Constitution are most germane in considering these issues? See generally Ely, *Democracy and Distrust* 116–25 (1980); Levinson, *Judicial Review and the Problem of the Comprehensible Constitution,* 59 Tex.L.Rev. 395, 413–15 (1981).

MOBILE v. BOLDEN

446 U.S. 55, 100 S.Ct. 1490, 64 L.Ed.2d 47 (1980).

JUSTICE STEWART announced the judgment of the Court and delivered an opinion in which THE CHIEF JUSTICE, JUSTICE POWELL, and JUSTICE REHNQUIST join.

The City of Mobile, Ala., has since 1911 been governed by a City Commission consisting of three members elected by the voters of the city at-large. [This] is the same basic electoral system that is followed by literally thousands of municipalities and other local governmental units throughout the Nation.

[The] constitutional objection to multimember districts is not and cannot be that, as such, they depart from apportionment on a population basis in violation of *Reynolds* and its progeny. Rather the focus in such cases has been on the lack of representation multimember districts afford various elements of the voting population in a system of representative legislative democracy. "Criticism [of multimember districts] is rooted in their winner-take-all aspects, their tendency to submerge minorities, [a] general preference for legislatures reflecting community interests as closely as possible and disenchantment with political parties and elections as devices to settle policy differences between contending interests." *Whitcomb v. Chavis,* 403 U.S. 124, 91 S.Ct. 1858, 29 L.Ed.2d 363 (1971).[a]

Despite repeated constitutional attacks upon multimember legislative districts, the Court has consistently held that they are not unconstitutional per se, e.g., *White v. Regester; Whitcomb; Burns v. Richardson; Fortson v. Dorsey,* 379 U.S. 433, 85 S.Ct. 498, 13 L.Ed.2d 401 (1965).[12] We have recognized, however, that such legislative apportionments could violate the Fourteenth Amendment if their purpose were invidiously to minimize or cancel out the voting potential of racial or ethnic minorities. To prove such a purpose it is not enough to show that the group allegedly discriminated against has not elected representatives in proportion to its numbers. A plaintiff must prove that the disputed plan was "conceived or operated as [a] purposeful device[ ] to further racial discrimination." *Whitcomb.*

This burden of proof is simply one aspect of the basic principle that only if there is purposeful discrimination can there be a violation of [equal protection]. See *Washington v. Davis; Arlington Heights; Personnel Adm'r v. Feeney,* [Sec. 2, III supra]. Although dicta may be drawn from a few of the Court's earlier opinions suggesting that disproportionate effects alone may establish a claim of unconstitutional racial vote dilution, the fact is that such a view is not supported by any decision of this Court.[13] More importantly, such a view is not consistent with the meaning of the Equal Protection Clause as it has been understood in a variety of other contexts involving alleged racial discrimination. *Davis* (employment); *Arlington Heights* (zoning); *Keyes,* [Sec. 2, IV supra] (public schools); *Akins v. Texas,* 325 U.S. 398, 65 S.Ct. 1276, 89 L.Ed. 1692 (1945) (jury selection).

In only one case has the Court sustained a claim that multimember legislative districts unconstitutionally diluted the voting strength of a discrete group. [*Regester*] upheld a constitutional challenge by Negroes and Mexican-Americans to parts of a legislative reapportionment plan adopted by the State of Texas. [T]he Court held that the plaintiffs had been able to "produce evidence to support the finding that the political processes leading to nomination and election were not equally open to participation by the group[s] in question." In so holding, the Court relied upon evidence in the record that included a long

a. On the issue generally, see Banzhaf, *Multi-Member Electoral Districts—Do They Violate the "One Man, One Vote" Principle,* 75 Yale L.J. 1309 (1966); Carpeneti, *Legislative Apportionment: Multi-member Districts and Fair Representation,* 120 U.Pa.L.Rev. 666 (1972); Tribe, *American Constitutional Law* 750 (1978).

12. We have made clear, however, that a court in formulating an apportionment [plan] should, as a general rule, not permit multimember legislative districts. * * * *Connor v. Finch.* [See *Wise v. Lipscomb,* 437 U.S. 535, 98 S.Ct. 2493, 57 L.Ed.2d 411 (1978), on whether a reapportionment plan was "court-devised" or "legislatively enacted."]

13. The dissenting opinion of Mr. Justice Marshall reads the Court's opinion in *Dorsey* to say that a claim of vote dilution under the Equal Protection Clause could rest on either discriminatory purpose or effect. [Although] the Court recognized that "designedly or otherwise," multimember districting schemes might, under the circumstances of a particular case, minimize the voting strength of a racial group, an issue as to the constitutionality of such an arrangement "[w]as not [presented]."

The phrase "designedly or otherwise" [was] repeated, also in dictum, in *Burns.* But the constitutional challenge to the multimember constituencies failed in that case because the plaintiffs demonstrated neither discriminatory purpose nor effect.

history of official discrimination against minorities as well as indifference to their needs and interests on the part of white elected officials. * * *

Regester is thus consistent with "the basic equal protection principle that the invidious quality of a law claimed to be racially discriminatory must ultimately be traced to a racially discriminatory purpose." [But] where the character of a law is readily explainable on grounds apart from race, as would nearly always be true where, as here, an entire system of local governance is brought into question, disproportionate impact alone cannot be decisive, and courts must look to other evidence to support a finding of discriminatory purpose. [I]t is clear that the evidence in the present case fell far short of showing that the appellants "conceived or operated [a] purposeful device[ ] to further racial discrimination." *Whitcomb.*

[T]he District Court [affirmed by the Court of Appeals] based its conclusion of unconstitutionality primarily on the fact that no Negro had ever been elected to the City Commission, apparently because of the pervasiveness of racially polarized voting in Mobile. The trial court also found that city officials had not been as responsive to the interests of Negroes as to those of white persons. On the basis of these findings, the court concluded that the political processes in Mobile were not equally open to Negroes, despite its seemingly inconsistent findings that there were no inhibitions against Negroes becoming candidates, and that in fact Negroes had registered and voted without hindrance. * * *

First, [i]t may be that Negro candidates have been defeated, but that fact alone does not work a constitutional deprivation.

Second, [evidence] of discrimination by white officials in Mobile is relevant only as the most tenuous and circumstantial evidence of the constitutional invalidity of the electoral system under which they attained their offices.

Third, the District Court and the Court of Appeals supported their conclusion by drawing upon the substantial history of official racial discrimination in Alabama. But past discrimination cannot, in the manner of original sin, condemn governmental action that is not itself unlawful. The ultimate question remains whether a discriminatory intent has been proved in a given [case].

Finally, the District Court and the Court of Appeals pointed to the mechanics of the at-large electoral system itself as proof that the votes of Negroes were being invidiously canceled out. But those features of that electoral system, such as the majority vote requirement, tend naturally to disadvantage any voting minority [and] are far from proof that the at-large electoral scheme represents purposeful discrimination against Negro voters.

We turn finally [to] Justice Marshall's dissenting opinion. The theory [appears] to be that every "political group," or at least every such group that is in the minority, has a federal constitutional right to elect candidates in proportion to its numbers.[22] Moreover, a political group's "right" to have its candidates elected is said to be a "fundamental interest," the infringement of which

22. The dissenting opinion seeks to disclaim this description of its theory by suggesting that a claim of vote dilution may require, in addition to proof of electoral defeat, some evidence of "historical and social factors" indicating that the group in question is without political influence. Putting to the side the evident fact that these gauzy sociological considerations have no constitutional basis, it remains far from certain that they could, in any principled manner, exclude the claims of any discrete political group that happens, for whatever reason, to elect fewer of its candidates than arithmetic indicates it might. Indeed, the putative limits are bound to prove illusory if the express purpose informing their application would be, as the dissent assumes, to redress the "inequitable distribution of political influence."

may be established without proof that a State has acted with the purpose of impairing anybody's access to the political process. This dissenting opinion finds the "right" infringed [because] no Negro has been elected to the Mobile City Commission.

Whatever appeal the dissenting opinion's view may have as a matter of political theory, it is not the law.[b] The Equal Protection Clause [does] not require proportional representation as an imperative of political organization. * * *

It is of course true that a law that impinges upon a fundamental right explicitly or implicitly secured by the Constitution is presumptively unconstitutional. See *Shapiro v. Thompson,* [Part II infra]. See also *San Antonio Ind. School Dist. v. Rodriguez,* [Part IV infra]. But plainly "[i]t is not the province of this Court to create substantive constitutional rights in the name of guaranteeing equal protection of the laws," id. [In] *Whitcomb,* the trial court had found that a multimember state legislative district had invidiously deprived Negroes and poor persons of rights guaranteed them by the Constitution, notwithstanding the absence of any evidence whatever of discrimination against them. Reversing the trial court, this Court said: "The District Court's holding, although on the facts of this case limited to guaranteeing one racial group representation, is not easily contained. It is expressive of the more general proposition that any group with distinctive interests must be represented in legislative halls if it is numerous enough to command at least one seat and represents a majority living in an area sufficiently compact to constitute a single-member district. This approach would make it difficult to reject claims of Democrats, Republicans, or members of any political [organization]. There are also union oriented workers, the university community, religious or ethnic groups occupying identifiable areas of our heterogeneous cities and urban areas. Indeed, it would be difficult for a great many, if not most, multi-member districts to survive analysis under the District Court's view unless combined with some voting arrangement such as proportional representation or cumulative voting aimed at providing representation for minority parties or interests. At the very least, affirmance [would] spawn endless litigation concerning the multi-member district systems now widely employed in this country." * * *

JUSTICE BLACKMUN, concurring in the result.

Assuming that proof of intent is a prerequisite to appellees' prevailing on their constitutional claim of vote dilution, I am inclined to agree with Mr. Justice White that, in this case, "the findings of the District Court amply support an inference of purposeful discrimination." I concur in the Court's judgment of reversal, however, because I believe that the relief afforded appellees by the District Court [ordering a new form of government "of a Mayor and a City Council with members elected from single-member districts"] was not commensurate with the sound exercise of judicial discretion. * * *

b. Consider Soifer, *Complacency and Constitutional Law,* 42 Ohio St.L.J. 383, 389–90 (1981): "It is forgotten, but not insignificant, that the group that Justice Stone identified first in his *Carolene Products* footnote as in need of special judicial concern were those persons without sufficient access to 'those political processes which can ordinarily be expected to bring about *repeal* of undesirable legislation.' That legislation already on the books might be particularly difficult to repeal seemed obvious and important in 1938. The Court now appears confident that, as a constitutional matter, whatever law is in place ought to remain there."

JUSTICE STEVENS, concurring in the judgment.

[While] I agree with Mr. Justice Stewart that no violation of respondents' constitutional rights has been demonstrated, my analysis of the issue proceeds along somewhat different lines.

[T]his case draws into question a political structure that treats all individuals as equals but adversely affects the political strength of a racially identifiable group. Although I am satisfied that such a structure may be challenged under the Fifteenth Amendment as well as under the Equal Protection Clause of the Fourteenth Amendment, I believe that under either provision it must be judged by a standard that allows the political process to function effectively. * * *

[No] case decided by this Court establishes a constitutional right to proportional representation for racial minorities. What *Gomillion* [Sec. 2, III supra] holds is that a sufficiently "uncouth" or irrational racial gerrymander violates the Fifteenth Amendment. [The] fact that the "gerrymander" condemned in *Gomillion* was equally vulnerable under both Amendments indicates that the essential holding of that case is applicable, not merely to gerrymanders directed against racial minorities, but to those aimed at religious, ethnic, economic and political groups as well.[7]

My conclusion that the same standard should be applied to racial groups as is applied to other groups leads me also to conclude that the standard cannot condemn every adverse impact on one or more political groups without spawning more dilution litigation than the judiciary can manage. [N]othing comparable to the mathematical yardstick used in apportionment cases is available to identify the difference between permissible and impermissible adverse impacts on the voting strength of political groups. * * *

In my view, the proper standard is suggested by three characteristics of the gerrymander condemned in *Gomillion:* (1) the 28-sided configuration [was] manifestly not the product of a routine or a traditional political decision; (2) it had a significant adverse impact on a minority group; and (3) it was unsupported by any neutral justification and thus was either totally irrational or entirely motivated by a desire to curtail the political strength of the minority. These characteristics suggest that a proper test should focus on the objective effects of the political decision rather than the subjective motivation of the decisionmaker. In this case, if the commission form of government in Mobile were extraordinary, or if it were nothing more than a vestige of history, with no greater justification than the grotesque figure in *Gomillion,* it would surely violate the Constitution. That conclusion would follow simply from its adverse impact on black voters plus the absence of any legitimate justification for the system, without reference to the subjective intent of the political body that has refused to alter it.

Conversely, I am also persuaded that a political decision that affects group voting rights may be valid even if it can be proved that irrational or invidious factors have played some part in its enactment or retention. The standard for testing the acceptability of such a decision must take into account the fact that

7. [See], e.g., *Whitcomb* (districts that are "conceived or operated as purposeful devices to further racial *or economic* discrimination" are prohibited by the Fourteenth Amendment) (emphasis supplied); *Dorsey* (an apportionment scheme would be invalid [if] it "operate[d] to minimize or cancel out the voting strength of racial *or political* elements of the voting population") (emphasis supplied).

[For the view that the right to "effective political representation" should be limited to racial groups under the fifteenth amendment and thus "avoid an uncontrolled expansion of the effectiveness principle to countless interest groups," see Note, *United Jewish Organizations v. Carey and the Need to Recognize Aggregate Voting Rights,* 87 Yale L.J. 571 (1978).]

the responsibility for drawing political boundaries is generally committed to the legislative process and that the process inevitably involves a series of compromises among different group interests. If the process is to work, it must reflect an awareness of group interests and it must tolerate some attempts to advantage or to disadvantage particular segments of the voting populace. [Accordingly], a political decision that is supported by valid and articulable justifications cannot be invalid simply because some participants in the decisionmaking process were motivated by a purpose to disadvantage a minority group.

The decision to retain the commission form of government in Mobile, Ala., is such a decision. [The] fact that these at-large systems characteristically place one or more minority groups at a significant disadvantage in the struggle for political power cannot invalidate all such systems. See *Whitcomb.* Nor can it be the law that such systems are valid when there is no evidence that they were instituted or maintained for discriminatory reasons, but that they may be selectively condemned on the basis of the subjective motivation of some of their supporters. A contrary view "would spawn endless litigation concerning the multimember districts now widely employed in this Country," and would entangle the judiciary in a voracious political thicket.

JUSTICE BRENNAN, dissenting.

I dissent because I agree with Mr. Justice Marshall that proof of discriminatory impact is sufficient in these cases. I also dissent because, even accepting the plurality's premise that discriminatory purpose must be shown, I agree with [Marshall and White, JJ.,] that the appellees have clearly met that burden.

JUSTICE WHITE, dissenting.

[Both] the District Court and the Court of Appeals properly found that an invidious discriminatory purpose could be inferred from the totality of facts in this case. The Court's cryptic rejection of their conclusions ignores the principles that an invidious discriminatory purpose can be inferred from objective factors of the kind relied on in *Regester* and that the trial courts are in a special position to make such intensely local appraisals.

[T]he plurality today rejects the inference of purposeful discrimination apparently because each of the factors relied upon by the courts below is alone insufficient to support the inference. [By] viewing each of the factors relied upon below in isolation, and ignoring the fact that racial bloc voting at the polls makes it impossible to elect a black commissioner under the at-large system, the plurality rejects the "totality of the circumstances" approach we endorsed in *Regester, Davis,* and *Arlington Heights* * * *.

JUSTICE MARSHALL, dissenting. * * *

The Court does not dispute the proposition that multimember districting can have the effect of submerging electoral minorities. [Further], we decided a series of vote-dilution cases under the Fourteenth Amendment that were designed to protect electoral minorities from precisely the combination of electoral laws and historical and social factors found in the present cases.[4] [Although] we

4. [T]hough municipalities must be accorded some discretion in arranging their affairs, see *Abate,* there is all the more reason to scrutinize assertions that municipal, rather than State, multi-member districting dilutes the vote of an electoral minority: "In statewide elections, it is possible that a large minority group in one multi-member district will be unable to elect any legislators, while in another multi-member district where the same group is a slight majority, they will elect the entire slate of legislators. [In] at-large elections, [t]here is no way to balance out the discrimination against a particular minority group because the entire city is one huge election district. The minority's loss is abso-

have held that multimember districts are not unconstitutional per se, there is simply no basis for the plurality's conclusion that under our prior cases proof of discriminatory intent is a necessary condition for the invalidation of multimember districting.

[Under] this line of cases, an electoral districting plan is invalid if it has the effect of affording an electoral minority "less opportunity [than] other residents in the district to participate in the political processes and to elect legislators of their choice," *Regester.* It is also apparent that the Court in *Regester* considered equal access to the political process as meaning more than merely allowing the minority the opportunity to vote. *Regester* stands for the proposition that an electoral system may not relegate an electoral minority to political impotence by diminishing the importance of its [vote].

The plurality fails to apply the discriminatory effect standard of *Regester* because that approach conflicts with what the plurality takes to be an elementary principle of law. "[O]nly if there is purposeful discrimination," announces the plurality, "can there be a violation of [equal protection]." That proposition [fails] to distinguish between two distinct lines of equal protection decisions: those involving suspect classifications, and those involving fundamental rights. * * *

Under the Equal Protection Clause, if a classification "impinges upon a fundamental right explicitly or implicitly protected by the [Constitution], strict judicial scrutiny" is required, *Rodriguez,* regardless of whether the infringement was intentional. As I will explain, our cases recognize a fundamental right to equal electoral participation that encompasses protection against vote dilution. Proof of discriminatory purpose is, therefore, not required to support a claim of vote dilution.[10] The plurality's erroneous conclusion to the contrary is the result of a failure to recognize the central distinction between *Regester* and *Davis:* the former involved an infringement of a constitutionally protected right, while the latter dealt with a claim of racially discriminatory distribution of an interest to which no citizen has a constitutional entitlement.[11] * * *

Reynolds and its progeny focused solely on the discriminatory *effects* of malapportionment. [In] the present cases, the alleged vote dilution, though caused by the combined effects of the electoral structure and social and historical factors rather than by unequal population distribution, is analytically the same concept: the unjustified abridgement of a fundamental right. It follows, then, that a showing of discriminatory intent is just as unnecessary under the vote-dilution approach adopted in *Dorsey* and applied in *Regester,* as it is under our reapportionment cases. * * *

lute." Berry & Dye, *The Discriminatory Effects of At-Large Elections,* 7 Fla.St.U.L.Rev. 85, 87 (1979). * * *

10. [Although] the right to vote is distinguishable for present purposes from the other fundamental rights our cases have recognized, surely the plurality would not require proof of discriminatory purpose in those cases. The plurality fails to articulate why the right to vote should receive such singular treatment. Furthermore, the plurality refuses to recognize the disutility of requiring proof of discriminatory purpose in fundamental rights cases. For example, it would make no sense to require such a showing when the question is whether a state statute regulating abortion violates the right of personal choice recognized in *Roe v. Wade.* The only logical inquiry is whether, regardless of the legislature's motive, the statute has the effect of infringing that right. See, e.g., *Planned Parenthood v. Danforth.*

11. [See] also Comment, *Proof of Racially Discriminatory Purpose Under the Equal Protection Clause,* 12 Harv.C.R.–C.L.L.Rev. 725, 758, n. 175 (1977); Note, *Racial Vote Dilution in Multimember Districts: The Constitutional Standard After Washington v. Davis,* 76 Mich. L.Rev. 694, 722–26 (1978); Comment, *Constitutional Challenges to Gerrymanders,* 45 U.Chi. L.Rev. 845, 869–77 (1978). * * *

The plurality's response is that my approach amounts to nothing less than a constitutional requirement of proportional representation for groups. That assertion amounts to nothing more than a red herring.[c] [Appellees] proved that no Negro had ever been elected to the Mobile City Commission, despite the fact that Negroes constitute about one-third of the electorate, and that the persistence of severe racial bloc voting made it highly unlikely that any Negro could be elected at-large in the foreseeable future. Contrary to the plurality's contention, however, I do not find unconstitutional vote dilution in this case simply because of that showing. The plaintiffs convinced the District Court that Mobile Negroes were unable to use alternative avenues of political influence. They showed that Mobile Negroes still suffered pervasive present effects of massive historical official and private discrimination, and that the city commission had been quite unresponsive to the needs of the minority community. Mobile has been guilty of such pervasive racial discrimination in hiring employees that extensive intervention by the Federal District Court has been required. Negroes are grossly underrepresented on city boards and committees. The city's distribution of public services is racially discriminatory. City officials and police were largely unmoved by Negro complaints about police brutality and "mock lynchings." The District Court concluded that "[t]his sluggish and timid response is another manifestation of the low priority given to the needs of the black citizens and of the [commissioners'] political fear of a white backlash vote when black citizens' needs are at stake."

[T]he protection against vote dilution recognized by our prior cases serves as a minimally intrusive guarantee of political survival for a discrete political minority that is effectively locked out of governmental decisionmaking processes. So understood, the doctrine hardly " 'create[s] substantive constitutional rights in the name of guaranteeing equal protection of the laws,' " [but] is a simple reflection of the basic principle that the Equal Protection Clause protects "[t]he right of a citizen to equal representation and to have his vote weighted equally with those of all other citizens." *Reynolds.*

[The] plurality's requirement of proof of *intentional discrimination* [may] represent an attempt to bury the legitimate concerns of the minority beneath the soil of a doctrine almost as impermeable as it is specious. If so, the superficial tranquility created by such measures can be but short-lived. If this Court refuses to honor our long-recognized principle that the Constitution "nullifies sophisticated as well as simple-minded modes of discrimination," it cannot expect the victims of discrimination to respect political channels of seeking redress. I dissent.

ROGERS v. LODGE, 458 U.S. 613, 102 S.Ct. 3272, 73 L.Ed.2d 1012 (1982), per WHITE, J., affirmed a decision that the at-large election system for a Georgia county Board of Commissioners violated equal protection: "The District Court [demonstrated] its understanding of the controlling standard by observing that a determination of discriminatory intent is 'a requisite to a finding of unconstitutional vote dilution' [and] concluded that the [system] 'although racially neutral when adopted, is being *maintained* for invidious purposes.' [For] the most part, the District Court dealt with the evidence in terms of the factors [that had been used by the district court in *Mobile*], but as the Court of Appeals stated: 'Judge

c. For the view that "PR is the only electoral system that can give equal representation to all groups," see Note, *The Constitutional Imperative of Proportional Representation,* 94 Yale L.J. 163 (1984).

Alaimo [did] not treat [those factors] as absolute, but rather considered them only to the extent that they were relevant to the question of discriminatory intent.' Although a tenable argument can be made to the contrary, we are not inclined to disagree with the Court of Appeals' conclusion that the District Court applied the proper legal standard. * * *

"The Court of Appeals [stated that the] District Court correctly anticipated *Mobile* and required appellees to prove that the at-large voting system was maintained [a] for a discriminatory purpose. The Court of Appeals also held that the District Court's findings not only were not clearly erroneous, but its conclusion that the at-large system was maintained for invidious purposes was 'virtually mandated by the overwhelming proof.' [This Court has] noted that issues of intent are commonly treated as factual matters [and] has frequently noted its reluctance to disturb findings of fact concurred in by two lower courts."

POWELL, J., joined by Rehnquist, J., dissented: "[T]he Court's opinion cannot be reconciled persuasively with [*Mobile*]. There are some variances in the largely sociological evidence presented in the two cases. But *Mobile* held that this *kind* of evidence was not enough. * * *

"The Court's decision today relies heavily on the capacity of the federal district courts—essentially free from any standards prepounded by this Court—to determine whether at-large voting systems are 'being maintained for the invidious purpose of diluting the voting strength of the black population.' Federal courts thus are invited to engage in deeply subjective inquiries into the motivations of local officials in structuring local governments. Inquiries of this kind not only can be 'unseemly,' they intrude the federal courts—with only the vaguest constitutional direction—into an area of intensely local and political concern.

"Emphasizing these considerations, Justice Stevens argues forcefully [that] subjective intent is irrelevant to the establishment of a case of racial vote [dilution].[b] I agree with much of what he says [but] would not accept this view. 'The central purpose of the Equal Protection Clause [is] the prevention of official conduct discriminating on the basis of race.' *Davis.* Because I am unwilling to abandon this central principle in cases of this kind, I cannot join Justice Stevens's opinion. [But] in the absence of proof of discrimination by reliance on the kind of objective factors identified by Justice Stevens, I would hold that the factors cited by the Court of Appeals are too attenuated as a matter of law to support an inference of discriminatory intent." [c]

DAVIS v. BANDEMER

478 U.S. 109, 106 S.Ct. 2797, 92 L.Ed.2d 85 (1986).

[Democrats challenged Indiana's 1981 state apportionment—enacted by Republican majorities in both houses of the legislature and signed by a Republican governor—on the ground that it "constituted a political gerrymander intended to disadvantage Democrats on a statewide basis." A majority of the Court, per White, J.—relying on cases such as *Baker* and *Reynolds* (indicating "the justiciability of claims going to the adequacy of

a. For commentary on the Court's handling of the intent issue, see Baker, *Outcome Equality or Equality of Respect: The Substantive Content of Equal Protection,* 131 U.Pa.L. Rev. 933, 983–84 (1983).

b. Stevens, J.'s long dissent expanded his views expressed in *Mobile.*

c. In 1982 Congress amended the Voting Rights Act of 1965, in a manner that has been interpreted to obviate the need for proof of discriminatory purpose.

state representation in state legislatures"); *Mobile, Whitcomb, Regester* and *Rogers* ("racial gerrymandering presents a justiciable equal protection claim"); and, particularly, *Gaffney v. Cummings* [a]—held that a "political gerrymandering claim [is] justiciable."]

JUSTICE WHITE announced the judgment of the Court and delivered [an] opinion in which JUSTICE BRENNAN, JUSTICE MARSHALL, and JUSTICE BLACKMUN joined * * *.

We [agree] with the District Court that in order to succeed the Bandemer plaintiffs were required to prove both intentional discrimination against an identifiable political group and an actual discriminatory effect on that group. [As] long as redistricting is done by a legislature, it should not be very difficult to prove that the likely political consequences of the reapportionment were intended.[11]

We do not accept, however, the District Court's legal and factual bases for concluding that the 1981 Act visited a sufficiently adverse effect on the appellees' constitutionally protected rights to make out a violation of the Equal Protection Clause. The District Court held that because any apportionment scheme that purposely prevents proportional representation is unconstitutional, Democratic voters need only show that their proportionate voting influence has been adversely affected. Our cases, however, clearly foreclose any claim that the Constitution requires proportional representation or that legislatures in reapportioning must draw district lines to come as near as possible to allocating seats to the contending parties in proportion to what their anticipated statewide vote will be. *Whitcomb; Regester.*

The typical election for legislative seats in the United States is conducted in described geographical districts, with the candidate receiving the most votes in each district winning the seat allocated to that district. If all or most of the districts are competitive, [even] a narrow statewide preference for either party would produce an overwhelming majority for the winning party in the state legislature. This consequence, however, is inherent in winner-take-all, district-based elections, and we cannot hold that such a reapportionment law would violate the Equal Protection Clause because the voters in the losing party do not have representation in the legislature in proportion to the statewide vote received by their party candidates. * * *

In cases involving individual multi-member districts, we have required a substantially greater showing of adverse effects than a mere lack of proportional

a. *Gaffney* ruled that the fact "that virtually every Senate and House district line [in Connecticut] was drawn with the conscious intent to create a districting plan that would achieve a rough approximation of the statewide political strengths of the Democratic and Republican Parties, the only two parties in the state large enough to elect legislators from discernible geographic areas" did not invalidate the plan.

11. That discriminatory intent may not be difficult to prove in this context does not, of course, mean that it need not be proved at all to succeed on such a claim. [Would (should) state constitutional speech and debate clause claims be respected in litigating the issue? For reflection on how the issue might be litigated, see Comment, *Politics and Purpose: Hide and Seek in the Gerrymandering Thicket After Davis v. Bandemer,* 136 U.Pa.L.Rev. 183, 184–85 (1987). See also Dixon, fn. d in *Reynolds* supra, at 322; Engstrom, *The Supreme Court and Equipopulous Gerrymandering: A Remaining Obstacle in the Quest for Fair and Effective Representation,* 1976 Ariz.St.L.J. 277. Cf. Voting Rights Act of 1965, fn. a, (burden of proof on state with respect to changes in districting); Halpin and Engstrom, *Racial Gerrymandering and Southern State Legislative Districting: Attorney General Determinations Under the Voting Rights Act,* 22 J.Pub.L. 37 (1973). For general commentary on the issue of purpose, see Baker, *Outcome Equality or Equality of Respect: The Substantive Content of Equal Protection,* 131 U.Pa.L.Rev. 933, 972–84 (1983)].

representation to support a finding of unconstitutional vote dilution. Only where there is evidence that excluded groups have "less opportunity to participate in the political processes and to elect candidates of their choice" have we refused to approve the use of multi-member districts. *Rogers.* See also *United Jewish Orgs. v. Carey; Regester; Whitcomb.* In these cases, we have also noted the lack of responsiveness by those elected to the concerns of the relevant groups. *Rogers; Regester.*[12]

These holdings rest on a conviction that the mere fact that a particular apportionment scheme makes it more difficult for a particular group in a particular district to elect the representatives of its choice does not render that scheme constitutionally infirm. This conviction, in turn, stems from a perception that the power to influence the political process is not limited to winning elections. An individual or a group of individuals who votes for a losing candidate is usually deemed to be adequately represented by the winning candidate and to have as much opportunity to influence that candidate as other voters in the district. We cannot presume in such a situation, without actual proof to the contrary, that the candidate elected will entirely ignore the interests of those voters. This is true even in a safe district where the losing group loses election after election. Thus, a group's electoral power is not unconstitutionally diminished by the simple fact of an appointment scheme that makes winning elections more difficult,[b] and a failure of proportional representation alone does not constitute impermissible discrimination under the Equal Protection Clause. See *Mobile v. Bolden,* n. 7 (Marshall, J., dissenting).

As with individual districts, where unconstitutional vote dilution is alleged in the form of statewide political gerrymandering, the mere lack of proportional representation will not be sufficient to prove unconstitutional discrimination. Again, without specific supporting evidence, a court cannot presume in such a case that those who are elected will disregard the disproportionately underrepresented group. Rather, unconstitutional discrimination occurs only when the electoral system is arranged in a manner that will consistently degrade a voter's or a group of voters' influence on the political process as a [whole].

In a challenge to an individual district, this inquiry focuses on the opportunity of members of the group to participate in party deliberations in the slating

12. Although these cases involved racial groups, we believe that the principles developed in these cases would apply equally to claims by political groups in individual districts. We note, however, that the elements necessary to a successful vote dilution claim may be more difficult to prove in relation to a claim by a political group. For example, historical patterns of exclusion from the political processes, evidence which would support a vote dilution claim, are in general more likely to be present for a racial group than for a political group.

b. Consider Alfange, "*Gerrymandering and the Constitution: Into the Thorns of the Thicket at Last,*" 1986 Sup.Ct.Rev. 175, 245–46: [It undoubtedly] "came as something of a surprise to the Republican National Committee to be told that whether their candidates are able to win elections is not essentially relevant to the question whether they have been victims of a gerrymander."

But consider Lowenstein, *Bandemer's Gap: Gerrymandering and Equal Protection,* in Toward Fair and Effective Representation 64 (Groffman ed. 1990): "As Professor Alfange acknowledges, it makes an enormous difference to a minority group whether their representatives regard them as 'enemies to be overcome or as constituents to be wooed in the next election.' Democrats represented by Republican legislators ordinarily fall within the latter category. Blacks, communists, and homosexuals are examples of groups that have sometimes fallen within the former category. If the plurality opinion is read as contemplating an action brought by a group suffering from that sort of discriminatory treatment, Justice White's statement about representation for supporters of losing candidates is not bewildering [at] all." For the contention that the plurality engages in a suspect classifications' analysis (not fundamental rights) and that the likely beneficiaries, if any, would not be major parties, see id.

and nomination of candidates, their opportunity to register and vote, and hence their chance to directly influence the election returns and to secure the attention of the winning candidate. Statewide, however, the inquiry centers on the voters' direct or indirect influence on the elections of the state legislature as a whole. And, as in individual district cases, an equal protection violation may be found only where the electoral system substantially disadvantages certain voters in their opportunity to influence the political process effectively. In this context, such a finding of unconstitutionality must be supported by evidence of continued frustration of the will of a majority of the voters or effective denial to a minority of voters of a fair chance to influence the political process.

Based on these views, we would reject the District Court's apparent holding that *any* interference with an opportunity to elect a representative of one's choice would be sufficient to allege or make out an equal protection violation, unless justified by some acceptable state interest that the State would be required to demonstrate. [S]uch a low threshold for legal action would invite attack on all or almost all reapportionment statutes. District-based elections hardly ever produce a perfect fit between votes and representation. [Inviting] attack on minor departures from some supposed norm would too much embroil the judiciary in second-guessing what has consistently been referred to as a political task for the legislature * * *.

The view that a prima facie case of illegal discrimination in reapportionment requires a showing of more than a *de minimis* effect is not unprecedented. Reapportionment cases involving the one person, one vote principle [provide] support for such a requirement. In the present, considerably more complex context, it is also appropriate to require allegations and proof that the challenged legislative plan has had or will have effects that are sufficiently serious to require intervention by the federal courts in state reapportionment decisions.

The District Court's findings do not satisfy this threshold condition to stating and proving a cause of action. In reaching its conclusion, the District Court relied primarily on the results of the 1982 elections: Democratic candidates for the State House of Representatives had received 51.9% of the votes cast statewide and Republican candidates 48.1%; yet, out of the 100 seats to be filled, Republican candidates won 57 and Democrats 43. In the Senate, 53.1% of the votes were cast for Democratic candidates and 46.9% for Republicans; of the 25 Senate seats to be filled, Republicans won 12 and Democrats 13. The court also relied upon the use of multi-member districts in Marion and Allen counties, where Democrats or those inclined to vote Democratic in 1982 amounted to 46.6% of the population of those counties but Republicans won 86 percent—18 of 21—seats allocated to the districts in those counties. These disparities were enough to require a neutral justification by the State, which in the eyes of the District Court was not forthcoming.[15]

15. The District Court apparently thought that the political group suffering discrimination was all those voters who voted for Democratic Assembly candidates in 1982. Judge Pell, in dissent, argued that the allegedly disfavored group should be defined as those voters who could be counted on to vote Democratic from election to election, thus excluding those who vote the Republican ticket from time to time. He would have counted the true believers by averaging the Democratic vote cast in two different elections for those statewide offices for which party-line voting is thought to be the rule and personality and issue-oriented factors are relatively unimportant. Although accepting Judge Pell's definition of Democratic voters would have strongly suggested that the 1981 reapportionment had no discriminatory effect at all, there was no response to his position. The appellees take up the challenge in this Court, claiming that Judge Pell chose the wrong election years for the purpose of averaging the Democratic votes. The dispute need not now be resolved.

Relying on a single election to prove unconstitutional discrimination is unsatisfactory. The District Court observed, and the parties do not disagree, that Indiana is a swing State. Voters sometimes prefer Democratic candidates, and sometimes Republican. The District Court did not find that because of the 1981 Act the Democrats could not in one of the next few elections secure a sufficient vote to take control of the assembly. Indeed, the District Court declined to hold that the 1982 election results were the predictable consequences of the 1981 Act and expressly refused to hold that those results were a reliable prediction of future ones. The District Court did not ask by what percentage the statewide Democratic vote would have had to increase to control either the House or the Senate. The appellants argue here, without a persuasive response from appellees, that had the Democratic candidates received an additional few percentage points of the votes cast statewide, they would have obtained a majority of the seats in both houses. Nor was there any finding that the 1981 reapportionment would consign the Democrats to a minority status in the Assembly throughout the 1980's or that the Democrats would have no hope of doing any better in the reapportionment that would occur after the 1990 census. Without findings of this nature, the District Court erred in concluding that the 1981 Act violated the Equal Protection Clause.

The District Court's discussion of the multi-member districts created by the 1981 Act does not undermine this conclusion. For the purposes of the statewide political gerrymandering claim, these districts appear indistinguishable from safe Republican and safe Democratic single-member districts. Simply showing that there are multi-member districts in the State and that those districts are constructed so as to be safely Republican or Democratic in no way bolsters the contention that there has been *statewide* discrimination against Democratic voters. It could be, were the necessary threshold effect to be shown, that multi-member districts could be demonstrated to be suspect on the ground that they are particularly useful in attaining impermissibly discriminatory ends; at this stage of the inquiry, however, the multi-member district evidence does not materially aid the appellees' case. * * *

In response to our approach, Justice Powell suggests an alternative method for evaluating equal protection claims of political gerrymandering. In his view, courts should look at a number of factors in considering these claims: the nature of the legislative procedures by which the challenged redistricting was accomplished and the intent behind the redistricting; the shapes of the districts and their conformity with political subdivision boundaries; and "evidence concerning population disparities and statistics tending to show vote dilution." [T]he crux of Justice Powell's analysis seems to be that—at least in some cases—the intentional drawing of district boundaries for partisan ends and for no other reason violates the Equal Protection Clause in and of itself. We disagree, however, with this conception of a constitutional violation. Specifically, even if a state legislature redistricts with the specific intention of disadvantaging one political party's election prospects, we do not believe that there has been an unconstitutional discrimination against members of that party unless the redistricting does in fact disadvantage it at the polls.

Moreover, as we discussed above, a mere lack of proportionate results in one election cannot suffice in this regard. [E]qual protection violations may be found only where a history (actual or projected) of disproportionate results appears in conjunction with ["strong indicia of lack of political power and the denial of fair representation."] The mere lack of control of the General Assembly after a single election does not rise to the requisite level. [But] Justice Powell's view would allow a constitutional violation to be found where the only proven effect on a political party's electoral power was disproportionate results in one (or possibly two) elections. * * *

In rejecting Justice Powell's approach, we do not mean to intimate that the factors he considers are entirely irrelevant. The election results obviously are relevant to a showing of the effects required to prove a political gerrymandering claim under our view. And the district configurations may be combined with vote projections to predict future election results, which are also relevant to the effects showing. The other factors, even if not relevant to the effects issue, might well be relevant to an equal protection claim. The equal protection argument would proceed along the following lines: If there were a discriminatory effect and a discriminatory intent, then the legislation would be examined for valid underpinnings. Thus, evidence of exclusive legislative process and deliberate drawing of district lines in accordance with accepted gerrymandering principles would be relevant to intent, and evidence of valid and invalid configuration would be relevant to whether the districting plan met legitimate state interests.

This course is consistent with our equal protection cases generally and is the course we follow here: We assumed that there was discriminatory intent, found that there was insufficient discriminatory effect to constitute an equal protection violation,[19] and therefore did not reach the question of the state interests (legitimate or otherwise) served by the particular districts as they were created by the legislature. Consequently, the valid or invalid configuration of the districts was an issue we did not need to consider.

* * * We recognize that our own view may be difficult of application. Determining when an electoral system has been "arranged in a manner that will consistently degrade a voter's or a group of voters' influence on the political process as a whole" is of necessity a difficult inquiry. Nevertheless, we believe that it recognizes the delicacy of intruding on this most political of legislative functions and is at the same time consistent with our prior cases regarding individual multi-member districts, which have formulated a parallel standard. * * *

JUSTICE POWELL, with whom JUSTICE STEVENS joins, concurring [on the issue of justiciability], and dissenting.

[T]he plurality expresses the view, with which I agree, that a partisan political gerrymander violates the Equal Protection Clause only on proof of "both intentional discrimination against an identifiable political group and an actual discriminatory effect on that group." The plurality acknowledges that the record in this case supports a finding that the challenged redistricting plan was adopted for the purpose of discriminating against Democratic voters. The plurality argues, however, that appellees failed to establish that their voting strength was diluted statewide despite uncontradicted proof that certain key districts were grotesquely gerrymandered to enhance the election prospects of Republican candidates. * * *

The Equal Protection Clause guarantees citizens that their state will govern them impartially. In the context of redistricting, that guarantee is of critical importance because the franchise provides most citizens their only voice in the legislative process. Since the contours of a voting district powerfully may affect

19. In most equal protection cases, it is true, a discriminatory effect will be readily apparent, and no heightened effect will be required, but that is the only real difference between this type of equal protection claim and others.

citizens' ability to exercise influence through their vote, district lines should be determined in accordance with neutral and legitimate criteria. When deciding where those lines will fall, the state should treat its voters as standing in the same position, regardless of their political beliefs or party affiliation. [*Reynolds*] contemplated that "one person, one vote" would be only one among several neutral factors that serve the constitutional mandate of fair and effective representation. * * *

The [most] basic flaw in the plurality's opinion is its failure to enunciate any standard that affords guidance to legislatures and courts.[10] [This] places the plurality in the curious position of inviting further litigation even as it appears to signal the "constitutional green light" to would-be gerrymanderers. * * *

A court should look first to the legislative process by which the challenged plan was adopted. Here, the District Court found that the procedures used in redistricting Indiana were carefully designed to exclude Democrats from participating in the legislative process [which] consisted of nothing more than the majority party's private application of computer technology to mapmaking. [T]he only data used in the computer program were precinct population, race of precinct citizens, precinct political complexion, and statewide party voting trends. * * *

Next, the District Court found [how] the mapmakers carved up counties, cities, and even townships in their effort to draw lines beneficial to the majority party. [The] redistricting dissects counties into strange shapes lacking in common interests, on one occasion even placing the seat of one county in a voting district composed of townships from other counties. Under these conditions, the District Court expressly found that "the potential for voter disillusion and nonparticipation is great," as voters are forced to focus their political activities in artificial electoral units. Intelligent voters, regardless of party affiliation, resent this sort of political manipulation of the electorate for no public purpose. * * *

[When] the plan was completed, Republican leaders announced that the House map was designed to yield 56 "safe" Republican seats and 30 Democratic seats, with the remainder being "tossups." Republicans expected that their Senate map would regularly produce 30 Republican seats and 8 to 10 Democratic seats so that Republicans would maintain their grip on the Senate even if Democrats won the remaining seats. In short, the record unequivocally demonstrates that in 1981 the Republican-dominated General Assembly deliberately sought to design a redistricting plan under which members of the Democratic party would be deprived of a fair opportunity to win control of the General Assembly at least until 1991, the date of the next redistricting. * * *

Appellees further demonstrated through a statistical showing that the House Plan debased the effectiveness of their votes [reciting the 1982 election statistics in White, J.'s opinion. Moreover, since] half of the Senate membership is up for election every two years, the only election results under the challenged plan available at trial [showed] that, of the seats up for election in 1982,

10. * * * I cannot agree, as the plurality suggests, that a standard requiring proof of "heightened effect," where invidious intent has been established directly, has support in any of our cases, or that an equal protection violation can be established "only where a history (actual or projected) of disproportionate results appears." If a racial minority established that the legislature adopted a redistricting law for no purpose other than to disadvantage that group, the plurality's new and erroneous standard would require plaintiffs to wait for the results of several elections, creating a history of discriminatory effect, before they can challenge the law in court.

Democrats were elected to 13 seats and Republicans to 12. [It] was appellees' contention that most of the Senate seats won by Democrats in 1982 were "safe" Democratic seats so that their party's success at the polls in that year was fully consistent with the statewide Republican gerrymander. This contention is borne out by the results of the 1984 Senate election. In that election, Democratic candidates received 42.3 percent of the vote, and Republicans 57.7 percent. Yet, of the 25 Senate positions up for election, only 7 were captured by Democrats.

The District Court found, and I agree, that appellants failed to justify the discriminatory impact of the plan by showing that the plan had a rational basis in permissible neutral criteria. [As] the plurality opinion makes clear, [a] colorable claim of discriminatory gerrymandering presents a justiciable controversy under the Equal Protection Clause. Federal courts in exercising their duty to adjudicate such claims should impose a heavy burden of proof on those who allege that a redistricting plan violates the Constitution. [T]his case presents a paradigm example of unconstitutional discrimination against the members of a political party that happened to be out of power. The well-grounded findings of the District Court to this effect have not been, and I believe cannot be, held clearly erroneous. * * * [25]

JUSTICE O'CONNOR, with whom THE CHIEF JUSTICE and JUSTICE REHNQUIST join, concurring in the judgment.

[T]he legislative business of apportionment is fundamentally a political affair, and challenges to the manner in which an apportionment has been carried out—by the very parties that are responsible for this process—present a political question in the truest sense of the term.

To turn these matters over to the federal judiciary is to inject the courts into the most heated partisan issues. It is predictable that the courts will respond by moving away from the nebulous standard a plurality of the Court fashions today and toward some form of rough proportional representation for all political groups. The consequences of this shift will be as immense as they are unfortunate. I do not believe, and the Court offers not a shred of evidence to suggest, that the Framers of the Constitution intended the judicial power to encompass the making of such fundamental choices about how this Nation is to be governed. Nor do I believe that the proportional representation towards which the Court's expansion of equal protection doctrine will lead is consistent with our history, our traditions, or our political institutions.[c] * * *

The step taken today is a momentous one, which if followed in the future can only lead to political instability and judicial malaise. [Federal] courts will have no alternative but to attempt to recreate the complex process of legislative apportionment in the context of adversary litigation in order to reconcile the competing claims of political, religious, ethnic, racial, occupational, and socioeconomic groups. Even if there were some way of limiting such claims to organized political parties, the fact remains that the losing party or the losing group of legislators in every reapportionment will now be invited to fight the battle anew in federal court. [The] Equal Protection Clause does not supply judicially

25. As is evident from the several opinions filed today, there is no "Court" for a standard that properly should be applied in determining whether a challenged redistricting plan is an unconstitutional partisan political gerrymander. The standard proposed by the plurality is explicitly rejected by two Justices, and three Justices also have expressed the view that the plurality's standard will "prove unmanageable and arbitrary." (O'Connor, J., joined by Burger, C.J., and Rehnquist, J., concurring in the judgment).

c. Burger, C.J.'s separate opinion, relying on Frankfurter, J.'s dissent in *Baker v. Carr*, is omitted.

manageable standards for resolving purely political gerrymandering claims, and no group right to an equal share of political power was ever intended by the Framers. [Unlike racial minorities], members of the Democratic and Republican parties cannot claim that they are a discrete and insular group vulnerable to exclusion from the political process by some dominant group: these political parties *are* the dominant groups, and the Court has offered no reason to believe that they are incapable of fending for themselves through the political process. Indeed, there is good reason to think that political gerrymandering is a self-limiting enterprise. See Cain, *The Reapportionment Puzzle* 151–159 (1984). In order to gerrymander, the legislative majority must weaken some of its safe seats, thus exposing its own incumbents to greater risks of defeat—risks they may refuse to accept past a certain point. Similarly, an overambitious gerrymander can lead to disaster for the legislative majority: because it has created more seats in which it hopes to win relatively narrow victories, the same swing in overall voting strength will tend to cost the legislative majority more and more seats as the gerrymander becomes more ambitious. More generally, each major party presumably has ample weapons at its disposal to conduct the partisan struggle that often leads to a partisan apportionment, but also often leads to a bipartisan one. * * *

Furthermore, the Court fails to explain why a bipartisan gerrymander—which is what was approved in *Gaffney*—affects individuals any differently than a partisan gerrymander. [As] the plurality acknowledges, the scheme upheld in *Gaffney* tended to "deny safe district minorities any realistic chance to elect their own representatives." If this bipartisan arrangement between two groups of self-interested legislators is constitutionally permissible, as I believe and as the Court held in *Gaffney,* then—in terms of the rights of individuals—it should be equally permissible for a legislative majority to employ the same means to pursue its own interests over the opposition of the other party.

* * * [The] Court has in effect decided that it is constitutionally acceptable for both parties to "waste" the votes of individuals through a bipartisan gerrymander, so long as the *parties* themselves are not deprived of their group voting strength to an extent that will exceed the plurality's threshold requirement. This choice confers greater rights on powerful political groups than on individuals; that cannot be the meaning of the Equal Protection Clause. * * *

Vote dilution analysis is far less manageable when extended to major political parties than if confined to racial minority groups. First, [d]esigning an apportionment plan that does not impair or degrade the voting strength of several groups is more difficult than designing a plan that does not have such an effect on one group for the simple reason that, as the number of criteria the plan must meet increases, the number of solutions that will satisfy those criteria will decrease. * * *

Second, while membership in a racial group is an immutable characteristic, voters can—and often do—move from one party to the other or support candidates from both parties. Consequently, the difficulty of measuring voting strength is heightened in the case of a major political party. * * *

Moreover, any such intervention is likely to move in the direction of proportional representation for political parties. This is clear by analogy to the problem that arises in racial gerrymandering cases: "in order to decide whether an electoral system has made it harder for minority voters to elect the candidates they prefer, a court must have an idea in mind of how hard it 'should' be for minority voters to elect their preferred candidates under an acceptable system." Any such norm must make some reference, even if only a loose one, to the relation between the racial minority group's share of the electorate and its share of the elected representatives. In order to implement the plurality's standard, it will thus be necessary for courts to adopt an analogous norm, in order to assess whether the voting strength of a political party has been "degraded" by an apportionment, either on a state-wide basis or in particular districts. Absent any such norm, the inquiry the plurality proposes would be so standardless as to make the adjudication of political gerrymandering claims impossible.

* * * [Because] the most easily measured indicia of political power relate solely to winning and losing elections, there is a grave risk that the plurality's various attempts to qualify and condition the group right the Court has created will gradually pale in importance. What is likely to remain is a loose form of proportionality, under which *some* deviations from proportionality are permissible, but any significant, persistent deviations from proportionality are suspect. Courts will be forced to look for some form of "undue" disproportionality with respect to electoral success if political gerrymandering claims are justiciable, because otherwise they will find their decisions turning on imponderables such as whether the legislators of one party have fairly represented the voters of the other.

Of course, in one sense a requirement of proportional representation, whether loose or absolute, is judicially manageable. If this Court were to declare that the Equal Protection Clause required proportional representation within certain fixed tolerances, I have no doubt that district courts would be able to apply this edict. The flaw in such a pronouncement, however, would be the use of the Equal Protection Clause as the vehicle for making a fundamental policy choice that is contrary to the intent of its Framers and to the traditions of this republic. The political question doctrine as articulated in *Baker* rightly requires that we refrain from making such policy choices in order to evade what would otherwise be a lack of judicially manageable standards. * * *

* * * [To] allow district courts to strike down apportionment plans on the basis of their prognostications as to the outcome of future elections or future apportionments invites "findings" on matters as to which neither judges nor anyone else can have any confidence. Once it is conceded that "a group's electoral power is not unconstitutionally diminished by the simple fact of an apportionment scheme that makes winning elections more difficult," the virtual impossibility of reliably predicting how difficult it will be to win an election in 2, or 4, or 10 years should, in my view, weigh in favor of holding such challenges nonjusticiable. Racial gerrymandering should remain justiciable, for the harms it engenders run counter to the central thrust of the Fourteenth Amendment. But no such justification can be given for judicial intervention on behalf of mainstream political parties, and the risks such intervention poses to our political institutions are unacceptable. * * *

Notes and Questions

1. Consider Tribe, *American Constitutional Law* 1083 (2d ed.1988): "Justice White's opinion for the Court on the justiciability issue [equated] the Court's decision to intervene in the case with the Court's determination in *Baker v. Carr* to hear claims relating to the disparate size of election districts. Yet the two kinds of intervention are surely distinct. Although the *Baker* Court did not

itself announce the one person, one vote rule, that rule was looming on the near horizon; the *Baker* Court had no reason to fear that no judicially manageable standard could be found. The Court in *Bandemer* had every reason to fear such an eventuality."

2. Is one person's gerrymander another person's good government? Consider R.H. Brown & Lowenstein, *A Democratic Perspective on Legislative Districting,* 6 J. of Law & Politics 673, 679 (1990): "The most common 'neutral' criterion Republicans try to impose [is] compactness. The usual way of levying a political attack on a districting plan is to show diagrams of selected oddly-shaped districts. This is supposed to prove that the plan is an outrageous gerrymander. * * * The real reason the Republicans promote the compactness requirement is that it tends to work systematically to their [benefit]. Inner-city areas tend to contain Democratic voters concentrated in extraordinarily high percentages. Many surrounding affluent areas are predominantly but not nearly so overwhelmingly Republican. Accordingly, it may be relatively easy to draw compact districts separating these areas and thereby to accomplish the objective of a Republican gerrymander—a small number of overwhelmingly democratic districts surrounded by a large number of much closer but still safely Republican districts." [d]

But cf. M. Shapiro, *Gerrymandering, Unfairness, and the Supreme Court,* 33 UCLA L.Rev. 227, 240 (1985): "If geography favors the Republicans in an ungerrymandered world, that is a purely fortuitous result, unforeseeable by either party when it chose its ideologies and clienteles. Such stacking ought to be considered extraneous to the goal of constraining the self-serving actions of the legislatures." [e] For a comprehensive attempt to show that the removal of politics from redistricting is an illusory goal with the conclusion that judges should keep out, see Lowenstein & Steinberg, *The Quest for Legislative Districting in the Public Interest: Elusive or Illusory,* 33 UCLA L.Rev. 1 (1985).[f] But see Groffman, *Criteria for Districting: A Social Science Perspective,* 33 UCLA L.Rev. 77 (1985).

3. Consider Schuck, fn. f supra, at 1372, 1375–76: "It is puzzling that the concern for [party] representation so evident in all of the [*Bandemer*] opinions [has] crested at this particular moment in our political history. * * * The partisan identification of American voters is probably weaker today than at any time since the founding of mass-based political parties * * *." Is the Court wasting judicial resources in *Bandemer?* Alternatively, does the existence of gerrymandering undercut the wisdom of the expending of judicial resources in *Reynolds?*

d. See Comment, *Politics and Purpose,* fn. 11 supra: "While the plaintiffs in [*Bandemer*] were Indiana Democrats, Republicans nationally hailed the justiciability of gerrymandering: they believed that Democrats, who control most state legislatures, have drawn state and congressional district lines to Democratic advantage. National Democrats, however, have minimized the impact of the decision, taking the view that the high equal protection threshold in [*Bandemer*] would prevent drastic restructuring." For some indication of the threshold's height, see *Badham v. Eu,* 694 F.Supp. 664 (N.D.Cal.1988), affirmed mem., 488 U.S. 1024, 109 S.Ct. 829, 102 L.Ed.2d 962 (1989) (California reapportionment plan not violated under *Bandemer* standards).

e. For Shapiro's opposition to judicial intervention, nonetheless, see id. at 252–56.

f. See also Schuck, *The Thickest Thicket: Partisan Gerrymandering and Judicial Regulation of Politics,* 87 Colum.L.Rev. 1325, 1337 (1987) (arguments against a structure permitting gerrymandering "overlook important complexities and values in our political life, project incomplete visions of democratic representation, and invite innovative political remedies that should not be mandated by our federal courts").

B. DENIAL OR QUALIFICATION OF THE RIGHT

CARRINGTON v. RASH, 380 U.S. 89, 85 S.Ct. 775, 13 L.Ed.2d 675 (1965), per STEWART, J., held a Texas provision, barring members of the military who moved to Texas from voting in state elections so long as they remained in the military, "an invidious discrimination": "We deal here with matters close to the core of our constitutional system." Only "where military personnel are involved has Texas been unwilling to develop more precise tests to determine the bona fides of an individual claiming to have actually made his home in the State long enough to vote." " 'Fencing out' from the franchise a sector of the population because of the way they may vote is constitutionally impermissible." [a]

HARPER v. VIRGINIA STATE BD. OF ELEC., 383 U.S. 663, 86 S.Ct. 1079, 16 L.Ed.2d 169 (1966), per DOUGLAS, J., overruling *Breedlove v. Suttles,* 302 U.S. 277, 58 S.Ct. 205, 82 L.Ed. 252 (1937), held that Virginia's $1.50 poll tax as "a prerequisite of voting" was "an 'invidious' discrimination": "[T]he right to vote in state elections is nowhere expressly mentioned" in the Constitution, but "once the franchise is [granted] lines may not be drawn which [violate equal protection].[3]"

"Long ago in *Yick Wo,* [Sec. 2, III supra], the Court referred to 'the political franchise of voting' as a 'fundamental political right, because preservative of all rights.' * * * Wealth, like race, creed, or color, is not germane to one's ability to participate intelligently in the electoral process. Lines drawn on the basis of wealth or property, like those of race, are traditionally disfavored. See *Edwards v. California,* 314 U.S. 160, 62 S.Ct. 164, 86 L.Ed. 119 (1941) (Jackson, J., concurring); *Griffin v. Illinois; Douglas v. California,* [Part III infra]. To introduce wealth or payment of a fee as a measure of a voter's qualifications is to introduce a capricious or irrelevant factor. * * *

"In determining what lines are unconstitutionally discriminatory, we have never been confined to historic notions of equality" and "notions of what constitutes equal treatment for purposes of the Equal Protection Clause *do* change [citing *Plessy* and *Brown,* Sec. 2, II supra]. Our conclusion, like that in *Reynolds,* is founded not on what we think governmental policy should be, but on what the Equal Protection Clause requires.

"We have long been mindful that where fundamental rights and liberties are asserted under the Equal Protection Clause, classifications which might invade or restrain them must be closely scrutinized and carefully confined. See, e.g., *Reynolds; Carrington.*"

BLACK, J., dissented: "[U]nder a proper interpretation of the Equal Protection Clause States are to have the broadest kind of leeway in areas where they have a general constitutional competence to act. [P]oll tax legislation can 'reasonably,' 'rationally' and without an 'invidious' or evil purpose to injure anyone be found to rest on a number of state policies including (1) the State's

a. Harlan, J., dissented: The classification was "rational" in treating such persons as "transients for voting purposes" because the "vast majority" will leave "when the military compulsion ends." Finally, Texas "could rationally decide to protect local politics against the influences of military voting strength." Warren, C.J., did not participate.

May a state single out certain groups (students) for a presumption of nonresidency (in the district in which they attend college)? See generally Note, *Student Voting and the Constitution,* 72 Colum.L.Rev. 162 (1972).

3. [While] the "Virginia poll tax was born of a desire to disenfranchise the Negro," we do not stop to determine whether [the] Virginia tax in its modern setting serves the same end.

desire to collect its revenue, and (2) its belief that voters who pay a poll tax will be interested in furthering the State's welfare when they vote. [And] history is on the side of 'rationality' of the State's poll tax policy. Property qualifications existed in the Colonies and were continued by many States after the Constitution was adopted. [The Court] seems to be using the old 'natural-law-due-process formula' to justify striking down state laws as violations of [equal protection]."

HARLAN, J., joined by Stewart, J., dissented: "The [equal protection] test evolved by this Court [is whether] a classification can be deemed to be founded on some rational and otherwise constitutionally permissible state [policy].[3] *Reynolds* [also] marked a departure from these traditional and wise principles. [I]t was probably accepted as sound political theory by a large percentage of Americans through most of our history, that people with some property have a deeper stake in community affairs, and are consequently more responsible, more educated, more knowledgeable, more worthy of [confidence. It] is all wrong, in my view, for the Court to adopt the political doctrines popularly accepted at a particular moment of our history and to declare all others to be irrational and invidious * * *."

KRAMER v. UNION FREE SCHOOL DISTRICT

395 U.S. 621, 89 S.Ct. 1886, 23 L.Ed.2d 583 (1969).

CHIEF JUSTICE WARREN delivered the opinion of the Court.

[§ 2012 of the New York Education Law] provides that in certain New York school districts residents [may] vote in the school district election only if they [or their spouse] (1) own (or lease) taxable real property within the district, or (2) are parents (or have custody of) children enrolled in the local public schools. Appellant, a bachelor who neither owns nor leases taxable real property, [claimed] § 2012 denied him equal protection * * *.

[I]t is important to note what is *not* at issue in this case. The requirements of § 2012 that school district voters must (1) be citizens of the United States, (2) be bona fide residents of the school district, and (3) be at least 21 years of age are not challenged. * * *

[S]tatutes distributing the franchise constitute the foundation of our representative society. Any unjustified discrimination in determining who may participate in political affairs or in the selection of public officials undermines the legitimacy of representative government. [Therefore,] if a [statute] grants the right to vote to some bona fide residents of requisite age and citizenship and denies the franchise to others, the Court must determine whether the exclusions are necessary to promote a compelling state interest. See *Carrington.*

[The] presumption of constitutionality and the approval given "rational" classifications in other types of enactments are based on an assumption that the institutions of state government are structured so as to represent fairly all the people. However, when the challenge to the statute is in effect a challenge of this basic assumption, the assumption can no longer serve as the basis for presuming constitutionality. And, the assumption is no less under attack because the legislature which decides who may participate at the various levels of political choice is fairly elected. * * *[10]

3. I think the somewhat different application of the Equal Protection Clause to racial discrimination cases finds justification in the fact that insofar as that clause may embody a particular value in addition to rationality, the historical origins of the Civil War Amendments might attribute to racial equality this special status. * * *

10. [See] *Avery v. Midland County.*

The need for exacting judicial scrutiny of statutes distributing the franchise is undiminished simply because, under a different statutory scheme, the offices subject to election might have been filled through appointment [11] [since] "once the franchise is granted to the electorate, lines may not be drawn which are inconsistent with [equal protection]." *Harper.*

Nor is the need for close judicial examination affected because the district [and] the school board do not have "general" legislative powers. Our exacting examination is necessitated not by the subject of the election [but] because some resident citizens are permitted to participate and some are not. * * *

Besides appellant and others who similarly live in their parents' homes, the statute also disenfranchises the following persons (unless they are parents or guardians of children enrolled in the district public school): senior citizens and others living with children or relatives; clergy, military personnel and others who live on tax-exempt property; boarders and lodgers; parents who neither own nor lease qualifying property and whose children are too young to attend school [or] attend private schools.

[A]ppellees argue that the State has a legitimate interest in limiting the franchise in school district elections [to] those "primarily interested in such elections" [and] that the State may reasonably and permissibly conclude that "property taxpayers" (including lessees of taxable property who share the tax burden through rent payments) and parents of the children enrolled in the district's schools are those "primarily interested" in school affairs. * * *

[A]ssuming, arguendo, that New York legitimately might limit the franchise in these school district elections to those "primarily interested in school affairs," close scrutiny of the § 2012 classifications demonstrates that they do not accomplish this purpose with sufficient precision to justify denying appellant the franchise.

[T]he classifications must be tailored so that the exclusion of appellant and members of his class is necessary to achieve the articulated state goal.[14] Section 2012 does not meet the exacting standard of precision [because it permits] inclusion of many persons who have, at best, a remote and indirect interest in school affairs and on the other hand, exclude[s] others who have a distinct and direct interest in the school meeting decisions.[15] * * * [a]

JUSTICE STEWART, with whom JUSTICE BLACK and JUSTICE HARLAN join, dissenting. * * *

Clearly a State may reasonably assume that its residents have a greater stake in the outcome of elections held within its boundaries than do other persons [and] that residents, being generally better informed regarding state

11. Similarly, no less a showing of a compelling justification for disenfranchising residents is required merely because the questions scheduled for the election need not have been submitted to the voters.

14. Of course, if the exclusions are necessary to promote the articulated state interest, we must then determine whether the interest promoted by limiting the franchise constitutes a compelling state interest. We do not reach that issue in this case.

15. For example, appellant resides with his parents in the school district, pays state and federal taxes and is interested in and affected by school board decisions [but] an uninterested unemployed young man who pays no state or federal taxes, but who rents an apartment in the district, can [vote].

a. See also *Cipriano v. Houma,* 395 U.S. 701, 89 S.Ct. 1897, 23 L.Ed.2d 647 (1969) (invalidating statute confining vote to property taxpayers in elections for issuance of municipal bonds by a municipal utility); *Phoenix v. Kolodziejski,* 399 U.S. 204, 90 S.Ct. 1990, 26 L.Ed.2d 523 (1970) (invalidating statute confining vote to real property taxpayers in elections for issuance of general obligation bonds for financing various municipal improvements).

affairs than are nonresidents, will be more likely [to] vote responsibly. And the same may be said of legislative assumptions regarding the electoral competence of adults and literate persons on the one hand, and of minors and illiterates on the other. It is clear, of course, that lines thus drawn cannot infallibly perform their intended legislative function. Just as "[i]lliterate people may be intelligent voters," nonresidents or minors might also in some instances be interested, informed, and intelligent participants in the electoral process. Persons who commute across a state line to work may well have a great stake in the affairs of the State in which they are employed; some college students under 21 may be both better informed and more passionately interested in political affairs than many adults. But such discrepancies are the inevitable concomitant of the line-drawing that is essential to lawmaking.[b] So long as the classification is rationally related to a permissible legislative end, therefore—as are residence, literacy, and age requirements imposed with respect to voting—there is no denial of equal protection.

Thus judged, the statutory classification involved here seems to me clearly to be valid [and] the Court does not really argue the contrary. Instead, it [asserts] that the traditional equal protection standard is [inapt]. But the asserted justification for applying [a stricter] standard cannot withstand analysis. [The] voting qualifications at issue have been promulgated not by Union Free School District, but by the New York State Legislature, and the appellant is of course fully able to participate in the election of representatives in that body. There is simply no claim whatever here that the state government is not "structured so as to represent fairly all the people," including the appellant.

[§ 2012] does not involve racial classifications [and] is not one that impinges upon a constitutionally protected right, and that consequently can be justified only by a "compelling" state interest. For "the Constitution of the United States does not confer the right of suffrage upon any one."

In any event, it seems to me that under *any* equal protection standard, short of a doctrinaire insistence that universal suffrage is somehow mandated by the Constitution, the appellant's claim must be rejected. * * *

SALYER LAND CO. v. TULARE LAKE BASIN WATER STORAGE DIST., 410 U.S. 719, 93 S.Ct. 1224, 35 L.Ed.2d 659 (1973), per REHNQUIST, J., upheld California statutes permitting only landowners to vote in "water storage districts" elections and apportioning votes according to the assessed valuation of the land within the districts. These districts planned projects for water acquisition, conservation and distribution; they were empowered to fix charges for use of water in proportion to services rendered; project costs were assessed against land in accordance with benefits accruing to each tract. Appellee district had a population of 77 (including 18 children), most employed by one of four corporations that farmed 85% of the land; there were also about 200 other small landowners; one of the corporations (Boswell Co.) held a majority of the votes.

"[Appellee], although vested with some typical governmental powers,[7] has relatively limited authority." Apart from water,[8] "it [does] not exercise what

b. See Lee, *Mr. Herbert Spencer and the Bachelor Stockbroker,* 15 Ariz.L.Rev. 457 (1973).

7. The board [can] condemn private property [and] cooperate (including contract) with other agencies, state and federal. Both general obligations bonds and interest-bearing warrants may be authorized.

8. Appellants strongly urge that districts [engage] in flood control activities [but these] are incident to the exercise of the district's might be thought of as 'normal governmental' authority, [and] its actions disproportionately affect landowners" because of the method of allocating project costs and service charges. "In short, there is no way that the economic burdens of district operations can fall on residents qua residents, and the operations of the districts primarily affect the land within their boundaries." Thus, relying on the language of *Avery* and *Hadley* that some elections might not come within the doctrine in *Reynolds* and *Kramer,* "we conclude that [appellee], by reason of its special limited purpose and of the disproportionate effect of its activities on landowners as a group, is the sort of exception to the [rule] contemplated."

Thus, the franchise restriction is valid unless " 'wholly irrelevant to achievement of the regulation's objectives.' No doubt residents within the district may be affected by its activities. But [California] could quite reasonably have concluded that the number of landowners and owners of sufficient amounts of acreage whose consent was necessary to organize the district would not have subjected their land to the lien of its possibly very substantial assessments unless they had a dominant voice in its control." [b] As to appellants' "reliance on the various decisions of this Court holding that wealth has no relation to resident-voter qualifications," because "the benefits and burdens to each landowner in the District are in proportion to the assessed value of the land," "we cannot say that the California legislative decision to permit voting in the same proportion is not rationally based." [c]

Douglas, J., joined by Brennan and Marshall, JJ., dissented: In the past, floods were averted by storing water in Buena Vista Lake. "But that was not done in the great 1969 flood" because the board—"dominated [by] Boswell Co.—voted 6–4 to table the motion" because it had an "agricultural lease in the Buena Vista Lake Basin and flooding it would have interfered" with its crops. As a result, the residence of one of the non-landowner appellants "was 15½ feet below the water level of the crest of the flood." "Measured by the *Hadley* test," the district "surely performs 'important governmental functions' which 'have sufficient impact throughout the district' to justify the application of the *Avery* principle. [The] result [here] is a corporate political kingdom undreamed of [by] our Constitution."

BALL v. JAMES, 451 U.S. 355, 101 S.Ct. 1811, 68 L.Ed.2d 150 (1981), per STEWART, J., applied *Salyer* to an Arizona water district which limited voting to landowners on a "one acre, one vote" basis. Although the district was formed for "storage, delivery, and conservation of water," it had become "a major generator and supplier of hydroelectric power in the State, [and] roughly 40% of the water it delivers goes to urban areas for nonagricultural uses." Although "the District has $290 million of general obligation bonds outstanding that are

primary functions of water storage and distribution.

b. Compare Note, 72 Mich.L.Rev. 868, 893–94 (1974): "[W]hether a unit provides an unusual or specialized service should not be determinative. [The] critical question is, rather, whether the impact on the citizens is so uniform that each citizen should participate equally in political decision-making. [*Salyer*] posed the choice as between a unit with specialized powers and disproportionate effects and a unit with general powers and equalized effects and ignored the possibility of a unit with specialized powers but equalized effects."

c. Compare 87 Harv.L.Rev. 100–01 (1973): "[*Salyer*] merely found that landowners were disproportionately affected 'as a group' and made no claim that some landowners were disproportionately affected relative to other landowners. It is unlikely that disproportionate effects on those within the landowner group could be found, since a large landowner, although assessed more on an absolute basis than a small landowner, receives proportionately larger benefits from district activities."

secured by a lien on lands owned by the voting members, [the] bonds have so far been serviced out of the District's electricity revenues, [and] all capital improvements have been financed by revenue bonds":

"[A]ppellees claim [that] the sheer size of the power operations and the great number of people they affect serve to transform the District into an entity of general governmental power. But no matter how great the number of nonvoting residents buying electricity from the District, the relationship between them and the District's power operations is essentially that between consumers and a business enterprise from which they buy. Nothing in the *Avery, Hadley,* or *Salyer* cases suggests that the volume of business or the breadth of economic effect of a venture undertaken by a government entity as an incident of its narrow and primary governmental public function can, of its own weight, subject the entity to the one-person-one-vote requirements of the *Reynolds* case.

"[The] voting landowners are the only residents [subject] to the acreage-based taxing power of the District, [and] the only residents who have ever committed capital to the District through stock assessments charged by the Association.[19] The *Salyer* opinion did not say that the selected class of voters for a special public entity must be the only parties at all affected by the operations of the entity, [but rather] whether the effect of the entity's operations on them was disproportionately greater than the effect on those seeking the vote.[20]"

WHITE, J., joined by Brennan, Marshall and Blackmun, JJ., dissented: The district's "power to set its own rates and other conditions of service"—"not subject to control by another state agency"—"constitutes important attributes of sovereignty. When combined with a consideration of the District's wide-ranging operations, [it] is clear that the District exercises broad governmental power. [Here] the landowners could not themselves afford to finance their own project and turned to a public agency [which] now subsidizes the storage and delivery of irrigation water for agricultural purposes by selling electricity to the public at prices that neither the voters nor any representative public agency has any right to control. Unlike the situation in *Salyer,* the financial burden of supplying irrigation water has been shifted from the landowners to the consumers of electricity. [T]he burdens placed upon the lands within the District are so minimal that they cannot possibly serve as a basis for limiting the franchise to property owners. * * *[11]"[a]

---

19. The Court of Appeals found it significant that 98% of the District's revenues come from sales of electricity, and only 2% from charges assessed for water deliveries. This fact in no way affects the constitutionality of the voting scheme. When the consumers of electricity supply those power revenues, they are simply buying electricity; they are neither committing capital to the District nor committing any of their property as security for the credit of the District.

20. The appellees, of course, are qualified voters in Arizona and so remain equal participants in the election of the state legislators who created and have the power to change the District.

[Powell, J., who joined the Court's opinion, emphasized "the importance [of] the Arizona Legislature's control over voting requirements for the [District. It] is large enough and the resources it manages are basic enough that the people will act through their elected legislature when further changes in the governance of the District are warranted. [For] this Court to dictate how the Board of the District must be elected would detract from the democratic process we profess to protect."]

11. [In] most situations involving a state agency or even a city, the state legislature and ultimately the people could exercise control since any municipal corporation is a creature of the State. The Fourteenth Amendment requires a far more direct sense of democratic participation in elective schemes which is not satisfied by the indirect and imprecise voter control suggested by the Court [in fn. 20] and by Justice Powell.

---

a. See note a on page 1141.

HOLT CIVIC CLUB v. TUSCALOOSA, 439 U.S. 60, 99 S.Ct. 383, 58 L.Ed.2d 292 (1978), per REHNQUIST, J., upheld the Alabama "police jurisdiction" statute, which extended a city's police and sanitary regulations and its business-licensing powers (at 1/2 the fees for city businesses) to residents of adjacent unincorporated communities, but did not permit them to vote in city elections: "[O]ur cases have uniformly recognized that a government unit may legitimately restrict the right to participate in its political processes to those who reside within its borders. See, e.g., *Dunn v. Blumstein,* [Part II infra]; *Kramer; Carrington.*[a] [A] city's decisions inescapably affect individuals living immediately outside its borders. The granting of building permits for highrise apartments, industrial plants, and the like on the city's fringe unavoidably contributes to problems of traffic congestion, school districting, and law enforcement immediately outside the city. A rate change in the city's sales or ad valorem tax could well have a significant impact on retailers and property values in areas bordering the city. The condemnation of real property on the city's edge for construction of a municipal [dump] would have obvious implications for neighboring nonresidents. [Yet] no one would suggest that nonresidents likely to be affected [have] a constitutional right to participate in the political processes bringing it about. * * *

"Thus stripped of its voting rights attire, the equal protection issue [is] whether the Alabama statutes [bear] some rational relationship to a legitimate state [purpose].[8]"

STEVENS, J., who joined the Court's opinion, added: "The powers of extraterritorial jurisdiction granted by the challenged statutes are limited. [Nor] is there any claim [that] residents of the police jurisdictions have been charged unreasonable costs for the services they receive."

BRENNAN, J., joined by White and Marshall, JJ., dissented: "[S]tate law characterizations of residency are not controlling for purposes of the Fourteenth Amendment. See, e.g., *Evans; Carrington.* [The] touchstone for determining whether a residency requirement is 'appropriately defined' derives from the purpose of such requirements, which, as stated in *Dunn,* is 'to preserve the basic conception of a political community.' * * *

"The residents of Tuscaloosa's police jurisdiction are vastly more affected by Tuscaloosa's decisionmaking processes than were the plaintiffs in either *Kramer* or *Cipriano* affected by the decisionmaking processes from which they had been unconstitutionally excluded. [The] Court today does [not] provide any standards for determining when those subjected to extraterritorial municipal legislation will have been 'governed enough' to trigger the protections of the Equal Protection Clause.[b]

a. For a careful analysis distinguishing *Ball* from *Salyer* on the ground that the system in *Salyer* (but not in *Ball*) distributed benefits and burdens in a way comporting with the way in which the vote was distributed, see Durchslag, *Salyer, Ball and Holt: Reappraising the Right to Vote in Terms of Political "Interest" and Vote Dilution,* 33 Case W.Res.L.Rev. 1 (1982).

a. Consider 93 Harv.L.Rev. 146–47 (1979): "There are severe constitutional restraints on extraterritorial exercises of direct governmental powers by states [that] ensure that individuals who do not reside in a state will not be forced to submit to its authority in important ways. As a result, nonresidents have little claim to a voice in a state's affairs. There are no comparable restraints on the extraterritorial exercise of municipal powers."

8. [We] do not have before us, of course, a situation in which a city has annexed outlying territory in all but name, and is exercising precisely the same governmental powers over residents of surrounding unincorporated territory as it does over those residing within its corporate limits. * * *

b. Consider Note, 68 Calif.L.Rev. 126, 145–46 (1980): "[Brennan, J.'s] call for full enfranchisement [is] fraught with constitutional difficulties. Holt residents had absolutely no cognizable interest in numerous functions con-

"[There] is a crystal distinction between those who reside in Tuscaloosa's police jurisdiction, and who are therefore subject to that city's police and sanitary ordinances, licensing fees, and the jurisdiction of its recorders' courts, and those who reside in neither the city nor its police jurisdiction, and who are thus merely affected by the indirect impact of the city's decisions. This distinction [is] consistent with, if not mandated by, the very conception of a political community underlying constitutional recognition of bona fide residency requirements." [c]

Notes and Questions

1. *"Remedial" or "reform" legislation "extending" the franchise.* (a) In KATZENBACH v. MORGAN, p. 1272 infra, Congress suspended state English literacy tests for voting for citizens "educated in American-flag schools (schools located within United States jurisdiction)." The Court held this was not "an invidious discrimination" against other foreign-language citizens. Because the statute "does not restrict or deny the franchise but in effect extends" it, "the principle that calls for the closest scrutiny of distinctions in laws *denying* fundamental rights is inapplicable; for the distinction challenged [is] presented only as a limitation on a reform measure aimed at eliminating an existing barrier to the exercise of the franchise. Rather, in deciding the constitutional propriety of the limitations in such a reform measure we are guided by the familiar principles that a 'statute is not invalid under the Constitution because it might have gone further than it did,' [and] that 'reform may take one step at a time, addressing itself to the phase of the problem which seems most acute to the legislative mind.' " [d]

(b) By what test does (should) the Court determine whether legislation "distributing the franchise" "restricts or denies" it rather than "extends" it? Is it that if the group given the vote had been excluded by the state, the exclusion would be held "necessary to promote a compelling state interest"? Or is the matter more complex? Did the *Morgan* statute "grant the right to vote to some bona fide residents of requisite age and citizenship and deny the franchise to others"?

Does "extension" of the right to vote "dilute" the voting rights of others? If so, should extensions be justified only by a "compelling state interest"? May a city extend the vote in local elections to all nonresidents who own property in the city? If so, under what standard should its refusal to extend it also to nonresidents who work in the city be judged? Should the "traditional" equal protection standard be applicable because use of the "stricter" standard would invalidate most classifications and the state might well then eliminate extensions altogether? Was such a choice realistically (constitutionally) available to

ducted by the City of Tuscaloosa. The grant of an equal voice to extraterritorials, regardless of laudable motives, would necessarily dilute the vote of Tuscaloosa's residents in important matters. [Thus,] a court should look for solutions that will enfranchise extraterritorials *only* to the extent of their interest in the city's affairs." See also Note, *Dilution of Residents' Votes by Extension of the Franchise to Certain Nonresidents,* 64 Ia.L.Rev. 722 (1979). See further note 1 infra.

c. Must an election on whether a city should annex an adjacent area include the citizens of both the city and the adjacent area? May it exclude persons who reside just outside both areas but who will be "affected"? See Notes, *Annexation Elections and the Right to Vote,* 20 U.C.L.A.L.Rev. 1093 (1973); *The Right to Vote in Municipal Annexations,* 88 Harv.L.Rev. 1571 (1975).

d. Douglas, J., reserved judgment on the question.

See also *Schilb v. Kuebel,* 404 U.S. 357, 92 S.Ct. 479, 30 L.Ed.2d 502 (1971) (bail reform law).

the state after *Reynolds*? *Carrington*? *Harper*? *Kramer*? *Salyer*? *Holt*? In some of these, but not all?

2. *Other laws "distributing the franchise."* (a) After *Kramer,* what of the validity of age, residency and literacy requirements for voting? Consider 83 Harv.L.Rev. 81 (1969): "[T]he danger of an impermissible selection is much less when the goal of a voting test is to select competent voters than when interest differences are involved. The Court refused to assume that some voters have no interest whatsoever, but it must acknowledge that some citizens, like two-year olds and the insane, are not competent. Since such cases of permissible exclusion can be conceived of, a competency classification cannot be termed impermissible in its general purpose." Does this "interest-competency" distinction adequately respond to Stewart, J.'s objections? If *all* 2-year-olds are incompetent, are *all* 17-year-olds? If not, would an 18-year-old voting qualification "meet the exacting standard of precision required of statutes which selectively distribute the franchise"? See *Oregon v. Mitchell,* p. 1281 infra; Notes, *Student Voting and Apportionment: The "Rotten Boroughs" of Academia,* 81 Yale L.J. 35 (1971); *Applying Equal Protection to Bona Fide Residence Requirements,* 59 Ia.L.Rev. 671 (1974). Assuming the continued validity of literacy tests, what of an *English* literacy requirement? Compare the opinions of Douglas and Harlan, JJ., in *Cardona v. Power,* 384 U.S. 672, 86 S.Ct. 1728, 16 L.Ed.2d 848 (1966).

(b) *Felons.* RICHARDSON v. RAMIREZ, 418 U.S. 24, 94 S.Ct. 2655, 41 L.Ed. 2d 551 (1974), per REHNQUIST, J.,—relying on § 2 of the fourteenth amendment—held California's disenfranchising felons not violative of equal protection: "[T]he express language of § 2 [and] the historical and judicial interpretation of the Amendment's applicability to state laws disenfranchising felons, is of controlling significance in distinguishing such laws from those other state limitations on the franchise which have been held [invalid. We] rest on the demonstrably sound proposition that § 1, in dealing with voting rights as it does, could not have been meant to bar outright a form of disenfranchisement which was expressly exempted from the less drastic sanction of reduced representation which § 2 imposed for other forms of disenfranchisement." [e]

3. *Burdensome Requirements.* (a) ROSARIO v. ROCKEFELLER, 410 U.S. 752, 93 S.Ct. 1245, 36 L.Ed.2d 1 (1973), concerned New York Election Law § 186, requiring voters to enroll in the party of their choice at least 30 days before the November general election in order to vote in the next party primary. This cutoff date "occurs approximately eight months prior to a presidential primary [and] 11 months prior to a nonpresidential primary." The Court, per STEWART, J., rejected the contention that § 186 denied petitioners "their right to vote in [the] primary and abridged their freedom to associate with the political party of their choice" under *Williams v. Rhodes,* Part C infra. The law "did not absolutely disenfranchise" petitioners; rather, their "plight [was caused] by their own failure to take timely steps to effect their enrollment."

The "important state goal" served by § 186's "lengthy" time period "is to inhibit party 'raiding,' whereby voters in sympathy with one party designate

e. Marshall, J., joined by Brennan, J., dissented, arguing that "§ 2 was not intended [to] be a limitation on the other sections of the Fourteenth Amendment" and that, under the "compelling state interest test," "the blanket disenfranchisement of ex-felons cannot stand." Douglas, J., dissented on procedural grounds. Consider Tribe, *American Constitutional Law* 771 (1978): "[§ 2] provides no warrant for circumscribing the reach of the equal protection clause [which] is not bound to the political theories of a particular era but draws much of its substance from changing social norms and evolving conceptions of equality."

themselves as voters of another party so as to influence or determine the results of the other party's primary." "Allowing enrollment any time after the general election would [not] put the voter in the unseemly position of asking to be enrolled in one party while at the same time intending to vote immediately for another." The "time limitation for enrollment is thus tied to a particularized legitimate purpose, and is in no sense invidious or arbitrary."

POWELL, J., joined by Douglas, Brennan and Marshall, JJ., dissented: "Deferment of a right [can] be tantamount to its denial. [The] majority does not identify the standard of scrutiny it applies" but its "formulation, though the terminology is somewhat stronger, resembles the traditional equal protection 'rational basis' test [rejected in *Kramer*]. The state interest here is hardly substantial enough to sustain the presumption, upon which the statute appears to be based, that most persons who change or declare party affiliation nearer than eight to 11 months to a party primary do so with intent to raid that primary. [Citizens] customarily choose a party and vote in its primary simply because it presents candidates and issues more responsive to their immediate concerns and aspirations. Such candidates or issues often are not apparent eight to 11 months before a primary."

(b) KUSPER v. PONTIKES, 414 U.S. 51, 94 S.Ct. 303, 38 L.Ed.2d 260 (1973), per STEWART, J., invalidated an Illinois statute prohibiting a person "from voting in the primary election of a political party if he has voted in the primary of any other party within the preceding 23 months": "The Illinois law, unlike that [in *Rosario,*] 'locks' voters into a preexisting party affiliation from one primary to the next, and the only way to break the 'lock' is to forego voting in *any* primary for a period of almost two years. [Far] from supporting the validity of the Illinois legislation, [*Rosario*] suggests that the asserted state interest [in preventing "raiding"] can be attained by less drastic means, which do not unnecessarily burden the exercise of constitutionally protected activity." Burger, C.J., concurred in the result. Blackmun and Rehnquist, JJ., dissented.

4. *Absentee ballots.* (a) McDONALD v. BOARD OF ELEC., 394 U.S. 802, 89 S.Ct. 1404, 22 L.Ed.2d 739 (1969), per WARREN, C.J., upheld an Illinois statute granting absentee ballots to designated classes but not to "unsentenced inmates awaiting trial." The Court applied "the more traditional standards [for] equal protection claims [because it is] not the right to vote that is at stake here but a claimed right to receive absentee ballots."[6] "Indeed, appellants' challenge seems to disclose not an arbitrary scheme or plan but [a] consistent and laudable state policy of adding, over a 50-year period, groups to the absentee [coverage]. That Illinois has not gone still further [should] not render void its remedial legislation, which need [not] 'strike at all evils at the same time.'"

(b) O'BRIEN v. SKINNER, 414 U.S. 524, 94 S.Ct. 740, 38 L.Ed.2d 702 (1974), per BURGER, C.J., held "wholly arbitrary" and thus violative of equal protection New York's denial of absentee ballots to persons being held for trial and to convicted misdemeanants. Since state law permitted absentee ballots to persons absent from their home county, those held in jail in a county other than their residence could vote, "yet persons confined for the same reason in the county of their residence are completely denied the ballot."[f] Blackmun, J., joined by

6. [T]he record is barren of any indication that the State might not, for instance, possibly furnish the jails with special polling booths or facilities on election day, or provide guarded transportation to the polls themselves for certain inmates, or entertain motions for temporary reductions in bail to allow some inmates to get to the polls on their own.

f. Marshall, J., joined by Douglas and Brennan, JJ., joined the Court's opinion, but would have invalidated the discrimination un-

Rehnquist, J., dissented, relying on *McDonald:* Since the state "need not have provided for *any* absentee registration or absentee voting," the "legislature traditionally has been allowed to take reform 'one step at a [time].' " [g]

C. RESTRICTIONS ON PARTIES AND CANDIDATES

WILLIAMS v. RHODES, 393 U.S. 23, 89 S.Ct. 5, 21 L.Ed.2d 24 (1968): To gain a place on the presidential election ballot, Ohio required new political parties to have an elaborate party structure, hold "a primary election conforming to detailed and rigorous standards," "obtain petitions signed by qualified electors totaling 15% of the number of ballots cast in the last preceding gubernatorial election," and file by Feb. 7 of the election year. Parties on previous ballots remained "simply by obtaining 10% of the votes in the last gubernatorial election."

The Court, per BLACK, J., held that "the totality of" these laws violated equal protection, placing "burdens on two different, although overlapping, kinds of rights—the right of individuals to associate for the advancement of political beliefs, and the right of qualified voters, regardless of their political persuasion, to cast their votes effectively. Both of [these] rank among our most precious freedoms. [In] determining whether the State has power to place such unequal burdens on minority groups where rights of this kind are at [stake,] 'only a compelling state interest in the regulation of a subject within the State's constitutional power to regulate can justify limiting First Amendment freedoms.' *NAACP v. Button,* 371 U.S. 415, 83 S.Ct. 328, 9 L.Ed.2d 405 (1963).

Ohio "does not merely favor a 'two-party system' " to "encourage compromise and political stability," but tends to give the Republicans and Democrats "a complete monopoly." Nor could the state interest in avoiding a "plurality winner" "justify the very severe restrictions." The "very early" filing requirement frustrated the state's interest in promoting cohesiveness of "disaffected" groups. In light of the "experience in many other States" where "a very low number of signatures, such as 1% of the electorate is required," Ohio's concern for voter confusion due to many parties on the ballot was too "remote." [a]

AMERICAN PARTY OF TEXAS v. WHITE, 415 U.S. 767, 94 S.Ct. 1296, 39 L.Ed.2d 744 (1974), per WHITE, J., upheld a method for candidates of "minority political parties" to get on the general election ballot. Candidates of "major" parties (those whose gubernatorial candidate polled more than 200,000 votes in the last general election) could obtain ballot position by being nominated in a primary election. But parties with less than 2% of the total gubernatorial vote in the preceding general election (or new parties) had to hold precinct, county and state nominating conventions and obtain signatures equaling at least 1% of persons voting in the last gubernatorial election (about 22,000 in 1972). Signatories could be persons participating in the precinct convention (required to be held on the same day as the major party primaries) or signing a petition within

der the "compelling state interest test." See 59 Corn.L.Rev. 1139 (1974).

g. May a state, after *Kramer,* deny absentee voting to persons unable to vote otherwise? What constitutes "inability" to vote? See generally Note, *The Submerged Constitutional Right to an Absentee Ballot,* 72 Mich.L. Rev. 157 (1973).

a. Harlan, J., concurred in the result. Stewart and White, JJ., dissented. Warren, C.J., dissented without reaching the merits. See generally Barton, *The General-Election Ballot: More Nominees or More Representative Nominees,* 22 Stan.L.Rev. 165 (1970).

55 days thereafter (ending 120 days before the general election). Each had to execute a notarized oath that he had not participated in any other party's primary or nomination process. These requirements "depend upon whether they are necessary to further compelling state interests," but "whether considered alone or in combination," they "are constitutionally valid measures, reasonably taken in pursuit of vital state objectives that cannot be served equally well in significantly less burdensome ways. * * * Texas 'in no way freezes the status quo,' [but] affords minority political parties a real and essentially equal opportunity for ballot qualification." [b] Douglas, J., dissented.

ANDERSON v. CELEBREZZE, 460 U.S. 780, 103 S.Ct. 1564, 75 L.Ed.2d 547 (1983), per STEVENS, J., held that Ohio's "early filing deadline"—requiring an independent candidate for President to file more than seven months before the November general election—violates the first and fourteenth amendment rights of voters and candidates: [7] "Although these rights of voters are fundamental, [the] state's important regulatory interests are generally sufficient to justify reasonable, nondiscriminatory restrictions.[9]

"Constitutional challenges to specific provisions of a State's election laws therefore cannot be resolved by any 'litmus-paper' test. [Instead], a court [must] first consider the character and magnitude of the asserted injury to the rights protected [and] then must identify and evaluate the precise interests put forward by the State as justifications for the burden imposed by its rule. In passing judgment, the Court must not only determine the legitimacy and strength of each of these interests; it also must consider the extent to which those interests make it necessary to burden the plaintiff's rights.[c]

b. See also *Munro v. Socialist Workers Party,* 479 U.S. 189, 107 S.Ct. 533, 93 L.Ed.2d 499 (1986) (upholding requirement that minor party candidates receive at least 1% of all votes cast for the office sought in primary in order to get on general election ballot).

7. In this case, we [do] not engage in a separate Equal Protection Clause analysis. We rely, however, on the analysis in a number of our prior election cases [which,] applying the "fundamental rights" strand of equal protection analysis, have identified the First and Fourteenth Amendment rights implicated by restrictions on the eligibility of voters and candidates, and have considered the degree to which the State's restrictions further legitimate state interests. See, e.g., *Williams.*

9. We have upheld generally-applicable and evenhanded restrictions that protect the integrity and reliability of the electoral process itself. The State has the undoubted right to require candidates to make a preliminary showing of substantial support in order to qualify for a place on the ballot, because it is both wasteful and confusing to encumber the ballot with the names of frivolous candidates. *Jenness v. Fortson,* 403 U.S. 431, 91 S.Ct. 1970, 29 L.Ed.2d 554 (1971); *American Texas Party.* * * *

c. Does *Anderson* employ the same standard of equal protection review as *Williams* and *American Texas Party*? Do the latter cases use the same standard? *Illinois Bd. of Elections v. Socialist Workers Party,* 440 U.S. 173, 99 S.Ct. 983, 59 L.Ed.2d 230 (1979), per Marshall, J., held a law—that "produced the incongruous result" of requiring new parties to get "substantially more signatures to gain access to the ballot" for an election in Chicago than for a statewide election—violative of equal protection because the classification was not "necessary to serve a compelling interest."

Blackmun, J., joined the opinion but expressed "my unrelieved discomfort with [using] as tests such easy phrases as 'compelling state interest' and 'least drastic [or restrictive] means.' I have never been able fully to appreciate just what a 'compelling state interest' is. If it means 'convincingly controlling,' or 'incapable of being overcome' upon any balancing process, then, of course, the test merely announces an inevitable result, and the test is no test at all. And, for me, 'least drastic means' is a slippery slope and also the signal of the result the Court has chosen to reach. A judge would be unimaginative indeed if he could not come up with something a little less 'drastic' or a little less 'restrictive' in almost any situation, and thereby enable himself to vote to strike legislation down."

Burger, C.J., concurred in the judgment. Rehnquist and Stevens, JJ., each also concurred in the judgment because the law bore

"[Unlike *Storer v. Brown,* 415 U.S. 724, 94 S.Ct. 1274, 39 L.Ed.2d 714 (1974), per White, J.,—which found a "compelling" interest for a California law barring independent candidates in general elections if they "had a registered affiliation with a qualified political party at any time within one year prior to the immediately preceding primary election" [d]—Ohio's] ballot access rule for presidential elections "has an impact beyond its own borders. Similarly, the State has a less important interest in regulating Presidential elections than statewide or local elections, because the outcome of the former will be largely determined by voters beyond the State's boundaries."

Ohio's rule "prevents persons who wish to be independent candidates from entering the significant political arena established in the State by a Presidential election campaign—and creating new political coalitions of Ohio voters—at any time after mid-to-late March. At this point developments in campaigns for the major-party nominations have only begun, and the major parties will not adopt their nominees and platforms for another five months. Candidates and supporters within the major parties thus have the political advantage of continued flexibility." As for the state's interest in "political stability"—e.g., preventing "a candidate's decision to abandon efforts to win the party primary and to run as an independent"—Ohio's law "is both too broad and too narrow. It is true that [petitioner John Anderson] had previously competed in party primaries [in other states] and then sought to run as an independent [in Ohio]. But the early deadline applies broadly to independent candidates who have not been affiliated in the recent past with any political party. On the other hand, as long as the decision to run is made before the March deadline, Ohio does not prohibit independent candidacies by persons formerly affiliated with a political party, or currently participating in intraparty competition in other States—regardless of the effect on the political party structure."

REHNQUIST, J., joined by White, Powell and O'Connor, JJ., dissented, believing the case governed by *Storer* and finding no support for the Court's conclusion that Ohio's law had a "substantial impact on nonparty candidates and their supporters": "The record shows that in 1980 five independent candidates submitted nominating petitions with the necessary 5,000 signatures by the March 20 deadline and thus qualified for the general election ballot in Ohio. [T]he Constitution does not require that a State allow any particular Presidential candidate to be on its ballot, and so long as the Ohio ballot access laws are rational and allow nonparty candidates reasonable access to the general election ballot, this Court should not interfere with Ohio's exercise of its Article II, § 1, cl. 2 power."

LUBIN v. PANISH, 415 U.S. 709, 94 S.Ct. 1315, 39 L.Ed.2d 702 (1974), per BURGER, C.J., held that California's requirement of a filing fee to get on a primary election ballot or to be a write-in candidate—in this case, 2% of the annual salary for the state office sought ($701.60)—as applied to indigents, violated "equal protection [and] rights of expression and association": "[T]he

no "rational" relationship to any state interest.

d. "The State's general policy is to have contending forces within the party employ the primary [to] finally settle their differences. The general election ballot is reserved for major struggles; it is not a forum for continuing intraparty feuds." Brennan, Douglas and Marshall, JJ., dissented.

What of a law forbidding a person to be a candidate of a political party if he was the candidate (or voted in the primary) of a different political party within the *four* preceding years? See *Lippitt v. Cipollone,* 404 U.S. 1032, 92 S.Ct. 729, 30 L.Ed.2d 725 (1972).

State's interest in keeping its ballots within manageable, understandable limits is of the highest order [but it] must be achieved by a means that does not unfairly or unnecessarily burden either a minority party's or an individual candidate's equally important interest in the continued availability of political opportunity. [V]oters can assert their preferences only through candidates or parties or both and it is this broad interest that must be weighed in the balance. [A] voter [cannot] be assured that a candidate to his liking will be on the ballot, but the process of qualifying candidates [may] not constitutionally be measured solely in dollars."

[The Court relied on *Bullock v. Carter,* 405 U.S. 134, 92 S.Ct. 849, 31 L.Ed.2d 92 (1972), per BURGER, C.J., invalidating a Texas statute requiring candidates to pay $50 plus their pro rata share of the costs of the election in order to get on the primary ballot, resulting in fees as high as $8,900: "Because the Texas [scheme] has a real and appreciable impact on the exercise of the franchise, and because this impact is related to the resources of the voters supporting a particular candidate, we conclude, as in *Harper,* that the laws must be 'closely scrutinized' and found reasonably necessary to the accomplishment of legitimate state [objectives]."] [e]

"[A] wealthy candidate with not the remotest chance of election may secure a place on the ballot by writing a check [but, due to filing fees], impecunious but serious candidates may be prevented from running. [W]e hold that in the absence of reasonable alternative means of ballot access, a State may [not] require from an indigent candidate filing fees he cannot pay."

As reasonable alternatives, states may "impose on minor political parties the precondition of demonstrating the existence of some reasonable quantum of voter [support]. See *American Party of Texas.* Similarly, a candidate who establishes that he cannot pay the [fee] may be required to demonstrate the 'seriousness' of his candidacy by persuading a substantial number of voters to sign a petition in his behalf." [f] But "the intimation that a write-in provision without the filing fee required by [California] would constitute 'an acceptable alternative' appears dubious at best." [g]

---

e. In *Bullock,* the Court rejected "the theory that since the candidates are availing themselves of the primary machinery, it is appropriate that they pay that share of the cost which they have occasioned. [A] primary system designed to give the voters some influence at the nominating stage should spread the cost among all of the voters in an attempt to distribute the influence without regard to wealth. Viewing the myriad governmental functions supported from general revenues, it is difficult to single out any of a higher order than the conduct of elections at all levels to bring forth those persons desired by their fellow citizens to govern. Without making light of the State's interest in husbanding its revenues, we fail to see such an element of necessity in the State's present means of financing primaries as to justify the resulting incursion on the prerogatives of voters."

What standard of equal protection review is employed in these opinions by Burger, C.J.?

f. May a state require that *only* those who cannot pay a filing fee demonstrate the "seriousness" of their candidacy? See Note, *The Constitutionality of Candidate Filing Fees,* 70 Mich.L.Rev. 558 (1972).

g. Douglas, J., joined the Court's opinion, adding: "Since classifications based on wealth are 'traditionally disfavored,' *Harper,* the State's inability to show a compelling interest in conditioning the right to run for office on payment of fees cannot stand."

Blackmun, J., joined by Rehnquist, J., concurred in part: "I would regard a write-in procedure, free of fee, as an acceptable alternative" because it "provides the indigent [with] as much ease of access to the ballot as the alternative of obtaining a large number of petition signatures in a relatively short time. See *Storer.*"

CLEMENTS v. FASHING, 457 U.S. 957, 102 S.Ct. 2836, 73 L.Ed. 508 (1982), held that Texas provisions, restricting a public official's ability to run for another office, do not violate equal protection. REHNQUIST, J., joined by Burger, C.J., and Powell and O'Connor, JJ., reasoned: "Far from recognizing candidacy as a 'fundamental right,' we have held that the existence of barriers to a candidate's access to the ballot 'does not of itself compel close scrutiny.' *Bullock*. [Our] ballot access cases, however, do focus on the degree to which the challenged restrictions operate as a mechanism to exclude certain classes of candidates from the electoral process. * * *

"One line of ballot access cases involves classifications based on wealth. In invalidating candidate filing-fee provisions, for example, we have departed from traditional equal protection analysis because such a 'system falls with unequal weight on voters, as well as candidates, according to their economic status.' *Bullock*. * * *

"The second line of ballot access cases involves classification schemes that impose burdens on new or small political parties or independent candidates. [T]he State may not act to maintain the 'status quo' by making it virtually impossible for any but the two major parties to achieve ballot positions for their candidates. See *Williams*. * * *

"It does not automatically follow, of course, that we must apply traditional equal protection principles in examining § 19 and § 65 merely because these restrictions on candidacy do not fall into the two patterns just described. But this fact does counsel against discarding traditional principles without first examining the nature of the interests that are affected and the extent of the burden these provisions place on candidacy. [§ 19] simply requires Baca to complete his four-year term as Justice of the Peace before he may be eligible for the Legislature. At most, therefore, Baca must wait two years—one election cycle—before he may run as a candidate for the legislature. [Unlike] filing fees or the level-of-support requirements, § 19 in no way burdens access to the political process by those who are outside the 'mainstream' of political life. * * *

"A 'waiting period' is hardly a significant barrier to candidacy. [See *Storer*.] We conclude that this sort of insignificant interference with access to the ballot need only rest on a rational predicate in order to survive a challenge under the Equal Protection Clause. * * *

"Finally, it is no argument that § 19 is invalid because it burdens only those officeholders who desire to run for the Legislature. [The] Equal Protection Clause allows the State to regulate 'one step at a time, addressing itself to the phase of the problem which seems most acute.' *Williamson v. Lee Optical Co.*"

STEVENS, J., concurred in the judgment: "I see no reason why a State may not provide that certain offices will be filled on a part-time basis and that others will be filled by persons who may not seek other office until they have fulfilled their duties in the first. There may be no explanation for these classifications that a federal judge would find to be 'rational.' But they do not violate the Equal Protection Clause because there is no federal requirement that a State fit the emoluments or the burdens of different elective state offices into any particular pattern."

BRENNAN, J., joined by White, Marshall and Blackmun, JJ., dissented: "Putting to one side the question of the proper level of equal protection scrutiny to be applied to these restrictions on candidacy for public office,[2] [neither] the State nor the plurality offers any justification for *differential* treatment of various classes of officeholders, and the search for such justification makes clear that the classifications embodied in these provisions lack any meaningful relationship to the State's asserted or supposed interests [and cannot] survive even minimal equal protection scrutiny.[7] "

II. DISCRIMINATION IN RESPECT TO TRAVEL

SHAPIRO v. THOMPSON

394 U.S. 618, 89 S.Ct. 1322, 22 L.Ed.2d 600 (1969).

JUSTICE BRENNAN delivered the opinion of the Court.

These three appeals [are from federal courts] holding unconstitutional [Conn., Pa. and D.C. statutes denying welfare] to residents [who] have not resided within their jurisdictions for at least one [year].

There is no dispute that the effect of the waiting-period requirement [is] to create two classes of needy resident families indistinguishable from each other except that one is composed of residents who have resided a year or more, and the second of residents who have resided less than a year, in the jurisdiction. [T]he second class is denied welfare aid upon which may depend the ability of the families to obtain the very means to subsist—food, shelter, and other necessities of life. [We] agree [that the statutes deny equal protection]. The interests which appellants assert are promoted by the classification either may not constitutionally be promoted by government or are not compelling governmental interests.

Primarily, appellants justify the waiting-period requirement as a protective device to preserve the fiscal integrity of state public assistance programs. It is asserted that people who require welfare assistance during their first year of residence in a State are likely to become continuing burdens on state welfare programs. Therefore, the argument runs, if such people can be deterred from entering the jurisdiction by denying them welfare benefits during the first year, state programs to assist long-time residents will not be impaired. [But] the

2. [Although] we have never defined candidacy as a fundamental right, we have clearly recognized that restrictions on candidacy impinge on First Amendment rights of candidates and voters. See, e.g., *Illinois Elections Bd.; Lubin; American Texas Party; Bullock; Williams.* With this consideration in mind, we have applied strict scrutiny in reviewing most restrictions on ballot access [because] of their impact on the First Amendment *rights* of candidates and voters, not because the *class* of candidates or voters that was burdened was somehow suspect. The plurality offers no explanation as to why the restrictions at issue here, which completely bar some candidates from running and require other candidates to give up their present employment, are less "substantial" in their impact on candidates and their supporters than, for example, the $700 filing fee at issue in *Lubin.*

[May a state require a minimum age for candidates? See 71 Mich.L.Rev. 854 (1973). May a state limit the number of terms an elected official may serve? May it place major party candidates (or incumbents) at the top of the ballot? See 63 Minn.L.Rev. 517 (1979). Is there a constitutional right to be a candidate? See Tribe, *American Constitutional Law* 775 (1978).]

7. * * * I agree with Justice Stevens that the State may define *many* of the "benefits and burdens of different elective state offices," in a dissimilar manner without offering an explanation for the classifications that a federal judge will find to be rational, so long as such classifications do not mask any racial or otherwise impermissible discrimination. But where the differential treatment concerns a restriction on the right to seek public office—a right protected by the First Amendment—that Amendment supplies the federal interest in equality that may be lacking where the State is simply determining salary, hours, or working conditions of its own employees.

purpose of inhibiting migration by needy persons into the State is constitutionally impermissible.

This Court long ago recognized that the nature of our Federal Union and our constitutional concepts of personal liberty unite to require that all citizens be free to travel throughout the length and breadth of our land uninhibited by statutes, rules, or regulations which unreasonably burden or restrict this movement. [See *United States v. Guest,* p. 1267 infra].

Alternatively, appellants argue that even if it is impermissible for a State to attempt to deter the entry of all indigents, the challenged classification may be justified as a permissible state attempt to discourage those indigents who would enter the State solely to obtain larger benefits. [But] a State may no more try to fence out those indigents who seek higher welfare benefits than it may try to fence out indigents generally. [W]e do not perceive why a mother who is seeking to make a new life for herself and her children should be regarded as less deserving because she considers, among other factors, the level of a State's public assistance. Surely such a mother is no less deserving than a mother who moves into a particular State in order to take advantage of its better educational facilities.

Appellants argue further that the challenged classification may be sustained as an attempt to distinguish between new and old residents on the basis of the contribution they have made to the community through the payment of taxes. [But this] would logically permit the State to bar new residents from schools, parks, and libraries or deprive them of police and fire protection. Indeed it would permit the State to apportion all benefits and services according to the past tax contributions of its citizens. The Equal Protection Clause prohibits such an apportionment of state services.[10]

We recognize that a State [may] legitimately attempt to limit its expenditures, whether for public assistance, public education, or any other program. But a State may not accomplish such a purpose by invidious distinctions between classes of its citizens. It could not, for example, reduce expenditures for education by barring indigent children from its schools. [Thus], appellants must do more than show that denying welfare benefits to new residents saves [money.]

Appellants next advance as justification [four] administrative and related governmental objectives allegedly served by the waiting-period requirement. * * *

At the outset, we reject appellants' argument that a mere showing of a rational relationship between the waiting period and these four admittedly permissible state objectives will suffice, [for] in moving from State to State or to the District of Columbia appellees were exercising a constitutional right, and any classification which serves to penalize the exercise of that right, unless shown to be necessary to promote a *compelling* governmental interest, is unconstitutional. Cf. *Skinner v. Oklahoma*; *Korematsu*; *Sherbert v. Verner*.

The argument that the waiting-period requirement facilitates budget predictability is wholly unfounded. The records in all three cases are utterly devoid of evidence [of use of] the one-year requirement as a means to predict the number of people who will require assistance in the budget year. * * *

10. We are not dealing here with state insurance programs which may legitimately tie the amount of benefits to the individual's contributions.

The argument that the waiting period serves as an administratively efficient rule of thumb for determining residency similarly will not withstand scrutiny. [Before] granting an application, the welfare authorities investigate the applicant [and] in the course of the inquiry necessarily learn the facts upon which to determine whether the applicant is a resident.

Similarly, there is no need for a State to use the one-year waiting period as a safeguard against fraudulent receipt of benefits; for less drastic means are available, and are employed * * *.

Pennsylvania suggests that the one-year waiting period is justified as a means of encouraging new residents to join the labor force promptly. But this logic would also require a similar waiting period for long-term [residents.]

We conclude therefore that appellants [have] no need to use the one-year requirement for the governmental purposes suggested. Thus, even under traditional equal protection tests [the classification] would seem irrational and unconstitutional. But [s]ince the classification here touches on the fundamental right of interstate movement, its constitutionality must be judged by the stricter standard of whether it promotes a *compelling* state interest. Under this standard, the waiting period requirement clearly violates the Equal Protection Clause.[21]

[The Court rejected the contention that Social Security Act § 402(b) approved imposition of one-year residence requirements. But] even if it could be argued that the constitutionality of § 402(b) is [in issue,] Congress may not authorize the States to violate the Equal Protection Clause. * * *

Affirmed.[a]

CHIEF JUSTICE WARREN with whom JUSTICE BLACK joins, dissenting.

[§ 402(b)] intended to authorize state residence requirements of up to one [year.] Congress, pursuant to its commerce power, has enacted a variety of restrictions upon interstate travel. It has taxed air and rail fares and [gasoline]. Many of the federal safety regulations of common carriers which cross state lines burden the right to travel. And Congress has prohibited by criminal statute interstate travel for certain purposes. * * *

The Court's right-to-travel cases lend little support to the view that congressional action is invalid merely because it burdens the right to travel. Most of our cases fall into two categories: those in which *state* imposed restrictions were involved, see e.g., *Edwards v. California,* and those concerning congressional decisions to remove impediments to interstate movement, see, e.g., [*Guest*]. *Aptheker v. Secretary of State,* is the only case in which this Court invalidated on a constitutional basis a congressionally imposed restriction. *Aptheker* also involved [a] claim that the congressional restriction compelled a potential traveler to choose between his right to travel and his First Amendment right of freedom of association. [*Aptheker*] thus contains two characteristics distinguishing it from the [instant case]: a combined infringement of two constitutionally protected rights and a flat prohibition upon travel. [Here], travel itself is not prohibited. Any burden inheres solely in the fact that a potential welfare

21. We imply no view of the validity of waiting period *or* residence requirements determining eligibility to vote, [for] tuition-free education, to obtain a license to practice a profession, to hunt or fish, [etc. These] may promote compelling state interests on the one hand, or, on the other, may not be penalties upon the exercise of the constitutional right of interstate travel.

a. Stewart, J., joined the Court's opinion, emphasizing that "the Court simply recognizes" that the statutes impinge upon "the constitutional right of interstate travel."

recipient might take into consideration the loss of welfare benefits for a limited period of time if he changes his residence. Not only is this burden of uncertain degree,[5] but appellees themselves assert there is evidence that few welfare recipients have in fact been deterred by residence requirements.

The insubstantiality of the restriction imposed by residence requirements must then be evaluated in light of the possible congressional reasons for such requirements. [Given] the apprehensions of many States that an increase in benefits without minimal residence requirements would result in an inability to provide an adequate welfare system, Congress deliberately adopted the intermediate course of a cooperative program. [Our] cases require only that Congress have a rational basis for finding that a chosen regulatory scheme is necessary to the furtherance of interstate commerce. See, e.g., *Katzenbach v. McClung,* 379 U.S. 294, 85 S.Ct. 377, 13 L.Ed.2d 290 (1964). I conclude that residence requirements can be imposed by Congress as an exercise of its power to control interstate commerce consistent with the constitutionally guaranteed right to travel. * * * [b]

JUSTICE HARLAN, dissenting. * * *

In upholding the equal protection argument, the Court has applied an equal protection doctrine of relatively recent vintage [—the] "compelling interest" doctrine [which constitutes] an increasingly significant exception to the long-established rule that a statute does not deny equal protection if it is rationally related to a legitimate governmental objective. The "compelling interest" doctrine has two branches. [The] "suspect" criteria [branch today] apparently has been further enlarged to include classifications based upon recent interstate movement, and perhaps those based upon the exercise of *any* constitutional [right].

I think that this branch of the "compelling interest" doctrine is sound when applied to racial classifications, for historically the Equal Protection Clause was largely a product of the desire to eradicate legal distinctions founded upon race. However, I believe that the more recent extensions have been unwise. [When] a classification is based upon the exercise of rights guaranteed against state infringement by the federal Constitution, then there is no need for any resort to the Equal Protection Clause; in such instances, this Court may properly and straightforwardly invalidate any undue burden upon those rights under the Fourteenth Amendment's Due Process Clause.

The second branch of the "compelling interest" principle is even more troublesome. For it has been held that a statutory classification is subject to the "compelling interest" test if the result of the classification may be to affect a "fundamental right," regardless of the basis of the classification. This rule was foreshadowed in *Skinner* [and] re-emerged in *Reynolds v. Sims,* [again] in *Carrington v. Rash* [and] was also an alternate ground in *Harper* and apparently was a basis of the holding in *Williams v. Rhodes.* It has reappeared today in the Court's cryptic suggestion that the "compelling interest" test is applicable merely because the result of the classification may be to deny the appellees "food, shelter, and other necessities of life," as well as in the Court's statement that "[s]ince the classification here touches on the fundamental right of inter-

5. [I]ndigents who are disqualified from categorical assistance by residence requirements are not left wholly without assistance. Each of the appellees in these cases found alternative sources of assistance * * *.

b. As to whether the "federalistic dimension" of the right to travel should limit Congress' power to affect it, see Karst, *The Fifth Amendment's Guarantee of Equal Protection,* 55 N.C.L.Rev. 541, 558–60 (1977).

state movement, its constitutionality must be judged by the stricter standard of whether it promotes a *compelling* state interest."

I think this branch [is] unfortunate because it creates an exception which threatens to swallow the standard equal protection rule. Virtually every state statute affects important rights. This Court has repeatedly held, for example, that the traditional equal protection standard is applicable to statutory classifications affecting such fundamental matters as the right to pursue a particular occupation, the right to receive greater or smaller wages or to work more or less hours, and the right to inherit property. Rights such as these are in principle indistinguishable from those involved here, and to extend the "compelling interest" rule to all cases in which such rights are affected would go far toward making this Court a "super-legislature." This branch of the doctrine is also unnecessary. When the right affected is one assured by the federal Constitution, any infringement can be dealt with under the Due Process Clause. But when a statute affects only matters not mentioned in the federal Constitution and is not arbitrary or irrational, I must reiterate that I know of nothing which entitles this Court to pick out particular human activities, characterize them as "fundamental," and give them added protection under an unusually stringent equal protection test. * * *

For reasons hereafter set forth, a legislature might rationally find that the imposition of a welfare residence requirement would aid in the accomplishment of at least four valid governmental objectives. It might also find that residence requirements have advantages not shared by other methods of achieving the same goals. [Thus], it cannot be said that the requirements are "arbitrary" or "lacking in rational justification." Hence, I can find no objection to these residence requirements under [equal protection].

The next issue [is] whether a one-year welfare residence requirement amounts to an undue burden upon the right of interstate travel [which I conclude] is a "fundamental" right [that] should be regarded as having its source in the Due Process Clause of the Fifth Amendment.

[In] my view, a number of considerations militate in favor of constitutionality. First, as just shown, four separate, legitimate governmental interests are furthered by residence requirements. Second, the impact of the requirements upon the freedom of individuals to travel interstate is indirect and, according to evidence put forward by the appellees themselves, insubstantial. Third, these are [cases] in which the States have acted within the terms of a limited authorization by the national government, and in which Congress itself has laid down a like rule for the District of Columbia. Fourth, the legislatures which enacted these statutes have been fully exposed to the arguments of the appellees as to why these residence requirements are unwise, and have rejected them. This is not, therefore, an instance in which legislatures have acted without mature deliberation.

Fifth, [the] field of welfare assistance is one in which there is a widely recognized need for fresh solutions and consequently for experimentation. Invalidation of welfare residence requirements might have the unfortunate consequence of discouraging the Federal and State Governments from establishing unusually generous welfare programs in particular areas on an experimental basis, because of fears that the program would cause an influx of persons seeking higher welfare payments. Sixth, [the] statutes come to us clothed with the authority of Congress and attended by a correspondingly heavy presumption of constitutionality. * * *

Notes and Questions

1. *Equal protection vs. due process.* If a state simply eliminated welfare, or granted lower payments than other states, would this "touch on the fundamental right of interstate movement" just as harshly as the programs in *Shapiro?* "Fence out indigents" at least as much? Would it be invalid under *Shapiro* "unless shown to be necessary to promote a *compelling* governmental interest"? See generally Harvith, *The Constitutionality of Residence Tests for General and Categorical Assistance Programs,* 54 Calif.L. Rev. 567, 593–95 (1966). Or does *Shapiro* deal only with "invidious distinctions between classes of citizens"? Does Harlan, J.'s contention—that "when the right affected is one assured by the Constitution, any infringement can be dealt with under the Due Process Clause"—render the *Shapiro* approach superfluous? [a] Or does *Shapiro's* equal protection analysis add another dimension to the problem by distinguishing between the state interest needed to justify (a) reducing expenditures generally, and (b) reducing expenditures by denying benefits to recent travellers? See *Chicago Police Dep't. v. Mosley.* See generally Reinstein, *The Welfare Cases: Fundamental Rights, The Poor, and the Burden of Proof in Constitutional Litigation,* 44 Temp.L.Q. 1, 36–40 (1970); Choper, Kamisar & Tribe, *The Supreme Court: Trends and Developments 1978–1979,* 263–64, 311–12 (1979).

2. *Residence requirements.* (a) After *Shapiro,* may a state deny welfare assistance to transients who have no intention of remaining permanently in the state? Did *Shapiro* not really involve "the interest in freedom of travel" but rather "only the narrower interest in freedom of interstate migration"—i.e., to "resettle, find a new job, and start a new life"? See Barrett, *Judicial Supervision of Legislative Classifications—A More Modest Role for Equal Protection,* 1976 B.Y.U.L.Rev. 89, 117. See also *Memorial Hosp. v. Maricopa Cty.,* note 3(b) infra. Consider Note, *Durational Residence Requirements from Shapiro Through Sosna,* 50 N.Y.U.L.Rev. 622, 675 (1975): "A classification scheme based [on] residency does not penalize exercise of the right to travel because it results in no denial of benefits or privileges: transient nonresidents remain eligible for benefits in the state in which they are residents." See also McCoy, *Recent Equal Protection Decisions—Fundamental Right to Travel or "Newcomers" as a Suspect Class?* 28 Vand.L.Rev. 987, 1016–23 (1975).

(b) DOE v. BOLTON, p. 165 supra, invalidated the residency requirement of the Georgia abortion law: "Just as the Privileges and Immunities Clause, Art. IV, § 2, protects persons who enter other States to ply their trade, so must it protect persons who enter Georgia seeking the medical services that are available there. A contrary holding would mean that a State could limit to its own residents the general medical care available within its borders." Is *Doe* consistent with the analysis in note (a) supra? Compare *Carrington v. Rash,* Part I, B supra.

(c) What of a residency requirement that affects both freedom of travel and freedom of interstate migration? McCARTHY v. PHILADELPHIA CIVIL SERVICE COM'N, 424 U.S. 645, 96 S.Ct. 1154, 47 L.Ed.2d 366 (1976), per curiam—involving a Philadelphia fireman who was terminated when he moved to New Jersey—held that "a municipal regulation requiring employees of the city [to] be

a. For support of this view, see Loewy, *A Different and More Viable Theory of Equal Protection,* 57 N.C.L.Rev. 1 (1978); Perry, *Modern Equal Protection: A Conceptualization and Appraisal,* 79 Colum.L.Rev. 1023 (1979).

residents of the city" did not impair the "right to travel interstate as defined in *Shapiro,*" which questioned neither "the validity of a condition placed upon municipal employment that a person be a resident *at the time* of his application,"[6] nor "the validity of appropriately defined and uniformly applied bona fide residence requirements."[b] Is *McCarthy* consistent with *Shapiro* and *Doe?*

(d) MARTINEZ v. BYNUM, 461 U.S. 321, 103 S.Ct. 1838, 75 L.Ed.2d 879 (1983), per POWELL, J., upheld Texas' denial of free public education to children who, apart from their parents or guardians, reside in the school district "for the sole purpose of attending" the public schools: "A bona fide residence requirement [with] respect to attendance in public free schools does not violate the Equal Protection Clause[7] [nor does it] burden or penalize the constitutional right of interstate travel, for any person is free to move to a State and to establish residence there. [A]t the very least, a school district generally would be justified in requiring school-age children or their parents to satisfy the traditional, basic residence criteria—i.e., to live in the district with a bona fide intention of remaining there—before it treated them as residents." Marshall, J., dissented, mainly on the ground that an "intention of remaining" is not a proper criterion for a bona fide residence requirement. Is *Martinez* consistent with *Shapiro* and *Doe?*

(e) May a state deny welfare to a person who has permanently left the state but who cannot obtain welfare elsewhere? CALIFANO v. GAUTIER TORRES, 435 U.S. 1, 98 S.Ct. 906, 55 L.Ed.2d 65 (1978), per curiam, upheld Social Security Act provisions, which made benefits available in the fifty states but not in Puerto Rico, as applied to U.S. residents who lost benefits when they moved to Puerto Rico. The lower court had "held that the Constitution requires that a person who travels to Puerto Rico must be given benefits superior to those enjoyed by other residents of Puerto Rico if the newcomer enjoyed those benefits in the State from which he came. This Court has never held that the constitutional right to travel embraces any such doctrine [which] would bid fair to destroy the independent power of each State [to] enact laws uniformly applicable to all of its residents."[c]

(f) After *Shapiro,* may a state adopt a "one-year-waiting-period" in which the newcomer receives no more welfare than in the state from which he came?

3. *Other waiting-period requirements.* (a) *Voting.* DUNN v. BLUMSTEIN, 405 U.S. 330, 92 S.Ct. 995, 31 L.Ed.2d 274 (1972), per MARSHALL, J., held that Tennessee's voting registration requirements—of residence in the state for one year and in the county for three months—violate equal protection. Although "States have the power to require that voters be bona fide residents of the relevant political subdivision," it is the "additional *durational* residence requirement which appellee challenges. [Here], whether we look to the benefit withheld by the classification (the opportunity to vote) or the basis for the classification (recent interstate travel)," the classification must be "*necessary* to promote a

6. Nor did [it] involve a public agency's relationship with its own employees which, of course, may justify greater control than over the citizenry at large. Cf. *Pickering v. Board of Educ.*; *Broadrick v. Oklahoma.*

b. Burger, C.J., and Brennan and Blackmun, JJ., would set the case for argument.

7. A bona fide residence requirement implicates no "suspect" classification, and therefore is not subject to strict scrutiny. Indeed, there is nothing invidiously discriminatory about a bona fide residence requirement if it is uniformly applied. Thus the question is simply whether there is a rational basis for it.

This view assumes, of course, that the "service" that the State would deny to nonresidents is not a fundamental right protected by the Constitution. * * *

c. Brennan, J., dissented. Marshall, J., would have set the case for full argument.

compelling governmental interest. [In] pursuing that important interest, the State cannot choose means which unnecessarily burden or restrict constitutionally protected activity."

First, as for the state's interest in "preventing fraud [by] keeping nonresidents from voting, [the] record is totally devoid of any evidence that durational residence requirements are in fact necessary to identify bona fide residents." Second, "the State cannot seriously maintain that it is 'necessary' to reside for a year in the State and three months in the county in order to be minimally knowledgeable about congressional, state or even purely local elections. [T]he conclusive presumptions of durational residence requirements are much too crude." [a]

BURGER, C.J., dissented: "It is no more a denial of Equal Protection for a State to require newcomers to be exposed to state and local problems for a reasonable period such as one year before voting, than it is to require children to wait 18 years before [voting.] Some lines must be drawn. To challenge such lines by the 'compelling state interest' standard is to condemn them all." [b]

(b) *Medical care.* MEMORIAL HOSPITAL v. MARICOPA COUNTY, 415 U.S. 250, 94 S.Ct. 1076, 39 L.Ed.2d 306 (1974), per MARSHALL, J., held an Arizona statute—requiring one year's residence in the county for indigents to receive nonemergency hospitalization or medical care at county expense—violative of equal protection: "Although any durational residence requirement impinges to some extent on the right to travel," *Shapiro* "did not declare such requirements to be per se unconstitutional." It is only a state classification that "operates to *penalize* [indigents] for exercising their right to migrate to and settle in that state" which "must be justified by a compelling state interest. [*Dunn*] found that the denial of the franchise, 'a fundamental political right,' was a penalty [and *Shapiro*] found denial of the basic 'necessities of life' to be a penalty. Nonetheless, the Court has declined to strike down state statutes requiring one year of residence as a condition to lower tuition at state institutions of higher education.[12] Whatever the ultimate parameters of the *Shapiro* penalty analysis, it is at least clear that medical care is as much 'a basic necessity of life' to an indigent as welfare assistance." For reasons similar to those in *Shapiro,* the state has not met its "heavy burden of justification." [c]

REHNQUIST, J., dissented: "[F]ees for use of transportation facilities such as taxes on airport users,[12] have been upheld [against] attacks based upon the right to travel. [T]he line to be derived from our prior cases is that some financial impositions on interstate travelers have such indirect or inconsequential impact

a. Blackmun, J., concurred in the result. Powell and Rehnquist, JJ., did not participate.

b. *Marston v. Lewis,* 410 U.S. 679, 93 S.Ct. 1211, 35 L.Ed.2d 627 (1973), per curiam, upheld Arizona's 50-day durational residency requirement for state and local elections as "necessary to permit preparation of accurate voter lists." *Burns v. Fortson,* 410 U.S. 686, 93 S.Ct. 1209, 35 L.Ed.2d 633 (1973), upheld a similar Georgia provision, noting that "the 50-day registration period approaches the outer constitutional limits in this area" (Blackmun, J., concurring only in the result because of objection to this statement).

Marshall, J., joined by Douglas and Brennan, JJ., dissented, observing that *Dunn* "held that a 30-day residency requirement provided the State with '[ample time to] complete whatever administrative tasks are necessary to prevent fraud' in the process of voter registration."

Compare *Rosario v. Rockefeller,* Part I, B supra.

12. See *Vlandis v. Kline* [Sec. 5 infra].

c. Burger, C.J., and Blackmun, J., concurred in the result. Douglas, J., filed a separate opinion: "So far as interstate travel per se is considered, I share the doubts of my Brother Rehnquist. [Here,] invidious discrimination against the poor [is] the critical issue."

12. See *Evansville-Vanderburgh Airport Auth. Dist. v. Delta Airlines,* 405 U.S. 707, 92 S.Ct. 1349, 31 L.Ed.2d 620 (1972).

on travel that they simply do not constitute the type of direct purposeful barriers struck down" in *Shapiro.* "The solicitude which the Court has shown in cases involving the right to vote, and the virtual denial of entry inherent in denial of welfare benefits—'the very means by which to live'—ought not be so casually extended to the alleged deprivation here. Rather the Court should examine, as it has done in the past, whether the challenged requirement erects a real and purposeful barrier to movement, [or] whether the effects on travel, viewed realistically, are merely incidental and remote."

(c) *Divorce.* SOSNA v. IOWA, 419 U.S. 393, 95 S.Ct. 553, 42 L.Ed.2d 532 (1975), per REHNQUIST, J., upheld a one-year residency requirement to file for divorce: The laws in *Shapiro* and *Maricopa* "were justified on the basis of budgetary or record-keeping considerations which were held insufficient to outweigh the constitutional claims of the individuals. But Iowa's divorce residency requirement is of a different stripe. [A] decree of divorce [will] affect [both spouses'] marital status and very likely their property rights. Where a married couple has minor children, a decree of divorce would usually include provisions for their custody and support. With consequences of such moment riding on a divorce decree issued by its courts, Iowa may insist that one seeking to initiate such a proceeding have the modicum of attachment to the State required here. Such a requirement additionally furthers the State's parallel interests in both avoiding officious intermeddling in matters in which another State has a paramount interest, and in minimizing the susceptibility of its own divorce decrees to collateral attack." [d]

MARSHALL, J., joined by Brennan, J., dissented, relying on *Boddie v. Connecticut,* Part III infra: The right to divorce "is of such fundamental importance" that the law "penalizes interstate travel within the meaning of *Shapiro, Dunn,* and *Maricopa.* [The] Court has not only declined to apply the 'compelling interest' test to this case, it has conjured up possible justifications for the State's restriction in a manner much more akin to the lenient standard" of equal protection review. A "simple requirement of domicile—physical presence plus intent to remain—[would] remove the rigid one-year barrier while permitting the State to restrict the availability of its divorce process to citizens who are genuinely its own." [e]

(d) *The decisions' rationale.* Do the cases explain how the Court determines whether a "waiting-period" requirement "operates to *penalize*" the right to travel? In both *Dunn* and *Maricopa* the Court conceded "that there is no evidence in the record before us that anyone was actually deterred from traveling by the challenged restriction [but] *Shapiro* did not rest upon a finding that denial of welfare actually deterred travel. Nor have other 'right to travel' [cases] always relied on the presence of actual deterrence." Consider 88 Harv.L. Rev. 117–18 (1974): "[T]he Court should consider the deterrent effect [rather] than attempt, as does Justice Marshall's 'penalty' analysis, to assess the importance of various state benefits to immigrants. Insofar as the validity of a given requirement depends upon the latter, what is being protected is not the right to travel, but the right to the withheld benefit."

d. White, J., dissented on procedural grounds.

e. For the view that "durational residency requirements for state benefits and services are permissible only to the extent they respond to a reasonable concern for proof of domiciliary intent," see W. Cohen, *Equal Treatment for Newcomers: The Core Meaning of National and State Citizenship,* 1 Const. Comment. 9 (1984).

Does the Court *presume* that withholding of certain benefits (but not others) deters travel? Would this explain the "basic necessity of life" emphasis in *Shapiro* and *Maricopa?* Does it account for the result in *Sosna?* In *Dunn?* Are *Shapiro* and *Maricopa* distinguishable from *Dunn* and *Sosna* because only the former tend to "fence out indigents" (*Shapiro;* cf. Douglas, J., in *Maricopa*)? [f] See Part III infra. Is *Dunn* explicable on other grounds? See Part I, B supra.

Should the decisions turn on whether residency requirements reflect a "reasonable concern for proof of domiciliary intent"? See Cohen, *Equal Treatment for Newcomers,* 1 Const.Comm. 9, 19 (1984).

(e) *Other problems.* What of the validity of waiting-period requirements to be eligible for public housing? To be a candidate for elective office? See Note, *Durational Residency Requirements for Candidates,* 40 U.Chi.L.Rev. 357 (1973). To be admitted to the bar? To obtain public employment? See Note, 67 Calif.L. Rev. 386 (1979).

4. *Length of residence requirements.* ZOBEL v. WILLIAMS, 457 U.S. 55, 102 S.Ct. 2309, 72 L.Ed.2d 672 (1982), per BURGER, C.J., held that Alaska's scheme of distributing its revenue from state-owned oil reserves to its citizens "in varying amounts, based on the length of each citizen's residence, violates the equal protection rights of newer state citizens." The Court held that two of Alaska's stated objectives—"creating a financial incentive for individuals to establish and maintain Alaska residence, and assuring prudent management of the [oil revenues] and the State's natural and mineral resources"—were "not rationally related to the distinctions Alaska seeks to draw." And, under *Shapiro,* the objective of rewarding "contributions of various kinds, both tangible and intangible, which residents have made during their years of residence," was "not a legitimate state purpose. [Such] reasoning could open the door to state apportionment of other rights, benefits and services according to length of residency. It would permit the states to divide citizens into expanding numbers of permanent classes. Such a result would be clearly impermissible."

BRENNAN, J., joined by Marshall, Blackmun and Powell, JJ., joined the Court's opinion, adding that "the Citizenship Clause of the Fourteenth Amendment [bars] degrees of citizenship based on length of residence. And the Equal Protection Clause would not tolerate such distinctions. In short, as much as the right to travel, equality of citizenship is of the essence in our republic. [Thus], discrimination on the basis of residence must be supported by a valid state interest independent of the discrimination itself. [L]ength of residence may, for example, be used to test the bona fides of citizenship—and allegiance and attachment may bear some rational relationship to a very limited number of legitimate state purposes. Cf. *Chimento v. Stark,* 353 F.Supp. 1211 (D.N.H.), affirmed, 414 U.S. 802, 94 S.Ct. 125, 38 L.Ed.2d 39 (1973) (seven year citizenship requirement to run for governor); U.S. Const., art. I, § 2, cl. 2, § 3, cl. 3; art. II, § 1, cl. 4. But those instances in which length of residence could provide a legitimate basis for distinguishing one citizen from another are rare."

O'CONNOR, J., concurred: "A desire to compensate citizens for their prior contributions is neither inherently invidious nor irrational. Under some circumstances, the objective may be wholly reasonable.[1] Even a generalized desire to

f. For the view that *Sosna* may be distinguished from *Shapiro* and *Maricopa* because of the absence of impermissible state "motivation," see Loewy, fn. a after *Shapiro,* at 38–39; Clark, *Legislative Motivation and Fundamental Rights in Constitutional Law,* 15 San Diego L.Rev. 953, 984–90 (1978).

1. A State, for example, might choose to divide its largesse among all persons who previously have contributed their time to volunreward citizens for past endurance, particularly in a State where years of hardship only recently have produced prosperity, is not innately improper. The difficulty is that plans enacted to further this objective necessarily treat new residents of a State less favorably than the longer-term residents who have past contributions to 'reward.' * * * Stripped to its essentials, the plan denies non-Alaskans settling in the State the same privileges afforded longer-term residents. The Privileges and Immunities Clause of Article IV [addresses] just this type of discrimination.

"* * * I believe [that] application of the Privileges and Immunities Clause to controversies involving the 'right to travel' would at least begin the task of reuniting this elusive right with the constitutional principles it embodies. [I] conclude that Alaska's disbursement scheme violates [the] Privileges and Immunities Clause" because there is nothing "to indicate that noncitizens constitute a peculiar source of the evil at which the statute is aimed" and no " 'substantial relationship' between the evil and the discrimination practiced against the noncitizens. *Hicklin v. Orbeck,* 437 U.S. 518, 98 S.Ct. 2482, 57 L.Ed.2d 397 (1978)."

REHNQUIST, J., dissented: "[T]he illegitimacy of a State's recognizing past contributions of its citizens has been established by the Court only in certain cases considering an infringement of the right to travel, and the majority itself rightly declines to apply the strict scrutiny analysis of those right-to-travel cases. The distribution scheme at issue in this case impedes no person's right to travel to and settle in Alaska; if anything, the prospect of receiving annual cash dividends would encourage immigration to Alaska." [g]

ATTORNEY GENERAL v. SOTO-LOPEZ, 476 U.S. 898, 106 S.Ct. 2317, 90 L.Ed.2d 899 (1986), held violative of equal protection a New York civil service employment preference for residents who served in the military during time of war and who were New York residents when they entered the service. BRENNAN, J., joined by Marshall, Blackmun and Powell, JJ., recognized that "the benefit sought here may not rise to the same level of importance as the necessities of life and the right to vote, [but such] a permanent deprivation of a significant benefit, based only on the fact of nonresidence at a past point in time, clearly operates to penalize appellees' for exercising their rights to migrate. [The] State has not met its heavy burden of proving that it has selected a means of pursuing a compelling state interest which does not impinge unnecessarily on constitutionally protected interests."

teer community organizations. If the State graded its dividends according to the number of years devoted to prior community service, it could be said that the State intended "to reward citizens for past contributions." Alternatively, a State might enact a tax credit for citizens who contribute to the State's ecology by building alternative fuel sources or establishing recycling plants. If the State made this credit retroactive, to benefit those citizens who launched these improvements before they became fashionable, the State once again would be rewarding past contributions. The Court's opinion would dismiss these objectives as wholly illegitimate. I would recognize them as valid goals and inquire only whether their implementation infringed any constitutionally protected interest.

g. See also *Hooper v. Bernalillo County Assessor,* 472 U.S. 612, 105 S.Ct. 2862, 86 L.Ed. 2d 487 (1985), per Burger, C.J., holding that a New Mexico property tax exemption for only those Vietnam veterans who were state residents before May 1976 "is not rationally related to the State's asserted legislative goal[s]," and thus "suffers the same constitutional flaw [as] *Zobel*": "[T]he Equal Protection Clause [forbids] the State to prefer established resident veterans over newcomers in [the] apportionment of an economic benefit."

Stevens, J., joined by Rehnquist and O'Connor, JJ., dissented: The classification "rationally furthers a legitimate state purpose. [The] need to budget for the future is itself a valid reason for [a limit] on the size of potential beneficiaries."

BURGER, C.J.—with whom White, J., agreed—concurred in the judgment because, under *Zobel* and *Hooper*—in which "we had no occasion to reach the issues whether the classifications would survive heightened scrutiny or whether the right to travel was violated"—"the statutory scheme cannot pass even the minimum rationality test."

O'CONNOR, J., joined by Rehnquist and Stevens, JJ., dissented, reasoning along the lines of her concurrence in *Zobel* and the dissents in *Zobel* and *Hooper:* "[F]inding that this scheme in theory or practical effect constitutes a 'penalty' on appellees' fundamental right to settle in New York or on their 'right to migrate' seems to me ephemeral, and completely unnecessary to safeguard the constitutional purpose of 'maintaining a Union rather than a mere "league of states."' *Zobel* (O'Connor, J., concurring in judgment). Thus, heightened scrutiny, either under the 'right to migrate' or the Equal Protection Clause is inappropriate. Under rational basis review, New York [is] attempting to say 'thank you' to those who personified New York's sacrifice and effort to 'do its part' in supporting this Nation's war efforts."

III. DISCRIMINATORY IMPACT ON THE POOR

Although the Warren Court had *stated* on several occasions that "lines drawn on the basis of wealth or property" "render a classification highly suspect," [a] the Burger Court observed in 1973 that the Court had "never held that wealth discrimination alone provides an adequate basis for invoking strict scrutiny," [b] and, in 1980, *Harris v. McRae,* p. 194 supra, said that "this Court has held repeatedly that poverty, standing alone, is not a suspect classification. See, e.g. *James v. Valtierra* [infra]." In fact, explicit (or "de jure") government discriminations against poor people are rare.

JAMES v. VALTIERRA, 402 U.S. 137, 91 S.Ct. 1331, 28 L.Ed.2d 678 (1971), per BLACK, J., upheld Art. 34 of the California constitution that no low-income public housing project could be developed unless approved by referendum in the locality: "Provisions for referendums demonstrate devotion to democracy, not to bias, discrimination, or prejudice." "California law reveals that persons advocating low-income housing have not been singled out for mandatory referendums [which] are required for approval of state constitutional amendments, for the issuance of general obligation long-term bonds by local governments, and for certain municipal territorial annexations." [c]

MARSHALL, J., joined by Brennan and Blackmun, JJ., dissented,[d] noting that under California law, "publicly assisted housing developments designed to accommodate the aged, veterans, state employees, persons of moderate income, or any class of citizens other than the poor, need not be approved by prior referenda. [Art. 34 is] an explicit classification on the basis of poverty—a suspect classification which demands exacting judicial scrutiny."

Notes and Questions

Should explicit discriminations against poor people be held "suspect"? Consider Michelman, *On Protecting the Poor Through the Fourteenth Amendment,* 83

a. *Harper v. Virginia Bd. of Elections* and *McDonald v. Board of Elec. Comm'rs,* Sec. 4, I, B infra.

b. *San Antonio Ind. School Dist. v. Rodriguez,* Sec. 4, IV infra.

c. If a statute forbade all minors, teachers, lawyers and blacks from serving on juries, would the statute explicitly discriminate against blacks and thus be "suspect"? See *Hunter v. Erickson,* Sec. 2, V supra.

d. Douglas, J., did not participate.

Harv.L.Rev. 7, 21 (1969): "[I]f money is power, then a class deliberately defined so as to include everyone who has less wealth or income than any person outside it may certainly be deemed [to] be especially susceptible to abuse by majoritarian process; and classification of 'the poor' as such, may, like classification of racial minorities as such, be popularly understood as a badge of inferiority. Especially is this so in light of the extreme difficulty of imagining proper governmental objectives which require for their achievement the explicit carving out, for relatively disadvantageous treatment, of a class defined by relative paucity of wealth or income." [e] Compare Winter, *Poverty, Economic Equality, and the Equal Protection Clause,* 1972 Sup.Ct.Rev. 41, 97–98: "Race is [the] basis of a stereotype which served as a systematic vehicle of governmental discrimination. Moreover, it is not a stereotype with a pretense at being related to individual merit, even though it [is] unalterable by the individual. [But] poverty is not absolutely unalterable for all those afflicted by it. The history of this nation is a history of virtually all of its people bettering themselves [economically].[f] Beyond that, [t]here simply has not been any legislation invoking a poverty classification even remotely resembling the widespread, official, racial segregation of schools and other facilities. To the contrary, there is an enormous amount of legislation [to] help the poor. [Finally], to the extent low income is related to low productivity—and it is to a large extent—poverty is not entirely unrelated to individual merit. One need not adopt productivity as the sole criterion of merit to say that poverty resulting from low productivity is far different from legal exclusion from public facilities because of one's race."

Several Warren Court decisions (in addition to *Harper v. Virginia Bd. of Elec.,* Part I, B supra) held that state laws or practices that operated to the disadvantage of poor people—in contrast to "de jure" discrimination against the poor—violated equal protection (and/or due process). Most of these rulings, as well as those of the Burger Court following this path, concern the question of whether states must waive fees (or provide certain services without charge) to poor people who could not otherwise effectively participate in criminal or civil litigation. These decisions are included in this section. Other kinds of laws that have a disproportionate impact on the poor are considered in the section that follows.

GRIFFIN v. ILLINOIS, 351 U.S. 12, 76 S.Ct. 585, 100 L.Ed. 891 (1956), held that a state must furnish an indigent criminal defendant with a free trial transcript (or its equivalent) if it were necessary for "adequate and effective

e. What result if the state were to make it a crime for a person without visible means of support to refuse employment? Bar welfare recipients from public housing because of the risk of rental nonpayment? May the state require welfare recipients to accept "suitable employment"? Job training? To disclose certain intimate personal details?

f. See also 85 Harv.L.Rev. 129 (1972): "The poor seem to be a less cohesive and less readily identifiable group than are racial minorities. Because the class of 'poor' is constantly in flux, the reinforced sense of stigma which characterizes de jure racial classifications is probably mitigated even where explicit wealth classifications are concerned."

Compare Clune, *The Supreme Court's Treatment of Wealth Discriminations Under the Fourteenth Amendment,* 1975 Sup.Ct.Rev. 289, 329–30: "[Poverty] is one of the most startlingly stable social phenomena (the strata of personal income have remained in uncannily stable ratios to each other for decades); it seems totally immune to political attack or even war; the disabilities and abilities associated with wealth are pervasive and among the most highly important on our scale of values. [Whether] or not some individuals escape is insignificant compared to those who do not. If the non-escapees are vulnerable and weak economically, socially, and politically, their situation is identical to another class whose individual members are less able to escape."

appellate review" of the conviction. BLACK, J., joined by Warren, C.J., and Douglas and Clark, JJ., found that "both equal protection and due process emphasize [that in] criminal trials a State can no more discriminate on account of poverty than on account of religion, race, or color. Plainly the ability to pay costs in advance bears no rational relationship to a defendant's guilt or innocence and could not be used as an excuse to deprive a defendant of a fair trial. [It] is true that a State is not required by the federal constitution to provide appellate [review]. See, e.g., *McKane v. Durston,* 153 U.S. 684, 687–88, 14 S.Ct. 913, 914–15, 38 L.Ed. 687 (1894). But that is not to say that a State that does grant appellate review can do so in a way that discriminates against some convicted defendants on account of their poverty. * * *

"All of the States now provide some method of appeal from criminal convictions, recognizing the importance of appellate review to a correct adjudication of guilt or innocence. [Thus] to deny adequate review to the poor means that many of them may lose their life, liberty or property because of unjust convictions which appellate courts would set aside. [There] can be no equal justice where the kind of trial a man gets depends on the amount of money he has." [a]

DOUGLAS v. CALIFORNIA, 372 U.S. 353, 83 S.Ct. 814, 9 L.Ed.2d 811 (1963), per DOUGLAS, J., relying on *Griffin,* held that a state must appoint counsel for an indigent for "the first appeal, granted as a matter of [statutory right] from a criminal conviction." It disapproved California's system of appointing counsel only when the appellate court made "an independent investigation of the record and determine[d] it would be of advantage to the defendant or helpful to [the] court": "[A] state can, consistently with the Fourteenth Amendment, provide for differences so long as the result does not amount to a denial of due process or an 'invidious discrimination.' Absolute equality is not [required]. But where the merits of the one and only appeal an indigent has as of right are decided without benefit of counsel, we think an unconstitutional line has been drawn between rich and poor.

"When an indigent is forced to run this gantlet of a preliminary showing of merit, the right to appeal does not comport with fair procedure. [There] is lacking that equality demanded by the Fourteenth Amendment where the rich man, who appeals as of right, enjoys the benefit of counsel's examination into the record, research of the law, and marshalling of arguments on his behalf, while the indigent, already burdened by a preliminary determination that his case is without merit, is forced to shift for himself. The indigent, where the record is unclear or the errors are hidden, has only the right to a meaningless ritual, while the rich man has a meaningful appeal."

HARLAN, J., joined by Stewart, J., dissented from the Court's reliance, as in *Griffin,* "on a blend of the Equal Protection and Due Process Clauses," believing that "this case should be judged solely under the Due Process Clause": "States,

a. Frankfurter, J., concurred in the result. Burton, Minton, Reed and Harlan, JJ., dissented.

For subsequent application of *Griffin,* see e.g., *Burns v. Ohio,* 360 U.S. 252, 79 S.Ct. 1164, 3 L.Ed.2d 1209 (1959) (indigent criminal defendant cannot be required to pay filing fee for appeal); *Long v. District Court,* 385 U.S. 192, 87 S.Ct. 362, 17 L.Ed.2d 290 (1966) (indigent must be furnished free transcript of state habeas corpus hearing for use on appeal from denial of habeas, although transcript not a sine qua non to access to appellate court). Cf. *Britt v. North Carolina,* 404 U.S. 226, 92 S.Ct. 431, 30 L.Ed.2d 400 (1971) (adequate alternative to transcript existed).

of course, are prohibited by the Equal Protection Clause from discriminating between 'rich' and 'poor' *as such* in the formulation and application of their laws. But it is a far different thing to suggest that this provision prevents the State from adopting a law of general applicability that may affect the poor more harshly than it does the rich, or, on the other hand, from making some effort to redress economic imbalances while not eliminating them entirely.

"Every financial exaction which the State imposes on a uniform basis is more easily satisfied by the well-to-do than by the indigent. Yet I take it that no one would dispute the constitutional power of the State to levy a uniform sales tax, to charge tuition at a state university, to fix rates for the purchase of water from a municipal corporation, to impose a standard fine for criminal violations, or to establish minimum bail for various categories of offenses. Nor could it be contended that the State may not classify as crimes acts which the poor are more likely to commit than are the rich. And surely, there would be no basis for attacking a state law which provided benefits for the needy simply because those benefits fell short of the goods or services that others could purchase for themselves.

"Laws such as these do not deny equal protection to the less fortunate for one essential reason: the Equal Protection Clause does not impose on the States 'an affirmative duty to lift the handicaps flowing from differences in economic circumstances.' To so construe it would be to read into the Constitution a philosophy of leveling that would be foreign to many of our basic concepts of the proper relations between government and society. [N]o matter how far the state rule might go in providing counsel for indigents, it could never be expected to satisfy an affirmative duty—if one existed—to place the poor on the same level as those who can afford the best legal talent available."

As for due process, "we have today held [that] there is an absolute right to the services of counsel at trial. *Gideon v. Wainwright,* 372 U.S. 335, 83 S.Ct. 792, 9 L.Ed.2d 799 (1963). But [a]ppellate review is in itself not required by the Fourteenth Amendment, [and] thus the question presented is the narrow one whether the State's rules with respect to the appointment of counsel are so arbitrary or unreasonable, *in the context of the particular appellate procedure that it has established,* as to require their invalidation." Clark, J., also dissented.[b]

ROSS v. MOFFITT, 417 U.S. 600, 94 S.Ct. 2437, 41 L.Ed.2d 341 (1974), per REHNQUIST, J., held that *Douglas* does not require counsel for discretionary state appeals or for applications for review in the Supreme Court: As for due process, "it is clear that the State need not provide any appeal at all. The fact that an appeal *has* been provided does not automatically mean that a State then acts unfairly by refusing to provide counsel to indigent defendants at every stage of the way. Unfairness results only if indigents are singled out by the State and denied meaningful access to that system because of their poverty. That question is more profitably considered under an equal protection analysis [which] 'does not require absolute equality or precisely equal advantages,' [but] does require that the state appellate system be 'free of unreasoned distinctions' and that indigents have an adequate opportunity to present their claims fairly within the adversarial system.

b. For exploration of the implications of *Griffin* and *Douglas,* see Kamisar & Choper, *The Right to Counsel in Minnesota: Some Field Findings and Legal-Policy Observations,* 48 Minn.L.Rev. 1, 7–14 (1963).

"[P]rior to his seeking discretionary review in the State Supreme Court, [respondent's] claims 'had once been presented by a lawyer and passed upon by an [intermediate] appellate court.' *Douglas.* We do not believe that it can be said, therefore, that [respondent] is denied meaningful access to the North Carolina Supreme Court simply because the State does not appoint counsel to aid him in seeking review in that court. At that stage he will have, at the very least, [a record] of trial proceedings, a brief on his behalf in the Court of Appeals setting forth his claims of error, and in many cases an opinion by the Court of Appeals disposing of his case. These materials, supplemented by whatever submission respondent may make pro se, would appear to provide the Supreme Court of North Carolina with an adequate basis on which to base its decision to grant or deny [review].

"This is not to say, of course, that a skilled lawyer [would] not prove helpful to any litigant able to employ him. An indigent defendant seeking review in the Supreme Court of North Carolina is therefore somewhat handicapped in comparison with a wealthy [defendant]. But both the opportunity to have counsel prepare an initial brief in the Court of Appeals and the nature of discretionary review in the Supreme Court of North Carolina make this relative handicap far less than the handicap borne by the indigent defendant denied counsel on his initial appeal as of right in *Douglas.* [The] duty of the State under our cases is not to duplicate the legal arsenal that may be privately retained by a criminal defendant, [but] only to assure the indigent defendant an adequate opportunity to present his claims fairly in the context of the State's appellate [process]."

DOUGLAS, J., joined by Brennan and Marshall, JJ., dissented: "The right to discretionary review is a substantial one, and one where a lawyer can be of significant assistance to an indigent defendant. It was correctly perceived below that the 'same concepts of fairness and equality, which require counsel in a first appeal of right, require counsel in other and subsequent discretionary appeals.' " [c]

TATE v. SHORT, 401 U.S. 395, 91 S.Ct. 668, 28 L.Ed.2d 130 (1971): An indigent accumulated $425 in fines for traffic offenses. Texas law provided only for fines but required that those unable to pay be incarcerated to satisfy their fines at the rate of $5 per day. The Court, per BRENNAN, J., reversed: Equal protection " 'requires that the statutory ceiling placed on imprisonment for any substantive offense be the same for all defendants irrespective of their economic status.' *Williams v. Illinois,* 399 U.S. 235, 90 S.Ct. 2018, 26 L.Ed.2d 586 (1970). [Thus, Texas cannot] limit the punishment to payment of the fine if one is able to pay it, yet convert the fine into a prison term for an [indigent]. Imprisonment in such a case is not imposed to further any penal objective of the State. * * *

"There are, however, other alternatives [such as procedures for paying fines in installments] to which the State may constitutionally resort to serve its concededly valid interest in enforcing payment of fines. [O]ur decision [should not] be understood as precluding imprisonment as an enforcement method when

c. See also *United States v. MacCollom,* 426 U.S. 317, 96 S.Ct. 2086, 48 L.Ed.2d 666 (1976) (5–4), relying on *Ross* to uphold provision of a free trial transcript for use in a collateral attack on a federal conviction only if a federal judge certifies that the claim is "not frivolous" and that the transcript is "needed to decide the issue."

See also *Lassiter v. Department of Social Servs.* (due process does not *always* require appointment of counsel for indigent parents in state suit to terminate parental status).

alternative means are unsuccessful despite the defendant's reasonable efforts to satisfy the fines by those means; the determination of the constitutionality of [that] must await the presentation of a concrete case." Black, J., concurred in the result.[a]

BEARDEN v. GEORGIA, 461 U.S. 660, 103 S.Ct. 2064, 76 L.Ed.2d 221 (1983), per O'CONNOR, J.,—noting that "due process and equal protection principles converge in these cases"—held that "it is fundamentally unfair" to "revoke a defendant's probation for failure to pay the imposed fine and restitution, absent evidence and findings that the defendant was somehow responsible for the failure or that alternative forms of punishment were inadequate": Probation "reflects a determination by the sentencing court that the State's penological interests do not require imprisonment. A probationer's failure to make reasonable efforts to repay his debt to society may indicate that this original determination needs reevaluation, [but 'only if alternate measures' such as 'extend[ing] the time for making payments, or reduc[ing] the fine, or direct[ing] that the probationer perform some form of labor or public service in lieu of the fine'] are not adequate to meet the State's interests in punishment and deterrence may the court imprison a probationer who has made sufficient bona fide efforts to pay." [b]

BODDIE v. CONNECTICUT, 401 U.S. 371, 91 S.Ct. 780, 28 L.Ed.2d 113 (1971), per HARLAN, J., sustained indigents' challenge to the state's requiring court fees and costs (averaging $60) in order to sue for divorce: "[M]arriage involves interests of basic importance in our society. [Without] a prior judicial imprimatur, individuals may freely enter into and rescind commercial contracts, for example, but we are unaware of any jurisdiction where private citizens may covenant for or dissolve marriages without state approval. [Thus], although they assert here due process rights as would-be plaintiffs, we think appellants' plight [is] akin to that of defendants faced with exclusion from the only forum effectively empowered to settle their disputes. [D]ue process requires, at a minimum, that absent a countervailing state interest of overriding significance, persons forced to settle their claims of right and duty through the judicial process must be given a meaningful opportunity to be heard." [d]

---

a. Harlan, J., concurred on the basis of his concurrence in *Williams* where he "dissociated" himself from the Court's "equal protection rationale" which, if "fully realized," "would require that the consequence of punishment be the same for all individuals."

Compare Clune, *The Supreme Court's Treatment of Wealth Discriminations Under the Fourteenth Amendment,* 1975 Sup.Ct.Rev. 289, 306: "The Court could require a schedule of fines fairly and thoughtfully designed to produce equal disutility on the average. One possibility would be a fine of an equal percentage of [earnings]. Such a system would go most of the way toward curing the wrong but would not represent a great interference with the states' systems of criminal justice."

b. White, J., joined by Burger, C.J., and Powell and Rehnquist, JJ., concurred on the ground that the sentencing judge had "automatically" imposed a "long prison term" rather than making "a good-faith effort to impose a jail sentence that in terms of the state's sentencing objectives will be roughly equivalent to the fine and restitution that the defendant failed to pay."

May an indigent accused be denied pretrial release if he is incapable of posting required bail? See *Bandy v. United States,* 81 S.Ct. 197, 5 L.Ed.2d 218 (1960) (Douglas, J., as Circuit Justice).

d. Douglas, J., and Brennan, J., concurred, but relied on the equal protection rationale of *Griffin.* Black, J., dissented.

UNITED STATES v. KRAS, 409 U.S. 434, 93 S.Ct. 631, 34 L.Ed.2d 626 (1973), per BLACKMUN, J., held that the Bankruptcy Act's conditioning the right to discharge on payment of $50 fees does not violate fifth amendment due process, including "equal protection": "[A] debtor, in theory, and often in actuality, may adjust his debts by negotiated agreement with his creditors. [Thus,] *Boddie's* emphasis on [judicial] exclusivity finds no counterpart in the bankrupt's situation." Moreover, unlike free speech or marriage, bankruptcy is not a "fundamental" right demanding "the lofty requirement of a compelling governmental interest before [it] may be significantly regulated." Bankruptcy legislation "is in the area of economics and social welfare. See *Dandridge v. Williams* [Part IV infra]." Thus, the standard is "rational justification"—and "the rational basis for the fee requirement is readily apparent": Congress' desire "to make the system self-sustaining and paid for by those who use [it]."

STEWART, J., joined by Douglas, Brennan and Marshall, JJ., dissented: "The bankrupt is bankrupt precisely for the reason that the State stands ready to exact all of his debts through garnishment, attachment, and the panoply of other creditor remedies. [I]n the unique situation of the indigent bankrupt the government provides the only effective means of his ever being free of these government imposed obligations. [While] the creditors of a bankrupt with assets might well desire to reach a compromise settlement, that possibility is foreclosed to the truly indigent bankrupt. [The] Court today holds that Congress may say that some of the poor are too poor even to go bankrupt." [e]

LITTLE v. STREATER, 452 U.S. 1, 101 S.Ct. 2202, 68 L.Ed.2d 627 (1981), per BURGER, C.J., held violative of due process Connecticut's refusal to pay the cost of blood grouping tests for indigent defendants in paternity actions. The Court stressed "the unique quality of blood grouping tests as a source of exculpatory evidence, the State's prominent role in the litigation,"—since the child was receiving welfare state law required the mother to institute the paternity action—"the 'quasi-criminal' overtones" of paternity proceedings, and the fact that state law made the defendant's testimony alone "insufficient to overcome the plaintiff's prima facie case": "Because appellant has no choice of an alternative forum and his interests, as well as those of the child, are constitutionally significant, this case is comparable to *Boddie* rather than to *Kras* and *Orwein.*"

Notes and Questions

1. *Access to courts in civil proceedings.* (a) *Defendants.* Do the decisions (especially *Boddie*) establish that persons made defendants in civil suits cannot be denied the opportunity to defend—whether as a matter of due process or equal protection—because of their inability to pay a state imposed fee? See Comment, *The Heirs of Boddie: Court Access for Indigents After Kras and Ortwein,* 8 Harv.Civ.Rts.—Civ.Lib.L.Rev. 571 (1973).

(b) *Plaintiffs.* To what extent do the decisions invalidate court access fees for indigent plaintiffs? Does *Boddie* forbid such fees in *all* situations where state law makes courts "the only forum effectively empowered to settle the

e. Douglas, J., joined by Brennan, J., as well as Marshall, J., also dissented.

See also *Ortwein v. Schwab,* 410 U.S. 656, 93 S.Ct. 1172, 35 L.Ed.2d 572 (1973), upholding a requirement that indigents appealing an adverse decision in a welfare hearing pay a $25 state appellate court filing fee. (For further discussion of indigents and appeals, see *Lindsey v. Normet,* Part IV infra.)

dispute"? Consider 85 Harv.L.Rev. 107 (1971): "Judicial approval is required to formalize legal relationships in [matters other than divorce]: adoption and custody of children, naturalization, change of a name, settlement of a decedent's estate, adjudication of incompetency, and awards of title to property in rem." Or do *Kras* (and *Ortwein*) also require that the right sought to be vindicated be "fundamental"? "Constitutional"? How do the cases line up in respect to these categories? Is the right to seek recovery for injury to person or property "fundamental"? See Part IV infra. For the view that access to courts generally may be a right derived from the first amendment, see Note, *A First Amendment Right to Access to the Courts for Indigents,* 82 Yale L.J. 1055 (1973); or a right analogous to voting, see Michelman, *The Supreme Court and Litigation Access Fees: The Right to Protect One's Rights—Part II,* 1974 Duke L.J. 527.

Is the "judicial exclusivity" factor—that for bankruptcy but not for divorce "effective alternatives for the adjustment of differences remain"—meaningful? Desirable as a constitutional principle? Consider 85 Harv.L.Rev. 108 (1971): "Much of the incentive for parties to agree to private resolution of a dispute is supplied by the threat that either may resort to the judicial process. Moreover, an agreement is of small value to a party unable to enforce its terms in court. Thus, although a tort claimant does have power to resolve his dispute with the tortfeasor while a divorce plaintiff does not, the likelihood of a settlement for a tort claimant too poor to get into court seems no greater than the possibility that the *Boddie* plaintiffs will obtain the funds necessary to obtain judicial relief." See also Goodpaster, *The Integration of Equal Protection, Due Process Standards, and the Indigent's Right of Free Access to the Courts,* 56 Ia.L.Rev. 223 (1970); Michelman, supra—*Part I,* 1973 Duke L.J. 1153, 1178–85.

2. *Other "payment requirements."* (a) May a state require indigents to pay a marriage license fee (n.b. the constitutional right of privacy)? A driver's license fee or interstate highway tolls or gasoline taxes (n.b. the constitutional right to travel)? May a state revoke the driver's license of an uninsured indigent who cannot post a security deposit after an accident? See Note, *Financial Responsibility Laws in Constitutional Perspective,* 61 Calif.L.Rev. 1072 (1973). Require a "court access fee" of an indigent plaintiff who seeks to enjoin an ordinance allegedly in violation of his first amendment rights? Require license fees from indigents to engage in certain occupations?

(b) May a public hospital deny abortions to indigents who cannot pay the established service charge? Cf. *Maher v. Roe,* Part IV infra. May a state charge a fee to all those who use public streets or parks for "free speech" purposes to defray costs of cleaning up, etc.? See *Cox v. New Hampshire.* Are these situations distinguishable from *Harper* because they do not simply condition the right on payment of a tax but reimburse the state for costs? Compare *Griffin, Douglas* and *Lubin v. Panish* (Part I, C supra).

(c) For further consideration, see note 2 after *Rodriguez,* Part IV infra. See generally Brudno, *Poverty, Inequality, and the Law* (1976).

IV. CONFINEMENT OF "FUNDAMENTAL RIGHTS"

DANDRIDGE v. WILLIAMS, 397 U.S. 471, 90 S.Ct. 1153, 25 L.Ed.2d 491 (1970): Maryland's Aid to Families with Dependent Children program gave most eligible families their computed "standard of need," but imposed a "maximum limitation" on the total amount any family could receive. The Court, per STEWART, J., held this did not violate equal protection: "[H]ere we deal with state regulation in the social and economic field, not affecting freedoms guaranteed by the Bill of Rights, and claimed to violate the Fourteenth Amendment only because the regulation results in some disparity in grants of welfare payments to the largest AFDC families.[16] In [this area] a State does not violate [equal protection] merely because the classifications made by its laws are imperfect." "It is enough that the State's action be rationally based and free from invidious discrimination."

"To be sure, [many cases] enunciating this [standard] have in the main involved state regulation of business or industry. The administration of public welfare assistance, by contrast, involves the most basic economic needs of impoverished human beings, [but] we can find no basis for applying a different constitutional standard. [By] combining a limit on the recipient's grant with permission to retain money earned, without reduction in the amount of the grant, Maryland provides an incentive to seek gainful employment. And by keeping the maximum family AFDC grants to the minimum wage a steadily employed head of a household receives, the State maintains some semblance of an equitable balance between families on welfare and those supported by an employed breadwinner.

"It is true that in some AFDC families there may be no person who is employable. It is also true that with respect to AFDC families whose determined standard of need is below the regulatory maximum, [the] employment incentive is absent. But the Equal Protection Clause does not require that a State must choose between attacking every aspect of a problem or not attacking the problem at all. [T]he intractable economic, social, and even philosophical problems presented by public welfare assistance programs are not the business of this Court."

MARSHALL, J., joined by Brennan, J., dissented:[a] "[T]he only distinction between those children with respect to whom assistance is granted and those [denied] is the size of the family into which the child permits himself to be born. [This] is grossly underinclusive in terms of the class which the AFDC program was designed to assist, namely *all* needy dependent children, [and requires] a persuasive justification * * *.

"The Court never undertakes to inquire for such a justification; rather it avoids the task by focusing upon the abstract dichotomy between two different approaches to equal protection problems which have been utilized by this Court.

"[The] cases relied on by the Court, in which a 'mere rationality' test was actually used, e.g., *Williamson v. Lee Optical Co.* [Sec. 1 supra], [involve] regulation of business interests. The extremes to which the Court has gone in dreaming up rational bases for state regulation in that area may in many instances be ascribed to a healthy revulsion from the Court's earlier excesses in using the Constitution to protect interests which have more than enough power to protect themselves in the legislative halls.[b] This case, involving the literally

16. Cf. *Shapiro,* where, by contrast, the Court found state interference with the constitutionally protected freedom of interstate travel.

a. Douglas, J., dissented on the ground (agreed to also by Marshall and Brennan, JJ.) that the Maryland law was inconsistent with the Social Security Act.

b. Compare Wilkinson, *The Supreme Court, the Equal Protection Clause, and the Three Faces of Constitutional Equality,* 61 Va. L.Rev. 945, 1008–09 (1975): "*Lochner* and cases like it arose precisely because business was not getting its way, because what were then thought traditional employer prerogatives were succumbing to a rising tide of social and regulatory legislation. Conversely, [the] legislative trend ever since the New Deal has been running more and more toward social welfare programs, [whose] stated purpose is to help the poor and less well off. Indiscrimivital interests of a powerless minority—poor families without breadwinners—is far removed from the area of business regulation, as the Court concedes. * * *

"In my view, equal protection analysis of this case is not appreciably advanced by the a priori definition of a 'right,' fundamental [and thus invoking the "compelling" test] or otherwise.[14] Rather, concentration must be placed upon the character of the classification in question, the relative importance to individuals in the class discriminated against of the governmental benefits which they do not receive, and the asserted state interests in support of the classification. * * *

"It is the individual interests here [that] most clearly distinguish this case from the 'business regulation' [cases]. AFDC support to needy dependent children provides the stuff which sustains those children's lives: food, clothing, shelter. And this Court has already recognized [that] when a benefit, even a 'gratuitous' benefit, is necessary to sustain life, stricter constitutional standards, both procedural[17] and substantive,[18] are applied to the deprivation of that benefit.

"Nor is the distinction upon which the deprivation is here based—the distinction between large and small families—one which readily commends [itself]. Indeed, governmental discrimination between children on the basis of a factor over which they have no control [bears] some resemblance to the classification between legitimate and illegitimate children which we condemned [in Sec. 3, III supra]."

On examination, the asserted state interests were either "arbitrary," impermissible, of "minimum rationality," "drastically overinclusive," or "grossly un-

nate application of [Marshall, J.'s] position, therefore, would invite the thought that the major change since *Lochner* is that the Court has switched political sides."

Is neutrality between these political sides desirable? Consider Balkin, *The Footnote,* 83 Nw.U.L.Rev. 275, 311: "The lesson of [repudiating] *Lochner* was that courts should not hinder legislatures from pursuing human rights through alteration of property rights; and that the state was responsible for the reproduction of disparities in economic power achieved through maintenance of the status quo. [By] understanding [the move away from *Lochner*], as the strict separation of political and economic liberty[,] the pluralist faith of *Carolene Products* reintroduced, at a new level, the very evil that *West Coast Hotel* found in *Lochner.* If the *Lochner* court had seen differences in economic status as natural and not seriously affecting human rights, so now *Carolene Products* saw differences in political power stemming from differences in economic power as prepolitical and not seriously threatening the purity of the democratic process."

14. Appellees do argue that their "fundamental rights" are infringed [and cite] *Skinner* for the proposition that the "right of procreation" is fundamental. [B]ut the effect of the maximum grant regulation upon the right of procreation is marginal and indirect at best, totally unlike the compulsory sterilization law [in] *Skinner.*

[T]he Court's insistence that equal protection analysis turns on the basis of a closed category of "fundamental rights" involves a curious value judgment. It is certainly difficult to believe that a person whose very survival is at stake would be comforted by the knowledge that his "fundamental" rights are preserved intact. * * *

17. See *Goldberg v. Kelly.*

18. [See] *Kirk v. Board of Regents,* 273 Cal. App.2d 430, 440–441, 78 Cal.Rptr. 260, 266–267 (1969), appeal dismissed, 396 U.S. 554, 90 S.Ct. 754, 24 L.Ed.2d 747 (1970), upholding a one-year residency requirement for tuition-free graduate education at state university, and distinguishing *Shapiro* on the ground that it "involved the immediate and pressing need for preservation of life and health of persons unable to live without public assistance, and their dependent children."

These cases and those cited n. 17, supra, suggest that whether or not there is a constitutional "right" to subsistence (as to which see n. 14, supra), deprivations of benefits necessary for subsistence will receive closer constitutional scrutiny, under both the Due Process and Equal Protection Clauses, than will deprivation of less essential forms of governmental entitlements.

derinclusive." "The existence of [other] alternatives [to satisfy asserted state interests] does not, of course, conclusively establish the invalidity of the maximum grant regulation. It is certainly relevant, however, in appraising the overall interest of the State in the maintenance of the regulation [against] a fundamental constitutional challenge." [c]

LINDSEY v. NORMET, 405 U.S. 56, 92 S.Ct. 862, 31 L.Ed.2d 36 (1972), per WHITE, J., employing the "traditional" equal protection standard, upheld an Oregon statute permitting a landlord to bring an expedited action for possession under certain circumstances. The Court rejected the contention "that the 'need for decent shelter' and the 'right to retain peaceful possession of one's home' are fundamental interests which are particularly important to the poor and which may be trenched upon only after the State demonstrates some superior interest": "We do not denigrate the importance of decent, safe and sanitary housing. But the Constitution does not provide judicial remedies for every social and economic ill. We are unable to perceive in that document any constitutional guarantee of access to dwellings of a particular quality or any recognition of the right of a tenant to occupy the real property of his landlord beyond the term of his [lease]. Absent constitutional mandate, the assurance of adequate housing and the definition of landlord-tenant relationships are legislative not judicial functions." Douglas, J., dissented on due process grounds; Brennan, J., dissented on procedural grounds; Powell and Rehnquist, JJ., did not participate.

The statute also required tenants who lost at trial to obtain special security for payment to the landlord, if he won on appeal. The Court found this "arbitrary and irrational" discrimination violative of equal protection: "The claim that the double-bond requirement operates to screen out frivolous appeals [not] only bars nonfrivolous appeals by those who are unable to post the bond but also allows meritless appeals by others who can afford the bond." [d] Douglas, J., agreed, but on the theory that housing was "fundamental" and thus the special statutory treatment must be justified by a "compelling interest."

SAN ANTONIO IND. SCHOOL DIST. v. RODRIGUEZ

411 U.S. 1, 93 S.Ct. 1278, 36 L.Ed.2d 16 (1973).

JUSTICE POWELL delivered the opinion of the Court.

This suit attacking the Texas system of financing public education was initiated by Mexican-American parents [as] a class action on behalf of school children throughout the State who are members of minority groups or who are poor and reside in school districts having a low property tax base. * * *

Recognizing the need for increased state funding to help offset disparities in local spending [because of sizable differences in the value of assessable property

c. See also *Richardson v. Belcher*, 404 U.S. 78, 92 S.Ct. 254, 30 L.Ed.2d 231 (1971), per Stewart, J., upholding a provision of the Social Security Act reducing disability benefits for those who receive state worker's compensation—but not for those who receive compensation from private insurance or from tort claim awards—as "rationally based." Douglas, J., and Marshall, J., joined by Brennan, J., dissented.

See generally Krislov, *The OEO Lawyers Fail to Constitutionalize a Right to Welfare: A Study in the Uses and Limits of the Judicial Process*, 58 Minn.L.Rev. 211 (1973).

d. Consider Note, 58 Va.L.Rev. 930, 941 (1972): "[T]hat the state's screening device for frivolous appeals is overinclusive and underinclusive does not in itself render the classification 'wholly irrelevant' to the goal of deterring frivolous appeals. [The] Court's analysis of the double-bond provision is essentially a balancing approach disguised in traditional 'rational relationship' terminology."

between local school districts,] the state legislature [established the] Minimum Foundation School Program [which] accounts for approximately half of the total educational expenditures in Texas. [It] calls for state and local contributions to a fund earmarked specifically for teacher salaries, operating expenses, and transportation costs. The State [finances] approximately [80%]. The districts' share, known as the Local Fund Assignment, is apportioned among the school districts under a formula designed to reflect each district's relative taxpaying ability. * * *

The school district in which appellees reside, [Edgewood,] has been compared throughout this litigation with the Alamo Heights [District. Edgewood] is situated in the core-city sector of San Antonio in a residential neighborhood that has little commercial or industrial property. [A]pproximately 90% of the student population is Mexican-American and over 6% is Negro. The average assessed property value per pupil is $5,960—the lowest in the metropolitan area—and the median family income ($4,686) is also the lowest. At an equalized tax rate of $1.05 per $100 of assessed property—the highest in the metropolitan area—the district contributed $26 to the education of each child for the 1967–1968 school year above its Local Fund Assignment for the Minimum Foundation Program. The Foundation Program contributed $222 per pupil for a state-local total of $248. Federal funds added another $108 for a total of $356 per pupil.

Alamo Heights is the most affluent school district in San Antonio. [Its] school population [has] only 18% Mexican-Americans and less than 1% Negroes. The assessed property value per pupil exceeds $49,000 and the median family income is $8,001. In 1967–1968 the local tax rate of $.85 per $100 of valuation yielded $333 per pupil over and above its contribution to the Foundation Program. Coupled with the $225 provided from that Program, the district was able to supply $558 per student. Supplemented by a $36 per pupil grant from federal sources, Alamo Heights spent $594 per pupil.

[M]ore recent partial statistics indicate that [the] trend of increasing state aid has been significant. For the 1970–1971 school year, the Foundation School Program allotment for Edgewood was $356 per [pupil and] Alamo Heights [received] $491 per [pupil].[35] These recent figures also reveal the extent to which these two districts' allotments were funded from their own required contributions to the Local Fund Assignment. Alamo Heights, because of its relative wealth, was required to contribute out of its local property tax collections approximately $100 per pupil, or about 20% of its Foundation grant. Edgewood, on the other hand, paid only $8.46 per pupil, which is about 2.4% of its grant. [Finding] that wealth is a "suspect" classification and that education is a "fundamental" interest, the District Court held that the Texas system could be sustained only if the State could show that it was premised upon some compelling state interest. * * *

35. [I]t is apparent that Alamo Heights has enjoyed a larger gain [due] to the emphasis in the State's allocation formula on the guaranteed minimum salaries for teachers. Higher salaries are guaranteed to teachers having more years of experience and possessing more advanced degrees. Therefore, Alamo Heights, which has a greater percentage of experienced personnel with advanced degrees, receives more State support. * * * Because more dollars have been given to districts that already spend more per pupil, such Foundation formulas have been described as "anti-equalizing." The formula, however, is anti-equalizing only if viewed in absolute terms. The percentage disparity between the two Texas districts is diminished substantially by State aid. Alamo Heights derived in 1967–1968 almost 13 times as much money from local taxes as Edgewood did. The State aid grants to each district in 1970–1971 lowered the ratio to approximately two to [one].

II. [The] wealth discrimination discovered [is] quite unlike any of the forms of wealth discrimination heretofore reviewed by this Court. [The] individuals who constituted the class discriminated against in our prior cases shared two distinguishing characteristics: because of their impecunity they were completely unable to pay for some desired benefit, and as a consequence, they sustained an absolute deprivation of a meaningful opportunity to enjoy that benefit [discussing *Griffin v. Illinois* and *Bullock v. Carter*]. *Douglas v. California* [provides] no relief for those on whom the burdens of paying for a criminal defense are, relatively speaking, great but not insurmountable. Nor does it deal with relative differences in the quality of counsel acquired by the less wealthy. [And] *Williams* and *Tate* [do] not touch on the question whether equal protection is denied to persons with relatively less money on whom designated fines impose heavier burdens. * * *

[Even] a cursory examination however, demonstrates that neither of the two distinguishing characteristics of wealth classifications can be found here. First, [there] is reason to believe that the poorest families are not necessarily clustered in the poorest property districts. A [recent] Connecticut study found, not surprisingly, that the poor were clustered around commercial and industrial areas—those same areas that provide the most attractive sources of property tax income for school districts. Whether a similar pattern would be discovered in Texas is not known, but there is no basis on the record [for] assuming [otherwise].

Second, [lack] of personal resources has not occasioned an absolute deprivation of the desired benefit. The argument here is not that the children [are] receiving no public education; rather, it is that they are receiving a poorer quality education [than] children in districts having more assessable wealth. [A] sufficient answer to appellees' argument is that at least where wealth is involved the Equal Protection Clause does not require absolute equality or precisely equal advantages. Nor indeed, in view of the infinite variables affecting the educational process, can any system assure equal quality of education except in the most relative sense. Texas asserts that the Minimum Foundation Program provides an "adequate" education for all children in the State. [No] proof was offered at trial persuasively discrediting or refuting the State's assertion. * * * [60]

[Appellees] sought to prove that a direct correlation exists between the wealth of families within each district and the expenditures therein for education. [But] appellees' proof [fails].

This brings us [to] the third way in which the classification scheme might be defined—*district* wealth discrimination. Since the only correlation indicated by the evidence is between district property wealth and expenditures, it may be argued that discrimination might be found without regard to the individual income characteristics of district residents. * * *

60. [If] elementary and secondary education were made available by the State only to those able to pay a tuition assessed against each pupil, there would be a clearly defined class of "poor" people—definable in terms of their inability to pay the prescribed sum—who would be absolutely precluded from receiving an education. That case would present a far more compelling set of circumstances for judicial assistance than [this one].

[Does this extend to higher education as well? See Strickman, *The Tuition-Poor, the Public University, and Equal Protection,* 29 U.Fla.L.Rev. 595 (1977). For the view that "*Dandridge* and its *progeny*" do not apply to situations involving "a total cut-off of welfare that approaches denial of subsistence," see Note, *Intermediate Equal Protection Scrutiny of Welfare Laws that Deny Subsistence,* 132 U.Pa.L.Rev. 1547 (1984).]

However described, it is clear that appellees' suit asks this Court to extend its most exacting scrutiny to review a system that allegedly discriminates against a large, diverse, and amorphous class, unified only by the common factor of residence in districts that happen to have less taxable wealth than other districts. The system of alleged discrimination and the class it defines have none of the traditional indicia of suspectness: the class is not saddled with such disabilities, or subjected to such a history of purposeful unequal treatment, or relegated to such a position of political powerlessness as to command extraordinary protection from the majoritarian political process.

We thus conclude that the Texas system does not operate to the peculiar disadvantage of any suspect class. But [recognizing] that this Court has never heretofore held that wealth discrimination alone provides an adequate basis for invoking strict scrutiny, appellees [also] assert that the State's system impermissibly interferes with the exercise of a "fundamental" right [requiring] the strict standard of judicial review. * * *

Nothing this Court holds today in any way detracts from our historic dedication to public education. [But] the importance of a service performed by the State does not determine whether it must be regarded as fundamental for purposes of examination under the Equal Protection Clause. [In *Shapiro,* the] right to interstate travel had long been recognized as a right of constitutional significance, and the Court's decision therefore did not require an ad hoc determination as to the social or economic importance of that right. *Lindsey* [as well as *Dandridge*] firmly reiterates that social importance is not the critical determinant for subjecting state legislation to strict scrutiny. * * *

The lesson of these cases [is that it] is not the province of this Court to create substantive constitutional rights in the name of guaranteeing equal protection of the laws. Thus the key to discovering whether education is "fundamental" is not to be found in comparisons of the relative societal significance of education as opposed to subsistence or housing [or] by weighing whether education is as important as the right to travel. Rather, the answer lies in assessing whether there is a right to education explicitly or implicitly guaranteed by the Constitution. *Dunn;*[74] *Skinner.*[76]

Education, of course, is not among the rights afforded explicit protection under [the] Constitution. Nor do we find any basis for saying it is implicitly so protected.[a] [But] appellees [contend] that education is distinguishable from other services and benefits provided by the State because it bears a peculiarly

74. *Dunn* fully canvasses this Court's voting rights cases and explains that "this Court has made clear that a citizen has a *constitutionally protected right* to participate in elections on an equal basis with other citizens in the jurisdiction." (emphasis supplied). The constitutional underpinnings of [this right] can no longer be doubted even though, as the Court noted in *Harper,* "the right to vote in state elections is nowhere expressly mentioned."

76. *Skinner* applied the standard of close scrutiny to a state law permitting forced sterilization of "habitual criminals." Implicit in the Court's opinion is the recognition that the right of procreation is among the rights of personal privacy protected under the Constitution. See *Roe v. Wade.*

a. For the view that education *is* "fundamental," see Coons, Clune & Sugarman, *Educational Opportunity: A Workable Constitutional Test for State Financial Structures,* 57 Calif.L.Rev. 305 (1969). As to housing, see Sager, *Tight Little Islands: Exclusionary Zoning, Equal Protection, and the Indigent,* 21 Stan.L.Rev. 767 (1969). As to various municipal services, see Ratner, *Inter-Neighborhood Denials of Equal Protection in the Provision of Municipal Services,* 4 Harv.Civ.Rts.—Civ.Lib. L.Rev. 1 (1968); Abascal, *Municipal Services and Equal Protection: Variations on a Theme by Griffin v. Illinois,* 20 Hast.L.J. 1367 (1969).

Massachusetts Bd. of Retirement v. Murgia (1976), Sec. 3, IV supra, held that a "right of governmental employment" is *not* fundamental.

close relationship to other rights and liberties accorded protection under the Constitution [in that] it is essential to the effective exercise of First Amendment freedoms and to intelligent utilization of the right to vote. In asserting a nexus between speech and education, appellees urge that the right to speak is meaningless unless the speaker is capable of articulating his thoughts intelligently and persuasively. [A] similar line of reasoning is pursued with respect to the right to [vote]: a voter cannot cast his ballot intelligently unless his reading skills and thought processes have been adequately developed.

We need not dispute any of these propositions. [Yet] we have never presumed to possess either the ability or the authority to guarantee to the citizenry the most *effective* speech or the most *informed* electoral choice. That these may be desirable goals [is] not to be doubted. [But] they are not values to be implemented by judicial intrusion into otherwise legitimate state activities.

Even if it were conceded that some identifiable quantum of education is a constitutionally protected prerequisite to the meaningful exercise of either right, we have no indication that the [present] system fails to provide each child with an opportunity to acquire the basic minimal skills [necessary]. Furthermore, the logical limitations on appellees' nexus theory are difficult * * *. Empirical examination might well buttress an assumption that the ill-fed, ill-clothed, and ill-housed are among the most ineffective participants in the political process and that they derive the least enjoyment from the benefits of the First Amendment. * * *

[The] present case, in another basic sense, is significantly different from any of the cases in which the Court has applied strict scrutiny [to] legislation touching upon constitutionally protected rights. [These] involved legislation which "deprived," "infringed," or "interfered" with the free exercise of some such fundamental personal right or liberty. [Every] step leading to the establishment of the system Texas utilizes today [was] implemented in an effort to *extend* public education and to improve its quality. Of course, every reform that benefits some more than others may be criticized for what it fails to accomplish. But we think it plain that, in substance, the thrust of the Texas system is affirmative and reformatory and, therefore, should be scrutinized under judicial principles sensitive to the nature of the State's efforts and to the rights reserved to the States under the Constitution.

[A] century of Supreme Court adjudication under the Equal Protection Clause affirmatively supports the application of the traditional standard of review, which requires only that the State's system be shown to bear some rational relationship to legitimate state purposes. This case represents [a] direct attack on the way in which Texas has chosen to raise and disburse state and local tax revenues. [This] Court has often admonished against such interferences with the State's fiscal policies under the Equal Protection Clause [and] we continue to acknowledge that the Justices of this Court lack both the expertise and the familiarity with local problems so necessary to the making of wise decisions with respect to the raising and disposition of public revenues. Yet we are urged to direct the States either to alter drastically the present system or to throw out the property tax altogether in favor of some other form of taxation. No scheme of taxation [has] yet been devised which is free of all discriminatory impact. In such a complex arena in which no perfect alternatives exist, the Court does well not to impose too rigorous a standard of scrutiny lest all local fiscal schemes become subjects of criticism under the Equal Protection Clause.

[T]his case also involves the most persistent and difficult questions of educational policy, another area in which this Court's lack of specialized knowledge and experience counsels against premature interference with the informed judgments made at the state and local levels. [On] even the most basic questions in this area the scholars and educational experts are divided. Indeed, one of the hottest sources of controversy concerns the extent to which there is a demonstrable correlation between educational expenditures and the quality of education—an assumed correlation underlying virtually every legal conclusion drawn by the District [Court].

It must be remembered also that every claim arising under the Equal Protection Clause has implications for the relationship between national and state power under our federal system. [I]t would be difficult to imagine a case having a greater potential impact on our federal system than the one now before us, in which we are urged to abrogate systems of financing public education presently in existence in virtually every State. * * *

III. [The] State's contribution, under the Minimum Foundation Program, was designed to provide an adequate minimum educational offering in every school in the State. [T]o fulfill its local Fund Assignment, every district must impose an ad valorem tax on property located within its borders. The Fund Assignment was designed to remain sufficiently low to assure that each district would have some ability to provide a more enriched educational program. [In] large measure, these additional local revenues are devoted to paying higher salaries to more teachers. Therefore, the primary distinguishing attributes of schools in property-affluent districts are lower pupil-teacher ratios and higher salary schedules.[101] [In] part, local control [means] freedom to devote more money to the education of one's children. Equally important, however, is the opportunity it offers for participation in the decision-making process that determines how those local tax dollars will be spent. [No] area of social concern stands to profit more from a multiplicity of viewpoints and from a diversity of approaches than does public education.

[While] it is no doubt true that reliance on local property taxation for school revenues provides less freedom of choice with respect to expenditures for some districts than for others,[107] the existence of "some inequality" in the manner in which the State's rationale is achieved is not alone a sufficient basis for striking down the entire system. [Nor] must the financing system fail because, as appellees suggest, other methods of satisfying the State's interest, which occasion "less drastic" disparities in expenditures, might be conceived. Only where state action impinges on the exercise of fundamental constitutional rights or liberties must it be found to have chosen the least restrictive alternative. It is also well

101. [As] previously noted, the extent to which the quality of education varies with expenditure per pupil is debated inconclusively by the most thoughtful students of public education. While all would agree that there is a correlation up to the point of providing the recognized essentials, [the] issues of greatest disagreement include the effect on the quality of education of pupil-teacher ratios and of higher teacher [salaries].

107. Mr. Justice White suggests in his dissent that the Texas system violates [equal protection] because the means it has selected to effectuate its interest in local autonomy fail to guarantee complete freedom of choice to every district. He places special emphasis on the statutory provision that establishes a maximum rate of $1.50 per $100 valuation at which a local school district may tax for school maintenance. The maintenance rate in Edgewood when this case was litigated [was] $.55 per $100, barely one-third of the allowable rate. (The tax rate of $1.05 per $100 is the equalized rate for maintenance and for the retirement of bonds.) Appellees do not claim that the ceiling presently bars desired tax increases in Edgewood or in any other Texas district. Therefore, the constitutionality of that statutory provision is not before [us].

to remember that even those districts that have reduced ability to make free decisions with respect to how much they spend on education still retain under the present system a large measure of authority as to how available funds will be allocated. They further enjoy the power to make numerous other decisions with respect to the operation of the schools.[108] The people of Texas may be justified in believing [that] along with increased control of the purse strings at the state level will go increased control over local policies.

[A]ny scheme of local taxation—indeed the very existence of identifiable local governmental units—requires the establishment of jurisdictional boundaries that are inevitably arbitrary. It is equally inevitable that some localities are going to be blessed with more taxable assets than others. Nor is local wealth a static quantity. Changes [may] result from any number of events, some of which local residents can and do influence. For instance, commercial and industrial enterprises may be encouraged to locate within a district by various actions—public and private.

Moreover, if local taxation for local expenditure is an unconstitutional method of providing for education then it may be an equally impermissible means of providing other necessary services customarily financed largely from local property taxes, including local police and fire protection, public health and hospitals, and public utility facilities of various kinds. [It has] never been within the constitutional prerogative of this Court to nullify statewide measures for financing public services merely because the burdens or benefits thereof fall unevenly depending upon the relative wealth of the political subdivisions in which citizens live.

[In] its essential characteristics the Texas plan for financing public education reflects what many educators for a half century have thought was an enlightened approach to a problem for which there is no perfect solution. We are unwilling to assume for ourselves a level of wisdom superior to that of legislators, scholars, and educational authorities in 49 States, especially where the alternatives proposed are only recently conceived and nowhere yet tested.

* * *

IV. [T]his Court's action today is not to be viewed as placing its judicial imprimatur on the status quo. The need is apparent for reform in tax systems which may well have relied too long and too heavily on the local property tax. And certainly innovative new thinking as to public education, its methods and its funding, is necessary to assure both a higher level of quality and greater uniformity of opportunity. These matters merit the continued attention of the scholars who already have contributed much by their challenges. But the ultimate solutions must come from the lawmakers and from the democratic pressures of those who elect them.

Reversed.[b]

JUSTICE BRENNAN, dissenting.

Although I agree with my Brother White that the Texas statutory scheme is devoid of any rational basis, [I] also record my disagreement with the Court's

108. Mr. Justice Marshall['s] assertion, that genuine local control does not exist in Texas, simply cannot be supported. It is abundantly refuted by the elaborate statutory division of responsibilities set out in the Texas Education Code. Although policy decision-making and supervision in certain areas are reserved to the State, the day-to-day authority over the "management and control" of all public elementary and secondary schools is squarely placed on the local school boards [listing a number of their specific powers].

b. The concurring opinion of Stewart, J., who joined the Court's opinion, is omitted.

rather distressing assertion that a right may be deemed "fundamental" for the purposes of equal protection analysis only if it is "explicitly or implicitly guaranteed by the Constitution." As my Brother Marshall convincingly demonstrates our prior cases stand for the proposition that "fundamentality" is, in large measure, a function of the right's importance in terms of the effectuation of those rights which are in fact constitutionally guaranteed. * * *

JUSTICE WHITE, with whom JUSTICE DOUGLAS and JUSTICE BRENNAN join, dissenting.

[T]his case would be quite different if it were true that the Texas system, while insuring minimum educational expenditures in every district through state funding, extends a meaningful option to all local districts to increase their per-pupil [expenditures. But for] districts with a low per-pupil real estate tax base [the] Texas system utterly fails to extend a realistic choice to parents, because the property tax, which is the only revenue-raising mechanism extended to school districts, is practically and legally unavailable. * * *

In order to equal the highest yield in any other Bexar County district, Alamo Heights would be required to tax at the rate of 68¢ per $100 of assessed valuation. Edgewood would be required to tax at the prohibitive rate of $5.76 per $100. But state law places a $1.50 per $100 ceiling on the maintenance tax [rate]. Requiring the State to establish only that unequal treatment is in furtherance of a permissible goal, without also requiring the State to show that the means chosen to effectuate that goal are rationally related to its achievement, makes equal protection analysis no more than an empty gesture. * * *

JUSTICE MARSHALL, with whom JUSTICE DOUGLAS, concurs, dissenting.

[T]he majority's holding can only be seen as a retreat from our historic commitment to equality of educational opportunity. [The issue] is not whether Texas is doing its best to ameliorate the worst features of a discriminatory scheme, but rather whether the scheme itself is in fact unconstitutionally discriminatory.[35] Authorities concerned with educational quality no doubt disagree as to the significance of variations in per pupil spending. [But it] is an inescapable fact that if one district has more funds available per pupil than another district, the former will have greater choice in educational [planning].

At the very least, in view of the substantial interdistrict disparities in funding, [the] burden of proving that these disparities do not in fact affect the quality of children's education must fall upon the appellants. Yet [they] have argued no more than that the relationship is ambiguous. * * *

Nor can I accept the appellants' apparent suggestion [that equal protection] cannot be offended by substantially unequal state treatment of persons who are similarly situated so long as the State provides everyone with some unspecified amount of education which evidently is "enough." [The] Equal Protection Clause is not addressed to the minimal sufficiency but rather to the unjustifiable inequalities of state action. [Even] if the Equal Protection Clause encompassed some theory of constitutional adequacy, discrimination in the provision of

35. * * * Texas' financing scheme is hardly remedial legislation of the type for which we have previously shown substantial tolerance. Such legislation may in fact extend the vote to "persons who otherwise would be denied it by state law," *Katzenbach v. Morgan,* or it may eliminate the evils of the private bail bondsman, *Schilb v. Kuebel* [Part I, B supra]. But those are instances in which a legislative body has sought to remedy problems for which it cannot be said to have been directly responsible. By contrast, [it] is the State's own scheme which has caused the funding problem, and, thus viewed, that scheme can hardly be deemed remedial.

educational opportunity would certainly seem to be a poor candidate for its application. Neither the majority nor appellants informs us how judicially manageable standards are to be derived for determining how much education is "enough" to excuse constitutional discrimination. [In] light of the data introduced before the District Court, the conclusion that the school children of property poor districts constitute a sufficient class for our purposes seems indisputable to me. [Whether] this discrimination, against [them] is violative of the Equal Protection Clause is the question to which we must now turn.

[The] Court apparently seeks to establish [that] equal protection cases fall into one of two neat categories which dictate the appropriate standard of review—strict scrutiny or mere rationality. But [a] principled reading of what this Court has done reveals that it has applied a spectrum of standards [which] clearly comprehends variations in the degree of care with which the Court will scrutinize particular classifications, depending [on] the constitutional and societal importance of the interest adversely affected and the recognized invidiousness of the basis upon which the particular classification is drawn.[c] * * *

I therefore cannot accept the majority's labored efforts to demonstrate that fundamental interests, which call for strict scrutiny of the challenged classification, encompass only established rights which we are somehow bound to recognize from the text of the Constitution itself. * * *[59]

I would like to know where the Constitution guarantees the right to procreate, *Skinner,* or the right to vote in state elections, e.g., *Reynolds v. Sims,*[60] or the right to an appeal from a criminal conviction, e.g., *Griffin.*[61] These are instances in which, due to the importance of the interests at stake, the Court has displayed a strong concern with the existence of discriminatory state treatment. But the Court has [never] indicated that these are interests which independently enjoy full-blown constitutional protection. * * *

The majority is, of course, correct when it suggests that the process of determining which interests are fundamental is a difficult one. But I do not think the problem is insurmountable. [The task] should be to determine the extent to which constitutionally guaranteed rights are dependent on interests not mentioned in the Constitution. As the nexus between the specific constitutional guarantee and the nonconstitutional interest draws closer, the nonconstitutional interest becomes more fundamental and the degree of judicial scrutiny

c. In *Vlandis v. Kline,* Sec. 5 infra,—decided after *Rodriquez* —White, J., stated that he, too, agreed that this has been the Court's approach in applying the equal protection clause. See also the dissent of Marshall, J., joined by Brennan and Blackmun, JJ., in *Cleburne v. Cleburne Living Center, Inc.,* Sec. 3, IV supra.

59. Indeed, the Court's theory would render the established concept of fundamental interests in the context of equal protection analysis superfluous, for the substantive constitutional right itself requires that this Court strictly scrutinize any asserted state interest for restricting or denying access to any particular guaranteed right.

60. It is interesting that in its effort to reconcile the state voting rights cases with its theory of fundamentality the majority can muster nothing more than the contention that "[t]he constitutional underpinnings of the *right to equal treatment in the voting process* can no longer be doubted." If, by this, the Court intends to recognize a substantive constitutional "right to equal treatment in the voting process" independent of the Equal Protection Clause, the source of such a right is certainly a mystery to me.

61. It is true that *Griffin* and *Douglas* also involved discrimination against [indigents]. But, as the majority points out, the Court has never deemed wealth discrimination alone to be sufficient to require strict judicial scrutiny; rather, such review of wealth classifications has been applied only where the discrimination affects an important individual interest, see, e.g., *Harper.* Thus, I believe *Griffin* and *Douglas* can only be understood as premised on a recognition of the fundamental importance of the criminal appellate process.

applied when the interest is infringed on a discriminatory basis must be adjusted accordingly. * * * Procreation is now understood to be important because of its interaction with the established constitutional right of privacy. The exercise of the state franchise is closely tied to basic civil and political rights inherent in the First Amendment. And access to criminal appellate processes enhances the integrity of the range of rights implicit in the Fourteenth Amendment guarantee of due process of law. Only if we closely protect the related interests from state discrimination do we ultimately ensure the integrity of the constitutional guarantee itself. This is the real lesson that must be taken from our previous decisions involving interests deemed to be fundamental.

The effect of the interaction of individual interests with established constitutional guarantees upon the degree of care exercised by this Court in reviewing state discrimination affecting such interests is amply illustrated [by] *Eisenstadt v. Baird,* [p. 425 supra]. [The] Court purported to test the statute under its traditional standard [but] clearly did not adhere to these highly tolerant standards of traditional rational review. [Yet] I think the Court's action was entirely appropriate for access to and use of contraceptives bears a close relationship to the individual's constitutional right of privacy.

A similar process of analysis with respect to the invidiousness of the basis on which a particular classification is drawn has also influenced the Court as to the appropriate degree of scrutiny to be accorded any particular case. [It] may be that all of [the] considerations, which make for particular judicial solicitude in the face of discrimination on the basis of race, nationality, or alienage, do not coalesce—or at least not to the same degree—in other forms of discrimination. Nevertheless, these considerations have undoubtedly influenced the care with which the Court has scrutinized other forms of discrimination. [Thus], in *Reed v. Reed,* [Sec. 3, II, A supra], the Court [resorted] to a more stringent standard of equal protection review than that employed in cases involving commercial matters. [T]he particularly invidious character of the classification caused the Court to pause and scrutinize with more than traditional care the rationality of state discrimination. Discrimination on the basis [of] sex posed for the Court the spectre of forms of discrimination which it implicitly recognized to have deep social and legal roots without necessarily having any basis in actual differences. Still, the Court's sensitivity to the invidiousness of the basis for discrimination is perhaps most apparent in its decisions protecting the interests of children born out of wedlock from discriminatory state action. [Sec. 3, III supra].

[In] the context of economic interests, we find that discriminatory state action is almost always sustained for such interests are generally far removed from constitutional guarantees. [But] the situation differs markedly when discrimination against important individual interests with constitutional implications and against particularly disadvantaged or powerless classes is involved.[d] The majority suggests, however, that a variable standard of review would give this Court the appearance of a "superlegislature." I cannot agree. Such an approach seems to me a part of the guarantees of our Constitution and of the historic experiences with oppression of and discrimination against discrete,

d. In *Massachusetts Bd. of Retirement v. Murgia,* Marshall, J., further explained his approach: "[T]here remain rights, not now classified as 'fundamental,' that remain vital to the flourishing of a free society, and classes, not now classified as 'suspect,' that are unfairly burdened by invidious discrimination unrelated to the individual worth of their members. Whatever we call these rights and classes, we simply cannot forgo all judicial protection against discriminatory legislation bearing upon them, but for the rare instances when the legislative choice can be termed 'wholly irrelevant' to the legislative goal."

powerless minorities which underlie that Document. In truth, the Court itself will be open to the criticism raised by the majority so long as it continues on its present course of effectively selecting in private which cases will be afforded special consideration without acknowledging the true basis of its action. [Such] obfuscated action may be appropriate to a political body such as a legislature, but it is not appropriate to this Court. Open debate of the bases for the Court's action is essential to the rationality and consistency of our decisionmaking process. * * *

[It] is true that this Court has never deemed the provision of free public education to be required by the Constitution. [But] the fundamental importance of education is amply indicated by the prior decisions of this Court, by the unique status accorded public education by our society, and by the close relationship between education and some of our most basic constitutional [values].

Education directly affects the ability of a child to exercise his First Amendment interests both as a source and as a receiver of information and [ideas]. Indeed, it has frequently been suggested that education is the dominant factor affecting political consciousness and participation.[72] * * * [74] [T]he issue is neither provision of the most *effective* speech nor of the most *informed* vote. Appellees do not now seek the best education Texas might provide [but] an end to state [discrimination].[75]

[We] are told that in every prior case involving a wealth classification, the members of the disadvantaged class have "shared two distinguishing characteristics: because of their impecunity they were completely unable to pay for some desired benefit, and as a consequence, they sustained an absolute deprivation of a meaningful opportunity to enjoy that benefit." I cannot agree. * * *

In *Harper,* the Court struck down [a] poll tax in toto; it did not order merely that those too poor to pay the tax be exempted; complete impecunity clearly was not determinative. [In] *Griffin* and *Douglas* [t]he right of appeal itself was not absolutely denied to those too poor to pay; but because of the cost of a transcript and of counsel, the appeal was a substantially less meaningful right for the poor than for the rich. [This] clearly encompassed degrees of discrimination on the basis of wealth which do not amount to outright denial of the affected right or interest.[77]

72. [I]t should be obvious that the political process, like most other aspects of social intercourse, is to some degree competitive. It is thus of little benefit to an individual from a property poor district to have "enough" education if those around him have more than "enough."

74. [Whatever] the severity of the impact of insufficient food or inadequate housing on a person's life, they have never been considered to bear the same direct and immediate relationship to constitutional concerns for free speech and for our political processes as education has long been recognized to bear. Perhaps, the best evidence of this fact is the unique status which has been accorded public education as the single public service nearly unanimously guaranteed in the constitutions of our States. Education, in terms of constitutional values, is much more analogous in my judgment, to the right to vote in state elections than to public welfare or public housing. [Indeed,] we have long recognized education as an essential step in providing the disadvantaged with the tools necessary to achieve economic self-sufficiency.

75. The majority's reliance on this Court's traditional deference to legislative bodies in matters of taxation falls wide of the mark [for] in this case we are presented with a claim [that] the revenue producing mechanism directly discriminates against the interests of some of the intended beneficiaries; and in contrast to the taxpayer suits, the interest adversely affected is of substantial constitutional and societal importance. * * *

77. Even putting aside its misreading of *Griffin* and *Douglas,* the Court fails to offer any reasoned constitutional basis for restricting cases involving wealth discrimination to instances in which there is an absolute deprivation of the interest affected. [Equal protection] guarantees equality of treatment of those persons who are similarly situated; it does not

This is not to say that the form of wealth classification in this case does not differ significantly from those recognized [in] previous [decisions. Here], the children of the disadvantaged Texas school districts are being discriminated against not necessarily because of [the] wealth of their families, but because of the taxable property wealth of the residents of the district in which they happen to live. The appropriate question, then, is whether the same degree of judicial solicitude and scrutiny that has previously been afforded wealth classifications is warranted here.

[That] wealth classifications alone have not necessarily been considered to bear the same high degree of suspectness as have classifications based on, for instance, race or alienage may be explainable on a number of grounds. The "poor" may not be seen as politically powerless as certain discrete and insular minority groups. Personal poverty may entail much the same social stigma as historically attached to certain racial or ethnic groups [but it] is not a permanent disability; its shackles may be escaped. Perhaps, most importantly, though, personal wealth may not necessarily share the general irrelevance as a basis for legislative action that race or nationality is recognized to have. While the "poor" have frequently been a legally disadvantaged group, it cannot be ignored that social legislation must frequently take cognizance of the economic status of our citizens. Thus, we have generally gauged the invidiousness of wealth classifications with an awareness of the importance of the interests being affected and the relevance of personal wealth to those interests.

When evaluated with these considerations in mind, it seems to me that discrimination on the basis of group wealth in this case likewise calls for careful judicial scrutiny. First, [it] bears no relationship whatsoever to the interest of Texas school children in the educational opportunity afforded them [by] Texas. Given the importance of that interest, we must be particularly sensitive to the invidious characteristics of any form of discrimination that is not clearly intended to serve it, as opposed to some other distinct state interest. Discrimination on the basis of group wealth may not, to be sure, reflect the social stigma frequently attached to personal poverty. Nevertheless, insofar as group wealth discrimination involves wealth over which the disadvantaged individual has no significant control,[83] it represents in fact a more serious basis of discrimination than does personal wealth. For such discrimination is no reflection of the individual's characteristics or his abilities. And thus—particularly in the context of a disadvantaged class composed of children—we have previously treated discrimination on a basis which the individual cannot control as constitutionally disfavored. Cf. *Weber; Levy,* [Sec. 3, III supra].

The disability of the disadvantaged class in this case extends as well into the political processes upon which we ordinarily rely as adequate for the protection and promotion of all interests. Here legislative reallocation of the State's property wealth must be sought in the face of inevitable opposition from significantly advantaged districts that have a strong vested interest in the preservation of the status [quo]. *Griffin, Douglas, Williams, Tate,* and our other prior cases have dealt with discrimination on the basis of indigency which was

merely bar some form of excessive discrimination between such persons. Outside the context of wealth discrimination, the Court's reapportionment decisions clearly indicate that relative discrimination is within the purview of the Equal Protection Clause. * * *

83. True, a family may move to escape a property poor school district, assuming it has the means to do so. But such a view would itself raise a serious constitutional question concerning an impermissible burdening of the right to travel, or, more precisely, the concomitant right to remain where one is.

attributable to the operation of the private sector. But we have no such simple de facto wealth discrimination here. The means for financing public education in Texas are selected and specified by the State. [At] the same time, governmentally imposed land use controls have undoubtedly encouraged and rigidified natural trends in the allocation of particular areas for residential or commercial use, and thus determined each district's amount of taxable property wealth. In short, this case, in contrast to the Court's previous wealth discrimination decisions, can only be seen as "unusual in the extent to which governmental action *is* the cause of the wealth classifications."

[Here] both the nature of the interest and the classification dictate close judicial [scrutiny. I] do not question that local control of public education, as an abstract matter, constitutes a very substantial state interest. [But] on this record, it is apparent that the State's purported concern with local control is offered primarily as an excuse rather than as a justification for interdistrict inequality.

In Texas statewide laws regulate [the] most minute details of local public education. For example, the State prescribes required courses. All textbooks must be submitted for state [approval]. The State has established the qualifications necessary for teaching in Texas public schools and the procedures for obtaining certification. The State has even legislated on the length of the school [day.]

Moreover, even if we accept Texas' general dedication to local control in educational matters, [i]f Texas had a system truly dedicated to local fiscal control one would expect the quality of the educational opportunity provided in each district to vary with the decision of the voters in that district as to the level of sacrifice they wish to make for public education. [But local] districts cannot choose to have the best education [by] imposing the highest tax rate. Instead, the quality of the educational opportunity offered by any particular district is largely determined by the amount of taxable property located in the district—a factor over which local voters can exercise no control.

The study introduced in the District Court showed a direct inverse relationship between equalized taxable district property wealth and district tax effort with the result that the property poor districts making the highest tax effort obtained the lowest per pupil yield. * * *

In my judgment, any substantial degree of scrutiny of the operation of the Texas financing scheme reveals that the State has selected means wholly inappropriate to secure its purported interest in assuring its school districts local fiscal control.[96] At the same time, appellees have pointed out a variety of alternative financing schemes which may serve the State's purported interest in local control as well as, if not better than, the present scheme without the current impairment of the educational opportunity of vast numbers of Texas schoolchildren.[98] * * *

96. [Although] my Brother White purports to reach this result by application of that lenient standard of mere rationality, [it] seems to be that the care with which he scrutinizes the practical effectiveness of the present local property tax as a device for affording local fiscal control reflects the application of a more stringent standard of [review].

98. * * * Central financing would leave in local hands the entire gamut of local educational policy-making—teachers, curriculum, school sites, the whole process of allocating resources among alternative educational objectives.

A second possibility is the much discussed theory of district power equalization put forth by Professors Coons, Clune, and Sugarman in their seminal work, *Private Wealth and Public Education* 201–242 (1970). Such a scheme would truly reflect a dedication to local fiscal

Notes and Questions

1. PAPASAN v. ALLAIN, 478 U.S. 265, 106 S.Ct. 2932, 92 L.Ed.2d 209 (1986), per WHITE, J., held that a complaint alleging an equal protection violation because of "a state decision to divide state resources unequally among school districts" should survive a motion to dismiss. *Rodriguez* was deemed to set the proper standard of review—rational basis—but was distinguished because it "did not purport to validate all funding variations that might result from a State's public school funding decision. It held merely that the variations that resulted from allowing local control over local property tax funding of the public schools were constitutionally permissible in that case."

POWELL, joined by Burger, C.J., and Rehnquist, J., dissented finding that the system was substantially similar to that upheld in *Rodriguez* and further maintaining that the variations in funding to local districts were *de minimis.*[g]

2. *Wealth classifications.* (a) Does *Rodriguez* hold that de facto discriminations against poor people are subject to "strict scrutiny" only if the classification involves a right "explicitly or implicitly guaranteed by the Constitution"? May *all* the prior "wealth discrimination" cases be explained on this basis? Or does the Court's fn. 60 suggest that a state payment requirement resulting in "an absolute deprivation" of an "important" (albeit not "fundamental") right requires "strict scrutiny"? If so, what are other "important" rights?

Is education unique because it is compulsory—i.e., is the state barred from requiring it and at the same time imposing a "user-fee" even on those who can't pay? May the public schools impose a charge for all textbooks, even against indigents? May any of the broad range of municipal services—fire and police, parks and recreation, etc.—be conditioned on a "user-fee"? How about water?

(b) *Affirmative obligation.* Suppose a state simply shut its public schools and left the task to private entrepreneurs? In what way is this different than the situation posited in fn. 60? Suppose a state simply shut off all relief and welfare assistance? Is this state action subject to "strict scrutiny" under equal protection? Or does this beg the "state action" issue?

May a state bar impoverished citizens from public housing? If not, may it charge rentals for all public housing that the impoverished can't afford? If not, may it simply not construct public housing, leaving the impoverished to fend for themselves? Or does government have the affirmative obligation to afford at least "minimum protection" (if not "equal protection") to all citizens in respect to those services that are "of such fundamental importance" that "severe

control. Under their system, each school district would receive a fixed amount of revenue per pupil for any particular level of tax effort regardless of the level of local property tax base. * * *

District wealth reapportionment is yet another alternative * * *.

A fourth possibility would be to remove commercial, industrial, and mineral property from local tax rolls, to tax this property on a state-wide basis, and to return the resulting revenues to the local districts in a fashion that would compensate for remaining variations in the local tax bases.

None of these particular alternatives are necessarily constitutionally compelled; rather, they indicate the breadth of choice which remains to the State if the present interdistrict disparities were eliminated.

[For a collection of further commentaries, emphasizing the varying complexities of school finance in constitutional adjudication, see Lockhart, Kamisar & Choper, *Constitutional Law: Cases—Comments—Questions* 1552–53 (4th ed. 1975).]

g. In response, White, J., stated: "We [decline] to append to the general requirements of an equal protection cause of action an additional threshold effects requirement." Compare *Bandemer,* p. 1124 supra.

deprivation" would otherwise result? See generally Michelman, *On Protecting the Poor Through the Fourteenth Amendment,* 83 Harv.L.Rev. 7 (1969). For the view that it is improper for the judiciary to decide issues of economic allocation, see Wilkinson, fn. b in *Dandridge;* Winter, fn. c in *Dandridge.* Compare generally Rawls, *A Theory of Justice* (1971) with Nozick, *Anarchy, State and Utopia* (1974).

Consider Bendich, *Privacy, Poverty, and the Constitution,* 54 Calif.L.Rev. 407, 420–21 (1966): "It would be perverse to say that one has a fundamental right to be assisted by a lawyer when charged with crime, but that he has no right to such food or medicine as might be required to keep him reasonably healthy and attentive during the process of his trial. [But] if a person charged with crime has a right to such assistance, on what principle is one innocent of such a charge to be denied equal access to assistance? [What] constitutional guarantees other than those which are bound up with the criminal law are denied to persons because of their poverty? Does the fourth amendment's guarantee of the right to be secure in one's person, papers, house, and effects presuppose housing for the people of America? If it does, then clearly the condition of being unable to pay rent can deprive one of this aspect of the right to privacy as effectively as the inability to pay counsel fees [deprives] one of the right to counsel." Are there *any* "constitutional guarantees" that can be effectively exercised without "minimally adequate" food, clothing and shelter? Without "minimally adequate" education and medical assistance? Is the state constitutionally obligated to provide its impoverished citizens "minimally adequate" political campaign expenses? "Minimally adequate" funds to travel throughout the country and abroad? How are the terms "minimally adequate" and "impoverished" to be defined? By whom? Of what relevance does the "cost-to-the-state" factor bear on the "compelling" justification inquiry?

May the state bar indigents from public parks? Golf courses? Opera houses? If not, may it charge a "user-fee"? May it decline to engage in such activities without subsidizing those persons who can't pay their own way? See generally Note, *Discrimination Against the Poor and the Fourteenth Amendment,* 81 Harv.L.Rev. 435 (1967).

(c) *Discrimination against fundamental rights.* MAHER v. ROE, p. 192 supra, per POWELL, J., held that Connecticut's refusal to give medicaid for nontherapeutic abortions, even though it gives medicaid for childbirth, does not violate equal protection: "The Constitution imposes no obligation on the States to pay the pregnancy-related medical expenses of indigent women, or indeed to pay any of the medical expenses of indigents.[5] But when a State decides to alleviate some of the hardships of poverty by providing medical care, the manner in which it dispenses benefits is subject to constitutional limitations. * * *

"This case involves no discrimination against a suspect class. An indigent woman desiring an abortion does not come within the limited category of disadvantaged classes so recognized by our cases. Nor does the fact that the impact of the regulation falls upon those who cannot pay lead to a different conclusion. In a sense, every denial of welfare to an indigent creates a wealth classification as compared to nonindigents who are able to pay for the desired goods or services. But this Court has never held that financial need alone

5. [Because] Connecticut has made no attempt to monopolize the means for terminating pregnancies through abortion the present case is easily distinguished from *Boddie.* [Does this similarly distinguish *Harper* and *Lubin v. Panish*?]

identifies a suspect [class]. See *Rodriguez; Dandridge.*[6] Accordingly, the central question in this case is whether the regulation 'impinges upon a fundamental right explicitly or implicitly protected by the Constitution.' "

In reasoning that "the Connecticut regulation places no obstacles—absolute or otherwise—in the pregnant woman's path to an abortion" the Court also found that "appellees' reliance on the penalty analysis of *Shapiro* and *Maricopa* is misplaced.[8]"

In rejecting the Court's distinction between a state's direct interference with a fundamental right and encouraging an alternative activity, BRENNAN, J., joined by Marshall and Blackmun, JJ., dissenting, added that "First Amendment decisions have consistently held [that] the compelling state interest test is applicable not only to outright denials but also to restraints that make exercise of those rights more difficult. See, e.g., *Sherbert.* [The] compelling state interest test has been applied in voting cases, even where only relatively small infringements upon voting power, such as dilution of voting strength caused by malapportionment, have been involved. [The] Connecticut scheme cannot be distinguished from other grants and withholdings of financial benefits that we have held unconstitutionally burdened a fundamental right.[a] [The] governing principle is the same [as in *Sherbert*], for Connecticut grants and withholds financial

6. [*Griffin* and *Douglas*] are grounded in the criminal justice system, a governmental monopoly in which participation is compelled. Cf. n. 5, supra. Our subsequent decisions have made it clear that the principles underlying *Griffin* and *Douglas* do not extend to legislative classifications generally.

[For incisive comparison of *Maher* with *Griffin* and *Douglas* —and with *Shapiro* (see fn. 8 infra)—see Brudno, *Wealth Discrimination in the Supreme Court: Equal Protection for the Poor from Griffin to Maher,* in Constitutional Government in America 229 (Collins ed. 1980).]

8. * * * Penalties are most familiar to the criminal law, where criminal sanctions are imposed as a consequence of proscribed conduct. *Shapiro* and *Maricopa* recognized that denial of welfare to one who had recently exercised the right to travel across state lines was sufficiently analogous to a criminal fine to justify strict judicial scrutiny.

If Connecticut denied general welfare benefits to all women who had obtained abortions and who were otherwise entitled to the benefits, we would have a close analogy to the facts in *Shapiro,* and strict scrutiny might be [appropriate]. But the claim here is that the State "penalizes" the woman's decision to have an abortion by refusing to pay for it. *Shapiro* and *Maricopa* did not hold that States would penalize the right to travel interstate by refusing to pay the bus fares of the indigent travelers. We find no support in the right to travel cases for the view that Connecticut must show a compelling interest for its decision not to fund elective abortions.

Sherbert v. Verner, similarly is inapplicable here. In addition, that case was decided in the significantly different context of a constitutionally imposed "governmental obligation of neutrality" originating in [the] Religion Clauses of the First Amendment.

a. Does the Connecticut regulation "discriminate against," rather than simply "burden," a fundamental right? Is there a constitutional difference? See note 1 after *Shapiro,* Part II supra. Consider 91 Harv.L.Rev. 144 (1977): "It can hardly be [that] the state could provide a free forum for indigents' speech only on the condition that no unpopular views be espoused, even though this policy would deny only the specific costs of exercising disfavored speech rights. Similarly, it is difficult to imagine that the Court would uphold a policy of providing free justices of the peace for intraracial but not racially mixed marriages, thereby declining to pay the specific costs of a disfavored but constitutionally protected union, notwithstanding that the state has merely made intraracial marriage a more attractive alternative without creating an obstacle to private marriage opportunities."

See also Brennan, J., dissenting in *Harris v. McRae* (1980), p. 194 supra (which relied on *Maher* to sustain denial of medicaid even for "medically necessary" abortions): "Whether the State withholds only the special costs of a disfavored option or penalizes the individual more broadly for the manner in which she exercises her choice, it cannot interfere with a constitutionally protected decision through the coercive use of governmental largess."

Did *Dandridge* uphold a policy of providing welfare to indigent parents only for sustaining four children and no more? If so, is the law in *Maher* distinguishable?

benefits in a manner that discourages significantly the exercise of a fundamental constitutional right. Indeed, the case for application of the principle actually is stronger than in *Sherbert* since appellees are all indigents and therefore even more vulnerable to the financial pressures imposed by the Connecticut regulations."

MARSHALL, J., dissented: "[*Rodriguez*] stated a test for analyzing discrimination on the basis of wealth that would, if fairly applied here, strike down the regulations. The Court there held that a wealth discrimination claim is made out by persons ['who] because of their impecunity [are] completely unable to pay for some desired benefit, and as a consequence [sustain] an absolute deprivation of a meaningful opportunity to enjoy that benefit.' Medicaid recipients are, almost by definition, 'completely unable to pay for' abortions, and are thereby completely denied 'a meaningful opportunity' to obtain them.[6]"

(d) Whatever the scope of "strict scrutiny" for de facto discriminations against (or among) poor people, does *Rodriguez* restrict the analysis to state action that imposes "payment requirements"? See *Jefferson v. Hackney* (1972), fn. a in *Washington v. Davis,* Sec. 2, III supra.

3. *"Implicitly guaranteed" rights.* (a) Apart from any issue of wealth discrimination, does *Rodriguez* suggest that there may be a "constitutional right" to a *minimum* education? E.g., must a state provide *some* meaningful education to mentally retarded children? To non-English speaking children? See Note, *The Constitutional Right of Bilingual Children to an Equal Educational Opportunity,* 47 So.Cal.L.Rev. 943 (1974).

(b) PLYLER v. DOE, 457 U.S. 202, 102 S.Ct. 2382, 72 L.Ed.2d 786 (1982), per BRENNAN, J., held that a Texas statute (§ 21.031) denying free public education to illegal alien children violated equal protection: "Persuasive arguments support the view that a State may withhold its beneficience from those whose very presence within the United States is the product of their own unlawful conduct. [But the children] in these cases 'can affect neither their parents' conduct nor their own status.' *Trimble v. Gordon,* [Sec. 3, III supra]. Even if the State found it expedient to control the conduct of adults by acting against their children, legislation directing the onus of a parent's misconduct against his children does not comport with fundamental conceptions of justice. * * * *Weber v. Aetna Casualty & Surety Co.* [Sec. 3, III supra].

"We reject the claim that 'illegal aliens' are a 'suspect class.' [U]ndocumented status is not irrelevant to any proper legislative goal. Nor is [it] an absolutely immutable characteristic since it is the product of conscious,

6. Application of the flexible equal protection standard [urged in Marshall, J.'s *Rodriguez* dissent] would allow the Court to strike down the regulations in these cases without calling into question laws funding public education or English language teaching in public schools. [See the majority's discussion of this point at p. 193 supra.] By permitting a court to weigh all relevant factors, the flexible standard does not logically require acceptance of any equal protection claim that is "identical in principle" under the traditional approach to those advanced here.

[Is there any way other than use of a "flexible equal protection standard" to distinguish *Maher* from the problems raised by the majority in respect to *Meyer* and *Pierce*? Consider Perry, *The Abortion Funding Cases: A Comment on the Supreme Court's Role in American Government,* 66 Geo.L.J. 1191, 1199–1200 (1978): "One need not disapprove of private schools to acknowledge the wisdom of providing free, public education. [But the state's decision in *Maher*] is recognizable solely as a disapproval of and an effort to discourage abortion." See also Perry, *Why the Supreme Court Was Plainly Wrong in the Hyde Amendment Case: A Brief Comment on Harris v. McRae,* 32 Stan.L.Rev. 1113 (1980). Tribe, *American Constitutional Law* 933 n. 77 (1978). Compare Fahy, *The Abortion Funding Cases: A Response to Professor Perry,* 67 Geo.L.J. 1205 (1979).]

indeed unlawful, action. But § 21.031 [imposes] its discriminatory burden on the basis of a legal characteristic over which children can have little control. It is thus difficult to conceive of a rational justification for penalizing these children for their presence within the United States. * * *

"Public education is not a 'right' granted to individuals by the Constitution. *Rodriguez.* But neither is it merely some governmental 'benefit' indistinguishable from other forms of social welfare legislation. Both the importance of education in maintaining our basic institutions, and the lasting impact of its deprivation on the life of the child, mark the distinction. [We] cannot ignore the significant social costs borne by our Nation when select groups are denied the means to absorb the values and skills upon which our social order rests.[20] [Thus], the discrimination contained in § 21.031 can hardly be considered rational unless it furthers some substantial goal of the State.

"* * * Faced with an equal protection challenge respecting the treatment of aliens, we agree that the courts must be attentive to congressional policy; the exercise of congressional power might well affect the State's prerogatives to afford differential treatment to a particular class of aliens. [But] there is no indication that the disability imposed by § 21.031 corresponds to any identifiable congressional policy. The State does not claim that the conservation of state educational resources was ever a congressional concern in restricting immigration. More importantly, the classification reflected in § 21.031 does not operate harmoniously within the federal program. [In] light of the discretionary federal power to grant relief from deportation, a State cannot realistically determine that any particular undocumented child will in fact be deported until after deportation proceedings have been completed. It would of course be most difficult for the State to justify a denial of education to a child enjoying an inchoate federal permission to remain.

"We are reluctant to impute to Congress the intention to withhold from these children, for so long as they are present in this country through no fault of their own, access to a basic education. In other contexts, undocumented status, coupled with some articulable federal policy, might enhance State authority with respect to the treatment of undocumented aliens. But in the area of special constitutional sensitivity presented by this case, and in the absence of any contrary indication fairly discernible in the present legislative record, we perceive no national policy that supports the State in denying these children an elementary education.[a] [We] therefore turn to the state objectives that are said to support § 21.031. * * *

"First, appellants appear to suggest that the State may seek to protect the State from an influx of illegal immigrants. While a State might have an interest in mitigating the potentially harsh economic effects of sudden shifts in population, [t]here is no evidence in the record suggesting that illegal entrants impose any significant burden on the State's economy. To the contrary, the available evidence suggests that illegal aliens underutilize public services, while contributing their labor to the local economy and tax money to the State fisc.

20. * * * Whatever the current status of these children, the courts below concluded that many will remain here permanently and that some indeterminate number will eventually become citizens. * * *

a. For the view that "the Court should have followed the lead of *Toll v. Moreno,* [Sec. 3, I supra], and used the Supremacy Clause" to hold the *Plyler* statute invalid because it was neither "sanctioned nor contemplated by Congress," see Choper, fn. e, p. 1065 supra, at 21–32. See also 96 Harv.L.Rev. 130 (1982). Compare Gerety, *Children in the Labyrinth: The Complexities of Plyler v. Doe,* 44 U.Pitt.L. Rev. 379, 380–87 (1983).

The dominant incentive for illegal entry [into] Texas is the availability of employment; few if any illegal immigrants come to this country [to] avail themselves of a free education. * * *

"Second, [appellants] suggest that undocumented children are appropriately singled out for exclusion because of the special burdens they impose on the State's ability to provide high quality public education. But the record in no way supports the claim [and], even if improvement in the quality of education were a likely result of barring some *number* of children from the schools of the State, the State must support its selection of *this* group as the appropriate target for exclusion. In terms of educational cost and need, however, undocumented children are 'basically indistinguishable' from legally resident alien children.

"Finally, appellants suggest that undocumented children are appropriately singled out because their unlawful presence within the United States renders them less likely than other children to remain within the boundaries of the State, and to put their education to productive social or political use within the State. Even assuming that such an interest is legitimate, it is an interest that is most difficult to quantify. The State has no assurance that any child, citizen or not, will employ the education provided by the State within the confines of the State's borders. In any event, the record is clear that many of the undocumented children disabled by this classification will remain in this country indefinitely, and that some will become lawful residents or citizens of the United States. It is difficult to understand precisely what the State hopes to achieve by promoting the creation and perpetuation of a subclass of illiterates within our boundaries, surely adding to the problems and costs of unemployment, welfare, and crime. It is thus clear that whatever savings might be achieved [are] wholly insubstantial in light of the costs involved to these children, the State, and the Nation."[b]

BLACKMUN, J., who joined the Court's opinion, concurred: "I joined [the] Court in *Rodriguez,* and I continue to believe that it provides the appropriate model for resolving most equal protection disputes. [But] I believe the Court's experience has demonstrated that the *Rodriguez* formulation does not settle every issue of 'fundamental rights' arising under the Equal Protection Clause. Only a pedant would insist that there are *no* meaningful distinctions among the multitude of social and political interests regulated by the States * * *. Children denied an education are placed at a permanent and insurmountable competitive [disadvantage]. And when those children are members of an identifiable group, that group—through the State's action—will have been converted into a discrete underclass. Other benefits provided by the State, such as housing and public assistance, are of course important: to an individual in immediate need, they may be more desirable than the right to be educated. But classifications involving the complete denial of education are in a sense unique, for they strike at the heart of equal protection values by involving the State in the creation of permanent class distinctions. Cf. *Rodriguez* (Marshall, J., dissenting). In a sense, then, denial of an education is the analogue of denial of the right to vote: the former relegates the individual to second-class social status; the latter places him at a permanent political disadvantage.

"This conclusion is fully consistent with *Rodriguez.* The Court there reserved judgment on the constitutionality of a state system that 'occasioned an

b. Marshall, J., joined the Court's opinion but emphasized "that the facts of these cases demonstrate the wisdom of rejecting a rigidified approach to equal protection analysis, and of employing" his suggested approach in *Dandridge* and *Rodriguez.*

absolute denial of educational opportunities to any of its children,' noting that 'no charge fairly could be made that the system [at issue in *Rodriguez*] fails to provide each child with an opportunity to acquire * * * basic minimal skills.' [In] such circumstances, the voting decisions suggest that the State must offer something more than a rational basis for its classification."

POWELL, J., who joined the Court's opinion, concurred "to emphasize the unique character of the case": "Although the analogy is not perfect, our holding today does find support in decisions of this Court with respect to the status of illegitimates. [Thus,] review in a case such as this is properly heightened. [These children] have been singled out for a lifelong penalty and stigma. A legislative classification that threatens the creation of an underclass of future citizens and residents cannot be reconciled with one of the fundamental purposes of the Fourteenth Amendment. In these unique circumstances, the Court properly may require that the State's interests be substantial and that the means bear a 'fair and substantial relation' to these interests.[3]"

BURGER, C.J., joined by White, Rehnquist and O'Connor, JJ., dissented: "[B]y patching together bits and pieces of what might be termed quasi-suspect-class and quasi-fundamental-rights analysis, the Court spins out a theory custom-tailored to the facts [and its] opinion rests on such a unique confluence of theories and rationales that it will likely stand for little beyond the results in these particular [cases].[c]

"[I]n some circumstances persons generally, and children in particular, may have little control over or responsibility for such things as their ill health, need for public assistance, or place of residence. Yet a state legislature is not barred from considering, for example, relevant differences between the mentally-healthy and the mentally-ill, or between the residents of different counties,[5] simply because these may be factors unrelated to individual choice or to any 'wrongdoing.' The Equal Protection Clause protects against arbitrary and irrational classifications, and against invidious discrimination stemming from prejudice and hostility; it is not an all-encompassing 'equalizer' designed to eradicate every distinction for which persons are not 'responsible.' * * *[d]

"The Court's analogy to cases involving discrimination against illegitimate children is grossly misleading. The State has not thrust any disabilities upon appellees due to their 'status of birth.' Cf. *Weber.* Rather, appellees' status is predicated upon the circumstances of their concededly illegal presence in this [country].

3. [I]n *Rodriguez* no group of children was singled out by the State and then penalized because of their parents' status. [Nor] was any group of children totally deprived of all education as in this case. If the resident children of illegal aliens were denied welfare assistance, made available by government to all other children who qualify, this also—in my opinion—would be an impermissible penalizing of children because of their parents' status.

c. See generally Hutchinson, *More Substantive Equal Protection? A Note on Plyler v. Doe,* 1982 Sup.Ct.Rev. 167.

5. Appellees "lack control" over their illegal residence in this country in the same sense as lawfully resident children lack control over the school district in which their parents reside. Yet in *Rodriguez,* [t]here was no suggestion [that] a child's "lack of responsibility" for his residence in a particular school district had any relevance to the proper standard of review of his [claims.]

d. Compare Choper, supra, at 29: "Although it is true that the children in *Rodriguez* had no effective choice as to where they lived, the statute in *Plyler* [is] much more stigmatizing. It [says] to a class of children that they are no good; that even though what is wrong with them is something over which they have no control, the state is going to penalize them nonetheless. I think [this] provided an effective doctrinal hook on which the Court could have more explicitly hung its decision."

"The central question in these cases, as in every equal protection case not involving truly fundamental rights 'explicitly or implicitly guaranteed by the Constitution,' *Rodriguez,* is whether there is some legitimate basis for a legislative distinction between different classes of persons. The fact that the distinction is drawn in legislation affecting access to public education—as opposed to legislation allocating other important governmental benefits, such as public assistance, health care, or housing—cannot make a difference in the level of scrutiny applied.

"Once it is conceded—as the Court does—that illegal aliens are not a suspect class, and that education is not a fundamental right, our inquiry should focus on and be limited to whether the legislative classification at issue bears a rational relationship to a legitimate state purpose. [I]t simply is not 'irrational' for a State to conclude that it does not have the same responsibility to provide benefits for persons whose very presence in the State and this country is illegal as it does to provide for persons lawfully present. * * *

"It is significant that the federal government has seen fit to exclude illegal aliens from numerous social welfare [programs]. Although these exclusions do not conclusively demonstrate the constitutionality of the State's use of the same classification for comparable purposes, at the very least they tend to support the rationality of excluding illegal alien residents of a State from such programs so as to preserve the State's finite revenues for the benefit of lawful residents. * * *

"Denying a free education to illegal alien children is not a choice I would make were I a legislator. Apart from compassionate considerations, the long-range costs of excluding any children from the public schools may well outweigh the costs of educating them. But [the] fact that there are sound *policy* arguments against the Texas legislature's choice does not render that choice an unconstitutional one. [While] the 'specter of a permanent caste' of illegal Mexican residents of the United States is indeed a disturbing one, it is but one segment of a larger problem, which is for the political branches to solve."

4. *Standards of equal protection review.* (a) Does Marshall, J.'s *Rodriguez* dissent demonstrate that the Court "has applied a spectrum of standards" as to "the degree of care with which it will scrutinize particular classifications"? In addition to *Papasan* and *Plyler* supra, see also fns. e and f following *New Orleans v. Dukes,* Sec. 1 supra; *Cleburne,* Sec. 3, IV supra.[a]

(b) UNITED STATES DEPT. OF AGRICULTURE v. MORENO, 413 U.S. 528, 93 S.Ct. 2821, 37 L.Ed.2d 782 (1973), per BRENNAN, J., applying " 'traditional' equal protection analysis," held that a provision of the Food Stamp Act—excluding "any household containing an individual who is unrelated to any other member of the household"—was "wholly without any rational basis": It "is clearly irrelevant to the stated purposes of the Act [which are to] raise levels of

a. For analysis urging that the Court use three levels of equal protection review and "should validate a statute [that "limits the exercise of a fundamental right by a class of persons"] only if the means used bear a factually demonstrable relationship to a state interest capable of withstanding analysis," see Nowak, *Realigning the Standard of Review Under the Equal Protection Guarantee—Prohibited, Neutral, and Permissive Classifications,* 62 Geo.L.J. 1071 (1974): "The Court will scrutinize the factual support for the legislation to determine whether its ends are capable of withstanding analysis and whether its means are rationally related to that end."

For analysis urging that the Court weigh the "*nature* of the affected interest" and the "*magnitude* of disadvantage" against the "*nature* of the state's interest" and the "relationship between *means and ends,*" see Simson, *A Method for Analyzing Discriminatory Effects Under the Equal Protection Clause,* 29 Stan.L. Rev. 663 (1977).

nutrition among low-income households. [Thus], the challenged classification must rationally further some legitimate governmental interest other than those specifically stated in the congressional 'declaration of policy.'

"[The] little legislative history [that] does exist" indicates that the provision "was intended to [prevent] 'hippie communes' from participating in the food stamp program. [But equal protection] at the very least mean[s] that a bare congressional desire to harm a politically unpopular group cannot constitute a *legitimate* governmental interest." Nor does the classification "operate so as rationally to further the prevention of fraud" because, under the Act, "two *unrelated* persons living together" may "avoid the 'unrelated person' exclusion simply by altering their living arrangements so as [to] create two separate 'households,' both of which are eligible for assistance. [Thus], in practical operation, the [provision] excludes from participation [not] those persons who are 'likely to abuse the program' but, rather, only those persons who are so desperately in need of aid that they cannot even afford to alter their living arrangements so as to retain their eligibility."

DOUGLAS, J., concurred: "I could not say that [this] provision has no 'rational' relation to control of fraud. We deal here, however, with the right of association, protected by the First Amendment." Thus, the classification "can be sustained only on a showing of a 'compelling' governmental interest."

REHNQUIST, J., joined by Burger, C.J., dissented: "Congress attacked the problem with a rather blunt instrument, [b]ut I do not think it is unreasonable for Congress to conclude that the basic unit which it was willing to support [with] food stamps is some variation on the family as we know it—a household consisting of related individuals. This unit provides a guarantee which is not provided by households containing unrelated individuals that the household exists for some purpose other than to collect federal food stamps.

"Admittedly, [the] limitation will make ineligible many households which have not been formed for the purpose of collecting federal food stamps, and will [not] wholly deny food stamps to those households which may have been formed in large part to take advantage of the program. But, as the Court concedes, 'traditional' equal protection analysis does not require that every classification be drawn with precise mathematical nicety." [b]

(c) MATHEWS v. DE CASTRO, 429 U.S. 181, 97 S.Ct. 431, 50 L.Ed.2d 389 (1976), per STEWART, J., relying on *Dandridge,* upheld a provision of the Social Security Act, granting benefits for a minor or dependent child in her care, to the wife (but not to the divorced former wife) of a man who is retired or disabled: "To be sure, the standard by which legislation ["providing for governmental payments of monetary benefits"] must be judged 'is not a toothless one,' *Mathews v. Lucas,* [Sec. 3, III supra]. But the challenged statute is entitled to a strong presumption of constitutionality. * * * Congress could have rationally as-

b. For invalidation of another Food Stamp Act provision, but on a different constitutional theory, see *United States Dept. of Agriculture v. Murry,* Sec. 5 infra. Compare Lyng v. Castillo, 477 U.S. 635, 106 S.Ct. 2727, 91 L.Ed.2d 527 (1986), per Stevens, J., holding that a Food Stamp Act provision—which treated "parents, children, and siblings who live together" *less* favorably than "distant relatives, or groups of unrelated persons who live together"—had a "rational basis": "Congress could reasonably determine that close relatives sharing a home—almost by definition—tend to purchase and prepare meals together while distant relatives and unrelated individuals might not be so inclined. [And] Congress might have reasoned that it would be somewhat easier for close relatives—again, almost by definition—to accommodate their living habits to a federal policy favoring common meal preparation than it would be for more distant relatives or unrelated persons to do so." Brennan, Marshall and White, JJ., dissented.

sumed that divorced husbands and wives depend less on each other for financial and other support than do couples who stay married." Marshall, J., concurred in the judgment.

SECTION 5. IRREBUTTABLE PRESUMPTIONS

A series of decisions in the early 1970s held that "permanent irrebuttable presumptions," which "have long been disfavored under the Due Process Clause," violated "procedural due process," *Vlandis,* infra. But, as the materials indicate, since the analysis of these cases is strikingly similar to the "fundamental rights" branch of equal protection, they are usefully studied here.

VLANDIS v. KLINE, 412 U.S. 441, 93 S.Ct. 2230, 37 L.Ed.2d 63 (1973): Connecticut imposed higher state university tuition on nonresidents. The Court, per STEWART, J., invalidated the statutory conclusive presumption that because the legal address of a student, if married, was outside the state at the time of application or, if unmarried, was outside the state at any point during the preceding year, he remains a nonresident for this purpose during the entire period of attendance at the university:

"*Bell v. Burson,* 402 U.S. 535, 91 S.Ct. 1586, 29 L.Ed.2d 90 (1971), involved a Georgia statute which provided that if an uninsured motorist was involved in an accident and could not post security for the amount of damages claimed, his driver's license must be suspended * * *. The Court held that since the State purported to be concerned with fault in suspending a driver's license, it could not, consistent with procedural due process, conclusively presume fault from the fact that the uninsured motorist was involved in an accident, and could not, therefore, suspend his driver's license without a hearing on that crucial factor.

"Likewise, in *Stanley v. Illinois,* 405 U.S. 645, 92 S.Ct. 1208, 31 L.Ed.2d 551 (1972), the Court [struck] Illinois' irrebuttable statutory presumption that all unmarried fathers are unqualified to raise their children. [T]he statute required the State, upon the death of the mother, to take custody of all such illegitimate [children]. It may be, the Court said, 'that most unmarried fathers are unsuitable and neglectful parents. [But] all unmarried fathers are not in this category; some are wholly suited to have custody of their children.' Hence, [the state] was required by the Due Process Clause to provide a hearing on that [issue].

"The same considerations obtain here. [S]ince Connecticut purports to be concerned with residency [it] is forbidden by the Due Process Clause to deny an individual the resident rates on the basis of a permanent and irrebuttable presumption of nonresidence, when that presumption is not necessarily or universally true in [fact]. Rather, standards of due process require that the State allow such an individual the opportunity to present evidence showing that he is a bona fide resident entitled to the in-state rates. [Our] holding today should in no wise [be] construed to deny a State the right to impose on a student, as one element in demonstrating bona fide residence, a reasonable durational residency requirement, which can be met while in student status.[9] " [a]

9. In *Starns v. Malkerson,* 326 F.Supp. 234 (D.Minn.1970), the District Court upheld a regulation of the University of Minnesota providing that no student could qualify as a resident for tuition purposes unless he had been a bona fide domiciliary of the State for at least a year immediately prior thereto. This Court affirmed summarily. [In] *Starns,* a student who applied to the University from out of State could rebut the presumption of nonresidency, after having lived in the State for one year, by presenting sufficient other evidence

a. See note a on page 1194.

BURGER, C.J., joined by Rehnquist, J., dissented: "[T]he Court applies 'strict scrutiny' [without] explaining why the statute impairs a genuine constitutional interest. [A]t least [*Stanley*] essayed to explain that the rights of fatherhood and family were regarded as 'essential' and 'basic civil rights of man.' [*Burson*] noted that revocation of a driver's license might impair the pursuit of a livelihood, thereby infringing 'important interests of the licensees.' [L]iterally thousands of state statutes create classifications permanent in duration, which are less than perfect, as all legislative classifications are, and might be improved on by individualized determinations so as to avoid the untoward results produced here due to the very unusual facts of this case. [F]or example, a State provides that a person may not be licensed to practice medicine or law unless he or she is a graduate of an accredited professional graduate school; a perfectly capable practitioner may as a consequence be barred 'permanently and irrebuttably' from pursuing his calling, without ever having an opportunity to prove his personal skills. [T]oday the Court makes an unchartered drift toward complications for the Due Process Clause comparable in scope and seriousness with those we are encountering in the equal protection area." [a]

UNITED STATES DEPT. OF AGRICULTURE v. MURRY, 413 U.S. 508, 93 S.Ct. 2832, 37 L.Ed.2d 767 (1973), per DOUGLAS, J., invalidated a federal statute that "any household which includes a member who has reached his eighteenth birthday and who is claimed as a dependent child for federal income tax purposes by a taxpayer who is not a member of an eligible household, shall be ineligible to participate in any food stamp program [during] the tax period such dependency is claimed and for a period of one year after the expiration of such tax period." The provision, a product of congressional concern about non-needy households participating in the food stamp program—and particularly about abuses of the program by "college students; children of wealthy parents"—created "an irrebuttable presumption often contrary to fact. It therefore lacks critical ingredients of due process found wanting in *Vlandis, Stanley,* and *Burson.*" [b]

CLEVELAND BD. OF EDUC. v. LaFLEUR, 414 U.S. 632, 94 S.Ct. 791, 39 L.Ed.2d 52 (1974), per STEWART, J., invalidated school board rules requiring pregnant teachers to take leave without pay at least five months—or, in a companion case from Virginia, four months—before the expected date of birth: "This Court has long recognized that freedom of personal choice in matters of

to show bona fide domicile within Minnesota. * * *

a. Marshall, J., joined by Brennan, J., joined the *Vlandis* opinion, except for "serious question as to the validity of [*Starns*] in light of" *Dunn* and *Shapiro,* Sec. 4, II supra. White, J., concurred in the judgment on the ground that "this bizarre pattern of discrimination [is] invidious and violates" equal protection: "[A]s the Court's assessment of the weight and value of the individual interest escalates, the less likely it is that mere administrative convenience and avoidance of hearings or investigations will be sufficient to justify what otherwise would appear to be irrational discriminations."

a. Rehnquist, J., joined by Burger, C.J., and Douglas, J., also dissented.

Compare Burger, C.J.'s opinion for the Court in *Jimenez v. Weinberger*—discussed in *Mathews v. Lucas,* Sec. 3, III supra—using an irrebuttable presumption-like rationale to hold a discrimination against some classes of illegitimate children violative of equal protection. Rehnquist, J., dissented.

b. Stewart and Marshall, JJ., joined the Court's opinion, but also concurred separately. Rehnquist, J., joined by Burger, C.J., and Powell, J., dissented; Blackmun, J., also dissented.

marriage and family life is one of the liberties protected by [due process. The] provisions amount to a conclusive presumption that every pregnant teacher who reaches the fifth or sixth month of pregnancy is physically incapable of continuing. There is no individualized determination by the teacher's doctor—or the school board's—as to any particular teacher's ability to continue at her job. [Because] the conclusive presumption [like] that in *Vlandis* [and *Stanley*], is neither 'necessarily nor universally true,' [it] is violative of the Due Process Clause [13] [which] requires the school boards to employ alternative administrative means, which do not so broadly infringe upon basic constitutional liberty, in support of their legitimate goals." [c]

REHNQUIST, J., joined by Burger, C.J., dissented from Stewart, J.'s enlisting "the Court in another quixotic engagement in his apparently unending war on irrebuttable presumptions. [All] legislation involves the drawing of lines, and the drawing of lines necessarily results in particular individuals who are disadvantaged by the line drawn being virtually indistinguishable for many purposes from those individuals who benefit from the legislative classification. The Court's disenchantment with 'irrebutable presumptions,' and its preference for 'individualized determination,' is in the last analysis nothing less than an attack upon the very notion of lawmaking itself."

Notes and Questions

1. *"Type" of due process.* (a) Is the "irrebuttable presumption" doctrine grounded in *procedural* or *substantive* due process? Consider Note, *The Conclusive Presumption Doctrine: Equal Process or Due Protection?,* 72 Mich.L.Rev. 800, 824 (1974): "The [cases] appear to be purely substantive in nature. First, the appellees admitted that the relevant statutory provisions had been properly applied [and], in effect, challenged the legislative fact-finding and demanded that new issues be made relevant. In essence, the Court required that the states extend benefits to those in the appellees' class; in procedural cases the Court does not expand the class of people entitled to receive the benefit but only deals with what procedures are necessary when affecting that interest." [d]

MICHAEL H. v. GERALD D., 491 U.S. 110, 109 S.Ct. 2333, 105 L.Ed.2d 91 (1989) upheld a California statute (§ 621) establishing an irrebuttable presumption (with narrow exceptions) that a child born to a married woman living with her husband, who is neither impotent nor sterile, is a child of the marriage. SCALIA, J., joined by Rehnquist, C.J., and O'Connor and Kennedy, JJ., argued that decisions such as *Stanley, Vlandis* and *LaFleur* did not "rest upon *procedural* due process. A conclusive presumption does, of course, foreclose the person

13. [We] are not dealing in these cases with maternity leave regulations requiring a termination of employment at some firm date during the last few weeks of pregnancy. We therefore have no occasion to decide whether such regulations might be justified by considerations not presented in these records—for example, widespread medical consensus about the "disabling" effect of pregnancy on a teacher's job performance during these latter days, or evidence showing that such firm cutoffs were the only reasonable method of avoiding the possibility of labor beginning while some teacher was in the classroom, or proof that adequate substitutes could not be procured without at least some minimal lead [time].

c. Powell, J., concurred in the result because "these regulations are invalid under rational basis standards of equal protection review." Douglas, J., concurred in the result.

d. In any event, is it clear that procedural due process is not at issue because neither *Vlandis* nor *Murry* concerned "property interests"—i.e., "interests that a person has already acquired in specific benefits," or interests to which a person has a "legitimate claim of entitlement" (*Board of Regents v. Roth*)? See Note, 72 Mich.L.Rev. at 816–21.

against whom it is invoked from demonstrating, in a particularized proceeding, that applying the presumption to him will in fact not further the lawful governmental policy the presumption is designed to effectuate. But the same can be said of any legal rule that establishes general classifications, whether framed in terms of a presumption or not. In this respect there is no difference between a rule which says that the marital husband shall be irrebuttably presumed to be the father, and a rule which says that the adulterous natural father shall not be recognized as the legal father. *Both* rules deny someone in Michael's situation a hearing on whether, in the particular circumstances of his case, California's policies would best be served by giving him parental rights. [Thus,] our 'irrebuttable presumption' cases must ultimately be analyzed as calling into question not the adequacy of procedures [but] the adequacy of the 'fit' between the classification and the policy that the classification serves."

BRENNAN, J., joined by Marshall and Blackmun, JJ., dissenting, responded "that the defect from which conclusive presumptions suffer is a *procedural* one: the State has declared a certain fact relevant, indeed controlling, yet has denied a particular class of litigants a hearing to establish that fact. [It] may be that all conclusive presumptions are, in a sense, substantive rules of law; but § 621 then belongs in that special category of substantive rules that presumes a fact relevant to a certain class of litigation, and it is that feature that renders § 621 suspect under our prior cases. To put the point differently, a conclusive presumption takes the form of 'no X's are Y's,' and is typically accompanied by a rule such as, 'and only Y's may obtain a driver's license.' (There would be no need for the presumption unless something hinged on the fact presumed.) Ignoring the fact that § 621 takes the form of 'no X's are Y's,' Gerald D. and the plurality fix upon the rule following § 621—only Y's may assert parental rights—and call § 621 a substantive rule of law. This strategy ignores both the form and the effect of § 621."

(b) Are the "irrebuttable presumption" cases limited to securing rights that are "explicitly or implicitly guaranteed by the Constitution" (*Rodriguez* Sec. 4, IV supra)—e.g., travel (*Vlandis*), procreation (*Stanley, LaFleur*), association (*Murry*)? Consider Bezanson, *Some Thoughts on the Emerging Irrebuttable Presumption Doctrine,* 7 Ind.L.Rev. 644, 652 (1974): "[The] doctrine seems to have substantive underpinnings, since it seems to be selectively applied to certain types of cases involving important, yet nonfundamental rights. *LaFleur* raised the difficult issue of whether sex-based discrimination is constitutionally suspect. *Vlandis* and *Murry* involved arguably new extensions of the right to travel, a matter which the Court may have preferred to leave untouched. *Stanley* was susceptible to analysis in terms of sex discrimination or the fundamental rights of procreation, privacy, or the like. But selective application of the doctrine to these 'quasi-fundamental' rights or interests can only be gleaned from what the Court has decided in fact, since the Court has made little effort to distinguish or identify in principle the scope of the doctrine's application. Indeed, the value of the doctrine seems to lie in the fact that it permits the Court to avoid the difficult policy issues raised in the cases." [e]

2. *Similarity to equal protection.* To what extent is the "irrebuttable presumption" doctrine no more than a substitute for equal protection analysis?

e. For efforts to limit the "irrebuttable presumption" approach to special types of situations, see Marshall, J., fn. b supra; Tribe, *American Constitutional Law* 1092–97 (1978); Gordon & Tenenbaum, *Conclusive Presumption Analysis: The Principle of Individual Opportunity,* 71 Nw.U.L.Rev. 579 (1977); Chase, *The Premature Demise of Irrebuttable Presumptions,* 47 U.Colo.L.Rev. 653 (1976).

Consider Note, *The Irrebuttable Presumption Doctrine in the Supreme Court,* 87 Harv.L.Rev. 1534, 1552 (1974): "When an equal protection decision requires that persons previously excluded from a benefit must now be included, an additional cost is of course incurred. But this is a cost inherent in the state's decision to award a certain benefit to a group of individuals. [But] when the Court requires that a hearing be given, [the] cost does not represent only benefits supplied to a group of individuals, but also includes a transaction cost in determining who is to receive benefits. [It] may impose substantial costs which a legislature never contemplated and would never have been willing to bear. The choice of classification by a legislature represents a judgment—one that could hardly be called irrational—that the increased accuracy of adjudication is not worth the increased expenditure of time and money." Compare Note, 46 U.Colo.L.Rev. 79, 102 (1974): "[T]he consequence of [the irrebuttable presumption] analysis is not as harsh as invalidating a classification under the usual equal protection analysis, since [t]he state is still left with a rebuttable presumption that it can use to shift the burden to an individual to come forward to refute the presumption in his case. The Court does not have to make the difficult decision to abolish the classification by making the statute operate either on everyone or on no one." See also Bartlett, *Pregnancy and the Constitution: The Uniqueness Trap,* 62 Calif.L.Rev. 1532, 1545–47 (1974): "The irrebuttable presumption model does not give an individual as much protection [as] under the strict scrutiny test of the equal protection and substantive due process models. An individual may be left with the burden of showing what others need not show. [U]nder this model, a statute like that in *Frontiero,* [Sec. 3, A supra,] [might] have been upheld, even though servicemen received [the] benefits without proving spousal dependency. [Moreover,] this opportunity to prove that one should not be restricted in a certain way does not mean that the factor which gave rise to the challenged presumption such as pregnancy, may not be weighed heavily in determining whether that individual belongs in the restricted group. [The] Court did not insist that pregnant teachers be treated the same as teachers with other temporary disabilities. They could be forced to prove their fitness to teach in order to remain in the classroom, even though other potentially unfit or disabled teachers need not do so."

3. *Limits on the doctrine.* (a) *Marshall v. United States,* 414 U.S. 417, 94 S.Ct. 700, 38 L.Ed.2d 618 (1974), per Burger, C.J., held that the Narcotic Rehabilitation Act—which authorizes judges to order treatment in lieu of imprisonment for addicts convicted of a federal offense, but excludes persons with two or more prior felony convictions—was "rational" and not violative of equal protection. *Usery v. Turner Elkhorn Mining Co.,* 428 U.S. 1, 96 S.Ct. 2882, 49 L.Ed.2d 752 (1976), per Marshall, J., held that the Federal Coal Mine Health and Safety Act—which presumes that a miner with pneumoconiosis is totally disabled and, if he dies, that his death was caused by this disease—was not "arbitrary and irrational" and thus not violative of due process. Both cases rejected irrebuttable presumption challenges. See also *N.Y.C. Transit Auth. v. Beazer,* Sec. 1 supra, finding "no merit" in such a challenge.

(b) To what extent does the doctrine survive *Salfi,* infra?

WEINBERGER v. SALFI

422 U.S. 749, 95 S.Ct. 2457, 45 L.Ed.2d 522 (1975).

JUSTICE REHNQUIST delivered the opinion of the Court.

[Within a month of appellee's marriage, her husband, who was allegedly "in apparent good health at the time of the marriage," suffered a heart attack and died five months later. Appellee filed] for mother's insurance benefits for herself and child's insurance benefits for her daughter by a previous marriage [which] were denied [on] the basis of the duration-of-relationship requirements of [the Act which] exclude surviving wives and stepchildren who had their respective relationships to a deceased wage earner for less than nine months prior to his death. * * *

The standard for testing the validity of Congress' Social Security classification was clearly stated in *Flemming v. Nestor,* 363 U.S. 603, 611, 80 S.Ct. 1367, 1373, 4 L.Ed.2d 1435 (1960): "Particularly when we deal with a withholding of a noncontractual benefit under a social welfare [program], we must recognize that the Due Process Clause can be thought to interpose a bar only if the statute manifests a patently arbitrary classification, utterly lacking in rational justification." [The Court cited similar language from *Dandridge,* Sec. 4, IV supra.]

We hold that [*Stanley,* which "referred to the fact that the 'rights to conceive and to raise one's children have been deemed "essential," ' " *Vlandis,* and *LaFleur,* which stated "that freedom of personal choice in matters of marriage and family life is one of the liberties protected" by due process] are not controlling on the issue before us now. Unlike the claims involved in *Stanley* and *LaFleur,* a noncontractual claim to receive funds from the public treasury enjoys no constitutionally protected status,[a] *Dandridge,* though of course Congress may not invidiously discriminate among such claimants on the basis of a "bare congressional desire to harm a politically unpopular group," *U.S. Dep't of Agriculture v. Moreno,* [Sec. 4, IV supra], or on the basis of criteria which bear no rational relation to a legitimate legislative goal. *Jimenez; Murry.* Unlike the statutory scheme in *Vlandis,* the Social Security Act does not purport to speak in terms of the bona fides of the parties to a marriage, but then make plainly relevant evidence of such bona fides inadmissible. As in *Starns,* [appellants] are completely free to present evidence that they meet the specified requirements; failing in this effort, their only constitutional claim is that the test they cannot meet is not so rationally related to a legitimate legislative objective that it can be used to deprive them of benefits available to those who do satisfy that test.

We think that the District Court's extension of the holdings of *Stanley, Vlandis* and *LaFleur* to the eligibility requirement in issue here would turn the doctrine of those cases into a virtual engine of destruction for countless legislative judgments which have heretofore been thought wholly consistent with [due process]. For example, the very section [which] authorizes an action such as this, [requires] that a claim be filed within 60 days after administrative remedies are exhausted. It is indisputable that this requirement places people who file their claims more than 60 days after exhaustion in a different "class" than

a. Consider Tribe, fn. e supra, at 1096: "*Salfi,* of course, did not involve the liberty interest in deciding whether, when, and whom to marry, because any claim that the duration-of-relationship rule in fact affected a particular marriage decision would in effect concede to the government the only issue to be addressed at any individualized hearing—i.e., whether the particular marriage was in fact entered into for purposes of obtaining social security benefits."

people who file their claims within the time limit. If we were to follow the District Court's analysis, we would first try to ascertain the congressional "purpose" behind the provision, and probably would conclude that it was to prevent stale claims from being asserted in court. We would then turn to the question of whether such a flat cutoff provision was necessary to protect the Secretary from stale claims, whether it would be possible to make individualized determinations as to any prejudice suffered by the Secretary as the result of an untimely filing, and whether or not an individualized hearing on that issue should be required in each case. This would represent a degree of judicial involvement in the legislative function which we have eschewed except in the most unusual circumstances * * *.

In *Williamson v. Lee Optical Co.,* [Sec. 1 supra, the] Court said: "The problem of legislative classification is a perennial one, admitting of no doctrinaire definition. Evils in the same field may be of different dimensions and proportions, requiring different remedies. Or so the legislature may think." * * *

If the Fifth and Fourteenth Amendments permit this latitude to legislative decisions regulating the private sector of the economy, they surely allow no less latitude in prescribing the conditions upon which funds shall be dispensed from the public treasury. *Dandridge* * * *.

Under those standards, the question raised is not whether a statutory provision precisely filters out those, and only those, who are in the factual position which generated the congressional concern reflected in the statute. Such a rule would ban all prophylactic [provisions]. Nor is the question whether the provision filters out a substantial part of the class which caused congressional concern, or whether it filters out more members of the class than nonmembers. The question is whether Congress, its concern having been reasonably aroused by the possibility of an abuse, [could] rationally have concluded both that a particular limitation or qualification would protect against its occurrence, and that the expense and other difficulties of individual determinations justified the inherent imprecision of a prophylactic rule. We conclude that the duration-of-relationship test meets this constitutional standard.

The danger of persons entering a marriage relationship not to enjoy its traditional benefits, but instead to enable one spouse to claim benefits upon the anticipated early death of the wage earner, has been recognized from the very beginning of the Social Security program. [The statute] undoubtedly excludes some surviving wives who married with no anticipation of shortly becoming widows, and it may be that appellee Salfi is among them. It likewise may be true that the requirement does not filter out every such claimant, if a wage earner lingers longer than anticipated, or in the case of illnesses which can be recognized as terminal more than nine months prior to death. But neither of these facts necessarily renders the statutory scheme unconstitutional.

While it is possible to debate the wisdom of excluding legitimate claimants in order to discourage sham relationships, and of relying on a rule which may not exclude some obviously sham arrangements, we think it clear that Congress could rationally choose to adopt such a course. Large numbers of people are eligible for these programs and are potentially subject to inquiry as to the validity of their relationships to wage earners. [Not] only does the prophylactic approach thus obviate the necessity for large number of individualized determinations, but it also protects large numbers of claimants who satisfy the rule from the uncertainties and delays of administrative inquiry into the circumstances of their marriages. Nor is it at all clear that individual determinations could effectively filter out sham arrangements, since neither marital intent, life expectancy nor knowledge of terminal illness has been shown by appellees to be reliably determinable. Finally, the very possibility of prevailing at a hearing could reasonably be expected to encourage sham relationships.

The administrative difficulties of individual eligibility determinations are without doubt matters which Congress may [consider]. In this sense, the duration-of-relationship requirement represents not merely a substantive policy determination that benefits should be awarded only on the basis of genuine marital relationships, but also a substantive policy determination that limited resources would not be well spent in making individual determinations. * * *

Reversed.

JUSTICE BRENNAN, with whom JUSTICE MARSHALL joins, dissenting.

[The] Court today distinguishes *Stanley* and *LaFleur* [because] both dealt with protected rights, while this case deals with "a noncontractual claim to receive funds from the public treasury [which] enjoys no constitutionally protected status." But *Vlandis* also dealt with a government benefit program. [The Court] attempts to wish away *Vlandis* by noting that "where Connecticut purported to be concerned with residency, it might not at the same time deny to one seeking to meet its test of residency the opportunity to show factors clearly bearing on the issue." [b]

Yet, the Connecticut statute in *Vlandis* did not set "residency," undefined, as the criteria of eligibility; it *defined* residency in certain ways. The definitions of "resident" were precisely parallel to the statute here, which defines "widow" and "child" in part by the number of months of marriage.

Similarly, *Murry* and *Jimenez* both dealt with conclusive presumptions contained in statutes setting out criteria for eligibility for government benefits. The Court distinguishes them as cases in which "the criteria bear no rational relation to a legitimate legislative goal." But if the assumptions in *Murry* and *Jimenez* were irrational, the presumption in this case is even more irrational. We have been presented with no evidence at all that the problem of collusive marriages is one which exists at all. Indeed, the very fact that Congress has continually moved back the amount of time required to avoid the irrebuttable presumption suggests that it found, for each time period set, that it was depriving deserving people of benefits without alleviating any real problem of collusion. There is no reason to believe that the nine-month period is any more likely to discard a high proportion of collusive marriages than the five-year, three-year, or one-year periods employed earlier.

The Court says: "The administrative difficulties of individual eligibility determinations are without doubt matters which Congress may [consider]." But, as we said in *Stanley:* "[T]he Constitution recognizes higher values than speed and efficiency. * * *"

b. *Elkins v. Moreno,* 435 U.S. 647, 98 S.Ct. 1338, 55 L.Ed.2d 614 (1978), per Brennan, J.—involving "in-state" status for tuition at the University of Maryland—avoided "a decision on the continuing vitality of *Vlandis.*" But *Turner v. Department of Employment Security,* 423 U.S. 44, 96 S.Ct. 249, 46 L.Ed.2d 181 (1975), per curiam, relied on *LaFleur* to invalidate a Utah law making "pregnant women ineligible for unemployment benefits for a period extending from 12 weeks before the expected date of childbirth until a date six weeks after childbirth." Burger, C.J., and Blackmun, J., would not have summarily disposed of the case. Rehnquist, J., dissented.

This is not to say [that] *all* statutory provisions based on assumptions about underlying facts are per se unconstitutional unless individual hearings are provided. But in this case, as in the others in which we have stricken down conclusive presumptions, it *is* possible to specify those factors which, if proven in a hearing, would disprove a rebuttable presumption. See, e.g., *Vlandis.* For example, persuasive evidence of good health at the time of marriage would be sufficient, I should think, to disprove that the marriage was collusive. Also, in this case, as in *Stanley* and *LaFleur,* the presumption, insofar as it precludes people as to whom the presumed fact is untrue from so proving, runs counter to the general legislative policy—here, providing true widows and children with survivors' benefits. And finally, the presumption here, like that in *Vlandis, Murry,* and *Jimenez,* involves a measure of social opprobrium; the assumption is that the individual has purposely undertaken to evade legitimate requirements. When these factors are present, I believe that the Government's interests in efficiency must be surrendered to the individual's interest in proving that the facts presumed are not true as to him. * * * [c]

c. The dissent of Douglas, J., is omitted.

Chapter 7

THE CONCEPT OF STATE ACTION

SECTION 1. INTRODUCTION

The "state action" doctrine has long established that, because of their language or history, most provisions of the Constitution that protect individual liberty—including those set forth in Art. 1, §§ 9 and 10, the Bill of Rights, and the fourteenth and fifteenth amendments—impose restrictions or obligations only on government. The subject received its first extensive treatment in the CIVIL RIGHTS CASES, 109 U.S. 3, 3 S.Ct. 18, 27 L.Ed. 835 (1883), which held, per BRADLEY, J., that neither the thirteenth nor fourteenth amendments empowered Congress to pass the Civil Rights Act of 1875, making racial discrimination unlawful in public accommodations (inns, public conveyances, places of public amusement, etc.)—"and no other ground of authority for its passage being suggested, it must necessarily be declared void." Although the issue presented did not simply concern the authority granted the *Court* under § 1 of the thirteenth and fourteenth amendments, but rather involved the scope of *Congress'* power under the final sections of these amendments to enforce their substantive provisions "by appropriate legislation" (a topic to be considered in detail in Ch. 8), the Court's discussion of "state action" remains the classic exposition of the doctrine.

The Court held that, under the fourteenth amendment, "it is state action of a particular character that is prohibited. Individual invasion of individual rights is not the subject-matter of the amendment. [It] nullifies and makes void all state legislation, and state action of every kind, which impairs the privileges and immunities of citizens of the United States, or which injures them in life, liberty, or property without due process of law, or which denies to any of them the equal protection of the laws. [T]he last section of the amendment invests congress with power [to] adopt appropriate legislation for correcting the effects of such prohibited state laws and state acts, and thus to render them effectually null, void, and innocuous. [It] does not authorize congress to create a code of municipal law for the regulation of private rights; but to provide modes of redress against the operation of state laws, and the action of state officers, executive or judicial, when these are subversive of the fundamental rights specified in the amendment. * * *

"An inspection of the [Civil Rights Act of 1875] shows that [it] proceeds ex directo to declare that certain acts committed by individuals shall be deemed offenses, and shall be prosecuted [by] the United States. It does not profess to be corrective of any constitutional wrong committed by the states; [it] applies equally to cases arising in states which have the justest laws respecting the personal rights of citizens, and whose authorities are ever ready to enforce such laws as to those which arise in states that may have violated the prohibition of the amendment. In other words, it steps into the domain of local jurisprudence, and lays down rules for the conduct of individuals in society towards each other * * *. [C]ivil rights, such as are guarantied by the constitution against state aggression, cannot be impaired by the wrongful acts of individuals, unsupported by state authority in the shape of laws, customs, or judicial or executive proceedings. The wrongful act of an individual, unsupported by any such authority, is simply a private wrong, or a crime of that individual * * *. An individual cannot deprive a man of his right to vote, to hold property, to buy and to sell, to sue in the courts, or to be a witness or a juror; he may, by force or fraud, interfere with the enjoyment of the right in a particular case; [but] unless protected in these wrongful acts by some shield of state law or state authority, he cannot destroy or injure the right; he will only render himself amenable to satisfaction or punishment; and amenable therefor to the laws of the state where the wrongful acts are committed. [The] abrogation and denial of rights, for which the states alone were or could be responsible, was the great seminal and fundamental wrong which was intended to be remedied."

The Court recognized that the thirteenth amendment "is not a mere prohibition of state laws establishing or upholding slavery, but an absolute declaration that slavery or involuntary servitude shall not exist in any part of the United States [and] that the power vested in congress to enforce the article by appropriate legislation, clothes congress with power to pass all laws necessary and proper for abolishing all badges and incidents of slavery, in the United States * * *. [T]he civil rights bill of 1866, passed in view of the thirteenth amendment, before the fourteenth was adopted, undertook to wipe out these burdens and disabilities, * * * namely, the same right to make and enforce contracts, to sue, be parties, give evidence, and to inherit, purchase, lease, sell, and convey property, as is enjoyed by white citizens. Whether this legislation was fully authorized by the thirteenth amendment alone, without the support which it afterwards received from the fourteenth amendment, after the adoption of which it was re-enacted with some additions, it is not necessary to inquire. It is referred to for the purpose of showing that at that time (in 1866) congress did not assume, under the authority given by the thirteenth amendment, to adjust what may be called the social rights of men and races in the community; but only to declare and vindicate those fundamental rights which appertain to the essence of citizenship, and the enjoyment or deprivation of which constitutes the essential distinction between freedom and slavery.

"[It] would be running the slavery argument into the ground to make it apply to every act of discrimination which a person may see fit to make as to the guests he will entertain, or as to the people he will take into his coach or cab or car, or admit to his concert or theater, or deal with in other matters of intercourse or business. Innkeepers and public carriers, by the laws of all the states, so far as we are aware, are bound, to the extent of their facilities, to furnish proper accommodation to all unobjectionable persons who in good faith apply for them. If the laws themselves make any unjust discrimination, amenable to the prohibitions of the fourteenth amendment, congress has full power to afford a remedy under that amendment and in accordance with it." [a]

a. In *Bell v. Maryland,* 378 U.S. 226, 84 S.Ct. 1814, 12 L.Ed.2d 822 (1964), Goldberg, J., joined by Warren, C.J., and Douglas, J., examining the "historical evidence" in detail, concluded that the *Civil Rights Cases* were based on the assumption of the framers of the fourteenth amendment that "under state law, when the Negro's disability as a citizen was removed, he would be assured the same public civil rights that the law had guaranteed white

HARLAN, J., dissented: "Was it the purpose of the nation [by the thirteenth amendment] simply to destroy the institution [of slavery], and remit the race, theretofore held in bondage, to the several states for such protection, in their civil rights, necessarily growing out of freedom, as those states, in their discretion, choose to provide? [S]ince slavery [was] the moving or principal cause of the adoption of that amendment, and since that institution rested wholly upon the inferiority, as a race, of those held in bondage, their freedom necessarily involved immunity from, and protection against, all discrimination against them, because of their race, in respect of such civil rights as belong to freemen of other races. Congress, therefore, under its express power to enforce that amendment, by appropriate legislation, may enact laws of a direct and primary character, operating upon states, their officers and agents, and also upon, at least, such individuals and corporations as exercise public functions and wield power and authority under the state. * * *

"It remains now to inquire what are the legal rights of colored persons in respect of the accommodations * * *.

"1. As to public conveyances on land and water. [In] *Olcott v. Sup'rs,* 16 Wall. 694, it was ruled that railroads [are] none the less public highways because controlled and owned by private corporations; that it is a part of the function of government to make and maintain highways for the conveyance of the public; that no matter who is the agent, and what is the agency, the function performed is *that of the state* * * *.

"Such being the relations these corporations hold to the public, it would seem that the right of a colored person to use an improved public highway, upon the terms accorded to freemen of other races, is as fundamental in the state of freedom, established in this country, as are any of the rights which my brethren concede to be so far fundamental as to be deemed the essence of civil freedom.

"2. As to inns. [The] authorities are sufficient to show that a keeper of an inn is in the exercise of a quasi public employment. The law gives him special privileges, and he is charged with certain duties and responsibilities to the public. The public nature of his employment forbids him from discriminating against any person asking admission as a guest on account of the race or color of that person.

"3. As to places of public amusement. [W]ithin the meaning of the act of 1875, [they] are such as are established and maintained under direct license of the law. [The] local government granting the license represents [the colored race] as well as all other races within its jurisdiction. A license from the public to establish a place of public amusement, imports, in law, equality of right, at such places, among all the members of that public.[b]"

Turning to the fourteenth amendment, "the first clause of the first section—'all persons born or naturalized in the United States, and subject to the

persons," and that "the duties of the proprietors of places of public accommodation would remain as they had long been and that the States would now be affirmatively obligated to insure that these rights ran to Negro as well as white citizens." Black, J., joined by Harlan and White, JJ., disagreed. Cf. Tribe, *American Constitutional Law* 1694 n. 14 (2d ed. 1988). See generally Frank & Munro, *The Original Understanding of "Equal Protection of the Laws,"* 1972 Wash.U.L.Q. 421, 468–72.

b. For general support of Harlan, J.'s thirteenth amendment view, see Kinoy, *The Constitutional Right of Negro Freedom,* 21 Rutg.L. Rev. 387 (1967). Although the Court has since ruled that the thirteenth amendment grants broad enforcement power to *Congress* (see p. 1289 infra), the Court has confined its use of the amendment, absent congressional legislation, to holding state peonage laws invalid. See *Memphis v. Greene,* p. 982 supra.

jurisdiction thereof, are citizens of the United States, and of the state wherein they reside'—is of a distinctly affirmative character. In its application to the colored race, previously liberated, it created and granted, as well citizenship of the United States, as citizenship of the state in which they respectively resided. [Further], they were brought, by this supreme act of the nation, within the direct operation of that provision of the constitution which declares that 'the citizens of each state shall be entitled to all privileges and immunities of citizens in the several states.' Article IV, § 2.

"The citizenship thus acquired [may be protected] by congressional legislation of a primary direct character; this, because the power of congress is not restricted to the enforcement of prohibitions upon state laws or state action. It is, in terms distinct and positive, to enforce 'the *provisions of this article*' of amendment * * * *all* of the provisions,—affirmative and prohibitive * * *.

"But what was secured to colored citizens of the United States—as between them and their respective states—by the grant to them of state citizenship? With what rights, privileges, or immunities did this grant from the nation invest them? There is one, if there be no others—exemption from race discrimination in respect of any civil right belonging to citizens of the white race in the same state [by] the state, or its officers, or by individuals, or corporations exercising public functions or authority * * *. It was perfectly well known that the great danger to the equal enjoyment by citizens of their rights, as citizens, was to be apprehended, not altogether from unfriendly state legislation, but from the hostile action of corporations and individuals in the states. * * *

"But if it were conceded that the power of congress could not be brought into activity until the rights specified in the act of 1875 had been abridged or denied by some state law or state action, I maintain that the decision of the court is erroneous. [In] every material sense applicable to the practical enforcement of the fourteenth amendment, railroad corporations, keepers of inns, and managers of places of public amusement are agents of the state, because amenable, in respect of their public duties and functions, to public regulation. * * * I agree that if one citizen chooses not to hold social intercourse with another, he is not and cannot be made amenable to the law for his conduct in that regard; for no legal right of a citizen is violated by the refusal of others to maintain merely social relations with him, even upon grounds of race. [The] rights which congress, by the act of 1875, endeavored to secure and protect are legal, not social, rights. The right, for instance, of a colored citizen to use the accommodations of a public highway upon the same terms as are permitted to white citizens is no more a social right than his right, under the law, to use the public streets of a city, or a town, or a turnpike road, or a public market, or a post-office, or his right to sit in a public building with others, of whatever race, for the purpose of hearing the political questions of the day discussed."

The basic doctrine of the *Civil Rights Cases* —that it is "state action" that is prohibited by the fourteenth amendment—has remained undisturbed. But the question of what constitutes "state action" has generated significant controversy. It is settled that the term comprehends statutes enacted by national, state and local legislative bodies and the official actions of all government officers. The more difficult problems arise when the conduct of private individuals or groups is challenged as being unconstitutional. Although—as will be pointed out in the materials that follow (see, e.g., note 7 after *Shelley v. Kraemer,* Sec. 3 infra)—it has often been argued that the inquiries are misperceived, the questions that the

Court has asked are whether the private actor (a) is performing a "government function," or (b) is sufficiently "involved with" or "encouraged by" the state so as to be held to the state's constitutional obligations. These subjects will be developed in the next two sections of this chapter.

Until the past few decades, most of the cases involved racial discrimination (or, occasionally, denial of free speech). But, as will be detailed in Ch. 8, the enactment and strengthening of federal (and state) civil rights statutes since the 1960s has largely mooted the problem of private racial discrimination. Further, with the growth under the equal protection clause of the number of "suspect" and "quasi-suspect" classifications (see Ch. 6, Sec. 3) and the expansion under the due process clause of the procedural rights that the state must afford persons before depriving them of liberty or property (see Ch. 3, Sec. 5), an increasing number of cases (as will be seen in the final section of this chapter) have involved attempts to require "private" adherence to these constitutional responsibilities.

SECTION 2. "GOVERNMENT FUNCTION"

SMITH v. ALLWRIGHT, 321 U.S. 649, 64 S.Ct. 757, 88 L.Ed. 987 (1944), held the fifteenth amendment forebade exclusion of blacks from primary elections conducted by the Democratic Party of Texas, pursuant to party resolution. The Court, per REED, J., relied heavily on a case from Louisiana, *United States v. Classic,* 313 U.S. 299, 61 S.Ct. 1031, 85 L.Ed. 1368 (1941), which held "that Section 4 of Article I of the Constitution authorized Congress to regulate primary as well as general elections, 'where the primary is by law made an integral part of the election machinery.'" *Classic* "makes clear that state delegation to a party of the power to fix the qualifications of primary elections is delegation of a state function that may make the party's action the action of the state." The Court added that the extensive statutory control of primary elections in Texas "makes the party which is required to follow these legislative directions an agency of the state in so far as it determines the participants in a primary election. [The] right to participate in the choice of elected officials without restriction by any state because of race [is] not to be nullified by a state through casting its electoral process in a form which permits a private organization to practice racial discrimination in the election." Frankfurter, J., concurred in the result. Roberts, J., dissented.

TERRY v. ADAMS, 345 U.S. 461, 73 S.Ct. 809, 97 L.Ed. 1152 (1953), involved the exclusion of blacks from the "pre-primary" elections of the Jaybird Democratic Association, an organization of all the white voters in a Texas county that was run like a regular political party and whose candidates since 1889 had nearly always run unopposed and won in the regular Democratic primary and the general election. The record showed "complete absence of any compliance with the state law or practice, or cooperation by or with the State." Although there was no majority opinion, the Court held the election subject to the fifteenth amendment.

BLACK, J., joined by Douglas and Burton, JJ., found that "the admitted party purpose" was "to escape the Fifteenth Amendment's command." The "Amendment excludes social or business clubs" but "no election machinery could be sustained if its purpose or effect was to deny Negroes on account of their race an effective voice in the governmental affairs." "The only election that has counted in this Texas county for more than fifty years has been that held by the

Jaybirds." "For a state to permit such a duplication of its election processes is to permit a flagrant abuse [of] the Fifteenth Amendment."

CLARK, J., joined by Vinson, C.J., and Reed and Jackson, JJ., described the Jaybirds as not merely a "private club" "organized to influence public candidacies or political action," but rather a "part and parcel of the Democratic Party, an organization existing under the auspices of Texas law. [W]hen a state structures its electoral apparatus in a form which devolves upon a political organization the uncontested choice of public officials, that organization itself, in whatever disguise, takes on those attributes of government which draw the Constitution's safeguards into play." [a]

Only MINTON, J., dissented: The Jaybird's activity "seems to differ very little from situations common in many other places [where] a candidate must obtain the approval of a religious group. [It] must be recognized that elections and other public business are influenced by all sorts of pressures from carefully organized groups. [Far] from the activities of these groups being properly labeled as state action, [they] are to be considered as attempts to influence or obtain state action." [b]

MARSH v. ALABAMA, 326 U.S. 501, 66 S.Ct. 276, 90 L.Ed. 265 (1946), held that "a State, consistently with the First and Fourteenth Amendments," cannot "impose criminal punishment on a person who undertakes to distribute religious literature on the premises of a company-owned town contrary to the wishes of the town's management." The town, owned by a shipbuilding company, had "all the characteristics of any other American town." Appellant, a Jehovah's Witness, was warned that she could not distribute the literature and when she refused to leave the sidewalk of the town's "business block," a deputy sheriff, who was paid by the company to serve as the town's policeman, arrested her and she was convicted of trespass.

The Court, per BLACK, J., reversed: Under *Lovell v. Griffin,* p. 599 supra, an ordinary municipality could not have barred appellant's activities, and the fact that "a single company had legal title to all the town" may not result in impairing "channels of communication" of its inhabitants or those persons passing through. "Ownership does not always mean absolute dominion. The more an owner, for his advantage, opens up his property for use by the public in general, the more do his rights become circumscribed by the statutory and constitutional rights of those who use it. Thus, the owners of privately held bridges, ferries, turnpikes and railroads may not operate them as freely as a farmer does his farm. Since these facilities are built and operated primarily to benefit the public and since their operation is essentially a public function, it is subject to state regulation." In balancing property rights against freedom of press and religion, "the latter occupy a preferred position" and the former do not "justify the State's permitting a

a. Frankfurter, J., stated that the "vital requirement is State responsibility" and found it as follows: "As a matter of practical politics," "we may assume" "those charged by State law with the duty of assuring all eligible voters an opportunity to participate in the selection of candidates at the primary—the county election officials who are normally leaders in their communities—participate by voting in the Jaybird primary" "and condone" "a wholly successful effort to withdraw significance from the State-prescribed primary, to subvert the operation of what is formally the law of the State for primaries in this county."

b. Are these examples distinguishable because "the only election that has counted in this Texas county for more than fifty years has been that held by the Jaybirds"? Because the fifteenth amendment outlawed discrimination *on the basis of race or color* with respect to the right to vote?

corporation to govern a community of citizens so as to restrict their fundamental liberties and the enforcement of such restraint by the application of a State statute." Frankfurter, J., concurred and Jackson, J., did not participate.

REED, J., joined by Vinson, C.J., and Burton, J., dissented, noting that "there was [no] objection to appellant's use of the nearby public highway and under our decisions she could rightfully have continued her activities [thirty feet parallel] from the spot she insisted upon using."

AMALGAMATED FOOD EMPLOYEES UNION v. LOGAN VALLEY PLAZA, 391 U.S. 308, 88 S.Ct. 1601, 20 L.Ed.2d 603 (1968), per MARSHALL, J.,—reasoning that a large privately owned shopping center was the "functional equivalent of the business district [involved] in *Marsh*"—held that it could not enjoin peaceful union picketing on its property against a store located in the shopping center. Black and White, JJ., dissented; Harlan, J., did not reach the merits.

Four years later, LLOYD CORP. v. TANNER, 407 U.S. 551, 92 S.Ct. 2219, 33 L.Ed.2d 131 (1972), per POWELL, J., held that a shopping center's refusal to permit antiwar handbilling on its premises was not state action violative of the first and fourteenth amendments. *Logan Valley* was distinguished on the grounds that the picketing there had been specifically directed to a store in the shopping center and the pickets had no other reasonable opportunity to reach their intended audience. *Marsh* was said to have "involved the assumption by a private enterprise of semi-official municipal functions as a delegate of the State. In effect, the owner of the company town was performing the full spectrum of municipal powers and stood in the shoes of the State. In the instant case there is no comparable assumption or exercise of municipal functions or power." Marshall, J., joined by Douglas, Brennan and Stewart, JJ., dissented, finding "no valid distinction" from *Logan Valley.*

Finally, HUDGENS v. NLRB, 424 U.S. 507, 96 S.Ct. 1029, 47 L.Ed.2d 196 (1976), per STEWART, J.,—involving picketing of a store in a shopping center by a union with a grievance against the store's warehouse (located elsewhere)—overruled *Logan Valley* on the ground that "*Lloyd* amounted to [its] total rejection."[a] MARSHALL, J., joined by Brennan, J., dissented: "*Logan Valley* [recognized] that the owner of the modern shopping center complex, by dedicating his property to public use as a business district, to some extent displaces the 'State' from control of historical First Amendment forums, and may acquire a virtual monopoly of places suitable for effective communication. The roadways, parking lots, and walkways of the modern shopping center may be as essential for effective speech as the streets and sidewalks in the municipal or company-owned town. [No] one would seriously question the legitimacy of the values of privacy and individual autonomy traditionally associated with privately owned property. [But] when a property owner opens his property to public use the force of those values diminishes." [c]

---

a. White, J., concurred in the result, finding that *Logan Valley* "does not cover the facts of this case. The pickets of the Butler Shoe Co. store [were] not purporting to convey information about the 'manner in which that particular [store] was being operated' but rather about the operation of a warehouse not located on the center's premises. The picketing was thus not 'directly related in its purpose to the use to which the shopping center property was being put.'" Stevens, J., did not participate.

c. For a decision that the free speech and petition provisions of the California constitution require that "shopping center owners per-

EVANS v. NEWTON, 382 U.S. 296, 86 S.Ct. 486, 15 L.Ed.2d 373 (1966): In 1911, Senator A.O. Bacon devised land to Macon, Ga., to be used as a park for whites only. After *Pennsylvania v. Board of Trusts,* 353 U.S. 230, 77 S.Ct. 806, 1 L.Ed.2d 792 (1957)—holding that there is "state action" when public officials act as trustees under a private will requiring racial discrimination—the city permitted blacks to use the park. When Bacon's heirs sued to remove the city as trustee, the Georgia courts accepted the city's resignation and appointed private individuals as trustees so that the trust's purpose would not fail.

The Court, per DOUGLAS, J., reversed. Although "when private individuals or groups are endowed by the State with powers or functions governmental in nature, they become agencies or instrumentalities of the State," nonetheless, "the range of government activities is broad and varied, and the fact that government has engaged in a particular activity does not necessarily mean that an individual entrepreneur or manager of the same kind of undertaking suffers the same constitutional inhibitions. While a State may not segregate public schools so as to exclude one or more religious groups, those sects may maintain their own parochial educational systems. *Pierce v. Society of Sisters,* [p. 144 supra]."

"If a testator wanted to leave a school or center for the use of one race only and in no way implicated the State in the supervision, control, or management of that facility, we assume arguendo that no constitutional difficulty would be encountered. This park, however, is in a different posture" because "for years it was an integral part" of the city's activities, assumedly "granted tax exemption" and "swept, manicured, watered, patrolled, and maintained by the city." "The momentum it acquired as a public facility is certainly not dissipated ipso facto by the appointment of 'private' trustees. So far as this record shows, there has been no change in municipal maintenance and concern over this facility. [If] the municipality remains entwined in the management or control of the park, it remains subject to the restraints of the Fourteenth Amendment."

"This conclusion is buttressed by the" fact that "the service rendered even by a private park of this character is municipal in nature," "more like a fire department or police department" than like "golf clubs, social centers, luncheon clubs, schools such as Tuskegee was at least in origin, and other like organizations in the private sector." "Mass recreation through the use of parks is plainly in the public domain and state courts that aid private parties to perform that public function on a segregated basis implicate the State in conduct proscribed by the Fourteenth Amendment. Like the streets of the company town in *Marsh,* the elective process of *Terry,* and the transit system of *Public Utilities Comm'n v. Pollak,*[c] the predominant character and purpose of this park are municipal." White, J., concurred on a separate ground.

HARLAN, J., joined by Stewart, J., dissented: The majority's "real holding" is not based on any state involvement in the park, but "because a privately operated park whose only criterion for exclusion is racial is within the 'public

mit expressive activity on their property," see *Robins v. Pruneyard Shopping Center,* 23 Cal. 3d 899, 153 Cal.Rptr. 854, 592 P.2d 341 (1979). For consideration under the National Labor Relations Act of the statutory right of unions to engage in communicative activity on the employer's premises, see *Eastex, Inc. v. NLRB,* 437 U.S. 556, 98 S.Ct. 2505, 57 L.Ed.2d 428 (1978); *Scott Hudgens,* 230 N.L.R.B. 414 (1977).

c. In *Public Utilities Com'n v. Pollak,* 343 U.S. 451, 72 S.Ct. 813, 96 L.Ed. 1068 (1952), a city transit company subject to public regulation was considered in "sufficiently close relation" with the government as to cause the Court to determine whether the company's playing of radio programs on buses violated due process.

domain.'" Precedent does "not support this novel state action theory." In *Pollak,* "state action was explicitly premised on the close legal regulation of the company by the public utilities commission and the commission's approval of the particular action under attack. The conclusion might alternatively have rested on the near-exclusive legal monopoly enjoyed by the company, but in all events nothing was rested on any 'public function' theory." In *Terry,* "none of the three prevailing opinions garnered a majority, and some commentators have simply concluded that the state action requirement was read out of the Fifteenth Amendment on that occasion." [d] *Marsh* is the "only Fourteenth Amendment case finding state action in the 'public function' performed by a technically private institution."

The failing of the majority's theory "can be shown by comparing [the] 'public function' of privately established schools with that of privately owned parks. Like parks, the purpose schools serve is important to the public. Like parks, private control exists, but there is also a very strong tradition of public control in this field. Like parks, schools may be available to almost anyone of one race or religion but to no others. Like parks, there are normally alternatives for those shut out but there may also be inconveniences and disadvantages caused by the restriction. Like parks, the extent of school intimacy varies greatly depending on the size and character of the institution." [e]

"While this process of analogy might be spun out to reach privately owned orphanages, libraries, garbage collection companies, detective agencies, and a host of other functions commonly regarded as nongovernmental though paralleling fields of governmental activity, the example of schools is, I think, sufficient to indicate the pervasive potentialities of this 'public function' theory of state action. It substitutes for the comparatively clear and concrete tests of state action a catch-phrase approach as vague and amorphous as it is far-reaching. [f] [And] it carries the seeds of transferring to federal authority vast areas of concerns whose regulation has wisely been left by the Constitution to the States." [g]

Notes and Questions

1. *Scope of the decisions.* (a) In *Marsh,* could the shipbuilding company discriminate against blacks in hiring production workers? In hiring peace officers or street cleaners for the town? In *Smith v. Allwright,* could the Democratic Party refuse to hire Jewish secretaries? In *Terry,* could the Jaybirds refuse to hire black secretaries? May "private organizations" that perform

d. Harlan, J., cited Lewis, *The Meaning of State Action,* 60 Colum.L.Rev. 1083, 1094 (1960), who argues that "voting is a purely governmental function. No private organization can decree that a majority vote shall entitle a candidate to public office, while most of the functions involved in [other] cases are those traditionally performed by private organizations or at least within their performance capabilities." See also Note, *The Strange Career of State Action Under the Fifteenth Amendment,* 74 Yale L.J. 1448, 1456–59 (1965).

e. For further consideration of "private schools," see note 3 after *Moose Lodge v. Irvis,* Sec. 3 infra.

f. Is there a "strong tradition" of private as well as public operation of parks in cities? Is it likely that, if Senator Bacon had not provided the park in *Evans,* the city would have provided its own? Is this approach too "vague and amorphous" to serve as a constitutional standard?

g. Black, J., believing that "the Georgia courts decided no federal constitutional question," agreed with the position also stated by Harlan, J.'s opinion that "the writ of certiorari should have been dismissed as improvidently granted."

For subsequent litigation in respect to this park, see *Evans v. Abney,* Sec. 3 infra.

"government functions" be subject to some constitutional limitations but not others?

(b) *Migrant labor camps.* A company that has a large commercial farm owns a "residential community" adjacent to it that is several miles from the nearest municipality. The "community" has duplex homes and apartments for about half of the 300 farmworkers (and their families) who work on the farm either seasonally or year-round. It also has a store that sells food, a cafeteria, and a recreation center. Does *Marsh* or *Hudgens* govern the question of whether the company may exclude union organizers from the "residential community"? See Note, *First Amendment and the Problem of Access to Migrant Labor Camps,* 67 Corn.L.Rev. 560 (1976).

(c) *Residential communities.* A company owns a "residential community, covering 129 acres and housing 12,000 family units made up of some 35,000 people, in 171 adjoining and 'interrelated' apartment houses." Does *Marsh* or *Hudgens* govern the question of whether the company may refuse to rent to blacks? May refuse to permit nonresidents to distribute political pamphlets in the apartment houses? On the privately owned "sidewalks" within the community? See *Watchtower Bible & Tract Society v. Metropolitan Life Ins. Co.,* 297 N.Y. 339, 79 N.E.2d 433 (1948), cert. denied, 335 U.S. 886, 69 S.Ct. 23, 93 L.Ed. 425 (1948).

(d) The "government function" issue is considered further in Sec. 4 infra.

2. *Statutory bargaining agents.* Suppose a labor union, acting as exclusive bargaining agent for all employees by authority of federal statute, does not bargain as strenuously for black employees? See generally Hale, *Force and the State: A Comparison of Political and Economic Compulsion,* 35 Colum.L.Rev. 149, 192–98 (1935). Consider Murphy, J. concurring in *Steele v. Louisville & N.R.R.,* 323 U.S. 192, 208, 65 S.Ct. 226, 234, 89 L.Ed. 173, 186 (1944): "While such a union is essentially a private organization, its power to represent and bind all members of a class or craft is derived solely from Congress. [I]t cannot be assumed that Congress meant to authorize the representative to act so to ignore the rights guaranteed by the Constitution. Otherwise the Act would bear the stigma of unconstitutionality under the Fifth Amendment." May such a union, although bargaining fairly for black employees, bar them from union membership?

3. *"Private" function.* (a) If the activities of private persons or groups may rise to the performance of a "government function," may certain official activities of government ever be considered the performance of a "private function"? Such as acting as trustee under a private will? Is the nature of the trust property relevant? In any case, does the state's official "entwinement" end the matter?

(b) If a privately owned amusement park contracts with a state deputy sheriff, who is regularly employed by the park, to enforce its racial segregation policy, may the state convict blacks, whom the deputy arrests when they refuse to leave the premises, for trespass? See *Griffin v. Maryland,* 378 U.S. 130, 84 S.Ct. 1770, 12 L.Ed.2d 754 (1964).

(c) *State university scholarship funds.* May a state university constitutionally award scholarships which the donor has designated for whites only? For persons of a particular religion only? If the donor personally selects the scholarship recipients each year and racially discriminates, may the university constitutionally admit those selected? Is there a "difference of substance" between these two situations? May a state university constitutionally solicit scholarships to be awarded on racial bases? See generally Note, *Constitutionality of Restricted Scholarships,* 33 N.Y.U.L.Rev. 604 (1958).

JACKSON v. METROPOLITAN EDISON CO.

419 U.S. 345, 95 S.Ct. 449, 42 L.Ed.2d 477 (1974).

JUSTICE REHNQUIST delivered the opinion of the Court.

Respondent [holds] a certificate of public convenience issued by the Pennsylvania Public Utility Commission empowering it to deliver electricity [and] is subject to extensive regulation by the Commission. Under a provision of its general tariff filed with the Commission, it has the right to discontinue service to any customer on reasonable notice of nonpayment of bills.

Petitioner [sued] Metropolitan [under] 42 U.S.C. § 1983, seeking damages for the termination and an injunction requiring Metropolitan to continue providing power to her residence until she had been afforded notice, a hearing, and an opportunity to pay any amounts found due. She urged that under state law she had an entitlement to reasonably continuous electrical service to her home and that Metropolitan's termination [was] "state action" depriving her of property in violation of the Fourteenth Amendment's guarantee of due process of law.

The District Court [and] Court of Appeals [found] an absence of state action.

[The] mere fact that a business is subject to state regulation does not by itself convert its action into that of the State for purposes of the Fourteenth Amendment. [It] may well be that acts of a heavily regulated utility with at least something of a governmentally protected monopoly will more readily be found to be "state" acts than will the acts of an entity lacking these characteristics. But the inquiry must be whether there is a sufficiently close nexus between the State and the challenged action of the regulated entity so that the action of the latter may be fairly treated as that of the State itself. * * *

Petitioner first argues that "state action" is present because of the monopoly status allegedly conferred upon Metropolitan by the State of Pennsylvania. As a factual matter, it may well be doubted that the State ever granted or guaranteed Metropolitan a monopoly.[8] But assuming that it had, this fact is not determinative * * *. In *Pollak,* where the Court dealt with the activities of the District of Columbia Transit Co., a congressionally established monopoly, we expressly disclaimed reliance on the monopoly status of the transit authority. * * *

Petitioner next urges that state action is present because respondent provides an essential public service [and] hence performs a "public function." We have, of course, found state action present in the exercise by a private entity of powers traditionally exclusively reserved to the State. See, e.g., *Terry v. Adams* (election); *Marsh* (company town); *Evans v. Newton* (municipal park). If we were dealing with the exercise by Metropolitan of some power delegated to it by the State which is traditionally associated with sovereignty, such as eminent domain, our case would be quite a different one. But while the Pennsylvania

8. [In] fact Metropolitan does face competition within portions of its service area from another private utility company and from municipal utility companies. Metropolitan was organized in 1874, 39 years before Pennsylvania's adoption of its first utility regulatory scheme in 1913. There is no indication that it faced any greater competition in 1912 than today. As petitioner admits, such public utility companies are natural monopolies created by the economic forces of high threshold capital requirements and virtually unlimited economy of scale. Regulation was superimposed on such natural monopolies as a substitute for competition and not to eliminate it * * *.

statute imposes an obligation to furnish service on regulated utilities, it imposes no such obligation on the State. * * *

Perhaps in recognition of the fact that the supplying of utility service is not traditionally the exclusive prerogative of the State, petitioner invites the expansion of the doctrine of this limited line of cases into a broad principle that all businesses "affected with the public interest" are state actors in all their actions.

We decline the invitation for reasons stated long ago in *Nebbia v. New York,* [p. 82 supra], in the course of rejecting a substantive due process attack on state legislation: "It is clear that there is no closed class or category of businesses affected with a public interest * * *. The phrase 'affected with a public interest' can, in the nature of things, mean no more than that an industry, for adequate reason is subject to control for the public good. * * *"

Doctors, optometrists, lawyers, Metropolitan, and Nebbia's upstate New York grocery selling a quart of milk are all in regulated businesses, providing arguably essential goods and services, "affected with a public interest." We do not believe that such a status converts their every action, absent more, into that of the State.

We also reject the notion that Metropolitan's termination is state action because the State "has specifically authorized and approved" the termination practice. In the instant case, Metropolitan filed with the Public Utility Commission a general tariff—a provision of which states Metropolitan's right to terminate service for nonpayment. This provision has appeared in Metropolitan's previously filed tariffs for many years and has never been the subject of a hearing or other scrutiny by the Commission.[11] Although the Commission did hold hearings on portions of Metropolitan's general tariff relating to a general rate increase, it never even considered the reinsertion of this provision in the newly filed general tariff. * * *

As a threshold matter, it is less than clear under state law that Metropolitan was even required to file this provision as part of its tariff or that the Commission would have had the power to disapprove it. * * *

The case most heavily relied on by petitioner is *Pollak.* There the Court dealt with the contention that Capital Transit's installation of a piped music system on its buses violated the First Amendment rights of the bus riders. [The] District of Columbia Public Utilities Commission, on its own motion, commenced an investigation of the effects of the piped music, and after a full hearing concluded [that] the practice "in fact, through the creation of better will among passengers, [tends] to improve the conditions under which the public ride." Here, on the other hand, there was no such imprimatur placed on the practice of Metropolitan about which petitioner complains. The nature of governmental regulation of private utilities is such that a utility may frequently be required by the state regulatory scheme to obtain approval for practices a business regulated in less detail would be free to institute without any approval from a regulatory body. Approval by a state utility commission of such a request from a regulated utility, where the commission has not put its own weight on the side of the proposed practice by ordering it, does not transmute a practice initiated by the utility and approved by the commission into "state action." At most, the Commission's failure to overturn this practice amounted to no more than a

11. Petitioner does not contest the fact that Metropolitan had this right at common law before the advent of regulation.

determination that a Pennsylvania utility was authorized to employ such a practice if it so desired. * * *

Affirmed.

JUSTICE DOUGLAS, dissenting.

* * * I agree that doctors, lawyers, and grocers are not transformed into state actors simply because they provide arguably essential goods and services and are regulated by the State. In the present case, however, respondent is not just one person among many; it is the only public utility furnishing electric power to the city. When power is denied a householder, the home, under modern conditions, is likely to become unlivable.

Respondent's procedures for termination of service may never have been subjected to the same degree of state scrutiny and approval, whether explicit or implicit, that was present in *Pollak.* [Yet] Pennsylvania has undertaken to regulate numerous aspects of respondent's operations in some detail, and a "hands-off" attitude of permissiveness or neutrality toward the operations in this case is at war with the state agency's functions of supervision over respondent's conduct in the area of servicing householders * * *.

JUSTICE MARSHALL, dissenting. * * *

Our state-action cases have repeatedly relied on several factors clearly presented by this case: a state-sanctioned monopoly; an extensive pattern of cooperation between the "private" entity and the State; and a service uniquely public in nature. Today the Court takes a major step in repudiating this line of authority. [Even] when the Court has not found state action based solely on the State's conferral of a monopoly, it has suggested that the monopoly factor weighs heavily in determining whether constitutional obligations can be imposed on formally private entities. See *Steele v. Louisville & Nashville R. Co.* * * *

The majority distinguishes this line of cases with a cryptic assertion that public utility companies are "natural monopolies." * * * Initially, it is far from obvious that an electric company would not be subject to competition if the market were unimpeded by governmental restrictions. Certainly the "start-up" costs of initiating electric service are substantial, but the rewards available in a relatively inelastic market might well be sufficient under the right circumstances to attract competitive investment. Instead, the State has chosen to forbid the high profit margins that might invite private competition or increase pressure for state ownership and operation of electric power facilities.

[To] invite inquiry into whether a particular state-sanctioned monopoly might have survived without the State's express approval grounds the analysis in hopeless speculation. Worse, this approach ignores important implications of the State's policy of utilizing private monopolies to provide electric service. Encompassed within this policy is the State's determination not to permit governmental competition with the selected private company, but to cooperate with and regulate the company in a multitude of ways to ensure that the company's service will be the functional equivalent of service provided by the State.

* * * I question the wisdom [of] focusing solely on the extent of state support for the particular activity under challenge. In cases where the State's only significant involvement is through financial support or limited regulation of the private entity, it may be well to inquire whether the State's involvement suggests state approval of the objectionable conduct. But where the State has so thoroughly insinuated itself into the operations of the enterprise, it should not

be fatal if the State has not affirmatively sanctioned the particular practice in question.

[I]t seems to me in any event that the State *has* given its approval to Metropolitan Edison's termination procedures. [That] it was not seriously questioned before approval does not mean that it was not approved. It suggests, instead, that the Commission was satisfied to permit the company to proceed in the termination area as it had done in the past. * * * Apparently, authorization and approval would require the kind of hearing that was held in *Pollak* * * *. I am afraid that the majority has in effect restricted *Pollak* to its facts if it has not discarded it altogether.

The fact that the Metropolitan Edison Co. supplies an essential public service that is in many communities supplied by the government weighs more heavily for me than for the majority. The Court * * * reads the "public function" argument too narrowly. [In] my view, utility service is traditionally identified with the State through universal public regulation or ownership to a degree sufficient to render it a "public function."

I agree with the majority that it requires more than a finding that a particular business is "affected with the public interest" before constitutional burdens can be imposed on that business. But when the activity in question is of such public importance that the State invariably either provides the service itself or permits private companies to act as state surrogates in providing it, much more is involved than just a matter of public interest. In those cases, the State has determined that if private companies wish to enter the field, they will have to surrender many of the prerogatives normally associated with private enterprise and behave in many ways like a governmental body. And when the State's regulatory scheme has gone that far, it seems entirely consistent to impose on the public utility the constitutional burdens normally reserved for the State.

Private parties performing functions affecting the public interest can often make a persuasive claim to be free of the constitutional requirements applicable to governmental institutions because of the value of preserving a private sector in which the opportunity for individual choice is maximized. See *Evans v. Newton*. Maintaining the private status of parochial schools * * * advances just this value. In the due process area, a similar value of diversity may often be furthered by allowing various private institutions the flexibility to select procedures that fit their particular needs. But it is hard to imagine any such interests that are furthered by protecting privately owned public utility companies from meeting the constitutional standards that would apply if the companies were state owned. The values of pluralism and diversity are simply not relevant when the private company is the only electric company in town. * * *

What is perhaps most troubling about the Court's opinion is that it would appear to apply to a broad range of claimed constitutional violations by the company. The Court has not adopted the notion, accepted elsewhere, that different standards should apply to state action analysis when different constitutional claims are presented. Thus, the majority's analysis would seemingly apply as well to a company that refused to extend service to Negroes, welfare recipients, or any other group that the company preferred, for its own reasons, not to serve. I cannot believe that this Court would hold that the State's involvement with the utility company was not sufficient to impose upon the company an obligation to meet the constitutional mandate of nondiscrimination. Yet nothing in the analysis of the majority opinion suggests otherwise.[a]

Notes and Questions

1. *The "power" theory.* (a) Of what significance should it be that Metropolitan was "the only public utility furnishing electricity to the city"? Might it be argued that the "power" held by certain organizations today was conceived by the framers of the fourteenth amendment to be only within the possession of government? That, under a "living Constitution," such "power" creates such a threat to individual freedom that it should fall within the purview of state action? See Note, *State Action: Theories for Applying Constitutional Restrictions to Private Activity,* 74 Colum.L.Rev. 656 (1974).

Is the "power theory" approach beyond the permissible bounds of constitutional interpretation? Does it extend to holding the only ice skating rink in town to the state's constitutional responsibilities? Or is it limited to an activity that "is of such public importance that the State invariably either provides the service itself or permits private companies to act as state surrogates in providing it"? Does this invoke the "public function"—or "government function"—approach (to be considered further in note 2 after *Flagg Bros. v. Brooks,* infra)? In any event, does *Jackson* preclude this line of analysis?

(b) Does (should) the "power theory" depend on state participation in conferring the status?

(i) *Corporations.* Consider Berle, *Constitutional Limitations on Corporate Activity—Protection of Personal Rights From Invasion Through Economic Power,* 100 U.Pa.L.Rev. 933, 942–43 (1952): "[A corporation should be] as subject to constitutional limitations which limit action as is the state itself. [The] preconditions of application are two: the undeniable fact that the corporation was created by the state and the existence of sufficient economic power concentrated in this vehicle to invade the constitutional right of an individual to a material degree. [The] principle is logical because [the] modern state has set up, and come to rely on, the corporate system to carry out functions for which in modern life by community demand the government is held ultimately responsible. * * * Instead of nationalizing the enterprise, this doctrine 'constitutionalizes' the operation." See also St. Antoine, *Color Blindness But Not Myopia: A New Look at State Action, Equal Protection, and "Private" Racial Discrimination,* 59 Mich.L.Rev. 993 (1961); A.S. Miller, *The Constitutional Law of the "Security State,"* 10 Stan.L.Rev. 620, 661–66 (1958). Does this rationale apply to *all* corporations? Should it be restricted to entities "created by the state"?

(ii) *Labor organizations.* Suppose a large powerful union, without statutory authority or assistance, becomes the exclusive bargaining agent in a particular industry. May it constitutionally discriminate against blacks? See generally Wellington, *The Constitution, The Labor Union, and "Governmental Action,"* 70 Yale L.J. 345, 346–50 (1961). If not, must such a union afford a member "due process" before expelling him? May such a union refuse to hire black secretaries?

a. Brennan, J., dissented on procedural grounds.

For a decision finding state action under the California constitution when a privately owned utility discriminates in hiring, see *Gay Law Students Ass'n v. Pacific Telephone & Telegraph Co.,* 24 Cal.3d 458, 156 Cal.Rptr. 14, 595 P.2d 592 (1979).

(c) Does the "power theory" aid in analyzing the last series of questions? Might it be argued, for example, that a particular industrial labor union has sufficient "power" in respect to job opportunities in the industry as to be constitutionally forbidden from racially discriminating among its members but insufficient power over general job opportunities as to be constitutionally barred from using a religious test for its office employees? That the "state's duty to take preventive action [or the "state action" issue] varies with the magnitude of the discrimination and the consequent problem it creates"? H. Friendly, *The Dartmouth College Case and the Public-Private Penumbra* 22 (1969). See generally Choper, *Thoughts on State Action: The "Government Function" and "Power Theory" Approaches, 1979 Wash.U.L.Q. 757; compare Leedes, State Action Limitations on Courts and Congressional Power,* 60 N.C.L.Rev. 747, 757–61 (1981).[b]

2. *Constitutional rights of "power holders."* (a) In COLUMBIA BROADCASTING SYSTEM v. DEMOCRATIC NAT'L COMM., p. 698 supra—in which the FCC had ruled that a broadcaster is not required to accept editorial advertisements—some justices addressed the question of whether the action of the broadcast licensee was "governmental action" for purposes of the first amendment. BURGER, C.J., joined by Stewart and Rehnquist, JJ., concluded that it was not: "The historic aversion to censorship led Congress [to] explicitly [prohibit] the Commission from interfering with the exercise of free speech over the broadcast frequencies * * *. [T]he Commission acts in essence as an 'overseer,' but the initial and primary responsibility for fairness, balance and objectivity rests with the licensee. * * * Moreover, the Commission has not fostered the licensee policy challenged here; it has simply declined to command particular action because it fell within the area of journalistic discretion. * * *

"Thus, it cannot be said that the government is a 'partner' to the action of the broadcast licensee complained of here. * * * [In *Pollak*], Congress had expressly authorized the agency to undertake plenary intervention into the affairs of the carrier and it was pursuant to that authorization that the agency investigated the challenged policy and approved [it]. A more basic distinction, [is] that *Pollak* was concerned with a transportation utility that itself derives no protection from the First Amendment.

"Were we to read the First Amendment to spell out governmental action in the circumstances presented here, few licensee decisions on the content of broadcasts or the processes of editorial evaluation would escape constitutional scrutiny. In this sensitive area so sweeping a concept of governmental action would go far in practical effect to undermine nearly a half century of unmistakable congressional purpose to maintain—no matter how difficult the task—essentially private broadcast journalism held only broadly accountable to public interest standards."

BRENNAN, J., joined by Marshall, J., disagreed: "[T]he public nature of the airwaves, the governmentally created preferred status of broadcast licensees, the pervasive federal regulation of broadcast programming, and the Commission's

b. For the view that the state action doctrine may be justified by values of private pluralism, see Schwarzschild, *Value Pluralism and the Constitution: In Defense of the State Action Doctrine,* 1988 Sup.Ct.Rev. 129, 146–47: "For a value pluralist, the essence of the doctrine is that it distinguishes between exercises of choice by the monopoly institutions of the state—which must conform to the Constitution—and exercises of choice by private persons acting, as private persons always do, with the protection of the state. This is an essential distinction for a society that wants to safeguard the diversity of its own values by limiting the reach of the constitutional norms that govern its public institutions."

specific approval of the challenged broadcaster policy combine in this case to bring the promulgation and enforcement of that policy within the orbit of constitutional imperatives. [Here], as in *Pollak,* the broadcast licensees operate 'under the regulatory supervision of [an] agency authorized by Congress.' And, again as in *Pollak,* that agency received 'protests' against the challenged policy and, after formal consideration, 'dismissed' the complaints on the ground that the 'public interest, convenience, and necessity' were not 'impaired' by that policy. Indeed, the argument for finding 'governmental action' here is even stronger than in *Pollak,* for this case concerns not an incidental activity of a bus company but, rather, the primary activity of the regulated entities—communication. * * * [12] "

(b) *Newspapers.* Is the conduct of the only newspaper in a metropolitan area "state action"? May it offer free "society news" space to whites only? May it refuse to hire black employees? After the *CBS* case, may a licensed broadcaster engage in such actions?

SECTION 3. STATE "INVOLVEMENT" OR "ENCOURAGEMENT"

SHELLEY v. KRAEMER

334 U.S. 1, 68 S.Ct. 836, 92 L.Ed. 1161 (1948).

CHIEF JUSTICE VINSON delivered the opinion of the Court.

[In two cases from Missouri and Michigan, petitioners were blacks who had purchased houses from whites despite the fact that the properties were subject to restrictive covenants, signed by most property owners in the block, providing that for a specified time (in one case fifty years from 1911) the property would be sold only to Caucasians. Respondents, owners of other property subject to the covenants, sued to enjoin the blacks from taking possession and to divest them of title. The state courts granted the relief.]

It cannot be doubted that among the civil rights intended to be protected from discriminatory state action by the Fourteenth Amendment are the rights to acquire, enjoy, own and dispose of property. Equality in the enjoyment of property rights was regarded by the framers of that Amendment as an essential pre-condition to the realization of other basic civil rights and liberties which the Amendment was intended to guarantee.[7] Thus, [42 U.S.C. § 1982] derived from § 1 of the Civil Rights Act of 1866 which was enacted by Congress while the Fourteenth Amendment was also under consideration, provides:

12. [W]here, as here, the Government has implicated itself in the actions of an otherwise private individual, that individual must exercise his own rights with due regard for the First Amendment rights of others. In other words, an accommodation of competing rights is required, and "balancing" [is] the result. * * *

I might also note that [a] finding of governmental involvement in this case does not in any sense command a similar conclusion with respect to newspapers. [The] decision as to who shall operate newspapers is made in the free market, not by Government fiat. The newspaper industry is not extensively regulated and, indeed, in light of the differences between the electronic and printed media, such regulation would violate the First Amendment with respect to newspapers. * * *

7. *Slaughter-House Cases* [p. 72 supra]. See Flack, *The Adoption of the Fourteenth Amendment.*

"All citizens of the United States shall have the same right, in every State and Territory, as is enjoyed by white citizens thereof to inherit, purchase, lease, sell, hold, and convey real and personal property." * * *

It is likewise clear that restrictions on the right of occupancy of the sort sought to be created by the private agreements in these cases could not be squared with the requirements of the Fourteenth Amendment if imposed by state statute or local ordinance. * * *

But the present cases [do] not involve action by state legislatures or city councils. Here the particular patterns of discrimination and the areas in which the restrictions are to operate, are determined, in the first instance, by the terms of agreements among private individuals. Participation of the State consists in the enforcement of the restrictions so defined. * * *

Since the decision of this Court in the *Civil Rights Cases,* the principle has become firmly embedded in our constitutional law that the action inhibited by the first section of the Fourteenth Amendment is only such action as may fairly be said to be that of the States. That Amendment erects no shield against merely private conduct, however discriminatory or wrongful.

We conclude, therefore, that the restrictive agreements standing alone cannot be regarded as a violation of any rights guaranteed to petitioners by the Fourteenth Amendment. So long as the purposes of those agreements are effectuated by voluntary adherence to their terms, it would appear clear that there has been no action by the State and the provisions of the Amendment have not been violated.

But here there was more. These are cases in which the purposes of the agreements were secured only by judicial enforcement by state courts of the restrictive terms of the agreements. * * *

That the action of state courts and of judicial officers in their official capacities is to be regarded as action of the State within the meaning of the Fourteenth Amendment, is a proposition which has long been established. [In] the *Civil Rights Cases,* this Court pointed out that the Amendment makes void "state action of every kind" which is inconsistent with the guaranties therein contained, and extends to manifestations of "state authority in the shape of laws, customs, or judicial or executive proceedings." * * *

One of the earliest applications of the prohibitions contained in the Fourteenth Amendment to action of state judicial officials occurred in cases in which Negroes had been excluded from jury service * * *. These cases demonstrate, also, the early recognition by this Court that state action in violation of the Amendment's provisions is equally repugnant to the constitutional commands whether directed by state statute or taken by a judicial official in the absence of statute. * * *

The action of state courts in imposing penalties or depriving parties of other substantive rights without providing adequate notice and opportunity to defend, has, of course, long been regarded as a denial of the due process of law guaranteed by the Fourteenth Amendment.

In numerous cases, this Court has reversed criminal convictions in state courts for failure of those courts to provide the essential ingredients of a fair hearing. Thus it has been held that convictions obtained in state courts under the domination of a mob are void. Convictions obtained by coerced confessions, by the use of perjured testimony known by the prosecution to be such, or without the effective assistance of counsel, have also been held to be exertions of state authority in conflict with the fundamental rights protected by the Fourteenth Amendment.

But the examples of state judicial action which have been held by this Court to violate the Amendment's commands are not restricted to situations in which the judicial proceedings were found in some manner to be procedurally unfair. It has been recognized that the action of state courts in enforcing a substantive common-law rule formulated by those courts, may result in the denial of rights guaranteed by the Fourteenth Amendment * * *. Thus, in *AFL v. Swing,* 1941, 312 U.S. 321, 61 S.Ct. 568, 85 L.Ed. 855, enforcement by state courts of the common-law policy of the State, which resulted in the restraining of peaceful picketing, was held to be state action of the sort prohibited by the Amendment's guaranties of freedom of discussion. In *Cantwell v. Connecticut,* 1940, 310 U.S. 296, 60 S.Ct. 900, 84 L.Ed. 1213, a conviction in a state court of the common-law crime of breach of the peace was, under the circumstances of the case, found to be a violation of the Amendment's commands relating to freedom of religion. In *Bridges v. California,* 1941, 314 U.S. 252, 62 S.Ct. 190, 86 L.Ed. 192, enforcement of the state's common-law rule relating to contempts by publication was held to be state action inconsistent with the prohibitions of the Fourteenth Amendment. * * *

We have no doubt that there has been state action in these cases in the full and complete sense of the phrase. The undisputed facts disclose that petitioners were willing purchasers of properties upon which they desired to establish homes. The owners of the properties were willing sellers; and contracts of sale were accordingly consummated. It is clear that but for the active intervention of the state courts, supported by the full panoply of state power, petitioners would have been free to occupy the properties in question without restraint.

These are not cases, as has been suggested, in which the States have merely abstained from action, leaving private individuals free to impose such discriminations as they see fit. Rather, these are cases in which the States have made available to such individuals the full coercive power of government to deny to petitioners, on the grounds of race or color, the enjoyment of property rights in premises which petitioners are willing and financially able to acquire and which the grantors are willing to sell. * * *

The enforcement of the restrictive agreements by the state courts in these cases was directed pursuant to the common-law policy of the States as formulated by those courts in earlier decisions. [The] judicial action in each case bears the clear and unmistakable imprimatur of the State. We have noted that previous decisions of this Court have established the proposition that judicial action is not immunized from the operation of the Fourteenth Amendment simply because it is taken pursuant to the state's common-law policy. Nor is the Amendment ineffective simply because the particular pattern of discrimination, which the State has enforced, was defined initially by the terms of a private agreement. State action, as that phrase is understood for the purposes of the Fourteenth Amendment, refers to exertions of state power in all forms. * * * We have noted that freedom from discrimination by the States in the enjoyment of property rights was among the basic objectives sought to be effectuated by the framers of the Fourteenth Amendment. That such discrimination has occurred in these cases is clear. * * *

Respondents urge, however, that since the state courts stand ready to enforce restrictive covenants excluding white persons[,] enforcement of covenants excluding colored persons may not be deemed a denial of equal protection of the laws to the colored persons who are thereby affected. This contention does not bear scrutiny. [The] rights created by the first section of the Fourteenth Amendment are, by its terms, guaranteed to the individual. The rights established are personal rights. It is, therefore, no answer to these petitioners to say that the courts may also be induced to deny white persons rights of ownership and occupancy on grounds of race or color. Equal protection of the laws is not achieved through indiscriminate imposition of inequalities. * * *

Reversed.

JUSTICE REED, JUSTICE JACKSON, and JUSTICE RUTLEDGE took no part in the consideration or decision of these cases.[a]

Notes and Questions

1. *Authority of prior decisions.* Do the cases holding that "judicial action is state action" call for the result in *Shelley*? Consider Comment, *The Impact of Shelley v. Kraemer on the State Action Concept*, 44 Calif.L.Rev. 718, 724 (1956): "In the cases exemplifying 'orthodox' judicial violation the prohibited activity [e.g., barring blacks from juries] was practiced by the judge himself. [But in *Shelley*] the discrimination originated with private persons." May this be said about "convictions obtained under the domination of a mob"?

As to those cases (*Swing, Cantwell, Bridges*) involving "the action of state courts in enforcing a substantive common-law rule," consider Comment, 45 Mich. L.Rev. 733, 742–43 (1947): "The difficulty of attributing the discrimination effected by the covenants to the enforcing tribunal is not to be escaped by pretending that it forms an element of the common law from which the right to enforcement is derived. The common law is simply the policy of the state in certain of its aspects, [and] that policy as seen in respect to these facts looks no further than to the protection of property and contract rights." Did the state policy in *Cantwell* look any further than to the protection of public tranquility? Did it, in *Bridges*, look any further than to the protection of the integrity of the court? For careful analysis, see Van Alstyne, *Mr. Justice Black, Constitutional Review, and the Talisman of State Action,* 1965 Duke L.J. 219.

Are the considerations in *Shelley* different from all of these cases because it involves equal protection rather than due process? Because these other cases involve the right of free speech? Should there be a distinction between civil suits and criminal prosecutions? Consider Comment, 45 Mich.L.Rev. 733, 746 (1947): "The theory of civil remedies is that the interest of the state in the protection of property and contract rights is ordinarily secondary to that of the individual citizen, that the extent to which the protection of the law is obtained for them is largely discretionary with him. [A] criminal statute is an expression of state policy of a much higher order. In theory, the state pursues purposes of its own in criminal legislation."

2. Is *Shelley* supportable because "so long as it is unconstitutional for a state to require racial segregation by zoning statutes [it] is equally unconstitutional for the state to bring it about by any other form of state action"? McGovney, *Racial Residential Segregation by State Court Enforcement of Restrictive Agreements, Covenants or Conditions in Deeds is Unconstitutional,* 33 Calif. L.Rev. 5, 30 (1945). Is the source of the discrimination the same in both instances? Or is this a variation of the "government function" approach?

a. For a history of the battle against restrictive covenants, see Vose, *NAACP Strategy in the Covenant Cases,* 6 W.Res.L.Rev. 101 (1955).

Consider Groner & Helfeld, *Race Discrimination in Housing,* 57 Yale L.J. 426, 454 (1948): "Where covenants do not presently cover entire areas, experience shows that, if encouraged by court enforcement, covenants do in time cover all of the area available for desirable residences." See also Ming, *Racial Restrictions and the Fourteenth Amendment: The Restrictive Covenant Cases,* 16 U.Chi.L.Rev. 203 (1949).

3. BARROWS v. JACKSON, 346 U.S. 249, 73 S.Ct. 1031, 97 L.Ed. 1586 (1953), held that an action by a co-covenantor to recover damages from a property owner who sold to a black was barred by equal protection. Would this suit, like the one in *Shelley,* involve "the full coercive power of government to deny [on] grounds of race [the] enjoyment of property rights"? Would the suit in *Barrows* have the same effect as a suit to enjoin a white property owner from breaching the covenant? See *Hurd v. Hodge,* 334 U.S. 24, 68 S.Ct. 847, 92 L.Ed. 1187 (1948).

4. *Other devices.* After *Shelley* and *Barrows,* consider the validity of:

(a) A deed conveying property on condition that if sold to a black it automatically reverts to the original grantor.

(i) Suppose the grantor sues to evict the purchasing black? Suppose the grantor retakes possession and the purchasing black sues to evict? Might a court deny relief in the latter situation on the ground that it had "merely abstained from action, leaving private individuals free to impose such discrimination as they see fit"?

(ii) Suppose a suit for declaratory judgment as to the validity of the reverter? If the reverter were declared invalid, could it be said "that the restrictive agreements standing alone cannot be regarded as a violation of [the] Fourteenth Amendment"? If it were declared valid, could a court deny the original grantor's suit to enjoin the black purchaser's taking possession? See generally Miller, *Racial Discrimination and Private Schools,* 41 Minn.L.Rev. 245, 276–80 (1957).

(b) A will devising property on condition that if the beneficiary marry a person "not born in the Hebrew faith" the property be paid over to someone else. Suppose the beneficiary marries a Catholic and the remainderman sues for the property?

(c) A child custody decree directing the father to pay private school tuition. Suppose the father refuses to pay because the school racially discriminates and the mother sues to enforce the decree.

5. *The limits of Shelley.* (a) Consider Comment, 44 Calif.L.Rev. 718, 733 (1956): "If obtaining court aid to carry out 'private' activity 'converts' such private action into 'state' action, then there could never be any private action in any practical sense. So entwined are our lives with the law that the logical result would be that almost *all* action, to be effective, must result in state action. Thus all private activity would be required to 'conform' with the standards of conduct imposed on the states by the fourteenth amendment."

(b) Evaluate the following analyses of *Shelley:*

(i) "[S]ince one's property rights in land are only powers delegated by higher state agencies [and] are legally effective only by virtue of authority granted by the state, then looking only to the face of the Fourteenth Amendment, it applies to all property [rights] used in a prohibited manner." Lathrop, *The Racial Covenant Cases,* 1948 Wis.L.Rev. 508, 515.

(ii) "[T]he *law* of contracts is not a matter of private agreement. The *agreements* entered may be classified as *private* affairs. However, when resort is had to a state court seeking enforcement for breach of such an agreement, it is the *law* of contracts which then must be invoked." Scanlan, *Racial Restriction in Real Estate—Property Values Versus Human Values,* 24 Not.D.Law. 157, 172–73 (1949).

(iii) "Professor Louis Pollak [*Racial Discrimination and Judicial Integrity,* 108 U.Pa.L.Rev. 1, 13 (1959)] would apply *Shelley* to prevent the state from enforcing a discrimination by one who does not wish to discriminate;[b] but he would allow the state to give its support to willing discrimination * * *. [H]is proposal requires important limitation of *Shelley,* and raises a number of possible objections. One may argue, for instance, that while the fourteenth amendment may perhaps protect an individual's 'liberty' to refuse to discriminate as it may protect another's liberty to discriminate, that hardly seems to be the focus of the equal protection clause. That clause seems to be designed to protect the victim against discrimination, not to protect an unwilling 'actor' against being compelled to discriminate. It would seem also an eccentric constitutional provision which protected the aggrieved against involuntary discrimination by private persons but not against voluntary private discrimination. Moreover, the distinction is offered as a definition of 'state action.' But whether the judgment of a court enforces a voluntary discrimination or compels a no-longer-voluntary discrimination, the discrimination is private in origin; in both cases it requires a court judgment to make the discrimination effective. * * * Finally, in *Shelley* itself, is it acceptable to think of the case as one in which the state was compelling discrimination by a grantor of property who no longer wished to discriminate? In essence, the state was enforcing discrimination by the other parties to the covenant." Henkin, *Shelley v. Kraemer: Notes for a Revised Opinion,* 110 U.Pa.L.Rev. 473, 477–78 & n. 10 (1962).

Compare Horowitz, *The Misleading Search for "State Action" Under the Fourteenth Amendment,* 30 So.Cal.L.Rev. 208, 213 (1957): "There is involved here a question of the degree of effect of different forms of state action on a prospective Negro buyer's opportunity to purchase and use land * * *. The state does not substantially deny the Negro that opportunity by *permitting* a private person to refuse to deal with him because of his race. This would be the situation where there was 'voluntary adherence' to the restrictive covenant by the landowner. But the state does to a far greater degree deny the Negro the opportunity to acquire land, because of his race, if it *compels* a landowner not to deal with the Negro. This is the situation where the state enforces the restrictive covenant after a landowner has decided not to adhere to it."

(iv) Since restraints on alienation of property are presumptively void, being valid generally only if the court finds the restraint a reasonable one and consistent with public policy, Restatement, *Property* § 406 (1944), was there state action in *Shelley* because the court placed its imprimatur on a racially discriminatory restraint? Might it be argued that, due to this, the source of discrimination was public rather than private? See Choper, *Thoughts on State Action,* 1979 Wash.U.L.Q. 757, 769–71.

(c) Consider Comment, 44 Calif.L.Rev. 718, 735 (1956): "It is submitted that the doctrine of judicial enforcement as interpreted by *Shelley* is applicable only

b. See *Moose Lodge v. Irvis,* infra, for this application of *Shelley*—in the only opinion of the Court (apart from *Barrows v. Jackson*) that has relied on *Shelley* to find state action. Cf. also fn. 10 in *Flagg Bros. v. Brooks,* Sec. 4 infra, and note 1 thereafter.

when the court action abets private discrimination which in the absence of such judicial aid would be ineffective. * * * Where the private activity, admitted in *Shelley* to be valid in itself, is already effective, it is not to be said that the court, recognizing or failing to abolish the activity, is itself an arm of the discrimination; the situation has remained the same, court action or no. It is only where the proponents of discrimination, unable to further their ends privately, seek court aid is the state itself causing discrimination under *Shelley*."

(i) Suppose plaintiff is denied relief in a breach of contract suit against a cemetery for refusing to bury a black because the burial lot purchase contract was restricted to Caucasians? What result under *Shelley*? Under the above theory? Would denial of plaintiff's cause of action make the discrimination "effective"? If the body had already been interred, could the cemetery obtain the court's aid in removing it?

(ii) Suppose a collective bargaining agreement authorizes discharge of employees for "just cause" and an employee is so discharged because he is black. What result in the employee's suit for reinstatement? See *Black v. Cutter Lab.*, 351 U.S. 292, 301–03, 76 S.Ct. 824, 828, 100 L.Ed. 1188, 1197 (1956) (dissenting opinion). What result in the employer's suit to restrain the employee from continuing to appear on the job?

(iii) Suppose a landlord seeks the court's aid to evict a tenant whose defense is that the eviction is solely on the grounds of race (or religion, or speech)? Suppose the tenant seeks to restrain the landlord from recovering possession of the leased premises? If the tenant refuses to give up possession and is forcibly evicted by the landlord, what result in the tenant's suit for assault? Would a desirable rule produce different results in the above situations?

(iv) What result in a suit by the state real estate board to revoke a broker's license for having sold property to a black contrary to the owner's instructions? In a suit by a citizen to force the state real estate board to revoke a broker's license for having refused to show property to blacks pursuant to the owner's instructions?

(v) At common law, no person who offered his property for sale could be enjoined from arbitrarily refusing to sell to another. Suppose an owner refuses to sell solely because of the buyer's race. Consider Huber, *Revolution in Private Law?* 6 S.C.L.Q. 8, 26 (1953): "It would seem, under *Shelley,* that he could bring suit alleging denial of equal protection of the laws. Even if the court wished to dismiss the suit as not stating a cause of action [it] would seem that the court could not do so without supporting the discrimination."

6. *Reconsideration of prior problems in light of Shelley.* (a) *Evans v. Newton.* (i) When the state court accepted the city's resignation and appointed private trustees to carry out the testator's discriminatory intent, was this state action that abetted otherwise private discrimination? If the city had not resigned and the state court had granted the relief sought to remove the city as trustee, would this be enforcing discrimination by one who did not wish to discriminate in violation of the *Shelley* rule?

If Senator Bacon had designated a private trustee who was unwilling or unable to act, a new trustee would be appointed by the court. 4 Scott, *Trusts* § 388 (2d ed. 1956). Would discrimination by such an appointee be state action? In most states, charitable trusts are enforced by the attorney general. Id. § 391. If Bacon's will had designated a private trustee who refused to discriminate, would an action by the attorney general to force the trustee to comply with terms of the trust violate equal protection? If the private trustee, in compliance with the terms, discriminates from the outset, would the attorney general's failure to seek to end the discrimination violate equal protection? What would be the effect of a court approving the trustee's accounts?

(ii) On remand, after *Evans,* the Georgia courts interpreted Senator Bacon's will and held that "because the park's segregated, whites-only character was an essential and inseparable part of the testator's plan," the "cy pres doctrine to amend the terms of the will by striking the racial restrictions" was inapplicable; that, therefore, the trust failed and the trust property "by operation of law reverted to the heirs of Senator Bacon." EVANS v. ABNEY, 396 U.S. 435, 90 S.Ct. 628, 24 L.Ed.2d 634 (1970), per BLACK, J., affirmed, finding that "the Georgia court had no alternative under its relevant trust laws, which are long standing and neutral with regard to race, but to end the Baconsfield trust": "[T]he Constitution imposes no requirement upon the Georgia court to approach Bacon's will any differently than it would approach any will creating any charitable trust of any kind. [T]here is not the slightest indication that any of the Georgia judges involved were motivated by racial animus or discriminatory intent of any sort in construing and enforcing Senator Bacon's will. Nor is there any indication that Senator Bacon in drawing up his will was persuaded or induced to include racial restrictions by the fact that such restrictions were permitted by the Georgia trust statutes." *Shelley* was "easily distinguishable" because here "the termination of the park was a loss shared equally by the white and Negro citizens of Macon."

BRENNAN, J., dissented: "For almost half a century Baconsfield has been a public park." When "a public facility would remain open but for the constitutional command that it be operated on a nonsegregated basis, the closing of that facility conveys an unambiguous message of community involvement in racial discrimination. [But] the Court finds that in this case it is not the State or city but 'a private party which is injecting the racially discriminatory motivation.' " Nonetheless, "this discriminatory closing is permeated with state action": "First, there is state action whenever a State enters into an arrangement which creates a private right to compel or enforce the reversion of a public facility" and, here, "in accepting title to the park," city officials agreed to that "if the city should ever incur a constitutional obligation to desegregate the park. [The] decision whether or not a public facility shall be operated in compliance with the Constitution is an essential *governmental* decision." Second, "nothing in the record suggests that after our decision in *Evans v. Newton* the City of Macon retracted its previous willingness to manage Baconsfield on a nonsegregated basis, or that the white beneficiaries of Senator Bacon's generosity were unwilling to share it with Negroes, rather than have the park revert to his heirs." Thus, contrary to *Shelley,* "this is a case of a state court's enforcement of a racial restriction to prevent willing parties from dealing with one another." Douglas, J., dissented; Marshall, J., did not participate.

(iii) Was the Georgia courts' action "a judicial choice between two incompatible terms of his will"—"(1) to keep Negroes out of the park; and (2) to keep Baconsfield a park forever"—thus, state action placing its imprimatur on racial discrimination (see note 5(b)(iv) supra)? Comment, 14 Kan.L.Rev. 613, 625 (1966).

(b) *De facto school segregation.* Consider Comment, 31 Mo.L.Rev. 391, 397 (1966): "[*Shelley*] stands for the proposition that the state may not give discriminatory acts of private persons the force of law. Does not the local school board violate that proposition when [it] assures private persons that if they are able to keep their neighborhoods segregated their schools will be segregated also." Does the school board thus also encourage private housing discrimination?

7. *The balancing approach.* Is the ultimate solution in *Shelley,* and other cases, a balancing of *all* of the particular interests involved? Consider Van Alstyne & Karst, *State Action,* 14 Stan.L.Rev. 3, 44–45 (1961): "[There has been] an attempt to discover or invent the *kind* of state connection which will satisfy the state action requirement. It is suggested, for example, that the state acts in the sense of the amendment when it coerces private discrimination, but not when it simply lends its aid to such racial discrimination as private individuals may choose to practice. [This analysis] perpetuates the untenable distinction between the state action requirement on the one hand and the balance of 'substantive' constitutional interests on the other. This way of looking at the problem [is] even more dangerous than the suggestion's other unfortunate aspect: its assumption that every private discrimination is invalid once the right formal state connection has been found." See also J. Williams, *Mulkey v. Reitman and State Action,* 14 U.C.L.A.L.Rev. 26 (1966).

Compare Henkin, note 5(b)(iii) supra at 496: "Generally, the equal protection clause precludes state enforcement of private discrimination. There is, however, a small area of liberty favored by the Constitution even over claims to equality. Rights of liberty and property, of privacy and voluntary association, must be balanced, in close cases, against the right not to have the state enforce discrimination against the victim. In the few instances in which the right to discriminate is protected or preferred by the Constitution, the state may enforce it." [c] Is it the contention that the inquiry is not whether state action is present but whether the state policy preference, expressed through its laws, between conflicting claims of individuals, denies equal protection?

Contrast Gilbert, *Theories of State Action as Applied to the "Sit-In" Cases,* 17 Ark.L.Rev. 147, 161 (1963): "The primary weakness in Henkin's approach would seem to be that the responsibility of the state arises from its *power* to act in a given situation. It would seem much sounder to impute responsibility where there is a *duty* on the part of the state to act. Thus, where traditional state functions, such as running elections or operating a town, are involved, the state would seem to have a duty to see that these activities are conducted in a constitutional manner. Beyond the area of state functions being performed by private enterprises, the state might have a duty to insure nondiscrimination by enterprises which occupy important positions of public interest. For example, if all the milk producers in an area refused to sell to Negroes, it would seem that the state would have a duty to insure that Negroes could purchase milk on equal terms with whites. In the case of the small corner diner, especially in an area which offers other sources of similar meals to the Negro, it would seem that the state has no duty to insure the Negro a meal there, even though the state would clearly have the power to do so. Here again, an ad hoc approach would be required."

See Horowitz, *Fourteenth Amendment Aspects of Racial Discrimination in "Private" Housing,* 52 Calif.L.Rev. 1, 12–20 (1964): "The determination of the constitutionality under the fourteenth amendment of state law permitting a private person to discriminate, on racial grounds, against another private person

c. See also Black, *"State Action," Equal Protection, and California's Proposition 14,* 81 Harv.L.Rev. 69, 83–109 (1967); Sengstock & Sengstock, *Discrimination: A Constitutional Dilemma,* 9 Wm. & M.L.Rev. 59 (1967).

in a specific fact situation requires consideration of various interdependent factors: the nature and degree of injury to the person discriminated against, the interest of the discriminator in being permitted to discriminate, and the interest of the discriminatee in having opportunity of access equal to that of other persons to the benefits of governmental assistance to the discriminator * * *. If there is extensive state participation and involvement related to the activities of the discriminator, it is more likely that those activities will be public in nature, with consequent public indignity and humiliation suffered by the person discriminated against, and more likely that denial of access to those activities will be of some significance to the discriminatee. [When] there is governmental assistance to the discriminator in carrying on his activities, and the assistance is being provided to further the purposes of a governmental program designed to provide benefits for the public or a permissible segment of the public, the effect of the discrimination is to deny to the discriminatee the opportunity to have equal opportunity of access to the benefits of the governmental program." [d]

Compare Choper, *Thoughts on State Action,* 1979 Wash.U.L.Q. 757, 762: "[The balancing approaches] contradict a central feature of the fourteenth amendment. Although its major purpose was to augment the authority of the national government to secure certain constitutional rights, its primary thrust was to accomplish this goal by outlawing deprivations of these rights by state governments and their legal structures rather than by the impact of private choice. By effectively obliterating the distinction between state action and private action, these theories eviscerate the fourteenth amendment's restriction on the authority of the national government vis-à-vis the states regarding the regulation of the myriad relationships that occur between one individual and another. [A]t the initiative of any litigant who is offended by another person's behavior, these theories would subject to the scrutiny of federal judges, under substantive constitutional standards customarily developed for measuring the actions of government, all sorts of private conduct that because of political constraints and collective good sense would probably never be mandated by law. Further, by permitting private actors to violate constitutional norms when they have a constitutionally protected liberty interest to do so, these theories would delegate to federal judges the power to implement the vague mandate of the due process clause in speaking the final word about the validity of virtually all transactions between individuals. In doing so, the national judiciary would be required to determine whether private conduct was constitutionally immune from government control even though, because of general political sensitivity to individual autonomy, such private conduct probably would never be regulated by the state." See also T. Lewis, *The Role of Law in Regulating Discrimination in Places of Public Accommodation,* 13 Buf.L.Rev. 402, 416–18 (1964).

Consider also Haber, *Notes on the Limits of Shelley v. Kraemer,* 18 Rutgers L.Rev. 811, 813, 824–25 (1964): "[I]t is dangerous to let any constitutional guarantee rest on an ad hoc balancing test. [I]t is extremely difficult to weigh liberty against equality; the outcome depends entirely on the views of the particular judges. While to some extent this must always be true in constitutional adjudications, it is nevertheless incumbent upon lawyers to develop a

d. For other discussions of a balancing approach, see Glennon & Nowak, *A Functional Analysis of the Fourteenth Amendment "State Action" Requirement,* 1976 Sup.Ct.Rev. 221; Quinn, *State Action: A Pathology and a Proposed Cure,* 64 Calif.L.Rev. 146 (1976); Thompson, *Piercing the Veil of State Action: The Revisionist Theory and a Mythical Application to Self-Help Repossession.* 1977 Wis.L.Rev. 1; Morris & Powe, *Constitutional & Statutory Rights to Open Housing,* 44 Wash.L.Rev. 1–56 (1968).

principle that will put some restraint even on the membership of the Supreme Court. * * *

"[T]he state can prohibit all racial discrimination. There is no liberty to discriminate. Whatever other incidents of property may be protected by the due process clause, the property and liberty protected by it occurring in the same amendment which guarantees the equal protection of the laws, does not include the right to treat people differently on the basis of their race and color."

Professor Haber would limit *Shelley* as follows: "the principle of state action as applied to judicial and police aid to private discrimination permits such aid only in the following instances: (1) Where the suit is by the victim and he seeks a new remedy based entirely on the discrimination, the state may deny the remedy. (2) Though this is doubtful, conceivably [the] state may also deny the remedy based on a contract voluntarily entered into with the discriminator by the victim of the discrimination or his privy, where the discriminator defends on the basis of a discriminatory provision in the contract. (3) The state may protect all property and personal rights of the discriminator other than the act of discrimination. (4) The state may even protect the act of discrimination provided it has offered the victim an adequate alternative remedy."

For recent consideration of "balancing," see Chemerinsky, *Rethinking State Action,* 80 Nw.U.L.Rev. 503 (1985); Marshall, *Diluting Constitutional Rights: Rethinking "Rethinking State Action,"* 80 Nw.U.L.Rev. 558 (1985); Chemerinsky, *More Is Not Less: A Rejoinder to Professor Marshall,* 80 Nw.U.L.Rev. 571 (1985).

8. *"Sit-in" cases.*[e] (a) In PETERSON v. GREENVILLE, 373 U.S. 244, 83 S.Ct. 1119, 10 L.Ed.2d 323 (1963), an ordinance forebade restaurants to seat whites and blacks together. The Court, per WARREN, C.J., reversed trespass convictions of black youths who, when denied service at a lunch counter, refused to leave: "[T]hese convictions cannot stand, even assuming [that] the manager would have acted as he did independently of the existence of the ordinance. [When] a state agency passes a law compelling persons to discriminate [such] a palpable violation of the Fourteenth Amendment cannot be saved by attempting to separate the mental urges of the discriminators."[f] Douglas, J., concurred.[g] HARLAN, J., noting "a clash of competing constitutional claims of a high order: liberty and equality," would have "the issue of state action" turn on the

e. In the early 1960s, the Court—employing a variety of doctrines, but never relying on *Shelley*—reversed a long series of trespass convictions of "sit-in" demonstrators who were protesting racial discrimination by restaurants and other businesses. The Civil Rights Act of 1964 largely mooted the constitutional problem of equal rights in public accommodations.

f. See also *Lombard v. Louisiana,* 373 U.S. 267, 83 S.Ct. 1122, 10 L.Ed.2d 338 (1963) (statements by city officials that sit-ins "would not be permitted" had "as much coercive effect as an ordinance"); *Robinson v. Florida,* 378 U.S. 153, 84 S.Ct. 1693, 12 L.Ed.2d 771 (1964) (state health regulations, requiring racially separate toilets in restaurants, impose "burdens bound to discourage the serving of the two races together").

If a statute requires private colleges to enact regulations for maintenance of order on campus, must such a college's procedures for dismissal of students comport with procedural due process?

g. See also Douglas, J.'s view that "state policy may be as effectively expressed in *customs* as in formal legislative, executive, or judicial action," *Garner v. Louisiana,* 368 U.S. 157, 82 S.Ct. 248, 7 L.Ed.2d 207 (1961) (concurring opinion) (cf. Karst & Van Alstyne, *Sit-Ins and State Action—Mr. Justice Douglas Concurring,* 14 Stan.L.Rev. 762 (1962)); and Brennan, J.'s view that *Peterson, Lombard,* and *Robinson* "together hold that a state policy of discouraging privately chosen integration or encouraging privately chosen segregation, even though the policy is expressed in a form nondiscriminatory on its face, is unconstitutional and taints the privately chosen segregation it seeks to bring about," *Adickes v. S.H. Kress & Co.,* 398 U.S. 144, 90 S.Ct. 1598, 26 L.Ed.2d 142 (1970) (separate opinion). See further, note 2 after *Reitman v. Mulkey,* infra.

"question of fact" whether the restaurant "might have preferred for reasons entirely of its own not to serve meals to Negroes along with whites, [or] whether the ordinance played some part in [the] decision to segregate." [h]

(b) In BELL v. MARYLAND, 378 U.S. 226, 84 S.Ct. 1814, 12 L.Ed.2d 822 (1964), GOLDBERG, J., joined by Warren, C.J., and Douglas, J., relying on the historical view in Sec. 1, fn. a, cited *Marsh, Shelley, Terry* and *Barrows* for the view that "a State, obligated under the Fourteenth Amendment to maintain a system of law in which Negroes are not denied protection in their claim to be treated as equal members of the community, may not use its criminal trespass laws to frustrate the constitutionally granted right. Nor, it should be added, may a State frustrate this right by legitimating a proprietor's attempt at self-help."

BLACK, J., joined by Harlan and White, JJ., dissented: Reliance on *Shelley* was "misplaced" because it established only these propositions: "(1) When an owner of property is willing to sell and a would-be purchaser is willing to buy, then the Civil Rights Act of 1866, which gives all persons the same right to 'inherit, lease, sell, hold, and convey' property, prohibits a State, whether through its legislature, executive, or judiciary, from preventing the sale on the grounds of the race or color of one of the parties. * * * (2) Once a person has become a property owner, then he [may] sell his property to whom he pleases and admit to that property whom he will; so long as *both* parties are willing parties, then the principles stated in *Buchanan v. Warley,* 245 U.S. 60, 38 S.Ct. 16, 62 L.Ed. 149 (1917) and *Shelley* protect this right. But equally, when one party is unwilling, as when the property owner chooses *not* to sell to a particular person or *not* to admit that person, [then] he is entitled to rely on the guarantee of due process of law [to] protect his free use and enjoyment of property and to know that only by valid legislation, passed pursuant to some constitutional grant of power, can anyone disturb this free use."

REITMAN v. MULKEY

387 U.S. 369, 87 S.Ct. 1627, 18 L.Ed.2d 830 (1967).

JUSTICE WHITE delivered the opinion of the Court.

[Section 26 of the California constitution], an initiated measure submitted to the people [in] a statewide ballot in 1964, provides in part as follows: "Neither the State nor any subdivision or agency thereof shall deny, limit or abridge, directly or indirectly, the right of any person, who is willing or desires to sell, lease or rent any part or all of his real property, to decline to sell, lease or rent such property to such person or persons as he, in his absolute discretion, chooses." The real property covered by § 26 is limited to residential property and contains an exception for state-owned real estate.

h. Consider T. Lewis, *The Sit-In Cases: Great Expectations,* 1963 Sup.Ct.Rev. 101, 110: "The Court [was] concerned with persons unknown and unknowable who might be affected by the cumulative pressure of such laws on a variety of proprietors in a variety of environments. [When] only the proprietor can know what his 'mental urges' are, and when even he might find difficulty in separating them, judicial review will be more effective for the mass of cases [if] the Court by the announcement of its rule makes it as certain as it can that proprietors and officials alike appreciate the precise status of segregation laws."

If federal law requires airlines to search passengers for weapons, should the issue of whether such a search by an airline employee is "state action" under the fourth and fourteenth amendments turn on whether the airlines would have conducted the searches regardless of the federal legislation?

[Respondents] sued under § 51 and § 52 of the California Civil Code [forbidding racial discrimination "in all business establishments"] alleging that petitioners had refused to rent them an apartment solely on account of their race. An injunction and damages were demanded. Petitioners moved for summary judgment on the ground that §§ 51 and 52 [had] been rendered null and void by the adoption of [§ 26] after the filing of the complaint. The trial court granted the motion [but the California Supreme Court held that § 26] was invalid as denying [equal protection].

We affirm the judgment [which] quite properly undertook to examine the constitutionality of § 26 in terms of its "immediate objective," its "ultimate impact" and its "historical context and the conditions existing prior to its enactment." Judgments such as these we have frequently undertaken ourselves. *Yick Wo v. Hopkins; Lombard v. Louisiana; Anderson v. Martin.* But here the California Supreme Court has addressed itself to these matters and we should give careful consideration to its views because they concern the purpose, scope, and operative effect of a provision of the California Constitution.

First, the court considered whether § 26 was concerned at all with private discriminations in residential housing. This involved a review of past efforts by the California Legislature to regulate such discriminations. The Unruh Act, on which respondents based their cases, was passed in 1959. [I]n 1963, came the Rumford Fair Housing Act * * * prohibiting racial discriminations in the sale or rental of any private dwelling containing more than four units. [§ 26's] immediate design and intent, the California court said, was "to overturn state laws that bore on the right of private sellers and lessors to discriminate," the Unruh and Rumford Acts, and "to forestall future state action that might circumscribe this right." * * *

Second, the court conceded that the State was permitted a neutral position with respect to private racial discriminations and that the State was not bound by the Federal Constitution to forbid them. But [the] court deemed it necessary to determine whether [§ 26] invalidly involved the State in racial discriminations in the housing market. Its conclusion was that it did.

To reach this result, the state court [reasoned] that a prohibited state involvement could be found "even where the state can be charged with only encouraging," rather than commanding discrimination. [To] the California court "[t]he instant case [was one]" wherein the State had taken affirmative action designed to make private discriminations legally possible. Section 26 was said to have changed the situation from one in which discriminatory practices were restricted "to one wherein it is encouraged, within the meaning of the cited decisions"; § 26 was legislative action "which authorized private discrimination" and made the State "at least a partner in the instant act of discrimination * * *." The court could "conceive of no other purpose for an application of section 26 aside from authorizing the perpetration of a purported private discrimination * * *." * * *

There is no sound reason for rejecting this judgment. [It] did not read either our cases or the Fourteenth Amendment as establishing an automatic constitutional barrier to the repeal of an existing law prohibiting racial discriminations in housing; nor did the court rule that a State may never put in statutory form an existing policy of neutrality with respect to private discriminations. [It] dealt with § 26 as though it expressly authorized and constitutionalized the private right to discriminate [and] the court assessed the ultimate impact of § 26 in the California environment and concluded that the section would encourage and significantly involve the State in private racial discrimination contrary to the Fourteenth Amendment.

The California court could very reasonably conclude that § 26 would and did have wider impact than a mere repeal of existing statutes. * * * Private discriminations in housing were now not only free from Rumford and Unruh but they also enjoyed a far different status than was true before the passage of those statutes. The right to discriminate, including the right to discriminate on racial grounds, was now embodied in the State's basic charter, immune from legislative, executive, or judicial regulation at any level of the state government. Those practicing racial discriminations need no longer rely solely on their personal choice. They could now invoke express constitutional authority, free from censure or interference of any kind from official sources. * * *

This Court has never attempted the "impossible task" of formulating an infallible test for determining whether the State "in any of its manifestations" has become significantly involved in private discriminations. [Here] the California court, armed as it was with the knowledge of the facts and circumstances concerning the passage and potential impact of § 26, and familiar with the milieu in which that provision would operate, has determined that the provision would involve the State in private racial discriminations to an unconstitutional degree. We accept this holding of the California court.

* * * Section 26 was intended to authorize, and does authorize, racial discrimination in the housing market. The right to discriminate is now one of the basic policies of the State. The California Supreme Court believes that the section will significantly encourage and involve the State in private discriminations. We have been presented with no persuasive considerations indicating that this judgment should be overturned.

Affirmed.[a]

JUSTICE HARLAN, whom JUSTICE BLACK, JUSTICE CLARK, and JUSTICE STEWART join, dissenting.

[A]ll that has happened is that California has effected a pro tanto repeal of its prior statutes forbidding private discrimination. This runs no more afoul of the Fourteenth Amendment than would have California's failure to pass any such antidiscrimination statutes in the first instance. The fact that such repeal was also accompanied by a constitutional prohibition against future enactment of such laws by the California Legislature cannot well be thought to affect, from a federal constitutional standpoint, the validity of what California has done. * * *

The Court attempts to fit § 26 within the coverage of the Equal Protection Clause by characterizing it as in effect an affirmative call to residents of California to discriminate. [But § 26] is neutral on its face, and it is only by in effect asserting that this requirement of passive official neutrality is camouflage that the Court is able to reach its conclusion. In depicting the provision as tantamount to active state encouragement of discrimination the Court essentially relies on the fact that the California Supreme Court so concluded. * * *

a. Douglas, J., joined the Court's opinion, adding that "we deal here with a problem in the realm of zoning, similar to the one we had in *Shelley*. [When] the state leaves [the zoning] function to private agencies or institutions [including real estate brokers who are state licensees], it suffers a governmental function to be performed under private auspices in a way the State itself may not act. The present case is therefore kin to *Terry v. Adams.*"

There is no disagreement whatever but that § 26 was meant to nullify California's fair-housing legislation and thus to remove from private residential property transactions the state-created impediment upon freedom of choice. [But there was no finding] that the defendants' actions were anything but the product of their own private choice. [There] were no findings as to the general effect of § 26. The Court declares that the California court "held the purpose and intent of § 26 was to authorize private racial discriminations in the housing market," but there is no supporting fact in the record for this characterization. * * *

A state enactment, particularly one that is simply permissive of private decision-making rather than coercive[,] should not be struck down [without] persuasive evidence of an invidious purpose or effect. [§ 26 is] a neutral provision restoring to the sphere of free choice, left untouched by the Fourteenth Amendment, private behavior within a limited area of the racial problem. The denial of equal protection emerges only from the conclusion reached by the Court that the implementation of a new policy of governmental neutrality [has] the effect of lending encouragement to those who wish to discriminate. In the context of the actual facts of the case, this conclusion appears to me to state only a truism: people who want to discriminate but were previously forbidden to do so by state law are now left free because the State has chosen to have no law on the subject at all. Obviously whenever there is a change in the law it will have resulted from the concerted activity of those who desire the change, and its enactment will allow those supporting the legislation to pursue their private goals.

A moment of thought will reveal the far-reaching possibilities of the Court's new doctrine, which I am sure the Court does not intend. Every act of private discrimination is either forbidden by state law or permitted by it. There can be little doubt that such permissiveness—whether by express constitutional or statutory provision, or implicit in the common law—to some extent "encourages" those who wish to discriminate to do so. Under this theory "state action" in the form of laws that do nothing more than passively permit private discrimination could be said to tinge *all* private discrimination with the taint of unconstitutional state encouragement. * * *

I think that this decision is not only constitutionally unsound, but in its practical potentialities short-sighted. Opponents of state antidiscrimination statutes are now in a position to argue that such legislation should be defeated because, if enacted, it may be unrepealable. More fundamentally, the doctrine underlying this decision may hamper, if not preclude, attempts to deal with the delicate and troublesome problems of race relations through the legislative process. * * *

Notes and Questions

1. *Court's rationale.* (a) What was the specific basis for § 26's invalidity? Was it that it "constitutionalized the private right to discriminate" in housing, making it "immune from legislative, executive, or judicial regulation at any level of state government"—thus making it much more difficult for minorities to get governmental antidiscrimination help? Would this call for the same result even if California had never enacted the Unruh or Rumford Acts? Suppose a state provides that *all* legislation requires approval by $^2/_3$ of the voters? All legislation having *anything* to do with the sale and purchase of real and personal property? Was § 26 a less "neutral provision"? Sufficiently "nonneutral"?

Was *this* the thrust of the opinion? If so, does *Reitman* hold that racial discrimination in housing by private individuals in California is "state action"?

(b) Or did the Court rest on the finding (whose finding?) that § 26, given "the milieu in which that provision would operate," "would involve the State in private racial discriminations to an unconstitutional degree"? If so, could "mere repeal of existing statutes" so operate? Failure to enact a proposed antidiscrimination law? The mere absence of an antidiscrimination law? Consider Cox, *The Warren Court* 45 (1968): "The truth would seem to be that the absence of legal restraints gives encouragement of a sort to anyone minded to engage in discrimination, and any defeat of proposed restraints after strong public debate will give moral support to some persons who might not otherwise have been ready to discriminate. The degree of support that is given seems likely to depend upon a congeries of factors far more diffuse and subtle than the differences between repeal of a statute and amendment of a constitution." Compare 42 Wash.L.Rev. 285 (1966). See generally C. Black, *"State Action," Equal Protection, and California's Proposition 14,* 81 Harv.L.Rev. 69 (1967); Kurland, *Egalitarianism and the Warren Court,* 68 Mich. 629, 668–70 (1970); Karst & Horowitz, *Reitman v. Mulkey: A Telophase of Substantive Equal Protection,* 1967 Sup.Ct.Rev. 39.

Suppose a school board rescinds a resolution of its predecessor that recognized the boards' responsibility for segregation and called for—but did not enact—any remedial action? See *Dayton Bd. of Educ. v. Brinkman,* 433 U.S. 406, 413–14, 97 S.Ct. 2766, 2772, 53 L.Ed.2d 851, 859 (1977).

2. *State "encouragement" or "authorization."* (a) To what extent does *Reitman* establish the principle that state law which *encourages* (or *authorizes*) private conduct results in "state action"? Is this the basis for Brennan, J.'s view in *Adickes*? What result if "a state passed a statute which provided that individuals shall have the legal right to engage in racial discrimination in their own homes"? J. Williams, *The Twilight of State Action,* 41 Texas L.Rev. 347, 384 (1963). Consider Burke & Reber, *State Action, Congressional Power and Creditors' Rights: An Essay on the Fourteenth Amendment,* 46 So.Cal.L.Rev. 1003, 1105–09 (1973): "[The] basic principle limiting the scope of the fourteenth amendment would be destroyed by equating state action with action authorized or encouraged by state law. [California] statutory law authorizes [the] use of force in self-defense; the disposition of real and personal property; [the] creation of a contractual relationship; [the] execution of a will; the formation of a corporation [etc.]. If state authority or encouragement is a valid state action test, then all of the above forms of private conduct would present fourteenth amendment equal protection and due process problems. [The] fallacy in the thesis [is] most readily apparent when one considers the impact of judicial law. It is almost impossible to consider any form of activity that is not somehow authorized by state decisional law. [As] long as the law is permissive in nature and leaves the initial decision to take the action entirely within the realm of private choice, neither the state nor the individual should be held constitutionally responsible under the fourteenth amendment. [Further], constitutional significance should not attach to such extraneous considerations as whether the law restates a long-standing law, clarifies an existing law, changes the law, creates entirely new law or repeals existing law. [First], the effect of a statute as a form of state law authorizing private conduct is precisely the same regardless of the statute's longevity * * *. Second, untoward consequences would follow from a holding that the statute is unconstitutional because of its newness or because it

repeals an existing law considered more socially desirable by the Court. Such a holding would constitutionally freeze into state law every form of social legislation or decisional or administrative law deemed constitutionally proper by the Court and would thereby discourage states from experimenting in this regard. It would also produce anomalous and illogical results since the identical private conduct authorized and encouraged by the identical statutory or judicial law would be valid in some states under the fourteenth amendment but invalid in others solely because of the age of the state law in each jurisdiction."

Compare Note, *State Action: Theories for Applying Constitutional Restrictions to Private Activity,* 74 Colum.L.Rev. 656, 665–66 (1974): "Statutes enlarging common law rights clearly amount to an increase of private powers, while mere statutory codification of common law rights does not amount to authorization [and the] argument that such 'authorizing' statutes involve government by increasing private powers implies that an increase in powers through expansion of common law rights effected by the courts will constitute a government grant of power. Since any particular decision expanding the previously existing common law would thus constitute 'authorization,' the question arises as against when present common law rights are to be measured. The most reasonable starting point for 'state action' cases arising under the fourteenth amendment would seem to be the common law as of adoption of that amendment." See also Horowitz & Karst, *The California Supreme Court and State Action Under the Fourteenth Amendment: The Leader Beclouds the Issue,* 21 U.C.L.A.L.Rev. 1421 (1974).

(b) The "state 'encouragement' or 'authorization' " issue is considered further in *Flagg Bros. v. Brooks,* Sec. 4 infra.

3. *Repeal of discriminatory legislation.* Recall *Lombard, Peterson* and *Robinson.* Suppose all official pronouncements *requiring* discrimination are repealed or retracted? Is subsequent "private" discrimination in respect to matters previously covered by official pronouncements "state action"? Is the state "significantly involved" because its repeals have now made "private discriminations legally possible"? Have they "authorized" and "encouraged" discrimination? Or is this "mere repeal of existing statutes"? Is discrimination more "authorized and encouraged" by repeal of laws requiring discrimination or by repeal of laws forbidding it?

MOOSE LODGE v. IRVIS

407 U.S. 163, 92 S.Ct. 1965, 32 L.Ed.2d 627 (1972).

JUSTICE REHNQUIST delivered the opinion of the Court.

Appellee Irvis, a Negro, [who] was refused service [as the guest of a member] by appellant Moose Lodge, [claimed] that because the Pennsylvania liquor board had issued appellant Moose Lodge a private club license that authorized the sale of alcoholic beverages on its premises, the refusal of service to him was "state action" * * *.

A three-judge district court [entered] a decree declaring invalid the liquor license issued to Moose Lodge "as long as it follows a policy of racial discrimination in its membership or operating policies or practices." * * *

Moose Lodge is a private club in the ordinary meaning of that term. [It] conducts all of its activities in a building that is owned by it. It is not publicly funded. Only members and guests are permitted in any lodge of the order; one may become a guest only by invitation * * *.

While the principle is easily stated, the question of whether particular discriminatory conduct is private, on the one hand, or amounts to "state action," on the other hand, frequently admits of no easy answer. "Only by sifting facts and weighing circumstances can the non-obvious involvement of the State in private conduct be attributed its true significance." *Burton v. Wilmington Parking Authority,* 365 U.S. 715, 81 S.Ct. 856, 6 L.Ed.2d 45 (1961).

[The] Court held in *Burton* that a private restaurant owner who refused service because of a customer's race violated the Fourteenth Amendment, where the restaurant was located in a building owned by a state-created parking authority and leased from the authority. The Court, after a comprehensive review of the relationship between the lessee and the parking authority concluded that the latter had "so far insinuated itself into a position of interdependence with Eagle [the restaurant owner] that it must be recognized as a joint participant in the challenged activity, which, on that account, cannot be considered to have been so 'purely private' as to fall without the scope of the Fourteenth Amendment."

The Court has never held, of course, that discrimination by an otherwise private entity would be violative of the Equal Protection Clause if the private entity receives any sort of benefit or service at all from the State, or if it is subject to state regulation in any degree whatever. Since state-furnished services include such necessities of life as electricity, water, and police and fire protection, such a holding would utterly emasculate the distinction between private as distinguished from State conduct set forth in *The Civil Rights Cases* and adhered to in subsequent decisions. Our holdings indicate that where the impetus for the discrimination is private, the State must have "significantly involved itself with invidious discriminations," *Reitman,* in order for the discriminatory action to fall within the ambit of the constitutional prohibition. * * *

In *Burton,* the Court's full discussion of the facts in its opinion indicates the significant differences between that case and this: "The land and building were publicly owned.[a] As an entity, the building was dedicated to 'public uses' in performance of the Authority's 'essential governmental functions.'[b] The costs of land acquisition, construction, and maintenance are defrayed entirely from donations by the City of Wilmington, from loans and revenue bonds and from the proceeds of rentals and parking services out of which the loans and bonds were payable. Assuming that the distinction would be significant, the commercially leased areas were not surplus state property, but constituted a physically and financially integral and, indeed, indispensable part of the State's plan to operate its project as a self-sustaining unit.[c] Upkeep and maintenance of the building, including necessary repairs, were responsibilities of the Authority and were payable out of public funds. It cannot be doubted that the peculiar relationship of the restaurant to the parking facility in which it is located confers on each an incidental variety of mutual benefits. Guests of the restaurant are afforded a

a. If the space has been leased to a law firm, could it constitutionally discriminate among its clients?

b. If the Authority had municipal immunity from tort liability, is Eagle liable for a customer's food poisoning?

c. "Other portions of the structure were leased to other tenants, including a bookstore, a retail jeweler, and a food store. Upon completion of the building, the Authority located at appropriate places thereon official signs indicating the public character of the building, and flew from mastheads on the roof both the state and national flags." *Burton.* Query: If Wilmington, instead of including rental space in the parking building, had relied on rental income from other of its properties located throughout the city to help finance the parking facility, could lessees of these properties refuse to do business with blacks?

convenient place to park their automobiles, even if they cannot enter the restaurant directly from the parking area. Similarly, its convenience for diners may well provide additional demand for the Authority's parking facilities.[d] Should any improvements effected in the leasehold by Eagle become part of the realty, there is no possibility of increased taxes being passed on to it since the fee is held by a tax-exempt government agency. Neither can it be ignored, especially in view of Eagle's affirmative allegation that for it to serve Negroes would injure its business, that profits earned by discrimination not only contribute to, but also are indispensable elements in, the financial success of a governmental agency."[e]

Here there is nothing approaching the symbiotic relationship between lessor and lessee that was present in *Burton* * * *. Far from apparently holding itself out as a place of public accommodation Moose Lodge quite ostentatiously proclaims the fact that it is not open to the public at large. Nor is it located and operated in such surroundings that although private in name, it discharges a function or performs a service that would otherwise in all likelihood be performed by the State. In short, while Eagle was a public restaurant in a public building, Moose Lodge is a private social club in a private building.

With the exception hereafter noted, the Pennsylvania Liquor Control Board plays absolutely no part in establishing or enforcing the membership or guest policies of the club which it licenses to serve liquor.[3] [The] only effect that the state licensing of Moose Lodge to serve liquor can be said to have on the right of any other Pennsylvanian to buy or be served liquor on premises other than those of Moose Lodge is that for some purposes club licenses are counted in the maximum number of licenses which may be issued in a given municipality. Basically each municipality has a quota of one retail license for each 1,500 inhabitants. Licenses issued to hotels, municipal golf courses and airport restaurants are not counted in this quota, nor are club licenses until the maximum number of retail licenses is reached. Beyond that point, neither additional retail licenses nor additional club licenses may be issued so long as the number of issued and outstanding retail licenses remains above the statutory maximum.

d. Suppose Eagle were located in a private building immediately adjacent to the public parking building?

e. *Burton* added: "It is irony amounting to grave injustice that in one part of a single building, erected and maintained with public funds by an agency of the State to serve a public purpose, all persons have equal rights, while in another portion, also serving the public, a Negro is a second-class citizen [but] at the same time fully enjoys equal access to nearby restaurants in wholly privately owned buildings. [I]n its lease with Eagle the Authority could have affirmatively required Eagle to discharge the responsibilities under the Fourteenth Amendment imposed upon the private enterprise as a consequence of state participation. But no State may effectively abdicate its responsibilities by either ignoring them or by merely failing to discharge them whatever the motive may be." Query: If the state sells surplus property without requiring its nondiscriminatory use because such a requirement would bring the city a lower price, may the purchaser constitutionally discriminate? If such a requirement were financially irrelevant but the state neglected to include it, may the buyer discriminate?

Harlan, J., joined by Whittaker, J., dissented: "The Court's opinion, by a process of first undiscriminatingly throwing together various factual bits and pieces and then undermining the resulting structure by an equally vague disclaimer, seems to me to leave completely at sea just what it is in this record that satisfies the requirement of 'state action.'" See generally T. Lewis, *Burton v. Wilmington Parking Authority—A Case Without Precedent,* 61 Colum.L.Rev. 1458 (1961).

3. Unlike the situation in *Public Utilities Comm'n v. Pollak,* where the regulatory agency had affirmatively approved the practice of the regulated entity after full investigation * * *.

The District Court was at pains to [note that] an applicant for a club license must make such physical alterations in its premises as the board may require, must file a list of the names and addresses of its members and employees, and must keep extensive financial records. The board is granted the right to inspect the licensed premises at any time * * *.

However detailed this type of regulation may be in some particulars, it cannot be said to in any way foster or encourage racial discrimination. Nor can it be said to make the State in any realistic sense a partner or even a joint venturer in the club's enterprise. The limited effect of the prohibition against obtaining additional club licenses when the maximum number of retail licenses allotted to a municipality has been issued, when considered together with the availability of liquor from hotel, restaurant, and retail licensees falls far short of conferring upon club licensees a monopoly in the dispensing of liquor * * *. We therefore hold that, with the exception hereafter noted, the operation of the regulatory scheme enforced by the Pennsylvania Liquor Control Board does not sufficiently implicate the State in the discriminatory guest policies of Moose Lodge * * *.

The District Court found that [Regulations § 113.09] of the Liquor Control Board adopted pursuant to statute affirmatively require that "every club licensee shall adhere to all the provisions of its constitution and by-laws." Appellant argues that the purpose of this provision "is purely and simply and plainly the prevention of subterfuge" * * *. There can be no doubt that the label "private club" can and has been used to evade both regulations of State and local liquor authorities, and statutes requiring places of public accommodation to serve all persons without regard to race, color, religion, or national origin. * * *

[The Moose constitution and by-laws limit membership and guest privileges to male Caucasians.]

Even though the Liquor Control Board regulation in question is neutral in its terms, the result of its application in a case where the constitution and by-laws of a club required racial discrimination would be to invoke the sanctions of the State to enforce a concededly discriminatory private rule. * * * *Shelley v. Kraemer* makes it clear that the application of state sanctions to enforce such a rule would violate the Fourteenth Amendment. * * *

Appellee was entitled to a decree enjoining the enforcement of § 113.09 [but] no more. The judgment of the District Court is reversed * * *.

JUSTICE DOUGLAS, with whom JUSTICE MARSHALL joins, dissenting.

My view of the First Amendment and the related guarantees of the Bill of Rights is that they create a zone of privacy which precludes government from interfering with private clubs or groups.[1] The associational rights which our system honors permits all white, all black, all brown, and all yellow clubs to be formed. [So] the fact that the Moose Lodge allows only Caucasians to join or come as guests is constitutionally irrelevant * * *. And the fact that a private club gets some kind of permit from the State or municipality does not make it ipso facto a public enterprise or undertaking, any more than the grant to a householder of a permit to operate an incinerator puts the householder in the public domain. We must therefore examine whether there are special

1. [There] was no occasion [below] to consider the question whether perhaps because of a role as a center of community activity, Moose Lodge No. 107 was in fact "private" for equal protection purposes. The decision today, therefore, leaves this question open.

circumstances involved in the Pennsylvania scheme which differentiate the liquor license possessed by Moose Lodge from the incinerator permit.

[The opinion then agrees with the Court's disposition of Regulations § 113.09]. But there is another flaw in the scheme not so easily cured. Liquor licenses in Pennsylvania [are] not freely available to those who meet racially neutral qualifications. There is a complex quota system, which the majority accurately describes. What the majority neglects to say is that the Harrisburg quota, where Moose Lodge No. 107 is located, has been full for many years. No more club licenses may be issued in that city.

This state-enforced scarcity of licenses restricts the ability of blacks to obtain liquor, for liquor is commercially available *only* at private clubs for a significant portion of each week.[3] [A] group desiring to form a nondiscriminatory club which would serve blacks must purchase a license held by an existing club, which can exact a monopoly price for the transfer. The availability of such a license is speculative at best, however, for, as Moose Lodge itself concedes, without a liquor license a fraternal organization would be hard-pressed to survive.

Thus, the State of Pennsylvania is putting the weight of its liquor license, concededly a valued and important adjunct to a private club, behind racial discrimination. * * *

JUSTICE BRENNAN, with whom JUSTICE MARSHALL joins, dissenting.

When Moose Lodge obtained its liquor license, the State of Pennsylvania became an active participant in the operation of the Lodge bar. Liquor licensing laws [are] primarily pervasive regulatory schemes under which the State dictates and continually supervises virtually every detail of the operation of the licensee's business. Very few, if any, other licensed businesses experience such complete state involvement. [The] opinion of the [court below] most persuasively demonstrates the "state action" present in this case: * * *

"[After describing the regulations, mentioned in the majority opinion, the court below continued:] It is only on compliance with these and numerous other requirements and if the Board is satisfied that the applicant is 'a person of good repute' and that the license will not be 'detrimental to the welfare, health, peace and morals of the inhabitants of the neighborhood,' that the license may issue.

"Once a license has been issued the licensee must comply with many detailed requirements or risk its suspension or revocation. He must in any event have it renewed periodically. Liquor licenses have been employed in Pennsylvania to regulate a wide variety of moral conduct, such as the presence and activities of homosexuals, performance by a topless dancer, lewd dancing, swearing, being noisy or disorderly. So broad is the state's power that the courts of Pennsylvania have upheld its restriction of freedom of expression of a licensee on the ground that in doing so it merely exercises its plenary power to attach conditions to the privilege of dispensing liquor which a licensee holds at the sufferance of the state. * * *" * * *[f]

3. Hotels and restaurants may serve liquor between 7:00 a.m. and 2:00 a.m. the next day, Monday through Saturday. On Sunday, such licensees are restricted to sales between 12:00 a.m. and 2:00 a.m., and between 1:00 p.m. and 10:00 p.m. * * * Club licensees, however, are permitted to sell liquor to members and guests from 7:00 a.m. to 3:00 a.m. the next day, seven-days-a-week. * * *

f. Irvis also complained to the Pennsylvania Human Rights Commission. *Commonwealth v. Loyal Order of Moose,* 448 Pa. 451, 294 A.2d 594, appeal dismissed, 409 U.S. 1052 (1972), upheld the Commission's ruling that the Harrisburg Moose Lodge was a "public accommodation" under state law and could not bar guests on the basis of race.

Notes and Questions

1. *Court's rationale.* Does *Moose Lodge* rest ultimately on a "balancing approach"? See Note, *State Action and the Burger Court,* 60 Va.L.Rev. 840 (1974). If so, consider Note, *Developing Legal Vistas for the Discouragement of Private Club Discrimination,* 58 Ia.L.Rev. 108, 139 (1972): "[In cases of] large, nationwide fraternal orders which are segregated pursuant to national constitutions, [there] is evidence that these clubs serve substantially economic interests. Furthermore, a glance at the membership requirement and size of these clubs indicates they are not closely knit clubs involving a high quotient of intimacy. They are certainly not primarily religious or political in nature. Hence, under the balancing approach, the associational rights asserted by these clubs would not seem strong."

2. *Burton vs. Moose Lodge.* Consider C. Stone, *Corporate Vices and Corporate Virtues: Do Public/Private Distinctions Matter?*, 130 U.Pa.L.Rev. 1441, 1449–1501 (1982): "[W]e should be readier to deem an actor 'public' when [it is 'symbolically public' and] when the preponderant costs of doing so will be imposed on the benefitting public at-large. * * * There are several ways to interpret the contrasting results in *Burton* and *Moose Lodge.* One way is to contrast the symbolic elements of the situation: after all, the parking authority building flew, quite literally, the flags of government. [Second,] in *Burton,* the government stood to capture essentially all the economic benefits of the discrimination, assuming perfect competition among bidders for the lease. Hence, the Court's decision prohibiting the arrangement eliminated from public revenues essentially the full measure of the ill-gotten gains. [T]he preponderant costs of setting a morally correct example will be borne by the public, which is exactly where they ought to lie. Note that the same consequence, the apportionment of essentially all 'fairness' costs on general revenues, would not result from a plaintiff's victory when the government is insuring mortgages, or guaranteeing loans, or is a regulatory licensor, as in *Moose Lodge.* [In] those situations, extending state action would concentrate costs on a distinct sub-group, a result that courts have been reluctant to decree."

3. *Private schools.* (a) NORWOOD v. HARRISON, 413 U.S. 455, 93 S.Ct. 2804, 37 L.Ed.2d 723 (1973), per BURGER, C.J., enjoined Mississippi's lending of textbooks to all students in public and private schools as applied to racially segregated private schools: "[T]hat the Constitution may compel toleration of private discrimination in some circumstances does not mean that it requires state support for such discrimination."

The textbook program, "enacted first in 1940, long before [there] was any occasion to have a policy or reason to foster the development of racially segregated private academies," may have been "motivated by [a] sincere interest in the educational welfare of all Mississippi children. But good intentions as to one valid objective do not serve to negate the State's involvement in violation of a constitutional duty. 'The existence of a permissible purpose cannot sustain an action that has an impermissible effect.' [citing school desegregation cases]." The lower court had found "that the textbook loans did not interfere with or impede the State's acknowledged duty to establish a unitary school system" since "the State's public schools are now fully unitary." The Court, although casting doubt on the finding, held it "irrelevant": "A State's constitutional obligation requires it to steer clear, not only of operating the old dual system of racially segregated schools, but also of giving significant aid to institutions that practice racial or other invidious discrimination."

Plaintiffs had failed to show that "any child enrolled in private school, if deprived of free textbooks, would withdraw from private school and subsequently enroll in the public schools." But "the Constitution does not permit the State to aid discrimination even when there is no precise causal relationship between state financial aid to a private school and the continued well-being of that school. A State may not grant the type of tangible financial aid here involved if that aid has a significant tendency to facilitate, reinforce, and support private discrimination. * * * Textbooks are a basic educational tool and, like tuition grants, they are provided only in connection with schools; they are to be distinguished from generalized services government might provide to schools in common with others. Moreover, the textbooks provided to private school students by the State in this case are a form of assistance readily available from sources entirely independent of the State—unlike, for example, 'such necessities of life as electricity, water, and police and fire protection.'" Douglas and Brennan, JJ., concurred in the result.

(b) In GILMORE v. MONTGOMERY, 417 U.S. 556, 94 S.Ct. 2416, 41 L.Ed.2d 304 (1974), a federal court enjoined the city's "permitting the use of public park recreational facilities by private segregated school groups and by other nonschool groups that racially discriminate in their membership." The Court, per BLACKMUN, J., modified the decree in part: It "was wholly proper for the city to be enjoined from permitting *exclusive* access to public recreational facilities by segregated private schools" (emphasis added), which had been "formed in reaction against" the federal court's school desegregation order. "[T]his assistance significantly tended to undermine the federal court order mandating [a] unitary school system in Montgomery."

But, "upon this record, we are unable to draw a conclusion as to whether the use of zoos, museums, parks, and other recreational facilities by private school groups *in common with others,* and by private nonschool organizations, involves government so directly in the actions of those users as to warrant" intervention (emphasis added). "It is possible that certain uses of city facilities will be judged to be in contravention of the parks [or school] desegregation order, [or] in some way to constitute impermissible 'state action' ascribing to the city the discriminatory actions of the groups."

The latter issue concerns "whether there is significant state involvement in the private discrimination alleged. * * * Traditional state monopolies, such as electricity, water, and police and fire protection—all generalized governmental services—do not by their mere provision constitute a showing of state involvement in invidious discrimination. *Norwood.* The same is true of a broad spectrum of municipal recreational facilities * * *.

"If, however, the city or other governmental entity rations otherwise freely accessible recreational facilities, the case for state action will naturally be stronger than if the facilities are simply available to all comers without condition or reservation. Here, for example, petitioners allege that the city engages in scheduling softball games for an all-white church league and provides balls, equipment, fields, and lighting. The city's role in that situation would be dangerously close to what was found to exist in *Burton* * * *." [a]

a. Brennan, J., concurred in part but would enjoin *any* "school-sponsored or directed uses of the city recreational facilities that enable private segregated schools to duplicate public school operations at public expense."

WHITE, J., joined by Douglas, J., concurred: "[T]he question is not whether there is state action, but whether the conceded action by the city, and hence by the State, is such that the State must be deemed to have denied the equal protection of the laws. In other words, by permitting a segregated school or group to use city-owned facilities, has the State furnished such aid to the group's segregated policies or become so involved in them that the State itself may fairly be said to have denied equal protection? Under *Burton,* it is perfectly clear that to violate the Equal Protection Clause the State itself need not make, advise, or authorize the private decision to discriminate that involves the State in the practice of segregation or would appear to do so in the minds of ordinary citizens." Marshall, J. generally agreed with White, J.

(c) *Significance of remedy.* In contrast to *Burton* (where plaintiff sought an injunction against Eagle Coffee Shoppe), since the only remedy sought in *Norwood* and *Gilmore* was against the state or city itself, did these cases really present any "state action" issue at all? Was the issue in *Moose Lodge* whether the club's refusal to serve Irvis constituted "state action"? Or was it whether Pennsylvania could grant a liquor license to a club that practiced racial discrimination? Are these constitutional issues the same? Consider R. Brown, *State Action Analysis of Tax Expenditures,* 11 Harv.Civ.Rts.-Civ.Lib.L. 97, 115–19 (1976): "[T]wo kinds of 'state action' cases should [be] distinguished: only in suits in which relief is sought against a private actor should the private actor's interests be taken into account. [Thus,] it is quite possible that a plaintiff proceeding under a state action theory might prevail in enjoining the government's action but fail in his efforts to enjoin the private activity." Compare McCoy, *Current State Action Theories, the Jackson Nexus Requirement, and Employee Discharges by Semi-Public and State-Aided Institutions,* 31 Vand.L. Rev. 785, 802 (1978): "Although this theoretical distinction has considerable superficial appeal, primarily because it is formulated in terms of balancing competing constitutional interests, closer inspection reveals no significant difference between the cases. [E]ither kind of suit presents the private actor with precisely the same basic option—either modify the private action to conform to fourteenth amendment standards or do without the state aid. In other words, the two kinds of suits are indistinguishable in terms of the private interest interfered with, and therefore they should not present significantly different standards for the level of state aid required." Contrast Brown, supra, at 119 n. 102: "It is of course true that the removal of the government aid will have a coercive effect on the private actor. In some cases the pressure to conform private behavior to constitutional standards generated by the loss of assistance will be as coercive as an injunction. In such a case, however, the fact that withdrawing the aid had a strong influence on private behavior would imply a high level of significance of government involvement with the private actor. In that case it would be appropriate to impose relief on the private actor as well as on the government, so the remedy distinction would not apply."

In any event, since the practices in *Norwood* and *Gilmore* were not shown to be "motivated" to perpetuate racial discrimination, can these decisions be squared with *Washington v. Davis,* p. 972 supra? Given the doctrines that (1) public financial aid to parochial schools violates the establishment clause if either the *purpose or effect* advances religion (Ch. 9, Sec. 1, II), whereas (2) a racially discriminatory *purpose* must exist for violation of the equal protection clause (Ch. 6, Sec. 2, III), can *Norwood* be squared with *Board of Educ. v. Allen* (p. 846 supra)? See Choper, *Thoughts on State Action,* 1979 Wash.U.L.Q. 757, 765–69.

(d) What results in *Norwood* and *Gilmore* if the remedy sought had been to compel the private schools to desegregate? Should some or all private schools be held to the requirements of the equal protection clause? [b]

(i) *Financial aid.* If private schools receive extensive financial aid from the state, does it result in state action only in respect to a specific activity being funded? Consider Comment, *Tax Incentives as State Action,* 122 U.Pa.L.Rev. 414, 436 (1973): "This [theory] incorrectly assumes that government involvement that bears directly upon a specific activity of an entity can be meaningfully distinguished from government involvement that serves more generally to perpetuate that entity as a whole. It is an inescapable fact that general government assistance which perpetuates an entity operates indirectly to perpetuate the specific activities of that entity." May a person whose sole source of income is public relief constitutionally refuse to sell his home to blacks?

(ii) *Public control.* Suppose the private schools' curriculum and admission policy are subject to state regulation? If a state statute regulates election procedures of all voluntary organizations, is a social club barred from racially discriminating? If the state provides private schools with extensive financial aid and strict regulation, are the schools "state functions"? If the state licenses all barber schools and requires that all barbers attend such schools, are the schools "state functions"?

(iii) *"Government function."* Even without state aid or regulation, does "the spirit of [the segregation decisions] support the argument that education is a matter of such vital public concern that any action taken in regard to it must be subject to the prohibitions of the fourteenth amendment"? 56 Colum.L.Rev. 285, 287 (1956). Consider Abernathy, *Expansion of the State Action Concept Under the Fourteenth Amendment,* 43 Corn.L.Q. 375, 407 (1958): "[T]he only purely privately operated functions which properly should be considered as governmental are those which are indispensable to the maintenance of democratic government. [S]uch a definition does not go so far as to cover operations which are merely useful or desirable as aids to a more efficient or intelligently controlled government. If these are to be included, then we are no better off than if we equate governmental action with operations affected with a public interest. Education is desirable and useful in a democratic system but it is not indispensable [in] the sense that access to the ballot and the processes of selecting public officials is." If the state closed all of its public schools, would that make private schools "indispensable to the maintenance of democratic government"? If so, would some (all) private schools be barred from racially (sexually, religiously) discriminating? [c]

4. *Tax exempt organizations.* May government give tax exemptions (or permit tax deductions for donations) to private schools, fraternal groups and charitable foundations that fail to adhere to fourteenth amendment requirements? See generally Bittker & Kaufman, *Taxes and Civil Rights: "Constitutionalizing" the Internal Revenue Code,* 82 Yale L.J. 51 (1972). Consider Note, *State Action and the United States Junior Chamber of Commerce,* 43 Geo.Wash. L.Rev. 1407, 1423–24 (1975): "[T]he Internal Revenue Code's tax exemptions for

b. See *Runyon v. McCrary,* p. 1290 infra, holding that a federal statute prohibits private schools from refusing to accept black students.

c. See generally Note, *The Wall of Racial Separation: The Role of Private and Parochial Schools in Racial Integration,* 43 N.Y.U.L.Rev. 514 (1968); Note, *Segregation Academies and State Action,* 82 Yale L.J. 1436 (1973); O'Neil, *Private Universities and Public Law,* 19 Buf.L. Rev. 155 (1970).

For further consideration of this issue, see note 2(b) after *Flagg Bros. v. Brooks,* Sec. 4 infra.

charitable organizations are based upon the theory that the Government is compensated for the loss of revenue by being relieved of the financial burden that would otherwise have to be met by appropriations of government funds. [Where] the private entity is thus acting as a surrogate for the government, any discrimination connected with the performance of public services, even if not affirmatively approved by the government, subjects the victims to discrimination that would not have occurred had the government performed the services directly. The government cannot avoid these constitutional limitations by delegating its functions to private entities, even if the delegation is well-intentioned." See also Parker, *Evans v. Newton and the Racially Restricted Charitable Trust,* 13 How.L.J. 223 (1967). Reconsider note 4(c) supra.

5. *Redevelopment housing.* Are major urban redevelopment housing projects, undertaken pursuant to statutory authority with benefit of public condemnation power and tax exemption, constitutionally barred from racially discriminating? If so, what about ordinary private housing projects that receive public "aid" in the form of water and sewage disposal, police and fire protection? See generally Comment, *Application of the Fourteenth Amendment to Builders of Private Housing,* 12 Kan.L.Rev. 426 (1964); Note, *Nondiscrimination Implications of Federal Involvement in Housing,* 19 Vand.L.Rev. 865 (1966); 17 J.Pub.L. 175 (1968). Is urban redevelopment distinguishable from a small private housing project because the former has the effect of racial zoning? Is this a restatement of the "government function" theory? Is the issue of "state action" affected if the claim is that the housing project evicted a tenant without affording procedural due process?

SECTION 4. RECENT DEVELOPMENTS

DeSHANEY v. WINNEBAGO DEP'T OF SOCIAL SERV.

489 U.S. 189, 109 S.Ct. 998, 103 L.Ed.2d 249 (1989).

CHIEF JUSTICE REHNQUIST delivered the opinion of the Court.

Petitioner is a boy who was beaten and permanently injured by his father [who had been divorced from his mother], with whom he lived. The respondents are social workers and other local officials who received complaints that petitioner was being abused by his father and had reason to believe that this was the case, but nonetheless did not act to remove petitioner from his father's custody. Petitioner [claimed that respondents'] failure to act deprived him of his liberty in violation of the Due Process Clause of [due process]. We hold that it did not.

[The] Winnebago County authorities first learned that Joshua DeShaney might be a victim of child abuse in January 1982, when his father's second wife complained to the police, at the time of their divorce, that he had previously "hit the boy causing marks and [was] a prime case for child abuse." The Winnebago County Department of Social Services (DSS) interviewed the father, but he denied the accusations, and DSS did not pursue them further. In January 1983, Joshua was admitted to a local hospital with multiple bruises and abrasions. The examining physician suspected child abuse and notified DSS, which immediately obtained an order from a Wisconsin juvenile court placing Joshua in the temporary custody of the hospital. Three days later, the county convened an ad hoc "Child Protection Team" [which] decided that there was insufficient evidence of child abuse to retain Joshua in the custody of the court. The Team did, however, decide to recommend several measures to protect Joshua, including enrolling him in a preschool program, providing his father with certain counselling services, and encouraging his father's girlfriend to move out of the home.

Randy DeShaney entered into a voluntary agreement with DSS in which he promised to cooperate with them in accomplishing these goals.

[A month after] the juvenile court dismissed the child protection case and returned Joshua to the custody of his father * * * emergency room personnel called the DSS caseworker handling Joshua's case to report that he had once again been treated for suspicious injuries. The caseworker concluded that there was no basis for action. For the next six months, the caseworker made monthly visits to the DeShaney home, during which she observed a number of suspicious injuries on Joshua's head; she also noticed that he had not been enrolled in school and that the girlfriend had not moved out. The caseworker dutifully recorded these incidents in her files, along with her continuing suspicions that someone in the DeShaney household was physically abusing Joshua, but she did nothing more. In November 1983, the emergency room notified DSS that Joshua had been treated once again for injuries that they believed to be caused by child abuse. On the caseworker's next two visits to the DeShaney home, she was told that Joshua was too ill to see her. Still DSS took no action.

In March 1984, Randy DeShaney beat 4-year-old Joshua so severely that he fell into a life-threatening coma. [H]e suffered brain damage so severe that he is expected to spend the rest of his life confined to an institution for the profoundly retarded. Randy DeShaney was subsequently tried and convicted of child abuse.

Joshua and his mother brought this action under 42 U.S.C. § 1983 [alleging] that respondents had deprived Joshua of his liberty without due process of law, in violation of his rights under the Fourteenth Amendment, by failing to intervene to protect him against a risk of violence at his father's hands of which they knew or should have known. The District Court granted summary judgment for respondents. The Court of Appeals for the Seventh Circuit affirmed.

[Petitioners] contend that the State deprived Joshua of his liberty interest in "free[dom] from unjustified intrusions on personal security" by failing to provide him with adequate protection against his father's violence. The claim is one invoking the substantive rather than procedural component of the Due Process Clause; petitioners do not claim that the State denied Joshua protection without according him appropriate procedural safeguards, but that it was categorically obligated to protect him in these circumstances.

But nothing in the language of the Due Process Clause itself requires the State to protect the life, liberty, and property of its citizens against invasion by private actors. The Clause is phrased as a limitation on the State's power to act, not as a guarantee of certain minimal levels of safety and security. [Nor] does history support such an expansive reading of the constitutional text. [The Clause's] purpose was to protect the people from the State, not to ensure that the State protected them from each other. The Framers were content to leave the extent of governmental obligation in the latter area to the democratic political processes.

Consistent with these principles, our cases have recognized that the Due Process Clauses generally confer no affirmative right to governmental aid, even where such aid may be necessary to secure life, liberty, or property interests of which the government itself may not deprive the individual. See e.g., *Harris v. McRae* [p. 194 supra] (no obligation to fund abortions or other medical services); *Lindsey v. Normet* [p. 1177 supra] (no obligation to provide adequate housing). [If] the Due Process Clause does not require the State to provide its citizens with particular protective services, it follows that the State cannot be held liable under the Clause for injuries that could have been averted had it chosen to provide them. As a general matter, then, we conclude that a State's failure to protect an individual against private violence simply does not constitute a violation of the Due Process Clause.

Petitioners contend, however, that even if the Due Process Clause imposes no affirmative obligation on the State to provide the general public with adequate protective services, such a duty may arise out of certain "special relationships" created or assumed by the State with respect to particular individuals [and] that such a "special relationship" existed here because the State knew that Joshua faced a special danger of abuse at his father's hands, and specifically proclaimed, by word and by deed, its intention to protect him against that danger. * * *

We reject this argument. It is true that in certain limited circumstances the Constitution imposes upon the State affirmative duties of care and protection with respect to particular individuals [discussing *Youngberg v. Romeo,* p. 271 supra; *Estelle v. Gamble,* 429 U.S. 97, 97 S.Ct. 285, 50 L.Ed.2d 251 (1976); and other cases.]

But these [cases] stand only for the proposition that when the State takes a person into its custody and holds him there against his will, the Constitution imposes upon it a corresponding duty to assume some responsibility for his safety and general well-being. [In] the substantive due process analysis, it is the State's affirmative act of restraining the individual's freedom to act on his own behalf—through incarceration, institutionalization, or other similar restraint of personal liberty—which is the "deprivation of liberty" triggering the protections of the Due Process Clause, not its failure to act to protect his liberty interests against harms inflicted by other means.

The *Estelle-Youngberg* analysis simply has no applicability in the present case. Petitioners concede that the harms Joshua suffered did not occur while he was in the State's custody, but while he was in the custody of his natural father, who was in no sense a state actor.[9] While the State may have been aware of the dangers that Joshua faced in the free world, it played no part in their creation, nor did it do anything to render him any more vulnerable to them. That the State once took temporary custody of Joshua does not alter the analysis, for when it returned him to his father's custody, it placed him in no worse position than that in which he would have been had it not acted at all; the State does not become the permanent guarantor of an individual's safety by having once offered him shelter. Under these circumstances, the State had no constitutional duty to protect Joshua.

It may well be that, by voluntarily undertaking to protect Joshua against a danger it concededly played no part in creating, the State acquired a duty under state tort law to provide him with adequate protection against that danger. [But] the claim here is based on the Due Process Clause of the Fourteenth Amendment, which, as we have said many times, does not transform every tort committed by a state actor into a constitutional violation. [Because] the State had no constitutional duty to protect Joshua against his father's violence, its failure to do so—though calamitous in hindsight—simply does not constitute a violation of the Due Process Clause.[10]

9. [Had] the State by the affirmative exercise of its power removed Joshua from free society and placed him in a foster home operated by its agents, we might have a situation sufficiently analogous to incarceration or institutionalization to give rise to an affirmative duty to protect. Indeed, several Courts of Appeals have [so held], by analogy to *Estelle* and *Youngberg.* * * * We express no view on the validity of this analogy, however, as it is not before us in the present case. [See Note 2, following this case.]

10. Because we conclude that the Due Process Clause did not require the State to protect Joshua from his father, we need not ad-

Judges and lawyers, like other humans, are moved by natural sympathy in a case like this to find a way for Joshua and his mother to receive adequate compensation for the grievous harm inflicted upon them. But before yielding to that impulse, it is well to remember once again that the harm was inflicted not by the State of Wisconsin, but by Joshua's father. The most that can be said of the state functionaries in this case is that they stood by and did nothing when suspicious circumstances dictated a more active role for them. In defense of them it must also be said that had they moved too soon to take custody of the son away from the father, they would likely have been met with charges of improperly intruding into the parent-child relationship, charges based on the same Due Process Clause that forms the basis for the present charge of failure to provide adequate protection.

The people of Wisconsin may well prefer a system of liability which would place upon the State and its officials the responsibility for failure to act in situations such as the present one. They may create such a system, if they do not have it already, by changing the tort law of the State in accordance with the regular law-making process. But they should not have it thrust upon them by this Court's expansion of the Due Process Clause of the Fourteenth Amendment.

JUSTICE BRENNAN, with whom JUSTICE MARSHALL and JUSTICE BLACKMUN join, dissenting. * * *

It may well be, as the Court decides, that the Due Process Clause as construed by our prior cases creates no general right to basic governmental services. That, however, is not the question presented here. [No one] has asked the Court to proclaim that, as a general matter, the Constitution safeguards positive as well as negative liberties. * * *

Because of the Court's initial fixation on the general principle that the Constitution does not establish positive rights, it is unable to appreciate our recognition in *Estelle* and *Youngberg* that this principle does not hold true in all circumstances.

[T]he fact of hospitalization was critical in *Youngberg* not because it rendered Romeo helpless to help himself, but because it separated him from other sources of aid that, we held, the State was obligated to replace. Unlike the Court, therefore, I am unable to see in *Youngberg* a neat and decisive divide between action and inaction.

Moreover, to the Court, the only fact that seems to count as an "affirmative act of restraining the individual's freedom to act on his own behalf" is direct physical control. I would not however, give *Youngberg* and *Estelle* such a stingy scope. I would recognize, as the Court apparently cannot, that "the State's knowledge of [an] individual's predicament [and] its expressions of intent to help him" can amount to a "limitation of his freedom to act on his own behalf" or to obtain help from others. Thus, I would read *Youngberg* and *Estelle* to stand for the much more generous proposition that, if a State cuts off private sources of aid and then refuses aid itself, it cannot wash its hands of the harm that results from its inaction.

Youngberg and *Estelle* are not alone in sounding this theme. In striking down a filing fee as applied to divorce cases brought by indigents, see *Boddie v. Connecticut* [p. 1166 supra] and in deciding that a local government could not entirely foreclose the opportunity to speak in a public forum, see e.g., *Schneider v. Irvington* [p. 641 supra], we have acknowledged that a State's actions—such as

dress respondents' alternative argument that the individual state actors lacked the requisite "state of mind" to make out a due process violation. * * *

the monopolization of a particular path of relief—may impose upon the State certain positive duties. Similarly, *Shelley v. Kraemer* and *Burton v. Wilmington Parking Authority* suggest that a State may be found complicit in an injury even if it did not create the situation that caused the harm.

[These] cases signal that a State's prior actions may be decisive in analyzing the constitutional significance of its inaction. I thus would locate the DeShaneys' claims within the framework of cases like *Youngberg* and *Estelle,* and more generally, *Boddie* and *Schneider,* by considering the actions that Wisconsin took with respect to Joshua.

Wisconsin has established a child-welfare system specifically designed to help children like Joshua. Wisconsin law places upon the local departments of social services such as respondent [a] duty to investigate reported instances of child abuse. While other governmental bodies and private persons are largely responsible for the reporting of possible cases of child abuse, Wisconsin law channels all such reports to the local departments of social services for evaluation and, if necessary, further action. [In] this way, Wisconsin law invites—indeed, directs—citizens and other governmental entities to depend on local departments of social services such as respondent to protect children from abuse.

The specific facts before us bear out this view of Wisconsin's system of protecting children. Each time someone voiced a suspicion that Joshua was being abused, that information was relayed to the Department for investigation and possible action. * * * As to the extent of the social worker's involvement in and knowledge of Joshua's predicament, her reaction to the news of Joshua's last and most devastating injuries is illuminating: "I just knew the phone would ring some day and Joshua would be dead."

Even more telling than these examples is the Department's control over the decision whether to take steps to protect a particular child from suspected abuse. While many different people contributed information and advice to this decision, it was up to the people at DSS to make the ultimate decision (subject to the approval of the local government's Corporation Counsel) whether to disturb the family's current arrangements. When Joshua first appeared at a local hospital with injuries signaling physical abuse, for example, it was DSS that made the decision to take him into temporary custody for the purpose of studying his situation—and it was DSS, acting in conjunction with the Corporation Counsel, that returned him to his father. Unfortunately for Joshua DeShaney, the buck effectively stopped with the Department.

In these circumstances, a private citizen, or even a person working in a government agency other than DSS, would doubtless feel that her job was done as soon as she had reported her suspicions of child abuse to DSS. [If] DSS ignores or dismisses these suspicions, no one will step in to fill the gap. Wisconsin's child-protection program thus effectively confined Joshua DeShaney within the walls of Randy DeShaney's violent home until such time as DSS took action to remove him. Conceivably, then, children like Joshua are made worse off by the existence of this program when the persons and entities charged with carrying it out fail to do their jobs.

It simply belies reality, therefore, to contend that the State "stood by and did nothing" with respect to Joshua. Through its child-protection program, the State actively intervened in Joshua's life and, by virtue of this intervention, acquired ever more certain knowledge that Joshua was in grave danger. These circumstances, in my view, plant this case solidly within the tradition of cases like *Youngberg* and *Estelle.*

[As] the Court today reminds us, "the Due Process Clause of the Fourteenth Amendment was intended to prevent government 'from abusing [its] power, or employing it as an instrument of oppression.' " My disagreement with the Court arises from its failure to see that inaction can be every bit as abusive of power as action, that oppression can result when a State undertakes a vital duty and then ignores it. * * *

JUSTICE BLACKMUN, dissenting.

Today, the Court purports to be the dispassionate oracle of the law, unmoved by "natural sympathy." But, in this pretense, the Court itself retreats into a sterile formalism which prevents it from recognizing either the facts of the case before it or the legal norms that should apply to those facts. As Justice Brennan demonstrates, the facts here involve not mere passivity, but active state intervention in the life of Joshua DeShaney—intervention that triggered a fundamental duty to aid the boy once the State learned of the severe danger to which he was exposed.

The Court fails to recognize this duty because it attempts to draw a sharp and rigid line between action and inaction. But such formalistic reasoning has no place in the interpretation of the broad and stirring clauses of the Fourteenth Amendment. Indeed, I submit that these clauses were designed, at least in part, to undue the formalistic legal reasoning that infected antebellum jurisprudence, which the late Professor Robert Cover analyzed so effectively in his significant work entitled *Justice Accused* (1975).

Like the antebellum judges who denied relief to fugitive slaves, the Court today claims that its decision, however harsh, is compelled by existing legal doctrine. On the contrary, the question presented by this case is an open one, and our Fourteenth Amendment precedents may be read more broadly or narrowly depending upon how one chooses to read them. Faced with the choice, I would adopt a "sympathetic" reading, one which comports with dictates of fundamental justice and recognizes that compassion need not be exiled from the province of judging. * * *

Poor Joshua! Victim of repeated attacks by an irresponsible, bullying, cowardly, and intemperate father, and abandoned by respondents who placed him in a dangerous predicament and who knew or learned what was going on, and yet did essentially nothing except, as the Court revealingly observes, "dutifully recorded these incidents in [their] files." It is a sad commentary upon American life, and constitutional principles—so full of late of patriotic fervor and proud proclamations about "liberty and justice for all," that this child, Joshua DeShaney, now is assigned to live out the remainder of his life profoundly retarded. Joshua and his mother, as petitioners here, deserve—but now are denied by this Court—the opportunity to have the facts of their case considered in the light of the constitutional protection that 42 U.S.C. § 1983 is meant to provide.

THE MEANING AND SIGNIFICANCE OF GOVERNMENT "INACTION"

Notes and Questions

1. *Government "inaction."* Consider Strauss, *Due Process, Government Inaction and Private Wrongs,* 1989 Sup.Ct.Rev. 53, 57–59: "Suppose that police officers learn that a murder is about to occur that they can prevent with minimal cost. [They] decide not to [intervene] because the targeted victim is

someone whom they believe is guilty of another crime. The officers would rather see him killed by private persons than brought to trial where, they fear, he might escape with an acquittal or a light sentence.

"This must be a case of government inaction, assuming that there is such a thing. The police officers did not instigate or facilitate the murder in any way, except to refrain from intervening. They did not make the victim worse off than he would have been if the officers had never become aware of the predicament.

"But it seems clear that this kind of government failure to act violates the Due Process Clause. A summary execution of a suspect by the authorities would be the clearest possible violation of the Due Process Clause. The hypothetical example is no different except for the fortuity that there were private persons who planned to do the murder. The *DeShaney* approach would allow the existence of that fortuity to make the difference between a flagrant violation of the Due Process Clause and an action that is not a constitutional violation at all. There is no reason to attack such significance to a fortuity.

"This hypothetical case is indistinguishable from *DeShaney,* at least as the Supreme Court viewed that case. In *DeShaney* social services workers, instead of police officers, failed to intervene to prevent private violence; that difference is immaterial. Of course, in *DeShaney,* the state of mind of the government officials was different. [Had] the Supreme Court decided *DeShaney* on the ground that the state officials lacked the necessary state of mind to violate the Constitution, the holding would be less vulnerable to criticism, and much less significant.

"But the Court [assumed] that the defendant's state of mind was sufficiently culpable to violate the Constitution [referring to fn. 10 of the majority opinion]. It ruled in favor of the officials on the ground that they had only engaged in inaction, not action. [U]nder *DeShaney,* child protective services employees would not violate the Due Process Clause even if they deliberately refuse to intervened because they wanted to see a child harmed (because of a grudge against a family or out of a bizarre belief that child abuse constitutes proper discipline, for example)."

2. *The exception for "custodial" situations.* Consider Strauss, supra, at 63–66: "[The *DeShaney* Court] explicitly left open the possibility that the state might have 'an affirmative duty to protect' a child in Joshua DeShaney's situation if the child were in a 'foster home operated by state agents.' [quoting from fn. 9 of the majority opinion]. [But] Joshua DeShaney's situation did not differ in any relevant respect from the situation of the persons to whom this exception applies. [The] state was, to a significant degree responsible for the fact that Joshua was in a family unit with his father. Even leaving aside the fact that Joshua lived with his father because of a court decree * * * the family unit is to a significant extent the product of state action.

"The government actively supports the family unit in countless ways. State law imposes support obligations on parents and gives them vast rights to control and direct their lives. State law bars strangers from intervening in the family except in extraordinary circumstances. Many state laws [are] designed to promote the establishment and maintenance of families. Through schools and many other media, the government promotes the family unit and reinforces the authority of the parents.

"* * * What is wrongful under the Due Process Clause, according [to] *DeShaney,* is to establish [prisons, state hospitals and other institutions] without taking care to protect those who are 'confined' within them. Since the state plays a role in establishing the family, it owes a duty of care to persons in Joshua DeShaney's position as well.

"It is also not an answer that children in a 'natural' family are not held in state custody against their will. The fact that the state has placed someone in the custody of a private party instead of in the custody of a state employee has no bearing on whether the state has placed the person in danger or has cut off that person's sources of private aid. And it is pointless, and probably meaningless, to ask whether an infant is in a family against his or her will."

3. *The deeper insights offered by Boddie v. Connecticut. Youngberg* and *Estelle,* observes Tribe, *The Curvature of Constitutional Space: What Lawyers Can Learn from Modern Physics,* 103 Harv.L.Rev. 1, 11 (1989), "seem to have lured Justice Brennan away from the perhaps deeper insights offered by *Boddie v. Connecticut.*" *Boddie* held that due process prohibits a state from denying those seeking divorce access to its courts solely because of inability to pay filing fees and costs. Consider Tribe at 12:

"[Although] Justice Brennan portrayed *Boddie* as a close parallel to *Youngberg* and *Estelle,* [there] is a fundamental distinction to be made between *Youngberg* and *Estelle* on the one hand, and *Boddie* on the other. In both *Youngberg* and *Estelle,* it was the state's institutionalization of a *particular individual* that had isolated that person from alternative means of fulfilling his or her basic needs. In *Boddie,* however, there had been no previous state action directed at the particular individual. It was the legal structure itself—combined, to be sure, with the economic and social circumstances of the individual—that had isolated the person from the fulfillment of an important need.

"[If] the law creates a state monopoly over the fulfillment of certain needs (dissolution of a failed marriage, protection from a violent parent) and thereby renders some, but not all, individuals particularly vulnerable, can the very act of creating this legal *structure* constitute state action violative of due process? Has the creation of a state monopoly over the fulfillment of a category of needs warped legal space itself in a cognizable fashion? *Boddie* answers 'yes,' at least where the state's interest in preserving that legal structure inviolate is sufficient to 'override the interest' of the plaintiff.

"Although Justice Brennan stressed *Youngberg* and *Estelle,* the spirit of his argument seems to derive from *Boddie.* [As] in *Boddie,* the governmental act in *DeShaney* that isolated Joshua—that is, the establishment of a legal structure that narrowly channeled all information and action in regard to child abuse—was not a force directed at Joshua personally; his isolation was a result of the simple juxtaposition of Wisconsin law and his personal situation. And, again as in *Boddie,* it was the monopoly created by the legal structure in *DeShaney* that made the plaintiff peculiarly vulnerable."

4. *Battered women's claims after DeShaney.* Do battered women's cases differ from child abuse? Are the duties of police officers clearer and more manageable than those of child welfare agencies? Does the state's grant of an order of protection unambiguously interpose the state in the private life of a battered woman? In cases of child abuse, the state is dealing with a minor and a child's individual liberty competes with the interests of the family relationship, but when a battered woman has received an order of protection, has the woman already severed the family unit? See generally Note, *Battered Women's Substantive Due Process Claims: Can Orders of Protection Deflect DeShaney?*, 65 N.Y.U.L.Rev. 1280 (1990).

RENDELL-BAKER v. KOHN

457 U.S. 830, 102 S.Ct. 2764, 73 L.Ed.2d 418 (1982).

CHIEF JUSTICE BURGER delivered the opinion of the Court.

[New Perspectives is a private school that] specializes in dealing with students who have experienced difficulty completing public high [schools]. In recent years, nearly all of the students at the school have been referred to it by the Brookline or Boston school committees, or by the Drug Rehabilitation Division of the Massachusetts Department of Mental Health.[1] The school issues high school diplomas certified by the Brookline School Committee. In recent years, public funds have accounted for at least 90%, and in one year 99%, of respondent's operating budget. There were approximately 50 students at the school in those years and none paid tuition.[2]

To be eligible for tuition funding under Chapter 766, the school must comply with a variety [of] detailed regulations concerning matters ranging from record-keeping to student-teacher ratios. Concerning personnel policies, [the] regulations require the school to maintain written job descriptions [and] statements describing personnel standards and procedures, but they impose few specific requirements.

[By] its contract with the Boston School Committee, [the] school must agree to carry out the individualized plan developed for each student referred to the school by the Committee. [The] school also has a contract with the State Drug Rehabilitation Division. [It] provides for reimbursement for services provided for students referred to the school [and] includes requirements concerning the services to be provided. Except for general requirements, such as an equal employment opportunity requirement, the agreement does not cover personnel policies.

[Petitioners were discharged by the school for, inter alia, supporting student criticisms against various school policies and sued under 42 U.S.C. § 1983.]

While five of the six petitioners were teachers at the school, petitioner Rendell-Baker was a vocational counselor hired under a grant from the federal Law Enforcement Assistance Administration, whose funds are distributed in Massachusetts through the State Committee on Criminal Justice. As a condition of the grant, the Committee on Criminal Justice must approve the school's initial hiring decisions. The purpose of this requirement is to insure that the school hires vocational counselors who meet the qualifications described in the school's grant proposal to the Committee; the Committee does not interview applicants for counselor positions.

1. Chapter 766, Mass.G.L., requires school committees to identify students with special needs and to develop suitable educational programs for such students. Mass.G.L. c. 71B, § 4 provides that school committees may "enter into an agreement with any public or private school, agency, or institution to provide the necessary special education" for these students. A student identified [may] remain in public school, if his parents object to a placement in a particular private school, unless he is especially disruptive or dangerous. Parents who object to placement in a particular private school may also elect to place their child in a private school of their choice; in such cases, they must pay the tuition.

2. Amicus curiae Massachusetts Association of 766 Approved Private Schools, Inc., of which the New Perspectives School is a member, informs the Court that many of its members have a student population which is more or less evenly divided between students referred and paid for by the State and students referred and paid for by their parents or guardians.

Rendell-Baker * * * demanded reinstatement or a hearing. The school agreed to apply a new policy, calling for appointment of a grievance committee, to consider her claims. Rendell-Baker also complained to the State Committee on Criminal Justice, which asked the school to provide a written explanation for her discharge. After the school complied, the Committee responded that it was satisfied with the explanation, but notified the school that it would not pay any back pay or other damage award Rendell-Baker might obtain from it as a result of her discharge. The Committee told Rendell-Baker that it had no authority to order a hearing, although it would refuse to approve the hiring of another counselor if the school disregarded its agreement to apply its new grievance procedure in her case. [The] core issue presented [is] not whether petitioners were discharged because of their speech or without adequate procedural protections, but whether the school's action in discharging them can fairly be seen as state action. * * *

In *Blum v. Yaretsky,* 457 U.S. 991, 102 S.Ct. 2777, 43 L.Ed.2d 534 (1982), [t]he Court considered whether certain nursing homes were state actors for the purpose of determining whether decisions regarding transfers of patients could be fairly attributed to the state, and hence be subjected to Fourteenth Amendment due process requirements. The challenged transfers primarily involved decisions, made by physicians and nursing home administrators, to move patients from "skilled nursing facilities" to less expensive "health related facilities." Like the New Perspectives School, the nursing homes were privately owned and operated. [T]he Court held that, "[A] State normally can be held responsible for a private decision only when it has exercised coercive power or has provided such significant encouragement, either overt or covert, that the choice must in law be deemed to be that of the State." In determining that the transfer decisions were not actions of the state, the Court considered each of the factors alleged by petitioners here to make the discharge decisions of the New Perspective School fairly attributable to the state.

First, the nursing homes, like the school, depended on the State for funds; the State subsidized the operating and capital costs of the nursing homes, and paid the medical expenses of more than 90% of the patients. * * *

The school, like the nursing homes, is not fundamentally different from many private corporations whose business depends primarily on contracts to build roads, bridges, dams, ships, or submarines for the government. Acts of such private contractors do not become acts of the government by reason of their significant or even total engagement in performing public contracts.

The school is also analogous to the public defender found not to be a state actor in *Polk County v. Dodson,* 454 U.S. 312, 102 S.Ct. 445, 70 L.Ed.2d 509 (1981). There we concluded that, although the State paid the public defender, her relationship with her client was "identical to that existing between any other lawyer and client." Here the relationship between the school and its teachers and counselors is not changed because the State pays the tuition of the students.

A second factor considered in *Blum* was the extensive regulation of the nursing homes by the State. There the State was indirectly involved in the transfer decisions challenged in that case because a primary goal of the State in regulating nursing homes was to keep costs down by transferring patients from intensive treatment centers to less expensive facilities when possible.[a] Both

a. Brennan, J., joined by Marshall, J., dissented in *Blum:* "[A]n accurate and realistic appraisal of the procedures actually employed in the State of New York leaves no doubt that not only has the State established the system of treatment levels and utilization review in state and federal regulations encouraged the nursing homes to transfer patients to less expensive facilities when appropriate. The nursing homes were extensively regulated in many other ways as well. The Court relied on *Jackson,* where we held that state regulation, even if "extensive and detailed," did not make a utility's actions state action.

Here the decisions to discharge the petitioners were not compelled or even influenced by any state regulation. Indeed, in contrast to the extensive regulation of the school generally, the various regulators showed relatively little interest in the school's personnel matters. The most intrusive personnel regulation promulgated by the various government agencies was the requirement that the Committee on Criminal Justice had the power to approve persons hired as vocational counselors. Such a regulation is not sufficient to make a decision to discharge, made by private management, state action.[6]

The third factor asserted to show that the school is a state actor is that it performs a "public function." However, our holdings have made clear that the relevant question [is] whether the function performed has been "traditionally the *exclusive* prerogative of the State." There can be no doubt that the education of maladjusted high school students is a public function, but that is only the beginning of the inquiry. Chapter 766 [demonstrates] that the State intends to provide services for such students at public expense. That legislative policy choice in no way makes these services the exclusive province of the State. Indeed, [until] recently the State had not undertaken to provide education for students who could not be served by traditional public schools. That a private entity performs a function which serves the public does not make its acts state action.[7]

Fourth, petitioners argue that there is a "symbiotic relationship" [as] in *Burton.* Such a claim was rejected in *Blum,* and we reject it here. In *Burton,* [i]n response to the argument that the restaurant's profits, and hence the State's financial position, would suffer if it did not discriminate, the Court concluded that this showed that the State profited from the restaurant's discriminatory conduct. [Here] the school's fiscal relationship with the State is not different from that of many contractors performing services for the government.[b] * * *

Affirmed.[c]

order to further its own fiscal goals, but that the State prescribes with as much precision as is possible the standards by which individual determinations are to be made. [The] Court thus fails to perceive the decisive involvement of the State in the private conduct challenged by the respondents."

6. [The] Committee had no power to hire or discharge a counselor who had the qualifications specified in the school's grant application. Moreover, the Committee did not take any part in discharging Rendell-Baker; on the contrary, it attempted to use leverage to aid her. [T]here is no evidence that the Committee had any authority to take even those steps.

7. There is no evidence that the State has attempted to avoid its constitutional duties by a sham arrangement which attempts to disguise provision of public services as acts of private parties. Cf. *Evans v. Newton.*

[Compare Brennan, J., joined by Marshall, J., dissenting in *Blum:* "For many, the totality of their social network is the nursing home community. Within that environment, the nursing home operator is the immediate authority, the provider of food, clothing, shelter, and health care, and, in every significant respect, the functional equivalent of a State. Cf. *Marsh.*"]

b. Does this adopt the "moral exemplar model" in note 2 after *Moose Lodge?*

c. White, J., concurred in the judgment (and in *Blum*): "For me, the critical factor is the absence of any allegation that the employment decision was itself based upon some rule of conduct or policy put forth by the State."

JUSTICE MARSHALL, with whom JUSTICE BRENNAN joins, dissenting.

[I]t is difficult to imagine a closer relationship between a government and a private enterprise. [The] school's very survival depends on the State. If the State chooses, it may exercise complete control over the school's operations simply by threatening to withdraw financial support if the school takes action that it considers objectionable. [Almost] every decision the school makes is substantially affected in some way by the State's regulations.[1]

The fact that the school is providing a substitute for public education is also an important indicium of state action. [Under Ch. 766], the State is *required* to provide a free education to all children, including those with special needs. Clearly, if the State had decided to provide the service itself, its conduct would be measured against constitutional standards. The State should not be permitted to avoid constitutional requirements simply by delegating its statutory duty to a private entity. * * *

* * * Petitioners claim that they were discharged because they supported student demands for increased responsibilities in school affairs. [If true,] the school has adopted a specific view of the sort of education that should be provided under the statute, and refuses to tolerate departures from that view. The State, by refusing to intervene, has effectively endorsed that view of its duties under Chapter 766. In short, because petitioners' criticism was directly addressed to the State's responsibilities under Chapter 766, a finding of state action is justified.

The majority repeatedly compares the school to a private contractor * * *. Although shipbuilders and dambuilders, like the school, may be dependent on government funds, they are not so closely supervised by the government. And unlike most private contractors, the school is performing a statutory duty of the State.

The majority [would] apparently concede that actions directly affecting the students could be treated as under color of state law, since the school is fulfilling the State's obligations to those children under Chapter 766. [But] the personnel decisions challenged here are related to the provision of Chapter 766 education. In any event, since the school is funded almost entirely by the State, is closely supervised by the State, and exists solely to perform the State's statutory duty to educate children with special needs—since the school is really just an arm of the State—its personnel decisions may appropriately be considered state action. * * *

In SAN FRANCISCO ARTS & ATHLETICS, INC. v. UNITED STATES OLYMPIC COMM., 483 U.S. 522, 107 S.Ct. 2971, 97 L.Ed.2d 427 (1987), respondent USOC, to which Congress granted the right to prohibit certain commercial and promotional uses of the word "Olympic," secured relief enjoining petitioner from calling its athletic competitions the "Gay Olympic Games." Petitioner claimed that USOC's enforcement discriminated in violation of equal protection. The Court, per POWELL, J.—relying mainly on *Rendell–Baker, Blum* and *Jackson*—held that USOC is not a "governmental actor."

BRENNAN, J., joined by Marshall, J.—and "largely" by O'Connor and Blackmun, JJ.—dissented on the basis of *Burton:* "The USOC and the Federal Government exist in a symbiotic relationship sufficient to provide a nexus

1. [By] analyzing the various indicia of state action separately, without considering their cumulative impact, the majority commits a fundamental error.

between the USOC's challenged action and the Government. First, as in *Burton,* the relationship here confers a variety of mutual benefits. [T]he Act gave the USOC authority and responsibilities that no private organization in this country had ever held. The Act also conferred substantial financial resources on the USOC, authorizing it to seek up to $16 million annually in grants from the Secretary of Commerce, and affording it unprecedented power to control the use of the word 'Olympic' and related emblems to raise additional funds. As a result of the Act, the United States obtained, for the first time in its history, an exclusive and effective organization to coordinate and administer all amateur athletics related to international competition, and to represent that program abroad.

"Second, in the eye of the public, both national and international, the connection between the decisions of the United States Government and those of the United States Olympic Committee is profound. The President of the United States has served as the Honorary President of the USOC. The national flag flies both literally and figuratively over the central product of the USOC, the United States Olympic Team. * * *

"If petitioner is correct in its allegation that the USOC has used its discretion to discriminate against certain groups, then the situation here, as in *Burton,* is that 'profits earned by discrimination not only contribute to, but also are indispensable elements in, the financial success of a governmental agency.' Indeed, the required nexus between the challenged action and the Government appears even closer here than in *Burton.* While in *Burton* the restaurant was able to pursue a policy of discrimination because the State had failed to impose upon it a policy of non-discrimination, the USOC could pursue its alleged policy of selective enforcement only because Congress *affirmatively* granted it power that it would not otherwise have to control the use of the word 'Olympic.' " [d]

FLAGG BROS., INC. v. BROOKS

436 U.S. 149, 98 S.Ct. 1729, 56 L.Ed.2d 185 (1978).

JUSTICE REHNQUIST delivered the opinion of the Court.

The question presented [is] whether a warehouseman's proposed sale of goods entrusted to him for storage, as permitted by New York Uniform Commercial Code § 7–210, is an action properly attributable to the State * * *.

[R]espondent Shirley Brooks and her family were evicted from their apartment in Mount Vernon, N.Y., on June 13, 1973. The city marshal arranged for

d. The Court responded that petitioner "has failed to demonstrate that the Federal Government can or does exert any influence over the exercise of the USOC's enforcement decisions. Absent proof of this type of 'close nexus between the [Government] and the challenged action of the [USOC],' the challenged action may not be 'fairly treated as that of the [Government] itself.' *Jackson.*"

Brennan, J., joined only by Marshall, J., also argued that unlike the entities in the cases relied on by the Court, "which merely provided public services, the USOC has been endowed by the Federal Government with the exclusive power to serve a unique national, administrative, adjudicative, and representational role"—"it represents this Nation to the world community." The Court responded that "absent the additional element of governmental control, this representational function can hardly be called traditionally governmental. All sorts of private organizations send 'national representatives' to participate in world competitions. Although many are of interest only to a select group, others, like the Davis Cup Competition, the America's Cup, and the Miss Universe Pageant, are widely viewed as involving representation of our country. The organizations that sponsor United States participation in these events all perform 'national representational,' as well as 'administrative [and] adjudicative role[s],' in selecting and presenting the national representatives."

Brooks' possessions to be stored by petitioner Flagg Brothers, Inc., in its warehouse. Brooks was informed of the cost of moving and storage, and she instructed the workmen to proceed, although she found the price too high. On August 25, 1973, after a series of disputes over the validity of the charges being claimed by petitioner Flagg Brothers, Brooks received a letter demanding that her account be brought up to date within 10 days "or your furniture will be sold." A series of subsequent letters from respondent and her attorneys produced no satisfaction.

Brooks thereupon initiated this class action in the District Court under 42 U.S.C. § 1983, seeking damages, an injunction against the threatened sale of her belongings, and the declaration that such a sale pursuant to § 7–210 would violate [due process]. She was later joined in her action by [Jones,] whose goods had been stored by Flagg Brothers following her eviction. [T]he District Court * * * dismissed the complaint [and] the Court of Appeals reversed. * * *

It must be noted that respondents have named no public officials as defendants in this action. The city marshal, who supervised their evictions, was dismissed from the case by the consent of all the parties. This total absence of overt official involvement plainly distinguishes this case from earlier decisions imposing procedural restrictions on creditors' remedies such as *North Georgia Finishing, Inc., v. Di-Chem, Inc.,* 419 U.S. 601, 95 S.Ct. 719, 42 L.Ed.2d 751 (1975); *Fuentes v. Shevin,* 407 U.S. 67, 92 S.Ct. 1983, 32 L.Ed.2d 556 (1972); *Sniadach v. Family Finance Corp.,* 395 U.S. 337, 89 S.Ct. 1820, 23 L.Ed.2d 349 (1969).[a] [While] as a factual matter any person with sufficient physical power may deprive a person of his property, only a State or a private person whose action "may be fairly treated as that of the State itself," *Jackson,* may deprive him of "an interest encompassed within the Fourteenth Amendment's protection," *Fuentes* * * *.

Respondents' primary contention is that New York has delegated to Flagg Brothers a power "traditionally exclusively reserved to the State." *Jackson.* They argue that the resolution of private disputes is a traditional function of civil government, and that the State in § 7–210 has delegated this function to Flagg Brothers. Respondents, however, have read too much into the language of

a. *Sniadach* held that a statute—authorizing a creditor to get a summons from a court clerk and thereby obtain prejudgment garnishment of a debtor's wages—violated due process because the statute did not provide the debtor with prior notice and opportunity for a hearing.

Fuentes held that a statute—authorizing a seller of goods under a conditional sales contract to get a writ from a court clerk and thereby obtain prejudgment repossession with the sheriff's help—violated due process because the statute did not provide the buyer with prior notice and opportunity for a hearing.

North Georgia Finishing held violative of due process a statute authorizing a creditor to obtain prejudgment garnishment of a debtor's assets by filing an affidavit with a court clerk stating reasons to fear that the property would otherwise be lost. The Court distinguished *Mitchell v. W.T. Grant Co.,* 416 U.S. 600, 94 S.Ct. 1895, 40 L.Ed.2d 406 (1974), which had upheld a statute that, without requiring prior notice to a buyer-debtor, permitted a seller-creditor holding a vendor's lien to secure a writ of sequestration and, having filed a bond, to cause the sheriff to take possession of the property at issue. *North Georgia Finishing* emphasized that under the sequestration statute in *Mitchell,* unlike the garnishment statute at bar, the writ "was issuable only by a judge upon the filing of an affidavit going beyond mere conclusory allegations and clearly setting out the facts entitling the creditor to sequestration" and that the *Mitchell* statute "expressly entitled the debtor to an immediate hearing after seizure and to dissolution of the writ absent proof by the creditor of the grounds on which the writ was issued."

For general discussion of these cases, see Scott, *Constitutional Regulation of Provisional Creditor Remedies: The Cost of Procedural Due Process,* 61 Va.L.Rev. 807 (1975); Silberman, *Shaffer v. Heitner: The End of an Era,* 53 N.Y.U.L.Rev. 33, 53–62 (1978).

our previous cases. While many functions have been traditionally performed by governments, very few have been "exclusively reserved to the State."

One such area has been elections. * * * *Terry v. Adams; Smith v. Allwright.* Although the rationale of these cases may be subject to some dispute, their scope is carefully defined. The doctrine does not reach to all forms of private political activity, but encompasses only state-regulated elections or elections conducted by organizations which in practice produce "the uncontested choice of public officials." *Terry* (Clark, J., concurring). * * *

A second line of cases under the public-function doctrine originated with *Marsh.* Just as the Texas Democratic Party in *Smith* and the Jaybird Democratic Association in *Terry* effectively performed the entire public function of selecting public officials, so too the Gulf Shipbuilding Corp. performed all the necessary municipal functions in the town of Chickasaw, Ala., which it owned. * * *

These two branches of the public-function doctrine have in common the feature of exclusivity.[8] Although the elections held by the Democratic Party and its affiliates were the only meaningful elections in Texas, and the streets owned by the Gulf Shipbuilding Corp. were the only streets in Chickasaw, the proposed sale by Flagg Brothers under § 7–210 is not the only means of resolving this purely private dispute. Respondent Brooks has never alleged that state law barred her from seeking a waiver of Flagg Brothers' right to sell her goods at the time she authorized their storage. Presumably, respondent Jones, who alleges that she never authorized the storage of her goods, could have sought to replevy her goods at any time under state law. The challenged statute itself provides a damages remedy against the warehouseman for violations of its provisions. This system of rights and remedies, recognizing the traditional place of private arrangements in ordering relationships in the commercial world,[9] can hardly be said to have delegated to Flagg Brothers an exclusive prerogative of the sovereign.[10]

8. Respondents also contend that *Evans v. Newton* establishes that the operation of a park for recreational purposes is an exclusively public function. We doubt that *Newton* intended to establish any such broad doctrine in the teeth of the experience of several American entrepreneurs who amassed great fortunes by operating parks for recreational purposes. We think *Newton* rests on a finding of ordinary state action under extraordinary circumstances. The Court's opinion emphasizes that the record showed "no change in the municipal maintenance and concern over this facility" after the transfer of title to private trustees. That transfer had not been shown to have eliminated the actual involvement of the city in the daily maintenance and care of the park.

9. Unlike the parade of horribles suggested by our Brother Stevens in dissent, this case does not involve state authorization of private breach of the peace.

10. [It] would intolerably broaden, beyond the scope of any of our previous cases, the notion of state action [to] hold that the mere existence of a body of property law in a State, whether decisional or statutory, itself amounted to "state action" even though no state process or state officials were ever involved in enforcing that body of law.

This situation is clearly distinguishable from cases such as *North Georgia Finishing; Fuentes;* and *Sniadach.* In each of those cases a government official participated in the physical deprivation of what had concededly been the constitutional plaintiff's property under state law before the deprivation occurred. The constitutional protection attaches not because, as in *North Georgia Finishing,* a clerk issued a ministerial writ out of the court, but because as a result of that writ the property of the debtor was seized and impounded by the affirmative command of the law of Georgia. The creditor in *North Georgia Finishing* had not simply sought to pursue the collection of his debt by private means permissible under Georgia law; he had invoked the authority of the Georgia court, which in turn had ordered the garnishee not to pay over money which previously had been the property of the debtor. See *Shelley v. Kraemer.* * * *

Whatever the particular remedies available under New York law, we do not consider a more detailed description of them necessary to our conclusion that the settlement of disputes between debtors and creditors is not traditionally an exclusive public function.[11] Creditors and debtors have had available to them historically a far wider number of choices than has one who would be an elected public official, or a member of Jehovah's Witnesses who wished to distribute literature in Chickasaw, Ala. * * * [12] This is true whether these commercial rights and remedies are created by statute or decisional law. To rely upon the historical antecedents of a particular practice would result in the constitutional condemnation in one State of a remedy found perfectly permissible in another.

[W]e would be remiss if we did not note that there are a number of state and municipal functions not covered by our election cases or governed by the reasoning of *Marsh* which have been administered with a greater degree of exclusivity by States and municipalities than has the function of so-called "dispute resolution." Among these are such functions as education, fire and police protection, and tax collection. We express no view as to the extent, if any, to which a city or State might be free to delegate to private parties the performance of such functions and thereby avoid the strictures of the Fourteenth Amendment. * * *

Respondents further urge that Flagg Brothers' proposed action is properly attributable to the State because the State has authorized and encouraged it in enacting § 7–210. Our cases state "that a State is responsible for [the] act of a private party when the State, by its law, has compelled the act." This Court, however, has never held that a State's mere acquiescence in a private action converts that action into that of the State. The Court rejected a similar argument in *Jackson* * * *. The clearest demonstration of this distinction appears in *Moose Lodge,* which held that the Commonwealth of Pennsylvania,

11. It may well be, as my Brother Stevens' dissent contends, that "[t]he power to order legally binding surrenders of property and the constitutional restrictions on that power are necessary correlatives in our system." But here New York, unlike Florida in *Fuentes,* Georgia in *North Georgia Finishing,* and Wisconsin in *Sniadach,* has not ordered respondents to surrender any property whatever. It has merely enacted a statute which provides that a warehouseman conforming to the provisions of the statute may convert his traditional lien into good title. There is no reason whatever to believe that either Flagg Brothers or respondents could not, if they wished, seek resort to the New York courts in order to either compel or prevent the "surrenders of property" to which that dissent refers, and that the compliance of Flagg Brothers with applicable New York property law would be reviewed after customary notice and hearing in such a proceeding.

The fact that such a judicial review of a self-help remedy is seldom encountered bears witness to the important part that such remedies have played in our system of property rights. This is particularly true of the warehouseman's lien, which is the source of this provision in the Uniform Commercial Code which is the law in 49 States and the District of Columbia. The lien in this case, particularly because it is burdened by procedural constraints and provides for a compensatory remedy and judicial relief against abuse, is not atypical of creditors' liens historically, whether created by statute or legislatively enacted. The conduct of private actors in relying on the rights established under these liens to resort to self-help remedies does not permit their conduct to be ascribed to the State.

12. This is not to say that dispute resolution between creditors and debtors involves a category of human affairs that is never subject to constitutional constraints. We merely address the public-function doctrine as respondents would apply it to this case.

Self-help of the type involved in this case is not significantly different from creditor remedies generally, whether created by common law or enacted by legislatures. New York's statute has done nothing more than authorize (and indeed limit)—without participation by any public official—what Flagg Brothers would tend to do, even in the absence of such authorization, i.e., dispose of respondents' property in order to free up its valuable storage space. The proposed sale pursuant to the lien in this case is not a significant departure from traditional private arrangements.

although not responsible for racial discrimination voluntarily practiced by a private club, could not by law require the club to comply with its own discriminatory rules. These cases clearly rejected the notion that our prior cases permitted the imposition of Fourteenth Amendment restraints on private action by the simple device of characterizing the State's inaction as "authorization" or "encouragement."

It is quite immaterial that the State has embodied its decision not to act in statutory form. If New York had no commercial statutes at all, its courts would still be faced with the decision whether to prohibit or to permit the sort of sale threatened here the first time an aggrieved bailor came before them for relief. A judicial decision to deny relief would be no less an "authorization" or "encouragement" of that sale than the legislature's decision embodied in this statute. [If] the mere denial of judicial relief is considered sufficient encouragement to make the State responsible for those private acts, all private deprivations of property would be converted into public acts whenever the State, for whatever reason, denies relief sought by the putative property owner. * * *

Here, the State of New York has not compelled the sale of a bailor's goods, but has merely announced the circumstances under which its courts will not interfere with a private sale. Indeed, the crux of respondents' complaint is not that the State *has* acted, but that it has *refused* to act. This statutory refusal to act is no different in principle from an ordinary statute of limitations whereby the State declines to provide a remedy for private deprivations of property after the passage of a given period of time. * * *

Reversed.

JUSTICE STEVENS, with whom JUSTICE WHITE and JUSTICE MARSHALL join, dissenting.

[The] question is whether a state statute which authorizes a private party to deprive a person of his property without his consent must meet the requirements of the Due Process Clause of the Fourteenth Amendment. This question must be answered in the affirmative unless the State has virtually unlimited power to transfer interests in private property without any procedural protections.

[Under the Court's] approach a State could enact laws authorizing private citizens to use self-help in countless situations without any possibility of federal challenge. A state statute could authorize the warehouseman to retain all proceeds of the lien sale, even if they far exceeded the amount of the alleged debt; it could authorize finance companies to enter private homes to repossess merchandise; or indeed, it could authorize "any person with sufficient physical power" to acquire and sell the property of his weaker neighbor. An attempt to challenge the validity of any such outrageous statute would be defeated by the reasoning the Court uses today: The Court's rationale would characterize action pursuant to such a statute as purely private action, which the State permits but does not compel, in an area not exclusively reserved to the State.

As these examples suggest, the distinctions between "permission" and "compulsion" on the one hand, and "exclusive" and "non-exclusive," on the other, cannot be determinative factors in state-action analysis. There is no great chasm between "permission" and "compulsion" requiring particular state action to fall within one or the other definitional camp. [In] this case, the State of New York, by enacting § 7–210 of the Uniform Commercial Code, has acted in the most effective and unambiguous way a State can act. This section specifically authorizes petitioner Flagg Brothers to sell respondents' possessions; it details the procedures that petitioner must follow; and it grants petitioner the power to convey good title to goods that are now owned by respondents to a third party.

* * * New York has authorized the warehouseman to perform what is clearly a state function. [P]etitioners have attempted to argue that the nonconsensual transfer of property rights is not a traditional function of the sovereign. The overwhelming historical evidence is to the contrary, however,[7] and the Court wisely does not adopt this position. Instead, the Court reasons that state action cannot be found because the State has not delegated to the warehouseman an *exclusive* sovereign function.[8] This distinction, however, is not consistent with our prior decisions on state action; is not even adhered to by the Court in this case;[10] and, most importantly, is inconsistent with the line of cases beginning with *Sniadach.*

Since *Sniadach* this Court has scrutinized various state statutes regulating the debtor-creditor relationship for compliance with the Due Process Clause. In each of these cases a finding of state action was a prerequisite to the Court's decision. The Court today seeks to explain these findings on the ground that in each case there was some element of "overt official involvement." [But] until today, this Court had never held that purely ministerial acts of "minor governmental functionaries" were sufficient to establish state action. The suggestion that this was the basis for due process review in *Sniadach, Fuentes,* and *North Georgia Finishing* marks a major and, in my judgment, unwise expansion of the state-action doctrine. The number of private actions in which a governmental functionary plays some ministerial role is legion;[12] to base due process review on the fortuity of such governmental intervention would demean the majestic purposes of the Due Process Clause.

7. The New York State courts have recognized that the execution of a lien is a traditional function of the State. See also 3 W. Blackstone, *Commentaries* §§ 7–11, pp. * 3–6, which notes that the right of self-help at common law was severely limited.

I fully agree with the Court that the decision of whether or not a statute is subject to due process scrutiny should not depend on " 'whether a particular class of creditor did or did not enjoy the same freedom to act in Elizabethan or Georgian England.' " Nonetheless some reference to history and well-settled practice is necessary to determine whether a particular action is a "traditional state function." * * *

8. As I understand the Court's notion of "exclusivity," the sovereign function here is not exclusive because there may be other state remedies, under different statutes or common-law theories, available to respondents. Even if I were to accept the notion that sovereign functions must be "exclusive," the Court's description of exclusivity is incomprehensible. The question is whether a particular action is a uniquely sovereign function, not whether state law forecloses any possibility of recovering for damages for such activity. For instance, it is clear that the maintenance of a police force is a unique sovereign function, and the delegation of police power to a private party will entail state action. Under the Court's analysis, however, there would be no state action if the State provided a remedy, such as an action for wrongful imprisonment, for the individual injured by the "private" policeman. This analysis is not based on "exclusivity," but on some vague, and highly inappropriate, notion that respondents should not complain about this state statute if the State offers them a glimmer of hope of redeeming their possessions, or at least the value of the goods, through some other state action. Of course, the availability of other state remedies may be relevant in determining whether the statute provides sufficient procedural protections under the Due Process Clause, but it is not relevant to the state-action issue.

10. As the Court is forced to recognize, its notion of exclusivity simply cannot be squared with the wide range of functions that are typically considered sovereign functions, such as "education, fire and police protection, and tax collection."

12. For instance, state officials often perform ministerial acts in the transferring of ownership in motor vehicles or real estate. It is difficult to believe that the Court would hold that all car sales are invested with state action.

Instead, cases such as *North Georgia Finishing* must be viewed as reflecting this Court's recognition of the significance of the State's role in defining *and controlling* the debtor-creditor relationship. [In *Fuentes*, the] statutes placed the state power to repossess property in the hands of an interested private party, just as the state statute in this case places the state power to conduct judicially binding sales in satisfaction of a lien in the hands of the warehouseman. "Private parties, serving their own private advantage, may unilaterally invoke state power to replevy goods from another. No state official participates in the decision to seek a writ; no state official reviews the basis for the claim to repossession; and no state official evaluates the need for immediate seizure. There is not even a requirement that the plaintiff provide any information to the court on these matters." Ibid. [Yet] the very defect that made the statutes in *Fuentes* and *North Georgia Finishing* unconstitutional—lack of state control—is, under today's decision, the factor that precludes constitutional review of the state statute. The Due Process Clause cannot command such incongruous results. If it is unconstitutional for a State to allow a private party to exercise a traditional state power because the state supervision of that power is purely mechanical, the State surely cannot immunize its actions from constitutional *scrutiny* by removing even the mechanical supervision.

Not only has the State removed its nominal supervision in this case, it has also authorized a private party to exercise a governmental power that is at least as significant as the power exercised in *Fuentes* or *North Georgia Finishing.* In *Fuentes,* the Florida statute allowed the debtor's property to be seized and held pending the outcome of the creditor's action for repossession. The property would not be finally disposed of until there was an adjudication of the underlying claim. Similarly, in *North Georgia Finishing,* the state statute provided for a garnishment procedure which deprived the debtor of the use of property in the garnishee's hands pending the outcome of litigation. The warehouseman's power under § 7–210 is far broader * * *.

Whether termed "traditional," "exclusive," or "significant," the state power to order binding, nonconsensual resolution of a conflict between debtor and creditor is exactly the sort of power with which the Due Process Clause is concerned. And the State's delegation of that power to a private party is, accordingly, subject to due process scrutiny. This, at the very least, is the teaching of *Sniadach, Fuentes,* and *North Georgia Finishing.*

It is important to emphasize that, contrary to the Court's apparent fears, this conclusion does not even remotely suggest that "all private deprivations of property [will] be converted into public acts whenever the State, for whatever reason, denies relief sought by the putative property owner." The focus is not on the private deprivation but on the state authorization. [The] State's conduct in this case takes the concrete form of a statutory enactment, and it is that statute that may be challenged.

[It] is only what the State itself has enacted that [respondents] may ask the federal court to review in a § 1983 case. If there should be a deviation from the state statute—such as a failure to give the notice required by the state law—the defect could be remedied by a state court and there would be no occasion for § 1983 relief. [Under] this approach, the federal courts do not have jurisdiction to review every foreclosure proceeding in which the debtor claims that there has been a procedural defect constituting a denial of due process of law. Rather, the federal district court's jurisdiction under § 1983 is limited to challenges to the constitutionality of the state procedure itself * * *.

Finally, it is obviously true that the overwhelming majority of disputes in our society are resolved in the private sphere. But it is no longer possible, if it ever was, to believe that a sharp line can be drawn between private and public actions. The Court['s] description of what is state action does not even attempt to reflect the concerns of the Due Process Clause, for the state-action doctrine is, after all, merely one aspect of this broad constitutional protection.

In the broadest sense, we expect government "to provide a reasonable and fair framework of rules which facilitate commercial transactions." This "framework of rules" is premised on the assumption that the State will control nonconsensual deprivations of property and that the State's control will, in turn, be subject to the restrictions of the Due Process Clause. * * * [b]

Notes and Questions

1. *Authority of prior decisions.* (a) Does the Court's use of *Shelley v. Kraemer* (in fn. 10) refute the dissent's objection that the Court's handling of the prior debtor-creditor decisions establishes the principle that "purely ministerial acts of minor governmental functionaries" constitute state action? If so, then would the Court have found state action in *Flagg Bros.* if the state courts had to be used to enforce the warehouseman's lien? Would this read *Shelley* for all it is worth? Does fn. 10 so read *Shelley*? In any event, is the dissent correct in complaining that "the very defect that made the statutes in *Fuentes* and *North Georgia Finishing* unconstitutional—lack of state control—is, under *Flagg Bros.,* the factor that precludes constitutional review of the state statute"?

(b) LUGAR v. EDMONDSON OIL CO., 457 U.S. 922, 102 S.Ct. 2744, 73 L.Ed. 2d 482 (1982), per White, J.,—involving a statute that authorized a creditor to file a petition with a court clerk and thus obtain a prejudgment attachment of a debtor's property which was executed by the sheriff—relied on all the debtor-creditor decisions as establishing the doctrine "that a private party's joint participation with state officials in the seizure of disputed property is sufficient to characterize that party as a 'state actor' for purposes of the Fourteenth Amendment." Powell, J., joined by Rehnquist and O'Connor, JJ., dissented: "It is unclear why a private party engages in state action when filing papers seeking an attachment of property, but not [when] summoning police to investigate a suspected crime." BURGER, C.J., also dissented.

(c) NATIONAL COLLEGIATE ATHLETIC ASS'N v. TARKANIAN, 488 U.S. 179, 109 S.Ct. 454, 102 L.Ed.2d 469 (1988): The NCAA is an association of virtually all colleges with major athletic programs, and its rules governing these programs are binding on its members. After its investigation that found 38 recruitment violations by the staff of the University of Nevada, Las Vegas (including 10 by Tarkanian, who was UNLV's basketball coach), NCAA imposed sanctions on UNLV and requested it to show cause why additional penalties should not be imposed if it failed to suspend Tarkanian. The Court, per STEVENS, J., conceded that UNLV's suspension of Tarkanian, which was clearly state action, "was influenced by the rules and recommendations of the NCAA," but held that this did not turn the NCAA's conduct into "state action" and thus the NCAA did not violate Tarkanian's right to procedural due process: Although, as a member of the NCAA, UNLV played a role in formulating its rules, "UNLV delegated no power to the NCAA to take specific action against any University employee. The commitment by UNLV to adhere to NCAA enforcement proce-

b. The separate dissent of Marshall, J., is omitted. Brennan, J., did not participate.

dures was enforceable only by sanctions that the NCAA might impose on UNLV," and which UNLV could choose to ignore by withdrawing from the NCAA. And even if "the power of the NCAA is so great that the UNLV had no practical alternative to compliance with its demands," "it does not follow that such a private party [is] acting under color of state law." Finally, "in the case before us the state and private parties' relevant interests do not coincide, as they did in *Burton;* rather, they have clashed throughout the investigation, the attempt to discipline Tarkanian, and this litigation. UNLV and the NCAA were antagonists, not joint participants, and the NCAA may not be deemed a state actor on this ground."

WHITE, J., joined by Brennan, Marshall and O'Connor, JJ.,—emphasizing that UNLV, a public university is a "state actor"—dissented: "[I]t was the NCAA's findings that Tarkanian had violated NCAA rules, made at NCAA-conducted hearings, all of which were agreed to by UNLV in its membership agreement with the NCAA, that resulted in Tarkanian's suspension by UNLV. On these facts, the NCAA was 'jointly engaged with [UNLV] officials in the challenged action,' and therefore was a state actor."

2. "*Governmental function.*" (a) *Dispute resolution.* Do you agree that the authority exercised by the warehouseman under the New York statute was not a "governmental function"? Consider 92 Harv.L.Rev. 128 (1978): "The exclusivity of the function's exercise may shed some light on this inquiry, but it does not give a final answer to the basic question. Regardless of the fact that there are many ways to go about resolving a private dispute, the ability to conclude unresolved disputes by making authoritative determinations of rights in property is central to our conception of government's role in society. If a state chose to assign part of its judicial function to private tribunals, giving them all the authority of trial courts, there would be little doubt that a vital attribute of sovereignty was involved."

What result in *Flagg Bros.* if the warehouseman's lien had not been "burdened by procedural constraints" and had not provided "for a compensatory remedy and judicial relief against abuse"?

(b) *Education.* Would (should) the Court hold that private schools perform a "government function"? If so, under what circumstances? Consider Choper, *Thoughts on State Action,* 1979 Wash.U.L.Q. 757, 778: "[I]t is clear that the operation of elementary and secondary schools is not an enterprise that is 'traditionally *exclusively* reserved to the State.' But a comprehensive survey of school districts in the United States would surely show that virtually all maintained at least one public elementary and secondary school unless, because of some peculiar development, the educational needs of the community's children were historically always met by a privately funded school. Such a school—or at least one of such schools if there are several in the hypothetical community (and which one is *the* one may present a nice question)—is, in effect, serving as a substitute for the conventional public school that the school district would otherwise provide. In this sense, it is performing a function 'traditionally *exclusively* reserved to the State.'"

3. *The limits (or lack of limits) of the state action concept.* Do you agree that "an ordinary statute of limitations whereby the State declines to provide a remedy for private deprivations of property after the passage of a given period of time" is *not* state action? If it *is* state action, then is New York's rule—that "its courts will not interfere with a private sale" pursuant to a warehouseman's lien—also state action? If so, is it not true that "all private deprivations of

property would be converted into public acts whenever the State, for whatever reason, denies relief sought by the putative property owner"? Of what relevance is it that "the State's conduct in *Flagg Bros.* takes the concrete form of a statutory enactment"? May a "state procedure" providing a "framework of rules which facilitate commercial transactions" be promulgated by common law as well as by statute? See generally Brest, *State Action and Liberal Theory: A Casenote on Flagg Brothers v. Brooks,* 130 U.Pa.L.Rev. 1296 (1982); Goodman, *Professor Brest on State Action and Liberal Theory,* 130 U.Pa.L.Rev. 1331–45 (1982).

Chapter 8

CONGRESSIONAL ENFORCEMENT OF CIVIL RIGHTS

The exercise of congressional authority under the commerce and spending powers to protect civil rights was examined in detail in Ch. 2, Secs. 2, V and 3, II. But the potentially most pervasive sources of federal legislative power to enforce personal liberty are found in the final sections of the thirteenth, fourteenth, and fifteenth amendments which grant Congress power to enforce the substantive provisions of these amendments "by appropriate legislation."

MODERN DEVELOPMENTS

SOUTH CAROLINA v. KATZENBACH, 383 U.S. 301, 86 S.Ct. 803, 15 L.Ed.2d 769 (1966): South Carolina challenged the Voting Rights Act of 1965 (enacted pursuant to § 2 of the fifteenth amendment)—"the heart of [which] is a complex scheme of stringent remedies aimed at areas where voting discrimination has been most flagrant." The Court, per WARREN, C.J., referred to "the voluminous legislative history" that showed, inter alia, "unremitting and ingenious defiance of the Constitution," the enactment of literacy tests in Alabama, Georgia, Louisiana, Mississippi, North Carolina, South Carolina, and Virginia, still in use, which, because of their various qualifications, "were specifically designed to prevent Negroes from voting." It pointed out that "discriminatory application of voting tests" "pursuant to a widespread 'pattern or practice' " "is now the principal method used to bar Negroes from the polls," and gave a number of illustrations; that "case-by-case litigation against voting discrimination" under federal statutes of 1957, 1960 and 1964 has "done little to cure the problem."

"As against the reserved powers of the States, Congress may use any rational means to effectuate the constitutional prohibition of racial discrimination in voting. [The] basic test to be applied in a case involving § 2 of the Fifteenth Amendment is the same as in all cases concerning the express powers of Congress with relation to the reserved powers of the [states.] 'Let the end be legitimate, let it be within the scope of the constitution, and all means which are appropriate, which are plainly adapted to that end, which are not prohibited, but consist with the letter and spirit of the constitution, are constitutional.' *McCulloch v. Maryland*, 17 U.S. (4 Wheat.) 316, 4 L.Ed. 579 (1819). We therefore reject South Carolina's argument that Congress may appropriately do no more than to forbid violations of the Fifteenth Amendment in general terms—that the task of fashioning specific remedies or of applying them to particular localities must necessarily be left entirely to the courts."

The "coverage formula" of the Act applied "to any State, or to any separate political subdivision [for] which two findings have been made: (1) the Attorney General has determined that on November 1, 1964, it maintained a 'test or device,' and (2) the Director of the Census has determined that less than 50% of its voting-age residents were registered on November 1, 1964, or voted in the presidential election of November 1964. These findings are not reviewable * * *. § 4(b). [T]he phrase 'test or device' means any requirement that a registrant or voter must '(1) demonstrate the ability to read, write, understand, or interpret any matter, (2) demonstrate any educational achievement or his knowledge of any particular subject, (3) possess good moral character, or (4) prove his qualifications by the voucher of registered voters or members of any other class.' § 4(c)." Statutory coverage was terminated by a so-called "bail out" provision—if the area obtained a judgment from a three-judge federal court in the District of Columbia "that tests and devices have not been used during the preceding five years to abridge the franchise on racial grounds." "In acceptable legislative fashion, Congress chose to limit its attention to the geographic areas where immediate action seemed necessary."

The areas covered, "for which there was evidence of actual voting discrimination,"—Alabama, Louisiana, Mississippi, Georgia, South Carolina and much of North Carolina—shared the "two characteristics incorporated by Congress into the coverage formula." "It was therefore permissible to impose the new remedies on the few remaining States and political subdivisions covered by the formula, at least in the absence of proof that they have been free of substantial voting discrimination in recent years." That there are excluded areas "for which there is evidence of voting discrimination by other means" is irrelevant: "Congress strengthened existing remedies for voting discrimination in other areas of the country. Legislation need not deal with all phases of a problem in the same way, so long as the distinctions drawn have some basis in political experience." "There are no States or political subdivisions exempted from coverage under § 4(b) in which the record reveals recent racial discrimination involving tests and devices. This fact confirms the rationality of the formula." The findings "which trigger application of the coverage formula" "consist of objective statistical determinations" and the termination procedure "serves as a partial substitute for direct judicial review."

In areas covered, § 4(a) suspended "literacy tests and similar voting qualifications for a period of five years from the last occurrence of substantial voting discrimination," and § 5 suspended "all new voting regulations pending review by [the Attorney General or a three-judge court in the District of Columbia] to determine whether their use would perpetuate voting discrimination." [a] Both were upheld as a "legitimate response to the problem," the Court recounting the evidence Congress had before it of prior discriminatory administration of old tests and use of new tests to evade court decrees. "Congress knew that continuance of the tests and devices in use at the present time, no matter how fairly administered in the future, would freeze the effect of past discrimination in favor of unqualified white registrants. Congress permissibly rejected the alternatives of requiring a complete re-registration of all voters, believing that this would be too harsh on many whites who had enjoyed the franchise for their

a. For examples of the Court's subsequent broad interpretation of "voting regulations" that are subject to the suspension provision of section 5, see *United Jewish Orgs. v. Carey,* p. 1279 supra (new or revised reapportionment plan); *Rome v. United States,* infra (election of officials "at large" rather than by district; annexation of adjacent area thus increasing number of eligible voters).

entire adult lives." [b]

UNITED STATES v. GUEST

383 U.S. 745, 86 S.Ct. 1170, 16 L.Ed.2d 239 (1966).

JUSTICE STEWART delivered the opinion of the Court.

[Defendants were indicted] for criminal conspiracy in violation of 18 U.S.C. § 241 [to] deprive Negro citizens of the free exercise and enjoyment of several specified rights secured by the Constitution and laws of the United States. The defendants [successfully] moved to dismiss the indictment on the ground that it did not charge an offense under the laws of the United States. [As] in *Price,* decided today, we deal here with issues of statutory construction, not with issues of constitutional power. * * * [a]

II. The second numbered paragraph of the indictment alleged that the defendants conspired to injure, oppress, threaten, and intimidate Negro citizens of the United States in the free exercise of enjoyment of: "The right to the equal utilization, without discrimination upon the basis of race, of public facilities in the vicinity of Athens, Georgia, owned, operated, or managed by [the State]." * * *

Unlike the indictment in *Price,* [the] indictment in the present case names no person alleged to have acted in any way under the color of state law. * * *

It is a commonplace that rights under the Equal Protection Clause itself arise only where there has been involvement of the State or of one acting under the color of its authority. [Here, one] of the means of accomplishing the object of the conspiracy, according to the indictment, was "By causing the arrest of Negroes by means of false reports that such Negroes had committed criminal acts." [The] allegation of the extent of official involvement in the present case is not clear. [But it] is broad enough to cover a charge of active connivance by agents of the State in the making of the "false reports," or other conduct amounting to official discrimination clearly sufficient to constitute denial of rights protected by the Equal Protection Clause. Although it is possible [that] the proof if the case goes trial, would disclose no cooperative action of that kind by officials of the State, the allegation is enough to prevent dismissal of this branch of the indictment.

III. The fourth numbered paragraph of the indictment alleged that the defendants conspired to injure, oppress, threaten, and intimidate Negro citizens of the United States in the free exercise and enjoyment of: "The right to travel freely to and from the State of Georgia." * * *

The District Court was in error in dismissing the indictment as to this paragraph. The constitutional right to travel from one State to another, and necessarily to use the highways and other instrumentalities of interstate commerce in doing so, occupies a position fundamental to the concept of our Federal Union. [See the Court's discussion, Ch. 7, Sec. 3.]

b. Black, J., agreed "with substantially all of the Court's opinion" but dissented in respect to § 5: "[I]f all the provisions of our Constitution which limit the power of the Federal Government and reserve other power to the States are to mean anything, they mean at least that the States have power to pass laws [without] first sending their officials hundreds of miles away to beg federal authorities to approve them."

a. *United States v. Price*, 383 U.S. 787, 86 S.Ct. 1152, 16 L.Ed.2d 267 (1966), unanimously held that "private persons, jointly engaged with state officers in the prohibited action, are acting 'under color' of law for the purposes of" 18 U.S.C.A. § 242.

This does not mean, of course, that every criminal conspiracy affecting an individual's right of free interstate passage is within the sanction of § 241. A specific intent to interfere with the federal right must be [proved]. Thus, for example, a conspiracy to rob an interstate traveler would not, of itself, violate § 241. But if the predominant purpose of the conspiracy is to impede or prevent the exercise of the right of interstate travel, or to oppress a person because of his exercise of that right, then, whether or not motivated by racial discrimination, the conspiracy becomes a proper object of the federal law under which the indictment in this case was brought. * * * [a]

Reversed and remanded.

JUSTICE CLARK, with whom JUSTICE BLACK and JUSTICE FORTAS join, concurring.

I join the opinion of the Court in this case but believe it worthwhile to comment on [Part II]. The Court's interpretation of the indictment clearly avoids the question whether Congress, by appropriate legislation, has the power to punish private conspiracies that interfere with Fourteenth Amendment rights, such as the right to utilize public facilities. My Brother Brennan, however, [suggests] that the Court indicates sub silentio that Congress does not have the power to outlaw such conspiracies. Although the Court specifically rejects any such connotation, it is, I believe, both appropriate and necessary under the circumstances here to say that there now can be no doubt that the specific language of § 5 empowers the Congress to enact laws punishing all conspiracies—with or without state action—that interfere with Fourteenth Amendment rights.

MR. JUSTICE HARLAN, concurring in part and dissenting in part.

I join [Part] II of the Court's opinion, but I cannot subscribe to Part III in its full sweep. To the extent that it is there held that § 241 reaches conspiracies, embracing only the action of private persons, [to] interfere with the right of citizens freely to engage in interstate travel, I am constrained to dissent. On the other hand, I agree that § 241 does embrace state interference with such interstate travel, and I therefore consider that this aspect of the indictment is sustainable on the reasoning of Part II of the Court's opinion. * * *

JUSTICE BRENNAN, with whom THE CHIEF JUSTICE and JUSTICE DOUGLAS join, concurring in part and dissenting in part.

* * * I do not agree [with the rationale] of Part II, which holds, as I read the opinion, that a conspiracy to interfere with the exercise of the right to equal utilization of state facilities is not within the meaning of § 241 [unless] discriminatory conduct by state officers is involved in the alleged conspiracy.

* * * I believe that § 241 reaches such a private conspiracy, not because the Fourteenth Amendment of its own force prohibits such a conspiracy, but because § 241, as an exercise of congressional power under § 5 of that Amendment, prohibits *all* conspiracies to interfere with the exercise of a "right * * * secured [by] the Constitution" and because the right to equal utilization of state facilities is a "right * * * secured [by] the Constitution" within the meaning of that phrase as used in § 241. * * *

a. The Civil Rights Act of 1968, 18 U.S.C.A. § 245(b), penalizes all persons who interfere etc. with "(2) any person because of his race, color, religion or national origin and because he is or has been * * * (E) traveling in or using any facility of interstate commerce, or using any vehicle, terminal, or facility of any common carrier by motor, rail, water, or air."

For me, the right to use state facilities without discrimination on the basis of race is, within the meaning of § 241, a right created by, arising under and dependent upon the Fourteenth Amendment and hence is a right "secured" by that Amendment. It finds its source in that Amendment. [The] Fourteenth Amendment commands the State to provide the members of all races with equal access to the public facilities it owns or manages, and the right of a citizen to use those facilities without discrimination on the basis of race is a basic corollary of this command. Whatever may be the status of the right to equal utilization of *privately owned facilities,* it must be emphasized that we are here concerned with the right to equal utilization of *public facilities owned or operated by or on behalf of the State.* * * *

In reversing the District Court's dismissal of the second numbered paragraph, I would therefore hold that proof at the trial of the conspiracy charged to the defendants in that paragraph will establish a violation of § 241 without regard to whether there is also proof that state law enforcement officers actively connived in causing the arrests of Negroes by means of false reports. * * *

A majority of the members of the Court[6] express the view today that § 5 empowers Congress to enact laws punishing *all* conspiracies to interfere with the exercise of Fourteenth Amendment rights, whether or not state officers or others acting under the color of state law are implicated in the conspiracy. * * * § 5 authorizes Congress to make laws that it concludes are reasonably necessary to protect a right created by and arising under that Amendment; and Congress is thus fully empowered to determine that punishment of private conspiracies interfering with the exercise of such a right is necessary to its full protection. * * *

I acknowledge that some of the decisions of this Court, most notably an aspect of the *Civil Rights Cases,* have declared that Congress' power under § 5 is confined to the adoption of "appropriate legislation for correcting the effects [of] prohibited state law and state [acts]." I do not accept—and a majority of the Court today rejects—this interpretation of § 5. It reduces the legislative power to enforce the provisions of the Amendment to that of the judiciary;[7] and it attributes a far too limited objective to the Amendment's sponsors.[8] [For amplification, see Brennan, J.'s opinion for the Court in *Katzenbach v. Morgan,* infra.]

Viewed in its proper perspective, § 5 appears as a positive grant of legislative power, authorizing Congress to exercise its discretion in fashioning remedies to achieve civil and political equality for all citizens. No one would deny [that]

6. The majority consists of the Justices joining my Brother Clark's opinion and the Justices joining this opinion. * * *

7. Congress, not the judiciary, was viewed as the more likely agency to implement fully the guarantees of equality, and thus it could be presumed the primary purpose of the Amendments was to augment the power of Congress, not the judiciary. See James, *The Framing of the Fourteenth Amendment* 184 (1956); Harris, *The Quest for Equality* 53–54 (1960); Frantz, *Congressional Power to Enforce the Fourteenth Amendment Against Private Acts,* 73 Yale L.J. 1353, 1356 (1964).

8. As the first Mr. Justice Harlan said in dissent in the *Civil Rights Cases:* "It was perfectly well known that the great danger to equal enjoyment by citizens of their rights, as citizens, was to be apprehended, not altogether from unfriendly state legislation, but from the hostile action of corporations and individuals in the states. And it is to be presumed that it was intended, by [§ 5], to clothe congress with power and authority to meet that danger."

[For the view that the fourteenth amendment's "Privileges or Immunities Clause (coupled with the § 5 Enforcement Clause)" was intended "as an authorization of Federal legislation to prohibit private racial discrimination if the states did not," see Lusky, *By What Right?* 181–203 (1975). See also Frantz, fn. 7 supra.]

Congress has the power to punish state officers who, in excess of their authority and in violation of state law, conspire to threaten, harass and murder Negroes for attempting to use [state] facilities. And I can find no principle of federalism nor word of the Constitution that denies Congress power to determine that in order adequately to protect the right to equal utilization of state facilities, it is also appropriate to punish other individuals—neither state officers nor acting in concert with state officers—who engage in the same brutal conduct for the same misguided purpose. * * *

Notes and Questions

1. *Interference with fourteenth (and fifteenth) amendment rights.* Are private persons, who intimidate state officials in an attempt to thwart their racial integration of schools, subject to prosecution under § 241? Private persons who intimidate black school children or their parents in an attempt to stop them from going to integrated schools? Who lynch a prisoner, thus preventing his fair trial by the state? Who intimidate blacks in an effort to prevent them from voting? Cf. note after *South Carolina v. Katzenbach.* Who detain a judge in an effort to prevent him from setting bail?

2. *Scope of congressional power under § 5.* (a) Do you agree with "a majority of the members of the Court" in *Guest* that "§ 5 empowers Congress to enact laws punishing *all* conspiracies to interfere with the exercise of Fourteenth Amendment rights, whether or not state officers or others acting under color of state law are implicated in the conspiracy"? Consider Feuerstein, *Civil Rights Crimes and the Federal Power to Punish Private Individuals for Interference With Federally Secured Rights,* 19 Vand.L.Rev. 641, 674–75 (1966): "[They] start with the proposition that there is a right to use state facilities without discrimination based upon race, when actually they are saying that there is a right to use state facilities without racial discrimination from any quarter—state or private. The traditional view of the equal protection clause is that it creates a right to be free of discrimination by the state. So defined, the right can only be infringed by state action, and legislation under § 5 must be directed at that infringement. Unfortunately, neither the Brennan nor the Clark opinion directly confronts this traditional approach." [b] Is the majority's rationale limited to "conspiracies" or is Congress empowered, beyond § 241, to penalize individual private acts? Does Brennan, J.'s rationale extend to "the right to equal utilization of *privately owned facilities*"?

(b) *Civil Rights Act of 1968.* 18 U.S.C.A. § 245(b): "Whoever, whether or not acting under color of law, by force or threat of force willfully injures, intimidates or interferes with, or attempts to injure, intimidate or interfere with—* * *

"(2) any person because of his race, color, religion or national origin and because he is or has been—

"(A) enrolling in or attending any public school or public college;

b. Compare Stevens, J., concurring in *Great American Fed. Sav. & Loan Ass'n v. Novotny,* 442 U.S. 366, 99 S.Ct. 2345, 60 L.Ed. 2d 957 (1979): "[I]f private persons take conspiratorial action that prevents or hinders the constituted authorities of any State from giving or securing equal treatment, the private persons would cause those authorities to violate the Fourteenth Amendment; [but if] private persons engage in purely private acts of discrimination, [they] do not violate the Equal Protection Clause of the Fourteenth Amendment. The rights secured by the Equal Protection and Due Process Clauses of the Fourteenth Amendment are rights to protection against unequal or unfair treatment by the State, not by private parties."

"(B) participating in or enjoying any benefit, service, privilege, program, facility or activity provided or administered by any State or subdivision thereof;

"(C) applying for or enjoying employment, or any perquisite thereof, by any private employer or any agency of any State or subdivision thereof, or joining or using the services or advantages of any labor organization, hiring hall, or employment agency;

"(D) serving, or attending upon any court of any State in connection with possible service, as a grand or petit juror; * * *

"(F) enjoying the goods, services, facilities, privileges, advantages, or accommodations of any inn, hotel, motel, or other establishment which provides lodging to transient guests, or of any restaurant, cafeteria, lunchroom, lunch counter, soda fountain, or other facility which serves the public and which is principally engaged in selling food or beverages for consumption on the premises, or of any gasoline station, or of any motion picture house, theater, concert hall, sports arena, stadium, or any other place of exhibition or entertainment which serves the public, or of any other establishment which serves the public and (i) which is located within the premises of any of the aforesaid establishments or within the premises of which is physically located any of the aforesaid establishments, and (ii) which holds itself out as serving patrons of such establishments; or * * *

"(5) any citizen because he is or has been, or in order to intimidate such citizen or any other citizen from lawfully aiding or encouraging other persons to participate, without discrimination on account of race, color, religion or national origin, in any of the benefits or activities described [or] participating lawfully in speech or peaceful assembly opposing any denial of the opportunity to so participate—

"shall be fined not more than $1,000, or imprisoned not more than one year, or both; and if bodily injury results shall be fined not more than $10,000, or imprisoned not more than ten years, or both; and if death results shall be subject to imprisonment for any term of years or for life. * * * Nothing in subparagraph (2)(F) * * * of this subsection shall apply to the proprietor of any establishment which provides lodging to transient guests, or to any employee acting on behalf of such proprietor, with respect to the enjoyment of the goods, services, facilities, privileges, advantages, or accommodations of such establishment if such establishment is located within a building which contains not more than five rooms for rent or hire and which is actually occupied by the proprietor as his residence."

(c) Suppose a private individual murders a black. It is clear that the *effect* (irrespective of the murderer's *intent*) is to prevent the victim's equal use of state facilities; that it prevents his right to vote, etc. These facts would be equally true if the victim were white. May the murderer be punished under § 241? Under a more narrowly drawn federal criminal statute? Consider Cox, *Constitutional Adjudication and the Promotion of Human Rights,* 80 Harv.L.Rev. 91, 116 (1966): "It seems unlikely that much constitutional significance will attach to distinctions in terms of intent. The differences between purpose, awareness that a consequence must follow, conscious indifference, and responsibility for the natural and probable consequences of an act are far too elusive to measure the scope of congressional power. Furthermore, if violence and intimidation are actually interfering with the right to vote or to enjoy state facilities, there is scant practical relevance in the wrongdoers' motivation. The suggestion was once made that the power of Congress to regulate local activities under the commerce clause depended upon the intent with which the activities were conducted, but the idea was shortly abandoned in favor of legislative or administrative determination of the practical effects on commerce."

Does congressional power fail in the above instance because "its authority is confined to instances in which there is a special relationship between the person injured and the state"? Because there is "an utter lack of proportion between the federal punishment [and] the federal interest in safeguarding enjoyment of the constitutional right"? Or is "the responsibility for the federal system" left to Congress: "possession of congressional power should not be confused with its exercise"? Id. at 116–17, 119.

KATZENBACH v. MORGAN

384 U.S. 641, 86 S.Ct. 1717, 16 L.Ed.2d 828 (1966).

JUSTICE BRENNAN delivered the opinion of the Court.

[Section] 4(e) of the Voting Rights Act of 1965 [provides] that no person who has successfully completed the sixth primary grade in a [school] accredited by the Commonwealth of Puerto Rico in which the language of instruction was other than English shall be denied the right to vote in any election because of his inability to read or write English. Appellees, registered voters in New York City, brought this suit to challenge the constitutionality of § 4(e) insofar as it pro tanto prohibits the enforcement of the election laws of New York requiring an ability to read and write English * * *.

Under the distribution of powers effected by the Constitution, [the] qualifications established by the States for voting for members of the most numerous branch of the state legislature also determine who may vote for United States Representatives and Senators, Art. I, § 2; Seventeenth Amendment. But, of course, the States have no power to grant or withhold the franchise on conditions that are forbidden by the Fourteenth Amendment * * *.

The Attorney General of New York argues that an exercise of congressional power under § 5 of the Fourteenth Amendment that prohibits the enforcement of a state [law] cannot be sustained as appropriate legislation to enforce the Equal Protection Clause unless the judiciary decides—even with the guidance of a congressional judgment—that the application of the English literacy requirement prohibited by § 4(e) is forbidden by the Equal Protection Clause itself. We disagree. Neither the language nor history of § 5 supports such a construction.[7] [A] construction of § 5 that would require a judicial determination that the enforcement of the state law precluded by Congress violated the Amendment, as a condition of sustaining the congressional enactment [would] confine the legislative power in this context to the insignificant role of abrogating only those state laws that the judicial branch was prepared to adjudge unconstitutional, or of merely informing the judgment of the judiciary by particularizing the "majestic generalities" of [§ 1]. Accordingly, our decision in *Lassiter v. Northampton Cty. Bd. of Elec.,* 360 U.S. 45, 79 S.Ct. 985, 3 L.Ed.2d 1072 (1959), sustaining the North Carolina English literacy requirement as not in all circumstances prohibited by the first sections of the Fourteenth and Fifteenth Amendments, [did] not present the question before us here: Without regard to whether the judiciary

7. For the historical evidence suggesting that the sponsors and supporters of the Amendment were primarily interested in augmenting the power of Congress, rather than the judiciary, see generally tenBroek, *The Antislavery Origins of the Fourteenth Amendment* 187–217 (1951). [But see Burt, *Miranda and Title II: A Morganatic Marriage,* 1969 Sup.Ct.Rev. 81–100.]

would find that the Equal Protection Clause itself nullifies New York's English literacy requirement as so applied, could Congress prohibit the enforcement of the state law by legislating under § 5? In answering this question, our task is limited to determining whether such legislation is, as required by § 5, appropriate legislation to enforce the Equal Protection Clause.

By including § 5 the draftsmen sought to grant to Congress [the] same broad powers expressed in the Necessary and Proper Clause.[9] The classic formulation of the reach of those powers was established by Chief Justice Marshall in *McCulloch v. Maryland* * * *. *Ex parte Virginia,* decided 12 years after the adoption of the Fourteenth Amendment, held that congressional power under § 5 had this same broad scope * * *. Section 2 of the Fifteenth Amendment grants Congress a similar power [and] we recently held in *South Carolina v. Katzenbach* that [the test was] the one formulated in *McCulloch.* * * * Correctly viewed, § 5 is a positive grant of legislative power authorizing Congress to exercise its discretion in determining whether and what legislation is needed to secure the guarantees of the Fourteenth Amendment. * * *[10]

There can be no doubt that § 4(e) may be regarded as an enactment to enforce the Equal Protection Clause. [S]pecifically, § 4(e) may be viewed as a measure to secure for the Puerto Rican community residing in New York nondiscriminatory treatment by government—both in the imposition of voting qualifications and the provision or administration of governmental services, such as public schools, public housing and law enforcement.

Section 4(e) may be readily seen as "plainly adapted" to furthering these aims of the Equal Protection Clause. The practical effect of § 4(e) is to prohibit New York from denying the right to vote to large segments of its Puerto Rican community [—the] right that is "preservative of all rights." This enhanced political power will be helpful in gaining nondiscriminatory treatment in public services for the entire Puerto Rican community.[11] Section 4(e) thereby enables the Puerto Rican minority better to obtain "perfect equality of civil rights and equal protection of the laws." [It] was for Congress, as the branch that made this judgment, to assess and weigh the various conflicting considerations—the risk or pervasiveness of the discrimination in governmental services, the effectiveness of eliminating the state restriction on the right to vote as a means of dealing with the evil, the adequacy or availability of alternative remedies, and the nature and significance of the state interests that would be affected by the

9. In fact, earlier drafts of the proposed Amendment employed the "necessary and proper" terminology to describe the scope of congressional power under the Amendment. The substitution of the "appropriate legislation" formula was never thought to have the effect of diminishing the scope of this congressional power. See, e.g., Cong. Globe, 42d Cong., 1st Sess., App. 83 * * *. [But see Note, *Theories of Federalism and Civil Rights,* 75 Yale L.J. 1007, 1046 n. 200 (1966). Compare discussion in *Argument: The Oral Argument Before the Supreme Court in Brown v. Board of Education of Topeka,* 1952–55, 93–94 (Friedman ed. 1969).]

10. Contrary to the suggestion of the dissent, § 5 does not grant Congress power to exercise discretion in the other direction and to enact "statutes so as in effect to dilute equal protection and due process decisions of this Court." We emphasize that Congress' power under § 5 is limited to adopting measures to enforce the guarantees of the Amendment; § 5 grants Congress no power to restrict, abrogate, or dilute these guarantees. Thus, for example, an enactment authorizing the States to establish racially segregated systems of education would not be—as required by § 5—a measure "to enforce" the Equal Protection Clause since that clause of its own force prohibits such state laws.

11. Cf. * * * *United States v. Darby,* 312 U.S. 100, 61 S.Ct. 451, 85 L.Ed. 609 (1941), that the power of Congress to regulate interstate commerce "extends to those activities intrastate which so affect interstate commerce or the exercise of the power of Congress over it as to make regulation of them appropriate means to the attainment of a legitimate end * * *."

nullification of the English literacy requirement * * *. It is not for us to review the congressional resolution of these factors. It is enough that we be able to perceive a basis upon which the Congress might resolve the conflict as it did. There plainly was such a [basis]. Any contrary conclusion would require us to be blind to the realities familiar to the legislators.

The result is no different if we confine our inquiry to the question whether § 4(e) was merely legislation aimed at the elimination of an invidious discrimination in establishing voter qualifications. We are told that New York's English literacy requirement originated in the desire to provide an incentive for non-English speaking immigrants to learn the English language and in order to assure the intelligent exercise of the franchise. Yet Congress might well have questioned, in light of the many exemptions provided,[13] and some evidence suggesting that prejudice played a prominent role in the enactment of the requirement,[14] whether these were actually the interests being served. Congress might have also questioned whether denial of a right deemed so precious and fundamental in our society was a necessary or appropriate means of encouraging persons to learn English, or of furthering the goal of an intelligent exercise of the franchise. Finally, Congress might well have concluded that as a means of furthering the intelligent exercise of the franchise, an ability to read or understand Spanish is as effective as ability to read English for those to whom Spanish-language newspapers and Spanish-language radio and television programs are available to inform them of election issues and governmental affairs.[16] Since Congress undertook to legislate so as to preclude the enforcement of the state law, and did so in the context of a general appraisal of literacy requirements for voting, see *South Carolina v. Katzenbach,* to which it brought a specially informed legislative competence,[17] it was Congress' prerogative to weigh these competing considerations. Here again, it is enough that we perceive a basis upon which Congress might predicate a judgment that the application of New York's English literacy requirement * * * constituted an invidious discrimination in violation of the Equal Protection Clause.

[The Court rejected the contention that the "American-flag schools" limitation itself violates "the letter and spirit of the Constitution"].

Reversed.

JUSTICE HARLAN, whom JUSTICE STEWART joins, dissenting.

[Harlan, J., first argued that the New York law was not forbidden by the equal protection clause itself.] I believe the Court has confused the issue of how much enforcement power Congress possesses under § 5 with the distinct issue of what questions are appropriate for congressional determination and what questions are essentially judicial in nature.

13. The principal exemption complained of is that for persons who had been eligible to vote before January 1, 1922.

14. This evidence consists in part of statements made in the Constitutional Convention first considering the English literacy requirement * * *. Congress was aware of this evidence. See, e.g., *Literacy Tests and Voter Requirements in Federal and State Elections,* Senate Hearings 507–513; *Voting Rights,* House Hearings 508–513.

16. See, e.g., 111 Cong.Rec. 10675 (May 20, 1965), 15102 (July 6, 1965), 15666 (July 9, 1965). The record in this case includes affidavits describing the nature of New York's two major Spanish-language newspapers [and] its three full-time Spanish-language radio stations and affidavits from those who have campaigned in Spanish speaking areas.

17. See, e.g., 111 Cong.Rec. 10676 (Senator Long of Louisiana and Senator Young), 10678 (Senator Holland) (May 20, 1965), drawing on their experience with voters literate in a language other than English. * * *

When recognized state violations of federal constitutional standards have occurred, Congress is of course empowered by § 5 to take appropriate remedial measures * * *. But it is a judicial question whether the condition with which Congress has thus sought to deal is in truth an infringement of the Constitution, something that is the necessary prerequisite to bringing the § 5 power into play at all. Thus, in *Ex parte Virginia,* involving a federal statute making it a federal crime to disqualify anyone from jury service because of race, the Court first held as a matter of constitutional law that "the Fourteenth Amendment secures [an] impartial jury trial, by jurors indifferently selected or chosen without discrimination against such jurors because of their color." Only then did the Court hold that to enforce this prohibition upon state discrimination, Congress could enact a criminal statute of the type under consideration. [In] *South Carolina v. Katzenbach,* [we] reviewed first the "voluminous legislative history" as well as judicial precedents supporting the basic congressional finding that the clear commands of the Fifteenth Amendment had been infringed by various state subterfuges. Given the existence of the evil, we held the remedial steps taken by the legislature under the Enforcement Clause of the Fifteenth Amendment to be a justifiable exercise of congressional initiative.

[The] question here is not whether the statute is appropriate remedial legislation to cure an established violation of a constitutional command, but whether there has in fact been an infringement of that constitutional command, that is, whether a particular state practice or, as here, a statute is so arbitrary or irrational as to offend the command of [equal protection]. That question is one for the judicial branch ultimately to determine. [In] view of [*Lassiter*], I do not think it is open to Congress to limit the effect of that decision as it has undertaken to do by § 4(e). In effect the Court reads § 5 of the Fourteenth Amendment as giving Congress the power to define the *substantive* scope of the Amendment. If that indeed be the true reach of § 5, then I do not see why Congress should not be able as well to exercise its § 5 "discretion" by enacting statutes so as in effect to dilute equal protection and due process decisions of this Court. In all such cases there is room for reasonable men to differ as to whether or not a denial of equal protection or due process has occurred, and the final decision is one of judgment. Until today this judgment has always been one for the judiciary to resolve.

I do not mean to suggest in what has been said that a legislative judgment of the type incorporated in § 4(e) is without any force whatsoever. Decisions on questions of equal protection and due process are based not on abstract logic, but on empirical foundations. To the extent "legislative facts" are relevant to a judicial determination, Congress is well equipped to investigate them, and such determinations are of course entitled to due respect.[a] In *South Carolina v. Katzenbach,* such legislative findings were made to show that racial discrimination in voting was actually occurring. Similarly, in *Heart of Atlanta Motel, Inc. v. United States,* and *Katzenbach v. McClung,* 379 U.S. 241 (1964), the congressional determination that racial discrimination in a clearly defined group of public accommodations did effectively impede interstate commerce was based on "voluminous testimony" which had been put before the Congress and in the context of which it passed remedial legislation.

a. For the view that "Congress cannot alter the *normative component* of a judicial decision" but that "the *empirical component* [is] the province of Congress," see Gordon, *The Nature and Uses of Congressional Power Under Section Five of the Fourteenth Amendment to Overcome Decisions of the Supreme Court,* 72 Nw.U.L.Rev. 656 (1977). See note 6(b) infra.

But no such factual data provide a legislative record supporting § 4(e)[9] by way of showing that Spanish-speaking citizens are fully as capable of making informed decisions in a New York election as are English-speaking citizens. Nor was there any showing whatever to support the Court's alternative argument that § 4(e) should be viewed as but a remedial measure designed to cure or assure against unconstitutional discrimination of other varieties, e.g., in "public schools, public housing and law enforcement" * * *.

Thus, we have [here] what can at most be called a legislative announcement that Congress believes a state law to entail an unconstitutional deprivation of equal protection. Although this kind of declaration is of course entitled to the most respectful consideration, coming as it does from a concurrent branch and one that is knowledgeable in matters of popular political participation, I do not believe it lessens our responsibility to decide the fundamental issue of whether in fact the state enactment violates federal constitutional rights.

In assessing the deference we should give to this kind of congressional expression of policy, it is relevant that the judiciary has always given to congressional enactments a presumption of validity. However, it is also a canon of judicial review that state statutes are given a similar presumption, [and] although it has been suggested that this Court should give somewhat more deference to Congress than to a State Legislature,[10] such a simple weighing of presumptions is hardly a satisfying way of resolving a matter that touches the distribution of state and federal power in an area so sensitive as that of the regulation of the franchise. Rather it should be recognized that while the Fourteenth Amendment is a "brooding omnipresence" over all state legislation, the substantive matters which it touches are all within the primary legislative competence of the States. Federal authority, legislative no less than judicial, does not intrude unless there has been a denial by state action of Fourteenth Amendment [limitations]. At least in the area of primary state concern a state statute that passes constitutional muster under the judicial standard of rationality should not be permitted to be set at naught by a mere contrary congressional pronouncement unsupported by a legislative record justifying that conclusion.

[To] hold, on this record, that § 4(e) overrides the New York literacy requirement seems to me tantamount to allowing the Fourteenth Amendment to swallow the State's constitutionally ordained primary authority in this field. For if Congress by what, as here, amounts to mere ipse dixit can set that otherwise permissible requirement partially at naught I see no reason why it could not also substitute its judgment for that of the States in other fields of their exclusive primary competence as well. * * *

Notes and Questions

1. *Congress and equal protection.* After *Morgan,* may Congress enact legislation prohibiting *all* state discrimination on the basis of alienage, illegitimacy and gender? Cf. Ch. 6, Sec. 3. Forbidding state discrimination against pushcart food vendors, opticians, debt adjustors and methadone users? Cf. Ch. 6, Sec. 1. Requiring that, in all instances in which state action has a racially disproportionate impact, the courts should balance the strength of the government interest against the disadvantage imposed on the racial minority? Cf. Ch.

9. There were no committee hearings or reports referring to this section, which was introduced from the floor during debate on the full Voting Rights Act.

10. See Thayer, *The Origin and Scope of the American Doctrine of Constitutional Law,* 7 Harv.L.Rev. 129, 154–155 (1893).

6, Sec. 2, IV. For the view that, since the Court "underenforces" the provisions of § 1 of the fourteenth amendment because of "institutional" reasons "based upon questions of propriety or capacity," Congress has "the authority to enact legislation which fills in that body's conception" of those provisions, see Sager, *Fair Measure: The Legal Status of Underenforced Constitutional Norms,* 91 Harv.L.Rev. 1212 (1978). For the view that "Congress may expand the judiciary's role by identifying additional suspect classes and fundamental rights and by increasing the level of scrutiny in specified types of equal protection cases," see Ross, *Legislative Enforcement of Equal Protection,* 72 Minn.L.Rev. 311, 335 (1987).

After *Morgan,* may Congress outlaw *all* age and residence requirements for voting? Consider Bickel, *The Voting Rights Cases,* 1966 Sup.Ct.Rev. 79, 100: "[S]uppose Congress decided that aliens or eighteen-year-olds or residents of New Jersey are being discriminated against in New York. The decision would be as plausible as the one concerning Spanish-speaking Puerto Ricans. Could Congress give these groups the vote? If Congress may freely bestow the vote as a means of curing other discriminations, which it fears may be practiced against groups deprived of the vote, essentially because of this deprivation and on the basis of no other evidence, then there is nothing left of state autonomy in setting qualifications for voting."

2. *Analogy to commerce power.* On the scope of Congress' power under the commerce clause, is Congress' discretion limited to determining what are "appropriate means" for regulating intrastate commerce that affects commerce in more than one state, or does it extend to determining *whether* intrastate commerce affects commerce in more than one state? See Comment, 20 Rutg.L.Rev. 826 (1966). Is the *Morgan* standard of judicial review of Congress' power under § 5 the same as the standard for reviewing Congress' power under the commerce clause? Consider Cox, p. 1271 supra, at 104: "Conclusory but qualifying phrases like 'reasonable relation' and 'rational' are notably absent from the opinion, in contrast to the public accommodations and voting rights cases where [the opinions] were limited by the need to use terms acceptable to a unanimous bench. It is sufficient that the law 'may be viewed' as a measure for securing equal protection and that the Court can 'perceive a basis' upon which Congress might predicate its judgment. The choice of words cannot have been casual. Evidently, the Court intends to validate any legislation under section 5—at least any legislation dealing with state action—without judging the substantiality of its relation to a permissible federal objective."

3. *Need for a "legislative record."* What of Harlan, J.'s suggestion that other broad exertions of congressional power have been sustained only on the basis of "factual data" or "voluminous testimony"? Consider Cox, supra, at 105: "[His view] is at odds with the presumption of constitutionality and with a long line of precedents holding that a statute must be judged constitutional if any set of facts which can reasonably be conceived would sustain it. No case has ever held that a record is constitutionally required. [The] principle is not merely one of deference to Congress or the states. It rests upon appreciation of the fact that the fundamental basis for legislative action is the knowledge, experience, and judgment of the people's representatives only a small part, or even none, of which may come from the hearings and reports of committees or debates upon the floor."

4. *Congress and due process.* After *Morgan,* may Congress impose the federal rules of civil and criminal procedure on the states on the ground that the

fourteenth amendment requires that due process be accorded all litigants and that in "its discretion" the federal rules are "needed to secure the guarantees of the Fourteenth Amendment"? Apart from "specific" constitutional prohibitions, under *Morgan,* what are the limits of congressional power? See generally Note, *Congressional Power to Enforce Due Process Rights,* 80 Colum.L.Rev. 1265 (1980).

5. *Congress and state action.* If *Morgan* gives Congress "the power to define the *substantive* scope" of equal protection (and due process), does it similarly permit Congress to determine the question of what constitutes "state action"? For example, might Congress, in "exercise of its discretion," determine that any judicial enforcement of racial discrimination shall be prohibited? That racial discrimination in the sale and rental of housing exists because of the failure of the states to make such discrimination illegal, and that this state "inaction" is state action under the fourteenth amendment that should "appropriately" be "remedied" by federal fair housing legislation? See fn. 8 in Brennan, J.'s opinion in *Guest.*

6. *Congressional dilution of fourteenth amendment rights.* (a) After *Morgan,* does Congress have power "to dilute equal protection and due process decisions" of the Court? Consider Cox, supra, at 106 n. 86: "According to the conventional theory [enunciated in fn. 10 of *Morgan*], the Court has invalidated state statutes under the due process and equal protection clauses only when no state of facts which can reasonably be conceived would sustain them. Where that is true, a congressional effort to withdraw the protection granted by the clause would lack the foundation of a reasonably conceivable set of facts and would therefore be just as invalid as the state legislation. But while that is true in the realm of economic regulation, the Court has often substituted its own evaluation of actual conditions in reviewing legislation dealing with 'preferred rights.' It is hard to see how the Court can consistently give weight to the congressional judgment in expanding the definition of equal protection in the area of human rights but refuse to give it weight in narrowing the definition where the definition depends upon appraisal of the facts." Does the "answer" lie in a theory that justifies judicial review principally on the need to afford protection to certain minority "rights" from the majority will? Consider W. Cohen, *Congressional Power to Interpret Due Process and Equal Protection,* 27 Stan.L.Rev. 603, 614 (1975): "[A] theory that distinguishes between congressional competence to make 'liberty' and 'federalism' judgments resolves the dilemma. A congressional judgment rejecting a judicial interpretation of the due process or equal protection clauses—an interpretation that had given the individual procedural or substantive protection from state and federal government alike—is entitled to no more deference than the identical decision of a state legislature.[b] Congress is no more immune to momentary passions of the majority than are the state legislatures. But a congressional judgment resolving at the national level an issue that could—without constitutional objection—be decided in the same way at the state level, ought normally to be binding on the courts, since Congress presumably reflects a balance between both national and state interests and hence is better able to adjust such conflicts." See also Choper, *Judicial Review and the National Political Process* 198–200 (1980).

In MISSISSIPPI UNIV. FOR WOMEN v. HOGAN, p. 1088 supra, "the State contended that Congress, in enacting [the] Education Amendments of 1972,

b. For the view that equal protection challenges to congressional action should be judged by a more lenient (but not "toothless") standard of review than state action, see Bohrer, *Bakke, Weber and Fullilove: Benign Discrimination and Congressional Power to Enforce the Fourteenth Amendment,* 56 Ind. L.J. 473 (1981).

expressly had authorized MUW to continue its single-sex admissions policy by exempting public undergraduate institutions that traditionally have used single-sex admissions policies from the gender discrimination prohibition of Title IX. Through that provision, the State argued, Congress limited the reach of the Fourteenth Amendment by exercising its power under § 5 of the Amendment." The Court, relying on fn. 10 of *Morgan,* responded: "Although we give deference to congressional decisions and classifications, neither Congress nor a State can validate a law that denies the rights guaranteed by the Fourteenth Amendment." The four dissenting justices did not address the issue.

(b) *Competence as to "facts."* Does *Miranda v. Arizona,* 384 U.S. 436, 86 S.Ct. 1602, 16 L.Ed.2d 694 (1966), rest on the *factual* assumption that there is "compulsion inherent in custodial surroundings" and thus "no statement obtained from the defendant can truly be the product of his free choice"? Does *Mapp v. Ohio,* p. 136 supra, rest on the *factual* assumption that the exclusionary rule is a "deterrent safeguard without insistence upon which the Fourth Amendment would have been reduced to 'a form of words' "? Does *Gideon v. Wainwright,* 372 U.S. 335, 83 S.Ct. 792, 9 L.Ed.2d 799 (1963), rest on the *factual* assumption that a person "who is too poor to hire a lawyer, cannot be assured a fair trial unless counsel is provided for him"? Does *Brown v. Board of Education,* p. 958 supra, rest on the *factual* assumption that racially "separate educational facilities are inherently unequal"? If so, may Congress, pursuant to § 5, find the *facts* to be otherwise and legislate a contrary rule? See S.Rep. No. 1097, 90th Cong., 2d Sess. 59–63 (1968).

(c) *Line-drawing.* What deference is owed congressional action, pursuant to § 5, that precisely defines (i) how long a delay constitutes denial of the "right to a speedy trial," see *Barker v. Wingo,* 407 U.S. 514, 92 S.Ct. 2182, 33 L.Ed.2d 101 (1972); (ii) how great a deviation from absolute population equality among legislative districts constitutes a violation of the "one person-one vote" requirement, see Ch. 6, Sec. 4, I, A?

(d) *Conflicting constitutional provisions.* May de facto racial segregation in the schools arguably violate equal protection; may use of racial criteria to alleviate de facto segregation arguably violate equal protection (see Ch. 6, Secs. 2, III and 2, V? If so, what deference is owed congressional action, pursuant to § 5, dealing with these matters? See opinion of White, J., in *Welsh v. United States,* p. 924 supra.

(e) *Rights vs. remedies.* May Congress, pursuant to § 5, withdraw (or replace) the "exclusionary rule" of *Mapp v. Ohio* on the ground that this does not "dilute" any substantive constitutional right but merely modifies a remedy for its violation? On similar analysis, may Congress forbid busing (or substitute alternatives) to remedy school segregation? See fn. a, p. 990 supra. Consider Note, *The Nixon Busing Bills and Constitutional Power,* 81 Yale L.J. 1542, 1570–71 (1972): "Because busing is one remedy among many, Bork [*Constitutionality of the President's Busing Proposals* 21–22 (1972)] argues [that the anti-busing bill] leaves intact the duty *Brown* imposed upon formerly segregated school districts. Such an argument creates an artificial distinction between rights and remedies; the right which cannot be vindicated is not a right at all, and the most that can be said for the distinction is that it may be useful where a right can be vindicated in several ways. [If] busing is in some cases—as it was in *Swann*—the only remedy that would produce desegregation in any real sense, then Bork's argument falls. The real question about the constitutionality of the busing bills is the question that Bork hesitates to answer directly: to what extent does the

Equal Protection Clause require that once segregated schools achieve a racial balance? *Swann,* of course, had a simple and direct answer: to the greatest extent possible." See also Rotunda, *Congressional Power to Restrict the Jurisdiction of the Lower Federal Courts and the Problem of School Busing,* 64 Geo.L.J. 839 (1976).

For the view that many judicial decisions implementing constitutional rights are not "true constitutional interpretations" but rather only "constitutional common law" rules that may be modified by Congress, see Monaghan, *Constitutional Common Law,* 89 Harv.L.Rev. 1 (1975). Compare Schrock & Welsh, *Reconsidering the Constitutional Common Law,* 91 Harv.L.Rev. 1117 (1978).

(f) *Definition of "dilution."* If Congress believed that more wrongdoers would be convicted and crime deterred by changing the *Miranda* rule, would such legislation "dilute" the due process rights of the accused, or "secure" the rights of the public generally not to be denied life or property without due process of law? Who should *ultimately* determine these issues? See generally Nathanson, *Congressional Power to Contradict the Supreme Court's Constitutional Decisions. Accommodation of Rights in Conflict,* 27 Wm. & M.L.Rev. 331 (1986).

(g) *"Human Life Bill."* What of the constitutionality of the following proposed statute, S. 158 and H.R. 900, 97th Cong., 1st Sess. (1981):

"Sec. 1. The Congress finds that present day scientific evidence indicates a significant likelihood that actual human life exists from conception.

"The Congress further finds that the fourteenth amendment to the Constitution of the United States was intended to protect all human beings.

"Upon the basis of these findings, and in the exercise of the powers of the Congress, including its power under section 5 of the fourteenth amendment to the Constitution of the United States, the Congress hereby declares that for the purpose of enforcing the obligation of the States under the fourteenth amendment not to deprive persons of life without due process of law, human life shall be deemed to exist from conception, without regard to race, sex, age, health, defect, or condition of dependency; and for this purpose 'person' shall include all human life as defined herein. * * *"[c]

(i) *Questions of "fact."* Do the issues of when "human life" begins and what is a "person" involve questions of fact? Consider Tribe, *Prepared Statement,* Hearings on S. 158 at 251: "Such questions [call] at bottom for normative judgments no less profound than those involved in defining 'liberty' or 'equality.' [They] entail 'question[s] to which science can provide no answer,' as the National Academy of Sciences itself acknowledged * * *. Congress cannot transform an issue of religion, morality, and law into one of fact by waving the magic wand of Section 5 [which] no more authorizes Congress to transmute a matter of values into a matter of scientific observation than it authorizes Congress to announce a mathematical formula for human freedom." See also Cox, *Prepared Statement,* id. at 340–41.

c. For argument in favor of its validity, see Galebach, *A Human Life Statute,* 7 Human Life Rev. 3 (1981), reprinted in Hearings on S. 158, before the Subcomm. on Separation of Powers of the Senate Comm. on the Judiciary, 97th Cong., 1st Sess. 205 (1981); Nagel, *Prepared Statement,* id. 321. For exhaustive consideration, see Estreicher, *Congressional Power and Constitutional Rights: Reflections on Proposed "Human Life" Legislation,* 68 Va.L.Rev. 333 (1982). For an "institutional" perspective, see Carter, *The Morgan "Power" and the Forced Reconsideration of Constitutional Decisions,* 53 U.Chi.L.Rev. 819 (1986).

(ii) *"Dilution" vs. "expansion."* Does the Bill dilute the right to an abortion? Consider Noonan, *Prepared Statement,* id. at 266–67: "In recognizing the unborn as persons, [the] Act treats no one unequally but gives equal protection to one class of humanity now unequally treated. * * * Necessarily, the expression of the rights of one class of human beings has an impact on the rights of others. The elimination of literacy tests in this way 'diluted' the voting rights of the literate. It is inescapable that congressional expression of the right to life will have an impact on the abortion right; but in the eyes of Congress, [there] will be a net gain for Fourteenth Amendment rights by the expansion and the attendant diminution."

OREGON v. MITCHELL

400 U.S. 112, 91 S.Ct. 260, 27 L.Ed.2d 272 (1970).

[In original jurisdiction suits, brought by Oregon and Texas against the Attorney General and by the United States against Arizona and Idaho, the states challenged Congress' power to enact Titles II and III of the Voting Rights Act Amendments of 1970. (1) Section 302 forbade states to deny any citizen, otherwise qualified to vote, the right to vote in any federal, state or local election "on account of age if such citizen is eighteen years of age or older." Black, Douglas, Brennan, White and Marshall, JJ., voted to uphold this provision as to federal elections; Burger, C.J., and Black, Harlan, Stewart and Blackmun, JJ., voted to hold it unconstitutional as to state and local elections. (2) Section 201 extended the Voting Rights Act of 1965 for an additional five years (to 1975) and also extended nationwide § 4(a)'s prohibition of "any test or device" (including literacy tests) "as a prerequisite for voting or registration." This was upheld unanimously.[a] (3) Sec. 202 abolished any state "durational residency requirement as a precondition to voting for President and Vice President"; it required the registration "of all duly qualified residents of such State who apply, not later than thirty days immediately prior to any presidential election," and the provision of "absentee ballots" to those "who may be absent [on] the day such election is held and who have applied therefor not later than seven days immediately prior to such election"; an "otherwise qualified" voter who changes state residency within thirty days of such election must be permitted to vote either "in person" or "by absentee ballot" "in the State or political subdivision in which he resided immediately prior to his removal." Only Harlan, J., voted to hold this provision invalid.]

JUSTICE BLACK, announcing the judgments of the Court in an opinion expressing his own view of the cases.

[T]he responsibility of the States for setting the qualifications of voters in congressional elections [in Art. I, § 2] was made subject to the power of Congress to make or alter such regulations [in Art. I, § 4].[b]

a. In 1975, the Act was amended to extend for an additional seven years, to make § 4(a)'s suspension of "any test or device" indefinite, and to greatly expand the geographic coverage (including, inter alia, areas with at least 5% language minorities) of the requirement that new voting regulations be reviewed by the Attorney General or a federal court. See generally Hunter, *The 1975 Voting Rights Act and Language Minorities,* 25 Cath.U.L.Rev. 250 (1976). The seven year extension was upheld in *Rome v. United States,* note 3 infra. In 1982, the Act's preclearance mechanism was extended for 25 years.

b. Could the substance of the 24th amendment, barring payment of a poll tax as a condition to vote in federal elections, have been enacted simply by a federal statute?

* * * Similarly, it is the prerogative of Congress to oversee the conduct of presidential and vice presidential elections and to set the qualifications for voters for electors for those offices. * * *

On the other hand, [n]o function is more essential to the separate and independent existence of the States [than] the power to determine within the limits of the Constitution the qualifications of their own voters for state, county, and municipal [offices].

In enacting the 18-year-old vote provisions of the Act now before the Court, Congress made no legislative findings that 21-year-old vote requirements were used by the States to disenfranchise voters on account of race. I seriously doubt that such a finding, if made, could be supported by substantial evidence. [On] the other hand, [i]n enacting the literacy test ban of Title II Congress had before it a long history of the discriminatory use of literacy tests to disfranchise voters on account of their race. [A]s to the Nation as a whole, Congress had before it statistics which demonstrate that voter registration and voter participation are consistently greater in States without literacy tests. [Finally in enacting the residency and absentee voting] regulations for national elections Congress was attempting to insure a fully effective voice to all citizens in national elections. What I said [about Congress' power to regulate federal elections] applies with equal force here. * * *

JUSTICE BRENNAN, JUSTICE WHITE, and JUSTICE MARSHALL dissent from the judgment insofar as it declares § 302 unconstitutional as applied to state and local elections * * *.

[Residency:] [A] durational residence requirement operates to penalize those persons, and only those persons, who have exercised their constitutional right of interstate migration. [I]n such a case, governmental action may withstand constitutional scrutiny only upon a clear showing that the burden imposed is necessary to protect a compelling and substantial governmental interest. *Shapiro v. Thompson* [p. 1150 supra]. [W]e find ample justification for the congressional conclusion that § 202 is a reasonable means for eliminating an unnecessary burden on the right of interstate migration. *Guest.*

[Age:] We believe there is serious question whether a statute [denying] the franchise to citizens [between] the ages of 18 and 21 could, in any event, withstand present scrutiny under the Equal Protection Clause. Regardless of the answer to this question, however, it is clear to us that proper regard for the special function of Congress in making determinations of legislative fact compels this Court to respect those determinations unless they are contradicted by evidence far stronger than anything that has been adduced in these cases. * * *

A. [W]hen exclusions from the franchise are challenged as violating [equal protection] "the Court must determine whether the exclusions are necessary to promote a compelling state interest."

In the present cases, the States justify exclusion of 18- to 21-year-olds from the voting rolls solely on the basis of the States' interests in promoting intelligent and responsible exercise of the franchise. [But no state] requires attendance at school beyond the age of 18. [T]hat 18-year-olds as a class may be less educated than some of their elders cannot justify restriction of the franchise for the States themselves have determined that this incremental education is irrelevant to voting qualifications.

[No] State seeking to uphold its denial of the franchise to 18-year-olds has adduced anything beyond the mere difference in age. [But] perhaps more important is the uniform experience of those States—Georgia since 1943, and Kentucky since 1955—that have permitted 18-year-olds to vote. [E]very person who spoke to the issue in either the House or Senate was agreed that 18-year-olds in both States were at least as interested, able, and responsible in voting as were their elders. * * *

B. [When] a state legislative classification is subjected to judicial challenge as violating the Equal Protection Clause, it comes before the courts cloaked by the presumption that the legislature has, as it should, acted within constitutional limitations. [But] this limitation on judicial review of state legislative classifications is a limitation stemming not from the Fourteenth Amendment itself, but from the nature of [the] judicial process [which] makes it an inappropriate forum for the determination of complex factual questions of the kind so often involved in constitutional adjudication. [Should Congress, however, pursuant to § 5] undertake an investigation in order to determine whether the factual basis necessary to support a state legislative discrimination actually exists, it need not stop once it determines that some reasonable men could believe the factual basis exists. Section 5 empowers Congress to make its own determination on the matter. See *Morgan.* It should hardly be necessary to add that if the asserted factual basis necessary to support a given state discrimination does not exist, § 5 of the Fourteenth Amendment vests Congress with power to remove the discrimination by appropriate means.

The scope of our review in such matters has been established by a long line of consistent decisions. * * * "[W]here we find that the legislators, in light of the facts and testimony before them, have a rational basis for finding a chosen regulatory scheme necessary [our] investigation is at an end." *Katzenbach v. McClung; Morgan.*[32] * * *

Finally, it is no answer to say that Title III intrudes upon a domain reserved to the States—the power to set qualifications for voting. It is no longer open to question that the Fourteenth Amendment applies to this, as to all other, exercises of state power. * * *

C. [T]he language of the Fourteenth Amendment [applies] on its face to all assertions of state power, however made. [I]t seems to us, the historical record will not bear the weight our Brother Harlan has placed upon it. [Our] reading of the historical background [results] in a somewhat imperfect picture of an era of constitutional confusion, confusion which the Amendment did little to resolve. [The opinion examines in some detail the historical setting, the "politics of the day," the changes in language of the proposed Amendment made in the Joint Congressional Committee on Reconstruction, and the "obscure" and sometimes "incongruous" statements made in congressional debates, campaign speeches and the press. It] suggests an alternative hypothesis: that the Amendment was framed by men who possessed differing views on the great question of the suffrage and [who] papered over their differences with the broad, elastic language of § 1 and left to future interpreters of their Amendment the task of

32. As we emphasized in *Morgan,* "§ 5 does not grant Congress power [to] enact 'statutes so as in effect to dilute equal protection and due process decisions of this Court.'" As indicated above, a decision of this Court striking down a state statute expresses, among other things, our conclusion that the legislative findings upon which the statute is based are so far wrong as to be unreasonable. Unless Congress were to unearth new evidence in its investigation, its identical findings on the identical issue would be no more reasonable than those of the state legislature.

resolving in accordance with future vision and future needs the issues which they left unresolved. * * *

In sum, Congress had ample evidence upon which it could have based the conclusion [under § 5] that exclusion of citizens 18 to 21 years of age from the franchise is wholly unnecessary to promote any legitimate interest the States may have in assuring intelligent and responsible voting. * * *

JUSTICE HARLAN, concurring in part and dissenting in part.

[Similar to his dissent in *Reynolds v. Sims,* [p. 1111 supra], Harlan, J., argued at length "that the history of the Fourteenth Amendment makes it clear beyond any reasonable doubt" that § 1 was never intended to "reach discriminatory voting qualifications," again emphasizing § 2—providing for reduced congressional representation for states denying 21-year old male citizens the right to vote.[c] [That] constitutional amendments were deemed necessary to bring about federal abolition of state restrictions on voting by reason of race (Amend. XV), sex (Amend. XIX), and, even with respect to federal elections, the failure to pay state poll taxes (Amend. XXIV), is itself forceful evidence of the common understanding in 1869, 1919, and 1962, respectively, that the Fourteenth Amendment did not empower Congress to legislate in these respects. * * *

[Although] Congress' expression of the view that it does have power to alter state suffrage qualifications is entitled to the most respectful consideration by the judiciary, [this] cannot displace the duty of this Court to make an independent determination whether Congress has exceeded its powers. The reason for this goes beyond Marshall's assertion that "It is emphatically the province and duty of the judicial department to say what the law is." *Marbury.*[86] It inheres in the structure of the constitutional system itself. Congress is subject to none of the institutional restraints imposed on judicial decisionmaking; it is controlled only by the political process. In Article V, the Framers expressed the view that the political restraints on Congress alone were an insufficient control over the process of constitution-making. The concurrence of two-thirds of each House and of three-fourths of the States was needed for the political check to be adequate. [Nor] is that structure adequately protected by a requirement that the judiciary be able to perceive a basis for the congressional interpretation, the only restriction laid down in *Morgan.*

It is suggested that the proper basis for the doctrine enunciated in *Morgan* lies in the relative fact-finding competence of Court, Congress, and state legislatures. [But the] disagreement in these cases revolves around the evaluation [of] largely uncontested factual material. On the assumption that maturity and experience are relevant to intelligent and responsible exercise of the elective franchise, are the immaturity and inexperience of the average 18-, 19-, or 20-year-old sufficiently serious to justify denying such a person a direct voice in decisions affecting his or her life? Whether or not this judgment is character-

c. "To be sure, one might argue that § 2 is simply a rhetorical flourish, and that the qualifications listed there are merely the ones which the Framers deemed to be consistent with the alleged prohibition of § 1. This argument is not only unreasonable on its face and untenable in light of the historical record; it is fatal to the validity of the reduction of the voting age [before] us.

"The only sensible explanation of § 2, therefore, is that the racial voter qualifications it was designed to penalize were understood to be permitted by § 1 * * *."

86. In fact, however, I do not understand how the doctrine of deference to rational constitutional interpretation by Congress, espoused by the majority in *Morgan,* is consistent with this statement of Chief Justice Marshall or with our reaffirmation of it in *Cooper v. Aaron* [p. 15 supra] * * *.

ized as "factual," it calls for striking a balance between incommensurate interests. Where the balance is to be struck depends ultimately on the values and the perspective of the decisionmaker. It is a matter as to which men of good will can and do reasonably differ.

I fully agree that judgments of the sort involved here are beyond the institutional competence and constitutional authority of the judiciary. [But judicial] deference is based, not on relative fact-finding competence, but on due regard for the decision of the body constitutionally appointed to decide. Establishment of voting qualifications is a matter for state legislatures. Assuming any authority at all, only when the Court can say with some confidence that the legislature has demonstrably erred in adjusting the competing interests is it justified in striking down the legislative judgment. * * *

The same considerations apply, and with almost equal force, to Congress' displacement of state decisions with its own ideas of wise policy. The sole distinction between Congress and the Court in this regard is that Congress, being an elective body, presumptively has popular authority for the value judgment it makes. But since the state legislature has a like authority, this distinction between Congress and the judiciary falls short of justifying a congressional veto on the state judgment. The perspectives and values of national legislators on the issue of voting qualifications are likely to differ from those of state legislators, but I see no reason a priori to prefer those of the national figures, whose collective decision, applying nationwide, is necessarily less able to take account of peculiar local conditions. Whether one agrees with this judgment or not, it is the one expressed by the Framers in leaving voter qualifications to the States. The Supremacy Clause does not, as my colleagues seem to argue, represent a judgment that federal decisions are superior to those of the States whenever the two may differ.

To be sure, my colleagues do not expressly say that Congress or this Court is empowered by the Constitution to substitute its own judgment for those of the States. However, before sustaining a state judgment they require a "clear showing that the burden imposed is necessary to protect a compelling and substantial governmental interest." [88] I should think that [if] my colleagues or a majority of Congress deem a given voting qualification undesirable as a matter of policy, they must consider that the state interests involved are not "compelling" or "substantial" or that they can be adequately protected in other ways. It follows that my colleagues must be prepared to hold invalid as a matter of federal constitutional law all state voting qualifications which they deem unwise, as well as all such qualifications which Congress reasonably deems unwise. For this reason, I find their argument subject to the same objection as if it explicitly acknowledged such a conclusion. * * *

JUSTICE STEWART, with whom THE CHIEF JUSTICE and JUSTICE BLACKMUN join, concurring in part and dissenting in part. * * *

[Literacy:] Because the justification for extending the ban on literacy tests to the entire Nation need not turn on whether literacy tests unfairly discriminate against Negroes in every State in the Union, Congress was not required to make state-by-state findings * * *. In the interests of uniformity, Congress

88. It might well be asked why this standard is not equally applicable to the congressional expansion of the franchise before us. Lowering of voter qualifications dilutes the voting power of those who could meet the higher standard, and it has been held that "the right of suffrage can be denied by a debasement or dilution of the weight of a citizen's vote just as effectively as by wholly prohibiting the free exercise of the franchise." *Reynolds v. Sims.* * * *

may paint with a much broader brush than may this Court, which must confine itself to the judicial function of deciding individual cases and controversies upon individual records. * * * Experience gained under the 1965 Act has now led Congress to conclude that it should go the whole distance. This approach to the problem is a rational one; consequently it is within [the] power of Congress under § 2 of the Fifteenth Amendment.[d] * * *

The Constitution withholds from Congress any general authority to change by legislation the qualifications for voters in federal elections. * * * Article I, § 2, and the Seventeenth Amendment prescribe [as] the federal standard the standard which each State has chosen for itself. * * *

Contrary to the submission of my Brother Black, Article I, § 4 does not create in the federal legislature the power to alter the constitutionally established qualifications to vote in congressional elections. [The] "manner" of holding elections can hardly be read to mean the *qualifications* for voters * * *. I am persuaded that the constitutional provisions discussed above are not sufficient to prevent Congress from protecting a person who exercises his constitutional right to enter and abide in any State in the Union from losing his opportunity to vote, when Congress may protect the right of interstate travel from other less fundamental disabilities. [The] power which Congress has exercised in enacting § 202 [is] confined to federal action against a particular problem clearly within the purview of congressional authority. * * *

[Age: Recent] decisions have established that state action regulating suffrage is not immune from the impact of the Equal Protection Clause. But we have been careful in those decisions to note the undoubted power of a State to establish a qualification for voting based on age. See, e.g., *Kramer*. Indeed, none of the opinions filed today suggest that the States have anything but a constitutionally unimpeachable interest in establishing some age qualification as such. Yet to test the power to establish an age qualification by the "compelling interest" standard is really to deny a State any choice at all, because no State could demonstrate a "compelling interest" in drawing the line with respect to age at one point rather than another. * * *[14]

Morgan does not hold that Congress has the power to determine what are and what are not "compelling state interests" for equal protection purposes. [*Morgan*] upheld the statute on two grounds: that Congress could conclude that enhancing the political power of the Puerto Rican community by conferring the right to vote was an appropriate means of remedying discriminatory treatment in public services; and that Congress could conclude that the New York statute was tainted by the impermissible purpose of denying the right to vote to Puerto Ricans, an undoubted invidious discrimination under the Equal Protection Clause. Both of these decisional grounds were far-reaching. The Court's opinion made clear that Congress could impose on the States a remedy for the denial of equal protection which elaborated upon the direct command of the Constitution, and that it could override state laws on the ground that they were in fact used as instruments of invidious discrimination even though a court in an individual lawsuit might not have reached that factual conclusion.

d. The opinion sustained the residency provision on a rationale similar to Brennan, J.'s.

14. [S]o long as a State does not set the voting age higher than 21, the reasonableness of its choice is confirmed by the very Fourteenth Amendment upon which the Government relies [see § 2].

But it is necessary to go much further to sustain § 302. The state laws which it invalidates do not invidiously discriminate against any discrete and insular minority. Unlike the statute considered in *Morgan,* § 302 is valid only if Congress has the power not only to provide the means of eradicating situations which amount to a violation of the Equal Protection Clause, but also to determine as a matter of substantive constitutional law what situations fall within the ambit of the clause, and what state interests are "compelling." * * * [e]

Notes and Questions

1. *Mitchell's "interpretation" of Morgan.* (a) To what extent do the opinions in *Mitchell* clarify (or cloud) the scope of Congress' power delineated in *Morgan*? Do either Brennan or Harlan, JJ., do more in *Mitchell* than restate their *Morgan* analyses? Do Black and Stewart, JJ., accurately "read" *Morgan*? Consider Cox, *The Role of Congress in Constitutional Determinations,* 40 U.Cin.L. Rev. 199, 237 (1971): "Justice Stewart's summary of *Morgan* [is] historically inaccurate: the New York literacy statute antedates by decades the arrival of numerous Puerto Ricans. Second, [the] *Morgan* opinion barely hints that Congress was concerned to ascribe a racist purpose to the New York lawmakers. [Finally], even by Justice Stewart's own account, the *Morgan* case sustained a congressional finding of substantive unconstitutionality and thus belies his later assertion that Congress lacks power to make a substantive determination of constitutional law." Do you agree? If Congress believed that "prejudice played a prominent role in the enactment" of the state literacy law in *Morgan,* is it important against which minority group the prejudice was directed? If this was the basis of Congress' "constitutional determination" in *Morgan,* is it the same kind of "substantive determination of constitutional law" by Congress that Brennan, J. sought to uphold in *Mitchell*?

(b) In any event, does Stewart, J.'s "reading" of *Morgan*—that Congress may "override state laws on the ground that they were in fact used as instruments of invidious discrimination"—mean that Congress may outlaw all "de facto" discriminations against "any discrete and insular minority"? Consider 85 Harv.L. Rev. 162 (1971): "Congress might be able to revamp a host of state benefit programs that impose particular disabilities on the poor on the rational basis that, in fact, a large fraction of the poor were blacks or members of ethnic minorities. [T]he literacy test analogy seems instructive: the class of citizens to whom the device was a serious obstacle was surely wider than merely blacks, yet Congress' conclusion that a large number of blacks were seriously disadvantaged [was] sufficient to uphold abolishing the practice under Congress' enforcement powers." Do you agree? Or does Stewart, J.'s "reading" of *Morgan* only comprehend congressional power over state laws it finds "tainted by [an] impermissible purpose"? See note 3 infra. See generally Choper, *Congressional Power to Expand Judicial Definitions of the Substantive Terms of the Civil War Amendments,* 67 Minn.L.Rev. 299, 328–34 (1982).

2. *Present status of Morgan.* In EEOC v. WYOMING, 460 U.S. 226, 103 S.Ct. 1054, 75 L.Ed.2d 18 (1983), BURGER, C.J., joined by Powell, Rehnquist and O'Connor, JJ., dissenting—after pointing out that the Court had rejected equal protection challenges to mandatory retirement schemes (p. 1104 supra)—denied that Congress had power under § 5 to apply the Age Discrimination in Employment Act to state hiring: "Allowing Congress [to] define rights wholly indepen-

e. Douglas, J.'s separate opinion, upholding all provisions, is omitted.

dently of our case law * * * fundamentally alters our scheme of government. Although the *South Carolina v. Katzenbach* line of cases may be read to allow Congress a degree of flexibility in deciding what the Fourteenth Amendment safeguards, I have always read *Mitchell* as finally imposing a limitation on the extent to which Congress may substitute its own judgment for that of the states and assume this Court's 'role of final arbiter,' (Harlan, J., dissenting)." [f]

3. *De facto discrimination.* (a) ROME v. UNITED STATES, 446 U.S. 156, 100 S.Ct. 1548, 64 L.Ed.2d 119 (1980), involved the Attorney General's refusal to approve, under § 5 of the Voting Rights Act, various changes in the city's electoral system and a number of city annexations. A federal court found that the city had not employed any discriminatory barriers to black voting or black candidacy in the past 17 years and that the city had proved that the electoral changes and annexations were not discriminatorily motivated, but that they were prohibited by the Act because they had a discriminatory effect. The Court, per MARSHALL, J., affirmed: "[T]he Act's ban on electoral changes that are discriminatory in effect is an appropriate method of promoting the purposes of the Fifteenth Amendment, even if it is assumed that § 1 of the Amendment prohibits only intentional discrimination in voting. [See *Mobile v. Bolden,* p. 981 supra.] Congress could rationally have concluded that, because electoral changes by jurisdictions with a demonstrable history of intentional racial discrimination in voting create the risk of purposeful discrimination, it was proper to prohibit changes that have a discriminatory impact. See *South Carolina v. Katzenbach.*"

REHNQUIST, J., joined by Stewart, J., dissented: Court today identifies the constitutional wrong which was the object of this congressional exercise of power as purposeful discrimination by local governments in structuring their political processes in an effort to reduce black voting strength. [What] the Court explicitly ignores is that in this case the city has proven that these changes are not discriminatory in purpose. * * *

"Congress had before it evidence that various governments were enacting electoral changes and annexing territory to prevent the participation of blacks in local government by measures other than outright denial of the franchise. [G]iven the difficulties of proving that an electoral change or annexation has been undertaken for the purpose of discriminating against blacks, Congress could properly conclude that as a remedial matter it was necessary to place the burden of proving lack of discriminatory purpose on the localities. See *South Carolina v. Katzenbach.* But all of this does not support the conclusion that Congress is acting remedially when it continues the presumption of purposeful discrimination even after the locality has disproved that presumption. Absent other circumstances, it would be a topsy-turvy judicial system which held that electoral changes which have been affirmatively proven to be permissible under the Constitution nonetheless violate the Constitution. [Thus,] the result of the Court's holding is that Congress effectively has the power to determine for itself that this conduct violates the Constitution. This result violates previously well-established distinctions between the Judicial Branch and the Legislative or Executive Branches of the Federal Government." Powell, J., dissented on narrower grounds.

f. For the view that "the scope of the definitional power" granted Congress in *Morgan,* "although by no means insignificant, may nonetheless be quite limited," see Choper, note 1(b) supra.

(b) Do you agree that *Rome* empowers Congress "to determine for itself [what] conduct violates the Constitution"? Consider Choper, note 1(b) supra, at 331–32: "[*Rome's*] rationale permits Congress to create a 'conclusive presumption' of racial motivation with respect to specified state or local practices that Congress finds have been widely or consistently employed for the purpose of disadvantaging racial minorities—and thus effectively authorizes a congressional conclusion that such practices violate the substance of the fourteenth amendment. But this is a much narrower license than empowering Congress to declare that all state or local rules with a racially disproportionate impact violate equal protection for that reason alone. [A] variety of factors make it extremely difficult for plaintiffs to prove that a state legislative or administrative body has acted with discriminatory intent and make it much more appropriate for Congress than for the judiciary to combat the problem of illicit motivation. Thus, there are powerful reasons for Congress to choose not to rely upon district judges for the highly sensitive task of ascertaining racially discriminatory intent on a case by case basis in respect to state of local schemes whose real purpose Congress has grounds to suspect. [*Rome*] did no more than recognize this reality when is [used] what is principally a remedial or prophylactic rationale."

JONES v. ALFRED H. MAYER CO.

392 U.S. 409, 88 S.Ct. 2186, 20 L.Ed.2d 1189 (1968).

JUSTICE STEWART delivered the opinion of the Court.

In this case we are called upon to determine the scope and the constitutionality [of] 42 U.S.C. § 1982.

[P]etitioners filed a complaint [that] respondents had refused to sell them a home [for] the sole reason that petitioner [is] a Negro. Relying in part upon § 1982, the petitioners sought injunctive and other relief. The [courts below] sustained the respondents' motion to dismiss [concluding] that § 1982 applies only to state action * * *.

On its [face] § 1982 appears to prohibit *all* discrimination against Negroes in the sale or rental of property—discrimination by private owners as well as discrimination by public authorities. * * * Stressing what they consider to be the revolutionary implications of so literal a reading of § 1982, the respondents argue that Congress cannot possibly have intended any such result. Our examination of the relevant history, however, persuades us that Congress meant exactly what it said. * * *

The remaining question is whether Congress has power under the Constitution to do what § 1982 purports to [do]. Our starting point is the Thirteenth Amendment, for it was pursuant to that constitutional provision that Congress originally enacted what is now § 1982. [It] has never been [doubted] "that the power vested in Congress to enforce the article by appropriate legislation," [*Civil Rights Cases,*] includes the power to enact laws "direct and primary, operating upon the acts of individuals, whether sanctioned by State legislation or not." Id. * * *

"By its own unaided force and effect," the Thirteenth Amendment "abolished slavery, and established universal freedom." *Civil Rights Cases.* Whether or not the Amendment *itself* did any more than that—a question not involved in this case—it is at least clear that the Enabling Clause of that Amendment empowered Congress to do much more.[a] For that clause clothed "Congress with power to pass *all laws necessary and proper for abolishing all badges and incidents of slavery in the United States.*" Ibid. (Emphasis added.)

Those who opposed passage of the Civil Rights Act of 1866 argued in effect that the Thirteenth Amendment merely authorized Congress to dissolve the legal bond by which the Negro slave was held to his master. Yet [the] majority leaders in Congress—who were, after all, the authors of the Thirteenth Amendment—had no doubt that its Enabling Clause contemplated the sort of positive legislation that was embodied in the 1866 Civil Rights Act. * * * Surely Congress has the power under the Thirteenth Amendment rationally to determine what are the badges and the incidents of slavery, and the authority to translate that determination into effective legislation. Nor can we say that the determination Congress has made is an irrational one. For this Court recognized long ago that, whatever else they may have encompassed, the badges and incidents of slavery—its "burdens and disabilities"—included restraints upon "those fundamental rights which are the essence of civil freedom, namely the same right [to] inherit, purchase, lease, sell and convey property, as is enjoyed by white citizens." *Civil Rights Cases.* Just as the Black Codes, enacted after the Civil War to restrict the free exercise of those rights, were substitutes for the slave system, so the exclusion of Negroes from white communities became a substitute for the Black Codes. And when racial discrimination herds men into ghettos and makes their ability to buy property turn on the color of their skin, then it too is a relic of slavery.

[At] the very least, the freedom that Congress is empowered to secure under the Thirteenth Amendment includes the freedom to buy whatever a white man can buy, the right to live wherever a white man can live. If Congress cannot say that being a free man means at least this much, then the Thirteenth Amendment made a promise the Nation cannot keep. * * *

Reversed.

JUSTICE HARLAN, whom JUSTICE WHITE joins, dissenting.

[In a lengthy opinion, Harlan, J., relied on statements in prior Supreme Court opinions, the use of the word "right" in § 1982, the legislative history and debates of the Civil Rights Act of 1866 and of companion legislation, and on the ethics of the times to demonstrate that the Court's construction of § 1982 was "open to the most serious doubt" if not "wholly untenable."][b]

RUNYON v. McCRARY, 427 U.S. 160, 96 S.Ct. 2586, 49 L.Ed.2d 415 (1976), per Stewart, J., relying on *Mayer's* interpretation of § 1982, held that § 1981, which guarantees equality in respect to contract rights, prohibits private schools—that were operated commercially and open to the public in that they engaged in general advertising to attract students—from refusing to accept blacks. POWELL, J., joined the opinion, but added that "choices, including those involved in entering into a contract, that are 'private' in the sense that they are not part of a commercial relationship offered generally or widely, and that reflect the selectivity exercised by an individual entering into a personal relationship, certainly were never intended to be restricted by" § 1981. Stevens, J., joined the Court's opinion, feeling bound by, but disagreeing with, the statutory

a. For discussion of the use of judicial power under § 1 of the amendment, see fn. b, p. 1204 supra.

b. The concurring opinion of Douglas, J., is omitted.

interpretation in *Mayer.* White, J., joined by Rehnquist, J., dissented on grounds of statutory interpretation.

Notes and Questions

1. *Scope of §§ 1982 and 1981.* (a) What other discriminations against blacks are presently prohibited by these provisions? Consider Henkin, *On Drawing Lines,* 82 Harv.L.Rev. 63, 85–86 (1968): "Will no bequest stand up which includes a racial discrimination since that would deprive Negroes of 'the same right [to] inherit'? Has there been an easier answer to [Senator Bacon's] will all this time while the Court struggled with theories of state action to find escape from his discrimination [see *Evans v. Newton* and *Evans v. Abney,* pp. 1209, 1225 supra.]? Indeed, does not the Court's reading render superfluous the Civil Rights Act of 1964? Title II of that Act provides that certain places of public accommodations may not discriminate on the basis of race in selling goods and services; the Court's construction of § 1982, when applied to personal property, renders the title (and its limitations) superfluous. Moreover, by the Court's technique of construction, the right 'to make and enforce contracts' guaranteed by [§ 1981] should prevent a restaurant or hotel management from refusing on grounds of race to 'make a contract' for service with a Negro. Indeed, that construction should prevent any employer from refusing 'to make a contract' of employment with a Negro; and the fair employment provisions of the 1964 Act likewise become superfluous, as does the entire struggle, since the days of the New Deal, to enact adequate fair employment legislation." [c]

(b) *Constitutionality.* Are the above racial discriminations "badges and incidents of slavery"? What of the practice by sellers of certain goods or services of charging blacks higher prices? See Note, *Discriminatory Housing Markets, Racial Unconscionability, and Section 1988,* 80 Yale L.J. 516 (1971). Is the initial question inaccurately stated? Do these instances "run the slavery argument into the ground" (*Civil Rights Cases*)?

Does the thirteenth amendment empower Congress to prohibit action that has a racially disproportionate impact, regardless of its purpose? Do §§ 1981–82 do so? See Note, *Section 1981: Discriminatory Purpose or Disproportionate Impact?* 80 Colum.L.Rev. 137 (1980); *Memphis v. Greene,* p. 982 supra.

2. To what extent does *Jones* empower Congress to define the terms of the Civil War amendments? For example, pursuant to § 2 of the thirteenth amendment, may Congress "rationally determine" that discriminations against groups other than blacks are "badges and incidents of slavery"? See *McDonald v. Santa Fe Trail Transp. Co.,* 427 U.S. 273, 96 S.Ct. 2574, 49 L.Ed.2d 493 (1976) ("Congress is authorized under [§ 2] to legislate in regard to 'every race and individual' "). Consider Note, *Jones v. Mayer: The Thirteenth Amendment and the Federal Anti-Discrimination Laws,* 69 Colum.L.Rev. 1019, 1025–26 (1969): "[T]he Court's conclusion that housing discrimination *today* is a badge or incident of slavery is itself a recognition that the 'slavery' referred to in the thirteenth amendment now encompasses the second class citizenship imposed on members of disparate minority groups. By doing so, the Court has implicitly interpreted 'slavery' as the word has come to mean. [A] victim's people need not have been enslaved in order to invoke its protection. He need only be suffering today under conditions that could reasonably be called symptoms of a slave society, inability to raise a family with dignity caused by unemployment, poor

c. Does § 1981 make the result in *Moose Lodge v. Irvis,* p. 1234 supra, incorrect? Or do other constitutional provisions (values) justify the decision?

schools and housing, and lack of a place in the body politic. By removing the time element from badges and incidents of slavery, an aggrieved party need not show a continuous link between his plight and actual slavery in order to benefit from the guarantees of the thirteenth amendment." [e] Compare Note, *The "New" Thirteenth Amendment: A Preliminary Analysis,* 82 Harv.L.Rev. 1294 (1969). Consider Choper, note 1(b) after *Morgan* at 313–14: "*Jones* need not be interpreted as conferring any *definitional* authority on Congress. Rather, it can be persuasively argued on either of two theories that the Court upheld the Civil Rights Act of 1866 as only a *remedial* exercise of Congress's enforcement power under the thirteenth amendment. First, 'slavery' may be regarded as a status to be defined by the Court, [and] the 'badges and incidents of slavery' may be regarded, not as elements of that definition, but as stigmas and disabilities related to slavery. [Thus] to say that Congress may rationally determine the badges and incidents of slavery is nothing more than to say that Congress may prohibit certain practices, although those practices themselves do not constitute slavery, when Congress rationally finds that their prohibition will help to *prevent* slavery.[83] Alternatively, since Congress's power under *Morgan*'s remedial branch encompasses eradicating the *effects* of constitutional violations as well as preventing future ones, the congressional prohibition in *Jones* may be readily sustained as an effort to eliminate the persistent legacies of the past condition of slavery."

3. *Self-executing force of thirteenth amendment.* Apart from federal legislation pursuant to § 2, are any (all) of the discriminations referred to above made unconstitutional by § 1 of "the Amendment *itself*"? If so, by what means should (can) the Court enforce § 1?

e. For the view that *McDonald* strongly supports this approach, see Calhoun, *The Thirteenth and Fourteenth Amendments: Constitutional Authority for Federal Legislation Against Private Sex Discrimination,* 61 Minn. L.Rev. 313 (1977). For criticism of *McDonald,* see Note, *The Thirteenth Amendment and Private Affirmative Action,* 89 Yale L.J. 399 (1979).

83. Engdahl, *Constitutional Power: Federal and State in a Nutshell* 247–48 (1974) (emphasis added).

Chapter 9

LIMITATIONS ON JUDICIAL POWER AND REVIEW

CASE OR CONTROVERSY

I. ADVISORY OPINIONS

MUSKRAT v. UNITED STATES, 219 U.S. 346, 31 S.Ct. 250, 55 L.Ed. 246 (1911): In 1902, Congress made a "final" allotment of lands to certain Cherokee Indians. Subsequent legislation increased the number of allottees. Congress then enacted a statute authorizing four named allottees under the 1902 act to bring suits against the United States in the court of claims with appeal to the Supreme Court, "on their own behalf and on behalf of all other Cherokee citizens" who were allottees under the 1902 act, "to determine the validity of any acts of Congress passed since the said act." For "the speedy disposition of the questions involved" such suits were to be given preference by the courts, and attorneys' fees were to be paid out of tribal funds held by the government if the subsequent legislation were held invalid. Suits were instituted and the court of claims sustained the validity of the subsequent legislation.

The Court, per DAY, J., held that "the jurisdiction conferred" was not "within the power of Congress, having in view the limitations of the judicial power, as established by the Constitution" because "the judicial power is limited to 'cases' and 'controversies.'" Art. III "does not extend the judicial power to every violation of the Constitution which may possibly take place." "By cases and controversies are intended the claims of litigants brought before the courts for determination by such regular proceedings as are established by law or custom for the protection or enforcement of rights, or the prevention, redress, or punishment of wrongs. [The] term implies the existence of present or possible adverse parties, whose contentions are submitted to the court for adjudication."

The Court pointed out that "as early as 1792, an act of Congress" authorized federal courts to decide certain pension claims against the government, subject to revision by the Secretary of War. *Case of Hayburn*, 2 U.S. (2 Dall.) 408, 1 L.Ed. 436 (1792), held that such duties were beyond the judicial power; "by the Constitution, neither the Secretary at War, nor any other executive officer, nor even the legislature, are authorized to sit as a court of errors on the judicial acts or opinions of this court." [a] In 1793, the Court, in response to a request by

a. Consider Currie, *Federal Courts* 9 (4th ed. 1990): "[Such cases are] most easily understood in terms of the independence of the courts. The Constitution protects the judges from indirect pressures on their decisions by guaranteeing them tenure during good behavior at an irreducible salary; to subject their decisions to executive review is a much more

President Washington and Secretary of State Jefferson, declined to offer its advice on "the construction of treaties, laws of nations and laws of the land, which the Secretary said were often presented under circumstances which '*do not give a cognizance of them to the tribunals of the country.*' "

The act in *Muskrat* was found to be nothing more "than an attempt to provide for a judicial determination, final in this court, of the constitutional validity of an act of Congress. [It] is true the United States is made a defendant to this action, but it has no interest adverse to the claimants. The object is not to assert a property right as against the government, or to demand compensation for alleged wrongs because of action upon its part. [The] judgment will not conclude private parties, when actual litigation brings to the court the question of the constitutionality of such legislation. In a legal sense the judgment [amounts] to no more than an expression of opinion upon the validity of the" 1902 act. "If such actions as are here attempted [are] sustained, the result will be that this court, instead of keeping within the limits of judicial power, and deciding cases or controversies arising between opposing parties, [will] be required to give opinions in the nature of advice concerning legislative action,—a function never conferred upon it by the Constitution."

Notes and Questions

1. *Pro's and con's of advisory opinions.* (a) Do you agree with the established principle that bars the Court from advising Congress on the constitutionality of legislation? Consider Note, *Advisory Opinions on the Constitutionality of Statutes,* 69 Harv.L.Rev. 1302, 1305 (1956): "Before it is successfully challenged, an unconstitutional statute may discourage legitimate activity; or, conversely, it may encourage reliance which, when the statute is invalidated, will [cause] injury to those who have based action upon it. Further [there] is frequently an unnecessary expenditure of time and money when the state enacts a statute, invalidates it in lengthy judicial proceedings, and subsequently must enact new legislation; this waste would seem particularly great when the government sets up elaborate machinery to implement a statute later held unconstitutional." See also Note, *The Case for an Advisory Function in the Federal Judiciary,* 50 Geo.L.J. 785, 799 (1962).

(b) Consider Comment, *The Advisory Opinion and the United States Supreme Court,* 5 Ford.L.Rev. 94, 108 (1936): "The advisory opinion, it is said [by Frankfurter, *A Note on Advisory Opinions,* 37 Harv.L.Rev. 1002 (1924)], would distort the entire focus of the judicial function in that it would require the Court to express its judgment on abortive issues without the benefit of all the relevant facts which, in crucial constitutional questions, are the very heart of the case. In addition, the operation of the device would debilitate the creative responsibility of the legislature in that it would tend to induce reliance upon the judiciary, depriving the former of submitting its convictions to the test of trial and error and of accumulating new facts for the vindication of its judgment which, a priori, may run counter to settled legal principles."

direct interference." But, "how far should this principle be carried? Congress, after all, can defeat any money judgment against the United States by failing to vote money to pay it; should the courts therefore refuse to entertain money actions against the Government? Since the President can refuse to enforce judgments against state officers or private litigants, should the courts decline to act at all?" Id. Should the Court refuse to interpret acts of Congress because the Court's decision may be negated by congressional revision? Decline to enforce the terms of executive regulations against executive officers because they may choose to amend or revoke the regulations? See *United States v. Nixon,* p. 210 supra.

(i) As to the "facts" argument, might this be cured by having Congress present the Court with a specific set of facts, real or assumed? Or by having the Court confine its opinion to the statute's application to what it considers the most common set of facts intended to be covered? In how many constitutional cases are the litigated facts crucial?

(ii) As to the "responsibility of the legislature" argument, might this be cured by limiting the advisory opinion to statutes fully considered and already passed by Congress? [a] Is there *any* answer to the point that the cumulative experience of a statute's operation may shed great light on its constitutionality? If not, is this sufficient to sustain the present advisory opinion practice?

(c) Is the opposition to advisory opinions justified by the necessity for "actual antagonistic assertion of rights by one individual against another"? Consider Note, 69 Harv.L.Rev. 1302, 1309–10 (1956): "Argument in advisory proceedings might in some situations provide more assistance to the court than would argument in a normal adversary proceeding. Representation of diversified interests might provide the justices with a more realistic perspective on the statute than representation of only two parties; and, unlike ordinary litigation where the prosecutor or plaintiff [may] be able to select an opponent with little interest in the proceeding or one who is peculiarly culpable, the parties seeking to appear will generally be strong antagonists."

(d) Consider Note, *Judicial Determinations in Nonadversary Proceedings,* 72 Harv.L.Rev. 723, 724 (1959): "The requirement that a specific injury have been suffered or that the danger of such injury be substantial [probably] has its basis, at least partially, in the belief that the respect in which the courts are held varies with the restraint exercised in deciding only the most critical questions." Is this "belief" founded on the premise that the Court's ability to preserve constitutional values is limited and should be reserved for situations in which it is absolutely necessary? If so, may occasions for some advisory opinions present such a necessity? Or should the enactments of popularly elected representatives be invalidated by a Court of lifetime appointees only when injury is imminent? Even when the popularly elected representatives request the Court's advice? Even when they believe that the withholding of such advice may produce very grave injuries?

2. *Mootness.* (a) Is the principle that "moot cases [are] beyond the judicial power" simply an application of the bar against advisory opinions? That "there is no case or controversy once the matter has been resolved"? Wright, *Federal Courts* 55 (4th ed. 1983). Or is the doctrine merely a judicially created rule for judicial economy? Of what significance is the point in litigation at which a case becomes moot? Compare the opinions of Rehnquist, C.J., and Scalia, J., in *Honig v. Doe,* 484 U.S. 305, 108 S.Ct. 592, 98 L.Ed.2d 686 (1988). See Note, *Cases Moot on Appeal: A Limit on the Judicial Power,* 103 U.Pa.L.Rev. 772 (1955).

(b) In DE FUNIS v. ODEGAARD, p. 1008 supra, petitioner was admitted to the University of Washington Law School after a state trial court had sustained his claim that the school's special admissions policy violated equal protection. The Washington supreme court reversed but its judgment was stayed. By the time the case was argued in the Supreme Court, petitioner had registered for the final term of his third year. Although the school stated that if its admissions

a. The Voting Rights Act Amendments of 1970, some of which were not to take effect until elections held in 1971, became law on June 22, 1970. Motions for leave to file suits within the Court's original jurisdiction, involving four states challenging the act's constitutionality, were granted on Oct. 6, 1970. The cases were argued on Oct. 19 and decided on Dec. 21, 1970. See *Oregon v. Mitchell,* p. 1281 supra.

policy were upheld, petitioner would be subject to it if he had to register for any additional terms, his present registration "would not be cancelled [regardless] of the outcome of this litigation." The Court, per curiam, held the case moot: "There is a line of decisions in this Court standing for the proposition that the 'voluntary cessation of allegedly illegal conduct does not deprive the tribunal of power to hear and determine the case, i.e., does not make the case moot,'" because "otherwise, 'the defendant is free to return to his old ways' * * *. But mootness in the present case depends not at all upon a 'voluntary cessation' of the admissions practices that were the subject of this litigation. It depends, instead, upon the simple fact that DeFunis is now in the final quarter of the final year of his course of study, and the settled and unchallenged policy of the Law School to permit him to complete the term for which he is now enrolled."

BRENNAN, J., joined by Douglas, White and Marshall, JJ., dissented: "Any number of unexpected events—illness, economic necessity, even academic failure—might prevent his graduation at the end of the term. Were that misfortune to befall, and were petitioner required to register for yet another term, the prospect that he would again face the hurdle of the admissions policy is real * * *.[b] Few constitutional questions in recent history have stirred as much debate, and they will not disappear. [Because] avoidance of repetitious litigation serves the public interest, that inevitability counsels against mootness determinations, as here, not compelled by the record."[c]

4. *Collusiveness.* The Court "will not hear collusive cases.[15] Though the rule is not in terms so confined, it is principally applied in constitutional cases, on the notion that 'it never was the thought that by means of a friendly suit, a party beaten in the legislature could transfer to the courts an inquiry as to the constitutionality of the legislative act.'[16] Even here application of the rule has not always been rigid—some of the most famous constitutional decisions have come in what now seem to have been collusive cases.[17]" Wright, supra, at 56.

II. STANDING AND RIPENESS

INTRODUCTORY NOTE

The doctrines of "standing" and "ripeness" both go to determining whether there is a dispute capable of and suitable for judicial resolution. These two issues frequently overlap, but may roughly be described as concerning (1) *who* may assert certain contentions (the claimant or someone else)—"standing," and (2) *when* (if ever) may these claims be asserted (now or at some subsequent time after other events have occurred)—"ripeness."

Both doctrines relate to whether there is a "case or controversy" under Art. III. But they also implicate "prudential" principles of "judicial self-restraint,"

b. In response to this point, the Court said: "But such speculative contingencies afford no basis for our passing on the substantive issues" in the absence of "evidence that this is a prospect of 'immediacy and reality.'"

c. "In rare instances the power to refrain from deciding moot cases has been used by the Court to avoid decision of an otherwise difficult matter. In [*Atherton Mills v. Johnston,* 259 U.S. 13, 42 S.Ct. 422, 66 L.Ed. 814 (1922), a law was challenged] regulating the labor of youths between the ages of 14 and 16. The Court held the case for two and a half years after argument, and then decided that since the plaintiff was by that time over 16, and no longer affected by the statute, the case was moot." Wright, *Federal Courts* 36 (2d ed. 1970).

15. *Lord v. Veazie,* 1850, 8 How. 251, 12 L.Ed. 1067.

16. *Chicago & G.T. Ry. Co. v. Wellman.* See also *U.S. v. Johnson,* 319 U.S. 302, 63 S.Ct. 1075, 87 L.Ed. 1413 (1943).

17. E.g., *Fletcher v. Peck,* [p. 68 supra]; *Dred Scott v. Sandford,* [discussed in *Plessy v. Ferguson,* p. 955 supra.

some perspective on which may be found in the following statement of the Court, per RUTLEDGE, J., in RESCUE ARMY v. MUNICIPAL COURT, 331 U.S. 549, 67 S.Ct. 1409, 91 L.Ed. 1666 (1947):

"[T]his Court has followed a policy of strict necessity in disposing of constitutional issues [which] has not been limited to jurisdictional determinations. For, in addition, 'the Court [has] developed, for its own governance in the cases confessedly within its jurisdiction, a series of rules under which it has avoided passing upon a large part of all the constitutional questions pressed upon it for decision.' [31] [Thus], constitutional issues affecting legislation will not be determined in friendly, non-adversary proceedings; in advance of the necessity of deciding them; in broader terms than are required by the precise facts to which the ruling is to be applied; if the record presents some other ground upon which the case may be disposed of; at the instance of one who fails to show that he is injured by the statute's operation, or who has availed himself of its [benefits].[a]

"[E]very application has been an instance of reluctance, indeed of refusal, to undertake the most important and the most delicate of the Court's [functions].

"Indeed in origin and in practical effects, though not in technical function, it is a corollary offshoot of the case and controversy rule. And often the line between applying the policy or the rule is very thin.[37] * * *

"The policy's ultimate foundations, some if not all of which also sustain the jurisdictional limitation, [are] found in the delicacy of that function, particularly in view of possible consequences for others stemming also from constitutional roots; the comparative finality of those consequences; the consideration due to the judgment of other repositories of constitutional power concerning the scope of their authority; the necessity, if government is to function constitutionally, for each to keep within its power, including the courts; the inherent limitations of the judicial process, arising especially from its largely negative character and limited resources of enforcement; withal in the paramount importance of constitutional adjudication in our system.

"[Its] execution has involved a continuous choice between the obvious advantages it produces [and] the very real disadvantages, for the assurance of rights, which deferring decision very often entails.[b] On the other hand it is not altogether speculative that a contrary policy of accelerated decision, might do equal or greater harm for the security of private rights * * *. For premature and relatively abstract decision, which such a policy would be most likely to promote, have their part too in rendering rights uncertain and insecure.

"* * * Time and experience [have] verified for both that the choice was wisely made. Any other indeed might have put an end to or seriously impaired

31. Brandeis, J., with whom Stone, Roberts and Cardozo, JJ., concurred in *Ashwander v. TVA*, 297 U.S. 288, concurring opinion at 346, 56 S.Ct. 466, 482, 80 L.Ed. 688.

a. One of the rules set forth by Brandeis, J., in *Ashwander* was that "when the validity of an act of the Congress is drawn in question, and even if a serious doubt of constitutionality is raised, it is a cardinal principle that this Court will first ascertain whether a construction of the statute is fairly possible by which the question may be avoided." For illustrations of this technique, see *Yates v. United States*, p. 408 supra; *Jones v. Alfred H. Mayer Co.*, p. 1289 supra. But compare *Marbury v. Madison*, p. 1 supra; *United States v. Robel*, p. 734 supra.

37. Indeed more than once the policy has been applied in order to avoid the necessity of deciding the "case or controversy" jurisdictional question, when constitutional issues were at stake on the merits * * *.

b. "Whether 'justiciability' exists, therefore, has most often turned on evaluating both the appropriateness of the issues for decision by courts and the hardship of denying judicial relief." Frankfurter, J., concurring in *Joint Anti-Fascist Refugee Committee v. McGrath*, 341 U.S. 123, 71 S.Ct. 624, 95 L.Ed. 817 (1951).

the distinctively American institution of judicial review.[38] " [c]

A. INJURY REQUIRED FOR STANDING; SUITS BY TAXPAYERS AND CITIZENS

In FROTHINGHAM v. MELLON, 262 U.S. 447, 43 S.Ct. 597, 67 L.Ed. 1078 (1923), a federal taxpayer contended that a federal statute providing funds to states undertaking programs to reduce maternal and infant mortality exceeded Congress' power, and "that the effect of the appropriations complained of will be to increase the burden of future taxation and thereby take her property without due process of law." The Court, per SUTHERLAND, J., dismissed "for want of jurisdiction." "The interest of a taxpayer of a municipality in the application of its moneys is direct and immediate and the remedy by injunction to prevent their misuse is not inappropriate." But a federal taxpayer's "interest in the moneys of the treasury [is] shared with millions of others, is comparatively minute and indeterminable, and the effect upon future taxation, of any payment out of the funds, so remote, fluctuating and uncertain, that no basis is afforded for an appeal to the preventive powers of a court of equity." [a] To permit such suits might result in attacks on "every other appropriation act and statute whose administration requires the outlay of public money * * *. The bare suggestion of such a result, with its attendant inconveniences, goes far to sustain the conclusion which we have reached, that a suit of this character cannot be maintained." A person asking the Court to hold a federal act unconstitutional "must be able to show, not only that the statute is invalid, but that he has sustained or is immediately in danger of sustaining some direct injury as the result of its enforcement, and not merely that he suffers in some indefinite way in common with people generally." Here, the complaint "is merely that [federal officials] will execute an act of Congress asserted to be unconstitutional; and this we are asked to prevent. To do so would be, not to decide a judicial controversy, but to assume a position of authority over the governmental acts of another and coequal department, an authority which plainly we do not possess."

In DOREMUS v. BOARD OF EDUC., 342 U.S. 429, 72 S.Ct. 394, 96 L.Ed. 475 (1952), a state court had held that Bible-reading in public schools was not an establishment of religion. The Court, per JACKSON, J., dismissed the appeal: Although municipal taxpayers have standing to enjoin "a measurable appropriation or disbursement of [municipal] funds occasioned solely by the activities complained of," there "is no allegation that this activity is supported by any

38. It is not without significance for the policy's validity that the periods when the power has been exercised most readily and broadly have been the ones in which this Court and the institution of judicial review have had their stormiest experiences. See e.g., Brant, *Storm Over the Constitution* (1936).

c. Consider Tribe, *American Constitutional Law* 110 (2d ed. 1988): "The Court's current formulation presents one aspect of the continuing debate over whether federal courts exist primarily to resolve concrete disputes among individual litigants, with the power to make constitutional decisions only a necessary incident to this role, or whether federal courts have a special responsibility, as the branch of government best able to develop a coherent interpretation of the Constitution, to engage in the exposition of constitutional norms, limited primarily by the requirement that they do so in the context of reasonably concrete disputes presented to them for review." See generally Bandes, *The Idea of a Case,* 42 Stan. L.Rev. 227 (1990).

a. *ASARCO Inc. v. Kadish,* 490 U.S. 605, 109 S.Ct. 2037, 104 L.Ed.2d 696 (1989), per Kennedy, J., held that the exception from the *Frothingham* rule for municipal taxpayers does not apply to state taxpayers: "we have refused to confer standing upon a state taxpayer absent a showing of 'direct injury,' pecuniary or otherwise." Brennan, J., joined by White, Marshall and Blackmun, JJ., did not join this part of the Court's opinion.

separate tax or paid for from any particular appropriation or that it adds any sum whatever to the cost of conducting the school." Although state courts may render advisory opinions on federal constitutional questions, "because our own jurisdiction is cast in terms of 'case or controversy,' we cannot * * *. The taxpayer's action can meet this test, but only when it is a good-faith pocketbook action." [b]

DOUGLAS, J., joined by Reed and Burton, JJ. dissented: "There is no group more interested in [the] public schools than the taxpayers who support them and the parents whose children attend them. [W]here the clash of interests is as real and as strong as it is here, it is odd indeed to hold there is no case or controversy within the meaning of art. III."

FLAST v. COHEN

392 U.S. 83, 88 S.Ct. 1942, 20 L.Ed.2d 947 (1968).

CHIEF JUSTICE WARREN delivered the opinion of the Court.

[As federal taxpayers, appellants sought to enjoin federal expenditures for parochial schools, alleging violation of the religion clauses of the first amendment. A three-judge federal court held that under *Frothingham* appellants lacked standing.]

The jurisdiction of federal courts is defined and limited by [Art. III]. Embodied in the words "cases" and "controversies" are two complementary but somewhat different limitations. In part those words limit the business of federal courts to questions presented in an adversary context and in a form historically viewed as capable of resolution through the judicial process. And in part those words define the role assigned to the judiciary in a tripartite allocation of power to assure that the federal courts will not intrude into areas committed to the other branches of government. Justiciability is the term of art employed to give expression to this dual limitation * * *.

[T]he Government's position is that the constitutional scheme of separation of powers, and the deference owed by the federal judiciary to the other two branches of government within that scheme, presents an absolute bar to taxpayer suits challenging the validity of federal spending programs.[17]

b. Consider Freund in *Supreme Court & Supreme Law* 35 (Cahn ed. 1954): "I think it is a needed change to make standing to raise a federal constitutional question, itself a federal question, so that it will be decided uniformly throughout the country. I disagree with *Doremus* in so far as it lets the state judgment stand and merely declines review. [T]he Court should have [held that] the petition should stand dismissed in the state court and the decree vacated so that it would not be a precedent even in the state court." Does *Doremus* "let the state judgment stand and merely decline review"? What action would the Court have taken if the New Jersey court had found the statute violative of the first amendment? See Tribe, *American Constitutional Law* 114 n. 20 (2d ed. 1988). See *Asarco Inc. v. Kadish* (Court has no jurisdiction to review state judgment under such circumstances).

See generally Murphy, *Supreme Court Review of Abstract State Court Decisions on Federal Law: A Justiciability Analysis,* 25 St.L.U. L.J. 473 (1981).

17. The logic of the Government's argument would compel it to concede that a taxpayer would lack standing even if Congress engaged in such palpably unconstitutional conduct as providing funds for the construction of churches for particular sects. The Government [contends] there might be individuals in society other than taxpayers who could invoke federal judicial power to challenge such unconstitutional appropriations. However, if as we conclude there are circumstances under which a taxpayer will be a proper and appropriate party to seek judicial review of federal statutes, the taxpayer's access to federal courts should not be barred because there might be at large in society a hypothetical plaintiff who might possibly bring such a suit.

Standing is an aspect of justiciability [and] there are at work in the standing doctrine the many subtle pressures which tend to cause policy considerations to blend into constitutional limitations. [The] fundamental aspect of standing is that it focuses on the party seeking to get his complaint before a federal court and not on the issues he wishes to have adjudicated. The "gist of the question of standing" is whether the party seeking relief has "alleged such a personal stake in the outcome of the controversy as to assure that concrete adverseness which sharpens the presentation of issues upon which the court so largely depends for illumination of difficult constitutional questions." *Baker v. Carr,* [p. 31 supra]. In other words, when standing is placed in issue in a case, the question is whether the person whose standing is challenged is a proper party to request an adjudication of a particular issue and not whether the issue itself is justiciable. Thus, a party may have standing in a particular case, but the federal court may nevertheless decline to pass on the merits of the case because, for example, it presents a political question. [The] question whether a particular person is a proper party to maintain the action does not, by its own force, raise separation of powers problems related to improper judicial interference in areas committed to other branches of the Federal Government. Such problems arise, if at all, only from the substantive issues the individual seeks to have adjudicated. Thus, in terms of Article III limitations on federal court jurisdiction, the question of standing is related only to whether the dispute sought to be adjudicated will be presented in an adversary context and in a form historically viewed as capable of judicial resolution. [A] taxpayer may or may not have the requisite personal stake in the outcome, depending upon the circumstances of the particular case. [I]n ruling on standing, it is both appropriate and necessary to look to the substantive issues [to] determine whether there is a logical nexus between the status asserted and the claim sought to be adjudicated [to] assure that [the litigant] is a proper and appropriate party to invoke federal judicial power [so as] to satisfy Article III requirements.

The nexus demanded of federal taxpayers has two aspects to it. First, the taxpayer must establish a logical link between that status and the type of legislative enactment attacked. Thus, a taxpayer will be a proper party to allege the unconstitutionality only of exercises of congressional power under the taxing and spending clause of Art. I, § 8, of the Constitution. It will not be sufficient to allege an incidental expenditure of tax funds in the administration of an essentially regulatory statute. This requirement is consistent with the limitation imposed upon state taxpayer standing in federal courts in *Doremus.* Secondly, the taxpayer must establish a nexus between that status and the precise nature of the constitutional infringement alleged. Under this requirement, the taxpayer must show that the challenged enactment exceeds specific constitutional limitations imposed upon the exercise of the congressional taxing and spending power and not simply that the enactment is generally beyond the powers delegated to Congress by Art. I, § 8. * * *

The taxpayer-appellants in this case have satisfied both nexuses * * *. Their constitutional challenge is made to an exercise by Congress of its power under Art. I, § 8, to spend for the general welfare, and the challenged program involves a substantial expenditure of federal tax funds. In addition, appellants have alleged that the challenged expenditures violate the Establishment and Free Exercise Clauses of the First Amendment. Our history vividly illustrates that one of the specific evils feared by those who drafted the Establishment Clause [was] that the taxing and spending power would be used to favor one religion over another or to support religion in general [and] that religious liberty ultimately would be the victim * * *. [T]hat clause of the First Amendment operates as a specific constitutional limitation upon the exercise by Congress of the taxing and spending power conferred by Art. I, § 8.

[The] taxpayer in *Frothingham* attacked a federal spending program and she, therefore, established the first nexus required. However, [she] alleged essentially that Congress, by enacting the challenged statute, had exceeded the general powers delegated to it by Art. I, § 8, and that Congress had thereby invaded the legislative province reserved to the States by the Tenth Amendment. To be sure, Mrs. Frothingham made the additional allegation that her tax liability would be increased as a result of the allegedly unconstitutional enactment, and she framed that allegation in terms of a deprivation of property without due process of law. However, the Due Process Clause of the Fifth Amendment does not protect taxpayers against increases in tax liability * * *. In essence, Mrs. Frothingham was attempting to assert the States' interest in their legislative prerogatives and not a federal taxpayer's interest in being free of taxing and spending in contravention of specific constitutional limitations imposed upon Congress' taxing and spending power.

We have noted that the Establishment Clause of the First Amendment does specifically limit the taxing and spending power conferred by Art. I, § 8. Whether the Constitution contains other specific limitations can be determined only in the context of future cases. [Under] such circumstances, we feel confident that the questions will be framed with the necessary specificity, that the issues will be contested with the necessary adverseness and that the litigation will be pursued with the necessary vigor to assure that the constitutional challenge will be made in a form traditionally thought to be capable of judicial resolution. We lack that confidence in cases such as *Frothingham* where a taxpayer seeks to employ a federal court as a forum in which to air his generalized grievances about the conduct of government or the allocation of power in the Federal System. * * *

Reversed.

JUSTICE DOUGLAS [who joined the Court's opinion], concurring. * * *

There has long been a school of thought here that the less the judiciary does, the better. It is often said that judicial intrusion should be infrequent, [but the] judiciary is an indispensable part of the operation of our federal system. With the growing complexities of government it is often the one and only place where effective relief can be obtained, [and] where wrongs to individuals are done by violation of specific guarantees, it is abdication for courts to close their [doors].

JUSTICE STEWART [who joined the Court's opinion], concurring.

[Because the Establishment Clause] plainly prohibits taxing and spending in aid of religion, every taxpayer can claim a personal constitutional right not to be taxed for the support of a religious institution. The present case is thus readily distinguishable from *Frothingham* * * *.[a]

JUSTICE HARLAN, dissenting.

[F]ederal taxpayers may, as taxpayers, contest the constitutionality of tax obligations imposed severally upon them by federal statute. Such a challenge may be made by way of defense to an action by the United States to recover the amount of a challenged tax debt, or to a prosecution for willful failure to pay [the tax].

a. The concurring opinion of Fortas, J., is omitted.

The lawsuits here and in *Frothingham* are fundamentally different. They present the question whether federal taxpayers qua taxpayers may, in suits in which they do not contest the validity of their previous or existing tax obligations, challenge the constitutionality of the uses for which Congress has authorized the expenditure of public funds. [The] relief available to such a plaintiff consists entirely of the vindication of rights held in common by all citizens. * * *

Surely it is plain that the rights and interests of taxpayers who contest the constitutionality of public expenditures are markedly different from those of "Hohfeldian" plaintiffs,[5] including those taxpayer-plaintiffs who challenge the validity of their own tax liabilities. We must recognize that these non-Hohfeldian plaintiffs complain [not] as taxpayers, but as "private attorneys-general." [These are] "public actions" brought to vindicate public rights.[7]

It does not, however, follow that suits brought by non-Hohfeldian plaintiffs are excluded by the "case or controversy" clause of [Art. III]. This and other federal courts have repeatedly held that individual litigants, acting as private attorneys-general, may have standing as "representatives of the public interest." *Scripps-Howard Radio v. FCC,* 316 U.S. 4, 15, 62 S.Ct. 875, 882, 86 L.Ed. 1229. See also *Associated Industries v. Ickes,* 134 F.2d 694 * * *.[b]

The Court's analysis consists principally of the observation that the requirements of standing are met if a taxpayer has the "requisite personal stake in the outcome" of his suit. [The] Court implements this standard with the declaration that taxpayers will be "deemed" to have the necessary personal interest if their suits satisfy two [criteria]. The difficulties with these criteria [are] that they are not in any sense a measurement of any plaintiff's interest in the outcome of any [suit.]

It is surely clear that a plaintiff's interest in the outcome of a suit in which he challenges the constitutionality of a federal expenditure is not made greater or smaller by the unconnected fact that the expenditure is, or is not, "incidental" to an "essentially regulatory program." * * * Presumably the Court does not believe that regulatory programs are necessarily less destructive of First Amendment rights, or that regulatory programs are necessarily less prodigal of public

5. The phrase is Professor Jaffe's, adopted, of course, from W. Hohfeld, *Fundamental Legal Conceptions* (1923). I have here employed the phrases "Hohfeldian" and "non-Hohfeldian" plaintiffs to mark the distinction between the personal and proprietary interests of the traditional plaintiff, and the representative and public interests of the plaintiff in a public action. * * *

7. Jaffe, *Judicial Control of Administrative Action* 483 (1965).

b. *Scripps-Howard* held that the Communications Act conferred standing on a radio station, as a "person aggrieved," to contest the FCC's grant of a license to an additional station: "The purpose of the Act was to protect the public interest in communications. [T]hese private litigants have standing [as] representatives of the public interest." Consider Jaffe, *Standing to Secure Judicial Review: Public Actions,* 74 Harv.L.Rev. 1265, 1314 (1961): "It might be argued that whatever the purported rationale [of] *Scripps-Howard,* a decision upholding the justiciability of a suit brought by a person of a very limited class which is in fact adversely affected is not a precedent for permitting actions by the unlimited class of citizen or taxpayer. But in *Associated Industries,* Judge Frank, following what he believed to be the rationale of [*Scripps-Howard*], did apply it to a consumer, a member of a class which is coterminous with the entire human population [and] characterized the appellant as a 'private Attorney General.' " Nonetheless, argues Davis, *Standing: Taxpayers and Others,* 35 U.Chi.L.Rev. 601, 616 (1968), "I think it entirely clear that the Court has always required 'economic and other personal interests' as the basis for standing, without exception." See his discussion of the cases, id. at 613–17. For the view that "the notion that the constitution demands injury to a personal interest as a prerequisite to attacks on allegedly unconstitutional action is historically unfounded," see Berger, *Standing to Sue in the Public Actions: Is it a Constitutional Requirement?* 78 Yale L.J. 816 (1969).

The issue of congressionally authorized standing is considered in this Part infra.

funds than are grants-in-aid, for both these general propositions are demonstrably false. * * *

The Court's second criterion is similarly unrelated to its standard for the determination of standing. The intensity of a plaintiff's interest in a suit is not measured, even obliquely, by the fact that the constitutional provision under which he claims is, or is not, a "specific limitation" upon Congress' spending powers. * * *

Although the Court does not altogether explain its position, the essence of its reasoning is evidently that a taxpayer's claim under the Establishment Clause is "not merely one of ultra vires," but instead asserts "an abridgment of individual religious liberty" * * *. Choper, *The Establishment Clause and Aid to Parochial Schools,* 56 Calif.L.Rev. 260, 276. [But] the Court has not adduced, historical evidence that properly permits the Court to distinguish, as it has here, among the Establishment Clause, the Tenth Amendment and the Due Process Clause of the Fifth Amendment as limitations upon Congress' taxing and spending powers. * * * [18]

[This] Court has previously held that individual litigants have standing to represent the public interest, despite their lack of economic or other personal interests, if Congress has appropriately authorized such suits.[c] I would adhere to that principle. Any hazards to the proper allocation of authority among the three branches of the Government would be substantially diminished if public actions had been pertinently authorized by Congress and the President. * * *

Notes and Questions

1. *The first nexus.* (a) After *Flast,* may a federal taxpayer challenge the issuance of a "commemorative Christmas postage stamp" as violating the establishment clause? Assuming the issuance "involves a substantial expenditure of federal tax funds," does it concern an "exercise of congressional power under the taxing and spending clause" or is it merely an "incidental expenditure of tax funds in the administration of an essentially regulatory" program? *Should* this question be relevant to the taxpayer's standing? Consider 82 Harv.L.Rev. 230 (1968): "If a governmental regulation does violate the establishment clause, a taxpayer would sustain a special injury to conscience by the expenditure of any revenues under the regulatory scheme. Therefore, taxpayers could be designated as properly adverse article III parties to sue to vindicate the public interest. But governmental regulatory action will usually encroach on the legally protected interests of a significant portion of the citizenry as well. Thus there is no justification for concluding that the establishment clause itself should be said to designate a special injury class of litigants as proper parties to challenge this category of governmental conduct." Is this analysis consistent with *Flast's* fn. 17?

(b) *The "pocketbook" injury requirement.* On the likely assumption that if this particular stamp is not issued some other one will be, does this activity—like

18. I have equal difficulty with the argument that the religious clauses of the First Amendment create a "personal constitutional right," held by all *citizens,* such that any *citizen* may, under those clauses, contest the constitutionality of federal expenditures. The essence of the argument would presumably be that freedom from establishment is a right that inheres in every citizen * * *. The Establishment Clause is, after all, only one of many provisions of the Constitution that might be characterized in this fashion. [I]t might even be urged that the Ninth and Tenth Amendments, since they are largely confirmatory of rights created elsewhere in the Constitution, were intended to declare the standing of individual citizens to contest the validity of governmental activities. * * *

c. See fn. b supra.

that in *Doremus*—not "add any sum whatever to the cost of conducting" the postal system? If so, is the establishment clause evil nonetheless present because the stamp issuance "involves a substantial expenditure of tax funds" allegedly "to favor one religion over another"? If the school authorities in *Doremus* had annually expended $100 ($10) for the purchase of Bibles, would "appellants [have] established the requisite special injury necessary to a taxpayer's case or controversy"? See Davis, *Standing: Taxpayers and Others,* 35 U.Chi. L.Rev. 601 (1968). Or may it be said that the Bible-reading resulted in the public school being "used to favor one religion over another or to support religion in general" and thus the "substantial expenditure of tax funds" for general operation of the schools was allegedly violative of the establishment clause? Should there be taxpayer standing in both cases? Do the above queries lead to the conclusion that in all these cases taxpayers are "non-Hohfeldian plaintiffs [suing] to vindicate public rights"?

2. *The second nexus.* Does *Flast* find *Frothingham* distinguishable because the different "substantive issues" involved make Flast but not Frothingham an "appropriate party [as a taxpayer] to invoke federal judicial power," i.e., Frothingham was attempting to assert the States' interest in their legislative prerogatives" whereas (as phrased by Stewart, J.) Flast was asserting "a personal constitutional right not to be taxed for the support of a religious institution"? That Flast did—but Frothingham did *not*—allegedly suffer a constitutionally prohibited injury?

Does Harlan, J., effectively refute the position that federal taxpayers hold a "personal constitutional right" under the establishment clause? If this "right" is *not to have money collected from the individual by taxation expended for religion by government,* is its existence denied by the fact that a suit to enjoin expenditures does not allege "that the contested expenditures will in any fashion affect the amount of the taxpayers' own existing or foreseeable tax obligations"?

Do all of these analyses speak to the merits rather than standing?

CONGRESSIONAL POWER TO CREATE STANDING

SIERRA CLUB v. MORTON, 405 U.S. 727, 92 S.Ct. 1361, 31 L.Ed.2d 636 (1972): A membership corporation with "a special interest in the conservation and sound maintenance of the national parks," relied on Administrative Procedure Act § 10 (authorizing judicial review by persons "suffering legal wrong" or "adversely affected or aggrieved") as permitting it, as a "representative of the public," to challenge construction of a recreation area in a national forest as violative of federal statutes for preservation of national parks, etc. The Court, per STEWART, J., denied standing: "[Where] Congress has authorized public officials to perform certain functions according to law, and has provided by statute for judicial review of those actions under certain circumstances, the inquiry as to standing must begin with a determination of whether the statute in question authorizes review at the behest of the plaintiff.[3] * * *

"The trend of cases arising under the APA and other statutes authorizing judicial review of federal agency action has been towards recognizing that injuries other than economic harm are sufficient to bring a person within the meaning of the statutory language, and towards discarding the notion that an injury that is widely shared is ipso facto not an injury sufficient to provide the basis for judicial review. We noted this development with approval in [*Associa-*

3. [W]here a dispute is otherwise justiciable, the question whether the litigant is a "proper party to request an adjudication of a particular issue," is one within the power of Congress to determine.

tion of Data Processing Service Organizations, Inc. v. Camp, 397 U.S. 150, 90 S.Ct. 827, 25 L.Ed.2d 184 (1970)] in saying that the interest alleged to have been injured 'may reflect "aesthetic, conservational, and recreational" as well as economic values.' But broadening the categories of injury that may be alleged in support of standing is a different matter from abandoning the requirement that the party seeking review must have himself suffered an injury." Here, "the Sierra Club failed to allege that it or its members [use the site in the national forest] for any purpose, much less that they use it in any way that would be significantly affected by the proposed" construction.[a]

TRAFFICANTE v. METROPOLITAN LIFE INS. CO., 409 U.S. 205, 93 S.Ct. 364, 34 L.Ed.2d 415 (1972), per DOUGLAS, J., held that tenants of an apartment complex had standing to complain that the owner racially discriminated in renting in violation of the Civil Rights Act of 1968. The Act gave "persons aggrieved" the right to sue—defined as "any person who claims to have been injured by a discriminatory housing practice." The tenants "claimed they had been injured in that (1) they had lost the social benefits of living in an integrated community; (2) they had missed business and professional advantages which would have accrued if they had lived with members of minority groups; (3) they had suffered embarrassment and economic damage in social, business, and professional activities from being 'stigmatized' as residents of a 'white ghetto.' "

Observing that "the role of 'private attorneys general' is not uncommon in modern legislative programs," the Court found that "the language of the Act is broad and inclusive" and "concluded that the words used showed 'a congressional intention to define standing as broadly as is permitted by [Art. III].' Individual injury or injury in fact to petitioners, the ingredient found missing in *Sierra Club,* is alleged here."[b]

UNITED STATES v. SCRAP, 412 U.S. 669, 93 S.Ct. 2405, 37 L.Ed.2d 254 (1973), per STEWART, J., held that appellee environmental groups, who challenged the ICC's failure to suspend a surcharge on railroad freight rates as violative of the ICC's statutory duties, had standing as persons "adversely affected or aggrieved" under the APA. Appellees alleged "that their members used the forests, streams, mountains, and other resources in the Washington metropolitan area for camping, hiking, fishing, and sightseeing." The Court was willing to follow an "attenuated line of causation to the eventual injury of which the appellees complained—a general rate increase would allegedly cause increased use of nonrecyclable commodities as compared to recyclable goods, thus resulting in the need to use more natural resources to produce such goods, some of which resources might be taken from the Washington area, and resulting in more refuse that might be discarded in national parks in the Washington area."

a. Douglas, J., dissented, contending for standing "in the name of the inanimate object about to be despoiled, defaced or invaded by roads and bulldozers and where injury is the subject of public outrage." (See C. Stone, *Should Trees Have Standing?—Toward Legal Rights for Natural Objects,* 45 So.Cal.L.Rev. 450 (1972)). Blackmun, J. dissented, calling (with Brennan, J.) for "an imaginative expansion of our traditional concepts of standing in order to enable an organization such as the Sierra Club, possessed, as it is, of pertinent, bona-fide and well-recognized attributes and purposes in the area of environment, to litigate environmental issues." (See Sedler, *Standing, Justiciability and All That: A Behavioral Analysis,* 25 Vand.L.Rev. 479 (1973)). Powell and Rehnquist, JJ., did not participate.

The Sierra Club subsequently amended its complaint and obtained standing by alleging its members' use of the national forest.

b. See also *Gladstone, Realtors v. Bellwood,* 441 U.S. 91, 99 S.Ct. 1601, 60 L.Ed.2d 66 (1979) (standing under Fair Housing Act).

WHITE, J., joined by Burger, C.J. and Rehnquist, J., dissented: "The allegations here do not satisfy the threshold requirement of injury in fact [for] a justiciable case or controversy. [T]he alleged injuries are so remote, speculative, and insubstantial" as to "no more qualify these appellees to litigate than allegations of a taxpayer that governmental expenditures will increase his taxes and have an impact on his pocketbook, or allegations that governmental decisions are offensive to reason or morals. [If] they are sufficient here, we are well on our way to permitting citizens at large to litigate any decisions of the Government which fall in an area of interest to them and with which they disagree."

Notes and Questions

1. *The cases' rationale.* Do *Sierra Club, Trafficante* and *SCRAP* establish that a litigant must have suffered "injury in fact" to satisfy the case-or-controversy requirement? Or does the Court's definition of "individual injury" in these cases in reality permit "citizens at large to litigate"? Consider Albert, *Standing to Challenge Administrative Action: An Inadequate Surrogate Claim for Relief,* 83 Yale L.J. 425, 489 (1974): "The interests of consumers and environmentalists, while held in common with many, are plainly not equivalent to a citizen's interest in good government. To the contrary, such interests, going to matters that affect the quality of life, leisure, and health, are as tangible and palpable as the typical fare for adjudication. People are injured in real and recognizable ways when action despoiling parks and woodlands is authorized, when a licensee with a poor or discriminatory broadcasting record is renewed, or when an agency fails to act upon unsafe regulated products. [If] litigants presenting these claims, as in *Sierra Club,* do not show injury to themselves from government action, Article III is a barrier. But there is nothing inherent in the nature of the interests or their shared character that raises problems under Article III."

2. *Congressional power and Art. III.* After *Frothingham,* could Congress authorize suit by *any* taxpayer to test the constitutionality of the Maternity Act? *Any* citizen? [c] What was the view of Harlan, J., in *Flast*? Would "such individuals demonstrate the necessary stake in the outcome to satisfy Article III requirements"? How could they if *Frothingham* did not present a "judicial controversy"? Do they suffer greater "injury in fact" than a federal officer who brings a criminal prosecution, or a civil action to enforce regulatory prohibitions, against a private individual? See Sedler, *Standing and the Burger Court: An Analysis and Some Proposals for Legislative Reform,* 30 Rutg.L.Rev. 863, 881–85 (1977). Consider Jaffe, *The Citizen as Litigant in Public Actions: The Non-Hohfeldian or Ideological Plaintiff,* 116 U.Pa.L.Rev. 1033, 1037–38 (1968): "[T]he very fact of [an "ideological plaintiff"] investing money in a lawsuit from which one is to acquire no further monetary profit argues, to my mind, a quite exceptional kind of interest, and one peculiarly indicative of a desire to say all that can be said in the support of one's contention. From this I would conclude that, insofar as the argument for a traditional plaintiff runs in terms of the need for effective advocacy, the argument is not persuasive." See also Tushnet, *The Sociology of Article III,* 93 Harv.L.Rev. 1698, 1711 (1980): "In a legal system based on precedent, a successful litigant benefits those in the future who can invoke the earlier decision, [yet] the present litigant cannot capture those

c. The Endangered Species Act, 16 U.S.C. § 1540(g), authorizes "any person" to enjoin violations. See *TVA v. Hill,* 437 U.S. 153, 98 S.Ct. 2279, 57 L.Ed.2d 117 (1978).

potential benefits. Thus, as a general proposition, it seems that rational Hohfeldian litigants should underinvest in their litigation. [On the other hand, studies] from the perspective of economics [and] sociology have demonstrated that ["ideological"] litigants who have a continuing interest in the substantive outcomes of litigation, and who have a continuing interest in the development of legal rules favorable to their position, are more likely to invest adequate resources and therefore to succeed in their litigation."

If the "ideological plaintiff" satisfies the case-or-controversy requirement, is there any lawsuit in which plaintiff is not "a proper party to request an adjudication of a particular issue"? Does restriction of standing to "traditional plaintiffs" serve other significant constitutional ends? Should there be standing for "public actions" irrespective of congressional authorization? See note 2 after *Allen v. Wright,* infra.

UNITED STATES v. RICHARDSON, 418 U.S. 166, 94 S.Ct. 2940, 41 L.Ed.2d 678 (1974), per BURGER, C.J., held that a federal taxpayer had no standing to contend that the Central Intelligence Agency Act, which provides that CIA appropriations and expenditures not be made public, violates Art. I, § 9, cl. 7—"a regular Statement of Account of the Receipts and Expenditures of all public money shall be published from time to time": Respondent "makes no claim that appropriated funds are being spent in violation of a 'specific constitutional limitation upon [the] taxing and spending power * * *.' Rather, he asks the courts to compel the Government to give him information on precisely how the CIA spends its funds [without which] he cannot intelligently follow the actions of Congress or the Executive, nor can he properly fulfill his obligations as a member of the electorate in voting for candidates seeking national office.

"This is surely the kind of a generalized grievance described in both *Frothingham* and *Flast* since the impact on him is plainly undifferentiated and 'common to all members of the public.' *Ex parte Levitt,* 302 U.S. 633, 58 S.Ct. 1, 82 L.Ed. 493 (1983).[a] While we can hardly dispute that this respondent has a genuine interest in the use of funds and that his interest may be prompted by his status as a taxpayer, he has not alleged that, as a taxpayer, he is in danger of suffering any particular concrete injury as a result of the operation of this statute. * * *[11]

"[T]he absence of any particular individual or class to litigate these claims gives support to the argument that the subject matter is committed to the surveillance of Congress, and ultimately to the political process. [T]hat the Constitution does not afford a judicial remedy does not, of course, completely disable the citizen * * *. Slow, cumbersome and unresponsive though the traditional electoral process may be thought at times, our system provides for changing members of the political branches when dissatisfied citizens convince a

a. *Levitt* held that a private individual had no standing to challenge the appointment of a Supreme Court justice as violative of Art. I, § 6, cl. 2.

11. Although we need not reach or decide precisely what is meant by "a regular Statement of Account," it [is] open to serious question whether the Framers of the Constitution ever imagined that general directives to the Congress or the Executive would be subject to enforcement by an individual citizen. [H]istorical analysis of the genesis of cl. 7 suggests that it was intended to permit some degree of secrecy of governmental operations. The ultimate weapon of enforcement available to the Congress would, of course, be the "power of the purse." Independent of the statute here challenged by respondent, Congress could grant standing to taxpayers or citizens, or both, limited, of course, by the "Cases" and "Controversies" provisions of Art. III. * * *

sufficient number of their fellow electors that elected representatives are delinquent in performing duties committed to them."

POWELL, J., who joined the Court's opinion, concurred: "[T]here can be little doubt about respondent's fervor in pursuing his case [and the] intensity of his interest appears to bear no relationship to the fact that, literally speaking, he is not challenging directly a congressional exercise of the taxing and spending power. On the other hand, [it] requires no great leap in reasoning to conclude that the Statement and Account Clause [is] inextricably linked to that power. And that clause might well be seen as a 'specific' limitation on congressional spending. Indeed, it could be viewed as the most democratic of limitations. Thus, although the Court's application of *Flast* to the instant case is probably literally correct, adherence to the *Flast* test in this instance suggests, as does *Flast* itself, that the test is not a sound or logical limitation on standing. [D]espite the diminution of standing requirements in the last decade, the Court has not broken with the traditional requirement that, in the absence of a specific statutory grant of the right of review, a plaintiff must allege some particularized injury that sets him apart from the man on the street. * * * [17]"

STEWART, J., joined by Marshall, J., dissented: "[Respondent] contends that the Statement and Account Clause gives him a right to receive the information and burdens the Government with a correlative duty to supply it. [When] a party is seeking a judicial determination that a defendant owes him an affirmative duty, it seems clear to me that he has standing to litigate the issue of the existence vel non of this duty once he shows that the defendant has declined to honor his claim. [Thus,] there is no necessity to resort to any extended analysis, such as the *Flast* nexus tests [which "were no more than a response to the problem of taxpayer standing to challenge federal legislation enacted in the exercise of the taxing and spending power."] Certainly, after *SCRAP*, it does not matter that those to whom the duty is owed may be many."

BRENNAN, J., dissented, relying on his dissent in *Reservists*, this Sec. infra: "Richardson plainly alleged injury in fact [in] respect of his right as a citizen to know how Congress was spending the public fisc [and] as a voter to receive information to aid his decision how and for whom to vote. These claims may ultimately fail on the merits, but Richardson has 'standing' to assert them."

SCHLESINGER v. RESERVISTS COMMITTEE TO STOP THE WAR, 418 U.S. 208, 94 S.Ct. 2925, 41 L.Ed.2d 706 (1974), per BURGER, C.J., held that respondents lacked standing as citizens to contend that the Secretary of Defense's permitting Members of Congress to be in the Armed Forces Reserve violated the Incompatibility Clause of Art. I, § 6, cl. 2—"No person holding any office under the United States shall be a Member of either House during his continuance in office." Respondents alleged injury because "nonobservance of [the] Clause deprives citizens of the faithful discharge of the legislative duties of Reservist members of Congress" since they would "be subject to the possibility of undue influence by the Executive Branch [and] possible inconsistent obligations." The Court responded:

17. *Baker v. Carr* may have a special claim to sui generis status. It was perhaps a necessary response to the manifest distortion of democratic principles practiced by malapportioned legislatures * * *. *Flast* may also have been a reaction to what appeared at the time as an immutable political logjam that included unsuccessful efforts to confer specific statutory grants of standing.

"[T]hat claimed nonobservance, standing alone, would adversely affect only the generalized interest of all citizens in constitutional governance, and that is an abstract injury. [T]he requirement of concrete injury [serves] the function of insuring that [constitutional] adjudication does not take place unnecessarily, [and] the framing of relief no more broad than required by the precise facts to which the court's ruling would be applied. This is especially important when the relief sought produces a confrontation with one of the coordinate branches of the government. [T]he fact that the adverse parties sharply conflicted in their interests and views and were supported by able briefs and arguments [is] not a substitute for the actual injury needed [to] focus litigation efforts and judicial decision-making. Moreover, [a] logical corollary to this approach would be the manifestly untenable view that the inadequacy of the presentation on the merits would be an appropriate basis for denying standing.[a] [Our] system of government leaves many crucial decisions to the political processes. The assumption that if respondents have no standing to sue, no one would have standing, is not a reason to find standing. See *Richardson*." [b]

STEWART, J., who joined the Court's opinion, concurred: "[U]nlike *Richardson*, the respondents do not allege that the petitioners have refused to perform an affirmative duty imposed upon them by the Constitution."

MARSHALL, J., dissented: Respondents' "specific interest"—"to have the Congress take all the steps necessary to terminate American involvement in Vietnam"—"is certainly not a 'general interest common to all members of the public.' [It] is a sad commentary on our priorities that a litigant who contends that a violation of a federal stature has interfered with his aesthetic appreciation of natural resources can have a claim heard by a federal court, see *SCRAP*, while one who contends that a violation of a specific provision of [the] Constitution has interfered with the effectiveness of expression protected by the First Amendment is turned away."

Notes and Questions

Nature of constitutional provision. (a) Did the claimants in *Reservists* and *Richardson* allege "concrete injury" or only "the generalized interest of all citizens in constitutional governance"? Consider Albert, *Justiciability and Theories of Judicial Review: A Remote Relationship*, 50 So.Cal.L.Rev. 1139, 1153 (1977): "[*Reservists* and *Richardson*] illustrate that the article III concept of 'injury in fact' [involves] a subtle judicial judgment founded upon a construction of the substantive constitutional mandate in issue. [In the Court's view, the Incompatibility Clause and the Statement and Account Clause] gave rise to no

a. See Davis, *Administrative Law Text* 427–28 (3d ed. 1972): "Standing should not depend upon the probable manner in which a party will present a case; it should depend only upon the question whether the plaintiff should be entitled to judicial assistance in order that justice may be done. Two simple illustrations, one at each pole, should suffice to show this: (1) The best law firm in the country, no matter how skillful its presentation to the court may be, *obviously* lacks standing to get an adjudication of an abstract question of law when neither it nor its client has any interest at stake. (2) An illiterate pauper who refuses legal assistance *obviously* has standing to challenge a $10 fine imposed on him, no matter how badly he may present his case."

b. The Court also denied respondents standing as taxpayers because they "did not challenge an enactment under Art. I, § 8, but rather the action of the Executive Branch." Douglas, J., dissented on this point because "Acts of Congress make various appropriations for the services of reservists" and the Incompatibility Clause " 'was designed as a specific bulwark against such potential abuses [and] operates as a specific constitutional limitation upon' such expenditures." Brennan, J., dissenting, also "would find the injury-in-fact requirement met by the respondents' taxpayer allegation."

definable legal interest, and therefore there was no immediacy or actuality to the alleged harms. But there is no objective calculus for saying that these harms are less immediate or real than injury to schoolchildren from unequal educational financing or to voters from unequal districting. What differs is the source of the judgment, the law on which the claim is founded. Hence, it was a choice between competing views of the unconstrued constitutional provisions in *Richardson* and *Reservists* that determined whether there was 'injury in fact.'" See also Fletcher, *The Structure of Standing,* 98 Yale L.J. 221, 271–72 (1988): "*Flast, Valley Forge* [infra], *Richardson,* and *Schlesinger* should not be seen as a group of 'federal taxpayer cases.' Rather they should be seen as cases involving three different provisions of the Constitution, [and the issue should be whether] the purposes of the particular clause at issue will be best served by permitting federal taxpayers to sue to enforce its obligations."

(b) Were *Reservists* and *Richardson* based on the judgment that enforcement of the Incompatibility Clause and the Statement and Account Clause should be left "to the political process"? That—as with the states' rights issue in *Frothingham* and unlike the establishment clause issue in *Flast*—no one has "standing to sue"? Consider Davis, *Administrative Law of the Seventies* 522–23 (1976): "The way to protect against too much government by judges is to limit *what* the judges decide, not to limit *who* can raise a question for a court to decide. [The] law of 'political question' is a much better judicial tool than the law of standing for deciding *what* the courts should decide." Compare Bogen, *Standing Up for Flast: Taxpayer and Citizen Standing to Raise Constitutional Issues,* 67 Ky.L.J. 147, 162 (1978–79): "If the constitutional provision in question is intended to protect a particular right from the majoritarian political process, the Court should not remand the plaintiff to those same processes. The critical question should center on the nature of the constitutional provision in question and whether the particular provision would be more effective if enforced by citizen suits." For the view that some constitutional rights are held "in personam" while others are held "in gross," see Note, *Toward a Coherent Doctrine of Standing,* 86 Colum.L.Rev. 564 (1986).

VALLEY FORGE CHRISTIAN COLLEGE v. AMERICANS UNITED FOR SEPARATION OF CHURCH AND STATE, INC., 454 U.S. 464, 102 S.Ct. 752, 70 L.Ed.2d 700 (1982), per REHNQUIST, J., held that respondents lacked standing as taxpayers or citizens to challenge, as violative of the establishment clause, the giving of surplus federal property to a church college that trained students "for Christian services as either ministers or laymen": "While the [power of judicial review] is a formidable means of vindicating individual rights, when employed unwisely or unnecessarily it is also the ultimate threat to the continued effectiveness of the federal courts in performing that role. '[R]epeated and essentially head-on confrontations between the life-tenured branch and the representative branches of government will not, in the long run, be beneficial to either. The public confidence essential to the former and the vitality critical to the latter may well erode if we do not exercise self-restraint in the utilization of our power to negative the actions of the other branches.' *Richardson* (Powell, J., concurring).[a] Proper regard for the complex nature of our constitutional structure requires neither that the judicial branch shrink from a confrontation with the other two coequal branches of the federal government, nor that it hospitably

a. See generally Brilmayer, *The Jurisprudence of Article III: Perspectives on the "Case or Controversy" Requirement,* 93 Harv.L.Rev. 297 (1979).

accept for adjudication claims of constitutional violation by other branches of government where the claimant has not suffered cognizable injury. * * * Art. III, which is every bit as important in its circumscription of the judicial power of the United States as in its granting of that power, is not merely a troublesome hurdle to be overcome if possible so as to reach the 'merits' of a lawsuit * * *.

"[R]espondents fail the first prong of the [*Flast*] test for taxpayer standing [in] two respects. First, the source of their complaint is not a congressional action, but a decision by HEW to transfer a parcel of federal property. *Flast* limited taxpayer standing to challenges directed 'only [at] exercises of congressional power.' Second, [the] property transfer [was] not an exercise of authority conferred by the taxing and spending clause of Art. I, § 8.[b] The authorizing legislation [was] an evident exercise of Congress' power under the Property Clause, Art. IV, § 3, cl. 2.

"[*Reservists* and *Richardson* cannot] be distinguished on the ground that the Incompatibility and Accounts Clauses are in some way less 'fundamental' than the Establishment Clause. Each establishes a norm of conduct which the federal government is bound to honor. [W]e know of no principled basis on which to create a hierarchy of constitutional values or a complementary 'sliding scale' of standing which might permit respondents to invoke the judicial power of the United States. 'The proposition that all constitutional provisions are enforceable by any citizen simply because citizens are the ultimate beneficiaries of those provisions has no boundaries.' *Reservists.*

"The complaint in this case shares a common deficiency with those in *Reservists* and *Richardson.* Although they claim that the Constitution has been violated, [they] fail to identify any personal injury suffered by the plaintiffs *as a consequence* of the alleged constitutional error, other than the psychological consequence presumably produced by observation of conduct with which one disagrees. That is not an injury sufficient to confer standing under Art. III, even though the disagreement is phrased in constitutional terms. It is evident that respondents are firmly committed to the constitutional principle of separation of church and State, but standing is not measured by the intensity of the litigant's interest or the fervor of his advocacy. * * *

"In reaching this conclusion, we do not retreat from our earlier holdings that standing may be predicated on noneconomic injury. See, e.g., *SCRAP, Data Processing Service.* We simply cannot see that respondents have alleged an *injury* of *any* kind, economic or otherwise, sufficient to confer standing.[22] [Their] claim of standing implicitly rests on the presumption that violations of the Establishment Clause typically will not cause injury sufficient to confer standing under the 'traditional' view of Art. III. But '[t]he assumption that if respondents have no standing to sue, no one would have standing, is not a reason to find standing.' *Reservists.* This view would convert standing into a requirement

b. For a recent decision applying the *Flast* exception against taxpayer standing to an exercise of Congress' power under the taxing and spending clause, see *Bowen v. Kendrick,* p. 867 supra.

22. [The] plaintiffs in *Schempp* [p. 828 supra] had standing, not because their complaint rested on the Establishment Clause—for as *Doremus* demonstrated, that is insufficient—but because impressionable schoolchildren were subjected to unwelcome religious exercises or were forced to assume special burdens to avoid them. Respondents have alleged no comparable injury. [See generally C. Black, *Religion, "Standing," and the Supreme Court's Role,* 13 J.Pub.L. 459 (1964); E. Brown, *Quis Custodiet Ipsos Custodes?—The School Prayer Cases,* 1963 Sup.Ct.Rev. 1; Choper, *Religion in the Public Schools: A Proposed Constitutional Standard,* 47 Minn.L.Rev. 329, 366–67 (1963); Dixon, *Religion, Schools, and the Open Society: A Socio-Constitutional Issue,* 13 J.Pub.L. 267 (1964).]

that must be observed only when satisfied. Moreover, we are unwilling to assume that injured parties are nonexistent simply because they have not joined respondents in their suit. * * * [26]"

BRENNAN, J., joined by Marshall and Blackmun, JJ.,[c] dissented: "The Court makes a fundamental mistake when it determines that a plaintiff has failed to satisfy [the] 'injury-in-fact' test, or indeed any other test of 'standing,' without first determining whether the Constitution [defines] injury, and creates a cause of action for redress of that injury, in precisely the circumstance presented to the Court.[5] [One] of the primary purposes of the Establishment Clause was to prevent the use of tax monies for religious purposes. *The taxpayer was the direct and intended beneficiary of the prohibition on financial aid to religion.* [It] may be that Congress can tax for *almost* any reason, or for no reason at all. There is, so far as I have been able to discern, but one constitutionally imposed limit on that authority. Congress cannot use tax money to support a church, or to encourage religion. [T]he history of the Establishment Clause [makes] this clear. History also makes it clear that the federal taxpayer is a singularly 'proper and appropriate party to invoke a federal court's jurisdiction' to challenge a federal bestowal of largesse as a violation of the Establishment Clause. Each, and indeed every, federal taxpayer suffers precisely the injury that the Establishment Clause guards against when the Federal Government directs that funds be taken from the pocketbooks of the citizenry and placed into the coffers of the ministry."

As for the fact that HEW transferred the property, "to be sure, the First Amendment is phrased as a restriction on Congress' legislative authority; this is only natural since the Constitution assigns the authority to legislate and appropriate only to the Congress. But it is difficult to conceive of an expenditure for which the last governmental actor, either implementing directly the legislative will, or acting within the scope of legislatively delegated authority, is not an Executive Branch official. The First Amendment binds the Government as a whole, regardless of which branch is at work in a particular instance.

"The Court's second purported distinction between this case and *Flast* is equally unavailing. [It] can make no constitutional difference [whether] the donation to the defendant here was in the form of a cash grant to build a facility, see *Tilton v. Richardson,* [p. 862 supra], or in the nature of a gift of property including a facility already [built.] Whether undertaken pursuant to the Property Clause or the Spending Clause, the breach of the Establishment Clause, and the relationship of the taxpayer to that breach, is precisely the same."

Notes and Questions

1. *Other "injured parties."* After *Valley Forge,* would a neighboring college, that alleges competitive disadvantage because of the federal grant of

26. Were we to recognize standing premised on an "injury" consisting solely of an alleged violation of a " 'personal constitutional right' to a government that does not establish religion," a principled consistency would dictate recognition of respondents' standing to challenge execution of every capital sentence on the basis of a personal right to a government that does not impose cruel and unusual punishment, or standing to challenge every affirmative action program on the basis of a personal right to a government that does not deny equal protection of the laws, to choose but two among as many possible examples as there are commands in the Constitution.

c. Stevens, J., dissented separately, agreeing with Brennan, J.

5. When the Constitution makes it clear that a particular person is to be protected from a particular form of government action, then that person has a "right" to be free of that action; when that right is infringed, then there is injury, and a personal stake, within the meaning of Article III.

property to Valley Forge Christian, have "an injury sufficient to confer standing"? If Mrs. Frothingham had refused to pay part of her federal income taxes and was prosecuted for income tax evasion, could she defend on the ground that the Maternity Act expenditures were beyond congressional power?

2. *Other constitutional provisions.* Apart from the establishment clause, are there any other "specific limitations on the taxing and spending power" that *taxpayers* have standing to enforce? Suppose Congress appropriated funds for racially segregated facilities? See McCoy & Nevins, *Standing and Adverseness in Challenges of Tax Exemptions for Discriminatory Private Schools,* 52 Ford.L. Rev. 441, 453–56 (1984). For polygraphs to be used on all criminal defendants? For a federal censorship office? For subsidies to some newspapers? For the administration of general loyalty oaths to all public employees? Assuming that all of these activities are unconstitutional, whose "rights" do they violate? Taxpayers' "rights"? How about an appropriation of "$50 to every member of the Republican Party"?

3. *State suits.* Are the Court's strictures on federal taxpayer and citizen standing also applicable to Supreme Court review of state taxpayer and citizen suits? Consider Scharpf, *Judicial Review and the Political Question: A Functional Analysis,* 75 Yale L.J. 517, 521 n. 12 (1966): "In *Frothingham,* the Court based its narrow interpretation of [the 'case and controversy'] requirement upon an understanding of the *federal* allocation of functions to the three departments of government: the Court's only legitimate function *within that framework* is to decide 'normal' cases and controversies, and any expansion of that concept would change this balance. [However, the] Constitution would seem to leave the states free to divide their functions of government differently, and to define the 'judicial power' of their own courts somewhat more broadly than [Art. III]. Thus, if a state permits its own courts to decide taxpayers' suits, and if a federal question should be determined by a state court in such a suit, it seems that the 'separation-of-powers' rationale should carry little or no weight for the Supreme Court's definition of what is a proper 'case and controversy' for purposes of appellate jurisdiction. In this situation 'case and controversy' might well have a more permissive content, protecting only the functional requisites for the correctness of the Court's constitutional decision: a well developed case, litigated by the best possible parties."

WARTH v. SELDIN

422 U.S. 490, 95 S.Ct. 2197, 45 L.Ed.2d 343 (1975).

JUSTICE POWELL delivered the opinion of the Court.

Petitioners, various organizations and individuals resident in the Rochester, New York, metropolitan area, brought this action [against] the Town of Penfield, an incorporated municipality adjacent to Rochester, and against members of Penfield's Zoning, Planning, and Town Boards. Petitioners claimed that the town's zoning [ordinance] effectively excluded persons of low and moderate income from living in the town, in contravention of petitioners' First, Ninth, and Fourteenth Amendment rights and in violation of 42 U.S.C. §§ 1981, 1982, and 1983. The [federal courts below held] that none of the plaintiffs [had standing].

In its constitutional dimension, standing imports justiciability: whether the plaintiff has made out a "case or controversy" between himself and the defendant within the meaning of Art. III. * * *

Apart from this minimum constitutional mandate, this Court has recognized other ["prudential"] limits on the class of persons who may invoke the courts' decisional and remedial powers. First, the Court has held that when the asserted harm is a "generalized grievance" shared in substantially equal measure by all or a large class of citizens, that harm alone normally does not warrant exercise of jurisdiction. E.g., *Reservists.* Second, even when the plaintiff has alleged injury sufficient to meet the "case or controversy" requirement, this Court has held that the plaintiff generally must assert his own legal rights and interests, and cannot rest his claim to relief on the legal rights or interests of third parties.[a] Without such limitations—closely related to Art. III concerns but essentially matters of judicial self-governance—the courts would be called upon to decide abstract questions of wide public significance even though other governmental institutions may be more competent to address the questions and even though judicial intervention may be unnecessary to protect individual rights.

Although standing in no way depends on the merits of the plaintiff's contention that particular conduct is illegal, e.g., *Flast,* it often turns on the nature and source of the claim asserted. The actual or threatened injury required by Art. III may exist solely by virtue of "statutes creating legal rights, the invasion of which creates standing * * *." See *Sierra Club.* Moreover, the source of the plaintiff's claim to relief assumes critical importance with respect to the prudential rules of standing * * *. Essentially, the standing question in such cases is whether the constitutional or statutory provision on which the claim rests properly can be understood as granting persons in the plaintiff's position a right to judicial relief.[12] In some circumstances, countervailing considerations may outweigh the concerns underlying the usual reluctance to exert judicial power when the plaintiff's claim to relief rests on the legal rights of third parties. In such instances, the Court has found, in effect, that the constitutional or statutory provision in question implies a right of action in the plaintiff. See *Pierce v. Society of Sisters* [Part B infra]. Moreover, Congress may grant an express right of action to persons who otherwise would be barred by prudential standing rules. Of course, Art. III's requirement remains: the plaintiff still must allege a distinct and palpable injury to himself, even if it is an injury shared by a large class of other possible litigants. E.g., *SCRAP.* But so long as this requirement is satisfied, persons to whom Congress has granted a right of action, either expressly or by clear implication, may have standing to seek relief on the basis of the legal rights and interests of others, and, indeed, may invoke the general public interest in support of their claim. E.g., *Sierra Club.* * * *

III. With these general considerations in mind, we turn first to the claims of petitioners Ortiz, Reyes, Sinkler, and Broadnax, each of whom asserts standing as a person of low or moderate income and, coincidentally, as a member of a minority racial or ethnic group. We must assume, taking the allegations of the complaint as true, that Penfield's zoning ordinance and the pattern of enforcement [have] the purpose and effect of excluding [such persons]. We also assume, for purposes here, that such intentional exclusionary practices, if proved in a

a. This topic is considered in Part B infra.

12. A similar standing issue arises when the litigant asserts the rights of third parties defensively, as a bar to judgment against him. E.g., *Barrows v. Jackson; McGowan v. Maryland* [Part B infra]. In such circumstances, there is no Art. III standing problem; but the prudential question is governed by considerations closely related to the question whether a person in the litigant's position would have a right of action on the claim.

proper case, would be adjudged violative of the constitutional and statutory rights of the persons excluded.

But the fact that these petitioners share attributes common to persons who may have been excluded from residence in the town is an insufficient predicate for the conclusion that petitioners themselves have been excluded, or that the respondents' assertedly illegal actions have violated their rights. Petitioners must allege and show that they personally have been injured * * *.

In their complaint, petitioners Ortiz, Reyes, Sinkler, and Broadnax alleged in conclusory terms that they are among the persons excluded by respondents' actions. None of them has ever resided in Penfield; each claims at least implicitly that he desires, or has desired, to do so. Each asserts, moreover, that he made some effort, at some time, to locate housing in Penfield that was at once within his means and adequate for his family's needs. Each claims that his efforts proved fruitless. We may assume, as petitioners alleged, that respondents' actions have contributed, perhaps substantially, to the cost of housing in Penfield. But there remains the question whether petitioners' inability to locate suitable housing in Penfield reasonably can be said to have resulted, in any concretely demonstrable way, from respondents' alleged constitutional and statutory infractions. Petitioners must allege facts from which it reasonably could be inferred that, absent the respondents' restrictive zoning practices, there is a substantial probability that they would have been able to purchase or lease in Penfield and that, if the court affords the relief requested, the asserted inability of petitioners will be removed.

We find the record devoid of the necessary allegations. [N]one of these petitioners has a present interest in any Penfield property; none is himself subject to the ordinance's strictures; and none has ever been denied a variance or permit by respondent officials. Instead, petitioners claim that respondents' enforcement of the ordinance against third parties—developers, builders, and the like—has had the consequence of precluding the construction of housing suitable to their needs at prices they might be able to afford. The fact that the harm to petitioners may have resulted indirectly does not in itself preclude standing. When a governmental prohibition or restriction imposed on one party causes specific harm to a third party, harm that a constitutional provision or statute was intended to prevent, the indirectness of the injury does not necessarily deprive the person harmed of standing to vindicate his rights. But it may make it substantially more difficult to meet the minimum requirement of Art. III: to establish that, in fact, the asserted injury was the consequence of the defendants' actions, or that prospective relief will remove the harm.

Here, by their own admission, realization of petitioners' desire to live in Penfield always has depended on the efforts and willingness of third parties to build low- and moderate-cost housing. The record specifically refers to only two such efforts: that of Penfield Better Homes Corporation, in late 1969, to obtain the rezoning of certain land in Penfield to allow the construction of subsidized cooperative townhouses that could be purchased by persons of moderate income; and a similar effort by O'Brien Homes, Inc., in late 1971. But the record is devoid of any indication that these projects or other like projects, would have satisfied petitioners needs at prices they could afford, or that, were the court to remove the obstructions attributable to respondents, such relief would benefit petitioners. Indeed, petitioners' descriptions of their individual financial situations and housing needs suggest precisely the contrary—that their inability to reside in Penfield is the consequence of the economics of the area housing market, rather than of respondents' assertedly illegal acts. In short, the facts alleged fail to support an actionable causal relationship between Penfield's zoning practices and petitioners' asserted injury.[18] * * *

V. We turn next to the standing problems presented by the petitioner associations * * *.

A. Petitioner Metro-Act [claims] that, as a result of the persistent pattern of exclusionary zoning [its] members who are Penfield residents are deprived of the benefits of living in a racially and ethnically integrated community. * * *

Metro-Act does not assert on behalf of its members any right of action under the 1968 Civil Rights [Act]. In this, we think, lies the critical distinction between *Trafficante* and the situation here. * * *

B. Petitioner Home Builders [asserted] standing to represent its member firms engaged in the development and construction of residential housing in the Rochester area, including Penfield. Home Builders alleged that the Penfield zoning restrictions [had] deprived some of its members of "substantial business opportunities and profits." * * *

Home Builders [can] have standing as the representative of its members only if it has alleged facts sufficient to make out a case or controversy had the members themselves brought suit. No such allegations were made. The complaint refers to no specific project of any of its members that is currently precluded either by the ordinance or by respondents' action in enforcing [it].

A like problem is presented with respect to petitioner Housing Council [which] includes in its membership "at least seventeen" groups that have been, are, or will be involved in the development of low- and moderate-cost housing. But, with one exception, the complaint does not suggest that any of these groups has focused its efforts on Penfield or has any specific plan to do so. [The] exception is the Penfield Better Homes Corporation. As we have observed above, it applied to respondents in late 1969 for a zoning variance to allow construction of a housing project designed for persons of moderate income. [It] is therefore possible that in 1969, or within a reasonable time thereafter, Better Homes itself and possibly Housing Council as its representative would have had standing to seek review of respondents' action. The complaint, however, does not allege that the Penfield Better Homes project remained viable in 1972 when this complaint was filed, or that respondents' actions continued to block a then current construction project. * * *

Affirmed.

JUSTICE BRENNAN, with whom JUSTICE WHITE and JUSTICE MARSHALL join, dissenting.

18. [We] also note that zoning laws and their provisions, long considered essential to effective urban planning, are peculiarly within the province of state and local legislative authorities. They are, of course, subject to judicial review in a proper case. But citizens dissatisfied with provisions of such laws need not overlook the availability of the normal democratic process.

[For a case in which a potential home buyer demonstrated a "substantial probability" that he would have been able to purchase if rezoning were granted and thus "adequately averred an 'actionable causal relationship' between the zoning practice and his asserted injury," see *Arlington Heights v. Metropolitan Housing Dev. Corp.*, 429 U.S. 252, 97 S.Ct. 555, 50 L.Ed.2d 450 (1977). See also *Duke Power Co. v. Carolina Environmental Study Group, Inc.*, Part C infra, finding a "substantial likelihood" of "a 'but for' causal connection" between the injuries alleged and the challenged government action. For a lenient application of this doctrine, upholding standing to raise a nonconstitutional claim, see *Bryant v. Yellen*, 447 U.S. 352, 100 S.Ct. 2232, 65 L.Ed.2d 184 (1980)].

[T]he opinion, which tosses out of court almost every conceivable kind of plaintiff who could be injured by the activity claimed to be unconstitutional, can be explained only by an indefensible hostility to the claim on the merits. [I]t is quite clear, when the record is viewed with dispassion, that at least three of the groups of plaintiffs have made allegations, and supported them with affidavits and documentary evidence, sufficient to survive a motion to dismiss for lack of standing.

[O]ne glaring defect of the Court's opinion is that it views each set of plaintiffs as if it were prosecuting a separate lawsuit, refusing to recognize that the interests are intertwined * * *. For example, the Court says that the low-income-minority plaintiffs have not alleged facts sufficient to show that but for the exclusionary practices claimed, they would be able to reside in Penfield. The Court then intimates that such a causal relationship could be shown only if "the initial focus [is] on a particular project." Later, the Court objects to the ability of the Housing Council to prosecute the suit on behalf of its member, Penfield Better Homes Corporation, *despite* the fact that Better Homes *had* displayed an interest in a particular project, because that project was no longer live. Thus, we must suppose that even if the low-income plaintiffs had alleged a desire to live in the Better Homes project, that allegation would be insufficient because it appears that particular project might never be built. The rights of low-income-minority plaintiffs who desire to live in a locality, then, seem to turn on the willingness of a third party to litigate the legality of preclusion of a particular project, despite the fact that the third party may have no economic incentive to incur the costs of litigation with regard to one project, and despite the fact that the low-income-minority plaintiff's interest is *not* to live in a particular project but to live somewhere in the town in a dwelling they can afford.

[In] effect, the Court tells the low-income-minority and building company plaintiffs they will not be permitted to prove what they have alleged—that they could and would build and live in the town if changes were made in the zoning ordinance and its application—because they have not succeeded in breaching, before the suit was filed, the very barriers which are the subject of the suit.[b]

Low-Income and Minority Plaintiffs. [P]laintiffs Ortiz, Broadnax, Reyes, and Sinkler alleged that "as a result" of respondents' exclusionary practices, they were unable, despite attempts, to find the housing they desired in Penfield, and consequently have incurred high commuting expenses, received poorer municipal services, and, in some instances, been relegated to live in substandard housing. * * *

Here, the very fact that, as the Court stresses, these petitioners' claim rests in part upon proving the intentions and capabilities of third parties to build in Penfield suitable housing which they can afford, coupled with the exclusionary character of the claim on the merits, makes it particularly inappropriate to assume that these petitioners' lack of specificity reflects a fatal weakness in their theory of causation. Obviously they cannot be expected, prior to discovery and trial, to know the future plans of building companies, the precise details of the housing market in Penfield, or everything which has transpired in 15 years

b. See also Tribe, *American Constitutional Law* 132 (2d ed. 1988): "[The] Court has not generally required identification of the specific transaction or project that would proceed unhindered but for a challenged rule or practice. Any contrary rule would confront excluded groups with a kind of Catch 22: the more severely and successfully exclusionary a challenged scheme is, the more difficult it would be to find insiders or developers willing to incur the inconvenience and expense of joining outsiders in designing a project or transaction that could meet any judicial test of specific identification."

of application of the Penfield zoning ordinance, including every housing plan suggested and refused. To require them to allege such facts is to require them to prove their case on paper in order to get into court at all, reverting to the form of fact-pleading long abjured in the federal courts. * * * [c]

SIMON v. EASTERN KY. WELFARE RIGHTS ORG., 426 U.S. 26, 96 S.Ct. 1917, 48 L.Ed.2d 450 (1976), per POWELL, J., held that respondents—including persons who had been denied hospital services because of their indigency—had no standing to sue the Secretary of the Treasury under APA § 10 on the ground that a new Revenue Ruling, which granted favorable tax treatment to hospitals despite their refusal to give full service to indigents, was contrary to the Internal Revenue Code: "[T]he constitutional standing requirement under [APA § 10 requires] allegations which, if true, would establish that the plaintiff had been injured in fact by the action he sought to have reviewed. [The] necessity that the plaintiff who seeks to invoke judicial power stand to profit in some personal interest remains an Art. III requirement." Relying on *Warth*, the Court reasoned that "Art. III still requires that a federal court act only to redress injury that fairly can be traced to the challenged action of the defendant, and not injury that results from the independent action of some third party not before the court.[a]

"The complaint here alleged only that petitioners, by the adoption of Revenue Ruling 69–545, had 'encouraged' hospitals to deny service to indigents. The implicit corollary of this allegation is that a grant of respondents' requested relief, resulting in a requirement that all hospitals serve indigents as a condition to favorable tax treatment, would 'discourage' hospitals from denying their services to respondents. But it [is] purely speculative whether the denials of service specified in the complaint fairly can be traced to petitioners' 'encouragement' or instead result from decisions made by the hospitals without regard to the tax implications.

"It is equally speculative whether the desired exercise of the court's remedial powers in this suit would result in the availability to respondents of such services. So far as the complaint sheds light, it is just as plausible that the hospitals to which respondents may apply for service would elect to forego favorable tax treatment to avoid the undetermined financial drain of an increase in the level of uncompensated services." Accordingly, the complaint should be dismissed.[b]

c. The dissent of Douglas, J., is omitted.

a. The Court recognized "Congress' power to create new interests the invasion of which will confer standing. See *Trafficante*. [But when] Congress has so acted, the requirements of Art. III remain: 'the plaintiff still must allege a distinct and palpable injury to himself, even if it is an injury shared by a large class of other possible litigants.' *Warth*. See also *SCRAP;* cf. *Sierra Club*."

Must the "distinct and palpable injury" alleged by plaintiff at the time suit is filed continue throughout the litigation? See *United States Parole Comm'n v. Geraghty*, fn. g, Part I, supra.

b. Stewart, J., joined the Court's opinion, adding "that I cannot now imagine a case, at least outside the First Amendment area, where a person whose own tax liability was not affected ever could have standing to litigate the federal tax liability of someone else."

See also *Los Angeles v. Lyons*, 461 U.S. 95, 103 S.Ct. 1660, 75 L.Ed.2d 675 (1983) (although person who was subject to allegedly unconstitutional "chokehold" by police after being stopped for traffic violation has standing to sue for damages, that does not constitute sufficiently real and immediate threat of future injury to justify federal injunctive relief). Marshall, J., joined by Brennan, Blackmun and Stevens, JJ., dissented. For criticism of *Lyons*, see Fallon, *Of Justiciability, Remedies, and Public Law Litigation: Notes on the Jurisprudence of Lyons*, 59 N.Y.U.L.Rev. 1 (1984); Tribe, *Constitutional Choices* 99 (1985).

BRENNAN, J., joined by Marshall, J., dissented from the Court's reasoning: "Any prudential, nonconstitutional considerations that underlay the Court's disposition of the injury in fact standing requirement in cases such as *Linda R.S.* and *Warth* are simply inapposite when review is sought under a congressionally enacted statute conferring standing and providing for judicial review. In such a case considerations respecting 'the allocation of power at the national level [and] a shift away from a democratic form of government,' *Richardson* (Powell, J., concurring), are largely ameliorated. * * *

"[T]here can be no doubt that respondents here, by demonstrating a connection between the disputed ruling and the hospitals affecting them, could have adequately served the policy implicated by the pleading requirement of *Sierra Club*—putting 'the decision as to whether review will be sought in the hands of those who have a direct stake in the outcome.' [But] the most disturbing aspect of today's opinion is the Court's insistence on resting its decision regarding standing squarely on the irreducible Art. III minimum of injury in fact, thereby effectively placing its holding beyond congressional power to rectify. Thus, any time Congress chooses to legislate in favor of certain interests by setting up a scheme of incentives for third parties, judicial review of administrative action that allegedly frustrates the congressionally intended objective will be denied, because any complainant will be required to make an almost impossible showing."

In ALLEN v. WRIGHT, 468 U.S. 737, 104 S.Ct. 3315, 82 L.Ed.2d 556 (1984), parents of black public school children in districts in the process of desegregating brought a "nationwide class action" seeking (1) a declaratory judgment that IRS guidelines and procedures were inadequate "to fulfill its obligation to deny tax-exempt status to racially discriminatory private schools," and (2) an injunction requiring the IRS to deny tax exemptions to a greater number of private schools. The Court, per O'CONNOR, J., held that respondents had no standing.

First, as for their "claim of stigmatic injury, or denigration, suffered by all members of a racial group when the Government discriminates on the basis of race," respondents "do not allege a stigmatic injury suffered as a direct result of having personally been denied equal treatment. [If] the abstract stigmatic injury were cognizable, standing would extend nationwide to all members of the particular racial groups against which the Government was alleged to be discriminating by its grant of tax exemption to a racially discriminatory school, regardless of the location of that school. * * * Constitutional limits on the role of federal courts preclude [this]."

Second, as for their claim "that the federal tax exemptions to racially discriminatory private schools in their communities impair their ability to have their public schools desegregated": "The diminished ability of respondent's children to receive a desegregated education would be fairly traceable to unlawful IRS grants of tax exemptions only if there were enough racially discriminatory private schools receiving tax exemptions in respondents' communities for withdrawal of those exemptions to make an appreciable difference in public-school integration. Respondents have made no such allegation."

STEVENS, J., joined by Blackmun, J., dissented: "If racially discriminatory private schools lose the 'cash grants' that flow from the operation of the statutes, the education they provide will become more expensive and hence less of their services will be purchased [, thus] reducing their competitiveness for parents seeking 'a racially segregated alternative' to public schools, which is what respondents have alleged many white parents in desegregating school districts seek. [Thus], the laws of economics * * * compel the conclusion that the injury respondents have alleged—the increased segregation of their children's schools because of the ready availability of private schools that admit whites only—will be redressed if these schools' operations are inhibited through the denial of preferential tax treatment.[6]" Brennan, J., also dissented.

Marshall, J., did not participate.

Notes and Questions

1. "*Causation.*" How broad are the consequences for the law of standing of the "causation" requirement imposed by *Warth, Eastern Ky.* and *Allen?* Consider 90 Harv.L.Rev. 210 (1976): "As a practical matter, the [requirement] will be largely insignificant in most cases in which private parties seek review of government actions. Where the plaintiff sues the government for an injury inflicted directly by an agency, it is axiomatic that any causation requirement is satisfied and that a court order to the government will affect the alleged harm. Indeed, only in those cases in which a plaintiff sues the government to complain of an injury suffered as a result of the impact of government action on third parties not before the court will the causation/relief issue arise."

2. *Congressional power and Art. III.* (a) Given *Trafficante* and *SCRAP,* to what extent does *Eastern Ky.* limit congressional power to grant standing? For example, suppose Congress authorized "any citizen" to challenge the constitutionality of armed forces reserve status for members of Congress (*Reservists*), or the constitutionality of the secrecy provisions of the CIA Act (*Richardson*)? Any citizen who alleges that such policies diminish his "ability to persuade a member of Congress to vote in a particular way"? Would such litigants allege "concrete harm" (*Reservists*)? A "distinct and palpable injury" (*Eastern Ky.,* fn. b)? What is the significance of *Warth's* categorizing the "generalized grievance" obstacle to standing as "prudential" rather than "constitutional"? See Bice, *Congress' Power to Confer Standing in the Federal Courts,* in Constitutional Government in America 291 (Collins ed. 1980); Nichol, *Standing on the Constitution: The Supreme Court and Valley Forge,* 61 N.C.L.Rev. 798 (1983).

(b) What result in *Eastern Ky.* if respondents had sued under a statute specifically conferring standing on such persons instead of under APA § 10 which authorizes judicial review only for persons "adversely affected or aggrieved by agency action"? What result after *Allen* if Congress authorizes "any member of a minority racial group" to challenge "any government discrimination against that group"? Compare Sunstein, *Standing and the Privatization of Public Law,* 88 Colum.L.Rev. 1432, 1464–69 (1988): "The central problem [is] how to characterize the relevant injury. [In *Eastern Ky.,*] for example, the plaintiffs might have characterized their injury as an impairment of the opportunity to obtain medical services under a regime undistorted by unlawful tax incentives. In *Allen,* the plaintiffs themselves argued that their injury should be characterized as the deprivation of an

6. [W]hile here the source of the causal nexus is the price that white parents must pay to obtain a segregated education, which is inextricably intertwined with the school's tax status, in *Eastern Ky.* the plaintiffs were seeking free care, which hospitals could decide not to provide for any number of reasons unrelated to their tax status. Moreover, in *Eastern Ky.,* the hospitals had to spend money in order to obtain charitable status. Therefore, they had an economic incentive to forego preferential treatment. [Here] the financial incentives run in only one direction.

opportunity to undergo desegregation in school systems unaffected by unlawful tax deductions. Thus recharacterized, the injuries are not speculative at all. [The] harm might be characterized broadly if the relevant source of law is designed to prohibit the injury thus characterized. A related route would be to ask straightforwardly whether Congress intended to confer on the plaintiff a right to bring suit. [Thus, if *Eastern Ky.*] was rightly decided, it was because the tax statutes have been interpreted so as to deny standing, not because of a problem with causation; and if people now thought to be indirectly or incidentally harmed by regulatory action or inaction are to be denied standing, it is because the denial is a sensible reading of congressional purposes in enacting regulatory legislation."

If Congress believes that the case-or-controversy requirement is satisfied, should (must) the Court defer (at least to some degree) to the legislative determination? See fn. b in *Trafficante;* cf. *Marbury v. Madison.* Even if the Court agrees that a congressionally authorized suit satisfies Art. III, must the Court decide it despite its own reservations based on "prudential" principles of "self-restraint"? See Monaghan, *Constitutional Adjudication: The Who and When,* 82 Yale L.J. 1363 (1973).

(c) Of what significance is the fact that the question presented—with or without congressional authorization—is constitutional (as in *Richardson* and *Reservists*) rather than one only of statutory interpretation (as in *Trafficante* and *SCRAP*)? That the Court "is asked to undertake constitutional adjudication, the most important and delicate of its responsibilities" (*Reservists*)? That the Court "has followed a policy of strict necessity in disposing of constitutional issues" (*Ashwander*)? Compare Scott, *Standing in the Supreme Court—A Functional Analysis,* 86 Harv.L.Rev. 645 (1973) with Broderick, *The Warth Optional Standing Doctrine: Return to Judicial Supremacy?* 25 Cath.U.L.Rev. 467 (1976). See note 4 after *Poe v. Ullman,* Part C infra.

B. ASSERTION OF THIRD PARTY RIGHTS

BARROWS v. JACKSON, 346 U.S. 249, 73 S.Ct. 1031, 97 L.Ed. 1586 (1953): A homeowner who had agreed with other homeowners in the neighborhood, by signing a restrictive covenant, not to sell her home to a Negro, broke the covenant and was sued for damages for breach by a co-covenantor. Earlier, *Shelley v. Kraemer*, p. 1218 supra, had held "that racial restrictive covenants could not be enforced [by injunction] against Negro purchasers because such enforcement would constitute state action denying equal protection of the laws to the Negroes."

The Court, per MINTON, J., first held that "if a state court awards damages for breach of a restrictive covenant, a prospective seller of restricted land will either refuse to sell to non-Caucausians or else will require non-Caucausians to pay a higher price," thus violating the equal protection rights of non-Caucausians. But "no non-Caucausian is before the Court," only the Caucausian signatories to the covenant.

"Ordinarily, one may not claim standing in this Court to vindicate the constitutional rights of some third party [even] though [the person before the Court] will suffer a direct substantial injury." "But in the instant case, we are faced with a unique situation in which it is the action of the state *court* which might result in a denial of constitutional rights and in which it would be difficult if not impossible for the persons whose rights are asserted to present their

;rievance before any court. Under the peculiar circumstances of this case, we ›elieve the reasons which underlie our rule denying standing to raise another's ·ights, which is only a rule of practice, are outweighed by the need to protect the 'undamental rights which would be denied by permitting the damages action to be maintained."

The Court observed that restrictive covenants are "widely condemned by the courts" and that the selling homeowner "is the only effective adversary of the unworthy covenant in its last stand.

GRISWOLD v. CONNECTICUT, p. 143 supra, held that birth control clinic officials convicted of abetting married persons in violating the same statute barring use of contraceptives, had standing to assert the constitutional rights of the married persons: "Certainly the accessory should have standing to assert that the offense which he is charged with assisting is not, or cannot constitutionally be a crime. [The] rights of husband and wife, pressed here, are likely to be diluted or adversely affected unless those rights are considered in a suit involving those who have this kind of confidential relation to them."

EISENSTADT v. BAIRD, p. 154 supra, held that a person, convicted for violating a statute forbidding distribution of contraceptive materials to unmarried persons, had standing to assert the constitutional rights of the unmarried persons: "Enforcement of the Massachusetts statute will materially impair the ability of single persons to obtain contraceptives."

Consider Hart & Wechsler's *The Federal Courts and the Federal System* 190 (2d ed. 1973): "Isn't the real question whether the constitutional right of unmarried persons to have contraceptives—if it exists—substantively implies constitutional protection against conviction for supplying contraceptives to such persons? [I]f the state cannot constitutionally prohibit unmarried persons from possessing and using contraceptives, the question whether it can nevertheless prohibit distribution to them depends, does it not, on the substantive scope and purpose of the constitutional policy involved? And doesn't the formulation of the issue in terms of whether a defendant has standing to raise the rights of recipients obscure the true nature of the issue?"

In SINGLETON v. WULFF, 428 U.S. 106, 96 S.Ct. 2868, 49 L.Ed.2d 826 (1976), BLACKMUN, J., joined by Brennan, White and Marshall, JJ., ruled that doctors—who alleged that they "provided, and anticipate providing abortions to welfare patients who are eligible for Medicaid"—had standing to challenge a statute denying Medicaid benefits for abortions: "[T]he Court has looked primarily to two factual elements to determine whether the [general rule against assertion of third party rights] should apply in a particular case. The first is the relationship of the litigant to the person whose right he seeks to assert. If the enjoyment of the right is inextricably bound up with the activity the litigant wishes to pursue, the court at least can be sure that its construction of the right is not unnecessary in the sense that the right's enjoyment will be unaffected by the outcome of the suit. Furthermore, the relationship between the litigant and the third party may be such that the former is fully, or very nearly, as effective a proponent of the right as the latter. [See *Griswold; Eisenstadt; Barrows.*] [a]

"The other factual element to which the Court has looked is the ability of the third party to assert his own right. [I]f there is some genuine obstacle to such assertion, [the] third party's absence from court loses its tendency to suggest that his right is not truly at stake, or truly important to him, and the party who is in court becomes by the default the right's best available proponent. [See *NAACP; Eisenstadt; Barrows.*] [6]

"Application of these principles to the present case quickly yields its proper result. The closeness of the relationship is patent. [A] woman cannot safely secure an abortion without the aid of a physician, and an impecunious woman cannot easily secure an abortion without the physician's being paid by the State. * * *

"As to the woman's assertion of her own rights, there are several obstacles. For one thing she may be chilled from such assertion by a desire to protect the very privacy of her decision from the publicity of a court suit. A second obstacle is [that in only] a few months, at the most, after the maturing of the decision to undergo an abortion, her right thereto will have been irrevocably lost, assuming, as it seems fair to assume, that unless the impecunious woman can establish Medicaid eligibility she must forgo abortion. It is true that these obstacles are not insurmountable. Suit may be brought under a pseudonym, as so frequently has been done. A woman who is no longer pregnant may nonetheless retain the right to litigate the point because it is 'capable of repetition yet evading review.' *Roe v. Wade.* And it may be that a class could be assembled, whose fluid membership always included some women with live claims. But if the assertion

a. For cases upholding the standing of sellers, in actions in which they were plaintiffs seeking declaratory and injunctive relief, see *Craig v. Boren,* p. 1073 supra (seller of beer has standing to assert males' equal protection claim against law prohibiting sale of beer to males under age 21 and females under age 18) and *Carey v. Population Services Intern.,* p. 155 supra (seller of contraceptives has standing to assert potential purchasers' right of privacy claims against law regulating distribution of contraceptives). These cases reasoned that if the sellers could not challenge the laws they would be deterred from selling the products and that this "would result indirectly in the violation of third parties' rights."

United States Department of Labor v. Triplett, 494 U.S. 715, 110 S.Ct. 1428, 108 L.Ed.2d 701 (1990), held that a lawyer who represented a claimant under the Black Lung Benefits Act had standing to challenge the Act's limits on attorneys fees as depriving the claimant's due process right to obtain legal representation: "When enforcement of a restriction against the litigant prevents a third party from entering into a relationship with the litigant (typically a contractual relationship), to which relationship the third party has a legal entitlement (typically a constitutional entitlement), third-party standing has been held to exist. See *Maryland v. Joseph H. Munson Co.,* 467 U.S. 947, 104 S.Ct. 2839, 81 L.Ed.2d 786 (1984) (professional fundraiser given third-party standing to challenge statute limiting its commission to 25 percent as a violation of clients' First Amendment right to hire him for a higher fee)."

6. Mr. Justice Powell objects [that] our prior cases allow assertion of third party rights only when such assertion by the third parties themselves would be "in all practicable terms impossible." Carefully analyzed, our cases do not go that far. The Negro real-estate purchaser in *Barrows,* if he could prove that the racial covenant alone stood in the way of his purchase (as presumably he could easily have done, given the amicable posture of the seller in that case), could surely have sought a declaration of its invalidity or an injunction against its enforcement. [But see note 1(c) supra.] The Association members in *NAACP* could have obtained a similar declaration or injunction, suing anonymously by the use of pseudonyms. The recipients of contraceptives in *Eisenstadt* (or their counterparts in *Griswold* and *Doe,* for that matter) could have sought similar relief as necessary to the enjoyment of their constitutional rights. The point is not that these were easy alternatives, but that they differed only in the degree of difficulty, if they differed at all, from the alternative in this case of the women themselves seeking a declaration or injunction that would force the State to pay the doctors for their abortions.

of the right is to be 'representative' to such an extent anyway, there seems little loss in terms of effective advocacy from allowing its assertion by a physician."

POWELL, J., joined by Burger, C.J., and Stewart and Rehnquist, JJ., * * * dissented: "[T]he 'obstacles' identified by the plurality as justifying departure from the general rule simply are not significant."

C. TIMING OF ADJUDICATION

LAIRD v. TATUM

408 U.S. 1, 92 S.Ct. 2318, 33 L.Ed.2d 154 (1972).

CHIEF JUSTICE BURGER delivered the opinion of the Court.

Respondents brought this class action in the District Court seeking declaratory and injunctive relief on their claim that their rights were being invaded by the Army's alleged "surveillance of lawful civilian political activity." * * *

The system put into operation as a result of the Army's 1967 experience [with civil disorders] consisted essentially of the collection of information about public activities that were thought to have at least some potential for civil disorder, the reporting of that information to Army Intelligence headquarters at Fort Holabird, Maryland, the dissemination of these reports from headquarters to major Army posts around the country, and the storage of the reported information in a computer data bank located at Fort Holabird. [T]he principal sources of information were the news media and publications in general circulation. Some of the information came from Army Intelligence agents who attended meetings that were open to the public and who wrote field reports describing the meetings, giving such data as the name of the sponsoring organization, the identity of speakers, the approximate number of persons in attendance, and an indication of whether any disorder occurred. And still other information was provided to the Army by civilian law enforcement agencies. * * *

By early 1970 [the] Army, in the course of a review of the system, ordered a significant reduction in its scope[:] "[R]eports [will] be limited [to] outbreaks of violence or incidents with a high potential for violence beyond the capability of state and local police and the National Guard to control. These reports [will] not be placed in a computer [and] are destroyed 60 days after publication or 60 days after the end of the disturbance. This limited reporting system will ensure that the Army is prepared to respond to whatever directions the President may issue in civil disturbance situations and without watching lawful activities of civilians." * * *[5]

In reversing, the Court of Appeals noted that [respondents] "freely admit that they complain of no specific action of the Army against them. [There] is no evidence of illegal or unlawful surveillance activities. [So] far as is yet shown, the information gathered is nothing more than a good newspaper reporter would

5. In the course of the oral argument, the District Judge [asked] what exactly it was in the Army's activities that tended to chill respondents and others in the exercise of their constitutional rights. Counsel responded that it was "precisely the threat in this case that *in some future civil disorder* of some kind, the Army is going to come in with its list of trouble-makers [and] go rounding up people and putting them in military prisons somewhere." (Emphasis added.) To this the court responded that "we still sit here with the writ of habeas corpus." At another point, counsel for respondents took a somewhat different approach in arguing that "*we're not quite sure exactly what they have in mind* and that is precisely what causes [the] chilling effect." (Emphasis added.)

be able to gather by attendance at public meetings and the clipping of articles from publications available on any newsstand."

[T]he Court of Appeals [also] had this to say: "[While respondents] do indeed argue that in the future it is possible that information relating to matters far beyond the responsibilities of the military may be misused by the military to the detriment of these [respondents], yet [respondents] do not attempt to establish this as a definitely foreseeable event, or to base their complaint on this ground. Rather, [respondents] contend that the *present existence of this system* of gathering and distributing information, allegedly far beyond the mission requirements of the Army, constitutes an impermissible burden on [respondents] and other persons similarly situated which exercises a *present inhibiting effect* on their full expression and utilization of their First Amendment rights." * * *

In recent years this Court has found in a number of cases that constitutional violations may arise from the deterrent, or "chilling," effect of governmental regulations that fall short of a direct prohibition against the exercise of First Amendment rights. E.g., *Keyishian v. Board of Regents,* [p. 734 supra]. In none of these cases, however, did the chilling effect arise merely from the individual's knowledge that a governmental agency was engaged in certain activities or from the individual's concomitant fear that, armed with the fruits of those activities, the agency might in the future take some *other* and additional action detrimental to that individual. Rather, in each of these cases, the challenged exercise of governmental power was regulatory, proscriptive, or compulsory in nature, and the complainant was either presently or prospectively subject to the regulations, proscriptions, or compulsions * * *.

[T]hese decisions have in no way eroded the "established principle that to entitle a private individual to invoke the judicial power to determine the validity of executive or legislative action he must show that he has sustained or is immediately in danger of sustaining a direct injury as the result of that action." The respondents do not meet this test; [their] alleged "chilling" effect may perhaps be seen as arising from respondents' very perception of the system as inappropriate to the Army's role under our form of government, or as arising from respondents' beliefs that it is inherently dangerous for the military to be concerned with activities in the civilian sector, or as arising from respondents' less generalized yet speculative apprehensiveness that the Army may at some future date misuse the information in some way that would cause direct harm to respondents.[7] Allegations of a subjective "chill" are not an adequate substitute for a claim of specific present objective harm or a threat of specific future harm; "the federal courts established pursuant to Article III of the Constitution do not render advisory opinions." *United Public Workers of America (C.I.O.) v. Mitchell,* 330 U.S. 75, 67 S.Ct. 556, 91 L.Ed. 754 (1947).

7. Not only have respondents left somewhat unclear the precise connection between the mere existence of the challenged system and their own alleged chill, but they have also cast considerable doubt on whether they themselves are in fact suffering from any such chill. [At] the oral argument before the District Court, counsel for respondents admitted that his clients were "not people, obviously, who are cowed and chilled"; indeed, they were quite willing "to open themselves up to public investigation and public scrutiny." But, counsel argued, these respondents must "represent millions of Americans not nearly as forward [and] courageous" as themselves. [Even] assuming a justiciable controversy, if respondents themselves are not chilled, but seek only to represent those "millions" whom they believe are so chilled, respondents clearly lack that "personal stake in the outcome of the controversy" essential to standing. [A] litigant "has standing to seek redress for injuries done to him, but may not seek redress for injuries done to others."

Stripped to its essentials, what respondents appear to be seeking is a broad scale investigation, conducted by themselves as private parties armed with the subpoena power of a federal district court and the power of cross-examination, to probe into the Army's intelligence-gathering activities, with the district court determining at the conclusion of that investigation the extent to which those activities may or may not be appropriate to the Army's mission. * * *

Carried to its logical end, this approach would have the federal courts as virtually continuing monitors of the wisdom and soundness of Executive action; such a role is appropriate for the Congress [not for] the judiciary, absent actual present or immediately threatened injury resulting from unlawful governmental action.

[O]n this record the respondents have not presented a case for resolution by the courts. * * *

Reversed.

JUSTICE DOUGLAS, with whom JUSTICE MARSHALL concurs, dissenting.

[When] refusal of the Court to pass on the constitutionality of an Act under the normal consideration of forbearance "would itself have an inhibitory effect on freedom of speech" then the Court will act. * * *

One need not wait to sue until he loses his job or until his reputation is defamed. To withhold standing to sue until that time arrives would in practical effect immunize from judicial scrutiny all surveillance activities regardless of their misuse and their deterrent effect. * * *

The present controversy is not a remote, imaginary conflict. Respondents were targets of the Army's surveillance. First, the surveillance was not casual but massive and comprehensive. Second, the intelligence reports were regularly and widely circulated and were exchanged with reports of the FBI, state and municipal police departments, and the CIA. Third, the Army's surveillance was not collecting material in public records but staking-out teams of agents, infiltrating undercover agents, creating command posts inside meetings, posing as press photographers and newsmen, posing as TV newsmen, posing as students, shadowing public figures.

Finally, [reports] of the Army have been "taken from the Intelligence Command's highly inaccurate civil disturbance teletype and filed in Army dossiers on persons who have held, or were being considered for, security clearances, thus contaminating what are supposed to be investigative reports with unverified gossip and rumor. This practice directly jeopardized the employment and employment opportunities of persons seeking sensitive positions with the federal government or defense industry."

[The] fact that since this litigation started the Army's surveillance may have been cut back is not an end of the matter. Whether there has been an actual cutback or whether the announcements are merely a ruse can be determined only after a hearing in the District Court. * * *[a]

Notes and Questions

1. *Consistency with prior decisions.* Could it be argued in *Tatum* (as Douglas, J., argued in dissent in *Mitchell*) that what respondents "propose to do is plain enough" and if they do so "it is clear that they will be discharged from

a. Brennan, J., joined by Stewart and Marshall, JJ., also dissented, agreeing with the Court of Appeals that the case was justiciable and respondents had standing.

their positions"? Consider 86 Harv.L.Rev. 134 (1972): "Granted, misuse in the *Tatum* situation is conjectural even after the protected activity is pursued, whereas injury for violation of a regulatory or prohibitive statute is clear and immediate. But the temptation to avoid the protected activity which risks unfavorable consequences may be no less when those consequences are undefined; indeed, it will be all the greater if the lack of definition implies the absence of an upward limit on injury."

To what extent did *Tatum* turn on the fact that respondents sought to speak not simply for themselves but for "millions of Americans not nearly as courageous"? Consider id. at 135: "Any decision on the merits would have required a court to weigh in some fashion the first amendment injury against the sufficiency of the Government's interest in military surveillance. Such an undertaking would have necessitated a determination of the relevance of the information gathered to the alleged governmental interest in the suppression of domestic insurrection without the application of blind force. Since the plaintiffs were bringing a class action seeking an injunction of all military surveillance activity and the destruction of all files unrelated to the Army's legitimate mission, this determination would have required consideration of an enormous bulk of information." Is this factor relevant to the discretionary exercise of declaratory judgment jurisdiction?

2. *Remote or hypothetical threat of injury.* (a) In O'SHEA v. LITTLETON, 414 U.S. 488, 94 S.Ct. 669, 38 L.Ed.2d 674 (1974), black and white residents who had protested racial discrimination in Cairo, Illinois obtained a federal injunction against state judicial officers, alleging a deliberate pattern of illegal bail, sentencing and jury fee practices against them due to their race and exercise of first amendment rights. Although some respondents "had actually been defendants in proceedings before petitioners and had suffered from the alleged unconstitutional practices," the Court, per WHITE, J., reversed: "Of course, past wrongs are evidence bearing on whether there is a real and immediate threat of repeated injury. [But] respondents here have not pointed to any imminent prosecutions contemplated against any of their number and they naturally do not suggest that any one of them expects to violate valid criminal laws. [Thus], the threat of injury from the alleged course of conduct they attack is simply too remote to satisfy the 'case or controversy' requirement and permit adjudication by a federal court." [b]

Even if there were "an existing case or controversy," however, "a proper balance in the concurrent operation of federal and state courts" precludes federal equitable relief. The decision below "would contemplate interruption of state proceedings to adjudicate assertions of noncompliance by petitioners. This seems to us nothing less than an ongoing federal audit of state criminal proceedings [that] is antipathetic to established principles of comity.[c] [Respondents] have failed, moreover, to establish the basic requisites of the issuance of equitable relief in these circumstances—the likelihood of substantial and imme-

b. For similar analysis, see *Rizzo v. Goode,* 423 U.S. 362, 96 S.Ct. 598, 46 L.Ed.2d 561 (1976).

c. Compare *Allee v. Medrano,* 416 U.S. 802, 94 S.Ct. 2191, 40 L.Ed.2d 566 (1974), upholding a federal injunction against state police disruption of unionization efforts. For fuller consideration of the delicacy of federal interference with state criminal proceedings, see Sec. 2, II infra. See also *Rizzo v. Goode,* fn. b, discussed at 90 Harv.L.Rev. 238 (1976), holding that "principles of equity, comity, and federalism" also restrict federal court supervision of state executive or administrative agencies—in this case, the disciplinary practices of a city police department.

See generally Meltzer, *Deterring Constitutional Violations by Law Enforcement Officials: Plaintiffs and Defendants as Private Attorneys General,* 88 Colum.L.Rev. 247 (1989).

diate irreparable injury, and the inadequacy of remedies at law. [I]f any of the respondents are ever prosecuted and face trial, or if they are illegally sentenced, there are available state and federal procedures which could provide relief from the wrongful conduct alleged"—e.g., direct review, collateral relief, and federal criminal prosecution of petitioners.[d]

(b) In DOE v. BOLTON, p. 436 supra, physicians with pregnant patients sought a federal declaratory judgment that a state criminal abortion statute deterred them from practicing their profession in violation of their constitutional rights. The Court, per BLACKMUN, J., held that they "present a justiciable controversy and do have standing despite the fact that the record does not disclose that any one of them has been prosecuted, or threatened with prosecution * * *. The physician is the one against whom these criminal statutes directly operate in the event he procures an abortion that does not meet the statutory exceptions and conditions. [They], therefore, assert a sufficiently direct threat of personal detriment. They should not be required to await and undergo a criminal prosecution as the sole means of seeking relief."

Is *Doe* consistent with *Tatum? O'Shea?*

POE v. ULLMAN

367 U.S. 497, 81 S.Ct. 1752, 6 L.Ed.2d 989 (1961).

JUSTICE FRANKFURTER announced the judgment of the Court and an opinion in which THE CHIEF JUSTICE, JUSTICE CLARK and JUSTICE WHITTAKER join.

These appeals challenge the constitutionality [of] Connecticut statutes [which] prohibit the use of contraceptive devices and the giving of medical advice in the use of such devices. In proceedings seeking declarations of law [brought by married couples and their doctor, the state] court has ruled that these statutes would be applicable in the case of married couples and even under claim that conception would constitute a serious threat to the health or life of the female spouse. * * *

Appellants' complaints [do] not clearly, and certainly do not in terms, allege that appellee Ullman threatens to prosecute [them]. The allegations are merely that, in the course of his public duty, he intends to prosecute any offenses against Connecticut law, and that he claims that use of and advice concerning contraceptives would constitute offenses. The lack of immediacy of the threat described by these allegations might alone raise serious questions of non-justiciability of appellants' claims. See *Mitchell.* But even were we to read the allegations to convey a clear threat of imminent prosecutions, we are not bound to accept as true all that is alleged on the face of the complaint and admitted, technically, by demurrer, any more than the Court is bound by stipulation of the parties. Formal agreement between parties that collides with plausibility is too fragile a foundation for indulging in constitutional adjudication.

The Connecticut law prohibiting the use of contraceptives has been on the State's books since 1879. During the more than three-quarters of a century since its enactment, a prosecution for its violation seems never to have been initiated, save in *State v. Nelson,* 126 Conn. 412, 11 A.2d 856. The circumstances of that case, decided in 1940, only prove the abstract character of what is before us. There, a test case was brought to determine the constitutionality of the Act as applied against two doctors and a nurse who had allegedly disseminated

d. Blackmun, J., concurred in the first part of the Court's opinion. Douglas, J., joined by Brennan and Marshall, JJ., dissented.

contraceptive information. After the Supreme Court of Errors sustained the legislation on appeal from a demurrer to the information, the State moved to dismiss the information. * * * We were advised by counsel for appellants that contraceptives are commonly and notoriously sold in Connecticut drug stores. Yet no prosecutions are recorded; and certainly such ubiquitous, open, public sales would more quickly invite the attention of enforcement officials than the conduct in which the present appellants wish to engage—the giving of private medical advice by a doctor to his individual patients, and their private use of the devices prescribed. The undeviating policy of nullification by Connecticut of its anticontraceptive laws throughout all the long years that they have been on the statute books bespeaks more than prosecutorial paralysis. What was said in another context is relevant here. "Deeply embedded traditional ways of carrying out state policy * * *"—or not carrying it out—"are often tougher and truer law than the dead words of the written text."

The restriction of our jurisdiction to cases and controversies within the meaning of Article III of the Constitution is not the sole limitation on the exercise of our appellate powers, especially in cases raising constitutional questions. The policy reflected in numerous cases and over a long period was thus summarized in the oft-quoted statement of Mr. Justice Brandeis: "The Court [has] developed, for its own governance in the cases confessedly within its jurisdiction, a series of rules under which it has avoided passing upon a large part of all the constitutional questions pressed upon it for decision." In part the rules summarized in the *Ashwander* opinion have derived from the historically defined, limited nature and function of courts and from the recognition that, within the framework of our adversary system, the adjudicatory process is most securely founded when it is exercised under the impact of a lively conflict between antagonistic demands, actively pressed, which make resolution of the controverted issue a practical necessity. * * *

These considerations press with special urgency in cases challenging legislative action or state judicial action as repugnant to the Constitution. [The] various doctrines of "standing," "ripeness," and "mootness," [are] but several manifestations—each having its own "varied application"—of the primary conception that federal judicial power is to be exercised to strike down legislation, whether state or federal, only at the instance of one who is himself immediately harmed, or immediately threatened with harm, by the challenged action. [It] was with respect to a state-originating declaratory judgment proceeding that we said [that] "the discretionary element characteristic of declaratory jurisdiction [offers] a convenient instrument for making * * * effective" the policy against premature constitutional decision. *Rescue Army v. Municipal Court,* [Part II supra, "Introductory Note"].

[If] the prosecutor expressly agrees not to prosecute, a suit against him for declaratory and injunctive relief is not such an adversary case as will be reviewed here. Eighty years of Connecticut history demonstrate a similar, albeit tacit agreement.

[W]e cannot accept, as the basis of constitutional adjudication, other than as chimerical the fear of enforcement of provisions that have during so many years gone uniformly and without exception unenforced.

Justiciability is of course not a legal concept with a fixed content or susceptible of scientific verification. Its utilization is the resultant of many subtle pressures, including the appropriateness of the issues for decision by this Court and the actual hardship to the litigants of denying them the relief sought.

Both these factors justify withholding adjudication of the constitutional issue raised under the circumstances and in the manner in which they are now before the Court.

Dismissed.

JUSTICE BLACK dissents because he believes that the constitutional questions should be reached and decided.

JUSTICE BRENNAN, concurring in the judgment.

[The] true controversy in this case is over the opening of birth-control clinics on a large scale; it is that which the State has prevented in the [past]. It will be time enough to decide the constitutional questions urged upon us when, if ever, that real controversy flares up again. * * *

JUSTICE DOUGLAS, dissenting.

[The] Court [goes] outside the record to conclude that there exists a "tacit agreement" that these statutes will not be enforced. No lawyer, I think, would advise his clients to rely on that "tacit agreement." No police official, I think, would feel himself bound by that "tacit agreement." After our national experience during the prohibition era, it would be absurd to pretend that all criminal statutes are adequately enforced. But that does not mean that bootlegging was the less a crime. * * *

When the Court goes outside the record to determine that Connecticut has adopted "The undeviating policy of nullification [of] its anti-contraceptive laws," it selects a particularly poor case in which to exercise such a novel power. This is not a law which is a dead letter. Twice since 1940, Connecticut has reenacted these laws as part of general statutory revisions. Consistently, bills to remove the statutes from the books have been rejected by the legislature. In short, the statutes—far from being the accidental left-overs of another era—are the center of a continuing controversy * * *.

[O]n oral argument, counsel for the appellee stated on his own knowledge that several proprietors had been prosecuted in the "minor police courts of Connecticut" after they had been "picked up" for selling contraceptives. The enforcement of criminal laws in minor courts has just as much impact as in those cases where appellate courts are resorted to. * * *

What are these people—doctor and patients—to do? Flout the law and go to prison? Violate the law surreptitiously and hope they will not get caught? By today's decision we leave them no other alternatives. It is not the choice they need have under the regime of the declaratory judgment * * *.

[On the merits, Douglas J., and Harlan, J., in his opinion that follows, argued that the statute was unconstitutional.]

JUSTICE HARLAN, dissenting.

[There] is no lack of "ripeness" [since] appellants have stated in their pleadings fully and unequivocally what it is that they intend to do; no clarifying or resolving contingency stands in their way before they may embark on that conduct. Thus there is no circumstance besides that of detection or prosecution to make remote the particular controversy. And it is clear beyond cavil that the mere fact that a controversy such as this is rendered still more unavoidable by an actual prosecution, is not *alone* sufficient to make the case too remote * * *.

[This] is not a feigned, hypothetical, friendly or colorable suit such as discloses "a want of a truly adversary contest." * * * I think both the plurality and concurring opinions confuse [the] predictive likelihood that, had [appellants] not brought themselves to appellee's attention, he would not enforce the statute against them, with some entirely suppositious "tacit agreement" not to prosecute, thereby ignoring the prosecutor's claim, asserted in these very proceedings, of a right, at his unbounded prosecutorial discretion, to enforce the statute. * * *

We are brought, then, to the precise failing in these proceedings which is said to justify refusal to exercise our mandatory appellate jurisdiction: that there has been but one recorded Connecticut case dealing with a *prosecution* under the statute. * * * I think it is pure conjecture, and indeed conjecture which to me seems contrary to realities, that an open violation of the statute by a doctor (or more obviously still by a birth-control clinic) would not result in a substantial threat of prosecution. Crucial to the opposite conclusion is the description of the 1940 prosecution instituted in *State v. Nelson* as a "test case" * * *. [T]he respect in which *Nelson* was a test case is only that it was brought for the purpose of making entirely clear the State's power and willingness to enforce against "*any* person, whether a physician or layman" (emphasis supplied), the statute and to eliminate from future cases the very doubt about the existence of these elements which had resulted in eight open birth-control clinics, and which would have made unfair the conviction of Nelson.

* * * I fear that the Court has indulged in a bit of sleight of hand to be rid of this case. It has treated the significance of the absence of prosecutions during the twenty years since *Nelson* as identical with that of the absence of prosecutions during the years before *Nelson*. It has ignored the fact that the very purpose of the *Nelson* prosecution was to change defiance into compliance. It has ignored the very possibility that this purpose may have been successful. * * *

The Court's disposition assumes that to decide the case now, in the absence of any consummated prosecutions, is unwise because it forces a difficult decision in advance of any exigent necessity therefor. [D]espite speculation as to a "tacit agreement" that this law will not be enforced, there is, of course, no suggestion of an estoppel against the State if it should attempt to prosecute appellants. Neither the plurality nor the concurring opinion suggests that appellants have some legally cognizable right not to be prosecuted if the statute is Constitutional. What is meant is simply that the appellants are more or less free to act without fear of prosecution because the prosecuting authorities of the State, in their discretion and at their whim, are, as a matter of prediction, unlikely to decide to prosecute.

Here is the core of my disagreement with the present disposition. [T]he most substantial claim which these married persons press is their right to enjoy the privacy of their marital relations free of the enquiry of the criminal law, whether it be in a prosecution of them or of a doctor whom they have consulted. And I cannot agree that their enjoyment of this privacy is not substantially impinged upon, when they are told that if they use contraceptives, indeed whether they do so or not, the only thing which stands between them and being forced to render criminal account of their marital privacy is the whim of the prosecutor. [Indeed] it appears that whereas appellants would surely have been entitled to review were this a new statute [the] State here is enabled to maintain at least some substantial measure of compliance with this statute and still obviate any review in this Court, by the device of purely discretionary prosecutorial inactivity. It seems to me to destroy the whole purpose of anticipatory relief to consider the prosecutor's discretion, once all legal and administrative channels have been cleared, as in any way analogous to those other contingencies which make remote a controversy presenting Constitutional claims. * * *

MR. JUSTICE STEWART, dissenting.

For the reasons so convincingly advanced by both Mr. Justice Douglas and Mr. Justice Harlan, I join them in dissenting from the dismissal of these appeals. * * *[a]

Notes and Questions

1. *The Court's rationale.* (a) Does *Poe* undermine the idea that law—good or bad—is to be obeyed? Or does it take the position that the Connecticut statutes were not really "*law*"? Does *Poe* ignore the fact that some (many?) people wish to (will?) obey the law simply because it is "the law," whether or not it will ever be enforced?

(b) Was the law not "a dead letter [because] consistently, bills to remove the statutes from the books have been rejected by the legislature"? Consider Bickel, *The Passive Virtues,* 75 Harv.L.Rev. 40, 63 (1961): "[G]reater strength must be mobilized to repeal a statute than to resist its enactment. When the law is consistently not enforced, the chance of mustering opposition sufficient to move the legislature is reduced to the vanishing point. For consistent failure to enforce is itself a political concession to the opposition, and will satisfy at least some portions of it. [The] unenforced statute is not, in the normal way, a continuing reflection of the balance of political pressures."

2. Is *Poe* distinguishable from *Epperson v. Arkansas,* p. 837 supra, where there was no record of enforcement of a forty year old statute making the teaching of evolution unlawful and, after her school adopted a textbook teaching evolution, a biology teacher sought a declaration that the statute was unconstitutional and an injunction against her dismissal?

3. *"Discretionary" dismissal of appeals.* Was the disposition in *Poe* inconsistent with the fact that the cases came to the Court on appeal, thus within the "obligatory jurisdiction" (Ch. 1, Sec. 4)? Consider Comment, *Threat of Enforcement—Prerequisite of a Judicial Controversy,* 62 Colum.L.Rev. 106, 126 (1962): "When an appeal is taken from a federal court decision, the Supreme Court, as the ultimate interpreter of federal law may derive its discretionary authority to deny adjudication from the nature of the injunction and declaratory judgment remedies. [B]ut it would seem that state construction of state remedies should be conclusively binding on the Supreme Court in the absence of article III objections. To justify discretion as an inherent power of the Court is equally unsatisfactory in view of the obligatory character of the appeal jurisdiction." Does this distinguish *Mitchell* from *Adler?*

Was the Court's refusal to decide *Poe* and *Socialist Labor Party* justified as commendable restraint in avoiding possibly unnecessary constitutional decision? Consider Note, *The Discretionary Power of the Supreme Court to Dismiss Appeals from State Courts,* 63 Colum.L.Rev. 688, 707 (1963): "[T]he assertion of discretion to refuse the jurisdiction that is given [by Congress] is inimical to fundamental postulates of principled judicial restraint; the declaration by the Court of such discretion itself violates the separation of powers philosophy upon which the Court has consistently relied. For by asserting power to make exceptions to its

a. For a further constitutional test, see *Griswold v. Connecticut,* p. 143 supra.

jurisdiction, the Court has assumed a power expressly delegated by the Constitution to Congress." See generally Gunther, *The Subtle Vices of the "Passive Virtues"—A Comment on Principle and Expediency in Judicial Review,* 64 Colum.L.Rev. 1 (1964). Does this argument draw an unrealistic dichotomy between (1) what Congress intended in conferring appeal jurisdiction and (2) the Court's rules of "self-limitation" from decision on the merits? See *Molinaro v. New Jersey,* 396 U.S. 365, 90 S.Ct. 498, 24 L.Ed.2d 586 (1970) (appeal dismissed because appellant was fugitive from justice); cf. *Ohio v. Wyandotte Chemicals Corp.,* 401 U.S. 493, 91 S.Ct. 1005, 28 L.Ed.2d 256 (1971) (declining to exercise statutorily granted original jurisdiction). Does it make an unwarranted assumption as to the clarity of the Constitution's allocation of power?

Consider Choper, *Judicial Review and the National Political Process* 406–09, 414 (1980): "[T]he Court should be hesitant to attribute an intention to the political branches that requires [it] to engage in the delicate process of constitutional adjudication despite the Justices' belief that it would be inappropriate or wasteful for the Court to do so. [This] suggested ground for nondecision would, of course, be unavailable if a clearly articulated legislative intent forbade a limiting construction of the jurisdictional statute. [In these circumstances, to] justify its deliberate refusal to decide some constitutional questions [the Court] should hold that political edicts to the contrary infringe 'the judicial Power of the United States.' Like all other constitutionally enumerated powers [this] clause implies those accessory powers necessary to its effective discharge, and final interpretation of its meaning belongs to the Supreme Court. [I]t is highly important to recognize the peculiar quality of the judicial assumption of power at issue. Viewed realistically, it is a judicial authority not to enhance the Court's power but rather to confine it, a course not of self-arrogation but rather one of self-denial—a capacity of the judiciary to refrain from exerting influence not wholly dissimilar (though the analogy is far from perfect) to whatever discretion the executive has to decline to enforce laws * * *."

*

Appendix A

THE JUSTICES OF THE SUPREME COURT

Originally prepared by JOHN J. COUND

Professor of Law, University of Minnesota

The data which follow, summarizing the prior public careers of those individuals who have served on the Supreme Court of the United States, are not presented with any notion that they did presage or now explain their judicial performance or constitutional philosophy. The experience which the justices have at any one time brought to bear upon the issues before the Court, however, seem worthy of interest, and may serve as a consideration in assessing charges that the Court has in particular cases rendered "ivory tower" decisions, unaware or heedless of "the realities."

Two conclusions are manifest. First, the diversity of distinguished experience which the bench of the Court has at all times reflected, always among its members and frequently in a single justice, is startling. William Howard Taft is unique, but surely few Americans have lived lives of diversified public service so rich as John Jay, Levi Woodbury, Lucius Q.C. Lamar, Charles Evans Hughes and Fred M. Vinson. Second, a broad background in public service has not assured prominence upon the Court, nor has its absence precluded it. Gabriel Duvall, with prior executive, legislative and judicial experience, was forgotten in the first edition of the *Dictionary of American Biography.* Samuel F. Miller and Joseph P. Bradley, with no prior public offices, surely stand among the front rank of the justices. (The interested student will find stimulation in Frankfurter, *The Supreme Court in the Mirror of Justice,* 105 U.Pa.L.Rev. 781 (1957), which treats particularly of the relevance of prior judicial office).

In the data, the first dates in parentheses are those of birth and death; these are followed by the name of the appointing President, and the dates of service on the Court. The state in which the justice was residing when appointed and his political affiliation at that time are then given. In detailing prior careers, I have followed chronological order, with two exceptions: I have listed first that a justice was a signer of the Declaration of Independence or the Federal Constitution, and I have indicated state legislative experience only once for each justice. I have not distinguished between different bodies in the state legislature, and I have omitted service in the Continental Congresses. Private practice, except where deemed especially signficant, and law teaching have been omitted, except where the justice was primarily engaged therein upon his appointment. (Blackmun, Burger, Douglas, Fortas, Holmes, Hughes, Kennedy, L.Q.C. Lamar, Lurton,

McReynolds, Murphy, Roberts, W. Rutledge, Stevens, Stone and Van Devanter in addition to Taft and Frankfurter, had all taught before going on the Court; Story, Strong and Wilson taught while on the court or after leaving it). The activity in which a justice was engaged upon appointment has been italicized. Figures in parentheses indicate years of service in the position. In only a few cases, a justice's extra-Court or post-Court activity has been indicated, or some other note made. An asterisk designates the Chief Justices.

For detailed information on the men who have served as members of the Supreme Court, see L. Friedman & F. Israel, eds., *The Justices of the United States Supreme Court 1789–1969: Their Lives and Major Opinions* (Chelsea House, 1969), and the bibliographical references collected therein.

The accompanying Table of Justices on pages [3] and [4] has been planned so that the composition of the Court at any time can be readily ascertained.

(This material has been compiled from a great number of sources, but special acknowledgment must be made to the *Dictionary of American Biography* (Charles Scribner's Sons), the A.N. Marquis Company works, and Ewing, *The Judges of the Supreme Court, 1789–1937* (University of Minnesota Press, 1938).)

BALDWIN, HENRY (1780–1844; Jackson 1830–1844). Pa.Dem.—U.S., House of Representatives (5). *Private practice.*

BARBOUR, PHILIP P. (1783–1841; Jackson, 1836–1841). Va.Dem.—Va., Legislature (2). U.S., House of Representatives (14). Va., Judge, General Court (2); President, State Constitutional Convention, 1829–30, *U.S., Judge, District Court (5).*

BLACK, HUGO L. (1886–1971; F.D. Roosevelt, 1937–1971). Ala.Dem.—Captain, Field Artillery, World War I. Ala., Judge, Police Court (1); County Solicitor (2). *U.S., Senate (10).*

BLACKMUN, HARRY A. (1908–____; Nixon, 1970–____). Minn.Rep.—Resident Counsel, Mayo Clinic, (10). *U.S., Judge, Court of Appeals (11).*

BLAIR, JOHN (1732–1800; Washington, 1789–1796). Va.Fed.—Signer, U.S. Constitution, 1787. Va., Legislature (9); Judge and Chief Justice, General Court (2), *Court of Appeals (9).* His opinion in *Commonwealth v. Caton,* 4 Call 5, 20 (Va.1782), is one of the earliest expressions of the doctrine of judicial review.

BLATCHFORD, SAMUEL (1820–1893; Arthur, 1882–1893). N.Y.Rep.—U.S., Judge, District Court (5); *Circuit Court (10).*

BRADLEY, JOSEPH P. (1803–1892; Grant, 1870–1892). N.J.Rep.—Actuary. *Private practice.*

BRANDEIS, LOUIS D. (1856–1941; Wilson, 1916–1939). Mass.Dem.—*Private practice.* Counsel, variously for the government, for industry, and "for the people", in numerous administrative and judicial proceedings, both state and federal.

BRENNAN, WILLIAM J. (1906–____; Eisenhower, 1956–____). N.J.Dem.—U.S. Army, World War II. N.J., Judge, Superior Court (1); Appellate Division (2); *Supreme Court (4).*

BREWER, DAVID J. (1837–1910; B. Harrison, 1889–1910). Kans.Rep.—Kans., Judge, County Criminal and Probate Court (1), District Court (4); County Attorney (1); Judge, Supreme Court (14), *U.S., Judge, Circuit Court (5).*

BROWN, HENRY, B. (1836–1913; B. Harrison, 1890–1906). Mich.Rep.—U.S., Assistant U.S. Attorney (5). Mich., Judge, Circuit Court (1). *U.S., Judge, District Court (15).*

1789	Jay	Rutledge, J.	Cushing	Wilson	Blair						1789
1790						Iredell					1790
1791		Johnson, T.									1791
1793		Paterson									1793
1795	Rutledge, J.										1795
1796	Ellsworth				Chase, Samuel						1796
1798				Washington							1798
1799						Moore					1799
1801	Marshall, J.										1801
1804						Johnson, W.					1804
1806		Livingston									1806
1807							Todd				1807
1811			Story		Duval						1811
1823		Thompson									1823
1826							Trimble				1826
1829							McLean				1829
1830				Baldwin							1830
1835						Wayne					1835
1836	Taney				Barbour						1836
1837								Catron	McKinley		1837
1841					Daniel						1841
1845		Nelson	Woodbury								1845
1846				Grier							1846
1851			Curtis								1851
1853									Campbell		1853
1858			Clifford								1858
1862					Miller		Swayne		Davis		1862
1863										Field	1863
1864	Chase, Salmon										1864
1865								*			1865
1867						*					1867
1870				Strong		Bradley					1870
1872		Hunt									1872
1874	Waite										1874
1877								Harlan			1877
1880				Woods							1880
1881			Gray				Matthews				1881
1882		Blatchford									1882
1888	Fuller			Lamar, L.							1888
1889							Brewer				1889
1890					Brown						1890
1892						Shiras					1892
1893				Jackson, H.							1893
1894		White, E.									1894
1895				Peckham							1895
1898									McKenna		1898
1902			Holmes								1902
1903						Day					1903
1906					Moody						1906

* Catron died in 1865, Wayne in 1867; their positions were abolished by Congress to prevent their being filled by President Johnson; a new position was created in 1869, which traditionally has been regarded as a re-creation of Wayne's seat.

1909				Lurton						1909
1910	White, E.	** Van Devanter			Lamar, J.		Hughes			1910
1912								Pitney		1912
1914				McReynolds						1914
1916					Brandeis		Clarke			1916
1921	Taft									1921
1922						Butler	Sutherland			1922
1923								Sanford		1923
1925									Stone	1925
1930	Hughes							Roberts		1930
1932			Cardozo							1932
1937		Black								1937
1938							Reed			1938
1939			Frankfurter		Douglas					1939
1940						Murphy				1940
1941	Stone			Byrnes					** Jackson, R.	1941
1943				Rutledge						1943
1945								Burton		1945
1946	Vinson									1946
1949				Minton		Clark				1949
1953	Warren									1953
1955									Harlan	1955
1956				Brennan						1956
1957							Whittaker			1957
1958								Stewart		1958
1962			Goldberg				White, B.			1962
1965			Fortas							1965
1966										1966
1967						Marshall, T.				1967
1968										1968
1969	Burger									1969
1970			Blackmun							1970
1972		Powell							Rehnquist	1972
1975					Stevens					1975
1981								O'Connor		1981
1982										1982
1983										1983
1986	Rehnquist								** Scalia	1986
1987										1987
1988		Kennedy								1988
1989										1989
1990				Souter						1990

** Fuller died in 1910 and White was named Chief Justice. Hughes resigned in 1941, and Stone was named Chief Justice. Burger resigned in 1986 and Rehnquist was named Chief Justice.

*BURGER, WARREN E. (1907–____; Nixon, 1969–____). Va.Rep.—U.S., Assistant Attorney General, Civil Division (3), *Judge, Court of Appeals (13).*

BURTON, HAROLD H. (1888–1964; Truman, 1945–1958). Ohio Rep.—Capt., U.S.A., World War I. Ohio, Legislature (2). Mayor, Cleveland, O. (5). *U.S., Senate (4).*

BUTLER, PIERCE (1866–1939; Harding, 1922–1939). Minn.Dem.—Minn., County Attorney (4). *Private practice.*

BYRNES, JAMES F. (1879–1972; F.D. Roosevelt, 1941–1942). S.C.Dem.—S.C., Solicitor, Circuit Court (2). U.S., House of Representatives (14); *Senate (12).* Resigned from the Court to become U.S. Director of Economic Stabilization.

CAMPBELL, JOHN A. (1811–1889; Pierce, 1853–1861). Ala.Dem.—*Private practice.* After his resignation, he became Assistant Secretary of War, C.S.A.

CARDOZO, BENJAMIN N. (1870–1938; Hoover, 1932–1938). N.Y.Dem.—N.Y., Judge, Supreme Court (6 weeks); Associate Judge and *Chief Judge, Court of Appeals (18).*

CATRON, JOHN (1778–1865; Van Buren, 1837–1865). Tenn.Dem.—Tenn., Judge and Chief Justice, Supreme Court of Errors and Appeals (10). *Private practice.*

*CHASE, SALMON P. (1808–1873; Lincoln 1864–1873). Ohio Rep.—U.S., Senate (6). Ohio, Governor (4). *U.S., Secretary of the Treasury (3).*

CHASE, SAMUEL (1741–1811; Washington, 1796–1811). Md.Fed.—Signer, U.S., Declaration of Independence, 1776. Md., Legislature (20); Chief Judge, Court of Oyer and Terminer (2), *General Court (5).* Impeached and acquitted, 1804–05.

CLARK, TOM C. (1899–1977; Truman, 1949–1967). Tex.Dem.—U.S. Army, World War I. Tex., Civil District Attorney (5). U.S., Assistant Attorney General (2), *Attorney General (4).*

CLARKE, JOHN H. (1857–1945; Wilson, 1916–1922). Ohio Dem.—*U.S. Judge, District Court (2).*

CLIFFORD, NATHAN (1803–1881; Buchanan, 1858–1881). Me.Dem.—Me., Legislature (4); Attorney General (4). U.S., House of Representatives (4); Attorney General (2); Minister Plenipotentiary to Mexico, 1848. *Private practice.*

CURTIS, BENJAMIN R. (1809–1874; Fillmore, 1851–1857). Mass.Whig.—Mass., Legislature (1). *Private practice.*

CUSHING, WILLIAM (1732–1810; Washington, 1789–1810). Mass.Fed.—Mass., Judge, Superior Court (3); Justice and *Chief Justice, Supreme Judicial Court (14).*

DANIEL, PETER V. (1784–1860; Van Buren, 1841–1860). Va.Dem.—Va., Legislature (3); Member, Privy Council (23). *U.S., Judge, District Court (5).*

DAVIS, DAVID (1815–1886; Lincoln, 1862–1877). Ill.Rep.—Ill., Legislature (2); *Judge, Circuit Court (14).* His resignation to become U.S. Senator upset the agreed-upon composition of the Hayes-Tilden Electoral Commission.

DAY, WILLIAM R. (1849–1923; T. Roosevelt, 1903–1922). Ohio Rep.—Ohio, Judge, Court of Common Pleas (4). U.S., Assistant Secretary of State (1), Secretary of State ($^1/_2$); Chairman, U.S. Peace Commissioners, 1898; *Judge, Circuit Court of Appeals (4).*

DOUGLAS, WILLIAM O. (1898–1980; F.D. Roosevelt, 1939–1975). Conn. Dem.—Pvt., U.S. Army, World War I. *U.S., Chairman, Securities and Exchange Commission (3).* His was the longest tenure in the history of the Court.

DUVAL(L), GABRIEL (1752–1844; Madison, 1811–1935). Md.Rep.—Declined to serve as delegate, U.S. Constitutional Convention, 1787. Md., State Council (3). U.S., House of Representatives (2). Md., Judge, General Court (6). *U.S., Comptroller of the Treasury (9).*

*ELLSWORTH, OLIVER (1745–1807; Washington, 1796–1800). Conn. Fed.—Delegate, U.S. Constitutional Convention, 1787. Conn., Legislature (2); Member, Governor's Council (4); Judge, Superior Court (5). *U.S., Senate (7).*

FIELD, STEPHEN J. (1816–1899; Lincoln, 1863–1897). Calif.Dem.—*Calif.,* Justice, and *Chief Justice, Supreme Court (6).*

FORTAS, ABE (1910–1982; L.B. Johnson, 1965–1969). Tenn.Dem.—U.S. Government attorney and consultant (A.A.A., S.E.C., P.W.A., Dep't of Interior (9); Undersecretary of Interior (4). *Private practice in Washington, D.C.* Nominated as Chief Justice; nomination withdrawn, 1968. Resigned.

FRANKFURTER, FELIX (1882–1965; F.D. Roosevelt, 1939–1962). Mass. Independent.—U.S., Assistant U.S. Attorney (4); Law Officer, War Department, Bureau of Insular Affairs (3); Assistant to Secretary of War (1). *Professor of Law (25).*

*FULLER, MELVILLE W. (1833–1910; Cleveland, 1888–1910). Ill.Dem.—Ill., Legislature (2). *Private practice.*

GOLDBERG, ARTHUR J. (1908–____; Kennedy, 1962–1965). Ill.Dem.—Major, U.S.A., World War II. General Counsel, USW–AFL–CIO (13). *U.S., Secretary of Labor (1).* Resigned to become Ambassador to U.N.

GRAY, HORACE (1828–1902; Arthur, 1881–1902). Mass.Rep.—*Mass.,* Associate Justice and *Chief Justice, Supreme Judicial Court (18).*

GRIER, ROBERT O. (1794–1870; Polk, 1846–1870). Pa.Dem.—*Pa., Presiding Judge, District Court (13).*

HARLAN, JOHN M. (1833–1911; Hayes, 1877–1911). Ky.Rep.—Ky., Judge, County Court (1). Col., Union Army, 1861–63. Ky., Attorney General (4). U.S., Member, President's Louisiana Commission, 1877. *Private practice.* Grandfather of:

HARLAN, JOHN M. (1899–1971; Eisenhower, 1955–1971). N.Y.Rep.—Col., U.S.A.A.F., World War II. N.Y. Chief Counsel, State Crime Commission (2). *U.S., Judge, Court of Appeals (1).*

HOLMES, OLIVER W., JR. (1841–1935; T. Roosevelt, 1902–1932). Mass. Rep.—Lt. Col., Mass. Volunteers, Civil War. *Mass.,* Associate Justice, and *Chief Justice, Supreme Judicial Court (20).*

*HUGHES, CHARLES E. (1862–1948; Taft, 1910–1916, and Hoover, 1930–1941). N.Y.Rep.—N.Y., Counsel, legislative committees investigating gas and insurance industries, 1905–06. U.S., Special Assistant to Attorney General for Coal Investigation, 1906. *N.Y., Governor (3).* [Between appointments to the Supreme Court: Presidential Nominee, Republican Party, 1916. U.S., Secretary of State (4). *Member, Permanent Court of Arbitration, The Hague (4). Judge, Permanent Court of International Justice (2).*] Chief Justice on second appointment.

HUNT, WARD (1810–1886; Grant, 1872–1882). N.Y.Rep.—N.Y., Legislature (2). Mayor of Utica, N.Y. (1). N.Y. Associate Judge, and Chief Judge, Court of Appeals (4); *Commissioner of Appeals (4).* He did not sit from 1879 to his retirement in 1882.

IREDELL, JAMES (1750–1799; Washington, 1790–1799). N.C.Fed.—Comptroller of Customs (6), Collector of Port (2), Edenton, N.C., N.C., Judge, Superior Court (1/2); Attorney General (2); Member, Council of State, 1787; *Reviser of Statutes (3).*

JACKSON, HOWELL E. (1832–1895; B. Harrison, 1893–1895). Tenn. Dem.—Tenn., Judge, Court of Arbitration (4); Legislature (1). U.S. Senate (5); *Judge, Circuit Court of Appeals (7).*

JACKSON, ROBERT H. (1892–1954; F.D. Roosevelt, 1941–1954). N.Y. Dem.—U.S., General Counsel, Bureau of Internal Revenue (2); Assistant Attorney General (2); Solicitor General (2); *Attorney General (1).*

*JAY, JOHN (1745–1829; Washington, 1789–1795). N.Y.Fed.—N.Y., Chief Justice, Supreme Court (2). U.S., Envoy to Spain (2); Commissioner, Treaty of Paris, 1782–83; Secretary for Foreign Affairs (6). Co-author, The Federalist.

JOHNSON, THOMAS (1732–1819; Washington, 1791–1793). Md.Fed.—Md., Brigadier-General, Militia (1); Legislature (5); Governor (2); *Chief Judge, General Court (1).*

JOHNSON, WILLIAM (1771–1834; Jefferson, 1804–1834). S.C.Rep.—S.C., Legislature (4); *Judge, Court of Common Pleas (6).*

KENNEDY, ANTHONY M. (1936–____); Reagan (1988–____); Calif.Rep.; U.S., *Judge, Court of Appeals* (11).

LAMAR, JOSEPH R. (1857–1916; Taft, 1910–1916). Ga.Dem.—Ga., Legislature (3); Commissioner to Codify Laws (3); Associate Justice, Supreme Court (4). *Private practice.*

LAMAR, LUCIUS Q.C. (1825–1893; Cleveland, 1888–1893). Miss.Dem.—Ga., Legislature (2). U.S., House of Representatives (4). Draftsman, Mississippi Ordinance of Secession, 1861. C.S.A., Lt. Col. (1); Commissioner to Russia (1); Judge-Advocate, III Corps. Army of No. Va. (1). U.S., House of Representatives (4); Senate (8); *Secretary of the Interior (3).*

LIVINGSTON, (HENRY) BROCKHOLST (1757–1823; Jefferson, 1806–1823). N.Y.Rep.—Lt. Col., Continental Army. *N.Y., Judge, Supreme Court (4).*

LURTON, HORACE H. (1844–1914; Taft, 1909–1914). Tenn.Dem.—Sgt. Major, C.S.A. Tenn., Chancellor (3); Associate Justice and Chief Justice, Supreme Court (7). *U.S., Judge, Circuit Court of Appeals (16).*

McKENNA, JOSEPH (1843–1926; McKinley, 1898–1925). Calif.Rep.—Calif., District Attorney (2); Legislature (2). U.S., House of Representatives (7); *Judge, Circuit Court of Appeals (5); Attorney General (1).*

McKINLEY, JOHN (1780–1852; Van Buren, 1837–1852). Ala.Dem.—Legislature (4). U.S., Senate (5); House of Representatives (2); *re-elected to Senate,* but appointed to Court before taking seat.

McLEAN, JOHN (1785–1861; Jackson, 1829–1861). Ohio Dem.—U.S., House of Representatives (4). Ohio, Judge, Supreme Court (6). U.S., Commissioner, General Land Office (1); *Postmaster-General (6).*

McREYNOLDS, JAMES C. (1862–1946; Wilson, 1914–1941). Tenn.Dem.—U.S., Assistant Attorney General (4); *Attorney General (1).*

*MARSHALL, JOHN (1755–1835; J. Adams, 1801–1835). Va.Fed.—Va., Legislature (7); U.S., Envoy to France (1); House of Representatives (1); *Secretary of State (1).*

MARSHALL, THURGOOD (1908–____; L.B. Johnson, 1967–1991). N.Y. Dem.—Counsel, Legal Defense and Educational Fund, NAACP (21). U.S., Judge, Court of Appeals (4); *Solicitor General (2).*

MATTHEWS, STANLEY (1824–1889; Garfield, 1881–1889). Ohio Rep.—Ohio, Judge, Court of Common Pleas (2); Legislature (3). U.S., District Attorney (3). Col., Ohio Volunteers. Ohio, Judge, Superior Court (2). Counsel before Hayes-Tilden Electoral Commission, 1877. U.S., Senate (2). *Private practice.* His first appointment to the Court by Hayes in 1881 was not acted upon by the Senate.

MILLER, SAMUEL F. (1816–1890; Lincoln, 1862–1890). Iowa Rep.—Physician. *Private practice.*

MINTON, SHERMAN (1890–1965; Truman, 1949–1956). Ind.Dem.—Capt., Inf., World War I. U.S., Senate (6); *Judge, Court of Appeals (8).*

MOODY, WILLIAM H. (1853–1917; T. Roosevelt, 1906–1910). Mass.Rep.—U.S., District Attorney (5), House of Representatives (7); Secretary of the Navy (2); *Attorney General (2).*

MOORE, ALFRED (1755–1810; J. Adams, 1799–1804). N.C.Fed.—N.C., Col. of Militia; Legislature (2); Attorney General (9). U.S. Commissioner, Treaty with Cherokee Nation (1); *N.C., Judge, Superior Court (1).*

MURPHY, FRANK (1893–1949; F.D. Roosevelt, 1940–1949). Mich.Dem.—Capt., Inf., World War I. U.S., Assistant U.S. Attorney (1). Mich., Judge, Recorder's Court (7). Mayor, Detroit, Mich. (3). U.S., Governor-General, and High Commissioner, P.I. (3). Mich., Governor (2). *U.S., Attorney General (1).*

NELSON, SAMUEL (1792–1873; Tyler, 1845–1872). N.Y.Dem.—N.Y., Judge, Circuit Court (8); Associate Justice, and *Chief Justice, Supreme Court (14).*

O'CONNOR, SANDRA DAY (1930–____; Reagan, 1981–____. Ariz.Rep.—Ariz., Assistant Attorney General (4); Legislature (6). Ariz., Judge, Superior Court (4); *Court of Appeals (2).*

PATERSON, WILLIAM (1745–1806; Washington, 1793–1806). N.J.Fed.—Signer, U.S. Constitution, 1787. N.J., Legislature (2); Attorney General (7). U.S., Senate (1). *N.J., Governor (3).* Reviser of English Pre-Revolutionary Statutes in Force in N.J.

PECKHAM, RUFUS W. (1838–1909; Cleveland, 1895–1909). N.Y.Dem.—N.Y., District Attorney (1); Justice, Supreme Court (3); *Associate Judge, Court of Appeals (9).*

PITNEY, MAHLON (1858–1924; Taft, 1912–1922). N.J.Rep.—U.S., House of Representatives (4). N.J., Legislature (2); Associate Justice, Supreme Court (7); Chancellor (4).

POWELL, LEWIS F. (1907–____; Nixon, 1972–____). Va.Dem.—Col., U.S. A.A.F., World War II. *Private practice.*

REED, STANLEY F. (1884–1980; F.D. Roosevelt, 1938–1957). Ky.Dem.—Ky., Legislature (4). 1st Lt., U.S.A., World War I. U.S., General Counsel, Federal Farm Board (3); General Counsel, Reconstruction Finance Corporation (3); *Solicitor General (3).*

REHNQUIST, WILLIAM H. (1924–____; Nixon, 1972–____). Ariz.Rep.—U.S.A.F., World War II. Law Clerk, Justice Jackson, 1952–53. *U.S., Assistant Attorney General (3).*

ROBERTS, OWEN J. (1875–1955; Hoover, 1930–1945). Pa.Rep.—Pa., Assistant District Attorney (3). U.S., Special Deputy Attorney General in Espionage Act Cases, World War I; Special Prosecutor, Oil Cases, 1924. *Private practice.*

*RUTLEDGE, JOHN (1739–1800; Washington, 1789–1791, and Washington, 1795). S.C.Fed.—Signer, U.S. Constitution, 1787. S.C., Legislature (18); Attorney General (1); President and Governor (6); *Chancellor (7).* [Between appointments to the Supreme Court: *S.C., Chief Justice, Court of Common Pleas and Sessions (4).*] He did not sit under his first appointment; he sat with a recess appointment as Chief Justice, but his regular appointment was rejected by the Senate.

RUTLEDGE, WILEY B. (1894–1949; F.D. Roosevelt, 1943–1949). Iowa Dem.—Mo., then Iowa, Member, National Conference of Commissioners on Uniform State Laws (10). *U.S., Judge, Court of Appeals (4).*

SANFORD, EDWARD T. (1865–1930; Harding, 1923–1930). Tenn.Rep.—U.S., Assistant Attorney General (1); *Judge, District Court (15).*

SCALIA, ANTONIN (1936–____); Reagan (1986–____); Va.Rep.—U.S., Assistant Attorney General (3); *Judge, Court of Appeals* (4).

SHIRAS, GEORGE (1832–1924; B. Harrison, 1892–1903). Pa.Rep. *Private practice.*

SOUTER, DAVID H. (1939–____); Bush (1990–____); N.H.Rep.; N.H., Deputy Attorney General (5); Attorney General (2); Associate Justice, Superior Court (5), Associate Justice, Supreme Court (7); U.S., *Judge, Court of Appeals* (5 mo.).

STEVENS, JOHN PAUL (1920–____; Ford, 1975–____). Ill.Independent.—U.S.N.R., World War II. Law Clerk, Justice Wiley Rutledge, 1947–48. *Judge, Court of Appeals (5).*

STEWART, POTTER (1915–1985; Eisenhower, 1958–1981). Ohio Rep.—Lt., U.S.N.R., World War II. *U.S., Judge, Court of Appeals (4).*

*STONE, HARLAN F. (1872–1946; Coolidge, later F.D. Roosevelt, 1925–1946). N.Y.Rep.—*U.S., Attorney General (1).* Chief Justice, 1941–1946.

STORY, JOSEPH (1779–1845; Madison, 1811–1845). Mass.Rep.—Mass., Legislature (5). U.S., House of Representatives (2). *Private practice.*

STRONG, WILLIAM (1808–1895; Grant, 1870–1880). Pa.Rep.—U.S., House of Representatives (4). Pa., Justice, Supreme Court (11). *Private practice.*

SUTHERLAND, GEORGE (1862–1942; Harding, 1922–1938). Utah Rep.—Utah, Legislature (4). U.S., House of Representatives (2); Senate (12). *Private practice.*

SWAYNE, NOAH H. (1804–1884; Lincoln, 1862–1881). Ohio Rep.—Ohio, County Attorney (4); Legislature (2). U.S., District Attorney (9). *Private practice.*

*TAFT, WILLIAM H. (1857–1930; Harding, 1921–1930). Conn.Rep.—U.S., Collector of Internal Revenue (1). Ohio, Judge, Superior Court (3). U.S., Solicitor General (2); Judge, Circuit Court of Appeals (8); Governor-General, P.I. (3); Secretary of War (4); President (4). *Professor of Law.*

*TANEY, ROGER B. (1777–1864; Jackson, 1836–1864). Md.Dem.—Md., Legislature (7); Attorney General (2). U.S., Attorney General (2), Secretary of the Treasury (3/4; rejected by the Senate). *Private practice.*

THOMPSON, SMITH (1768–1843; Monroe, 1823–1843). N.Y.Rep.—N.Y., Legislature (2); Associate Justice, and Chief Justice, Supreme Court (16). *U.S., Secretary of the Navy (4).*

TODD, THOMAS (1765–1826; Jefferson, 1807–1826). Ky.Rep.—*Ky., Judge, and Chief Justice, Court of Appeals (6).*

TRIMBLE, ROBERT (1777–1828; J.Q. Adams, 1826–1828). Ky.Rep.—Ky., Legislature (2). Judge, Court of Appeals (2). U.S., District Attorney (4); *Judge, District Court (9).*

VAN DEVANTER, WILLIS (1859–1941; Taft, 1910–1937). Wyo.Rep.—Wyo., Legislature (2); Chief Justice, Supreme Court (1). U.S., Assistant Attorney General (Interior Department) (6); *Judge, Circuit Court of Appeals (7).*

*VINSON, FRED M. (1890–1953; Truman, 1946–1953). Ky.Dem.—Ky., Commonwealth Attorney (3). U.S., House of Representatives (14); Judge, Court of Appeals (5); Director, Office of Economic Stabilization (2); Federal Loan Administrator (1 mo.); Director, Office of War Mobilization and Reconversion (3 mo.); *Secretary of the Treasury (1).*

*WAITE, MORRISON R. (1816–1888; Grant, 1874–1888). Ohio Rep.—Ohio, Legislature (2). Counsel for United States, U.S.—Gr. Brit. Arbitration ("Alabama" Claims), 1871–72. *Private practice.*

*WARREN, EARL (1891–1974; Eisenhower, 1953–1969). Calif.Rep.—1st Lt., Inf., World War I. Deputy City Attorney (1); Deputy District Attorney (5); District Attorney (14); Attorney General (4); *Governor (10).*

WASHINGTON, BUSHROD (1762–1829; J. Adams, 1798–1829). Pa.Fed.—Va., Legislature (1). *Private practice.*

WAYNE, JAMES M. (1790–1867; Jackson, 1835–1867). Ga.Dem.—Ga., Officer, Hussars, War of 1812; Legislature (2). Mayor of Savannah, Ga. (2). Ga., Judge, Superior Court (5). *U.S., House of Representatives (6).*

WHITE, BYRON R. (1917–____; Kennedy, 1962–____). Colo.Dem.—U.S. N.R., World War II. Law Clerk, Chief Justice Vinson, 1946–47. *U.S., Deputy Attorney General (1).*

*WHITE, EDWARD D. (1845–1921; Cleveland, later Taft, 1894–1921). La. Dem.—La., Legislature (4); Justice, Supreme Court (2). *U.S., Senate (3).* Chief Justice, 1910–1921.

WHITTAKER, CHARLES E. (1901–1973; Eisenhower, 1957–1962). Mo. Rep.—U.S., Judge, District Court (2); *Court of Appeals (1).*

WILSON, JAMES (1724–1798; Washington, 1789–1798). Pa.Fed.—Signer, U.S. Declaration of Independence, 1776, and U.S. Constitution, 1787. Although he was strongly interested in western-land development companies for several years prior to his appointment, his primary activity in the period immediately preceding his appointment was in obtaining ratification of the Federal and Pennsylvania Constitutions.

WOODBURY, LEVI (1789–1851; Polk, 1845–1851). N.H. Dem.—N.H., Associate Justice, Superior Court (6); Governor (2); Legislature (1). U.S., Senate (6); Secretary of the Navy (3); Secretary of the Treasury (7); *Senate (4).*

WOODS, WILLIAM B. (1824–1887; Hayes, 1880–1887). Ga.Rep.—Mayor, Newark, O. (1). Ohio, Legislature (4). Brevet Major General, U.S. Vol., Civil War. Ala., Chancellor (1). *U.S., Judge, Circuit Court (11).*

Appendix B

THE CONSTITUTION OF THE UNITED STATES

PREAMBLE

We the People of the United States, in Order to form a more perfect Union, establish Justice, insure domestic Tranquility, provide for the common defence, promote the general Welfare, and secure the Blessings of Liberty to ourselves and our Posterity, do ordain and establish this Constitution for the United States of America.

ARTICLE I

Section 1. All legislative Powers herein granted shall be vested in a Congress of the United States, which shall consist of a Senate and House of Representatives.

Section 2. [1] The House of Representatives shall be composed of Members chosen every second Year by the People of the several States, and the Electors in each State shall have the Qualifications requisite for Electors of the most numerous Branch of the State Legislature.

[2] No Person shall be a Representative who shall not have attained to the Age of twenty five Years, and been seven Years a Citizen of the United States, and who shall not, when elected, be an Inhabitant of that State in which he shall be chosen.

[3] Representatives and direct Taxes shall be apportioned among the several States which may be included within this Union, according to their respective Numbers, which shall be determined by adding to the whole Number of free Persons, including those bound to Service for a Term of Years, and excluding Indians not taxed, three fifths of all other Persons. The actual Enumeration shall be made within three Years after the first Meeting of the Congress of the United States, and within every subsequent Term of ten Years, in such Manner as they shall by Law direct. The Number of Representatives shall not exceed one for every thirty Thousand, but each State shall have at Least one Representative; and until such enumeration shall be made, the State of New Hampshire shall be entitled to chuse three, Massachusetts eight, Rhode Island and Providence Plantations one, Connecticut five, New York six, New Jersey four, Pennsylvania eight, Delaware one, Maryland six, Virginia ten, North Carolina five, South Carolina five, and Georgia three.

[4] When vacancies happen in the Representation from any State, the Executive Authority thereof shall issue Writs of Election to fill such Vacancies.

[5] The House of Representatives shall chuse their Speaker and other Officers; and shall have the sole Power of Impeachment.

Section 3. [1] The Senate of the United States shall be composed of two Senators from each State, chosen by the Legislature thereof, for six Years; and each Senator shall have one Vote.

[2] Immediately after they shall be assembled in Consequence of the first Election, they shall be divided as equally as may be into three Classes. The Seats of the Senators of the first Class shall be vacated at the Expiration of the Second Year, of the second Class at the Expiration of the fourth Year, and of the third Class at the Expiration of the sixth Year, so that one third may be chosen every second Year; and if Vacancies happen by Resignation, or otherwise, during the Recess of the Legislature of any State, the Executive thereof may make temporary Appointments until the next Meeting of the Legislature, which shall then fill such Vacancies.

[3] No Person shall be a Senator who shall not have attained to the Age of thirty Years, and been nine Years a Citizen of the United States, and who shall not, when elected, by an Inhabitant of that State for which he shall be chosen.

[4] The Vice President of the United States shall be President of the Senate, but shall have no Vote, unless they be equally divided.

[5] The Senate shall chuse their other Officers, and also a President pro tempore, in the Absence of the Vice President, or when he shall exercise the Office of President of the United States.

[6] The Senate shall have the sole Power to try all Impeachments. When sitting for that Purpose, they shall be on Oath or Affirmation. When the President of the United States is tried, the Chief Justice shall preside: And no Person shall be convicted without the Concurrence of two thirds of the Members present.

[7] Judgment in Cases of Impeachment shall not extend further than to removal from Office, and disqualification to hold and enjoy any Office of honor, Trust, or Profit under the United States: but the Party convicted shall nevertheless be liable and subject to Indictment, Trial, Judgment, and Punishment, according to Law.

Section 4. [1] The Times, Places and Manner of holding Elections for Senators and Representatives, shall be prescribed in each State by the Legislature thereof; but the Congress may at any time by Law make or alter such Regulations, except as to the Places of chusing Senators.

[2] The Congress shall assemble at least once in every Year, and such Meeting shall be on the first Monday in December, unless they shall by Law appoint a different Day.

Section 5. [1] Each House shall be the Judge of the Elections, Returns, and Qualifications of its own Members, and a Majority of each shall constitute a Quorum to do Business; but a smaller Number may adjourn from day to day, and may be authorized to compel the Attendance of absent Members, in such Manner, and under such Penalties as each House may provide.

[2] Each House may determine the Rules of its Proceedings, punish its Members for disorderly Behavior, and, with the Concurrence of two thirds, expel a Member.

[3] Each House shall keep a Journal of its Proceedings, and from time to time publish the same, excepting such Parts as may in their Judgment require

Secrecy; and the Yeas and Nays of the Members of either House on any question shall, at the Desire of one fifth of those Present, be entered on the Journal.

[4] Neither House, during the Session of Congress, shall without the Consent of the other, adjourn for more than three days, nor to any other Place than that in which the two Houses shall be sitting.

Section 6. [1] The Senators and Representatives shall receive a Compensation for their Services, to be ascertained by Law, and paid out of the Treasury of the United States. They shall in all Cases, except Treason, Felony and Breach of the Peace, be privileged from Arrest during their Attendance at the Session of their respective Houses, and in going to and returning from the same; and for any Speech or Debate in either House, they shall not be questioned in any other Place.

[2] No Senator or Representative shall, during the Time for which he was elected, be appointed to any civil Office under the Authority of the United States, which shall have been created, or the Emoluments whereof shall have been increased during such time; and no Person holding any Office under the United States, shall be a Member of either House during his Continuance in Office.

Section 7. [1] All Bills for raising Revenue shall originate in the House of Representatives; but the Senate may propose or concur with Amendments as on other Bills.

[2] Every Bill which shall have passed the House of Representatives and the Senate, shall, before it become a Law, be presented to the President of the United States; If he approve he shall sign it, but if not he shall return it, with his Objections to the House in which it shall have originated, who shall enter the Objections at large on their Journal, and proceed to reconsider it. If after such Reconsideration two thirds of that House shall agree to pass the Bill, it shall be sent together with the Objections, to the other House, by which it shall likewise be reconsidered, and if approved by two thirds of that House, it shall become a Law. But in all such Cases the Votes of both Houses shall be determined by yeas and Nays, and the Names of the Persons voting for and against the Bill shall be entered on the Journal of each House respectively. If any Bill shall not be returned by the President within ten Days (Sundays excepted) after it shall have been presented to him, the Same shall be a Law, in like Manner as if he had signed it, unless the Congress by their Adjournment prevent its Return in which Case it shall not be a Law.

[3] Every Order, Resolution, or Vote, to Which the Concurrence of the Senate and House of Representatives may be necessary (except on a question of Adjournment) shall be presented to the President of the United States; and before the Same shall take Effect, shall be approved by him, or being disapproved by him, shall be repassed by two thirds of the Senate and House of Representatives, according to the Rules and Limitations prescribed in the Case of a Bill.

Section 8. [1] The Congress shall have Power To lay and collect Taxes, Duties, Imposts and Excises, to pay the Debts and provide for the common Defence and general Welfare of the United States; but all Duties, Imposts and Excises shall be uniform throughout the United States;

[2] To borrow money on the credit of the United States;

[3] To regulate Commerce with foreign Nations, and among the several States, and with the Indian Tribes;

[4] To establish an uniform Rule of Naturalization, and uniform Laws on the subject of Bankruptcies throughout the United States;

[5] To coin Money, regulate the Value thereof, and of foreign Coin, and fix the Standard of Weights and Measures;

[6] To provide for the Punishment of counterfeiting the Securities and current Coin of the United States;

[7] To Establish Post Offices and Post Roads;

[8] To promote the Progress of Science and useful Arts, by securing for limited Times to Authors and Inventors the exclusive Right to their respective Writings and Discoveries;

[9] To constitute Tribunals inferior to the supreme Court;

[10] To define and punish Piracies and Felonies committed on the high Seas, and Offenses against the Law of Nations;

[11] To declare War, grant Letters of Marque and Reprisal, and make Rules concerning Captures on Land and Water;

[12] To raise and support Armies, but no Appropriation of Money to that Use shall be for a longer Term than two Years;

[13] To provide and maintain a Navy;

[14] To make Rules for the Government and Regulation of the land and naval Forces;

[15] To provide for calling forth the Militia to execute the Laws of the Union, suppress Insurrections and repel Invasions;

[16] To provide for organizing, arming, and disciplining, the Militia, and for governing such Part of them as may be employed in the Service of the United States, reserving to the States respectively, the Appointment of the Officers, and the Authority of training the Militia according to the discipline prescribed by Congress;

[17] To exercise exclusive Legislation in all Cases whatsoever, over such District (not exceeding ten Miles square) as may, by Cession of particular States, and the Acceptance of Congress, become the Seat of the Government of the United States, and to exercise like Authority over all Places purchased by the Consent of the Legislature of the State in which the Same shall be, for the Erection of Forts, Magazines, Arsenals, dock-Yards, and other needful Buildings;—And

[18] To make all Laws which shall be necessary and proper for carrying into Execution the foregoing Powers, and all other Powers vested by this Constitution in the Government of the United States, or in any Department or Officer thereof.

Section 9. [1] The Migration or Importation of Such Persons as any of the States now existing shall think proper to admit, shall not be prohibited by the Congress prior to the Year one thousand eight hundred and eight, but a Tax or duty may be imposed on such Importation, not exceeding ten dollars for each Person.

[2] The privilege of the Writ of Habeas Corpus shall not be suspended, unless when in Cases of Rebellion or Invasion the public Safety may require it.

[3] No Bill of Attainder or ex post facto Law shall be passed.

[4] No Capitation, or other direct, Tax shall be laid, unless in Proportion to the Census or Enumeration herein before directed to be taken.

[5] No Tax or Duty shall be laid on Articles exported from any State.

[6] No Preference shall be given by any Regulation of Commerce or Revenue to the Ports of one State over those of another: nor shall Vessels bound to, or from, one State be obliged to enter, clear, or pay Duties in another.

[7] No money shall be drawn from the Treasury, but in Consequence of Appropriations made by Law; and a regular Statement and Account of the Receipts and Expenditures of all public Money shall be published from time to time.

[8] No Title of Nobility shall be granted by the United States: And no Person holding any Office of Profit or Trust under them, shall, without the Consent of the Congress, accept of any present, Emolument, Office, or Title, of any kind whatever, from any King, Prince, or foreign State.

Section 10. [1] No State shall enter into any Treaty, Alliance, or Confederation; grant Letters of Marque and Reprisal; coin Money; emit Bills of Credit; make any Thing but gold and silver Coin a Tender in Payment of Debts; pass any Bill of Attainder, ex post facto Law, or Law impairing the Obligation of Contracts, or grant any Title of Nobility.

[2] No State shall, without the Consent of the Congress, lay any Imposts or Duties on Imports or Exports, except what may be absolutely necessary for executing it's inspection Laws: and the net Produce of all Duties and Imposts, laid by any State on Imports or Exports, shall be for the Use of the Treasury of the United States; and all such Laws shall be subject to the Revision and Controul of the Congress.

[3] No State shall, without the Consent of Congress, lay any Duty of Tonnage, keep Troops, or Ships of War in time of Peace, enter into any Agreement or Compact with another State, or with a foreign Power, or engage in War, unless actually invaded, or in such imminent Danger as will not admit of delay.

ARTICLE II

Section 1. [1] The executive Power shall be vested in a President of the United States of America. He shall hold his Office during the Term of four Years, and, together with the Vice President, chosen for the same Term, be elected, as follows:

[2] Each State shall appoint, in such Manner as the Legislature thereof may direct, a Number of Electors, equal to the whole Number of Senators and Representatives to which the State may be entitled in the Congress; but no Senator or Representative, or Person holding an Office of Trust or Profit under the United States, shall be appointed an Elector.

[3] The Electors shall meet in their respective States, and vote by Ballot for two Persons, of whom one at least shall not be an Inhabitant of the same State with themselves. And they shall make a List of all the Persons voted for, and of the Number of Votes for each; which List they shall sign and certify, and transmit sealed to the Seat of the Government of the United States, directed to the President of the Senate. The President of the Senate shall, in the Presence of the Senate and House of Representatives, open all the Certificates, and the Votes shall then be counted. The Person having the greatest Number of Votes shall be the President, if such Number be a Majority of the whole Number of Electors appointed; and if there be more than one who have such Majority, and have an equal Number of Votes, then the House of Representatives shall

immediately chuse by Ballot one of them for President; and if no Person have a Majority, then from the five highest on the List the said House shall in like Manner chuse the President. But in chusing the President, the Votes shall be taken by States the Representation from each State having one Vote; A quorum for this Purpose shall consist of a Member or Members from two thirds of the States, and a Majority of all the States shall be necessary to a Choice. In every Case, after the Choice of the President, the Person having the greater Number of Votes of the Electors shall be the Vice President. But if there should remain two or more who have equal Votes, the Senate shall chuse from them by Ballot the Vice President.

[4] The Congress may determine the Time of chusing the Electors, and the Day on which they shall give their Votes; which Day shall be the same throughout the United States.

[5] No person except a natural born Citizen, or a Citizen of the United States, at the time of the Adoption of this Constitution, shall be eligible to the Office of President; neither shall any Person be eligible to that Office who shall not have attained to the Age of thirty five Years, and been fourteen Years a Resident within the United States.

[6] In case of the removal of the President from Office, or of his Death, Resignation or Inability to discharge the Powers and Duties of the said Office, the Same shall devolve on the Vice President, and the Congress may by Law provide for the Case of Removal, Death, Resignation or Inability, both of the President and Vice President, declaring what Officer shall then act as President, and such Officer shall act accordingly, until the Disability be removed, or a President shall be elected.

[7] The President shall, at stated Times, receive for his Services, a Compensation, which shall neither be increased nor diminished during the Period for which he shall have been elected, and he shall not receive within that Period any other Emolument from the United States, or any of them.

[8] Before he enter on the Execution of his Office, he shall take the following Oath or Affirmation: "I do solemnly swear (or affirm) that I will faithfully execute the Office of President of the United States, and will to the best of my Ability, preserve, protect and defend the Constitution of the United States."

Section 2. [1] The President shall be Commander in Chief of the Army and Navy of the United States, and of the militia of the several States, when called into the actual Service of the United States; he may require the Opinion, in writing, of the principal Officer in each of the Executive Departments, upon any Subject relating to the Duties of their respective Offices, and he shall have Power to grant Reprieves and Pardons for Offenses against the United States, except in Cases of Impeachment.

[2] He shall have Power, by and with the Advice and Consent of the Senate to make Treaties, provided two thirds of the Senators present concur; and he shall nominate, and by and with the Advice and Consent of the Senate, shall appoint Ambassadors, other public Ministers and Consuls, Judges of the supreme Court, and all other Officers of the United States, whose Appointments are not herein otherwise provided for, and which shall be established by Law; but the Congress may by Law vest the Appointment of such inferior Officers, as they think proper, in the President alone, in the Courts of Law, or in the Heads of Departments.

[3] The President shall have Power to fill up all Vacancies that may happen during the Recess of the Senate, by granting Commissions which shall expire at the End of their next Session.

Section 3. He shall from time to time give to the Congress Information of the State of the Union, and recommend to their Consideration such Measures as he shall judge necessary and expedient; he may, on extraordinary Occasions, convene both Houses, or either of them, and in Case of Disagreement between them, with Respect to the Time of Adjournment, he may adjourn them to such Time as he shall think proper; he shall receive Ambassadors and other public Ministers; he shall take Care that the Laws be faithfully executed, and shall Commission all the Officers of the United States.

Section 4. The President, Vice President and all civil Officers of the United States, shall be removed from Office on Impeachment for, and Conviction of, Treason, Bribery, or other high Crimes and Misdemeanors.

Article III

Section 1. The judicial Power of the United States, shall be vested in one supreme Court, and in such inferior Courts as the Congress may from time to time ordain and establish. The Judges, both of the supreme and inferior Courts, shall hold their Offices during good Behaviour, and shall, at stated Times, receive for their Services a Compensation, which shall not be diminished during their Continuance in Office.

Section 2. [1] The judicial Power shall extend to all Cases, in Law and Equity, arising under this Constitution, the Laws of the United States, and Treaties made, or which shall be made, under their Authority;—to all Cases affecting Ambassadors, other public Ministers and Consuls;—to all Cases of admiralty and maritime Jurisdiction;—to Controversies to which the United States shall be a Party;—to Controversies between two or more States;—between a State and Citizens of another State;—between Citizens of different States;—between Citizens of the same State claiming Lands under the Grants of different States, and between a State, or the Citizens thereof, and foreign States, Citizens or Subjects.

[2] In all Cases affecting Ambassadors, other public Ministers and Consuls, and those in which a State shall be a Party, the supreme Court shall have original Jurisdiction. In all the other Cases before mentioned, the supreme Court shall have appellate Jurisdiction, both as to Law and Fact, with such Exceptions, and under such Regulations as the Congress shall make.

[3] The trial of all Crimes, except in Cases of Impeachment, shall be by Jury; and such Trial shall be held in the State where the said Crimes shall have been committed; but when not committed within any State, the Trial shall be at such Place or Places as the Congress may by Law have directed.

Section 3. [1] Treason against the United States, shall consist only in levying War against them, or, in adhering to their Enemies, giving them Aid and Comfort. No Person shall be convicted of Treason unless on the Testimony of two Witnesses to the same overt Act, or on Confession in open Court.

[2] The Congress shall have Power to declare the Punishment of Treason, but no Attainder of Treason shall work Corruption of Blood, or Forfeiture except during the Life of the Person attainted.

ARTICLE IV

Section 1. Full Faith and Credit shall be given in each State to the public Acts, Records, and judicial Proceedings of every other State. And the Congress may by general Laws prescribe the Manner in which such Acts, Records and Proceedings shall be proved, and the Effect thereof.

Section 2. [1] The Citizens of each State shall be entitled to all Privileges and Immunities of Citizens in the several States.

[2] A Person charged in any State with Treason, Felony, or other Crime, who shall flee from Justice, and be found in another State, shall on demand of the executive Authority of the State from which he fled, be delivered up, to be removed to the State having Jurisdiction of the Crime.

[3] No Person held to Service or Labour in one State, under the Laws thereof, escaping into another, shall, in Consequence of any Law or Regulation therein, be discharged from such Service or Labour, but shall be delivered up on Claim of the Party to whom such Service or Labour may be due.

Section 3. [1] New States may be admitted by the Congress into this Union; but no new State shall be formed or erected within the Jurisdiction of any other State; nor any State be formed by the Junction of two or more States, or Parts of States, without the Consent of the Legislatures of the States concerned as well as of the Congress.

[2] The Congress shall have Power to dispose of and make all needful Rules and Regulations respecting the Territory or other Property belonging to the United States; and nothing in this Constitution shall be so construed as to Prejudice any Claims of the United States, or of any particular State.

Section 4. The United States shall guarantee to every State in this Union a Republican Form of Government, and shall protect each of them against Invasion; and on Application of the Legislature, or of the Executive (when the Legislature cannot be convened) against domestic Violence.

ARTICLE V

The Congress, whenever two thirds of both Houses shall deem it necessary, shall propose Amendments to this Constitution, or, on the Application of the Legislatures of two thirds of the several States, shall call a Convention for proposing Amendments, which, in either Case, shall be valid to all Intents and Purposes, as part of this Constitution, when ratified by the Legislatures of three fourths of the several States, or by Conventions in three fourths thereof, as the one or the other Mode of Ratification may be proposed by the Congress; Provided that no Amendment which may be made prior to the Year One thousand eight hundred and eight shall in any Manner affect the first and fourth Clauses in the Ninth Section of the first Article; and that no State, without its Consent, shall be deprived of its equal Suffrage in the Senate.

ARTICLE VI

[1] All Debts contracted and Engagements entered into, before the Adoption of this Constitution shall be as valid against the United States under this Constitution, as under the Confederation.

[2] This Constitution, and the Laws of the United States which shall be made in Pursuance thereof; and all Treaties made, or which shall be made, under the Authority of the United States, shall be the supreme Law of the Land;

and the Judges in every State shall be bound thereby, any Thing in the Constitution or Laws of any State to the Contrary notwithstanding.

[3] The Senators and Representatives before mentioned, and the Members of the several State Legislatures, and all executive and judicial Officers, both of the United States and of the several States, shall be bound by Oath or Affirmation, to support this Constitution; but no religious Test shall ever be required as a Qualification to any Office or public Trust under the United States.

Article VII

The Ratification of the Conventions of nine States shall be sufficient for the Establishment of this Constitution between the States so ratifying the Same.

ARTICLES IN ADDITION TO, AND AMENDMENT OF, THE CONSTITUTION OF THE UNITED STATES OF AMERICA, PROPOSED BY CONGRESS, AND RATIFIED BY THE LEGISLATURES OF THE SEVERAL STATES PURSUANT TO THE FIFTH ARTICLE OF THE ORIGINAL CONSTITUTION.

Amendment I [1791]

Congress shall make no law respecting an establishment of religion, or prohibiting the free exercise thereof; or abridging the freedom of speech, or of the press; or the right of the people peaceably to assemble, and to petition the Government for a redress of grievances.

Amendment II [1791]

A well regulated Militia, being necessary to the security of a free State, the right of the people to keep and bear Arms, shall not be infringed.

Amendment III [1791]

No Soldier shall, in time of peace be quartered in any house, without the consent of the Owner, nor in time of war, but in a manner to be prescribed by law.

Amendment IV [1791]

The right of the people to be secure in their persons, houses, papers, and effects, against unreasonable searches and seizures, shall not be violated, and no Warrants shall issue, but upon probable cause, supported by Oath or affirmation and particularly describing the place to be searched, and the persons or things to be seized.

Amendment V [1791]

No person shall be held to answer for a capital, or otherwise infamous crime, unless on a presentment or indictment of a Grand Jury, except in cases arising in the land or naval forces, or in the Militia, when in actual service in time of War or public danger; nor shall any person be subject for the same offence to be twice put in jeopardy of life or limb; nor shall be compelled in any criminal case to be a witness against himself, nor be deprived of life, liberty, or property, without due process of law; nor shall private property be taken for public use, without just compensation.

Amendment VI [1791]

In all criminal prosecutions, the accused shall enjoy the right to a speedy and public trial, by an impartial jury of the State and district wherein the crime shall have been committed, which district shall have been previously ascertained by law, and to be informed of the nature and cause of the accusation; to be confronted with the witnesses against him; to have compulsory process for obtaining witnesses in his favor, and to have the Assistance of Counsel for his defence.

AMENDMENT VII [1791]

In Suits at common law, where the value in controversy shall exceed twenty dollars, the right of trial by jury shall be preserved, and no fact tried by jury, shall be otherwise re-examined in any Court of the United States, than according to the rules of the common law.

AMENDMENT VIII [1791]

Excessive bail shall not be required, nor excessive fines imposed, nor cruel and unusual punishments inflicted.

AMENDMENT IX [1791]

The enumeration in the Constitution, of certain rights, shall not be construed to deny or disparage others retained by the people.

AMENDMENT X [1791]

The powers not delegated to the United States by the Constitution, nor prohibited by it to the States, are reserved to the States respectively, or to the people.

AMENDMENT XI [1798]

The Judicial power of the United States shall not be construed to extend to any suit in law or equity, commenced or prosecuted against one of the United States by Citizens of another State, or by Citizens or Subjects of any Foreign State.

AMENDMENT XII [1804]

The Electors shall meet in their respective states and vote by ballot for President and Vice-President, one of whom, at least, shall not be an inhabitant of the same state with themselves; they shall name in their ballots the person voted for as President, and in distinct ballots the person voted for as Vice-President, and they shall make distinct lists of all persons voted for as President, and of all persons voted for as Vice-President, and of the number of votes for each, which lists they shall sign and certify, and transmit sealed to the seat of the government of the United States, directed to the President of the Senate;—The President of the Senate shall, in the presence of the Senate and House of Representatives, open all the certificates and the votes shall then be counted;—The person having the greatest number of votes for President, shall be the President, if such number be a majority of the whole number of Electors appointed; and if no person have such majority, then from the persons having the highest numbers not exceeding three on the list of those voted for as President, the House of Representatives shall choose immediately, by ballot, the President. But in choosing the President, the votes shall be taken by states, the representation from each state having one vote; a quorum for this purpose shall consist of a member or members from two-thirds of the states, and a majority of all the states shall be necessary to a choice. And if the House of Representatives shall not choose a President whenever the right of choice shall devolve upon them before the fourth day of March next following, then the Vice-President shall act as President, as in the case of the death or other constitutional disability of the President.—The person having the greatest number of votes as

Vice-President, shall be the Vice-President, if such number be a majority of the whole number of Electors appointed, and if no person have a majority, then from the two highest numbers on the list, the Senate shall choose the Vice-President; a quorum for the purpose shall consist of two-thirds of the whole number of Senators, and a majority of the whole number shall be necessary to a choice. But no person constitutionally ineligible to the office of President shall be eligible to that of Vice-President of the United States.

AMENDMENT XIII [1865]

Section 1. Neither slavery nor involuntary servitude, except as a punishment for crime whereof the party shall have been duly convicted, shall exist within the United States, or any place subject to their jurisdiction.

Section 2. Congress shall have power to enforce this article by appropriate legislation.

AMENDMENT XIV [1868]

Section 1. All persons born or naturalized in the United States, and subject to the jurisdiction thereof, are citizens of the United States and of the State wherein they reside. No State shall make or enforce any law which shall abridge the privileges or immunities of citizens of the United States; nor shall any State deprive any person of life, liberty, or property, without due process of law; nor deny to any person within its jurisdiction the equal protection of the laws.

Section 2. Representatives shall be apportioned among the several States according to their respective numbers, counting the whole number of persons in each State, excluding Indians not taxed. But when the right to vote at any election for the choice of electors for President and Vice President of the United States, Representatives in Congress, the Executive and Judicial officers of a State, or the members of the Legislature thereof, is denied to any of the male inhabitants of such State, being twenty-one years of age, and citizens of the United States, or in any way abridged, except for participation in rebellion, or other crime, the basis of representation therein shall be reduced in the proportion which the number of such male citizens shall bear to the whole number of male citizens twenty-one years of age in such State.

Section 3. No person shall be a Senator or Representative in Congress, or elector of President and Vice President, or hold any office, civil or military, under the United States, or under any State, who having previously taken an oath, as a member of Congress, or as an officer of the United States, or as a member of any State legislature, or as an executive or judicial officer of any State, to support the Constitution of the United States, shall have engaged in insurrection or rebellion against the same, or given aid or comfort to the enemies thereof. But Congress may by a vote of two-thirds of each House, remove such disability.

Section 4. The validity of the public debt of the United States, authorized by law, including debts incurred for payment of pensions and bounties for services in suppressing insurrection or rebellion, shall not be questioned. But neither the United States nor any State shall assume or pay any debt or obligation incurred in aid of insurrection or rebellion against the United States, or any claim for the loss or emancipation of any slave; but all such debts, obligations and claims shall be held illegal and void.

Section 5. The Congress shall have power to enforce, by appropriate legislation, the provisions of this article.

AMENDMENT XV [1870]

Section 1. The right of citizens of the United States to vote shall not be denied or abridged by the United States or by any State on account of race, color, or previous condition of servitude.

Section 2. The Congress shall have power to enforce this article by appropriate legislation.

AMENDMENT XVI [1913]

The Congress shall have power to lay and collect taxes on incomes, from whatever source derived, without apportionment among the several States, and without regard to any census or enumeration.

AMENDMENT XVII [1913]

[1] The Senate of the United States shall be composed of two Senators from each State, elected by the people thereof, for six years; and each Senator shall have one vote. The electors in each State shall have the qualifications requisite for electors of the most numerous branch of the State legislatures.

[2] When vacancies happen in the representation of any State in the Senate, the executive authority of such State shall issue writs of election to fill such vacancies: *Provided,* That the legislature of any State may empower the executive thereof to make temporary appointments until the people fill the vacancies by election as the legislature may direct.

[3] This amendment shall not be so construed as to affect the election or term of any Senator chosen before it becomes valid as part of the Constitution.

AMENDMENT XVIII [1919]

Section 1. After one year from the ratification of this article the manufacture, sale, or transportation of intoxicating liquors within, the importation thereof into, or the exportation thereof from the United States and all territory subject to the jurisdiction thereof for beverage purposes is hereby prohibited.

Section 2. The Congress and the several States shall have concurrent power to enforce this article by appropriate legislation.

Section 3. This article shall be inoperative unless it shall have been ratified as an amendment to the Constitution by the legislatures of the several States, as provided in the Constitution, within seven years from the date of the submission hereof to the States by the Congress.

AMENDMENT XIX [1920]

[1] The right of citizens of the United States to vote shall not be denied or abridged by the United States or by any State on account of sex.

[2] Congress shall have power to enforce this article by appropriate legislation.

AMENDMENT XX [1933]

Section 1. The terms of the President and Vice President shall end at noon on the 20th day of January, and the terms of Senators and Representatives at noon on the 3d day of January, of the years in which such terms would have ended if this article had not been ratified; and the terms of their successors shall then begin.

Section 2. The Congress shall assemble at least once in every year, and such meeting shall begin at noon on the 3d day of January, unless they shall by law appoint a different day.

Section 3. If, at the time fixed for the beginning of the term of the President, the President elect shall have died, the Vice President elect shall become President. If the President shall not have been chosen before the time fixed for the beginning of his term, or if the President elect shall have failed to qualify, then the Vice President elect shall act as President until a President shall have qualified; and the Congress may by law provide for the case wherein neither a President elect nor a Vice President elect shall have qualified, declaring who shall then act as President, or the manner in which one who is to act shall be selected, and such person shall act accordingly until a President or Vice President shall have qualified.

Section 4. The Congress may by law provide for the case of the death of any of the persons from whom the House of Representatives may choose a President whenever the right of choice shall have devolved upon them, and for the case of the death of any of the persons from whom the Senate may choose a Vice President whenever the right of choice shall have devolved upon them.

Section 5. Sections 1 and 2 shall take effect on the 15th day of October following the ratification of this article.

Section 6. This article shall be inoperative unless it shall have been ratified as an amendment to the Constitution by the legislatures of three-fourths of the several States within seven years from the date of its submission.

Amendment XXI [1933]

Section 1. The eighteenth article of amendment to the Constitution of the United States is hereby repealed.

Section 2. The transportation or importation into any State, Territory, or possession of the United States for delivery or use therein of intoxicating liquors, in violation of the laws thereof, is hereby prohibited.

Section 3. This article shall be inoperative unless it shall have been ratified as an amendment to the Constitution by conventions in the several States, as provided in the Constitution, within seven years from the date of the submission hereof to the States by the Congress.

Amendment XXII [1951]

Section 1. No person shall be elected to the office of the President more than twice, and no person who has held the office of President, or acted as President, for more than two years of a term to which some other person was elected President shall be elected to the office of President more than once. But this Article shall not apply to any person holding the office of President when this Article was proposed by the Congress, and shall not prevent any person who may be holding the office of President, or acting as President, during the term within which this Article becomes operative from holding the office of President or acting as President during the remainder of such term.

Section 2. This article shall be inoperative unless it shall have been ratified as an amendment to the Constitution by the legislatures of three-fourths of the several States within seven years from the date of its submission to the States by the Congress.

AMENDMENT XXIII [1961]

Section 1. The District constituting the seat of Government of the United States shall appoint in such manner as the Congress may direct:

A number of electors of President and Vice President equal to the whole number of Senators and Representatives in Congress to which the District would be entitled if it were a State, but in no event more than the least populous state; they shall be in addition to those appointed by the states, but they shall be considered, for the purposes of the election of President and Vice President, to be electors appointed by a state; and they shall meet in the District and perform such duties as provided by the twelfth article of amendment.

Section 2. The Congress shall have power to enforce this article by appropriate legislation.

AMENDMENT XXIV [1964]

Section 1. The right of citizens of the United States to vote in any primary or other election for President or Vice President, for electors for President or Vice President, or for Senator or Representative in Congress, shall not be denied or abridged by the United States or any State by reason of failure to pay any poll tax or other tax.

Section 2. The Congress shall have power to enforce this article by appropriate legislation.

AMENDMENT XXV [1967]

Section 1. In case of the removal of the President from office or of his death or resignation, the Vice President shall become President.

Section 2. Whenever there is a vacancy in the office of the Vice President, the President shall nominate a Vice President who shall take office upon confirmation by a majority vote of both Houses of Congress.

Section 3. Whenever the President transmits to the President pro tempore of the Senate and the Speaker of the House of Representatives his written declaration that he is unable to discharge the powers and duties of his office, and until he transmits to them a written declaration to the contrary, such powers and duties shall be discharged by the Vice President as Acting President.

Section 4. Whenever the Vice President and a majority of either the principal officers of the executive departments or of such other body as Congress may by law provide, transmit to the President pro tempore of the Senate and the Speaker of the House of Representatives their written declaration that the President is unable to discharge the powers and duties of his office, the Vice President shall immediately assume the powers and duties of the office as Acting President.

Thereafter, when the President transmits to the President pro tempore of the Senate and the Speaker of the House of Representatives his written declaration that no inability exists, he shall resume the powers and duties of his office unless the Vice President and a majority of either the principal officers of the executive department or of such other body as Congress may by law provide, transmit within four days to the President pro tempore of the Senate and the Speaker of the House of Representatives their written declaration that the President is unable to discharge the powers and duties of his office. Thereupon Congress shall decide the issue, assembling within forty-eight hours for that purpose if not in session. If the Congress, within twenty-one days after receipt of the latter written declaration, or, if Congress is not in session, within twenty-one days after Congress is required to assemble, determines by two-thirds vote of both Houses that the President is unable to discharge the powers and duties of his office, the Vice President shall continue to discharge the same as Acting President; otherwise, the President shall resume the powers and duties of his office.

AMENDMENT XXVI [1971]

Section 1. The right of citizens of the United States, who are eighteen years of age or older, to vote shall not be denied or abridged by the United States or by any State on account of age.

Section 2. The Congress shall have power to enforce this article by appropriate legislation.

Index

References are to Pages

†